T H E
1986
Elias Baseball
Analyst

THE
1986
Elias Baseball Analyst

Seymour Siwoff, Steve Hirdt & Peter Hirdt

COLLIER BOOKS
Macmillan Publishing Company
New York
COLLIER MACMILLAN PUBLISHERS
London

Copyright © 1986 by Elias Sports Bureau Inc.

All rights reserved. No part of this book may be reproduced or transmitted
in any form or by any means, electronic or mechanical, including photocopying,
recording or by any information storage and retrieval system, without permission
in writing from the Publisher.

Macmillan Publishing Company
866 Third Avenue, New York, N.Y. 10022
Collier Macmillan Canada, Inc.

"The Library of Congress has cataloged this
serial publication as follows:".

The . . . Elias baseball analyst. — 1985-   — New York :
  Collier Books, c1985-

        v. ; 28 cm.

    Annual.
    Re-arrangement of material issued in a series of computerized reports called:
The Player analysis.
    Produced by the Elias Sports Bureau.
    Editors for 1985–   by S. Siwoff, S. Hirdt, and P. Hirdt.

    1. Baseball—United States—Statistics—Periodicals.   2. National League of
Professional Baseball Clubs—Statistics—Periodicals.   3. Baseball—Statistics—
    1. Baseball—United States—Statistics—Periodicals.   2. National League of
Periodicals.   4. Baseball—Miscellanea—Periodicals.   I. Siwoff, Seymour.
II. Hirdt, Steve.   III. Hirdt, Peter. IV. Elias Sports Bureau.   V. Player analysis.
VI. Title: Baseball analyst.
GV877.E44   85-643022
                    796.357'0973—dc19
                                                          AACR 2   MARC-S

ISBN 0-02-081430-5

Macmillan books are available at special discounts
for bulk purchases for sales promotions, premiums,
fund-raising, or educational use. For details, contact:

    Special Sales Director
    Macmillan Publishing Company
    866 Third Avenue
    New York, N.Y. 10022

10 9 8 7 6 5 4 3 2 1

Printed in the United States of America

Contents

ACKNOWLEDGMENTS

The three names on the cover do not sufficiently cover the matter of authorship of this book. In the truest sense, everyone currently employed at the Elias Sports Bureau has helped in its preparation, and we would also like to recognize the work of former employees in this regard. Even among them, there are some who must be singled out not only for their tangible contributions, but for their commitment to the project.

The assistant author is Tom Hirdt, who not only contributed many original ideas and research techniques, but also made a major contribution to the text. We could never have produced a book of this quality without his enthusiasm, common sense, and support. Tommy Hirdt meant no less to us than Tommy Herr meant to the Cardinals.

Christopher Thorn, Larry Meisner, Warren Bannerman, and Dick Hata have the ability to communicate not only with people, but with machines, and their computer skills allowed our data to reach these pages swiftly and accurately.

John Chymczuk and John Labombarda were our chief researchers; we also drew upon the talents of Rocky Avakian, Jay Chesler, Lino Gutierrez, Santo Labombarda, Paul Mort, Bob Rosen, Andrew Thorn, and Gilbert Traub.

Once again, Jeff Neuman drew the short straw over at Macmillan and served as our editor, which in our case means not only correcting our grammar, but more importantly letting us know if we're going off the deep end statistically, or even heading toward the pier. With the major-league career of the former Oakland and Boston catcher apparently at an end, our Jeff takes his rightful place as the only Jeff Neuman in baseball. And, believe us, this one is more than a .224 hitter.

We also say thanks to Casey Lee, Fred Richardson, Bob Keefe, and Jackie Dickens, who have once again made important contributions to the *Analyst*.

THE
1986
Elias Baseball
Analyst

I
Introduction

INTRODUCTION

We're back again with our second edition, and to old friends and new, we're glad you joined us. For those familiar with last year's first edition of the *Analyst*, treat the next few paragraphs as a refresher course, because we'd like to tell the rest of you a little bit about ourselves and our book.

When we published the first edition of *The Elias Baseball Analyst* last year, we were proud—not only of our own work and that of our colleagues at the Elias Sports Bureau, to whom the project was a consuming passion, but also of the fine work done by people outside our office who helped us immeasurably in our first year in print.

We were especially proud to see that the book was received by the public in the spirit in which it was intended: to become the most exhaustive analysis of player and team performance ever set between two covers, while being presented in a style that would make it "user-friendly" even to casual baseball fans. We intended it to be neither high-brow nor low-brow—and while any form of human endeavor is laced with imperfections, we were pleased that the comments made about the book generally upheld our original belief that the media and the public were as anxious to absorb this type of material as we were to publish it.

The Elias Bureau has been in the business of recording baseball statistics since the days when Babe Ruth was a pitcher. The company's trademark has always been accuracy, a quality that was first honed back when stats were entered by hand on color-coded tally sheets, and one that has made the transition to the era of microchips. In the early seventies, we began to assemble the structure of a computer system that would digest play-by-play details from every major-league game and assimilate them into various categories for purposes of analysis. By 1975 that system was functional, and following that season, a group of reports known as *The Player Analysis* was first produced.

Those reports included breakdowns of player and team performance statistics that are essentially the same as those featured in this book. They identified for the first time how each batter and pitcher did with runners in scoring position, or in the late innings of close games, or against opposing left-handers, or in any

of many other meaningful situations. The reports were marketed to what was presumed to be the most interested audience—the major-league teams themselves. While some teams weren't interested, others were able to evaluate their players and those of other teams through the prism of the statistics produced in *The Player Analysis*.

While we considered the project an artistic success, we were also aware that many people following baseball didn't want to know any more about the sport than they already knew. That's all right; one of the beauties of the game is that it can be enjoyed on many different levels, and the statistical level is certainly a specialized one. But at the same time, the growing sophistication of an even greater portion of the public demanded that we make our material available to as wide an audience as possible. So last year we celebrated the tenth anniversary of our project by publishing *The 1985 Elias Baseball Analyst*, a book that contained the best of the material we had formerly provided to the teams themselves, as well as many features created especially for the book.

To everyone who contacted us about the book, we offer our gratitude. Many nice things were said and written about it by some very knowledgeable people, and the response that we received from fans and members of the media encouraged us to publish it again this year. Many offered suggestions on how to improve the book, and to those who did, our special thanks. Indeed, we have included several new elements in the 1986 *Analyst*, some based on that response. But our overriding philosophy continues to be as we expressed it last year: to present accurate information in an understandable language. We feel sure that any baseball fan will learn something every time he opens the book.

So much for the old news; the new news is that the book is somewhat expanded from its 1985 form. It is 32 pages thicker, and we have used much of that additional space to expand the material in a couple of areas that proved to be very popular last year. The first of these is the "Loves to face, Hates to face" references in the Batter and Pitcher Sections, which list, for each batter and pitcher, opposing players who have proved to be particularly easy or difficult for him to handle. We were inundated with requests for more of that type of information, and so we have introduced an entire section in this year's book, "Batter/Pitcher Matchups," which details how some of the game's greatest players have done in individual confrontations against everyone they've faced for five or more at bats.

The other new section deals with a rather popular statistical commodity known as records. Traditional record books contain traditional records—most home runs in a season, most doubles in a career, most innings pitched in a game. This year's *Analyst* contains a section of "Single-Season and Career Leaders" that lists the best performances not in home runs, doubles, or innings pitched, but in various categories compiled only since the inception of *The Player Analysis* in 1975. Who's been the best hitter during that time against left-handed pitchers? Who had the best single-season batting average in Late-Inning Pressure Situations? Who has been the most efficient batter at driving in runners from scoring position? Or from first base? All the top performances from the 1985 season can be judged in relation to those of the previous ten years, for pitchers as well as batters. And this section allows us to recognize outstanding performances of seasons from the recent past, in order to broaden the frame of reference for contemporary players.

Throughout the rest of the book, you will notice many additions to the formats we used last year. To take one example, the comments for each player in the Batter and Pitcher Sections indicate record and near-record performances not listed in the Leaders Section. We have not only indicated how many double-play ground balls each pitcher threw, but also how many double-play opportunities he had (batters faced with a runner on first and less than two outs). With that information, we can determine who's the best at getting the crucial DP. That information has also been included for batters with unusually high or low averages. And we have not only expanded the scope of the ground outs-to-air outs ratio (which we introduced last year for pitchers) to batters, but in the Atlanta Braves essay on page 97, you'll find an interesting application of this statistic which could well change the way a manager makes out his lineup and selects his pinch-hitters and relief pitchers.

We feel that this year's *Analyst* surpasses the standards we set for ourselves in our initial edition a year ago. We hope you'll agree. Come inside—the show's about to start.

II
Team Section

Team Section

The Team Section consists of comments and statistics for each of the twenty-six major-league teams. The examples here, and in all of the section introductions, are from the 1984 season.

WON-LOST RECORD BY STARTING POSITION

DETROIT 104-58	C	1B	2B	3B	SS	LF	CF	RF	P	DH	Leadoff	Relief	Starts
Glenn Abbott	-	-	-	-	-	-	-	-	4-4	-	-	2-3	4-4
Rod Allen	-	-	-	-	-	-	-	-	-	10-0	-	-	10-0
Doug Bair	-	-	-	-	-	-	-	-	0-1	-	-	26-20	0-1
Doug Baker	-	-	3-1	-	16-11	-	-	-	-	-	-	-	19-12
Juan Berenguer	-	-	-	-	-	-	-	-	15-12	-	-	0-4	15-12
Dave Bergman	-	50-17	-	-	-	0-1	-	-	-	-	2-2	-	50-18
Tom Brookens	-	-	9-10	17-5	12-10	-	-	-	-	-	2-3	-	38-25
Marty Castillo	12-16	-	-	10-4	-	-	-	-	-	-	-	-	22-20
Scotty Earl	-	-	5-3	-	-	-	-	-	-	-	2-1	-	5-3
Darrell Evans	-	24-19	-	7-7	-	-	-	-	-	42-11	-	-	73-37
Barbaro Garbey	-	30-21	10-4	-	-	1-1	-	-	-	8-4	2-1	-	49-30
Kirk Gibson	-	-	-	-	-	-	82-46	-	-	3-3	-	-	85-49
Johnny Grubb	-	-	-	-	-	18-4	2-1	-	15-11	-	-	-	35-16
Willie Hernandez	-	-	-	-	-	-	-	-	-	-	-	63-17	0-0
Larry Herndon	-	-	-	-	-	61-37	-	-	-	-	-	-	61-37
Howard Johnson	-	-	60-38	0-1	-	-	-	-	-	0-2	1-0	-	60-41
Ruppert Jones	-	-	-	-	-	23-15	13-7	-	-	2-0	-	-	38-22
Rusty Kuntz	-	-	-	-	-	2-5	19-9	-	-	1-2	8-7	-	22-16

The first table following the team comments is the Won-Lost Record by Starting Position chart. This chart lists, for each player on a team, the team's won-lost record in games started by that player at each position, in the leadoff spot in the lineup, and in games in which a pitcher appeared in relief. (This last is included to give some insight into how the manager chose to use his relief staff.) The players are listed in alphabetical order.

Following this table is a series of eight charts detailing the performance of each player and pitcher on the team who played at least semiregularly. Included are all players who had at least 200 plate appearances in the season, all pitchers who faced at least 250 batters, and selected individuals who did not meet the standard but were still significant enough to merit inclusion.

Overall Batting Compared to Late Inning Pressure Situations

		BA	Rank	SA	Rank	OBA	Rank	HR %	Rank	BB %	Rank	SO %	Rank	RDI %	Rank
Dave Bergman	Overall	.273	67	.417	65	.351	47	2.58	76	10.44	39	12.66	76	.350	16
	Pressure	.351	16	.703	3	.419	24	8.11	7	11.36	47	13.64	86	.357	42
Tom Brookens	Overall	.246	121	.397	83	.306	120	2.23	89	7.51	89	13.04	82	.350	16
	Pressure	.389	--	.778	--	.421	--	5.56	--	4.55	--	9.09	--	.200	--
Marty Castillo	Overall	.234	--	.383	--	.285	--	2.84	--	6.45	--	21.29	--	.204	154
	Pressure	.000	--	.000	--	.182	--	0.00	--	18.18	--	36.36	--	.000	--
Darrell Evans	Overall	.232	136	.384	95	.353	46	3.99	42	15.94	4	14.49	103	.310	48
	Pressure	.146	159	.146	162	.241	146	0.00	114	10.91	51	14.55	97	.083	164
Barbaro Garbey	Overall	.287	38	.391	88	.325	83	1.53	110	4.89	138	10.06	46	.389	4
	Pressure	.342	20	.500	28	.375	43	2.63	79	5.00	133	7.50	22	.111	153
Kirk Gibson	Overall	.282	52	.516	9	.363	28	5.08	20	10.31	41	16.86	131	.280	95
	Pressure	.250	93	.516	25	.351	59	6.25	17	12.00	43	17.33	118	.200	118
Johnny Grubb	Overall	.267	78	.432	60	.395	4	4.55	27	16.67	2	16.67	124	.176	--
	Pressure	.242	103	.424	60	.409	27	6.06	19	22.73	2	15.91	107	.200	118
Larry Herndon	Overall	.280	56	.400	78	.333	69	1.72	102	7.17	98	14.13	98	.225	142
	Pressure	.318	31	.409	67	.400	32	2.27	85	12.00	43	14.00	91	.385	30
Howard Johnson	Overall	.248	118	.394	86	.324	84	3.38	57	9.95	44	16.67	124	.294	74
	Pressure	.186	147	.356	98	.226	151	5.08	28	4.76	136	12.70	75	.176	134
Ruppert Jones	Overall	.284	49	.516	8	.346	55	5.58	13	8.86	67	19.83	152	.367	9
	Pressure	.194	138	.333	106	.211	155	2.78	75	2.63	153	26.32	160	.200	118
Chet Lemon	Overall	.287	40	.495	21	.358	37	3.93	44	8.89	66	14.46	102	.293	77
	Pressure	.259	86	.328	112	.419	23	1.72	101	18.67	6	10.67	52	.357	42
Team Average	Overall	.271	4	.432	2	.342	1	3.31	1	9.44	2	14.76	13	.287	7
	Pressure	.263	5	.417	3	.351	2	3.67	2	11.60	2	14.25	6	.250	12
League Average	Overall	.264		.398		.326		2.54		8.26		13.32		.284	
	Pressure	.257		.384		.327		2.59		9.06		14.55		.277	

Column Headings Information

BA	Batting Average
SA	Slugging Average
OBA	On-Base Average
HR%	Home Run Percentage (home runs per 100 at bats)
BB%	Base-on-Balls Percentage (bases on balls per 100 plate appearances)
SO%	Strikeout Percentage (strikeouts per 100 plate appearances)
RDI%	Percentage of Runners Driven In

Each chart provides a statistical breakdown of player performance in a selected category. For each category, the player's average or percentage is given, along with his ranking within the league. This enables us to see at a glance that while Kirk Gibson ranked ninth in the league in slugging overall in 1984, he ranked 25th in pressure situations (see below). Rankings in each category are listed for the 158 players and 131 pitchers with the most plate appearances or batters faced in the category (plus ties) in the American League, and the top 134 batters and 115 pitchers (plus ties) in the National League. If a player does not qualify under this standard, no ranking is listed. (For a more detailed description of the methods used in determining the number of qualifiers for a given category, see the introduction to the Leaders Section.)

The batter charts list breakdowns against left-handed and right-handed pitching, performance with bases empty and runners on base, and overall performance for the season compared with performance in pressure situations (all at bats occurring in the seventh inning or later with the score tied or the batter's team trailing by one, two, or three runs, or four runs with the bases loaded).

The final batter chart lists miscellaneous comparisons for each player, giving his batting average on grass fields and artificial turf; in home games and in road games; with runners in scoring position and with runners in scoring position and two out; on-base average leading off an inning; and the percentage of runners he drove in from third base with less than two out. (For players who played for more than one team in a league, all totals are combined. The "home" totals for Bo Diaz, for example, include all games played in Philadelphia when he was with the Phillies, and all games played in Cincinnati while he was with the Reds.)

On each chart, following the individual batter totals, are the team's averages for each category, and the team's ranking within the league. For purposes of comparison, the overall league average is also included.

The pitcher charts list breakdowns against left-handed and right-handed batters, performance with bases empty and runners on base, and overall performance for the season compared with performance in pressure situations (against all batters in the seventh inning or later with the score tied or the pitcher's team leading or trailing by one or two runs).

The final pitcher chart lists miscellaneous comparisons for each pitcher giving his opponents' batting average on grass fields and artificial turf; in home games and in road games; with runners in scoring position and with runners in scoring position and two out; and opponents' on-base average leading off an inning.

On each chart, following the individual pitcher statistics, are the team's averages for each category, and the team's ranking within the league. For purposes of comparison, the overall league average is also included.

For a detailed discussion of the use of opposing batters' records to examine pitching performance, see the introduction to the Pitcher Section.

American League

BALTIMORE ORIOLES

The big news in Baltimore last season was the return of Earl Weaver to the Orioles' dugout. After an absence of two-and-a-half years, Weaver replaced his own successor, Joe Altobelli, on June 14, with Baltimore seven games behind the division-leading Blue Jays. Weaver's Orioles made their debut in a weekend series against Milwaukee, and the results were as devastating as a Navratilova opening-round rout: 9–3, 7–5, 9–1. *No mas!* Combined with Boston's sweep of Toronto, Weaver's band had sliced a game a day from the Blue Jays' lead, one-two-three, and nearly halved Toronto's margin in less than 48 hours.

Euphoric Baltimoreans were reminded of Super Bowl V, when Earl Morrall relieved a battered Johnny Unitas and rallied the Colts, the *Baltimore* Colts, to a fourth-quarter comeback victory. There was every reason to hope that Weaver's return would incite the O's to another division title. It wasn't to be; the Orioles never came closer to the Blue Jays than they were on that Monday, when they woke up four games back.

This is not to say that Weaver's return was a failure. For one thing, Baltimore extended their streak of consecutive winning seasons to 18, snapping a tie with the Chicago White Sox (1951–67) for the second-longest in major league history, behind the great New York Yankees dynasty (39 consecutive seasons). The Orioles can be proud to have nurtured a streak of excellence nearly unrivaled in professional sports. And, of course, that streak began in Earl's first year as manager of the Orioles.

Nevertheless, Weaver's comeback kindled some criticism that his return would delay the rebuilding of a team that had grown old, that he would let past loyalties stand in the way of progress. Nothing could be further from the truth. Weaver in fact used the second half of the season a kind of laboratory, challenging some of his own time-tested techniques, finding out just what some of his new players could do, and experimenting at the expense of several of his trusted soldiers of the past.

Shortly after Weaver's arrival, the Orioles acquired Alan Wiggins, which hastened the demotion to Rochester of Lenn Sakata, one of Earl's favored role players in the early 1980s, and represented the *de facto* end of Rich Dauer's days as an everyday player. Rick Dempsey, Weaver's alter ego on the field, was reduced to part-time status by the elevation of Floyd Rayford to a full-time starting role. Gary Roenicke kept his starting job against lefties, but he would be dealt away in December, severing yet another link to the earlier clubs. Cal Ripken and Eddie Murray were unaffected by the managerial change, of course, but even Fred Lynn felt the sting of Weaver's whip: An everyday starter under Altobelli, due in part to Lee Lacy's missing the first month of the season, Lynn started only 22 of 44 games against left-handers under Weaver.

The Rayford move, more than any other, typified Weaver's willingness to challenge old assumptions and test his players' limits. During parts of three seasons in the majors, Rayford was a seldom-used utility infielder. His value increased in 1984 when he added catchers' equipment to his bag of tricks, but even then, he was considered a one-way player, batting against right-handed pitchers only when he could slip out of the dugout unnoticed. No one ever doubted his ability to hit southpaws, however, as these career statistics indicate:

Floyd Rayford	AB	H	2B	3B	HR	BB	SO	BA	SA	OBA
vs. LHP	351	105	15	0	19	21	73	.299	.504	.338

Weaver not only used Rayford as his everyday third baseman against left-handers, but, lacking a left-handed hitting catcher, also used him to spell Dempsey behind the plate against right-handers. By season's end, Rayford proved he could hit all pitching, and he started all but three Orioles games after August 1. During his first three major league seasons, Rayford had just seven hits in 70 at bats against righties. But notice in the following figures how he improved with increased activity against right-handers:

Vs. RHP	AB	H	2B	3B	HR	BB	SO	BA	SA	OBA
1980	8	0	0	0	0	0	2	.000	.000	.000
1982	35	3	0	0	2	2	9	.086	.257	.135
1983	27	4	1	0	0	3	5	.148	.185	.226
1984	144	32	10	0	1	7	32	.222	.313	.271
1985	219	63	13	1	6	5	45	.288	.438	.302

In several other similar moves, Weaver went against past evidence to try to discover for himself what his players' future roles might be. He resurrected John Shelby, the centerfielder for whom the Orioles had forsaken Al Bumbry a few years earlier. Shelby, a switch-hitter, had been an inadequate hitter from the left side earlier in his career—.226 through the 1984 season. That didn't stop Earl from using him even against right-handers, and Shelby hit .309 as a left-handed batter last season. Another switch-hitting outfielder, Mike Young, has the kind of powerful bat Weaver can't resist. Though he was seldom used against right-handers by Altobelli, Young played nearly every day during the second half of the season, and completed the year with 28 home runs, 16 from the left side. It's probably too soon to say that Weaver will shift to a set lineup, away from his pattern of platooning and pinch-hitting, but last season's experiments gave him a great deal of new information about his players. It's going to be interesting to see what the little genius does with it all.

Man Bites Dog: Baltimore Faces Pitching Problems

Weaver may have spent so much time tinkering with his lineup last season because he was so exasperated trying to solve his pitching woes. Consistent starting pitching had been a Baltimore trademark since the days of McNally, Palmer, and Cuellar. Throughout the 1970s, the Orioles had a seemingly never-ending supply of pitchers to fill in around them. Pat Dobson left, Doyle Alexander replaced him. Then came Ross Grimsley and Wayne Garland, soon to be followed by Mike Torrez. Rudy May and Ken Holtzman arrived, followed by Dennis Martinez. And Scott McGregor. And Mike Flanagan. And Mike Boddicker. And Storm Davis. But last season that all ended.

Baltimore finished eighth in the American League with an ERA of 4.38, the first time a Weaver-managed Orioles team had not finished among the top half of the American League teams. They allowed nearly one hundred more runs last season than they had in 1984, although the staff was basically unchanged. And to make matters worse, more than half of that difference occurred in the first inning. Baltimore allowed only 63 first-inning runs in 1984, the lowest total in the American League; last season that skied to 117 runs, second-highest in the league. Scott McGregor allowed 27 runs in the first inning, the highest total in either league, and Dennis Martinez (26) and Storm Davis (24) followed close behind.

Despite the league's second-highest run total, the Orioles scored first in only 74 games last season, tying them with California and Minnesota for second-worst in the league. The following tables illustrate the difference that scoring the first run makes:

Scoring Game's First Run				Allowing Game's First Run			
	W	L	Pct.		W	L	Pct.
Toronto	61	19	.763	Toronto	38	43	.469
Chicago	59	21	.738	**Baltimore**	38	49	.437
Kansas City	65	24	.730	New York	23	32	.418
California	54	20	.730	California	36	52	.409
Seattle	56	22	.718	Detroit	25	44	.362
Minnesota	53	21	.716	Kansas City	26	47	.356
Boston	60	24	.714	Oakland	33	64	.340
New York	74	32	.698	Milwaukee	29	57	.337
Oakland	44	21	.677	Chicago	26	56	.317
Detroit	59	33	.641	Minnesota	24	64	.273
Baltimore	45	29	.608	Boston	21	57	.269
Milwaukee	42	33	.560	Texas	21	62	.253
Texas	41	37	.526	Cleveland	20	60	.250
Cleveland	40	42	.488	Seattle	18	66	.214
Totals	753	378	.666	Totals	378	753	.334

The importance of the first run is massive: it gives a typical American League team a two-to-one edge on its opponent. In addition, the worst team in the league after scoring first is still better than the best team in the league when the opponents score first. Were it not for their potent offense, Baltimore would have suffered much greater losses from their poor first-inning pitching.

Many Baltimore games last season resembled the Apollo Creed–Rocky Balboa rematch. The Orioles usually hit the canvas first, but just like in the "Rocky" movies, they kept coming back. And a major factor was their major-league leading total in Weaver's favorite category: they hit 33 three-run homers. Both the Orioles and their opponents held the lead at some point in 85 different games, by far the highest total in the majors. The following table lists each team's record in games in which both teams held the lead at some point—come-from-behind victories and blown-lead losses. And like in the movies, Baltimore was usually ahead at the final bell; as their percentage shows, they gained more from their ability to come back than they lost from their problems holding onto a lead:

	G	W	L	Pct.		G	W	L	Pct.
Baltimore	85	48	37	.565	Atlanta	64	32	32	.500
Boston	69	33	36	.478	Chicago	72	38	34	.528
California	69	42	27	.609	Cincinnati	67	42	25	.627
Chicago	63	34	29	.540	Houston	70	37	33	.529
Cleveland	80	27	53	.338	Los Angeles	70	42	28	.600
Detroit	68	31	37	.456	Montreal	58	29	29	.500
Kansas City	68	32	36	.471	New York	57	32	25	.561
Milwaukee	76	36	40	.474	Philadelphia	68	33	35	.485
Minnesota	61	32	29	.525	Pittsburgh	71	25	46	.352
New York	75	39	36	.520	St. Louis	61	35	26	.574
Oakland	67	40	27	.597	San Diego	70	30	40	.429
Seattle	54	27	27	.500	San Francisco	78	28	50	.359
Texas	70	26	44	.371					
Toronto	69	40	29	.580					

Dog Bites Man: Ripken at Shortstop

Cal Ripken has now played every inning of every game in each of the past three complete seasons. The every-inning streak (not to be confused with his concurrent consecutive-*game* streak) actually started on June 5, 1982, so Ripken will start the 1986 season having played 5,445 consecutive innings. Again, we wonder, why?

Does it make sense never to rest one of your most valuable players? Does it make sense to needlessly expose him to injury in a lopsided game? Does it make sense to have had no one else on your roster play shortstop all season long? No, no, and no, respectively.

Sometimes players and teams get caught up in pursuit of records and achievements which are hollow and spurious. Sometimes these pursuits are trivial and harmless, but at other times they can run counter to the team's best interests. In his prime, Pete Rose was quoted as saying that he could be of the most benefit to his team by leading the league in runs, hits, or doubles. Although you might be put off by Rose's repeated use of the vertical pronoun, at least you could catch his drift. But then, when asked if he, like other players, would benefit from an occasional rest, he would turn his initial logical statement around by replying that such a rest would hurt his chances to lead the league in runs, hits, or doubles. Huh?

Remember back in 1980, when Billy Martin was managing the A's and he decided that, come hell or high water, Rick Langford was going to complete every game he started? He did just that, for a period of 22 consecutive games, from May 23 through September 12. But it was a record of will, not skill: Martin's will, not Langford's skill. To keep the streak going, Martin had Langford pitch all 14 innings of a game against Cleveland, winning 6–5. In that game, Langford took a 5–0 lead into the ninth inning before allowing the Indians to tie it up. Notwithstanding the fact that the A's had a weak bullpen that year, would a pitcher without a streak in progress have been allowed to stay in such a game? Langford's subsequent arm troubles only add fuel to the fire.

This sort of thing happens more often in football. Take the NFL record for consecutive games catching a pass: 127 by Harold Carmichael. That record is hollow enough to begin with, since players with pass-catching streaks can, and often do, extend their streaks with meaningless receptions within a yard or two of the line of scrimmage—in either direction. And one reception in the course of a game is hardly an achievement for any receiver who weighs less than 300 pounds. But a few years ago, when Mel Gray was challenging Carmichael's record, Gray's team, the Cardinals, actually declined a five-yard penalty in order to let a three-yard Gray reception stand, because acceptance of the penalty would statistically wipe out the catch. And in another game, with the Cardinals leading narrowly in the dying moments and the Eagles out of time outs, but with Gray having not yet caught a pass, the Cardinals' quarterback attempted to hit Gray with a quick pass, which was nearly intercepted. Winning a game was made subordinate to the streak.

The wisdom of continuing a consecutive-game playing streak in any sport can be questioned any time a team would be better off in the long term by a player's absence than by his presence. This includes giving rest to players so that they will be fresh later on. It was Leo Durocher, when managing the Cubs, who decided one day that Billy Williams's consecutive-game playing streak had gone far enough. Durocher sat Williams out, and purposely kept him out, just so that Williams, Durocher, and the team would no longer have that sword hanging over their heads.

Ripken's consecutive-*innings* streak compounds the already silly situation manufactured by a consecutive-game streak. Ripken is a marvelous ballplayer whose skills will be appreciated—perhaps even more appreciated—without having a record of will hanging like an albatross around his neck. Maybe Earl will take a page out of Leo's book, and say that enough is enough.

WON-LOST RECORD BY STARTING POSITION

BALTIMORE 83-78	C	1B	2B	3B	SS	LF	CF	RF	P	DH	Leadoff	Relief	Starts
Don Aase	-	-	-	-	-	-	-	-	-	-	-	26-28	-
Eric Bell	-	-	-	-	-	-	-	-	-	-	-	0-4	-
Mike Boddicker	-	-	-	-	-	-	-	-	13-19	-	-	-	13-19
Fritz Connally	-	1-0	-	12-15	-	-	-	-	-	1-0	-	-	14-15
Rich Dauer	-	-	32-31	4-4	-	-	-	-	-	-	-	-	36-35
Storm Davis	-	-	-	-	-	-	-	-	16-12	-	-	0-3	16-12
Rick Dempsey	57-56	-	-	-	-	-	-	-	-	-	-	-	57-56
Ken Dixon	-	-	-	-	-	-	-	-	10-8	-	-	2-14	10-8
Jim Dwyer	-	-	-	-	-	16-20	-	16-9	-	0-1	9-6	-	32-30
Mike Flanagan	-	-	-	-	-	-	-	-	7-8	-	-	-	7-8
Dan Ford	-	-	-	-	-	-	-	-	-	10-6	5-5	-	10-6
Wayne Gross	-	0-5	-	30-27	-	-	-	-	-	1-3	-	-	31-35
John Habyan	-	-	-	-	-	-	-	-	-	-	-	1-1	-
Brad Havens	-	-	-	-	-	-	-	-	0-1	-	-	2-5	0-1
Leo Hernandez	-	-	-	-	-	-	-	-	0-4	-	-	-	0-4
Phil Huffman	-	-	-	-	-	-	-	-	1-0	-	-	0-1	1-0
Lee Lacy	-	-	-	-	-	-	-	51-61	-	3-1	16-20	-	54-62
John Lowenstein	-	-	-	-	-	1-3	-	-	-	2-2	-	-	3-5
Fred Lynn	-	-	-	-	-	-	62-59	-	-	-	-	-	62-59
Dennis Martinez	-	-	-	-	-	-	-	-	17-14	-	-	1-1	17-14
Tippy Martinez	-	-	-	-	-	-	-	-	-	-	-	14-35	-
Scott McGregor	-	-	-	-	-	-	-	-	19-15	-	-	0-1	19-15
Eddie Murray	-	82-72	-	-	-	-	-	-	-	0-2	-	-	82-74
Joe Nolan	3-1	-	-	-	-	-	-	-	-	0-1	-	-	3-2
Tom O'Malley	-	-	-	2-1	-	-	-	-	-	-	-	-	2-1
Al Pardo	12-10	-	-	-	-	-	-	-	-	-	-	-	12-10
Kelly Paris	-	-	1-1	-	-	-	-	-	-	0-1	-	-	1-2
Floyd Rayford	11-11	-	-	35-31	-	-	-	-	-	-	2-3	-	46-42
Cal Ripken	-	-	-	-	83-78	-	-	-	-	-	-	-	83-78
Gary Roenicke	-	-	-	-	-	26-19	0-2	3-3	-	2-2	-	-	31-26
Lenn Sakata	-	-	11-11	-	-	-	-	-	-	-	2-1	-	11-11
Larry Sheets	-	0-1	-	-	-	-	-	3-3	-	48-38	-	-	51-42
John Shelby	-	-	-	-	-	0-1	21-17	4-0	-	0-1	8-5	-	25-19
Nat Snell	-	-	-	-	-	-	-	-	-	-	-	14-29	-
Sammy Stewart	-	-	-	-	-	-	-	-	0-1	-	-	21-34	0-1
Bill Swaggerty	-	-	-	-	-	-	-	-	-	-	-	0-1	-
Alan Wiggins	-	-	39-35	-	-	-	-	-	-	-	39-35	-	39-35
Mike Young	-	-	-	-	-	40-35	-	6-2	-	16-16	2-3	-	62-53

Batting vs. Left and Right Handed Pitchers

		BA	Rank	SA	Rank	OBA	Rank	HR %	Rank	BB %	Rank	SO %	Rank
Fritz Connally	vs. Lefties	.279	63	.382	100	.402	10	1.47	102	15.66	8	13.25	91
	vs. Righties	.159	--	.295	--	.255	--	4.55	--	11.54	--	19.23	--
Rich Dauer	vs. Lefties	.247	108	.358	117	.322	101	2.47	81	9.68	60	3.23	3
	vs. Righties	.173	158	.205	158	.245	155	0.00	152	7.80	87	2.84	1
Rick Dempsey	vs. Lefties	.325	16	.529	20	.403	9	4.46	44	11.54	36	22.53	145
	vs. Righties	.200	149	.312	143	.299	117	2.44	86	12.18	24	19.33	141
Jim Dwyer	vs. Lefties	.000	--	.000	--	.000	--	0.00	--	0.00	--	00.00	--
	vs. Righties	.250	96	.401	77	.354	41	3.02	69	13.55	14	10.99	52
Wayne Gross	vs. Lefties	.250	--	1.000	--	.400	--	25.00	--	16.67	--	0.00	--
	vs. Righties	.235	118	.413	69	.368	21	4.69	27	17.44	4	18.60	137
Lee Lacy	vs. Lefties	.313	26	.470	44	.375	26	3.01	65	8.11	88	15.68	108
	vs. Righties	.282	43	.377	94	.327	74	1.23	122	6.76	105	18.59	136
Fred Lynn	vs. Lefties	.242	121	.379	104	.312	111	2.61	79	9.41	63	24.71	152
	vs. Righties	.275	53	.485	20	.352	45	6.44	6	10.95	37	17.16	119
Eddie Murray	vs. Lefties	.286	53	.502	25	.384	14	4.93	34	13.50	20	12.24	75
	vs. Righties	.303	14	.534	7	.382	15	5.53	15	11.82	27	8.86	31
Floyd Rayford	vs. Lefties	.336	7	.650	2	.359	46	8.57	1	3.42	147	16.44	114
	vs. Righties	.288	31	.438	50	.302	110	2.74	80	2.21	157	19.91	143
Cal Ripken	vs. Lefties	.272	70	.436	69	.346	66	2.97	67	10.09	55	6.14	16
	vs. Righties	.286	37	.484	22	.347	49	4.55	29	8.98	64	11.02	53
Gary Roenicke	vs. Lefties	.209	146	.453	59	.347	64	6.98	9	17.84	5	12.21	73
	vs. Righties	.245	--	.472	--	.322	--	5.66	--	9.84	--	16.39	--
Larry Sheets	vs. Lefties	.118	--	.176	--	.273	--	0.00	--	17.39	--	21.74	--
	vs. Righties	.270	59	.457	41	.326	77	5.47	16	7.10	98	13.91	86
John Shelby	vs. Lefties	.244	115	.378	106	.262	147	2.44	83	2.38	154	25.00	154
	vs. Righties	.309	--	.472	--	.336	--	4.07	--	3.85	--	17.69	--
Alan Wiggins	vs. Lefties	.314	25	.390	95	.395	13	0.00	131	10.74	45	4.13	6
	vs. Righties	.269	60	.326	132	.329	71	0.00	152	7.48	91	5.14	4
Mike Young	vs. Lefties	.293	46	.547	14	.335	84	6.63	14	6.19	121	17.53	123
	vs. Righties	.260	77	.491	18	.356	38	5.95	8	11.61	30	22.58	150
Team Average	vs. Lefties	.271	3	.456	1	.346	4	4.21	1	10.13	4	14.62	11
	vs. Righties	.259	7	.417	4	.330	4	3.71	1	9.52	2	14.62	13
League Average	vs. Lefties	.266		.416		.333		2.91		8.95		13.77	
	vs. Righties	.259		.401		.324		2.78		8.49		13.56	

Batting with Runners on Base and Bases Empty

		BA	Rank	SA	Rank	OBA	Rank	HR %	Rank	BB %	Rank	SO %	Rank
Rich Dauer	Runners On	.202	150	.250	154	.280	145	0.00	142	9.18	79	4.08	4
	Bases Empty	.202	150	.274	151	.272	144	1.61	109	8.09	70	2.21	1
Rick Dempsey	Runners On	.305	33	.521	16	.366	49	4.79	29	8.90	87	23.56	151
	Bases Empty	.210	141	.308	142	.328	66	2.05	99	14.41	9	18.34	132
Jim Dwyer	Runners On	.282	64	.476	41	.380	24	3.88	50	13.01	29	11.38	66
	Bases Empty	.223	128	.338	125	.331	60	2.31	92	13.91	13	11.26	50
Wayne Gross	Runners On	.175	154	.275	152	.347	76	2.50	80	20.59	3	18.63	138
	Bases Empty	.270	48	.511	13	.383	9	6.57	5	15.43	5	17.90	126
Lee Lacy	Runners On	.312	28	.407	84	.367	46	1.51	103	8.81	91	17.18	126
	Bases Empty	.280	31	.410	66	.326	74	2.05	100	6.07	111	17.89	125
Fred Lynn	Runners On	.260	97	.450	57	.356	60	6.00	12	13.81	23	17.57	129
	Bases Empty	.266	59	.448	40	.323	78	4.44	41	7.43	81	21.56	146
Eddie Murray	Runners On	.361	3	.647	1	.438	4	6.02	11	13.25	26	9.15	39
	Bases Empty	.243	105	.420	63	.333	54	4.73	36	11.67	24	10.83	46
Floyd Rayford	Runners On	.322	20	.530	14	.329	96	5.37	20	1.30	157	18.18	136
	Bases Empty	.295	16	.514	11	.321	84	4.76	35	3.67	147	18.81	135
Cal Ripken	Runners On	.291	52	.465	46	.360	54	3.68	54	10.47	51	8.72	36
	Bases Empty	.274	44	.472	29	.334	53	4.37	45	8.29	68	10.16	42
Gary Roenicke	Runners On	.260	95	.604	3	.362	53	9.38	1	14.41	19	10.17	52
	Bases Empty	.186	154	.349	117	.327	69	4.65	37	17.31	2	15.38	104
Larry Sheets	Runners On	.274	74	.452	56	.331	92	5.48	19	8.02	107	11.11	62
	Bases Empty	.253	95	.434	51	.317	89	4.95	29	7.54	79	17.09	120
John Shelby	Runners On	.293	--	.520	--	.329	--	5.33	--	4.94	--	16.05	--
	Bases Empty	.277	37	.385	94	.293	122	2.31	92	2.26	157	23.31	154
Alan Wiggins	Runners On	.333	7	.409	83	.392	15	0.00	142	8.33	101	1.85	1
	Bases Empty	.263	68	.322	136	.335	59	0.00	148	8.81	59	6.17	7
Mike Young	Runners On	.296	44	.566	7	.377	29	6.63	8	10.71	45	18.75	140
	Bases Empty	.256	85	.472	28	.325	76	5.91	10	8.57	64	22.14	150
Team Average	Runners On	.284	1	.469	1	.356	1	4.30	1	10.37	2	13.55	
	Bases Empty	.248	10	.401	7	.320	8	3.57	2	9.22	3	15.44	9
League Average	Runners On	.271		.416		.338		2.85		9.26		13.25	
	Bases Empty	.254		.397		.318		2.80		8.14		13.92	

Overall Batting Compared to Late Inning Pressure Situations

		BA	Rank	SA	Rank	OBA	Rank	HR %	Rank	BB %	Rank	SO %	Rank	RDI %	Rank
Rich Dauer	Overall	.202	155	.264	154	.275	148	0.96	129	8.55	73	2.99	1	.200	--
	Pressure	.118	--	.118	--	.118	--	0.00	--	0.00	--	0.00	--	.000	--
Rick Dempsey	Overall	.254	99	.406	88	.345	50	3.31	61	11.90	30	20.71	149	.318	48
	Pressure	.171	149	.293	124	.286	118	2.44	77	14.00	30	24.00	146	.286	--
Jim Dwyer	Overall	.249	106	.399	95	.353	36	3.00	73	13.50	16	11.31	50	.324	43
	Pressure	.344	13	.563	10	.500	2	3.13	56	23.81	2	14.29	82	.455	12
Wayne Gross	Overall	.235	134	.424	69	.369	17	5.07	17	17.42	2	18.18	133	.118	163
	Pressure	.184	143	.316	113	.225	149	2.63	69	5.00	124	20.00	133	.100	155
Lee Lacy	Overall	.293	22	.409	82	.343	52	1.83	105	7.22	103	17.59	124	.262	113
	Pressure	.297	40	.453	44	.378	33	4.69	38	10.81	56	16.22	100	.167	128
Fred Lynn	Overall	.263	78	.449	41	.339	63	5.13	15	10.43	40	19.69	140	.285	88
	Pressure	.231	104	.481	34	.333	73	7.69	11	13.33	35	23.33	143	.214	111
Eddie Murray	Overall	.297	16	.523	4	.383	6	5.32	13	12.41	24	10.04	42	.428	4
	Pressure	.333	15	.682	3	.400	23	9.09	4	10.67	57	8.00	23	.636	1
Floyd Rayford	Overall	.306	9	.521	5	.324	84	5.01	19	2.69	156	18.55	136	.214	143
	Pressure	.268	64	.585	8	.333	73	7.32	12	8.89	79	24.44	149	.250	87
Cal Ripken	Overall	.282	39	.469	25	.347	47	4.05	44	9.33	57	9.47	37	.378	9
	Pressure	.292	43	.528	23	.366	41	6.94	15	10.98	54	9.76	37	.250	87
Gary Roenicke	Overall	.218	151	.458	30	.342	57	6.67	4	16.06	4	13.14	77	.364	19
	Pressure	.043	--	.174	--	.185	--	4.35	--	14.81	--	14.81	--	.167	--
Larry Sheets	Overall	.262	81	.442	49	.323	90	5.18	14	7.76	92	14.40	98	.330	35
	Pressure	.235	102	.412	71	.291	116	5.88	25	7.27	101	20.00	133	.273	78
John Shelby	Overall	.283	38	.434	57	.307	121	3.41	60	3.27	154	20.56	147	.333	31
	Pressure	.200	130	.286	127	.222	150	0.00	113	2.78	143	25.00	150	.250	87
Alan Wiggins	Overall	.285	35	.349	130	.353	38	0.00	154	8.66	68	4.78	2	.339	29
	Pressure	.308	32	.346	94	.438	9	0.00	113	18.18	7	3.03	4	.400	22
Mike Young	Overall	.273	59	.513	11	.348	43	6.22	6	9.52	52	20.63	148	.293	73
	Pressure	.222	114	.426	66	.311	93	5.56	30	11.48	52	18.03	118	.333	55
Team Average	Overall	.263	8	.430	1	.336	3	3.88	1	9.72	3	14.62	12	.303	4
	Pressure	.239	11	.423	1	.323	9	4.66	1	11.08	2	15.29	12	.311	2
League Average	Overall	.261		.406		.327		2.82		8.63		13.62		.287	
	Pressure	.253		.381		.323		2.74		9.11		14.40		.273	

Additional Miscellaneous Batting Comparisons

	Grass Surface BA	Rank	Artificial Surface BA	Rank	Home Games BA	Rank	Road Games BA	Rank	Runners in Scoring Position BA	Rank	Runners in Scoring Pos and Two Outs BA	Rank	Leading Off Inning OBA	Rank	Runners on 3B with less than 2 Outs RDI %	Rank
Rich Dauer	.198	152	.220	--	.178	154	.224	135	.184	--	.182	139	.313	89	.300	155
Rick Dempsey	.257	88	.235	109	.235	122	.273	48	.289	61	.205	128	.330	70	.722	25
Jim Dwyer	.231	135	.342	--	.212	147	.283	28	.362	6	.440	1	.333	59	.538	97
Wayne Gross	.250	104	.171	153	.225	134	.243	112	.200	148	.111	--	.339	54	.333	--
Lee Lacy	.296	25	.268	62	.308	25	.277	41	.313	31	.245	78	.274	128	.742	18
Fred Lynn	.269	62	.238	104	.272	69	.255	90	.240	115	.196	134	.327	75	.739	19
Eddie Murray	.294	28	.312	14	.296	38	.298	12	.370	5	.347	13	.350	41	.794	8
Floyd Rayford	.305	18	.316	--	.322	16	.291	19	.259	98	.278	49	.338	55	.467	132
Cal Ripken	.286	38	.258	70	.289	44	.275	45	.327	17	.273	52	.313	86	.750	13
Gary Roenicke	.233	133	.125	--	.250	99	.183	155	.298	49	.357	10	.286	119	.625	--
Larry Sheets	.254	95	.311	16	.276	61	.247	105	.276	77	.226	104	.313	86	.682	40
John Shelby	.275	53	.417	--	.245	110	.320	5	.317	--	.333	--	.317	82	.400	146
Alan Wiggins	.286	39	.282	--	.253	95	.316	6	.388	3	.421	3	.341	49	.615	62
Mike Young	.286	39	.208	137	.278	59	.269	56	.291	58	.215	115	.328	74	.600	66
Team Average	.265	5	.249	12	.261	8	.265	3	.288	2	.260	4	.317	8	.655	1
League Average	.262		.259		.266		.256		.268		.248		.321		.587	

Pitching vs. Left and Right Handed Batters

		BA	Rank	SA	Rank	OBA	Rank	HR %	Rank	BB %	Rank	SO %	Rank
Don Aase	vs. Lefties	.238	36	.345	32	.306	34	2.38	55	9.04	66	15.43	37
	vs. Righties	.279	100	.403	70	.354	102	1.30	11	10.11	102	21.35	11
Mike Boddicker	vs. Lefties	.294	98	.405	66	.375	103	1.77	35	10.29	84	11.65	78
	vs. Righties	.275	93	.360	36	.342	89	1.46	14	9.38	92	19.53	17
Storm Davis	vs. Lefties	.258	61	.394	60	.346	79	1.67	30	11.92	100	14.60	42
	vs. Righties	.252	58	.355	32	.300	41	1.60	20	6.19	39	9.73	116
Ken Dixon	vs. Lefties	.226	24	.378	50	.310	40	2.68	67	10.76	91	14.17	47
	vs. Righties	.251	56	.413	79	.313	58	4.06	111	7.62	65	17.88	28
Mike Flanagan	vs. Lefties	.306	--	.388	--	.346	--	0.00	--	5.66	--	13.21	--
	vs. Righties	.296	113	.502	126	.353	99	4.81	124	7.67	67	10.74	103
Dennis Martinez	vs. Lefties	.273	75	.459	95	.344	77	3.61	99	10.25	83	9.34	108
	vs. Righties	.305	123	.487	123	.354	102	4.72	120	5.14	21	7.71	128
Tippy Martinez	vs. Lefties	.198	6	.311	18	.250	5	0.94	15	6.72	32	21.01	10
	vs. Righties	.302	121	.469	116	.404	131	4.32	114	15.03	131	11.40	95
Scott McGregor	vs. Lefties	.260	62	.520	122	.286	19	6.78	130	3.76	3	10.22	97
	vs. Righties	.289	109	.456	108	.347	92	3.53	94	8.31	76	9.60	117
Nate Snell	vs. Lefties	.276	78	.376	48	.327	56	1.66	29	7.11	38	6.09	125
	vs. Righties	.245	50	.319	14	.303	47	0.49	5	7.14	49	12.95	80
Sammy Stewart	vs. Lefties	.252	55	.413	68	.367	97	2.61	63	15.52	125	13.00	59
	vs. Righties	.240	41	.362	38	.304	48	3.66	101	8.21	74	14.64	57
Team Average	vs. Lefties	.263	8	.410	8	.339	11	2.60	4	10.21	13	12.40	8
	vs. Righties	.275	14	.420	12	.338	12	3.18	13	8.32	10	13.19	10
League Average	vs. Lefties	.265		.408		.333		2.74		9.21		12.94	
	vs. Righties	.259		.404		.322		2.88		8.19		14.14	

Pitching with Runners on Base and Bases Empty

		BA	Rank	SA	Rank	OBA	Rank	HR %	Rank	BB %	Rank	SO %	Rank
Don Aase	Runners On	.290	96	.426	81	.366	106	2.96	78	10.55	93	20.10	7
	Bases Empty	.222	22	.314	12	.287	30	0.65	2	8.38	71	16.17	34
Mike Boddicker	Runners On	.270	68	.336	18	.347	81	0.79	8	10.11	88	14.25	48
	Bases Empty	.300	121	.430	94	.373	118	2.40	54	9.70	94	15.73	39
Storm Davis	Runners On	.303	108	.437	87	.378	117	2.11	47	10.74	97	11.96	79
	Bases Empty	.221	21	.332	20	.285	28	1.29	14	8.25	67	12.74	72
Ken Dixon	Runners On	.261	53	.416	74	.352	85	3.10	84	12.27	112	14.50	45
	Bases Empty	.223	23	.381	48	.285	26	3.41	91	7.49	59	16.67	33
Mike Flanagan	Runners On	.301	107	.545	127	.325	44	6.29	131	3.16	2	11.39	90
	Bases Empty	.294	116	.442	100	.371	115	2.54	60	10.41	101	10.86	94
Dennis Martinez	Runners On	.299	103	.506	120	.360	96	4.80	123	9.55	80	6.05	132
	Bases Empty	.280	104	.451	105	.341	93	3.68	104	6.95	48	10.32	108
Tippy Martinez	Runners On	.271	70	.393	62	.346	79	2.86	73	10.91	98	15.15	39
	Bases Empty	.250	59	.422	89	.347	94	3.13	84	12.93	122	14.97	47
Scott McGregor	Runners On	.283	87	.472	103	.341	72	3.77	101	8.70	59	10.87	97
	Bases Empty	.282	105	.469	111	.329	80	4.56	120	6.40	37	8.91	120
Nate Snell	Runners On	.275	76	.371	37	.340	71	1.12	16	8.96	64	11.94	80
	Bases Empty	.246	54	.324	16	.291	34	0.97	7	5.45	20	7.73	127
Sammy Stewart	Runners On	.262	55	.380	49	.355	89	2.53	56	12.85	117	13.89	55
	Bases Empty	.230	30	.393	63	.316	66	3.77	108	10.78	108	13.75	60
Team Average	Runners On	.283	10	.429	10	.355	12	2.91	9	10.21	11	12.96	9
	Bases Empty	.259	10	.406	9	.325	10	2.92	9	8.34	9	12.72	11
League Average	Runners On	.271		.416		.338		2.85		9.26		13.25	
	Bases Empty	.254		.397		.318		2.80		8.14		13.92	

Overall Pitching Compared to Late Inning Pressure Situations

		BA	Rank	SA	Rank	OBA	Rank	HR %	Rank	BB %	Rank	SO %	Rank
Don Aase	Overall	.258	62	.373	36	.330	69	1.86	26	9.56	87	18.31	13
	Pressure	.244	49	.335	35	.331	62	1.44	35	11.48	86	14.75	49
Mike Boddicker	Overall	.286	106	.385	47	.361	111	1.64	20	9.90	93	15.02	44
	Pressure	.247	52	.438	92	.373	96	5.62	124	15.52	120	13.79	57
Storm Davis	Overall	.256	58	.376	39	.325	61	1.63	19	9.33	82	12.40	78
	Pressure	.211	20	.316	23	.244	8	2.63	67	4.65	13	13.95	54
Ken Dixon	Overall	.237	23	.394	52	.311	45	3.29	94	9.37	84	15.81	30
	Pressure	.295	100	.364	49	.380	102	0.00	1	11.76	89	9.80	98
Mike Flanagan	Overall	.297	114	.485	123	.352	99	4.12	118	7.39	47	11.08	100
	Pressure	.286	90	.429	88	.286	23	2.86	79	0.00	1	8.33	111
Dennis Martinez	Overall	.288	109	.472	119	.349	91	4.11	117	7.98	56	8.62	124
	Pressure	.288	95	.424	82	.328	60	1.69	45	6.25	28	10.94	90
Tippy Martinez	Overall	.261	71	.407	66	.346	90	2.99	78	11.86	113	15.06	42
	Pressure	.235	41	.407	75	.347	79	3.70	97	14.58	116	12.50	70
Scott McGregor	Overall	.283	101	.470	116	.334	78	4.25	121	7.35	46	9.73	118
	Pressure	.306	108	.417	81	.359	87	1.39	32	7.23	37	9.64	101
Nate Snell	Overall	.260	67	.345	19	.314	46	1.04	3	7.13	39	9.74	117
	Pressure	.262	66	.328	29	.328	61	1.64	42	8.82	55	16.18	37
Sammy Stewart	Overall	.246	38	.387	49	.336	79	3.15	89	11.85	111	13.82	55
	Pressure	.271	77	.382	64	.355	84	2.78	76	11.05	82	13.95	54
Team Average	Overall	.270	12	.416	10	.338	12	2.91	7	9.19	12	12.83	9
	Pressure	.264	10	.381	6	.343	11	2.39	5	10.52	11	13.07	10
League Average	Overall	.261		.406		.327		2.82		8.63		13.62	
	Pressure	.258		.392		.332		2.71		9.52		14.05	

Additional Miscellaneous Pitching Comparisons

	Grass Surface		Artificial Surface		Home Games		Road Games		Runners in Scoring Position		Runners in Scoring Pos and Two Outs		Leading Off Inning	
	BA	Rank	BA	Rank	BA	Rank	BA	Rank	BA	Rank	BA	Rank	OBA	Rank
Don Aase	.253	56	.286	93	.252	65	.267	73	.308	108	.380	129	.333	80
Mike Boddicker	.280	94	.319	118	.270	89	.301	110	.237	30	.194	28	.370	115
Storm Davis	.250	48	.295	102	.234	26	.278	87	.329	120	.341	122	.267	14
Ken Dixon	.247	43	.188	7	.246	49	.221	15	.246	42	.194	26	.277	23
Mike Flanagan	.302	112	.241	--	.328	130	.277	86	.269	70	.211	38	.330	77
Dennis Martinez	.288	105	.283	89	.301	116	.278	88	.287	92	.288	100	.316	64
Tippy Martinez	.262	73	.257	--	.248	53	.279	89	.296	97	.310	114	.317	65
Scott McGregor	.272	86	.333	123	.281	101	.284	93	.287	91	.224	52	.344	93
Nate Snell	.254	60	.293	101	.254	68	.266	71	.301	100	.233	59	.264	12
Sammy Stewart	.242	37	.273	77	.239	38	.255	48	.270	73	.276	91	.377	118
Team Average	.267	9	.284	12	.264	10	.275	12	.283	11	.261	10	.322	7
League Average	.262		.259		.256		.266		.268		.248		.321	

BOSTON RED SOX

Imagine, if you will, a natural habitat exhibit at a major metropolitan zoo. Three foxes, foiled in their attempt to turn the duck in the pond into an impromptu lunch, retreat into the woods to formulate a new plan. They huddle for a minute, and map out an unspoken football chalkboard of Xs and Os. Having settled on a game plan, the foxes confidently approach the pond, splash into the water, and swim the exact same patterns as they had last time. The duck again makes all the right moves at the right moments, and again, foiled in their attempt to turn the duck in the pond into an impromptu lunch, the foxes retreat into the woods. . . .

Time after time, day after day, year after year. Same foxes, same duck, same result: duck wins, no lunch. But New Englanders need not go to the zoo to see this little drama unfold. Pastoral Fenway Park has staged the same play every summer for decades. The chalkboard discussion goes something like this:

"Well, we came pretty close last season, and we scored a lot of runs, but we could sure use some pitching."

"But we've got the Green Monster down the left-field line. Let's go for one more power hitter."

"Okay. Let's break for an impromptu lunch."

Think about it for a moment. Can you remember the last state-of-the-art starting pitcher the Red Sox traded for? Five years ago, the Sox traded for an already past his peak Frank Tanana in a shotgun trade for Fred Lynn, who held the threat of impending free agency over the heads of the front office. Before that, Boston packaged some loose parts for Dennis Eckersley (in 1978) and Ferguson Jenkins (in 1975). But in neither case did Boston fortify its pitching staff by sacrificing offense. The same can be said of the signings of free agents Mike Torrez and Steve Renko, who helped, but not enough. So the recent trades—of John Tudor for Mike Easler, Dennis Eckersley for Bill Buckner, and Bob Ojeda for a pair of minor-league pitchers and change—present two questions: Does a powerful lineup make a team more effective in a hitters' park like Fenway than in a typical stadium? And have the Sox overdosed on power, with the consequent imbalance between batting and pitching doing more harm than good? The following table contains just about all the information needed to answer those questions:

Year	Home Runs				Games Won		
	Own	Opp.	Diff.	Home	Road	Total	Diff.
1961	112	157	−45	50	26	76	+24
1962	146	159	−13	39	37	76	+2
1963	171	152	+19	44	32	76	+12
1964	186	178	+8	45	27	72	+18
1965	165	158	+7	34	28	62	+6
1966	145	164	−19	40	32	72	+8
1967	158	142	+16	49	43	92	+6
1968	125	115	+10	46	40	86	+6
1969	197	155	+42	46	41	87	+5
1970	203	156	+47	52	35	87	+17
1971	161	136	+25	47	38	85	+9
1972	124	101	+23	52	33	85	+19
1973	147	158	−11	48	41	89	+7
1974	109	126	−17	46	38	84	+8
1975	134	145	−11	47	48	95	−1
1976	134	109	+25	46	37	83	+9
1977	213	158	+55	51	46	97	+5
1978	172	137	+35	59	40	99	+19
1979	194	133	+61	51	40	91	+11
1980	162	129	+33	36	47	83	−11
1981	90	90	—	30	29	59	+1
1982	136	155	−19	49	40	89	+9
1983	142	158	−16	38	40	78	−2
1984	181	141	+40	41	45	86	−4
1985	162	130	+32	43	38	81	+5
Totals	3869	3542	+327	1129	941	2070	+188
Averages	157	144	+13	46	38	84	+8

(Averages treat the strike-shortened 1981 season as though it were two-thirds of a season.)

Let's assume that a powerful home-run hitting team plays better in a small home-run hitters' park like Fenway Park than in a cavernous place like Cleveland Stadium. If our assumption is correct, then the difference between the Red Sox' home and road performance should grow as their power increases. The years in which Boston played significantly better at home than on the road correspond pretty well to the years in which they hit more home runs than their average. So it does seem that the Boston front office has been justified in trying to take advantage of their hitters' stadium with an emphasis on home-run hitters. But has it been an overemphasis?

Clearly, there has been a tendency for the Red Sox to stretch the gap between their home and road records as their power increases—

despite the imbalance in 1961, when Boston had their lowest relative home run total of the quarter-century and their *greatest* home-road differential. But the tendency is greater if you consider not only the number of home runs hit by the Red Sox, but the number hit by their opponents as well. The column which lists the difference between those two totals corresponds much more closely to the difference between Boston's home and road records than the Red Sox' home-run totals alone. And that makes a lot of sense: If power is an important ingredient in winning at Fenway Park, then preventing the opposition's home runs must be as important as hitting your own.

A comparison of the home-run totals for Boston and their opponents leaves little doubt that Boston has stressed offense, frequently at the expense of their pitching. It is difficult to judge Boston's power relative to the rest of the American League precisely because they play half their games each season in Fenway Park. But if we evaluate Red Sox batters and pitchers of the past 25 seasons based on road-game totals alone, negating the effect of the home park, we can place them properly within the context of the league in general. And during that quarter of a century, Boston batters have outslugged the league (that is, hit more home runs than the league average) *in road games* in 18 of 25 seasons. But Red Sox pitchers have allowed fewer than the league average only eight times. So the question remains: Have the Red Sox gained more from their emphasis on offense than they have lost by their corresponding de-emphasis of pitching? And the startling answer for all you Sox Trashers out there is yes!

Over the past 25 years, Boston's overall record has a much stronger correlation to their own home-run totals (relative to the league) than to their opponents' totals. Let's spell it out: The Red Sox' power plays—trades over the last five years for Tony Armas, Mike Easler, and Bill Buckner—have gained them more at Fenway Park than they have cost them on the road. This suggests that the law of diminishing returns would not apply to Boston's home-run total until they had saturated their entire lineup with Palookas at every position—and that those foxes may yet lunch on duck soup!

Two things should be noted. First, despite the trades of Tudor and Eckersley, last season's Boston team threw fewer home-run balls (130) than any pitching staff in the American League except that of the World Champion Kansas City Royals (103). Boston pitching staffs on the whole have been subpar over the past 25 years, but last season's staff was among their best. And second, last season was unusual in another respect: More home runs were hit in Red Sox road games than in games at Fenway Park for only the third time in the last 20 years, and by the largest margin since 1936. Those two items may not necessarily be unrelated, and it will be interesting to watch during the 1986 season whether these unusual situations recur. A recurrence could indicate that after nearly three-quarters of a century, pitchers have learned how to work in Fenway Park, negating the power advantage we've just described. But we wouldn't bet on it.

Life in the Slow Lane

The emphasis on power throughout Red Sox history has sapped not only their pitching, but also their speed. Always playing for the big inning, Boston has snubbed run-building plays like sacrifice bunts and stolen bases with a Goliath-like arrogance. The Sox have not led the majors in bunts since 1946 (when they won the American League pennant), or in steals since 1935. In fact, Boston has had the fewest stolen bases in the American League in five of the last seven seasons.

The purpose here is not to condemn Boston for decades-old strategies which are totally appropriate to their ballpark. Rather, we'd like to analyze with some new statistics whether the Sox' lack

of base-running aggressiveness has had a ripple effect throughout other areas of play, two in particular. First, does Boston go first-to-third on singles less frequently than a typical team? And second, why does Boston ground into so many double plays?

The Red Sox have been roundly criticized over the past few seasons for playing baseball on the local track. Rarely, it is said, do Red Sox base-runners take an extra base on a single, score from first on a double, or break up a double play on a hit-and-run ground out. The following table shows the number of singles which each American League team hit last season with a runner on first, and the number of times that runner reached third safely on the hit. (The records are divided into winning-or-tied situations and losing situations; the score has a dramatic impact on base-running strategy.)

Team	Winning or Tied				Losing			
	No.	Adv.	Pct.	Rank	No.	Adv.	Pct.	Rank
Baltimore	207	66	.319	11	113	20	.177	14
Boston	256	88	.344	9	133	35	.263	12
California	190	74	.389	2	111	30	.270	11
Chicago	183	70	.383	5	88	31	.352	4
Cleveland	200	58	.290	13	152	46	.303	7
Detroit	182	64	.352	7	120	33	.275	9T
Kansas City	188	57	.303	12	105	33	.314	5
Milwaukee	214	72	.336	10	145	44	.303	6
Minnesota	200	74	.370	6	120	33	.275	9T
New York	223	100	.448	1	96	37	.385	2
Oakland	186	65	.349	8	151	54	.358	3
Seattle	164	47	.287	14	125	27	.216	13
Texas	180	69	.383	4	128	36	.281	8
Toronto	208	81	.389	3	79	31	.392	1

Get ready to take that smug smile off your face. While Boston ranked near the bottom of the league last season in taking third base on singles, the Red Sox' lowly 1985 ranking is *not* typical of their performance over the past ten years. Here is where the Sox ranked among American League teams in those categories each year since 1976, with an average rank of 5th in a 14-team league:

Winning/Tied	1985	1984	1983	1982	1981	1980	1979	1978	1977	1976
Percentage	.344	.409	.327	.357	.398	.367	.358	.420	.445	.406
Rank	9	2	8	9	4	7	7	2	2	3

Losing	1985	1984	1983	1982	1981	1980	1979	1978	1977	1976
Percentage	.263	.336	.301	.277	.330	.319	.333	.310	.407	.324
Rank	12	2	6	9	6	5	2	3	2	3

In general, the Don Zimmer–managed teams (mid-1976 to mid-1980) appear to have been more aggressive on the bases than Ralph Houk's teams (1981–84). Last season's Red Sox, the most conservative of the past ten, may have been responding to the style of current manager John McNamara, whose past teams (the Angels, Reds, and Padres) also ranked consistently near the bottoms of their leagues. But the picture is not nearly what we expected to find, as is so often the case when we find a new way to look at an old chestnut of a topic.

The other area we can now look at is that of double-play ground outs. The American League has compiled records on double-play ground outs since 1940. In 1954, Boston centerfielder Jackie Jensen set a league record by grounding into 32 double plays. The record stood for 30 years; in 1984, Jim Rice broke the mark. And last season he broke it again.

In 1982, the Red Sox set an all-time major-league record with a team total of 171 GIDPs. The next season, they equalled their own record. Without a doubt, the Boston Red Sox of the 1980s are to double plays what the 1930s New York Yankees were to home runs. But why? The following figures clearly indicate that, on the whole, the Red Sox are victims of circumstances, though not necessarily ones beyond their control.

The table below lists the 1985 American League individual leaders in GIDP opportunities: the number of times a batter came to the plate with a runner on first base and less than two out. Notice that four of the league's top five are from the Red Sox, and that among those four players only Wade Boggs is a prolific ground-ball hitter. Remember, the average ground out-to-air out ratio (G/A) in the American League is 1.09.

Player, Team	Opp.	GIDP	Pct.	G/A
Mattingly, N.Y.	173	15	8.7	0.85
Buckner, Bos.	171	16	9.4	0.72
Rice, Bos.	171	35	20.5	1.19
Boggs, Bos.	164	20	12.2	1.56
Evans, Bos.	161	16	9.9	1.02

What was true for the individual Red Sox was also true for the team as a whole. While the Red Sox did lead the league last year in GIDPs, they also led in GIDP opportunities, and by a substantial margin. And their ratio of GIDPs to opportunities was actually lower than that of the World Champion Royals. (As it happens, the team that had the second-highest total of opportunities also had the second-lowest percentage of GIDPs. Sorry, New England, but that team was the Yankees.)

	Opp.	GIDP	Pct.
Seattle	1162	147	12.7
Milwaukee	1168	145	12.4
Kansas City	1028	125	12.2
Boston	1351	164	12.1
Texas	1127	136	12.1
Cleveland	1153	139	12.0
California	1205	138	11.6
Baltimore	1166	132	11.3
Chicago	1066	119	11.0
Oakland	1160	128	11.0
Toronto	1109	121	10.9
Minnesota	1166	117	10.0
New York	1217	119	9.8
Detroit	1074	81	7.5

Can the Red Sox' perennially high GIDP totals be explained? Start with the fact that, year after year, the Sox have a lot of runners on base. They don't steal bases or advance on bunts, so those runners remain in place. And they play in a park that promotes double plays (see the California Angels essay). Under those conditions, it apparently doesn't take much to set records. Can they be explained away? No, of course not. But they should be accepted as part of the price of playing in Fenway Park. Really, folks, their GIDP performance isn't as bad as you think.

WON-LOST RECORD BY STARTING POSITION

BOSTON 81-81	C	1B	2B	3B	SS	LF	CF	RF	P	DH	Leadoff	Relief	Starts
Tony Armas	-	-	-	-	-	4-4	35-34	2-0	-	4-14	-	-	45-52
Marty Barrett	-	-	74-75	-	-	-	-	-	-	-	2-5	-	74-75
Wade Boggs	-	-	-	80-79	-	-	-	-	-	-	21-25	-	80-79
Dennis Boyd	-	-	-	-	-	-	-	-	19-16	-	-	-	19-16
Mike Brown	-	-	-	-	-	-	-	-	0-1	-	-	0-1	0-1
Bill Buckner	-	80-81	-	-	-	-	-	-	-	-	1-4	-	80-81
Mark Clear	-	-	-	-	-	-	-	-	-	-	-	9-32	-
Roger Clemens	-	-	-	-	-	-	-	-	8-7	-	-	-	8-7
Steve Crawford	-	-	-	-	-	-	-	-	1-0	-	-	25-18	1-0
Jim Dorsey	-	-	-	-	-	-	-	-	0-1	-	-	0-1	0-1
Mike Easler	-	-	-	-	-	11-7	-	1-1	-	66-63	-	-	78-71
Dwight Evans	-	-	-	-	-	-	-	74-77	-	4-3	38-34	-	78-80
Rich Gedman	67-62	-	-	-	-	-	-	-	-	-	-	-	67-62
Mike Greenwell	-	-	-	-	-	0-4	-	1-1	-	-	-	-	1-5
Jackie Gutierrez	-	-	-	-	31-51	-	-	-	-	-	-	-	31-51
Glenn Hoffman	-	-	0-1	1-0	50-30	-	-	-	-	-	-	-	51-31
Bruce Hurst	-	-	-	-	-	-	-	-	14-17	-	-	1-3	14-17
Ed Jurak	-	-	-	0-2	-	-	-	-	-	-	-	-	0-2
Bruce Kison	-	-	-	-	-	-	-	-	5-4	-	-	4-9	5-4
Tim Lollar	-	-	-	-	-	-	-	-	5-5	-	-	3-3	5-5
Steve Lyons	-	-	-	-	-	44-43	-	-	-	-	15-11	-	44-43
Tom McCarthy	-	-	-	-	-	-	-	-	-	-	-	0-3	-
Rick Miller	-	-	-	-	-	-	2-0	-	-	-	-	-	2-0
Charlie Mitchell	-	-	-	-	-	-	-	-	-	-	-	0-2	-
Reid Nichols	-	-	-	-	-	-	2-4	0-1	-	-	2-1	-	2-5
Al Nipper	-	-	-	-	-	-	12-13	-	-	-	-	-	12-13
Bob Ojeda	-	-	-	-	-	-	-	-	9-12	-	-	9-8	9-12
Jim Rice	-	-	-	-	-	64-65	-	-	-	6-1	-	-	70-66
Kevin Romine	-	-	-	-	-	2-1	-	1-1	-	-	2-1	-	3-2
Dave Sax	5-6	-	-	-	-	-	-	-	-	-	-	-	5-6
Jeff Sellers	-	-	-	-	-	-	-	-	3-1	-	-	-	3-1
Bob Stanley	-	-	-	-	-	-	-	-	-	-	-	25-23	-
Dave Stapleton	-	1-0	7-5	-	-	-	-	-	-	1-0	-	-	9-5
Marc Sullivan	9-13	-	-	-	-	-	-	-	-	-	-	-	9-13
Mike Trujillo	-	-	-	-	-	-	-	-	4-3	-	-	7-13	4-3
Rob Woodward	-	-	-	-	-	-	-	-	1-1	-	-	0-3	1-1

Batting vs. Left and Right Handed Pitchers

		BA	Rank	SA	Rank	OBA	Rank	HR %	Rank	BB %	Rank	SO %	Rank
Tony Armas	vs. Lefties	.336	7	.636	3	.377	24	6.43	15	6.62	112	15.89	112
	vs. Righties	.224	131	.445	48	.251	151	5.71	11	3.09	153	25.48	156
Marty Barrett	vs. Lefties	.274	69	.341	128	.356	51	0.00	131	11.40	37	3.63	4
	vs. Righties	.262	73	.343	123	.326	79	1.35	115	8.19	81	10.36	48
Wade Boggs	vs. Lefties	.347	4	.441	66	.418	5	0.94	121	10.00	57	8.75	31
	vs. Righties	.377	1	.495	16	.465	1	1.36	114	13.90	12	7.72	25
Bill Buckner	vs. Lefties	.291	48	.404	85	.311	112	1.74	96	3.29	148	4.94	9
	vs. Righties	.302	15	.470	31	.333	65	2.71	82	4.62	137	5.04	2
Mike Easler	vs. Lefties	.277	65	.364	113	.345	68	1.16	115	8.76	73	26.80	155
	vs. Righties	.256	86	.433	58	.316	93	3.54	55	8.24	79	17.62	125
Dwight Evans	vs. Lefties	.271	72	.518	23	.416	7	7.06	8	19.63	3	12.15	72
	vs. Righties	.260	81	.430	62	.363	26	3.80	47	13.58	13	14.91	100
Rich Gedman	vs. Lefties	.244	111	.348	124	.299	124	1.48	101	6.76	109	18.24	128
	vs. Righties	.314	6	.534	6	.384	8	4.41	33	9.80	49	12.75	71
Jackie Gutierrez	vs. Lefties	.206	148	.278	146	.235	153	0.00	131	3.77	144	11.32	56
	vs. Righties	.225	130	.270	150	.258	148	1.12	124	4.19	141	13.09	77
Glenn Hoffman	vs. Lefties	.304	35	.519	22	.349	62	5.06	31	6.74	110	11.24	53
	vs. Righties	.265	66	.375	95	.341	56	1.00	130	8.19	82	12.93	73
Steve Lyons	vs. Lefties	.269	75	.358	116	.338	79	1.49	100	9.46	62	18.92	131
	vs. Righties	.263	70	.359	112	.318	89	1.32	117	7.46	92	14.93	101
Jim Rice	vs. Lefties	.258	88	.470	43	.363	40	4.64	42	14.53	16	8.94	33
	vs. Righties	.304	13	.494	17	.343	54	5.06	21	5.83	121	13.75	84
Team Average	vs. Lefties	.283	1	.429	3	.352	1	2.73	9	9.49	5	12.31	3
	vs. Righties	.282	1	.429	2	.344	1	2.88	7	8.42	6	12.89	5
League Average	vs. Lefties	.266		.416		.333		2.91		8.95		13.77	
	vs. Righties	.259		.401		.324		2.78		8.49		13.56	

Batting with Runners on Base and Bases Empty

		BA	Rank	SA	Rank	OBA	Rank	HR %	Rank	BB %	Rank	SO %	Rank
Tony Armas	Runners On	.232	138	.409	81	.269	148	4.42	35	5.58	136	22.84	150
	Bases Empty	.294	19	.608	1	.324	77	7.35	2	3.29	152	21.13	143
Marty Barrett	Runners On	.251	117	.325	131	.332	90	0.87	125	10.11	57	7.58	25
	Bases Empty	.277	36	.356	114	.338	47	0.99	124	8.46	66	8.76	31
Wade Boggs	Runners On	.387	1	.493	29	.476	2	0.70	133	14.45	18	7.08	20
	Bases Empty	.352	1	.466	35	.430	1	1.63	108	11.22	26	8.83	33
Bill Buckner	Runners On	.330	9	.495	27	.357	58	3.30	62	4.92	142	4.37	6
	Bases Empty	.268	57	.400	78	.293	123	1.47	114	3.40	150	5.67	3
Mike Easler	Runners On	.258	99	.426	73	.321	106	2.46	81	9.03	82	18.77	141
	Bases Empty	.265	61	.401	77	.328	65	3.09	68	7.91	73	21.75	147
Dwight Evans	Runners On	.258	100	.422	74	.374	35	3.64	55	15.38	14	13.91	97
	Bases Empty	.266	60	.480	23	.382	10	5.56	15	15.27	6	14.29	84
Rich Gedman	Runners On	.317	25	.491	31	.393	14	2.17	87	10.94	43	13.21	87
	Bases Empty	.276	41	.478	25	.333	54	4.85	31	7.22	90	15.12	96
Jackie Gutierrez	Runners On	.168	156	.226	155	.190	158	0.73	132	2.65	153	15.23	108
	Bases Empty	.268	54	.319	138	.308	101	0.72	136	5.48	125	9.59	37
Glenn Hoffman	Runners On	.229	141	.328	130	.293	140	0.76	130	7.05	116	13.46	92
	Bases Empty	.318	6	.493	17	.388	60	3.38	60	8.48	65	11.52	52
Steve Lyons	Runners On	.253	111	.342	126	.316	111	1.90	93	8.94	85	16.20	118
	Bases Empty	.272	46	.371	103	.326	72	0.94	127	6.96	96	15.22	101
Jim Rice	Runners On	.294	48	.448	58	.351	69	3.34	60	8.85	89	12.68	79
	Bases Empty	.287	26	.534	7	.346	30	6.88	4	7.81	75	11.90	56
Team Average	Runners On	.282	2	.417	8	.348	4	2.35	12	9.35	5	12.41	3
	Bases Empty	.283	1	.439	1	.345	1	3.25	3	8.21	6	12.99	3
League Average	Runners On	.271		.416		.338		2.85		9.26		13.25	
	Bases Empty	.254		.397		.318		2.80		8.14		13.92	

Overall Batting Compared to Late Inning Pressure Situations

		BA	Rank	SA	Rank	OBA	Rank	HR %	Rank	BB %	Rank	SO %	Rank	RDI %	Rank
Tony Armas	Overall	.265	74	.514	9	.298	134	5.97	8	4.39	147	21.95	150	.255	114
	Pressure	.194	135	.274	135	.194	156	1.61	97	0.00	154	25.81	154	.222	104
Marty Barrett	Overall	.266	70	.343	133	.336	64	0.94	132	9.21	64	8.22	26	.263	110
	Pressure	.253	81	.316	112	.344	60	0.00	113	12.09	43	10.99	50	.100	155
Wade Boggs	Overall	.368	1	.478	22	.450	1	1.23	122	12.66	20	8.05	24	.372	14
	Pressure	.395	3	.420	65	.495	4	0.00	113	16.00	16	5.00	10	.226	103
Bill Buckner	Overall	.299	14	.447	44	.325	82	2.38	90	4.17	148	5.01	4	.370	17
	Pressure	.333	15	.529	22	.359	47	3.45	52	4.26	132	3.19	6	.353	48
Mike Easler	Overall	.262	80	.412	79	.325	83	2.82	77	8.40	77	20.44	145	.250	119
	Pressure	.241	92	.310	114	.302	100	1.15	111	8.33	84	25.00	150	.118	145
Dwight Evans	Overall	.263	79	.454	34	.378	9	4.70	30	15.32	6	14.11	88	.236	129
	Pressure	.225	112	.483	33	.336	72	7.87	9	13.08	37	14.95	89	.154	135
Rich Gedman	Overall	.295	18	.484	19	.362	24	3.61	53	8.99	67	14.21	93	.344	25
	Pressure	.362	6	.551	14	.457	5	4.35	40	14.29	28	14.29	82	.500	7
Jackie Gutierrez	Overall	.218	150	.273	152	.250	156	0.73	136	4.04	150	12.46	64	.175	160
	Pressure	.172	148	.172	155	.226	148	0.00	113	6.06	116	15.15	90	.200	117
Glenn Hoffman	Overall	.276	49	.416	76	.343	53	2.15	99	7.79	91	12.46	65	.287	84
	Pressure	.282	51	.436	52	.364	44	2.56	71	8.70	81	15.22	92	.400	22
Steve Lyons	Overall	.264	75	.358	120	.322	94	1.35	114	7.82	90	15.65	109	.204	152
	Pressure	.254	79	.356	89	.343	62	1.69	95	11.76	46	11.76	57	.353	48
Rick Miller	Overall	.333	--	.378	--	.392	--	0.00	--	9.80	--	11.76	--	.400	--
	Pressure	.200	--	.250	--	.273	--	0.00	--	9.09	--	13.64	--	.182	122
Jim Rice	Overall	.291	23	.487	15	.349	42	4.95	23	8.39	78	12.34	61	.330	34
	Pressure	.263	68	.526	24	.298	108	7.89	7	5.95	117	19.05	128	.458	11
Team Average	Overall	.282	1	.429	2	.347	1	2.83	6	8.75	6	12.71	3	.289	8
	Pressure	.275	1	.417	3	.345	1	3.16	4	9.34	6	14.01	8	.255	11
League Average	Overall	.261		.406		.327		2.82		8.63		13.62		.287	
	Pressure	.253		.381		.323		2.74		9.11		14.40		.273	

Additional Miscellaneous Batting Comparisons

	Grass Surface BA	Rank	Artificial Surface BA	Rank	Home Games BA	Rank	Road Games BA	Rank	Runners in Scoring Position BA	Rank	Runners in Scoring Pos and Two Outs BA	Rank	Leading Off Inning OBA	Rank	Runners on 3B with less than 2 Outs RDI %	Rank
Tony Armas	.269	63	.246	88	.289	45	.245	107	.274	82	.250	68	.344	46	.500	106
Marty Barrett	.278	51	.202	140	.275	64	.257	85	.262	93	.274	50	.372	23	.484	124
Wade Boggs	.363	1	.389	1	.418	1	.322	4	.392	2	.373	7	.468	1	.677	42
Bill Buckner	.302	22	.282	48	.299	35	.299	10	.320	22	.292	42	.295	114	.735	21
Mike Easler	.259	87	.278	51	.249	105	.275	46	.248	111	.211	122	.347	44	.581	79
Dwight Evans	.267	71	.240	98	.277	60	.249	99	.177	153	.211	121	.377	16	.500	106
Rich Gedman	.308	12	.217	129	.335	8	.256	87	.317	25	.308	33	.315	83	.519	103
Jackie Gutierrez	.237	127	.137	157	.214	146	.222	138	.099	158	.079	157	.313	86	.421	144
Glenn Hoffman	.284	42	.233	113	.256	90	.293	16	.260	96	.250	68	.373	19	.563	86
Steve Lyons	.267	69	.245	89	.264	80	.264	71	.283	67	.250	68	.305	101	.500	106
Jim Rice	.304	20	.224	125	.350	5	.232	129	.341	10	.328	22	.383	13	.551	92
Team Average	.288	1	.251	10	.301	1	.265	4	.280	4	.260	3	.356	1	.557	13
League Average	.262		.259		.266		.256		.268		.248		.321		.587	

Pitching vs. Left and Right Handed Batters

		BA	Rank	SA	Rank	OBA	Rank	HR %	Rank	BB %	Rank	SO %	Rank
Dennis Boyd	vs. Lefties	.231	29	.334	26	.272	10	1.70	31	4.95	13	14.22	46
	vs. Righties	.300	119	.478	120	.349	95	3.51	91	7.11	48	12.85	81
Mark Clear	vs. Lefties	.244	42	.256	2	.437	130	0.00	1	24.37	131	22.69	8
	vs. Righties	.211	11	.289	6	.348	94	0.88	6	15.00	130	20.00	15
Roger Clemens	vs. Lefties	.248	47	.297	13	.308	35	0.50	5	8.14	50	14.93	38
	vs. Righties	.204	7	.302	11	.297	37	2.47	50	10.22	103	22.04	7
Steve Crawford	vs. Lefties	.301	103	.421	73	.353	86	1.09	19	7.80	45	12.68	62
	vs. Righties	.276	94	.397	62	.321	65	1.72	25	6.35	43	16.93	35
Bruce Hurst	vs. Lefties	.281	84	.425	77	.337	69	3.27	92	7.19	39	23.35	7
	vs. Righties	.271	88	.442	96	.325	73	3.53	93	7.20	55	18.61	25
Bruce Kison	vs. Lefties	.332	129	.519	121	.403	126	3.21	89	10.85	93	9.43	107
	vs. Righties	.211	11	.298	10	.251	6	1.75	26	4.84	14	19.35	18
Tim Lollar	vs. Lefties	.208	10	.342	30	.309	39	2.50	59	12.14	101	24.29	4
	vs. Righties	.261	74	.450	103	.375	124	3.64	98	15.31	132	13.42	71
Al Nipper	vs. Lefties	.274	76	.421	74	.378	105	2.68	66	13.64	116	8.81	110
	vs. Righties	.238	40	.371	43	.322	67	1.90	34	9.42	93	14.96	55
Bob Ojeda	vs. Lefties	.315	119	.449	92	.346	78	1.57	28	4.48	7	18.66	18
	vs. Righties	.262	75	.383	49	.322	66	1.87	31	7.82	70	14.34	59
Bob Stanley	vs. Lefties	.248	50	.354	37	.324	53	2.48	58	10.75	90	12.37	69
	vs. Righties	.225	28	.356	33	.279	19	1.88	32	5.75	32	13.22	76
Mike Trujillo	vs. Lefties	.306	108	.428	79	.361	93	1.16	21	8.38	54	6.28	123
	vs. Righties	.333	130	.452	104	.369	122	2.82	69	3.72	5	3.72	133
Team Average	vs. Lefties	.268	9	.388	4	.337	8	1.93	1	9.33	8	13.41	7
	vs. Righties	.263	9	.403	6	.326	9	2.59	3	8.06	8	15.37	4
League Average	vs. Lefties	.265		.408		.333		2.74		9.21		12.94	
	vs. Righties	.259		.404		.322		2.88		8.19		14.14	

Pitching with Runners on Base and Bases Empty

		BA	Rank	SA	Rank	OBA	Rank	HR %	Rank	BB %	Rank	SO %	Rank
Dennis Boyd	Runners On	.266	61	.414	73	.294	21	2.87	74	3.96	5	13.00	72
	Bases Empty	.258	76	.386	53	.314	61	2.23	43	7.23	53	14.01	53
Mark Clear	Runners On	.224	17	.288	3	.389	123	0.80	9	18.90	132	21.34	6
	Bases Empty	.227	--	.253	--	.389	--	0.00	--	20.00	--	21.05	--
Roger Clemens	Runners On	.218	13	.317	9	.294	20	2.11	47	9.94	85	19.88	9
	Bases Empty	.234	37	.288	8	.309	52	0.90	6	8.54	73	17.07	29
Steve Crawford	Runners On	.304	112	.418	76	.364	104	0.54	3	8.96	65	13.68	60
	Bases Empty	.272	94	.399	67	.308	51	2.31	48	4.95	17	15.93	38
Bruce Hurst	Runners On	.293	99	.474	106	.331	52	3.79	102	5.22	14	19.90	8
	Bases Empty	.259	77	.415	83	.324	75	3.26	90	8.58	74	19.09	11
Bruce Kison	Runners On	.208	6	.377	46	.278	10	3.83	105	9.09	69	15.79	33
	Bases Empty	.343	130	.451	106	.392	125	1.14	10	6.88	47	12.17	79
Tim Lollar	Runners On	.240	28	.406	69	.313	31	3.69	99	9.97	86	14.47	47
	Bases Empty	.260	79	.446	103	.402	129	3.11	83	18.72	131	16.76	32
Al Nipper	Runners On	.253	44	.377	48	.340	70	2.20	50	10.97	100	10.03	103
	Bases Empty	.258	75	.411	79	.358	107	2.35	49	11.93	117	13.45	64
Bob Ojeda	Runners On	.266	63	.387	52	.346	80	2.02	43	10.58	94	17.75	19
	Bases Empty	.278	101	.403	74	.312	57	1.67	23	4.50	13	13.23	68
Bob Stanley	Runners On	.281	85	.377	45	.370	107	0.68	4	11.93	110	7.39	126
	Bases Empty	.200	9	.337	22	.239	2	3.43	93	4.89	16	17.93	27
Mike Trujillo	Runners On	.290	94	.426	82	.323	40	2.73	67	4.59	9	6.12	130
	Bases Empty	.353	131	.455	107	.410	131	1.20	11	7.65	60	3.83	131
Team Average	Runners On	.267	7	.407	6	.332	5	2.50	3	8.59	5	14.21	5
	Bases Empty	.263	12	.388	6	.330	13	2.16	2	8.60	11	14.81	4
League Average	Runners On	.271		.416		.338		2.85		9.26		13.25	
	Bases Empty	.254		.397		.318		2.80		8.14		13.92	

Overall Pitching Compared to Late Inning Pressure Situations

		BA	Rank	SA	Rank	OBA	Rank	HR %	Rank	BB %	Rank	SO %	Rank
Dennis Boyd	Overall	.261	72	.397	57	.306	36	2.49	51	5.92	14	13.60	57
	Pressure	.345	126	.507	118	.394	109	4.05	100	7.32	39	8.54	110
Mark Clear	Overall	.225	13	.275	2	.389	128	0.50	1	19.31	131	21.24	6
	Pressure	.294	99	.431	89	.500	130	1.96	48	27.27	130	12.99	64
Roger Clemens	Overall	.228	15	.299	5	.303	29	1.37	13	9.09	78	18.18	15
	Pressure	.412	--	.588	--	.474	--	5.88	--	10.00	--	5.00	--
Steve Crawford	Overall	.289	110	.409	70	.338	80	1.40	15	7.11	37	14.72	46
	Pressure	.302	104	.426	85	.383	103	1.55	38	11.92	93	16.56	31
Bruce Hurst	Overall	.273	89	.439	96	.327	65	3.48	101	7.19	43	19.42	10
	Pressure	.370	129	.647	128	.419	122	5.88	125	6.82	35	13.64	59
Bruce Kison	Overall	.274	90	.413	76	.332	74	2.51	54	8.04	59	14.07	51
	Pressure	.200	12	.289	16	.250	10	2.22	54	6.12	27	16.33	35
Tim Lollar	Overall	.250	47	.427	90	.361	112	3.39	98	14.65	129	15.70	32
	Pressure	.342	124	.658	130	.480	129	2.63	67	19.61	128	11.76	80
Al Nipper	Overall	.256	59	.396	54	.350	92	2.28	41	11.50	107	11.92	87
	Pressure	.250	54	.441	95	.307	46	4.41	107	6.58	31	11.84	79
Bob Ojeda	Overall	.273	88	.396	56	.327	64	1.81	24	7.15	40	15.20	41
	Pressure	.267	72	.367	51	.371	94	1.11	23	13.51	109	11.71	84
Bob Stanley	Overall	.237	20	.355	26	.303	27	2.18	37	8.33	65	12.78	69
	Pressure	.206	17	.317	24	.278	22	2.29	57	8.87	56	13.71	58
Mike Trujillo	Overall	.320	127	.440	99	.365	117	2.00	30	6.07	16	5.01	131
	Pressure	.341	122	.415	79	.400	111	0.00	1	6.67	32	8.89	108
Team Average	Overall	.265	8	.397	5	.331	8	2.31	2	8.60	8	14.54	4
	Pressure	.286	14	.438	13	.365	14	2.90	10	10.60	13	12.56	12
League Average	Overall	.261		.406		.327		2.82		8.63		13.62	
	Pressure	.258		.392		.332		2.71		9.52		14.05	

Additional Miscellaneous Pitching Comparisons

	Grass Surface BA	Rank	Artificial Surface BA	Rank	Home Games BA	Rank	Road Games BA	Rank	Runners in Scoring Position BA	Rank	Runners in Scoring Pos and Two Outs BA	Rank	Leading Off Inning OBA	Rank
Dennis Boyd	.259	69	.276	82	.267	87	.253	46	.252	51	.239	67	.286	32
Mark Clear	.226	15	.219	--	.198	--	.244	35	.233	28	.159	11	.370	--
Roger Clemens	.245	41	.184	5	.250	57	.203	6	.167	3	.195	29	.343	91
Steve Crawford	.305	115	.210	17	.326	129	.265	69	.311	111	.300	108	.309	54
Bruce Hurst	.276	90	.250	52	.284	104	.263	66	.254	53	.270	83	.351	99
Bruce Kison	.281	96	.253	58	.304	119	.258	54	.209	15	.278	92	.404	124
Tim Lollar	.253	59	.200	--	.244	45	.256	53	.203	10	.194	26	.367	111
Al Nipper	.258	66	.248	49	.256	73	.255	49	.264	62	.283	98	.368	113
Bob Ojeda	.271	83	.292	100	.263	78	.290	101	.283	88	.233	60	.335	83
Bob Stanley	.226	14	.283	89	.261	77	.213	11	.306	105	.302	111	.284	30
Mike Trujillo	.333	130	.240	35	.310	124	.330	124	.306	105	.294	104	.410	127
Team Average	.269	11	.241	2	.272	13	.257	3	.264	6	.255	8	.334	12
League Average	.262		.259		.256		.266		.268		.248		.321	

CALIFORNIA ANGELS

The Last Shall (Almost) Be First

Can a team which has its league's lowest batting average win the pennant? Before you answer, consider this: It has not been done since 1906, when the Chicago White Sox won the American League pennant despite a last-place .230 batting average. Of course, that team's pitching staff, led by Frank Owen, Nick Altrock, Ed Walsh, and ERA leader Doc White, compiled a league-leading 1.76 ERA.

For nearly eighty years since, no league champion has finished last in its league in batting average. During the era of divisional play, only two teams have won their half-pennants while trailing the division in batting average; they were the 1973 New York Mets and 1974 Oakland A's, and neither finished last in the entire league. But it nearly happened last season, when the Angels and Royals battled to the final weekend not only for the American League's Western Division title, but also for the league's lowest batting average. Each team grabbed one of those titles: Kansas City won the division title by one game, ánd California finished last in batting by a margin of fewer than six hits over almost 5,500 at bats.

Several conditions contributed to California's unusually high position in the standings despite their low batting average. First, their total of 732 runs ranked seventh in the American League, despite their poor batting average. Frequently, the team with the league's lowest batting average also has its lowest slugging percentage; that has been the case in 10 of the last 17 years, but was not so with the Angels, who ranked 10th in slugging. Second, the 14 American League teams were separated by fewer than 32 batting average points, or one hit per 31 at bats, the narrowest range since 1978. In fact, the Angels were the first team to finish last in batting with an average above the .250 mark since 1973, when Milwaukee trailed the league with a .253 average. Third, Kansas City and California stood substantially above the rest of the West in earned run average. They were the only teams in the division with averages below four runs per game; the other five teams had a composite 4.43 mark.

California's pitching also presented a paradox. Compare the batting statistics compiled against the Angels' pitching staff last season to the league average:

	R	H	2B	3B	HR	BB	SO	BA	SA	OBA
Vs. Angels	703	1453	252	36	171	514	767	.263	.414	.326
A.L. Avg.	737	1442	254	38	156	533	841	.261	.406	.327

California struck out significantly fewer batters, but in nearly every other respect the figures above resemble each other like the Smith brothers. But look at the exceptions: The Angels allowed 15 *more* home runs, but opponents scored 34 *fewer* runs than against the average American League team. One missing figure might clarify the success of the California pitchers: The Angels made 202 double plays last season, the highest total in either league since 1980; the league average was 159. Only three other teams have reached the 200-mark in the 20 years since Pittsburgh established an all-time National League record with 215 DPs in 1966. (The all-time major league record of 217 was set in 1949 by the Philadelphia Athletics.)

Must double plays be considered an integral part of the evaluation of a pitching staff? After all, if a league-leading total can compensate for 15 home runs—as it apparently did in the case of the 1985 Angels—shouldn't it be accorded greater respect? The following figures present some suggestive but as yet inconclusive support.

Pete Palmer and John Thorn, in their book *The Hidden Game Of Baseball,* present a formula for calculating the number of runs a team can be expected to score from the basic components of its offense (singles, doubles, walks, and so on). According to the authors, the estimate falls within 20 runs in roughly two of three cases, and is the most accurate tool devised for such estimations. Based upon the statistics compiled against California pitchers last season, Angels opponents might have been expected to score 723 runs, 20 more than they actually scored. Do the extra double plays account for this difference? Well, the double-play leaders in each league over the past five seasons have frequently fallen substantially short of their expected runs-allowed totals:

	N.L. Leader	Act.	Exp.	A.L. Leader	Act.	Exp.
1985	Atlanta	781	778	California	703	723
1984	St. Louis	645	631	New York	679	703
1983	Atlanta	640	672	California	779	781
1982	Atlanta	702	685	Milwaukee	717	740
1981	San Diego	455	474	Milwaukee	459	456

Four of the ten teams have allowed 20 or more runs fewer than predicted by Palmer's Linear Weights formulas. It seems plausible, then, that this state-of-the-art formula, which deduces run totals so accurately for the vast majority of teams, is insensitive to those few teams that turn an extreme number of double plays. And that the Angels were able to compensate (and then some) for their opponents' total of 171 home runs—only four fewer than the highest total allowed in the league—with their 43–double-play advantage.

A New Park Effect

Players, fans, and the media have long been aware of the effect of stadiums on baseball statistics. Speculation on how many home runs a certain player might hit if he played his home games in Fenway Park, for instance, has always provided a good topic for discussion. Unfortunately, for many years the discussion seldom strayed beyond home runs. Ironically, as distinctions among ballparks have apparently dwindled, the unique features of each have been given more notice, and their effects examined more closely. Despite the advent of synthetic playing surfaces and cookie-cutter configurations, the remaining characteristics of various stadiums that affect the way the game is played there, and consequently the statistics in those games, are scrutinized today as never before.

Just as certain stadiums enhance or inhibit the likelihood of a home run (like Fenway Park or the Astrodome), or a double (like the Metrodome—see the Minnesota Twins essay for more on this), there are also those which produce more or fewer double plays. Does this mean that we should view California's league-leading performance in double plays the way we view Wade Boggs's batting average, or Bob Horner's home-run totals?

A study of American League double-play ground outs over the past three seasons illustrates the phenomenon of double-play–promoting and double-play–inhibiting ballparks. The scope of the study is limited to double play ground outs (GIDPs) because they not only constitute roughly 80 percent of all double plays, but are also more likely to be affected by the individual characteristics and biases of particular stadiums. These biases include the amount of foul territory, the size and contour of the outfield, and the likelihood that teams will play for the big inning, disdaining plays such as sacrifice bunts and stolen bases, which trade an out for a base and reduce the number of double plays. Such attitudes affect the double-play totals at fields like Fenway Park and Wrigley Field. And, in fact, Anaheim Stadium is one of the parks that *inhibits* double plays.

The accompanying table shows the number of double play ground outs in every regular-season game since 1983 for each American League team, divided into their home-game and road-game totals. Remember that for any given team, the home-road comparison is not compromised by the specific characteristics of that team. When considering the Angels, for example, their high double-play total should be divided somewhat evenly between home and road games. If not, the ballpark may be responsible.

Team	Home	Road	Home Diff.
Baltimore	439	395	+11.1%
Boston	453	407	+11.3%
California	433	452	−4.2%
Chicago	373	359	+3.9%
Cleveland	418	402	+4.0%
Detroit	320	356	−10.1%
Kansas City	387	407	−4.9%
Milwaukee	412	410	+0.5%
Minnesota	348	390	−10.8%
New York	398	439	−9.3%
Oakland	381	361	+5.5%
Seattle	368	367	+0.3%
Texas	391	358	+9.2%
Toronto	343	361	−5.0%

It is unlikely that the wide disparity between the home and road totals of six of the 14 teams can be attributed to chance alone. Memorial Stadium in Baltimore, Fenway Park in Boston, and Arlington Stadium in Texas significantly increase the double-play rate. Three fields clearly seem to inhibit double plays: the Metrodome, Tiger Stadium, and Yankee Stadium. And Anaheim Stadium tends in that direction as well. Last season, when the Angels led all major-league teams with 202 twin killings, they divided their double plays almost evenly between home and road games, but their opponents made 68 at Anaheim Stadium, 102 in California's road games.

What makes the Angels so prolific at turning double plays that they can approach the all-time record despite an uncooperative playing field? Not their pitching staff, which had a collective ratio of 1.13 ground outs per air out. That ranked fifth among the 14 American League teams, but was only slightly higher than the league average of 1.09. Nor do Angels pitchers put enough runners on base to create an abundance of GIDP opportunities (runner on first base, less than two outs). In fact, they rank only sixth in the league in defensive GIDP opportunities. But California is the most proficient in terms of GIDP percentage:

Team	Def. GIDP Opportunities	Def. GIDP	Pct.
California	1169	162	13.9
New York	1127	143	12.7
Baltimore	1204	146	12.1
Toronto	1080	127	11.8
Detroit	1056	124	11.7
Boston	1225	138	11.3
Kansas City	1128	126	11.2
Texas	1116	124	11.1
Chicago	1125	123	10.9
Milwaukee	1143	125	10.9
Seattle	1233	129	10.5
Cleveland	1240	123	9.9
Minnesota	1098	108	9.8
Oakland	1208	113	9.4

Having eliminated the possible mitigating factors, the credit for California's league-leading double-play total must rightfully go to their infield. More specifically, to shortstop Dick Schofield, since neither second baseman Bobby Grich nor third baseman Doug DeCinces can any longer be considered superior fielders. Perhaps we who don't see Schofield every day have finally discovered why the Angels have been willing to support his .206 batting average for the past two seasons, the lowest mark by any everyday player in either league during that time. It could be that Schofield did as much for California's starting rotation last season as Donnie Moore.

Surface Considerations

Before concluding a discussion of the double-play tendencies of specific stadiums, it is worth noting the strong disparity between the American League's 10 grass fields and its four carpeted surfaces. Three of the four carpeted fields tend to suppress the incidence of GIDPs, while the Kingdome appears to have little or no effect. Of course, the speed at which ground balls reach infielders on artificial surfaces undoubtedly affords them a greater opportunity to turn two. But that is negated and then some by the balls that bound through so quickly that no infielder can handle them. This explains why the National League, with half its fields unnatural, places an emphasis on quicker infielders (of the Ozzie Smith type), while American League teams, in a league with only four synthetic surfaces and generally smaller fields, favor stronger offensive players with lesser defensive skills (say, Cal Ripken and Alan Trammell). This would hold especially true for teams in the Eastern Division, since they play only 25 games each season on carpets, with the exception of the Toronto Blue Jays, who play at carpeted Exhibition Stadium. And their shortstop is what type, ladies and gentlemen?

WON-LOST RECORD BY STARTING POSITION

CALIFORNIA 90-72	C	1B	2B	3B	SS	LF	CF	RF	P	DH	Leadoff	Relief	Starts
Juan Beniquez		21-17				7-8	16-12	6-5		1-0	9-5		51-42
Bob Boone	76-61												76-61
Mike Brown								23-8		0-3	1-0		23-11
John Candelaria									8-5				8-5
Rod Carew		60-49									19-16		60-49
Pat Clements												16-25	
Stu Cliburn												21-23	
Doug Corbett												13-17	
Doug DeCinces				66-45						2-1			68-46
Brian Downing						68-50				8-13	13-13		76-63
Alan Fowlkes												1-1	
Craig Gerber					17-13								17-13
Bobby Grich		6-5	64-45	5-6						4-2			79-58
George Hendrick								6-6		1-0			7-6
Al Holland												3-12	
Jack Howell				19-21									19-21
Reggie Jackson								43-38		27-19			70-57
Tommy John									2-4			1-5	2-4
Ruppert Jones						14-14	8-6	11-12		25-16	4-4		58-48
Pat Keedy						1-0							1-0
Bob Kipper									0-1			0-1	0-1
Rufino Linares										7-5			7-5
Urbano Lugo								6-4				2-8	6-4
Tony Mack									0-1				0-1
Kirk McCaskill									17-12			0-1	17-12
Darrell Miller						1-0	1-3			1-2			3-5
Donnie Moore												50-15	
Jerry Narron	14-11									4-2			18-13
Gary Pettis							64-54				38-33		64-54
Gus Polidor													0-
Ron Romanick									20-11				20-11
Luis Sanchez												6-20	
Dick Schofield					73-59						2-0		73-59
Daryl Sconiers		3-1								9-9			12-10
Jim Slaton									11-13			2-3	11-13
D. W. Smith												0-4	
Don Sutton									2-3				2-3
Devon White						1-0							1-0
Rob Wilfong			26-27							1-0	4-1		27-27
Mike Witt									20-15				20-15
Geoff Zahn									4-3				4-3

Batting vs. Left and Right Handed Pitchers

		BA	Rank	SA	Rank	OBA	Rank	HR %	Rank	BB %	Rank	SO %	Rank
Juan Beniquez	vs. Lefties	.356	2	.540	16	.414	8	3.45	57	7.77	93	5.70	12
	vs. Righties	.266	64	.329	130	.327	73	0.84	135	7.12	97	13.11	78
Bob Boone	vs. Lefties	.259	86	.326	132	.331	88	0.74	126	8.92	70	5.73	13
	vs. Righties	.243	109	.314	142	.295	126	1.23	121	6.34	113	7.16	21
Mike C. Brown	vs. Lefties	.325	15	.550	12	.372	29	5.00	32	6.90	107	11.49	59
	vs. Righties	.205	--	.274	--	.227	--	0.00	--	1.30	--	14.29	--
Rod Carew	vs. Lefties	.264	84	.283	145	.371	32	0.00	131	13.18	22	17.83	126
	vs. Righties	.285	38	.365	106	.371	20	0.59	141	12.08	25	6.17	13
Doug DeCinces	vs. Lefties	.244	113	.449	63	.345	71	4.72	39	13.51	19	12.84	87
	vs. Righties	.243	108	.437	52	.304	105	4.67	28	7.94	86	15.29	104
Brian Downing	vs. Lefties	.262	85	.483	38	.343	73	4.65	40	11.56	35	11.56	60
	vs. Righties	.264	69	.399	80	.384	10	3.45	60	13.06	18	9.03	36
Bobby Grich	vs. Lefties	.265	81	.442	65	.372	29	3.40	60	14.45	17	15.03	102
	vs. Righties	.232	122	.340	125	.348	48	2.41	88	14.07	9	12.81	72
Reggie Jackson	vs. Lefties	.221	134	.398	88	.355	54	3.54	54	17.39	6	31.88	158
	vs. Righties	.262	72	.516	10	.362	27	6.63	5	13.40	15	23.33	152
Ruppert Jones	vs. Lefties	.174	--	.370	--	.255	--	4.35	--	9.26	--	22.22	--
	vs. Righties	.239	113	.458	40	.338	58	5.54	14	12.94	19	17.41	122
Gary Pettis	vs. Lefties	.281	60	.331	131	.370	33	0.00	131	12.73	26	17.58	124
	vs. Righties	.247	105	.319	141	.336	59	0.33	149	11.68	29	27.35	157
Dick Schofield	vs. Lefties	.259	87	.354	122	.323	100	1.36	108	6.51	115	10.65	49
	vs. Righties	.199	150	.320	139	.269	142	2.06	96	7.34	95	15.90	110
Rob Wilfong	vs. Lefties	.143	--	.429	--	.174	--	9.52	--	3.70	--	25.93	--
	vs. Righties	.194	155	.240	156	.250	152	1.02	128	6.94	100	11.57	60
Team Average	vs. Lefties	.265	8	.409	10	.347	3	2.78	8	10.65	2	14.25	8
	vs. Righties	.245	14	.376	12	.327	5	2.82	8	10.22	1	14.46	12
League Average	vs. Lefties	.266		.416		.333		2.91		8.95		13.77	
	vs. Righties	.259		.401		.324		2.78		8.49		13.56	

Batting with Runners on Base and Bases Empty

		BA	Rank	SA	Rank	OBA	Rank	HR %	Rank	BB %	Rank	SO %	Rank
Juan Beniquez	Runners On	.313	26	.453	54	.380	25	3.35	59	8.61	93	7.66	27
	Bases Empty	.297	12	.392	88	.351	21	0.86	132	6.37	108	11.95	57
Bob Boone	Runners On	.257	104	.307	140	.297	130	0.46	141	5.56	137	6.75	16
	Bases Empty	.240	111	.326	132	.313	94	1.65	107	8.58	63	6.72	11
Rod Carew	Runners On	.288	56	.335	128	.413	9	0.59	137	17.05	7	5.53	10
	Bases Empty	.275	43	.352	115	.342	38	0.37	145	8.97	58	11.63	54
Doug DeCinces	Runners On	.245	125	.472	44	.317	110	6.02	10	9.45	70	17.72	134
	Bases Empty	.242		.408	69	.316	90	3.32	61	9.83	45	11.11	49
Brian Downing	Runners On	.300	41	.515	20	.385	21	5.29	.21	10.37	53	11.85	69
	Bases Empty	.235	118	.358	112	.360	17	2.73	77	14.29	10	8.29	28
Bobby Grich	Runners On	.255	107	.373	111	.377	28	1.96	92	15.48	12	12.70	80
	Bases Empty	.233	121	.371	102	.339	46	3.27	62	13.17	15	14.11	82
Reggie Jackson	Runners On	.271	77	.532	13	.376	30	6.88	6	14.73	16	24.42	155
	Bases Empty	.236	117	.446	42	.346	29	4.96	28	14.13	12	26.50	157
Ruppert Jones	Runners On	.287	59	.539	12	.374	36	5.62	17	12.15	31	18.69	139
	Bases Empty	.185	155	.370	105	.289	130	5.21	20	12.81	16	17.36	121
Gary Pettis	Runners On	.262	89	.323	132	.346	78	0.61	136	11.17	37	21.83	148
	Bases Empty	.254	88	.323	135	.348	25	0.00	148	12.54	18	25.71	155
Dick Schofield	Runners On	.218	146	.356	122	.309	119	1.60	100	9.17	80	13.10	85
	Bases Empty	.220	132	.312	141	.270	146	2.00	101	5.24	128	14.98	94
Rob Wilfong	Runners On	.253	113	.289	148	.312	117	1.20	114	7.92	108	11.88	70
	Bases Empty	.149	158	.239	154	.197	158	2.24	97	5.63	121	14.08	81
Team Average	Runners On	.266	11	.420	6	.349	3	3.39	2	10.77	1	14.21	12
	Bases Empty	.239	14	.360	14	.320	7	2.37	12	10.00	1	14.55	12
League Average	Runners On	.271		.416		.338		2.85		9.26		13.25	
	Bases Empty	.254		.397		.318		2.80		8.14		13.92	

Overall Batting Compared to Late Inning Pressure Situations

		BA	Rank	SA	Rank	OBA	Rank	HR %	Rank	BB %	Rank	SO %	Rank	RDI %	Rank
Juan Beniquez	Overall	.304	10	.418	72	.364	22	1.95	102	7.39	98	10.00	41	.230	133
	Pressure	.239	97	.284	130	.292	114	0.00	113	6.67	107	12.00	62	.227	102
Bob Boone	Overall	.248	109	.317	146	.306	123	1.09	124	7.12	104	6.73	14	.278	94
	Pressure	.316	25	.351	92	.412	19	0.00	113	14.49	26	8.70	29	.526	6
Mike C. Brown	Overall	.268	--	.418	--	.304	--	2.61	--	4.27	--	12.80	--	.245	123
	Pressure	.111	--	.111	--	.111	--	0.00	--	0.00	--	10.00	--	.400	--
Rod Carew	Overall	.280	42	.345	132	.371	11	0.45	145	12.36	25	9.07	34	.305	60
	Pressure	.214	121	.250	142	.353	51	0.00	113	16.90	13	8.45	28	.333	55
Doug DeCinces	Overall	.244	118	.440	52	.317	105	4.68	31	9.63	48	14.55	99	.297	70
	Pressure	.259	71	.352	91	.375	35	1.85	89	13.64	32	15.15	90	.235	99
Brian Downing	Overall	.263	77	.427	65	.371	13	3.85	48	12.58	22	9.84	39	.369	18
	Pressure	.290	46	.478	36	.367	40	4.35	40	8.64	83	11.11	51	.308	65
Bobby Grich	Overall	.242	122	.372	116	.355	34	2.71	84	14.19	13	13.49	80	.277	95
	Pressure	.270	61	.317	110	.343	63	0.00	113	9.72	67	13.89	77	.353	48
Reggie Jackson	Overall	.252	100	.487	16	.360	26	5.87	9	14.42	10	25.51	157	.314	53
	Pressure	.136	158	.153	159	.320	84	0.00	113	21.33	3	30.67	158	.267	84
Ruppert Jones	Overall	.231	137	.447	43	.328	79	5.40	11	12.50	23	17.98	128	.265	108
	Pressure	.216	119	.471	39	.365	42	5.88	25	18.18	7	19.70	131	.267	84
Jerry Narron	Overall	.220	--	.364	--	.280	--	3.79	--	7.69	--	11.89	--	.212	--
	Pressure	.226	111	.452	45	.250	141	6.45	21	3.13	141	18.75	124	.357	45
Gary Pettis	Overall	.257	94	.323	143	.347	46	0.23	151	12.02	26	24.22	155	.248	122
	Pressure	.261	69	.326	102	.382	31	0.00	113	15.79	17	28.07	156	.200	117
Dick Schofield	Overall	.219	147	.331	141	.287	143	1.83	106	7.06	105	14.11	88	.210	147
	Pressure	.167	150	.278	133	.231	147	2.78	64	7.32	100	14.63	86	.273	78
Rob Wilfong	Overall	.189	158	.258	155	.243	157	1.84	103	6.58	117	13.17	78	.226	139
	Pressure	.237	99	.289	125	.256	138	0.00	113	2.44	147	4.88	9	.273	78
Team Average	Overall	.251	14	.386	11	.333	4	2.81	7	10.35	1	14.40	11	.279	9
	Pressure	.232	13	.327	14	.326	6	1.68	13	11.60	1	15.27	11	.294	5
League Average	Overall	.261		.406		.327		2.82		8.63		13.62		.287	
	Pressure	.253		.381		.323		2.74		9.11		14.40		.273	

Additional Miscellaneous Batting Comparisons

	Grass Surface BA	Rank	Artificial Surface BA	Rank	Home Games BA	Rank	Road Games BA	Rank	Runners in Scoring Position BA	Rank	Runners in Scoring Pos and Two Outs BA	Rank	Leading Off Inning OBA	Rank	Runners on 3B with less than 2 Outs RDI %	Rank
Juan Beniquez	.322	4	.217	129	.327	12	.279	37	.278	76	.222	106	.333	59	.364	153
Bob Boone	.253	97	.217	129	.235	121	.259	79	.250	109	.236	93	.325	77	.519	103
Mike C. Brown	.272	58	.250	--	.231	--	.295	--	.227	--	.241	87	.276	--	.500	106
Rod Carew	.275	54	.299	26	.279	58	.281	33	.313	32	.218	111	.366	27	.824	3
Doug DeCinces	.254	96	.210	135	.264	79	.224	136	.254	106	.302	35	.276	124	.679	41
Brian Downing	.251	103	.317	12	.241	116	.284	27	.311	33	.246	76	.374	18	.700	29
Bobby Grich	.242	116	.244	94	.250	99	.234	123	.240	116	.176	--	.331	66	.478	128
Jack Howell	.169	157	.462	--	.159	--	.235	--	.212	--	.241	85	.235	--	.833	--
Reggie Jackson	.251	102	.260	69	.218	143	.285	24	.289	59	.227	101	.333	59	.393	149
Ruppert Jones	.223	141	.271	58	.256	91	.211	150	.220	131	.356	11	.294	115	.625	58
Gary Pettis	.252	98	.277	52	.231	129	.276	43	.281	69	.140	152	.345	45	.526	101
Dick Schofield	.213	147	.254	76	.219	139	.219	141	.214	136	.273	52	.303	102	.467	132
Rob Wilfong	.196	153	.158	--	.205	150	.178	156	.255	103			.260	144	.750	--
Team Average	.248	13	.261	4	.244	14	.257	7	.259	11	.243	8	.328	3	.565	10
League Average	.262		.259		.266		.256		.268		.248		.321		.587	

Pitching vs. Left and Right Handed Batters

		BA	Rank	SA	Rank	OBA	Rank	HR %	Rank	BB %	Rank	SO %	Rank
John Candelaria	vs. Lefties	.156	--	.244	--	.152	--	2.22	--	0.00	--	36.17	--
	vs. Righties	.284	103	.459	110	.359	109	2.70	61	9.45	94	14.17	61
Pat Clements	vs. Lefties	.240	39	.380	54	.327	57	3.00	81	9.48	70	11.21	86
	vs. Righties	.198	--	.250	--	.285	--	0.86	--	10.69	--	4.58	--
Stu Cliburn	vs. Lefties	.291	95	.432	82	.365	94	3.38	97	10.71	88	9.52	104
	vs. Righties	.207	9	.263	2	.238	3	0.00	1	3.52	4	14.10	62
Urbano Lugo	vs. Lefties	.315	117	.478	105	.382	112	2.81	75	9.50	72	14.00	49
	vs. Righties	.221	25	.382	48	.287	24	3.68	103	6.62	44	9.27	121
Kirk McCaskill	vs. Lefties	.278	80	.420	72	.339	70	2.70	69	8.65	59	10.20	98
	vs. Righties	.234	34	.394	59	.295	33	3.69	104	7.02	47	15.73	44
Donnie Moore	vs. Lefties	.200	8	.270	4	.247	4	1.00	17	5.91	21	18.64	19
	vs. Righties	.277	96	.408	76	.307	52	3.80	105	4.06	8	15.74	43
Ron Romanick	vs. Lefties	.280	83	.461	97	.333	64	3.90	109	7.71	42	6.83	121
	vs. Righties	.279	99	.434	91	.334	83	3.81	106	7.16	51	8.75	123
Luis Sanchez	vs. Lefties	.313	115	.530	126	.396	119	4.35	116	12.69	106	14.93	39
	vs. Righties	.254	61	.467	114	.313	59	3.28	89	7.46	64	10.45	108
Jim Slaton	vs. Lefties	.297	100	.479	107	.379	107	3.30	94	11.75	99	8.31	116
	vs. Righties	.270	83	.461	112	.325	75	4.49	117	7.43	63	10.47	107
Don Sutton	vs. Lefties	.244	43	.373	46	.294	25	2.94	78	6.68	30	13.15	55
	vs. Righties	.261	72	.397	64	.303	46	2.77	64	5.82	34	9.48	119
Mike Witt	vs. Lefties	.263	66	.375	47	.332	62	2.12	48	9.01	64	14.04	48
	vs. Righties	.218	20	.342	22	.296	34	2.63	58	9.75	96	20.97	13
Geoff Zahn	vs. Lefties	.353	--	.647	--	.421	--	5.88	--	10.53	--	5.26	--
	vs. Righties	.292	111	.485	122	.350	96	3.08	81	8.28	75	8.97	122
Team Average	vs. Lefties	.276	12	.427	10	.342	12	3.02	10	9.16	7	11.69	12
	vs. Righties	.250	3	.402	5	.311	5	3.16	10	7.56	5	13.16	11
League Average	vs. Lefties	.265		.408		.333		2.74		9.21		12.94	
	vs. Righties	.259		.404		.322		2.88		8.19		14.14	

Pitching with Runners on Base and Bases Empty

		BA	Rank	SA	Rank	OBA	Rank	HR %	Rank	BB %	Rank	SO %	Rank
John Candelaria	Runners On	.271	69	.398	66	.294	19	2.54	61	3.08	1	16.15	28
	Bases Empty	.255	69	.443	102	.351	100	2.68	65	11.70	115	18.71	15
Pat Clements	Runners On	.232	--	.358	--	.318	--	3.16	--	9.91	--	6.31	--
	Bases Empty	.207	14	.273	4	.294	38	0.83	4	10.29	100	8.82	123
Stu Cliburn	Runners On	.246	33	.317	10	.297	24	1.20	17	6.95	32	13.90	54
	Bases Empty	.237	41	.345	27	.288	31	1.55	20	6.25	32	10.58	103
Urbano Lugo	Runners On	.241	31	.368	35	.280	12	1.50	23	4.83	11	11.03	95
	Bases Empty	.298	119	.486	121	.383	123	4.42	118	10.68	106	12.62	73
Kirk McCaskill	Runners On	.300	104	.500	118	.358	92	4.48	115	8.28	50	11.35	91
	Bases Empty	.231	31	.348	28	.293	37	2.26	44	7.69	62	13.51	61
Donnie Moore	Runners On	.203	4	.273	2	.252	3	1.60	28	6.13	20	16.04	29
	Bases Empty	.269	91	.396	64	.298	43	3.05	79	3.90	6	18.54	16
Ron Romanick	Runners On	.265	58	.395	65	.327	45	2.94	77	8.50	55	9.35	111
	Bases Empty	.290	111	.485	120	.339	91	4.49	119	6.69	44	6.49	129
Luis Sanchez	Runners On	.313	117	.600	131	.374	110	5.22	127	9.92	84	11.45	89
	Bases Empty	.254	66	.402	71	.336	89	2.46	56	10.22	99	13.87	56
Jim Slaton	Runners On	.275	77	.429	84	.331	53	1.62	29	7.86	43	8.57	120
	Bases Empty	.291	112	.502	125	.373	116	5.57	127	11.23	110	9.86	113
Don Sutton	Runners On	.260	50	.377	47	.304	30	2.40	53	6.28	23	12.30	76
	Bases Empty	.248	55	.390	58	.295	39	3.14	86	6.24	31	10.75	98
Mike Witt	Runners On	.247	37	.388	54	.320	36	2.83	72	9.50	79	15.61	35
	Bases Empty	.240	44	.341	24	.313	58	2.00	31	9.23	85	18.29	21
Team Average	Runners On	.264	6	.411	7	.323	3	2.82	6	7.97	2	12.45	10
	Bases Empty	.262	11	.416	11	.328	12	3.30	13	8.63	12	12.44	12
League Average	Runners On	.271		.416		.338		2.85		9.26		13.25	
	Bases Empty	.254		.397		.318		2.80		8.14		13.92	

Overall Pitching Compared to Late Inning Pressure Situations

		BA	Rank	SA	Rank	OBA	Rank	HR %	Rank	BB %	Rank	SO %	Rank
John Candelaria	Overall	.262	75	.423	88	.327	63	2.62	61	7.97	55	17.61	20
	Pressure	.400	--	1.400	--	.333	--	20.00	--	0.00	--	0.00	--
Pat Clements	Overall	.218	--	.310	--	.305	--	1.85	--	10.12	--	7.69	--
	Pressure	.226	32	.250	8	.343	74	0.00	--	13.86	112	9.90	97
Stu Cliburn	Overall	.241	30	.332	11	.292	19	1.39	14	6.58	--	12.15	82
	Pressure	.222	25	.328	30	.297	33	1.59	40	8.88	57	11.21	88
Doug Corbett	Overall	.274	--	.447	--	.348	--	3.91	--	9.85	--	11.82	--
	Pressure	.304	107	.536	121	.388	107	4.35	105	12.20	99	9.76	99
Urbano Lugo	Overall	.274	91	.436	94	.341	83	3.18	90	8.26	62	11.97	86
	Pressure	.273	--	.591	--	.360	--	9.09	--	11.54	--	11.54	--
Kirk McCaskill	Overall	.258	63	.408	67	.319	54	3.14	88	7.93	54	12.64	74
	Pressure	.333	118	.500	114	.357	85	3.70	97	1.79	2	7.14	118
Donnie Moore	Overall	.237	22	.336	13	.275	7	2.34	44	5.04	8	17.27	22
	Pressure	.255	61	.363	48	.287	25	2.62	66	4.45	11	16.10	38
Ron Romanick	Overall	.280	99	.449	102	.334	77	3.86	113	7.46	50	7.70	129
	Pressure	.259	64	.448	98	.295	32	3.45	94	4.84	15	6.45	123
Luis Sanchez	Overall	.283	103	.498	128	.354	104	3.80	109	10.07	95	12.69	72
	Pressure	.209	19	.395	67	.277	20	4.65	114	8.51	51	19.15	19
Jim Slaton	Overall	.284	105	.470	118	.355	105	3.86	112	9.77	90	9.30	120
	Pressure	.206	15	.353	43	.325	59	2.94	88	12.20	99	7.32	117
Don Sutton	Overall	.253	52	.385	46	.298	22	2.86	71	6.26	21	11.35	95
	Pressure	.302	103	.397	69	.323	57	1.59	40	2.99	7	5.97	127
Mike Witt	Overall	.243	34	.360	31	.316	49	2.35	45	9.34	83	17.16	23
	Pressure	.204	13	.336	36	.318	52	3.54	95	14.18	113	16.42	34
Team Average	Overall	.263	7	.414	9	.326	6	3.09	12	8.34	6	12.44	12
	Pressure	.253	5	.399	8	.320	4	3.13	12	8.56	3	12.40	13
League Average	Overall	.261		.406		.327		2.82		8.63		13.62	
	Pressure	.258		.392		.332		2.71		9.52		14.05	

Additional Miscellaneous Pitching Comparisons

	Grass Surface BA	Rank	Artificial Surface BA	Rank	Home Games BA	Rank	Road Games BA	Rank	Runners in Scoring Position BA	Rank	Runners in Scoring Pos and Two Outs BA	Rank	Leading Off Inning OBA	Rank
John Candelaria	.261	72	.267	--	.305	121	.221	14	.274	--	.267	--	.315	61
Pat Clements	.212	7	.259	--	.173	3	.289	--	.302	--	.273	--	.278	24
Stu Cliburn	.239	31	.247	48	.242	42	.240	29	.248	46	.200	30	.356	101
Doug Corbett	.274	89	.273	--	.267	--	.281	--	.304	--	.360	--	.270	--
Urbano Lugo	.278	92	.254	59	.255	70	.291	102	.197	7	.167	--	.345	94
Kirk McCaskill	.263	76	.221	21	.249	56	.267	74	.255	54	.183	22	.325	75
Donnie Moore	.236	24	.241	36	.224	15	.250	42	.219	19	.185	23	.286	31
Ron Romanick	.269	82	.339	124	.276	94	.284	95	.257	56	.250	74	.358	103
Luis Sanchez	.302	111	.235	30	.308	--	.267	72	.354	129	.432	132	.309	56
Jim Slaton	.286	103	.278	84	.267	86	.302	111	.260	58	.271	87	.369	114
Don Sutton	.239	30	.305	110	.235	33	.269	79	.260	59	.224	50	.281	26
Mike Witt	.243	38	.246	46	.247	52	.239	27	.241	34	.237	62	.338	85
Geoff Zahn	.275	--	.321	120	.275	--	.321	--	.206	--	.118	--	.341	--
Team Average	.260	6	.274	10	.256	7	.270	9	.258	5	.249	7	.334	13
League Average	.262		.259		.256		.266		.268		.248		.321	

CHICAGO WHITE SOX

The White Sox finished 85–77 last season, up 11 games from their dreadful 1984 season for the biggest gain by any team in the American League. The bulk of the turnaround was on offense; they scored 736 runs and allowed 720, compared to 679 and 736 by the 1984 model. The increase of 57 runs is hard to figure from their traditional statistics:

	BA	SA	OBA	2B	3B	HR	BB	SB
1984 White Sox	.247	.395	.314	225	38	172	523	109
1985 White Sox	.253	.392	.315	247	37	146	471	108

Sure, the team batting average rose by six points, but that would seem to be more than offset by the large decreases in home runs and walks. The slugging and on-base averages were nearly identical. So where in the world did those 57 additional runs come from?

The simple answer is that the '85 White Sox hit extraordinarily well with runners in scoring position. They batted .294 with runners on second or third, the highest such batting average by any team in the majors. Most teams show a marginal improvement in their batting averages at such times (league average: .268 with runners in scoring position, .261 overall), but the Sox took matters to another plateau.

In fact, Chicago's performance last season earned the team a spot in the *Player Analysis* record book. What the White Sox did in 1985, better than any major league team since we started compiling the information in 1975, was to overachieve at the key moments. Their batting average with runners in scoring position was 41 points higher than their overall batting average for the season (.253). The top ten such performances since 1975:

	Overall BA	Scor. Pos. BA	Improvement (in Points)
1985 White Sox	.253	.294	+41
1981 Brewers	.257	.293	+36
1977 Cardinals	.270	.305	+35
1975 Red Sox	.275	.309	+34
1982 Cubs	.260	.290	+30
1978 Cardinals	.249	.277	+28
1976 Pirates	.267	.292	+25
1981 Twins	.240	.265	+25
1985 Orioles	.263	.288	+25
1981 A's	.247	.271	+24

As you can see from the charts listed on the next pages, nearly every regular player on the team batted higher with runners in scoring position than without. The run-producing effect of that combination of opportunistic hitters was impressive. Look at the comparative 1985 statistics of these three teams:

	BA	SA	OBA	2B	3B	HR	BB	SB
White Sox	.253	.392	.315	247	37	146	471	108
Tigers	.253	.424	.318	254	45	202	526	75
Mariners	.255	.412	.326	277	38	171	564	94

Would you guess from those numbers that the White Sox (736 runs) would outscore both Detroit (729) and Seattle (719)? Maybe you would if you knew that with runners in scoring position, the team batting averages were White Sox, .294; Tigers, .240; and Mariners, .261.

While opportunistic hitting was a key factor for last year's White Sox, there is plenty of room for improvement in other areas of the team in 1986. The White Sox were never really in the pennant race during the second half of last season. Their six-game deficit at year's end represents the closest they came to the top after the brief players' strike in early August.

Last year was a year of change for the White Sox. Gone from the 1984 squad were Greg Luzinski, Vance Law, and LaMarr Hoyt, three key actors in the '83 division-winning drama. Throughout the season, Tony LaRussa kept tinkering as he tried to balance the sometimes contradictory objectives of winning today and building for the future. That led to trial and error at several positions, a process that went on for much of the summer.

The "Won-Lost by Starting Position" table below shows that at four of the nine everyday positions (including DH, excluding pitcher), no White Sox player started the majority of the team's 163 games. At second base, Julio Cruz led the way with 74 starts (including one in a tie game); in left field, it was Rudy Law with 65; Daryl Boston was the most frequent centerfielder, but he started only 60 times; and Ron Kittle led designated hitters with 51 starts. That's highly unusual for a major-league team. The 13 other American League teams combined had only 12 everyday positions without a majority starter; the 12 National League teams had a combined total of only 15. And no team other than the White Sox had as many as four such positions.

How the Sox fill those four positions will be pivotal to the team's chances in 1986. Kittle, who had 12 home runs and 30 RBIs in his last 30 games of '85, seems sure of a spot, either in left field or as DH. He was the subject of a "He's gotta play" pronouncement from announcer-turned-executive Hawk Harrelson.

Second base and center field may prove to be more difficult. Boston, rather than Law, will probably get first crack at center; he has hit 60 home runs in the minors over the past three and a half seasons, but he wasn't up to the task last year at this time. Wayne Tolleson, acquired from Texas in December with Dave Schmidt for Scott Fletcher, may wind up at second; he hit .313 in 323 at bats last season. Another candidate is Tim Hulett, who made only one error in 28 games there last year before being shifted to third. Julio Cruz, possessor of a .213 average over the past two years, is unlikely to keep the job.

LaRussa has been on the hot seat for years, but never is the job of a manager so tenuous as it is after having provided a taste of success. LaRussa served up that taste with a first-place finish in '83. But since divisional play began in 1969, only two managers—Earl Weaver and Chuck Tanner—have survived three consecutive no-title seasons after having won a division championship.

Are the Sox in the Wrong League?

The Chicago pitching staff led the American League with 1,023 strikeouts last season, the most by any team in the league since 1973, when the introduction of the DH eliminated the opportunity for pitchers to strike out other pitchers. It was also the first time since

1953, and only the fourth time ever, that the White Sox led the A.L. in strikeouts. Nevertheless, Chicago finished in the middle of the pack in runs allowed (720) and earned run average (4.07).

Strikeouts have always been treated deferentially by baseball statisticians. Pitchers' strikeouts have been a part of the baseball box-scores since Amos Rusie was a pup, while corresponding figures for batters have appeared in the official averages since the early years of this century. Similar accord, however, has never been granted to other methods of making an out. (There are more than 50 such methods according to the latest baseball rule book, although not too many baserunners have been called out lately for running the bases in reverse order.) With the introduction of ground out and air out information in this book, perhaps that imbalance is easing.

Ground outs and air outs notwithstanding, does the strikeout merit the special attention it has historically received? Is a pitching staff composed primarily of strikeout pitchers more likely to be a top-notch staff than a nonstrikeout staff?

The numbers argue in favor of high-strikeout staffs being better than low-strikeout staffs. These charts show where the team that led the league in strikeouts has finished in runs allowed in every season since 1900:

American League (since 1901)

	Yrs.	1st	2nd	3rd	4th	5th	6th	7th	8th	9th	10th
8-team league	60	14	22	6	12	2	1	2	1	—	—
10-team league	8	0	0	2	0	0	3	2	1	0	0
12-team league	8	0	0	1	1	1	3	0	2	0	0
14-team league	9	1	0	0	1	1	2	0	3	1	0

National League (since 1900)

	Yrs.	1st	2nd	3rd	4th	5th	6th	7th	8th	9th	10th
8-team league	62	20	14	7	8	1	8	4	0	—	—
10-team league	7	3	0	1	0	0	1	2	0	0	0
12-team league	17	7	2	1	1	2	1	0	2	0	1

Conversely, the team finishing last in the league in strikeouts has allowed the fewest runs in its league only six times, but has allowed the most runs 40 times.

If chance were the sole determining factor, the average number of times that the team striking out the most batters would also lead the league in fewest runs allowed would be about 10 in each major league. The actual figures are 15 in the American, 30 in the National. Perhaps more impressively, the team leading in strikeouts finished either first or second in the league in fewest runs allowed 44 percent of the time in the American League, and 53 percent in the National.

Of particular interest is the divergent pattern that has developed in recent baseball history between the two leagues. The correlation between leading the league in Ks and ranking first or second in runs allowed has been increasing in the National League, while it has almost disappeared from the American League. Over the past 25 years, only one American League team, the 1981 Yankees, has done both, while it has been accomplished 12 times in the National League: by the Dodgers in 1963, '66, and '74; the Reds in 1964; the Astros in 1980 and '81; and the Mets in 1970, '71, '73, '76, and '85.

Could this be one piece of statistical evidence that the National League has become a fastball league and the American League a curveball league? It is certainly true that the dominant pitching team in the American League over the past 25 years has been the Orioles, whose management and pitching coaches, notably Harry Brecheen and George Bamberger, have historically stressed control and pitch-variety over sheer speed; no Orioles staff has ever led the league in strikeouts. The dominant National League staffs during that same span, the Dodgers and to a lesser degree the Mets, have reached the top on the wings of home-grown fastball pitchers. The current Dodgers' staff, led by Valenzuela and Hershiser, obviously does not fit that mold, but even they ranked first and third in strikeouts the past two seasons. But limiting ourselves to the double-leaders listed above, we're talking about staffs led by Koufax, Drysdale, Seaver, Koosman, Ryan, and Gooden.

With Britt Burns traded to the Yankees, the White Sox have lost a pitcher who contributed 172 strikeouts in 34 starts last season. In return, they got Joe Cowley, whose career strikeout rate is within a tenth of a strikeout per nine innings of Burns's. Assuming that Seaver, Floyd Bannister, and Gene Nelson pitch the bulk of Chicago's innings, the staff could very well be dominated by strikeout pitchers again And to complete the picture, what ex-pitcher has agreed to lend his expertise to LaRussa as a "pitching consultant," even while continuing to broadcast the team's games? That old National League sidewinder Don Drysdale himself. Here's hoping that the 'Winder has more success crossing the league/style continuum than Bamberger did when he strayed into the National League to manage the Mets.

WON-LOST RECORD BY STARTING POSITION

CHICAGO 85-77	C	1B	2B	3B	SS	LF	CF	RF	P	DH	Leadoff	Relief	Starts
Juan Agosto												24-29	-
Harold Baines								85-73					85-73
Floyd Bannister									14-19				14-19
Daryl Boston							29-31						29-31
Britt Burns									21-13			1-1	21-13
John Cangelosi						0-1					2-3		0-1
Ed Correa									1-0			1-3	1-0
Julio Cruz			37-36										37-36
Joel Davis									7-4			1-0	7-4
Joe DeSa		2-4								3-1			5-5
Richard Dotson									4-5			3-7	4-5
Bob Fallon												1-3	-
Steve Fireovid													-
Carlton Fisk	65-54									14-14	13-7		79-68
Scott Fletcher			9-6	21-18	16-15								46-39
Oscar Gamble										25-18			25-18
Mark Gilbert						1-0	2-2	0-1			2-2		3-3
Jerry Don Gleaton												14-17	-
Ozzie Guillen					69-62						4-4		69-62
Jerry Hairston						1-1				13-10			14-11
Marc Hill	12-16												12-16
Tim Hulett			7-13	52-43									59-56
Bob James												50-19	-
Al Jones												3-2	-
Ron Kittle						31-23				24-27			55-50
Rudy Law						30-34	16-15				44-46		46-49
Bryan Little			32-22	0-1							1-1		32-23
Tim Lollar									7-6			1-4	7-6
Bill Long									1-2			0-1	1-2
Gene Nelson									8-10			14-14	8-10
Reid Nichols						5-5	12-5	0-1			16-9		17-11
Tom Paciorek		3-2				11-7		0-2		4-3			18-14
Mark Ryal						4-5	1-0				3-5		5-5
Luis Salazar		4-2		12-15		2-2	25-24					1-1	43-42
Tom Seaver									19-14				19-14
Joel Skinner	8-7												8-7
Dan Spillner												20-29	-
Mike Squires												5-6	-
Mike Stanton												2-4	-
Bruce Tanner									2-2				2-2
Greg Walker		76-69								2-4			78-73
Dave Wehrmeister												12-11	-

Batting vs. Left and Right Handed Pitchers

		BA	Rank	SA	Rank	OBA	Rank	HR %	Rank	BB %	Rank	SO %	Rank
Harold Baines	vs. Lefties	.341	6	.465	48	.368	34	2.76	74	4.76	136	14.29	98
	vs. Righties	.293	25	.468	32	.338	57	3.78	49	6.71	108	12.12	63
Daryl Boston	vs. Lefties	.118	--	.118	--	.211	--	0.00	--	10.00	--	20.00	--
	vs. Righties	.237	114	.349	118	.276	135	1.40	109	5.26	129	17.54	124
Julio Cruz	vs. Lefties	.250	101	.319	136	.360	43	0.00	131	14.71	12	10.29	44
	vs. Righties	.144	--	.144	--	.233	--	0.00	--	8.96	--	19.40	--
Carlton Fisk	vs. Lefties	.251	98	.464	50	.329	90	4.92	35	8.21	86	14.29	90
	vs. Righties	.231	124	.500	13	.316	91	7.78	2	8.47	72	11.92	67
Scott Fletcher	vs. Lefties	.298	38	.381	102	.374	27	1.19	112	9.03	61	15.48	105
	vs. Righties	.203	148	.218	157	.279	133	0.00	152				
Oscar Gamble	vs. Lefties	.125	--	.125	--	.125	--	0.00	--	0.00	--	12.50	68
	vs. Righties	.207	146	.329	131	.364	23	2.86	77	19.32	2	10.42	47
Ozzie Guillen	vs. Lefties	.211	144	.244	153	.228	155	0.00	131	1.04	157	16.48	116
	vs. Righties	.287	35	.384	90	.305	103	0.25	150	2.64	155	6.24	15
Tim Hulett	vs. Lefties	.296	41	.428	72	.354	56	1.26	110	8.52	77	19.92	144
	vs. Righties	.250	96	.339	126	.304	108	1.27	119	5.75	123	22.16	142
Ron Kittle	vs. Lefties	.236	126	.459	55	.323	98	6.76	11	10.78	44	22.00	149
	vs. Righties	.225	129	.472	28	.276	136	6.93	3	5.20	131	22.00	149
Rudy Law	vs. Lefties	.360	--	.480	--	.360	--	0.00	--	0.00	--	3.70	--
	vs. Righties	.252	94	.367	104	.308	98	1.10	126	6.75	107	9.75	44
Bryan Little	vs. Lefties	.000	--	.000	--	.222	--	0.00	--	11.11	--	33.33	--
	vs. Righties	.258	82	.352	115	.351	47	1.10	125	11.68	28	8.41	30
Reid Nichols	vs. Lefties	.282	58	.419	78	.344	72	1.71	97	9.02	68	9.77	40
	vs. Righties	.242	--	.242	--	.359	--	0.00	--	12.50	--	10.00	--
Tom Paciorek	vs. Lefties	.282	57	.306	139	.326	93	0.00	131	6.52	114	15.22	107
	vs. Righties	.162	--	.162	--	.220	--	0.00	--	4.88	--	19.51	--
Luis Salazar	vs. Lefties	.246	109	.398	89	.268	142	2.34	85	3.28	149	16.39	113
	vs. Righties	.244	107	.410	71	.267	145	3.85	44	3.53	151	17.65	126
Greg Walker	vs. Lefties	.230	129	.388	97	.257	150	2.19	89	3.66	145	13.07	76
	vs. Righties	.270	58	.483	23	.331	68	4.78	25	8.06	83	20.94	136
Team Average	vs. Lefties	.268	5	.395	13	.327	8	2.21	12	7.85	12	14.47	10
	vs. Righties	.247	13	.391	10	.309	14	2.89	6	7.68	13	13.55	8
League Average	vs. Lefties	.266		.416		.333		2.91		8.95		13.77	
	vs. Righties	.259		.401		.324		2.78		8.49		13.56	

Batting with Runners on Base and Bases Empty

		BA	Rank	SA	Rank	OBA	Rank	HR %	Rank	BB %	Rank	SO %	Rank
Harold Baines	Runners On	.337	6	.521	15	.370	42	4.21	43	6.16	127	13.20	86
	Bases Empty	.284	28	.417	64	.327	71	2.72	78	5.97	113	12.50	63
Daryl Boston	Runners On	.244	126	.322	134	.296	132	1.11	117	7.07	114	17.17	125
	Bases Empty	.218	135	.338	126	.255	150	1.41	116	4.70	136	18.12	128
Julio Cruz	Runners On	.172	155	.222	156	.252	154	0.00	142	9.82	60	15.18	106
	Bases Empty	.215	138	.237	155	.329	62	0.00	148	13.29	14	14.56	90
Carlton Fisk	Runners On	.287	58	.603	4	.371	40	8.02	2	10.71	45	10.00	50
	Bases Empty	.199	152	.399	82	.279	139	5.88	11	6.47	103	15.59	105
Scott Fletcher	Runners On	.287	57	.313	137	.366	47	0.00	142	10.56	49	9.86	46
	Bases Empty	.237	115	.306	145	.311	97	1.08	121	9.71	47	16.02	108
Ozzie Guillen	Runners On	.278	72	.351	123	.295	136	0.00	142	1.92	156	5.29	8
	Bases Empty	.269	50	.364	106	.289	131	0.34	146	2.62	155	8.20	26
Tim Hulett	Runners On	.258	101	.335	127	.322	104	0.65	134	8.38	100	20.67	147
	Bases Empty	.275	42	.400	78	.326	75	1.67	106	5.81	118	17.05	118
Ron Kittle	Runners On	.193	151	.398	93	.250	155	6.21	9	6.82	121	23.86	153
	Bases Empty	.257	81	.518	9	.328	63	7.34	3	7.88	74	20.75	139
Rudy Law	Runners On	.260	96	.382	105	.308	121	0.00	142	5.76	131	9.35	40
	Bases Empty	.258	75	.371	104	.313	95	1.50	113	6.60	99	9.38	36
Bryan Little	Runners On	.273	75	.403	90	.352	67	1.30	108	10.64	48	8.51	33
	Bases Empty	.234	120	.297	146	.341	42	0.90	130	12.40	19	10.08	40
Luis Salazar	Runners On	.255	106	.436	66	.293	139	4.03	48	5.78	130	12.72	82
	Bases Empty	.236	116	.376	100	.244	155	2.25	96	1.11	158	21.11	142
Greg Walker	Runners On	.285	61	.513	22	.350	70	4.56	33	9.52	65	13.61	94
	Bases Empty	.237	114	.408	68	.275	142	3.55	55	4.49	142	16.85	116
Team Average	Runners On	.270	8	.421	4	.332	10	2.95	6	8.47	13	12.92	7
	Bases Empty	.242	12	.372	11	.302	13	2.47	11	7.18	12	14.54	11
League Average	Runners On	.271		.416		.338		2.85		9.26		13.25	
	Bases Empty	.254		.397		.318		2.80		8.14		13.92	

Overall Batting Compared to Late Inning Pressure Situations

		BA	Rank	SA	Rank	OBA	Rank	HR %	Rank	BB %	Rank	SO %	Rank	RDI %	Rank
Harold Baines	Overall	.309	8	.467	27	.348	44	3.44	59	6.06	127	12.84	72	.362	21
	Pressure	.355	9	.605	6	.417	16	3.95	43	9.52	68	10.71	48	.333	55
Daryl Boston	Overall	.228	140	.332	140	.271	150	1.29	118	5.65	134	17.74	127	.176	159
	Pressure	.194	134	.333	99	.216	154	2.78	64	2.63	145	23.68	145	.167	--
Julio Cruz	Overall	.197	156	.231	158	.297	135	0.00	154	11.85	31	14.81	104	.174	161
	Pressure	.259	71	.296	120	.412	19	0.00	113	20.59	4	11.76	57	.429	16
Carlton Fisk	Overall	.238	130	.488	14	.320	100	6.81	3	8.39	79	13.06	76	.333	31
	Pressure	.286	49	.532	19	.341	67	6.49	20	6.98	104	13.95	78	.375	32
Scott Fletcher	Overall	.256	97	.309	147	.332	71	0.66	139	10.06	45	13.51	82	.373	11
	Pressure	.270	59	.297	119	.308	95	0.00	113	5.00	124	20.00	133	.385	30
Ozzie Guillen	Overall	.273	61	.358	121	.291	139	0.20	153	2.34	158	7.02	16	.230	133
	Pressure	.370	5	.425	60	.418	15	0.00	113	7.50	97	3.75	7	.176	124
Jerry Hairston	Overall	.243	--	.343	--	.371	--	1.43	--	16.57	--	10.29	--	.380	--
	Pressure	.326	21	.419	67	.420	13	0.00	113	14.00	30	10.00	40	.211	114
Tim Hulett	Overall	.268	66	.375	113	.324	85	1.27	120	6.86	112	18.54	135	.269	102
	Pressure	.231	104	.308	116	.259	134	1.92	86	3.57	136	25.00	150	.000	158
Ron Kittle	Overall	.230	139	.467	28	.295	136	6.86	2	7.43	97	22.06	152	.316	50
	Pressure	.149	156	.213	151	.259	134	2.13	82	11.11	53	31.48	159	.333	--
Rudy Law	Overall	.259	86	.374	114	.311	110	1.03	127	6.32	121	9.37	35	.315	51
	Pressure	.289	47	.356	90	.333	73	0.00	113	4.08	133	8.16	24	.167	128
Bryan Little	Overall	.250	104	.340	134	.345	48	1.06	125	11.66	32	9.42	36	.433	3
	Pressure	.214	--	.214	--	.313	--	0.00	--	12.50	--	6.25	--	.333	--
Reid Nichols	Overall	.273	--	.380	--	.347	--	1.33	--	9.83	--	9.83	--	.354	--
	Pressure	.286	--	.429	--	.304	--	4.76	--	4.17	--	8.33	--	.250	87
Tom Paciorek	Overall	.246	--	.262	--	.293	--	0.00	--	6.02	--	16.54	--	.278	--
	Pressure	.211	--	.211	--	.286	--	0.00	--	4.76	--	33.33	--	.200	117
Luis Salazar	Overall	.245	114	.404	90	.267	152	3.06	72	3.40	152	17.00	122	.303	61
	Pressure	.269	62	.442	50	.296	111	1.92	86	3.39	139	11.86	60	.222	104
Greg Walker	Overall	.258	89	.454	33	.309	114	3.99	45	6.77	114	15.38	108	.302	64
	Pressure	.259	74	.529	21	.300	104	7.06	14	5.56	121	20.00	133	.321	63
Team Average	Overall	.253	12	.392	10	.315	13	2.67	10	7.74	13	13.84	9	.313	1
	Pressure	.265	3	.397	4	.328	5	2.53	9	7.99	11	14.90	10	.272	8
League Average	Overall	.261		.406		.327		2.82		8.63		13.62		.287	
	Pressure	.253		.381		.323		2.74		9.11		14.40		.273	

Additional Miscellaneous Batting Comparisons

	Grass Surface BA	Rank	Artificial Surface BA	Rank	Home Games BA	Rank	Road Games BA	Rank	Runners in Scoring Position BA	Rank	Runners in Scoring Pos and Two Outs BA	Rank	Leading Off Inning OBA	Rank	Runners on 3B with less than 2 Outs RDI %	Rank
Harold Baines	.319	7	.244	91	.283	55	.335	2	.346	9	.370	8	.330	69	.667	47
Daryl Boston	.217	144	.279	--	.175	155	.267	63	.196	149	.217	113	.276	125	.667	--
Julio Cruz	.188	155	.243	--	.140	159	.230	131	.183	152	.182	139	.274	126	.375	--
Carlton Fisk	.225	139	.302	21	.203	151	.272	51	.336	14	.328	24	.270	132	.514	105
Scott Fletcher	.234	131	.351	7	.225	135	.283	29	.306	38	.296	39	.296	109	.667	47
Oscar Gamble	.193	154	.375	--	.190	--	.212	--	.270	--	.313	--	.378	--	.833	--
Ozzie Guillen	.287	36	.182	151	.279	57	.267	61	.305	39	.172	145	.274	127	.438	142
Jerry Hairston	.256	89	.174	--	.277	--	.213	--	.324	19	.238	90	.265	--	.700	29
Tim Hulett	.260	85	.311	15	.251	97	.285	25	.250	109	.255	64	.298	106	.563	86
Ron Kittle	.228	138	.238	104	.241	115	.217	144	.256	101	.250	68	.295	113	.550	93
Rudy Law	.268	65	.207	138	.271	70	.247	104	.304	40	.379	5	.306	100	.550	93
Bryan Little	.267	70	.148	--	.320	17	.170	158	.319	23	.188	--	.385	--	.750	13
Reid Nichols	.299	23	.130	--	.329	--	.221	--	.344	--	.353	--	.373	20	.455	137
Luis Salazar	.249	105	.224	123	.260	85	.232	128	.272	85	.344	14	.273	129	.500	106
Greg Walker	.255	91	.275	54	.266	77	.250	97	.285	65	.257	62	.307	97	.483	126
Team Average	.254	11	.250	11	.248	13	.258	6	.294	1	.282	1	.302	13	.576	7
League Average	.262		.259		.266		.256		.268		.248		.321		.587	

Pitching vs. Left and Right Handed Batters

		BA	Rank	SA	Rank	OBA	Rank	HR %	Rank	BB %	Rank	SO %	Rank
Juan Agosto	vs. Lefties	.214	15	.316	20	.310	41	1.02	18	9.65	75	16.67	29
	vs. Righties	.207	--	.276	--	.277	--	1.72	--	9.09	--	15.15	--
Floyd Bannister	vs. Lefties	.301	104	.548	129	.360	91	4.11	114	8.02	47	16.67	29
	vs. Righties	.253	59	.423	84	.339	88	3.64	98	11.36	118	22.32	6
Britt Burns	vs. Lefties	.240	40	.396	63	.279	14	3.90	108	5.36	16	19.64	13
	vs. Righties	.242	46	.385	54	.312	55	2.87	75	9.02	89	17.91	27
Joel Davis	vs. Lefties	.288	90	.404	65	.335	67	1.28	24	7.06	36	10.59	91
	vs. Righties	.215	18	.364	39	.301	42	3.31	90	10.22	104	13.87	64
Richard Dotson	vs. Lefties	.290	93	.477	104	.372	102	3.74	103	9.02	65	13.11	57
	vs. Righties	.229	--	.281	--	.269	--	1.04	--	5.77	--	16.35	--
Bob James	vs. Lefties	.236	33	.297	14	.283	17	0.51	7	6.48	27	20.37	11
	vs. Righties	.216	19	.309	13	.253	9	1.96	36	4.09	10	20.00	15
Gene Nelson	vs. Lefties	.249	52	.440	87	.334	66	3.89	107	10.54	87	14.63	41
	vs. Righties	.267	79	.470	117	.353	98	4.33	115	10.32	105	16.62	39
Tom Seaver	vs. Lefties	.249	51	.363	39	.314	46	2.15	49	8.46	57	16.15	32
	vs. Righties	.246	53	.386	55	.293	31	2.76	63	5.29	25	10.57	105
Dan Spillner	vs. Lefties	.210	11	.427	78	.272	9	4.03	112	7.97	46	10.87	89
	vs. Righties	.266	78	.402	68	.332	82	2.34	44	9.17	91	10.83	101
Team Average	vs. Lefties	.258	4	.403	6	.322	3	2.77	6	8.21	2	16.33	1
	vs. Righties	.255	6	.407	8	.331	11	3.01	7	9.71	14	16.51	1
League Average	vs. Lefties	.265		.408		.333		2.74		9.21		12.94	
	vs. Righties	.259		.404		.322		2.88		8.19		14.14	

Pitching with Runners on Base and Bases Empty

		BA	Rank	SA	Rank	OBA	Rank	HR %	Rank	BB %	Rank	SO %	Rank
Juan Agosto	Runners On	.253	--	.385	--	.330	--	2.20	--	10.09	--	10.09	--
	Bases Empty	.179	2	.228	1	.263	9	0.81	3	8.76	79	20.44	8
Floyd Bannister	Runners On	.269	67	.489	113	.359	93	5.14	126	12.53	114	19.30	11
	Bases Empty	.257	72	.415	84	.331	82	2.74	69	9.45	89	22.87	4
Britt Burns	Runners On	.247	39	.425	80	.332	54	4.06	108	11.50	105	17.91	16
	Bases Empty	.239	43	.365	37	.289	33	2.44	55	6.32	36	18.42	18
Joel Davis	Runners On	.268	66	.402	68	.328	48	2.68	63	8.73	60	7.94	124
	Bases Empty	.248	57	.376	46	.315	63	1.82	27	8.29	70	14.92	48
Richard Dotson	Runners On	.385	--	.500	--	.425	--	1.28	--	5.68	--	15.91	--
	Bases Empty	.184	3	.312	11	.261	7	3.20	89	8.70	78	13.77	59
Bob James	Runners On	.250	41	.332	15	.280	11	1.53	24	4.13	6	21.56	5
	Bases Empty	.202	10	.276	5	.257	6	0.99	9	6.42	38	18.81	13
Gene Nelson	Runners On	.211	7	.346	24	.315	34	2.53	56	11.89	109	17.48	21
	Bases Empty	.294	115	.538	129	.367	113	5.31	125	9.24	87	14.29	52
Tom Seaver	Runners On	.272	72	.384	50	.340	69	1.81	33	8.85	63	11.46	88
	Bases Empty	.233	35	.368	39	.282	22	2.81	72	5.75	24	14.78	50
Dan Spillner	Runners On	.277	79	.387	51	.363	100	1.46	21	12.20	111	10.37	102
	Bases Empty	.224	24	.428	92	.271	14	3.98	113	6.07	28	11.21	91
Team Average	Runners On	.270	8	.418	8	.347	10	3.03	11	10.45	13	15.45	1
	Bases Empty	.246	5	.397	8	.312	4	2.85	7	8.14	5	17.21	1
League Average	Runners On	.271		.416		.338		2.85		9.26		13.25	
	Bases Empty	.254		.397		.318		2.80		8.14		13.92	

Overall Pitching Compared to Late Inning Pressure Situations

		BA	Rank	SA	Rank	OBA	Rank	HR %	Rank	BB %	Rank	SO %	Rank
Juan Agosto	Overall	.210	--	.294	--	.292	--	1.40	--	9.35	--	15.85	--
	Pressure	.172	7	.276	14	.270	14	2.30	58	10.68	81	11.65	85
Floyd Bannister	Overall	.262	74	.445	101	.343	85	3.72	107	10.78	104	21.34	5
	Pressure	.348	127	.576	123	.450	127	6.06	126	16.25	123	17.50	25
Britt Burns	Overall	.242	33	.387	50	.306	34	3.05	82	8.37	66	18.22	14
	Pressure	.171	6	.317	25	.209	3	4.88	117	4.60	12	21.84	8
Joel Davis	Overall	.256	60	.386	48	.320	55	2.17	34	8.47	70	12.05	84
	Pressure	.313	112	.531	119	.405	114	3.13	83	13.16	105	18.42	23
Jerry Don Gleaton	Overall	.316	--	.453	--	.382	--	2.56	--	9.63	--	16.30	--
	Pressure	.243	47	.351	42	.300	36	2.70	71	7.32	39	14.63	50
Bob James	Overall	.226	14	.303	7	.268	3	1.25	7	5.28	9	20.18	8
	Pressure	.229	35	.318	26	.275	17	1.55	38	5.92	23	18.82	20
Gene Nelson	Overall	.259	64	.456	107	.344	87	4.13	120	10.42	101	15.71	31
	Pressure	.256	62	.463	103	.408	115	4.88	117	17.92	126	19.81	18
Tom Seaver	Overall	.248	43	.374	38	.304	31	2.44	46	6.95	32	13.49	60
	Pressure	.252	58	.378	61	.353	82	1.68	44	12.06	95	12.77	66
Dan Spillner	Overall	.246	37	.411	74	.310	41	2.96	77	8.73	74	10.85	106
	Pressure	.371	130	.661	131	.473	128	6.45	128	15.79	122	9.21	105
Mike Stanton	Overall	.283	--	.446	--	.397	--	3.61	--	14.50	--	14.50	--
	Pressure	.283	89	.609	126	.411	119	8.70	131	17.54	125	12.28	73
Dave Wehrmeister	Overall	.241	--	.372	--	.304	--	2.76	--	6.29	--	20.13	--
	Pressure	.306	109	.367	52	.358	86	0.00	1	5.56	21	20.37	14
Team Average	Overall	.256	4	.406	6	.327	7	2.92	8	9.15	11	16.44	1
	Pressure	.259	9	.407	10	.340	10	3.10	11	10.30	10	16.10	3
League Average	Overall	.261		.406		.327		2.82		8.63		13.62	
	Pressure	.258		.392		.332		2.71		9.52		14.05	

Additional Miscellaneous Pitching Comparisons

	Grass Surface BA	Rank	Artificial Surface BA	Rank	Home Games BA	Rank	Road Games BA	Rank	Runners in Scoring Position BA	Rank	Runners in Scoring Pos and Two Outs BA	Rank	Leading Off Inning OBA	Rank
Juan Agosto	.217	10	.125	--	.226	16	.185	--	.250	--	.290	101	.268	16
Floyd Bannister	.265	79	.250	52	.243	43	.277	85	.239	31	.172	18	.342	90
Britt Burns	.240	32	.256	62	.234	28	.250	42	.205	11	.207	35	.269	19
Joel Davis	.246	42	.286	93	.246	49	.265	70	.291	--	.231	--	.289	37
Richard Dotson	.229	18	.424	--	.234	29	.328	--	.283	--	.304	--	.232	6
Bob James	.227	16	.218	19	.237	35	.214	12	.252	49	.217	46	.267	15
Gene Nelson	.250	49	.347	125	.234	27	.286	96	.207	13	.161	13	.403	123
Tom Seaver	.250	52	.227	26	.270	88	.230	18	.219	18	.250	74	.273	20
Dan Spillner	.258	67	.186	6	.295	110	.191	4	.301	101	.275	89	.289	36
Mike Stanton	.286	--	.280	87	.151	--	.387	--	.350	128	.346	--	.297	--
Team Average	.256	4	.258	6	.254	6	.258	4	.243	1	.222	2	.315	4
League Average	.262		.259		.256		.266		.268		.248		.321	

CLEVELAND INDIANS

The litany of Cleveland baseball is by now familiar. No pennants since 1954. No pennant race since 1959. Twenty-five consecutive seasons finishing 14 or more games behind the league or division leader (excluding the 1981 season).

Ah, but there have been bad times, too.

Hardly a man is now alive who remembers the summer of '99, when the city's major-league representative was called the Spiders, not the Indians, and played in the 12-team National League. That team won 20 games and lost 134, a percentage of .130, the worst in the 110-year history of major-league baseball. And the team was just hitting its stride when the season ended, losing 40 of their last 41 games.

Some day, when the going gets tough, thumb through the *Baseball Encyclopedia* until you reach the Spiders' final National League season. Take a look at that pitching staff: Cold Water Jim Hughey, the ace right-hander, was 4–30 with a 5.41 ERA. He was backed up by Charlie Knepper (4–22)—clearly one of the best pitchers of his day, since his .154 percentage was markedly superior to the team's .130—and by Frank Bates, 1–18, believed to have later gone into the motel business.

Spalding's Official Base Ball Guide for 1900 looked upon the Spiders' pitching roster with alarm, noting that because Cleveland used the scandalously high total of 14 pitchers during the season, "if anything in the way of a lesson in club management was taught by the season's management of 1899, it was the folly of carrying a large corps of pitchers."

Hmmm, must have been an early-day stats-squirrel: look at some numbers, jump to the wrong conclusion. In fact, there was a more devious method to the Spiders' sadness. A small conflict of interest existed in the National League that year: A pair of brothers, Frank DeHaas Robison and Stanley Robison, owned both the Cleveland and St. Louis franchises. (Not that such a thing was all that uncommon: Similar double-ownerships affected the Baltimore and Brooklyn franchises, and for a time, Louisville and Pittsburgh.) The Robisons figured that by transferring the Spiders' best players to St. Louis, they would have a chance to win the pennant there before larger crowds than were likely in Cleveland. The Spiders had finished a respectable 81–68 in 1898, but none of their regular players or starting pitchers returned to Cleveland in '99; all but one wound up in St. Louis. The plan didn't work—St. Louis finished in fifth place in 1899—but among the players whom the Spiders lost were future Hall-of-Famers Jesse Burkett, Bobby Wallace, and a pitcher named Cy Young, who had gone 25–14 in 1898 to win the Dwight Gooden Award.

Following the 1899 season, the National League dropped the Cleveland, Louisville, Baltimore, and Washington franchises to get down to the eight-city league that remained intact until 1953. Three of those four cities became a part of the first American League season in 1901, although the Baltimore team was moved to New York two years later. For the Indians, there was one pennant (1920) in 47 seasons, followed by two more within seven years. There have been 17 managers in the 31 seasons since then, and the 102 losses accumulated last season equal the team record.

There are no quick fixes to be had. Contemporary baseball men are unlikely to allow St. Louis to make belated amends by sending Cleveland Willie McGee, Ozzie Smith, and John Tudor. The executive in charge of making the Indians a contender is named Bavasi, not Robison. And he is from a stock that stresses youth, patience, and development. The 4.91 ERA compiled by the Tribe last season was the highest in the majors since the 5.04 turned in by the 1962 Mets. It took the Mets seven more years to build a championship team. Can the Indians speed up that timetable? Well, they do have one truly remarkable player with a very useful specialty. . . .

The Tabler Tables

How often have you heard the phrase, "He rewrote the record book?" Every generation, it seems, has had a few outstanding players who have set so many records, whose achievements were so numerous and superior, that the record book indeed was rewritten to include their accomplishments. Their names read like a Cooperstown guide book: Babe Ruth; Ty Cobb; Walter Johnson; Ted Williams; Sandy Koufax; Pat Tabler.

Well, maybe not Tabler. And we didn't really rewrite the book on his particular specialty: hitting with the bases loaded. But that's only because there was no book on bases-loaded performance; one look at Tabler's extraordinary success with the bags full and we had to create one. Ruth and Cobb may have rewritten the book; Tabler wrote a new one all his own!

What, exactly, are we talking about? Entering the 1985 season, Tabler had the best batting average with the bases loaded in the majors over the previous ten seasons. And all he did last season was tack on another six hits in seven at bats. His career statistics with the bases loaded, including his totals of plate appearances and runs responsible for (see the explanation in the Batter Section introduction):

Year	PA	AB	H	2B	3B	HR	RRF	BB	SO	BA	SA	OBA
1981	1	1	0	0	0	0	0	0	1	.000	.000	.000
1982	1	0	0	0	0	0	2	0	0	—	—	.000
1983	22	19	11	0	2	0	25	1	3	.579	.789	.545
1984	13	9	5	1	0	1	14	3	1	.556	1.000	.615
1985	7	7	6	1	1	1	15	0	0	.857	1.714	.857
Totals	44	36	22	2	3	2	56	4	5	.611	1.000	.591

Compiling similar statistics for every player required a reexamination of our play-by-play data, and we took that opportunity to explore several related topics. Check the table on page 404 for a list of the Bases-Loaded Top 25. And read on for an examination of the bases-loaded situation unlike any other ever published.

Say your team trails by five runs going to the bottom of the ninth. Most of the crowd has gone, most of the rest are leaving. Do you stick around for the final out, or try to beat what's left of the traffic? First, consider the fact that only one half-inning in 110 produces at least five runs. For National League teams, the story is even worse —only one five-or-more-run inning in 135, and no team had more than 13 during the entire 1985 season. But what's this? While you were computing, your boys have loaded the bases with none out! How does that affect their chances of winning?

The none-out, bases-loaded situation increases the likelihood of a five-run inning more than 16 times. While the typical team loads the bases before its first out only once every 87 innings, those situations produce nearly 20 percent of all innings of five runs or more. On average, a team will parlay that situation into 2.5 runs; nonetheless, more than one-third will score no more than once, and the most common outcome is a single score. Here is the breakdown of runs scored following a none-out, bases-loaded situation last season:

Run Total	0	1	2	3	4	5	6	7	8	9	10	Total Inns.
American League	22	65	50	39	24	18	13	3	3	2	1	240
National League	27	48	30	37	26	14	2	6	1	1	1	193
Totals	49	113	80	76	50	32	15	9	4	3	2	433

The bases-loaded situation creates some stark but understandable changes in batter-pitcher dynamics. The most noticeable statistical change is a rise in batting average, from an overall .257 in the majors last season to .274 with the bags full. But that is merely cosmetic; batters are not charged with at bats for sacrifice flies ("scoring fly balls," for you Vin Scully fans), which are 10 times more common with the bases loaded than without. Award an at bat for all sac flies and the bases-loaded batting average of .254 falls one point below the new overall mark of .255 (with sacrifice flies treated as outs).

More significant is the decline in the rate of bases on balls, especially with less than two outs. Only one batter in 20 walks with the bases full and less than two outs, compared to an overall major league average of one in 12. Pitchers are also more likely to keep the ball down, in hopes of a double play. The ratio of ground outs to air outs increases from a major league average of 1.16 overall to 1.32 with the bases loaded, most but not all of which is a result of the increased likelihood of double-play ground outs.

Tabler's success, given all of those factors, is still somewhat unexpected; he hardly fits the profile of the typical bases-loaded overachiever. With pitchers forced to put the ball over the plate, and trying to keep their pitches down, players who hit significantly better with the bases loaded tend to be free swingers, with much higher than average home run and strikeout ratios. They also tend to be fly-ball hitters rather than ground-ball hitters. (Fly-ball hitters hit better against ground-ball pitchers. For more on this topic, see the Atlanta Braves essay.) None of those labels applies to Tabler.

Since we first compiled *The Player Analysis* in 1975, 277 players have batted at least 50 times with the bases loaded. From them, we extracted the 27 players—the top 10 percent—who demonstrated the most significant improvement with the bags full. We found an unusually high incidence of home-run hitters; among them, 11 players (41 percent) have overall career home-run percentages in the top 25 percent of all players (at least 3.5 home runs per 100 at bats); a 12th, Dusty Baker, just missed . Here are the career batting averages with the bases loaded for the group of 27; the home-run hitters are noted with asterisks:

	Bases Loaded BA	Overall BA	Diff.
Biff Pocoroba	.435	.257	.178
* Eddie Murray	.445	.298	.147
* Lee May	.402	.256	.146
* Ellis Valentine	.417	.278	.139
Dale Berra	.375	.238	.137
Lou Brock	.423	.286	.137
* Ken Singleton	.417	.284	.133
* Oscar Gamble	.392	.268	.124
Bill Madlock	.430	.308	.122
* Rico Carty	.404	.287	.117
Jay Johnstone	.400	.285	.115
Bill Russell	.380	.265	.115
Roy Howell	.370	.262	.108
Dave Concepcion	.374	.272	.102
* Richie Zisk	.382	.282	.100
Willie Randolph	.372	.274	.098
* Jason Thompson	.360	.262	.098
Darrell Porter	.338	.249	.089
Dusty Baker	.364	.279	.085
Steve Yeager	.303	.222	.081
Chris Chambliss	.361	.280	.081
* Don Baylor	.343	.263	.080
* Greg Luzinski	.354	.274	.080
Steve Garvey	.379	.300	.079
Dan Ford	.356	.270	.076
* Reggie Jackson	.339	.263	.076
Garry Maddox	.354	.282	.072

Finally, we'd like to give you a look at the first edition of the Bases-Loaded Record Book, honoring the outstanding individual bases-loaded performances over the past 11 seasons, and dedicated to Mr. Tabler.

Most hits in a season: 11, by six players—Steve Garvey and Larry Hisle in 1977, Chris Chambliss in 1978, Willie McGee in 1982, Tabler in 1983, and Hubie Brooks in 1985.

Most RRFs per plate appearance in a season: 2.50, Terry Crowley in 1977, with three two-run singles and a grand-slam home run in four appearances.

Most total plate appearances without a strikeout: 37, Dick Davis. Most total walks: 19, Sixto Lezcano and Pete Rose.

And now the underside:

Most total at bats without a hit: 20, Nelson Norman. Most career plate appearances without an RRF: 8, Danny Cox and Kevin Gross. Highest strikeout percentage: .380, Rick Monday (24 for 63).

All this doesn't mean that if Pat Tabler is coming up with the bases loaded, you'd do best to walk him intentionally. But it does mean that if there are runners on second and third and Tabler is on deck, you should think at least twice before you walk *anyone* to face him.

WON-LOST RECORD BY STARTING POSITION

CLEVELAND 60-102	C	1B	2B	3B	SS	LF	CF	RF	P	DH	Leadoff	Relief	Starts
Benny Ayala						8-11				1-1			9-12
Chris Bando	15-42												15-42
Jeff Barkley												3-18	-
Rick Behenna									1-3				1-3
Butch Benton	9-13												9-13
Tony Bernazard			52-89										52-89
Bert Blyleven									10-13				10-13
Brett Butler							53-95				43-84		53-95
Ernie Camacho												0-2	-
Joe Carter		4-3				33-68	0-1	4-7		2-4		1-3	43-83
Carmen Castillo								21-28		3-4			24-32
Ed Clark									0-3			8-20	0-3
Keith Creel									4-4			1-6	4-4
Jamie Easterly									5-2			11-32	5-2
Mike Fischlin			6-7		1-4								7-11
Julio Franco			2-6		57-92					0-1			59-99
Mel Hall						4-9				2-2			6-11
Mike Hargrove		28-42											28-42
Neal Heaton									11-22			0-3	11-22
Brook Jacoby				58-100									58-100
Mike Jeffcoat												1-8	-
Johnnie LeMaster					2-6								2-6
Otis Nixon						10-13	7-6			1-0	16-15		18-19
Jerry Reed									1-4			14-14	1-4
Jose Roman									0-3			0-2	0-3
Roman Romero									4-6			0-9	4-6
Vern Ruhle									4-12			9-17	4-12
Don Schulze									4-14			0-1	4-14
Roy Smith									4-7			0-1	4-7
Pat Tabler		28-55	2-2							6-11			36-68
Rich Thompson												12-45	-
Andre Thornton										42-79			42-79
Dave Von Ohlen												11-15	-
George Vukovich						5-1		35-67					40-68
Tom Waddell									6-3			17-23	6-3
Curt Wardle									6-6			1-2	6-6
Jerry Willard	36-47									1-0			37-47
Jim Wilson		0-2								2-0			2-2

Batting vs. Left and Right Handed Pitchers

		BA	Rank	SA	Rank	OBA	Rank	HR %	Rank	BB %	Rank	SO %	Rank
Benny Ayala	vs. Lefties	.275	67	.464	51	.301	123	2.90	70	4.11	142	17.81	125
	vs. Righties	.000	--	.000	--	.125	--	0.00	--	12.50	--	50.00	--
Chris Bando	vs. Lefties	.169	156	.236	155	.211	157	0.00	131	5.15	132	11.34	57
	vs. Righties	.107	--	.107	--	.255	--	0.00	--	16.67	--	9.80	--
Tony Bernazard	vs. Lefties	.258	89	.313	138	.364	39	0.00	131	14.57	14	9.27	35
	vs. Righties	.280	49	.435	56	.359	31	2.96	73	10.98	36	13.55	80
Brett Butler	vs. Lefties	.332	10	.430	71	.378	22	0.52	106	7.04	106	7.04	24
	vs. Righties	.302	17	.432	59	.376	17	1.01	129	10.60	41	5.96	9
Joe Carter	vs. Lefties	.248	106	.391	94	.303	120	3.11	62	6.86	108	16.57	118
	vs. Righties	.268	61	.418	66	.296	123	3.05	67	3.74	148	12.93	73
Carmen Castillo	vs. Lefties	.270	73	.557	10	.328	91	7.83	4	7.20	104	21.60	138
	vs. Righties	.203	--	.304	--	.247	--	2.90	--	2.74	--	17.81	--
Julio Franco	vs. Lefties	.286	53	.408	84	.340	78	2.04	91	7.44	99	12.56	80
	vs. Righties	.289	30	.368	101	.344	52	0.45	145	7.79	88	9.63	42
Mike Hargrove	vs. Lefties	.091	--	.091	--	.300	--	0.00	--	22.58	--	3.23	--
	vs. Righties	.302	16	.374	97	.378	16	0.38	147	10.85	39	9.49	39
Brook Jacoby	vs. Lefties	.276	66	.459	55	.335	85	4.86	37	8.37	80	17.24	122
	vs. Righties	.273	55	.411	70	.319	87	2.61	85	6.75	106	18.52	134
Pat Tabler	vs. Lefties	.312	27	.416	79	.353	58	1.95	92	6.51	115	10.65	49
	vs. Righties	.252	95	.344	121	.301	114	0.80	137	5.93	119	13.70	82
Andre Thornton	vs. Lefties	.268	77	.451	62	.358	47	5.23	26	12.85	25	11.73	65
	vs. Righties	.221	133	.386	89	.275	137	4.55	29	7.16	96	16.12	113
George Vukovich	vs. Lefties	.143	--	.190	--	.200	--	0.00	--	4.35	--	26.09	--
	vs. Righties	.255	87	.367	102	.302	111	2.04	97	6.60	109	14.86	99
Jerry Willard	vs. Lefties	.146	--	.188	--	.222	--	0.00	--	7.27	--	36.36	--
	vs. Righties	.294	23	.421	64	.355	40	2.78	79	8.60	70	13.98	87
Team Average	vs. Lefties	.260	12	.389	14	.320	13	2.48	10	8.08	11	14.19	7
	vs. Righties	.267	4	.383	11	.326	6	1.93	13	8.02	11	12.97	6
League Average	vs. Lefties	.266		.416		.333		2.91		8.95		13.77	
	vs. Righties	.259		.401		.324		2.78		8.49		13.56	

Batting with Runners on Base and Bases Empty

		BA	Rank	SA	Rank	OBA	Rank	HR %	Rank	BB %	Rank	SO %	Rank
Chris Bando	Runners On	.115	158	.141	158	.228	157	0.00	142	12.77	30	8.51	33
	Bases Empty	.158	--	.200	--	.238	--	0.00	--	9.52	--	12.38	--
Tony Bernazard	Runners On	.281	65	.366	117	.382	23	0.89	123	13.97	21	9.93	48
	Bases Empty	.268	54	.435	48	.342	40	3.26	63	10.10	39	14.66	92
Brett Butler	Runners On	.328	13	.444	61	.390	16	1.52	102	9.52	65	3.03	2
	Bases Empty	.303	10	.425	58	.370	14	0.51	142	9.43	49	8.05	23
Joe Carter	Runners On	.273	75	.418	75	.314	112	2.27	85	5.79	129	14.05	98
	Bases Empty	.253	94	.401	76	.285	137	3.72	49	3.91	146	14.23	83
Carmen Castillo	Runners On	.227	--	.440	--	.275	--	5.33	--	5.00	--	23.75	--
	Bases Empty	.257	81	.477	27	.314	93	6.42	7	5.93	114	17.80	124
Julio Franco	Runners On	.301	37	.404	88	.355	62	1.37	107	8.18	104	9.39	42
	Bases Empty	.276	40	.360	110	.332	58	0.58	140	7.24	89	11.53	53
Mike Hargrove	Runners On	.330	10	.385	102	.426	7	0.92	121	14.50	17	9.92	47
	Bases Empty	.257	80	.331	131	.333	54	0.00	148	10.26	34	8.21	27
Brook Jacoby	Runners On	.297	42	.480	38	.350	71	4.03	47	8.47	97	17.59	130
	Bases Empty	.255	86	.381	97	.301	110	2.70	79	6.20	110	18.59	133
Pat Tabler	Runners On	.302	36	.413	78	.337	84	1.68	98	5.64	133	11.79	68
	Bases Empty	.253	93	.338	127	.309	100	0.89	131	6.56	100	13.11	70
Andre Thornton	Runners On	.267	79	.521	17	.327	97	6.91	5	8.98	83	14.29	100
	Bases Empty	.209	144	.307	143	.283	138	2.87	75	9.29	52	14.87	93
George Vukovich	Runners On	.240	131	.403	89	.295	138	3.06	70	7.34	111	14.68	103
	Bases Empty	.248	101	.307	144	.290	129	0.84	134	5.56	122	17.06	119
Jerry Willard	Runners On	.246	124	.377	107	.313	115	3.08	68	8.11	105	16.89	123
	Bases Empty	.288	24	.388	93	.349	22	1.76	104	8.60	62	18.28	130
Team Average	Runners On	.278	4	.414	9	.338	6	2.56	10	8.62	11	12.42	4
	Bases Empty	.255	5	.363	13	.313	10	1.75	13	7.57	11	14.09	7
League Average	Runners On	.271		.416		.338		2.85		9.26		13.25	
	Bases Empty	.254		.397		.318		2.80		8.14		13.92	

Overall Batting Compared to Late Inning Pressure Situations

		BA	Rank	SA	Rank	OBA	Rank	HR %	Rank	BB %	Rank	SO %	Rank	RDI %	Rank
Chris Bando	Overall	.139	--	.173	--	.234	--	0.00	--	11.06	--	10.55	--	.255	115
	Pressure	.143	--	.143	--	.172	--	0.00	--	3.33	--	10.00	--	.250	87
Tony Bernazard	Overall	.274	56	.404	89	.361	25	2.20	97	11.92	29	12.44	63	.282	89
	Pressure	.291	45	.430	55	.333	73	2.33	78	6.45	114	13.98	79	.308	65
Brett Butler	Overall	.311	7	.431	60	.377	10	0.85	134	9.46	53	6.31	9	.292	75
	Pressure	.195	133	.220	150	.267	130	0.00	113	8.79	80	5.49	12	.167	128
Joe Carter	Overall	.262	82	.409	80	.298	132	3.07	71	4.78	140	14.15	92	.275	96
	Pressure	.296	41	.394	77	.315	88	2.82	63	2.67	144	13.33	72	.174	126
Julio Franco	Overall	.288	28	.381	107	.343	54	0.94	131	7.68	95	10.53	46	.320	45
	Pressure	.200	130	.250	142	.273	127	0.00	113	9.09	77	5.68	14	.250	87
Mike Hargrove	Overall	.285	36	.352	126	.370	14	0.35	148	11.96	27	8.90	33	.371	16
	Pressure	.304	35	.326	102	.385	28	0.00	113	11.54	51	13.46	73	.222	104
Brook Jacoby	Overall	.274	58	.426	67	.324	87	3.30	63	7.25	102	18.13	132	.286	85
	Pressure	.229	106	.289	126	.286	118	1.20	109	7.69	93	16.48	102	.118	145
Pat Tabler	Overall	.275	55	.371	117	.321	98	1.24	121	6.15	124	12.53	67	.407	5
	Pressure	.214	121	.321	105	.267	130	0.00	113	4.92	126	8.20	25	.273	78
Andre Thornton	Overall	.236	132	.408	86	.304	126	4.77	28	9.14	65	14.59	101	.356	23
	Pressure	.224	113	.493	28	.284	121	8.96	6	8.11	90	9.46	32	.308	65
George Vukovich	Overall	.244	117	.350	129	.292	138	1.84	103	6.38	119	15.96	112	.238	127
	Pressure	.241	96	.278	132	.259	134	0.00	113	2.47	146	23.46	144	.154	135
Jerry Willard	Overall	.270	65	.383	103	.333	69	2.33	91	8.38	80	17.66	125	.268	105
	Pressure	.347	11	.531	20	.421	12	4.08	42	12.07	44	6.90	17	.318	64
Team Average	Overall	.265	4	.385	12	.324	9	2.10	13	8.04	11	13.35	6	.301	6
	Pressure	.242	10	.340	13	.296	14	1.85	12	6.99	14	12.74	1	.230	14
League Average	Overall	.261		.406		.327		2.82		8.63		13.62		.287	
	Pressure	.253		.381		.323		2.74		9.11		14.40		.273	

Additional Miscellaneous Batting Comparisons

	Grass Surface BA	Rank	Artificial Surface BA	Rank	Home Games BA	Rank	Road Games BA	Rank	Runners in Scoring Position BA	Rank	Runners in Scoring Pos and Two Outs BA	Rank	Leading Off Inning OBA	Rank	Runners on 3B with less than 2 Outs RDI %	Rank
Chris Bando	.132	158	.182	--	.140	158	.137	--	.130	157	.154	149	.256	--	.857	--
Tony Bernazard	.291	32	.193	149	.301	33	.248	103	.262	95	.241	87	.331	68	.538	97
Brett Butler	.306	16	.340	9	.329	11	.295	14	.351	8	.244	79	.352	39	.571	83
Joe Carter	.267	72	.234	111	.267	75	.256	86	.244	112	.220	107	.294	115	.688	35
Carmen Castillo	.232	134	.303	--	.282	--	.221	139	.176	--	.333	--	.383	12	.250	--
Julio Franco	.306	14	.194	148	.306	26	.271	53	.292	56	.286	44	.339	53	.585	76
Mike Hargrove	.303	21	.200	141	.302	32	.269	58	.321	21	.214	118	.382	14	.857	1
Brook Jacoby	.256	90	.374	3	.271	72	.277	40	.237	119	.235	94	.322	80	.674	46
Otis Nixon	.247	109	.083	--	.275	--	.204	--	.182	--	.100	--	.348	42	.500	--
Pat Tabler	.288	34	.150	--	.326	13	.215	145	.340	12	.208	125	.278	123	.840	2
Andre Thornton	.230	136	.275	53	.231	129	.242	115	.309	34	.255	65	.269	138	.613	64
George Vukovich	.247	110	.230	118	.231	127	.257	83	.241	114	.246	75	.287	118	.611	65
Jerry Willard	.272	59	.262	67	.272	68	.268	59	.227	125	.156	148	.395	9	.600	66
Team Average	.267	3	.252	8	.279	3	.252	10	.270	6	.234	12	.319	6	.639	2
League Average	.262		.259		.266		.256		.268		.248		.321		.587	

Pitching vs. Left and Right Handed Batters

		BA	Rank	SA	Rank	OBA	Rank	HR %	Rank	BB %	Rank	SO %	Rank
Bryan Clark	vs. Lefties	.378	--	.573	--	.446	--	4.88	--	10.64	--	12.77	--
	vs. Righties	.278	97	.420	82	.364	118	2.37	45	12.24	123	6.12	131
Keith Creel	vs. Lefties	.298	101	.473	103	.340	71	3.05	82	5.56	19	11.81	76
	vs. Righties	.293	--	.457	--	.368	--	2.59	--	11.28	--	10.53	--
Jamie Easterly	vs. Lefties	.270	71	.296	12	.351	85	0.00	1	10.45	86	13.43	53
	vs. Righties	.261	73	.414	80	.358	107	3.61	96	12.96	126	13.29	73
Neal Heaton	vs. Lefties	.304	106	.435	83	.367	96	1.24	23	8.70	60	10.87	89
	vs. Righties	.296	114	.445	99	.361	114	2.58	56	8.68	84	8.41	126
Jerry Reed	vs. Lefties	.289	91	.496	118	.329	58	5.19	128	5.44	18	6.80	122
	vs. Righties	.203	5	.341	20	.268	16	3.62	97	7.14	49	17.53	30
Ramon Romero	vs. Lefties	.276	--	.382	--	.356	--	2.63	--	11.49	--	18.39	--
	vs. Righties	.276	94	.529	129	.391	128	6.32	131	13.46	127	10.58	104
Vern Ruhle	vs. Lefties	.270	70	.395	61	.314	45	2.73	72	6.16	24	10.14	100
	vs. Righties	.297	115	.441	95	.335	85	3.81	107	5.08	19	10.16	111
Don Schulze	vs. Lefties	.355	131	.496	117	.379	106	2.63	64	3.72	2	6.20	124
	vs. Righties	.278	97	.426	86	.328	77	2.37	45	5.35	27	11.76	92
Roy Smith	vs. Lefties	.328	127	.542	128	.371	100	4.58	122	6.94	34	5.56	127
	vs. Righties	.313	126	.443	97	.348	93	1.53	17	4.96	17	14.18	60
Rick Thompson	vs. Lefties	.304	105	.488	113	.390	118	3.20	88	12.93	111	2.72	131
	vs. Righties	.302	120	.444	98	.404	130	2.12	39	12.50	124	11.21	98
Dave Von Ohlen	vs. Lefties	.302	--	.372	--	.375	--	2.33	--	9.43	--	5.66	--
	vs. Righties	.283	102	.383	52	.353	97	1.67	22	10.49	109	6.29	130
Tom Waddell	vs. Lefties	.276	77	.502	119	.361	92	5.91	129	11.49	97	8.09	117
	vs. Righties	.219	22	.406	74	.258	10	3.65	100	5.08	20	14.41	58
Curt Wardle	vs. Lefties	.310	112	.581	130	.397	122	3.88	105	12.34	103	18.18	20
	vs. Righties	.274	92	.494	124	.358	108	4.72	120	11.65	119	15.18	50
Team Average	vs. Lefties	.294	14	.447	14	.355	14	2.89	8	8.60	4	10.59	14
	vs. Righties	.272	13	.432	14	.340	13	3.20	14	8.83	11	11.65	14
League Average	vs. Lefties	.265		.408		.333		2.74		9.21		12.94	
	vs. Righties	.259		.404		.322		2.88		8.19		14.14	

Pitching with Runners on Base and Bases Empty

		BA	Rank	SA	Rank	OBA	Rank	HR %	Rank	BB %	Rank	SO %	Rank
Bryan Clark	Runners On	.347	129	.554	128	.413	129	4.96	125	10.64	95	7.80	125
	Bases Empty	.277	100	.392	60	.369	114	1.54	19	12.75	121	8.72	124
Keith Creel	Runners On	.300	104	.473	104	.359	94	1.82	34	9.38	75	14.06	52
	Bases Empty	.292	114	.460	109	.349	99	3.65	103	7.38	57	8.72	124
Jamie Easterly	Runners On	.263	56	.395	64	.332	58	3.16	86	9.21	71	13.60	61
	Bases Empty	.264	84	.356	35	.382	122	1.72	25	15.46	129	13.04	70
Neal Heaton	Runners On	.263	56	.392	61	.322	39	2.11	46	7.64	38	8.80	119
	Bases Empty	.328	127	.487	123	.397	127	2.51	59	9.61	92	9.00	119
Jerry Reed	Runners On	.290	95	.439	88	.339	68	2.80	71	7.32	37	13.01	71
	Bases Empty	.217	17	.404	76	.270	13	5.42	126	5.62	22	11.80	85
Ramon Romero	Runners On	.261	54	.369	36	.381	119	1.80	32	14.07	124	15.56	36
	Bases Empty	.288	109	.576	130	.381	121	7.91	130	11.88	116	10.63	101
Vern Ruhle	Runners On	.321	122	.492	114	.363	102	4.15	109	6.94	31	9.26	112
	Bases Empty	.258	74	.368	38	.297	42	2.68	64	4.75	14	10.76	96
Don Schulze	Runners On	.314	118	.459	98	.356	90	2.70	64	5.29	15	7.21	127
	Bases Empty	.330	128	.472	114	.357	106	2.36	50	3.62	4	9.95	111
Roy Smith	Runners On	.353	130	.526	122	.388	122	3.45	94	6.15	21	9.23	115
	Bases Empty	.295	117	.466	110	.335	88	2.74	70	5.81	25	10.32	107
Rick Thompson	Runners On	.328	124	.497	117	.427	131	2.73	67	14.35	125	6.09	131
	Bases Empty	.267	88	.412	80	.356	103	2.29	46	10.07	95	10.74	99
Tom Waddell	Runners On	.228	22	.431	85	.297	25	4.57	118	9.25	72	13.22	68
	Bases Empty	.262	82	.471	113	.320	73	4.89	122	7.38	56	9.43	117
Curt Wardle	Runners On	.333	127	.639	132	.392	126	6.39	132	9.38	75	13.28	66
	Bases Empty	.237	40	.404	75	.348	97	2.63	62	14.23	125	18.73	14
Team Average	Runners On	.292	14	.454	13	.357	13	3.08	12	9.39	8	10.68	14
	Bases Empty	.272	14	.426	13	.336	14	3.06	11	8.16	6	11.67	14
League Average	Runners On	.271		.416		.338		2.85		9.26		13.25	
	Bases Empty	.254		.397		.318		2.80		8.14		13.92	

Overall Pitching Compared to Late Inning Pressure Situations

Player		BA	Rank	SA	Rank	OBA	Rank	HR %	Rank	BB %	Rank	SO %	Rank
Jeff Barkley	Overall	.243	--	.388	--	.308	--	3.29	--	8.62	--	17.24	--
	Pressure	.333	118	.472	106	.432	125	2.78	76	14.89	119	6.38	124
Bryan Clark	Overall	.311	124	.470	117	.390	129	3.19	91	11.72	109	8.28	126
	Pressure	.262	65	.357	45	.360	88	2.38	59	13.46	108	9.62	102
Keith Creel	Overall	.296	113	.466	112	.354	103	2.83	70	8.30	64	11.19	99
	Pressure	.200	--	.400	--	.227	--	5.00	--	4.55	--	13.64	--
Jamie Easterly	Overall	.264	76	.376	41	.356	106	2.47	50	12.18	115	13.33	63
	Pressure	.253	59	.301	18	.343	74	1.20	25	12.12	97	14.14	52
Neal Heaton	Overall	.298	100	.443	100	.362	116	2.32	42	8.69	72	8.90	121
	Pressure	.315	114	.548	122	.393	108	4.11	102	10.47	78	6.98	120
Jerry Reed	Overall	.245	36	.418	83	.298	21	4.40	122	6.31	23	12.29	81
	Pressure	.282		.487	112	.345	77	5.13	121	9.20	61	12.64	69
Ramon Romero	Overall	.276	95	.484	122	.381	124	5.20	131	12.88	123	12.88	68
	Pressure	.182	--	.455	--	.182	--	9.09	--	0.00	--	0.00	--
Vern Ruhle	Overall	.283	102	.417	82	.324	58	3.25	93	5.64	10	10.15	112
	Pressure	.270	75	.381	63	.338	69	3.17	87	9.86	74	5.63	129
Don Schulze	Overall	.322	129	.466	113	.357	107	2.52	55	4.43	6	8.62	123
	Pressure	.243	47	.405	74	.300	36	2.70	71	7.50	41	7.50	116
Roy Smith	Overall	.321	128	.492	127	.359	109	3.05	83	5.96	15	9.82	116
	Pressure	.333	--	.519	--	.357	--	3.70	--	3.45	--	6.90	--
Rick Thompson	Overall	.303	119	.462	110	.398	131	2.55	58	12.66	122	7.92	128
	Pressure	.319	115	.460	101	.416	120	2.65	70	13.38	106	6.34	125
Dave Von Ohlen	Overall	.288	--	.380	--	.358	--	1.84	--	10.20	--	6.12	--
	Pressure	.500	131	.500	114	.655	131	0.00	1	30.56	131	2.78	131
Tom Waddell	Overall	.246	40	.453	104	.309	39	4.74	128	8.28	63	11.25	97
	Pressure	.264	68	.438	91	.313	49	3.31	91	6.72	34	12.69	68
Curt Wardle	Overall	.284	104	.519	129	.369	119	4.47	124	11.85	112	16.06	28
	Pressure	.291	97	.608	125	.378	101	6.33	127	11.70	88	22.34	7
Team Average	Overall	.281	14	.438	14	.346	14	3.07	11	8.74	9	11.21	14
	Pressure	.280	12	.419	12	.358	13	2.87	8	10.58	12	9.98	14
League Average	Overall	.261		.406		.327		2.82		8.63		13.62	
	Pressure	.258		.392		.332		2.71		9.52		14.05	

Additional Miscellaneous Pitching Comparisons

Player	Grass Surface BA	Rank	Artificial Surface BA	Rank	Home Games BA	Rank	Road Games BA	Rank	Runners in Scoring Position BA	Rank	Runners in Scoring Pos and Two Outs BA	Rank	Leading Off Inning OBA	Rank
Bryan Clark	.325	128	.231	--	.312	126	.310	115	.375	131	.371	127	.317	65
Keith Creel	.300	110	.143	--	.310	124	.275	--	.197	6	.226	54	.313	60
Jamie Easterly	.264	77	.264	71	.212	10	.300	107	.265	64	.294	104	.359	105
Neal Heaton	.296	107	.309	113	.271	90	.330	125	.254	52	.226	54	.362	109
Jerry Reed	.230	19	.319	119	.222	--	.263	65	.298	--	.250	--	.194	2
Ramon Romero	.272	85	.318	--	.240	40	.310	116	.279	86	.231	--	.348	98
Vern Ruhle	.281	95	.291	99	.251	61	.306	113	.327	117	.238	66	.287	33
Don Schulze	.330	129	.267	--	.297	112	.360	130	.330	122	.282	97	.408	126
Roy Smith	.316	123	.355	--	.302	117	.345	--	.302	102	.281	96	.309	55
Rick Thompson	.313	121	.262	69	.319	128	.290	100	.336	123	.281	95	.385	120
Dave Von Ohlen	.257	64	.600	--	.354	--	.261	60	.304	--	.346	--	.349	--
Tom Waddell	.241	35	.267	74	.235	32	.261	60	.270	71	.200	30	.360	107
Curt Wardle	.306	117	.236	32	.252	64	.314	120	.303	103	.176	21	.339	86
Team Average	.279	14	.293	14	.265	11	.297	14	.294	14	.260	9	.329	10
League Average	.262		.259		.256		.266		.268		.248		.321	

DETROIT TIGERS

Last winter, the word *dynasty* was restored to the baseball vocabulary. Time was when the word provoked images of Ruth, Gehrig, DiMaggio, and Mantle. But in the baseball world of the 1980s, back-to-back titles constitutes a notable streak, and the mention of *dynasty* only diverts discussion away from Ruth and Gehrig to Linda Evans and Joan Collins. In the wake of the Detroit Tigers' spectacular romp over the rest of the American League during the 1984 season and their devastating post-season performance, though, talk again was of a dynasty. The parley was as follows: the largest margin of victory in the American League's Eastern Division since 1970 (15 games), by a team whose top players were only approaching their 30s (Whitaker, Trammell, Gibson, and Parrish), with an equally young pitching staff (Morris, Petry, and Hernandez), and several highly-touted young players to be added (Chris Pittaro, Nelson Simmons, and Randy O'Neal). The logical conclusion: dynasty. The inevitable result: futility.

The facts are well-known. Over the past five seasons, the 10 American League division titles have been won by nine different teams. Kansas City has won the Western Division championship in each of the past two seasons, the first American League team to repeat as a division champion since the New York Yankees of 1980 and '81. No team has won the American League pennant in consecutive seasons since the Yankees of 1977 and '78. Five different teams have won the past five league titles for the first time since the 1940s.

The story is no different in the National League. No fewer than 10 of its 12 teams have won division titles in the past seven seasons. No team has won consecutive division titles since 1978, when Philadelphia and Los Angeles each successfully defended their titles. No team has successfully defended the NL pennant since the Cincinnati Reds in 1976.

On a year-to-year basis, contemporary baseball has not been without its budding dynasties. Last year, we noted, "With rare exceptions, defending championship teams look good enough on paper to repeat. . . . and the (1985) Tigers look as solid as any defending champion since. . . . the 1983 Orioles." Inevitably, those teams have stumbled, opening the door for the next budding dynasty. And we are left to conclude that the great teams of today pale by comparison to those of eras gone by. Or are we?

Stephen Jay Gould, in his book *The Flamingo's Smile*, tackles a similar puzzle in his discussion of the extinction of the .400 hitter. Gould, a natural scientist and then some who occasionally turns his brilliance to the study of baseball, maintains that the commonly cited factors (among them relief pitching, night games, and the extended schedule) fail to adequately explain declining batting averages among the best hitters, because recent league averages have remained fairly constant, and at roughly the level of the decade from 1911 to 1920. In that decade, the author points out, American League–leading averages dipped below .380 just twice.

Gould contends that to explain the extinction of .400 hitters, we must study the systems in which they once flourished. And, he continues, the evolution of this system we call baseball has generated such refinements as improved defensive positioning and execution, and the development of new unorthodox pitches, which have dulled the brilliance of today's most illustrious performers. As Gould says, "The best now (meet) an opposition too finely honed to its own perfection to permit the extremes of achievement that characterized a more casual age."

The same theory can be applied to explain the volatility in the standings of both leagues over the past decade (and the resultant extinction of dynastic teams) as merely an extension of a half-century-old trend. Over the past 50 years, the talent gap between the best and worst teams has gradually but steadily shrunk, not because today's best teams are historically inferior, but because the overall level of play has risen to a point at which it is practically impossible for a given team to dominate its opposition continually the way the great teams of the past did. As a result, with even a modest improvement, a team can climb rapidly in the standings past the pack of roughly equivalent teams.

During this time, teams have experimented with different innovations. Some, like the expanded use of the bullpen, have worked; others, like Charlie O. Finley's pinch-running specialists, have not. Unsuccessful teams have emulated the innovations of consistent winners, narrowing the margin between the best and the worst without shrinking the *talent* gap between the teams. As the successful innovations are spread among all teams throughout baseball, the distinctions between teams are blurred. Talent will never be equally distributed among the major-league teams, but a team's overall performance also depends on strategy and, to a certain extent, streakiness and luck. And there are no copyrights on strategy.

The following table shows the standard deviation of team winning percentages over each of the past five decades, and illustrates the spread between teams. You don't need an understanding of *Principia Mathematica* to see that the variation between teams has decreased progressively during that time:

1940–49	.093
1950–59	.087
1960–69	.079
1970–79	.072
1980–85	.068

In practical terms, the theory suggests that a given team, the the 1984 Detroit Tigers for example, can dominate its division or league over a limited period, but that such a period represents only an exceptional streak by a good team, like a .300 hitter who hits .400 for a month or so. Just as that .300 hitter will find it impossible to maintain a .400 average for two months, it is unlikely that the team will extend its temporary dominance over the course of more than a single season. In the case of the Tigers, the peak period lasted for only a few months, but was so exceptional that no team could catch them. Remember, Detroit won 35 of its first 40 games, but had only the second-best record in their division during the second half of the 1984 season. And never during the 1985 season did Detroit even approach its form of that phenomenal stretch a year earlier.

No Relief In Sight

The reasons for Detroit's decline were many, but were nowhere as apparent as in the bullpen. During the 1984 championship season, Willie Hernandez became the second relief pitcher ever named the American League's Most Valuable Player, and for good reason: Detroit did not lose a single game in which they led after the eighth inning. Hernandez did not fail in a save situation until the final weekend of the regular season, long after the Tigers had wrapped up the division title. And Sparky Anderson reprised his fabled role as Captain Hook, making a full-time setup man of Aurelio Lopez, whose job it was to take the ball from the starting pitcher, frequently as early as the sixth inning, and deliver it to Hernandez in the eighth or ninth, along with the same lead he had inherited.

Lopez performed so well that despite one of the league's best starting rotations—they ranked fourth with a 3.88 ERA—Tigers starters completed seven innings only 59 times, the lowest total in the league. And in games in which their starters failed to pitch seven innings, normally an indication of failure, the Tigers compiled a 59–44 record, compared to a .333 winning percentage by other AL teams. But last season, the failure of Lopez and Hernandez even to approach their 1984 performances spelled disaster for Detroit. The Tigers lost seven games last season in which they led after eight innings, the second-highest total in the American League. Hernandez was the pitcher of record in five of them. And the failure of Lopez to provide the same service last season as a year earlier is evident in the following figures:

Starting Pitchers	1984 Total (Rank)	W–L	Pct.	1985 Total (Rank)	W–L	Pct.
7 innings or more	59 (14)	45–14	.763	75 (3)	55–20	.787
Less than 7 innings	103 (1)	59–44	.573	87 (11T)	29–57	.337

Last season, only Boston and Minnesota had fewer seven-inning starts than Detroit. Anderson lost confidence in Lopez, and his starters were forced to get the game to Hernandez by themselves. Detroit's record in games in which the starters failed to go seven fell from a league-leading .573 to .337, only slightly above the league average of .281.

On the offensive side of the ledger, the problems were less obvious, but no less significant. Great seasons by Darrell Evans and Lou Whitaker more than offset a subpar season for Alan Trammell, while players like Lance Parrish, Kirk Gibson, and Chet Lemon approximated their 1984 seasons. Nevertheless, Detroit scored 100 fewer runs last season than a year earlier, and the decline can be traced largely to the lack of production from the faceless Detroit irregulars, a group which had played a significant part in the 1984 season. What had made Detroit look primed to repeat was their strength up the middle and in right field; that strength masked the weaknesses at the traditional hitting positions of left field, third base, first base, and designated hitter. Evans's great comeback helped, but the rest of the group holding down those spots fell off sharply. Compare the performances of the following players, who started a nearly equal number of games in each of the past two seasons. The statistics include only games which the players started:

	1984					1985			
Player	GS	BA	HR	RBI	Player	GS	BA	HR	RBI
Bergman	68	.274	6	33	Bergman	33	.164	3	6
Brookens	63	.249	5	22	Brookens	137	.233	7	45
Garbey	79	.284	5	41	Garbey	59	.270	5	24
Herndon	98	.266	4	35	Herndon	110	.247	11	32
Johnson	101	.253	12	44	Pittaro	21	.259	0	7
Jones	60	.279	11	33	Sanchez	29	.250	4	8
Totals	469	.267	43	208	Simmons	67	.239	9	31
					Totals	456	.240	39	153

The loss of Howard Johnson's home runs from the third-base mix was balanced by the acquisition of Walt Terrell. But the loss of Ruppert Jones was a difficult pill for the Tigers to swallow. They let Jones go as a free agent, and he turned in a solid season for the California Angels. He hit 21 homers and drove in 67 runs, starting 106 games and playing all three outfield positions as well as designated hitter. Although Jones has never hit left-handed pitching very well, neither has Larry Herndon hit right-handed pitching, and the two might have provided Sparky with a classic lefty-righty platoon in the outfield, comparable to the Lowenstein-Roenicke tandem of the 1983 Orioles. The batting averages below are misleading; don't overlook the extra-base hit and walk totals. Last season's statistics:

	AB	H	2B	3B	HR	BB	SO	BA	SA	OBA
Herndon vs. LH	155	41	3	5	7	20	23	.265	.484	.347
Jones vs. RH	343	82	16	1	19	52	70	.239	.458	.338
Totals	498	123	19	6	26	72	93	.247	.466	.341

Detroit's most significant action at the winter meetings this past December was to acquire Dave Collins from Oakland for Barbaro Garbey. Even if Collins does not become an everyday starter for the Tigers, he hits better from the left side than the right (for both average and power), and could eventually complement Herndon as Jones might have. Here is how Collins has batted since 1980:

	AB	H	2B	3B	HR	BB	SO	BA	SA	OBA
Batting Right-Handed	649	169	28	7	1	51	57	.260	.330	.319
Batting Left-Handed	1832	524	74	29	15	176	246	.286	.383	.352

Clearly, one trade will not restore to the Tigers their 1984 lustre, but the deal does address one of last season's major problems, and the one most easily remedied. It's not possible to go out and buy another Hernandez-quality reliever, and even if it were, Detroit would rather hope that their own Hernandez recaptures his 1984 brilliance. But a useful role-player like Collins might be all Detroit needs to shore up its starting lineup and get back into the thick of the American League East race.

WON-LOST RECORD BY STARTING POSITION

DETROIT 84-77	C	1B	2B	3B	SS	LF	CF	RF	P	DH	Leadoff	Relief	Starts
Doug Bair	-	-	-	-	-	-	-	-	2-1	-	-	5-13	2-1
Doug Baker	-	-	-	-	3-3	-	-	-	-	-	-	-	3-3
Juan Berenguer	-	-	-	-	-	-	-	-	6-7	-	-	1-17	6-7
Dave Bergman	-	13-20	-	-	-	-	-	-	-	-	0-1	-	13-20
Tom Brookens	-	-	1-1	67-67	0-1	-	-	-	-	-	2-7	-	68-69
Chuck Cary	-	-	-	-	-	-	-	-	-	-	-	5-11	-
Marty Castillo	6-13	-	-	3-2	-	-	-	-	-	-	-	-	9-15
Darrell Evans	-	58-43	-	1-3	-	-	-	-	-	14-19	-	-	73-65
Doug Flynn	-	-	2-8	-	2-3	-	-	-	-	-	-	-	4-11
Barbaro Garbey	-	11-12	-	-	-	5-5	-	4-6	-	11-5	-	-	31-28
Kirk Gibson	-	-	-	-	-	-	8-10	71-54	-	2-6	-	-	81-70
Johnny Grubb	-	-	-	-	-	7-5	-	1-1	-	17-14	-	-	25-20
Willie Hernandez	-	-	-	-	-	-	-	-	-	-	-	48-26	-
Larry Herndon	-	-	-	-	-	56-54	-	-	-	-	-	-	56-54
Rusty Kuntz	-	-	-	-	-	-	-	-	-	-	-	-	0-
Mike Laga	-	2-2	-	-	-	-	-	-	-	2-3	-	-	4-5
Chet Lemon	-	-	-	-	-	-	76-67	-	-	-	-	-	76-67
Aurelio Lopez	-	-	-	-	-	-	-	-	-	-	-	19-32	-
Scotti Madison	-	-	-	-	-	-	-	-	-	2-1	-	-	2-1
Mickey Mahler	-	-	-	-	-	-	-	-	0-2	-	-	1-0	0-2
Bob Melvin	12-13	-	-	-	-	-	-	-	-	-	-	-	12-13
Jack Morris	-	-	-	-	-	-	-	-	21-14	-	-	-	21-14
Randy O'Neal	-	-	-	-	-	-	-	-	6-6	-	-	6-10	6-6
Lance Parrish	66-51	-	-	-	-	-	-	-	-	9-13	-	-	75-64
Dan Petry	-	-	-	-	-	-	-	-	17-17	-	-	-	17-17
Chris Pittaro	-	-	1-2	13-5	-	-	-	-	-	-	-	-	14-7
Alejandro Sanchez	-	-	-	-	-	2-2	-	4-8	-	7-6	-	-	13-16
Bill Scherrer	-	-	-	-	-	-	-	-	-	-	-	16-32	-
Nelson Simmons	-	-	-	-	-	14-11	-	4-8	-	20-10	-	-	38-29
Bob Stoddard	-	-	-	-	-	-	-	-	-	-	-	1-7	-
Frank Tanana	-	-	-	-	-	-	-	-	11-9	-	-	-	11-9
Walt Terrell	-	-	-	-	-	-	-	-	19-15	-	-	-	19-15
Alan Trammell	-	-	-	-	79-70	-	-	-	-	-	2-3	-	79-70
Jim Weaver	-	-	-	-	-	-	-	-	-	-	-	-	-
Lou Whitaker	-	-	80-66	-	-	-	-	-	-	-	80-66	-	80-66
Milt Wilcox	-	-	-	-	-	-	-	-	2-6	-	-	-	2-6

Batting vs. Left and Right Handed Pitchers

		BA	Rank	SA	Rank	OBA	Rank	HR %	Rank	BB %	Rank	SO %	Rank
Dave Bergman	vs. Lefties	.200	--	.200	--	.333	--	0.00	--	16.67	--	0.00	--
	vs. Righties	.178	156	.259	152	.247	153	2.22	91	8.61	69	9.93	46
Tom Brookens	vs. Lefties	.290	49	.481	39	.350	61	2.47	81	8.29	84	11.60	62
	vs. Righties	.211	145	.322	135	.238	157	0.93	134	3.52	152	16.72	115
Darrell Evans	vs. Lefties	.208	147	.467	46	.275	138	7.50	5	8.33	81	21.97	140
	vs. Righties	.260	79	.535	5	.379	15	8.05	1	16.02	5	12.12	63
Barbaro Garbey	vs. Lefties	.268	76	.420	77	.320	103	2.90	70	6.00	124	13.33	92
	vs. Righties	.242	--	.323	--	.284	--	2.02	--	5.50	--	15.60	--
Kirk Gibson	vs. Lefties	.224	133	.424	75	.297	128	4.12	50	8.76	73	26.80	155
	vs. Righties	.314	7	.557	4	.392	7	5.35	18	11.34	33	17.86	129
Johnny Grubb	vs. Lefties	.000	--	.000	--	.000	--	0.00	--	0.00	--	00.00	--
	vs. Righties	.248	101	.405	75	.346	51	3.27	64	13.19	17	12.64	70
Larry Herndon	vs. Lefties	.265	82	.484	34	.347	65	4.52	43	11.30	39	12.99	88
	vs. Righties	.233	121	.331	128	.269	141	1.74	102	4.30	140	18.54	135
Chet Lemon	vs. Lefties	.322	19	.564	8	.378	21	5.37	23	8.54	76	19.51	133
	vs. Righties	.242	110	.389	86	.316	91	2.72	81	7.54	89	14.84	98
Lance Parrish	vs. Lefties	.305	33	.563	9	.372	29	5.96	18	10.40	50	9.83	41
	vs. Righties	.261	74	.447	46	.304	107	4.77	26	5.39	127	17.10	117
Alejandro Sanchez	vs. Lefties	.298	38	.536	17	.298	127	5.95	19	0.00	158	30.95	157
	vs. Righties	.163	--	.327	--	.163	--	2.04	--	0.00	--	26.53	--
Nelson Simmons	vs. Lefties	.250	--	.458	--	.315	--	6.25	--	9.26	--	12.96	--
	vs. Righties	.236	116	.389	85	.304	106	3.45	60	9.25	57	14.98	103
Alan Trammell	vs. Lefties	.250	101	.364	114	.324	97	2.17	90	9.71	59	7.28	25
	vs. Righties	.261	75	.387	88	.307	100	2.14	93	6.36	112	11.86	61
Lou Whitaker	vs. Lefties	.228	130	.324	133	.323	98	1.38	107	11.70	34	13.45	93
	vs. Righties	.295	21	.498	14	.374	19	4.09	38	11.32	34	6.23	14
Team Average	vs. Lefties	.260	11	.446	2	.326	12	3.87	2	8.71	7	16.21	14
	vs. Righties	.251	11	.415	5	.315	12	3.52	2	8.35	7	14.33	11
League Average	vs. Lefties	.266		.416		.333		2.91		8.95		13.77	
	vs. Righties	.259		.401		.324		2.78		8.49		13.56	

Batting with Runners on Base and Bases Empty

		BA	Rank	SA	Rank	OBA	Rank	HR %	Rank	BB %	Rank	SO %	Rank
Tom Brookens	Runners On	.223	144	.308	139	.263	150	0.47	140	5.15	141	15.45	110
	Bases Empty	.248	100	.427	56	.287	134	2.19	98	5.19	130	14.53	88
Darrell Evans	Runners On	.290	53	.580	5	.419	8	8.00	3	18.07	5	12.05	73
	Bases Empty	.220	133	.479	24	.310	99	7.87	1	11.59	25	15.94	107
Barbaro Garbey	Runners On	.241	130	.277	151	.282	142	0.00	142	5.65	132	16.94	124
	Bases Empty	.272	47	.472	30	.326	73	4.80	34	5.93	115	11.85	55
Kirk Gibson	Runners On	.320	24	.520	18	.395	12	3.13	66	11.07	42	19.54	144
	Bases Empty	.262	71	.517	10	.339	45	6.46	6	10.19	36	21.21	145
Larry Herndon	Runners On	.212	148	.282	149	.282	143	1.18	115	8.95	84	19.47	143
	Bases Empty	.265	65	.449	39	.308	102	3.68	50	5.54	123	14.53	88
Chet Lemon	Runners On	.253	110	.439	64	.323	101	4.07	45	8.06	106	16.13	115
	Bases Empty	.274	45	.439	46	.343	36	3.04	72	7.65	78	16.21	110
Lance Parrish	Runners On	.295	47	.492	30	.353	65	5.04	27	8.56	95	13.70	95
	Bases Empty	.254	89	.467	34	.295	119	5.15	23	5.19	129	16.23	111
Nelson Simmons	Runners On	.291	50	.515	21	.353	65	5.83	15	10.08	58	12.61	78
	Bases Empty	.203	148	.324	134	.272	145	2.70	79	8.64	61	16.05	109
Alan Trammell	Runners On	.264	85	.366	118	.321	105	1.63	99	7.88	110	13.36	89
	Bases Empty	.253	91	.390	91	.306	105	2.51	87	6.99	94	8.29	29
Lou Whitaker	Runners On	.312	27	.507	23	.399	10	4.39	37	13.31	24	8.47	32
	Bases Empty	.262	69	.431	52	.342	39	2.97	74	10.38	32	7.73	20
Team Average	Runners On	.261	12	.419	7	.329	13	3.29	4	9.20	7	15.77	14
	Bases Empty	.248	11	.427	2	.310	11	3.86	1	7.90	8	14.22	10
League Average	Runners On	.271		.416		.338		2.85		9.26		13.25	
	Bases Empty	.254		.397		.318		2.80		8.14		13.92	

Overall Batting Compared to Late Inning Pressure Situations

		BA	Rank	SA	Rank	OBA	Rank	HR %	Rank	BB %	Rank	SO %	Rank	RDI %	Rank
Dave Bergman	Overall	.179	--	.257	--	.250	--	2.14	--	8.92	--	9.55	--	.147	--
	Pressure	.237	99	.342	98	.286	118	2.63	69	7.14	102	16.67	103	.125	143
Tom Brookens	Overall	.237	131	.375	112	.277	147	1.44	112	5.17	105	14.94	105	.263	111
	Pressure	.250	82	.321	105	.300	104	0.00	113	6.56	109	9.84	39	.400	22
Darrell Evans	Overall	.248	110	.519	6	.356	32	7.92	1	14.31	11	14.31	95	.299	67
	Pressure	.254	80	.687	1	.351	56	13.43	1	12.99	24	10.39	44	.385	30
Barbaro Garbey	Overall	.257	93	.380	109	.305	124	2.53	86	5.79	131	14.29	94	.268	103
	Pressure	.227	109	.295	122	.292	114	2.27	80	8.33	84	18.75	124	.357	45
Kirk Gibson	Overall	.287	29	.518	7	.364	21	4.99	22	10.60	38	20.45	146	.337	30
	Pressure	.257	76	.459	42	.349	58	5.41	31	12.79	41	19.77	132	.222	104
Johnny Grubb	Overall	.245	--	.400	--	.342	--	3.23	--	13.04	--	13.59	--	.275	97
	Pressure	.179	147	.286	127	.250	141	3.57	49	9.38	72	18.75	124	.125	143
Larry Herndon	Overall	.244	116	.385	102	.298	133	2.71	83	6.89	111	16.49	121	.213	144
	Pressure	.187	140	.253	140	.265	132	1.33	104	9.52	68	28.57	157	.167	128
Chet Lemon	Overall	.265	73	.439	55	.334	68	3.48	57	7.83	89	16.17	117	.248	121
	Pressure	.282	51	.423	62	.341	67	2.56	71	8.24	87	17.65	112	.400	22
Lance Parrish	Overall	.273	60	.479	21	.323	89	5.10	16	6.83	113	15.00	106	.286	85
	Pressure	.210	126	.383	84	.238	145	4.94	36	2.30	149	18.39	120	.308	65
Alejandro Sanchez	Overall	.248	--	.459	--	.248	--	4.51	--	0.00	--	29.32	--	-.103	--
	Pressure	.280	--	.680	--	.280	--	12.00	--	0.00	--	28.00	--	.000	158
Nelson Simmons	Overall	.239	127	.402	91	.306	122	3.98	46	9.25	60	14.59	100	.288	81
	Pressure	.129	159	.161	157	.282	122	0.00	113	17.95	11	23.08	142	.400	--
Alan Trammell	Overall	.258	90	.380	108	.312	109	2.15	100	7.37	99	10.47	43	.266	107
	Pressure	.213	123	.238	145	.297	109	0.00	113	10.87	55	14.13	81	.250	87
Lou Whitaker	Overall	.279	44	.456	31	.362	23	3.45	58	11.41	33	7.99	23	.306	58
	Pressure	.269	62	.385	81	.383	29	2.56	71	15.63	19	11.46	55	.273	78
Team Average	Overall	.253	11	.424	5	.318	12	3.62	2	8.45	7	14.88	13	.264	12
	Pressure	.230	14	.370	10	.305	13	3.50	3	9.73	5	17.26	14	.258	9
League Average	Overall	.261		.406		.327		2.82		8.63		13.62		.287	
	Pressure	.253		.381		.323		2.74		9.11		14.40		.273	

Additional Miscellaneous Batting Comparisons

	Grass Surface BA	Rank	Artificial Surface BA	Rank	Home Games BA	Rank	Road Games BA	Rank	Runners in Scoring Position BA	Rank	Runners in Scoring Pos and Two Outs BA	Rank	Leading Off Inning OBA	Rank	Runners on 3B with less than 2 Outs RDI %	Rank
Dave Bergman	.168	--	.238	--	.167	--	.194	--	.038	--	.111	--	.269	134	.571	--
Tom Brookens	.241	117	.218	128	.233	123	.241	116	.271	86	.321	29	.252	146	.500	106
Darrell Evans	.245	112	.263	66	.244	112	.251	95	.276	78	.280	48	.341	49	.484	124
Barbaro Garbey	.263	78	.233	--	.239	117	.282	32	.210	141	.229	99	.309	95	.500	106
Kirk Gibson	.312	9	.160	155	.311	23	.264	70	.308	36	.255	65	.412	5	.667	47
Johnny Grubb	.252	99	.188	--	.228	132	.278	--	.225	--	.250	68	.408	7	.556	--
Larry Herndon	.245	111	.238	104	.256	89	.234	123	.186	151	.209	124	.340	51	.278	157
Chet Lemon	.261	84	.286	43	.288	47	.245	108	.230	123	.215	115	.336	57	.588	71
Lance Parrish	.287	35	.204	139	.280	56	.267	62	.274	81	.244	80	.235	151	.588	71
Nelson Simmons	.244	114	.211	--	.271	71	.203	152	.288	62	.242	83	.230	152	.818	4
Alan Trammell	.264	75	.229	120	.287	48	.230	130	.207	144	.194	135	.296	111	.677	42
Lou Whitaker	.262	82	.371	4	.267	74	.291	20	.293	54	.297	38	.365	28	.737	20
Team Average	.256	8	.238	14	.259	9	.248	11	.240	14	.236	11	.315	10	.566	9
League Average	.262		.259		.266		.256		.268		.248		.321		.587	

Pitching vs. Left and Right Handed Batters

		BA	Rank	SA	Rank	OBA	Rank	HR %	Rank	BB %	Rank	SO %	Rank
Doug Bair	vs. Lefties	.289	91	.456	94	.387	114	2.22	51	14.02	118	10.28	95
	vs. Righties	.275	--	.412	--	.336	--	0.98	--	8.55	--	16.24	--
Juan Berenguer	vs. Lefties	.305	107	.448	91	.389	116	2.96	79	12.39	104	17.52	24
	vs. Righties	.204	6	.383	51	.286	23	3.59	95	10.00	98	21.58	10
Willie Hernandez	vs. Lefties	.171	1	.229	1	.193	1	0.95	16	1.82	1	17.27	26
	vs. Righties	.224	26	.399	66	.252	7	4.20	113	3.93	7	18.69	22
Aurelio Lopez	vs. Lefties	.224	21	.306	17	.324	52	2.04	44	13.07	113	15.91	35
	vs. Righties	.271	86	.541	131	.335	86	6.63	132	8.87	86	12.32	88
Jack Morris	vs. Lefties	.223	20	.341	29	.310	42	2.06	45	11.18	95	17.76	23
	vs. Righties	.226	30	.338	17	.302	44	2.43	48	8.96	88	17.70	29
Randy O'Neal	vs. Lefties	.236	32	.340	28	.298	29	2.09	47	8.33	52	13.89	51
	vs. Righties	.245	49	.397	65	.326	76	2.65	60	10.47	107	12.79	82
Dan Petry	vs. Lefties	.222	19	.347	33	.306	33	2.67	65	10.79	92	9.51	106
	vs. Righties	.211	16	.345	24	.258	11	2.84	71	5.30	26	13.73	66
Bill Scherrer	vs. Lefties	.200	8	.286	7	.306	32	2.86	76	12.20	102	21.95	9
	vs. Righties	.283	101	.455	107	.387	127	4.83	125	14.77	129	10.80	102
Frank Tanana	vs. Lefties	.227	26	.447	90	.253	7	4.67	125	3.77	4	19.50	14
	vs. Righties	.272	90	.427	87	.323	69	3.07	80	6.82	45	17.11	33
Walt Terrell	vs. Lefties	.247	46	.323	23	.309	38	0.40	4	8.42	55	11.47	81
	vs. Righties	.267	80	.388	56	.357	106	1.93	35	11.29	117	15.53	47
Team Average	vs. Lefties	.236	1	.347	1	.311	1	1.96	2	9.87	11	14.74	2
	vs. Righties	.245	2	.397	4	.310	4	3.15	9	8.32	9	15.95	2
League Average	vs. Lefties	.265		.408		.333		2.74		9.21		12.94	
	vs. Righties	.259		.404		.322		2.88		8.19		14.14	

Pitching with Runners on Base and Bases Empty

		BA	Rank	SA	Rank	OBA	Rank	HR %	Rank	BB %	Rank	SO %	Rank
Juan Berenguer	Runners On	.307	114	.473	105	.400	128	3.33	90	13.81	121	17.13	22
	Bases Empty	.227	27	.382	50	.300	47	3.18	88	9.47	90	20.99	7
Willie Hernandez	Runners On	.241	30	.373	42	.273	8	2.53	56	5.11	13	15.91	31
	Bases Empty	.189	5	.339	23	.209	1	3.86	111	2.09	2	20.08	9
Aurelio Lopez	Runners On	.275	75	.451	94	.361	98	4.58	119	12.90	118	9.68	107
	Bases Empty	.229	29	.423	90	.301	48	4.57	121	8.81	80	18.13	25
Jack Morris	Runners On	.225	20	.327	13	.297	23	2.03	44	8.77	61	16.67	25
	Bases Empty	.224	25	.350	30	.314	60	2.37	53	11.27	112	18.52	17
Randy O'Neal	Runners On	.297	102	.391	58	.353	86	1.56	25	9.27	73	13.25	67
	Bases Empty	.206	13	.350	32	.283	23	2.80	71	9.28	88	13.50	62
Dan Petry	Runners On	.251	43	.399	67	.319	35	3.54	96	8.99	66	11.01	96
	Bases Empty	.199	8	.317	14	.266	12	2.30	47	8.10	47	11.51	89
Bill Scherrer	Runners On	.265	59	.393	63	.393	127	4.27	111	16.67	130	14.00	53
	Bases Empty	.233	34	.376	47	.315	65	3.76	106	10.74	107	16.78	31
Frank Tanana	Runners On	.281	84	.452	95	.351	84	2.97	81	9.92	83	16.43	26
	Bases Empty	.254	67	.418	88	.285	27	3.58	100	3.97	8	18.23	23
Walt Terrell	Runners On	.274	73	.359	28	.335	61	0.78	6	8.11	48	11.04	94
	Bases Empty	.241	45	.343	26	.325	76	1.26	12	10.95	109	15.03	46
Team Average	Runners On	.260	3	.383	3	.334	6	2.33	2	9.95	10	13.92	6
	Bases Empty	.227	1	.366	1	.294	1	2.75	6	8.42	10	16.44	2
League Average	Runners On	.271		.416		.338		2.85		9.26		13.25	
	Bases Empty	.254		.397		.318		2.80		8.14		13.92	

Overall Pitching Compared to Late Inning Pressure Situations

		BA	Rank	SA	Rank	OBA	Rank	HR %	Rank	BB %	Rank	SO %	Rank
Doug Bair	Overall	.281	--	.432	--	.360	--	1.56	--	11.16	--	13.39	--
	Pressure	.172	7	.172	2	.273	16	0.00	1	11.76	89	20.59	13
Juan Berenguer	Overall	.259	66	.419	86	.343	84	3.24	92	11.32	106	19.34	11
	Pressure	.250	54	.344	40	.400	111	3.13	83	20.00	129	15.00	46
Willie Hernandez	Overall	.210	5	.353	25	.236	2	3.32	96	3.37	2	18.31	12
	Pressure	.207	18	.369	54	.231	6	4.56	113	2.75	4	16.86	27
Aurelio Lopez	Overall	.250	47	.436	93	.330	70	4.57	125	10.82	105	13.98	52
	Pressure	.229	34	.393	66	.339	71	4.29	104	13.77	111	16.77	29
Jack Morris	Overall	.225	12	.340	16	.307	37	2.22	39	10.21	97	17.73	17
	Pressure	.232	39	.325	28	.306	45	1.32	28	9.83	70	13.87	56
Randy O'Neal	Overall	.240	28	.365	33	.310	40	2.34	43	9.28	81	13.40	62
	Pressure	.304	--	.478	--	.360	--	4.35	--	7.69	--	11.54	--
Dan Petry	Overall	.217	10	.346	21	.285	11	2.74	65	8.42	69	11.33	96
	Pressure	.132	2	.207	4	.222	5	1.65	43	10.37	76	10.37	95
Bill Scherrer	Overall	.248	46	.384	44	.354	102	4.00	115	13.71	127	15.38	37
	Pressure	.278	83	.444	97	.383	104	4.44	108	13.39	107	12.50	70
Frank Tanana	Overall	.264	77	.430	91	.310	43	3.36	97	6.28	22	17.53	21
	Pressure	.266	71	.453	99	.338	69	4.69	115	9.59	65	16.44	33
Walt Terrell	Overall	.255	57	.350	23	.330	68	1.04	4	9.66	89	13.22	64
	Pressure	.295	100	.443	96	.386	106	3.41	93	11.32	85	12.26	74
Team Average	Overall	.240	1	.373	1	.311	2	2.58	3	9.06	10	15.37	2
	Pressure	.221	1	.350	2	.301	1	3.21	13	9.80	9	15.05	4
League Average	Overall	.261		.406		.327		2.82		8.63		13.62	
	Pressure	.258		.392		.332		2.71		9.52		14.05	

Additional Miscellaneous Pitching Comparisons

	Grass Surface		Artificial Surface		Home Games		Road Games		Runners in Scoring Position		Runners in Scoring Pos and Two Outs		Leading Off Inning	
	BA	Rank	BA	Rank	BA	Rank	BA	Rank	BA	Rank	BA	Rank	OBA	Rank
Doug Bair	.288	--	.269	76	.240	--	.326	--	.328	118	.379	128	.326	--
Juan Berenguer	.262	75	.246	45	.286	105	.230	17	.345	126	.368	125	.293	40
Willie Hernandez	.208	5	.220	20	.167	2	.258	56	.279	84	.250	74	.213	3
Aurelio Lopez	.249	47	.257	--	.253	67	.241	--	.312	112	.271	86	.325	74
Jack Morris	.238	28	.156	1	.249	54	.207	8	.239	31	.211	38	.316	62
Randy O'Neal	.253	55	.156	--	.288	106	.212	9	.288	93	.270	84	.306	52
Dan Petry	.216	9	.224	23	.213	11	.222	16	.276	80	.321	115	.241	7
Bill Scherrer	.256	62	.174	--	.240	40	.256	52	.234	29	.128	5	.323	72
Frank Tanana	.258	68	.304	108	.266	83	.262	62	.246	39	.210	37	.301	47
Walt Terrell	.241	33	.327	122	.215	12	.297	105	.264	63	.216	45	.303	51
Team Average	.240	1	.244	3	.237	2	.244	1	.275	10	.264	12	.286	1
League Average	.262		.259		.256		.266		.268		.248		.321	

KANSAS CITY ROYALS

For all fans of the overlooked and the underdog, there was poetic justice in the team from Kansas City winning it all in 1985. All through the summer, all the talk was of the ultimate media Series: Yankees–Mets, Dodgers–Angels, or any combination matching New York and Los Angeles. Then, when the Blue Jays clinched the division title and went on to a 3–1 lead in the Championship Series, the stories were about the prospect of the first Series involving a Canadian team.

Even after the Royals came back to defeat Toronto, they still weren't given their proper due. Then what we heard was about Whitey coming back to beat his old team, about Tudor and Joaquin, about Coleman and the Killer Tarp. It was almost predictable that even after matching the most decisive final-game victory in World Series history, the Royals would awaken the next morning to read more about Whitey and Denkinger, Joaquin and Denkinger, and Tudor and the dugout fan.

Well, what about Howser? That's Dick Howser; H-O-W-S-E-R. He was a semistory early during post-season play, after the Royals dropped the first two playoff games in Toronto to extend his streak of consecutive post-season losses to eleven. But after directing the Royals over the Blue Jays in the last three games of that series— games in which managerial decisions proved pivotal—he reverted to his usual lower-than-low profile. Typically, the one moment in which he had the nation's attention followed a loss: the Game 2 loss when he kept Charlie Leibrandt in the game and lost a 2–0 ninth-inning lead while Dan Quisenberry warmed up. He was rightly saluted for his class in submitting to a dugout interview with Reggie Jackson immediately after the game. But why, after the Series was won, wasn't there more written about Howser's rallying the Royals, and less about the Cardinals' collapse?

What's especially strange about all this is that on the surface, the Royals would seem to be everything that America wants in a team— and more. They've honed the role of the Silky Sullivan come-from-behind winner to perfection. For two straight seasons, the Royals have staged dramatic second-half comebacks to capture the American League West title, clinching matters on the season's final weekend in each instance.

But maybe what's kept them from becoming true media darlings is their failure to project any sense of fury and strain in overcoming the first-place team. Howser and the Royals convey an image of cool confidence; they approach the pennant chase like a seasoned marathoner, methodically letting the others set the pace, knowing exactly when to make a move to the front, and passing the pack in the final 400 meters. Then, in the post-race interview, we see nary a trace of sweat on the runner's face, and marvel at the poise and calm which seems to permeate the runner's being. It sometimes seems as if the Royals gather in Fort Myers every spring to lay out their master plan, get the kinks out during the spring months, and leave a wake-up call for the week after the All-Star Game.

But not every move they make is scripted. In both 1984 and '85, Howser made key changes on the fly that contributed to their division titles.

In 1984, Howser vacillated early on about his shortstop, as neither the incumbent, U.L. Washington, nor the challenger, Onix Concepcion, could take charge. To complicate matters, both were injured for much of the first half. But following the All-Star break, Howser installed Concepcion on an everyday basis, and reaped the rewards when Onix produced the best post-break batting average in the majors (.370) among players with 125 or more plate appearances.

In 1985, shortstop was a season-long problem, Buddy Biancalana's post-season heroics notwithstanding. But one problem that was worked out was the DH spot. Jorge Orta and Hal McRae platooned during the first part of the season, with undistinguished results. The importance of the position was compounded because not only did the Royals use their DH in the cleanup position against right-handers, but that player also had to "protect" the position of George Brett, the number-three hitter. Actually, the DHs afforded Brett about as much protection as Neville Chamberlain gave to Czechoslovakia: Brett had been walked intentionally 18 times through games of July 21.

The night of July 22 proved to be a turning point for the Royals. Before their game against the Yankees that night, Howser made his decision: He would install McRae, batting .205 at the time, as the regular designated hitter against both types of pitching. Since the Yankees were starting a left-hander, Dennis Rasmussen, the decision was not immediately apparent, but would be before the end of the game. The Yankees took a 3–0 lead, but the Royals tied the score in the fifth. Right-handed Rich Bordi replaced Rasmussen, and with two outs, the bases loaded, and the score tied, McRae was due up, batting .138 (4 for 29) for the season against right-handers. Howser could have used Orta or Pat Sheridan to pinch-hit for McRae, as he had done seven times up to that point; it was not yet Righetti time. But he stuck with McRae, who delivered a two-run single to left-center. Kansas City won, 5–4. Chalk up another one for Howser.

The longer he stayed with McRae, the hotter Hal got. It took the Royals 43 games to dislodge the Angels from first place, but by September 6 they had done it. McRae started 40 of those 43 games, hitting cleanup in 38 of them, batting .297 and slugging .466, with 37 runs batted in. Against right-handers, the Royals played .622 ball (23–14) with McRae as the DH, compared to .539 (41–35) with others, principally Orta, in that role. The performance of their starting DHs against right-handers was as follows:

	Date	Record	Pos.	GB	Record To End of Season
1984	July 18	40–51	6th	8	44–27
1985	July 22	46–44	4th	7.5	45–27

	Through July 21						July 22 to End					
	GS	W–L	BA	SA	HR	RBI	GS	W–L	BA	SA	HR	RBI
Orta	63	34–29	.275	.389	2	35	11	6–5	.243	.432	2	5
McRae	0	0–0	.000	.000	0	0	37	23–14	.285	.438	4	31
Others*	0	0–0	.000	.000	0	0	2	1–1	.167	.667	1	2

* Brett and Motley, one game each, during the final week of the season.

It wasn't just McRae who turned his season around that night; it also marked the night that Dan Quisenberry rediscovered how to get out left-handed batters. Quisenberry's performance during the season almost mirrored, and may well have been responsible for, that of the team. And his success, or lack of it, was tied to his performance against left-handed batters. Throughout his career, Quis had always had a larger than normal disparity in the statistics of opposing left-handers and right-handers:

| | Quisenberry vs. Left-Handed Batters | | | | | | Quisenberry vs. Right-Handed Batters | | | | | |
	AB	H	BB	SO	BA	SA	AB	H	BB	SO	BA	SA
1979	44	16	6	4	.364	.568	107	26	1	9	.243	.364
1980	243	72	16	11	.296	.399	244	57	11	26	.234	.303
1981	114	34	12	9	.298	.351	115	25	3	11	.217	.304
1982	239	62	7	16	.259	.381	261	64	5	30	.245	.330
1983	262	68	7	20	.260	.340	253	50	4	28	.198	.289
1984	276	73	8	17	.264	.359	213	48	4	24	.225	.324
Totals	1178	325	56	77	.276	.374	1193	270	28	128	.226	.315

Since his rookie season, he had always kept the left-handers within reasonable bounds, while gobbling up the righties. But during the first half of the 1985 season, left-handers battered Quis as if he were a rookie again. It was only after he got the lefties under control that he and the team flourished:

LHB vs. Quisenberry	AB	H	2B	3B	HR	BA	SA
Through July 21	148	53	12	1	2	.361	.493
July 22 to End	123	33	4	1	2	.268	.366

The Royals had the second-lowest team earned run average in the American League last season, despite a terribly disappointing regular-season performance by their top pitcher of the previous season, Bud Black. Black finished 17–12 with a 3.12 ERA in 1984, allowed the fewest base runners per nine innings among American League starters, and had the league's lowest ERA over the last seven weeks of the season. He earned the 1985 opening day assignment, symbolic of the reigning ace of the staff, and defeated Toronto. He then won only four games in 17 starts over the next three months.

The Royals clearly needed someone else to take charge, and the savior proved to be baby-faced Bret Saberhagen, who emerged as the best young pitcher in the American League. He battled Orel Hershiser all season for the right to the title, "Most Unappreciated Pitcher as a Result of Being Born Around the Same Time as Dwight Gooden." He was supported by Leibrandt, Mark Gubicza, and Danny Jackson; the latter two saw 21 of their 28 combined victories saved by Quisenberry. The overall quality of their starting rotation was critical, since only the deepest of pitching staffs could compensate for the problems of its ace in sufficient degree to win a division title. There have been 84 division or league regular-season titles contested over the past 25 years; only two other times has a team finished the regular season in first place despite having its opening-day starter finish five games or more below .500. In both cases, the team was pitching-rich Baltimore: in 1974, compensating for a 7–12 Jim Palmer, and in 1983, when Dennis Martinez went 7–16.

Balboni's Ballpark

Steve Balboni for Mike Armstrong will turn out to be one of the major steals of the 1980s, but that's old hat for the Royals. This is the same organization that has in the past come up with Hal McRae for Richie Scheinblum and Roger Nelson, Amos Otis for Joe Foy, Fred Patek and others for a bag of shells, John Mayberry for Jim York and Lance Clemons, and Larry Gura for Fran Healy.

Balboni spent six years in the Yankees organization, and despite getting into only 69 games in pinstripes, he seemed destined to be the man who would persuade the Yankees to shrink Death Valley. Then Mr. Steinbrenner's "baseball people" looked up one day and saw a first baseman named Mattingly; for Balboni, it was goodbye Columbus, hello Kansas City. For very little cost, the Royals received a player who has now hammered 64 home runs in two seasons in mid-America.

That Balboni has produced those numbers, despite playing half of his games in Royals Stadium, has surprised a lot of people. The stadium opened in 1973, and had yielded an average of only 97 home runs per season up to the time of the Balboni trade. (The Royals averaged only 46 of those 97 homers.)

Not that Balboni hasn't been handicapped by the distant dimensions of his adopted home. There were more home runs hit in every other stadium in the American League than there were in Kansas City last season; the average was 155, but only 110 were hit in Royals Stadium. That statistic is not big news in itself; this is the third time in the past five years that Royals Stadium has seen the fewest homers. What is noteworthy, however, is that, besides Balboni's 36 home runs, George Brett hit 30. It is rare enough for a team playing in the stadium that allows the fewest home runs in its league to have one 30-home-run hitter; it has only happened nine times in baseball history, and the nine are listed below. But notice that the 1985 Royals were the first team whose stadium ranked last in homers allowed ever to have two 30-home run producers on its roster:

Season	Player, Team	HR	Home HR	Road HR
1953	Eddie Mathews, Mil.	47	17	30
1958	Frank Thomas, Pitt.	35	9	26
1958	Gus Triandos, Balt.	30	13	17
1961	Dick Stuart, Pitt.	35	16	19
1967	Jim Wynn, Hou.	37	15	22
1970	Willie Stargell, Pitt.	31	13	18
1973	Frank Robinson, Cal.	30	16	14
1985	Steve Balboni, K.C.	36	17	19
1985	George Brett, K.C.	30	15	15

Balboni did hit 17 home runs at home, the most by any player in the 13-year history of the ballpark. But his two-year home/road breakdown suggests that, although it has boosted his totals of doubles and triples, Royals Stadium has reduced his home-run output at the rate of five per season:

Balboni 1984–85	AB	H	2B	3B	HR	RRF	BB	SO	BA	SA
Home	522	124	34	3	27	83	40	138	.238	.469
Road	516	129	17	1	37	84	57	167	.250	.502

What does it mean in terms of wins and losses? In the two years before Balboni arrived, the Royals played like a championship team at home, but an also-ran on the road. A gap of more than 200 points stood between their home and road winning percentages:

| | Home Games | | Road Games | |
	W–L	Pct.	W–L	Pct.
1982–83	101–61	.623	68–94	.420
1984–85	94–69	.577	81–80	.503

Since the addition of Balboni, the Royals' home-field advantage has lessened a bit, but they've more than made up for it on the road. Balboni's power gives them one more weapon at their disposal when they get away from their spacious, carpeted home. And, of course, they've won a division title and a World Series in his two seasons with the club. Well worth Mike Armstrong, no?

WON-LOST RECORD BY STARTING POSITION

KANSAS CITY	91-71	C	1B	2B	3B	SS	LF	CF	RF	P	DH	Leadoff	Relief	Starts
Steve Balboni		-	90-69	-	-	-	-	-	-	-	-	-	-	90-69
Joe Beckwith		-	-	-	-	-	-	-	-	-	-	-	15-34	-
Buddy Biancalana		-	-	-	30-18	-	-	-	-	-	-	-	-	30-18
Bud Black		-	-	-	-	-	-	-	15-18	-	-	-	-	15-18
George Brett		-	-	-	87-65	-	-	-	-	-	1-0	-	-	88-65
Onix Concepcion		-	-	-	-	61-48	-	-	-	-	-	1-0	-	61-48
Steve Farr		-	-	-	-	-	-	-	2-1	-	-	5-8	2-1	
Tony Ferreira		-	-	-	-	-	-	-	-	-	-	0-2	-	
Mark Gubicza		-	-	-	-	-	-	-	14-14	-	-	1-0	14-14	
Larry Gura		-	-	-	-	-	-	-	-	-	-	1-2	-	
Bob Hegman		-	-	-	-	-	-	-	-	-	-	-	0-	
Mark Huismann		-	-	-	-	-	-	-	-	-	-	2-7	-	
Dane Iorg		-	1-1	-	0-1	-	8-3	-	11-8	-	-	-	-	20-13
Danny Jackson		-	-	-	-	-	-	-	18-14	-	-	-	18-14	
Lynn Jones		-	-	-	-	-	1-0	8-5	6-8	-	-	1-0	-	15-13
Mike Jones		-	-	-	-	-	-	-	0-1	-	-	8-24	0-1	
Mike LaCoss		-	-	-	-	-	-	-	-	-	-	6-15	-	
Dave Leeper		-	-	-	-	-	0-1	-	2-4	-	-	0-1	-	2-5
Charlie Leibrandt		-	-	-	-	-	-	-	18-15	-	-	-	18-15	
Dennis Leonard		-	-	-	-	-	-	-	-	-	-	1-1	-	
Hal McRae		-	-	-	-	-	-	-	48-34	-	-	-	48-34	
Omar Moreno		-	-	-	-	-	7-2	3-4	-	-	7-2	-	10-6	
Darryl Motley		-	-	-	-	-	16-14	-	38-25	2-3	-	-	56-42	
Jorge Orta		-	-	-	-	-	-	-	-	40-34	-	-	40-34	
Greg Pryor		-	-	9-6	4-5	0-4	-	-	-	-	-	-	13-15	
Jamie Quirk		9-6	-	-	-	-	-	-	-	-	-	-	9-6	
Dan Quisenberry		-	-	-	-	-	-	-	-	-	-	58-26	-	
Bret Saberhagen		-	-	-	-	-	-	-	24-8	-	-	-	24-8	
Larry Scranton		-	-	-	0-1	-	-	-	-	-	-	-	0-1	
Pat Sheridan		-	-	-	-	-	31-22	-	-	-	-	-	31-22	
Lonnie Smith		-	-	-	-	66-53	-	-	-	-	11-6	-	66-53	
Jim Sundberg		61-46	-	-	-	-	-	-	-	-	-	-	61-46	
John Wathan		21-19	0-1	-	-	-	-	-	-	-	-	-	21-20	
Frank White		-	-	82-65	-	-	-	-	-	-	-	-	82-65	
Willie Wilson		-	-	-	-	-	76-64	-	-	-	71-62	-	76-64	

Batting vs. Left and Right Handed Pitchers

		BA	Rank	SA	Rank	OBA	Rank	HR %	Rank	BB %	Rank	SO %	Rank
Steve Balboni	vs. Lefties	.220	135	.421	76	.312	110	4.88	36	11.83	32	24.73	153
	vs. Righties	.252	91	.498	15	.305	104	6.42	7	6.30	114	25.21	155
George Brett	vs. Lefties	.330	12	.550	13	.395	12	5.24	25	10.45	49	6.82	21
	vs. Righties	.337	3	.604	1	.456	2	5.57	13	17.98	3	7.64	24
Onix Concepcion	vs. Lefties	.217	138	.255	152	.263	146	0.00	131	6.09	123	8.70	30
	vs. Righties	.197	153	.240	155	.251	150	0.96	132	3.85	145	8.12	29
Lynn Jones	vs. Lefties	.172	154	.195	158	.221	156	0.00	131	4.12	141	8.25	28
	vs. Righties	.262	--	.338	--	.314	--	0.00	--	5.56	--	9.72	--
Hal McRae	vs. Lefties	.233	128	.467	46	.345	70	5.33	24	14.69	13	11.30	54
	vs. Righties	.282	42	.435	57	.353	44	3.53	56	9.38	56	13.02	75
Darryl Motley	vs. Lefties	.255	93	.478	41	.295	131	4.97	33	5.20	131	11.56	61
	vs. Righties	.198	152	.365	108	.230	158	4.05	41	3.83	146	15.74	109
Jorge Orta	vs. Lefties	.083	--	.083	--	.083	--	0.00	--	0.00	--	38.46	--
	vs. Righties	.274	54	.396	82	.326	80	1.39	111	6.94	101	7.26	23
Pat Sheridan	vs. Lefties	.071	--	.143	--	.071	--	0.00	--	0.00	--	37.50	--
	vs. Righties	.240	112	.349	117	.323	84	1.56	107	10.55	43	14.68	95
Lonnie Smith	vs. Lefties	.293	45	.414	81	.350	60	1.43	105	8.28	85	12.10	71
	vs. Righties	.240	111	.344	120	.308	99	1.30	118	8.21	80	14.66	94
Jim Sundberg	vs. Lefties	.217	137	.452	61	.268	141	6.09	16	6.45	117	12.10	70
	vs. Righties	.258	83	.349	116	.325	81	1.19	123	8.83	66	18.37	133
Frank White	vs. Lefties	.247	107	.446	64	.277	136	5.42	22	4.02	143	10.92	52
	vs. Righties	.249	100	.401	78	.287	131	3.27	62	4.93	133	15.73	108
Willie Wilson	vs. Lefties	.293	47	.409	83	.316	106	0.61	128	3.49	146	15.12	105
	vs. Righties	.272	56	.408	74	.316	94	0.68	138	4.89	135	14.47	93
Team Average	vs. Lefties	.250	14	.413	8	.308	14	3.42	3	7.68	13	12.61	4
	vs. Righties	.252	10	.396	8	.315	11	2.55	11	7.79	12	14.25	10
League Average	vs. Lefties	.266		.416		.333		2.91		8.95		13.77	
	vs. Righties	.259		.401		.324		2.78		8.49		13.56	

Batting with Runners on Base and Bases Empty

		BA	Rank	SA	Rank	OBA	Rank	HR %	Rank	BB %	Rank	SO %	Rank
Steve Balboni	Runners On	.262	92	.485	37	.325	100	5.77	16	8.56	95	23.63	152
	Bases Empty	.229	123	.471	31	.292	125	6.18	8	7.30	86	26.22	156
George Brett	Runners On	.367	2	.615	2	.497	1	5.88	14	21.96	1	8.45	31
	Bases Empty	.313	7	.565	5	.388	8	5.17	21	10.30	33	6.50	9
Onix Concepcion	Runners On	.258	101	.298	144	.301	125	0.81	128	2.76	152	7.59	26
	Bases Empty	.168	157	.211	158	.225	157	0.53	141	5.88	116	8.82	32
Hal McRae	Runners On	.307	32	.540	11	.395	12	5.52	18	13.02	28	7.81	29
	Bases Empty	.210	142	.357	113	.299	113	3.18	65	10.73	30	16.95	117
Darryl Motley	Runners On	.242	129	.433	69	.275	147	4.46	34	4.68	143	14.62	102
	Bases Empty	.208	146	.398	83	.245	154	4.42	42	4.22	144	13.50	74
Jorge Orta	Runners On	.242	128	.379	106	.296	131	1.86	94	7.18	112	8.84	38
	Bases Empty	.295	17	.388	92	.342	37	0.72	137	6.04	112	8.05	24
Pat Sheridan	Runners On	.183	153	.280	150	.261	152	1.22	112	9.47	68	24.21	154
	Bases Empty	.258	78	.371	101	.338	48	1.61	109	10.07	40	10.79	45
Lonnie Smith	Runners On	.249	119	.402	91	.330	95	1.78	96	11.17	37	15.74	112
	Bases Empty	.262	70	.344	121	.316	92	1.08	121	6.31	109	12.62	64
Jim Sundberg	Runners On	.254	109	.348	124	.323	101	1.45	104	9.43	73	17.61	133
	Bases Empty	.240	110	.402	75	.298	114	3.49	56	7.26	88	15.73	106
Frank White	Runners On	.281	68	.389	100	.314	113	1.81	95	4.56	145	12.86	83
	Bases Empty	.228	124	.430	54	.265	148	5.26	17	4.74	134	15.32	103
Willie Wilson	Runners On	.307	31	.438	65	.350	72	0.52	139	4.33	147	15.87	113
	Bases Empty	.264	67	.395	87	.300	111	0.73	135	4.61	139	14.06	79
Team Average	Runners On	.267	10	.414	10	.336	8	2.74	8	9.15	8	13.71	11
	Bases Empty	.241	13	.392	8	.296	14	2.84	7	6.75	14	13.83	6
League Average	Runners On	.271		.416		.338		2.85		9.26		13.25	
	Bases Empty	.254		.397		.318		2.80		8.14		13.92	

Overall Batting Compared to Late Inning Pressure Situations

		BA	Rank	SA	Rank	OBA	Rank	HR %	Rank	BB %	Rank	SO %	Rank	RDI %	Rank
Steve Balboni	Overall	.243	119	.477	23	.307	120	6.00	7	7.85	88	25.08	156	.210	146
	Pressure	.314	26	.686	2	.385	27	9.30	3	9.38	72	25.00	150	.160	134
George Brett	Overall	.335	2	.585	1	.436	2	5.45	10	15.49	5	7.37	20	.358	22
	Pressure	.311	30	.475	37	.500	1	1.64	96	26.74	1	5.81	15	.421	18
Onix Concepcion	Overall	.204	154	.245	156	.255	155	0.64	141	4.58	143	8.31	28	.205	150
	Pressure	.100	--	.100	--	.250	--	0.00	--	12.00	--	12.00	--	.000	--
Dane Iorg	Overall	.223	--	.331	--	.268	--	0.77	--	5.80	--	11.59	--	.340	--
	Pressure	.154	--	.192	--	.241	--	0.00	--	10.34	--	20.69	--	.111	149
Lynn Jones	Overall	.211	--	.257	--	.261	--	0.00	--	4.73	--	8.88	--	.243	--
	Pressure	.147	157	.176	154	.143	159	0.00	113	0.00	154	14.29	82	.111	149
Hal McRae	Overall	.259	85	.450	39	.349	41	4.38	38	11.92	28	13.97	87	.376	10
	Pressure	.282	51	.462	41	.429	11	5.13	33	19.61	5	13.73	75	.333	55
Darryl Motley	Overall	.222	145	.413	78	.257	154	4.44	34	4.41	146	13.97	87	.235	131
	Pressure	.215	120	.323	104	.221	151	1.54	99	1.47	152	14.71	87	.240	98
Jorge Orta	Overall	.267	69	.383	103	.317	104	1.33	116	6.67	116	8.48	30	.310	55
	Pressure	.206	129	.294	123	.275	126	2.94	61	9.52	68	16.67	109	.286	75
Pat Sheridan	Overall	.228	141	.335	138	.307	119	1.46	111	9.83	46	16.24	118	.210	148
	Pressure	.265	66	.382	85	.359	46	0.00	113	12.82	40	17.95	116	.143	--
Lonnie Smith	Overall	.257	95	.366	118	.321	97	1.34	115	8.23	83	13.86	85	.223	142
	Pressure	.234	103	.319	108	.321	82	0.00	113	9.43	71	16.98	109	.136	139
Jim Sundberg	Overall	.245	112	.381	105	.308	117	2.72	82	8.11	86	16.46	120	.230	135
	Pressure	.382	4	.545	15	.375	35	3.64	48	0.00	154	15.25	93	.357	45
John Wathan	Overall	.234	--	.324	--	.319	--	0.69	--	10.30	--	9.09	--	.163	--
	Pressure	.250	--	.292	--	.333	--	0.00	--	10.34	--	6.90	--	.100	155
Frank White	Overall	.249	107	.414	77	.284	144	3.91	47	4.67	142	14.33	96	.289	79
	Pressure	.313	27	.425	59	.337	71	2.50	74	3.53	137	8.24	26	.300	71
Willie Wilson	Overall	.278	46	.408	83	.316	106	0.66	140	4.52	144	14.64	103	.282	89
	Pressure	.298	38	.369	88	.318	85	0.00	113	2.27	150	15.91	97	.333	55
Team Average	Overall	.252	13	.401	9	.313	14	2.80	8	7.76	12	13.78	8	.266	11
	Pressure	.262	4	.390	7	.331	4	2.25	10	8.96	9	14.67	9	.241	12
League Average	Overall	.261		.406		.327		2.82		8.63		13.62		.287	
	Pressure	.253		.381		.323		2.74		9.11		14.40		.273	

Additional Miscellaneous Batting Comparisons

	Grass Surface BA	Rank	Artificial Surface BA	Rank	Home Games BA	Rank	Road Games BA	Rank	Runners in Scoring Position BA	Rank	Runners in Scoring Pos and Two Outs BA	Rank	Leading Off Inning OBA	Rank	Runners on 3B with less than 2 Outs RDI %	Rank
Steve Balboni	.251	100	.239	103	.253	96	.233	125	.220	131	.192	137	.302	103	.500	106
Buddy Biancalana	.176	--	.195	146	.184	--	.194	--	.160	--	.231	--	.314	85	.400	--
George Brett	.306	13	.352	6	.368	3	.298	11	.340	11	.396	4	.426	3	.676	45
Onix Concepcion	.240	121	.178	152	.201	152	.206	151	.254	107	.220	110	.203	157	.583	77
Dane Iorg	.211	--	.233	112	.210	--	.235	--	.279	--	.133	--	.333	--	.583	77
Lynn Jones	.164	--	.242	95	.225	--	.194	--	.161	--	.133	--	.243	--	.800	--
Hal McRae	.241	119	.273	57	.267	76	.252	93	.314	29	.245	77	.365	29	.750	13
Omar Moreno	.171	--	.296	30	.308	--	.141	--	.233	--	.250	--	.233	--	.250	--
Darryl Motley	.221	142	.223	126	.230	131	.214	147	.207	145	.243	81	.265	141	.478	128
Jorge Orta	.295	--	.250	83	.275	66	.259	78	.263	92	.213	119	.368	26	.800	7
Greg Pryor	.260	--	.188	150	.226	--	.217	--	.125	--	.083	--	.233	--	.000	--
Pat Sheridan	.151	--	.283	45	.286	50	.176	157	.173	154	.136	153	.184	159	.462	135
Lonnie Smith	.294	29	.236	108	.231	128	.283	31	.202	147	.217	113	.333	59	.481	127
Jim Sundberg	.234	132	.252	81	.250	99	.240	117	.268	88	.256	63	.311	92	.500	106
John Wathan	.197	--	.262	68	.274	--	.194	--	.200	--	.250	--	.237	--	.200	--
Frank White	.260	86	.241	97	.242	113	.256	88	.289	60	.333	17	.270	132	.375	152
Willie Wilson	.289	33	.271	59	.275	65	.281	35	.295	52	.228	100	.312	91	.750	13
Team Average	.250	12	.253	7	.259	10	.244	13	.255	12	.237	10	.302	14	.566	8
League Average	.262		.259		.266		.256		.268		.248		.321		.587	

Pitching vs. Left and Right Handed Batters

		BA	Rank	SA	Rank	OBA	Rank	HR %	Rank	BB %	Rank	SO %	Rank
Joe Beckwith	vs. Lefties	.299	102	.478	106	.380	110	4.46	121	11.54	98	16.48	31
	vs. Righties	.246	54	.341	21	.291	29	0.95	8	4.82	13	21.93	8
Bud Black	vs. Lefties	.267	69	.364	41	.303	31	1.14	20	4.76	9	14.81	40
	vs. Righties	.269	82	.407	75	.328	78	2.38	47	7.18	52	13.51	69
Mark Gubicza	vs. Lefties	.253	56	.391	58	.329	59	2.37	54	9.58	74	13.08	58
	vs. Righties	.219	22	.339	18	.305	49	1.71	24	10.84	114	12.95	79
Danny Jackson	vs. Lefties	.272	73	.367	44	.350	84	0.63	8	10.00	80	17.78	22
	vs. Righties	.258	65	.359	35	.322	68	0.93	7	8.13	73	11.50	94
Mike Jones	vs. Lefties	.292	--	.472	--	.404	--	4.17	--	16.48	--	10.99	--
	vs. Righties	.243	47	.385	53	.330	80	1.78	27	12.06	122	11.06	99
Charlie Leibrandt	vs. Lefties	.250	53	.348	35	.294	26	1.96	40	5.43	17	13.12	56
	vs. Righties	.247	55	.358	34	.303	45	1.87	30	7.35	61	10.37	109
Dan Quisenberry	vs. Lefties	.317	123	.435	84	.350	82	1.48	26	4.86	12	5.90	126
	vs. Righties	.236	38	.308	12	.244	4	1.69	23	0.82	1	15.16	51
Bret Saberhagen	vs. Lefties	.242	41	.363	40	.280	15	2.79	74	5.21	15	16.95	28
	vs. Righties	.240	42	.349	27	.260	12	1.33	12	2.54	2	17.01	34
Team Average	vs. Lefties	.262	7	.386	3	.324	4	2.20	3	8.26	3	13.81	4
	vs. Righties	.254	5	.367	1	.309	3	1.63	1	7.06	2	13.67	9
League Average	vs. Lefties	.265		.408		.333		2.74		9.21		12.94	
	vs. Righties	.259		.404		.322		2.88		8.19		14.14	

Pitching with Runners on Base and Bases Empty

		BA	Rank	SA	Rank	OBA	Rank	HR %	Rank	BB %	Rank	SO %	Rank
Joe Beckwith	Runners On	.288	93	.424	79	.343	77	2.72	66	7.69	39	19.71	10
	Bases Empty	.250	59	.375	45	.317	68	2.17	35	7.92	64	19.31	10
Bud Black	Runners On	.274	74	.391	60	.328	49	2.29	52	6.87	30	16.28	27
	Bases Empty	.264	83	.402	73	.319	71	1.98	30	6.50	41	11.79	86
Mark Gubicza	Runners On	.248	40	.363	31	.330	51	1.48	22	10.22	89	13.74	59
	Bases Empty	.232	33	.372	42	.311	56	2.49	58	10.07	95	12.53	75
Danny Jackson	Runners On	.267	64	.376	44	.332	54	0.91	11	8.82	62	11.23	92
	Bases Empty	.257	73	.350	31	.326	77	0.85	5	8.29	69	13.87	55
Mike Jones	Runners On	.254	46	.421	78	.333	59	1.59	26	11.69	107	11.04	93
	Bases Empty	.261	80	.400	70	.375	120	3.48	96	15.44	128	11.03	93
Charlie Leibrandt	Runners On	.219	14	.329	14	.277	9	1.92	38	7.09	33	11.49	87
	Bases Empty	.267	89	.374	43	.317	69	1.87	28	6.79	45	10.63	100
Dan Quisenberry	Runners On	.268	65	.335	17	.303	28	0.79	7	4.73	10	10.55	101
	Bases Empty	.291	113	.417	87	.300	45	2.36	52	1.17	1	9.73	114
Bret Saberhagen	Runners On	.217	12	.304	5	.248	2	1.28	19	4.36	7	14.83	41
	Bases Empty	.254	65	.387	54	.284	25	2.66	63	3.92	7	18.23	24
Team Average	Runners On	.254	2	.364	1	.315	2	1.63	1	8.12	3	13.52	7
	Bases Empty	.259	9	.381	4	.314	7	2.01	1	7.03	2	13.88	6
League Average	Runners On	.271		.416		.338		2.85		9.26		13.25	
	Bases Empty	.254		.397		.318		2.80		8.14		13.92	

Overall Pitching Compared to Late Inning Pressure Situations

		BA	Rank	SA	Rank	OBA	Rank	HR %	Rank	BB %	Rank	SO %	Rank
Joe Beckwith	Overall	.269	83	.399	60	.330	71	2.45	47	7.80	52	19.51	9
	Pressure	.303	105	.441	94	.376	99	1.97	50	9.83	70	20.81	11
Bud Black	Overall	.268	82	.398	58	.323	57	2.11	33	6.67	27	13.79	56
	Pressure	.253	60	.333	32	.321	56	0.00	1	8.99	58	12.36	72
Steve Farr	Overall	.245	--	.353	--	.344	--	1.44	--	12.20	--	21.95	--
	Pressure	.325	116	.500	114	.438	126	2.50	61	14.58	116	18.75	22
Mark Gubicza	Overall	.238	25	.368	32	.319	53	2.09	32	10.13	96	13.03	66
	Pressure	.286	90	.469	105	.375	98	4.08	101	12.50	102	16.07	39
Danny Jackson	Overall	.261	70	.361	32	.328	67	0.87	2	8.51	71	12.77	70
	Pressure	.298	102	.426	83	.353	83	0.00	1	7.77	42	11.65	85
Mike Jones	Overall	.257	61	.411	73	.353	100	2.49	52	13.45	125	11.03	101
	Pressure	.241	45	.426	84	.349	80	5.56	123	13.64	110	6.06	126
Mike LaCoss	Overall	.304	--	.416	--	.411	--	1.24	--	15.03	--	13.47	--
	Pressure	.265	69	.408	77	.333	63	2.04	53	9.09	60	21.82	9
Charlie Leibrandt	Overall	.248	44	.356	27	.301	24	1.89	27	6.92	31	10.99	102
	Pressure	.286	90	.484	108	.363	89	4.40	106	9.62	66	13.46	60
Dan Quisenberry	Overall	.280	98	.376	40	.301	25	1.57	18	3.01	1	10.15	112
	Pressure	.277	81	.366	50	.302	40	1.54	36	3.22	9	10.53	93
Bret Saberhagen	Overall	.241	29	.357	29	.271	4	2.17	35	4.08	5	16.97	25
	Pressure	.236	43	.396	68	.277	21	4.72	116	5.26	18	18.42	23
Team Average	Overall	.257	5	.374	2	.315	3	1.85	1	7.51	1	13.72	7
	Pressure	.277	11	.408	11	.336	9	2.28	2	7.69	1	14.35	8
League Average	Overall	.261		.406		.327		2.82		8.63		13.62	
	Pressure	.258		.392		.332		2.71		9.52		14.05	

Additional Miscellaneous Pitching Comparisons

	Grass Surface		Artificial Surface		Home Games		Road Games		Runners in Scoring Position		Runners in Scoring Pos and Two Outs		Leading Off Inning	
	BA	Rank	BA	Rank	BA	Rank	BA	Rank	BA	Rank	BA	Rank	OBA	Rank
Joe Beckwith	.342	--	.237	33	.249	55	.301	108	.252	49	.274	88	.321	71
Bud Black	.251	54	.279	86	.278	97	.258	55	.291	95	.270	84	.312	58
Steve Farr	.143	--	.256	64	.264	80	.172	--	.220	--	.105	--	.394	--
Mark Gubicza	.234	22	.241	37	.224	14	.253	47	.277	81	.217	47	.302	48
Mark Huismann	.300	--	.204	14	.214	--	.227	--	.167	--	.250	--	.250	--
Danny Jackson	.287	104	.244	42	.253	66	.269	77	.246	40	.224	50	.288	34
Mike Jones	.270	--	.250	52	.252	63	.263	64	.273	76	.268	82	.393	121
Mike LaCoss	.227	--	.358	128	.326	--	.280	--	.375	131	.333	--	.385	--
Charlie Leibrandt	.277	91	.229	27	.246	47	.249	41	.223	21	.219	49	.319	69
Dan Quisenberry	.307	118	.263	70	.267	84	.296	104	.223	20	.200	30	.295	44
Bret Saberhagen	.238	29	.243	39	.235	31	.248	38	.227	24	.162	15	.276	21
Team Average	.266	7	.251	5	.252	5	.262	6	.256	4	.229	3	.307	2
League Average	.262		.259		.256		.266		.268		.248		.321	

MILWAUKEE BREWERS

"Now let's throw it back to Al Michaels for the starting lineups."

"Thanks, Fernando. Here's the lineup the Brewers will use today to try to get some runs for their 25-game winner Juan Nieves in the opening game of the 1991 World Series. Third baseman Randy Ready will lead it off for Milwaukee. He'll be followed by centerfielder Glenn Braggs. Eighteen-year veteran Robin Yount will play left field and bat third. First baseman Billy Joe Robidoux is in the cleanup spot, and he's followed by catcher B.J. Surhoff. Alan Cartwright will play right field and bat sixth. Carlos Ponce, the designated hitter, will bat seventh. Batting eighth and playing shortstop, Earnest Riles. And batting ninth, their amazing 50-year-old second baseman, Pete Rose. . . ."

"Mr. Uecker, can you hear me? Wake up, Mr. Uecker."

"Grrrbllhmphh."

"Mr. Uecker, you must have fallen asleep while you were waiting."

"Mmrrrmph. I guess you're right. You know, I had the craziest dream. That Pete Rose—I love 'im!"

Wishful thinking or a psychic dream? That is a key question for Brewers fans who have endured three disappointing and often depressing seasons since losing the 1982 World Series to the St. Louis Cardinals. But there is help on the horizon. What began as a ripple four years ago has grown into a powerful wave threatening to roll over the American League within a few years. That good news is based upon the recent success of Milwaukee's minor-league teams.

Three years ago, the Paintsville Brewers won the championship of the Appalachian Rookie League. A year later, the Stockton Ports, another Milwaukee affiliate including many Paintsville graduates, won a first-half division title in the California League (Class A). Last season, many of those same players advanced to Class AA ball and, playing for the El Paso Diablos, finished with the Texas League's best record by far, before losing in the playoff finals. Should the players from El Paso graduate to the Triple-A level and win a title there, they will cap a rare achievement, one that suggests the Milwaukee Brewers may be one of baseball's strongest teams within five years.

An examination of minor-league standings since 1969 showed that only four organizations won rookie-league titles followed within two years by one or more Class AA championships, and then a Triple-A title in the next three years. (For our purposes, "titles" represented the league's best regular-season record, not a victory in a short playoff series.) Those parent organizations have subsequently remained among the most successful in the majors. Kansas City experienced such a streak from 1973 through 1977; Detroit from 1974 through 1979; the New York Yankees from 1979 through 1984; and the Los Angeles Dodgers from 1980 through 1983.

These periods of development do not involve a single set of players rising through the minor-league ranks together, and arriving at their major-league manager's doorstep to announce, "We're here. Order the World Series rings." Instead, they represent a four- or five-year period of organization-wide excellence, during which players who started their professional careers within a year or two of one another are promoted through the system, each at his own pace, eventually reaching the major-league team at around the same time.

The development of the Tigers is an excellent example of that process. Lance Parrish, Tim Corcoran, and Bob Sykes were members of the Bristol team that had the best record in the Appalachian League in 1974. (Sykes, a successful minor-league pitcher with just a 23–26 lifetime record in the big leagues, played a vital role in building not one but two World Champions: Detroit traded him to St. Louis for Aurelio Lopez in 1978, and the Cardinals later traded him to the Yankees for Willie McGee.) Two years later, they made some new friends at Montgomery: Jack Morris, Steve Kemp, Tom Brookens, and, later in the season, Alan Trammell. Together they won the first of two consecutive Southern League championships; for the second they were joined by Lou Whitaker. By the late 1970s, all had reached the parent Tigers. From the 1979 Evansville team, which went on to win the American Association title, Detroit plucked Dan Petry at midseason. The rest is history.

Kansas City affiliates had the best records in two of the three rookie leagues in 1973. Kingsport of the Appalachian League produced U.L. Washington; Ruppert Jones cut his teeth at Billings of the Pioneer League, where Bob McClure was the leader in wins. Jamie Quirk and John Wathan joined the bandwagon a year later at Jacksonville of the Southern League. Three years later, Omaha of the American Association groomed Willie Wilson and Clint Hurdle for the Royals teams that won division titles in 1978 and 1980.

The Yankees won so many championships at different levels from 1979 through 1981 that tracing the player development is pointless. But they did illustrate another aspect of these streaks, one we touched on when discussing Detroit. Frequently, the players produced during these periods never play for the parent team, but nevertheless become essential pieces in the puzzle. The Yankees have made an art of using promising minor leaguers as bait for established major leaguers. Pitcher Pete Filson was a key in the deal that brought Butch Wynegar from Minnesota. Pat Tabler, Fred Toliver, and Otis Nixon, all developed during those three years, were bartered for Jay Howell, Ken Griffey, and Toby Harrah respectively. The process is continuous: Tabler was traded to the Cubs for Bill Caudill (who was immediately sent to Seattle with Bobby Brown and Gene Nelson for Shane Rawley, who in turn ended up going to Philadelphia for Marty Bystrom) and Jay Howell, who was packaged with several other young players to Oakland for Rickey Henderson. This is every bit as legitimate a use of the farm system as is developing a Don Mattingly.

Although Los Angeles technically qualifies for a period of player development beginning in 1980, no players from the 1980 rookie team at Lethbridge have contributed to the Dodgers' success, so we won't waste any time on them.

The success of two of the other three teams after their periods of peak development has been enormous. Detroit and Kansas City both had winning percentages above .550 for the five years immediately following their productive periods, and they have maintained that excellence beyond those five years. They faced each other, of course, in the '84 A.L. playoffs. The third team, the Yankees, should reap the benefits of their own successful program over the next few years. But, looking beyond that, we may see the Brewers' foamy heads rising to the top of the league once again, if their youngsters eventually fulfill their promise at the major-league level.

Their Triple-A performance will provide a good indication of what is to come. The El Paso team of last season will for the most part be promoted to Vancouver of the Pacific Coast League this season, where they will try to match their winning performances in the lower minor-league levels. Some exceptions may even make the jump directly to the big leagues. Regardless, there will be a lot of unfamiliar names in Milwaukee boxscores this season, but don't let that alarm you. Last season's Vancouver Canadians, a group one year ahead of Milwaukee's prime prospects, won the PCL playoffs, and many of their graduates will undoubtedly be the Brewers' advance men, laying the foundation, along with Riles, Ready, Higuera, and others, for what is to come.

In China, They'd Call It the Year of the Gopher

Last season, Milwaukee's offensive statistics were nearly identical to those of their opponents, with one exception. Unfortunately, that exception was the single most important category: home runs. Notice in the figures below that Milwaukee had 26 more singles and a few more doubles and triples than their opponents last season, which more than compensated for 51 fewer walks and hit batters. But Milwaukee was out-scored by 112 runs:

	AB	H	1B	2B	3B	HR	HP	BB	SO
Brewers	5568	1467	1072	250	44	101	19	462	746
Opponents	5577	1510	1046	247	42	175	33	499	777

That 74-homer deficit was the largest in the American League in more than 20 years. The Kansas City Athletics allowed 199 home runs in 1962 and hit only 116, a difference of 83 home runs. (The Athletics had an excuse of sorts. They played in Kansas City's Municipal Stadium, which during the first 10 years of major-league baseball there increased the home-run rate by more than 50 percent over the league average. On top of that, the left-field fence was moved in 17 feet prior to the 1962 season to aid their power-poor offense. But their opponents were better equipped to exploit the new dimensions than the A's were; the K.C. outfield of Gino Cimoli, Bobby Del Greco, and Manny Jimenez wouldn't remind anyone of Rice, Armas, and Evans under any circumstances. Club President Charlie O. Finley was so appalled by his team's lack of power that for several seasons he kept lowering the fences and moving them closer, until he finally got fed up and moved to Oakland, much to the gratitude of his shell-shocked pitchers.

The Milwaukee pitchers have no such defense. Although County Stadium has been considered a home-run hitters' park for the past three decades, that mistaken impression has resulted only because of the great sluggers who have played there, from Hank Aaron, Eddie Mathews, and Joe Adcock, to Gorman Thomas, Ben Oglivie, and Ted Simmons. County Stadium is definitely a pitchers' park, making the performance of the Brewers' pitchers all the more remarkable. Although the feat of allowing 174 home runs was truly

a team effort—regular starting pitchers Ray Burris, Danny Darwin, Moose Haas, and Ted Higuera allowed more than 20 each—no one was more responsible than Darwin, who tied Scott McGregor for the league lead by throwing 34 gopher balls.

How did Darwin manage to allow 34 home runs in a park like County Stadium? He didn't; only 12 of the home runs against Darwin were hit at County Stadium, leaving a total of 22 home runs against him in road games.

It's interesting that any baseball fan can recite a litany of home-run statistics about batters, but hardly any about pitchers; official statistics on home runs allowed were not even compiled until the 1950s. That oversight reflects, in part, the origins of the game, when home runs were so rare that it was barely worth the effort to keep track of them. But some vestigial traces of the prejudice against pitching statistics still remain today. This is still the only book you will find that presents information on doubles and triples hit against a pitcher, or the number of double-play ground balls allowed.

We bring this up because the 22 home runs against Darwin on the road was among the highest totals in the 11 seasons for which we have play-by-play data. But who knew? In fact, only one pitcher since 1975 has allowed more road home runs in a single season. But let's not limit ourselves to road games; what follows is a mini-record book for pitchers' home-run statistics since 1975:

Most home runs: 41, Phil Niekro (1979); 40, Ferguson Jenkins (1979); 38, Matt Keough (1982); 37, Ferguson Jenkins (1975), Jack Morris (1982), and Dan Petry (1983).

Most home-game home runs: 22, Gaylord Perry (Seattle, 1982); 21, Ray Burris (Chicago Cubs, 1977), Jerry Ujdur (Detroit, 1982), and Ken Schrom (Minnesota, 1985); 20, Buzz Capra (Atlanta, 1977), Phil Niekro (Atlanta, 1979 and 1980), Glenn Abbott (Seattle, 1980), Dennis Martinez (Baltimore, 1982), John Tudor (Boston, 1983), and Luis Leal (Toronto, 1984).

Most road-game home runs: 26, Matt Keough (1982); 22, Ferguson Jenkins (1979) and Danny Darwin (1985); 21, Phil Niekro (1979) and Dan Petry (1983).

Most home runs by right-handed batters: 31, Mike Caldwell (1983); 30, Frank Viola (1983) and John Tudor (1983); 28, Bill Travers (1979) and Tom Browning (1985).

Most home runs by left-handed batters: 23, LaMarr Hoyt (1984) and Mike Smithson (1984); 22, Jack Morris (1982); 21, Ferguson Jenkins (1975) and Dan Petry (1983).

Most home runs with runners on base: 21, Matt Keough (1982) and Jack Morris (1982); 18, Larry Gura (1982); 17, Dennis Leonard (1979), Floyd Bannister (1985), and John Butcher (1985).

Most home runs in Late-Inning Pressure Situations: 12, Bob Lacey (1977); 11, Ron Davis (1982) and Willie Hernandez (1985); 10, Bill Campbell (1975), Oscar Zamora (1975), Jim Palmer (1977), Ron Davis (1984), and Bruce Sutter (1985).

Finally, before we put the topic to rest, a tip of the hat to the 1964 Athletics and the 1982 Twins: the only teams in baseball history to allow 200 or more home runs in a season (220 and 208, respectively). Hey, Blue Moon Odom, Diego Segui, John O'Donoghue, Bobby Castillo, Brad Havens, Terry Felton, and all the rest—this one's for you.

WON-LOST RECORD BY STARTING POSITION

MILWAUKEE 71-90	C	1B	2B	3B	SS	LF	CF	RF	P	DH	Leadoff	Relief	Starts
Mark Brouhard	-	-	-	-	-	2-6	-	8-13	-	1-0	-	0-1	11-19
Ray Burris	-	-	-	-	-	-	-	-	12-16	-	-	0-1	12-16
Bobby Clark	-	-	-	-	-	-	8-9	2-5	-	-	-	-	10-14
Jaime Cocanower	-	-	-	-	-	-	-	-	7-8	-	-	1-8	7-8
Cecil Cooper	-	55-68	-	-	-	-	-	-	-	9-21	-	-	64-89
Danny Darwin	-	-	-	-	-	-	-	-	10-19	-	-	4-6	10-19
Mike Felder	-	-	-	-	-	-	5-8	-	-	-	5-8	-	5-8
Rollie Fingers	-	-	-	-	-	-	-	-	-	-	-	25-22	-
Jim Gantner	-	-	50-71	10-8	-	-	-	-	-	-	1-1	-	60-79
Bob Gibson	-	-	-	-	-	-	-	-	0-1	-	-	22-18	0-1
Brian Giles	-	-	5-3	-	7-4	-	-	-	-	-	-	-	12-7
Moose Haas	-	-	-	-	-	-	-	-	12-14	-	-	0-1	12-14
Ted Higuera	-	-	-	-	-	-	-	-	17-13	-	-	0-2	17-13
Paul Householder	-	-	-	-	-	1-0	14-15	23-24	-	-	-	-	38-39
Dave Huppert	3-5	-	-	-	-	-	-	-	-	-	-	-	3-5
Dion James	-	-	-	-	-	-	2-9	-	-	1-	-	-0	3-9
Jim Kern	-	-	-	-	-	-	-	-	-	-	-	0-5	-
Pete Ladd	-	-	-	-	-	-	-	-	-	-	-	7-22	-
Tim Leary	-	-	-	-	-	-	-	-	1-4	-	-	-	1-4
Brad Lesley	-	-	-	-	-	-	-	-	-	-	-	1-4	-
Doug Loman	-	-	-	-	-	-	3-5	2-6	-	-	-	-	5-11
Rick Manning	-	-	-	-	-	-	21-23	7-5	-	-	-	-	28-28
Bob McClure	-	-	-	-	-	-	-	-	0-1	-	-	11-26	0-1
Paul Molitor	-	-	-	60-73	-	-	-	-	-	1-3	57-68	-	61-76
Charlie Moore	43-53	-	-	-	-	-	-	1-1	-	-	-	-	44-54
Ben Oglivie	-	-	-	-	-	17-19	-	23-28	-	3-1	-	-	43-48
Carlos Ponce	-	3-2	-	-	-	1-4	-	1-0	-	2-1	-	-	7-7
Chuck Porter	-	-	-	-	-	-	-	-	1-0	-	-	0-5	1-0
Randy Ready	-	-	1-1	1-6	-	16-16	1-2	-	-	1-0	2-5	-	20-25
Earnest Riles	-	-	-	-	49-64	-	-	-	-	1-0	5-4	-	50-64
Billy Joe Robidoux	-	3-1	-	-	-	2-7	-	-	-	1-0	-	-	6-8
Ed Romero	-	-	15-15	0-1	15-22	0-1	-	3-6	-	-	-	-	33-45
Bill Schroeder	19-27	1-0	-	-	-	-	-	-	-	1-3	-	-	21-30
Ray Searage	-	-	-	-	-	-	-	-	-	-	-	9-24	-
Ted Simmons	6-5	9-18	-	0-2	-	-	-	-	-	45-54	-	-	60-79
Pete Vuckovich	-	-	-	-	-	-	-	-	9-13	-	-	-	9-13
Rick Waits	-	-	-	-	-	-	-	-	-	-	-	5-19	-
Bill Wegman	-	-	-	-	-	-	-	-	2-1	-	-	-	2-1
Robin Yount	-	0-1	-	-	-	32-37	18-21	-	-	5-7	1-4	-	55-66

Batting vs. Left and Right Handed Pitchers

		BA	Rank	SA	Rank	OBA	Rank	HR %	Rank	BB %	Rank	SO %	Rank
Mark Brouhard	vs. Lefties	.253	95	.398	90	.295	130	1.20	111	5.62	127	22.47	144
	vs. Righties	.280	--	.360	--	.308	--	0.00	--	0.00	--	23.08	--
Bobby Clark	vs. Lefties	.243	119	.286	143	.299	125	0.00	131	7.79	92	14.29	98
	vs. Righties	.174	--	.174	--	.208	--	0.00	--	4.17	--	33.33	--
Cecil Cooper	vs. Lefties	.321	21	.498	27	.360	54	2.87	72	5.70	125	11.40	58
	vs. Righties	.280	48	.436	54	.303	109	2.37	89	3.81	147	11.43	56
Jim Gantner	vs. Lefties	.329	13	.372	109	.368	35	0.00	131	5.06	134	6.18	17
	vs. Righties	.220	135	.306	145	.270	140	1.39	110	6.08	117	7.85	28
Paul Householder	vs. Lefties	.304	34	.487	31	.357	48	4.35	45	7.94	89	18.25	129
	vs. Righties	.228	127	.375	95	.297	120	3.26	65	8.37	75	18.23	130
Rick Manning	vs. Lefties	.235	--	.353	--	.297	--	2.94	--	8.11	--	16.22	--
	vs. Righties	.214	141	.286	148	.259	147	0.55	143	5.67	125	6.70	18
Paul Molitor	vs. Lefties	.324	17	.464	52	.384	15	2.79	73	8.50	79	9.50	38
	vs. Righties	.285	40	.383	91	.343	53	1.26	120	8.37	76	13.80	85
Charlie Moore	vs. Lefties	.285	56	.366	112	.367	37	0.00	131	10.64	46	9.93	43
	vs. Righties	.204	147	.252	154	.243	156	0.00	152	4.90	134	15.92	111
Ben Oglivie	vs. Lefties	.213	141	.387	99	.238	152	2.67	76	2.44	153	15.85	110
	vs. Righties	.312	8	.455	42	.384	9	3.01	71	11.22	35	12.18	65
Randy Ready	vs. Lefties	.250	101	.369	111	.289	133	1.19	112	5.49	128	8.79	32
	vs. Righties	.278	--	.402	--	.343	--	0.00	--	8.26	--	13.76	--
Earnest Riles	vs. Lefties	.241	123	.298	140	.310	115	0.00	131	8.18	87	15.09	104
	vs. Righties	.306	12	.414	67	.353	42	1.63	104	6.85	103	8.93	34
Ed Romero	vs. Lefties	.192	153	.242	154	.266	144	0.00	131	8.77	72	4.39	8
	vs. Righties	.289	27	.342	124	.357	35	0.00	152	9.52	51	8.93	34
Bill Schroeder	vs. Lefties	.293	--	.586	--	.323	--	8.62	--	4.84	--	24.19	--
	vs. Righties	.221	134	.331	129	.277	134	2.21	92	6.08	116	31.08	158
Ted Simmons	vs. Lefties	.307	31	.500	26	.380	19	4.22	48	10.64	46	5.85	14
	vs. Righties	.257	84	.356	113	.324	82	1.38	112	9.16	65	5.20	5
Robin Yount	vs. Lefties	.300	37	.453	60	.357	48	2.67	76	8.93	69	11.31	55
	vs. Righties	.266	64	.437	51	.335	60	3.48	58	9.47	53	10.31	47
Team Average	vs. Lefties	.277	2	.405	11	.333	6	2.15	13	7.55	14	12.00	2
	vs. Righties	.257	8	.365	14	.312	13	1.65	14	7.48	14	12.17	1
League Average	vs. Lefties	.266		.416		.333		2.91		8.95		13.77	
	vs. Righties	.259		.401		.324		2.78		8.49		13.56	

Batting with Runners on Base and Bases Empty

		BA	Rank	SA	Rank	OBA	Rank	HR %	Rank	BB %	Rank	SO %	Rank
Cecil Cooper	Runners On	.322	19	.505	26	.349	73	2.61	76	5.36	139	7.74	28
	Bases Empty	.265	61	.410	65	.296	117	2.47	88	3.55	149	15.09	95
Jim Gantner	Runners On	.251	116	.311	138	.309	120	0.91	122	7.11	113	7.11	22
	Bases Empty	.257	83	.339	124	.294	121	0.99	125	4.69	137	7.50	19
Paul Householder	Runners On	.248	120	.431	71	.320	107	4.38	38	9.09	81	16.88	122
	Bases Empty	.265	61	.407	70	.320	85	3.09	68	7.43	82	19.43	136
Rick Manning	Runners On	.229	140	.323	133	.282	144	2.08	91	6.73	123	8.65	35
	Bases Empty	.208	145	.275	150	.252	152	0.00	148	5.51	124	7.87	21
Paul Molitor	Runners On	.300	39	.361	120	.375	33	0.56	138	11.16	39	10.70	57
	Bases Empty	.295	15	.429	55	.347	28	2.27	95	7.03	93	13.35	73
Charlie Moore	Runners On	.222	145	.293	147	.276	146	0.00	142	6.88	120	11.11	62
	Bases Empty	.242	107	.291	149	.299	112	0.00	148	7.11	91	16.24	112
Ben Oglivie	Runners On	.328	12	.555	8	.389	17	5.11	24	11.11	41	11.11	62
	Bases Empty	.265	65	.363	108	.327	67	1.47	114	8.07	71	14.35	85
Randy Ready	Runners On	.291	51	.443	62	.333	89	1.27	110	5.62	134	13.48	93
	Bases Empty	.245	--	.343	--	.306	--	0.00	--	8.11	--	9.91	--
Earnest Riles	Runners On	.296	45	.374	110	.354	63	0.99	118	8.19	103	9.48	43
	Bases Empty	.278	35	.380	98	.327	68	1.22	119	6.46	104	12.17	58
Ed Romero	Runners On	.301	38	.359	121	.368	44	0.00	142	9.24	77	7.56	24
	Bases Empty	.216	137	.264	153	.288	132	0.00	148	9.20	53	6.75	12
Bill Schroeder	Runners On	.253	111	.418	77	.322	103	5.06	26	8.89	88	27.78	158
	Bases Empty	.235	119	.400	78	.267	147	3.48	57	3.33	151	30.00	158
Ted Simmons	Runners On	.289	54	.395	96	.370	41	1.75	97	12.03	34	3.76	3
	Bases Empty	.260	73	.407	71	.319	87	2.67	81	7.67	77	6.75	12
Robin Yount	Runners On	.321	22	.486	35	.379	26	3.21	65	9.45	70	10.63	56
	Bases Empty	.238	112	.403	74	.308	103	3.23	64	9.16	55	10.62	44
Team Average	Runners On	.279	3	.397	13	.337	7	1.96	14	8.33	14	10.87	1
	Bases Empty	.252	9	.365	12	.305	12	1.71	14	6.84	13	13.12	4
League Average	Runners On	.271		.416		.338		2.85		9.26		13.25	
	Bases Empty	.254		.397		.318		2.80		8.14		13.92	

Overall Batting Compared to Late Inning Pressure Situations

		BA	Rank	SA	Rank	OBA	Rank	HR %	Rank	BB %	Rank	SO %	Rank	RDI %	Rank
Cecil Cooper	Overall	.293	21	.456	32	.322	92	2.54	85	4.45	145	11.42	52	.364	19
	Pressure	.356	8	.425	58	.378	34	1.15	111	3.30	140	13.19	71	.391	29
Jim Gantner	Overall	.254	98	.327	142	.300	131	0.96	130	5.76	132	7.33	19	.245	124
	Pressure	.256	77	.317	111	.326	79	1.22	108	9.38	72	9.38	31	.167	128
Paul Householder	Overall	.258	92	.418	73	.320	101	3.68	52	8.21	84	18.24	134	.188	156
	Pressure	.308	32	.423	62	.321	82	1.92	86	1.89	151	16.98	109	.118	145
Rick Manning	Overall	.218	152	.296	150	.265	153	0.93	133	6.06	127	8.23	27	.230	136
	Pressure	.150	155	.250	142	.150	158	2.50	74	0.00	154	7.50	20	.250	87
Paul Molitor	Overall	.297	15	.408	85	.356	31	1.74	107	8.41	76	12.46	65	.281	91
	Pressure	.312	29	.442	51	.365	43	1.30	106	7.95	91	14.77	88	.294	74
Charlie Moore	Overall	.232	136	.292	151	.288	142	0.00	154	6.99	108	13.73	84	.252	117
	Pressure	.241	92	.259	138	.279	124	0.00	113	4.84	127	9.68	35	.261	86
Ben Oglivie	Overall	.290	24	.440	54	.354	35	2.93	76	9.39	56	12.94	73	.404	6
	Pressure	.245	88	.396	75	.310	94	3.77	46	6.56	109	18.03	118	.500	7
Randy Ready	Overall	.265	72	.387	100	.318	103	0.55	143	7.00	107	11.50	55	.373	13
	Pressure	.212	124	.333	99	.257	137	3.03	59	5.56	121	16.67	103	.417	20
Earnest Riles	Overall	.286	33	.377	110	.339	62	1.12	123	7.27	101	10.91	48	.317	49
	Pressure	.217	118	.261	137	.280	123	0.00	113	6.49	113	10.39	44	.286	75
Ed Romero	Overall	.251	102	.303	149	.321	96	0.00	154	9.22	62	7.09	18	.328	39
	Pressure	.333	15	.444	49	.415	18	0.00	113	11.63	50	4.65	8	.222	104
Bill Schroeder	Overall	.242	121	.407	87	.290	140	4.12	40	5.71	133	29.05	158	.255	115
	Pressure	.276	57	.414	69	.313	92	3.45	52	6.25	115	21.88	138	.375	32
Ted Simmons	Overall	.273	62	.402	93	.342	58	2.27	95	9.63	49	5.41	5	.305	59
	Pressure	.247	85	.424	61	.323	80	3.53	50	9.28	75	8.25	27	.424	17
Robin Yount	Overall	.277	47	.442	50	.342	55	3.22	65	9.30	59	10.63	47	.340	28
	Pressure	.191	137	.213	151	.344	61	0.00	113	17.74	12	11.29	54	.333	55
Team Average	Overall	.263	7	.379	14	.319	11	1.81	14	7.50	14	12.11	1	.294	7
	Pressure	.253	8	.346	12	.312	12	1.57	14	7.42	13	13.23	4	.296	4
League Average	Overall	.261		.406		.327		2.82		8.63		13.62		.287	
	Pressure	.253		.381		.323		2.74		9.11		14.40		.273	

Additional Miscellaneous Batting Comparisons

	Grass Surface BA	Rank	Artificial Surface BA	Rank	Home Games BA	Rank	Road Games BA	Rank	Runners in Scoring Position BA	Rank	Runners in Scoring Pos and Two Outs BA	Rank	Leading Off Inning OBA	Rank	Runners on 3B with less than 2 Outs RDI %	Rank
Cecil Cooper	.296	26	.282	48	.285	52	.301	8	.298	50	.227	103	.371	24	.805	6
Jim Gantner	.247	107	.286	43	.238	119	.271	52	.238	118	.218	111	.269	134	.640	55
Paul Householder	.248	106	.306	18	.239	117	.273	49	.205	146	.212	120	.329	72	.500	106
Rick Manning	.199	151	.289	40	.218	142	.217	143	.216	135	.071	158	.235	150	.667	--
Paul Molitor	.306	15	.257	72	.323	15	.276	43	.280	71	.264	57	.377	17	.556	91
Charlie Moore	.237	128	.214	133	.254	93	.211	149	.223	128	.220	107	.243	148	.476	130
Ben Oglivie	.293	30	.270	--	.319	18	.265	68	.299	48	.268	56	.330	71	.786	10
Randy Ready	.272	57	.244	90	.265	--	.265	67	.333	--	.350	--	.304	--	.667	--
Earnest Riles	.297	24	.235	110	.332	9	.239	119	.292	55	.315	32	.340	51	.632	57
Ed Romero	.262	83	.189	--	.258	87	.244	110	.300	44	.208	125	.302	104	.778	--
Bill Schroeder	.243	115	.235	--	.212	148	.278	--	.209	142	.211	--	.311	--	.600	66
Ted Simmons	.279	49	.242	95	.283	54	.264	73	.284	66	.293	40	.257	145	.487	122
Robin Yount	.285	41	.214	133	.309	24	.242	114	.278	75	.262	58	.227	153	.722	25
Team Average	.266	4	.252	9	.272	5	.255	8	.263	9	.241	9	.303	12	.630	3
League Average	.262		.259		.266		.256		.268		.248		.321		.587	

Pitching vs. Left and Right Handed Batters

		BA	Rank	SA	Rank	OBA	Rank	HR %	Rank	BB %	Rank	SO %	Rank
Ray Burris	vs. Lefties	.236	34	.431	80	.292	22	3.61	100	7.09	37	11.39	83
	vs. Righties	.313	125	.497	125	.364	117	3.87	109	7.29	58	10.50	106
Jaime Cocanower	vs. Lefties	.288	88	.365	43	.404	127	0.86	12	16.01	127	4.27	130
	vs. Righties	.259	68	.349	26	.360	112	1.89	33	11.07	116	12.65	84
Danny Darwin	vs. Lefties	.270	72	.459	96	.343	75	4.07	113	9.70	76	10.55	93
	vs. Righties	.238	39	.404	72	.270	17	4.09	112	4.27	11	16.85	37
Rollie Fingers	vs. Lefties	.317	121	.485	112	.381	111	3.96	110	9.57	73	5.22	128
	vs. Righties	.233	--	.414	--	.282	--	4.31	--	6.35	--	14.29	--
Bob Gibson	vs. Lefties	.246	45	.423	76	.343	76	4.23	115	13.17	114	11.38	84
	vs. Righties	.270	84	.392	58	.361	113	2.12	39	12.00	121	15.11	52
Moose Haas	vs. Lefties	.260	63	.389	56	.291	21	2.99	80	4.29	6	10.57	92
	vs. Righties	.260	69	.433	90	.283	20	3.67	102	3.16	3	12.97	78
Ted Higuera	vs. Lefties	.236	35	.378	49	.293	24	2.36	53	7.04	35	19.01	16
	vs. Righties	.234	36	.372	44	.289	27	2.85	72	7.24	56	13.66	67
Bob McClure	vs. Lefties	.240	38	.365	42	.295	28	3.13	85	6.60	28	16.98	27
	vs. Righties	.288	107	.470	118	.355	105	2.97	79	8.71	85	14.77	56
Pete Vuckovich	vs. Lefties	.311	113	.422	75	.376	104	1.78	36	9.13	68	9.52	104
	vs. Righties	.284	104	.507	127	.371	123	5.33	128	9.65	95	11.97	91
Rick Waits	vs. Lefties	.310	--	.479	--	.410	--	1.41	--	14.29	--	11.90	--
	vs. Righties	.357	132	.460	111	.393	129	1.59	19	5.88	35	10.29	110
Team Average	vs. Lefties	.273	10	.427	11	.338	10	3.15	13	8.91	6	10.75	13
	vs. Righties	.269	12	.422	13	.326	8	3.13	8	7.36	3	13.86	8
League Average	vs. Lefties	.265		.408		.333		2.74		9.21		12.94	
	vs. Righties	.259		.404		.322		2.88		8.19		14.14	

Pitching with Runners on Base and Bases Empty

		BA	Rank	SA	Rank	OBA	Rank	HR %	Rank	BB %	Rank	SO %	Rank
Ray Burris	Runners On	.280	82	.433	86	.341	73	2.76	70	8.53	57	11.60	84
	Bases Empty	.267	86	.478	117	.315	62	4.33	116	6.29	35	10.56	104
Jaime Cocanower	Runners On	.245	32	.305	6	.359	95	0.43	1	14.74	127	8.07	123
	Bases Empty	.307	124	.415	85	.410	130	2.36	50	12.45	119	8.43	126
Danny Darwin	Runners On	.285	89	.480	109	.338	66	4.70	120	7.95	45	14.25	49
	Bases Empty	.235	38	.402	72	.289	32	3.69	105	6.50	40	13.18	69
Bob Gibson	Runners On	.247	38	.367	34	.332	54	2.53	56	11.52	106	11.52	86
	Bases Empty	.272	94	.439	98	.373	119	3.47	95	13.43	123	15.42	41
Moose Haas	Runners On	.304	109	.460	99	.343	75	3.13	85	6.50	27	8.94	118
	Bases Empty	.237	39	.383	51	.255	3	3.41	92	2.14	3	13.33	66
Ted Higuera	Runners On	.228	21	.345	22	.282	13	2.41	54	7.25	35	13.29	65
	Bases Empty	.239	42	.390	56	.295	40	2.98	77	7.18	50	15.29	42
Bob McClure	Runners On	.260	48	.487	112	.337	64	4.55	117	10.11	87	14.61	42
	Bases Empty	.287	108	.399	68	.339	90	1.69	24	6.25	32	16.15	35
Pete Vuckovich	Runners On	.295	100	.475	107	.374	112	3.50	95	10.34	91	10.78	98
	Bases Empty	.300	120	.456	108	.373	117	3.60	101	8.60	76	10.75	97
Rick Waits	Runners On	.321	121	.443	90	.392	125	1.89	37	10.66	96	9.02	116
	Bases Empty	.363	--	.495	--	.408	--	1.10	--	7.14	--	13.27	--
Team Average	Runners On	.277	9	.422	9	.343	9	2.90	8	9.29	7	11.87	12
	Bases Empty	.266	13	.426	14	.323	8	3.31	14	7.04	3	13.01	10
League Average	Runners On	.271		.416		.338		2.85		9.26		13.25	
	Bases Empty	.254		.397		.318		2.80		8.14		13.92	

Overall Pitching Compared to Late Inning Pressure Situations

		BA	Rank	SA	Rank	OBA	Rank	HR %	Rank	BB %	Rank	SO %	Rank
Ray Burris	Overall	.272	85	.461	109	.325	60	3.73	108	7.18	42	10.98	103
	Pressure	.246	50	.377	59	.292	31	3.28	90	5.97	24	13.43	61
Jaime Cocanower	Overall	.274	94	.357	28	.383	125	1.35	12	13.67	126	8.24	127
	Pressure	.238	44	.357	45	.333	63	2.38	59	12.24	101	12.24	75
Danny Darwin	Overall	.254	54	.432	92	.308	38	4.08	116	7.07	36	13.60	58
	Pressure	.276	80	.428	87	.333	63	2.76	75	8.48	50	12.73	67
Rollie Fingers	Overall	.272	--	.447	--	.329	--	4.15	--	7.88	--	9.96	--
	Pressure	.288	94	.489	113	.367	92	5.04	120	11.11	83	9.26	104
Bob Gibson	Overall	.260	68	.405	64	.353	101	3.02	81	12.50	119	13.52	59
	Pressure	.222	25	.407	75	.321	55	4.44	108	11.80	92	14.91	47
Moose Haas	Overall	.260	69	.410	72	.287	12	3.31	95	3.75	3	11.71	88
	Pressure	.309	110	.636	127	.345	77	7.27	129	5.17	17	6.90	122
Ted Higuera	Overall	.235	19	.373	37	.290	14	2.77	67	7.21	44	14.53	48
	Pressure	.265	69	.361	47	.303	43	2.72	74	5.13	16	14.10	53
Pete Ladd	Overall	.315	--	.467	--	.347	--	2.72	--	4.95	--	10.89	--
	Pressure	.290	96	.484	109	.303	42	3.23	88	3.03	8	9.09	107
Bob McClure	Overall	.274	92	.440	97	.338	81	3.01	79	8.11	60	15.41	36
	Pressure	.279	85	.368	53	.319	54	0.00	1	5.41	20	14.86	48
Ray Searage	Overall	.338	--	.438	--	.422	--	1.25	--	12.70	--	19.05	--
	Pressure	.350	128	.463	102	.418	121	1.25	27	10.64	80	20.21	15
Pete Vuckovich	Overall	.298	116	.464	111	.374	121	3.56	104	9.39	85	10.76	108
	Pressure	.333	--	.467	--	.355	--	3.33	--	3.23	--	6.45	--
Team Average	Overall	.271	13	.424	12	.331	11	3.14	13	8.03	3	12.51	11
	Pressure	.286	13	.445	14	.349	12	3.34	14	8.78	5	12.78	11
League Average	Overall	.261		.406		.327		2.82		8.63		13.62	
	Pressure	.258		.392		.332		2.71		9.52		14.05	

Additional Miscellaneous Pitching Comparisons

	Grass Surface BA	Rank	Artificial Surface BA	Rank	Home Games BA	Rank	Road Games BA	Rank	Runners in Scoring Position BA	Rank	Runners in Scoring Pos and Two Outs BA	Rank	Leading Off Inning OBA	Rank
Ray Burris	.260	71	.417	131	.251	60	.306	112	.243	35	.243	70	.268	18
Jaime Cocanower	.279	93	.258	65	.277	96	.271	80	.226	23	.262	80	.398	122
Danny Darwin	.248	44	.310	114	.246	48	.261	59	.251	48	.236	61	.288	34
Rollie Fingers	.282	99	.234	--	.305	--	.246	36	.300	--	.303	112	.313	--
Bob Gibson	.250	49	.296	103	.276	95	.242	32	.272	75	.200	30	.367	111
Moose Haas	.253	58	.301	106	.256	71	.268	76	.308	108	.217	47	.318	67
Ted Higuera	.243	39	.201	12	.254	69	.220	13	.262	61	.246	73	.290	38
Pete Ladd	.321	--	.298	104	.341	--	.293	--	.286	90	.194	--	.471	--
Bob McClure	.268	81	.346	--	.292	108	.248	40	.279	84	.333	117	.295	42
Ray Searage	.376	131	.148	--	.385	--	.250	--	.328	118	.344	123	.361	--
Pete Vuckovich	.298	108	.298	105	.282	102	.313	117	.296	97	.302	110	.347	97
Rick Waits	.323	126	.424	--	.366	--	.322	122	.344	125	.320	--	.468	--
Team Average	.269	12	.278	11	.276	14	.266	7	.273	9	.262	11	.324	9
League Average	.262		.259		.256		.266		.268		.248		.321	

MINNESOTA TWINS

The 1985 All-Star Game at the Metrodome provided a classic example of what happens when myth and reputation collide with cold, hard fact. The Twins' ballpark hosted only the third mid-season classic without a home run since 1967. The other two were played at fields which were subsequently altered to increase home-run production: the Astrodome and San Diego/Jack Murphy Stadium. Televised before a national audience of millions of baseball fans, the game should have cast doubt on the stadium's "Homerdome" label. Nevertheless, the reputation survived intact. Rather than saying, "All those sluggers and no home runs. And we thought it was a hitters' park," people's overriding reaction was, "Boy, were those pitchers lucky to get out of there alive." Myth 1, Fact 0.

This is not to say that the Metrodome should be considered a characterless ballpark. The Metrodome is among the most idiosyncratic fields in either league, but for reasons that have nothing to do with home runs. And its unique character was put on conspicuous display in that same All-Star Game, while all America watched but refused to see.

Third inning, two outs, Steve Garvey on first base. Dale Murphy lofts a lazy single to shallow center field. Rickey Henderson charges the ball to hold Garvey at second, then freezes as it leaps off the Metrodome carpet like Greg Louganis off the springboard. Henderson spins, retreats, backhands the ball over his shoulder, pivots, and soft-tosses it to second base. Murphy has already reached the bag for a stand-up double. A Metrodome double. Two-base hits are 24 percent more common at the Metrodome than at an average American League ballpark, and are the single largest factor contributing to the nearly 10 percent increase in scoring at the home of the Twins.

The simplest method for comparing the Metrodome to a typical stadium is to compare the composite statistics from Twins home games to Twins road games. Over the course of a season, Minnesota plays a roughly equal number of home and road games against each American League opponent—13 games against California, six at home, seven on the road; 13 against Kansas City, seven at home, six on the road, etc. Over the four-year period since the opening of the Metrodome, even those little discrepancies are evened out, so that we can compare a set of games played at the Metrodome to a set played by the same teams at a cross-section of stadiums and consider the differences as evidence of what makes the Metrodome unique. Here are the composite four-year batting lines for both teams from all Minnesota Twins games:

	G	AB	R	H	2B	3B	HR	BB	SO	SB
Metrodome	327	22540	3077	6099	1186	194	632	2025	3278	349
Road Games	321	21741	2765	5657	923	190	606	2003	2965	296

The most significant differences between those two sets of games are in runs scored and doubles. The teams averaged 9.4 runs per game and one double per 19 at bats at the Metrodome, 8.6 runs per game and one double per 24 at bats in Minnesota's road games. The scoring increase is directly related to the increase in doubles, since the differences in the other statistics are minimal and are totally

within the statistically expected range of variation. But, ironically, those high-scoring Metrodome games are precisely what perpetuate the Homerdome myth.

The figures speak for themselves: home runs have been 0.6 percent more common at the Metrodome, doubles 23.9 percent more frequent. By the way, if you remain skeptical because there were 26 more home runs hit at the Metrodome than on the road, notice that there have been six more games and nearly 800 more at bats there as well. The Metrodome produces one home run every 35.7 at bats, compared to one every 35.9 at bats in road games. Even if that were a significant difference—and it isn't—would such a margin warrant the Homerdome nickname? And how did that misnomer arise in the first place?

During 1982, the first season of play at the Metrodome, there were more home runs (191) hit there than in Twins road games (165). Not a conclusive margin, considering that the stadium had just opened, but the stadium was under scrutiny right from opening night: In the first game ever played there, Seattle defeated Minnesota 11–7, in a game with 12 extra-base hits, five of them homers. Compound that premiere with the relative obscurity of the game's stars, and the tag seemed a natural. But who knew four years ago that Gary Gaetti was a *bona fide* home run hitter, not just another rookie exploiting this new stadium for a cheap pair of opening night home runs? Time has proven that Gaetti probably had a lot more to do with those home runs than the park.

Following the first season, Twins management made a change for the benefit of their fans: After a year of sweltering without air conditioning, climate control was introduced for the 1983 season. Whether or not this had anything to do with it, the home-run statistics have changed markedly:

	1982			1983–85		
	AB	HR	Pct.	AB	HR	Pct.
Metrodome	5543	191	3.45	16997	441	2.59
Road Games	5517	165	2.99	16224	441	2.72

Home runs have decreased since 1982 by 18 percent overall, due largely to the improvement of Minnesota's pitching staff. But the split has been anything but even: Round-trippers have fallen by 25 percent at the Metrodome, but by only 9 percent in road games. Either the Metrodome's first season produced an uncharacteristically high home-run total in 1982, which only time has allowed us to interpret, or the park has actually suppressed home runs since then. In either case, the Homerdome label is erroneous: during three subsequent seasons, the home-run percentage is actually five percent higher in Twins road games than at home. Even worse, the tag is misleading. It has clouded our appreciation of some of Minnesota's fine young hitters, notably Kent Hrbek and Tom Brunansky. Notice in the following statistics that while both players show the Metrodome's bias towards doubles, neither player has padded his home-run totals at home. While Hrbek has hit for an extremely high average at home, Brunansky appears to have been penalized by his home park:

(See chart on following page)

Kent Hrbek	AB	H	2B	3B	HR	BB	SO	BA	SA	OBA
Metrodome	1149	375	73	13	43	132	167	.326	.525	.395
Elsewhere	1117	293	56	1	45	116	167	.262	.435	.332

Tom Brunansky	AB	H	2B	3B	HR	BB	SO	BA	SA	OBA
Metrodome	1054	261	56	7	44	131	185	.248	.439	.331
Elsewhere	1118	274	47	3	66	137	201	.245	.470	.331

Ten years ago, a misconception about a baseball stadium would have been unimportant. But with today's level of sophistication, and the awareness of the effect that different ballparks can have on a player's performance, it is crucial that we base those evaluations on correct information. And this Homerdome thing has just gone too far. We promise not to go through all this again next season; that is, unless we hear more of that Homerdome bull this summer. (And if you think we're tired of hearing how easy it is to hit homers there, how do you think Brunansky feels?)

Great Expectations

Two steps forward, one step back. Do it once, you're ahead of the game; twice, you're on a roll. But does it work as well in baseball, where even the slightest wobble is noted with disapproval, and a step backwards frequently costs the manager his job, as it did Billy Gardner last season?

Following two seasons of considerable improvement, Minnesota took a step back last season, and before you could say "Steinbrenner," Gardner was gone and Ray Miller had taken his place. Gardner seemed to be the victim of expectations raised by Minnesota's dramatic rise of the previous two seasons. Was the step back a natural part of a team's progression from the depths, a result of their having played over their heads? Or had Gardner taken Minnesota as far as he could?

To examine the issue, we found five teams from the past 30 seasons who matched the recent pattern of the Twins. We had expected to find that this pattern was fairly common, but surprisingly, there were very few teams with similar up-up-down (but not too far down) patterns, especially at the same caliber of play—moving across the .500 line and back. For each of the six teams listed below, the year given is their crossroads year, the third year of their up-up-down pattern. Year 0 is their bottom year, the year that preceded the pattern; years 1 and 2 are the two steps up; year 3 is the step down; year 4 is the next season, the one the Twins are now facing. The last record given is for the five seasons after they reached the crossroads, with their number of above-.500 seasons among the five in parentheses:

Team	Year 0	Year 1	Year 2	Year 3	Year 4	Next 5 Seasons
1958 Orioles	57–97	69–85	76–76	74–79	74–80	421–373 .530 (3)
1969 Yankees	70–89	72–90	83–79	80–81	93–69	423–380 .527 (4)
1970 Astros	69–93	72–90	81–81	79–83	79–83	390–410 .488 (3)
1971 Angels	67–95	71–91	86–76	76–86	75–80	370–432 .461 (1)
1975 Rangers	54–100	57–105	84–76	79–83	76–86	416–393 .514 (3)
1985 Twins	60–102	70–92	81–81	77–85		

All the teams above qualified by sliding below the .500 mark following two seasons that pushed them up to or beyond the break-even point. While you might think that the four-game drop for the Twins last year was just a small step compared to the giant leap made in the previous two seasons, it was actually typical of the group, and two of those five teams slipped even further back in the next season, while one compiled the same below-.500 record. But a look at the cumulative performances of those teams over five years indicates that, on the whole, their rebuilding programs emerged intact from a few shaky seasons. The table illustrates that it is very difficult to gauge the direction of a team fitting this pattern.

There is one team among the five that bears a striking resemblance to last season's Twins. The 1975 Texas Rangers had a young lineup, with Jeff Burroughs (24), Toby Harrah (26), Mike Hargrove (25), Roy Howell (21), and Jim Sundberg (24) to complement more established players like Jim Spencer and designated hitter Cesar Tovar who, like last season's Minnesota DH Roy Smalley, was his team's only everyday starter past the age of 30. Note the similarity to the ages of Minnesota's regulars: Brunansky (24), Puckett (24), Salas (24), Hrbek (25), and Gaetti (26).

Both teams had set lineups expected to remain more or less intact for several years. But the '75 Rangers had a problem on the mound: 129 of their 162 games were started by pitchers past the age of 30, including Gaylord Perry (36), Bill Hands (35), and Clyde Wright (34). They knew that those arms might wear out, and they felt forced to trade to ease those fears. One of those trades sent Smalley (with others and a truckload of cash) to Minnesota for Danny Thompson and Bert Blyleven. Ironically, Blyleven was the pitcher whom the Twins acquired last season to complement their own group of starters, a much younger crew including Frank Viola (25), John Butcher (28), and Mike Smithson (30).

After a losing 1976 season, Texas signed Doyle Alexander as a free agent, but then hit the panic button. They traded Burroughs, who had had an off season, to Atlanta for five players who failed to make an impact. Despite a successful 1977 season, there remained a lingering suspicion that the gap between Texas and division champion Kansas City might have been closed by a slugger like Burroughs, who drilled 41 home runs that season for the Braves.

As with the Rangers of the late 1970s, the success or failure of Minnesota's pitching will probably determine the Twins' fortunes over the next few seasons. But unlike Texas, who saw their options limited by the age of their staff, Minnesota has a starting rotation with several young pitchers. Viola has proven his worth, but following unexpectedly poor seasons by Butcher and Smithson, Minnesota must decide whether they, along with Blyleven, make up a rotation capable of winning a pennant. Regardless, by assembling a lineup of talented young players, the Twins have bought themselves time to make that decision and act accordingly. In the baseball world of the 1980s, the clock is always ticking. But thanks to the policies—farsighted, shortsighted, or just plain cheap—of former owner Calvin Griffith, Minnesota is one team that, at least temporarily, can ignore the running meter.

WON-LOST RECORD BY STARTING POSITION

MINNESOTA 77-85	C	1B	2B	3B	SS	LF	CF	RF	P	DH	Leadoff	Relief	Starts
Bert Blyleven	.	.	.	.	.	.	.	.	8-6	.	.	.	8-6
Mark Brown	.	.	.	.	.	.	.	.	.	.	.	0-6	-
Tom Brunansky	.	.	.	.	.	.	0-1	71-80	.	.	.	.	71-81
Dennis Burtt	.	.	.	.	.	.	.	.	2-0	.	.	0-3	2-0
Randy Bush	.	0-1	.	.	.	.	14-15	.	2-1	12-14	.	.	28-31
John Butcher	.	.	.	.	.	.	.	.	14-19	.	.	1-0	14-19
Ron Davis	.	.	.	.	.	.	.	.	.	.	32-25	.	-
Dave Engle	7-5	.	.	.	.	.	1-1	.	.	13-20	.	.	21-26
Alvaro Espinoza	.	.	.	.	10-11	.	.	.	.	.	.	.	10-11
Frank Eufemia	.	.	.	.	.	.	.	.	.	.	.	12-27	-
Pete Filson	.	.	.	.	.	.	.	.	1-5	.	.	13-21	1-5
Mark Funderburk	.	0-1	.	.	.	.	2-1	.	.	7-6	.	.	9-8
Gary Gaetti	.	1-0	.	62-81	.	.	2-2	.	.	.	.	.	65-83
Greg Gagne	.	.	.	.	47-45	.	.	.	.	1-0	.	.	48-45
Mickey Hatcher	.	2-2	.	.	.	.	44-49	.	.	6-5	.	.	52-56
Steve Howe	.	.	.	.	.	.	.	.	.	.	.	2-11	-
Kent Hrbek	.	70-77	.	.	.	.	.	.	1-1	.	.	.	71-78
Tom Klawitter	.	.	.	.	.	.	.	.	1-1	.	.	0-5	1-1
Tim Laudner	21-32	.	.	.	.	.	.	.	.	.	.	.	21-32
Steve Lombardozzi	.	.	13-7	.	.	.	.	.	.	.	.	.	13-7
Rick Lysander	.	.	.	.	.	.	.	.	0-1	.	.	7-27	0-1
Dave Meier	.	.	.	.	.	.	10-15	1-0	1-0	.	1-0	.	12-15
Mark Portugal	.	.	.	.	.	.	.	.	1-3	.	.	1-1	1-3
Kirby Puckett	.	.	.	.	.	.	.	76-84	.	.	76-84	.	76-84
Jeff Reed	1-1	.	.	.	.	.	.	.	.	.	.	.	1-1
Mark Salas	48-47	.	.	.	.	.	.	.	.	1-1	.	0-3	49-48
Ken Schrom	.	.	.	.	.	.	.	.	12-14	.	.	.	12-14
Roy Smalley	.	0-1	.	10-3	16-23	.	.	.	.	25-21	.	.	51-48
Mike Smithson	.	.	.	.	.	.	.	.	18-19	.	.	.	18-19
Mike Stenhouse	.	4-3	.	.	.	.	4-2	.	3-4	9-16	.	.	20-25
Tim Teufel	.	.	57-70	.	.	.	.	.	.	.	.	.	57-70
Frank Viola	.	.	.	.	.	.	.	.	20-16	.	.	.	20-16
Curt Wardle	.	.	.	.	.	.	.	.	.	.	.	10-25	-
Ron Washington	.	.	7-8	5-1	4-6	.	.	.	.	2-1	0-1	.	18-16
Len Whitehouse	.	.	.	.	.	.	.	.	.	.	.	1-4	-
Rich Yett	.	.	.	.	.	.	.	.	0-1	.	.	.	0-1

Batting vs. Left and Right Handed Pitchers

		BA	Rank	SA	Rank	OBA	Rank	HR %	Rank	BB %	Rank	SO %	Rank
Tom Brunansky	vs. Lefties	.214	140	.379	103	.302	122	2.75	75	11.79	33	9.91	42
	vs. Righties	.255	88	.481	24	.328	72	5.71	11	10.48	45	14.81	97
Randy Bush	vs. Lefties	.083	--	.167	--	.214	--	0.00	--	14.29	--	0.00	--
	vs. Righties	.248	103	.464	35	.327	75	4.50	32	8.76	67	11.95	62
Dave Engle	vs. Lefties	.295	42	.581	5	.383	16	6.67	12	12.50	28	11.67	64
	vs. Righties	.194	--	.239	--	.253	--	0.00	--	8.00	--	18.67	--
Gary Gaetti	vs. Lefties	.206	149	.349	123	.272	140	3.43	59	7.25	102	16.58	119
	vs. Righties	.265	67	.436	53	.314	96	3.64	52	5.54	126	13.73	83
Greg Gagne	vs. Lefties	.244	113	.354	121	.265	145	0.79	124	3.01	152	18.05	127
	vs. Righties	.211	144	.289	147	.289	129	0.60	140	8.47	73	17.46	123
Mickey Hatcher	vs. Lefties	.280	61	.379	105	.312	109	0.76	125	4.96	135	2.84	2
	vs. Righties	.282	44	.359	110	.307	101	0.64	139	2.76	154	5.83	8
Kent Hrbek	vs. Lefties	.256	91	.402	86	.324	96	3.02	64	9.13	65	16.89	120
	vs. Righties	.289	28	.464	34	.365	22	3.81	46	10.51	44	11.19	54
Tim Laudner	vs. Lefties	.270	73	.487	31	.341	76	6.09	16	9.09	66	21.97	140
	vs. Righties	.163	--	.184	--	.163	--	0.00	--	0.00	--	32.00	--
Dave Meier	vs. Lefties	.282	58	.372	110	.356	52	1.28	109	10.34	52	6.90	22
	vs. Righties	.192	--	.269	--	.417	--	0.00	--	23.08	--	15.38	--
Kirby Puckett	vs. Lefties	.356	3	.525	21	.383	18	1.83	94	4.33	139	10.39	46
	vs. Righties	.256	85	.320	138	.306	102	0.00	152	6.04	118	12.28	66
Mark Salas	vs. Lefties	.190	--	.238	--	.320	--	0.00	--	16.00	--	16.00	--
	vs. Righties	.307	11	.472	27	.333	62	2.65	84	3.92	144	9.24	37
Roy Smalley	vs. Lefties	.236	127	.333	129	.349	62	0.00	131	15.12	10	15.12	105
	vs. Righties	.263	71	.418	65	.359	32	3.80	48	12.84	20	14.21	89
Mike Stenhouse	vs. Lefties	.200	--	.400	--	.200	--	0.00	--	0.00	--	40.00	--
	vs. Righties	.224	132	.333	127	.333	62	2.87	76	14.22	8	7.84	27
Tim Teufel	vs. Lefties	.200	150	.267	150	.288	134	0.74	126	10.83	43	12.74	85
	vs. Righties	.288	32	.458	39	.357	35	3.01	70	9.14	59	14.75	96
Ron Washington	vs. Lefties	.294	43	.471	42	.338	79	1.47	102	6.58	113	7.89	27
	vs. Righties	.254	--	.328	--	.278	--	0.00	--	4.11	--	12.33	--
Team Average	vs. Lefties	.265	7	.411	9	.327	10	2.38	11	8.45	8	12.88	5
	vs. Righties	.263	5	.404	7	.326	7	2.64	9	8.07	10	12.63	4
League Average	vs. Lefties	.266		.416		.333		2.91		8.95		13.77	
	vs. Righties	.259		.401		.324		2.78		8.49		13.56	

Batting with Runners on Base and Bases Empty

		BA	Rank	SA	Rank	OBA	Rank	HR %	Rank	BB %	Rank	SO %	Rank
Tom Brunansky	Runners On	.232	137	.418	76	.307	122	4.29	40	10.94	44	15.50	111
	Bases Empty	.251	97	.477	26	.332	59	5.23	18	10.87	28	10.87	47
Randy Bush	Runners On	.223	143	.402	92	.299	126	3.57	56	9.45	70	12.60	77
	Bases Empty	.254	90	.492	18	.341	43	4.92	30	8.70	60	10.14	41
Gary Gaetti	Runners On	.234	136	.369	114	.288	141	3.28	64	5.62	134	17.60	132
	Bases Empty	.256	84	.440	45	.311	96	3.80	46	6.45	106	12.32	62
Greg Gagne	Runners On	.239	133	.299	143	.266	149	0.00	142	4.11	149	16.44	120
	Bases Empty	.214	139	.333	130	.290	128	1.26	117	7.95	72	18.75	134
Mickey Hatcher	Runners On	.297	43	.397	95	.320	108	0.96	119	3.60	150	4.50	7
	Bases Empty	.268	56	.336	129	.298	115	0.43	143	3.27	153	5.31	2
Kent Hrbek	Runners On	.262	90	.434	68	.358	57	4.12	44	13.10	27	13.42	91
	Bases Empty	.291	22	.451	37	.346	31	3.07	71	7.37	84	12.75	67
Kirby Puckett	Runners On	.323	18	.460	50	.376	31	1.21	113	6.81	122	10.75	58
	Bases Empty	.269	52	.343	122	.303	107	0.23	147	4.73	135	12.26	61
Mark Salas	Runners On	.323	17	.479	39	.348	75	2.40	83	4.49	146	9.55	45
	Bases Empty	.280	32	.440	44	.319	88	2.59	85	4.90	132	9.80	38
Roy Smalley	Runners On	.286	60	.398	93	.384	22	1.24	111	14.14	20	16.23	119
	Bases Empty	.238	113	.405	72	.337	49	4.41	44	12.64	17	13.03	69
Mike Stenhouse	Runners On	.303	35	.461	48	.438	5	5.26	22	19.79	4	6.25	13
	Bases Empty	.165	--	.243	--	.239	--	0.97	--	8.85	--	10.62	--
Tim Teufel	Runners On	.263	87	.368	115	.330	94	1.58	101	9.46	69	14.41	101
	Bases Empty	.258	77	.422	62	.339	44	2.87	75	9.85	43	13.87	76
Team Average	Runners On	.269	9	.405	12	.331	11	2.39	11	8.62	10	13.55	10
	Bases Empty	.260	4	.408	6	.322	5	2.69	10	7.84	9	12.02	1
League Average	Runners On	.271		.416		.338		2.85		9.26		13.25	
	Bases Empty	.254		.397		.318		2.80		8.14		13.92	

Overall Batting Compared to Late Inning Pressure Situations

		BA	Rank	SA	Rank	OBA	Rank	HR %	Rank	BB %	Rank	SO %	Rank	RDI %	Rank
Tom Brunansky	Overall	.242	123	.448	42	.320	102	4.76	29	10.91	36	13.21	79	.262	112
	Pressure	.243	91	.486	32	.341	65	7.14	13	13.41	34	7.32	18	.350	53
Randy Bush	Overall	.239	126	.449	40	.321	99	4.27	39	9.06	66	11.32	51	.299	66
	Pressure	.182	144	.273	136	.217	153	2.27	80	4.35	131	10.87	49	.167	128
Dave Engle	Overall	.256	--	.448	--	.333	--	4.07	--	10.77	--	14.36	--	.242	125
	Pressure	.240	--	.240	--	.286	--	0.00	--	7.14	--	17.86	--	.400	22
Gary Gaetti	Overall	.246	111	.409	81	.301	130	3.57	54	6.09	126	14.64	102	.211	145
	Pressure	.292	42	.446	47	.403	22	3.08	57	15.38	21	6.41	16	.133	141
Greg Gagne	Overall	.225	142	.317	145	.279	145	0.68	137	6.21	122	17.70	126	.239	126
	Pressure	.292	--	.333	--	.393	--	0.00	--	13.79	--	20.69	--	1.000	--
Mickey Hatcher	Overall	.282	41	.365	119	.308	116	0.68	138	3.43	151	4.93	3	.300	65
	Pressure	.218	117	.236	146	.246	144	0.00	113	3.45	138	1.72	1	.211	114
Kent Hrbek	Overall	.278	45	.444	47	.351	39	3.54	55	10.06	44	13.06	75	.329	37
	Pressure	.288	48	.342	97	.388	26	1.37	103	12.94	39	17.65	112	.348	54
Tim Laudner	Overall	.238	--	.396	--	.292	--	4.27	--	6.59	--	24.73	--	.204	151
	Pressure	.182	--	.318	--	.250	--	0.00	--	7.69	--	34.62	--	.167	--
Kirby Puckett	Overall	.288	27	.385	101	.330	76	0.58	142	5.51	136	11.69	57	.350	24
	Pressure	.325	22	.446	48	.380	32	1.20	109	6.52	111	22.83	140	.364	40
Mark Salas	Overall	.300	12	.458	29	.332	70	2.50	88	4.71	141	9.69	38	.223	141
	Pressure	.319	24	.447	46	.340	69	2.13	82	4.00	134	10.00	40	.278	77
Roy Smalley	Overall	.258	91	.402	92	.357	30	3.09	69	13.27	18	14.38	97	.273	99
	Pressure	.246	87	.351	92	.353	51	1.75	93	14.71	25	16.18	99	.304	69
Mike Stenhouse	Overall	.223	143	.335	137	.330	77	2.79	78	13.88	14	8.61	31	.277	--
	Pressure	.424	1	.545	15	.513	1	3.03	59	15.38	21	2.56	3	.364	40
Tim Teufel	Overall	.260	83	.399	96	.335	65	2.30	93	9.68	47	14.11	88	.298	68
	Pressure	.206	128	.286	127	.265	133	1.59	98	5.71	119	18.57	123	.118	145
Team Average	Overall	.264	6	.407	7	.326	6	2.56	11	8.19	9	12.71	4	.276	10
	Pressure	.262	5	.363	11	.337	2	1.99	11	9.83	4	13.81	6	.286	6
League Average	Overall	.261		.406		.327		2.82		8.63		13.62		.287	
	Pressure	.253		.381		.323		2.74		9.11		14.40		.273	

Additional Miscellaneous Batting Comparisons

	Grass Surface BA	Rank	Artificial Surface BA	Rank	Home Games BA	Rank	Road Games BA	Rank	Runners in Scoring Position BA	Rank	Runners in Scoring Pos and Two Outs BA	Rank	Leading Off Inning OBA	Rank	Runners on 3B with less than 2 Outs RDI %	Rank
Tom Brunansky	.200	150	.265	64	.254	94	.229	132	.227	125	.176	144	.291	117	.585	75
Randy Bush	.256	--	.231	114	.250	99	.224	134	.234	121	.194	136	.308	96	.615	62
Dave Engle	.263	--	.252	81	.244	--	.267	--	.300	44	.259	59	.364	--	.429	143
Mark Funderburk	.200	--	.378	2	.259	--	.349	--	.381	--	.125	--	.417	--	.833	--
Gary Gaetti	.244	113	.248	87	.261	84	.232	127	.235	120	.197	133	.271	130	.520	102
Greg Gagne	.221	--	.228	121	.232	124	.219	142	.303	42	.206	127	.260	143	.462	135
Mickey Hatcher	.237	124	.306	19	.299	34	.260	75	.295	53	.250	68	.205	156	.545	96
Kent Hrbek	.240	120	.299	27	.312	22	.240	118	.264	91	.211	122	.331	67	.659	53
Tim Laudner	.169	--	.290	37	.309	--	.188	154	.191	150	.231	96	.367	--	.286	156
Dave Meier	.231	--	.288	41	.270	--	.254	--	.182	--	.154	--	.217	--	.500	--
Kirby Puckett	.271	61	.298	28	.324	14	.251	96	.318	24	.328	21	.320	81	.714	27
Mark Salas	.293	--	.304	20	.315	20	.280	36	.234	122	.200	130	.269	134	.455	137
Roy Smalley	.264	77	.254	75	.249	107	.267	60	.242	113	.227	101	.350	40	.667	47
Mike Stenhouse	.210	--	.231	114	.232	125	.214	--	.297	--	.375	6	.196	158	.286	--
Tim Teufel	.239	122	.273	55	.276	63	.244	109	.272	84	.282	47	.361	30	.696	33
Ron Washington	.245	--	.293	34	.304	--	.242	--	.257	--	.214	--	.500	--	.636	56
Team Average	.244	14	.275	1	.281	2	.246	12	.265	8	.231	13	.305	11	.578	6
League Average	.262		.259		.266		.256		.268		.248		.321		.587	

Pitching vs. Left and Right Handed Batters

		BA	Rank	SA	Rank	OBA	Rank	HR %	Rank	BB %	Rank	SO %	Rank
Bert Blyleven	vs. Lefties	.258	60	.362	38	.311	44	1.71	32	6.71	31	16.00	34
	vs. Righties	.212	17	.340	19	.261	13	2.60	57	5.57	30	18.69	23
John Butcher	vs. Lefties	.290	94	.463	98	.324	54	3.06	83	4.71	8	11.07	88
	vs. Righties	.286	106	.446	100	.325	74	2.70	61	4.94	16	9.38	120
Ron Davis	vs. Lefties	.233	31	.379	52	.343	74	2.59	61	14.29	120	24.29	4
	vs. Righties	.228	31	.374	46	.324	72	3.25	87	10.34	106	26.21	1
Frank Eufemia	vs. Lefties	.255	58	.353	36	.315	47	0.00	1	8.11	48	12.61	63
	vs. Righties	.246	52	.467	114	.307	51	5.74	130	8.63	82	11.51	93
Pete Filson	vs. Lefties	.273	74	.418	71	.319	51	2.73	71	6.61	29	11.57	79
	vs. Righties	.241	44	.395	60	.299	40	3.83	108	7.72	69	9.82	115
Rick Lysander	vs. Lefties	.315	118	.491	115	.370	99	2.78	73	8.33	52	10.00	101
	vs. Righties	.297	116	.352	29	.355	104	0.00	1	8.45	78	9.86	114
Ken Schrom	vs. Lefties	.283	85	.470	102	.350	83	4.67	126	9.78	77	8.70	112
	vs. Righties	.259	67	.482	121	.313	57	4.61	118	7.40	62	13.50	70
Mike Smithson	vs. Lefties	.288	89	.467	99	.333	63	3.33	95	5.78	20	11.08	87
	vs. Righties	.245	50	.350	28	.329	79	1.47	15	9.03	90	12.47	85
Frank Viola	vs. Lefties	.287	87	.454	93	.325	55	3.24	91	4.76	9	12.99	60
	vs. Righties	.262	76	.397	63	.312	56	2.49	52	6.88	46	12.68	83
Team Average	vs. Lefties	.282	13	.446	13	.334	7	3.10	11	7.24	1	12.31	10
	vs. Righties	.257	7	.405	7	.318	6	2.91	5	7.94	7	12.92	12
League Average	vs. Lefties	.265		.408		.333		2.74		9.21		12.94	
	vs. Righties	.259		.404		.322		2.88		8.19		14.14	

Pitching with Runners on Base and Bases Empty

		BA	Rank	SA	Rank	OBA	Rank	HR %	Rank	BB %	Rank	SO %	Rank
Bert Blyleven	Runners On	.246	34	.357	27	.303	29	1.86	35	7.87	44	14.49	46
	Bases Empty	.234	36	.350	29	.282	21	2.22	41	5.14	18	18.89	12
John Butcher	Runners On	.317	120	.530	124	.361	99	5.33	128	6.34	26	7.16	128
	Bases Empty	.271	93	.409	78	.300	46	1.38	18	3.77	5	12.45	76
Ron Davis	Runners On	.217	11	.349	25	.335	62	3.29	88	14.36	126	26.60	1
	Bases Empty	.253	--	.425	--	.330	--	2.30	--	8.25	--	22.68	--
Frank Eufemia	Runners On	.286	90	.505	119	.350	82	4.76	121	9.84	81	9.84	105
	Bases Empty	.218	--	.336	--	.273	--	1.68	--	7.03	--	14.06	--
Pete Filson	Runners On	.222	15	.359	29	.271	6	3.59	97	6.52	28	9.24	113
	Bases Empty	.275	98	.436	97	.333	84	3.43	94	8.11	66	11.26	90
Rick Lysander	Runners On	.304	111	.448	92	.364	105	1.60	27	9.15	70	10.56	100
	Bases Empty	.306	--	.378	--	.358	--	0.90	--	7.50	--	9.17	--
Ken Schrom	Runners On	.281	86	.465	102	.333	59	4.15	110	8.24	49	12.94	73
	Bases Empty	.267	87	.482	118	.333	83	4.92	123	8.96	82	9.67	115
Mike Smithson	Runners On	.284	88	.456	97	.339	67	3.35	92	7.26	36	10.66	99
	Bases Empty	.261	81	.393	61	.326	78	2.03	32	7.11	49	12.36	77
Frank Viola	Runners On	.290	97	.447	91	.332	57	3.28	87	5.77	17	9.24	114
	Bases Empty	.252	62	.384	52	.304	50	2.23	42	6.87	46	15.18	45
Team Average	Runners On	.283	11	.463	14	.341	8	3.93	14	8.16	4	11.34	13
	Bases Empty	.258	8	.396	7	.314	5	2.31	3	7.19	4	13.65	7
League Average	Runners On	.271		.416		.338		2.85		9.26		13.25	
	Bases Empty	.254		.397		.318		2.80		8.14		13.92	

Overall Pitching Compared to Late Inning Pressure Situations

		BA	Rank	SA	Rank	OBA	Rank	HR %	Rank	BB %	Rank	SO %	Rank
Bert Blyleven	Overall	.239	26	.353	24	.290	15	2.08	31	6.23	20	17.12	24
	Pressure	.188	10	.250	8	.253	11	0.69	18	6.92	36	15.09	45
John Butcher	Overall	.289	112	.455	105	.325	59	2.90	74	4.82	7	10.30	111
	Pressure	.248	53	.337	37	.276	18	1.98	51	2.80	6	11.21	88
Ron Davis	Overall	.230	16	.377	42	.333	76	2.93	76	12.28	116	25.26	1
	Pressure	.211	20	.342	39	.303	41	2.63	67	9.55	64	24.16	4
Frank Eufemia	Overall	.250	47	.415	79	.310	44	3.13	87	8.40	68	12.00	85
	Pressure	.234	40	.377	58	.298	34	2.60	64	8.24	46	11.76	80
Pete Filson	Overall	.251	51	.402	62	.305	32	3.50	103	7.39	48	10.34	109
	Pressure	.247	51	.315	22	.276	19	1.37	30	3.95	10	9.21	105
Steve Howe	Overall	.333	--	.440	--	.372	--	1.19	--	7.45	--	10.64	--
	Pressure	.273	78	.333	32	.333	63	0.00	1	8.33	47	5.56	130
Rick Lysander	Overall	.305	121	.415	80	.362	114	1.27	9	8.40	67	9.92	115
	Pressure	.344	125	.656	129	.400	111	3.13	83	8.33	47	8.33	111
Ken Schrom	Overall	.272	86	.476	120	.333	75	4.64	127	8.69	73	10.90	104
	Pressure	.105	1	.158	1	.164	1	1.75	46	6.35	29	14.29	51
Mike Smithson	Overall	.270	84	.418	84	.331	72	2.56	59	7.17	41	11.67	89
	Pressure	.288	93	.438	93	.373	97	1.37	30	10.47	78	8.14	113
Frank Viola	Overall	.268	80	.410	71	.315	48	2.66	63	6.42	25	12.75	71
	Pressure	.204	14	.259	10	.271	15	0.00	1	8.47	49	15.25	44
Team Average	Overall	.268	10	.424	11	.326	5	3.00	9	7.61	2	12.64	10
	Pressure	.235	3	.369	5	.303	2	2.35	4	8.07	2	14.48	7
League Average	Overall	.261		.406		.327		2.82		8.63		13.62	
	Pressure	.258		.392		.332		2.71		9.52		14.05	

Additional Miscellaneous Pitching Comparisons

	Grass Surface BA	Rank	Artificial Surface BA	Rank	Home Games BA	Rank	Road Games BA	Rank	Runners in Scoring Position BA	Rank	Runners in Scoring Pos and Two Outs BA	Rank	Leading Off Inning OBA	Rank
Bert Blyleven	.237	27	.243	40	.239	37	.239	26	.247	44	.237	64	.283	29
Dennis Burtt	.196	--	.204	14	.204	--	.196	--	.200	--	.125	--	.367	--
John Butcher	.257	65	.313	116	.300	113	.276	84	.330	121	.352	124	.318	68
Ron Davis	.217	--	.238	34	.230	21	.231	20	.229	26	.237	64	.390	--
Frank Eufemia	.190	--	.273	78	.233	25	.275	--	.279	86	.172	18	.265	--
Pete Filson	.226	--	.260	68	.256	72	.243	33	.202	9	.083	2	.231	5
Steve Howe	.500	--	.316	117	.313	--	.400	--	.516	--	.462	--	.125	--
Rick Lysander	.306	--	.304	109	.229	--	.357	128	.338	124	.382	130	.407	125
Mark Portugal	.375	--	.247	47	.263	--	.281	--	.182	--	.333	--	.423	--
Ken Schrom	.323	125	.254	60	.264	79	.289	99	.275	79	.216	44	.358	104
Mike Smithson	.273	88	.268	75	.265	81	.274	82	.284	89	.232	58	.308	53
Frank Viola	.254	61	.275	81	.267	85	.268	75	.323	115	.337	121	.302	49
Team Average	.267	8	.269	8	.261	9	.277	13	.289	13	.264	13	.320	6
League Average	.262		.259		.256		.266		.268		.248		.321	

NEW YORK YANKEES

He doesn't have a nickname like "The Refrigerator" or "One Tough Dominican." He doesn't appear on commercials for light beer, model bikini underwear, or trade quips with late-night talk show hosts. He plays when he's hurt, he doesn't complain when less talented teammates steal the headlines, and he works in the media center of planet earth; he is the Most Valuable Player in the American League, he is frequently compared to Lou Gehrig, and he could be this season's contender for baseball's next can't-miss Hall of Famer. Why is it, then, that through the entire 1985 season, no one—absolutely no one—called Don Mattingly the best player in baseball?

It's a wise sports fan who is skeptical about players glorified by the same media machine that gave the world Clint Hartung, Ron Blomberg, Bobby Murcer, and Lee Mazzilli, not to mention Tucker Frederickson, Richard Todd, Spencer Haywood, and Bob McAdoo. But Don Mattingly has not only failed to benefit from the usual hype surrounding New York players, he actually seems to have been stigmatized by it. Remember early last season when it was Rickey Henderson who was being touted as the best player in baseball? In retrospect, we can see that the label was being applied prematurely to an excellent player having a spectacular six-week run. And Henderson's streak occurred relatively early in the season, at a time when lasting impressions are formed. Later in the season, after Henderson had come back to earth, Mattingly was accused of building his RBI total simply by batting in the middle of one of the most dangerous orders in the major leagues: "Yeah, he drives in a lot of runs, but who wouldn't with Henderson on second all the time?" "And he gets all those good pitches to hit, with Dave Winfield and Don Baylor coming up behind him." Fact: Mattingly not only led the American League with 145 RBIs last season, but was also the only American League regular to drive in at least 40 percent of the runners in scoring position when he came to bat; his career percentage of 37.2 is the highest in the majors over the past 11 seasons. Sure, he drove in more runs with the Yankees than he would have for the Rangers. But he also drove in more runs for the Yankees than any other player in baseball would have.

Mattingly has also had to face the accusation that he has developed a "Yankee Stadium swing," and it's hard to deny that: He hit 22 home runs and drove in 87 runs at the Stadium, both league-leading home-game totals. But only one American League player (Eddie Murray, by a margin of three) had more *road-game* RBIs than Mattingly, and only three had higher batting averages on the road.

Mattingly is quite simply an exceptional ballplayer. Perhaps not the next Lou Gehrig, but a future Hall of Famer? Could be. And very possibly the best player in baseball today. There—somebody said it!

Starting Over

Dave Righetti's assignment to the bullpen two years ago was certainly one of the most unconventional management decisions of the 1980s. Faced with the loss of Rich Gossage to the San Diego Padres, and unable to swing a deal for a gold-medal reliever like Bruce Sutter, George Steinbrenner's "baseball people" decided that their young star left-hander, who had no-hit the Boston Red Sox the previous season, would from that day forward hang his hat in the bullpen. And so it has been.

The decision was accorded the respect usually reserved for campaign promises and used car ads. Righetti himself said, "Ninety-nine percent of the people I've talked to think the move is crazy. But the one percent who count think it's good." And for two years since then, the baseball world has waited in vain for Righetti's return from exile. All Righetti has done during that time is save 60 games, more than any other American League pitcher except Dan Quisenberry (81) and Willie Hernandez (63). As a result, it has become nearly impossible to overcome a late-inning deficit against the Yankees. During the two seasons Righetti has worked in short relief, New York has lost a total of seven games in which they led after eight innings; they lost six during the 1983 season alone—Gossage's last in New York.

As early as the start of the 1985 season, many skeptics were willing to admit that the move had merit. Some, in fact, hailed it as innovative and tried to copy it. Pittsburgh moved John Candelaria from their apparently deep starting rotation to the bullpen, and Boston transferred (relegated was no longer the appropriate word) Bob Ojeda. It is noteworthy that while Righetti continued to prosper as a reliever for the Yankees, neither the Candy Man nor Bobby O flourished in the bullpen; both now wear different uniforms. So the debate continues: Can a top-shelf starting pitcher contribute more to his team from the bullpen than from the starting rotation?

The arithmetic involved in such a study is straightforward. The loss that a team incurs when it drops a top pitcher from its rotation (and replaces him with its sixth-best starter) must be compared to the gain from adding a top-flight reliever. If gain exceeds loss, you win. If loss exceeds gain, well, you can talk to the Pirates or Red Sox about that.

The following table compares the winning percentages of each team in games started by their most successful starting pitchers to that in games not started by one of their five most frequent starters. The Yankees' "Won-Lost Record By Starting Position" table shows that they were most successful with Ron Guidry starting (23–10). When pitchers other than their five regulars (Guidry, Joe Cowley, Phil Niekro, Dennis Rasmussen, and Ed Whitson) started, the Yankees had a 12–11 record. Had Guidry been dispatched to the bullpen, his rotation spot would likely have been taken by some combination of those 12–11 pitchers. The difference in winning percentage between Guidry and his replacements (.175), multiplied by 32 starts (every fifth game over the course of a 162-game season), results in 5.6 fewer wins, a typical margin.

Team	Top Starter	Sub.	Difference Pct.	Wins	Team	Top Starter	Sub.	Difference Pct.	Wins
Balt.	16–12	8–10	.127	4.1	Atl.	20–19	12–16	.084	2.7
Bos.	19–16	19–16	.000	0.0	Chi.	16–9	18–32	.280	9.0
Cal.	20–11	14–16	.178	5.7	Cin.	26–12	15–11	.107	3.4
Chi.	21–13	16–15	.102	3.2	Hou.	22–13	8–7	.095	3.0
Clev.	10–13	25–35	.018	0.6	L.A.	25–9	4–8	.402	12.9
Det.	21–14	10–15	.200	6.4	Mtl.	23–9	11–26	.421	13.5
K.C.	24–8	2–2	.250	8.0	N.Y.	28–7	11–7	.189	6.0
Mil.	17–13	11–15	.144	4.6	Phil.	16–15	6–17	.255	8.2
Minn.	20–16	5–11	.243	7.8	Pitt.	13–13	10–23	.197	6.3
N.Y.	23–10	12–11	.175	5.6	St.L.	24–12	2–3	.267	8.5
Oak.	18–11	15–22	.215	6.9	S.D.	19–12	4–5	.168	5.4
Sea.	19–15	12–18	.159	5.1	S.F.	14–14	9–19	.214	5.7
Tex.	14–20	19–32	.039	1.3					
Tor.	20–12	16–4	−.175	−5.6					

The question then becomes: Can the addition of a top pitcher to the bullpen offset the loss which results from his departure from the starting rotation? In some cases, yes; in most, no. As a general rule, the difference is slight. As the following figures indicate, most teams do not blow enough late-inning leads to justify the typical loss of six wins from the starting rotation. Since the current vogue is to use a bullpen stopper only to protect a lead, let's examine the following table, which shows the number of games each team lost last season in which it led after seven innings, games in which the team probably relied upon its top reliever to hold its lead. (Because relief stoppers are used infrequently in tied games, and rarely when their teams trail, a team's record in games *tied* after seven innings bears little correlation to the quality of its best reliever, and accordingly such games have been ignored.)

Baltimore	11		Atlanta	9
Boston	7		Chicago	3
California	7		Cincinnati	2
Chicago	5		Houston	8
Cleveland	9		Los Angeles	5
Detroit	10		Montreal	7
Kansas City	11		New York	4
Milwaukee	8		Philadelphia	6
Minnesota	7		Pittsburgh	10
New York	4		St. Louis	1
Oakland	3		San Diego	3
Seattle	2		San Francisco	11
Texas	8			
Toronto	13			

Since the profit margin is so slim, there must be other compelling reasons for a team to do the Righetti shuffle, based primarily on factors that make that team different from the norm. For instance, rather than move its number one starter from the rotation, a team may find it appropriate to transfer its second or third starter, as was the case with Righetti. The Yankees switched him to the bullpen not only to replace Gossage, but also to ease the arm problems that had troubled him as a starter. They might also try a second- or third-line starter who had worked successfully from the bullpen earlier in his career (say, Shane Rawley), or who has pitched extremely well over the first few innings of his starts but not thereafter. Ironically, this was the case with both Candelaria and Ojeda in the 1984 season. (Our Pitcher Section shows how each pitcher fared last season on his first pass through the batting order, his second pass, and against all subsequent batters. You can make your own evaluations of bullpen candidates based on those figures.) If you can gain as much in the bullpen with a secondary starter as you can with your top man, you reduce the cost to your rotation.

Second, teams may be more willing to make the switch with a starting pitcher who they feel has underachieved. Again, Righetti is a prime example. In 1982, he had more strikeouts than hits allowed, a rare achievement for a starting pitcher. The following season, he allowed less than one hit per inning, with a strikeout-to-walk ratio of nearly 3.00. But over those two seasons, he won only 25 games. What did the Yankees have to lose by sending this hard-luck starter to the pen? (Sound familiar, Jose DeLeon? Pittsburgh might simply have made the right move with the wrong man.)

Third, teams with deep starting rotations, deep enough to keep a potential full-time starter in long relief, have less to lose by using him to replace a top-shelf starter, who can then be moved to the bullpen. Once more, the Yankees serve as an example. After Righetti became a reliever, they were able to select his replacement from among Ray Fontenot, Bob Shirley, Dennis Rasmussen, John Montefusco, and Joe Cowley. Eventually, Cowley found his way into the rotation, and New York won all 11 games he started in 1984. Notice in the chart above that Toronto had an exceptional record with makeshift starters last season. (Consult the Blue Jays' "Won-Lost Record By Starting Position" table for the records of the specific pitchers involved.) Cleveland, Texas, Atlanta, and Houston all had competent additional starters as well—at least, as compared to their regular rotations.

The conclusion, then, is that in certain unique instances, moving your top starter to the bullpen can be advantageous. But the risk is substantial, the profit margin slim, and the proper conditions rare. Nevertheless, the Yankees spotted the appropriate set of conditions, and were bold enough to make the move. But let other teams beware. This move is not for everyone.

F/T Mgr, Gd Sal, No Exp Req

What do 1985 World Series managers Dick Howser and Whitey Herzog have in common with Lou Piniella? All were given their first major-league managerial jobs without prior experience in the minor leagues. We all know that players who went right to the majors have excelled: Hall of Famers Mel Ott, Sandy Koufax, and Al Kaline, as well as Cooperstown contender Dave Winfield, are among those who never played in the bushes. But what about managers? Big league managers without minor league experience are neither as rare nor as successful. Are the teams that appoint first-time managers taking a risk?

Thirty of the 121 major-league managers who managed at least ten games since 1969 took their first jobs without experience either in a minor league dugout or with another major league team. Of the 10 who assumed their positions in spring training, as will Piniella, seven improved their teams' records from the previous season. Counted among the three who failed to improve their teams is Yogi Berra, who led the 1964 Yankees to the American League title, but won fewer games than Ralph Houk had in 1963. Among the recent managers who took new positions to start a season, 28 of 38 (74%) led their teams to improved records, a rate insignificantly higher than the first-timers.

Among the inexperienced managers, nine have won at least a division title during their careers. Five won them for their first employers, all of them within their first two seasons: Yogi Berra, Alvin Dark, Jim Fregosi, Howser, and Harvey Kuenn. Compare those figures to the statistics compiled during that time by managers who had honed their skills at the minor-league level:

	Mgrs.	Winners	Won With First Team
Experience	91	24 (26%)	16 (18%)
No Experience	30	9 (30%)	5 (17%)

Managers without minor-league experience have been as successful as those with it, and have been able to compete with their more experienced counterparts even as rookies. Should Piniella fail, the temptation will be to blame his inexperience. It ain't necessarily so.

WON-LOST RECORD BY STARTING POSITION

NEW YORK 97-64	C	1B	2B	3B	SS	LF	CF	RF	P	DH	Leadoff	Relief	Starts
Neil Allen	-	-	-	-	-	-	-	-	-	-	-	9-8	-
Mike Armstrong	-	-	-	-	-	-	-	-	-	-	-	2-7	-
Don Baylor	-	-	-	-	-	-	-	-	-	74-52	-	-	74-52
Dale Berra	-	-	-	22-11	-	-	-	-	-	-	-	-	22-11
Juan Bonilla	-	-	1-2	-	-	-	-	-	-	-	-	-	1-2
Rich Bordi	-	-	-	-	-	-	-	-	2-1	-	-	20-28	2-1
Scott Bradley	0-3	-	-	-	-	-	-	-	-	5-4	-	-	5-7
Marty Bystrom	-	-	-	-	-	-	-	-	4-4	-	-	-	4-4
Don Cooper	-	-	-	-	-	-	-	-	-	-	-	3-4	-
Henry Cotto	-	-	-	-	-	5-3	6-1	-	-	-	-	-	11-4
Joe Cowley	-	-	-	-	-	-	-	16-10	-	-	-	1-3	16-10
Juan Espino	2-1	-	-	-	-	-	-	-	-	-	-	-	2-1
Brian Fisher	-	-	-	-	-	-	-	-	-	-	-	37-18	-
Ken Griffey	-	-	-	-	-	54-36	2-1	0-1	-	5-2	-	-	61-40
Ron Guidry	-	-	-	-	-	-	-	-	23-10	-	-	1-0	23-10
Ron Hassey	41-24	0-1	-	-	-	-	-	-	-	1-1	-	-	42-26
Rickey Henderson	-	-	-	-	-	1-2	82-55	-	-	0-1	83-58	-	83-58
Rex Hudler	-	1-0	7-8	-	-	-	-	-	-	-	-	-	8-8
Vic Mata	-	-	-	-	-	-	-	0-1	-	-	-	-	0-1
Don Mattingly	-	96-63	-	-	-	-	-	-	-	-	-	-	96-63
Bobby Meacham	-	-	-	-	92-61	-	-	-	-	-	0-1	-	92-61
John Montefusco	-	-	-	-	-	-	-	-	1-0	-	-	0-2	1-0
Omar Moreno	-	-	-	-	-	2-1	5-6	2-0	-	-	2-3	-	9-7
Dale Murray	-	-	-	-	-	-	-	-	-	-	-	0-3	-
Joe Niekro	-	-	-	-	-	-	-	-	2-1	-	-	-	2-1
Phil Niekro	-	-	-	-	-	-	-	-	19-14	-	-	-	19-14
Mike Pagliarulo	-	-	-	56-40	-	-	-	-	-	-	-	-	56-40
Dan Pasqua	-	-	-	-	-	11-6	-	4-1	-	10-4	-	-	25-11
Willie Randolph	-	-	87-54	-	-	-	-	-	-	-	12-1	-	87-54
Dennis Rasmussen	-	-	-	-	-	-	-	-	8-8	-	-	0-6	8-8
Dave Righetti	-	-	-	-	-	-	-	-	-	-	-	50-24	-
Andre Robertson	-	-	2-0	19-13	5-3	-	-	-	-	-	-	-	26-16
Billy Sample	-	-	-	-	-	24-16	2-1	-	-	-	0-1	-	26-17
Rod Scurry	-	-	-	-	-	-	-	-	-	-	-	3-2	-
Bob Shirley	-	-	-	-	-	-	-	-	3-5	-	-	21-19	3-5
Keith Smith	-	-	-	-	-	-	-	-	-	19-11	-	-	19-11
Ed Whitson	-	-	-	-	-	-	-	-	19-11	-	-	-	19-11
Dave Winfield	-	-	-	-	-	-	-	91-61	-	2-0	-	-	93-61
Butch Wynegar	54-36	-	-	-	-	-	-	-	-	-	-	-	54-36

Batting vs. Left and Right Handed Pitchers

		BA	Rank	SA	Rank	OBA	Rank	HR %	Rank	BB %	Rank	SO %	Rank
Don Baylor	vs. Lefties	.254	94	.492	29	.377	25	5.70	21	13.50	20	12.66	82
	vs. Righties	.215	140	.387	87	.297	121	4.23	37	6.12	115	18.35	132
Dale Berra	vs. Lefties	.241	122	.345	126	.298	126	1.15	116	7.29	101	13.54	94
	vs. Righties	.182	--	.227	--	.182	--	0.00	--	0.00	--	31.82	--
Ken Griffey	vs. Lefties	.243	118	.346	125	.278	135	1.87	93	5.22	129	9.57	39
	vs. Righties	.284	41	.450	44	.347	50	2.42	87	9.41	55	10.75	50
Ron Hassey	vs. Lefties	.167	--	.188	--	.259	--	0.00	--	11.11	--	9.26	--
	vs. Righties	.324	5	.580	2	.393	6	5.94	9	9.02	62	6.56	17
Rickey Henderson	vs. Lefties	.361	1	.656	1	.487	1	6.67	12	19.91	2	11.95	68
	vs. Righties	.292	26	.447	47	.383	11	3.27	63	12.62	22	8.88	32
Don Mattingly	vs. Lefties	.288	51	.568	7	.328	92	6.82	10	6.16	122	5.48	11
	vs. Righties	.348	2	.567	3	.400	4	4.38	34	8.74	68	5.75	7
Bobby Meacham	vs. Lefties	.225	132	.267	149	.313	108	0.00	131	9.09	66	19.09	132
	vs. Righties	.214	141	.265	151	.295	124	0.34	148	9.83	48	17.34	120
Mike Pagliarulo	vs. Lefties	.157	--	.275	--	.267	--	3.92	--	9.84	--	36.07	--
	vs. Righties	.252	92	.468	32	.333	62	5.17	20	10.43	46	17.11	118
Dan Pasqua	vs. Lefties	.133	--	.133	--	.188	--	0.00	--	6.25	--	18.75	--
	vs. Righties	.218	137	.459	38	.300	115	6.77	4	10.00	47	23.33	153
Willie Randolph	vs. Lefties	.315	24	.414	80	.418	6	1.10	119	14.55	15	4.23	7
	vs. Righties	.253	89	.323	134	.361	28	0.95	133	14.06	10	7.81	26
Andre Robertson	vs. Lefties	.320	22	.390	96	.346	67	1.00	120	4.67	137	15.89	111
	vs. Righties	.360	--	.520	--	.407	--	4.00	--	3.45	--	24.14	--
Billy Sample	vs. Lefties	.307	32	.377	107	.357	48	0.88	123	6.30	118	6.30	19
	vs. Righties	.200	--	.200	--	.231	--	0.00	--	3.70	--	7.41	--
Dave Winfield	vs. Lefties	.251	99	.470	45	.343	74	4.65	40	12.50	28	10.89	51
	vs. Righties	.287	34	.471	30	.320	86	3.83	45	4.76	136	15.65	106
Butch Wynegar	vs. Lefties	.216	139	.317	137	.360	42	1.44	104	18.50	4	14.45	101
	vs. Righties	.229	126	.324	133	.351	46	1.76	101	15.84	6	8.91	33
Team Average	vs. Lefties	.266	6	.420	4	.350	2	3.09	6	10.80	1	11.97	1
	vs. Righties	.268	3	.428	3	.341	2	3.30	3	9.43	3	12.60	3
League Average	vs. Lefties	.266		.416		.333		2.91		8.95		13.77	
	vs. Righties	.259		.401		.324		2.78		8.49		13.56	

Batting with Runners on Base and Bases Empty

		BA	Rank	SA	Rank	OBA	Rank	HR %	Rank	BB %	Rank	SO %	Rank
Don Baylor	Runners On	.265	83	.493	28	.371	39	5.12	23	10.45	52	16.79	121
	Bases Empty	.202	149	.378	99	.294	120	4.58	39	8.11	69	15.20	100
Ken Griffey	Runners On	.281	66	.452	55	.340	82	2.86	71	9.54	63	9.54	44
	Bases Empty	.268	58	.399	81	.321	83	1.75	105	7.32	85	11.38	51
Ron Hassey	Runners On	.264	84	.405	87	.355	61	3.31	61	11.59	35	7.97	30
	Bases Empty	.322	4	.596	2	.381	11	6.16	9	7.50	80	6.25	8
Rickey Henderson	Runners On	.337	5	.489	32	.433	6	4.21	42	15.58	10	9.96	49
	Bases Empty	.303	11	.529	8	.411	4	4.48	40	14.89	7	9.93	39
Don Mattingly	Runners On	.321	23	.549	9	.373	37	5.08	25	9.54	64	4.09	5
	Bases Empty	.326	3	.585	3	.369	15	5.64	14	5.83	117	7.22	18
Bobby Meacham	Runners On	.252	115	.301	142	.331	93	0.00	142	8.57	94	15.36	109
	Bases Empty	.188	153	.235	156	.276	141	0.39	144	10.49	31	20.63	138
Mike Pagliarulo	Runners On	.231	139	.488	33	.326	98	6.88	7	12.11	32	18.42	137
	Bases Empty	.245	103	.409	67	.322	79	3.64	53	8.98	57	20.82	140
Willie Randolph	Runners On	.246	123	.303	141	.337	83	0.95	120	11.42	36	7.09	21
	Bases Empty	.297	13	.395	86	.414	3	1.05	123	16.33	4	6.12	6
Dave Winfield	Runners On	.281	67	.473	43	.345	79	4.42	36	9.32	75	12.71	81
	Bases Empty	.269	51	.468	33	.310	98	3.80	46	5.67	120	15.22	102
Butch Wynegar	Runners On	.237	134	.375	108	.368	45	2.63	75	17.20	6	10.75	58
	Bases Empty	.210	142	.268	152	.344	34	0.64	139	16.93	3	12.17	59
Team Average	Runners On	.273	7	.428	3	.350	2	3.34	3	10.26	3	11.95	2
	Bases Empty	.262	3	.423	4	.339	2	3.13	4	9.67	2	12.72	2
League Average	Runners On	.271		.416		.338		2.85		9.26		13.25	
	Bases Empty	.254		.397		.318		2.80		8.14		13.92	

Overall Batting Compared to Late Inning Pressure Situations

		BA	Rank	SA	Rank	OBA	Rank	HR %	Rank	BB %	Rank	SO %	Rank	RDI %	Rank
Don Baylor	Overall	.231	138	.430	62	.330	75	4.82	27	9.22	62	15.96	112	.330	36
	Pressure	.276	55	.553	13	.313	91	7.89	7	4.82	129	12.05	63	.500	7
Ken Griffey	Overall	.274	57	.425	68	.331	73	2.28	94	8.42	75	10.47	44	.308	56
	Pressure	.227	109	.318	109	.299	107	1.52	101	10.39	61	10.39	44	.364	40
Ron Hassey	Overall	.296	17	.509	12	.369	16	4.87	26	9.40	55	7.05	17	.298	69
	Pressure	.270	59	.486	31	.341	65	5.41	31	9.76	66	9.76	37	.364	40
Rickey Henderson	Overall	.314	4	.516	8	.419	6	4.39	36	15.14	7	9.94	40	.272	101
	Pressure	.276	55	.421	64	.389	24	3.95	43	15.56	20	10.00	40	.174	126
Don Mattingly	Overall	.324	3	.567	2	.371	12	5.37	12	7.70	94	5.64	6	.400	7
	Pressure	.313	27	.542	17	.353	51	6.25	23	5.88	118	1.96	2	.407	21
Bobby Meacham	Overall	.218	149	.266	153	.302	129	0.21	152	9.54	51	18.02	129	.263	109
	Pressure	.190	139	.222	149	.250	141	0.00	113	6.85	106	21.92	139	.444	13
Mike Pagliarulo	Overall	.239	125	.442	48	.324	85	5.00	21	10.34	41	19.77	141	.314	52
	Pressure	.212	125	.385	81	.317	86	5.77	27	11.67	49	20.00	133	.375	32
Willie Randolph	Overall	.276	50	.356	124	.382	7	1.01	128	14.24	12	6.53	10	.229	137
	Pressure	.229	107	.229	148	.308	95	0.00	113	10.00	63	8.75	30	.214	111
Dave Winfield	Overall	.275	54	.471	24	.328	80	4.11	41	7.55	96	13.93	86	.372	15
	Pressure	.244	89	.384	83	.293	113	3.49	51	6.52	111	19.57	129	.440	14
Butch Wynegar	Overall	.223	144	.320	144	.356	33	1.62	109	17.07	3	11.47	53	.225	140
	Pressure	.283	50	.491	30	.415	17	5.66	28	18.46	6	12.31	66	.600	4
Team Average	Overall	.267	3	.425	4	.344	2	3.22	3	9.94	2	12.36	2	.304	3
	Pressure	.255	7	.396	5	.325	8	3.65	2	9.24	8	13.05	2	.346	1
League Average	Overall	.261		.406		.327		2.82		8.63		13.62		.287	
	Pressure	.253		.381		.323		2.74		9.11		14.40		.273	

Additional Miscellaneous Batting Comparisons

	Grass Surface BA	Rank	Artificial Surface BA	Rank	Home Games BA	Rank	Road Games BA	Rank	Runners in Scoring Position BA	Rank	Runners in Scoring Pos and Two Outs BA	Rank	Leading Off Inning OBA	Rank	Runners on 3B with less than 2 Outs RDI %	Rank
Don Baylor	.225	140	.266	63	.216	144	.244	110	.281	70	.271	55	.298	106	.676	44
Ken Griffey	.283	45	.225	122	.292	43	.259	80	.269	87	.220	107	.341	48	.788	9
Ron Hassey	.320	5	.167	154	.330	10	.270	55	.227	125	.179	141	.369	25	.692	34
Rickey Henderson	.316	8	.308	17	.305	29	.322	3	.288	63	.250	68	.418	4	.684	37
Don Mattingly	.328	2	.298	29	.336	7	.311	7	.316	27	.354	12	.356	33	.732	22
Bobby Meacham	.214	146	.240	100	.169	156	.264	72	.260	97	.254	67	.306	99	.559	90
Mike Pagliarulo	.237	125	.255	74	.242	114	.238	121	.262	94	.293	40	.314	84	.474	131
Dan Pasqua	.208	148	.217	--	.218	--	.197	--	.296	--	.462	--	.250	--	.400	--
Willie Randolph	.268	64	.313	13	.262	83	.286	22	.218	134	.111	155	.448	2	.576	80
Billy Sample	.311	10	.150	--	.264	--	.313	--	.393	--	.375	--	.314	--	.857	--
Dave Winfield	.282	47	.240	98	.285	51	.266	65	.316	28	.324	27	.389	10	.648	54
Butch Wynegar	.220	143	.244	92	.196	153	.252	92	.214	136	.286	44	.296	110	.385	150
Team Average	.269	2	.254	6	.267	7	.268	2	.270	7	.259	5	.356	2	.624	4
League Average	.262		.259		.266		.256		.268		.248		.321		.587	

Pitching vs. Left and Right Handed Batters

		BA	Rank	SA	Rank	OBA	Rank	HR %	Rank	BB %	Rank	SO %	Rank
Rich Bordi	vs. Lefties	.309	111	.442	88	.372	101	2.42	56	8.70	60	11.41	82
	vs. Righties	.209	10	.270	4	.252	8	0.47	3	5.63	31	18.61	24
Joe Cowley	vs. Lefties	.228	27	.399	64	.347	80	4.44	120	14.85	124	11.88	72
	vs. Righties	.220	24	.428	88	.297	38	5.60	129	8.93	87	17.50	31
Brian Fisher	vs. Lefties	.225	22	.289	10	.302	30	1.16	21	9.90	78	19.79	12
	vs. Righties	.207	8	.266	3	.245	5	1.09	9	5.03	18	23.62	5
Ron Guidry	vs. Lefties	.212	13	.348	34	.241	3	4.35	116	4.08	5	14.29	44
	vs. Righties	.256	64	.402	69	.285	22	2.51	54	4.06	9	13.74	65
Phil Niekro	vs. Lefties	.261	64	.432	81	.366	95	3.86	104	14.34	122	12.60	64
	vs. Righties	.226	29	.383	50	.311	54	3.08	82	10.48	108	19.13	19
Dennis Rasmussen	vs. Lefties	.255	--	.408	--	.305	--	3.06	--	6.67	--	17.14	--
	vs. Righties	.255	63	.404	73	.334	84	2.48	51	10.80	113	13.89	63
Dave Righetti	vs. Lefties	.196	5	.277	5	.308	35	0.89	13	13.74	117	24.43	3
	vs. Righties	.259	66	.346	25	.320	64	1.40	13	8.41	77	18.69	21
Bob Shirley	vs. Lefties	.212	14	.267	3	.250	5	0.68	10	5.13	14	19.23	15
	vs. Righties	.272	89	.370	42	.316	62	1.51	16	6.21	40	8.62	125
Ed Whitson	vs. Lefties	.311	114	.481	110	.342	72	2.93	77	4.76	9	10.28	96
	vs. Righties	.307	124	.453	106	.362	115	2.92	76	7.84	71	15.69	45
Team Average	vs. Lefties	.253	3	.398	5	.328	5	3.27	14	10.02	12	14.09	3
	vs. Righties	.251	4	.385	3	.307	2	2.59	2	7.45	4	15.59	3
League Average	vs. Lefties	.265		.408		.333		2.74		9.21		12.94	
	vs. Righties	.259		.404		.322		2.88		8.19		14.14	

Pitching with Runners on Base and Bases Empty

		BA	Rank	SA	Rank	OBA	Rank	HR %	Rank	BB %	Rank	SO %	Rank
Rich Bordi	Runners On	.287	92	.389	55	.350	83	1.27	18	9.29	74	12.02	78
	Bases Empty	.228	28	.315	13	.272	15	1.37	17	5.17	19	18.10	26
Joe Cowley	Runners On	.189	2	.365	33	.313	32	4.50	116	15.24	129	15.99	30
	Bases Empty	.246	53	.440	99	.335	86	5.19	124	10.60	104	13.01	71
Brian Fisher	Runners On	.214	9	.301	4	.262	4	1.73	31	6.32	25	17.89	17
	Bases Empty	.217	18	.255	3	.284	24	0.54	1	8.46	72	25.37	2
Ron Guidry	Runners On	.247	35	.410	71	.271	7	3.32	89	3.88	4	12.92	74
	Bases Empty	.249	58	.381	49	.280	18	2.58	61	4.18	12	14.40	51
Phil Niekro	Runners On	.250	41	.388	53	.355	88	2.87	75	13.90	122	17.80	18
	Bases Empty	.241	47	.424	91	.330	81	3.95	112	11.56	114	13.94	54
Dennis Rasmussen	Runners On	.324	123	.462	101	.376	113	2.07	45	8.43	52	13.86	56
	Bases Empty	.213	16	.370	41	.297	41	2.98	76	10.65	105	15.21	44
Dave Righetti	Runners On	.261	51	.332	16	.329	50	0.47	2	9.47	78	18.52	13
	Bases Empty	.219	20	.321	15	.301	49	2.14	34	10.53	103	22.49	5
Bob Shirley	Runners On	.261	52	.337	20	.293	18	1.09	15	4.93	12	15.27	37
	Bases Empty	.242	48	.330	19	.292	36	1.32	16	6.58	42	9.88	112
Ed Whitson	Runners On	.346	128	.540	126	.364	103	3.81	103	3.86	3	11.58	85
	Bases Empty	.280	103	.413	81	.340	92	2.22	40	7.87	63	13.45	64
Team Average	Runners On	.261	5	.397	4	.324	4	2.70	5	8.88	6	14.76	3
	Bases Empty	.245	3	.386	5	.310	3	3.00	10	8.29	8	15.10	3
League Average	Runners On	.271		.416		.338		2.85		9.26		13.25	
	Bases Empty	.254		.397		.318		2.80		8.14		13.92	

Overall Pitching Compared to Late Inning Pressure Situations

		BA	Rank	SA	Rank	OBA	Rank	HR %	Rank	BB %	Rank	SO %	Rank
Rich Bordi	Overall	.253	53	.346	20	.306	33	1.33	10	6.99	33	15.42	35
	Pressure	.340	121	.481	107	.421	123	2.83	78	11.11	83	11.90	77
Joe Cowley	Overall	.224	11	.412	75	.327	62	4.93	130	12.43	117	14.18	50
	Pressure	.224	30	.373	55	.307	46	4.48	111	9.21	62	15.79	42
Brian Fisher	Overall	.216	9	.277	3	.273	6	1.12	5	7.42	49	21.74	4
	Pressure	.213	22	.310	19	.291	29	1.94	47	9.83	70	24.28	3
Ron Guidry	Overall	.248	45	.392	51	.277	8	2.86	71	4.07	4	13.84	54
	Pressure	.269	74	.356	44	.290	28	0.96	22	2.78	5	12.96	65
Phil Niekro	Overall	.245	35	.409	69	.341	82	3.50	102	12.57	120	15.60	33
	Pressure	.293	98	.586	124	.397	110	8.62	130	14.71	118	11.76	80
Dennis Rasmussen	Overall	.255	56	.405	65	.327	66	2.63	62	9.79	91	14.69	47
	Pressure	.281	86	.375	57	.343	73	3.13	83	8.57	52	11.43	80
Dave Righetti	Overall	.241	31	.327	10	.316	50	1.26	8	9.96	94	20.35	7
	Pressure	.250	54	.321	27	.323	58	1.12	24	9.84	73	20.66	12
Bob Shirley	Overall	.251	50	.333	12	.293	20	1.22	6	5.83	11	12.33	80
	Pressure	.227	33	.273	13	.289	27	0.00	1	7.84	43	10.78	92
Ed Whitson	Overall	.309	123	.469	114	.350	95	2.92	75	6.10	17	12.62	75
	Pressure	.240	--	.440	--	.269	--	4.00	--	3.85	--	19.23	--
Team Average	Overall	.252	3	.391	4	.316	4	2.88	6	8.54	7	14.95	3
	Pressure	.256	6	.368	4	.327	6	2.43	6	9.26	6	16.84	1
League Average	Overall	.261		.406		.327		2.82		8.63		13.62	
	Pressure	.258		.392		.332		2.71		9.52		14.05	

Additional Miscellaneous Pitching Comparisons

	Grass Surface		Artificial Surface		Home Games		Road Games		Runners in Scoring Position		Runners in Scoring Pos and Two Outs		Leading Off Inning	
	BA	Rank	BA	Rank	BA	Rank	BA	Rank	BA	Rank	BA	Rank	OBA	Rank
Rich Bordi	.241	35	.350	127	.227	19	.284	94	.270	72	.255	77	.268	17
Marty Bystrom	.281	97	.286	--	.282	--	.282	--	.258	--	.333	--	.444	--
Joe Cowley	.218	11	.258	65	.216	13	.230	19	.148	1	.161	13	.316	63
Brian Fisher	.211	6	.241	38	.236	34	.188	2	.240	33	.173	20	.302	50
Ron Guidry	.253	57	.200	11	.252	62	.243	34	.243	36	.237	63	.309	57
Phil Niekro	.250	53	.223	22	.238	36	.252	44	.247	45	.256	78	.332	79
Dennis Rasmussen	.273	87	.184	4	.275	93	.239	28	.315	113	.333	117	.343	91
Dave Righetti	.230	20	.333	--	.231	23	.253	55	.256	55	.212	41	.293	39
Bob Shirley	.248	45	.333	--	.226	18	.288	98	.205	12	.226	56	.330	78
Ed Whitson	.310	119	.306	111	.303	118	.314	119	.345	127	.276	90	.345	94
Team Average	.252	2	.251	4	.245	3	.258	5	.251	3	.234	5	.323	8
League Average	.262		.259		.256		.266		.268		.248		.321	

OAKLAND A'S

The Oakland A's dealt away two major stars a year ago. They first sent Rickey Henderson to the Yankees, and three days later traded reliever Bill Caudill to Toronto. Infielder Tony Phillips summarized the team's catch-22 situation with Henderson by saying, "They (the A's) had to do what they had to do. (Henderson) was looking for a long-term contract. But I'm not sure he will ever be replaced by the A's." The Caudill trade then doubled the stakes.

A comparison of Oakland's leadoff statistics for the past two seasons confirms Phillips's worst fears. The A's failed miserably to keep the top spot in their batting order productive after the departure of Henderson. First-place hitters in the A's lineup last season had a lower on-base average than those of any other team. The composite statistics of all of Oakland's leadoff hitters, compared to a year earlier, with Henderson usually in the first position:

	AB	R	H	2B	3B	HR	RBI	BB	SO	SB	BA	SA	OBA
1984	642	124	180	31	6	17	72	96	112	70	.280	.427	.376
1985	711	93	183	30	7	4	53	37	66	38	.257	.336	.293

Oakland's first-place hitters reached base only 86 times while leading off 292 innings last season (29.5%), the lowest average in the American League. And the A's scored in just 73 of those 292 innings (25.0%), a last-place average in a category in which Oakland had led the league in '84. Alfredo Griffin and Dave Collins, Oakland's leadoff hitters (in 72 and 69 games, respectively), both acquired in the Caudill trade, proved Phillips's point: As a leadoff hitter at least, Henderson was impossible to replace.

But the A's were a veteran team looking to prove that there was more to their offense than one star, no matter how flashy. Despite the loss of Henderson, Oakland scored 19 more runs than they had in '84, and ranked fifth in the American League with 757 runs, their highest total since 1975.

There were many heroes. Mike Davis was the league's best player during the month of April, and finished the season with a .287 batting average, 24 home runs, and 82 RBIs, compared to .230, 9, and 46 a year earlier. The A's also retrieved Dusty Baker and Steve Henderson from the baseball scrap heap; they both made significant contributions. And let's not forget that Oakland had made similarly successful salvage efforts before the 1984 season, when they added the prodigal Bruce Bochte and the orphaned Dave Kingman. Apparently, some of the Al Davis philosophy has rubbed off on his former Bay Area housemates; before the Oakland Raiders moved to Los Angeles, Davis kept them at the top of the AFC's Western Division by running a last-chance house for players like Lyle Alzado, John Matuszak, and Jim Plunkett, all of whom now wear Super Bowl rings.

One More for the Road

Playing 83 games at the Oakland Coliseum made it all the more unlikely that the A's would maintain a strong attack without Henderson. Their rankings in scoring and allowing runs—fifth in runs, twelfth in runs allowed—would normally indicate a team that plays in a hitters' park. But nothing could be further from the truth. In fact, their offense was even stronger than it appeared last season, and their pitching was even worse.

Oakland Coliseum is the most extreme pitchers' park in the American League. With the increased awareness of stadium biases, that should go without saying, but it seems that most of the attention to those biases has been directed toward parks that increase offense rather those those that silence it. No A.L. stadium has a reputation for stifling runs equal to those of Fenway Park, the Metrodome, and Tiger Stadium for doing the opposite.

The following tables show the runs scored per game by each American League team, overall, at home, and on the road. Oakland ranks twelfth at home, third on the road. They also led the league with a .272 road-game batting average:

All Games		Home Games		Road Games	
New York	5.21	New York	5.14	New York	5.28
Baltimore	5.08	Boston	5.12	Baltimore	5.05
Boston	4.91	Baltimore	5.11	**Oakland**	4.93
Toronto	4.71	Toronto	4.95	Boston	4.70
Oakland	4.67	Minnesota	4.85	Chicago	4.60
Detroit	4.53	Detroit	4.77	Seattle	4.54
California	4.52	Cleveland	4.69	Toronto	4.48
Chicago	4.52	California	4.68	California	4.36
Cleveland	4.50	Milwaukee	4.60	Cleveland	4.31
Seattle	4.44	Texas	4.45	Detroit	4.29
Minnesota	4.35	Chicago	4.43	Kansas City	4.13
Milwaukee	4.29	**Oakland**	4.41	Milwaukee	3.98
Kansas City	4.24	Kansas City	4.35	Minnesota	3.82
Texas	3.83	Seattle	4.34	Texas	3.22

The next table compares the number of runs per game scored by both teams over the past four seasons in each team's home games to those scored in their road games. (The 1982 starting point corresponds to the opening of the Metrodome, which completed the current set of American League parks.) As you can see, the average in A's road games is 1.13 runs per game higher than at the Coliseum, the only reduction greater than one run per game.

	Runs Per Game		
	Home	Road	Diff.
Boston	9.90	8.77	+12.9%
Minnesota	9.41	8.61	+9.3%
Toronto	9.10	8.41	+8.2%
Cleveland	9.53	9.10	+4.7%
Chicago	9.15	8.78	+4.2%
Seattle	8.88	8.57	+3.6%
Texas	8.34	8.23	+1.3%
Kansas City	8.72	8.69	+0.3%
California	8.89	9.05	−1.8%
Detroit	8.78	9.07	−3.2%
Baltimore	8.79	9.24	−4.9%
New York	8.57	9.46	−9.4%
Milwaukee	8.72	9.67	−9.8%
Oakland	8.81	9.94	−11.4%

Now you can tell your friends how the Oakland Coliseum hurts hitters nearly as much as Fenway Park helps them. Unless, of course, one of your friends is Tony Armas, who has been well aware of the difference for several years now. His career statistics at each:

Tony Armas	AB	H	2B	3B	HR	BB	SO	BA	SA	OBA
at Fenway Park	836	235	44	7	53	50	162	.281	.541	.320
at Oakland Coliseum	1349	322	46	11	60	72	336	.239	.423	.275

The key player acquired in the Henderson trade, at least on a short-term basis, was Jay Howell, both for what he did and for what he enabled them to do. Oakland was gambling that Howell could fill the hole they then created by trading Bill Caudill for Griffin and Collins. And a large hole it was: Caudill ranked second in the league to Dan Quisenberry with 36 saves in 1984. This would be Howell's first shot at the fireman role; his job with the Yankees in '84 had been as the set-up man, trying to preserve a sixth- or seventh-inning lead and deliver it to Dave Righetti in the ninth. Now Howell would be the final line of defense.

The move was an overwhelming success. Oakland lost only three games in which they led after seven innings last season, the second-lowest total in the league. (Check the Toronto Blue Jays essay for a complete listing of those statistics.) That figure was not only much lower than the totals of blown leads in the pre-Caudill days, but lower even than Oakland's total with Caudill in the bullpen in 1984. The A's record in games in which they led after seven innings has been improving steadily over the past four seasons, as they rebuild their bullpen from its previous neglect:

Year	W	L	Pct.	Saves Leader
1982	53	11	.828	Dave Beard (11)
1983	54	10	.844	Dave Beard (10)
1984	57	4	.934	Bill Caudill (36)
1985	56	3	.949	Jay Howell (29)

Set 'Em Up, Joe. . . .Er, Steve

Howell's ability to make a successful transition to stopper demonstrates the increased importance teams have placed on finding a talented pitcher to fill the set-up relief role. Formerly a graveyard spot for pitchers trying to work their way into shape or out of the doghouse, the set-up man is now often a potential star reliever on a deep staff. Aurelio Lopez was every bit as important to the Tigers' bullpen in the set-up role in '84 as Willie Hernandez was as a closer; Hernandez himself had been plucked by Detroit from the set-up role behind Al Holland in Philadelphia prior to the season. And it was just five years ago that Ron Davis pioneered the role of advance man for Rich Gossage in New York; Davis, of course, went on to become Minnesota's *numero uno* in the bullpen.

But few teams have two top-of-the-line relief pitchers, enabling them to reserve a bullpen ace for the set-up spot. For teams that

don't have relief staffs with the depth of the '84 Tigers, the set-up role has become a proving ground for young relievers, a logical consequence of the increasing number of pitchers being groomed in the minors for a career in the bullpen. Such was the case with Oakland's rookie Steve Ontiveros last season.

Ontiveros was recalled in mid-June, and it wasn't long before he assumed the set-up role for Howell. The accompanying table lists the leaders in each league in save set-ups, which we defined as a relief appearance of at least one inning which immediately precedes a save. Notice that Ontiveros wasn't the only rookie to handle that position successfully last season; rookies are indicated by asterisks:

A.L. Leaders		N.L. Leaders	
*Fisher, N.Y.	8	*Burke, Mtl.	13
Lavelle, Tor.	8	Franco, Cin.	9
Atherton, Oak.	7	Dedmon, Atl.	8
Acker, Tor.	6	Dawley, Hou.	7
Bordi, N.Y.	6	Frazier, Chi.	7
*Ontiveros, Oak.	6	Hume, Cin.	7
*Clements, Cal.	6	*Carman, Phil.	6
		*McDowell, N.Y.	5

Ontiveros didn't lead the A's in save set-ups, but only because he didn't inherit the role from Keith Atherton until mid-season. Atherton had all seven of his save set-ups before the All-Star break, Ontiveros all but one of his in the second half of the season. We'll hear his name more often this season, but, as fans of mediocre San Francisco and Chicago infielders recall, we've heard it before, too. (What's next, an infielder named Jim Duffalo?)

One Tough Situation

Those of you with critical minds might be thinking something like this: "So Oakland had a poor pitching staff last season. They play in a pitchers' park. Their late-inning relief was excellent. Their set-up men were among the league leaders. Woof! Those starting pitchers must be awful!" Well, you're absolutely right.

A's starters compiled an ERA of 5.41 in road games. That might not seem so bad if you live in Cleveland (Indians starters had a 6.68 road-game ERA), or Seattle (5.89 for the Mariners), but it ranked behind everyone else, nearly a run above the league average of 4.56. For a team with the run-scoring capability of Oakland, that rotation may be all that stands in the way of a pennant chase. That fact was not lost on Oakland's front office, which confronted the problem in a typical manner last winter. Think about it this way: A team with a growing reputation as a haven for outcast players needs a starting pitcher. Only one name comes to mind. Welcome to Oakland, Mr. Andujar.

WON-LOST RECORD BY STARTING POSITION

OAKLAND 77-85	C	1B	2B	3B	SS	LF	CF	RF	P	DH	Leadoff	Relief	Starts
Keith Atherton	·											21-35	·
Dusty Baker	·	26-27	·	·	·	13-9	·	1-2	·	7-5	·	·	47-43
Tim Birtsas	·	·							13-12	·	·	0-4	13-12
Bruce Bochte	·	46-56				·	·	·	·	·	·	·	46-56
Jose Canseco	· ·	·			·	4-7	·	5-9	·		·	·	9-16
Chris Codiroli						·	·	·	18-19	·	·	·	18-19
Dave Collins					·	39-47	·	·	·	·	36-33	·	39-47
Tim Conroy	·	·	·	·	·	·	·	·	0-2	·	·	4-10	0-2
Mike Davis	·	·	·	·	·	0-1	5-11	63-63	·	·	·	·	68-75
Mike Gallego	·	·	8-17	1-1	·	·	·	·	·	·	·	·	9-18
Alfredo Griffin	·	·	·	·	77-85	·	·	·	·	·	30-42	·	77-85
Mike Heath	40-54	·	·	5-4	·	2-2	·	5-7	·	·	·	·	52-67
Steve Henderson	·	·	·	·	·	19-19	·	3-4	·	0-1	7-9	·	22-24
Donnie Hill	·	·	59-53	·	·	·	·	·	·	·	·	·	59-53
Jay Howell	·	·	·	·	·	·	·	·	·	·	·	43-20	·
Tommy John	·	·	·	·	·	·	·	·	4-7	·	·	·	4-7
Jeff Kaiser	·	·	·	·	·	·	·	·	·	·	·	2-13	·
Steve Kiefer	·	·	·	9-10	·	·	·	·	·	·	·	·	9-10
Dave Kingman	·	5-2	·	·	·	·	·	·	·	70-79	·	·	75-81
Bill Krueger	·	·	·	·	·	·	·	·	9-14	·	·	2-7	9-14
Rick Langford	·	·	·	·	·	·	·	·	1-2	·	·	5-15	1-2
Carney Lansford	·	·	·	48-49	·	·	·	·	·	·	·	·	48-49
Steve McCatty	·	·	·	·	·	·	·	·	6-3	·	·	2-19	6-3
Dan Meyer	·	·	·	·	·	·	·	·	·	·	·	·	·
Steve Mura	·	·	·	·	·	·	·	·	0-1	·	·	5-17	0-1
Dwayne Murphy	·	·	·	·	·	·	72-74	·	·	·	4-1	·	72-74
Charlie O'Brien	1-1	·	·	·	·	·	·	·	·	·	·	·	1-1
Steve Ontiveros	·	·	·	·	·	·	·	·	·	·	·	24-15	·
Tony Phillips	·	·	3-6	11-20	·	·	·	·	·	·	·	·	14-26
Rob Picciolo	·	·	7-9	3-1	·	·	·	·	·	·	·	·	10-10
Jose Rijo	·	·	·	·	·	·	·	·	4-5	·	·	2-1	4-5
Don Sutton	·	·	·	·	·	·	·	·	18-11	·	·	·	18-11
Tom Tellmann	·	·	·	·	·	·	·	·	·	·	·	1-10	·
Mickey Tettleton	36-30	·	·	·	·	·	·	·	·	·	·	·	36-30
Mike Warren	·	·	·	·	·	·	·	·	2-4	·	·	2-8	2-4
Curt Young	·	·	·	·	·	·	·	2-5	·	·	·	1-11	2-5

Batting vs. Left and Right Handed Pitchers

		BA	Rank	SA	Rank	OBA	Rank	HR %	Rank	BB %	Rank	SO %	Rank
Dusty Baker	vs. Lefties	.250	101	.396	91	.355	55	3.47	56	14.20	18	12.43	78
	vs. Righties	.281	45	.472	26	.361	29	4.52	31	11.45	31	11.45	57
Bruce Bochte	vs. Lefties	.333	9	.611	4	.438	3	7.41	6	15.63	9	17.19	121
	vs. Righties	.289	29	.414	68	.356	37	2.70	83	9.51	52	11.46	58
Dave Collins	vs. Lefties	.218	136	.287	142	.260	148	1.15	116	5.21	130	6.25	18
	vs. Righties	.260	76	.363	109	.315	95	1.03	127	7.45	93	9.63	41
Mike Davis	vs. Lefties	.271	71	.484	34	.335	83	5.16	27	7.65	95	21.76	139
	vs. Righties	.293	24	.485	21	.353	43	4.08	40	8.53	71	14.29	90
Alfredo Griffin	vs. Lefties	.326	14	.401	87	.337	81	0.53	129	2.05	155	4.10	5
	vs. Righties	.246	106	.302	146	.270	139	0.23	151	3.55	150	9.31	38
Mike Heath	vs. Lefties	.285	55	.490	30	.341	75	3.31	61	8.33	81	13.69	95
	vs. Righties	.232	123	.365	107	.298	118	2.81	78	8.33	77	12.35	67
Steve Henderson	vs. Lefties	.321	20	.457	57	.373	28	1.43	105	7.84	90	15.03	103
	vs. Righties	.245	--	.321	--	.322	--	1.89	--	10.00	--	18.33	--
Donnie Hill	vs. Lefties	.250	101	.284	144	.306	117	0.00	131	7.77	94	11.65	63
	vs. Righties	.295	22	.370	98	.326	78	0.98	131	4.50	139	6.31	16
Dave Kingman	vs. Lefties	.244	112	.483	36	.325	95	7.39	7	11.33	38	15.76	109
	vs. Righties	.236	117	.389	84	.302	112	4.09	39	8.42	74	17.71	127
Carney Lansford	vs. Lefties	.237	125	.359	115	.266	143	2.29	86	4.29	140	5.00	10
	vs. Righties	.296	20	.463	36	.332	67	3.70	50	4.11	142	6.85	20
Dwayne Murphy	vs. Lefties	.197	151	.374	108	.297	129	4.76	38	12.57	27	22.86	146
	vs. Righties	.247	104	.410	72	.357	33	3.46	59	13.96	11	18.69	138
Rob Picciolo	vs. Lefties	.323	18	.387	98	.333	86	1.61	99	1.59	156	12.70	83
	vs. Righties	.200	--	.225	--	.220	--	0.00	--	2.44	--	21.95	--
Mickey Tettleton	vs. Lefties	.213	143	.344	127	.304	118	1.64	98	10.00	57	22.86	146
	vs. Righties	.267	62	.353	114	.360	30	1.33	116	11.93	26	24.43	154
Team Average	vs. Lefties	.268	4	.416	6	.327	9	3.12	5	8.15	10	14.28	9
	vs. Righties	.262	6	.394	9	.324	8	2.62	10	8.18	8	13.66	9
League Average	vs. Lefties	.266		.416		.333		2.91		8.95		13.77	
	vs. Righties	.259		.401		.324		2.78		8.49		13.56	

Batting with Runners on Base and Bases Empty

		BA	Rank	SA	Rank	OBA	Rank	HR %	Rank	BB %	Rank	SO %	Rank
Dusty Baker	Runners On	.267	81	.460	49	.376	32	4.67	31	15.47	13	9.39	41
	Bases Empty	.269	49	.425	59	.344	33	3.63	54	10.23	35	13.95	78
Bruce Bochte	Runners On	.342	4	.571	6	.396	11	5.98	13	8.42	98	10.89	61
	Bases Empty	.258	76	.338	128	.346	32	1.25	118	11.76	22	13.24	72
Dave Collins	Runners On	.300	39	.385	104	.354	64	0.77	129	7.89	109	10.53	54
	Bases Empty	.225	127	.325	133	.274	143	1.20	120	6.39	107	7.89	22
Mike Davis	Runners On	.280	69	.458	51	.348	74	3.81	51	9.36	74	17.98	135
	Bases Empty	.293	21	.505	15	.347	27	4.82	33	7.42	83	15.13	97
Alfredo Griffin	Runners On	.296	46	.393	98	.296	134	0.81	127	1.15	158	6.49	15
	Bases Empty	.253	92	.292	148	.286	135	0.00	148	4.43	143	8.59	30
Mike Heath	Runners On	.275	73	.427	72	.351	68	2.81	72	10.70	47	11.16	65
	Bases Empty	.233	122	.395	85	.285	136	3.10	67	6.50	102	14.08	80
Steve Henderson	Runners On	.329	11	.447	59	.363	52	1.18	115	5.43	138	14.13	99
	Bases Empty	.278	33	.398	84	.355	19	1.85	103	10.74	29	17.36	121
Donnie Hill	Runners On	.325	16	.406	85	.356	59	0.63	135	5.26	140	6.84	17
	Bases Empty	.258	79	.313	140	.297	116	0.86	133	5.28	127	8.13	25
Dave Kingman	Runners On	.226	142	.385	103	.295	135	4.24	41	9.26	76	17.59	131
	Bases Empty	.249	99	.447	41	.322	82	5.83	12	9.36	51	16.67	114
Carney Lansford	Runners On	.333	7	.547	10	.364	50	4.67	31	4.14	148	5.33	9
	Bases Empty	.243	104	.359	111	.278	140	2.39	91	4.18	145	6.84	15
Dwayne Murphy	Runners On	.215	147	.346	125	.346	77	3.07	69	16.49	9	20.00	146
	Bases Empty	.247	102	.441	43	.335	50	4.41	43	11.08	27	19.76	137
Mickey Tettleton	Runners On	.250	118	.295	146	.359	55	0.00	142	13.89	22	25.00	157
	Bases Empty	.252	96	.390	90	.333	54	2.44	89	9.42	50	23.19	153
Team Average	Runners On	.277	5	.421	5	.339	5	2.87	7	8.77	9	13.42	8
	Bases Empty	.255	6	.387	10	.314	9	2.71	9	7.72	10	14.19	8
League Average	Runners On	.271		.416		.338		2.85		9.26		13.25	
	Bases Empty	.254		.397		.318		2.80		8.14		13.92	

Overall Batting Compared to Late Inning Pressure Situations

		BA	Rank	SA	Rank	OBA	Rank	HR %	Rank	BB %	Rank	SO %	Rank	RDI %	Rank
Dusty Baker	Overall	.268	67	.440	53	.359	27	4.08	42	12.63	21	11.87	58	.294	71
	Pressure	.345	12	.621	5	.433	10	6.90	16	13.43	33	11.94	61	.304	69
Bruce Bochte	Overall	.295	20	.439	56	.367	62	3.30	62	10.34	42	12.24	60	.319	47
	Pressure	.338	14	.492	29	.419	14	3.08	57	12.16	42	12.16	65	.188	121
Dave Collins	Overall	.251	103	.346	131	.303	127	1.06	126	6.94	110	8.85	32	.325	41
	Pressure	.265	66	.279	131	.333	73	0.00	113	7.69	93	12.82	68	.353	48
Mike Davis	Overall	.287	31	.484	17	.348	45	4.39	36	8.28	82	16.39	119	.342	27
	Pressure	.244	89	.419	67	.301	103	4.65	39	7.37	99	18.95	127	.150	137
Alfredo Griffin	Overall	.270	104	.332	139	.290	141	0.33	149	3.10	155	7.74	22	.322	44
	Pressure	.191	137	.213	151	.210	155	0.00	113	2.88	142	12.50	67	.216	110
Mike Heath	Overall	.250	104	.408	84	.313	108	2.98	75	8.33	81	12.80	71	.330	33
	Pressure	.222	114	.319	107	.253	140	2.78	64	3.90	135	11.69	56	.353	48
Steve Henderson	Overall	.301	11	.420	71	.358	28	1.55	110	8.45	74	15.96	114	.474	1
	Pressure	.281	54	.344	96	.351	55	0.00	113	10.53	58	15.79	96	.615	3
Donnie Hill	Overall	.285	37	.351	127	.321	95	0.76	135	5.28	138	7.57	21	.373	12
	Pressure	.273	58	.345	95	.355	50	1.82	92	9.86	64	5.63	13	.375	32
Dave Kingman	Overall	.238	129	.417	75	.309	115	5.07	18	9.31	58	17.12	123	.303	63
	Pressure	.247	86	.481	35	.359	47	7.79	10	15.05	23	13.98	79	.105	153
Carney Lansford	Overall	.277	48	.429	64	.311	111	3.24	64	4.17	149	6.25	8	.293	72
	Pressure	.185	141	.278	133	.237	146	1.85	89	4.76	130	9.52	34	.250	87
Dwayne Murphy	Overall	.233	135	.400	94	.340	61	3.82	50	13.57	15	19.87	142	.235	130
	Pressure	.192	136	.372	86	.297	109	5.13	33	11.96	45	19.57	129	.111	149
Tony Phillips	Overall	.280	--	.453	--	.331	--	2.48	--	7.30	--	19.10	--	.273	--
	Pressure	.208	--	.333	--	.259	--	0.00	--	7.14	--	21.43	--	.375	32
Mickey Tettleton	Overall	.251	101	.351	128	.344	51	1.42	113	11.38	34	23.98	154	.183	157
	Pressure	.258	75	.419	66	.343	63	3.23	55	10.53	58	18.42	121	.143	--
Team Average	Overall	.264	5	.401	8	.325	8	2.78	9	8.17	10	13.85	10	.312	2
	Pressure	.251	9	.372	9	.319	10	2.98	6	8.70	10	13.89	7	.255	10
League Average	Overall	.261		.406		.327		2.82		8.63		13.62		.287	
	Pressure	.253		.381		.323		2.74		9.11		14.40		.273	

Additional Miscellaneous Batting Comparisons

	Grass Surface BA	Rank	Artificial Surface BA	Rank	Home Games BA	Rank	Road Games BA	Rank	Runners in Scoring Position BA	Rank	Runners in Scoring Pos and Two Outs BA	Rank	Leading Off Inning OBA	Rank	Runners on 3B with less than 2 Outs RDI %	Rank
Dusty Baker	.262	80	.302	23	.248	108	.286	23	.256	102	.273	52	.282	121	.813	5
Bruce Bochte	.309	11	.230	117	.314	21	.277	39	.300	44	.243	81	.344	47	.667	47
Dave Collins	.251	101	.250	83	.232	54	.270	54	.313	30	.297	37	.297	108	.688	35
Mike Davis	.286	37	.290	38	.276	62	.296	13	.280	72	.258	60	.348	43	.593	70
Alfredo Griffin	.274	56	.253	78	.257	88	.283	30	.303	41	.235	94	.268	139	.683	39
Mike Heath	.255	94	.231	114	.244	111	.256	89	.322	20	.319	30	.352	37	.600	66
Steve Henderson	.293	31	.345	--	.250	99	.351	1	.426	1	.300	--	.333	59	.765	12
Donnie Hill	.268	68	.354	5	.268	73	.300	9	.337	13	.333	17	.309	94	.560	89
Dave Kingman	.235	130	.252	80	.223	138	.252	94	.219	133	.188	138	.301	105	.619	61
Carney Lansford	.278	50	.270	60	.302	31	.250	97	.259	99	.344	14	.250	147	.440	141
Dwayne Murphy	.229	137	.253	78	.215	145	.249	100	.211	139	.200	130	.333	59	.500	106
Tony Phillips	.284	43	.231	--	.288	--	.273	--	.205	--	.000	--	.381	--	1.000	--
Mickey Tettleton	.255	92	.211	--	.245	109	.257	82	.212	138	.136	153	.396	8	.500	106
Team Average	.265	6	.263	3	.256	12	.272	1	.276	5	.251	6	.315	9	.607	5
League Average	.262		.259		.266		.256		.268		.248		.321		.587	

Pitching vs. Left and Right Handed Batters

		BA	Rank	SA	Rank	OBA	Rank	HR %	Rank	BB %	Rank	SO %	Rank
Keith Atherton	vs. Lefties	.258	59	.436	85	.349	81	3.68	102	12.70	107	13.23	54
	vs. Righties	.211	14	.417	81	.267	15	4.93	126	7.32	60	21.14	12
Tim Birtsas	vs. Lefties	.221	18	.379	51	.342	73	3.16	87	14.41	123	10.17	99
	vs. Righties	.242	45	.423	83	.354	101	3.52	92	14.62	128	16.21	41
Chris Codiroli	vs. Lefties	.248	49	.380	53	.294	27	2.09	46	6.21	25	11.84	75
	vs. Righties	.271	87	.430	89	.346	90	3.23	84	10.00	98	10.87	100
Jay Howell	vs. Lefties	.254	57	.313	19	.318	49	0.50	6	8.93	63	16.07	33
	vs. Righties	.270	85	.374	45	.314	61	2.30	43	5.79	33	16.84	38
Tommy John	vs. Lefties	.310	--	.393	--	.352	--	1.19	--	6.59	--	9.89	--
	vs. Righties	.337	131	.515	128	.387	126	2.96	78	7.19	54	5.23	132
Bill Krueger	vs. Lefties	.317	122	.439	86	.397	120	2.44	57	11.35	96	7.09	120
	vs. Righties	.266	77	.401	67	.338	87	2.11	37	9.94	97	8.63	124
Rick Langford	vs. Lefties	.294	96	.495	116	.358	89	4.59	123	9.17	69	8.33	115
	vs. Righties	.231	--	.355	--	.256	--	2.48	--	3.15	--	8.66	--
Steve McCatty	vs. Lefties	.277	79	.446	89	.379	107	2.70	69	13.22	115	9.20	109
	vs. Righties	.293	112	.435	92	.359	110	3.26	88	8.61	81	9.57	118
Steve Ontiveros	vs. Lefties	.216	16	.321	22	.277	12	1.49	27	7.33	40	8.67	113
	vs. Righties	.128	1	.192	1	.187	1	1.60	21	5.97	37	17.16	32
Jose Rijo	vs. Lefties	.280	82	.488	113	.379	107	4.00	111	12.84	109	25.68	1
	vs. Righties	.195	--	.265	--	.254	--	0.88	--	7.26	--	21.77	--
Mike Warren	vs. Lefties	.329	128	.776	131	.477	131	11.76	131	19.27	130	17.43	25
	vs. Righties	.211	11	.360	36	.313	59	2.63	58	12.69	125	21.64	9
Curt Young	vs. Lefties	.208	--	.354	--	.269	--	4.17	--	5.77	--	5.77	--
	vs. Righties	.331	129	.690	133	.407	132	9.15	133	11.73	120	9.88	113
Team Average	vs. Lefties	.261	5	.411	9	.333	6	2.91	9	9.53	10	12.23	11
	vs. Righties	.257	8	.413	10	.330	10	3.18	12	9.64	13	12.53	13
League Average	vs. Lefties	.265		.408		.333		2.74		9.21		12.94	
	vs. Righties	.259		.404		.322		2.88		8.19		14.14	

Pitching with Runners on Base and Bases Empty

		BA	Rank	SA	Rank	OBA	Rank	HR %	Rank	BB %	Rank	SO %	Rank
Keith Atherton	Runners On	.204	5	.419	77	.290	16	4.84	124	11.06	101	17.05	23
	Bases Empty	.255	68	.430	93	.317	67	4.00	114	8.26	68	18.35	20
Tim Birtsas	Runners On	.216	10	.372	39	.336	63	3.03	83	14.79	128	18.66	12
	Bases Empty	.255	71	.448	104	.365	111	3.79	110	14.41	126	12.06	80
Chris Codiroli	Runners On	.247	36	.361	30	.298	26	1.86	36	7.13	34	11.64	83
	Bases Empty	.268	90	.435	95	.334	85	3.17	87	8.66	77	11.19	92
Jay Howell	Runners On	.254	45	.321	11	.321	38	1.04	14	9.05	68	16.74	24
	Bases Empty	.269	92	.363	36	.311	55	1.65	22	5.70	23	16.06	34
Tommy John	Runners On	.367	131	.507	121	.418	130	2.00	41	8.38	51	8.38	121
	Bases Empty	.304	123	.471	112	.349	98	2.94	74	5.96	26	4.59	130
Bill Krueger	Runners On	.280	83	.411	72	.343	76	2.18	49	9.03	67	9.35	110
	Bases Empty	.273	97	.407	77	.357	105	2.17	35	11.26	111	7.42	128
Rick Langford	Runners On	.222	--	.389	--	.293	--	3.33	--	8.91	--	7.92	--
	Bases Empty	.286	107	.443	101	.315	64	3.57	99	4.11	10	8.90	121
Steve McCatty	Runners On	.301	106	.485	110	.381	120	4.29	112	10.94	99	8.33	122
	Bases Empty	.272	96	.396	65	.356	104	1.78	26	10.47	102	10.47	106
Steve Ontiveros	Runners On	.149	1	.198	1	.198	1	0.83	10	6.02	19	12.03	77
	Bases Empty	.196	6	.312	10	.265	11	2.17	35	7.28	54	13.25	67
Jose Rijo	Runners On	.238	27	.314	8	.328	47	0.95	12	10.48	92	23.39	2
	Bases Empty	.241	46	.436	96	.318	70	3.76	106	10.14	97	24.32	3
Mike Warren	Runners On	.282	--	.541	--	.422	--	7.06	--	19.27	--	17.43	--
	Bases Empty	.246	52	.535	128	.358	108	6.14	128	12.69	120	21.64	6
Curt Young	Runners On	.319	--	.611	--	.405	--	6.94	--	11.90	--	7.14	--
	Bases Empty	.288	110	.602	131	.354	102	8.47	131	9.23	86	10.00	109
Team Average	Runners On	.261	4	.407	5	.336	7	2.86	7	10.28	12	12.40	11
	Bases Empty	.257	6	.417	12	.327	11	3.23	12	9.02	13	12.41	13
League Average	Runners On	.271		.416		.338		2.85		9.26		13.25	
	Bases Empty	.254		.397		.318		2.80		8.14		13.92	

Overall Pitching Compared to Late Inning Pressure Situations

		BA	Rank	SA	Rank	OBA	Rank	HR %	Rank	BB %	Rank	SO %	Rank
Keith Atherton	Overall	.231	17	.425	89	.303	30	4.40	123	9.66	88	17.70	19
	Pressure	.242	46	.427	86	.335	68	3.82	99	12.15	98	18.78	21
Tim Birtsas	Overall	.238	24	.415	78	.352	98	3.45	100	14.58	128	15.06	42
	Pressure	.364	--	.636	--	.417	--	9.09	--	7.69	--	15.38	--
Chris Codiroli	Overall	.259	65	.403	63	.319	52	2.61	60	8.00	58	11.38	92
	Pressure	.229	37	.398	70	.319	53	3.61	96	11.58	87	9.47	103
Jay Howell	Overall	.261	73	.341	17	.316	51	1.33	11	7.49	51	16.43	27
	Pressure	.258	63	.338	38	.305	44	1.34	29	6.40	29	16.46	32
Tommy John	Overall	.331	131	.486	124	.379	123	2.54	57	7.05	35	6.30	130
	Pressure	.370	--	.630	--	.379	--	3.70	--	3.23	--	0.00	--
Bill Krueger	Overall	.276	96	.409	68	.351	96	2.18	36	10.24	98	8.31	125
	Pressure	.207	--	.276	--	.258	--	0.00	--	6.45	--	3.23	--
Steve McCatty	Overall	.286	107	.440	97	.368	118	3.01	79	10.70	103	9.40	119
	Pressure	.303	106	.485	110	.410	118	3.03	81	14.29	114	7.14	118
Steve Ontiveros	Overall	.174	1	.259	1	.234	1	1.54	16	6.69	28	12.68	73
	Pressure	.159	5	.206	3	.221	4	0.79	19	7.30	38	13.14	63
Jose Rijo	Overall	.239	27	.382	43	.322	56	2.52	56	10.29	100	23.90	3
	Pressure	.267	72	.400	72	.333	63	3.33	92	8.57	52	20.00	16
Team Average	Overall	.259	6	.412	8	.331	9	3.07	10	9.59	13	12.41	13
	Pressure	.245	4	.360	3	.319	3	2.29	3	9.69	8	13.24	9
League Average	Overall	.261		.406		.327		2.82		8.63		13.62	
	Pressure	.258		.392		.332		2.71		9.52		14.05	

Additional Miscellaneous Pitching Comparisons

	Grass Surface BA	Rank	Artificial Surface BA	Rank	Home Games BA	Rank	Road Games BA	Rank	Runners in Scoring Position BA	Rank	Runners in Scoring Pos and Two Outs BA	Rank	Leading Off Inning OBA	Rank
Keith Atherton	.223	12	.276	82	.209	9	.256	51	.181	4	.125	4	.341	88
Tim Birtsas	.245	40	.191	9	.239	39	.237	25	.216	16	.149	9	.366	110
Chris Codiroli	.256	63	.273	79	.231	23	.284	92	.290	94	.266	81	.340	87
Jay Howell	.249	46	.366	--	.260	75	.263	66	.265	67	.160	12	.256	9
Tommy John	.311	120	.415	130	.293	109	.357	129	.309	110	.244	72	.362	108
Bill Krueger	.282	98	.245	43	.281	99	.272	81	.297	99	.279	94	.429	129
Rick Langford	.232	21	.367	129	.204	--	.299	106	.264	--	.286	99	.254	8
Steve McCatty	.285	102	.291	98	.315	127	.262	63	.320	114	.214	42	.346	96
Steve Mura	.206	4	.275	80	.187	--	.252	--	.222	--	.250	--	.306	--
Steve Ontiveros	.179	2	.149	--	.155	1	.198	5	.138	--	.214	42	.279	25
Jose Rijo	.229	17	.280	87	.247	--	.234	23	.247	43	.207	35	.448	131
Mike Warren	.250	49	.314	--	.250	57	.275	--	.246	40	.080	1	.264	--
Curt Young	.284	101	.371	--	.301	115	.299	--	.333	--	.350	--	.327	--
Team Average	.252	3	.289	13	.245	4	.272	11	.266	7	.220	1	.337	14
League Average	.262		.259		.256		.266		.268		.248		.321	

SEATTLE MARINERS

Can you identify this promising pitcher by his statistics? He is young, around 27 years old, and although he has pitched exclusively for losing teams, only six American League pitchers have won more games over the past four seasons: Jack Morris, Ron Guidry, Dan Petry, Dave Stieb, Charlie Hough, and Scott McGregor. And of all the A.L. pitchers who have started at least 100 games since 1982, only Dave Stieb has compiled a lower ERA. The statistics:

Year	W	L	ERA	GS	CG	SHO	IP	H	BB	SO
1982	12	13	3.43	35	5	3	247.0	225	77	209
1983	11	15	3.27	32	5	2	203.2	178	79	130
1984	17	10	3.40	33	5	2	225.0	188	118	204
1985	17	10	3.46	34	14	2	247.0	230	70	155
Totals	57	48	3.39	134	29	9	922.2	821	344	698

Still don't know? These are the composite statistics of the Seattle Mariners' Annual Promising Young Pitcher: Floyd Bannister in 1982, Matt Young in 1983, Mark Langston in 1984, and Mike Moore last season. For four seasons in a row, Seattle has developed a young pitcher who appeared to be on the brink of stardom-plus. Judging by the figures above, Seattle could have had the league's best pitching staff by now had those pitchers fulfilled their potential. But Young and Langston took the express train to oblivion, and Bannister, who signed with Chicago as a free agent in 1983, also failed to live up to those great expectations. Here are the statistics of each of those pitchers since the seasons above:

	W	L	ERA	GS	CG	SHO	IP	H	BB	SO
Bannister										
1983	16	10	3.35	34	5	2	217.1	191	71	193
1984	14	11	4.83	33	4	0	218.0	211	80	152
1985	10	14	4.87	34	4	1	210.2	211	100	198
Young										
1984	6	8	5.72	22	1	0	113.1	141	57	73
1985	12	19	4.91	35	5	2	218.1	242	76	136
Langston										
1985	7	14	5.47	24	2	0	126.2	122	91	72
Totals	65	76	4.73	182	21	5	1104.1	1118	475	824

The starting rotation will likely determine Seattle's success, or lack of it, in the 1986 season. With the rapid development of young hitters like Alvin Davis, Jim Presley, and Phil Bradley, and the resurrection of long-ball threat Gorman Thomas, the Mariners finally have a lineup capable of supporting a reasonably equipped pitching staff. But unless Young or Langston regains his earlier form, and Moore can at least approach the numbers he put on the board last season, Seattle again faces a hopeless situation. Last season Seattle's starters, with the exception of Moore, were dreadful. Compare Moore's outstanding figures with what was "accomplished" by all of Seattle's other starting pitchers:

Starter	W	L	ERA	GS	CG	SHO	IP	H	R	ER	HR	BB	SO
Moore	17	10	3.47	34	14	2	246.1	228	100	95	18	70	154
Others	35	70	5.73	128	9	3	679.2	764	472	433	82	352	386

Seattle's pitching problems, oddly enough, led them to deal away a pitcher during the off-season. The Mariners traded reliever Ed Vande Berg to Los Angeles for Steve Yeager. Vande Berg was coveted by several teams at the winter meetings in December, and, according to the law of supply and demand, one would have expected that Seattle could extract a greater bounty than a 37-year-old catcher with gimpy knees and a .228 career batting average (.214 since 1978, including .198 against right-handed pitching). But Seattle was determined to acquire a veteran catcher to work with their young pitching staff.

Timing was the key to understanding the deal; it was made just two months after Kansas City's victory in the 1985 World Series. Seattle is apparently trying to mirror the move made by the Royals a year earlier, when Kansas City acquired Jim Sundberg, a 34-year-old catcher with a .238 average over the previous three seasons, to handle their own staff of young pitchers. There's no questions that everybody loves a winner, but in baseball it traditionally goes a step further: Everybody copies a winner. But what if Kansas City had lost Game 5 of the American League playoffs to Toronto, and Sundberg and his buddies had spent the winter still needing their American Express cards wherever they traveled? Wouldn't Vande Berg have fetched a different and more lucrative return at the winter market? That question will be posed all summer long if Yeager can't match the performance of his American League alter ego, and coax the potential from even one of Seattle's once-promising pitchers.

You Always Hurt the One You Love

One interesting side aspect of the Yeager trade, as well as several others made during the off-season, is the performance of catchers who bat against former teammates. With everything we've learned about the guessing games played by pitchers and catchers against hitters, it would seem that a pitcher's ex-catcher would have a distinct advantage hitting against him, wouldn't it? Well, to put it simply, he does.

Since so many winter transactions involved catchers—the Yeager trade, Ozzie Virgil to the Braves, Ron Hassey to the White Sox, Dann Bilardello to the Phillies, Alex Trevino to the Dodgers—we decided to take a look at matchups of catchers and pitchers who faced each other at least five times before playing together, and at least another five times after being separated. We found 14 such combinations over the past 11 years: Gary Allenson and Brian Downing vs. Frank Tanana; Carlton Fisk vs. Dennis Eckersley and Mike Torrez; Steve Nicosia vs. Larry McWilliams; Darrell Porter vs. Doug Bird; Ted Simmons vs. Jamie Easterly and Don Sutton; Jim Sundberg vs. Doyle Alexander, Bert Blyleven, Sutton, and Tanana; and Butch Wynegar vs. Alexander and Tommy John. Apparently, the rapport that develops when a catcher learns to think with his pitchers doesn't evaporate when they're divorced, and the settlement terms clearly favor the catcher thereafter. The composite batting lines from those matchups, before and after, follow:

	AB	H	2B	3B	HR	BB	SO	BA	SA	OBA
Before	235	46	10	2	6	27	37	.196	.332	.283
After	178	50	12	0	6	10	17	.281	.449	.323

If we limit our study to batter-pitcher matchups involving 10 or more at bats both before and after, the difference is even greater—

.156 vs. .304, and all seven of those combinations produced higher averages after than before. Among the outstanding individual splits: Downing vs. Tanana (2-for-19 before, 8-for-24, 3 HR after); Fisk vs. Torrez (7-for-25 before, 5-for-7 after); and Sundberg vs. Blyleven (1-for-16 before, 5-for-16 after).

Although the Dodgers may have saved themselves some grief by sending Yeager to the American League, Seattle may derive a bonus from the deal, because Yeager will now be batting against many of the pitchers he handled for Los Angeles: Joe Beckwith, Burt Hooton, Charlie Hough, Tommy John, and Don Sutton. We'll keep you posted.

Star Search

We mentioned earlier that Seattle's lineup houses a number of excellent young hitters, specifically Alvin Davis, Jim Presley, and Phil Bradley. But while first Davis and then Presley captured most of the attention, Bradley, one of the league's leading hitters during his first two seasons, has been largely ignored. Consider the statistics that each player has compiled over the past two seasons:

Player	AB	R	H	2B	3B	HR	RBI	RDI%	BB	SO	SB	BA	SA	OBA
Bradley	963	149	289	45	12	26	112	.276	89	190	43	.300	.453	.368
Davis	1145	158	327	67	4	45	194	.305	187	149	6	.286	.469	.386
Presley	821	98	214	45	2	38	120	.287	50	163	3	.261	.459	.301

We wouldn't want to have to choose from among them at this early stage of their careers; who wouldn't love to have all three? We would, however, like to call your attention to Bradley, who seems to have been denied appropriate acclaim only because of the notice given his equally talented teammates. And because time may prove him to be the best of the bunch.

When two or more young teammates develop at the same time, it's not unusual for the public to focus its attention on the wrong man. Sometimes, the error is merely in not recognizing a pair as equals. Tom Brunansky, eclipsed by the shadow of Minnesota teammate Kent Hrbek, has become the most obscure home run threat in baseball. Dale Murphy's promising rookie-season totals of 23 home runs and 79 RBIs were blurred in the focus on Bob Horner, who stepped off the Arizona State campus and posted similar figures in 60 fewer games than Murphy in 1978. These errors of judgment aren't limited to small media markets or second-division teams

either. Thurman Munson labored under a similar burden early in his career, playing before fans who expected Bobby Murcer to be the Yankees' next MVP. Munson turned out to be the one.

In other cases, however, the more heralded player fizzles as his teammate rises. Given a choice today between Ron Kittle and Greg Walker, would any sane general manager choose Kittle? But following the 1983 season, when Kittle blasted 35 home runs and drove in 100 runs, Kittle was treated like the heir to the throne, Walker like the prince consort. A decade ago, Fred Lynn and Jim Rice arrived simultaneously in Boston. Lynn was the American League's MVP as a rookie in 1975, and Rice has battled since then to shake the stigma of being "the other rookie," despite his obviously superior talents. It took several years for most of the baseball community to appreciate the skill of Paul Blair, and nearly as long to realize that his teammate Curt Blefary would never fulfill the potential he suggested when both were rookies with the Baltimore Orioles in 1965.

Remember Sonny Jackson? He broke in at shortstop with Houston in 1966, and during that rookie season, *The Sporting News* had this to say: "It may be that Sonny, if he reaches that potential of greatness which is only inches away, will be a player who can move the audience by the sheer skill, grace, and speed he displays on the field." After Braves general manager Paul Richards traded for Jackson following a disappointing (.237) sophomore season, he defended the shortstop's poor season by citing his injuries, and said, "Jackson had an off year, but in 1966 you couldn't have gotten him for a Honus Wagner." We're not talking here about Reggie Jackson. Or Shoeless Joe Jackson. Hell, we're not even talking about Michael Jackson! And while Paul Richards was expending all that effort to pry Jackson away, few noticed that his double-play partner was a pretty fair prospect named Joe Morgan. Little Joe remained underappreciated for years, especially by Houston, who would eventually deal to Cincinnati this one player you might not want to trade even-up for Honus Wagner.

We're not trying to say that we expect Alvin Davis or Jim Presley to suffer a fate similar to Jackson's or Blefary's—but you never can tell. We just want you to be aware that there's another star on the Seattle horizon, one shining just as bright. Which one is going to be one of the all-time greats? Let's not be in too much of a hurry to make up our minds; our collective track record leaves something to be desired.

WON-LOST RECORD BY STARTING POSITION

SEATTLE 74-88	C	1B	2B	3B	SS	LF	CF	RF	P	DH	Leadoff	Relief	Starts
Salome Barojas	-	-	-	-	-	-	-	-	0-4	-	-	3-10	0-4
Jim Beattie	-	-	-	-	-	-	-	-	8-7	-	-	0-3	8-7
Karl Best	-	-	-	-	-	-	-	-	-	-	-	7-8	-
Barry Bonnell	-	1-2	-	-	-	2-3	-	5-5	-	2-0	-	-	10-10
Phil Bradley	-	-	-	-	-	57-67	13-14	1-7	-	-	0-1	-	71-88
Ivan Calderon	-	0-1	-	-	-	15-17	-	11-9	-	1-0	-	-	27-27
Al Chambers	-	-	-	-	-	-	-	-	-	-	-	-	-
Darnell Coles	-	-	-	2-0	4-8	0-1	-	-	-	0-1	0-1	-	6-10
Al Cowens	-	-	-	-	-	-	-	51-58	-	2-2	-	-	53-60
Alvin Davis	-	72-82	-	-	-	-	-	-	-	-	-	-	72-82
Dave Geisel	-	-	-	-	-	-	-	-	-	-	-	3-9	-
Dave Henderson	-	-	-	-	-	-	55-64	6-9	-	-	-	-	61-73
Bob Kearney	42-53	-	-	-	-	-	-	-	-	-	-	-	42-53
Mark Langston	-	-	-	-	-	-	-	-	10-14	-	-	-	10-14
Jack Lazorko	-	-	-	-	-	-	-	-	-	-	-	5-10	-
Jim Lewis	-	-	-	-	-	-	-	-	0-1	-	-	0-1	0-1
Bob Long	-	-	-	-	-	-	-	-	-	-	-	2-26	-
Paul Mirabella	-	-	-	-	-	-	-	-	-	-	-	2-8	-
Mike Moore	-	-	-	-	-	-	-	19-15	-	-	-	0-1	19-15
Mike Morgan	-	-	-	-	-	-	-	-	1-1	-	-	-	1-1
John Moses	-	-	-	-	-	6-10	-	-	-	-	-	-	6-10
Ricky Nelson	-	-	-	-	-	-	-	-	-	-	-	-	-
Edwin Nunez	-	-	-	-	-	-	-	-	-	-	-	40-30	-
Spike Owen	-	-	-	-	53-58	-	-	-	-	-	1-3	-	53-58
Jack Perconte	-	-	54-68	-	-	-	-	-	-	-	54-68	-	54-68
Ken Phelps	-	1-3	-	-	-	-	-	-	-	7-15	-	-	8-18
Jim Presley	-	-	-	69-85	-	-	-	-	-	-	-	-	69-85
Domingo Ramos	-	-	6-4	1-1	11-16	-	-	-	-	-	13-10	-	18-21
Harold Reynolds	-	-	14-16	-	-	-	-	-	-	-	6-5	-	14-16
Donnie Scott	25-23	-	-	-	-	-	-	-	-	-	-	-	25-23
Brian Snyder	-	-	-	-	-	-	-	-	3-3	-	-	3-6	3-3
Mike Stanton	-	-	-	-	-	-	-	-	-	-	-	7-17	-
Billy Swift	-	-	-	-	-	-	-	-	11-10	-	-	1-1	11-10
Danny Tartabull	-	-	-	2-2	6-6	-	-	-	-	-	-	-	8-8
Gorman Thomas	-	-	-	-	-	-	-	-	-	62-70	-	-	62-70
Roy Thomas	-	-	-	-	-	-	-	-	-	-	-	12-28	-
Dave Tobik	-	-	-	-	-	-	-	-	-	-	-	2-6	-
Dave Valle	7-12	-	-	-	-	-	-	-	-	-	-	-	7-12
Ed Vande Berg	-	-	-	-	-	-	-	-	-	-	-	30-46	-
Bill Wilkinson	-	-	-	-	-	-	-	-	0-2	-	-	-	0-2
Frank Wills	-	-	-	-	-	-	-	-	7-11	-	-	1-5	7-11
Matt Young	-	-	-	-	-	-	-	-	15-20	-	-	1-1	15-20

Batting vs. Left and Right Handed Pitchers

		BA	Rank	SA	Rank	OBA	Rank	HR %	Rank	BB %	Rank	SO %	Rank
Phil Bradley	vs. Lefties	.267	78	.483	36	.337	82	5.11	29	8.59	75	20.71	135
	vs. Righties	.312	9	.503	12	.375	18	3.66	51	7.36	94	17.05	116
Ivan Calderon	vs. Lefties	.296	40	.535	18	.383	17	4.23	47	12.35	30	22.22	143
	vs. Righties	.281	46	.504	11	.331	69	3.60	53	5.92	120	17.76	128
Al Cowens	vs. Lefties	.264	83	.486	33	.331	87	3.57	53	9.55	61	7.01	23
	vs. Righties	.266	63	.436	55	.300	115	2.88	75	4.55	138	13.64	81
Alvin Davis	vs. Lefties	.239	124	.358	118	.340	77	2.27	87	13.11	24	12.62	81
	vs. Righties	.308	10	.478	25	.399	5	3.48	57	13.38	16	9.55	40
Dave Henderson	vs. Lefties	.280	61	.439	67	.345	69	2.27	87	7.59	97	13.10	90
	vs. Righties	.227	128	.370	99	.298	119	2.97	72	9.00	63	20.68	146
Bob Kearney	vs. Lefties	.196	152	.320	135	.257	149	3.09	63	5.66	126	10.38	45
	vs. Righties	.264	68	.370	100	.287	130	1.44	108	2.27	156	21.82	148
Spike Owen	vs. Lefties	.256	92	.356	120	.302	121	1.11	118	6.25	119	9.38	36
	vs. Righties	.260	80	.378	93	.329	70	1.91	100	9.43	54	6.06	12
Jack Perconte	vs. Lefties	.242	120	.273	147	.320	104	0.00	131	10.14	54	9.46	37
	vs. Righties	.272	57	.365	105	.341	55	0.57	142	8.88	65	5.58	6
Jim Presley	vs. Lefties	.344	5	.573	6	.398	11	5.10	30	8.52	77	12.50	79
	vs. Righties	.249	99	.450	43	.295	125	4.84	24	6.46	110	17.37	121
Domingo Ramos	vs. Lefties	.145	157	.200	157	.242	151	0.00	131	11.11	40	12.70	83
	vs. Righties	.221	--	.274	--	.280	--	0.88	--	7.87	--	11.81	--
Donnie Scott	vs. Lefties	.250	--	.429	--	.290	--	3.57	--	6.25	--	25.00	--
	vs. Righties	.217	139	.344	122	.272	138	1.91	99	7.51	90	19.08	139
Gorman Thomas	vs. Lefties	.211	145	.493	28	.326	94	8.55	2	14.92	11	23.20	148
	vs. Righties	.217	138	.431	61	.332	66	5.72	10	14.50	7	21.37	147
Team Average	vs. Lefties	.253	13	.417	5	.331	7	3.33	4	10.13	3	14.66	12
	vs. Righties	.256	9	.410	6	.324	9	3.01	4	8.71	5	15.46	14
League Average	vs. Lefties	.266		.416		.333		2.91		8.95		13.77	
	vs. Righties	.259		.401		.324		2.78		8.49		13.56	

Batting with Runners on Base and Bases Empty

		BA	Rank	SA	Rank	OBA	Rank	HR %	Rank	BB %	Rank	SO %	Rank
Phil Bradley	Runners On	.311	29	.487	34	.387	20	3.30	63	9.24	78	18.79	142
	Bases Empty	.291	23	.505	14	.348	26	4.62	38	6.50	101	17.50	123
Ivan Calderon	Runners On	.261	93	.446	60	.337	85	2.17	87	9.52	65	16.19	117
	Bases Empty	.305	9	.568	4	.359	18	5.08	26	7.03	92	21.88	148
Al Cowens	Runners On	.262	91	.413	79	.313	114	2.43	82	7.05	117	8.81	37
	Bases Empty	.268	53	.484	21	.308	103	3.66	52	5.38	75	13.85	75
Alvin Davis	Runners On	.264	86	.406	86	.372	38	2.76	73	15.21	15	11.97	72
	Bases Empty	.306	8	.469	32	.389	6	3.40	58	11.68	23	9.24	35
Dave Henderson	Runners On	.267	80	.394	97	.319	109	2.54	78	6.98	118	15.89	114
	Bases Empty	.218	136	.383	95	.302	109	3.01	73	10.07	41	21.14	144
Bob Kearney	Runners On	.270	78	.362	119	.297	128	1.42	106	1.96	155	13.73	96
	Bases Empty	.220	134	.348	119	.260	149	2.44	89	4.62	138	21.97	149
Spike Owen	Runners On	.257	103	.386	101	.303	123	1.43	105	6.37	125	7.01	19
	Bases Empty	.259	74	.363	107	.335	52	1.89	102	10.17	37	6.78	14
Jack Perconte	Runners On	.243	127	.254	153	.312	116	0.00	142	8.82	90	6.86	18
	Bases Empty	.276	38	.391	89	.349	24	0.66	138	9.47	48	6.51	10
Jim Presley	Runners On	.261	94	.463	47	.325	99	4.67	30	9.80	61	15.20	107
	Bases Empty	.288	25	.502	16	.322	81	5.11	25	4.56	141	16.72	115
Domingo Ramos	Runners On	.241	--	.293	--	.292	--	0.00	--	7.35	--	10.29	--
	Bases Empty	.173	156	.227	157	.254	151	0.91	129	9.84	44	13.11	70
Donnie Scott	Runners On	.224	--	.408	--	.250	--	3.95	--	4.71	--	22.35	--
	Bases Empty	.220	131	.321	137	.292	126	0.92	128	9.17	54	18.33	131
Gorman Thomas	Runners On	.208	149	.476	40	.343	80	8.00	3	16.88	8	22.73	149
	Bases Empty	.222	130	.423	61	.316	91	5.13	24	12.03	21	21.05	141
Team Average	Runners On	.256	13	.407	11	.330	12	3.14	5	9.75	4	15.15	13
	Bases Empty	.255	7	.417	5	.322	4	3.07	5	8.60	4	15.30	13
League Average	Runners On	.271		.416		.338		2.85		9.26		13.25	
	Bases Empty	.254		.397		.318		2.80		8.14		13.92	

Overall Batting Compared to Late Inning Pressure Situations

		BA	Rank	SA	Rank	OBA	Rank	HR %	Rank	BB %	Rank	SO %	Rank	RDI %	Rank
Barry Bonnell	Overall	.243	--	.342	--	.282	--	0.90	--	5.13	--	16.24	--	.182	--
	Pressure	.222	--	.444	--	.300	--	3.70	--	10.00	--	16.67	--	.333	55
Phil Bradley	Overall	.300	13	.498	13	.365	20	4.06	43	7.70	93	18.07	130	.281	92
	Pressure	.304	35	.554	12	.350	57	6.52	18	6.93	105	16.83	108	.375	32
Ivan Calderon	Overall	.286	33	.514	9	.349	40	3.81	51	8.15	85	19.31	139	.281	93
	Pressure	.300	37	.633	4	.382	30	10.00	2	11.76	46	17.65	112	.167	--
Al Cowens	Overall	.265	71	.451	37	.310	112	3.10	68	6.16	123	11.50	54	.325	42
	Pressure	.250	82	.433	53	.303	98	5.00	35	7.58	95	16.67	103	.438	15
Alvin Davis	Overall	.287	30	.441	51	.381	8	3.11	67	13.29	17	10.49	45	.273	99
	Pressure	.259	71	.309	115	.368	39	0.00	113	14.74	24	9.47	33	.136	139
Dave Henderson	Overall	.241	124	.388	99	.310	113	2.79	79	8.63	71	18.71	137	.288	83
	Pressure	.311	31	.541	18	.363	45	6.76	17	7.41	98	18.52	122	.211	114
Bob Kearney	Overall	.243	120	.354	125	.277	146	1.97	101	3.37	153	18.10	131	.190	154
	Pressure	.297	39	.432	54	.316	87	2.70	67	2.44	147	24.39	148	.333	--
Spike Owen	Overall	.259	88	.372	115	.322	93	1.70	108	8.65	69	6.87	15	.268	105
	Pressure	.156	152	.156	158	.296	111	0.00	113	16.07	15	14.29	82	.364	40
Jack Perconte	Overall	.264	76	.340	135	.335	66	0.41	146	9.23	61	6.64	13	.190	155
	Pressure	.327	20	.473	38	.439	8	0.00	113	16.42	14	7.46	19	.000	158
Ken Phelps	Overall	.207	--	.466	--	.343	--	7.76	--	17.14	--	23.57	--	.209	--
	Pressure	.185	141	.296	120	.333	73	3.70	47	18.18	7	24.24	147	.300	71
Jim Presley	Overall	.275	52	.484	18	.324	88	4.91	25	7.04	106	16.00	115	.274	98
	Pressure	.179	146	.256	139	.256	139	1.28	107	9.20	76	22.99	141	.133	141
Donnie Scott	Overall	.222	146	.357	122	.275	149	2.16	98	7.32	100	20.00	143	.233	132
	Pressure	.182	144	.455	43	.182	157	6.06	24	0.00	154	12.12	64	.000	158
Gorman Thomas	Overall	.215	153	.450	38	.330	74	6.61	5	14.63	9	21.95	150	.237	128
	Pressure	.154	154	.231	147	.273	127	1.54	99	14.10	29	16.67	103	.231	100
Team Average	Overall	.255	9	.412	6	.326	7	3.10	4	9.12	4	15.23	14	.256	14
	Pressure	.237	12	.377	8	.315	11	3.11	5	10.26	3	17.22	13	.237	13
League Average	Overall	.261		.406		.327		2.82		8.63		13.62		.287	
	Pressure	.253		.381		.323		2.74		9.11		14.40		.273	

Additional Miscellaneous Batting Comparisons

	Grass Surface BA	Rank	Artificial Surface BA	Rank	Home Games BA	Rank	Road Games BA	Rank	Runners in Scoring Position BA	Rank	Runners in Scoring Pos and Two Outs BA	Rank	Leading Off Inning OBA	Rank	Runners on 3B with less than 2 Outs RDI %	Rank
Barry Bonnell	.283	--	.215	132	.217	--	.275	--	.200	--	.167	--	.348	--	.429	--
Phil Bradley	.320	6	.287	42	.305	28	.294	15	.302	43	.242	84	.336	58	.500	106
Ivan Calderon	.270	--	.294	32	.297	36	.273	49	.327	18	.100	--	.488	--	.588	71
Al Cowens	.262	81	.268	61	.284	53	.249	101	.308	35	.327	25	.327	76	.621	60
Alvin Davis	.280	48	.292	36	.293	40	.281	34	.275	79	.239	89	.389	11	.625	58
Dave Henderson	.203	149	.265	65	.249	106	.233	126	.291	57	.274	50	.286	119	.550	93
Bob Kearney	.252	--	.237	107	.238	120	.248	102	.295	51	.304	34	.269	134	.167	158
Spike Owen	.214	--	.281	50	.274	67	.238	120	.280	73	.333	17	.373	22	.588	71
Jack Perconte	.306	17	.239	102	.251	98	.277	38	.255	104	.236	92	.336	56	.563	86
Ken Phelps	.188	--	.221	127	.214	--	.200	--	.139	--	.071	--	.280	--	.500	--
Jim Presley	.264	76	.283	46	.264	81	.288	21	.273	83	.284	46	.311	93	.531	99
Domingo Ramos	.195	--	.198	144	.196	--	.196	153	.229	--	.222	--	.224	154	.455	137
Harold Reynolds	.162	--	.134	158	.136	--	.156	--	.148	--	.083	--	.294	--	.333	--
Donnie Scott	.182	--	.244	93	.263	82	.174	--	.267	90	.250	--	.239	--	.467	132
Gorman Thomas	.247	108	.199	143	.207	149	.223	137	.162	156	.164	146	.353	35	.486	123
Team Average	.254	10	.256	5	.258	11	.253	9	.261	10	.247	7	.326	4	.514	14
League Average	.262		.259		.266		.256		.268		.248		.321		.587	

Pitching vs. Left and Right Handed Batters

		BA	Rank	SA	Rank	OBA	Rank	HR %	Rank	BB %	Rank	SO %	Rank
Salome Barojas	vs. Lefties	.323	125	.516	120	.429	129	3.23	90	15.93	126	4.42	129
	vs. Righties	.292	110	.408	77	.368	121	2.50	53	10.95	115	16.06	42
Jim Beattie	vs. Lefties	.313	116	.480	108	.401	125	3.33	95	12.99	112	11.86	73
	vs. Righties	.319	128	.458	109	.367	120	2.78	65	6.33	42	15.19	49
Mark Langston	vs. Lefties	.228	--	.392	--	.344	--	3.80	--	15.05	--	18.28	--
	vs. Righties	.260	69	.463	113	.380	125	4.75	123	15.91	133	11.36	96
Mike Moore	vs. Lefties	.226	23	.337	27	.285	18	1.75	34	7.64	41	15.45	36
	vs. Righties	.272	91	.389	57	.319	63	2.15	42	5.96	36	15.01	54
Edwin Nunez	vs. Lefties	.211	12	.388	55	.309	37	4.61	124	12.43	105	11.86	73
	vs. Righties	.254	60	.411	78	.296	35	3.24	86	5.97	37	18.41	26
Bill Swift	vs. Lefties	.308	109	.485	111	.383	113	2.69	68	10.07	81	8.05	118
	vs. Righties	.243	48	.290	7	.307	53	0.48	4	7.69	68	13.25	74
Roy Thomas	vs. Lefties	.176	3	.284	6	.319	50	2.03	43	16.76	128	11.89	71
	vs. Righties	.225	27	.343	23	.288	26	2.81	67	8.50	79	24.00	3
Ed Vande Berg	vs. Lefties	.246	44	.331	25	.333	64	0.85	11	10.95	94	11.68	77
	vs. Righties	.298	117	.447	101	.365	119	2.13	41	10.06	101	11.32	97
Frank Wills	vs. Lefties	.287	86	.469	101	.387	115	3.88	105	14.05	119	12.42	66
	vs. Righties	.240	42	.395	61	.323	71	4.00	110	10.64	111	12.34	87
Matt Young	vs. Lefties	.264	67	.304	15	.335	68	0.68	9	8.43	56	23.49	6
	vs. Righties	.286	105	.439	94	.346	91	3.10	83	7.90	72	12.36	86
Team Average	vs. Lefties	.262	6	.404	7	.348	13	2.62	5	11.20	14	13.47	6
	vs. Righties	.267	11	.409	9	.340	14	2.93	6	9.45	12	14.15	7
League Average	vs. Lefties	.265		.408		.333		2.74		9.21		12.94	
	vs. Righties	.259		.404		.322		2.88		8.19		14.14	

Pitching with Runners on Base and Bases Empty

		BA	Rank	SA	Rank	OBA	Rank	HR %	Rank	BB %	Rank	SO %	Rank
Salome Barojas	Runners On	.286	90	.486	111	.374	109	4.76	121	12.80	116	9.60	108
	Bases Empty	.324	--	.426	--	.416	--	0.93	--	13.60	--	12.00	--
Jim Beattie	Runners On	.398	132	.556	129	.444	132	3.01	82	7.84	42	15.69	34
	Bases Empty	.248	56	.398	66	.335	87	3.11	82	11.54	113	11.54	87
Mark Langston	Runners On	.257	47	.410	70	.363	101	2.70	64	13.58	120	13.58	62
	Bases Empty	.253	63	.486	122	.385	124	6.23	129	17.63	130	11.54	87
Mike Moore	Runners On	.278	80	.389	56	.314	33	1.94	39	5.63	16	14.83	40
	Bases Empty	.227	26	.342	25	.291	35	1.92	29	7.68	61	15.52	40
Edwin Nunez	Runners On	.265	60	.428	83	.324	42	3.61	98	8.47	53	13.76	57
	Bases Empty	.205	12	.374	44	.280	19	4.09	115	9.52	91	16.93	30
Bill Swift	Runners On	.278	80	.374	43	.376	114	1.01	13	12.50	113	10.00	104
	Bases Empty	.279	102	.415	86	.329	79	2.21	39	6.16	30	10.62	102
Roy Thomas	Runners On	.222	16	.363	31	.360	97	2.96	80	18.64	131	18.08	14
	Bases Empty	.188	4	.283	7	.255	4	2.09	33	7.21	52	18.27	22
Ed Vande Berg	Runners On	.272	71	.391	59	.354	87	1.99	40	11.86	108	11.86	81
	Bases Empty	.278	--	.398	--	.345	--	0.93	--	8.40	--	10.92	--
Frank Wills	Runners On	.296	101	.493	115	.373	108	4.43	113	11.43	104	9.39	109
	Bases Empty	.243	49	.392	59	.348	96	3.53	98	13.51	124	14.86	49
Matt Young	Runners On	.304	110	.449	93	.378	118	3.41	93	9.85	82	13.05	70
	Bases Empty	.267	85	.393	62	.319	72	2.17	35	6.61	43	15.23	43
Team Average	Runners On	.288	13	.439	11	.365	14	3.00	10	10.55	14	12.98	8
	Bases Empty	.246	4	.381	3	.324	9	2.64	4	9.85	14	14.62	5
League Average	Runners On	.271		.416		.338		2.85		9.26		13.25	
	Bases Empty	.254		.397		.318		2.80		8.14		13.92	

Overall Pitching Compared to Late Inning Pressure Situations

		BA	Rank	SA	Rank	OBA	Rank	HR %	Rank	BB %	Rank	SO %	Rank
Salome Barojas	Overall	.305	122	.455	106	.395	130	2.82	69	13.20	124	10.80	107
	Pressure	.500	--	.500	--	.600	--	0.00	--	20.00	--	0.00	--
Jim Beattie	Overall	.316	126	.469	115	.385	126	3.06	84	9.85	92	13.43	61
	Pressure	.000	--	.000	--	.143	--	0.00	--	14.29	--	28.57	--
Karl Best	Overall	.207		.273		.250		0.83		4.69		25.00	
	Pressure	.178	9	.267	11	.196	2	2.22	54	2.17	3	28.26	1
Mark Langston	Overall	.255	55	.451	103	.375	122	4.59	126	15.77	130	12.48	77
	Pressure	.154	--	.154	--	.313	--	0.00	--	18.75	--	12.50	--
Robert Long	Overall	.210		.392		.302		4.90		10.49		17.90	
	Pressure	.150	3	.225	5	.261	12	2.50	61	13.04	104	21.74	10
Mike Moore	Overall	.247	41	.360	30	.300	23	1.93	28	6.89	30	15.26	40
	Pressure	.223	29	.277	15	.288	26	0.00	1	8.00	45	16.80	28
Edwin Nunez	Overall	.234	18	.401	61	.302	26	3.86	111	8.99	76	15.34	39
	Pressure	.231	38	.410	78	.301	38	4.49	112	9.04	59	11.86	78
Bill Swift	Overall	.279	97	.398	59	.350	93	1.70	21	9.02	77	10.34	110
	Pressure	.222	25	.333	32	.314	50	2.22	54	9.62	66	5.77	128
Roy Thomas	Overall	.202	3	.316	8	.303	28	2.45	48	12.47	118	18.18	15
	Pressure	.154	4	.246	7	.286	23	1.54	36	15.58	121	23.38	6
Ed Vande Berg	Overall	.274	93	.394	53	.350	94	1.54	16	10.47	102	11.49	91
	Pressure	.277	82	.398	70	.408	115	1.20	25	17.14	124	16.19	36
Frank Wills	Overall	.266	79	.437	95	.359	110	3.93	114	12.57	79	12.38	79
	Pressure	.341	122	.415	79	.408	117	0.00	1	12.00	94	10.00	96
Matt Young	Overall	.282	100	.416	81	.344	86	2.68	64	7.99	57	14.30	49
	Pressure	.281	86	.313	20	.367	91	0.00	1	10.00	75	10.91	91
Team Average	Overall	.265	9	.407	7	.343	13	2.80	5	10.18	14	13.87	6
	Pressure	.233	2	.338	1	.327	7	1.88	1	11.52	14	14.96	5
League Average	Overall	.261		.406		.327		2.82		8.63		13.62	
	Pressure	.258		.392		.332		2.71		9.52		14.05	

Additional Miscellaneous Pitching Comparisons

	Grass Surface BA	Rank	Artificial Surface BA	Rank	Home Games BA	Rank	Road Games BA	Rank	Runners in Scoring Position BA	Rank	Runners in Scoring Pos and Two Outs BA	Rank	Leading Off Inning OBA	Rank
Salome Barojas	.298	--	.308	112	.283	103	.333	--	.265	64	.297	106	.333	80
Jim Beattie	.448	--	.253	56	.244	46	.430	131	.415	133	.257	79	.372	116
Karl Best	.140	--	.244	41	.253	--	.130	--	.143	--	.100	--	.259	--
Dave Geisel	.340	--	.288	97	.262	--	.338	--	.388	--	.409	--	.364	--
Mark Langston	.262	74	.250	52	.272	91	.240	31	.244	38	.333	117	.356	101
Jack Lazorko	.320	--	.278	84	.292	--	.290	--	.333	--	.364	--	.333	--
Robert Long	.222	--	.202	13	.155	--	.264	--	.209	--	.190	--	.303	--
Mike Moore	.241	34	.250	51	.257	74	.234	22	.265	66	.293	103	.265	13
Edwin Nunez	.236	26	.233	29	.228	20	.240	29	.273	76	.204	34	.312	59
Brian Snyder	.314	--	.301	106	.310	--	.298	--	.277	--	.304	--	.474	--
Bill Swift	.266	80	.286	93	.300	114	.256	50	.270	74	.300	108	.359	106
Roy Thomas	.224	13	.178	2	.188	5	.213	10	.266	68	.135	8	.298	46
Ed Vande Berg	.258	--	.284	91	.304	119	.246	37	.250	47	.150	10	.333	80
Frank Wills	.299	109	.246	44	.250	57	.286	97	.261	60	.170	17	.377	117
Matt Young	.324	127	.267	73	.260	76	.313	118	.325	116	.371	126	.336	84
Team Average	.276	13	.259	7	.259	8	.272	10	.289	12	.279	14	.329	11
League Average	.262		.259		.256		.266		.268		.248		.321	

TEXAS RANGERS

The bad news is that the Rangers lost seven more games in 1985 than in 1984. The worse news is that they lost seven more games in 1984 than in 1983. The worst news is that in 1983, they finished 22 games out of first.

By the time Bobby Valentine replaced Doug Rader as manager on May 17, the Rangers were already 14 games below .500. The team wound up 62–99, with an unplayed rainout possibly sparing them their first 100-loss season since 1973. (All right, trivia fans, what two certified Grade A geniuses managed the Rangers to that 57–105 debacle in '73? Take your time; the answer will be at the end of this essay.) In an urban area that takes as much pride in its athletic teams as any in America—so much so that it has convinced the entire nation that its football team is America's team—the Rangers' sorry record sticks out: no championships of any kind, not even a division title or a minipennant in the strike season, in the team's history.

In fact, with the Blue Jays having won the American League East title last season, only two of the 26 major-league teams have never played in a post-season game: the Rangers and the Seattle Mariners. The Rangers' streak goes back to their life in Washington, in the 1961–62 wave of expansion that produced the Angels, the Mets, and the Astros (nee Colt .45s). Those three teams, along with the four teams born in 1969, have all grown out of the "expansion" stage, through the teenage years, and into maturity. Some, like the Mets, have already won a title, fallen, and resurged. But the Rangers seem to be an expansion team in perpetuity, always rebuilding, forever changing managers and front office personnel. Uneasy lies the head that wears the crown: Rader was fired after 30 months as manager, and that's the longest tenure any manager has enjoyed since the team moved to Texas.

The Rangers scored the fewest runs in the American League last season; that's not unusual for a last-place team, but what was unusual was the distance between their total of 617 runs and that of the Royals, who scored 687 for the next-lowest total. That distance of 70 runs between the last-place and next-to-last teams in runs scored is akin to the distance between Neptune and Pluto. There have been only two larger gulfs in the American League over the past 50 years: in 1983, when Seattle finished 81 runs behind Texas, and in '53, when the Browns trailed the Philadelphia Athletics by 77 runs.

That problem shows up clearly in the distribution of the runs that Texas did score. Ever see someone take out a thick wad of bills from his wallet, but upon closer inspection you see they're all singles? The Rangers had that kind of George Washington offense in 1985, one run at a time.

The following chart illustrates the problem. It summarizes how many times each American League team scored each number of runs in an inning last season.

	Total Runs	1 Run	2 Runs	3 Runs	4 Runs	5 Runs	6 Runs	7 Runs	8 Runs	9 Runs
N.Y.	839	242	120	63	14	9	6	2	1	1
Balt.	818	205	108	49	19	11	11	5	1	0*
Bos.	800	242	113	47	27	7	2	4	1	0
Tor.	759	228	103	45	26	10	6	0	0	0
Oak.	757	222	99	44	29	10	4	1	1	0
Chi.	736	222	102	50	20	7	4	3	0	0
Cal.	732	218	103	52	19	11	2	0	0	1
Clev.	729	185	118	43	18	12	4	1	2	0
Det.	729	231	106	50	17	7	4	0	0	1
Sea.	719	195	111	43	28	8	1	1	1	0
Minn.	705	213	102	43	19	8	3	1	1	0*
Mil.	690	205	98	41	18	8	5	1	1	1
K.C.	687	227	101	50	14	8	2	0	0	0
Tex.	617	218	93	34	16	7	2	0	0	0
Avg.	737	218	106	47	20	9	4	1	1	0

* also one 10-run inning

Texas finished right at the league average in the number of innings scoring exactly one run. The trouble arose in attempting to sustain a rally, or in producing the hit that could drive in more than one run. The team finished 12 percent below the league average in two-run innings, and an even more damaging 28 percent below the league average in three-run innings.

Earl Weaver's dreams about three-run homers and big innings have been well chronicled. But preventing your opponents from having those kinds of innings is as important as having them yourself. Unfortunately for the '85 Rangers, they were also too generous in allowing multiple-run innings. They held the opposition below the league average in the number of one-run innings, but they yielded more than the league average in every other denomination, and even though the differences between Texas's figures and the league average are not stark, they do add up: The Rangers allowed 48 more runs than the average American League team.

Here's a listing of the runs allowed in an inning by each of the American League pitching staffs last year:

	Total Runs	1 Run	2 Runs	3 Runs	4 Runs	5 Runs	6 Runs	7 Runs	8 Runs	9 Runs
Tor.	588	198	106	29	12	5	3	0	0	0
K.C.	639	216	100	35	14	3	4	2	0	1
N.Y.	660	207	120	28	13	8	5	1	0	0
Det.	688	217	79	40	19	11	6	1	0	1*
Cal.	703	211	97	53	14	11	2	0	2	0
Bos.	720	223	120	40	18	5	3	2	1	0
Chi.	720	218	104	46	30	3	1	1	1	0
Balt.	764	232	97	50	20	12	4	1	1	1
Minn.	782	214	96	54	33	10	3	2	0	0
Tex.	785	215	108	51	22	10	8	1	1	0
Oak.	787	232	110	53	17	9	3	4	1	1
Mil.	802	220	113	59	21	14	3	1	0	0
Sea.	818	217	103	56	23	12	7	1	2	0*
Clev.	861	233	124	60	28	10	4	2	0	0
Avg.	737	218	106	47	20	9	4	1	1	0

* also one 10-run inning

Don't Raise the Fences, Lower the Field

How many times have you heard well-meaning fans of a particular team urge their team's management to alter the dimensions of its playing field? Bring in the fences, push 'em back, raise them, lower them. The object is generally to make it easier or harder to hit home runs, but the effect is usually thought of only in relation to how it will affect the home team's batters.

For example, every time the Yankees acquire a right-handed slugger (the most recent being Dave Winfield and Don Baylor), the cry goes up to reduce the mammoth distances in left-center. But consideration is rarely given to the effect that such alterations would have on the opposition, or on the home team's pitching staff. For all teams considering such changes, a study of the recent history of the Texas Rangers is a must.

Arlington Stadium has been home to the Rangers since the team moved to Texas in 1972, and it was always regarded as a pitchers' park. From 1972 through 1983, the Rangers hit an average of 48 home runs a year at home, 59 a year on the road; they allowed 54 a year at home, 60 on the road. In other words, 14 percent fewer home runs were hit in Rangers games at Arlington Stadium than in their games everywhere else in the American League.

In 1984, the Rangers erected an enormous scoreboard, rising 29 feet above the back row of the outfield general admission area and circling the ballpark. Besides the entertainment and commercial value of the board, it had the effect of blocking the winds that had thwarted the best efforts of power hitters for more than a decade.

Although the home runs have come more frequently since the erection of the scoreboard, the results have been disastrous for the Rangers. Here are the pertinent figures on the subject, beginning with 1983, the year before the change was made:

	Home Games				Road Games			
		Tex.	Opp.			Tex.	Opp.	
	W–L	HR	HR		W–L	HR	HR	
1983	44–37	45	33		33–48	61	64	
1984	34–46	55	70		35–46	65	78	
1985	37–43	76	102		25–56	53	71	

The home-run output at Arlington Stadium increased from 78 in 1983 to 125 in 1984, and to 178 in 1985. But of the 100-home-run increase from 1983 to 1985, the Rangers hit only 31, while the opposition hit 69.

The erection of a scoreboard, of course, is a more permanent measure than moving a chain link fence a few feet one way or the other. So the Rangers will have to live with the board, and they may even learn to like its effect. Whether they do or not may depend on the progress of rookie outfielder Pete Incaviglia, who had 48 home runs and 143 RBIs in 75 games at Oklahoma State University last year. Incaviglia was obtained by the Rangers from Montreal after he balked at playing with the Expos, and he may not even make Texas's opening day roster. But the mere fact that he is on the horizon lends a sense of excitement to the Rangers that has been missing for years.

The Lower Third

Picture the executive offices of a major television network. The ratings for its entertainment programs are low, and the guilty shows must be identified and eliminated.

"We've got to get rid of 'Bubbles for Bertha,'" says one mucky-muck. "It's shown on Sunday night, when viewing audiences are high. Its ratings look OK, but they're a bit below those of the shows on the other networks.'

"Maybe so," counters another executive, "but Saturday night is a problem, too. We've got to do something about 'My Friend Gus' and 'The Byzantine Hour.' They're killing us!"

"You're wrong," says the first one. "Saturday night ratings are always low, because fewer people are home, so you don't expect to get the same numbers from those shows as you get from your Sunday shows. 'Bertha' has got to go."

"You don't expect the same numbers from Saturday," concludes his colleague, "and maybe our lead-in shows aren't the greatest, but there are still minimum standards that apply. And 'Gus' and 'The Byzantines' don't even meet those! The other networks have almost doubled us, and the best that they've got against us is 'The Lighter Side of Sweatshops.'"

Standards and expectations are different depending on circumstances. While asserting that all men are created equal, the Declaration of Independence makes no promises about opportunity. So it is with a batting order in baseball.

The bottom part of the order doesn't share an equal burden of run-producing responsibilities with the meat of the order, but that doesn't mean that any level of offense is acceptable from the lower spots. The seven-eight-nine spots in the order have two responsibilities that form an important bridge between the heart of the order and the top: They have to deliver the runners left on by the meat of the lineup, and they have to get on base to help set things up for the top of the order. Run production is a chain reaction in which all the lineup positions become interdependent; nonetheless, there are levels of acceptable offense even for those from whom the least is expected. And if the least was expected of the bottom of the Rangers' order in 1985, it certainly delivered; in the grand tradition of Mario Mendoza and Nelson Norman, it didn't produce runs, and it didn't start rallies.

First, the run production. Here are the average RBI figures for the American League last season, based on batting order position, compared with the Rangers' figures for each spot. (Remember that these figures include all players who appeared in each spot during the season, not just the primary players.)

	1st	2nd	3rd	4th	5th	6th	7th	8th	9th
A.L. Avg.	62	77	103	106	83	79	71	62	53
Texas	52	74	86	92	70	76	48	49	31
Deficit	−10	−3	−17	−14	−13	−3	−23	−13	−22

The Rangers fell below the league average in each of the nine batting positions, but the most serious deficiencies are at the tail of the order. Collectively, the seventh, eighth, and ninth spots fell 31 percent below the league average for runs batted in.

Now about starting rallies: When leading off an inning, the Rangers' seventh spot was no day at the beach, either. Of all the batting positions in the American League (126 total positions—nine for each of the 14 teams), the Rangers' seventh position was the least likely one, when leading off an inning, to produce runs: it led off 124 innings, and the team scored in only 18 of them. To take it one step further: When the seven spot led off an inning with an out, which it did 86 times, the Rangers scored in just five innings.

The only player to hit well in the lower third of the lineup was Wayne Tolleson, who batted .326 in 70 games in those three spots. For his troubles, he was traded to Chicago over the winter.

(Oh, yes, that question about 1973. The two managers for Texas that year were Whitey Herzog and Billy Martin. Just the kind of calm, reasonable guys you want to travel around the country with while you're losing 105 games.)

WON-LOST RECORD BY STARTING POSITION

TEXAS 62-99	C	1B	2B	3B	SS	LF	CF	RF	P	DH	Leadoff	Relief	Starts
Alan Bannister	-	1-0	2-3	-	-	5-2	-	0-3	-	6-9	4-2	-	14-17
Buddy Bell	-	-	-	29-53	-	-	-	-	-	-	-	-	29-53
Tommy Boggs	-	-	-	-	-	-	-	-	-	-	-	0-4	-
Glenn Brummer	16-15	-	-	-	-	-	-	-	-	-	-	-	16-15
Steve Buechele	-	-	-	28-40	-	-	-	-	-	-	-	-	28-40
Nick Capra	-	-	-	-	-	-	0-3	-	-	-	0-1	-	0-3
Glen Cook	-	-	-	-	-	-	-	-	3-4	-	-	0-2	3-4
Tommy Dunbar	-	-	-	-	-	3-8	-	0-1	-	6-9	1-4	-	9-18
Jose Guzman	-	-	-	-	-	-	-	-	3-2	-	-	-	3-2
Toby Harrah	-	-	46-73	-	-	-	-	-	-	-	14-23	-	46-73
Greg Harris	-	-	-	-	-	-	-	-	-	-	-	19-39	-
Dwayne Henry	-	-	-	-	-	-	-	-	-	-	-	6-10	-
Burt Hooton	-	-	-	-	-	-	-	-	8-12	-	-	2-7	8-12
Charlie Hough	-	-	-	-	-	-	-	-	14-20	-	-	-	14-20
Cliff Johnson	-	-	-	-	-	-	-	-	-	31-50	-	-	31-50
Bobby Jones	-	1-0	-	-	-	1-2	-	5-6	-	4-3	-	-	11-11
Jeff Kunkel	-	-	-	-	1-0	-	-	-	-	-	-	-	1-0
Mike Mason	-	-	-	-	-	-	-	-	11-19	-	-	0-8	11-19
Oddibe McDowell	-	-	-	-	-	-	38-60	-	-	1-2	33-54	-	39-62
Dale Murray	-	-	-	-	-	-	-	-	-	-	-	0-1	-
Dickie Noles	-	-	-	-	-	-	-	-	4-9	-	-	4-11	4-9
Pete O'Brien	-	56-97	-	-	-	-	-	-	-	-	-	-	56-97
Larry Parrish	-	-	-	1-0	-	-	-	27-42	-	10-12	-	-	38-54
Gene Petralli	8-23	-	-	-	-	-	-	-	-	-	-	-	8-23
Luis Pujols	-	-	-	-	-	-	-	-	-	-	-	-	-
Dave Rozema	-	-	-	-	-	-	-	-	2-2	-	-	13-17	2-2
Jeff Russell	-	-	-	-	-	-	-	-	6-7	-	-	-	6-7
Dave Schmidt	-	-	-	-	-	-	-	-	2-2	-	-	11-36	2-2
Bob Sebra	-	-	-	-	-	-	-	-	0-4	-	-	1-2	0-4
Don Slaught	38-61	-	-	-	-	-	-	-	-	-	-	-	38-61
Bill Stein	-	4-2	-	3-4	-	-	-	-	-	0-2	-	-	7-8
Dave Stewart	-	-	-	-	-	-	-	-	1-4	-	-	4-33	1-4
Rick Surhoff	-	-	-	-	-	-	-	-	-	-	-	4-3	-
Frank Tanana	-	-	-	-	-	-	-	-	4-9	-	-	-	4-9
Wayne Tolleson	-	-	8-11	1-2	25-42	-	-	-	-	-	6-13	-	34-55
Ellis Valentine	-	-	-	-	-	-	-	3-2	-	1-3	-	-	4-5
Duane Walker	-	-	-	-	-	4-4	-	6-14	-	1-7	-	-	11-25
Gary Ward	-	-	-	-	-	49-83	9-10	-	-	1-0	-	-	59-93
Chris Welsh	-	-	-	-	-	-	-	-	2-4	-	-	1-18	2-4
Curtis Wilkerson	-	-	6-12	-	36-57	-	-	-	-	-	-	4-2	42-69
Matt Williams	-	-	-	-	-	-	-	-	2-1	-	-	1-2	2-1
George Wright	-	-	-	-	-	15-26	21-31	-	-	1-2	-	-	37-59
Ricky Wright	-	-	-	-	-	-	-	-	-	-	-	2-3	-

Batting vs. Left and Right Handed Pitchers

		BA	Rank	SA	Rank	OBA	Rank	HR %	Rank	BB %	Rank	SO %	Rank
Alan Bannister	vs. Lefties	.244	115	.268	148	.311	113	0.00	131	8.89	71	12.22	74
	vs. Righties	.300	--	.475	--	.391	--	2.50	--	12.77	--	12.77	--
Buddy Bell	vs. Lefties	.289	50	.382	101	.356	52	0.00	131	10.34	52	2.30	1
	vs. Righties	.219	136	.321	137	.292	127	1.69	103	9.09	60	7.20	22
Steve Buechele	vs. Lefties	.267	79	.427	73	.304	119	4.00	51	5.06	133	16.46	115
	vs. Righties	.194	154	.319	140	.255	149	2.08	94	6.37	111	15.92	112
Toby Harrah	vs. Lefties	.310	29	.465	49	.448	2	3.52	55	20.77	1	12.02	69
	vs. Righties	.248	102	.346	119	.423	3	1.57	105	22.19	1	11.24	55
Bobby Jones	vs. Lefties	.000	--	.000	--	.143	--	0.00	--	14.29	--	42.86	--
	vs. Righties	.234	119	.367	103	.291	128	3.91	43	7.09	99	19.15	140
Oddibe McDowell	vs. Lefties	.244	115	.431	70	.311	113	2.44	83	7.19	105	24.46	151
	vs. Righties	.237	115	.431	60	.301	113	5.30	19	8.31	78	16.29	114
Pete O'Brien	vs. Lefties	.225	131	.296	141	.289	132	1.18	114	8.33	81	13.02	89
	vs. Righties	.285	39	.517	9	.364	23	4.95	23	11.45	32	6.05	11
Larry Parrish	vs. Lefties	.245	110	.532	19	.321	102	8.51	3	10.38	51	19.81	134
	vs. Righties	.250	96	.397	81	.312	97	3.57	54	7.97	85	20.29	145
Don Slaught	vs. Lefties	.287	52	.426	74	.351	59	2.97	67	6.25	119	14.29	98
	vs. Righties	.277	51	.421	63	.322	85	2.07	95	5.04	132	9.69	43
Wayne Tolleson	vs. Lefties	.253	96	.356	119	.275	139	0.00	131	3.23	150	11.83	66
	vs. Righties	.335	4	.390	83	.380	14	0.42	146	6.87	102	13.36	79
Duane Walker	vs. Lefties	.167	--	.167	--	.167	--	0.00	--	0.00	--	16.67	--
	vs. Righties	.175	157	.310	144	.268	144	3.97	42	10.56	42	19.72	142
Gary Ward	vs. Lefties	.301	36	.511	24	.354	57	3.98	52	7.81	91	14.06	96
	vs. Righties	.281	46	.400	79	.318	88	1.92	98	5.38	128	15.70	107
Curtis Wilkerson	vs. Lefties	.279	64	.395	92	.367	36	0.00	131	11.00	41	9.00	34
	vs. Righties	.234	120	.281	149	.268	143	0.00	152	3.73	149	18.31	131
George Wright	vs. Lefties	.172	155	.221	156	.231	154	0.00	131	7.46	98	14.18	97
	vs. Righties	.199	151	.253	153	.246	154	0.83	136	5.75	123	11.49	59
Team Average	vs. Lefties	.264	9	.395	12	.334	5	2.12	14	9.09	6	14.07	6
	vs. Righties	.249	12	.375	13	.317	10	2.52	12	8.72	4	13.46	7
League Average	vs. Lefties	.266		.416		.333		2.91		8.95		13.77	
	vs. Righties	.259		.401		.324		2.78		8.49		13.56	

Batting with Runners on Base and Bases Empty

Name		BA	Rank	SA	Rank	OBA	Rank	HR %	Rank	BB %	Rank	SO %	Rank
Buddy Bell	Runners On	.247	122	.321	135	.311	118	0.00	142	8.74	92	6.01	12
	Bases Empty	.225	126	.351	116	.304	106	2.65	83	10.12	38	5.95	5
Steve Buechele	Runners On	.247	121	.371	113	.299	127	3.37	58	6.19	126	13.40	90
	Bases Empty	.200	151	.346	120	.252	153	2.31	92	5.76	119	17.99	127
Toby Harrah	Runners On	.322	21	.476	42	.461	3	3.50	57	20.73	2	10.36	53
	Bases Empty	.241	109	.340	123	.415	2	1.58	112	22.26	1	12.20	60
Oddibe McDowell	Runners On	.192	152	.329	129	.259	153	2.74	74	8.38	99	19.76	145
	Bases Empty	.265	64	.488	20	.330	61	5.38	16	7.72	76	18.25	129
Pete O'Brien	Runners On	.255	105	.409	82	.334	88	2.55	77	11.15	40	7.12	23
	Bases Empty	.278	34	.492	19	.349	23	5.02	27	9.94	42	9.04	34
Larry Parrish	Runners On	.254	108	.410	80	.332	91	4.05	46	10.20	55	17.35	127
	Bases Empty	.243	106	.457	36	.296	118	5.78	13	6.99	95	23.12	152
Don Slaught	Runners On	.279	71	.390	99	.335	87	1.30	108	5.95	128	11.90	71
	Bases Empty	.280	30	.450	38	.327	70	3.17	66	4.95	131	10.40	43
Wayne Tolleson	Runners On	.263	87	.316	136	.296	133	0.75	131	4.64	144	13.25	88
	Bases Empty	.347	2	.426	57	.392	5	0.00	148	6.86	98	12.75	66
Gary Ward	Runners On	.289	55	.431	70	.342	81	2.51	79	8.27	102	16.17	116
	Bases Empty	.285	27	.435	47	.320	86	2.54	86	4.57	140	14.52	86
Curtis Wilkerson	Runners On	.234	135	.298	144	.295	137	0.00	142	6.90	119	15.17	105
	Bases Empty	.250	98	.314	139	.292	124	0.00	148	4.80	133	16.40	113
George Wright	Runners On	.159	157	.172	157	.241	156	0.00	142	9.77	62	12.07	74
	Bases Empty	.212	140	.292	147	.241	156	0.94	126	3.62	148	12.67	65
Team Average	Runners On	.254	14	.367	14	.323	14	1.97	13	9.25	6	12.92	6
	Bases Empty	.253	8	.391	9	.321	6	2.73	8	8.50	5	14.20	9
League Average	Runners On	.271		.416		.338		2.85		9.26		13.25	
	Bases Empty	.254		.397		.318		2.80		8.14		13.92	

Overall Batting Compared to Late Inning Pressure Situations

Name		BA	Rank	SA	Rank	OBA	Rank	HR %	Rank	BB %	Rank	SO %	Rank	RDI %	Rank
Buddy Bell	Overall	.236	133	.335	136	.308	117	1.28	119	9.40	54	5.98	7	.250	119
	Pressure	.255	78	.426	57	.314	90	2.13	82	7.84	92	15.69	95	.250	87
Steve Buechele	Overall	.219	147	.356	123	.271	151	2.74	80	5.93	129	16.10	116	.200	153
	Pressure	.261	--	.435	--	.320	--	4.35	--	4.00	--	8.00	--	.400	--
Toby Harrah	Overall	.270	64	.389	98	.432	3	2.27	95	21.69	1	11.52	56	.343	26
	Pressure	.328	18	.508	26	.440	7	4.92	37	15.79	17	11.84	59	.400	22
Bobby Jones	Overall	.224	--	.351	--	.284	--	3.73	--	7.43	--	20.27	--	.327	40
	Pressure	.250	82	.523	25	.353	51	9.09	4	11.76	46	13.73	75	.200	117
Oddibe McDowell	Overall	.239	128	.431	61	.304	125	4.43	35	7.96	87	18.81	138	.206	149
	Pressure	.208	127	.396	75	.300	104	5.66	28	9.84	65	16.39	101	.105	153
Pete O'Brien	Overall	.267	68	.452	36	.342	56	3.84	49	10.53	39	8.09	25	.319	46
	Pressure	.160	151	.253	140	.278	125	2.67	68	14.44	27	11.11	51	.214	111
Larry Parrish	Overall	.249	108	.434	58	.314	107	4.91	24	8.64	70	20.16	144	.252	118
	Pressure	.261	69	.500	27	.358	49	6.52	18	13.21	36	26.42	155	.375	32
Don Slaught	Overall	.280	43	.423	70	.331	72	2.33	92	5.41	137	11.08	49	.293	74
	Pressure	.328	19	.414	69	.371	38	1.72	94	4.84	127	9.68	35	.182	122
Bill Stein	Overall	.253	--	.354	--	.272	--	1.27	--	1.23	--	18.52	--	.257	--
	Pressure	.263	--	.316	--	.300	--	0.00	--	5.00	--	15.00	--	.625	2
Wayne Tolleson	Overall	.313	5	.381	106	.353	37	0.31	150	5.92	130	12.96	74	.179	158
	Pressure	.353	10	.471	39	.389	24	1.96	85	5.56	121	11.11	51	.222	104
Gary Ward	Overall	.287	32	.433	59	.329	78	2.53	87	6.11	125	15.20	107	.303	61
	Pressure	.241	92	.333	99	.302	100	2.30	79	8.33	84	15.63	94	.250	87
Curtis Wilkerson	Overall	.244	115	.308	148	.293	137	0.00	154	5.57	135	15.95	111	.227	138
	Pressure	.417	2	.583	9	.451	6	0.00	113	5.66	120	7.55	21	.556	5
George Wright	Overall	.190	157	.242	157	.241	158	0.55	144	6.33	120	12.41	62	.172	162
	Pressure	.155	153	.172	155	.219	152	0.00	113	7.58	95	7.58	22	.111	149
Team Average	Overall	.253	10	.381	13	.322	10	2.41	12	8.83	5	13.64	7	.263	13
	Pressure	.261	6	.394	6	.333	3	2.96	7	9.28	7	13.10	3	.272	7
League Average	Overall	.261		.406		.327		2.82		8.63		13.62		.287	
	Pressure	.253		.381		.323		2.74		9.11		14.40		.273	

Additional Miscellaneous Batting Comparisons

Name	Grass Surface BA	Rank	Artificial Surface BA	Rank	Home Games BA	Rank	Road Games BA	Rank	Runners in Scoring Position BA	Rank	Runners in Scoring Pos and Two Outs BA	Rank	Leading Off Inning OBA	Rank	Runners on 3B with less than 2 Outs RDI %	Rank
Buddy Bell	.241	118	.209	136	.226	133	.247	105	.238	117	.152	150	.382	15	.684	37
Steve Buechele	.216	145	.235	--	.218	140	.220	140	.255	104	.318	31	.333	59	.500	106
Toby Harrah	.266	73	.292	35	.289	46	.254	91	.329	15	.241	85	.409	6	.731	23
Bobby Jones	.237	--	.150	--	.247	--	.189	--	.227	--	.143	151	.250	--	.786	10
Oddibe McDowell	.237	126	.250	83	.266	78	.212	148	.207	143	.200	130	.324	79	.400	146
Pete O'Brien	.275	52	.229	119	.292	42	.243	113	.257	100	.179	143	.265	140	.714	27
Larry Parrish	.239	123	.295	31	.218	141	.285	26	.210	140	.205	128	.271	131	.571	83
Don Slaught	.295	27	.200	141	.293	41	.265	66	.253	108	.179	141	.280	122	.571	83
Wayne Tolleson	.324	3	.250	83	.354	4	.262	74	.222	129	.237	91	.360	31	.667	--
Gary Ward	.284	44	.302	22	.344	6	.235	122	.317	26	.300	36	.373	21	.500	106
Curtis Wilkerson	.255	93	.197	145	.225	136	.260	75	.222	129	.225	105	.324	78	.385	150
George Wright	.182	156	.240	100	.158	157	.215	146	.163	155	.159	147	.215	155	.333	154
Team Average	.256	9	.240	13	.267	6	.240	14	.250	13	.226	14	.325	5	.560	12
League Average	.262		.259		.266		.256		.268		.248		.321		.587	

Pitching vs. Left and Right Handed Batters

		BA	Rank	SA	Rank	OBA	Rank	HR %	Rank	BB %	Rank	SO %	Rank
Greg Harris	vs. Lefties	.175	2	.286	9	.257	8	1.94	39	9.09	67	25.11	2
	vs. Righties	.199	3	.293	9	.290	28	1.57	18	10.05	100	24.20	1
Burt Hooton	vs. Lefties	.295	99	.527	125	.359	90	4.92	127	9.49	71	12.54	65
	vs. Righties	.300	118	.447	102	.331	81	2.11	37	4.78	12	9.96	112
Charlie Hough	vs. Lefties	.226	25	.343	31	.290	20	2.22	51	7.76	44	14.23	45
	vs. Righties	.202	4	.332	16	.275	18	2.82	68	8.60	80	13.42	72
Mike Mason	vs. Lefties	.279	81	.416	70	.356	87	2.60	62	10.73	89	9.60	103
	vs. Righties	.304	122	.473	119	.363	116	3.24	85	8.67	83	12.04	90
Dickie Noles	vs. Lefties	.339	130	.468	100	.398	124	2.15	49	8.14	49	11.24	85
	vs. Righties	.234	33	.364	40	.287	25	2.80	66	5.22	24	13.04	77
Dave Rozema	vs. Lefties	.262	65	.393	59	.311	43	3.14	86	6.31	26	7.77	119
	vs. Righties	.318	127	.452	105	.359	111	2.55	55	5.36	28	15.48	48
Jeff Russell	vs. Lefties	.322	124	.534	127	.390	117	3.42	98	10.30	85	14.55	43
	vs. Righties	.328	--	.517	--	.385	--	4.31	--	7.69	--	15.38	--
Dave Schmidt	vs. Lefties	.232	30	.369	45	.278	13	1.79	37	6.04	23	13.74	52
	vs. Righties	.261	71	.329	15	.306	50	1.86	29	6.32	41	12.07	89
Dave Stewart	vs. Lefties	.323	126	.524	124	.408	128	3.66	101	12.89	110	12.37	67
	vs. Righties	.219	21	.424	85	.285	21	4.64	119	7.19	53	23.95	4
Chris Welsh	vs. Lefties	.229	28	.294	11	.276	11	0.92	14	6.03	22	12.07	70
	vs. Righties	.360	133	.592	132	.419	133	4.74	122	7.66	66	7.23	129
Team Average	vs. Lefties	.273	11	.436	12	.338	9	3.11	12	8.70	5	13.60	5
	vs. Righties	.265	10	.418	11	.326	7	3.17	11	7.78	6	14.56	6
League Average	vs. Lefties	.265		.408		.333		2.74		9.21		12.94	
	vs. Righties	.259		.404		.322		2.88		8.19		14.14	

Pitching with Runners on Base and Bases Empty

		BA	Rank	SA	Rank	OBA	Rank	HR %	Rank	BB %	Rank	SO %	Rank
Greg Harris	Runners On	.214	8	.352	26	.298	27	2.52	55	10.33	90	22.28	3
	Bases Empty	.168	1	.248	2	.256	5	1.26	13	9.02	83	26.32	1
Burt Hooton	Runners On	.290	98	.462	100	.345	78	3.33	90	8.51	56	13.19	69
	Bases Empty	.302	122	.509	126	.347	95	3.78	109	6.43	39	9.97	110
Charlie Hough	Runners On	.225	19	.345	23	.321	37	2.53	56	12.63	115	14.52	44
	Bases Empty	.210	15	.334	21	.262	8	2.48	57	5.57	21	13.47	63
Mike Mason	Runners On	.316	119	.441	89	.374	111	2.56	62	9.39	77	14.09	51
	Bases Empty	.285	106	.476	116	.352	101	3.53	97	8.90	81	9.36	118
Dickie Noles	Runners On	.330	125	.455	96	.385	121	2.00	41	5.91	18	11.82	82
	Bases Empty	.255	70	.389	55	.313	59	2.83	73	7.46	58	12.31	78
Dave Rozema	Runners On	.331	126	.529	123	.391	124	4.46	114	8.00	47	9.71	106
	Bases Empty	.251	61	.330	18	.281	20	1.57	21	4.02	9	12.56	74
Jeff Russell	Runners On	.306	113	.532	125	.378	116	4.03	107	11.11	102	18.06	15
	Bases Empty	.341	129	.522	127	.397	128	3.62	102	7.28	54	11.92	83
Dave Schmidt	Runners On	.266	62	.343	21	.327	46	0.70	5	8.64	58	14.20	50
	Bases Empty	.231	32	.355	34	.263	10	2.69	67	4.12	11	11.86	84
Dave Stewart	Runners On	.235	25	.477	108	.337	64	5.37	130	13.33	119	21.67	4
	Bases Empty	.307	125	.476	115	.365	110	3.01	78	7.18	50	13.81	57
Chris Welsh	Runners On	.312	115	.497	116	.377	115	3.82	104	7.95	46	6.82	129
	Bases Empty	.319	126	.485	119	.366	112	3.07	80	6.29	34	10.86	95
Team Average	Runners On	.284	12	.453	12	.353	11	3.51	13	9.72	9	14.93	2
	Bases Empty	.258	7	.407	10	.314	6	2.88	8	7.00	1	13.48	8
League Average	Runners On	.271		.416		.338		2.85		9.26		13.25	
	Bases Empty	.254		.397		.318		2.80		8.14		13.92	

Overall Pitching Compared to Late Inning Pressure Situations

		BA	Rank	SA	Rank	OBA	Rank	HR %	Rank	BB %	Rank	SO %	Rank
Greg Harris	Overall	.186	2	.290	4	.273	5	1.76	22	9.56	86	24.67	2
	Pressure	.218	24	.347	41	.298	35	2.59	63	9.22	63	23.96	5
Dwayne Henry	Overall	.211	--	.303	--	.274	--	0.00	--	8.14	--	23.26	--
	Pressure	.264	67	.377	60	.310	48	0.00	1	6.67	32	20.00	16
Burt Hooton	Overall	.297	115	.489	125	.346	89	3.59	106	7.33	45	11.36	93
	Pressure	.400	--	.500	--	.429	--	0.00	--	4.76	--	4.76	--
Charlie Hough	Overall	.215	8	.338	15	.283	10	2.50	53	8.15	61	13.85	53
	Pressure	.235	42	.374	56	.302	39	2.61	65	7.94	44	16.67	30
Mike Mason	Overall	.299	118	.461	108	.362	115	3.10	86	9.13	79	11.50	90
	Pressure	.270	76	.459	100	.426	124	2.70	71	18.75	127	10.42	94
Dickie Noles	Overall	.289	111	.418	85	.346	88	2.46	49	6.76	29	12.09	83
	Pressure	.222	25	.400	72	.314	50	4.44	108	11.76	89	11.76	80
Dave Rozema	Overall	.287	108	.420	87	.332	73	2.87	73	5.88	13	11.23	98
	Pressure	.326	117	.500	114	.364	90	3.26	89	6.00	25	8.00	115
Jeff Russell	Overall	.324	130	.527	130	.388	127	3.82	110	9.15	80	14.92	45
	Pressure	.167	--	.250	--	.231	--	0.00	--	7.14	--	35.71	--
Dave Schmidt	Overall	.246	39	.350	22	.292	16	1.82	25	6.18	19	12.92	67
	Pressure	.225	31	.292	17	.266	13	0.83	20	5.34	19	15.27	43
Dave Stewart	Overall	.273	87	.476	121	.351	97	4.13	119	10.25	99	17.73	18
	Pressure	.278	83	.486	111	.369	93	4.17	103	12.79	103	8.14	113
Chris Welsh	Overall	.316	125	.491	126	.371	120	3.44	99	7.12	38	8.83	122
	Pressure	.263	--	.421	--	.333	--	5.26	--	9.52	--	9.52	--
Team Average	Overall	.269	11	.426	13	.331	10	3.14	14	8.20	5	14.12	5
	Pressure	.256	7	.401	9	.324	5	2.66	7	8.73	4	16.32	2
League Average	Overall	.261		.406		.327		2.82		8.63		13.62	
	Pressure	.258		.392		.332		2.71		9.52		14.05	

Additional Miscellaneous Pitching Comparisons

	Grass Surface BA	Rank	Artificial Surface BA	Rank	Home Games BA	Rank	Road Games BA	Rank	Runners in Scoring Position BA	Rank	Runners in Scoring Pos and Two Outs BA	Rank	Leading Off Inning OBA	Rank
Greg Harris	.164	1	.347	125	.183	4	.190	3	.191	5	.087	3	.175	1
Burt Hooton	.303	113	.255	61	.281	100	.315	121	.277	82	.231	57	.328	76
Charlie Hough	.215	8	.216	18	.226	17	.206	7	.217	17	.192	25	.277	22
Mike Mason	.304	114	.265	72	.307	123	.291	103	.278	83	.278	92	.384	119
Dickie Noles	.283	100	.353	--	.296	111	.281	91	.358	130	.328	116	.324	73
Dave Rozema	.289	106	.261	--	.292	107	.281	90	.306	105	.243	71	.282	28
Jeff Russell	.318	124	.391	--	.357	131	.276	83	.304	104	.387	131	.435	130
Dave Schmidt	.236	23	.286	93	.235	30	.260	58	.224	22	.239	68	.228	4
Dave Stewart	.265	78	.310	115	.278	98	.269	78	.228	25	.133	7	.410	128
Chris Welsh	.313	121	.324	121	.307	122	.322	123	.292	96	.333	117	.297	45
Team Average	.268	10	.272	9	.271	12	.266	8	.266	8	.243	6	.314	3
League Average	.262		.259		.256		.266		.268		.248		.321	

TORONTO BLUE JAYS

Everyone knows why Toronto lost to Kansas City in last season's American League Championship Series, eh? The Blue Jays couldn't beat left-handed pitching, and were no match for Danny Jackson, Bud Black, and Charlie Leibrandt. It didn't take a degree in computer science to interpret the statistics: Last season, Toronto had a fantastic 75–36 record against right-handed pitchers, but were 24–26 against left-handers. So what's wrong with the conclusion that Kansas City's lefties spoiled the Blue Jays' title bid? The fact is that while the Jays couldn't buy a win against left-handed pitchers on the road, they left southpaws for dead at Exhibition Stadium, site of those final two playoffs defeats. The following figures indicate that this has been the case for the past four seasons:

	Vs. Left-Handers		Vs. Right-Handers	
Year	Home	Road	Home	Road
1982	19–15	16–29	25–22	18–18
1983	20–11	10–20	28–22	31–20
1984	19–8	13–10	30–24	27–31
1985	17–10	7–16	37–16	38–20
Totals	75–44	46–75	120–84	114–89
	(.630)	(.380)	(.588)	(.562)

The difference between the Blue Jays' home and road records against left-handers since 1982 is staggering. But during that time, the margin was never larger than last season. There's no denying that Jackson, Black, and Leibrandt ruined Toronto's pennant hopes, but to blame the two decisive losses at Exhibition Stadium on the Blue Jays' incompetence against southpaws is akin to holding Dwight Gooden responsible for the Mets' three-game deficit in the N.L. East. Well, he lost four games, didn't he?

Fixing A Hole

For their first six years of existence, the Blue Jays had barely a moment's worry about their relief pitching. It's not that they had a superior relief staff; it's just that they had a few other frivolous things to take care of—like the starting lineup, the pitching rotation, managers, coaches, that sort of thing. But ever since Toronto achieved respectability a few years ago, no problem has been more urgent or received greater attention than the failings of the bullpen.

The Blue Jays thought Dennis Lamp would solve the problem, but adding him to the staff in 1984 did nothing to improve the situation. In fact, it got worse. So for the 1985 season, Toronto traded for not one but two of baseball's most effective relievers: Bill Caudill, who ranked second to Dan Quisenberry with 36 saves in '84, and Gary Lavelle, one of the National League's top left-handed relief pitchers for a decade. In addition, they plucked reliever Tom Henke from Texas in the now-defunct free-agent compensation draft. He began the year in Syracuse, but joined the Jays in mid-season, and was impressive enough to steal the nickname "The Terminator" from Canada's other stopper, National League saves leader Jeff Reardon. (Does this make Reardon the ExTerminator?) This time, the Jays appeared certain to have resolved their bullpen crisis, which would go a long way toward narrowing the 15-game gap between themselves and the defending champion Tigers.

Casual fans outside Toronto might even assume that they won their division title last season largely because of their improved bullpen. Nothing could be further from the truth. For the third consecutive season, the Blue Jays lost more games that they led after seven innings than any other team in either league. Toronto won the pennant despite their relievers, not on account of them. Compare their records over the past four seasons in games they led after seven:

Year	W	L	Pct.
1982	56	8	.875
1983	65	12	.844
1984	61	15	.803
1985	82	13	.863

Those records don't look too shabby, but most teams win about nine out of 10 games in which they lead entering the eighth; teams with the best bullpens win about 19 out of 20. The following table illustrates just how poorly Toronto has protected late leads compared to other American League teams, not only last season, but over the four years since 1982:

1985				1982–1985			
Team	W	L	Pct.	Team	W	L	Pct.
Seattle	57	2	.966	Seattle	220	17	.928
New York	79	4	.952	Chicago	286	23	.926
Oakland	56	3	.949	Kansas City	282	23	.925
Chicago	68	5	.932	New York	277	25	.917
Boston	70	7	.909	Detroit	290	28	.912
California	70	7	.909	Boston	268	26	.912
Minnesota	62	7	.899	Minnesota	241	24	.909
Kansas City	77	11	.875	Baltimore	281	33	.895
Milwaukee	54	8	.871	California	268	33	.890
Detroit	65	10	.867	Oakland	220	28	.887
Toronto	82	13	.863	Milwaukee	247	33	.882
Baltimore	62	11	.849	Texas	212	29	.880
Texas	45	8	.849	Cleveland	216	33	.867
Cleveland	48	9	.842	**Toronto**	264	48	.846
Totals	895	105	.895	Totals	3572	403	.899

With Very Little Help From My Friends

No one has suffered more on account of Toronto's bullpen than Dave Stieb. Stieb has been among the American League's most consistent pitchers during the 1980s. He has the league's lowest ERA over the past five seasons among pitchers with at least 100 starts (2.95), and during that time, his ERA has never exceeded 3.25. Stieb has won 75 games during those five years; only three American League pitchers have won more: Jack Morris, Ron Guidry, and Dan Petry. Despite that, Stieb has battled the label of underachiever: never played on a pennant winner, never won 20 games, never this, never that. And during Toronto's championship season, that hum grew into a chorus.

Despite his league-leading ERA, Stieb won only 14 games, the fewest by an ERA leader on a division or league champion since 1958, when Whitey Ford won only 14 games (against seven losses) for the Yankees despite a 2.01 ERA. For those who wondered how such a talented pitcher could win so few games for so good a team, the answer is simple: bad luck. Stieb was the victim, not the perpetrator. Consider the evidence.

Thirty starts, give or take a few, are not nearly enough to overcome an unlucky streak. (Fantasy-league managers planning to spend big bucks on the previous season's winningest pitchers will want to pay strict attention here.) While the single biggest factor in a pitcher's won-lost record is his own performance, his team's support—batting, fielding, and relief pitching—are all vital elements as well.

What portion of a starting pitcher's record depends on circumstances beyond his control? For the sake of argument, let's not even consider the effect of a trade from a contender to a cellar-dweller, or vice versa. The following study deals with all pitchers over the past four seasons who meet the following criteria: (1) they started at least 30 games in consecutive seasons; (2) they played for the same team in those seasons; and (3) they had ERAs in those seasons that differed by no more than 0.40 runs. Those rules are designed to include only pitchers who performed equally well for two consecutive seasons under equivalent circumstances.

We found 35 such pairs of seasons; as expected, the stats for the group as a whole differed little from year to year. The pitchers won an average of 15.6 games with a .591 winning percentage in Year 1, and 14.7 games with a .562 percentage in Year 2. But there was considerable variation in the figures for individual pitchers, whose differences in games won (Year-1 Wins minus Year-2 Wins) are summarized in the following table:

Difference	−8	−7	−6	−5	−4	−3	−2	−1	0	+1	+2	+3	+4	+5	+6	+7
Pitchers	2	0	3	1	1	5	2	5	5	3	1	2	1	2	1	1

Remember, we have only included pitchers with nearly equal ERAs for the same team in consecutive seasons. You'd expect only minor differences in wins, but only a little over one-third of the pitchers came within a single win of their previous season's total. Nearly that many varied by four wins or more. The statistical shape of the distribution implies that over the course of many seasons, only 40% of all pitchers who meet the strict criteria we established would come within two wins of their first-season totals in their second seasons.

(Incidentally, all of our conclusions remained unchanged when we examined winning percentage differential instead of total wins. The variations in winning percentage factored out the differences from year to year in games started, but the results were the same, and it was an awful lot easier to explain without the decimal points.)

Let's examine Dave Stieb's 1985 performance in light of those figures. First, you should know that Stieb, whom we earlier called one of the most consistent American League pitchers, was the only pitcher in either league to meet our criteria in each of the past three pairs of consecutive seasons. Since 1982, he has started at least 30

games in every season, and his year-to-year ERAs have never varied by more than four-tenths of a run:

Year	GS	W–L	Pct.	ERA
1982	38	17–14	.548	3.25
1983	36	17–12	.586	3.04
1984	35	16–8	.667	2.83
1985	36	14–13	.519	2.48

The differences between Stieb's records in 1984 and 1985 are within normal limits, even considering the difference in winning percentages. Stieb's percentage was .148 lower last season than a year earlier; roughly 25 percent of all pitchers working under similar year-to-year circumstances would drop even further. So, despite all the negative reaction to Stieb's disappointing season, his 14–13 record might only indicate that he was the victim of bad luck. If that's the case, we shouldn't be too surprised if he rebounds with a 20-win season in 1986. And a look at the figures clearly calls for an indictment of the Blue Jays for lack of support *in re* David Andrew Stieb.

First, lack of batting support: Toronto gave Stieb slightly fewer runs to work with than their average, scoring 4.44 runs a game in Stieb's 36 starts, 4.79 for their other starting pitchers; they scored two or fewer runs for Stieb nine times. Second, lack of fielding support: Blue Jays errors led to 16 unearned runs charged to Stieb; only six American League pitchers allowed more. Twenty-seven percent of Toronto's unearned runs were charged to Stieb, who accounted for only 18 percent of their innings pitched. Third, and most damning, lack of relief support: No fewer than six times last season, Blue Jays relievers blew leads that Stieb had delivered to them. No starting pitcher has the right to expect flawless relief help, but as we described above, Toronto had one of the American League's most wasteful bullpens.

Despite his league-leading ERA, Stieb was unable to overcome the cumulative effect of Toronto's failure to adequately support him. Stieb suffered the slings and arrows of outrageous fortune, and found himself accused of vague character flaws to explain his seemingly illogical won-lost record. (His demeanor did little to dissuade such talk.) It's an ironic byproduct of the contemporary baseball era, when every aspect of play is scrutinized, that the word *unlucky* has been discarded. As a result, Stieb is denied the kind of understanding accorded Whitey Ford in the more innocent 1950s. Late in that 1958 season we discussed earlier, Dan Daniel, one of the most respected baseball writers of his day, wrote, "Ford, a truly great hurler, has been jinxed year after year. Always there is the promise of his first 20-game season, and always something happens." Although they may have lacked our analytical sophistication, baseball fans of 30 years ago probably understood a pitcher like Dave Stieb a lot better than we, in our search for answers, allow ourselves to.

WON-LOST RECORD BY STARTING POSITION

TORONTO 99-62	C	1B	2B	3B	SS	LF	CF	RF	P	DH	Leadoff	Relief	Starts
Jim Acker	-	-	-	-	-	-	-	-	-	-	-	36-25	-
Willie Aikens	-	-	-	-	-	-	-	-	-	5-1	-	-	5-1
Doyle Alexander	-	-	-	-	-	-	-	-	22-14	-	-	-	22-14
Gary Allenson	7-4	-	-	-	-	-	-	-	-	-	-	-	7-4
Jesse Barfield	-	-	-	-	-	-	6-1	88-57	-	-	-	-	94-58
George Bell	-	-	-	-	-	-	98-59	-	-	-	-	-	98-59
Jeff Burroughs	-	-	-	-	-	-	-	-	-	29-25	-	-	29-25
Bill Caudill	-	-	-	-	-	-	-	-	-	-	-	41-26	-
John Cerutti	-	-	-	-	-	-	-	-	0-1	-	-	0-3	0-1
Jim Clancy	-	-	-	-	-	-	-	-	16-7	-	-	-	16-7
Stan Clarke	-	-	-	-	-	-	-	-	-	-	-	1-3	-
Steve Davis	-	-	-	-	-	-	-	-	4-1	-	-	1-4	4-1
Tony Fernandez	-	-	-	-	98-60	-	-	-	-	-	13-8	-	98-60
Cecil Fielder	-	12-12	-	-	-	-	-	-	-	-	-	-	12-12
Tom Filer	-	-	-	-	-	-	-	-	9-0	-	-	0-2	9-0
Damaso Garcia	-	-	86-56	-	-	-	-	-	-	-	86-54	-	86-56
Kelly Gruber	-	-	-	1-1	-	-	-	-	-	-	-	-	1-1
Jeff Hearron	0-2	-	-	-	-	-	-	-	-	-	-	-	0-2
Tom Henke	-	-	-	-	-	-	-	-	-	-	-	22-6	-
Garth Iorg	-	-	12-5	29-28	-	-	-	-	-	-	-	-	41-33
Cliff Johnson	-	1-2	-	-	-	-	-	-	-	7-6	-	-	8-8
Jimmy Key	-	-	-	-	-	-	-	-	20-12	-	-	1-2	20-12
Dennis Lamp	-	-	-	-	-	-	-	-	0-1	-	-	28-24	0-1
Gary Lavelle	-	-	-	-	-	-	-	-	-	-	-	47-22	-
Rick Leach	-	3-1	-	-	-	0-1	-	0-1	-	-	-	-	3-3
Luis Leal	-	-	-	-	-	-	-	-	8-6	-	-	0-1	8-6
Manny Lee	-	-	1-1	-	1-2	-	-	-	-	-	-	-	2-3
Buck Martinez	18-14	-	-	-	-	-	-	-	-	-	-	-	18-14
Len Matuszek	-	1-0	-	-	-	-	-	-	-	24-15	-	-	25-15
Lloyd Moseby	-	-	-	-	-	-	93-58	-	-	-	-	-	93-58
Rance Mulliniks	-	-	-	69-33	-	-	-	-	-	-	-	-	69-33
Ron Musselman	-	-	-	-	-	-	-	-	3-1	-	-	9-12	3-1
Steve Nicosia	1-2	-	-	-	-	-	-	-	-	-	-	-	1-2
Al Oliver	-	-	-	-	-	-	-	-	-	33-15	-	-	33-15
Ron Shepherd	-	-	-	-	-	1-0	0-3	1-0	-	-	-	-	2-3
Dave Stieb	-	-	-	-	-	-	-	-	17-19	-	-	-	17-19
Lou Thornton	-	-	-	-	-	0-2	10-4	-	-	-	-	-	10-6
Willie Upshaw	-	82-47	-	-	-	-	-	-	-	1-0	-	-	83-47
Mitch Webster	-	-	-	-	-	-	-	-	-	-	-	-	-
Ernie Whitt	73-40	-	-	-	-	-	-	-	-	-	-	-	73-40

Batting vs. Left and Right Handed Pitchers

Player		BA	Rank	SA	Rank	OBA	Rank	HR %	Rank	BB %	Rank	SO %	Rank
Jesse Barfield	vs. Lefties	.309	30	.541	15	.379	20	4.35	45	10.64	46	23.83	149
	vs. Righties	.277	50	.533	8	.363	25	5.42	17	10.88	38	23.08	151
George Bell	vs. Lefties	.252	97	.463	53	.314	107	5.14	28	7.59	96	12.24	75
	vs. Righties	.288	33	.489	19	.335	61	4.33	35	5.81	122	14.19	88
Jeff Burroughs	vs. Lefties	.266	80	.455	58	.378	23	4.20	49	15.70	7	12.79	86
	vs. Righties	.229	--	.354	--	.327	--	0.00	--	12.73	--	25.45	--
Tony Fernandez	vs. Lefties	.294	44	.412	82	.366	38	0.00	131	10.05	56	6.39	20
	vs. Righties	.286	36	.378	92	.327	76	0.54	144	5.26	129	6.77	19
Cecil Fielder	vs. Lefties	.319	23	.551	11	.360	44	5.80	20	6.67	111	21.33	137
	vs. Righties	.200	--	.200	--	.333	--	0.00	--	16.67	--	0.00	--
Damaso Garcia	vs. Lefties	.251	100	.333	129	.276	137	0.91	122	3.06	151	7.42	26
	vs. Righties	.299	19	.402	76	.317	90	1.57	158	2.01	158	6.03	10
Garth Iorg	vs. Lefties	.310	28	.480	40	.361	41	2.50	80	7.37	100	5.99	15
	vs. Righties	.318	--	.443	--	.351	--	2.27	--	5.26	--	13.68	--
Cliff Johnson	vs. Lefties	.330	11	.438	68	.419	4	1.79	95	13.18	22	12.40	77
	vs. Righties	.230	125	.409	73	.296	122	4.28	36	7.99	84	14.93	102
Buck Martinez	vs. Lefties	.138	158	.264	151	.206	158	3.45	57	7.22	103	8.25	28
	vs. Righties	.333	--	.667	--	.438	--	8.33	--	18.75	--	25.00	--
Len Matuszek	vs. Lefties	.200	--	.200	--	.200	--	0.00	--	0.00	--	20.00	--
	vs. Righties	.212	143	.322	136	.261	146	1.37	113	6.83	104	14.29	90
Lloyd Moseby	vs. Lefties	.256	90	.393	93	.330	89	2.99	66	9.20	64	18.39	130
	vs. Righties	.260	78	.449	45	.355	39	3.14	66	12.71	21	10.51	49
Rance Mulliniks	vs. Lefties	.227	--	.318	--	.393	--	0.00	--	21.43	--	14.29	--
	vs. Righties	.299	18	.462	37	.382	12	2.91	74	12.28	23	12.53	69
Al Oliver	vs. Lefties	.235	--	.529	--	.235	--	5.88	--	0.00	--	23.53	--
	vs. Righties	.253	90	.359	111	.287	132	2.35	90	3.93	143	5.06	3
Willie Upshaw	vs. Lefties	.275	68	.462	54	.309	116	2.92	69	4.40	138	16.48	117
	vs. Righties	.276	52	.439	49	.357	34	3.03	68	10.67	40	10.93	51
Ernie Whitt	vs. Lefties	.213	141	.320	134	.318	105	2.67	76	12.22	31	24.44	150
	vs. Righties	.252	93	.472	29	.324	83	5.04	22	9.60	50	9.87	45
Team Average	vs. Lefties	.263	10	.416	7	.326	11	2.81	7	8.33	9	14.67	13
	vs. Righties	.272	2	.431	1	.334	3	2.90	5	8.18	9	12.39	2
League Average	vs. Lefties	.266		.416		.333		2.91		8.95		13.77	
	vs. Righties	.259		.401		.324		2.78		8.49		13.56	

Batting with Runners on Base and Bases Empty

		BA	Rank	SA	Rank	OBA	Rank	HR %	Rank	BB %	Rank	SO %	Rank
Jesse Barfield	Runners On	.279	70	.507	24	.366	48	4.80	28	12.08	33	24.53	156
	Bases Empty	.297	14	.558	6	.372	13	5.16	22	9.80	46	22.48	151
George Bell	Runners On	.253	114	.441	63	.297	129	3.91	49	6.43	124	11.58	67
	Bases Empty	.294	18	.512	12	.354	20	5.21	19	6.46	105	15.17	99
Jeff Burroughs	Runners On	.259	98	.435	67	.369	43	2.35	84	15.53	11	17.48	128
	Bases Empty	.255	87	.425	60	.363	16	3.77	48	14.52	8	14.52	86
Tony Fernandez	Runners On	.283	62	.371	112	.336	86	0.83	126	7.06	115	6.32	14
	Bases Empty	.293	20	.404	73	.344	35	0.00	148	6.88	97	6.88	16
Damaso Garcia	Runners On	.283	63	.367	116	.301	124	0.88	126	2.07	154	5.81	11
	Bases Empty	.281	29	.382	96	.303	108	1.60	111	2.59	156	6.99	17
Garth Iorg	Runners On	.304	34	.457	52	.374	34	2.17	87	10.19	56	10.83	60
	Bases Empty	.320	5	.480	22	.342	41	2.67	81	3.23	154	5.81	4
Cliff Johnson	Runners On	.327	14	.506	25	.389	18	3.70	52	10.22	54	12.90	84
	Bases Empty	.208	147	.348	118	.290	127	3.38	59	9.09	56	15.15	98
Lloyd Moseby	Runners On	.309	30	.519	19	.378	27	3.70	52	10.04	59	12.19	75
	Bases Empty	.223	129	.361	109	.322	80	2.64	84	12.28	20	14.58	91
Rance Mulliniks	Runners On	.326	15	.486	36	.388	19	2.17	87	10.56	50	10.56	55
	Bases Empty	.276	38	.434	49	.380	12	3.07	70	14.29	10	13.91	77
Al Oliver	Runners On	.240	132	.375	108	.263	151	3.13	66	3.03	151	10.10	51
	Bases Empty	.264	--	.374	--	.302	--	2.20	--	4.17	--	3.13	--
Willie Upshaw	Runners On	.293	49	.467	45	.358	56	2.18	86	8.91	86	14.73	104
	Bases Empty	.261	72	.430	53	.328	64	3.68	50	8.36	67	11.04	48
Ernie Whitt	Runners On	.266	82	.457	52	.363	51	4.35	39	13.30	25	12.39	76
	Bases Empty	.228	124	.434	49	.287	133	4.82	32	7.29	87	12.96	68
Team Average	Runners On	.274	6	.429	2	.335	9	2.68	9	8.50	12	12.80	5
	Bases Empty	.265	2	.423	3	.328	3	3.01	6	8.03	7	13.54	5
League Average	Runners On	.271		.416		.338		2.85		9.26		13.25	
	Bases Empty	.254		.397		.318		2.80		8.14		13.92	

Overall Batting Compared to Late Inning Pressure Situations

		BA	Rank	SA	Rank	OBA	Rank	HR %	Rank	BB %	Rank	SO %	Rank	RDI %	Rank
Jesse Barfield	Overall	.289	25	.536	3	.369	15	5.01	20	10.78	37	23.37	153	.306	57
	Pressure	.291	44	.557	11	.349	58	6.33	22	8.14	89	17.44	111	.176	124
George Bell	Overall	.275	53	.479	20	.327	81	4.61	32	6.45	118	13.49	81	.289	80
	Pressure	.359	7	.590	7	.412	19	3.85	45	7.06	103	12.94	69	.400	22
Jeff Burroughs	Overall	.257	96	.429	63	.366	19	3.14	66	14.98	8	15.86	110	.290	78
	Pressure	.229	107	.400	74	.308	95	2.86	62	10.26	62	17.95	116	.143	138
Tony Fernandez	Overall	.289	26	.390	97	.340	60	0.35	147	6.96	109	6.63	12	.285	87
	Pressure	.305	34	.390	78	.374	37	0.00	113	8.70	81	13.04	70	.333	55
Damaso Garcia	Overall	.282	40	.377	111	.302	128	1.33	116	2.39	157	6.54	11	.329	38
	Pressure	.267	65	.387	80	.273	127	1.33	104	1.27	153	5.06	11	.370	39
Garth Iorg	Overall	.313	6	.469	26	.358	29	2.43	89	6.73	115	8.33	29	.291	77
	Pressure	.323	23	.387	79	.323	81	0.00	113	0.00	154	3.13	5	.200	--
Cliff Johnson	Overall	.260	84	.417	74	.334	67	3.52	56	9.59	50	14.15	91	.395	8
	Pressure	.241	95	.370	87	.288	117	1.85	89	6.67	107	10.00	40	.500	7
Lloyd Moseby	Overall	.259	87	.426	66	.345	49	3.08	70	11.34	35	13.58	83	.288	82
	Pressure	.237	99	.303	117	.315	89	0.00	113	8.99	78	13.48	74	.421	18
Rance Mulliniks	Overall	.295	19	.454	35	.383	5	2.73	81	12.88	19	12.65	68	.440	2
	Pressure	.200	130	.300	118	.340	69	2.50	74	18.00	10	16.00	98	.273	78
Al Oliver	Overall	.251	--	.374	--	.282	--	2.67	--	3.59	--	6.67	--	.314	54
	Pressure	.286	--	.571	--	.318	--	9.52	--	4.55	--	4.55	--	.500	--
Willie Upshaw	Overall	.275	51	.447	45	.342	59	2.99	74	8.62	72	12.75	70	.291	76
	Pressure	.239	97	.403	73	.301	102	1.49	102	8.22	88	17.81	115	.300	71
Ernie Whitt	Overall	.245	113	.444	46	.323	91	4.61	33	10.11	43	12.69	69	.268	103
	Pressure	.220	116	.407	72	.303	98	3.39	54	10.45	60	10.45	47	.231	100
Team Average	Overall	.269	2	.425	3	.331	5	2.87	5	8.24	8	13.21	5	.301	5
	Pressure	.269	2	.423	2	.326	7	2.60	8	7.44	12	13.40	5	.303	3
League Average	Overall	.261		.406		.327		2.82		8.63		13.62		.287	
	Pressure	.253		.381		.323		2.74		9.11		14.40		.273	

Additional Miscellaneous Batting Comparisons

	Grass Surface BA	Rank	Artificial Surface BA	Rank	Home Games BA	Rank	Road Games BA	Rank	Runners in Scoring Position BA	Rank	Runners in Scoring Pos and Two Outs BA	Rank	Leading Off Inning OBA	Rank	Runners on 3B with less than 2 Outs RDI %	Rank
Jesse Barfield	.282	46	.294	33	.286	49	.292	18	.281	68	.328	22	.352	38	.444	140
George Bell	.305	19	.255	73	.255	92	.293	17	.275	80	.215	117	.329	73	.576	80
Jeff Burroughs	.164	--	.300	25	.294	39	.226	133	.286	64	.231	96	.362	--	.500	106
Tony Fernandez	.271	60	.302	24	.306	27	.274	47	.300	44	.324	28	.355	34	.419	145
Cecil Fielder	.280	--	.327	10	.300	--	.324	--	.286	--	.429	--	.545	--	.857	--
Damaso Garcia	.268	66	.290	39	.303	30	.260	75	.308	36	.339	16	.296	112	.576	80
Garth Iorg	.263	--	.347	8	.378	2	.266	64	.329	16	.333	17	.265	141	.375	--
Cliff Johnson	.263	79	.253	77	.250	99	.269	57	.355	7	.327	26	.237	149	.700	29
Buck Martinez	.206	--	.138	156	.200	--	.136	--	.150	--	.200	--	.242	--	.400	146
Len Matuszek	.232	--	.195	147	.164	--	.256	--	.216	--	.292	42	.267	--	.700	29
Lloyd Moseby	.236	129	.273	56	.258	86	.259	81	.279	74	.231	96	.352	36	.531	99
Rance Mulliniks	.268	66	.318	11	.316	19	.276	42	.381	4	.361	9	.357	32	.750	13
Al Oliver	.244	--	.257	71	.244	--	.257	--	.348	--	.423	2	.405	--	.556	--
Willie Upshaw	.265	74	.282	47	.297	37	.257	84	.267	89	.258	61	.313	89	.667	47
Ernie Whitt	.274	55	.224	124	.223	137	.265	69	.229	124	.111	155	.306	98	.727	24
Team Average	.262	7	.274	2	.275	4	.264	5	.284	3	.271	2	.319	7	.563	11
League Average	.262		.259		.266		.256		.268		.248		.321		.587	

Pitching vs. Left and Right Handed Batters

		BA	Rank	SA	Rank	OBA	Rank	HR %	Rank	BB %	Rank	SO %	Rank
Jim Acker	vs. Lefties	.308	110	.390	57	.398	123	1.37	25	12.79	108	8.72	111
	vs. Righties	.234	37	.354	31	.323	70	2.86	73	10.61	110	13.64	68
Doyle Alexander	vs. Lefties	.264	68	.416	69	.330	61	3.11	84	8.22	51	9.97	102
	vs. Righties	.268	81	.375	47	.297	36	2.43	49	3.86	6	16.41	40
Bill Caudill	vs. Lefties	.248	48	.407	67	.397	120	4.42	119	18.88	129	13.99	50
	vs. Righties	.179	2	.293	8	.222	2	2.86	73	5.19	23	16.88	36
Jim Clancy	vs. Lefties	.251	54	.396	62	.316	48	1.96	40	8.87	62	10.28	94
	vs. Righties	.230	32	.435	92	.265	14	4.35	116	4.90	15	15.10	53
Jimmy Key	vs. Lefties	.178	4	.306	16	.233	2	2.55	60	6.94	33	17.92	21
	vs. Righties	.251	57	.403	71	.295	32	2.83	70	5.56	29	7.91	127
Dennis Lamp	vs. Lefties	.238	37	.320	21	.292	23	1.74	33	7.73	43	12.37	67
	vs. Righties	.255	62	.352	30	.293	30	1.85	28	5.17	22	18.97	20
Gary Lavelle	vs. Lefties	.220	17	.330	24	.330	60	3.30	93	14.29	120	18.75	17
	vs. Righties	.211	15	.286	5	.298	39	1.24	10	10.75	112	15.59	46
Luis Leal	vs. Lefties	.316	120	.522	123	.368	98	4.41	118	8.55	58	8.55	114
	vs. Righties	.289	108	.533	130	.353	100	5.19	127	7.28	57	13.25	75
Ron Musselman	vs. Lefties	.294	97	.480	109	.356	87	1.96	40	10.17	82	12.71	61
	vs. Righties	.274	--	.321	--	.347	--	0.00	--	10.17	--	11.86	--
Dave Stieb	vs. Lefties	.198	7	.286	7	.281	16	1.79	37	9.92	79	11.50	80
	vs. Righties	.234	35	.367	41	.302	43	2.96	77	7.30	59	20.80	14
Team Average	vs. Lefties	.245	2	.381	2	.317	2	2.81	7	9.50	9	12.34	9
	vs. Righties	.241	1	.371	2	.296	1	2.65	4	6.82	1	14.88	5
League Average	vs. Lefties	.265		.408		.333		2.74		9.21		12.94	
	vs. Righties	.259		.404		.322		2.88		8.19		14.14	

Pitching with Runners on Base and Bases Empty

		BA	Rank	SA	Rank	OBA	Rank	HR %	Rank	BB %	Rank	SO %	Rank
Jim Acker	Runners On	.260	49	.373	40	.324	43	2.96	78	8.47	53	13.76	57
	Bases Empty	.276	99	.368	39	.392	126	1.32	15	14.92	127	8.84	122
Doyle Alexander	Runners On	.276	78	.390	57	.323	41	2.28	51	6.24	22	14.55	43
	Bases Empty	.259	78	.400	69	.309	53	3.10	81	6.09	29	12.02	81
Bill Caudill	Runners On	.200	3	.336	19	.293	17	4.00	106	11.33	103	13.33	64
	Bases Empty	.219	19	.352	33	.320	74	3.13	84	12.24	118	17.69	28
Jim Clancy	Runners On	.235	26	.417	75	.264	5	3.74	100	4.48	8	13.43	63
	Bases Empty	.245	51	.413	82	.310	54	2.68	65	8.59	75	11.96	82
Jimmy Key	Runners On	.225	18	.373	41	.287	15	2.90	76	7.69	39	8.97	117
	Bases Empty	.243	50	.390	57	.279	17	2.70	68	4.78	15	10.48	105
Dennis Lamp	Runners On	.240	29	.372	38	.286	14	2.73	67	6.73	29	15.87	32
	Bases Empty	.254	64	.307	9	.298	44	0.98	8	5.96	26	16.06	37
Gary Lavelle	Runners On	.233	24	.325	12	.343	74	1.67	30	13.91	123	15.23	38
	Bases Empty	.197	7	.280	6	.279	16	2.27	45	10.20	98	18.37	19
Luis Leal	Runners On	.313	116	.571	130	.357	91	5.36	129	6.30	24	12.60	75
	Bases Empty	.296	118	.497	124	.364	109	4.40	117	9.09	84	9.66	116
Dave Stieb	Runners On	.229	23	.306	7	.294	22	1.29	20	7.69	39	17.65	20
	Bases Empty	.203	11	.329	17	.287	29	2.95	75	9.61	93	13.80	58
Team Average	Runners On	.247	1	.378	2	.306	1	2.68	4	7.77	1	14.36	4
	Bases Empty	.240	2	.373	2	.306	2	2.75	5	8.27	7	13.23	9
League Average	Runners On	.271		.416		.338		2.85		9.26		13.25	
	Bases Empty	.254		.397		.318		2.80		8.14		13.92	

Overall Pitching Compared to Late Inning Pressure Situations

		BA	Rank	SA	Rank	OBA	Rank	HR %	Rank	BB %	Rank	SO %	Rank
Jim Acker	Overall	.268	81	.371	35	.358	108	2.18	37	11.62	108	11.35	94
	Pressure	.310	111	.380	62	.386	105	2.00	52	10.43	77	6.96	121
Doyle Alexander	Overall	.266	78	.396	55	.315	47	2.78	68	6.15	18	13.03	65
	Pressure	.336	120	.533	120	.377	100	4.92	119	6.06	26	12.12	76
Bill Caudill	Overall	.209	4	.344	18	.306	35	3.56	105	11.78	110	15.49	34
	Pressure	.250	54	.432	90	.344	76	5.30	122	12.10	96	15.92	40
Jim Clancy	Overall	.241	32	.414	77	.292	18	3.09	85	7.02	34	12.52	76
	Pressure	.444	--	.556	--	.444	--	0.00	--	0.00	--	11.11	--
Tom Henke	Overall	.206	--	.312	--	.245	--	2.84	--	5.23	--	27.45	--
	Pressure	.206	16	.330	31	.245	9	3.09	82	4.81	14	27.88	2
Jimmy Key	Overall	.237	21	.384	45	.282	9	2.77	66	5.84	12	9.93	114
	Pressure	.214	23	.271	12	.291	30	1.43	34	9.76	69	9.76	99
Dennis Lamp	Overall	.247	42	.338	14	.292	17	1.80	23	6.34	24	15.96	29
	Pressure	.191	11	.235	6	.236	7	0.87	21	5.69	22	17.07	26
Gary Lavelle	Overall	.214	7	.302	6	.310	42	1.98	29	12.08	114	16.78	26
	Pressure	.229	36	.314	21	.343	72	1.96	48	14.29	114	15.87	41
Luis Leal	Overall	.303	120	.528	131	.361	113	4.80	129	7.92	53	10.89	105
	Pressure	.444	--	1.222	--	.545	--	22.22	--	18.18	--	9.09	--
Ron Musselman	Overall	.284	--	.399	--	.352	--	0.96	--	10.17	--	12.29	--
	Pressure	.313	112	.469	104	.371	94	0.00	1	8.57	52	8.57	109
Dave Stieb	Overall	.213	6	.320	9	.290	13	2.28	40	8.83	75	15.36	38
	Pressure	.273	78	.392	65	.350	81	1.40	33	9.70	68	13.33	62
Team Average	Overall	.243	2	.375	3	.306	1	2.72	4	8.06	4	13.71	8
	Pressure	.258	8	.385	7	.331	8	2.87	9	9.54	7	14.57	6
League Average	Overall	.261		.406		.327		2.82		8.63		13.62	
	Pressure	.258		.392		.332		2.71		9.52		14.05	

Additional Miscellaneous Pitching Comparisons

	Grass Surface BA	Rank	Artificial Surface BA	Rank	Home Games BA	Rank	Road Games BA	Rank	Runners in Scoring Position BA	Rank	Runners in Scoring Pos and Two Outs BA	Rank	Leading Off Inning OBA	Rank
Jim Acker	.336	--	.226	25	.204	8	.333	126	.259	57	.292	102	.456	132
Doyle Alexander	.306	116	.249	50	.243	44	.301	109	.268	69	.224	53	.295	41
Bill Caudill	.230	--	.199	10	.189	6	.231	21	.233	27	.128	5	.295	43
Jim Clancy	.271	84	.209	16	.199	7	.263	68	.273	76	.298	107	.353	100
Steve Davis	.190	--	.232	28	.261	--	.147	--	.286	--	.286	--	.344	--
Tom Filer	.277	--	.189	8	.163	--	.291	--	.321	--	.000	--	.360	--
Tom Henke	.095	--	.253	56	.219	--	.191	--	.240	--	.273	--	.281	--
Jimmy Key	.260	70	.224	24	.230	22	.248	39	.208	14	.242	69	.263	11
Dennis Lamp	.236	24	.256	63	.266	82	.235	24	.243	37	.211	38	.281	27
Gary Lavelle	.252	--	.182	3	.156	--	.259	57	.153	2	.162	15	.262	10
Luis Leal	.333	--	.285	92	.273	92	.336	127	.367	--	.400	--	.342	89
Ron Musselman	.315	--	.259	67	.232	--	.309	114	.276	--	.303	112	.404	--
Dave Stieb	.184	3	.236	31	.247	51	.187	1	.199	8	.186	24	.319	70
Team Average	.256	5	.234	1	.230	1	.255	2	.244	2	.234	4	.315	5
League Average	.262		.259		.256		.266		.268		.248		.321	

National League

ATLANTA BRAVES

Atlanta Stadium. Mention it at the National Pitchers Convention and watch out for flying stones. Mention it to a group of hitters, and watch them drool. The Braves play in one of baseball's most notorious home-run ballparks. Perhaps for that reason, Atlanta has loaded its pitching staff with guys who keep the ball down, on the premise that ground balls rarely clear the fences. A sound strategy to counter opposing batters who see Atlanta Stadium as a great place to fatten their home run totals? Oddly enough, no. Quite the opposite.

In last year's *Analyst,* we presented a new statistic for the first time: the Ground Outs-to-Air Outs Ratio. For every pitcher listed in the Pitcher Section, we gave his figure for the season and for his career, and we have done the same in this edition as well. And since we last chatted, we have uncovered a simple yet essential fact that will raise the level of your armchair managing, one that will make a knowledge of individual players' G/A ratios an indispensable part of your understanding of baseball, whether you are a fan, a player, or a manager.

According to a study of our play-by-play data for the past 11 seasons, the outcomes of head-to-head matchups between batters and pitchers are heavily influenced by the G/A tendencies of the players involved. Matchups of likenesses (e.g., ground-ball hitters vs. ground-ball pitchers) favor pitchers. Matchups of opposites favor batters. Remember this by noting that the same is true of lefty-righty matchups: likenesses (e.g., left-handed batters vs. left-handed pitchers) favor pitchers, opposites favor batters. Moreover, the batting average variations found by grouping batters and pitchers by their G/A ratios are nearly as substantial as those found when players are grouped by "handedness." As a point of reference, remember these figures: left-handed batters last season hit .251 against left-handed pitchers and .266 against right-handers; right-handed batters hit .261 against lefties, .247 against northpaws.

Last summer, we looked at 10 years of play-by-play data, and chose as our study groups all batters with at least 1,000 plate appearances during that time and all pitchers who had faced 1,000 or more batters. We ranked the batters and pitchers according their G/A ratios, saved the highest and lowest 25 percent of each group, and discarded the rest. Type "A" batters and type "A" pitchers were the groups which tended toward hitting or inducing ground balls; the type "B" groups tended toward air outs. The summary of more than half a million head-to-head matchups between members of our two control groups follows, with expected marks based upon the career statistics of the individual players included in each group:

	Opposing Pitchers	
"A" Batters	"A"	"B"
Actual BA	.268	.265
Expected BA	.277	.261

	Opposing Pitchers	
"B" Batters	"A"	"B"
Actual BA	.272	.247
Expected BA	.265	.248

Notice that fly-ball hitters and pitchers are expected to produce comparatively lower batting averages than ground ballers. The "B" groups are top-heavy with home run hitters (including Mike Schmidt, Gorman Thomas, Tom Brunansky) and strikeout pitchers (Jeff Reardon, Bill Caudill, Steve Bedrosian). There is a greater variation among the ground-ball groups. For lists of the twenty-five most extreme hitters and pitchers over the past eleven seasons, see the career leaders lists on pages 403 and 410.

The discovery of these trends has has greater implications for Atlanta than for most other teams, because the Braves' pitching staff was more loaded with ground-ball pitchers than any other in the major leagues last season, especially in the bullpen. National League team G/A ratios follow; the Braves' tendency toward ground outs is so pronounced that the gap between Atlanta and the second-place Cubs is greater than that between the Cubs and the ninth-place Astros:

Atlanta	1.67	St. Louis	1.21
Chicago	1.40	Houston	1.18
Los Angeles	1.40	New York	1.12
San Francisco	1.27	Cincinnati	1.02
Montreal	1.27	San Diego	1.02
Pittsburgh	1.26	League Avg.	1.24
Philadelphia	1.24		

Because Braves pitchers tend so heavily toward ground balls, type "B" hitters as a group hit much better against Atlanta than type "A" hitters. The following table includes the National League players with the highest and lowest G/A ratios among qualifying batters (502 or more plate appearances). Qualifying batters hit 26 points higher against the Braves last season than against the league in general. While our 10 type "A" hitters increased their averages by only 10 points per player, the middle group (players close to the league average, not listed below) fattened up by an average of 29 points, and type "B" hitters added nearly 36 points per player to their averages. The four largest differences below all belong to type "B" players, fly-ball hitters against Atlanta's ground-ball pitching staff.

	Type "A" Hitters				Type "B" Hitters		
	Vs.	Vs.			Vs.	Vs.	
Player	N.L.	Atl.	Diff.	Player	N.L.	Atl.	Diff.
McGee	.353	.306	−47	Schmidt	.277	.323	+46
Backman	.273	.313	+40	Clark	.281	.389	+108
Sax	.279	.318	+39	Carter	.281	.366	+85
Gwynn	.317	.375	+58	Guerrero	.320	.286	−34
Templeton	.282	.238	−44	Foster	.263	.267	+4
Cruz	.300	.303	+3	Landreaux	.268	.339	+71
Coleman	.267	.304	+37	Wallach	.260	.250	−10
Oester	.295	.281	−14	Moreland	.307	.275	−32
Smith	.276	.310	+34	Madlock	.275	.315	+40
Santana	.257	.256	−1	Marshall	.293	.370	+77

Some of the ground out/fly out fallout is intriguing. For instance, most opposing managers loaded their lineups with right-handed batters when facing Zane Smith, the only left-handed pitcher in Atlanta's rotation. But Smith has a tendency toward ground balls so pronounced that managers might be better off stacking their lineups not with right-handed hitters but with fly ball hitters, right-handed or not. For example, Terry Puhl of the Astros (who doubled in his only at bat vs. Smith last season) and Ken Landreaux of the Dodgers (1-for-2 vs. Smith in 1985) are left-handed fly-ball swingers who might have more success against Smith than some right-handed ground-ball hitters. Consider the following breakdowns of batters opposing Smith last season:

	AB	H	2B	3B	HR	BB	SO	BA	SA	OBA
Left Handed Batters	81	23	2	0	0	8	24	.284	.309	.348
Right-Handed Batters	450	112	27	6	4	72	61	.249	.362	.356
Ground-Ball Hitters	236	58	9	3	2	38	42	.246	.335	.350
Fly-Ball Hitters	295	77	20	3	2	42	43	.261	.369	.358

Batters in the table above are divided into ground-ball and fly-ball hitters according to whether their 1985 G/A ratios fell above or below the National League average of 1.242 ground outs per air out. Not surprisingly, considering the results of our study, fly-ball hitters as a group hit better against Smith than right-handed hitters.

Bedrock Assumptions

With the exception of Dave Schuler, who faced only 50 batters, no Atlanta pitcher had a lower G/A ratio last season than Steve Bedrosian. Although his 1.04 average was the highest of his career, it was still far below the league average. And despite our suggestion that ground-ball pitchers may be at a disadvantage against teams visiting Atlanta, enemy fly balls are apparently as welcome in Atlanta as Ted Turner is at a CBS board meeting; Bedrosian was sent to Philadelphia in an off-season trade for catcher Ozzie Virgil.

Since moving to Atlanta in 1966, the Braves have rarely surrendered a starting pitcher for an everyday player. Atlanta was burned (remember, Scarlett?) in 1973 when they shipped Pat Dobson to the Yankees for a care package of Triple-A disappointments, and again two years later when they traded Ron Reed, with a decade worth of pitching left in his right arm, for Elias Sosa and played-out Ray Sadecki. For ten years after, the Braves bartered a rotation pitcher for an everyday slugger only once, when they tossed Carl Morton and Rogelio Moret into the dowry for Jeff Burroughs following the 1976 season. But last winter they relinquished Bedrosian, albeit reluctantly, for Virgil, who fills a long-standing need behind the plate. Before examining that years-long void, though, a few words on the past reluctance of the Braves not only to deal a starting pitcher, but also to admit the need for another slugger.

To understand the Braves' attitude, you must understand Atlanta Stadium, a.k.a. Fenway South. Playing in a stadium which promotes home runs, the Braves' run-scoring potential has been overestimated. For two decades this ballpark illusion has damaged the reputations of their pitchers; this is clear in the following table, which shows the Braves' leaguewide *home-game* ranking since 1976 in batting (runs scored) and pitching (runs allowed):

	1976	1977	1978	1979	1980	1981	1982	1983	1984	1985
Batting	5	2	5	7	6	10	2	1	7	6
Pitching	12	12	12	12	6	4	11	6	10	12

During that period, Atlanta has an average home-game rank of fifth in batting and tenth in pitching, apparently supporting the popular notion that the Braves' pitching has been weak but their offense adequate. But to net out the effect of Atlanta Stadium, let's examine the same table when applied only to road games:

	1976	1977	1978	1979	1980	1981	1982	1983	1984	1985
Batting	9	12	12	11	11	7	6	1	10	9
Pitching	5	12	8	5	10	7	4	2.5	1.5	9

Road statistics provide an unbiased picture, and the situation here is nearly reversed. Over the past ten seasons, Atlanta's average National League rank in road-game scoring is ninth, and in road-game pitching, sixth. But during that time, Atlanta has conducted a virtually never-ending search for pitchers, sometimes at the expense of their lineup (Gary Matthews for Bob Walk, Brett Butler and Brook Jacoby for Len Barker), other times dipping into Ted Turner's wallet (John Montefusco, Terry Forster, Pete Falcone, Bruce Sutter). The Braves' policy has been exactly the opposite of that of the Boston Red Sox, who have tended to neglect their pitching staff while looking for sluggers in an attempt to take advantage of their own home-run ballpark. (See the Boston essay for a discussion of the success of Boston's efforts.) But finally, Atlanta has reversed their philosophy, and as a result, they have added Ozzie Virgil to their anemic attack.

The Backstop's Here

A lack of production from behind the plate has hurt the Braves for more than 10 years. As we pointed out last year, no Atlanta catcher has hit 10 home runs or driven in 50 runs in a season since Earl Williams in 1972. Since then, the names of Braves backstops indicate the futility of their attempts to fill the hole: Oates, Correll, Pocoroba, Nahorodny, Nolan, Sinatro. Rick Cerone was acquired last season, but only added to the problem. Compare the performance of Atlanta's starting catchers last season (who also included Bruce Benedict and Larry Owen) to the National League average:

Starting Catchers	AB	R	H	2B	3B	HR	RBI	BB	SB	BA	SA	OBA
Atlanta Braves	537	34	115	18	0	5	53	55	0	.214	.276	.287
N.L. Average	552	55	132	24	2	15	69	59	3	.239	.369	.313

So the acquisition of Virgil for Steve Bedrosian, a pitcher reportedly considered untouchable just one year earlier, and promising outfielder Milt Thompson (whose 3.65 G/A ratio, the highest in the majors among players with at least 100 plate appearances last season, made him particularly unsuited to Atlanta Stadium), addresses several problems which have characterized the Braves for more than a decade. It bolsters their lineup at its weakest position with an established hitter to complement Dale Murphy and Bob Horner, and indicates a willingness to part with a pitcher in order to satisfy a more pressing need. Bedrosian may indeed thrive away from Atlanta Stadium, but our guess is that the Braves will benefit from the deal regardless.

WON-LOST RECORD BY STARTING POSITION

ATLANTA 66-96	C	1B	2B	3B	SS	LF	CF	RF	P	Leadoff	Relief	Starts
Len Barker	-	-	-	-	-	-	-	-	3-15	-	0-2	3-15
Steve Bedrosian	-	-	-	-	-	-	-	-	15-22	-	-	15-22
Bruce Benedict	28-39	-	-	-	-	-	-	-	-	-	-	28-39
Rick Camp	-	-	-	-	-	-	-	-	1-1	-	12-52	1-1
Rick Cerone	26-50	-	-	-	-	-	-	-	-	-	-	26-50
Chris Chambliss	-	12-15	-	-	-	-	-	-	-	-	-	12-15
Jeff Dedmon	-	-	-	-	-	-	-	-	-	-	19-41	-
Terry Forster	-	-	-	-	-	-	-	-	-	-	12-34	-
Gene Garber	-	-	-	-	-	-	-	-	-	-	15-44	-
Albert Hall	-	-	-	-	-	-	0-1	-	-	0-1	-	0-1
Terry Harper	-	-	-	-	-	-	47-75	-	2-0	-	-	49-75
Bob Horner	-	38-47	-	14-26	-	-	-	-	-	-	-	52-73
Glenn Hubbard	-	-	53-77	-	-	-	-	-	-	-	-	53-77
Joe Johnson	-	-	-	-	-	-	-	-	8-6	-	0-1	8-6
Brad Komminsk	-	-	-	-	-	11-9	-	24-30	-	12-16	-	35-39
Rick Mahler	-	-	-	-	-	-	-	-	20-19	-	-	20-19
Craig McMurtry	-	-	-	-	-	-	-	-	1-5	-	1-10	1-5
Dale Murphy	-	-	-	-	-	-	66-95	-	-	-	-	66-95
Ken Oberkfell	-	-	4-8	43-58	-	-	-	-	-	-	-	47-66
Larry Owen	12-7	-	-	-	-	-	-	-	-	-	-	12-7
Pascual Perez	-	-	-	-	-	-	-	-	6-16	-	-	6-16
Gerald Perry	-	16-34	-	-	-	-	-	-	-	1-0	-	16-34
Johnny Rabb	-	-	-	-	-	-	-	-	-	-	-	-
Rafael Ramirez	-	-	-	-	52-78	-	-	-	-	9-11	-	52-78
Paul Runge	-	-	-	8-11	2-1	-	-	-	-	-	-	10-12
Dave Schuler	-	-	-	-	-	-	-	-	-	-	0-9	-
Steve Shields	-	-	-	-	-	-	-	-	2-4	-	1-16	2-4
Zane Smith	-	-	-	-	-	-	-	-	10-8	-	7-17	10-8
Bruce Sutter	-	-	-	-	-	-	-	-	-	-	44-14	-
Andres Thomas	-	-	-	-	2-0	-	-	-	-	2-	-0	2-0
Milt Thompson	-	-	-	-	-	8-12	-	6-10	-	14-22	-	14-22
Claudell Washington	-	-	-	-	-	-	-	34-56	-	26-43	-	34-56
Paul Zuvella	-	-	9-11	1-1	10-17	-	-	-	-	2-3	-	20-29

Batting vs. Left and Right Handed Pitchers

		BA	Rank	SA	Rank	OBA	Rank	HR %	Rank	BB %	Rank	SO %	Rank
Bruce Benedict	vs. Lefties	.190	128	.224	131	.304	89	0.00	108	13.04	26	0.00	1
	vs. Righties	.207	126	.233	133	.268	128	0.00	120	7.74	77	7.14	14
Rick Cerone	vs. Lefties	.198	122	.275	123	.253	124	1.10	90	7.07	89	7.07	15
	vs. Righties	.225	118	.283	123	.304	97	1.05	92	10.14	42	8.29	24
Chris Chambliss	vs. Lefties	.194	--	.250	--	.286	--	0.00	--	11.90	--	14.29	--
	vs. Righties	.246	91	.351	91	.313	85	2.24	57	8.84	63	10.88	51
Terry Harper	vs. Lefties	.221	105	.395	58	.280	112	4.65	23	7.94	80	14.29	78
	vs. Righties	.288	29	.413	52	.352	45	2.81	43	8.22	69	13.88	76
Bob Horner	vs. Lefties	.298	23	.553	8	.354	38	6.21	8	8.43	74	8.43	24
	vs. Righties	.252	80	.472	14	.323	69	5.28	9	9.67	53	11.60	58
Glenn Hubbard	vs. Lefties	.229	99	.278	120	.335	61	0.69	101	14.20	19	9.66	33
	vs. Righties	.234	110	.332	101	.313	84	1.36	79	9.23	57	11.01	53
Brad Komminsk	vs. Lefties	.214	111	.324	100	.289	104	1.65	78	9.27	64	20.49	119
	vs. Righties	.246	93	.331	103	.350	47	0.85	99	13.77	20	21.01	129
Dale Murphy	vs. Lefties	.333	5	.552	10	.440	3	5.46	13	16.06	8	19.27	113
	vs. Righties	.286	31	.533	5	.364	31	6.24	4	11.13	35	20.04	123
Ken Oberkfell	vs. Lefties	.243	83	.287	117	.323	71	0.00	108	9.16	66	13.74	75
	vs. Righties	.283	34	.387	73	.372	20	1.01	94	11.44	33	5.87	11
Gerald Perry	vs. Lefties	.171	--	.244	--	.190	--	2.44	--	2.38	--	21.43	--
	vs. Righties	.223	120	.279	124	.300	105	1.02	93	10.00	49	8.64	27
Rafael Ramirez	vs. Lefties	.240	86	.323	101	.271	117	0.00	108	4.39	121	10.24	41
	vs. Righties	.253	76	.338	95	.272	126	1.33	81	2.82	132	10.77	49
Paul Runge	vs. Lefties	.222	102	.356	84	.352	41	2.22	66	15.79	9	15.79	93
	vs. Righties	.214	--	.214	--	.346	--	0.00	--	16.98	--	16.98	--
Milt Thompson	vs. Lefties	.143	--	.143	--	.143	--	0.00	--	0.00	--	20.00	--
	vs. Righties	.315	10	.381	75	.354	43	0.00	120	3.93	129	18.54	114
Claudell Washington	vs. Lefties	.206	118	.365	77	.261	122	1.59	79	7.25	88	26.09	129
	vs. Righties	.290	28	.472	15	.358	40	4.18	18	9.41	55	12.90	71
Paul Zuvella	vs. Lefties	.250	77	.309	108	.320	75	0.00	108	9.33	62	6.67	10
	vs. Righties	.254	74	.303	115	.305	94	0.00	120	6.67	93	6.67	13
Team Average	vs. Lefties	.237	12	.355	11	.309	10	2.26	9	9.31	3	14.73	5
	vs. Righties	.250	8	.367	9	.318	7	2.29	5	8.72	4	13.19	4
League Average	vs. Lefties	.250		.374		.317		2.26		8.65		14.84	
	vs. Righties	.253		.374		.320		2.12		8.62		14.28	

Batting with Runners on Base and Bases Empty

		BA	Rank	SA	Rank	OBA	Rank	HR %	Rank	BB %	Rank	SO %	Rank
Bruce Benedict	Runners On	.227	112	.278	124	.287	121	0.00	115	8.04	92	4.46	4
	Bases Empty	.180	133	.189	133	.272	115	0.00	120	10.40	28	5.60	8
Rick Cerone	Runners On	.243	90	.331	99	.314	92	1.47	74	10.26	64	6.41	10
	Bases Empty	.192	131	.233	132	.263	120	0.68	108	8.13	50	9.38	29
Chris Chambliss	Runners On	.203	133	.278	123	.304	99	1.27	78	13.04	34	9.78	49
	Bases Empty	.264	--	.374	--	.309	--	2.20	--	6.19	--	13.40	--
Terry Harper	Runners On	.246	86	.388	73	.324	85	4.02	26	9.84	70	17.72	118
	Bases Empty	.280	32	.422	38	.330	53	2.99	39	6.60	77	10.76	40
Bob Horner	Runners On	.258	77	.537	4	.342	64	6.56	3	11.97	44	10.56	58
	Bases Empty	.276	42	.460	24	.324	63	4.60	16	6.25	82	10.55	38
Glenn Hubbard	Runners On	.216	122	.268	128	.295	108	0.53	109	9.25	76	12.78	72
	Bases Empty	.245	88	.349	91	.340	39	1.61	92	12.28	21	8.77	22
Brad Komminsk	Runners On	.223	118	.286	117	.346	61	0.89	93	15.94	11	23.91	133
	Bases Empty	.229	106	.351	86	.293	102	1.60	78	7.80	56	18.54	108
Dale Murphy	Runners On	.324	12	.604	1	.401	17	6.83	2	11.80	45	20.19	128
	Bases Empty	.281	29	.485	16	.377	8	5.33	9	13.33	13	19.49	119
Ken Oberkfell	Runners On	.239	97	.347	93	.340	65	1.14	82	13.04	34	8.70	35
	Bases Empty	.297	12	.369	73	.374	11	0.42	116	9.06	40	7.55	16
Gerald Perry	Runners On	.223	117	.291	115	.289	119	1.94	66	8.77	80	14.91	88
	Bases Empty	.207	123	.259	127	.277	111	0.74	107	8.78	41	7.43	15
Rafael Ramirez	Runners On	.279	50	.403	63	.294	111	0.88	95	2.92	133	8.33	32
	Bases Empty	.228	108	.287	123	.256	128	0.88	101	3.66	128	12.11	55
Milt Thompson	Runners On	.328	--	.328	--	.350	--	0.00	--	3.28	--	14.75	--
	Bases Empty	.290	15	.379	66	.333	47	0.00	120	3.79	124	20.45	123
Claudell Washington	Runners On	.271	59	.414	55	.373	36	3.01	44	14.56	23	17.72	119
	Bases Empty	.279	36	.475	20	.325	59	4.15	21	6.01	91	13.43	69
Paul Zuvella	Runners On	.235	105	.321	105	.287	120	0.00	115	6.59	114	6.59	11
	Bases Empty	.266	51	.294	122	.328	56	0.00	120	8.40	48	6.72	12
Team Average	Runners On	.246	9	.376	8	.321	10	2.51	3	9.83	5	14.19	10
	Bases Empty	.246	9	.353	10	.310	7	2.10	8	8.16	4	13.26	1
League Average	Runners On	.258		.381		.332		2.19		9.74		13.69	
	Bases Empty	.248		.369		.309		2.14		7.75		15.05	

Overall Batting Compared to Late Inning Pressure Situations

		BA	Rank	SA	Rank	OBA	Rank	HR %	Rank	BB %	Rank	SO %	Rank	RDI %	Rank
Bruce Benedict	Overall	.202	132	.231	133	.279	126	0.00	127	9.28	54	5.06	7	.261	85
	Pressure	.147	129	.147	133	.216	126	0.00	92	7.50	91	10.00	30	.000	--
Rick Cerone	Overall	.216	127	.280	129	.288	117	1.06	99	9.18	57	7.91	18	.235	106
	Pressure	.233	90	.279	104	.333	67	0.00	92	11.76	39	3.92	2	.400	10
Chris Chambliss	Overall	.235	--	.329	--	.307	--	1.76	--	9.52	--	11.64	--	.310	40
	Pressure	.176	123	.255	116	.250	117	1.96	63	8.93	68	17.86	93	.167	109
Terry Harper	Overall	.264	66	.407	55	.327	68	3.46	33	8.12	73	14.02	79	.293	62
	Pressure	.286	42	.455	35	.375	34	3.90	30	11.24	43	10.11	32	.214	89
Bob Horner	Overall	.267	61	.499	12	.333	56	5.59	7	9.26	56	10.56	41	.315	36
	Pressure	.325	19	.650	2	.400	24	8.75	3	11.11	44	7.78	17	.258	63
Glenn Hubbard	Overall	.232	115	.314	118	.321	71	1.14	94	10.94	37	10.55	40	.240	103
	Pressure	.204	105	.278	108	.358	47	1.85	65	17.14	12	7.14	15	.188	102
Brad Komminsk	Overall	.227	118	.327	111	.314	84	1.33	88	11.08	34	20.70	128	.243	100
	Pressure	.188	116	.250	118	.304	89	0.00	92	14.04	19	22.81	123	.067	131
Dale Murphy	Overall	.300	13	.539	4	.388	11	6.01	4	12.64	21	19.80	123	.335	20
	Pressure	.296	37	.459	33	.434	8	4.08	28	19.67	3	20.49	112	.379	17
Ken Oberkfell	Overall	.272	46	.359	86	.359	35	0.73	109	10.81	41	8.05	19	.254	92
	Pressure	.181	121	.194	129	.280	100	0.00	92	10.98	46	7.32	16	.174	108
Gerald Perry	Overall	.214	128	.273	130	.282	124	1.26	90	8.78	65	10.69	44	.145	133
	Pressure	.238	82	.302	88	.300	91	1.59	70	8.57	69	14.29	68	.471	3
Rafael Ramirez	Overall	.248	95	.333	107	.272	132	0.88	106	3.36	132	10.59	42	.285	68
	Pressure	.292	42	.404	52	.330	72	1.12	83	5.26	117	11.58	46	.400	10
Milt Thompson	Overall	.302	--	.363	--	.339	--	0.00	--	3.63	--	18.65	--	.175	--
	Pressure	.415	1	.512	19	.467	1	0.00	92	6.67	100	15.56	79	.111	121
Claudell Washington	Overall	.276	38	.455	22	.342	47	3.77	29	9.07	59	14.97	89	.265	81
	Pressure	.213	98	.263	114	.276	105	1.25	77	8.05	80	20.69	113	.200	96
Paul Zuvella	Overall	.253	85	.305	122	.311	90	0.00	127	7.62	85	6.67	10	.083	--
	Pressure	.167	--	.208	--	.231	--	0.00	--	7.14	--	3.57	--	.000	133
Team Average	Overall	.246	10	.363	10	.315	8	2.28	5	8.91	4	13.68	3	.256	10
	Pressure	.244	11	.352	9	.333	4	2.20	6	11.10	1	13.57	2	.237	10
League Average	Overall	.252		.374		.319		2.16		8.63		14.45		.273	
	Pressure	.253		.368		.325		2.17		9.26		15.10		.257	

Additional Miscellaneous Batting Comparisons

	Grass Surface BA	Rank	Artificial Surface BA	Rank	Home Games BA	Rank	Road Games BA	Rank	Runners in Scoring Position BA	Rank	Runners in Scoring Pos and Two Outs BA	Rank	Leading Off Inning OBA	Rank	Runners on 3B with less than 2 Outs RDI %	Rank
Bruce Benedict	.225	106	.140	--	.263	73	.150	136	.255	80	.308	24	.333	52	.545	90
Rick Cerone	.230	103	.178	--	.219	120	.214	115	.258	78	.250	66	.200	135	.571	75
Chris Chambliss	.217	115	.280	--	.226	--	.244	87	.244	88	.174	116	.317	--	.692	23
Terry Harper	.269	53	.250	84	.286	46	.242	88	.254	81	.279	40	.302	87	.520	102
Bob Horner	.267	56	.268	56	.269	65	.265	55	.252	83	.217	84	.333	52	.697	22
Glenn Hubbard	.240	88	.209	126	.250	89	.213	116	.238	91	.255	64	.404	10	.440	123
Brad Komminsk	.223	109	.237	99	.204	124	.254	78	.254	81	.143	127	.344	48	.500	105
Dale Murphy	.294	29	.318	12	.299	31	.302	12	.329	17	.365	7	.408	9	.538	99
Ken Oberkfell	.294	30	.211	124	.301	26	.241	90	.211	112	.267	54	.390	16	.444	122
Gerald Perry	.220	111	.197	--	.226	116	.198	126	.164	132	.138	129	.288	95	.333	--
Rafael Ramirez	.266	59	.200	130	.294	37	.206	123	.260	76	.281	39	.279	104	.591	66
Paul Runge	.209	120	.250	--	.205	--	.229	--	.136	--	.200	--	.435	--	.250	--
Milt Thompson	.326	5	.211	--	.326	11	.276	38	.265	--	.263	--	.383	22	.667	--
Claudell Washington	.281	44	.265	59	.277	58	.275	39	.274	62	.225	79	.327	63	.769	11
Paul Zuvella	.230	101	.400	--	.209	122	.320	--	.175	--	.174	116	.429	3	.000	--
Team Average	.250	8	.233	12	.256	6	.236	10	.242	11	.244	5	.332	2	.538	11
League Average	.251		.254		.256		.248		.257		.235		.315		.576	

Pitching vs. Left and Right Handed Batters

		BA	Rank	SA	Rank	OBA	Rank	HR %	Rank	BB %	Rank	SO %	Rank
Len Barker	vs. Lefties	.302	99	.500	109	.392	102	4.32	114	12.77	95	12.77	47
	vs. Righties	.269	--	.385	--	.336	--	2.31	--	8.84	--	15.65	--
Steve Bedrosian	vs. Lefties	.283	82	.444	98	.386	98	3.38	106	14.32	106	9.33	81
	vs. Righties	.226	37	.303	18	.309	56	1.02	11	10.09	87	20.40	24
Rick Camp	vs. Lefties	.269	67	.328	37	.364	89	0.40	11	13.18	97	6.76	105
	vs. Righties	.257	75	.390	77	.331	80	2.90	90	8.06	60	10.62	96
Jeff Dedmon	vs. Lefties	.229	30	.319	32	.380	96	0.69	18	19.23	115	12.09	54
	vs. Righties	.293	108	.408	89	.347	98	2.30	60	7.18	47	9.74	102
Terry Forster	vs. Lefties	.225	--	.366	--	.329	--	2.82	--	13.41	--	14.63	--
	vs. Righties	.220	27	.353	48	.296	44	3.33	93	9.94	84	14.62	66
Gene Garber	vs. Lefties	.246	46	.349	45	.293	33	1.54	60	5.61	16	15.42	35
	vs. Righties	.284	100	.403	85	.335	86	2.84	83	6.67	35	16.92	48
Joe Johnson	vs. Lefties	.288	91	.455	104	.331	60	3.21	102	6.47	24	10.59	71
	vs. Righties	.282	99	.418	94	.340	91	2.26	56	6.60	34	8.12	112
Rick Mahler	vs. Lefties	.262	58	.372	62	.308	40	1.29	49	6.42	22	9.12	86
	vs. Righties	.276	96	.435	100	.335	87	3.61	98	7.92	58	10.23	99
Craig McMurtry	vs. Lefties	.344	113	.594	115	.453	114	3.13	101	16.53	111	10.74	69
	vs. Righties	.264	--	.402	--	.323	--	3.45	--	7.07	--	15.15	--
Pascual Perez	vs. Lefties	.302	97	.467	105	.400	107	2.83	99	14.29	104	11.11	67
	vs. Righties	.291	106	.440	101	.369	111	2.29	59	10.45	90	14.43	68
Steve Shields	vs. Lefties	.362	115	.500	109	.420	110	3.29	104	8.88	58	10.06	76
	vs. Righties	.265	--	.393	--	.353	--	3.42	--	11.97	--	8.45	--
Zane Smith	vs. Lefties	.284	84	.309	26	.348	74	0.00	1	8.70	55	26.09	4
	vs. Righties	.249	65	.362	58	.356	104	0.89	10	13.36	110	11.32	91
Bruce Sutter	vs. Lefties	.242	41	.366	56	.322	51	3.11	100	9.73	70	9.19	84
	vs. Righties	.289	104	.500	112	.333	83	4.44	113	5.58	21	17.77	37
Team Average	vs. Lefties	.279	11	.412	11	.359	12	2.32	10	11.04	12	10.81	11
	vs. Righties	.264	12	.394	11	.336	12	2.48	8	9.19	10	13.40	11
League Average	vs. Lefties	.262		.374		.330		1.73		9.17		12.66	
	vs. Righties	.246		.374		.311		2.44		8.28		15.62	

Pitching with Runners on Base and Bases Empty

		BA	Rank	SA	Rank	OBA	Rank	HR %	Rank	BB %	Rank	SO %	Rank
Len Barker	Runners On	.291	98	.461	103	.363	94	3.55	103	9.82	57	14.72	44
	Bases Empty	.285	106	.437	103	.372	112	3.31	103	12.21	108	13.37	71
Steve Bedrosian	Runners On	.277	86	.406	80	.384	104	2.83	88	14.32	105	12.79	61
	Bases Empty	.239	45	.350	43	.322	81	1.74	49	10.66	98	16.28	43
Rick Camp	Runners On	.248	48	.291	10	.337	69	0.39	2	10.89	73	8.91	98
	Bases Empty	.280	101	.432	102	.361	107	2.97	94	10.53	94	8.27	109
Jeff Dedmon	Runners On	.260	63	.367	55	.379	100	1.78	44	15.64	112	8.06	105
	Bases Empty	.268	91	.369	69	.343	100	1.34	29	9.64	86	14.46	58
Terry Forster	Runners On	.267	71	.465	106	.350	84	4.95	113	11.76	84	15.13	41
	Bases Empty	.183	4	.267	8	.269	17	1.67	45	10.45	93	14.18	63
Gene Garber	Runners On	.247	45	.377	60	.324	47	2.60	79	9.84	59	16.39	30
	Bases Empty	.276	98	.373	73	.305	57	1.84	52	3.10	4	15.93	45
Joe Johnson	Runners On	.295	103	.468	108	.348	81	4.32	111	6.92	16	10.06	86
	Bases Empty	.278	99	.412	91	.327	87	1.55	41	6.25	36	8.65	106
Rick Mahler	Runners On	.269	77	.390	72	.335	65	2.58	78	8.80	41	9.26	95
	Bases Empty	.268	90	.408	89	.312	66	2.23	68	6.00	33	9.90	99
Craig McMurtry	Runners On	.277	87	.465	106	.353	85	2.97	91	10.57	70	14.63	47
	Bases Empty	.341	--	.549	--	.443	--	3.66	--	14.43	--	10.31	--
Pascual Perez	Runners On	.301	105	.454	101	.407	113	2.73	84	15.04	108	13.27	57
	Bases Empty	.294	110	.456	108	.366	110	2.45	78	10.13	90	11.89	82
Steve Shields	Runners On	.393	115	.557	114	.473	115	4.10	109	13.82	104	7.24	107
	Bases Empty	.259	74	.367	65	.314	72	2.72	90	6.92	45	11.32	90
Zane Smith	Runners On	.252	55	.352	42	.347	79	0.80	9	11.51	81	15.13	40
	Bases Empty	.256	71	.356	45	.361	106	0.71	9	13.76	111	11.93	81
Bruce Sutter	Runners On	.259	61	.426	88	.318	40	4.32	112	6.99	18	8.60	99
	Bases Empty	.274	97	.447	105	.337	92	3.35	104	8.16	67	18.37	84
Team Average	Runners On	.275	12	.405	11	.361	12	2.59	11	11.30	12	11.63	11
	Bases Empty	.268	11	.401	11	.336	12	2.25	7	8.99	12	12.65	11
League Average	Runners On	.258		.381		.332		2.19		9.74		13.69	
	Bases Empty	.248		.369		.309		2.14		7.75		15.05	

Overall Pitching Compared to Late Inning Pressure Situations

		BA	Rank	SA	Rank	OBA	Rank	HR %	Rank	BB %	Rank	SO %	Rank
Len Barker	Overall	.288	104	.449	107	.367	109	3.42	108	11.04	94	14.03	60
	Pressure	.000	--	.000	--	.000	--	0.00	--	0.00	--	16.67	--
Steve Bedrosian	Overall	.254	66	.373	65	.349	97	2.19	64	12.24	101	14.77	51
	Pressure	.414	116	.448	95	.485	116	0.00	1	9.09	56	6.06	106
Rick Camp	Overall	.263	80	.358	44	.348	95	1.62	34	10.72	90	8.61	107
	Pressure	.284	86	.365	58	.357	79	0.68	27	9.94	66	11.11	81
Jeff Dedmon	Overall	.264	83	.368	59	.363	106	1.57	31	13.00	107	10.88	88
	Pressure	.260	70	.346	45	.384	95	0.96	33	16.28	110	9.30	89
Terry Forster	Overall	.222	16	.357	41	.307	40	3.17	102	11.07	95	14.62	54
	Pressure	.244	53	.412	82	.308	46	4.20	99	8.40	44	13.74	64
Gene Garber	Overall	.264	83	.375	69	.313	51	2.16	63	6.11	14	16.14	38
	Pressure	.280	81	.381	68	.361	81	1.79	54	10.05	67	14.57	52
Joe Johnson	Overall	.285	103	.435	104	.336	81	2.70	96	6.54	19	9.26	101
	Pressure	.235	--	.235	--	.278	--	0.00	--	5.26	--	5.26	--
Rick Mahler	Overall	.268	89	.401	90	.321	61	2.37	75	7.12	29	9.64	96
	Pressure	.238	48	.357	51	.312	50	2.38	72	9.57	62	7.45	99
Pascual Perez	Overall	.297	111	.455	111	.386	113	2.58	90	12.58	102	12.58	76
	Pressure	.429	--	.500	--	.400	--	0.00	--	0.00	--	12.50	--
Steve Shields	Overall	.320	115	.454	110	.390	114	3.35	107	10.29	83	9.32	100
	Pressure	.320	--	.640	--	.357	--	8.00	--	7.14	--	7.14	--
Zane Smith	Overall	.254	65	.354	35	.354	102	0.75	4	12.68	103	13.47	69
	Pressure	.130	3	.130	2	.254	16	0.00	1	13.43	95	13.43	66
Bruce Sutter	Overall	.267	88	.437	105	.328	72	3.81	113	7.59	39	13.61	66
	Pressure	.280	82	.468	99	.342	70	4.59	104	7.72	30	11.38	79
Team Average	Overall	.271	12	.403	11	.347	12	2.40	10	10.07	12	12.17	11
	Pressure	.268	11	.388	10	.344	10	2.42	10	9.78	6	11.35	12
League Average	Overall	.252		.374		.319		2.16		8.63		14.45	
	Pressure	.249		.363		.326		2.12		9.92		15.33	

Additional Miscellaneous Pitching Comparisons

	Grass Surface BA	Rank	Artificial Surface BA	Rank	Home Games BA	Rank	Road Games BA	Rank	Runners in Scoring Position BA	Rank	Runners in Scoring Pos and Two Outs BA	Rank	Leading Off Inning OBA	Rank
Len Barker	.305	104	.204	--	.289	99	.284	--	.329	111	.257	76	.429	115
Steve Bedrosian	.259	67	.242	43	.272	87	.238	36	.235	41	.226	52	.336	80
Rick Camp	.284	91	.202	11	.291	100	.233	30	.270	72	.325	111	.387	105
Jeff Dedmon	.276	85	.219	--	.278	90	.250	50	.287	89	.222	45	.390	108
Terry Forster	.203	10	.295	--	.199	13	.263	--	.305	--	.345	114	.115	--
Gene Garber	.270	81	.239	--	.284	94	.237	35	.278	80	.222	45	.253	11
Joe Johnson	.321	112	.138	--	.310	109	.267	81	.267	66	.283	90	.307	56
Rick Mahler	.262	69	.285	91	.255	70	.281	95	.252	54	.240	65	.301	54
Craig McMurtry	.279	86	.556	--	.272	--	.350	--	.302	100	.308	105	.489	--
Pascual Perez	.305	107	.277	83	.307	107	.287	100	.252	53	.196	34	.394	110
Steve Shields	.335	114	.273	--	.321	112	.318	112	.413	115	.333	112	.299	49
Zane Smith	.245	56	.278	86	.270	83	.237	34	.241	46	.186	23	.392	109
Bruce Sutter	.299	102	.178	2	.314	111	.212	14	.290	96	.205	37	.354	89
Team Average	.278	12	.250	4	.281	12	.260	7	.276	11	.250	10	.342	12
League Average	.251		.254		.248		.256		.257		.235		.315	

CHICAGO CUBS

Chicago is a city not unprepared for adversity. It has survived Mrs. O'Leary's cow, the Valentine's Day Massacre, the departure of the football Cardinals, the 1968 Democratic National Convention, and Dave Kingman in left field. To be a Chicago sports fan falls on the torture scale somewhere between root canal work and a Pia Zadora film festival. Many are resigned to this fate with grim humor. Following the second game of the 1984 National League Championship Series, Cubs fan and ABC News commentator George Will noted Chicago's two-games-to-none lead over the Padres by saying, "We all know that means it will be the Padres in five."

Will was correct, of course, and we hope his pain was eased by his anticipation of the inevitable. But the whole year to follow was surely an equal torture. The playoff defeat was humane—quick, decisive, total. But Chicago's 1985 season was cruel and unusual—slow, painful, without a sharp onset or a final gasp. While a dazed Cubs fan, after the playoff loss to San Diego, might have asked, "What happened?" he could only struggle back to his feet following the 1985 season and hopefully ask, "Is it over yet?"

Cubs manager Jim Frey began the 1985 season with the same game plan he had a year earlier. Dallas Green had laid the groundwork by re-signing Chicago's three free-agent pitchers: Cy Young Award winner Rick Sutcliffe, Dennis Eckersley, and Steve Trout. By opening day, Frey was ready to field nearly the same lineup as the one he had used day in and day out in 1984; only shortstop Larry Bowa had been replaced, by rookie Shawon Dunston. When the Dunston experiment was abandoned in early May, Bowa was ready to step back in. But unlike a year earlier, when the Cubs remained consistent and sound throughout the season, the lineup was soon shattered by injuries. The starting lineup that the Cubs used 46 times in 1984 and throughout the playoffs against San Diego started only six games together during the first half of the 1985 season. And the tide of injuries would continue all year.

Bob Dernier and Gary Matthews both spent time on the disabled list before the All-Star break, and while Dave Lopes filled in capably for both, the rest of Chicago's outfield depth was reduced by injuries. Brian Dayett missed most of the season, and Gary Woods and Billy Hatcher also spent two weeks apiece on the shelf. Although never officially disabled, Ryne Sandberg missed 10 days in early June, and Jody Davis missed two weeks later in the month. Players like Chris Speier, Richie Hebner, Thad Bosley, and Steve Lake, who had figured to be little more than pinch-hitters, were thrust into the Cubs' lineup. Even if their pitchers had stayed healthy, the Cubs would have had a lot to worry about, but might have remained afloat. But the injuries that knocked out the starting rotation made the other problems seem insignificant.

Rick Sutcliffe was injured in late May, returned for a month, and then was disabled again. When he next returned, Steve Trout went on the disabled list. By the time Trout returned, Sutcliffe (yet again), Dick Ruthven, Dennis Eckersley, and Scott Sanderson had all been lost. During a 10-day stretch from August 14 through August 23, all five members of Chicago's April starting rotation were disabled at the same time. For more than one month, from August 10 through September 11, the Cubs were unable to start any two pitchers from their top five in consecutive games. Chicago went 12-19 with a 5.06 ERA during that period, and fell from 10 to 17 games back.

At first glance, it would seem foolish to say that injuries cost the Cubs a shot at the division title, considering that they finished 23.5 games behind the Cardinals. But this was an extraordinarily severe set of circumstances. The Cubs lost a total of 494 man-days to the disabled list; on any given day during the season, Chicago was likely to have three disabled players. Add in the games lost by Sandberg and Davis, who remained on the active roster, factor in the quality of the players lost and Chicago's standing before the storm, and it seems quite plausible to say that they could have made a run at the title were it not for the injuries.

The Cubs used only five starters during the first seven weeks of the season: Sutcliffe, Trout, Eckersley, and Sanderson, with Dick Ruthven as a spot starter. To that point, the Cubs had no reason to think they would surrender their Eastern Division title without a battle. On the morning of May 20, Chicago had a 21-13 record, good for second place in the division, one-and-one-half games behind New York. And despite the handicap of playing their home games at Wrigley Field, the Cubs' team ERA of 2.52 was the best in the league. Shortly thereafter, first one by one, then in bunches, their pitchers fell by the wayside, and with them, Chicago's hopes for another title. To see how much this cost them, compare the performances of their top five to that of the others. Had the regular rotation been able to start 30 games apiece, they would have kept Larry Gura, Johnny Abrego, and Derek Botelho in the bullpen, if not in Iowa:

Starters	W	L	ERA	GS	CG	IP	H	BB	SO
Eckersley	11	7	3.08	25	6	169.1	145	19	117
Ruthven	4	7	4.63	15	0	79.2	90	35	22
Sanderson	5	6	3.12	19	2	121.0	100	27	80
Sutcliffe	8	8	3.18	20	6	130.0	119	44	102
Trout	9	7	3.39	24	3	140.2	142	63	44
Top Five	37	35	3.41	103	17	640.2	596	188	365
Others	12	26	5.24	59	3	330.0	402	110	149

From Out of Nowhere—and Back Again

Few teams in National League history have won a title—league or division—and finished more than 20 games behind in the following season with a record below the .500 mark. Only six teams prior to last year's Cubs have done it, none since the San Francisco Giants of the early 1970s. The following table lists those teams, along with their performances after the fall:

		One Season After Title				Two Seasons After Title				Next Pennant (Wait in
Year	Team	W	L	Pct.	GB	W	L	Pct.	GB	years)
1917	Brooklyn	70	81	.464	26.5	57	69	.452	25.5	1920 (3)
1949	Boston	75	79	.487	22	83	71	.539	8	1957 (8)
1951	Philadelphia	73	81	.474	23.5	87	67	.565	9.5	1976 (25)
1967	Los Angeles	73	89	.452	28.5	76	86	.469	21	1974 (7)
1970	Atlanta	76	86	.469	26	82	80	.506	8	1982 (12)
1972	San Francisco	69	86	.445	26.5	88	74	.543	11	— (13+)
1985	**Chicago**	77	84	.478	23.5	—	—	—	—	—

Only one team rebounded to win a title within three seasons of its unsuccessful title defense. Three failed to win another pennant for more than a decade, and those are the only three teams listed above who, like the 1983 Chicago team, finished more than 10 games behind the league or division leader in the seasons preceding their titles. The bottom line: teams that came from nowhere to win a title but slid back to mediocrity the following season were unable to rebound quickly from that slide.

The Layoff Effect

Let's consider more closely another aspect of the pitching injuries that precipitated their slide back to the lower levels of the NL East. We illustrated Chicago's problem in a table above; the Cubs were forced to play 59 games with starting pitchers other than the five who began the season in their rotation. And while it is true that four of those five (Ruthven being the exception) pitched well in their limited action, a survey of pitchers returning from injuries indicates that for most pitchers there is a long period of recuperation as they pitch themselves back into shape. Based upon those figures, it is safe to say that Chicago lost not only quantity (those 59 games started by inferior pitchers), but also quality.

Cubs fans will recall that following his first return from the disabled list last season, Rick Sutcliffe pitched a five-hit shutout against the Pirates. Although he failed to win any of his next three starts, Sutcliffe compiled a 1.88 ERA in those games, and followed with a complete-game victory over the Mets. But Sutcliffe is hardly typical in his immediate return to form, perhaps because he had not injured his arm, but had pulled a muscle in his leg. Most starting pitchers travel a much longer, rockier path to recovery. Although nine of the 33 starting pitchers who returned last season following time on the disabled list won their first starts, the typical pitcher did not win until his third start. The following table illustrates the progress a pitcher makes after his return:

Start	1st	2nd	3rd	4th	5th
Number of pitchers	33	32	30	25	22
Less than 5 innings	14 (42%)	11 (34%)	10 (33%)	6 (24%)	4 (18%)
7 innings or more	5 (15%)	8 (25%)	11 (37%)	9 (36%)	10 (45%)

The percentage of starters failing to complete at least five innings decreases for each of the returning pitchers' first five starts, and the percentage of those lasting at least seven innings gradually increases

during that time. Of course, there is also a survival-of-the-fittest effect: Fewer pitchers reach each subsequent start along the way, and presumably it is the best that struggle through. But it appears safe to conclude that a typical pitcher will struggle for at least three games following a return from the disabled list, and even for those who continue to pitch in rotation, a total return to previous form may not occur for as many as five starts.

Those who manage fantasy-league baseball teams will realize the implications. The tenuous nature of the physical condition of these pitchers makes their first few starts highly unpredictable. Even a pitcher's first start after returning cannot be used as a reliable guide to future performance; pitchers who failed to complete five innings in their first starts actually pitched better in their second starts than did those who lasted seven or more innings in their returns:

1st Start Distance	GS	W	L	ERA	IP	H	ER	BB	SO
5 innings or less	14	4	3	4.65	69.2	71	36	21	33
7 innings or more	4	0	2	5.16	22.2	27	13	8	8

Even more pronounced, and more astounding, are the composite second-start performances divided according to first-start decisions (i.e., first-start winners vs. first-start losers):

1st Start Decision	GS	W	L	ERA	IP	H	ER	BB	SO
First-Start Winners	8	1	4	4.37	47.1	55	23	19	23
First-Start Losers	12	5	1	4.19	62.1	53	29	23	28

Fantasy-league managers who participate in leagues that hold a new draft every season, with no recall from the previous season's rosters, would be well-advised not to reactivate pitchers returning from the disabled list during the season, and to rid themselves of those pitchers if they are able to trade for value. And if you can work a trade after a victorious return performance, the figures above indicate that you may well be able to extract a high price for a potentially unreliable pitcher.

Incidentally, there is no evidence that starting pitchers regain their form more quickly if they work their way back by pitching in relief. Several pitchers last season used the bullpen as a halfway house, pitching in relief at least once before returning to the starting rotation: they were Len Barker, Bruce Kison, Jerry Koosman, Rick Langford, Larry McWilliams, Zane Smith, and Curt Young. Those pitchers no differently than the rest of the group, not only in their first starts but also over the course of their first five starts.

WON-LOST RECORD BY STARTING POSITION

CHICAGO 77-84	C	1B	2B	3B	SS	LF	CF	RF	P	Leadoff	Relief	Starts
Johnny Abrego	-	-	-	-	-	-	-	-	3-2	-	0-1	3-2
Jay Baller	-	-	-	-	-	-	-	-	0-4	-	9-7	0-4
Dave Beard	-	-	-	-	-	-	-	-	-	-	2-7	-
Thad Bosley	-	-	-	-	-	7-17	0-1	3-2	-	2-4	-	10-20
Derek Botelho	-	-	-	-	-	-	-	-	3-4	-	0-4	3-4
Larry Bowa	-	-	-	-	34-26	-	-	-	-	-	-	34-26
Warren Brusstar	-	-	-	-	-	-	-	-	-	-	18-33	-
Ron Cey	-	-	-	66-71	-	-	-	-	-	-	-	66-71
Jody Davis	63-65	-	-	-	-	-	-	-	-	-	-	63-65
Brian Dayett	-	-	-	-	-	1-2	-	-	-	-	-	1-2
Bob Dernier	-	-	-	-	-	-	58-53	-	-	58-53	-	58-53
Shawon Dunston	-	-	-	-	34-36	-	-	-	-	0-2	-	34-36
Leon Durham	-	66-77	-	-	-	-	-	-	-	-	-	66-77
Dennis Eckersley	-	-	-	-	-	-	-	-	16-9	-	-	16-9
Steve Engel	-	-	-	-	-	-	-	-	3-5	-	1-2	3-5
Ray Fontenot	-	-	-	-	-	-	-	-	8-15	-	5-10	8-15
George Frazier	-	-	-	-	-	-	-	-	-	-	15-36	-
Dave Gumpert	-	-	-	-	-	-	-	-	-	-	3-6	-
Larry Gura	-	-	-	-	-	-	-	-	0-4	-	0-1	0-4
Billy Hatcher	-	-	-	-	-	5-4	10-15	2-1	-	10-12	-	17-20
Richie Hebner	-	5-4	-	4-3	-	-	-	-	-	-	-	9-7
Darrin Jackson	-	-	-	-	-	-	0-4	-	-	-	-	0-4
Steve Lake	14-19	-	-	-	-	-	-	-	-	-	-	14-19
Dave Lopes	-	-	1-1	-	-	20-15	9-10	7-4	-	7-11	-	37-30
Gary Matthews	-	-	-	-	-	40-44	-	-	-	-	-	40-44
Ron Meridith	-	-	-	-	-	-	-	-	-	-	8-24	-
Keith Moreland	-	6-3	-	5-3	-	-	-	63-76	-	-	-	74-82
Dave Owen	-	-	0-1	0-1	-	-	-	-	-	-	-	0-2
Reggie Patterson	-	-	-	-	-	-	-	-	4-0	-	0-3	4-0
Jon Perlman	-	-	-	-	-	-	-	-	-	-	1-5	-
Dick Ruthven	-	-	-	-	-	-	-	-	4-11	-	0-5	4-11
Ryne Sandberg	-	-	70-81	-	-	-	-	-	-	-	-	70-81
Scott Sanderson	-	-	-	-	-	-	-	-	10-9	-	-	10-9
Lee Smith	-	-	-	-	-	-	-	-	-	-	46-18	-
Lary Sorensen	-	-	-	-	-	-	-	-	1-2	-	7-34	1-2
Chris Speier	-	-	7-3	1-5	9-21	-	-	-	-	-	-	17-29
Rick Sutcliffe	-	-	-	-	-	-	-	-	11-9	-	-	11-9
Steve Trout	-	-	-	-	-	-	-	-	14-10	-	-	14-10
Chico Walker	-	-	-	-	-	-	-	0-1	-	0-1	-	0-1
Gary Woods	-	-	-	-	-	4-2	0-1	2-0	-	-	0-1	6-3

Batting vs. Left and Right Handed Pitchers

		BA	Rank	SA	Rank	OBA	Rank	HR %	Rank	BB %	Rank	SO %	Rank
Thad Bosley	vs. Lefties	.000	--	.000	--	.000	--	0.00	--	0.00	--	60.00	--
	vs. Righties	.337	3	.526	8	.401	8	4.00	22	10.15	41	13.20	74
Ron Cey	vs. Lefties	.221	103	.443	37	.312	83	5.74	11	11.59	40	21.74	122
	vs. Righties	.235	108	.397	64	.317	77	3.97	24	9.86	52	17.84	108
Jody Davis	vs. Lefties	.235	93	.470	29	.291	99	4.35	27	7.87	81	11.81	60
	vs. Righties	.232	113	.379	76	.302	103	3.27	33	9.29	56	16.63	97
Bob Dernier	vs. Lefties	.288	30	.373	71	.348	46	0.00	108	8.21	78	5.97	9
	vs. Righties	.242	99	.296	119	.303	102	0.28	116	7.49	82	9.30	35
Shawon Dunston	vs. Lefties	.222	--	.356	--	.255	--	2.22	--	4.26	--	10.64	--
	vs. Righties	.268	54	.395	67	.321	71	1.46	76	7.56	80	16.44	95
Leon Durham	vs. Lefties	.268	55	.425	45	.340	53	3.15	47	9.93	54	21.99	123
	vs. Righties	.287	30	.477	13	.363	36	4.10	21	10.73	36	14.59	85
Billy Hatcher	vs. Lefties	.225	--	.250	--	.244	--	0.00	--	2.38	--	2.38	--
	vs. Righties	.252	79	.407	58	.304	99	1.63	74	5.15	118	8.09	20
Dave Lopes	vs. Lefties	.239	87	.467	31	.346	49	5.43	14	14.02	22	11.21	52
	vs. Righties	.306	15	.432	39	.401	9	3.28	32	14.22	14	11.47	55
Gary Matthews	vs. Lefties	.232	97	.402	55	.340	54	4.88	19	14.43	18	10.31	43
	vs. Righties	.236	107	.407	56	.370	23	4.17	19	16.98	6	20.38	124
Keith Moreland	vs. Lefties	.315	14	.460	34	.415	5	2.42	62	14.97	17	6.80	11
	vs. Righties	.305	17	.434	38	.363	33	2.38	53	8.85	62	9.23	32
Ryne Sandberg	vs. Lefties	.276	46	.434	40	.339	56	3.29	44	8.93	69	14.29	78
	vs. Righties	.315	11	.527	6	.372	21	4.60	13	8.32	68	14.46	83
Chris Speier	vs. Lefties	.333	5	.515	13	.378	20	4.55	25	7.79	83	11.69	56
	vs. Righties	.204	128	.276	125	.258	131	0.66	106	6.75	92	15.34	88
Team Average	vs. Lefties	.252	6	.400	2	.322	4	3.00	1	9.39	1	15.38	10
	vs. Righties	.255	7	.387	3	.324	5	2.65	1	9.01	3	15.10	10
League Average	vs. Lefties	.250		.374		.317		2.26		8.65		14.84	
	vs. Righties	.253		.374		.320		2.12		8.62		14.28	

Batting with Runners on Base and Bases Empty

		BA	Rank	SA	Rank	OBA	Rank	HR %	Rank	BB %	Rank	SO %	Rank
Thad Bosley	Runners On	.328	--	.578	--	.423	--	6.25	--	15.38	--	15.38	--
	Bases Empty	.328	7	.474	21	.371	15	2.59	47	6.45	79	13.71	73
Ron Cey	Runners On	.239	96	.446	39	.357	50	5.41	10	15.04	20	18.42	122
	Bases Empty	.227	111	.378	67	.279	110	3.60	29	6.04	90	19.13	114
Jody Davis	Runners On	.206	130	.358	85	.306	98	2.75	49	12.84	38	13.23	79
	Bases Empty	.254	78	.436	32	.294	100	4.17	20	5.38	106	17.56	101
Bob Dernier	Runners On	.233	106	.286	117	.318	88	0.00	115	10.63	57	6.88	17
	Bases Empty	.262	58	.327	102	.313	74	0.30	118	6.37	81	9.14	25
Shawon Dunston	Runners On	.268	63	.330	100	.336	67	1.03	86	9.91	68	14.41	85
	Bases Empty	.255	74	.425	37	.292	105	1.96	65	4.97	114	16.15	94
Leon Durham	Runners On	.274	56	.449	38	.385	26	3.85	28	15.47	13	15.47	97
	Bases Empty	.289	17	.477	18	.334	46	3.90	27	6.38	80	17.02	98
Billy Hatcher	Runners On	.179	--	.214	--	.250	--	0.00	--	4.55	--	3.03	--
	Bases Empty	.280	31	.449	26	.313	75	1.87	70	4.46	120	8.93	23
Dave Lopes	Runners On	.273	57	.529	6	.377	34	7.44	1	14.97	21	6.80	15
	Bases Empty	.292	13	.377	69	.388	5	1.30	88	13.48	12	15.17	88
Gary Matthews	Runners On	.264	70	.488	20	.395	20	5.79	5	17.11	7	17.76	120
	Bases Empty	.215	118	.350	89	.338	40	3.39	32	15.71	3	17.62	102
Keith Moreland	Runners On	.329	11	.477	26	.385	25	2.68	51	9.65	73	7.60	24
	Bases Empty	.284	25	.401	53	.363	20	2.08	63	10.77	27	9.85	33
Ryne Sandberg	Runners On	.274	55	.496	16	.344	62	4.76	17	9.76	72	12.20	68
	Bases Empty	.328	6	.510	8	.378	7	3.92	24	7.51	63	16.06	92
Chris Speier	Runners On	.253	79	.407	59	.278	126	3.30	40	4.00	130	15.00	90
	Bases Empty	.236	99	.307	117	.307	80	0.79	103	9.29	37	13.57	71
Team Average	Runners On	.248	8	.396	3	.331	7	3.20	1	10.85	1	13.78	8
	Bases Empty	.259	1	.386	2	.317	2	2.39	3	7.71	8	16.27	11
League Average	Runners On	.258		.381		.332		2.19		9.74		13.69	
	Bases Empty	.248		.369		.309		2.14		7.75		15.05	

Overall Batting Compared to Late Inning Pressure Situations

		BA	Rank	SA	Rank	OBA	Rank	HR %	Rank	BB %	Rank	SO %	Rank	RDI %	Rank
Thad Bosley	Overall	.328	4	.511	8	.391	8	3.89	26	9.90	48	14.36	85	.333	--
	Pressure	.373	4	.647	4	.407	20	7.84	7	5.56	115	18.52	99	.286	--
Ron Cey	Overall	.232	116	.408	54	.316	78	4.40	16	10.28	45	18.79	122	.227	113
	Pressure	.266	62	.430	42	.363	46	5.06	17	12.09	37	18.68	102	.176	106
Jody Davis	Overall	.232	114	.400	60	.300	105	3.53	32	8.96	62	15.49	94	.227	114
	Pressure	.120	132	.213	128	.205	129	2.67	42	9.41	62	22.35	119	.217	88
Bob Dernier	Overall	.254	83	.316	116	.315	81	0.21	121	7.68	83	8.45	20	.233	108
	Pressure	.263	63	.281	102	.364	43	0.00	92	13.24	25	8.82	24	.154	116
Shawon Dunston	Overall	.260	76	.388	73	.310	92	1.60	85	6.99	96	15.44	92	.224	115
	Pressure	.217	--	.261	--	.240	--	0.00	--	3.85	--	15.38	--	.250	--
Leon Durham	Overall	.282	23	.465	19	.357	36	3.87	27	10.54	44	16.31	101	.318	33
	Pressure	.256	66	.488	26	.315	82	4.88	19	7.87	85	17.98	95	.333	25
Richie Hebner	Overall	.217	--	.308	--	.266	--	2.50	--	5.47	--	11.72	--	.333	21
	Pressure	.234	87	.298	89	.280	101	2.13	57	6.00	107	18.00	96	.350	22
Dave Lopes	Overall	.284	21	.444	26	.383	15	4.00	25	14.15	53	11.38	53	.322	31
	Pressure	.296	36	.593	8	.387	30	7.41	8	12.70	31	9.52	28	.238	75
Gary Matthews	Overall	.235	111	.406	56	.362	33	4.36	17	16.30	4	17.68	113	.269	79
	Pressure	.189	115	.243	122	.295	94	0.00	92	13.64	22	25.00	130	.235	78
Keith Moreland	Overall	.307	10	.440	29	.374	19	2.39	55	10.19	46	8.70	23	.349	15
	Pressure	.311	28	.444	39	.363	45	1.11	85	7.84	87	10.78	41	.439	6
Ryne Sandberg	Overall	.305	11	.504	9	.364	28	4.27	20	8.47	69	14.41	86	.283	70
	Pressure	.368	5	.598	7	.433	9	4.60	22	9.18	65	14.29	68	.417	8
Chris Speier	Overall	.243	100	.349	92	.295	110	1.83	69	7.08	93	14.17	82	.304	49
	Pressure	.340	14	.553	13	.396	28	6.38	12	9.09	66	14.55	72	.333	25
Team Average	Overall	.254	7	.390	1	.323	4	2.73	1	9.10	3	15.17	10	.267	8
	Pressure	.262	3	.406	1	.333	3	3.27	1	9.37	7	16.72	11	.286	3
League Average	Overall	.252		.374		.319		2.16		8.63		14.45		.273	
	Pressure	.253		.368		.325		2.17		9.26		15.10		.257	

Additional Miscellaneous Batting Comparisons

	Grass Surface BA	Rank	Artificial Surface BA	Rank	Home Games BA	Rank	Road Games BA	Rank	Runners in Scoring Position BA	Rank	Runners in Scoring Pos and Two Outs BA	Rank	Leading Off Inning OBA	Rank	Runners on 3B with less than 2 Outs RDI %	Rank
Thad Bosley	.323	7	.340	--	.361	3	.289	--	.286	--	.083	--	.375	25	.600	59
Ron Cey	.248	80	.193	133	.261	77	.206	121	.246	86	.250	66	.306	84	.409	126
Jody Davis	.239	91	.212	123	.255	85	.206	120	.161	133	.111	133	.261	119	.684	24
Bob Dernier	.249	77	.266	58	.278	57	.230	108	.208	117	.174	116	.307	81	.545	90
Shawon Dunston	.273	51	.235	102	.299	30	.204	124	.233	99	.133	--	.339	51	.583	68
Leon Durham	.307	15	.226	110	.331	9	.239	97	.286	44	.286	36	.321	70	.583	68
Billy Hatcher	.230	102	.280	--	.229	112	.278	--	.212	--	.250	--	.288	94	.364	133
Richie Hebner	.209	121	.241	--	.209	--	.226	--	.222	--	.200	--	.278	--	.846	3
Steve Lake	.123	--	.185	--	.178	--	.135	--	.161	--	.053	--	.391	--	.545	90
Dave Lopes	.267	57	.316	14	.282	50	.285	30	.267	71	.310	21	.384	21	.571	75
Gary Matthews	.262	66	.184	135	.264	72	.214	114	.224	109	.160	122	.275	108	.647	38
Keith Moreland	.320	10	.274	46	.340	8	.272	48	.335	9	.306	27	.355	38	.634	47
Ryne Sandberg	.319	12	.275	45	.304	22	.307	11	.284	49	.268	52	.417	6	.565	84
Chris Speier	.238	92	.254	--	.223	119	.264	58	.302	30	.350	--	.279	105	.571	75
Team Average	.263	4	.234	11	.274	1	.235	11	.249	10	.219	10	.314	7	.568	9
League Average	.251		.254		.256		.248		.257		.235		.315		.576	

Pitching vs. Left and Right Handed Batters

Name		BA	Rank	SA	Rank	OBA	Rank	HR %	Rank	BB %	Rank	SO %	Rank
Jay Baller	vs. Lefties	.268	65	.382	68	.326	55	0.81	25	8.03	46	10.22	75
	vs. Righties	.247	--	.584	--	.310	--	9.09	--	6.98	--	19.77	--
Derek Botelho	vs. Lefties	.311	104	.556	114	.380	97	4.44	115	9.00	61	12.00	55
	vs. Righties	.286	--	.452	--	.394	--	4.76	--	13.59	--	10.68	--
Warren Brusstar	vs. Lefties	.282	81	.419	91	.372	94	1.61	62	12.24	90	9.52	80
	vs. Righties	.299	110	.477	109	.365	109	3.45	96	9.05	75	10.05	101
Dennis Eckersley	vs. Lefties	.258	55	.416	88	.284	23	3.42	107	3.25	5	11.54	62
	vs. Righties	.199	12	.285	12	.223	2	1.28	16	2.45	2	23.93	13
Steve Engel	vs. Lefties	.200	--	.250	--	.273	--	0.00	--	8.70	--	13.04	--
	vs. Righties	.308	113	.546	115	.386	113	5.41	115	11.21	95	12.15	87
Ray Fontenot	vs. Lefties	.182	4	.247	5	.264	11	1.30	50	10.00	74	20.00	15
	vs. Righties	.310	114	.493	111	.354	103	4.19	107	6.30	29	9.11	106
George Frazier	vs. Lefties	.307	102	.486	108	.413	109	3.57	110	14.29	104	11.90	56
	vs. Righties	.292	107	.448	104	.404	115	3.90	103	14.81	114	13.76	76
Dick Ruthven	vs. Lefties	.328	108	.484	107	.378	95	2.15	78	8.45	52	6.57	106
	vs. Righties	.266	83	.386	74	.343	93	1.27	14	10.61	93	6.70	115
Scott Sanderson	vs. Lefties	.243	43	.470	106	.296	35	3.98	113	7.19	33	13.31	44
	vs. Righties	.207	15	.319	24	.231	3	1.60	27	3.47	3	21.29	22
Lee Smith	vs. Lefties	.266	62	.401	75	.324	54	2.08	77	8.02	45	23.58	7
	vs. Righties	.214	25	.357	51	.283	31	2.98	91	8.11	62	33.51	1
Lary Sorensen	vs. Lefties	.329	109	.517	113	.390	100	2.80	98	9.20	63	6.13	111
	vs. Righties	.228	38	.351	45	.281	30	2.34	62	4.69	10	12.50	81
Rick Sutcliffe	vs. Lefties	.270	68	.410	84	.331	59	2.05	76	7.89	43	16.92	25
	vs. Righties	.211	21	.319	23	.279	26	2.79	80	8.13	64	20.14	25
Steve Trout	vs. Lefties	.269	--	.373	--	.347	--	1.49	--	10.39	--	10.39	--
	vs. Righties	.271	91	.356	50	.347	97	1.53	24	10.50	91	6.87	114
Team Average	vs. Lefties	.281	12	.432	12	.343	9	2.44	12	8.55	5	12.28	9
	vs. Righties	.263	11	.413	12	.326	11	3.10	12	8.26	7	13.90	10
League Average	vs. Lefties	.262		.374		.330		1.73		9.17		12.66	
	vs. Righties	.246		.374		.311		2.44		8.28		15.62	

Pitching with Runners on Base and Bases Empty

Name		BA	Rank	SA	Rank	OBA	Rank	HR %	Rank	BB %	Rank	SO %	Rank
Jay Baller	Runners On	.257	--	.365	--	.341	--	1.35	--	11.24	--	12.36	--
	Bases Empty	.262	80	.516	114	.306	58	5.56	115	5.22	19	14.93	53
Warren Brusstar	Runners On	.331	113	.531	113	.417	114	3.45	99	12.85	97	12.29	71
	Bases Empty	.255	67	.379	76	.317	77	1.96	57	7.78	62	7.19	112
Dennis Eckersley	Runners On	.201	9	.346	35	.238	2	2.80	87	3.86	3	17.60	24
	Bases Empty	.243	52	.355	44	.262	9	2.14	65	2.32	2	17.63	37
Ray Fontenot	Runners On	.306	108	.460	102	.347	77	3.57	104	6.01	10	9.54	90
	Bases Empty	.286	107	.463	109	.339	94	4.00	110	7.41	55	11.38	89
George Frazier	Runners On	.293	100	.449	100	.407	112	3.40	98	15.22	110	14.67	46
	Bases Empty	.306	113	.483	112	.410	115	4.08	111	13.87	112	10.98	95
Dick Ruthven	Runners On	.280	90	.440	95	.330	56	2.29	68	7.92	29	6.44	111
	Bases Empty	.320	115	.438	104	.395	114	1.18	17	11.05	102	6.84	113
Scott Sanderson	Runners On	.228	23	.356	46	.269	7	2.01	55	6.32	12	14.37	50
	Bases Empty	.228	30	.431	101	.268	16	3.45	107	5.23	20	17.97	34
Lee Smith	Runners On	.231	26	.390	71	.295	20	2.75	85	8.37	34	24.63	4
	Bases Empty	.253	62	.371	71	.314	71	2.25	69	7.73	60	31.96	2
Lary Sorensen	Runners On	.278	89	.436	92	.355	88	2.26	65	9.82	57	7.36	106
	Bases Empty	.271	94	.420	98	.313	67	2.76	91	4.17	11	11.46	86
Rick Sutcliffe	Runners On	.237	34	.356	45	.321	43	2.58	77	11.01	74	19.82	14
	Bases Empty	.243	51	.369	67	.292	36	2.33	73	5.90	31	17.70	36
Steve Trout	Runners On	.272	81	.349	40	.343	74	0.86	11	10.29	67	6.99	109
	Bases Empty	.270	93	.365	59	.350	104	2.05	59	10.64	97	7.60	110
Team Average	Runners On	.273	11	.429	12	.340	10	3.00	12	9.23	4	12.80	9
	Bases Empty	.269	12	.414	12	.329	11	2.70	12	7.69	5	13.59	10
League Average	Runners On	.258		.381		.332		2.19		9.74		13.69	
	Bases Empty	.248		.369		.309		2.14		7.75		15.05	

Overall Pitching Compared to Late Inning Pressure Situations

		BA	Rank	SA	Rank	OBA	Rank	HR %	Rank	BB %	Rank	SO %	Rank
Jay Baller	Overall	.260	--	.460	--	.320	--	4.00	--	7.62	--	13.90	--
	Pressure	.228	40	.404	79	.297	41	3.51	93	9.23	58	21.54	17
Warren Brusstar	Overall	.292	107	.453	109	.368	110	2.68	95	10.40	84	9.83	95
	Pressure	.283	85	.384	70	.349	75	1.01	34	8.26	39	10.09	85
Dennis Eckersley	Overall	.229	25	.352	32	.254	2	2.37	74	2.86	2	17.62	30
	Pressure	.293	89	.448	95	.323	58	1.72	51	3.13	43	15.63	43
Ray Fontenot	Overall	.294	109	.462	114	.342	91	3.82	114	6.81	26	10.59	90
	Pressure	.346	111	.481	102	.391	96	3.70	94	6.74	23	5.62	109
George Frazier	Overall	.299	112	.466	115	.409	115	3.74	112	14.57	114	12.89	73
	Pressure	.315	103	.535	114	.436	112	6.30	113	16.88	112	8.75	92
Ron Meridith	Overall	.301	--	.432	--	.382	--	1.70	--	11.48	--	11.00	--
	Pressure	.306	99	.367	62	.404	103	0.00	1	13.79	97	17.24	32
Dick Ruthven	Overall	.299	113	.439	106	.362	105	1.74	41	9.44	73	6.63	115
	Pressure	.400	--	.400	--	.438	--	0.00	--	6.25	--	6.25	--
Scott Sanderson	Overall	.228	24	.405	94	.268	7	2.96	99	5.63	11	16.67	35
	Pressure	.136	5	.136	3	.174	1	0.00	1	4.17	7	16.67	36
Lee Smith	Overall	.242	43	.381	74	.305	38	2.50	83	8.06	45	28.21	1
	Pressure	.246	57	.406	80	.315	53	2.90	83	8.77	52	29.87	2
Lary Sorensen	Overall	.274	97	.427	101	.331	77	2.55	87	6.76	25	9.58	98
	Pressure	.306	98	.389	72	.375	86	0.00	1	8.24	37	8.24	94
Rick Sutcliffe	Overall	.240	41	.364	57	.304	37	2.42	80	8.01	44	18.58	23
	Pressure	.234	45	.406	81	.258	17	4.69	105	3.03	3	16.67	36
Steve Trout	Overall	.270	92	.358	43	.347	94	1.52	29	10.48	85	7.32	112
	Pressure	.400	115	.600	115	.438	113	0.00	1	6.25	20	12.50	73
Team Average	Overall	.271	11	.420	12	.333	11	2.83	12	8.38	5	13.24	9
	Pressure	.278	12	.423	12	.350	12	2.65	11	9.51	4	16.42	4
League Average	Overall	.252		.374		.319		2.16		8.63		14.45	
	Pressure	.249		.363		.326		2.12		9.92		15.33	

Additional Miscellaneous Pitching Comparisons

	Grass Surface BA	Rank	Artificial Surface BA	Rank	Home Games BA	Rank	Road Games BA	Rank	Runners in Scoring Position BA	Rank	Runners in Scoring Pos and Two Outs BA	Rank	Leading Off Inning OBA	Rank
Jay Baller	.291	98	.227	26	.296	--	.225	24	.191	--	.160	--	.280	--
Derek Botelho	.295	100	.321	--	.309	--	.288	--	.196	--	.250	--	.333	--
Warren Brusstar	.288	94	.303	--	.322	113	.265	74	.323	109	.289	91	.278	27
Dennis Eckersley	.226	30	.232	31	.228	38	.229	28	.226	31	.246	71	.289	35
Steve Engel	.294	99	.304	--	.282	93	.316	--	.327	--	.355	116	.382	--
Ray Fontenot	.305	105	.248	50	.308	108	.274	86	.307	103	.319	109	.358	95
George Frazier	.286	93	.338	115	.284	95	.318	113	.293	98	.298	98	.373	101
Ron Meridith	.297	101	.333	--	.297	101	.308	--	.228	--	.148	--	.333	--
Reggie Patterson	.265	73	.230	--	.265	--	.230	--	.156	--	.200	--	.300	--
Dick Ruthven	.307	108	.270	--	.301	102	.297	106	.236	43	.205	37	.446	116
Scott Sanderson	.225	28	.237	36	.229	39	.226	25	.212	19	.190	26	.282	30
Lee Smith	.242	51	.241	41	.238	52	.247	46	.174	5	.120	2	.342	82
Lary Sorensen	.265	75	.295	98	.288	97	.261	68	.313	106	.348	115	.238	7
Rick Sutcliffe	.224	25	.274	82	.227	35	.250	50	.195	10	.121	3	.295	47
Steve Trout	.275	84	.258	61	.272	86	.269	82	.265	64	.180	21	.374	102
Team Average	.273	11	.264	10	.278	11	.263	10	.255	6	.233	6	.333	10
League Average	.251		.254		.248		.256		.257		.235		.315	

CINCINNATI REDS

| | With 3 Days
Between Starts | | | With 4 Days
Between Starts | | |
Pitcher	GS	W–L	ERA	GS	W–L	ERA
Browning	23	15–3	3.07	10	5–3	3.65
Soto	19	7–8	2.69	11	2–7	5.35
Tibbs	23	8–11	3.52	5	1–1	4.76
Others	21	5–7	4.72	11	3–4	4.62
Totals	86	35–29	3.45	37	11–15	4.60

Manager of the Year. The award is annually bestowed upon the manager whose team exceeds its preseason forecasts by the greatest margin. Whose preseason forecasts? Why, whoever bestows the award, of course! We all do it: you, me, the baseball writers association, whoever. We underestimate a team's performance, and credit the gap between our lowly expectations and its lofty accomplishments not to the improvement of key players, or to deals yet to come which we could know nothing about, or to our own poor judgment. No, we credit the improvement to the manager. And by those standards, Pete Rose was an ideal candidate for 1985 National League Manager of the Year for most of us. He led the Reds to a second-place finish in the National League's Western Division, after Cincinnati had been written off by many.

Little does it matter that Dave Parker returned to his MVP form after four years of hibernation. Or that Cincinnati filled two painful cavities with mid-season deals for Buddy Bell and Bo Diaz, giving the team their first legitimate major-league catcher since Johnny Bench. Or that few listened when we told you last spring that "there is more cause for optimism. . . . the number of young pitchers is encouraging. . . . no staff in the majors is so poised for a turnaround as Cincinnati's promising group." Regardless, Cincinnati was perceived as a second-division team. They finished in second place. Therefore, Rose should be Manager of the Year. Q.E.D.

The Three-Day Rest (Kaat's Pause)

While we think Rose was given a free ride because most observers failed to anticipate Cincinnati's revival, he did share in at least one major decision which played a vital role in the team's turnaround: the choice of Jim Kaat as pitching coach. Kaat is a proponent of the four-man rotation, which has been out of vogue since the 1960s. And, of course, he was accustomed to frequent work during his own long major-league career.

Kaat flourished working every fourth day for the Minnesota Twins during the mid-1960s, in a rotation that included Mudcat Grant, Jim Perry, and Camilo Pascual, among others. Kaat led the league in games started in both 1965 and '66, and in wins with 25 in '66; 16 of those wins were on three days' rest. Nearly a decade later, then in his mid-30s, Kaat was still thriving on work, this time for the Chicago White Sox. He and knuckleballer Wilbur Wood pitched a total of almost 1,200 innings for the Sox over a two-year period. Kaat lasted in the majors until he was nearly 45 years old, and pitched in more games than anyone in big-league history except Hoyt Wilhelm, Lindy McDaniel, Cy Young, and Sparky Lyle.

Not everyone on the Reds agreed with the wisdom of a four-man rotation. In fact, the experiment was abandoned briefly in late May when the schedule became less accommodating and Mario Soto became an outspoken critic of the three-day rest. But even Kaat's most prominent adversary pitched far better with only three days between starts than with four. And ultimately, not even Soto could dispute its success.

No one seemed to thrive on the work as much as Tom Browning. Pitching nearly every fourth day after the All-Star break, he was the National League's winningest pitcher, with 13 victories during the second half of the season. He made 12 starts, winning all but one, during an incredible 47-day stretch after the brief players' strike in August. The kicker: For that no-decision start, he had an extra day of rest.

Some might say it was Browning's tough luck to hit the big leagues shortly after Dwight Gooden. Or at the same time as Vince Coleman. But, deprived of the attention he deserved, Browning was left to develop without the pressures which would otherwise have accompanied his effort to become the first rookie 20-game winner since 1954, when Bob Grim won 20 for the New York Yankees. It seemed that no one outside Cincinnati realized that Browning had a chance to win 20 until he had already won 19.

Browning and the other starting pitchers benefitted not only from the four-man rotation, but also from a bullpen which clung to leads as if they were treated with pine tar. Cincinnati lost only two games last season in which they led after eight innings, and only *three* in which they led after the sixth, five fewer than the average of the other 11 National League teams. The Reds won 20 of their 24 games in which the score was tied after eight innings. How valuable were those wins? The following chart shows that in games tied after eight innings, essentially extra-inning games, Cincinnati was five games better than even the second-best team. These games alone gave Cincinnati a 12-game edge over the Dodgers. Had the Reds simply split those games, they would have finished in fourth place at the .500 mark. Had the Dodgers simply split their own games tied after eight, there would have been no Western Division pennant race.

| | Games Tied
After Eight | | |
	W	L	GB
Cincinnati	20	4	—
Montreal	14	8	5
St. Louis	9	7	7
San Francisco	14	12	7
Chicago	6	6	8
New York	12	12	8
Philadelphia	10	11	8.5
Atlanta	9	11	9
San Diego	7	9	9
Houston	6	12	11
Pittsburgh	6	13	11.5
Los Angeles	7	15	12

It should also be noted that the Reds had an astonishing record in one-run games. They were 39–18 in one-run games, 50–54 in all other games. This pattern is very unusual; the next-best overall record for a club with a sub-.500 record in games decided by more than one run was Chicago's 77–84 mark. (For a further discussion of one-run records, see the Philadelphia Phillies essay.)

Trouble In Roseland?

Rose's most dominant characteristic in his year and a half as Reds manager has been his faith in veteran players. Following the dismissal of Vern Rapp in August 1984, Rose quickly restored Dave Concepcion to his old position at shortstop; Rapp had moved him to third base to make room for Tom Foley, a move Concepcion publicly criticized. Rapp had also opened a position at first base for Nick Esasky by trading veteran Dan Driessen. But the 44-year-old Rose then displaced Esasky at first himself, except on those days when he started Tony Perez, at 43 the second-oldest player in the league.

Last season nearly every personnel decision was made in favor of older players. Outfielders Eric Davis and Duane Walker were dispatched—Davis to the minors, Walker to the Texas Rangers—to clear a starting position for 34-year-old Cesar Cedeno, who started more for Rose in April than he had in his first two months under Rapp. Bell and Diaz were brought in, Bell putting Esasky temporarily on the bench, Diaz displacing the crew of mediocrities—but younger mediocrities—who had been sharing the catching job. By season's end, Rose had assembled a favorite starting lineup that he used in 24 of the Reds' final 54 games before their elimination from the pennant race; it contained only two players under the age of 30:

Pos.	Player	Age
1B	Pete Rose	44
2B	Ron Oester	29
3B	Buddy Bell	34
SS	Dave Concepcion	37
LF	Nick Esasky	25
CF	Eddie Milner	30
RF	Dave Parker	34
C	Bo Diaz	32

One tough decision Rose will face is the disposition of last season's first baseman. Even last year, when for some the Ty Cobb chase was in itself justification for Rose to start regularly at first base, not everyone agreed it was best for the Reds. Not even all the Reds agreed it was best for the Reds. Gary Redus on Pete Rose: "All he can do is hit singles. He thinks he's helping the club hitting .265, but we'd have more speed and power without him." (Redus's comments can be fairly viewed as echoing W. C. Fields's, "On the whole, I'd rather be in Philadelphia.")

Manager Rose's indulgence of player Rose was no more pronounced than Philadelphia's indulgence of him in 1983 when, playing for two different managers (Pat Corrales and Paul Owens), he started 113 games, and subbed in 38 others, in left field and at first base, on a National League championship team. And while Rose might not have carried a very dangerous piece of lumber to the plate last season, his 1983 performance was even worse:

Year	AB	R	H	2B	3B	HR	RBI	BB	SO	SB	CS	BA	SA	OBA
1983	493	52	121	14	3	0	45	52	28	7	7	.245	.286	.316
1985	405	60	107	12	2	2	46	86	35	8	1	.264	.319	.395

Rose's performance last season can look acceptable only by comparison to his own 1983 statistics. Over the past five seasons, exactly four National League players have had seasons with fewer than 20 extra-base hits and more than 500 plate appearances, and only Rose has done it twice. The other three—Ozzie Smith in 1981, Bill Russell in 1983, and Steve Sax in 1985—were all middle infielders, and therefore did not keep a more productive bat on the bench.

As Redus so eagerly pointed out, Rose could have put Nick Esasky at first base for the Reds, freeing left field for Gary himself, for Eric Davis, or for anyone else who could reach the Riverfront fences. Look at how the typical National League starting first baseman compares to Rose over the course of the 110 starts Rose made last season:

Player	AB	H	2B	3B	HR	RBI	BB	SO	SB	BA	SA	OBA
Rose	397	106	12	2	2	46	85	35	8	.267	.322	.398
N.L. Avg.	401	108	20	2	13	54	50	57	3	.269	.422	.349

There was an obvious lack of power with Rose in the lineup, and only a fool would argue that Rose compensated with his 35 additional walks for the 19 extra-base hits by which he fell short of the league average. And yet, in all fairness, we must point out one crucial entry in the Reds' table of Won-Lost Records by Starting Position: the Reds were 17 games above .500 with Pete in the starting lineup, 26–26 with other starting first basemen. And among those others was Tony Perez, whose .346 batting average in 45 starts raised the Cincinnati composite for starting first basemen to .285, 16 points higher than the league average.

There does come a time for all of us to pass the baton, and that time will come shortly for Rose and Perez. And the question of who's on first will be pretty irrelevant if Dave Parker fails to match last season's performance, or Mario Soto does not rebound from an off season, or the bullpen is merely good rather than exceptional.

Cincinnati's success last season is, to a degree, vindication of Rose's preference for veterans. Nevertheless, a one-year turnaround of such proportions is rarely accomplished by a veteran team. Since 1969, only 25 teams have increased their win total by 15 or more in a single season, and none had a starting lineup nearly as old as that of the 1985 Reds. The only remotely similar (i.e., old) team to reverse its form was the 1984 Chicago Cubs. While the Cubs' subsequent decline can be attributed in part to the many injuries to their pitchers last season, the Reds may have invited the same problems this winter by acquiring veteran pitchers Bill Gullickson and John Denny, both coming off recent injury problems. The ultimate test of Rose as a manager will be the 1986 season, when he must prod his aging regulars not to one last burst of glory, but to repeat the burst they achieved in '85.

Murphy's Law of Statistics

You might have noticed that there is a new statistic being used to evaluate starting pitchers, the Quality Start. A starting pitcher who completes at least six innings and allows three or fewer runs is credited with a Quality Start. It is said that this figure tells us things that we would not have known otherwise. For instance, the three National League pitchers with the most Quality Starts last season were Dwight Gooden, Orel Hershiser, and John Tudor. Who could possibly have known that otherwise? Ah, blessed serendipity—Quality Starts appeared at the time when we needed it most.

Prompted by the deserved acclaim for the Quality Start and some impassioned letters from the National Committee for Batters' Equality, the Elias Sports Bureau spared no expense this winter in order to develop a similar statistic for batters. Thousands of man-hours of laborious research and millions of computer calculations later, we are proud to announce the result: Quality At Bats. Any time a batter hits the ball and reaches base safely, without benefit of a misplay, he is awarded a Quality At Bat.

It would be nice if we could tell you that the development of the Quality At Bat was a completely successful venture. But Murphy's Law struck here at Elias in February. The development of the Quality At Bat, it turns out, came one year too late. We discovered that last season Pete Rose broke the all-time career record for Quality At Bats, a record which had stood for nearly 60 years. Imagine what drama could have resulted from the chase as Rose closed in on the decades-old record. Had we only known a year ago what we know now, we could have ensured that so momentous an occasion would not have happened in such lamentable obscurity.

WON-LOST RECORD BY STARTING POSITION

CINCINNATI 89-72	C	1B	2B	3B	SS	LF	CF	RF	P	Leadoff	Relief	Starts
Buddy Bell				41-25								41-25
Dann Bilardello	15-15											15-15
Tom Browning									26-12			26-12
Bob Buchanan											3-10	
Cesar Cedeno		2-3			22-21	0-3		1-1		0-3		25-28
Dave Concepcion					83-62							83-62
Eric Davis						0-3	15-5	1-0		12-7		16-8
Bo Diaz	27-20											27-20
Nick Esasky		0-2		26-25		32-21						58-48
Tom Foley			5-8		4-6							9-14
John Franco											43-24	
Tom Hume											23-32	
Alan Knicely	23-19											23-19
Wayne Krenchicki				20-22								20-22
Andy McGaffigan									8-7			8-7
Eddie Milner							58-49					58-49
Rob Murphy										45-42	0-2	
Paul O'Neill						0-2						0-2
Ron Oester			84-63									84-63
Dave Parker								86-71		1-0		86-71
Frank Pastore									4-2		2-9	4-2
Tony Perez		24-21										24-21
Ted Power											47-16	
Joe Price									5-3		6-12	5-3
Gary Redus						19-11	14-15			30-20		33-26
Ron Robinson									6-6		10-11	6-6
Pete Rose		63-46										63-46
Wade Rowdon			2-0									2-0
Tom Runnells			0-1		2-4							2-5
Mike Smith											1-1	
Mario Soto									18-18			18-18
John Stuper									8-5			8-5
Jay Tibbs									14-19		5-14	14-19
Dave Van Gorder	24-18										0-1	24-18
Max Venable						13-11	2-0			1-0		15-11
Duane Walker					3-3			1-0				4-3
Carl Willis											3-8	

Batting vs. Left and Right Handed Pitchers

		BA	Rank	SA	Rank	OBA	Rank	HR %	Rank	BB %	Rank	SO %	Rank
Buddy Bell	vs. Lefties	.250	77	.361	81	.321	74	1.39	83	9.88	55	8.64	27
	vs. Righties	.206	127	.371	80	.307	93	2.86	41	12.81	23	9.85	40
Dave Concepcion	vs. Lefties	.244	82	.359	82	.322	73	2.56	55	10.34	50	12.07	65
	vs. Righties	.255	72	.319	108	.312	86	0.74	104	7.17	85	10.31	46
Eric Davis	vs. Lefties	.264	61	.604	1	.316	78	9.43	1	7.02	90	29.82	133
	vs. Righties	.232	--	.449	--	.264	--	4.35	--	4.05	--	29.73	--
Bo Diaz	vs. Lefties	.233	95	.350	86	.329	67	0.00	108	12.86	29	2.86	2
	vs. Righties	.249	88	.379	77	.298	107	2.82	42	6.22	98	11.92	62
Nick Esasky	vs. Lefties	.298	25	.518	12	.375	24	4.96	17	10.63	46	19.38	114
	vs. Righties	.243	98	.438	33	.309	88	5.15	10	7.89	72	23.36	133
Wayne Krenchicki	vs. Lefties	.200	--	.200	--	.250	--	0.00	--	7.69	--	15.38	--
	vs. Righties	.276	42	.405	60	.377	17	2.45	52	14.06	16	9.38	36
Eddie Milner	vs. Lefties	.213	--	.234	--	.327	--	0.00	--	14.29	--	14.29	--
	vs. Righties	.259	67	.360	87	.343	51	0.74	105	11.42	34	4.96	8
Ron Oester	vs. Lefties	.277	45	.338	94	.312	81	0.00	108	5.06	115	15.82	94
	vs. Righties	.302	20	.370	83	.369	24	0.26	117	10.09	44	9.39	37
Dave Parker	vs. Lefties	.279	40	.443	36	.305	39	3.48	39	2.86	132	17.62	106
	vs. Righties	.327	5	.601	1	.390	11	6.22	5	9.50	54	8.88	29
Tony Perez	vs. Lefties	.331	7	.508	15	.393	12	4.84	20	10.00	53	9.29	31
	vs. Righties	.322	--	.390	--	.403	--	0.00	--	11.94	--	13.43	--
Gary Redus	vs. Lefties	.242	84	.367	76	.366	29	1.56	81	15.58	13	17.53	105
	vs. Righties	.263	61	.466	18	.367	29	3.39	31	14.18	15	17.73	106
Pete Rose	vs. Lefties	.347	3	.408	52	.467	1	0.00	108	18.33	3	5.00	4
	vs. Righties	.253	75	.306	112	.385	14	0.56	110	17.01	5	7.26	15
Max Venable	vs. Lefties	.000	--	.000	--	.000	--	0.00	--	0.00	--	12.50	--
	vs. Righties	.302	19	.442	25	.328	64	0.00	120	4.35	124	11.59	57
Team Average	vs. Lefties	.253	4	.372	8	.321	5	2.30	8	8.82	7	15.60	11
	vs. Righties	.256	6	.378	6	.329	3	2.02	8	9.59	1	13.29	5
League Average	vs. Lefties	.250		.374		.317		2.26		8.65		14.84	
	vs. Righties	.253		.374		.320		2.12		8.62		14.28	

Batting with Runners on Base and Bases Empty

		BA	Rank	SA	Rank	OBA	Rank	HR %	Rank	BB %	Rank	SO %	Rank
Buddy Bell	Runners On	.246	85	.492	17	.326	79	4.24	22	11.03	53	8.09	28
	Bases Empty	.194	130	.256	130	.297	93	0.78	105	12.84	17	10.81	41
Dave Concepcion	Runners On	.211	127	.274	127	.274	129	1.27	78	7.52	99	10.15	51
	Bases Empty	.282	28	.372	71	.345	36	1.24	91	8.47	46	11.30	47
Bo Diaz	Runners On	.271	58	.385	76	.327	76	1.04	85	7.34	102	8.26	30
	Bases Empty	.227	110	.362	80	.292	103	2.84	41	8.44	47	10.39	37
Nick Esasky	Runners On	.260	75	.481	25	.325	82	5.52	9	8.25	86	18.45	123
	Bases Empty	.263	55	.453	25	.337	42	4.74	15	9.30	36	24.81	132
Wayne Krenchicki	Runners On	.276	53	.395	69	.406	11	2.63	52	18.37	4	8.16	29
	Bases Empty	.268	--	.392	--	.336	--	2.06	--	9.35	--	11.21	--
Eddie Milner	Runners On	.245	87	.310	112	.326	80	0.65	104	11.11	52	6.67	13
	Bases Empty	.258	65	.366	77	.350	30	0.67	110	12.06	22	5.59	7
Ron Oester	Runners On	.305	25	.385	77	.405	12	0.47	112	15.06	19	11.20	64
	Bases Empty	.288	21	.345	94	.314	72	0.00	120	3.69	127	11.08	45
Dave Parker	Runners On	.337	9	.573	2	.401	16	5.57	8	9.89	69	10.44	57
	Bases Empty	.285	23	.529	6	.324	62	5.13	13	4.85	116	12.73	58
Tony Perez	Runners On	.378	1	.489	18	.453	2	2.22	55	13.21	31	10.38	55
	Bases Empty	.280	--	.452	--	.337	--	4.30	--	7.92	--	10.89	--
Gary Redus	Runners On	.230	110	.414	52	.333	69	3.45	36	13.46	28	15.38	95
	Bases Empty	.264	52	.415	41	.384	6	1.89	67	15.71	4	18.85	110
Pete Rose	Runners On	.275	54	.335	97	.424	5	0.60	107	20.09	3	7.76	26
	Bases Empty	.256	71	.307	118	.372	13	0.42	117	14.89	7	6.38	10
Team Average	Runners On	.265	5	.393	4	.344	2	2.47	4	10.66	2	12.79	4
	Bases Empty	.248	7	.364	8	.314	4	1.83	10	8.35	2	14.84	7
League Average	Runners On	.258		.381		.332		2.19		9.74		13.69	
	Bases Empty	.248		.369		.309		2.14		7.75		15.05	

Overall Batting Compared to Late Inning Pressure Situations

		BA	Rank	SA	Rank	OBA	Rank	HR %	Rank	BB %	Rank	SO %	Rank	RDI %	Rank
Buddy Bell	Overall	.219	124	.368	81	.311	88	2.43	52	11.97	23	9.51	33	.265	81
	Pressure	.091	133	.121	134	.162	135	0.00	92	7.89	84	13.16	62	.154	116
Dave Concepcion	Overall	.252	88	.330	109	.314	82	1.25	91	8.06	76	10.81	46	.229	110
	Pressure	.210	101	.270	111	.268	112	1.00	90	7.96	83	12.39	55	.313	42
Bo Diaz	Overall	.245	97	.371	79	.307	98	2.11	63	7.98	78	9.51	32	.433	1
	Pressure	.268	59	.415	48	.348	56	2.44	50	10.64	49	10.64	39	.333	25
Nick Esasky	Overall	.262	71	.465	20	.332	60	5.08	11	8.84	64	21.98	130	.301	54
	Pressure	.211	99	.461	32	.274	107	7.89	6	8.14	76	27.91	133	.250	64
Wayne Krenchicki	Overall	.272	48	.393	70	.369	21	2.31	58	13.66	16	9.76	36	.273	78
	Pressure	.231	91	.282	100	.333	67	0.00	92	13.33	24	11.11	44	.222	83
Eddie Milner	Overall	.254	82	.347	97	.342	48	0.66	112	11.73	24	5.96	8	.252	94
	Pressure	.254	69	.286	96	.347	58	0.00	92	10.81	47	5.41	9	.364	20
Ron Oester	Overall	.295	17	.361	84	.354	39	0.19	124	8.73	66	11.13	51	.236	105
	Pressure	.382	3	.461	31	.433	9	0.00	92	8.25	74	9.28	26	.167	109
Dave Parker	Overall	.312	8	.551	3	.365	26	5.35	9	7.49	87	11.53	56	.369	7
	Pressure	.385	2	.635	5	.438	6	4.17	25	8.57	69	12.38	54	.438	7
Tony Perez	Overall	.328	3	.470	17	.396	4	3.28	36	10.63	42	10.63	43	.403	4
	Pressure	.343	12	.371	67	.439	5	0.00	92	14.63	18	12.20	52	.222	83
Gary Redus	Overall	.252	87	.415	47	.366	24	2.44	50	14.92	8	17.63	112	.304	49
	Pressure	.250	73	.364	68	.377	33	0.00	92	16.36	13	21.82	115	.250	64
Pete Rose	Overall	.264	67	.319	113	.395	5	0.49	118	17.17	1	6.99	12	.331	23
	Pressure	.290	45	.290	93	.388	29	0.00	92	13.75	21	8.75	23	.261	61
Dave Van Gorder	Overall	.238	--	.325	--	.280	--	1.32	--	5.42	--	11.45	--	.362	9
	Pressure	.158	--	.158	--	.200	--	0.00	--	5.00	--	10.00	--	.429	--
Team Average	Overall	.255	6	.376	7	.327	3	2.10	9	9.37	2	13.93	6	.285	4
	Pressure	.272	1	.382	4	.342	1	1.96	7	9.60	4	14.14	4	.289	2
League Average	Overall	.252		.374		.319		2.16		8.63		14.45		.273	
	Pressure	.253		.368		.325		2.17		9.26		15.10		.257	

Additional Miscellaneous Batting Comparisons

	Grass Surface BA	Rank	Artificial Surface BA	Rank	Home Games BA	Rank	Road Games BA	Rank	Runners in Scoring Position BA	Rank	Runners in Scoring Pos and Two Outs BA	Rank	Leading Off Inning OBA	Rank	Runners on 3B with less than 2 Outs RDI %	Rank
Buddy Bell	.178	126	.236	100	.246	96	.194	128	.231	102	.152	123	.295	89	.563	86
Dave Concepcion	.244	84	.255	77	.271	63	.233	101	.206	119	.152	123	.400	11	.583	68
Bo Diaz	.273	--	.234	104	.301	27	.201	125	.352	6	.320	18	.224	132	.917	1
Nick Esasky	.297	24	.244	93	.230	111	.290	20	.286	44	.196	104	.313	77	.600	59
Wayne Krenchicki	.279	--	.269	53	.309	18	.224	--	.259	77	.257	60	.333	--	.583	68
Eddie Milner	.250	75	.255	78	.247	93	.261	62	.263	74	.256	63	.347	47	.450	121
Ron Oester	.225	106	.323	10	.304	23	.285	29	.269	66	.179	113	.331	59	.760	12
Dave Parker	.301	22	.317	13	.308	19	.316	7	.360	4	.310	23	.373	28	.628	50
Tony Perez	.267	--	.358	4	.369	2	.275	42	.388	3	.316	20	.340	50	.857	2
Gary Redus	.205	123	.272	48	.289	41	.207	118	.294	36	.357	8	.350	46	.400	127
Pete Rose	.263	61	.265	62	.255	83	.273	47	.269	66	.303	30	.372	29	.656	33
Dave Van Gorder	.239	--	.238	98	.273	--	.203	--	.311	25	.250	--	.231	--	.800	7
Max Venable	.208	--	.306	17	.325	--	.236	--	.250	--	.200	--	.300	--	.750	--
Team Average	.236	9	.263	3	.270	3	.241	8	.271	4	.225	8	.315	6	.613	1
League Average	.251		.254		.256		.248		.257		.235		.315		.576	

Pitching vs. Left and Right Handed Batters

		BA	Rank	SA	Rank	OBA	Rank	HR %	Rank	BB %	Rank	SO %	Rank
Tom Browning	vs. Lefties	.223	25	.277	11	.282	21	0.68	17	6.71	27	19.51	17
	vs. Righties	.249	66	.403	84	.300	50	3.34	94	6.75	38	13.38	80
John Franco	vs. Lefties	.176	3	.224	2	.222	2	1.18	43	4.17	9	15.63	33
	vs. Righties	.253	70	.353	47	.340	90	1.49	22	11.58	101	14.79	65
Tom Hume	vs. Lefties	.250	47	.371	61	.371	92	1.72	68	16.31	110	9.22	83
	vs. Righties	.207	14	.322	26	.270	20	2.87	87	6.32	30	19.47	29
Andy McGaffigan	vs. Lefties	.275	73	.357	51	.342	70	0.97	33	9.09	62	17.32	22
	vs. Righties	.208	16	.329	29	.263	15	1.34	18	5.59	22	26.71	6
Frank Pastore	vs. Lefties	.288	89	.388	69	.333	63	1.25	46	5.75	19	12.64	50
	vs. Righties	.287	--	.372	--	.338	--	0.00	--	7.59	--	12.41	--
Ted Power	vs. Lefties	.224	27	.320	33	.349	75	0.80	24	15.48	108	7.74	96
	vs. Righties	.230	43	.280	9	.317	62	0.62	7	11.23	96	16.04	56
Joe Price	vs. Lefties	.333	--	.509	--	.375	--	3.51	--	7.58	--	9.09	--
	vs. Righties	.214	24	.385	73	.279	27	4.28	110	8.65	69	22.12	20
Ron Robinson	vs. Lefties	.302	98	.447	99	.353	80	2.33	84	7.30	36	11.59	61
	vs. Righties	.212	22	.354	49	.266	17	3.03	92	6.82	40	22.27	18
Mario Soto	vs. Lefties	.209	13	.370	60	.304	39	3.74	111	11.89	89	17.17	24
	vs. Righties	.214	23	.353	46	.276	24	2.75	77	7.81	55	23.43	15
John Stuper	vs. Lefties	.322	107	.408	82	.396	106	1.15	39	11.76	87	6.37	108
	vs. Righties	.287	103	.402	83	.324	74	2.87	86	5.70	23	10.96	92
Jay Tibbs	vs. Lefties	.267	64	.390	72	.336	65	1.16	41	9.54	68	9.13	85
	vs. Righties	.256	72	.362	56	.315	60	2.28	58	8.30	65	12.11	88
Team Average	vs. Lefties	.257	4	.376	6	.334	8	1.91	8	10.23	11	12.60	5
	vs. Righties	.242	7	.376	8	.302	3	2.74	11	7.79	5	16.48	4
League Average	vs. Lefties	.262		.374		.330		1.73		9.17		12.66	
	vs. Righties	.246		.374		.311		2.44		8.28		15.62	

Pitching with Runners on Base and Bases Empty

		BA	Rank	SA	Rank	OBA	Rank	HR %	Rank	BB %	Rank	SO %	Rank
Tom Browning	Runners On	.240	38	.413	83	.300	25	3.20	94	8.14	32	12.09	76
	Bases Empty	.248	58	.366	61	.296	40	2.78	92	5.82	28	15.77	46
John Franco	Runners On	.236	33	.291	9	.325	51	1.35	26	10.56	69	12.78	62
	Bases Empty	.233	38	.345	41	.304	52	1.46	37	9.25	81	16.74	41
Tom Hume	Runners On	.220	18	.341	33	.312	33	2.44	73	11.19	76	14.69	45
	Bases Empty	.228	29	.341	40	.314	70	2.40	76	10.11	89	15.43	49
Andy McGaffigan	Runners On	.257	60	.382	65	.340	71	1.39	27	9.64	54	25.30	3
	Bases Empty	.241	47	.321	28	.288	31	0.94	13	6.19	35	18.14	31
Ted Power	Runners On	.257	59	.349	39	.356	89	0.66	5	12.83	96	12.30	70
	Bases Empty	.194	9	.239	2	.303	51	0.75	11	13.55	109	12.26	79
Joe Price	Runners On	.267	71	.416	84	.347	78	2.97	91	12.20	87	15.45	37
	Bases Empty	.224	27	.413	92	.265	11	4.90	114	5.30	21	21.85	16
Ron Robinson	Runners On	.266	68	.416	85	.318	39	3.47	101	7.18	19	11.79	78
	Bases Empty	.254	65	.392	80	.306	60	2.08	64	6.98	47	20.54	19
Mario Soto	Runners On	.202	10	.359	48	.298	22	3.26	96	12.22	88	21.27	11
	Bases Empty	.217	22	.363	56	.285	29	3.22	100	8.36	70	19.66	21
John Stuper	Runners On	.358	114	.489	111	.385	105	2.27	66	6.00	9	7.00	108
	Bases Empty	.256	70	.333	35	.336	91	1.93	56	10.78	100	10.34	97
Jay Tibbs	Runners On	.283	93	.389	69	.333	59	1.67	39	7.56	21	6.59	110
	Bases Empty	.245	56	.367	64	.320	79	1.72	47	10.04	87	13.71	67
Team Average	Runners On	.260	8	.397	9	.329	7	2.48	10	9.35	6	13.25	7
	Bases Empty	.240	3	.361	5	.304	5	2.37	10	8.33	9	16.19	4
League Average	Runners On	.258		.381		.332		2.19		9.74		13.69	
	Bases Empty	.248		.369		.309		2.14		7.75		15.05	

Overall Pitching Compared to Late Inning Pressure Situations

		BA	Rank	SA	Rank	OBA	Rank	HR %	Rank	BB %	Rank	SO %	Rank
Tom Browning	Overall	.245	48	.384	77	.297	30	2.94	98	6.74	24	14.31	57
	Pressure	.225	37	.324	34	.286	27	1.41	40	7.79	32	11.69	77
John Franco	Overall	.234	33	.322	20	.313	50	1.41	23	9.83	77	14.99	47
	Pressure	.222	33	.313	27	.290	36	1.45	43	8.31	40	15.34	46
Tom Hume	Overall	.224	20	.341	28	.313	49	2.41	78	10.57	86	15.11	45
	Pressure	.227	39	.364	56	.297	40	3.79	97	7.53	28	16.44	38
Andy McGaffigan	Overall	.247	50	.346	29	.309	41	1.12	13	7.65	40	21.17	13
	Pressure	.200	--	.267	--	.250	--	0.00	--	5.88	--	5.88	--
Ted Power	Overall	.227	23	.297	11	.331	76	0.70	3	13.16	109	12.28	80
	Pressure	.252	66	.332	38	.344	71	0.93	32	12.25	88	11.07	82
Joe Price	Overall	.242	44	.414	98	.301	34	4.10	115	8.39	54	18.98	17
	Pressure	.222	--	.333	--	.300	--	3.70	--	9.68	--	16.13	--
Ron Robinson	Overall	.259	73	.402	91	.311	46	2.66	94	7.06	28	16.78	34
	Pressure	.200	17	.309	25	.241	9	1.82	55	5.17	12	13.79	63
Mario Soto	Overall	.211	11	.361	51	.290	24	3.24	104	9.86	79	20.28	16
	Pressure	.243	52	.383	69	.323	59	2.61	78	10.53	70	14.29	58
John Stuper	Overall	.303	114	.405	93	.358	103	2.09	54	8.56	57	8.80	105
	Pressure	.300	--	.350	--	.364	--	0.00	--	8.33	--	8.33	--
Jay Tibbs	Overall	.262	79	.377	70	.326	70	1.69	38	8.94	65	10.56	91
	Pressure	.296	91	.481	102	.415	108	1.85	58	16.42	111	8.96	91
Team Average	Overall	.248	6	.376	7	.315	6	2.41	11	8.77	7	14.92	5
	Pressure	.244	5	.359	6	.318	4	2.05	6	9.50	3	13.18	10
League Average	Overall	.252		.374		.319		2.16		8.63		14.45	
	Pressure	.249		.363		.326		2.12		9.92		15.33	

Additional Miscellaneous Pitching Comparisons

	Grass Surface		Artificial Surface		Home Games		Road Games		Runners in Scoring Position		Runners in Scoring Pos and Two Outs		Leading Off Inning	
	BA	Rank	BA	Rank	BA	Rank	BA	Rank	BA	Rank	BA	Rank	OBA	Rank
Tom Browning	.224	27	.254	57	.265	77	.225	21	.269	69	.267	84	.280	28
John Franco	.231	35	.236	34	.199	14	.278	92	.244	47	.255	74	.347	86
Tom Hume	.221	21	.225	24	.254	67	.196	5	.225	29	.275	88	.263	16
Andy McGaffigan	.284	--	.238	38	.237	51	.263	71	.264	63	.256	75	.347	86
Frank Pastore	.216	--	.310	106	.322	114	.239	--	.328	--	.290	92	.327	--
Ted Power	.267	77	.213	14	.222	32	.234	31	.228	34	.222	45	.314	63
Joe Price	.269	--	.232	29	.276	88	.200	7	.281	84	.185	--	.311	61
Ron Robinson	.230	34	.273	80	.266	78	.252	56	.282	86	.260	79	.299	51
Mario Soto	.198	8	.218	19	.217	25	.206	10	.181	7	.167	10	.308	57
John Stuper	.236	42	.335	113	.344	115	.265	76	.374	114	.270	85	.422	114
Jay Tibbs	.258	66	.263	69	.256	72	.267	80	.288	91	.234	60	.322	71
Team Average	.234	3	.254	7	.258	10	.238	1	.265	9	.238	7	.318	6
League Average	.251		.254		.248		.256		.257		.235		.315	

HOUSTON ASTROS

Last season marked the twentieth anniversary of the opening of the Houston Astrodome, the stadium that gave us inappropriately plush seats, a constant one-mile-per-hour "wind," and the unwelcome new excuse, "I lost it in the roof." While it may lack the charm or the history of Yankee Stadium, Judge Roy Hofheinz's pleasure dome shares at least one characteristic with the House that Ruth Built: no one has ever hit a fair ball out of either park.

The coming of indoor baseball precipitated an almost comical chain of events, one that led to the game of today being played so often on God's own green plastic. To review quickly: Pitcher throws ball. Batter hits ball in air. Outfielder looks up for ball, sees only glass and glare; no ball. Outfielder complains. Crew paints glass, blocking sun from outfielder's eyes. Also from grass; grass dies. New, improved grass is developed by Monsanto, avoiding such old-fashioned materials as chlorophyll. It is dubbed Astroturf. A new age dawns.

While the stuff was first used for indoor play, it proved to have an important benefit for the outdoor game as well: It was easier to maintain than grass, especially after a heavy rain, reducing the chance of a costly rainout. It spread like plastic crabgrass around the National League, which soon reached its current state in which half the fields are artificial and half are natural. And it seemed to change the game, too; in last season's League Championship Series, the grass-bound Dodgers battled the turf-tough Cardinals in a series scored like a tennis match: the Dodgers held serve on their home grass, the Cardinals matched them by holding their own on their speedy carpet, and then took the series by breaking serve in Game 6 in L.A.

If the surface of the field really creates substantially different conditions of play, we would expect teams to craft themselves to the game they play at home. The new, spacious, synthetically paved stadiums dictate a game based on speed and defense; they turn cannon shots to center into 400-foot fly outs, and singles to left- or right-center into extra-base hits in the gaps. Teams that play in older ballparks, with their grass fields and shorter fences, can still play a power game. Because the league's fields are split down the middle, a team can safely build for its park, knowing that a sizable percentage of its road games will be played in parks similar to its own.

Last year's Cardinals are a perfect example of this trend, but they are only the latest example; the classic prototype teams were the Astros of the late 1970s. The Astros spent that decade stressing speed and pitching, and why not? They had the most experience with conditions, and presumably had the chance to learn what worked and what didn't. Entering the 1985 season, the Astros hadn't hit 100 homers in a season since 1977, or fallen below 100 steals since 1973; the streaks were the longest and second-longest, respectively, in the league. In addition, no Astros batter has hit more than 20 home runs in a season since '74. While no other artificial turf team has deemphasized power to quite that extent, the stolen base and home-run totals of National League teams last season, broken down by home surface, show the extent to which this division has taken hold:

Carpeted Home Fields			Grass Home Fields		
	SB	HR		SB	HR
St. Louis	314	87	Chicago	182	150
Montreal	169	118	Los Angeles	136	129
Cincinnati	159	114	New York	117	134
Philadelphia	122	141	San Francisco	99	115
Pittsburgh	110	80	Atlanta	72	126
Houston	96	121	San Diego	60	109
Totals	970	661	Totals	666	763

Teams that play their home games on a rug stole 46 percent more bases than their grass-field counterparts, and hit 15 percent fewer homers. These are offensive choices, based on what a team feels it must do to win, given the peculiarities of its home park and the general conditions of the league. But how does this relate to winning? Are the choices being made sensibly? Can teams really exploit these conditions with custom-crafted personnel? Is the game of baseball being divided down the middle? The surprising answer is a definite no.

If it were true that the grass game and the plastic game were becoming two separate sports, we would expect teams to have a large home-field advantage over teams from opposite surfaces, and a much reduced advantage over those with like fields. A survey of National League games over the past 10 seasons indicates that this is nowhere near the case: Road teams actually play a little better in parks with surfaces that differ from their own. The home-field advantage has nothing to do with the composition of that field. The following table shows the composite records of National League home teams over the last 10 seasons, divided into games against opponents with like home surfaces and those with different home surfaces:

	Home Teams vs. Teams With Like Surfaces			Home Teams vs. Teams With Different Surfaces		
Year	W	L	Pct.	W	L	Pct.
1976	233	200	.538	278	261	.516
1977	249	183	.576	298	242	.552
1978	268	181	.597	288	234	.552
1979	241	203	.543	278	247	.530
1980	260	183	.587	296	233	.560
1981	161	128	.557	185	166	.527
1982	232	212	.523	267	261	.506
1983	226	218	.509	305	223	.578
1984	232	212	.523	273	254	.518
1985	238	205	.537	281	246	.533
Totals	2340	1925	.549	2749	2367	.537

On the whole, these figures demonstrate that the entire question of tailoring your personnel to grass or artificial turf has been greatly exaggerated. The truth, amply displayed by the evidence above, is that since the home-field advantage is greater against teams from like surfaces, the stadiums differ *within* each group at least as much as they do *between* groups. New York's Shea Stadium is a difficult hitters' park, and thus, despite its grass field, is closer in spirit to synthetically turfed Olympic Stadium in Montreal than to a hitters' haven like grassy Atlanta Stadium. The impression created by last season's playoffs notwithstanding, baseball is baseball, whether it's played on grass, carpets, or just plain dirt. The traditionalists who cry that artificial turf has created a synthetic spinoff of their beloved game are missing the point. The smell of new-Zambonied turf may be less pleasing than that of new-mowed grass, but turf's effect on the game is no greater, and thus no different, than that of Fenway's Green Monster, Candlestick's roller-coaster infield, Yankee Stadium's old Death Valley, or Oakland's enormous foul territory.

Even So, There's No Place like Dome

To every trend, there are exceptions. To this one, the Astros are a distinct exception. Over the past 10 years, the Astros have exploited their advantage over grass-field teams to a significant degree. It's not hard to see why the Astrodome poses a unique problem for grass-based teams with their power-based offenses: the Dome is the toughest home-run park in baseball, one that makes even the outer reaches of Busch Stadium look like the ivied walls of Wrigley by comparison. Houston's home advantage, ample over teams from carpeted fields, is vast over teams with grassy homes:

	Astros at Home vs. Teams With Grass Fields			Astros at Home vs. Teams With Carpeted Fields		
Year	W	L	Pct.	W	L	Pct.
1976	28	18	.609	18	18	.500
1977	25	20	.556	21	15	.583
1978	23	16	.590	27	15	.643
1979	33	15	.688	19	14	.576
1980	37	11	.771	18	15	.545
1981	23	9	.719	8	11	.421
1982	22	26	.458	21	12	.636
1983	30	19	.612	16	17	.485
1984	24	24	.500	19	14	.576
1985	26	22	.543	18	15	.545
Totals	271	180	.601	185	146	.559

Over the past four years, the Astros have gradually but steadily moved away from their speed-based offense of the '70s to become a team built around power hitters. Go back for a moment to the chart showing each team's stolen base and home-run totals from last season. The most surprising numbers are those of the Astros, who broke both of their major streaks: those of consecutive years above 100 steals and below 100 homers. They seem to be moving deliberately and methodically away from the formula that led to their one-and-a-half divisional titles in 1980 and '81. And as they do, their home advantage over grass teams has shrunk dramatically. From 1976 to 1981, their home record was .655 against grass teams; since then, it has fallen to .528. In that time, their home edge over other carpeted teams has stayed virtually the same, rising marginally from .558 to .561. The importance of their advantage over grass teams in the Dome cannot be overestimated; during that six-year period (1976–81), the Astros were 80 games over .500 at home against grass teams, 45 games under .500 *in all their other games*.

The implications are serious. The Astros have chosen to fly in the face of one of the most powerful stadium biases in the game. Our discussion of the Boston Red Sox implied that, given a home as unusual as Fenway Park, they cannot go too far in customizing their team for that park. The Astrodome is every bit as unusual a park as Fenway, in the opposite direction. The Astros are making a great mistake if they think they can club their opponents into submission, dismissing the formula that worked so well in the past.

The Envelope, Please

It isn't awarded every year, like the Most Valuable Player or Cy Young awards. It's meant to be an honor, but seems more like a consolation prize, like its cousin, "Miss Congeniality." Not all players are eligible: Reggie Jackson and Darryl Strawberry never had a chance. But there is probably no title in the game that clings to a player more tenaciously that that of "The Most Underrated Player in Baseball."

Calling a player underrated does more for the nominator than for the nominee—it's an important measure of our sophistication as baseball fans, a label that shouts, "Look at what I know that you don't!" But by the middle of last season, even the TV weathergirl filling in for the sports guy at 11 knew enough to say, "Houston 4, Cincinnati 3, on a home run by Jose Cruz, *the most underrated player in baseball.*" Arrrgh!

The award is informal—it just kind of attaches itself to someone and stays there until it either wears away or is passed on to another deserving soul. In the mid-1960s, it was Hank Aaron. In the early 1970s, Joe Rudi. Then came Al Oliver's turn, and then Eddie Murray's. And now the title has been passed on to Jose Cruz. Make no mistake: Cruz is a great player. Given a few years at Wrigley Field or Atlanta Stadium, he might have posted numbers every bit as lofty as those of Murray or Dale Murphy. So why has he been overlooked for so long?

(1) *He plays for the Astros.* Far from the major media markets, far from the pennant races, unencumbered by a rabid following, the Astros play most of their games in blissful obscurity. It's hard to gain a national reputation without national attention, and Cruz has had only two shots at the fame that accompanies post-season glory, one of them in the first round of the expanded 1981 playoffs. Typically, Cruz batted .343 for the two series.

(2) *He plays in the Astrodome.* All together now: "The Astrodome is the worst hitters' park in baseball." Enough said.

(3) *He has a simple name.* Hank Aaron, Joe Rudi, Al Oliver, Eddie Murray, Jose Cruz. Simple, straightforward, and unmemorable. Nobody ever called Jerry Dybzynski underrated, right? Cruz, in fact, is the only one of the group whose last name isn't really a first name. Unfortunately for him, though. . .

(4). . .*his last name is Cruz.* Prior to 1970, there had never been a player named Cruz in the major leagues. Since then we've had Jose and his brothers Hector (also known as Heity) and Tommy (also known as Cirilio), Henry, Julio, Todd, and Victor. Jose tried to clear the stage for himself by sending his brothers to play in Japan, but it still took a long time to get the Cruzes sorted out, and to realize that Jose was the one worth noticing.

But there's an underside to the title, too: By the time America proclaims a new "Most Underrated Player in Baseball," he probably isn't any more. Last season, Cruz received so much attention for being underrated that he drew notice away from some of his teammates who were having pretty fair seasons of their own. Glenn Davis hit 20 home runs in just 350 at bats. And Kevin Bass had more extra-base hits than Cruz, but got less press than Randy Bass did for his Triple Crown season in Japan. Cruz might not even have been the most underrated player *on his own team*.

So what's ahead for The Most Underrated Player in Baseball? At age 38, Cruz is likely to miss the biggest fringe benefit that accompanies the award—a long and lucrative period of being overrated. But considering the fact that Cruz has been getting better as he gets older, he may well be around long enough to pass on the torch to the next simply-named player laboring far from the major media markets. Are you listening, Phil Bradley?

WON-LOST RECORD BY STARTING POSITION

HOUSTON 83-79	C	1B	2B	3B	SS	LF	CF	RF	P	Leadoff	Relief	Starts
Alan Ashby	24-31	-	-	-	-	-	-	-	-	-	-	24-31
Mark Bailey	55-41	-	-	-	-	-	-	-	-	-	-	55-41
Kevin Bass	-	-	-	-	-	2-4	55-46	11-12	-	2-2	-	68-62
Eric Bullock	-	-	-	-	-	1-2	-	-	-	1-1	-	1-2
Enos Cabell	-	15-14	-	-	-	-	-	-	-	-	-	15-14
Jeff Calhoun	-	-	-	-	-	-	-	-	-	-	15-29	-
Jose Cruz	-	-	-	-	-	69-68	-	-	-	-	-	69-68
Glenn Davis	-	47-41	-	-	-	-	-	4-4	-	-	-	51-45
Bill Dawley	-	-	-	-	-	-	-	-	-	-	18-31	-
Jim Deshaies	-	-	-	-	-	-	-	-	-	-	0-2	-
Frank DiPino	-	-	-	-	-	-	-	-	-	-	25-29	-
Bill Doran	-	-	71-74	-	-	-	-	-	-	66-67	-	71-74
Ty Gainey	-	-	-	-	-	-	3-3	0-1	-	-	-	3-4
Phil Garner	-	-	5-4	51-52	-	-	-	-	-	-	-	56-56
Jeff Heathcock	-	-	-	-	-	-	-	-	5-2	-	3-4	5-2
Chris Jones	-	-	-	-	-	-	-	-	-	-	-	-
Charlie Kerfeld	-	-	-	-	-	-	-	-	3-3	-	4-1	3-3
Bob Knepper	-	-	-	-	-	-	-	-	19-18	-	-	19-18
Mark Knudson	-	-	-	-	-	-	-	-	0-2	-	-	0-2
Mike Madden	-	-	-	-	-	-	-	-	-	-	0-13	-
Ron Mathis	-	-	-	-	-	-	-	-	3-5	-	3-12	3-5
John Mizerock	4-7	-	-	-	-	-	-	-	-	-	-	4-7
Jerry Mumphrey	-	-	-	-	-	-	25-30	29-29	-	-	-	54-59
Joe Niekro	-	-	-	-	-	-	-	-	11-21	-	-	11-21
Jim Pankovits	-	-	7-1	-	0-1	7-3	-	12-5	-	3-1	-	26-10
Bert Pena	-	-	-	2-0	3-1	-	-	-	-	-	-	5-1
Terry Puhl	-	-	-	-	-	-	26-26	-	-	1-2	-	26-26
Craig Reynolds	-	-	-	-	44-45	-	-	-	-	-	-	44-45
German Rivera	-	-	-	6-3	-	-	-	-	-	-	-	6-3
Mark Ross	-	-	-	-	-	-	-	-	-	-	2-6	-
Nolan Ryan	-	-	-	-	-	-	-	-	20-15	-	-	20-15
Mike Scott	-	-	-	-	-	-	-	-	22-13	-	0-1	22-13
Dave Smith	-	-	-	-	-	-	-	-	-	-	40-24	-
Julio Solano	-	-	-	-	-	-	-	-	-	-	3-17	-
Harry Spilman	-	4-10	-	-	-	-	-	-	-	-	-	4-10
Dickie Thon	-	-	-	-	36-32	-	-	-	-	10-6	-	36-32
Tim Tolman	-	1-0	-	-	-	2-1	-	1-1	-	-	-	4-2
Denny Walling	-	16-14	-	24-24	-	2-1	-	0-1	-	-	-	42-40

Batting vs. Left and Right Handed Pitchers

		BA	Rank	SA	Rank	OBA	Rank	HR %	Rank	BB %	Rank	SO %	Rank
Alan Ashby	vs. Lefties	.288	31	.409	51	.377	22	3.03	48	12.99	27	11.69	56
	vs. Righties	.276	41	.472	16	.355	42	4.88	12	10.07	46	12.95	72
Mark Bailey	vs. Lefties	.290	29	.435	39	.413	6	3.23	46	16.67	7	16.67	100
	vs. Righties	.250	83	.375	78	.375	19	2.88	40	16.67	7	17.86	109
Kevin Bass	vs. Lefties	.311	15	.553	9	.359	33	4.57	24	5.49	109	13.08	70
	vs. Righties	.241	100	.341	94	.284	67	1.88	67	5.22	116	9.28	33
Jose Cruz	vs. Lefties	.277	44	.405	54	.306	87	2.27	64	4.31	122	15.09	86
	vs. Righties	.315	12	.441	28	.377	16	1.23	88	9.22	59	10.89	52
Glenn Davis	vs. Lefties	.278	42	.563	6	.346	48	8.33	3	8.75	71	15.00	83
	vs. Righties	.267	57	.413	51	.323	70	3.88	25	5.65	110	19.13	118
Bill Doran	vs. Lefties	.300	20	.461	33	.383	17	2.30	63	12.10	34	11.29	53
	vs. Righties	.280	37	.418	44	.350	48	2.49	50	10.02	48	10.02	43
Phil Garner	vs. Lefties	.268	53	.368	75	.318	76	0.45	107	7.44	84	13.22	73
	vs. Righties	.267	55	.428	40	.317	78	2.06	63	6.08	100	15.21	87
Jerry Mumphrey	vs. Lefties	.241	85	.293	116	.323	72	0.00	108	11.54	41	10.90	47
	vs. Righties	.293	24	.441	29	.331	62	2.57	47	5.72	108	12.05	65
Jim Pankovits	vs. Lefties	.235	93	.330	97	.279	113	2.61	54	5.74	106	13.11	72
	vs. Righties	.263	--	.333	--	.382	--	1.75	--	14.49	--	18.84	--
Terry Puhl	vs. Lefties	.294	28	.382	67	.342	52	0.00	52	6.33	100	10.13	40
	vs. Righties	.278	39	.437	35	.343	52	1.59	75	9.22	58	10.64	48
Craig Reynolds	vs. Lefties	.315	--	.407	--	.339	--	0.00	--	3.57	--	19.64	--
	vs. Righties	.265	59	.391	70	.285	116	1.23	89	2.94	131	5.59	10
Dickie Thon	vs. Lefties	.272	51	.383	66	.324	69	2.47	60	7.39	85	15.34	87
	vs. Righties	.213	--	.303	--	.253	--	2.25	--	5.21	--	23.96	--
Denny Walling	vs. Lefties	.267	--	.289	--	.298	--	0.00	--	4.26	--	21.28	--
	vs. Righties	.270	53	.410	54	.318	75	2.33	55	7.03	88	4.89	7
Team Average	vs. Lefties	.268	1	.402	1	.327	1	2.32	5	7.97	10	15.19	9
	vs. Righties	.257	4	.379	5	.315	8	2.07	6	7.53	12	13.41	6
League Average	vs. Lefties	.250		.374		.317		2.26		8.65		14.84	
	vs. Righties	.253		.374		.320		2.12		8.62		14.28	

Batting with Runners on Base and Bases Empty

		BA	Rank	SA	Rank	OBA	Rank	HR %	Rank	BB %	Rank	SO %	Rank
Alan Ashby	Runners On	.282	46	.372	82	.380	29	1.28	77	12.90	36	8.60	34
	Bases Empty	.279	35	.505	9	.350	31	6.31	7	9.76	31	15.45	90
Mark Bailey	Runners On	.343	8	.503	14	.478	1	4.20	24	20.22	2	16.39	106
	Bases Empty	.206	124	.317	108	.315	70	2.12	62	13.70	11	18.26	106
Kevin Bass	Runners On	.259	76	.429	48	.317	90	3.57	32	6.40	117	12.80	73
	Bases Empty	.276	41	.425	36	.313	73	2.54	48	4.52	117	9.34	28
Jose Cruz	Runners On	.311	19	.457	35	.369	40	1.57	72	8.87	79	12.77	71
	Bases Empty	.290	16	.400	54	.331	51	1.72	73	5.84	93	12.34	57
Glenn Davis	Runners On	.309	22	.487	22	.374	35	4.61	20	8.52	83	14.77	87
	Bases Empty	.242	90	.465	23	.299	89	6.57	4	5.61	102	19.63	120
Bill Doran	Runners On	.297	30	.431	45	.383	28	2.56	53	12.88	37	9.44	44
	Bases Empty	.282	26	.436	31	.351	28	2.35	56	9.67	32	11.08	46
Phil Garner	Runners On	.262	74	.391	71	.322	86	0.99	90	7.89	93	15.79	98
	Bases Empty	.272	46	.406	46	.314	71	1.53	80	5.78	96	13.00	61
Jerry Mumphrey	Runners On	.310	21	.438	41	.379	32	1.97	64	11.02	54	10.17	52
	Bases Empty	.249	82	.361	82	.282	109	1.66	75	4.37	122	13.10	64
Terry Puhl	Runners On	.351	5	.532	5	.404	13	0.00	115	8.60	82	9.68	46
	Bases Empty	.239	95	.342	95	.299	88	1.71	74	7.87	55	11.02	44
Craig Reynolds	Runners On	.270	60	.377	80	.293	113	0.63	105	3.53	132	8.82	39
	Bases Empty	.273	45	.405	50	.292	104	1.36	87	2.65	132	6.64	11
Dickie Thon	Runners On	.286	42	.429	48	.333	69	3.06	42	7.34	102	17.43	116
	Bases Empty	.229	105	.307	116	.276	113	1.96	65	6.13	88	19.02	111
Denny Walling	Runners On	.289	36	.437	42	.333	69	2.96	45	7.33	104	6.00	9
	Bases Empty	.257	69	.367	76	.304	82	1.43	84	6.25	82	7.59	17
Team Average	Runners On	.273	3	.404	1	.339	5	2.16	6	8.90	11	13.88	9
	Bases Empty	.252	5	.376	4	.305	8	2.18	7	6.76	12	14.27	4
League Average	Runners On	.258		.381		.332		2.19		9.74		13.69	
	Bases Empty	.248		.369		.309		2.14		7.75		15.05	

Overall Batting Compared to Late Inning Pressure Situations

		BA	Rank	SA	Rank	OBA	Rank	HR %	Rank	BB %	Rank	SO %	Rank	RDI %	Rank
Alan Ashby	Overall	.280	32	.450	24	.363	30	4.23	21	11.11	33	12.50	64	.340	--
	Pressure	.314	24	.629	6	.405	23	8.57	4	13.95	20	11.63	47	.500	--
Mark Bailey	Overall	.265	65	.398	64	.389	10	3.01	39	16.67	3	17.41	109	.313	38
	Pressure	.245	77	.408	49	.422	13	4.08	28	21.88	2	20.31	111	.462	4
Kevin Bass	Overall	.269	57	.427	38	.315	80	2.97	41	5.33	119	10.82	47	.275	77
	Pressure	.319	21	.500	23	.380	31	4.17	25	7.50	91	12.50	56	.250	64
Jose Cruz	Overall	.300	15	.426	39	.349	41	1.65	81	7.29	89	12.54	65	.406	3
	Pressure	.279	49	.382	62	.364	43	1.47	73	11.69	40	14.29	68	.533	1
Glenn Davis	Overall	.271	50	.474	16	.332	57	5.71	6	6.92	98	17.44	110	.306	46
	Pressure	.122	131	.220	127	.163	134	2.44	50	4.44	122	26.67	132	.200	96
Bill Doran	Overall	.287	20	.434	33	.362	32	2.42	53	10.81	40	10.50	39	.291	64
	Pressure	.208	104	.338	76	.284	98	2.60	46	9.89	60	16.48	88	.310	43
Phil Garner	Overall	.268	58	.400	61	.317	76	1.30	89	6.73	101	14.26	84	.288	66
	Pressure	.292	43	.500	23	.366	41	4.17	25	9.76	61	15.85	84	.400	10
Jerry Mumphrey	Overall	.277	36	.396	65	.329	67	1.80	74	7.58	86	11.68	58	.336	19
	Pressure	.277	54	.338	73	.314	84	0.00	92	5.71	114	10.00	30	.263	60
Terry Puhl	Overall	.284	22	.418	45	.343	46	1.03	101	8.18	71	10.45	38	.300	--
	Pressure	.350	--	.400	--	.440	--	0.00	--	15.38	--	11.54	--	.500	--
Craig Reynolds	Overall	.272	47	.393	69	.293	115	1.06	100	3.03	134	7.58	15	.222	116
	Pressure	.238	82	.286	96	.284	99	0.00	92	5.88	109	10.29	35	.056	132
Dickie Thon	Overall	.251	90	.355	87	.299	107	2.39	54	6.62	104	18.38	121	.317	35
	Pressure	.250	--	.357	--	.300	--	3.57	--	6.67	--	33.33	--	.250	--
Denny Walling	Overall	.270	54	.394	67	.316	79	2.03	64	6.68	103	6.95	11	.355	12
	Pressure	.200	107	.233	124	.250	117	0.00	92	6.25	106	12.50	56	.000	133
Team Average	Overall	.261	2	.388	2	.320	6	2.17	7	7.70	12	14.10	8	.294	2
	Pressure	.251	8	.374	7	.325	8	2.59	5	9.30	8	15.87	9	.296	1
League Average	Overall	.252		.374		.319		2.16		8.63		14.45		.273	
	Pressure	.253		.368		.325		2.17		9.26		15.10		.257	

Additional Miscellaneous Batting Comparisons

	Grass Surface BA	Rank	Artificial Surface BA	Rank	Home Games BA	Rank	Road Games BA	Rank	Runners in Scoring Position BA	Rank	Runners in Scoring Pos and Two Outs BA	Rank	Leading Off Inning OBA	Rank	Runners on 3B with less than 2 Outs RDI %	Rank
Alan Ashby	.247	82	.306	18	.321	--	.252	79	.300	--	.308	--	.267	114	.556	--
Mark Bailey	.318	13	.246	90	.263	73	.267	54	.308	29	.286	36	.317	75	.500	105
Kevin Bass	.281	43	.263	65	.250	89	.287	25	.267	71	.323	16	.311	78	.480	116
Jose Cruz	.266	60	.315	15	.310	17	.291	19	.331	14	.317	19	.357	36	.710	20
Glenn Davis	.214	116	.304	19	.317	15	.231	106	.316	22	.173	119	.363	33	.619	52
Bill Doran	.328	4	.268	55	.283	49	.291	18	.278	57	.279	41	.332	58	.636	44
Phil Garner	.296	25	.256	76	.272	62	.264	59	.245	87	.212	92	.323	68	.586	67
Jerry Mumphrey	.293	32	.270	51	.305	20	.254	75	.277	58	.233	74	.294	91	.846	3
Jim Pankovits	.304	--	.222	116	.274	--	.216	111	.250	--	.217	83	.262	--	.667	--
Terry Puhl	.333	--	.275	41	.325	14	.211	--	.317	--	.150	125	.077	--	.600	59
Craig Reynolds	.326	6	.254	81	.230	110	.314	8	.241	90	.292	35	.304	85	.500	105
Mike Scott	.095	--	.176	--	.179	--	.121	--	.167	--	.200	--	.214	--	.545	90
Dickie Thon	.307	16	.221	117	.190	131	.308	9	.333	10	.308	24	.263	118	.500	105
Denny Walling	.320	10	.248	89	.260	78	.280	34	.322	20	.286	36	.263	116	.680	27
Team Average	.274	1	.255	6	.263	4	.260	3	.271	3	.248	4	.302	10	.596	2
League Average	.251		.254		.256		.248		.257		.235		.315		.576	

Pitching vs. Left and Right Handed Batters

		BA	Rank	SA	Rank	OBA	Rank	HR %	Rank	BB %	Rank	SO %	Rank
Jeff Calhoun	vs. Lefties	.155	--	.207	--	.215	--	1.72	--	7.35	--	23.53	--
	vs. Righties	.273	93	.349	44	.346	96	0.58	4	9.95	85	16.23	55
Bill Dawley	vs. Lefties	.258	54	.364	55	.333	63	2.27	83	9.80	72	10.46	73
	vs. Righties	.261	78	.379	71	.342	92	2.48	68	11.34	99	16.49	53
Frank DiPino	vs. Lefties	.344	--	.500	--	.442	--	3.13	--	15.19	--	8.86	--
	vs. Righties	.220	26	.346	41	.321	71	2.34	61	12.40	105	16.80	50
Jeff Heathcock	vs. Lefties	.190	7	.298	18	.236	5	2.38	86	5.56	15	4.44	115
	vs. Righties	.272	--	.512	--	.319	--	5.60	--	5.88	--	15.44	--
Charlie Kerfeld	vs. Lefties	.329	110	.425	93	.444	113	1.37	55	17.78	114	11.11	67
	vs. Righties	.220	--	.253	--	.284	--	1.10	--	8.74	--	19.42	--
Bob Knepper	vs. Lefties	.261	57	.409	83	.287	28	2.61	92	4.00	8	16.80	27
	vs. Righties	.272	92	.412	90	.313	58	2.20	52	5.50	18	12.35	83
Ron Mathis	vs. Lefties	.250	47	.375	63	.322	50	0.78	22	10.14	76	7.43	100
	vs. Righties	.329	115	.529	114	.379	112	3.87	102	7.02	46	13.45	79
Joe Niekro	vs. Lefties	.271	69	.379	65	.369	91	2.37	85	13.35	99	7.88	94
	vs. Righties	.224	34	.337	31	.289	39	2.86	84	8.12	63	17.31	44
Nolan Ryan	vs. Lefties	.246	45	.337	42	.317	45	1.20	44	9.53	67	20.55	14
	vs. Righties	.234	50	.340	34	.319	67	1.59	26	9.78	83	21.92	21
Mike Scott	vs. Lefties	.217	18	.289	13	.289	30	0.70	19	8.90	60	12.63	51
	vs. Righties	.254	71	.442	103	.317	64	4.27	109	8.43	67	17.31	43
Dave Smith	vs. Lefties	.233	33	.302	21	.286	26	0.86	27	6.35	21	8.73	90
	vs. Righties	.237	52	.299	16	.274	21	1.13	13	4.76	11	15.34	60
Team Average	vs. Lefties	.249	3	.344	4	.326	4	1.52	6	10.18	10	12.42	7
	vs. Righties	.257	10	.394	10	.318	9	2.57	10	7.88	6	16.16	6
League Average	vs. Lefties	.262		.374		.330		1.73		9.17		12.66	
	vs. Righties	.246		.374		.311		2.44		8.28		15.62	

Pitching with Runners on Base and Bases Empty

		BA	Rank	SA	Rank	OBA	Rank	HR %	Rank	BB %	Rank	SO %	Rank
Jeff Calhoun	Runners On	.243	41	.330	21	.328	53	1.94	52	11.48	80	13.11	58
	Bases Empty	.244	54	.299	22	.299	48	0.00	1	7.30	54	22.63	11
Bill Dawley	Runners On	.304	106	.437	93	.391	106	2.96	90	12.72	93	12.72	63
	Bases Empty	.222	25	.316	26	.289	33	1.90	53	8.62	75	14.94	52
Frank DiPino	Runners On	.294	102	.476	109	.406	111	3.97	108	15.19	109	15.19	39
	Bases Empty	.211	18	.303	23	.298	45	1.32	26	11.11	103	14.62	57
Jeff Heathcock	Runners On	.136	--	.247	--	.193	--	3.70	--	5.56	--	13.33	--
	Bases Empty	.305	112	.539	115	.346	102	4.69	113	5.88	29	9.56	102
Bob Knepper	Runners On	.275	85	.404	77	.330	57	1.60	36	7.62	24	12.70	64
	Bases Empty	.267	89	.417	95	.295	39	2.67	87	3.60	7	13.04	75
Ron Mathis	Runners On	.305	107	.435	91	.362	93	2.29	69	8.50	36	9.80	88
	Bases Empty	.283	103	.480	111	.343	100	2.63	84	8.43	71	11.45	87
Joe Niekro	Runners On	.219	17	.296	12	.316	37	1.50	29	12.22	88	11.25	82
	Bases Empty	.267	87	.400	85	.339	95	3.44	106	9.50	85	13.76	65
Nolan Ryan	Runners On	.245	44	.365	54	.326	52	1.63	38	10.00	62	20.45	12
	Bases Empty	.235	40	.319	27	.311	65	1.23	19	9.39	84	21.92	15
Mike Scott	Runners On	.241	39	.351	41	.315	36	2.22	62	9.59	53	18.08	21
	Bases Empty	.231	35	.370	70	.294	38	2.54	80	8.08	66	12.75	76
Dave Smith	Runners On	.229	24	.313	18	.267	5	1.20	18	5.03	5	11.17	84
	Bases Empty	.244	54	.283	13	.294	37	0.79	12	5.88	29	14.71	55
Team Average	Runners On	.253	5	.368	5	.328	6	1.97	4	9.85	8	14.48	5
	Bases Empty	.254	8	.380	10	.315	9	2.32	9	7.89	6	14.87	8
League Average	Runners On	.258		.381		.332		2.19		9.74		13.69	
	Bases Empty	.248		.369		.309		2.14		7.75		15.05	

Overall Pitching Compared to Late Inning Pressure Situations

		BA	Rank	SA	Rank	OBA	Rank	HR %	Rank	BB %	Rank	SO %	Rank
Jeff Calhoun	Overall	.243	46	.313	16	.313	48	0.87	6	9.27	70	18.15	25
	Pressure	.265	71	.333	39	.336	66	0.85	30	9.70	63	17.16	33
Bill Dawley	Overall	.259	74	.372	63	.338	85	2.39	76	10.66	88	13.83	64
	Pressure	.241	51	.352	48	.366	83	2.78	81	15.83	107	14.39	56
Frank DiPino	Overall	.248	52	.381	75	.350	99	2.52	85	13.07	108	14.89	48
	Pressure	.305	97	.445	93	.409	105	3.13	89	14.10	101	14.10	62
Bob Knepper	Overall	.271	93	.412	97	.310	42	2.25	68	5.31	7	12.89	72
	Pressure	.309	102	.515	109	.347	73	4.41	101	5.48	15	10.96	83
Ron Mathis	Overall	.293	108	.459	113	.352	101	2.47	81	8.46	56	10.66	89
	Pressure	.323	106	.419	84	.432	111	0.00	1	16.22	109	8.11	95
Joe Niekro	Overall	.247	49	.357	39	.329	74	2.63	83	10.70	89	12.65	75
	Pressure	.280	83	.493	104	.368	84	6.67	114	11.49	82	12.64	71
Nolan Ryan	Overall	.239	39	.339	27	.318	58	1.40	22	9.66	76	21.26	12
	Pressure	.236	46	.374	66	.287	29	3.25	92	5.11	11	21.90	16
Mike Scott	Overall	.235	35	.363	54	.302	35	2.42	79	8.68	58	14.86	49
	Pressure	.108	2	.169	4	.205	4	1.54	46	10.96	76	12.33	75
Dave Smith	Overall	.235	37	.300	12	.279	14	1.02	11	5.40	8	12.70	74
	Pressure	.230	41	.302	22	.272	21	1.35	39	5.04	10	12.61	72
Team Average	Overall	.254	7	.375	6	.321	8	2.17	7	8.78	8	14.70	6
	Pressure	.252	8	.374	7	.330	8	2.76	12	9.87	8	14.42	8
League Average	Overall	.252		.374		.319		2.16		8.63		14.45	
	Pressure	.249		.363		.326		2.12		9.92		15.33	

Additional Miscellaneous Pitching Comparisons

	Grass Surface		Artificial Surface		Home Games		Road Games		Runners in Scoring Position		Runners in Scoring Pos and Two Outs		Leading Off Inning	
	BA	Rank	BA	Rank	BA	Rank	BA	Rank	BA	Rank	BA	Rank	OBA	Rank
Jeff Calhoun	.137	--	.274	81	.242	57	.245	42	.270	71	.188	24	.237	6
Bill Dawley	.310	109	.238	39	.242	56	.278	89	.289	92	.304	103	.372	100
Frank DiPino	.270	81	.236	35	.237	49	.256	62	.288	90	.294	95	.319	68
Jeff Heathcock	.234	39	.243	44	.217	--	.248	49	.140	--	.176	--	.293	43
Charlie Kerfeld	.238	--	.287	92	.286	--	.242	--	.262	--	.176	--	.489	--
Bob Knepper	.249	58	.278	86	.278	89	.263	72	.268	68	.243	68	.337	81
Ron Mathis	.346	115	.272	78	.267	81	.336	116	.309	104	.270	85	.411	112
Joe Niekro	.226	29	.259	63	.254	68	.241	38	.230	38	.216	42	.311	60
Nolan Ryan	.304	103	.218	20	.220	28	.266	78	.233	39	.224	49	.351	88
Mike Scott	.241	48	.232	30	.195	10	.276	88	.256	58	.217	43	.265	17
Dave Smith	.206	--	.243	44	.235	45	.236	--	.209	18	.173	15	.310	59
Julio Solano	.172	--	.287	92	.317	--	.209	--	.135	--	.059	--	.455	--
Team Average	.255	9	.253	6	.247	6	.262	8	.253	5	.230	5	.333	11
League Average	.251		.254		.248		.256		.257		.235		.315	

LOS ANGELES DODGERS

The Dodgers won another division title last season, and they did it the old-fashioned way—with pitching. From Sandy Koufax and Don Drysdale, the torch has been passed: Bill Singer, Don Sutton, Andy Messersmith, and Tommy John are all a part of the legacy of Los Angeles pitching that has dominated the National League for nearly three decades. Now Fernando Valenzuela, Orel Hershiser, and Bob Welch have formed the next generation of great Dodgers starters. The Dodgers have won half of the National League's team ERA titles since moving west 28 years ago, and have won at least a division title in nine of those 14 league-leading seasons. One of baseball's most worn adages explains their success: Good pitching stops good hitting.

In the most recent Elias survey of overused sports cliches, "Good pitching stops good hitting" ranked ahead of "Drive for show, and putt for dough," and a close second to "You can throw (emotion, the home-field advantage, etc.) out the window in this one." And the reason that good pitching stops good hitting is, of course, that "pitching is 70 percent of baseball" (fourth in our survey), right? Well, we decided to take a look at this hoary axiom, and we found that while the best pitchers don't render the best hitters helpless, they do more than neutralize those big bats.

We instructed our computer to scan our 1985 database, and to summarize the performance of last summer's National League All-Star team against a select group of 12 pitchers: the league's top five winners (Dwight Gooden, John Tudor, Joaquin Andujar, Tom Browning, and Orel Hershiser); other qualifying pitchers with ERAs below 2.50 (Rick Reuschel, Welch, and Valenzuela); and the top four relievers in saves (Jeff Reardon, Lee Smith, Ted Power, and Dave Smith). The results, along with a proportional slice of their composite overall performance for the season for comparison purposes, look like this:

Player	AB	H	2B	3B	HR	BB	SO	BA	SA	OBA
Gary Carter	80	15	1	0	1	4	7	.188	.238	.235
Jack Clark	49	14	1	2	3	10	11	.286	.571	.407
Jose Cruz	68	13	0	0	0	6	14	.191	.191	.257
Steve Garvey	95	18	7	0	0	3	21	.189	.263	.225
Pedro Guerrero	42	13	3	0	4	8	9	.310	.667	.431
Tony Gwynn	90	27	4	0	2	6	3	.300	.411	.351
Tommy Herr	60	17	3	0	0	8	7	.283	.333	.357
Terry Kennedy	81	17	2	0	0	16	16	.210	.235	.210
Willie McGee	59	23	3	2	1	2	9	.390	.559	.410
Dale Murphy	83	29	6	0	4	11	18	.349	.566	.421
Graig Nettles	57	15	2	0	1	11	9	.263	.351	.382
Dave Parker	84	22	2	0	5	5	12	.262	.464	.303
Tony Pena	58	10	0	0	0	4	7	.172	.172	.226
Tim Raines	70	24	5	0	1	13	9	.343	.457	.452
Pete Rose	51	10	0	0	0	9	5	.196	.196	.328
Ryne Sandberg	85	26	7	0	0	7	14	.306	.388	.359
Ozzie Smith	54	12	0	0	0	7	3	.222	.222	.311
Darryl Strawberry	54	12	1	0	2	5	14	.222	.352	.283
Garry Templeton	76	18	2	0	0	10	16	.237	.263	.326
Ozzie Virgil	66	15	2	0	0	8	18	.227	.258	.307
Tim Wallach	68	20	4	0	4	1	8	.294	.529	.314
Glenn Wilson	96	24	5	1	0	6	22	.250	.323	.294
Vs. Selected Pitchers	1526	394	60	5	28	144	252	.258	.359	.324
Vs. All Pitchers	1508	436	77	12	48	160	208	.289	.451	.357

The .258 composite batting average is just two points lower than the overall league batting average (excluding pitchers). But don't overlook the drop in power: this elite group, which includes five of the six leading home-run hitters in the league, had its home-run output cut nearly in half. In fact, the number of *singles* hit by the group actually *increased* by two; the dropoff of 42 hits resulted from the loss of 44 extra-base hits.

The run-scoring implications of this power shortage are extreme. To demonstrate, let's treat this group, playing a full schedule against those pitchers, as a regular National League team. We'll add in a representative team's worth of pitchers' batting (pitchers hit .140 overall, .129 against the Gooden Group), extrapolate the performance over 162 games, and look at their composite batting statistics, along with their rank in this hypothetical 13-team National League:

AB	R	H	2B	3B	HR	BB	SO	BA	SA	OBA
5548	605	1382	207	17	97	505	1015	.249	.345	.311
	(11)		(13)	(13)	(11)	(10)	(12)	(8)	(13)	(10)

By applying Pete Palmer's Linear Weights formula to the hit, extra-base hit, and walk totals above, we can estimate that our All-Star batting team (with a typical set of pitchers batting in the ninth spot throughout the season) would score an average of 3.73 runs per game against the superpitchers. Only two National League teams had lower scoring averages last season: the two last-place teams, Pittsburgh and San Francisco. Our team of All-Star batters, given an average pitching staff, would probably win about 74 games if they played a full 162-game schedule against Gooden, Tudor, and the rest. Against a normally representative group of National League pitchers, they would have scored an average of more than five runs per game, and won roughly 107 games.

The results support the old axiom, but seem a little extreme. After all, it's hard to imagine a team with an outfield of Pedro Guerrero, Willie McGee, and Dave Parker at or near the bottom of any league in so many areas, regardless of the quality of the opposing pitchers. So we repeated the study, using the 1985 American League All-Star team, and a group of opposing pitchers selected in the same manner as the National League group: Ron Guidry, Bret Saberhagen, Frank Viola, Britt Burns, Bert Blyleven, Mike Moore, Doyle Alexander, and Charlie Leibrandt for wins (the last four tied for fifth); Dan Quisenberry, Bob James, Donnie Moore, and Willie Hernandez for saves; and Dave Stieb for his ERA under 2.50. The results were similar to those found with the National League statistics. Here is the 162-game composite batting line of our AL batting stars, with their league ranks had they been added as a fifteenth team:

AB	R	H	2B	3B	HR	BB	SO	BA	SA	OBA
5689	726	1566	221	36	154	419	795	.275	.408	.324
	(10)		(13)	(9)	(9)	(15)	(4)	(2)	(7)	(9)

Based upon its run-scoring potential, this composite team might be expected to win 80 of 162 games playing with a typical American League pitching staff: not quite as poor as the NL team, but then there are no Goodens on the American League superstaff. More significantly, the pattern of offensive reduction is quite similar. For both leagues, the All-Star batters compiled respectable batting averages, but the top pitchers robbed those batters of their power—not only home runs, but doubles and triples as well—and on-base potential.

So: Does good pitching stop good hitting? Not completely, but it sure does quiet it down.

With the Greatest of E's

The Dodgers' most serious problem last season was defense. They led the National League with 166 errors, and made fewer double plays (131) than any other team except Pittsburgh. No National League team since the 1971 San Francisco Giants had won their division while leading the league in errors. Had Los Angeles defeated St. Louis in last season's National League Championship Series, the Dodgers would have been the first team since the 1925 Pittsburgh Pirates to lead the league in errors and still win the pennant.

How good might the Dodgers have been with a solid defense behind them? We don't mean to frighten their Western Division opponents, but the Dodgers were devastating in games in which they committed fewer than two errors. And their defense has plenty of room for improvement. Let's look at the Dodgers' 1985 record according to the number of errors made:

Errors	W	L	Pct.
0	48	17	.738
1	31	23	.574
2	12	12	.500
3+	4	15	.211

No team in the National League last season had a record as sensitive to errors as the Dodgers'. It's only because the Dodgers made two or more errors in more than one-quarter of their games that there was a Western Division pennant race at all. Los Angeles ranked second in the National League with 43 multi-error games, only one fewer than league-leading Houston, but 10 above the league average. How many games did defense cost Los Angeles last season? This is a somewhat primitive tool, but let's project the Dodgers' winning percentage at each "error level" according to the number of games a typical team would play at that level:

Dodgers Winning Pct. at Each Error Level		N.L. Average Games at Each Error Level	
.73846 with 0 errors	×	74.32 games =	54.9 wins
.57407 with 1 error	×	54.28 games =	31.2 wins
.50000 with 2 errors	×	23.05 games =	11.5 wins
.21053 with 3+ errors	×	10.35 games =	2.2 wins
		162 games =	99.8 wins

According to these figures, with an average National League defense the Dodgers might have won 100 games last season. In fact, Los Angeles won five fewer. That's the price you pay for cutting your defense budget.

Clark/Van Slyke Revisited

We don't want to beat a dead horse here. And we're not looking to second-guess Tommy Lasorda's decision to pitch to Jack Clark, rather than walk him and face Andy Van Slyke, in the sixth game of last season's National League Championship Series. But the decision has caused more than a few Dodgers fans to toss and turn in their sleep, muttering, "Walk that sucker!" into their pillows, so we thought we'd take a look at what Lasorda could have known beforehand, and what he might have done with the knowledge.

First, for those who have forgotten, and for Dodgers fans who have suppressed the memory (remember, it might hurt, but you'll never get over it if you don't confront it), a review of the situation. St. Louis leads three games to two. The Dodgers lead Game 6, 5–4, going to the top of the ninth, on the strength of Mike Marshall's home run in the bottom of the eighth. With two outs, and runners on second and third, Clark comes to the plate with Van Slyke on deck. You would walk Clark and pitch to Van Slyke? What if you knew their career batting statistics against Niedenfuer:

Player	AB	H	2B	3B	HR	BB	SO	BA	SA	OBA
Clark	17	4	0	0	0	1	4	.235	.235	.278
Van Slyke	5	3	0	0	1	1	2	.600	1.200	.667

Based upon those figures, Lasorda's decision looks pretty sound. That is, if you are willing to base a decision on Van Slyke's five at bats, or even Clark's 18 appearances, regardless of how they might have fared. The figures which we consider more telling, hindsight notwithstanding, are these, which represent the Late-Inning Pressure performances of Clark and Van Slyke for the past three seasons:

Player	AB	H	2B	3B	HR	BB	SO	BA	SA	OBA	RDI%
Clark	171	59	11	1	6	32	36	.345	.526	.446	.400
Van Slyke	163	40	7	3	3	24	34	.245	.380	.344	.250

Over the past three seasons, Clark has driven in 40 percent of the runners in scoring position in Late-Inning Pressure Situations, to rank third among National League players with at least 20 runners driven in (behind Ozzie Virgil and Tony Gwynn). Additionally, in Late-Inning Pressure Situations with two outs and runners in scoring position—the most detailed and pressured situation that we track—Clark's average since 1983 is .333 (7 for 21), while Van Slyke has only a pair of singles in 18 at bats.

Computers can never replace managers, because no amount of statistics can eliminate the need for judgment. Lasorda judged that the righty-vs.-righty conditions dictated pitching to Clark. The two hitters' performances against Niedenfuer weigh in on that side of the argument. We would have been determined not to let Clark beat us, but that's our judgment. If he had walked Clark, and Van Slyke had driven in the winning runs, someone—not us, of course—would have shown how the stats proved that he should have pitched to Clark. We don't think the stats prove anything; we just hope they spice up the discussion, and help to ease those sleepless nights.

WON-LOST RECORD BY STARTING POSITION

LOS ANGELES 95-67	C	1B	2B	3B	SS	LF	CF	RF	P	Leadoff	Relief	Starts
Dave Anderson	-	-	1-0	26-13	11-9	-	-	-	-	18-6	-	38-22
Bob Bailor	-	-	2-4	8-10	2-0	-	-	-	-	-	-	12-14
Sid Bream	-	8-6	-	-	-	-	-	-	-	-	-	8-6
Tom Brennan	-	-	-	-	-	-	-	-	0-4	-	1-7	0-4
Greg Brock	-	70-47	-	-	-	-	-	-	-	-	-	70-47
Ralph Bryant	-	-	-	-	-	-	-	-	-	-	-	-
Enos Cabell	-	7-5	-	19-10	-	-	-	2-1	-	-	-	28-16
Bobby Castillo	-	-	-	-	-	-	-	-	4-1	-	4-26	4-1
Carlos Diaz	-	-	-	-	-	-	-	-	-	-	13-33	-
Mariano Duncan	-	-	9-7	-	71-49	-	-	-	-	50-32	-	80-56
Jose Gonzalez	-	-	-	-	-	-	-	0-1	-	-	-	0-1
Pedro Guerrero	-	4-6	-	23-21	-	48-23	4-5	-	-	-	-	79-55
Orel Hershiser	-	-	)	-	-	-	-	-	25-9	-	1-1	25-9
Brian Holton	-	-	-	-	-	-	-	-	-	-	2-1	-
Rick Honeycutt	-	-	-	-	-	-	-	-	11-14	-	2-4	11-14
Steve Howe	-	-	-	-	-	-	-	-	-	-	5-14	-
Ken Howell	-	-	-	-	-	-	-	-	-	-	31-25	-
Jay Johnstone	-	-	-	-	-	-	-	-	-	-	-	-
Ken Landreaux	-	-	-	-	-	1-2	65-43	2-2	-	1-2	-	68-47
Bill Madlock	-	-	-	19-13	-	-	-	-	-	-	-	19-13
Candy Maldonado	-	-	-	-	-	4-2	24-17	-	-	-	-	28-19
Mike Marshall	-	4-3	-	-	-	-	-	71-54	-	-	-	75-57
Len Matuszek	-	2-0	-	-	-	9-7	-	-	-	-	-	11-7
Tom Niedenfuer	-	-	-	-	-	-	-	-	-	-	39-25	-
Al Oliver	-	-	-	-	-	7-10	-	-	-	-	-	7-10
Stu Pederson	-	-	-	-	-	-	-	-	-	-	-	0-
Alejandro Pena	-	-	-	-	-	-	-	-	0-1	-	0-1	0-1
Dennis Powell	-	-	-	-	-	-	-	-	0-2	-	3-11	0-2
Mike Ramsey	-	-	1-1	1-0	-	-	-	-	-	-	-	2-1
Jerry Reuss	-	-	-	-	-	-	-	-	18-15	-	0-1	18-15
Gilberto Reyes	-	-	-	-	-	-	-	-	-	-	-	0-
R. J. Reynolds	-	-	-	-	-	9-13	2-2	17-7	-	2-2	-	28-22
Bill Russell	-	-	4-1	-	10-9	9-6	-	-	-	-	1-1	23-16
Steve Sax	-	-	78-54	-	-	-	-	-	-	23-24	-	78-54
Mike Scioscia	78-53	-	-	-	-	-	-	-	-	-	-	78-53
Franklin Stubbs	-	-	-	-	-	-	-	-	-	-	-	-
Fernando Valenzuela	-	-	-	-	-	-	-	-	18-17	-	-	18-17
Bob Welch	-	-	-	-	-	-	-	-	19-4	-	-	19-4
Terry Whitfield	-	-	-	-	-	8-4	-	3-2	-	-	-	11-6
Reggie Williams	-	-	-	-	-	-	-	-	-	-	-	-
Steve Yeager	17-14	-	-	-	-	-	-	-	-	-	-	17-14

Batting vs. Left and Right Handed Pitchers

		BA	Rank	SA	Rank	OBA	Rank	HR %	Rank	BB %	Rank	SO %	Rank
Dave Anderson	vs. Lefties	.194	123	.313	107	.333	62	2.99	50	16.87	6	10.84	45
	vs. Righties	.201	129	.266	128	.299	106	1.30	85	11.73	31	18.44	112
Greg Brock	vs. Lefties	.176	130	.255	127	.222	132	1.96	71	5.45	110	20.91	121
	vs. Righties	.274	49	.494	10	.363	35	5.65	6	12.44	29	12.69	69
Enos Cabell	vs. Lefties	.298	21	.398	57	.371	27	0.55	106	10.40	48	8.42	22
	vs. Righties	.240	103	.299	116	.282	120	0.65	107	5.45	112	11.52	56
Mariano Duncan	vs. Lefties	.286	35	.429	43	.332	64	2.20	67	6.06	103	17.68	107
	vs. Righties	.224	119	.297	118	.275	124	0.53	112	6.16	99	18.48	113
Pedro Guerrero	vs. Lefties	.304	19	.556	7	.413	7	6.67	5	15.63	12	10.63	44
	vs. Righties	.327	6	.585	3	.425	2	6.82	3	13.78	19	12.11	66
Ken Landreaux	vs. Lefties	.186	129	.339	93	.246	126	3.39	40	5.97	105	20.90	120
	vs. Righties	.279	38	.414	50	.320	72	2.36	54	6.30	96	5.00	9
Bill Madlock	vs. Lefties	.278	41	.405	53	.366	28	2.53	58	12.57	30	12.02	63
	vs. Righties	.273	50	.400	62	.335	60	2.25	56	6.60	94	7.87	18
Candy Maldonado	vs. Lefties	.232	96	.363	80	.301	92	2.98	51	9.09	68	16.58	99
	vs. Righties	.200	--	.244	--	.234	--	0.00	--	4.17	--	18.75	--
Mike Marshall	vs. Lefties	.287	33	.490	20	.349	45	5.10	16	9.14	67	27.43	131
	vs. Righties	.296	21	.526	7	.339	56	5.54	8	5.40	114	22.88	132
Bill Russell	vs. Lefties	.318	12	.365	78	.402	10	0.00	108	12.12	33	5.05	5
	vs. Righties	.202	--	.250	--	.261	--	0.00	--	6.45	--	4.30	--
Steve Sax	vs. Lefties	.215	109	.278	120	.324	70	0.69	101	14.04	21	7.02	13
	vs. Righties	.305	16	.334	99	.365	30	0.00	120	7.89	72	8.16	22
Mike Scioscia	vs. Lefties	.253	74	.345	89	.337	57	1.15	89	10.38	49	5.66	7
	vs. Righties	.307	14	.439	32	.424	3	1.75	71	15.71	8	3.57	4
Steve Yeager	vs. Lefties	.202	119	.245	128	.235	129	0.00	108	4.08	123	17.35	103
	vs. Righties	.222	--	.296	--	.281	--	0.00	--	9.09	--	21.21	--
Team Average	vs. Lefties	.247	8	.357	10	.316	7	2.13	10	8.96	5	14.75	6
	vs. Righties	.267	2	.393	1	.333	2	2.44	3	8.52	6	13.08	2
League Average	vs. Lefties	.250		.374		.317		2.26		8.65		14.84	
	vs. Righties	.253		.374		.320		2.12		8.62		14.28	

Batting with Runners on Base and Bases Empty

		BA	Rank	SA	Rank	OBA	Rank	HR %	Rank	BB %	Rank	SO %	Rank
Dave Anderson	Runners On	.165	134	.206	134	.281	124	1.03	86	13.56	26	10.17	52
	Bases Empty	.226	113	.339	99	.333	47	2.42	55	13.19	14	20.83	126
Greg Brock	Runners On	.288	37	.510	9	.380	30	5.77	6	13.11	33	14.34	84
	Bases Empty	.217	117	.374	70	.286	108	3.91	25	8.73	43	14.68	85
Enos Cabell	Runners On	.296	31	.401	64	.367	42	0.70	102	10.00	67	8.75	37
	Bases Empty	.254	76	.316	109	.304	81	0.52	114	6.76	72	10.63	39
Mariano Duncan	Runners On	.250	82	.367	83	.291	118	1.67	70	5.26	125	16.27	105
	Bases Empty	.241	92	.327	103	.294	97	0.79	104	6.57	78	19.22	116
Pedro Guerrero	Runners On	.304	27	.509	10	.423	6	5.36	11	17.20	6	10.39	56
	Bases Empty	.335	3	.635	1	.421	1	7.98	3	11.59	25	12.91	60
Ken Landreaux	Runners On	.241	93	.354	89	.294	111	1.03	88	7.59	98	6.70	14
	Bases Empty	.286	22	.439	29	.323	64	3.48	31	5.28	108	7.26	14
Bill Madlock	Runners On	.270	61	.389	72	.355	53	2.21	56	9.81	71	8.30	31
	Bases Empty	.279	37	.411	43	.337	43	2.44	54	7.37	65	9.94	34
Candy Maldonado	Runners On	.227	112	.309	113	.309	95	0.00	115	10.71	55	16.07	100
	Bases Empty	.224	114	.362	79	.268	118	4.31	19	5.69	100	17.89	104
Mike Marshall	Runners On	.304	26	.506	13	.351	55	4.45	21	6.96	108	19.78	125
	Bases Empty	.284	24	.524	7	.333	47	6.27	8	6.19	85	28.52	133
Bill Russell	Runners On	.274	--	.290	--	.370	--	0.00	--	13.16	--	5.26	--
	Bases Empty	.252	81	.318	107	.310	76	0.00	120	6.90	69	4.31	3
Steve Sax	Runners On	.281	48	.329	101	.366	43	0.48	111	11.38	49	7.32	22
	Bases Empty	.277	40	.309	113	.341	38	0.00	120	8.52	45	8.20	19
Mike Scioscia	Runners On	.348	7	.439	40	.447	3	0.53	108	14.71	22	2.94	1
	Bases Empty	.256	72	.405	48	.375	9	2.48	51	14.58	9	4.86	5
Team Average	Runners On	.269	4	.384	7	.343	3	2.00	8	9.74	8	12.43	2
	Bases Empty	.254	3	.381	3	.316	3	2.60	2	7.79	6	14.53	6
League Average	Runners On	.258		.381		.332		2.19		9.74		13.69	
	Bases Empty	.248		.369		.309		2.14		7.75		15.05	

Overall Batting Compared to Late Inning Pressure Situations

		BA	Rank	SA	Rank	OBA	Rank	HR %	Rank	BB %	Rank	SO %	Rank	RDI %	Rank
Dave Anderson	Overall	.199	133	.281	128	.310	91	1.81	73	13.36	18	16.03	97	.203	125
	Pressure	.240	--	.360	--	.367	--	4.00	--	15.63	--	12.50	--	.000	--
Greg Brock	Overall	.251	89	.438	31	.332	59	4.79	13	10.89	39	14.52	87	.259	87
	Pressure	.164	128	.230	125	.227	125	1.64	68	7.46	93	22.39	120	.100	124
Enos Cabell	Overall	.272	49	.352	89	.332	62	0.60	115	8.17	72	9.81	37	.291	65
	Pressure	.263	63	.281	102	.311	86	0.00	92	6.56	102	9.84	29	.250	64
Mariano Duncan	Overall	.244	98	.340	101	.293	114	1.07	98	6.13	111	18.23	120	.215	118
	Pressure	.183	120	.283	99	.242	122	1.67	67	5.80	113	24.64	129	.111	121
Pedro Guerrero	Overall	.320	5	.577	1	.422	1	6.78	2	14.29	11	11.70	59	.298	56
	Pressure	.306	30	.677	1	.419	15	9.68	2	16.22	15	10.81	42	.368	19
Ken Landreaux	Overall	.268	59	.405	58	.311	87	2.49	48	6.26	108	7.02	18	.255	91
	Pressure	.267	61	.317	82	.323	76	0.00	92	7.58	90	10.61	38	.000	133
Bill Madlock	Overall	.275	41	.402	59	.345	45	2.34	57	8.49	68	9.19	29	.265	83
	Pressure	.344	11	.422	45	.379	32	1.11	85	4.17	125	5.21	6	.306	45
Candy Maldonado	Overall	.225	119	.338	103	.288	118	2.35	56	8.09	75	17.02	105	.203	124
	Pressure	.214	97	.429	43	.250	117	7.14	9	4.44	122	22.22	118	.000	133
Mike Marshall	Overall	.293	18	.515	6	.342	49	5.41	8	6.56	105	24.29	133	.318	34
	Pressure	.296	38	.479	27	.324	75	5.63	15	4.00	127	18.67	101	.333	25
Al Oliver	Overall	.253	--	.316	--	.294	--	0.00	--	5.88	--	12.94	--	.308	--
	Pressure	.429	--	.643	--	.400	--	0.00	--	0.00	--	13.33	--	.308	44
Bill Russell	Overall	.260	--	.308	--	.333	--	0.00	--	9.38	--	4.69	--	.271	--
	Pressure	.321	--	.357	--	.387	--	0.00	--	8.82	--	5.88	--	.214	89
Steve Sax	Overall	.279	34	.318	114	.352	40	0.20	122	9.80	50	7.80	16	.308	43
	Pressure	.299	34	.403	53	.351	51	1.49	72	8.00	81	8.00	18	.200	96
Mike Scioscia	Overall	.296	16	.420	44	.407	2	1.63	84	14.64	9	3.99	2	.323	29
	Pressure	.254	67	.407	51	.353	51	1.69	66	12.50	34	5.56	12	.214	89
Terry Whitfield	Overall	.260	--	.413	--	.300	--	2.88	--	5.45	--	24.55	--	.324	--
	Pressure	.300	32	.550	14	.317	80	5.00	18	2.44	133	14.63	73	.333	25
Team Average	Overall	.261	3	.382	5	.328	2	2.34	4	8.66	6	13.59	2	.271	6
	Pressure	.267	2	.404	2	.326	7	2.74	4	7.88	11	14.60	5	.228	11
League Average	Overall	.252		.374		.319		2.16		8.63		14.45		.273	
	Pressure	.253		.368		.325		2.17		9.26		15.10		.257	

Additional Miscellaneous Batting Comparisons

	Grass Surface		Artificial Surface		Home Games		Road Games		Runners in Scoring Position		Runners in Scoring Pos and Two Outs		Leading Off Inning		Runners on 3B with less than 2 Outs	
	BA	Rank	BA	Rank	BA	Rank	BA	Rank	BA	Rank	BA	Rank	OBA	Rank	RDI %	Rank
Dave Anderson	.199	124	.200	--	.189	132	.209	117	.185	127	.097	134	.307	82	.467	119
Bob Bailor	.242	87	.259	--	.185	--	.321	--	.174	--	.000	--	.240	--	.625	--
Greg Brock	.249	78	.257	73	.251	88	.251	81	.283	51	.211	94	.238	127	.500	105
Enos Cabell	.296	27	.242	95	.269	66	.275	45	.270	65	.209	95	.279	103	.714	17
Mariano Duncan	.240	89	.255	79	.240	100	.247	86	.227	105	.189	107	.298	88	.385	130
Pedro Guerrero	.304	19	.359	3	.311	16	.330	5	.250	84	.259	59	.427	4	.567	83
Ken Landreaux	.284	38	.226	111	.247	93	.286	28	.168	131	.140	128	.236	128	.679	28
Bill Madlock	.295	28	.259	71	.292	39	.259	66	.290	39	.268	52	.388	17	.643	41
Candy Maldonado	.222	110	.235	--	.194	129	.255	73	.204	121	.074	135	.333	52	.625	--
Mike Marshall	.298	23	.279	38	.303	25	.284	31	.296	34	.343	9	.321	69	.568	82
Bill Russell	.288	35	.162	--	.326	13	.193	129	.375	--	.421	--	.325	--	.714	--
Steve Sax	.257	68	.333	6	.226	117	.329	6	.310	27	.213	88	.354	40	.483	115
Mike Scioscia	.323	8	.224	113	.297	34	.295	14	.324	19	.340	10	.384	20	.542	98
Steve Yeager	.213	118	.188	--	.222	--	.190	--	.143	--	.077	--	.281	--	.667	--
Team Average	.261	5	.259	5	.255	7	.266	1	.256	6	.219	11	.312	8	.574	7
League Average	.251		.254		.256		.248		.257		.235		.315		.576	

Pitching vs. Left and Right Handed Batters

		BA	Rank	SA	Rank	OBA	Rank	HR %	Rank	BB %	Rank	SO %	Rank
Bobby Castillo	vs. Lefties	.212	15	.356	49	.303	37	1.92	73	11.76	87	23.53	8
	vs. Righties	.243	60	.434	98	.359	107	4.61	114	14.84	115	15.93	57
Carlos Diaz	vs. Lefties	.203	--	.313	--	.203	--	3.13	--	0.00	--	21.54	--
	vs. Righties	.238	54	.363	59	.290	40	2.08	46	6.90	41	22.61	16
Orel Hershiser	vs. Lefties	.222	24	.289	14	.281	20	0.63	15	7.46	40	13.77	41
	vs. Righties	.186	7	.252	4	.249	7	1.27	15	6.74	37	19.77	28
Rick Honeycutt	vs. Lefties	.219	23	.329	38	.272	18	0.00	1	7.23	35	16.87	26
	vs. Righties	.267	87	.397	81	.329	77	1.92	38	8.32	66	10.25	98
Ken Howell	vs. Lefties	.185	6	.245	4	.268	12	0.66	16	10.00	74	21.18	12
	vs. Righties	.229	40	.373	68	.304	53	4.22	108	9.68	81	26.34	9
Tom Niedenfuer	vs. Lefties	.224	24	.363	54	.284	24	2.49	89	7.34	37	22.02	10
	vs. Righties	.222	28	.276	8	.250	9	0.54	3	4.06	5	27.41	4
Jerry Reuss	vs. Lefties	.282	79	.369	59	.308	41	1.94	74	3.70	6	9.26	82
	vs. Righties	.257	73	.365	62	.310	57	1.56	25	6.97	44	9.55	105
Fernando Valenzuela	vs. Lefties	.233	34	.344	43	.291	31	1.84	71	7.69	41	19.23	18
	vs. Righties	.210	20	.282	11	.285	32	1.34	17	9.39	78	18.66	34
Bob Welch	vs. Lefties	.214	16	.291	15	.254	8	0.92	30	4.87	13	14.90	37
	vs. Righties	.237	53	.435	99	.291	41	4.35	111	5.52	19	13.50	78
Team Average	vs. Lefties	.221	1	.311	1	.279	1	1.24	2	7.35	1	16.20	1
	vs. Righties	.241	5	.355	3	.302	4	2.16	2	7.78	4	16.20	5
League Average	vs. Lefties	.262		.374		.330		1.73		9.17		12.66	
	vs. Righties	.246		.374		.311		2.44		8.28		15.62	

Pitching with Runners on Base and Bases Empty

		BA	Rank	SA	Rank	OBA	Rank	HR %	Rank	BB %	Rank	SO %	Rank
Bobby Castillo	Runners On	.274	83	.558	115	.404	110	6.19	115	17.61	115	15.49	36
	Bases Empty	.196	10	.280	12	.277	24	1.40	33	10.06	88	22.01	13
Carlos Diaz	Runners On	.185	3	.331	22	.255	3	3.23	95	8.57	37	22.86	6
	Bases Empty	.261	79	.367	63	.285	30	1.67	45	3.23	5	22.04	12
Orel Hershiser	Runners On	.210	12	.296	11	.281	13	1.22	20	8.89	43	15.09	42
	Bases Empty	.203	13	.258	4	.258	8	0.74	10	6.01	34	17.35	38
Rick Honeycutt	Runners On	.271	79	.425	87	.344	76	2.34	71	10.44	68	10.84	85
	Bases Empty	.254	64	.364	57	.305	56	1.22	18	6.55	41	11.40	88
Ken Howell	Runners On	.230	25	.338	25	.301	27	2.70	83	8.98	45	22.16	8
	Bases Empty	.189	6	.290	16	.275	22	2.37	75	10.58	96	25.40	5
Tom Niedenfuer	Runners On	.245	43	.355	43	.290	17	1.94	51	6.47	13	27.06	1
	Bases Empty	.208	15	.299	20	.253	6	1.30	24	5.31	22	22.86	9
Jerry Reuss	Runners On	.255	58	.360	50	.313	34	2.17	59	8.20	33	11.20	83
	Bases Empty	.263	83	.368	66	.308	61	1.23	21	5.42	25	8.32	108
Fernando Valenzuela	Runners On	.251	52	.341	32	.313	35	1.81	45	8.72	40	16.78	28
	Bases Empty	.190	7	.260	6	.267	15	1.17	16	9.37	83	20.09	20
Bob Welch	Runners On	.195	5	.274	4	.270	8	0.88	13	6.98	17	15.50	35
	Bases Empty	.243	50	.408	87	.273	21	3.50	108	4.08	10	13.43	70
Team Average	Runners On	.246	2	.365	4	.313	2	2.26	8	8.85	3	15.93	2
	Bases Empty	.226	1	.324	1	.281	1	1.60	1	6.77	3	16.40	3
League Average	Runners On	.258		.381		.332		2.19		9.74		13.69	
	Bases Empty	.248		.369		.309		2.14		7.75		15.05	

Overall Pitching Compared to Late Inning Pressure Situations

		BA	Rank	SA	Rank	OBA	Rank	HR %	Rank	BB %	Rank	SO %	Rank
Bobby Castillo	Overall	.230	29	.402	92	.337	83	3.52	109	13.62	112	18.94	18
	Pressure	.304	--	.522	--	.448	--	4.35	--	20.69	--	24.14	--
Carlos Diaz	Overall	.230	28	.352	33	.272	12	2.30	71	5.52	10	22.39	10
	Pressure	.234	44	.351	47	.289	33	2.60	76	7.06	26	23.53	10
Orel Hershiser	Overall	.206	6	.272	4	.267	4	0.92	7	7.14	30	16.47	36
	Pressure	.174	11	.279	16	.260	18	2.33	69	8.25	38	18.56	24
Rick Honeycutt	Overall	.261	77	.388	81	.321	62	1.66	35	8.17	48	11.17	86
	Pressure	.185	--	.259	--	.267	--	0.00	--	9.68	--	12.90	--
Steve Howe	Overall	.319	--	.404	--	.353	--	2.13	--	4.81	--	10.58	--
	Pressure	.244	54	.317	29	.319	57	2.44	73	8.33	41	14.58	50
Ken Howell	Overall	.208	8	.312	15	.287	21	2.52	86	9.83	78	23.88	7
	Pressure	.221	31	.319	30	.312	49	2.45	74	11.49	81	22.98	13
Tom Niedenfuer	Overall	.223	18	.321	19	.268	6	1.55	30	5.78	12	24.58	6
	Pressure	.245	55	.355	50	.300	43	1.63	48	7.09	27	24.63	7
Jerry Reuss	Overall	.260	75	.365	58	.310	43	1.61	32	6.57	20	9.51	99
	Pressure	.278	77	.352	48	.328	61	1.85	58	6.78	24	8.47	93
Fernando Valenzuela	Overall	.214	13	.292	8	.286	19	1.42	24	9.11	67	18.76	20
	Pressure	.167	10	.210	5	.245	10	0.72	28	9.43	61	14.47	55
Bob Welch	Overall	.225	21	.359	47	.272	11	2.56	88	5.19	6	14.22	59
	Pressure	.220	29	.280	18	.250	11	0.00	1	3.85	6	7.69	97
Team Average	Overall	.234	1	.341	1	.295	1	1.87	3	7.65	3	16.20	2
	Pressure	.226	2	.323	1	.298	1	1.86	4	8.90	1	19.45	1
League Average	Overall	.252		.374		.319		2.16		8.63		14.45	
	Pressure	.249		.363		.326		2.12		9.92		15.33	

Additional Miscellaneous Pitching Comparisons

	Grass Surface BA	Rank	Artificial Surface BA	Rank	Home Games BA	Rank	Road Games BA	Rank	Runners in Scoring Position BA	Rank	Runners in Scoring Pos and Two Outs BA	Rank	Leading Off Inning OBA	Rank
Tom Brennan	.288	94	.750	--	.207	--	.446	--	.415	--	.438	--	.387	--
Bobby Castillo	.236	43	.205	--	.213	21	.252	54	.289	93	.311	107	.242	9
Carlos Diaz	.227	32	.237	36	.209	19	.246	43	.203	16	.111	--	.282	29
Orel Hershiser	.188	4	.268	76	.160	2	.258	65	.214	20	.229	54	.276	24
Rick Honeycutt	.234	36	.325	111	.236	48	.290	103	.318	108	.321	110	.318	67
Steve Howe	.321	111	.313	--	.325	--	.315	--	.394	--	.313	--	.350	--
Ken Howell	.208	13	.208	--	.218	26	.197	6	.280	83	.250	73	.342	82
Tom Niedenfuer	.234	38	.187	9	.251	66	.184	1	.237	44	.229	56	.177	1
Dennis Powell	.281	87	.200	--	.296	--	.233	--	.290	--	.333	--	.407	--
Jerry Reuss	.255	63	.272	79	.244	58	.272	84	.225	30	.229	54	.293	42
Fernando Valenzuela	.208	12	.230	27	.202	15	.225	23	.228	33	.188	25	.257	12
Bob Welch	.235	41	.198	10	.241	55	.203	8	.180	6	.171	12	.276	25
Team Average	.229	1	.250	5	.221	1	.248	3	.251	4	.240	8	.282	1
League Average	.251		.254		.248		.256		.257		.235		.315	

MONTREAL EXPOS

When the New York Mets speak of their friends to the North, they don't so much mean the whole nation of Canada as the few among them responsible for exporting Gary Carter to the States a year ago. But while the Mets are congratulating themselves for international grand larceny, the Expos no doubt are smiling over the exchange rate. They picked up four players—Hubie Brooks, Mike Fitzgerald, Herm Winningham and Floyd Youmans—all of whom made contributions to Montreal's surprising third-place finish last season.

The Carter trade is the first between two National League teams in more than a decade in which a team acquired three everyday starters for a single player. (Winningham actually had 79 starts—fewer than half of Montreal's games, but 30 more than any other Expo started in center.) Curiously, the Expos and Mets were the teams involved in the last such trade, in 1972, when Montreal sent Rusty Staub to New York for Tim Foli, Mike Jorgensen, and Ken Singleton, all of whom cracked the Expos' starting lineup. And this time, as a bonus, they also got promising pitcher Floyd Youmans, whose potential may be realized sooner than even Montreal hoped.

Not everything about the Carter deal went well for the Expos. Winningham did not prove to be the everyday centerfielder Montreal had sought. He started only three games last season against left-handed pitchers, sitting down while the likes of Jim Wohlford, Miguel Dilone, and Mitch Webster faced the southpaws. And if the Expos had envisioned a batting order in which Winningham would follow leadoff hitter Tim Raines to terrorize opposing teams on the basepaths, they quickly learned that Winningham didn't reach base often enough to steal too many. By the end of April, Herman had toted his .297 on-base average to the seventh spot in the Expos' batting order. Whether he will improve with time is debatable; the Expos may have tipped their hand on Winningham's future late last season when he started only 20 of the team's final 50 games.

Catcher Mike Fitzgerald was another disappointment, and as with Winningham, the degree of the Expos' dissatisfaction can be measured by the players they used ahead of him late last season: thrift-shop receivers like Sal Butera, Steve Nicosia, Mike O'Berry, and Ned Yost. They may have been more popular in the Montreal clubhouse than Carter, but they hardly conjured up on-field images of Cochrane, Dickey, and Bench.

Still, even if neither Winningham nor Fitzgerald starts another game for Montreal, the Expos may be able to justify the trade on the basis of the performances of Brooks and, eventually, Youmans. The latter demonstrated his potential late last season with an ERA of 2.45 after the All-Star break, which ranked fifth among National League pitchers with at least 10 starts. And Brooks's 1985 performance exceeded the wildest dreams of Expos fans, and probably gave Mets fans a few fitful nights.

Brooks started 153 games at shortstop, where he had never started a game in the majors until the previous August. He drove in 100 runs, the highest total by a National League shortstop since 1960, when Ernie Banks had 117 RBIs for the Cubs. Brooks's total, ironically, tied him for sixth in the league with Carter. And he did it playing his home games at Olympic Stadium, a notorious pitchers' park where Brooks had a career batting average of .202 with no home runs in 92 at bats as a visitor with the Mets.

The sudden emergence of Hubie Brooks as one of the league's leading run producers presents a terrific case study of the mixture of talent and circumstances that puts a man near the top of the RBI lists. To begin with, Brooks had proven himself in his five seasons with the Mets to be one of the National League's leading hitters with runners in scoring position; in 1983, he topped the league with a .354 mark. His statistics:

Year	AB	H	2B	3B	HR	RRF	BB	SO	BA	SA	OBA
1980	23	7	1	1	0	9	2	3	.304	.435	.385
1981	91	23	6	1	0	33	12	17	.253	.341	.321
1982	106	25	3	1	0	35	14	25	.236	.283	.323
1983	144	51	9	1	2	52	9	21	.354	.472	.396
1984	128	35	8	1	1	57	28	23	.273	.375	.399
1985	175	55	12	3	5	88	14	26	.314	.503	.354
Totals	667	196	39	8	8	274	79	115	.294	.412	.363

Obviously, the talent is there. And the circumstances? Well, the Expos gave Brooks a chance the Mets never did when they made him their cleanup hitter against left-handed pitchers until the Dan Driessen trade on August 1, and against everyone thereafter. The fourth spot in Montreal's lineup, behind Raines, Vance Law, and Andre Dawson, provided ample opportunity for Brooks to produce; he had 60 more opportunities to drive in runners from scoring position last season than he had a year earlier batting sixth for the Mets.

The more general question is, are the league leaders in RBIs those who bat in the most favorable lineup positions for the highest-scoring teams (that is, those who have the most opportunities to drive runners home), or those who are most efficient at bringing in the runners they find on base when they come to bat, however numerous or scarce they may be? The tables below list the National League leaders in those three areas: RBIs, Opportunities (runners in scoring position when each player came to bat, excluding his at bats that resulted in walks, hit batters, and sacrifice bunts), and RDI Percentage (the percentage of runners in scoring position driven in):

Runs Batted In		Opportunities From Scoring Position		RDI Percentage From Scoring Position	
Parker, Cin.	125	Moreland, Chi.	238	Diaz, Phil.-Cin.	.433
Murphy, Atl.	111	Herr, St.L.	232	Herr, St.L.	.409
Herr, St.L.	110	Wilson, Phil.	217	Cruz, Hou.	.406
Moreland, Chi.	106	Brooks, Mtl.	214	Perez, Cin.	.403
Wilson, Phil.	102	Pendleton, St.L.	213	Strawberry, N.Y.	.369
Brooks, Mtl.	100	Parker, Cin.	206	Parker, Cin.	.369
Carter, N.Y.	100	Hernandez, N.Y.	203	Hernandez, N.Y.	.360
Marshall, L.A.	95	McGee, St.L.	197	McGee, St.L.	.355
Schmidt, Phil.	93	Kennedy, S.D.	195	Brooks, Mtl.	.355
Dawson, Mtl.	91	Garvey, S.D.	191	Walling, Hou.	.355
Hernandez, N.Y.	91				

Statistical tests that measure the correspondence between different categories indicate a strong relationship between RBIs and RDI percentage, but an even stronger one between RBIs and opportunities from scoring position. The lists above illustrate that: Six of the seven players with at least 200 opportunities were among the top ten in RBIs, and none of the opportunity leaders drove in fewer than 69 runs. But several of the percentage leaders did not even approach that total. To take an extreme example from just below the top ten, Tim Flannery of the Padres drove in 34 percent of the runners in scoring position when he came to bat, but because he batted in the leadoff spot—and for a team with the National League's poorest-hitting pitchers—there were only 107 of them, and Flannery had just 40 RBIs for the season.

It is rare for a player to squander so many chances that he would rank among the league leaders in opportunities but not RBIs. For instance, in 1984, Lance Parrish of the Detroit Tigers came to bat with 220 opportunities to drive in runners from scoring position, the second-highest total in the American League that year. Although his RDI percentage of .214 ranked near the bottom of the league, Parrish hit 33 home runs and drove in 65 base runners for an impressive total of 98 RBIs, despite a major league-leading total of 173 runners left in scoring position (LISPs). The all-time *Player Analysis* LISP record holder (since 1975, that is) is Tony Perez, who left 184 of the 268 runners he found in scoring position on base in 1975. Last season's major-league LISP leader was Julio Franco (166), who not coincidentally also led in opportunities (244). Here are the major-league leaders:

	LISPs
Julio Franco	166
Keith Moreland	155
Terry Pendleton	149
Mike Easler	147
Glenn Wilson	144
Jim Rice	140
Dave Winfield	140
Brook Jacoby	140
Steve Balboni	139
Bill Buckner	138
Hubie Brooks	138

Let's look at the Carter-Brooks swap in light of all these statistics. Although most people would probably guess that the cleanup position in the Mets' order provides more RBI opportunities than the same spot for the Expos, it was Brooks who was the beneficiary of more favorable situations. And if we apply the rates at which each player drove in those base runners to the number of opportunities they would have had playing for their former teams, we can make a theoretical projection of RBIs for each had there been no trade. (Of course, Brooks would never have been promoted to the cleanup position on a team that included Hernandez, Strawberry, and Foster, but what the heck. . . .)

Gary Carter (batting cleanup for 1985 Expos)

RDI Pct. From Scoring Position	.313 × 214 opportunities =	67 RBIs
RDI Pct. From First Base	.078 × 204 opportunities =	16 RBIs
Home Runs		= 32 RBIs
		= 115 Projected RBIs

Hubie Brooks (batting cleanup for 1985 Mets)

RDI Pct. From Scoring Position	.355 × 176 opportunities =	62 RBIs
RDI Pct. From First Base	.054 × 193 opportunities =	10 RBIs
Home Runs		= 13 RBIs
		= 85 Projected RBIs

Platoon, Halt!

Terry Francona made his major-league debut for Montreal in 1981. Among the 284 players who have batted at least 1,000 times during those five seasons, Francona ranks 33rd with a .290 batting average. Granted, he does not hit with a lot of power, and he walks about as frequently as Raymond Burr's Ironside. But he has other desirable qualities: He rarely strikes out (ranking ninth among those 284 players since 1981), and almost never grounds into a double play (his 1 GIDP in 51 GIDP opportunities was the third best rate in the majors last season). Still, Francona has batted only 1,005 times in his career, because he has been labelled a lefty platoon player who can't hit left-handed pitching. During his five seasons with the Expos, he has started only 14 games against southpaws, just one last season, and has batted against them only 133 times. But as you can see from the statistics below, he has been anything but unsuccessful against lefties:

Year	PA	AB	H	2B	3B	HR	RRF	BB	SO	BA	SA	OBA
1981	9	9	6	0	0	0	1	0	0	.667	.667	.667
1982	32	28	9	1	0	0	3	4	4	.321	.357	.406
1983	22	20	2	0	0	0	0	2	2	.100	.100	.182
1984	42	41	14	2	0	0	2	0	4	.341	.390	.341
1985	28	26	11	1	0	0	7	1	4	.423	.462	.444
Totals	133	124	42	4	0	0	13	7	14	.339	.371	.374

You can nitpick all you want with those figures—no power, insufficient evidence, whatever—and we will agree that the stats are inconclusive. But it seems absurd that for five seasons Francona has been flat-out denied an opportunity to prove himself against left-handed pitchers. Lest you think (as we once did) that Francona has inflated his totals by playing only against mediocre southpaws and absolutely never against the better left-handers, the following figures will be nothing less than shocking. We selected an elite subset of left-handers, all pitchers who over the past five seasons had at least 25 wins and a winning percentage above .500—no meatballs need apply. Not surprisingly, Francona has faced only 14 of those pitchers, but these are guys who normally eat left-handed batters for lunch: Dave Dravecky, Pete Falcone, Willie Hernandez, Al Holland, Dave LaPoint, Gary Lavelle, Charlie Leibrandt, Larry McWilliams, Jesse Orosco, Joe Price, Mark Thurmond, Steve Trout, John Tudor, and Fernando Valenzuela. And how Francona has tattooed them! He has hit them far better than the lesser southpaws he has faced:

	PA	AB	H	2B	3B	HR	BB	SO	BA	SA	OBA
Vs. Elite Group	60	54	22	1	0	0	5	5	.407	.426	.458
Vs. Meatball Lefties	73	70	20	3	0	0	2	9	.286	.329	.306

Given a full shot to play everyday, maybe Francona would fall flat on his face. But consider this a plea for him and the other Franconas of baseball: Ron Hassey (.271 career batting average against lefties), Denny Walling (.262), Tim Corcoran (.281), and the Expos' own Scot Thompson (.284), all of whom have hit well in their few chances against left-handed pitchers. All we are saying is give them a chance.

WON-LOST RECORD BY STARTING POSITION

MONTREAL 84-77	C	1B	2B	3B	SS	LF	CF	RF	P	Leadoff	Relief	Starts
Skeeter Barnes	-	-	-	1-0	-	0-1	-	0-1	-	-	-	1-2
Hubie Brooks	-	-	-	-	81-72	-	-	-	-	-	-	81-72
Tim Burke	-	-	-	-	-	-	-	-	-	-	35-43	-
Sal Butera	19-21	-	-	-	-	-	-	-	-	-	0-1	19-21
Andre Dawson	-	-	-	-	-	-	11-10	59-49	-	-	-	70-59
Miguel Dilone	-	-	-	-	-	2-3	6-4	-	-	2-3	-	8-7
John Dopson	-	-	-	-	-	-	-	-	-	0-3	1-	-3
Dan Driessen	-	46-38	-	-	-	-	-	-	-	-	-	46-38
Mike Fitzgerald	55-38	-	-	-	-	-	-	-	-	-	-	55-38
Doug Flynn	-	-	-	-	-	-	-	-	-	-	-	-
Terry Francona	-	13-24	-	-	-	2-3	-	8-11	-	-	-	23-38
Doug Frobel	-	-	-	-	-	-	0-1	1-2	-	-	-	1-3
Andres Galarraga	-	12-7	-	-	-	-	-	-	-	-	-	12-7
Ed Glynn	-	-	-	-	-	-	-	-	-	-	0-3	-
Dick Grapenthin	-	-	-	-	-	-	-	-	-	-	1-4	-
Bill Gullickson	-	-	-	-	-	-	-	-	16-13	-	-	16-13
Joe Hesketh	-	-	-	-	-	-	-	-	16-9	-	-	16-9
Roy Johnson	-	-	-	-	-	-	0-1	-	-	-	-	0-1
Bill Laskey	-	-	-	-	-	-	-	-	1-6	-	0-4	1-6
Vance Law	-	9-6	66-54	2-4	-	-	-	-	-	-	-	77-64
Gary Lucas	-	-	-	-	-	-	-	-	-	-	15-34	-
Mickey Mahler	-	-	-	-	-	-	-	-	2-5	-	1-1	2-5
Fred Manrique	-	-	0-1	1-0	0-1	-	-	-	-	1-1	-	1-2
Al Newman	-	-	2-4	-	-	-	-	-	-	-	-	2-4
Steve Nicosia	6-9	0-1	-	-	-	-	-	-	-	-	-	6-10
Mike O'Berry	3-6	-	-	-	-	-	-	-	-	-	-	3-6
Jack O'Connor	-	-	-	-	-	-	-	-	0-1	-	5-14	0-1
David Palmer	-	-	-	-	-	-	-	-	12-11	-	0-1	12-11
Tim Raines	-	-	-	-	-	75-68	-	-	-	75-68	-	75-68
Jeff Reardon	-	-	-	-	-	-	-	-	-	-	52-11	-
Bert Roberge	-	-	-	-	-	-	-	-	-	-	12-30	-
Steve Rogers	-	-	-	-	-	-	-	-	3-4	-	0-1	3-4
Dan Schatzeder	-	-	-	-	-	-	-	-	6-9	-	4-5	6-9
Razor Shines	-	4-0	-	-	-	-	-	-	-	-	0-1	4-0
Bryn Smith	-	-	-	-	-	-	-	-	23-9	-	-	23-9
Randy St. Claire	-	-	-	-	-	-	-	-	-	-	11-31	-
Scot Thompson	-	0-1	-	-	-	-	-	1-0	-	-	-	1-1
Tim Wallach	-	-	-	80-72	-	-	-	-	-	-	-	80-72
U. L. Washington	-	-	16-18	0-1	3-4	-	-	-	-	1-0	-	19-23
Mitch Webster	-	-	-	-	-	-	27-22	2-2	-	-	3-2	29-24
Herm Winningham	-	-	-	-	-	-	40-39	-	-	2-3	-	40-39
Jim Wohlford	-	-	-	-	-	5-2	-	13-12	-	-	-	18-14
Ned Yost	1-3	-	-	-	-	-	-	-	-	-	-	1-3
Floyd Youmans	-	-	-	-	-	-	-	-	5-7	-	1-1	5-7

Batting vs. Left and Right Handed Pitchers

		BA	Rank	SA	Rank	OBA	Rank	HR %	Rank	BB %	Rank	SO %	Rank
Hubie Brooks	vs. Lefties	.310	16	.476	28	.361	31	2.14	69	6.93	94	10.89	46
	vs. Righties	.251	81	.385	74	.287	114	2.15	61	4.44	123	12.67	68
Andre Dawson	vs. Lefties	.275	47	.515	14	.303	91	5.99	9	3.43	127	16.00	95
	vs. Righties	.246	92	.412	53	.292	113	3.59	27	5.82	107	16.20	92
Mike Fitzgerald	vs. Lefties	.237	91	.268	125	.336	58	0.00	108	13.27	24	15.04	85
	vs. Righties	.192	131	.298	117	.278	122	2.53	49	10.09	45	16.67	98
Terry Francona	vs. Lefties	.423	--	.462	--	.444	--	0.00	--	3.57	--	14.29	--
	vs. Righties	.251	82	.337	97	.285	117	0.78	100	4.10	127	2.99	2
Doug Frobel	vs. Lefties	.167	--	.167	--	.250	--	0.00	--	10.00	--	25.00	--
	vs. Righties	.193	130	.272	126	.308	90	0.88	97	13.97	17	18.38	111
Vance Law	vs. Lefties	.245	81	.384	65	.353	40	2.52	59	13.76	23	12.17	67
	vs. Righties	.275	44	.414	49	.376	18	1.67	73	13.89	18	16.90	102
Tim Raines	vs. Lefties	.275	48	.438	38	.351	42	3.37	41	10.89	43	8.42	22
	vs. Righties	.340	2	.491	11	.428	1	1.26	87	12.74	25	9.29	34
Scot Thompson	vs. Lefties	.500	--	.750	--	.500	--	0.00	--	0.00	--	0.00	--
	vs. Righties	.216	123	.252	130	.241	133	0.00	120	3.42	130	11.64	59
Tim Wallach	vs. Lefties	.256	70	.423	47	.287	107	2.98	51	4.49	119	10.11	39
	vs. Righties	.262	63	.461	19	.319	74	4.24	17	6.83	91	13.90	77
U.L. Washington	vs. Lefties	.190	127	.316	104	.244	127	1.27	86	6.98	92	19.77	118
	vs. Righties	.289	--	.377	--	.341	--	0.00	--	7.32	--	13.01	--
Mitch Webster	vs. Lefties	.322	10	.578	3	.361	42	6.67	5	6.19	102	15.46	89
	vs. Righties	.238	105	.418	45	.316	80	4.10	20	10.22	40	13.14	73
Herm Winningham	vs. Lefties	.217	--	.283	--	.224	--	2.17	--	2.00	--	32.00	--
	vs. Righties	.241	101	.323	106	.308	89	0.75	102	9.15	61	18.98	116
Jim Wohlford	vs. Lefties	.213	112	.306	111	.303	90	0.93	95	11.38	42	11.38	54
	vs. Righties	.059	--	.059	--	.158	--	0.00	--	10.53	--	21.05	--
Team Average	vs. Lefties	.254	3	.392	3	.310	8	2.59	2	7.41	12	13.87	1
	vs. Righties	.244	11	.367	8	.311	11	1.98	9	8.45	8	14.84	9
League Average	vs. Lefties	.250		.374		.317		2.26		8.65		14.84	
	vs. Righties	.253		.374		.320		2.12		8.62		14.28	

Batting with Runners on Base and Bases Empty

		BA	Rank	SA	Rank	OBA	Rank	HR %	Rank	BB %	Rank	SO %	Rank
Hubie Brooks	Runners On	.294	33	.433	44	.331	73	1.73	69	5.36	124	12.93	76
	Bases Empty	.247	87	.396	57	.290	107	2.53	49	5.07	112	11.34	48
Andre Dawson	Runners On	.287	41	.510	7	.343	63	5.58	7	7.75	97	16.20	103
	Bases Empty	.227	111	.385	64	.248	130	3.24	36	2.45	133	16.08	93
Mike Fitzgerald	Runners On	.217	121	.252	133	.349	58	0.00	115	17.69	5	9.52	45
	Bases Empty	.200	126	.311	112	.258	126	2.78	42	6.19	85	21.13	127
Terry Francona	Runners On	.317	13	.358	86	.368	41	0.00	115	7.41	100	5.19	7
	Bases Empty	.228	109	.342	97	.242	131	1.27	90	1.24	134	3.11	1
Vance Law	Runners On	.250	82	.405	61	.364	47	1.82	68	15.16	17	16.25	104
	Bases Empty	.278	38	.405	49	.372	14	2.01	64	12.79	18	14.83	86
Tim Raines	Runners On	.290	35	.401	65	.398	18	1.23	80	15.08	18	9.05	42
	Bases Empty	.332	4	.504	10	.408	4	2.18	60	10.94	26	9.01	24
Tim Wallach	Runners On	.264	72	.464	30	.326	81	4.68	19	7.20	106	10.61	59
	Bases Empty	.257	68	.440	27	.297	92	3.29	34	5.38	105	14.45	81
U.L. Washington	Runners On	.299	29	.414	52	.361	49	0.00	115	9.28	75	10.31	54
	Bases Empty	.208	122	.302	120	.250	129	0.94	100	5.36	107	20.54	125
Mitch Webster	Runners On	.253	78	.414	52	.320	87	3.45	36	9.18	77	15.31	93
	Bases Empty	.288	20	.536	5	.346	35	6.40	5	8.09	51	13.24	67
Herm Winningham	Runners On	.233	107	.276	125	.306	97	0.00	115	10.37	61	21.48	131
	Bases Empty	.240	94	.342	96	.290	106	1.53	81	6.67	73	20.48	124
Team Average	Runners On	.254	7	.375	9	.329	8	2.06	7	9.76	6	13.35	6
	Bases Empty	.242	10	.375	5	.297	11	2.26	5	6.89	11	15.44	9
League Average	Runners On	.258		.381		.332		2.19		9.74		13.69	
	Bases Empty	.248		.369		.309		2.14		7.75		15.05	

Overall Batting Compared to Late Inning Pressure Situations

		BA	Rank	SA	Rank	OBA	Rank	HR %	Rank	BB %	Rank	SO %	Rank	RDI %	Rank
Hubie Brooks	Overall	.269	56	.413	49	.310	93	2.15	62	5.21	121	12.12	61	.355	12
	Pressure	.295	39	.381	63	.327	73	0.95	91	4.55	121	15.45	78	.304	47
Andre Dawson	Overall	.255	79	.444	25	.295	111	4.35	18	5.09	124	16.14	99	.330	25
	Pressure	.259	65	.420	46	.315	82	2.47	48	7.87	85	22.47	122	.316	39
Mike Fitzgerald	Overall	.207	130	.288	126	.297	108	1.69	78	11.14	32	16.13	98	.329	26
	Pressure	.211	99	.289	94	.268	110	2.63	43	7.32	95	19.51	107	.222	83
Terry Francona	Overall	.267	62	.349	91	.299	106	0.71	110	4.05	130	4.05	3	.293	61
	Pressure	.254	67	.305	84	.290	95	0.00	92	4.84	119	4.84	4	.391	14
Doug Frobel	Overall	.189	--	.258	--	.301	--	0.76	--	13.46	--	19.23	--	.286	--
	Pressure	.194	113	.250	118	.356	48	0.00	92	19.15	5	19.15	106	.222	83
Vance Law	Overall	.266	63	.405	57	.369	23	1.93	66	13.85	15	15.46	93	.212	121
	Pressure	.282	48	.397	56	.367	40	0.00	92	11.96	38	17.39	92	.265	59
Tim Raines	Overall	.320	6	.475	15	.405	3	1.91	67	12.18	22	9.02	27	.248	97
	Pressure	.348	9	.438	41	.410	19	1.12	83	9.90	59	5.94	13	.158	114
Scot Thompson	Overall	.224	--	.266	--	.248	--	0.00	--	3.33	--	11.33	--	.261	--
	Pressure	.164	127	.164	131	.197	131	0.00	92	4.17	125	13.89	65	.250	64
Tim Wallach	Overall	.260	75	.450	23	.310	94	3.87	28	6.16	109	12.80	68	.305	47
	Pressure	.209	102	.352	70	.263	114	3.30	36	7.07	98	12.12	50	.320	36
U.L. Washington	Overall	.249	93	.352	88	.301	101	0.52	117	7.18	91	15.79	96	.259	88
	Pressure	.250	73	.275	110	.333	67	0.00	92	11.11	44	24.44	128	.231	81
Mitch Webster	Overall	.274	44	.486	14	.335	54	5.19	10	8.55	67	14.10	81	.302	52
	Pressure	.171	124	.400	55	.216	126	5.71	14	5.26	117	13.16	62	.125	--
Herm Winningham	Overall	.237	110	.317	115	.297	109	0.96	103	8.12	74	20.87	129	.213	120
	Pressure	.200	107	.311	83	.265	113	2.22	54	8.00	81	26.00	131	.083	127
Jim Wohlford	Overall	.192	--	.272	--	.284	--	0.80	--	11.27	--	12.68	--	.341	--
	Pressure	.125	--	.208	--	.323	--	0.00	--	21.88	--	9.38	--	.222	83
Team Average	Overall	.247	8	.375	8	.310	11	2.17	6	8.13	10	14.54	9	.271	7
	Pressure	.253	7	.355	8	.311	10	1.54	10	7.84	12	14.82	7	.263	6
League Average	Overall	.252		.374		.319		2.16		8.63		14.45		.273	
	Pressure	.253		.368		.325		2.17		9.26		15.10		.257	

Additional Miscellaneous Batting Comparisons

	Grass Surface BA	Rank	Artificial Surface BA	Rank	Home Games BA	Rank	Road Games BA	Rank	Runners in Scoring Position BA	Rank	Runners in Scoring Pos and Two Outs BA	Rank	Leading Off Inning OBA	Rank	Runners on 3B with less than 2 Outs RDI %	Rank
Hubie Brooks	.282	40	.264	64	.281	52	.260	64	.314	23	.325	15	.354	39	.714	17
Sal Butera	.174	--	.216	120	.143	--	.239	--	.211	--	.000	--	.276	--	.714	--
Andre Dawson	.284	37	.243	94	.249	91	.261	62	.331	12	.370	6	.223	133	.475	118
Mike Fitzgerald	.291	--	.188	134	.166	134	.258	70	.238	91	.304	29	.284	99	.619	52
Terry Francona	.254	--	.271	49	.279	56	.258	69	.293	37	.239	71	.197	136	.625	51
Doug Frobel	.179	--	.197	132	.212	--	.175	134	.226	--	.278	--	.297	--	1.000	--
Vance Law	.255	70	.270	52	.263	73	.268	50	.224	108	.224	80	.359	35	.367	132
Tim Raines	.304	18	.326	9	.346	6	.295	15	.237	94	.220	82	.391	14	.500	105
Scot Thompson	.253	73	.179	--	.169	--	.262	--	.250	--	.214	--	.211	--	.500	105
Tim Wallach	.267	54	.257	72	.257	82	.263	61	.275	61	.212	89	.329	62	.600	59
U.L. Washington	.311	14	.210	125	.190	--	.289	22	.300	31	.240	70	.289	--	.556	--
Mitch Webster	.328	--	.250	84	.247	--	.290	21	.261	75	.273	44	.412	8	.750	--
Herm Winningham	.253	73	.231	105	.191	130	.287	26	.197	125	.125	131	.355	37	.611	55
Jim Wohlford	.138	--	.208	127	.169	--	.212	--	.278	--	.235	--	.242	--	.700	21
Team Average	.264	3	.241	10	.238	11	.255	6	.253	7	.234	7	.320	4	.568	8
League Average	.251		.254		.256		.248		.257		.235		.315		.576	

Pitching vs. Left and Right Handed Batters

		BA	Rank	SA	Rank	OBA	Rank	HR %	Rank	BB %	Rank	SO %	Rank
Tim Burke	vs. Lefties	.253	51	.360	52	.355	81	1.61	62	13.57	100	12.67	49
	vs. Righties	.166	3	.268	7	.233	4	2.55	70	5.34	13	22.52	17
Bill Gullickson	vs. Lefties	.282	80	.362	53	.338	66	0.83	26	8.19	49	7.44	99
	vs. Righties	.258	77	.365	63	.288	36	1.52	23	3.93	4	10.67	95
Joe Hesketh	vs. Lefties	.215	17	.269	9	.270	17	1.08	36	6.80	29	16.50	29
	vs. Righties	.224	33	.343	37	.281	28	1.92	37	7.38	52	18.64	35
Bill Laskey	vs. Lefties	.277	75	.419	89	.351	77	2.70	96	10.65	82	7.69	97
	vs. Righties	.289	105	.481	110	.331	82	3.83	101	5.35	14	10.69	94
Gary Lucas	vs. Lefties	.271	--	.414	--	.311	--	2.86	--	5.26	--	14.47	--
	vs. Righties	.243	59	.359	55	.315	61	2.21	54	9.62	80	9.62	104
Mickey Mahler	vs. Lefties	.278	--	.278	--	.300	--	0.00	--	5.00	--	10.00	--
	vs. Righties	.223	31	.338	32	.326	75	1.91	34	12.57	108	16.39	54
David Palmer	vs. Lefties	.265	61	.325	35	.348	73	0.37	10	11.18	86	19.08	20
	vs. Righties	.235	51	.309	21	.331	81	1.65	28	11.62	104	16.90	49
Jeff Reardon	vs. Lefties	.210	14	.287	12	.274	19	2.21	82	8.04	47	15.08	36
	vs. Righties	.208	18	.306	20	.263	16	2.08	46	6.37	31	23.57	14
Bert Roberge	vs. Lefties	.259	56	.379	66	.353	79	0.86	27	11.11	84	9.63	79
	vs. Righties	.209	--	.336	--	.248	--	2.99	--	4.83	--	14.48	--
Steve Rogers	vs. Lefties	.314	106	.407	81	.429	111	1.16	42	16.82	112	8.41	92
	vs. Righties	.348	--	.435	--	.361	--	0.00	--	2.78	--	12.50	--
Dan Schatzeder	vs. Lefties	.220	--	.237	--	.266	--	0.00	--	6.15	--	18.46	--
	vs. Righties	.266	84	.459	107	.319	68	3.93	104	7.38	51	14.21	70
Bryn Smith	vs. Lefties	.241	37	.313	28	.268	14	0.24	9	3.85	7	11.76	57
	vs. Righties	.224	32	.346	42	.268	19	2.64	74	5.36	15	16.74	50
Randy St. Claire	vs. Lefties	.276	74	.388	70	.356	82	1.72	68	11.11	84	8.89	88
	vs. Righties	.257	74	.340	35	.314	59	0.69	8	6.92	43	8.18	110
Floyd Youmans	vs. Lefties	.217	19	.269	8	.324	53	0.57	13	13.73	101	16.67	28
	vs. Righties	.186	--	.314	--	.328	--	1.96	--	16.54	--	15.75	--
Team Average	vs. Lefties	.260	5	.344	3	.329	6	1.09	1	9.28	7	12.41	8
	vs. Righties	.237	3	.361	4	.299	2	2.34	6	7.64	3	15.59	7
League Average	vs. Lefties	.262		.374		.330		1.73		9.17		12.66	
	vs. Righties	.246		.374		.311		2.44		8.28		15.62	

Pitching with Runners on Base and Bases Empty

		BA	Rank	SA	Rank	OBA	Rank	HR %	Rank	BB %	Rank	SO %	Rank
Tim Burke	Runners On	.188	4	.277	5	.285	15	1.57	32	10.04	63	17.03	27
	Bases Empty	.217	23	.335	37	.291	35	2.61	82	8.27	68	18.90	23
Bill Gullickson	Runners On	.267	73	.372	59	.322	44	1.04	15	8.06	30	5.97	114
	Bases Empty	.273	96	.357	47	.309	62	1.24	22	4.72	17	11.32	90
Joe Hesketh	Runners On	.260	62	.410	82	.309	29	2.00	54	6.67	14	18.67	20
	Bases Empty	.202	11	.287	14	.263	10	1.66	44	7.63	58	18.07	32
Bill Laskey	Runners On	.328	112	.504	112	.379	100	3.45	99	7.69	25	8.42	100
	Bases Empty	.254	63	.413	93	.316	74	3.13	98	8.36	69	9.66	101
Gary Lucas	Runners On	.233	28	.301	15	.336	68	1.94	52	13.18	102	9.30	93
	Bases Empty	.264	84	.426	99	.297	43	2.70	89	4.52	15	12.26	79
David Palmer	Runners On	.262	65	.346	36	.354	86	1.69	40	11.47	79	17.20	25
	Bases Empty	.241	48	.292	18	.327	86	0.36	5	11.33	105	18.77	24
Jeff Reardon	Runners On	.242	40	.348	38	.322	45	2.27	66	9.87	60	19.08	18
	Bases Empty	.187	5	.259	5	.230	1	2.07	62	5.39	23	18.63	26
Bert Roberge	Runners On	.262	66	.477	110	.325	50	3.74	105	8.13	31	8.94	97
	Bases Empty	.210	16	.266	7	.280	27	0.70	7	7.64	59	14.65	56
Dan Schatzeder	Runners On	.220	19	.327	20	.266	4	1.89	50	6.11	11	15.56	32
	Bases Empty	.286	107	.494	113	.343	98	4.33	112	7.97	63	14.34	60
Bryn Smith	Runners On	.235	30	.324	19	.272	9	1.54	30	4.74	4	12.26	72
	Bases Empty	.231	34	.333	35	.266	12	1.38	32	4.52	16	15.63	47
Randy St. Claire	Runners On	.271	80	.364	53	.356	89	0.85	10	11.35	78	9.93	87
	Bases Empty	.261	77	.359	50	.314	69	1.41	34	6.54	40	7.19	111
Floyd Youmans	Runners On	.200	8	.300	14	.329	55	2.50	74	16.22	113	14.19	52
	Bases Empty	.210	17	.274	11	.322	82	0.00	1	13.66	110	18.03	33
Team Average	Runners On	.252	3	.361	3	.324	3	1.82	3	9.34	5	13.08	8
	Bases Empty	.243	6	.349	2	.302	4	1.81	3	7.53	4	15.16	6
League Average	Runners On	.258		.381		.332		2.19		9.74		13.69	
	Bases Empty	.248		.369		.309		2.14		7.75		15.05	

Overall Pitching Compared to Late Inning Pressure Situations

		BA	Rank	SA	Rank	OBA	Rank	HR %	Rank	BB %	Rank	SO %	Rank
Tim Burke	Overall	.204	5	.309	14	.288	23	2.14	60	9.11	68	18.01	27
	Pressure	.193	14	.302	23	.288	32	2.48	75	9.75	64	16.10	41
Bill Gullickson	Overall	.271	94	.363	56	.315	55	1.16	15	6.19	15	8.96	104
	Pressure	.250	62	.333	39	.333	63	0.00	1	10.91	74	5.45	110
Joe Hesketh	Overall	.222	17	.331	24	.279	16	1.78	46	7.28	34	18.28	24
	Pressure	.318	104	.432	90	.400	100	0.00	1	11.54	83	19.23	23
Bill Laskey	Overall	.283	102	.449	108	.342	90	3.26	105	8.08	46	9.15	103
	Pressure	.194	15	.226	8	.235	6	0.00	1	5.56	16	2.78	114
Gary Lucas	Overall	.251	59	.375	67	.314	54	2.39	77	8.45	55	10.92	87
	Pressure	.303	96	.440	92	.364	82	2.75	80	8.87	53	11.29	80
Jack O'Connor	Overall	.239	--	.364	--	.330	--	1.14	--	12.26	--	15.09	--
	Pressure	.135	4	.216	7	.238	8	2.70	79	11.36	79	31.82	1
David Palmer	Overall	.250	56	.317	18	.340	88	0.98	8	11.39	97	18.03	26
	Pressure	.261	--	.348	--	.320	--	0.00	--	4.00	--	24.00	--
Jeff Reardon	Overall	.209	10	.295	10	.269	9	2.15	62	7.30	36	18.82	19
	Pressure	.212	26	.280	17	.286	28	1.69	50	9.06	55	18.49	25
Bert Roberge	Overall	.232	31	.356	38	.299	32	2.00	50	7.86	43	12.14	82
	Pressure	.224	36	.357	51	.283	26	3.06	88	6.48	22	15.74	42
Dan Schatzeder	Overall	.259	72	.426	99	.311	47	3.33	106	7.19	32	14.85	50
	Pressure	.273	74	.424	87	.333	63	3.03	86	8.11	35	5.41	111
Bryn Smith	Overall	.232	32	.330	23	.268	5	1.44	26	4.61	4	14.27	58
	Pressure	.154	6	.231	10	.200	3	1.92	63	5.36	13	14.29	58
Randy St. Claire	Overall	.265	85	.362	52	.333	79	1.15	14	8.84	61	8.50	108
	Pressure	.247	60	.321	31	.358	80	0.00	1	14.29	103	6.12	105
Floyd Youmans	Overall	.206	7	.285	7	.325	68	1.08	12	14.80	115	16.31	37
	Pressure	.273	74	.394	74	.400	100	3.03	86	17.50	113	17.50	28
Team Average	Overall	.247	4	.354	4	.312	4	1.81	2	8.33	4	14.24	8
	Pressure	.230	3	.330	3	.311	2	1.86	5	9.83	7	15.30	7
League Average	Overall	.252		.374		.319		2.16		8.63		14.45	
	Pressure	.249		.363		.326		2.12		9.92		15.33	

Additional Miscellaneous Pitching Comparisons

	Grass Surface		Artificial Surface		Home Games		Road Games		Runners in Scoring Position		Runners in Scoring Pos and Two Outs		Leading Off Inning	
	BA	Rank	BA	Rank	BA	Rank	BA	Rank	BA	Rank	BA	Rank	OBA	Rank
Tim Burke	.184	2	.215	16	.225	33	.189	4	.147	2	.134	5	.380	103
Bill Gullickson	.321	113	.251	53	.221	31	.321	114	.266	65	.264	83	.365	98
Joe Hesketh	.208	11	.226	25	.228	37	.217	18	.226	32	.264	82	.239	8
Bill Laskey	.252	60	.317	108	.304	105	.264	73	.327	110	.264	81	.323	73
Gary Lucas	.255	--	.250	52	.239	53	.266	79	.281	85	.222	--	.286	31
Mickey Mahler	.184	3	.263	67	.250	--	.212	16	.238	--	.412	--	.420	--
David Palmer	.198	7	.262	65	.256	71	.243	40	.252	52	.261	80	.290	38
Jeff Reardon	.269	80	.185	8	.209	18	.209	11	.276	77	.190	26	.192	3
Bert Roberge	.286	--	.221	21	.215	24	.252	54	.260	60	.243	69	.277	26
Steve Rogers	.370	--	.320	110	.333	--	.326	--	.304	--	.273	--	.385	--
Dan Schatzeder	.265	74	.257	60	.237	49	.290	105	.228	34	.194	32	.382	104
Bryn Smith	.245	55	.225	23	.210	20	.253	58	.258	59	.244	70	.316	65
Randy St. Claire	.234	--	.279	88	.287	96	.248	48	.278	79	.294	95	.292	41
Floyd Youmans	.268	79	.179	3	.176	5	.228	27	.158	3	.190	26	.291	39
Team Average	.255	8	.244	1	.236	4	.257	5	.250	3	.241	9	.318	5
League Average	.251		.254		.248		.256		.257		.235		.315	

NEW YORK METS

To the degree that a team's season is a mosaic of individual games, the Mets' 1985 season may have been the most colorful tableau offered by any major league team in years. Some highlights:

The season opener, Dwight Gooden against Joaquin Andujar, won by Gary Carter's extra-inning home run in his first game with the team, before his new home fans.

The 18-inning win over Pittsburgh in April, which featured Chuck Tanner's eight-man infield against Wally Backman, a series of defensive heroics by Carter, and a huffing-and-puffing catch by Rusty Staub in right field that prevented the Pirates from taking an 18th-inning lead. (It was Rusty's only defensive chance of the season, and came despite the Mets' novel strategy of "platooning" him by having him in left field against left-handed hitters and right field against righties.)

The 26–7 loss at Philadelphia in June, a game in which the Mets trailed 16–0 after two quarters, er, innings.

The 19-inning July 4 game in Atlanta, the latest-ending game (3:55 a.m.) in the history of the major leagues. It was prolonged by two two-out, two-strike, extra-inning home runs by the Braves, including one by pitcher Rick Camp—at the time, possessor of the worst career batting average in the major leagues—in the 18th inning.

Three memorable matchups between Gooden and Fernando Valenzuela, including an early-September classic that stretched through 12 scoreless innings before the Mets won in the 13th.

A pair of three-homer games by Darryl Strawberry (in Chicago) and Carter (in San Diego).

All of those games *preceded* the excruciating pennant race showdowns with the Cardinals during the final weeks: First three one-run games in New York in the middle of the month, each of them a classic, including Tudor–Gooden, 0–0 through nine innings, won by Cesar Cedeno's home run off Jesse Orosco in the tenth; then the three-game set in St. Louis the final week, which featured Tudor against Darling, 0–0 through nine innings, won by Strawberry's home run off Ken Dayley and the scoreboard clock in the eleventh; Gooden's 24th victory the next night; and the 4–3 St. Louis victory in the finale, with Vince Coleman digging Keith Hernandez's double out of the bullpen to keep Len Dykstra from scoring. (For more on that game, see the Cardinals essay.)

To the gourmet Mets fan, the flavor of the 162-game season was delightful, notwithstanding the bitter dessert of finishing second to the Cardinals. Unfortunately, one can't taste the pleasures of a distant feast forever; the hard reality for the Mets is that after two consecutive second-place finishes, and with the Yankees across the bridge resurgent, the pressure to win in 1986 will be immense.

But let's not forget how far the team has come during Davey Johnson's two seasons as manager. The Mets are only the second team in the history of the major leagues to follow two 90-loss seasons with two 90-win seasons. Johnson came in as manager right at the turnaround point. The other team to do it was the Brewers, and a curious irony links their effort with that of the Mets. Milwaukee had 90-loss seasons in 1976 and 1977, and 90-win seasons in 1978 and 1979. They, too, changed managers at the turnaround

point, with George Bamberger taking the helm. The same Bamberger set the stage for Johnson's record by managing the Mets to a 90-loss season in '82, and getting a good jump on the 90-loss season of '83; he quit in June of that year, and Frank Howard finished out the year.

The Mets have had the best cumulative record in their division—indeed, in the entire league—over the past two seasons. Since the introduction of divisional play in 1969, and excluding the 1981 season soiled by the players' strike, only one major-league team has had its division's best two-year record without finishing first in either year: the Montreal Expos of 1979–80, who were beaten out by Pittsburgh and Philadelphia, respectively. (In 1981, of course, that same fate befell the Reds within the span of a single calendar year: They finished second in both halves of the split season, but didn't make the expanded playoffs.)

That the Expos were able to win the second-half pennant in the N.L. East in 1981, and to defeat the Phillies in the miniplayoff, was not enough to dissolve the image of perpetual bridesmaids that has haunted the Expos to this day. And should the Mets again fail to win in 1986, it is this image that will haunt the team in general and, however unfairly, Gary Carter in particular, given his pivotal position on both those Expos and the current Mets.

Davey Johnson received deserved acclaim following the 1984 season for changing his lineup to produce more runs. The changes were especially noticeable at the top of the batting order, where Wally Backman, who replaced Brian Giles as the second baseman, also supplanted Mookie Wilson as the leadoff man. The Mets, who had scored only 575 runs in 1983, wound up with 652 runs in 1984.

Curiously, though, the team's total of runs scored in the first inning, when the Backman/Wilson switch might have been expected to produce the greatest results, was not affected: 73 first-inning runs in 1983, 72 in 1984. In 1985, however, with the addition of Carter to the lineup in the cleanup spot, the Mets became the National League's best first-inning team, with 104 runs. (The complete list of first-inning runs for the league is in the San Diego essay.) And, if you check the "Won-Lost by Starting Position" chart, you'll see that Johnson was willing to adjust when the Mets struggled with Backman leading off, even if that meant restoring Wilson to the leadoff spot.

The Mets also knew how to make the most of their first-inning production. They were 39–8 in games in which they scored in the first inning—the best such record by any team in either league. The overall National League won-lost percentage for teams scoring in the first inning was .631; the Mets exceeded that mark by 199 percentage points.

The Mets have never been a heavy-hitting team. When they finished third in the league in runs scored last season, it was the highest such finish in their history. But how they scored the runs was just as big a story, and finally provided the answer to a Mets fan's prayers: New York had the most powerful middle of the batting order in the National League.

The Mets had more than 100 RBIs from each of the fourth, fifth, and sixth positions in their batting order last season. Getting 100 from the cleanup spot is hardly surprising; five of the twelve National League teams did that. But only one other team, the Reds, got 100 RBIs from the fifth position, and no other team in the league had 100 from the six hole.

During the course of the season, 10 different players batted fifth or sixth in the Mets' order. Carter and Ron Gardenhire had a single start each; Tom Paciorek had four; Clint Hurdle and Howard Johnson, eight each; Ray Knight, 16; and John Christensen, 17. Danny Heep, who filled in during Strawberry's injury and at other times, had 61; Strawberry himself had 91. And the player who had the most starts in those very productive positions was George Foster with 117.

This is intriguing because, outside of the efforts of the volunteer "K" counters during Dwight Gooden's starts, the most popular pastime at Shea Stadium last season seemed to be getting on George Foster. Now admittedly, Foster's inclusion in the "highest-paid" lists that clutter the baseball landscape is partly to blame. For a certain segment of the fans, the attitude seems to be that if your name is up there with Mike Schmidt's and Eddie Murray's, you should produce numbers like Schmidt and Murray. Foster didn't make things easier on himself through his performance with the game on the line: he batted just .132 in Late-Inning Pressure Situations. Then, too, his cautious approach to outfielding does not evoke the memory of Pete Reiser.

But those deficiencies obscure Foster's major contributions to the team's run production. What the Mets got from Foster in 1985 was a season of 21 home runs and 77 runs batted in, despite his starting only 119 games. (He batted fifth 41 times, mostly while Strawberry was hurt, sixth 76 times, and cleanup twice.) Foster drove in 31 percent of his teammates from scoring position, a rate somewhat below those of Hernandez and Strawberry, but the equal of Carter's. He also batted .284 and slugged .474 with runners in scoring position, his best marks since his days in Cincinnati. The upshot of it all was that the New York lineup was the most productive in the league in the five and six slots in the batting order:

Fifth Batting Position	BA	SA	HR	RBI
Mets	.272	.494*	35*	102*
N.L. Avg.	.260	.410	18	86

Sixth Batting Position	BA	SA	HR	RBI
Mets	.257	.452*	26*	103*
N.L. Avg.	.246	.380	17	74

* led National League (or tied for lead)

With Hernandez, Carter, Strawberry, and Foster in the starting lineup, the Mets played .700 ball (49 wins, 21 losses). In the other 92 games, New York was 49–43 (.533).

Johnson's timing in taking over the Mets' managerial job was impeccable: His rookie year was also Gooden's first in the majors. But that circumstance was not just accidental; Johnson had reportedly lobbied for Gooden's inclusion on the opening-day roster throughout spring training in '84, and finally prevailed. Within six weeks of the start of that season, Johnson had jettisoned three veteran pitchers (Mike Torrez, Dick Tidrow, and Craig Swan), allowing Gooden and Darling to inherit their innings.

Last season, Johnson surprised (some may say shocked) Sid Fernandez with a spring demotion to Tidewater, and the final results here, too, were impressive. After his recall in May, Fernandez went on to have the best strikeout and hit rates among National League starters; his rate of 5.71 hits per nine innings ranks seventh in

major-league history. In June, Rick Aguilera was promoted from Tidewater, and Johnson stuck him right into the rotation. While the results (10–7, 3.24) were not of Goodenite proportions, they were impressive for any mortal 23-year-old.

It's curious, then, that despite Johnson's golden touch with the pitching staff, the Mets' most troublesome moments in 1985 were provided by the inconsistency of their relief pitching, especially their ace of seasons past, Jesse Orosco. Orosco had established himself among relief pitchers' royalty in '84, when he saved 31 games as the Mets became contenders. His saves total declined to 17 last year— an unusual but not unprecedented drop. (Eleven of the 34 pitchers who have had 30-save seasons have experienced a decline at least as large as Orosco's the next season.) But Orosco didn't have a terrible year. He was 8–6 with a 2.73 ERA in 54 appearances. He allowed only 66 hits in 79 innings, and opponents batted only .224 against him for the season, and even lower (.186) with runners in scoring position.

But hidden among those numbers were poor performances scattered throughout the season. There were nine missed save opportunities (four of which resulted in "vultured victories" for Orosco), and seven games that he entered with the score tied, but let the enemy take the lead (another of his victories came in one of these games). In a five-week period in June and early July, Orosco did not save any games, lost a lead or a tie six times, and suffered the indignity of allowing four runs in one inning in mopping up the 26–7 game. Then in September, he allowed game-tying or go-ahead home runs in three successive appearances against the Dodgers and Cardinals.

Above all, Orosco's availability always seemed to be in question, and although the Mets never came out and said that he was injured, Johnson's use of him seemed to leave no other reasonable conclusion. There was a nine-day stretch without an appearance in late May, a seven-day layoff in the middle of June, one appearance (for two batters) in 15 days surrounding the All-Star Game, another eight days off in early August (including the two days of the players' strike), and another seven-day vacation later that month. That's five occasions on which Orosco wasn't used for seven days or more. Among the 34 pitchers who have had 30-save seasons since 1969, only one other pitcher has ever had five inactive weeks the next season, and that one, Bill Campbell, had admitted arm problems in 1978. (Excluding Orosco and Campbell, the other 32 pitchers had a combined total of only 47 inactive weeks.)

The emergence of rookie Roger McDowell made Orosco's troubles a little easier to take. During the first two months of the season, he relieved in 16 games in which the Mets were leading or tied, and held the lead or tie in all 16. But the accumulation of innings throughout the season may have taken its toll on an arm only one year removed from the surgeon's knife; McDowell blew five save opportunities within 23 days during September, including three within five days at the end of the month.

The Orosco–McDowell combination was reminiscent of the pairing of Orosco and Doug Sisk in 1984. Orosco was at his most effective when Sisk was sharing the stopper's burden, particularly in the first half of the season. It could well be that Orosco is that rare bullpen closer who needs not so much a set-up man as a co-stopper to keep him rested. McDowell's late-season woes raise doubts about whether he can be that man. Mets fans can only hope for season-long health and effectiveness from Orosco and McDowell or, failing that, yet another great pitcher to be pulled out of Davey Johnson's cap.

WON-LOST RECORD BY STARTING POSITION

NEW YORK 98-64	C	1B	2B	3B	SS	LF	CF	RF	P	Leadoff	Relief	Starts
Rick Aguilera	-	-	-	-	-	-	-	-	10-9	-	2-0	10-9
Wally Backman	-	-	72-50	-	-	-	-	-	-	25-24	-	72-50
Billy Beane	-	-	-	-	-	0-1	-	-	-	-	-	0-1
Bruce Berenyi	-	-	-	-	-	-	-	-	2-1	-	-	2-1
Terry Blocker	-	-	-	-	-	1-1	0-1	-	-	-	-	1-2
Larry Bowa	-	-	2-1	-	1-2	-	-	-	-	-	-	3-3
Gary Carter	85-54	6-0	-	-	-	-	-	0-1	-	-	-	91-55
Kelvin Chapman	-	-	22-12	-	-	-	-	-	-	2-4	-	22-12
John Christensen	-	-	-	-	-	2-1	-	16-9	-	-	-	18-10
Ron Darling	-	-	-	-	-	-	-	-	23-12	-	1-0	23-12
Len Dykstra	-	-	-	-	-	-	37-16	-	-	35-14	-	37-16
Sid Fernandez	-	-	-	-	-	-	-	-	13-13	-	-	13-13
George Foster	-	-	-	-	-	75-44	-	-	-	-	-	75-44
Ron Gardenhire	-	-	1-1	2-0	5-4	-	-	-	-	-	-	8-5
Wes Gardner	-	-	-	-	-	-	-	-	-	-	0-9	-
Dwight Gooden	-	-	-	-	-	-	-	-	28-7	-	-	28-7
Tom Gorman	-	-	-	-	-	-	-	-	1-1	-	8-24	1-1
Danny Heep	-	0-2	-	-	-	20-16	2-4	10-16	-	-	-	32-38
Keith Hernandez	-	91-61	-	-	-	-	-	-	-	-	-	91-61
Clint Hurdle	6-6	-	-	-	-	0-1	-	3-3	-	-	-	9-10
Howard Johnson	-	-	56-37	3-2	-	-	-	-	-	-	-	59-39
Ray Knight	-	-	1-0	40-27	-	-	-	-	-	-	-	41-27
Bill Latham	-	-	-	-	-	-	-	-	1-2	-	0-4	1-2
Terry Leach	-	-	-	-	-	-	-	-	3-1	-	7-11	3-1
Ed Lynch	-	-	-	-	-	-	-	-	13-16	-	0-2	13-16
Roger McDowell	-	-	-	-	-	-	-	-	1-1	-	38-22	1-1
Randy Myers	-	-	-	-	-	-	-	-	-	-	0-1	-
Randy Niemann	-	-	-	-	-	-	-	-	/	-	0-4	-
Jesse Orosco	-	-	-	-	-	-	-	-	-	-	37-17	-
Tom Paciorek	-	1-1	-	-	-	-	-	13-8	-	-	-	14-9
Ronn Reynolds	7-4	-	-	-	-	-	-	-	-	-	-	7-4
Joe Sambito	-	-	-	-	-	-	-	-	-	-	1-7	-
Rafael Santana	-	-	-	-	89-56	-	-	-	-	-	-	89-56
Calvin Schiraldi	-	-	-	-	-	-	-	-	3-1	-	1-5	3-1
Doug Sisk	-	-	-	-	-	-	-	-	-	-	14-28	-
Rusty Staub	-	-	-	-	-	-	-	-	-	-	-	-
Darryl Strawberry	-	-	-	-	-	14-11	56-27	-	-	-	-	70-38
Mookie Wilson	-	-	-	-	-	-	45-32	-	-	36-22	-	45-32

Batting vs. Left and Right Handed Pitchers

		BA	Rank	SA	Rank	OBA	Rank	HR %	Rank	BB %	Rank	SO %	Rank
Wally Backman	vs. Lefties	.122	133	.153	133	.207	133	0.00	108	8.61	73	17.22	101
	vs. Righties	.324	7	.409	55	.359	39	0.26	118	5.44	113	10.87	50
Larry Bowa	vs. Lefties	.238	90	.325	99	.271	118	0.00	108	4.65	118	12.79	69
	vs. Righties	.231	114	.291	121	.280	121	0.00	120	6.08	101	7.43	16
Gary Carter	vs. Lefties	.329	8	.566	5	.429	4	5.94	10	15.33	15	3.83	3
	vs. Righties	.250	83	.438	33	.320	73	5.65	6	7.80	74	9.68	38
Kelvin Chapman	vs. Lefties	.172	131	.188	132	.230	130	0.00	108	5.63	108	8.45	26
	vs. Righties	.188	--	.250	--	.235	--	0.00	--	5.88	--	17.65	--
John Christensen	vs. Lefties	.200	121	.365	78	.299	93	3.53	36	12.37	31	15.46	89
	vs. Righties	.143	--	.179	--	.314	--	0.00	--	19.44	--	22.22	--
Len Dykstra	vs. Lefties	.268	54	.321	102	.349	44	0.00	108	9.38	61	10.94	48
	vs. Righties	.250	83	.333	100	.335	61	0.56	111	11.48	32	8.13	21
George Foster	vs. Lefties	.271	52	.468	30	.358	34	4.79	22	12.09	35	14.42	81
	vs. Righties	.258	69	.455	23	.311	87	4.55	14	6.92	89	19.38	120
Danny Heep	vs. Lefties	.265	57	.327	98	.356	36	0.00	108	11.86	39	13.56	74
	vs. Righties	.284	32	.441	26	.337	59	3.15	37	8.13	70	7.72	17
Keith Hernandez	vs. Lefties	.315	13	.415	49	.358	35	1.15	88	6.67	96	8.77	28
	vs. Righties	.303	18	.441	26	.403	6	2.10	62	14.61	11	8.56	26
Howard Johnson	vs. Lefties	.156	132	.299	113	.241	128	3.90	31	10.23	51	23.86	127
	vs. Righties	.263	60	.417	48	.315	82	2.56	48	7.35	84	16.76	101
Ray Knight	vs. Lefties	.259	65	.418	48	.285	108	3.53	36	3.35	130	11.73	58
	vs. Righties	.149	--	.178	--	.198	--	0.00	--	6.31	--	9.91	--
Tom Paciorek	vs. Lefties	.337	4	.424	46	.378	21	1.09	91	6.06	103	8.08	20
	vs. Righties	.083	--	.083	--	.120	--	0.00	--	0.00	--	24.00	--
Rafael Santana	vs. Lefties	.265	57	.301	112	.313	80	0.00	108	6.60	97	8.02	19
	vs. Righties	.252	77	.303	114	.284	119	0.30	114	4.26	125	10.51	47
Darryl Strawberry	vs. Lefties	.256	69	.506	16	.348	47	7.05	4	12.36	32	25.28	128
	vs. Righties	.291	27	.591	2	.414	5	7.59	1	17.47	4	17.47	105
Mookie Wilson	vs. Lefties	.295	27	.490	21	.361	30	2.68	53	9.64	58	12.05	64
	vs. Righties	.261	66	.372	79	.305	95	1.06	90	5.97	104	15.92	91
Team Average	vs. Lefties	.252	7	.378	6	.319	6	2.43	3	8.77	8	13.92	3
	vs. Righties	.260	3	.390	2	.326	4	2.41	4	8.72	5	13.98	8
League Average	vs. Lefties	.250		.374		.317		2.26		8.65		14.84	
	vs. Righties	.253		.374		.320		2.12		8.62		14.28	

Batting with Runners on Base and Bases Empty

		BA	Rank	SA	Rank	OBA	Rank	HR %	Rank	BB %	Rank	SO %	Rank
Wally Backman	Runners On	.311	20	.388	74	.356	52	0.49	110	6.69	113	12.13	67
	Bases Empty	.248	83	.315	110	.296	95	0.00	120	5.97	92	12.84	59
Larry Bowa	Runners On	.204	132	.276	126	.248	134	0.00	115	5.41	123	9.01	41
	Bases Empty	.259	64	.328	101	.301	87	0.00	120	5.69	100	9.76	32
Gary Carter	Runners On	.288	40	.483	23	.393	21	5.17	14	13.93	25	6.81	16
	Bases Empty	.275	43	.493	14	.335	44	6.34	6	7.74	60	7.74	18
Len Dykstra	Runners On	.228	111	.337	94	.291	116	1.09	84	8.41	85	5.61	8
	Bases Empty	.271	48	.326	104	.367	19	0.00	120	12.65	20	10.84	42
George Foster	Runners On	.276	52	.487	21	.365	46	5.03	15	12.02	43	16.74	110
	Bases Empty	.253	79	.439	30	.303	85	4.35	18	6.64	74	17.71	103
Danny Heep	Runners On	.313	16	.509	10	.362	48	3.57	32	8.46	84	8.46	33
	Bases Empty	.258	66	.358	83	.326	57	1.89	67	9.14	38	9.14	26
Keith Hernandez	Runners On	.317	14	.463	31	.403	15	1.93	67	13.42	29	7.03	19
	Bases Empty	.302	10	.404	51	.369	18	1.50	83	9.49	34	10.03	35
Howard Johnson	Runners On	.227	114	.348	92	.304	99	2.21	57	10.58	59	17.79	121
	Bases Empty	.255	75	.433	33	.295	96	3.37	33	5.45	104	18.64	109
Ray Knight	Runners On	.226	115	.411	57	.246	135	4.03	25	3.73	131	11.19	63
	Bases Empty	.211	120	.259	128	.256	127	0.68	109	5.13	110	10.90	43
Rafael Santana	Runners On	.236	100	.286	116	.277	127	0.45	113	5.44	122	7.11	20
	Bases Empty	.272	47	.314	111	.308	79	0.00	120	4.92	115	11.38	49
Darryl Strawberry	Runners On	.303	28	.545	3	.420	7	6.18	4	16.89	8	17.35	115
	Bases Empty	.256	73	.567	3	.363	21	8.37	2	14.34	10	23.11	130
Mookie Wilson	Runners On	.214	124	.286	117	.276	128	0.00	115	8.06	90	16.13	101
	Bases Empty	.307	8	.493	13	.358	24	2.67	45	7.41	64	13.17	66
Team Average	Runners On	.261	6	.399	2	.336	6	2.60	2	9.84	4	12.77	3
	Bases Empty	.253	4	.374	6	.314	5	2.27	4	7.84	5	14.92	8
League Average	Runners On	.258		.381		.332		2.19		9.74		13.69	
	Bases Empty	.248		.369		.309		2.14		7.75		15.05	

Overall Batting Compared to Late Inning Pressure Situations

		BA	Rank	SA	Rank	OBA	Rank	HR %	Rank	BB %	Rank	SO %	Rank	RDI %	Rank
Wally Backman	Overall	.273	45	.344	99	.320	73	0.19	123	6.27	107	12.54	66	.250	95
	Pressure	.292	41	.338	73	.338	64	0.00	92	6.58	101	13.16	62	.200	96
Larry Bowa	Overall	.234	113	.304	123	.276	130	0.00	127	5.56	115	9.40	31	.197	130
	Pressure	.208	--	.208	--	.240	--	0.00	--	3.70	--	18.52	--	.125	--
Gary Carter	Overall	.281	29	.488	13	.365	25	5.77	5	10.90	38	7.27	14	.313	38
	Pressure	.289	46	.458	34	.366	42	4.82	20	10.75	48	8.60	22	.320	36
Len Dykstra	Overall	.254	80	.331	108	.338	52	0.42	119	10.99	36	8.79	25	.229	111
	Pressure	.286	--	.393	--	.323	--	0.00	--	6.25	--	12.50	--	.429	--
George Foster	Overall	.263	69	.460	21	.331	63	4.65	14	9.13	58	17.26	108	.309	41
	Pressure	.132	130	.176	130	.189	132	1.47	73	6.76	99	24.32	127	.333	25
Danny Heep	Overall	.280	31	.421	42	.341	51	2.58	47	8.85	63	8.85	26	.349	14
	Pressure	.269	58	.423	44	.344	60	3.85	31	11.48	42	6.56	14	.286	50
Keith Hernandez	Overall	.309	9	.430	36	.384	13	1.69	79	11.29	28	8.65	22	.360	10
	Pressure	.354	7	.451	37	.432	12	1.22	78	12.63	33	12.63	58	.333	25
Howard Johnson	Overall	.242	102	.393	68	.300	104	2.83	43	7.94	79	18.22	119	.256	90
	Pressure	.279	50	.574	10	.353	51	6.56	11	10.14	58	20.29	110	.214	89
Ray Knight	Overall	.218	125	.328	110	.252	133	2.21	61	4.48	129	11.03	49	.301	53
	Pressure	.196	112	.304	85	.213	128	2.17	56	2.13	134	8.51	21	.111	121
Rafael Santana	Overall	.257	78	.302	124	.295	112	0.19	125	5.14	123	9.57	34	.203	126
	Pressure	.237	85	.263	113	.275	106	0.00	92	4.82	120	14.46	71	.188	102
Rusty Staub	Overall	.267	--	.400	--	.400	--	2.22	--	18.18	--	7.27	--	.286	--
	Pressure	.292	--	.500	--	.393	--	4.17	--	14.29	--	10.71	--	.273	55
Darryl Strawberry	Overall	.277	35	.557	2	.389	9	7.38	1	15.53	7	20.43	127	.369	6
	Pressure	.237	84	.576	9	.333	67	10.17	1	13.04	27	30.43	134	.286	50
Mookie Wilson	Overall	.276	39	.424	41	.331	64	1.78	75	7.63	84	14.17	83	.241	102
	Pressure	.278	51	.537	15	.371	36	5.56	16	12.70	31	15.87	85	.100	124
Team Average	Overall	.257	4	.385	3	.323	5	2.41	3	8.74	5	13.96	7	.274	5
	Pressure	.245	10	.377	6	.308	12	2.91	3	8.40	10	15.93	10	.250	8
League Average	Overall	.252		.374		.319		2.16		8.63		14.45		.273	
	Pressure	.253		.368		.325		2.17		9.26		15.10		.257	

Additional Miscellaneous Batting Comparisons

	Grass Surface		Artificial Surface		Home Games		Road Games		Runners in Scoring Position		Runners in Scoring Pos and Two Outs		Leading Off Inning		Runners on 3B with less than 2 Outs	
	BA	Rank	BA	Rank	BA	Rank	BA	Rank	BA	Rank	BA	Rank	OBA	Rank	RDI %	Rank
Wally Backman	.275	48	.268	56	.259	79	.286	27	.324	18	.273	44	.304	85	.650	37
Larry Bowa	.267	57	.122	--	.280	53	.187	131	.211	112	.143	--	.259	123	.417	125
Gary Carter	.293	31	.253	82	.266	68	.295	16	.331	12	.271	47	.375	25	.656	33
Kelvin Chapman	.152	133	.212	--	.141	--	.205	--	.167	--	.211	--	.205	--	.750	--
John Christensen	.159	131	.258	--	.159	--	.227	--	.194	--	.211	--	.320	--	.000	--
Len Dykstra	.243	86	.284	--	.239	102	.268	52	.207	118	.265	55	.330	61	.600	59
George Foster	.253	72	.285	30	.262	76	.264	57	.284	48	.305	28	.269	112	.517	104
Dwight Gooden	.275	47	.083	--	.255	--	.196	--	.269	--	.286	--	.194	--	.286	--
Danny Heep	.276	46	.291	26	.288	42	.275	45	.276	59	.259	57	.286	97	.684	24
Keith Hernandez	.283	39	.364	2	.284	48	.331	4	.312	24	.296	34	.385	19	.805	6
Howard Johnson	.223	108	.280	36	.229	113	.254	77	.200	123	.208	97	.286	97	.722	15
Ray Knight	.214	117	.231	--	.197	128	.236	98	.281	55	.214	86	.231	129	.636	44
Tom Paciorek	.296	26	.222	--	.356	--	.211	--	.269	--	.273	--	.091	--	.667	--
Rafael Santana	.238	94	.301	22	.235	103	.279	36	.208	116	.161	121	.320	71	.464	120
Darryl Strawberry	.306	17	.219	119	.298	33	.259	67	.330	16	.326	14	.324	66	.545	90
Mookie Wilson	.287	36	.256	75	.329	10	.232	104	.246	85	.235	73	.378	23	.438	124
Team Average	.254	6	.262	4	.253	9	.261	2	.264	5	.248	3	.316	5	.575	6
League Average	.251		.254		.256		.248		.257		.235		.315		.576	

Pitching vs. Left and Right Handed Batters

		BA	Rank	SA	Rank	OBA	Rank	HR %	Rank	BB %	Rank	SO %	Rank
Rick Aguilera	vs. Lefties	.241	38	.330	39	.310	42	1.34	52	8.80	57	14.80	38
	vs. Righties	.275	95	.408	88	.317	65	2.15	49	5.84	24	14.40	69
Ron Darling	vs. Lefties	.241	36	.354	47	.323	52	1.74	70	10.71	83	14.72	39
	vs. Righties	.230	44	.366	64	.320	70	2.90	89	11.15	94	17.31	44
Sid Fernandez	vs. Lefties	.163	1	.326	36	.222	2	2.17	79	7.00	31	40.00	1
	vs. Righties	.185	6	.298	14	.289	38	2.38	63	12.48	107	23.93	12
Dwight Gooden	vs. Lefties	.203	11	.249	6	.260	10	0.53	12	7.15	32	21.79	11
	vs. Righties	.198	11	.298	15	.246	6	2.39	64	5.56	20	29.78	2
Tom Gorman	vs. Lefties	.250	--	.423	--	.291	--	3.85	--	5.26	--	10.53	--
	vs. Righties	.287	102	.460	108	.349	100	4.00	105	8.82	71	15.29	61
Terry Leach	vs. Lefties	.291	93	.443	97	.352	78	1.27	48	8.89	59	7.78	95
	vs. Righties	.200	--	.280	--	.241	--	1.60	--	4.41	--	16.91	--
Ed Lynch	vs. Lefties	.274	71	.436	95	.295	34	3.25	103	2.86	4	7.03	103
	vs. Righties	.238	55	.347	43	.268	18	1.91	36	4.07	6	9.67	103
Roger McDowell	vs. Lefties	.235	35	.319	30	.287	28	0.88	29	6.50	25	9.76	77
	vs. Righties	.225	35	.344	38	.286	33	2.87	85	7.78	54	17.04	46
Jesse Orosco	vs. Lefties	.200	--	.200	--	.238	--	0.00	--	4.69	--	23.44	--
	vs. Righties	.230	42	.345	39	.318	66	2.55	70	11.61	102	19.85	26
Doug Sisk	vs. Lefties	.306	100	.403	77	.392	101	1.49	59	12.34	92	5.84	113
	vs. Righties	.278	97	.377	69	.368	110	0.62	6	11.23	96	9.09	107
Team Average	vs. Lefties	.244	2	.344	2	.302	2	1.59	7	7.57	2	14.87	2
	vs. Righties	.231	1	.351	2	.303	5	2.34	5	8.98	9	18.42	1
League Average	vs. Lefties	.262		.374		.330		1.73		9.17		12.66	
	vs. Righties	.246		.374		.311		2.44		8.28		15.62	

Pitching with Runners on Base and Bases Empty

		BA	Rank	SA	Rank	OBA	Rank	HR %	Rank	BB %	Rank	SO %	Rank
Rick Aguilera	Runners On	.283	93	.383	67	.338	70	1.11	17	7.69	25	15.87	31
	Bases Empty	.242	49	.361	53	.298	44	2.17	66	7.02	48	13.71	66
Ron Darling	Runners On	.216	15	.302	16	.302	28	1.30	24	10.67	71	15.56	32
	Bases Empty	.250	59	.402	86	.336	90	3.05	96	11.13	104	16.36	42
Sid Fernandez	Runners On	.196	6	.266	3	.300	26	0.93	14	12.99	101	23.23	5
	Bases Empty	.173	2	.322	30	.267	14	3.14	99	10.90	101	28.07	4
Dwight Gooden	Runners On	.180	1	.219	1	.228	1	0.55	3	5.36	7	26.02	2
	Bases Empty	.213	20	.299	21	.269	19	1.76	50	7.13	50	24.67	8
Ed Lynch	Runners On	.249	50	.383	66	.268	6	2.17	58	3.00	2	11.33	81
	Bases Empty	.260	76	.397	84	.289	34	2.84	93	3.77	8	6.50	114
Roger McDowell	Runners On	.227	22	.389	70	.300	24	3.78	106	9.39	50	12.68	65
	Bases Empty	.232	36	.295	19	.277	25	0.70	8	5.61	26	14.19	62
Jesse Orosco	Runners On	.213	14	.280	7	.293	19	1.83	46	10.27	66	21.62	10
	Bases Empty	.237	41	.359	49	.315	73	2.29	72	10.27	92	19.18	22
Doug Sisk	Runners On	.313	109	.442	97	.398	108	1.84	48	11.64	83	6.35	112
	Bases Empty	.263	82	.323	31	.355	105	0.00	1	11.84	107	9.21	104
Team Average	Runners On	.237	1	.341	1	.305	1	1.76	2	8.71	1	16.81	1
	Bases Empty	.236	2	.353	3	.301	3	2.19	6	8.14	8	16.98	2
League Average	Runners On	.258		.381		.332		2.19		9.74		13.69	
	Bases Empty	.248		.369		.309		2.14		7.75		15.05	

Overall Pitching Compared to Late Inning Pressure Situations

		BA	Rank	SA	Rank	OBA	Rank	HR %	Rank	BB %	Rank	SO %	Rank
Rick Aguilera	Overall	.258	71	.370	61	.314	52	1.75	42	7.30	35	14.60	55
	Pressure	.103	1	.103	1	.188	2	0.00	1	9.09	56	18.18	26
Ron Darling	Overall	.235	36	.360	48	.321	64	2.31	72	10.93	92	16.01	39
	Pressure	.278	79	.400	77	.381	92	1.74	52	13.87	100	12.41	74
Sid Fernandez	Overall	.181	2	.302	13	.279	15	2.35	73	11.68	99	26.28	3
	Pressure	.182	12	.364	56	.250	11	4.55	102	8.33	41	27.08	5
Dwight Gooden	Overall	.201	4	.270	2	.254	3	1.32	19	6.48	17	25.16	5
	Pressure	.232	42	.298	21	.295	38	1.32	38	8.33	41	24.40	9
Tom Gorman	Overall	.277	--	.450	--	.335	--	3.96	--	7.93	--	14.10	--
	Pressure	.247	58	.397	76	.276	23	4.11	98	3.80	5	12.66	70
Ed Lynch	Overall	.256	68	.392	84	.281	18	2.59	91	3.47	3	8.37	110
	Pressure	.278	77	.528	113	.289	34	5.56	110	2.56	1	5.13	113
Roger McDowell	Overall	.230	26	.332	25	.286	20	1.91	49	7.17	31	13.57	67
	Pressure	.212	25	.292	19	.274	22	1.15	35	7.90	33	11.68	78
Jesse Orosco	Overall	.224	19	.315	17	.303	36	2.03	52	10.27	82	20.54	15
	Pressure	.220	30	.308	24	.306	45	1.76	53	10.94	75	22.27	15
Doug Sisk	Overall	.291	105	.389	82	.379	112	1.01	10	11.73	100	7.62	111
	Pressure	.300	94	.362	54	.393	97	0.77	29	12.50	89	7.24	100
Team Average	Overall	.237	2	.348	2	.302	2	2.01	5	8.38	6	16.91	1
	Pressure	.241	4	.333	4	.316	3	1.78	2	9.75	5	15.44	6
League Average	Overall	.252		.374		.319		2.16		8.63		14.45	
	Pressure	.249		.363		.326		2.12		9.92		15.33	

Additional Miscellaneous Pitching Comparisons

	Grass Surface		Artificial Surface		Home Games		Road Games		Runners in Scoring Position		Runners in Scoring Pos and Two Outs		Leading Off Inning	
	BA	Rank	BA	Rank	BA	Rank	BA	Rank	BA	Rank	BA	Rank	OBA	Rank
Rick Aguilera	.222	22	.302	103	.219	27	.281	94	.262	62	.241	66	.272	22
Ron Darling	.249	59	.180	4	.249	62	.214	17	.194	9	.193	31	.289	36
Sid Fernandez	.180	1	.184	7	.175	4	.186	2	.198	12	.175	18	.261	14
Dwight Gooden	.198	9	.208	12	.191	7	.211	13	.144	1	.133	4	.265	18
Tom Gorman	.241	49	.361	--	.245	--	.315	--	.250	--	.194	--	.353	--
Terry Leach	.268	78	.161	--	.239	--	.232	--	.245	--	.200	--	.345	85
Ed Lynch	.238	44	.303	104	.230	41	.284	97	.216	22	.208	39	.263	15
Roger McDowell	.223	24	.255	58	.226	34	.235	32	.245	48	.190	26	.294	44
Jesse Orosco	.253	61	.168	1	.262	76	.188	3	.186	8	.136	6	.328	79
Doug Sisk	.274	83	.333	112	.304	104	.281	93	.349	113	.304	103	.314	63
Team Average	.231	2	.249	2	.232	3	.241	2	.234	1	.206	1	.288	2
League Average	.251		.254		.248		.256		.257		.235		.315	

PHILADELPHIA PHILLIES

He wanted to tighten the defense; it was done. He wanted to strengthen the bullpen; it was done. The one thing that John Felske forget to tell his Phillies when he took over as manager for the 1985 season was simply to hit the ball; that wasn't done.

Oh, they hit it occasionally, and sometimes far. But not often enough. After leading the National League with a .266 batting average in 1984, the Phillies fell to .245 to finish 11th in the league in '85. And despite 141 home runs—the second-most in the league—they managed to finish only seventh in the league in runs scored. Blend in the problems brought on by having two starting pitchers who were born during the Roosevelt Administration, and you have the Phillies' first losing season since 1974.

For Want of a Run, the Game Was Lost

The Phillies were a .500 team in 1985—if you only count games in which the margin of victory was more than a single run. But in contests decided by the "minimum margin" (don't you miss those old *Sporting News* headlines?), the Phillies were only 23–35 (.397).

For as long as anyone can remember, a team's record in one-run games has been regarded as a poor-man's barometer to its overall ability. How many times have you read or heard it said of a team with a good record in one-run games, "That's the mark of a championship team"? Probably about as many times as you've heard the lament that a lousy record in one-run games is "the sign of a bad ball club."

Maybe it's because the one-run record is one of the first "analytical" stats we all learned about, but the notion of the importance of one-run games is one of baseball's most persistent myths. Those who first started keeping track of them must have done so with the intent of measuring teams' records in games which were reasonably up for grabs throughout the contest, even in the final innings. In that sense, it's true that the good teams win more one-run games than do the bad teams. Of course, they win more of *all* games than bad teams.

But what about the generalization that it's their mark in one-run games that separates the champions from the rest? Is it true that the differences in the quality of teams shows up most sharply in one-run games? To find the answer, let's look at a decade's worth of records for the National League, breaking down the results of each game by the margin of victory.

From 1975 through 1984, there were 9,381 National League games played to a decision. It is convenient both from a mathematical point of view and from a baseball sense to group those games into three categories: There were 3,111 games decided by one run (33.2 percent); 3,256 games decided by two or three runs (34.7 percent); and 3,014 games decided by four or more runs (32.1 percent). The number of games within each group is quite close, and the percentages within any one season don't stray far from the norm established for the 10-year period.

The following table lists the collective won-lost percentages for all National League teams, 1975–84, broken down according to the quality of the team and the margin of victory in each game. (There were five teams that finished with .500 records; since it seemed inappropriate to include them in either the above- or below-.500 groups, and they formed too small a sample to list separately, they have not been included. In 1975, the Cubs and Expos tied for last place; their records have been split evenly between the two bottom groups. Finally, for 1981, combined won-lost records were used, ignoring the split season.)

	One-Run Games	Two- or Three- Run Games	Four-or-More- Run Games	Overall Record
First-Place Teams	.547	.573	.638	.587
Above .500, but not First	.532	.544	.542	.539
Below .500, but not Last	.480	.464	.437	.461
Last-Place Teams	.436	.404	.384	.409

The best teams do *not* dominate the one-run games. In terms of won-lost percentage, each of the four groups of teams collapsed toward the middle in games decided by a single run. And the more lopsided the game became, the more of a spread developed between the different groups, with the largest spread in games decided by four or more runs.

Of the 20 division-winning teams, only five had a higher won-lost percentage in one-run games than in all other games combined. But 17 of those same 20 division winners had a higher percentage in games decided by four or more runs than in all other games combined.

When you think about it, isn't it pretty obvious? If the whole point about one-run games is that they're up for grabs, then shouldn't the real mark of a great team be their ability to break open those games and put them out of reach? It seems natural enough, but it hasn't been recognized, for two reasons. First, it doesn't sound good to talk about winning by a blowout; players and managers like to feel that they "earn their money" in close games, which, they like to remind us, aren't just games, but tests of character. Blowout games, on the other hand, are frequently derided as aberrant "laughers". The other reason is that there is a column for won-lost records in one-run games listed in so many newspapers, but there is no corresponding column for blowout games.

We're not saying here that it isn't important to win the close games. A game is a game, regardless of the final margin. What we are saying is that a team's overall won-lost record owes much more to the team's performance in blowout games than to its record in one-run games.

Now that we've got that general rule straightened out, it's time to turn back to the Phillies, and to put that rule aside: despite their sub-.500 record, the Phils' won-lost percentage in one-run games was 66 percentage points worse than their overall percentage. And it was exactly reflective of the type of team they were. Here are the final National League standings for 1985, with each team's record broken down by margin of victory:

(See chart on following page)

139

	One-Run Games		Two- or Three- Run Games		Four-or-More- Run Games		Overall Record	
	W–L	Pct.	W–L	Pct.	W–L	Pct.	W–L	Pct.
St. Louis	28–19	.596	25–24	.510	48–18	.727	101–61	.623
New York	33–31	.516	27–8	.771	38–25	.603	98–64	.605
Los Angeles	28–20	.583	27–21	.583	40–26	.606	95–67	.586
Cincinnati	39–18	.684	27–28	.491	23–26	.469	89–72	.553
Montreal	23–24	.489	34–22	.607	27–31	.466	84–77	.522
Houston	25–21	.543	27–31	.466	31–27	.534	83–79	.512
San Diego	31–30	.508	26–25	.510	26–24	.520	83–79	.512
Chicago	27–21	.563	23–32	.418	27–31	.466	77–84	.478
Philadelphia	23–35	.397	28–25	.528	24–27	.471	75–87	.463
Atlanta	18–24	.429	26–28	.481	22–44	.333	66–96	.407
San Francisco	22–36	.379	21–35	.375	19–29	.396	62–100	.383
Pittsburgh	20–38	.345	19–31	.380	18–35	.340	57–104	.354

In a one-run loss, the little things that are a part of winning baseball are magnified to a maddening degree. The importance of a particular misplay, a bullpen malfunction, or a strikeout in a situation that demanded contact is heightened. And while other teams may have committed more errors or blown more leads, the 1985 Phillies were the whiff kings by a mile.

Swish!

When you plot the batters' strikeouts for the 12 National League teams for 1985, this is the distribution you get:

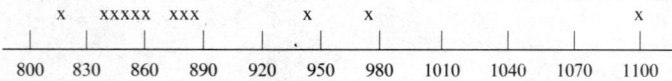

One guess who that mark way over there on the right represents. With 1,095 strikeouts for the season, the Phillies beat by 11 their league-leading total of a year earlier, and amassed the highest total in the majors since the Ivan Murrell Padres of 1970. The three leading run-producers on the team—Mike Schmidt, Juan Samuel, and Glenn Wilson—each struck out 100 or more times, while their fourth-leading run-producer, Von Hayes, stopped at 99.

A strikeout total of 1,000 or higher would be unusual for most major-league teams, but not for the Phillies. Their link to that figure began in 1960, the year that manager Eddie Sawyer, apparently prescient, resigned following an opening-day loss in Cincinnati. Just six years after Roger Bannister broke the four-minute barrier for the mile, those Phils, led by rookie Pancho Herrera, broke the four-figure barrier for strikeouts with a 154-game total of 1,054.

Aided by the expanded schedule, the Los Angeles Angels broke the Phillies' record in 1961 (curiously, some other record received an asterisk's attention that season); the Mets took care of the league record in 1963. But the Phils came back strong; they surpassed the 1,000 mark six times within the seven years from 1965 through 1971.

Then, in 1972, baseball changed. After 48 team-seasons of 1,000 or more strikeouts over the preceding dozen years, there was only one—the 1977 Padres—over the next ten. (In the American League, the DH, introduced in 1973, was partly to blame.) Then the Mets, pesky challengers to Philadelphia's reign as strikeout king, did it in 1982; they did it again, along with the Reds, in 1983. The Mets and Phils, neck and neck now, both topped the M-K mark (as Roman statisticians used to say) in 1984. That left each of those teams with eight 1,000-strikeout seasons, sharing the major-league record; the Phils claimed it all for themselves last September 22. And they did it with a flourish: Dennis Eckersley struck out the side—Schmidt, Wilson, and Ozzie Virgil—in the fourth inning of that game, with Virgil putting them over the top.

What do 1,000 strikeouts mean? In the 1960s and '70s, teams of varying stripes struck out that often. Four division- or pennant-winners did it within a five-year span from 1967 to 1971. Three of those teams—the '67 Red Sox, and '71 A's and Giants—compensated by finishing above the league average in home runs, stolen bases, and walks; the fourth, the '69 Mets, did not depend on their offense. But since 1977, when it resurfaced after an absence of five years, a 1,000-strikeout season has been an indicator of a poor team; only one of the seven teams finished above .500.

Despite the attention paid to their strikeouts, the Phillies had more general problems on offense in 1985. Their batting average declined by 21 points, their walk total by 28, and their stolen-base count by 64 from the previous season. Net result: 53 fewer runs scored, and six more losses.

The Phillies finished 26 games back last season, and no team since the 1961 Reds has won a National League pennant or division title a year after finishing 25 or more games out. This winter, though, the team made trades to directly address the areas where they fell off last season, acquiring outfielders Gary Redus and Milt Thompson, and adding veterans Tom Hume and Steve Bedrosian to help young Don Carman (52 hits allowed in 86 1/3 innings last year) in the bullpen. If the starting pitching comes through, the Phillies could surprise some people in 1986. And if not, there's always the chance for another 1,000-strikeout year.

(Read more about it: For further information on strikeouts, consult local library listings under "Browne, Byron.")

WON-LOST RECORD BY STARTING POSITION

PHILADELPHIA 75-87	C	1B	2B	3B	SS	LF	CF	RF	P	Leadoff	Relief	Starts
Luis Aguayo	-	-	0-3	1-2	17-19	-	-	-	-	0-5	-	18-24
Larry Andersen	-	-	-	-	-	-	-	-	-	-	14-43	-
Steve Carlton	-	-	-	-	-	-	-	-	4-12	-	-	4-12
Don Carman	-	-	-	-	-	-	-	-	-	-	37-34	-
Rocky Childress	-	-	-	-	-	-	-	-	0-1	-	4-11	0-1
Tim Corcoran	-	13-25	-	-	-	-	-	0-1	-	-	-	13-26
Darren Daulton	11-16	-	-	-	-	-	-	-	-	-	-	11-16
John Denny	-	-	-	-	-	-	-	-	15-18	-	-	15-18
Bo Diaz	7-13	-	-	-	-	-	-	-	-	-	-	7-13
Tom Foley	-	-	-	-	20-23	-	-	-	-	-	-	20-23
Kiko Garcia	-	-	-	-	-	-	-	-	-	-	-	-
Greg Gross	-	1-0	-	-	-	11-15	-	0-5	-	3-3	-	12-20
Kevin Gross	-	-	-	-	-	-	-	-	16-15	-	3-4	16-15
Von Hayes	-	-	-	-	-	12-10	50-68	1-1	-	5-6	-	63-79
Al Holland	-	-	-	-	-	-	-	-	-	-	1-2	-
Charles Hudson	-	-	-	-	-	-	-	-	13-13	-	2-10	13-13
Steve Jeltz	-	-	-	-	32-38	-	-	-	-	-	-	32-38
Alan Knicely	-	-	-	-	-	-	-	-	-	-	-	-
Jerry Koosman	-	-	-	-	-	-	-	-	11-7	-	0-1	11-7
Garry Maddox	-	-	-	-	-	-	25-19	-	-	2-2	-	25-19
Shane Rawley	-	-	-	-	-	-	-	-	14-17	-	3-2	14-17
Dave Rucker	-	-	-	-	-	-	-	-	2-1	-	9-27	2-1
John Russell	-	6-8	-	-	-	23-23	-	-	-	-	-	29-31
Juan Samuel	-	-	75-84	-	-	-	-	-	-	44-40	-	75-84
Mike Schmidt	-	53-52	-	18-31	-	-	-	-	-	-	-	71-83
Rick Schu	-	-	-	56-54	-	-	-	-	-	2-2	-	56-54
Dave Shipanoff	-	-	-	-	-	-	-	-	-	-	8-18	-
Dave Stewart	-	-	-	-	-	-	-	-	-	-	0-4	-
Jeff Stone	-	-	-	-	-	29-37	-	-	-	19-27	-	29-37
Rick Surhoff	-	-	-	-	-	-	-	-	-	-	1-1	-
Kent Tekulve	-	-	-	-	-	-	-	-	-	-	29-29	-
Derrel Thomas	-	-	-	-	6-7	0-2	-	-	-	0-2	-	6-9
Fred Toliver	-	-	-	-	-	-	-	-	0-3	-	3-5	0-3
Ozzie Virgil	57-58	-	-	-	-	-	-	-	-	-	-	57-58
Glenn Wilson	-	-	-	-	-	-	-	74-80	-	-	-	74-80
John Wockenfuss	-	2-2	-	-	-	-	-	-	-	-	-	2-2
Pat Zachry	-	-	-	-	-	-	-	-	-	-	2-8	-

Batting vs. Left and Right Handed Pitchers

		BA	Rank	SA	Rank	OBA	Rank	HR %	Rank	BB %	Rank	SO %	Rank
Luis Aguayo	vs. Lefties	.190	126	.286	118	.329	66	1.59	79	14.10	20	10.26	42
	vs. Righties	.333	--	.578	--	.408	--	4.90	--	9.02	--	14.75	--
Tim Corcoran	vs. Lefties	.211	--	.211	--	.200	--	0.00	--	0.00	--	20.00	--
	vs. Righties	.215	124	.264	129	.323	68	0.00	120	14.57	13	8.04	19
Tom Foley	vs. Lefties	.200	--	.200	--	.238	--	0.00	--	4.76	--	19.05	--
	vs. Righties	.248	90	.362	85	.304	98	1.43	77	7.49	83	11.45	54
Greg Gross	vs. Lefties	.333	--	.333	--	.500	--	0.00	--	30.00	--	10.00	--
	vs. Righties	.258	68	.313	109	.368	27	0.00	120	14.87	10	4.10	5
Von Hayes	vs. Lefties	.229	98	.338	95	.291	102	2.55	56	8.09	79	19.65	115
	vs. Righties	.276	43	.421	43	.348	49	2.18	59	10.13	43	14.01	78
Steve Jeltz	vs. Lefties	.194	124	.226	130	.324	68	0.00	108	15.79	9	19.74	117
	vs. Righties	.187	132	.216	134	.262	130	0.00	120	9.21	60	26.32	134
Alan Knicely	vs. Lefties	.212	113	.308	109	.276	116	1.92	72	8.62	72	18.97	111
	vs. Righties	.257	70	.425	42	.325	66	3.54	28	8.66	66	21.26	130
Garry Maddox	vs. Lefties	.272	50	.386	60	.309	84	1.75	74	5.69	107	9.76	35
	vs. Righties	.202	--	.288	--	.250	--	1.92	--	5.31	--	12.39	--
John Russell	vs. Lefties	.221	104	.411	50	.315	79	4.21	29	12.04	36	26.85	130
	vs. Righties	.215	--	.388	--	.246	--	4.13	--	3.97	--	34.13	--
Juan Samuel	vs. Lefties	.239	88	.386	61	.266	120	2.54	57	3.85	125	19.71	116
	vs. Righties	.275	45	.457	21	.318	76	3.00	39	4.99	119	19.96	122
Mike Schmidt	vs. Lefties	.284	37	.484	25	.391	13	3.87	32	15.22	16	16.30	97
	vs. Righties	.274	47	.551	4	.369	26	6.85	2	12.80	24	18.87	115
Rick Schu	vs. Lefties	.280	39	.477	27	.349	43	3.03	48	9.52	59	15.65	91
	vs. Righties	.239	104	.324	105	.303	100	1.06	91	7.74	76	17.74	107
Jeff Stone	vs. Lefties	.294	--	.353	--	.351	--	0.00	--	8.11	--	21.62	--
	vs. Righties	.261	64	.335	98	.300	104	1.30	83	4.90	121	17.14	103
Ozzie Virgil	vs. Lefties	.238	89	.385	62	.307	86	3.28	45	9.49	60	13.87	76
	vs. Righties	.250	83	.451	24	.339	55	4.93	11	10.40	39	19.08	117
Glenn Wilson	vs. Lefties	.287	34	.485	23	.330	65	3.51	38	6.49	99	11.89	62
	vs. Righties	.270	52	.400	61	.303	100	1.83	68	4.95	120	20.43	125
Team Average	vs. Lefties	.240	10	.375	7	.309	11	2.42	4	9.13	4	17.09	12
	vs. Righties	.247	9	.386	4	.313	9	2.64	2	8.41	9	18.20	12
League Average	vs. Lefties	.250		.374		.317		2.26		8.65		14.84	
	vs. Righties	.253		.374		.320		2.12		8.62		14.28	

Batting with Runners on Base and Bases Empty

		BA	Rank	SA	Rank	OBA	Rank	HR %	Rank	BB %	Rank	SO %	Rank
Luis Aguayo	Runners On	.338	--	.569	--	.439	--	3.08	--	13.95	--	12.79	--
	Bases Empty	.240	93	.400	54	.333	47	4.00	22	8.77	42	13.16	65
Tim Corcoran	Runners On	.143	135	.194	135	.266	133	0.00	115	15.20	16	8.80	38
	Bases Empty	.298	--	.333	--	.372	--	0.00	--	10.64	--	9.57	--
Tom Foley	Runners On	.210	129	.320	106	.295	110	2.00	62	10.71	55	14.29	83
	Bases Empty	.260	62	.347	92	.293	101	0.67	112	4.46	121	11.46	51
Greg Gross	Runners On	.282	--	.352	--	.391	--	0.00	--	15.73	--	3.37	--
	Bases Empty	.245	89	.286	124	.362	22	0.00	120	15.52	5	5.17	6
Von Hayes	Runners On	.265	69	.376	81	.348	60	2.04	60	11.62	47	13.38	81
	Bases Empty	.262	60	.415	40	.320	67	2.46	52	7.93	54	17.28	99
Steve Jeltz	Runners On	.220	119	.264	130	.327	76	0.00	115	13.39	30	24.11	134
	Bases Empty	.162	134	.181	134	.241	132	0.00	120	9.48	35	24.14	131
Garry Maddox	Runners On	.244	88	.322	104	.297	107	0.00	115	7.84	95	7.84	27
	Bases Empty	.234	100	.352	85	.269	117	3.13	38	3.73	125	13.43	70
John Russell	Runners On	.223	116	.426	51	.291	116	5.32	12	8.74	81	24.27	135
	Bases Empty	.213	119	.377	68	.267	119	3.28	35	6.87	70	35.88	134
Juan Samuel	Runners On	.267	65	.450	37	.292	115	3.88	27	2.90	134	20.65	129
	Bases Empty	.262	59	.427	35	.309	77	2.22	58	5.77	97	19.40	118
Mike Schmidt	Runners On	.264	73	.429	47	.377	33	3.15	41	15.48	12	17.10	113
	Bases Empty	.288	19	.620	2	.373	12	8.47	1	11.64	24	19.10	113
Rick Schu	Runners On	.232	108	.297	114	.312	94	0.72	100	10.32	62	16.13	101
	Bases Empty	.263	57	.410	45	.321	66	2.16	61	7.28	67	17.55	100
Jeff Stone	Runners On	.235	103	.353	90	.270	131	2.35	54	4.40	129	19.78	125
	Bases Empty	.279	34	.330	100	.325	61	0.56	113	5.76	99	16.75	96
Ozzie Virgil	Runners On	.218	120	.378	78	.301	103	3.63	31	10.45	60	15.45	96
	Bases Empty	.270	49	.476	27	.354	27	5.15	12	9.89	30	19.39	117
Glenn Wilson	Runners On	.268	64	.465	29	.297	106	3.52	35	4.90	127	17.65	117
	Bases Empty	.281	30	.389	62	.323	65	1.23	92	5.81	94	18.31	107
Team Average	Runners On	.240	11	.374	10	.314	11	2.46	5	9.74	7	17.13	12
	Bases Empty	.249	6	.390	1	.310	6	2.66	1	7.73	7	18.47	12
League Average	Runners On	.258		.381		.332		2.19		9.74		13.69	
	Bases Empty	.248		.369		.309		2.14		7.75		15.05	

Overall Batting Compared to Late Inning Pressure Situations

		BA	Rank	SA	Rank	OBA	Rank	HR %	Rank	BB %	Rank	SO %	Rank	RDI %	Rank
Luis Aguayo	Overall	.279	33	.467	18	.378	17	3.64	31	11.00	35	13.00	71	.302	--
	Pressure	.300	32	.467	30	.400	24	3.33	34	10.26	56	15.38	77	.143	--
Tim Corcoran	Overall	.214	128	.258	131	.312	85	0.00	127	13.24	19	9.13	28	.238	104
	Pressure	.167	125	.262	115	.296	93	0.00	92	16.36	13	5.45	11	.259	62
Darren Daulton	Overall	.204	--	.369	--	.311	--	3.88	--	13.45	--	31.09	--	.158	--
	Pressure	.143	--	.143	--	.294	--	0.00	--	17.65	--	29.41	--	.000	133
Tom Foley	Overall	.240	105	.336	105	.294	113	1.20	92	7.06	94	12.64	67	.281	72
	Pressure	.271	57	.375	66	.314	85	2.08	61	5.88	109	15.69	81	.286	50
Greg Gross	Overall	.260	74	.314	119	.374	20	0.00	127	15.61	5	4.39	4	.265	--
	Pressure	.250	73	.295	91	.400	24	0.00	92	19.30	4	5.26	7	.182	104
Von Hayes	Overall	.263	70	.398	62	.332	58	2.28	60	9.58	61	15.54	95	.282	71
	Pressure	.277	55	.383	60	.352	53	2.13	57	10.38	52	17.92	94	.194	101
Steve Jeltz	Overall	.189	134	.219	134	.283	123	0.00	127	11.40	27	24.12	132	.222	116
	Pressure	.188	--	.250	--	.188	--	0.00	--	0.00	--	11.76	--	.333	--
Alan Knicely	Overall	.242	--	.388	--	.310	--	3.03	--	8.65	--	20.54	--	.321	32
	Pressure	.375	--	.583	--	.407	--	4.17	--	7.14	--	17.86	--	.167	--
Garry Maddox	Overall	.239	107	.339	102	.281	125	1.83	69	5.51	116	11.02	48	.286	67
	Pressure	.178	122	.244	121	.260	115	2.22	54	7.84	87	11.76	49	.000	133
John Russell	Overall	.218	126	.398	63	.278	128	4.17	22	7.69	82	30.77	134	.182	131
	Pressure	.200	--	.229	--	.222	--	0.00	--	2.78	--	44.44	--	.167	--
Juan Samuel	Overall	.264	68	.436	32	.303	100	2.87	42	4.65	128	19.89	124	.275	76
	Pressure	.278	51	.500	23	.340	62	4.44	23	5.94	108	19.80	109	.379	17
Mike Schmidt	Overall	.277	37	.532	5	.375	18	6.01	3	13.49	17	18.14	118	.296	59
	Pressure	.318	22	.648	5	.406	21	7.95	5	12.87	30	18.81	103	.320	36
Rick Schu	Overall	.252	86	.373	77	.318	75	1.68	80	8.32	70	17.07	106	.198	129
	Pressure	.239	81	.254	117	.311	87	0.00	92	8.11	77	14.86	75	.182	104
Jeff Stone	Overall	.265	64	.337	104	.307	96	1.14	95	5.32	120	17.73	114	.103	134
	Pressure	.200	--	.314	--	.222	--	2.86	--	2.70	--	21.62	--	.000	--
Ozzie Virgil	Overall	.246	96	.432	35	.330	65	4.46	15	10.14	47	17.60	111	.231	109
	Pressure	.218	95	.333	78	.326	74	2.56	47	12.90	29	23.66	125	.231	81
Glenn Wilson	Overall	.275	48	.424	40	.311	89	2.30	59	5.38	118	18.00	115	.336	18
	Pressure	.311	29	.573	11	.333	67	5.83	13	3.70	130	23.15	124	.306	45
Team Average	Overall	.245	11	.383	4	.312	9	2.57	2	8.61	7	17.89	12	.265	9
	Pressure	.255	6	.396	3	.331	5	2.94	2	9.62	3	18.25	12	.246	9
League Average	Overall	.252		.374		.319		2.16		8.63		14.45		.273	
	Pressure	.253		.368		.325		2.17		9.26		15.10		.257	

Additional Miscellaneous Batting Comparisons

	Grass Surface BA	Rank	Artificial Surface BA	Rank	Home Games BA	Rank	Road Games BA	Rank	Runners in Scoring Position BA	Rank	Runners in Scoring Pos and Two Outs BA	Rank	Leading Off Inning OBA	Rank	Runners on 3B with less than 2 Outs RDI %	Rank
Luis Aguayo	.238	--	.293	25	.287	45	.269	49	.400	--	.167	120	.315	76	.800	7
Tim Corcoran	.189	--	.221	118	.183	133	.260	--	.141	134	.133	130	.422	5	.600	59
Tom Foley	.151	134	.287	28	.296	36	.193	130	.232	100	.214	86	.333	52	.714	17
Greg Gross	.340	--	.224	113	.263	--	.258	68	.244	--	.278	--	.353	43	.750	--
Von Hayes	.227	104	.276	40	.288	44	.240	93	.291	38	.212	89	.333	52	.629	49
Steve Jeltz	.079	--	.215	121	.202	125	.175	133	.208	115	.259	57	.273	110	.500	--
Alan Knicely	.157	--	.281	33	.272	--	.214	--	.289	41	.308	24	.341	49	.667	--
Garry Maddox	.149	--	.263	65	.241	99	.236	99	.236	95	.200	100	.254	125	.571	75
John Russell	.182	--	.227	109	.265	70	.162	135	.184	128	.200	100	.261	119	.222	--
Juan Samuel	.262	65	.265	61	.248	92	.280	35	.268	69	.300	33	.325	65	.519	103
Mike Schmidt	.282	41	.275	44	.279	55	.275	44	.282	54	.215	85	.367	30	.657	32
Rick Schu	.195	125	.275	43	.269	67	.241	91	.235	98	.270	48	.362	34	.583	68
Jeff Stone	.232	99	.280	35	.280	54	.248	85	.176	130	.179	114	.350	45	.200	--
Derrel Thomas	.125	--	.224	115	.196	--	.220	--	.313	--	.500	--	.227	--	.333	--
Ozzie Virgil	.164	130	.275	42	.252	87	.241	92	.236	95	.120	132	.354	41	.571	75
Glenn Wilson	.267	54	.277	39	.292	38	.257	71	.287	43	.241	69	.365	31	.651	36
Team Average	.220	12	.254	8	.253	10	.238	9	.250	9	.225	9	.329	3	.596	3
League Average	.251		.254		.256		.248		.257		.235		.315		.576	

Pitching vs. Left and Right Handed Batters

		BA	Rank	SA	Rank	OBA	Rank	HR %	Rank	BB %	Rank	SO %	Rank
Larry Andersen	vs. Lefties	.309	103	.415	87	.403	108	1.63	66	12.41	93	11.72	59
	vs. Righties	.247	61	.377	69	.287	35	1.85	32	4.62	8	19.08	31
Steve Carlton	vs. Lefties	.233	--	.256	--	.298	--	0.00	--	8.33	--	10.42	--
	vs. Righties	.251	67	.373	67	.357	105	2.03	43	13.88	111	12.18	85
Don Carman	vs. Lefties	.218	20	.299	19	.269	15	1.15	39	5.32	14	22.34	9
	vs. Righties	.161	1	.263	6	.275	23	2.44	67	13.31	109	26.61	7
John Denny	vs. Lefties	.285	85	.388	71	.356	83	1.32	51	9.75	71	10.33	74
	vs. Righties	.279	98	.396	79	.328	76	2.06	44	6.80	39	14.43	67
Kevin Gross	vs. Lefties	.242	40	.354	48	.329	58	0.94	32	10.27	77	17.25	23
	vs. Righties	.262	79	.369	65	.322	73	2.02	40	8.03	59	17.36	42
Charles Hudson	vs. Lefties	.273	70	.419	90	.344	71	2.39	87	9.67	69	10.61	70
	vs. Righties	.230	45	.404	86	.293	42	3.79	100	8.07	61	18.83	33
Jerry Koosman	vs. Lefties	.319	--	.426	--	.333	--	0.00	--	0.00	--	16.67	--
	vs. Righties	.271	90	.459	106	.337	88	4.12	106	8.83	72	13.51	77
Shane Rawley	vs. Lefties	.231	31	.319	31	.320	47	2.20	81	10.48	81	13.33	43
	vs. Righties	.252	68	.364	61	.322	72	2.11	48	9.41	79	12.37	82
Dave Rucker	vs. Lefties	.208	12	.347	44	.268	13	1.39	57	8.24	50	12.94	45
	vs. Righties	.301	112	.451	105	.390	114	2.21	55	12.45	106	11.32	90
Kent Tekulve	vs. Lefties	.297	94	.398	73	.366	90	1.56	61	8.45	52	8.45	91
	vs. Righties	.226	36	.327	28	.302	51	1.89	33	9.73	82	15.14	62
Team Average	vs. Lefties	.269	8	.385	8	.344	10	1.42	4	9.72	8	12.67	4
	vs. Righties	.253	9	.384	9	.324	10	2.48	9	9.45	12	15.42	8
League Average	vs. Lefties	.262		.374		.330		1.73		9.17		12.66	
	vs. Righties	.246		.374		.311		2.44		8.28		15.62	

Pitching with Runners on Base and Bases Empty

		BA	Rank	SA	Rank	OBA	Rank	HR %	Rank	BB %	Rank	SO %	Rank
Larry Andersen	Runners On	.264	67	.396	75	.344	75	2.08	56	9.64	54	18.07	22
	Bases Empty	.284	105	.390	78	.336	89	1.42	35	6.58	42	13.16	73
Steve Carlton	Runners On	.238	35	.360	49	.333	59	1.83	46	12.12	86	12.12	74
	Bases Empty	.259	75	.356	46	.365	109	1.72	48	14.29	113	11.82	83
Don Carman	Runners On	.181	2	.283	8	.278	12	1.57	33	11.54	82	19.23	15
	Bases Empty	.176	3	.267	8	.269	18	2.42	77	10.75	99	30.65	3
John Denny	Runners On	.284	96	.392	73	.343	73	1.75	42	8.70	39	12.17	73
	Bases Empty	.280	102	.392	81	.342	97	1.63	43	7.99	64	12.45	77
Kevin Gross	Runners On	.245	42	.361	51	.324	49	1.22	21	10.26	65	15.53	34
	Bases Empty	.256	69	.361	52	.327	85	1.57	42	8.52	73	18.66	26
Charles Hudson	Runners On	.282	92	.442	96	.350	82	2.60	79	9.32	48	14.41	48
	Bases Empty	.231	33	.390	79	.296	42	3.42	105	8.56	74	14.82	54
Jerry Koosman	Runners On	.266	69	.461	104	.335	66	5.19	114	9.39	51	14.92	43
	Bases Empty	.283	104	.451	106	.337	93	2.58	81	6.75	44	13.10	74
Shane Rawley	Runners On	.233	27	.340	29	.310	31	2.20	61	10.08	64	12.53	66
	Bases Empty	.261	78	.373	72	.330	88	2.06	60	9.13	80	12.45	78
Dave Rucker	Runners On	.291	99	.444	99	.362	92	2.65	81	11.05	75	9.39	91
	Bases Empty	.265	86	.408	88	.361	108	1.36	30	11.83	106	14.20	61
Kent Tekulve	Runners On	.248	49	.380	63	.348	80	2.19	60	12.57	91	14.37	49
	Bases Empty	.267	87	.340	39	.313	67	1.33	28	5.63	27	10.00	98
Team Average	Runners On	.261	9	.390	8	.337	9	2.16	5	10.30	10	13.81	6
	Bases Empty	.256	10	.379	9	.326	10	2.03	5	8.91	11	14.91	7
League Average	Runners On	.258		.381		.332		2.19		9.74		13.69	
	Bases Empty	.248		.369		.309		2.14		7.75		15.05	

Overall Pitching Compared to Late Inning Pressure Situations

		BA	Rank	SA	Rank	OBA	Rank	HR %	Rank	BB %	Rank	SO %	Rank
Larry Andersen	Overall	.274	96	.393	86	.340	89	1.75	43	8.18	49	15.72	41
	Pressure	.299	93	.429	88	.329	62	1.95	64	4.32	9	17.28	31
Steve Carlton	Overall	.249	53	.358	42	.349	98	1.78	45	13.22	110	11.97	84
	Pressure	.167	--	.167	--	.375	--	0.00	--	22.22	--	0.00	--
Don Carman	Overall	.178	1	.274	5	.273	13	2.05	53	11.11	96	25.44	4
	Pressure	.157	7	.239	12	.250	11	1.52	45	10.53	70	29.39	3
John Denny	Overall	.282	100	.392	85	.342	92	1.68	37	8.32	52	12.32	79
	Pressure	.250	62	.367	60	.313	52	1.67	49	8.70	50	14.49	54
Kevin Gross	Overall	.251	58	.361	50	.326	69	1.42	25	9.28	71	17.30	31
	Pressure	.282	84	.372	65	.380	91	0.00	1	13.83	98	14.89	48
Charles Hudson	Overall	.252	63	.412	96	.319	59	3.08	100	8.88	62	14.65	53
	Pressure	.248	61	.362	56	.319	56	2.86	82	9.24	59	11.76	76
Jerry Koosman	Overall	.276	98	.455	111	.336	82	3.62	111	7.85	42	13.86	63
	Pressure	.269	--	.538	--	.286	--	3.85	--	3.57	--	14.29	--
Shane Rawley	Overall	.249	54	.359	46	.321	65	2.12	59	9.54	75	12.49	77
	Pressure	.271	73	.458	97	.338	69	5.08	108	8.96	54	16.42	39
Dave Rucker	Overall	.279	99	.426	100	.361	104	2.01	51	11.43	98	11.71	85
	Pressure	.279	80	.508	107	.375	86	4.92	106	13.33	94	13.33	67
Dave Shipanoff	Overall	.231	--	.371	--	.309	--	2.10	--	9.88	--	16.05	--
	Pressure	.222	34	.400	77	.327	60	2.22	68	14.55	104	12.73	69
Kent Tekulve	Overall	.258	70	.359	45	.330	75	1.74	40	9.17	69	12.23	81
	Pressure	.277	76	.391	73	.354	78	2.17	67	10.33	69	9.86	86
Team Average	Overall	.259	10	.384	10	.331	10	2.09	6	9.55	11	14.40	7
	Pressure	.250	6	.378	9	.328	7	2.37	9	10.39	11	15.93	5
League Average	Overall	.252		.374		.319		2.16		8.63		14.45	
	Pressure	.249		.363		.326		2.12		9.92		15.33	

Additional Miscellaneous Pitching Comparisons

	Grass Surface		Artificial Surface		Home Games		Road Games		Runners in Scoring Position		Runners in Scoring Pos and Two Outs		Leading Off Inning	
	BA	Rank	BA	Rank	BA	Rank	BA	Rank	BA	Rank	BA	Rank	OBA	Rank
Larry Andersen	.311	--	.263	71	.255	69	.298	108	.247	49	.190	26	.354	90
Steve Carlton	.240	45	.252	54	.205	16	.286	99	.222	25	.195	33	.421	113
Don Carman	.172	--	.180	5	.142	1	.212	15	.214	21	.231	57	.299	50
Rocky Childress	.290	--	.336	114	.321	--	.333	--	.298	--	.240	--	.387	--
John Denny	.253	62	.294	97	.288	98	.275	87	.253	56	.294	94	.342	82
Kevin Gross	.312	110	.230	28	.245	59	.256	62	.247	49	.146	9	.296	48
Charles Hudson	.285	92	.242	42	.258	73	.247	45	.230	36	.209	40	.286	33
Jerry Koosman	.270	--	.277	84	.281	92	.270	83	.238	45	.139	7	.362	97
Shane Rawley	.240	46	.253	55	.250	63	.248	47	.201	15	.226	53	.295	45
Dave Rucker	.323	--	.266	74	.266	78	.305	109	.272	74	.225	51	.356	93
Dave Shipanoff	.218	--	.239	40	.222	--	.239	--	.261	--	.250	--	.257	--
Kent Tekulve	.265	--	.256	59	.271	85	.242	39	.235	40	.234	60	.300	52
Team Average	.268	10	.255	8	.255	9	.263	11	.242	2	.219	2	.321	7
League Average	.251		.254		.248		.256		.257		.235		.315	

PITTSBURGH PIRATES

No team in baseball suffered a more inglorious 1985 season than the Pittsburgh Pirates. Chosen by some to win the National League's Eastern Division (don't worry, we won't name names), the Pirates accumulated more than 100 losses to finish last for a second consecutive season. The previous winter's acquisitions, George Hendrick and Sixto Lezcano among them, were schlepped through the summer doldrums like a ball-and-chain on a 100-degree day. Perennially reliable performers like Jason Thompson and Bill Madlock endured subpar seasons, costing the former his starting spot and buying the latter a one-way ticket out of town. Pitching, the brightest spot during a dreary 1984 season, was a disaster. Forget that Rick Reuschel won 14 games with a 2.27 ERA; the fact that Pittsburgh was desperate enough to resurrect his long-forgotten carcass tells you all you need to know.

As bad as the season was on the field, it was probably worse off the field, with rumors of impending arrests and franchise shifts flying from the start of the season. We don't want to minimize the importance of those things, but there's been more than enough written about them already. With your indulgence, we'll stick to the things we all can see: the games played on the field. Between the white lines, as they said in a simpler age.

Typical of Pittsburgh's problems last season was the lack of production by their outfielders. In last year's *Analyst* we showed that Pirates starting outfielders had hit only 24 home runs in 1984 while driving in only 165 runs, both the lowest totals in the National League. Last season they were even worse. The composite statistics for the starting outfielders of all National League teams last season:

Team	AB	H	2B	3B	HR	RBI	BA	SA	OBA
St. Louis	1883	552	80	37	28	201	.293	.420	.350
Los Angeles	1774	508	89	11	72	261	.286	.471	.346
Atlanta	1871	515	76	15	71	242	.275	.446	.348
Houston	1871	511	101	14	36	227	.273	.400	.324
New York	1824	494	86	17	69	254	.271	.450	.346
Montreal	1815	489	77	24	47	201	.269	.416	.333
Cincinnati	1890	508	97	20	66	259	.269	.446	.335
San Diego	1831	491	83	12	42	199	.268	.395	.336
Chicago	1820	488	79	8	41	203	.268	.388	.347
Philadelphia	1858	483	90	15	38	227	.260	.386	.311
Pittsburgh	1797	464	81	14	22	158	.258	.356	.316
San Francisco	1869	471	74	13	46	200	.252	.379	.319
N.L. Average	1842	498	84	17	48	219	.270	.413	.334

More unexpected was the ineffectiveness of Pittsburgh's pitching staff. Despite the Pirates' disappointing 1984 season, few foresaw the problems that developed last season, if only because they seemed so sound on the mound. The 1984 staff led the National League in ERA—a first for a last-place team—and had one of the deepest starting rotations in the majors: John Candelaria, Jose DeLeon, Larry McWilliams, Rick Rhoden, and John Tudor, with Lee Tunnell and Don Robinson held in reserve. The rest is history: Tudor was traded for George Hendrick, Candelaria went to the bullpen, McWilliams hurt his arm, DeLeon spent the season in the twilight zone, and Rhoden was left holding the bag. When the smoke cleared, Pittsburgh's staff had earned another distinction: it became

the first in major-league history to sink from first place in ERA to last place in a single season.

Most of those problems can be explained, except for the enigma of Jose DeLeon. Three seasons ago, DeLeon appeared to be the most promising development in Pittsburgh since pollution control. He pitched into the seventh inning without allowing a hit in three of his first seven starts, and finished the season with a 7–3 record and 118 strikeouts in 108 innings. But shortly before the first anniversary of his major-league debut, something went wrong. Drastically wrong. Compare his first 29 starts for Pittsburgh to those since then; the figures look absurd:

	W–L	GS	CG	IP	H	BB	SO	ERA
7/23/83–7/12/84	13–7	29	6	209.2	152	97	201	2.83
7/17/84–10/4/85	3–28	39	3	253.1	208	131	219	4.73

Certain aspects of DeLeon's decline and fall are apparent in those numbers; others are hidden, and some defy explanation. The obvious: DeLeon's ratio of hits to innings has always been good, and even last season he ranked ninth in the NL with his rate of 7.64 hits per nine innings. But his average was substantially lower during his first calendar year (6.52 per nine innings) than it has been since (7.39). So, too, his walks-to-innings ratio—4.16 before, 4.76 after. The hidden: DeLeon has pitched consistently well throughout his three seasons with the bases empty, but in runners-on-base situations, the statistics of batters facing DeLeon have improved markedly:

Year	Situation	AB	H	2B	3B	HR	BB	SO	BA	SA	OBA
1983	Bases Empty	215	44	9	4	3	28	67	.205	.326	.299
	Runners on	168	31	4	2	2	19	51	.185	.268	.263
1984	Bases Empty	416	84	14	2	6	56	102	.202	.288	.298
	Runners on	270	63	13	3	4	36	51	.233	.348	.321
1985	Bases Empty	330	71	13	2	6	60	86	.215	.321	.339
	Runners on	267	67	7	3	9	29	63	.251	.401	.322

The inexplicable: DeLeon has maintained a ratio of strikeouts to hits allowed of more than one, which is to say that he has struck out more batters than he has allowed hits, even since his dramatic turnaround a year and a half ago. This is not a commonly cited statistic, and for good reason—it's a freak stat that has no real application to the game. But it is one of those pointers which invariably indicates power pitchers of the highest caliber. Consider this: Only four pitchers have started more than 50 games over the past three seasons with more strikeouts than hits allowed. When the group gathers to discuss its accomplishments, will Dwight Gooden, Nolan Ryan, and Mario Soto allow DeLeon to use the front door?

Whether DeLeon can shift out of reverse is questionable, but one thing is certain: He can't do it without better support from his teammates. Although his 4.70 ERA last season would have made him a loser regardless, the Pirates made matters worse by scoring only 58 runs in DeLeon's 25 starts. This has been a key element in DeLeon's form reversal; during the first 29 starts of his career, Pittsburgh scored an average of 3.93 runs per game; since then, he has received just 2.54 runs per game. Still, we can't help feeling that a pitcher with a 2.83 ERA would have more reason to complain of nonsupport than one who's blown up to 4.73.

My, But We're Having a Long Spring This Year!

Despite 104 losses last season, there is reason for hope in Pittsburgh. For one thing, there is only one direction to go—in the ever-changing baseball world of the 1980s, consecutive hundred-loss seasons have gone the way of football drop kicks, low-scoring hockey games, and undisputed boxing champions. No National League team has reached the century mark in two straight years since the San Diego Padres of 1973 and 1974. More positive, and even encouraging, were the happenings at Three Rivers Stadium late last season.

The home team resembled the Pirates of previous seasons in name only. For Pirates fans who still occasionally wear the lucky shirts they had on when Bill Mazeroski won the seventh game of the 1960 World Series, Bream, Khalifa, and Orsulak are hardly the stuff of dreams, but for those willing to consider the first five months of the 1985 season merely an extension of spring training, and the final four weeks of the season a preview of the 1986 season, the results had to make the winter a wee bit more bearable.

Certainly no team underwent more changes during the 1985 season than Pittsburgh. The Pirates' opening-day lineup made its last starting appearance together on April 19. By September, four of those starters—Bill Madlock, Tim Foli, Doug Frobel, and George Hendrick—were gone, and two others, Jason Thompson and Marvell Wynne, lost their starting spots by season's end. Only catcher Tony Pena and second baseman Johnny Ray were everyday starters throughout the entire season. Winter acquisitions Steve Kemp and Sixto Lezcano, who had designs on at least part-time starting roles, contributed little and were relegated to the bench. While some accused the Pirates of chop-shop management—dismantling the pieces, and selling them to the highest bidders—it was clear by late in the season that, like any sensible corporate heads, the Pirates' front office had sold off their weak divisions to create a more streamlined and efficient core.

Their philosophy was similar to that of the Minnesota Twins in the early 1980s. Twins owner Cal Griffith figured he could just as easily lose 100 games without high-salaried name players—Rod Carew, Butch Wynegar, Roy Smalley, Jerry Koosman, and Doug Corbett—as with them, so he traded them for parts of his team of the future: Ken Landreaux (eventually traded for Mickey Hatcher), Ron Davis, and Tom Brunansky, among others. Three years later, the Twins were making the kinds of deals associated with teams reaching the threshold of championships, acquiring Bert Blyleven or signing Steve Howe, for instance. (No one ever said the process was foolproof.) Pittsburgh's performance last September indicates that the Pirates may be headed down that same road. It's a long trip, but at least they're headed in the right direction.

The symbolic end of Pittsburgh's eight-month spring training was the arrival of Sid Bream, the final piece in the reassembled Pirates puzzle, who made his first start for them on September 12. From then on, manager Chuck Tanner went with a fairly steady lineup, but one unlike the one envisioned a few months earlier: Bream at first base, Ray at second, Sammy Khalifa at shortstop, and either Denny Gonzalez (vs. right-handers) or Jim Morrison (vs. southpaws) at third base; Mike Brown, R. J. Reynolds, and either Gonzalez or Joe Orsulak in the outfield; Pena behind the plate. The Pirates split their 26 games after the arrival of Bream, but with some

combination or other consisting solely of the players mentioned above in the starting lineup, they won 9 of 13. During those final four weeks of the season, Pittsburgh ranked third in the National League with a .278 composite batting average, second with 33 stolen bases, and fourth with an average of 5.15 runs per game. They placed two batters among the league's top ten for the period: Orsulak (5th at .359) and Ray (9th at .337), with Mike Brown also topping the .300 mark. Steve Kemp (4 for 9) and Lee Mazzilli (3 for 8) provided excellent pinch-hitting.

Despite all this, few Pirates rooters were able to say, "I have seen the future, and it works." One by-product of the Pirates' season-long ineptitude was the sparse attendance at Three Rivers Stadium while the seeds for '86 were being planted. The Pirates drew only slightly more than 50,000 fans for their final 10 home dates. Having taken steps to turn the team around, the next task for Pirates management will be to win their fans back.

The Long Goodbye

Regardless of whether they return to Three Rivers Stadium, Pirates fans won't have Chuck Tanner to kick around anymore. The Pirates' manager since 1977, and the head of the 1979 Fa-mi-leee, has left Pittsburgh for a brave new world in Atlanta. He left a year too late.

Few managers with careers as long and successful as Tanner's have ever suffered through seasons as bad as that which the Bucco manager endured in 1985. Only eight others have withstood 100-loss seasons after 1,000 career victories: four of them, Lou Boudreau, Leo Durocher, Jimmy Dykes, and Ralph Houk, barely edged their toes over the century mark. The others are listed in the following table, which shows the losingest seasons ever by managers who had already won 1,000 games:

Year	Manager, Team	W	L
1962	Casey Stengel, N.Y. (NL)	40	120
1916	Connie Mack, Phil. (AL)	36	117
1935	Bill McKechnie, Bos. (NL)	38	115
1963	Casey Stengel, N.Y. (NL)	51	111
1915	Connie Mack, Phil. (AL)	43	109
1964	Casey Stengel, N.Y. (NL)	53	109
1920	Connie Mack, Phil. (AL)	48	106
1943	Connie Mack, Phil. (AL)	49	105
1946	Connie Mack, Phil. (AL)	49	105
1905	Ned Hanlon, Bklyn. (NL)	48	104
1919	Connie Mack, Phil. (AL)	36	104
1985	Chuck Tanner, Pitt. (NL)	57	104

A technique we like to use in this book is to look at a contemporary event in terms of its historical precedents, trying to divine the future based upon those past parallels. The indicators make it simple to project Tanner's future: nine of the other 11 seasons in the table above were turned in by managers who remained active to very advanced ages and had extremely white hair and wrinkled faces. Based upon those observations, we expect a white and wrinkled Chuck Tanner to still be managing when "Rocky LXVI" hits the nation's theaters.

WON-LOST RECORD BY STARTING POSITION

PITTSBURGH 57-104	C	1B	2B	3B	SS	LF	CF	RF	P	Leadoff	Relief	Starts
Bill Almon	-	1-2	-	2-2	10-21	5-16	1-1	-	-	10-26	-	19-42
Rafael Belliard	-	-	-	2-5	-	-	-	-	-	-	-	2-5
Mike Bielecki	-	-	-	-	-	-	-	-	2-5	-	-	2-5
Sid Bream	-	12-11	-	-	-	-	-	-	-	-	1-4	12-11
Mike Brown	-	-	-	-	-	-	-	23-32	-	-	-	23-32
John Candelaria	-	-	-	-	-	-	-	-	-	-	16-21	-
Pat Clements	-	-	-	-	-	-	-	-	-	-	10-17	-
Trench Davis	-	-	-	-	-	-	0-2	-	-	-	-	0-2
Jose DeLeon	-	-	-	-	-	-	-	-	4-21	-	3-3	4-21
Jerry Dybzinski	-	-	-	-	0-1	-	-	-	-	-	-	0-1
Tim Foli	-	-	-	-	3-5	-	-	-	-	-	-	3-5
Doug Frobel	-	-	-	-	-	3-6	4-10	-	-	-	-	7-16
Denny Gonzalez	-	-	1-3	9-8	-	5-8	-	-	-	0-1	-	15-19
Cecilio Guante	-	-	-	-	-	-	-	-	-	-	16-47	-
George Hendrick	-	-	-	-	-	-	-	24-40	-	-	-	24-40
Al Holland	-	-	-	-	-	-	-	-	-	-	9-29	-
Steve Kemp	-	-	-	-	-	23-38	-	-	-	-	-	23-38
Sam Khalifa	-	-	-	35-59	-	-	-	-	-	-	-	35-59
Bob Kipper	-	-	-	-	-	-	-	-	1-3	-	1-0	1-3
Ray Krawczyk	-	-	-	-	-	-	-	-	-	-	0-8	-
Johnnie LeMaster	-	-	-	-	7-13	-	-	-	-	0-1	-	7-13
Sixto Lezcano	-	-	-	-	-	5-12	-	3-9	-	-	-	8-21
Scott Loucks	-	-	-	-	-	-	-	0-1	-	-	-	0-1
Bill Madlock	-	3-6	-	33-64	-	-	-	-	-	-	-	36-70
Lee Mazzilli	-	3-9	-	-	-	0-1	0-2	-	-	-	-	3-12
Larry McWilliams	-	-	-	-	-	-	-	-	9-10	-	1-10	9-10
Jim Morrison	-	-	7-5	13-30	-	-	-	-	-	-	-	20-35
Joe Orsulak	-	-	-	-	-	3-12	29-34	3-12	-	25-30	-	35-58
Junior Ortiz	4-16	-	-	-	-	-	-	-	-	-	-	4-16
Tony Pena	53-88	-	-	-	-	-	-	-	-	-	-	53-88
Johnny Ray	-	-	49-96	-	-	-	-	-	-	13-22	-	49-96
Rick Reuschel	-	-	-	-	-	-	-	-	13-13	-	4-1	13-13
R. J. Reynolds	-	-	-	-	-	13-11	2-5	-	-	0-1	-	15-16
Rick Rhoden	-	-	-	-	-	-	-	-	12-23	-	-	12-23
Don Robinson	-	-	-	-	-	-	-	-	2-4	-	11-27	2-4
Rod Scurry	-	-	-	-	-	-	-	-	-	-	4-26	-
Kent Tekulve	-	-	-	-	-	-	-	-	-	-	0-3	-
Jason Thompson	-	38-76	-	-	-	-	-	-	-	-	-	38-76
Dave Tomlin	-	-	-	-	-	-	-	-	-	-	0-1	-
Lee Tunnell	-	-	-	-	-	-	-	-	9-14	-	0-1	9-14
Bob Walk	-	-	-	-	-	-	-	-	3-6	-	-	3-6
Jim Winn	-	-	-	-	-	-	-	-	2-5	-	2-21	2-5
Marvell Wynne	-	-	-	-	-	-	25-60	-	-	9-23	-	25-60

Batting vs. Left and Right Handed Pitchers

		BA	Rank	SA	Rank	OBA	Rank	HR %	Rank	BB %	Rank	SO %	Rank
Bill Almon	vs. Lefties	.277	43	.431	42	.336	59	2.19	68	7.28	87	18.54	110
	vs. Righties	.262	--	.393	--	.322	--	2.80	--	8.94	--	26.83	--
Mike C. Brown	vs. Lefties	.356	1	.492	19	.406	9	1.69	76	7.81	82	10.94	48
	vs. Righties	.322	8	.521	9	.386	13	2.74	44	10.06	47	11.83	60
George Hendrick	vs. Lefties	.202	120	.273	124	.252	125	0.00	108	6.54	98	13.08	71
	vs. Righties	.248	89	.338	96	.294	110	1.27	86	6.47	95	16.47	96
Steve Kemp	vs. Lefties	.214	--	.250	--	.250	--	0.00	--	6.06	--	18.18	--
	vs. Righties	.255	73	.361	86	.326	65	0.96	95	9.87	51	20.60	127
Sammy Khalifa	vs. Lefties	.264	60	.356	83	.343	51	0.00	108	10.78	44	7.84	18
	vs. Righties	.227	117	.305	113	.293	111	0.86	98	8.68	65	18.11	110
Sixto Lezcano	vs. Lefties	.215	110	.342	91	.376	23	3.80	33	19.80	2	8.91	29
	vs. Righties	.189	--	.216	--	.423	--	0.00	--	28.85	--	15.38	--
Jim Morrison	vs. Lefties	.266	56	.349	88	.287	105	0.92	96	3.48	126	13.91	77
	vs. Righties	.244	97	.341	93	.270	127	2.22	58	2.82	133	19.72	121
Joe Orsulak	vs. Lefties	.215	108	.231	129	.224	131	0.00	108	1.41	133	7.04	14
	vs. Righties	.316	9	.392	68	.363	34	0.00	120	6.85	90	6.03	12
Tony Pena	vs. Lefties	.258	68	.344	90	.309	85	1.32	84	6.79	95	9.88	38
	vs. Righties	.246	94	.367	84	.275	123	2.03	64	4.24	126	12.00	64
Johnny Ray	vs. Lefties	.253	73	.335	96	.291	100	0.59	104	5.41	111	9.73	34
	vs. Righties	.283	33	.392	69	.338	58	1.42	78	7.71	79	1.28	1
R.J. Reynolds	vs. Lefties	.261	62	.369	74	.287	105	0.00	108	3.42	128	7.69	17
	vs. Righties	.292	25	.407	57	.345	50	1.33	82	7.06	87	15.69	90
Jason Thompson	vs. Lefties	.260	63	.350	87	.374	25	2.44	61	15.65	11	15.65	91
	vs. Righties	.233	112	.391	71	.367	28	3.23	34	17.78	3	10.20	44
Marvell Wynne	vs. Lefties	.252	76	.306	110	.278	114	0.90	98	3.39	129	16.10	96
	vs. Righties	.181	134	.235	132	.232	134	0.44	113	5.71	109	11.84	61
Team Average	vs. Lefties	.246	9	.334	12	.309	9	1.29	12	8.36	9	13.91	2
	vs. Righties	.247	10	.353	11	.311	10	1.55	11	8.46	7	13.76	7
League Average	vs. Lefties	.250		.374		.317		2.26		8.65		14.84	
	vs. Righties	.253		.374		.320		2.12		8.62		14.28	

Batting with Runners on Base and Bases Empty

		BA	Rank	SA	Rank	OBA	Rank	HR %	Rank	BB %	Rank	SO %	Rank
Bill Almon	Runners On	.242	91	.453	36	.292	114	5.26	13	7.27	105	22.73	132
	Bases Empty	.289	18	.389	60	.354	26	0.67	110	8.54	44	21.95	128
Sid Bream	Runners On	.236	102	.333	98	.352	54	1.39	75	15.38	14	16.48	107
	Bases Empty	.224	--	.461	--	.263	--	6.58	--	5.00	--	11.25	--
Mike C. Brown	Runners On	.292	34	.458	33	.372	38	2.08	59	12.07	42	12.93	75
	Bases Empty	.367	1	.560	4	.410	2	2.75	43	6.84	71	10.26	36
George Hendrick	Runners On	.230	109	.317	108	.281	125	0.79	98	7.19	107	15.83	99
	Bases Empty	.231	103	.308	115	.275	114	0.77	106	5.80	95	14.49	82
Steve Kemp	Runners On	.237	99	.280	122	.318	88	0.00	115	11.71	46	17.12	114
	Bases Empty	.259	63	.392	59	.316	69	1.40	85	7.74	60	22.58	129
Sammy Khalifa	Runners On	.211	126	.268	129	.313	93	0.81	97	12.82	39	16.67	109
	Bases Empty	.254	77	.350	90	.303	83	0.51	115	6.64	75	14.22	79
Jim Morrison	Runners On	.282	47	.336	96	.299	105	0.91	92	2.54	135	13.56	82
	Bases Empty	.231	102	.351	88	.259	125	2.24	57	3.60	129	20.14	122
Joe Orsulak	Runners On	.236	101	.283	121	.284	122	0.00	115	6.71	112	4.70	6
	Bases Empty	.330	5	.404	52	.369	16	0.00	120	5.57	103	6.97	13
Tony Pena	Runners On	.239	95	.352	91	.271	130	2.17	58	4.72	128	11.42	66
	Bases Empty	.256	70	.367	75	.294	98	1.58	79	5.11	111	11.41	50
Johnny Ray	Runners On	.266	68	.386	75	.324	84	1.29	76	8.24	87	4.49	5
	Bases Empty	.280	33	.368	74	.325	60	1.11	94	6.23	84	3.12	2
R.J. Reynolds	Runners On	.308	23	.406	60	.350	56	0.70	103	6.10	119	15.24	92
	Bases Empty	.263	56	.387	63	.309	78	1.03	97	5.77	98	11.54	52
Jason Thompson	Runners On	.286	42	.460	32	.435	4	4.23	23	21.54	1	9.76	48
	Bases Empty	.202	125	.305	119	.303	84	1.88	69	12.70	19	13.93	77
Marvell Wynne	Runners On	.214	125	.260	131	.270	132	0.00	115	6.76	111	10.81	61
	Bases Empty	.199	127	.257	129	.233	134	0.97	99	3.72	126	14.88	87
Team Average	Runners On	.245	10	.341	12	.323	9	1.49	12	10.31	3	13.46	7
	Bases Empty	.248	8	.351	11	.301	10	1.46	12	6.94	10	14.08	3
League Average	Runners On	.258		.381		.332		2.19		9.74		13.69	
	Bases Empty	.248		.369		.309		2.14		7.75		15.05	

Overall Batting Compared to Late Inning Pressure Situations

		BA	Rank	SA	Rank	OBA	Rank	HR %	Rank	BB %	Rank	SO %	Rank	RDI %	Rank
Bill Almon	Overall	.270	52	.414	48	.330	66	2.46	49	8.03	77	22.26	131	.253	93
	Pressure	.341	13	.512	19	.460	2	2.44	50	18.00	10	22.00	116	.125	--
Sid Bream	Overall	.230	--	.399	--	.310	--	4.05	--	10.53	--	14.04	--	.271	--
	Pressure	.240	--	.440	--	.333	--	4.00	--	13.33	--	23.33	--	.333	25
Mike C. Brown	Overall	.332	2	.512	7	.391	7	2.44	50	9.44	52	11.59	57	.307	45
	Pressure	.242	--	.364	--	.265	--	3.03	--	2.86	--	11.43	--	.083	127
George Hendrick	Overall	.230	117	.313	120	.278	127	0.78	108	6.50	106	15.16	90	.247	98
	Pressure	.167	125	.229	126	.200	130	0.00	92	4.00	127	22.00	116	.000	133
Steve Kemp	Overall	.250	91	.347	94	.317	77	0.85	107	9.40	53	20.30	126	.229	111
	Pressure	.362	6	.511	21	.400	24	0.00	92	5.88	109	21.57	114	.154	116
Sammy Khalifa	Overall	.238	108	.319	112	.307	95	0.63	114	9.26	55	15.26	91	.303	51
	Pressure	.271	56	.339	72	.338	63	0.00	92	8.57	69	17.14	91	.083	127
Sixto Lezcano	Overall	.207	--	.302	--	.392	--	2.59	--	22.88	--	11.11	--	.171	--
	Pressure	.184	119	.289	94	.354	50	2.63	43	18.75	8	10.42	37	.071	130
Lee Mazzilli	Overall	.282	--	.376	--	.425	--	0.85	--	19.73	--	11.56	--	.200	--
	Pressure	.333	15	.407	50	.438	7	0.00	92	15.38	16	10.77	40	.211	93
Jim Morrison	Overall	.254	81	.344	98	.277	129	1.64	82	3.11	133	17.12	107	.215	119
	Pressure	.234	87	.383	60	.280	101	4.26	24	5.88	109	15.69	81	.167	109
Joe Orsulak	Overall	.300	14	.365	82	.341	50	0.00	127	5.96	112	6.19	9	.202	127
	Pressure	.215	96	.246	120	.278	103	0.00	92	8.11	77	5.41	9	.333	25
Tony Pena	Overall	.249	92	.361	85	.284	122	1.83	71	4.94	127	11.41	54	.260	86
	Pressure	.196	111	.278	107	.238	124	2.06	62	5.50	116	11.01	43	.290	49
Johnny Ray	Overall	.274	43	.375	76	.325	70	1.18	93	7.06	95	3.68	1	.331	22
	Pressure	.242	79	.303	86	.321	78	0.00	92	10.53	50	5.26	7	.240	73
R.J. Reynolds	Overall	.282	25	.395	66	.327	69	0.89	105	5.91	113	13.17	73	.346	16
	Pressure	.302	31	.524	17	.323	76	1.59	70	2.99	132	22.39	120	.238	75
Jason Thompson	Overall	.241	103	.378	74	.369	22	2.99	40	11.84	60	15.73	83	.313	37
	Pressure	.222	94	.292	92	.371	37	1.39	75	19.10	6	15.73	83	.238	75
Marvell Wynne	Overall	.205	131	.258	132	.247	134	0.59	116	4.96	126	13.22	75	.175	132
	Pressure	.254	69	.286	96	.288	96	0.00	92	4.35	124	10.14	33	.158	114
Team Average	Overall	.247	9	.347	12	.311	10	1.47	12	8.43	8	13.81	5	.252	11
	Pressure	.251	9	.339	11	.325	9	1.14	12	9.59	5	13.94	3	.208	12
League Average	Overall	.252		.374		.319		2.16		8.63		14.45		.273	
	Pressure	.253		.368		.325		2.17		9.26		15.10		.257	

Additional Miscellaneous Batting Comparisons

	Grass Surface BA	Rank	Artificial Surface BA	Rank	Home Games BA	Rank	Road Games BA	Rank	Runners in Scoring Position BA	Rank	Runners in Scoring Pos and Two Outs BA	Rank	Leading Off Inning OBA	Rank	Runners on 3B with less than 2 Outs RDI %	Rank
Bill Almon	.208	122	.299	24	.345	7	.206	121	.232	100	.194	105	.391	15	.571	75
Sid Bream	.185	--	.265	60	.214	--	.239	95	.268	68	.273	44	.250	--	.286	--
Mike C. Brown	.323	--	.333	6	.296	35	.364	1	.317	21	.407	2	.446	1	.611	55
Denny Gonzalez	.200	--	.229	107	.206	--	.246	--	.257	--	.375	--	.306	--	.250	--
George Hendrick	.159	--	.257	74	.242	98	.215	112	.286	44	.263	56	.281	101	.563	86
Steve Kemp	.254	--	.248	87	.275	59	.231	105	.200	123	.207	98	.276	107	.818	5
Sammy Khalifa	.173	128	.259	70	.255	86	.219	110	.205	120	.147	126	.259	122	.636	44
Sixto Lezcano	.222	--	.200	130	.227	--	.180	--	.143	--	.083	--	.424	--	.667	--
Lee Mazzilli	.140	--	.365	1	.327	--	.250	--	.233	--	.200	--	.483	--	.200	--
Jim Morrison	.262	--	.252	83	.258	81	.250	83	.238	91	.231	75	.241	126	.381	131
Joe Orsulak	.226	105	.322	11	.370	1	.239	94	.211	112	.209	95	.387	18	.545	90
Tony Pena	.212	119	.262	67	.246	95	.252	80	.267	71	.212	89	.288	95	.545	90
Johnny Ray	.248	79	.284	31	.291	40	.259	65	.296	33	.333	11	.293	92	.600	59
R.J. Reynolds	.281	42	.282	32	.300	29	.267	53	.298	32	.270	48	.307	82	.583	68
Jason Thompson	.349	2	.203	129	.200	126	.289	23	.308	28	.279	41	.282	100	.722	15
Marvell Wynne	.155	132	.225	112	.234	105	.179	132	.235	97	.250	66	.260	121	.400	127
Team Average	.223	11	.255	7	.260	5	.234	12	.250	8	.242	6	.312	9	.534	12
League Average	.251		.254		.256		.248		.257		.235		.315		.576	

Pitching vs. Left and Right Handed Batters

		BA	Rank	SA	Rank	OBA	Rank	HR %	Rank	BB %	Rank	SO %	Rank
Mike Bielecki	vs. Lefties	.257	53	.404	78	.341	69	2.75	97	10.40	80	7.20	102
	vs. Righties	.258	--	.394	--	.417	--	3.03	--	20.93	--	15.12	--
John Candelaria	vs. Lefties	.204	--	.265	--	.200	--	0.00	--	0.00	--	34.00	--
	vs. Righties	.297	109	.525	113	.352	102	4.43	112	7.82	56	16.76	51
Jose DeLeon	vs. Lefties	.277	76	.414	86	.389	99	2.46	88	15.04	107	13.86	40
	vs. Righties	.189	8	.304	19	.278	25	2.56	73	10.53	92	28.25	3
Cecilio Guante	vs. Lefties	.289	92	.447	100	.394	104	1.97	75	13.26	98	12.71	48
	vs. Righties	.166	4	.253	5	.222	1	0.83	9	6.06	25	26.14	10
Al Holland	vs. Lefties	.246	--	.377	--	.286	--	2.90	--	6.33	--	22.78	--
	vs. Righties	.229	41	.369	66	.299	47	1.91	34	9.04	74	16.95	47
Larry McWilliams	vs. Lefties	.329	111	.500	109	.393	103	2.63	93	6.98	30	11.63	60
	vs. Righties	.274	94	.416	92	.365	108	1.68	29	11.62	103	8.71	109
Rick Reuschel	vs. Lefties	.224	28	.308	25	.283	22	0.93	31	7.37	38	10.48	72
	vs. Righties	.208	17	.280	10	.261	14	1.03	12	6.19	28	24.05	11
Rick Rhoden	vs. Lefties	.306	101	.425	92	.360	85	1.39	58	7.40	39	11.21	65
	vs. Righties	.285	101	.442	102	.345	95	2.80	81	7.22	48	15.92	58
Don Robinson	vs. Lefties	.242	42	.291	16	.339	67	0.00	1	12.63	94	15.79	32
	vs. Righties	.266	82	.420	95	.330	79	2.90	88	7.89	57	15.35	59
Lee Tunnell	vs. Lefties	.274	72	.375	63	.372	93	1.61	62	13.10	96	8.97	87
	vs. Righties	.228	39	.362	57	.281	29	2.76	79	6.91	42	17.45	40
Bob Walk	vs. Lefties	.281	78	.367	57	.326	56	0.78	22	6.43	23	12.86	46
	vs. Righties	.245	--	.378	--	.308	--	2.04	--	8.33	--	20.37	--
Jim Winn	vs. Lefties	.288	90	.349	46	.350	76	1.37	55	8.75	56	6.25	110
	vs. Righties	.243	58	.319	25	.329	78	1.39	19	10.24	89	7.23	113
Team Average	vs. Lefties	.275	10	.381	7	.350	11	1.48	5	10.03	9	12.49	6
	vs. Righties	.241	6	.374	7	.313	8	2.28	3	8.96	8	17.68	2
League Average	vs. Lefties	.262		.374		.330		1.73		9.17		12.66	
	vs. Righties	.246		.374		.311		2.44		8.28		15.62	

Pitching with Runners on Base and Bases Empty

		BA	Rank	SA	Rank	OBA	Rank	HR %	Rank	BB %	Rank	SO %	Rank
Jose DeLeon	Runners On	.251	53	.401	76	.322	46	3.37	97	9.42	52	20.45	12
	Bases Empty	.215	21	.321	29	.339	96	1.82	51	15.31	114	21.94	14
Cecilio Guante	Runners On	.196	7	.313	17	.298	23	1.23	22	12.31	90	17.95	23
	Bases Empty	.226	28	.339	38	.288	32	1.30	25	6.40	39	22.80	10
Al Holland	Runners On	.255	--	.388	--	.319	--	1.02	--	9.32	--	11.02	--
	Bases Empty	.219	24	.359	51	.275	23	3.13	97	7.25	51	25.36	6
Larry McWilliams	Runners On	.253	56	.378	61	.354	86	1.72	41	12.59	92	8.99	96
	Bases Empty	.309	114	.475	110	.383	113	1.93	55	9.31	82	9.31	103
Rick Reuschel	Runners On	.224	21	.298	13	.312	32	0.78	8	10.77	72	16.50	29
	Bases Empty	.211	19	.290	17	.246	4	1.10	15	4.20	12	18.70	25
Rick Rhoden	Runners On	.293	101	.404	78	.364	95	1.33	25	8.41	35	13.79	56
	Bases Empty	.298	111	.455	107	.343	99	2.69	88	6.40	38	13.37	71
Don Robinson	Runners On	.286	97	.405	79	.378	98	2.38	72	12.82	95	12.82	59
	Bases Empty	.230	32	.328	34	.296	41	0.98	14	7.62	56	17.94	35
Lee Tunnell	Runners On	.269	76	.433	90	.358	91	3.48	102	11.91	85	12.34	69
	Bases Empty	.239	46	.326	32	.306	59	1.33	27	8.79	76	13.64	68
Bob Walk	Runners On	.282	--	.376	--	.340	--	1.18	--	8.25	--	17.53	--
	Bases Empty	.255	68	.369	68	.305	54	1.42	35	6.62	43	15.23	50
Jim Winn	Runners On	.283	95	.370	58	.383	103	1.57	33	13.25	103	9.27	94
	Bases Empty	.252	61	.307	24	.303	49	1.23	19	6.29	37	4.57	115
Team Average	Runners On	.268	10	.397	10	.354	11	2.24	7	11.25	11	14.67	3
	Bases Empty	.246	7	.362	6	.309	8	1.72	2	7.92	7	16.18	5
League Average	Runners On	.258		.381		.332		2.19		9.74		13.69	
	Bases Empty	.248		.369		.309		2.14		7.75		15.05	

Overall Pitching Compared to Late Inning Pressure Situations

		BA	Rank	SA	Rank	OBA	Rank	HR %	Rank	BB %	Rank	SO %	Rank
John Candelaria	Overall	.275	--	.464	--	.319	--	3.38	--	6.11	--	20.52	--
	Pressure	.233	43	.367	60	.270	20	2.00	65	5.42	14	22.89	14
Pat Clements	Overall	.289	--	.415	--	.358	--	1.48	--	9.80	--	11.11	--
	Pressure	.324	108	.423	86	.410	106	0.00	1	12.94	92	7.06	102
Jose DeLeon	Overall	.231	30	.357	40	.332	78	2.51	84	12.71	104	21.29	11
	Pressure	.324	107	.500	105	.397	98	2.94	84	11.11	77	20.99	19
Cecilio Guante	Overall	.214	12	.328	22	.293	25	1.27	17	8.99	66	20.67	14
	Pressure	.214	27	.323	33	.306	44	1.49	44	10.82	73	17.32	30
Al Holland	Overall	.235	34	.372	62	.295	28	2.21	66	8.20	50	18.75	21
	Pressure	.295	90	.438	91	.348	74	1.90	62	7.63	29	15.25	47
Larry McWilliams	Overall	.283	101	.429	102	.369	111	1.83	47	10.92	91	9.15	111
	Pressure	.290	88	.419	84	.421	109	3.23	90	18.42	114	5.26	112
Rick Reuschel	Overall	.215	14	.293	9	.271	10	0.99	9	6.73	23	17.85	29
	Pressure	.255	67	.368	63	.313	51	1.89	60	7.76	31	15.52	44
Rick Rhoden	Overall	.296	103	.433	103	.352	100	2.10	56	7.31	37	13.56	68
	Pressure	.343	110	.514	108	.425	110	1.43	41	12.05	87	18.07	27
Don Robinson	Overall	.255	67	.363	55	.334	80	1.61	33	10.05	80	15.55	42
	Pressure	.239	49	.341	41	.335	65	1.45	42	11.32	78	16.35	40
Rod Scurry	Overall	.236	--	.371	--	.337	--	2.25	--	13.33	--	20.48	--
	Pressure	.210	24	.371	64	.279	25	3.23	90	8.70	50	23.19	12
Lee Tunnell	Overall	.251	59	.369	60	.327	71	2.19	65	10.09	81	13.10	71
	Pressure	.205	19	.359	53	.295	39	5.13	109	11.36	79	20.45	20
Jim Winn	Overall	.266	86	.334	26	.340	87	1.38	20	9.51	74	6.75	114
	Pressure	.318	104	.341	42	.412	107	0.00	1	11.76	85	7.84	96
Team Average	Overall	.255	8	.377	8	.329	9	1.94	4	9.41	10	15.50	4
	Pressure	.267	10	.390	11	.344	11	1.81	3	10.17	10	16.71	3
League Average	Overall	.252		.374		.319		2.16		8.63		14.45	
	Pressure	.249		.363		.326		2.12		9.92		15.33	

Additional Miscellaneous Pitching Comparisons

	Grass Surface		Artificial Surface		Home Games		Road Games		Runners in Scoring Position		Runners in Scoring Pos and Two Outs		Leading Off Inning	
	BA	Rank	BA	Rank	BA	Rank	BA	Rank	BA	Rank	BA	Rank	OBA	Rank
Mike Bielecki	.214	--	.277	85	.313	--	.190	--	.302	--	.400	117	.370	--
John Candelaria	.213	--	.311	107	.279	--	.272	--	.235	42	.182	22	.378	--
Pat Clements	.500	--	.261	64	.275	--	.303	--	.350	--	.368	--	.394	--
Jose DeLeon	.219	19	.235	33	.215	23	.253	57	.253	55	.143	8	.369	99
Cecilio Guante	.220	20	.211	13	.198	12	.230	29	.200	13	.179	20	.287	34
Al Holland	.277	--	.223	22	.186	6	.314	--	.267	66	.300	100	.268	20
Larry McWilliams	.283	90	.282	90	.311	110	.258	67	.280	81	.290	92	.389	107
Rick Reuschel	.215	17	.216	18	.208	17	.226	26	.222	25	.258	77	.236	5
Rick Rhoden	.282	89	.301	100	.302	103	.288	102	.306	102	.294	95	.387	106
Don Robinson	.227	31	.263	67	.269	82	.244	41	.286	88	.224	49	.260	13
Rod Scurry	.274	--	.216	17	.226	--	.240	37	.408	--	.417	118	.250	--
Lee Tunnell	.266	76	.248	48	.247	60	.256	61	.282	87	.239	64	.326	75
Bob Walk	.269	--	.265	73	.295	--	.258	66	.280	--	.250	--	.311	61
Jim Winn	.250	--	.270	77	.243	--	.278	90	.260	61	.219	44	.354	91
Team Average	.254	7	.256	9	.252	7	.259	6	.278	12	.264	12	.328	9
League Average	.251		.254		.248		.256		.257		.235		.315	

ST. LOUIS CARDINALS

From anticipated also-rans to surprising contenders, to dominating division champions, to heroic playoff victors, to disappointing World Series spoilsports—the 1985 Cardinals truly captured the attention of the nation in all their various guises.

The Cardinals' compelling season actually started well before opening day; the real beginning was on December 7, 1984, a date now forgotten, but one that many felt would live in infamy for the Cards. That was the day on which Bruce Sutter, the all-world relief star, signed with the Braves as a free agent. Sutter had accounted for 127 of the Cardinals' 158 saves during his four seasons with them, and in the wake of his departure, the bullpen cupboard looked bare.

Just five days after Sutter signed with Atlanta, however, the Cardinals' fortunes began to turn, as they acquired John Tudor from the Pirates. Then, in February, the Redbirds got Jack Clark from the Giants. Tudor won 21 games, Clark hit 22 home runs, and both of their former clubs finished last, losing 100 or more games.

No pennant- or division-winning team had acquired both a 20-game winner and a 20-home-run hitter in trades during the previous off-season since the 1961 Reds. (Cincinnati picked up Joey Jay from the Braves and Gene Freese from the White Sox on the same day, December 15, 1960; Jay won 21 games and Freese hit 26 homers for the pennant-winning Reds.)

Still, while Tudor and Clark were regarded as good players, their reputations last spring were a mile short of what they are as you read this. Blend in the fact that Willie McGee and Tommy Herr were not yet doing their impressions of Tris Speaker and Charlie Gehringer, and the fact that Danny Cox's career major-league record was only 9–11, and you can understand why Cardinals fans might have felt uneasy at the start of the season.

That uneasy feeling was reinforced when the Cardinals became the first National League team since the '43 Cardinals to begin a season with back-to-back extra-inning losses. But older Cardinal fans may have recalled that their team of 42 years earlier, which lost consecutive 1–0 extra-inning games at Cincinnati to open the season, went on to win 105 games and take the National League pennant before losing the World Series. Thoughts of such events taking place in 1985, however, would have been regarded as pipe dreams.

Things started to look up less than 10 days later. That's when the Cardinals made their other significant acquisition of 1985, not from Pittsburgh or San Francisco, but from Louisville. Vince Coleman arrived from Triple-A on Thursday, April 18, in time for the Cardinals' eighth game of the season. By Sunday afternoon, he was tied for the league lead in stolen bases; he took the lead for good on April 25, and was never headed.

'Cause Champs Like Us, Baby, We Were Born to Run

Much has been made of the Cardinals' team speed being the primary factor in their success. St. Louis wasn't the first team ever to run its way to a pennant, and won't be the last, but speed teams are constantly under criticism for, among other things, not being able to come from behind; not being capable of producing the big inning; and playing poorly on grass fields. Well, the Cardinals took care of all three criticisms:

(1) The Cardinals won 11 of the 60 games in which they trailed going into the seventh inning—the second-best rate in the National League. (Don't be fooled by the "11-of-60" figure; the overall league percentage for teams trailing going into the seventh was .122; the Cardinals' percentage was .183. Only the Dodgers, with .190 on a record of 11–47, were better.)

(2) The Cardinals produced 84 innings of three or more runs, the most by any National League team. (The league average was 70; curiously, the team leading the league in home runs, Chicago, had exactly 70.)

(3) The Cardinals had a better record on grass fields (27–15, .643) than they did on artificial surfaces (74–46, .617).

Don't count on this little rebuttal to lay to rest those misconceptions. You see, when the Cardinals won the pennant in 1982 with a speed team, they also came back well (exactly the same 11–49 record when trailing after six), produced big innings (76 of at least three runs), and played better on grass than on plastic (27–15, .643, as opposed to 65–55, .542). But even with a World Series victory in 1982, people didn't revise their opinions about the capabilities of such a team, so a little old National League pennant, even with 101 victories, is unlikely to sway anybody this time.

Rob from the Rich, Rob More from the Poor

The Cardinals went about amassing their 101 victories less like a deft pickpocket than like a bullying thug; St. Louis beat up on the weak sisters of the National League to an extraordinary degree. The Cards went 15–3 against Pittsburgh, 10–2 against San Francisco, and 9–3 against Atlanta, for a combined mark of 34–8 (.810) against the three National League teams with won-lost percentages below .450. Here are the records of all 12 National League teams, broken down according to the quality of the opponent:

	Vs. Teams above .550		Vs. Teams .450–.550		Vs. Teams below .450		Total	
	W–L	Pct.	W–L	Pct.	W–L	Pct.	W–L	Pct.
St. Louis	22–20	.524	45–33	.577	34–8	.810	101–61	.623
New York	21–21	.500	49–29	.628	28–14	.667	98–64	.605
Montreal	29–31	.483	30–30	.500	25–16	.610	84–77	.522
Chicago	18–41	.305	33–27	.550	26–16	.619	77–84	.478
Philadelphia	28–32	.467	28–32	.467	19–23	.452	75–87	.463
Pittsburgh	18–42	.300	30–47	.390	9–15	.375	57–104	.354
Los Angeles	25–17	.595	38–34	.528	32–16	.667	95–67	.586
Cincinnati	16–26	.381	41–30	.577	32–16	.667	89–72	.553
Houston	23–37	.383	29–25	.537	31–17	.646	83–79	.512
San Diego	28–32	.467	24–30	.444	31–17	.646	83–79	.512
Atlanta	17–43	.283	33–39	.458	16–14	.533	66–96	.407
San Francisco	19–41	.317	26–46	.361	17–13	.567	62–100	.383

The chart documents that the Cardinals dominated the sub-.450 teams to a greater degree than any other National League team last year. But was that won-lost breakdown typical or atypical of a team finishing in first place?

To answer that question, we compared the Cardinals' breakdown last season with similar breakdowns for all National League division-winning teams over the previous 10 seasons. (The 1981 strike season is excluded, so the composite totals represent 18 team-years.) The results are revealing.

	Vs. Teams above .550		Vs. Teams .450–.550		Vs. Teams below .450		Total	
18-team Composite	234–211	.526	1004–747	.573	471–247	.656	1709–1205	.586
1985 Cardinals	22–20	.524	45–33	.577	34–8	.810	101–61	.623

The Cardinals matched the performance of the composite of the division winners against the plus-.550 group and against the middle group. It was against the lower rung of teams that they made their mark, and they had to; the typical division winner didn't have a .605 team breathing down its neck all year. You have to go back to the 1963 Dodgers to find the last National League division- or pennant-winner with an .800 won-lost percentage against sub-.450 teams. Only ten of the 101 N.L. pennant- or division-winners since 1900 (excluding 1981) have played that well against the bottom of the league. The Cardinals won the pennant because of their remarkable performance against sub-.450 teams, a performance that was far from typical. We often hear of teams that were successful because they won the games they had to win. We usually think that refers to games against other contenders; as the '85 Cardinals demonstrated, that's not necessarily the case.

The Bullpen By Committee

As a public service, we were going to refrain from any reference to what emerged as one of last season's new baseball cliches, its own version of the BBC, the Bullpen By Committee. But just this once, we'll discuss it, and then you can go on to the rest of the book, secure in the knowledge that you won't encounter the phrase again. (In fact, if you're still reeling from the countless references to the Committee during last August, September, and October, you're excused and can go on to the San Diego essay right now.)

What the overuse of that buzzphrase did was to obscure the very different capabilities and strategic uses of the individuals Whitey Herzog counted on so often down the stretch and in post-season play. Herzog replaced Sutter not with one man, but with four: Ken Dayley and Ricky Horton, the left-handers, and Jeff Lahti and Todd Worrell, the right-handers. True, they formed a bullpen. But a committee? Is a batting order called an "Offense By Committee"? Of course not, yet each player has specific strengths and is used, in some cases, for specialized purposes.

The image evoked by lumping the four key relievers together was that of a ball being tossed into the air, and whichever of the four came down with it heading for the mound. It's too late to undo much of the damage here, but for historical purposes, here are the particular strengths, weaknesses and uses of each pitcher:

Dayley is a strikeout pitcher who was frequently used in small doses to get out particular batters. From September 1 until the end of the regular season, eight of his 12 appearances lasted less than an inning.

Horton was more likely to be the long man as needed, pitching three or more innings nine times during the season. He also started three games in September. Compared with Dayley, who throws over the top, Horton is more of a sidearmer, and accordingly is more effective against left-handed batters than Dayley.

Lahti was the closer for most of the season, and led National League relievers in the ratio of double-play grounders to innings pitched. He was so good at keeping the ball away from left-handed power hitters that from June 7 until the end of the season, lefty swingers had only two extra-base hits against him, both of them doubles. He did not allow a home run to a left-handed batter all year.

Worrell, called up from Louisville on August 27, was usually used as a closer and, including post-season play, had 26 strikeouts in 32 2/3 innings.

Herzog's mastery in playing the left-right game is what pulled the whole fabric together and made it work. In the Cardinals' most important game of the regular season, the 4–3 victory over the Mets on October 3 that kept New York from pulling into a tie for first with three to play, it was Herzog who had the upper hand over Davey Johnson. Look at how Herzog was able to orchestrate the key matchups in the late innings:

Seventh inning, 4–2 St. Louis lead, no outs, one on: Herzog brought in Dayley to replace starter Danny Cox. That turned Mookie Wilson around to the right side; Wilson struck out. Tom Paciorek struck out pinch-hitting for Wally Backman, a good left-handed bat who would be missed later in the game. Keith Hernandez then doubled, setting up. . . .

Seventh inning, 4–2 St. Louis lead, two outs, two on: Worrell came in to face Gary Carter, who popped out to the infield with the tying runs in scoring position.

Eighth inning, 4–3 St. Louis lead, one out, one on: After the Mets had scored once, and with the tying run on first, Danny Heep was announced to bat for Rafael Santana. Herzog responded with Horton. That left Johnson with the options of letting Heep bat (.234 career vs. left-handers), or wasting him in favor of Ray Knight (1-for-16 as a pinch-hitter in 1985). Johnson went with Knight, who flied to short center; he then had to leave up weak-hitting Ron Gardenhire, who had replaced Backman on a double switch. Gardenhire, who hadn't had a major-league hit in two months, struck out.

Ninth inning, 4–3 St. Louis lead, two out, one on: With the tying run again on base and Carter coming up, Herzog went to Lahti, who retired Carter on a soft fly to right to end the game.

Four individuals, each operating at peak efficiency, each doing the things he does best. Does that sound like any committee that you've ever known?

Now, as we promised, not another word about the BBC. (But we're not making *any* promises about "One Tough Dominican"!)

WON-LOST RECORD BY STARTING POSITION

ST. LOUIS 101-61	C	1B	2B	3B	SS	LF	CF	RF	P	Leadoff	Relief	Starts
Neil Allen	-	-	-	-	-	-	-	-	0-1	-	4-18	0-1
Joaquin Andujar	-	-	-	-	-	-	-	-	22-16	-	-	22-16
Doug Bair	-	-	-	-	-	-	-	-	-	-	0-2	-
Joe Boever	-	-	-	-	-	-	-	-	-	-	3-10	-
Steve Braun	-	-	-	-	-	1-1	-	0-3	-	-	-	1-4
Bill Campbell	-	-	-	-	-	-	-	-	-	-	21-29	-
Cesar Cedeno	-	10-6	-	-	-	-	-	1-0	-	-	-	11-6
Jack Clark	-	74-47	-	-	-	-	-	2-2	-	-	-	76-49
Vince Coleman	-	-	-	-	-	86-44	5-4	5-5	-	96-53	-	96-53
Danny Cox	-	-	-	-	-	-	-	-	23-12	-	-	23-12
Ken Dayley	-	-	-	-	-	-	-	-	-	-	30-27	-
Ivan DeJesus	-	-	-	5-2	2-2	-	-	-	-	-	-	7-4
Curt Ford	-	-	-	-	-	0-1	0-0	1-0	-	0-1	-	1-1
Bob Forsch	-	-	-	-	-	-	-	-	12-7	-	4-11	12-7
Brian Harper	-	-	-	2-1	-	1-0	-	1-1	-	-	-	4-2
Andy Hassler	-	-	-	-	-	-	-	-	-	-	2-8	-
Tom Herr	-	-	99-59	-	-	-	-	-	-	2-3	-	99-59
Ricky Horton	-	-	-	-	-	-	-	2-1	-	-	18-28	2-1
Art Howe	-	-	-	-	-	-	-	-	-	-	-	-
Randy Hunt	1-2	-	-	-	-	-	-	-	-	-	-	1-2
Mike Jorgensen	-	17-8	-	-	-	-	-	-	-	-	-	17-8
Matt Keough	-	-	-	-	-	-	-	0-1	-	-	2-1	0-1
Kurt Kepshire	-	-	-	-	-	-	-	18-11	-	-	1-2	18-11
Jeff Lahti	-	-	-	-	-	-	-	-	-	-	34-18	-
Tito Landrum	-	-	-	-	-	1-0	-	20-17	-	1-0	-	21-17
Mike Lavalliere	6-5	-	-	-	-	-	-	-	-	-	-	6-5
Tom Lawless	-	-	2-2	6-1	-	-	-	-	-	-	-	8-3
Willie McGee	-	-	-	-	-	-	95-51	-	-	1-1	-	95-51
Tom Nieto	51-29	-	-	-	-	-	-	-	-	-	-	51-29
Terry Pendleton	-	-	-	88-57	-	-	-	-	-	-	-	88-57
Pat Perry	-	-	-	-	-	-	-	-	-	-	3-3	-
Darrell Porter	43-25	-	-	-	-	-	-	-	-	-	-	43-25
Lonnie Smith	-	-	-	-	-	12-15	-	-	-	1-3	-	12-15
Ozzie Smith	-	-	-	-	99-59	-	-	-	-	-	-	99-59
John Tudor	-	-	-	-	-	-	-	-	24-12	-	-	24-12
Andy Van Slyke	-	-	-	-	-	-	1-6	71-33	-	-	-	72-39
Todd Worrell	-	-	-	-	-	-	-	-	-	-	12-5	-

Batting vs. Left and Right Handed Pitchers

		BA	Rank	SA	Rank	OBA	Rank	HR %	Rank	BB %	Rank	SO %	Rank
Cesar Cedeno	vs. Lefties	.319	11	.496	18	.390	14	3.70	35	9.74	56	8.44	25
	vs. Righties	.267	56	.398	63	.308	91	2.48	51	5.20	117	16.76	100
Jack Clark	vs. Lefties	.324	9	.597	2	.467	1	6.47	7	21.67	1	11.11	50
	vs. Righties	.261	65	.459	20	.355	41	4.29	16	12.50	27	19.32	119
Vince Coleman	vs. Lefties	.237	92	.341	92	.284	110	0.00	108	6.19	101	17.26	102
	vs. Righties	.282	35	.332	102	.338	57	0.24	119	7.73	78	16.31	94
Tom Herr	vs. Lefties	.283	38	.373	72	.333	62	1.42	82	7.30	86	5.58	6
	vs. Righties	.313	13	.440	30	.402	7	1.30	84	13.61	21	9.07	31
Mike Jorgensen	vs. Lefties	.300	--	.300	--	.417	--	0.00	--	14.29	--	0.00	--
	vs. Righties	.186	133	.245	131	.371	22	0.00	120	21.97	2	20.45	126
Tito Landrum	vs. Lefties	.265	59	.394	59	.353	39	2.27	64	12.00	37	18.00	108
	vs. Righties	.345	--	.586	--	.367	--	3.45	--	3.23	--	9.68	--
Willie McGee	vs. Lefties	.348	2	.571	4	.372	26	3.33	42	4.48	120	22.87	125
	vs. Righties	.356	1	.468	17	.390	12	0.75	103	5.59	111	8.16	23
Tom Nieto	vs. Lefties	.210	115	.266	126	.285	109	0.00	108	9.29	63	12.14	66
	vs. Righties	.240	102	.295	120	.324	67	0.00	120	8.78	64	13.51	75
Terry Pendleton	vs. Lefties	.228	101	.298	114	.257	123	1.17	87	3.87	124	11.60	55
	vs. Righties	.245	96	.309	108	.298	108	0.77	101	7.13	86	12.83	70
Darrell Porter	vs. Lefties	.184	--	.289	--	.295	--	2.63	--	13.64	--	20.45	--
	vs. Righties	.228	116	.436	37	.342	54	4.46	15	14.58	12	16.25	93
Ozzie Smith	vs. Lefties	.298	23	.484	24	.407	8	3.73	34	15.38	14	7.18	16
	vs. Righties	.266	58	.309	111	.330	63	0.00	120	8.33	67	3.10	3
Andy Van Slyke	vs. Lefties	.111	134	.148	134	.158	134	0.00	108	5.17	113	18.97	111
	vs. Righties	.281	36	.481	12	.360	38	3.51	29	10.55	38	10.31	45
Team Average	vs. Lefties	.257	2	.382	4	.326	2	1.91	11	9.33	2	15.11	7
	vs. Righties	.268	1	.377	7	.340	1	1.44	12	9.55	2	13.17	3
League Average	vs. Lefties	.250		.374		.317		2.26		8.65		14.84	
	vs. Righties	.253		.374		.320		2.12		8.62		14.28	

Batting with Runners on Base and Bases Empty

		BA	Rank	SA	Rank	OBA	Rank	HR %	Rank	BB %	Rank	SO %	Rank
Cesar Cedeno	Runners On	.354	4	.497	15	.395	19	3.40	39	7.36	101	9.82	50
	Bases Empty	.228	107	.389	60	.299	91	2.68	44	7.32	66	15.85	91
Jack Clark	Runners On	.283	45	.506	12	.379	31	4.72	18	14.08	24	16.61	108
	Bases Empty	.278	39	.498	12	.408	3	5.26	10	17.25	2	16.47	95
Vince Coleman	Runners On	.253	80	.320	107	.301	102	0.00	115	6.54	115	13.08	77
	Bases Empty	.274	44	.342	98	.328	55	0.23	119	7.53	62	18.20	105
Tom Herr	Runners On	.357	3	.483	24	.411	8	1.02	89	10.06	66	6.61	12
	Bases Empty	.248	84	.351	87	.348	33	1.66	76	12.93	16	9.20	27
Tito Landrum	Runners On	.306	24	.471	27	.372	37	3.53	34	9.47	74	20.00	127
	Bases Empty	.250	--	.382	--	.337	--	1.32	--	11.63	--	12.79	--
Willie McGee	Runners On	.360	2	.510	8	.404	14	1.98	63	7.83	96	12.46	70
	Bases Empty	.348	2	.499	11	.369	17	1.39	86	3.23	130	13.75	74
Tom Nieto	Runners On	.267	66	.336	96	.356	51	0.00	115	10.14	65	12.32	69
	Bases Empty	.190	132	.234	131	.260	123	0.00	120	8.00	53	13.33	68
Terry Pendleton	Runners On	.250	82	.311	111	.295	109	0.71	101	6.23	118	11.15	62
	Bases Empty	.229	104	.301	121	.276	112	1.08	95	6.06	89	13.80	75
Darrell Porter	Runners On	.206	131	.327	102	.331	74	2.80	48	16.15	10	16.92	111
	Bases Empty	.233	101	.481	17	.338	41	5.26	10	12.99	15	16.88	97
Ozzie Smith	Runners On	.295	32	.357	87	.386	23	0.88	96	12.45	41	4.03	3
	Bases Empty	.261	61	.365	78	.330	52	1.29	89	9.06	39	4.68	41
Andy Van Slyke	Runners On	.235	103	.407	58	.326	78	2.94	46	11.54	48	14.53	86
	Bases Empty	.282	27	.468	22	.344	37	3.18	37	8.30	49	8.30	20
Team Average	Runners On	.274	2	.387	6	.344	1	1.60	11	9.70	9	13.16	5
	Bases Empty	.257	2	.372	7	.328	1	1.59	11	9.29	1	14.34	5
League Average	Runners On	.258		.381		.332		2.19		9.74		13.69	
	Bases Empty	.248		.369		.309		2.14		7.75		15.05	

Overall Batting Compared to Late Inning Pressure Situations

		BA	Rank	SA	Rank	OBA	Rank	HR %	Rank	BB %	Rank	SO %	Rank	RDI %	Rank
Steve Braun	Overall	.239	--	.343	--	.342	--	1.49	--	12.66	--	11.39	--	.316	--
	Pressure	.344	--	.531	--	.432	--	3.13	--	13.51	--	8.11	--	.417	8
Cesar Cedeno	Overall	.291	19	.443	27	.347	43	3.04	38	7.34	88	12.84	69	.305	48
	Pressure	.298	35	.561	12	.344	60	7.02	10	6.45	104	11.29	45	.240	73
Jack Clark	Overall	.281	30	.502	11	.393	6	4.98	12	15.60	6	16.54	102	.327	27
	Pressure	.333	15	.517	18	.459	3	3.33	34	18.92	7	18.92	105	.333	25
Vince Coleman	Overall	.267	60	.335	106	.320	72	0.16	126	7.23	90	16.62	103	.262	84
	Pressure	.243	78	.338	75	.300	91	0.00	92	7.14	97	16.67	89	.526	2
Brian Harper	Overall	.250	--	.327	--	.273	--	0.00	--	3.64	--	5.45	--	.269	--
	Pressure	.333	--	.429	--	.348	--	0.00	--	4.35	--	4.35	--	.273	55
Tom Herr	Overall	.302	12	.416	46	.379	16	1.34	87	11.49	25	7.90	17	.409	2
	Pressure	.314	25	.442	40	.371	35	3.49	33	8.16	75	5.10	5	.267	58
Mike Jorgensen	Overall	.196	--	.250	--	.375	--	0.00	--	21.23	--	18.49	--	.224	--
	Pressure	.182	--	.227	--	.379	--	0.00	--	23.33	--	20.00	--	.250	64
Tito Landrum	Overall	.280	--	.429	--	.356	--	2.48	--	10.50	--	16.57	--	.245	99
	Pressure	.313	26	.469	29	.405	22	3.13	38	13.16	26	18.42	98	.100	124
Willie McGee	Overall	.353	1	.503	10	.384	14	1.63	83	5.21	121	13.19	74	.355	11
	Pressure	.321	20	.506	22	.345	59	3.70	32	3.57	131	16.67	89	.391	14
Tom Nieto	Overall	.225	120	.281	127	.305	99	0.00	127	9.03	61	12.85	70	.323	30
	Pressure	.258	--	.258	--	.343	--	0.00	--	11.11	--	13.89	--	.250	64
Terry Pendleton	Overall	.240	106	.306	121	.285	120	0.89	104	6.15	110	12.46	63	.300	55
	Pressure	.253	71	.402	54	.316	81	1.15	81	8.33	73	19.79	108	.280	54
Darrell Porter	Overall	.221	122	.413	50	.335	55	4.17	22	14.44	10	16.90	104	.275	75
	Pressure	.186	118	.279	104	.239	123	2.33	53	6.52	103	15.22	76	.400	10
Ozzie Smith	Overall	.276	40	.361	83	.355	38	1.12	96	10.57	43	4.39	4	.278	74
	Pressure	.230	92	.276	109	.302	90	1.15	81	9.28	64	8.25	19	.167	109
Andy Van Slyke	Overall	.259	77	.439	30	.335	53	3.07	37	9.89	49	11.37	52	.281	73
	Pressure	.190	114	.238	123	.271	108	0.00	92	8.57	69	12.86	61	.211	93
Team Average	Overall	.264	1	.379	6	.335	1	1.59	11	9.48	1	13.80	4	.300	1
	Pressure	.261	4	.378	5	.335	2	1.87	9	9.67	2	14.62	6	.272	4
League Average	Overall	.252		.374		.319		2.16		8.63		14.45		.273	
	Pressure	.253		.368		.325		2.17		9.26		15.10		.257	

Additional Miscellaneous Batting Comparisons

	Grass Surface BA	Rank	Artificial Surface BA	Rank	Home Games BA	Rank	Road Games BA	Rank	Runners in Scoring Position BA	Rank	Runners in Scoring Pos and Two Outs BA	Rank	Leading Off Inning OBA	Rank	Runners on 3B with less than 2 Outs RDI %	Rank
Cesar Cedeno	.301	21	.286	29	.355	4	.234	100	.349	7	.270	48	.265	115	.571	75
Jack Clark	.392	1	.239	97	.231	109	.332	3	.285	47	.226	78	.436	2	.609	58
Vince Coleman	.259	67	.271	50	.305	21	.231	107	.283	50	.323	16	.351	44	.550	88
Tom Herr	.302	20	.302	21	.303	24	.301	13	.333	10	.303	30	.374	27	.734	13
Mike Jorgensen	.143	--	.214	122	.196	--	.197	--	.186	--	.125	--	.429	--	.500	--
Tito Landrum	.279	--	.280	37	.329	--	.239	96	.283	52	.182	110	.310	--	.444	--
Willie McGee	.345	3	.356	5	.353	5	.353	2	.391	2	.377	4	.364	32	.658	31
Tom Nieto	.194	--	.236	101	.244	97	.206	119	.288	42	.257	60	.278	106	.647	38
Terry Pendleton	.255	71	.234	103	.228	114	.251	82	.256	79	.257	62	.263	117	.614	54
Darrell Porter	.165	129	.248	88	.255	84	.196	127	.227	105	.192	106	.415	7	.550	88
Ozzie Smith	.262	63	.281	34	.298	32	.254	74	.268	70	.269	51	.353	42	.611	55
Andy Van Slyke	.235	96	.269	54	.301	28	.225	109	.244	89	.207	98	.331	60	.645	40
Team Average	.266	2	.264	1	.274	2	.256	5	.274	2	.251	2	.337	1	.593	5
League Average	.251		.254		.256		.248		.257		.235		.315		.576	

Pitching vs. Left and Right Handed Batters

		BA	Rank	SA	Rank	OBA	Rank	HR %	Rank	BB %	Rank	SO %	Rank
Joaquin Andujar	vs. Lefties	.300	95	.405	79	.357	84	1.21	45	8.09	48	7.54	98
	vs. Righties	.223	30	.322	27	.286	34	1.71	30	6.52	33	12.18	86
Bill Campbell	vs. Lefties	.227	29	.299	20	.321	49	1.03	35	12.28	91	11.40	63
	vs. Righties	.232	49	.345	40	.275	22	2.82	82	4.49	7	17.95	36
Danny Cox	vs. Lefties	.264	59	.382	67	.313	43	1.62	65	6.79	28	11.25	64
	vs. Righties	.239	56	.382	72	.288	37	2.56	72	6.18	27	15.06	64
Ken Dayley	vs. Lefties	.313	105	.400	74	.341	68	1.25	46	4.65	11	24.42	6
	vs. Righties	.240	57	.341	36	.297	46	0.60	5	7.57	53	22.16	19
Bob Forsch	vs. Lefties	.241	39	.296	17	.299	36	0.00	1	7.69	41	5.88	112
	vs. Righties	.269	88	.430	96	.337	89	3.56	97	8.67	70	10.12	100
Ricky Horton	vs. Lefties	.219	21	.238	3	.270	16	0.00	1	5.98	20	16.24	30
	vs. Righties	.266	86	.406	87	.347	99	2.18	50	10.19	88	15.09	63
Kurt Kepshire	vs. Lefties	.301	96	.454	103	.363	88	3.35	105	9.51	66	7.21	101
	vs. Righties	.232	46	.339	33	.320	69	2.19	51	11.48	100	12.30	84
Jeff Lahti	vs. Lefties	.256	52	.337	41	.360	86	0.00	1	14.00	102	7.00	104
	vs. Righties	.248	64	.364	60	.299	48	1.82	31	6.70	36	18.99	32
John Tudor	vs. Lefties	.203	10	.264	7	.244	7	1.35	53	4.49	10	28.21	3
	vs. Righties	.210	19	.288	13	.249	8	1.41	20	4.64	9	13.80	74
Team Average	vs. Lefties	.265	7	.362	5	.324	3	1.32	3	8.00	3	11.62	10
	vs. Righties	.234	2	.348	1	.293	1	2.08	1	7.19	2	14.13	9
League Average	vs. Lefties	.262		.374		.330		1.73		9.17		12.66	
	vs. Righties	.246		.374		.311		2.44		8.28		15.62	

Pitching with Runners on Base and Bases Empty

		BA	Rank	SA	Rank	OBA	Rank	HR %	Rank	BB %	Rank	SO %	Rank
Joaquin Andujar	Runners On	.254	57	.358	47	.320	42	1.62	37	7.72	27	8.33	102
	Bases Empty	.265	85	.365	59	.321	80	1.37	31	6.93	46	11.18	92
Bill Campbell	Runners On	.239	37	.339	28	.333	59	2.75	86	11.19	77	14.18	53
	Bases Empty	.223	26	.315	25	.257	7	1.54	40	4.41	14	16.18	44
Danny Cox	Runners On	.234	29	.363	52	.272	11	2.25	64	5.28	6	12.81	60
	Bases Empty	.262	80	.394	82	.318	78	2.01	58	7.28	53	13.54	69
Ken Dayley	Runners On	.280	90	.368	57	.333	59	0.00	1	7.75	28	19.01	19
	Bases Empty	.246	--	.352	--	.287	--	1.64	--	5.43	--	27.13	--
Bob Forsch	Runners On	.275	84	.378	62	.350	83	1.55	31	9.91	61	8.11	104
	Bases Empty	.248	57	.376	75	.304	53	2.51	79	7.25	51	8.70	105
Ricky Horton	Runners On	.270	78	.340	30	.376	97	0.71	6	12.92	98	11.80	77
	Bases Empty	.238	43	.363	55	.279	26	2.07	62	5.39	23	18.63	27
Kurt Kepshire	Runners On	.323	111	.442	98	.403	109	1.84	49	12.93	99	8.37	101
	Bases Empty	.229	31	.361	54	.299	47	3.23	101	9.07	79	11.03	94
Jeff Lahti	Runners On	.235	31	.341	31	.336	67	0.76	7	12.99	100	14.29	51
	Bases Empty	.269	--	.370	--	.304	--	1.68	--	4.80	--	15.20	--
John Tudor	Runners On	.212	13	.279	6	.272	10	1.23	22	7.20	20	13.85	55
	Bases Empty	.207	14	.287	15	.237	2	1.48	38	3.28	6	16.98	39
Team Average	Runners On	.253	4	.354	2	.326	5	1.51	1	9.45	7	11.85	10
	Bases Empty	.241	4	.353	4	.289	2	1.98	4	6.06	1	14.18	9
League Average	Runners On	.258		.381		.332		2.19		9.74		13.69	
	Bases Empty	.248		.369		.309		2.14		7.75		15.05	

Overall Pitching Compared to Late Inning Pressure Situations

		BA	Rank	SA	Rank	OBA	Rank	HR %	Rank	BB %	Rank	SO %	Rank
Neil Allen	Overall	.283	--	.425	--	.373	--	2.65	--	12.59	--	7.41	--
	Pressure	.245	56	.377	67	.400	100	3.77	96	19.72	116	5.63	108
Joaquin Andujar	Overall	.260	76	.362	53	.321	60	1.47	27	7.28	33	9.94	93
	Pressure	.209	23	.327	35	.336	66	1.82	55	14.18	102	6.72	104
Bill Campbell	Overall	.230	27	.326	21	.294	27	2.09	55	7.78	41	15.19	44
	Pressure	.217	28	.267	15	.290	35	0.00	1	8.45	45	15.49	45
Danny Cox	Overall	.251	57	.382	76	.300	33	2.11	58	6.47	16	13.25	70
	Pressure	.306	100	.468	98	.353	77	1.61	47	7.04	25	9.86	86
Ken Dayley	Overall	.263	80	.360	49	.311	45	0.81	5	6.64	22	22.88	9
	Pressure	.287	87	.366	59	.346	72	0.61	25	8.20	36	24.59	8
Bob Forsch	Overall	.258	69	.377	71	.322	66	2.15	61	8.29	51	8.47	109
	Pressure	.400	--	.520	--	.483	--	4.00	--	10.00	--	0.00	--
Ricky Horton	Overall	.251	62	.353	34	.324	67	1.50	28	8.90	63	15.45	43
	Pressure	.258	69	.315	28	.383	94	0.00	1	14.55	104	14.55	53
Kurt Kepshire	Overall	.264	82	.391	83	.339	86	2.72	97	10.58	87	9.99	92
	Pressure	.341	109	.477	100	.383	93	4.55	102	6.25	20	14.58	50
Jeff Lahti	Overall	.251	59	.355	37	.321	63	1.20	16	9.32	72	14.70	52
	Pressure	.247	59	.310	26	.308	48	0.63	26	8.05	34	14.37	57
John Tudor	Overall	.209	9	.285	6	.249	1	1.40	21	4.61	5	15.91	40
	Pressure	.236	47	.327	35	.270	19	1.82	55	4.31	8	14.66	49
Todd Worrell	Overall	.215	--	.405	--	.273	--	2.53	--	7.95	--	19.32	--
	Pressure	.226	38	.415	83	.288	31	1.89	60	8.47	46	16.95	35
Team Average	Overall	.246	3	.354	3	.305	3	1.79	1	7.49	2	13.19	10
	Pressure	.256	9	.353	5	.335	9	1.46	1	10.04	9	14.10	9
League Average	Overall	.252		.374		.319		2.16		8.63		14.45	
	Pressure	.249		.363		.326		2.12		9.92		15.33	

Additional Miscellaneous Pitching Comparisons

	Grass Surface		Artificial Surface		Home Games		Road Games		Runners in Scoring Position		Runners in Scoring Pos and Two Outs		Leading Off Inning	
	BA	Rank	BA	Rank	BA	Rank	BA	Rank	BA	Rank	BA	Rank	OBA	Rank
Neil Allen	.265	--	.291	96	.114	--	.359	--	.378	--	.231	--	.269	--
Joaquin Andujar	.291	97	.248	49	.249	61	.272	85	.272	75	.241	67	.321	70
Bill Campbell	.159	--	.259	62	.236	46	.225	22	.220	23	.171	12	.276	23
Danny Cox	.264	71	.247	47	.251	65	.251	53	.222	24	.232	59	.323	72
Ken Dayley	.205	--	.287	94	.262	75	.265	75	.273	76	.314	108	.286	31
Bob Forsch	.244	54	.262	66	.236	46	.283	96	.317	107	.298	98	.271	21
Ricky Horton	.240	--	.254	56	.259	74	.246	44	.292	97	.302	101	.318	66
Kurt Kepshire	.209	15	.290	95	.307	106	.224	20	.345	112	.171	11	.327	78
Jeff Lahti	.257	--	.249	51	.194	--	.285	98	.163	4	.174	16	.283	--
John Tudor	.193	6	.214	15	.197	11	.223	19	.224	28	.236	62	.217	4
Team Average	.235	4	.249	3	.239	5	.252	4	.257	8	.227	4	.291	3
League Average	.251		.254		.248		.256		.257		.235		.315	

SAN DIEGO PADRES

Take It from the Top

A look at the fall of the San Diego Padres from the top of the National League in 1984 to last season's mediocrity must begin at the top of their batting order. Alan Wiggins was the Padres' catalyst during their championship season, batting .258 with 75 walks, stealing 70 bases, and scoring 106 runs, setting the table for Tony Gwynn and Steve Garvey from the leadoff spot. In 1984, the Padres scored 93 runs in the first inning to rank fifth in the National League. Last season, San Diego's first-inning production fell by nearly one-third to the lowest total in either league. They scored 10 fewer first-inning runs than the second-worst National League team:

New York	104	Cincinnati	75
St. Louis	98	Los Angeles	75
Chicago	91	Montreal	75
Philadelphia	90	San Francisco	75
Atlanta	85	Houston	73
Pittsburgh	81	**San Diego**	63

Can one player be responsible for such a drastic turnaround? Let's take a look at the changes throughout the Padres' order precipitated by the loss of Wiggins. There was no way to replace Wiggins's speed in the leadoff spot; San Diego fell from fifth in the National League with 152 stolen bases in 1984 to last with 60 steals last season. But at the plate, San Diego's platoon of Tim Flannery and Jerry Royster was a match made in role players' heaven. Flannery has hit better against right-handed pitchers than left-handers in each of his seven seasons in the majors; despite an overall career batting average of .255, he has never hit higher than .172 against southpaws. During those seven years, Royster had a higher batting average against right-handers only twice, in each case by a margin of less than two hits. Their career batting statistics:

Flannery	AB	H	2B	3B	HR	BA	SA	OBA
Vs. Left-Handers	195	29	5	2	0	.149	.195	.211
Vs. Right-Handers	1334	361	46	16	6	.271	.343	.340

Royster	AB	H	2B	3B	HR	BA	SA	OBA
Vs. Left-Handers	1174	308	56	14	11	.262	.362	.327
Vs. Right-Handers	2479	605	81	19	17	.244	.313	.309

Wiggins	AB	H	2B	3B	HR	BA	SA	OBA
Vs. Left-Handers	545	165	30	2	4	.303	.387	.365
Vs. Right-Handers	1157	285	24	14	0	.246	.291	.326

At first glance, the Padres seem not to have lost much with the substitution of Flannery and Royster for Wiggins at second base. With the unavoidable exception of that steep decline in stolen bases —and, as a result, runs scored—the production from the composite of all starting second basemen for San Diego last season not only surpasses that of their championship season a year earlier, but would have equalled last season's National League average were it not for Wiggins's own horrible April:

Second Basemen	AB	R	H	2B	3B	HR	RBI	BB	SB	BA
1984 Padres	620	107	159	20	7	3	35	76	68	.256
1985 Padres	585	73	158	25	3	5	59	82	8	.270
1985 N.L. Avg.	614	81	165	29	5	9	63	61	23	.269

But when we examine the situation more closely, the effect of the loss of Wiggins's speed rolls like a tidal wave through the top of the Padres' batting order. First, let's compare the Flannery-Royster platoon not to the National League's other starting second basemen, but to its other leadoff hitters:

Leadoff Batters	AB	R	H	2B	3B	HR	RBI	BB	SB	BA	OBA
Atlanta	693	84	172	32	10	12	44	59	23	.248	.308
Chicago	682	96	172	32	3	6	38	63	43	.252	.318
Cincinnati	652	108	153	28	11	14	57	89*	64	.235	.327
Houston	673	102	191	34	7	17*	74*	81	22	.284	.359
Los Angeles	689	99	168	25	8	7	54	60	50	.244	.304
Montreal	650	127*	206*	36*	13*	13	46	85	78	.317*	.397*
New York	674	102	179	23	10	8	61	73	33	.266	.338
Philadelphia	704*	96	183	28	10	14	66	38	45	.260	.301
Pittsburgh	681	87	179	32	6	9	55	37	31	.263	.302
St. Louis	688	119	184	23	10	1	44	57	114*	.267	.325
San Diego	666	83	172	26	6	5	60	72	20	.258	.336
San Francisco	666	95	166	17	8	12	59	59	39	.249	.316
N.L. Average	677	100	177	28	9	10	55	64	47	.262	.328

Even with an on-base average above the league norm, the Padres' leadoff men ranked last in the league in stolen bases and runs scored, despite being followed in the batting order by two of baseball's best run producers, Gwynn and Garvey. During his four seasons in the major leagues, Gwynn has batted .339 with runners in scoring position, a mark exceeded during that time by only two players, Wade Boggs (.371) and Al Oliver (.339). He has driven in exactly one-third of all runners in scoring position when he came to bat, to rank among the top ten percent of all players since 1982 with at least 100 opportunities. Last season, with Flannery, Royster, and occasionally Garry Templeton hitting ahead of him, Gwynn batted 277 times with runners on base, only two times fewer than in 1984. But without Wiggins and his ability to put himself in scoring position, 56 percent of Gwynn's plate appearances with runners on base last season occurred with a man on first only, compared to just 37 percent a year earlier. Batting behind Wiggins in 1984, Gwynn came up 54 more times with a runner in scoring position.

Although the absence of Wiggins from San Diego's lineup is responsible for most of that difference, the Padres also had by far the worst-hitting ninth position in the National League last season with a .121 batting average, 50 points lower than the league mark and a stunning 32 points lower than the eleventh-place Atlanta Braves. A year earlier, Padres pitchers ranked second in the league in batting average.

Can the decline in Gwynn's overall batting average from .351 in 1984 to .317 last season be attributed to pitchers serving him fewer fastballs with Flannery on first base than with Wiggins there? There are some statistics to indicate that this might be the case, but the evidence is inconclusive. While it is not unusual for a player to suffer a 34-point single-season drop in batting average, especially following such a superb season, his bases-empty average dropped by only an insignificant margin of 15 points. Gwynn's drop from .406 with runners on base in 1984 to .337 last season is responsible for three-quarters of the decline in his overall average. This might mean that

Gwynn was seeing different pitches last year with runners on base than he had in '84; then again, it might not.

Steve Garvey, who has batted third in San Diego's order throughout most of the past two seasons, was also affected by the loss of Wiggins. During 1984, Garvey had 66 opportunities to drive in a runner from third base with less than two outs, compared to only 38 last season. Those other runners were still on base last season, but they were further from home: Garvey came to bat with 10 more runners on first base and 16 more on second base last season than in 1984.

The bottom line? On the surface, Flannery and Royster did an entirely adequate job replacing him at second, but Wiggins's main value had never been as a second baseman—which, in fact, he had never been in the majors prior to '84. Wiggins was moved to second to keep his unique skills as a leadoff man in the lineup, and Flanneroyster could do nothing to fill the vacuum his departure left behind. Let's look at one final measure, which quantifies in a different way Wiggins's talent as San Diego's table setter. The following table shows the Padres' performance over the past three seasons when the first-place hitter in their batting order led off an inning. (Wiggins was the starting leadoff batter in only 52 games in 1983; Bobby Brown had 50 games at leadoff, Luis Salazar had 30, and Gene Richards had 29 to account for all but one of San Diego's starts that year.)

Year	Total Inns.	Scoring Inns.	Pct.	(Rank)	Total Runs	Runs per Inn.	(Rank)
1985	347	99	28.5	(9th)	158	0.46	(12th)
1984	318	94	29.6	(8th)	172	0.54	(7th)
1983	328	96	29.3	(9th)	152	0.46	(11th)

Winning Streaks and Beyond

During the 24 years from 1961 through 1984, only 11 pitchers won more than 10 consecutive decisions during a single season, and by the turn of the century, nearly half of those pitchers will be enshrined in Cooperstown: Sandy Koufax (who did it twice), Bob Gibson, Don Drysdale, Steve Carlton, and Tom Seaver. It is an accomplishment rarely achieved even by pitchers of the highest caliber. But during the 1985 season, no fewer than four NL pitchers had winning streaks of at least 11 decisions: Dwight Gooden, John Tudor, and San Diego teammates Andy Hawkins and LaMarr Hoyt.

Mets fans, of course, have already started work on Gooden's plaque. But Hoyt, Tudor, and Hawkins began their 1985 seasons without Cooperstown credentials, and even last season, the San Diego pitchers gave little indication before or after their winning streaks that they were anything more than useful starting pitchers. Since the Padres' lineup includes Steve Garvey and Graig Nettles, two of the oldest regulars in the National League, and their bullpen stopper (Goose Gossage) still relies on heat at age 36, it is clear that over the next five years, San Diego's starting rotation must remain among the league's elite if they are to have any chance of competing with the best of the West.

Can the Padres expect Hawkins and Hoyt to be a major factor through the late 1980s? A study of recent National League pitching performances suggests that their futures may be more cloudy than bright. The following table lists all pitchers with winning streaks of 10 or more decisions from 1961 through 1984.

Year	Pitcher	Streak	W–L	"C"	"D"	"E"
1962	Sanford, S.F.	16	24–7	8–7	16–13	26
1968	Gibson, St.L.	15	22–9	7–9	20–13	59
1984	Sutcliffe, Chi.	14	20–6	6–6	8–8	—
1972	Carlton, Phil.	15	27–10	12–10	13–20	44
1971	Ellis, Pitt.	13	19–9	6–9	15–7	39
1975	Hooton, L.A.	12	18–9	6–9	11–15	42
1962	Drysdale, L.A.	11	25–9	14–9	19–17	60
1964	Koufax, L.A.	11	19–5	8–5	26–8	—
1965	Koufax, L.A.	11	26–8	15–8	27–9	—
1972	Pappas, Chi.	11	17–7	6–7	7–12	—
1979	Seaver, Cin.	11	16–6	5–6	10–8	29
1961	Spahn, Mil.	10	21–13	11–13	18–14	47
1966	Marichal, S.F.	10	25–6	15–6	14–10	61
1968	Marichal, S.F.	10	26–9	16–9	21–11	51
1969	Seaver, N.Y.	10	25–7	15–7	18–12	59
1970	Gibson, St.L.	10	23–7	13–7	16–13	47
1970	Simpson, Cin.	10	14–3	4–3	4–7	15
1978	Blue, S.F.	10	18–10	8–10	14–14	36

Column C indicates the record of each pitcher during his streak season without the streak included, and column D, his record in the season following the streak. Notice the strong relationship between games won in columns C and D, and the even stronger correspondence between wins in column C and column E, which shows each pitcher's win total during the three seasons following the streak season. (Sutcliffe has insufficient data for column E, while Koufax and Pappas retired before reaching the third season after their streaks.)

From those statistics, we can make a reasonable forecast for the near future for Hawkins and Hoyt, and a not terribly optimistic one at that. Neither pitcher compiled a winning record for the portions of last season other than his streak. Without their 11-game streaks, Hawkins was 7–8, Hoyt 5–8. From the table above, those with losing records in column C had an average record in the following season of 14–12, compared to 17–12 for those with winning records. But notice that none of those pitchers had a column C record as poor as Hoyt's, and based upon their specific records last season, Hawkins and Hoyt are not likely to combine for more than 70 wins over the next three seasons; a total of 60 would be more likely.

So much for statistics. It should be noted that Hoyt suffered from shoulder soreness through the final two months of last season, and his performance this season will depend in large part on whether he can rebound from that problem. Hoyt himself said late last season that he'd be "surprised if (the 1986) season were not the best of my career." We observed last year that, in winning their division, San Diego had enjoyed unusual good health—and their rivals unusual ill health—in 1984. The Padres will need that kind of fortune from Hoyt, from Gossage, from Garvey and Nettles yet again, and from all the rest if they are to regain the Western Division title.

WON-LOST RECORD BY STARTING POSITION

SAN DIEGO 83-79	C	1B	2B	3B	SS	LF	CF	RF	P	Leadoff	Relief	Starts
Kurt Bevacqua			15-16									15-16
Bruce Bochy	13-15											13-15
Greg Booker											2-15	
Bobby Brown						2-0	2-0	1-1		1-0		5-1
Al Bumbry						3-3	2-2			3-5		5-5
Jerry Davis						1-1	1-6			2-2		2-7
Luis DeLeon											9-20	
Miguel Dilone						1-1	3-3	1-0		5-4		5-4
Dave Dravecky								14-17			0-3	14-17
Tim Flannery			52-49							31-30		52-49
Steve Garvey		83-79										83-79
Goose Gossage											39-11	
Tony Gwynn							80-72					80-72
Andy Hawkins									20-13			20-13
LaMarr Hoyt									19-12			19-12
Roy Lee Jackson									1-1		6-14	1-1
Terry Kennedy	70-64											70-64
Craig Lefferts											19-41	
Carmelo Martinez						76-74						76-74
Lance McCullers											11-10	
Kevin McReynolds							76-74					76-74
Graig Nettles				63-60								63-60
Bob Patterson											0-3	
Mario Ramirez		1-1		6-4								7-5
Edwin Rodriguez												
Jerry Royster			24-26	5-3	0-4					17-17		29-33
Eric Show									18-17			18-17
Tim Stoddard											9-35	
Garry Templeton					77-71					18-18		77-71
Mark Thurmond									8-15		6-7	8-15
Gene Walter											5-10	
Alan Wiggins			6-3							6-3		6-3
Ed Wojna									3-4		1-7	3-4

Batting vs. Left and Right Handed Pitchers

		BA	Rank	SA	Rank	OBA	Rank	HR %	Rank	BB %	Rank	SO %	Rank
Kurt Bevacqua	vs. Lefties	.253	75	.385	63	.384	16	3.30	43	17.86	4	9.82	36
	vs. Righties	.213	--	.277	--	.278	--	0.00	--	9.09	--	10.91	--
Bruce Bochy	vs. Lefties	.274	49	.466	32	.312	82	5.48	12	5.13	114	23.08	126
	vs. Righties	.256	--	.410	--	.293	--	5.13	--	4.76	--	28.57	--
Tim Flannery	vs. Lefties	.162	--	.243	--	.262	--	0.00	--	9.52	--	9.52	--
	vs. Righties	.294	23	.352	90	.399	10	0.29	115	13.04	22	8.45	25
Steve Garvey	vs. Lefties	.297	26	.502	17	.345	50	4.31	28	6.99	91	9.17	30
	vs. Righties	.274	46	.396	66	.305	96	1.80	70	4.04	128	9.79	39
Tony Gwynn	vs. Lefties	.288	32	.351	85	.354	37	0.98	93	8.41	75	5.75	8
	vs. Righties	.331	4	.436	36	.369	25	0.96	96	5.84	106	4.49	6
Terry Kennedy	vs. Lefties	.259	66	.374	70	.283	111	2.04	70	3.29	131	27.63	132
	vs. Righties	.262	62	.371	80	.308	92	1.82	69	6.30	97	14.53	84
Carmelo Martinez	vs. Lefties	.247	80	.452	35	.379	18	4.82	21	17.73	5	11.82	61
	vs. Righties	.256	71	.425	41	.353	44	3.74	26	12.53	26	14.25	81
Kevin McReynolds	vs. Lefties	.260	64	.370	73	.340	55	1.73	75	10.66	45	11.17	51
	vs. Righties	.223	121	.371	82	.266	129	3.07	38	5.25	115	14.08	79
Graig Nettles	vs. Lefties	.216	106	.433	41	.294	98	4.12	30	10.09	52	17.43	104
	vs. Righties	.274	48	.417	47	.382	15	3.21	35	15.02	9	9.85	40
Jerry Royster	vs. Lefties	.298	21	.425	44	.385	15	1.66	77	11.90	38	9.52	32
	vs. Righties	.235	--	.368	--	.303	--	2.94	--	9.09	--	14.29	--
Garry Templeton	vs. Lefties	.254	72	.316	105	.291	101	0.56	105	4.66	117	15.03	84
	vs. Righties	.295	22	.407	58	.351	46	1.36	80	7.94	71	14.64	86
Team Average	vs. Lefties	.253	5	.379	5	.322	3	2.31	7	8.86	6	13.94	4
	vs. Righties	.256	5	.363	10	.318	6	1.82	10	8.09	11	12.76	1
League Average	vs. Lefties	.250		.374		.317		2.26		8.65		14.84	
	vs. Righties	.253		.374		.320		2.12		8.62		14.28	

Batting with Runners on Base and Bases Empty

		BA	Rank	SA	Rank	OBA	Rank	HR %	Rank	BB %	Rank	SO %	Rank
Kurt Bevacqua	Runners On	.215	123	.354	88	.337	66	3.80	29	16.16	9	9.09	43
	Bases Empty	.271	--	.339	--	.368	--	0.00	--	13.24	--	11.76	--
Tim Flannery	Runners On	.349	6	.457	34	.411	9	0.78	99	8.05	91	8.72	36
	Bases Empty	.247	85	.282	125	.375	10	0.00	120	14.98	6	8.47	21
Steve Garvey	Runners On	.264	71	.366	84	.307	96	1.59	71	5.54	121	7.00	18
	Bases Empty	.297	11	.488	15	.329	54	3.53	30	4.49	119	12.08	54
Tony Gwynn	Runners On	.337	10	.404	62	.384	27	1.18	81	6.86	109	3.61	21
	Bases Empty	.302	9	.411	42	.350	29	0.82	102	6.60	76	5.84	9
Terry Kennedy	Runners On	.288	39	.401	66	.332	72	1.95	65	6.50	116	16.97	112
	Bases Empty	.236	98	.345	93	.271	116	1.82	71	4.51	118	19.10	112
Carmelo Martinez	Runners On	.288	38	.465	28	.366	45	3.70	30	10.32	63	12.81	74
	Bases Empty	.221	115	.406	47	.359	23	4.43	17	17.63	1	13.98	78
Kevin McReynolds	Runners On	.281	49	.431	45	.348	59	2.69	50	9.15	78	13.22	78
	Bases Empty	.194	129	.319	106	.237	133	2.63	46	4.98	113	13.08	63
Graig Nettles	Runners On	.279	51	.398	67	.370	39	1.49	73	13.19	32	10.64	60
	Bases Empty	.247	86	.439	28	.357	25	5.02	14	14.64	8	12.14	56
Jerry Royster	Runners On	.311	18	.433	43	.407	10	1.11	83	13.51	27	7.21	21
	Bases Empty	.264	52	.396	56	.335	45	2.52	50	9.66	33	13.07	62
Garry Templeton	Runners On	.314	15	.412	56	.389	22	0.98	91	11.30	50	15.06	91
	Bases Empty	.263	54	.357	84	.294	99	1.17	93	3.92	123	14.57	83
Team Average	Runners On	.277	1	.387	5	.341	4	1.81	10	8.55	12	12.26	1
	Bases Empty	.239	11	.355	9	.303	9	2.10	8	8.18	3	13.87	2
League Average	Runners On	.258		.381		.332		2.19		9.74		13.69	
	Bases Empty	.248		.369		.309		2.14		7.75		15.05	

Overall Batting Compared to Late Inning Pressure Situations

		BA	Rank	SA	Rank	OBA	Rank	HR %	Rank	BB %	Rank	SO %	Rank	RDI %	Rank
Kurt Bevacqua	Overall	.239	--	.348	--	.349	--	2.17	--	14.97	--	10.18	--	.364	8
	Pressure	.316	23	.395	57	.413	17	0.00	92	14.89	17	12.77	60	.304	47
Tim Flannery	Overall	.281	27	.341	100	.386	12	0.26	120	12.72	20	8.55	21	.336	17
	Pressure	.250	73	.324	79	.350	55	0.00	92	12.20	36	12.20	52	.176	106
Steve Garvey	Overall	.281	26	.430	37	.318	74	2.60	46	5.01	125	9.59	35	.309	42
	Pressure	.233	89	.282	101	.250	117	0.00	92	1.85	135	13.89	65	.333	25
Tony Gwynn	Overall	.317	7	.408	53	.364	27	0.96	102	6.71	102	4.92	6	.283	69
	Pressure	.347	10	.453	36	.415	16	2.11	60	10.38	52	8.49	20	.346	23
Terry Kennedy	Overall	.261	73	.372	78	.301	103	1.88	68	5.49	117	18.05	116	.308	43
	Pressure	.294	40	.376	65	.348	56	1.18	80	7.61	89	14.13	67	.286	50
Carmelo Martinez	Overall	.253	84	.434	34	.362	34	4.09	24	14.26	12	13.44	77	.266	80
	Pressure	.253	72	.389	58	.321	79	3.16	37	9.35	63	10.28	34	.344	24
Kevin McReynolds	Overall	.234	112	.371	80	.290	116	2.66	45	6.98	97	13.15	72	.292	63
	Pressure	.198	110	.279	104	.258	116	0.00	92	7.37	94	14.74	74	.167	109
Graig Nettles	Overall	.261	72	.420	43	.363	29	3.41	34	13.98	14	11.46	55	.297	58
	Pressure	.242	79	.364	68	.338	65	3.03	39	12.99	28	10.39	36	.200	96
Jerry Royster	Overall	.281	28	.410	52	.363	31	2.01	65	11.15	31	10.80	45	.383	5
	Pressure	.333	15	.528	16	.432	11	2.78	41	13.64	22	4.55	3	.250	64
Garry Templeton	Overall	.282	24	.377	75	.332	61	1.10	97	6.88	99	14.77	88	.331	23
	Pressure	.268	59	.341	71	.355	49	1.22	78	10.42	51	15.63	80	.136	119
Team Average	Overall	.255	5	.368	9	.320	7	1.98	10	8.34	9	13.15	1	.285	3
	Pressure	.258	5	.346	10	.326	6	1.36	11	8.94	9	13.05	1	.256	7
League Average	Overall	.252		.374		.319		2.16		8.63		14.45		.273	
	Pressure	.253		.368		.325		2.17		9.26		15.10		.257	

Additional Miscellaneous Batting Comparisons

	Grass Surface BA	Rank	Artificial Surface BA	Rank	Home Games BA	Rank	Road Games BA	Rank	Runners in Scoring Position BA	Rank	Runners in Scoring Pos and Two Outs BA	Rank	Leading Off Inning OBA	Rank	Runners on 3B with less than 2 Outs RDI %	Rank
Kurt Bevacqua	.243	85	.229	--	.246	--	.233	--	.282	53	.400	3	.357	--	.667	29
Miguel Dilone	.185	--	.211	--	.211	--	.186	--	.250	--	.200	--	.271	111	1.000	--
Tim Flannery	.289	34	.264	63	.273	61	.288	24	.356	5	.333	11	.320	72	.733	14
Steve Garvey	.293	33	.249	86	.284	47	.279	37	.289	40	.310	21	.320	73	.684	24
Tony Gwynn	.323	9	.300	23	.326	12	.307	10	.270	64	.255	65	.393	13	.565	84
Terry Kennedy	.238	93	.331	8	.233	106	.292	17	.296	35	.224	81	.216	134	.523	101
Carmelo Martinez	.270	52	.205	128	.273	60	.233	103	.231	102	.183	109	.319	74	.484	114
Kevin McReynolds	.220	112	.273	47	.235	103	.233	102	.311	26	.303	32	.289	93	.643	41
Graig Nettles	.244	83	.302	20	.258	80	.265	56	.280	56	.230	76	.323	67	.667	29
Jerry Royster	.256	69	.370	--	.288	42	.275	43	.396	1	.417	1	.326	64	.786	10
Garry Templeton	.273	50	.308	16	.281	51	.283	32	.330	15	.333	11	.275	109	.654	35
Team Average	.252	7	.263	2	.253	8	.257	4	.277	1	.259	1	.292	12	.595	4
League Average	.251		.254		.256		.248		.257		.235		.315		.576	

Pitching vs. Left and Right Handed Batters

		BA	Rank	SA	Rank	OBA	Rank	HR %	Rank	BB %	Rank	SO %	Rank
Dave Dravecky	vs. Lefties	.267	63	.322	34	.320	46	1.11	37	7.22	34	24.74	5
	vs. Righties	.247	62	.358	53	.296	45	2.39	65	6.42	32	10.40	97
Rich Gossage	vs. Lefties	.252	50	.313	27	.291	32	0.76	21	5.63	17	16.20	31
	vs. Righties	.204	13	.237	3	.250	9	0.00	1	5.42	16	17.47	39
Andy Hawkins	vs. Lefties	.269	66	.402	76	.332	61	2.18	80	8.64	54	6.26	109
	vs. Righties	.265	81	.388	75	.303	52	2.02	42	5.10	12	8.16	111
LaMarr Hoyt	vs. Lefties	.286	87	.412	85	.303	38	2.56	90	2.67	1	6.46	107
	vs. Righties	.232	47	.357	52	.252	11	2.40	66	2.05	1	13.85	72
Roy Lee Jackson	vs. Lefties	.169	2	.221	1	.220	1	0.00	1	4.82	12	9.64	78
	vs. Righties	.288	--	.545	--	.364	--	6.06	--	11.25	--	25.00	--
Craig Lefferts	vs. Lefties	.191	8	.270	10	.255	9	1.12	38	8.00	44	20.00	15
	vs. Righties	.266	85	.417	93	.333	83	2.75	78	8.98	73	11.43	89
Eric Show	vs. Lefties	.287	88	.453	101	.362	87	3.45	108	10.29	78	8.76	89
	vs. Righties	.194	10	.312	22	.259	13	2.70	75	7.30	50	21.02	23
Tim Stoddard	vs. Lefties	.286	86	.367	58	.395	105	1.02	34	15.97	109	11.76	57
	vs. Righties	.257	76	.390	76	.344	94	1.47	21	11.25	98	17.50	38
Mark Thurmond	vs. Lefties	.250	47	.304	23	.327	57	0.00	1	9.35	65	12.15	53
	vs. Righties	.300	111	.414	91	.351	101	2.06	44	7.01	45	9.07	108
Ed Wojna	vs. Lefties	.279	77	.453	102	.344	72	3.49	109	8.33	51	8.33	93
	vs. Righties	.345	--	.512	--	.424	--	3.57	--	10.78	--	9.80	--
Team Average	vs. Lefties	.269	9	.396	10	.329	5	2.35	11	8.09	4	10.08	12
	vs. Righties	.249	8	.370	6	.303	6	2.32	4	6.83	1	13.27	12
League Average	vs. Lefties	.262		.374		.330		1.73		9.17		12.66	
	vs. Righties	.246		.374		.311		2.44		8.28		15.62	

Pitching with Runners on Base and Bases Empty

		BA	Rank	SA	Rank	OBA	Rank	HR %	Rank	BB %	Rank	SO %	Rank
Dave Dravecky	Runners On	.238	36	.348	37	.283	14	2.51	76	5.62	8	12.36	68
	Bases Empty	.257	72	.358	48	.310	63	2.07	61	7.12	49	11.73	85
Rich Gossage	Runners On	.261	64	.339	27	.310	30	0.87	12	7.58	22	11.36	80
	Bases Empty	.202	12	.226	1	.239	3	0.00	1	3.98	9	21.02	17
Andy Hawkins	Runners On	.248	46	.338	26	.317	38	1.21	19	9.37	49	5.57	115
	Bases Empty	.278	100	.430	100	.317	76	2.65	86	5.02	18	8.42	107
LaMarr Hoyt	Runners On	.315	110	.465	105	.333	59	2.93	89	2.72	1	8.16	103
	Bases Empty	.233	39	.346	42	.251	5	2.26	70	2.20	1	10.83	96
Craig Lefferts	Runners On	.252	54	.385	68	.320	41	2.22	63	8.92	44	17.20	26
	Bases Empty	.238	44	.366	62	.303	50	2.33	73	8.51	72	11.17	93
Eric Show	Runners On	.223	20	.344	34	.297	21	2.31	70	9.02	46	15.29	38
	Bases Empty	.257	73	.415	94	.325	83	3.62	109	8.82	77	13.84	64
Tim Stoddard	Runners On	.267	70	.408	81	.379	100	2.50	74	15.23	111	13.91	54
	Bases Empty	.272	--	.351	--	.352	--	0.00	--	10.94	--	16.41	--
Mark Thurmond	Runners On	.298	104	.423	86	.392	107	1.40	28	12.73	94	9.36	92
	Bases Empty	.287	109	.376	74	.311	64	1.91	54	3.08	3	9.85	100
Team Average	Runners On	.259	7	.382	7	.325	4	2.22	6	8.71	2	11.62	12
	Bases Empty	.255	9	.378	8	.305	6	2.41	11	6.29	2	12.32	12
League Average	Runners On	.258		.381		.332		2.19		9.74		13.69	
	Bases Empty	.248		.369		.309		2.14		7.75		15.05	

Overall Pitching Compared to Late Inning Pressure Situations

		BA	Rank	SA	Rank	OBA	Rank	HR %	Rank	BB %	Rank	SO %	Rank
Greg Booker	Overall	.247	--	.432	--	.376	--	3.70	--	16.67	--	6.86	--
	Pressure	.240	50	.480	101	.375	86	8.00	115	18.75	115	0.00	116
Luis DeLeon	Overall	.267	--	.425	--	.325	--	4.11	--	6.13	--	19.02	--
	Pressure	.378	114	.689	116	.408	104	8.89	116	5.77	18	13.46	65
Dave Dravecky	Overall	.249	55	.354	36	.299	31	2.24	67	6.51	18	11.99	83
	Pressure	.297	92	.516	110	.375	86	6.25	112	10.81	72	9.46	88
Rich Gossage	Overall	.226	22	.272	3	.269	8	0.35	1	5.52	9	16.88	33
	Pressure	.206	21	.237	11	.250	11	0.00	1	5.67	17	17.00	34
Andy Hawkins	Overall	.267	87	.395	87	.317	57	2.10	56	6.82	27	7.24	113
	Pressure	.300	94	.500	105	.398	99	5.00	107	13.68	96	1.05	115
LaMarr Hoyt	Overall	.261	78	.386	79	.280	17	2.48	82	2.38	1	9.89	94
	Pressure	.208	22	.323	32	.232	5	2.08	66	3.00	2	7.00	103
Roy Lee Jackson	Overall	.224	--	.371	--	.289	--	2.80	--	7.98	--	17.18	--
	Pressure	.255	68	.447	94	.352	76	4.26	100	12.50	89	21.43	18
Craig Lefferts	Overall	.244	47	.375	68	.311	44	2.28	70	8.70	59	13.91	62
	Pressure	.252	65	.342	43	.316	54	1.29	37	8.62	49	13.22	68
Lance McCullers	Overall	.195	--	.322	--	.296	--	2.54	--	11.27	--	19.01	--
	Pressure	.221	32	.349	46	.337	68	2.33	69	12.96	93	20.37	21
Eric Show	Overall	.243	45	.387	80	.314	53	3.10	101	8.90	64	14.43	56
	Pressure	.224	35	.388	71	.287	30	2.35	71	8.51	47	10.64	84
Tim Stoddard	Overall	.269	91	.380	73	.366	108	1.28	18	13.26	111	15.05	46
	Pressure	.372	113	.526	112	.474	115	1.28	36	16.16	108	7.07	101
Mark Thurmond	Overall	.291	106	.395	88	.347	93	1.70	39	7.43	38	9.63	97
	Pressure	.250	62	.344	44	.294	37	0.00	1	5.80	19	17.39	29
Gene Walter	Overall	.158	--	.211	--	.235	--	0.00	--	9.30	--	20.93	--
	Pressure	.161	8	.226	8	.235	6	0.00	1	8.57	48	25.71	6
Team Average	Overall	.257	9	.380	9	.313	5	2.33	9	7.32	1	12.02	12
	Pressure	.251	7	.375	8	.322	6	2.29	8	9.31	2	12.92	11
League Average	Overall	.252		.374		.319		2.16		8.63		14.45	
	Pressure	.249		.363		.326		2.12		9.92		15.33	

Additional Miscellaneous Pitching Comparisons

	Grass Surface		Artificial Surface		Home Games		Road Games		Runners in Scoring Position		Runners in Scoring Pos and Two Outs		Leading Off Inning	
	BA	Rank	BA	Rank	BA	Rank	BA	Rank	BA	Rank	BA	Rank	OBA	Rank
Luis DeLeon	.290	96	.136	--	.295	--	.247	--	.415	--	.400	--	.412	--
Dave Dravecky	.256	65	.233	32	.240	54	.257	64	.250	51	.236	63	.290	37
Rich Gossage	.209	14	.278	--	.193	9	.250	50	.267	--	.281	89	.188	2
Andy Hawkins	.262	70	.281	89	.270	84	.262	70	.222	25	.178	19	.326	76
LaMarr Hoyt	.260	68	.263	72	.279	91	.237	33	.295	99	.270	85	.248	10
Roy Lee Jackson	.222	22	.229	--	.227	--	.221	--	.147	--	.176	--	.385	--
Craig Lefferts	.224	26	.314	--	.234	43	.255	60	.310	105	.310	106	.295	46
Lance McCullers	.213	16	.125	--	.225	--	.132	--	.270	--	.318	--	.345	--
Eric Show	.243	52	.245	46	.230	40	.255	59	.206	17	.173	14	.303	55
Tim Stoddard	.246	57	.328	--	.200	--	.321	115	.289	93	.211	41	.355	92
Mark Thurmond	.282	88	.317	109	.267	80	.314	110	.306	101	.333	112	.300	52
Ed Wojna	.305	106	.345	--	.290	--	.338	--	.345	--	.238	--	.364	--
Team Average	.254	6	.266	11	.252	8	.262	9	.266	10	.251	11	.302	4
League Average	.251		.254		.248		.256		.257		.235		.315	

SAN FRANCISCO GIANTS

"San Francisco can say this is the finest ballpark in America. It is truly a magnificent stadium."

Those words were delivered on April 12, 1960, on the occasion of the Giants' first game in Candlestick Park. The speaker was the vice president of the United States, Richard M. Nixon, addressing the crowd at home-plate ceremonies dedicating the park. Given what fans who went there were later to find out about "the 'Stick," Nixon's comment ranks right up there with "You won't have Nixon to kick around anymore" as a prediction.

Candlestick has been a part of the American sports scene for 26 years. During that time, it has been the scene of one World Series, two All-Star Games, and one National League Championship Series. It has also been home to both the Oakland Raiders (in 1961) and the San Francisco 49ers (since 1971). Like an aging movie queen striving for youth, the stadium has undergone frequent face-lifts. There have been configuration changes, the erection of additional outfield double-deck stands to combat the wind, and the installation and subsequent removal of artificial turf. But the whole facelift process has been unable to do anything about the problems that have plagued the park since its infancy, best symbolized by the wind that blew Stu Miller off the mound during the nationally televised 1961 All-Star Game, when the park was just a year and a half old.

Through it all, the stadium has been abused, vilified, and ridiculed by players, fans, and media. In recent years, the Giants have tried various promotional ideas to attract more fans to Candlestick. A few years ago, there was a clever campaign seeking to draw hardy fans who could withstand the rugged conditions; anyone who stayed through an extra-inning night game was presented with a badge of honor upon leaving the stadium—the Croix de Candlestick. Then last year, the Giants tried to avoid the unpleasant conditions at Candlestick at night by scheduling 64 of their 81 games in the daytime, the largest number of day games scheduled by a major-league team, except the Cubs, in recent years.

Unfortunately, the daytime schedule did not have the desired effect on either the attendance or the Giants' play. A loss to the Braves on the final day of the season spoiled the team's proud record of having been the only team among the 16 pre-expansion franchises never to suffer a 100-loss season. Only Pittsburgh and Cleveland lost more games; only Pittsburgh and Cleveland drew fewer fans.

The Giants had the lowest batting average (.233) and scored the fewest runs (3.4 per game) in the major leagues last season, but before the fingers are pointed at ex-manager Jim Davenport, ex-general manager Tom Haller, or owner Bob Lurie, consider the effect of Candlestick itself on those puny figures. Candlestick Park depressed batting averages to a greater extent than any stadium in the National League last season. The Giants hit 21 points higher on the road than they did at home; their opponents batted 38 points higher in their own parks than they did at the 'Stick:

	At Candlestick Park				On The Road			
	BA	SA	R/G	HR	BA	SA	R/G	HR
Giants	.222	.339	3.27	58	.243	.356	3.59	57
Opponents	.229	.346	3.79	67	.267	.403	4.53	58
Totals	.226	.343	7.06	125	.255	.379	8.12	115

Even though nine percent more home runs were hit in San Francisco than in Giants' road games, the overall effect of the 'Stick was a 29-point drop in composite batting average, and a 1.06 drop in the rate of runs per game. Here's how those figures stack up against the other stadiums in the National League (ranked according to the effect of the home park on batting average):

	Composite In Home Games			Composite In Road Games			Effect of Home Park		
	BA	SA	R/G	BA	SA	R/G	BA	SA	R/G
Chicago	.276	.443	10.15	.249	.366	7.32	+27	+77	+2.83
Atlanta	.269	.399	9.47	.248	.366	7.98	+21	+33	+1.49
Cincinnati	.264	.392	8.72	.239	.359	7.86	+25	+33	+0.86
Pittsburgh	.256	.371	8.26	.246	.354	7.59	+10	+17	+0.67
Philadelphia	.254	.391	8.49	.250	.376	8.05	+4	+15	+0.44
St. Louis	.256	.363	7.57	.254	.369	8.72	+2	−6	−1.15
San Diego	.253	.381	7.95	.259	.367	7.75	−6	+14	+0.20
Houston	.255	.364	8.28	.261	.399	8.96	−6	−35	−0.68
New York	.242	.354	7.38	.251	.379	8.21	−9	−25	−0.83
Montreal	.237	.347	7.27	.256	.381	8.50	−19	−34	−1.23
Los Angeles	.238	.334	7.01	.257	.389	8.56	−19	−55	−1.55
San Francisco	.226	.343	7.06	.255	.379	8.12	−29	−36	−1.06

While other stadiums had a greater effect on run-scoring and power, none sapped batting averages as much as Candlestick. What's curious, though, is that while such stadiums as Olympic Stadium and Shea Stadium have had that effect for years, Candlestick has not. Here's another look at the collected offensive statistics of the Giants and their opponents, this time comparing the previous four seasons to the 1985 figures:

	Composite In Home Games			Composite In Road Games			Effect of Home Park		
	BA	SA	R/G	BA	SA	R/G	BA	SA	R/G
1981–84	.260	.370	8.41	.261	.385	8.59	−1	−15	−0.18
1985	.226	.343	7.06	.255	.379	8.12	−29	−36	−1.06

The unusual total of 64 day games that the Giants played in 1985 may have been responsible for a dramatic change in the statistical tilt of the ballpark, away from one that was "batting average–neutral," to borrow a phrase from Congressman Rostenkowski, to one that only a pitcher could love. (From 1981–84, the Giants played an average of 40 home day games a season, pro-rating the total for strike-shortened 1981.) The curiosity, of course, is that the park revered as the ultimate hitter's park—and the one that gave hitters their biggest boost in batting average last season—is Wrigley Field in Chicago, where, rumor has it, all games are played in the daytime. So the two parks in which the most day games were played came in first and last on the same list.

Perhaps, however, the day games are only a coincidental factor. There is one other element that inexorably links those two fields: Of all National League stadiums, Candlestick and Wrigley are the two where the wind has the most visible continuing impact. The wind doesn't *always* blow out at Wrigley, but when it does, it seems to produce high-scoring games. Since 1960, there have been 318 double-digit scores at Wrigley Field, but only 174 at Candlestick, where the wind rarely blows out. And on any discomfort scale, the windiest day at Wrigley can't compete with the typical day at Candlestick. For the batter standing at the plate, wiping tears from his eyes, dirt billowing into his face, calling time out while papers swirl across the infield, might not the thought, "Let's get this over with," creep into his mind? Bobby Murcer has as much as admitted that he felt that way during the two years he played for the Giants. If the Giants do actually move from Candlestick Point, they will be saying good-bye to what will be one of the least-missed parks in the history of the game.

National League GIDPs by Park

We discussed at length in the California Angels essay the tendencies of certain parks to increase or decrease the likelihood of double-play ground-outs. One noticeable trend throughout the American League was that grass fields generally increased GIDPs, while artificial turf tended to suppress them. That holds true for the National League stadiums as well, with two significant exceptions: Dodger Stadium, with its hard, crushed-brick infield surface, and Candlestick Park, which inhibits double plays more than any other stadium in either league.

Those who have watched baseball at Candlestick know that ground balls there frequently take twists and turns more associated with a miniature-golf course than a major-league infield. As we mentioned earlier, the Giants experimented with artificial turf at Candlestick during the 1970s, but since 1979 they have played on a surface of natural grass that produces some rather unnatural results. There were 12 percent more errors last season in Giants home games than Giants road games, and no one found turning double plays an easy task. The following table lists the number of double-play ground-outs over the past three seasons for each National League team, divided into their home-game and road-game totals:

Team	Home	Road	Diff.
Atlanta	453	388	+16.8%
Chicago	388	321	+20.9%
Cincinnati	319	340	−6.2%
Houston	355	337	+5.3%
Los Angeles	312	355	−12.1%
Montreal	350	335	+4.5%
New York	359	395	−9.1%
Philadelphia	347	356	−2.5%
Pittsburgh	367	354	+3.7%
St. Louis	361	408	−11.5%
San Diego	388	348	+11.5%
San Francisco	319	381	−16.3%

This Year's Model

The Giants made the first big deal of the off-season, trading Dave LaPoint and two youngsters to the Tigers in October for Juan Berenguer and catcher Bob Melvin. LaPoint was 7–17 with a 3.52 ERA in his one season with the Giants, but in his 17 losses, San Francisco scored a total of only 29 runs. That total is low, even for the Giants.

For some reason, we can't help but think about the parallels between the careers of LaPoint and the Cardinals' John Tudor. Each was born in upstate New York (LaPoint in Glens Falls, Tudor in Schenectady), each throws left-handed, each was traded (LaPoint by the Cardinals, Tudor by the Red Sox) following four straight seasons over the .500 mark. Each then lasted only one season with his new team (Tudor with the 1984 Pirates, LaPoint with the 1985 Giants), suffered through a last-place finish, and was traded again. LaPoint's career ERA is 3.79 and his career strikeout rate is 5.3 per nine innings; Tudor had those *exact same numbers* at the time he was traded to St. Louis last year. Both the Pirates and the Giants received a veteran player and a young catcher in return for Tudor and LaPoint, respectively.

The Pirates struck out in trading Tudor to the Cardinals last season. The big man the Pirates received, George Hendrick, didn't last the season in Pittsburgh. Roger Craig has seen Berenguer pitch well before, on the Tigers in '84, but for the Giants, long criticized for their tendency to give away outfielders, the ultimate indignity would be for the 1986 LaPoint to pitch like the 1985 Tudor.

WON-LOST RECORD BY STARTING POSITION

SAN FRANCISCO 62-100	C	1B	2B	3B	SS	LF	CF	RF	P	Leadoff	Relief	Starts
Rick Adams	-	-	1-2	5-5	6-13	-	-	-	-	1-1	-	12-20
Vida Blue	-	-	-	-	-	-	-	-	10-10	-	4-9	10-10
Bob Brenly	37-65	1-2	-	5-11	-	-	-	-	-	-	-	43-78
Chris Brown	-	-	-	45-75	-	-	-	-	-	-	-	45-75
Chili Davis	-	-	-	-	-	-	16-20	35-55	-	-	-	51-75
Mark Davis	-	-	-	-	-	-	-	-	0-1	-	27-49	0-1
Rob Deer	-	1-6	-	-	-	5-10	-	4-12	-	-	-	10-28
Dan Driessen	-	20-27	-	-	-	-	-	-	-	-	-	20-27
Scott Garrelts	-	-	-	-	-	-	-	-	-	-	29-45	
Dan Gladden	-	-	-	-	6-6	38-68	-	-	-	44-74	-	44-74
Jim Gott	-	-	-	-	-	-	-	-	9-17	-	-	9-17
David Green	-	26-46	-	-	-	-	-	4-4	-	-	-	30-50
Atlee Hammaker	-	-	-	-	-	-	-	-	12-17	-	-	12-17
Mike Jeffcoat	-	-	-	-	-	-	-	-	0-1	-	0-18	0-1
Mike Krukow	-	-	-	-	-	-	-	-	14-14	-	-	14-14
Duane Kuiper	-	-	-	-	-	-	-	-	-	-	-	
Dave LaPoint	-	-	-	-	-	-	-	-	8-23	-	-	8-23
Bill Laskey	-	-	-	-	-	-	-	-	7-12	-	-	7-12
Johnnie LeMaster	-	-	-	2-3	-	-	-	-	-	-	-	2-3
Jeff Leonard	-	-	-	-	46-76	2-0	-	-	-	-	-	48-76
Roger Mason	-	-	-	-	-	-	-	-	2-3	-	-	2-3
Greg Minton	-	-	-	-	-	-	-	-	-	-	18-50	-
Bobby Moore	-	-	-	-	-	-	-	-	-	-	0-11	-
Matt Nokes	4-9	-	-	-	-	-	-	-	-	-	-	4-9
Gary Rajsich	-	8-11	-	-	-	-	-	-	-	-	-	8-11
Jeff Robinson	-	-	-	-	-	-	-	-	-	-	0-8	-
Ron Roenicke	-	-	-	-	-	3-5	0-3	7-12	-	2-2	-	10-20
Scot Thompson	-	6-8	-	-	-	-	-	-	-	-	-	6-8
Alex Trevino	21-26	-	-	-	-	-	-	-	-	-	-	21-26
Manny Trillo	-	-	42-72	0-1	-	-	-	-	-	-	-	42-73
Jose Uribe	-	-	-	53-84	-	-	-	-	-	4-6	-	53-84
Colin Ward	-	-	-	-	-	-	-	-	0-2	-	0-4	0-2
Brad Wellman	-	-	13-13	7-7	1-0	-	-	-	-	1-0	-	21-20
Frank Williams	-	-	-	-	-	-	-	-	-	-	13-36	-
Mike Woodard	-	-	6-13	-	-	-	-	-	-	2-4	-	6-13
Joel Youngblood	-	-	-	0-1	-	2-3	6-9	12-17	-	8-13	-	20-30

Batting vs. Left and Right Handed Pitchers

		BA	Rank	SA	Rank	OBA	Rank	HR %	Rank	BB %	Rank	SO %	Rank
Bob Brenly	vs. Lefties	.193	125	.377	69	.298	95	5.26	15	12.88	28	6.82	12
	vs. Righties	.230	115	.396	65	.316	79	3.99	23	10.72	37	14.21	80
Chris Brown	vs. Lefties	.209	116	.400	56	.298	94	4.55	25	8.87	70	14.52	82
	vs. Righties	.292	26	.457	22	.361	37	3.42	30	7.54	81	16.76	99
Chili Davis	vs. Lefties	.248	79	.314	106	.296	96	0.95	94	6.96	93	16.52	98
	vs. Righties	.277	40	.439	31	.363	32	3.19	36	12.39	30	12.61	67
Rob Deer	vs. Lefties	.209	117	.522	11	.289	103	8.96	2	10.53	47	31.58	134
	vs. Righties	.168	--	.274	--	.279	--	2.11	--	13.51	--	42.34	--
Dan Driessen	vs. Lefties	.284	36	.379	68	.317	77	1.05	92	4.90	116	11.76	59
	vs. Righties	.234	111	.344	92	.313	83	2.01	65	10.00	49	8.67	28
Dan Gladden	vs. Lefties	.259	66	.320	103	.335	60	0.68	103	9.70	57	12.73	68
	vs. Righties	.237	106	.358	88	.295	109	1.69	72	6.06	102	14.39	82
David Green	vs. Lefties	.211	114	.275	122	.277	115	0.92	96	8.33	76	22.50	124
	vs. Righties	.270	51	.389	72	.315	81	2.16	60	5.97	104	15.42	89
Jeff Leonard	vs. Lefties	.255	71	.489	22	.266	119	4.96	17	1.40	134	15.38	88
	vs. Righties	.235	109	.355	89	.274	125	2.73	45	4.90	122	21.91	131
Ron Roenicke	vs. Lefties	.278	--	.333	--	.316	--	0.00	--	5.26	--	5.26	--
	vs. Righties	.252	78	.417	46	.420	4	2.61	46	22.52	1	17.22	104
Alex Trevino	vs. Lefties	.308	17	.481	26	.393	11	1.92	72	13.11	25	9.84	37
	vs. Righties	.171	--	.371	--	.256	--	4.76	--	10.17	--	15.25	--
Manny Trillo	vs. Lefties	.229	100	.282	119	.294	97	0.76	100	8.28	77	8.28	21
	vs. Righties	.222	122	.291	122	.285	115	0.63	108	7.78	75	8.89	30
Jose Uribe	vs. Lefties	.216	107	.296	115	.263	99	0.80	99	5.26	112	14.29	78
	vs. Righties	.245	95	.322	107	.293	112	0.57	109	6.05	103	10.00	42
Brad Wellman	vs. Lefties	.324	--	.471	--	.333	--	0.00	--	0.00	--	5.26	--
	vs. Righties	.214	125	.271	127	.252	132	0.00	120	2.67	134	20.67	128
Joel Youngblood	vs. Lefties	.308	17	.385	63	.379	18	1.28	85	9.20	65	18.39	109
	vs. Righties	.250	83	.329	104	.343	52	1.97	66	12.50	27	11.93	63
Team Average	vs. Lefties	.238	11	.358	9	.301	12	2.31	6	7.59	11	15.18	8
	vs. Righties	.231	12	.345	12	.299	12	2.06	7	8.20	10	16.10	11
League Average	vs. Lefties	.250		.374		.317		2.26		8.65		14.84	
	vs. Righties	.253		.374		.320		2.12		8.62		14.28	

Batting with Runners on Base and Bases Empty

		BA	Rank	SA	Rank	OBA	Rank	HR %	Rank	BB %	Rank	SO %	Rank
Bob Brenly	Runners On	.238	98	.427	50	.335	68	4.88	16	12.82	39	9.74	47
	Bases Empty	.210	121	.370	72	.297	94	3.99	23	10.32	29	13.87	76
Chris Brown	Runners On	.313	16	.489	19	.386	24	3.41	38	8.08	89	18.69	124
	Bases Empty	.242	91	.410	44	.317	68	3.91	26	7.75	59	14.44	80
Chili Davis	Runners On	.240	94	.398	68	.350	57	3.06	42	15.35	15	15.35	94
	Bases Empty	.291	14	.421	39	.348	32	2.46	53	8.06	52	11.94	53
Dan Driessen	Runners On	.211	128	.256	132	.301	104	0.45	114	11.15	51	8.85	40
	Bases Empty	.270	50	.430	34	.325	58	2.96	40	7.19	68	9.59	31
Dan Gladden	Runners On	.252	81	.314	109	.316	91	0.63	105	5.88	120	11.23	65
	Bases Empty	.239	96	.362	81	.302	86	1.75	72	7.75	58	15.24	89
David Green	Runners On	.241	92	.286	117	.304	101	0.89	93	7.87	94	14.96	89
	Bases Empty	.253	80	.385	65	.299	90	2.20	59	6.19	85	20.10	121
Jeff Leonard	Runners On	.243	89	.393	70	.283	123	2.93	47	5.10	126	21.18	130
	Bases Empty	.239	97	.392	58	.261	122	3.73	28	2.90	131	19.20	115
Manny Trillo	Runners On	.269	62	.311	110	.330	75	0.00	115	8.16	88	7.65	25
	Bases Empty	.197	128	.275	126	.262	121	1.06	96	7.77	57	9.39	30
Jose Uribe	Runners On	.266	67	.326	103	.325	83	0.00	115	6.83	110	7.32	22
	Bases Empty	.219	116	.308	114	.260	124	1.03	98	5.19	109	13.64	72
Joel Youngblood	Runners On	.286	42	.378	79	.366	44	2.04	60	10.62	58	13.27	80
	Bases Empty	.258	67	.326	105	.347	34	1.52	82	12.00	23	14.67	84
Team Average	Runners On	.239	12	.348	11	.313	12	1.96	9	9.00	10	15.36	11
	Bases Empty	.229	12	.348	12	.290	12	2.22	6	7.38	9	16.22	10
League Average	Runners On	.258		.381		.332		2.19		9.74		13.69	
	Bases Empty	.248		.369		.309		2.14		7.75		15.05	

Overall Batting Compared to Late Inning Pressure Situations

		BA	Rank	SA	Rank	OBA	Rank	HR %	Rank	BB %	Rank	SO %	Rank	RDI %	Rank
Bob Brenly	Overall	.220	123	.391	72	.311	86	4.32	19	11.29	29	12.28	62	.256	89
	Pressure	.187	117	.336	77	.269	109	4.67	21	9.02	67	9.02	25	.242	72
Chris Brown	Overall	.271	51	.442	28	.345	44	3.70	30	7.88	81	16.18	100	.325	28
	Pressure	.351	8	.479	28	.419	14	2.13	57	10.38	52	18.87	104	.314	41
Chili Davis	Overall	.270	53	.412	51	.349	42	2.70	44	11.25	30	13.43	76	.296	60
	Pressure	.235	86	.321	80	.367	39	2.47	48	17.17	11	12.12	50	.385	16
Rob Deer	Overall	.185	--	.377	--	.283	--	4.94	--	12.30	--	37.97	--	.186	--
	Pressure	.079	135	.158	132	.186	133	2.63	43	11.63	41	51.16	135	.286	--
Dan Driessen	Overall	.243	99	.351	90	.314	83	1.83	72	9.06	60	9.24	30	.234	107
	Pressure	.333	15	.449	38	.413	18	2.90	40	12.50	34	3.75	1	.316	39
Dan Gladden	Overall	.243	101	.347	96	.307	97	1.39	86	7.13	92	13.90	78	.297	57
	Pressure	.202	106	.298	89	.276	104	1.06	88	6.36	105	18.18	97	.233	80
David Green	Overall	.248	94	.347	95	.301	102	1.70	77	6.85	100	18.07	117	.209	122
	Pressure	.311	27	.377	64	.368	38	1.64	68	7.25	96	15.94	86	.357	21
Jeff Leonard	Overall	.241	104	.393	71	.272	131	3.35	35	3.95	131	20.15	125	.248	96
	Pressure	.278	51	.389	59	.337	66	1.11	85	8.08	79	16.16	87	.125	120
Gary Rajsich	Overall	.165	--	.231	--	.296	--	0.00	--	15.45	--	20.00	--	.216	--
	Pressure	.091	133	.091	135	.268	110	0.00	92	18.60	9	18.60	100	.600	--
Ron Roenicke	Overall	.256	--	.406	--	.408	--	2.26	--	20.59	--	15.88	--	.190	--
	Pressure	.290	44	.419	47	.452	4	0.00	92	23.26	1	11.63	47	.455	5
Manny Trillo	Overall	.224	121	.288	125	.287	119	0.67	111	7.92	80	8.71	24	.208	123
	Pressure	.200	107	.267	112	.286	97	1.33	76	10.34	55	12.64	59	.235	78
Jose Uribe	Overall	.237	109	.315	117	.285	121	0.63	113	5.85	114	11.11	50	.200	128
	Pressure	.208	103	.302	87	.248	121	1.04	89	3.77	129	9.43	27	.211	93
Joel Youngblood	Overall	.270	54	.348	93	.355	37	1.74	76	11.41	26	14.07	80	.243	101
	Pressure	.226	93	.321	81	.305	88	1.89	64	10.17	57	23.73	126	.273	55
Team Average	Overall	.233	12	.348	11	.299	12	2.12	8	8.05	11	15.87	11	.248	12
	Pressure	.230	12	.326	12	.309	11	1.89	8	9.38	6	15.80	8	.272	5
League Average	Overall	.252		.374		.319		2.16		8.63		14.45		.273	
	Pressure	.253		.368		.325		2.17		9.26		15.10		.257	

Additional Miscellaneous Batting Comparisons

	Grass Surface BA	Rank	Artificial Surface BA	Rank	Home Games BA	Rank	Road Games BA	Rank	Runners in Scoring Position BA	Rank	Runners in Scoring Pos and Two Outs BA	Rank	Leading Off Inning OBA	Rank	Runners on 3B with less than 2 Outs RDI %	Rank
Bob Brenly	.218	114	.228	108	.227	115	.214	113	.216	110	.200	100	.267	113	.478	117
Chris Brown	.277	45	.254	80	.266	69	.275	41	.337	8	.373	5	.333	52	.526	100
Chili Davis	.263	62	.290	27	.265	70	.275	40	.204	121	.182	110	.308	79	.630	48
Rob Deer	.174	127	.220	--	.159	--	.213	--	.121	--	.056	--	.441	--	.400	127
Dan Driessen	.262	64	.229	106	.233	107	.255	72	.196	126	.211	93	.378	24	.576	74
Dan Gladden	.237	95	.260	69	.232	108	.254	76	.214	111	.237	72	.308	80	.800	7
David Green	.233	98	.296	--	.207	123	.283	33	.182	129	.200	100	.280	102	.500	105
Jeff Leonard	.240	90	.244	92	.239	101	.242	89	.226	107	.175	115	.258	124	.545	90
Ron Roenicke	.250	75	.273	--	.274	--	.233	--	.121	--	.250	--	.500	--	.444	--
Alex Trevino	.248	81	.136	--	.250	--	.178	--	.156	--	.182	110	.300	--	.500	--
Manny Trillo	.219	113	.240	96	.200	126	.249	84	.229	104	.184	108	.294	90	.643	41
Jose Uribe	.235	97	.245	91	.214	121	.263	60	.271	63	.226	77	.227	131	.333	134
Brad Wellman	.231	100	.243	--	.226	118	.247	--	.263	--	.211	--	.227	130	.625	--
Joel Youngblood	.274	49	.260	68	.271	64	.268	51	.276	59	.276	43	.394	12	.500	105
Team Average	.230	10	.241	9	.222	12	.243	7	.221	12	.208	12	.295	11	.542	10
League Average	.251		.254		.256		.248		.257		.235		.315		.576	

Pitching vs. Left and Right Handed Batters

		BA	Rank	SA	Rank	OBA	Rank	HR %	Rank	BB %	Rank	SO %	Rank
Vida Blue	vs. Lefties	.200	9	.307	24	.286	26	2.67	95	9.30	64	20.93	13
	vs. Righties	.248	63	.431	97	.359	106	3.71	99	14.75	113	17.42	41
Mark Davis	vs. Lefties	.184	5	.316	29	.231	4	2.63	93	5.65	18	31.45	2
	vs. Righties	.232	48	.358	54	.317	63	3.41	95	9.97	86	26.98	5
Scott Garrelts	vs. Lefties	.231	31	.302	22	.314	44	0.59	14	10.36	79	19.17	19
	vs. Righties	.172	5	.214	1	.300	49	0.47	2	14.56	112	26.44	8
Jim Gott	vs. Lefties	.245	44	.357	50	.321	48	1.36	54	9.94	73	11.14	66
	vs. Righties	.264	80	.399	82	.307	55	2.20	53	6.06	25	13.80	73
Atlee Hammaker	vs. Lefties	.219	21	.333	40	.239	6	1.90	72	2.73	3	15.45	34
	vs. Righties	.253	69	.396	78	.305	54	2.75	76	7.30	49	13.76	75
Mike Krukow	vs. Lefties	.283	82	.442	96	.333	62	2.60	91	6.70	26	17.94	21
	vs. Righties	.189	9	.299	16	.237	5	2.54	69	5.44	17	19.43	30
Dave LaPoint	vs. Lefties	.264	60	.406	80	.284	24	3.77	112	2.70	2	12.61	52
	vs. Righties	.269	89	.396	80	.335	85	2.02	40	9.16	76	13.94	71
Greg Minton	vs. Lefties	.353	114	.432	94	.462	115	0.72	20	17.71	113	5.71	114
	vs. Righties	.222	29	.335	30	.294	43	2.26	57	9.24	77	10.84	93
Frank Williams	vs. Lefties	.342	112	.504	112	.436	112	1.71	67	14.18	103	13.48	42
	vs. Righties	.164	2	.230	2	.259	12	1.97	39	8.47	68	19.77	27
Team Average	vs. Lefties	.262	6	.386	9	.331	7	1.95	9	9.13	6	14.62	3
	vs. Righties	.240	4	.368	5	.313	7	2.47	7	9.34	11	16.66	3
League Average	vs. Lefties	.262		.374		.330		1.73		9.17		12.66	
	vs. Righties	.246		.374		.311		2.44		8.28		15.62	

Pitching with Runners on Base and Bases Empty

		BA	Rank	SA	Rank	OBA	Rank	HR %	Rank	BB %	Rank	SO %	Rank
Vida Blue	Runners On	.250	51	.431	89	.324	48	4.17	110	9.80	56	19.22	16
	Bases Empty	.232	37	.395	83	.367	111	3.04	95	17.24	115	16.93	40
Mark Davis	Runners On	.278	88	.439	94	.332	58	3.89	107	6.70	15	22.49	7
	Bases Empty	.172	1	.273	10	.266	13	2.64	85	10.55	95	32.81	1
Scott Garrelts	Runners On	.206	11	.256	2	.342	72	0.56	4	16.67	114	21.93	9
	Bases Empty	.191	8	.250	3	.270	20	0.49	6	8.85	78	24.78	7
Jim Gott	Runners On	.268	75	.396	74	.328	54	2.13	57	8.58	38	9.70	89
	Bases Empty	.244	53	.364	58	.305	55	1.51	39	7.76	61	14.40	59
Atlee Hammaker	Runners On	.236	32	.335	23	.290	16	1.57	33	7.59	23	11.72	79
	Bases Empty	.254	66	.418	96	.299	46	3.27	102	5.91	32	15.60	48
Mike Krukow	Runners On	.218	16	.356	44	.292	18	3.17	93	8.84	42	19.21	17
	Bases Empty	.251	60	.385	77	.284	28	2.20	67	4.20	12	18.28	30
Dave LaPoint	Runners On	.268	74	.368	56	.333	59	1.76	43	9.28	47	12.11	75
	Bases Empty	.270	92	.420	97	.325	84	2.61	82	7.63	57	15.06	51
Greg Minton	Runners On	.272	82	.337	24	.378	99	1.09	16	14.91	107	6.14	113
	Bases Empty	.273	95	.409	90	.347	103	2.27	71	10.20	91	11.73	84
Frank Williams	Runners On	.248	47	.381	64	.364	96	2.65	82	14.58	106	12.50	67
	Bases Empty	.237	42	.327	33	.316	75	1.28	23	8.05	65	20.69	18
Team Average	Runners On	.255	6	.374	6	.332	8	2.27	9	10.19	9	14.59	4
	Bases Empty	.241	5	.374	7	.309	7	2.31	8	8.54	10	17.08	1
League Average	Runners On	.258		.381		.332		2.19		9.74		13.69	
	Bases Empty	.248		.369		.309		2.14		7.75		15.05	

Overall Pitching Compared to Late Inning Pressure Situations

		BA	Rank	SA	Rank	OBA	Rank	HR %	Rank	BB %	Rank	SO %	Rank
Vida Blue	Overall	.240	40	.411	95	.348	95	3.55	110	13.94	113	17.94	28
	Pressure	.208	--	.375	--	.333	--	4.17	--	16.13	--	25.81	--
Mark Davis	Overall	.219	15	.346	30	.294	26	3.19	103	8.82	60	28.17	2
	Pressure	.190	13	.331	37	.277	24	3.72	95	9.25	60	28.83	4
Scott Garrelts	Overall	.198	3	.253	1	.306	39	0.52	2	12.78	106	23.35	8
	Pressure	.197	16	.246	13	.319	55	0.44	24	14.80	106	23.47	11
Jim Gott	Overall	.254	64	.377	72	.315	56	1.76	44	8.11	47	12.40	78
	Pressure	.357	112	.429	88	.438	113	0.00	1	11.76	85	5.88	107
Atlee Hammaker	Overall	.247	51	.386	78	.295	29	2.61	92	6.59	21	14.03	61
	Pressure	.206	20	.294	20	.308	46	2.94	84	12.82	91	7.69	97
Mike Krukow	Overall	.238	38	.373	66	.287	22	2.57	89	6.09	13	18.66	22
	Pressure	.163	9	.212	6	.250	11	0.00	1	10.08	68	14.29	58
Dave LaPoint	Overall	.269	90	.398	89	.329	73	2.25	69	8.35	53	13.77	65
	Pressure	.309	101	.519	111	.378	90	6.17	111	9.89	65	14.29	58
Greg Minton	Overall	.272	95	.372	64	.364	107	1.67	36	12.74	105	8.73	106
	Pressure	.271	72	.396	75	.372	85	2.60	77	13.85	99	9.09	90
Frank Williams	Overall	.242	42	.349	31	.338	84	1.86	48	11.01	93	16.98	32
	Pressure	.200	17	.255	14	.299	42	0.91	31	11.63	84	20.16	22
Team Average	Overall	.247	5	.374	5	.319	7	2.29	8	9.27	9	15.97	3
	Pressure	.225	1	.326	2	.320	5	2.18	7	11.78	12	18.55	2
League Average	Overall	.252		.374		.319		2.16		8.63		14.45	
	Pressure	.249		.363		.326		2.12		9.92		15.33	

Additional Miscellaneous Pitching Comparisons

	Grass Surface		Artificial Surface		Home Games		Road Games		Runners in Scoring Position		Runners in Scoring Pos and Two Outs		Leading Off Inning	
	BA	Rank	BA	Rank	BA	Rank	BA	Rank	BA	Rank	BA	Rank	OBA	Rank
Vida Blue	.241	47	.231	--	.214	22	.278	91	.290	95	.231	57	.360	96
Mark Davis	.235	40	.183	6	.228	36	.211	12	.271	73	.205	36	.323	74
Scott Garrelts	.191	5	.231	--	.193	8	.203	9	.200	13	.109	1	.320	69
Jim Gott	.234	37	.302	102	.221	30	.287	101	.255	57	.222	45	.327	77
Atlee Hammaker	.242	50	.263	70	.231	42	.265	77	.270	70	.246	72	.267	19
Mike Krukow	.229	33	.266	75	.221	29	.262	69	.196	11	.174	17	.308	58
Dave LaPoint	.255	64	.301	101	.250	63	.290	104	.230	37	.202	35	.356	94
Roger Mason	.243	53	.000	--	.176	--	.297	--	.304	--	.250	--	.281	--
Greg Minton	.265	72	.295	98	.234	44	.298	107	.280	81	.258	78	.395	111
Frank Williams	.216	18	.304	105	.169	3	.316	111	.277	78	.303	102	.292	40
Team Average	.240	5	.270	12	.229	2	.267	12	.255	7	.226	3	.323	8
League Average	.251		.254		.248		.256		.257		.235		.315	

III
Batter Section

Batter Section

The Batter Section is an alphabetical listing of every player who had at least 200 plate appearances in either the American or the National League last season. Also included are key players who did not meet the 200-plate-appearance requirement. Players are listed alphabetically within each league, followed by the totals for each team and the league as a whole.

Column Headings Information

Don Baylor
New York Yankees   AB H 2B 3B HR RRF BB SO BA SA OBA

AB	At Bats
H	Hits
2B	Doubles
3B	Triples
HR	Home Runs
RRF	Runs Responsible For (See below)
BB	Bases on Balls
SO	Strikeouts
BA	Batting Average
SA	Slugging Average
OBA	On-Base Average

For each player, information is provided in eleven offensive categories. The only one that may be unfamiliar is RRF, *Runs Responsible For*. RRF includes official runs batted in, but also includes all other plays on which runners score following a batter's action, even if no RBI is officially given. (Examples include a runner scoring from third on a ground-ball double play, a runner scoring as a result of a fielder's error on a batted ball, or a batter hitting a triple and scoring on an error on the same play. Runs scored on such plays as a wild pitch or an error resulting from a pickoff attempt are not credited to the batter.)

Season Summary Information

Season	493	129	29	1	27	91	38	68	.262	.489	.341
vs. Left-Handed Pitchers	188	53	9	0	9	38	18	27	.282	.473	.366
vs. Right-Handed Pitchers	305	76	20	1	18	53	20	41	.249	.498	.326
Home	223	55	11	0	10	43	18	38	.247	.430	.325
Road	270	74	18	1	17	48	20	30	.274	.537	.354
Grass	409	106	26	0	21	79	33	57	.259	.477	.336
Artificial Turf	84	23	3	1	6	12	5	11	.274	.548	.365
April	74	16	6	0	3	7	0	9	.216	.419	.244
May	75	21	4	0	6	12	10	12	.280	.573	.386
June	87	23	3	0	7	24	11	9	.264	.540	.360
July	88	22	6	0	3	11	6	10	.250	.420	.316
August	98	25	4	1	5	21	7	14	.255	.469	.333
Sept./Oct.	71	22	6	0	3	16	4	14	.310	.521	.402

Each player's seasonal performance is broken down into a variety of special categories. The first line for each player gives his totals for the whole season. This is followed by breakdowns of his performance against left- and right-handed pitchers, in home and road games, on grass fields and on artificial turf, and in each month. (For players who played for more than one team within a league, all totals are combined. The "home" totals for Bo Diaz, for example, include all games he played in Philadelphia while with the Phillies, and all games played in Cincinnati while with the Reds.)

Leading Off Inn.	107	25	5	0	6	6	8	16	.234	.449	.311
Bases Empty	221	57	11	1	14	14	18	29	.258	.507	.339
Runners On	272	72	18	0	13	77	20	39	.265	.474	.343
Runners/Scor. Pos.	140	35	9	0	3	51	13	15	.250	.379	.337
Runners On/2 Out	133	29	6	0	5	26	11	19	.218	.376	.325
Scor. Pos./2 Out	60	11	2	0	0	12	7	7	.183	.217	.319

Following these breakdowns, each batter's performance is divided into specific game situations. Totals are given for each batter when he led off an inning, when he batted with the bases empty, and with runners on base. These are followed by his performance with runners in scoring position (on second or third base, or both), with runners on base and two out, and with runners in scoring position and two out.

Late Inning Pressure	90	23	6	1	3	13	5	13	.256	.444	.299
Leading Off	18	5	2	0	1	1	0	2	.278	.556	.316
Bases Empty	42	12	5	1	2	2	1	7	.286	.595	.318
Runners On	48	11	1	0	1	11	4	6	.229	.313	.283
Runners/Scor. Pos.	26	7	1	0	1	11	3	2	.269	.423	.333

The next group shows the batter's performance in late-inning pressure situations: any plate appearances occurring in the seventh inning or later with the score tied or with the batter's team trailing by one, two, or three runs (or four runs if the bases are loaded).

Each player's totals are listed for all late-inning pressure situations, then broken out for his performance when leading off an inning, with bases empty, with runners on base, and with runners in scoring position.

DRIVING IN RUNS	0 Out	1 Out	2 Out	Total	
From 1B	3/37	5/77	10/109	18/223	8%
From 2B	4/17	12/50	7/51	23/118	19%
From 3B	3/3	16/23	4/20	23/46	50%
Scoring Position	7/20	28/73	11/71	46/164	28%
Scor. Pos. %	35%	38%	15%	28%	
Driving In Runners from 3B with Less than Two Out:		19/26	73%		

The next section, labeled "Driving In Runs," is a measure of the player's ability to drive in runners from each base with every possible number of outs. For every combination of outs and bases, two numbers are listed: the first is the number of RRFs credited to the batter for bringing home runners from that base; the second is the total number of opportunities the batter faced for that situation. (For example, the notation "14/31" under runners on second with two out would mean that the player batted 31 times with runners on second and two out

and drove home 14 of the runners.) Plate appearances that result in a base on balls, hit batsman, sacrifice bunt, or an award of first base through catcher's interference are not treated as "opportunities" if they do not result in a run.

If there is more than one runner on base, the batter is charged with an "opportunity" to drive in each base runner. A single with the bases loaded that scores only the runner from third is an opportunity and an RRF for the "From 3B" line, but an unsuccessful opportunity for the "From 2B" and "From 1B" lines. (The exception to this is when a base on balls, hit batsman, sacrifice bunt, or award through interference results in a run. A walk with the bases loaded would result in an RRF and an opportunity for the "From 3B" line, but would not be charged as an unsuccessful opportunity for the other two.)

Also given are the total number of runners driven in (RRFs) from each base, followed by the percentage of successful opportunities; runners driven in from scoring position (combining the "From 3B" and "From 2B" lines); the percentage of runs driven in for each number of outs; and a line summarizing the batter's performance driving in runners from third with less than two out.

Following the "Driving In Runs" information are comments for each player. Included are the pitchers each batter loves to face and hates to face. The statistics listed for each individual match-up are from regular season games since 1975.

American League

Tony Armas

Boston Red Sox	AB	H	2B	3B	HR	RRF	BB	SO	BA	SA	OBA
Season	385	102	17	5	23	64	18	90	.265	.514	.298
vs. Left-Handed Pitchers	140	47	9	3	9	23	10	24	.336	.636	.377
vs. Right-Handed Pitchers	245	55	8	2	14	41	8	66	.224	.445	.251
Home	173	50	7	3	11	30	11	26	.289	.555	.332
Road	212	52	10	2	12	34	7	64	.245	.481	.268
Grass	316	85	14	5	20	56	16	74	.269	.535	.305
Artificial Turf	69	17	3	0	3	8	2	16	.246	.420	.264
April	85	21	4	1	6	18	2	15	.247	.529	.261
May	101	23	3	0	7	11	3	25	.228	.465	.250
June	6	3	1	0	1	1	0	1	.500	1.167	.500
July	9	2	0	0	1	1	0	3	.222	.556	.222
August	78	21	5	1	3	14	1	20	.269	.474	.280
Sept./Oct.	106	32	4	3	5	19	12	26	.302	.538	.372
Leading Off Inn.	85	26	3	3	7	7	4	17	.306	.659	.344
Bases Empty	204	60	11	4	15	15	7	45	.294	.608	.324
Runners On	181	42	6	1	8	49	11	45	.232	.409	.269
Runners/Scor. Pos.	106	29	3	1	3	39	11	28	.274	.406	.328
Runners On/2 Out	72	15	4	0	2	17	6	14	.208	.347	.269
Scor. Pos./2 Out	44	11	2	0	1	15	6	8	.250	.364	.340
Late Inning Pressure	62	12	2	0	1	5	0	16	.194	.274	.194
Leading Off	9	1	0	0	0	0	0	3	.111	.111	.111
Bases Empty	37	8	2	0	1	1	0	10	.216	.351	.216
Runners On	25	4	0	0	0	4	0	6	.160	.160	.160
Runners/Scor. Pos.	15	3	0	0	0	4	0	4	.200	.200	.200

DRIVING IN RUNS	0 Out	1 Out	2 Out	Total	
From 1B	3/34	1/47	2/57	6/138	4%
From 2B	2/17	5/36	7/27	14/80	18%
From 3B	1/5	14/25	6/27	21/57	37%
Scoring Position	3/22	19/61	13/54	35/137	26%
Scor. Pos. %	14%	31%	24%	26%	
Driving In Runners from 3B with Less than Two Out:			15/30	50%	

Loves to face: Bert Blyleven (.435, 10-for-23)
Hates to face: Mike Smithson (.077, 2-for-26)
Fly-ball hitter: 0.84 G/A ratio last season. Career: 0.96. . . . Has batted under .200 in Late-Inning Pressure Situations in each of last three seasons. Career average: .236. . . . Only 200-home run hitter in major league history who has more career homers (213) than walks (206), and 38 of those walks have been intentional. . . . Struck out 36 times between bases on balls from May 15 to August 29. . . . Has batted over .300 in day games in each of last two seasons. . . . Has struck out 22 times in 83 career at bats with the bases loaded. . . . Last year's left/right breakdown was unusual; coming into 1985, had batted .250 and slugged .418 vs. lefties, .248 and .470 vs. righties.

Harold Baines

Chicago White Sox	AB	H	2B	3B	HR	RRF	BB	SO	BA	SA	OBA
Season	640	198	29	3	22	116	42	89	.309	.467	.348
vs. Left-Handed Pitchers	217	74	7	1	6	31	11	33	.341	.465	.368
vs. Right-Handed Pitchers	423	124	22	2	16	85	31	56	.293	.468	.338
Home	315	89	16	1	13	62	21	40	.283	.463	.324
Road	325	109	13	2	9	54	21	49	.335	.471	.371
Grass	554	177	28	3	18	102	40	73	.319	.478	.363
Artificial Turf	86	21	1	0	4	14	2	16	.244	.395	.250
April	73	26	3	0	4	13	5	6	.356	.562	.397
May	85	16	4	0	0	9	9	12	.188	.235	.260
June	106	30	6	1	2	15	11	20	.283	.415	.342
July	107	34	4	0	3	21	6	19	.318	.439	.360
August	129	45	6	2	5	30	4	14	.349	.543	.366
Sept./Oct.	140	47	6	0	8	28	7	18	.336	.550	.358
Leading Off Inn.	100	29	2	1	2	2	6	12	.290	.390	.330
Bases Empty	331	94	15	1	9	9	21	44	.284	.417	.327
Runners On	309	104	14	2	13	107	21	45	.337	.521	.370
Runners/Scor. Pos.	182	63	7	1	11	98	16	35	.346	.577	.383
Runners On/2 Out	110	43	7	1	6	44	8	15	.391	.636	.432
Scor. Pos./2 Out	73	27	3	0	6	40	7	12	.370	.658	.425
Late Inning Pressure	76	27	8	1	3	13	8	9	.355	.605	.417
Leading Off	15	6	0	1	1	1	0	2	.400	.733	.400
Bases Empty	42	13	3	1	2	2	2	4	.310	.571	.341
Runners On	34	14	5	0	1	11	6	5	.412	.647	.500
Runners/Scor. Pos.	20	7	2	0	1	9	5	4	.350	.600	.480

DRIVING IN RUNS	0 Out	1 Out	2 Out	Total	
From 1B	1/48	7/87	11/71	19/206	9%
From 2B	7/29	11/53	14/50	32/132	24%
From 3B	9/15	21/30	13/30	43/75	57%
Scoring Position	16/44	32/83	27/80	75/207	36%
Scor. Pos. %	36%	39%	34%	36%	
Driving In Runners from 3B with Less than Two Out:			30/45	67%	

Loves to face: Steve Crawford (.636, 7-for-11, 1 HR)
Hates to face: Floyd Bannister (0-for-11, 5 SO)
.346 batting average with runners in scoring position led team; Chicago's batters hit 41 points higher in those situations than overall last season (see White Sox essay). . . . Led A.L. with .391 average with runners on base and two outs. . . . One of two A.L. players (Don Mattingly was the other) with at least 20 home runs and a .300 batting average in both 1984 and '85. . . . Led A.L. rightfielders with 158 games started. . . . Hit .330 at home, .282 on the road in '84; reversed the pattern in '85. . . . Collected 109 hits in road games, second in A.L. to Boggs's 110, and led league with .335 road batting average. . . . What number comes next in this series? Baines's yearly batting averages vs. left-handers: .159 in 1980, then .320, .282, .234, .278, .341. . . . Has hit at least one grand-slam home run in each of last four seasons.

Dusty Baker

Oakland As	AB	H	2B	3B	HR	RRF	BB	SO	BA	SA	OBA
Season	343	92	15	1	14	53	50	47	.268	.440	.359
vs. Left-Handed Pitchers	144	36	6	0	5	18	24	21	.250	.396	.355
vs. Right-Handed Pitchers	199	56	9	1	9	35	26	26	.281	.472	.361
Home	161	40	5	1	5	19	22	21	.248	.385	.339
Road	182	52	10	0	9	34	28	26	.286	.489	.376
Grass	290	76	12	1	11	38	39	42	.262	.424	.348
Artificial Turf	53	16	3	0	3	15	11	5	.302	.528	.409
April	25	7	1	0	2	12	8	4	.280	.560	.441
May	53	15	3	0	3	9	4	8	.283	.509	.333
June	60	18	0	1	4	10	10	9	.300	.533	.400
July	68	23	4	0	4	10	5	8	.338	.574	.378
August	79	19	3	0	1	8	15	10	.241	.316	.358
Sept./Oct.	58	10	4	0	0	4	8	8	.172	.241	.273
Leading Off Inn.	78	17	2	0	1	1	7	21	.218	.282	.282
Bases Empty	193	52	7	1	7	7	22	30	.269	.425	.344
Runners On	150	40	8	0	7	46	28	17	.267	.460	.376
Runners/Scor. Pos.	90	23	5	0	6	43	17	11	.256	.511	.364
Runners On/2 Out	71	19	5	0	4	23	9	7	.268	.507	.350
Scor. Pos./2 Out	55	15	4	0	4	23	4	6	.273	.564	.322
Late Inning Pressure	58	20	4	0	4	13	9	8	.345	.621	.433
Leading Off	5	1	1	0	0	0	1	2	.200	.400	.333
Bases Empty	26	10	2	0	1	1	2	3	.385	.577	.429
Runners On	32	10	2	0	3	12	7	5	.313	.656	.436
Runners/Scor. Pos.	17	5	2	0	2	10	7	3	.294	.765	.500

DRIVING IN RUNS	0 Out	1 Out	2 Out	Total	
From 1B	1/24	3/43	3/50	7/117	6%
From 2B	0/9	3/20	8/39	11/68	16%
From 3B	5/6	8/10	8/25	21/41	51%
Scoring Position	5/15	11/30	16/64	32/109	29%
Scor. Pos. %	33%	37%	25%	29%	
Driving In Runners from 3B with Less than Two Out:			13/16	81%	

Loves to face: Gary Lavelle (.433, 13-for-30)
Hates to face: Ron Guidry (0-for-10)
.345 batting average in Late-Inning Pressure Situations was his highest in 11 years of *The Player Analysis*. . . . Intriguing totals with bases loaded: 1975–82: .416 (37-for-89); 1983–85: .111 (2-for-18). . . . Batted .412 (7-for-17) as a pinch-hitter last season. . . . Started 51 of 54 games in which A's faced left-handed starters, 39 of 108 against right-handers, mostly in July and August. . . . Batted .057 (2-for-35) in 11 games vs. New York last season. . . . Made his major-league debut with the Braves at age 19 on Sept. 7, 1968, pinch-hitting for a man 10 years his senior—Phil Niekro.

Steve Balboni

Kansas City Royals	AB	H	2B	3B	HR	RRF	BB	SO	BA	SA	OBA
Season	600	146	28	2	36	89	52	166	.243	.477	.307
vs. Left-Handed Pitchers	164	36	9	0	8	15	22	46	.220	.421	.312
vs. Right-Handed Pitchers	436	110	19	2	28	74	30	120	.252	.498	.305
Home	304	77	21	1	17	45	23	73	.253	.497	.308
Road	296	69	7	1	19	44	29	93	.233	.456	.305
Grass	227	57	7	1	16	36	23	71	.251	.502	.325
Artificial Turf	373	89	21	1	20	53	29	95	.239	.461	.295
April	78	21	3	0	5	14	0	21	.269	.500	.269
May	105	26	4	0	3	11	10	27	.248	.371	.319
June	94	22	5	0	5	12	11	31	.234	.447	.308
July	98	29	7	0	8	19	8	28	.296	.612	.358
August	103	21	4	2	6	16	8	22	.204	.456	.261
Sept./Oct.	122	27	5	0	9	17	15	37	.221	.484	.312
Leading Off Inn.	131	34	10	0	8	8	8	36	.260	.519	.302
Bases Empty	340	78	17	1	21	21	27	97	.229	.471	.292
Runners On	260	68	11	1	15	68	25	69	.262	.485	.325
Runners/Scor. Pos.	150	33	1	1	8	50	18	43	.220	.400	.299
Runners On/2 Out	123	26	6	0	3	22	11	38	.211	.333	.287
Scor. Pos./2 Out	73	14	0	0	3	19	9	24	.192	.315	.289
Late Inning Pressure	86	27	6	1	8	15	9	24	.314	.686	.385
Leading Off	21	8	3	0	3	3	2	8	.381	.952	.435
Bases Empty	47	15	4	0	6	6	4	14	.319	.787	.373
Runners On	39	12	2	1	2	9	5	10	.308	.564	.400
Runners/Scor. Pos.	23	5	0	1	1	6	4	5	.217	.435	.357

DRIVING IN RUNS	0 Out	1 Out	2 Out	Total	
From 1B	5/48	6/46	5/92	16/186	9%
From 2B	6/25	5/41	10/56	21/122	17%
From 3B	3/8	9/16	4/30	16/54	30%
Scoring Position	9/33	14/57	14/86	37/176	21%
Scor. Pos. %	27%	25%	16%	21%	
Driving In Runners from 3B with Less than Two Out:			12/24	50%	

Loves to face: Moose Haas (.556, 5-for-9, 1 HR)
Hates to face: Mike Warren (0-for-5, 5 SO)
Led American League with 15 extra-base hits in Late-Inning Pressure Situations last season, one shy of the *Player Analysis* record shared by George Foster ('78), Dave Parker ('79), Bruce Bochte ('80), Dave Winfield ('80), and Lance Parrish ('83). . . . Hit 19 home runs on the road to tie Darrell Evans for A.L. lead. . . . One of six A.L. players to hit at least one home run vs. every opposing club last season. . . . 166 strikeouts was 9th-highest season total in major-league history. . . . Has had 60 career post-season at bats without an extra-base hit; averages one XBH every 9.3 at bats in regular season. . . . Career average of .238 against both left-handers and right-handers, with slightly better power numbers against lefties. . . . Has only two home runs in 94 career at bats at Yankee Stadium.

Jesse Barfield

Toronto Blue Jays	AB	H	2B	3B	HR	RRF	BB	SO	BA	SA	OBA
Season	539	156	34	9	27	86	66	143	.289	.536	.369
vs. Left-Handed Pitchers	207	64	17	2	9	29	25	56	.309	.541	.379
vs. Right-Handed Pitchers	332	92	17	7	18	57	41	87	.277	.533	.363
Home	255	73	16	5	15	50	33	71	.286	.565	.368
Road	284	83	18	4	12	36	33	72	.292	.511	.371
Grass	209	59	12	3	10	31	30	48	.282	.512	.379
Artificial Turf	330	97	22	6	17	55	36	95	.294	.552	.363
April	71	17	2	0	3	11	6	23	.239	.394	.308
May	86	27	6	1	7	14	12	26	.314	.651	.394
June	87	19	2	1	2	12	13	22	.218	.333	.324
July	91	25	5	2	6	14	11	19	.275	.571	.365
August	96	35	12	4	2	17	12	24	.365	.635	.431
Sept./Oct.	108	33	7	1	7	18	12	29	.306	.583	.375
Leading Off Inn.	130	38	9	1	6	6	11	24	.292	.515	.352
Bases Empty	310	92	21	6	16	16	34	78	.297	.558	.372
Runners On	229	64	13	3	11	70	32	65	.279	.507	.366
Runners/Scor. Pos.	135	38	6	1	9	61	24	39	.281	.541	.387
Runners On/2 Out	95	31	9	2	5	34	11	26	.326	.621	.402
Scor. Pos./2 Out	61	20	5	1	5	30	8	17	.328	.689	.414
Late Inning Pressure	79	23	2	2	5	9	7	15	.291	.557	.349
Leading Off	23	5	0	0	1	1	1	3	.217	.348	.250
Bases Empty	54	16	2	2	3	3	3	9	.296	.574	.333
Runners On	25	7	0	0	2	6	4	6	.280	.520	.379
Runners/Scor. Pos.	16	4	0	0	2	6	4	2	.250	.625	.400

DRIVING IN RUNS	0 Out	1 Out	2 Out	Total	
From 1B	1/38	3/61	6/61	10/160	6%
From 2B	3/14	7/37	12/41	22/92	24%
From 3B	3/9	13/27	10/29	26/65	40%
Scoring Position	6/23	20/64	22/70	48/157	31%
Scor. Pos. %	26%	31%	31%	31%	
Driving In Runners from 3B with Less than Two Out:			16/36	44%	

Loves to face: Britt Burns (.389, 14-for-36, 4 HR)
Hates to face: Dan Spillner (0-for-11, 6 SO)
Broke out of platoon shell with 152-start season, exactly double his total of the previous season. . . . 44 career home runs vs. left-handers, 44 vs. right-handers. . . . Batting average with runners in scoring position (.281) was highest of his career. . . . Led major-league outfielders in assists (22) and double plays (8). . . . Career rate of 12.2 assists per 100 games in outfield is highest among active players (minimum: 500 games). . . . Career batting figures at Exhibition Stadium: batting .282, slugging .562, 59 home runs; on road: batting .253, slugging .408, 29 home runs. . . . Has homered in every A.L. stadium except Tiger Stadium. . . . Career batting average of .342 in Late-Inning Pressure Situations with two outs and runners on base.

Marty Barrett

Boston Red Sox	AB	H	2B	3B	HR	RRF	BB	SO	BA	SA	OBA
Season	534	142	26	0	5	56	56	50	.266	.343	.336
vs. Left-Handed Pitchers	164	45	11	0	0	18	22	7	.274	.341	.356
vs. Right-Handed Pitchers	370	97	15	0	5	38	34	43	.262	.343	.326
Home	265	73	15	0	3	26	27	35	.275	.366	.341
Road	269	69	11	0	2	30	29	15	.257	.320	.330
Grass	450	125	23	0	4	49	50	45	.278	.356	.350
Artificial Turf	84	17	3	0	1	7	6	5	.202	.274	.256
April	64	15	1	0	1	6	9	6	.234	.297	.324
May	65	18	6	0	0	8	7	3	.277	.369	.342
June	93	28	4	0	1	14	11	8	.301	.376	.377
July	94	29	3	0	2	13	13	9	.309	.404	.393
August	107	25	6	0	1	7	9	14	.234	.318	.293
Sept./Oct.	111	27	6	0	0	8	7	10	.243	.297	.292
Leading Off Inn.	119	38	8	0	2	2	10	11	.319	.437	.372
Bases Empty	303	84	15	0	3	3	28	29	.277	.356	.338
Runners On	231	58	11	0	2	53	28	21	.251	.325	.332
Runners/Scor. Pos.	141	37	5	0	2	51	20	15	.262	.340	.349
Runners On/2 Out	108	31	6	0	2	33	11	8	.287	.398	.353
Scor. Pos./2 Out	73	20	3	0	2	31	10	6	.274	.397	.361
Late Inning Pressure	79	20	5	0	0	3	11	10	.253	.316	.344
Leading Off	22	6	1	0	0	0	2	4	.273	.318	.333
Bases Empty	51	15	3	0	0	0	6	8	.294	.353	.368
Runners On	28	5	2	0	0	3	5	2	.179	.250	.303
Runners/Scor. Pos.	18	3	1	0	0	2	2	1	.167	.222	.250

DRIVING IN RUNS	0 Out	1 Out	2 Out	Total	
From 1B	0/34	0/61	5/76	5/171	3%
From 2B	2/19	3/35	13/55	18/109	17%
From 3B	6/10	9/21	13/35	28/66	42%
Scoring Position	8/29	12/56	26/90	46/175	26%
Scor. Pos. %	28%	21%	29%	26%	
Driving In Runners from 3B with Less than Two Out:			15/31	48%	

Loves to face: Mike Boddicker (.471, 8-for-17)
Hates to face: Joe Beckwith (0-for-8)
Led A.L. second basemen in games (155), starts (149), putouts (355), and double plays (110). . . . Career batting average of .320, and on-base average of .372, when leading off an inning. . . . Career batting averages: .259 with runners on base, .291 with the bases empty. . . . Has hit only one of his eight career home runs against a left-handed pitcher: May 11, 1984, off Larry Gura. . . . Career rate of 28 percent of runners driven in from scoring position in nonpressure situations, but only 17 percent in Late-Inning Pressure Situations. . . . Plays home games in what may be baseball's most nostalgic ballpark, where his career average is .296, but likes the great indoors, too: career batting average of .348 at the Metrodome, .350 at the Kingdome.

Don Baylor

New York Yankees	AB	H	2B	3B	HR	RRF	BB	SO	BA	SA	OBA
Season	477	110	24	1	23	92	52	90	.231	.430	.330
vs. Left-Handed Pitchers	193	49	13	0	11	39	32	30	.254	.492	.377
vs. Right-Handed Pitchers	284	61	11	1	12	53	20	60	.215	.387	.297
Home	231	50	14	0	12	51	22	44	.216	.433	.315
Road	246	60	10	1	11	41	30	46	.244	.427	.345
Grass	413	93	23	0	17	76	44	78	.225	.404	.322
Artificial Turf	64	17	1	1	6	16	8	12	.266	.594	.380
April	65	17	5	0	2	9	9	9	.262	.431	.368
May	91	23	4	1	7	26	10	16	.253	.549	.364
June	78	13	1	0	3	11	9	16	.167	.295	.264
July	71	22	3	0	6	22	8	14	.310	.606	.388
August	75	14	7	0	1	11	9	17	.187	.320	.330
Sept./Oct.	97	21	4	0	4	13	7	18	.216	.381	.280
Leading Off Inn.	125	26	1	1	6	6	12	23	.208	.376	.298
Bases Empty	262	53	8	1	12	12	24	45	.202	.378	.294
Runners On	215	57	16	0	11	80	28	45	.265	.493	.371
Runners/Scor. Pos.	139	39	12	0	7	70	22	30	.281	.518	.382
Runners On/2 Out	101	31	7	0	7	37	14	22	.307	.584	.435
Scor. Pos./2 Out	70	19	5	0	5	32	11	17	.271	.557	.400
Late Inning Pressure	76	21	3	0	6	14	4	10	.276	.553	.313
Leading Off	28	5	0	0	2	2	0	5	.179	.393	.179
Bases Empty	54	13	1	0	5	5	1	8	.241	.537	.255
Runners On	22	8	2	0	1	9	3	2	.364	.591	.429
Runners/Scor. Pos.	10	5	1	0	1	9	2	0	.500	.900	.533

DRIVING IN RUNS	0 Out	1 Out	2 Out	Total	
From 1B	1/29	3/58	6/64	10/151	7%
From 2B	6/20	6/43	16/52	28/115	24%
From 3B	6/10	17/24	8/30	31/64	48%
Scoring Position	12/30	23/67	24/82	59/179	33%
Scor. Pos. %	40%	34%	29%	33%	
Driving In Runners from 3B with Less than Two Out:			23/34	68%	

Loves to face: Bob Stanley (.348, 16-for-46, 2 HR)
Hates to face: Mike Witt (0-for-10, 4 SO)
Fly-ball hitter: 0.56 G/A ratio was 4th-lowest in majors last season (minimum: 200 PA). Career average: 0.65. . . . Hit by pitch 24 times in '85, tying A.L. record; also boosted career total to 192, breaking Minnie Minoso's A.L. career mark. . . . Before Baylor joined team, no Yankee had led A.L. in that category since four players did it from 1945–48: Crosetti, Henrich, Rizzuto, DiMaggio. . . . One of six players to hit at least one home run vs. every opposing A.L. club last season. . . . Batting average in Late-Inning Pressure Situations has been higher than overall batting average in eight of last 11 seasons. . . . Has batted .317 with runners on base in LIP situations since 1975. . . . Batting .417 (15-for-36) with the bases loaded since joining New York in 1983. . . . Started all 65 games vs. left-handers in '85, but only 61 of 97 against right-handers.

Buddy Bell

Texas Rangers	AB	H	2B	3B	HR	RRF	BB	SO	BA	SA	OBA
Season	313	74	13	3	4	34	33	21	.236	.335	.308
vs. Left-Handed Pitchers	76	22	3	2	0	11	9	2	.289	.382	.356
vs. Right-Handed Pitchers	237	52	10	1	4	23	24	19	.219	.321	.292
Home	155	35	5	1	2	16	19	16	.226	.310	.311
Road	158	39	8	2	2	18	14	5	.247	.361	.305
Grass	270	65	12	3	4	32	28	20	.241	.352	.310
Artificial Turf	43	9	1	0	0	2	5	1	.209	.233	.292
April	76	18	2	1	0	10	6	4	.237	.289	.289
May	89	29	7	1	4	12	13	3	.326	.562	.417
June	104	21	4	1	0	9	6	8	.202	.260	.241
July	44	6	0	0	0	3	8	6	.136	.136	.264
August	0	0	0	0	0	0	0	0	.000	.000	.000
Sept./Oct.	0	0	0	0	0	0	0	0	.000	.000	.000
Leading Off Inn.	51	17	3	1	3	3	4	5	.333	.608	.382
Bases Empty	151	34	5	1	4	4	17	10	.225	.351	.304
Runners On	162	40	8	2	0	30	16	11	.247	.321	.311
Runners/Scor. Pos.	84	20	5	2	0	28	11	8	.238	.345	.320
Runners On/2 Out	49	8	1	1	0	6	5	5	.163	.224	.241
Scor. Pos./2 Out	33	5	1	1	0	6	5	3	.152	.242	.263
Late Inning Pressure	47	12	1	2	1	4	4	8	.255	.426	.314
Leading Off	8	4	0	1	1	1	1	1	.500	1.125	.556
Bases Empty	24	6	0	1	1	1	2	4	.250	.458	.308
Runners On	23	6	1	1	0	3	2	4	.261	.391	.320
Runners/Scor. Pos.	10	3	1	1	0	3	2	2	.300	.600	.417

DRIVING IN RUNS	0 Out	1 Out	2 Out	Total	
From 1B	1/31	3/57	1/36	5/124	4%
From 2B	2/15	5/26	5/26	12/67	18%
From 3B	5/9	8/10	0/14	13/33	39%
Scoring Position	7/24	13/36	5/40	25/100	25%
Scor. Pos. %	29%	36%	13%	25%	
Driving In Runners from 3B with Less than Two Out:			13/19	68%	

Loves to face: Mike Armstrong (.667, 4-for-6, 3 HR)
Hates to face: Chris Codiroli (0-for-12)
Figures above are for A.L. only. . . . Within the scope of a single season, led A.L. third basemen and finished last among N.L. third basemen in the same category: assists per nine innings (minimum: 300 innings in each case). . . . Led A.L. third basemen with rate of 2.43, but transition to a new league, new hitters, a new pitching staff, and artificial surface saw his rate drop to 1.61 after trade to Reds. . . . In 1984, had finished 2d in A.L. in that category, just .001 assist per nine innings behind George Brett. . . . For more on Bell, see National League batters.

George Bell

Toronto Blue Jays	AB	H	2B	3B	HR	RRF	BB	SO	BA	SA	OBA
Season	607	167	28	6	28	97	43	90	.275	.479	.327
vs. Left-Handed Pitchers	214	54	8	2	11	31	18	29	.252	.463	.314
vs. Right-Handed Pitchers	393	113	20	4	17	66	25	61	.288	.489	.335
Home	286	73	16	2	10	49	27	46	.255	.430	.321
Road	321	94	12	4	18	48	16	44	.293	.523	.333
Grass	243	74	11	2	13	38	14	32	.305	.527	.344
Artificial Turf	364	93	17	4	15	59	29	58	.255	.448	.317
April	74	23	1	1	5	11	7	15	.311	.554	.378
May	104	25	8	1	3	14	4	19	.240	.423	.266
June	112	34	3	2	6	19	4	17	.304	.527	.336
July	99	26	6	0	5	22	11	12	.263	.475	.333
August	101	31	4	0	8	23	9	13	.307	.584	.379
Sept./Oct.	117	28	6	2	1	8	8	14	.239	.350	.286
Leading Off Inn.	136	36	5	1	6	6	11	23	.265	.449	.329
Bases Empty	326	96	12	4	17	17	23	54	.294	.512	.354
Runners On	281	71	16	2	11	80	20	36	.253	.441	.297
Runners/Scor. Pos.	160	44	9	2	7	69	14	24	.275	.488	.319
Runners On/2 Out	128	24	4	2	3	25	10	20	.188	.320	.252
Scor. Pos./2 Out	79	17	2	2	2	21	9	16	.215	.367	.295
Late Inning Pressure	78	28	7	1	3	12	6	11	.359	.590	.412
Leading Off	19	6	3	0	1	1	1	2	.316	.632	.381
Bases Empty	52	18	5	1	2	2	3	7	.346	.596	.393
Runners On	26	10	2	0	1	10	3	4	.385	.577	.448
Runners/Scor. Pos.	17	7	1	0	1	10	3	3	.412	.647	.500

DRIVING IN RUNS	0 Out	1 Out	2 Out	Total	
From 1B	5/46	5/78	5/80	15/204	7%
From 2B	6/21	12/46	10/55	28/122	23%
From 3B	6/10	13/23	7/32	26/65	40%
Scoring Position	12/31	25/69	17/87	54/187	29%
Scor. Pos. %	39%	36%	20%	29%	
Driving In Runners from 3B with Less than Two Out:			19/33	58%	

Loves to face: Dennis Boyd (.583, 7-for-12, 1 HR)
Hates to face: Al Nipper (.176, 3-for-17)
Ranks 6th in 11-year history of *The Player Analysis* with .327 career batting average in Late-Inning Pressure Situations (minimum: 200 PA). . . . Fly-ball hitter: 0.73 G/A ratio last season. Career: 0.81. . . . Career RDI percentage from scoring position increases from 27 percent in nonpressure situations to 35 percent in Late-Inning Pressure Situations; .353 career LIP batting average with runners on base. . . . 18 home runs on road was 3d-highest total in A.L. . . . Led A.L. leftfielders with 157 games started. . . . Career batting averages: .282 vs. left-handers, .273 vs. right-handers. . . . Inherits from former teammate Willie Aikens the distinction of being the active major leaguer with the most career at bats (1488) and no sacrifice bunts. Aikens, who defined this category, had 2492. . . . Of all the places not to hit: his career batting average at the Metrodome is .153 (9-for-59).

Juan Beniquez

California Angels	AB	H	2B	3B	HR	RRF	BB	SO	BA	SA	OBA
Season	411	125	13	5	8	47	34	46	.304	.418	.364
vs. Left-Handed Pitchers	174	62	6	4	6	21	15	11	.356	.540	.414
vs. Right-Handed Pitchers	237	63	7	1	2	26	19	35	.266	.329	.327
Home	214	70	6	3	6	32	20	20	.327	.467	.386
Road	197	55	7	2	2	15	14	26	.279	.365	.340
Grass	342	110	13	5	7	43	29	37	.322	.450	.382
Artificial Turf	69	15	0	0	1	4	5	9	.217	.261	.270
April	54	14	1	0	3	8	4	8	.259	.444	.322
May	81	22	1	0	1	9	4	7	.272	.321	.306
June	91	31	2	3	1	8	7	7	.341	.462	.396
July	65	17	2	0	0	2	4	8	.262	.292	.314
August	50	16	1	1	2	10	7	5	.320	.500	.404
Sept./Oct.	70	25	6	1	1	10	8	11	.357	.514	.430
Leading Off Inn.	90	26	4	1	0	0	5	13	.289	.356	.333
Bases Empty	232	69	10	3	2	2	16	30	.297	.392	.351
Runners On	179	56	3	2	6	45	18	16	.313	.453	.380
Runners/Scor. Pos.	108	30	1	1	4	35	8	9	.278	.417	.331
Runners On/2 Out	52	15	0	0	0	8	10	5	.288	.288	.413
Scor. Pos./2 Out	36	8	0	0	0	8	4	3	.222	.222	.300
Late Inning Pressure	67	16	3	0	0	9	5	9	.239	.284	.292
Leading Off	12	2	1	0	0	0	1	3	.167	.250	.231
Bases Empty	32	7	1	0	0	0	3	5	.219	.250	.286
Runners On	35	9	2	0	0	9	2	4	.257	.314	.297
Runners/Scor. Pos.	21	5	0	0	0	5	0	2	.238	.238	.238

DRIVING IN RUNS	0 Out	1 Out	2 Out	Total	
From 1B	5/34	4/50	0/38	9/122	7%
From 2B	3/21	10/42	6/31	19/94	20%
From 3B	3/5	5/17	2/10	10/32	31%
Scoring Position	6/26	15/59	8/41	29/126	23%
Scor. Pos. %	23%	25%	20%	23%	
Driving In Runners from 3B with Less than Two Out:			8/22	36%	

Loves to face: Willie Hernandez (.571, 4-for-7)
Hates to face: Aurelio Lopez (.167, 2-for-12, 5 SO)
Did not commit an error in 120 chances in the outfield last season, but fell 37 games short of meeting the 108-game minimum to qualify for individual league fielding championship. . . . Ground-ball hitter: 1.43 G/A ratio last season. . . . One of two A.L. players (along with teammate Ruppert Jones) to start at least 10 games at each outfield position last year. . . . Was in starting lineup at five different positions last season—1B, LF, CF, RF, and DH. . . . Batting average vs. left-handers (.356) was 2d-highest in A.L. . . . Batting average over last three seasons (.315) is 4th-highest in major leagues (minimum: 1000 AB). . . . Has batted for higher average on grass fields than on artificial surfaces in each of last five seasons. . . . Led A.L. with .368 batting average in day games.

Tony Bernazard

Cleveland Indians	AB	H	2B	3B	HR	RRF	BB	SO	BA	SA	OBA
Season	500	137	26	3	11	64	69	72	.274	.404	.361
vs. Left-Handed Pitchers	128	33	7	0	0	10	22	14	.258	.313	.364
vs. Right-Handed Pitchers	372	104	19	3	11	54	47	58	.280	.435	.359
Home	246	74	16	2	4	29	34	35	.301	.431	.383
Road	254	63	10	1	7	35	35	37	.248	.378	.339
Grass	412	120	25	2	10	56	59	58	.291	.434	.378
Artificial Turf	88	17	1	1	1	8	10	14	.193	.261	.276
April	50	18	2	1	3	7	4	4	.360	.620	.400
May	63	15	6	0	1	8	10	14	.238	.381	.338
June	86	23	3	1	2	13	11	17	.267	.395	.351
July	92	25	5	0	2	8	13	9	.272	.391	.368
August	98	25	5	0	2	12	12	11	.255	.367	.330
Sept./Oct.	111	31	5	1	1	16	19	17	.279	.369	.385
Leading Off Inn.	110	29	8	2	2	2	11	20	.264	.427	.331
Bases Empty	276	74	15	2	9	9	31	45	.268	.435	.342
Runners On	224	63	11	1	2	55	38	27	.281	.366	.382
Runners/Scor. Pos.	130	34	6	1	1	48	33	19	.262	.346	.405
Runners On/2 Out	87	20	4	0	0	20	26	14	.230	.276	.407
Scor. Pos./2 Out	54	13	2	0	0	17	24	9	.241	.278	.474
Late Inning Pressure	86	25	6	0	2	11	6	13	.291	.430	.333
Leading Off	25	8	3	0	1	1	2	6	.320	.560	.370
Bases Empty	52	16	4	0	2	2	3	12	.308	.500	.345
Runners On	34	9	2	0	0	9	3	1	.265	.324	.316
Runners/Scor. Pos.	21	5	1	0	0	8	3	0	.238	.286	.320

DRIVING IN RUNS	0 Out	1 Out	2 Out	Total	
From 1B	1/45	4/52	4/59	9/156	6%
From 2B	5/24	9/41	7/36	21/101	21%
From 3B	7/11	7/15	9/29	23/55	42%
Scoring Position	12/35	16/56	16/65	44/156	28%
Scor. Pos. %	34%	29%	25%	28%	
Driving In Runners from 3B with Less than Two Out:			14/26	54%	

Loves to face: Bud Black (.419, 13-for-31)
Hates to face: Mark Clear (1-for-14, 5 SO)
First Tribe second-sacker to belt for double-digits in round-trippers since Eddie Leon clouted 10 in 1970; boy, that felt good. . . . Admittedly, recent competition has not been overwhelming at that position (Duane Kuiper and Jack Perconte, among others). . . . Hit Indians' only extra-inning homer last year (July 21, beating Dan Spillner). . . . Career batting average of .217 with two outs and runners in scoring position. . . . Over last two seasons, hitless in 23 at bats with two outs and runners on base in Late-Inning Pressure Situations. . . . Has hit 38 of his 44 career homers batting left-handed. Last one from right side: Aug. 15, 1984, off Jimmy Key. . . . 98-point edge on grass last season is not indicative of past performance. Career averages through 1984: .248 on grass fields, .264 on plastic.

Buddy Biancalana

Kansas City Royals	AB	H	2B	3B	HR	RRF	BB	SO	BA	SA	OBA
Season	138	26	5	1	1	7	17	34	.188	.261	.277
vs. Left-Handed Pitchers	27	7	1	0	0	1	2	3	.259	.296	.310
vs. Right-Handed Pitchers	111	19	4	1	1	6	15	31	.171	.252	.270
Home	76	14	4	1	1	6	10	18	.184	.303	.279
Road	62	12	1	0	0	1	7	16	.194	.210	.275
Grass	51	9	1	0	0	1	4	14	.176	.196	.236
Artificial Turf	87	17	4	1	1	6	13	20	.195	.299	.300
April	29	4	0	0	1	4	4	11	.138	.241	.242
May	5	0	0	0	0	0	0	2	.000	.000	.000
June	16	2	1	0	0	0	1	3	.125	.188	.176
July	36	7	0	0	0	0	3	3	.194	.194	.256
August	15	5	2	1	0	0	4	2	.333	.600	.474
Sept./Oct.	37	8	2	0	0	3	5	13	.216	.270	.310
Leading Off Inn.	46	11	1	1	0	0	5	11	.239	.304	.314
Bases Empty	86	18	3	1	0	0	8	21	.209	.267	.277
Runners On	52	8	2	0	1	7	9	13	.154	.250	.279
Runners/Scor. Pos.	25	4	1	0	1	6	6	5	.160	.320	.323
Runners On/2 Out	25	5	1	0	1	4	4	7	.200	.360	.310
Scor. Pos./2 Out	13	3	0	0	1	3	2	3	.231	.462	.333
Late Inning Pressure	12	2	0	0	0	0	3	4	.167	.167	.333
Leading Off	3	2	0	0	0	0	0	1	.667	.667	.667
Bases Empty	7	2	0	0	0	0	2	2	.286	.286	.444
Runners On	5	0	0	0	0	0	1	2	.000	.000	.167
Runners/Scor. Pos.	1	0	0	0	0	0	1	0	.000	.000	.500

DRIVING IN RUNS	0 Out	1 Out	2 Out	Total	
From 1B	0/8	0/14	2/16	2/38	5%
From 2B	0/3	0/6	1/12	1/21	5%
From 3B	0/0	2/5	0/3	2/8	25%
Scoring Position	0/3	2/11	1/15	3/29	10%
Scor. Pos. %	0%	18%	7%	10%	
Driving In Runners from 3B with Less than Two Out:			2/5	40%	

Loves to face: Dave Stewart (.667, 2-for-3, 1 2B, 1 HR)
Hates to face: Phil Niekro (0-for-6, 4 SO)
Had not started seven consecutive games all season until the seven games of the A.L. Championship Series. . . . Received first intentional walk of career from Bill Campbell in Game Seven of World Series; do you think Joaquin would have followed those orders? . . . Possessor of lowest batting average (.191) in major leagues over past two seasons (minimum: 300 PA). . . . Career batting averages: .219 vs. left-handers, .187 vs. right-handers. . . . 15 of 17 career extra-base hits, including all three of his home runs, have been hit from the left side of the plate. . . . From The Elias Book of Lists: American League Stadiums in which Buddy Biancalana Has Not Had a Hit: Tiger Stadium, County Stadium, Yankee Stadium, Arlington Stadium. . . . No, not Royals Stadium, wise guy; he has all of 28 there.

Bruce Bochte

Oakland As	AB	H	2B	3B	HR	RRF	BB	SO	BA	SA	OBA
Season	424	125	17	1	14	64	49	58	.295	.439	.367
vs. Left-Handed Pitchers	54	18	3	0	4	12	10	11	.333	.611	.438
vs. Right-Handed Pitchers	370	107	14	1	10	52	39	47	.289	.414	.356
Home	204	64	13	0	6	31	21	26	.314	.466	.378
Road	220	61	4	1	8	33	28	32	.277	.414	.357
Grass	350	108	17	1	11	53	39	45	.309	.457	.378
Artificial Turf	74	17	0	0	3	11	10	13	.230	.351	.318
April	56	19	2	0	0	8	2	3	.339	.375	.362
May	56	20	3	0	0	7	11	8	.357	.411	.463
June	60	17	4	0	3	9	7	6	.283	.500	.358
July	72	22	0	0	4	15	9	9	.306	.472	.383
August	83	23	4	0	3	15	12	17	.277	.434	.365
Sept./Oct.	97	24	4	1	4	10	8	15	.247	.433	.305
Leading Off Inn.	84	23	6	0	0	0	9	10	.274	.345	.344
Bases Empty	240	62	10	0	3	3	32	36	.258	.338	.346
Runners On	184	63	7	1	11	61	17	22	.342	.571	.396
Runners/Scor. Pos.	100	30	2	1	3	42	14	11	.300	.430	.383
Runners On/2 Out	63	22	3	1	7	25	7	8	.349	.762	.414
Scor. Pos./2 Out	37	9	2	1	1	12	6	5	.243	.432	.349
Late Inning Pressure	65	22	4	0	2	8	9	9	.338	.492	.419
Leading Off	22	8	2	0	0	0	3	3	.364	.455	.440
Bases Empty	36	13	3	0	0	0	6	4	.361	.444	.452
Runners On	29	9	1	0	2	8	3	5	.310	.552	.375
Runners/Scor. Pos.	13	3	0	0	1	5	3	3	.231	.462	.375

DRIVING IN RUNS	0 Out	1 Out	2 Out	Total	
From 1B	2/36	4/56	8/40	14/132	11%
From 2B	7/24	5/24	6/26	18/74	24%
From 3B	8/8	6/13	4/18	18/39	46%
Scoring Position	15/32	11/37	10/44	36/113	32%
Scor. Pos. %	47%	30%	23%	32%	
Driving In Runners from 3B with Less than Two Out:			14/21	67%	

Loves to face: Mark Clear (.368, 7-for-19, 1 HR)
Hates to face: Bret Saberhagen (.071, 1-for-14, 5 SO)
Has batted for a higher average with runners on base than with the bases empty in nine of last ten seasons. Batting averages since 1975: .308 with runners on base, .267 with the bases empty. . . . Career batting average of .337 with runners in scoring position in Late-Inning Pressure Situations. . . . Started 98 of 108 games against right-handers, but only four starts against southpaws. Maybe he deserves better: .270 batting average vs. lefties since 1975. . . . Was batting .307 on Sept. 29, but went 1-for-his-last-19 to fall below .300. . . . Annual won-lost records of Bochte's major-league teams: 68–94, 72–89, 76–86, 73–91 (pro-rated record; traded in mid-season), 56–104, 67–95, 59–103, 44–65, 76–86, a now-understandable year off, and 77–85 in each of the last two years with Oakland; just .475 to most of you, but the best that Bruce has ever played on.

Bob Boone

California Angels	AB	H	2B	3B	HR	RRF	BB	SO	BA	SA	OBA
Season	460	114	17	0	5	56	37	35	.248	.317	.306
vs. Left-Handed Pitchers	135	35	6	0	1	15	14	9	.259	.326	.331
vs. Right-Handed Pitchers	325	79	11	0	4	41	23	26	.243	.314	.295
Home	221	52	5	0	0	33	21	22	.235	.258	.305
Road	239	62	12	0	5	23	16	13	.259	.372	.306
Grass	391	99	16	0	5	52	32	33	.253	.332	.310
Artificial Turf	69	15	1	0	0	4	5	2	.217	.232	.280
April	55	10	1	0	0	4	5	3	.182	.200	.246
May	66	21	0	0	0	9	6	9	.318	.318	.375
June	80	23	4	0	3	13	7	4	.288	.450	.360
July	83	17	3	0	1	6	4	4	.205	.277	.241
August	72	15	2	0	0	9	8	4	.208	.236	.288
Sept./Oct.	104	28	7	0	1	15	7	11	.269	.365	.313
Leading Off Inn.	104	25	4	0	3	3	10	6	.240	.365	.325
Bases Empty	242	58	9	0	4	4	23	18	.240	.326	.313
Runners On	218	56	8	0	1	52	14	17	.257	.307	.297
Runners/Scor. Pos.	132	33	4	0	0	47	12	10	.250	.280	.304
Runners On/2 Out	113	26	4	0	0	21	10	12	.230	.265	.293
Scor. Pos./2 Out	72	17	2	0	0	20	8	8	.236	.264	.313
Late Inning Pressure	57	18	2	0	0	10	10	6	.316	.351	.412
Leading Off	14	4	1	0	0	0	2	1	.286	.357	.375
Bases Empty	33	10	1	0	0	0	5	3	.303	.333	.395
Runners On	24	8	1	0	0	10	5	3	.333	.375	.433
Runners/Scor. Pos.	16	6	0	0	0	10	5	2	.375	.375	.500

DRIVING IN RUNS	0 Out	1 Out	2 Out	Total	
From 1B	2/24	2/56	2/88	6/168	4%
From 2B	1/6	11/46	12/57	24/109	22%
From 3B	4/6	10/21	7/26	21/53	40%
Scoring Position	5/12	21/67	19/83	45/162	28%
Scor. Pos. %	42%	31%	23%	28%	
Driving In Runners from 3B with Less than Two Out:			14/27	52%	

Loves to face: Luis Leal (.455, 10-for-22, 1 HR)
Hates to face: Jim Clancy (.095, 2-for-21)
Oldest catcher in majors last season (37), but led A.L. catchers in games (147) and starts (137); started 46 of the Angels' 47 games against southpaws. . . . 1,664 career games at catcher, 9th-most in major-league history; a 100-game season in 1986 would send him past Yogi Berra, Bill Dickey, Ted Simmons (probably), Ray Schalk, and Johnny Bench. . . . Scored the fewest runs (37) of any player to qualify for A.L. batting title last season. . . . Batted .077 (1-for-13) with the bases loaded last year. . . . Walk/strikeout ratios over past 11 years: 1.74 vs. left-handers, 0.87 vs. right-handers. . . . Has hit .218 (36-for-165) in Late-Inning Pressure Situations with runners on base since 1975. . . . Career batting average of .171 at Royals Stadium, the only A.L. ballpark in which he has not had an extra-base hit.

Wade Boggs

Boston Red Sox	AB	H	2B	3B	HR	RRF	BB	SO	BA	SA	OBA
Season	653	240	42	3	8	81	96	61	.368	.478	.450
vs. Left-Handed Pitchers	213	74	12	1	2	29	24	21	.347	.441	.418
vs. Right-Handed Pitchers	440	166	30	2	6	52	72	40	.377	.495	.465
Home	311	130	24	2	6	40	51	38	.418	.566	.503
Road	342	110	18	1	2	41	45	23	.322	.398	.401
Grass	545	198	33	2	7	69	81	51	.363	.470	.448
Artificial Turf	108	42	9	1	1	12	15	10	.389	.519	.463
April	83	25	3	0	1	8	15	11	.301	.373	.400
May	101	32	4	1	0	15	15	10	.317	.376	.405
June	101	38	12	0	1	7	17	6	.376	.525	.475
July	103	40	8	0	2	16	16	12	.388	.524	.471
August	123	49	7	0	3	15	13	11	.398	.528	.460
Sept./Oct.	142	56	8	2	1	20	20	11	.394	.500	.472
Leading Off Inn.	136	54	12	0	2	2	18	13	.397	.529	.468
Bases Empty	369	130	24	0	6	6	47	37	.352	.466	.430
Runners On	284	110	18	3	2	75	49	24	.387	.493	.476
Runners/Scor. Pos.	158	62	9	2	2	73	32	15	.392	.513	.490
Runners On/2 Out	102	38	6	0	0	30	22	9	.373	.431	.484
Scor. Pos./2 Out	75	28	5	0	0	30	17	7	.373	.440	.489
Late Inning Pressure	81	32	2	0	0	7	16	5	.395	.420	.495
Leading Off	13	8	1	0	0	0	5	0	.615	.692	.722
Bases Empty	36	14	1	0	0	0	6	2	.389	.417	.476
Runners On	45	18	1	0	0	7	10	3	.400	.422	.509
Runners/Scor. Pos.	27	10	0	0	0	7	8	3	.370	.370	.514

DRIVING IN RUNS	0 Out	1 Out	2 Out	Total	
From 1B	3/73	0/68	0/62	3/203	1%
From 2B	8/33	11/36	18/60	37/129	29%
From 3B	6/7	15/24	12/28	33/59	56%
Scoring Position	14/40	26/60	30/88	70/188	37%
Scor. Pos. %	35%	43%	34%	37%	
Driving In Runners from 3B with Less than Two Out:			21/31	68%	

Loves to face: Tom Tellmann (1.000, 7-for-7, 1 HR)
Hates to face: Matt Young (0-for-14)
Ground-ball hitter: 1.56 G/A ratio last season. Career: 1.38. . . . Batted over .300 against every A.L. club except Cleveland (.275, 14-for-51). . . . Career batting averages: .373 vs. right-handers, .300 vs. left-handers. . . . Improved batting average vs. left-handed pitchers 107 points from 1984 to '85. . . . Batted .188 (3-for-16) with the bases loaded last season; had batted .483 (14-for-29) until last year. . . . Batting average with runners in scoring position has been higher than overall batting average in each of four seasons with Boston. . . . Failed to reach base safely in only eight games in which he played last season. . . . Yes, he hit only one fair popup to an infielder all year (Doyle Alexander made him do it on Sept. 26), but he also hit four foul popups caught by an infielder or catcher.

Daryl Boston

Chicago White Sox	AB	H	2B	3B	HR	RRF	BB	SO	BA	SA	OBA
Season	232	53	13	1	3	16	14	44	.228	.332	.271
vs. Left-Handed Pitchers	17	2	0	0	0	0	2	4	.118	.118	.211
vs. Right-Handed Pitchers	215	51	13	1	3	16	12	40	.237	.349	.276
Home	97	17	3	0	1	3	5	21	.175	.237	.214
Road	135	36	10	1	2	13	9	23	.267	.400	.313
Grass	189	41	11	1	1	12	13	36	.217	.302	.266
Artificial Turf	43	12	2	0	2	4	1	8	.279	.465	.295
April	48	14	4	1	0	5	2	5	.292	.417	.320
May	52	8	1	0	1	1	6	12	.154	.231	.241
June	63	13	3	0	2	6	3	18	.206	.349	.242
July	0	0	0	0	0	0	0	0	.000	.000	.000
August	0	0	0	0	0	0	0	0	.000	.000	.000
Sept./Oct.	69	18	5	0	0	4	3	9	.261	.333	.288
Leading Off Inn.	55	13	4	0	0	0	3	15	.236	.309	.276
Bases Empty	142	31	9	1	2	3	7	27	.218	.338	.255
Runners On	90	22	4	0	1	13	7	17	.244	.322	.296
Runners/Scor. Pos.	46	9	2	0	1	11	4	9	.196	.304	.255
Runners On/2 Out	38	10	2	0	0	6	3	7	.263	.316	.317
Scor. Pos./2 Out	23	5	2	0	0	6	3	4	.217	.304	.308
Late Inning Pressure	36	7	2	0	1	2	1	9	.194	.333	.216
Leading Off	10	3	1	0	0	0	0	2	.300	.400	.300
Bases Empty	24	5	2	0	1	1	0	5	.208	.417	.208
Runners On	12	2	0	0	0	1	1	4	.167	.167	.231
Runners/Scor. Pos.	6	1	0	0	0	1	1	2	.167	.167	.286

DRIVING IN RUNS	0 Out	1 Out	2 Out	Total	
From 1B	1/12	1/31	1/29	3/72	4%
From 2B	1/6	1/15	2/16	4/37	11%
From 3B	1/1	1/2	3/11	5/14	36%
Scoring Position	2/7	2/17	5/27	9/51	18%
Scor. Pos. %	29%	12%	19%	18%	
Driving In Runners from 3B with Less than Two Out:			2/3	67%	

Loves to face: Charlie Hough (.500, 7-for-14)
Hates to face: Kirk McCaskill (0-for-6)
To counterbalance Boston Red Sox, who usually hit better at home, this Boston hits better on the road: Daryl hit 92 points higher on road than at home last season, 3d-largest such difference in A.L. . . . Started 44 of Chicago's first 48 games against right-handers. Got off strong, going 12-for-26 (.462) in his first seven starts, but went 5-for-55 (.091) in next 18, greasing the skids for his demotion to Buffalo on June 30. . . . Recalled in September, and started 16 of team's last 21 games against righties. . . . Did not start against a left-hander for the Sox; 3-for-34 against southpaws in parts of two seasons in majors. . . . Hitless in six career at bats, with three strikeouts, in bases-loaded situations.

Phil Bradley

Seattle Mariners	AB	H	2B	3B	HR	RRF	BB	SO	BA	SA	OBA
Season	641	192	33	8	26	90	55	129	.300	.498	.365
vs. Left-Handed Pitchers	176	47	7	2	9	24	17	41	.267	.483	.337
vs. Right-Handed Pitchers	465	145	26	6	17	66	38	88	.312	.503	.375
Home	321	98	18	4	15	43	30	58	.305	.526	.376
Road	320	94	15	4	11	47	25	71	.294	.469	.353
Grass	244	78	11	3	9	39	19	51	.320	.500	.372
Artificial Turf	397	114	22	5	17	51	36	78	.287	.496	.360
April	85	26	6	2	5	16	7	7	.306	.600	.366
May	93	31	5	2	2	9	10	17	.333	.495	.417
June	116	37	7	1	4	17	6	22	.319	.500	.358
July	101	28	1	1	2	7	7	22	.277	.366	.333
August	117	32	7	2	5	14	8	28	.274	.496	.331
Sept./Oct.	129	38	7	0	8	27	17	33	.295	.535	.385
Leading Off Inn.	119	34	7	2	2	2	7	22	.286	.429	.336
Bases Empty	368	107	18	5	17	17	26	70	.291	.505	.348
Runners On	273	85	15	3	9	73	29	59	.311	.487	.387
Runners/Scor. Pos.	159	48	5	3	5	63	21	41	.302	.465	.392
Runners On/2 Out	98	26	7	3	4	29	16	21	.265	.520	.374
Scor. Pos./2 Out	62	15	2	3	3	25	13	18	.242	.516	.382
Late Inning Pressure	92	28	3	1	6	20	7	17	.304	.554	.350
Leading Off	25	5	1	0	1	1	1	9	.200	.360	.231
Bases Empty	52	12	1	0	4	4	2	13	.231	.481	.259
Runners On	40	16	2	1	2	16	5	4	.400	.650	.457
Runners/Scor. Pos.	26	11	1	1	2	16	4	2	.423	.769	.484

DRIVING IN RUNS	0 Out	1 Out	2 Out	Total	
From 1B	2/56	3/56	6/69	11/181	6%
From 2B	9/34	6/42	13/50	28/126	22%
From 3B	10/15	8/21	6/23	24/59	41%
Scoring Position	19/49	14/63	19/73	52/185	28%
Scor. Pos. %	39%	22%	26%	28%	
Driving In Runners from 3B with Less than Two Out:			18/36	50%	

Loves to face: Ray Burris (.556, 5-for-9)
Hates to face: Tommy John (.143, 1-for-7)
Second player in history, and first since Cap Anson in 1884, to hit 20 or more home runs the year after a 300-AB season with no homers. Anson's circumstances were extraordinary: his home field had a right-field fence estimated at less than 250 feet from home plate. Before 1884, balls hit over it were ground-rule doubles, but that year the White Stockings (probably Anson himself) had them changed to home runs. Chicago hit 142 home runs that year (131 at home); the old record had been 34. *The Boston Herald* observed, "That over-the-fence rule is a perfect sham and burlesque." Most of today's Seattle pitchers would agree, and go along with a reinstatement of the old rule. ... Oh, yes—Bradley: career batting averages of .320 with runners on base, .282 with the bases empty; .241 vs. left-handers, .324 vs. right-handers.

Tom Brookens

Detroit Tigers	AB	H	2B	3B	HR	RRF	BB	SO	BA	SA	OBA
Season	485	115	34	6	7	47	27	78	.237	.375	.277
vs. Left-Handed Pitchers	162	47	13	3	4	18	15	21	.290	.481	.350
vs. Right-Handed Pitchers	323	68	21	3	3	29	12	57	.211	.322	.238
Home	232	54	17	4	3	22	12	40	.233	.379	.270
Road	253	61	17	2	4	25	15	38	.241	.372	.283
Grass	407	98	28	4	7	43	24	66	.241	.381	.282
Artificial Turf	78	17	6	2	0	4	3	12	.218	.346	.247
April	26	10	2	1	0	5	2	1	.385	.538	.429
May	75	18	6	2	0	7	4	10	.240	.373	.278
June	89	22	7	1	3	10	7	15	.247	.449	.299
July	93	20	7	1	1	5	7	16	.215	.344	.270
August	97	20	6	0	2	8	4	18	.206	.330	.238
Sept./Oct.	105	25	6	1	1	12	3	18	.238	.343	.259
Leading Off Inn.	104	24	7	1	1	1	3	17	.231	.346	.252
Bases Empty	274	68	23	4	6	6	15	42	.248	.427	.287
Runners On	211	47	11	2	1	41	12	36	.223	.308	.263
Runners/Scor. Pos.	118	32	6	1	0	38	5	20	.271	.339	.298
Runners On/2 Out	82	24	5	2	0	18	6	14	.293	.402	.341
Scor. Pos./2 Out	53	17	1	1	0	17	3	11	.321	.377	.357
Late Inning Pressure	56	14	4	0	0	6	4	6	.250	.321	.300
Leading Off	11	3	0	0	0	0	0	0	.273	.273	.273
Bases Empty	34	8	3	0	0	0	2	3	.235	.324	.278
Runners On	22	6	1	0	0	6	2	3	.273	.318	.333
Runners/Scor. Pos.	14	5	1	0	0	6	2	1	.357	.429	.438

DRIVING IN RUNS	0 Out	1 Out	2 Out	Total	
From 1B	1/32	1/58	2/60	4/150	3%
From 2B	2/13	7/41	12/43	21/97	22%
From 3B	2/3	9/19	4/18	15/40	38%
Scoring Position	4/16	16/60	16/61	36/137	26%
Scor. Pos. %	25%	27%	26%	26%	
Driving In Runners from 3B with Less than Two Out:			11/22	50%	

Loves to face: Tim Birtsas (.667, 4-for-6, 1 3B, 2 HR)
Hates to face: Ken Schrom (.067, 1-for-15)
Mid-eighties successor to the "Mendoza Line": Brookens is only major-league player who has batted below .250, with at least 200 at bats, each of past five seasons. Honorable mention to Wayne Gross, who would be there with Brookens but for a .251 season in '82. ... Committed 23 errors at third base last season, tied with Tim Hulett for most in majors. ... Started 88 of 111 games vs. right-handers, 49 of 50 vs. left-handers. ... Large difference in career batting averages: .279 vs. left-handers, .219 vs. right-handers. ... Career batting average of .199 on artificial surfaces. ... Batting average with runners in scoring position has been higher than overall batting average in four of last five seasons. ... Fly-ball hitter: 0.82 G/A ratio last season. Career: 0.90.

George Brett

Kansas City Royals	AB	H	2B	3B	HR	RRF	BB	SO	BA	SA	OBA
Season	550	184	38	5	30	113	103	49	.335	.585	.436
vs. Left-Handed Pitchers	191	63	10	1	10	39	23	15	.330	.550	.395
vs. Right-Handed Pitchers	359	121	28	4	20	74	80	34	.337	.604	.456
Home	285	105	21	4	15	66	59	23	.368	.628	.469
Road	265	79	17	1	15	47	44	26	.298	.540	.400
Grass	206	63	10	1	15	38	37	22	.306	.583	.415
Artificial Turf	344	121	28	4	15	75	66	27	.352	.587	.449
April	68	19	4	1	2	10	18	3	.279	.456	.430
May	103	36	8	1	6	22	13	8	.350	.621	.415
June	65	21	4	1	0	9	14	6	.323	.415	.443
July	95	41	5	1	7	25	20	10	.432	.726	.534
August	96	35	10	1	7	21	19	10	.365	.708	.458
Sept./Oct.	123	32	7	0	8	26	19	12	.260	.512	.358
Leading Off Inn.	107	37	10	2	8	8	14	6	.346	.701	.426
Bases Empty	329	103	24	4	17	17	38	24	.313	.565	.388
Runners On	221	81	14	1	13	96	65	25	.367	.615	.497
Runners/Scor. Pos.	147	50	9	1	7	80	60	24	.340	.558	.512
Runners On/2 Out	67	26	2	1	2	26	29	5	.388	.537	.577
Scor. Pos./2 Out	48	19	2	1	0	22	27	4	.396	.479	.618
Late Inning Pressure	61	19	7	0	1	12	23	5	.311	.475	.500
Leading Off	15	5	2	0	1	1	8	3	.333	.667	.583
Bases Empty	36	8	4	0	1	1	12	3	.222	.417	.429
Runners On	25	11	3	0	0	11	11	2	.440	.560	.595
Runners/Scor. Pos.	16	7	2	0	0	10	11	2	.438	.563	.643

DRIVING IN RUNS	0 Out	1 Out	2 Out	Total	
From 1B	5/37	11/51	4/43	20/131	15%
From 2B	4/33	14/51	11/36	29/120	24%
From 3B	8/12	17/25	9/19	34/56	61%
Scoring Position	12/45	31/76	20/55	63/176	36%
Scor. Pos. %	27%	41%	36%	36%	
Driving In Runners from 3B with Less than Two Out:			25/37	68%	

Loves to face: Dan Petry (.464, 13-for-28, 5 HR, 1.214 SA)
Hates to face: Roger Clemens (.083, 1-for-12)
Would love to see Ed Vande Berg sign a lifetime contract with the Dodgers; Brett was hitless in 14 career at bats vs. the former Mariner. ... After a quiet World Series, tied a Game Seven record, shared by Max Carey, Ripper Collins, and Willie Stargell, with four hits. ... Led A.L. in batting for the months of May and July. ... Batting averages vs. left-handed pitchers (.330) and with runners in scoring position (.396) were his highest in past 11 years (in 1980, when he hit .390 overall, he batted only .318 vs. southpaws). ... Scoring-position batting average was higher than overall batting average for the first time since 1980. ... Batting .529 (9-for-17) with the bases loaded over last two seasons. ... Walked intentionally 31 times last season, two shy of Ted Williams's A.L. record. ... Batting averages since 1975: .285 on grass fields, .345 on artificial surfaces.

Tom Brunansky

Minnesota Twins	AB	H	2B	3B	HR	RRF	BB	SO	BA	SA	OBA
Season	567	137	28	4	27	90	71	86	.242	.448	.320
vs. Left-Handed Pitchers	182	39	11	2	5	24	25	21	.214	.379	.302
vs. Right-Handed Pitchers	385	98	17	2	22	66	46	65	.255	.481	.328
Home	287	73	13	2	12	47	35	38	.254	.439	.326
Road	280	64	15	2	15	43	36	48	.229	.457	.313
Grass	205	41	10	1	12	30	28	30	.200	.434	.294
Artificial Turf	362	96	18	3	15	60	43	56	.265	.456	.334
April	70	23	4	0	6	17	16	8	.329	.643	.438
May	97	31	3	2	6	17	17	10	.320	.577	.410
June	94	20	5	0	5	17	14	14	.213	.426	.315
July	100	19	5	2	2	9	7	16	.190	.340	.239
August	94	17	3	0	2	8	6	15	.181	.277	.228
Sept./Oct.	112	27	8	0	6	22	11	23	.241	.473	.299
Leading Off Inn.	137	30	6	2	5	5	14	13	.219	.401	.291
Bases Empty	287	72	14	3	15	15	35	35	.251	.477	.332
Runners On	280	65	14	1	12	75	36	51	.232	.418	.307
Runners/Scor. Pos.	150	34	11	0	3	56	22	32	.227	.360	.303
Runners On/2 Out	141	28	7	0	5	26	18	30	.199	.355	.289
Scor. Pos./2 Out	74	13	6	0	2	20	10	19	.176	.338	.274
Late Inning Pressure	70	17	2	0	5	14	11	6	.243	.486	.341
Leading Off	16	3	0	0	2	2	2	0	.188	.563	.278
Bases Empty	38	7	0	0	3	3	5	2	.184	.421	.279
Runners On	32	10	2	0	2	11	6	4	.313	.563	.410
Runners/Scor. Pos.	15	6	1	0	1	9	6	3	.400	.667	.545

DRIVING IN RUNS	0 Out	1 Out	2 Out	Total	
From 1B	4/33	4/85	7/94	15/212	7%
From 2B	3/21	7/40	9/50	19/111	17%
From 3B	10/11	14/30	5/31	29/72	40%
Scoring Position	13/32	21/70	14/81	48/183	26%
Scor. Pos. %	41%	30%	17%	26%	
Driving In Runners from 3B with Less than Two Out:			24/41	59%	

Loves to face: Salome Barojas (.500, 7-for-14, 5 HR)
Hates to face: Aurelio Lopez (0-for-15)
Was leading the A.L. in batting with .362 average on morning of May 25; from May 25 to the end of the season, his .206 average was the lowest in the majors (among players with at least 3.1 plate appearances per team's games). ... Fly-ball hitter: 0.58 G/A ratio was 5th-lowest in majors last season (minimum: 200 PA). Career average: 0.74. ... Career batting averages in Late-Inning Pressure Situations: .315 with runners on base (40-for-127), .144 with the bases empty (27-for-188); must be goin' for the pump with no one on. ... Yearly batting averages vs. left-handed pitchers since 1983: .302, .239, .214. ... Career walk/strikeout ratio of 1.10 vs. lefties, 0.57 vs. righties. ... Has hit fewer home runs at the Metrodome than on road in each of four seasons with Twins; annual home/road breakdowns: 10/10 in 1982, then 8/20, 14/18, 12/15.

Bill Buckner

Boston Red Sox	AB	H	2B	3B	HR	RRF	BB	SO	BA	SA	OBA
Season	673	201	46	3	16	112	30	36	.299	.447	.325
vs. Left-Handed Pitchers	230	67	10	2	4	38	8	12	.291	.404	.311
vs. Right-Handed Pitchers	443	134	36	1	12	74	22	24	.302	.470	.333
Home	328	98	22	2	6	53	12	22	.299	.433	.322
Road	345	103	24	1	10	59	18	14	.299	.461	.329
Grass	563	170	41	3	13	90	26	30	.302	.455	.329
Artificial Turf	110	31	5	0	3	22	4	6	.282	.409	.308
April	81	24	6	0	2	12	5	3	.296	.444	.333
May	104	34	8	0	3	14	6	5	.327	.490	.360
June	106	26	5	0	2	13	5	8	.245	.349	.274
July	108	31	9	0	4	22	1	5	.287	.481	.295
August	123	34	8	2	2	20	4	5	.276	.423	.300
Sept./Oct.	151	52	10	1	3	31	9	10	.344	.483	.374
Leading Off Inn.	142	37	8	3	3	3	7	7	.261	.423	.295
Bases Empty	340	91	24	3	5	5	12	20	.268	.400	.293
Runners On	333	110	22	0	11	107	18	16	.330	.495	.357
Runners/Scor. Pos.	169	54	15	0	10	99	11	7	.320	.586	.344
Runners On/2 Out	133	42	15	0	5	36	7	8	.316	.541	.359
Scor. Pos./2 Out	72	21	10	0	4	31	5	4	.292	.597	.346
Late Inning Pressure	87	29	8	0	3	12	4	3	.333	.529	.359
Leading Off	27	10	4	0	1	1	2	1	.370	.630	.414
Bases Empty	52	17	6	0	1	1	2	1	.327	.500	.352
Runners On	35	12	2	0	2	11	2	2	.343	.571	.368
Runners/Scor. Pos.	14	5	2	0	1	9	0	0	.357	.714	.333

DRIVING IN RUNS	0 Out	1 Out	2 Out	Total	
From 1B	3/52	5/111	7/108	15/271	6%
From 2B	6/29	15/54	14/54	35/137	26%
From 3B	12/18	24/31	10/33	46/82	56%
Scoring Position	18/47	39/85	24/87	81/219	37%
Scor. Pos. %	38%	46%	28%	37%	
Driving In Runners from 3B with Less than Two Out:			36/49	73%	

Loves to face: Nate Snell (.571, 4-for-7, 1 HR)
Hates to face: Joe Cowley (.056, 1-for-18)
Yearly batting averages with runners in scoring position since 1981: .430, .341, .220, .325, .320. . . . Has batted for higher average with runners on base than with the bases empty in eight of last nine seasons; he's been over .300 with runners on base in each of those eight years. . . . Broke his own major-league record for first basemen with 184 assists last season. He had set the record of 161 with Cubs in '83. . . . Led A.L. first basemen with 161 games started. . . . Drove in 17 base runners with 16 home runs last season, 2d-highest average in A.L. . . . Finished last season with 11-game hitting streak to raise batting average to .299, one hit shy of .300 mark. . . . Topped 100-RBI mark for the second time with career-high total of 110. . . . Career batting average of .436 (24-for-55) at Memorial Stadium.

Jeff Burroughs

Toronto Blue Jays	AB	H	2B	3B	HR	RRF	BB	SO	BA	SA	OBA
Season	191	49	9	3	6	29	34	36	.257	.429	.366
vs. Left-Handed Pitchers	143	38	5	2	6	24	27	22	.266	.455	.378
vs. Right-Handed Pitchers	48	11	4	1	0	5	7	14	.229	.354	.327
Home	85	25	6	3	4	16	13	15	.294	.576	.388
Road	106	24	3	0	2	13	21	21	.226	.311	.349
Grass	61	10	2	0	1	6	12	11	.164	.246	.293
Artificial Turf	130	39	7	3	5	23	22	25	.300	.515	.401
April	35	9	2	1	1	5	3	6	.257	.457	.316
May	36	13	1	0	2	9	12	4	.361	.556	.510
June	30	4	0	0	0	2	5	5	.133	.133	.250
July	47	14	3	1	2	7	9	10	.298	.532	.411
August	32	7	2	1	0	5	5	6	.219	.344	.324
Sept./Oct.	11	2	1	0	1	1	0	5	.182	.545	.182
Leading Off Inn.	40	10	1	0	2	2	7	6	.250	.425	.362
Bases Empty	106	27	6	0	4	4	18	18	.255	.425	.363
Runners On	85	22	3	3	2	25	16	18	.259	.435	.369
Runners/Scor. Pos.	49	14	3	2	2	24	11	10	.286	.551	.403
Runners On/2 Out	38	8	2	1	1	12	7	10	.211	.395	.333
Scor. Pos./2 Out	26	6	2	1	1	12	5	6	.231	.500	.355
Late Inning Pressure	35	8	1	1	1	4	4	7	.229	.400	.308
Leading Off	11	3	1	0	0	0	0	1	.273	.364	.273
Bases Empty	19	5	1	0	1	1	1	3	.263	.474	.300
Runners On	16	3	0	1	0	3	3	4	.188	.313	.316
Runners/Scor. Pos.	10	2	0	0	0	2	2	2	.200	.200	.333

DRIVING IN RUNS	0 Out	1 Out	2 Out	Total	
From 1B	1/17	1/19	3/26	5/62	8%
From 2B	0/5	4/15	4/18	8/38	21%
From 3B	2/3	4/9	4/12	10/24	42%
Scoring Position	2/8	8/24	8/30	18/62	29%
Scor. Pos. %	25%	33%	27%	29%	
Driving In Runners from 3B with Less than Two Out:			6/12	50%	

Loves to face: Bryan Clark (.556, 5-for-9, 2 HR)
Hates to face: Bob McClure (.071, 1-for-14)
One of five A.L. players with two pinch-hit homers last season, but was 3-for-30 on the year as a pinch-hitter. . . . Last home run against a right-hander: June 12, 1984, off Tom Waddell. . . . Started first 48 games in which Jays faced a left-hander, but lack of production in those games (17 RBIs in 135 at bats) convinced Toronto to re-acquire Cliff Johnson in late August; Burroughs didn't start against a southpaw the rest of the season. . . . Has batted .203 in Late-Inning Pressure Situations over past three seasons. . . . Career total of 240 home runs is three more than Gus Zernial's, two fewer than Hack Wilson's. Overall career statistical line is somewhat similar to Bill Nicholson's (Cubs and Phillies in '40s and '50s), or, for younger fans, Deron Johnson's.

Steve Buechele

Texas Rangers	AB	H	2B	3B	HR	RRF	BB	SO	BA	SA	OBA
Season	219	48	6	3	6	21	14	38	.219	.356	.271
vs. Left-Handed Pitchers	75	20	1	1	3	7	4	13	.267	.427	.304
vs. Right-Handed Pitchers	144	28	5	2	3	14	10	25	.194	.319	.255
Home	110	24	4	1	5	14	5	21	.218	.409	.256
Road	109	24	2	2	1	7	9	17	.220	.303	.286
Grass	185	40	4	2	6	20	12	35	.216	.357	.270
Artificial Turf	34	8	2	1	0	1	2	3	.235	.353	.278
April	0	0	0	0	0	0	0	0	.000	.000	.000
May	0	0	0	0	0	0	0	0	.000	.000	.000
June	0	0	0	0	0	0	0	0	.000	.000	.000
July	39	9	0	0	0	1	4	7	.231	.231	.302
August	76	17	3	2	1	5	6	17	.224	.355	.298
Sept./Oct.	104	22	3	1	5	15	4	14	.212	.404	.239
Leading Off Inn.	55	15	3	1	2	2	5	5	.273	.473	.333
Bases Empty	130	26	4	3	3	3	8	25	.200	.346	.252
Runners On	89	22	2	0	3	18	6	13	.247	.371	.299
Runners/Scor. Pos.	51	13	1	0	1	13	4	8	.255	.333	.316
Runners On/2 Out	37	12	2	0	3	11	4	2	.324	.622	.390
Scor. Pos./2 Out	22	7	1	0	1	6	3	2	.318	.500	.400
Late Inning Pressure	23	6	1	0	1	4	1	2	.261	.435	.320
Leading Off	10	2	1	0	0	0	0	0	.200	.300	.200
Bases Empty	14	3	1	0	0	0	0	2	.214	.286	.214
Runners On	9	3	0	0	1	4	1	0	.333	.667	.455
Runners/Scor. Pos.	5	1	0	0	0	2	1	0	.200	.200	.429

DRIVING IN RUNS	0 Out	1 Out	2 Out	Total	
From 1B	0/16	0/28	3/26	3/70	4%
From 2B	0/7	2/17	3/18	5/42	12%
From 3B	0/1	5/9	2/8	7/18	39%
Scoring Position	0/8	7/26	5/26	12/60	20%
Scor. Pos. %	0%	27%	19%	20%	
Driving In Runners from 3B with Less than Two Out:			5/10	50%	

Loves to face: Mike Moore (.500, 3-for-6, 1 2B, 1 HR)
Hates to face: Joe Beckwith (0-for-6)
Ground-ball hitter: 1.38 G/A ratio last season. . . . Recalled after the Buddy Bell trade, started 68 of Rangers' last 72 games at third. . . . Averaged 2.12 assists per nine innings (league average: 2.04). . . . Homered in back-to-back games twice last season. . . . Grounded into 11 double plays in 48 opportunities last season, 3d-highest rate in A.L. (minimum: 5 GIDPs), and about double the league average rate. . . . Otherwise developed a positive profile in his half-season, doing his best hitting with runners on base. . . . Played mostly second base in first three minor-league seasons, but was switched to third at Oklahoma City last year. . . . Drafted by White Sox in first round out of high school in 1979, did not sign, and attended Stanford, where he was John Elway's roommate; Rangers selected him in 5th round of 1982 draft.

Randy Bush

Minnesota Twins	AB	H	2B	3B	HR	RRF	BB	SO	BA	SA	OBA
Season	234	56	13	3	10	36	24	30	.239	.449	.321
vs. Left-Handed Pitchers	12	1	1	0	0	0	2	0	.083	.167	.214
vs. Right-Handed Pitchers	222	55	12	3	10	36	22	30	.248	.464	.327
Home	136	34	9	2	5	22	16	15	.250	.456	.335
Road	98	22	4	1	5	14	8	15	.224	.439	.300
Grass	78	20	4	1	5	12	7	12	.256	.526	.326
Artificial Turf	156	36	9	2	5	24	17	18	.231	.410	.318
April	5	1	0	0	1	2	1	0	.200	.800	.333
May	58	16	3	1	5	13	4	9	.276	.621	.317
June	31	2	1	0	0	1	0	3	.065	.097	.121
July	64	16	4	1	3	9	7	9	.250	.484	.329
August	45	14	5	1	1	8	10	7	.311	.533	.446
Sept./Oct.	31	7	0	0	0	3	2	2	.226	.226	.294
Leading Off Inn.	47	11	4	1	2	2	4	5	.234	.489	.308
Bases Empty	122	31	9	1	6	6	12	14	.254	.492	.341
Runners On	112	25	4	2	4	30	12	16	.223	.402	.299
Runners/Scor. Pos.	64	15	3	2	3	28	9	10	.234	.484	.329
Runners On/2 Out	45	8	1	0	1	8	7	7	.178	.267	.302
Scor. Pos./2 Out	31	6	1	0	1	8	6	5	.194	.323	.342
Late Inning Pressure	44	8	1	0	1	4	2	5	.182	.273	.217
Leading Off	8	1	0	0	0	0	0	1	.125	.125	.125
Bases Empty	19	5	1	0	1	1	0	1	.263	.474	.263
Runners On	25	3	0	0	0	3	2	4	.120	.120	.185
Runners/Scor. Pos.	13	2	0	0	0	3	0	2	.154	.154	.154

DRIVING IN RUNS	0 Out	1 Out	2 Out	Total	
From 1B	0/20	2/32	1/36	3/88	3%
From 2B	1/8	8/22	4/26	13/56	23%
From 3B	1/4	7/9	2/8	10/21	48%
Scoring Position	2/12	15/31	6/34	23/77	30%
Scor. Pos. %	17%	48%	18%	30%	
Driving In Runners from 3B with Less than Two Out:			8/13	62%	

Loves to face: Steve McCatty (.438, 7-for-16, 1 HR)
Hates to face: Dennis Boyd (.067, 1-for-15, 5 SO)
Fly-ball hitter: 0.65 G/A ratio, 8th-lowest in A.L. last season (minimum: 200 PA). Career average: 0.74. . . . Batted .125 (4-for-32) as a pinch-hitter last season, .400 (8-for-20) in '84. . . . Candidate for title of Most Strictly Platooned Player, recently abdicated by John Lowenstein: only 39 plate appearances against lefties in four seasons with Twins. Career batting averages: .243 vs. right-handers, .091 (3-for-33) against left-handers. Had his first extra-base hit against a southpaw last July 18, a double off Dennis Rasmussen. . . . Until last season, had always hit better with runners on base (.279) than with the bases empty (.205). . . . No one has ever confused him with Reggie: Twins had 2–8 record in games in which he homered. . . . Has homered in every A.L. ballpark except Anaheim Stadium; career batting average there is .139 (5-for-36).

Brett Butler

Cleveland Indians	AB	H	2B	3B	HR	RRF	BB	SO	BA	SA	OBA
Season	591	184	28	14	5	52	63	42	.311	.431	.377
vs. Left-Handed Pitchers	193	64	8	4	1	17	15	15	.332	.430	.378
vs. Right-Handed Pitchers	398	120	20	10	4	35	48	27	.302	.432	.376
Home	289	95	12	7	1	26	26	14	.329	.429	.382
Road	302	89	16	7	4	26	37	28	.295	.434	.372
Grass	494	151	22	11	5	48	50	36	.306	.425	.369
Artificial Turf	97	33	6	3	0	4	13	6	.340	.464	.418
April	73	20	3	2	0	6	8	8	.274	.370	.341
May	110	33	8	2	1	10	6	8	.300	.436	.342
June	105	34	9	2	1	12	9	4	.324	.476	.374
July	109	31	1	2	0	6	9	9	.284	.330	.336
August	78	27	2	4	3	12	11	6	.346	.590	.427
Sept./Oct.	116	39	5	2	0	6	20	7	.336	.414	.434
Leading Off Inn.	229	67	15	4	0	0	21	19	.293	.393	.352
Bases Empty	393	119	24	9	2	2	41	35	.303	.425	.370
Runners On	198	65	4	5	3	50	22	7	.328	.444	.390
Runners/Scor. Pos.	111	39	4	2	2	44	17	5	.351	.477	.427
Runners On/2 Out	71	20	2	1	1	17	11	2	.282	.380	.378
Scor. Pos./2 Out	41	10	2	0	0	14	7	1	.244	.293	.354
Late Inning Pressure	82	16	2	0	0	4	8	5	.195	.220	.267
Leading Off	18	3	1	0	0	0	1	3	.167	.222	.211
Bases Empty	43	7	2	0	0	0	4	4	.163	.209	.234
Runners On	39	9	0	0	0	4	4	1	.231	.231	.302
Runners/Scor. Pos.	22	5	0	0	0	4	2	0	.227	.227	.292

DRIVING IN RUNS	0 Out	1 Out	2 Out	Total	
From 1B	3/35	1/55	2/52	6/142	4%
From 2B	2/22	8/39	7/24	17/85	20%
From 3B	3/5	13/23	7/24	23/52	44%
Scoring Position	5/27	21/62	14/48	40/137	29%
Scor. Pos. %	19%	34%	29%	29%	
Driving In Runners from 3B with Less than Two Out:			16/28	57%	

Loves to face: Dennis Lamp (.833, 5-for-6)
Hates to face: John Candelaria (0-for-9, 4 SO)
Yearly batting averages with runners in scoring position since 1982: .163, .238, .346, .351. One of two A.L. regulars to bat over .340 in those situations in both 1984 and '85; the other was Rance Mulliniks. . . . Even better with the sacks full: .414 (12-for-29) with the bases loaded over past two seasons. . . . First Cleveland player since Al Smith (1954–55) to score 100 or more runs in two consecutive seasons. . . . Batted .332 against left-handers; among non-platooned lefty batters, only major-leaguers to do better were Wade Boggs and Harold Baines. . . . Has hit 12 of his 13 career home runs against right-handers. Only one against a lefty: August 17 last year, off Frank Tanana. . . . Averaged 3.10 putouts per nine innings last season, 4th-most among A.L. outfielders (minimum: 300 innings).

Ivan Calderon

Seattle Mariners	AB	H	2B	3B	HR	RRF	BB	SO	BA	SA	OBA
Season	210	60	16	4	8	28	19	45	.286	.514	.349
vs. Left-Handed Pitchers	71	21	6	1	3	11	10	18	.296	.535	.383
vs. Right-Handed Pitchers	139	39	10	3	5	17	9	27	.281	.504	.331
Home	111	33	8	1	6	16	10	21	.297	.550	.358
Road	99	27	8	3	2	12	9	24	.273	.475	.339
Grass	74	20	4	3	1	9	8	18	.270	.446	.341
Artificial Turf	136	40	12	1	7	19	11	27	.294	.551	.353
April	13	2	0	0	0	0	2	1	.154	.154	.313
May	49	14	3	1	5	12	5	9	.286	.694	.364
June	58	16	6	1	1	5	5	10	.276	.466	.333
July	79	25	7	2	2	10	7	22	.316	.532	.368
August	11	3	0	0	0	1	0	3	.273	.273	.273
Sept./Oct.	0	0	0	0	0	0	0	0	.000	.000	.000
Leading Off Inn.	41	19	2	2	2	2	2	3	.463	.756	.488
Bases Empty	118	36	7	3	6	6	9	28	.305	.568	.359
Runners On	92	24	9	1	2	22	10	17	.261	.446	.337
Runners/Scor. Pos.	49	16	5	0	2	20	6	8	.327	.551	.404
Runners On/2 Out	21	3	0	0	1	3	5	5	.143	.286	.308
Scor. Pos./2 Out	10	1	0	0	1	3	3	3	.100	.400	.308
Late Inning Pressure	30	9	1	0	3	5	4	6	.300	.633	.382
Leading Off	6	3	1	0	1	1	0	0	.500	1.167	.500
Bases Empty	17	5	1	0	2	2	1	3	.294	.706	.333
Runners On	13	4	0	0	1	3	3	3	.308	.538	.438
Runners/Scor. Pos.	5	2	0	0	1	3	2	0	.400	1.000	.571

DRIVING IN RUNS	0 Out	1 Out	2 Out	Total	
From 1B	1/19	2/31	1/19	4/69	6%
From 2B	2/12	3/17	0/8	5/37	14%
From 3B	1/2	9/15	1/3	11/20	55%
Scoring Position	3/14	12/32	1/11	16/57	28%
Scor. Pos. %	21%	38%	9%	28%	
Driving In Runners from 3B with Less than Two Out:			10/17	59%	

Loves to face: Bud Black (.667, 4-for-6, 3 2B)
Hates to face: Mike Smithson (.100, 1-for-10)
Ground-ball hitter: 1.49 G/A ratio last season. Career: 1.58. . . . Started in exactly one-third of Mariners' 162 games. His season ended during players' strike, when doctors discovered a broken bone in his left wrist, explaining season-long pain. . . . Injury in same wrist forced him onto disabled list after brief trial with Mariners toward end of 1984 season. . . . Solid 10-week period from May 22 up to the strike: started 47 of Seattle's 67 games, batting .298 during that span. . . . Did not play enough to qualify in our rankings (page 364), but .488 on-base average when leading off inning was higher than league leaders in both leagues (Wade Boggs, .468; Mike Brown, .446).

Rod Carew

California Angels	AB	H	2B	3B	HR	RRF	BB	SO	BA	SA	OBA
Season	443	124	17	3	2	43	64	47	.280	.345	.371
vs. Left-Handed Pitchers	106	28	2	0	0	9	17	23	.264	.283	.371
vs. Right-Handed Pitchers	337	96	15	3	2	34	47	24	.285	.365	.371
Home	219	61	8	1	1	20	34	15	.279	.338	.374
Road	224	63	9	2	1	23	30	32	.281	.353	.369
Grass	346	95	11	2	1	31	45	36	.275	.327	.357
Artificial Turf	97	29	6	1	1	12	19	11	.299	.412	.419
April	79	23	5	1	0	13	15	9	.291	.380	.411
May	23	4	1	0	1	1	6	0	.174	.348	.345
June	50	11	0	0	0	9	7	5	.220	.220	.316
July	101	27	4	0	0	6	6	11	.267	.307	.308
August	94	31	3	0	1	5	16	9	.330	.394	.427
Sept./Oct.	96	28	4	2	0	9	14	13	.292	.375	.378
Leading Off Inn.	114	36	7	2	0	0	8	17	.316	.412	.366
Bases Empty	273	75	12	3	1	1	27	35	.275	.352	.342
Runners On	170	49	5	0	1	42	37	12	.288	.335	.413
Runners/Scor. Pos.	112	35	5	0	0	39	26	8	.313	.357	.439
Runners On/2 Out	70	15	0	0	0	15	19	7	.214	.214	.382
Scor. Pos./2 Out	54	13	0	0	0	14	12	5	.241	.241	.379
Late Inning Pressure	56	12	2	0	0	6	12	6	.214	.250	.353
Leading Off	13	4	1	0	0	0	3	1	.308	.385	.438
Bases Empty	28	6	1	0	0	0	5	5	.214	.250	.333
Runners On	28	6	1	0	0	6	7	1	.214	.250	.371
Runners/Scor. Pos.	17	3	1	0	0	6	4	1	.176	.235	.333

DRIVING IN RUNS	0 Out	1 Out	2 Out	Total	
From 1B	1/29	0/33	1/41	2/103	2%
From 2B	4/22	7/29	6/42	17/93	18%
From 3B	8/8	6/9	8/18	22/35	63%
Scoring Position	12/30	13/38	14/60	39/128	30%
Scor. Pos. %	40%	34%	23%	30%	
Driving In Runners from 3B with Less than Two Out:			14/17	82%	

Loves to face: Mike Brown (1.000, 5-for-5)
Hates to face: Don Sutton (.059, 1-for-17)
Has hit for a higher average with runners on base than with bases empty in nine of last 11 seasons. . . . One more figure for his critics to munch on: eleven years of bases-loaded data shows that Carew has batted .388 and slugged .647 in those situations, and hasn't struck out in 38 bases-loaded appearances over past four years. . . . Batted under .300 vs. right-handers in '85 for first time in 11 years of *The Player Analysis*. . . . Started only 21 of 47 games in which Angels faced a left-hander last season, but more for reasons of rest than ineffectiveness: during closing weeks of pennant race, he started nine of 11 games against lefties, batting .351 in those games. . . . Has been caught stealing 187 times in career, most among active players and 12 shy of A.L. record held by Bert Campaneris. . . . No surprise that he's a ground-ball hitter: 1.82 G/A ratio last season, 1.89 since 1975.

Joe Carter

Cleveland Indians	AB	H	2B	3B	HR	RRF	BB	SO	BA	SA	OBA
Season	489	128	27	0	15	60	25	74	.262	.409	.298
vs. Left-Handed Pitchers	161	40	8	0	5	12	12	29	.248	.391	.303
vs. Right-Handed Pitchers	328	88	19	0	10	48	13	45	.268	.418	.296
Home	247	66	15	0	5	26	18	39	.267	.389	.320
Road	242	62	12	0	10	34	7	35	.256	.430	.276
Grass	412	110	24	0	13	53	22	63	.267	.420	.305
Artificial Turf	77	18	3	0	2	7	3	11	.234	.351	.263
April	50	9	3	0	1	9	3	17	.180	.300	.218
May	76	18	2	0	1	9	2	10	.237	.303	.256
June	82	23	5	0	4	9	9	10	.280	.488	.352
July	83	16	2	0	0	4	3	18	.193	.217	.221
August	66	16	5	0	2	5	5	4	.242	.409	.306
Sept./Oct.	132	46	10	0	7	24	3	15	.348	.583	.362
Leading Off Inn.	106	29	2	0	5	5	2	19	.274	.434	.294
Bases Empty	269	68	10	0	10	10	11	40	.253	.401	.285
Runners On	220	60	17	0	5	50	14	34	.273	.418	.314
Runners/Scor. Pos.	123	30	10	0	2	42	9	21	.244	.374	.287
Runners On/2 Out	83	21	3	0	3	15	7	13	.253	.398	.319
Scor. Pos./2 Out	50	11	2	0	2	12	6	8	.220	.380	.304
Late Inning Pressure	71	21	1	0	2	6	2	10	.296	.394	.315
Leading Off	19	5	0	0	1	1	0	3	.263	.421	.263
Bases Empty	39	10	1	0	2	2	2	6	.256	.436	.293
Runners On	32	11	0	0	0	4	0	4	.344	.344	.344
Runners/Scor. Pos.	21	7	0	0	0	4	0	3	.333	.333	.333

DRIVING IN RUNS	0 Out	1 Out	2 Out	Total	
From 1B	2/49	2/58	2/58	6/165	4%
From 2B	4/20	3/35	5/39	12/94	13%
From 3B	3/5	19/27	5/16	27/48	56%
Scoring Position	7/25	22/62	10/55	39/142	27%
Scor. Pos. %	28%	35%	18%	27%	
Driving In Runners from 3B with Less than Two Out:			22/32	69%	

Loves to face: Ron Davis (.625, 5-for-8, 1 HR)
Hates to face: Ron Romanick (0-for-12)
Achieved a perverse sort of perfection last season by starting at least one game in each of the nine batting order spots: leadoff, 4 games; second, 8; third, 10; cleanup, 3; fifth, 8; sixth, 23; seventh, 38; eighth, 31; and ninth, 1. Take that, Tim McCarver, who mentioned during a World Series broadcast that he had batted in all nine spots during his *career*. . . . Also started at five different positions last season: 1B, LF, CF, RF, and DH. . . . Batted .348 after Sept. 1, 2d in A.L. to Wade Boggs's .394. . . . Career batting averages: .276 on grass fields, .196 on artificial surfaces. . . . Career batting average of .353 (18-for-51) in Late-Inning Pressure Situations with runners on base. . . . Stolen base percentage of .800 (24-of-30) was 6th-best in A.L. last year (minimum: 20 SB).

Dave Collins

Oakland As	AB	H	2B	3B	HR	RRF	BB	SO	BA	SA	OBA
Season	379	95	16	4	4	34	29	37	.251	.346	.303
vs. Left-Handed Pitchers	87	19	3	0	1	9	5	6	.218	.287	.260
vs. Right-Handed Pitchers	292	76	13	4	3	25	24	31	.260	.363	.315
Home	190	44	5	1	1	12	18	20	.232	.284	.300
Road	189	51	11	3	3	22	11	17	.270	.407	.305
Grass	319	80	13	3	3	28	26	35	.251	.339	.307
Artificial Turf	60	15	3	1	1	6	3	2	.250	.383	.281
April	82	24	1	0	1	10	6	6	.293	.341	.337
May	99	21	5	3	1	7	5	12	.212	.354	.248
June	76	20	4	0	0	3	5	7	.263	.316	.313
July	42	9	2	0	1	3	2	3	.214	.333	.250
August	43	9	2	0	1	8	5	3	.209	.326	.286
Sept./Oct.	37	12	2	1	0	3	6	6	.324	.432	.419
Leading Off Inn.	142	33	6	2	1	1	13	11	.232	.324	.297
Bases Empty	249	56	12	2	3	3	17	21	.225	.325	.274
Runners On	130	39	4	2	1	31	12	16	.300	.385	.354
Runners/Scor. Pos.	67	21	0	1	1	30	11	8	.313	.388	.390
Runners On/2 Out	59	18	2	1	0	11	5	6	.305	.373	.359
Scor. Pos./2 Out	37	11	0	1	0	11	4	6	.297	.351	.366
Late Inning Pressure	68	18	1	0	0	6	6	10	.265	.279	.333
Leading Off	22	5	1	0	0	0	2	3	.227	.273	.292
Bases Empty	41	9	1	0	0	0	2	5	.220	.244	.256
Runners On	27	9	0	0	0	6	4	5	.333	.333	.438
Runners/Scor. Pos.	13	5	0	0	0	6	4	1	.385	.385	.529

DRIVING IN RUNS	0 Out	1 Out	2 Out	Total	
From 1B	0/24	2/39	1/37	3/100	3%
From 2B	2/8	3/14	5/23	10/45	22%
From 3B	5/6	6/10	5/19	16/35	46%
Scoring Position	7/14	9/24	10/42	26/80	33%
Scor. Pos. %	50%	38%	24%	33%	
Driving In Runners from 3B with Less than Two Out:			11/16	69%	

Loves to face: Jim Slaton (.457, 16-for-35)
Hates to face: Bob Stanley (0-for-20, 5 SO)
Will start his 12th big-league season with his 7th big-league team, the Tigers; no repeaters yet, and has never been traded in the middle of a season. Major-league record is 10 teams, shared by Tommy Davis, Bob Miller, and Ken Brett. . . . Started 66 of Oakland's first 82 games last year, but only 20 of last 80; didn't start against a left-hander after July 8. . . . Career batting average of .301 in Late-Inning Pressure Situations; it's .325 in those same situations with runners in scoring position. . . . Ground-ball hitter: 1.40 G/A ratio last season. Career: 1.21. . . . Sting like a butterfly: has a career batting average of .384 in 112 at bats against knuckleballers (17-for-37 against Charlie Hough, 16-for-45 vs. Phil Niekro, 10-for-30 vs. Joe Niekro).

Onix Concepcion

Kansas City Royals	AB	H	2B	3B	HR	RRF	BB	SO	BA	SA	OBA
Season	314	64	5	1	2	22	16	29	.204	.245	.255
vs. Left-Handed Pitchers	106	23	2	1	0	7	7	10	.217	.255	.263
vs. Right-Handed Pitchers	208	41	3	0	2	15	9	19	.197	.240	.251
Home	144	29	4	1	1	11	8	11	.201	.264	.268
Road	170	35	1	0	1	11	8	18	.206	.229	.244
Grass	129	31	1	0	0	10	5	14	.240	.248	.272
Artificial Turf	185	33	4	1	2	12	11	15	.178	.243	.244
April	36	6	0	0	1	2	0	4	.167	.250	.189
May	71	13	1	0	0	6	4	7	.183	.197	.224
June	54	9	1	0	0	4	5	5	.167	.185	.262
July	47	13	1	0	0	2	0	7	.277	.298	.292
August	57	13	2	1	0	3	3	4	.228	.298	.279
Sept./Oct.	49	10	0	0	1	5	4	2	.204	.265	.278
Leading Off Inn.	71	12	1	0	0	0	3	6	.169	.183	.203
Bases Empty	190	32	3	1	1	1	12	18	.168	.211	.225
Runners On	124	32	2	0	1	21	4	11	.258	.298	.301
Runners/Scor. Pos.	71	18	1	0	0	17	2	5	.254	.268	.299
Runners On/2 Out	63	17	0	0	0	7	4	3	.270	.270	.324
Scor. Pos./2 Out	41	9	0	0	0	7	2	2	.220	.220	.273
Late Inning Pressure	20	2	0	0	0	0	3	3	.100	.100	.250
Leading Off	4	0	0	0	0	0	0	2	.000	.000	.000
Bases Empty	14	2	0	0	0	0	2	2	.143	.143	.250
Runners On	6	0	0	0	0	0	1	1	.000	.000	.250
Runners/Scor. Pos.	4	0	0	0	0	0	1	0	.000	.000	.333

DRIVING IN RUNS	0 Out	1 Out	2 Out	Total	
From 1B	2/17	0/30	0/45	2/92	2%
From 2B	0/7	3/17	3/30	6/54	11%
From 3B	0/1	7/11	4/17	11/29	38%
Scoring Position	0/8	10/28	7/47	17/83	20%
Scor. Pos. %	0%	36%	15%	20%	
Driving In Runners from 3B with Less than Two Out:			7/12	58%	

Loves to face: John Butcher (.500, 5-for-10)
Hates to face: Frank Viola (0-for-13)
Led A.L. shortstops with 3.47 assists per nine innings (league average: 2.96, Buddy Biancalana averaged 3.35); finished 2d to Cal Ripken in same category in 1984. . . . Hitless in 11 of last 12 games he started last season, undoubtedly a factor in Howser's choice of Biancalana for post-season play. . . . Ratio of 1.92 ground outs-to-air outs was 5th-highest A.L. last season (minimum: 200 PA). Career average: 1.39. . . . 1985 batting average peaked at .214 on Sept. 6. . . . Some unusual career batting average breakdowns: .271 with runners on base, .212 with the bases empty; .254 vs. right-handers, .205 vs. left-handers. . . . Hitless in 18 at bats vs. Seattle last season. . . . Three career home runs; only one off a left-hander came on first pitch he saw in 1984 season, off Ron Guidry on opening day.

Cecil Cooper

Milwaukee Brewers	AB	H	2B	3B	HR	RRF	BB	SO	BA	SA	OBA
Season	631	185	39	8	16	105	30	77	.293	.456	.322
vs. Left-Handed Pitchers	209	67	13	3	6	49	13	26	.321	.498	.360
vs. Right-Handed Pitchers	422	118	26	5	10	56	17	51	.280	.436	.303
Home	309	88	19	4	6	56	17	36	.285	.430	.315
Road	322	97	20	4	10	49	13	41	.301	.481	.329
Grass	521	154	31	6	13	88	23	63	.296	.453	.323
Artificial Turf	110	31	8	2	3	17	7	14	.282	.473	.322
April	65	19	4	0	0	6	2	8	.292	.354	.324
May	95	32	5	6	1	19	4	11	.337	.547	.353
June	107	33	8	2	3	20	4	10	.308	.505	.327
July	112	29	7	0	2	13	5	7	.259	.375	.292
August	113	38	8	0	5	27	4	17	.336	.540	.356
Sept./Oct.	139	34	7	0	5	20	11	24	.245	.403	.296
Leading Off Inn.	97	31	8	1	1	1	6	15	.320	.454	.371
Bases Empty	324	86	19	2	8	8	12	51	.265	.410	.296
Runners On	307	99	20	6	8	97	18	26	.322	.505	.349
Runners/Scor. Pos.	168	50	13	3	4	84	13	17	.298	.482	.330
Runners On/2 Out	115	27	2	4	2	30	7	14	.235	.374	.279
Scor. Pos./2 Out	75	17	2	1	2	26	4	10	.227	.360	.266
Late Inning Pressure	87	31	3	0	1	12	3	12	.356	.425	.378
Leading Off	25	7	1	0	0	0	3	5	.280	.320	.357
Bases Empty	45	12	2	0	0	0	3	11	.267	.311	.313
Runners On	42	19	1	0	1	12	0	1	.452	.548	.452
Runners/Scor. Pos.	19	8	0	0	1	11	0	0	.421	.579	.421

DRIVING IN RUNS	0 Out	1 Out	2 Out	Total	
From 1B	2/48	8/100	7/79	17/227	7%
From 2B	7/31	11/43	14/57	32/131	24%
From 3B	13/17	20/24	7/26	40/67	60%
Scoring Position	20/48	31/67	21/83	72/198	36%
Scor. Pos. %	42%	46%	25%	36%	
Driving In Runners from 3B with Less than Two Out:			33/41	80%	

Loves to face: Rick Langford (.463, 19-for-41, 4 HR)
Hates to face: Ray Burris (0-for-11)
With a week to go in season, was batting .304 with 99 RBIs; went 0-for-22 to finish at .293 with 99 RBIs. . . . Batted .462 (6-for-13) with the bases loaded last season; four of his six hits went for extra bases, and he wound up with 20 RRFs in the 13 appearances (league average: .73 RRF per bases-loaded PA). . . . One of three active players with .300 career batting average, at least 200 home runs, and at least 1,000 RBIs (others: Al Oliver, Jim Rice). . . . Career strikeout rate of one every 9.4 at bats is 5th-lowest, and walk rate of one every 16.8 at bats is 4th-lowest, among the 36 active players with 200 or more homers. . . . Has batted for a higher average with runners on base than with bases empty in seven of last eight seasons. . . . 1985 LIP batting average with runners on base increased 306 points from his 11-year low of .146 (6-for-41) in '84.

Al Cowens

Seattle Mariners	AB	H	2B	3B	HR	RRF	BB	SO	BA	SA	OBA
Season	452	120	32	5	14	73	30	56	.265	.451	.310
vs. Left-Handed Pitchers	140	37	10	3	5	23	15	11	.264	.486	.331
vs. Right-Handed Pitchers	312	83	22	2	9	50	15	45	.266	.436	.300
Home	211	60	12	1	8	37	19	22	.284	.464	.341
Road	241	60	20	4	6	36	11	34	.249	.440	.282
Grass	187	49	17	4	6	30	9	24	.262	.492	.298
Artificial Turf	265	71	15	1	8	43	21	32	.268	.423	.318
April	75	27	5	1	4	11	3	9	.360	.613	.385
May	71	9	5	0	0	7	4	13	.127	.197	.177
June	37	9	2	0	3	9	3	7	.243	.541	.300
July	92	25	6	3	2	21	4	6	.272	.467	.299
August	100	25	6	0	3	16	10	14	.250	.400	.318
Sept./Oct.	77	25	8	1	2	9	6	7	.325	.532	.373
Leading Off Inn.	99	29	9	1	3	3	5	14	.293	.495	.327
Bases Empty	246	66	22	2	9	9	14	36	.268	.484	.308
Runners On	206	54	10	3	5	64	16	20	.262	.413	.313
Runners/Scor. Pos.	120	37	10	2	3	59	14	13	.308	.500	.374
Runners On/2 Out	84	24	7	2	1	28	9	13	.286	.452	.362
Scor. Pos./2 Out	55	18	7	2	1	28	8	9	.327	.582	.422
Late Inning Pressure	60	15	2	0	3	11	5	11	.250	.433	.303
Leading Off	18	6	0	0	2	2	1	3	.333	.667	.368
Bases Empty	36	10	1	0	2	2	2	6	.278	.472	.316
Runners On	24	5	1	0	1	9	3	5	.208	.375	.286
Runners/Scor. Pos.	12	4	1	0	1	9	3	2	.333	.667	.438

DRIVING IN RUNS	0 Out	1 Out	2 Out	Total	
From 1B	2/37	4/60	3/61	9/158	6%
From 2B	3/18	5/38	14/48	22/104	21%
From 3B	7/10	11/19	9/18	27/47	57%
Scoring Position	10/28	16/57	23/66	49/151	32%
Scor. Pos. %	36%	28%	35%	32%	
Driving In Runners from 3B with Less than Two Out:			18/29	62%	

Loves to face: Chris Codiroli (.500, 5-for-10)
Hates to face: Jay Howell (0-for-9)
April batting average of .360 was 2d-best in A.L. . . . Batted .533 (8-for-15) with the bases loaded last season. . . . A good clutch hitter, he has batted over .300 in Late-Inning Pressure Situations with runners in scoring position in four of last five seasons. . . . Grounded into 23 double plays in 102 opportunities (runner on first, less than two outs) last season, 4th-highest rate in A.L. (minimum: 5 GIDPs; league average: one GIDP every 8.9 opportunities). . . . Shared A.L. Calvin Coolidge "I Do Not Choose to Run" Award; one of two A.L. players with at least 400 at bats last season, but no stolen bases and no times caught stealing. This from a player who stole 119 bases in 11 previous major-league seasons.

Julio Cruz

Chicago White Sox	AB	H	2B	3B	HR	RRF	BB	SO	BA	SA	OBA
Season	234	46	2	3	0	15	32	40	.197	.231	.297
vs. Left-Handed Pitchers	116	29	2	3	0	10	20	14	.250	.319	.360
vs. Right-Handed Pitchers	118	17	0	0	0	5	12	26	.144	.144	.233
Home	86	12	0	2	0	3	15	16	.140	.186	.267
Road	148	34	2	1	0	12	17	24	.230	.257	.315
Grass	197	37	2	3	0	12	27	34	.188	.228	.284
Artificial Turf	37	9	0	0	0	3	5	6	.243	.243	.364
April	50	10	1	0	0	3	9	10	.200	.220	.317
May	19	3	0	0	0	2	4	1	.158	.158	.304
June	65	12	0	0	0	1	10	13	.185	.185	.312
July	21	3	1	1	0	3	2	3	.143	.286	.217
August	38	9	0	1	0	4	2	4	.237	.289	.275
Sept./Oct.	41	9	0	1	0	2	5	9	.220	.268	.304
Leading Off Inn.	52	7	0	1	0	0	10	9	.135	.173	.274
Bases Empty	135	29	1	1	0	0	21	23	.215	.237	.329
Runners On	99	17	1	2	0	15	11	17	.172	.222	.252
Runners/Scor. Pos.	60	11	0	1	0	13	8	13	.183	.217	.275
Runners On/2 Out	47	6	0	1	0	9	7	10	.128	.170	.241
Scor. Pos./2 Out	33	6	0	1	0	9	5	9	.182	.242	.289
Late Inning Pressure	27	7	1	0	0	6	7	4	.259	.296	.412
Leading Off	4	1	0	0	0	0	4	0	.250	.250	.625
Bases Empty	10	3	1	0	0	0	5	3	.300	.400	.533
Runners On	17	4	0	0	0	6	2	1	.235	.235	.316
Runners/Scor. Pos.	11	4	0	0	0	6	1	1	.364	.364	.417

DRIVING IN RUNS	0 Out	1 Out	2 Out	Total	
From 1B	0/15	2/19	1/27	3/61	5%
From 2B	0/7	1/16	4/23	5/46	11%
From 3B	0/1	3/7	4/15	7/23	30%
Scoring Position	0/8	4/23	8/38	12/69	17%
Scor. Pos. %	0%	17%	21%	17%	
Driving In Runners from 3B with Less than Two Out:			3/8	38%	

Loves to face: Frank Tanana (.372, 16-for-43, 2 HR)
Hates to face: Bill Krueger (0-for-16)
Set a *Player Analysis* record last season for most at bats against right-handed pitchers without an extra-base hit (118). . . . Early-season knee problems put him on disabled list in mid-May; despite those three weeks, he still started 43 of Chicago's 70 games up to the end of June. He started only 31 of 93 games thereafter (and only three were against right-handers). . . . Ground-ball hitter: 1.81 G/A ratio was 9th-highest in A.L. last season (minimum: 200 PA). Career average: 1.73. . . . Career batting averages with runners in scoring position: .310 with less than two outs, .197 with two outs. . . . Has batted over .300 in Late-Inning Pressure Situations with runners in scoring position in each of last four seasons. Career average: .325. . . . Career stolen base percentage of .816 ranks 4th among active players (minimum: 100 SB).

Rich Dauer

Baltimore Orioles	AB	H	2B	3B	HR	RRF	BB	SO	BA	SA	OBA
Season	208	42	7	0	2	15	20	7	.202	.264	.275
vs. Left-Handed Pitchers	81	20	3	0	2	10	9	3	.247	.358	.322
vs. Right-Handed Pitchers	127	22	4	0	0	5	11	4	.173	.205	.245
Home	101	18	3	0	1	8	11	2	.178	.238	.259
Road	107	24	4	0	1	7	9	5	.224	.290	.291
Grass	167	33	4	0	2	12	17	5	.198	.257	.276
Artificial Turf	41	9	3	0	0	3	3	2	.220	.293	.273
April	35	6	2	0	0	4	7	3	.171	.229	.310
May	68	16	2	0	1	2	5	3	.235	.309	.288
June	48	9	1	0	0	3	5	0	.188	.208	.278
July	24	7	1	0	1	3	1	0	.292	.458	.320
August	9	1	1	0	0	1	0	0	.111	.222	.111
Sept./Oct.	24	3	0	0	0	2	2	1	.125	.125	.192
Leading Off Inn.	47	14	3	0	2	2	1	1	.298	.489	.313
Bases Empty	124	25	3	0	2	2	11	3	.202	.274	.272
Runners On	84	17	4	0	0	13	9	4	.202	.250	.280
Runners/Scor. Pos.	38	7	1	0	0	10	3	2	.184	.211	.244
Runners On/2 Out	36	6	1	0	0	6	5	0	.167	.194	.268
Scor. Pos./2 Out	22	4	1	0	0	6	2	0	.182	.227	.250
Late Inning Pressure	17	2	0	0	0	0	0	0	.118	.118	.118
Leading Off	4	1	0	0	0	0	0	0	.250	.250	.250
Bases Empty	15	2	0	0	0	0	0	0	.133	.133	.133
Runners On	2	0	0	0	0	0	0	0	.000	.000	.000
Runners/Scor. Pos.	0	0	0	0	0	0	0	0	.000	.000	.000

DRIVING IN RUNS	0 Out	1 Out	2 Out	Total	
From 1B	0/18	3/20	1/27	4/65	6%
From 2B	1/4	0/8	4/19	5/31	16%
From 3B	1/2	2/8	1/4	4/14	29%
Scoring Position	2/6	2/16	5/23	9/45	20%
Scor. Pos. %	33%	13%	22%	20%	
Driving In Runners from 3B with Less than Two Out:			3/10	30%	

Loves to face: Britt Burns (.421, 16-for-38, 2 HR)
Hates to face: Tom Seaver (0-for-13)
Not the guy you want up there with the bases loaded. He's hitless in 11 bases-loaded at bats over the past two years; in 1984, he set a *Player Analysis* record for most bases-loaded plate appearances (9) without driving in a run. How about a little more pressure? With the bases loaded and two outs, he's 0-for-13 over the past five years. Well, maybe he'll get a walk? Uh-uh: only one walk in 92 career plate appearances with the bases loaded. Where's Terry Crowley when you need him? . . . Dauer has batted below .190 with runners in scoring position in each of last three seasons. . . . Started 55 of Orioles' first 75 games, but only 16 of 86 (eight of them at third) after Baltimore acquired Alan Wiggins. . . . Struck out only once in 123 plate appearances after May 27. No strikeouts in 45 career appearances vs. Geoff Zahn.

Alvin Davis

Seattle Mariners	AB	H	2B	3B	HR	RRF	BB	SO	BA	SA	OBA
Season	578	166	33	1	18	80	90	71	.287	.441	.381
vs. Left-Handed Pitchers	176	42	9	0	4	24	27	26	.239	.358	.340
vs. Right-Handed Pitchers	402	124	24	1	14	56	63	45	.308	.478	.399
Home	297	87	15	1	11	42	50	31	.293	.461	.393
Road	281	79	18	0	7	38	40	40	.281	.420	.369
Grass	218	61	13	0	7	33	24	30	.280	.436	.352
Artificial Turf	360	105	20	1	11	47	66	41	.292	.444	.398
April	64	19	2	0	1	4	13	5	.297	.375	.410
May	82	20	4	0	3	10	14	13	.244	.402	.357
June	104	26	5	0	2	18	13	10	.250	.356	.333
July	104	36	4	0	2	12	13	8	.346	.442	.412
August	100	35	9	0	4	14	14	10	.350	.560	.430
Sept./Oct.	124	30	9	1	6	22	23	25	.242	.476	.358
Leading Off Inn.	128	40	9	0	4	4	16	11	.313	.477	.389
Bases Empty	324	99	20	0	11	11	43	34	.306	.469	.389
Runners On	254	67	13	1	7	69	47	37	.264	.406	.372
Runners/Scor. Pos.	149	41	7	0	6	64	30	24	.275	.443	.385
Runners On/2 Out	89	22	3	0	3	28	17	16	.247	.382	.368
Scor. Pos./2 Out	67	16	2	0	3	28	11	13	.239	.403	.346
Late Inning Pressure	81	21	4	0	0	3	14	9	.259	.309	.368
Leading Off	21	6	1	0	0	0	1	1	.286	.333	.318
Bases Empty	48	16	4	0	0	0	7	4	.333	.417	.418
Runners On	33	5	0	0	0	3	7	5	.152	.152	.300
Runners/Scor. Pos.	17	2	0	0	0	3	5	4	.118	.118	.318

DRIVING IN RUNS	0 Out	1 Out	2 Out	Total	
From 1B	4/48	3/73	4/58	11/179	6%
From 2B	3/22	7/50	11/59	21/131	16%
From 3B	4/7	16/25	10/24	30/56	54%
Scoring Position	7/29	23/75	21/83	51/187	27%
Scor. Pos. %	24%	31%	25%	27%	
Driving In Runners from 3B with Less than Two Out:			20/32	63%	

Loves to face: Mike Smithson (.462, 6-for-13, 2 HR)
Hates to face: Bert Blyleven (.042, 1-for-24, 7 SO)
Had batted higher against left-handers (.286) than against right-handers (.283) in 1984. . . . Career strikeout rate of one every nine plate appearances, but has yet to strike out in 36 plate appearances with the bases loaded. . . . Seattle had a record of 14–4 in games in which he homered. . . . No home runs in Late-Inning Pressure Situations last season; only A.L. player with as many homers as Davis to be similarly blanked in LIPS was Reggie Jackson. . . . 4th player in history to draw 90 or more walks in each of first two seasons in majors; the others were Ferris Fain (1947–48), Ted Williams (1939–40), and Roy Thomas (1899–1900). Think Roy had the *Analyst* in mind? . . . Career at the Kingdome: batting .294, slugging .507, 26 home runs; on the road: .277, .431 and 19. . . . Fly-ball hitter: 0.79 G/A ratio last season. Career: 0.91.

Mike Davis

Oakland As	AB	H	2B	3B	HR	RRF	BB	SO	BA	SA	OBA
Season	547	157	34	1	24	86	50	99	.287	.484	.348
vs. Left-Handed Pitchers	155	42	9	0	8	27	13	37	.271	.484	.335
vs. Right-Handed Pitchers	392	115	25	1	16	59	37	62	.293	.485	.353
Home	246	68	15	1	12	42	27	46	.276	.492	.349
Road	301	89	19	0	12	44	23	53	.296	.478	.347
Grass	447	128	26	1	19	69	44	80	.286	.477	.352
Artificial Turf	100	29	8	0	5	17	6	19	.290	.520	.330
April	77	25	6	0	9	24	4	14	.325	.753	.361
May	69	21	3	0	3	9	14	11	.304	.478	.422
June	110	34	9	0	2	12	11	18	.309	.445	.374
July	92	22	6	0	5	16	8	9	.239	.467	.300
August	106	32	7	1	3	15	8	20	.302	.472	.351
Sept./Oct.	93	23	3	0	2	10	5	27	.247	.344	.286
Leading Off Inn.	130	38	10	0	7	7	10	24	.292	.531	.348
Bases Empty	311	91	21	0	15	15	25	51	.293	.505	.347
Runners On	236	66	13	1	9	71	25	48	.280	.458	.348
Runners/Scor. Pos.	132	37	8	1	5	62	15	29	.280	.470	.353
Runners On/2 Out	92	23	1	1	3	24	12	21	.250	.380	.343
Scor. Pos./2 Out	62	16	1	1	2	22	10	17	.258	.403	.370
Late Inning Pressure	86	21	3	0	4	8	7	18	.244	.419	.301
Leading Off	25	4	0	0	1	1	1	3	.160	.280	.192
Bases Empty	47	10	1	0	3	3	1	6	.213	.426	.229
Runners On	39	11	2	0	1	5	6	12	.282	.410	.378
Runners/Scor. Pos.	19	3	1	0	0	3	5	8	.158	.211	.333

DRIVING IN RUNS	0 Out	1 Out	2 Out	Total	
From 1B	3/51	3/68	3/61	9/180	5%
From 2B	7/23	12/33	12/47	31/103	30%
From 3B	5/8	11/19	6/25	22/52	42%
Scoring Position	12/31	23/52	18/72	53/155	34%
Scor. Pos. %	39%	44%	25%	34%	
Driving In Runners from 3B with Less than Two Out:			16/27	59%	

Loves to face: Charlie Hough (.414, 12-for-29)
Hates to face: Jimmy Key (0-for-8, 4 SO)
Led A.L. with nine home runs and 23 RBIs in April; held A.L. home run lead until May 25. . . . Did most of that in the 7th spot in the batting order; cooled off when he was moved up in the lineup. Totals for 38 games batting 7th: .369 batting average, 14 home runs, 36 RBIs. . . . Has driven in 41.2 percent of runners from scoring position with less than two outs in his 6-year career, the 2d-best rate by any major leaguer over the past 11 seasons (minimum: 20 RRF). . . . Career batting averages with runners in scoring position: .343 with less than two outs, .203 with two outs. . . . Percentage of runners driven in from scoring position last season decreased from 34 percent in nonpressure situations to 15 percent in Late-Inning Pressure Situations. . . . Oakland was 17–5 when he homered. . . . Fly-ball hitter: 0.89 G/A ratio last season.

Doug DeCinces
California Angels

	AB	H	2B	3B	HR	RRF	BB	SO	BA	SA	OBA
Season	427	104	22	1	20	82	47	71	.244	.440	.317
vs. Left-Handed Pitchers	127	31	6	1	6	26	20	19	.244	.449	.345
vs. Right-Handed Pitchers	300	73	16	0	14	56	27	52	.243	.437	.304
Home	208	55	12	1	12	44	25	32	.264	.505	.345
Road	219	49	10	0	8	38	22	39	.224	.379	.290
Grass	327	83	19	1	18	68	41	46	.254	.483	.335
Artificial Turf	100	21	3	0	2	14	6	25	.210	.300	.255
April	80	19	4	0	4	16	10	11	.238	.438	.330
May	25	4	0	0	1	3	2	4	.160	.280	.214
June	93	25	6	0	2	14	13	13	.269	.398	.355
July	91	26	7	0	5	19	9	14	.286	.527	.343
August	54	10	3	0	1	10	6	12	.185	.296	.262
Sept./Oct.	84	20	2	1	7	20	7	17	.238	.536	.297
Leading Off Inn.	99	23	6	0	1	1	6	9	.232	.323	.276
Bases Empty	211	51	14	0	7	7	23	26	.242	.408	.316
Runners On	216	53	8	1	13	75	24	45	.245	.472	.317
Runners/Scor. Pos.	126	32	4	0	9	62	22	25	.254	.500	.353
Runners On/2 Out	93	20	3	0	5	26	17	16	.215	.409	.348
Scor. Pos./2 Out	55	12	2	0	4	22	16	8	.218	.473	.403
Late Inning Pressure	54	14	2	0	1	6	9	10	.259	.352	.375
Leading Off	13	4	1	0	0	0	2	2	.308	.385	.400
Bases Empty	29	7	1	0	0	0	4	4	.241	.276	.333
Runners On	25	7	1	0	1	6	5	6	.280	.440	.419
Runners/Scor. Pos.	15	4	1	0	1	6	5	4	.267	.533	.450

DRIVING IN RUNS	0 Out	1 Out	2 Out	Total	
From 1B	4/39	5/62	6/71	15/172	9%
From 2B	3/19	10/45	9/38	22/102	22%
From 3B	7/7	12/21	5/25	24/53	45%
Scoring Position	10/26	22/66	14/63	46/155	30%
Scor. Pos. %	38%	33%	22%	30%	
Driving In Runners from 3B with Less than Two Out:		19/28	68%		

Loves to face: Mike Moore (.536, 15-for-28, 6 HR)
Hates to face: Don Aase (.059, 1-for-17, 1 HR)
Yearly batting averages since 1982: .301, .281, .269, .244. Only one other active player has had a decline of 10 or more points in each of last three seasons (minimum: 200 AB in each)—Robin Yount. ... Walk/strikeout ratio over past 11 seasons is 1.11 vs. left-handers, 0.53 vs. right-handers. ... Has batted for a higher average in day games than in night games in nine of last 10 seasons. ... Not a two-out hitter: over last 11 years, has batted .294 with runners in scoring position and less than two outs, .237 in those same situations with two outs. ... Drove in 18 base runners with 20 home runs, tied for 6th-highest average in A.L. ... Has driven in just two fewer runs than Ron Cey over the past five years, yet is often omitted from discussions of power-hitting third basemen.

Rick Dempsey
Baltimore Orioles

	AB	H	2B	3B	HR	RRF	BB	SO	BA	SA	OBA
Season	362	92	19	0	12	54	50	87	.254	.406	.345
vs. Left-Handed Pitchers	157	51	11	0	7	33	21	41	.325	.529	.403
vs. Right-Handed Pitchers	205	41	8	0	5	21	29	46	.200	.312	.299
Home	179	42	10	0	4	27	30	50	.235	.358	.346
Road	183	50	9	0	8	27	20	37	.273	.454	.343
Grass	311	80	15	0	11	50	45	78	.257	.412	.351
Artificial Turf	51	12	4	0	1	4	5	9	.235	.373	.304
April	59	18	2	0	4	18	9	12	.305	.542	.397
May	63	13	1	0	0	3	12	21	.206	.222	.329
June	58	11	4	0	1	6	6	11	.190	.310	.266
July	61	18	7	0	1	6	6	17	.295	.459	.358
August	60	16	1	0	4	11	7	17	.267	.483	.348
Sept./Oct.	61	16	4	0	2	10	10	9	.262	.426	.366
Leading Off Inn.	86	21	5	0	1	1	11	18	.244	.337	.330
Bases Empty	195	41	7	0	4	4	33	42	.210	.308	.328
Runners On	167	51	12	0	8	50	17	45	.305	.521	.366
Runners/Scor. Pos.	90	26	9	0	3	40	13	23	.289	.489	.371
Runners On/2 Out	70	16	4	0	2	13	6	21	.229	.371	.289
Scor. Pos./2 Out	44	9	3	0	2	13	6	14	.205	.409	.300
Late Inning Pressure	41	7	2	0	1	4	7	12	.171	.293	.286
Leading Off	16	4	1	0	0	0	3	5	.250	.313	.368
Bases Empty	31	5	2	0	0	0	6	9	.161	.226	.297
Runners On	10	2	0	0	1	4	1	3	.200	.500	.250
Runners/Scor. Pos.	5	0	0	0	0	2	1	1	.000	.000	.143

DRIVING IN RUNS	0 Out	1 Out	2 Out	Total	
From 1B	1/33	4/40	2/55	7/128	5%
From 2B	5/14	8/27	8/39	21/80	26%
From 3B	2/3	11/15	1/12	14/30	47%
Scoring Position	7/17	19/42	9/51	35/110	32%
Scor. Pos. %	41%	45%	18%	32%	
Driving In Runners from 3B with Less than Two Out:		13/18	72%		

Loves to face: Tommy John (.394, 13-for-33, 1 HR)
Hates to face: Bob Stanley (.071, 1-for-14)
Batted 125 points higher vs. left-handers than vs. right-handers last season, the largest platoon difference of any kind among A.L. batters (minimum: 100 AB against each). The .325 average vs. southpaws was his highest in the 11 years of *The Player Analysis*. ... Fly-ball hitter: 0.63 G/A ratio was 8th-lowest in majors last season (minimum: 200 PA). Career average: 0.91. ... Attention, Earl: Since 1981, Dempsey is hitless in 16 at bats with two outs and the bases loaded; he has batted .067 (3-for-45) in such situations in the last 11 years. ... Total of 12 home runs last season was his highest at any level of professional ball. ... Who'd have figured this? Only 2 GIDPs in 86 opportunities last season, 2d-lowest rate among A.L. players with at least 50 opportunities; only Ken Griffey's was better.

Brian Downing
California Angels

	AB	H	2B	3B	HR	RRF	BB	SO	BA	SA	OBA
Season	520	137	23	1	20	91	78	61	.263	.427	.371
vs. Left-Handed Pitchers	172	45	14	0	8	31	23	23	.262	.483	.343
vs. Right-Handed Pitchers	348	92	9	1	12	60	55	38	.264	.399	.384
Home	249	60	11	0	10	46	43	29	.241	.406	.362
Road	271	77	12	1	10	45	35	32	.284	.446	.379
Grass	419	105	19	0	17	72	69	51	.251	.418	.364
Artificial Turf	101	32	4	1	3	19	9	10	.317	.465	.400
April	71	20	3	0	1	15	17	9	.282	.366	.440
May	75	14	2	0	3	11	14	6	.187	.333	.319
June	69	13	5	0	0	6	5	9	.188	.261	.256
July	90	25	3	0	5	16	12	17	.278	.478	.371
August	103	38	5	1	8	26	12	8	.369	.670	.454
Sept./Oct.	112	27	5	0	3	17	18	12	.241	.366	.351
Leading Off Inn.	127	35	4	0	7	7	18	11	.276	.472	.374
Bases Empty	293	69	12	0	8	8	50	29	.235	.358	.360
Runners On	227	68	11	1	12	83	28	32	.300	.515	.385
Runners/Scor. Pos.	135	42	8	1	8	73	21	18	.311	.563	.405
Runners On/2 Out	88	27	3	1	5	36	13	12	.307	.534	.408
Scor. Pos./2 Out	63	19	2	1	3	31	11	10	.302	.508	.421
Late Inning Pressure	69	20	4	0	3	13	7	9	.290	.478	.367
Leading Off	17	7	1	0	2	2	3	1	.412	.824	.500
Bases Empty	32	11	3	0	2	2	6	2	.344	.625	.462
Runners On	37	9	1	0	1	11	1	7	.243	.351	.275
Runners/Scor. Pos.	23	4	0	0	0	8	0	6	.174	.174	.200

DRIVING IN RUNS	0 Out	1 Out	2 Out	Total	
From 1B	3/42	3/61	6/62	12/165	7%
From 2B	6/19	7/38	13/44	26/101	26%
From 3B	9/13	12/17	12/29	33/59	56%
Scoring Position	15/32	19/55	25/73	59/160	37%
Scor. Pos. %	47%	35%	34%	37%	
Driving In Runners from 3B with Less than Two Out:		21/30	70%		

Loves to face: Bryan Clark (.545, 6-for-11)
Hates to face: Jim Clancy (.080, 2-for-25, 6 SO)
Only major leaguer who has batted at least 30 points higher on road than at home in each of past three seasons (minimum: 200 PA each year). Composite for three years: road .287, home .239. Over same period, his teammates have hit .253 at Anaheim, .252 on the road. ... August batting average of .369 was 4th-best in A.L. ... Has batted .300 or better with two outs and runners in scoring position in four of last five seasons. ... Shares *Player Analysis* record of 15 home runs leading off an inning; Downing did it in '82, Dave Lopes in '79. ... Committed two errors last season, lowering his career fielding percentage in 605 outfield games to .997, the highest among active players with at least 500 games. (For the record books, the official minimum is 1,000 games; Terry Puhl holds that mark with .993.)

Jim Dwyer
Baltimore Orioles

	AB	H	2B	3B	HR	RRF	BB	SO	BA	SA	OBA
Season	233	58	8	3	7	36	37	31	.249	.399	.353
vs. Left-Handed Pitchers	1	0	0	0	0	0	0	1	.000	.000	.000
vs. Right-Handed Pitchers	232	58	8	3	7	36	37	30	.250	.401	.354
Home	113	24	4	2	1	20	20	11	.212	.310	.333
Road	120	34	4	1	6	16	17	20	.283	.483	.372
Grass	195	45	8	3	4	30	34	25	.231	.364	.346
Artificial Turf	38	13	0	0	3	6	3	6	.342	.579	.390
April	32	9	1	1	0	5	2	4	.281	.375	.324
May	61	19	0	0	4	10	8	9	.311	.508	.391
June	65	15	2	0	3	12	9	6	.231	.400	.333
July	24	6	1	0	0	4	2	2	.250	.292	.308
August	21	4	2	2	0	4	5	3	.190	.476	.346
Sept./Oct.	30	5	2	0	0	1	11	7	.167	.233	.381
Leading Off Inn.	58	14	3	0	2	2	8	5	.241	.397	.333
Bases Empty	130	29	6	0	3	3	21	17	.223	.338	.331
Runners On	103	29	2	3	4	33	16	14	.282	.476	.380
Runners/Scor. Pos.	58	21	1	3	3	31	9	10	.362	.638	.449
Runners On/2 Out	42	14	1	1	3	19	7	4	.333	.619	.429
Scor. Pos./2 Out	25	11	1	1	2	17	5	2	.440	.800	.533
Late Inning Pressure	32	11	2	1	1	7	10	6	.344	.563	.500
Leading Off	7	0	0	0	0	0	3	0	.000	.000	.300
Bases Empty	18	7	2	0	1	1	6	1	.389	.667	.542
Runners On	14	4	0	1	0	6	4	5	.286	.429	.444
Runners/Scor. Pos.	9	3	0	1	0	6	2	3	.333	.556	.455

DRIVING IN RUNS	0 Out	1 Out	2 Out	Total	
From 1B	1/26	1/24	4/30	6/80	8%
From 2B	1/13	3/14	9/22	13/49	27%
From 3B	4/7	3/6	3/9	10/22	45%
Scoring Position	5/20	6/20	12/31	23/71	32%
Scor. Pos. %	25%	30%	39%	32%	
Driving In Runners from 3B with Less than Two Out:		7/13	54%		

Loves to face: Joe Cowley (.308, 4-for-13, 3 HR)
Hates to face: Ron Romanick (.071, 1-for-14)
Led majors last year with .440 batting average with runners in scoring position and two outs. ... Started 47 of first 56 games in which Birds faced a right-hander, but only 15 of the last 47. ... Had much the same pattern of play in 1984: only seven of his 43 starts that year came after the All-Star Game. ... Batted .356 with runners in scoring position over past three seasons. ... Has 15 hits in his last 39 at bats with the bases loaded. ... Batted .192 (5-for-26) as a pinch-hitter last season. ... Ratio of 0.67 ground outs-to-air outs was 9th-lowest in A.L. last season (minimum: 200 PA). Career average: 0.62. ... What does he have in common with Mel Ott, Roger Maris, Brooks Robinson, and Mickey Lolich (among others)? Each hit a home run in his first World Series at bat.

Mike Easler

Boston Red Sox	AB	H	2B	3B	HR	RRF	BB	SO	BA	SA	OBA
Season	568	149	29	4	16	76	53	129	.262	.412	.325
vs. Left-Handed Pitchers	173	48	9	0	2	18	17	52	.277	.364	.345
vs. Right-Handed Pitchers	395	101	20	4	14	58	36	77	.256	.433	.316
Home	273	68	17	3	4	31	24	75	.249	.377	.311
Road	295	81	12	1	12	45	29	54	.275	.444	.337
Grass	478	124	26	4	14	68	44	117	.259	.418	.320
Artificial Turf	90	25	3	0	2	8	9	12	.278	.378	.350
April	76	16	4	0	4	9	7	21	.211	.421	.271
May	95	24	3	1	3	10	8	17	.253	.400	.311
June	98	31	7	0	1	14	9	25	.316	.418	.374
July	96	25	6	2	3	13	10	20	.260	.458	.343
August	99	25	5	0	2	15	7	23	.253	.364	.296
Sept./Oct.	104	28	4	1	3	15	12	23	.269	.413	.342
Leading Off Inn.	132	38	4	1	4	4	11	28	.288	.424	.347
Bases Empty	324	86	10	2	10	11	28	77	.265	.401	.328
Runners On	244	63	19	2	6	65	25	52	.258	.426	.321
Runners/Scor. Pos.	153	38	13	1	4	59	17	34	.248	.425	.315
Runners On/2 Out	112	25	6	1	1	24	16	23	.223	.321	.320
Scor. Pos./2 Out	76	16	4	1	1	24	10	14	.211	.329	.302
Late Inning Pressure	87	21	1	1	1	4	8	24	.241	.310	.302
Leading Off	22	4	0	0	0	0	3	7	.182	.182	.280
Bases Empty	56	14	0	0	1	1	4	14	.250	.304	.300
Runners On	31	7	1	1	0	3	4	10	.226	.323	.306
Runners/Scor. Pos.	12	1	0	1	0	3	2	5	.083	.250	.200

DRIVING IN RUNS	0 Out	1 Out	2 Out	Total	
From 1B	2/29	5/64	3/78	10/171	6%
From 2B	2/20	9/48	13/60	24/128	19%
From 3B	3/7	15/24	7/37	25/68	37%
Scoring Position	5/27	24/72	20/97	49/196	25%
Scor. Pos. %	19%	33%	21%	25%	
Driving In Runners from 3B with Less than Two Out:			18/31	58%	

Loves to face: Pete Ladd (.571, 4-for-7, 2 HR)
Hates to face: Jack Morris (.071, 1-for-14, 6 SO)
.262 batting average was his lowest at any level of organized ball since 1970, when the 19-year-old Hit Man batted .252 for the Cocoa Astros in the Florida State League. (That must have been a pitchers' league. Four other guys who are still around played in the FSL that year: Rick Burleson hit .220, Joel Youngblood .222, Dan Driessen .223, and Ivan DeJesus .232). . . . Easler's Fenway Park batting average dropped from .375 in 1984 to .249 last season. Home run production at Fenway dropped from 16 (one every 18.7 at bats) in '84 to four (one every 68.3 at bats) in '85. . . . Five grand-slam homers in 39 bases-loaded at bats since 1982. . . . Has homered in every A.L. ballpark except Memorial Stadium. . . . Even at .262, he outhit his brother-in-law, Cliff Johnson, for the sixth straight year.

Darrell Evans

Detroit Tigers	AB	H	2B	3B	HR	RRF	BB	SO	BA	SA	OBA
Season	505	125	17	0	40	97	85	85	.248	.519	.356
vs. Left-Handed Pitchers	120	25	4	0	9	23	11	29	.208	.467	.275
vs. Right-Handed Pitchers	385	100	13	0	31	74	74	56	.260	.535	.379
Home	242	59	7	0	21	48	45	41	.244	.533	.362
Road	263	66	10	0	19	49	40	44	.251	.506	.350
Grass	425	104	14	0	31	80	75	67	.245	.496	.358
Artificial Turf	80	21	3	0	9	17	10	18	.263	.638	.344
April	48	9	2	0	1	2	4	3	.188	.292	.250
May	75	22	2	0	7	16	10	12	.293	.600	.376
June	85	24	5	0	6	14	21	11	.282	.553	.421
July	93	17	1	0	8	20	20	16	.183	.452	.333
August	91	19	4	0	7	18	16	21	.209	.484	.327
Sept./Oct.	113	34	3	0	11	27	14	22	.301	.619	.375
Leading Off Inn.	117	30	0	0	14	14	15	17	.256	.615	.341
Bases Empty	305	67	7	0	24	24	40	55	.220	.479	.310
Runners On	200	58	10	0	16	73	45	30	.290	.580	.419
Runners/Scor. Pos.	116	32	6	0	7	54	29	19	.276	.509	.415
Runners On/2 Out	85	22	5	0	3	20	26	14	.259	.424	.438
Scor. Pos./2 Out	50	14	3	0	2	18	19	10	.280	.460	.478
Late Inning Pressure	67	17	2	0	9	16	10	8	.254	.687	.351
Leading Off	18	6	0	0	5	5	2	4	.333	1.167	.400
Bases Empty	47	11	1	0	7	7	5	6	.234	.702	.308
Runners On	20	6	1	0	2	9	5	2	.300	.650	.440
Runners/Scor. Pos.	10	4	0	0	2	9	5	1	.400	1.000	.600

DRIVING IN RUNS	0 Out	1 Out	2 Out	Total	
From 1B	5/32	9/51	3/65	17/148	11%
From 2B	2/14	9/33	8/38	19/85	22%
From 3B	3/6	12/25	6/18	21/49	43%
Scoring Position	5/20	21/58	14/56	40/134	30%
Scor. Pos. %	25%	36%	25%	30%	
Driving In Runners from 3B with Less than Two Out:			15/31	48%	

Loves to face: Ron Guidry (1.000, 2-for-2, 2 HR)
Hates to face: Rod Scurry (0-for-14, 6 SO)
At 38, the oldest A.L. player ever to hit 40 homers, breaking Babe Ruth's mark (age 37 in 1932). . . . First Detroit player to lead A.L. in homers since Hank Greenberg in 1946. . . . First 40-home run hitter since 1973 to have fewer than 100 RBIs. Hank Aaron and Davey Johnson both hit 40 with fewer than 100 for the '73 Braves while Evans, their teammate, set career highs with 41 homers and 104 RBIs. . . . 0.55 G/A ratio was 2d-lowest in majors last season (minimum: 200 PA). Career average: 0.67. . . . Led majors with nine home runs in Late-Inning Pressure Situations. . . . Batted 131 points higher in day games (.338) than at night (.207) last season, biggest such difference in A.L. (minimum: 200 PA). . . . Hit seven home runs vs. New York last season, five of them in a three-game series in Tiger Stadium (Sept. 17–19).

Dwight Evans

Boston Red Sox	AB	H	2B	3B	HR	RRF	BB	SO	BA	SA	OBA
Season	617	162	29	1	29	82	114	105	.263	.454	.378
vs. Left-Handed Pitchers	170	46	6	0	12	29	42	26	.271	.518	.416
vs. Right-Handed Pitchers	447	116	23	1	17	53	72	79	.260	.430	.363
Home	292	81	18	0	14	37	49	49	.277	.483	.382
Road	325	81	11	1	15	45	65	56	.249	.428	.375
Grass	513	137	27	1	23	67	94	86	.267	.458	.381
Artificial Turf	104	25	2	0	6	15	20	19	.240	.433	.362
April	75	16	4	0	2	7	23	12	.213	.347	.394
May	96	17	5	0	2	6	24	16	.177	.292	.347
June	83	25	3	0	5	13	17	15	.301	.518	.412
July	109	30	1	0	3	11	16	24	.275	.367	.367
August	113	30	9	1	7	20	13	17	.265	.549	.344
Sept./Oct.	141	44	7	0	10	25	21	21	.312	.574	.406
Leading Off Inn.	180	53	9	1	11	11	23	29	.294	.539	.377
Bases Empty	342	91	14	1	19	19	62	58	.266	.480	.382
Runners On	275	71	15	0	10	63	52	47	.258	.422	.374
Runners/Scor. Pos.	141	25	3	0	3	47	33	28	.177	.262	.328
Runners On/2 Out	112	29	8	0	4	28	22	22	.259	.438	.381
Scor. Pos./2 Out	71	15	3	0	3	25	15	15	.211	.380	.349
Late Inning Pressure	89	20	2	0	7	18	14	16	.225	.483	.336
Leading Off	18	6	1	0	1	1	3	2	.333	.556	.455
Bases Empty	44	9	1	0	2	2	7	9	.205	.364	.327
Runners On	45	11	1	0	5	16	7	7	.244	.600	.345
Runners/Scor. Pos.	30	4	1	0	1	8	6	6	.133	.267	.282

DRIVING IN RUNS	0 Out	1 Out	2 Out	Total	
From 1B	4/65	3/73	4/75	11/213	5%
From 2B	1/16	3/45	13/52	17/113	15%
From 3B	5/10	13/26	7/29	25/65	38%
Scoring Position	6/26	16/71	20/81	42/178	24%
Scor. Pos. %	23%	23%	25%	24%	
Driving In Runners from 3B with Less than Two Out:			18/36	50%	

Loves to face: Ken Schrom (.600, 6-for-10, 1 HR)
Hates to face: Luis Sanchez (0-for-15)
In space of one year, batting average with runners in scoring position dropped from .331 (his highest over past 11 years) to .177 (his lowest over same span). Batted with virtually the same number of runners in scoring position in 1985 (178) as in '84 (175), but RBI total fell from 104 to 78. . . . Batted .059 (1-for-17) with the bases loaded last season; that one hit saved him the ignominy of matching the *Player Analysis* record of 0-for-17, set in 1979 by the one San Pedro de Macoris player you don't hear much about any more: Nelson Norman. . . . They used to call it a salary drive: From Aug. 14 to the end of the season, Evans hit 17 home runs in 51 games, the most home runs by any major leaguer over that span.

Tony Fernandez

Toronto Blue Jays	AB	H	2B	3B	HR	RRF	BB	SO	BA	SA	OBA
Season	564	163	31	10	2	55	43	41	.289	.390	.340
vs. Left-Handed Pitchers	194	57	13	5	0	17	22	14	.294	.412	.366
vs. Right-Handed Pitchers	370	106	18	5	2	38	21	27	.286	.378	.327
Home	265	81	22	6	1	24	23	16	.306	.445	.366
Road	299	82	9	4	1	31	20	25	.274	.341	.318
Grass	236	64	5	2	1	21	14	23	.271	.322	.311
Artificial Turf	328	99	26	8	1	34	29	18	.302	.439	.361
April	68	18	3	1	0	5	2	5	.265	.338	.296
May	89	24	4	1	1	12	7	5	.270	.371	.320
June	95	34	7	3	1	13	9	6	.358	.526	.419
July	99	20	4	0	0	5	7	6	.202	.242	.252
August	97	31	7	3	0	13	10	8	.320	.454	.383
Sept./Oct.	116	36	6	2	0	7	8	11	.310	.397	.355
Leading Off Inn.	143	43	12	4	0	0	11	10	.301	.441	.355
Bases Empty	324	95	22	7	0	0	24	24	.293	.404	.344
Runners On	240	68	9	3	2	55	19	17	.283	.371	.336
Runners/Scor. Pos.	140	42	7	2	1	51	16	13	.300	.400	.371
Runners On/2 Out	95	31	6	1	0	28	12	5	.326	.411	.407
Scor. Pos./2 Out	68	22	5	0	0	26	12	6	.324	.397	.432
Late Inning Pressure	82	25	3	2	0	10	8	12	.305	.390	.374
Leading Off	18	5	2	0	0	0	2	4	.278	.389	.381
Bases Empty	42	13	2	1	0	0	6	7	.310	.405	.408
Runners On	40	12	1	1	0	10	2	5	.300	.375	.333
Runners/Scor. Pos.	21	6	0	0	0	8	2	4	.286	.286	.348

DRIVING IN RUNS	0 Out	1 Out	2 Out	Total	
From 1B	0/37	2/71	2/60	4/168	2%
From 2B	2/20	8/40	15/49	25/109	23%
From 3B	2/5	11/26	11/32	24/63	38%
Scoring Position	4/25	19/66	26/81	49/172	28%
Scor. Pos. %	16%	29%	32%	28%	
Driving In Runners from 3B with Less than Two Out:			13/31	42%	

Loves to face: Joe Beckwith (1.000, 3-for-3)
Hates to face: Bud Black (.083, 1-for-12)
Had more walks than strikeouts for 2d straight season, due more to a low strikeout total than an overabundance of walks. There must be "DON'T WALK" signs all over San Pedro de Macoris: besides Fernandez's moderate total of 43, townmate Mariano Duncan had only 38 in 620 plate appearances, Juan Samuel 33 in 709, Rafael Ramirez 20 in 595, Rafael Santana 29 (12 of them intentional) in 564, and Alfredo Griffin 20 in 646. . . . June batting average of .358 was 3d-highest in A.L. . . . Led A.L. shortstops in assists (478) and chances accepted (761). . . . Career batting averages: .297 with the bases empty, .263 with runners on base, .249 with runners in scoring position. . . . All five career home runs have been hit from the left side. . . . Has batted over .300 leading off innings in each of past two seasons. . . . Ground-ball hitter: 1.44 G/A ratio last season.

Carlton Fisk

Chicago White Sox	AB	H	2B	3B	HR	RRF	BB	SO	BA	SA	OBA
Season	543	129	23	1	37	108	52	81	.238	.488	.320
vs. Left-Handed Pitchers	183	46	12	0	9	34	17	22	.251	.464	.329
vs. Right-Handed Pitchers	360	83	11	1	28	74	35	59	.231	.500	.316
Home	271	55	9	1	20	51	31	42	.203	.465	.294
Road	272	74	14	0	17	57	21	39	.272	.511	.346
Grass	457	103	18	1	36	101	49	73	.225	.505	.314
Artificial Turf	86	26	5	0	1	7	3	8	.302	.395	.355
April	55	17	4	0	4	14	5	7	.309	.600	.377
May	80	21	2	0	8	18	5	12	.263	.588	.322
June	87	15	1	0	6	10	7	14	.172	.391	.270
July	92	21	5	1	9	23	12	13	.228	.598	.321
August	108	24	4	0	6	19	10	20	.222	.426	.306
Sept./Oct.	121	31	7	0	4	24	13	15	.256	.413	.343
Leading Off Inn.	132	24	4	0	7	7	10	28	.182	.371	.270
Bases Empty	306	61	7	0	18	18	22	53	.199	.399	.279
Runners On	237	68	16	1	19	90	30	28	.287	.603	.371
Runners/Scor. Pos.	128	43	13	1	8	67	24	15	.336	.641	.438
Runners On/2 Out	103	31	6	0	13	46	18	10	.301	.738	.415
Scor. Pos./2 Out	58	19	5	0	5	29	14	6	.328	.672	.473
Late Inning Pressure	77	22	2	1	5	14	6	12	.286	.532	.341
Leading Off	25	8	1	0	2	2	1	3	.320	.600	.370
Bases Empty	54	12	1	0	3	3	4	8	.222	.407	.288
Runners On	23	10	1	1	2	11	2	4	.435	.826	.462
Runners/Scor. Pos.	12	6	1	1	0	7	2	3	.500	.750	.533

DRIVING IN RUNS	0 Out	1 Out	2 Out	Total	
From 1B	2/44	6/62	11/74	19/180	11%
From 2B	3/15	9/39	13/40	25/94	27%
From 3B	5/9	13/26	9/27	27/62	44%
Scoring Position	8/24	22/65	22/67	52/156	33%
Scor. Pos. %	33%	34%	33%	33%	
Driving In Runners from 3B with Less than Two Out:			18/35	51%	

Loves to face: Dan Quisenberry (.429, 9-for-21, 1 HR)
Hates to face: Jack Morris (.057, 2-for-35, 9 SO)
What's more amazing for a 36-year-old catcher, 37 home runs or 17 stolen bases? Both are records for his age/position.... Left field's thataway, Pudge: he has played only eight of his 1702 major-league games there.... Has had 100 hits at Comiskey Park over past two seasons, 55 for extra bases, 31 of them homers.... One of only five players to have hit 100 home runs for the White Sox in their 85-year history. That's as many 100-home run hitters as the Angels have had in their 25 years, or the Royals in their 17. (The Brewers, in 17 years, have had seven).... One of two A.L. catchers with two putouts on one play last year; Buck Martinez's was more spectacular, as he broke his leg in the middle of it, but Fisk's had the virtue of being on national TV.... Fly-ball hitter: 0.77 G/A ratio last season. Career: 0.80.

Scott Fletcher

Chicago White Sox	AB	H	2B	3B	HR	RRF	BB	SO	BA	SA	OBA
Season	301	77	8	1	2	31	35	47	.256	.309	.332
vs. Left-Handed Pitchers	168	50	6	1	2	14	21	23	.298	.381	.374
vs. Right-Handed Pitchers	133	27	2	0	0	17	14	24	.203	.218	.279
Home	142	32	3	0	0	17	22	26	.225	.246	.327
Road	159	45	5	1	2	14	13	21	.283	.365	.337
Grass	244	57	6	1	1	27	28	41	.234	.279	.311
Artificial Turf	57	20	2	0	1	4	7	6	.351	.439	.422
April	39	10	1	0	0	5	6	11	.256	.282	.356
May	74	15	2	0	0	7	7	10	.203	.230	.272
June	34	10	1	0	0	2	4	7	.294	.324	.368
July	48	10	0	0	0	5	4	5	.208	.208	.269
August	56	17	0	0	2	4	5	9	.304	.411	.355
Sept./Oct.	50	15	4	1	0	8	9	5	.300	.420	.407
Leading Off Inn.	74	17	2	0	2	2	7	10	.230	.338	.296
Bases Empty	186	44	5	1	2	2	20	33	.237	.306	.311
Runners On	115	33	3	0	0	29	15	14	.287	.313	.366
Runners/Scor. Pos.	62	19	2	0	0	29	12	8	.306	.339	.413
Runners On/2 Out	45	11	0	0	0	11	6	7	.244	.244	.333
Scor. Pos./2 Out	27	8	0	0	0	11	6	5	.296	.296	.424
Late Inning Pressure	37	10	1	0	0	5	2	8	.270	.297	.308
Leading Off	9	1	0	0	0	0	0	4	.111	.111	.111
Bases Empty	16	3	1	0	0	0	0	4	.188	.250	.188
Runners On	21	7	0	0	0	5	2	4	.333	.333	.391
Runners/Scor. Pos.	13	4	0	0	0	5	2	2	.308	.308	.400

DRIVING IN RUNS	0 Out	1 Out	2 Out	Total	
From 1B	0/23	1/22	0/29	1/74	1%
From 2B	2/7	3/17	8/21	13/45	29%
From 3B	3/4	9/14	3/12	15/30	50%
Scoring Position	5/11	12/31	11/33	28/75	37%
Scor. Pos. %	45%	39%	33%	37%	
Driving In Runners from 3B with Less than Two Out:			12/18	67%	

Loves to face: Ted Higuera (.545, 6-for-11, 1 HR)
Hates to face: Mike Mason (0-for-9, 4 SO)
Traded to Texas over the offseason. Rangers are getting a player with a .312 career batting average with runners in scoring position, .227 at all other times.... Yearly percentage of runners driven in from scoring position, starting with 1983: 30.7, 33.3, 37.3.... Batted .306 after All-Star break last season.... Only major-leaguer to play 30 or more games at second base, third base, and shortstop last season.... LaRussa liked him against left-handers, starting him in 49 of Chicago's 54 games against southpaws.... Ground-ball hitter: 1.75 G/A ratio was 10th-highest in A.L. last season (minimum: 200 PA). Career average: 1.52.... Tough one to explain to the kids: batted .029 (1-for-34) vs. Cleveland last year.

Julio Franco

Cleveland Indians	AB	H	2B	3B	HR	RRF	BB	SO	BA	SA	OBA
Season	636	183	33	4	6	93	54	74	.288	.381	.343
vs. Left-Handed Pitchers	196	56	12	0	4	23	16	27	.286	.408	.340
vs. Right-Handed Pitchers	440	127	21	4	2	70	38	47	.289	.368	.344
Home	307	94	16	1	3	50	22	32	.306	.394	.354
Road	329	89	17	3	3	43	32	42	.271	.368	.332
Grass	533	163	28	4	6	87	48	62	.306	.407	.362
Artificial Turf	103	20	5	0	0	6	6	12	.194	.243	.239
April	67	27	6	0	1	14	12	6	.403	.537	.482
May	103	24	5	1	1	8	8	16	.233	.330	.283
June	98	24	6	0	0	11	6	10	.245	.306	.295
July	116	32	4	0	1	12	8	9	.276	.336	.323
August	117	38	4	0	3	26	5	12	.325	.436	.355
Sept./Oct.	135	38	8	3	0	22	15	21	.281	.385	.351
Leading Off Inn.	103	29	7	0	0	0	8	12	.282	.350	.339
Bases Empty	344	95	19	2	2	2	27	43	.276	.360	.332
Runners On	292	88	14	2	4	91	27	31	.301	.404	.355
Runners/Scor. Pos.	195	57	8	2	2	84	21	20	.292	.385	.350
Runners On/2 Out	103	28	6	1	2	29	10	14	.272	.408	.342
Scor. Pos./2 Out	77	22	5	1	2	28	9	9	.286	.455	.360
Late Inning Pressure	80	16	0	2	0	10	8	5	.200	.250	.273
Leading Off	14	1	0	0	0	0	1	0	.071	.071	.133
Bases Empty	43	7	0	1	0	0	2	2	.163	.209	.200
Runners On	37	9	0	1	0	10	6	3	.243	.297	.349
Runners/Scor. Pos.	30	7	0	1	0	9	5	3	.233	.300	.343

DRIVING IN RUNS	0 Out	1 Out	2 Out	Total	
From 1B	2/69	3/54	3/56	8/179	4%
From 2B	10/40	7/44	11/57	28/141	20%
From 3B	19/24	19/41	12/38	50/103	49%
Scoring Position	29/64	26/85	23/95	78/244	32%
Scor. Pos. %	45%	31%	24%	32%	
Driving In Runners from 3B with Less than Two Out:			38/65	58%	

Loves to face: Bud Black (.462, 12-for-26, 1 HR)
Hates to face: Dan Quisenberry (0-for-12)
90 RBIs last season sound impressive, but are somewhat mitigated by fact that he led majors with 244 opportunities to drive in runners from scoring position, the highest total in A.L. since 1979, when Don Baylor had 257 and drove in 139 runs.... Has batted for a higher average with runners on base than he has with the bases empty in each of his four big league seasons. Career batting averages: .272 with the bases empty, .295 with runners on base, .311 with runners in scoring position.... Yearly batting averages in Late-Inning Pressure Situations since 1983: .265, .226, .200.... April batting average of .403 led A.L.... Had lowest fielding percentage (.949) of any major league shortstop last season (minimum: 100 games).... Lowest career batting average at any A.L. Stadium is .181 (13-for-72) at the Metrodome.

Gary Gaetti

Minnesota Twins	AB	H	2B	3B	HR	RRF	BB	SO	BA	SA	OBA
Season	560	138	31	0	20	64	37	89	.246	.409	.301
vs. Left-Handed Pitchers	175	36	7	0	6	10	14	32	.206	.349	.272
vs. Right-Handed Pitchers	385	102	24	0	14	54	23	57	.265	.436	.314
Home	280	73	16	0	10	31	17	48	.261	.425	.309
Road	280	65	15	0	10	33	20	41	.232	.393	.293
Grass	217	53	11	0	8	28	17	27	.244	.406	.311
Artificial Turf	343	85	20	0	12	36	20	62	.248	.411	.294
April	75	21	8	0	3	14	11	15	.280	.507	.372
May	93	26	5	0	4	15	13	20	.280	.462	.382
June	78	16	7	0	2	5	2	11	.205	.372	.225
July	105	27	4	0	3	13	0	18	.257	.381	.257
August	80	17	4	0	2	7	7	9	.213	.338	.300
Sept./Oct.	129	31	3	0	6	10	4	16	.240	.403	.269
Leading Off Inn.	120	26	8	0	4	4	6	15	.217	.383	.271
Bases Empty	316	81	22	0	12	12	22	42	.256	.440	.311
Runners On	244	57	9	0	8	52	15	47	.234	.369	.288
Runners/Scor. Pos.	132	31	7	0	3	42	10	26	.235	.356	.301
Runners On/2 Out	111	20	4	0	3	24	6	24	.180	.297	.235
Scor. Pos./2 Out	66	13	4	0	1	20	4	15	.197	.303	.264
Late Inning Pressure	65	19	4	0	2	4	12	5	.292	.446	.403
Leading Off	15	4	2	0	0	0	3	2	.267	.400	.389
Bases Empty	44	17	4	0	2	2	9	2	.386	.614	.491
Runners On	21	2	0	0	0	2	3	3	.095	.095	.208
Runners/Scor. Pos.	11	2	0	0	0	2	3	2	.182	.182	.357

DRIVING IN RUNS	0 Out	1 Out	2 Out	Total	
From 1B	2/45	1/56	6/78	9/179	5%
From 2B	2/21	4/34	10/53	16/108	15%
From 3B	7/8	6/17	5/28	18/53	34%
Scoring Position	9/29	10/51	15/81	34/161	21%
Scor. Pos. %	31%	20%	19%	21%	
Driving In Runners from 3B with Less than Two Out:			13/25	52%	

Loves to face: Floyd Bannister (.440, 11-for-25, 5 HR)
Hates to face: Roy Thomas (.083, 1-for-12, 5 SO)
Home run totals in last four seasons: 25, 21, 5, 20.... Some pretty poor career numbers in Late-Inning Pressure Situations, the worst being his rate of 15.2 percent of runners driven in from scoring position. That's the lowest rate by any player in the 11-year history of *The Player Analysis* (minimum: 75 opportunities).... Has never homered in 122 LIP at bats with a runner on base.... Led A.L. third basemen in putouts (146) and double plays (31).... 115 doubles in four seasons; could wind up in the all-time top 30 with around 500 if the Metrodome's roof holds out.... Career batting average of .182 (16-for-88) at Yankee Stadium.... Has missed only seven games over past three years; stop chuckling, Cal, Jr.

Greg Gagne

Minnesota Twins	AB	H	2B	3B	HR	RRF	BB	SO	BA	SA	OBA
Season	293	66	15	3	2	24	20	57	.225	.317	.279
vs. Left-Handed Pitchers	127	31	7	2	1	10	4	24	.244	.354	.265
vs. Right-Handed Pitchers	166	35	8	1	1	14	16	33	.211	.289	.289
Home	142	33	10	2	0	13	12	22	.232	.331	.297
Road	151	33	5	1	2	11	8	35	.219	.305	.261
Grass	104	23	4	1	2	8	7	24	.221	.337	.274
Artificial Turf	189	43	11	2	0	16	13	33	.228	.307	.282
April	63	19	6	1	0	6	7	7	.302	.429	.380
May	32	9	2	0	0	2	3	6	.281	.344	.343
June	60	13	2	1	2	7	3	14	.217	.383	.262
July	65	12	4	1	0	4	3	13	.185	.277	.221
August	4	0	0	0	0	0	0	3	.000	.000	.000
Sept./Oct.	69	13	1	0	0	5	4	14	.188	.203	.237
Leading Off Inn.	67	13	4	0	1	1	6	9	.194	.299	.260
Bases Empty	159	34	9	2	2	2	14	33	.214	.333	.290
Runners On	134	32	6	1	0	22	6	24	.239	.299	.266
Runners/Scor. Pos.	76	23	5	1	0	21	3	14	.303	.395	.317
Runners On/2 Out	55	11	2	0	0	6	3	10	.200	.236	.241
Scor. Pos./2 Out	34	7	2	0	0	6	2	7	.206	.265	.250
Late Inning Pressure	24	7	1	0	0	3	4	6	.292	.333	.393
Leading Off	7	2	0	0	0	0	3	2	.286	.286	.500
Bases Empty	13	3	0	0	0	0	3	5	.231	.231	.375
Runners On	11	4	1	0	0	3	1	1	.364	.455	.417
Runners/Scor. Pos.	3	3	1	0	0	3	0	0	1.000	1.333	1.000

DRIVING IN RUNS	0 Out	1 Out	2 Out	Total	
From 1B	1/24	0/29	0/35	1/88	1%
From 2B	4/18	5/21	6/29	15/68	22%
From 3B	2/5	4/8	0/7	6/20	30%
Scoring Position	6/23	9/29	6/36	21/88	24%
Scor. Pos. %	26%	31%	17%	24%	
Driving In Runners from 3B with Less than Two Out:			6/13	46%	

Loves to face: Frank Tanana (.667, 4-for-6, 1 HR)
Hates to face: Danny Jackson (0-for-10)
Averaged 3.08 assists per nine innings; that's slightly above the league average (2.96), but it looks very impressive compared to the other Minnesota shortstop—Roy Smalley averaged only 2.42. . . . Hit his only two career home runs in the same series at Texas (June 13–16). . . . Suffered through a 33-game RBI drought from July 13 to Sept. 16; we mean *suffered*, as he spent three weeks on disabled list in late August with back spasms. . . . Fly-ball hitter: 0.71 G/A ratio last season. . . . Yankees originally drafted him in 5th round in 1979; 14 rounds later, they got around to picking Don Mattingly. Traded to Twins with Ron Davis and Paul Boris for Roy Smalley, who eventually took circuitous route back to Twin Cities.

Barbaro Garbey

Detroit Tigers	AB	H	2B	3B	HR	RRF	BB	SO	BA	SA	OBA
Season	237	61	9	1	6	29	15	37	.257	.380	.305
vs. Left-Handed Pitchers	138	37	7	1	4	15	9	20	.268	.420	.320
vs. Right-Handed Pitchers	99	24	2	0	2	14	6	17	.242	.323	.284
Home	134	32	4	1	4	19	9	19	.239	.373	.284
Road	103	29	5	0	2	10	6	18	.282	.388	.333
Grass	194	51	7	1	5	24	15	31	.263	.387	.319
Artificial Turf	43	10	2	0	1	5	0	6	.233	.349	.233
April	21	4	0	0	0	1	1	2	.190	.190	.227
May	26	11	3	0	1	4	0	7	.423	.654	.444
June	30	6	1	0	2	5	6	3	.200	.433	.333
July	79	21	2	0	2	13	4	13	.266	.367	.299
August	63	13	2	0	0	2	3	9	.206	.238	.250
Sept./Oct.	18	6	1	1	1	4	1	3	.333	.667	.368
Leading Off Inn.	52	14	0	0	6	6	3	8	.269	.615	.309
Bases Empty	125	34	5	1	6	6	8	16	.272	.472	.326
Runners On	112	27	4	0	0	23	7	21	.241	.277	.282
Runners/Scor. Pos.	62	13	3	0	0	23	6	13	.210	.258	.274
Runners On/2 Out	50	13	2	0	0	10	4	9	.260	.300	.315
Scor. Pos./2 Out	35	8	2	0	0	10	4	7	.229	.286	.308
Late Inning Pressure	44	10	0	0	1	6	4	9	.227	.295	.292
Leading Off	12	3	0	0	1	1	1	2	.250	.500	.308
Bases Empty	26	6	0	0	1	1	3	3	.231	.346	.310
Runners On	18	4	0	0	0	5	1	6	.222	.222	.263
Runners/Scor. Pos.	12	4	0	0	0	5	1	3	.333	.333	.385

DRIVING IN RUNS	0 Out	1 Out	2 Out	Total	
From 1B	0/22	1/30	0/37	1/89	1%
From 2B	0/3	3/18	7/29	10/50	20%
From 3B	0/3	9/15	3/14	12/32	38%
Scoring Position	0/6	12/33	10/43	22/82	27%
Scor. Pos. %	0%	36%	23%	27%	
Driving In Runners from 3B with Less than Two Out:			9/18	50%	

Loves to face: Tim Lollar (1.000, 3-for-3, 1 HR)
Hates to face: Phil Niekro (0-for-5)
Broke into the majors with five pinch-hits in his first six pinch-hit at bats. Since then, his pinch-hit batting average is .132 (5-for-38). . . . Averaged one home run per 8.7 at bats leading off innings last season, topped only by Darrell Evans (one every 8.4 at bats) among players with 50 or more leadoff plate appearances. . . . Might have some tough batting practice sessions: Garbey is 0-for-8 with four strikeouts against new Oakland teammate Tim Birtsas. . . . In two seasons with Detroit, started 108 of 120 games against left-handers, but only 30 of 203 against right-handers. . . . Had led A.L. in 1984 in batting average with two outs and runners on base (.393), but didn't approach that mark last year.

Jim Gantner

Milwaukee Brewers	AB	H	2B	3B	HR	RRF	BB	SO	BA	SA	OBA
Season	523	133	15	4	5	46	33	42	.254	.327	.300
vs. Left-Handed Pitchers	164	54	5	1	0	15	9	11	.329	.372	.368
vs. Right-Handed Pitchers	359	79	10	3	5	31	24	31	.220	.306	.270
Home	261	62	6	2	4	27	14	23	.238	.322	.274
Road	262	71	9	2	1	19	19	19	.271	.332	.325
Grass	425	105	12	4	5	41	28	36	.247	.329	.293
Artificial Turf	98	28	3	0	0	5	5	6	.286	.316	.333
April	57	8	1	1	0	4	4	7	.140	.193	.197
May	79	23	4	1	1	11	3	6	.291	.405	.313
June	102	33	3	0	2	14	8	6	.324	.412	.373
July	97	20	2	0	0	5	10	4	.206	.227	.284
August	73	16	2	0	2	6	3	9	.219	.329	.244
Sept./Oct.	115	33	3	2	0	6	5	10	.287	.348	.328
Leading Off Inn.	122	27	3	1	0	0	7	9	.221	.262	.269
Bases Empty	304	78	12	2	3	3	15	24	.257	.339	.294
Runners On	219	55	3	2	2	43	18	18	.251	.311	.309
Runners/Scor. Pos.	122	29	1	1	1	38	14	13	.238	.287	.312
Runners On/2 Out	88	21	0	0	1	14	11	10	.239	.273	.323
Scor. Pos./2 Out	55	12	0	0	0	12	9	7	.218	.218	.328
Late Inning Pressure	82	21	2	0	1	4	9	9	.256	.317	.326
Leading Off	22	5	1	0	0	0	1	2	.227	.273	.261
Bases Empty	52	15	2	0	1	1	5	6	.288	.385	.351
Runners On	30	6	0	0	0	3	4	3	.200	.200	.286
Runners/Scor. Pos.	15	3	0	0	0	3	4	1	.200	.200	.350

DRIVING IN RUNS	0 Out	1 Out	2 Out	Total	
From 1B	1/44	3/57	1/61	5/162	3%
From 2B	4/24	4/32	7/36	15/92	16%
From 3B	5/7	11/18	5/30	21/55	38%
Scoring Position	9/31	15/50	12/66	36/147	24%
Scor. Pos. %	29%	30%	18%	24%	
Driving In Runners from 3B with Less than Two Out:			16/25	64%	

Loves to face: Tom Waddell (.833, 5-for-6, 2 HR)
Hates to face: Dan Quisenberry (.063, 1-for-16, 10 ground outs)
Astonishing left/right breakdown last season: Left-handed batter hit 109 points higher vs. left-handers than right-handers, the largest "backward" disparity by any major-league player (minimum: 100 AB against each). This was the first season in which he batted for higher average vs. left-handers than against right-handers; previous high vs. lefties was .289 in 1982. . . . Career batting averages: .269 on grass fields, .312 on artificial surfaces. . . . Yearly batting averages with runners in scoring position since 1982: .353, .283, .272, .238. . . . Career defensive rate of 77.5 double plays per 100 games, best rate by any active second baseman (minimum: 150 games). . . . Has never driven in a runner from first base in Late-Inning Pressure Situations (138 career opportunities).

Damaso Garcia

Toronto Blue Jays	AB	H	2B	3B	HR	RRF	BB	SO	BA	SA	OBA
Season	600	169	25	4	8	69	15	41	.282	.377	.302
vs. Left-Handed Pitchers	219	55	10	1	2	15	7	17	.251	.333	.276
vs. Right-Handed Pitchers	381	114	15	3	6	54	8	24	.299	.402	.317
Home	300	91	16	4	4	48	12	19	.303	.423	.334
Road	300	78	9	0	4	21	3	22	.260	.330	.269
Grass	224	60	5	0	4	19	1	18	.268	.344	.273
Artificial Turf	376	109	20	4	4	50	14	23	.290	.396	.319
April	86	18	4	0	1	5	4	4	.209	.291	.244
May	109	38	5	1	0	19	3	8	.349	.413	.368
June	119	32	3	3	1	16	1	7	.269	.370	.285
July	115	35	6	0	2	16	3	4	.304	.409	.328
August	84	24	3	0	0	2	0	7	.286	.321	.286
Sept./Oct.	87	22	4	0	4	11	4	11	.253	.437	.283
Leading Off Inn.	237	63	9	2	2	3	8	20	.266	.346	.296
Bases Empty	374	105	16	2	6	7	10	27	.281	.382	.303
Runners On	226	64	9	2	2	62	5	14	.283	.367	.301
Runners/Scor. Pos.	133	41	7	2	1	59	4	10	.308	.414	.331
Runners On/2 Out	99	28	2	1	1	27	5	7	.283	.354	.324
Scor. Pos./2 Out	62	21	2	1	0	25	4	6	.339	.403	.388
Late Inning Pressure	75	20	4	1	1	12	1	4	.267	.387	.273
Leading Off	12	1	0	0	0	0	1	1	.083	.083	.154
Bases Empty	35	5	1	0	1	1	1	2	.143	.257	.167
Runners On	40	15	3	1	0	11	0	2	.375	.500	.366
Runners/Scor. Pos.	22	9	2	1	0	11	0	1	.409	.591	.391

DRIVING IN RUNS	0 Out	1 Out	2 Out	Total	
From 1B	1/39	2/52	3/63	6/154	4%
From 2B	3/15	9/38	11/44	23/97	24%
From 3B	7/11	12/22	12/34	31/67	46%
Scoring Position	10/26	21/60	23/78	54/164	33%
Scor. Pos. %	38%	35%	29%	33%	
Driving In Runners from 3B with Less than Two Out:			19/33	58%	

Loves to face: Ray Burris (.583, 7-for-12)
Hates to face: Rick Waits (.045, 1-for-22)
RBIs equal opportunities times execution; it's the E equals mc squared of baseball statistics. Last season, Garcia batted with 164 runners in scoring position, the most he's ever seen out there, and he batted .317 in those situations, the best such mark of his career. Result? A career-high 65 RBIs. . . . May batting average of .349 was 2d-best in A.L. . . . Career batting averages: .268 with runners on base, .298 with the bases empty. . . . Career rate of 2.9 walks per 100 plate appearances is 3d-lowest among active players (minimum: 500 PA). . . . Had five hits (in 12 at bats) with two outs and the bases loaded last season, tying Reggie Jackson for A.L. lead. . . . Over career, has hit 28 points higher on artificial turf than on grass, 29 points higher in day games than at night.

Rich Gedman

Boston Red Sox	AB	H	2B	3B	HR	RRF	BB	SO	BA	SA	OBA
Season	498	147	30	5	18	84	50	79	.295	.484	.362
vs. Left-Handed Pitchers	135	33	6	1	2	30	10	27	.244	.348	.299
vs. Right-Handed Pitchers	363	114	24	4	16	54	40	52	.314	.534	.384
Home	248	83	16	4	9	54	21	33	.335	.540	.386
Road	250	64	14	1	9	30	29	46	.256	.428	.338
Grass	429	132	28	4	15	79	42	64	.308	.497	.369
Artificial Turf	69	15	2	1	3	5	8	15	.217	.406	.316
April	65	19	4	0	1	8	5	16	.292	.400	.338
May	80	25	6	3	3	9	8	13	.313	.575	.375
June	76	22	7	0	1	17	8	14	.289	.421	.353
July	80	27	4	1	3	13	12	7	.338	.525	.436
August	87	25	5	0	5	16	8	16	.287	.517	.347
Sept./Oct.	110	29	4	1	5	21	9	13	.264	.455	.325
Leading Off Inn.	121	32	6	0	5	5	9	18	.264	.438	.315
Bases Empty	268	74	11	2	13	13	21	44	.276	.478	.333
Runners On	230	73	19	3	5	71	29	35	.317	.491	.393
Runners/Scor. Pos.	123	39	8	2	4	63	22	17	.317	.512	.415
Runners On/2 Out	108	34	10	0	4	39	14	20	.315	.519	.393
Scor. Pos./2 Out	65	20	4	0	3	33	14	10	.308	.508	.430
Late Inning Pressure	69	25	4	0	3	12	12	12	.362	.551	.457
Leading Off	21	5	0	0	1	1	3	4	.238	.381	.333
Bases Empty	42	14	1	0	2	2	3	8	.333	.500	.378
Runners On	27	11	3	0	1	10	9	4	.407	.630	.556
Runners/Scor. Pos.	12	6	2	0	1	10	8	0	.500	.917	.700

DRIVING IN RUNS	0 Out	1 Out	2 Out	Total	
From 1B	1/43	3/52	9/74	13/169	8%
From 2B	6/16	7/32	12/52	25/100	25%
From 3B	5/8	9/19	14/27	28/54	52%
Scoring Position	11/24	16/51	26/79	53/154	34%
Scor. Pos. %	46%	31%	33%	34%	
Driving In Runners from 3B with Less than Two Out:			14/27	52%	

Loves to face: Richard Dotson (.440, 11-for-25, 2 HR)
Hates to face: Dennis Martinez (0-for-15)
Career .305 hitter at Fenway; over last two seasons has hit .328 with 25 homers in home games, .238 with 17 home runs in road games. He's getting to like the pressure: yearly batting averages in Late-Inning Pressure Situations since 1982: .179, .200, .278, .362. Career average: .250. . . . Has hit 50 of 53 career home runs off right-handers. . . . Hit for cycle vs. Toronto on Sept. 18, driving in seven runs in the process. In the post-war era, only three other catchers have cycled in a major league game: Randy Hundley, Charlie Moore, and Carlton Fisk. . . . Stole first two bases of his major-league career last year: one was on the sneak-end of a double steal, but the other was legit, against Dickie Noles and Don Slaught of Texas. . . . Led A.L. catchers in assists (78) and errors (15) last season.

Kirk Gibson

Detroit Tigers	AB	H	2B	3B	HR	RRF	BB	SO	BA	SA	OBA
Season	581	167	37	5	29	101	71	137	.287	.518	.364
vs. Left-Handed Pitchers	170	38	9	2	7	23	17	52	.224	.424	.297
vs. Right-Handed Pitchers	411	129	28	3	22	78	54	85	.314	.557	.392
Home	286	89	21	1	18	55	35	58	.311	.580	.384
Road	295	78	16	4	11	46	36	79	.264	.458	.345
Grass	487	152	33	4	26	86	63	102	.312	.556	.389
Artificial Turf	94	15	4	1	3	15	8	35	.160	.319	.234
April	73	17	1	1	2	12	8	14	.233	.356	.301
May	83	26	6	1	5	16	8	22	.313	.590	.389
June	108	33	9	1	9	24	13	23	.306	.657	.371
July	94	29	5	0	3	16	11	22	.309	.457	.376
August	114	32	6	2	4	12	14	31	.281	.474	.364
Sept./Oct.	109	30	10	0	6	21	17	25	.275	.532	.370
Leading Off Inn.	84	27	5	1	5	5	12	17	.321	.583	.412
Bases Empty	325	85	14	3	21	22	37	77	.262	.517	.339
Runners On	256	82	23	2	8	79	34	60	.320	.520	.395
Runners/Scor. Pos.	133	41	11	1	6	67	26	32	.308	.541	.407
Runners On/2 Out	93	25	6	2	5	30	14	18	.269	.538	.370
Scor. Pos./2 Out	55	14	3	1	3	22	10	11	.255	.509	.379
Late Inning Pressure	74	19	1	1	4	10	11	17	.257	.459	.349
Leading Off	21	8	1	1	2	2	1	3	.381	.810	.409
Bases Empty	45	11	1	1	3	3	3	12	.244	.511	.292
Runners On	29	8	0	0	1	7	8	5	.276	.379	.421
Runners/Scor. Pos.	21	5	0	0	1	7	7	5	.238	.381	.414

DRIVING IN RUNS	0 Out	1 Out	2 Out	Total	
From 1B	3/38	4/86	8/67	15/191	8%
From 2B	7/20	6/41	12/41	25/102	25%
From 3B	6/12	20/27	5/25	31/64	48%
Scoring Position	13/32	26/68	17/66	56/166	34%
Scor. Pos. %	41%	38%	26%	34%	
Driving In Runners from 3B with Less than Two Out:			26/39	67%	

Loves to face: Phil Niekro (.438, 7-for-16, 3 HR)
Hates to face: Bud Black (0-for-11, 5 SO)
Hit 90 points higher vs. right-handers than vs. left-handers last season, the most by any A.L. left-handed batter with at least 100 at bats against each. . . . Career batting average vs. left-handers: .248. . . . Led A.L. with nine homers in June. . . . One of six players to hit at least one home run vs. every opposing A.L. club last season. . . . Batting average in Late-Inning Pressure Situations has been lower than overall batting average in six of seven seasons in majors. . . . Career batting averages: .287 on grass fields, .218 on artificial surfaces. . . . Stolen base percentage of .882 (30 of 34) was 3d-best in A.L. last season (minimum: 20 SB). . . . 6-for-12 with bases loaded last season, 15-for-45 in his career, but no grand-slam homers.

Bobby Grich

California Angels	AB	H	2B	3B	HR	RRF	BB	SO	BA	SA	OBA
Season	479	116	17	3	13	58	81	77	.242	.372	.355
vs. Left-Handed Pitchers	147	39	7	2	5	23	25	26	.265	.442	.372
vs. Right-Handed Pitchers	332	77	10	1	8	35	56	51	.232	.340	.348
Home	248	62	7	1	7	36	39	38	.250	.371	.356
Road	231	54	10	2	6	22	42	39	.234	.372	.354
Grass	401	97	14	2	10	48	70	63	.242	.362	.359
Artificial Turf	78	19	3	1	3	10	11	14	.244	.423	.337
April	62	22	1	0	2	9	15	8	.355	.468	.481
May	83	16	4	1	1	8	11	7	.193	.301	.287
June	65	12	1	0	1	6	12	10	.185	.246	.312
July	88	24	5	1	1	11	10	11	.273	.386	.347
August	78	16	3	0	3	9	8	15	.205	.359	.287
Sept./Oct.	103	26	3	1	5	15	25	26	.252	.447	.408
Leading Off Inn.	126	29	3	0	4	4	18	19	.230	.349	.331
Bases Empty	275	64	9	1	9	9	42	45	.233	.371	.339
Runners On	204	52	8	2	4	49	39	32	.255	.373	.377
Runners/Scor. Pos.	121	29	4	1	2	42	28	21	.240	.339	.383
Runners On/2 Out	88	20	4	1	1	19	18	16	.227	.330	.364
Scor. Pos./2 Out	57	14	2	1	1	18	14	12	.246	.368	.394
Late Inning Pressure	63	17	3	0	0	6	7	10	.270	.317	.343
Leading Off	19	4	1	0	0	0	1	5	.211	.263	.250
Bases Empty	34	7	1	0	0	0	2	6	.206	.235	.250
Runners On	29	10	2	0	0	6	5	4	.345	.414	.441
Runners/Scor. Pos.	17	6	0	0	0	6	3	3	.353	.353	.450

DRIVING IN RUNS	0 Out	1 Out	2 Out	Total	
From 1B	2/31	3/58	2/62	7/151	5%
From 2B	0/10	11/37	10/44	21/91	23%
From 3B	3/5	8/18	6/23	17/46	37%
Scoring Position	3/15	19/55	16/67	38/137	28%
Scor. Pos. %	20%	35%	24%	28%	
Driving In Runners from 3B with Less than Two Out:			11/23	48%	

Loves to face: Gene Nelson (.692, 9-for-13)
Hates to face: Danny Jackson (.063, 1-for-16, 5 SO)
Committed only two errors last season, lifting career fielding percentage at second base to .9841, 2d-highest in major-league history behind Jerry Lumpe's .9844; Grich can pass Lumpe if he handles his first 127 chances of 1986 errorlessly. But even if he overthrows King Lumpe, Grich's reign will be little more than an interregnum; Rich Dauer stands just 36 games short of the 1,000-game minimum needed to qualify for the record, and his percentage is .987. . . . April batting average of .355 was 4th-best in A.L. . . . Batting average vs. right-handers has decreased in five of his last six seasons to 11-year low of .234. . . . Career rate of 74.7 double plays per 100 games at second base, 2d-highest among active players (minimum: 150 games).

Ken Griffey

New York Yankees	AB	H	2B	3B	HR	RRF	BB	SO	BA	SA	OBA
Season	438	120	28	4	10	73	41	51	.274	.425	.331
vs. Left-Handed Pitchers	107	26	5	0	2	20	6	11	.243	.346	.278
vs. Right-Handed Pitchers	331	94	23	4	8	53	35	40	.284	.450	.347
Home	195	57	12	3	6	35	21	26	.292	.477	.359
Road	243	63	16	1	4	38	20	25	.259	.383	.307
Grass	367	104	21	4	9	63	35	43	.283	.436	.340
Artificial Turf	71	16	7	0	1	10	6	8	.225	.366	.282
April	59	15	3	2	0	7	5	5	.254	.373	.308
May	61	17	6	0	3	15	6	10	.279	.525	.329
June	59	14	3	1	0	8	7	4	.237	.322	.309
July	96	26	3	0	3	16	9	14	.271	.396	.333
August	89	25	5	0	0	10	4	7	.281	.337	.309
Sept./Oct.	74	23	8	1	4	17	10	11	.311	.608	.388
Leading Off Inn.	76	22	5	1	1	1	6	6	.289	.421	.341
Bases Empty	228	61	14	2	4	4	18	28	.268	.399	.321
Runners On	210	59	14	2	6	69	23	23	.281	.452	.340
Runners/Scor. Pos.	134	36	5	2	5	65	20	18	.269	.448	.346
Runners On/2 Out	69	17	3	2	1	14	10	9	.246	.391	.342
Scor. Pos./2 Out	50	11	1	2	1	13	9	7	.220	.380	.339
Late Inning Pressure	66	15	3	0	1	11	8	8	.227	.318	.299
Leading Off	8	0	0	0	0	0	0	2	.000	.000	.000
Bases Empty	33	9	2	0	0	0	2	5	.273	.333	.314
Runners On	33	6	1	0	1	11	6	3	.182	.303	.286
Runners/Scor. Pos.	14	2	0	0	1	10	6	2	.143	.357	.348

DRIVING IN RUNS	0 Out	1 Out	2 Out	Total	
From 1B	2/49	6/55	3/39	11/143	8%
From 2B	7/41	9/36	6/34	22/111	20%
From 3B	11/13	15/20	4/25	30/58	52%
Scoring Position	18/54	24/56	10/59	52/169	31%
Scor. Pos. %	33%	43%	17%	31%	
Driving In Runners from 3B with Less than Two Out:			26/33	79%	

Loves to face: Joaquin Andujar (.417, 15-for-36, 1 HR)
Hates to face: Neal Heaton (0-for-12)
.320 career batting average in Late-Inning Pressure Situations puts him 10th in 11-year history of *The Player Analysis* (minimum: 200 PA); with the additional pressure of runners in scoring position in LIP, his 11-year average is .342. . . . Other 11-year batting averages: .290 vs. left-handers, .305 vs. right-handers. Batted .393 vs. left-handers in 1976, the highest mark by a lefty against a lefty in last 11 years. . . . Batted .583 (7-for-12) with the bases loaded last season to lead A.L. (minimum: 10 at bats). . . . Drove in 11 base runners with 10 home runs, highest rate in A.L. . . . Career batting average of .391 at Fenway Park. . . . Led A.L. in double-play avoidance last season, grounding into only two in 106 opportunities (runner on first, less than two outs; minimum: 50 opportunities).

Alfredo Griffin

Oakland As	AB	H	2B	3B	HR	RRF	BB	SO	BA	SA	OBA
Season	614	166	18	7	2	68	20	50	.270	.332	.290
vs. Left-Handed Pitchers	187	61	5	3	1	27	4	8	.326	.401	.337
vs. Right-Handed Pitchers	427	105	13	4	1	41	16	42	.246	.302	.270
Home	292	75	6	3	0	35	10	26	.257	.298	.277
Road	322	91	12	4	2	33	10	24	.283	.363	.302
Grass	515	141	16	5	2	61	18	45	.274	.336	.294
Artificial Turf	99	25	2	2	0	7	2	5	.253	.313	.267
April	69	21	2	0	0	8	6	5	.304	.333	.360
May	84	23	3	1	1	20	2	10	.274	.369	.284
June	105	32	2	2	1	15	5	10	.305	.390	.333
July	98	19	2	2	0	9	1	6	.194	.255	.198
August	126	37	4	1	0	9	5	10	.294	.341	.318
Sept./Oct.	132	34	5	1	0	7	1	9	.258	.311	.261
Leading Off Inn.	183	41	6	0	0	0	11	14	.224	.257	.268
Bases Empty	367	93	12	1	0	0	17	33	.253	.292	.286
Runners On	247	73	6	6	2	68	3	17	.296	.393	.296
Runners/Scor. Pos.	145	44	3	5	1	65	3	9	.303	.414	.303
Runners On/2 Out	103	23	1	2	1	22	2	8	.223	.301	.238
Scor. Pos./2 Out	68	16	1	2	0	20	2	4	.235	.309	.257
Late Inning Pressure	94	18	0	1	0	8	3	13	.191	.213	.210
Leading Off	16	3	0	0	0	0	2	3	.188	.188	.278
Bases Empty	47	7	0	0	0	0	2	7	.149	.149	.184
Runners On	47	11	0	1	0	8	1	6	.234	.277	.235
Runners/Scor. Pos.	29	7	0	1	0	8	1	3	.241	.310	.242

DRIVING IN RUNS	0 Out	1 Out	2 Out	Total	
From 1B	1/46	3/54	4/76	8/176	5%
From 2B	3/17	10/43	8/49	21/109	19%
From 3B	8/11	20/30	9/30	37/71	52%
Scoring Position	11/28	30/73	17/79	58/180	32%
Scor. Pos. %	39%	41%	22%	32%	
Driving In Runners from 3B with Less than Two Out:			28/41	68%	

Loves to face: Matt Young (.643, 9-for-14)
Hates to face: Brad Havens (.067, 1-for-15, 5 SO)
Drove in 32.2 percent of runners from scoring position, by far the highest rate of his career (previous high: 26.1 in '82), leading to career-high 64 RBIs. . . . Career batting average of .118 (4-for-34) with the bases loaded and two outs. . . . Has not walked twice in same game since Aug. 4, 1983. . . . Averaged 2.87 assists per nine innings, slightly below league average, but an improvement from his league-low 2.56 with Toronto in '84. . . . The only A.L. player to start 162 games last season, and the first Oakland shortstop since Bert Campaneris in '68 to play more than 150 games, suggesting that when one tough Dominican takes the mound for the A's this season, he'll find another behind him at short. (There are five references to One Tough Dominican in this book. Did you spot them all? Send your list to the Center for Cliche Control, Shawnee Mission, Kansas.)

Ozzie Guillen

Chicago White Sox	AB	H	2B	3B	HR	RRF	BB	SO	BA	SA	OBA
Season	491	134	21	9	1	34	12	36	.273	.358	.291
vs. Left-Handed Pitchers	90	19	1	1	0	10	1	10	.211	.244	.228
vs. Right-Handed Pitchers	401	115	20	8	1	24	11	26	.287	.384	.305
Home	244	68	7	7	1	21	7	17	.279	.377	.298
Road	247	66	14	2	0	13	5	19	.267	.340	.285
Grass	425	122	20	9	1	32	12	30	.287	.384	.308
Artificial Turf	66	12	1	0	0	2	0	6	.182	.197	.182
April	58	16	2	0	0	4	3	4	.276	.310	.306
May	77	16	0	1	0	4	2	4	.208	.234	.228
June	77	16	2	0	0	1	2	7	.208	.234	.228
July	73	25	9	2	0	12	2	5	.342	.521	.368
August	96	32	4	1	1	7	2	6	.333	.427	.347
Sept./Oct.	110	29	4	5	0	6	1	10	.264	.391	.270
Leading Off Inn.	130	32	5	1	0	0	5	14	.246	.300	.274
Bases Empty	297	80	13	6	1	1	8	25	.269	.364	.289
Runners On	194	54	8	3	0	33	4	11	.278	.351	.295
Runners/Scor. Pos.	105	32	2	3	0	32	4	6	.305	.381	.333
Runners On/2 Out	100	19	3	2	0	15	2	7	.190	.260	.206
Scor. Pos./2 Out	58	10	0	2	0	14	2	4	.172	.241	.200
Late Inning Pressure	73	27	2	1	0	3	6	3	.370	.425	.418
Leading Off	17	11	1	0	0	0	2	0	.647	.706	.684
Bases Empty	40	19	2	1	0	0	3	1	.475	.575	.512
Runners On	33	8	0	0	0	3	3	2	.242	.242	.306
Runners/Scor. Pos.	16	4	0	0	0	3	3	1	.250	.250	.368

DRIVING IN RUNS	0 Out	1 Out	2 Out	Total	
From 1B	0/30	1/38	3/66	4/134	3%
From 2B	7/17	3/24	6/43	16/84	19%
From 3B	2/4	5/12	6/26	13/42	31%
Scoring Position	9/21	8/36	12/69	29/126	23%
Scor. Pos. %	43%	22%	17%	23%	
Driving In Runners from 3B with Less than Two Out:			7/16	44%	

Loves to face: Bruce Kison (1.000, 4-for-4)
Hates to face: Mike Witt (0-for-6, 2 SO)
One of only two rookies to play in 150 or more games last season, and the only one not to be run over by a tarpaulin. . . . At 21, was youngest player to appear in an A.L. opening-day lineup last season. . . . Drew one walk every 42.8 plate appearances, lowest rate among A.L. regulars (is he *sure* he's not from San Pedro de Macoris?). . . . Led A.L. shortstops with .980 fielding percentage, becoming the second straight A.L. rookie to accomplish that feat (minimum: 100 games). Dick Schofield led in '84, becoming the first rookie in league history to lead shortstops in fielding. . . . His .647 average leading off innings in Late-Inning Pressure Situations was a *Player Analysis* record (minimum: 15 PA). . . . Likes those historic ballparks: batted .500 (8-for-16) at Fenway Park and .450 (9-for-20) at Yankee Stadium.

Wayne Gross

Baltimore Orioles	AB	H	2B	3B	HR	RRF	BB	SO	BA	SA	OBA
Season	217	51	8	0	11	19	46	48	.235	.424	.369
vs. Left-Handed Pitchers	4	1	0	0	1	3	1	0	.250	1.000	.400
vs. Right-Handed Pitchers	213	50	8	0	10	16	45	48	.235	.413	.368
Home	102	23	2	0	9	11	28	24	.225	.510	.392
Road	115	28	6	0	2	8	18	24	.243	.348	.346
Grass	176	44	6	0	10	14	38	40	.250	.455	.383
Artificial Turf	41	7	2	0	1	5	8	8	.171	.293	.306
April	45	11	3	0	2	3	13	14	.244	.444	.414
May	42	7	1	0	1	4	8	13	.167	.262	.300
June	54	19	4	0	5	8	13	5	.352	.704	.478
July	37	7	0	0	1	2	5	6	.189	.270	.286
August	16	5	0	0	1	1	2	2	.313	.500	.389
Sept./Oct.	23	2	0	0	1	1	5	8	.087	.217	.250
Leading Off Inn.	55	14	1	0	3	3	7	12	.255	.436	.339
Bases Empty	137	37	6	0	9	9	25	29	.270	.511	.383
Runners On	80	14	2	0	2	10	21	19	.175	.275	.347
Runners/Scor. Pos.	45	9	1	0	2	10	12	12	.200	.356	.368
Runners On/2 Out	34	5	1	0	0	2	10	6	.147	.176	.341
Scor. Pos./2 Out	18	2	1	0	0	2	5	5	.111	.167	.304
Late Inning Pressure	38	7	2	0	1	2	2	8	.184	.316	.225
Leading Off	12	1	0	0	0	0	0	5	.083	.083	.083
Bases Empty	22	4	2	0	1	1	2	7	.182	.409	.250
Runners On	16	3	0	0	0	1	0	1	.188	.188	.188
Runners/Scor. Pos.	9	2	0	0	0	1	0	0	.222	.222	.222

DRIVING IN RUNS	0 Out	1 Out	2 Out	Total	
From 1B	0/17	2/19	0/25	2/61	3%
From 2B	0/9	3/16	2/16	5/41	12%
From 3B	1/1	0/2	0/7	1/10	10%
Scoring Position	1/10	3/18	2/23	6/51	12%
Scor. Pos. %	10%	17%	9%	12%	
Driving In Runners from 3B with Less than Two Out:			1/3	33%	

Loves to face: Bob Stanley (.434, 11-for-26, 1 HR)
Hates to face: Frank Tanana (.050, 1-for-20)
Some strange patterns for this fellow. . . . Since 1982, batting averages in day games: .301, .298, .306, .297; same four years in night games: .225, .192, .175, .209. During that span he has hit 26 of his 54 home runs in daylight, despite nearly twice as many at bats at night. . . . While we're at it, here's another teaser: career batting averages with runners in scoring position: .286 with less than two outs, .187 with two outs. . . . Drove in over 30 percent of runners from scoring position in both '83 and '84, but dropped to 11.8 percent last season, the 5th-lowest mark in *Player Analysis* history (minimum: 50 opportunities). . . . Has had only 12 plate appearances vs. left-handed pitchers in two seasons with Orioles, but did hit home run off Oakland southpaw Jeff Kaiser last June.

Jackie Gutierrez

Boston Red Sox	AB	H	2B	3B	HR	RRF	BB	SO	BA	SA	OBA
Season	275	60	5	2	2	23	12	37	.218	.273	.250
vs. Left-Handed Pitchers	97	20	3	2	0	8	4	12	.206	.278	.235
vs. Right-Handed Pitchers	178	40	2	0	2	15	8	25	.225	.270	.258
Home	131	28	3	2	0	15	5	17	.214	.267	.241
Road	144	32	2	0	2	8	7	20	.222	.278	.258
Grass	224	53	5	2	2	22	10	30	.237	.304	.268
Artificial Turf	51	7	0	0	0	1	2	7	.137	.137	.170
April	57	12	0	2	1	8	4	3	.211	.333	.262
May	67	18	2	0	0	5	2	9	.269	.299	.290
June	4	1	0	0	0	2	0	1	.250	.250	.250
July	19	3	0	0	0	1	1	5	.158	.158	.200
August	88	22	2	0	1	6	5	9	.250	.307	.290
Sept./Oct.	40	4	1	0	0	1	0	10	.100	.125	.098
Leading Off Inn.	65	19	1	0	0	0	2	5	.292	.308	.313
Bases Empty	138	37	4	0	1	1	8	14	.268	.319	.308
Runners On	137	23	1	2	1	22	4	23	.168	.226	.190
Runners/Scor. Pos.	81	8	0	1	0	19	3	14	.099	.123	.129
Runners On/2 Out	56	7	1	1	0	7	1	9	.125	.179	.140
Scor. Pos./2 Out	38	3	0	1	0	7	1	6	.079	.132	.103
Late Inning Pressure	29	5	0	0	0	2	2	5	.172	.172	.226
Leading Off	7	2	0	0	0	0	0	0	.286	.286	.286
Bases Empty	19	4	0	0	0	0	1	3	.211	.211	.250
Runners On	10	1	0	0	0	2	1	2	.100	.100	.182
Runners/Scor. Pos.	8	0	0	0	0	2	1	2	.000	.000	.111

DRIVING IN RUNS	0 Out	1 Out	2 Out	Total	
From 1B	1/26	1/32	1/32	3/90	3%
From 2B	2/14	2/23	3/29	7/66	11%
From 3B	3/7	5/12	2/12	10/31	32%
Scoring Position	5/21	7/35	5/41	17/97	18%
Scor. Pos. %	24%	20%	12%	18%	
Driving In Runners from 3B with Less than Two Out:			8/19	42%	

Loves to face: Mark Gubicza (.467, 7-for-15)
Hates to face: Frank Viola (.063, 1-for-16)
Only major league player (minimum: 200 PA) who batted 100 points higher with the bases empty than with runners on base last season. . . . Ground-ball hitter: 1.90 G/A ratio was 6th-highest in A.L. last season (minimum: 200 PA). Career average: 1.96. . . . Played 99 games at short; made only three errors in his first 51 games, then 20 errors in his last 48, including six in his last four games of season. . . . Only player in majors who batted below .100 with runners in scoring position. . . . Somewhat resistible force vs. immovable object: Gutierrez, who has never played a position other than shortstop in the major leagues, has been traded to Baltimore, home of Cal Ripken, the play-'em-all shortstop. . . . Maybe they'll rest Ripken in Cleveland: Gutierrez has career batting average of .432 (16-for-37) there.

Jerry Hairston

Chicago White Sox	AB	H	2B	3B	HR	RRF	BB	SO	BA	SA	OBA
Season	140	34	8	0	2	23	29	18	.243	.343	.371
vs. Left-Handed Pitchers	34	11	1	0	1	10	7	6	.324	.441	.442
vs. Right-Handed Pitchers	106	23	7	0	1	13	22	12	.217	.311	.348
Home	65	18	7	0	0	10	15	11	.277	.385	.407
Road	75	16	1	0	2	13	14	7	.213	.307	.340
Grass	117	30	7	0	2	22	27	16	.256	.368	.388
Artificial Turf	23	4	1	0	0	1	2	2	.174	.217	.286
April	10	3	0	0	0	2	2	2	.300	.300	.417
May	23	5	1	0	1	6	6	2	.217	.391	.355
June	22	5	0	0	1	4	2	1	.227	.364	.308
July	35	9	3	0	0	4	11	4	.257	.343	.435
August	22	6	3	0	0	2	6	4	.273	.409	.429
Sept./Oct.	28	6	1	0	0	5	2	5	.214	.250	.281
Leading Off Inn.	31	6	3	0	0	0	3	6	.194	.290	.265
Bases Empty	80	16	6	0	2	2	9	9	.200	.350	.289
Runners On	60	18	2	0	0	21	20	9	.300	.333	.459
Runners/Scor. Pos.	37	12	0	0	0	20	13	4	.324	.324	.473
Runners On/2 Out	28	5	0	0	0	9	9	4	.179	.179	.395
Scor. Pos./2 Out	21	5	0	0	0	9	8	2	.238	.238	.467
Late Inning Pressure	43	14	4	0	0	4	7	5	.326	.419	.420
Leading Off	10	5	2	0	0	0	0	2	.500	.700	.500
Bases Empty	21	6	3	0	0	0	1	2	.286	.429	.318
Runners On	22	8	1	0	0	4	6	3	.364	.409	.500
Runners/Scor. Pos.	15	5	0	0	0	4	4	2	.333	.333	.474

DRIVING IN RUNS	0 Out	1 Out	2 Out	Total	
From 1B	0/12	1/20	1/17	2/49	4%
From 2B	1/4	3/9	4/17	8/30	27%
From 3B	1/2	6/8	4/10	11/20	55%
Scoring Position	2/6	9/17	8/27	19/50	38%
Scor. Pos. %	33%	53%	30%	38%	
Driving In Runners from 3B with Less than Two Out:			7/10	70%	

Loves to face: Tippy Martinez (.800, 4-for-5)
Hates to face: Mike Witt (0-for-10)
Led A.L. with 69 pinch-hit appearances (.264, 18-for-53). . . . 11-year batting averages: .304 with runners on base, .222 with the bases empty. . . . Batted .326 in Late-Inning Pressure Situations last season to raise his career LIP average from .200 to .220. . . . Batting average from the right side of the plate (.324) was a career high, from the left side (.217) was his lowest since 1976. . . . Percentage of runners driven in from scoring position over last three seasons is 33 percent in nonpressure situations, 14 percent in Late-Inning Pressure Situations. . . . Career batting average of .464 (13-for-28) at the Kingdome, .094 (3-for-32) at County Stadium. . . . Groundball hitter: 1.38 G/A ratio last season.

Mike Hargrove

Cleveland Indians	AB	H	2B	3B	HR	RRF	BB	SO	BA	SA	OBA
Season	284	81	14	1	1	29	39	29	.285	.352	.370
vs. Left-Handed Pitchers	22	2	0	0	0	4	7	1	.091	.091	.300
vs. Right-Handed Pitchers	262	79	14	1	1	25	32	28	.302	.374	.378
Home	139	42	7	1	0	17	19	14	.302	.367	.384
Road	145	39	7	0	1	12	20	15	.269	.338	.358
Grass	234	71	13	1	1	26	34	22	.303	.380	.390
Artificial Turf	50	10	1	0	0	3	5	7	.200	.220	.273
April	19	4	1	0	0	1	2	2	.211	.263	.273
May	29	6	1	0	0	0	9	6	.207	.241	.395
June	41	12	3	0	0	4	4	4	.293	.366	.356
July	36	8	2	1	1	4	5	2	.222	.417	.317
August	51	16	1	0	0	7	9	7	.314	.333	.417
Sept./Oct.	108	35	6	0	0	13	10	8	.324	.380	.381
Leading Off Inn.	58	16	3	0	0	0	10	5	.276	.328	.382
Bases Empty	175	45	11	1	0	0	20	16	.257	.331	.333
Runners On	109	36	3	0	1	29	19	13	.330	.385	.426
Runners/Scor. Pos.	56	18	2	0	0	27	15	8	.321	.357	.458
Runners On/2 Out	42	8	1	0	0	9	8	5	.190	.214	.320
Scor. Pos./2 Out	28	6	1	0	0	9	7	4	.214	.250	.371
Late Inning Pressure	46	14	1	0	0	2	6	7	.304	.326	.385
Leading Off	14	4	0	0	0	0	2	1	.286	.286	.375
Bases Empty	26	7	1	0	0	0	3	4	.269	.308	.345
Runners On	20	7	0	0	0	2	3	3	.350	.350	.435
Runners/Scor. Pos.	8	2	0	0	0	2	3	1	.250	.250	.455

DRIVING IN RUNS	0 Out	1 Out	2 Out	Total	
From 1B	0/21	2/29	0/25	2/75	3%
From 2B	3/11	2/11	5/20	10/42	24%
From 3B	5/5	7/9	4/14	16/28	57%
Scoring Position	8/16	9/20	9/34	26/70	37%
Scor. Pos. %	50%	45%	26%	37%	
Driving In Runners from 3B with Less than Two Out:			12/14	86%	

Loves to face: Jim Beattie (.344, 11-for-32, 12 BB, .523 OBA)
Hates to face: Dave Righetti (.056, 1-for-18, 5 SO)
Has hit for higher average with runners in scoring position than overall in each of last eight seasons; six of those scoring-position averages have been over .300. . . . His bases-loaded figures would impress even teammate Tabler: batting .368 over past 11 years, and drew six bases-loaded walks in '83 (at bats that must have taken 15 minutes apiece), a *Player Analysis* record. . . . Hargrove (85.7 percent) and Tabler (84.0) ranked one-two in A.L. in driving in runners from third base with less than two outs. . . . Has seen less and less action against left-handers, whom he once hit well. Last three years: .277 in 141 at bats, .185 in 81, .091 in 22. . . . Last home run against a southpaw: July 31, 1982, off Mike Caldwell. . . . Career on-base average (.396) is 3d-highest among active players (minimum: 500 at bats).

Toby Harrah

Texas Rangers	AB	H	2B	3B	HR	RRF	BB	SO	BA	SA	OBA
Season	396	107	18	1	9	48	113	60	.270	.389	.432
vs. Left-Handed Pitchers	142	44	7	0	5	25	38	22	.310	.465	.448
vs. Right-Handed Pitchers	254	63	11	1	4	23	75	38	.248	.346	.423
Home	187	54	9	0	5	24	59	24	.289	.417	.458
Road	209	53	9	1	4	24	54	36	.254	.364	.407
Grass	331	88	12	0	8	37	97	49	.266	.375	.433
Artificial Turf	65	19	6	1	1	11	16	11	.292	.462	.422
April	59	19	4	0	1	7	20	6	.322	.441	.494
May	68	18	2	1	1	4	29	15	.265	.368	.485
June	79	24	0	0	4	15	20	9	.304	.456	.446
July	74	20	4	0	1	6	18	10	.270	.365	.419
August	75	17	4	0	2	13	19	15	.227	.360	.375
Sept./Oct.	41	9	4	0	0	3	7	5	.220	.317	.327
Leading Off Inn.	110	29	7	0	1	1	27	22	.264	.355	.409
Bases Empty	253	61	13	0	4	4	73	40	.241	.340	.415
Runners On	143	46	5	1	5	44	40	20	.322	.476	.461
Runners/Scor. Pos.	82	27	3	1	3	39	23	12	.329	.500	.455
Runners On/2 Out	42	12	1	0	2	13	16	7	.286	.452	.492
Scor. Pos./2 Out	29	7	0	0	2	12	11	5	.241	.448	.463
Late Inning Pressure	61	20	2	0	3	12	12	9	.328	.508	.440
Leading Off	18	4	0	0	1	1	3	7	.222	.389	.333
Bases Empty	34	7	1	0	1	1	7	8	.206	.324	.357
Runners On	27	13	1	0	2	11	5	1	.481	.741	.545
Runners/Scor. Pos.	11	5	0	0	0	6	3	1	.455	.455	.533

DRIVING IN RUNS	0 Out	1 Out	2 Out	Total	
From 1B	1/39	1/34	1/25	3/98	3%
From 2B	3/22	4/20	4/24	11/66	17%
From 3B	11/15	8/11	6/13	25/39	64%
Scoring Position	14/37	12/31	10/37	36/105	34%
Scor. Pos. %	38%	39%	27%	34%	
Driving In Runners from 3B with Less than Two Out:			19/26	73%	

Loves to face: Jim Clancy (.370, 10-for-27, 4 HR)
Hates to face: Dave Righetti (.100, 2-for-20, 7 SO)
Ranked 2d in A.L. with 113 walks last season, while .432 on-base average was 3d-highest. . . . On-base average leading off innings has been .400 or better in four of last five seasons. . . . Batting average with runners in scoring position (.329) was his highest in last 11 years. . . . Drew at least one walk in 16 consecutive games from April 20 to May 11, six games short of the major-league record held by Roy Cullenbine. Harrah's streak was broken when he singled as a pinch-hitter in his only at bat on May 12. Two days later he started another walk streak that stretched 11 games. . . . Has homered in every current A.L. ballpark except the Metrodome. . . . Fly-ball hitter: 0.73 G/A ratio last season. Career: 0.98. . . . Started only six of Rangers' last 26 games, as manager Valentine looked at others.

Ron Hassey

New York Yankees	AB	H	2B	3B	HR	RRF	BB	SO	BA	SA	OBA
Season	267	79	16	1	13	42	28	21	.296	.509	.369
vs. Left-Handed Pitchers	48	8	1	0	0	1	6	5	.167	.188	.259
vs. Right-Handed Pitchers	219	71	15	1	13	41	22	16	.324	.580	.393
Home	115	38	7	0	3	14	16	10	.330	.470	.421
Road	152	41	9	1	10	28	12	11	.270	.539	.327
Grass	225	72	14	1	13	39	23	18	.320	.564	.388
Artificial Turf	42	7	2	0	0	3	5	3	.167	.214	.271
April	9	3	0	0	0	0	0	1	.333	.333	.333
May	22	7	1	0	1	6	2	0	.318	.500	.375
June	52	17	7	1	3	6	7	6	.327	.673	.407
July	74	16	4	0	1	6	6	6	.216	.311	.301
August	41	14	1	0	5	12	2	6	.341	.732	.372
Sept./Oct.	69	22	3	0	3	12	11	2	.319	.493	.413
Leading Off Inn.	64	23	3	0	7	7	1	5	.359	.734	.369
Bases Empty	146	47	11	1	9	9	12	10	.322	.596	.381
Runners On	121	32	5	0	4	33	16	11	.264	.405	.355
Runners/Scor. Pos.	75	17	2	0	3	31	9	8	.227	.373	.318
Runners On/2 Out	54	10	2	0	2	12	7	8	.185	.333	.290
Scor. Pos./2 Out	39	7	2	0	2	12	5	7	.179	.385	.289
Late Inning Pressure	37	10	2	0	2	6	4	4	.270	.486	.341
Leading Off	8	4	0	0	1	1	1	0	.500	.875	.556
Bases Empty	19	6	1	0	1	1	3	1	.316	.526	.409
Runners On	18	4	1	0	1	5	1	3	.222	.444	.263
Runners/Scor. Pos.	9	2	0	0	1	5	1	1	.222	.556	.300

DRIVING IN RUNS	0 Out	1 Out	2 Out	Total	
From 1B	1/18	1/28	2/35	4/81	5%
From 2B	0/7	8/23	4/26	12/56	21%
From 3B	3/3	6/10	4/15	13/28	46%
Scoring Position	3/10	14/33	8/41	25/84	30%
Scor. Pos. %	30%	42%	20%	30%	
Driving In Runners from 3B with Less than Two Out:			9/13	69%	

Loves to face: Ken Dixon (.800, 4-for-5, 1 HR)
Hates to face: Don Sutton (.053, 1-for-19)
Slugging average vs. right-handers (.580) was 2d among A.L. semi-regulars to George Brett's .604. . . . Batted .305 with 13 home runs and 42 RBIs in 68 games as a starter last season. . . . Batting average vs. left-handers (.167) was a career low, while batting average vs. right-handers (.324) was a career high. Even with those figures, though, Hassey's career log is surprisingly balanced: .276 vs. right-handers, and .271 vs. lefties. . . . Batted 60 points higher at home than he did on road last season, but hit only three of his 13 home runs in The Bronx. Leaves Yankee Stadium with career mark of .343 with four homers there, but has also hit well at Comiskey Park: .333 (18-for-54), and three homers (all in a two-game series there last August). . . . The legacy of Niekro: Hassey was charged with 15 passed balls last season, most in A.L.

Mickey Hatcher

Minnesota Twins	AB	H	2B	3B	HR	RRF	BB	SO	BA	SA	OBA
Season	444	125	28	0	3	52	16	23	.282	.365	.308
vs. Left-Handed Pitchers	132	37	10	0	1	14	7	4	.280	.379	.312
vs. Right-Handed Pitchers	312	88	18	0	2	38	9	19	.282	.359	.307
Home	244	73	20	0	1	34	9	11	.299	.393	.325
Road	200	52	8	0	2	18	7	12	.260	.330	.287
Grass	156	37	4	0	2	15	6	10	.237	.301	.270
Artificial Turf	288	88	24	0	1	37	10	13	.306	.399	.329
April	87	27	6	0	2	9	0	2	.310	.448	.307
May	112	34	5	0	0	13	6	7	.304	.348	.339
June	91	25	6	0	0	6	5	6	.275	.341	.313
July	32	9	2	0	0	9	0	2	.281	.344	.324
August	76	16	5	0	1	9	4	3	.211	.316	.250
Sept./Oct.	46	14	4	0	0	6	1	3	.304	.391	.313
Leading Off Inn.	75	13	2	0	1	1	3	5	.173	.240	.205
Bases Empty	235	63	13	0	1	1	8	13	.268	.336	.298
Runners On	209	62	15	0	2	51	8	10	.297	.397	.320
Runners/Scor. Pos.	122	36	10	0	1	46	7	7	.295	.402	.328
Runners On/2 Out	81	21	6	0	1	19	3	5	.259	.370	.286
Scor. Pos./2 Out	60	15	5	0	0	17	3	4	.250	.333	.286
Late Inning Pressure	55	12	1	0	0	4	2	1	.218	.236	.246
Leading Off	14	3	1	0	0	0	1	0	.214	.286	.267
Bases Empty	30	8	1	0	0	0	1	0	.267	.300	.290
Runners On	25	4	0	0	0	4	1	1	.160	.160	.192
Runners/Scor. Pos.	17	3	0	0	0	4	1	1	.176	.176	.222

DRIVING IN RUNS	0 Out	1 Out	2 Out	Total	
From 1B	3/47	2/44	2/49	7/140	5%
From 2B	3/15	5/28	7/38	15/81	19%
From 3B	6/11	12/22	9/26	27/59	46%
Scoring Position	9/26	17/50	16/64	42/140	30%
Scor. Pos. %	35%	34%	25%	30%	
Driving In Runners from 3B with Less than Two Out:			18/33	55%	

Loves to face: Don Sutton (.600, 6-for-10, 1 HR)
Hates to face: Ray Burris (0-for-12)
What a turnaround with the bases loaded: 0-for-15 in his first four years in majors, but 15-for-34 (.441) over past three seasons, with 31 RRFs in 25 plate appearances. . . . Yearly batting averages in Late-Inning Pressure Situations since 1983: .431, .348, .218. . . . Career averages of .282 against left-handers, .281 against right-handers. . . . Career batting average of .310 at the Metrodome. . . . Ground-ball hitter: 1.57 G/A ratio last season. Career: 1.20. . . . One of two A.L. players with at least 400 at bats last season but no stolen bases and no times caught stealing (see Al Cowens). . . . Started 41 of 58 games against left-handers, 67 of 104 against righties. . . . His next walk will be the 100th of his major league career; it has taken him seven seasons and 647 games to get to 99.

Mike Heath

Oakland As	AB	H	2B	3B	HR	RRF	BB	SO	BA	SA	OBA
Season	436	109	18	6	13	62	41	63	.250	.408	.313
vs. Left-Handed Pitchers	151	43	10	3	5	23	14	23	.285	.490	.341
vs. Right-Handed Pitchers	285	66	8	3	8	39	27	40	.232	.365	.298
Home	209	51	8	1	8	38	17	26	.244	.407	.301
Road	227	58	10	5	5	24	24	37	.256	.410	.324
Grass	345	88	12	3	12	51	32	47	.255	.412	.318
Artificial Turf	91	21	6	3	1	11	9	16	.231	.396	.297
April	72	19	3	2	4	15	7	8	.264	.528	.325
May	82	16	1	0	1	5	8	14	.195	.244	.267
June	70	21	2	2	3	12	5	10	.300	.514	.342
July	66	19	2	1	2	6	6	7	.288	.439	.342
August	87	14	5	0	0	6	11	14	.161	.218	.263
Sept./Oct.	59	20	5	1	3	18	4	10	.339	.610	.375
Leading Off Inn.	96	28	5	2	4	4	9	12	.292	.510	.352
Bases Empty	258	60	12	3	8	8	18	39	.233	.395	.285
Runners On	178	49	6	3	5	54	23	24	.275	.427	.351
Runners/Scor. Pos.	90	29	4	2	2	46	18	11	.322	.478	.420
Runners On/2 Out	85	21	4	1	1	22	11	12	.247	.353	.333
Scor. Pos./2 Out	47	15	3	1	1	21	9	5	.319	.489	.429
Late Inning Pressure	72	16	1	0	2	9	3	9	.222	.319	.253
Leading Off	13	4	0	0	1	1	1	1	.308	.538	.357
Bases Empty	45	12	1	0	2	2	2	6	.267	.422	.298
Runners On	27	4	0	0	0	7	1	3	.148	.148	.179
Runners/Scor. Pos.	15	3	0	0	0	7	1	1	.200	.200	.250

DRIVING IN RUNS	0 Out	1 Out	2 Out	Total	
From 1B	2/31	5/46	4/67	11/144	8%
From 2B	3/14	6/24	11/38	20/76	26%
From 3B	3/4	9/16	6/19	18/39	46%
Scoring Position	6/18	15/40	17/57	38/115	33%
Scor. Pos. %	33%	38%	30%	33%	
Driving In Runners from 3B with Less than Two Out:			12/20	60%	

Loves to face: Ed Vande Berg (.714, 5-for-7, 1 HR)
Hates to face: Juan Berenguer (0-for-13)
Cardinals have acquired an effective hitter, especially against left-handed pitchers or when there's a chance to knock in a run. . . . Career batting average is an unassuming .250, but it's 38 points above that against left-handers (26 points below against right-handers). . . . Has hit over .300 with runners in scoring position in three of the past four seasons, boosting career scoring-position average to .282. . . . He'll be operating in the high-speed world of the National League, where the average team had 1.21 attempted steals per game last year (A.L. average: .96 attempts per team per game). . . . Good athlete who has played 174 games in outfield, 29 at third base, and even an inning at shortstop.

Dave Henderson

Seattle Mariners	AB	H	2B	3B	HR	RRF	BB	SO	BA	SA	OBA
Season	502	121	28	2	14	68	48	104	.241	.388	.310
vs. Left-Handed Pitchers	132	37	10	1	3	19	11	19	.280	.439	.345
vs. Right-Handed Pitchers	370	84	18	1	11	49	37	85	.227	.370	.298
Home	253	63	11	2	8	37	28	44	.249	.403	.330
Road	249	58	17	0	6	31	20	60	.233	.373	.289
Grass	192	39	11	0	4	22	16	46	.203	.323	.263
Artificial Turf	310	82	17	2	10	46	32	58	.265	.429	.338
April	74	19	2	1	2	7	4	12	.257	.392	.295
May	76	23	5	0	4	13	7	16	.303	.526	.357
June	85	19	5	0	0	11	10	15	.224	.282	.313
July	69	13	1	0	3	10	7	13	.188	.333	.260
August	74	16	4	1	1	7	9	19	.216	.338	.310
Sept./Oct.	124	31	11	0	4	20	11	29	.250	.435	.316
Leading Off Inn.	121	31	6	1	5	5	4	21	.256	.446	.286
Bases Empty	266	58	16	2	8	8	30	63	.218	.383	.302
Runners On	236	63	12	0	6	60	18	41	.267	.394	.319
Runners/Scor. Pos.	134	39	8	0	4	53	15	20	.291	.440	.362
Runners On/2 Out	108	30	5	0	2	31	8	17	.278	.380	.333
Scor. Pos./2 Out	73	20	3	0	2	29	7	11	.274	.397	.346
Late Inning Pressure	74	23	2	0	5	10	6	15	.311	.541	.363
Leading Off	19	8	0	0	2	2	0	2	.421	.737	.421
Bases Empty	41	16	1	0	4	4	4	6	.390	.707	.444
Runners On	33	7	1	0	1	6	2	9	.212	.333	.257
Runners/Scor. Pos.	17	4	1	0	1	6	2	2	.235	.471	.316

DRIVING IN RUNS	0 Out	1 Out	2 Out	Total	
From 1B	3/43	3/65	4/79	10/187	5%
From 2B	4/19	4/27	14/53	22/99	22%
From 3B	3/5	8/15	11/34	22/54	41%
Scoring Position	7/24	12/42	25/87	44/153	29%
Scor. Pos. %	29%	29%	29%	29%	
Driving In Runners from 3B with Less than Two Out:			11/20	55%	

Loves to face: Tippy Martinez (.714, 5-for-7, 2 HR)
Hates to face: Bert Blyleven (0-for-14)
Broke out of past platoon status to start 134 games, a career high, including 119 in center. . . . Didn't do as well against right-handers this year, however, as he had in the past on a part-time basis (batted .250, slugged .424 against righties, 1981–84). . . . Batting average reached post-April high of .317 at climax of 14-game hitting streak on May 19, but descended rapidly thereafter; last saw .260 on June 30. . . . Career batting average of .133 (4-for-30) with the bases loaded. . . . Has batted over .300 in Late-Inning Pressure Situations for two straight seasons. . . . Has homered in every current A.L. ballpark except Tiger Stadium, where his career batting average is .183. . . . Fly-ball hitter: 0.87 G/A ratio last season. Career: 0.75.

Rickey Henderson

New York Yankees	AB	H	2B	3B	HR	RRF	BB	SO	BA	SA	OBA
Season	547	172	28	5	24	73	99	65	.314	.516	.419
vs. Left-Handed Pitchers	180	65	13	2	12	25	45	27	.361	.656	.487
vs. Right-Handed Pitchers	367	107	15	3	12	48	54	38	.292	.447	.383
Home	246	75	12	1	8	23	46	31	.305	.459	.416
Road	301	97	16	4	16	50	53	34	.322	.561	.422
Grass	456	144	25	4	21	61	82	52	.316	.526	.419
Artificial Turf	91	28	3	1	3	12	17	13	.308	.462	.417
April	34	6	0	0	1	5	5	2	.176	.265	.275
May	82	28	6	2	2	10	15	9	.341	.537	.455
June	113	47	4	2	6	17	14	10	.416	.646	.477
July	103	36	7	0	7	15	17	12	.350	.621	.438
August	96	26	3	0	4	13	17	13	.271	.427	.377
Sept./Oct.	119	29	8	1	4	13	31	19	.244	.429	.401
Leading Off Inn.	230	71	16	5	10	10	41	27	.309	.552	.418
Bases Empty	357	108	23	5	16	16	63	42	.303	.529	.411
Runners On	190	64	5	0	8	57	36	23	.337	.489	.433
Runners/Scor. Pos.	118	34	3	0	3	45	28	18	.288	.390	.411
Runners On/2 Out	95	25	2	0	3	23	11	15	.263	.379	.340
Scor. Pos./2 Out	68	17	1	0	2	20	9	14	.250	.353	.338
Late Inning Pressure	76	21	0	1	3	7	14	9	.276	.421	.389
Leading Off	22	6	0	1	0	0	4	1	.273	.364	.385
Bases Empty	48	15	0	1	3	3	9	6	.313	.542	.421
Runners On	28	6	0	0	0	4	5	3	.214	.214	.333
Runners/Scor. Pos.	19	4	0	0	0	4	3	2	.211	.211	.318

DRIVING IN RUNS	0 Out	1 Out	2 Out	Total	
From 1B	4/34	2/37	3/57	9/128	7%
From 2B	4/16	6/30	8/51	18/97	19%
From 3B	2/4	11/15	9/31	22/50	44%
Scoring Position	6/20	17/45	17/82	40/147	27%
Scor. Pos. %	30%	38%	21%	27%	
Driving In Runners from 3B with Less than Two Out:			13/19	68%	

Loves to face: Jimmy Key (.462, 6-for-13, 3 HR)
Hates to face: Luis Leal (.100, 2-for-20, 8 SO)
Most runs scored (146) by a major leaguer since Ted Williams scored 150 in 1949. . . . Led A.L. in batting in June. . . . Ranked 6th in A.L. in road homers, tied for 4th in homers vs. left-handers. . . . Batting average vs. left-handers (.361) led majors, and was highest of his career. . . . One of six A.L. players to hit at least one home run vs. every opposing club last season. . . . In his career, has homered in every current A.L. park except Fenway. . . . After only seven seasons, leads all active players with 573 stolen bases; Lou Brock had 334 stolen bases after his first seven seasons. Needs 14 steals to surpass Maury Wills's career total. . . . Successful on 88.9 percent of steal attempts last season, best rate of career. . . . Averaged 3.24 putouts per nine innings last season, highest among major-league outfielders (minimum: 300 innings).

Steve Henderson

Oakland As	AB	H	2B	3B	HR	RRF	BB	SO	BA	SA	OBA
Season	193	58	8	3	3	34	18	34	.301	.420	.358
vs. Left-Handed Pitchers	140	45	7	3	2	23	12	23	.321	.457	.373
vs. Right-Handed Pitchers	53	13	1	0	1	11	6	11	.245	.321	.322
Home	96	24	4	2	1	13	10	16	.250	.365	.318
Road	97	34	4	1	2	21	8	18	.351	.474	.400
Grass	164	48	7	3	3	28	14	30	.293	.427	.346
Artificial Turf	29	10	1	0	0	6	4	4	.345	.379	.424
April	4	2	0	0	0	2	1	1	.500	.500	.600
May	31	10	1	1	0	6	2	3	.323	.419	.364
June	33	10	2	0	0	5	5	2	.303	.364	.385
July	29	8	0	1	0	2	3	6	.276	.345	.344
August	33	10	1	0	1	9	3	9	.303	.424	.361
Sept./Oct.	63	18	4	1	2	10	4	13	.286	.476	.328
Leading Off Inn.	53	15	2	1	2	2	4	11	.283	.472	.333
Bases Empty	108	30	3	2	2	2	13	21	.278	.398	.355
Runners On	85	28	5	1	1	32	5	13	.329	.447	.363
Runners/Scor. Pos.	47	20	4	1	0	29	5	6	.426	.553	.472
Runners On/2 Out	23	7	2	0	0	5	5	5	.304	.391	.429
Scor. Pos./2 Out	10	3	1	0	0	5	5	2	.300	.400	.533
Late Inning Pressure	32	9	2	0	0	10	4	6	.281	.344	.351
Leading Off	9	2	0	0	0	0	1	2	.222	.222	.300
Bases Empty	16	3	0	0	0	0	2	3	.188	.188	.278
Runners On	16	6	2	0	0	10	2	3	.375	.500	.421
Runners/Scor. Pos.	9	4	1	0	0	10	2	0	.444	.556	.500

DRIVING IN RUNS	0 Out	1 Out	2 Out	Total	
From 1B	0/21	4/24	0/16	4/61	7%
From 2B	4/11	5/17	2/7	11/35	31%
From 3B	7/7	6/10	3/5	16/22	73%
Scoring Position	11/18	11/27	5/12	27/57	47%
Scor. Pos. %	61%	41%	42%	47%	
Driving In Runners from 3B with Less than Two Out:			13/17	76%	

Loves to face: Joe Niekro (.393, 11-for-28)
Hates to face: Phil Niekro (.140, 6-for-43, 11 SO)
Try and explain that. . . . Only player in majors last year to bat over .400 with runners in scoring position. . . . Also A.L.'s best hitter in road games last season, and the only A.L. player who batted 100 points higher on road than at home (minimum: 200 PA); six players hit 100 points higher the other way. . . . Ground-ball hitter: 2.65 G/A ratio was highest in A.L. last season (minimum: 200 PA). Career average: 2.04, a rate typical of middle infielders and leadoff batters. . . . Started only five of A's 108 games vs. right-handers last season, 41 of 54 against left-handers. Career batting averages: .305 vs. lefties, .269 vs. right-handers. . . . Has batted .438 (21-for-48) in Late-Inning Pressure Situations with runners in scoring position over past four seasons, 3d-highest mark in majors during that time (minimum: 40 AB).

Donnie Hill

Oakland As	AB	H	2B	3B	HR	RRF	BB	SO	BA	SA	OBA
Season	393	112	13	2	3	53	23	33	.285	.351	.321
vs. Left-Handed Pitchers	88	22	3	0	0	12	8	12	.250	.284	.306
vs. Right-Handed Pitchers	305	90	10	2	3	41	15	21	.295	.370	.326
Home	190	51	6	2	0	20	12	17	.268	.321	.309
Road	203	61	7	0	3	33	11	16	.300	.379	.333
Grass	314	84	8	2	0	39	20	27	.268	.306	.309
Artificial Turf	79	28	5	0	3	14	3	6	.354	.532	.373
April	70	16	1	1	1	7	3	4	.229	.314	.260
May	67	18	0	0	1	9	2	11	.269	.313	.286
June	79	19	1	1	0	13	8	4	.241	.278	.310
July	74	23	2	0	1	10	5	6	.311	.378	.346
August	103	36	9	0	0	14	5	8	.350	.437	.376
Sept./Oct.	0	0	0	0	0	0	0	0	.000	.000	.000
Leading Off Inn.	92	25	3	0	1	1	5	5	.272	.337	.309
Bases Empty	233	60	7	0	2	2	13	20	.258	.313	.297
Runners On	160	52	6	2	1	51	10	13	.325	.406	.356
Runners/Scor. Pos.	98	33	5	1	1	48	6	10	.337	.439	.361
Runners On/2 Out	69	23	2	1	1	22	2	8	.333	.435	.352
Scor. Pos./2 Out	45	15	1	0	1	20	1	5	.333	.422	.348
Late Inning Pressure	55	15	1	0	1	4	7	4	.273	.345	.355
Leading Off	19	8	1	0	1	1	2	1	.421	.632	.476
Bases Empty	45	12	1	0	1	1	3	4	.267	.356	.313
Runners On	10	3	0	0	0	3	4	0	.300	.300	.500
Runners/Scor. Pos.	7	2	0	0	0	3	2	0	.286	.286	.444

DRIVING IN RUNS	0 Out	1 Out	2 Out	Total	
From 1B	2/21	1/46	3/47	6/114	5%
From 2B	5/14	7/29	12/38	24/81	30%
From 3B	6/11	8/14	6/12	20/37	54%
Scoring Position	11/25	15/43	18/50	44/118	37%
Scor. Pos. %	44%	35%	36%	37%	
Driving In Runners from 3B with Less than Two Out:			14/25	56%	

Loves to face: Doyle Alexander (.417, 5-for-12, 2 HR)
Hates to face: Bruce Hurst (0-for-15)
.2850 batting average was 2d-highest among regular A.L. second basemen last season; Alan Wiggins (.2852) nosed him out for that honor. . . . The fact that Hill hit as well as he did was impressive, considering that it was a change-of-position year for him; previously a shortstop, he had played only 22 games at second in his four pro seasons. . . . Fielding percentage of .973 was lowest in A.L. at second (minimum: 100 games). . . . Career batting averages: .238 with the bases empty, .307 with runners on base, .324 with runners in scoring position. . . . First career home run was hit at Oakland Coliseum in 1983. All six since were hit on road. . . . Hit safely in 17 consecutive games, Aug. 8–23, longest streak by an Oakland player last season. . . . Collected 14 of his 48 RBIs vs. Seattle last season. . . . Fly-ball hitter: 0.88 G/A ratio last season.

Larry Herndon

Detroit Tigers	AB	H	2B	3B	HR	RRF	BB	SO	BA	SA	OBA
Season	442	108	12	7	12	37	33	79	.244	.385	.298
vs. Left-Handed Pitchers	155	41	3	5	7	19	20	23	.265	.484	.347
vs. Right-Handed Pitchers	287	67	9	2	5	18	13	56	.233	.331	.269
Home	211	54	7	3	7	20	16	28	.256	.417	.308
Road	231	54	5	4	5	17	17	51	.234	.355	.288
Grass	379	93	10	5	12	35	31	70	.245	.393	.303
Artificial Turf	63	15	2	2	0	2	2	9	.238	.333	.262
April	67	16	4	1	1	4	4	8	.239	.373	.282
May	73	17	3	1	3	6	9	14	.233	.425	.317
June	97	23	1	2	1	6	6	18	.237	.320	.282
July	84	24	3	0	4	11	4	15	.286	.464	.315
August	72	17	1	2	1	3	3	15	.236	.347	.276
Sept./Oct.	49	11	0	1	2	7	7	9	.224	.388	.321
Leading Off Inn.	101	31	4	4	4	4	4	10	.307	.545	.340
Bases Empty	272	72	8	6	10	10	16	42	.265	.449	.308
Runners On	170	36	4	1	2	27	17	37	.212	.282	.282
Runners/Scor. Pos.	86	16	1	0	1	24	13	17	.186	.233	.290
Runners On/2 Out	74	17	2	0	1	16	9	17	.230	.297	.313
Scor. Pos./2 Out	43	9	1	0	0	14	8	8	.209	.233	.333
Late Inning Pressure	75	14	2	0	1	4	8	24	.187	.253	.265
Leading Off	12	1	0	0	1	1	0	3	.083	.333	.083
Bases Empty	48	8	1	0	1	1	3	17	.167	.250	.216
Runners On	27	6	1	0	0	3	5	7	.222	.259	.344
Runners/Scor. Pos.	12	3	0	0	0	3	2	3	.250	.250	.357

DRIVING IN RUNS	0 Out	1 Out	2 Out	Total	
From 1B	0/24	1/55	1/60	2/139	1%
From 2B	0/13	4/25	8/33	12/71	17%
From 3B	2/6	3/12	6/19	11/37	30%
Scoring Position	2/19	7/37	14/52	23/108	21%
Scor. Pos. %	11%	19%	27%	21%	
Driving In Runners from 3B with Less than Two Out:			5/18	28%	

Loves to face: John Candelaria (.459, 17-for-37, 3 HR)
Hates to face: Jim Clancy (0-for-18)
Given a chance to be full-time leftfielder last season: started all but two of Tigers' 50 games against lefties, and 53 of first 66 against right-handers, but then reverted to platoon status, starting only nine of last 45 games against right-handers. . . . Batting average vs. left-handers (.265) was under .300 for first time since 1980. Career marks: .301 vs. left-handers, .259 vs. right-handers. . . . Annual batting averages with runners in scoring position since 1983: .320, .231, .186. . . . Drove in only two base runners with 12 home runs last season, tied for 2d-lowest rate in A.L. . . . Drove in only 27.8 percent of runners from third with less than two outs, 2d-lowest rate in majors last year. . . . Has drawn six walks in 31 times up with the bases loaded over last two seasons. . . . Has homered in every current A.L. ballpark except Exhibition Stadium.

Glenn Hoffman

Boston Red Sox	AB	H	2B	3B	HR	RRF	BB	SO	BA	SA	OBA
Season	279	77	17	2	6	36	25	40	.276	.416	.343
vs. Left-Handed Pitchers	79	24	5	0	4	15	6	10	.304	.519	.349
vs. Right-Handed Pitchers	200	53	12	2	2	21	19	30	.265	.375	.341
Home	129	33	9	1	2	17	17	20	.256	.388	.349
Road	150	44	8	1	4	19	8	20	.293	.440	.337
Grass	236	67	15	2	5	27	22	32	.284	.428	.352
Artificial Turf	43	10	2	0	1	9	3	8	.233	.349	.292
April	16	4	2	0	0	1	0	0	.250	.375	.250
May	15	5	1	0	1	1	5	3	.333	.600	.524
June	93	23	5	2	1	17	3	15	.247	.376	.278
July	75	20	4	0	1	6	5	12	.267	.360	.313
August	6	0	0	0	0	0	0	1	.000	.000	.000
Sept./Oct.	74	25	5	0	3	11	12	9	.338	.527	.435
Leading Off Inn.	68	21	5	0	1	1	6	9	.309	.426	.373
Bases Empty	148	47	11	0	5	5	14	19	.318	.493	.388
Runners On	131	30	6	2	1	31	11	21	.229	.328	.293
Runners/Scor. Pos.	73	19	3	1	1	30	4	14	.260	.370	.296
Runners On/2 Out	64	16	4	2	0	17	6	11	.250	.375	.324
Scor. Pos./2 Out	40	10	2	1	0	16	2	10	.250	.350	.286
Late Inning Pressure	39	11	3	0	1	5	4	7	.282	.436	.364
Leading Off	7	1	1	0	0	0	2	2	.143	.286	.400
Bases Empty	19	7	2	0	1	1	2	4	.368	.632	.455
Runners On	20	4	1	0	0	4	2	3	.200	.250	.273
Runners/Scor. Pos.	7	3	0	0	0	4	1	1	.429	.429	.500

DRIVING IN RUNS	0 Out	1 Out	2 Out	Total	
From 1B	0/11	0/37	3/51	3/99	3%
From 2B	0/7	4/21	7/32	11/60	18%
From 3B	1/1	8/15	7/18	16/34	47%
Scoring Position	1/8	12/36	14/50	27/94	29%
Scor. Pos. %	13%	33%	28%	29%	
Driving In Runners from 3B with Less than Two Out:			9/16	56%	

Loves to face: Bob Shirley (.667, 4-for-6)
Hates to face: Britt Burns (.048, 1-for-21, 10 SO)
Started season on the bench (three starts in first 41 games), then replaced Jackie Gutierrez, starting Boston's next 53 games; made only three errors during that span. Reclaimed the job in late August after shoulder injury; with Gutierrez traded, stands as the incumbent entering '86. . . . Assists per nine innings and chances accepted were virtually equal for the two shortstops, but Hoffman had decisive edges in double plays (61 to 47) and fewer errors (10 to 23); hardly explains the won-lost disparity (31–51 with Gutierrez starting, 50–30 with Hoffman). . . . Batting average vs. left-handers (.304) was his highest since 1980, when as a rookie he hit .309 against southpaws. In between he hit .224 vs. lefties. . . . Batted .500 (6-for-12) with the bases loaded last season. . . . Ground-ball hitter: 1.47 G/A ratio last season. Career: 1.19.

Paul Householder

Milwaukee Brewers	AB	H	2B	3B	HR	RRF	BB	SO	BA	SA	OBA
Season	299	77	15	0	11	35	27	60	.258	.418	.320
vs. Left-Handed Pitchers	115	35	6	0	5	13	10	23	.304	.487	.357
vs. Right-Handed Pitchers	184	42	9	0	6	22	17	37	.228	.375	.297
Home	134	32	8	0	3	14	16	24	.239	.366	.320
Road	165	45	7	0	8	21	11	36	.273	.461	.320
Grass	250	62	14	0	9	29	26	50	.248	.412	.318
Artificial Turf	49	15	1	0	2	6	1	10	.306	.449	.333
April	22	4	1	0	1	5	6	8	.182	.364	.357
May	30	9	3	0	0	1	3	4	.300	.400	.364
June	27	7	0	0	0	1	1	7	.259	.259	.276
July	58	15	2	0	1	2	4	12	.259	.345	.306
August	56	8	2	0	1	6	3	12	.143	.232	.186
Sept./Oct.	106	34	7	0	8	20	10	17	.321	.613	.385
Leading Off Inn.	74	19	2	0	4	4	8	15	.257	.446	.329
Bases Empty	162	43	8	0	5	5	13	34	.265	.407	.320
Runners On	137	34	7	0	6	30	14	26	.248	.431	.320
Runners/Scor. Pos.	78	16	3	0	3	23	10	16	.205	.359	.300
Runners On/2 Out	65	16	3	0	2	12	4	15	.246	.385	.300
Scor. Pos./2 Out	33	7	1	0	0	8	3	8	.212	.242	.297
Late Inning Pressure	52	16	3	0	1	3	1	9	.308	.423	.321
Leading Off	15	4	0	0	1	1	0	3	.267	.467	.267
Bases Empty	32	13	3	0	1	1	1	5	.406	.594	.424
Runners On	20	3	0	0	0	2	0	4	.150	.150	.150
Runners/Scor. Pos.	15	1	0	0	0	2	0	3	.067	.067	.067

DRIVING IN RUNS	0 Out	1 Out	2 Out	Total	
From 1B	1/19	3/33	2/51	6/103	6%
From 2B	1/13	3/29	2/26	6/68	9%
From 3B	2/5	4/7	6/16	12/28	43%
Scoring Position	3/18	7/36	8/42	18/96	19%
Scor. Pos. %	17%	19%	19%	19%	
Driving In Runners from 3B with Less than Two Out:			6/12	50%	

Loves to face: Tim Lollar (.421, 8-for-19, 3 HR)
Hates to face: Vern Ruhle (0-for-11, 4 SO)
Started only one-quarter of Milwaukee's first 68 games, but after June 29, started in 60 of 93. Batting average was still down at .223 with 30 days left in season, but with everyday play he boosted it to .258. . . . Had .613 slugging average after Sept. 1, 5th-best in A.L., up there with big boys Thornton, Kittle, Mattingly, and Darrell Evans. . . . Had hit for power in minor leagues (66 homers in last four minor-league seasons), but despite two years as regular with Reds (417 and 380 at bats) had not reached double-digits in homers in the majors before. . . . Career batting average of .192 (5-for-26) with the bases loaded. . . . Career batting averages: .275 batting right-handed, .220 batting left-handed. . . . Has batted for a higher average in day games than in night games in each of past five seasons; last year: .298 day, .239 night.

Kent Hrbek

Minnesota Twins	AB	H	2B	3B	HR	RRF	BB	SO	BA	SA	OBA
Season	593	165	31	2	21	95	67	87	.278	.444	.351
vs. Left-Handed Pitchers	199	51	9	1	6	25	20	37	.256	.402	.324
vs. Right-Handed Pitchers	394	114	22	1	15	70	47	50	.289	.464	.365
Home	314	98	21	2	10	61	34	45	.312	.487	.378
Road	279	67	10	0	11	34	33	42	.240	.394	.322
Grass	208	50	5	0	7	24	19	33	.240	.365	.303
Artificial Turf	385	115	26	2	14	71	48	54	.299	.486	.377
April	76	16	4	1	3	11	14	8	.211	.408	.341
May	115	30	7	0	3	20	5	16	.261	.400	.289
June	85	25	5	0	3	9	12	16	.294	.459	.378
July	81	16	0	0	4	17	12	17	.198	.346	.309
August	104	38	6	0	3	17	8	13	.365	.510	.411
Sept./Oct.	132	40	9	1	5	21	16	17	.303	.500	.373
Leading Off Inn.	123	36	9	0	5	5	6	12	.293	.488	.331
Bases Empty	326	95	20	1	10	11	26	45	.291	.451	.346
Runners On	267	70	11	1	11	84	41	42	.262	.434	.358
Runners/Scor. Pos.	148	39	8	1	6	70	27	19	.264	.453	.372
Runners On/2 Out	91	22	1	1	4	22	13	15	.242	.407	.337
Scor. Pos./2 Out	57	12	1	1	2	17	9	7	.211	.368	.318
Late Inning Pressure	73	21	1	0	1	10	11	15	.288	.342	.388
Leading Off	24	5	0	0	0	0	0	4	.208	.208	.240
Bases Empty	45	14	1	0	0	0	2	8	.311	.333	.354
Runners On	28	7	0	0	1	10	9	7	.250	.357	.432
Runners/Scor. Pos.	17	5	0	0	1	10	5	4	.294	.471	.455

DRIVING IN RUNS	0 Out	1 Out	2 Out	Total	
From 1B	4/42	8/87	5/58	17/187	9%
From 2B	5/25	11/42	9/41	25/108	23%
From 3B	5/7	22/34	4/21	31/62	50%
Scoring Position	10/32	33/76	13/62	56/170	33%
Scor. Pos. %	31%	43%	21%	33%	
Driving In Runners from 3B with Less than Two Out:			27/41	66%	

Loves to face: Dan Quisenberry (.571, 8-for-14, 2 HR)
Hates to face: Bob McClure (0-for-10, 3 SO)
Don't say anything bad about the Metrodome around Hrbek, or you may get a hrap in the teeth: Kent is a mild-mannered hitter on the road (batting .263, slugging .438 for career), but turns into a Superman at dome (.324 and .520). Last year's home-batting and home-slugging averages were his *lowest* in four full years in the majors. . . . His road batting average has declined every year; since 1982: .285, .270, .263, .240. . . . Hit three grand-slam homers last year, tying Eddie Murray for major-league lead. . . . Career batting averages: .282 with the bases empty, .308 with runners on base, .323 with runners in scoring position. . . . Hit game-winning home run in major-league debut at Yankee Stadium in 1981, but career batting average there is only .150, his lowest at any A.L. ballpark.

Tim Hulett

Chicago White Sox	AB	H	2B	3B	HR	RRF	BB	SO	BA	SA	OBA
Season	395	106	19	4	5	38	30	81	.268	.375	.324
vs. Left-Handed Pitchers	159	47	7	4	2	17	15	29	.296	.428	.354
vs. Right-Handed Pitchers	236	59	12	0	3	21	15	52	.250	.339	.304
Home	195	49	8	4	2	15	17	41	.251	.364	.315
Road	200	57	11	0	3	23	13	40	.285	.385	.333
Grass	334	87	18	4	5	31	27	70	.260	.383	.321
Artificial Turf	61	19	1	0	0	7	3	11	.311	.328	.344
April	15	5	1	0	0	2	0	3	.333	.400	.333
May	57	22	1	2	2	11	1	6	.386	.579	.417
June	94	20	6	1	0	5	7	21	.213	.298	.265
July	87	23	4	1	1	9	11	23	.264	.368	.356
August	62	9	2	0	0	2	9	17	.145	.177	.250
Sept./Oct.	80	27	5	0	2	9	2	11	.338	.475	.354
Leading Off Inn.	91	25	6	1	1	1	2	16	.275	.396	.298
Bases Empty	240	66	12	3	4	4	15	44	.275	.400	.326
Runners On	155	40	7	1	1	34	15	37	.258	.335	.322
Runners/Scor. Pos.	88	22	5	0	1	31	12	27	.250	.341	.330
Runners On/2 Out	73	22	3	0	0	17	7	19	.301	.342	.363
Scor. Pos./2 Out	51	13	2	0	0	16	7	16	.255	.294	.345
Late Inning Pressure	52	12	1	0	1	1	2	14	.231	.308	.259
Leading Off	11	5	0	0	0	0	0	2	.455	.455	.455
Bases Empty	30	11	1	0	1	1	1	6	.367	.500	.387
Runners On	22	1	0	0	0	0	1	8	.045	.045	.087
Runners/Scor. Pos.	11	0	0	0	0	0	1	5	.000	.000	.083

DRIVING IN RUNS	0 Out	1 Out	2 Out	Total	
From 1B	1/23	2/38	2/40	5/101	5%
From 2B	3/13	1/19	9/35	13/67	19%
From 3B	2/4	7/12	6/21	15/37	41%
Scoring Position	5/17	8/31	15/56	28/104	27%
Scor. Pos. %	29%	26%	27%	27%	
Driving In Runners from 3B with Less than Two Out:			9/16	56%	

Loves to face: Dennis Martinez (.667, 4-for-6, 1 HR)
Hates to face: Dave Stieb (0-for-6, 3 SO)
Played in 141 games last season, 2d among A.L. rookies behind teammate Ozzie Guillen's 150. . . . After playing second base in the minors, played only 28 games there for Sox, but 115 at third. . . . Fielding percentage of .924 was lowest among major-league third basemen (minimum: 100 games), but he averaged an impressive 2.20 assists per nine innings playing behind a high-strikeout pitching staff (league average: 2.04). . . . Batting average of .045 (1-for-22) with runners on base in LIP situations was lowest in majors last year (minimum: 20 PA); some pretty good players have gone 20 or more at bats without a hit in that category over the past 11 years: Toby Harrah (0-for-23 in '84) and Fred Lynn (0-for-21 in '81). . . . Fly-ball hitter: 0.73 G/A ratio last year.

Dane Iorg

Kansas City Royals	AB	H	2B	3B	HR	RRF	BB	SO	BA	SA	OBA
Season	130	29	9	1	1	21	8	16	.223	.331	.268
vs. Left-Handed Pitchers	0	0	0	0	0	0	0	0	.000	.000	.000
vs. Right-Handed Pitchers	130	29	9	1	1	21	8	16	.223	.331	.268
Home	62	13	3	1	0	8	4	5	.210	.290	.258
Road	68	16	6	0	1	13	4	11	.235	.368	.278
Grass	57	12	3	0	1	11	1	10	.211	.316	.224
Artificial Turf	73	17	6	1	0	10	7	6	.233	.342	.300
April	7	1	0	0	0	0	1	2	.143	.143	.250
May	27	5	2	0	1	5	2	2	.185	.370	.241
June	12	1	0	0	0	0	1	2	.083	.083	.154
July	36	9	2	1	0	9	0	4	.250	.361	.250
August	39	10	4	0	0	5	4	4	.256	.359	.326
Sept./Oct.	9	3	1	0	0	2	0	2	.333	.444	.333
Leading Off Inn.	22	6	1	1	0	0	2	2	.273	.409	.333
Bases Empty	59	11	3	1	1	1	5	6	.186	.322	.250
Runners On	71	18	6	0	0	20	3	10	.254	.338	.284
Runners/Scor. Pos.	43	12	4	0	0	19	3	5	.279	.372	.326
Runners On/2 Out	19	3	0	0	0	3	0	2	.158	.158	.158
Scor. Pos./2 Out	15	2	0	0	0	3	0	1	.133	.133	.133
Late Inning Pressure	26	4	1	0	0	1	3	6	.154	.192	.241
Leading Off	5	1	0	0	0	0	0	0	.200	.200	.200
Bases Empty	10	2	1	0	0	0	1	1	.200	.300	.273
Runners On	16	2	0	0	0	1	2	5	.125	.125	.222
Runners/Scor. Pos.	9	1	0	0	0	1	2	2	.111	.111	.273

DRIVING IN RUNS	0 Out	1 Out	2 Out	Total	
From 1B	1/15	2/22	0/12	3/49	6%
From 2B	4/11	3/10	2/11	9/32	28%
From 3B	3/5	4/7	1/6	8/18	44%
Scoring Position	7/16	7/17	3/17	17/50	34%
Scor. Pos. %	44%	41%	18%	34%	
Driving In Runners from 3B with Less than Two Out:			7/12	58%	

Loves to face: Doyle Alexander (.500, 5-for-10, 1 HR)
Hates to face: Richard Dotson (.071, 1-for-14)
He didn't surprise *us* with his game-winning hit in the ninth inning of Game Six; nor did he shock anyone who studied last year's *Analyst*. . . . Cardinals led 1–0, one out, bases loaded, right-hander Todd Worrell pitching—a veritable definition of the Dane Iorg situation: career batting averages of .467 (14-for-30) with the bases loaded, .321 with runners in scoring position, and .326 in Late-Inning Pressure Situations with runners in scoring position. . . . Has faced right-handers in 92 percent of career plate appearances, and reached his own Nirvana last year, when he didn't see a left-hander all season. Career batting averages: .287 vs. right-handers, .205 vs. left-handers. . . . Started 33 games last season, but only one (final day of season) after Aug. 28. . . . Ground-ball hitter: 1.76 G/A ratio last season.

Garth Iorg

Toronto Blue Jays	AB	H	2B	3B	HR	RRF	BB	SO	BA	SA	OBA
Season	288	90	22	1	7	39	21	26	.313	.469	.358
vs. Left-Handed Pitchers	200	62	17	1	5	25	16	13	.310	.480	.361
vs. Right-Handed Pitchers	88	28	5	0	2	14	5	13	.318	.443	.351
Home	119	45	10	0	5	20	8	9	.378	.588	.417
Road	169	45	12	1	2	19	13	17	.266	.385	.317
Grass	118	31	9	1	1	11	9	14	.263	.381	.313
Artificial Turf	170	59	13	0	6	28	12	12	.347	.529	.390
April	30	9	1	0	1	5	2	2	.300	.433	.344
May	39	13	3	0	0	2	6	1	.333	.410	.422
June	41	13	4	0	1	4	1	4	.317	.488	.333
July	38	10	3	0	0	5	5	2	.263	.342	.349
August	67	20	5	1	1	13	7	8	.299	.448	.360
Sept./Oct.	73	25	6	0	4	10	0	9	.342	.589	.342
Leading Off Inn.	67	17	4	0	2	2	1	3	.254	.403	.265
Bases Empty	150	48	12	0	4	4	5	9	.320	.480	.342
Runners On	138	42	10	1	3	35	16	17	.304	.457	.374
Runners/Scor. Pos.	73	24	5	1	2	30	11	11	.329	.507	.412
Runners On/2 Out	66	22	6	1	1	19	5	9	.333	.500	.380
Scor. Pos./2 Out	39	13	3	1	1	17	3	7	.333	.538	.381
Late Inning Pressure	31	10	2	0	0	2	0	1	.323	.387	.323
Leading Off	7	3	0	0	0	0	0	0	.429	.429	.429
Bases Empty	19	6	1	0	0	0	0	1	.316	.368	.316
Runners On	12	4	1	0	0	2	0	0	.333	.417	.333
Runners/Scor. Pos.	4	1	0	0	0	1	0	0	.250	.250	.250

DRIVING IN RUNS	0 Out	1 Out	2 Out	Total	
From 1B	0/19	3/32	4/45	7/96	7%
From 2B	2/10	6/22	8/29	16/61	26%
From 3B	0/4	3/4	6/17	9/25	36%
Scoring Position	2/14	9/26	14/46	25/86	29%
Scor. Pos. %	14%	35%	30%	29%	
Driving In Runners from 3B with Less than Two Out:			3/8	38%	

Loves to face: Frank Viola (.394, 13-for-33, 2 HR)
Hates to face: Danny Darwin (0-for-16, 6 SO)
Career batting average in Late-Inning Pressure Situations (.329) ranks 5th in 11-year history of *The Player Analysis* (minimum: 200 PA). . . . But has only .175 career batting average (7-for-40) with the bases loaded. . . . Had hit only nine major-league home runs before last September, when he belted four within 24 days. . . . Batted 112 points higher at home than on road, 3d-largest difference in A.L. last season (minimum: 200 PA). His slugging average at home was 3d-highest in A.L. . . . Batted .318 against right-handers, a career high, and hit homers against Joe Beckwith and Oil Can Boyd, the first two he has ever hit against righties. . . . Iorg family has career average of .394 (39-for-99) in Late-Inning Pressure Situations with two outs and runners on base. Take that, Waners, DiMaggios, and Delahantys, wherever you are!

Reggie Jackson

California Angels	AB	H	2B	3B	HR	RRF	BB	SO	BA	SA	OBA
Season	460	116	27	0	27	87	78	138	.252	.487	.360
vs. Left-Handed Pitchers	113	25	8	0	4	19	24	44	.221	.398	.355
vs. Right-Handed Pitchers	347	91	19	0	23	68	54	94	.262	.516	.362
Home	225	49	10	0	15	45	38	70	.218	.462	.328
Road	235	67	17	0	12	42	40	68	.285	.511	.391
Grass	383	96	24	0	25	80	61	115	.251	.509	.353
Artificial Turf	77	20	3	0	2	7	17	23	.260	.377	.394
April	57	12	1	0	3	10	5	15	.211	.386	.274
May	57	17	5	0	4	10	14	16	.298	.596	.437
June	82	20	6	0	4	16	17	29	.244	.463	.374
July	85	27	4	0	6	16	12	20	.318	.576	.402
August	90	19	6	0	3	16	14	25	.211	.378	.314
Sept./Oct.	89	21	5	0	7	19	16	33	.236	.528	.355
Leading Off Inn.	101	23	4	0	4	4	15	32	.228	.386	.333
Bases Empty	242	57	15	0	12	12	40	75	.236	.446	.346
Runners On	218	59	12	0	15	75	38	63	.271	.532	.376
Runners/Scor. Pos.	114	33	7	0	8	58	28	26	.289	.561	.424
Runners On/2 Out	100	26	5	0	7	35	16	30	.260	.520	.362
Scor. Pos./2 Out	58	14	4	0	3	26	12	15	.241	.466	.371
Late Inning Pressure	59	8	1	0	0	4	16	23	.136	.153	.320
Leading Off	13	1	0	0	0	0	3	5	.077	.077	.250
Bases Empty	30	5	1	0	0	0	7	12	.167	.200	.324
Runners On	29	3	0	0	0	4	9	11	.103	.103	.316
Runners/Scor. Pos.	13	2	0	0	0	4	7	4	.154	.154	.450

DRIVING IN RUNS	0 Out	1 Out	2 Out	Total	
From 1B	1/37	7/63	9/79	17/179	9%
From 2B	7/15	6/22	8/47	21/84	25%
From 3B	2/10	9/18	11/25	22/53	42%
Scoring Position	9/25	15/40	19/72	43/137	31%
Scor. Pos. %	36%	38%	26%	31%	
Driving In Runners from 3B with Less than Two Out:			11/28	39%	

Loves to face: Doyle Alexander (.487, 19-for-39, 4 HR)
Hates to face: Dave Righetti (.056, 1-for-18, 8 SO)
Not too hot against Bret Saberhagen, either (0-for-17). . . . Yearly batting averages in Late-Inning Pressure Situations since 1981: .333, .276, .221, .188, .136. LIP batting average of .166 (with only one home run in 139 AB) over past two seasons is 3d-lowest in majors during that period (minimum: 100 AB). . . . RDI percentage from scoring position in LIP Situations has been lower than in nonpressure situations in eight of last nine seasons. . . . Needs 44 homers to move into second place on all-time A.L. home run list: Ruth 708, Killebrew 573, Mantle 536, Reggie 530. . . . Ranks 2d among active players in RBIs (Reggie, 1601; Tony Perez, 1623) and total bases (Reggie, 1013; Pete Rose, 1031). . . . Averaged 1.61 putouts per nine innings last season, lowest rate among A.L. outfielders (minimum: 300 innings).

Brook Jacoby

Cleveland Indians	AB	H	2B	3B	HR	RRF	BB	SO	BA	SA	OBA
Season	606	166	26	3	20	89	48	120	.274	.426	.324
vs. Left-Handed Pitchers	185	51	7	0	9	29	17	35	.276	.459	.335
vs. Right-Handed Pitchers	421	115	19	3	11	60	31	85	.273	.411	.319
Home	303	82	14	3	9	46	25	58	.271	.426	.323
Road	303	84	12	0	11	43	23	62	.277	.426	.324
Grass	515	132	22	3	16	75	42	104	.256	.404	.310
Artificial Turf	91	34	4	0	4	14	6	16	.374	.549	.404
April	73	17	2	0	1	8	6	9	.233	.301	.288
May	96	32	4	0	3	15	9	16	.333	.469	.387
June	100	29	6	0	6	21	9	24	.290	.530	.339
July	99	26	3	1	1	6	10	21	.263	.343	.327
August	104	30	3	0	4	18	9	19	.288	.433	.345
Sept./Oct.	134	32	8	2	5	21	5	31	.239	.440	.264
Leading Off Inn.	117	35	5	0	4	4	4	21	.299	.444	.322
Bases Empty	333	85	13	1	9	9	22	66	.255	.381	.301
Runners On	273	81	13	2	11	80	26	54	.297	.480	.350
Runners/Scor. Pos.	156	37	9	0	5	64	21	32	.237	.391	.315
Runners On/2 Out	103	28	6	1	4	29	13	22	.272	.466	.353
Scor. Pos./2 Out	68	16	3	0	2	23	9	10	.235	.368	.325
Late Inning Pressure	83	19	2	0	1	3	7	15	.229	.289	.286
Leading Off	17	6	1	0	0	0	1	2	.353	.412	.389
Bases Empty	52	12	2	0	1	1	3	9	.231	.327	.273
Runners On	31	7	0	0	0	2	4	6	.226	.226	.306
Runners/Scor. Pos.	15	1	0	0	0	2	3	2	.067	.067	.211

DRIVING IN RUNS	0 Out	1 Out	2 Out	Total	
From 1B	2/57	4/64	7/72	13/193	7%
From 2B	6/28	3/41	10/47	19/116	16%
From 3B	14/20	15/23	8/37	37/80	46%
Scoring Position	20/48	18/64	18/84	56/196	29%
Scor. Pos. %	42%	28%	21%	29%	
Driving In Runners from 3B with Less than Two Out:			29/43	67%	

Loves to face: Mike Mason (.600, 6-for-10, 1 HR)
Hates to face: Tom Seaver (0-for-10)
Look, a record is a record: he was the only player in the majors last season to start in 100 losing games. Brook: see Bruce Bochte; things could be worse. . . . Missed last six weeks of '84 season with fractured hand but came back strong: had 606 at bats without getting hit by a pitch, 83 at bats short of the major-league record for that sort of thing, held by that toughest of targets, Sandy Alomar. . . . Batting average of .374 on artificial surfaces last season was 2d-highest in majors among players who were just visiting; Wade Boggs led with .389. . . . Career batting average of .206 in Late-Inning Pressure Situations. . . . Career batting averages: .290 vs. left-handers, .257 vs. right-handers. . . . A terror in Canada: .405 batting average and five home runs in 37 career at bats at Exhibition Stadium.

Cliff Johnson

Rangers/Blue Jays	AB	H	2B	3B	HR	RRF	BB	SO	BA	SA	OBA
Season	369	96	17	1	13	67	40	59	.260	.417	.334
vs. Left-Handed Pitchers	112	37	6	0	2	15	17	16	.330	.438	.419
vs. Right-Handed Pitchers	257	59	11	1	11	52	23	43	.230	.409	.296
Home	172	43	5	1	9	44	23	32	.250	.448	.343
Road	197	53	12	0	4	23	17	27	.269	.391	.326
Grass	278	73	12	1	12	56	32	45	.263	.442	.343
Artificial Turf	91	23	5	0	1	11	8	14	.253	.341	.307
April	68	19	4	0	4	15	6	11	.279	.515	.347
May	84	18	4	0	3	17	12	10	.214	.369	.317
June	40	12	3	1	2	8	5	4	.300	.575	.378
July	20	9	2	0	0	4	1	4	.450	.550	.476
August	87	18	4	0	3	12	8	16	.207	.356	.274
Sept./Oct.	70	20	0	0	1	11	8	14	.286	.329	.354
Leading Off Inn.	87	13	2	0	3	3	9	15	.149	.276	.237
Bases Empty	207	43	8	0	7	7	21	35	.208	.348	.290
Runners On	162	53	9	1	6	60	19	24	.327	.506	.389
Runners/Scor. Pos.	93	33	7	0	4	53	10	16	.355	.559	.402
Runners On/2 Out	77	26	6	0	2	25	9	14	.338	.494	.407
Scor. Pos./2 Out	52	17	5	0	1	22	6	10	.327	.481	.397
Late Inning Pressure	54	13	4	0	1	9	4	6	.241	.370	.288
Leading Off	14	2	1	0	0	0	0	2	.143	.214	.143
Bases Empty	34	6	3	0	0	0	3	3	.176	.265	.243
Runners On	20	7	1	0	1	9	1	3	.350	.550	.364
Runners/Scor. Pos.	11	5	1	0	1	9	0	2	.455	.818	.417

DRIVING IN RUNS	0 Out	1 Out	2 Out	Total	
From 1B	0/24	6/39	3/42	9/105	9%
From 2B	5/9	6/24	15/38	26/71	37%
From 3B	5/5	9/15	5/23	19/43	44%
Scoring Position	10/14	15/39	20/61	45/114	39%
Scor. Pos. %	71%	38%	33%	39%	
Driving In Runners from 3B with Less than Two Out:			14/20	70%	

Loves to face: Dennis Rasmussen (.700, 7-for-10)
Hates to face: Steve Crawford (0-for-11, 5 SO)
Drove in 12 runs in 12 games vs. Toronto last season before rejoining Jays for stretch drive. Season batting average peaked at .282 with a three-hit game vs. once and future teammates, Aug. 2. . . . Drove in 36.6 percent of runners from second base, highest in majors since Bill Buckner set *Player Analysis* record of 41.8 in 1981 (minimum: 25 RRF). . . . Has hit for higher average with runners on base than with the bases empty in each of last four seasons, capping things with 119-point differential last year, largest in A.L. (minimum: 200 PA). . . . One of six A.L. players with a 100-point disparity between batting averages vs. left-handers and right-handers last season. . . . Over last 11 years, has hit .290 vs. left-handers, .236 vs. right-handers. Home run rates are closer: one every 18.4 at bats vs. lefties, one every 21.8 vs. righties.

Ruppert Jones

California Angels	AB	H	2B	3B	HR	RRF	BB	SO	BA	SA	OBA
Season	389	90	17	2	21	68	57	82	.231	.447	.328
vs. Left-Handed Pitchers	46	8	1	1	2	10	5	12	.174	.370	.255
vs. Right-Handed Pitchers	343	82	16	1	19	58	52	70	.239	.458	.338
Home	180	46	8	1	10	33	32	38	.256	.478	.364
Road	209	44	9	1	11	35	25	44	.211	.421	.295
Grass	319	71	12	1	18	52	51	72	.223	.436	.328
Artificial Turf	70	19	5	1	3	16	6	10	.271	.500	.329
April	36	11	5	0	2	8	7	11	.306	.611	.409
May	61	15	2	0	4	15	18	10	.246	.475	.413
June	66	14	1	0	5	10	7	18	.212	.455	.288
July	74	26	4	0	6	15	12	9	.351	.649	.442
August	85	18	4	1	3	15	10	17	.212	.388	.295
Sept./Oct.	67	6	1	1	1	5	3	17	.090	.179	.129
Leading Off Inn.	97	20	2	0	8	8	12	20	.206	.474	.294
Bases Empty	211	39	6	0	11	11	31	42	.185	.370	.289
Runners On	178	51	11	2	10	57	26	40	.287	.539	.374
Runners/Scor. Pos.	100	22	2	1	3	37	15	27	.220	.350	.316
Runners On/2 Out	74	22	5	1	6	27	10	14	.297	.635	.381
Scor. Pos./2 Out	44	10	0	0	3	17	7	10	.227	.432	.333
Late Inning Pressure	51	11	2	1	3	9	12	13	.216	.471	.365
Leading Off	19	4	0	0	2	2	1	3	.211	.526	.250
Bases Empty	33	7	1	0	2	2	5	6	.212	.424	.316
Runners On	18	4	1	1	1	7	7	7	.222	.556	.440
Runners/Scor. Pos.	14	3	1	0	1	6	5	5	.214	.500	.421

DRIVING IN RUNS	0 Out	1 Out	2 Out	Total	
From 1B	3/28	4/47	9/54	16/129	12%
From 2B	0/14	4/29	7/34	11/77	14%
From 3B	2/5	13/19	5/16	20/40	50%
Scoring Position	2/19	17/48	12/50	31/117	26%
Scor. Pos. %	11%	35%	24%	26%	
Driving In Runners from 3B with Less than Two Out:			15/24	63%	

Loves to face: Dan Quisenberry (.500, 4-for-8, 1 HR)
Hates to face: Rod Scurry (.063, 1-for-16)
One of two A.L. players to start at least 10 games at each outfield position last season.... Batted 102 points higher with runners on base than with bases empty, 4th-highest such difference in A.L.... Has hit for a higher average with runners on base than with the bases empty in seven of last eight years.... July batting average of .351 was 6th-highest in A.L.... Started 23 games in cleanup spot: batted .312 and slugged .649, with six home runs, 18 RBIs, and four game-winners; Angels were 17–6 in those games.... Hitless in 13 at bats as a pinch-hitter last season. Last pinch-hit: Sept. 2, 1984, while playing for Detroit.... Career batting averages: .269 vs. right-handers, .212 vs. left-handers.... Has homered in every current A.L. ballpark except Memorial Stadium, where he has a career batting average of .172.

Bob Kearney

Seattle Mariners	AB	H	2B	3B	HR	RRF	BB	SO	BA	SA	OBA
Season	305	74	14	1	6	29	11	59	.243	.354	.277
vs. Left-Handed Pitchers	97	19	3	0	3	9	6	11	.196	.320	.257
vs. Right-Handed Pitchers	208	55	11	1	3	20	5	48	.264	.370	.287
Home	160	38	9	1	2	17	4	31	.238	.344	.263
Road	145	36	5	0	4	12	7	28	.248	.366	.292
Grass	115	29	3	0	3	10	6	19	.252	.357	.301
Artificial Turf	190	45	11	1	3	19	5	40	.237	.353	.263
April	34	1	0	0	0	3	3	4	.029	.029	.108
May	34	6	2	0	0	1	2	10	.176	.235	.222
June	72	19	2	1	4	14	2	13	.264	.486	.299
July	73	30	6	0	2	7	3	9	.411	.575	.442
August	79	14	4	0	0	3	1	20	.177	.228	.188
Sept./Oct.	13	4	0	0	0	1	0	3	.308	.308	.357
Leading Off Inn.	50	12	1	0	2	2	2	15	.240	.380	.269
Bases Empty	164	36	9	0	4	4	8	38	.220	.348	.260
Runners On	141	38	5	1	2	25	3	21	.270	.362	.297
Runners/Scor. Pos.	88	26	3	1	2	24	1	11	.295	.420	.315
Runners On/2 Out	66	18	3	0	1	14	2	10	.273	.364	.314
Scor. Pos./2 Out	46	14	2	0	1	14	1	5	.304	.413	.347
Late Inning Pressure	37	11	2	0	1	3	1	10	.297	.432	.316
Leading Off	4	0	0	0	0	0	0	2	.000	.000	.000
Bases Empty	26	7	2	0	1	1	0	6	.269	.462	.269
Runners On	11	4	0	0	0	2	1	4	.364	.364	.417
Runners/Scor. Pos.	4	1	0	0	0	2	1	1	.250	.250	.400

DRIVING IN RUNS	0 Out	1 Out	2 Out	Total	
From 1B	0/13	3/35	0/43	3/91	3%
From 2B	1/11	3/24	8/30	12/65	18%
From 3B	0/4	3/14	5/22	8/40	20%
Scoring Position	1/15	6/38	13/52	20/105	19%
Scor. Pos. %	7%	16%	25%	19%	
Driving In Runners from 3B with Less than Two Out:			3/18	17%	

Loves to face: Bruce Kison (3-for-3, 2 2B, 1 HR)
Hates to face: Dennis Rasmussen (0-for-11)
Made 95 starts at catcher until a Walt Terrell pitch fractured his wrist, ending his season on Sept. 6.... Led major-league catchers in fielding percentage (.995) last season; his three errors all came within an eight-game span in early June.... Delivered only three of 18 runners from third base with less than two outs last season; that rate of 17 percent is the lowest in the 11 years that we've been keeping the data (minimum: 15 opportunities).... Nearly set another record: his ratio of 9.6 strikeouts per walk vs. right-handed pitchers last season was 2d-highest in majors over past 11 years (minimum: 40 SO).... Got his first hit of 1985 on his 2d at bat; got his 2d hit on his 36th at bat.... Batting average with runners in scoring position was higher than overall batting average for first time in career.

Dave Kingman

Oakland As	AB	H	2B	3B	HR	RRF	BB	SO	BA	SA	OBA
Season	592	141	16	0	30	96	62	114	.238	.417	.309
vs. Left-Handed Pitchers	176	43	3	0	13	38	23	32	.244	.483	.325
vs. Right-Handed Pitchers	416	98	13	0	17	58	39	82	.236	.389	.302
Home	278	62	10	0	14	45	35	58	.223	.410	.312
Road	314	79	6	0	16	51	27	56	.252	.424	.305
Grass	481	113	14	0	26	86	56	94	.235	.426	.313
Artificial Turf	111	28	2	0	4	10	6	20	.252	.378	.288
April	75	17	4	0	4	12	12	12	.227	.440	.333
May	95	27	2	0	7	18	12	21	.284	.526	.364
June	108	24	1	0	8	24	8	23	.222	.454	.277
July	108	27	5	0	3	9	5	16	.250	.380	.278
August	105	25	2	0	4	18	12	21	.238	.371	.322
Sept./Oct.	101	21	2	0	4	15	13	21	.208	.347	.288
Leading Off Inn.	145	36	4	0	9	9	10	28	.248	.462	.301
Bases Empty	309	77	7	0	18	18	32	57	.249	.447	.322
Runners On	283	64	9	0	12	78	30	57	.226	.385	.295
Runners/Scor. Pos.	146	32	4	0	6	63	20	29	.219	.370	.299
Runners On/2 Out	133	27	3	0	6	30	20	28	.203	.361	.307
Scor. Pos./2 Out	69	13	0	0	3	21	15	16	.188	.319	.333
Late Inning Pressure	77	19	0	0	6	9	14	13	.247	.481	.359
Leading Off	20	5	0	0	4	4	4	3	.250	.850	.375
Bases Empty	43	13	0	0	5	5	8	7	.302	.651	.412
Runners On	34	6	0	0	1	4	6	6	.176	.265	.293
Runners/Scor. Pos.	15	1	0	0	0	2	5	3	.067	.067	.286

DRIVING IN RUNS	0 Out	1 Out	2 Out	Total	
From 1B	2/47	4/82	7/88	13/217	6%
From 2B	7/18	3/39	9/47	19/104	18%
From 3B	7/12	19/30	8/29	34/71	48%
Scoring Position	14/30	22/69	17/76	53/175	30%
Scor. Pos. %	47%	32%	22%	30%	
Driving In Runners from 3B with Less than Two Out:			26/42	62%	

Loves to face: Matt Young (.714, 5-for-7, 3 HR)
Hates to face: Ron Romanick (0-for-18, 4 SO)
Has homered in every current major-league stadium except Memorial and County.... Last year's home-run rate of one every 19.7 at bats, good for you or me, was poorest of his 15-year career.... Homered twice in a game only once last year. His homers were not exactly an inspiration for his teammates: Oakland went 13–16 in games in which he homered, the most "home run losses" by any player in majors.... 11-year totals with the bases loaded: batting .266, slugging .681, with 12 home runs and 101 RRFs in 113 plate appearances; 23 strikeouts and only three run-scoring walks.... In two years with A's, has batted .300 and slugged .551 in day games, .222 and .401 at night.... Fly-ball hitter: 0.72 G/A ratio last season.... His 62 walks last season were a career-high.

Ron Kittle

Chicago White Sox	AB	H	2B	3B	HR	RRF	BB	SO	BA	SA	OBA
Season	379	87	12	0	26	63	31	92	.230	.467	.295
vs. Left-Handed Pitchers	148	35	3	0	10	25	18	37	.236	.459	.323
vs. Right-Handed Pitchers	231	52	9	0	16	38	13	55	.225	.472	.276
Home	199	48	8	0	12	29	15	42	.241	.462	.300
Road	180	39	4	0	14	34	16	50	.217	.472	.290
Grass	316	72	11	0	19	49	28	77	.228	.443	.297
Artificial Turf	63	15	1	0	7	14	3	15	.238	.587	.284
April	30	4	2	0	0	3	3	11	.133	.200	.212
May	53	10	0	0	5	8	4	17	.189	.472	.259
June	65	15	3	0	3	7	6	15	.231	.415	.301
July	20	2	1	0	0	1	2	4	.100	.150	.182
August	102	26	2	0	6	11	9	27	.255	.451	.321
Sept./Oct.	109	30	4	0	12	33	7	18	.275	.642	.328
Leading Off Inn.	79	17	2	0	4	4	7	19	.215	.392	.295
Bases Empty	218	56	9	0	16	16	19	50	.257	.518	.328
Runners On	161	31	3	0	10	47	12	42	.193	.398	.250
Runners/Scor. Pos.	78	20	3	0	5	37	5	23	.256	.487	.294
Runners On/2 Out	71	13	1	0	4	20	5	17	.183	.366	.237
Scor. Pos./2 Out	36	9	1	0	2	16	4	10	.250	.444	.325
Late Inning Pressure	47	7	0	0	1	4	6	17	.149	.213	.259
Leading Off	14	1	0	0	0	0	2	8	.071	.071	.188
Bases Empty	34	3	0	0	0	0	5	15	.088	.088	.225
Runners On	13	4	0	0	1	4	1	2	.308	.538	.357
Runners/Scor. Pos.	6	2	0	0	1	4	0	1	.333	.833	.333

DRIVING IN RUNS	0 Out	1 Out	2 Out	Total	
From 1B	2/26	2/45	3/56	7/127	6%
From 2B	3/9	3/24	7/26	13/59	22%
From 3B	5/7	6/13	6/16	17/36	47%
Scoring Position	8/16	9/37	13/42	30/95	32%
Scor. Pos. %	50%	24%	31%	32%	
Driving In Runners from 3B with Less than Two Out:			11/20	55%	

Loves to face: Jim Clancy (.500, 8-for-16, 4 HR)
Hates to face: Mike Boddicker (0-for-12, 6 SO)
Hit 12 home runs after Sept. 1 to tie Don Mattingly for A.L. lead, and led A.L. with six game-winning RBIs during that span.... One home run every 14.4 at bats vs. right-handers, 2d-best rate among A.L. right-handed batters.... 0-for-9 with seven strikeouts as a pinch-hitter last season.... Poor numbers in Late-Inning Pressure Situations: his .168 career batting average is the lowest of any player (minimum: 200 PA) in the 11-year history of *The Player Analysis*. And career strikeout rate of one every 3.3 plate appearances in LIP situations is also worst in majors over same span.... Annual batting averages with runners on base since 1983: .270, .250, .193.... Only 1.87 putouts per nine innings last year, 3d-lowest rate among A.L. outfielders (minimum: 300 innings).... Has homered in every A.L. park except Memorial Stadium.

Lee Lacy

Baltimore Orioles	AB	H	2B	3B	HR	RRF	BB	SO	BA	SA	OBA
Season	492	144	22	4	9	50	39	95	.293	.409	.343
vs. Left-Handed Pitchers	166	52	9	1	5	16	15	29	.313	.470	.375
vs. Right-Handed Pitchers	326	92	13	3	4	34	24	66	.282	.377	.327
Home	250	77	13	0	3	23	20	55	.308	.396	.358
Road	242	67	9	4	6	27	19	40	.277	.421	.328
Grass	436	129	22	2	9	43	36	91	.296	.417	.349
Artificial Turf	56	15	0	2	0	7	3	4	.268	.339	.300
April	0	0	0	0	0	0	0	0	.000	.000	.000
May	77	20	2	0	0	7	3	13	.260	.286	.284
June	111	36	5	1	3	11	6	24	.324	.468	.353
July	107	39	5	2	1	13	10	19	.364	.477	.417
August	105	29	5	0	5	14	9	19	.276	.467	.333
Sept./Oct.	92	20	5	1	0	5	11	20	.217	.293	.305
Leading Off Inn.	103	26	4	2	2	2	3	15	.252	.388	.274
Bases Empty	293	82	12	4	6	6	19	56	.280	.410	.326
Runners On	199	62	10	0	3	44	20	39	.312	.407	.367
Runners/Scor. Pos.	115	36	3	0	3	41	16	25	.313	.417	.384
Runners On/2 Out	75	18	3	0	1	12	9	16	.240	.320	.321
Scor. Pos./2 Out	49	12	1	0	1	11	7	12	.245	.327	.339
Late Inning Pressure	64	19	1	0	3	5	8	12	.297	.453	.378
Leading Off	12	3	0	0	0	0	0	0	.250	.250	.250
Bases Empty	40	12	1	0	2	2	2	8	.300	.475	.333
Runners On	24	7	0	0	1	3	6	4	.292	.417	.438
Runners/Scor. Pos.	10	2	0	0	1	3	5	3	.200	.500	.471

DRIVING IN RUNS	0 Out	1 Out	2 Out	Total	
From 1B	1/41	1/50	1/49	3/140	2%
From 2B	0/13	5/40	6/38	11/91	12%
From 3B	2/6	21/25	4/23	27/54	50%
Scoring Position	2/19	26/65	10/61	38/145	26%
Scor. Pos. %	11%	40%	16%	26%	
Driving In Runners from 3B with Less than Two Out:			23/31	74%	

Loves to face: Gary Lavelle (.423, 11-for-26, 1 HR)
Hates to face: Walt Terrell (0-for-9, 4 SO)
Played first game on May 13 after missing 28 games due to springtime injury, and was batted in leadoff spot by Joe Altobelli. After Weaver took over, however, Earl noted that Lacy hardly ever walks (about once every 14 plate appearances, and even less when he leads off an inning), and dropped him to number two, where he batted .306 in 79 starts.... First game at Tiger Stadium was memorable: one home run to lead off the game, another to win it in the 11th inning (June 10).... Batted over .310 with runners in scoring position for third time in past four seasons.... Over last 11 years, has driven in only 21 percent of runners from scoring position in Late-Inning Pressure Situations.

Carney Lansford

Oakland As	AB	H	2B	3B	HR	RRF	BB	SO	BA	SA	OBA
Season	401	111	18	2	13	47	18	27	.277	.429	.311
vs. Left-Handed Pitchers	131	31	5	1	3	12	6	7	.237	.359	.266
vs. Right-Handed Pitchers	270	80	13	1	10	35	12	20	.296	.463	.332
Home	205	62	10	1	7	26	6	11	.302	.463	.321
Road	196	49	8	1	6	21	12	16	.250	.393	.300
Grass	338	94	13	1	13	43	14	21	.278	.438	.308
Artificial Turf	63	17	5	1	0	4	4	6	.270	.381	.324
April	85	19	1	1	1	8	6	4	.224	.294	.280
May	95	27	5	0	6	14	5	10	.284	.526	.320
June	115	33	4	0	5	16	4	7	.287	.452	.314
July	92	30	8	1	1	9	2	5	.326	.467	.344
August	3	0	0	0	0	0	1	0	.000	.000	.250
Sept./Oct.	11	2	0	0	0	0	0	1	.182	.182	.182
Leading Off Inn.	79	16	3	0	2	2	5	6	.203	.316	.250
Bases Empty	251	61	7	2	6	6	11	18	.243	.359	.278
Runners On	150	50	11	0	7	41	7	9	.333	.547	.364
Runners/Scor. Pos.	85	22	7	0	3	33	7	6	.259	.447	.313
Runners On/2 Out	52	17	5	0	3	19	2	2	.327	.596	.364
Scor. Pos./2 Out	32	11	3	0	1	15	2	2	.344	.531	.400
Late Inning Pressure	54	10	2	0	1	6	3	6	.185	.278	.237
Leading Off	11	2	0	0	0	0	3	3	.182	.182	.357
Bases Empty	29	3	0	0	0	0	3	5	.103	.103	.188
Runners On	25	7	2	0	1	6	0	1	.280	.480	.296
Runners/Scor. Pos.	18	4	1	0	1	6	0	1	.222	.444	.250

DRIVING IN RUNS	0 Out	1 Out	2 Out	Total	
From 1B	1/37	1/26	3/35	5/98	5%
From 2B	2/17	3/21	7/21	12/59	20%
From 3B	7/11	4/14	6/15	17/40	43%
Scoring Position	9/28	7/35	13/36	29/99	29%
Scor. Pos. %	32%	20%	36%	29%	
Driving In Runners from 3B with Less than Two Out:			11/25	44%	

Loves to face: Milt Wilcox (.434, 23-for-53, 5 HR)
Hates to face: Don Sutton (0-for-8, 2 SO)
Failed by 11 games to meet 108-game requirement for individual league fielding championship. His .976 percentage at third base would have been good enough to top the leader, Rance Mulliniks (.971).... But his rate of only 1.29 assists per nine innings was dreadful; the league average for third basemen was 2.04, and among players who fielded 300 innings at third, the next-lowest rate was 1.74, by Mulliniks. ... Batting .429 (15-for-35) with the bases loaded since 1981.... Oakland had a 10–1 record in games in which he homered.... Has hit for a higher average against right-handed pitchers than he has against left-handers in three of last four seasons, leaving him with career marks of .306 vs. left-handers, .288 vs. right-handers.... Has homered in every current A.L. ballpark except Yankee Stadium.

Rudy Law

Chicago White Sox	AB	H	2B	3B	HR	RRF	BB	SO	BA	SA	OBA
Season	390	101	21	6	4	36	27	40	.259	.374	.311
vs. Left-Handed Pitchers	25	9	1	1	0	4	0	1	.360	.480	.360
vs. Right-Handed Pitchers	365	92	20	5	4	32	27	39	.252	.367	.308
Home	192	52	12	1	4	14	14	19	.271	.406	.322
Road	198	49	9	5	0	22	13	21	.247	.343	.300
Grass	332	89	19	4	4	28	25	36	.268	.386	.324
Artificial Turf	58	12	2	2	0	8	2	4	.207	.310	.233
April	42	10	2	0	1	4	5	5	.238	.357	.319
May	69	15	6	0	1	4	4	10	.217	.348	.260
June	82	26	6	2	0	9	6	7	.317	.439	.371
July	38	7	2	1	0	5	2	3	.184	.289	.244
August	66	17	1	2	1	6	5	7	.258	.379	.310
Sept./Oct.	93	26	4	1	1	8	5	8	.280	.376	.320
Leading Off Inn.	167	42	8	2	3	3	11	17	.251	.377	.306
Bases Empty	267	69	14	2	4	4	19	27	.258	.371	.313
Runners On	123	32	7	4	0	32	8	13	.260	.382	.308
Runners/Scor. Pos.	79	24	7	3	0	31	5	9	.304	.468	.349
Runners On/2 Out	47	12	2	2	0	13	5	6	.255	.383	.327
Scor. Pos./2 Out	29	11	2	2	0	13	4	4	.379	.586	.455
Late Inning Pressure	45	13	3	0	0	2	2	4	.289	.356	.333
Leading Off	14	7	2	0	0	0	0	2	.500	.643	.533
Bases Empty	25	11	3	0	0	0	1	3	.440	.560	.481
Runners On	20	2	0	0	0	2	1	1	.100	.100	.143
Runners/Scor. Pos.	12	2	0	0	0	2	1	1	.167	.167	.231

DRIVING IN RUNS	0 Out	1 Out	2 Out	Total	
From 1B	0/16	1/33	2/28	3/77	4%
From 2B	2/17	5/22	8/23	15/62	24%
From 3B	2/4	9/16	3/10	14/30	47%
Scoring Position	4/21	14/38	11/33	29/92	32%
Scor. Pos. %	19%	37%	33%	32%	
Driving In Runners from 3B with Less than Two Out:			11/20	55%	

Loves to face: Kirk McCaskill (.625, 5-for-8)
Hates to face: Ray Burris (.036, 1-for-28)
Fifth in A.L. last season with .379 average with runners in scoring position and two outs.... Batting average with runners in scoring position has been higher than overall average in each of last four seasons.... Stolen base percentage of .829 (29 of 35) was 5th-best in A.L. last season (minimum: 20 SB).... Has batted above .300 vs. left-handed pitchers in three of last four seasons, but the exception was 1984's .202 average. Maybe that's why he was permitted to start only four games against lefties last year, despite higher career batting average vs. left-handers (.274) than vs. right-handers (.272).... Career batting average of .358 (29-for-81) at County Stadium.... Ground-ball hitter: 1.43 G/A ratio last season. Career: 1.38.

Chet Lemon

Detroit Tigers	AB	H	2B	3B	HR	RRF	BB	SO	BA	SA	OBA
Season	517	137	28	4	18	68	45	93	.265	.439	.334
vs. Left-Handed Pitchers	149	48	8	2	8	26	14	32	.322	.564	.378
vs. Right-Handed Pitchers	368	89	20	2	10	42	31	61	.242	.389	.316
Home	243	70	12	3	9	37	20	41	.288	.473	.348
Road	274	67	16	1	9	31	25	52	.245	.409	.321
Grass	433	113	21	3	14	54	36	76	.261	.420	.328
Artificial Turf	84	24	7	1	4	14	9	17	.286	.536	.365
April	68	19	8	0	0	6	3	8	.279	.397	.329
May	81	20	3	1	1	8	11	14	.247	.346	.351
June	65	19	3	1	3	11	1	10	.292	.508	.299
July	105	27	7	1	0	3	8	21	.257	.343	.316
August	82	19	2	0	5	13	6	12	.232	.439	.301
Sept./Oct.	116	33	5	1	9	27	16	28	.284	.578	.381
Leading Off Inn.	112	33	6	1	4	4	6	19	.295	.473	.336
Bases Empty	296	81	18	2	9	9	25	53	.274	.439	.343
Runners On	221	56	10	2	9	59	20	40	.253	.439	.323
Runners/Scor. Pos.	122	28	6	1	4	46	13	27	.230	.393	.312
Runners On/2 Out	102	24	6	0	6	33	12	23	.235	.471	.328
Scor. Pos./2 Out	65	14	3	0	4	27	8	16	.215	.446	.320
Late Inning Pressure	78	22	5	0	2	11	7	15	.282	.423	.341
Leading Off	17	9	2	0	1	1	0	2	.529	.824	.529
Bases Empty	48	13	4	0	1	1	2	10	.271	.417	.300
Runners On	30	9	1	0	1	10	5	5	.300	.433	.400
Runners/Scor. Pos.	15	5	1	0	0	8	2	4	.333	.400	.412

DRIVING IN RUNS	0 Out	1 Out	2 Out	Total	
From 1B	2/39	3/53	8/75	13/167	8%
From 2B	2/20	6/33	11/49	19/102	19%
From 3B	4/6	6/11	8/30	18/47	38%
Scoring Position	6/26	12/44	19/79	37/149	25%
Scor. Pos. %	23%	27%	24%	25%	
Driving In Runners from 3B with Less than Two Out:			10/17	59%	

Loves to face: Bob McClure (.625, 10-for-16)
Hates to face: Bill Caudill (0-for-9, 2 SO)
Severe left/right differences over past two years: batting .357, slugging .605 vs. left-handers; .234 and .396 vs. right-handers. In nine major-league seasons before 1984, had hit better against righties (.283) than lefties (.277).... Batting .419 (13-for-31) with the bases loaded since '83.... Has driven in 38 percent of runners from scoring position in Late-Inning Pressure Situations over past three years.... Made three of his four errors last season in a single game at California, Aug. 25. On Aug. 26, 1984, Lemon was hit on the head by a fly ball at Anaheim and missed nine starts. Chet has not yet announced whether he'll accompany Tigers to Anaheim for Aug. 28–31 series this year.... He's on a roll: hit two homers in 1985 season finale. ... Over last four years, Lemon has six stolen bases, 18 caught stealings.

Bryan Little

Chicago White Sox	AB	H	2B	3B	HR	RRF	BB	SO	BA	SA	OBA
Season	188	47	9	1	2	28	26	21	.250	.340	.345
vs. Left-Handed Pitchers	6	0	0	0	0	1	1	3	.000	.000	.222
vs. Right-Handed Pitchers	182	47	9	1	2	27	25	18	.258	.352	.351
Home	100	32	5	0	2	16	13	13	.320	.430	.391
Road	88	15	4	1	0	12	13	8	.170	.239	.295
Grass	161	43	8	1	2	26	23	19	.267	.366	.362
Artificial Turf	27	4	1	0	0	2	3	2	.148	.185	.250
April	0	0	0	0	0	0	0	0	.000	.000	.000
May	8	3	1	0	0	0	1	0	.375	.500	.444
June	9	3	0	0	0	1	4	2	.333	.333	.538
July	43	9	0	1	0	5	4	5	.209	.256	.286
August	59	19	4	0	2	13	12	6	.322	.492	.437
Sept./Oct.	69	13	4	0	0	9	5	8	.188	.246	.256
Leading Off Inn.	32	8	1	0	0	0	6	3	.250	.281	.385
Bases Empty	111	26	4	0	1	1	16	13	.234	.297	.341
Runners On	77	21	5	1	1	27	10	8	.273	.403	.352
Runners/Scor. Pos.	47	15	4	1	1	27	6	6	.319	.511	.375
Runners On/2 Out	25	4	1	0	0	4	7	4	.160	.200	.364
Scor. Pos./2 Out	16	3	1	0	0	4	4	3	.188	.250	.350
Late Inning Pressure	14	3	0	0	0	1	2	1	.214	.214	.313
Leading Off	7	1	0	0	0	0	1	0	.143	.143	.250
Bases Empty	10	1	0	0	0	0	2	0	.100	.100	.250
Runners On	4	2	0	0	0	1	0	1	.500	.500	.500
Runners/Scor. Pos.	3	1	0	0	0	1	0	1	.333	.333	.333

DRIVING IN RUNS	0 Out	1 Out	2 Out	Total	
From 1B	0/16	0/21	0/13	0/50	0%
From 2B	3/8	4/15	2/10	9/33	27%
From 3B	8/8	7/12	2/7	17/27	63%
Scoring Position	11/16	11/27	4/17	26/60	43%
Scor. Pos. %	69%	41%	24%	43%	
Driving In Runners from 3B with Less than Two Out:			15/20	75%	

Loves to face: Dickie Noles (.625, 5-for-8)
Hates to face: Marty Bystrom (.059, 1-for-17)
Had widest home/road batting average disparity among A.L. players last season (minimum: 200 PA). . . . A nominal switch-hitter, but is seen batting right-handed about as often as Harold Baines; started 55 of Chicago's 109 games against right-handers, but none against lefties. . . . Career averages: .198 batting right-handed, .259 batting left-handed. . . . Career batting averages: .241 with bases empty, .266 with runners on base, .293 with runners in scoring position. . . . Had the game-winning RBI in Chicago's final two games last season, matching his total for his previous six months' work. . . . Hit two home runs last season for first time at any level in pro ball. . . . Ground-ball hitter: 1.63 G/A ratio last season. Career: 1.58. . . . Think this is easy? In 1984, he stranded all 42 base runners on second base when he batted.

Fred Lynn

Baltimore Orioles	AB	H	2B	3B	HR	RRF	BB	SO	BA	SA	OBA
Season	448	118	12	1	23	69	53	100	.263	.449	.339
vs. Left-Handed Pitchers	153	37	7	1	4	19	16	42	.242	.379	.312
vs. Right-Handed Pitchers	295	81	5	0	19	50	37	58	.275	.485	.352
Home	217	59	8	0	14	39	24	49	.272	.502	.343
Road	231	59	4	1	9	30	29	51	.255	.398	.335
Grass	364	98	9	0	20	57	41	82	.269	.459	.340
Artificial Turf	84	20	3	1	3	12	12	18	.238	.405	.333
April	72	23	2	0	3	8	8	13	.319	.472	.383
May	94	24	3	0	5	18	15	19	.255	.447	.358
June	91	21	1	0	5	15	5	19	.231	.407	.265
July	83	24	1	1	4	13	5	22	.289	.470	.333
August	68	13	4	0	2	5	12	19	.191	.338	.309
Sept./Oct.	40	13	1	0	4	10	8	8	.325	.650	.429
Leading Off Inn.	98	24	2	1	3	3	11	23	.245	.378	.327
Bases Empty	248	66	10	1	11	11	20	58	.266	.448	.323
Runners On	200	52	2	0	12	58	33	42	.260	.450	.356
Runners/Scor. Pos.	100	24	0	0	8	49	20	22	.240	.480	.349
Runners On/2 Out	92	18	1	0	3	19	17	21	.196	.304	.321
Scor. Pos./2 Out	56	11	0	0	3	18	11	13	.196	.357	.328
Late Inning Pressure	52	12	1	0	4	9	8	14	.231	.481	.333
Leading Off	16	2	0	0	1	1	2	8	.125	.313	.222
Bases Empty	34	8	1	0	2	2	2	12	.235	.441	.278
Runners On	18	4	0	0	2	7	6	2	.222	.556	.417
Runners/Scor. Pos.	13	3	0	0	2	7	5	1	.231	.692	.444

DRIVING IN RUNS	0 Out	1 Out	2 Out	Total	
From 1B	5/41	2/48	4/77	11/166	7%
From 2B	1/11	5/24	8/43	14/78	18%
From 3B	6/9	11/14	4/22	21/45	47%
Scoring Position	7/20	16/38	12/65	35/123	28%
Scor. Pos. %	35%	42%	18%	28%	
Driving In Runners from 3B with Less than Two Out:			17/23	74%	

Loves to face: Don Schulze (.538, 7-for-13, 1 HR)
Hates to face: Mike Moore (.080, 2-for-25, 9 SO)
Led A.L. with six 9th-inning home runs last season; three of them were in Late-Inning Pressure Situations. His LIP batting average has been lower than his overall batting average in 10 out of 11 years of *The Player Analysis* (11-year LIP average: .240). . . . More 11-year averages: .299 on grass fields, .237 on artificial turf. . . . Drove in only two runs in his first 14 games last season. RBI drought of 12 games (April 12–24) was his longest of the season. . . . Struck out 100 times for first time in career; to reach 100, he had to whiff in his last three at bats of the season, and he did. . . . Tom Seaver fanned him four times in a game, July 14. . . . Played 128 games last season; has been in majors since August 1974, but has played 150 games in a season only once: 1978.

Steve Lyons

Boston Red Sox	AB	H	2B	3B	HR	RRF	BB	SO	BA	SA	OBA
Season	371	98	14	3	5	30	32	64	.264	.358	.322
vs. Left-Handed Pitchers	67	18	1	1	1	6	7	14	.269	.358	.338
vs. Right-Handed Pitchers	304	80	13	2	4	24	25	50	.263	.359	.318
Home	193	51	8	1	4	19	17	35	.264	.378	.322
Road	178	47	6	2	1	11	15	29	.264	.337	.321
Grass	318	85	11	2	4	27	24	57	.267	.352	.317
Artificial Turf	53	13	3	1	1	3	8	7	.245	.396	.349
April	4	1	0	0	0	1	1	0	.250	.250	.400
May	16	4	0	0	2	4	1	1	.250	.625	.294
June	92	24	3	0	0	6	9	8	.261	.293	.330
July	90	27	5	0	1	6	10	19	.300	.389	.366
August	84	23	2	1	1	7	5	14	.274	.357	.311
Sept./Oct.	85	19	4	2	1	6	6	22	.224	.353	.275
Leading Off Inn.	110	28	6	1	1	1	7	18	.255	.355	.305
Bases Empty	213	58	11	2	2	2	16	35	.272	.371	.326
Runners On	158	40	3	1	3	28	16	29	.253	.342	.316
Runners/Scor. Pos.	92	26	2	1	2	26	11	14	.283	.391	.349
Runners On/2 Out	65	13	1	0	0	7	6	11	.200	.215	.268
Scor. Pos./2 Out	36	9	1	0	0	7	6	6	.250	.278	.357
Late Inning Pressure	59	15	3	0	1	7	8	8	.254	.356	.343
Leading Off	15	4	3	0	0	0	1	2	.267	.467	.313
Bases Empty	33	7	3	0	1	1	3	4	.212	.394	.278
Runners On	26	8	0	0	0	6	5	4	.308	.308	.419
Runners/Scor. Pos.	16	8	0	0	0	6	3	1	.500	.500	.579

DRIVING IN RUNS	0 Out	1 Out	2 Out	Total	
From 1B	1/25	1/42	0/46	2/113	2%
From 2B	3/14	3/34	4/30	10/78	13%
From 3B	4/7	6/13	3/15	13/35	37%
Scoring Position	7/21	9/47	7/45	23/113	20%
Scor. Pos. %	33%	19%	16%	20%	
Driving In Runners from 3B with Less than Two Out:			10/20	50%	

Loves to face: Urbano Lugo (.750, 3-for-4)
Hates to face: Charlie Hough (0-for-3, 3 SO)
For Boston fans who still haven't gotten over the trade of Fred Lynn, Sox brought up the closest thing to him—alphabetically, that is. . . . Didn't start his first game until May 27, but from then on started 77 of 91 games against right-handers, and 11 of 30 against left-handers. . . . Stolen base percentage of .571 (12 of 21) was lowest among A.L. players with 10 or more steals. . . . Batted .154 (2-for-13) as a pinch-hitter last season. . . . Four of his five career home runs have been hit at Fenway Park, the other in the Kingdome. . . . Batted .222 (2-for-9) with the bases loaded. The Red Sox had the most bases-loaded at bats in the A.L. by far; they had 160, and Baltimore was next with 132. The Sox hit .256 with the bags full; that ranked 13th—the league average was .285.

Rick Manning

Milwaukee Brewers	AB	H	2B	3B	HR	RRF	BB	SO	BA	SA	OBA
Season	216	47	9	1	2	19	14	19	.218	.296	.265
vs. Left-Handed Pitchers	34	8	1	0	1	4	3	6	.235	.353	.297
vs. Right-Handed Pitchers	182	39	8	1	1	15	11	13	.214	.286	.259
Home	101	22	3	1	1	6	5	9	.218	.297	.255
Road	115	25	6	0	1	13	9	10	.217	.296	.274
Grass	171	34	5	1	1	12	9	14	.199	.257	.239
Artificial Turf	45	13	4	0	1	7	5	5	.289	.444	.360
April	23	6	0	0	0	1	1	1	.261	.261	.292
May	24	9	3	0	0	3	0	3	.375	.500	.375
June	55	9	2	1	0	2	3	5	.164	.236	.207
July	33	8	0	0	1	3	5	3	.242	.333	.342
August	41	7	1	0	0	1	2	3	.171	.195	.209
Sept./Oct.	40	8	3	0	1	9	3	4	.200	.350	.256
Leading Off Inn.	49	10	2	1	0	0	2	2	.204	.286	.235
Bases Empty	120	25	6	1	0	0	7	10	.208	.275	.252
Runners On	96	22	3	0	2	19	7	9	.229	.323	.282
Runners/Scor. Pos.	51	11	2	0	1	17	5	5	.216	.314	.286
Runners On/2 Out	49	8	1	0	1	5	5	7	.163	.245	.241
Scor. Pos./2 Out	28	2	0	0	0	3	4	5	.071	.071	.188
Late Inning Pressure	40	6	1	0	1	4	0	3	.150	.250	.150
Leading Off	6	0	0	0	0	0	0	0	.000	.000	.000
Bases Empty	22	2	1	0	0	0	0	2	.091	.136	.091
Runners On	18	4	0	0	1	4	0	1	.222	.389	.222
Runners/Scor. Pos.	8	1	0	0	0	2	0	0	.125	.125	.125

DRIVING IN RUNS	0 Out	1 Out	2 Out	Total	
From 1B	0/15	1/19	1/35	2/69	3%
From 2B	1/5	4/12	0/19	5/36	14%
From 3B	1/1	5/8	3/16	9/25	36%
Scoring Position	2/6	9/20	3/35	14/61	23%
Scor. Pos. %	33%	45%	9%	23%	
Driving In Runners from 3B with Less than Two Out:			6/9	67%	

Loves to face: Luis Sanchez (.833, 5-for-6)
Hates to face: Ron Guidry (.075, 3-for-40, 11 SO)
Not including strike season, Manning's teams have finished season an average of 22.65 games behind division leaders; closest race he has experienced was in 1983, when Brewers, who were only two and a half games behind when they acquired Manning in June, finished fifth, 11 games behind Baltimore. . . . Started 54 of 106 games against right-handers, only two against lefties. At bats against left-handers have dwindled from over 200 in 1982 and '83, to 80 in '84, to 34 last year. . . . Batting average of .071 with two outs and runners in scoring position was lowest in majors last year. . . . Made errors in each of his last two starts of the season, the first time since 1982 that he has had errors in consecutive games. Those errors reduced his 1985 fielding percentage to .976, lowest of his career. . . . Ground-ball hitter: 1.59 G/A ratio last season. Career: 1.45.

Don Mattingly

New York Yankees	AB	H	2B	3B	HR	RRF	BB	SO	BA	SA	OBA
Season	652	211	48	3	35	150	56	41	.324	.567	.371
vs. Left-Handed Pitchers	264	76	20	0	18	67	18	16	.288	.568	.328
vs. Right-Handed Pitchers	388	135	28	3	17	83	38	25	.348	.567	.400
Home	318	107	21	1	22	89	24	21	.336	.616	.374
Road	334	104	27	2	13	61	32	20	.311	.521	.368
Grass	548	180	40	2	29	130	51	33	.328	.568	.379
Artificial Turf	104	31	8	1	6	20	5	8	.298	.567	.324
April	72	22	7	1	0	14	2	5	.306	.431	.325
May	99	31	6	0	5	27	12	6	.313	.525	.377
June	108	29	7	1	1	14	9	8	.269	.380	.317
July	113	38	11	1	6	27	11	4	.336	.611	.383
August	118	46	8	0	11	26	12	6	.390	.737	.447
Sept./Oct.	142	45	9	0	12	42	10	12	.317	.634	.357
Leading Off Inn.	98	31	10	1	6	6	5	8	.316	.622	.356
Bases Empty	337	110	24	3	19	19	21	26	.326	.585	.369
Runners On	315	101	24	0	16	131	35	15	.321	.549	.373
Runners/Scor. Pos.	174	55	14	0	4	100	29	8	.316	.466	.385
Runners On/2 Out	94	28	10	0	1	37	14	4	.298	.436	.389
Scor. Pos./2 Out	65	23	9	0	1	36	13	3	.354	.538	.462
Late Inning Pressure	96	30	4	0	6	22	6	2	.313	.542	.353
Leading Off	14	3	1	0	1	1	1	1	.214	.500	.267
Bases Empty	51	17	1	0	2	2	1	2	.333	.471	.346
Runners On	45	13	3	0	4	20	5	0	.289	.622	.360
Runners/Scor. Pos.	26	8	2	0	1	14	5	0	.308	.500	.419

DRIVING IN RUNS	0 Out	1 Out	2 Out	Total	
From 1B	11/76	11/87	7/63	29/226	13%
From 2B	8/41	8/40	11/41	27/122	22%
From 3B	19/24	22/32	18/37	59/93	63%
Scoring Position	27/65	30/72	29/78	86/215	40%
Scor. Pos. %	42%	42%	37%	40%	
Driving In Runners from 3B with Less than Two Out:			41/56	73%	

Loves to face: Curt Wardle (.625, 5-for-8, 2 2B, 1 HR)
Hates to face: Matt Young (.200, 3-for-16, 6 SO)
First player since Ted Williams in 1957 to hit more than 30 home runs in a season while striking out fewer than 50 times. . . . Led majors last season with 18 home runs off left-handers; also led with 22 homers at home. . . . Amazingly, has only one extra-base hit, a double, in 49 career plate appearances with the bases loaded. . . . Career batting averages: .296 (one homer every 21.5 at bats) vs. left-handers, .337 (one homer every 27.3 at bats) vs. right-handers. . . . Career batting average of .458 (27-for-59) at the Oakland Coliseum, a pitchers' park for everyone else. . . . Selected in 19th round of 1979 draft. Teams were too busy stocking up for their touch football leagues: Jay Schroeder (1st round), Dan Marino (4th), and John Elway (18th) were all selected by various teams ahead of Mattingly.

Oddibe McDowell

Texas Rangers	AB	H	2B	3B	HR	RRF	BB	SO	BA	SA	OBA
Season	406	97	14	5	18	44	36	85	.239	.431	.304
vs. Left-Handed Pitchers	123	30	6	4	3	8	10	34	.244	.431	.311
vs. Right-Handed Pitchers	283	67	8	1	15	36	26	51	.237	.431	.301
Home	203	54	4	3	10	25	15	35	.266	.463	.323
Road	203	43	10	2	8	19	21	50	.212	.399	.286
Grass	346	82	10	4	15	37	31	70	.237	.419	.305
Artificial Turf	60	15	4	1	3	7	5	15	.250	.500	.299
April	0	0	0	0	0	0	0	0	.000	.000	.000
May	48	8	2	1	0	10	1	9	.167	.250	.192
June	105	26	5	1	3	10	7	20	.248	.400	.295
July	108	28	3	2	8	13	7	31	.259	.546	.310
August	90	21	4	0	3	4	13	17	.233	.378	.330
Sept./Oct.	55	14	0	1	4	7	8	8	.255	.509	.359
Leading Off Inn.	155	38	7	3	6	6	17	32	.245	.445	.324
Bases Empty	260	69	10	3	14	14	22	52	.265	.488	.330
Runners On	146	28	4	2	4	30	14	33	.192	.329	.259
Runners/Scor. Pos.	82	17	1	2	2	24	10	25	.207	.341	.287
Runners On/2 Out	60	10	1	2	1	12	7	16	.167	.300	.254
Scor. Pos./2 Out	40	8	0	2	0	9	5	13	.200	.300	.289
Late Inning Pressure	53	11	1	0	3	7	6	10	.208	.396	.300
Leading Off	12	2	0	0	1	1	2	2	.167	.417	.286
Bases Empty	28	7	0	0	2	2	3	5	.250	.464	.344
Runners On	25	4	1	0	1	5	3	5	.160	.320	.250
Runners/Scor. Pos.	14	2	0	0	0	2	2	4	.143	.143	.250

DRIVING IN RUNS	0 Out	1 Out	2 Out	Total	
From 1B	2/29	1/32	3/38	6/99	6%
From 2B	2/12	4/23	5/30	11/65	17%
From 3B	4/6	2/9	3/17	9/32	28%
Scoring Position	6/18	6/32	8/47	20/97	21%
Scor. Pos. %	33%	19%	17%	21%	
Driving In Runners from 3B with Less than Two Out:			6/15	40%	

Loves to face: Marty Bystrom (1.000, 2-for-2, 1 HR)
Hates to face: Frank Wills (0-for-9)
Hit for cycle on July 23 at age 22 and 10 months, the youngest A.L. player to do it since Jim Fregosi (22 and three) in 1964. Only other A.L. players to hit for cycle before 23d birthday: Joe Cronin, Joe DiMaggio, and Vic Wertz. Youngest ever in majors: Mel Ott (20 and two) in 1929. . . . Played first major-league game on May 19, after hitting .400 in 31 games at Oklahoma City. . . . Despite spotting the league six weeks, wound up leading A.L. rookies in homers (18) and stolen bases (25). . . . Homered in six of eight games, July 22–30, and in four of six games from Aug. 31 to Sept. 5. . . . Selected six times in various amateur baseball drafts before Rangers finally signed him: Cardinals, Jan. '81; Rangers, June '81; Yankees, Jan. '82; Blue Jays, June '82; Twins, June '83; Rangers, June '84.

Hal McRae

Kansas City Royals	AB	H	2B	3B	HR	RRF	BB	SO	BA	SA	OBA
Season	320	83	19	0	14	73	44	45	.259	.450	.349
vs. Left-Handed Pitchers	150	35	11	0	8	31	26	20	.233	.467	.345
vs. Right-Handed Pitchers	170	48	8	0	6	42	18	25	.282	.435	.353
Home	165	44	11	0	7	40	21	24	.267	.461	.349
Road	155	39	8	0	7	33	23	21	.252	.439	.348
Grass	133	32	8	0	4	23	17	17	.241	.391	.327
Artificial Turf	187	51	11	0	10	50	27	28	.273	.492	.364
April	10	2	1	0	0	2	4	1	.200	.300	.400
May	43	8	2	0	1	2	6	4	.186	.302	.286
June	30	9	2	0	4	15	7	2	.300	.767	.432
July	70	19	3	0	4	20	3	7	.271	.486	.311
August	89	25	5	0	2	21	13	17	.281	.404	.369
Sept./Oct.	78	20	6	0	3	13	11	14	.256	.449	.348
Leading Off Inn.	66	19	6	0	3	3	7	11	.288	.515	.365
Bases Empty	157	33	8	0	5	5	19	30	.210	.357	.299
Runners On	163	50	11	0	9	68	25	15	.307	.540	.395
Runners/Scor. Pos.	105	33	6	0	4	54	15	10	.314	.486	.393
Runners On/2 Out	80	21	4	0	4	28	15	11	.263	.463	.379
Scor. Pos./2 Out	53	13	2	0	0	18	9	8	.245	.283	.355
Late Inning Pressure	39	11	1	0	2	7	10	7	.282	.462	.429
Leading Off	7	3	0	0	0	0	2	3	.429	.429	.556
Bases Empty	19	8	0	0	1	1	4	4	.421	.579	.522
Runners On	20	3	1	0	1	6	6	3	.150	.350	.346
Runners/Scor. Pos.	12	3	1	0	1	6	5	2	.250	.583	.471

DRIVING IN RUNS	0 Out	1 Out	2 Out	Total	
From 1B	2/20	3/36	7/49	12/105	11%
From 2B	3/12	9/27	9/36	21/75	28%
From 3B	5/5	13/19	8/26	26/50	52%
Scoring Position	8/17	22/46	17/62	47/125	38%
Scor. Pos. %	47%	48%	27%	38%	
Driving In Runners from 3B with Less than Two Out:			18/24	75%	

Loves to face: Neal Heaton (.556, 10-for-18, 2 HR)
Hates to face: Mark Langston (0-for-8, 2 SO)
Batted 97 points higher with runners on base than with the bases empty, 5th-largest such difference in A.L. . . . Despite being platooned over first half of season, wound up hitting 49 points higher vs. right-handers than vs. southpaws; batting average vs. left-handers (.233) was his lowest in 11 years of *The Player Analysis*. . . . For 2d consecutive season, had major improvement over latter half of season: in 1984, hit 74 points higher following All-Star Game; in 1985, 87 points higher. What's ironic is that in '84, he began year as full-time DH and only blossomed after being platooned; reverse was true in '85. . . . Batted .091 (2-for-22) vs. Baltimore last season, but both of his hits were home runs. . . . Batted .167 (4-for-24) as a pinch-hitter; batted only three times in that role during World Series (an out, a walk, a hit-by-pitch).

Bobby Meacham

New York Yankees	AB	H	2B	3B	HR	RRF	BB	SO	BA	SA	OBA
Season	481	105	16	2	1	50	54	102	.218	.266	.302
vs. Left-Handed Pitchers	187	42	6	1	0	18	20	42	.225	.267	.313
vs. Right-Handed Pitchers	294	63	10	1	1	32	34	60	.214	.265	.295
Home	231	39	5	1	1	17	23	59	.169	.212	.247
Road	250	66	11	1	0	33	31	43	.264	.316	.352
Grass	406	87	12	1	1	42	46	97	.214	.256	.298
Artificial Turf	75	18	4	1	0	8	8	5	.240	.320	.321
April	55	15	2	0	0	7	9	11	.273	.309	.375
May	73	20	6	0	0	14	15	15	.274	.356	.407
June	81	13	2	0	0	7	10	20	.160	.185	.253
July	77	20	1	2	0	6	5	13	.260	.325	.310
August	90	19	2	0	1	9	6	18	.211	.267	.268
Sept./Oct.	105	18	3	0	0	7	9	25	.171	.200	.241
Leading Off Inn.	108	24	3	1	1	1	13	20	.222	.296	.306
Bases Empty	255	48	5	2	1	1	30	59	.188	.235	.276
Runners On	226	57	11	0	0	49	24	43	.252	.301	.331
Runners/Scor. Pos.	127	33	7	0	0	46	18	26	.260	.315	.362
Runners On/2 Out	108	27	6	0	0	19	10	25	.250	.306	.331
Scor. Pos./2 Out	59	15	4	0	0	18	10	15	.254	.322	.389
Late Inning Pressure	63	12	2	0	0	4	5	16	.190	.222	.250
Leading Off	19	3	1	0	0	0	2	7	.158	.211	.238
Bases Empty	44	5	1	0	0	0	4	15	.114	.136	.188
Runners On	19	7	1	0	0	4	1	1	.368	.421	.400
Runners/Scor. Pos.	7	4	0	0	0	4	1	0	.571	.571	.625

DRIVING IN RUNS	0 Out	1 Out	2 Out	Total	
From 1B	1/33	2/51	2/81	5/165	3%
From 2B	1/15	7/38	9/45	17/98	17%
From 3B	7/11	12/23	8/35	27/69	39%
Scoring Position	8/26	19/61	17/80	44/167	26%
Scor. Pos. %	31%	31%	21%	26%	
Driving In Runners from 3B with Less than Two Out:			19/34	56%	

Loves to face: Bill Krueger (.500, 5-for-10)
Hates to face: Dave Stieb (.143, 2-for-14, 6 SO)
Batted more times with the bases loaded than any A.L. player last season (25); he also led the league in bases-loaded strikeouts (7) and bases-loaded walks (4). . . . Averaged 2.60 assists per nine innings, 2d-lowest rate in majors among shortstops (minimum: 300 innings); old Yankee buddy Roy Smalley kept him out of the cellar. . . . Made 13 of his 24 errors against Baltimore and Boston. . . . Tied with Gary Pettis for fewest extra-base hits (19) among A.L. batting qualifiers last year. . . . Home/road batting figures were a reversal from 1984's .318 at home, .193 on road. . . . Career batting average of .171 in Late-Inning Pressure Situations. . . . 102 strikeouts were most by a Yankee middle infielder since Frank Crosetti (105 in 1937). . . . Career batting average of .031 (1-for-32) at the Kingdome.

Paul Molitor

Milwaukee Brewers	AB	H	2B	3B	HR	RRF	BB	SO	BA	SA	OBA
Season	576	171	28	3	10	52	54	80	.297	.408	.356
vs. Left-Handed Pitchers	179	58	8	1	5	19	17	19	.324	.464	.384
vs. Right-Handed Pitchers	397	113	20	2	5	33	37	61	.285	.383	.343
Home	257	83	15	2	6	33	25	31	.323	.467	.382
Road	319	88	13	1	4	19	29	49	.276	.361	.334
Grass	471	144	25	2	7	43	44	61	.306	.412	.364
Artificial Turf	105	27	3	1	3	9	10	19	.257	.390	.319
April	71	23	2	0	1	7	10	12	.324	.394	.402
May	90	25	5	1	1	8	10	11	.278	.389	.347
June	107	37	8	1	5	16	13	18	.346	.579	.413
July	120	32	5	0	1	7	9	7	.267	.333	.321
August	45	12	1	0	0	4	2	12	.267	.289	.298
Sept./Oct.	143	42	7	1	2	10	10	20	.294	.399	.340
Leading Off Inn.	233	76	13	2	5	5	19	26	.326	.464	.377
Bases Empty	396	117	22	2	9	9	30	57	.295	.429	.347
Runners On	180	54	6	1	1	43	24	23	.300	.361	.375
Runners/Scor. Pos.	107	30	4	1	0	39	19	19	.280	.336	.377
Runners On/2 Out	83	23	2	0	0	18	13	10	.277	.301	.375
Scor. Pos./2 Out	53	14	2	0	0	18	11	9	.264	.302	.391
Late Inning Pressure	77	24	5	1	1	7	7	13	.312	.442	.365
Leading Off	23	9	2	0	0	0	2	1	.391	.478	.440
Bases Empty	53	16	4	0	1	1	4	8	.302	.434	.351
Runners On	24	8	1	1	0	6	3	5	.333	.458	.393
Runners/Scor. Pos.	14	3	1	1	0	6	3	5	.214	.429	.333

DRIVING IN RUNS	0 Out	1 Out	2 Out	Total	
From 1B	3/32	3/47	0/55	6/134	4%
From 2B	2/16	6/30	11/43	19/89	21%
From 3B	5/8	5/10	7/21	17/39	44%
Scoring Position	7/24	11/40	18/64	36/128	28%
Scor. Pos. %	29%	28%	28%	28%	
Driving In Runners from 3B with Less than Two Out:			10/18	56%	

Loves to face: Dave Righetti (.407, 11-for-27, 1 HR)
Hates to face: Mike Moore (0-for-14)
Mr. Bases-Empty Homer: of his last 23 home runs, 22 have been solo shots. . . . Leadoff batter in his first 115 starts last year, but surrendered that spot to Mike Felder in September. . . . June batting average of .346 was 5th-highest in A.L. . . . Career batting averages: .299 with runners on base, .278 with runners on base, .275 with runners in scoring position. . . . Has batted for a higher average vs. left-handers than against right-handers in each of last seven seasons (batted 10 points higher vs. righties as rookie in 1978). Career breakdown: .316 vs. left-handers, .281 right-handers. . . . Has homered in every current A.L. ballpark except Arlington Stadium. . . . Career batting average of .336 at Fenway Park.

Charlie Moore

Milwaukee Brewers	AB	H	2B	3B	HR	RRF	BB	SO	BA	SA	OBA
Season	349	81	13	4	0	33	27	53	.232	.292	.288
vs. Left-Handed Pitchers	123	35	6	2	0	15	15	14	.285	.366	.367
vs. Right-Handed Pitchers	226	46	7	2	0	18	12	39	.204	.252	.243
Home	169	43	8	4	0	18	9	29	.254	.349	.294
Road	180	38	5	0	0	15	18	24	.211	.239	.283
Grass	279	66	12	4	0	27	19	44	.237	.308	.287
Artificial Turf	70	15	1	0	0	6	8	9	.214	.229	.295
April	17	4	2	0	0	3	1	2	.235	.353	.278
May	62	17	4	2	0	5	8	13	.274	.403	.366
June	79	18	2	0	0	7	6	12	.228	.253	.282
July	74	12	1	1	0	8	5	12	.162	.203	.213
August	45	12	2	0	0	1	5	5	.267	.311	.340
Sept./Oct.	72	18	2	1	0	9	2	9	.250	.306	.270
Leading Off Inn.	70	14	2	0	0	0	4	13	.200	.229	.243
Bases Empty	182	44	7	1	0	0	14	32	.242	.291	.299
Runners On	167	37	6	3	0	33	13	21	.222	.293	.276
Runners/Scor. Pos.	94	21	5	2	0	31	10	10	.223	.319	.295
Runners On/2 Out	75	16	2	2	0	14	4	11	.213	.293	.253
Scor. Pos./2 Out	50	11	2	2	0	14	4	5	.220	.340	.278
Late Inning Pressure	58	14	1	0	0	7	3	6	.241	.259	.279
Leading Off	9	1	0	0	0	0	1	2	.111	.111	.200
Bases Empty	26	5	0	0	0	0	2	4	.192	.192	.250
Runners On	32	9	1	0	0	7	1	2	.281	.313	.303
Runners/Scor. Pos.	20	4	1	0	0	6	1	1	.200	.250	.238

DRIVING IN RUNS	0 Out	1 Out	2 Out	Total	
From 1B	2/28	1/40	2/53	5/121	4%
From 2B	3/10	3/26	6/39	12/75	16%
From 3B	2/3	8/18	6/15	16/36	44%
Scoring Position	5/13	11/44	12/54	28/111	25%
Scor. Pos. %	38%	25%	22%	25%	
Driving In Runners from 3B with Less than Two Out:			10/21	48%	

Loves to face: Jim Beattie (.471, 8-for-17)
Hates to face: Dan Petry (.037, 1-for-27)
Occupation: catcher, 1973–81; outfielder, 1982–84; catcher: 1985. Not too many catchers become regular outfielders; even fewer return to their original position. Yogi Berra did it, but he was never the Yankees' *regular* catcher in his reincarnation there. . . . Maybe it's not advisable, after all: Moore had the lowest fielding percentage (.977) of any major-league catcher last season (minimum: 80 games). . . . No home runs in 349 at bats; only one A.L. player had more at bats without a homer: Curtis Wilkerson, 360. But it's more surprising from Moore, who had 32 homers over the 10 previous years. . . . Has had only two extra-base hits (both doubles) in 83 plate appearances with the bases loaded in the last 11 years. . . . Gimme that ol' time religion: career batting average of .346 at Fenway Park, .170 at Royals Stadium.

Lloyd Moseby

Toronto Blue Jays	AB	H	2B	3B	HR	RRF	BB	SO	BA	SA	OBA
Season	584	151	30	7	18	75	76	91	.259	.426	.345
vs. Left-Handed Pitchers	234	60	11	0	7	22	24	48	.256	.393	.330
vs. Right-Handed Pitchers	350	91	19	7	11	53	52	43	.260	.449	.355
Home	283	73	16	5	11	48	38	43	.258	.466	.344
Road	301	78	14	2	7	27	38	48	.259	.389	.347
Grass	225	53	9	2	6	19	33	33	.236	.373	.338
Artificial Turf	359	98	21	5	12	56	43	58	.273	.460	.350
April	71	20	4	0	3	8	14	12	.282	.465	.395
May	98	24	8	3	1	9	13	20	.245	.418	.339
June	110	26	6	1	1	11	15	13	.236	.336	.323
July	86	17	5	1	1	8	11	18	.198	.314	.296
August	103	31	3	2	4	17	9	13	.301	.485	.365
Sept./Oct.	116	33	4	0	8	22	14	15	.284	.526	.359
Leading Off Inn.	105	26	3	1	4	4	17	17	.248	.410	.352
Bases Empty	341	76	12	4	9	9	48	57	.223	.361	.322
Runners On	243	75	18	3	9	66	28	34	.309	.519	.378
Runners/Scor. Pos.	122	34	6	3	4	49	17	21	.279	.475	.363
Runners On/2 Out	87	21	4	1	2	20	11	14	.241	.379	.333
Scor. Pos./2 Out	52	12	2	1	1	16	9	11	.231	.365	.355
Late Inning Pressure	76	18	3	1	0	8	8	12	.237	.303	.315
Leading Off	24	5	0	0	0	0	2	3	.208	.208	.269
Bases Empty	48	11	1	0	0	0	4	7	.229	.250	.302
Runners On	28	7	2	1	0	8	4	5	.250	.393	.333
Runners/Scor. Pos.	14	5	1	1	0	8	3	4	.357	.571	.429

DRIVING IN RUNS	0 Out	1 Out	2 Out	Total	
From 1B	5/60	5/51	4/57	14/168	8%
From 2B	2/22	10/32	8/42	20/96	21%
From 3B	5/8	12/24	5/18	22/50	44%
Scoring Position	7/30	22/56	13/60	42/146	29%
Scor. Pos. %	23%	39%	22%	29%	
Driving In Runners from 3B with Less than Two Out:			17/32	53%	

Loves to face: Dan Quisenberry (.500, 10-for-20)
Hates to face: Britt Burns (.129, 4-for-31, 11 SO)
Home run totals in his six years in the majors: 9, 9, 9, 18, 18, 18. Pencil him in for 27 this year. . . . Toronto had a 14–3 record in games in which he homered. . . . For first time in his career, batted higher in United States than in Canada, albeit by a single point. . . . Subject of subtle but helpful lineup change by Bobby Cox: Moseby batted 3d against right-handers through July 6, but batted only .233 with 21 RBIs in those 48 games. Cox then moved him to 2d, where he also batted against lefties; in the remaining 46 games against right-handed starters, he hit .259 with 28 RBIs. . . . Batting .571 (8-for-14) with the bases loaded over past two seasons, with 22 RRFs in 18 plate appearances. . . . Has homered in every current A.L. ballpark except Royals Stadium, Quisenberry notwithstanding.

Darryl Motley

Kansas City Royals	AB	H	2B	3B	HR	RRF	BB	SO	BA	SA	OBA
Season	383	85	20	1	17	52	18	57	.222	.413	.257
vs. Left-Handed Pitchers	161	41	10	1	8	23	9	20	.255	.478	.295
vs. Right-Handed Pitchers	222	44	10	0	9	29	9	37	.198	.365	.230
Home	187	43	11	1	6	24	9	25	.230	.396	.264
Road	196	42	9	0	11	28	9	32	.214	.429	.251
Grass	154	34	8	0	8	22	6	24	.221	.429	.253
Artificial Turf	229	51	12	1	9	30	12	33	.223	.402	.260
April	69	13	4	0	2	4	5	8	.188	.333	.253
May	59	13	4	0	2	7	1	9	.220	.390	.226
June	49	15	0	0	4	9	2	6	.306	.551	.327
July	61	14	4	0	2	10	1	16	.230	.393	.254
August	50	11	3	1	3	10	3	6	.220	.500	.259
Sept./Oct.	95	19	5	0	4	12	6	12	.200	.379	.245
Leading Off Inn.	98	23	6	1	5	5	3	16	.235	.469	.265
Bases Empty	226	47	11	1	10	10	10	32	.208	.398	.245
Runners On	157	38	9	0	7	42	8	25	.242	.433	.275
Runners/Scor. Pos.	92	19	4	0	5	34	5	16	.207	.413	.243
Runners On/2 Out	62	15	2	0	4	18	3	15	.242	.468	.277
Scor. Pos./2 Out	37	9	1	0	4	17	3	11	.243	.595	.300
Late Inning Pressure	65	14	4	0	1	7	1	10	.215	.323	.221
Leading Off	17	3	3	0	0	0	0	0	.176	.353	.176
Bases Empty	35	8	4	0	1	1	0	3	.229	.429	.229
Runners On	30	6	0	0	0	6	1	7	.200	.200	.212
Runners/Scor. Pos.	19	4	0	0	0	6	1	4	.211	.211	.227

DRIVING IN RUNS	0 Out	1 Out	2 Out	Total	
From 1B	2/26	2/50	3/45	7/121	6%
From 2B	1/17	4/29	6/29	11/75	15%
From 3B	2/4	9/19	5/17	16/40	40%
Scoring Position	3/21	13/48	11/46	27/115	23%
Scor. Pos. %	14%	27%	24%	23%	
Driving In Runners from 3B with Less than Two Out:			11/23	48%	

Loves to face: Frank Viola (.421, 8-for-19, 3 HR)
Hates to face: John Butcher (.067, 1-for-15)
No one may ever top Bill Mazeroski for a dramatic home run in Game Seven of a World Series, but his homer has overshadowed subsequent seventh-game homers, each of which put a team ahead to stay, game-winning RBI-style: by Lou Johnson (1965), Roberto Clemente (1971), Bert Campaneris (1973), Willie Stargell (1979), and Darryl Motley (1985). . . . Motley started 48 of 49 games against left-handers, but only 50 of 113 (44 percent) against righties; he had started 70 percent of games against right-handers in 1984. . . . Career batting average of .524 (11-for-21) with the bases loaded. . . . Despite only 17 home runs last year, managed to hit at least one against every opposing A.L. team except Oakland. . . . Yearly batting averages in Late-Inning Pressure Situations since 1983: .313, .230, .215.

Rance Mulliniks

Toronto Blue Jays	AB	H	2B	3B	HR	RRF	BB	SO	BA	SA	OBA
Season	366	108	26	1	10	58	55	54	.295	.454	.383
vs. Left-Handed Pitchers	22	5	2	0	0	1	6	4	.227	.318	.393
vs. Right-Handed Pitchers	344	103	24	1	10	57	49	50	.299	.462	.382
Home	174	55	15	1	4	26	28	25	.316	.483	.407
Road	192	53	11	0	6	32	27	29	.276	.427	.360
Grass	168	45	10	0	5	29	25	25	.268	.417	.357
Artificial Turf	198	63	16	1	5	29	30	29	.318	.485	.404
April	47	9	4	0	1	5	8	12	.191	.340	.309
May	50	22	5	0	1	15	10	9	.440	.600	.525
June	68	18	3	0	2	10	13	8	.265	.397	.373
July	70	27	8	0	3	11	5	4	.386	.629	.421
August	59	13	1	1	3	8	6	11	.220	.424	.288
Sept./Oct.	72	19	5	0	0	9	13	10	.264	.333	.376
Leading Off Inn.	70	16	5	0	3	3	14	11	.229	.429	.357
Bases Empty	228	63	13	1	7	7	38	37	.276	.434	.380
Runners On	138	45	13	0	3	51	17	17	.326	.486	.388
Runners/Scor. Pos.	84	32	10	0	2	48	13	8	.381	.571	.441
Runners On/2 Out	46	16	2	0	1	16	7	9	.348	.457	.434
Scor. Pos./2 Out	36	13	2	0	1	16	5	7	.361	.500	.439
Late Inning Pressure	40	8	1	0	1	5	9	8	.200	.300	.340
Leading Off	14	5	0	0	1	1	3	3	.357	.571	.471
Bases Empty	25	7	0	0	1	1	6	6	.280	.400	.419
Runners On	15	1	1	0	0	4	3	2	.067	.133	.211
Runners/Scor. Pos.	9	1	1	0	0	4	2	1	.111	.222	.250

DRIVING IN RUNS	0 Out	1 Out	2 Out	Total	
From 1B	1/27	2/32	1/27	4/86	5%
From 2B	6/17	9/23	6/27	21/67	31%
From 3B	7/8	8/12	8/13	23/33	70%
Scoring Position	13/25	17/35	14/40	44/100	44%
Scor. Pos. %	52%	49%	35%	44%	
Driving In Runners from 3B with Less than Two Out:			15/20	75%	

Loves to face: Don Sutton (.571, 12-for-21, 1 HR)
Hates to face: Tom Seaver (0-for-15, 6 SO)
May be the toughest hitter in baseball when there's an opportunity to knock in a run: .381 batting average with runners in scoring position was 4th-highest in A.L. last season; in 1984, he finished 2d in A.L. in that category with .372 average. . . . Only clutch figure not up to snuff was his Late-Inning Pressure mark of .200; even including this year's average, however, his LIP mark since 1983 is .307. . . . Has batted over .300 with runners on base in each of last three seasons. . . . Usual platoon stuff: started only two games against left-handers last season; started all but two against righties. . . . Drove in 69.7 percent of runners from third base, highest A.L. average in *Player Analysis* history (minimum: 20 RRF). . . . Ground-ball hitter: 1.82 G/A ratio was 7th-highest in A.L. last year (minimum: 200 PA). Career average: 1.63.

Dwayne Murphy

Oakland As	AB	H	2B	3B	HR	RRF	BB	SO	BA	SA	OBA
Season	523	122	21	3	20	63	84	123	.233	.400	.340
vs. Left-Handed Pitchers	147	29	3	1	7	20	22	40	.197	.374	.297
vs. Right-Handed Pitchers	376	93	18	2	13	43	62	83	.247	.410	.357
Home	242	52	12	1	5	22	39	54	.215	.335	.326
Road	281	70	9	2	15	41	45	69	.249	.456	.353
Grass	424	97	15	3	18	54	71	100	.229	.406	.341
Artificial Turf	99	25	6	0	2	9	13	23	.253	.374	.339
April	69	13	3	0	3	6	20	14	.188	.362	.367
May	78	18	3	0	3	7	11	15	.231	.385	.337
June	91	22	4	0	6	11	14	20	.242	.484	.349
July	84	19	4	1	3	15	17	24	.226	.405	.356
August	109	26	4	1	1	12	13	31	.239	.321	.315
Sept./Oct.	92	24	3	1	4	12	9	19	.261	.446	.327
Leading Off Inn.	103	25	8	1	5	5	13	25	.243	.485	.333
Bases Empty	295	73	14	2	13	13	37	66	.247	.441	.335
Runners On	228	49	7	1	7	50	47	57	.215	.346	.346
Runners/Scor. Pos.	128	27	3	1	3	39	28	29	.211	.320	.344
Runners On/2 Out	93	20	4	1	5	22	22	23	.215	.441	.371
Scor. Pos./2 Out	55	11	1	1	3	16	13	12	.200	.418	.353
Late Inning Pressure	78	15	0	1	4	7	11	18	.192	.372	.297
Leading Off	17	4	0	1	2	2	2	3	.235	.706	.350
Bases Empty	54	12	0	1	3	3	5	10	.222	.426	.300
Runners On	24	3	0	0	1	4	6	8	.125	.250	.290
Runners/Scor. Pos.	12	0	0	0	0	2	4	4	.000	.000	.235

DRIVING IN RUNS	0 Out	1 Out	2 Out	Total	
From 1B	2/35	1/57	5/60	8/152	5%
From 2B	1/22	7/35	6/37	14/94	15%
From 3B	2/5	13/25	6/25	21/55	38%
Scoring Position	3/27	20/60	12/62	35/149	23%
Scor. Pos. %	11%	33%	19%	23%	
Driving In Runners from 3B with Less than Two Out:			15/30	50%	

Loves to face: Dan Petry (.387, 12-for-21, 4 HR)
Hates to face: Ron Davis (0-for-12, 6 SO)
RBI total suffered from absence of Rickey Henderson, falling from 88 to 59. In 1984, Murphy batted with 171 runners in scoring position; last year, that figure fell to 149. . . . What's the opposite of a plateau? Yearly batting averages with two outs and runners in scoring position since 1981: .357, .270, .229, .222, .200. . . . One of four major leaguers to have struck out 100 times in each of past four years (others: Reggie Jackson, Dale Murphy, Mike Schmidt—nice group!); last season's 123 whiffs were a career high. . . . Has now batted below .200 against left-handers twice in the past three years, but started 40 of Oakland's 54 games against left-handers last season. . . . You thought that Eddie Gaedel was good? Murphy pinch-hit four times last season and had four walks.

Eddie Murray

Baltimore Orioles	AB	H	2B	3B	HR	RRF	BB	SO	BA	SA	OBA
Season	583	173	37	1	31	128	84	68	.297	.523	.383
vs. Left-Handed Pitchers	203	58	14	0	10	41	32	29	.286	.502	.384
vs. Right-Handed Pitchers	380	115	23	1	21	87	52	39	.303	.534	.382
Home	291	86	19	0	15	66	49	29	.296	.515	.396
Road	292	87	18	1	16	62	35	39	.298	.531	.369
Grass	506	149	34	0	27	111	74	61	.294	.522	.382
Artificial Turf	77	24	3	1	4	17	10	7	.312	.532	.386
April	52	13	1	0	4	12	6	7	.250	.500	.350
May	101	29	9	1	2	19	10	12	.287	.455	.345
June	96	30	7	0	5	20	14	9	.313	.542	.389
July	103	29	6	0	7	30	16	10	.282	.544	.372
August	100	34	5	0	6	25	19	13	.340	.570	.442
Sept./Oct.	131	38	9	0	7	22	19	17	.290	.519	.380
Leading Off Inn.	143	37	6	0	6	6	19	21	.259	.427	.350
Bases Empty	317	77	11	0	15	15	42	39	.243	.420	.333
Runners On	266	96	26	1	16	113	42	29	.361	.647	.438
Runners/Scor. Pos.	138	51	15	0	11	96	25	19	.370	.717	.448
Runners On/2 Out	142	49	10	1	5	41	25	18	.345	.535	.446
Scor. Pos./2 Out	72	25	6	0	4	35	16	11	.347	.597	.472
Late Inning Pressure	66	22	5	0	6	25	8	6	.333	.682	.400
Leading Off	11	1	0	0	0	0	2	2	.091	.091	.231
Bases Empty	36	5	0	0	2	2	4	4	.139	.306	.225
Runners On	30	17	5	0	4	23	4	2	.567	1.133	.600
Runners/Scor. Pos.	15	9	4	0	3	20	2	0	.600	1.467	.611

DRIVING IN RUNS	0 Out	1 Out	2 Out	Total	
From 1B	7/45	7/63	9/104	23/212	11%
From 2B	9/23	11/36	17/60	37/119	31%
From 3B	12/16	15/18	10/20	37/54	69%
Scoring Position	21/39	26/54	27/80	74/173	43%
Scor. Pos. %	54%	48%	34%	43%	
Driving In Runners from 3B with Less than Two Out:			27/34	79%	

Loves to face: Britt Burns (.441, 15-for-34, 3 HR)
Hates to face: Joe Cowley (.071, 1-for-14, 1 HR)
Batting averages with runners on base (.361) and runners in scoring position (.370) were the best of a career marked by superb clutch performance. . . . Owns .445 career batting average (53-for-119, 12 doubles, 12 home runs) with the bases loaded; 172 RRFs in 151 plate appearances. Career bases-loaded slugging average of .866 is the best over the last 11 years (minimum: 50 AB). . . . Only player to have hit a grand-slam homer in each of last five years. . . . Career average of .324 in Late-Inning Pressure Situations, .407 when you blend in the phrase "with runners in scoring position," .424 when you also add in the words "and two outs". . . . Drove in 14 of 22 runners (63.6 percent) from scoring position in LIP Situations, best rate in majors last season. . . . With all that, has not hit a 9th-inning home run in 499 games since 1982.

Pete O'Brien

Texas Rangers	AB	H	2B	3B	HR	RRF	BB	SO	BA	SA	OBA
Season	573	153	34	3	22	95	69	53	.267	.452	.342
vs. Left-Handed Pitchers	169	38	6	0	2	21	16	25	.225	.296	.289
vs. Right-Handed Pitchers	404	115	28	3	20	74	53	28	.285	.517	.364
Home	277	81	18	0	12	58	35	26	.292	.487	.367
Road	296	72	16	3	10	37	34	27	.243	.419	.318
Grass	477	131	29	0	18	80	58	43	.275	.449	.350
Artificial Turf	96	22	5	3	4	15	11	10	.229	.469	.303
April	67	10	2	1	2	9	9	6	.149	.299	.247
May	100	24	5	0	3	9	9	8	.240	.380	.303
June	94	27	7	0	3	14	14	15	.287	.457	.378
July	99	26	6	0	5	23	9	9	.263	.475	.318
August	102	35	10	2	2	17	6	9	.343	.539	.373
Sept./Oct.	111	31	4	0	7	23	22	6	.279	.505	.393
Leading Off Inn.	87	15	5	0	3	3	11	8	.172	.333	.265
Bases Empty	299	83	19	0	15	15	33	30	.278	.492	.349
Runners On	274	70	15	3	7	80	36	23	.255	.409	.334
Runners/Scor. Pos.	148	38	9	2	4	69	24	16	.257	.426	.343
Runners On/2 Out	111	23	7	2	1	25	13	11	.207	.333	.296
Scor. Pos./2 Out	67	12	4	1	1	21	10	8	.179	.313	.286
Late Inning Pressure	75	12	1	0	2	8	13	10	.160	.253	.278
Leading Off	14	1	0	0	1	1	4	1	.071	.286	.278
Bases Empty	43	7	1	0	2	2	7	6	.163	.326	.280
Runners On	32	5	0	0	0	6	6	4	.156	.156	.275
Runners/Scor. Pos.	23	4	0	0	0	6	4	2	.174	.174	.276

DRIVING IN RUNS	0 Out	1 Out	2 Out	Total	
From 1B	0/41	6/80	9/80	15/201	7%
From 2B	7/21	11/45	10/45	28/111	25%
From 3B	9/10	16/25	5/36	30/71	42%
Scoring Position	16/31	27/70	15/81	58/182	32%
Scor. Pos. %	52%	39%	19%	32%	
Driving In Runners from 3B with Less than Two Out:			25/35	71%	

Loves to face: Mike Smithson (.545, 6-for-11, 3 HR)
Hates to face: Willie Hernandez (0-for-15, 4 SO)
92 RBIs last season were the most by any first baseman in the history of the Senators II/Rangers franchise, which began in 1961. . . . Too good to keep secret: in researching the previous note, we ran across the following regular first basemen for the Senators: 1961, Dale Long; 1962, Harry Bright; 1963, Bobo (son of Tiny) Osborne; 1964, Moose Skowron; 1965, Dick Nen. . . . Hit nine 1st-inning home runs last year to lead A.L. . . . Hit lefties well as a rookie (.262 in 141 at bats in 1983), but has fallen off (.213, .225) the past two years. Lefties have also muted his power: slugging .460 with one home run every 29 at bats vs. right-handers; slugging .318, one every 94 vs. southpaws. . . . Career batting averages with runners in scoring position: .341 with less than two outs, .209 with two outs. . . . Has homered in every A.L. park except Yankee Stadium.

Ben Oglivie

Milwaukee Brewers	AB	H	2B	3B	HR	RRF	BB	SO	BA	SA	OBA
Season	341	99	17	2	10	66	37	51	.290	.440	.354
vs. Left-Handed Pitchers	75	16	5	1	2	15	2	13	.213	.387	.238
vs. Right-Handed Pitchers	266	83	12	1	8	51	35	38	.312	.455	.384
Home	160	51	11	2	4	37	12	23	.319	.488	.363
Road	181	48	6	0	6	29	25	28	.265	.398	.346
Grass	304	89	17	2	9	61	31	45	.293	.451	.352
Artificial Turf	37	10	0	0	1	5	6	6	.270	.351	.372
April	53	10	2	0	0	4	4	14	.189	.226	.259
May	60	15	2	0	1	7	4	7	.250	.333	.292
June	59	16	3	0	2	10	10	11	.271	.424	.366
July	72	30	7	1	3	22	12	6	.417	.667	.488
August	77	24	3	1	3	20	6	11	.312	.494	.341
Sept./Oct.	20	4	0	0	1	3	1	2	.200	.350	.273
Leading Off Inn.	88	25	4	0	2	2	6	17	.284	.398	.330
Bases Empty	204	54	11	0	3	3	18	32	.265	.363	.327
Runners On	137	45	6	2	7	63	19	19	.328	.555	.389
Runners/Scor. Pos.	87	26	4	1	3	53	14	9	.299	.471	.366
Runners On/2 Out	60	17	2	1	2	17	10	10	.283	.450	.394
Scor. Pos./2 Out	41	11	1	1	1	14	7	5	.268	.415	.388
Late Inning Pressure	53	13	2	0	2	8	4	11	.245	.396	.310
Leading Off	16	6	0	0	2	2	1	3	.375	.750	.412
Bases Empty	37	7	0	0	2	2	2	8	.189	.351	.231
Runners On	16	6	2	0	0	6	2	3	.375	.500	.474
Runners/Scor. Pos.	10	4	2	0	0	6	2	1	.400	.600	.538

DRIVING IN RUNS	0 Out	1 Out	2 Out	Total	
From 1B	2/24	6/36	4/37	12/97	12%
From 2B	3/16	8/21	5/27	16/64	25%
From 3B	7/8	15/20	6/17	28/45	62%
Scoring Position	10/24	23/41	11/44	44/109	40%
Scor. Pos. %	42%	56%	25%	40%	
Driving In Runners from 3B with Less than Two Out:			22/28	79%	

Loves to face: Dan Quisenberry (.500, 6-for-12, 2 HR)
Hates to face: Dave Schmidt (0-for-14)
Batting average with runners on base (.328) was his highest in the 11 years that we have been recording it. Unfortunately, he had fewer at bats in such situations (137) than in any year since 1975.... Also had fewer than 100 at bats against left-handers for first time since 1979; started only 10 of Brewers' 55 games against left-handers last season.... July batting average of .417 was 2d-best in A.L.... Batting average against right-handers was his highest in past 11 years.... Last big year was 1982 (34 home runs); has hit 35 home runs in three years since then.... Stop me before I run again: no stolen bases, eight times caught stealing, in past two seasons.

Al Oliver

Toronto Blue Jays	AB	H	2B	3B	HR	RRF	BB	SO	BA	SA	OBA
Season	187	47	6	1	5	23	7	13	.251	.374	.282
vs. Left-Handed Pitchers	17	4	2	0	1	3	0	4	.235	.529	.235
vs. Right-Handed Pitchers	170	43	4	1	4	20	7	9	.253	.359	.287
Home	86	21	4	0	1	7	5	5	.244	.326	.293
Road	101	26	2	1	4	16	2	8	.257	.416	.272
Grass	86	21	2	1	2	12	1	6	.244	.360	.253
Artificial Turf	101	26	4	0	3	11	6	7	.257	.386	.306
April	0	0	0	0	0	0	0	0	.000	.000	.000
May	0	0	0	0	0	0	0	0	.000	.000	.000
June	0	0	0	0	0	0	0	0	.000	.000	.000
July	58	16	2	0	3	10	2	0	.276	.466	.300
August	69	17	3	0	2	5	4	10	.246	.377	.297
Sept./Oct.	60	14	1	1	0	8	1	3	.233	.283	.246
Leading Off Inn.	40	15	1	0	2	2	1	2	.375	.550	.405
Bases Empty	91	24	4	0	2	2	4	3	.264	.374	.302
Runners On	96	23	2	1	3	21	3	10	.240	.375	.263
Runners/Scor. Pos.	46	16	1	1	3	21	2	4	.348	.609	.375
Runners On/2 Out	47	14	0	1	2	14	2	4	.298	.468	.327
Scor. Pos./2 Out	26	11	0	1	2	14	1	2	.423	.731	.444
Late Inning Pressure	21	6	0	0	2	4	1	1	.286	.571	.318
Leading Off	7	4	0	0	2	2	0	0	.571	1.429	.571
Bases Empty	13	4	0	0	2	2	0	0	.308	.769	.308
Runners On	8	2	0	0	0	2	1	1	.250	.250	.333
Runners/Scor. Pos.	3	2	0	0	0	2	1	0	.667	.667	.750

DRIVING IN RUNS	0 Out	1 Out	2 Out	Total	
From 1B	0/15	0/22	2/31	2/68	3%
From 2B	0/3	1/10	5/16	6/29	21%
From 3B	0/0	5/9	5/13	10/22	45%
Scoring Position	0/3	6/19	10/29	16/31	31%
Scor. Pos. %	0%	32%	34%	31%	
Driving In Runners from 3B with Less than Two Out:			5/9	56%	

Loves to face: Bob Stanley (.556, 10-for-18, 1 HR)
Hates to face: Neil Allen (.071, 1-for-14)
Figures above are for A.L. only.... Had not hit a home run in his last 178 games in N.L. before connecting in his first game with the Blue Jays. Went on to hit five home runs in his first 26 games upon returning to A.L.... Combined-leagues average was .252, the first time since 1975 that he did not hit .300.... Career total of hits (2,743) ranks 3d among active players; career total of doubles (529) is 2d to Pete Rose.... Has batted over .300 with runners in scoring position in each of last eight seasons.... Dodgers' leftfielder and number three hitter on opening day last season; mid-season trade to Toronto for Len Matuszek earns Philadelphia the "I told you so" award, since they traded both of them away before the start of the season.... First major-league hit came off Jim Bunning, Sept. 23, 1968.

Jorge Orta

Kansas City Royals	AB	H	2B	3B	HR	RRF	BB	SO	BA	SA	OBA
Season	300	80	21	1	4	47	22	28	.267	.383	.317
vs. Left-Handed Pitchers	12	1	0	0	0	0	0	5	.083	.083	.083
vs. Right-Handed Pitchers	288	79	21	1	4	47	22	23	.274	.396	.326
Home	142	39	11	0	1	19	12	12	.275	.373	.329
Road	158	41	10	1	3	28	10	16	.259	.392	.306
Grass	112	33	8	1	1	20	8	11	.295	.411	.344
Artificial Turf	188	47	13	0	3	27	14	17	.250	.367	.301
April	67	20	7	0	1	8	2	4	.299	.448	.319
May	59	16	4	0	1	13	6	4	.271	.390	.343
June	72	17	4	0	0	9	4	9	.236	.292	.273
July	43	12	3	1	0	8	3	3	.279	.395	.319
August	17	4	0	0	0	0	2	3	.235	.235	.350
Sept./Oct.	42	11	3	0	2	9	5	5	.262	.476	.333
Leading Off Inn.	62	19	5	0	0	0	5	3	.306	.387	.368
Bases Empty	139	41	10	0	1	1	9	12	.295	.388	.342
Runners On	161	39	11	1	3	46	13	16	.242	.379	.296
Runners/Scor. Pos.	99	26	7	1	2	43	10	8	.263	.414	.325
Runners On/2 Out	75	18	4	0	1	12	4	9	.240	.333	.288
Scor. Pos./2 Out	47	10	2	0	0	9	4	6	.213	.255	.288
Late Inning Pressure	34	7	0	0	1	6	4	7	.206	.294	.275
Leading Off	8	0	0	0	0	0	0	0	.000	.000	.000
Bases Empty	17	2	0	0	0	0	0	3	.118	.118	.118
Runners On	17	5	0	0	1	6	4	4	.294	.471	.391
Runners/Scor. Pos.	11	3	0	0	1	6	4	3	.273	.545	.412

DRIVING IN RUNS	0 Out	1 Out	2 Out	Total	
From 1B	2/20	2/49	3/52	7/121	6%
From 2B	2/10	10/36	7/31	19/77	25%
From 3B	3/3	13/17	1/19	17/39	44%
Scoring Position	5/13	23/53	8/50	36/116	31%
Scor. Pos. %	38%	43%	16%	31%	
Driving In Runners from 3B with Less than Two Out:			16/20	80%	

Loves to face: Bruce Kison (.833, 5-for-6, 1 HR)
Hates to face: Steve McCatty (.111, 3-for-27, 8 SO)
Started Royals' first 63 games against right-handers last season; was then replaced by Hal McRae, and started only two games from July 22 to Sept. 19.... Lost in the shuffle of the Denkinger World Series call: give Orta credit for hitting that little roller to Jack Clark; Todd Worrell was working on a streak of six consecutive strikeouts carried over from Game Five.... Only 41 plate appearances vs. left-handers over past four years; last extra-base hit against a southpaw was in 1981.... Here's an eight-year schneid: Orta is 0-for-14 with the bases loaded and two outs since 1978 (two bases-loaded walks in 1979 are the only blemishes on that record).... Yearly batting averages in Late-Inning Pressure Situations since 1983: .432, .333, .206.

Spike Owen

Seattle Mariners	AB	H	2B	3B	HR	RRF	BB	SO	BA	SA	OBA
Season	352	91	10	6	6	38	34	27	.259	.372	.322
vs. Left-Handed Pitchers	90	23	6	0	1	11	6	9	.256	.356	.302
vs. Right-Handed Pitchers	262	68	4	6	5	27	28	18	.260	.378	.329
Home	201	55	7	3	3	19	20	16	.274	.383	.338
Road	151	36	3	3	3	19	14	11	.238	.358	.301
Grass	117	25	3	3	2	14	11	10	.214	.342	.281
Artificial Turf	235	66	7	3	4	24	23	17	.281	.387	.342
April	59	11	3	0	0	2	5	5	.186	.237	.250
May	55	11	0	1	1	6	9	7	.200	.291	.308
June	78	25	2	3	2	8	8	4	.321	.500	.384
July	38	11	3	0	0	4	3	3	.289	.368	.333
August	63	16	1	0	0	9	7	4	.254	.270	.329
Sept./Oct.	59	17	1	2	3	9	2	4	.288	.525	.311
Leading Off Inn.	90	26	3	0	2	2	12	4	.289	.389	.373
Bases Empty	212	55	6	2	4	4	24	16	.259	.363	.335
Runners On	140	36	4	4	2	34	10	11	.257	.386	.303
Runners/Scor. Pos.	75	21	2	1	1	28	6	7	.280	.373	.325
Runners On/2 Out	65	18	2	1	1	16	5	4	.277	.385	.329
Scor. Pos./2 Out	36	12	1	0	1	15	2	3	.333	.444	.368
Late Inning Pressure	45	7	0	0	0	4	9	8	.156	.156	.296
Leading Off	13	1	0	0	0	0	3	1	.077	.077	.250
Bases Empty	32	4	0	0	0	0	8	5	.125	.125	.300
Runners On	13	3	0	0	0	4	1	3	.231	.231	.286
Runners/Scor. Pos.	9	3	0	0	0	4	1	1	.333	.333	.400

DRIVING IN RUNS	0 Out	1 Out	2 Out	Total	
From 1B	0/10	4/40	2/44	6/94	6%
From 2B	1/7	2/28	6/26	9/61	15%
From 3B	1/1	9/16	7/19	17/36	47%
Scoring Position	2/8	11/44	13/45	26/97	27%
Scor. Pos. %	25%	25%	29%	27%	
Driving In Runners from 3B with Less than Two Out:			10/17	59%	

Loves to face: Dave Schmidt (.778, 7-for-9, 1 HR)
Hates to face: Ken Schrom & Frank Tanana (0-for-17 vs. each)
Averaged 3.37 assists per nine innings last season, 2d-highest among A.L. shortstops (Onix Concepcion led with 3.47).... Finally had first two-error game of major-league career in his 332d game at shortstop, Sept. 15 vs. Chicago.... Had 11 steals until he was disabled with pulled hamstring muscle in mid-July; returned Aug. 2, but had no stolen bases thereafter.... Career batting average of .179 in Late-Inning Pressure Situations.... Career batting average of .158 at Anaheim Stadium, the only A.L. ballpark in which he has never had an extra-base hit.... First-round draft choice in 1982, he was 6th player selected; Dwight Gooden was 5th. Three other shortstops were chosen among top seven: Cubs' Shawon Dunston (1st), Toronto's August Schmidt (2d), Pirates' Sam Khalifa (7th).

Mike Pagliarulo

New York Yankees	AB	H	2B	3B	HR	RRF	BB	SO	BA	SA	OBA
Season	380	91	16	2	19	63	45	86	.239	.442	.324
vs. Left-Handed Pitchers	51	8	0	0	2	9	6	22	.157	.275	.267
vs. Right-Handed Pitchers	329	83	16	2	17	54	39	64	.252	.468	.333
Home	178	43	5	1	8	30	20	39	.242	.416	.320
Road	202	48	11	1	11	33	25	47	.238	.465	.328
Grass	329	78	15	2	15	53	35	71	.237	.432	.315
Artificial Turf	51	13	1	0	4	10	10	15	.255	.510	.377
April	31	8	3	0	1	5	8	6	.258	.452	.410
May	45	6	1	0	1	11	7	11	.133	.222	.268
June	70	17	4	0	3	7	9	12	.243	.429	.329
July	75	21	2	1	5	14	3	17	.280	.533	.313
August	76	20	2	1	7	15	12	18	.263	.592	.364
Sept./Oct.	83	19	4	0	2	11	6	22	.229	.349	.289
Leading Off Inn.	94	22	4	0	3	3	10	17	.234	.372	.314
Bases Empty	220	54	8	2	8	8	22	51	.245	.409	.322
Runners On	160	37	8	0	11	55	23	35	.231	.488	.326
Runners/Scor. Pos.	84	22	4	0	5	41	17	21	.262	.488	.381
Runners On/2 Out	65	16	3	0	7	31	14	17	.246	.615	.380
Scor. Pos./2 Out	41	12	3	0	3	23	11	13	.293	.585	.442
Late Inning Pressure	52	11	0	0	3	7	7	12	.212	.385	.317
Leading Off	21	4	0	0	1	1	2	4	.190	.333	.292
Bases Empty	36	6	0	0	2	2	3	9	.167	.333	.250
Runners On	16	5	0	0	1	5	4	3	.313	.500	.450
Runners/Scor. Pos.	7	2	0	0	0	3	1	2	.286	.286	.375

DRIVING IN RUNS	0 Out	1 Out	2 Out	Total	
From 1B	2/31	2/46	7/47	11/124	9%
From 2B	3/13	4/22	10/31	17/66	26%
From 3B	5/10	4/9	7/20	16/39	41%
Scoring Position	8/23	8/31	17/51	33/105	31%
Scor. Pos. %	35%	26%	33%	31%	
Driving In Runners from 3B with Less than Two Out:			9/19	47%	

Loves to face: Bret Saberhagen (.333, 3-for-9, 2 HR)
Hates to face: Dan Petry (0-for-12, 3 SO)
Since joining the Yankees in July 1984, has started 152 out of 153 games against right-handers, but only one (last April 29 against Frank Tanana) against a lefty.... Has hit only .185 against left-handers (15-for-81, two home runs) in major-league career, but even that doesn't explain the infamous episode of last Sept. 18, when Billy Martin told him to bat *right-handed* against left-hander Mickey Mahler with runners on second and third and two outs in a 2–2 game. Pags, who had struck out twice previously, fanned again, and the Yankees went on to lose.... Career breakdown: .224 with the bases empty, .257 with runners on base, .270 with runners in scoring position.... Fly-ball hitter: 0.78 G/A ratio last season.... Averaged only 1.76 assists per nine innings, 3d-lowest rate among A.L. third basemen last year (minimum: 300 innings).

Lance Parrish

Detroit Tigers	AB	H	2B	3B	HR	RRF	BB	SO	BA	SA	OBA
Season	549	150	27	1	28	99	41	90	.273	.479	.323
vs. Left-Handed Pitchers	151	46	10	1	9	27	18	17	.305	.563	.372
vs. Right-Handed Pitchers	398	104	17	0	19	72	23	73	.261	.447	.304
Home	268	75	14	1	11	44	26	51	.280	.463	.341
Road	281	75	13	0	17	55	15	39	.267	.495	.306
Grass	456	131	25	1	25	87	40	73	.287	.511	.344
Artificial Turf	93	19	2	0	3	12	1	17	.204	.323	.213
April	66	17	3	0	2	12	3	4	.258	.394	.286
May	105	32	6	0	5	18	4	19	.305	.505	.327
June	107	30	3	0	4	19	13	19	.280	.421	.355
July	55	7	2	0	2	7	4	10	.127	.273	.200
August	109	34	9	1	10	29	12	17	.312	.688	.374
Sept./Oct.	107	30	4	0	5	14	5	21	.280	.458	.319
Leading Off Inn.	139	25	10	0	4	4	9	28	.180	.338	.235
Bases Empty	291	74	17	0	15	15	16	50	.254	.467	.295
Runners On	258	76	10	1	13	84	25	40	.295	.492	.353
Runners/Scor. Pos.	157	43	4	0	6	63	17	30	.274	.414	.335
Runners On/2 Out	130	37	7	1	5	36	14	19	.285	.469	.354
Scor. Pos./2 Out	78	19	3	0	3	26	9	15	.244	.397	.322
Late Inning Pressure	81	17	2	0	4	13	2	16	.210	.383	.238
Leading Off	26	3	0	0	1	1	0	7	.115	.231	.115
Bases Empty	51	9	1	0	3	3	0	12	.176	.373	.176
Runners On	30	8	1	0	1	10	2	4	.267	.400	.333
Runners/Scor. Pos.	22	7	1	0	0	8	2	3	.318	.364	.375

DRIVING IN RUNS	0 Out	1 Out	2 Out	Total	
From 1B	1/31	7/63	9/82	17/176	10%
From 2B	2/25	10/46	14/55	26/126	21%
From 3B	7/14	13/20	8/29	28/63	44%
Scoring Position	9/39	23/66	22/84	54/189	29%
Scor. Pos. %	23%	35%	26%	29%	
Driving In Runners from 3B with Less than Two Out:			20/34	59%	

Loves to face: Bruce Hurst (.579, 11-for-19, 6 HR)
Hates to face: Dennis Lamp (.129, 4-for-31, 13 SO)
Had 98 RBIs, same as 1984, despite drop in runners in scoring position when he batted, from 220 to 189. How'd he do it? He raised his batting average at those times from .217 to .274.... One of five major-leaguers to average 30 homers over past five years.... Slugging average vs. left-handers has been above .500 five times in last eight years.... Over last three years, has hit 52 homers on the road, 36 at Tiger Stadium.... Favorite place seems to be Anaheim, where his career average is .345 (48-for-139), with 10 home runs.... Missed 13 games due to back injury, July 11–26. During that stretch, Tigers lost seven straight to right-handed starters.... In the five weeks following his return to the lineup (July 27–Sept. 1), he drove in 33 runs in 34 games and did not go more than two straight games without an RBI.

Larry Parrish

Texas Rangers	AB	H	2B	3B	HR	RRF	BB	SO	BA	SA	OBA
Season	346	86	11	1	17	53	33	77	.249	.434	.314
vs. Left-Handed Pitchers	94	23	3	0	8	22	11	21	.245	.532	.321
vs. Right-Handed Pitchers	252	63	8	1	9	31	22	56	.250	.397	.312
Home	188	41	4	1	8	32	18	43	.218	.378	.285
Road	158	45	7	0	9	21	15	34	.285	.500	.349
Grass	285	68	8	1	14	46	26	65	.239	.421	.303
Artificial Turf	61	18	3	0	3	7	7	12	.295	.492	.368
April	71	22	1	0	5	15	4	12	.310	.535	.347
May	83	16	3	0	0	4	10	27	.193	.229	.280
June	98	24	3	0	8	19	12	21	.245	.520	.330
July	17	2	0	1	0	1	1	4	.118	.235	.167
August	0	0	0	0	0	0	0	0	.000	.000	.000
Sept./Oct.	77	22	4	0	4	14	6	13	.286	.494	.333
Leading Off Inn.	91	21	5	0	3	3	5	28	.231	.385	.271
Bases Empty	173	42	5	1	10	10	13	43	.243	.457	.296
Runners On	173	44	6	0	7	43	20	34	.254	.410	.332
Runners/Scor. Pos.	100	21	3	0	3	34	13	24	.210	.330	.302
Runners On/2 Out	75	17	1	0	3	14	10	17	.227	.360	.318
Scor. Pos./2 Out	44	9	0	0	0	8	6	11	.205	.205	.300
Late Inning Pressure	46	12	2	0	3	8	7	14	.261	.500	.358
Leading Off	19	5	1	0	0	0	1	4	.263	.316	.300
Bases Empty	29	7	1	0	0	0	3	8	.241	.276	.313
Runners On	17	5	1	0	3	8	4	6	.294	.882	.429
Runners/Scor. Pos.	7	2	0	0	2	6	3	3	.286	1.143	.500

DRIVING IN RUNS	0 Out	1 Out	2 Out	Total	
From 1B	1/24	3/48	3/52	7/124	6%
From 2B	1/6	4/33	4/30	9/69	13%
From 3B	3/7	13/21	4/18	20/46	43%
Scoring Position	4/13	17/54	8/48	29/115	25%
Scor. Pos. %	31%	31%	17%	25%	
Driving In Runners from 3B with Less than Two Out:			16/28	57%	

Loves to face: Floyd Bannister (.452, 14-for-31, 5 HR)
Hates to face: Willie Hernandez (.083, 1-for-12, 4 SO)
Drove in 29 runs in August, 2d-most in A.L.... Has batted for higher average with runners on base than with the bases empty in five of last six seasons.... Has also has batted for higher average against right-handers than against left-handers in five of last six seasons. During that time, however, his home run rate is greater against southpaws.... 1985 batting average with runners in scoring position (.210) was his lowest in 11 years of *The Player Analysis*.... Averaged 1.70 putouts per nine innings last season, 2d-lowest rate among A.L. outfielders (minimum: 300 innings); lowest? See Jackson, Reggie.... May have reached that DH threshold: Did not play the field after returning from disabled list in September, and Pete Incaviglia is on his way.

Jack Perconte

Seattle Mariners	AB	H	2B	3B	HR	RRF	BB	SO	BA	SA	OBA
Season	485	128	17	7	2	26	50	36	.264	.340	.335
vs. Left-Handed Pitchers	132	32	2	1	0	6	15	14	.242	.273	.320
vs. Right-Handed Pitchers	353	96	15	6	2	20	35	22	.272	.365	.341
Home	247	62	8	3	2	13	22	22	.251	.332	.316
Road	238	66	9	4	0	13	28	14	.277	.349	.354
Grass	180	55	7	3	0	12	17	11	.306	.378	.367
Artificial Turf	305	73	10	4	2	14	33	25	.239	.318	.317
April	56	13	3	0	0	1	2	6	.232	.286	.259
May	89	20	5	2	1	2	4	6	.225	.360	.263
June	91	26	3	0	0	7	9	3	.286	.319	.356
July	34	4	0	1	0	2	2	3	.118	.176	.167
August	85	27	2	1	0	5	15	6	.318	.365	.420
Sept./Oct.	130	38	4	3	1	9	18	12	.292	.392	.380
Leading Off Inn.	199	53	13	5	2	3	20	15	.266	.412	.336
Bases Empty	304	84	15	7	2	3	32	22	.276	.391	.349
Runners On	181	44	2	0	0	23	18	14	.243	.254	.312
Runners/Scor. Pos.	102	26	1	0	0	23	11	6	.255	.265	.328
Runners On/2 Out	85	21	1	0	0	12	10	5	.247	.259	.326
Scor. Pos./2 Out	55	13	0	0	0	12	7	2	.236	.236	.323
Late Inning Pressure	55	18	4	2	0	0	11	5	.327	.473	.439
Leading Off	15	4	2	0	0	0	3	1	.267	.400	.389
Bases Empty	36	13	3	2	0	0	6	1	.361	.556	.452
Runners On	19	5	1	0	0	0	5	4	.263	.316	.417
Runners/Scor. Pos.	12	4	0	0	0	0	2	1	.333	.333	.429

DRIVING IN RUNS	0 Out	1 Out	2 Out	Total	
From 1B	0/36	0/35	0/49	0/120	0%
From 2B	1/10	1/28	4/45	6/83	7%
From 3B	3/5	6/11	8/22	17/38	45%
Scoring Position	4/15	7/39	12/67	23/121	19%
Scor. Pos. %	27%	18%	18%	19%	
Driving In Runners from 3B with Less than Two Out:			9/16	56%	

Loves to face: Brian Fisher (1.000, 4-for-4)
Hates to face: Ken Schrom (.091, 1-for-11)
Stolen base percentage of .939 (31 of 33) was best in majors last year (minimum: 20 SB); starts 1986 with streak of 27 consecutive steals. Only catcher to catch him was Buck Martinez (with Jim Clancy pitching); the other caught stealing came on a pickoff by Geoff Zahn.... Batted .233 in first 67 games, then was unexpectedly sent to minors; recalled a month later, he batted .302 in 58 games to season's end.... Left-handed batter whose career average against lefties (.274) is higher than his average vs. righties (.272).... Hit first two career home runs in 1985, both leading off bottom of first inning at the Kingdome.... Drove in none of 120 runners from first base last season, tying George Wright for worst mark in A.L., and had undisputed worst record in majors at driving in runners from second base: 6 of 83, 7.2 percent (minimum: 40 opportunities).

Gary Pettis

California Angels	AB	H	2B	3B	HR	RRF	BB	SO	BA	SA	OBA
Season	443	114	10	8	1	34	62	125	.257	.323	.347
vs. Left-Handed Pitchers	139	39	5	1	0	13	21	29	.281	.331	.370
vs. Right-Handed Pitchers	304	75	5	7	1	21	41	96	.247	.319	.336
Home	182	42	5	4	0	13	31	48	.231	.302	.340
Road	261	72	5	4	1	21	31	77	.276	.337	.353
Grass	349	88	6	7	1	27	52	97	.252	.318	.347
Artificial Turf	94	26	4	1	0	7	10	28	.277	.340	.346
April	73	21	2	3	0	6	15	22	.288	.397	.409
May	62	12	2	1	0	2	11	18	.194	.258	.315
June	92	25	1	0	1	6	10	34	.272	.315	.340
July	4	1	0	0	0	0	0	1	.250	.250	.250
August	97	20	2	0	0	6	15	26	.206	.227	.313
Sept./Oct.	115	35	3	4	0	14	11	24	.304	.400	.362
Leading Off Inn.	149	35	3	4	0	0	25	46	.235	.309	.345
Bases Empty	279	71	9	5	0	0	40	82	.254	.323	.348
Runners On	164	43	1	3	1	34	22	43	.262	.323	.346
Runners/Scor. Pos.	96	27	1	1	1	32	13	27	.281	.344	.360
Runners On/2 Out	73	22	1	1	1	21	13	19	.301	.384	.407
Scor. Pos./2 Out	45	16	1	1	1	21	6	9	.356	.489	.431
Late Inning Pressure	46	12	1	1	0	3	9	16	.261	.326	.382
Leading Off	15	5	1	1	0	0	4	5	.333	.533	.474
Bases Empty	32	9	1	1	0	0	5	12	.281	.375	.378
Runners On	14	3	0	0	0	3	4	4	.214	.214	.389
Runners/Scor. Pos.	8	1	0	0	0	3	1	4	.125	.125	.222

DRIVING IN RUNS	0 Out	1 Out	2 Out	Total	
From 1B	0/30	2/40	4/50	6/120	5%
From 2B	0/10	1/27	11/33	12/70	17%
From 3B	4/6	6/13	5/20	15/39	38%
Scoring Position	4/16	7/40	16/53	27/109	25%
Scor. Pos. %	25%	18%	30%	25%	
Driving In Runners from 3B with Less than Two Out:			10/19	53%	

Loves to face: Rick Thompson (1.000, 3-for-3, 1 3B)
Hates to face: Mike Boddicker (0-for-9)
Ratio of 2.40 ground outs-to-air outs was 3d-highest in majors last season (minimum: 200 PA). Career average: 2.35. . . . Tied with Bobby Meacham for fewest extra-base hits (19) among players who qualified for A.L. batting title last season. . . . No home runs in 305 career at bats vs. left-handers; seven against right-handers. . . . Career batting average of .556 (5-for-9) with the bases loaded. . . . Successful in his first 22 stolen base attempts last season. First time caught was on a Joe Cowley-Butch Wynegar pitchout, May 30. . . . Held lead in A.L. stolen base race through games until June 22, when Rickey Henderson passed him by. . . . Averaged 3.14 putouts per nine innings last season, 3d-highest rate among A.L. outfielders (minimum: 300 innings).

Jim Presley

Seattle Mariners	AB	H	2B	3B	HR	RRF	BB	SO	BA	SA	OBA
Season	570	157	33	1	28	85	44	100	.275	.484	.324
vs. Left-Handed Pitchers	157	54	10	1	8	26	15	22	.344	.573	.398
vs. Right-Handed Pitchers	413	103	23	0	20	59	29	78	.249	.450	.295
Home	296	78	17	1	12	35	25	50	.264	.449	.320
Road	274	79	16	0	16	50	19	50	.288	.522	.328
Grass	220	58	10	0	13	41	13	42	.264	.486	.298
Artificial Turf	350	99	23	1	15	44	31	58	.283	.483	.339
April	72	15	3	0	6	13	9	12	.208	.500	.293
May	95	28	7	0	4	11	5	16	.295	.495	.330
June	95	31	6	0	6	17	9	21	.326	.579	.381
July	101	33	4	0	7	13	9	21	.327	.574	.382
August	102	25	6	1	2	15	3	16	.245	.382	.266
Sept./Oct.	105	25	7	0	3	16	9	14	.238	.390	.288
Leading Off Inn.	129	38	7	0	6	6	3	19	.295	.488	.311
Bases Empty	313	90	19	0	16	16	15	55	.288	.502	.322
Runners On	257	67	14	1	12	69	29	45	.261	.463	.325
Runners/Scor. Pos.	128	35	11	1	5	55	21	23	.273	.492	.354
Runners On/2 Out	105	27	6	1	5	30	11	20	.257	.476	.328
Scor. Pos./2 Out	67	19	6	1	3	26	9	12	.284	.537	.368
Late Inning Pressure	78	14	3	0	1	3	8	20	.179	.256	.256
Leading Off	21	4	1	0	1	1	0	5	.190	.381	.190
Bases Empty	45	8	3	0	1	1	2	11	.178	.311	.213
Runners On	33	6	0	0	0	2	6	9	.182	.182	.308
Runners/Scor. Pos.	13	2	0	0	0	2	6	3	.154	.154	.421

DRIVING IN RUNS	0 Out	1 Out	2 Out	Total	
From 1B	3/61	5/62	3/73	11/196	6%
From 2B	2/24	5/32	12/47	19/103	18%
From 3B	8/14	9/18	10/33	27/65	42%
Scoring Position	10/38	14/50	22/80	46/168	27%
Scor. Pos. %	26%	28%	28%	27%	
Driving In Runners from 3B with Less than Two Out:			17/32	53%	

Loves to face: Jeff Russell (1.000, 2-for-2, 1 2B, 1 HR)
Hates to face: Jack Morris (0-for-11, 4 SO)
Mariners' leading hitter against left-handers, and 5th-best in A.L. . . . His .344 mark against southpaws is surprising in light of .167 average against them in 1984. . . . Hit home runs in four consecutive games twice last season (April 10–13, June 8–11). . . . Grounded into 29 double plays in 132 opportunities last season; his GIDP total was 3d-highest in the A.L., and his rate ranked 5th (minimum: 5 GIDPs). . . . Batted .320 in Seattle victories, .238 in losses last year. . . . In two seasons, has batted only .156 in Late-Inning Pressure Situations with runners on base. . . . Went down to his last at bat in final game of season before joining the Century Club for strikeouts. Joel Davis of the White Sox initiated him.

Tony Phillips

Oakland As	AB	H	2B	3B	HR	RRF	BB	SO	BA	SA	OBA
Season	161	45	12	2	4	19	13	34	.280	.453	.331
vs. Left-Handed Pitchers	58	21	3	0	2	10	2	4	.362	.517	.383
vs. Right-Handed Pitchers	103	24	9	2	2	9	11	30	.233	.417	.304
Home	73	21	8	1	2	10	6	17	.288	.507	.342
Road	88	24	4	1	2	9	7	17	.273	.409	.323
Grass	148	42	11	1	4	17	12	30	.284	.453	.335
Artificial Turf	13	3	1	1	0	2	1	4	.231	.462	.286
April	0	0	0	0	0	0	0	0	.000	.000	.000
May	0	0	0	0	0	0	0	0	.000	.000	.000
June	0	0	0	0	0	0	0	0	.000	.000	.000
July	0	0	0	0	0	0	0	0	.000	.000	.000
August	26	7	2	0	0	0	3	5	.269	.346	.345
Sept./Oct.	135	38	10	2	4	19	10	29	.281	.474	.329
Leading Off Inn.	40	14	3	0	2	2	2	6	.350	.575	.381
Bases Empty	102	34	7	1	3	3	9	22	.333	.510	.387
Runners On	59	11	5	1	1	16	4	12	.186	.356	.234
Runners/Scor. Pos.	39	8	3	0	1	14	3	7	.205	.359	.256
Runners On/2 Out	30	1	0	1	0	2	3	8	.033	.100	.121
Scor. Pos./2 Out	20	0	0	0	0	1	2	5	.000	.000	.091
Late Inning Pressure	24	5	3	0	0	4	2	6	.208	.333	.259
Leading Off	5	2	2	0	0	0	0	0	.400	.800	.400
Bases Empty	13	4	2	0	0	0	1	3	.308	.462	.357
Runners On	11	1	1	0	0	4	1	3	.091	.182	.154
Runners/Scor. Pos.	5	1	1	0	0	4	1	2	.200	.400	.286

DRIVING IN RUNS	0 Out	1 Out	2 Out	Total	
From 1B	1/8	1/9	1/18	3/35	9%
From 2B	1/6	6/11	1/16	8/33	24%
From 3B	1/1	3/3	0/7	4/11	36%
Scoring Position	2/7	9/14	1/23	12/44	27%
Scor. Pos. %	29%	64%	4%	27%	
Driving In Runners from 3B with Less than Two Out:			4/4	100%	

Loves to face: Ron Guidry (.429, 12-for-28, 1 HR)
Hates to face: Milt Wilcox (0-for-14)
Fractured a bone in his foot in a winter workout, then re-fractured it in his second spring game, on March 25. Did not play first regular-season game until Aug. 22. . . . When he did rejoin team, he was used mostly at third base, where he had played only four major-league games before last year. . . . Oakland's regular number-two hitter over last month, batting .286 with 16 RBIs in 27 games in that spot. . . . Career batting averages with runners in scoring position: .327 with less than two outs, .195 with two outs. . . . Tied *Player Analysis* record for most hitless at bats (20) with two outs and runners in scoring position. Co-holder: Mike Stenhouse (1984). . . . Had batted for a higher average with runners on base than with the bases empty in each of three previous seasons. . . . Career batting average of .083 (1-for-12) with the bases loaded.

Kirby Puckett

Minnesota Twins	AB	H	2B	3B	HR	RRF	BB	SO	BA	SA	OBA
Season	691	199	29	13	4	76	41	87	.288	.385	.330
vs. Left-Handed Pitchers	219	78	11	7	4	34	10	24	.356	.525	.383
vs. Right-Handed Pitchers	472	121	18	6	0	42	31	63	.256	.320	.306
Home	352	114	19	6	2	41	26	41	.324	.429	.374
Road	339	85	10	7	2	35	15	46	.251	.339	.283
Grass	255	69	8	4	1	25	10	39	.271	.345	.299
Artificial Turf	436	130	21	9	3	51	31	48	.298	.408	.348
April	91	30	3	2	1	17	2	9	.330	.440	.344
May	117	32	4	4	0	16	8	13	.274	.376	.331
June	109	28	4	2	1	10	4	9	.257	.358	.289
July	112	30	4	2	1	9	11	12	.268	.366	.331
August	115	30	2	2	0	9	6	18	.261	.313	.295
Sept./Oct.	147	49	12	1	1	15	10	26	.333	.449	.377
Leading Off Inn.	282	78	10	3	1	1	18	31	.277	.344	.320
Bases Empty	443	119	18	6	1	1	22	57	.269	.343	.303
Runners On	248	80	11	7	3	75	19	30	.323	.460	.376
Runners/Scor. Pos.	154	49	9	7	3	75	11	21	.318	.526	.365
Runners On/2 Out	99	33	2	5	1	33	11	15	.333	.485	.405
Scor. Pos./2 Out	67	22	2	5	1	33	8	10	.328	.552	.408
Late Inning Pressure	83	27	1	3	1	16	6	21	.325	.446	.380
Leading Off	18	7	0	0	0	0	2	2	.389	.389	.450
Bases Empty	45	13	0	1	0	0	2	13	.289	.333	.319
Runners On	38	14	1	2	1	16	4	8	.368	.579	.444
Runners/Scor. Pos.	26	7	0	2	1	16	4	6	.269	.538	.394

DRIVING IN RUNS	0 Out	1 Out	2 Out	Total	
From 1B	0/35	4/71	6/67	10/173	6%
From 2B	4/20	12/53	12/45	28/118	24%
From 3B	5/7	15/21	14/31	34/59	58%
Scoring Position	9/27	27/74	26/76	62/177	35%
Scor. Pos. %	33%	36%	34%	35%	
Driving In Runners from 3B with Less than Two Out:			20/28	71%	

Loves to face: Ed Whitson (.625, 5-for-8)
Hates to face: Danny Jackson (0-for-13, 12 ground outs)
Major consistency here: his 1985 batting averages when leading off an inning, with runners on base, with two outs and runners in scoring position, at the Metrodome, and on artificial turf games are all within two points of his 1984 figures in those categories. . . . Career batting averages: .323 with runners on base, .275 with the bases empty. . . . Ground-ball hitter: 2.35 G/A ratio was 4th-highest in majors last season (minimum: 200 PA). Career average: 2.01. . . . One of six A.L. players with a disparity of at least 100 points between batting averages vs. left-handers and right-handers. . . . Started more games in leadoff spot (160) than any other major-leaguer. . . . Led majors in outfield putouts (465) last season; his rate per nine innings (2.98), however, was only 8th-best in A.L.

Willie Randolph

New York Yankees	AB	H	2B	3B	HR	RRF	BB	SO	BA	SA	OBA
Season	497	137	21	2	5	43	85	39	.276	.356	.382
vs. Left-Handed Pitchers	181	57	10	1	2	11	31	9	.315	.414	.418
vs. Right-Handed Pitchers	316	80	11	1	3	32	54	30	.253	.323	.361
Home	221	58	12	1	3	23	45	16	.262	.367	.387
Road	276	79	9	1	2	20	40	23	.286	.348	.377
Grass	414	111	19	1	5	38	72	33	.268	.355	.377
Artificial Turf	83	26	2	1	0	5	13	6	.313	.361	.408
April	60	14	3	0	0	1	9	5	.233	.283	.333
May	92	30	2	2	1	9	18	5	.326	.424	.436
June	95	22	3	0	0	9	16	11	.232	.263	.339
July	99	35	4	0	2	15	9	2	.354	.455	.396
August	101	21	5	0	0	6	18	8	.208	.257	.333
Sept./Oct.	50	15	4	0	2	3	15	8	.300	.500	.478
Leading Off Inn.	119	39	7	2	2	2	26	8	.328	.471	.448
Bases Empty	286	85	15	2	3	3	56	21	.297	.395	.414
Runners On	211	52	6	0	2	40	29	18	.246	.303	.337
Runners/Scor. Pos.	119	26	4	0	1	38	20	11	.218	.277	.331
Runners On/2 Out	79	13	1	0	0	9	15	9	.165	.177	.320
Scor. Pos./2 Out	54	6	1	0	0	9	12	6	.111	.130	.304
Late Inning Pressure	70	16	0	0	0	3	8	7	.229	.229	.308
Leading Off	15	3	0	0	0	0	2	3	.200	.200	.294
Bases Empty	46	12	0	0	0	0	5	7	.261	.261	.333
Runners On	24	4	0	0	0	3	3	0	.167	.167	.259
Runners/Scor. Pos.	12	1	0	0	0	3	3	0	.083	.083	.267

DRIVING IN RUNS	0 Out	1 Out	2 Out	Total	
From 1B	1/46	1/58	0/48	2/152	1%
From 2B	4/18	4/34	4/42	12/94	13%
From 3B	5/9	14/24	4/26	23/59	39%
Scoring Position	9/27	18/58	8/68	35/153	23%
Scor. Pos. %	33%	31%	12%	23%	
Driving In Runners from 3B with Less than Two Out:			19/33	58%	

Loves to face: Scott McGregor (.371, 23-for-62, 2 HR)
Hates to face: Bill Caudill (.091, 1-for-11)
On-base average when leading off inning (.448) was 2d-highest in majors last season (leader: Wade Boggs, .468). ... Rate of 3.44 walks for every strikeout against left-handed pitchers was best in A.L. last season, and that's a Randolph specialty: over the past 11 years, he owns four of the top five A.L. season rates in that category. ... Batting average with runners in scoring position (.218) was the lowest of his career, in a year in which he had a career-high at bat total (119) in such situations. ... Batted .111 with runners in scoring position to rank 3d from the bottom in A.L., exactly the same spot he occupied in 1984, when he batted .098 in the category. ... Batting average in Late-Inning Pressure Situations has been lower than overall average in each of last eight seasons. ... Ended season with 50-game errorless streak, his longest since 63-gamer in 1982.

Randy Ready

Milwaukee Brewers	AB	H	2B	3B	HR	RRF	BB	SO	BA	SA	OBA
Season	181	48	9	5	1	27	14	23	.265	.387	.318
vs. Left-Handed Pitchers	84	21	5	1	1	10	5	8	.250	.369	.289
vs. Right-Handed Pitchers	97	27	4	4	0	17	9	15	.278	.402	.343
Home	83	22	6	2	0	12	7	13	.265	.386	.319
Road	98	26	3	3	1	15	7	10	.265	.388	.318
Grass	136	37	7	3	1	20	9	18	.272	.390	.318
Artificial Turf	45	11	2	2	0	7	5	5	.244	.378	.320
April	13	4	1	0	0	1	2	2	.308	.385	.375
May	0	0	0	0	0	0	0	0	.000	.000	.000
June	0	0	0	0	0	0	0	0	.000	.000	.000
July	0	0	0	0	0	0	0	0	.000	.000	.000
August	55	13	2	0	1	5	4	6	.236	.327	.283
Sept./Oct.	113	31	6	5	0	21	8	15	.274	.416	.328
Leading Off Inn.	41	9	4	0	0	0	5	4	.220	.317	.304
Bases Empty	102	25	8	1	0	0	9	11	.245	.343	.306
Runners On	79	23	1	4	1	27	5	12	.291	.443	.333
Runners/Scor. Pos.	42	14	1	1	0	19	4	8	.333	.405	.375
Runners On/2 Out	32	12	1	3	0	12	1	5	.375	.594	.412
Scor. Pos./2 Out	20	7	1	0	0	8	1	4	.350	.400	.381
Late Inning Pressure	33	7	1	0	1	7	2	6	.212	.333	.257
Leading Off	6	0	0	0	0	0	0	2	.000	.000	.000
Bases Empty	15	1	0	0	0	0	1	3	.067	.067	.125
Runners On	18	6	1	0	1	7	1	3	.333	.556	.368
Runners/Scor. Pos.	11	5	1	0	0	5	0	2	.455	.545	.455

DRIVING IN RUNS	0 Out	1 Out	2 Out	Total	
From 1B	1/17	1/19	4/22	6/58	10%
From 2B	2/5	3/15	5/14	10/34	29%
From 3B	2/2	4/7	3/8	9/17	53%
Scoring Position	4/7	7/22	8/22	19/51	37%
Scor. Pos. %	57%	32%	36%	37%	
Driving In Runners from 3B with Less than Two Out:			6/9	67%	

Loves to face: Ed Whitson (1.000, 4-for-4)
Hates to face: Dave Stieb (0-for-6)
Started season with Brewers and had game-winning RBI in first game he played. Went on disabled list on April 30 (bruised heel), and was sent to Vancouver upon his recovery in mid-June; recalled after the players' strike, and had another game-winning RBI in first game back, Aug. 10. ... Started 41 of Milwaukee's last 56 games; including his April tour of duty, was in starting lineup at five different positions last season: 2B, 3B, LF, RF, and DH. ... Versatility extended to the batting order: in 45 starts, he was listed everywhere in the lineup except 3d and 4th. ... One of six A.L. players to have a 5-for-5 game last season, he did so in a losing effort against New York on Sept. 10. ... Career batting average of .347 in 72 at bats with runners in scoring position.

Floyd Rayford

Baltimore Orioles	AB	H	2B	3B	HR	RRF	BB	SO	BA	SA	OBA
Season	359	110	21	1	18	50	10	69	.306	.521	.324
vs. Left-Handed Pitchers	140	47	8	0	12	22	5	24	.336	.650	.359
vs. Right-Handed Pitchers	219	63	13	1	6	28	5	45	.288	.438	.302
Home	177	57	9	1	6	23	4	33	.322	.486	.337
Road	182	53	12	0	12	27	6	36	.291	.555	.312
Grass	321	98	19	1	17	46	10	61	.305	.530	.325
Artificial Turf	38	12	2	0	1	4	0	8	.316	.447	.316
April	4	1	0	0	0	0	0	0	.250	.250	.250
May	12	5	1	0	0	1	0	2	.417	.500	.417
June	31	11	3	0	2	5	1	11	.355	.645	.375
July	76	23	5	0	2	7	1	14	.303	.447	.312
August	105	35	3	1	6	15	4	14	.333	.552	.358
Sept./Oct.	131	35	9	0	8	22	4	28	.267	.519	.287
Leading Off Inn.	79	26	9	0	6	6	1	16	.329	.671	.338
Bases Empty	210	62	16	0	10	10	8	41	.295	.514	.321
Runners On	149	48	5	1	8	40	2	28	.322	.530	.329
Runners/Scor. Pos.	81	21	3	0	2	26	2	20	.259	.370	.274
Runners On/2 Out	57	17	3	1	4	20	1	12	.298	.596	.310
Scor. Pos./2 Out	36	10	2	0	1	13	1	9	.278	.417	.297
Late Inning Pressure	41	11	4	0	3	5	4	11	.268	.585	.333
Leading Off	8	2	1	0	1	1	0	4	.250	.750	.250
Bases Empty	29	9	4	0	2	2	2	9	.310	.655	.355
Runners On	12	2	0	0	1	3	2	2	.167	.417	.286
Runners/Scor. Pos.	7	1	0	0	1	3	2	2	.143	.571	.333

DRIVING IN RUNS	0 Out	1 Out	2 Out	Total	
From 1B	4/28	1/45	5/41	10/114	9%
From 2B	2/12	2/27	7/28	11/67	16%
From 3B	3/5	4/10	3/16	10/31	32%
Scoring Position	5/17	6/37	10/44	21/98	21%
Scor. Pos. %	29%	16%	23%	21%	
Driving In Runners from 3B with Less than Two Out:			7/15	47%	

Loves to face: Jimmy Key (.714, 5-for-7, 2 HR)
Hates to face: Floyd Bannister (.091, 1-for-11, 4 SO)
Weaver found him lying around collecting dust and put him to work, with dynamite results. After starting only two games against left-handers under Altobelli, started 30 of 31 games vs. southpaws after the All-Star break and wound up leading A.L. with rate of one home run every 11.7 at bats against them; his .650 slugging average against southpaws was 2d-highest in majors, after Rickey Henderson's .656. ... Career home run rate of one every 18.5 at bats against left-handers is roughly equivalent to career rates (against all pitchers) of Ernie Banks and Mel Ott. ... Homered in two consecutive games four times over the back half of last season. ... Likes those old-time ballparks: .455 (15-for-33) career at Fenway Park, four home runs in 37 at bats at Tiger Stadium. ... Rate of 6.9 strikeouts per walk was highest in A.L. last season (minimum: 50 SO).

Jim Rice

Boston Red Sox	AB	H	2B	3B	HR	RRF	BB	SO	BA	SA	OBA
Season	546	159	20	3	27	107	51	75	.291	.487	.349
vs. Left-Handed Pitchers	151	39	9	1	7	18	26	16	.258	.470	.363
vs. Right-Handed Pitchers	395	120	11	2	20	89	25	59	.304	.494	.343
Home	274	96	13	3	11	66	20	44	.350	.540	.391
Road	272	63	7	0	16	41	31	31	.232	.434	.309
Grass	461	140	17	3	24	95	39	64	.304	.510	.356
Artificial Turf	85	19	3	0	3	12	12	11	.224	.365	.313
April	83	23	2	0	4	17	12	13	.277	.446	.368
May	106	27	2	0	5	13	4	16	.255	.415	.283
June	104	36	6	1	5	21	9	13	.346	.567	.395
July	106	21	1	0	4	19	7	14	.198	.321	.246
August	86	20	3	1	3	12	15	13	.233	.395	.343
Sept./Oct.	61	32	6	1	6	25	4	6	.525	.951	.545
Leading Off Inn.	106	35	4	0	8	8	8	9	.330	.594	.383
Bases Empty	247	71	8	1	17	17	21	32	.287	.534	.346
Runners On	299	88	12	2	10	90	30	43	.294	.448	.351
Runners/Scor. Pos.	164	56	9	0	6	79	25	27	.341	.506	.412
Runners On/2 Out	103	28	3	0	3	29	18	14	.272	.388	.380
Scor. Pos./2 Out	61	20	1	0	1	25	14	11	.328	.393	.453
Late Inning Pressure	76	20	2	0	6	20	5	16	.263	.526	.298
Leading Off	24	5	1	0	2	2	1	5	.208	.500	.240
Bases Empty	36	8	1	0	4	4	1	5	.222	.583	.243
Runners On	40	12	1	0	2	16	4	11	.300	.475	.340
Runners/Scor. Pos.	18	6	0	0	2	15	4	5	.333	.667	.400

DRIVING IN RUNS	0 Out	1 Out	2 Out	Total	
From 1B	2/61	5/104	4/78	11/243	5%
From 2B	8/34	12/54	14/43	34/131	26%
From 3B	12/20	15/29	8/29	35/78	45%
Scoring Position	20/54	27/83	22/72	69/209	33%
Scor. Pos. %	37%	33%	31%	33%	
Driving In Runners from 3B with Less than Two Out:			27/49	55%	

Loves to face: Brad Havens (.600, 9-for-15, 3 HR)
Hates to face: Danny Darwin (.119, 5-for-42, 1 XBH, 11 SO)
Batting average vs. left-handers (.258) was lowest of career, and under .300 for only 2d time (other: 1982). ... Batting average in Late-Inning Pressure Situations has been lower than overall average in each of last seven years. ... Grounded into 35 double plays, one shy of major-league record he set in 1984; had 31 of them in first 94 games, but then added only four more in last 46 games, and didn't play after Sept. 20. ... 118-point home-over-road batting differential was highest among A.L. every-day players. ... Strikeout rate last season was lowest of his career; among active players who average better than a homer every 20 at bats, only Eddie Murray and Bob Horner have lower career strikeout rates. ... Since 1975, has 116 RRFs in 151 plate appearances with bases loaded (.77 per PA; 1985 major-league average: .73).

Earnest Riles

Milwaukee Brewers	AB	H	2B	3B	HR	RRF	BB	SO	BA	SA	OBA
Season	448	128	12	7	5	50	36	54	.286	.377	.339
vs. Left-Handed Pitchers	141	34	2	3	0	12	13	24	.241	.298	.310
vs. Right-Handed Pitchers	307	94	10	4	5	38	23	30	.306	.414	.353
Home	226	75	9	3	2	27	18	29	.332	.425	.381
Road	222	53	3	4	3	23	18	25	.239	.329	.298
Grass	367	109	10	6	4	41	28	49	.297	.390	.348
Artificial Turf	81	19	2	1	1	9	8	5	.235	.321	.303
April	0	0	0	0	0	0	0	0	.000	.000	.000
May	33	12	1	0	1	5	0	4	.364	.485	.353
June	95	22	2	3	1	14	8	12	.232	.347	.288
July	81	26	3	1	1	6	9	7	.321	.420	.389
August	106	36	1	3	1	17	5	12	.340	.434	.377
Sept./Oct.	133	32	5	0	1	8	14	19	.241	.301	.313
Leading Off Inn.	101	31	4	2	0	0	5	10	.307	.386	.340
Bases Empty	245	68	8	4	3	3	17	32	.278	.380	.327
Runners On	203	60	4	3	2	47	19	22	.296	.374	.354
Runners/Scor. Pos.	106	31	0	2	2	44	7	13	.292	.387	.333
Runners On/2 Out	81	25	2	1	1	24	9	11	.309	.395	.378
Scor. Pos./2 Out	54	17	0	1	1	23	5	7	.315	.407	.373
Late Inning Pressure	69	15	3	0	0	4	5	8	.217	.261	.280
Leading Off	15	5	1	0	0	0	0	1	.333	.400	.333
Bases Empty	40	10	3	0	0	0	1	4	.250	.325	.286
Runners On	29	5	0	0	0	4	4	4	.172	.172	.273
Runners/Scor. Pos.	13	3	0	0	0	4	0	2	.231	.231	.231

DRIVING IN RUNS	0 Out	1 Out	2 Out	Total	
From 1B	0/40	3/53	3/55	6/148	4%
From 2B	0/12	7/31	13/42	20/85	24%
From 3B	3/5	9/14	7/19	19/38	50%
Scoring Position	3/17	16/45	20/61	39/123	32%
Scor. Pos. %	18%	36%	33%	32%	
Driving In Runners from 3B with Less than Two Out:			12/19	63%	

Loves to face: Don Schulze (1.000, 2-for-2, 1 2B, 1 HR)
Hates to face: Mike Boddicker (0-for-10)
Recalled from Vancouver on May 14 and started all but 18 of Milwaukee's remaining games. . . . Batted .315 with runners in scoring position and two outs, 2d among A.L. rookies; Steve Buechele hit .318. . . . Hit 93 points higher at County Stadium than on road, largest differential by any Brewers' player since 1980, when Ben Oglivie hit 100 points better at home. . . . Started in every batting order position except the 4th and 8th slots last season, but was not used in the same slot in more than six consecutive games. . . . Ground-ball hitter: 1.62 G/A ratio last season. . . . According to one of those *USA Today* lists, George Bamberger thinks Riles is the best two-strike hitter that he has seen. At least 54 times last season, he wasn't.

Cal Ripken

Baltimore Orioles	AB	H	2B	3B	HR	RRF	BB	SO	BA	SA	OBA
Season	642	181	32	5	26	116	67	68	.282	.469	.347
vs. Left-Handed Pitchers	202	55	13	1	6	31	23	14	.272	.436	.346
vs. Right-Handed Pitchers	440	126	19	4	20	85	44	54	.286	.484	.347
Home	311	90	13	1	15	54	41	33	.289	.482	.371
Road	331	91	19	4	11	62	26	35	.275	.456	.323
Grass	545	156	25	4	21	94	64	59	.286	.462	.358
Artificial Turf	97	25	7	1	5	22	3	9	.258	.505	.277
April	70	18	3	1	2	14	12	8	.257	.414	.366
May	105	31	7	1	7	24	10	12	.295	.581	.347
June	107	29	4	0	2	14	8	11	.271	.364	.319
July	115	30	4	1	6	24	10	14	.261	.470	.315
August	106	30	8	1	1	17	14	11	.283	.406	.369
Sept./Oct.	139	43	6	1	8	23	13	12	.309	.540	.366
Leading Off Inn.	130	38	8	1	5	5	4	10	.292	.485	.313
Bases Empty	343	94	17	3	15	15	31	38	.274	.472	.334
Runners On	299	87	15	2	11	101	36	30	.291	.465	.360
Runners/Scor. Pos.	165	54	8	1	6	85	23	19	.327	.497	.396
Runners On/2 Out	116	32	6	1	5	33	16	13	.276	.474	.364
Scor. Pos./2 Out	66	18	4	1	2	26	11	10	.273	.455	.377
Late Inning Pressure	72	21	2	0	5	13	9	8	.292	.528	.366
Leading Off	17	5	1	0	1	1	1	0	.294	.529	.333
Bases Empty	37	11	1	0	3	3	3	4	.297	.568	.350
Runners On	35	10	1	0	2	10	6	4	.286	.486	.381
Runners/Scor. Pos.	21	7	1	0	1	8	3	4	.333	.524	.400

DRIVING IN RUNS	0 Out	1 Out	2 Out	Total	
From 1B	2/48	7/92	6/83	15/223	7%
From 2B	9/33	10/43	12/47	31/123	25%
From 3B	12/13	21/31	10/29	43/73	59%
Scoring Position	21/46	31/74	22/76	74/196	38%
Scor. Pos. %	46%	42%	29%	38%	
Driving In Runners from 3B with Less than Two Out:			33/44	75%	

Loves to face: Gene Nelson (.700, 7-for-10, 2 2B, 2 3B, 2 HR)
Hates to face: Joe Cowley (.067, 1-for-15, 6 SO)
Rate of assists per nine innings declined from league-leading 3.65 in 1984 to 2.99 last year; could that be the sign of a tired shortstop? . . . Career batting average of .324 in Late-Inning Pressure Situations; that jumps to .371 when you add the phrase "with runners in scoring position". . . . Very little career left/right difference: .292 (one home run every 23 at bats) against left-handers; .290 (one every 24 at bats) vs. right-handers. . . . Has 11 hits in his last 31 at bats with the bases loaded. . . . Streak of 603 consecutive games is 19th-longest in major-league history; he could move into the top ten if he plays in every game again this season. (Sandy Alomar once played in 648 consecutive games, and Omar Moreno in 503. Why?)

Andre Robertson

New York Yankees	AB	H	2B	3B	HR	RRF	BB	SO	BA	SA	OBA
Season	125	41	5	0	2	17	6	24	.328	.416	.358
vs. Left-Handed Pitchers	100	32	4	0	1	14	5	17	.320	.390	.346
vs. Right-Handed Pitchers	25	9	1	0	1	3	1	7	.360	.520	.407
Home	70	28	3	0	2	11	5	15	.400	.529	.434
Road	55	13	2	0	0	6	1	9	.236	.273	.259
Grass	112	37	3	0	2	15	6	24	.330	.411	.367
Artificial Turf	13	4	2	0	0	2	0	0	.308	.462	.286
April	0	0	0	0	0	0	0	0	.000	.000	.000
May	8	2	0	0	2	2	0	3	.250	1.000	.250
June	9	5	0	0	0	3	0	2	.556	.556	.556
July	33	11	3	0	0	4	3	2	.333	.424	.395
August	29	11	0	0	0	4	2	8	.379	.379	.419
Sept./Oct.	46	12	2	0	0	4	1	9	.261	.304	.271
Leading Off Inn.	27	10	2	0	0	0	2	4	.370	.444	.414
Bases Empty	65	22	3	0	2	2	5	12	.338	.477	.394
Runners On	60	19	2	0	0	15	1	12	.317	.350	.317
Runners/Scor. Pos.	37	12	1	0	0	15	0	7	.324	.351	.308
Runners On/2 Out	22	7	1	0	0	5	0	5	.318	.364	.318
Scor. Pos./2 Out	13	5	1	0	0	5	0	3	.385	.462	.385
Late Inning Pressure	13	6	0	0	0	1	0	3	.462	.462	.462
Leading Off	4	2	0	0	0	0	0	1	.500	.500	.500
Bases Empty	9	4	0	0	0	0	0	2	.444	.444	.444
Runners On	4	2	0	0	0	1	0	1	.500	.500	.500
Runners/Scor. Pos.	1	1	0	0	0	1	0	0	1.000	1.000	1.000

DRIVING IN RUNS	0 Out	1 Out	2 Out	Total	
From 1B	0/11	0/16	0/16	0/43	0%
From 2B	1/8	3/14	3/8	7/30	23%
From 3B	1/3	5/5	2/5	8/13	62%
Scoring Position	2/11	8/19	5/13	15/43	35%
Scor. Pos. %	18%	42%	38%	35%	
Driving In Runners from 3B with Less than Two Out:			6/8	75%	

Loves to face: Moose Haas (.714, 5-for-7)
Hates to face: Dave Stieb (0-for-13)
Knee injury a week before opening day kept him out of action until May 29. . . . Made odd starts at second, short, and third until first week of August, when he replaced Dale Berra as third baseman against left-handed pitchers. (That was right after Berra's imitation of Babe Herman on the basepaths resulted in a double tag-out at the plate by Carlton Fisk.) Starting third baseman in team's last 26 games against lefties, batting .319 in those games. . . . Career batting averages: .287 with bases empty, .206 with runners on base, .202 with runners in scoring position. . . . Batted .389 in day games last season. Career breakdown: .295 in day games, .234 in night games. . . . Career batting average of .309 in Late-Inning Pressure Situations. . . . Ground-ball hitter: 1.48 G/A ratio last season. Career: 1.28.

Gary Roenicke

Baltimore Orioles	AB	H	2B	3B	HR	RRF	BB	SO	BA	SA	OBA
Season	225	49	9	0	15	46	44	36	.218	.458	.342
vs. Left-Handed Pitchers	172	36	6	0	12	37	38	26	.209	.453	.347
vs. Right-Handed Pitchers	53	13	3	0	3	9	6	10	.245	.472	.322
Home	116	29	3	0	9	28	19	17	.250	.509	.353
Road	109	20	6	0	6	18	25	19	.183	.404	.331
Grass	193	45	7	0	14	42	39	32	.233	.487	.357
Artificial Turf	32	4	2	0	1	4	5	4	.125	.281	.243
April	29	4	0	0	3	8	2	7	.138	.448	.188
May	39	12	5	0	1	7	7	5	.308	.513	.404
June	30	9	1	0	2	3	8	4	.300	.533	.447
July	45	6	0	0	4	10	10	4	.133	.400	.291
August	37	5	1	0	2	5	9	5	.135	.324	.304
Sept./Oct.	45	13	2	0	3	13	8	11	.289	.533	.389
Leading Off Inn.	54	9	1	0	2	2	9	4	.167	.296	.286
Bases Empty	129	24	3	0	6	6	27	24	.186	.349	.327
Runners On	96	25	6	0	9	40	17	12	.260	.604	.362
Runners/Scor. Pos.	57	17	5	0	5	31	11	9	.298	.649	.394
Runners On/2 Out	45	15	2	0	5	22	11	7	.333	.711	.464
Scor. Pos./2 Out	28	10	1	0	3	17	8	4	.357	.714	.500
Late Inning Pressure	23	1	0	0	1	2	4	4	.043	.174	.185
Leading Off	9	0	0	0	0	0	0	2	.000	.000	.000
Bases Empty	15	0	0	0	0	0	2	3	.000	.000	.118
Runners On	8	1	0	0	1	2	2	1	.125	.500	.300
Runners/Scor. Pos.	6	1	0	0	1	2	1	1	.167	.667	.286

DRIVING IN RUNS	0 Out	1 Out	2 Out	Total	
From 1B	2/13	0/21	5/36	7/70	10%
From 2B	2/9	5/16	8/24	15/49	31%
From 3B	2/3	3/5	4/9	9/17	53%
Scoring Position	4/12	8/21	12/33	24/66	36%
Scor. Pos. %	33%	38%	36%	36%	
Driving In Runners from 3B with Less than Two Out:			5/8	63%	

Loves to face: Pete Filson (.625, 5-for-8, 1 HR)
Hates to face: Jamie Easterly (.063, 1-for-16)
One of three major-league players to have hit a grand-slam home run in each of past four seasons (others: Harold Baines and Eddie Murray, who has a five-year streak). Now has hit five career grand slams, as many as Duke Snider and two more than Al Kaline. . . . Yearly batting averages since 1982: .270, .260, .224, .218. . . . Despite lowest overall batting average of his career, batting average with runners in scoring position (.298) was 2d-highest of career. . . . Batting average with runners on base has been higher than with the bases empty in each of last five seasons. . . . Batted .103 (3-for-29) as a pinch-hitter last year. . . . Had more at bats at Yankee Stadium that at any road park while with Orioles, batting .254 there with four home runs in 122 at bats.

Ed Romero

Milwaukee Brewers	AB	H	2B	3B	HR	RRF	BB	SO	BA	SA	OBA
Season	251	63	11	1	0	23	26	20	.251	.303	.321
vs. Left-Handed Pitchers	99	19	5	0	0	6	10	5	.192	.242	.266
vs. Right-Handed Pitchers	152	44	6	1	0	17	16	15	.289	.342	.357
Home	128	33	5	1	0	10	11	13	.258	.313	.317
Road	123	30	6	0	0	13	15	7	.244	.293	.326
Grass	214	56	9	1	0	23	22	20	.262	.313	.331
Artificial Turf	37	7	2	0	0	0	4	0	.189	.243	.268
April	30	7	1	0	0	7	7	2	.233	.267	.378
May	37	6	1	0	0	1	2	3	.162	.189	.205
June	13	5	1	0	0	3	2	1	.385	.462	.467
July	23	1	0	0	0	0	2	3	.043	.043	.120
August	82	31	5	1	0	8	7	7	.378	.463	.427
Sept./Oct.	66	13	3	0	0	4	6	4	.197	.242	.264
Leading Off Inn.	57	13	3	1	0	0	6	4	.228	.316	.302
Bases Empty	148	32	5	1	0	0	15	11	.216	.264	.288
Runners On	103	31	6	0	0	23	11	9	.301	.359	.368
Runners/Scor. Pos.	50	15	4	0	0	22	9	4	.300	.380	.407
Runners On/2 Out	41	11	3	0	0	8	4	4	.268	.341	.333
Scor. Pos./2 Out	24	5	2	0	0	7	4	2	.208	.292	.321
Late Inning Pressure	36	12	4	0	0	2	5	2	.333	.444	.415
Leading Off	6	1	0	0	0	0	1	0	.167	.167	.286
Bases Empty	17	5	2	0	0	0	2	1	.294	.412	.368
Runners On	19	7	2	0	0	2	3	1	.368	.474	.455
Runners/Scor. Pos.	8	1	1	0	0	2	1	1	.125	.250	.222

DRIVING IN RUNS	0 Out	1 Out	2 Out	Total	
From 1B	1/20	0/27	1/31	2/78	3%
From 2B	1/10	5/12	2/17	8/39	21%
From 3B	2/3	5/6	5/13	12/22	55%
Scoring Position	3/13	10/18	7/30	20/61	33%
Scor. Pos. %	23%	56%	23%	33%	
Driving In Runners from 3B with Less than Two Out:			7/9	78%	

Loves to face: Dennis Martinez (.538, 7-for-13)
Hates to face: Mike Mason (0-for-11)
Ground-ball champion: 0.53 G/A ratio was lowest in the majors last season (minimum: 200 PA). Career average: 0.77. . . . Starting second baseman for most of August when Jim Gantner was hurt; .378 batting average that month was 3d-highest in A.L. . . . Good clutch statistics: has batted over .300 in Late-Inning Pressure Situations in each of last four seasons. Career LIP batting average is .328. . . . Career breakdown: .240 with bases empty, .280 with runners on base, .290 with runners in scoring position. . . . Has hit only one home run in 713 career plate appearances vs. right-handed pitchers (Oct. 5, 1980, off Rick Langford). . . . Drove in two runners from first base last season, matching his total for six previous seasons. . . . Career average of .326 (14-for-43) in his new home, Fenway Park; has hit 20 percent of his career homers there. That's right, one of five.

Luis Salazar

Chicago White Sox	AB	H	2B	3B	HR	RRF	BB	SO	BA	SA	OBA
Season	327	80	18	2	10	49	12	60	.245	.404	.267
vs. Left-Handed Pitchers	171	42	12	1	4	28	6	30	.246	.398	.268
vs. Right-Handed Pitchers	156	38	6	1	6	21	6	30	.244	.410	.267
Home	150	39	9	1	4	23	9	26	.260	.413	.298
Road	177	41	9	1	6	26	3	34	.232	.395	.240
Grass	269	67	15	1	8	45	12	52	.249	.401	.276
Artificial Turf	58	13	3	1	2	4	0	8	.224	.414	.224
April	44	9	0	0	2	8	2	7	.205	.341	.239
May	40	5	1	0	1	5	1	10	.125	.225	.140
June	40	7	1	0	2	3	4	8	.175	.350	.250
July	48	15	4	0	1	12	1	8	.313	.458	.314
August	92	26	7	1	1	8	3	15	.283	.413	.305
Sept./Oct.	63	18	5	1	3	13	1	12	.286	.540	.292
Leading Off Inn.	76	20	4	2	2	2	1	13	.263	.447	.273
Bases Empty	178	42	9	2	4	4	2	38	.236	.376	.244
Runners On	149	38	9	0	6	45	10	22	.255	.436	.293
Runners/Scor. Pos.	81	22	5	0	3	36	7	11	.272	.444	.312
Runners On/2 Out	54	14	1	0	4	22	7	9	.259	.500	.344
Scor. Pos./2 Out	32	11	1	0	2	18	6	5	.344	.563	.447
Late Inning Pressure	52	14	4	1	1	6	2	7	.269	.442	.296
Leading Off	12	4	1	1	0	0	1	2	.333	.583	.385
Bases Empty	25	8	2	1	0	0	1	4	.320	.480	.346
Runners On	27	6	2	0	1	6	1	3	.222	.407	.250
Runners/Scor. Pos.	17	4	1	0	0	4	0	2	.235	.294	.235

DRIVING IN RUNS	0 Out	1 Out	2 Out	Total	
From 1B	2/32	4/39	3/35	9/106	8%
From 2B	2/15	4/28	9/23	15/66	23%
From 3B	5/8	4/10	6/15	15/33	45%
Scoring Position	7/23	8/38	15/38	30/99	30%
Scor. Pos. %	30%	21%	39%	30%	
Driving In Runners from 3B with Less than Two Out:			9/18	50%	

Loves to face: Jay Howell (1.000, 2-for-2, 1 HR)
Hates to face: Rod Scurry (.063, 1-for-16, 7 SO)
Started 50 of 54 games against left-handers last season, but only 36 of 109 against right-handers. . . . Career batting average of .299 in Late-Inning Pressure Situations. . . . Leading off innings is not his thing: .278 career on-base average in those situations; in two years with White Sox, has led off 138 innings and drawn a total of two walks. Nevertheless, he was Chicago's leadoff batter nine times last season. . . . Walked twice in a game only once last season, April 27 vs. Yankees, but one of those was intentional, and the other was issued by someone named Don Cooper. . . . Batting average vs. left-handed pitchers (.246) was the lowest of his career. . . . Career batting average of .209 (9-for-43) with the bases loaded. . . . Batted .400 (6-for-15) as a pinch-hitter last season.

Mark Salas

Minnesota Twins	AB	H	2B	3B	HR	RRF	BB	SO	BA	SA	OBA
Season	360	108	20	5	9	41	18	37	.300	.458	.332
vs. Left-Handed Pitchers	21	4	1	0	0	1	4	4	.190	.238	.320
vs. Right-Handed Pitchers	339	104	19	5	9	40	14	33	.307	.472	.333
Home	203	64	11	5	6	25	10	23	.315	.507	.346
Road	157	44	9	0	3	16	8	14	.280	.395	.315
Grass	123	36	8	0	2	12	6	11	.293	.407	.331
Artificial Turf	237	72	12	5	7	29	12	26	.304	.485	.333
April	30	11	1	1	1	4	0	3	.367	.567	.367
May	79	24	3	2	0	6	3	11	.304	.392	.329
June	51	17	1	0	1	6	2	4	.333	.412	.352
July	61	20	6	0	1	9	5	7	.328	.475	.373
August	59	11	2	1	2	7	4	6	.186	.356	.246
Sept./Oct.	80	25	7	1	4	9	4	6	.313	.575	.345
Leading Off Inn.	100	24	5	2	4	4	4	11	.240	.450	.269
Bases Empty	193	54	12	2	5	5	10	20	.280	.440	.319
Runners On	167	54	8	3	4	36	8	17	.323	.479	.348
Runners/Scor. Pos.	94	22	4	2	2	29	8	12	.234	.383	.286
Runners On/2 Out	66	23	2	1	4	17	4	3	.348	.591	.386
Scor. Pos./2 Out	40	8	0	1	2	12	4	3	.200	.400	.273
Late Inning Pressure	47	15	1	1	1	8	2	5	.319	.447	.340
Leading Off	19	2	0	0	0	0	0	2	.105	.105	.105
Bases Empty	25	5	0	0	0	0	1	2	.200	.200	.231
Runners On	22	10	1	1	1	8	1	3	.455	.727	.458
Runners/Scor. Pos.	13	3	1	0	0	5	1	3	.231	.308	.267

DRIVING IN RUNS	0 Out	1 Out	2 Out	Total	
From 1B	1/30	2/45	4/44	7/119	6%
From 2B	2/9	4/33	6/33	12/75	16%
From 3B	3/4	7/18	3/15	13/37	35%
Scoring Position	5/13	11/51	9/48	25/112	22%
Scor. Pos. %	38%	22%	19%	22%	
Driving In Runners from 3B with Less than Two Out:			10/22	45%	

Loves to face: Jim Clancy (.667, 4-for-6, 1 HR)
Hates to face: Dave Stieb (0-for-7, 2 SO)
Only major-league rookie with at least 200 at bats who batted .300 last season; yes, Joe Orsulak, we're serious. . . . First Twins catcher to hit .300 and catch at least half of team's games since Earl Battey hit .302 in 1961, their first year in Minnesota. . . . Started 97 of 104 games against right-handers last season, but his next start against a left-hander will be his first. . . . Batted .323 with runners on base, highest average on the team and also the highest by any rookie in the majors last season. . . . Ratio of 0.70 ground outs-to-air outs was 10th-lowest in A.L. last season (minimum: 200 PA). Career average: 0.71. . . . Had career minor-league batting average of .260 in six seasons in Cardinals' system; drafted by Twins at 1984 winter meetings.

Dick Schofield

California Angels	AB	H	2B	3B	HR	RRF	BB	SO	BA	SA	OBA
Season	438	96	19	3	8	43	35	70	.219	.331	.287
vs. Left-Handed Pitchers	147	38	6	1	2	11	11	18	.259	.354	.323
vs. Right-Handed Pitchers	291	58	13	2	6	32	24	52	.199	.320	.269
Home	219	48	8	1	5	22	12	41	.219	.333	.269
Road	219	48	11	2	3	21	23	29	.219	.329	.305
Grass	367	78	14	2	7	36	26	60	.213	.319	.274
Artificial Turf	71	18	5	1	1	7	9	10	.254	.394	.354
April	73	17	1	1	4	12	7	14	.233	.438	.309
May	64	10	3	0	1	6	3	13	.156	.250	.214
June	70	13	3	0	0	2	6	12	.186	.229	.266
July	63	11	2	0	2	6	8	10	.175	.302	.268
August	77	19	7	1	1	11	6	10	.247	.403	.306
Sept./Oct.	91	26	3	1	0	6	5	11	.286	.341	.337
Leading Off Inn.	88	19	2	0	0	1	9	13	.216	.239	.303
Bases Empty	250	55	8	0	5	7	14	40	.220	.312	.270
Runners On	188	41	11	3	3	36	21	30	.218	.356	.309
Runners/Scor. Pos.	98	21	5	2	1	30	11	18	.214	.337	.304
Runners On/2 Out	84	14	2	0	1	13	14	18	.167	.226	.300
Scor. Pos./2 Out	50	7	1	0	1	13	9	10	.140	.220	.295
Late Inning Pressure	36	6	1	0	1	5	3	6	.167	.278	.231
Leading Off	5	2	0	0	0	0	0	0	.400	.400	.400
Bases Empty	22	5	1	0	1	2	1	3	.227	.409	.261
Runners On	14	1	0	0	0	3	2	3	.071	.071	.188
Runners/Scor. Pos.	7	1	0	0	0	3	2	1	.143	.143	.333

DRIVING IN RUNS	0 Out	1 Out	2 Out	Total	
From 1B	1/31	6/50	1/61	8/142	6%
From 2B	1/12	6/31	5/40	12/83	14%
From 3B	2/5	5/10	6/21	13/36	36%
Scoring Position	3/17	11/41	11/61	25/119	21%
Scor. Pos. %	18%	27%	18%	21%	
Driving In Runners from 3B with Less than Two Out:			7/15	47%	

Loves to face: Jaime Cocanower (.667, 4-for-6, 1 HR)
Hates to face: Danny Darwin (0-for-11, 4 SO)
Lowest career batting average (.206) of any active player with at least 1000 plate appearances; with runners on base, it's even lower (.176). . . . How did Craig Gerber feel on April 18 when Schofield pinch-hit for him? . . . But even a stopped clock is right twice a day: he batted .323 (10-for-31) in 11 games against Kansas City last season, has a career batting average of .300 (12-for-40) at Cleveland Stadium, and has hit three home runs in 51 career at bats at Comiskey Park. . . . His eight home runs last year were the most for an Angels shortstop since 1970, when Jim Fregosi had 22. . . . Averaged .82 double plays per nine innings, best rate in A.L. (league average: .65). . . . Stole 11 bases last season, one fewer than his father had in his 19-year major-league career. Now we understand why they called him "Ducky."

Bill Schroeder

Milwaukee Brewers	AB	H	2B	3B	HR	RRF	BB	SO	BA	SA	OBA
Season	194	47	8	0	8	25	12	61	.242	.407	.290
vs. Left-Handed Pitchers	58	17	2	0	5	14	3	15	.293	.586	.323
vs. Right-Handed Pitchers	136	30	6	0	3	11	9	46	.221	.331	.277
Home	104	22	6	0	2	9	5	36	.212	.327	.257
Road	90	25	2	0	6	16	7	25	.278	.500	.330
Grass	177	43	8	0	7	22	11	55	.243	.407	.292
Artificial Turf	17	4	0	0	1	3	1	6	.235	.412	.278
April	53	13	1	0	5	14	5	21	.245	.547	.300
May	29	8	2	0	1	2	0	11	.276	.448	.300
June	16	3	0	0	1	2	4	5	.188	.375	.350
July	26	9	2	0	1	5	1	5	.346	.538	.393
August	52	11	2	0	0	1	2	12	.212	.250	.241
Sept./Oct.	18	3	1	0	0	1	0	7	.167	.222	.167
Leading Off Inn.	41	10	2	0	2	2	3	13	.244	.439	.311
Bases Empty	115	27	7	0	4	4	4	36	.235	.400	.267
Runners On	79	20	1	0	4	21	8	25	.253	.418	.322
Runners/Scor. Pos.	43	9	0	0	3	18	6	17	.209	.419	.294
Runners On/2 Out	36	10	0	0	1	5	6	12	.278	.361	.381
Scor. Pos./2 Out	19	4	0	0	1	5	4	7	.211	.368	.348
Late Inning Pressure	29	8	1	0	1	4	2	7	.276	.414	.313
Leading Off	10	2	1	0	0	0	1	5	.200	.300	.273
Bases Empty	19	5	1	0	0	0	1	5	.263	.316	.300
Runners On	10	3	0	0	1	4	1	2	.300	.600	.333
Runners/Scor. Pos.	7	2	0	0	1	4	1	2	.286	.714	.333

DRIVING IN RUNS	0 Out	1 Out	2 Out	Total	
From 1B	0/9	3/25	0/30	3/64	5%
From 2B	1/6	3/16	3/14	7/36	19%
From 3B	1/2	5/8	1/9	7/19	37%
Scoring Position	2/8	8/24	4/23	14/55	25%
Scor. Pos. %	25%	33%	17%	25%	
Driving In Runners from 3B with Less than Two Out:			6/10	60%	

Loves to face: Charlie Hough (.667, 4-for-6, 2 HR)
Hates to face: Walt Terrell (0-for-6, 6 SO)
On disabled list from May 15 to June 14 with a strained right elbow, active for a week, then back onto the DL until after All-Star Game. Even then, was used sparingly over the second half of the season, starting only 24 games until Sept. 7, when he went out for the year to have surgery on the elbow. . . . Has hit 19 of his 25 career home runs with the bases empty. . . . Has career rate of one home run every 12.6 at bats against lefties (12 home runs in 151 at bats). . . . Down the ladder career batting averages: .261 with bases empty, .210 with runners on base, .148 with runners in scoring position. . . . Career batting average of .317 (20-for-63) in Late-Inning Pressure Situations, .421 (8-for-19) in LIP with runners on base.

Donnie Scott

Seattle Mariners	AB	H	2B	3B	HR	RRF	BB	SO	BA	SA	OBA
Season	185	41	13	0	4	25	15	41	.222	.357	.275
vs. Left-Handed Pitchers	28	7	2	0	1	6	2	8	.250	.429	.290
vs. Right-Handed Pitchers	157	34	11	0	3	19	13	33	.217	.344	.272
Home	99	26	9	0	3	20	10	19	.263	.444	.324
Road	86	15	4	0	1	5	5	22	.174	.256	.215
Grass	66	12	4	0	1	4	5	18	.182	.288	.236
Artificial Turf	119	29	9	0	3	21	10	23	.244	.395	.295
April	13	5	0	0	2	9	2	1	.385	.846	.438
May	48	8	2	0	0	4	2	11	.167	.208	.196
June	23	3	1	0	0	1	1	5	.130	.174	.160
July	23	4	3	0	0	1	2	8	.174	.304	.240
August	23	10	4	0	1	6	2	6	.435	.739	.480
Sept./Oct.	55	11	3	0	1	4	6	10	.200	.309	.274
Leading Off Inn.	44	9	3	0	1	1	2	9	.205	.341	.239
Bases Empty	109	24	8	0	1	1	11	22	.220	.321	.292
Runners On	76	17	5	0	3	24	4	19	.224	.408	.250
Runners/Scor. Pos.	45	12	3	0	2	20	3	14	.267	.467	.288
Runners On/2 Out	34	7	1	0	2	8	2	7	.206	.412	.250
Scor. Pos./2 Out	20	5	0	0	1	5	2	6	.250	.400	.318
Late Inning Pressure	33	6	3	0	2	4	0	4	.182	.455	.182
Leading Off	10	3	1	0	1	1	0	0	.300	.700	.300
Bases Empty	18	3	1	0	1	1	0	2	.167	.389	.167
Runners On	15	3	2	0	1	3	0	2	.200	.533	.200
Runners/Scor. Pos.	7	1	1	0	0	0	0	1	.143	.286	.143

DRIVING IN RUNS	0 Out	1 Out	2 Out	Total	
From 1B	0/12	4/21	2/24	6/57	11%
From 2B	1/8	2/13	1/15	4/36	11%
From 3B	2/7	5/8	3/9	10/24	42%
Scoring Position	3/15	7/21	4/24	14/60	23%
Scor. Pos. %	20%	33%	17%	23%	
Driving In Runners from 3B with Less than Two Out:			7/15	47%	

Loves to face: Ken Schrom (.444, 4-for-9, 1 HR)
Hates to face: Don Schulze (0-for-9)
How many switch-hitting backup catchers do you know? . . . Despite batting from both sides, was used much more frequently against right-handers (42 starts) than against left-handers (six). . . . Random facts about backup catchers: Joe Garagiola's last major-league hit was a double off Robin Roberts. . . . Bob Montgomery's first major-league home run was hit off Jim Palmer. . . . Charlie Silvera was eligible for 42 World Series games and played in one; Arndt Jorgens did even better: 23 Series games watched, none played. . . . Pat Corrales, who never had a pinch-hit in his major-league career, once batted for Hal McRae in a World Series game.

Larry Sheets

Baltimore Orioles	AB	H	2B	3B	HR	RRF	BB	SO	BA	SA	OBA
Season	328	86	8	0	17	53	28	52	.262	.442	.323
vs. Left-Handed Pitchers	17	2	1	0	0	4	4	5	.118	.176	.273
vs. Right-Handed Pitchers	311	84	7	0	17	49	24	47	.270	.457	.326
Home	170	47	5	0	5	26	16	27	.276	.394	.344
Road	158	39	3	0	12	27	12	25	.247	.494	.300
Grass	283	72	6	0	12	44	23	46	.254	.403	.314
Artificial Turf	45	14	2	0	5	9	5	6	.311	.689	.380
April	39	11	2	0	3	8	4	5	.282	.564	.349
May	59	21	3	0	4	11	5	9	.356	.610	.400
June	75	16	0	0	2	14	6	12	.213	.293	.280
July	47	8	1	0	1	3	7	8	.170	.255	.278
August	46	14	1	0	4	11	3	7	.304	.587	.347
Sept./Oct.	62	16	1	0	3	6	3	11	.258	.419	.303
Leading Off Inn.	64	18	3	0	4	4	3	12	.281	.516	.313
Bases Empty	182	46	6	0	9	9	15	34	.253	.434	.317
Runners On	146	40	2	0	8	44	13	18	.274	.452	.331
Runners/Scor. Pos.	76	21	1	0	5	37	8	10	.276	.487	.341
Runners On/2 Out	57	15	0	0	4	13	5	10	.263	.474	.323
Scor. Pos./2 Out	31	7	0	0	2	9	3	6	.226	.419	.294
Late Inning Pressure	51	12	0	0	3	7	4	11	.235	.412	.291
Leading Off	13	4	0	0	0	0	1	3	.308	.308	.357
Bases Empty	31	7	0	0	1	1	3	6	.226	.323	.294
Runners On	20	5	0	0	2	6	1	5	.250	.550	.286
Runners/Scor. Pos.	11	3	0	0	2	6	0	2	.273	.818	.273

DRIVING IN RUNS	0 Out	1 Out	2 Out	Total	
From 1B	0/28	4/45	2/44	6/117	5%
From 2B	2/10	6/22	4/24	12/56	21%
From 3B	4/8	11/14	3/13	18/35	51%
Scoring Position	6/18	17/36	7/37	30/91	33%
Scor. Pos. %	33%	47%	19%	33%	
Driving In Runners from 3B with Less than Two Out:			15/22	68%	

Loves to face: Ron Romanick (.625, 5-for-8, 1 HR)
Hates to face: Charlie Hough (0-for-6)
Ranked 3d among major-league rookies with 17 home runs, trailing Oddibe McDowell (18) and Glenn Davis (20). . . . Started 93 of Birds' 103 games against right-handers, but none against left-handers last season. . . . Two hits vs. left-handers were a single off Jeff Kaiser and a double off Pete Filson. . . . Started only seven games in the field, and only one of those came after April 18. . . . Hit 12 of 17 home runs on the road; his teammates hit 98 at home and 99 on the road. . . . Hit the first of the Orioles' league-leading six pinch-hit home runs on April 19. One of five A.L. players to hit two pinch-hit homers last season. . . . Ground-ball hitter: 1.56 G/A ratio last season. . . . Did not steal a base last season, and has a total of just two in 604 professional games.

John Shelby

Baltimore Orioles	AB	H	2B	3B	HR	RRF	BB	SO	BA	SA	OBA
Season	205	58	6	2	7	28	7	44	.283	.434	.307
vs. Left-Handed Pitchers	82	20	3	1	2	9	2	21	.244	.378	.262
vs. Right-Handed Pitchers	123	38	3	1	5	19	5	23	.309	.472	.336
Home	102	25	2	1	4	15	3	23	.245	.402	.267
Road	103	33	4	1	3	13	4	21	.320	.466	.346
Grass	193	53	6	1	7	27	7	40	.275	.425	.300
Artificial Turf	12	5	0	1	0	1	0	4	.417	.583	.417
April	0	0	0	0	0	0	0	0	.000	.000	.000
May	0	0	0	0	0	0	0	0	.000	.000	.000
June	29	11	2	0	2	5	1	5	.379	.655	.400
July	48	8	0	1	0	4	1	14	.167	.208	.184
August	42	13	2	0	1	8	0	7	.310	.429	.310
Sept./Oct.	86	26	2	1	4	11	5	18	.302	.488	.341
Leading Off Inn.	62	19	1	1	3	3	1	11	.306	.500	.317
Bases Empty	130	36	3	1	3	3	3	31	.277	.385	.293
Runners On	75	22	3	1	4	25	4	13	.293	.520	.329
Runners/Scor. Pos.	41	13	3	1	0	17	2	7	.317	.439	.349
Runners On/2 Out	30	12	1	0	2	12	2	6	.400	.633	.438
Scor. Pos./2 Out	18	6	1	0	0	8	2	4	.333	.389	.400
Late Inning Pressure	35	7	1	1	0	2	1	9	.200	.286	.222
Leading Off	9	2	0	1	0	0	0	3	.222	.444	.222
Bases Empty	23	5	1	1	0	0	1	7	.217	.348	.250
Runners On	12	2	0	0	0	2	0	2	.167	.167	.167
Runners/Scor. Pos.	7	2	0	0	0	2	0	2	.286	.286	.286

DRIVING IN RUNS	0 Out	1 Out	2 Out	Total	
From 1B	1/11	1/26	2/24	4/61	7%
From 2B	2/6	3/12	3/12	8/30	27%
From 3B	2/2	2/8	5/11	9/21	43%
Scoring Position	4/8	5/20	8/23	17/51	33%
Scor. Pos. %	50%	25%	35%	33%	
Driving In Runners from 3B with Less than Two Out:			4/10	40%	

Loves to face: Tommy John (.700, 7-for-10, 1 HR)
Hates to face: John Butcher (.067, 1-for-15)
Recalled from minors just before Weaver replaced Altobelli as manager, and played little until Fred Lynn was injured in late August. Shelby then started 26 consecutive games in center field, batting .303 during that time. . . . Averaged 3.15 putouts per nine innings last season, 2d-highest rate among A.L. outfielders (minimum: 300 innings); Rickey Henderson led with 3.24. . . . Career batting average of .421 (8-for-19) with the bases loaded; 22 RRFs in 22 plate appearances. . . . Has batted for higher average in road games than in home games in each of last three seasons; his .320 mark on road last season was 5th-best in A.L. among semi-regulars. . . . Batting average with runners in scoring position (.317) was highest of career. . . . Career batting average of .219 in Late-Inning Pressure Situations, .182 in LIP with runners on base.

Pat Sheridan

Kansas City Royals	AB	H	2B	3B	HR	RRF	BB	SO	BA	SA	OBA
Season	206	47	9	2	3	19	23	38	.228	.335	.307
vs. Left-Handed Pitchers	14	1	1	0	0	1	0	6	.071	.143	.071
vs. Right-Handed Pitchers	192	46	8	2	3	18	23	32	.240	.349	.323
Home	98	28	7	0	2	12	9	16	.286	.418	.343
Road	108	19	2	2	1	7	14	22	.176	.259	.276
Grass	86	13	2	2	0	6	12	20	.151	.221	.263
Artificial Turf	120	34	7	0	3	13	11	18	.283	.417	.341
April	68	16	2	1	0	4	7	10	.235	.294	.307
May	49	8	2	0	2	7	8	10	.163	.327	.281
June	35	11	2	1	1	3	5	6	.314	.514	.415
July	19	3	0	0	0	1	2	4	.158	.158	.238
August	5	2	0	0	0	0	0	0	.400	.400	.400
Sept./Oct.	30	7	3	0	0	4	1	8	.233	.333	.250
Leading Off Inn.	44	4	0	0	0	0	5	7	.091	.091	.184
Bases Empty	124	32	6	1	2	2	14	15	.258	.371	.338
Runners On	82	15	3	1	1	17	9	23	.183	.280	.261
Runners/Scor. Pos.	52	9	2	0	1	14	4	18	.173	.269	.228
Runners On/2 Out	29	4	1	0	0	4	4	10	.138	.172	.242
Scor. Pos./2 Out	22	3	1	0	0	4	3	9	.136	.182	.240
Late Inning Pressure	34	9	2	1	0	1	5	7	.265	.382	.359
Leading Off	10	3	0	0	0	0	2	3	.300	.300	.417
Bases Empty	21	8	2	1	0	0	3	5	.381	.571	.458
Runners On	13	1	0	0	0	1	2	2	.077	.077	.200
Runners/Scor. Pos.	5	0	0	0	0	1	1	1	.000	.000	.167

DRIVING IN RUNS	0 Out	1 Out	2 Out	Total	
From 1B	3/22	0/19	0/20	3/61	5%
From 2B	1/10	2/11	2/17	5/38	13%
From 3B	3/8	3/5	2/11	8/24	33%
Scoring Position	4/18	5/16	4/28	13/62	21%
Scor. Pos. %	22%	31%	14%	21%	
Driving In Runners from 3B with Less than Two Out:			6/13	46%	

Loves to face: Jim Slaton (.857, 6-for-7)
Hates to face: Danny Darwin (.050, 1-for-20)
0-for-15 with runners in scoring position in 12 post-season games last year. . . . His first major-league home run tied a game in the ninth inning against Milt Wilcox in May 1983. His next Late-Inning Pressure home run came in Game Two of the '85 League Championship Series, to tie the game in the ninth, this time off Tom Henke. . . . Had lowest on-base average when leading off inning (.184) in majors last year. That's definitely not his specialty: his career on-base average leading off innings (.257) is lower than his overall career *batting* average (.267). . . . Spent 45 days on disabled list last season and started only 53 games, all but one against right-handers. . . . Ground-ball hitter: 1.67 G/A ratio last season. Career: 1.50.

Nelson Simmons

Detroit Tigers	AB	H	2B	3B	HR	RRF	BB	SO	BA	SA	OBA
Season	251	60	11	0	10	35	26	41	.239	.402	.306
vs. Left-Handed Pitchers	48	12	1	0	3	11	5	7	.250	.458	.315
vs. Right-Handed Pitchers	203	48	10	0	7	24	21	34	.236	.389	.304
Home	133	36	3	0	7	22	15	20	.271	.451	.338
Road	118	24	8	0	3	13	11	21	.203	.347	.269
Grass	213	52	7	0	9	32	24	31	.244	.404	.315
Artificial Turf	38	8	4	0	1	3	2	10	.211	.395	.250
April	4	0	0	0	0	0	0	0	.000	.000	.000
May	59	15	4	0	2	8	5	6	.254	.424	.308
June	33	8	2	0	1	4	4	10	.242	.394	.324
July	0	0	0	0	0	0	0	0	.000	.000	.000
August	66	16	3	0	4	12	4	6	.242	.470	.278
Sept./Oct.	89	21	2	0	3	11	13	19	.236	.360	.330
Leading Off Inn.	58	11	2	0	2	2	3	6	.190	.328	.230
Bases Empty	148	30	6	0	4	4	14	26	.203	.324	.272
Runners On	103	30	5	0	6	31	12	15	.291	.515	.353
Runners/Scor. Pos.	52	15	3	0	2	23	9	6	.288	.462	.369
Runners On/2 Out	55	13	1	0	4	14	3	5	.236	.473	.276
Scor. Pos./2 Out	33	8	1	0	2	10	2	2	.242	.455	.286
Late Inning Pressure	31	4	1	0	0	2	7	9	.129	.161	.282
Leading Off	7	1	0	0	0	0	1	2	.143	.143	.250
Bases Empty	22	3	1	0	0	0	4	8	.136	.182	.269
Runners On	9	1	0	0	0	2	3	1	.111	.111	.308
Runners/Scor. Pos.	3	1	0	0	0	2	2	0	.333	.333	.500

DRIVING IN RUNS	0 Out	1 Out	2 Out	Total	
From 1B	2/19	1/22	3/40	6/81	7%
From 2B	2/7	1/9	6/28	9/44	20%
From 3B	3/4	6/7	1/11	10/22	45%
Scoring Position	5/11	7/16	7/39	19/66	29%
Scor. Pos. %	45%	44%	18%	29%	
Driving In Runners from 3B with Less than Two Out:			9/11	82%	

Loves to face: Roy Smith (1.000, 3-for-3, 2 HR)
Hates to face: Kirk McCaskill (0-for-7)
First career home run came as a pinch-hitter on May 4 and was hit off his namesake. No, not Curt Simmons, Gene Nelson. . . . Hit more homers in rookie season than any Nelson or any Simmons in baseball history: Rocky had four, Ricky had five, Ted had three, and Hall-of-Famer Al had eight. . . . Started season on disabled list, later was sent to minors for seven weeks. . . . From Aug. 13 to end of season, started 43 of 51 games that Tigers played. . . . One of only five major-league rookies to reach double figures in home runs last season. . . . Drove in 81.8 percent of runners from third base with less than two outs, 4th-best rate in A.L. . . . Batted .129 in Late-Inning Pressure Situations, lowest in A.L. last season. Good company, though: 2d-lowest was Reggie Jackson, .136.

Ted Simmons

Milwaukee Brewers	AB	H	2B	3B	HR	RRF	BB	SO	BA	SA	OBA
Season	528	144	28	2	12	79	57	32	.273	.402	.342
vs. Left-Handed Pitchers	166	51	11	0	7	30	20	11	.307	.500	.380
vs. Right-Handed Pitchers	362	93	17	2	5	49	37	21	.257	.356	.324
Home	251	71	13	1	8	41	24	19	.283	.438	.344
Road	277	73	15	1	4	38	33	13	.264	.368	.340
Grass	437	122	25	1	9	63	47	28	.279	.403	.348
Artificial Turf	91	22	3	1	3	16	10	4	.242	.396	.314
April	66	17	2	0	1	9	9	4	.258	.333	.347
May	81	25	3	0	0	13	7	5	.309	.346	.360
June	87	16	9	0	2	9	7	5	.184	.356	.250
July	97	27	5	2	5	19	12	7	.278	.526	.351
August	73	25	3	0	3	15	12	7	.342	.507	.430
Sept./Oct.	124	34	6	0	1	14	10	4	.274	.347	.328
Leading Off Inn.	132	28	9	0	3	3	8	8	.212	.348	.257
Bases Empty	300	78	16	2	8	8	25	22	.260	.407	.319
Runners On	228	66	12	0	4	71	32	10	.289	.395	.370
Runners/Scor. Pos.	162	46	8	0	3	67	26	7	.284	.389	.373
Runners On/2 Out	106	28	7	0	2	32	16	3	.264	.387	.361
Scor. Pos./2 Out	82	24	6	0	2	31	12	2	.293	.439	.383
Late Inning Pressure	85	21	6	0	3	19	9	8	.247	.424	.323
Leading Off	21	2	1	0	0	0	3	4	.095	.143	.208
Bases Empty	50	11	3	0	2	2	5	6	.220	.400	.304
Runners On	35	10	3	0	1	17	4	2	.286	.457	.350
Runners/Scor. Pos.	26	9	3	0	1	17	4	1	.346	.577	.419

DRIVING IN RUNS	0 Out	1 Out	2 Out	Total	
From 1B	1/35	2/55	6/66	9/156	6%
From 2B	2/15	13/47	19/61	34/123	28%
From 3B	3/10	16/29	5/28	24/67	36%
Scoring Position	5/25	29/76	24/89	58/190	31%
Scor. Pos. %	20%	38%	27%	31%	
Driving In Runners from 3B with Less than Two Out:			19/39	49%	

Loves to face: Roy Smith (.800, 4-for-5)
Hates to face: Floyd Bannister (.059, 1-for-17)
Career strikeout rate of one every 13.4 at bats is lowest among active players with 200 or more home runs. . . . His 464 career doubles are the most in baseball history by a player who spent most of his career as a catcher. . . . Has grounded into 278 double plays, 50 short of Hank Aaron's major-league record. But Jim Rice is at 252 and surging. . . . Recovered from terrible 1984 season, raising batting average by 52 points and slugging average by 102. . . . If Rusty Staub retires, Simmons inherits the active presidency of the Society for Intentional Walks, with 176. . . . Batting average with runners in scoring position has been higher than his overall batting average in each of last six seasons. . . . Has not walked with the bases loaded in 67 plate appearances in A.L.

Don Slaught

Texas Rangers	AB	H	2B	3B	HR	RRF	BB	SO	BA	SA	OBA
Season	343	96	17	4	8	41	20	41	.280	.423	.331
vs. Left-Handed Pitchers	101	29	5	0	3	13	7	16	.287	.426	.351
vs. Right-Handed Pitchers	242	67	12	4	5	28	13	25	.277	.421	.322
Home	181	53	10	2	4	18	12	21	.293	.436	.347
Road	162	43	7	2	4	23	8	20	.265	.407	.312
Grass	288	85	15	3	7	36	16	34	.295	.441	.341
Artificial Turf	55	11	2	1	1	5	4	7	.200	.327	.279
April	67	18	1	1	1	5	2	8	.269	.358	.300
May	65	13	1	0	2	8	5	4	.200	.308	.268
June	85	23	7	1	1	8	7	11	.271	.412	.326
July	11	5	1	1	0	2	2	1	.455	.727	.538
August	12	3	1	0	1	3	2	2	.250	.583	.400
Sept./Oct.	103	34	6	1	3	15	2	15	.330	.495	.361
Leading Off Inn.	76	17	5	0	1	1	6	8	.224	.329	.280
Bases Empty	189	53	10	2	6	6	10	21	.280	.450	.327
Runners On	154	43	7	2	2	35	10	20	.279	.390	.335
Runners/Scor. Pos.	75	19	4	1	0	27	7	12	.253	.333	.317
Runners On/2 Out	64	15	3	1	0	17	5	7	.234	.313	.300
Scor. Pos./2 Out	39	7	2	1	0	16	4	6	.179	.282	.256
Late Inning Pressure	58	19	2	0	1	4	3	6	.328	.414	.371
Leading Off	7	1	0	0	0	0	0	0	.143	.143	.143
Bases Empty	29	10	1	0	0	0	1	1	.345	.379	.367
Runners On	29	9	1	0	1	4	2	5	.310	.448	.375
Runners/Scor. Pos.	11	2	1	0	0	2	1	3	.182	.273	.250

DRIVING IN RUNS	0 Out	1 Out	2 Out	Total	
From 1B	1/34	4/36	4/43	9/113	8%
From 2B	1/10	2/15	7/24	10/49	20%
From 3B	1/4	7/10	6/19	14/33	42%
Scoring Position	2/14	9/25	13/43	24/82	29%
Scor. Pos. %	14%	36%	30%	29%	
Driving In Runners from 3B with Less than Two Out:			8/14	57%	

Loves to face: Matt Young (.550, 11-for-20)
Hates to face: Bert Blyleven (0-for-23)
Batted everywhere in Texas starting lineup except leadoff and cleanup. . . . Career batting average (.282) ranks 3d among active players with at least 200 games caught, behind Ted Simmons (.287) and Tony Pena (.285). . . . No place like home, wherever it is: despite trade from Kansas City to Texas, still hit higher at home than on road last season, keeping his record perfect—four years in major leagues, four years hitting better at home. . . . One difference between Kansas City and Texas: he batted 21 times with the bases loaded in 1984, only four times last year. . . . Had six consecutive multiple-hit games (Sept. 8–13). . . . Career batting average of .303 in Late-Inning Pressure Situations. . . . Career breakdown: .310 vs. left-handers, .268 vs. right-handers.

Roy Smalley

Minnesota Twins	AB	H	2B	3B	HR	RRF	BB	SO	BA	SA	OBA
Season	388	100	20	0	12	48	60	65	.258	.402	.357
vs. Left-Handed Pitchers	72	17	7	0	0	9	13	13	.236	.333	.349
vs. Right-Handed Pitchers	316	83	13	0	12	39	47	52	.263	.418	.359
Home	201	50	11	0	7	32	30	34	.249	.408	.348
Road	187	50	9	0	5	16	30	31	.267	.396	.367
Grass	148	39	6	0	4	14	25	25	.264	.385	.368
Artificial Turf	240	61	14	0	8	34	35	40	.254	.413	.350
April	59	15	3	0	1	5	10	7	.254	.356	.362
May	75	24	4	0	3	11	13	12	.320	.493	.420
June	65	19	5	0	1	9	11	13	.292	.415	.390
July	62	14	4	0	3	10	12	9	.226	.435	.347
August	51	10	1	0	3	5	8	14	.196	.392	.317
Sept./Oct.	76	18	3	0	1	8	6	10	.237	.316	.293
Leading Off Inn.	87	22	6	0	4	4	13	10	.253	.460	.350
Bases Empty	227	54	8	0	10	10	33	34	.238	.405	.337
Runners On	161	46	12	0	2	38	27	31	.286	.398	.384
Runners/Scor. Pos.	91	22	6	0	1	33	21	22	.242	.341	.377
Runners On/2 Out	66	19	4	0	1	14	9	12	.288	.394	.373
Scor. Pos./2 Out	44	10	3	0	0	11	8	9	.227	.295	.346
Late Inning Pressure	57	14	3	0	1	8	10	11	.246	.351	.353
Leading Off	13	3	1	0	1	1	1	3	.231	.538	.286
Bases Empty	30	4	1	0	1	1	6	6	.133	.267	.278
Runners On	27	10	2	0	0	7	4	5	.370	.444	.438
Runners/Scor. Pos.	15	5	1	0	0	7	3	2	.333	.400	.421

DRIVING IN RUNS	0 Out	1 Out	2 Out	Total	
From 1B	1/24	1/49	4/47	6/120	5%
From 2B	4/15	5/26	6/31	15/72	21%
From 3B	3/3	9/15	3/20	15/38	39%
Scoring Position	7/18	14/41	9/51	30/110	27%
Scor. Pos. %	39%	34%	18%	27%	
Driving In Runners from 3B with Less than Two Out:			12/18	67%	

Loves to face: Ed Whitson (.667, 4-for-6)
Hates to face: Rick Langford (.140, 6-for-43, 14 SO)
Averaged only 2.42 assists per nine innings last season, lowest rate among major-league shortstops (minimum: 300 innings); Twins' other shortstop, Greg Gagne, averaged 3.08.... Fly-ball hitter: 0.55 G/A ratio was 3d-lowest in majors last season (minimum: 200 PA). Career average: 0.91.... Drove in only two base runners with 12 home runs, tied for 2d-lowest average in A.L.... After 11 seasons in majors, has for first time shown dominance from one side of the plate for two straight years. Not only did he hit higher from left side in both '84 and '85, but 21 of his 23 home runs have come from that side over last two years.... Through 1984, had homered once every 36.4 at bats vs. left-handers, once every 36.7 at bats vs. right-handers.

Lonnie Smith

Kansas City Royals	AB	H	2B	3B	HR	RRF	BB	SO	BA	SA	OBA
Season	448	115	23	4	6	41	41	69	.257	.366	.321
vs. Left-Handed Pitchers	140	41	11	0	2	13	13	19	.293	.414	.350
vs. Right-Handed Pitchers	308	74	12	4	4	28	28	50	.240	.344	.308
Home	225	52	10	4	2	20	24	30	.231	.338	.307
Road	223	63	13	0	4	21	17	39	.283	.395	.336
Grass	160	47	12	0	3	13	10	27	.294	.425	.339
Artificial Turf	288	68	11	4	3	28	31	42	.236	.333	.312
April	0	0	0	0	0	0	0	0	.000	.000	.000
May	42	8	1	0	0	1	5	7	.190	.214	.292
June	94	20	4	4	1	13	13	17	.213	.372	.303
July	79	26	8	0	1	5	12	7	.329	.468	.424
August	104	25	3	0	2	10	7	19	.240	.327	.296
Sept./Oct.	129	36	7	0	2	12	4	19	.279	.380	.299
Leading Off Inn.	97	31	7	0	1	1	2	9	.320	.423	.333
Bases Empty	279	73	14	0	3	3	19	38	.262	.344	.316
Runners On	169	42	9	4	3	38	22	31	.249	.402	.330
Runners/Scor. Pos.	104	21	4	4	0	29	16	21	.202	.317	.302
Runners On/2 Out	74	16	3	3	2	17	9	17	.216	.419	.301
Scor. Pos./2 Out	46	10	2	3	0	12	7	11	.217	.391	.321
Late Inning Pressure	47	11	2	1	0	5	5	9	.234	.319	.321
Leading Off	7	3	0	0	0	0	1	1	.429	.429	.500
Bases Empty	20	5	0	0	0	0	2	2	.250	.250	.348
Runners On	27	6	2	1	0	5	3	7	.222	.370	.300
Runners/Scor. Pos.	20	3	0	1	0	4	1	5	.150	.250	.190

DRIVING IN RUNS	0 Out	1 Out	2 Out	Total	
From 1B	1/26	2/29	5/48	8/103	8%
From 2B	1/19	3/23	8/34	12/76	16%
From 3B	7/12	6/15	2/18	15/45	33%
Scoring Position	8/31	9/38	10/52	27/121	22%
Scor. Pos. %	26%	24%	19%	22%	
Driving In Runners from 3B with Less than Two Out:			13/27	48%	

Loves to face: Phil Niekro (.500, 14-for-28, 1 HR)
Hates to face: Bill Swift (0-for-11, 4 SO)
Figures above are for A.L. only.... Yearly batting averages with runners in scoring position since 1982: .341, .286, .231, .197 (including both leagues in 1985).... First player in World Series history to oppose the team with which he started the season. ... More than a coincidence? Has played with three different Series-winning teams. All three took the crown in his first 100-game season with them; two, the Phillies and Royals, had never won a Series before, and the Cardinals hadn't won in 15 years. ... Had stolen base rate of .667 (12 of 18) with St. Louis last season, .851 (40 of 47) with Royals.... Career fielding percentage (.960) is 2d-lowest among active outfielders (minimum: 500 games); only Kingman's is lower. But his career rate of 10.2 assists per nine innings is 3d-highest among same group, and those assists don't even count the times when Lonnie throws the ball to himself.

Mike Stenhouse

Minnesota Twins	AB	H	2B	3B	HR	RRF	BB	SO	BA	SA	OBA
Season	179	40	5	0	5	22	29	18	.223	.335	.330
vs. Left-Handed Pitchers	5	1	1	0	0	0	0	2	.200	.400	.200
vs. Right-Handed Pitchers	174	39	4	0	5	22	29	16	.224	.333	.333
Home	95	22	3	0	2	11	20	10	.232	.326	.362
Road	84	18	2	0	3	11	9	8	.214	.345	.290
Grass	62	13	1	0	2	6	7	6	.210	.323	.290
Artificial Turf	117	27	4	0	3	16	22	12	.231	.342	.350
April	20	5	1	0	1	3	2	1	.250	.450	.318
May	26	4	2	0	1	2	9	2	.154	.346	.371
June	18	5	1	0	1	3	1	2	.278	.500	.316
July	37	10	0	0	1	3	6	3	.270	.351	.372
August	34	6	0	0	0	3	5	5	.176	.176	.282
Sept./Oct.	44	10	1	0	1	8	6	5	.227	.318	.314
Leading Off Inn.	48	7	0	0	1	1	3	8	.146	.208	.196
Bases Empty	103	17	5	0	1	1	10	12	.165	.243	.239
Runners On	76	23	0	0	4	21	19	6	.303	.461	.438
Runners/Scor. Pos.	37	11	0	0	2	16	8	4	.297	.459	.413
Runners On/2 Out	38	14	0	0	1	13	5	2	.368	.447	.442
Scor. Pos./2 Out	24	9	0	0	1	12	3	2	.375	.500	.444
Late Inning Pressure	33	14	1	0	1	5	6	1	.424	.545	.513
Leading Off	8	2	0	0	0	0	1	1	.250	.250	.333
Bases Empty	18	5	1	0	0	0	1	1	.278	.333	.316
Runners On	15	9	0	0	1	5	5	0	.600	.800	.700
Runners/Scor. Pos.	8	4	0	0	1	5	3	0	.500	.875	.636

DRIVING IN RUNS	0 Out	1 Out	2 Out	Total	
From 1B	1/15	1/14	2/29	4/58	7%
From 2B	1/4	0/4	5/20	6/28	21%
From 3B	1/3	1/4	5/12	7/19	37%
Scoring Position	2/7	1/8	10/32	13/47	28%
Scor. Pos. %	29%	13%	31%	28%	
Driving In Runners from 3B with Less than Two Out:			2/7	29%	

Loves to face: Brian Fisher (.667, 2-for-3)
Hates to face: Walt Terrell (0-for-10)
Raised average from .183 in 1984 to .223 last year, but his clutch figures made a quantum leap: from .156 to .424 in Late-Inning Pressure Situations, from .196 to .297 with runners in scoring position, from 0-for-20 (a *Player Analysis* record) to .375 with runners in scoring position and two outs.... Started 45 of 104 games against right-handers; zippo against left-handers.... Career batting average is .150 (3-for-20) vs. lefties.... Batted .217 (5-for-23) as a pinch-hitter last year.... Hitless in nine career at bats with the bases loaded.... His father, Dave, is a member of one of the most exclusive clubs in America: Stenhouse Sr., Vida Blue, and Dave Stieb are the only men in the country who have been A.L. starting pitchers in All-Star Games won by that league in the last quarter-century.

Jim Sundberg

Kansas City Royals	AB	H	2B	3B	HR	RRF	BB	SO	BA	SA	OBA
Season	367	90	12	4	10	36	33	67	.245	.381	.308
vs. Left-Handed Pitchers	115	25	4	1	7	16	8	15	.217	.452	.268
vs. Right-Handed Pitchers	252	65	8	3	3	20	25	52	.258	.349	.325
Home	188	47	5	3	2	14	11	36	.250	.340	.294
Road	179	43	7	1	8	22	22	31	.240	.425	.322
Grass	137	32	7	1	5	18	15	25	.234	.409	.307
Artificial Turf	230	58	5	3	5	18	18	42	.252	.365	.308
April	61	13	2	1	1	3	5	8	.213	.328	.273
May	80	23	3	1	4	15	3	12	.288	.500	.310
June	76	18	2	2	3	7	7	15	.237	.434	.301
July	74	16	0	0	0	8	10	15	.216	.216	.306
August	31	10	4	0	1	1	4	7	.323	.548	.417
Sept./Oct.	45	10	1	0	1	2	4	10	.222	.311	.286
Leading Off Inn.	100	29	6	0	3	3	3	17	.290	.440	.311
Bases Empty	229	55	9	2	8	8	18	39	.240	.402	.298
Runners On	138	35	3	2	2	28	15	28	.254	.348	.323
Runners/Scor. Pos.	82	22	2	2	1	25	10	18	.268	.378	.340
Runners On/2 Out	60	14	1	1	1	13	7	9	.233	.333	.313
Scor. Pos./2 Out	39	10	0	1	1	12	5	6	.256	.385	.341
Late Inning Pressure	55	21	1	1	2	7	0	9	.382	.545	.375
Leading Off	22	7	1	0	0	0	0	4	.318	.364	.318
Bases Empty	36	13	1	1	2	2	0	5	.361	.611	.361
Runners On	19	8	0	0	0	5	0	4	.421	.421	.400
Runners/Scor. Pos.	11	5	0	0	0	5	0	2	.455	.455	.417

DRIVING IN RUNS	0 Out	1 Out	2 Out	Total	
From 1B	0/24	1/30	2/40	3/94	3%
From 2B	1/11	4/28	3/29	8/68	12%
From 3B	2/6	6/10	7/16	15/32	47%
Scoring Position	3/17	10/38	10/45	23/100	23%
Scor. Pos. %	18%	26%	22%	23%	
Driving In Runners from 3B with Less than Two Out:			8/16	50%	

Loves to face: Scott McGregor (.381, 16-for-42, 1 HR)
Hates to face: Bryan Clark (.063, 1-for-15)
1,607 career games as a catcher puts him 12th on all-time list. Two ahead of him are active (Ted Simmons, 1,737; Bob Boone, 1,664); six of the nine others are in the Hall of Fame, with Johnny Bench sure to join them.... Boone and Sundberg have had parallel careers; each has a career .253 average coming into 1986, with Boone having outslugged Sundberg by .353 to .350.... Home run off Doyle Alexander in Game Three of Championship Series was another example of a catcher haunting a former battery-mate (see Seattle essay).... Hit only two home runs in his last 81 home games while with Texas, but has knocked out two in his six games at Arlington Stadium since being traded away.... One for the ages: over the past 11 years, in Late-Inning Pressure Situations with less than two outs, Sundberg is 0-for-134 trying to drive in runners from first base.

Pat Tabler

Cleveland Indians	AB	H	2B	3B	HR	RRF	BB	SO	BA	SA	OBA
Season	404	111	18	3	5	60	27	55	.275	.371	.321
vs. Left-Handed Pitchers	154	48	7	0	3	23	11	18	.312	.416	.353
vs. Right-Handed Pitchers	250	63	11	3	2	37	16	37	.252	.344	.301
Home	218	71	11	0	5	37	13	25	.326	.445	.366
Road	186	40	7	3	0	23	14	30	.215	.285	.269
Grass	364	105	18	3	5	55	22	45	.288	.396	.330
Artificial Turf	40	6	0	0	0	5	5	10	.150	.150	.244
April	78	25	4	1	1	15	6	7	.321	.436	.365
May	80	20	1	2	0	9	5	10	.250	.313	.294
June	85	23	2	0	1	10	4	11	.271	.329	.311
July	86	22	5	0	1	13	4	14	.256	.349	.297
August	75	21	6	0	2	13	8	13	.280	.440	.341
Sept./Oct.	0	0	0	0	0	0	0	0	.000	.000	.000
Leading Off Inn.	93	23	7	0	0	0	3	14	.247	.323	.278
Bases Empty	225	57	11	1	2	2	16	32	.253	.338	.309
Runners On	179	54	7	2	3	58	11	23	.302	.413	.337
Runners/Scor. Pos.	106	36	6	2	2	56	7	13	.340	.491	.371
Runners On/2 Out	79	18	2	1	2	18	7	10	.228	.354	.291
Scor. Pos./2 Out	48	10	1	1	1	16	4	7	.208	.333	.269
Late Inning Pressure	56	12	4	1	0	3	3	5	.214	.321	.267
Leading Off	14	4	3	0	0	0	1	3	.286	.500	.375
Bases Empty	38	7	3	1	0	0	3	4	.184	.316	.262
Runners On	18	5	1	0	0	3	0	1	.278	.333	.278
Runners/Scor. Pos.	10	3	1	0	0	3	0	0	.300	.400	.300

DRIVING IN RUNS	0 Out	1 Out	2 Out	Total	
From 1B	1/33	1/51	3/52	5/136	4%
From 2B	6/15	10/29	8/32	24/76	32%
From 3B	7/7	14/18	5/22	26/47	55%
Scoring Position	13/22	24/47	13/54	50/123	41%
Scor. Pos. %	59%	51%	24%	41%	
Driving In Runners from 3B with Less than Two Out:			21/25	84%	

Loves to face: Ted Higuera (.556, 5-for-9)
Hates to face: Luis Leal (0-for-9)
Looking for bases-loaded totals? See the Tabler Tables in the Indians essay. . . . OK, just one bases-loaded stat here: he has accumulated 26.3 percent of his career RRFs in bases loaded situations, which account for 2.6 percent of his career plate appearances. . . . His season ended early due to knee surgery; last game: Aug. 31. Until then, had started 54 of 79 games vs. right-handers, and all 50 vs. left-handers. . . . Career batting averages: .258 with the bases empty, .296 with runners on base, .331 with runners in scoring position. Average with runners in scoring position has been higher than overall average in each of five big-league seasons. . . . Drove in 37 of 69 runners from scoring position with less than two outs, highest A.L. mark since 1980 (minimum: 20 RRF). . . . Indians were 5–0 in games in which he homered; now if he were only Dale Murphy. . . .

Tim Teufel

Minnesota Twins	AB	H	2B	3B	HR	RRF	BB	SO	BA	SA	OBA
Season	434	113	24	3	10	53	48	70	.260	.399	.335
vs. Left-Handed Pitchers	135	27	6	0	1	13	17	20	.200	.267	.288
vs. Right-Handed Pitchers	299	86	18	3	9	40	31	50	.288	.458	.357
Home	221	61	12	1	6	34	21	37	.276	.421	.340
Road	213	52	12	2	4	19	27	33	.244	.376	.331
Grass	163	39	11	2	3	14	21	29	.239	.387	.328
Artificial Turf	271	74	13	1	7	39	27	41	.273	.406	.340
April	70	20	3	0	1	14	5	10	.286	.371	.338
May	86	24	3	1	2	12	8	19	.279	.407	.340
June	78	21	6	0	1	4	10	9	.269	.385	.352
July	77	19	4	1	1	6	14	11	.247	.364	.359
August	67	16	3	1	1	5	8	12	.239	.358	.320
Sept./Oct.	56	13	5	0	4	12	3	9	.232	.536	.283
Leading Off Inn.	99	30	7	0	4	4	8	8	.303	.495	.361
Bases Empty	244	63	13	3	7	7	27	38	.258	.422	.339
Runners On	190	50	11	0	3	46	21	32	.263	.368	.330
Runners/Scor. Pos.	103	28	5	0	2	41	14	18	.272	.379	.347
Runners On/2 Out	70	20	3	0	1	11	8	13	.286	.371	.359
Scor. Pos./2 Out	39	11	0	0	1	10	5	6	.282	.359	.364
Late Inning Pressure	63	13	2	0	1	4	4	13	.206	.286	.265
Leading Off	9	1	0	0	0	0	2	0	.111	.111	.273
Bases Empty	29	7	0	0	1	1	2	5	.241	.345	.313
Runners On	34	6	2	0	0	3	2	8	.176	.235	.222
Runners/Scor. Pos.	15	2	0	0	0	2	1	4	.133	.133	.188

DRIVING IN RUNS	0 Out	1 Out	2 Out	Total	
From 1B	1/34	4/51	1/50	6/135	4%
From 2B	3/20	9/38	4/31	16/89	18%
From 3B	6/11	10/12	5/12	21/35	60%
Scoring Position	9/31	19/50	9/43	37/124	30%
Scor. Pos. %	29%	38%	21%	30%	
Driving In Runners from 3B with Less than Two Out:			16/23	70%	

Loves to face: Jim Gott (1.000, 2-for-2, 1 HR)
Hates to face: Geoff Zahn (.056, 1-for-18)
German scholars avidly await resumption of the confrontations between Gott and the Teufel. . . . Batted 88 points higher against right-handed pitchers than he did against lefties last season, largest such imbalance among A.L. right-handed batters. What makes that especially intriguing is that Mets acquired him ostensibly to platoon with Wally Backman at second base, playing against left-handers. . . . Career averages are less radical: .267 vs. right-handers, .259 vs. left-handers. . . . Getting prepped for New York: batted .351 vs. Yankees last season, and has career mark of .467 (7-for-15) against Tom Seaver. . . . Has hit 21 of his 27 career home runs indoors (18 at the Metrodome, three at the Kingdome). If he can do that at the Astrodome, long a house of horrors for his new teammates, it may inspire devil worship among Mets fans everywhere.

Mickey Tettleton

Oakland As	AB	H	2B	3B	HR	RRF	BB	SO	BA	SA	OBA
Season	211	53	12	0	3	15	28	59	.251	.351	.344
vs. Left-Handed Pitchers	61	13	5	0	1	2	7	16	.213	.344	.304
vs. Right-Handed Pitchers	150	40	7	0	2	13	21	43	.267	.353	.360
Home	110	27	4	0	1	9	14	35	.245	.309	.336
Road	101	26	8	0	2	6	14	24	.257	.396	.353
Grass	192	49	11	0	3	14	24	56	.255	.359	.341
Artificial Turf	19	4	1	0	0	1	4	3	.211	.263	.375
April	4	0	0	0	0	0	1	1	.000	.000	.200
May	13	3	1	0	0	2	1	2	.231	.308	.286
June	45	14	3	0	1	2	8	8	.311	.444	.415
July	63	16	3	0	2	5	11	20	.254	.397	.373
August	25	2	0	0	0	1	1	11	.080	.080	.115
Sept./Oct.	61	18	5	0	0	5	6	17	.295	.377	.368
Leading Off Inn.	45	16	6	0	2	2	2	11	.356	.622	.396
Bases Empty	123	31	8	0	3	3	13	32	.252	.390	.333
Runners On	88	22	4	0	0	12	15	27	.250	.295	.359
Runners/Scor. Pos.	52	11	4	0	0	12	11	18	.212	.288	.349
Runners On/2 Out	33	6	2	0	0	2	9	11	.182	.242	.357
Scor. Pos./2 Out	22	3	2	0	0	2	6	8	.136	.227	.321
Late Inning Pressure	31	8	2	0	1	2	4	7	.258	.419	.343
Leading Off	9	4	2	0	1	1	1	1	.444	1.000	.500
Bases Empty	20	6	2	0	1	1	3	4	.300	.550	.391
Runners On	11	2	0	0	0	1	1	3	.182	.182	.250
Runners/Scor. Pos.	6	0	0	0	0	1	0	2	.000	.000	.000

DRIVING IN RUNS	0 Out	1 Out	2 Out	Total	
From 1B	1/20	0/20	0/23	1/63	2%
From 2B	0/7	3/14	2/18	5/39	13%
From 3B	2/4	4/8	0/9	6/21	29%
Scoring Position	2/11	7/22	2/27	11/60	18%
Scor. Pos. %	18%	32%	7%	18%	
Driving In Runners from 3B with Less than Two Out:			6/12	50%	

Loves to face: Gene Nelson & Vern Ruhle (1.000, 2-for-2 vs. each)
Hates to face: Dennis Boyd (.143, 1-for-7, 3 SO)
Offers striking contrast with Tabler: hitless in seven career at bats, including four strikeouts, in bases-loaded situations. . . . Started only four games during April and May, but 62 of 116 after that. . . . Oakland played .545 ball (36–30) with Tettleton catching, .426 (40–56) with Heath. . . . Batted .263 (in 76 at bats) in 1984, .251 last year; both averages are higher than his best minor-league mark (.249 at Modesto in the California League in '82). . . . Ground-ball hitter: 1.56 G/A ratio last season. Career: 1.37. . . . Career averages: .276 batting left-handed, .211 batting right-handed. . . . Finished strong, batting .366 in his last 14 games, raising average from .224 to its final .251. . . . Made two errors in second start of season, May 4, and only two more the rest of the season.

Gorman Thomas

Seattle Mariners	AB	H	2B	3B	HR	RRF	BB	SO	BA	SA	OBA
Season	484	104	16	1	32	89	84	126	.215	.450	.330
vs. Left-Handed Pitchers	152	32	4	0	13	38	27	42	.211	.493	.326
vs. Right-Handed Pitchers	332	72	12	1	19	51	57	84	.217	.431	.332
Home	251	52	7	1	16	46	50	65	.207	.434	.337
Road	233	52	9	0	16	43	34	61	.223	.468	.323
Grass	162	40	7	0	14	34	31	44	.247	.549	.371
Artificial Turf	322	64	9	1	18	55	53	82	.199	.401	.310
April	66	18	1	0	6	16	12	11	.273	.561	.380
May	43	7	1	0	3	6	6	10	.163	.395	.265
June	55	14	2	0	3	10	18	18	.255	.455	.438
July	106	24	3	0	11	21	17	25	.226	.566	.333
August	91	15	3	0	5	15	11	26	.165	.363	.252
Sept./Oct.	123	26	6	1	4	21	20	36	.211	.374	.324
Leading Off Inn.	114	28	4	1	8	8	19	29	.246	.509	.353
Bases Empty	234	52	9	1	12	12	32	56	.222	.423	.316
Runners On	250	52	7	0	20	77	52	70	.208	.476	.343
Runners/Scor. Pos.	148	24	4	0	10	57	33	42	.162	.392	.310
Runners On/2 Out	110	22	2	0	11	31	25	32	.200	.518	.348
Scor. Pos./2 Out	67	11	1	0	6	21	11	17	.164	.448	.282
Late Inning Pressure	65	10	2	0	1	7	11	13	.154	.231	.273
Leading Off	13	4	1	0	1	1	2	2	.308	.615	.400
Bases Empty	28	8	2	0	1	1	3	3	.286	.464	.355
Runners On	37	2	0	0	0	6	8	10	.054	.054	.217
Runners/Scor. Pos.	19	2	0	0	0	6	4	4	.105	.105	.250

DRIVING IN RUNS	0 Out	1 Out	2 Out	Total	
From 1B	3/43	5/64	7/71	15/178	8%
From 2B	3/24	8/41	7/48	18/113	16%
From 3B	8/16	10/21	6/27	24/64	38%
Scoring Position	11/40	18/62	13/75	42/177	24%
Scor. Pos. %	28%	29%	17%	24%	
Driving In Runners from 3B with Less than Two Out:			18/37	49%	

Loves to face: Bruce Hurst (.421, 8-for-19, 4 HR)
Hates to face: Mark Clear (.063, 1-for-16)
Dramatic comeback from surgery-shortened 1984 season (.157, one home run in 108 at bats). . . . All 32 home runs last year came as DH, 2d-highest DH total in 13-year history of the rule; the record is 35 by Dave Kingman in '84. . . . Led A.L. with 11 home runs in July. . . . Fly-ball hitter: 0.88 G/A ratio last season. Career: 0.76. . . . Lowest career batting average (.227) of any active player with at least 100 home runs. . . . As a group, A.L. DHs batted only .240 last season, by far the lowest DH average since the introduction of the rule in 1973 (previous low: .247 in 1981). Meanwhile, the total of 333 DH homers was the highest ever, although by a margin of only 11 over 1984, and the total of DH stolen bases was an all-time low of 43. The eight DHs with the most at bats in the league last season were all 34 or older by season's end.

Andre Thornton

Cleveland Indians	AB	H	2B	3B	HR	RRF	BB	SO	BA	SA	OBA
Season	461	109	13	0	22	89	47	75	.236	.408	.304
vs. Left-Handed Pitchers	153	41	4	0	8	31	23	21	.268	.451	.358
vs. Right-Handed Pitchers	308	68	9	0	14	58	24	54	.221	.386	.275
Home	221	51	6	0	12	49	24	32	.231	.421	.302
Road	240	58	7	0	10	40	23	43	.242	.396	.305
Grass	392	90	8	0	22	82	39	67	.230	.418	.295
Artificial Turf	69	19	5	0	0	7	8	8	.275	.348	.351
April	17	2	0	0	0	1	0	6	.118	.118	.118
May	87	15	0	0	1	8	6	15	.172	.207	.223
June	58	6	0	0	2	5	8	12	.103	.207	.209
July	87	18	3	0	3	17	15	13	.207	.345	.317
August	101	32	1	0	7	22	7	14	.317	.535	.358
Sept./Oct.	111	36	9	0	9	36	11	15	.324	.649	.382
Leading Off Inn.	136	30	2	0	3	3	9	22	.221	.301	.269
Bases Empty	244	51	3	0	7	7	25	40	.209	.307	.283
Runners On	217	58	10	0	15	82	22	35	.267	.521	.327
Runners/Scor. Pos.	123	38	9	0	8	68	15	22	.309	.577	.368
Runners On/2 Out	94	23	4	0	8	32	10	18	.245	.543	.317
Scor. Pos./2 Out	55	14	4	0	4	24	7	10	.255	.545	.339
Late Inning Pressure	67	15	0	0	6	14	6	7	.224	.493	.284
Leading Off	21	4	0	0	1	1	1	2	.190	.333	.227
Bases Empty	45	10	0	0	2	2	3	4	.222	.356	.271
Runners On	22	5	0	0	4	12	3	3	.227	.773	.308
Runners/Scor. Pos.	10	3	0	0	2	8	1	3	.300	.900	.333

DRIVING IN RUNS	0 Out	1 Out	2 Out	Total	
From 1B	2/34	6/62	6/55	14/151	9%
From 2B	5/17	11/39	10/38	26/94	28%
From 3B	7/9	12/22	8/24	27/55	49%
Scoring Position	12/26	23/61	18/62	53/149	36%
Scor. Pos. %	46%	38%	29%	36%	
Driving In Runners from 3B with Less than Two Out:			19/31	61%	

Loves to face: Ted Higuera (.500, 5-for-10, 2 HR)
Hates to face: Jay Howell (0-for-10)
Started season on disabled list; first game: April 25. . . . From then on, started 67 of 93 games against right-handers, and all but one game against left-handers. . . . Before All-Star break: 56 games, .177, six home runs; after break: 68 games, .286, 16 home runs. . . . Led A.L. in slugging (.649) after Sept. 1; 35 RBIs during same span was 2d-most in league behind Don Mattingly. . . . Had highest scoring-position batting average in the 11 years that we've been keeping track. . . . Needs three home runs to become fourth Cleveland player to accumulate 200 homers; needs 30 to break Earl Averill's team record of 226. That's the 2d-lowest team home run record among the 16 original franchises; only the White Sox have a lower record: 154 by Bill Melton.

Wayne Tolleson

Texas Rangers	AB	H	2B	3B	HR	RRF	BB	SO	BA	SA	OBA
Season	323	101	9	5	1	18	21	46	.313	.381	.353
vs. Left-Handed Pitchers	87	22	5	2	0	6	3	11	.253	.356	.275
vs. Right-Handed Pitchers	236	79	4	3	1	12	18	35	.335	.390	.380
Home	178	63	4	3	0	11	13	24	.354	.410	.394
Road	145	38	5	2	1	7	8	22	.262	.345	.301
Grass	275	89	8	4	1	17	19	39	.324	.393	.365
Artificial Turf	48	12	1	1	0	1	2	7	.250	.313	.280
April	13	5	0	0	0	1	0	2	.385	.385	.385
May	44	14	0	0	0	0	0	3	.318	.318	.318
June	54	17	4	0	0	1	9	8	.315	.389	.406
July	58	21	1	0	1	8	5	8	.362	.431	.413
August	74	24	3	3	0	5	2	13	.324	.446	.342
Sept./Oct.	80	20	1	2	0	3	5	12	.250	.313	.291
Leading Off Inn.	85	28	2	1	0	0	4	13	.329	.376	.360
Bases Empty	190	66	7	4	0	0	14	26	.347	.426	.392
Runners On	133	35	2	1	1	18	7	20	.263	.316	.296
Runners/Scor. Pos.	72	16	0	0	1	16	4	9	.222	.264	.256
Runners On/2 Out	59	17	1	1	0	9	4	9	.288	.339	.333
Scor. Pos./2 Out	38	9	0	0	0	8	2	5	.237	.237	.275
Late Inning Pressure	51	18	1	1	1	6	3	6	.353	.471	.389
Leading Off	12	8	0	0	0	0	2	0	.667	.667	.714
Bases Empty	27	12	1	0	0	0	3	4	.444	.481	.500
Runners On	24	6	0	1	1	6	0	2	.250	.458	.250
Runners/Scor. Pos.	15	4	0	0	1	5	0	2	.267	.467	.267

DRIVING IN RUNS	0 Out	1 Out	2 Out	Total	
From 1B	1/24	0/35	1/36	2/95	2%
From 2B	0/12	3/22	3/26	6/60	10%
From 3B	0/0	4/6	5/18	9/24	38%
Scoring Position	0/12	7/28	8/44	15/84	18%
Scor. Pos. %	0%	25%	18%	18%	
Driving In Runners from 3B with Less than Two Out:			4/6	67%	

Loves to face: Mike Flanagan (.667, 4-for-6, 1 HR)
Hates to face: Jack Morris (.091, 1-for-11, 4 SO)
Added 100 points to his overall batting average from 1984 to '85, but batting average from the right side of the plate fell from .271 to .253. His left-handed average of .335 was a 145-point improvement. . . . Ground-ball hitter: 2.33 G/A ratio was 5th-highest in majors last season (minimum: 200 PA). Career average: 1.81. . . . Career percentage of runners driven in from scoring position (16.6) is lowest among active non-pitchers (minimum: 100 opportunities). . . . Career averages: .275 with the bases empty, .211 with runners on base, .169 with runners in scoring position. . . . Batted .354 at Arlington Stadium last season (4th-best in A.L. at home), but home is now Comiskey Park, where his career average is .229, with no extra-base hits in 48 at bats.

Alan Trammell

Detroit Tigers	AB	H	2B	3B	HR	RRF	BB	SO	BA	SA	OBA
Season	605	156	21	7	13	64	50	71	.258	.380	.312
vs. Left-Handed Pitchers	184	46	5	2	4	19	20	15	.250	.364	.324
vs. Right-Handed Pitchers	421	110	16	5	9	45	30	56	.261	.387	.307
Home	296	85	10	2	7	39	28	32	.287	.405	.347
Road	309	71	11	5	6	25	22	39	.230	.356	.278
Grass	500	132	16	6	12	57	44	55	.264	.392	.322
Artificial Turf	105	24	5	1	1	7	6	16	.229	.324	.265
April	76	23	2	3	4	15	8	6	.303	.566	.365
May	107	26	4	0	2	5	6	13	.243	.336	.278
June	109	33	6	1	1	10	6	15	.303	.404	.342
July	94	20	3	1	1	10	11	13	.213	.298	.296
August	117	28	3	1	3	12	10	16	.239	.359	.295
Sept./Oct.	102	26	3	1	2	12	9	8	.255	.363	.313
Leading Off Inn.	107	26	1	3	4	4	8	8	.243	.421	.296
Bases Empty	359	91	10	6	9	9	27	32	.253	.390	.306
Runners On	246	65	11	1	4	55	23	39	.264	.366	.321
Runners/Scor. Pos.	140	29	2	1	2	48	16	21	.207	.279	.277
Runners On/2 Out	102	22	3	0	2	22	13	17	.216	.304	.304
Scor. Pos./2 Out	67	13	1	0	2	21	9	9	.194	.299	.289
Late Inning Pressure	80	17	2	0	0	7	10	13	.213	.238	.297
Leading Off	9	0	0	0	0	0	2	1	.000	.000	.182
Bases Empty	38	7	2	0	0	0	3	5	.184	.237	.244
Runners On	42	10	0	0	0	7	7	8	.238	.238	.340
Runners/Scor. Pos.	25	3	0	0	0	7	5	6	.120	.120	.258

DRIVING IN RUNS	0 Out	1 Out	2 Out	Total	
From 1B	3/62	2/44	1/72	6/178	3%
From 2B	3/28	2/33	10/49	15/110	14%
From 3B	10/12	11/19	9/28	30/59	51%
Scoring Position	13/40	13/52	19/77	45/169	27%
Scor. Pos. %	33%	25%	25%	27%	
Driving In Runners from 3B with Less than Two Out:			21/31	68%	

Loves to face: Ray Burris (.545, 6-for-11, 3 HR)
Hates to face: Mike Mason (0-for-10)
Batted 50 times more than in 1984, but had 18 fewer hits, 10 fewer walks, eight fewer RBIs, six fewer runs scored, and five fewer stolen bases. . . . Average with runners in scoring position was lowest of his career, as was his average against left-handed pitching. . . . Career bases-loaded average of .366; it's .420 (29-for-69) over the past seven years. . . . Owns 2d-highest fielding percentage (.9767) among all shortstops in A.L. history; can break Mark Belanger's record (.9769) if he handles first 42 chances of season without error. . . . Rate of 2.71 assists per nine innings dropped slightly from last year's 2.85; only Meacham and Smalley had lower rates among shortstops with 300 or more innings. . . . Has homered in every A.L. park except Comiskey Park and Yankee Stadium. . . . Fly-ball hitter: 0.60 G/A ratio last season. Career: 0.84.

Willie Upshaw

Toronto Blue Jays	AB	H	2B	3B	HR	RRF	BB	SO	BA	SA	OBA
Season	501	138	31	5	15	68	48	71	.275	.447	.342
vs. Left-Handed Pitchers	171	47	11	3	5	34	8	30	.275	.462	.309
vs. Right-Handed Pitchers	330	91	20	2	10	34	40	41	.276	.439	.357
Home	236	70	19	3	6	35	26	36	.297	.479	.366
Road	265	68	12	2	9	33	22	35	.257	.419	.320
Grass	200	53	10	0	9	27	15	29	.265	.450	.326
Artificial Turf	301	85	21	5	6	41	33	42	.282	.445	.352
April	74	20	6	1	4	12	4	13	.270	.541	.321
May	92	19	4	1	1	17	10	13	.207	.304	.288
June	106	24	5	0	3	10	15	15	.226	.358	.325
July	92	30	7	1	2	16	11	14	.326	.489	.398
August	81	26	5	1	3	8	4	9	.321	.519	.353
Sept./Oct.	56	19	4	1	2	5	4	7	.339	.554	.383
Leading Off Inn.	119	31	7	1	5	5	8	12	.261	.462	.313
Bases Empty	272	71	14	1	10	10	25	33	.261	.430	.328
Runners On	229	67	17	4	5	58	23	38	.293	.467	.358
Runners/Scor. Pos.	131	35	9	3	1	47	20	17	.267	.405	.357
Runners On/2 Out	101	24	9	1	1	24	9	17	.238	.376	.313
Scor. Pos./2 Out	66	17	5	1	0	21	8	6	.258	.364	.338
Late Inning Pressure	67	16	4	2	1	9	6	13	.239	.403	.301
Leading Off	18	5	1	1	0	0	1	3	.278	.444	.316
Bases Empty	41	9	2	1	1	1	2	6	.220	.390	.256
Runners On	26	7	2	1	0	8	4	7	.269	.423	.367
Runners/Scor. Pos.	15	3	1	0	0	6	4	3	.200	.267	.368

DRIVING IN RUNS	0 Out	1 Out	2 Out	Total	
From 1B	4/32	1/63	4/63	9/158	6%
From 2B	2/14	9/42	12/38	23/94	24%
From 3B	2/4	12/17	7/36	21/57	37%
Scoring Position	4/18	21/59	19/74	44/151	29%
Scor. Pos. %	22%	36%	26%	29%	
Driving In Runners from 3B with Less than Two Out:			14/21	67%	

Loves to face: Mike Warren (.556, 5-for-9, 2 HR)
Hates to face: Ron Guidry (.091, 2-for-22, 8 SO)
Once again hit left-handers about as well as right-handers. Career batting averages: .274 vs. lefties (903 at bats), .271 vs. righties. . . . It was rather startling, then, to see him platooned over last half of season: he started all 32 games against southpaws before the All-Star break, but only four of 27 after, yielding to Cecil Fielder. . . . Jays had a 13–1 record in games in which he homered. . . . Has hit 63 of 88 career home runs with the bases empty. . . . Career strikeout rates: overall, one every 7.1 plate appearances; with bases loaded, one every 3.9 appearances. Has averaged only .65 RRF per bases-loaded appearance (1985 A.L. average: .74). . . . Batting average with runners on base was highest of his career. . . . Has homered in every A.L. stadium outside of Milwaukee.

George Vukovich

Cleveland Indians

	AB	H	2B	3B	HR	RRF	BB	SO	BA	SA	OBA
Season	434	106	22	0	8	45	30	75	.244	.350	.292
vs. Left-Handed Pitchers	42	6	2	0	0	1	2	12	.143	.190	.200
vs. Right-Handed Pitchers	392	100	20	0	8	44	28	63	.255	.367	.302
Home	212	49	7	0	4	23	12	36	.231	.321	.269
Road	222	57	15	0	4	22	18	39	.257	.378	.314
Grass	373	92	20	0	6	35	24	66	.247	.349	.290
Artificial Turf	61	14	2	0	2	10	6	9	.230	.361	.304
April	63	15	1	0	0	6	6	10	.238	.254	.304
May	70	24	4	0	1	7	4	10	.343	.443	.373
June	77	15	4	0	0	4	5	10	.195	.247	.244
July	56	13	1	0	3	12	3	10	.232	.411	.267
August	70	17	6	0	1	8	6	16	.243	.371	.295
Sept./Oct.	98	22	6	0	3	8	6	19	.224	.378	.276
Leading Off Inn.	96	24	1	0	2	2	5	16	.250	.323	.287
Bases Empty	238	59	8	0	2	2	14	43	.248	.307	.290
Runners On	196	47	14	0	6	43	16	32	.240	.403	.295
Runners/Scor. Pos.	108	26	6	0	4	37	14	17	.241	.407	.323
Runners On/2 Out	95	21	7	0	2	19	6	16	.221	.358	.267
Scor. Pos./2 Out	61	15	4	0	1	17	5	9	.246	.361	.303
Late Inning Pressure	79	19	3	0	0	4	2	19	.241	.278	.259
Leading Off	17	3	1	0	0	0	1	5	.176	.235	.222
Bases Empty	42	11	2	0	0	0	2	11	.262	.310	.295
Runners On	37	8	1	0	0	4	0	8	.216	.243	.216
Runners/Scor. Pos.	23	4	1	0	0	4	0	4	.174	.217	.174

DRIVING IN RUNS	0 Out	1 Out	2 Out	Total	
From 1B	1/30	4/51	2/69	7/150	5%
From 2B	1/12	3/29	6/41	10/82	12%
From 3B	4/8	7/10	9/26	20/44	45%
Scoring Position	5/20	10/39	15/67	30/126	24%
Scor. Pos. %	25%	26%	22%	24%	
Driving In Runners from 3B with Less than Two Out:		11/18	61%		

Loves to face: Mike Moore (.588, 10-for-17)
Hates to face: Joe Niekro (0-for-11, 3 SO)
Batting average fell 60 points from 1984. . . . Started all but two of Indians' 104 games against right-handers, but in only six of 58 against left-handers. . . . Career .207 batter against lefties (179 at bats), with only home run coming against Tippy Martinez in 1983. . . . Career batting average of .350 (14-for-40) with the bases loaded; .378 over the past four years. . . . Has driven in only 20.4 percent of runners from scoring position in Late-Inning Pressure Situations in his career; 15.4 percent last year. . . . Favorite road parks: Arlington Stadium (17-for-45, two home runs), the Metrodome (three home runs in 40 at bats). But has only five hits in 45 at bats at Yankee Stadium.

Greg Walker

Chicago White Sox

	AB	H	2B	3B	HR	RRF	BB	SO	BA	SA	OBA
Season	601	155	38	4	24	93	44	100	.258	.454	.309
vs. Left-Handed Pitchers	183	42	17	0	4	25	7	40	.230	.388	.257
vs. Right-Handed Pitchers	418	113	21	4	20	68	37	60	.270	.483	.331
Home	293	78	22	4	11	47	21	61	.266	.481	.319
Road	308	77	16	0	13	46	23	39	.250	.429	.300
Grass	521	133	34	4	19	84	40	92	.255	.445	.309
Artificial Turf	80	22	4	0	5	9	4	8	.275	.513	.310
April	73	20	4	2	2	10	3	12	.274	.466	.303
May	84	26	4	0	4	12	7	16	.310	.500	.363
June	100	24	8	0	7	24	9	13	.240	.530	.309
July	98	26	9	1	2	13	13	16	.265	.439	.345
August	115	26	7	0	2	16	6	19	.226	.339	.268
Sept./Oct.	131	33	6	1	7	18	6	24	.252	.473	.285
Leading Off Inn.	167	43	14	1	5	5	12	36	.257	.443	.307
Bases Empty	338	80	20	1	12	12	16	60	.237	.408	.275
Runners On	263	75	18	3	12	81	28	40	.285	.513	.350
Runners/Scor. Pos.	144	41	10	2	5	63	19	22	.285	.486	.361
Runners On/2 Out	122	32	4	0	8	36	16	20	.262	.492	.348
Scor. Pos./2 Out	74	19	3	0	2	24	14	11	.257	.378	.375
Late Inning Pressure	85	22	5	0	6	19	5	18	.259	.529	.300
Leading Off	20	3	1	0	0	0	3	7	.150	.200	.261
Bases Empty	49	8	2	0	2	2	3	12	.163	.327	.212
Runners On	36	14	3	0	4	17	2	6	.389	.806	.421
Runners/Scor. Pos.	24	9	3	0	1	11	2	5	.375	.625	.423

DRIVING IN RUNS	0 Out	1 Out	2 Out	Total	
From 1B	1/28	8/80	8/79	17/187	9%
From 2B	1/12	17/48	12/48	30/108	28%
From 3B	5/8	9/21	8/35	22/64	34%
Scoring Position	6/20	26/69	20/83	52/172	30%
Scor. Pos. %	30%	38%	24%	30%	
Driving In Runners from 3B with Less than Two Out:			14/29	48%	

Loves to face: Bob Stanley (.833, 5-for-6, 2 HR)
Hates to face: Matt Young (0-for-4, 4 SO)
First major leaguer to play in 163 games since Al Oliver and Steve Garvey did it in 1980; first White Sox player to lead A.L. in games played since Ken (the S.S.) Henderson, the whirlpool king, did it in 1974. . . . First White Sox first baseman to hit 20 or more home runs two years in a row since Roy Sievers in 1960–61. . . . One of six players to hit at least one home run vs. every opposing A.L. club last season. . . . Has batted over .280 both with runners on base and with runners in scoring position in each of three seasons with Sox. . . . That .230 average against left-handers is his best in three years in majors, but strikeout/walk ratio of 5.71 against lefties was highest in A.L. last year (minimum: 25 SO).

Gary Ward

Texas Rangers

	AB	H	2B	3B	HR	RRF	BB	SO	BA	SA	OBA
Season	593	170	28	7	15	73	39	97	.287	.433	.329
vs. Left-Handed Pitchers	176	53	10	3	7	29	15	27	.301	.511	.354
vs. Right-Handed Pitchers	417	117	18	4	8	44	24	70	.281	.400	.318
Home	282	97	15	5	10	52	15	45	.344	.539	.375
Road	311	73	13	2	5	21	24	52	.235	.338	.288
Grass	497	141	22	6	14	67	29	88	.284	.437	.321
Artificial Turf	96	29	6	1	1	6	10	9	.302	.417	.368
April	78	23	3	1	2	11	2	13	.295	.436	.313
May	103	26	8	1	2	13	12	11	.252	.408	.330
June	109	34	6	1	1	16	6	14	.312	.413	.345
July	89	22	3	1	1	7	5	21	.247	.337	.281
August	95	27	1	2	5	15	5	12	.284	.495	.324
Sept./Oct.	119	38	7	1	4	11	9	26	.319	.496	.364
Leading Off Inn.	156	55	7	3	5	5	5	15	.353	.532	.373
Bases Empty	354	101	14	6	9	9	17	54	.285	.435	.320
Runners On	239	69	14	1	6	64	22	43	.289	.431	.342
Runners/Scor. Pos.	142	45	11	0	5	60	19	32	.317	.500	.386
Runners On/2 Out	101	26	1	0	2	24	13	18	.257	.327	.342
Scor. Pos./2 Out	70	21	1	0	2	24	12	15	.300	.400	.402
Late Inning Pressure	87	21	2	0	2	7	8	15	.241	.333	.302
Leading Off	27	9	0	0	1	1	3	6	.333	.444	.400
Bases Empty	57	14	0	0	1	1	6	12	.246	.298	.317
Runners On	30	7	2	0	1	6	2	3	.233	.400	.273
Runners/Scor. Pos.	14	3	1	0	1	5	2	1	.214	.500	.294

DRIVING IN RUNS	0 Out	1 Out	2 Out	Total	
From 1B	2/54	4/60	2/78	8/192	4%
From 2B	3/26	15/39	8/49	26/114	23%
From 3B	2/5	10/19	12/27	24/51	47%
Scoring Position	5/31	25/58	20/76	50/165	30%
Scor. Pos. %	16%	43%	26%	30%	
Driving In Runners from 3B with Less than Two Out:			12/24	50%	

Loves to face: Ron Guidry (.364, 20-for-55, 4 HR)
Hates to face: Bill Caudill (.071, 1-for-14)
Batted .237 under Doug Rader over first five weeks of season, batting mostly second in the order; when Valentine took over, he moved Ward to fifth, where his average bloomed. . . . Has batted .300 or higher with two outs and runners in scoring position in each of last four seasons. . . . Hit a career-high .344 at home, and .302 on the four artificial-turf fields; toughest times came on grass fields on the road (.205). . . . Has driven in 29.8 percent of runners from scoring position in nonpressure situations, but only 19.8 percent in Late-Inning Pressure Situations. . . . Batting .375 (9-for-24) with the bases loaded since joining Texas. . . . Rangers were 12–3 in games in which he hit a home run. . . . Committed 10 errors last season, one behind A.L. outfield leaders George Bell and Kirk Gibson.

Lou Whitaker

Detroit Tigers

	AB	H	2B	3B	HR	RRF	BB	SO	BA	SA	OBA
Season	609	170	29	8	21	74	80	56	.279	.456	.362
vs. Left-Handed Pitchers	145	33	4	2	2	15	20	23	.228	.324	.323
vs. Right-Handed Pitchers	464	137	25	6	19	59	60	33	.295	.498	.374
Home	303	81	13	3	11	43	42	30	.267	.439	.352
Road	306	89	16	5	10	31	38	26	.291	.474	.372
Grass	512	134	20	6	19	63	71	48	.262	.436	.350
Artificial Turf	97	36	9	2	2	11	9	8	.371	.567	.430
April	61	21	3	1	2	8	7	7	.344	.525	.400
May	101	31	5	0	3	11	16	5	.307	.446	.407
June	109	31	5	0	7	18	15	12	.284	.523	.368
July	116	40	8	3	3	12	12	10	.345	.543	.406
August	106	24	4	2	4	13	15	8	.226	.415	.328
Sept./Oct.	116	23	4	2	2	12	15	14	.198	.319	.286
Leading Off Inn.	248	69	12	3	8	8	32	17	.278	.448	.365
Bases Empty	404	106	22	5	12	12	47	35	.262	.431	.342
Runners On	205	64	7	3	9	62	33	21	.312	.507	.399
Runners/Scor. Pos.	116	34	4	2	5	52	28	15	.293	.491	.416
Runners On/2 Out	102	30	4	1	5	33	19	13	.294	.500	.405
Scor. Pos./2 Out	64	19	3	1	3	28	17	10	.297	.516	.444
Late Inning Pressure	78	21	3	0	2	9	15	11	.269	.385	.383
Leading Off	21	4	0	0	1	1	7	3	.190	.333	.393
Bases Empty	42	11	3	0	1	1	10	6	.262	.405	.404
Runners On	36	10	0	0	1	8	5	5	.278	.361	.357
Runners/Scor. Pos.	19	6	0	0	0	6	4	3	.316	.316	.417

DRIVING IN RUNS	0 Out	1 Out	2 Out	Total	
From 1B	2/28	2/48	5/58	9/134	7%
From 2B	2/9	5/36	13/48	20/93	22%
From 3B	2/5	12/14	10/32	24/51	47%
Scoring Position	4/14	17/50	23/80	44/144	31%
Scor. Pos. %	29%	34%	29%	31%	
Driving In Runners from 3B with Less than Two Out:			14/19	74%	

Loves to face: Dan Quisenberry (.480, 12-for-25)
Hates to face: Bob McClure (.071, 1-for-14, 6 SO)
Like consistency? Whitaker's career batting averages: .283 with bases empty, .282 with runners on base, .284 with runners in scoring position. . . . 21 homers last season were the most ever by a Detroit second baseman. Tigers were 17–3 in games when Whitaker homered. . . . Except for one day in July, batting average remained above .300 from start of season through Aug. 30. Then it dipped below, never to see .300 again. . . . Batting averages against left-handers since 1982: .299, .307, .230, .228. . . . Career average of .349 with the bases loaded. . . . Hit by pitch twice last season, the first time that has happened to him; in 4,743 career plate appearances, he has been hit six times. . . . Chris Pittaro notwithstanding, Whitaker has never played a major-league game anywhere but second base.

Frank White

Kansas City Royals	AB	H	2B	3B	HR	RRF	BB	SO	BA	SA	OBA
Season	563	140	25	1	22	70	28	86	.249	.414	.284
vs. Left-Handed Pitchers	166	41	6	0	9	27	7	19	.247	.446	.277
vs. Right-Handed Pitchers	397	99	19	1	13	43	21	67	.249	.401	.287
Home	297	72	13	0	9	36	14	41	.242	.377	.277
Road	266	68	12	1	13	34	14	45	.256	.455	.292
Grass	223	58	9	1	12	33	7	36	.260	.471	.281
Artificial Turf	340	82	16	0	10	37	21	50	.241	.376	.286
April	52	10	4	0	3	5	2	11	.192	.442	.222
May	98	24	5	1	4	16	7	7	.245	.439	.292
June	97	22	0	0	2	9	4	14	.227	.289	.257
July	99	26	3	0	7	19	4	17	.263	.505	.295
August	99	27	7	0	2	13	4	17	.273	.404	.298
Sept./Oct.	118	31	6	0	4	8	7	20	.263	.415	.304
Leading Off Inn.	143	35	4	0	5	5	5	23	.245	.378	.270
Bases Empty	342	78	13	1	18	18	17	55	.228	.430	.265
Runners On	221	62	12	0	4	52	11	31	.281	.389	.314
Runners/Scor. Pos.	128	37	7	0	3	50	7	16	.289	.414	.324
Runners On/2 Out	82	27	5	0	2	28	6	10	.329	.463	.375
Scor. Pos./2 Out	54	18	3	0	1	26	5	6	.333	.444	.390
Late Inning Pressure	80	25	3	0	2	8	3	7	.313	.425	.337
Leading Off	21	8	0	0	2	2	1	2	.381	.667	.409
Bases Empty	45	15	1	0	2	2	1	3	.333	.489	.348
Runners On	35	10	2	0	0	6	2	4	.286	.343	.324
Runners/Scor. Pos.	19	5	2	0	0	6	2	1	.263	.368	.333

DRIVING IN RUNS	0 Out	1 Out	2 Out	Total	
From 1B	0/39	0/67	2/53	2/159	1%
From 2B	0/19	10/42	14/38	24/99	24%
From 3B	2/8	10/24	10/28	22/60	37%
Scoring Position	2/27	20/66	24/66	46/159	29%
Scor. Pos. %	7%	30%	36%	29%	
Driving In Runners from 3B with Less than Two Out:			12/32	38%	

Loves to face: Joe Cowley (1.000, 2-for-2, 2 HR)
Hates to face: Moose Haas (.096, 5-for-52)
Batted in each batting order slot except the 1st and 9th positions last season, but he took care of those two earlier in his career. That's an impressive feat of versatility, impressive to everyone except Joe Carter. . . . Grand slam off Dennis Rasmussen on July 10 is his only home run in 191 regular-season at bats at Yankee Stadium; he also had one in Game Three of 1980 Championship Series. . . . Failed to drive in a runner from first base with less than two outs in 106 opportunities, 10 short of the *Player Analysis* record: 116, by Thurman Munson in 1975. . . . Started A.L.'s only triple play of 1985 by catching a looping liner hit by Rickey Henderson.

Ernie Whitt

Toronto Blue Jays	AB	H	2B	3B	HR	RRF	BB	SO	BA	SA	OBA
Season	412	101	21	2	19	67	47	59	.245	.444	.323
vs. Left-Handed Pitchers	75	16	2	0	2	8	11	22	.213	.320	.318
vs. Right-Handed Pitchers	337	85	19	2	17	59	36	37	.252	.472	.324
Home	197	44	13	1	7	28	27	33	.223	.406	.319
Road	215	57	8	1	12	39	20	26	.265	.479	.326
Grass	175	48	6	0	12	35	18	22	.274	.514	.340
Artificial Turf	237	53	15	2	7	32	29	37	.224	.392	.310
April	45	11	4	0	1	6	3	5	.244	.400	.292
May	61	21	4	0	5	17	3	7	.344	.656	.375
June	70	19	6	0	3	11	8	6	.271	.486	.346
July	73	19	2	2	4	12	10	11	.260	.507	.357
August	70	16	3	0	2	10	9	11	.229	.357	.313
Sept./Oct.	93	15	2	0	4	11	14	19	.161	.312	.269
Leading Off Inn.	87	19	7	0	3	3	11	6	.218	.402	.306
Bases Empty	228	52	14	0	11	11	18	32	.228	.434	.287
Runners On	184	49	7	2	8	56	29	27	.266	.457	.363
Runners/Scor. Pos.	109	25	3	0	5	44	22	16	.229	.394	.353
Runners On/2 Out	73	12	3	0	3	14	16	15	.164	.329	.315
Scor. Pos./2 Out	45	5	1	0	1	8	14	9	.111	.200	.322
Late Inning Pressure	59	13	3	1	2	7	7	7	.220	.407	.303
Leading Off	14	2	0	0	2	2	2	1	.143	.571	.250
Bases Empty	35	6	2	0	2	2	2	5	.171	.400	.216
Runners On	24	7	1	1	0	5	5	2	.292	.417	.414
Runners/Scor. Pos.	13	3	0	0	0	3	5	1	.231	.231	.444

DRIVING IN RUNS	0 Out	1 Out	2 Out	Total	
From 1B	4/32	5/50	6/46	15/128	12%
From 2B	5/17	7/36	3/29	15/82	18%
From 3B	6/9	10/13	2/19	18/41	44%
Scoring Position	11/26	17/49	5/48	33/123	27%
Scor. Pos. %	42%	35%	10%	27%	
Driving In Runners from 3B with Less than Two Out:			16/22	73%	

Loves to face: Richard Dotson (.385, 10-for-26, 3 HR)
Hates to face: Tippy Martinez (0-for-11, 4 SO)
Pressed into increased duty after platoonmate Buck Martinez broke his leg on July 9; started 62 of 77 games from then until division was clinched on Oct. 5, and got into nine other games as a pinch-hitter or substitute catcher. Of necessity, a dozen of those starts were against left-handers; he batted .212 in those games, while the team went 6–6. . . . Hit two homers off lefties last year, taking Matt Young and Ron Guidry deep; only previous home run off a left-hander came off Grant Jackson in 1982. . . . Career batting average is .300 (24-for-80) in Late-Inning Pressure Situations with runners in scoring position. . . . Has homered in every current A.L. ballpark except Royals Stadium, where he has a career batting average of .133.

Alan Wiggins

Baltimore Orioles	AB	H	2B	3B	HR	RRF	BB	SO	BA	SA	OBA
Season	298	85	11	4	0	23	29	16	.285	.349	.353
vs. Left-Handed Pitchers	105	33	6	1	0	8	13	5	.314	.390	.395
vs. Right-Handed Pitchers	193	52	5	3	0	15	16	11	.269	.326	.329
Home	146	37	6	1	0	12	15	8	.253	.308	.323
Road	152	48	5	3	0	11	14	8	.316	.388	.381
Grass	259	74	9	4	0	22	25	12	.286	.351	.351
Artificial Turf	39	11	2	0	0	1	4	4	.282	.333	.364
April	0	0	0	0	0	0	0	0	.000	.000	.000
May	0	0	0	0	0	0	0	0	.000	.000	.000
June	0	0	0	0	0	0	0	0	.000	.000	.000
July	85	23	5	1	0	9	8	5	.271	.353	.340
August	109	31	3	2	0	7	13	6	.284	.349	.366
Sept./Oct.	104	31	3	1	0	7	8	5	.298	.346	.348
Leading Off Inn.	118	31	6	1	0	0	13	7	.263	.331	.341
Bases Empty	205	54	8	2	0	0	20	14	.263	.322	.335
Runners On	93	31	3	2	0	23	9	2	.333	.409	.392
Runners/Scor. Pos.	49	19	1	2	0	23	7	2	.388	.490	.464
Runners On/2 Out	33	11	0	1	0	10	5	1	.333	.394	.421
Scor. Pos./2 Out	19	8	0	1	0	10	5	1	.421	.526	.542
Late Inning Pressure	26	8	1	0	0	4	6	1	.308	.346	.438
Leading Off	6	2	1	0	0	0	2	1	.333	.500	.500
Bases Empty	14	5	1	0	0	0	4	1	.357	.429	.500
Runners On	12	3	0	0	0	4	2	0	.250	.250	.357
Runners/Scor. Pos.	9	3	0	0	0	4	1	0	.333	.333	.400

DRIVING IN RUNS	0 Out	1 Out	2 Out	Total	
From 1B	0/19	1/25	1/21	2/65	3%
From 2B	1/6	3/16	3/16	7/38	18%
From 3B	2/5	6/8	6/11	14/24	58%
Scoring Position	3/11	9/24	9/27	21/62	34%
Scor. Pos. %	27%	38%	33%	34%	
Driving In Runners from 3B with Less than Two Out:			8/13	62%	

Loves to face: John Candelaria (.353, 6-for-17, 1 HR)
Hates to face: Walt Terrell (.091, 1-for-11)
Figures above are for A.L. only. . . . Averaged only 2.59 assists per nine innings, lowest rate among A.L. second basemen (minimum: 300 innings). . . . Committed 10 errors in final 28 games after 30-game errorless streak from July 28 to Aug. 31. . . . Committed all 14 of his errors on grass fields. . . . Ground-ball hitter: 1.62 G/A ratio last season. Career: 2.01. . . . Batted .388 with runners in scoring position to rank 3d in A.L. . . . Career batting averages: .303 batting right-handed, .246 batting left-handed. His four career home runs were all hit in San Diego, from right side of plate. . . . Orioles' stolen-base record is 57 by Luis Aparicio in 1964; the Earl Weaver record is 44 by Al Bumbry in 1980. . . . With 30 stolen bases last season, Wiggins joined Bumbry and Don Baylor as the only players to enjoy 30-steal seasons under Earl.

Rob Wilfong

California Angels	AB	H	2B	3B	HR	RRF	BB	SO	BA	SA	OBA
Season	217	41	3	0	4	16	16	32	.189	.258	.243
vs. Left-Handed Pitchers	21	3	0	0	2	3	1	7	.143	.429	.174
vs. Right-Handed Pitchers	196	38	3	0	2	13	15	25	.194	.240	.250
Home	88	18	2	0	2	8	6	10	.205	.295	.253
Road	129	23	1	0	2	8	10	22	.178	.233	.236
Grass	179	35	3	0	4	15	15	21	.196	.279	.256
Artificial Turf	38	6	0	0	0	1	1	11	.158	.158	.175
April	14	2	0	0	0	0	4	1	.143	.143	.333
May	75	15	1	0	0	7	5	12	.200	.213	.247
June	46	7	0	0	2	3	2	8	.152	.283	.188
July	49	11	1	0	2	4	1	5	.224	.367	.240
August	22	4	1	0	0	1	1	6	.182	.227	.208
Sept./Oct.	11	2	0	0	0	1	3	0	.182	.182	.357
Leading Off Inn.	48	11	2	0	1	1	2	8	.229	.333	.260
Bases Empty	134	20	3	0	3	3	8	20	.149	.239	.197
Runners On	83	21	0	0	1	13	8	12	.253	.289	.312
Runners/Scor. Pos.	47	12	0	0	1	13	8	5	.255	.319	.351
Runners On/2 Out	36	7	0	0	1	8	3	6	.194	.278	.256
Scor. Pos./2 Out	22	6	0	0	1	8	3	3	.273	.409	.360
Late Inning Pressure	38	9	2	0	0	3	1	2	.237	.289	.256
Leading Off	13	4	2	0	0	0	1	1	.308	.462	.357
Bases Empty	22	5	2	0	0	0	1	2	.227	.318	.261
Runners On	16	4	0	0	0	3	0	0	.250	.250	.250
Runners/Scor. Pos.	11	3	0	0	0	3	0	0	.273	.273	.273

DRIVING IN RUNS	0 Out	1 Out	2 Out	Total	
From 1B	0/14	0/20	0/24	0/58	0%
From 2B	0/12	2/12	3/12	5/36	14%
From 3B	1/1	2/3	4/13	7/17	41%
Scoring Position	1/13	4/15	7/25	12/53	23%
Scor. Pos. %	8%	27%	28%	23%	
Driving In Runners from 3B with Less than Two Out:			3/4	75%	

Loves to face: Aurelio Lopez (.412, 7-for-17, 1 HR)
Hates to face: Tom Seaver (0-for-12)
Nice alphabetical segue from Wiggins: Wilfong led A.L. second basemen with 3.86 assists per nine innings, aiding the Angels' major-league leading total of 202 double plays. . . . Batted 104 points higher with runners on base than with the bases empty last season; among A.L. players (minimum: 200 PA), only Cliff Johnson and Eddie Murray had greater imbalances of that type. . . . Batting average with runners in scoring position has been higher than his overall batting average in each of last four years. . . . Batting average vs. left-handed pitchers has been above .200 only once (.333 in 1979). Career averages: .166 vs. left-handers, .265 vs. right-handers. . . . No GIDPs despite 42 opportunities last season, the most opportunities without a GIDP in the majors.

Curtis Wilkerson

Texas Rangers	AB	H	2B	3B	HR	RRF	BB	SO	BA	SA	OBA
Season	360	88	11	6	0	23	22	63	.244	.308	.293
vs. Left-Handed Pitchers	86	24	6	2	0	5	11	9	.279	.395	.367
vs. Right-Handed Pitchers	274	64	5	4	0	18	11	54	.234	.281	.268
Home	160	36	4	1	0	9	8	26	.225	.263	.267
Road	200	52	7	5	0	14	14	37	.260	.345	.313
Grass	294	75	9	5	0	19	17	51	.255	.320	.303
Artificial Turf	66	13	2	1	0	4	5	12	.197	.258	.250
April	46	9	1	0	0	2	5	11	.196	.217	.269
May	71	19	3	2	0	3	3	14	.268	.366	.297
June	51	13	0	1	0	4	4	11	.255	.294	.316
July	52	13	1	1	0	4	3	7	.250	.308	.304
August	48	11	1	0	0	1	2	8	.229	.250	.260
Sept./Oct.	92	23	5	2	0	9	5	12	.250	.348	.300
Leading Off Inn.	103	30	2	3	0	0	4	17	.291	.369	.324
Bases Empty	236	59	7	4	0	0	12	41	.250	.314	.292
Runners On	124	29	4	2	0	23	10	22	.234	.298	.295
Runners/Scor. Pos.	72	16	3	2	0	21	8	12	.222	.319	.298
Runners On/2 Out	57	11	3	2	0	13	8	9	.193	.316	.292
Scor. Pos./2 Out	40	9	2	2	0	12	6	5	.225	.375	.326
Late Inning Pressure	48	20	4	2	0	6	3	4	.417	.583	.451
Leading Off	19	8	1	1	0	0	0	4	.421	.579	.421
Bases Empty	38	15	3	1	0	0	0	4	.395	.526	.395
Runners On	10	5	1	1	0	6	3	0	.500	.800	.615
Runners/Scor. Pos.	7	4	1	1	0	6	2	0	.571	1.000	.667

DRIVING IN RUNS	0 Out	1 Out	2 Out	Total	
From 1B	0/19	0/33	2/39	2/91	2%
From 2B	2/7	2/20	5/28	9/55	16%
From 3B	2/5	3/8	6/20	11/33	33%
Scoring Position	4/12	5/28	11/48	20/88	23%
Scor. Pos. %	33%	18%	23%	23%	
Driving In Runners from 3B with Less than Two Out:			5/13	38%	

Loves to face: Jim Clancy (.625, 5-for-8)
Hates to face: Don Sutton (0-for-10, 3 SO)
Committed 21 errors last season; that's nothing to brag about, except that in 1984, he had 24 errors *before the All-Star break*. . . . Increased his rate of assists per nine innings from 2.84 in '84 to 3.03 in '85. . . . Ground-ball hitter: 1.59 G/A ratio last season. Career: 1.85. . . . Batting average in Late-Inning Pressure Situations (.417) was 2d-highest in majors last year (leader: Mike Stenhouse, .424). . . . Has never driven in a runner from first base (113 career opportunities). . . Down, down, down: career batting averages of .248 with the bases empty, .235 with runners on base, .213 with runners in scoring position, .170 with runners in scoring position and two outs. . . . One hitter whom the scoreboard hasn't helped: his only career home run was hit in 1984 at the Metrodome off John Butcher; he's 0-for-408 in Arlington.

Jerry Willard

Cleveland Indians	AB	H	2B	3B	HR	RRF	BB	SO	BA	SA	OBA
Season	300	81	13	0	7	40	28	59	.270	.383	.333
vs. Left-Handed Pitchers	48	7	2	0	0	5	4	20	.146	.188	.222
vs. Right-Handed Pitchers	252	74	11	0	7	35	24	39	.294	.421	.355
Home	136	37	4	0	4	23	10	30	.272	.390	.320
Road	164	44	9	0	3	17	18	29	.268	.378	.344
Grass	239	65	8	0	6	31	23	48	.272	.381	.337
Artificial Turf	61	16	5	0	1	9	5	11	.262	.393	.318
April	25	4	2	0	0	1	4	4	.160	.240	.276
May	3	0	0	0	0	0	0	0	.000	.000	.000
June	70	19	5	0	1	9	8	8	.271	.386	.346
July	44	13	3	0	0	2	5	14	.295	.364	.367
August	53	16	1	0	0	10	4	11	.302	.321	.345
Sept./Oct.	105	29	2	0	6	18	7	22	.276	.467	.327
Leading Off Inn.	66	20	3	0	1	1	10	12	.303	.394	.395
Bases Empty	170	49	8	0	3	3	16	34	.288	.388	.349
Runners On	130	32	5	0	4	37	12	25	.246	.377	.313
Runners/Scor. Pos.	75	17	2	0	0	27	7	13	.227	.253	.298
Runners On/2 Out	46	7	1	0	1	11	7	6	.152	.239	.264
Scor. Pos./2 Out	32	5	1	0	0	9	4	4	.156	.188	.250
Late Inning Pressure	49	17	3	0	2	13	7	4	.347	.531	.421
Leading Off	12	3	1	0	0	0	3	1	.250	.333	.400
Bases Empty	26	8	1	0	0	0	5	2	.308	.346	.419
Runners On	23	9	2	0	2	13	2	2	.391	.739	.423
Runners/Scor. Pos.	17	6	1	0	0	8	2	1	.353	.412	.400

DRIVING IN RUNS	0 Out	1 Out	2 Out	Total	
From 1B	2/27	4/34	1/29	7/90	8%
From 2B	3/18	5/26	5/22	13/66	20%
From 3B	2/6	7/9	4/16	13/31	42%
Scoring Position	5/24	12/35	9/38	26/97	27%
Scor. Pos. %	21%	34%	24%	27%	
Driving In Runners from 3B with Less than Two Out:			9/15	60%	

Loves to face: Frank Wills (.625, 5-for-8, 1 HR)
Hates to face: Charlie Hough (.111, 1-for-9, 3 SO)
Started 71 of Indians' 104 games against right-handers, but only 13 of 58 against lefties. . . . Fanned 20 times in 48 at bats against lefties, 2d-highest A.L. rate over past 11 years (minimum: 20 SO). . . . Only major-league home run against a lefty was not off a pitcher but an outfielder/first baseman/quarterback, Toronto's Rick Leach, who was mopping up a game in August 1984 when Willard connected. . . . Has hit nine of 17 career home runs in 8th or 9th inning. . . . Career batting average of .175 (17-for-97) with two outs and runners on base. . . . Boosted his batting average to .270, the highest it had been since June 16, by going 3-for-4 on the final day of season.

Willie Wilson

Kansas City Royals	AB	H	2B	3B	HR	RRF	BB	SO	BA	SA	OBA
Season	605	168	25	21	4	44	29	94	.278	.408	.316
vs. Left-Handed Pitchers	164	48	10	3	1	12	6	26	.293	.409	.316
vs. Right-Handed Pitchers	441	120	15	18	3	32	23	68	.272	.408	.316
Home	302	83	12	14	1	23	14	52	.275	.417	.313
Road	303	85	13	7	3	21	15	42	.281	.399	.319
Grass	232	67	10	6	3	16	8	29	.289	.422	.315
Artificial Turf	373	101	15	15	1	28	21	65	.271	.399	.316
April	82	27	2	5	0	6	5	15	.329	.476	.382
May	119	29	6	4	2	6	3	18	.244	.412	.260
June	104	29	4	3	0	7	10	19	.279	.375	.348
July	121	39	6	2	2	10	3	11	.322	.455	.339
August	108	28	2	5	0	12	5	19	.259	.370	.298
Sept./Oct.	71	16	5	2	0	3	3	12	.225	.352	.267
Leading Off Inn.	239	65	11	10	2	2	13	36	.272	.427	.312
Bases Empty	413	109	15	15	3	3	20	61	.264	.395	.300
Runners On	192	59	10	6	1	41	9	33	.307	.438	.350
Runners/Scor. Pos.	105	31	7	3	1	38	8	18	.295	.448	.359
Runners On/2 Out	80	17	3	2	1	17	7	18	.213	.338	.284
Scor. Pos./2 Out	57	13	3	1	1	16	6	13	.228	.368	.302
Late Inning Pressure	84	25	4	1	0	8	2	14	.298	.369	.318
Leading Off	21	6	1	0	0	0	0	4	.286	.333	.286
Bases Empty	49	14	2	1	0	0	1	9	.286	.367	.300
Runners On	35	11	2	0	0	8	1	5	.314	.371	.342
Runners/Scor. Pos.	19	7	2	0	0	8	1	3	.368	.474	.409

DRIVING IN RUNS	0 Out	1 Out	2 Out	Total	
From 1B	0/31	3/62	4/61	7/154	5%
From 2B	1/6	5/28	4/38	10/72	14%
From 3B	5/6	10/14	8/25	23/45	51%
Scoring Position	6/12	15/42	12/63	33/117	28%
Scor. Pos. %	50%	36%	19%	28%	
Driving In Runners from 3B with Less than Two Out:			15/20	75%	

Loves to face: Mike Brown (.778, 7-for-9)
Hates to face: Dave Stewart (.067, 1-for-15)
Muscling up: Inside-the-park home runs had accounted for 13 of his 17 career four-baggers through the 1984 season, but all four of his homers last season were "outside-the-park" shots. . . . Batting average leading off innings (.272) was his lowest since 1978. . . . Another bold Howser move: Wilson was dropped from usual leadoff position spot to the second slot in the batting order for last week of the Royals' pennant drive and stayed in that spot throughout the post-season. Sept. 29 marked the first time since Aug. 14, 1979, that Wilson was in the starting lineup in a position other than leadoff, a total of 828 games under three different Kansas City managers. . . . Career batting average of .222 (12-for-54) with the bases loaded. . . . Career batting average of .367 at Fenway Park.

Dave Winfield

New York Yankees	AB	H	2B	3B	HR	RRF	BB	SO	BA	SA	OBA
Season	633	174	34	6	26	122	52	96	.275	.471	.328
vs. Left-Handed Pitchers	215	54	11	3	10	39	31	27	.251	.470	.343
vs. Right-Handed Pitchers	418	120	23	3	16	83	21	69	.287	.471	.320
Home	298	85	19	1	15	65	27	42	.285	.507	.343
Road	335	89	15	5	11	57	25	54	.266	.439	.315
Grass	529	149	28	4	24	107	46	78	.282	.486	.337
Artificial Turf	104	25	6	2	2	15	6	18	.240	.394	.282
April	70	18	2	1	2	6	6	11	.257	.400	.312
May	105	27	6	1	3	20	8	16	.257	.419	.307
June	105	36	3	0	4	23	4	14	.343	.486	.364
July	106	32	7	1	6	21	12	16	.302	.557	.373
August	109	25	7	2	6	26	15	18	.229	.495	.323
Sept./Oct.	138	36	9	1	5	26	7	21	.261	.449	.295
Leading Off Inn.	123	43	11	0	5	5	8	18	.350	.561	.389
Bases Empty	316	85	23	2	12	12	19	51	.269	.468	.310
Runners On	317	89	11	4	14	110	33	45	.281	.473	.345
Runners/Scor. Pos.	187	59	8	2	10	98	25	29	.316	.540	.389
Runners On/2 Out	124	38	4	3	7	40	13	22	.306	.556	.372
Scor. Pos./2 Out	74	24	3	2	4	31	12	16	.324	.581	.419
Late Inning Pressure	86	21	3	0	3	16	6	18	.244	.384	.293
Leading Off	19	5	0	0	1	1	2	5	.263	.421	.333
Bases Empty	46	9	3	0	1	1	3	9	.196	.326	.245
Runners On	40	12	0	0	2	15	3	9	.300	.450	.349
Runners/Scor. Pos.	20	6	0	0	1	12	1	6	.300	.450	.333

DRIVING IN RUNS	0 Out	1 Out	2 Out	Total	
From 1B	2/35	4/93	7/78	13/206	6%
From 2B	8/24	14/61	15/51	37/136	27%
From 3B	10/15	25/39	11/33	46/87	53%
Scoring Position	18/39	39/100	26/84	83/223	37%
Scor. Pos. %	46%	39%	31%	37%	
Driving In Runners from 3B with Less than Two Out:			35/54	65%	

Loves to face: Jim Clancy (.429, 9-for-21, 4 HR)
Hates to face: Luis Sanchez (0-for-11, 3 SO)
Yankees had a record of 21–3 in games in which he homered. . . . One of six A.L. players to hit two extra-inning home runs; his were the only two hit by the Yankees last season. . . . Batting average in Late-Inning Pressure Situations has been lower than overall batting average in each of five seasons with Yankees; composite LIP average over that span is .252. . . . Batted with the bases loaded 17 times last season (his highest total in A.L.) but hit only .133 (2-for-15) with two walks and two singles. . . . Batting average vs. left-handed pitchers (.251) was his lowest over the past 11 years; has hit for a higher average against right-handers than he has against left-handers for two straight seasons. . . . Highest career batting average at any A.L. park is .373 at Cleveland Stadium, where he has also homered with the greatest frequency (one per 10.6 at bats).

George Wright

Texas Rangers	AB	H	2B	3B	HR	RRF	BB	SO	BA	SA	OBA
Season	363	69	13	0	2	19	25	49	.190	.242	.241
vs. Left-Handed Pitchers	122	21	6	0	0	9	10	19	.172	.221	.231
vs. Right-Handed Pitchers	241	48	7	0	2	10	15	30	.199	.253	.246
Home	158	25	3	0	2	6	11	25	.158	.215	.213
Road	205	44	10	0	0	13	14	24	.215	.263	.262
Grass	313	57	10	0	2	17	19	42	.182	.233	.228
Artificial Turf	50	12	3	0	0	2	6	7	.240	.300	.321
April	60	10	2	0	0	2	4	3	.167	.200	.219
May	54	10	1	0	0	2	7	4	.185	.204	.279
June	0	0	0	0	0	0	0	0	.000	.000	.000
July	72	12	3	0	0	7	4	11	.167	.208	.205
August	94	23	4	0	2	5	6	12	.245	.351	.290
Sept./Oct.	83	14	3	0	0	3	4	19	.169	.205	.207
Leading Off Inn.	75	13	4	0	1	1	4	4	.173	.267	.215
Bases Empty	212	45	11	0	2	2	8	28	.212	.292	.241
Runners On	151	24	2	0	0	17	17	21	.159	.172	.241
Runners/Scor. Pos.	80	13	1	0	0	17	12	9	.163	.175	.266
Runners On/2 Out	72	11	1	0	0	8	6	10	.153	.167	.218
Scor. Pos./2 Out	44	7	1	0	0	8	4	4	.159	.182	.229
Late Inning Pressure	58	9	1	0	0	2	5	5	.155	.172	.219
Leading Off	19	1	0	0	0	0	2	1	.053	.053	.143
Bases Empty	34	6	1	0	0	0	3	4	.176	.206	.243
Runners On	24	3	0	0	0	2	2	1	.125	.125	.185
Runners/Scor. Pos.	16	1	0	0	0	2	0	1	.063	.063	.059

DRIVING IN RUNS	0 Out	1 Out	2 Out	Total	
From 1B	0/29	0/36	0/55	0/120	0%
From 2B	0/13	3/16	4/33	7/62	11%
From 3B	5/7	1/11	4/19	10/37	27%
Scoring Position	5/20	4/27	8/52	17/99	17%
Scor. Pos. %	25%	15%	15%	17%	
Driving In Runners from 3B with Less than Two Out:			6/18	33%	

Loves to face: Willie Hernandez (.800, 4-for-5)
Hates to face: Milt Wilcox (0-for-14)
Only major-league player who batted below .200 against both left-handers and right-handers last season (minimum: 100 AB against each).... Switch-hitter, started two-thirds of Rangers' games against left-handers and 56 percent of them against right-handers.... Seems to be forgetting how to hit southpaws; annual averages since 1982: .305, .251, .197, .172. Last home run against a lefty: Aug. 18, 1984, off Bud Black.... Percentage of runners driven in from scoring position (17.2) was lowest of career.... Did not drive in a runner from first base in 120 opportunities last season, tying Jack Perconte for league's biggest 0-for.... Career batting average of .342 (13-for-38) with the bases loaded.... Has homered in every A.L. ballpark except Memorial Stadium.

Butch Wynegar

New York Yankees	AB	H	2B	3B	HR	RRF	BB	SO	BA	SA	OBA
Season	309	69	15	0	5	33	64	43	.223	.320	.356
vs. Left-Handed Pitchers	139	30	8	0	2	12	32	25	.216	.317	.360
vs. Right-Handed Pitchers	170	39	7	0	3	21	32	18	.229	.324	.351
Home	158	31	8	0	2	13	33	22	.196	.285	.333
Road	151	38	7	0	3	20	31	21	.252	.358	.379
Grass	268	59	13	0	3	25	55	39	.220	.302	.352
Artificial Turf	41	10	2	0	2	8	9	4	.244	.439	.380
April	60	19	4	0	1	8	7	6	.317	.433	.388
May	81	16	2	0	2	12	18	11	.198	.296	.343
June	45	12	2	0	1	4	6	3	.267	.378	.353
July	20	1	1	0	0	0	3	4	.050	.100	.174
August	59	15	6	0	0	8	17	12	.254	.356	.416
Sept./Oct.	44	6	0	0	1	1	13	7	.136	.205	.333
Leading Off Inn.	60	10	2	0	0	0	11	11	.167	.200	.296
Bases Empty	157	33	6	0	1	1	32	23	.210	.268	.344
Runners On	152	36	9	0	4	32	32	20	.237	.375	.368
Runners/Scor. Pos.	84	18	4	0	2	26	23	15	.214	.333	.380
Runners On/2 Out	61	18	7	0	2	13	16	6	.295	.508	.442
Scor. Pos./2 Out	35	10	2	0	2	12	13	4	.286	.514	.479
Late Inning Pressure	53	15	2	0	3	10	12	8	.283	.491	.415
Leading Off	16	3	0	0	0	0	2	2	.188	.188	.278
Bases Empty	35	7	1	0	1	1	6	5	.200	.314	.317
Runners On	18	8	1	0	2	9	6	3	.444	.833	.583
Runners/Scor. Pos.	8	4	1	0	1	7	4	2	.500	1.000	.667

DRIVING IN RUNS	0 Out	1 Out	2 Out	Total	
From 1B	0/31	3/40	2/40	5/111	5%
From 2B	2/14	2/21	8/31	12/66	18%
From 3B	5/9	5/17	1/10	11/36	31%
Scoring Position	7/23	7/38	9/41	23/102	23%
Scor. Pos. %	30%	18%	22%	23%	
Driving In Runners from 3B with Less than Two Out:			10/26	38%	

Loves to face: Bert Blyleven (.438, 7-for-16, 1 HR)
Hates to face: Mark Gubicza (0-for-11, 3 SO)
Hitless in 10 at bats with the bases loaded last season, the most at bats without a hit by any player in the majors.... Started 52 of team's first 59 games, but an injury, a cool bat, and a hot Ron Hassey combined to limit him to 38 starts the rest of the way.... Biggest hit of year was two-out, 9th-inning homer off Tom Henke to tie score on final Friday of season, prolonging Yankees' hopes for division title; Yankees went on to win that game but were eliminated the next day.... Three of his last four home runs have been hit in Late-Inning Pressure Situations.... Percentage of runners driven in from scoring position in LIP (60.0, 4th-best in A.L.) was higher than in nonpressure situations (18.5) for first time since 1979.... Has homered in every current A.L. ballpark except Fenway Park.

Mike Young

Baltimore Orioles	AB	H	2B	3B	HR	RRF	BB	SO	BA	SA	OBA
Season	450	123	22	1	28	83	48	104	.273	.513	.348
vs. Left-Handed Pitchers	181	53	8	1	12	30	12	34	.293	.547	.335
vs. Right-Handed Pitchers	269	70	14	0	16	53	36	70	.260	.491	.356
Home	216	60	9	1	15	42	33	49	.278	.537	.377
Road	234	63	13	0	13	41	15	55	.269	.491	.319
Grass	378	108	16	1	26	72	44	83	.286	.540	.364
Artificial Turf	72	15	6	0	2	11	4	21	.208	.375	.260
April	60	13	3	0	2	6	9	17	.217	.367	.329
May	43	10	3	0	2	7	4	14	.233	.442	.298
June	31	8	1	1	1	5	3	6	.258	.452	.324
July	91	29	6	0	6	14	8	22	.319	.582	.374
August	94	28	5	0	11	34	11	18	.298	.702	.374
Sept./Oct.	131	35	4	0	6	17	13	27	.267	.435	.342
Leading Off Inn.	106	28	4	0	8	8	9	30	.264	.528	.328
Bases Empty	254	65	10	0	15	15	24	62	.256	.472	.325
Runners On	196	58	12	1	13	68	24	42	.296	.566	.377
Runners/Scor. Pos.	117	34	6	1	7	55	18	28	.291	.538	.387
Runners On/2 Out	91	21	7	0	2	23	13	21	.231	.374	.327
Scor. Pos./2 Out	65	14	4	0	2	22	10	17	.215	.369	.320
Late Inning Pressure	54	12	2	0	3	10	7	11	.222	.426	.311
Leading Off	12	3	1	0	2	2	1	4	.250	.833	.308
Bases Empty	34	6	1	0	2	2	2	6	.176	.382	.222
Runners On	20	6	1	0	1	8	5	5	.300	.500	.440
Runners/Scor. Pos.	10	3	1	0	0	6	3	4	.300	.400	.462

DRIVING IN RUNS	0 Out	1 Out	2 Out	Total	
From 1B	1/35	10/51	3/70	14/156	9%
From 2B	4/18	7/26	12/48	23/92	25%
From 3B	5/6	7/14	6/28	18/48	38%
Scoring Position	9/24	14/40	18/76	41/140	29%
Scor. Pos. %	38%	35%	24%	29%	
Driving In Runners from 3B with Less than Two Out:			12/20	60%	

Loves to face: Jim Beattie (.714, 5-for-7, 2 HR)
Hates to face: Mike Moore (.118, 2-for-17, 8 SO)
Monthly breakdown illustrates how he came on toward end of season; had 32 RBIs in August to lead A.L., and his 11 home runs that month tied Don Mattingly for A.L. lead.... Instant lightning: career slugging average of .521 when leading off innings.... Career breakdown with runners in scoring position: .354 with less than two outs, .211 with two outs.... Shuttled between DH and outfield until Aug. 31. From then on, was Orioles' regular leftfielder, starting all 36 games.... Until he hit 17 for the Orioles in '84, had never hit more than 16 homers in a season in organized baseball.... Has struck out 214 times in last two seasons, highest two-year total by Baltimore player since Lee May in 1977–78.

Robin Yount

Milwaukee Brewers	AB	H	2B	3B	HR	RRF	BB	SO	BA	SA	OBA
Season	466	129	26	3	15	73	49	56	.277	.442	.342
vs. Left-Handed Pitchers	150	45	7	2	4	22	15	19	.300	.453	.357
vs. Right-Handed Pitchers	316	84	19	1	11	51	34	37	.266	.437	.335
Home	243	75	17	1	11	50	30	25	.309	.523	.382
Road	223	54	9	2	4	23	19	31	.242	.354	.297
Grass	410	117	23	2	15	67	46	48	.285	.461	.355
Artificial Turf	56	12	3	1	0	6	3	8	.214	.304	.246
April	77	19	3	1	0	4	6	10	.247	.312	.298
May	72	25	1	1	6	21	7	10	.347	.639	.388
June	106	28	8	0	0	14	10	16	.264	.340	.328
July	107	33	9	0	4	15	6	8	.308	.505	.345
August	100	23	5	1	5	19	20	11	.230	.450	.355
Sept./Oct.	4	1	0	0	0	0	0	1	.250	.250	.250
Leading Off Inn.	110	18	4	0	0	0	9	9	.164	.200	.227
Bases Empty	248	59	13	2	8	8	25	29	.238	.403	.308
Runners On	218	70	13	1	7	65	24	27	.321	.486	.379
Runners/Scor. Pos.	115	32	7	1	1	50	15	18	.278	.383	.343
Runners On/2 Out	75	21	4	0	3	19	16	8	.280	.453	.419
Scor. Pos./2 Out	42	11	3	0	1	14	9	6	.262	.405	.404
Late Inning Pressure	47	9	1	0	0	6	11	7	.191	.213	.344
Leading Off	16	1	0	0	0	0	1	1	.063	.063	.118
Bases Empty	28	5	0	0	0	0	4	3	.179	.179	.281
Runners On	19	4	1	0	0	6	7	4	.211	.263	.414
Runners/Scor. Pos.	11	3	0	0	0	6	3	1	.273	.273	.375

DRIVING IN RUNS	0 Out	1 Out	2 Out	Total	
From 1B	5/48	1/59	4/50	10/157	6%
From 2B	3/17	7/43	7/28	17/88	19%
From 3B	4/5	22/31	5/17	31/53	58%
Scoring Position	7/22	29/74	12/45	48/141	34%
Scor. Pos. %	32%	39%	27%	34%	
Driving In Runners from 3B with Less than Two Out:			26/36	72%	

Loves to face: Roger Clemens (.625, 5-for-8, 2 HR)
Hates to face: Mark Clear (.071, 1-for-15, 5 SO)
Batting averages in the last four seasons—.331, .308, .298, .277— make him one of two active players with a decline of 10 or more points in batting average each of the last three seasons (minimum: 200 AB in each).... Didn't play a game at shortstop last season; played left field until July 11, then moved over to center.... Batted leadoff in five games, 2d in 59 games, 3d once, and 4th 56 times.... On-base average when leading off inning stood 7th from the bottom in A.L.... Batting .370 with the bases loaded over past eight years.... Has batted over .300 at County Stadium in seven of last eight years.... Batted .191 in Late-Inning Pressure Situations last season, his lowest mark over the past 11 seasons.... Fly-ball hitter: 0.81 G/A ratio last season. Career: 0.97.

Baltimore Orioles

	AB	H	2B	3B	HR	RRF	BB	SO	BA	SA	OBA
Season	5517	1451	234	22	214	808	604	908	.263	.430	.336
vs. Left-Handers	1851	502	96	6	78	280	212	306	.271	.456	.346
vs. Right-Handers	3666	949	138	16	136	528	392	602	.259	.417	.330
Home	2697	703	110	7	103	408	334	450	.261	.421	.342
Road	2820	748	124	15	111	400	270	458	.265	.438	.329
Grass	4715	1251	196	16	186	690	527	783	.265	.432	.339
Artificial Turf	802	200	38	6	28	118	77	125	.249	.416	.316
April	628	155	23	2	25	97	87	115	.247	.409	.340
May	887	233	42	2	30	127	105	154	.263	.416	.338
June	901	236	37	2	33	128	90	134	.262	.417	.329
July	979	263	43	6	35	144	92	163	.269	.432	.331
August	943	259	41	6	43	158	109	146	.275	.468	.351
Sept./Oct.	1179	305	48	4	48	154	121	196	.259	.428	.328
Leading Off Inn.	1318	342	60	6	49	49	107	206	.259	.426	.317
Bases Empty	3168	785	124	11	113	113	323	541	.248	.401	.320
Runners On	2349	666	110	11	101	695	281	367	.284	.469	.356
Runners/Scor. Pos.	1280	369	60	8	58	582	182	227	.288	.484	.369
Runners On/2 Out	1009	265	43	5	37	258	141	171	.263	.425	.354
Scor. Pos./2 Out	597	155	27	3	23	219	99	116	.260	.430	.366
Late Inning Pressure	686	164	26	2	32	101	87	120	.239	.423	.323
Leading Off	169	33	7	1	5	5	17	38	.195	.337	.269
Bases Empty	425	94	18	1	17	17	46	82	.221	.388	.297
Runners On	261	70	8	1	15	84	41	38	.268	.479	.362
Runners/Scor. Pos.	145	41	7	1	11	75	26	25	.283	.572	.382

DRIVING IN RUNS	0 Out	1 Out	2 Out	Total	
From 1B	26/429	45/624	48/759	119/1812	7%
From 2B	42/202	71/363	109/474	222/1039	21%
From 3B	62/92	126/195	63/233	251/520	48%
Scoring Position	104/294	197/558	172/707	473/1559	30%
Scor. Pos. %	35%	35%	24%	30%	
Driving In Runners from 3B with Less than Two Out:			188/287	66%	

Love to face: Jim Beattie (11–3 against him)
Hate to face: Doyle Alexander (4–9 against him overall, 0–5 with Toronto)
Led A.L. in home runs for only 2d time in 32 years in Baltimore; only five of 17 major-league teams that hit 200 or more home runs have won league or division pennant. . . . Scored five or more runs in 29 innings, highest total in either league. . . . Gap of 21 points between batting average with runners on base and overall mark was largest in majors last season. . . . Batting average with runners in scoring position represents Baltimore's highest mark in the 11-year history of *The Player Analysis*. . . . It's tougher to hit a triple at Memorial Stadium than at Pimlico Race Track: only 11 were hit there last season, and Baltimore trailed the A.L. with a total of 22, the 6th time in the past nine seasons that the O's have finished last.

California Angels

	AB	H	2B	3B	HR	RRF	BB	SO	BA	SA	OBA
Season	5442	1364	215	31	153	724	648	902	.251	.386	.333
vs. Left-Handers	1580	419	70	13	44	222	195	261	.265	.409	.347
vs. Right-Handers	3862	945	145	18	109	502	453	641	.245	.376	.327
Home	2570	627	93	13	75	368	332	416	.244	.378	.332
Road	2872	737	122	18	78	356	316	486	.257	.393	.333
Grass	4438	1102	177	24	132	610	543	732	.248	.388	.332
Artificial Turf	1004	262	38	7	21	114	105	170	.261	.375	.336
April	730	187	25	5	21	105	111	123	.256	.390	.359
May	789	172	26	3	20	94	104	125	.218	.335	.310
June	933	233	34	5	22	112	108	164	.250	.368	.330
July	916	246	40	2	32	117	84	123	.269	.421	.331
August	960	236	42	4	27	133	111	166	.246	.382	.327
Sept./Oct.	1114	290	48	12	31	163	130	201	.260	.408	.340
Leading Off Inn.	1313	330	47	8	31	32	138	212	.251	.370	.328
Bases Empty	3082	737	125	14	73	75	345	502	.239	.360	.320
Runners On	2360	627	90	17	80	649	303	400	.266	.420	.349
Runners/Scor. Pos.	1372	355	45	9	44	540	213	229	.259	.401	.354
Runners On/2 Out	995	248	30	5	35	270	158	181	.249	.395	.357
Scor. Pos./2 Out	641	156	15	3	22	231	114	113	.243	.379	.362
Late Inning Pressure	715	166	26	3	12	91	98	129	.232	.327	.326
Leading Off	176	46	10	2	4	4	24	30	.261	.409	.350
Bases Empty	393	88	16	2	6	7	48	67	.224	.321	.310
Runners On	322	78	10	1	6	84	50	62	.242	.335	.346
Runners/Scor. Pos.	197	45	3	0	5	76	34	40	.228	.320	.342

DRIVING IN RUNS	0 Out	1 Out	2 Out	Total	
From 1B	26/403	40/631	48/713	114/1747	7%
From 2B	28/186	83/419	106/488	217/1093	20%
From 3B	50/82	106/194	80/257	236/533	44%
Scoring Position	78/268	189/613	186/745	453/1626	28%
Scor. Pos. %	29%	31%	25%	28%	
Driving In Runners from 3B with Less than Two Out:			156/276	57%	

Love to face: John Butcher (6–2 against him)
Hate to face: Bert Blyleven (12–24 against him)
Recaptured A.L. lead in Gene Mauch's favorite statistical category, sacrifice bunts (99), the 4th time in past five years that Angels have led A.L. in that specialty. Ten of Mauch's last 14 teams have led their league in sacrifices. . . . Team of ground-ball hitters: G/A ratio of 1.23 was highest in A.L. last season. . . . Led the majors with nine wins in games in which they trailed after eight innings, including seven at home. . . . Led A.L. with 648 walks, the first team since the 1960 Tigers to have the league's lowest batting average and the most walks. . . . Started 10 different players in cleanup position last season, tying Texas and San Francisco for major-league lead.

Boston Red Sox

	AB	H	2B	3B	HR	RRF	BB	SO	BA	SA	OBA
Season	5720	1615	292	31	162	784	562	816	.282	.429	.347
vs. Left-Handers	1758	498	90	11	48	247	189	245	.283	.429	.352
vs. Right-Handers	3962	1117	202	20	114	537	373	571	.282	.429	.344
Home	2767	832	166	21	73	408	261	414	.301	.455	.361
Road	2953	783	126	10	89	376	301	402	.265	.405	.333
Grass	4785	1380	256	28	136	678	468	688	.288	.439	.351
Artificial Turf	935	235	36	3	26	106	94	128	.251	.380	.322
April	716	184	32	3	22	96	83	105	.257	.402	.330
May	901	244	43	5	27	100	88	126	.271	.420	.336
June	907	271	54	3	18	133	88	117	.299	.424	.361
July	922	259	41	3	25	123	94	136	.281	.413	.348
August	1033	280	55	6	28	135	85	155	.271	.417	.326
Sept./Oct.	1241	377	67	11	42	197	124	177	.304	.477	.367
Leading Off Inn.	1347	405	72	9	46	46	110	176	.301	.470	.356
Bases Empty	3078	870	152	15	100	101	277	438	.283	.439	.345
Runners On	2642	745	140	16	62	683	285	378	.282	.417	.348
Runners/Scor. Pos.	1475	413	73	9	39	611	196	226	.280	.421	.355
Runners On/2 Out	1091	286	66	4	22	276	134	157	.262	.390	.344
Scor. Pos./2 Out	685	178	36	3	16	253	103	104	.260	.391	.357
Late Inning Pressure	824	227	37	1	26	106	88	132	.275	.417	.345
Leading Off	200	60	14	0	7	7	22	30	.300	.475	.375
Bases Empty	458	127	23	0	15	15	36	72	.277	.426	.333
Runners On	366	100	14	1	11	91	52	60	.273	.407	.358
Runners/Scor. Pos.	200	54	7	1	6	78	37	32	.270	.405	.374

DRIVING IN RUNS	0 Out	1 Out	2 Out	Total	
From 1B	21/478	25/731	39/779	85/1988	4%
From 2B	43/230	82/447	124/524	249/1201	21%
From 3B	59/102	137/250	90/300	286/652	44%
Scoring Position	102/332	219/697	214/824	535/1853	29%
Scor. Pos. %	31%	31%	26%	29%	
Driving In Runners from 3B with Less than Two Out:			196/352	56%	

Love to face: Jim Clancy (12–5 against him)
Hate to face: Bob McClure (2–7 against him)
Won their 16th A.L. batting title, tying Detroit for the all-time league record. Boston has led the league seven times since Detroit last led in 1961. . . . Again had fewest steals (66) in A.L. (5th time in seven years), but don't sneeze at that total: Sox stole just 38 and 30 in the two previous seasons, under Ralph Houk. . . . Committed most errors (145) in A.L. for 1st time since 1954; no, Don Buddin was not the shortstop on that team, it was Milt Bolling (stop nodding, Jonathan Schwartz). . . . Starting lineup of Gedman; Buckner, Barrett, Boggs, Hoffman; Rice, Lyons, Evans, and Easler was used 39 times, highest total in A.L. It was also the losingest lineup combination in league, with a record of 11–21. . . . Slugging average with runners on base was highest in majors since 1982, when Milwaukee compiled .476 mark.

Chicago White Sox

	AB	H	2B	3B	HR	RRF	BB	SO	BA	SA	OBA
Season	5470	1386	247	37	146	721	471	843	.253	.392	.315
vs. Left-Handers	1764	472	81	13	39	232	154	284	.268	.395	.327
vs. Right-Handers	3706	914	166	24	107	489	317	559	.247	.391	.309
Home	2641	656	124	23	74	350	249	421	.248	.397	.314
Road	2829	730	123	14	72	371	222	422	.258	.388	.316
Grass	4649	1181	221	34	122	630	431	737	.254	.395	.319
Artificial Turf	821	205	26	3	24	91	40	106	.250	.376	.291
April	608	161	25	3	14	82	55	96	.265	.385	.327
May	806	179	25	3	25	92	64	120	.222	.354	.281
June	922	213	40	4	23	98	95	161	.231	.358	.308
July	876	217	50	8	16	131	95	137	.248	.378	.325
August	1058	285	46	7	28	137	86	161	.269	.405	.326
Sept./Oct.	1200	331	61	12	40	181	76	168	.276	.447	.321
Leading Off Inn.	1334	319	64	10	28	28	108	217	.239	.365	.302
Bases Empty	3202	774	139	20	79	80	250	506	.242	.372	.302
Runners On	2268	612	108	17	67	641	221	337	.270	.421	.332
Runners/Scor. Pos.	1265	372	68	12	37	556	157	211	.294	.455	.365
Runners On/2 Out	968	252	36	6	36	281	110	151	.260	.421	.338
Scor. Pos./2 Out	595	168	25	5	18	237	92	102	.282	.432	.381
Late Inning Pressure	751	199	34	4	19	92	67	125	.265	.397	.328
Leading Off	186	58	9	2	3	3	15	36	.312	.430	.373
Bases Empty	427	107	22	3	9	9	34	74	.251	.379	.312
Runners On	324	92	12	1	10	83	33	51	.284	.420	.348
Runners/Scor. Pos.	191	55	7	1	3	67	25	35	.288	.382	.367

DRIVING IN RUNS	0 Out	1 Out	2 Out	Total	
From 1B	12/365	39/593	48/630	99/1588	6%
From 2B	40/177	72/363	112/419	224/959	23%
From 3B	50/81	116/207	85/271	251/559	45%
Scoring Position	90/258	188/570	197/690	475/1518	31%
Scor. Pos. %	35%	33%	29%	31%	
Driving In Runners from 3B with Less than Two Out:			166/288	58%	

Love to face: Bob Stanley (9–4 against him; so why try to trade for him?)
Hate to face: Dave Stieb (3–12 against him)
Committed fewest errors in A.L. (111) for first time since 1962, the team's last Aparicio-Fox season. . . . Scored in only 18.6 percent of innings in which 3d-position batters led off, 3d-lowest rate by any batting order position in A.L., and especially low for the 3d position (league average: 27.4). . . . Left only 1,009 runners on base, lowest total in A.L. since 1966, when the Kansas City Athletics stranded 995 runners. . . . Had major leagues' highest batting average in Late-Inning Pressure Situations with runners on base. . . . Gambling base runners: with Chicago trailing last season, Chicago runners went from first to third on 16 of 29 two-out singles (55.2%), the highest A.L. average in *Player Analysis* history, excluding Texas's mark (55.6%) in the strike-shortened 1981 season.

Cleveland Indians

	AB	H	2B	3B	HR	RRF	BB	SO	BA	SA	OBA
Season	5527	1465	254	31	116	714	492	817	.265	.385	.324
vs. Left-Handers	1696	441	79	7	42	206	152	267	.260	.389	.320
vs. Right-Handers	3831	1024	175	24	74	508	340	550	.267	.383	.326
Home	2711	756	127	17	52	371	231	379	.279	.396	.334
Road	2816	709	127	14	64	343	261	438	.252	.375	.315
Grass	4698	1256	219	27	99	622	419	697	.267	.389	.326
Artificial Turf	829	209	35	4	17	92	73	120	.252	.366	.312
April	667	175	32	4	7	86	65	101	.262	.354	.323
May	865	212	37	6	9	87	67	134	.245	.333	.297
June	888	220	45	3	19	108	78	127	.248	.369	.308
July	948	242	34	5	17	96	82	139	.255	.355	.316
August	976	274	40	5	26	143	90	142	.281	.412	.340
Sept./Oct.	1183	342	66	8	38	194	110	174	.289	.455	.350
Leading Off Inn.	1339	356	64	7	23	23	100	195	.266	.376	.319
Bases Empty	3140	801	139	18	55	55	258	480	.255	.363	.313
Runners On	2387	664	115	13	61	659	234	337	.278	.414	.338
Runners/Scor. Pos.	1379	373	71	8	29	570	178	205	.270	.397	.345
Runners On/2 Out	964	233	44	5	27	236	115	148	.242	.382	.324
Scor. Pos./2 Out	620	145	29	3	15	202	89	94	.234	.363	.330
Late Inning Pressure	809	196	26	4	15	83	62	113	.242	.340	.296
Leading Off	197	47	10	0	4	4	17	33	.239	.350	.306
Bases Empty	467	106	16	2	8	8	35	71	.227	.321	.284
Runners On	342	90	10	2	7	75	27	42	.263	.365	.314
Runners/Scor. Pos.	203	47	5	2	2	60	20	22	.232	.305	.295

DRIVING IN RUNS	0 Out	1 Out	2 Out	Total	
From 1B	19/455	32/604	37/639	88/1698	5%
From 2B	48/235	73/387	86/441	207/1063	19%
From 3B	77/110	139/228	85/286	301/624	48%
Scoring Position	125/345	212/615	171/727	508/1687	30%
Scor. Pos. %	36%	34%	24%	30%	
Driving In Runners from 3B with Less than Two Out:			216/338	64%	

Love to face: Jim Beattie (8–3 against him)
Hate to face: Moose Haas (4–11 against him)
Tied for 9th in the A.L. in runs scored, but had the fewest one-run innings of any team in the league (185).... Ranked 2d in A.L. in batting during month of September (.289), led league during month of October (.311).... Scored 196 runs in the 297 innings led off by the first-place hitter in batting order (0.66 runs per inning). Only one team in majors had a higher average: the Rickey Henderson-led New York Yankees (0.72). Cleveland's first-place hitters had a composite batting average of .302, second only to the Yankees' .315.... Batting average with runners in scoring position exceeded overall mark by only five points, following 20-point edges in the two previous seasons.

Detroit Tigers

	AB	H	2B	3B	HR	RRF	BB	SO	BA	SA	OBA
Season	5575	1413	254	45	202	723	526	926	.253	.424	.318
vs. Left-Handers	1630	424	74	20	63	210	159	296	.260	.446	.326
vs. Right-Handers	3945	989	180	25	139	513	367	630	.251	.415	.315
Home	2742	711	121	20	108	382	274	427	.259	.436	.325
Road	2833	702	133	25	94	341	252	499	.248	.412	.311
Grass	4690	1202	205	36	177	623	468	751	.256	.429	.324
Artificial Turf	885	211	49	9	25	100	58	175	.238	.399	.287
April	635	165	29	11	13	74	52	74	.260	.402	.315
May	911	242	49	5	33	111	74	159	.266	.439	.324
June	941	244	43	6	40	131	106	152	.259	.445	.332
July	963	231	42	6	27	113	88	162	.240	.380	.304
August	1013	246	46	9	43	128	93	166	.243	.433	.308
Sept./Oct.	1112	285	45	8	46	166	113	213	.256	.435	.324
Leading Off Inn.	1343	345	54	17	59	59	107	174	.257	.454	.315
Bases Empty	3265	809	146	31	126	127	281	506	.248	.427	.310
Runners On	2310	604	108	14	76	596	245	420	.261	.419	.329
Runners/Scor. Pos.	1290	310	52	8	35	485	171	260	.240	.374	.322
Runners On/2 Out	1025	255	47	7	34	257	126	185	.249	.408	.333
Scor. Pos./2 Out	632	149	24	4	20	213	92	122	.236	.381	.336
Late Inning Pressure	801	184	24	2	28	96	88	156	.230	.370	.305
Leading Off	202	51	4	2	13	13	17	34	.252	.485	.311
Bases Empty	480	107	18	2	18	18	41	92	.223	.381	.284
Runners On	321	77	6	0	10	78	47	64	.240	.352	.333
Runners/Scor. Pos.	186	45	3	0	3	64	35	45	.242	.306	.352

DRIVING IN RUNS	0 Out	1 Out	2 Out	Total	
From 1B	22/379	35/591	47/718	104/1688	6%
From 2B	22/173	59/383	109/479	190/1035	18%
From 3B	43/82	116/199	67/259	226/540	42%
Scoring Position	65/255	175/582	176/738	416/1575	26%
Scor. Pos. %	25%	30%	24%	26%	
Driving In Runners from 3B with Less than Two Out:			159/281	57%	

Love to face: Rick Waits (14–2 against him)
Hate to face: Bret Saberhagen (2–7 against him)
Had lowest fielding percentage in A.L. (.977) for first time since 1947, when Eddie Lake made 43 errors at shortstop.... Batting average in Late-Inning Pressure Situations represents Detroit's lowest mark in the 11-year history of *The Player Analysis*.... Team of fly-ball hitters: G/A ratio of 0.90 was lowest in majors last season.... Grounded into only 81 double plays, lowest total in A.L. since 1967, when the Kansas City Athletics had 79 GIDPs.... Batting average with runners in scoring position was 3d-lowest in A.L. over last six full seasons.... Tigers are 3d consecutive A.L. team to have league's lowest batting average in both Late-Inning Pressure Situations and with runners in scoring position. Seattle did it in 1983, California in 1984.

Kansas City Royals

	AB	H	2B	3B	HR	RRF	BB	SO	BA	SA	OBA
Season	5500	1384	261	49	154	678	473	840	.252	.401	.313
vs. Left-Handers	1579	394	82	7	54	196	134	220	.250	.413	.308
vs. Right-Handers	3921	990	179	42	100	482	339	620	.252	.396	.315
Home	2757	714	144	35	67	353	239	395	.259	.410	.320
Road	2743	670	117	14	87	325	234	445	.244	.392	.306
Grass	2122	530	93	13	68	258	169	342	.250	.402	.308
Artificial Turf	3378	854	168	36	86	420	304	498	.253	.400	.316
April	664	156	29	8	17	64	55	104	.235	.380	.297
May	905	223	46	7	26	120	75	119	.246	.399	.303
June	889	217	32	11	20	99	88	141	.244	.372	.314
July	937	263	44	5	31	140	75	139	.281	.438	.339
August	925	245	51	12	23	119	85	146	.265	.421	.329
Sept./Oct.	1180	280	59	6	37	136	95	191	.237	.392	.296
Leading Off Inn.	1371	355	75	16	37	37	80	198	.259	.418	.302
Bases Empty	3272	789	153	31	93	93	238	488	.241	.392	.296
Runners On	2228	595	108	18	61	585	235	352	.267	.414	.336
Runners/Scor. Pos.	1337	341	58	14	34	498	176	221	.255	.396	.339
Runners On/2 Out	923	224	34	7	22	218	114	166	.243	.366	.330
Scor. Pos./2 Out	607	144	18	6	12	187	90	112	.237	.346	.340
Late Inning Pressure	756	198	34	6	17	85	77	126	.262	.390	.331
Leading Off	190	52	10	0	6	6	17	35	.274	.421	.337
Bases Empty	423	112	20	4	13	13	34	66	.265	.423	.322
Runners On	333	86	14	2	4	72	43	60	.258	.348	.341
Runners/Scor. Pos.	199	50	7	2	3	65	37	32	.251	.352	.364

DRIVING IN RUNS	0 Out	1 Out	2 Out	Total	
From 1B	24/374	35/563	39/623	98/1560	6%
From 2B	27/208	76/387	89/444	192/1039	18%
From 3B	47/84	116/204	68/261	231/549	42%
Scoring Position	74/292	192/591	157/705	423/1588	27%
Scor. Pos. %	25%	32%	22%	27%	
Driving In Runners from 3B with Less than Two Out:			163/288	57%	

Love to face: Frank Tanana (20–6 against him)
Hate to face: Ron Guidry (4–14 against him)
Ranked 2d in A.L. last season with 114 RBIs by designated hitters, by far the most for any A.L. team that has been forced to play the Series without a DH.... Lost only seven home games to left-handed pitchers last season.... Year-by-year batting averages with runners in scoring position, starting with 1982: .296, .285, .260, .255.... Had losing record (18–25) and A.L.'s lowest batting average in day games (.239, 10 points lower than 13th-place Baltimore).... Had league's lowest batting average after September 1.... Dick Howser is the 5th manager since 1900 to lead his team into post-season competition four times in his first six seasons. The others: Frank Chance, Sparky Anderson, Earl Weaver, and Dick Williams.

Milwaukee Brewers

	AB	H	2B	3B	HR	RRF	BB	SO	BA	SA	OBA
Season	5568	1467	250	44	101	682	462	746	.263	.379	.319
vs. Left-Handers	1862	516	86	16	40	246	156	248	.277	.405	.333
vs. Right-Handers	3706	951	164	28	61	436	306	498	.257	.365	.312
Home	2708	737	137	26	50	364	216	361	.272	.397	.325
Road	2860	730	113	18	51	318	246	385	.255	.361	.314
Grass	4642	1234	214	36	86	580	377	631	.266	.383	.320
Artificial Turf	926	233	36	8	15	102	85	115	.252	.356	.315
April	642	154	25	3	8	72	62	111	.240	.326	.307
May	813	239	39	13	13	114	57	105	.294	.422	.337
June	938	248	49	7	17	119	82	125	.264	.386	.322
July	954	249	44	6	19	108	83	99	.261	.379	.320
August	958	262	38	6	22	135	75	131	.273	.395	.323
Sept./Oct.	1263	315	55	9	22	134	103	175	.249	.359	.309
Leading Off Inn.	1344	334	65	9	17	17	101	177	.249	.348	.303
Bases Empty	3165	796	153	22	54	54	233	447	.252	.365	.305
Runners On	2403	671	97	22	47	628	229	299	.279	.397	.337
Runners/Scor. Pos.	1360	358	58	12	22	545	167	183	.263	.372	.334
Runners On/2 Out	1016	261	34	11	16	228	114	142	.257	.359	.335
Scor. Pos./2 Out	642	155	22	5	9	199	85	88	.241	.333	.333
Late Inning Pressure	829	210	36	1	13	90	69	123	.253	.346	.312
Leading Off	211	47	7	0	3	3	17	35	.223	.299	.281
Bases Empty	486	114	21	0	8	8	36	77	.235	.327	.290
Runners On	343	96	15	1	5	82	33	46	.280	.373	.341
Runners/Scor. Pos.	195	50	11	1	3	76	21	25	.256	.369	.323

DRIVING IN RUNS	0 Out	1 Out	2 Out	Total	
From 1B	20/425	37/639	38/707	95/1771	5%
From 2B	32/199	81/393	102/470	215/1062	20%
From 3B	57/87	139/224	72/269	268/580	46%
Scoring Position	89/286	220/617	174/739	483/1642	29%
Scor. Pos. %	31%	36%	24%	29%	
Driving In Runners from 3B with Less than Two Out:			196/311	63%	

Love to face: Floyd Bannister (8–3 against him)
Hate to face: Ron Romanick (1–6 against him)
Did not win a road game in which they trailed after seven innings.... Led A.L. in batting during the month of May.... Used 114 different starting lineup combinations last season, highest total in A.L.... Had A.L.'s fewest home runs for 2d consecutive season. No A.L. team has trailed for three years running since the Los Angeles/California Angels of 1963–65.... Have had fewest strikeouts in A.L. for three consecutive seasons.... Have batted .270 or better with runners on base in each of the past eight seasons.... Milwaukee runners went from first to third on only 31 of 121 singles, 25.6%, *while the Brewers were winning*, the lowest average in the league. A.L. average: 35.4%.

Minnesota Twins

	AB	H	2B	3B	HR	RRF	BB	SO	BA	SA	OBA
Season	5509	1453	282	41	141	696	502	779	.264	.407	.326
vs. Left-Handers	1723	457	93	18	41	194	162	247	.265	.411	.327
vs. Right-Handers	3786	996	189	23	100	502	340	532	.263	.404	.326
Home	2833	795	166	22	71	403	260	378	.281	.430	.342
Road	2676	658	116	19	70	293	242	401	.246	.382	.310
Grass	2014	491	81	14	53	215	185	302	.244	.377	.309
Artificial Turf	3495	962	201	27	88	481	317	477	.275	.424	.336
April	697	198	40	5	22	106	72	81	.284	.451	.351
May	925	264	43	10	24	131	92	128	.285	.431	.351
June	840	205	43	3	19	81	74	116	.244	.370	.307
July	946	234	44	9	25	123	90	147	.247	.392	.313
August	920	228	40	8	18	100	87	140	.248	.367	.316
Sept./Oct.	1181	324	72	6	33	155	87	167	.274	.429	.323
Leading Off Inn.	1327	332	69	9	37	37	98	146	.250	.399	.305
Bases Empty	3085	801	161	24	83	84	264	405	.260	.408	.322
Runners On	2424	652	121	17	58	612	238	374	.269	.405	.331
Runners/Scor. Pos.	1392	369	81	14	30	532	160	237	.265	.408	.335
Runners On/2 Out	1015	250	36	7	24	219	98	173	.246	.367	.315
Scor. Pos./2 Out	644	149	26	7	13	191	72	115	.231	.354	.313
Late Inning Pressure	703	184	21	4	14	89	79	111	.262	.363	.337
Leading Off	168	38	5	0	3	3	17	20	.226	.310	.301
Bases Empty	390	98	12	1	8	8	37	57	.251	.349	.319
Runners On	313	86	9	3	6	81	42	54	.275	.380	.358
Runners/Scor. Pos.	175	48	4	2	4	75	30	35	.274	.389	.376

DRIVING IN RUNS	0 Out	1 Out	2 Out	Total	
From 1B	21/400	34/640	41/690	96/1730	6%
From 2B	36/204	82/403	88/465	206/1072	19%
From 3B	60/90	125/230	66/263	251/583	43%
Scoring Position	96/294	207/633	154/728	457/1655	28%
Scor. Pos. %	33%	33%	21%	28%	
Driving In Runners from 3B with Less than Two Out:			185/320	58%	

Love to face: Dave Stieb (9–5 against him)
Hate to face: Ron Guidry (4–16 against him)
Tied Oakland for major-league lead with 14 wins in games in which they trailed after six innings. . . . Won 33 of 36 home games in which they scored the first run, including 19 in a row from the start of the season. All three losses came within three-week period (August 10–30). . . . Tied for A.L. lead with 166 home-game doubles; tied for next-to-last with 116 road-game doubles. See Twins' team essay for more details. . . . Led league in batting average during April, ranked 2d during May, then ranked among bottom three teams in June, July, and August. . . . No sissies here: hitters in 3-4-5 spots in batting order had only one sacrifice bunt last season. (Baltimore's 3-4-5 hitters had none.). . . . Team of fly-ball hitters: G/A ratio of 1.02 was 2d-lowest in majors last season.

New York Yankees

	AB	H	2B	3B	HR	RRF	BB	SO	BA	SA	OBA
Season	5458	1458	272	31	176	821	620	771	.267	.425	.344
vs. Left-Handers	2005	534	103	10	62	286	250	277	.266	.420	.350
vs. Right-Handers	3453	924	169	21	114	535	370	494	.268	.428	.341
Home	2595	692	125	12	92	405	303	375	.267	.430	.345
Road	2863	766	147	19	84	416	317	396	.268	.420	.343
Grass	4632	1248	231	23	150	703	531	666	.269	.426	.346
Artificial Turf	826	210	41	8	26	118	89	105	.254	.418	.332
April	615	161	32	5	7	64	63	74	.262	.364	.331
May	872	237	46	6	30	161	119	122	.272	.442	.364
June	925	247	37	5	22	118	97	124	.267	.389	.335
July	959	275	51	8	38	154	92	117	.287	.475	.351
August	966	258	50	3	37	153	121	149	.267	.440	.354
Sept./Oct.	1121	280	56	4	42	171	128	185	.250	.419	.328
Leading Off Inn.	1281	359	70	13	44	44	142	168	.280	.458	.356
Bases Empty	3001	787	153	23	94	94	324	426	.262	.423	.339
Runners On	2457	671	119	8	82	727	296	345	.273	.428	.350
Runners/Scor. Pos.	1424	384	68	4	43	622	222	221	.270	.414	.362
Runners On/2 Out	998	260	50	5	34	269	131	163	.261	.423	.356
Scor. Pos./2 Out	649	168	34	4	22	235	111	120	.259	.425	.377
Late Inning Pressure	768	196	20	2	28	104	80	113	.255	.396	.325
Leading Off	195	43	3	1	6	6	17	38	.221	.338	.286
Bases Empty	470	116	11	2	16	16	40	78	.247	.381	.307
Runners On	298	80	9	0	12	88	40	35	.268	.419	.351
Runners/Scor. Pos.	150	41	4	0	6	74	29	18	.273	.420	.382

DRIVING IN RUNS	0 Out	1 Out	2 Out	Total	
From 1B	27/441	37/647	44/658	108/1746	6%
From 2B	47/235	78/401	106/469	231/1105	21%
From 3B	77/119	144/235	84/304	305/658	46%
Scoring Position	124/354	222/636	190/773	536/1763	30%
Scor. Pos. %	35%	35%	25%	30%	
Driving In Runners from 3B with Less than Two Out:			221/354	62%	

Love to face: Scott McGregor (11–6 against him, six wins in a row)
Hate to face: Mike Flanagan (7–12 against him, six losses in a row)
Scored 839 runs to lead the A.L. for 24th time, but for the 1st time since 1962. . . . Led A.L. in stolen bases for 1st time since 1938, which was also the last time any team led the A.L. in runs and steals in the same season. . . . Thanks, Rickey: Led majors with 132 first-inning runs; finished 9th in majors with 96 a year earlier. . . . Led the majors with 216 multi-run innings. . . . Faced more left-handed starting pitchers than any other team in majors (65), but had a better record in those games (40–25) than vs. right-handed starters (57–39). . . . Won 39 of 42 home games in which they scored in the first inning. . . . Hit eight more home runs at Yankee Stadium than in road games, but scored 17 more runs on the road than at home.

Oakland A's

	AB	H	2B	3B	HR	RRF	BB	SO	BA	SA	OBA
Season	5581	1475	230	34	155	740	508	861	.264	.401	.325
vs. Left-Handers	1729	464	70	12	54	252	157	275	.268	.416	.327
vs. Right-Handers	3852	1011	160	22	101	488	351	586	.262	.394	.324
Home	2655	680	110	15	66	340	251	412	.256	.383	.321
Road	2926	795	120	19	89	400	257	449	.272	.417	.329
Grass	4607	1219	184	26	132	614	430	718	.265	.402	.327
Artificial Turf	974	256	46	8	23	126	78	143	.263	.397	.316
April	699	185	24	4	26	114	76	77	.265	.422	.336
May	853	225	30	5	26	113	79	131	.264	.402	.326
June	983	274	37	6	33	136	93	127	.279	.429	.342
July	913	241	39	6	26	109	76	122	.264	.405	.319
August	998	250	45	4	14	124	97	179	.251	.346	.315
Sept./Oct.	1135	300	55	9	30	144	87	225	.264	.408	.316
Leading Off Inn.	1357	351	66	6	39	39	107	201	.259	.402	.315
Bases Empty	3244	827	133	15	88	88	272	500	.255	.387	.314
Runners On	2337	648	97	19	67	652	236	361	.277	.421	.339
Runners/Scor. Pos.	1302	360	55	13	34	564	163	199	.276	.417	.348
Runners On/2 Out	978	243	36	9	32	245	113	158	.248	.402	.328
Scor. Pos./2 Out	597	150	21	7	17	205	81	99	.251	.395	.343
Late Inning Pressure	838	210	23	2	25	96	84	134	.251	.372	.319
Leading Off	209	60	9	1	10	10	24	29	.287	.483	.363
Bases Empty	496	126	13	1	16	16	42	73	.254	.381	.314
Runners On	342	84	10	1	9	80	42	61	.246	.360	.327
Runners/Scor. Pos.	183	39	6	1	4	69	35	32	.213	.322	.333

DRIVING IN RUNS	0 Out	1 Out	2 Out	Total	
From 1B	20/428	33/613	44/670	97/1711	6%
From 2B	47/206	76/344	96/436	219/986	22%
From 3B	73/104	122/217	73/252	268/573	47%
Scoring Position	120/310	198/561	169/688	487/1559	31%
Scor. Pos. %	39%	35%	25%	31%	
Driving In Runners from 3B with Less than Two Out:			195/321	61%	

Love to face: Dave Rozema (9–1 against him)
Hate to face: Scott McGregor (3–10 against him)
Only major-league team that, over the past three years, has scored a run every time its leadoff batter reached third base (22 of 22); no other team has done it for even two years. . . . Turned the fewest double plays in the A.L. (137) for the 6th time in the past 11 years. . . . Batting average with runners in scoring position represents Oakland's highest mark in the 11-year history of *The Player Analysis*. . . . Only A.L. team to hit for a higher batting average with runners on base than with the bases empty in each of those 11 seasons. . . . Ranked 7th in A.L. with 155 home runs, but hit only nine in the first inning, lowest total in the league. . . . Update from last year's *Analyst*: A's have made 70 errors and only 52 double plays on artificial turf over the past three seasons.

Seattle Mariners

	AB	H	2B	3B	HR	RRF	BB	SO	BA	SA	OBA
Season	5521	1410	277	38	171	709	564	942	.255	.412	.326
vs. Left-Handers	1562	395	83	9	52	222	179	259	.253	.417	.331
vs. Right-Handers	3959	1015	194	29	119	487	385	683	.256	.410	.324
Home	2781	718	138	19	92	358	304	447	.258	.421	.333
Road	2740	692	139	19	79	351	260	495	.253	.404	.318
Grass	2096	533	103	17	65	281	200	380	.254	.413	.320
Artificial Turf	3425	877	174	21	106	428	364	562	.256	.412	.329
April	696	165	27	4	27	86	73	82	.237	.404	.311
May	830	200	45	6	27	95	77	153	.241	.407	.308
June	930	249	46	6	28	131	105	152	.268	.420	.344
July	980	266	42	8	32	126	89	167	.271	.429	.332
August	947	235	51	5	23	111	91	172	.248	.385	.315
Sept./Oct.	1138	295	66	9	34	160	129	216	.259	.423	.336
Leading Off Inn.	1328	352	75	12	38	39	113	200	.265	.425	.326
Bases Empty	3097	789	170	23	95	96	293	521	.255	.417	.322
Runners On	2424	621	107	15	76	613	271	421	.256	.407	.330
Runners/Scor. Pos.	1392	364	65	9	42	524	185	255	.261	.412	.344
Runners On/2 Out	994	245	43	7	35	258	132	172	.246	.409	.338
Scor. Pos./2 Out	644	159	27	6	23	226	89	116	.247	.415	.343
Late Inning Pressure	771	183	30	3	24	84	90	151	.237	.377	.315
Leading Off	197	48	10	0	9	9	13	38	.244	.431	.290
Bases Empty	449	112	22	2	16	16	41	78	.249	.414	.312
Runners On	322	71	8	1	8	68	49	73	.220	.326	.319
Runners/Scor. Pos.	172	42	5	1	6	63	35	31	.244	.390	.363

DRIVING IN RUNS	0 Out	1 Out	2 Out	Total	
From 1B	21/425	40/633	39/679	100/1737	6%
From 2B	34/218	56/404	99/492	189/1114	17%
From 3B	52/94	109/219	84/269	245/582	42%
Scoring Position	86/312	165/623	183/761	434/1696	26%
Scor. Pos. %	28%	26%	24%	26%	
Driving In Runners from 3B with Less than Two Out:			161/313	51%	

Love to face: Bud Black (5–1 against him)
Hate to face: Doyle Alexander (5–11, 0–6 with the Blue Jays)
Lost 61 games in which they never held a lead, highest total in the A.L. . . . Designated hitters batted .211, lowest DH mark in 13-year history of rule, except for Twins' .208 average in strike-shortened 1981 season. . . . Runners on first base advanced to third base on only nine of 39 singles while the Mariners were losing (23.1%), the third time in the past five seasons that Seattle has had the A.L.'s lowest average. . . . Had 193 multi-run innings last season, compared to 195 one-run innings, the 2d-highest ratio in A.L. Baltimore split its 410 scoring innings right down the middle: 205 one-run and 205 multi-run innings. . . . Have batted for a higher batting average with runners on base than with the bases empty in each of their nine seasons.

Texas Rangers

	AB	H	2B	3B	HR	RRF	BB	SO	BA	SA	OBA
Season	5361	1359	213	41	129	606	530	819	.253	.381	.322
vs. Left-Handers	1554	411	74	15	33	181	159	246	.264	.395	.334
vs. Right-Handers	3807	948	139	26	96	425	371	573	.249	.375	.317
Home	2603	696	97	20	76	350	270	398	.267	.408	.338
Road	2758	663	116	21	53	256	260	421	.240	.355	.307
Grass	4516	1156	168	31	115	529	446	696	.256	.383	.324
Artificial Turf	845	203	45	10	14	77	84	123	.240	.367	.309
April	637	162	20	4	15	80	60	79	.254	.369	.320
May	894	217	38	6	16	86	111	119	.243	.352	.329
June	938	244	44	7	22	112	105	124	.260	.392	.336
July	895	218	28	7	18	98	84	158	.244	.351	.309
August	912	243	39	9	22	96	81	143	.266	.401	.327
Sept./Oct.	1085	275	44	8	36	134	89	174	.253	.408	.312
Leading Off Inn.	1306	340	55	13	34	34	122	202	.260	.400	.325
Bases Empty	3079	779	122	25	84	84	288	481	.253	.391	.321
Runners On	2282	580	91	16	45	522	242	338	.254	.367	.323
Runners/Scor. Pos.	1267	317	54	10	24	451	166	215	.250	.365	.330
Runners On/2 Out	949	219	35	9	14	199	115	145	.231	.331	.316
Scor. Pos./2 Out	606	137	22	7	7	173	89	98	.226	.320	.327
Late Inning Pressure	812	212	26	5	24	96	85	120	.261	.394	.333
Leading Off	206	55	5	2	6	6	22	30	.267	.398	.338
Bases Empty	476	121	15	2	10	10	46	75	.254	.357	.324
Runners On	336	91	11	3	14	86	39	45	.271	.446	.345
Runners/Scor. Pos.	171	43	6	2	6	66	27	23	.251	.415	.346

DRIVING IN RUNS	0 Out	1 Out	2 Out	Total	
From 1B	11/416	33/609	35/654	79/1679	5%
From 2B	27/176	67/359	83/434	177/969	18%
From 3B	51/82	102/191	67/269	220/542	41%
Scoring Position	78/258	169/550	150/703	397/1511	26%
Scor. Pos. %	30%	31%	21%	26%	
Driving In Runners from 3B with Less than Two Out:	153/273	56%			

Love to face: Floyd Bannister (9–5 against him)
Hate to face: Storm Davis (0–7 against him)
Batting average with two outs and runners on base was lowest in A.L. since Yankees hit .222 in 1982. . . . Could this be the first team in the history of baseball to play an entire season without winning a day game at home? Of course, they did only play six. . . . Opening-day lineup combination (Slaught; O'Brien, Harrah, Bell, Wilkerson; Ward, G. Wright, Jones, and Johnson) lost and was never used again. . . . Hit only 11 home runs with more than one runner on base, lowest total in either league. . . . Ranked last in A.L. with 26 come-from-behind wins. . . . Maybe they should trade for Tabler: the Rangers ranked a solid last in batting with the bases loaded last season. How solid? Their .178 average was 107 points below the league average, and 78 points behind 13th-place Boston.

Toronto Blue Jays

	AB	H	2B	3B	HR	RRF	BB	SO	BA	SA	OBA
Season	5508	1482	281	53	158	747	503	807	.269	.425	.331
vs. Left-Handers	1992	524	105	16	56	243	184	324	.263	.416	.326
vs. Right-Handers	3516	958	176	37	102	504	319	483	.272	.431	.334
Home	2635	724	162	33	75	391	272	391	.275	.447	.343
Road	2873	758	119	20	83	356	231	416	.264	.406	.320
Grass	2208	579	90	12	70	283	188	320	.262	.409	.322
Artificial Turf	3300	903	191	41	88	464	315	487	.274	.438	.337
April	676	166	33	5	22	85	58	116	.246	.407	.308
May	865	244	48	9	23	137	88	126	.282	.438	.347
June	977	251	47	11	23	125	97	125	.257	.398	.325
July	955	258	54	7	29	135	89	127	.270	.432	.335
August	925	262	49	13	26	131	79	141	.283	.449	.342
Sept./Oct.	1110	301	50	8	35	134	92	172	.271	.425	.325
Leading Off Inn.	1311	336	66	11	37	38	111	166	.256	.408	.319
Bases Empty	3118	826	154	28	94	95	274	462	.265	.423	.328
Runners On	2390	656	127	25	64	652	229	345	.274	.429	.335
Runners/Scor. Pos.	1346	382	73	18	38	565	171	205	.284	.449	.357
Runners On/2 Out	1002	260	54	12	22	260	106	159	.259	.403	.335
Scor. Pos./2 Out	646	175	35	10	15	230	89	110	.271	.426	.364
Late Inning Pressure	731	197	31	12	19	95	60	108	.269	.423	.326
Leading Off	189	49	7	1	8	8	14	28	.259	.434	.317
Bases Empty	429	112	18	6	14	14	30	66	.261	.429	.314
Runners On	302	85	13	6	5	81	30	42	.281	.414	.342
Runners/Scor. Pos.	167	49	6	2	3	68	27	24	.293	.407	.383

DRIVING IN RUNS	0 Out	1 Out	2 Out	Total	
From 1B	23/421	33/610	46/640	102/1671	6%
From 2B	34/181	89/381	107/445	230/1007	23%
From 3B	50/84	121/220	83/295	254/599	42%
Scoring Position	84/265	210/601	190/740	484/1606	30%
Scor. Pos. %	32%	35%	26%	30%	
Driving In Runners from 3B with Less than Two Out:	171/304	56%			

Love to face: Frank Viola (8–0 against him)
Hate to face: Bob Stanley (6–11 against him)
Set A.L. *Player Analysis* record with a .320 batting average in Late-Inning Pressure Situations with runners on base in 1984. Ranked 2d last season. . . . Led A.L. in triples for 3d consecutive season. Kansas City had a six-season streak snapped in 1981. League record: seven straight years, by the Washington Senators (1931–37), and they didn't even play on artificial turf! . . . Used 40 different starting lineup combinations last season, fewest in A.L. . . . No Toronto batter was hit by a pitch in 34 games after August 28. . . . 61–19 record in games in which they scored the first run was the best in A.L. last season. Won 59 games in which their opponents never led, tying Kansas City for league lead.

American League

	AB	H	2B	3B	HR	RRF	BB	SO	BA	SA	OBA
Season	77257	20182	3562	528	2178	10153	7465	11777	.261	.406	.327
vs. Left-Handers	24285	6451	1186	173	706	3217	2442	3755	.266	.416	.333
vs. Right-Handers	52972	13731	2376	355	1472	6936	5023	8022	.259	.401	.324
Home	37695	10041	1820	283	1074	5251	3796	5664	.266	.415	.334
Road	39562	10141	1742	245	1104	4902	3669	6113	.256	.396	.320
Grass	54812	14362	2438	337	1591	7316	5382	8443	.262	.406	.329
Artificial Turf	22445	5820	1124	191	587	2837	2083	3334	.259	.405	.324
April	9310	2374	396	66	246	1211	972	1338	.255	.391	.326
May	12116	3131	557	86	329	1568	1200	1821	.258	.400	.326
June	12912	3352	588	79	339	1631	1306	1911	.260	.396	.328
July	13143	3462	596	86	370	1717	1213	1936	.263	.406	.327
August	13534	3563	633	97	380	1803	1290	2137	.263	.409	.328
Sept./Oct.	16242	4300	792	114	514	2223	1484	2634	.265	.422	.328
Leading Off Inn.	18619	4856	902	146	519	522	1544	2638	.261	.409	.321
Bases Empty	43996	11170	2024	300	1231	1239	3920	6703	.254	.397	.318
Runners On	33261	9012	1538	228	947	8914	3545	5074	.271	.416	.338
Runners/Scor. Pos.	18881	5067	881	148	509	7645	2507	3094	.268	.412	.347
Runners On/2 Out	13927	3501	588	99	390	3474	1707	2271	.251	.392	.336
Scor. Pos./2 Out	8805	2188	361	73	232	3001	1295	1509	.248	.385	.348
Late Inning Pressure	10794	2726	394	51	296	1308	1114	1761	.253	.381	.323
Leading Off	2695	687	110	12	87	87	253	454	.255	.401	.322
Bases Empty	6269	1540	245	28	174	175	546	1028	.246	.377	.308
Runners On	4525	1186	149	23	122	1133	568	733	.262	.386	.342
Runners/Scor. Pos.	2534	649	81	16	65	976	418	419	.256	.378	.355

DRIVING IN RUNS	0 Out	1 Out	2 Out	Total	
From 1B	293/5839	498/8728	593/9559	1384/24126	6%
From 2B	507/2830	1045/5434	1416/6480	2968/14744	20%
From 3B	808/1293	1718/3013	1067/3788	3593/8094	44%
Scoring Position	1315/4123	2763/8447	2483/10268	6561/22838	29%
Scor. Pos. %	32%	33%	24%	29%	
Driving In Runners from 3B with Less than Two Out:	2526/4306	59%			

Loves to face: National League West (6–3 in World Series against them)
Hates to face: National League (2–21 in last 23 All-Star Games)
Teams scored in 51.7 percent of innings when leadoff batter reached base; 16.4 percent of innings when leadoff batter was put out. . . . That 51.7 includes home runs, and also breaks down this way: 42.7 percent when leadoff batter reached first, 65.7 percent when he reached second, 92.6 percent when he reached third. . . . Teams scoring the first run won 66.6 percent of games played to a decision, and in roughly six of seven cases (86 percent), that team never trailed in the game. In lower-scoring National League, edges were slightly greater for teams drawing first blood: 67.8 percent to win game, 86.1 percent never to fall behind. . . . Statistical similarity between 1984 and 1985 standings was greatest in any pair of consecutive seasons since 1978–79. But did anyone notice the stronger similarity between last season's standings and those of 1937?

National League

Luis Aguayo

Philadelphia Phillies	AB	H	2B	3B	HR	RRF	BB	SO	BA	SA	OBA
Season	165	46	7	3	6	22	22	26	.279	.467	.378
vs. Left-Handed Pitchers	63	12	1	1	1	4	11	8	.190	.286	.329
vs. Right-Handed Pitchers	102	34	6	2	5	18	11	18	.333	.578	.408
Home	87	25	5	2	4	16	9	16	.287	.529	.388
Road	78	21	2	1	2	6	13	10	.269	.397	.366
Grass	42	10	1	0	2	5	7	6	.238	.405	.340
Artificial Turf	123	36	6	3	4	17	15	20	.293	.488	.390
April	6	0	0	0	0	1	0	1	.000	.000	.000
May	45	10	0	1	2	6	8	12	.222	.400	.351
June	18	5	2	1	0	2	3	0	.278	.500	.435
July	21	6	0	0	0	0	1	4	.286	.286	.318
August	32	11	2	1	0	5	8	7	.344	.469	.476
Sept./Oct.	43	14	3	0	4	8	2	2	.326	.674	.370
Leading Off Inn.	47	10	1	1	2	2	6	6	.213	.404	.315
Bases Empty	100	24	2	1	4	4	10	15	.240	.400	.333
Runners On	65	22	5	2	2	18	12	11	.338	.569	.439
Runners/Scor. Pos.	35	14	3	2	0	14	9	6	.400	.600	.510
Runners On/2 Out	29	7	1	1	0	3	7	8	.241	.345	.389
Scor. Pos./2 Out	18	3	0	1	0	3	6	6	.167	.278	.375
Late Inning Pressure	30	9	2	0	1	3	4	6	.300	.467	.400
Leading Off	11	3	1	0	0	0	3	1	.273	.364	.429
Bases Empty	19	6	1	0	0	0	4	4	.316	.368	.458
Runners On	11	3	1	0	1	3	0	2	.273	.636	.273
Runners/Scor. Pos.	7	2	1	0	0	1	0	2	.286	.429	.286

DRIVING IN RUNS	0 Out	1 Out	2 Out	Total	
From 1B	1/18	2/11	0/23	3/52	6%
From 2B	1/7	1/7	1/11	3/25	12%
From 3B	4/5	4/5	2/8	10/18	56%
Scoring Position	5/12	5/12	3/19	13/43	30%
Scor. Pos. %	42%	42%	16%	30%	
Driving In Runners from 3B with Less than Two Out:			8/10	80%	

Loves to face: Mike Scott (.400, 4-for-10, 1 HR)
Hates to face: Mario Soto (0-for-8)
Drove in the winning runs in three of the Phillies' last ten victories last season. . . . Hit more home runs in September (four) than he had in any previous season in the majors. . . . Career batting averages: .305 with runners on base, .231 with the bases empty; .242 vs. left-handers, .273 vs. right-handers. . . . Career on-base percentage of .440 in 25 leadoff appearances in Late-Inning Pressure Situations. . . . Has two career home runs vs. left-handed pitchers: his first major-league home run, off Pete Falcone in 1980, and his most recent shot, off Sid Fernandez on September 24, 1985. . . . Phillies lost all five games in which he started and batted leadoff.

Bill Almon

Pittsburgh Pirates	AB	H	2B	3B	HR	RRF	BB	SO	BA	SA	OBA
Season	244	66	17	0	6	31	22	61	.270	.414	.330
vs. Left-Handed Pitchers	137	38	12	0	3	12	11	28	.277	.431	.336
vs. Right-Handed Pitchers	107	28	5	0	3	19	11	33	.262	.393	.322
Home	113	39	11	0	3	17	11	28	.345	.522	.408
Road	131	27	6	0	3	14	11	33	.206	.321	.262
Grass	77	16	5	0	2	10	5	17	.208	.351	.250
Artificial Turf	167	50	12	0	4	21	17	44	.299	.443	.366
April	30	8	1	0	0	6	2	8	.267	.300	.313
May	84	23	5	0	1	10	9	26	.274	.369	.337
June	43	14	3	0	3	8	5	9	.326	.605	.396
July	27	8	2	0	0	0	1	5	.296	.370	.321
August	19	3	2	0	1	1	3	7	.158	.421	.273
Sept./Oct.	41	10	4	0	1	6	2	6	.244	.415	.289
Leading Off Inn.	82	29	8	0	1	1	4	16	.354	.488	.391
Bases Empty	149	43	12	0	1	1	14	36	.289	.389	.354
Runners On	95	23	5	0	5	30	8	25	.242	.453	.292
Runners/Scor. Pos.	56	13	4	0	2	24	3	16	.232	.411	.258
Runners On/2 Out	47	10	1	0	2	12	4	10	.213	.362	.275
Scor. Pos./2 Out	31	6	1	0	1	10	1	7	.194	.323	.219
Late Inning Pressure	41	14	4	0	1	3	9	11	.341	.512	.460
Leading Off	11	6	3	0	0	0	2	2	.545	.818	.615
Bases Empty	25	11	4	0	0	0	7	4	.440	.600	.563
Runners On	16	3	0	0	1	3	2	7	.188	.375	.278
Runners/Scor. Pos.	8	1	0	0	0	1	1	4	.125	.125	.222

DRIVING IN RUNS	0 Out	1 Out	2 Out	Total	
From 1B	3/24	1/19	2/36	6/79	8%
From 2B	2/5	1/17	3/28	6/50	12%
From 3B	2/4	6/10	5/11	13/25	52%
Scoring Position	4/9	7/27	8/39	19/75	25%
Scor. Pos. %	44%	26%	21%	25%	
Driving In Runners from 3B with Less than Two Out:			8/14	57%	

Loves to face: Dan Schatzeder (.571, 4-for-7, 1 HR)
Hates to face: John Denny (.083, 3-for-36, 13 SO)
Batted .261 in 61 games as a starter, .346 (9-for-26) in 27 games as a substitute (including 5-for-14 as a pinch-hitter). . . . Has played with six different teams since 1979. . . . The only N.L. player to start at least one game at five different positions last season (1B, 3B, SS, LF, and CF). . . . Has batted .300 or better in three of the last four seasons in Late-Inning Pressure Situations. . . . Pirates had a record of 1–5 in games in which he homered. . . . Hit two grand slams last season, quite a reversal from past bases-loaded performance: .228 (13-for-57), no home runs, two walks, and 16 strikeouts from 1975–84. . . . Batted 139 points higher in home games than road games, largest difference in N.L. (minimum: 200 PA). . . . Career batting average of .172 at Shea Stadium (no home runs in 134 AB).

Dave Anderson

Los Angeles Dodgers	AB	H	2B	3B	HR	RRF	BB	SO	BA	SA	OBA
Season	221	44	6	0	4	21	35	42	.199	.281	.310
vs. Left-Handed Pitchers	67	13	2	0	2	6	14	9	.194	.313	.333
vs. Right-Handed Pitchers	154	31	4	0	2	15	21	33	.201	.266	.299
Home	106	20	2	0	1	7	18	23	.189	.236	.312
Road	115	24	4	0	3	14	17	19	.209	.322	.308
Grass	171	34	4	0	4	14	26	31	.199	.292	.308
Artificial Turf	50	10	2	0	0	7	9	11	.200	.240	.317
April	49	8	0	0	1	2	5	7	.163	.224	.241
May	0	0	0	0	0	0	0	0	.000	.000	.000
June	74	16	2	0	1	7	14	15	.216	.284	.348
July	71	16	4	0	2	9	11	17	.225	.366	.325
August	0	0	0	0	0	0	0	0	.000	.000	.000
Sept./Oct.	27	4	0	0	0	3	5	3	.148	.148	.281
Leading Off Inn.	63	11	4	0	1	1	11	19	.175	.286	.307
Bases Empty	124	28	5	0	3	3	19	30	.226	.339	.333
Runners On	97	16	1	0	1	18	16	12	.165	.206	.281
Runners/Scor. Pos.	54	10	1	0	0	15	13	8	.185	.204	.338
Runners On/2 Out	43	6	0	0	0	5	8	3	.140	.140	.275
Scor. Pos./2 Out	31	3	0	0	0	4	8	3	.097	.097	.282
Late Inning Pressure	25	6	0	0	1	1	5	4	.240	.360	.367
Leading Off	6	0	0	0	0	0	0	1	.000	.000	.000
Bases Empty	17	5	0	0	1	1	2	3	.294	.471	.368
Runners On	8	1	0	0	0	0	3	1	.125	.125	.364
Runners/Scor. Pos.	4	0	0	0	0	0	2	1	.000	.000	.333

DRIVING IN RUNS	0 Out	1 Out	2 Out	Total	
From 1B	1/23	0/22	2/30	3/75	4%
From 2B	1/3	3/12	2/25	6/40	15%
From 3B	3/3	4/12	1/14	8/29	28%
Scoring Position	4/6	7/24	3/39	14/69	20%
Scor. Pos. %	67%	29%	8%	20%	
Driving In Runners from 3B with Less than Two Out:			7/15	47%	

Loves to face: Bob Knepper (.500, 7-for-14)
Hates to face: Dan Schatzeder (0-for-9)
Fly-ball hitter: 0.78 G/A ratio last season, 9th-lowest in N.L. (minimum: 200 PA). Career average: 0.91. . . . Eight of his nine errors were committed on grass fields. . . . Shifted to third base when he lost his starting shortstop position to Mariano Duncan; averaged 2.61 assists per nine innings there last season, highest rate among N.L. third basemen (minimum: 300 innings). . . . Career batting averages: .245 vs. left-handers, .211 vs. right-handers; .205 on grass fields, .270 on artificial surfaces. . . . Has hit .146 at San Diego Stadium, .135 at Candlestick Park. . . . Batting average of .172 in Late-Inning Pressure Situations over past three seasons is 2d-lowest in N.L. during that time (minimum: 100 PA).

Alan Ashby

Houston Astros	AB	H	2B	3B	HR	RRF	BB	SO	BA	SA	OBA
Season	189	53	8	0	8	26	24	27	.280	.450	.363
vs. Left-Handed Pitchers	66	19	2	0	2	7	10	9	.288	.409	.377
vs. Right-Handed Pitchers	123	34	6	0	6	19	14	18	.276	.472	.355
Home	78	25	5	0	3	9	13	10	.321	.500	.424
Road	111	28	3	0	5	17	11	17	.252	.414	.317
Grass	81	20	2	0	5	14	8	13	.247	.457	.315
Artificial Turf	108	33	6	0	3	12	16	14	.306	.444	.397
April	44	11	4	0	1	4	4	10	.250	.409	.313
May	38	11	2	0	1	6	7	5	.289	.421	.391
June	41	13	1	0	2	4	5	7	.317	.488	.391
July	39	12	1	0	1	4	4	5	.308	.410	.386
August	0	0	0	0	0	0	0	0	.000	.000	.000
Sept./Oct.	27	6	0	0	3	8	4	0	.222	.556	.323
Leading Off Inn.	54	10	1	0	2	2	6	9	.185	.315	.267
Bases Empty	111	31	4	0	7	7	12	19	.279	.505	.350
Runners On	78	22	4	0	1	19	12	8	.282	.372	.380
Runners/Scor. Pos.	40	12	3	0	1	19	7	6	.300	.450	.396
Runners On/2 Out	25	7	2	0	0	8	5	2	.280	.360	.419
Scor. Pos./2 Out	13	4	2	0	0	8	2	1	.308	.462	.400
Late Inning Pressure	35	11	2	0	3	8	6	5	.314	.629	.405
Leading Off	7	1	0	0	1	1	2	1	.143	.571	.333
Bases Empty	21	8	1	0	3	3	3	4	.381	.857	.458
Runners On	14	3	1	0	0	5	3	1	.214	.286	.333
Runners/Scor. Pos.	6	2	1	0	0	5	2	0	.333	.500	.444

DRIVING IN RUNS	0 Out	1 Out	2 Out	Total	
From 1B	1/26	0/15	1/23	2/64	3%
From 2B	3/11	1/10	4/11	8/32	25%
From 3B	3/6	2/3	3/6	8/15	53%
Scoring Position	6/17	3/13	7/17	16/47	34%
Scor. Pos. %	35%	23%	41%	34%	
Driving In Runners from 3B with Less than Two Out:			5/9	56%	

Loves to face: Doug Bair (4-for-4, 1 2B, 1 3B)
Hates to face: Tom Hume (.095, 2-for-21)
Ground-ball hitter: 2.16 G/A ratio last season, 2d-highest in N.L. (minimum: 200 PA). Career average: 1.57. . . . Missed seven weeks due to broken finger suffered on July 28. Proved he was fully recovered by driving in eight runs (four with a grand slam) in October, second-most in N.L. . . . Was hitless in 16 consecutive bases-loaded situations since 1981 before connecting for grand slam off Ed Wojna on October 5. . . . Career batting averages: .203 batting right-handed, .254 batting left-handed. . . . Grounded into 9 double plays in 44 opportunities last season, 10th-highest average among N.L. players (minimum: 5 GIDP). . . . What do you do with two switch-hitting catchers? Pick 'em at random, it seems: Ashby started 20 games vs. left-handers, 35 vs. right-handers; Bailey started 36 vs. LHP, 60 vs. RHP.

Wally Backman

New York Mets	AB	H	2B	3B	HR	RRF	BB	SO	BA	SA	OBA
Season	520	142	24	5	1	38	36	72	.273	.344	.320
vs. Left-Handed Pitchers	131	16	4	0	0	7	13	26	.122	.153	.207
vs. Right-Handed Pitchers	389	126	20	5	1	31	23	46	.324	.409	.359
Home	251	65	13	3	0	17	19	35	.259	.335	.311
Road	269	77	11	2	1	21	17	37	.286	.353	.328
Grass	378	104	18	3	1	28	23	53	.275	.347	.318
Artificial Turf	142	38	6	2	0	10	13	19	.268	.338	.325
April	52	16	1	2	0	3	5	6	.308	.404	.368
May	62	11	2	0	0	1	4	12	.177	.210	.224
June	69	18	1	0	0	3	8	6	.261	.275	.338
July	97	33	5	2	1	11	6	14	.340	.464	.375
August	116	37	9	1	0	13	6	12	.319	.414	.350
Sept./Oct.	124	27	6	0	0	7	7	22	.218	.266	.265
Leading Off Inn.	149	39	10	2	0	0	9	16	.262	.356	.304
Bases Empty	314	78	15	3	0	0	20	43	.248	.315	.296
Runners On	206	64	9	2	1	38	16	29	.311	.388	.356
Runners/Scor. Pos.	108	35	6	1	1	34	10	18	.324	.426	.372
Runners On/2 Out	81	22	4	1	0	13	7	13	.272	.346	.330
Scor. Pos./2 Out	55	15	3	1	0	12	6	10	.273	.364	.344
Late Inning Pressure	65	19	3	0	0	4	5	10	.292	.338	.338
Leading Off	19	8	1	0	0	0	2	1	.421	.474	.476
Bases Empty	41	13	2	0	0	0	2	5	.317	.366	.349
Runners On	24	6	1	0	0	4	3	5	.250	.292	.321
Runners/Scor. Pos.	16	4	1	0	0	4	2	4	.250	.313	.316

DRIVING IN RUNS	0 Out	1 Out	2 Out	Total	
From 1B	1/40	2/44	1/43	4/127	3%
From 2B	2/14	6/28	5/42	13/84	15%
From 3B	3/5	10/15	7/28	20/48	42%
Scoring Position	5/19	16/43	12/70	33/132	25%
Scor. Pos. %	26%	37%	17%	25%	
Driving In Runners from 3B with Less than Two Out:			13/20	65%	

Loves to face: Rick Mahler (.500, 11-for-22)
Hates to face: Fernando Valenzuela (0-for-16, 5 SO)
Ground-ball hitter: 1.99 G/A ratio last season, 4th-highest in N.L. (minimum: 200 PA). Career average: 2.42 (leads active players). . . . July batting average of .340 was 6th-highest in N.L. . . . Led N.L. second basemen with .989 fielding percentage. . . . Tied with Nolan Ryan for N.L. lead in sacrifice hits (14). . . . Combined with Kelvin Chapman for a batting average of .343 (12-for-35) in pinch-hitting roles. Most of those at bats were not in pressure situations; they resulted from Mets' second-base platoon. . . . Batted 202 points higher vs. right-handers than left-handers, largest difference in N.L. (minimum: 100 PA vs. each). . . . Career batting averages: .134 vs. left-handers, .304 vs. right-handers. . . . Grounded into three double plays in 100 opportunities last season, 3d-lowest average in N.L. (minimum: 50 opportunities).

Mark Bailey

Houston Astros	AB	H	2B	3B	HR	RRF	BB	SO	BA	SA	OBA
Season	332	88	14	0	10	46	67	70	.265	.398	.389
vs. Left-Handed Pitchers	124	36	6	0	4	21	25	25	.290	.435	.413
vs. Right-Handed Pitchers	208	52	8	0	6	25	42	45	.250	.375	.375
Home	171	45	8	0	4	24	35	34	.263	.380	.388
Road	161	43	6	0	6	22	32	36	.267	.416	.390
Grass	88	28	4	0	3	12	23	20	.318	.466	.460
Artificial Turf	244	60	10	0	7	34	44	50	.246	.373	.361
April	25	4	1	0	0	4	5	2	.160	.200	.290
May	52	12	0	0	1	9	8	12	.231	.288	.333
June	55	22	5	0	4	12	11	11	.400	.709	.500
July	55	13	2	0	1	2	11	14	.236	.327	.364
August	78	21	3	0	4	14	14	17	.269	.462	.380
Sept./Oct.	67	16	3	0	0	5	18	14	.239	.284	.407
Leading Off Inn.	88	19	7	0	2	2	13	16	.216	.364	.317
Bases Empty	189	39	9	0	4	4	30	40	.206	.317	.315
Runners On	143	49	5	0	6	42	37	30	.343	.503	.478
Runners/Scor. Pos.	78	24	3	0	3	36	32	19	.308	.462	.505
Runners On/2 Out	60	21	4	0	0	14	18	17	.350	.417	.506
Scor. Pos./2 Out	35	10	3	0	0	14	17	11	.286	.371	.519
Late Inning Pressure	49	12	2	0	2	8	14	13	.245	.408	.422
Leading Off	16	5	2	0	1	1	3	3	.313	.625	.421
Bases Empty	27	6	2	0	2	2	7	8	.222	.519	.382
Runners On	22	6	0	0	0	6	7	5	.273	.273	.467
Runners/Scor. Pos.	10	4	0	0	0	6	5	2	.400	.400	.600

DRIVING IN RUNS	0 Out	1 Out	2 Out	Total	
From 1B	3/32	3/33	0/44	6/109	6%
From 2B	3/12	5/26	7/29	15/67	22%
From 3B	3/6	5/10	7/13	15/29	52%
Scoring Position	6/18	10/36	14/42	30/96	31%
Scor. Pos. %	33%	28%	33%	31%	
Driving In Runners from 3B with Less than Two Out:			8/16	50%	

Loves to face: LaMarr Hoyt (.500, 6-for-12)
Hates to face: Kevin Gross (.125, 1-for-8, 4 SO)
Batted .321 in day games, .247 in night games. . . . Led N.L. with 19 passed balls, but 12 of them were with knuckleballer Joe Niekro on the mound—and Bailey only caught six of his starts. . . . Niekro was the only pitcher caught primarily by either Bailey or Ashby. . . . Career batting averages: .259 at the Astrodome, .217 on the road; .259 batting right-handed, .227 batting left-handed. . . . Astros had a record of 8–2 in games in which he hit a home run. . . . Drove in 11 base runners with 10 home runs, 2d-highest average in N.L. . . . Batted 137 points higher with runners on base than with the bases empty, largest difference in N.L. (minimum: 200 PA). . . . Grounded into 16 double plays in 74 opportunities last season, 6th-highest average among N.L. players (minimum: 5 GIDP).

Kevin Bass

Houston Astros	AB	H	2B	3B	HR	RRF	BB	SO	BA	SA	OBA
Season	539	145	27	5	16	70	31	63	.269	.427	.315
vs. Left-Handed Pitchers	219	68	15	4	10	32	13	31	.311	.553	.359
vs. Right-Handed Pitchers	320	77	12	1	6	38	18	32	.241	.341	.284
Home	264	66	11	1	9	37	20	30	.250	.402	.307
Road	275	79	16	4	7	33	11	33	.287	.451	.323
Grass	178	50	12	2	4	19	7	22	.281	.438	.316
Artificial Turf	361	95	15	3	12	51	24	41	.263	.421	.315
April	49	12	1	0	2	7	3	7	.245	.388	.288
May	56	14	0	0	3	9	3	5	.250	.411	.283
June	114	26	9	0	2	9	2	8	.228	.360	.241
July	100	27	3	1	3	11	7	14	.270	.410	.336
August	83	20	5	1	2	15	4	15	.241	.398	.281
Sept./Oct.	137	46	9	3	4	19	12	14	.336	.533	.397
Leading Off Inn.	114	32	6	3	3	3	5	13	.281	.465	.311
Bases Empty	315	87	13	5	8	8	15	31	.276	.425	.313
Runners On	224	58	14	0	8	62	16	32	.259	.429	.317
Runners/Scor. Pos.	135	36	7	0	4	49	7	23	.267	.407	.308
Runners On/2 Out	95	27	7	0	4	25	6	8	.284	.484	.333
Scor. Pos./2 Out	62	20	4	0	3	22	3	6	.323	.532	.354
Late Inning Pressure	72	23	4	0	3	11	6	10	.319	.500	.380
Leading Off	23	9	1	0	0	0	1	4	.391	.435	.417
Bases Empty	47	15	2	0	0	0	3	7	.319	.362	.373
Runners On	25	8	2	0	3	11	3	3	.320	.760	.393
Runners/Scor. Pos.	11	3	1	0	0	4	2	2	.273	.364	.385

DRIVING IN RUNS	0 Out	1 Out	2 Out	Total	
From 1B	3/33	7/55	2/63	12/151	8%
From 2B	5/20	6/41	14/43	25/104	24%
From 3B	2/5	10/20	5/24	17/49	35%
Scoring Position	7/25	16/61	19/67	42/153	27%
Scor. Pos. %	28%	26%	28%	27%	
Driving In Runners from 3B with Less than Two Out:			12/25	48%	

Loves to face: Tom Niedenfuer (.556, 5-for-9, 1 HR)
Hates to face: Pascual Perez (0-for-11, 3 SO)
Something fishy here: 3-for-3 against Steve Trout (and he can't wait to feast on Bob Kipper). . . . Led N.L. outfielders with a .994 fielding percentage. . . . September batting average of .333 was ninth-highest in N.L. . . . Had only three home runs in 291 at bats vs. left-handed pitchers through the 1984 season. . . . Career batting average of .308 with two outs and runners in scoring position. . . . Batted 70 points higher vs. left-handers than right-handers, 4th-largest difference in N.L. (minimum: 100 PA vs. each). . . . Career batting averages: .337 at Dodger Stadium, .172 at Atlanta Stadium. . . . Career batting average of .308 with 2 outs and runners in scoring position. . . . Has walked only six times leading off 283 innings in his career, 5th-lowest percentage in 11-year history of *The Player Analysis* (minimum: 200 PA).

Buddy Bell

Cincinnati Reds	AB	H	2B	3B	HR	RRF	BB	SO	BA	SA	OBA
Season	247	54	15	2	6	37	34	27	.219	.368	.311
vs. Left-Handed Pitchers	72	18	3	1	1	10	8	7	.250	.361	.321
vs. Right-Handed Pitchers	175	36	12	1	5	27	26	20	.206	.371	.307
Home	118	29	10	2	4	24	14	10	.246	.466	.323
Road	129	25	5	0	2	13	20	17	.194	.279	.300
Grass	73	13	2	0	1	6	10	12	.178	.247	.274
Artificial Turf	174	41	13	2	5	31	24	15	.236	.420	.327
April	0	0	0	0	0	0	0	0	.000	.000	.000
May	0	0	0	0	0	0	0	0	.000	.000	.000
June	0	0	0	0	0	0	0	0	.000	.000	.000
July	45	11	2	1	0	4	6	7	.244	.333	.333
August	98	19	6	0	2	11	15	12	.194	.316	.301
Sept./Oct.	104	24	7	1	4	22	13	8	.231	.433	.311
Leading Off Inn.	53	10	3	0	0	0	8	11	.189	.245	.295
Bases Empty	129	25	5	0	1	1	19	16	.194	.256	.297
Runners On	118	29	10	2	5	36	15	11	.246	.492	.326
Runners/Scor. Pos.	65	15	5	0	3	28	13	5	.231	.446	.350
Runners On/2 Out	52	11	7	0	3	14	6	5	.212	.519	.293
Scor. Pos./2 Out	33	5	4	0	1	9	5	3	.152	.364	.263
Late Inning Pressure	33	3	1	0	0	2	3	5	.091	.121	.162
Leading Off	8	1	0	0	0	0	1	2	.125	.125	.222
Bases Empty	16	2	0	0	0	0	1	2	.125	.125	.176
Runners On	17	1	1	0	0	2	2	3	.059	.118	.150
Runners/Scor. Pos.	9	1	1	0	0	2	2	3	.111	.222	.250

DRIVING IN RUNS	0 Out	1 Out	2 Out	Total	
From 1B	3/20	1/27	5/35	9/82	11%
From 2B	1/9	6/18	3/28	10/55	18%
From 3B	2/5	7/11	3/12	12/28	43%
Scoring Position	3/14	13/29	6/40	22/83	27%
Scor. Pos. %	21%	45%	15%	27%	
Driving In Runners from 3B with Less than Two Out:			9/16	56%	

Loves to face: LaMarr Hoyt (.452, 14-for-31, 1 HR)
Hates to face: Bob Welch (0-for-10)
Figures above are for N.L. only. . . . Drove in 21 runs in 22 games from September 8–30. . . . Has hit for a higher average with runners on base than he has with the bases empty for six consecutive seasons. Batting averages during that time: .308 with runners on, .271 with the bases empty. . . . Has batted over .300 on artificial surfaces in seven of his last nine seasons. . . . Averaged 1.61 assists per nine innings last season, lowest rate among N.L. third basemen (minimum: 300 innings). . . . Last season's combined-league .270 batting average was his lowest vs. left-handed pitchers over the past 11 seasons.

Bruce Benedict

Atlanta Braves	AB	H	2B	3B	HR	RRF	BB	SO	BA	SA	OBA
Season	208	42	6	0	0	20	22	12	.202	.231	.279
vs. Left-Handed Pitchers	58	11	2	0	0	4	9	0	.190	.224	.304
vs. Right-Handed Pitchers	150	31	4	0	0	16	13	12	.207	.233	.268
Home	95	25	3	0	0	10	8	3	.263	.295	.324
Road	113	17	3	0	0	10	14	9	.150	.177	.242
Grass	151	34	4	0	0	16	12	7	.225	.252	.285
Artificial Turf	57	8	2	0	0	4	10	5	.140	.175	.265
April	12	1	0	0	0	0	0	0	.083	.083	.083
May	36	8	1	0	0	2	8	2	.222	.250	.364
June	24	5	0	0	0	0	5	2	.208	.208	.345
July	43	11	1	0	0	4	4	1	.256	.279	.333
August	36	9	1	0	0	9	3	2	.250	.278	.308
Sept./Oct.	57	8	3	0	0	5	2	5	.140	.193	.164
Leading Off Inn.	48	12	0	0	0	0	6	1	.250	.250	.333
Bases Empty	111	20	1	0	0	0	13	7	.180	.189	.272
Runners On	97	22	5	0	0	20	9	5	.227	.278	.287
Runners/Scor. Pos.	55	14	4	0	0	20	6	4	.255	.327	.317
Runners On/2 Out	40	10	2	0	0	11	3	2	.250	.300	.302
Scor. Pos./2 Out	26	8	1	0	0	11	1	2	.308	.346	.333
Late Inning Pressure	34	5	0	0	0	0	3	4	.147	.147	.216
Leading Off	9	3	0	0	0	0	1	0	.333	.333	.400
Bases Empty	22	4	0	0	0	0	2	4	.182	.182	.250
Runners On	12	1	0	0	0	0	1	0	.083	.083	.154
Runners/Scor. Pos.	7	1	0	0	0	0	0	0	.143	.143	.143

DRIVING IN RUNS	0 Out	1 Out	2 Out	Total	
From 1B	0/19	1/27	1/30	2/76	3%
From 2B	1/6	1/21	6/21	8/48	17%
From 3B	1/3	5/8	4/10	10/21	48%
Scoring Position	2/9	6/29	10/31	18/69	26%
Scor. Pos. %	22%	21%	32%	26%	
Driving In Runners from 3B with Less than Two Out:			6/11	55%	

Loves to face: David Palmer (.462, 6-for-13)
Hates to face: Bryn Smith (.143, 3-for-21)
Batted 113 points higher in home games than road games, 5th-largest difference in N.L. (minimum: 200 PA). . . . Road game batting averages, year by year since 1981: .296, .267, .259, .206, .150. . . . Career batting average of .323 with the bases loaded. . . . Batted 69 times without a strikeout against left-handed pitchers last season, the highest total in the 11-year history of *The Player Analysis*. . . . Career batting average of .188 at Dodger Stadium (no home runs in 154 AB). . . . Six hits in 50 at bats (.120) in Late-Inning Pressure Situations with runners on base over the past three seasons. . . . Has driven in only 4 of 14 runners from third with less than two outs in Late-Inning Pressure Situations.

Thad Bosley

Chicago Cubs	AB	H	2B	3B	HR	RRF	BB	SO	BA	SA	OBA
Season	180	59	6	3	7	28	20	29	.328	.511	.391
vs. Left-Handed Pitchers	5	0	0	0	0	0	0	3	.000	.000	.000
vs. Right-Handed Pitchers	175	59	6	3	7	28	20	26	.337	.526	.401
Home	97	35	5	0	4	18	14	13	.361	.536	.434
Road	83	24	1	3	3	10	6	16	.289	.482	.337
Grass	130	42	5	1	5	20	14	20	.323	.492	.384
Artificial Turf	50	17	1	2	2	8	6	9	.340	.560	.411
April	5	1	0	1	0	2	1	0	.200	.600	.286
May	23	5	2	0	0	2	2	5	.217	.304	.280
June	44	11	1	0	1	1	5	10	.250	.341	.327
July	24	11	2	1	1	4	2	3	.458	.750	.500
August	34	15	0	0	4	9	4	1	.441	.794	.500
Sept./Oct.	50	16	1	1	1	10	6	10	.320	.440	.386
Leading Off Inn.	55	20	2	2	2	2	1	6	.364	.582	.375
Bases Empty	116	38	4	2	3	3	8	17	.328	.474	.371
Runners On	64	21	2	1	4	25	12	12	.328	.578	.423
Runners/Scor. Pos.	35	10	0	1	1	17	8	5	.286	.429	.400
Runners On/2 Out	20	5	0	0	2	5	4	5	.250	.550	.375
Scor. Pos./2 Out	12	1	0	0	0	1	1	4	.083	.083	.154
Late Inning Pressure	51	19	2	0	4	8	3	10	.373	.647	.407
Leading Off	18	6	1	0	1	1	0	3	.333	.556	.333
Bases Empty	35	11	2	0	2	2	1	7	.314	.543	.333
Runners On	16	8	0	0	2	6	2	3	.500	.875	.556
Runners/Scor. Pos.	7	2	0	0	0	2	1	1	.286	.286	.375

DRIVING IN RUNS	0 Out	1 Out	2 Out	Total	
From 1B	1/13	3/25	2/13	6/51	12%
From 2B	0/2	5/13	0/8	5/23	22%
From 3B	4/7	5/8	1/7	10/22	45%
Scoring Position	4/9	10/21	1/15	15/45	33%
Scor. Pos. %	44%	48%	7%	33%	
Driving In Runners from 3B with Less than Two Out:			9/15	60%	

Loves to face: Jeff Lahti (.800, 4-for-5)
Hates to face: John Denny (.125, 1-for-8, 4 SO)
Fly-ball hitter: 0.94 G/A ratio last season. . . . Led N.L. in pinch-hits (20) in '85. . . . Started 30 games last season, his highest total since 1980, when he started 31 games for White Sox. Personal record: 55, with Sox in '78. . . . Career batting averages: .301 with 2 outs and runners on base; .474 (9-for-19) with the bases loaded. . . . Prototype of Wrigley Field player: .313 career batting average in day games, .251 in night games; .349 at Wrigley. . . . Has batted only nine times vs. left-handed pitchers over the past three seasons. Career batting averages: .199 (with one extra-base hit in 171 AB) vs. left-handers, .290 vs. right-handers.

Larry Bowa

Cubs/Mets	AB	H	2B	3B	HR	RRF	BB	SO	BA	SA	OBA
Season	214	50	7	4	0	15	13	22	.234	.304	.276
vs. Left-Handed Pitchers	80	19	3	2	0	9	4	11	.238	.325	.271
vs. Right-Handed Pitchers	134	31	4	2	0	6	9	11	.231	.291	.280
Home	107	30	4	3	0	6	7	16	.280	.374	.325
Road	107	20	3	1	0	9	6	6	.187	.234	.228
Grass	165	44	6	4	0	12	8	18	.267	.352	.301
Artificial Turf	49	6	1	0	0	3	5	4	.122	.143	.200
April	13	4	2	0	0	0	0	4	.308	.462	.308
May	37	6	1	0	0	4	1	3	.162	.189	.184
June	49	9	0	0	0	1	4	3	.184	.184	.241
July	70	21	3	2	0	4	2	7	.300	.400	.319
August	33	8	0	2	0	4	4	3	.242	.364	.324
Sept./Oct.	12	2	1	0	0	2	2	2	.167	.250	.286
Leading Off Inn.	56	13	3	1	0	0	2	5	.232	.321	.259
Bases Empty	116	30	4	2	0	0	7	12	.259	.328	.301
Runners On	98	20	3	2	0	15	6	10	.204	.276	.248
Runners/Scor. Pos.	57	12	3	2	0	15	4	6	.211	.333	.258
Runners On/2 Out	42	7	1	1	0	7	2	3	.167	.238	.205
Scor. Pos./2 Out	21	3	1	1	0	7	2	1	.143	.286	.217
Late Inning Pressure	24	5	0	0	0	1	1	5	.208	.208	.240
Leading Off	6	1	0	0	0	0	0	1	.167	.167	.167
Bases Empty	14	3	0	0	0	0	1	3	.214	.214	.267
Runners On	10	2	0	0	0	1	0	2	.200	.200	.200
Runners/Scor. Pos.	7	1	0	0	0	1	0	1	.143	.143	.143

DRIVING IN RUNS	0 Out	1 Out	2 Out	Total	
From 1B	0/15	0/27	2/34	2/76	3%
From 2B	2/10	1/20	3/17	6/47	13%
From 3B	2/4	3/8	2/7	7/19	37%
Scoring Position	4/14	4/28	5/24	13/66	20%
Scor. Pos. %	29%	14%	21%	20%	
Driving In Runners from 3B with Less than Two Out:			5/12	42%	

Loves to face: Dave LaPoint (.529, 9-for-17)
Hates to face: Neil Allen (.087, 2-for-23)
Batted .275 in day games, .169 in night games. . . . Committed an error on the first ball hit to him after joining Mets. . . . Appearance at second base on September 13 was his first there since June 25, 1970. . . . Has never hit a home run in a Late-Inning Pressure Situation. . . . Bound for Cooperstown glory? You'll get some arguments, but not here. Bowa has played more games at shortstop than any player in major-league history except Luis Aparicio. The all-time leaders: Aparicio (2,581), Bowa (2,222), Luke Appling (2,218), and Rabbit Maranville (2,154). The other three are all Hall of Famers. . . . Don't think those guys substantially outhit Bowa, either: Appling (.310 career batting average), Aparicio (.262), Bowa (.260), Maranville (.258). . . . Could field his position, run the bases, and he played for winners. . . . That's a Hall of Famer.

Sid Bream

Dodgers/Pirates	AB	H	2B	3B	HR	RRF	BB	SO	BA	SA	OBA
Season	148	34	7	0	6	21	18	24	.230	.399	.310
vs. Left-Handed Pitchers	41	7	0	0	1	5	4	9	.171	.244	.244
vs. Right-Handed Pitchers	107	27	7	0	5	16	14	15	.252	.458	.333
Home	56	12	2	0	2	9	8	10	.214	.357	.303
Road	92	22	5	0	4	12	10	14	.239	.424	.314
Grass	65	12	0	0	4	8	10	14	.185	.369	.289
Artificial Turf	83	22	7	0	2	13	8	10	.265	.422	.326
April	44	5	0	0	3	6	7	9	.114	.318	.231
May	4	1	0	0	0	0	0	0	.250	.250	.250
June	4	1	0	0	0	0	0	1	.250	.250	.250
July	1	0	0	0	0	0	0	0	.000	.000	.000
August	0	0	0	0	0	0	0	0	.000	.000	.000
Sept./Oct.	95	27	7	0	3	15	11	14	.284	.453	.355
Leading Off Inn.	34	7	1	0	4	4	2	3	.206	.588	.250
Bases Empty	76	17	3	0	5	5	4	9	.224	.461	.263
Runners On	72	17	4	0	1	16	14	15	.236	.333	.352
Runners/Scor. Pos.	41	11	2	0	0	13	14	8	.268	.317	.439
Runners On/2 Out	36	9	2	0	1	10	7	7	.250	.389	.372
Scor. Pos./2 Out	22	6	1	0	0	7	7	4	.273	.318	.448
Late Inning Pressure	25	6	2	0	1	4	4	7	.240	.440	.333
Leading Off	9	2	0	0	0	0	0	1	.222	.222	.222
Bases Empty	16	5	1	0	1	1	1	3	.313	.563	.353
Runners On	9	1	1	0	0	3	3	4	.111	.222	.308
Runners/Scor. Pos.	6	1	1	0	0	3	3	4	.167	.333	.400

DRIVING IN RUNS	0 Out	1 Out	2 Out	Total	
From 1B	0/8	0/21	2/20	2/49	4%
From 2B	0/4	4/13	3/17	7/34	21%
From 3B	0/0	2/7	4/7	6/14	43%
Scoring Position	0/4	6/20	7/24	13/48	27%
Scor. Pos. %	0%	30%	29%	27%	
Driving In Runners from 3B with Less than Two Out:			2/7	29%	

Loves to face: Bill Laskey (.429, 3-for-7, 1 HR)
Hates to face: Dennis Eckersley (0-for-5)
Started at first base in each of the Dodgers' first 14 games last season. . . . Batted .132 with three home runs and six RBIs in 24 games with Los Angeles, .284 with three home runs and 15 RBIs in 26 games with Pittsburgh. . . . Led N.L. first basemen with an average of 0.93 assists per nine innings (minimum: 300 innings). . . . One extra-base hit in 43 career at bats vs. left-handed pitchers: a home run off Bob Knepper on April 16. . . . Nine hits in 29 career at bats (.310) with two outs and runners in scoring position. . . . Pirates won 11 of 21 games started by both Bream and R.J. Reynolds, acquired from Dodgers for Bill Madlock.

Bob Brenly

San Francisco Giants	AB	H	2B	3B	HR	RRF	BB	SO	BA	SA	OBA
Season	440	97	16	1	19	58	57	62	.220	.391	.311
vs. Left-Handed Pitchers	114	22	3	0	6	14	17	9	.193	.377	.298
vs. Right-Handed Pitchers	326	75	13	1	13	44	40	53	.230	.396	.316
Home	225	51	10	1	9	30	27	29	.227	.400	.310
Road	215	46	6	0	10	28	30	33	.214	.381	.313
Grass	339	74	13	1	14	44	41	47	.218	.386	.305
Artificial Turf	101	23	3	0	5	14	16	15	.228	.406	.331
April	58	9	1	1	2	3	7	7	.155	.310	.246
May	50	10	3	0	2	4	6	8	.200	.380	.286
June	92	26	5	0	5	17	12	9	.283	.500	.374
July	81	17	4	0	4	12	10	16	.210	.407	.293
August	63	13	0	0	4	7	8	10	.206	.397	.296
Sept./Oct.	96	22	3	0	2	15	14	12	.229	.323	.327
Leading Off Inn.	120	24	4	0	5	5	11	14	.200	.358	.267
Bases Empty	276	58	9	1	11	11	32	43	.210	.370	.297
Runners On	164	39	7	0	8	47	25	19	.238	.427	.335
Runners/Scor. Pos.	102	22	3	0	4	37	21	16	.216	.363	.344
Runners On/2 Out	71	18	5	0	3	18	12	8	.254	.451	.361
Scor. Pos./2 Out	50	10	2	0	2	15	12	8	.200	.360	.355
Late Inning Pressure	107	20	1	0	5	14	11	11	.187	.336	.269
Leading Off	34	8	0	0	3	3	2	3	.235	.500	.278
Bases Empty	64	11	0	0	4	4	6	8	.172	.359	.254
Runners On	43	9	1	0	1	10	5	3	.209	.302	.292
Runners/Scor. Pos.	29	6	1	0	0	8	4	3	.207	.241	.303

DRIVING IN RUNS	0 Out	1 Out	2 Out	Total	
From 1B	0/29	5/43	3/52	8/124	6%
From 2B	3/16	5/27	7/34	15/77	19%
From 3B	3/5	8/18	5/21	16/44	36%
Scoring Position	6/21	13/45	12/55	31/121	26%
Scor. Pos. %	29%	29%	22%	26%	
Driving In Runners from 3B with Less than Two Out:			11/23	48%	

Loves to face: Andy Hawkins (.800, 8-for-10, 1 HR)
Hates to face: Danny Cox (0-for-9)
Fly-ball hitter: 0.79 G/A ratio last season. . . . Swings right-handed, but has hit for a higher batting average vs. right-handers than left-handers in each of the past three seasons. His marks during those three seasons: .223 vs. left-handers, .262 vs. right-handers. . . . Batting average with runners in scoring position, year by year since 1983: .253, .246, .216; in Late-Inning Pressure Situations: .318, .250, .187. . . . Two hits in 20 career at bats with 2 outs and the bases loaded. . . . Career batting average of .373 at Atlanta Stadium (5 home runs in 75 AB). . . . Has hit five home runs in 54 at bats at Shea Stadium. . . . Has hit a home run in every current National League stadium except Dodger Stadium (73 AB).

Greg Brock

Los Angeles Dodgers	AB	H	2B	3B	HR	RRF	BB	SO	BA	SA	OBA
Season	438	110	19	0	21	67	54	72	.251	.438	.332
vs. Left-Handed Pitchers	102	18	2	0	2	11	6	23	.176	.255	.222
vs. Right-Handed Pitchers	336	92	17	0	19	56	48	49	.274	.494	.363
Home	219	55	9	0	7	33	26	37	.251	.388	.331
Road	219	55	10	0	14	34	28	35	.251	.489	.333
Grass	333	83	14	0	17	56	36	55	.249	.444	.322
Artificial Turf	105	27	5	0	4	11	18	17	.257	.419	.363
April	15	2	0	0	0	0	1	2	.133	.133	.188
May	78	18	2	0	6	14	8	12	.231	.487	.302
June	89	24	4	0	5	9	13	11	.270	.483	.363
July	99	32	3	0	5	24	6	21	.323	.505	.362
August	81	16	5	0	0	2	9	13	.198	.259	.275
Sept./Oct.	76	18	5	0	5	18	17	13	.237	.500	.372
Leading Off Inn.	95	18	3	0	4	4	6	13	.189	.347	.238
Bases Empty	230	50	9	0	9	9	22	37	.217	.374	.286
Runners On	208	60	10	0	12	58	32	35	.288	.510	.380
Runners/Scor. Pos.	113	32	3	0	8	50	18	16	.283	.522	.376
Runners On/2 Out	89	22	4	0	5	21	23	14	.247	.461	.402
Scor. Pos./2 Out	57	12	2	0	2	15	14	8	.211	.351	.366
Late Inning Pressure	61	10	1	0	1	3	5	15	.164	.230	.227
Leading Off	13	2	0	0	1	1	0	3	.154	.385	.154
Bases Empty	31	5	0	0	1	1	0	6	.161	.258	.161
Runners On	30	5	1	0	0	2	5	9	.167	.200	.286
Runners/Scor. Pos.	16	3	0	0	0	2	2	4	.188	.188	.278

DRIVING IN RUNS	0 Out	1 Out	2 Out	Total	
From 1B	4/45	3/52	4/59	11/156	7%
From 2B	5/17	7/30	7/43	19/90	21%
From 3B	3/7	8/15	5/23	16/45	36%
Scoring Position	8/24	15/45	12/66	35/135	26%
Scor. Pos. %	33%	33%	18%	26%	
Driving In Runners from 3B with Less than Two Out:			11/22	50%	

Loves to face: Frank Pastore (.700, 7-for-10, 1 HR)
Hates to face: Bob Knepper (.071, 1-for-14)
Batted 98 points higher vs. right-handers than left-handers, 2d-largest difference in N.L. (minimum: 100 PA vs. each). . . . Batting average vs. left-handers has declined in each season while average vs. right-handers has increased. Career batting averages: .201 vs. lefties, .242 vs. righties. . . . Dodgers had a record of 17–2 in games in which he hit a home run. . . . Drove in 20 base runners with 21 home runs, 4th-highest average in N.L. . . . Batted 12 times without a hit in Late-Inning Pressure Situations with 2 outs and runners on base, highest total in majors last season. . . . Career batting averages: .156 at Veterans Stadium (no home runs in 45 AB), .151 at Candlestick Park (no home runs in 73 AB). . . . No triples in 587 career at bats at Dodger Stadium.

Hubie Brooks

Montreal Expos	AB	H	2B	3B	HR	RRF	BB	SO	BA	SA	OBA
Season	605	163	34	7	13	100	34	79	.269	.413	.310
vs. Left-Handed Pitchers	187	58	15	2	4	29	14	22	.310	.476	.361
vs. Right-Handed Pitchers	418	105	19	5	9	71	20	57	.251	.385	.287
Home	278	78	23	3	4	55	12	40	.281	.428	.313
Road	327	85	11	4	9	45	22	39	.260	.401	.307
Grass	170	48	5	3	4	17	12	17	.282	.418	.328
Artificial Turf	435	115	29	4	9	83	22	62	.264	.411	.303
April	71	22	4	1	0	13	5	7	.310	.394	.350
May	94	21	3	1	3	9	2	8	.223	.372	.255
June	106	30	7	0	2	17	6	23	.283	.406	.333
July	107	23	5	0	2	16	6	14	.215	.318	.252
August	99	31	5	4	3	21	6	10	.313	.535	.346
Sept./Oct.	128	36	10	1	3	24	9	17	.281	.445	.326
Leading Off Inn.	137	44	12	2	3	3	7	14	.321	.504	.354
Bases Empty	316	78	17	3	8	8	17	38	.247	.396	.290
Runners On	289	85	17	4	5	92	17	41	.294	.433	.331
Runners/Scor. Pos.	175	55	12	3	5	88	14	26	.314	.503	.354
Runners On/2 Out	138	44	8	2	3	39	9	19	.319	.471	.365
Scor. Pos./2 Out	83	27	6	1	3	37	8	11	.325	.530	.385
Late Inning Pressure	105	31	2	2	1	10	5	17	.295	.381	.327
Leading Off	32	14	1	1	0	0	1	6	.438	.531	.455
Bases Empty	62	19	1	1	1	1	1	11	.306	.403	.317
Runners On	43	12	1	1	0	9	4	6	.279	.349	.340
Runners/Scor. Pos.	22	6	0	1	0	8	4	3	.273	.364	.385

DRIVING IN RUNS	0 Out	1 Out	2 Out	Total	
From 1B	3/43	3/73	5/88	11/204	5%
From 2B	1/20	14/55	14/57	29/132	22%
From 3B	4/7	26/35	17/40	47/82	57%
Scoring Position	5/27	40/90	31/97	76/214	36%
Scor. Pos. %	19%	44%	32%	36%	
Driving In Runners from 3B with Less than Two Out:			30/42	71%	

Loves to face: Rick Honeycutt (.600, 9-for-15)
Hates to face: Cecilio Guante (0-for-10)
Despite his performance against Guante, which included 0-for-5 last season, Brooks batted .365 with four home runs and 23 RBIs vs. Pittsburgh in '85. . . . Drove in 100th run in season finale at Shea Stadium. . . . Only N.L. shortstop to start in the cleanup position last season. He did it 95 times. . . . Batted .647 (11-for-17, 4 doubles, 2 homers) with the bases loaded last season, tying *Player Analysis* record for bases-loaded hits. . . . Career batting averages: .299 vs. left-handers, .261 vs. right-handers. . . . Averaged 2.89 assists per nine innings last season, 3d-lowest rate among N.L. shortstops (minimum: 300 innings). . . . Career batting averages: .348 in Dodger Stadium; .173 in Veterans Stadium.

Chris Brown

San Francisco Giants	AB	H	2B	3B	HR	RRF	BB	SO	BA	SA	OBA
Season	432	117	20	3	16	65	38	78	.271	.442	.345
vs. Left-Handed Pitchers	110	23	6	0	5	10	11	18	.209	.400	.298
vs. Right-Handed Pitchers	322	94	14	3	11	55	27	60	.292	.457	.361
Home	203	54	14	1	5	33	19	36	.266	.419	.341
Road	229	63	6	2	11	32	19	42	.275	.463	.349
Grass	318	88	18	1	10	51	26	59	.277	.434	.348
Artificial Turf	114	29	2	2	6	14	12	19	.254	.465	.336
April	44	11	2	1	0	4	6	8	.250	.341	.353
May	85	19	2	1	2	12	3	19	.224	.341	.267
June	73	21	6	1	3	10	6	13	.288	.521	.358
July	90	29	6	0	5	16	8	15	.322	.556	.390
August	69	21	1	0	3	9	5	12	.304	.449	.368
Sept./Oct.	71	16	3	0	3	14	10	11	.225	.394	.337
Leading Off Inn.	100	26	4	2	6	6	9	19	.260	.520	.333
Bases Empty	256	62	9	2	10	10	22	41	.242	.410	.317
Runners On	176	55	11	1	6	55	16	37	.313	.489	.386
Runners/Scor. Pos.	104	35	5	0	6	51	11	27	.337	.558	.420
Runners On/2 Out	74	29	7	1	1	28	8	19	.392	.554	.464
Scor. Pos./2 Out	51	19	3	0	1	24	6	15	.373	.490	.448
Late Inning Pressure	94	33	2	2	2	14	11	20	.351	.479	.419
Leading Off	21	7	0	1	1	1	3	4	.333	.571	.417
Bases Empty	56	19	1	1	2	2	6	11	.339	.500	.403
Runners On	38	14	1	1	0	12	5	9	.368	.447	.442
Runners/Scor. Pos.	27	10	1	0	0	11	3	8	.370	.407	.433

DRIVING IN RUNS	0 Out	1 Out	2 Out	Total	
From 1B	0/26	3/48	7/44	10/118	8%
From 2B	2/12	7/32	8/27	17/71	24%
From 3B	3/4	7/15	12/30	22/49	45%
Scoring Position	5/16	14/47	20/57	39/120	33%
Scor. Pos. %	31%	30%	35%	33%	
Driving In Runners from 3B with Less than Two Out:			10/19	53%	

Loves to face: Scott Sanderson (.714, 5-for-7)
Hates to face: Dave Dravecky (0-for-8, 4 SO)
Ground-ball hitter: 1.62 G/A ratio last season. . . . July batting average of .322 was tenth-highest in N.L. . . . Led N.L. third basemen with .971 fielding percentage. . . . Batted .243 in day games, .307 in night games. . . . Hit by 11 pitches in 1985 (most in N.L.). . . . Batted 83 points higher vs. right-handers than left-handers, 4th-largest difference in N.L. (minimum: 100 PA vs. each). . . . Grounded into 19 double plays in 79 opportunities last season, 3d-highest average among N.L. players (minimum: 5 GIDP). . . . Ranked 2d among major-league rookies with 61 RBIs, three fewer than Glenn Davis of Houston.

Mike Brown

Pittsburgh Pirates	AB	H	2B	3B	HR	RRF	BB	SO	BA	SA	OBA
Season	205	68	18	2	5	34	22	27	.332	.512	.391
vs. Left-Handed Pitchers	59	21	5	0	1	10	5	7	.356	.492	.406
vs. Right-Handed Pitchers	146	47	13	2	4	24	17	20	.322	.521	.386
Home	98	29	10	0	3	16	12	17	.296	.490	.369
Road	107	39	8	2	2	18	10	10	.364	.533	.412
Grass	31	10	0	0	2	4	5	3	.323	.516	.417
Artificial Turf	174	58	18	2	3	30	17	24	.333	.511	.387
April	0	0	0	0	0	0	0	0	.000	.000	.000
May	0	0	0	0	0	0	0	0	.000	.000	.000
June	0	0	0	0	0	0	0	0	.000	.000	.000
July	0	0	0	0	0	0	0	0	.000	.000	.000
August	85	29	9	0	0	11	2	13	.341	.447	.348
Sept./Oct.	120	39	9	2	5	23	20	14	.325	.558	.418
Leading Off Inn.	52	21	8	0	3	3	4	5	.404	.731	.446
Bases Empty	109	40	12	0	3	3	8	12	.367	.560	.410
Runners On	96	28	6	2	2	31	14	15	.292	.458	.372
Runners/Scor. Pos.	60	19	3	1	2	28	10	12	.317	.500	.397
Runners On/2 Out	40	14	1	2	1	11	3	6	.350	.550	.395
Scor. Pos./2 Out	27	11	1	1	1	10	2	5	.407	.630	.448
Late Inning Pressure	33	8	1	0	1	3	1	4	.242	.364	.265
Leading Off	10	4	0	0	1	1	0	4	.400	.700	.400
Bases Empty	17	5	0	0	1	1	0	4	.294	.471	.294
Runners On	16	3	1	0	0	2	1	4	.188	.250	.235
Runners/Scor. Pos.	10	1	0	0	0	1	1	3	.100	.100	.182

DRIVING IN RUNS	0 Out	1 Out	2 Out	Total	
From 1B	1/21	3/29	2/29	6/79	8%
From 2B	2/11	2/18	5/15	9/44	20%
From 3B	1/4	10/14	3/13	14/31	45%
Scoring Position	3/15	12/32	8/28	23/75	31%
Scor. Pos. %	20%	38%	29%	31%	
Driving In Runners from 3B with Less than Two Out:			11/18	61%	

Loves to face: Tom Browning (.571, 4-for-7)
Hates to face: Tim Burke (0-for-4)
Figures above are for N.L. only. . . . Ground-ball hitter: 1.56 G/A ratio last season. . . . August batting average of .341 was 4th-highest in N.L. . . . Hit safely in 18 of 19 games for Pittsburgh from August 21 to September 10. . . . Career batting average of .341 leading off innings, with 19 extra-base hits in 126 at bats. . . . Batted 75 points lower with runners on base than with the bases empty, 4th-largest difference in N.L. (minimum: 200 PA). . . . Career batting averages: .271 with runners on base, .301 with the bases empty. . . . Career batting average of .158 (3-for-19) with the bases loaded. . . . Averaged 1.61 putouts per nine innings last season, 4th-lowest rate among N.L. outfielders (minimum: 300 innings).

Gary Carter

New York Mets	AB	H	2B	3B	HR	RRF	BB	SO	BA	SA	OBA
Season	555	156	17	1	32	102	69	46	.281	.488	.365
vs. Left-Handed Pitchers	219	72	11	1	13	38	40	10	.329	.566	.429
vs. Right-Handed Pitchers	336	84	6	0	19	64	29	36	.250	.438	.320
Home	263	70	9	0	12	42	34	23	.266	.437	.355
Road	292	86	8	1	20	60	35	23	.295	.534	.373
Grass	389	114	11	1	25	77	48	34	.293	.519	.375
Artificial Turf	166	42	6	0	7	25	21	12	.253	.416	.342
April	62	15	3	0	3	6	10	5	.242	.435	.355
May	82	20	4	0	2	17	14	9	.244	.366	.361
June	103	32	2	1	6	12	10	8	.311	.524	.383
July	95	25	2	0	2	15	9	9	.263	.347	.333
August	88	24	4	0	6	16	8	5	.273	.523	.333
Sept./Oct.	125	40	2	0	13	36	18	10	.320	.648	.403
Leading Off Inn.	151	51	5	0	11	11	8	9	.338	.589	.375
Bases Empty	284	78	6	1	18	18	24	24	.275	.493	.335
Runners On	271	78	11	0	14	84	45	22	.288	.483	.393
Runners/Scor. Pos.	154	51	6	0	8	71	37	14	.331	.526	.459
Runners On/2 Out	117	27	4	0	6	33	29	14	.231	.419	.392
Scor. Pos./2 Out	70	19	3	0	4	28	22	7	.271	.486	.452
Late Inning Pressure	83	24	2	0	4	14	10	8	.289	.458	.366
Leading Off	29	9	1	0	1	1	2	2	.310	.448	.355
Bases Empty	43	13	1	0	2	2	5	5	.302	.465	.375
Runners On	40	11	1	0	2	12	5	3	.275	.450	.356
Runners/Scor. Pos.	21	6	1	0	1	10	3	2	.286	.476	.375

DRIVING IN RUNS	0 Out	1 Out	2 Out	Total	
From 1B	1/47	8/75	6/71	15/193	8%
From 2B	2/18	11/46	14/58	27/122	22%
From 3B	4/10	17/22	7/22	28/54	52%
Scoring Position	6/28	28/68	21/80	55/176	31%
Scor. Pos. %	21%	41%	26%	31%	
Driving In Runners from 3B with Less than Two Out:			21/32	66%	

Loves to face: Atlee Hammaker (.529, 9-for-17, 1 HR)
Hates to face: Don Robinson (.068, 3-for-44)
First N.L. player since Ted Kluszewski in 1956 to hit more than 30 home runs while striking out fewer than 50 times. . . . Batted .343 and led N.L. with 13 home runs and 34 RBIs in September. . . . Five homers at San Diego (Sept. 3–4) tied major-league record for home runs in consecutive games. . . . Carter's first five home runs at Shea Stadium last season all drove in game-winning runs. Mets won all 11 home games in which he homered. . . . Led N.L. with 13 home runs off left-handed pitchers. . . . Has batted higher with men on base than with the bases empty in each of the last eight seasons. . . . Batting .438 (14-for-32, 4 HR) with the bases loaded since 1983. Has connected for at least one grand slam in seven of the last eight years.

Enos Cabell

Astros/Dodgers	AB	H	2B	3B	HR	RRF	BB	SO	BA	SA	OBA
Season	335	91	19	1	2	38	30	36	.272	.352	.332
vs. Left-Handed Pitchers	181	54	13	1	1	18	21	17	.298	.398	.371
vs. Right-Handed Pitchers	154	37	6	0	1	20	9	19	.240	.299	.282
Home	182	49	12	0	1	21	18	22	.269	.352	.335
Road	153	42	7	1	1	17	12	14	.275	.353	.327
Grass	186	55	8	1	1	24	15	22	.296	.366	.348
Artificial Turf	149	36	11	0	1	14	15	14	.242	.336	.311
April	45	13	4	0	0	4	0	4	.289	.378	.289
May	36	7	0	1	1	4	4	6	.194	.333	.275
June	50	13	4	0	1	6	11	4	.260	.400	.393
July	67	16	1	0	0	6	6	9	.239	.254	.301
August	68	18	5	0	0	7	3	6	.265	.338	.296
Sept./Oct.	69	24	5	0	0	11	6	7	.348	.420	.400
Leading Off Inn.	64	15	2	0	0	0	4	9	.234	.266	.279
Bases Empty	193	49	9	0	1	1	14	22	.254	.316	.304
Runners On	142	42	10	1	1	37	16	14	.296	.401	.367
Runners/Scor. Pos.	89	24	5	1	1	35	13	9	.270	.382	.363
Runners On/2 Out	59	17	7	1	0	14	7	5	.288	.441	.364
Scor. Pos./2 Out	43	9	3	1	0	12	6	4	.209	.326	.306
Late Inning Pressure	57	15	1	0	0	6	4	6	.263	.281	.311
Leading Off	11	0	0	0	0	0	2	3	.000	.000	.154
Bases Empty	29	6	0	0	0	0	2	3	.207	.207	.258
Runners On	28	9	1	0	0	6	2	3	.321	.357	.367
Runners/Scor. Pos.	17	2	0	0	0	5	2	2	.118	.118	.211

DRIVING IN RUNS	0 Out	1 Out	2 Out	Total	
From 1B	0/23	1/29	3/31	4/83	5%
From 2B	1/13	5/23	5/34	11/70	16%
From 3B	5/6	10/15	6/19	21/40	53%
Scoring Position	6/19	15/38	11/53	32/110	29%
Scor. Pos. %	32%	39%	21%	29%	
Driving In Runners from 3B with Less than Two Out:			15/21	71%	

Loves to face: Bob Ojeda (.556, 5-for-9, 1 HR)
Hates to face: Bill Gullickson (0-for-10)
Batted .455 (5-for-13) vs. Houston after being traded to L.A. . . . Only one home run in 337 career at bats at Dodger Stadium. . . . Hitless in 23 at bats in Late-Inning Pressure Situations with two outs and runners in scoring position since 1981. . . . Career batting averages: .330 at Three Rivers Stadium, .316 at Riverfront Stadium. . . . Has batted .321 vs. left-handed pitchers over the past three seasons, 4th-highest mark in majors during that same time (minimum: 150 hits). . . . Has hit only one home run in 258 at bats in Late-Inning Pressure Situations over the past four seasons. . . . Batted .209 with two outs and runners in scoring position last season, equaling his *highest* mark since 1981. . . . Ranks second in career hits among players named Enos.

Cesar Cedeno

Reds/Cardinals	AB	H	2B	3B	HR	RRF	BB	SO	BA	SA	OBA
Season	296	86	16	1	9	50	24	42	.291	.443	.347
vs. Left-Handed Pitchers	135	43	9	0	5	25	15	13	.319	.496	.390
vs. Right-Handed Pitchers	161	43	7	1	4	25	9	29	.267	.398	.308
Home	138	49	9	1	5	29	9	18	.355	.543	.391
Road	158	37	7	0	4	21	15	24	.234	.354	.309
Grass	83	25	6	0	2	13	9	11	.301	.446	.376
Artificial Turf	213	61	10	1	7	37	15	31	.286	.441	.335
April	68	18	4	0	0	6	7	10	.265	.324	.338
May	57	12	4	0	0	10	4	11	.211	.281	.270
June	37	9	2	0	2	6	4	7	.243	.459	.317
July	37	9	2	0	1	5	3	5	.243	.378	.317
August	26	7	1	0	1	5	1	3	.269	.423	.296
Sept./Oct.	71	31	3	1	5	18	5	6	.437	.718	.468
Leading Off Inn.	63	13	6	0	1	1	4	13	.206	.349	.265
Bases Empty	149	34	10	1	4	4	12	26	.228	.389	.299
Runners On	147	52	6	0	5	46	12	16	.354	.497	.395
Runners/Scor. Pos.	83	29	4	0	2	39	10	8	.349	.470	.406
Runners On/2 Out	61	15	3	0	1	12	6	11	.246	.344	.313
Scor. Pos./2 Out	37	10	2	0	0	10	5	5	.270	.324	.357
Late Inning Pressure	57	17	1	1	4	12	4	7	.298	.561	.344
Leading Off	12	3	0	0	1	1	1	4	.250	.500	.308
Bases Empty	26	8	1	1	2	2	3	6	.308	.654	.379
Runners On	31	9	0	0	2	10	1	1	.290	.484	.313
Runners/Scor. Pos.	19	5	0	0	0	6	1	1	.263	.263	.300

DRIVING IN RUNS	0 Out	1 Out	2 Out	Total	
From 1B	1/27	6/43	2/34	9/104	9%
From 2B	3/13	8/24	4/30	15/67	22%
From 3B	3/8	9/13	5/17	17/38	45%
Scoring Position	6/21	17/37	9/47	32/105	30%
Scor. Pos. %	29%	46%	19%	30%	
Driving In Runners from 3B with Less than Two Out:			12/21	57%	

Loves to face: Steve Engel (1.000, 7-for-7, 1 HR)
Hates to face: Orel Hershiser (0-for-13)
Fly-ball hitter: 0.81 G/A ratio last season. . . . 1985 pinch-hit batting average of .400 (10-for-25) was 2d-highest in N.L. (minimum: 20 pinch-hit at bats). . . . Batted .241 with three home runs and 30 RBIs in 83 games with Cincinnati, .434 with six home runs and 19 RBIs in 28 games with St. Louis. . . . Has batted over .300 vs. left-handers in five of the last six seasons. . . . Batted 126 points higher with runners on base than with the bases empty, 2d-largest difference in N.L. (minimum: 200 PA). . . . Batting average of .349 with runners in scoring position last season was his highest in the 11 years of *The Player Analysis*. . . . Batted higher on grass fields than artificial surfaces last season for the first time since 1974. . . . Batting average of .360 at Busch Stadium since 1975.

Rick Cerone

Atlanta Braves	AB	H	2B	3B	HR	RRF	BB	SO	BA	SA	OBA
Season	282	61	9	0	3	27	29	25	.216	.280	.288
vs. Left-Handed Pitchers	91	18	4	0	1	10	7	7	.198	.275	.253
vs. Right-Handed Pitchers	191	43	5	0	2	17	22	18	.225	.283	.304
Home	151	33	6	0	3	20	16	10	.219	.318	.290
Road	131	28	3	0	0	7	13	15	.214	.237	.286
Grass	209	48	8	0	3	24	23	14	.230	.311	.304
Artificial Turf	73	13	1	0	0	3	6	11	.178	.192	.241
April	56	15	0	0	2	6	5	3	.268	.375	.328
May	48	10	1	0	0	2	5	5	.208	.229	.278
June	16	4	0	0	0	3	0	2	.250	.250	.235
July	59	11	3	0	0	5	2	6	.186	.237	.210
August	52	12	2	0	1	8	10	6	.231	.327	.359
Sept./Oct.	51	9	3	0	0	3	7	3	.176	.235	.276
Leading Off Inn.	57	9	2	0	1	1	3	5	.158	.246	.200
Bases Empty	146	28	3	0	1	1	13	15	.192	.233	.263
Runners On	136	33	6	0	2	26	16	10	.243	.331	.314
Runners/Scor. Pos.	66	17	2	0	1	23	11	6	.258	.333	.346
Runners On/2 Out	57	13	3	0	1	11	7	6	.228	.333	.313
Scor. Pos./2 Out	32	8	0	0	1	10	7	4	.250	.344	.385
Late Inning Pressure	43	10	2	0	0	5	6	2	.233	.279	.333
Leading Off	12	3	1	0	0	0	1	0	.250	.333	.308
Bases Empty	26	5	1	0	0	0	3	1	.192	.231	.300
Runners On	17	5	1	0	0	5	3	1	.294	.353	.381
Runners/Scor. Pos.	6	2	1	0	0	5	2	0	.333	.500	.444

DRIVING IN RUNS	0 Out	1 Out	2 Out	Total	
From 1B	0/25	2/44	2/40	4/109	4%
From 2B	1/9	3/24	5/24	9/57	16%
From 3B	1/3	7/11	3/14	11/28	39%
Scoring Position	2/12	10/35	8/38	20/85	24%
Scor. Pos. %	17%	29%	21%	24%	
Driving In Runners from 3B with Less than Two Out:			8/14	57%	

Loves to face: John Tudor (.462, 6-for-13, 1 HR)
Hates to face: Jim Gott (0-for-7, 3 SO)
Hit 14 home runs, drove in 85 runs in 1980; 14 HR, 109 RBIs in five seasons since. . . . Has batted .219 over past four seasons, 4th-lowest average in majors during that time (minimum: 1,000 PA). . . . Has hit over .250 only once in his 11-year major-league career—.277 in (when else?) 1980. . . . Four hits in 27 at bats (.148) with the bases loaded over the past five seasons, .199 with two outs and runners on base during that same period. . . . One bright spot: 12 hits in 26 at bats (.462) in Late-Inning Pressure Situations with runners in scoring position since 1982.

Ron Cey

Chicago Cubs	AB	H	2B	3B	HR	RRF	BB	SO	BA	SA	OBA
Season	500	116	18	2	22	63	58	106	.232	.408	.316
vs. Left-Handed Pitchers	122	27	6	0	7	13	16	30	.221	.443	.312
vs. Right-Handed Pitchers	378	89	12	2	15	50	42	76	.235	.397	.317
Home	238	62	6	1	15	45	33	44	.261	.483	.354
Road	262	54	12	1	7	18	25	62	.206	.340	.279
Grass	355	88	11	1	18	50	44	64	.248	.437	.335
Artificial Turf	145	28	7	1	4	13	14	42	.193	.338	.267
April	56	8	0	0	2	7	4	17	.143	.250	.194
May	88	25	4	1	7	14	14	19	.284	.591	.388
June	93	18	2	0	3	6	17	27	.194	.312	.318
July	75	18	4	0	1	2	7	12	.240	.333	.313
August	94	32	7	1	4	16	7	9	.340	.564	.392
Sept./Oct.	94	15	1	0	5	18	9	22	.160	.330	.240
Leading Off Inn.	126	33	4	0	8	8	8	19	.262	.484	.306
Bases Empty	278	63	12	0	10	10	18	57	.227	.378	.279
Runners On	222	53	6	2	12	53	40	49	.239	.446	.357
Runners/Scor. Pos.	114	28	3	2	9	47	28	30	.246	.544	.393
Runners On/2 Out	84	19	1	1	5	25	25	18	.226	.440	.409
Scor. Pos./2 Out	52	13	1	1	5	25	18	12	.250	.596	.443
Late Inning Pressure	79	21	1	0	4	7	11	17	.266	.430	.363
Leading Off	24	9	1	0	3	3	3	5	.375	.792	.444
Bases Empty	49	13	1	0	3	3	4	10	.265	.469	.321
Runners On	30	8	0	0	1	4	7	7	.267	.367	.421
Runners/Scor. Pos.	15	4	0	0	1	4	6	4	.267	.467	.500

DRIVING IN RUNS	0 Out	1 Out	2 Out	Total	
From 1B	4/55	2/54	5/58	11/167	7%
From 2B	0/16	6/33	6/39	12/88	14%
From 3B	5/7	4/15	9/22	18/44	41%
Scoring Position	5/23	10/48	15/61	30/132	23%
Scor. Pos. %	22%	21%	25%	23%	
Driving In Runners from 3B with Less than Two Out:			9/22	41%	

Loves to face: Vida Blue (.407, 11-for-27, 5 2B, 4 HR)
Hates to face: Frank DiPino (0-for-10)
Fly-ball hitter: 0.80 G/A ratio last season. . . . Batted .306 vs. ground-ball pitchers last season, .179 vs. fly-ball pitchers. . . . Seven home runs in May were tied for 2d-most in N.L. . . . August batting average of .340 was 5th-highest in N.L. . . . Committed 21 errors at third base last season (most in N.L.) after leading the league in fielding percentage the previous year. . . . Batted .260 in day games, .185 in night games. . . . Went 37 consecutive games without a home run from June 10 and July 27, the longest home-run drought of his career. . . . Don't talk to him about cookie-cutter stadiums; batting averages since 1975 of .321 at Riverfront Stadium, .189 at Three Rivers Stadium.

Chris Chambliss

Atlanta Braves	AB	H	2B	3B	HR	RRF	BB	SO	BA	SA	OBA
Season	170	40	7	0	3	22	18	22	.235	.329	.307
vs. Left-Handed Pitchers	36	7	2	0	0	6	5	6	.194	.250	.286
vs. Right-Handed Pitchers	134	33	5	0	3	16	13	16	.246	.351	.313
Home	84	19	2	0	1	8	8	9	.226	.286	.290
Road	86	21	5	0	2	14	10	13	.244	.372	.323
Grass	120	26	3	0	3	16	14	14	.217	.317	.296
Artificial Turf	50	14	4	0	0	6	4	8	.280	.360	.333
April	53	11	3	0	0	5	5	7	.208	.264	.276
May	26	8	2	0	0	4	1	3	.308	.385	.321
June	33	3	0	0	0	1	5	6	.091	.091	.211
July	29	10	2	0	1	5	2	3	.345	.517	.387
August	9	1	0	0	1	2	2	2	.111	.444	.273
Sept./Oct.	20	7	0	0	1	5	3	1	.350	.500	.435
Leading Off Inn.	39	11	1	0	1	1	2	7	.282	.385	.317
Bases Empty	91	24	4	0	2	2	6	13	.264	.374	.309
Runners On	79	16	3	0	1	20	12	9	.203	.278	.304
Runners/Scor. Pos.	45	11	2	0	0	18	8	4	.244	.289	.352
Runners On/2 Out	35	6	0	0	0	5	5	5	.171	.171	.275
Scor. Pos./2 Out	23	4	0	0	0	5	2	3	.174	.174	.240
Late Inning Pressure	51	9	1	0	1	5	5	10	.176	.255	.250
Leading Off	15	2	0	0	0	0	0	3	.133	.133	.133
Bases Empty	29	6	1	0	1	1	3	4	.207	.345	.281
Runners On	22	3	0	0	0	4	2	6	.136	.136	.208
Runners/Scor. Pos.	18	3	0	0	0	4	2	4	.167	.167	.250

DRIVING IN RUNS	0 Out	1 Out	2 Out	Total	
From 1B	0/13	1/20	0/22	1/55	2%
From 2B	0/6	4/11	4/21	8/38	21%
From 3B	3/3	6/10	1/7	10/20	50%
Scoring Position	3/9	10/21	5/28	18/58	31%
Scor. Pos. %	33%	48%	18%	31%	
Driving In Runners from 3B with Less than Two Out:			9/13	69%	

Loves to face: Frank Pastore (.450, 18-for-40, 3 HR)
Hates to face: Fernando Valenzuela (.091, 3-for-33, 8 SO)
Batted .250 in 27 games as a starter, .212 as a substitute; .361 in day games, .165 in night games. . . . Started only three games after the All-Star break. . . . Five hits in his last eight at bats as a pinch-hitter. . . . His last 17 home runs have been hit off right-handed pitchers. Last homer vs. a left-hander: July 31, 1983, off Mark Thurmond. . . . Has hit for a higher average on artificial surfaces than he has on grass fields in six of the last seven seasons. . . . Career batting averages: .351 at Veterans Stadium, .340 at Busch Stadium.

Jack Clark

St. Louis Cardinals	AB	H	2B	3B	HR	RRF	BB	SO	BA	SA	OBA
Season	442	124	26	3	22	88	83	88	.281	.502	.393
vs. Left-Handed Pitchers	139	45	9	1	9	35	39	20	.324	.597	.467
vs. Right-Handed Pitchers	303	79	17	2	13	53	44	68	.261	.459	.355
Home	225	52	14	1	8	35	36	44	.231	.409	.335
Road	217	72	12	2	14	53	47	44	.332	.599	.450
Grass	120	47	4	2	9	35	30	17	.392	.683	.516
Artificial Turf	322	77	22	1	13	53	53	71	.239	.435	.343
April	68	19	6	0	3	13	16	11	.279	.500	.417
May	95	30	6	1	7	27	15	12	.316	.621	.409
June	100	27	4	1	5	17	13	25	.270	.480	.354
July	91	27	6	0	5	20	19	20	.297	.527	.414
August	62	14	4	1	1	8	15	15	.226	.371	.372
Sept./Oct.	26	7	0	0	1	3	5	5	.269	.385	.387
Leading Off Inn.	109	34	5	1	9	9	23	15	.312	.624	.436
Bases Empty	209	58	11	1	11	11	44	42	.278	.498	.408
Runners On	233	66	15	2	11	77	39	46	.283	.506	.379
Runners/Scor. Pos.	137	39	10	2	6	65	33	31	.285	.518	.411
Runners On/2 Out	106	26	4	0	5	26	22	25	.245	.425	.375
Scor. Pos./2 Out	62	14	3	0	2	20	18	16	.226	.371	.400
Late Inning Pressure	60	20	3	1	2	9	14	14	.333	.517	.459
Leading Off	20	6	1	0	0	0	1	4	.300	.350	.333
Bases Empty	35	11	2	0	1	1	3	8	.314	.457	.368
Runners On	25	9	1	1	1	8	11	6	.360	.600	.556
Runners/Scor. Pos.	13	4	0	1	0	6	8	3	.308	.462	.571

DRIVING IN RUNS	0 Out	1 Out	2 Out	Total	
From 1B	4/43	5/50	4/62	13/155	8%
From 2B	3/14	5/33	9/47	17/94	18%
From 3B	9/12	19/34	8/22	36/68	53%
Scoring Position	12/26	24/67	17/69	53/162	33%
Scor. Pos. %	46%	36%	25%	33%	
Driving In Runners from 3B with Less than Two Out:			28/46	61%	

Loves to face: Lee Smith (.500, 10-for-20, 2 HR)
Hates to face: Bruce Berenyi (.088, 3-for-34, 9 SO)
Fly-ball hitter: 0.70 G/A ratio last season, 6th-lowest in N.L. (minimum: 200 PA). Career average: 0.91. . . . Seven home runs in May were tied for 2d-most in N.L. . . . Had most errors (14) and lowest fielding percentage (.988) of any N.L. first baseman (minimum: 100 games). . . . Batted .332 in road games (2d-highest in N.L.) and led N.L. with a .392 average on grass fields. Career batting averages: .276 on grass, .280 on artificial surfaces; .304 vs. left-handers, .267 vs. right-handers; .300 leading off innings. . . . Batted .413 vs. the Giants, his highest average vs. any opponent. . . . Has batted over .300 in Late-Inning Pressure Situations in each of the last three seasons. . . . Career batting averages: .322 at Three Rivers Stadium, .319 at Shea Stadium.

Vince Coleman

St. Louis Cardinals	AB	H	2B	3B	HR	RRF	BB	SO	BA	SA	OBA
Season	636	170	20	10	1	42	50	115	.267	.335	.320
vs. Left-Handed Pitchers	211	50	10	6	0	14	14	39	.237	.341	.284
vs. Right-Handed Pitchers	425	120	10	4	1	28	36	76	.282	.332	.338
Home	315	96	11	6	1	23	25	40	.305	.387	.356
Road	321	74	9	4	0	19	25	75	.231	.283	.285
Grass	174	45	5	4	0	12	8	42	.259	.333	.290
Artificial Turf	462	125	15	6	1	30	42	73	.271	.335	.331
April	50	15	3	1	0	6	5	6	.300	.400	.364
May	104	27	4	1	1	5	9	21	.260	.346	.319
June	110	27	1	2	0	6	12	16	.245	.291	.320
July	100	29	3	3	0	3	7	22	.290	.380	.333
August	123	33	4	3	0	6	4	30	.268	.350	.291
Sept./Oct.	149	39	5	0	0	16	13	20	.262	.295	.321
Leading Off Inn.	277	79	10	5	0	0	28	56	.285	.357	.351
Bases Empty	442	121	13	7	1	1	36	87	.274	.342	.328
Runners On	194	49	7	3	0	41	14	28	.253	.320	.301
Runners/Scor. Pos.	127	36	3	2	0	40	10	19	.283	.339	.333
Runners On/2 Out	91	24	2	1	0	21	5	14	.264	.308	.302
Scor. Pos./2 Out	62	20	0	1	0	21	5	11	.323	.355	.373
Late Inning Pressure	74	18	5	1	0	11	6	14	.243	.338	.300
Leading Off	21	3	2	0	0	0	2	8	.143	.238	.217
Bases Empty	43	7	2	0	0	0	4	13	.163	.209	.234
Runners On	31	11	3	1	0	11	2	1	.355	.516	.394
Runners/Scor. Pos.	18	8	2	1	0	11	2	1	.444	.667	.500

DRIVING IN RUNS	0 Out	1 Out	2 Out	Total	
From 1B	2/30	0/37	0/44	2/111	2%
From 2B	3/16	4/37	12/51	19/104	18%
From 3B	5/8	6/12	8/21	19/41	46%
Scoring Position	8/24	10/49	20/72	38/145	26%
Scor. Pos. %	33%	20%	28%	26%	
Driving In Runners from 3B with Less than Two Out:			11/20	55%	

Loves to face: Scott Sanderson (.714, 5-for-7, 1 2B, 2 3B)
Hates to face: Ed Lynch (0-for-9)
Also hates to face: Tarp jokes.... Ground-ball hitter: 1.65 G/A ratio last season.... Batted .326 vs. ground-ball pitchers last season, .221 vs. fly-ball pitchers.... Coleman's on-base percentage against Montreal (.205) was his lowest vs. any opponent. But he made the most of it: stole 15 bases in 15 attempts vs. the Expos.... First rookie (and fourth player) to steal 100 bases; also set rookie record for caught stealing (25).... Most strikeouts (115) of any N.L. player with 10 or fewer homers.... Stole more than one base in a game 28 times.... Season batting average did not fluctuate more than 15 points from July 4 to season's end.... Batted .228 in day games, .291 in night games.... Grounded into three double plays in 78 opportunities last season, 5th-lowest average in N.L. (minimum: 50 opportunities).

Dave Concepcion

Cincinnati Reds	AB	H	2B	3B	HR	RRF	BB	SO	BA	SA	OBA
Season	560	141	19	2	7	50	50	67	.252	.330	.314
vs. Left-Handed Pitchers	156	38	6	0	4	9	18	21	.244	.359	.322
vs. Right-Handed Pitchers	404	103	13	2	3	41	32	46	.255	.319	.312
Home	273	74	10	2	1	22	28	32	.271	.333	.342
Road	287	67	9	0	6	28	22	35	.233	.328	.288
Grass	176	43	5	0	3	9	8	20	.244	.324	.281
Artificial Turf	384	98	14	2	4	41	42	47	.255	.333	.329
April	71	17	4	0	2	5	5	8	.239	.380	.289
May	93	25	6	1	2	8	4	14	.269	.419	.306
June	93	28	4	0	1	9	11	5	.301	.376	.371
July	81	18	0	0	1	7	15	11	.222	.259	.347
August	99	22	2	0	1	9	7	13	.222	.273	.280
Sept./Oct.	123	31	3	1	0	12	8	16	.252	.293	.293
Leading Off Inn.	114	39	4	0	1	1	11	15	.342	.404	.400
Bases Empty	323	91	13	2	4	4	30	40	.282	.372	.345
Runners On	237	50	6	0	3	46	20	27	.211	.274	.274
Runners/Scor. Pos.	136	28	2	0	2	42	17	19	.206	.265	.296
Runners On/2 Out	96	12	1	0	1	14	9	14	.125	.167	.208
Scor. Pos./2 Out	66	10	0	0	1	14	8	11	.152	.197	.253
Late Inning Pressure	100	21	3	0	1	12	9	14	.210	.270	.268
Leading Off	24	5	0	0	1	1	3	6	.208	.333	.296
Bases Empty	65	12	2	0	1	1	6	10	.185	.262	.254
Runners On	35	9	1	0	0	11	3	4	.257	.286	.293
Runners/Scor. Pos.	25	5	0	0	0	10	1	4	.200	.200	.207

DRIVING IN RUNS	0 Out	1 Out	2 Out	Total	
From 1B	2/38	1/63	1/61	4/162	2%
From 2B	3/18	10/44	7/54	20/116	17%
From 3B	4/5	10/19	5/30	19/54	35%
Scoring Position	7/23	20/63	12/84	39/170	23%
Scor. Pos. %	30%	32%	14%	23%	
Driving In Runners from 3B with Less than Two Out:			14/24	58%	

Loves to face: Bob Knepper (.362, 34-for-94)
Hates to face: Danny Cox (.095, 2-for-21)
Ground-ball hitter: 1.71 G/A ratio last season.... Committed 11 errors in 46 games on grass fields, 13 errors in 109 games on the rug.... Hitless in six at bats as a pinch-hitter last season, one hit in his 19 pinch-hit at bats since 1984.... Averaged 2.80 assists per nine innings last season, 2d-lowest rate among N.L. shortstops (minimum: 300 innings).... Batted 71 points lower with runners on base than with the bases empty, 5th-largest difference in N.L. (minimum: 200 PA).... Career batting average of .189 at Olympic Stadium.... Grounded into 23 double plays in 107 opportunities last season, 7th-highest rate among N.L. players (minimum: 5 GIDP).

Tim Corcoran

Philadelphia Phillies	AB	H	2B	3B	HR	RRF	BB	SO	BA	SA	OBA
Season	182	39	6	1	0	23	29	20	.214	.258	.312
vs. Left-Handed Pitchers	19	4	0	0	0	3	0	4	.211	.211	.200
vs. Right-Handed Pitchers	163	35	6	1	0	20	29	16	.215	.264	.323
Home	109	20	3	0	0	12	20	15	.183	.211	.299
Road	73	19	3	1	0	11	9	5	.260	.329	.333
Grass	37	7	2	0	0	4	4	3	.189	.243	.256
Artificial Turf	145	32	4	1	0	19	25	17	.221	.262	.326
April	44	15	3	0	0	5	5	3	.341	.409	.408
May	54	10	1	0	0	5	9	7	.185	.204	.292
June	18	3	0	1	0	5	2	2	.167	.278	.227
July	30	6	1	0	0	3	4	4	.200	.233	.278
August	19	1	0	0	0	1	4	3	.053	.053	.217
Sept./Oct.	17	4	1	0	0	4	5	1	.235	.294	.391
Leading Off Inn.	37	11	1	0	0	0	8	3	.297	.324	.422
Bases Empty	84	25	3	0	0	0	10	9	.298	.333	.372
Runners On	98	14	3	1	0	23	19	11	.143	.194	.266
Runners/Scor. Pos.	64	9	1	1	0	21	13	5	.141	.188	.262
Runners On/2 Out	36	5	0	1	0	6	9	3	.139	.194	.311
Scor. Pos./2 Out	30	4	0	1	0	6	7	3	.133	.200	.297
Late Inning Pressure	42	7	2	1	0	9	9	3	.167	.262	.296
Leading Off	5	1	1	0	0	0	2	0	.200	.400	.429
Bases Empty	15	3	1	0	0	0	2	2	.200	.267	.294
Runners On	27	4	1	1	0	9	7	1	.148	.259	.297
Runners/Scor. Pos.	20	2	0	1	0	8	4	0	.100	.200	.222

DRIVING IN RUNS	0 Out	1 Out	2 Out	Total	
From 1B	1/17	1/33	1/19	3/69	4%
From 2B	2/8	1/22	2/23	5/53	9%
From 3B	2/3	10/17	3/11	15/31	48%
Scoring Position	4/11	11/39	5/34	20/84	24%
Scor. Pos. %	36%	28%	15%	24%	
Driving In Runners from 3B with Less than Two Out:			12/20	60%	

Loves to face: Dennis Eckersley (.524, 11-for-21)
Hates to face: Rich Gossage (0-for-7)
Hitless in 13 at bats vs. San Francisco last season.... Career batting averages: .281 vs. left-handers (one extra-base hit per 15 AB), .270 vs. right-handers (one XBH per 17 AB), yet only 13 percent of his plate appearances have been vs. left-handed pitchers.... Career batting average of .379 (11-for-29) with the bases loaded. Has never struck out with the bases full (34 PA).... Batted 155 points lower with runners on base than with the bases empty, largest difference in N.L. (minimum: 200 PA).... Batted .365 with runners on base in '84.... Career batting average of .195 with two outs and runners on base.

Jose Cruz

Houston Astros	AB	H	2B	3B	HR	RRF	BB	SO	BA	SA	OBA
Season	544	163	34	4	9	85	43	74	.300	.426	.349
vs. Left-Handed Pitchers	220	61	11	1	5	46	10	35	.277	.405	.306
vs. Right-Handed Pitchers	324	102	23	3	4	39	33	39	.315	.441	.377
Home	255	79	15	2	1	38	19	31	.310	.396	.355
Road	289	84	19	2	8	47	24	43	.291	.453	.344
Grass	173	46	11	1	5	32	13	25	.266	.428	.316
Artificial Turf	371	117	23	3	4	53	30	49	.315	.426	.365
April	81	26	3	1	0	10	4	10	.321	.383	.353
May	85	29	7	1	4	14	6	12	.341	.588	.385
June	72	18	1	0	1	7	2	18	.250	.306	.270
July	105	26	6	1	1	14	12	10	.248	.352	.322
August	101	37	11	0	0	22	8	13	.366	.475	.409
Sept./Oct.	100	27	6	1	3	18	11	11	.270	.440	.339
Leading Off Inn.	149	48	6	0	1	1	8	21	.322	.383	.357
Bases Empty	290	84	13	2	5	5	18	38	.290	.400	.331
Runners On	254	79	21	2	4	80	25	36	.311	.457	.369
Runners/Scor. Pos.	142	47	13	2	2	73	21	23	.331	.493	.410
Runners On/2 Out	117	37	8	0	2	25	14	25	.316	.436	.389
Scor. Pos./2 Out	63	20	3	0	1	21	11	16	.317	.413	.419
Late Inning Pressure	68	19	4	0	1	11	9	11	.279	.382	.364
Leading Off	14	5	1	0	0	0	0	2	.357	.429	.357
Bases Empty	36	10	3	0	0	0	2	5	.278	.361	.316
Runners On	32	9	1	0	1	11	7	6	.281	.406	.410
Runners/Scor. Pos.	12	6	1	0	1	11	6	3	.500	.833	.667

DRIVING IN RUNS	0 Out	1 Out	2 Out	Total	
From 1B	2/29	5/72	4/72	11/173	6%
From 2B	5/15	19/45	9/45	33/105	31%
From 3B	7/10	15/21	10/24	32/55	58%
Scoring Position	12/25	34/66	19/69	65/160	41%
Scor. Pos. %	48%	52%	28%	41%	
Driving In Runners from 3B with Less than Two Out:			22/31	71%	

Loves to face: Jay Tibbs (.450, 9-for-20)
Hates to face: Jeff Reardon (0-for-9)
Ground-ball hitter: 1.72 G/A ratio last season.... May batting average of .341 was tied with Bill Doran for 4th-highest in N.L.; August average of .366 ranked 3d in league.... Equaled career high mark of 34 doubles.... Astros had a record of 8–1 in games in which he hit a home run.... Has hit 28 of his last 29 home runs on the road.... Set personal high with .400 RDI percentage from scoring position; that jumped to .533 in Late-Inning Pressure Situations.... Has batted higher vs. right-handed pitchers than left-handers in eight of the past nine seasons. During that time: .268 vs. lefties, .315 vs. righties.... Has batted .429 (12-for-28, 2 HR) with the bases loaded since 1983.

Chili Davis

San Francisco Giants	AB	H	2B	3B	HR	RRF	BB	SO	BA	SA	OBA
Season	481	130	25	2	13	58	62	74	.270	.412	.349
vs. Left-Handed Pitchers	105	26	4	0	1	12	8	19	.248	.314	.296
vs. Right-Handed Pitchers	376	104	21	2	12	46	54	55	.277	.439	.363
Home	234	62	12	0	7	30	28	34	.265	.406	.335
Road	247	68	13	2	6	28	34	40	.275	.417	.363
Grass	350	92	14	1	11	42	45	53	.263	.403	.341
Artificial Turf	131	38	11	1	2	16	17	21	.290	.435	.372
April	64	17	3	0	2	14	5	14	.266	.406	.306
May	81	25	9	0	4	11	15	12	.309	.568	.417
June	98	23	2	1	1	6	6	11	.235	.306	.271
July	101	28	4	1	1	8	13	12	.277	.366	.360
August	90	24	5	0	4	15	19	17	.267	.456	.391
Sept./Oct.	47	13	2	0	1	4	4	8	.277	.383	.333
Leading Off Inn.	111	28	1	1	3	3	9	14	.252	.360	.308
Bases Empty	285	83	14	1	7	7	25	37	.291	.421	.348
Runners On	196	47	11	1	6	51	37	37	.240	.398	.350
Runners/Scor. Pos.	98	20	5	0	3	40	29	21	.204	.347	.366
Runners On/2 Out	75	19	4	1	3	18	15	14	.253	.453	.378
Scor. Pos./2 Out	44	8	2	0	1	11	11	9	.182	.295	.345
Late Inning Pressure	81	19	1	0	2	8	17	12	.235	.321	.367
Leading Off	22	7	0	0	1	1	3	1	.318	.455	.400
Bases Empty	55	13	0	0	1	1	8	7	.236	.291	.333
Runners On	26	6	1	0	1	7	9	5	.231	.385	.429
Runners/Scor. Pos.	11	4	1	0	1	7	7	3	.364	.727	.611

DRIVING IN RUNS	0 Out	1 Out	2 Out	Total	
From 1B	4/36	2/59	5/48	11/143	8%
From 2B	2/14	5/27	4/32	11/73	15%
From 3B	10/11	7/16	6/15	23/42	55%
Scoring Position	12/25	12/43	10/47	34/115	30%
Scor. Pos. %	48%	28%	21%	30%	
Driving In Runners from 3B with Less than Two Out:			17/27	63%	

Loves to face: Jesse Orosco (.615, 8-for-13, 1 HR)
Hates to face: Jeff Lahti (0-for-10)
Over the past two seasons has averaged one home run per 72.3 at bats vs. left-handers (.253 BA), one home run per 24.6 at bats vs. right-handers (.304 BA). . . . Five hits in his last seven at bats with the bases loaded. . . . Career batting averages: .337 at San Diego Stadium (8 HR in 104 AB), .325 at Riverfront Stadium; .165 at the Astrodome, .196 at Dodger Stadium. . . . Giants lost 25 of the 36 games he didn't start last season. . . . Career batting average of .361 in Late-Inning Pressure Situations with runners in scoring position. Has driven in 35.4 percent of runners in scoring position in Late-Inning Pressure Situations.

Glenn Davis

Houston Astros	AB	H	2B	3B	HR	RRF	BB	SO	BA	SA	OBA
Season	350	95	11	0	20	65	27	68	.271	.474	.332
vs. Left-Handed Pitchers	144	40	5	0	12	33	14	24	.278	.563	.346
vs. Right-Handed Pitchers	206	55	6	0	8	32	13	44	.267	.413	.323
Home	164	52	5	0	8	31	11	34	.317	.494	.367
Road	186	43	6	0	12	34	16	34	.231	.457	.303
Grass	126	27	4	0	6	20	10	18	.214	.389	.275
Artificial Turf	224	68	7	0	14	45	17	50	.304	.522	.366
April	0	0	0	0	0	0	0	0	.000	.000	.000
May	0	0	0	0	0	0	0	0	.000	.000	.000
June	47	11	0	0	1	3	2	8	.234	.298	.265
July	78	21	2	0	7	21	7	21	.269	.564	.356
August	93	24	6	0	3	15	8	13	.258	.419	.324
Sept./Oct.	132	39	3	0	9	26	10	26	.295	.523	.347
Leading Off Inn.	83	25	4	0	8	8	6	16	.301	.639	.363
Bases Empty	198	48	5	0	13	13	12	42	.242	.465	.299
Runners On	152	47	6	0	7	52	15	26	.309	.487	.374
Runners/Scor. Pos.	98	31	4	0	4	45	9	17	.316	.480	.372
Runners On/2 Out	70	16	0	0	3	18	5	15	.229	.357	.280
Scor. Pos./2 Out	52	9	0	0	1	14	3	13	.173	.231	.218
Late Inning Pressure	41	5	1	0	1	3	2	12	.122	.220	.163
Leading Off	13	3	0	0	1	1	1	1	.231	.462	.286
Bases Empty	25	3	0	0	1	1	1	6	.120	.240	.154
Runners On	16	2	1	0	0	2	1	6	.125	.188	.176
Runners/Scor. Pos.	9	2	1	0	0	2	1	3	.222	.333	.300

DRIVING IN RUNS	0 Out	1 Out	2 Out	Total	
From 1B	1/30	4/33	2/35	7/98	7%
From 2B	4/15	8/24	9/39	21/78	27%
From 3B	5/8	8/13	4/25	17/46	37%
Scoring Position	9/23	16/37	13/64	38/124	31%
Scor. Pos. %	39%	43%	20%	31%	
Driving In Runners from 3B with Less than Two Out:			13/21	62%	

Loves to face: Craig Lefferts (.571, 4-for-7, 3 2B, 1 HR)
Hates to face: Mario Soto (0-for-11, 4 SO)
Led major-league rookies in home runs (20) and RBIs (64) despite playing only 100 games. . . . Eight home runs in September were fifth most in N.L. . . . One of nine players to hit at least one home run vs. every opposing N.L. club last season. . . . Hit 12 home runs off left-handed pitchers, 2d-most in N.L. . . . Despite his name, he's not exactly Mr. Outside: career batting averages of .299 in the Astrodome, .227 in road games. . . . Late-Inning Pressure performance was nearly as bad in limited action in 1984: two hits, five strikeouts in 14 at bats. . . . Strong candidate to become first Houston player to surpass 20-home-run mark since Cesar Cedeno in 1974. Two others have hit exactly 20 since then: Cliff Johnson (1975) and Dickie Thon (1983).

Jody Davis

Chicago Cubs	AB	H	2B	3B	HR	RRF	BB	SO	BA	SA	OBA
Season	482	112	30	0	17	59	48	83	.232	.400	.300
vs. Left-Handed Pitchers	115	27	12	0	5	11	10	15	.235	.470	.291
vs. Right-Handed Pitchers	367	85	18	0	12	48	38	68	.232	.379	.302
Home	259	66	15	0	10	36	28	40	.255	.429	.325
Road	223	46	15	0	7	23	20	43	.206	.368	.269
Grass	364	87	21	0	13	42	34	56	.239	.404	.303
Artificial Turf	118	25	9	0	4	17	14	27	.212	.390	.291
April	54	15	5	0	2	4	4	8	.278	.481	.328
May	81	18	4	0	1	12	9	16	.222	.309	.293
June	68	19	6	0	3	19	6	12	.279	.500	.333
July	90	18	2	0	3	6	4	11	.200	.322	.234
August	80	14	6	0	3	6	12	11	.175	.363	.280
Sept./Oct.	109	28	7	0	5	12	13	25	.257	.459	.336
Leading Off Inn.	111	26	5	0	3	3	4	19	.234	.360	.261
Bases Empty	264	67	15	0	11	11	15	49	.254	.436	.294
Runners On	218	45	15	0	6	48	33	34	.206	.358	.306
Runners/Scor. Pos.	112	18	6	0	2	37	20	20	.161	.268	.279
Runners On/2 Out	102	14	4	0	2	14	10	19	.137	.235	.214
Scor. Pos./2 Out	63	7	1	0	2	13	6	15	.111	.222	.188
Late Inning Pressure	75	9	1	0	2	8	8	19	.120	.213	.205
Leading Off	16	3	0	0	0	0	1	6	.188	.188	.235
Bases Empty	40	5	0	0	1	1	2	11	.125	.200	.167
Runners On	35	4	1	0	1	7	6	8	.114	.229	.244
Runners/Scor. Pos.	20	3	1	0	0	5	4	4	.150	.200	.292

DRIVING IN RUNS	0 Out	1 Out	2 Out	Total	
From 1B	3/33	5/64	2/75	10/172	6%
From 2B	4/14	5/30	8/51	17/95	18%
From 3B	2/3	11/16	2/27	15/46	33%
Scoring Position	6/17	16/46	10/78	32/141	23%
Scor. Pos. %	35%	35%	13%	23%	
Driving In Runners from 3B with Less than Two Out:			13/19	68%	

Loves to face: Shane Rawley (.438, 7-for-16, 4 2B, 2 HR)
Hates to face: Steve Bedrosian (0-for-11, 6 SO)
Career batting averages of .207 with two outs and runners in scoring position, .203 in Late-Inning Pressure Situations, .185 in LIP with runners on base. . . . Has hit 48 career home runs at Wrigley Field, 28 in road games. . . . Higher batting average vs. left-handed pitchers than right-handed pitchers in all five major-league seasons. Career marks: .279 vs. lefties, .246 vs. righties. . . . Hitless in nine at bats with two outs and the bases loaded last season. Had four hits in seven at bats in the same situation in 1984. . . . Career batting averages: .354 at Dodger Stadium, .175 at the Astrodome.

Andre Dawson

Montreal Expos	AB	H	2B	3B	HR	RRF	BB	SO	BA	SA	OBA
Season	529	135	27	2	23	95	29	92	.255	.444	.295
vs. Left-Handed Pitchers	167	46	8	1	10	33	6	28	.275	.515	.303
vs. Right-Handed Pitchers	362	89	19	1	13	62	23	64	.246	.412	.292
Home	253	63	8	1	11	44	17	44	.249	.419	.297
Road	276	72	19	1	12	51	12	48	.261	.467	.294
Grass	155	44	11	1	8	36	4	27	.284	.523	.301
Artificial Turf	374	91	16	1	15	59	25	65	.243	.412	.293
April	70	23	2	0	5	13	3	8	.329	.571	.365
May	98	23	9	0	2	17	7	14	.235	.388	.280
June	61	13	3	0	2	10	1	14	.213	.361	.238
July	87	24	3	0	1	9	6	15	.276	.345	.333
August	104	30	7	1	4	23	4	17	.288	.490	.306
Sept./Oct.	109	22	3	1	9	23	8	24	.202	.495	.254
Leading Off Inn.	99	19	5	0	3	3	3	16	.192	.333	.223
Bases Empty	278	63	13	2	9	9	7	46	.227	.385	.248
Runners On	251	72	14	0	14	86	22	46	.287	.510	.343
Runners/Scor. Pos.	154	51	10	0	10	76	18	26	.331	.591	.392
Runners On/2 Out	76	25	9	0	4	33	10	15	.329	.605	.407
Scor. Pos./2 Out	54	20	7	0	2	28	8	12	.370	.611	.452
Late Inning Pressure	81	21	7	0	2	15	7	20	.259	.420	.315
Leading Off	24	5	1	0	1	1	1	7	.208	.375	.240
Bases Empty	38	10	3	0	1	1	1	8	.263	.421	.282
Runners On	43	11	4	0	1	14	6	12	.256	.419	.340
Runners/Scor. Pos.	30	8	4	0	1	14	5	9	.267	.500	.361

DRIVING IN RUNS	0 Out	1 Out	2 Out	Total	
From 1B	1/49	4/76	5/42	10/167	6%
From 2B	7/31	12/52	14/39	33/122	27%
From 3B	12/18	7/22	10/26	29/66	44%
Scoring Position	19/49	19/74	24/65	62/188	33%
Scor. Pos. %	39%	26%	37%	33%	
Driving In Runners from 3B with Less than Two Out:			19/40	48%	

Loves to face: Shane Rawley (.435, 10-for-23, 3 2B, 4 HR)
Hates to face: Dennis Eckersley (.077, 2-for-26)
Fly-ball hitter: 0.95 G/A ratio last season. . . . Has batted higher in day games than night games in each of his 10 major-league seasons. Last season: .332 in day games, .207 in night games. Career batting averages: .307 and .263. . . . Last season, Dawson averaged one home run per 12.8 at bats in daylight, compared to one every 46.3 at bats at night. . . . Six RBIs in 5th inning at Wrigley Field on Sept. 24 tied major-league record for RBIs in an inning. . . . Career batting averages: .347 at Wrigley, .325 in Atlanta (with 14 HR in 212 AB). . . . Career batting averages: .300 on grass fields, .272 on artificial turf. . . . Hit 15 of his 23 home runs against three clubs: Cardinals (6), Cubs (5), and Pirates (4). Only four of his homers were hit against Western Division teams.

Bob Dernier

Chicago Cubs	AB	H	2B	3B	HR	RRF	BB	SO	BA	SA	OBA
Season	469	119	20	3	1	22	40	44	.254	.316	.315
vs. Left-Handed Pitchers	118	34	6	2	0	11	11	8	.288	.373	.348
vs. Right-Handed Pitchers	351	85	14	1	1	11	29	36	.242	.296	.303
Home	230	64	12	1	1	9	16	20	.278	.352	.328
Road	239	55	8	2	0	13	24	24	.230	.280	.302
Grass	345	86	18	1	1	17	25	32	.249	.316	.303
Artificial Turf	124	33	2	2	0	5	15	12	.266	.315	.345
April	62	16	1	0	0	1	7	6	.258	.274	.333
May	106	27	6	1	0	8	9	14	.255	.330	.316
June	26	8	0	1	0	1	1	4	.308	.385	.333
July	53	10	3	0	0	5	5	4	.189	.245	.254
August	95	24	4	0	1	2	5	8	.253	.326	.287
Sept./Oct.	127	34	6	1	0	5	13	8	.268	.331	.345
Leading Off Inn.	189	49	10	1	0	0	13	17	.259	.323	.307
Bases Empty	336	88	15	2	1	1	23	33	.262	.327	.313
Runners On	133	31	5	1	0	21	17	11	.233	.286	.318
Runners/Scor. Pos.	77	16	3	1	0	21	15	8	.208	.273	.333
Runners On/2 Out	68	13	3	1	0	10	9	5	.191	.265	.286
Scor. Pos./2 Out	46	8	2	1	0	10	8	3	.174	.261	.296
Late Inning Pressure	57	15	1	0	0	2	9	6	.263	.281	.364
Leading Off	15	4	0	0	0	0	1	0	.267	.267	.313
Bases Empty	38	10	0	0	0	0	3	5	.263	.263	.317
Runners On	19	5	1	0	0	2	6	1	.263	.316	.440
Runners/Scor. Pos.	12	2	0	0	0	2	6	1	.167	.167	.444

DRIVING IN RUNS	0 Out	1 Out	2 Out	Total	
From 1B	0/21	0/24	0/44	0/89	0%
From 2B	1/5	4/21	5/38	10/64	16%
From 3B	1/3	5/8	5/15	11/26	42%
Scoring Position	2/8	9/29	10/53	21/90	23%
Scor. Pos. %	25%	31%	19%	23%	
Driving In Runners from 3B with Less than Two Out:			6/11	55%	

Loves to face: Len Barker (.625, 5-for-8)
Hates to face: Charles Hudson (.042, 1-for-24)
Ground-ball hitter: 1.40 G/A ratio last season. . . . Fewest RBIs (21) of any major leaguer to qualify for 1985 batting championship. . . . After committing 13 errors in his first 458 games in the outfield, Dernier committed eight errors in 30 games from August 31 to October 4. . . . First four major-league home runs were hit off left-handed pitchers (all in 1982). Since then, all five home runs have come against right-handers. . . . Did not drive in any runners from first base in 89 opportunities last season, largest oh-fer in N.L. . . . Career batting average of .178 at Shea Stadium. . . . Career batting average of .167 with bases loaded.

Bo Diaz

Phillies/Reds	AB	H	2B	3B	HR	RRF	BB	SO	BA	SA	OBA
Season	237	58	13	1	5	36	21	25	.245	.371	.307
vs. Left-Handed Pitchers	60	14	5	1	0	13	9	2	.233	.350	.329
vs. Right-Handed Pitchers	177	44	8	0	5	23	12	23	.249	.379	.298
Home	103	31	7	0	4	23	8	12	.301	.485	.354
Road	134	27	6	1	1	13	13	13	.201	.284	.270
Grass	66	18	4	0	1	8	6	4	.273	.379	.333
Artificial Turf	171	40	9	1	4	28	15	21	.234	.368	.296
April	13	2	0	0	0	3	0	1	.154	.154	.154
May	0	0	0	0	0	0	0	0	.000	.000	.000
June	35	6	3	0	0	7	2	3	.171	.257	.216
July	24	8	2	1	2	9	4	3	.333	.750	.429
August	74	15	3	0	0	5	7	11	.203	.243	.272
Sept./Oct.	91	27	5	0	3	12	8	7	.297	.451	.353
Leading Off Inn.	72	13	2	0	2	2	4	7	.181	.292	.224
Bases Empty	141	32	5	1	4	4	13	16	.227	.362	.292
Runners On	96	26	8	0	1	32	8	9	.271	.385	.327
Runners/Scor. Pos.	54	19	5	0	0	29	4	6	.352	.444	.393
Runners On/2 Out	42	10	1	0	1	11	5	5	.238	.333	.333
Scor. Pos./2 Out	25	8	1	0	0	9	3	3	.320	.360	.414
Late Inning Pressure	41	11	1	1	1	4	5	5	.268	.415	.348
Leading Off	15	2	0	0	1	1	0	3	.133	.333	.133
Bases Empty	28	9	1	1	1	1	3	4	.321	.536	.387
Runners On	13	2	0	0	0	3	2	1	.154	.154	.267
Runners/Scor. Pos.	7	1	0	0	0	3	2	1	.143	.143	.333

DRIVING IN RUNS	0 Out	1 Out	2 Out	Total	
From 1B	1/16	0/27	1/31	2/74	3%
From 2B	2/6	7/20	3/16	12/42	29%
From 3B	3/4	8/8	6/13	17/25	68%
Scoring Position	5/10	15/28	9/29	29/67	43%
Scor. Pos. %	50%	54%	31%	43%	
Driving In Runners from 3B with Less than Two Out:			11/12	92%	

Loves to face: Lee Smith (.600, 6-for-10)
Hates to face: Nolan Ryan (0-for-18)
Ground-ball hitter: 1.41 G/A ratio last season. . . . Had career high batting average (.352) with runners in scoring position last season. . . . Drove in 52.6% of runners from scoring position with less than two outs, 6th-highest average in 11-year history of *The Player Analysis* (minimum: 20 RRF). . . . Last nine home runs have been hit off right-handed pitchers. Last homer vs. a left-hander: August 18, 1983, off Gary Lucas. . . . Career batting averages: .359 at Wrigley Field, .148 at Dodger Stadium. . . . Grounded into 11 double plays in 47 opportunities last season, 4th-highest average among N.L. players (minimum: 5 GIDP).

Bill Doran

Houston Astros	AB	H	2B	3B	HR	RRF	BB	SO	BA	SA	OBA
Season	578	166	31	6	14	60	71	69	.287	.434	.362
vs. Left-Handed Pitchers	217	65	14	3	5	24	30	28	.300	.461	.383
vs. Right-Handed Pitchers	361	101	17	3	9	36	41	41	.280	.418	.350
Home	269	76	20	5	5	28	40	29	.283	.450	.372
Road	309	90	11	1	9	32	31	40	.291	.421	.354
Grass	183	60	7	1	6	24	22	24	.328	.475	.396
Artificial Turf	395	106	24	5	8	36	49	45	.268	.415	.347
April	70	17	5	0	0	3	11	9	.243	.314	.346
May	85	29	3	1	3	7	11	9	.341	.506	.412
June	116	29	4	0	4	14	12	12	.250	.388	.318
July	105	33	9	0	1	11	8	14	.314	.429	.357
August	102	32	7	2	5	18	14	12	.314	.569	.397
Sept./Oct.	100	26	3	3	1	7	15	13	.260	.380	.353
Leading Off Inn.	244	67	13	1	4	4	21	29	.275	.385	.332
Bases Empty	383	108	24	4	9	9	41	47	.282	.436	.351
Runners On	195	58	7	2	5	51	30	22	.297	.431	.383
Runners/Scor. Pos.	108	30	4	2	2	44	26	13	.278	.407	.403
Runners On/2 Out	92	28	3	1	2	21	19	11	.304	.424	.423
Scor. Pos./2 Out	61	17	2	1	2	21	18	7	.279	.443	.443
Late Inning Pressure	77	16	4	0	2	13	9	15	.208	.338	.284
Leading Off	14	2	0	0	0	0	4	3	.143	.143	.333
Bases Empty	39	11	3	0	1	1	7	10	.282	.436	.391
Runners On	38	5	1	0	1	12	2	5	.132	.237	.167
Runners/Scor. Pos.	21	4	0	0	1	11	1	3	.190	.333	.208

DRIVING IN RUNS	0 Out	1 Out	2 Out	Total	
From 1B	3/27	2/55	2/56	7/138	5%
From 2B	1/11	7/29	9/51	17/91	19%
From 3B	1/2	13/20	8/21	22/43	51%
Scoring Position	2/13	20/49	17/72	39/134	29%
Scor. Pos. %	15%	41%	24%	29%	
Driving In Runners from 3B with Less than Two Out:			14/22	64%	

Loves to face: John Franco (.857, 6-for-7)
Hates to face: Mario Soto (.098, 4-for-41, 6 SO)
Batting average of .341 during month of May was tied with Jose Cruz for 4th-highest in N.L. . . . Batted .426 last season vs. New York. . . . Career batting averages: .302 on grass, .261 on artificial surfaces, .259 in the Astrodome. . . . Career batting average of .464 (26-for-56) at Wrigley Field. . . . Year-by-year road-game batting averages since 1983: .292, .288, .292. . . . Has not drawn a walk in 31 career plate appearances with the bases loaded. . . . Career batting average of .196 in Late-Inning Pressure Situations with runners on base, .175 in LIP with runners in scoring position. . . . Only player with four extra-base hits against Dwight Gooden.

Dan Driessen

Expos/Giants	AB	H	2B	3B	HR	RRF	BB	SO	BA	SA	OBA
Season	493	120	26	0	9	49	50	51	.243	.351	.314
vs. Left-Handed Pitchers	95	27	6	0	1	9	5	12	.284	.379	.317
vs. Right-Handed Pitchers	398	93	20	0	8	40	45	39	.234	.344	.313
Home	262	61	14	0	4	29	30	27	.233	.332	.308
Road	231	59	12	0	5	20	20	24	.255	.372	.320
Grass	214	56	11	0	7	23	21	19	.262	.411	.326
Artificial Turf	279	64	15	0	2	26	29	32	.229	.305	.304
April	64	19	6	0	2	6	7	6	.297	.484	.366
May	84	21	3	0	3	10	9	5	.250	.393	.323
June	80	18	4	0	1	9	8	10	.225	.313	.289
July	84	20	5	0	0	2	9	8	.238	.298	.326
August	86	17	4	0	2	9	6	13	.198	.314	.250
Sept./Oct.	95	25	4	0	1	13	11	9	.263	.337	.336
Leading Off Inn.	123	39	8	0	7	7	11	11	.317	.553	.378
Bases Empty	270	73	19	0	8	8	21	28	.270	.430	.325
Runners On	223	47	7	0	1	41	29	23	.211	.256	.301
Runners/Scor. Pos.	138	27	2	0	1	38	22	13	.196	.232	.301
Runners On/2 Out	115	27	3	0	0	13	13	11	.235	.261	.318
Scor. Pos./2 Out	71	15	1	0	0	11	11	7	.211	.225	.317
Late Inning Pressure	69	23	2	0	2	9	10	3	.333	.449	.413
Leading Off	19	8	1	0	2	2	1	2	.421	.789	.450
Bases Empty	42	17	2	0	2	2	7	2	.405	.595	.490
Runners On	27	6	0	0	0	7	3	1	.222	.222	.290
Runners/Scor. Pos.	16	4	0	0	0	6	2	1	.250	.250	.316

DRIVING IN RUNS	0 Out	1 Out	2 Out	Total	
From 1B	0/23	1/61	2/71	3/155	2%
From 2B	5/14	2/38	6/52	13/104	13%
From 3B	5/8	14/25	5/21	24/54	44%
Scoring Position	10/22	16/63	11/73	37/158	23%
Scor. Pos. %	45%	25%	15%	23%	
Driving In Runners from 3B with Less than Two Out:			19/33	58%	

Loves to face: Jeff Dedmon (.500, 5-for-10, 1 HR)
Hates to face: Fernando Valenzuela (.091, 3-for-33)
Batted .269 in day games, .224 in night games. . . . Hitless in his 23 at bats as a pinch-hitter since April 8, 1984. Was hitless in 12 pinch-hit at bats while with the Expos. . . . Batted .381 in five games vs. Montreal after being traded to the Giants. . . . Three hits in his last 28 at bats with the bases loaded. . . . Last season's .284 mark against left-handed pitchers was his highest vs. southpaws since batting .294 in 1981. He hit .195 vs. lefties during three intervening seasons. . . . Has hit 62 of his last 69 home runs off right-handed pitchers. . . . RDI percentage of .234 from scoring position was his personal low during 11-year *Player Analysis* history.

Mariano Duncan

Los Angeles Dodgers	AB	H	2B	3B	HR	RRF	BB	SO	BA	SA	OBA
Season	562	137	24	6	6	44	38	113	.244	.340	.293
vs. Left-Handed Pitchers	182	52	10	2	4	16	12	35	.286	.429	.332
vs. Right-Handed Pitchers	380	85	14	4	2	28	26	78	.224	.297	.275
Home	275	66	13	2	1	17	16	53	.240	.313	.286
Road	287	71	11	4	5	27	22	60	.247	.366	.300
Grass	417	100	17	4	4	33	26	80	.240	.329	.287
Artificial Turf	145	37	7	2	2	11	12	33	.255	.372	.310
April	62	16	4	0	2	2	5	10	.258	.419	.313
May	62	15	2	0	0	2	5	23	.242	.274	.299
June	95	22	5	0	0	4	6	11	.232	.284	.272
July	89	21	5	2	1	7	3	17	.236	.371	.277
August	114	31	3	2	2	10	4	24	.272	.386	.297
Sept./Oct.	140	32	5	2	1	19	15	28	.229	.314	.304
Leading Off Inn.	204	46	5	1	1	1	19	46	.225	.275	.298
Bases Empty	382	92	18	3	3	3	27	79	.241	.327	.294
Runners On	180	45	6	3	3	41	11	34	.250	.367	.291
Runners/Scor. Pos.	110	25	2	2	2	36	8	20	.227	.336	.270
Runners On/2 Out	66	13	2	2	2	16	5	11	.197	.379	.254
Scor. Pos./2 Out	53	10	2	1	2	15	5	8	.189	.377	.259
Late Inning Pressure	60	11	1	1	1	4	4	17	.183	.283	.242
Leading Off	17	2	1	0	0	0	3	3	.118	.176	.250
Bases Empty	34	6	1	0	1	1	4	9	.176	.294	.263
Runners On	26	5	0	1	0	3	0	8	.192	.269	.214
Runners/Scor. Pos.	14	0	0	0	0	2	0	4	.000	.000	.000

DRIVING IN RUNS	0 Out	1 Out	2 Out	Total	
From 1B	0/38	4/53	3/41	7/132	5%
From 2B	2/12	8/38	7/46	17/96	18%
From 3B	4/7	6/19	4/22	14/48	29%
Scoring Position	6/19	14/57	11/68	31/144	22%
Scor. Pos. %	32%	25%	16%	22%	
Driving In Runners from 3B with Less than Two Out:			10/26	38%	

Loves to face: Dave Dravecky (.636, 7-for-11, 1 HR)
Hates to face: Mike Scott (.067, 1-for-15)
Had lowest fielding percentage (.954) of any N.L. shortstop (minimum: 100 games); ranked in the middle of the pack (7th of 16) in assists per nine innings with 3.26 (minimum: 300 innings). . . . Batted .280 in day games, .229 in night games. . . . Successful in 83 percent (38 of 46) of his attempted steals last season. Only Bruce Benedict was able to catch him twice. . . . Dodgers won all six games in which he hit a home run. . . . Batted 14 times without a hit in Late-Inning Pressure Situations with runners in scoring position, highest total in majors last season, and drove in only two of 12 runners from scoring position in those at bats.

Shawon Dunston

Chicago Cubs	AB	H	2B	3B	HR	RRF	BB	SO	BA	SA	OBA
Season	250	65	12	4	4	18	19	42	.260	.388	.310
vs. Left-Handed Pitchers	45	10	3	0	1	4	2	5	.222	.356	.255
vs. Right-Handed Pitchers	205	55	9	4	3	14	17	37	.268	.395	.321
Home	147	44	7	3	3	8	15	25	.299	.449	.362
Road	103	21	5	1	1	10	4	17	.204	.301	.231
Grass	165	45	8	3	3	8	15	30	.273	.412	.331
Artificial Turf	85	20	4	1	1	10	4	12	.235	.341	.267
April	48	11	3	1	0	2	2	3	.229	.333	.260
May	24	3	1	0	1	2	5	10	.125	.292	.276
June	0	0	0	0	0	0	0	0	.000	.000	.000
July	0	0	0	0	0	0	0	0	.000	.000	.000
August	47	9	1	1	0	3	0	6	.191	.255	.191
Sept./Oct.	131	42	7	2	3	11	12	23	.321	.473	.372
Leading Off Inn.	59	18	3	2	1	1	3	10	.305	.475	.339
Bases Empty	153	39	9	4	3	3	8	26	.255	.425	.292
Runners On	97	26	3	0	1	15	11	16	.268	.330	.336
Runners/Scor. Pos.	43	10	1	0	0	13	8	9	.233	.256	.340
Runners On/2 Out	34	6	1	0	0	3	4	6	.176	.206	.263
Scor. Pos./2 Out	15	2	0	0	0	3	4	3	.133	.133	.316
Late Inning Pressure	23	5	1	0	0	1	1	4	.217	.261	.240
Leading Off	7	2	1	0	0	0	1	0	.286	.429	.375
Bases Empty	15	3	1	0	0	0	1	2	.200	.267	.250
Runners On	8	2	0	0	0	1	0	2	.250	.250	.222
Runners/Scor. Pos.	2	1	0	0	0	1	0	1	.500	.500	.333

DRIVING IN RUNS	0 Out	1 Out	2 Out	Total	
From 1B	0/27	1/22	0/30	1/79	1%
From 2B	1/8	2/19	2/15	5/42	12%
From 3B	1/2	6/10	1/4	8/16	50%
Scoring Position	2/10	8/29	3/19	13/58	22%
Scor. Pos. %	20%	28%	16%	22%	
Driving In Runners from 3B with Less than Two Out:			7/12	58%	

Loves to face: John Denny (.500, 5-for-10, 1 2B, 2 3B)
Hates to face: Dave Shipanoff (0-for-5, 4 SO)
Ground-ball hitter: 1.48 G/A ratio last season. . . . Batted .350 vs. ground-ball pitchers last season, .173 vs. fly-ball pitchers. . . . Youngest batter to appear on an N.L. opening day roster. . . . September batting average of .330 was 11th-highest in N.L. . . . Batted .286 in day games, .200 in night games. . . . Committed nine errors in 23 games before his demotion in May, eight errors in 51 games after being recalled in August. . . . Averaged 3.72 assists per nine innings last season, highest rate among N.L. shortstops (minimum: 300 innings).

Leon Durham

Chicago Cubs	AB	H	2B	3B	HR	RRF	BB	SO	BA	SA	OBA
Season	542	153	32	2	21	79	64	99	.282	.465	.357
vs. Left-Handed Pitchers	127	34	8	0	4	24	14	31	.268	.425	.340
vs. Right-Handed Pitchers	415	119	24	2	17	55	50	68	.287	.477	.363
Home	257	85	21	1	15	52	37	34	.331	.595	.414
Road	285	68	11	1	6	27	27	65	.239	.347	.304
Grass	378	116	26	1	16	58	48	55	.307	.508	.384
Artificial Turf	164	37	6	1	5	21	16	44	.226	.366	.294
April	52	13	3	0	2	6	3	10	.250	.423	.291
May	88	21	3	1	4	14	13	18	.239	.432	.337
June	104	34	7	0	2	15	10	16	.327	.452	.383
July	98	27	7	0	3	9	15	13	.276	.439	.372
August	76	26	4	1	4	12	8	15	.342	.579	.405
Sept./Oct.	124	32	8	0	6	23	15	27	.258	.468	.338
Leading Off Inn.	119	30	9	0	4	4	12	26	.252	.429	.321
Bases Empty	308	89	20	1	12	12	21	56	.289	.477	.334
Runners On	234	64	12	1	9	67	43	43	.274	.449	.385
Runners/Scor. Pos.	140	40	8	1	8	63	37	29	.286	.529	.433
Runners On/2 Out	116	32	6	1	5	33	24	18	.276	.474	.400
Scor. Pos./2 Out	70	20	4	1	4	31	24	15	.286	.543	.468
Late Inning Pressure	82	21	7	0	4	16	7	16	.256	.488	.315
Leading Off	18	5	3	0	0	0	1	3	.278	.444	.316
Bases Empty	47	11	3	0	1	1	1	8	.234	.362	.250
Runners On	35	10	4	0	3	15	6	8	.286	.657	.390
Runners/Scor. Pos.	20	6	3	0	3	14	6	5	.300	.900	.462

DRIVING IN RUNS	0 Out	1 Out	2 Out	Total	
From 1B	2/37	2/50	5/83	9/170	5%
From 2B	7/25	5/28	13/48	25/101	25%
From 3B	3/7	11/17	10/29	24/53	45%
Scoring Position	10/32	16/45	23/77	49/154	32%
Scor. Pos. %	31%	36%	30%	32%	
Driving In Runners from 3B with Less than Two Out:			14/24	58%	

Loves to face: Pascual Perez (.429, 9-for-21, 6 HR)
Hates to face: Bob Forsch (.048, 1-for-21)
Also loves to face the man the Cubs gave up to get him, Bruce Sutter (.467, 7-for-15, 3 HR). . . . June batting average of .327 was 7th-highest in N.L. . . . Career batting average of .301 with runners in scoring position. . . . Has 12 hits in 22 at bats with the bases loaded since 1983. Batted seven times with two outs and the bases loaded last season: 3-for-3 with four walks. . . . Has hit a home run at every current National League stadium except Dodger Stadium (96 career AB). . . . Has .311 career batting average, 61 home runs at Wrigley Field; .261 average, 35 home runs elsewhere. . . . Has hit 82 of 96 career home runs vs. right-handed pitchers.

Len Dykstra

New York Mets	AB	H	2B	3B	HR	RRF	BB	SO	BA	SA	OBA
Season	236	60	9	3	1	19	30	24	.254	.331	.338
vs. Left-Handed Pitchers	56	15	3	0	0	5	6	7	.268	.321	.349
vs. Right-Handed Pitchers	180	45	6	3	1	14	24	17	.250	.333	.335
Home	109	26	4	1	0	8	14	12	.239	.294	.323
Road	127	34	5	2	1	11	16	12	.268	.362	.352
Grass	169	41	6	3	0	13	23	17	.243	.314	.330
Artificial Turf	67	19	3	0	1	6	7	7	.284	.373	.360
April	0	0	0	0	0	0	0	0	.000	.000	.000
May	13	5	0	0	1	3	0	1	.385	.615	.385
June	17	3	0	1	0	1	1	6	.176	.294	.222
July	106	25	4	0	0	11	13	10	.236	.274	.320
August	76	21	3	1	0	3	11	6	.276	.342	.368
Sept./Oct.	24	6	2	1	0	1	5	1	.250	.417	.379
Leading Off Inn.	83	20	4	0	0	0	11	11	.241	.289	.330
Bases Empty	144	39	6	1	0	0	21	18	.271	.326	.367
Runners On	92	21	3	2	1	19	9	6	.228	.337	.291
Runners/Scor. Pos.	58	12	2	1	0	16	6	3	.207	.276	.273
Runners On/2 Out	46	15	2	2	0	9	7	2	.326	.457	.415
Scor. Pos./2 Out	34	9	1	1	0	8	5	2	.265	.353	.359
Late Inning Pressure	28	8	3	0	0	3	2	4	.286	.393	.323
Leading Off	8	2	1	0	0	0	2	0	.250	.375	.400
Bases Empty	17	4	2	0	0	0	2	4	.235	.353	.316
Runners On	11	4	1	0	0	3	0	0	.364	.455	.333
Runners/Scor. Pos.	6	2	1	0	0	3	0	0	.333	.500	.286

DRIVING IN RUNS	0 Out	1 Out	2 Out	Total	
From 1B	0/12	1/17	1/24	2/53	4%
From 2B	0/4	2/15	4/29	6/48	13%
From 3B	1/1	5/9	4/12	10/22	45%
Scoring Position	1/5	7/24	8/41	16/70	23%
Scor. Pos. %	20%	29%	20%	23%	
Driving In Runners from 3B with Less than Two Out:			6/10	60%	

Loves to face: Bob Knepper (.500, 3-for-6)
Hates to face: Derek Botelho (0-for-6)
Mets were 21 games above the .500 mark with Dykstra starting and batting leadoff, compared to 14 above with Mookie Wilson, and one above with Wally Backman. . . . Collected the bulk of his 19 RBIs vs. Atlanta (7) and Cincinnati (6). . . . Averaged 2.84 putouts per nine innings last season, 3d-highest rate among N.L. outfielders (minimum: 300 innings). . . . Got his home run in second major-league at bat, vs. Mario Soto on May 3. Finished season with a streak of 234 consecutive at bats without a home run. . . . Batted .326 with two outs and runners on base, .130 with less than two outs and runners on base.

Nick Esasky

Cincinnati Reds	AB	H	2B	3B	HR	RRF	BB	SO	BA	SA	OBA
Season	413	108	21	0	21	70	41	102	.262	.465	.332
vs. Left-Handed Pitchers	141	42	10	0	7	22	17	31	.298	.518	.375
vs. Right-Handed Pitchers	272	66	11	0	14	48	24	71	.243	.438	.309
Home	196	45	13	0	7	29	12	45	.230	.403	.276
Road	217	63	8	0	14	41	29	57	.290	.521	.378
Grass	138	41	6	0	9	27	21	39	.297	.536	.398
Artificial Turf	275	67	15	0	12	43	20	63	.244	.429	.297
April	60	16	5	0	3	12	7	16	.267	.500	.338
May	72	14	3	0	1	13	10	15	.194	.278	.289
June	35	12	2	0	1	5	9	8	.343	.486	.500
July	31	8	2	0	3	6	2	9	.258	.613	.303
August	108	31	4	0	7	15	6	24	.287	.519	.330
Sept./Oct.	107	27	5	0	6	19	7	30	.252	.467	.302
Leading Off Inn.	117	29	4	0	5	5	10	28	.248	.410	.313
Bases Empty	232	61	11	0	11	11	24	64	.263	.453	.337
Runners On	181	47	10	0	10	59	17	38	.260	.481	.325
Runners/Scor. Pos.	112	32	8	0	7	52	13	27	.286	.545	.357
Runners On/2 Out	72	17	3	0	4	19	7	21	.236	.444	.321
Scor. Pos./2 Out	46	9	1	0	2	14	6	17	.196	.348	.302
Late Inning Pressure	76	16	1	0	6	13	7	24	.211	.461	.274
Leading Off	25	3	0	0	1	1	1	10	.120	.240	.154
Bases Empty	46	8	1	0	3	3	3	19	.174	.391	.224
Runners On	30	8	0	0	3	10	4	5	.267	.567	.343
Runners/Scor. Pos.	19	6	0	0	3	10	3	4	.316	.789	.391

DRIVING IN RUNS	0 Out	1 Out	2 Out	Total	
From 1B	3/34	2/47	4/48	9/129	7%
From 2B	8/24	6/32	7/29	21/85	25%
From 3B	6/6	9/19	4/23	19/48	40%
Scoring Position	14/30	15/51	11/52	40/133	30%
Scor. Pos. %	47%	29%	21%	30%	
Driving In Runners from 3B with Less than Two Out:			15/25	60%	

Loves to face: Fernando Valenzuela (.429, 9-for-21)
Hates to face: Jose DeLeon (0-for-14, 8 SO)
Batted .218 in day games, .286 in night games. Career averages: .218 and .251.... Batted .474 with four homers and 15 RBIs in 14 games vs. Atlanta last season.... Career statistics at Atlanta Stadium are a .459 batting average, .967 slugging average, .553 on-base average, and 8 home runs in 61 AB.... Other ballparks: 3-for-33 at Wrigley Field, 3-for-28 at Shea Stadium. No homers at either.... Hit two extra-inning home runs last season.... Career batting averages: .287 vs. left-handed pitchers, .217 vs. right-handers.... Career batting average of .298 in Late-Inning Pressure Situations with runners in scoring position.

Mike Fitzgerald

Montreal Expos	AB	H	2B	3B	HR	RRF	BB	SO	BA	SA	OBA
Season	295	61	7	1	5	35	38	55	.207	.288	.297
vs. Left-Handed Pitchers	97	23	3	0	0	7	15	17	.237	.268	.336
vs. Right-Handed Pitchers	198	38	4	1	5	28	23	38	.192	.298	.278
Home	163	27	2	1	3	15	19	32	.166	.245	.253
Road	132	34	5	0	2	20	19	23	.258	.341	.351
Grass	55	16	1	0	2	11	7	7	.291	.418	.365
Artificial Turf	240	45	6	1	3	24	31	48	.188	.258	.282
April	52	14	3	0	0	6	11	8	.269	.327	.397
May	67	12	0	0	0	6	9	11	.179	.179	.282
June	51	9	0	0	3	4	4	14	.176	.353	.236
July	67	11	2	0	2	10	8	12	.164	.284	.260
August	52	14	2	1	0	8	6	9	.269	.346	.333
Sept./Oct.	6	1	0	0	0	1	0	1	.167	.167	.143
Leading Off Inn.	75	17	1	0	2	2	6	17	.227	.320	.284
Bases Empty	180	36	3	1	5	5	12	41	.200	.311	.258
Runners On	115	25	4	0	0	30	26	14	.217	.252	.349
Runners/Scor. Pos.	63	15	3	0	0	29	24	12	.238	.286	.424
Runners On/2 Out	41	8	2	0	0	10	18	3	.195	.244	.441
Scor. Pos./2 Out	23	7	2	0	0	10	16	3	.304	.391	.590
Late Inning Pressure	38	8	0	0	1	3	3	8	.211	.289	.268
Leading Off	10	5	0	0	1	1	1	3	.500	.800	.545
Bases Empty	24	7	0	0	1	1	2	6	.292	.417	.346
Runners On	14	1	0	0	0	2	1	2	.071	.071	.133
Runners/Scor. Pos.	8	1	0	0	0	2	1	2	.125	.125	.222

DRIVING IN RUNS	0 Out	1 Out	2 Out	Total	
From 1B	0/20	2/34	1/29	3/83	4%
From 2B	2/8	3/25	3/14	8/47	17%
From 3B	6/9	7/12	6/14	19/35	54%
Scoring Position	8/17	10/37	9/28	27/82	33%
Scor. Pos. %	47%	27%	32%	33%	
Driving In Runners from 3B with Less than Two Out:			13/21	62%	

Loves to face: Bruce Sutter (.750, 3-for-4, 1 2B, 1 HR)
Hates to face: Steve Bedrosian (0-for-11)
Batted .095 vs. New York last season, his worst average vs. any N.L. opponent.... Career batting average of .203 at Shea Stadium.... Even worse at Olympic Stadium (.169).... Batted .247 in day games, .188 in night games last season.... Career batting average of .328 with two outs and runners in scoring position.... Only two home runs and no triples in 243 career at bats vs. left-handed pitchers.... Career RDI percentage of .544 from third base, .316 from scoring position, both well above N.L. averages (.439 and .273 respectively).... Expos were 17 games above .500 in games he started, 10 games below with other starting catchers.

Tim Flannery

San Diego Padres	AB	H	2B	3B	HR	RRF	BB	SO	BA	SA	OBA
Season	384	108	14	3	1	40	58	39	.281	.341	.386
vs. Left-Handed Pitchers	37	6	1	1	0	1	4	4	.162	.243	.262
vs. Right-Handed Pitchers	347	102	13	2	1	39	54	35	.294	.352	.399
Home	165	45	5	1	1	17	30	17	.273	.333	.402
Road	219	63	9	2	0	23	28	22	.288	.347	.373
Grass	263	76	8	2	1	26	38	22	.289	.346	.394
Artificial Turf	121	32	6	1	0	14	20	17	.264	.331	.369
April	29	9	1	0	0	1	2	0	.310	.345	.375
May	67	18	5	1	0	8	9	5	.269	.373	.364
June	65	16	1	2	1	9	10	6	.246	.369	.388
July	83	25	4	0	0	7	13	10	.301	.349	.398
August	73	23	3	0	0	10	9	9	.315	.356	.398
Sept./Oct.	67	17	0	0	0	5	15	9	.254	.254	.386
Leading Off Inn.	144	27	4	0	0	0	25	15	.188	.215	.320
Bases Empty	255	63	9	0	0	0	46	26	.247	.282	.375
Runners On	129	45	5	3	1	40	12	13	.349	.457	.411
Runners/Scor. Pos.	87	31	2	3	1	38	8	9	.356	.483	.414
Runners On/2 Out	71	27	2	1	1	21	4	10	.380	.479	.429
Scor. Pos./2 Out	54	18	1	1	1	21	3	9	.333	.444	.390
Late Inning Pressure	68	17	3	1	0	3	10	10	.250	.324	.350
Leading Off	24	4	1	0	0	0	2	6	.167	.208	.231
Bases Empty	48	12	3	0	0	0	7	8	.250	.313	.345
Runners On	20	5	0	1	0	3	3	2	.250	.350	.360
Runners/Scor. Pos.	13	3	0	1	0	3	1	1	.231	.385	.313

DRIVING IN RUNS	0 Out	1 Out	2 Out	Total	
From 1B	1/16	2/25	0/40	3/81	4%
From 2B	3/7	2/23	13/45	18/75	24%
From 3B	3/3	8/12	7/17	18/32	56%
Scoring Position	6/10	10/35	20/62	36/107	34%
Scor. Pos. %	60%	29%	32%	34%	
Driving In Runners from 3B with Less than Two Out:			11/15	73%	

Loves to face: Ed Lynch (.714, 5-for-7, 1 HR)
Hates to face: Mario Soto (.111, 2-for-18, 8 SO)
Batted .279 in 101 games started, .320 (8-for-25) in 25 games off the bench.... Set career highs in batting average, games, at bats, runs, hits, doubles, and RBIs.... Batted 102 points higher with runners on base than with the bases empty, 5th-largest difference in N.L. (minimum: 200 PA).... Career batting averages: .149 vs. left-handers (one extra-base hit per 28 AB), .271 vs. right-handers (one XBH per 20 AB).... Averaged 2.76 assists per nine innings last season, 3d-lowest rate among N.L. second basemen (minimum: 300 innings); sharp contrast with his platoon partner Royster.... Career batting average of .167 at Three Rivers Stadium.... Career batting averages: .226 in day games, .267 in night games.

Tom Foley

Reds/Phillies	AB	H	2B	3B	HR	RRF	BB	SO	BA	SA	OBA
Season	250	60	13	1	3	25	19	34	.240	.336	.294
vs. Left-Handed Pitchers	40	8	0	0	0	1	2	8	.200	.200	.238
vs. Right-Handed Pitchers	210	52	13	1	3	24	17	26	.248	.362	.304
Home	115	34	11	0	2	15	13	10	.296	.443	.367
Road	135	26	2	1	1	10	6	24	.193	.244	.227
Grass	86	13	0	0	1	5	4	14	.151	.186	.189
Artificial Turf	164	47	13	1	2	20	15	20	.287	.415	.346
April	20	2	0	0	0	1	0	7	.100	.100	.100
May	44	9	1	1	0	1	1	6	.205	.273	.222
June	11	2	1	0	0	3	1	1	.182	.273	.250
July	14	4	2	0	0	2	2	1	.286	.429	.375
August	72	19	5	0	2	9	7	8	.264	.417	.329
Sept./Oct.	89	24	4	0	1	9	8	11	.270	.348	.330
Leading Off Inn.	70	22	5	0	1	1	2	8	.314	.429	.333
Bases Empty	150	39	10	0	1	1	7	18	.260	.347	.293
Runners On	100	21	3	1	2	24	12	16	.210	.320	.295
Runners/Scor. Pos.	56	13	3	0	2	23	10	9	.232	.393	.348
Runners On/2 Out	46	7	1	0	1	8	8	8	.152	.239	.278
Scor. Pos./2 Out	28	6	1	0	1	8	7	3	.214	.357	.371
Late Inning Pressure	48	13	0	1	1	7	3	8	.271	.375	.314
Leading Off	13	6	0	0	0	0	0	2	.462	.462	.462
Bases Empty	28	9	0	0	0	0	1	4	.321	.321	.345
Runners On	20	4	0	1	1	7	2	4	.200	.450	.273
Runners/Scor. Pos.	12	3	0	0	1	6	1	3	.250	.500	.308

DRIVING IN RUNS	0 Out	1 Out	2 Out	Total	
From 1B	1/18	1/27	1/31	3/76	4%
From 2B	0/6	2/13	2/19	4/38	11%
From 3B	3/4	7/10	4/12	14/26	54%
Scoring Position	3/10	9/23	6/31	18/64	28%
Scor. Pos. %	30%	39%	19%	28%	
Driving In Runners from 3B with Less than Two Out:			10/14	71%	

Loves to face: Rich Gossage (1.000, 2-for-2, 1 HR)
Hates to face: Fernando Valenzuela (0-for-9, 4 SO)
Career batting averages: .209 in day games, .261 in night games; .264 with runners on base, .224 with the bases empty.... Batting average with runners on base has decreased in each of his three seasons in the major leagues: .324, .292, .210.... All eight of his career home runs have been hit off right-handed pitchers.... No extra-base hits in 40 at bats vs. southpaws last season, tied for highest total in majors.... Only extra-base hit of his career against a left-handed pitcher was his first major-league extra-base hit: a double off Mike Chris (Giants pitcher; you remember, don't you?) in April of 1983.... Career batting average of .346 at his new home, Veterans Stadium; .128 at Dodger Stadium.

George Foster

New York Mets	AB	H	2B	3B	HR	RRF	BB	SO	BA	SA	OBA
Season	452	119	24	1	21	77	46	87	.263	.460	.331
vs. Left-Handed Pitchers	188	51	10	0	9	36	26	31	.271	.468	.358
vs. Right-Handed Pitchers	264	68	14	1	12	41	20	56	.258	.455	.311
Home	225	59	12	1	9	41	26	41	.262	.444	.341
Road	227	60	12	0	12	36	20	46	.264	.476	.321
Grass	308	78	16	1	12	51	37	56	.253	.429	.334
Artificial Turf	144	41	8	0	9	26	9	31	.285	.528	.325
April	44	11	3	0	3	8	6	15	.250	.523	.340
May	74	16	4	0	4	10	3	12	.216	.432	.244
June	80	20	3	0	4	13	10	14	.250	.438	.337
July	81	22	6	0	4	23	10	18	.272	.494	.352
August	84	23	5	0	2	10	6	15	.274	.405	.322
Sept./Oct.	89	27	3	1	4	13	11	13	.303	.494	.379
Leading Off Inn.	87	19	2	0	3	3	6	14	.218	.345	.269
Bases Empty	253	64	12	1	11	11	18	48	.253	.439	.303
Runners On	199	55	12	0	10	66	28	39	.276	.487	.365
Runners/Scor. Pos.	116	33	4	0	6	55	20	26	.284	.474	.387
Runners On/2 Out	80	25	6	0	5	29	11	11	.313	.575	.409
Scor. Pos./2 Out	59	18	2	0	4	25	8	8	.305	.542	.406
Late Inning Pressure	68	9	0	0	1	6	5	18	.132	.176	.189
Leading Off	15	2	0	0	0	0	1	4	.133	.133	.188
Bases Empty	41	5	0	0	1	1	2	10	.122	.195	.163
Runners On	27	4	0	0	0	5	3	8	.148	.148	.226
Runners/Scor. Pos.	14	3	0	0	0	5	3	5	.214	.214	.333

DRIVING IN RUNS	0 Out	1 Out	2 Out	Total	
From 1B	1/37	6/62	6/59	13/158	8%
From 2B	3/15	7/29	11/44	21/88	24%
From 3B	8/10	7/19	7/22	22/51	43%
Scoring Position	11/25	14/48	18/66	43/139	31%
Scor. Pos. %	44%	29%	27%	31%	
Driving In Runners from 3B with Less than Two Out:			15/29	52%	

Loves to face: Dave Dravecky (.625, 10-for-16, 1 HR)
Hates to face: Lee Tunnell (.053, 1-for-19)
Fly-ball hitter: 0.80 G/A ratio last season. . . . Ranks 6th in the N.L. in homers over the past three years. . . . Batted .462 (6-for-13) with the bases loaded last season. . . . Two hits in last 18 at bats at Atlanta Stadium, following 95-for-250 streak (.380) over nine-year period. . . . Had batted .289 in Late-Inning Pressure Situations in first three seasons with Mets. . . . No extra-base hits in 62 at bats in Late-Inning Pressure Situations with runners on base over the past two seasons. . . . Related stat: has not driven in a base runner from first base in LIP since 1983 (0-for-54 since then). . . . But has driven in 27 of 69 runners from scoring position in LIP Situations over the past three seasons (.391).

Terry Francona

Montreal Expos	AB	H	2B	3B	HR	RRF	BB	SO	BA	SA	OBA
Season	281	75	15	1	2	34	12	12	.267	.349	.299
vs. Left-Handed Pitchers	26	11	1	0	0	7	1	4	.423	.462	.444
vs. Right-Handed Pitchers	255	64	14	1	2	27	11	8	.251	.337	.285
Home	122	34	6	1	0	15	9	6	.279	.344	.333
Road	159	41	9	0	2	19	3	6	.258	.352	.272
Grass	71	18	5	0	2	12	1	2	.254	.408	.264
Artificial Turf	210	57	10	1	0	22	11	10	.271	.329	.311
April	16	6	0	0	0	2	2	1	.375	.375	.444
May	26	6	2	1	0	3	1	0	.231	.385	.259
June	50	10	2	0	0	7	3	3	.200	.240	.259
July	32	11	1	0	1	6	1	2	.344	.469	.364
August	73	26	6	0	1	11	3	4	.356	.479	.382
Sept./Oct.	84	16	4	0	0	5	2	2	.190	.238	.209
Leading Off Inn.	66	13	4	0	1	1	0	4	.197	.303	.197
Bases Empty	158	36	10	1	2	2	2	5	.228	.342	.242
Runners On	123	39	5	0	0	32	10	7	.317	.358	.368
Runners/Scor. Pos.	82	24	2	0	0	28	9	6	.293	.317	.363
Runners On/2 Out	57	15	2	0	0	15	5	4	.263	.298	.323
Scor. Pos./2 Out	46	11	1	0	0	12	5	4	.239	.261	.314
Late Inning Pressure	59	15	3	0	0	11	3	3	.254	.305	.290
Leading Off	13	4	0	0	0	0	0	2	.308	.308	.308
Bases Empty	30	5	0	0	0	0	1	2	.167	.167	.194
Runners On	29	10	3	0	0	11	2	1	.345	.448	.387
Runners/Scor. Pos.	21	8	2	0	0	10	2	1	.381	.476	.435

DRIVING IN RUNS	0 Out	1 Out	2 Out	Total	
From 1B	1/21	1/28	3/39	5/88	6%
From 2B	0/4	5/21	5/29	10/54	19%
From 3B	2/7	8/9	7/22	17/38	45%
Scoring Position	2/11	13/30	12/51	27/92	29%
Scor. Pos. %	18%	43%	24%	29%	
Driving In Runners from 3B with Less than Two Out:			10/16	63%	

Loves to face: Eric Show (.438, 7-for-16, 1 HR)
Hates to face: Doug Bair (0-for-6, 3 SO)
Career batting averages: .339 vs. left-handers, .283 vs. right-handers. So why have 87 percent of his plate appearances been vs. right-handed pitchers? . . . Has hit for a higher average with men on base than he has with the bases empty in four of his five seasons in the majors. Career batting averages: .316 with runners on, .271 with the bases empty. . . . Led off 66 innings without a walk last season, highest total in either league. . . . Career totals: four leadoff walks in 202 career leadoff appearances, but 3-for-35 in Late-Inning Pressure Situations. . . . Grounded into one double play in 51 opportunities last season, 2d-lowest average in N.L. (minimum: 50 opportunities).

Phil Garner

Houston Astros	AB	H	2B	3B	HR	RRF	BB	SO	BA	SA	OBA
Season	463	124	23	10	6	55	34	72	.268	.400	.317
vs. Left-Handed Pitchers	220	59	9	5	1	19	18	32	.268	.368	.318
vs. Right-Handed Pitchers	243	65	14	5	5	36	16	40	.267	.428	.317
Home	232	63	13	2	2	24	19	31	.272	.371	.325
Road	231	61	10	8	4	31	15	41	.264	.429	.309
Grass	135	40	9	7	4	22	7	19	.296	.556	.331
Artificial Turf	328	84	14	3	2	33	27	53	.256	.335	.312
April	56	14	4	0	1	5	4	10	.250	.375	.295
May	99	24	3	3	1	13	10	17	.242	.364	.312
June	90	20	4	2	2	13	6	13	.222	.378	.265
July	61	15	1	0	0	6	5	13	.246	.262	.303
August	49	18	2	1	0	3	3	8	.367	.449	.396
Sept./Oct.	108	33	9	4	2	15	6	11	.306	.519	.350
Leading Off Inn.	92	27	6	1	1	1	4	12	.293	.413	.323
Bases Empty	261	71	15	4	4	4	16	36	.272	.406	.314
Runners On	202	53	8	6	2	51	18	36	.262	.391	.322
Runners/Scor. Pos.	106	26	5	3	1	43	12	18	.245	.377	.315
Runners On/2 Out	80	18	3	1	1	17	8	15	.225	.325	.295
Scor. Pos./2 Out	52	11	3	0	1	16	6	10	.212	.327	.293
Late Inning Pressure	72	21	2	2	3	15	8	13	.292	.500	.366
Leading Off	16	5	1	0	0	0	1	3	.313	.375	.353
Bases Empty	38	8	1	0	2	2	3	7	.211	.395	.268
Runners On	34	13	1	2	1	13	5	6	.382	.618	.463
Runners/Scor. Pos.	15	6	1	0	0	8	4	2	.400	.467	.500

DRIVING IN RUNS	0 Out	1 Out	2 Out	Total	
From 1B	2/40	6/56	2/55	10/151	7%
From 2B	1/11	6/28	6/37	13/76	17%
From 3B	6/10	11/19	8/27	25/56	45%
Scoring Position	7/21	17/47	14/64	38/132	29%
Scor. Pos. %	33%	36%	22%	29%	
Driving In Runners from 3B with Less than Two Out:			17/29	59%	

Loves to face: Mark Davis (.421, 8-for-19, 2 HR)
Hates to face: Craig McMurtry (0-for-14)
Had lowest fielding percentage (.932) of any N.L. third baseman last season (minimum: 100 games). . . . Slight variation in batting averages vs. right-handed and left-handed pitchers is indicative of his career breakdown: .262 vs. lefties, .262 vs. righties. . . . Has batted over .300 in Late-Inning Pressure Situations with runners on base in each of the last three seasons. Career average of .310 in LIP with runners in scoring position. . . . Has driven in 28 of 72 runners from scoring position (.389) in LIP over the past three seasons. . . . Drew two bases-loaded walks last season, after only one in previous 10 years. . . . Other players who played for the '74 A's and saw action last year: Reggie Jackson, Vida Blue, Claudell Washington, Rollie Fingers, and Manny Trillo.

Steve Garvey

San Diego Padres	AB	H	2B	3B	HR	RRF	BB	SO	BA	SA	OBA
Season	654	184	34	6	17	85	35	67	.281	.430	.318
vs. Left-Handed Pitchers	209	62	14	1	9	27	16	21	.297	.502	.345
vs. Right-Handed Pitchers	445	122	20	5	8	58	19	46	.274	.396	.305
Home	313	89	17	3	10	42	22	34	.284	.454	.331
Road	341	95	17	3	7	43	13	33	.279	.408	.306
Grass	485	142	26	5	17	67	26	51	.293	.472	.330
Artificial Turf	169	42	8	1	0	18	9	16	.249	.308	.284
April	79	24	4	0	3	10	1	10	.304	.468	.313
May	108	34	5	2	4	17	2	9	.315	.509	.321
June	120	24	4	0	5	14	9	16	.200	.358	.254
July	111	27	8	1	1	13	2	11	.243	.360	.270
August	101	32	5	1	3	15	10	6	.317	.475	.372
Sept./Oct.	135	43	8	2	1	16	11	15	.319	.430	.372
Leading Off Inn.	117	34	5	3	4	4	5	8	.291	.487	.320
Bases Empty	340	101	21	4	12	12	16	43	.297	.488	.329
Runners On	314	83	13	2	5	73	19	24	.264	.366	.307
Runners/Scor. Pos.	166	48	8	1	5	71	15	14	.289	.440	.340
Runners On/2 Out	97	24	5	0	0	22	12	9	.247	.299	.342
Scor. Pos./2 Out	58	18	4	0	0	22	9	8	.310	.379	.403
Late Inning Pressure	103	24	5	0	0	11	2	15	.233	.282	.250
Leading Off	23	6	1	0	0	0	0	1	.261	.304	.261
Bases Empty	48	11	3	0	0	0	0	7	.229	.292	.229
Runners On	55	13	2	0	0	11	2	8	.236	.273	.267
Runners/Scor. Pos.	25	7	1	0	0	11	1	5	.280	.320	.286

DRIVING IN RUNS	0 Out	1 Out	2 Out	Total	
From 1B	1/60	5/96	3/75	9/231	4%
From 2B	4/32	10/56	11/44	25/132	19%
From 3B	8/13	18/25	8/21	34/59	58%
Scoring Position	12/45	28/81	19/65	59/191	31%
Scor. Pos. %	27%	35%	29%	31%	
Driving In Runners from 3B with Less than Two Out:			26/38	68%	

Loves to face: Bob Welch (.435, 10-for-23, 1 HR)
Hates to face: Orel Hershiser (.063, 1-for-16, 6 SO)
Dropped a foul popup off the bat of Bob Brenly on April 15 to snap his 193-game errorless streak, a major-league record for first basemen. . . . Had handled N.L. record of 1,633 consecutive chances at first base without an error, dating back to June 1983. . . . 343 plate appearances with runners on base were his most since 1975 despite Gwynn's decline in on-base production and the Padres' loss of Wiggins. . . . Led off 161 innings without a walk in 1982, highest total in 11-year history of *The Player Analysis*. . . . Batted .241 in day games last season, .303 in night games. . . . Only one home run in his last 349 at bats at the Astrodome. . . . Batted .340 in Late-Inning Pressure Situations from 1975 through 1980, .249 in five seasons since then.

Dan Gladden

San Francisco Giants	AB	H	2B	3B	HR	RRF	BB	SO	BA	SA	OBA
Season	502	122	15	8	7	47	40	78	.243	.347	.307
vs. Left-Handed Pitchers	147	38	4	1	1	8	16	21	.259	.320	.335
vs. Right-Handed Pitchers	355	84	11	7	6	39	24	57	.237	.358	.295
Home	254	59	7	4	6	26	22	42	.232	.362	.306
Road	248	63	8	4	1	21	18	36	.254	.331	.307
Grass	371	88	12	4	6	38	31	61	.237	.340	.306
Artificial Turf	131	34	3	4	1	9	9	17	.260	.366	.308
April	73	22	3	0	1	11	5	15	.301	.384	.350
May	100	20	1	4	0	5	9	18	.200	.290	.270
June	92	16	3	1	1	4	4	9	.174	.261	.216
July	85	21	2	1	0	11	8	14	.247	.294	.333
August	53	13	2	1	0	2	6	8	.245	.321	.333
Sept./Oct.	99	30	4	1	5	14	8	14	.303	.515	.355
Leading Off Inn.	204	49	7	3	6	6	18	39	.240	.392	.308
Bases Empty	343	82	12	6	6	6	29	57	.239	.362	.302
Runners On	159	40	3	2	1	41	11	21	.252	.314	.316
Runners/Scor. Pos.	98	21	2	1	1	39	9	14	.214	.286	.295
Runners On/2 Out	78	19	1	1	1	25	5	12	.244	.321	.314
Scor. Pos./2 Out	59	14	0	1	1	24	4	7	.237	.322	.308
Late Inning Pressure	94	19	2	2	1	9	7	20	.202	.298	.276
Leading Off	12	2	0	0	0	0	2	2	.167	.167	.333
Bases Empty	53	14	1	2	0	0	3	11	.264	.358	.316
Runners On	41	5	1	0	1	9	4	9	.122	.220	.229
Runners/Scor. Pos.	26	4	1	0	1	9	4	5	.154	.308	.258

DRIVING IN RUNS	0 Out	1 Out	2 Out	Total	
From 1B	0/17	1/39	4/41	5/97	5%
From 2B	0/4	3/30	12/47	15/81	19%
From 3B	0/0	12/15	8/22	20/37	54%
Scoring Position	0/4	15/45	20/69	35/118	30%
Scor. Pos. %	0%	33%	29%	30%	
Driving In Runners from 3B with Less than Two Out:			12/15	80%	

Loves to face: Jeff Dedmon (.800, 4-for-5)
Hates to face: Andy Hawkins (0-for-8, 3 SO)
Batted .234 in 118 games as starter, .393 (11-for-28) in 24 games off the bench. . . . Batted .263 in day games, .219 in night games. . . . Had strong start and finish in 1985: batted .301 in April; hit three home runs in October. . . . Career batting average of .450 at Veterans Stadium. . . . Has hit all but one of 12 career home runs at Candlestick Park. . . . Only one home run in 165 career at bats in Late-Inning Pressure Situations. . . . Career batting average of .191 in LIP with runners on base. . . . No walks, no strikeouts in 20 career plate appearances with the bases loaded.

David Green

San Francisco Giants	AB	H	2B	3B	HR	RRF	BB	SO	BA	SA	OBA
Season	294	73	10	2	5	21	22	58	.248	.347	.301
vs. Left-Handed Pitchers	109	23	4	0	1	4	10	27	.211	.275	.277
vs. Right-Handed Pitchers	185	50	6	2	4	17	12	31	.270	.389	.315
Home	135	28	4	1	3	10	8	30	.207	.319	.250
Road	159	45	6	1	2	11	14	28	.283	.371	.343
Grass	223	52	6	2	4	15	15	44	.233	.332	.279
Artificial Turf	71	21	4	0	1	6	7	14	.296	.394	.367
April	37	3	0	0	0	1	6	12	.081	.081	.209
May	46	12	5	0	0	3	2	9	.261	.370	.286
June	57	9	0	1	1	2	2	9	.158	.246	.186
July	72	27	3	1	2	5	4	11	.375	.528	.408
August	41	13	1	0	2	7	5	9	.317	.488	.404
Sept./Oct.	41	9	1	0	0	3	3	8	.220	.244	.267
Leading Off Inn.	70	16	2	0	3	3	5	15	.229	.386	.280
Bases Empty	182	46	8	2	4	4	12	39	.253	.385	.299
Runners On	112	27	2	0	1	17	10	19	.241	.286	.304
Runners/Scor. Pos.	55	10	0	0	0	14	8	12	.182	.182	.288
Runners On/2 Out	46	11	2	0	0	7	6	8	.239	.283	.327
Scor. Pos./2 Out	30	6	0	0	0	6	4	5	.200	.200	.294
Late Inning Pressure	61	19	1	0	1	6	5	11	.311	.377	.368
Leading Off	15	3	0	0	0	0	0	2	.200	.200	.200
Bases Empty	41	13	1	0	1	1	1	10	.317	.415	.333
Runners On	20	6	0	0	0	5	4	1	.300	.300	.423
Runners/Scor. Pos.	10	4	0	0	0	5	4	0	.400	.400	.563

DRIVING IN RUNS	0 Out	1 Out	2 Out	Total	
From 1B	1/19	0/37	1/27	2/83	2%
From 2B	0/2	2/19	2/21	4/42	10%
From 3B	1/1	5/11	4/13	10/25	40%
Scoring Position	1/3	7/30	6/34	14/67	21%
Scor. Pos. %	33%	23%	18%	21%	
Driving In Runners from 3B with Less than Two Out:			6/12	50%	

Loves to face: Donnie Moore (.750, 3-for-4)
Hates to face: Bob James (0-for-5, 2 SO)
Ground-ball hitter: 1.71 G/A ratio last season. . . . Batted .210 in day games, .299 in night games last season. . . . Yearly batting averages with runners in scoring position since 1982: .373, .308, .234, .182. . . . Batting average vs. left-handed pitchers has declined dramatically in each of the past three seasons (.289, .256, .211), but performance vs. right-handers has been consistent (.281, .275, .270). Career batting averages are .254 vs. left-handers, .276 vs. right-handers. . . . Has hit .311 in Late-Inning Pressure Situations with runners on base over his career. . . . Has not walked leading off 61 career innings in LIP Situations. . . . Giants were 3–6 in games started by Green, Blue, and Brown; alas, that combo was never permitted to clash with the Reds.

Greg Gross

Philadelphia Phillies	AB	H	2B	3B	HR	RRF	BB	SO	BA	SA	OBA
Season	169	44	5	2	0	15	32	9	.260	.314	.374
vs. Left-Handed Pitchers	6	2	0	0	0	2	3	1	.333	.333	.500
vs. Right-Handed Pitchers	163	42	5	2	0	13	29	8	.258	.313	.368
Home	76	20	3	2	0	8	17	7	.263	.355	.389
Road	93	24	2	0	0	7	15	2	.258	.280	.361
Grass	53	18	2	0	0	5	7	1	.340	.377	.417
Artificial Turf	116	26	3	2	0	10	25	8	.224	.284	.357
April	23	5	2	0	0	2	1	0	.217	.304	.250
May	27	5	0	1	0	1	3	4	.185	.259	.267
June	34	11	1	0	0	5	13	0	.324	.353	.490
July	40	10	1	1	0	4	6	4	.250	.325	.348
August	44	13	1	0	0	3	7	1	.295	.318	.392
Sept./Oct.	1	0	0	0	0	0	2	0	.000	.000	.667
Leading Off Inn.	43	10	1	0	0	0	8	2	.233	.256	.353
Bases Empty	98	24	2	1	0	0	18	6	.245	.286	.362
Runners On	71	20	3	1	0	15	14	3	.282	.352	.391
Runners/Scor. Pos.	41	10	2	0	0	13	7	1	.244	.293	.340
Runners On/2 Out	28	7	3	0	0	7	10	3	.250	.357	.447
Scor. Pos./2 Out	18	5	2	0	0	6	5	1	.278	.389	.435
Late Inning Pressure	44	11	2	0	0	2	11	3	.250	.295	.400
Leading Off	13	4	1	0	0	0	5	0	.308	.385	.500
Bases Empty	27	7	1	0	0	0	7	1	.259	.296	.412
Runners On	17	4	1	0	0	2	4	2	.235	.294	.381
Runners/Scor. Pos.	9	1	1	0	0	2	3	1	.111	.222	.333

DRIVING IN RUNS	0 Out	1 Out	2 Out	Total	
From 1B	1/13	0/19	1/16	2/48	4%
From 2B	0/9	1/10	5/17	6/36	17%
From 3B	3/5	3/3	1/5	7/13	54%
Scoring Position	3/14	4/13	6/22	13/49	27%
Scor. Pos. %	21%	31%	27%	27%	
Driving In Runners from 3B with Less than Two Out:			6/8	75%	

Loves to face: Rick Mahler (.667, 6-for-9)
Hates to face: Greg Minton (0-for-10)
Ground-ball hitter: 1.45 G/A ratio last season. . . . Has hit only one home run in his career off of a left-handed pitcher: September 26, 1977, off Jim Kaat at Wrigley Field. . . . No home runs in 596 career at bats in Late-Inning Pressure Situations. . . . Has hit six career home runs: five in 1977, none since 1979; three in Atlanta, three at Wrigley Field. . . . Batted .349 in day games, .208 in night games last season. Career averages: .305 and .279. . . . Has batted only 124 times (four extra-base hits, all doubles) vs. left-handed pitchers in seven seasons with Philadelphia. . . . Ideal pinch-hitter: career batting average of .325 in Late-Inning Pressure Situations with two outs and runners on base.

Pedro Guerrero

Los Angeles Dodgers	AB	H	2B	3B	HR	RRF	BB	SO	BA	SA	OBA
Season	487	156	22	2	33	91	83	68	.320	.577	.422
vs. Left-Handed Pitchers	135	41	5	1	9	24	25	17	.304	.556	.413
vs. Right-Handed Pitchers	352	115	17	1	24	67	58	51	.327	.585	.425
Home	257	80	9	0	13	42	45	34	.311	.498	.416
Road	230	76	13	2	20	49	38	34	.330	.665	.429
Grass	342	104	12	0	17	55	61	48	.304	.488	.413
Artificial Turf	145	52	10	2	16	36	22	20	.359	.786	.444
April	74	19	2	0	2	9	12	11	.257	.365	.367
May	94	26	5	1	2	9	11	11	.277	.415	.361
June	93	32	3	0	15	27	15	14	.344	.860	.436
July	63	29	7	1	4	13	15	7	.460	.794	.563
August	92	26	3	0	8	25	19	16	.283	.576	.405
Sept./Oct.	71	24	2	0	2	8	11	9	.338	.451	.427
Leading Off Inn.	125	39	4	1	5	5	24	14	.312	.480	.427
Bases Empty	263	88	14	1	21	21	35	39	.335	.635	.421
Runners On	224	68	8	1	12	70	48	29	.304	.509	.423
Runners/Scor. Pos.	120	30	2	0	8	55	38	25	.250	.467	.421
Runners On/2 Out	107	32	3	0	7	31	25	10	.299	.523	.440
Scor. Pos./2 Out	58	15	1	0	4	22	19	8	.259	.483	.449
Late Inning Pressure	62	19	1	2	6	16	12	8	.306	.677	.419
Leading Off	17	4	0	1	1	1	5	2	.235	.529	.409
Bases Empty	31	10	1	1	3	3	5	4	.323	.710	.417
Runners On	31	9	0	1	3	13	7	4	.290	.645	.421
Runners/Scor. Pos.	15	3	0	0	1	8	7	3	.200	.400	.455

DRIVING IN RUNS	0 Out	1 Out	2 Out	Total	
From 1B	2/25	6/59	8/67	16/151	11%
From 2B	2/12	7/34	6/39	15/85	18%
From 3B	3/6	14/24	10/26	27/56	48%
Scoring Position	5/18	21/58	16/65	42/141	30%
Scor. Pos. %	28%	36%	25%	30%	
Driving In Runners from 3B with Less than Two Out:			17/30	57%	

Loves to face: Kevin Gross (.600, 9-for-15, 1 HR)
Hates to face: Dennis Eckersley (0-for-9)
Fly-ball hitter: 0.78 G/A ratio last season. . . . Hit 15 home runs in June to tie major-league record held by Babe Ruth, Bob Johnson, and Roger Maris. . . . Hit eight of his 33 home runs vs. Houston. . . . Tied Gary Carter for N.L. lead with 20 road-game home runs. . . . Career batting average of .314 in Late-Inning Pressure Situations. . . . Averaged 2.53 assists per nine innings at third last season, 4th-highest rate among N.L. third basemen (minimum: 300 innings). . . . Career batting averages: .282 in day games, .316 in night games. . . . Career batting average of .407, with 12 home runs in 135 at bats, at Atlanta Stadium. . . . Other ballparks: .373 at Busch Stadium, .367 at Olympic Stadium.

Tony Gwynn

San Diego Padres	AB	H	2B	3B	HR	RRF	BB	SO	BA	SA	OBA
Season	622	197	29	5	6	49	45	33	.317	.408	.364
vs. Left-Handed Pitchers	205	59	5	1	2	14	19	13	.288	.351	.354
vs. Right-Handed Pitchers	417	138	24	4	4	35	26	20	.331	.436	.369
Home	316	103	14	4	3	24	20	17	.326	.424	.368
Road	306	94	15	1	3	25	25	16	.307	.392	.360
Grass	462	149	21	4	5	36	31	26	.323	.418	.366
Artificial Turf	160	48	8	1	1	13	14	7	.300	.381	.358
April	74	22	5	2	1	4	5	2	.297	.459	.342
May	102	29	8	2	0	5	9	7	.284	.402	.348
June	122	41	5	0	3	15	2	6	.336	.451	.347
July	99	29	5	0	0	5	5	9	.293	.343	.333
August	103	34	3	0	0	3	8	5	.330	.359	.378
Sept./Oct.	122	42	3	1	2	17	16	4	.344	.434	.417
Leading Off Inn.	105	37	7	2	0	0	7	8	.352	.457	.393
Bases Empty	367	111	25	3	3	3	26	23	.302	.411	.350
Runners On	255	86	4	2	3	46	19	10	.337	.404	.384
Runners/Scor. Pos.	111	30	1	1	0	38	10	6	.270	.297	.328
Runners On/2 Out	94	31	3	1	0	16	9	2	.330	.383	.394
Scor. Pos./2 Out	55	14	1	0	0	14	6	2	.255	.273	.328
Late Inning Pressure	95	33	4	0	2	13	11	9	.347	.453	.415
Leading Off	19	8	1	0	0	0	3	4	.421	.474	.500
Bases Empty	49	20	3	0	2	2	6	8	.408	.592	.473
Runners On	46	13	1	0	0	11	5	1	.283	.304	.353
Runners/Scor. Pos.	22	5	0	0	0	10	3	1	.227	.227	.320

DRIVING IN RUNS	0 Out	1 Out	2 Out	Total	
From 1B	2/81	2/51	2/60	6/192	3%
From 2B	4/17	5/26	5/36	14/79	18%
From 3B	1/4	12/19	9/25	22/48	46%
Scoring Position	5/21	17/45	14/61	36/127	28%
Scor. Pos. %	24%	38%	23%	28%	
Driving In Runners from 3B with Less than Two Out:			13/23	57%	

Loves to face: Jeff Robinson (.750, 9-for-12)
Hates to face: Dan Schatzeder (0-for-9)
Ground-ball hitter: 1.94 G/A ratio last season, 6th-highest in N.L. (minimum: 200 PA). Career average: 2.01. . . . Year by year batting averages in Late-Inning Pressure Situations, starting with 1983: .340, .361, .347. . . . Career batting average of .367 in Late-Inning Pressure Situations with runners in scoring position. . . . Has driven in 30 of 72 base runners from scoring position (.417) in those situations. . . . Batted .281 in day games, .335 in night games last season. . . . Batted .556 (5-for-9) with the bases loaded last season, .542 (13-for-24) for career, but with no extra-base hits. . . . Stolen base percentage of .560 (14-of-25) last season was 2d-lowest among players with 10 or more stolen bases.

Terry Harper

Atlanta Braves	AB	H	2B	3B	HR	RRF	BB	SO	BA	SA	OBA
Season	492	130	15	2	17	74	44	76	.264	.407	.327
vs. Left-Handed Pitchers	172	38	6	0	8	29	15	27	.221	.395	.280
vs. Right-Handed Pitchers	320	92	9	2	9	45	29	49	.288	.413	.352
Home	248	71	9	0	9	40	23	41	.286	.431	.350
Road	244	59	6	2	8	34	21	35	.242	.381	.303
Grass	372	100	11	2	13	62	33	56	.269	.414	.331
Artificial Turf	120	30	4	0	4	12	11	20	.250	.383	.316
April	24	6	1	1	1	6	1	3	.250	.500	.280
May	85	24	5	1	3	12	7	15	.282	.471	.351
June	101	22	1	0	2	14	15	18	.218	.287	.319
July	103	31	2	0	7	24	4	19	.301	.524	.327
August	96	18	1	0	4	10	11	10	.188	.323	.271
Sept./Oct.	83	29	5	0	0	8	6	11	.349	.410	.393
Leading Off Inn.	120	32	7	1	7	7	6	15	.267	.517	.302
Bases Empty	268	75	10	2	8	8	19	31	.280	.422	.330
Runners On	224	55	5	0	9	66	25	45	.246	.388	.324
Runners/Scor. Pos.	126	32	5	0	4	56	14	24	.254	.389	.329
Runners On/2 Out	104	29	4	0	6	37	8	24	.279	.490	.330
Scor. Pos./2 Out	68	19	4	0	3	31	4	17	.279	.471	.319
Late Inning Pressure	77	22	4	0	3	10	10	9	.286	.455	.375
Leading Off	16	7	3	0	2	2	0	0	.438	1.000	.438
Bases Empty	40	14	4	0	2	2	2	1	.350	.600	.381
Runners On	37	8	0	0	1	8	8	8	.216	.297	.370
Runners/Scor. Pos.	24	4	0	0	0	6	5	4	.167	.167	.310

DRIVING IN RUNS	0 Out	1 Out	2 Out	Total	
From 1B	2/39	1/64	8/77	11/180	6%
From 2B	2/13	8/36	14/58	24/107	22%
From 3B	5/7	8/18	9/25	22/50	44%
Scoring Position	7/20	16/54	23/83	46/157	29%
Scor. Pos. %	35%	30%	28%	29%	
Driving In Runners from 3B with Less than Two Out:			13/25	52%	

Loves to face: Tom Gorman (.500, 3-for-6, 2 HR)
Hates to face: Vida Blue (.095, 2-for-21)
Batted .311 vs. ground-ball pitchers last season, .227 vs. fly-ball pitchers. . . . One of nine players to hit at least one home run vs. every opposing N.L. club last season, and one of two players in either league to hit three extra-inning home runs. The other was Tony Pena. . . . Batted .180 but had three game-winning RBIs vs. the Giants last season. . . . Batting .301 (37-for-123) with two outs and runners in scoring position since 1982. . . . Batted 67 points higher vs. right-handers than left-handers, 5th-largest difference in N.L. (minimum: 100 PA vs. each). . . . Has batted higher against right-handed pitchers than left-handers in each of the last three seasons. . . . Career batting average of .140 at Veterans Stadium.

Von Hayes

Philadelphia Phillies	AB	H	2B	3B	HR	RRF	BB	SO	BA	SA	OBA
Season	570	150	30	4	13	72	61	99	.263	.398	.332
vs. Left-Handed Pitchers	157	36	5	0	4	19	14	34	.229	.338	.291
vs. Right-Handed Pitchers	413	114	25	4	9	53	47	65	.276	.421	.348
Home	278	80	13	4	12	43	32	41	.288	.493	.360
Road	292	70	17	0	1	29	29	58	.240	.308	.306
Grass	150	34	10	0	0	10	13	26	.227	.293	.287
Artificial Turf	420	116	20	4	13	62	48	73	.276	.436	.348
April	71	26	4	1	1	12	9	12	.366	.493	.432
May	92	25	7	0	2	10	17	19	.272	.413	.382
June	66	11	0	0	3	11	9	13	.167	.303	.263
July	100	28	7	3	4	19	11	18	.280	.530	.348
August	115	30	9	0	3	14	9	23	.261	.417	.315
Sept./Oct.	126	30	3	0	0	6	6	14	.238	.262	.273
Leading Off Inn.	110	32	7	2	2	2	7	12	.291	.445	.333
Bases Empty	325	85	20	3	8	8	28	61	.262	.415	.320
Runners On	245	65	10	1	5	64	33	38	.265	.376	.348
Runners/Scor. Pos.	151	44	8	1	4	61	28	22	.291	.437	.393
Runners On/2 Out	101	20	3	0	2	22	15	17	.198	.287	.302
Scor. Pos./2 Out	66	14	3	0	2	22	12	11	.212	.348	.333
Late Inning Pressure	94	26	4	0	2	9	11	19	.277	.383	.352
Leading Off	27	7	0	0	0	0	3	5	.259	.259	.333
Bases Empty	52	13	3	0	1	1	5	13	.250	.365	.316
Runners On	42	13	1	0	1	8	6	6	.310	.405	.396
Runners/Scor. Pos.	25	9	1	0	1	8	5	5	.360	.520	.467

DRIVING IN RUNS	0 Out	1 Out	2 Out	Total	
From 1B	1/41	4/48	3/71	8/160	5%
From 2B	1/23	11/42	11/54	23/119	19%
From 3B	11/15	11/20	5/23	27/58	47%
Scoring Position	12/38	22/62	16/77	50/177	28%
Scor. Pos. %	32%	35%	21%	28%	
Driving In Runners from 3B with Less than Two Out:			22/35	63%	

Loves to face: Kurt Kepshire (.429, 6-for-14, 2 HR)
Hates to face: John Franco (0-for-8, 3 SO)
Became first player in major-league history to hit two first-inning home runs in one game (June 11 against New York; the 26–7 game, naturally). . . . Phillies lost all 10 games in which he started and batted cleanup. . . . Only player in majors to start at least 10 games each batting leadoff and batting cleanup. . . . Started games at all three outfield positions for a fourth consecutive season. . . . Drove in 14 runs vs. the Expos last season. . . . Yearly batting averages with two outs and runners in scoring position since 1981: .350, .294, .255, .232, .212. . . . Career batting average of .182 (10 for 55) with the bases loaded. . . . Career batting average of .364 at Busch Stadium.

Richie Hebner

Chicago Cubs	AB	H	2B	3B	HR	RRF	BB	SO	BA	SA	OBA
Season	120	26	2	0	3	23	7	15	.217	.308	.266
vs. Left-Handed Pitchers	6	1	0	0	0	2	0	3	.167	.167	.167
vs. Right-Handed Pitchers	114	25	2	0	3	21	7	12	.219	.316	.270
Home	67	14	1	0	2	8	5	11	.209	.313	.274
Road	53	12	1	0	1	15	2	4	.226	.302	.255
Grass	91	19	1	0	3	14	7	14	.209	.319	.273
Artificial Turf	29	7	1	0	0	9	0	1	.241	.276	.241
April	9	3	0	0	0	3	0	0	.333	.333	.333
May	17	4	0	0	1	5	3	2	.235	.412	.350
June	25	6	1	0	0	9	2	2	.240	.280	.296
July	21	8	0	0	0	3	0	1	.381	.381	.409
August	31	3	0	0	1	1	1	7	.097	.194	.125
Sept./Oct.	17	2	1	0	1	2	1	3	.118	.353	.167
Leading Off Inn.	16	3	0	0	0	0	2	3	.188	.188	.278
Bases Empty	48	11	0	0	2	2	4	5	.229	.354	.288
Runners On	72	15	2	0	1	21	3	10	.208	.278	.250
Runners/Scor. Pos.	45	10	2	0	1	21	1	4	.222	.333	.239
Runners On/2 Out	24	4	0	0	1	5	1	4	.167	.292	.231
Scor. Pos./2 Out	15	3	0	0	1	5	0	2	.200	.400	.200
Late Inning Pressure	47	11	0	0	1	8	3	9	.234	.298	.280
Leading Off	4	0	0	0	0	0	0	2	.000	.000	.000
Bases Empty	17	4	0	0	1	1	2	3	.235	.412	.316
Runners On	30	7	0	0	0	7	1	6	.233	.233	.258
Runners/Scor. Pos.	16	4	0	0	0	7	0	1	.250	.250	.250

DRIVING IN RUNS	0 Out	1 Out	2 Out	Total	
From 1B	0/13	1/23	1/19	2/55	4%
From 2B	1/8	3/16	2/12	6/36	17%
From 3B	4/6	7/7	1/5	12/18	67%
Scoring Position	5/14	10/23	3/17	18/54	33%
Scor. Pos. %	36%	43%	18%	33%	
Driving In Runners from 3B with Less than Two Out:			11/13	85%	

Loves to face: Tom Hume (.647, 11-for-17, 2 HR)
Hates to face: Mario Soto (0-for-14)
Fly-ball hitter: 0.93 G/A ratio last season. . . . Drove in 12 runs as a pinch-hitter, tied with Terry Whitfield for most in N.L. . . . Seven of his 22 RBIs last season were vs. the Expos. . . . Has not hit a home run off a left-handed pitcher since September 7, 1983, vs. Randy Jones. . . . Has faced left-handers only 15 times over the past two seasons. . . . Batting averages since 1975: .335 at Wrigley Field, .173 at Dodger Stadium, .194 at the Astrodome. . . . Has played for five teams over the past nine years, but has more home runs at home than on the road in eight of those nine seasons (the only exception: 1984, one HR at home, one on the road). . . . During that time: 61 homers at home, 21 on the road. . . . Set a record in '84 by appearing in his eighth National League Championship Series.

Danny Heep

New York Mets	AB	H	2B	3B	HR	RRF	BB	SO	BA	SA	OBA
Season	271	76	17	0	7	44	27	27	.280	.421	.341
vs. Left-Handed Pitchers	49	13	3	0	0	12	7	8	.265	.327	.356
vs. Right-Handed Pitchers	222	63	14	0	7	32	20	19	.284	.441	.337
Home	118	34	5	0	2	13	13	15	.288	.381	.361
Road	153	42	12	0	5	31	14	12	.275	.451	.326
Grass	192	53	12	0	4	26	22	20	.276	.401	.349
Artificial Turf	79	23	5	0	3	18	5	7	.291	.468	.322
April	27	7	2	0	0	5	2	3	.259	.333	.310
May	56	15	5	0	1	8	7	6	.268	.411	.338
June	84	22	3	0	4	13	8	9	.262	.440	.316
July	38	13	3	0	1	6	3	5	.342	.500	.381
August	30	9	3	0	0	2	3	1	.300	.400	.364
Sept./Oct.	36	10	1	0	1	10	4	3	.278	.389	.366
Leading Off Inn.	61	16	3	0	1	1	2	5	.262	.361	.286
Bases Empty	159	41	7	0	3	3	16	16	.258	.358	.326
Runners On	112	35	10	0	4	41	11	11	.313	.509	.362
Runners/Scor. Pos.	58	16	5	0	1	34	8	7	.276	.414	.342
Runners On/2 Out	46	13	5	0	1	14	5	5	.283	.457	.365
Scor. Pos./2 Out	27	7	3	0	0	12	4	2	.259	.370	.375
Late Inning Pressure	52	14	2	0	2	8	7	4	.269	.423	.344
Leading Off	10	3	1	0	0	0	1	0	.300	.400	.364
Bases Empty	30	7	2	0	0	0	3	1	.233	.300	.303
Runners On	22	7	0	0	2	8	4	3	.318	.591	.393
Runners/Scor. Pos.	8	1	0	0	0	4	3	3	.125	.125	.308

DRIVING IN RUNS	0 Out	1 Out	2 Out	Total	
From 1B	1/22	5/31	2/36	8/89	9%
From 2B	0/9	5/21	7/23	12/53	23%
From 3B	6/9	7/10	4/11	17/30	57%
Scoring Position	6/18	12/31	11/34	29/83	35%
Scor. Pos. %	33%	39%	32%	35%	
Driving In Runners from 3B with Less than Two Out:			13/19	68%	

Loves to face: Jeff Reardon (.615, 8-for-13)
Hates to face: Bill Gullickson (.050, 1-for-20)
Fly-ball hitter: 0.84 G/A ratio last season. . . . Batting average of .276 with runners in scoring position was the highest of his career. Career average: .211. . . . Batted .700 (7-for-10, 1 BB) with the bases loaded last season, a *Player Analysis* N.L. record (minimum: 10 AB). . . . Has never hit a home run against a left-handed pitcher (195 career PA). . . . Career batting averages: .343 at Olympic Stadium, .137 at Candlestick Park, .152 at Riverfront Stadium. . . . Grounded into 12 double plays in 58 opportunities last season, 9th-highest average among N.L. players (minimum: 5 GIDP). . . . Career batting average of .113 in Late-Inning Pressure Situations with runners in scoring position.

George Hendrick

Pittsburgh Pirates	AB	H	2B	3B	HR	RRF	BB	SO	BA	SA	OBA
Season	256	59	15	0	2	26	18	42	.230	.313	.278
vs. Left-Handed Pitchers	99	20	7	0	0	8	7	14	.202	.273	.252
vs. Right-Handed Pitchers	157	39	8	0	2	18	11	28	.248	.338	.294
Home	149	36	6	0	0	16	13	23	.242	.282	.301
Road	107	23	9	0	2	10	5	19	.215	.355	.246
Grass	69	11	4	0	1	2	1	12	.159	.261	.171
Artificial Turf	187	48	11	0	1	24	17	30	.257	.332	.314
April	64	14	4	0	1	6	7	9	.219	.328	.292
May	71	16	3	0	0	4	5	14	.225	.268	.276
June	64	17	5	0	1	11	4	12	.266	.391	.300
July	57	12	3	0	0	5	2	7	.211	.263	.237
August	0	0	0	0	0	0	0	0	.000	.000	.000
Sept./Oct.	0	0	0	0	0	0	0	0	.000	.000	.000
Leading Off Inn.	51	10	2	0	0	0	6	9	.196	.235	.281
Bases Empty	130	30	7	0	1	1	8	20	.231	.308	.275
Runners On	126	29	8	0	1	25	10	22	.230	.317	.281
Runners/Scor. Pos.	77	22	3	0	0	23	6	10	.286	.325	.326
Runners On/2 Out	52	11	4	0	0	10	6	10	.212	.288	.293
Scor. Pos./2 Out	38	10	3	0	0	10	4	5	.263	.342	.333
Late Inning Pressure	48	8	3	0	0	0	2	11	.167	.229	.200
Leading Off	8	1	1	0	0	0	0	2	.125	.250	.125
Bases Empty	24	4	2	0	0	0	0	6	.167	.250	.167
Runners On	24	4	1	0	0	0	2	5	.167	.208	.231
Runners/Scor. Pos.	13	3	0	0	0	0	1	2	.231	.231	.286

DRIVING IN RUNS	0 Out	1 Out	2 Out	Total	
From 1B	0/24	1/36	0/35	1/95	1%
From 2B	2/11	2/22	8/29	12/62	19%
From 3B	2/4	7/12	2/15	11/31	35%
Scoring Position	4/15	9/34	10/44	23/93	25%
Scor. Pos. %	27%	26%	23%	25%	
Driving In Runners from 3B with Less than Two Out:			9/16	56%	

Loves to face: Rod Scurry (.667, 8-for-12, 3 HR)
Hates to face: Doyle Alexander (.136, 3-for-22, 1 HR)
Figures above are for N.L. only. . . . Left the National League with fond memories of the following stadiums: Riverfront (.346 career batting average), Atlanta (.323), Three Rivers (.319), and San Diego (.305). . . . Four hits in 30 at bats with two outs and the bases loaded since 1977. . . . Has batted .164 in Late-Inning Pressure Situations over the past two seasons. . . . Batting .298 with runners in scoring position over the past seven seasons. . . . Stranded all 17 base runners in scoring position in Late-Inning Pressure Situations last season, after 3-for-14 performance in 1984.

Keith Hernandez

New York Mets	AB	H	2B	3B	HR	RRF	BB	SO	BA	SA	OBA
Season	593	183	34	4	10	96	77	59	.309	.430	.384
vs. Left-Handed Pitchers	260	82	15	1	3	41	19	25	.315	.415	.358
vs. Right-Handed Pitchers	333	101	19	3	7	55	58	34	.303	.441	.403
Home	285	81	12	1	4	47	39	31	.284	.375	.365
Road	308	102	22	3	6	49	38	28	.331	.481	.402
Grass	406	115	20	2	7	66	54	47	.283	.394	.363
Artificial Turf	187	68	14	2	3	30	23	12	.364	.508	.431
April	68	21	3	0	0	12	11	4	.309	.353	.405
May	87	21	3	0	4	10	16	10	.241	.414	.356
June	100	22	5	1	0	8	12	11	.220	.290	.298
July	102	40	12	1	4	29	18	8	.392	.647	.475
August	112	30	5	0	0	15	5	15	.268	.313	.297
Sept./Oct.	124	49	6	2	2	22	15	11	.395	.524	.457
Leading Off Inn.	118	38	5	1	2	2	12	11	.322	.432	.385
Bases Empty	334	101	15	2	5	5	35	37	.302	.404	.369
Runners On	259	82	19	2	5	91	42	22	.317	.463	.403
Runners/Scor. Pos.	173	54	13	2	3	81	38	19	.312	.462	.419
Runners On/2 Out	99	30	8	0	3	31	16	8	.303	.475	.405
Scor. Pos./2 Out	71	21	5	0	1	25	15	6	.296	.408	.425
Late Inning Pressure	82	29	3	1	1	10	12	12	.354	.451	.432
Leading Off	23	12	1	1	0	0	1	3	.522	.652	.542
Bases Empty	50	19	1	1	0	0	4	8	.380	.440	.426
Runners On	32	10	2	0	1	10	8	4	.313	.469	.439
Runners/Scor. Pos.	19	5	0	0	1	9	8	4	.263	.421	.464

DRIVING IN RUNS	0 Out	1 Out	2 Out	Total	
From 1B	3/30	6/65	4/52	13/147	9%
From 2B	4/23	12/58	18/50	34/131	26%
From 3B	11/15	22/26	6/31	39/72	54%
Scoring Position	15/38	34/84	24/81	73/203	36%
Scor. Pos. %	39%	40%	30%	36%	
Driving In Runners from 3B with Less than Two Out:			33/41	80%	

Loves to face: Mike Scott (.388, 19-for-49, 5 HR)
Hates to face: Dan Schatzeder (.146, 6-for-41)
Player of the Month for July, led N.L. in batting average (.392), hits (40), RBIs (29), and GW-RBIs (8). . . . Had three 5-hit games last season. . . . Has batted over .300 with runners on base in each of the last seven seasons, for a .333 average during that period. . . . Managed to put aside his crossword puzzles long enough to hit .333 with five GW-RBIs against the Cardinals since coming to the Mets. . . . Has driven in more than 35 percent of runners in scoring position in six of the past nine seasons. . . . Batting .190 (4-for-21) with the bases loaded since 1983. . . . Mets won nine of the 10 games in which he hit a home run. . . . Career batting average of .343 at San Diego Stadium. . . . Only one home run in 203 career at bats at the Astrodome.

Tom Herr

St. Louis Cardinals	AB	H	2B	3B	HR	RRF	BB	SO	BA	SA	OBA
Season	596	180	38	3	8	116	80	55	.302	.416	.379
vs. Left-Handed Pitchers	212	60	10	0	3	31	17	13	.283	.373	.333
vs. Right-Handed Pitchers	384	120	28	3	5	85	63	42	.313	.440	.402
Home	287	87	20	2	4	58	36	19	.303	.429	.375
Road	309	93	18	1	4	58	44	36	.301	.405	.383
Grass	172	52	9	1	3	31	19	24	.302	.419	.370
Artificial Turf	424	128	29	2	5	85	61	31	.302	.415	.383
April	69	27	5	1	0	14	14	5	.391	.493	.494
May	95	34	6	0	1	26	9	12	.358	.453	.398
June	104	32	8	0	2	24	9	14	.308	.442	.360
July	94	24	4	0	0	14	14	8	.255	.298	.345
August	106	34	8	2	1	15	14	6	.321	.462	.393
Sept./Oct.	128	29	7	0	4	23	20	10	.227	.375	.329
Leading Off Inn.	86	19	4	0	1	1	20	8	.221	.302	.374
Bases Empty	302	75	14	1	5	5	45	32	.248	.351	.348
Runners On	294	105	24	2	3	111	35	23	.357	.483	.411
Runners/Scor. Pos.	183	61	12	2	2	101	31	15	.333	.454	.408
Runners On/2 Out	95	33	6	1	1	32	12	6	.347	.463	.426
Scor. Pos./2 Out	66	20	4	1	0	29	10	4	.303	.394	.403
Late Inning Pressure	86	27	2	0	3	13	8	5	.314	.442	.371
Leading Off	15	2	0	0	0	0	2	1	.133	.133	.278
Bases Empty	49	12	1	0	2	2	5	2	.245	.388	.327
Runners On	37	15	1	0	1	11	3	3	.405	.514	.429
Runners/Scor. Pos.	22	7	0	0	0	8	2	2	.318	.318	.346

DRIVING IN RUNS	0 Out	1 Out	2 Out	Total	
From 1B	4/41	6/76	3/49	13/166	8%
From 2B	7/34	13/51	11/44	31/129	24%
From 3B	13/19	34/45	17/39	64/103	62%
Scoring Position	20/53	47/96	28/83	95/232	41%
Scor. Pos. %	38%	49%	34%	41%	
Driving In Runners from 3B with Less than Two Out:			47/64	73%	

Loves to face: Tom Gorman (.600, 9-for-15, 2 HR)
Hates to face: Ron Darling (.048, 1-for-21, 1 HR)
Batted .326 in day games, .287 in night games. . . . Batting average at season's end (.302) was at its lowest point of the season. . . . Had never hit a home run in a Late-Inning Pressure Situation entering last season. His three LIP home runs in '85 were hit all after August 18. . . . Batted 109 points higher with runners on base than with the bases empty, 4th-largest difference in N.L. (minimum: 200 PA). . . . Batted .343 with runners on base in 1983 but drove in only 31 runs that season. Big difference between '83 and '85 lies in his number of opportunities in such situations (161 in 1983, 348 in 1985). . . . Batting average vs. left-handed pitchers has dropped in each of the last two seasons from career-high .292 in 1983. . . . Career batting average of .351 at Three Rivers Stadium.

Bob Horner

Atlanta Braves	AB	H	2B	3B	HR	RRF	BB	SO	BA	SA	OBA
Season	483	129	25	3	27	95	50	57	.267	.499	.333
vs. Left-Handed Pitchers	161	48	11	0	10	35	15	15	.298	.553	.354
vs. Right-Handed Pitchers	322	81	14	3	17	60	35	42	.252	.472	.323
Home	219	59	19	2	13	53	23	27	.269	.553	.333
Road	264	70	6	1	14	42	27	30	.265	.455	.333
Grass	341	91	22	2	17	66	37	42	.267	.493	.336
Artificial Turf	142	38	3	1	10	29	13	15	.268	.514	.327
April	49	9	4	0	1	6	3	5	.184	.327	.231
May	70	19	3	0	3	11	7	4	.271	.443	.338
June	99	29	7	1	7	22	9	9	.293	.596	.342
July	82	31	6	1	9	28	9	13	.378	.805	.441
August	89	24	3	0	3	16	11	12	.270	.404	.347
Sept./Oct.	94	17	2	1	4	12	11	14	.181	.351	.264
Leading Off Inn.	104	30	4	0	7	7	7	13	.288	.529	.333
Bases Empty	239	66	9	1	11	11	16	27	.276	.460	.324
Runners On	244	63	16	2	16	84	34	30	.258	.537	.342
Runners/Scor. Pos.	127	32	8	1	7	60	23	20	.252	.496	.353
Runners On/2 Out	113	25	7	0	5	27	19	16	.221	.416	.333
Scor. Pos./2 Out	60	13	4	0	2	19	13	9	.217	.383	.356
Late Inning Pressure	80	26	3	1	7	22	10	7	.325	.650	.400
Leading Off	11	4	1	0	1	1	1	0	.364	.727	.417
Bases Empty	35	13	1	0	1	1	5	3	.371	.486	.450
Runners On	45	13	2	1	6	21	5	4	.289	.778	.360
Runners/Scor. Pos.	27	4	1	1	1	11	3	3	.148	.370	.233

DRIVING IN RUNS	0 Out	1 Out	2 Out	Total	
From 1B	3/44	12/71	6/79	21/194	11%
From 2B	1/14	7/37	9/43	17/94	18%
From 3B	4/9	19/24	7/22	30/55	55%
Scoring Position	5/23	26/61	16/65	47/149	32%
Scor. Pos. %	22%	43%	25%	32%	
Driving In Runners from 3B with Less than Two Out:			23/33	70%	

Loves to face: Fernando Valenzuela (.439, 18-for-41, 4 HR)
Hates to face: Mario Soto (.127, 8-for-63, 14 SO)
Has never hit a grand slam (61 career bases-loaded at bats), and holds the all-time major-league record for homers (188) by a hitter who can say that. ... Handled 950 chances at first base without committing an error in 1985. Prior to last season, Horner had committed seven errors in 451 chances (.984) in 47 games at first. ... Fielding percentage of .887 at third base was the worst in N.L. (minimum: 15 games). ... Had league's 2d-lowest assists per nine innings rate at third last year (1.72), but tied for 8th of 16 at first (0.70). ... Hit seven home runs and drove in 19 runs vs. Phillies last season. ... Batting .347 (51-for-147) in Late-Inning Pressure Situations since 1983. ... Career home-run totals: 122 at Atlanta Stadium, 66 in road games.

Glenn Hubbard

Atlanta Braves	AB	H	2B	3B	HR	RRF	BB	SO	BA	SA	OBA
Season	439	102	21	0	5	41	56	54	.232	.314	.321
vs. Left-Handed Pitchers	144	33	4	0	1	11	25	17	.229	.278	.335
vs. Right-Handed Pitchers	295	69	17	0	4	30	31	37	.234	.332	.313
Home	232	58	9	0	3	24	25	27	.250	.328	.323
Road	207	44	12	0	2	17	31	27	.213	.300	.318
Grass	329	79	12	0	5	36	34	40	.240	.322	.312
Artificial Turf	110	23	9	0	0	5	22	14	.209	.291	.346
April	47	11	3	0	0	2	10	5	.234	.298	.368
May	56	15	2	0	1	7	5	5	.268	.357	.328
June	85	17	4	0	2	9	15	9	.200	.318	.314
July	79	17	5	0	1	12	9	8	.215	.316	.297
August	62	15	1	0	0	4	9	11	.242	.258	.329
Sept./Oct.	110	27	6	0	1	7	8	16	.245	.327	.314
Leading Off Inn.	94	29	8	0	3	3	15	6	.309	.489	.404
Bases Empty	249	61	14	0	4	4	35	25	.245	.349	.340
Runners On	190	41	7	0	1	37	21	29	.216	.268	.295
Runners/Scor. Pos.	105	25	4	0	1	35	12	16	.238	.305	.301
Runners On/2 Out	78	19	2	0	1	16	6	17	.244	.308	.298
Scor. Pos./2 Out	47	12	1	0	1	16	5	11	.255	.340	.327
Late Inning Pressure	54	11	1	0	1	4	12	5	.204	.278	.358
Leading Off	18	6	0	0	1	1	5	0	.333	.500	.478
Bases Empty	35	7	1	0	1	1	7	1	.200	.314	.333
Runners On	19	4	0	0	0	3	5	4	.211	.211	.400
Runners/Scor. Pos.	11	2	0	0	0	3	4	3	.182	.182	.400

DRIVING IN RUNS	0 Out	1 Out	2 Out	Total	
From 1B	1/36	1/52	3/50	5/138	4%
From 2B	3/18	5/32	7/34	15/84	18%
From 3B	2/7	9/18	5/20	16/45	36%
Scoring Position	5/25	14/50	12/54	31/129	24%
Scor. Pos. %	20%	28%	22%	24%	
Driving In Runners from 3B with Less than Two Out:			11/25	44%	

Loves to face: Ted Power (.636, 7-for-11)
Hates to face: Guys named Smith (see below)
Five hits in 53 career at bats against pitchers named Smith: 0-for-17 vs. Bryn, 3-for-19 vs. Dave, 2-for-16 vs. Lee, and 0-for-1 vs. Mike. ... Fly-ball hitter: 0.87 G/A ratio last season. ... Led N.L. second basemen in total chances (888) and turned more double plays (127) than any N.L. second baseman since Dave Cash's 141 in 1974). ... Averaged 4.25 assists per nine innings, highest rate among N.L. second basemen (minimum: 300 innings). ... Tied major-league record for assists by a second baseman in one game with 12 vs. San Diego on April 14. ... Batted .178 in day games, .258 in night games last season. Career averages: .221 and .252. ... Has hit a home run at every current N.L. stadium except Olympic Stadium (.168 career batting average in 95 AB).

Steve Jeltz

Philadelphia Phillies	AB	H	2B	3B	HR	RRF	BB	SO	BA	SA	OBA
Season	196	37	4	1	0	13	26	55	.189	.219	.283
vs. Left-Handed Pitchers	62	12	2	0	0	6	12	15	.194	.226	.324
vs. Right-Handed Pitchers	134	25	2	1	0	7	14	40	.187	.216	.262
Home	99	20	4	1	0	9	10	24	.202	.263	.273
Road	97	17	0	0	0	4	16	31	.175	.175	.292
Grass	38	3	0	0	0	2	4	7	.079	.079	.167
Artificial Turf	158	34	4	1	0	11	22	48	.215	.253	.309
April	52	11	0	0	0	5	4	14	.212	.212	.263
May	40	7	0	0	0	2	5	10	.175	.175	.267
June	48	7	2	0	0	2	6	17	.146	.188	.241
July	49	12	2	1	0	4	10	11	.245	.327	.373
August	0	0	0	0	0	0	0	0	.000	.000	.000
Sept./Oct.	7	0	0	0	0	0	1	3	.000	.000	.125
Leading Off Inn.	40	8	1	0	0	0	4	8	.200	.225	.273
Bases Empty	105	17	2	0	0	0	11	28	.162	.181	.241
Runners On	91	20	2	1	0	13	15	27	.220	.264	.327
Runners/Scor. Pos.	48	10	1	1	0	13	8	15	.208	.271	.316
Runners On/2 Out	43	11	0	1	0	7	9	13	.256	.302	.385
Scor. Pos./2 Out	27	7	0	1	0	7	7	8	.259	.333	.412
Late Inning Pressure	16	3	1	0	0	1	0	2	.188	.250	.188
Leading Off	3	0	0	0	0	0	0	1	.000	.000	.000
Bases Empty	8	0	0	0	0	0	0	2	.000	.000	.000
Runners On	8	3	1	0	0	1	0	0	.375	.500	.375
Runners/Scor. Pos.	2	1	0	0	0	1	0	0	.500	.500	.500

DRIVING IN RUNS	0 Out	1 Out	2 Out	Total	
From 1B	0/17	0/25	1/31	1/73	1%
From 2B	1/7	2/12	3/19	6/38	16%
From 3B	0/2	3/4	3/10	6/16	38%
Scoring Position	1/9	5/16	6/29	12/54	22%
Scor. Pos. %	11%	31%	21%	22%	
Driving In Runners from 3B with Less than Two Out:			3/6	50%	

Loves to face: Scott Sanderson (.667, 2-for-3)
Hates to face: Dennis Eckersley (0-for-9)
Ground-ball hitter: 2.74 G/A ratio was highest in majors last season (minimum: 200 PA). Career average: 2.82. ... Career batting average of .303 (10-for-33) with two outs and runners in scoring position. ... Five hits (all singles) in 53 career at bats on grass fields for an .094 average; .215 on artificial surfaces. ... Committed three errors on opening day, and eight in first 19 games before 46-game errorless streak, only 13 short of single-season N.L. record set by Roger Metzger in 1976. ... Career batting averages: .227 with runners on base, .163 with the bases empty. ... No doubles or triples in 133 career at bats away from Veterans Stadium.

Howard Johnson

New York Mets	AB	H	2B	3B	HR	RRF	BB	SO	BA	SA	OBA
Season	389	94	18	4	11	52	34	78	.242	.393	.300
vs. Left-Handed Pitchers	77	12	0	1	3	8	9	21	.156	.299	.241
vs. Right-Handed Pitchers	312	82	18	3	8	44	25	57	.263	.417	.315
Home	188	43	7	2	5	30	19	36	.229	.367	.297
Road	201	51	11	2	6	22	15	42	.254	.418	.303
Grass	264	59	10	4	8	38	26	57	.223	.383	.290
Artificial Turf	125	35	8	0	3	14	8	21	.280	.416	.321
April	46	7	1	0	0	4	7	12	.152	.174	.264
May	55	9	0	1	1	5	5	8	.164	.255	.230
June	60	14	2	0	1	3	3	18	.233	.317	.270
July	84	25	6	0	4	19	7	11	.298	.512	.340
August	56	16	3	1	2	8	10	13	.286	.482	.394
Sept./Oct.	88	23	6	2	3	13	2	16	.261	.477	.278
Leading Off Inn.	71	16	5	0	1	1	6	14	.225	.338	.286
Bases Empty	208	53	12	2	7	7	12	41	.255	.433	.295
Runners On	181	41	6	2	4	45	22	37	.227	.348	.304
Runners/Scor. Pos.	100	20	5	0	1	35	17	21	.200	.280	.306
Runners On/2 Out	84	20	3	1	4	25	10	15	.238	.440	.319
Scor. Pos./2 Out	53	11	3	0	1	18	6	10	.208	.321	.288
Late Inning Pressure	61	17	4	1	4	8	7	14	.279	.574	.353
Leading Off	15	4	1	0	1	1	3	3	.267	.533	.389
Bases Empty	35	13	3	1	3	3	3	6	.371	.771	.421
Runners On	26	4	1	0	1	5	4	8	.154	.308	.267
Runners/Scor. Pos.	14	2	1	0	0	3	2	4	.143	.214	.250

DRIVING IN RUNS	0 Out	1 Out	2 Out	Total	
From 1B	1/36	2/40	5/63	8/139	6%
From 2B	1/14	3/30	8/40	12/84	14%
From 3B	6/7	7/11	8/27	21/45	47%
Scoring Position	7/21	10/41	16/67	33/129	26%
Scor. Pos. %	33%	24%	24%	26%	
Driving In Runners from 3B with Less than Two Out:			13/18	72%	

Loves to face: Nolan Ryan (1.000, 3-for-3)
Hates to face: Tom Browning (0-for-9)
Fly-ball hitter: 0.65 G/A ratio last season, 3d-lowest in N.L. last season (minimum: 200 PA). Career average: 0.73. ... Grand slam off Danny Cox on Sept. 10 immediately followed a bench-clearing altercation involving George Foster and Cox. ... Career batting averages: .197 (one HR per 39.6 AB) batting right-handed, .269 (one HR per 30.7 AB) batting left-handed. ... Mets won 10 of the 11 games in which he hit a home run. ... Has hit three extra-inning homers over the past two seasons. ... An all-time record? Scored four runs after entering game in *ninth* inning on July 4 at Atlanta.

Steve Kemp

Pittsburgh Pirates	AB	H	2B	3B	HR	RRF	BB	SO	BA	SA	OBA
Season	236	59	13	2	2	21	25	54	.250	.347	.317
vs. Left-Handed Pitchers	28	6	1	0	0	3	2	6	.214	.250	.250
vs. Right-Handed Pitchers	208	53	12	2	2	18	23	48	.255	.361	.326
Home	102	28	6	0	1	15	15	24	.275	.363	.358
Road	134	31	7	2	1	6	10	30	.231	.336	.283
Grass	71	18	6	1	1	1	5	15	.254	.408	.303
Artificial Turf	165	41	7	1	1	20	20	39	.248	.321	.323
April	25	6	1	1	0	4	1	4	.240	.360	.269
May	55	14	3	0	0	5	11	17	.255	.309	.373
June	59	9	2	0	0	6	7	15	.153	.186	.235
July	44	14	4	0	2	5	3	5	.318	.545	.354
August	28	5	2	1	0	0	2	8	.179	.321	.233
Sept./Oct.	25	11	1	0	0	1	1	5	.440	.480	.462
Leading Off Inn.	55	13	2	0	2	2	3	12	.236	.382	.276
Bases Empty	143	37	9	2	2	2	12	35	.259	.392	.316
Runners On	93	22	4	0	0	19	13	19	.237	.280	.318
Runners/Scor. Pos.	55	11	1	0	0	17	10	11	.200	.218	.304
Runners On/2 Out	37	8	2	0	0	7	5	6	.216	.270	.310
Scor. Pos./2 Out	29	6	1	0	0	6	4	6	.207	.241	.303
Late Inning Pressure	47	17	3	2	0	3	3	11	.362	.511	.400
Leading Off	9	6	2	0	0	0	1	1	.667	.889	.700
Bases Empty	27	12	2	2	0	0	1	6	.444	.667	.464
Runners On	20	5	1	0	0	3	2	5	.250	.300	.318
Runners/Scor. Pos.	12	2	0	0	0	2	2	3	.167	.167	.286

DRIVING IN RUNS	0 Out	1 Out	2 Out	Total	
From 1B	1/14	0/28	2/28	3/70	4%
From 2B	0/7	2/18	2/17	4/42	10%
From 3B	2/3	7/8	3/17	12/28	43%
Scoring Position	2/10	9/26	5/34	16/70	23%
Scor. Pos. %	20%	35%	15%	23%	
Driving In Runners from 3B with Less than Two Out:			9/11	82%	

Loves to face: Steve Trout (.727, 8-for-11, 1 HR)
Hates to face: Kevin Gross (0-for-7)
Led N.L. outfielders with 106 errorless chances last season. . . . Batting average with runners in scoring position (.200) was the lowest of his nine-year career. . . . Career batting averages of .306 in day games, .267 in night games; .262 (one extra-base hit per 14.9 AB) vs. left-handed pitchers, .289 (one XBH per 10.8 AB) vs. right-handers. . . . RDI percentage from scoring position: .350 from 1977 through 1982, .266 in three seasons since then; .207 in Late-Inning Pressure Situations over the past five seasons.

Sammy Khalifa

Pittsburgh Pirates	AB	H	2B	3B	HR	RRF	BB	SO	BA	SA	OBA
Season	320	76	14	3	2	34	34	56	.238	.319	.307
vs. Left-Handed Pitchers	87	23	4	2	0	7	11	8	.264	.356	.343
vs. Right-Handed Pitchers	233	53	10	1	2	27	23	48	.227	.305	.293
Home	165	42	12	0	1	16	21	30	.255	.345	.335
Road	155	34	2	3	1	18	13	26	.219	.290	.276
Grass	81	14	2	0	1	11	4	13	.173	.235	.212
Artificial Turf	239	62	12	3	1	23	30	43	.259	.347	.337
April	0	0	0	0	0	0	0	0	.000	.000	.000
May	0	0	0	0	0	0	0	0	.000	.000	.000
June	23	8	3	0	0	0	2	4	.348	.478	.400
July	93	20	3	0	1	9	7	7	.215	.280	.270
August	95	19	4	1	1	9	7	17	.200	.295	.250
Sept./Oct.	109	29	4	2	0	16	18	28	.266	.339	.364
Leading Off Inn.	77	17	5	2	1	1	4	14	.221	.377	.259
Bases Empty	197	50	10	3	1	1	14	30	.254	.350	.303
Runners On	123	26	4	0	1	33	20	26	.211	.268	.313
Runners/Scor. Pos.	73	15	2	0	1	32	17	14	.205	.274	.340
Runners On/2 Out	47	8	0	0	0	8	14	9	.170	.170	.361
Scor. Pos./2 Out	34	5	0	0	0	8	13	6	.147	.147	.383
Late Inning Pressure	59	16	2	1	0	2	6	12	.271	.339	.338
Leading Off	17	4	0	1	0	0	1	3	.235	.353	.278
Bases Empty	37	11	1	1	0	0	5	5	.297	.378	.381
Runners On	22	5	1	0	0	2	1	7	.227	.273	.261
Runners/Scor. Pos.	11	1	0	0	0	1	1	4	.091	.091	.167

DRIVING IN RUNS	0 Out	1 Out	2 Out	Total	
From 1B	1/26	1/35	0/31	2/92	2%
From 2B	2/8	6/25	4/29	12/62	19%
From 3B	3/6	11/16	4/15	18/37	49%
Scoring Position	5/14	17/41	8/44	30/99	30%
Scor. Pos. %	36%	41%	18%	30%	
Driving In Runners from 3B with Less than Two Out:			14/22	64%	

Loves to face: Ricky Horton (.750, 3-for-4, 1 3B)
Hates to face: Roger McDowell (0-for-4, 3 SO)
Youngest everyday player in N.L. last season, seven weeks older than his A.L. counterpart, Ozzie Guillen. . . . Three N.L. pitchers last season were younger: Dwight Gooden, Floyd Youmans, and Lance McCullers. . . . Made first major-league start on June 25, and started all but one Pittsburgh game thereafter. . . . Drove in only one of 12 base runners from scoring position in Late-Inning Pressure Situations. . . . Hit only two home runs in 1,134 minor-league at bats, but two more in half-season in majors. . . . No kidding: Khalifa's father, Rashad, instructed NBC's Ahmad Rashad in Islam. . . . Does that make Sammy spiritually related to Bill Cosby?

Terry Kennedy

San Diego Padres	AB	H	2B	3B	HR	RRF	BB	SO	BA	SA	OBA
Season	532	139	27	1	10	78	31	102	.261	.372	.301
vs. Left-Handed Pitchers	147	38	8	0	3	25	5	42	.259	.374	.283
vs. Right-Handed Pitchers	385	101	19	1	7	53	26	60	.262	.371	.308
Home	279	65	12	1	7	41	16	52	.233	.358	.274
Road	253	74	15	0	3	37	15	50	.292	.387	.331
Grass	399	95	20	1	9	57	26	78	.238	.361	.283
Artificial Turf	133	44	7	0	1	21	5	24	.331	.406	.355
April	68	11	1	0	4	9	5	15	.162	.353	.216
May	84	31	6	0	2	23	5	14	.369	.512	.404
June	99	22	6	1	1	12	6	22	.222	.333	.264
July	98	29	7	0	2	16	1	14	.296	.429	.303
August	89	20	4	0	0	11	4	16	.225	.270	.258
Sept./Oct.	94	26	3	0	1	7	10	21	.277	.340	.346
Leading Off Inn.	120	22	4	0	1	1	5	21	.183	.242	.216
Bases Empty	275	65	13	1	5	5	13	55	.236	.345	.271
Runners On	257	74	14	0	5	73	18	47	.288	.401	.332
Runners/Scor. Pos.	159	47	9	0	5	70	18	30	.296	.447	.363
Runners On/2 Out	117	27	3	0	3	25	10	26	.231	.333	.291
Scor. Pos./2 Out	76	17	1	0	3	23	10	18	.224	.355	.314
Late Inning Pressure	85	25	4	0	1	12	7	13	.294	.376	.348
Leading Off	17	3	0	0	0	0	1	3	.176	.176	.222
Bases Empty	44	10	1	0	1	1	2	7	.227	.318	.261
Runners On	41	15	3	0	0	11	5	6	.366	.439	.435
Runners/Scor. Pos.	29	8	2	0	0	11	5	6	.276	.345	.382

DRIVING IN RUNS	0 Out	1 Out	2 Out	Total	
From 1B	1/41	4/68	3/79	8/188	4%
From 2B	6/19	12/40	13/58	31/117	26%
From 3B	8/10	15/34	6/34	29/78	37%
Scoring Position	14/29	27/74	19/92	60/195	31%
Scor. Pos. %	48%	36%	21%	31%	
Driving In Runners from 3B with Less than Two Out:			23/44	52%	

Loves to face: Joe Price (.500, 13-for-26, 2 HR)
Hates to face: Alejandro Pena (.063, 1-for-16, 1 HR)
Led N.L with .369 batting average during the month of May. . . . Topped 100-strikeout mark for the first time in his career, after flirting with it for each of three previous seasons (91, 89, 99). . . . Career batting average of .320 in Late-Inning Pressure Situations with runners on base. . . . Career with the bases loaded: .246 (15-for-61), one walk, 15 strikeouts. . . . Career batting average of .351 at Veterans Stadium. . . . Has driven in only one base runner from first base in Late-Inning Pressure Situations over the past three seasons. . . . Ratio of 8.40 strikeouts per walk vs. left-handed pitchers was highest in majors last season (minimum: 25 SO), but lower than his average a year earlier (14.0 SO per BB). . . . No triples in 1,455 career at bats in road games.

Ray Knight

New York Mets	AB	H	2B	3B	HR	RRF	BB	SO	BA	SA	OBA
Season	271	59	12	0	6	39	13	32	.218	.328	.252
vs. Left-Handed Pitchers	170	44	9	0	6	29	6	21	.259	.418	.285
vs. Right-Handed Pitchers	101	15	3	0	0	10	7	11	.149	.178	.198
Home	127	25	6	0	4	23	7	19	.197	.339	.234
Road	144	34	6	0	2	16	6	13	.236	.319	.268
Grass	206	44	9	0	6	34	8	25	.214	.345	.240
Artificial Turf	65	15	3	0	0	5	5	7	.231	.277	.288
April	17	3	0	0	0	1	1	2	.176	.176	.250
May	39	7	3	0	2	8	5	5	.179	.410	.267
June	67	11	3	0	1	3	1	11	.164	.254	.174
July	40	14	4	0	1	12	1	5	.350	.525	.357
August	49	10	0	0	1	7	2	5	.204	.265	.231
Sept./Oct.	59	14	2	0	1	8	3	4	.237	.322	.274
Leading Off Inn.	47	7	1	0	0	0	4	5	.149	.170	.231
Bases Empty	147	31	4	0	1	1	8	17	.211	.259	.256
Runners On	124	28	8	0	5	38	5	15	.226	.411	.246
Runners/Scor. Pos.	64	18	4	0	3	32	3	11	.281	.484	.292
Runners On/2 Out	47	8	2	0	1	10	3	7	.170	.277	.220
Scor. Pos./2 Out	28	6	0	0	1	9	2	5	.214	.321	.267
Late Inning Pressure	46	9	2	0	1	3	1	4	.196	.304	.213
Leading Off	8	1	0	0	0	0	0	1	.125	.125	.125
Bases Empty	28	7	1	0	0	0	1	3	.250	.286	.276
Runners On	18	2	1	0	1	3	0	1	.111	.333	.111
Runners/Scor. Pos.	7	1	1	0	0	1	0	0	.143	.286	.143

DRIVING IN RUNS	0 Out	1 Out	2 Out	Total	
From 1B	3/24	3/39	2/35	8/98	8%
From 2B	0/10	4/19	4/21	8/50	16%
From 3B	3/6	11/16	3/11	17/33	52%
Scoring Position	3/16	15/35	7/32	25/83	30%
Scor. Pos. %	19%	43%	22%	30%	
Driving In Runners from 3B with Less than Two Out:			14/22	64%	

Loves to face: Steve Bedrosian (.529, 9-for-17, 2 HR)
Hates to face: Kent Tekulve (.077, 2-for-26)
Committed one error in 27 games on artificial surfaces, six errors in 63 games on grass fields. . . . Batting average with runners in scoring position (.281) was his highest since 1979, when he hit .325 in such situations. . . . Batted 110 points higher vs. left-handers than right-handers, largest difference in N.L. (minimum: 100 PA vs. each). . . . Career batting averages: .291 on grass fields, .266 on artificial surfaces. . . . Averaged 1.66 assists per nine innings last season, 2d-lowest rate among N.L. third basemen (minimum: 300 innings). . . . Grounded into 17 double plays in 64 opportunities last season, 2d-highest average among N.L. players (minimum: 5 GIDP). . . . Has homered at every current N.L. stadium except Olympic Stadium (118 career AB). . . . Career batting average of .376 at Atlanta Stadium (8 HR in 218 AB).

Brad Komminsk

Atlanta Braves	AB	H	2B	3B	HR	RRF	BB	SO	BA	SA	OBA
Season	300	68	12	3	4	24	38	71	.227	.327	.314
vs. Left-Handed Pitchers	182	39	7	2	3	13	19	42	.214	.324	.289
vs. Right-Handed Pitchers	118	29	5	1	1	11	19	29	.246	.331	.350
Home	162	33	9	3	1	11	24	41	.204	.315	.309
Road	138	35	3	0	3	13	14	30	.254	.341	.320
Grass	224	50	10	3	4	19	29	56	.223	.348	.313
Artificial Turf	76	18	2	0	0	5	9	15	.237	.263	.318
April	68	16	1	0	0	5	6	12	.235	.250	.297
May	32	8	1	0	0	3	8	11	.250	.281	.390
June	70	15	2	2	0	4	7	12	.214	.300	.295
July	35	5	1	0	0	0	5	9	.143	.171	.250
August	52	15	5	1	2	6	7	14	.288	.538	.367
Sept./Oct.	43	9	2	0	2	6	5	13	.209	.395	.292
Leading Off Inn.	86	23	7	2	1	1	9	18	.267	.430	.344
Bases Empty	188	43	8	3	3	3	16	38	.229	.351	.293
Runners On	112	25	4	0	1	21	22	33	.223	.286	.346
Runners/Scor. Pos.	63	16	2	0	1	20	13	19	.254	.333	.372
Runners On/2 Out	37	10	1	0	1	8	8	11	.270	.378	.400
Scor. Pos./2 Out	21	3	0	0	1	8	4	7	.143	.286	.280
Late Inning Pressure	48	9	1	1	0	1	8	13	.188	.250	.304
Leading Off	16	7	1	1	0	0	1	2	.438	.625	.471
Bases Empty	27	8	1	1	0	0	1	4	.296	.407	.321
Runners On	21	1	0	0	0	1	7	9	.048	.048	.286
Runners/Scor. Pos.	13	1	0	0	0	1	6	6	.077	.077	.368

DRIVING IN RUNS	0 Out	1 Out	2 Out	Total	
From 1B	0/20	1/34	1/28	2/82	2%
From 2B	1/12	5/25	1/16	7/53	13%
From 3B	3/3	3/9	5/9	11/21	52%
Scoring Position	4/15	8/34	6/25	18/74	24%
Scor. Pos. %	27%	24%	24%	24%	
Driving In Runners from 3B with Less than Two Out:			6/12	50%	

Loves to face: Scott Sanderson (.571, 4-for-7, 1 HR)
Hates to face: Rick Honeycutt (0-for-15)
Main beneficiary of Dale Murphy's hot April: ranked second in the league in runs scored for the month before reality set in. . . . Batted .281 with three homers in 34 day games, .201 with one home run in 72 night games. . . . Home run on August 11 was his first of the season after a drought of 257 plate appearances. . . . Did not drive in a run in 34 games from June 13 to August 9. . . . Career batting averages: .247 with runners on base, .193 with the bases empty; .204 on grass fields, .253 on artificial surfaces. . . . Stolen base percentage of .556 (10 of 18) last season was the lowest among all players with 10 or more steals. . . . No triples in 315 career at bats in road games. . . . Braves were four games below the .500 mark in his 74 starts, 31–57 when he didn't start.

Wayne Krenchicki

Cincinnati Reds	AB	H	2B	3B	HR	RRF	BB	SO	BA	SA	OBA
Season	173	47	9	0	4	25	28	20	.272	.393	.369
vs. Left-Handed Pitchers	10	2	0	0	0	2	1	2	.200	.200	.250
vs. Right-Handed Pitchers	163	45	9	0	4	23	27	18	.276	.405	.377
Home	97	30	7	0	2	15	18	14	.309	.443	.414
Road	76	17	2	0	2	10	10	6	.224	.329	.310
Grass	43	12	0	0	2	7	7	4	.279	.419	.380
Artificial Turf	130	35	9	0	2	18	21	16	.269	.385	.366
April	11	2	0	0	0	0	3	2	.182	.182	.357
May	35	8	2	0	0	2	5	7	.229	.286	.325
June	53	20	5	0	3	12	10	8	.377	.642	.469
July	31	9	2	0	0	3	2	0	.290	.355	.333
August	13	0	0	0	0	1	3	1	.000	.000	.188
Sept./Oct.	30	8	0	0	1	7	5	2	.267	.367	.361
Leading Off Inn.	38	10	4	0	1	1	4	4	.263	.447	.333
Bases Empty	97	26	6	0	2	2	10	12	.268	.392	.336
Runners On	76	21	3	0	2	23	18	8	.276	.395	.406
Runners/Scor. Pos.	58	15	3	0	2	23	11	6	.259	.414	.366
Runners On/2 Out	39	9	2	0	2	15	11	5	.231	.436	.400
Scor. Pos./2 Out	35	9	2	0	2	15	7	4	.257	.486	.381
Late Inning Pressure	39	9	2	0	0	5	6	5	.231	.282	.333
Leading Off	6	1	0	0	0	0	1	1	.167	.167	.286
Bases Empty	16	5	0	0	0	0	2	1	.313	.313	.389
Runners On	23	4	2	0	0	5	4	4	.174	.261	.296
Runners/Scor. Pos.	17	2	2	0	0	5	2	2	.118	.235	.211

DRIVING IN RUNS	0 Out	1 Out	2 Out	Total	
From 1B	0/6	0/21	3/26	3/53	6%
From 2B	1/8	0/10	8/27	9/45	20%
From 3B	1/4	6/8	2/9	9/21	43%
Scoring Position	2/12	6/18	10/36	18/66	27%
Scor. Pos. %	17%	33%	28%	27%	
Driving In Runners from 3B with Less than Two Out:			7/12	58%	

Loves to face: Dennis Eckersley (.467, 7-for-15)
Hates to face: Dick Ruthven (0-for-7)
Started an 0-for-17 slump the day the Reds acquired Buddy Bell. . . . Pinch-hit a grand slam homer off Alejandro Pena on October 4. . . . Hit home runs in consecutive games for the first time in his career (June 27–28). . . . Batted .324 in day games last season, .238 in night games; career: .324 day, .249 night. . . . Career batting average of .315 leading off innings. . . . Career batting averages: .210 (no extra-base hits in 62 at bats) vs. left-handers, .278 vs. right-handers. . . . Only 11 players in *Player Analysis* history have more at bats vs. southpaws without an XBH: nine pitchers, Chris Arnold, and World Series immortal Jim Mason. . . . One hit in 25 career at bats at the Astrodome; 2-for-21 at Olympic Stadium. . . . Career batting average of .429 (18-for-42) at San Diego Stadium.

Ken Landreaux

Los Angeles Dodgers	AB	H	2B	3B	HR	RRF	BB	SO	BA	SA	OBA
Season	482	129	26	2	12	54	33	37	.268	.405	.311
vs. Left-Handed Pitchers	59	11	3	0	2	5	4	14	.186	.339	.246
vs. Right-Handed Pitchers	423	118	23	2	10	49	29	23	.279	.414	.320
Home	223	55	10	0	2	20	17	24	.247	.318	.294
Road	259	74	16	2	10	34	16	13	.286	.479	.326
Grass	349	99	17	0	8	34	22	29	.284	.401	.321
Artificial Turf	133	30	9	2	4	20	11	8	.226	.414	.286
April	54	9	3	0	3	4	1	5	.167	.389	.182
May	76	19	5	1	0	6	1	5	.250	.342	.260
June	78	22	4	0	1	8	8	1	.282	.372	.341
July	74	26	5	0	3	11	6	7	.351	.541	.390
August	76	24	4	0	3	12	6	2	.316	.487	.365
Sept./Oct.	124	29	5	1	2	13	11	17	.234	.339	.292
Leading Off Inn.	86	18	3	0	3	3	3	6	.209	.349	.236
Bases Empty	287	82	14	0	10	10	16	22	.286	.439	.323
Runners On	195	47	12	2	2	44	17	15	.241	.354	.294
Runners/Scor. Pos.	119	20	5	1	2	40	11	10	.168	.277	.230
Runners On/2 Out	70	12	5	1	0	14	9	6	.171	.271	.266
Scor. Pos./2 Out	50	7	3	0	0	11	8	5	.140	.200	.259
Late Inning Pressure	60	16	3	0	0	2	5	7	.267	.317	.323
Leading Off	12	4	1	0	0	0	0	0	.333	.417	.333
Bases Empty	34	10	1	0	0	0	2	1	.294	.324	.333
Runners On	26	6	2	0	0	2	3	6	.231	.308	.310
Runners/Scor. Pos.	16	1	0	0	0	0	3	4	.063	.063	.211

DRIVING IN RUNS	0 Out	1 Out	2 Out	Total	
From 1B	1/38	0/38	4/45	5/121	4%
From 2B	1/17	7/40	5/37	13/94	14%
From 3B	6/9	13/19	4/19	23/47	49%
Scoring Position	7/26	20/59	9/56	36/141	26%
Scor. Pos. %	27%	34%	16%	26%	
Driving In Runners from 3B with Less than Two Out:			19/28	68%	

Loves to face: Ron Robinson (.467, 7-for-15, 1 HR)
Hates to face: Dennis Eckersley (.040, 1-for-25, 1 HR)
Fly-ball hitter: 0.83 G/A ratio last season. . . . Did not strike out in 50 plate appearances vs. San Diego last season. . . . Ten of his 12 home runs were solo shots. Drove in only two base runners with 12 homers, lowest average in N.L. (minimum: 10 HR). . . . Career batting averages: .235 vs. left-handers, .280 vs. right-handers. . . . Had batted .326 with two outs and runners in scoring position over three previous seasons before 1985 disaster. . . . Has hit a home run at every current N.L. stadium except Shea (91 career AB). . . . Did not drive in any of 17 base runners from scoring position in Late-Inning Pressure Situations last season. Was 0-for-9 in 1981.

Tito Landrum

St. Louis Cardinals	AB	H	2B	3B	HR	RRF	BB	SO	BA	SA	OBA
Season	161	45	8	2	4	22	19	30	.280	.429	.356
vs. Left-Handed Pitchers	132	35	6	1	3	20	18	27	.265	.394	.353
vs. Right-Handed Pitchers	29	10	2	1	1	2	1	3	.345	.586	.367
Home	73	24	5	2	2	15	12	12	.329	.534	.424
Road	88	21	3	0	2	7	7	18	.239	.341	.295
Grass	43	12	1	0	2	4	5	7	.279	.442	.354
Artificial Turf	118	33	7	2	2	18	14	23	.280	.424	.356
April	3	0	0	0	0	0	1	0	.000	.000	.250
May	6	3	0	0	2	3	0	1	.500	1.500	.500
June	32	10	2	1	0	2	4	2	.313	.438	.389
July	39	12	2	0	0	4	5	9	.308	.359	.386
August	50	14	4	1	1	9	2	10	.280	.460	.308
Sept./Oct.	31	6	0	0	1	4	7	8	.194	.290	.342
Leading Off Inn.	25	5	3	0	0	0	4	5	.200	.320	.310
Bases Empty	76	19	5	1	1	1	10	11	.250	.382	.337
Runners On	85	26	3	1	3	21	9	19	.306	.471	.372
Runners/Scor. Pos.	46	13	1	1	1	15	9	12	.283	.413	.400
Runners On/2 Out	36	8	0	1	0	5	3	5	.222	.278	.282
Scor. Pos./2 Out	22	4	0	1	0	5	3	5	.182	.273	.280
Late Inning Pressure	32	10	2	0	1	2	5	7	.313	.469	.405
Leading Off	6	3	2	0	0	0	1	1	.500	.833	.571
Bases Empty	18	7	2	0	1	1	2	4	.389	.667	.450
Runners On	14	3	0	0	0	1	3	3	.214	.214	.353
Runners/Scor. Pos.	8	1	0	0	0	1	3	2	.125	.125	.364

DRIVING IN RUNS	0 Out	1 Out	2 Out	Total	
From 1B	1/12	4/24	0/27	5/63	8%
From 2B	1/8	3/11	3/14	7/33	21%
From 3B	1/4	3/5	2/11	6/20	30%
Scoring Position	2/12	6/16	5/25	13/53	25%
Scor. Pos. %	17%	38%	20%	25%	
Driving In Runners from 3B with Less than Two Out:			4/9	44%	

Loves to face: Mark Thurmond (.750, 3-for-4)
Hates to face: Steve Carlton (.148, 4-for-27)
Career batting averages of .263 (one HR per 52 AB) vs. left-handers, .292 (one HR in 178 career AB) vs. right-handers. . . . One walk per 12 plate appearances vs. lefties, one per 22 PA vs. righties. . . . Home run off Bill Laskey (Aug. 16) is his only big-league homer off a right-handed pitcher. . . . Career batting averages: .306 on grass fields, .253 on artificial surfaces. . . . Six hits, including three home runs, in 11 career at bats at Atlanta Stadium. . . . Has batted .324 in Late-Inning Pressure Situations over the past three seasons. . . . Year-by-year batting averages with two outs and runners on base, starting with 1980: .222, .250, .222, .222, .222, .222.

Vance Law

Montreal Expos	AB	H	2B	3B	HR	RRF	BB	SO	BA	SA	OBA
Season	519	138	30	6	10	57	86	96	.266	.405	.369
vs. Left-Handed Pitchers	159	39	10	0	4	11	26	23	.245	.384	.353
vs. Right-Handed Pitchers	360	99	20	6	6	46	60	73	.275	.414	.376
Home	247	65	17	2	5	27	53	47	.263	.409	.393
Road	272	73	13	4	5	30	33	49	.268	.401	.344
Grass	137	35	6	1	5	21	13	26	.255	.423	.314
Artificial Turf	382	103	24	5	5	36	73	70	.270	.398	.387
April	56	16	3	0	0	4	7	14	.286	.339	.365
May	68	14	4	0	0	4	12	14	.206	.265	.321
June	101	24	5	2	4	18	18	23	.238	.446	.350
July	94	27	7	2	2	8	17	14	.287	.468	.396
August	90	25	4	2	2	9	12	13	.278	.433	.365
Sept./Oct.	110	32	7	0	2	14	20	18	.291	.409	.397
Leading Off Inn.	93	27	1	1	4	4	9	16	.290	.452	.359
Bases Empty	299	83	14	3	6	6	44	51	.278	.405	.372
Runners On	220	55	16	3	4	51	42	45	.250	.405	.364
Runners/Scor. Pos.	143	32	6	2	1	39	31	32	.224	.315	.350
Runners On/2 Out	73	18	5	2	2	22	10	17	.247	.452	.337
Scor. Pos./2 Out	58	13	4	2	0	17	6	15	.224	.362	.297
Late Inning Pressure	78	22	5	2	0	10	11	16	.282	.397	.367
Leading Off	15	5	0	1	0	0	0	5	.333	.467	.333
Bases Empty	42	13	2	2	0	0	4	8	.310	.452	.370
Runners On	36	9	3	0	0	10	7	8	.250	.333	.364
Runners/Scor. Pos.	29	7	2	0	0	10	7	5	.241	.310	.378

DRIVING IN RUNS	0 Out	1 Out	2 Out	Total	
From 1B	4/40	3/54	5/42	12/136	9%
From 2B	5/31	4/41	8/40	17/112	15%
From 3B	4/8	7/22	7/23	18/53	34%
Scoring Position	9/39	11/63	15/63	35/165	21%
Scor. Pos. %	23%	17%	24%	21%	
Driving In Runners from 3B with Less than Two Out:			11/30	37%	

Loves to face: Shane Rawley (.714, 5-for-7, 2 2B, 1 3B)
Hates to face: Bob Ojeda (.067, 1-for-15)
Started 120 games at second base last season, compared to 33 in his first four major-league seasons combined. ... Committed six errors in 36 games on grass fields, six errors in 111 games on artificial turf. ... Expos won all 10 games in which he homered last season. ... Career batting average of .244 with runners in scoring position: .304 in Late-Inning Pressure Situations, .236 in unpressured situations. ... One home run per 36 career at bats vs. left-handed pitchers, one per 70 AB vs. right-handers. ... Had driven in 30.3 percent of runners in scoring position during three previous seasons.

Jeff Leonard

San Francisco Giants	AB	H	2B	3B	HR	RRF	BB	SO	BA	SA	OBA
Season	507	122	20	3	17	65	21	107	.241	.393	.272
vs. Left-Handed Pitchers	141	36	8	2	7	15	2	22	.255	.489	.266
vs. Right-Handed Pitchers	366	86	12	1	10	50	19	85	.235	.355	.274
Home	238	57	5	1	8	24	8	53	.239	.370	.263
Road	269	65	15	2	9	41	13	54	.242	.413	.279
Grass	388	93	10	1	16	55	16	84	.240	.394	.271
Artificial Turf	119	29	10	2	1	10	5	23	.244	.387	.274
April	69	11	3	0	1	7	3	25	.159	.246	.194
May	95	22	5	1	1	9	6	22	.232	.337	.277
June	117	33	2	2	7	16	6	16	.282	.513	.315
July	101	27	4	0	5	13	4	17	.267	.455	.295
August	46	12	2	0	2	7	2	13	.261	.435	.292
Sept./Oct.	79	17	4	0	1	13	0	14	.215	.304	.225
Leading Off Inn.	118	29	4	0	5	5	2	18	.246	.407	.258
Bases Empty	268	64	9	1	10	10	8	53	.239	.392	.261
Runners On	239	58	11	2	7	55	13	54	.243	.393	.283
Runners/Scor. Pos.	133	30	5	1	4	45	8	37	.226	.368	.273
Runners On/2 Out	103	22	2	1	2	16	6	30	.214	.311	.264
Scor. Pos./2 Out	63	11	2	1	2	16	2	21	.175	.333	.212
Late Inning Pressure	90	25	5	1	1	7	8	16	.278	.389	.337
Leading Off	24	7	1	0	0	0	0	7	.292	.333	.292
Bases Empty	50	14	2	1	0	0	1	11	.280	.360	.294
Runners On	40	11	3	0	1	7	7	5	.275	.425	.383
Runners/Scor. Pos.	14	2	1	0	0	3	4	2	.143	.214	.333

DRIVING IN RUNS	0 Out	1 Out	2 Out	Total	
From 1B	1/43	8/60	1/59	10/162	6%
From 2B	4/27	9/32	8/51	21/110	19%
From 3B	5/6	7/16	5/21	17/43	40%
Scoring Position	9/33	16/48	13/72	38/153	25%
Scor. Pos. %	27%	33%	18%	25%	
Driving In Runners from 3B with Less than Two Out:			12/22	55%	

Loves to face: Steve Trout (.529, 9-for-17, 2 HR)
Hates to face: Mario Soto (.103, 4-for-39, 23 SO)
Fly-ball hitter: 0.78 G/A ratio last season, 10th-lowest in N.L. (minimum: 200 PA). Career average: 1.06. ... Batted .298 vs. ground-ball pitchers last season, .197 vs. fly-ball pitchers. ... Highest batting average (.339) in the major leagues vs. left-handed pitchers from 1981 through '84. ... Career batting averages: .298 (one HR per 24.4 AB) vs. left-handed pitchers, .257 (one HR per 45.5 AB) vs. right-handers. ... Two walks in 143 plate appearances vs. lefties is lowest N.L. ratio since 1983, when Brian Harper drew one walk in 103 PA vs. southpaws. ... Career average of .219 in Late-Inning Pressure Situations with runners in scoring position. ... Has hit a home run at every N.L. stadium except Olympic Stadium (68 career AB). ... Year-by-year RDI percentage from scoring position, starting with 1981: .408, .366, .318, .280, .248.

Dave Lopes

Chicago Cubs	AB	H	2B	3B	HR	RRF	BB	SO	BA	SA	OBA
Season	275	78	11	0	11	46	46	37	.284	.444	.383
vs. Left-Handed Pitchers	92	22	6	0	5	16	15	12	.239	.467	.346
vs. Right-Handed Pitchers	183	56	5	0	6	30	31	25	.306	.432	.401
Home	131	37	6	0	6	23	26	20	.282	.466	.396
Road	144	41	5	0	5	23	20	17	.285	.424	.370
Grass	180	48	9	0	8	33	33	31	.267	.450	.377
Artificial Turf	95	30	2	0	3	13	13	6	.316	.432	.394
April	25	8	0	0	1	5	4	1	.320	.440	.414
May	51	17	1	0	3	15	15	9	.333	.529	.464
June	72	20	2	0	2	6	13	10	.278	.389	.388
July	57	17	4	0	3	12	6	6	.298	.526	.365
August	45	7	2	0	0	1	6	8	.156	.200	.255
Sept./Oct.	25	9	2	0	2	7	2	3	.360	.680	.407
Leading Off Inn.	73	20	2	0	1	1	13	15	.274	.342	.384
Bases Empty	154	45	7	0	2	2	24	27	.292	.377	.388
Runners On	121	33	4	0	9	44	22	10	.273	.529	.377
Runners/Scor. Pos.	75	20	2	0	7	39	19	6	.267	.573	.402
Runners On/2 Out	42	15	1	0	6	21	11	4	.357	.810	.491
Scor. Pos./2 Out	29	9	1	0	4	16	9	3	.310	.759	.474
Late Inning Pressure	54	16	4	0	4	12	8	6	.296	.593	.387
Leading Off	13	3	1	0	0	0	2	4	.231	.308	.333
Bases Empty	27	8	3	0	0	0	4	5	.296	.407	.387
Runners On	27	8	1	0	4	12	4	1	.296	.778	.387
Runners/Scor. Pos.	19	5	1	0	2	8	3	0	.263	.632	.364

DRIVING IN RUNS	0 Out	1 Out	2 Out	Total	
From 1B	1/21	0/44	6/27	7/92	8%
From 2B	2/10	5/23	6/23	13/56	23%
From 3B	4/7	8/14	3/10	15/31	48%
Scoring Position	6/17	13/37	9/33	28/87	32%
Scor. Pos. %	35%	35%	27%	32%	
Driving In Runners from 3B with Less than Two Out:			12/21	57%	

Loves to face: Rick Honeycutt (.636, 7-for-11)
Hates to face: Mario Soto (.143, 3-for-21)
Ground-ball hitter: 1.41 G/A ratio last season. ... Batted .359 vs. ground-ball pitchers last season, .218 vs. fly-ball pitchers. ... Was successful on all 17 stolen base attempts on artificial surfaces last season. Has stolen 28 consecutive bases on carpets since August 8, 1982, when Sal Butera nailed him at the Metrodome. Butera caught Lopes again last season, but it was on the dirt infield at Wrigley. ... One of three N.L. players to start at least 10 games at each outfield position last season. ... On-base percentage of .383 was the highest of his 14-year career. ... Batted for a higher average against right-handed pitchers than he did against left-handers for the first time since 1975. 11-year batting averages: .293 vs. lefties, .249 vs. righties.

Garry Maddox

Philadelphia Phillies	AB	H	2B	3B	HR	RRF	BB	SO	BA	SA	OBA
Season	218	52	8	1	4	23	13	26	.239	.339	.281
vs. Left-Handed Pitchers	114	31	7	0	2	16	7	12	.272	.386	.309
vs. Right-Handed Pitchers	104	21	1	1	2	7	6	14	.202	.288	.250
Home	112	27	5	1	2	10	7	12	.241	.357	.283
Road	106	25	3	0	2	13	6	14	.236	.321	.278
Grass	47	7	1	0	1	4	2	9	.149	.234	.196
Artificial Turf	171	45	7	1	3	19	11	17	.263	.368	.304
April	18	7	1	0	1	4	2	3	.389	.611	.476
May	41	8	2	0	0	3	2	8	.195	.244	.233
June	52	16	1	1	1	8	4	2	.308	.423	.351
July	42	9	2	0	0	2	0	3	.214	.262	.209
August	18	3	0	0	0	2	0	3	.167	.167	.167
Sept./Oct.	47	9	2	0	2	4	5	7	.191	.362	.264
Leading Off Inn.	60	13	2	0	1	1	2	6	.217	.300	.254
Bases Empty	128	30	3	0	4	4	5	18	.234	.352	.269
Runners On	90	22	5	1	0	19	8	8	.244	.322	.297
Runners/Scor. Pos.	55	13	4	1	0	19	6	6	.236	.345	.297
Runners On/2 Out	43	9	2	0	0	6	4	4	.209	.256	.277
Scor. Pos./2 Out	25	5	2	0	0	6	3	3	.200	.280	.286
Late Inning Pressure	45	8	0	0	1	1	4	6	.178	.244	.260
Leading Off	16	5	0	0	0	0	1	1	.313	.313	.389
Bases Empty	26	6	0	0	1	1	1	3	.231	.346	.286
Runners On	19	2	0	0	0	0	3	3	.105	.105	.227
Runners/Scor. Pos.	11	0	0	0	0	0	3	1	.000	.000	.214

DRIVING IN RUNS	0 Out	1 Out	2 Out	Total	
From 1B	0/11	1/22	0/27	1/60	2%
From 2B	2/11	2/10	3/20	7/41	17%
From 3B	2/5	6/9	3/8	11/22	50%
Scoring Position	4/16	8/19	6/28	18/63	29%
Scor. Pos. %	25%	42%	21%	29%	
Driving In Runners from 3B with Less than Two Out:			8/14	57%	

Loves to face: Rick Mahler (.500, 7-for-14)
Hates to face: Ted Power (0-for-11)
Fly-ball hitter: 0.90 G/A ratio last season. ... Batted .313 vs. ground-ball pitchers last season, .176 vs. fly-ball pitchers. ... Batted .273 in day games, .224 in night games. ... Since 1980 has averaged one home run per 34.8 at bats in day games, one homer per 73.8 at bats in night games. ... Batted .481 with seven RBIs vs. Montreal last season. ... Has batted .137 (20-for-145) in Late-Inning Pressure Situations since 1983. ... Batted 70 points higher vs. right-handers than left-handers, 4th-largest difference in N.L. (minimum: 100 PA vs. each). ... Has batted .146 at Dodger Stadium over past seven seasons.

Bill Madlock

Pirates/Dodgers	AB	H	2B	3B	HR	RRF	BB	SO	BA	SA	OBA
Season	513	141	27	1	12	59	49	53	.275	.402	.345
vs. Left-Handed Pitchers	158	44	8	0	4	26	23	22	.278	.405	.366
vs. Right-Handed Pitchers	355	97	19	1	8	33	26	31	.273	.400	.335
Home	250	73	14	0	6	34	30	27	.292	.420	.373
Road	263	68	13	1	6	25	19	26	.259	.384	.317
Grass	220	65	9	0	6	24	18	18	.295	.418	.357
Artificial Turf	293	76	18	1	6	35	31	35	.259	.389	.336
April	63	11	5	0	0	4	3	5	.175	.254	.212
May	85	23	6	0	2	4	9	9	.271	.412	.347
June	85	21	5	1	1	6	9	10	.247	.365	.326
July	89	23	6	0	3	14	9	11	.258	.427	.330
August	78	23	1	0	4	15	9	7	.295	.462	.374
Sept./Oct.	113	40	4	0	2	16	10	11	.354	.442	.417
Leading Off Inn.	114	40	7	0	5	5	7	10	.351	.544	.388
Bases Empty	287	80	15	1	7	7	23	31	.279	.411	.337
Runners On	226	61	12	0	5	52	26	22	.270	.389	.355
Runners/Scor. Pos.	131	38	6	0	0	40	19	15	.290	.336	.390
Runners On/2 Out	88	23	3	0	1	15	11	9	.261	.330	.350
Scor. Pos./2 Out	56	15	1	0	0	13	9	6	.268	.286	.379
Late Inning Pressure	90	31	4	0	1	12	4	5	.344	.422	.379
Leading Off	24	14	3	0	1	1	1	1	.583	.833	.600
Bases Empty	49	19	3	0	1	1	1	3	.388	.510	.400
Runners On	41	12	1	0	0	11	3	2	.293	.317	.356
Runners/Scor. Pos.	27	9	1	0	0	11	3	1	.333	.370	.419

DRIVING IN RUNS	0 Out	1 Out	2 Out	Total	
From 1B	1/37	5/59	1/59	7/155	5%
From 2B	1/18	8/42	6/44	15/104	14%
From 3B	6/9	12/19	7/19	25/47	53%
Scoring Position	7/27	20/61	13/63	40/151	26%
Scor. Pos. %	26%	33%	21%	26%	
Driving In Runners from 3B with Less than Two Out:			18/28	64%	

Loves to face: Mark Davis (.500, 9-for-18, 3 HR)
Hates to face: Greg Minton (.105, 2-for-19)
Fly-ball hitter: 0.89 G/A ratio last season.... September batting average of .340 was seventh-highest in N.L.... Batted .352 with five home runs vs. New York last season.... Seemed to revive nicely once he got over the bends: batted .251 in 110 games with Pittsburgh, .360 in 34 games with the Dodgers.... Batting .563 (9-for-16) with the bases loaded over the last two seasons.... Led N.L. with six hits in Late-Inning Pressure Situations with 2 outs and runners in scoring position last season.... Has batted .337 at his new home, Dodger Stadium, over the past 10 seasons, .343 at Veterans Stadium during that same time.... Drove in 86.1 percent of runners from third base in 1976, still the *Player Analysis* record.

Candy Maldonado

Los Angeles Dodgers	AB	H	2B	3B	HR	RRF	BB	SO	BA	SA	OBA
Season	213	48	7	1	5	21	19	40	.225	.338	.288
vs. Left-Handed Pitchers	168	39	5	1	5	19	17	31	.232	.363	.301
vs. Right-Handed Pitchers	45	9	2	0	0	2	2	9	.200	.244	.234
Home	103	20	2	0	2	10	11	22	.194	.272	.270
Road	110	28	5	1	3	11	8	18	.255	.400	.305
Grass	162	36	4	0	4	16	15	31	.222	.321	.287
Artificial Turf	51	12	3	1	1	5	4	9	.235	.392	.291
April	42	9	1	0	2	4	3	9	.214	.381	.267
May	30	3	1	0	0	2	1	7	.100	.133	.125
June	17	4	0	0	0	0	3	2	.235	.235	.350
July	42	10	0	0	2	5	5	8	.238	.381	.319
August	32	7	1	0	1	2	3	5	.219	.344	.286
Sept./Oct.	50	15	4	1	0	8	4	9	.300	.420	.352
Leading Off Inn.	44	14	0	0	3	3	1	6	.318	.523	.333
Bases Empty	116	26	1	0	5	5	7	22	.224	.362	.268
Runners On	97	22	6	1	0	16	12	18	.227	.309	.309
Runners/Scor. Pos.	49	10	4	0	0	13	9	11	.204	.286	.322
Runners On/2 Out	40	4	3	0	0	6	5	8	.100	.175	.200
Scor. Pos./2 Out	27	2	1	0	0	4	5	7	.074	.111	.219
Late Inning Pressure	42	9	0	0	3	3	2	10	.214	.429	.250
Leading Off	6	3	0	0	2	2	0	0	.500	1.500	.500
Bases Empty	23	7	0	0	3	3	0	5	.304	.696	.304
Runners On	19	2	0	0	0	0	2	5	.105	.105	.190
Runners/Scor. Pos.	10	0	0	0	0	0	2	4	.000	.000	.167

DRIVING IN RUNS	0 Out	1 Out	2 Out	Total	
From 1B	1/18	1/26	2/25	4/69	6%
From 2B	2/8	1/10	3/21	6/39	15%
From 3B	2/3	3/5	1/12	6/20	30%
Scoring Position	4/11	4/15	4/33	12/59	20%
Scor. Pos. %	36%	27%	12%	20%	
Driving In Runners from 3B with Less than Two Out:			5/8	63%	

Loves to face: Frank DiPino (.714, 5-for-7)
Hates to face: Shane Rawley (1-for-15)
Career batting averages of .254 vs. left-handers, .179 vs. right-handers. Nine of his eleven career homers have been against lefties.... Last home run off a right-handed pitcher: June 22, 1984, vs. Rick Camp.... Ten of his eleven home runs have been hit with the bases empty; only home run with runners on base was his first major-league HR, on August 15, 1983 vs. Fred Breining.... Five home runs in 105 career at bats in Late-Inning Pressure Situations, six in 440 nonpressured AB.... Career batting average of .211 (8-for-38, 1 HR) in Candlestick Park.... One hit in 18 career at bats at Olympic Stadium; career batting average of .417 (10-for-24) at Atlanta Stadium.... Has never hit a triple at Dodger Stadium (262 career AB).

Mike Marshall

Los Angeles Dodgers	AB	H	2B	3B	HR	RRF	BB	SO	BA	SA	OBA
Season	518	152	27	2	28	95	37	137	.293	.515	.342
vs. Left-Handed Pitchers	157	45	8	0	8	30	16	48	.287	.490	.349
vs. Right-Handed Pitchers	361	107	19	2	20	65	21	89	.296	.526	.339
Home	261	79	14	1	15	48	17	70	.303	.536	.345
Road	257	73	13	1	13	47	20	67	.284	.494	.338
Grass	389	116	16	1	19	69	24	101	.298	.491	.340
Artificial Turf	129	36	11	1	9	26	13	36	.279	.589	.345
April	79	23	2	0	4	9	9	24	.291	.468	.364
May	91	23	5	0	4	15	7	20	.253	.440	.300
June	48	11	2	0	2	8	5	19	.229	.396	.302
July	55	19	4	0	3	12	2	13	.345	.582	.379
August	104	28	5	0	4	14	6	27	.269	.433	.306
Sept./Oct.	141	48	9	2	11	37	8	34	.340	.667	.382
Leading Off Inn.	98	26	3	0	6	6	7	25	.265	.480	.321
Bases Empty	271	77	12	1	17	17	18	83	.284	.524	.333
Runners On	247	75	15	1	11	78	19	54	.304	.506	.351
Runners/Scor. Pos.	142	42	9	1	7	67	13	30	.296	.521	.350
Runners On/2 Out	109	36	9	1	7	43	12	21	.330	.624	.402
Scor. Pos./2 Out	70	24	7	1	3	34	8	13	.343	.600	.418
Late Inning Pressure	71	21	1	0	4	12	3	14	.296	.479	.324
Leading Off	21	9	0	0	1	1	0	2	.429	.571	.429
Bases Empty	45	14	1	0	1	1	1	9	.311	.400	.326
Runners On	26	7	0	0	3	11	2	5	.269	.615	.321
Runners/Scor. Pos.	15	5	0	0	2	9	2	3	.333	.733	.412

DRIVING IN RUNS	0 Out	1 Out	2 Out	Total	
From 1B	0/40	4/67	8/73	12/180	7%
From 2B	2/19	4/36	18/50	24/105	23%
From 3B	8/10	13/27	10/31	31/68	46%
Scoring Position	10/29	17/63	28/81	55/173	32%
Scor. Pos. %	34%	27%	35%	32%	
Driving In Runners from 3B with Less than Two Out:			21/37	57%	

Loves to face: Len Barker (.500, 8-for-16, 3 HR)
Hates to face: Rick Mahler (.100, 2-for-20)
Fly-ball hitter: 0.94 G/A ratio last season.... Averaged one strikeout per 4.1 plate appearances (worst rate among N.L. regulars).... Batted .171 with no walks and 14 strikeouts in 41 plate appearances vs. Montreal last season.... Was thrown out 10 times in 13 stolen base attempts last season.... Batted .240 in day games, .316 in night games.... Yearly batting averages vs. left-handers since 1982: .211, .238, .278, .287.... No triples in 466 career at bats vs. southpaws.... Batting average with runners in scoring position (.296) exceeded his overall season average (.293) for the first time in his career.... Career batting average of .370 at Wrigley Field (4 HR in 46 AB).

Carmelo Martinez

San Diego Padres	AB	H	2B	3B	HR	RRF	BB	SO	BA	SA	OBA
Season	514	130	28	1	21	76	87	82	.253	.434	.362
vs. Left-Handed Pitchers	166	41	10	0	8	25	36	24	.247	.452	.379
vs. Right-Handed Pitchers	348	89	18	1	13	51	51	58	.256	.425	.353
Home	256	70	10	1	15	46	49	39	.273	.496	.390
Road	258	60	18	0	6	30	38	43	.233	.372	.333
Grass	382	103	19	1	18	64	68	59	.270	.466	.379
Artificial Turf	132	27	9	0	3	12	19	23	.205	.341	.309
April	42	12	2	0	3	9	6	9	.286	.548	.367
May	88	25	9	1	4	16	9	15	.284	.545	.354
June	102	24	4	0	3	10	15	14	.235	.363	.333
July	87	18	4	0	3	9	15	11	.207	.356	.327
August	88	23	6	0	3	13	15	17	.261	.432	.369
Sept./Oct.	107	28	3	0	5	19	27	16	.262	.430	.412
Leading Off Inn.	111	19	4	1	3	3	24	21	.171	.306	.319
Bases Empty	271	60	12	1	12	12	58	46	.221	.406	.359
Runners On	243	70	16	0	9	64	29	36	.288	.465	.366
Runners/Scor. Pos.	130	30	5	0	4	51	20	23	.231	.362	.333
Runners On/2 Out	95	25	6	0	4	27	15	17	.263	.453	.369
Scor. Pos./2 Out	60	11	2	0	2	21	12	12	.183	.317	.329
Late Inning Pressure	95	24	4	0	3	16	10	11	.253	.389	.321
Leading Off	21	3	0	0	0	0	5	3	.143	.143	.308
Bases Empty	46	9	0	0	2	2	7	7	.196	.326	.302
Runners On	49	15	4	0	1	14	3	4	.306	.449	.340
Runners/Scor. Pos.	27	7	1	0	1	13	2	2	.259	.407	.300

DRIVING IN RUNS	0 Out	1 Out	2 Out	Total	
From 1B	3/48	4/64	6/70	13/182	7%
From 2B	2/14	8/37	9/41	19/92	21%
From 3B	6/12	9/19	8/35	23/66	35%
Scoring Position	8/26	17/56	17/76	42/158	27%
Scor. Pos. %	31%	30%	22%	27%	
Driving In Runners from 3B with Less than Two Out:			15/31	48%	

Loves to face: Jerry Reuss (.545, 6-for-11)
Hates to face: Scott Sanderson (0-for-9)
Fly-ball hitter: 0.89 G/A ratio last season.... Did not appear in a game in which he was not in the starting lineup last season.... Batted .207 in day games, .274 in night games.... Has batted for a higher average with runners on base than with runners in scoring position in each of his three seasons in majors.... Career batting average of .194 with two outs and runners in scoring position.... Padres had a record of 16–3 in games in which he hit a home run last season, 9–4 in 1984.... Career batting average of .149 (7-for-47) at Olympic Stadium.... Career: has driven in only 42 of 80 runners from third base with less than two outs (52.5%).... Career RDI percentage of .397 from scoring position in Late-Inning Pressure Situations.

Gary Matthews

Chicago Cubs	AB	H	2B	3B	HR	RRF	BB	SO	BA	SA	OBA
Season	298	70	12	0	13	44	59	64	.235	.406	.362
vs. Left-Handed Pitchers	82	19	2	0	4	10	14	10	.232	.402	.340
vs. Right-Handed Pitchers	216	51	10	0	9	34	45	54	.236	.407	.370
Home	125	33	6	0	8	23	27	31	.264	.504	.396
Road	173	37	6	0	5	21	32	33	.214	.335	.337
Grass	195	51	8	0	13	37	42	42	.262	.503	.390
Artificial Turf	103	19	4	0	0	7	17	22	.184	.223	.306
April	55	13	2	0	2	7	12	10	.236	.382	.382
May	32	6	0	0	2	5	6	8	.188	.375	.308
June	19	6	1	0	0	3	7	5	.316	.368	.481
July	34	8	2	0	3	9	10	4	.235	.559	.409
August	89	18	5	0	1	7	13	21	.202	.292	.301
Sept./Oct.	69	19	2	0	5	13	11	16	.275	.522	.383
Leading Off Inn.	63	13	2	0	2	2	6	15	.206	.333	.275
Bases Empty	177	38	6	0	6	6	33	37	.215	.350	.338
Runners On	121	32	6	0	7	38	26	27	.264	.488	.395
Runners/Scor. Pos.	76	17	3	0	4	30	17	17	.224	.421	.361
Runners On/2 Out	37	9	3	0	1	8	9	7	.243	.405	.404
Scor. Pos./2 Out	25	4	1	0	0	5	7	6	.160	.200	.364
Late Inning Pressure	37	7	2	0	0	4	6	11	.189	.243	.295
Leading Off	10	2	0	0	0	0	1	3	.200	.200	.273
Bases Empty	19	3	0	0	0	0	2	5	.158	.158	.238
Runners On	18	4	2	0	0	4	4	6	.222	.333	.348
Runners/Scor. Pos.	13	3	2	0	0	4	3	5	.231	.385	.353

DRIVING IN RUNS	0 Out	1 Out	2 Out	Total	
From 1B	1/22	3/25	2/24	6/71	8%
From 2B	4/18	5/27	3/22	12/67	18%
From 3B	4/7	7/10	2/9	13/26	50%
Scoring Position	8/25	12/37	5/31	25/93	27%
Scor. Pos. %	32%	32%	16%	27%	
Driving In Runners from 3B with Less than Two Out:			11/17	65%	

Loves to face: John Franco (.800, 4-for-5, 1 HR)
Hates to face: Bryn Smith (.040, 1-for-25)
Fly-ball hitter: 0.90 G/A ratio last season. . . . Batted .249 in day games, .215 in night games. . . . Has hit only one home run in 151 at bats in Late-Inning Pressure Situations since 1983 (regular-season only). Quite an about-face: batted .341 with 10 homers in LIP from 1977 to 1979. . . . Averaged 1.64 putouts per nine innings last season, 5th-lowest rate among N.L. outfielders (minimum: 300 innings). . . . Has batted .320 at Atlanta Stadium since 1975; .354 at Three Rivers and .178 with no home runs at the Astrodome since '79. . . . Hitless in five at bats (three strikeouts) with the bases loaded last season.

Lee Mazzilli

Pittsburgh Pirates	AB	H	2B	3B	HR	RRF	BB	SO	BA	SA	OBA
Season	117	33	8	0	1	10	29	17	.282	.376	.425
vs. Left-Handed Pitchers	17	5	0	0	0	2	5	3	.294	.294	.455
vs. Right-Handed Pitchers	100	28	8	0	1	8	24	14	.280	.390	.419
Home	49	16	3	0	0	5	12	4	.327	.388	.459
Road	68	17	5	0	1	5	17	13	.250	.368	.400
Grass	43	6	2	0	1	3	7	7	.140	.256	.260
Artificial Turf	74	27	6	0	0	7	22	10	.365	.446	.510
April	5	1	1	0	0	0	5	2	.200	.400	.600
May	31	10	2	0	1	7	9	5	.323	.484	.475
June	36	10	3	0	0	1	8	4	.278	.361	.409
July	21	4	0	0	0	0	2	2	.190	.190	.261
August	12	4	1	0	0	0	1	2	.333	.417	.385
Sept./Oct.	12	4	1	0	0	2	4	2	.333	.417	.500
Leading Off Inn.	25	10	2	0	1	1	4	6	.400	.600	.483
Bases Empty	62	17	4	0	1	1	15	11	.274	.387	.416
Runners On	55	16	4	0	0	9	14	6	.291	.364	.435
Runners/Scor. Pos.	30	7	1	0	0	7	11	4	.233	.267	.439
Runners On/2 Out	26	8	2	0	0	5	7	1	.308	.385	.455
Scor. Pos./2 Out	15	3	1	0	0	4	6	1	.200	.267	.429
Late Inning Pressure	54	18	4	0	0	4	10	7	.333	.407	.438
Leading Off	13	6	2	0	0	0	2	3	.462	.615	.533
Bases Empty	27	9	3	0	0	0	4	4	.333	.444	.419
Runners On	27	9	1	0	0	4	6	3	.333	.370	.455
Runners/Scor. Pos.	16	5	0	0	0	4	4	2	.313	.313	.450

DRIVING IN RUNS	0 Out	1 Out	2 Out	Total	
From 1B	1/11	0/11	1/20	2/42	5%
From 2B	1/4	1/8	0/9	2/21	10%
From 3B	0/1	1/4	4/9	5/14	36%
Scoring Position	1/5	2/12	4/18	7/35	20%
Scor. Pos. %	20%	17%	22%	20%	
Driving In Runners from 3B with Less than Two Out:			1/5	20%	

Loves to face: Rick Camp (.533, 8-for-15, 1 HR)
Hates to face: Andy Hawkins (0-for-13)
Ground-ball hitter: 1.63 G/A ratio last season. . . . Appeared in 72 games as a pinch-hitter last season (most in major leagues). . . . Batted .240 in 15 games as starter, .313 in 77 games off the bench. . . . Did not start a game after July 19. . . . Yearly batting averages in Late-Inning Pressure Situations since 1981: .177, .178, .222, .274, .333. . . . Has batted for a higher average with runners on base than he has with the bases empty in nine of 10 seasons in majors. Missed by three hits in 1980. . . . Last 10 home runs have been hit batting left-handed. Last homer batting right-handed was July 25, 1982, off Detroit's Pat Underwood. . . . Has struck out 17 times in 54 career at bats with the bases loaded. . . . Career batting average of .336 at Dodger Stadium.

Willie McGee

St. Louis Cardinals	AB	H	2B	3B	HR	RRF	BB	SO	BA	SA	OBA
Season	612	216	26	18	10	85	34	86	.353	.503	.384
vs. Left-Handed Pitchers	210	73	12	7	7	34	10	51	.348	.571	.372
vs. Right-Handed Pitchers	402	143	14	11	3	51	24	35	.356	.468	.390
Home	283	100	11	7	3	34	10	38	.353	.473	.370
Road	329	116	15	11	7	51	24	48	.353	.529	.395
Grass	171	59	10	4	3	23	14	25	.345	.503	.392
Artificial Turf	441	157	16	14	7	62	20	61	.356	.503	.381
April	37	11	0	2	0	6	2	8	.297	.405	.333
May	109	38	6	4	2	16	9	15	.349	.532	.395
June	107	37	3	4	0	13	5	15	.346	.449	.368
July	110	39	9	2	3	13	3	18	.355	.555	.368
August	101	44	4	4	1	19	5	10	.436	.584	.458
Sept./Oct.	148	47	4	2	4	18	10	20	.318	.453	.361
Leading Off Inn.	107	37	7	3	0	0	3	16	.346	.467	.364
Bases Empty	359	125	19	10	5	5	12	51	.348	.499	.369
Runners On	253	91	7	8	5	80	22	35	.360	.510	.404
Runners/Scor. Pos.	169	66	7	7	4	77	14	21	.391	.586	.426
Runners On/2 Out	99	33	4	4	4	33	6	10	.333	.576	.371
Scor. Pos./2 Out	77	29	4	4	3	31	4	7	.377	.649	.407
Late Inning Pressure	81	26	2	2	3	13	3	14	.321	.506	.345
Leading Off	20	4	0	0	0	0	0	4	.200	.200	.200
Bases Empty	51	14	2	0	2	2	1	10	.275	.431	.288
Runners On	30	12	0	2	1	11	2	4	.400	.633	.438
Runners/Scor. Pos.	20	8	0	2	0	9	1	2	.400	.600	.429

DRIVING IN RUNS	0 Out	1 Out	2 Out	Total	
From 1B	1/47	0/32	3/53	4/132	3%
From 2B	8/37	11/39	15/58	34/134	25%
From 3B	12/19	13/19	11/25	36/63	57%
Scoring Position	20/56	24/58	26/83	70/197	36%
Scor. Pos. %	36%	41%	31%	36%	
Driving In Runners from 3B with Less than Two Out:			25/38	66%	

Loves to face: Mike Scott (.611, 11-for-18)
Hates to face: Jeff Reardon (.111, 2-for-18)
Ground-ball hitter: 2.10 G/A ratio last season, 3d-highest in N.L. (minimum: 200 PA). Career average: 2.02. . . . Had five consecutive singles vs. Gooden in 1984, and 10 hits in 15 at bats during one stretch from '84 through early '85. . . . Lowest batting average vs. any opposing club last season was .275 vs. Los Angeles. . . . Career breakdown shows a lower average but more power from the right-hand side of the plate (.299 BA, .456 SA) than from the left-hand side (.312 BA, .402 SA). . . . Career with the bases loaded: .385 (20-for-52), one walk, 12 strikeouts. . . . Career batting averages: .343 in day games, .291 in night games. . . . Career batting average of .386 at Riverfront Stadium (.614 slugging average). . . . Grounded into three double plays in 88 opportunities last season, 4th-lowest average in N.L. (minimum: 50 opportunities).

Kevin McReynolds

San Diego Padres	AB	H	2B	3B	HR	RRF	BB	SO	BA	SA	OBA
Season	564	132	24	4	15	78	43	81	.234	.371	.290
vs. Left-Handed Pitchers	173	45	6	2	3	31	21	22	.260	.370	.340
vs. Right-Handed Pitchers	391	87	18	2	12	47	22	59	.223	.371	.266
Home	264	62	9	3	6	36	19	43	.235	.360	.282
Road	300	70	15	1	9	42	24	38	.233	.380	.297
Grass	414	91	13	4	12	56	34	67	.220	.357	.280
Artificial Turf	150	41	11	0	3	22	9	14	.273	.407	.319
April	69	16	4	0	1	10	7	9	.232	.333	.295
May	98	26	3	0	6	22	8	13	.265	.480	.327
June	109	30	5	2	1	13	8	16	.275	.385	.328
July	98	15	3	1	3	14	3	12	.153	.296	.186
August	71	17	3	0	2	7	5	13	.239	.366	.289
Sept./Oct.	119	28	6	1	2	12	12	18	.235	.353	.303
Leading Off Inn.	126	30	4	2	4	4	9	13	.238	.397	.289
Bases Empty	304	59	10	2	8	8	16	42	.194	.319	.237
Runners On	260	73	14	2	7	70	27	39	.281	.431	.348
Runners/Scor. Pos.	148	46	8	1	6	64	18	25	.311	.500	.384
Runners On/2 Out	121	34	3	1	5	33	16	18	.281	.446	.370
Scor. Pos./2 Out	76	23	2	1	4	30	14	11	.303	.513	.418
Late Inning Pressure	86	17	5	1	0	8	7	14	.198	.279	.258
Leading Off	18	5	2	0	0	0	1	2	.278	.389	.316
Bases Empty	45	9	4	0	0	0	2	8	.200	.289	.234
Runners On	41	8	1	1	0	8	5	6	.195	.268	.283
Runners/Scor. Pos.	25	5	0	1	0	6	2	5	.200	.280	.259

DRIVING IN RUNS	0 Out	1 Out	2 Out	Total	
From 1B	3/46	3/64	5/85	11/195	6%
From 2B	2/20	9/43	12/58	23/121	19%
From 3B	3/7	15/21	11/29	29/57	51%
Scoring Position	5/27	24/64	23/87	52/178	29%
Scor. Pos. %	19%	38%	26%	29%	
Driving In Runners from 3B with Less than Two Out:			18/28	64%	

Loves to face: Rick Honeycutt (.692, 9-for-13, 1 HR)
Hates to face: Mark Davis (0-for-13)
Fly-ball hitter: 0.94 G/A ratio last season. . . . Led N.L. outfielders in putouts (430) and total chances (445); averaged 2.94 putouts per nine innings last season, 2d-highest rate among N.L. outfielders (minimum: 300 innings). . . . Matched 75-RBI output of 1984 despite 39-point drop in overall batting average. Avoided decline in run production by improving batting average with runners in scoring position from .303 in '84. . . . Career batting averages: .282 with runners on base, .229 with the bases empty. . . . Has hit a home run at every current N.L. stadium except Three Rivers Stadium (.194 batting average in 36 AB).

Eddie Milner

Cincinnati Reds	AB	H	2B	3B	HR	RRF	BB	SO	BA	SA	OBA
Season	453	115	19	7	3	35	61	31	.254	.347	.342
vs. Left-Handed Pitchers	47	10	1	0	0	2	8	8	.213	.234	.327
vs. Right-Handed Pitchers	406	105	18	7	3	33	53	23	.259	.360	.343
Home	223	55	12	4	1	12	31	16	.247	.350	.336
Road	230	60	7	3	2	23	30	15	.261	.343	.347
Grass	116	29	3	2	1	13	14	6	.250	.336	.336
Artificial Turf	337	86	16	5	2	22	47	25	.255	.350	.344
April	33	10	2	0	0	2	3	2	.303	.364	.361
May	86	15	0	0	0	2	14	5	.174	.174	.287
June	74	20	4	1	0	10	9	7	.270	.351	.349
July	76	22	5	2	0	4	9	5	.289	.408	.360
August	74	21	4	2	0	6	10	3	.284	.392	.372
Sept./Oct.	110	27	4	2	3	11	16	9	.245	.400	.341
Leading Off Inn.	173	43	8	1	2	2	25	12	.249	.341	.347
Bases Empty	298	77	16	5	2	2	41	19	.258	.366	.350
Runners On	155	38	3	2	1	33	20	12	.245	.310	.326
Runners/Scor. Pos.	95	25	2	1	1	32	14	9	.263	.337	.348
Runners On/2 Out	62	15	2	1	0	13	7	5	.242	.306	.319
Scor. Pos./2 Out	43	11	1	1	0	13	4	3	.256	.326	.319
Late Inning Pressure	63	16	2	0	0	4	8	4	.254	.286	.347
Leading Off	22	3	2	0	0	0	4	3	.136	.227	.296
Bases Empty	38	8	2	0	0	0	7	3	.211	.263	.348
Runners On	25	8	0	0	0	4	1	1	.320	.320	.346
Runners/Scor. Pos.	11	3	0	0	0	4	1	1	.273	.273	.333

DRIVING IN RUNS	0 Out	1 Out	2 Out	Total	
From 1B	0/23	1/42	1/36	2/101	2%
From 2B	3/13	6/32	6/35	15/80	19%
From 3B	4/8	5/12	6/19	15/39	38%
Scoring Position	7/21	11/44	12/54	30/119	25%
Scor. Pos. %	33%	25%	22%	25%	
Driving In Runners from 3B with Less than Two Out:			9/20	45%	

Loves to face: Frank Williams (.750, 6-for-8)
Hates to face: Craig McMurtry (.050, 1-for-20)
Fly-ball hitter: 0.93 G/A ratio last season. . . . Batted .309 vs. ground-ball pitchers last season, .217 vs. fly-ball pitchers. . . . Strikeout rate of one per 16.8 plate appearances was 5th-best in N.L. . . . Stole nine bases in nine attempts vs. Atlanta last season. . . . Career batting averages: .226 vs. left-handers, .262 vs. right-handers. . . . Has hit 21 of 23 career home runs off right-handed pitchers. . . . Last season's batting averages with runners on base (.245) and runners in scoring position (.263) are both career highs. . . . Led N.L. outfielders with an average of 3.07 putouts per nine innings last season. . . . Career batting average of .169 at Dodger Stadium.

Keith Moreland

Chicago Cubs	AB	H	2B	3B	HR	RRF	BB	SO	BA	SA	OBA
Season	587	180	30	3	14	108	68	58	.307	.440	.374
vs. Left-Handed Pitchers	124	39	7	1	3	17	22	10	.315	.460	.415
vs. Right-Handed Pitchers	463	141	23	2	11	91	46	48	.305	.434	.363
Home	300	102	16	2	11	63	37	27	.340	.517	.411
Road	287	78	14	1	3	45	31	31	.272	.359	.336
Grass	412	132	20	2	12	75	52	43	.320	.466	.394
Artificial Turf	175	48	10	1	2	33	16	15	.274	.377	.327
April	62	17	3	0	1	13	6	7	.274	.371	.324
May	90	28	4	0	2	16	14	9	.311	.422	.400
June	103	32	7	0	3	17	16	11	.311	.466	.400
July	91	22	4	1	2	12	11	13	.242	.374	.314
August	113	38	8	0	2	12	5	9	.336	.460	.370
Sept./Oct.	128	43	4	2	4	38	16	9	.336	.492	.407
Leading Off Inn.	123	34	7	0	4	4	15	11	.276	.431	.355
Bases Empty	289	82	14	1	6	6	35	32	.284	.401	.363
Runners On	298	98	16	2	8	102	33	26	.329	.477	.385
Runners/Scor. Pos.	197	66	13	2	4	93	23	16	.335	.482	.389
Runners On/2 Out	153	46	5	0	3	42	14	17	.301	.392	.359
Scor. Pos./2 Out	108	33	3	0	1	37	11	12	.306	.361	.370
Late Inning Pressure	90	28	9	0	1	20	8	11	.311	.444	.363
Leading Off	22	7	2	0	0	0	1	2	.318	.409	.348
Bases Empty	49	14	3	0	1	1	5	8	.286	.408	.364
Runners On	41	14	6	0	0	19	3	3	.341	.488	.362
Runners/Scor. Pos.	32	12	6	0	0	19	3	2	.375	.563	.395

DRIVING IN RUNS	0 Out	1 Out	2 Out	Total	
From 1B	2/31	5/69	3/85	10/185	5%
From 2B	10/26	12/49	22/83	44/158	28%
From 3B	5/10	21/31	13/39	39/80	49%
Scoring Position	15/36	33/80	35/122	83/238	35%
Scor. Pos. %	42%	41%	29%	35%	
Driving In Runners from 3B with Less than Two Out:			26/41	63%	

Loves to face: Rick Rhoden (.447, 17-for-38, 1 HR)
Hates to face: Mike Krukow (.097, 3-for-31)
Fly-ball hitter: 0.87 G/A ratio last season. . . . Batted .433 with 18 RBIs vs. Philadelphia last season. . . . Led N.L. with 238 opportunities to drive in runners from scoring position. . . . Has hit for a higher average with runners on base than with the bases empty in each of his six full seasons. Career breakdowns: .303 with men on base, .275 with the bases empty; .320 vs. left-handers, .278 vs. right-handers. . . . 45 of his 71 home runs (63 percent) have been hit at Wrigley Field. . . . Cubs had a 10–3 record in games in which he hit a home run. . . . Led N.L. with 33 hits with 2 outs and runners in scoring position, highest total in either league since 1979, when Dave Winfield had 33. Thurman Munson holds 11-year *Player Analysis* record (36 in 1975). . . . Career batting averages: .379 at Shea Stadium, .359 at Three Rivers Stadium.

Jim Morrison

Pittsburgh Pirates	AB	H	2B	3B	HR	RRF	BB	SO	BA	SA	OBA
Season	244	62	10	0	4	22	8	44	.254	.344	.277
vs. Left-Handed Pitchers	109	29	6	0	1	9	4	16	.266	.349	.287
vs. Right-Handed Pitchers	135	33	4	0	3	13	4	28	.244	.341	.270
Home	132	34	6	0	2	9	3	22	.258	.348	.277
Road	112	28	4	0	2	13	5	22	.250	.339	.277
Grass	42	11	3	0	0	3	2	6	.262	.333	.289
Artificial Turf	202	51	7	0	4	19	6	38	.252	.347	.275
April	20	7	1	0	0	0	3	6	.350	.400	.435
May	53	13	1	0	0	3	1	11	.245	.264	.255
June	45	11	3	0	0	2	0	9	.244	.311	.239
July	35	7	2	0	0	4	1	2	.200	.257	.243
August	28	7	1	0	2	6	2	4	.250	.500	.300
Sept./Oct.	63	17	2	0	2	7	1	12	.270	.397	.277
Leading Off Inn.	53	12	2	0	1	1	1	11	.226	.321	.241
Bases Empty	134	31	7	0	3	3	5	28	.231	.351	.259
Runners On	110	31	3	0	1	19	3	16	.282	.336	.299
Runners/Scor. Pos.	63	15	1	0	1	18	2	11	.238	.302	.261
Runners On/2 Out	42	12	2	0	0	5	1	5	.286	.333	.318
Scor. Pos./2 Out	26	6	1	0	0	5	1	5	.231	.269	.286
Late Inning Pressure	47	11	1	0	2	4	3	8	.234	.383	.280
Leading Off	11	2	0	0	0	0	0	2	.182	.182	.182
Bases Empty	25	5	1	0	1	1	2	5	.200	.360	.259
Runners On	22	6	0	0	1	3	1	3	.273	.409	.304
Runners/Scor. Pos.	12	3	0	0	1	3	1	2	.250	.500	.308

DRIVING IN RUNS	0 Out	1 Out	2 Out	Total	
From 1B	1/17	0/28	0/29	1/74	1%
From 2B	1/7	3/20	4/22	8/49	16%
From 3B	5/10	3/11	1/9	9/30	30%
Scoring Position	6/17	6/31	5/31	17/79	22%
Scor. Pos. %	35%	19%	16%	22%	
Driving In Runners from 3B with Less than Two Out:			8/21	38%	

Loves to face: Joe Price (.692, 9-for-13)
Hates to face: Dennis Eckersley (.160, 4-for-25)
Fly-ball hitter: 0.64 G/A ratio last season, 2d-lowest in N.L. (minimum: 200 PA). Career average: 0.89. . . . Handled more chances (71) at shortstop without committing an error than anyone in N.L. in 1985. . . . Batted .264 in 55 games as a starter, .188 in 37 games off the bench. . . . Career batting averages of .252 with runners on base, .273 with the bases empty. . . . Has batted .207 for his career with two outs and runners in scoring position. . . . Career batting average of .390 at Wrigley Field, .133 (4-for-30) at the Astrodome. . . . Career RDI percentage of .156 from scoring position in Late-Inning Pressure Situations.

Jerry Mumphrey

Houston Astros	AB	H	2B	3B	HR	RRF	BB	SO	BA	SA	OBA
Season	444	123	25	2	8	64	37	57	.277	.396	.329
vs. Left-Handed Pitchers	133	32	7	0	0	13	18	17	.241	.293	.323
vs. Right-Handed Pitchers	311	91	18	2	8	51	19	40	.293	.441	.331
Home	200	61	14	1	4	28	21	23	.305	.445	.369
Road	244	62	11	1	4	36	16	34	.254	.357	.294
Grass	140	41	4	1	4	26	10	22	.293	.421	.340
Artificial Turf	304	82	21	1	4	38	27	35	.270	.385	.323
April	71	18	3	2	0	9	9	7	.254	.352	.338
May	79	21	3	0	2	15	6	4	.266	.380	.307
June	44	12	2	0	2	7	1	7	.273	.455	.283
July	69	23	6	0	0	5	6	13	.333	.420	.382
August	90	22	6	0	1	9	12	17	.244	.344	.333
Sept./Oct.	91	27	5	0	3	19	3	9	.297	.451	.316
Leading Off Inn.	103	26	5	0	2	2	6	8	.252	.359	.294
Bases Empty	241	60	15	0	4	4	11	33	.249	.361	.282
Runners On	203	63	10	2	4	60	26	24	.310	.438	.379
Runners/Scor. Pos.	119	33	5	2	2	54	20	15	.277	.403	.366
Runners On/2 Out	89	24	4	2	2	21	15	14	.270	.427	.375
Scor. Pos./2 Out	60	14	3	2	2	21	11	9	.233	.450	.352
Late Inning Pressure	65	18	4	0	0	5	4	7	.277	.338	.314
Leading Off	17	4	3	0	0	0	1	1	.235	.412	.278
Bases Empty	36	13	3	0	0	0	1	3	.361	.444	.378
Runners On	29	5	1	0	0	5	3	4	.172	.207	.242
Runners/Scor. Pos.	17	2	1	0	0	5	1	3	.118	.176	.158

DRIVING IN RUNS	0 Out	1 Out	2 Out	Total	
From 1B	4/45	1/39	4/60	9/144	6%
From 2B	4/22	6/28	12/43	22/93	24%
From 3B	3/6	19/20	3/21	25/47	53%
Scoring Position	7/28	25/48	15/64	47/140	34%
Scor. Pos. %	25%	52%	23%	34%	
Driving In Runners from 3B with Less than Two Out:			22/26	85%	

Loves to face: Kent Tekulve (.529, 9-for-17)
Hates to face: Bruce Sutter (.077, 2-for-26, 6 SO)
Ground-ball hitter: 1.77 G/A ratio last season, 9th-highest in N.L. (minimum: 200 PA). Career average: 1.77. . . . Batting average from the right side of the plate (.293) was his lowest since 1978; career batting averages of .301 batting right-handed, .259 batting left-handed. . . . Batted for a higher average in road games than in home games in each of his first five full seasons, with St. Louis and San Diego, but reversed that trend in New York and Houston. He has now batted over .300 in his home ballpark in each of the last five seasons. . . . Career batting averages: .336 at Candlestick Park, .308 at the Astrodome, two of toughest hitters' parks in majors; only .252 at new home, Wrigley Field. . . . Career breakdown of Late-Inning Pressure Situations: .227 with runners on base, .328 with the bases empty.

Dale Murphy

Atlanta Braves	AB	H	2B	3B	HR	RRF	BB	SO	BA	SA	OBA
Season	616	185	32	2	37	114	90	141	.300	.539	.388
vs. Left-Handed Pitchers	183	61	8	1	10	31	35	42	.333	.552	.440
vs. Right-Handed Pitchers	433	124	24	1	27	83	55	99	.286	.533	.364
Home	308	92	15	1	19	60	53	61	.299	.539	.401
Road	308	93	17	1	18	54	37	80	.302	.539	.374
Grass	459	135	21	1	30	84	67	96	.294	.540	.384
Artificial Turf	157	50	11	1	7	30	23	45	.318	.535	.399
April	71	27	8	0	9	30	10	13	.380	.873	.451
May	96	28	2	0	4	9	11	18	.292	.438	.364
June	109	25	5	0	5	15	19	33	.229	.413	.341
July	101	31	7	2	9	27	19	26	.307	.683	.413
August	114	34	3	0	7	14	10	26	.298	.509	.352
Sept./Oct.	125	40	7	0	3	19	21	25	.320	.448	.419
Leading Off Inn.	126	39	3	1	9	9	21	23	.310	.563	.408
Bases Empty	338	95	11	2	18	18	52	76	.281	.485	.377
Runners On	278	90	21	0	19	96	38	65	.324	.604	.401
Runners/Scor. Pos.	140	46	12	0	11	74	27	37	.329	.650	.424
Runners On/2 Out	91	30	8	0	6	38	22	22	.330	.615	.465
Scor. Pos./2 Out	52	19	6	0	5	33	17	15	.365	.769	.522
Late Inning Pressure	98	29	4	0	4	22	24	25	.296	.459	.434
Leading Off	25	5	0	0	1	1	9	7	.200	.320	.412
Bases Empty	45	9	1	0	1	1	13	12	.200	.289	.379
Runners On	53	20	3	0	3	21	11	13	.377	.604	.484
Runners/Scor. Pos.	24	9	2	0	2	16	10	7	.375	.708	.559

DRIVING IN RUNS	0 Out	1 Out	2 Out	Total	
From 1B	5/49	7/81	9/64	21/194	11%
From 2B	5/26	7/41	14/41	26/108	24%
From 3B	5/9	16/30	9/20	30/59	51%
Scoring Position	10/35	23/71	23/61	56/167	34%
Scor. Pos. %	29%	32%	38%	34%	
Driving In Runners from 3B with Less than Two Out:			21/39	54%	

Loves to face: Bill Laskey (.524, 11-for-21, 5 HR)
Hates to face: Dave Stewart (.063, 1-for-16)
Also loves to face Dave Rucker (5-for-5). . . . Had twice as many RBIs (32) as any other player in N.L. as of May 2. . . . Held N.L. RBI lead from April 11 through September 3. . . . Led N.L. in runs (118), walks (90), and strikeouts (141). . . . Hit 11 first-inning home runs last season, most in N.L. . . . Drove in 21 runners from first base last season, tying Glenn Wilson and teammate Bob Horner for N.L. lead. . . . Led majors with 20 hits in Late-Inning Pressure Situations with runners on base last season. Steve Garvey holds 11-year *Player Analysis* record (24 in 1975). . . . Career batting average of .335 at Wrigley Field, .185 at Three Rivers Stadium. . . . Has hit 132 of 237 career home runs at Atlanta Stadium, but over past three seasons has hit 55 in road games, 54 in home games.

Graig Nettles

San Diego Padres	AB	H	2B	3B	HR	RRF	BB	SO	BA	SA	OBA
Season	440	115	23	1	15	62	72	59	.261	.420	.363
vs. Left-Handed Pitchers	97	21	9	0	4	14	11	19	.216	.433	.294
vs. Right-Handed Pitchers	343	94	14	1	11	48	61	40	.274	.417	.382
Home	217	56	10	0	6	35	35	28	.258	.387	.358
Road	223	59	13	1	9	27	37	31	.265	.453	.368
Grass	311	76	14	0	12	44	55	40	.244	.405	.355
Artificial Turf	129	39	9	1	3	18	17	19	.302	.457	.384
April	33	9	1	0	1	2	10	4	.273	.394	.442
May	80	20	4	0	3	12	20	12	.250	.413	.400
June	74	12	1	0	4	10	14	8	.162	.338	.292
July	79	28	4	1	3	11	14	14	.354	.544	.452
August	93	23	7	0	3	14	7	13	.247	.419	.297
Sept./Oct.	81	23	6	0	1	13	7	8	.284	.395	.337
Leading Off Inn.	115	27	3	1	5	5	15	16	.235	.409	.323
Bases Empty	239	59	8	1	12	12	41	34	.247	.439	.357
Runners On	201	56	15	0	3	50	31	25	.279	.398	.370
Runners/Scor. Pos.	125	35	9	0	2	46	22	15	.280	.400	.380
Runners On/2 Out	95	21	6	0	3	23	21	14	.221	.379	.362
Scor. Pos./2 Out	61	14	4	0	2	20	15	8	.230	.393	.382
Late Inning Pressure	66	16	2	0	2	6	10	8	.242	.364	.338
Leading Off	19	2	0	0	0	0	3	4	.105	.105	.227
Bases Empty	38	8	0	0	2	2	5	6	.211	.368	.302
Runners On	28	8	2	0	0	4	5	2	.286	.357	.382
Runners/Scor. Pos.	16	4	1	0	0	4	4	1	.250	.313	.381

DRIVING IN RUNS	0 Out	1 Out	2 Out	Total	
From 1B	0/29	1/47	3/60	4/136	3%
From 2B	3/22	5/30	11/43	19/95	20%
From 3B	8/10	10/17	6/23	24/50	48%
Scoring Position	11/32	15/47	17/66	43/145	30%
Scor. Pos. %	34%	32%	26%	30%	
Driving In Runners from 3B with Less than Two Out:			18/27	67%	

Loves to face: Jeff Robinson (.556, 5-for-9, 2 HR)
Hates to face: Mike Krukow (.056, 1-for-18)
Only major-league player to hit for a higher average with men on base than with the bases empty in each of the last eleven seasons. 11-year batting averages: .284 with men on base, .230 with the bases empty. . . . July batting average of .354 was 5th-highest in N.L. . . . Committed 13 errors in 102 games on grass fields, two errors in 35 games on artificial surfaces. . . . Has not hit N.L. left-handers well, batting .178 vs. southpaws in two seasons with the Padres, compared to .263 vs. right-handers. . . . Has not hit a triple in 768 at bats vs. lefties since 1980. . . . Hit 12 solo home runs last season. Drove in only three base runners with 15 homers, 3d-lowest average in N.L. . . . Has hit a home run at every current N.L. stadium except Three Rivers Stadium, but has hit .400 there (12-for-30).

Tom Nieto

St. Louis Cardinals	AB	H	2B	3B	HR	RRF	BB	SO	BA	SA	OBA
Season	253	57	10	2	0	35	26	37	.225	.281	.305
vs. Left-Handed Pitchers	124	26	5	1	0	14	13	17	.210	.266	.285
vs. Right-Handed Pitchers	129	31	5	1	0	21	13	20	.240	.295	.324
Home	127	31	6	1	0	19	13	16	.244	.307	.319
Road	126	26	4	1	0	16	13	21	.206	.254	.291
Grass	62	12	2	1	0	8	10	8	.194	.258	.324
Artificial Turf	191	45	8	1	0	27	16	29	.236	.288	.298
April	17	6	0	0	0	3	3	1	.353	.353	.450
May	41	9	1	0	0	8	5	9	.220	.244	.304
June	74	18	2	1	0	11	4	9	.243	.297	.300
July	60	11	2	1	0	9	7	12	.183	.250	.279
August	27	4	1	0	0	0	1	3	.148	.185	.179
Sept./Oct.	34	9	4	0	0	4	6	3	.265	.382	.375
Leading Off Inn.	47	8	2	0	0	0	7	5	.170	.213	.278
Bases Empty	137	26	4	1	0	0	12	20	.190	.234	.260
Runners On	116	31	6	1	0	35	14	17	.267	.336	.356
Runners/Scor. Pos.	80	23	2	1	0	33	12	9	.288	.338	.380
Runners On/2 Out	44	11	2	0	0	12	10	7	.250	.295	.389
Scor. Pos./2 Out	35	9	0	0	0	11	10	5	.257	.257	.422
Late Inning Pressure	31	8	0	0	0	3	4	5	.258	.258	.343
Leading Off	4	1	0	0	0	0	1	1	.250	.250	.400
Bases Empty	15	4	0	0	0	0	3	3	.267	.267	.389
Runners On	16	4	0	0	0	3	1	2	.250	.250	.294
Runners/Scor. Pos.	12	3	0	0	0	3	1	2	.250	.250	.308

DRIVING IN RUNS	0 Out	1 Out	2 Out	Total	
From 1B	1/17	2/30	1/22	4/69	6%
From 2B	2/9	7/28	7/26	16/63	25%
From 3B	5/6	6/11	4/16	15/33	45%
Scoring Position	7/15	13/39	11/42	31/96	32%
Scor. Pos. %	47%	33%	26%	32%	
Driving In Runners from 3B with Less than Two Out:			11/17	65%	

Loves to face: Sid Fernandez (.667, 4-for-6, 1 HR)
Hates to face: Bob Welch (0-for-6)
Ground-ball hitter: 1.42 G/A ratio last season. . . . Should Jerry Koosman hang 'em up, it won't be soon enough for Nieto, hitless in 16 at bats against the The Kooz. . . . No extra-base hits in 41 career at bats in Late-Inning Pressure Situations, the most LIP at bats without an XBH among active players. . . . Career batting averages: .277 with runners on base, .209 with the bases empty, .283 with runners in scoring position. . . . Cardinals had a .638 winning percentage in his 80 starts last season, but he started only three of 13 post-season games (two wins and a loss). . . . Hit three home runs in 1984, all in night games with runners on base.

Ken Oberkfell

Atlanta Braves	AB	H	2B	3B	HR	RRF	BB	SO	BA	SA	OBA
Season	412	112	19	4	3	36	51	38	.272	.359	.359
vs. Left-Handed Pitchers	115	28	3	1	0	8	12	18	.243	.287	.323
vs. Right-Handed Pitchers	297	84	16	3	3	28	39	20	.283	.387	.372
Home	209	63	9	2	2	21	32	14	.301	.392	.402
Road	203	49	10	2	1	15	19	24	.241	.325	.311
Grass	303	89	15	4	3	28	39	29	.294	.399	.380
Artificial Turf	109	23	4	0	0	8	12	9	.211	.248	.298
April	32	6	1	1	0	1	3	2	.188	.281	.257
May	57	17	1	1	0	5	3	4	.298	.351	.328
June	89	28	5	1	1	9	8	7	.315	.427	.367
July	75	19	5	1	0	8	16	9	.253	.347	.398
August	78	26	4	0	2	8	9	9	.333	.462	.416
Sept./Oct.	81	16	3	0	0	5	12	7	.198	.235	.316
Leading Off Inn.	92	28	5	0	0	0	10	5	.304	.359	.390
Bases Empty	236	70	12	1	1	1	24	20	.297	.369	.374
Runners On	176	42	7	3	2	35	27	18	.239	.347	.340
Runners/Scor. Pos.	95	20	3	3	1	32	20	8	.211	.337	.347
Runners On/2 Out	76	19	3	3	0	17	13	8	.250	.368	.360
Scor. Pos./2 Out	45	12	1	3	0	16	11	2	.267	.422	.411
Late Inning Pressure	72	13	1	0	0	4	9	6	.181	.194	.280
Leading Off	19	4	1	0	0	0	1	1	.211	.263	.286
Bases Empty	39	7	1	0	0	0	6	3	.179	.205	.304
Runners On	33	6	0	0	0	4	3	3	.182	.182	.250
Runners/Scor. Pos.	18	2	0	0	0	4	3	0	.111	.111	.238

DRIVING IN RUNS	0 Out	1 Out	2 Out	Total	
From 1B	0/27	2/57	2/54	4/138	3%
From 2B	3/13	3/27	7/34	13/74	18%
From 3B	1/3	7/15	8/22	16/40	40%
Scoring Position	4/16	10/42	15/56	29/114	25%
Scor. Pos. %	25%	24%	27%	25%	
Driving In Runners from 3B with Less than Two Out:			8/18	44%	

Loves to face: Bruce Berenyi (.471, 8-for-17)
Hates to face: Nolan Ryan (.111, 3-for-27)
August batting average of .333 was 7th-highest in N.L. . . . Batted .189 in day games, .309 in night games. Career averages: .269 and .294. . . . Did not commit an error in 34 games on artificial surfaces last season. . . . Has walked nine times in 59 career plate appearances with the bases loaded (14-for-47, .298). . . . Has hit 14 of his 15 career home runs vs. right-handed pitchers. His only home run against a left-hander was on August 29, 1981, off Chris Welsh. . . . 1985 performance in Late-Inning Pressure Situations was by far the worst of his career. He batted over .300 in LIP for five consecutive years with the Cardinals (1979–83), and has a career LIP batting average of .287. . . . Career batting average of .313 in Atlanta, .186 at Candlestick.

Ron Oester

Cincinnati Reds	AB	H	2B	3B	HR	RRF	BB	SO	BA	SA	OBA
Season	526	155	26	3	1	36	51	65	.295	.361	.354
vs. Left-Handed Pitchers	148	41	7	1	0	8	8	25	.277	.338	.312
vs. Right-Handed Pitchers	378	114	19	2	1	28	43	40	.302	.370	.369
Home	270	82	16	2	0	16	22	28	.304	.378	.354
Road	256	73	10	1	1	20	29	37	.285	.344	.354
Grass	151	34	5	0	1	14	16	25	.225	.278	.296
Artificial Turf	375	121	21	3	0	22	35	40	.323	.395	.378
April	49	10	3	0	0	5	5	10	.204	.265	.273
May	67	25	5	1	0	5	8	5	.373	.478	.440
June	98	27	7	1	0	8	6	9	.276	.367	.311
July	93	30	6	0	0	4	8	10	.323	.387	.376
August	98	31	4	1	0	7	8	9	.316	.378	.364
Sept./Oct.	121	32	1	0	1	7	16	22	.264	.298	.348
Leading Off Inn.	126	39	5	1	0	0	4	11	.310	.365	.331
Bases Empty	313	90	16	1	0	0	12	36	.288	.345	.314
Runners On	213	65	10	2	1	36	39	29	.305	.385	.405
Runners/Scor. Pos.	108	29	2	1	0	30	30	17	.269	.306	.413
Runners On/2 Out	91	21	4	1	1	10	23	16	.231	.330	.386
Scor. Pos./2 Out	39	7	0	1	0	6	19	8	.179	.231	.448
Late Inning Pressure	89	34	5	1	0	3	8	9	.382	.461	.433
Leading Off	19	9	0	1	0	0	1	3	.474	.579	.500
Bases Empty	54	24	3	1	0	0	1	7	.444	.537	.455
Runners On	35	10	2	0	0	3	7	2	.286	.343	.405
Runners/Scor. Pos.	17	3	0	0	0	3	6	1	.176	.176	.391

DRIVING IN RUNS	0 Out	1 Out	2 Out	Total	
From 1B	2/45	0/50	3/73	5/168	3%
From 2B	2/20	3/39	4/30	9/89	10%
From 3B	10/11	9/14	2/13	21/38	55%
Scoring Position	12/31	12/53	6/43	30/127	24%
Scor. Pos. %	39%	23%	14%	24%	
Driving In Runners from 3B with Less than Two Out:			19/25	76%	

Loves to face: Kevin Gross (.545, 6-for-11)
Hates to face: Steve Bedrosian (.111, 3-for-27, 6 SO)
Ground-ball hitter: 1.63 G/A ratio last season. . . . Batted .246 in day games, .318 in night games. . . . Set career-high marks in both hits and walks last season. . . . First two major-league home runs were hit against left-handed pitchers in 1980. Since then, 27 of his 29 homers have been hit off right-handers. . . . Unusually large margin between grass and artificial-turf batting averages last season. Career breakdown through 1984: .265 on grass fields, .259 on artificial surfaces. . . . Career batting average of .296 in Late-Inning Pressure Situations. . . . Highest season batting average with two outs and runners in scoring position was .210 in 1983. Career average in such situations is .189. . . . Has struck out 16 times in 49 career at bats with the bases loaded. . . . Career batting average of .322 at Candlestick Park, .168 at Shea Stadium, .186 at the Astrodome.

Dave Parker

Cincinnati Reds	AB	H	2B	3B	HR	RRF	BB	SO	BA	SA	OBA
Season	635	198	42	4	34	128	52	80	.312	.551	.365
vs. Left-Handed Pitchers	201	56	10	1	7	40	6	37	.279	.443	.305
vs. Right-Handed Pitchers	434	142	32	3	27	88	46	43	.327	.601	.390
Home	312	96	21	1	16	67	24	35	.308	.535	.356
Road	323	102	21	3	18	61	28	45	.316	.567	.373
Grass	193	58	11	0	12	31	17	30	.301	.544	.362
Artificial Turf	442	140	31	4	22	97	35	50	.317	.554	.366
April	75	21	4	0	0	5	4	7	.280	.333	.316
May	107	36	10	1	8	29	8	6	.336	.673	.379
June	100	32	5	0	6	23	15	12	.320	.550	.407
July	100	26	3	2	5	19	8	16	.260	.480	.321
August	115	30	9	1	4	13	6	21	.261	.461	.295
Sept./Oct.	138	53	11	0	11	39	11	18	.384	.703	.433
Leading Off Inn.	113	39	11	1	7	7	5	11	.345	.646	.373
Bases Empty	312	89	24	2	16	16	16	42	.285	.529	.324
Runners On	323	109	18	2	18	112	36	38	.337	.573	.401
Runners/Scor. Pos.	172	62	11	1	10	92	30	24	.360	.610	.449
Runners On/2 Out	115	37	6	0	5	36	21	11	.322	.504	.426
Scor. Pos./2 Out	71	22	5	0	3	32	20	9	.310	.507	.462
Late Inning Pressure	96	37	10	1	4	20	9	13	.385	.635	.438
Leading Off	27	11	4	0	1	1	0	3	.407	.667	.407
Bases Empty	50	19	5	1	2	2	1	7	.380	.640	.392
Runners On	46	18	5	0	2	18	8	6	.391	.630	.481
Runners/Scor. Pos.	27	11	3	0	1	16	8	5	.407	.630	.543

DRIVING IN RUNS	0 Out	1 Out	2 Out	Total	
From 1B	5/62	9/108	4/75	18/245	7%
From 2B	6/23	16/54	14/52	36/129	28%
From 3B	8/13	19/30	13/34	40/77	52%
Scoring Position	14/36	35/84	27/86	76/206	37%
Scor. Pos. %	39%	42%	31%	37%	
Driving In Runners from 3B with Less than Two Out:			27/43	63%	

Loves to face: Greg Minton (.588, 10-for-17)
Hates to face: Craig Lefferts (0-for-14)
Led N.L. with .386 batting average in September. . . . Also led the league with 80 extra-base hits last season, highest total since Mike Schmidt had 81 in 1980. . . . Tied Glenn Wilson for N.L. lead with 15 extra-base hits in Late-Inning Pressure Situations, two short of *Player Analysis* record, which Parker set in 1979. . . . Has batted for a higher average with runners on base than with the bases empty in seven of the last eight years. . . . Has batted .400 (20-for-50) with the bases loaded since 1983. . . . Parker and George Brett start the 1986 season with identical career totals in games (1,617) and RBIs (977). . . . Career batting average of .304 is 5th-highest among active players with at least 5,000 at bats.

Joe Orsulak

Pittsburgh Pirates	AB	H	2B	3B	HR	RRF	BB	SO	BA	SA	OBA
Season	397	119	14	6	0	21	26	27	.300	.365	.341
vs. Left-Handed Pitchers	65	14	1	0	0	6	1	5	.215	.231	.224
vs. Right-Handed Pitchers	332	105	13	6	0	15	25	22	.316	.392	.363
Home	184	68	5	5	0	12	13	11	.370	.451	.408
Road	213	51	9	1	0	9	13	16	.239	.291	.282
Grass	93	21	5	0	0	2	6	7	.226	.280	.273
Artificial Turf	304	98	9	6	0	19	20	20	.322	.391	.362
April	40	15	4	1	0	2	4	1	.375	.525	.432
May	32	4	1	0	0	3	2	3	.125	.156	.194
June	66	22	1	1	0	1	4	4	.333	.379	.371
July	44	10	0	0	0	2	3	4	.227	.227	.277
August	94	28	4	1	0	5	2	6	.298	.362	.303
Sept./Oct.	121	40	4	3	0	8	11	9	.331	.413	.386
Leading Off Inn.	131	44	3	2	0	0	10	13	.336	.389	.387
Bases Empty	270	89	8	6	0	0	16	20	.330	.404	.369
Runners On	127	30	6	0	0	21	10	7	.236	.283	.284
Runners/Scor. Pos.	76	16	3	0	0	20	9	4	.211	.250	.281
Runners On/2 Out	69	15	4	0	0	12	2	5	.217	.275	.239
Scor. Pos./2 Out	43	9	2	0	0	11	2	3	.209	.256	.244
Late Inning Pressure	65	14	2	0	0	7	6	4	.215	.246	.278
Leading Off	21	2	0	0	0	0	1	2	.095	.095	.136
Bases Empty	43	5	0	0	0	0	1	3	.116	.116	.136
Runners On	22	9	2	0	0	7	5	1	.409	.500	.500
Runners/Scor. Pos.	16	6	2	0	0	7	5	1	.375	.500	.500

DRIVING IN RUNS	0 Out	1 Out	2 Out	Total	
From 1B	0/16	0/21	2/46	2/83	2%
From 2B	1/11	2/20	6/35	9/66	14%
From 3B	1/3	5/8	4/17	10/28	36%
Scoring Position	2/14	7/28	10/52	19/94	20%
Scor. Pos. %	14%	25%	19%	20%	
Driving In Runners from 3B with Less than Two Out:			6/11	55%	

Loves to face: Rick Sutcliffe (.727, 8-for-11)
Hates to face: Jim Gott (0-for-5)
Only major leaguer to start at least 15 games at each outfield postion last season. . . . Don't include him in your list of rookies to hit .300. His 1985 season batting average was actually .2997. . . . Just think of the fuss we'd have caused if Ted Williams had sat out that doubleheader in '41! . . .Career batting average of .342 at Three Rivers Stadium. . . . Batted 131 points higher in home games than road games, 2d-largest difference in N.L. (minimum: 200 PA), but had no homers in 228 career at bats at home. . . . Batted 94 points lower with runners on base than with the bases empty, 2d-largest difference in N.L. (minimum: 200 PA). . . . Career: one walk and a pair of singles leading off 26 innings in LIP Situations. . . . Has driven in only two runners from first base in 104 career opportunities.

Tony Pena

Pittsburgh Pirates	AB	H	2B	3B	HR	RRF	BB	SO	BA	SA	OBA
Season	546	136	27	2	10	62	29	67	.249	.361	.284
vs. Left-Handed Pitchers	151	39	7	0	2	10	11	16	.258	.344	.309
vs. Right-Handed Pitchers	395	97	20	2	8	52	18	51	.246	.367	.275
Home	280	69	15	2	2	34	21	32	.246	.336	.294
Road	266	67	12	0	8	28	8	35	.252	.387	.274
Grass	137	29	4	0	4	8	6	21	.212	.328	.245
Artificial Turf	409	107	23	2	6	54	23	46	.262	.372	.297
April	63	17	3	0	1	4	8	5	.270	.365	.347
May	89	18	3	0	1	10	1	15	.202	.270	.209
June	103	37	6	1	3	14	4	10	.359	.524	.376
July	90	19	2	0	2	6	6	11	.211	.300	.260
August	93	19	3	0	1	12	5	16	.204	.269	.242
Sept./Oct.	108	26	10	1	2	16	5	10	.241	.407	.274
Leading Off Inn.	126	32	11	1	1	1	6	15	.254	.381	.288
Bases Empty	316	81	18	1	5	5	17	38	.256	.367	.294
Runners On	230	55	9	1	5	57	12	29	.239	.352	.271
Runners/Scor. Pos.	135	36	6	1	4	54	7	21	.267	.415	.293
Runners On/2 Out	102	21	4	0	3	20	3	11	.206	.333	.229
Scor. Pos./2 Out	66	14	3	0	3	19	2	6	.212	.394	.235
Late Inning Pressure	97	19	2	0	2	12	6	12	.196	.278	.238
Leading Off	31	7	1	0	1	1	0	5	.226	.355	.226
Bases Empty	60	11	1	0	1	1	2	8	.183	.250	.210
Runners On	37	8	1	0	1	11	4	4	.216	.324	.279
Runners/Scor. Pos.	21	5	0	0	1	11	3	3	.238	.381	.308

DRIVING IN RUNS	0 Out	1 Out	2 Out	Total	
From 1B	2/42	3/66	3/75	8/183	4%
From 2B	1/20	11/41	8/44	20/105	19%
From 3B	6/9	12/24	6/31	24/64	38%
Scoring Position	7/29	23/65	14/75	44/169	26%
Scor. Pos. %	24%	35%	19%	26%	
Driving In Runners from 3B with Less than Two Out:			18/33	55%	

Loves to face: Bob Knepper (.400, 12-for-30, 2 HR)
Hates to face: John Tudor (0-for-9)
Ground-ball hitter: 1.58 G/A ratio last season. . . . June batting average of .359 was highest in N.L. . . . Batted .111 (2-for-18) last season with the bases loaded. Has never walked in 76 career plate appearances with the bases full. . . . Career batting average of .293 in Late-Inning Pressure Situations despite .213 mark over past two seasons. . . . Pirates had a record of 7–2 in games in which he homered. . . . Tied Terry Harper for major-league lead with three extra-inning home runs. . . . Career batting averages: .367 at Riverfront Stadium, .349 at Wrigley Field. . . . Career batting averages: .303 vs. left-handed pitchers, .279 vs. right-handers. . . . Year-by-year batting averages in day games, starting with 1982: .397, .328, .308, .222.

Terry Pendleton

St. Louis Cardinals	AB	H	2B	3B	HR	RRF	BB	SO	BA	SA	OBA
Season	559	134	16	3	5	77	37	75	.240	.306	.285
vs. Left-Handed Pitchers	171	39	6	0	2	24	7	21	.228	.298	.257
vs. Right-Handed Pitchers	388	95	10	3	3	53	30	54	.245	.309	.298
Home	272	62	8	3	3	35	17	30	.228	.313	.273
Road	287	72	8	0	2	42	20	45	.251	.300	.297
Grass	153	39	4	0	1	25	10	22	.255	.301	.297
Artificial Turf	406	95	12	3	4	52	27	53	.234	.308	.281
April	73	17	3	0	1	10	6	18	.233	.315	.291
May	105	29	5	0	0	19	5	11	.276	.324	.306
June	51	6	0	0	1	5	2	5	.118	.176	.151
July	96	22	2	0	1	8	4	13	.229	.281	.257
August	96	21	3	0	2	14	9	13	.219	.313	.283
Sept./Oct.	138	39	3	3	0	21	11	15	.283	.348	.336
Leading Off Inn.	116	29	5	0	1	1	2	18	.250	.319	.263
Bases Empty	279	64	11	0	3	3	18	41	.229	.301	.276
Runners On	280	70	5	3	2	74	19	34	.250	.311	.295
Runners/Scor. Pos.	176	45	3	3	2	73	13	22	.256	.341	.302
Runners On/2 Out	114	26	3	2	1	29	8	15	.228	.316	.279
Scor. Pos./2 Out	74	19	2	2	1	28	4	10	.257	.378	.295
Late Inning Pressure	87	22	6	2	1	11	8	19	.253	.402	.316
Leading Off	21	8	4	0	1	1	0	4	.381	.714	.381
Bases Empty	44	14	6	0	1	1	3	8	.318	.523	.362
Runners On	43	8	0	2	0	10	5	11	.186	.279	.271
Runners/Scor. Pos.	23	5	0	2	0	10	4	5	.217	.391	.333

DRIVING IN RUNS	0 Out	1 Out	2 Out	Total	
From 1B	0/45	1/69	6/75	7/189	4%
From 2B	8/35	8/45	12/61	28/141	20%
From 3B	12/17	15/27	9/28	36/72	50%
Scoring Position	20/52	23/72	21/89	64/213	30%
Scor. Pos. %	38%	32%	24%	30%	
Driving In Runners from 3B with Less than Two Out:			27/44	61%	

Loves to face: Jose DeLeon (.563, 9-for-16)
Hates to face: Nolan Ryan (.077, 1-for-13, 5 SO)
Ground-ball hitter: 1.73 G/A ratio last season, 10th-highest in N.L. (minimum: 200 PA). Career average: 1.67. . . . Batted .277 in day games, .215 in night games. . . . Batted .444 (8-for-18) with the bases loaded last season, hitting a pair of grand slams. . . . Averaged 2.55 assists per nine innings last season, 3d-highest rate among N.L. third basemen (minimum: 300 innings). . . . Career batting average of .382 at Wrigley Field. . . . Career batting averages in Late-Inning Pressure Situations: .200 with runners on base, .324 with the bases empty. . . . Has drawn only four walks leading off 161 innings in his career.

Tony Perez

Cincinnati Reds	AB	H	2B	3B	HR	RRF	BB	SO	BA	SA	OBA
Season	183	60	8	0	6	34	22	22	.328	.470	.396
vs. Left-Handed Pitchers	124	41	4	0	6	25	14	13	.331	.508	.393
vs. Right-Handed Pitchers	59	19	4	0	0	9	8	9	.322	.390	.403
Home	103	38	6	0	4	27	10	9	.369	.544	.421
Road	80	22	2	0	2	7	12	13	.275	.375	.366
Grass	60	16	1	0	2	4	5	12	.267	.383	.323
Artificial Turf	123	44	7	0	4	30	17	10	.358	.512	.430
April	4	1	0	0	0	0	1	2	.250	.250	.400
May	19	10	1	0	4	13	5	1	.526	1.211	.625
June	39	9	1	0	0	4	3	5	.231	.256	.279
July	35	11	4	0	0	5	4	4	.314	.429	.385
August	42	16	0	0	1	6	5	6	.381	.452	.438
Sept./Oct.	44	13	2	0	1	6	4	4	.295	.409	.354
Leading Off Inn.	43	12	2	0	0	0	4	5	.279	.326	.340
Bases Empty	93	26	4	0	4	4	8	11	.280	.452	.337
Runners On	90	34	4	0	2	30	14	11	.378	.489	.453
Runners/Scor. Pos.	49	19	2	0	2	29	10	7	.388	.551	.475
Runners On/2 Out	39	12	2	0	0	9	9	5	.308	.359	.438
Scor. Pos./2 Out	19	6	2	0	0	9	7	2	.316	.421	.500
Late Inning Pressure	35	12	1	0	0	4	6	5	.343	.371	.439
Leading Off	9	4	1	0	0	0	3	1	.444	.556	.583
Bases Empty	12	4	1	0	0	0	4	1	.333	.417	.500
Runners On	23	8	0	0	0	4	2	4	.348	.348	.400
Runners/Scor. Pos.	16	5	0	0	0	4	2	4	.313	.313	.389

DRIVING IN RUNS	0 Out	1 Out	2 Out	Total	
From 1B	2/18	1/19	0/27	3/64	5%
From 2B	3/11	1/11	5/17	9/39	23%
From 3B	4/4	8/10	4/9	16/23	70%
Scoring Position	7/15	9/21	9/26	25/62	40%
Scor. Pos. %	47%	43%	35%	40%	
Driving In Runners from 3B with Less than Two Out:			12/14	86%	

Loves to face: Bryn Smith (1.000, 4-for-4, 2 2B, 1 HR)
Hates to face: Mark Davis (0-for-9)
Batted .346 in 45 games as a starter, .208 in 27 games off the bench. . . . Has the most RBIs (1,623) among active major leaguers, but should lose that distinction to Reggie Jackson (1,601) sometime in 1986. . . . Reds won all six games in which he hit a home run. . . . Ranked last among N.L. first basemen with an average of 0.54 assists per nine innings (minimum: 300 innings). . . . Has batted .309 in Late-Inning Pressure Situations over the past three seasons. . . . Minor blot: drove in only four base runners in Late-Inning Pressure Situations last season, all from third base.

Gerald Perry

Atlanta Braves	AB	H	2B	3B	HR	RRF	BB	SO	BA	SA	OBA
Season	238	51	5	0	3	15	23	28	.214	.273	.282
vs. Left-Handed Pitchers	41	7	0	0	1	4	1	9	.171	.244	.190
vs. Right-Handed Pitchers	197	44	5	0	2	11	22	19	.223	.279	.300
Home	137	31	4	0	3	14	11	13	.226	.321	.282
Road	101	20	1	0	0	1	12	15	.198	.208	.283
Grass	177	39	5	0	3	14	15	19	.220	.299	.280
Artificial Turf	61	12	0	0	0	1	8	9	.197	.197	.290
April	32	4	0	0	0	3	1	5	.125	.125	.152
May	88	22	3	0	1	4	8	6	.250	.318	.313
June	18	3	0	0	0	1	4	1	.167	.167	.304
July	19	1	0	0	0	1	5	3	.053	.053	.250
August	31	9	0	0	0	1	2	4	.290	.290	.333
Sept./Oct.	50	12	2	0	2	5	3	9	.240	.400	.283
Leading Off Inn.	60	13	1	0	1	1	6	3	.217	.283	.288
Bases Empty	135	28	4	0	1	1	13	11	.207	.259	.277
Runners On	103	23	1	0	2	14	10	17	.223	.291	.289
Runners/Scor. Pos.	55	9	1	0	1	11	10	9	.164	.236	.288
Runners On/2 Out	44	7	1	0	1	6	5	5	.159	.250	.245
Scor. Pos./2 Out	29	4	1	0	1	6	5	4	.138	.276	.265
Late Inning Pressure	63	15	1	0	1	11	6	10	.238	.302	.300
Leading Off	16	2	0	0	0	0	4	2	.125	.125	.300
Bases Empty	34	3	0	0	0	0	4	4	.088	.088	.184
Runners On	29	12	1	0	1	11	2	6	.414	.552	.438
Runners/Scor. Pos.	13	8	1	0	0	8	2	2	.615	.692	.625

DRIVING IN RUNS	0 Out	1 Out	2 Out	Total	
From 1B	2/22	0/25	0/28	2/75	3%
From 2B	1/8	2/17	3/24	6/49	12%
From 3B	1/2	1/4	2/14	4/20	20%
Scoring Position	2/10	3/21	5/38	10/69	14%
Scor. Pos. %	20%	14%	13%	14%	
Driving In Runners from 3B with Less than Two Out:			2/6	33%	

Loves to face: Mike Krukow (.833, 5-for-6, 2 HR)
Hates to face: Dave Dravecky (0-for-6)
The National League's answer to Joe Carter: started at least one game in each of the first eight spots in the batting order last season. . . . Talk about going 0-for-a-month: Perry was hitless from June 17 to July 27 (but had just 24 at bats in that time). . . . Career batting averages: .210 vs. left-handed pitchers, .261 vs. right-handers. . . . Career batting average of .351 (20-for-57) in Late-Inning Pressure Situations with runners on base. . . . One hit in 20 career at bats at the Astrodome; 2-for-24 at Riverfront Stadium. . . . Has hit 19 career doubles, none in 130 at bats on artificial surfaces. . . . Has drawn 21 walks and struck out only seven times leading off 156 innings during three-year career.

Darrell Porter

St. Louis Cardinals	AB	H	2B	3B	HR	RRF	BB	SO	BA	SA	OBA
Season	240	53	12	2	10	36	41	48	.221	.413	.335
vs. Left-Handed Pitchers	38	7	1	0	1	5	6	9	.184	.289	.295
vs. Right-Handed Pitchers	202	46	11	2	9	31	35	39	.228	.436	.342
Home	102	26	6	2	4	18	17	23	.255	.471	.364
Road	138	27	6	0	6	18	24	25	.196	.370	.313
Grass	79	13	5	0	3	8	13	14	.165	.342	.283
Artificial Turf	161	40	7	2	7	28	28	34	.248	.447	.359
April	13	2	0	0	0	0	1	2	.154	.154	.214
May	49	6	1	1	2	6	10	8	.122	.306	.267
June	2	0	0	0	0	0	0	0	.000	.000	.000
July	22	7	4	0	2	5	3	4	.318	.773	.400
August	71	16	3	0	3	17	15	15	.225	.394	.360
Sept./Oct.	83	22	4	1	3	8	12	19	.265	.446	.361
Leading Off Inn.	53	15	5	0	3	3	11	10	.283	.547	.415
Bases Empty	133	31	10	1	7	7	20	26	.233	.481	.338
Runners On	107	22	2	1	3	29	21	22	.206	.327	.331
Runners/Scor. Pos.	66	15	2	1	3	29	17	15	.227	.424	.376
Runners On/2 Out	39	6	1	0	1	9	11	7	.154	.256	.340
Scor. Pos./2 Out	26	5	1	0	1	9	9	4	.192	.346	.400
Late Inning Pressure	43	8	1	0	1	6	3	7	.186	.279	.239
Leading Off	12	1	0	0	0	0	2	1	.083	.083	.214
Bases Empty	24	3	1	0	0	0	2	5	.125	.167	.192
Runners On	19	5	0	0	1	6	1	2	.263	.421	.300
Runners/Scor. Pos.	10	4	0	0	1	6	1	0	.400	.700	.455

DRIVING IN RUNS	0 Out	1 Out	2 Out	Total	
From 1B	0/18	2/29	2/23	4/70	6%
From 2B	0/9	5/22	3/20	8/51	16%
From 3B	0/1	11/19	3/9	14/29	48%
Scoring Position	0/10	16/41	6/29	22/80	28%
Scor. Pos. %	0%	39%	21%	28%	
Driving In Runners from 3B with Less than Two Out:			11/20	55%	

Loves to face: Mike Krukow (.483, 14-for-29, 4 2B, 2 3B, 5 HR)
Hates to face: Lee Tunnell (.063, 1-for-16)
Nine extra-base hits in his last 17 at bats vs. Krukow. . . . Drove in two or more runs in four consecutive games (August 10–15). . . . Liability at the plate with two men out: eleven-year batting averages with runners on base: .290 with less than two outs, .225 with two outs; with runners in scoring position: .278 with less than 2 outs, .221 with two outs. . . . Has not batted above .200 with two outs and runners in scoring position since 1981. . . . Has hit a home run at every current N.L. stadium except Atlanta Stadium (64 career AB). . . . Has driven in 63.6 percent of runners from third base with less than two outs since 1975, including 25 of 34 (73.5%) in Late-Inning Pressure Situations.

Terry Puhl

Houston Astros	AB	H	2B	3B	HR	RRF	BB	SO	BA	SA	OBA
Season	194	55	14	3	2	23	18	23	.284	.418	.343
vs. Left-Handed Pitchers	68	20	4	1	0	12	5	8	.294	.382	.342
vs. Right-Handed Pitchers	126	35	10	2	2	11	13	15	.278	.437	.343
Home	123	40	9	2	1	16	10	13	.325	.455	.375
Road	71	15	5	1	1	7	8	10	.211	.352	.288
Grass	27	9	4	1	1	7	4	4	.333	.667	.406
Artificial Turf	167	46	10	2	1	16	14	19	.275	.377	.332
April	30	11	1	1	0	7	7	2	.367	.467	.487
May	87	24	8	1	2	10	6	14	.276	.460	.319
June	41	11	2	0	0	4	2	2	.268	.317	.295
July	13	2	0	0	0	0	0	2	.154	.154	.154
August	23	7	3	1	0	2	3	3	.304	.522	.385
Sept./Oct.	0	0	0	0	0	0	0	0	.000	.000	.000
Leading Off Inn.	26	2	0	0	0	0	0	4	.077	.077	.077
Bases Empty	117	28	6	0	2	2	10	14	.239	.342	.299
Runners On	77	27	8	3	0	21	8	9	.351	.532	.404
Runners/Scor. Pos.	41	13	4	0	0	17	6	6	.317	.415	.392
Runners On/2 Out	33	7	5	0	0	6	4	3	.212	.364	.316
Scor. Pos./2 Out	20	3	2	0	0	5	3	3	.150	.250	.292
Late Inning Pressure	20	7	1	0	0	2	4	3	.350	.400	.440
Leading Off	3	0	0	0	0	0	0	0	.000	.000	.000
Bases Empty	13	5	0	0	0	0	0	1	.385	.385	.385
Runners On	7	2	1	0	0	2	4	2	.286	.429	.500
Runners/Scor. Pos.	3	1	0	0	0	2	3	1	.333	.333	.571

DRIVING IN RUNS	0 Out	1 Out	2 Out	Total	
From 1B	3/24	1/11	2/25	6/60	10%
From 2B	2/7	3/9	3/15	8/31	26%
From 3B	2/3	4/7	1/9	7/19	37%
Scoring Position	4/10	7/16	4/24	15/50	30%
Scor. Pos. %	40%	44%	17%	30%	
Driving In Runners from 3B with Less than Two Out:			6/10	60%	

Loves to face: Ed Lynch (.571, 8-for-14)
Hates to face: John Denny (.087, 2-for-23)
Fly-ball hitter: 0.66 G/A ratio last season, 7th-lowest in N.L. (minimum: 200 PA). Career average: 0.98.... All-time major-league leader in fielding percentage by an outfielder at .993 (minimum: 1,000 games).... Batted 112 points higher with runners on base than with the bases empty, 3d-largest difference in N.L. (minimum: 200 PA).... Reached base only twice leading off 26 innings last season; that's an on-base average of .077, the lowest in either league (minimum: 25 PA).... Batted .483 (14-for-29) in day games, .248 in night games last season.... Has hit a home run at every current N.L. stadium except Candlestick Park (226 career AB).... Did not ground into a double play in 39 opportunities last season, highest total among N.L. players without a GIDP.

Tim Raines

Montreal Expos	AB	H	2B	3B	HR	RRF	BB	SO	BA	SA	OBA
Season	575	184	30	13	11	41	81	60	.320	.475	.405
vs. Left-Handed Pitchers	178	49	5	3	6	17	22	17	.275	.438	.351
vs. Right-Handed Pitchers	397	135	25	10	5	24	59	43	.340	.491	.428
Home	280	97	17	11	4	18	48	28	.346	.529	.446
Road	295	87	13	2	7	23	33	32	.295	.424	.364
Grass	161	49	8	1	5	18	19	21	.304	.460	.376
Artificial Turf	414	135	22	12	6	23	62	39	.326	.481	.416
April	78	21	4	2	0	4	4	4	.269	.372	.301
May	78	20	2	3	2	6	12	12	.256	.436	.363
June	107	37	3	2	2	7	11	11	.346	.467	.403
July	107	30	4	1	1	2	16	11	.280	.364	.384
August	100	39	8	2	3	11	15	7	.390	.600	.470
Sept./Oct.	105	37	9	3	3	11	23	15	.352	.581	.465
Leading Off Inn.	249	76	13	6	3	3	34	30	.305	.442	.391
Bases Empty	413	137	24	10	9	9	51	42	.332	.504	.408
Runners On	162	47	6	3	2	32	30	18	.290	.401	.398
Runners/Scor. Pos.	93	22	4	3	1	29	26	7	.237	.376	.398
Runners On/2 Out	69	19	4	1	0	14	12	8	.275	.362	.383
Scor. Pos./2 Out	50	11	3	1	0	13	11	4	.220	.320	.361
Late Inning Pressure	89	31	5	0	1	4	10	6	.348	.438	.410
Leading Off	26	9	2	0	0	0	1	1	.346	.423	.370
Bases Empty	58	22	4	0	1	1	4	2	.379	.500	.419
Runners On	31	9	1	0	0	3	6	4	.290	.323	.395
Runners/Scor. Pos.	15	2	1	0	0	3	3	1	.133	.200	.263

DRIVING IN RUNS	0 Out	1 Out	2 Out	Total	
From 1B	0/28	1/37	1/51	2/116	2%
From 2B	2/11	6/28	7/41	15/80	19%
From 3B	2/4	5/10	6/19	13/33	39%
Scoring Position	4/15	11/38	13/60	28/113	25%
Scor. Pos. %	27%	29%	22%	25%	
Driving In Runners from 3B with Less than Two Out:			7/14	50%	

Loves to face: Charles Hudson (.524, 11-for-21)
Hates to face: Shane Rawley (.071, 1-for-14)
August batting average of .390 was 2d-highest in N.L.... Hitless in seven at bats as a pinch-hitter last season.... Reached base safely in 38 of his last 39 starts.... Hit two home runs at New York on October 4 to tie his single-season career-high for homers.... Nine of his 11 home runs were solo shots. Drove in only two base runners with 11 home runs, 2d-lowest average in N.L.... Yearly batting averages in Late-Inning Pressure Situations since 1981: .372, .376, .360, .283, .348. Career LIP average: .340.... Walked as leadoff batter in 34 innings last season, highest total in N.L. since 1979, when Billy North (38) and Dave Lopes (35) both exceeded that figure.... Career batting average of .380 at Candlestick Park, .377 at Busch Stadium.

Rafael Ramirez

Atlanta Braves	AB	H	2B	3B	HR	RRF	BB	SO	BA	SA	OBA
Season	568	141	25	4	5	60	20	63	.248	.333	.272
vs. Left-Handed Pitchers	192	46	10	3	0	28	9	21	.240	.323	.271
vs. Right-Handed Pitchers	376	95	15	1	5	32	11	42	.253	.338	.272
Home	272	80	13	2	4	33	12	26	.294	.401	.321
Road	296	61	12	2	1	27	8	37	.206	.270	.225
Grass	413	110	19	2	5	45	15	42	.266	.358	.290
Artificial Turf	155	31	6	2	0	15	5	21	.200	.265	.222
April	82	20	1	1	1	5	3	7	.244	.317	.271
May	94	27	8	0	0	12	3	8	.287	.372	.309
June	101	25	5	1	2	14	3	13	.248	.376	.267
July	94	28	2	1	1	6	6	6	.298	.372	.337
August	118	31	7	0	0	16	4	14	.263	.322	.285
Sept./Oct.	79	10	2	1	1	7	1	15	.127	.215	.134
Leading Off Inn.	124	31	3	1	0	0	5	13	.250	.290	.279
Bases Empty	342	78	7	2	3	3	13	43	.228	.287	.256
Runners On	226	63	18	2	2	57	7	20	.279	.403	.294
Runners/Scor. Pos.	131	34	9	1	1	49	5	12	.260	.366	.277
Runners On/2 Out	82	24	8	1	1	26	3	9	.293	.451	.318
Scor. Pos./2 Out	64	18	5	1	1	23	3	8	.281	.438	.313
Late Inning Pressure	89	26	5	1	1	18	5	11	.292	.404	.330
Leading Off	19	4	0	0	0	0	2	0	.211	.211	.286
Bases Empty	47	11	1	0	0	0	2	8	.234	.255	.265
Runners On	42	15	4	1	1	18	3	3	.357	.571	.400
Runners/Scor. Pos.	26	9	2	0	0	13	3	2	.346	.423	.414

DRIVING IN RUNS	0 Out	1 Out	2 Out	Total	
From 1B	4/58	1/48	5/55	10/161	6%
From 2B	3/25	9/35	11/50	23/110	21%
From 3B	3/5	10/17	9/26	22/48	46%
Scoring Position	6/30	19/52	20/76	45/158	28%
Scor. Pos. %	20%	37%	26%	28%	
Driving In Runners from 3B with Less than Two Out:			13/22	59%	

Loves to face: Nolan Ryan (.333, 14-for-42, 2 HR)
Hates to face: Scott Sanderson (.095, 2-for-21)
Led N.L. shortstops in errors, 32, for the fifth straight season—the longest streak in the history of the league.... Dynasty appeared safe at the start of last season with trade of '84 co-leader Dale Berra to American League, but a new group of contenders emerged, led by young Mariano Duncan (27 errors at short, another two at second base) and convert Hubie Brooks (28 errors).... Toughest man in N.L. to walk last season: one BB per 29.8 plate appearances.... Successful on 25 percent of stolen base attempts last season (league average: 69.6 percent).... Career breakdowns: .291 vs. left-handers, .258 vs. right-handers; .290 in day games, .257 in night games.... Has driven in 33 of 84 runners from scoring position in Late-Inning Pressure Situations over past three seasons (39.3%).

Johnny Ray

Pittsburgh Pirates	AB	H	2B	3B	HR	RRF	BB	SO	BA	SA	OBA
Season	594	163	33	3	7	74	46	24	.274	.375	.325
vs. Left-Handed Pitchers	170	43	9	1	1	15	10	18	.253	.335	.291
vs. Right-Handed Pitchers	424	120	24	2	6	59	36	6	.283	.392	.338
Home	278	81	19	2	3	39	27	12	.291	.406	.353
Road	316	82	14	1	4	35	19	12	.259	.348	.299
Grass	161	40	6	1	2	14	10	7	.248	.335	.289
Artificial Turf	433	123	27	2	5	60	36	17	.284	.390	.338
April	74	18	4	0	0	8	2	1	.243	.297	.260
May	97	31	8	0	1	6	5	5	.320	.433	.353
June	112	26	4	1	2	14	4	5	.232	.339	.261
July	93	23	6	1	2	8	5	6	.247	.398	.280
August	85	24	4	1	0	11	10	3	.282	.353	.358
Sept./Oct.	133	41	7	0	2	27	20	4	.308	.406	.396
Leading Off Inn.	149	38	5	0	1	1	8	4	.255	.309	.293
Bases Empty	361	101	16	2	4	4	24	12	.280	.368	.325
Runners On	233	62	17	1	3	70	22	12	.266	.386	.324
Runners/Scor. Pos.	152	45	11	0	3	66	20	7	.296	.428	.369
Runners On/2 Out	80	25	9	0	3	35	9	3	.313	.538	.382
Scor. Pos./2 Out	63	21	6	0	3	34	8	2	.333	.571	.408
Late Inning Pressure	99	24	6	0	0	13	12	6	.242	.303	.321
Leading Off	24	8	0	0	0	0	1	1	.333	.333	.360
Bases Empty	49	12	2	0	0	0	3	2	.245	.286	.288
Runners On	50	12	4	0	0	13	9	4	.240	.320	.350
Runners/Scor. Pos.	39	10	3	0	0	13	9	3	.256	.333	.388

DRIVING IN RUNS	0 Out	1 Out	2 Out	Total	
From 1B	4/44	0/51	5/44	9/139	6%
From 2B	4/26	6/43	16/47	26/116	22%
From 3B	6/11	15/24	11/24	32/59	54%
Scoring Position	10/37	21/67	27/71	58/175	33%
Scor. Pos. %	27%	31%	38%	33%	
Driving In Runners from 3B with Less than Two Out:			21/35	60%	

Loves to face: Andy Hawkins (.632, 12-for-19)
Hates to face: Rick Sutcliffe (.043, 1-for-23)
May batting average of .320 was seventh-highest in N.L.... Started 96 losing games last season, highest total in N.L.... Strikeout rate of one per 27.2 plate appearances was best in N.L.... Six strikeouts in 467 plate appearances vs. right-handed pitchers was not only best average (1.3%) in either league last season, but in 11-year history of *The Player Analysis* as well.... Batted .406 with 13 RBIs during October, earning him the final N.L. Player of the Month award.... Career batting averages of .251 vs. left-handers, .296 vs. right-handers. Home run off Bob Knepper on May 22 was the first (and only) of his career against a left-handed pitcher.... Has struck out only twice in 94 career at bats at Riverfront Stadium.

Gary Redus

Cincinnati Reds	AB	H	2B	3B	HR	RRF	BB	SO	BA	SA	OBA
Season	246	62	14	4	6	30	44	52	.252	.415	.366
vs. Left-Handed Pitchers	128	31	6	2	2	12	24	27	.242	.367	.366
vs. Right-Handed Pitchers	118	31	8	2	4	18	20	25	.263	.466	.367
Home	135	39	10	2	4	16	25	28	.289	.481	.404
Road	111	23	4	2	2	14	19	24	.207	.333	.321
Grass	73	15	3	1	2	11	12	16	.205	.356	.314
Artificial Turf	173	47	11	3	4	19	32	36	.272	.439	.388
April	8	4	0	0	0	2	6	1	.500	.500	.714
May	46	14	3	1	1	4	6	11	.304	.478	.385
June	94	21	7	2	3	17	16	16	.223	.436	.339
July	43	10	2	0	1	4	7	11	.233	.349	.340
August	33	9	1	1	0	0	5	4	.273	.364	.368
Sept./Oct.	22	4	1	0	1	3	4	9	.182	.364	.308
Leading Off Inn.	87	20	3	1	3	3	16	20	.230	.391	.350
Bases Empty	159	42	9	3	3	3	30	36	.264	.415	.384
Runners On	87	20	5	1	3	27	14	16	.230	.414	.333
Runners/Scor. Pos.	51	15	5	1	2	25	8	10	.294	.549	.383
Runners On/2 Out	47	11	1	1	2	14	7	4	.234	.426	.333
Scor. Pos./2 Out	28	10	1	1	2	14	4	3	.357	.679	.438
Late Inning Pressure	44	11	3	1	0	4	9	12	.250	.364	.377
Leading Off	12	3	0	0	0	0	3	3	.250	.250	.400
Bases Empty	23	6	0	1	0	0	6	6	.261	.348	.414
Runners On	21	5	3	0	0	4	3	6	.238	.381	.333
Runners/Scor. Pos.	13	3	3	0	0	4	1	4	.231	.462	.286

DRIVING IN RUNS	0 Out	1 Out	2 Out	Total	
From 1B	0/14	1/13	1/32	2/59	3%
From 2B	2/10	4/12	4/25	10/47	21%
From 3B	1/2	3/8	7/12	11/22	50%
Scoring Position	3/12	7/20	11/37	21/69	30%
Scor. Pos. %	25%	35%	30%	30%	
Driving In Runners from 3B with Less than Two Out:			4/10	40%	

Loves to face: Steve Trout (.500, 5-for-10)
Hates to face: Andy Hawkins (.053, 1-for-19)
Fly-ball hitter: 0.61 G/A ratio last season, lowest in N.L. (minimum: 200 PA). Career average: 0.60. . . . Started only 15 games after the All-Star break. . . . Three-run homer on September 15 accounted for all of his RBIs after July 22. . . . Batting average with runners in scoring position (.294) was the highest of his career. . . . Reds won all six games in which he hit a home run last season. . . . Did not ground into a double play in 32 opportunities last season, 2d-highest total among N.L. players without a GIDP. . . . Has driven in only six base runners from first base in 252 career opportunities.

Craig Reynolds

Houston Astros	AB	H	2B	3B	HR	RRF	BB	SO	BA	SA	OBA
Season	379	103	18	8	4	33	12	30	.272	.393	.293
vs. Left-Handed Pitchers	54	17	3	1	0	3	2	11	.315	.407	.339
vs. Right-Handed Pitchers	325	86	15	7	4	30	10	19	.265	.391	.285
Home	191	44	8	3	1	16	9	17	.230	.319	.264
Road	188	59	10	5	3	17	3	13	.314	.468	.323
Grass	95	31	5	2	2	12	3	5	.326	.484	.343
Artificial Turf	284	72	13	6	2	21	9	25	.254	.363	.276
April	36	10	1	0	2	4	4	3	.278	.472	.350
May	80	25	4	2	0	9	2	5	.313	.413	.321
June	59	15	2	2	1	6	3	7	.254	.407	.290
July	73	20	3	1	0	6	2	8	.274	.342	.293
August	65	18	5	0	1	2	1	4	.277	.400	.288
Sept./Oct.	66	15	3	3	0	6	0	3	.227	.364	.227
Leading Off Inn.	78	23	4	2	2	2	1	4	.295	.474	.304
Bases Empty	220	60	10	5	3	3	6	15	.273	.405	.292
Runners On	159	43	8	3	1	30	6	15	.270	.377	.293
Runners/Scor. Pos.	83	20	5	1	1	26	4	9	.241	.361	.270
Runners On/2 Out	70	21	4	1	0	15	2	3	.300	.386	.319
Scor. Pos./2 Out	48	14	2	1	0	14	0	2	.292	.375	.292
Late Inning Pressure	63	15	3	0	0	1	4	7	.238	.286	.284
Leading Off	19	6	2	0	0	0	0	2	.316	.421	.316
Bases Empty	37	11	2	0	0	0	3	4	.297	.351	.350
Runners On	26	4	1	0	0	1	1	3	.154	.192	.185
Runners/Scor. Pos.	14	2	1	0	0	1	1	1	.143	.214	.200

DRIVING IN RUNS	0 Out	1 Out	2 Out	Total	
From 1B	2/38	2/35	2/44	6/117	5%
From 2B	1/12	2/16	8/40	11/68	16%
From 3B	4/9	3/5	4/17	11/31	35%
Scoring Position	5/21	5/21	12/57	22/99	22%
Scor. Pos. %	24%	24%	21%	22%	
Driving In Runners from 3B with Less than Two Out:			7/14	50%	

Loves to face: Pascual Perez (.500, 8-for-16, 3 HR)
Hates to face: Rick Mahler (.087, 2-for-23)
Fly-ball hitter: 0.81 G/A ratio last season. . . . 32 RBIs in 379 at bats last season; Houston pitchers had 30 RBIs in 360 at bats. . . . May batting average of .310 was 10th-highest in N.L. . . . Had five game-winning RBIs in September. . . . Hit three of his four home runs last season were against Atlanta. . . . Career batting average of .219 with 2 outs and runners on base. . . . Career batting average of .317 leading off innings in Late-Inning Pressure Situations. . . . Has hit 26 of his 29 career home runs vs. right-handed pitchers. His home-run rate vs. southpaws is one every 287.7 at bats. . . . Has not driven in a runner from first base in Late-Inning Pressure Situations in 82 opportunities since 1979.

R.J. Reynolds

Dodgers/Pirates	AB	H	2B	3B	HR	RRF	BB	SO	BA	SA	OBA
Season	337	95	15	7	3	42	22	49	.282	.395	.327
vs. Left-Handed Pitchers	111	29	6	3	0	13	4	9	.261	.369	.287
vs. Right-Handed Pitchers	226	66	9	4	3	29	18	40	.292	.407	.345
Home	150	45	10	3	1	18	14	25	.300	.427	.365
Road	187	50	5	4	2	24	8	24	.267	.369	.294
Grass	160	45	8	1	0	20	10	29	.281	.344	.322
Artificial Turf	177	50	7	6	3	22	12	20	.282	.441	.332
April	12	3	1	0	0	0	0	1	.250	.333	.250
May	92	26	5	2	0	13	4	11	.283	.380	.306
June	48	12	2	0	0	7	5	10	.250	.292	.327
July	25	6	2	1	0	3	2	5	.240	.400	.296
August	30	8	0	1	0	2	2	4	.267	.333	.313
Sept./Oct.	130	40	5	3	3	17	9	18	.308	.462	.357
Leading Off Inn.	70	18	2	2	1	1	5	9	.257	.386	.307
Bases Empty	194	51	10	4	2	2	12	24	.263	.387	.309
Runners On	143	44	5	3	1	40	10	25	.308	.406	.350
Runners/Scor. Pos.	84	25	4	2	1	38	7	16	.298	.429	.347
Runners On/2 Out	51	18	3	0	0	14	5	8	.353	.412	.421
Scor. Pos./2 Out	37	10	2	0	0	13	5	6	.270	.324	.372
Late Inning Pressure	63	19	3	4	1	6	2	15	.302	.524	.323
Leading Off	15	5	1	1	1	1	1	4	.333	.733	.375
Bases Empty	39	11	2	3	1	1	2	9	.282	.564	.317
Runners On	24	8	1	1	0	5	0	6	.333	.458	.333
Runners/Scor. Pos.	17	6	1	1	0	5	0	5	.353	.529	.353

DRIVING IN RUNS	0 Out	1 Out	2 Out	Total	
From 1B	1/32	1/32	1/30	3/94	3%
From 2B	2/12	7/20	6/27	15/59	25%
From 3B	3/6	11/18	7/21	21/45	47%
Scoring Position	5/18	18/38	13/48	36/104	35%
Scor. Pos. %	28%	47%	27%	35%	
Driving In Runners from 3B with Less than Two Out:			14/24	58%	

Loves to face: Craig Lefferts (.800, 4-for-5)
Hates to face: Dave Dravecky (0-for-9)
Ground-ball hitter: 1.52 G/A ratio last season. . . . Batted .290 in 81 games in the starting lineup. . . . Batted .308 in 31 games with Pirates. . . . Yearly batting averages with runners on base since 1983: .172, .253, .308. . . . One of three N.L. players to start at least 10 games at all three outfield positions last season. . . . Batted .236 in day games, .308 in night games last season. . . . Career batting average of .306 with two outs and runners on base. . . . Career batting average of .302 in Late-Inning Pressure Situations. . . . One walk per 33 career plate appearances batting left-handed, one per 15 PA batting right-handed.

Pete Rose

Cincinnati Reds	AB	H	2B	3B	HR	RRF	BB	SO	BA	SA	OBA
Season	405	107	12	2	2	47	86	35	.264	.319	.395
vs. Left-Handed Pitchers	49	17	3	0	0	5	11	3	.347	.408	.467
vs. Right-Handed Pitchers	356	90	9	2	2	42	75	32	.253	.306	.385
Home	196	50	5	2	0	22	47	12	.255	.301	.404
Road	209	57	7	0	2	25	39	23	.273	.335	.386
Grass	114	30	1	0	2	12	17	14	.263	.325	.359
Artificial Turf	291	77	11	2	0	35	69	21	.265	.316	.408
April	59	15	2	0	0	6	7	4	.254	.288	.333
May	71	21	4	1	1	6	16	6	.296	.423	.440
June	66	20	2	0	0	10	15	3	.303	.333	.432
July	59	14	3	0	0	8	17	5	.237	.288	.397
August	73	17	1	0	0	9	11	7	.233	.247	.333
Sept./Oct.	77	20	0	1	1	8	20	10	.260	.325	.414
Leading Off Inn.	72	18	3	0	1	1	14	5	.250	.333	.372
Bases Empty	238	61	5	2	1	1	42	18	.256	.307	.372
Runners On	167	46	7	0	1	46	44	17	.275	.335	.424
Runners/Scor. Pos.	108	29	5	0	1	44	40	9	.269	.343	.461
Runners On/2 Out	58	16	4	0	1	16	13	6	.276	.397	.425
Scor. Pos./2 Out	33	10	3	0	1	15	12	3	.303	.485	.511
Late Inning Pressure	69	20	0	0	0	6	11	7	.290	.290	.388
Leading Off	17	6	0	0	0	0	0	2	.353	.353	.353
Bases Empty	35	10	0	0	0	0	3	4	.286	.286	.342
Runners On	34	10	0	0	0	6	8	3	.294	.294	.429
Runners/Scor. Pos.	21	6	0	0	0	6	8	2	.286	.286	.483

DRIVING IN RUNS	0 Out	1 Out	2 Out	Total	
From 1B	0/24	1/39	2/38	3/101	3%
From 2B	2/13	6/42	6/24	14/79	18%
From 3B	6/7	15/25	7/16	28/48	58%
Scoring Position	8/20	21/67	13/40	42/127	33%
Scor. Pos. %	40%	31%	33%	33%	
Driving In Runners from 3B with Less than Two Out:			21/32	66%	

Loves to face: Bob Welch (.415, 22-for-53)
Hates to face: Dave Dravecky (0-for-7)
Ground-ball hitter: 1.62 G/A ratio last season. . . . Struck out in five consecutive games prior to tying the Cobb record. He had not done that since he struck out in seven straight games in May 1968. . . . Has only one hit in 11 at bats as a pinch-hitter since returning to Cincinnati. . . . Did not go more than seven consecutive games without an RBI last season. . . . Batting average with runners in scoring position (.269) was his lowest in 11 years of *The Player Analysis*. . . . Hitless in six at bats with the bases loaded last season, but walked four times to drive in runs. Has walked with the bases loaded more than any other player (19 times) since 1975. . . . His only career grand slam was hit in 1964 off Dallas Green.

Jerry Royster

San Diego Padres	AB	H	2B	3B	HR	RRF	BB	SO	BA	SA	OBA
Season	249	70	13	2	5	31	32	31	.281	.410	.363
vs. Left-Handed Pitchers	181	54	12	1	3	20	25	20	.298	.425	.385
vs. Right-Handed Pitchers	68	16	1	1	2	11	7	11	.235	.368	.303
Home	118	34	7	1	4	16	16	17	.288	.466	.378
Road	131	36	6	1	1	15	16	14	.275	.359	.349
Grass	195	50	8	1	4	23	23	26	.256	.369	.336
Artificial Turf	54	20	5	1	1	8	9	5	.370	.556	.453
April	31	5	1	0	0	3	0	3	.161	.194	.161
May	39	12	4	1	0	6	4	5	.308	.462	.372
June	49	18	4	0	1	8	12	7	.367	.510	.492
July	27	6	2	0	0	1	3	1	.222	.296	.313
August	25	6	1	0	1	3	3	5	.240	.400	.310
Sept./Oct.	78	23	1	1	3	10	10	10	.295	.449	.375
Leading Off Inn.	86	22	4	0	3	3	9	13	.256	.407	.326
Bases Empty	159	42	7	1	4	4	17	23	.264	.396	.335
Runners On	90	28	6	1	1	27	15	8	.311	.433	.407
Runners/Scor. Pos.	53	21	5	0	1	26	10	6	.396	.547	.477
Runners On/2 Out	39	14	3	1	1	13	7	1	.359	.564	.457
Scor. Pos./2 Out	24	10	2	0	1	12	5	1	.417	.625	.517
Late Inning Pressure	36	12	2	1	1	5	6	2	.333	.528	.432
Leading Off	11	3	2	0	1	1	1	1	.273	.727	.333
Bases Empty	19	8	2	0	1	1	2	2	.421	.684	.476
Runners On	17	4	0	1	0	4	4	0	.235	.353	.391
Runners/Scor. Pos.	10	2	0	0	0	3	1	0	.200	.200	.250

DRIVING IN RUNS	0 Out	1 Out	2 Out	Total	
From 1B	0/10	1/32	2/27	3/69	4%
From 2B	0/5	2/14	5/16	7/35	20%
From 3B	1/1	10/13	5/11	16/25	64%
Scoring Position	1/6	12/27	10/27	23/60	38%
Scor. Pos. %	17%	44%	37%	38%	
Driving In Runners from 3B with Less than Two Out:			11/14	79%	

Loves to face: Jeff Reardon (.556, 5-for-9)
Hates to face: Nolan Ryan (0-for-12, 4 SO)
One hit in 10 at bats as a pinch-hitter last season. His lone pinch-hit was a game-winner to cap a 4-run 9th-inning rally vs. Houston on August 8. . . . Since 1983 has batted .533 (8-for-15, three doubles, one home run) with the bases loaded; he hit that home run in his only bases-loaded at bat of 1985. . . . Last season's grass/artificial breakdown was a reversal. Career through 1984: .259 on grass fields, .217 on artificial surfaces. . . . Has batted for a higher average in home games than he has in road games in nine of the last 10 seasons. . . . Averaged 3.58 assists per nine innings last season, 2d-highest rate among N.L. second basemen (minimum: 300 innings). . . . Career batting averages: .176 at Shea Stadium, .184 at Olympic Stadium, .207 at Dodger Stadium.

John Russell

Philadelphia Phillies	AB	H	2B	3B	HR	RRF	BB	SO	BA	SA	OBA
Season	216	47	12	0	9	23	18	72	.218	.398	.278
vs. Left-Handed Pitchers	95	21	6	0	4	11	13	29	.221	.411	.315
vs. Right-Handed Pitchers	121	26	6	0	5	12	5	43	.215	.388	.246
Home	117	31	8	0	6	18	10	39	.265	.487	.323
Road	99	16	4	0	3	5	8	33	.162	.293	.224
Grass	44	8	2	0	2	2	5	21	.182	.364	.265
Artificial Turf	172	39	10	0	7	21	13	51	.227	.407	.281
April	28	4	2	0	0	0	3	13	.143	.214	.226
May	15	5	2	0	1	3	8	7	.333	.667	.565
June	24	3	0	0	0	1	1	6	.125	.125	.160
July	48	15	3	0	3	11	4	12	.313	.563	.365
August	48	10	5	0	1	1	0	16	.208	.375	.208
Sept./Oct.	53	10	0	0	4	7	2	18	.189	.415	.218
Leading Off Inn.	42	8	3	0	1	1	4	13	.190	.333	.261
Bases Empty	122	26	8	0	4	4	9	47	.213	.377	.267
Runners On	94	21	4	0	5	19	9	25	.223	.426	.291
Runners/Scor. Pos.	49	9	2	0	4	17	5	18	.184	.469	.259
Runners On/2 Out	37	9	2	0	4	15	7	8	.243	.622	.364
Scor. Pos./2 Out	25	5	1	0	3	13	5	7	.200	.600	.333
Late Inning Pressure	35	7	1	0	0	1	1	16	.200	.229	.222
Leading Off	6	1	0	0	0	0	1	4	.167	.167	.286
Bases Empty	18	2	0	0	0	0	1	12	.111	.111	.158
Runners On	17	5	1	0	0	1	0	4	.294	.353	.294
Runners/Scor. Pos.	5	1	0	0	0	1	0	2	.200	.200	.200

DRIVING IN RUNS	0 Out	1 Out	2 Out	Total	
From 1B	0/20	0/23	4/24	4/67	6%
From 2B	0/7	1/9	4/20	5/36	14%
From 3B	0/2	2/7	3/10	5/19	26%
Scoring Position	0/9	3/16	7/30	10/55	18%
Scor. Pos. %	0%	19%	23%	18%	
Driving In Runners from 3B with Less than Two Out:			2/9	22%	

Loves to face: Mark Thurmond (.444, 4-for-9, 2 HR)
Hates to face: Rick Sutcliffe (0-for-7, 5 SO)
Opened season as Phillies' starting first baseman. Committed two errors on opening night vs. Atlanta, batted .143 with no RBIs for the month of April, and was sitting on the bench by May 1. . . . Career batting averages: .297 at Veterans Stadium, .164 in road games. . . . Batted .277 vs. ground-ball pitchers last season, .154 vs. fly-ball pitchers. . . . Phillies won eight of nine games in which he hit a home run. . . . Averaged 1.35 putouts per nine innings last season, 2d-lowest rate among N.L. outfielders (minimum: 300 innings). . . . Struck out 43 times in 126 plate appearances vs. right-handed pitchers last season (34.1%), second-highest average in 11-year history of *The Player Analysis* (minimum: 40 SO). Highest average was also last season: 42.3% by Rob Deer. . . . Three hits in 30 career at bats at Three Rivers Stadium.

Juan Samuel

Philadelphia Phillies	AB	H	2B	3B	HR	RRF	BB	SO	BA	SA	OBA
Season	663	175	31	13	19	78	33	141	.264	.436	.303
vs. Left-Handed Pitchers	197	47	8	3	5	22	8	41	.239	.386	.266
vs. Right-Handed Pitchers	466	128	23	10	14	56	25	100	.275	.457	.318
Home	327	81	12	6	8	33	21	69	.248	.394	.298
Road	336	94	19	7	11	45	12	72	.280	.476	.307
Grass	172	45	6	4	8	20	6	42	.262	.483	.289
Artificial Turf	491	130	25	9	11	58	27	99	.265	.420	.307
April	81	22	2	2	1	5	2	22	.272	.383	.286
May	110	25	6	1	3	12	5	23	.227	.382	.261
June	118	34	7	3	2	12	5	25	.288	.449	.328
July	99	26	5	2	4	18	8	25	.263	.475	.321
August	123	37	4	3	7	22	3	22	.301	.553	.315
Sept./Oct.	132	31	7	2	2	9	10	24	.235	.364	.299
Leading Off Inn.	194	51	14	3	6	6	15	36	.263	.459	.325
Bases Empty	405	106	26	7	9	9	25	84	.262	.427	.309
Runners On	258	69	5	6	10	69	8	57	.267	.450	.292
Runners/Scor. Pos.	153	41	2	5	6	59	8	31	.268	.464	.308
Runners On/2 Out	99	27	2	2	7	36	5	26	.273	.545	.314
Scor. Pos./2 Out	70	21	0	2	5	32	5	16	.300	.571	.355
Late Inning Pressure	90	25	6	1	4	18	6	20	.278	.500	.340
Leading Off	13	3	1	1	0	0	3	4	.231	.462	.474
Bases Empty	41	9	3	1	0	0	4	9	.220	.341	.333
Runners On	49	16	3	0	4	18	2	11	.327	.633	.346
Runners/Scor. Pos.	25	11	2	0	2	14	2	4	.440	.760	.464

DRIVING IN RUNS	0 Out	1 Out	2 Out	Total	
From 1B	2/44	4/73	3/59	9/176	5%
From 2B	2/22	8/51	18/59	28/132	21%
From 3B	4/9	10/18	8/23	22/50	44%
Scoring Position	6/31	18/69	26/82	50/182	27%
Scor. Pos. %	19%	26%	32%	27%	
Driving In Runners from 3B with Less than Two Out:			14/27	52%	

Loves to face: Greg Minton (.600, 6-for-10)
Hates to face: Orel Hershiser (.067, 1-for-15)
Led N.L. second basemen in games (159) and putouts (389); reduced errors from 33 in '84 to 15. . . . Tied major-league record for second basemen with 12 assists vs. New York on April 20. . . . Shared N.L. lead in strikeouts (141) with Dale Murphy. . . . Had .251 average while batting in the leadoff slot, .272 average when batting second, and .290 when dropped down to third. . . . Hit home runs in all three games of series at Wrigley Field (August 16–18). Had back-to-back 4-hit games in the same series. . . . Career batting averages of .256 vs. right-handers, .274 vs. left-handers. . . . Career batting averages: .379 at Riverfront Stadium, .370 at Olympic Stadium, .367 at Dodger Stadium. . . . No home runs in 81 career at bats at Busch Stadium (.185 batting average).

Ryne Sandberg

Chicago Cubs	AB	H	2B	3B	HR	RRF	BB	SO	BA	SA	OBA
Season	609	186	31	6	26	85	57	97	.305	.504	.364
vs. Left-Handed Pitchers	152	42	9	0	5	14	15	24	.276	.434	.339
vs. Right-Handed Pitchers	457	144	22	6	21	71	42	73	.315	.527	.372
Home	293	89	16	4	17	43	32	56	.304	.560	.371
Road	316	97	15	2	9	42	25	41	.307	.453	.357
Grass	427	136	24	6	23	63	41	72	.319	.564	.377
Artificial Turf	182	50	7	0	3	22	16	25	.275	.363	.333
April	73	14	4	0	2	4	3	14	.192	.329	.224
May	107	33	4	2	4	8	9	14	.308	.495	.362
June	85	26	4	0	3	7	7	12	.306	.459	.366
July	107	38	6	1	6	20	12	20	.355	.598	.413
August	117	36	6	0	5	21	7	21	.308	.487	.347
Sept./Oct.	120	39	7	3	6	25	19	16	.325	.583	.411
Leading Off Inn.	107	40	9	1	6	6	8	18	.374	.645	.417
Bases Empty	357	117	19	2	14	14	29	62	.328	.510	.378
Runners On	252	69	12	4	12	71	28	35	.274	.496	.344
Runners/Scor. Pos.	134	38	7	3	5	52	19	22	.284	.493	.367
Runners On/2 Out	93	24	5	1	4	25	9	16	.258	.462	.330
Scor. Pos./2 Out	56	15	2	1	2	18	5	11	.268	.446	.339
Late Inning Pressure	87	32	6	1	4	16	9	14	.368	.598	.433
Leading Off	20	8	1	0	3	3	2	3	.400	.900	.455
Bases Empty	46	17	3	0	3	3	5	9	.370	.630	.431
Runners On	41	15	3	1	1	13	4	5	.366	.561	.435
Runners/Scor. Pos.	23	10	3	1	1	13	2	3	.435	.783	.500

DRIVING IN RUNS	0 Out	1 Out	2 Out	Total	
From 1B	5/57	5/57	5/56	15/170	9%
From 2B	5/25	9/40	9/48	23/113	20%
From 3B	4/8	9/15	7/16	20/39	51%
Scoring Position	9/33	18/55	16/64	43/152	28%
Scor. Pos. %	27%	33%	25%	28%	
Driving In Runners from 3B with Less than Two Out:			13/23	57%	

Loves to face: Lee Tunnell (.526, 10-for-19, 2 HR)
Hates to face: Bryn Smith (.094, 3-for-32, 9 SO)
Stole 11 bases in 11 attempts vs. the Expos. . . . Yearly batting averages in Late-Inning Pressure Situations since 1982: .173, .281, .279, .368. . . . Career batting averages of .288 with runners on base, .287 with the bases empty, .286 with runners in scoring position. . . . Has hit .193 at Olympic Stadium. . . . Career batting average of .311 at Wrigley Field, .265 on the road. . . . Averaged 3.37 assists per nine innings last season, 3d-highest rate among N.L. second basemen. . . . Career: one home run per 65 at bats vs. left-handed pitchers, one per 37 at bats vs. right-handers. . . . Has driven in 15 of 17 runners from third base with less than two outs in Late-Inning Pressure Situations.

Rafael Santana

New York Mets	AB	H	2B	3B	HR	RRF	BB	SO	BA	SA	OBA
Season	529	136	19	1	1	33	29	54	.257	.302	.295
vs. Left-Handed Pitchers	196	52	5	1	0	8	14	17	.265	.301	.313
vs. Right-Handed Pitchers	333	84	14	0	1	25	15	37	.252	.303	.284
Home	264	62	8	0	0	15	10	26	.235	.265	.262
Road	265	74	11	1	1	18	19	28	.279	.340	.326
Grass	366	87	12	0	0	19	15	36	.238	.270	.267
Artificial Turf	163	49	7	1	1	14	14	18	.301	.374	.354
April	55	10	2	0	1	6	5	6	.182	.273	.250
May	84	19	2	0	0	2	3	10	.226	.250	.253
June	92	29	4	0	0	10	4	5	.315	.359	.340
July	100	26	3	0	0	6	2	9	.260	.290	.275
August	85	25	2	0	0	4	2	11	.294	.318	.307
Sept./Oct.	113	27	6	1	0	5	13	13	.239	.310	.317
Leading Off Inn.	148	44	7	1	0	0	5	12	.297	.358	.320
Bases Empty	309	84	11	1	0	0	16	37	.272	.314	.308
Runners On	220	52	8	0	1	33	13	17	.236	.286	.277
Runners/Scor. Pos.	125	26	5	0	0	29	11	13	.208	.248	.268
Runners On/2 Out	96	19	4	0	0	10	10	7	.198	.240	.274
Scor. Pos./2 Out	62	10	3	0	0	8	8	6	.161	.210	.257
Late Inning Pressure	76	18	2	0	0	3	4	12	.237	.263	.275
Leading Off	20	4	0	0	0	0	1	2	.200	.200	.238
Bases Empty	52	13	0	0	0	0	3	8	.250	.250	.291
Runners On	24	5	2	0	0	3	1	4	.208	.292	.240
Runners/Scor. Pos.	15	3	1	0	0	3	0	3	.200	.267	.200

DRIVING IN RUNS	0 Out	1 Out	2 Out	Total	
From 1B	0/34	1/63	2/71	3/168	2%
From 2B	3/19	5/28	3/43	11/90	12%
From 3B	2/7	11/21	5/25	18/53	34%
Scoring Position	5/26	16/49	8/68	29/143	20%
Scor. Pos. %	19%	33%	12%	20%	
Driving In Runners from 3B with Less than Two Out:			13/28	46%	

Loves to face: Gary Lucas (.800, 4-for-5)
Hates to face: Steve Carlton (0-for-9, 4 SO)
Ground-ball hitter: 1.51 G/A ratio last season. . . . June batting average of .315 was 10th-highest in N.L. . . . Led N.L. shortstops with 301 putouts. . . . Averaged 2.66 assists per nine innings last season, lowest rate among N.L. shortstops (minimum: 300 innings). . . . Career batting average of .312 leading off innings. . . . Career batting averages: .231 with runners on base, .280 with the bases empty; .223 in day games, .282 in night games. . . . Has driven in only three runners from first base in 213 career opportunities. . . . Drove in only 18 of 53 runners from third base last season (34.0%), tied with Vance Law for lowest average in N.L. (minimum: 50 opportunities).

Mike Schmidt

Philadelphia Phillies	AB	H	2B	3B	HR	RRF	BB	SO	BA	SA	OBA
Season	549	152	31	5	33	96	87	117	.277	.532	.375
vs. Left-Handed Pitchers	155	44	13	0	6	18	28	30	.284	.484	.391
vs. Right-Handed Pitchers	394	108	18	5	27	78	59	87	.274	.551	.369
Home	265	74	18	1	14	44	42	49	.279	.513	.379
Road	284	78	13	4	19	52	45	68	.275	.549	.372
Grass	149	42	8	3	10	26	19	40	.282	.577	.359
Artificial Turf	400	110	23	2	23	70	68	77	.275	.515	.381
April	65	14	2	0	2	9	10	16	.215	.338	.308
May	84	18	5	0	4	13	11	19	.214	.417	.302
June	96	26	7	1	3	12	13	20	.271	.458	.358
July	96	27	4	1	6	14	14	19	.281	.531	.373
August	96	31	7	1	8	23	16	16	.323	.667	.422
Sept./Oct.	112	36	6	2	10	25	23	27	.321	.679	.441
Leading Off Inn.	133	40	11	0	12	12	13	36	.301	.654	.367
Bases Empty	295	85	21	1	25	25	39	64	.288	.620	.373
Runners On	254	67	10	4	8	71	48	53	.264	.429	.377
Runners/Scor. Pos.	149	42	4	2	8	65	37	32	.282	.497	.415
Runners On/2 Out	112	22	5	2	0	20	23	29	.196	.277	.333
Scor. Pos./2 Out	65	14	2	1	0	17	19	17	.215	.277	.393
Late Inning Pressure	88	28	4	2	7	18	13	19	.318	.648	.406
Leading Off	19	6	0	0	3	3	3	7	.316	.789	.409
Bases Empty	53	16	2	0	6	6	6	13	.302	.679	.373
Runners On	35	12	2	2	1	12	7	6	.343	.600	.452
Runners/Scor. Pos.	23	6	1	2	1	11	5	4	.261	.609	.393

DRIVING IN RUNS	0 Out	1 Out	2 Out	Total	
From 1B	4/49	4/57	5/76	13/182	7%
From 2B	5/22	7/41	9/52	21/115	18%
From 3B	11/15	12/20	6/19	29/54	54%
Scoring Position	16/37	19/61	15/71	50/169	30%
Scor. Pos. %	43%	31%	21%	30%	
Driving In Runners from 3B with Less than Two Out:			23/35	66%	

Loves to face: Bob Knepper (.387, 24-for-62, 6 2B, 2 3B, 6 HR)
Hates to face: Cecilio Guante (.111, 2-for-18, 10 SO)
Fly-ball hitter: 0.68 G/A ratio last season, 5th-lowest in N.L. (minimum: 200 PA). Career average: 0.69. . . . Career slugging percentage of .535 is highest among active players. . . . 458 home runs ranks 9th on all-time N.L. list. Needs 18 more to pass Musial and Stargell (both with 475) and 45 more to catch Eddie Mathews at 503. . . . Career total of 1,265 walks ranks 3d among players active in 1985. . . . Has batted above .300 in Late-Inning Pressure Situations in five of the last six seasons. . . . Tied Bob Horner for N.L. lead with seven LIP home runs last season. . . . Continued assault on Wrigley Field with four more home runs in 35 at bats last season. Career totals: 44 HR in 415 AB.

Steve Sax

Los Angeles Dodgers	AB	H	2B	3B	HR	RRF	BB	SO	BA	SA	OBA
Season	488	136	8	4	1	47	54	43	.279	.318	.352
vs. Left-Handed Pitchers	144	31	4	1	1	11	24	12	.215	.278	.324
vs. Right-Handed Pitchers	344	105	4	3	0	36	30	31	.305	.334	.365
Home	239	54	4	0	1	17	30	22	.226	.255	.317
Road	249	82	4	4	0	30	24	21	.329	.378	.386
Grass	350	90	5	1	1	31	43	29	.257	.286	.341
Artificial Turf	138	46	3	3	0	16	11	14	.333	.399	.383
April	1	0	0	0	0	0	0	0	.000	.000	.000
May	85	20	2	1	0	3	13	9	.235	.282	.337
June	93	21	0	0	0	7	9	9	.226	.226	.294
July	98	32	3	0	1	14	8	8	.327	.388	.383
August	91	24	2	0	0	8	7	10	.264	.286	.323
Sept./Oct.	120	39	1	3	0	15	17	7	.325	.383	.404
Leading Off Inn.	143	39	3	0	0	0	17	10	.273	.294	.354
Bases Empty	278	77	3	3	0	0	26	25	.277	.309	.341
Runners On	210	59	5	1	1	47	28	18	.281	.329	.366
Runners/Scor. Pos.	113	35	4	1	0	45	21	9	.310	.363	.413
Runners On/2 Out	88	17	2	1	1	17	20	11	.193	.273	.349
Scor. Pos./2 Out	47	10	2	1	0	15	16	5	.213	.298	.422
Late Inning Pressure	67	20	2	1	1	5	6	6	.299	.403	.351
Leading Off	22	9	1	0	0	0	3	3	.409	.455	.480
Bases Empty	38	13	1	1	0	0	4	5	.342	.421	.405
Runners On	29	7	1	0	1	5	2	1	.241	.379	.281
Runners/Scor. Pos.	12	3	0	0	0	3	1	1	.250	.250	.286

DRIVING IN RUNS	0 Out	1 Out	2 Out	Total	
From 1B	0/32	0/63	2/63	2/158	1%
From 2B	0/11	16/43	6/37	22/91	24%
From 3B	3/9	11/20	8/23	22/52	42%
Scoring Position	3/20	27/63	14/60	44/143	31%
Scor. Pos. %	15%	43%	23%	31%	
Driving In Runners from 3B with Less than Two Out:			14/29	48%	

Loves to face: Steve Carlton (.423, 11-for-26)
Hates to face: Eric Show (0-for-18)
Ground-ball hitter: 1.95 G/A ratio last season, 5th-highest in N.L. (minimum: 200 PA). Career average: 1.89. . . . Had most errors (22) and lowest fielding percentage (.969) among major-league second basemen (minimum: 100 games). . . . Averaged 2.74 assists per nine innings last season, 2d-lowest rate among N.L. second basemen (minimum: 300 innings). . . . Fewest extra-base hits (13) of any major leaguer to qualify for 1985 batting championship. . . . Batted .232 in 47 games in the leadoff spot, .316 in 84 games batting 8th in the order. . . . Batted 98 points higher vs. right-handers than left-handers last season, largest difference among right-handed N.L. batters (minimum: 100 PA vs. each). . . . Has not hit a home run in 672 at bats in day games since 1981, when he hit two in the span of 17 day-game at bats.

Rick Schu

Philadelphia Phillies	AB	H	2B	3B	HR	RRF	BB	SO	BA	SA	OBA
Season	416	105	21	4	7	27	38	78	.252	.373	.318
vs. Left-Handed Pitchers	132	37	10	2	4	9	14	23	.280	.477	.349
vs. Right-Handed Pitchers	284	68	11	2	3	18	24	55	.239	.324	.303
Home	175	47	9	2	2	12	20	25	.269	.377	.344
Road	241	58	12	2	5	15	18	53	.241	.369	.299
Grass	118	23	3	1	4	6	9	29	.195	.339	.258
Artificial Turf	298	82	18	3	3	21	29	49	.275	.386	.341
April	0	0	0	0	0	0	0	0	.000	.000	.000
May	11	2	0	0	0	0	0	5	.182	.182	.250
June	99	25	5	2	0	5	8	19	.253	.343	.315
July	74	23	5	0	2	3	8	14	.311	.459	.378
August	97	28	3	2	4	12	8	19	.289	.485	.343
Sept./Oct.	135	27	8	0	1	7	14	21	.200	.281	.275
Leading Off Inn.	106	32	9	1	4	4	8	12	.302	.519	.362
Bases Empty	278	73	17	3	6	6	22	53	.263	.410	.321
Runners On	138	32	4	1	1	21	16	25	.232	.297	.312
Runners/Scor. Pos.	81	19	3	0	0	18	12	16	.235	.272	.333
Runners On/2 Out	52	15	2	1	1	11	7	8	.288	.423	.373
Scor. Pos./2 Out	37	10	1	0	0	8	4	6	.270	.297	.341
Late Inning Pressure	67	16	1	0	0	2	6	11	.239	.254	.311
Leading Off	20	5	1	0	0	0	3	4	.250	.300	.375
Bases Empty	47	11	1	0	0	0	4	9	.234	.255	.308
Runners On	20	5	0	0	0	2	2	2	.250	.250	.318
Runners/Scor. Pos.	10	3	0	0	0	2	1	0	.300	.300	.364

DRIVING IN RUNS	0 Out	1 Out	2 Out	Total	
From 1B	0/30	0/33	2/32	2/95	2%
From 2B	1/16	2/20	6/29	9/65	14%
From 3B	2/5	5/7	2/14	9/26	35%
Scoring Position	3/21	7/27	8/43	18/91	20%
Scor. Pos. %	14%	26%	19%	20%	
Driving In Runners from 3B with Less than Two Out:			7/12	58%	

Loves to face: Danny Cox (.462, 6-for-13)
Hates to face: Jose DeLeon (0-for-7, 4 SO)
Fly-ball hitter: 0.93 G/A ratio last season. . . . Did not drive in a run in 25 games from June 18 to July 20. . . . No home runs in 72 career at bats in Late-Inning Pressure Situations. . . . Hit one home run in 294 at bats in night games last season, six in 135 at bats in day games. . . . Phillies were two games above the .500 mark in Schu's 110 starts, 14 games below without him in the starting lineup. . . . Two errors in 88 chances on grass fields, 18 errors in 209 chances on carpets. . . . Ranked 3d among N.L. rookies with 32 extra-base hits, but played 19 games fewer than leader Chris Brown (39), 30 fewer than runner-up Mariano Duncan (36).

Mike Scioscia

Los Angeles Dodgers	AB	H	2B	3B	HR	RRF	BB	SO	BA	SA	OBA
Season	429	127	26	3	7	54	77	21	.296	.420	.407
vs. Left-Handed Pitchers	87	22	5	0	1	9	11	6	.253	.345	.337
vs. Right-Handed Pitchers	342	105	21	3	6	45	66	15	.307	.439	.424
Home	202	60	11	0	1	27	40	10	.297	.366	.415
Road	227	67	15	3	6	27	37	11	.295	.467	.399
Grass	313	101	19	2	6	40	58	15	.323	.454	.431
Artificial Turf	116	26	7	1	1	14	19	6	.224	.328	.338
April	51	15	2	1	0	6	7	3	.294	.373	.377
May	82	17	2	1	2	8	7	5	.207	.329	.270
June	59	19	4	0	1	13	18	2	.322	.441	.494
July	59	19	5	0	1	11	9	2	.322	.458	.406
August	64	21	6	0	1	5	19	4	.328	.469	.482
Sept./Oct.	114	36	7	1	2	11	17	5	.316	.447	.414
Leading Off Inn.	88	19	3	1	5	5	23	7	.216	.443	.384
Bases Empty	242	62	12	3	6	6	42	14	.256	.405	.375
Runners On	187	65	14	0	1	48	35	7	.348	.439	.447
Runners/Scor. Pos.	105	34	8	0	0	44	24	5	.324	.400	.444
Runners On/2 Out	77	27	10	0	0	24	19	1	.351	.481	.485
Scor. Pos./2 Out	50	17	6	0	0	22	13	0	.340	.460	.484
Late Inning Pressure	59	15	4	1	1	5	9	4	.254	.407	.353
Leading Off	13	3	1	1	0	0	3	2	.231	.462	.375
Bases Empty	35	9	2	1	0	0	6	3	.257	.371	.366
Runners On	24	6	2	0	1	5	3	1	.250	.458	.333
Runners/Scor. Pos.	12	3	2	0	0	3	1	1	.250	.417	.308

DRIVING IN RUNS	0 Out	1 Out	2 Out	Total	
From 1B	1/28	0/59	2/55	3/142	2%
From 2B	4/12	5/37	11/39	20/88	23%
From 3B	3/7	10/17	10/21	23/45	51%
Scoring Position	7/19	15/54	21/60	43/133	32%
Scor. Pos. %	37%	28%	35%	32%	
Driving In Runners from 3B with Less than Two Out:			13/24	54%	

Loves to face: Ed Lynch (.500, 7-for-14, 1 HR)
Hates to face: Jay Tibbs (0-for-11)
Ranked 8th in N.L. in batting average during June, 9th during August. . . . Walk/strikeout ratio of 3.67 was highest in N.L. since 1976, when Dave Cash had 54 BB and 13 SO for 4.15 (minimum: 50 BB). . . . Had an on-base average of .561 in 17 games vs. the Braves last season. Three of his seven home runs were hit at Atlanta-Fulton County Stadium. . . . 1985 batting average peaked at .307 on September 14. . . . Home run at Dodger Stadium on July 31 was his first there since July 20, 1982. . . . Career batting averages of .297 with runners on base, .244 with the bases empty. Has batted over .300 with runners on base in four of his six seasons in majors. . . . Career breakdown: .287 on grass fields, .210 on artificial surfaces. . . . Career batting averages: .340 at Atlanta Stadium, .337 at Candlestick Park; .154 at the Astrodome.

Ozzie Smith

St. Louis Cardinals	AB	H	2B	3B	HR	RRF	BB	SO	BA	SA	OBA
Season	537	148	22	3	6	60	65	27	.276	.361	.355
vs. Left-Handed Pitchers	161	48	12	0	6	21	30	14	.298	.484	.407
vs. Right-Handed Pitchers	376	100	10	3	0	39	35	13	.266	.309	.330
Home	258	77	13	2	2	30	37	14	.298	.388	.389
Road	279	71	9	1	4	30	28	13	.254	.337	.321
Grass	145	38	6	0	1	15	17	6	.262	.324	.340
Artificial Turf	392	110	16	3	5	45	48	21	.281	.375	.360
April	63	12	1	1	1	5	8	2	.190	.286	.282
May	91	28	3	0	1	11	10	5	.308	.374	.376
June	93	24	5	0	1	6	6	4	.258	.344	.303
July	86	25	5	1	1	9	4	3	.291	.407	.330
August	94	26	4	0	0	10	12	4	.277	.319	.364
Sept./Oct.	110	33	4	1	2	19	25	9	.300	.409	.423
Leading Off Inn.	119	33	6	1	1	1	14	6	.277	.370	.353
Bases Empty	310	81	16	2	4	4	31	16	.261	.365	.330
Runners On	227	67	6	1	2	56	34	11	.295	.357	.386
Runners/Scor. Pos.	127	34	1	1	2	51	29	8	.268	.339	.399
Runners On/2 Out	91	24	2	0	1	18	20	4	.264	.319	.402
Scor. Pos./2 Out	52	14	1	0	1	16	19	2	.269	.346	.465
Late Inning Pressure	87	20	1	0	1	7	9	8	.230	.276	.302
Leading Off	18	4	0	0	0	0	3	0	.222	.222	.333
Bases Empty	51	12	1	0	1	1	4	3	.235	.314	.291
Runners On	36	8	0	0	0	6	5	5	.222	.222	.317
Runners/Scor. Pos.	24	5	0	0	0	6	3	4	.208	.208	.296

DRIVING IN RUNS	0 Out	1 Out	2 Out	Total	
From 1B	1/41	3/55	4/66	8/162	5%
From 2B	4/23	6/38	8/42	18/103	17%
From 3B	3/7	19/29	5/23	27/59	46%
Scoring Position	7/30	25/67	13/65	45/162	28%
Scor. Pos. %	23%	37%	20%	28%	
Driving In Runners from 3B with Less than Two Out:			22/36	61%	

Loves to face: Dan Schatzeder (.476, 10-for-21, 2 HR)
Hates to face: David Palmer (.045, 1-for-22)
Ground-ball hitter: 1.56 G/A ratio last season. . . . Led N.L. shortstops in fielding percentage (.983) for the fourth time in last five years. . . . Strikeout rate of one per 22.8 plate appearances was 3d-best in N.L. . . . Ratio of 6.25 walks per strikeout vs. left-handers in 1984 was highest in 11-year history of *The Player Analysis* (minimum: 25 BB). Last season's mark against lefties (2.14) ranked 2nd in N.L. to Gary Carter. . . . Bases-loaded strikeout vs. Steve Trout on October 5 was his first strikeout in 95 career plate appearances with the bags full. . . . Career batting average of .217 at San Diego Stadium. . . . Still looking for his first *regular-season* home run batting left-handed.

Chris Speier

Chicago Cubs	AB	H	2B	3B	HR	RRF	BB	SO	BA	SA	OBA
Season	218	53	11	0	4	26	17	34	.243	.349	.295
vs. Left-Handed Pitchers	66	22	3	0	3	15	6	9	.333	.515	.378
vs. Right-Handed Pitchers	152	31	8	0	1	11	11	25	.204	.276	.258
Home	112	25	5	0	1	19	8	14	.223	.295	.273
Road	106	28	6	0	3	7	9	20	.264	.406	.319
Grass	151	36	8	0	2	22	15	21	.238	.331	.304
Artificial Turf	67	17	3	0	2	4	2	13	.254	.388	.275
April	7	2	1	0	0	1	1	0	.286	.429	.333
May	31	6	1	0	1	1	6	8	.194	.323	.324
June	79	20	5	0	2	10	3	15	.253	.392	.277
July	46	11	3	0	0	3	5	6	.239	.304	.314
August	36	8	1	0	1	5	1	5	.222	.333	.243
Sept./Oct.	19	6	0	0	0	6	1	0	.316	.316	.350
Leading Off Inn.	55	11	2	0	1	1	6	9	.200	.291	.279
Bases Empty	127	30	6	0	1	1	13	19	.236	.307	.307
Runners On	91	23	5	0	3	25	4	15	.253	.407	.278
Runners/Scor. Pos.	53	16	3	0	2	23	3	6	.302	.472	.328
Runners On/2 Out	34	9	3	0	0	9	3	9	.265	.353	.324
Scor. Pos./2 Out	20	7	1	0	0	9	3	2	.350	.400	.435
Late Inning Pressure	47	16	1	0	3	10	5	8	.340	.553	.396
Leading Off	12	4	0	0	1	1	1	1	.333	.583	.385
Bases Empty	28	9	1	0	1	1	5	4	.321	.464	.424
Runners On	19	7	0	0	2	9	0	4	.368	.684	.350
Runners/Scor. Pos.	12	5	0	0	1	7	0	3	.417	.667	.385

DRIVING IN RUNS	0 Out	1 Out	2 Out	Total	
From 1B	0/11	1/29	0/25	1/65	2%
From 2B	0/7	4/21	4/16	8/44	18%
From 3B	3/3	5/11	5/11	13/25	52%
Scoring Position	3/10	9/32	9/27	21/69	30%
Scor. Pos. %	30%	28%	33%	30%	
Driving In Runners from 3B with Less than Two Out:			8/14	57%	

Loves to face: Dwight Gooden (.625, 5-for-8, 3 BB)
Hates to face: Bob Welch (0-for-11)
Batted .221 in day games, .290 in night games. . . . Batted 129 points higher vs. left-handed pitchers than right-handers last season, his largest disparity in 11 years of *The Player Analysis.* Composite averages during that time: .245 vs. lefties, .242 vs. righties. . . . Has batted under .200 five of the last eight years in Late-Inning Pressure Situations. . . . Averaged 3.68 assists per nine innings last season, 3d-highest rate among N.L. shortstops (minimum: 300 innings). . . . Only N.L. player to start at least five games at second base, third base, and shortstop last season. . . . Has batted .122 (10-for-82) at Riverfront Stadium since 1979. . . . One hit in his last 20 at bats at San Diego Stadium.

Jeff Stone

Philadelphia Phillies	AB	H	2B	3B	HR	RRF	BB	SO	BA	SA	OBA
Season	264	70	4	3	3	13	15	50	.265	.337	.307
vs. Left-Handed Pitchers	34	10	2	0	0	2	3	8	.294	.353	.351
vs. Right-Handed Pitchers	230	60	2	3	3	11	12	42	.261	.335	.300
Home	143	40	1	2	2	11	13	26	.280	.357	.340
Road	121	30	3	1	1	2	2	24	.248	.314	.266
Grass	82	19	2	0	0	1	2	17	.232	.256	.259
Artificial Turf	182	51	2	3	3	12	13	33	.280	.374	.328
April	60	18	0	2	2	5	6	10	.300	.467	.364
May	68	13	0	0	0	2	2	12	.191	.191	.214
June	36	10	1	0	0	1	3	6	.278	.306	.333
July	0	0	0	0	0	0	0	0	.000	.000	.000
August	31	9	1	1	0	2	0	5	.290	.387	.290
Sept./Oct.	69	20	2	0	1	3	4	17	.290	.362	.338
Leading Off Inn.	94	29	1	2	0	0	5	15	.309	.362	.350
Bases Empty	179	50	2	2	1	1	11	32	.279	.330	.325
Runners On	85	20	2	1	2	12	4	18	.235	.353	.270
Runners/Scor. Pos.	51	9	0	1	2	10	1	13	.176	.333	.192
Runners On/2 Out	38	8	1	1	1	7	3	8	.211	.368	.268
Scor. Pos./2 Out	28	5	0	1	1	7	0	8	.179	.357	.179
Late Inning Pressure	35	7	1	0	1	2	1	8	.200	.314	.222
Leading Off	7	1	0	0	0	0	1	0	.143	.143	.250
Bases Empty	23	5	0	0	1	1	1	2	.217	.348	.250
Runners On	12	2	1	0	0	1	0	6	.167	.250	.167
Runners/Scor. Pos.	5	0	0	0	0	0	0	2	.000	.000	.000

DRIVING IN RUNS	0 Out	1 Out	2 Out	Total	
From 1B	1/11	1/19	2/24	4/54	7%
From 2B	0/9	1/11	3/23	4/43	9%
From 3B	0/1	1/4	1/10	2/15	13%
Scoring Position	0/10	2/15	4/33	6/58	10%
Scor. Pos. %	0%	13%	12%	10%	
Driving In Runners from 3B with Less than Two Out:			1/5	20%	

Loves to face: Ed Lynch (.600, 6-for-10, 2 HR)
Hates to face: Orel Hershiser (0-for-10)
Two home runs off Lynch were hit in successive innings on April 20. He hit only one other all season. . . . Ground-ball hitter: 1.48 G/A ratio last season. . . . Batted .325 with three home runs and 10 RBIs in 29 day games, .241 with no homers and one RBI in 59 night games. . . . Career batting average of .297 with runners on base: .253 with runners in scoring position, .370 with a runner on first base only. . . . Averaged 1.47 putouts per nine innings last season, 3d-lowest rate among N.L. outfielders (minimum: 300 innings). . . . Six plate appearances with the bases loaded without an RRF was highest total in N.L. last season. . . . Career batting averages: .336 at Veterans Stadium, .275 in road games. . . . Drove in only six of 58 runners from scoring position last season (10.3%), lowest N.L. average in *Player Analysis* history (minimum: 50 opportunities).

Darryl Strawberry

New York Mets	AB	H	2B	3B	HR	RRF	BB	SO	BA	SA	OBA
Season	393	109	15	4	29	81	73	96	.277	.557	.389
vs. Left-Handed Pitchers	156	40	4	1	11	28	22	45	.256	.506	.348
vs. Right-Handed Pitchers	237	69	11	3	18	53	51	51	.291	.591	.414
Home	188	56	10	1	14	47	33	41	.298	.585	.399
Road	205	53	5	3	15	34	40	55	.259	.532	.381
Grass	265	81	12	3	19	63	46	65	.306	.589	.408
Artificial Turf	128	28	3	1	10	18	27	31	.219	.492	.353
April	68	16	2	0	6	12	6	17	.235	.529	.297
May	25	4	0	1	0	0	5	3	.160	.240	.300
June	8	1	0	0	0	0	1	3	.125	.125	.222
July	89	27	4	1	6	23	21	25	.303	.573	.432
August	96	30	3	1	9	24	19	22	.313	.646	.426
Sept./Oct.	107	31	6	1	8	22	21	26	.290	.589	.405
Leading Off Inn.	95	22	4	2	7	7	13	27	.232	.537	.324
Bases Empty	215	55	9	2	18	18	36	58	.256	.567	.363
Runners On	178	54	6	2	11	63	37	38	.303	.545	.420
Runners/Scor. Pos.	91	30	3	1	9	56	30	20	.330	.681	.484
Runners On/2 Out	78	24	5	0	3	27	24	20	.308	.487	.471
Scor. Pos./2 Out	43	14	2	0	3	25	21	11	.326	.581	.547
Late Inning Pressure	59	14	2	0	6	11	9	21	.237	.576	.333
Leading Off	16	5	1	0	1	1	2	7	.313	.563	.389
Bases Empty	33	10	1	0	5	5	6	11	.303	.788	.410
Runners On	26	4	1	0	1	6	3	10	.154	.308	.233
Runners/Scor. Pos.	11	1	1	0	0	4	2	4	.091	.182	.214

DRIVING IN RUNS	0 Out	1 Out	2 Out	Total	
From 1B	2/39	4/46	5/65	11/150	7%
From 2B	2/15	8/23	10/35	20/73	27%
From 3B	2/6	10/16	9/16	21/38	55%
Scoring Position	4/21	18/39	19/51	41/111	37%
Scor. Pos. %	19%	46%	37%	37%	
Driving In Runners from 3B with Less than Two Out:			12/22	55%	

Loves to face: Eric Show (.500, 9-for-18, 3 HR)
Hates to face: Mike Krukow (.059, 1-for-17, 8 SO)
Led N.L. with nine home runs in August; he didn't have that many *RBIs* in August 1984, when he went homerless. . . . The Mets were 32 games above the .500 mark in Strawberry's 108 starts, five above without him in the starting lineup. . . . Hit 11 home runs off left-handed pitchers, the most by a left-handed batter in N.L. last season. . . . Career batting averages: .237 vs. left-handers, .272 vs. right-handers. . . . Batted .311 in day games, .257 in night games. . . . Five hits (two homers) in seven at bats with the bases loaded last season. . . . Yearly batting averages with runners in scoring position since 1983: .202, .261, .330. . . . Career batting average of .157 in Late-Inning Pressure Situations with runners in scoring position.

Garry Templeton

San Diego Padres	AB	H	2B	3B	HR	RRF	BB	SO	BA	SA	OBA
Season	546	154	30	2	6	55	41	88	.282	.377	.332
vs. Left-Handed Pitchers	177	45	8	0	1	16	9	29	.254	.316	.291
vs. Right-Handed Pitchers	369	109	22	2	5	39	32	59	.295	.407	.351
Home	267	75	14	2	4	24	15	41	.281	.393	.319
Road	279	79	16	0	2	31	26	47	.283	.362	.343
Grass	403	110	21	2	6	39	27	69	.273	.380	.319
Artificial Turf	143	44	9	0	0	16	14	19	.308	.371	.365
April	60	11	6	0	0	7	7	7	.183	.283	.269
May	95	28	6	0	3	12	2	22	.295	.453	.303
June	101	36	4	1	0	10	6	13	.356	.416	.398
July	80	25	6	1	0	8	16	11	.313	.413	.423
August	103	23	1	0	2	6	8	17	.223	.291	.279
Sept./Oct.	107	31	7	0	1	12	2	18	.290	.383	.303
Leading Off Inn.	141	33	6	1	1	1	7	18	.234	.312	.275
Bases Empty	342	90	16	2	4	4	14	52	.263	.357	.294
Runners On	204	64	14	0	2	51	27	36	.314	.412	.389
Runners/Scor. Pos.	109	36	7	0	1	45	26	17	.330	.422	.449
Runners On/2 Out	92	28	8	0	1	23	20	17	.304	.424	.429
Scor. Pos./2 Out	51	17	5	0	0	19	20	8	.333	.431	.521
Late Inning Pressure	82	22	3	0	1	4	10	15	.268	.341	.355
Leading Off	15	6	0	0	0	0	2	1	.400	.400	.500
Bases Empty	49	17	2	0	1	1	4	6	.347	.449	.407
Runners On	33	5	1	0	0	3	6	9	.152	.182	.282
Runners/Scor. Pos.	19	3	0	0	0	3	6	5	.158	.158	.360

DRIVING IN RUNS	0 Out	1 Out	2 Out	Total	
From 1B	2/33	0/50	5/70	7/153	5%
From 2B	2/11	6/31	9/37	17/79	22%
From 3B	3/4	14/22	8/22	25/48	52%
Scoring Position	5/15	20/53	17/59	42/127	33%
Scor. Pos. %	33%	38%	29%	33%	
Driving In Runners from 3B with Less than Two Out:			17/26	65%	

Loves to face: Craig McMurtry (.579, 11-for-19)
Hates to face: Jesse Orosco (.071, 1-for-14)
Ground-ball hitter: 1.91 G/A ratio last season, 7th-highest in N.L. (minimum: 200 PA). Career average: 1.80. . . . June batting average of .356 was 2nd-highest in N.L. . . . Was walked intentionally four times in a 12-inning game vs. Pittsburgh on July 5. Since 1955, the first year in which intentional walks were officially compiled, only Roger Maris had accomplished this feat (also in a 12-inning game). . . . 14 of his 16 walks in July were intentional. . . . Career batting averages: .317 with runners on base, .269 with the bases empty. . . . Career .300 hitter on artificial surfaces. . . . Has hit a home run in every current N.L. stadium except the Astrodome (213 career AB). . . . Only player in N.L. history to lead the league in triples three straight years (1977–79); hit 69 triples in 713 games with the Cardinals, 15 in 563 games with the Padres.

Jason Thompson

Pittsburgh Pirates	AB	H	2B	3B	HR	RRF	BB	SO	BA	SA	OBA
Season	402	97	17	1	12	62	84	58	.241	.378	.369
vs. Left-Handed Pitchers	123	32	2	0	3	20	23	23	.260	.350	.374
vs. Right-Handed Pitchers	279	65	15	1	9	42	61	35	.233	.391	.367
Home	215	43	9	0	9	40	47	38	.200	.367	.338
Road	187	54	8	1	3	22	37	20	.289	.390	.406
Grass	106	37	7	0	3	17	17	11	.349	.500	.439
Artificial Turf	296	60	10	1	9	45	67	47	.203	.334	.346
April	67	16	4	0	2	9	11	11	.239	.388	.346
May	58	15	2	0	4	17	10	8	.259	.500	.352
June	79	19	3	1	3	12	11	10	.241	.418	.330
July	81	22	3	0	1	8	19	10	.272	.346	.410
August	86	21	4	0	2	14	26	14	.244	.360	.420
Sept./Oct.	31	4	1	0	0	2	7	5	.129	.161	.289
Leading Off Inn.	110	21	7	0	3	3	14	21	.191	.336	.282
Bases Empty	213	43	10	0	4	4	31	34	.202	.305	.303
Runners On	189	54	7	1	8	58	53	24	.286	.460	.435
Runners/Scor. Pos.	107	33	4	0	4	47	34	15	.308	.458	.462
Runners On/2 Out	105	26	4	1	4	30	24	16	.248	.419	.388
Scor. Pos./2 Out	61	17	2	0	2	24	15	9	.279	.410	.421
Late Inning Pressure	72	16	2	0	1	7	17	14	.222	.292	.371
Leading Off	22	3	1	0	0	0	4	7	.136	.182	.269
Bases Empty	39	6	1	0	1	1	6	9	.154	.256	.267
Runners On	33	10	1	0	0	6	11	5	.303	.333	.477
Runners/Scor. Pos.	17	5	0	0	0	5	9	3	.294	.294	.538

DRIVING IN RUNS	0 Out	1 Out	2 Out	Total	
From 1B	1/31	2/38	6/61	9/130	7%
From 2B	2/16	6/26	14/53	22/95	23%
From 3B	5/8	8/10	6/18	19/36	53%
Scoring Position	7/24	14/36	20/71	41/131	31%
Scor. Pos. %	29%	39%	28%	31%	
Driving In Runners from 3B with Less than Two Out:			13/18	72%	

Loves to face: Rick Mahler (.529, 9-for-17, 2 HR)
Hates to face: Bill Gullickson (.140, 6-for-43)
Walked in 11 consecutive games (July 30–August 11), four games short of N.L. record held by Darrell Evans. . . . Batted .273 in day games, .224 in night games. Career averages: .289 and .248. . . . Has batted above .300 with runners in scoring position in four of the last eight seasons. Career average: .286. . . . Drove in 11 base runners with 12 home runs, 5th-highest average in N.L. . . . Career batting average of .169 at Riverfront Stadium. . . . Career RDI percentage from scoring position of .342 in Late-Inning Pressure Situations ranks 8th in the 11-year history of *The Player Analysis.*

Dickie Thon

Houston Astros	AB	H	2B	3B	HR	RRF	BB	SO	BA	SA	OBA
Season	251	63	6	1	6	29	18	50	.251	.355	.299
vs. Left-Handed Pitchers	162	44	6	0	4	18	13	27	.272	.383	.324
vs. Right-Handed Pitchers	89	19	0	1	2	11	5	23	.213	.303	.253
Home	121	23	2	1	3	12	9	20	.190	.298	.246
Road	130	40	4	0	3	17	9	30	.308	.408	.348
Grass	88	27	3	0	1	13	7	23	.307	.375	.351
Artificial Turf	163	36	3	1	5	16	11	27	.221	.344	.270
April	40	8	0	0	0	2	3	11	.200	.200	.256
May	18	4	1	0	0	0	1	4	.222	.278	.263
June	43	7	1	0	0	1	1	13	.163	.186	.182
July	42	17	3	0	2	7	0	8	.405	.619	.405
August	44	10	0	1	2	10	4	6	.227	.409	.292
Sept./Oct.	64	17	1	0	2	9	9	8	.266	.375	.347
Leading Off Inn.	76	17	2	0	1	1	4	15	.224	.289	.263
Bases Empty	153	35	3	0	3	3	10	31	.229	.307	.276
Runners On	98	28	3	1	3	26	8	19	.286	.429	.333
Runners/Scor. Pos.	54	18	2	1	2	24	6	10	.333	.519	.387
Runners On/2 Out	40	12	0	1	1	12	6	4	.300	.425	.391
Scor. Pos./2 Out	26	8	0	1	1	12	5	3	.308	.500	.419
Late Inning Pressure	28	7	0	0	1	3	2	10	.250	.357	.300
Leading Off	12	3	0	0	0	0	0	3	.250	.250	.250
Bases Empty	21	5	0	0	0	0	1	7	.238	.238	.273
Runners On	7	2	0	0	1	3	1	3	.286	.714	.375
Runners/Scor. Pos.	4	2	0	0	1	3	0	1	.500	1.250	.500

DRIVING IN RUNS	0 Out	1 Out	2 Out	Total	
From 1B	0/22	1/24	2/29	3/75	4%
From 2B	3/12	2/11	5/14	10/37	27%
From 3B	2/4	4/8	4/14	10/26	38%
Scoring Position	5/16	6/19	9/28	20/63	32%
Scor. Pos. %	31%	32%	32%	32%	
Driving In Runners from 3B with Less than Two Out:			6/12	50%	

Loves to face: Rick Rhoden (.556, 5-for-9, 2 HR)
Hates to face: Bruce Sutter (0-for-9)
Ground-ball hitter: 1.38 G/A ratio last season. . . . Batted .194 vs. ground-ball pitchers last season, .321 vs. fly-ball pitchers. . . . 1985 strikeout rate of one per five at bats was worst of his career. . . . Career batting averages: .301 with runners on base, .260 with the bases empty; .293 vs. left-handers, .265 vs. right-handers. . . . Batting average with runners in scoring position (.333) was his highest in any full major-league season. . . . Career batting average of .379 (22-for-58) in Late-Inning Pressure Situations with runners in scoring position. . . . Batted 118 points higher in road games than home games, largest difference in N.L. (minimum: 200 PA); may have had trouble seeing indoors, since his pre-beaning averages with Houston were .304 at home, .260 on the road. . . . Career batting average of .413 at Shea Stadium.

Manny Trillo

San Francisco Giants	AB	H	2B	3B	HR	RRF	BB	SO	BA	SA	OBA
Season	451	101	16	2	3	30	40	44	.224	.288	.287
vs. Left-Handed Pitchers	131	30	4	0	1	8	12	12	.229	.282	.294
vs. Right-Handed Pitchers	320	71	12	2	2	22	28	32	.222	.291	.285
Home	230	46	9	0	1	12	20	22	.200	.252	.266
Road	221	55	7	2	2	18	20	22	.249	.326	.310
Grass	351	77	13	0	3	25	34	36	.219	.282	.289
Artificial Turf	100	24	3	2	0	5	6	8	.240	.310	.283
April	59	16	3	0	0	4	7	6	.271	.322	.343
May	98	20	2	1	0	5	6	10	.204	.245	.250
June	99	21	5	0	0	5	10	12	.212	.263	.291
July	75	22	1	0	3	10	7	5	.293	.427	.349
August	68	12	2	1	0	4	3	6	.176	.235	.211
Sept./Oct.	52	10	3	0	0	2	7	5	.192	.250	.288
Leading Off Inn.	78	18	3	0	1	1	7	10	.231	.308	.294
Bases Empty	284	56	11	1	3	3	24	29	.197	.275	.262
Runners On	167	45	5	1	0	27	16	15	.269	.311	.330
Runners/Scor. Pos.	96	22	2	1	0	23	15	10	.229	.271	.327
Runners On/2 Out	66	14	1	0	0	11	10	8	.212	.227	.316
Scor. Pos./2 Out	49	9	0	0	0	10	9	6	.184	.184	.310
Late Inning Pressure	75	15	2	0	1	5	9	11	.200	.267	.286
Leading Off	23	5	1	0	1	1	5	4	.217	.391	.357
Bases Empty	51	11	1	0	1	1	7	5	.216	.294	.310
Runners On	24	4	1	0	0	4	2	6	.167	.208	.231
Runners/Scor. Pos.	16	4	1	0	0	4	2	5	.250	.313	.333

DRIVING IN RUNS	0 Out	1 Out	2 Out	Total	
From 1B	2/45	1/21	1/32	4/98	4%
From 2B	2/15	2/22	5/32	9/69	13%
From 3B	1/3	8/11	4/23	13/37	35%
Scoring Position	3/18	10/33	9/55	22/106	21%
Scor. Pos. %	17%	30%	16%	21%	
Driving In Runners from 3B with Less than Two Out:			9/14	64%	

Loves to face: Mike Krukow (.476, 10-for-21, 1 HR)
Hates to face: Mike Scott (.045, 1-for-22)
Fly-ball hitter: 0.93 G/A ratio last season. . . . Fewest runs scored (36) of any major-league player to qualify for 1985 batting championship. . . . Overall batting average has declined in each of the past six seasons, from a career-high of .292 in 1980 to a low of .224 last season. . . . Has 163 plate appearances with the bases loaded since 1975, more than any player in the 11 years of *The Player Analysis*, but has never hit a grand slam home run. . . . Holds *Player Analysis* single-season record for batting average in Late-Inning Pressure Situations—.466 in 1981; his LIP average is .255 in four seasons since then.

Jose Uribe

San Francisco Giants	AB	H	2B	3B	HR	RRF	BB	SO	BA	SA	OBA
Season	476	113	20	4	3	29	30	57	.237	.315	.285
vs. Left-Handed Pitchers	125	27	7	0	1	10	7	19	.216	.296	.263
vs. Right-Handed Pitchers	351	86	13	4	2	19	23	38	.245	.322	.293
Home	248	53	13	2	2	12	19	23	.214	.306	.272
Road	228	60	7	2	1	17	11	34	.263	.325	.300
Grass	366	86	18	3	2	21	24	40	.235	.317	.284
Artificial Turf	110	27	2	1	1	8	6	17	.245	.309	.291
April	42	10	3	0	0	0	0	3	.238	.310	.238
May	89	18	3	1	1	4	4	12	.202	.292	.245
June	95	19	6	3	0	7	6	11	.200	.326	.248
July	81	23	3	0	0	6	7	10	.284	.321	.348
August	83	21	2	0	0	5	6	9	.253	.277	.303
Sept./Oct.	86	22	3	0	2	7	7	12	.256	.360	.312
Leading Off Inn.	117	18	2	1	1	1	11	16	.154	.214	.227
Bases Empty	292	64	11	3	3	3	16	42	.219	.308	.260
Runners On	184	49	9	1	0	26	14	15	.266	.326	.325
Runners/Scor. Pos.	96	26	6	0	0	23	14	8	.271	.333	.369
Runners On/2 Out	91	20	6	0	0	16	7	8	.220	.286	.283
Scor. Pos./2 Out	53	12	4	0	0	14	7	3	.226	.302	.328
Late Inning Pressure	96	20	4	1	1	5	4	10	.208	.302	.248
Leading Off	28	5	0	0	0	0	3	4	.179	.179	.258
Bases Empty	61	12	1	1	1	1	4	8	.197	.295	.246
Runners On	35	8	3	0	0	4	0	2	.229	.314	.250
Runners/Scor. Pos.	15	5	2	0	0	4	0	2	.333	.467	.333

DRIVING IN RUNS	0 Out	1 Out	2 Out	Total	
From 1B	1/26	0/41	2/66	3/133	2%
From 2B	2/10	2/25	9/45	13/80	16%
From 3B	2/5	3/10	5/20	10/35	29%
Scoring Position	4/15	5/35	14/65	23/115	20%
Scor. Pos. %	27%	14%	22%	20%	
Driving In Runners from 3B with Less than Two Out:			5/15	33%	

Loves to face: Ed Lynch (.417, 5-for-12)
Hates to face: LaMarr Hoyt (0-for-6, 3 SO)
One of six major-league rookies to start at least half his team's games at shortstop this season. The others: Mariano Duncan (Dodgers), Sammy Khalifa (Pirates), Ozzie Guillen (White Sox), Earnest Riles (Brewers), and Greg Gagne (Twins). . . . And to think this was supposed to be the year of Shawon Dunston (who started only 70 games for the Cubs). . . . Most games by a Giants shortstop (145) since Chris Speier (150 in 1973). . . . Went 35 consecutive games without an RBI (July 18–August 26). . . . Grounded into only five double plays in 76 opportunities. . . . Three hits in 26 career at bats at Veterans Stadium.

Andy Van Slyke

St. Louis Cardinals	AB	H	2B	3B	HR	RRF	BB	SO	BA	SA	OBA
Season	424	110	25	6	13	62	47	54	.259	.439	.335
vs. Left-Handed Pitchers	54	6	2	0	0	4	3	11	.111	.148	.158
vs. Right-Handed Pitchers	370	104	23	6	13	58	44	43	.281	.481	.360
Home	193	58	15	4	5	25	26	22	.301	.497	.386
Road	231	52	10	2	8	37	21	32	.225	.390	.291
Grass	119	28	7	0	5	20	12	19	.235	.420	.303
Artificial Turf	305	82	18	6	8	42	35	35	.269	.446	.348
April	60	17	5	1	0	5	10	8	.283	.400	.394
May	62	20	4	1	5	16	6	7	.323	.661	.391
June	61	17	7	1	1	8	8	11	.279	.475	.362
July	61	7	1	1	0	6	7	9	.115	.164	.206
August	86	22	3	1	5	16	5	11	.256	.488	.297
Sept./Oct.	94	27	5	1	2	11	11	8	.287	.426	.358
Leading Off Inn.	115	32	8	2	5	5	9	9	.278	.513	.331
Bases Empty	220	62	14	3	7	7	20	20	.282	.468	.344
Runners On	204	48	11	3	6	55	27	34	.235	.407	.326
Runners/Scor. Pos.	119	29	6	2	4	49	25	24	.244	.429	.372
Runners On/2 Out	88	17	3	1	3	21	15	15	.193	.352	.311
Scor. Pos./2 Out	58	12	2	0	1	16	13	11	.207	.293	.352
Late Inning Pressure	63	12	3	0	0	4	6	9	.190	.238	.271
Leading Off	22	5	1	0	0	0	0	1	.227	.273	.227
Bases Empty	36	8	2	0	0	0	3	2	.222	.278	.300
Runners On	27	4	1	0	0	4	3	7	.148	.185	.233
Runners/Scor. Pos.	16	2	0	0	0	4	2	6	.125	.125	.222

DRIVING IN RUNS	0 Out	1 Out	2 Out	Total	
From 1B	1/37	2/47	3/55	6/139	4%
From 2B	1/19	6/26	6/41	13/86	15%
From 3B	7/9	13/22	8/29	28/60	47%
Scoring Position	8/28	19/48	14/70	41/146	28%
Scor. Pos. %	29%	40%	20%	28%	
Driving In Runners from 3B with Less than Two Out:			20/31	65%	

Loves to face: Ed Lynch (.500, 11-for-22, 1 HR)
Hates to face: Floyd Youmans (0-for-11)
Yearly batting averages in Late-Inning Pressure Situations since 1983: .319, .245, .190. Career average: .245. . . . Career batting averages: .196 (one extra-base hit per 14.8 at bats) vs. left-handers, .264 (one XBH per 10.6 AB) vs. right-handers. . . . Has hit 26 of his 28 career home runs vs. right-handed pitchers. Last homer against a left-hander was on September 5, 1983, off Bob Owchinko. . . . Career batting average of .196 with two outs and runners on base. . . . Batted .091 (1-for-11) with the bases loaded last season; no extra-base hits in 22 career at bats with bags full. . . . Career batting average of .364 at Atlanta Stadium, .151 at Olympic Stadium. . . . Did not start any games in the infield last season for the first time in his three-year career.

Ozzie Virgil

Philadelphia Phillies	AB	H	2B	3B	HR	RRF	BB	SO	BA	SA	OBA
Season	426	105	16	3	19	57	49	85	.246	.432	.330
vs. Left-Handed Pitchers	122	29	4	1	4	15	13	19	.238	.385	.307
vs. Right-Handed Pitchers	304	76	12	2	15	42	36	66	.250	.451	.339
Home	214	54	10	3	7	25	31	46	.252	.425	.355
Road	212	51	6	0	12	32	18	39	.241	.439	.303
Grass	110	18	1	0	8	20	10	24	.164	.391	.236
Artificial Turf	316	87	15	3	11	37	39	61	.275	.446	.362
April	54	17	2	0	3	9	2	7	.315	.519	.351
May	79	22	5	0	3	9	14	19	.278	.456	.389
June	69	18	2	0	4	9	5	13	.261	.464	.311
July	74	21	4	1	1	9	10	13	.284	.405	.376
August	66	15	2	1	5	10	9	14	.227	.515	.333
Sept./Oct.	84	12	1	1	3	11	9	19	.143	.286	.226
Leading Off Inn.	101	28	4	1	6	6	10	16	.277	.515	.354
Bases Empty	233	63	10	1	12	12	26	51	.270	.476	.354
Runners On	193	42	6	2	7	45	23	34	.218	.378	.301
Runners/Scor. Pos.	110	26	4	1	2	34	18	21	.236	.345	.338
Runners On/2 Out	77	10	2	0	1	11	13	18	.130	.195	.256
Scor. Pos./2 Out	50	6	2	0	0	9	10	10	.120	.160	.267
Late Inning Pressure	78	17	3	0	2	9	12	22	.218	.333	.326
Leading Off	22	4	1	0	1	1	1	6	.182	.364	.217
Bases Empty	42	8	2	0	1	1	7	13	.190	.310	.306
Runners On	36	9	1	0	1	8	5	9	.250	.361	.349
Runners/Scor. Pos.	21	5	0	0	0	6	4	6	.238	.238	.346

DRIVING IN RUNS	0 Out	1 Out	2 Out	Total	
From 1B	3/40	3/40	1/50	7/130	5%
From 2B	3/17	7/38	3/32	13/87	15%
From 3B	4/6	8/15	6/26	18/47	38%
Scoring Position	7/23	15/53	9/58	31/134	23%
Scor. Pos. %	30%	28%	16%	23%	
Driving In Runners from 3B with Less than Two Out:			12/21	57%	

Loves to face: Don Robinson (.467, 7-for-15, 2 HR)
Hates to face: Sid Fernandez (0-for-13)
Led N.L. catchers with a .994 fielding percentage. . . . Career batting averages: .200 on grass fields, .263 on artificial surfaces. . . . Career percentage of runners driven in from scoring position increases from .224 in unpressured situations to .371 in Late-Inning Pressure Situations. . . . Career batting average of .367 (18-for-49) in Late-Inning Pressure Situations with runners in scoring position. . . . Most sluggers would welcome a trade to Atlanta Stadium. Not Ozzie: four hits in 38 career at bats, no home runs. . . . No triples in 575 career at bats in road games, and none in 305 at bats on grass fields.

Tim Wallach

Montreal Expos	AB	H	2B	3B	HR	RRF	BB	SO	BA	SA	OBA
Season	569	148	36	3	22	85	38	79	.260	.450	.310
vs. Left-Handed Pitchers	168	43	13	0	5	23	8	18	.256	.423	.287
vs. Right-Handed Pitchers	401	105	23	3	17	62	30	61	.262	.461	.319
Home	272	70	18	1	9	45	25	39	.257	.430	.322
Road	297	78	18	2	13	40	13	40	.263	.468	.297
Grass	161	43	11	1	8	22	11	20	.267	.497	.316
Artificial Turf	408	105	25	2	14	63	27	59	.257	.431	.307
April	73	23	7	1	1	12	3	7	.315	.479	.338
May	93	25	7	0	2	11	8	12	.269	.409	.324
June	86	23	7	2	1	7	8	12	.267	.430	.326
July	98	23	5	0	5	21	7	17	.235	.439	.296
August	95	21	4	0	3	15	5	15	.221	.358	.272
Sept./Oct.	124	33	6	0	10	19	7	16	.266	.556	.311
Leading Off Inn.	140	40	15	1	4	4	9	18	.286	.493	.329
Bases Empty	334	86	22	3	11	11	19	51	.257	.440	.297
Runners On	235	62	14	0	11	74	19	28	.264	.464	.326
Runners/Scor. Pos.	138	38	10	0	8	63	18	18	.275	.522	.360
Runners On/2 Out	105	26	5	0	4	28	7	14	.248	.410	.313
Scor. Pos./2 Out	66	14	3	0	3	23	7	9	.212	.394	.307
Late Inning Pressure	91	19	4	0	3	12	7	12	.209	.352	.263
Leading Off	18	6	4	0	0	0	0	3	.333	.556	.333
Bases Empty	48	11	4	0	2	2	2	8	.229	.438	.260
Runners On	43	8	0	0	1	10	5	4	.186	.256	.265
Runners/Scor. Pos.	21	4	0	0	1	9	5	3	.190	.333	.333

DRIVING IN RUNS	0 Out	1 Out	2 Out	Total	
From 1B	3/36	4/54	6/72	13/162	8%
From 2B	4/21	10/37	8/43	22/101	22%
From 3B	8/11	10/19	10/33	28/63	44%
Scoring Position	12/32	20/56	18/76	50/164	30%
Scor. Pos. %	38%	36%	24%	30%	
Driving In Runners from 3B with Less than Two Out:			18/30	60%	

Loves to face: Rick Aguilera (.636, 7-for-11, 4 2B)
Hates to face: Dwight Gooden (.053, 1-for-19, 11 SO)
Fly-ball hitter: 0.83 G/A ratio last season. . . . Led N.L. third basemen in games started (152), putouts (148), assists (383), and double plays (34). . . . Hit 10 home runs in September, 2d-most in N.L. . . . Career batting averages: .299 leading off innings; .182 with the bases loaded. . . . Batting average with runners in scoring position (.275) was the highest of his career. . . . No triples in 404 career at bats in Late-Inning Pressure Situations. . . . Career batting average of .222 in LIP with runners on base. . . . RDI percentage of .305 from scoring position last season was highest of his major-league career.

Denny Walling

Houston Astros	AB	H	2B	3B	HR	RRF	BB	SO	BA	SA	OBA
Season	345	93	20	1	7	47	25	26	.270	.394	.316
vs. Left-Handed Pitchers	45	12	1	0	0	6	2	10	.267	.289	.298
vs. Right-Handed Pitchers	300	81	19	1	7	41	23	16	.270	.410	.318
Home	181	47	12	1	2	22	13	14	.260	.370	.306
Road	164	46	8	0	5	25	12	12	.280	.421	.326
Grass	103	33	4	0	4	19	7	4	.320	.476	.357
Artificial Turf	242	60	16	1	3	28	18	22	.248	.360	.298
April	55	21	5	0	1	10	4	1	.382	.527	.424
May	80	20	6	0	1	8	3	10	.250	.363	.274
June	62	12	2	0	1	6	3	2	.194	.274	.227
July	42	11	2	0	1	4	5	6	.262	.381	.340
August	68	19	3	1	1	10	6	5	.279	.397	.333
Sept./Oct.	38	10	2	0	2	9	4	2	.263	.474	.326
Leading Off Inn.	73	17	8	0	1	1	3	8	.233	.384	.263
Bases Empty	210	54	14	0	3	3	14	17	.257	.367	.304
Runners On	135	39	6	1	4	44	11	9	.289	.437	.333
Runners/Scor. Pos.	90	29	4	1	2	40	8	7	.322	.456	.363
Runners On/2 Out	50	13	1	0	2	16	4	2	.260	.400	.315
Scor. Pos./2 Out	35	10	1	0	0	12	4	1	.286	.314	.359
Late Inning Pressure	60	12	2	0	0	0	4	8	.200	.233	.250
Leading Off	18	3	1	0	0	0	1	4	.167	.222	.211
Bases Empty	37	10	1	0	0	0	3	6	.270	.297	.325
Runners On	23	2	1	0	0	0	1	2	.087	.130	.125
Runners/Scor. Pos.	9	0	0	0	0	0	1	1	.000	.000	.100

DRIVING IN RUNS	0 Out	1 Out	2 Out	Total	
From 1B	0/21	0/28	2/30	2/79	3%
From 2B	3/11	6/29	8/28	17/68	25%
From 3B	5/6	12/19	4/14	21/39	54%
Scoring Position	8/17	18/48	12/42	38/107	36%
Scor. Pos. %	47%	38%	29%	36%	
Driving In Runners from 3B with Less than Two Out:			17/25	68%	

Loves to face: Danny Cox (.526, 10-for-19)
Hates to face: Andy McGaffigan (0-for-9)
Ground-ball hitter: 1.56 G/A ratio last season. . . . Enjoyed career-high season in home runs (7) and RBIs (45); also in at bats (previous high was 284 in 1980). . . . Career batting averages: .292 with runners on base, .254 with the bases empty. . . . Has hit 25 of his 28 career home runs vs. right-handed pitchers. His last two home runs agianst lefties were hit during a four-day period in 1983, off John Candelaria and Craig Lefferts. . . . Career batting averages: .389 at Busch Stadium, .336 at Atlanta Stadium. . . . Total of 47 plate appearances vs. left-handed pitchers last season was 2d-*highest* of his major-league career; he faced 55 southpaws in 1980.

Claudell Washington

Atlanta Braves	AB	H	2B	3B	HR	RRF	BB	SO	BA	SA	OBA
Season	398	110	14	6	15	44	40	66	.276	.455	.342
vs. Left-Handed Pitchers	63	13	3	2	1	8	5	18	.206	.365	.261
vs. Right-Handed Pitchers	335	97	11	4	14	36	35	48	.290	.472	.358
Home	191	53	7	2	4	18	16	29	.277	.398	.337
Road	207	57	7	4	11	26	24	37	.275	.507	.348
Grass	285	80	11	3	9	27	27	50	.281	.435	.344
Artificial Turf	113	30	3	3	6	17	13	16	.265	.504	.339
April	64	18	5	1	0	5	7	8	.281	.391	.352
May	91	25	2	0	4	10	5	11	.275	.429	.313
June	62	17	1	1	5	9	4	14	.274	.565	.313
July	73	21	3	3	1	5	8	14	.288	.452	.361
August	35	9	1	0	1	2	10	5	.257	.371	.422
Sept./Oct.	73	20	2	1	4	13	6	14	.274	.493	.329
Leading Off Inn.	151	44	7	1	7	7	7	20	.291	.490	.327
Bases Empty	265	74	11	4	11	11	17	38	.279	.475	.325
Runners On	133	36	3	2	4	33	23	28	.271	.414	.373
Runners/Scor. Pos.	73	20	2	1	1	26	20	14	.274	.370	.421
Runners On/2 Out	64	17	3	0	2	13	15	12	.266	.406	.405
Scor. Pos./2 Out	40	9	2	0	1	11	13	9	.225	.350	.415
Late Inning Pressure	80	17	1	0	1	5	7	18	.213	.263	.276
Leading Off	20	6	0	0	0	0	0	4	.300	.300	.300
Bases Empty	47	11	1	0	1	1	0	8	.234	.319	.234
Runners On	33	6	0	0	0	4	7	10	.182	.182	.325
Runners/Scor. Pos.	18	4	0	0	0	4	6	4	.222	.222	.417

DRIVING IN RUNS	0 Out	1 Out	2 Out	Total	
From 1B	2/25	2/36	2/47	6/108	6%
From 2B	1/7	2/17	6/30	9/54	17%
From 3B	4/5	6/8	3/16	13/29	45%
Scoring Position	5/12	8/25	9/46	22/83	27%
Scor. Pos. %	42%	32%	20%	27%	
Driving In Runners from 3B with Less than Two Out:			10/13	77%	

Loves to face: Lary Sorensen (.448, 13-for-29, 1 HR)
Hates to face: Nolan Ryan (.141, 11-for-78, 33 SO)
Batted .329 vs. ground-ball pitchers last season, .236 vs. fly-ball pitchers. . . . Hit .356 with three home runs vs. New York last season. . . . Last season's day/night batting average breakdown (.336 day, .253 night) was counter to his career trend: .263 in day games, .285 at night. . . . Had batted .335 in Late-Inning Pressure Situations over three previous seasons before slipping in '85. . . . Drove in only four base runners with 15 homers, 4th-lowest average in N.L. . . . Has batted .198 with the bases loaded since 1975, lowest mark among the 47 players with at least 100 bases-loaded at bats during that period. . . . Averaged 1.34 putouts per nine innings last season, lowest rate among N.L. outfielders (minimum: 300 innings). . . . Only player to hit for the cycle against Gooden—in a career, not in one game.

U.L. Washington

Montreal Expos	AB	H	2B	3B	HR	RRF	BB	SO	BA	SA	OBA
Season	193	48	9	4	1	17	15	33	.249	.352	.301
vs. Left-Handed Pitchers	79	15	5	1	1	8	6	17	.190	.316	.244
vs. Right-Handed Pitchers	114	33	4	3	0	9	9	16	.289	.377	.341
Home	79	15	3	0	1	7	8	16	.190	.266	.261
Road	114	33	6	4	0	10	7	17	.289	.412	.331
Grass	74	23	4	3	0	10	5	12	.311	.446	.354
Artificial Turf	119	25	5	1	1	7	10	21	.210	.294	.269
April	23	10	0	0	0	1	1	1	.435	.435	.458
May	62	17	3	2	0	9	2	9	.274	.387	.292
June	29	11	3	2	0	4	4	5	.379	.621	.455
July	25	4	1	0	1	3	3	4	.160	.320	.250
August	41	5	2	0	0	0	5	8	.122	.171	.217
Sept./Oct.	13	1	0	0	0	0	0	6	.077	.077	.077
Leading Off Inn.	37	10	2	1	0	0	1	9	.270	.378	.289
Bases Empty	106	22	3	2	1	1	6	23	.208	.302	.250
Runners On	87	26	6	2	0	16	9	10	.299	.414	.361
Runners/Scor. Pos.	50	15	4	2	0	16	4	6	.300	.460	.345
Runners On/2 Out	33	8	3	2	0	8	3	4	.242	.455	.306
Scor. Pos./2 Out	25	6	2	2	0	8	0	3	.240	.480	.240
Late Inning Pressure	40	10	1	0	0	3	5	11	.250	.275	.333
Leading Off	11	3	0	0	0	0	1	4	.273	.273	.333
Bases Empty	21	4	0	0	0	0	2	8	.190	.190	.261
Runners On	19	6	1	0	0	3	3	3	.316	.368	.409
Runners/Scor. Pos.	12	3	0	0	0	3	1	2	.250	.250	.308

DRIVING IN RUNS	0 Out	1 Out	2 Out	Total	
From 1B	0/21	0/19	1/15	1/55	2%
From 2B	0/11	3/8	4/20	7/39	18%
From 3B	0/1	5/8	3/10	8/19	42%
Scoring Position	0/12	8/16	7/30	15/58	26%
Scor. Pos. %	0%	50%	23%	26%	
Driving In Runners from 3B with Less than Two Out:			5/9	56%	

Loves to face: Dennis Eckersley (.409, 9-for-22)
Hates to face: LaMarr Hoyt (.091, 2-for-22)
Ground-ball hitter: 1.58 G/A ratio last season. . . . Struck out seven times in his last 11 appearances as a pinch-hitter. . . . Batted .333 before the All-Star break, .127 after. . . . Did not drive in a run in 28 games after July 28. . . . Has hit 23 of his 27 career home runs from the right side of the plate. His last homer batting left-handed was September 26, 1982, off Matt Keough. . . . Batting average with runners on base last season was his highest since 1978. . . . Career batting average of .340 with runners on base in Late-Inning Pressure Situations. . . . Batted 99 points higher in road games than home games, 5th-largest difference in N.L. (minimum: 200 PA).

Mitch Webster

Montreal Expos	AB	H	2B	3B	HR	RRF	BB	SO	BA	SA	OBA
Season	212	58	8	2	11	30	20	33	.274	.486	.335
vs. Left-Handed Pitchers	90	29	3	1	6	19	6	15	.322	.578	.361
vs. Right-Handed Pitchers	122	29	5	1	5	11	14	18	.238	.418	.316
Home	81	20	3	2	3	12	5	10	.247	.444	.287
Road	131	38	5	0	8	18	15	23	.290	.511	.363
Grass	64	21	2	0	4	11	5	14	.328	.547	.377
Artificial Turf	148	37	6	2	7	19	15	19	.250	.459	.317
April	0	0	0	0	0	0	0	0	.000	.000	.000
May	0	0	0	0	0	0	0	0	.000	.000	.000
June	20	6	2	1	1	2	1	2	.300	.650	.333
July	68	14	2	1	3	6	2	10	.206	.397	.225
August	35	6	0	0	1	5	6	6	.171	.257	.293
Sept./Oct.	89	32	4	0	6	17	11	15	.360	.607	.430
Leading Off Inn.	46	16	1	0	3	3	5	6	.348	.565	.412
Bases Empty	125	36	5	1	8	8	11	18	.288	.536	.346
Runners On	87	22	3	1	3	22	9	15	.253	.414	.320
Runners/Scor. Pos.	46	12	2	0	2	18	7	8	.261	.435	.352
Runners On/2 Out	40	10	1	1	1	10	4	5	.250	.400	.318
Scor. Pos./2 Out	22	6	1	0	1	9	4	3	.273	.455	.385
Late Inning Pressure	35	6	2	0	2	4	2	5	.171	.400	.216
Leading Off	9	2	0	0	1	1	0	2	.222	.556	.222
Bases Empty	20	4	1	0	1	1	0	2	.200	.400	.200
Runners On	15	2	1	0	1	3	2	3	.133	.400	.235
Runners/Scor. Pos.	8	1	1	0	0	1	2	1	.125	.250	.300

DRIVING IN RUNS	0 Out	1 Out	2 Out	Total	
From 1B	1/14	1/18	1/26	3/58	5%
From 2B	0/5	2/15	5/16	7/36	19%
From 3B	2/3	4/5	3/9	9/17	53%
Scoring Position	2/8	6/20	8/25	16/53	30%
Scor. Pos. %	25%	30%	32%	30%	
Driving In Runners from 3B with Less than Two Out:			6/8	75%	

Loves to face: Bob Knepper (.571, 4-for-7, 2 HR)
Hates to face: Kevin Gross (0-for-12)
Figures above are for N.L. only. . . . Fly-ball hitter: 0.76 G/A ratio last season, 7th-lowest in N.L. (minimum: 200 PA). Career average: 0.74. . . . Batted .340 vs. ground-ball pitchers last season, .212 vs. fly-ball pitchers. . . . Three of his six September home runs were hit in successive games at Candlestick Park. . . . Batted .368 with seven home runs in 24 day games for Montreal, .229 with four homers in 50 night games. . . . Career batting average of .159 in Late-Inning Pressure Situations. . . . Has hit .303 for his career batting right-handed, .234 batting left-handed; .365 in day games, .221 in night games. . . . Drove in only three base runners with 11 home runs (eight solo shots), 5th-lowest average in N.L. . . . Eight hits in 17 career at bats at Wrigley Field.

Glenn Wilson

Philadelphia Phillies	AB	H	2B	3B	HR	RRF	BB	SO	BA	SA	OBA
Season	608	167	39	5	14	108	35	117	.275	.424	.311
vs. Left-Handed Pitchers	171	49	16	0	6	33	12	22	.287	.485	.330
vs. Right-Handed Pitchers	437	118	23	5	8	75	23	95	.270	.400	.303
Home	301	88	19	4	7	62	19	52	.292	.452	.329
Road	307	79	20	1	7	46	16	65	.257	.397	.292
Grass	161	43	10	0	5	24	9	38	.267	.422	.304
Artificial Turf	447	124	29	5	9	84	26	79	.277	.425	.313
April	62	17	3	2	2	16	2	12	.274	.484	.288
May	98	26	5	1	2	16	5	26	.265	.398	.301
June	101	26	9	2	3	24	6	21	.257	.475	.299
July	107	27	5	0	2	14	7	16	.252	.355	.298
August	106	31	6	0	3	18	11	22	.292	.434	.353
Sept./Oct.	134	40	11	0	2	20	4	20	.299	.425	.312
Leading Off Inn.	139	45	11	1	0	0	9	25	.324	.417	.365
Bases Empty	324	91	21	1	4	4	20	63	.281	.389	.323
Runners On	284	76	18	4	10	104	15	54	.268	.465	.297
Runners/Scor. Pos.	174	50	11	4	6	92	9	34	.287	.500	.311
Runners On/2 Out	116	29	5	1	5	41	8	20	.250	.440	.298
Scor. Pos./2 Out	79	19	4	1	4	37	5	14	.241	.468	.286
Late Inning Pressure	103	32	9	0	6	22	4	25	.311	.573	.333
Leading Off	27	11	3	0	0	0	1	6	.407	.519	.429
Bases Empty	60	20	6	0	3	3	2	15	.333	.583	.355
Runners On	43	12	3	0	3	19	2	10	.279	.558	.304
Runners/Scor. Pos.	27	8	2	0	1	13	1	6	.296	.481	.310

DRIVING IN RUNS	0 Out	1 Out	2 Out	Total	
From 1B	5/57	6/71	10/80	21/208	10%
From 2B	8/31	11/48	14/62	33/141	23%
From 3B	10/15	18/28	12/33	40/76	53%
Scoring Position	18/46	29/76	26/95	73/217	34%
Scor. Pos. %	39%	38%	27%	34%	
Driving In Runners from 3B with Less than Two Out:			28/43	65%	

Loves to face: Frank Williams (.714, 5-for-7, 1 HR)
Hates to face: Len Barker (0-for-9)
Ground-ball hitter: 1.50 G/A ratio last season. . . . Had 61 RBIs in home games last season, 3d-most in N.L. . . . Led N.L. outfielders in assists (18), major-league outfielders in errors (12). . . . Drove in 14 runs during a 5-game span, June 9–13. . . . Batted .302 with 55 RBIs in 68 games batting fifth in the order. . . . Batting average with runners in scoring position (.287) was the highest of his career. . . . Career batting average of .156 (7-for-45) with the bases loaded. . . . Career breakdowns: .290 vs. left-handers, .260 vs. right-handers. . . . Drove in 17 base runners with 14 home runs, highest average in the major leagues last season (minimum: 10 HR).

Mookie Wilson

New York Mets	AB	H	2B	3B	HR	RRF	BB	SO	BA	SA	OBA
Season	337	93	16	8	6	28	28	52	.276	.424	.331
vs. Left-Handed Pitchers	149	44	7	5	4	14	16	20	.295	.490	.361
vs. Right-Handed Pitchers	188	49	9	3	2	14	12	32	.261	.372	.305
Home	152	50	7	2	2	15	17	20	.329	.441	.396
Road	185	43	9	6	4	13	11	32	.232	.411	.274
Grass	216	62	9	2	4	19	22	32	.287	.403	.353
Artificial Turf	121	31	7	6	2	9	6	20	.256	.463	.289
April	61	16	5	2	0	3	4	10	.262	.410	.308
May	85	26	3	2	1	7	5	13	.306	.424	.344
June	76	16	3	0	2	8	5	11	.211	.329	.259
July	1	0	0	0	0	0	0	0	.000	.000	.000
August	0	0	0	0	0	0	0	0	.000	.000	.000
Sept./Oct.	114	35	5	4	3	10	14	18	.307	.500	.380
Leading Off Inn.	113	34	7	2	3	3	14	12	.301	.478	.378
Bases Empty	225	69	14	5	6	6	18	32	.307	.493	.358
Runners On	112	24	2	3	0	22	10	20	.214	.286	.276
Runners/Scor. Pos.	69	17	2	3	0	22	8	11	.246	.362	.321
Runners On/2 Out	46	9	0	0	0	9	7	7	.196	.196	.302
Scor. Pos./2 Out	34	8	0	0	0	9	6	5	.235	.235	.350
Late Inning Pressure	54	15	3	1	3	4	8	10	.278	.537	.371
Leading Off	24	8	2	1	2	2	3	4	.333	.750	.407
Bases Empty	39	12	3	1	3	3	5	7	.308	.667	.386
Runners On	15	3	0	0	0	1	3	3	.200	.200	.333
Runners/Scor. Pos.	7	2	0	0	0	1	2	1	.286	.286	.444

DRIVING IN RUNS	0 Out	1 Out	2 Out	Total	
From 1B	0/21	2/27	0/25	2/73	3%
From 2B	1/8	3/18	6/27	10/53	19%
From 3B	4/6	3/10	3/14	10/30	33%
Scoring Position	5/14	6/28	9/41	20/83	24%
Scor. Pos. %	36%	21%	22%	24%	
Driving In Runners from 3B with Less than Two Out:			7/16	44%	

Loves to face: Ken Dayley (.438, 7-for-16, 1 HR)
Hates to face: Andy Hawkins (0-for-13)
Ground-ball hitter: 1.82 G/A ratio last season, 8th-highest in N.L. (minimum: 200 PA). Career average: 1.74. . . . Mets' late-inning outfield of Wilson, Dykstra, and Strawberry had Mookie in left field for the first time since 1980. . . . Has batted for a higher average on grass fields than on artificial surfaces in each of his six big-league seasons. Career batting averages: .285 on grass, .251 on artificial surfaces. . . . Averaged 2.78 putouts per nine innings last season, 5th-highest rate in N.L., 2d-highest rate on Mets (Dykstra: 2.84). . . . Batted eight times with bases loaded without an RRF in 1981, highest N.L. total in 11-year history of *The Player Analysis*. . . . Batted 93 points lower with runners on base than with the bases empty, 3d-largest difference in N.L. (minimum: 200 PA). . . . Career batting average of .179 at San Diego Stadium.

Herm Winningham

Montreal Expos	AB	H	2B	3B	HR	RRF	BB	SO	BA	SA	OBA
Season	312	74	6	5	3	21	28	72	.237	.317	.297
vs. Left-Handed Pitchers	46	10	0	0	1	4	1	16	.217	.283	.224
vs. Right-Handed Pitchers	266	64	6	5	2	17	27	56	.241	.323	.308
Home	162	31	1	4	0	10	20	36	.191	.247	.277
Road	150	43	5	1	3	11	8	36	.287	.393	.319
Grass	87	22	1	1	2	5	6	27	.253	.356	.298
Artificial Turf	225	52	5	4	1	16	22	45	.231	.302	.296
April	40	9	0	0	1	4	4	7	.225	.300	.295
May	65	19	2	2	1	3	11	15	.292	.431	.395
June	46	11	0	0	0	3	2	17	.239	.239	.271
July	45	15	1	2	1	7	2	11	.333	.511	.340
August	67	13	2	1	0	2	4	11	.194	.254	.239
Sept./Oct.	49	7	1	0	0	2	5	11	.143	.163	.218
Leading Off Inn.	73	24	3	1	2	2	3	10	.329	.479	.355
Bases Empty	196	47	5	3	3	3	14	43	.240	.342	.290
Runners On	116	27	1	2	0	18	14	29	.233	.276	.306
Runners/Scor. Pos.	61	12	0	0	0	16	12	13	.197	.197	.312
Runners On/2 Out	40	9	0	1	0	4	3	8	.225	.275	.279
Scor. Pos./2 Out	24	3	0	0	0	3	3	6	.125	.125	.222
Late Inning Pressure	45	9	2	0	1	2	4	13	.200	.311	.265
Leading Off	11	4	1	0	1	1	0	1	.364	.727	.364
Bases Empty	27	6	1	0	1	1	1	7	.222	.370	.250
Runners On	18	3	1	0	0	1	3	6	.167	.222	.286
Runners/Scor. Pos.	10	2	0	0	0	1	2	3	.200	.200	.333

DRIVING IN RUNS	0 Out	1 Out	2 Out	Total	
From 1B	1/23	0/32	1/30	2/85	2%
From 2B	1/16	1/13	2/20	4/49	8%
From 3B	4/7	7/11	1/8	12/26	46%
Scoring Position	5/23	8/24	3/28	16/75	21%
Scor. Pos. %	22%	33%	11%	21%	
Driving In Runners from 3B with Less than Two Out:			11/18	61%	

Loves to face: Dave Smith (1.000, 2-for-2, 1 2B)
Hates to face: Bobby Castillo (.143, 1-for-7, 5 SO)
Grounded into only one double play in 61 GIDP situations last season, lowest average in majors (minimum: 50 opportunities). . . . Was successful in 10 consecutive stolen base attempts (June 12–August 12). . . . All three of his home runs were hit in day games. . . . Eight hits in 15 career at bats at Veterans Stadium. . . . No doubles or triples in 48 career at bats vs. left-handed pitchers. . . . No home runs in 172 career at bats at Olympic Stadium. . . . Drove in only two of 27 base runners in Late-Inning Pressure Situations last season, both from third base. He was 0-for-8 from second base, 0-for-14 from first base.

Marvell Wynne

Pittsburgh Pirates	AB	H	2B	3B	HR	RRF	BB	SO	BA	SA	OBA
Season	337	69	6	3	2	17	18	48	.205	.258	.247
vs. Left-Handed Pitchers	111	28	1	1	1	9	4	19	.252	.306	.278
vs. Right-Handed Pitchers	226	41	5	2	1	8	14	29	.181	.235	.232
Home	158	37	3	2	1	10	14	20	.234	.297	.297
Road	179	32	3	1	1	7	4	28	.179	.223	.201
Grass	97	15	3	0	0	4	3	19	.155	.186	.180
Artificial Turf	240	54	3	3	2	13	15	29	.225	.288	.273
April	30	7	0	0	0	0	1	6	.233	.233	.258
May	75	14	1	1	1	4	3	7	.187	.267	.218
June	58	17	3	1	0	5	4	5	.293	.379	.349
July	101	22	2	1	0	6	6	19	.218	.257	.262
August	62	8	0	0	1	2	4	7	.129	.177	.182
Sept./Oct.	11	1	0	0	0	0	0	4	.091	.091	.091
Leading Off Inn.	100	23	3	1	0	0	4	17	.230	.280	.260
Bases Empty	206	41	4	1	2	2	8	32	.199	.257	.233
Runners On	131	28	2	2	0	15	10	16	.214	.260	.270
Runners/Scor. Pos.	68	16	2	1	0	14	7	8	.235	.294	.307
Runners On/2 Out	52	12	1	1	0	8	7	3	.231	.288	.322
Scor. Pos./2 Out	32	8	1	0	0	7	6	2	.250	.281	.368
Late Inning Pressure	63	16	2	0	0	3	3	7	.254	.286	.288
Leading Off	15	6	1	0	0	0	1	1	.400	.467	.438
Bases Empty	34	10	1	0	0	0	2	6	.294	.324	.333
Runners On	29	6	1	0	0	3	1	1	.207	.241	.233
Runners/Scor. Pos.	16	3	1	0	0	3	0	1	.188	.250	.188

DRIVING IN RUNS	0 Out	1 Out	2 Out	Total	
From 1B	0/24	0/36	1/37	1/97	1%
From 2B	1/10	2/21	2/23	5/54	9%
From 3B	0/1	4/9	5/16	9/26	35%
Scoring Position	1/11	6/30	7/39	14/80	18%
Scor. Pos. %	9%	20%	18%	18%	
Driving In Runners from 3B with Less than Two Out:		4/10	40%		

Loves to face: Bob Knepper (.556, 5-for-9, 1 2B, 1 3B, 1 HR)
Hates to face: Dwight Gooden (0-for-15, 5 SO)
Ground-ball hitter: 1.50 G/A ratio last season.... Ended season with one hit in his last 27 at bats.... Has hit eight of his nine career home runs against right-handed pitchers. His only homer vs. a lefty was off Knepper.... No home runs in 217 career at bats in Late-Inning Pressure Situations.... One hit in his last 12 at bats with the bases loaded.... Batted 71 points higher vs. left-handers than right-handers, 3d-largest difference among N.L. left-handed batters (minimum: 100 PA vs. each).... Batted .149 in day games, .236 in night games last season.... Career batting averages: .139 at Riverfront Stadium, .149 at Atlanta Stadium.... Had Mets not traded him and prospect LaSchelle Tarver, they could have an outfield of Marvell, Mookie, and LaSchelle; of course, they'd have to bring in Phil Spector as manager.

Joel Youngblood

San Francisco Giants	AB	H	2B	3B	HR	RRF	BB	SO	BA	SA	OBA
Season	230	62	6	0	4	24	30	37	.270	.348	.355
vs. Left-Handed Pitchers	78	24	3	0	1	3	8	16	.308	.385	.379
vs. Right-Handed Pitchers	152	38	3	0	3	21	22	21	.250	.329	.343
Home	107	29	4	0	1	13	12	21	.271	.336	.345
Road	123	33	2	0	3	11	18	16	.268	.358	.364
Grass	157	43	6	0	2	16	21	29	.274	.350	.360
Artificial Turf	73	19	0	0	2	8	9	8	.260	.342	.345
April	16	2	0	0	0	0	3	3	.125	.125	.263
May	19	4	1	0	0	2	2	5	.211	.263	.286
June	57	12	0	0	0	2	4	8	.211	.211	.262
July	29	13	1	0	1	2	4	4	.448	.586	.515
August	71	19	2	0	2	12	11	11	.268	.380	.366
Sept./Oct.	38	12	2	0	1	8	6	6	.316	.447	.413
Leading Off Inn.	63	20	1	0	1	1	8	8	.317	.381	.394
Bases Empty	132	34	3	0	2	2	18	22	.258	.326	.347
Runners On	98	28	3	0	2	22	12	15	.286	.378	.366
Runners/Scor. Pos.	58	16	3	0	2	22	11	11	.276	.431	.394
Runners On/2 Out	43	12	1	0	2	12	5	10	.279	.442	.354
Scor. Pos./2 Out	29	8	1	0	2	12	5	8	.276	.517	.382
Late Inning Pressure	53	12	2	0	1	5	6	14	.226	.321	.305
Leading Off	16	3	0	0	0	1	2	.188	.188	.235	
Bases Empty	32	7	1	0	0	0	4	8	.219	.250	.306
Runners On	21	5	1	0	1	5	2	6	.238	.429	.304
Runners/Scor. Pos.	10	2	1	0	1	5	2	4	.200	.600	.333

DRIVING IN RUNS	0 Out	1 Out	2 Out	Total	
From 1B	0/12	1/24	2/26	3/62	5%
From 2B	1/3	2/20	5/24	8/47	17%
From 3B	1/2	5/10	3/11	9/23	39%
Scoring Position	2/5	7/30	8/35	17/70	24%
Scor. Pos. %	40%	23%	23%	24%	
Driving In Runners from 3B with Less than Two Out:		6/12	50%		

Loves to face: Steve Trout (.615, 8-for-13, 1 HR)
Hates to face: Alejandro Pena (.067, 1-for-15)
Hit two of his four home runs at the Astrodome last season.... Career batting average of .217 with two outs and runners in scoring position.... Career batting averages: .325 at Wrigley Field, .199 at Riverfront Stadium.... Has hit for a higher batting average vs. left-handed pitchers than right-handers in six of the past seven seasons. Missed by one point in 1981, when he batted .350 against righties. Composites since 1979: .301 vs. lefties, .261 vs. righties.... RDI percentage of .241 from scoring position was his lowest mark since 1977.... No grand slam home runs in 71 career at bats with the bases loaded.

Paul Zuvella

Atlanta Braves	AB	H	2B	3B	HR	RRF	BB	SO	BA	SA	OBA
Season	190	48	8	1	0	5	16	14	.253	.305	.311
vs. Left-Handed Pitchers	68	17	4	0	0	1	7	5	.250	.309	.320
vs. Right-Handed Pitchers	122	31	4	1	0	4	9	9	.254	.303	.305
Home	115	24	3	0	0	1	10	10	.209	.235	.272
Road	75	24	5	1	0	4	6	4	.320	.413	.370
Grass	165	38	8	1	0	5	13	13	.230	.291	.287
Artificial Turf	25	10	0	0	0	0	3	1	.400	.400	.464
April	9	2	1	0	0	0	0	1	.222	.333	.222
May	22	3	0	0	0	0	2	5	.136	.136	.208
June	18	8	0	0	0	1	0	0	.444	.444	.474
July	44	4	0	0	0	1	2	3	.091	.091	.130
August	31	9	3	1	0	2	3	4	.290	.452	.353
Sept./Oct.	66	22	4	0	0	2	8	1	.333	.394	.405
Leading Off Inn.	45	17	1	0	0	0	4	1	.378	.422	.429
Bases Empty	109	29	3	0	0	0	10	8	.266	.294	.328
Runners On	81	19	5	1	0	5	6	6	.235	.321	.287
Runners/Scor. Pos.	40	7	1	0	0	4	3	2	.175	.200	.233
Runners On/2 Out	43	10	4	0	0	4	2	3	.233	.326	.267
Scor. Pos./2 Out	23	4	1	0	0	4	2	1	.174	.217	.240
Late Inning Pressure	24	4	1	0	0	0	2	1	.167	.208	.231
Leading Off	7	3	0	0	0	0	1	0	.429	.429	.500
Bases Empty	13	3	0	0	0	0	2	0	.231	.231	.333
Runners On	11	1	1	0	0	0	0	1	.091	.182	.091
Runners/Scor. Pos.	7	0	0	0	0	0	0	0	.000	.000	.000

DRIVING IN RUNS	0 Out	1 Out	2 Out	Total	
From 1B	0/13	1/17	0/33	1/63	2%
From 2B	0/6	0/9	2/17	2/32	6%
From 3B	0/3	0/3	2/10	2/16	13%
Scoring Position	0/9	0/12	4/27	4/48	8%
Scor. Pos. %	0%	0%	15%	8%	
Driving In Runners from 3B with Less than Two Out:		0/6	0%		

Loves to face: Jay Tibbs (.800, 4-for-5)
Hates to face: Doug Sisk (0-for-6)
Ground-ball hitter: 1.55 G/A ratio last season.... Seven hits in 10 at bats vs. Cincinnati last season, hitless in 12 at bats vs. Philadelphia.... Only N.L. player to start at least 20 games at second base and shortstop last season.... Batted 111 points higher in road games than home games, 2d-largest difference in N.L. (minimum: 200 PA).... Seven hits in 11 career at bats at Riverfront Stadium; 0-for-14 at Shea Stadium.... Stranded all 18 base runners in Late-Inning Pressure Situations last season: nine from scoring position, nine from first base. ... Career batting averages: .276 in day games, .221 in night games.

Atlanta Braves

	AB	H	2B	3B	HR	RRF	BB	SO	BA	SA	OBA
Season	5526	1359	213	28	126	628	553	849	.246	.363	.315
vs. Left-Handers	1723	409	68	9	39	204	182	288	.237	.355	.309
vs. Right-Handers	3803	950	145	19	87	424	371	561	.250	.367	.318
Home	2771	709	119	14	65	335	287	400	.256	.379	.326
Road	2755	650	94	14	61	293	266	449	.236	.347	.303
Grass	4094	1025	162	20	98	478	401	610	.250	.372	.318
Artificial Turf	1432	334	51	8	28	150	152	239	.233	.339	.306
April	642	153	28	4	14	77	55	81	.238	.360	.298
May	866	224	32	2	16	85	75	113	.259	.356	.318
June	963	223	33	7	24	115	108	162	.232	.355	.306
July	950	243	38	9	31	130	94	152	.256	.413	.325
August	938	240	34	3	21	105	99	158	.256	.366	.328
Sept./Oct.	1167	276	48	3	20	116	122	183	.237	.334	.311
Leading Off Inn.	1355	367	58	7	39	39	116	179	.271	.410	.332
Bases Empty	3136	770	106	17	66	66	280	455	.246	.353	.310
Runners On	2390	589	107	11	60	562	273	394	.246	.376	.321
Runners/Scor. Pos.	1301	315	59	6	30	473	186	219	.242	.366	.329
Runners On/2 Out	1012	248	49	4	25	245	130	178	.245	.375	.332
Scor. Pos./2 Out	628	153	29	4	17	219	94	114	.244	.384	.342
Late Inning Pressure	910	222	30	4	20	112	117	143	.244	.352	.333
Leading Off	227	66	10	1	5	5	27	22	.291	.410	.371
Bases Empty	499	119	17	1	8	8	54	65	.238	.325	.317
Runners On	411	103	13	3	12	104	63	78	.251	.384	.351
Runners/Scor. Pos.	232	51	7	1	3	77	49	40	.220	.297	.353

DRIVING IN RUNS	0 Out	1 Out	2 Out	Total	
From 1B	20/443	34/645	42/716	96/1804	5%
From 2B	22/179	57/380	97/488	176/1047	17%
From 3B	35/67	113/208	81/261	229/536	43%
Scoring Position	57/246	170/588	178/749	405/1583	26%
Scor. Pos. %	23%	29%	24%	26%	
Driving In Runners from 3B with Less than Two Out:			148/275	54%	

Love to face: Bill Gullickson (8–3 against him)
Hate to face: Eric Show (1–8 against him)
Blowout victims: Lost 44 games by four or more runs last season to lead N.L.; over past 30 N.L. seasons, only 1974 Padres (53) and 1962-63-64-65 Mets have lost more games by margins so large. . . . Only major-league team with a better road record (34–47) than home record (32–49) last year. The last time so few teams were better on the road was 1978, when there were none. . . . Also the only team not to hit a grand-slam homer last season. . . . Lowest batting average in majors vs. left-handers (.237) last year; 13–28 record vs. lefties was 2d-worst to Pirates' 14–32. . . . Lost 17 of 23 home games vs. left-handers. . . . Led N.L. in making double plays for 3d time in past four years. A function of talent or opportunity? Both; had the most opportunities in the league, and 2d-best rate.

Cincinnati Reds

	AB	H	2B	3B	HR	RRF	BB	SO	BA	SA	OBA
Season	5431	1385	249	34	114	663	576	856	.255	.376	.327
vs. Left-Handers	1523	386	62	7	35	188	151	267	.253	.372	.321
vs. Right-Handers	3908	999	187	27	79	475	425	589	.256	.378	.329
Home	2679	723	150	22	49	340	282	388	.270	.397	.340
Road	2752	662	99	12	65	323	294	468	.241	.356	.314
Grass	1642	388	53	4	44	177	160	286	.236	.354	.306
Artificial Turf	3789	997	196	30	70	486	416	570	.263	.386	.336
April	647	145	27	2	9	58	57	128	.224	.314	.287
May	884	230	47	8	23	129	100	135	.260	.410	.337
June	881	237	46	5	20	129	113	127	.269	.401	.351
July	861	212	40	6	12	83	93	131	.246	.348	.321
August	972	238	39	5	15	98	90	152	.245	.342	.309
Sept./Oct.	1186	323	50	8	35	166	123	183	.272	.417	.341
Leading Off Inn.	1331	336	61	7	28	28	118	217	.252	.372	.315
Bases Empty	3123	774	145	23	57	57	286	508	.248	.364	.314
Runners On	2308	611	104	11	57	606	290	348	.265	.393	.344
Runners/Scor. Pos.	1347	365	62	4	36	537	221	215	.271	.403	.367
Runners On/2 Out	963	219	44	3	23	217	141	157	.227	.351	.330
Scor. Pos./2 Out	609	137	25	3	14	191	110	109	.225	.345	.348
Late Inning Pressure	869	236	35	5	17	102	95	140	.272	.382	.342
Leading Off	225	61	10	1	5	5	20	44	.271	.391	.333
Bases Empty	491	134	20	4	9	9	47	89	.273	.385	.338
Runners On	378	102	15	1	8	93	48	51	.270	.378	.347
Runners/Scor. Pos.	221	55	10	0	4	83	39	39	.249	.348	.353

DRIVING IN RUNS	0 Out	1 Out	2 Out	Total	
From 1B	22/400	25/591	33/646	80/1637	5%
From 2B	38/206	82/407	88/467	208/1080	19%
From 3B	62/90	125/215	73/257	260/562	46%
Scoring Position	100/296	207/622	161/724	468/1642	29%
Scor. Pos. %	34%	33%	22%	29%	
Driving In Runners from 3B with Less than Two Out:			187/305	61%	

Love to face: Dick Ruthven (16–6 against him)
Hate to face: Bob Welch (6–13 against him)
Increased run production from 627 in 1984 to 677 in 1985, despite scoring in virtually the same number of innings: 374 in '84, 373 in '85. Biggest portion of increase: six more three-run innings, seven more four-run innings. . . . Hit 50 percent of home runs with runners on base, highest rate in N.L. . . . Won 12 of 15 extra-inning games last season, best in N.L. and best by Reds since their 5–0 mark in 1948. . . . Won 10 games in which they trailed going into 8th inning (tied Angels for major-league lead). . . . Related note: Reds batted .272 in Late-Inning Pressure Situations, highest in N.L.; in 1984, team batted .222 in LIP, lowest in majors. . . . Only N.L. team to have scored in every inning in which leadoff batter reached third base (9 of 9); league average: 82.8 percent.

Chicago Cubs

	AB	H	2B	3B	HR	RRF	BB	SO	BA	SA	OBA
Season	5492	1397	239	28	150	662	562	937	.254	.390	.323
vs. Left-Handers	1334	336	67	5	40	162	141	231	.252	.400	.322
vs. Right-Handers	4158	1061	172	23	110	500	421	706	.255	.387	.324
Home	2746	752	126	16	98	385	313	455	.274	.438	.348
Road	2746	645	113	12	52	277	249	482	.235	.342	.298
Grass	3852	1013	173	20	122	486	413	639	.263	.413	.334
Artificial Turf	1640	384	66	8	28	176	149	298	.234	.335	.298
April	582	135	24	2	13	56	49	95	.232	.347	.290
May	862	208	31	5	28	114	115	166	.241	.386	.331
June	951	236	43	1	20	98	102	181	.248	.359	.320
July	914	241	48	5	22	103	88	136	.264	.399	.327
August	982	255	44	5	27	110	79	152	.260	.397	.315
Sept./Oct.	1201	322	49	10	40	181	129	207	.268	.425	.340
Leading Off Inn.	1342	347	67	7	34	34	108	229	.259	.395	.314
Bases Empty	3176	822	146	15	76	76	266	561	.259	.386	.317
Runners On	2316	575	93	13	74	586	296	376	.248	.396	.331
Runners/Scor. Pos.	1331	332	55	12	45	512	213	221	.249	.410	.347
Runners On/2 Out	997	223	35	5	30	222	137	169	.224	.359	.320
Scor. Pos./2 Out	629	138	18	5	20	195	104	114	.219	.359	.332
Late Inning Pressure	826	216	36	1	27	113	88	157	.262	.406	.333
Leading Off	207	58	11	0	8	8	20	38	.280	.449	.344
Bases Empty	472	119	18	0	13	13	44	92	.252	.373	.319
Runners On	354	97	18	1	14	100	44	65	.274	.449	.352
Runners/Scor. Pos.	209	59	16	1	8	87	35	34	.282	.483	.381

DRIVING IN RUNS	0 Out	1 Out	2 Out	Total	
From 1B	19/390	29/589	33/677	81/1656	5%
From 2B	37/195	72/382	90/495	199/1072	19%
From 3B	46/84	116/201	68/249	230/534	43%
Scoring Position	83/279	188/583	158/744	429/1606	27%
Scor. Pos. %	30%	32%	21%	27%	
Driving In Runners from 3B with Less than Two Out:			162/285	57%	

Love to face: Bob Knepper (10–6 against him)
Hate to face: Nolan Ryan (3–13 against him)
Scored 112 more runs at home than on road last season, largest such disparity in majors, and a large one even by recent Wrigley Field standards: Cubs were +66 at home in '84, +67 in '83, +28 in '82, +62 in '80. (They were +108 in '81, but played 11 more games at home because of the you-know-what). . . . Led N.L. in home runs for only 3d time in past 55 years. . . . Only team in the majors to use the same starting players (excluding pitchers) in its first and last games in '85. . . . Faced fewest left-handed starters (41) of any N.L. team; 25–16 in those games. . . . No apparent advantage in day games on the road (7–18); batted only .219 in road day games to rank last in N.L. in that category; league average in that category is .249, and if you eliminate other teams' road games at Wrigley Field, the average is .239.

Houston Astros

	AB	H	2B	3B	HR	RRF	BB	SO	BA	SA	OBA
Season	5582	1457	261	42	121	695	477	873	.261	.388	.320
vs. Left-Handers	2152	576	105	17	50	287	191	364	.268	.402	.327
vs. Right-Handers	3430	881	156	25	71	408	286	509	.257	.379	.315
Home	2746	721	143	19	47	326	263	402	.263	.380	.328
Road	2836	736	118	23	74	369	214	471	.260	.396	.312
Grass	1699	465	73	16	50	251	133	276	.274	.424	.326
Artificial Turf	3883	992	188	26	71	444	344	597	.255	.372	.317
April	672	173	32	4	7	71	62	97	.257	.348	.321
May	921	241	39	9	22	123	72	135	.262	.395	.312
June	964	235	42	4	23	104	73	139	.244	.367	.295
July	945	246	40	3	18	102	78	177	.260	.366	.321
August	893	250	56	7	19	128	85	143	.280	.422	.342
Sept./Oct.	1187	312	52	15	32	167	107	182	.263	.413	.325
Leading Off Inn.	1367	347	67	7	30	30	92	193	.254	.379	.302
Bases Empty	3218	812	147	21	70	70	234	494	.252	.376	.305
Runners On	2364	645	114	21	51	625	243	379	.273	.404	.339
Runners/Scor. Pos.	1369	371	65	13	29	551	184	240	.271	.401	.351
Runners On/2 Out	1019	269	50	7	19	233	124	178	.264	.383	.347
Scor. Pos./2 Out	657	163	27	6	12	209	99	122	.248	.362	.347
Late Inning Pressure	772	194	31	2	20	99	82	140	.251	.374	.325
Leading Off	197	49	11	0	4	4	17	33	.249	.365	.308
Bases Empty	439	118	19	0	10	10	42	83	.269	.380	.337
Runners On	333	76	12	2	10	89	40	57	.228	.366	.310
Runners/Scor. Pos.	166	43	7	0	6	75	29	28	.259	.410	.358

DRIVING IN RUNS	0 Out	1 Out	2 Out	Total	
From 1B	26/436	35/565	32/683	93/1684	6%
From 2B	40/198	81/374	105/488	226/1060	21%
From 3B	55/96	122/201	76/275	253/572	44%
Scoring Position	95/294	203/575	181/763	479/1632	29%
Scor. Pos. %	32%	35%	24%	29%	
Driving In Runners from 3B with Less than Two Out:			177/297	60%	

Love to face: Mark Davis (6–1 against him)
Hate to face: Dwight Gooden (1–6 against him)
First Houston team not to steal at least 100 bases (excluding 1981) since Leo Durocher's 1973 crew. . . . Only N.L. team with slugging average above .400 with runners on base. . . . Led N.L. in doubles (261); no team that plays home games on a grass field has led N.L. in doubles since 1970 Giants. . . . Led N.L. with 17 home runs and 74 RBIs from leadoff position; league averages: 10 homers, 55 RBIs. Also led league with 14 homers and 67 RBIs from 8th batting position; league averages: six home runs, 53 RBIs. . . . Highest N.L. batting average (.268) vs. left-handers. Four of their five switch-hitters hit better against left-handers, so who gets traded? Jerry Mumphrey, the one who hits righties better, to the Cubs.

Los Angeles Dodgers

	AB	H	2B	3B	HR	RRF	BB	SO	BA	SA	OBA
Season	5502	1434	226	28	129	663	539	846	.261	.382	.328
vs. Left-Handers	1691	418	64	7	36	184	172	283	.247	.357	.316
vs. Right-Handers	3811	1016	162	21	93	479	367	563	.267	.393	.333
Home	2686	685	106	4	47	299	276	420	.255	.350	.326
Road	2816	749	120	24	82	364	263	426	.266	.413	.329
Grass	4052	1059	149	12	90	479	394	632	.261	.371	.328
Artificial Turf	1450	375	77	16	39	184	145	214	.259	.414	.327
April	698	158	24	1	18	55	60	110	.226	.341	.290
May	881	205	36	7	15	78	69	139	.233	.341	.288
June	821	211	29	0	25	107	101	120	.257	.384	.339
July	912	272	45	6	22	137	85	139	.298	.433	.358
August	923	230	39	3	20	96	86	142	.249	.363	.314
Sept./Oct.	1267	358	53	11	29	190	138	196	.283	.410	.354
Leading Off Inn.	1316	316	37	6	32	32	130	203	.240	.350	.312
Bases Empty	3155	802	122	16	82	82	268	500	.254	.381	.316
Runners On	2347	632	104	12	47	581	271	346	.269	.384	.343
Runners/Scor. Pos.	1349	345	55	6	28	512	195	216	.256	.368	.344
Runners On/2 Out	1023	243	50	6	25	236	149	145	.238	.371	.339
Scor. Pos./2 Out	663	145	33	3	12	194	115	99	.219	.332	.339
Late Inning Pressure	767	205	24	9	21	86	68	126	.267	.404	.326
Leading Off	194	55	5	3	6	6	18	26	.284	.433	.344
Bases Empty	437	122	11	5	12	12	32	68	.279	.410	.328
Runners On	330	83	13	4	9	74	36	58	.252	.397	.323
Runners/Scor. Pos.	186	41	7	1	4	58	29	38	.220	.333	.318

DRIVING IN RUNS	0 Out	1 Out	2 Out	Total	
From 1B	17/391	18/606	40/682	75/1679	4%
From 2B	23/158	78/403	94/509	195/1070	18%
From 3B	47/84	140/242	75/291	262/617	42%
Scoring Position	70/242	218/645	169/800	457/1687	27%
Scor. Pos. %	29%	34%	21%	27%	
Driving In Runners from 3B with Less than Two Out:		187/326		57%	

Love to face: Vida Blue (11–4 against him)
Hate to face: Dan Schatzeder (2–7 against him)
Run total jumped from 580 to 682, largest one-season improvement in N.L. (excluding 1981) since 1978–79 Cardinals.... Led N.L. in sacrifices for 3d time in past four years.... Hit 45 of first 57 homers with bases empty, but only 37 of last 72 came that way.... Anomaly of the year, follow it closely: Dodgers hit 35 more home runs on road than at home, the biggest difference in the history of baseball in a season when the team's *pitchers* allowed more home runs *at home*. (L.A. pitchers allowed 54 at Dodger Stadium, 48 on the road.) In other words, this was not simply a case of the ballpark severely limiting the number of home runs hit there in a particular season, *a la* Griffith Stadium, Forbes Field, or the Astrodome. Maybe Lasorda should make the team travel to Dodger Stadium by bus.

Montreal Expos

	AB	H	2B	3B	HR	RRF	BB	SO	BA	SA	OBA
Season	5429	1342	242	49	118	617	492	880	.247	.375	.310
vs. Left-Handers	1696	431	82	10	44	200	139	260	.254	.392	.310
vs. Right-Handers	3733	911	160	39	74	417	353	620	.244	.367	.311
Home	2580	615	120	27	45	293	274	437	.238	.358	.313
Road	2849	727	122	22	73	324	218	443	.255	.390	.308
Grass	1499	396	63	13	49	197	115	244	.264	.422	.315
Artificial Turf	3930	946	179	36	69	420	377	636	.241	.357	.309
April	664	186	31	5	10	75	53	86	.280	.387	.333
May	870	204	39	9	14	85	83	130	.234	.348	.302
June	948	223	41	10	16	102	76	182	.235	.350	.293
July	942	222	38	7	19	95	84	152	.236	.351	.302
August	883	236	43	12	20	116	80	125	.267	.411	.327
Sept./Oct.	1122	271	50	6	39	144	116	205	.242	.401	.312
Leading Off Inn.	1345	355	72	14	31	31	107	203	.264	.407	.320
Bases Empty	3192	773	145	32	72	72	237	531	.242	.375	.297
Runners On	2237	569	97	17	46	545	255	349	.254	.375	.329
Runners/Scor. Pos.	1349	341	60	12	30	485	201	219	.253	.382	.344
Runners On/2 Out	951	237	45	11	16	218	114	153	.249	.370	.333
Scor. Pos./2 Out	645	151	34	8	9	190	91	113	.234	.353	.332
Late Inning Pressure	845	214	35	6	13	88	73	138	.253	.355	.311
Leading Off	224	71	11	3	6	6	9	42	.317	.473	.343
Bases Empty	489	125	19	4	10	10	29	80	.256	.372	.297
Runners On	356	89	16	2	3	78	44	58	.250	.331	.328
Runners/Scor. Pos.	218	56	11	2	2	72	36	36	.257	.353	.355

DRIVING IN RUNS	0 Out	1 Out	2 Out	Total	
From 1B	15/364	20/552	32/600	67/1516	4%
From 2B	27/198	69/373	86/464	182/1035	18%
From 3B	57/93	109/199	84/270	250/562	44%
Scoring Position	84/291	178/572	170/734	432/1597	27%
Scor. Pos. %	29%	31%	23%	27%	
Driving In Runners from 3B with Less than Two Out:		166/292		57%	

Love to face: Pascual Perez (6–0 against him)
Hate to face: Jerry Reuss (5–20 against him)
Only N.L. team to finish above .500 despite allowing more runs than it scored; that counterbalanced 1984, when Expos scored more runs than they allowed, and finished 78–83.... N.L.'s best batting average in day games (.268), but its worst at night (.234); 38–24 in day games, 46–53 at night.... 8th-place hitters batted only .200, the worst average by any N.L. team in any of the 1-through-8 spots.... Also had lowest batting (.226) and slugging (.359) averages in 5th batting position.... Used 44 players during the season, most by any team in the majors.

New York Mets

	AB	H	2B	3B	HR	RRF	BB	SO	BA	SA	OBA
Season	5549	1425	239	35	134	682	546	872	.257	.385	.323
vs. Left-Handers	2185	550	90	13	53	266	216	343	.252	.378	.319
vs. Right-Handers	3364	875	149	22	81	416	330	529	.260	.390	.326
Home	2659	672	111	13	58	338	279	411	.253	.370	.324
Road	2890	753	128	22	76	344	267	461	.261	.399	.323
Grass	3867	984	161	21	93	486	390	603	.254	.379	.323
Artificial Turf	1682	441	78	14	41	196	156	269	.262	.398	.324
April	626	142	27	4	13	68	65	116	.227	.345	.303
May	807	177	28	5	16	80	83	127	.219	.326	.290
June	978	235	33	3	24	93	86	153	.240	.354	.303
July	991	277	56	4	24	164	107	151	.280	.417	.348
August	948	266	45	6	21	113	83	137	.281	.407	.338
Sept./Oct.	1199	328	50	13	36	164	122	188	.274	.427	.341
Leading Off Inn.	1356	349	59	8	28	28	114	190	.257	.375	.316
Bases Empty	3166	802	127	20	72	72	270	514	.253	.374	.314
Runners On	2383	623	112	15	62	610	276	358	.261	.399	.336
Runners/Scor. Pos.	1361	359	62	9	35	523	215	220	.264	.400	.357
Runners On/2 Out	1025	256	54	5	26	252	149	150	.250	.388	.348
Scor. Pos./2 Out	660	164	29	3	16	214	120	96	.248	.374	.368
Late Inning Pressure	824	202	29	4	24	88	78	148	.245	.377	.308
Leading Off	215	62	9	2	5	5	20	33	.288	.419	.349
Bases Empty	489	128	17	3	15	15	39	84	.262	.401	.316
Runners On	335	74	12	1	9	73	39	64	.221	.343	.297
Runners/Scor. Pos.	177	36	8	1	3	59	29	35	.203	.311	.305

DRIVING IN RUNS	0 Out	1 Out	2 Out	Total	
From 1B	15/404	41/601	44/691	100/1696	6%
From 2B	21/178	72/382	109/505	202/1065	19%
From 3B	54/92	119/209	73/272	246/573	43%
Scoring Position	75/270	191/591	182/777	448/1638	27%
Scor. Pos. %	28%	32%	23%	27%	
Driving In Runners from 3B with Less than Two Out:		173/301		57%	

Love to face: Rick Reuschel (19–10 against him)
Hate to face: John Denny (5–16 against him)
Scored 15 or more runs in four games in July, most by N.L. team in one month since 1930. In 23 previous seasons, Mets had only five such games.... Faced the most left-handed starters (63) of any N.L. team, but went 41–22 in those games.... For 2d straight year (the only times in team history), they drew the most intentional walks (88) in N.L.... Batted only .203 with runners in scoring position in Late-Inning Pressure Situations, lowest in N.L.... Fell five home runs short of club record of 139 set in 1962; Frank Thomas led that team with 34, Marv Throneberry was second with 16.... Pitching staff combined for .185 batting average and 54 sacrifice bunts (N.L. highs).

Phila. Phillies

	AB	H	2B	3B	HR	RRF	BB	SO	BA	SA	OBA
Season	5477	1343	238	47	141	659	527	1095	.245	.383	.312
vs. Left-Handers	1532	367	80	8	37	177	157	294	.240	.375	.309
vs. Right-Handers	3945	976	158	39	104	482	370	801	.247	.386	.313
Home	2696	681	125	29	72	348	292	511	.253	.401	.326
Road	2781	662	113	18	69	311	235	584	.238	.366	.298
Grass	1441	317	49	8	45	148	112	332	.220	.359	.277
Artificial Turf	4036	1026	189	39	96	511	415	763	.254	.392	.324
April	637	164	22	7	12	80	52	131	.257	.370	.312
May	850	186	34	4	17	85	99	198	.219	.328	.301
June	909	220	42	11	17	112	89	168	.242	.369	.311
July	910	234	43	10	26	121	90	169	.257	.412	.323
August	977	260	48	9	38	141	92	194	.266	.450	.330
Sept./Oct.	1194	279	49	6	31	120	105	235	.234	.363	.298
Leading Off Inn.	1337	359	71	11	35	35	109	220	.269	.417	.329
Bases Empty	3160	786	150	22	84	84	266	636	.249	.390	.310
Runners On	2317	557	88	25	57	575	261	459	.240	.374	.314
Runners/Scor. Pos.	1366	341	55	19	37	514	185	275	.250	.399	.332
Runners On/2 Out	968	210	32	10	24	224	139	207	.217	.345	.316
Scor. Pos./2 Out	632	142	21	8	16	201	103	135	.225	.359	.334
Late Inning Pressure	884	225	37	5	26	111	97	184	.255	.396	.331
Leading Off	212	59	9	1	4	4	30	40	.278	.387	.381
Bases Empty	494	122	20	2	14	14	52	109	.247	.381	.326
Runners On	390	103	17	3	12	97	45	75	.264	.415	.337
Runners/Scor. Pos.	224	58	9	3	6	80	32	41	.259	.406	.344

DRIVING IN RUNS	0 Out	1 Out	2 Out	Total	
From 1B	20/427	29/558	38/658	87/1643	5%
From 2B	30/221	64/378	93/486	187/1085	17%
From 3B	58/97	116/195	68/244	242/536	45%
Scoring Position	88/318	180/573	161/730	429/1621	26%
Scor. Pos. %	28%	31%	22%	26%	
Driving In Runners from 3B with Less than Two Out:		174/292		60%	

Love to face: Nolan Ryan (10–6 against him)
Hate to face: Bryn Smith (4–8 against him)
Won their last 31 games in which their pitchers allowed fewer than three runs (league average: .830).... Grass-fields batting average (.220) was lowest in majors. ... Committed 22 fewer errors, turned 30 more double plays than they had in 1984. ... Scored 53 fewer runs than the year before; a drop in one- and two-run innings was responsible for 51 runs of the 53-run decline.... Batted .217 with two outs and runners on base, lowest in majors last year.

Pittsburgh Pirates

	AB	H	2B	3B	HR	RRF	BB	SO	BA	SA	OBA
Season	5436	1340	251	28	80	556	514	842	.247	.347	.311
vs. Left-Handers	1622	399	68	6	21	154	152	253	.246	.334	.309
vs. Right-Handers	3814	941	183	22	59	402	362	589	.247	.353	.311
Home	2626	683	134	15	39	309	293	408	.260	.367	.333
Road	2810	657	117	13	41	247	221	434	.234	.328	.289
Grass	1438	320	60	2	24	109	114	222	.223	.317	.279
Artificial Turf	3998	1020	191	26	56	447	400	620	.255	.358	.322
April	612	142	31	2	5	52	64	84	.232	.314	.303
May	876	205	39	1	11	85	82	155	.234	.318	.299
June	946	240	44	7	15	94	82	149	.254	.363	.312
July	901	211	37	2	12	72	78	124	.234	.320	.295
August	919	220	44	4	16	98	84	149	.239	.348	.302
Sept./Oct.	1182	322	56	12	21	155	124	181	.272	.393	.341
Leading Off Inn.	1372	361	74	9	26	26	95	213	.263	.387	.312
Bases Empty	3160	783	149	20	46	46	236	479	.248	.351	.301
Runners On	2276	557	102	8	34	510	278	363	.245	.341	.323
Runners/Scor. Pos.	1350	338	55	4	21	460	207	225	.250	.344	.343
Runners On/2 Out	986	236	45	4	16	215	125	147	.239	.342	.327
Scor. Pos./2 Out	660	160	27	1	13	198	97	102	.242	.345	.342
Late Inning Pressure	965	242	44	4	11	84	106	154	.251	.339	.325
Leading Off	253	80	17	1	4	4	20	38	.316	.439	.366
Bases Empty	544	140	27	4	8	8	45	81	.257	.366	.315
Runners On	421	102	17	0	3	76	61	73	.242	.304	.336
Runners/Scor. Pos.	254	61	8	0	2	70	52	44	.240	.295	.365

DRIVING IN RUNS	0 Out	1 Out	2 Out	Total	
From 1B	16/403	19/558	27/653	62/1614	4%
From 2B	24/189	68/398	92/507	184/1094	17%
From 3B	45/84	105/197	80/269	230/550	42%
Scoring Position	69/273	173/595	172/776	414/1644	25%
Scor. Pos. %	25%	29%	22%	25%	
Driving In Runners from 3B with Less than Two Out:			150/281	53%	

Love to face: Mike Scott (7–0 against him)
Hate to face: Mario Soto (4–13 against him)
Tough times for the Commonwealth: first time since 1956–57 that Pirates and Phillies have had consecutive nonwinning seasons. Recently, these two teams have risen and fallen together; Pirates have had only three nonwinning seasons since 1975 (breaking '81 season into two halves): 1981 (2d half), 1984, and 1985. Phillies also have had only three nonwinning seasons—the same three. . . . Pinch-hitters batted .286 with .412 on-base average; both figures were highest in N.L. . . . Only team in majors to lose every game in which it trailed going into 9th; they haven't won one of those before the home folks since July 21, 1983. . . . Made fewest double plays (127) in N.L. for first time since 1956—Bill Mazeroski's rookie year. . . . Only N.L. team that didn't use any lineup combination at least 10 times last year.

St Louis Cardinals

	AB	H	2B	3B	HR	RRF	BB	SO	BA	SA	OBA
Season	5467	1446	245	59	87	728	586	853	.264	.379	.335
vs. Left-Handers	1779	458	86	17	34	232	187	303	.257	.382	.326
vs. Right-Handers	3688	988	159	42	53	496	399	550	.268	.377	.340
Home	2633	721	126	36	36	350	283	378	.274	.390	.344
Road	2834	725	119	23	51	378	303	475	.256	.368	.328
Grass	1493	397	64	12	30	205	160	255	.266	.385	.338
Artificial Turf	3974	1049	181	47	57	523	426	598	.264	.376	.334
April	625	164	30	8	5	79	83	94	.262	.360	.352
May	908	251	39	8	22	147	97	149	.276	.410	.345
June	905	232	43	10	10	113	75	132	.256	.359	.314
July	864	221	42	8	13	99	84	148	.256	.368	.321
August	967	256	45	13	15	130	98	154	.265	.385	.331
Sept./Oct.	1198	322	46	12	22	160	149	176	.269	.382	.348
Leading Off Inn.	1295	335	68	13	22	22	149	206	.259	.382	.337
Bases Empty	3026	777	143	31	48	48	311	480	.257	.372	.328
Runners On	2441	669	102	28	39	680	275	373	.274	.387	.344
Runners/Scor. Pos.	1530	419	59	23	26	626	227	257	.274	.393	.360
Runners On/2 Out	997	245	34	11	17	245	126	154	.246	.353	.332
Scor. Pos./2 Out	677	170	22	9	9	220	106	117	.251	.350	.353
Late Inning Pressure	804	210	35	7	15	96	88	133	.261	.378	.335
Leading Off	205	48	14	0	2	2	18	37	.234	.332	.299
Bases Empty	453	116	28	1	9	9	46	79	.256	.382	.327
Runners On	351	94	7	6	6	87	42	54	.268	.373	.345
Runners/Scor. Pos.	213	56	3	6	2	78	32	34	.263	.362	.355

DRIVING IN RUNS	0 Out	1 Out	2 Out	Total	
From 1B	16/388	28/558	34/588	78/1534	5%
From 2B	45/247	84/411	102/505	231/1163	20%
From 3B	74/124	163/276	89/292	326/692	47%
Scoring Position	119/371	247/687	191/797	557/1855	30%
Scor. Pos. %	32%	36%	24%	30%	
Driving In Runners from 3B with Less than Two Out:			237/400	59%	

Love to face: Tom Hume (10–1 against him)
Hate to face: David Palmer (3–7 against him)
Blowout bullies: Won 48 games by four or more runs last season, most in N.L.; over past 36 years, only 1975 Reds (48) and 1971 Pirates (51) have won as many games by margins that large. Modern N.L. record is 56 by 1902 Pirates. . . . Led N.L. with .337 on-base average when leading off inning; also led league by scoring in 55.5 percent of innings when the first batter reached base. . . . Only major-league team without a two-homer game from any of its hitters last season. . . . Led N.L. in fielding for 4th time in past five years. . . . Have beaten Mets in season series in each of past four years, tying for longest current series domination in N.L. (others: Dodgers over Braves, Dodgers over Reds, Padres over Giants).

San Diego Padres

	AB	H	2B	3B	HR	RRF	BB	SO	BA	SA	OBA
Season	5507	1405	241	28	109	634	513	809	.255	.368	.320
vs. Left-Handers	1820	461	84	9	42	210	181	285	.253	.379	.322
vs. Right-Handers	3687	944	157	19	67	424	332	524	.256	.363	.318
Home	2649	671	105	18	64	312	256	402	.253	.379	.320
Road	2858	734	136	10	45	322	257	407	.257	.359	.319
Grass	4037	1018	161	23	94	469	383	615	.252	.373	.318
Artificial Turf	1470	387	80	5	15	165	130	194	.263	.355	.323
April	620	143	29	2	13	63	49	88	.231	.347	.286
May	902	247	54	7	23	130	77	136	.274	.426	.332
June	1009	253	38	6	23	119	99	149	.251	.369	.321
July	905	221	44	4	13	92	80	122	.244	.345	.309
August	904	230	36	2	17	97	80	144	.254	.355	.314
Sept./Oct.	1167	311	40	7	20	133	128	170	.266	.364	.339
Leading Off Inn.	1326	300	49	11	24	24	120	179	.226	.334	.292
Bases Empty	3136	748	132	17	66	66	280	475	.239	.355	.303
Runners On	2371	657	109	11	43	568	233	334	.277	.387	.341
Runners/Scor. Pos.	1330	369	59	6	30	515	169	206	.277	.398	.355
Runners On/2 Out	1045	271	42	5	21	239	131	171	.259	.369	.346
Scor. Pos./2 Out	656	170	25	2	16	217	107	116	.259	.377	.367
Late Inning Pressure	881	227	36	3	12	93	89	130	.258	.346	.326
Leading Off	214	53	8	0	2	2	23	35	.248	.313	.324
Bases Empty	486	129	19	0	11	11	44	80	.265	.372	.328
Runners On	395	98	17	3	1	82	45	50	.248	.314	.324
Runners/Scor. Pos.	225	52	8	2	1	77	27	36	.231	.298	.308

DRIVING IN RUNS	0 Out	1 Out	2 Out	Total	
From 1B	14/424	27/592	33/734	74/1750	4%
From 2B	28/171	64/358	104/483	196/1012	19%
From 3B	46/77	127/214	81/275	254/566	45%
Scoring Position	74/248	191/572	185/758	450/1578	29%
Scor. Pos. %	30%	33%	24%	29%	
Driving In Runners from 3B with Less than Two Out:			173/291	59%	

Love to face: Dan Schatzeder (5–0 against him)
Hate to face: Vida Blue (1–10 against him)
Used their basic starting lineup combination (eight starters at specific positions, regardless of batting order) 69 times last year, by far the most in majors: Kennedy; Garvey, Flannery, Nettles, Templeton; Martinez, McReynolds, Gwynn. No other N.L. team had even half that many starts by one combination. . . . Won all six 1–0 games, the most 1–0 wins without any losses by an N.L. team since the 1913 Philadelphia Phillies won seven. . . . Hit 38 points higher with runners on base than with bases empty, largest such difference in majors. . . . Finished last in league in steals (60) for 1st time in club history. . . . Pitchers batted a collective .094, only N.L. staff below .100 (league BA for pitchers: .140). . . . Pinch-hitters weren't much better: they hit .173, lowest in N.L.

San Francisco Giants

	AB	H	2B	3B	HR	RRF	BB	SO	BA	SA	OBA
Season	5420	1263	217	31	115	552	488	962	.233	.348	.299
vs. Left-Handers	1385	329	63	4	32	120	117	234	.238	.358	.301
vs. Right-Handers	4035	934	154	27	83	432	371	728	.231	.345	.299
Home	2643	588	109	13	58	264	234	449	.222	.339	.288
Road	2777	675	108	18	57	288	254	513	.243	.356	.310
Grass	3985	917	154	17	91	407	367	698	.230	.346	.298
Artificial Turf	1435	346	63	14	24	145	121	264	.241	.355	.302
April	596	124	21	2	7	50	46	123	.208	.285	.268
May	869	193	44	9	14	83	65	167	.222	.342	.278
June	1016	217	34	10	22	84	87	162	.214	.332	.279
July	913	249	36	4	22	103	84	152	.273	.393	.338
August	830	200	29	3	23	92	84	157	.241	.366	.315
Sept./Oct.	1196	280	53	3	27	140	122	201	.234	.351	.307
Leading Off Inn.	1364	320	45	7	40	40	108	231	.235	.366	.295
Bases Empty	3282	753	128	21	73	73	263	578	.229	.348	.290
Runners On	2138	510	89	10	42	479	225	384	.239	.348	.313
Runners/Scor. Pos.	1213	268	46	4	25	413	174	251	.221	.327	.319
Runners On/2 Out	969	217	42	4	20	211	109	203	.224	.337	.309
Scor. Pos./2 Out	621	129	23	2	12	180	83	138	.208	.309	.308
Late Inning Pressure	1059	244	27	7	20	103	114	192	.230	.326	.309
Leading Off	281	69	4	1	8	8	21	46	.246	.352	.303
Bases Empty	659	157	14	5	12	12	55	120	.238	.329	.301
Runners On	400	87	13	2	8	91	59	72	.218	.320	.321
Runners/Scor. Pos.	214	51	9	0	5	80	45	45	.238	.350	.367

DRIVING IN RUNS	0 Out	1 Out	2 Out	Total	
From 1B	10/356	31/509	39/620	80/1485	5%
From 2B	22/152	52/328	80/458	154/938	16%
From 3B	43/66	87/174	71/252	201/492	41%
Scoring Position	65/218	139/502	151/710	355/1430	25%
Scor. Pos. %	30%	28%	21%	25%	
Driving In Runners from 3B with Less than Two Out:			130/240	54%	

Love to face: Fernando Valenzuela (11–7 against him)
Hate to face: Bob Welch (2–15 against him)
.233 batting average was lowest in 103-year history of the team. . . . Had worst artificial-surface record (11–31) in majors, including 0–11 vs. left-handers on turf, 0–9 in one-run games on turf, and 1–17 vs. West on turf. . . . Batted N.L.-low .227 in day games, after leading league with .281 in daylight in 1984. . . . Batting average of .221 with runners in scoring position was lowest such average by any team in a full season since *The Player Analysis* began in 1975; Mets hit .214 in strike-abbreviated 1981. . . . Had 33 home runs from 7-8-9 spots in batting order, tying Cubs for N.L. lead. . . . Starting outfielders batted only .252, lowest in N.L.; in 1984, starting outfielders batted .307, best in N.L.

National League

	AB	H	2B	3B	HR	RRF	BB	SO	BA	SA	OBA
Season	65818	16596	2861	437	1424	7739	6373	10674	.252	.374	.319
vs. Left-Handers	20442	5120	919	112	463	2384	1986	3405	.250	.374	.317
vs. Right-Handers	45376	11476	1942	325	961	5355	4387	7269	.253	.374	.320
Home	32114	8221	1474	226	678	3899	3332	5061	.256	.379	.326
Road	33704	8375	1387	211	746	3840	3041	5613	.248	.369	.311
Grass	33099	8299	1322	168	830	3892	3142	5412	.251	.376	.317
Artificial Turf	32719	8297	1539	269	594	3847	3231	5262	.254	.372	.321
April	7621	1829	326	43	126	784	695	1233	.240	.344	.304
May	10496	2571	462	74	221	1224	1017	1750	.245	.366	.312
June	11291	2762	468	74	239	1270	1091	1824	.245	.363	.312
July	11008	2849	507	68	234	1301	1045	1753	.259	.381	.324
August	11136	2881	502	72	252	1324	1040	1807	.259	.385	.322
Sept./Oct.	14266	3704	596	106	352	1836	1485	2307	.260	.390	.330
Leading Off Inn.	16106	4092	728	107	369	369	1366	2463	.254	.381	.315
Bases Empty	37930	9402	1640	255	812	812	3197	6211	.248	.369	.309
Runners On	27888	7194	1221	182	612	6927	3176	4463	.258	.381	.332
Runners/Scor. Pos.	16196	4163	692	118	372	6121	2377	2764	.257	.383	.346
Runners On/2 Out	11955	2874	522	75	262	2757	1574	2012	.240	.362	.332
Scor. Pos./2 Out	7737	1822	313	54	166	2428	1229	1375	.235	.354	.343
Late Inning Pressure	10406	2637	399	57	226	1175	1095	1785	.253	.368	.325
Leading Off	2654	731	119	13	59	59	243	434	.275	.397	.339
Bases Empty	5952	1529	229	29	131	131	529	1030	.257	.371	.320
Runners On	4454	1108	170	28	95	1044	566	755	.249	.363	.332
Runners/Scor. Pos.	2539	619	103	17	46	896	434	450	.244	.352	.348

DRIVING IN RUNS	0 Out	1 Out	2 Out	Total	
From 1B	210/4826	336/6924	427/7948	973/19698	5%
From 2B	357/2292	843/4574	1140/5855	2340/12721	18%
From 3B	622/1054	1442/2531	919/3207	2983/6792	44%
Scoring Position	979/3346	2285/7105	2059/9062	5323/19513	27%
Scor. Pos. %	29%	32%	23%	27%	
Driving In Runners from 3B with Less than Two Out:		2064/3585	58%		

Loves to face: American League (21–2 in last 23 All-Star Games)
Hates to face: American League West (1–4 in World Series against them)
.252 batting average was lowest for N.L. since 1972 (.248). . . . Despite ballyhooed early-season lack of offense, run production for season was 7,899, compared with 7,894 in 1984. . . . Pirates and Giants both lost over 100 games; the last time two N.L. teams lost 100 in a nonexpansion year was 1928. . . . Teams scored in 48.9 percent of innings when leadoff batter reached base; 14.6 percent of innings when leadoff batter was put out. . . . That 48.9 figure breaks down this way: 41.3 percent when leadoff batter reached first, 62.5 percent when he reached second, 82.8 percent when he reached third, and—something of an anticlimax—in all 369 innings in which leadoff batter homered. . . . Rate of 1.68 stolen bases per game was the lowest in N.L. since 1979.

IV
Pitcher Section

Pitcher Section

The Pitcher Section is an alphabetical listing of every pitcher who faced at least 250 batters in either the American or the National League last season. Also included are several key pitchers who did not face the required 250 batters. Pitchers are listed alphabetically within each league, followed by the totals for each team and the league as a whole.

Column Headings Information

Bert Blyleven
Cleveland Indians   W–L ERA AB H HR BB SO BA SA OBA

W-L	Won-Lost Record
ERA	Earned-Run Average
AB	At Bats
H	Hits
HR	Home Runs
BB	Bases on Balls
SO	Strikeouts
BA	Batting Average
SA	Slugging Average
OBA	On-Base Average

In addition to the expected categories for pitchers (won-lost record, ERA, walks, and strikeouts), this book includes a unique perspective on each pitcher's season: the batting performance of the league against him. While this method may be unfamiliar at first, it enables us to look at the pitcher and his abilities in fascinating detail.

By compiling pitching statistics in this way, we can examine a pitcher's performance in the same "within the game" contexts we've used to look at batters. To take one example, we're all familiar with platoon differentials for batters; we know that some right-handed batters are far more effective against left-handed pitchers than they are against righties. The same must be true of pitchers, but because the specific information was never available before, who knew how big those differences were? Well,

we know now, and the differences can be huge: from 1976 thorugh 1984, to take one extreme case, right-handed batters hit .221 against Dennis Eckersley, while left-handed batters hit .282. Facing a .061-point difference in Eckersley's effectiveness, a manager should think twice about letting him face a lefty hitter in a clutch situation.

Moreover, by looking at the opponents' batting figures with runners on base or in scoring position, we can show conclusively for the first time who are those underrated pitchers who may give up a lot of hits or home runs, but rarely give them up with men on or in clutch situations. And we can also see those pitchers who (whisper the word, please) fold under the same pressure. (Bear in mind that overall batting averages increase with men on base. This makes any pitcher who holds opponents to a lower average with runners on all the more impressive.)

Season Summary Information

Season	19-7	2.87	910	204	19	74	170	.224	.330	.285
vs. Left-Handed Batters			475	95	7	42	93	.200	.282	.269
vs. Right-Handed Batters			435	109	12	32	77	.251	.382	.302
Home	10-2	3.23	468	118	10	30	86	.252	.357	.297
Road	9-5	2.50	442	86	9	44	84	.195	.301	.272
Grass	14-6	3.06	702	163	16	59	128	.232	.343	.291
Artificial Turf	5-1	2.22	208	41	3	15	42	.197	.284	.264
Day	6-4	3.04	374	91	9	33	66	.243	.364	.304
Night	13-3	2.74	536	113	10	41	104	.211	.306	.271
April	3-1	3.00	132	32	2	11	31	.242	.364	.301
May	1-1	4.26	103	29	1	13	20	.282	.379	.356
June	2-1	3.26	114	25	4	10	15	.219	.342	.291
July	4-1	2.93	163	32	7	16	30	.196	.337	.269
August	5-1	2.51	173	38	2	14	27	.220	.277	.282
Sept./Oct.	4-2	2.23	225	48	3	10	47	.213	.316	.249

Each pitcher's seasonal performance is broken down into a variety of special categories. The first line for each pitcher gives his totals for the whole season. This is followed by breakdowns of his performance against left- and right-handed hitters, in home and road games, on grass fields and on artificial turf, in day games and in night games, and by month. (For pitchers who pitched for more than one team within a league, all totals are combined. The "home" totals for Bert Blyleven, for example, include all games he pitched in Cleveland while with the Indians, and all games he pitched in Minnesota while with the Twins.

Leading Off Inn.	240	59	6	14	37	.246	.367	.287
Bases Empty	560	125	11	42	107	.223	.321	.28
Runners On	350	79	8	32	63	.226	.343	.290
Runners/Scor. Pos.	178	40	4	21	41	.225	.343	.30
Runners On/2 Out	152	30	3	14	31	.197	.309	.278
Scor. Pos./2 Out	89	20	2	9	20	.225	.371	.310

Following these breakdowns, each pitcher's performance is divided into specific game situations. Totals are given for each pitcher against batters who led off an inning, against players batting with the bases empty, and with runners on base. These are followed by his performance with runners in scoring position (on second or third base, or both), with runners on base and two out, and with runners in scoring position and two out.

Late Inning Pressure	79	19	2	11	19	.241	.342	.333
Leading Off	24	7	1	3	5	.292	.458	.370
Bases Empty	53	12	1	8	15	.226	.321	.328
Runners On	26	7	1	3	4	.269	.385	.345
Runners/Scor. Pos.	10	1	0	3	2	.100	.100	.308

The next group shows the pitcher's performance in late-inning pressure situations, which are defined a little differently for pitchers than they are for batters. For pitchers, late-inning pressure is defined as any situation occurring in the seventh inning or later with the score tied, or with his team leading or trailing by one or two runs.

Each pitcher's totals are listed for all late-inning pressure situations, then broken out for his performance when facing a leadoff batter, with the bases empty, with runners on base, and with runners in scoring position.

First 9 Batters	240	50	2	27	44	.208	.288	.288
Second 9 Batters	362	81	8	23	75	.224	.340	.272
All Batters Thereafter	308	73	9	24	51	.237	.351	.297

The last set of breakdowns tracks a pitcher's performance throughout each appearance by listing the opponents' batting record according to the number of batters he has faced, regardless of when he entered the game. This allows us to spotlight those pitchers who get stronger as the game progresses, and to pick out those who can breeze through the order once, but falter the second or third time around.

Following the statistics for each pitcher are a series of comments, beginning with the batter each pitcher loves to face and hates to face. The statistics listed for each individual match-up are from regular season games in the last ten years. Contained within the comments for each pitcher is his "Ground outs-to-air outs" ratio, which consists of his total of ground outs divided by outs on balls hit in the air. (Also included are plays in which the batter reaches base on an error.) An average figure, appropriately enough, is roughly 1.000, although a slight majority of pitchers exceeds that figure. (The median is 1.040.) Pitchers with ratios below 0.750 have their games charted by NASA; those above 1.500 receive hate mail from burrowing animals.

American League

Don Aase

Baltimore Orioles	W–L	ERA	AB	H	HR	BB	SO	BA	SA	OBA
Season	10-6	3.78	322	83	6	35	67	.258	.373	.330
vs. Left-Handed Batters			168	40	4	17	29	.238	.345	.306
vs. Right-Handed Batters			154	43	2	18	38	.279	.403	.354
Home	8-2	3.61	206	52	2	22	42	.252	.330	.326
Road	2-4	4.11	116	31	4	13	25	.267	.448	.336
Grass	9-6	3.82	273	69	5	30	56	.253	.366	.327
Artificial Turf	1-0	3.55	49	14	1	5	11	.286	.408	.345
Day	3-0	4.71	78	21	1	10	13	.269	.372	.348
Night	7-6	3.49	244	62	5	25	54	.254	.373	.324
April	2-0	8.22	30	10	1	5	3	.333	.533	.417
May	2-2	3.38	51	14	1	4	10	.275	.392	.327
June	0-1	7.43	56	23	0	5	10	.411	.482	.453
July	2-2	2.95	73	14	0	9	14	.192	.247	.280
August	2-0	1.93	54	13	2	5	13	.241	.389	.305
Sept./Oct.	2-1	1.96	58	9	2	7	17	.155	.310	.246
Leading Off Inn.			64	16	1	8	6	.250	.391	.333
Bases Empty			153	34	1	14	27	.222	.314	.287
Runners On			169	49	5	21	40	.290	.426	.366
Runners/Scor. Pos.			107	33	4	15	28	.308	.477	.389
Runners On/2 Out			68	24	3	7	14	.353	.529	.413
Scor. Pos./2 Out			50	19	3	5	9	.380	.620	.436
Late Inning Pressure			209	51	3	28	36	.244	.335	.331
Leading Off			44	11	1	4	5	.250	.409	.313
Bases Empty			99	22	1	9	13	.222	.323	.287
Runners On			110	29	2	19	23	.264	.345	.366
Runners/Scor. Pos.			70	17	1	14	17	.243	.329	.360
First 9 Batters			288	75	6	32	58	.260	.385	.332
Second 9 Batters			34	8	0	3	9	.235	.265	.308
All Batters Thereafter			0	0	0	0	0	.000	.000	.000

Loves to face: Doug DeCinces (.059, 1-for-17)
Hates to face: Don Mattingly (.800, 4-for-5, 1 HR)
Ground outs-to-air outs ratio: 0.95 last season, 0.99 for career. . . . Additional statistics: 13 double-play ground outs in 93 opportunities, 17 doubles, 1 triple allowed in 88.0 innings last season. . . . Oil on troubled waters: opponents have batted .309 with runners in scoring position, and .366 with runners in scoring position and two outs, over past two years. . . . Has been more effective vs. left-handers than vs. right-handers in every season since '81. . . . Hasn't allowed two home runs in a game in 90 appearances since May 6, 1982, when Ken Singleton and Gary Roenicke got him while he was still with Angels. . . . Faced more batters in Late-Inning Pressure Situations last season than any other in major-league career, but opponents' LIP batting average was 2d-highest of career.

Jim Acker

Toronto Blue Jays	W–L	ERA	AB	H	HR	BB	SO	BA	SA	OBA
Season	7-2	3.23	321	86	7	43	42	.268	.371	.358
vs. Left-Handed Batters			146	45	2	22	15	.308	.390	.398
vs. Right-Handed Batters			175	41	5	21	27	.234	.354	.323
Home	3-1	1.96	162	33	4	20	24	.204	.284	.293
Road	4-1	4.69	159	53	3	23	18	.333	.459	.422
Grass	4-1	4.35	122	41	1	20	11	.336	.418	.434
Artificial Turf	3-1	2.60	199	45	6	23	31	.226	.342	.308
Day	2-2	4.11	136	37	3	19	19	.272	.368	.361
Night	5-0	2.63	185	49	4	24	23	.265	.373	.355
April	1-0	1.08	62	17	0	7	3	.274	.306	.348
May	0-0	3.93	66	16	3	7	14	.242	.409	.320
June	3-2	3.77	54	14	0	10	4	.259	.259	.375
July	1-0	0.90	38	9	1	3	6	.237	.368	.286
August	1-0	4.50	37	14	0	7	3	.378	.432	.489
Sept./Oct.	1-0	4.76	64	16	3	9	12	.250	.453	.351
Leading Off Inn.			65	22	2	14	6	.338	.492	.456
Bases Empty			152	42	2	27	16	.276	.368	.392
Runners On			169	44	5	16	26	.260	.373	.324
Runners/Scor. Pos.			85	22	1	9	12	.259	.318	.330
Runners On/2 Out			76	25	2	6	12	.329	.434	.378
Scor. Pos./2 Out			48	14	0	2	7	.292	.292	.320
Late Inning Pressure			100	31	2	12	8	.310	.380	.386
Leading Off			21	6	1	5	0	.286	.429	.423
Bases Empty			50	15	1	9	4	.300	.380	.417
Runners On			50	16	1	3	4	.320	.380	.352
Runners/Scor. Pos.			23	7	0	1	2	.304	.304	.320
First 9 Batters			272	73	7	40	35	.268	.375	.362
Second 9 Batters			46	11	0	3	7	.239	.261	.314
All Batters Thereafter			3	2	0	0	0	.667	1.667	.667

Loves to face: Tony Armas (.083, 1-for-12)
Hates to face: Ted Simmons (.625, 5-for-8, 2 2B)
Ground outs-to-air outs ratio: 1.94 last season, 2.24 for career. . . . Additional statistics: 16 double-play ground outs in 92 opportunities (8th-highest rate in A.L.), 8 doubles, 2 triples allowed in 86.1 innings last season. . . . Opponents' on-base average leading off innings was highest in majors last season. . . . Has allowed a batting average above .300 in Late-Inning Pressure Situations in each of three years with Toronto. . . . Opponents have .424 career average (14-for-33) with the bases loaded, but no grand slams. . . . Has allowed 13 of 17 career home runs to right-handed batters, but lefties were killing him toward the end of the season (.375 after Aug. 1). . . . Collected eight of Blue Jays' first 20 saves last season, but only two of 27 after June 2.

Doyle Alexander

Toronto Blue Jays	W–L	ERA	AB	H	HR	BB	SO	BA	SA	OBA
Season	17-10	3.45	1008	268	28	67	142	.266	.396	.315
vs. Left-Handed Batters			515	136	16	47	57	.264	.416	.330
vs. Right-Handed Batters			493	132	12	20	85	.268	.375	.297
Home	11-5	2.83	609	148	17	43	92	.243	.371	.296
Road	6-5	4.48	399	120	11	24	50	.301	.434	.344
Grass	4-4	4.64	301	92	8	19	36	.306	.422	.347
Artificial Turf	13-6	2.98	707	176	20	48	106	.249	.385	.301
Day	5-4	3.49	344	88	9	26	44	.256	.390	.313
Night	12-6	3.43	664	180	19	41	98	.271	.399	.315
April	3-0	3.06	134	32	5	12	25	.239	.381	.306
May	3-2	5.91	150	50	8	10	20	.333	.560	.383
June	1-2	4.66	142	43	5	8	16	.303	.486	.342
July	3-2	3.05	180	52	4	14	32	.289	.406	.344
August	3-2	3.18	197	52	3	5	19	.264	.355	.281
Sept./Oct.	4-2	2.01	205	39	3	18	30	.190	.254	.258
Leading Off Inn.			258	64	9	14	30	.248	.415	.295
Bases Empty			613	159	19	40	79	.259	.400	.309
Runners On			395	109	9	27	63	.276	.390	.323
Runners/Scor. Pos.			209	56	4	18	39	.268	.373	.322
Runners On/2 Out			165	39	2	13	33	.236	.309	.292
Scor. Pos./2 Out			98	22	1	8	19	.224	.306	.283
Late Inning Pressure			122	41	6	8	16	.336	.533	.377
Leading Off			37	12	3	1	3	.324	.622	.342
Bases Empty			83	26	6	5	13	.313	.578	.352
Runners On			39	15	0	3	3	.385	.436	.429
Runners/Scor. Pos.			18	7	0	2	1	.389	.500	.450
First 9 Batters			302	75	5	16	54	.248	.348	.289
Second 9 Batters			294	83	11	24	37	.282	.456	.345
All Batters Thereafter			412	110	12	27	51	.267	.388	.311

Loves to face: Bobby Meacham (.083, 1-for-12)
Hates to face: Scott Fletcher (.462, 6-for-13)
Ground outs-to-air outs ratio: 0.80 last season, 0.95 for career. . . . Additional statistics: 15 double-play ground outs in 180 opportunities, 41 doubles, 3 triples allowed in 260.2 innings last season. . . . Ranked 9th among A.L. pitchers with an average of 7.24 innings per start. . . . Allowed 14 first-inning runs in 36 starts last season. . . . Batting support: 4.25 runs per start. . . . Allowed 11 steals in 14 attempts with Whitt catching; only one (by Rickey Henderson) in seven with Martinez catching. . . . Ranked 8th in A.L. with an average of 2.31 walks per nine innings. . . . Home-game ERA was 5th-lowest in A.L. last season. . . . Over last five years, opponents are 3-for-28 with the bases loaded, and he has not walked in a run.

Keith Atherton

Oakland As	W–L	ERA	AB	H	HR	BB	SO	BA	SA	OBA
Season	4-7	4.30	386	89	17	42	77	.231	.425	.303
vs. Left-Handed Batters			163	42	6	24	25	.258	.436	.349
vs. Right-Handed Batters			223	47	11	18	52	.211	.417	.267
Home	2-2	3.92	206	43	9	25	47	.209	.398	.292
Road	2-5	4.75	180	46	8	17	30	.256	.456	.317
Grass	3-5	4.13	328	73	15	38	68	.223	.412	.301
Artificial Turf	1-2	5.28	58	16	2	4	9	.276	.500	.317
Day	1-1	4.17	133	29	4	12	32	.218	.353	.279
Night	3-6	4.37	253	60	13	30	45	.237	.462	.316
April	1-2	4.91	64	13	5	7	12	.203	.531	.278
May	1-0	2.30	58	12	2	6	11	.207	.345	.281
June	1-2	3.57	85	22	3	12	20	.259	.435	.347
July	1-0	7.98	61	21	0	9	9	.344	.475	.423
August	0-2	4.50	47	11	2	6	10	.234	.383	.321
Sept./Oct.	0-1	3.38	71	10	5	2	15	.141	.366	.162
Leading Off Inn.			82	24	5	6	16	.293	.512	.341
Bases Empty			200	51	8	18	40	.255	.430	.317
Runners On			186	38	9	24	37	.204	.419	.290
Runners/Scor. Pos.			94	17	3	22	23	.181	.351	.325
Runners On/2 Out			80	17	5	12	15	.213	.488	.315
Scor. Pos./2 Out			48	6	2	11	11	.125	.333	.288
Late Inning Pressure			157	38	6	22	34	.242	.427	.335
Leading Off			38	16	4	2	7	.421	.789	.450
Bases Empty			87	27	4	7	17	.310	.529	.362
Runners On			70	11	2	15	17	.157	.300	.306
Runners/Scor. Pos.			33	6	1	13	11	.182	.364	.413
First 9 Batters			330	72	14	37	68	.218	.409	.294
Second 9 Batters			54	16	3	4	9	.296	.519	.345
All Batters Thereafter			2	1	0	1	0	.500	.500	.667

Loves to face: Cal Ripken (0-for-9)
Hates to face: Rance Mulliniks (.571, 4-for-7, 1 HR)
Ground outs-to-air outs ratio: 0.44 last season, lowest in A.L.; 0.48 for career, lowest in majors over past 11 seasons (minimum: 1,000 batters faced). . . . Additional statistics: 5 double-play ground outs in 93 opportunities (9th-lowest rate in A.L.), 22 doubles, 1 triple allowed in 104.2 innings last season. . . . Who was last reliever to allow 17 home runs in a season? Oscar Zamora of Cubs in 1975. The A.L. record is 23, by John Wyatt in 1964; N.L. record, 19 by Bill Henry in 1959. Atherton allowed 17 in 17 separate games, the most shocking being Dick Schofield's grand slam on April 12. . . . Opponents have .162 career batting average with runners in scoring position and two outs, 3d-lowest in past 11 years (minimum: 150 batters faced). . . . But with runners in scoring position and *less than* two outs, opponents' average is .333.

Floyd Bannister

Chicago White Sox	W–L	ERA	AB	H	HR	BB	SO	BA	SA	OBA
Season	10-14	4.87	806	211	30	100	198	.262	.445	.343
vs. Left-Handed Batters			146	44	6	13	27	.301	.548	.360
vs. Right-Handed Batters			660	167	24	87	171	.253	.423	.339
Home	5-6	3.61	354	86	13	45	98	.243	.418	.328
Road	5-8	5.90	452	125	17	55	100	.277	.467	.355
Grass	8-12	4.70	638	169	24	81	161	.265	.451	.346
Artificial Turf	2-2	5.53	168	42	6	19	37	.250	.423	.332
Day	1-3	4.95	137	35	3	19	28	.255	.416	.342
Night	9-11	4.85	669	176	27	81	170	.263	.451	.343
April	0-3	6.08	93	28	4	12	19	.301	.516	.393
May	3-1	2.75	146	32	3	18	42	.219	.342	.303
June	2-2	6.33	104	32	2	12	24	.308	.452	.375
July	0-2	3.79	149	36	5	24	34	.242	.383	.343
August	1-4	5.40	148	38	8	19	35	.257	.520	.337
Sept./Oct.	4-2	5.80	166	45	8	15	44	.271	.482	.335
Leading Off Inn.			204	56	7	19	46	.275	.475	.342
Bases Empty			475	122	13	50	121	.257	.415	.331
Runners On			331	89	17	50	77	.269	.489	.359
Runners/Scor. Pos.			205	49	11	33	54	.239	.463	.336
Runners On/2 Out			128	24	8	25	32	.188	.391	.325
Scor. Pos./2 Out			87	15	7	18	24	.172	.437	.321
Late Inning Pressure			66	23	4	13	14	.348	.576	.450
Leading Off			20	5	0	2	8	.250	.350	.318
Bases Empty			41	13	0	4	12	.317	.390	.378
Runners On			25	10	4	9	2	.400	.880	.543
Runners/Scor. Pos.			15	6	4	7	1	.400	1.200	.565
First 9 Batters			274	59	10	27	72	.215	.387	.286
Second 9 Batters			252	72	7	41	67	.286	.448	.385
All Batters Thereafter			280	80	13	32	59	.286	.500	.353

Loves to face: Harold Baines (0-for-11, 5 SO)
Hates to face: Larry Parrish (.452, 14-for-31, 5 HR)
Ground outs-to-air outs ratio: 0.89 last season, 0.90 for career. . . . Additional statistics: 20 double-play ground outs in 159 opportunities, 46 doubles (tied for 6th-most in A.L.), 6 triples allowed in 210.2 innings last season. . . . Total of 82 extra-base hits allowed was 3d-highest in A.L. . . . Allowed 18 first-inning runs in 34 starts last season. . . . Batting support: 4.56 runs per start. . . . Led A.L. with an average of 8.46 strikeouts per nine innings. . . . Has allowed 30 or more home runs in three of last four seasons, the first major leaguer to do that since Ferguson Jenkins (1972–73–75). . . . Allowed 17 home runs with runners on base last season, tying John Butcher for major-league lead. He was the only pitcher to allow three grand-slams last season, and all three (by Brook Jacoby, Eddie Murray, and Cecil Cooper) came with two outs.

Salome Barojas

Seattle Mariners	W–L	ERA	AB	H	HR	BB	SO	BA	SA	OBA
Season	0-5	5.98	213	65	6	33	27	.305	.455	.395
vs. Left-Handed Batters			93	30	3	18	5	.323	.516	.429
vs. Right-Handed Batters			120	35	3	15	22	.292	.408	.368
Home	0-3	4.40	120	34	2	21	13	.283	.392	.387
Road	0-2	8.18	93	31	4	12	14	.333	.538	.406
Grass	0-1	8.16	57	17	3	10	11	.298	.526	.397
Artificial Turf	0-4	5.17	156	48	3	23	16	.308	.429	.394
Day	0-1	1.35	21	2	0	9	5	.095	.190	.367
Night	0-4	6.65	192	63	6	24	22	.328	.484	.399
April	0-2	6.17	45	12	2	13	6	.267	.467	.431
May	0-3	6.57	104	36	2	11	10	.346	.471	.405
June	0-0	1.00	29	3	0	5	9	.103	.138	.229
July	0-0	9.82	35	14	2	4	2	.400	.657	.462
August			0	0	0	0	0	.000	.000	.000
Sept./Oct.			0	0	0	0	0	.000	.000	.000
Leading Off Inn.			47	11	0	7	5	.234	.298	.333
Bases Empty			108	35	1	17	15	.324	.426	.416
Runners On			105	30	5	16	12	.286	.486	.374
Runners/Scor. Pos.			68	18	3	13	9	.265	.441	.373
Runners On/2 Out			49	14	4	7	6	.286	.531	.375
Scor. Pos./2 Out			37	11	3	7	5	.297	.541	.409
Late Inning Pressure			8	4	0	2	0	.500	.500	.600
Leading Off			3	1	0	0	0	.333	.333	.333
Bases Empty			5	2	0	1	0	.400	.400	.500
Runners On			3	2	0	1	0	.667	.667	.750
Runners/Scor. Pos.			3	2	0	0	0	.667	.667	.667
First 9 Batters			125	37	5	21	16	.296	.488	.395
Second 9 Batters			67	21	0	7	11	.313	.358	.378
All Batters Thereafter			21	7	1	5	0	.333	.571	.444

Loves to face: Rich Dauer (0-for-13)
Hates to face: Tom Brunansky (.500, 7-for-14, 5 HR)
Ground outs-to-air outs ratio: 1.19 last season, 1.59 for career. . . . Additional statistics: 2 double-play ground outs in 50 opportunities (6th-lowest rate in A.L.), 12 doubles, 1 triple allowed in 52.2 innings last season. . . . Career left/right balance unbecoming a relief pitcher: .304 vs. left-handers, .224 vs. right-handers; last year, though, the door was open to all comers. . . . Entered 1985 season having never committed an error in major leagues, but that streak ended on May 17. . . . Had never allowed a grand-slam homer, but that streak was ended by Harold Baines on July 2. . . . Had never lived in Canada, but that streak ended on July 29, when he was optioned to Calgary.

Jim Beattie

Seattle Mariners	W–L	ERA	AB	H	HR	BB	SO	BA	SA	OBA
Season	5-6	7.29	294	93	9	33	45	.316	.469	.385
vs. Left-Handed Batters			150	47	5	23	21	.313	.480	.401
vs. Right-Handed Batters			144	46	4	10	24	.319	.458	.367
Home	4-2	4.75	180	44	5	19	26	.244	.383	.320
Road	1-4	12.52	114	49	4	14	19	.430	.605	.488
Grass	1-3	13.74	96	43	4	12	15	.448	.635	.505
Artificial Turf	4-3	4.91	198	50	5	21	30	.253	.389	.327
Day	2-2	5.40	72	18	0	8	14	.250	.319	.321
Night	3-4	7.96	222	75	9	25	31	.338	.518	.406
April	0-2	13.06	48	18	2	7	4	.375	.583	.466
May	2-2	4.95	144	40	4	13	25	.278	.410	.338
June	1-0	19.06	31	15	2	5	4	.484	.774	.556
July	1-1	5.63	32	9	1	3	5	.281	.406	.333
August	1-1	4.50	39	11	0	5	7	.282	.359	.356
Sept./Oct.			0	0	0	0	0	.000	.000	.000
Leading Off Inn.			69	20	1	9	8	.290	.391	.372
Bases Empty			161	40	5	21	21	.248	.398	.335
Runners On			133	53	4	12	24	.398	.556	.444
Runners/Scor. Pos.			82	34	2	7	14	.415	.561	.448
Runners On/2 Out			46	11	0	3	9	.239	.239	.300
Scor. Pos./2 Out			35	9	0	1	7	.257	.257	.297
Late Inning Pressure			6	0	0	1	2	.000	.000	.143
Leading Off			2	0	0	0	1	.000	.000	.000
Bases Empty			6	0	0	1	2	.000	.000	.143
Runners On			0	0	0	0	0	.000	.000	.000
Runners/Scor. Pos.			0	0	0	0	0	.000	.000	.000
First 9 Batters			137	43	5	15	19	.314	.489	.382
Second 9 Batters			91	31	1	11	14	.341	.451	.404
All Batters Thereafter			66	19	3	7	12	.288	.455	.365

Loves to face: Jim Sundberg (.100, 2-for-20)
Hates to face: Mike Young (.714, 5-for-7, 2 HR)
Ground outs-to-air outs ratio: 0.93 last season, 1.32 for career. . . . Additional statistics: 5 double-play ground outs in 80 opportunities, 16 doubles, 1 triple allowed in 70.1 innings last season. . . . Average of 4.27 innings per start was lowest among A.L. pitchers (minimum: 15 GS). . . . Allowed 17 first-inning runs in 15 starts last season. . . . Batting support: 6.07 runs per start, 2d-highest average in A.L. (minimum: 15 GS). . . . Opposing batters hit 150 points higher with runners on base than with the bases empty, largest difference in A.L. last season (minimum: 100 AB in both situations). . . . ERA of 7.29 was highest in majors among pitchers with at least 15 starts. . . . First pitcher in the 11-year history of *The Player Analysis* to allow an opposing batting average above .400 in road games (minimum: 100 AB).

Joe Beckwith

Kansas City Royals	W–L	ERA	AB	H	HR	BB	SO	BA	SA	OBA
Season	1-5	4.07	368	99	9	32	80	.269	.399	.330
vs. Left-Handed Batters			157	47	7	21	30	.299	.478	.380
vs. Right-Handed Batters			211	52	2	11	50	.246	.341	.291
Home	0-3	3.34	225	56	6	20	45	.249	.387	.313
Road	1-2	5.30	143	43	3	12	35	.301	.420	.356
Grass	0-1	6.67	111	38	3	8	26	.342	.477	.387
Artificial Turf	1-4	3.04	257	61	6	24	54	.237	.366	.305
Day	0-2	4.18	110	33	5	8	23	.300	.518	.358
Night	1-3	4.03	258	66	4	24	57	.256	.349	.318
April	1-1	0.66	49	9	0	4	15	.184	.204	.245
May	0-1	6.35	74	31	2	8	11	.419	.608	.476
June	0-2	2.65	62	14	0	8	17	.226	.306	.314
July	0-0	7.36	46	14	1	8	8	.304	.413	.418
August	0-1	6.32	59	16	4	2	15	.271	.508	.297
Sept./Oct.	0-0	2.18	78	15	2	2	14	.192	.308	.213
Leading Off Inn.			78	21	2	5	16	.269	.423	.321
Bases Empty			184	46	4	16	39	.250	.375	.317
Runners On			184	53	5	16	41	.288	.424	.343
Runners/Scor. Pos.			115	29	2	15	31	.252	.348	.331
Runners On/2 Out			88	27	1	8	16	.307	.409	.371
Scor. Pos./2 Out			62	17	0	8	13	.274	.323	.357
Late Inning Pressure			152	46	3	17	36	.303	.441	.376
Leading Off			38	12	2	1	8	.316	.553	.333
Bases Empty			78	24	3	7	17	.308	.513	.372
Runners On			74	22	0	10	19	.297	.365	.381
Runners/Scor. Pos.			51	14	0	10	16	.275	.353	.393
First 9 Batters			307	79	7	25	70	.257	.371	.317
Second 9 Batters			61	20	2	7	10	.328	.541	.397
All Batters Thereafter			0	0	0	0	0	.000	.000	.000

Loves to face: Ron Kittle (0-for-4, 3 SO)
Hates to face: The Brothers Iorg (Dane 2-for-2; Garth 2-for-2, 1 HR)
Ground outs-to-air outs ratio: 1.11 last season, 1.24 for career (0.95 vs. left-handed batters, 1.55 vs. right-handers). . . . Additional statistics: 8 double-play ground outs in 78 opportunities, 19 doubles, 1 triple allowed in 95.0 innings last season. . . . Dale Murphy is hitless in 14 career at bats vs. Beckwith, his highest 0-for against any pitcher (also Beckwith's highest 0-for vs. any batter). . . . Total of 80 strikeouts in relief ranked 5th in A.L. . . . Brutal with bases loaded last season: opponents were 6-for-11, with a double, a triple, and two grand-slams. . . . Earned his annual save on April 28 at Boston. . . . Opponents have .308 career batting average in Late-Inning Pressure Situations with runners on base. . . . Opposing left-handed batters hit one home run per 26 at bats over past two seasons, one per 59 AB from 1980–83.

Juan Berenguer

Detroit Tigers	W–L	ERA	AB	H	HR	BB	SO	BA	SA	OBA
Season	5-6	5.59	370	96	12	48	82	.259	.419	.343
vs. Left-Handed Batters			203	62	6	29	41	.305	.448	.389
vs. Right-Handed Batters			167	34	6	19	41	.204	.383	.286
Home	3-4	7.82	196	56	9	29	41	.286	.495	.376
Road	2-2	3.28	174	40	3	19	41	.230	.333	.305
Grass	4-5	5.81	309	81	11	39	65	.262	.424	.344
Artificial Turf	1-1	4.50	61	15	1	9	17	.246	.393	.338
Day	2-4	7.07	147	47	4	20	30	.320	.503	.396
Night	3-2	4.70	223	49	8	28	52	.220	.363	.307
April	0-1	8.00	39	14	2	4	5	.359	.538	.419
May	1-2	6.43	54	17	1	8	11	.315	.463	.391
June	1-0	5.40	40	7	2	11	8	.175	.325	.346
July	0-0	1.50	20	2	1	0	5	.100	.250	.100
August	1-0	5.75	82	22	1	9	23	.268	.390	.344
Sept./Oct.	2-3	5.29	135	34	5	16	30	.252	.437	.331
Leading Off Inn.			88	18	2	11	16	.205	.341	.293
Bases Empty			220	50	7	23	51	.227	.382	.300
Runners On			150	46	5	25	31	.307	.473	.400
Runners/Scor. Pos.			87	30	3	14	17	.345	.529	.425
Runners On/2 Out			65	19	2	8	12	.292	.415	.370
Scor. Pos./2 Out			38	14	2	5	7	.368	.579	.442
Late Inning Pressure			32	8	1	8	6	.250	.344	.400
Leading Off			8	1	0	3	1	.125	.125	.364
Bases Empty			20	4	1	4	5	.200	.350	.333
Runners On			12	4	0	4	1	.333	.333	.500
Runners/Scor. Pos.			6	2	0	3	0	.333	.333	.556
First 9 Batters			200	60	8	29	47	.300	.480	.386
Second 9 Batters			110	22	3	10	23	.200	.327	.267
All Batters Thereafter			60	14	1	9	12	.233	.383	.329

Loves to face: Mike Heath (0-for-13)
Hates to face: Pete Rose (.800, 4-for-5)
Ground outs-to-air outs ratio: 0.66 last season, 0.63 for career. . . . Additional statistics: 2 double-play ground outs in 74 opportunities (2d-lowest rate in A.L.), 15 doubles, 4 triples allowed in 95.0 innings last season. . . . Allowed 11 first-inning runs in 13 starts last season. . . . Batting support: 5.00 runs per start. . . . Left-handers' batting average: .232 from 1978 to 1984, .305 last season. . . . Opponents' average with runners in scoring position: .204 in 1983 (when his ERA was 3.14); .231 in 1984 (3.48); .345 last season (5.59). That's a pretty big difference; think of it this way: .345 is Willie Keeler's lifetime average; .231 belongs to Ozzie Virgil—the current coach, not the current catcher.

Tim Birtsas

Oakland As	W–L	ERA	AB	H	HR	BB	SO	BA	SA	OBA
Season	10-6	4.01	521	124	18	91	94	.238	.415	.352
vs. Left-Handed Batters			95	21	3	17	12	.221	.379	.342
vs. Right-Handed Batters			426	103	15	74	82	.242	.423	.354
Home	4-2	3.16	247	59	8	39	46	.239	.393	.344
Road	6-4	4.81	274	65	10	52	48	.237	.434	.359
Grass	8-6	4.13	453	111	15	80	77	.245	.417	.359
Artificial Turf	2-0	3.26	68	13	3	11	17	.191	.397	.304
Day	5-1	4.65	146	31	7	23	27	.212	.432	.326
Night	5-5	3.75	375	93	11	68	67	.248	.408	.362
April			0	0	0	0	0	.000	.000	.000
May	1-1	3.50	65	17	1	13	18	.262	.400	.395
June	3-1	4.09	123	30	0	25	23	.244	.309	.369
July	3-0	2.32	114	27	3	18	14	.237	.377	.343
August	3-3	4.07	153	30	10	19	27	.196	.458	.283
Sept./Oct.	0-1	7.27	66	20	4	16	12	.303	.591	.434
Leading Off Inn.			135	38	3	17	18	.281	.407	.366
Bases Empty			290	74	11	49	41	.255	.448	.365
Runners On			231	50	7	42	53	.216	.372	.336
Runners/Scor. Pos.			116	25	4	30	27	.216	.405	.373
Runners On/2 Out			87	18	3	20	19	.207	.402	.355
Scor. Pos./2 Out			47	7	1	16	9	.149	.319	.365
Late Inning Pressure			11	4	1	1	2	.364	.636	.417
Leading Off			4	2	0	1	0	.500	.500	.600
Bases Empty			6	4	1	1	0	.667	1.167	.714
Runners On			5	0	0	0	2	.000	.000	.000
Runners/Scor. Pos.			4	0	0	0	2	.000	.000	.000
First 9 Batters			205	52	4	42	45	.254	.395	.379
Second 9 Batters			161	33	3	33	27	.205	.335	.342
All Batters Thereafter			155	39	11	16	22	.252	.523	.322

Loves to face: Rick Dempsey (0-for-4, 3 SO)
Hates to face: Tom Brookens (.667, 4-for-6, 2 HR)
Ground outs-to-air outs ratio: 0.73 last season, his first in majors. . . . Additional statistics: 14 double-play ground outs in 128 opportunities, 24 doubles, 7 triples (tied for 6th-most in A.L.) allowed in 141.1 innings last season. . . . Average of 5.37 innings per start was 9th-lowest in A.L. (minimum: 15 GS). . . . Allowed 14 first-inning runs in 25 starts last season. . . . Batting support: 4.72 runs per start. . . . Don't load the bases on him: opponents were 1-for-17 *with 10 strikeouts* in those situations last year; that's the most bases-loaded Ks by an A.L. pitcher since 1978, when Mark Littell had 14 to tie the *Player Analysis* record set by Nolan Ryan in 1977. . . . Didn't make his first start until May 23, but was one of three A.L. rookies to win 10 or more games last season.

Bud Black

Kansas City Royals	W–L	ERA	AB	H	HR	BB	SO	BA	SA	OBA
Season	10-15	4.33	805	216	17	59	122	.268	.398	.323
vs. Left-Handed Batters			176	47	2	9	28	.267	.364	.303
vs. Right-Handed Batters			629	169	15	50	94	.269	.407	.328
Home	6-7	4.38	425	118	4	37	50	.278	.379	.341
Road	4-8	4.28	380	98	13	22	72	.258	.418	.302
Grass	4-7	4.46	299	75	11	19	58	.251	.415	.300
Artificial Turf	6-8	4.26	506	141	6	40	64	.279	.387	.336
Day	4-6	4.56	283	74	8	25	53	.261	.420	.327
Night	6-9	4.21	522	142	9	34	69	.272	.385	.321
April	2-1	2.37	140	32	0	11	16	.229	.286	.283
May	3-3	3.57	150	32	8	10	17	.213	.393	.276
June	0-4	5.14	116	35	2	9	21	.302	.448	.359
July	2-3	6.37	121	37	3	11	24	.306	.438	.368
August	1-3	4.41	144	46	1	12	25	.319	.431	.371
Sept./Oct.	2-1	4.89	134	34	3	6	19	.254	.403	.291
Leading Off Inn.			200	52	7	11	22	.260	.445	.312
Bases Empty			455	120	9	32	58	.264	.402	.319
Runners On			350	96	8	27	64	.274	.391	.328
Runners/Scor. Pos.			189	55	3	20	36	.291	.407	.358
Runners On/2 Out			134	32	4	14	21	.239	.358	.315
Scor. Pos./2 Out			74	20	1	12	16	.270	.351	.372
Late Inning Pressure			75	19	0	8	11	.253	.333	.321
Leading Off			23	8	0	0	2	.348	.478	.348
Bases Empty			48	15	0	1	5	.313	.417	.327
Runners On			27	4	0	7	6	.148	.185	.314
Runners/Scor. Pos.			15	3	0	6	5	.200	.267	.409
First 9 Batters			275	79	7	19	46	.287	.418	.337
Second 9 Batters			259	65	3	18	35	.251	.367	.307
All Batters Thereafter			271	72	7	22	41	.266	.406	.324

Loves to face: Kirk Gibson (0-for-11, 5 SO)
Hates to face: Chet Lemon (.556, 10-for-18, 1 HR)
Ground outs-to-air outs ratio: 1.08 last season, 1.06 for career (0.87 on grass surfaces, 1.20 on artificial turf). . . . Additional statistics: 13 double-play ground outs in 169 opportunities, 45 doubles (tied for 8th-most in A.L.), 4 triples allowed in 205.2 innings last season. . . . Allowed 17 first-inning runs in 33 starts last season. . . . Batting support: 3.85 runs per start, 7th-lowest average in A.L. (minimum: 15 GS). . . . Average of 5.79 walks per nine innings was 3d-highest among that same group. . . . Record of 10–15 included 4–0 mark against Cleveland, but 4–9 against teams finishing at or above .500. . . . Three post-season relief appearances were his first in that role since '82. . . . Did not react well to position as Royals' top starter, but will have considerably less pressure on him in '86, thanks to Messers. Saberhagen, Jackson, and Leibrandt.

Bert Blyleven

Indians/Twins	W–L	ERA	AB	H	HR	BB	SO	BA	SA	OBA
Season	17-16	3.16	1106	264	23	75	206	.239	.353	.290
vs. Left-Handed Batters			644	166	11	47	112	.258	.362	.311
vs. Right-Handed Batters			462	98	12	28	94	.212	.340	.261
Home	11-9	2.91	641	153	7	38	126	.239	.332	.286
Road	6-7	3.49	465	111	16	37	80	.239	.381	.297
Grass	11-11	3.16	765	181	16	52	145	.237	.349	.290
Artificial Turf	6-5	3.15	341	83	7	23	61	.243	.361	.292
Day	5-3	3.01	340	85	6	29	57	.250	.356	.310
Night	12-13	3.22	766	179	17	46	149	.234	.351	.282
April	0-2	5.64	126	41	4	11	16	.325	.492	.374
May	3-3	2.58	173	41	2	7	36	.237	.312	.273
June	4-2	1.93	186	36	3	15	38	.194	.290	.254
July	2-4	3.76	194	45	5	16	39	.232	.381	.306
August	4-2	2.41	218	48	4	11	37	.220	.312	.255
Sept./Oct.	4-3	3.64	209	53	5	15	40	.254	.373	.307
Leading Off Inn.			286	71	6	12	58	.248	.367	.283
Bases Empty			675	158	15	37	136	.234	.350	.282
Runners On			431	106	8	38	70	.246	.357	.303
Runners/Scor. Pos.			247	61	6	25	45	.247	.381	.310
Runners On/2 Out			180	38	5	22	32	.211	.344	.297
Scor. Pos./2 Out			118	28	3	17	20	.237	.373	.333
Late Inning Pressure			144	27	1	11	24	.188	.250	.253
Leading Off			41	7	0	2	8	.171	.195	.227
Bases Empty			94	17	0	6	20	.181	.223	.245
Runners On			50	10	1	5	4	.200	.300	.268
Runners/Scor. Pos.			27	5	1	5	3	.185	.333	.303
First 9 Batters			310	71	6	18	65	.229	.335	.275
Second 9 Batters			300	77	6	24	48	.257	.360	.314
All Batters Thereafter			496	116	11	33	93	.234	.359	.285

Loves to face: Alvin Davis (.042, 1-for-24)
Hates to face: Craig Reynolds (.467, 7-for-15)
Ground outs-to-air outs ratio: 0.94 last season, 1.22 for career. . . . Additional statistics: 21 double-play ground outs in 194 opportunities, 45 doubles (tied for 8th-most in A.L.), 6 triples allowed in 293.2 innings last season. . . . Led A.L. pitchers with an average of 7.94 innings per start; pitched into the 8th inning in 26 of his last 27 starts. . . . Allowed 13 first-inning runs in 37 starts last season. . . . Batting support: 4.05 runs per start. . . . Led A.L. in complete games for first time, with league's highest total (24) since 1980. Completed 65 percent of his starts, compared to overall A.L. rate of 16 percent, N.L. rate of 14 percent. . . . Was 12–2 vs. teams that finished the season with losing records, 5–14 vs. teams at or above the .500 mark. . . . Allowed one home run every 12.8 innings, 7th-best rate in A.L. last season. . . . Next start will be 500th of his career.

Mike Boddicker

Baltimore Orioles	W–L	ERA	AB	H	HR	BB	SO	BA	SA	OBA
Season	12-17	4.07	794	227	13	89	135	.286	.385	.361
vs. Left-Handed Batters			452	133	8	53	60	.294	.405	.375
vs. Right-Handed Batters			342	94	5	36	75	.275	.360	.342
Home	5-9	3.40	392	106	9	48	69	.270	.388	.354
Road	7-8	4.77	402	121	4	41	66	.301	.383	.368
Grass	9-16	3.89	678	190	13	80	113	.280	.382	.358
Artificial Turf	3-1	5.20	116	37	0	9	22	.319	.405	.378
Day	4-4	3.44	205	62	2	15	38	.302	.380	.356
Night	8-13	4.28	589	165	11	74	97	.280	.387	.362
April	3-1	3.09	118	32	1	19	24	.271	.356	.377
May	3-2	3.71	129	35	3	13	19	.271	.364	.338
June	2-4	5.24	173	45	2	24	23	.260	.353	.352
July	2-4	3.76	156	43	4	15	30	.276	.397	.347
August	2-2	4.30	118	37	0	8	22	.314	.381	.362
Sept./Oct.	0-4	3.97	100	35	3	10	17	.350	.490	.405
Leading Off Inn.			194	58	6	19	35	.299	.464	.370
Bases Empty			416	125	10	45	73	.300	.430	.373
Runners On			378	102	3	44	62	.270	.336	.347
Runners/Scor. Pos.			224	53	1	36	43	.237	.281	.340
Runners On/2 Out			141	33	1	21	25	.234	.284	.337
Scor. Pos./2 Out			103	20	1	18	20	.194	.243	.314
Late Inning Pressure			89	22	5	18	16	.247	.438	.373
Leading Off			24	6	1	5	7	.250	.417	.400
Bases Empty			58	12	3	9	12	.207	.397	.324
Runners On			31	10	2	9	4	.323	.516	.452
Runners/Scor. Pos.			16	4	1	9	2	.250	.438	.481
First 9 Batters			263	70	4	19	44	.266	.338	.325
Second 9 Batters			243	72	2	31	41	.296	.407	.376
All Batters Thereafter			288	85	7	39	50	.295	.410	.379

Loves to face: George Bell (0-for-16, 6 SO)
Hates to face: Darrell Evans (.556, 5-for-9)
Ground outs-to-air outs ratio: 1.20 last season (previous low was 1.74), 1.61 for career. . . . Additional statistics: 27 double-play ground outs in 200 opportunities, 36 doubles, 2 triples allowed in 203.1 innings last season. . . . Allowed 14 first-inning runs in 32 starts. . . . Batting support: 4.44 runs per start. . . . Allowed one home run every 15.6 innings last season, 4th-best rate in A.L. . . . Opponents' career batting average in Late-Inning Pressure Situations (.198) is lowest among starting pitchers over past 11 years. . . . Knocked out inside five innings eight times last year. . . . Who put a curse on 1984's ERA leaders? Boddicker's numbers are reflected above, coming off a 20–11, 2.79 year in '84. But he was lucky compared to Dodgers' Alejandro Pena (12–6, 2.48 in 1984), who missed most of '85 following surgery and wound up throwing only 4.1 innings.

Rich Bordi

New York Yankees	W–L	ERA	AB	H	HR	BB	SO	BA	SA	OBA
Season	6-8	3.21	376	95	5	29	64	.253	.346	.306
vs. Left-Handed Batters			165	51	4	16	21	.309	.442	.372
vs. Right-Handed Batters			211	44	1	13	43	.209	.270	.252
Home	4-3	2.57	207	47	3	14	28	.227	.319	.274
Road	2-5	4.07	169	48	2	15	36	.284	.379	.344
Grass	6-6	2.86	336	81	5	19	55	.241	.333	.282
Artificial Turf	0-2	6.30	40	14	0	10	9	.350	.450	.471
Day	3-2	2.70	156	33	3	12	25	.212	.314	.269
Night	3-6	3.62	220	62	2	17	39	.282	.368	.332
April	1-0	1.04	32	8	0	1	4	.250	.281	.273
May	0-0	4.32	32	9	1	3	4	.281	.438	.343
June	0-1	1.69	99	21	3	4	18	.212	.333	.248
July	1-2	5.60	69	20	0	11	12	.290	.377	.383
August	2-2	2.70	36	7	0	3	8	.194	.250	.256
Sept./Oct.	2-3	3.71	108	30	1	7	18	.278	.361	.319
Leading Off Inn.			91	20	2	6	18	.220	.352	.268
Bases Empty			219	50	3	12	42	.228	.315	.272
Runners On			157	45	2	17	22	.287	.389	.350
Runners/Scor. Pos.			89	24	1	12	15	.270	.360	.346
Runners On/2 Out			76	25	1	7	10	.329	.447	.386
Scor. Pos./2 Out			47	12	0	5	8	.255	.340	.327
Late Inning Pressure			106	36	3	14	15	.340	.481	.421
Leading Off			30	11	1	3	3	.367	.567	.424
Bases Empty			62	22	2	4	8	.355	.532	.403
Runners On			44	14	1	10	7	.318	.409	.444
Runners/Scor. Pos.			26	7	0	8	4	.269	.308	.441
First 9 Batters			270	70	4	21	44	.259	.370	.312
Second 9 Batters			78	16	1	5	16	.205	.269	.253
All Batters Thereafter			28	9	0	3	4	.321	.321	.387

Loves to face: Floyd Rayford (0-for-6, 3 SO)
Hates to face: Doug DeCinces (.667, 2-for-3, 2 HR)
Ground outs-to-air outs ratio: 0.92 last season, 1.05 for career. . . . Additional statistics: 5 double-play ground outs in 70 opportunities, 14 doubles, 3 triples allowed in 98.0 innings last season. . . . 100-point left/right imbalance came on the heels of 1984 season in which both left-handers and right-handers hit .242 against him. . . . Poor results in Late-Inning Pressure Situations were in line with past performances in those situations (.335 career BA). . . . Didn't walk more than two batters in any of 51 appearances last season. . . . Coincidence or no? Two of his three starts last season came in September against the Orioles; he split the decisions, but held the O's to a .216 batting average, striking out 10. Over the winter, he was traded to the Orioles in the Gary Roenicke deal.

Dennis Boyd

Boston Red Sox	W–L	ERA	AB	H	HR	BB	SO	BA	SA	OBA
Season	15-13	3.70	1045	273	26	67	154	.261	.397	.306
vs. Left-Handed Batters			589	136	10	31	89	.231	.334	.272
vs. Right-Handed Batters			456	137	16	36	65	.300	.478	.349
Home	11-8	3.76	606	162	18	45	94	.267	.422	.316
Road	4-5	3.62	439	111	8	22	60	.253	.362	.293
Grass	14-13	3.71	929	241	26	63	140	.259	.403	.306
Artificial Turf	1-0	3.64	116	32	0	4	14	.276	.353	.311
Day	5-5	3.32	322	85	5	16	51	.264	.385	.296
Night	10-8	3.87	723	188	21	51	103	.260	.402	.311
April	2-1	3.58	143	34	3	12	30	.238	.385	.301
May	3-3	1.58	170	40	1	16	31	.235	.300	.302
June	4-2	3.99	181	49	7	14	22	.271	.453	.320
July	2-3	4.47	189	45	8	8	27	.238	.397	.269
August	0-2	4.84	177	56	3	8	17	.316	.435	.348
Sept./Oct.	4-2	3.66	185	49	4	9	27	.265	.405	.299
Leading Off Inn.			265	63	4	17	34	.238	.340	.286
Bases Empty			627	162	14	49	95	.258	.386	.314
Runners On			418	111	12	18	59	.266	.414	.294
Runners/Scor. Pos.			222	56	7	10	26	.252	.410	.276
Runners On/2 Out			175	42	6	6	28	.240	.394	.269
Scor. Pos./2 Out			109	26	5	3	14	.239	.450	.259
Late Inning Pressure			148	51	6	12	14	.345	.507	.394
Leading Off			41	13	1	2	3	.317	.390	.349
Bases Empty			91	26	5	9	10	.286	.473	.350
Runners On			57	25	1	3	4	.439	.561	.467
Runners/Scor. Pos.			33	13	1	2	1	.394	.576	.429
First 9 Batters			285	72	6	23	48	.253	.375	.312
Second 9 Batters			295	73	8	13	48	.247	.407	.280
All Batters Thereafter			465	128	12	31	58	.275	.404	.319

Loves to face: Steve Balboni (0-for-13, 4 SO)
Hates to face: Dave Henderson (.556, 5-for-9, 2 2B, 1 HR)
Ground outs-to-air outs ratio: 1.08 last season, 1.06 for career. . . . Additional statistics: 16 double-play ground outs in 198 opportunities, 52 doubles (most in A.L.), 6 triples allowed in 272.1 innings last year. . . . Ranked 3d in A.L. with 7.78 innings per start, pitching into 7th inning in all but two of 35 starts. . . . Maybe he shouldn't pitch so long so often: has been hit at career .417 clip in Late-Inning Pressure Situations with runners on base. . . . Total of 84 extra-base hits allowed was tied for most in majors; 54 came at home, 3d-highest such total in majors over 11 years. . . . Allowed 20 first-inning runs in 35 starts last season. . . . Batting support: 5.09 runs per start. . . . Ranked 6th in A.L. with rate of 2.2 walks per nine innings. . . . Had most wins (15) by a Boston right-hander since 1979, when Eckersley, Stanley, and Torrez each had more.

Britt Burns

Chicago White Sox	W–L	ERA	AB	H	HR	BB	SO	BA	SA	OBA
Season	18-11	3.96	852	206	26	79	172	.242	.387	.306
vs. Left-Handed Batters			154	37	6	9	33	.240	.396	.279
vs. Right-Handed Batters			698	169	20	70	139	.242	.385	.312
Home	10-6	3.76	436	102	13	45	99	.234	.383	.305
Road	8-5	4.19	416	104	13	34	73	.250	.392	.307
Grass	16-9	3.89	762	183	25	71	159	.240	.390	.305
Artificial Turf	2-2	4.63	90	23	1	8	13	.256	.367	.313
Day	6-1	2.89	206	45	7	13	40	.218	.359	.267
Night	12-10	4.24	646	161	19	66	132	.249	.396	.318
April	3-1	3.13	88	22	1	7	13	.250	.364	.305
May	3-3	3.62	138	30	3	14	39	.217	.312	.288
June	1-2	3.53	132	32	4	13	24	.242	.386	.315
July	4-1	3.40	179	36	9	19	37	.201	.391	.279
August	3-1	5.63	157	43	6	16	28	.274	.427	.339
Sept./Oct.	4-3	4.20	158	43	3	10	31	.272	.424	.314
Leading Off Inn.			226	55	8	8	47	.243	.407	.269
Bases Empty			532	127	13	36	105	.239	.365	.289
Runners On			320	79	13	43	67	.247	.425	.332
Runners/Scor. Pos.			171	35	7	29	44	.205	.386	.312
Runners On/2 Out			139	33	6	22	38	.237	.432	.342
Scor. Pos./2 Out			87	18	3	17	27	.207	.368	.337
Late Inning Pressure			82	14	4	4	19	.171	.317	.209
Leading Off			25	4	2	0	6	.160	.400	.160
Bases Empty			66	9	3	4	15	.136	.273	.186
Runners On			16	5	1	0	4	.313	.500	.313
Runners/Scor. Pos.			8	3	1	0	0	.375	.750	.375
First 9 Batters			274	62	1	30	62	.226	.307	.305
Second 9 Batters			263	61	8	25	57	.232	.380	.300
All Batters Thereafter			315	83	17	24	53	.263	.463	.312

Loves to face: Glenn Hoffman (.048, 1-for-21, 10 SO)
Hates to face: Jesse Barfield (.389, 14-for-36, 4 HR)
Ground outs-to-air outs ratio: 1.04 last season, 0.89 for career. . . . Additional statistics: 20 double-play ground outs in 165 opportunities, 36 doubles, 5 triples allowed in 227.0 innings last year. . . . Allowed 13 first-inning runs in 34 starts in '85. . . . Batting support: 5.15 runs per start. . . . Ranked 3d in A.L. with 6.82 strikeouts per nine innings. . . . Owns distinction of being winning pitcher in Yogi's final (to this point, anyway) game as Yankee manager, April 28. It was Burns's only relief win of year. . . . Opponents' career batting averages: lefties .251, righties .251. . . . Opponents' .171 average in Late-Inning Pressure Situations was 2d-best for an A.L. starter in '85; Dan Petry led with .132. . . . First pitcher coming off a season of 18 or more wins that Yankees have acquired in an off-season trade (as opposed to free-agent signing) since they got Sad Sam Jones from Red Sox in 1921.

Ray Burris

Milwaukee Brewers	W–L	ERA	AB	H	HR	BB	SO	BA	SA	OBA
Season	9-13	4.81	670	182	25	53	81	.272	.461	.325
vs. Left-Handed Batters			360	85	13	28	45	.236	.431	.292
vs. Right-Handed Batters			310	97	12	25	36	.313	.497	.364
Home	7-7	4.46	415	104	12	32	54	.251	.402	.307
Road	2-6	5.37	255	78	13	21	27	.306	.557	.355
Grass	9-11	4.43	622	162	24	50	78	.260	.442	.316
Artificial Turf	0-2	10.80	48	20	1	3	3	.417	.708	.442
Day	3-4	6.24	219	65	11	18	24	.297	.498	.347
Night	6-9	4.15	451	117	14	35	57	.259	.443	.314
April	1-3	2.00	104	22	3	7	9	.212	.365	.259
May	2-1	3.86	111	31	1	7	15	.279	.405	.328
June	1-2	4.45	113	28	2	8	17	.248	.398	.294
July	1-2	4.91	102	32	6	9	10	.314	.549	.366
August	4-1	3.07	155	39	8	10	22	.252	.439	.301
Sept./Oct.	0-4	14.73	85	30	5	12	8	.353	.671	.433
Leading Off Inn.			174	43	4	5	15	.247	.431	.268
Bases Empty			416	111	18	28	47	.267	.478	.315
Runners On			254	71	7	25	34	.280	.433	.341
Runners/Scor. Pos.			144	35	5	20	19	.243	.410	.331
Runners On/2 Out			115	28	3	16	21	.243	.383	.341
Scor. Pos./2 Out			70	17	2	12	13	.243	.386	.361
Late Inning Pressure			61	15	2	4	9	.246	.377	.292
Leading Off			17	3	0	0	2	.176	.235	.176
Bases Empty			40	12	2	1	3	.300	.475	.317
Runners On			21	3	0	3	6	.143	.190	.250
Runners/Scor. Pos.			12	0	0	3	4	.000	.000	.200
First 9 Batters			235	65	8	15	26	.277	.472	.316
Second 9 Batters			202	60	7	15	25	.297	.480	.347
All Batters Thereafter			233	57	10	23	30	.245	.433	.315

Loves to face: Rudy Law (.036, 1-for-28)
Hates to face: Mike Easler (.389, 14-for-36, 5 HR)
Ground outs-to-air outs ratio: 0.81 last season, 0.96 for career. . . . Additional statistics: 9 double-play ground outs in 105 opportunities, 32 doubles, 10 triples (tied for 3d-most in A.L.) allowed in 170.1 innings in '85. . . . Allowed 20 first-inning runs in 28 starts last year. . . . Batting support: 4.54 runs per start. . . . Opposing right-handed batters hit 77 points higher than left-handers, 5th-largest difference in A.L. last season (minimum: 100 AB each way). . . . One of four active pitchers with career ERAs above 4.00 and at least 100 wins; others: Dick Ruthven, Milt Wilcox, Dennis Martinez. . . . Has allowed only two grand-slam homers in career: to Hank Aaron in 1974 and to Bill Robinson (current Mets coach) in 1982. Robinson also hit the first home run Burris allowed in majors, in 1973; the second was hit by current Mets manager Davey Johnson.

John Butcher

Minnesota Twins	W–L	ERA	AB	H	HR	BB	SO	BA	SA	OBA
Season	11-14	4.98	828	239	24	43	92	.289	.455	.325
vs. Left-Handed Batters			458	133	14	23	54	.290	.463	.324
vs. Right-Handed Batters			370	106	10	20	38	.286	.446	.325
Home	6-8	5.60	437	131	17	23	54	.300	.508	.339
Road	5-6	4.32	391	108	7	20	38	.276	.396	.309
Grass	5-5	3.42	362	93	6	19	35	.257	.359	.293
Artificial Turf	6-9	6.29	466	146	18	24	57	.313	.530	.349
Day	3-5	6.75	186	54	6	9	16	.290	.484	.318
Night	8-9	4.47	642	185	18	34	76	.288	.447	.327
April	3-1	2.30	152	31	1	8	22	.204	.270	.242
May	1-2	5.24	144	45	5	7	18	.313	.514	.349
June	1-4	7.00	147	48	4	7	14	.327	.503	.361
July	3-3	4.97	170	51	6	9	15	.300	.494	.333
August	1-2	3.67	108	30	4	6	14	.278	.417	.319
Sept./Oct.	2-2	7.71	107	34	4	6	9	.318	.551	.350
Leading Off Inn.			212	62	0	8	21	.292	.410	.318
Bases Empty			509	138	7	20	66	.271	.409	.300
Runners On			319	101	17	23	26	.317	.530	.361
Runners/Scor. Pos.			188	62	8	15	15	.330	.516	.367
Runners On/2 Out			140	48	8	7	10	.343	.564	.383
Scor. Pos./2 Out			91	32	6	6	6	.352	.571	.404
Late Inning Pressure			101	25	2	3	12	.248	.337	.276
Leading Off			32	8	0	0	3	.250	.250	.250
Bases Empty			79	18	1	0	9	.228	.304	.228
Runners On			22	7	1	3	3	.318	.455	.423
Runners/Scor. Pos.			13	5	1	2	2	.385	.615	.467
First 9 Batters			279	82	7	14	38	.294	.466	.326
Second 9 Batters			241	69	5	16	20	.286	.432	.328
All Batters Thereafter			308	88	12	13	34	.286	.464	.321

Loves to face: Reggie Jackson (.087, 2-for-23)
Hates to face: Don Baylor (.381, 8-for-21, 3 HR)
Ground outs-to-air outs ratio: 1.25 last season, 1.41 for career. . . . Additional statistics: 15 double-play ground outs in 140 opportunities, 44 doubles, 11 triples (tied for most in A.L.) allowed in 207.2 innings last season. . . . Total of 79 extra-base hits allowed was 7th-highest in A.L. . . . Allowed 23 first-inning runs (tied for 9th-most in A.L.) in 33 starts last season. . . . Batting support: 4.76 runs per start. . . . Ranked 4th in A.L. with 1.86 walks per nine innings. . . . Allowed 17 home runs with runners on base last season, tying Floyd Bannister for major-league lead, but each of those 17 was hit with only one base runner. Only one of the 28 homers Butcher has given up in his career has come with more than one man on: a May 22, 1983 three-run shot by Glenn Wilson. . . . Knocked out of nine starts before the fifth inning last year.

John Candelaria

California Angels	W–L	ERA	AB	H	HR	BB	SO	BA	SA	OBA
Season	7-3	3.80	267	70	7	24	53	.262	.423	.327
vs. Left-Handed Batters			45	7	1	0	17	.156	.244	.152
vs. Right-Handed Batters			222	63	6	24	36	.284	.459	.359
Home	2-2	7.02	131	40	5	10	26	.305	.511	.363
Road	5-1	0.96	136	30	2	14	27	.221	.338	.291
Grass	6-2	4.14	222	58	5	21	46	.261	.414	.331
Artificial Turf	1-1	2.19	45	12	2	3	7	.267	.467	.306
Day	2-0	2.40	55	13	0	7	13	.236	.255	.313
Night	5-3	4.18	212	57	7	17	40	.269	.467	.330
April			0	0	0	0	0	.000	.000	.000
May			0	0	0	0	0	.000	.000	.000
June			0	0	0	0	0	.000	.000	.000
July			0	0	0	0	0	.000	.000	.000
August	3-1	6.20	98	30	3	13	21	.306	.469	.386
Sept./Oct.	4-2	2.53	169	40	4	11	32	.237	.396	.290
Leading Off Inn.			64	14	2	8	12	.219	.391	.315
Bases Empty			149	38	4	20	32	.255	.443	.351
Runners On			118	32	3	4	21	.271	.398	.294
Runners/Scor. Pos.			62	17	2	2	12	.274	.419	.294
Runners On/2 Out			51	13	1	1	10	.255	.392	.269
Scor. Pos./2 Out			30	8	1	0	8	.267	.400	.267
Late Inning Pressure			5	2	1	0	0	.400	1.400	.333
Leading Off			2	1	0	0	0	.500	1.500	.500
Bases Empty			5	2	1	0	0	.400	1.400	.400
Runners On			0	0	0	0	0	.000	.000	.000
Runners/Scor. Pos.			0	0	0	0	0	.000	.000	.000
First 9 Batters			104	29	2	12	22	.279	.433	.359
Second 9 Batters			95	23	2	7	18	.242	.389	.298
All Batters Thereafter			68	18	3	5	13	.265	.456	.316

Loves to face: Brett Butler (0-for-9, 4 SO)
Hates to face: Larry Herndon (.459, 17-for-37, 3 HR)
Figures above are for A.L. only. . . . Ground outs-to-air outs ratio: 0.92 last season, 0.88 for career. . . . Additional statistics: 8 double-play ground outs in 106 opportunities, 26 doubles, 7 triples allowed in 125.1 innings last season. . . . Allowed 8 first-inning runs in 13 starts last year. . . . Batting support: 5.38 runs per start. . . . One of the top ten stats of the year: combining totals with Pirates and Angels, he struck out 34 left-handed batters and walked none. . . . Combined two-league strike-out percentage vs. lefties (35.1) was 4th-highest in *Player Analysis* history. He set the record himself (40.5) in 1983. . . . Also set another one last year by facing 97 left-handed batters without walking any, more than doubling the old record of 48 batters, set by Paul Siebert in 1977. . . . Opponents have .198 career batting average with runners in scoring position and two outs.

Bill Caudill

Toronto Blue Jays	W–L	ERA	AB	H	HR	BB	SO	BA	SA	OBA
Season	4-6	2.99	253	53	9	35	46	.209	.344	.306
vs. Left-Handed Batters			113	28	5	27	20	.248	.407	.397
vs. Right-Handed Batters			140	25	4	8	26	.179	.293	.222
Home	2-2	2.97	132	25	6	17	23	.189	.341	.283
Road	2-4	3.00	121	28	3	18	23	.231	.347	.331
Grass	0-3	3.04	87	20	2	12	16	.230	.333	.324
Artificial Turf	4-3	2.96	166	33	7	23	30	.199	.349	.297
Day	2-1	2.96	87	17	4	13	17	.195	.356	.301
Night	2-5	3.00	166	36	5	22	29	.217	.337	.309
April	3-2	6.28	52	12	3	5	12	.231	.442	.305
May	1-1	1.74	39	7	1	6	5	.179	.282	.283
June	0-0	0.79	39	8	1	5	9	.205	.282	.289
July	0-1	3.38	41	11	1	6	7	.268	.366	.354
August	0-2	3.72	35	7	2	5	7	.200	.400	.300
Sept./Oct.	0-0	1.38	47	8	1	8	6	.170	.277	.304
Leading Off Inn.			52	9	1	8	12	.173	.269	.295
Bases Empty			128	28	4	18	26	.219	.352	.320
Runners On			125	25	5	17	20	.200	.336	.293
Runners/Scor. Pos.			73	17	4	11	8	.233	.425	.326
Runners On/2 Out			61	6	1	10	10	.098	.148	.225
Scor. Pos./2 Out			39	5	1	7	6	.128	.205	.261
Late Inning Pressure			132	33	7	19	25	.250	.432	.344
Leading Off			27	6	1	4	8	.222	.407	.323
Bases Empty			65	16	3	9	15	.246	.415	.338
Runners On			67	17	4	10	10	.254	.448	.350
Runners/Scor. Pos.			45	14	4	8	6	.311	.600	.411
First 9 Batters			251	53	9	35	46	.211	.347	.308
Second 9 Batters			2	0	0	0	0	.000	.000	.000
All Batters Thereafter			0	0	0	0	0	.000	.000	.000

Loves to face: Gary Ward (.071, 1-for-14, 6 SO)
Hates to face: Alvin Davis (2-for-2, 1 2B, 1 HR)
Ground outs-to-air outs ratio: 0.55 last season (4th-lowest in A.L.), 0.62 for career. . . . Additional statistics: 3 double-play ground outs in 61 opportunities (8th-lowest rate in A.L.), 7 doubles, 0 triples allowed in 69.1 innings; allowed nine stolen bases in 10 attempts. . . . Career rate of 8.38 strikeouts per nine innings ranks 5th among active pitchers (minimum: 250 SO). . . . Opponents have .177 career batting average with runners on base and two outs, 3d-lowest over past 11 years (minimum: 250 batters faced in that situation). . . . Had 12 straight scoreless appearances from Aug. 23 until division title was won. Nevertheless, became second pitcher ever to appear in 60 or more games during regular season, but none in his team's post-season play. The other was Eddie Fisher of 1966 Orioles, who didn't need much relief in Series that year.

Jim Clancy

Toronto Blue Jays	W–L	ERA	AB	H	HR	BB	SO	BA	SA	OBA
Season	9-6	3.78	485	117	15	37	66	.241	.414	.292
vs. Left-Handed Batters			255	64	5	25	29	.251	.396	.316
vs. Right-Handed Batters			230	53	10	12	37	.230	.435	.265
Home	4-1	2.53	166	33	4	10	26	.199	.343	.243
Road	5-5	4.48	319	84	11	27	40	.263	.451	.317
Grass	3-4	4.87	255	69	8	22	28	.271	.463	.324
Artificial Turf	6-2	2.67	230	48	7	15	38	.209	.361	.256
Day	3-2	3.96	199	50	7	19	28	.251	.442	.312
Night	6-4	3.66	286	67	8	18	38	.234	.395	.278
April	0-0	3.60	18	3	1	1	1	.167	.333	.211
May	1-2	5.96	101	29	6	10	20	.287	.505	.348
June	3-2	4.19	148	38	5	13	16	.257	.459	.311
July	3-0	2.05	108	20	2	7	9	.185	.306	.235
August			0	0	0	0	0	.000	.000	.000
Sept./Oct.	2-2	3.14	110	27	1	6	20	.245	.391	.282
Leading Off Inn.			122	34	2	14	14	.279	.443	.353
Bases Empty			298	73	8	28	39	.245	.413	.310
Runners On			187	44	7	9	27	.235	.417	.264
Runners/Scor. Pos.			88	24	3	5	16	.273	.466	.296
Runners On/2 Out			81	22	3	6	12	.272	.494	.322
Scor. Pos./2 Out			47	14	2	3	9	.298	.574	.340
Late Inning Pressure			9	4	0	0	1	.444	.556	.444
Leading Off			3	1	0	0	0	.333	.333	.333
Bases Empty			6	2	0	0	0	.333	.333	.333
Runners On			3	2	0	0	1	.667	1.000	.667
Runners/Scor. Pos.			1	0	0	0	1	.000	.000	.000
First 9 Batters			188	47	5	13	29	.250	.426	.293
Second 9 Batters			187	41	8	15	28	.219	.412	.277
All Batters Thereafter			110	29	2	9	9	.264	.400	.317

Loves to face: Darrell Evans (.067, 1-for-15, 5 SO)
Hates to face: Ron Kittle (.500, 8-for-16, 4 HR)
Ground outs-to-air outs ratio: 0.68 last season, 1.00 for career. . . . Additional statistics: 6 double-play ground outs in 76 opportunities, 29 doubles, 5 triples allowed in 128.2 innings last season. . . . Allowed 8 first-inning runs in 23 starts last season. . . . Batting support: 5.22 runs per start, 9th-highest average in A.L. (minimum: 15 GS). . . . Won-lost breakdown: 8–1 against teams that finished below .500, 1–5 against teams that finished at or above .500. . . . Career rate of one home run every 35 at bats by right-handed batters, one every 48 by left-handers. . . . Has faced 2,871 batters with runners on base, highest total among active pitchers who have never balked. . . . Opponents' batting average in Late-Inning Pressure Situations, year by year starting in 1981: .226, .276, .289, .344, .444.

Bryan Clark

Cleveland Indians	W–L	ERA	AB	H	HR	BB	SO	BA	SA	OBA
Season	3-4	6.32	251	78	8	34	24	.311	.470	.390
vs. Left-Handed Batters			82	31	4	10	12	.378	.573	.446
vs. Right-Handed Batters			169	47	4	24	12	.278	.420	.364
Home	1-0	5.52	125	39	3	13	7	.312	.440	.374
Road	2-4	7.11	126	39	5	21	17	.310	.500	.405
Grass	1-3	6.79	212	69	7	30	18	.325	.491	.406
Artificial Turf	2-1	4.09	39	9	1	4	6	.231	.359	.302
Day	0-1	7.41	63	20	2	12	4	.317	.524	.416
Night	3-3	5.91	188	58	6	22	20	.309	.452	.381
April			0	0	0	0	0	.000	.000	.000
May	1-1	5.68	52	16	2	7	2	.308	.462	.390
June	0-0	5.54	52	17	2	4	8	.327	.500	.362
July	0-1	5.40	30	7	1	7	3	.233	.433	.378
August	0-1	6.38	75	24	3	8	6	.320	.520	.386
Sept./Oct.	2-1	8.71	42	14	0	8	5	.333	.381	.440
Leading Off Inn.			56	13	0	7	5	.232	.286	.317
Bases Empty			130	36	2	19	13	.277	.392	.369
Runners On			121	42	6	15	11	.347	.554	.413
Runners/Scor. Pos.			72	27	4	6	8	.375	.639	.413
Runners On/2 Out			53	18	1	3	4	.340	.434	.375
Scor. Pos./2 Out			35	13	1	0	4	.371	.514	.371
Late Inning Pressure			42	11	1	7	5	.262	.357	.360
Leading Off			9	3	0	3	0	.333	.444	.500
Bases Empty			19	5	0	3	1	.263	.316	.364
Runners On			23	6	1	4	4	.261	.391	.357
Runners/Scor. Pos.			11	2	1	4	1	.182	.455	.375
First 9 Batters			170	55	5	21	17	.324	.488	.394
Second 9 Batters			72	19	3	12	7	.264	.431	.369
All Batters Thereafter			9	4	0	1	0	.444	.444	.500

Loves to face: Willie Wilson (0-for-9)
Hates to face: Jeff Burroughs (.556, 5-for-9, 2 HR)
Ground outs-to-air outs ratio: 1.51 last season, 1.72 for career. . . . Additional statistics: 10 double-play ground outs in 65 opportunities, 12 doubles, 2 triples allowed in 62.2 innings last season. . . . Opponents have batted .341 and .340 with runners on base and two outs in the past two years. . . . Came to majors in 1981 looking like he would be a specialist against left-handers, but has had trouble with everyone in recent years. Annual opponents' batting averages: left-handers .191, .203, .298, .314, .378; right-handers .193, .256, .248, .358, .278. . . . Started three games last year, didn't get to fifth inning in any, and had a 9.26 ERA in those games. . . . Allowed a grand slam to Reggie Jackson last season; Reggie's last three grand slams have come against left-handers.

Mark Clear

Boston Red Sox	W–L	ERA	AB	H	HR	BB	SO	BA	SA	OBA
Season	1-3	3.72	200	45	1	50	55	.225	.275	.389
vs. Left-Handed Batters			86	21	0	29	27	.244	.256	.437
vs. Right-Handed Batters			114	24	1	21	28	.211	.289	.348
Home	1-0	3.09	81	16	0	18	23	.198	.210	.343
Road	0-3	4.18	119	29	1	32	32	.244	.319	.419
Grass	1-2	3.69	168	38	1	38	46	.226	.280	.377
Artificial Turf	0-1	3.86	32	7	0	12	9	.219	.250	.444
Day	0-1	4.37	88	21	0	21	28	.239	.295	.387
Night	1-2	3.27	112	24	1	29	27	.214	.259	.390
April	0-0	5.63	35	10	0	8	9	.286	.343	.432
May	1-1	1.69	36	7	0	8	14	.194	.194	.370
June	0-0	4.82	34	7	0	11	5	.206	.235	.413
July	0-0	0.98	61	10	0	10	20	.164	.197	.288
August	0-2	11.37	22	8	1	12	6	.364	.591	.571
Sept./Oct.	0-0	3.00	12	3	0	1	1	.250	.250	.308
Leading Off Inn.			39	10	0	7	7	.256	.256	.370
Bases Empty			75	17	0	19	20	.227	.253	.389
Runners On			125	28	1	31	35	.224	.288	.389
Runners/Scor. Pos.			90	21	1	24	27	.233	.322	.408
Runners On/2 Out			52	9	1	14	18	.173	.250	.348
Scor. Pos./2 Out			44	7	1	12	15	.159	.250	.339
Late Inning Pressure			51	15	1	21	10	.294	.431	.500
Leading Off			11	4	0	2	0	.364	.364	.462
Bases Empty			19	7	0	5	1	.368	.421	.520
Runners On			32	8	1	16	9	.250	.438	.490
Runners/Scor. Pos.			25	8	1	13	6	.320	.560	.537
First 9 Batters			176	39	1	48	48	.222	.267	.396
Second 9 Batters			24	6	0	2	7	.250	.333	.333
All Batters Thereafter			0	0	0	0	0	.000	.000	.000

Loves to face: Reggie Jackson (.083, 1-for-12, 8 SO)
Hates to face: Pete O'Brien (.800, 4-for-5)
Ground outs-to-air outs ratio: 1.15 last season, 0.85 for career. . . . Additional statistics: 8 double-play ground outs in 70 opportunities, 7 doubles, 0 triples allowed in 55.2 innings last season. . . . Rate of 8.89 strikeouts per nine innings was 2d-highest among A.L. relievers (minimum: 30 relief games); his career rate of 8.86 ranks 3d among active pitchers (minimum: 250 SO) behind Dwight Gooden and Nolan Ryan. . . . One extra-base hit allowed in 86 at bats vs. left-handed batters last season was 2d-lowest rate in A.L. over past 11 years (minimum: 100 BFP); hasn't allowed a home run to a lefty in 226 at bats since Kirk Gibson hit one on Sept. 18, 1983. . . . Rate of 8.08 walks per nine innings was highest in majors in '85; career average of 6.33 is highest among active pitchers (minimum: 200 BB).

Roger Clemens

Boston Red Sox	W–L	ERA	AB	H	HR	BB	SO	BA	SA	OBA
Season	7-5	3.29	364	83	5	37	74	.228	.299	.303
vs. Left-Handed Batters			202	50	1	18	33	.248	.297	.308
vs. Right-Handed Batters			162	33	4	19	41	.204	.302	.297
Home	4-2	3.73	192	48	3	16	39	.250	.313	.316
Road	3-3	2.83	172	35	2	21	35	.203	.285	.289
Grass	5-3	3.23	261	64	3	25	55	.245	.295	.316
Artificial Turf	2-2	3.45	103	19	2	12	19	.184	.311	.270
Day	2-3	4.04	133	33	2	16	26	.248	.308	.333
Night	5-2	2.87	231	50	3	21	48	.216	.294	.285
April	2-2	3.10	104	19	2	11	25	.183	.240	.261
May	4-2	3.65	166	39	3	15	36	.235	.331	.310
June	0-0	3.60	40	11	0	4	5	.275	.300	.333
July	0-0	4.50	17	8	0	1	1	.471	.529	.474
August	1-1	1.64	37	6	0	6	7	.162	.216	.279
Sept./Oct.			0	0	0	0	0	.000	.000	.000
Leading Off Inn.			96	27	1	8	16	.281	.344	.343
Bases Empty			222	52	2	21	42	.234	.288	.309
Runners On			142	31	3	16	32	.218	.317	.294
Runners/Scor. Pos.			84	14	1	10	23	.167	.238	.250
Runners On/2 Out			58	9	1	7	13	.155	.259	.246
Scor. Pos./2 Out			41	8	1	4	8	.195	.341	.267
Late Inning Pressure			17	7	1	2	1	.412	.588	.474
Leading Off			5	2	0	1	0	.400	.400	.500
Bases Empty			11	4	1	2	0	.364	.636	.462
Runners On			6	3	0	0	1	.500	.500	.500
Runners/Scor. Pos.			3	1	0	0	1	.333	.333	.333
First 9 Batters			117	28	1	15	32	.239	.282	.341
Second 9 Batters			120	25	2	12	18	.208	.275	.276
All Batters Thereafter			127	30	2	10	24	.236	.339	.292

Loves to face: Jim Gantner (0-for-10)
Hates to face: Robin Yount (.625, 5-for-8, 2 HR)
Ground outs-to-air outs ratio: 0.96 last season, 0.97 for career. . . . Additional statistics: 4 double-play ground outs in 68 opportunities, 9 doubles, 1 triple allowed in 98.1 innings last season. . . . Allowed 0 first-inning runs in 15 starts, lowest rate in A.L. last season (minimum: 15 GS). . . . Batting support: 4.07 runs per start. . . . Disabled from July 8 to Aug. 3, and again from Aug. 21 to end of season. . . . In brief career, has allowed 14 home runs in 409 at bats vs. right-handers, but only four in 493 at bats vs. left-handers. . . . Staying power is suspect: .339 opponents' batting average in Late-Inning Pressure Situations in his two years with Sox. Has struck out only four of 62 batters in LIP, compared to one for every 4.7 batters faced otherwise. . . . Drafted but not signed by Mets in June 1981.

Stu Cliburn

California Angels	W–L	ERA	AB	H	HR	BB	SO	BA	SA	OBA
Season	9-3	2.09	361	87	5	26	48	.241	.332	.292
vs. Left-Handed Batters			148	43	5	18	16	.291	.432	.365
vs. Right-Handed Batters			213	44	0	8	32	.207	.263	.238
Home	7-2	2.36	182	44	2	9	24	.242	.313	.281
Road	2-1	1.82	179	43	3	17	24	.240	.352	.303
Grass	8-3	2.10	280	67	5	18	31	.239	.336	.287
Artificial Turf	1-0	2.05	81	20	0	8	17	.247	.321	.311
Day	5-2	1.59	141	29	2	6	17	.206	.270	.242
Night	4-1	2.43	220	58	3	20	31	.264	.373	.324
April	1-0	2.25	29	5	0	2	5	.172	.172	.226
May	0-1	1.32	52	15	0	1	7	.288	.346	.302
June	2-0	2.18	74	16	2	11	2	.216	.365	.318
July	1-1	3.75	44	14	0	8	5	.318	.432	.426
August	4-0	0.88	108	21	1	3	20	.194	.250	.214
Sept./Oct.	1-1	3.86	54	16	2	1	9	.296	.444	.309
Leading Off Inn.			83	25	2	6	10	.301	.434	.356
Bases Empty			194	46	3	13	22	.237	.345	.288
Runners On			167	41	2	13	26	.246	.317	.297
Runners/Scor. Pos.			101	25	1	10	17	.248	.337	.310
Runners On/2 Out			69	15	1	6	11	.217	.319	.280
Scor. Pos./2 Out			45	9	1	6	7	.200	.356	.294
Late Inning Pressure			189	42	3	19	24	.222	.328	.297
Leading Off			48	16	1	3	7	.333	.438	.385
Bases Empty			108	28	1	8	14	.259	.343	.316
Runners On			81	14	2	11	10	.173	.309	.272
Runners/Scor. Pos.			47	8	1	10	7	.170	.340	.316
First 9 Batters			285	72	4	20	38	.253	.340	.302
Second 9 Batters			71	14	1	6	10	.197	.296	.260
All Batters Thereafter			5	1	0	0	0	.200	.400	.200

Loves to face: Robin Yount (0-for-3, 2 SO)
Hates to face: Jim Sundberg (3-for-3)
Ground outs-to-air outs ratio: 1.24 last season, 1.22 for career. . . . Additional statistics: 11 double-play ground outs in 77 opportunities, 14 doubles, 2 triples allowed in 99.0 innings last season. . . . Ranked 3d among A.L. relief pitchers with a 2.09 ERA last season (minimum: 30 relief games). . . . Faced 227 right-handed batters last season without allowing a home run, highest total in A.L. since 1975, when Sparky Lyle faced 256. . . . Persevered through five years in Pirates' minors (26–31, 4.03 ERA) and three more in Angels' system (19–23, 3.96) before reaching majors for one inning in September 1984. . . . Given all that, he was a rather unlikely candidate to pitch 54 percent of his 1985 innings in Late-Inning Pressure Situations. . . . Faced nine or more batters in all six of his saves.

Jaime Cocanower

Milwaukee Brewers	W–L	ERA	AB	H	HR	BB	SO	BA	SA	OBA
Season	6-8	4.33	445	122	6	73	44	.274	.357	.383
vs. Left-Handed Batters			233	67	2	45	12	.288	.365	.404
vs. Right-Handed Batters			212	55	4	28	32	.259	.349	.360
Home	5-3	4.02	238	66	3	34	25	.277	.366	.367
Road	1-5	4.70	207	56	3	39	19	.271	.348	.400
Grass	6-5	3.89	348	97	4	52	36	.279	.356	.380
Artificial Turf	0-3	5.88	97	25	2	21	8	.258	.361	.393
Day	2-2	4.21	143	43	0	15	10	.301	.336	.374
Night	4-6	4.39	302	79	6	58	34	.262	.368	.387
April			0	0	0	0	0	.000	.000	.000
May			0	0	0	0	0	.000	.000	.000
June	1-0	2.36	95	19	3	19	13	.200	.347	.339
July	1-1	5.89	72	21	0	11	6	.292	.347	.381
August	2-2	5.40	98	28	1	17	11	.286	.367	.397
Sept./Oct.	2-5	4.31	180	54	2	26	14	.300	.361	.400
Leading Off Inn.			100	29	0	17	14	.290	.340	.398
Bases Empty			212	65	5	31	21	.307	.415	.410
Runners On			233	57	1	42	23	.245	.305	.359
Runners/Scor. Pos.			146	33	1	29	17	.226	.281	.346
Runners On/2 Out			93	23	0	17	12	.247	.301	.364
Scor. Pos./2 Out			61	16	0	14	10	.262	.328	.400
Late Inning Pressure			42	10	1	6	6	.238	.357	.333
Leading Off			12	2	0	1	3	.167	.167	.231
Bases Empty			28	6	0	3	5	.214	.250	.290
Runners On			14	4	1	3	1	.286	.571	.412
Runners/Scor. Pos.			8	3	1	3	1	.375	.875	.545
First 9 Batters			177	51	3	25	21	.288	.384	.385
Second 9 Batters			136	30	1	27	14	.221	.279	.361
All Batters Thereafter			132	41	2	21	9	.311	.402	.403

Loves to face: George Brett (0-for-9)
Hates to face: Dick Schofield (.667, 4-for-6, 1 HR)
Ground outs-to-air outs ratio: 2.15 last season (8th-highest in A.L.), 2.38 for career. . . . Additional statistics: 19 double-play ground outs in 130 opportunities, 19 doubles, 0 triples allowed in 116.1 innings last season. . . . Allowed 12 first-inning runs in 15 starts last season. . . . Batting support: 4.47 runs per start. . . . Average of 5.65 walks per nine innings was 4th-highest among A.L. starters (minimum: 15 GS). . . . Career rate of 3.28 strikeouts per nine innings is 6th-lowest among active pitchers (minimum: 250 innings). . . . Has faced 683 right-handed batters in his career without allowing a triple. . . . Threw a wild pitch in each of eight consecutive games in June and July, a feat even more impressive when you consider that he pitched less than four innings in six of those games.

Chris Codiroli

Oakland As	W–L	ERA	AB	H	HR	BB	SO	BA	SA	OBA
Season	14-14	4.46	881	228	23	78	111	.259	.403	.319
vs. Left-Handed Batters			479	119	10	32	61	.248	.380	.294
vs. Right-Handed Batters			402	109	13	46	50	.271	.430	.346
Home	9-4	3.60	416	96	12	43	52	.231	.373	.303
Road	5-10	5.28	465	132	11	35	59	.284	.430	.333
Grass	12-11	4.41	731	187	20	69	90	.256	.397	.321
Artificial Turf	2-3	4.70	150	41	3	9	21	.273	.433	.307
Day	8-1	3.80	267	61	9	28	32	.228	.393	.301
Night	6-13	4.76	614	167	14	50	79	.272	.407	.326
April	2-1	3.21	105	22	1	9	15	.210	.276	.272
May	4-1	4.64	161	38	4	15	21	.236	.391	.309
June	2-1	4.95	145	43	5	13	18	.297	.469	.352
July	0-5	3.86	163	41	3	15	17	.252	.374	.317
August	2-2	4.46	146	36	4	16	21	.247	.397	.319
Sept./Oct.	4-4	5.35	161	48	6	10	19	.298	.472	.330
Leading Off Inn.			214	55	7	25	26	.257	.439	.340
Bases Empty			504	135	16	48	62	.268	.435	.334
Runners On			377	93	7	30	49	.247	.361	.298
Runners/Scor. Pos.			200	58	4	22	31	.290	.405	.348
Runners On/2 Out			156	39	1	19	19	.250	.327	.331
Scor. Pos./2 Out			94	25	0	16	15	.266	.319	.373
Late Inning Pressure			83	19	3	11	9	.229	.398	.319
Leading Off			21	5	1	6	2	.238	.476	.407
Bases Empty			51	12	1	7	4	.235	.392	.328
Runners On			32	7	2	4	5	.219	.406	.306
Runners/Scor. Pos.			15	3	0	4	3	.200	.200	.368
First 9 Batters			295	68	6	33	41	.231	.339	.308
Second 9 Batters			300	79	7	17	38	.263	.413	.301
All Batters Thereafter			286	81	10	28	32	.283	.458	.347

Loves to face: Tom Brookens (.071, 1-for-14)
Hates to face: Andre Thornton (6-for-6, 1 HR)
Ground outs-to-air outs ratio: 1.25 last season, 1.34 for career. . . . Additional statistics: 14 double-play ground outs in 167 opportunities, 46 doubles (tied for 6th-most in A.L.), 6 triples allowed in 226.0 innings last season. . . . Allowed 20 first-inning runs in 37 starts last season. . . . Batting support: 4.78 runs per start. . . . Tied for 2d in A.L. with eight day-game wins. . . . Career record of 18–9 in day games (including 12 wins in his last 13 decisions), 15–23 in night games. But all four complete games last season came in night games. . . . His error on July 8 snapped Oakland's streak of nine straight errorless games, a team record. He was also the last guy to make an error before the streak began. . . . Career record of 19–12 at Oakland Coliseum, 14–20 in road games. . . . Opposing batting average of .304 with runners in scoring position is 2d-highest among active pitchers (minimum: 500 PA).

Joe Cowley

New York Yankees	W–L	ERA	AB	H	HR	BB	SO	BA	SA	OBA
Season	12-6	3.95	588	132	29	85	97	.224	.412	.327
vs. Left-Handed Batters			338	77	15	60	48	.228	.399	.347
vs. Right-Handed Batters			250	55	14	25	49	.220	.428	.297
Home	4-2	3.25	245	53	10	35	45	.216	.363	.317
Road	8-4	4.48	343	79	19	50	52	.230	.446	.333
Grass	10-3	3.39	491	107	18	74	89	.218	.363	.325
Artificial Turf	2-3	7.03	97	25	11	11	8	.258	.660	.333
Day	5-3	3.15	246	51	10	44	41	.207	.366	.331
Night	7-3	4.55	342	81	19	41	56	.237	.444	.323
April	0-1	4.19	66	14	4	12	11	.212	.424	.329
May	4-1	3.41	116	25	4	14	23	.216	.336	.305
June	2-1	3.63	60	11	3	9	15	.183	.333	.300
July	3-1	4.39	102	23	6	12	5	.225	.461	.310
August	1-1	4.28	102	26	4	15	18	.255	.451	.356
Sept./Oct.	2-1	3.86	142	33	8	23	25	.232	.437	.343
Leading Off Inn.			153	36	7	15	19	.235	.392	.316
Bases Empty			366	90	19	44	54	.246	.440	.335
Runners On			222	42	10	41	43	.189	.365	.313
Runners/Scor. Pos.			122	18	4	26	25	.148	.303	.289
Runners On/2 Out			100	21	6	18	24	.210	.440	.331
Scor. Pos./2 Out			62	10	2	15	18	.161	.339	.325
Late Inning Pressure			67	15	3	7	12	.224	.373	.307
Leading Off			20	7	0	1	2	.350	.400	.409
Bases Empty			48	13	2	1	8	.271	.417	.300
Runners On			19	2	1	6	4	.105	.263	.320
Runners/Scor. Pos.			8	0	0	5	2	.000	.000	.385
First 9 Batters			209	43	9	43	33	.206	.368	.344
Second 9 Batters			192	40	8	21	34	.208	.359	.292
All Batters Thereafter			187	49	12	21	30	.262	.513	.341

Loves to face: Kirby Puckett (.083, 1-for-12, 6 SO)
Hates to face: Frank White (2-for-2, 2 HR)
Ground outs-to-air outs ratio: 0.76 last season, 0.74 for career. . . . Additional statistics: 9 double-play ground outs in 115 opportunities, 17 doubles, 3 triples allowed in 159.2 innings last season. . . . Allowed 15 first-inning runs in 26 starts last season. . . . Batting support: 5.15 runs per start, 10th-highest average in A.L. (minimum: 15 GS). . . . Yankees may miss Cowley against some "big guns" on division rivals. Career vs. Cowley: Armas .067 (1-for-15), Buckner .056 (1-for-18), Murray .071 (1-for-14), Ripken .067 (1-for-15). . . . Has led A.L. pitchers in batting average with runners in scoring position in each of past two seasons. . . . Career winning percentage of .688 (22–10) ranks 5th among active pitchers with at least 20 wins. . . . Career rate of one home run allowed every 6.28 innings is 3d-worst among active pitchers (minimum: 20 HR).

Steve Crawford

Boston Red Sox	W–L	ERA	AB	H	HR	BB	SO	BA	SA	OBA
Season	6-5	3.76	357	103	5	28	58	.289	.409	.338
vs. Left-Handed Batters			183	55	2	16	26	.301	.421	.353
vs. Right-Handed Batters			174	48	3	12	32	.276	.397	.321
Home	2-1	5.94	138	45	2	10	25	.326	.442	.372
Road	4-4	2.50	219	58	3	18	33	.265	.388	.317
Grass	5-4	4.19	295	90	4	21	48	.305	.417	.351
Artificial Turf	1-1	2.00	62	13	1	7	10	.210	.371	.278
Day	3-1	4.36	127	36	2	5	21	.283	.425	.311
Night	3-4	3.41	230	67	3	23	37	.291	.400	.352
April	2-2	5.00	72	21	2	2	9	.292	.431	.311
May	1-0	1.84	50	10	0	3	8	.200	.260	.245
June	1-0	0.00	33	7	0	2	10	.212	.273	.257
July	0-0	4.76	43	13	1	5	8	.302	.419	.375
August	1-2	4.03	89	29	1	10	13	.326	.483	.382
Sept./Oct.	1-1	5.28	70	23	1	6	10	.329	.457	.382
Leading Off Inn.			77	21	0	4	11	.273	.351	.309
Bases Empty			173	47	4	9	29	.272	.399	.308
Runners On			184	56	1	19	29	.304	.418	.364
Runners/Scor. Pos.			119	37	0	13	21	.311	.420	.370
Runners On/2 Out			75	21	1	8	17	.280	.373	.349
Scor. Pos./2 Out			50	15	0	8	12	.300	.360	.397
Late Inning Pressure			129	39	2	18	25	.302	.426	.383
Leading Off			28	9	0	2	5	.321	.429	.367
Bases Empty			61	18	1	4	11	.295	.426	.338
Runners On			68	21	1	14	14	.309	.426	.417
Runners/Scor. Pos.			44	16	0	10	10	.364	.477	.464
First 9 Batters			278	85	4	22	49	.306	.432	.354
Second 9 Batters			67	15	1	5	7	.224	.343	.274
All Batters Thereafter			12	3	0	1	2	.250	.250	.308

Loves to face: Cliff Johnson (0-for-11, 5 SO)
Hates to face: Andre Thornton (.556, 5-for-9, 2 HR)
Ground outs-to-air outs ratio: 1.51 last season, 1.80 for career. ... Additional statistics: 13 double-play ground outs in 91 opportunities, 22 doubles, 3 triples allowed in 91.0 innings last season. ... Allowed 46 runs in relief last season, 6th-highest total in A.L. ... Has faced 561 batters with runners on base during his career, and has not committed a balk. ... Career home run average: one for every 59 at bats vs. left-handed hitters, one for every 32 at bats vs. right-handers. ... Dear John McNamara: This guy is *not* your bullpen stopper. He has retired only 19 of 42 batters faced during his career in Late-Inning Pressure Situations with two outs and runners in scoring position, our most detailed and crucial category. Opposing batters have hit .441 with five extra-base hits. Sincerely, Elias Sports Bureau.

Keith Creel

Cleveland Indians	W–L	ERA	AB	H	HR	BB	SO	BA	SA	OBA
Season	2-5	4.79	247	73	7	23	31	.296	.466	.354
vs. Left-Handed Batters			131	39	4	8	17	.298	.473	.340
vs. Right-Handed Batters			116	34	3	15	14	.293	.457	.368
Home	1-4	5.35	145	45	4	9	18	.310	.490	.346
Road	1-1	4,05	102	28	3	14	13	.275	.431	.364
Grass	2-5	4.95	240	72	7	22	30	.300	.471	.357
Artificial Turf	0-0	0.00	7	1	0	1	1	.143	.286	.250
Day	1-1	3.60	72	19	2	9	8	.264	.444	.345
Night	1-4	5.36	175	54	5	14	23	.309	.474	.358
April			0	0	0	0	0	.000	.000	.000
May	0-3	4.88	109	33	5	12	11	.303	.486	.360
June	0-2	7.56	72	26	2	8	8	.361	.583	.427
July			0	0	0	0	0	.000	.000	.000
August			0	0	0	0	0	.000	.000	.000
Sept./Oct.	2-0	2.04	66	14	0	3	12	.212	.303	.257
Leading Off Inn.			59	15	2	4	5	.254	.390	.313
Bases Empty			137	40	5	11	13	.292	.460	.349
Runners On			110	33	2	12	18	.300	.473	.359
Runners/Scor. Pos.			61	12	0	8	10	.197	.295	.280
Runners On/2 Out			42	11	1	9	8	.262	.429	.404
Scor. Pos./2 Out			31	7	0	6	5	.226	.323	.368
Late Inning Pressure			20	4	1	1	3	.200	.400	.227
Leading Off			6	1	0	0	0	.167	.333	.167
Bases Empty			14	4	1	0	1	.286	.571	.286
Runners On			6	0	0	1	2	.000	.000	.125
Runners/Scor. Pos.			5	0	0	1	1	.000	.000	.143
First 9 Batters			110	34	4	13	16	.309	.545	.372
Second 9 Batters			80	26	2	4	8	.325	.450	.365
All Batters Thereafter			57	13	1	6	7	.228	.333	.302

Loves to face: George Wright (.143, 1-for-7, 2 SO)
Hates to face: Wayne Tolleson (3-for-3)
Ground outs-to-air outs ratio: 0.49 last season (2d-lowest in A.L.), 0.78 for career. ... Additional statistics: 2 double-play ground outs in 58 opportunities (4th-lowest rate in A.L.), 15 doubles, 3 triples allowed in 62.0 innings last season. ... Has finished 15 games in career, but has no saves. ... Faced five batters with the bases loaded last season, and no runs were scored. ... Career average of one home run allowed every 6.03 innings is 2d-worst among active pitchers (minimum: 20 HR). ... Had allowed 21 of 25 home runs to right-handed batters in two previous major-league seasons. ... Opposing hitters have a career .301 batting average. Only two pitchers active last season have career averages above .300 and have faced more batters than Creel: Mike Morgan and Don Schulze.

Danny Darwin

Milwaukee Brewers	W–L	ERA	AB	H	HR	BB	SO	BA	SA	OBA
Season	8-18	3.80	834	212	34	65	125	.254	.432	.308
vs. Left-Handed Batters			418	113	17	46	50	.270	.459	.343
vs. Right-Handed Batters			416	99	17	19	75	.238	.404	.270
Home	2-10	2.85	362	89	12	31	62	.246	.403	.305
Road	6-8	4.54	472	123	22	34	63	.261	.453	.311
Grass	7-16	3.56	750	186	28	62	111	.248	.416	.305
Artificial Turf	1-2	6.10	84	26	6	3	14	.310	.571	.333
Day	2-10	4.11	298	77	14	25	50	.258	.453	.315
Night	6-8	3.64	536	135	20	40	75	.252	.420	.304
April	2-1	2.73	110	19	2	4	10	.173	.291	.202
May	1-3	5.22	157	42	7	15	21	.268	.478	.329
June	3-3	3.33	177	45	8	14	29	.254	.435	.316
July	0-5	2.93	173	49	6	17	25	.283	.451	.342
August	1-3	3.24	126	29	6	7	25	.230	.405	.276
Sept./Oct.	1-3	6.26	91	28	5	8	15	.308	.516	.352
Leading Off Inn.			210	52	9	12	27	.248	.448	.288
Bases Empty			515	121	19	36	73	.235	.402	.289
Runners On			319	91	15	29	52	.285	.480	.338
Runners/Scor. Pos.			187	47	6	20	31	.251	.406	.313
Runners On/2 Out			141	35	6	15	20	.248	.440	.325
Scor. Pos./2 Out			89	21	5	12	14	.236	.472	.333
Late Inning Pressure			145	40	4	14	21	.276	.428	.333
Leading Off			40	11	1	1	7	.275	.425	.293
Bases Empty			91	27	2	4	12	.297	.451	.326
Runners On			54	13	2	10	9	.241	.389	.343
Runners/Scor. Pos.			33	5	0	7	6	.152	.212	.279
First 9 Batters			291	70	15	20	58	.241	.447	.286
Second 9 Batters			231	68	12	17	27	.294	.502	.349
All Batters Thereafter			312	74	7	28	40	.237	.365	.298

Loves to face: Garth Iorg (0-for-16, 6 SO)
Hates to face: Roy Smalley (.391, 9-for-23, 4 HR)
Ground outs-to-air outs ratio: 0.81 last season, 0.87 for career. ... Additional statistics: 15 double-play ground outs in 142 opportunities, 38 doubles, 4 triples allowed in 217.2 innings last season. ... Total of 76 extra-base hits allowed was 10th-highest in A.L. ... Allowed 12 first-inning runs in 29 starts last season. ... Batting support: 3.38 runs per start, 3d-lowest average in A.L. (minimum: 15 GS). ... Only A.L. pitcher to lose 10 home games last season, but ERA at County Stadium was A.L.'s 6th-best home-game mark. ... Has faced 98 batters in bases-loaded situations during career without allowing a grand salami, 2d to Andujar (124) among active A.L. pitchers. ... Opposing batters have hit for a higher average with runners on base than with the bases empty in each of his eight seasons in majors. Career averages: .286 with runners on, .226 with bases empty.

Joel Davis

Chicago White Sox	W–L	ERA	AB	H	HR	BB	SO	BA	SA	OBA
Season	3-3	4.16	277	71	6	26	37	.256	.386	.320
vs. Left-Handed Batters			156	45	2	12	18	.288	.404	.335
vs. Right-Handed Batters			121	26	4	14	19	.215	.364	.301
Home	2-1	3.97	130	32	3	16	20	.246	.369	.331
Road	1-2	4.34	147	39	3	10	17	.265	.401	.310
Grass	3-1	3.67	207	51	5	22	31	.246	.372	.319
Artificial Turf	0-2	5.71	70	20	1	4	6	.286	.429	.324
Day	1-1	4.91	100	26	3	8	16	.260	.420	.315
Night	2-2	3.74	177	45	3	18	21	.254	.367	.323
April			0	0	0	0	0	.000	.000	.000
May			0	0	0	0	0	.000	.000	.000
June			0	0	0	0	0	.000	.000	.000
July			0	0	0	0	0	.000	.000	.000
August	1-2	4.73	122	30	2	15	19	.246	.369	.331
Sept./Oct.	2-1	3.69	155	41	4	11	18	.265	.400	.311
Leading Off Inn.			69	15	1	7	12	.217	.333	.289
Bases Empty			165	41	3	15	27	.248	.376	.315
Runners On			112	30	3	11	10	.268	.402	.328
Runners/Scor. Pos.			55	16	1	7	5	.291	.400	.359
Runners On/2 Out			49	10	0	7	4	.204	.245	.304
Scor. Pos./2 Out			26	6	0	5	2	.231	.269	.355
Late Inning Pressure			32	10	1	5	7	.313	.531	.405
Leading Off			9	3	0	2	3	.333	.444	.455
Bases Empty			20	4	0	3	6	.200	.300	.304
Runners On			12	6	1	2	1	.500	.917	.571
Runners/Scor. Pos.			10	6	1	1	1	.600	1.100	.636
First 9 Batters			97	18	0	10	13	.186	.268	.259
Second 9 Batters			89	24	3	3	11	.270	.382	.298
All Batters Thereafter			91	29	3	13	13	.319	.516	.404

Loves to face: Charlie Moore (0-for-6, 2 SO)
Hates to face: Mike Gallego (.750, 3-for-4, 1 HR)
Ground outs-to-air outs ratio: 1.11 last season, his first in majors. ... Additional statistics: 3 double-play ground outs in 49 opportunities, 10 doubles, 4 triples allowed in 71.1 innings last season. ... Allowed 4 first-inning runs in 11 starts last season. ... Batting support: 4.91 runs per start. ... Defensive support was excellent as well: allowed only one unearned run. ... Made major-league debut at age 20, but wasn't even the youngest pitcher on his team. Ed Correa was youngest player in majors last season—this from the team that gave the world the baby staff of Britt Burns, Steve Trout, and Richard Dotson in 1980. ... Earned run average was 2.79 for first five innings of each of his 12 starts, 9.18 from the sixth inning on.

Ron Davis

Minnesota Twins	W–L	ERA	AB	H	HR	BB	SO	BA	SA	OBA
Season	2-6	3.48	239	55	7	35	72	.230	.377	.333
vs. Left-Handed Batters			116	27	3	20	34	.233	.379	.343
vs. Right-Handed Batters			123	28	4	15	38	.228	.374	.324
Home	1-0	1.97	122	28	2	17	42	.230	.320	.321
Road	1-6	4.96	117	27	5	18	30	.231	.436	.345
Grass	1-4	3.81	92	20	3	10	23	.217	.370	.318
Artificial Turf	1-2	3.26	147	35	4	25	49	.238	.381	.343
Day	0-0	2.81	61	14	1	9	22	.230	.328	.324
Night	2-6	3.70	178	41	6	26	50	.230	.393	.336
April	1-1	5.40	23	5	1	6	7	.217	.348	.400
May	0-4	7.43	53	14	3	10	18	.264	.509	.388
June	0-0	2.00	31	5	0	4	7	.161	.290	.270
July	1-0	0.00	40	7	0	4	14	.175	.200	.250
August	0-0	2.61	39	10	1	3	12	.256	.333	.310
Sept./Oct.	0-1	3.14	53	14	2	8	14	.264	.472	.355
Leading Off Inn.			35	10	0	4	11	.286	.314	.390
Bases Empty			87	22	2	8	22	.253	.425	.330
Runners On			152	33	5	27	50	.217	.349	.335
Runners/Scor. Pos.			118	27	5	20	41	.229	.398	.336
Runners On/2 Out			66	15	3	17	22	.227	.424	.393
Scor. Pos./2 Out			59	14	3	14	19	.237	.458	.384
Late Inning Pressure			152	32	4	17	43	.211	.342	.303
Leading Off			23	5	0	3	8	.217	.217	.357
Bases Empty			63	16	2	3	16	.254	.476	.309
Runners On			89	16	2	14	27	.180	.247	.299
Runners/Scor. Pos.			69	14	2	11	21	.203	.290	.313
First 9 Batters			234	53	7	34	71	.226	.376	.327
Second 9 Batters			5	2	0	1	1	.400	.400	.571
All Batters Thereafter			0	0	0	0	0	.000	.000	.000

Loves to face: Dwayne Murphy (0-for-12, 6 SO)
Hates to face: Joe Carter (.625, 5-for-8, 1 HR)
Ground outs-to-air outs ratio: 1.41 last season (highest since 1.59 in his rookie year of '79; 0.64 in '84), 0.93 for career. ... Additional statistics: 4 double-play ground outs in 67 opportunities, 6 doubles, 4 triples allowed in 64.2 innings last season. ... Average of 10.02 strikeouts per nine innings was highest among A.L. relievers (minimum: 30 relief games). ... Has finished 74.9 percent of his relief appearances, 6th-highest career average among active pitchers (minimum: 50 GF). ... Excellent season in Late-Inning Pressure Situations in '85 followed three consistently ineffective ones. Opponents' LIP batting averages: 1982, .272; '83, .272; '84, .286. ... Career strikeout averages: 14.9 per 100 left-handed batters faced, 22.6 per 100 right-handers. ... Has lost 12 road games since his last loss at the Metrodome (June 22, 1984).

Storm Davis

Baltimore Orioles	W–L	ERA	AB	H	HR	BB	SO	BA	SA	OBA
Season	10-8	4.53	673	172	11	70	93	.256	.376	.325
vs. Left-Handed Batters			360	93	6	49	60	.258	.394	.346
vs. Right-Handed Batters			313	79	5	21	33	.252	.355	.300
Home	5-5	4.53	338	79	6	37	51	.234	.364	.310
Road	5-3	4.52	335	93	5	33	42	.278	.388	.341
Grass	10-6	4.35	585	146	9	53	87	.250	.366	.312
Artificial Turf	0-2	5.73	88	26	2	17	6	.295	.443	.406
Day	0-3	6.69	163	51	6	14	18	.313	.528	.369
Night	10-5	3.90	510	121	5	56	75	.237	.327	.312
April	1-0	7.23	90	25	1	13	11	.278	.400	.369
May	2-1	3.44	134	32	1	19	19	.239	.336	.329
June	1-3	4.93	139	38	2	12	17	.273	.396	.331
July	1-2	4.44	100	21	2	14	9	.210	.340	.307
August	3-1	4.15	134	35	2	10	27	.261	.351	.310
Sept./Oct.	2-1	3.32	76	21	3	2	10	.276	.474	.304
Leading Off Inn.			170	38	3	10	15	.224	.329	.267
Bases Empty			389	86	5	35	54	.221	.332	.285
Runners On			284	86	6	35	39	.303	.437	.378
Runners/Scor. Pos.			170	56	4	26	26	.329	.471	.412
Runners On/2 Out			123	37	1	14	13	.301	.398	.377
Scor. Pos./2 Out			82	28	1	14	8	.341	.463	.438
Late Inning Pressure			38	8	1	2	6	.211	.316	.244
Leading Off			11	4	1	1	0	.364	.727	.417
Bases Empty			26	5	1	1	3	.192	.346	.222
Runners On			12	3	0	1	3	.250	.250	.286
Runners/Scor. Pos.			4	1	0	1	1	.250	.250	.333
First 9 Batters			243	66	3	27	34	.272	.370	.344
Second 9 Batters			206	61	4	25	26	.296	.447	.373
All Batters Thereafter			224	45	4	18	33	.201	.317	.258

Loves to face: Kirk Gibson (.063, 1-for-16)
Hates to face: Bill Schroeder (.583, 7-for-12)
Ground outs-to-air outs ratio: 1.11 last season, 1.13 for career. ... Additional statistics: 16 double-play ground outs in 133 opportunities, 38 doubles, 5 triples allowed in 175.0 innings last season. ... Allowed 24 first-inning runs (8th-most in A.L.) in 28 starts last season. ... Batting support: 5.39 runs per start, 7th-highest average in A.L. (minimum: 15 GS). ... Allowed one home run every 15.9 innings, 3d-best rate in A.L. last season. ... Allowed two home runs (Ron Hassey, Ken Griffey) in final start of 1985, first time in 78 appearances, 71 of them starts, that he had allowed two homers. ... Opponents hit 82 points higher with runners on base than with the bases empty last season, highest such difference among pitchers with 20 or more starts. ... Career winning percentage of .616 (45–28) ranks 4th among active pitchers with at least 40 wins.

Ken Dixon

Baltimore Orioles	W–L	ERA	AB	H	HR	BB	SO	BA	SA	OBA
Season	8-4	3.67	607	144	20	64	108	.237	.394	.311
vs. Left-Handed Batters			336	76	9	41	54	.226	.378	.310
vs. Right-Handed Batters			271	68	11	23	54	.251	.413	.313
Home	5-3	4.28	390	96	15	41	61	.246	.415	.320
Road	3-1	2.59	217	48	5	23	47	.221	.355	.295
Grass	6-4	3.92	511	126	18	54	87	.247	.409	.320
Artificial Turf	2-0	2.36	96	18	2	10	21	.188	.313	.264
Day	1-3	5.31	160	47	7	14	28	.294	.500	.349
Night	7-1	3.12	447	97	13	50	80	.217	.356	.298
April	1-0	1.15	55	8	0	5	13	.145	.145	.217
May	3-2	5.53	108	30	4	10	20	.278	.472	.339
June	0-1	6.65	92	31	6	6	15	.337	.576	.374
July	1-0	3.90	101	23	2	11	17	.228	.376	.316
August	1-0	2.20	113	21	4	14	21	.186	.319	.276
Sept./Oct.	2-1	2.70	138	31	4	18	22	.225	.384	.312
Leading Off Inn.			156	36	7	9	29	.231	.404	.277
Bases Empty			381	85	13	31	69	.223	.381	.285
Runners On			226	59	7	33	39	.261	.416	.352
Runners/Scor. Pos.			138	34	5	25	27	.246	.399	.358
Runners On/2 Out			99	21	2	14	21	.212	.283	.310
Scor. Pos./2 Out			67	13	2	11	17	.194	.299	.308
Late Inning Pressure			44	13	0	6	5	.295	.364	.380
Leading Off			12	1	0	2	2	.083	.083	.214
Bases Empty			30	6	0	3	5	.200	.267	.273
Runners On			14	7	0	3	0	.500	.571	.588
Runners/Scor. Pos.			11	4	0	3	0	.364	.364	.500
First 9 Batters			247	60	11	24	59	.243	.453	.314
Second 9 Batters			202	48	5	21	29	.238	.361	.309
All Batters Thereafter			158	36	4	19	20	.228	.342	.309

Loves to face: Lance Parrish (0-for-6, 3 SO)
Hates to face: Ron Hassey (.800, 4-for-5, 1 HR)
Ground outs-to-air outs ratio: 0.67 last season, 0.73 for career. ... Additional statistics: 7 double-play ground outs in 102 opportunities, 29 doubles, 3 triples allowed in 162.0 innings last season. ... Allowed 11 first-inning runs in 18 starts last season. ... Batting support: 5.22 runs per start, 8th-highest average in A.L. (minimum: 15 GS). ... Ranked 7th in A.L. with an average of 8.00 hits per nine innings. ... Ranked 10th in A.L. with an average of 6.00 strikeouts per nine innings. ... ERA on artificial turf ranked 5th in A.L. ... Attention, Civil War buff Keith Hernandez: Orioles exploded for six runs in sixth inning on August 19 to help Dixon to a complete-game victory over Texas Ranger Mike Mason.

Jamie Easterly

Cleveland Indians	W–L	ERA	AB	H	HR	BB	SO	BA	SA	OBA
Season	4-1	3.92	364	96	9	53	58	.264	.376	.356
vs. Left-Handed Batters			115	31	0	14	18	.270	.296	.351
vs. Right-Handed Batters			249	65	9	39	40	.261	.414	.358
Home	3-0	3.00	151	32	3	29	18	.212	.298	.341
Road	1-1	4.70	213	64	6	24	40	.300	.432	.367
Grass	4-0	3.97	292	77	7	45	43	.264	.370	.362
Artificial Turf	0-1	3.72	72	19	2	8	15	.264	.403	.329
Day	1-1	6.68	124	39	3	22	24	.315	.444	.418
Night	3-0	2.66	240	57	6	31	34	.238	.342	.321
April	1-0	3.38	49	10	1	7	12	.204	.286	.304
May	0-0	1.98	51	13	1	6	5	.255	.333	.345
June	0-0	0.63	49	9	1	11	8	.184	.245	.344
July	0-0	3.09	37	7	0	6	6	.189	.216	.319
August	2-0	2.81	57	14	1	10	7	.246	.316	.348
Sept./Oct.	1-1	7.58	121	43	5	13	20	.355	.562	.403
Leading Off Inn.			80	21	2	12	13	.263	.363	.359
Bases Empty			174	46	3	32	27	.264	.356	.382
Runners On			190	50	6	21	31	.263	.395	.332
Runners/Scor. Pos.			102	27	5	17	17	.265	.471	.354
Runners On/2 Out			80	20	5	11	17	.250	.488	.341
Scor. Pos./2 Out			51	15	5	10	10	.294	.667	.410
Late Inning Pressure			83	21	1	12	14	.253	.301	.343
Leading Off			19	4	1	3	2	.211	.368	.318
Bases Empty			44	11	1	7	5	.250	.318	.353
Runners On			39	10	0	5	9	.256	.282	.333
Runners/Scor. Pos.			20	5	0	5	3	.250	.300	.357
First 9 Batters			235	59	5	36	34	.251	.349	.354
Second 9 Batters			81	18	1	11	17	.222	.296	.309
All Batters Thereafter			48	19	3	6	7	.396	.646	.446

Loves to face: Lee Lacy (0-for-10)
Hates to face: Juan Beniquez (.636, 7-for-11)
Ground outs-to-air outs ratio: 1.55 last season, 1.92 for career. ... Additional statistics: 11 double-play ground outs in 109 opportunities, 12 doubles, 1 triple allowed in 98.2 innings last season. ... Ranked 5th among A.L. relief pitchers with a 2.25 ERA last season (minimum: 30 relief games). ... Average of 6.47 hits per nine innings was 4th-lowest among that group. ... Career total of 36 starts is 2d-highest among pitchers without a complete game. ... Career average of 4.70 walks per nine innings is 8th-highest among active pitchers (minimum: 200 BB). ... Relieved in 43 games last season, 2d-highest total among A.L. pitchers without a save. Career totals: 14 saves in 299 relief appearances. ... Opponents have batted .307 in Late-Inning Pressure Situations with runners on base vs. Easterly over past 11 seasons.

Frank Eufemia

Minnesota Twins	W–L	ERA	AB	H	HR	BB	SO	BA	SA	OBA
Season	4-2	3.79	224	56	7	21	30	.250	.415	.310
vs. Left-Handed Batters			102	26	0	9	14	.255	.353	.315
vs. Right-Handed Batters			122	30	7	12	16	.246	.467	.307
Home	3-0	3.08	133	31	1	12	22	.233	.323	.293
Road	1-2	4.94	91	25	6	9	8	.275	.549	.337
Grass	0-1	0.50	63	12	1	6	5	.190	.286	.257
Artificial Turf	4-1	5.15	161	44	6	15	25	.273	.466	.331
Day	1-1	6.20	78	24	4	9	8	.308	.577	.371
Night	3-1	2.61	146	32	3	12	22	.219	.329	.277
April			0	0	0	0	0	.000	.000	.000
May	0-0	0.00	23	4	0	0	2	.174	.217	.174
June	1-0	4.05	49	13	2	7	12	.265	.429	.351
July	2-1	2.45	67	16	2	3	7	.239	.373	.271
August	0-1	5.25	43	11	0	4	4	.256	.349	.353
Sept./Oct.	1-0	6.35	42	12	3	4	5	.286	.643	.340
Leading Off Inn.			44	8	0	5	8	.182	.250	.265
Bases Empty			119	26	2	9	18	.218	.336	.273
Runners On			105	30	5	12	12	.286	.505	.350
Runners/Scor. Pos.			68	19	4	11	6	.279	.500	.366
Runners On/2 Out			45	9	2	7	7	.200	.378	.308
Scor. Pos./2 Out			29	5	1	7	3	.172	.276	.333
Late Inning Pressure			77	18	2	7	10	.234	.377	.298
Leading Off			20	4	0	1	4	.200	.250	.238
Bases Empty			53	11	0	1	8	.208	.283	.222
Runners On			24	7	2	6	2	.292	.583	.433
Runners/Scor. Pos.			14	4	2	5	0	.286	.714	.474
First 9 Batters			205	52	7	19	28	.254	.420	.313
Second 9 Batters			19	4	0	2	2	.211	.368	.286
All Batters Thereafter			0	0	0	0	0	.000	.000	.000

Loves to face: Steve Balboni (0-for-2, 2 SO)
Hates to face: Brook Jacoby (3-for-3, 1 2B, 1 3B)
Ground outs-to-air outs ratio: 1.40 last season, his first in majors. . . . Additional statistics: 8 double-play ground outs in 42 opportunities, 12 doubles, 2 triples allowed in 61.2 innings last season. . . . Can anyone think of an ex-major leaguer with all five vowels in his last name? While we're at it, how about the ex-big leaguer with each of the first eight letters of the alphabet in his full name? . . . Makings of a Dennis Martinez: right-handed pitcher who allowed all seven home runs to right-handed batters. . . . Another foil for the Homerdome myth (see page 59): Allowed one HR in 133 at bats there, six in 91 at bats in road games. . . . Won all three decisions with a 1.46 ERA in his first 22 games; 1-2, 7.30 ERA in his last 19 games. . . . Answer to the first: Ed Figueroa; answer to the second: Frenchy Bordagaray.

Pete Filson

Minnesota Twins	W–L	ERA	AB	H	HR	BB	SO	BA	SA	OBA
Season	4-5	3.67	371	93	13	30	42	.251	.402	.305
vs. Left-Handed Batters			110	30	3	8	14	.273	.418	.319
vs. Right-Handed Batters			261	63	10	22	28	.241	.395	.299
Home	4-2	3.34	223	57	7	16	25	.256	.386	.305
Road	0-3	4.15	148	36	6	14	17	.243	.426	.305
Grass	0-2	4.34	106	24	5	10	15	.226	.406	.288
Artificial Turf	4-3	3.38	265	69	8	20	27	.260	.400	.312
Day	2-0	3.13	91	21	3	8	9	.231	.396	.293
Night	2-5	3.84	280	72	10	22	33	.257	.404	.309
April	0-0	0.00	5	1	0	0	0	.200	.200	.200
May	2-2	4.50	110	25	2	11	10	.227	.318	.293
June	1-3	5.31	87	27	7	6	8	.310	.609	.355
July	0-0	1.80	51	10	3	4	10	.196	.373	.255
August	1-0	3.55	51	13	0	3	7	.255	.314	.296
Sept./Oct.	0-0	2.16	67	17	1	6	7	.254	.373	.315
Leading Off Inn.			86	16	1	5	13	.186	.279	.231
Bases Empty			204	56	7	18	25	.275	.436	.333
Runners On			167	37	6	12	17	.222	.359	.271
Runners/Scor. Pos.			84	17	2	9	8	.202	.298	.274
Runners On/2 Out			72	12	3	5	7	.167	.333	.221
Scor. Pos./2 Out			36	3	0	4	4	.083	.083	.175
Late Inning Pressure			73	18	1	3	7	.247	.315	.276
Leading Off			21	3	0	0	2	.143	.190	.143
Bases Empty			47	11	1	1	5	.234	.319	.250
Runners On			26	7	0	2	2	.269	.308	.321
Runners/Scor. Pos.			14	3	0	2	1	.214	.214	.313
First 9 Batters			226	54	7	21	29	.239	.363	.304
Second 9 Batters			89	25	3	3	9	.281	.438	.304
All Batters Thereafter			56	14	3	6	4	.250	.500	.313

Loves to face: Butch Wynegar (0-for-10)
Hates to face: Gary Roenicke (.625, 5-for-8, 1 HR)
Ground outs-to-air outs ratio: 0.71 last season, 0.74 for career. . . . Additional statistics: 2 double-play ground outs in 80 opportunities (lowest rate in A.L.), 13 doubles, 2 triples allowed in 95.2 innings last season. . . . Ranked 8th among A.L. relief pitchers with a 2.43 ERA last season (minimum: 30 relief games). . . . Had a 1-5 record with a 6.06 ERA in six starts last season; 3-0, 2.43 in 34 relief appearances. . . . Career record of 11-4 at the Metrodome, 3-9 (including four losses since his last win) in road games. . . . Followed the first and only complete game of his career (June 7) with a 2d-inning knockout at the hands of the Texas Rangers, the first of three consecutive losses. . . . Opposing batters have a career batting average of .176 with two outs and runners in scoring position.

Brian Fisher

New York Yankees	W–L	ERA	AB	H	HR	BB	SO	BA	SA	OBA
Season	4-4	2.38	357	77	4	29	85	.216	.277	.273
vs. Left-Handed Batters			173	39	2	19	38	.225	.289	.302
vs. Right-Handed Batters			184	38	2	10	47	.207	.266	.245
Home	3-3	2.75	208	49	2	15	49	.236	.288	.286
Road	1-1	1.90	149	28	2	14	36	.188	.262	.256
Grass	4-4	2.62	299	63	3	27	71	.211	.268	.275
Artificial Turf	0-0	1.13	58	14	1	2	14	.241	.328	.262
Day	0-2	3.43	154	43	2	11	42	.279	.364	.325
Night	4-2	1.68	203	34	2	18	43	.167	.212	.234
April			0	0	0	0	0	.000	.000	.000
May	2-0	2.29	69	15	0	6	12	.217	.232	.280
June	0-2	3.38	86	22	1	10	18	.256	.326	.330
July	0-0	0.68	46	7	1	3	14	.152	.217	.200
August	2-1	2.08	81	20	1	7	20	.247	.321	.307
Sept./Oct.	0-1	2.75	75	13	1	3	21	.173	.253	.205
Leading Off Inn.			77	17	1	9	19	.221	.260	.302
Bases Empty			184	40	1	17	51	.217	.255	.284
Runners On			173	37	3	12	34	.214	.301	.262
Runners/Scor. Pos.			100	24	3	9	17	.240	.360	.297
Runners On/2 Out			75	15	1	8	10	.200	.293	.277
Scor. Pos./2 Out			52	9	1	5	6	.173	.269	.246
Late Inning Pressure			155	33	3	17	42	.213	.310	.291
Leading Off			38	8	1	5	11	.211	.289	.302
Bases Empty			88	19	1	9	27	.216	.284	.289
Runners On			67	14	2	8	15	.209	.343	.293
Runners/Scor. Pos.			37	8	2	7	8	.216	.432	.341
First 9 Batters			298	61	3	22	74	.205	.258	.253
Second 9 Batters			52	15	1	7	10	.288	.404	.373
All Batters Thereafter			7	1	0	0	1	.143	.143	.143

Loves to face: Kirk Gibson (0-for-3, 3 SO)
Hates to face: Jack Perconte (4-for-4)
Ground outs-to-air outs ratio: 1.04 last season, his first in majors. . . . Additional statistics: 10 double-play ground outs in 83 opportunities, 8 doubles, 1 triple allowed in 98.1 innings last season (lowest rate of extra-base hits per 100 at bats among A.L. pitchers facing at least 200 batters). . . . Ranked 8th among A.L. relief pitchers with a 2.38 ERA last season (minimum: 30 relief games). . . . Total of 85 strikeouts in relief ranked 4th in A.L. . . . New York's newest crosstown rivalry? Fisher led A.L. rookies with 14 saves; Roger McDowell led N.L. rookies with 17. No other rookie pitcher had more than eight. . . . Tied Gary Lavelle for A.L. lead with eight save set-ups (relief appearances of at least one inning immediately preceding a save).

Mike Flanagan

Baltimore Orioles	W–L	ERA	AB	H	HR	BB	SO	BA	SA	OBA
Season	4-5	5.13	340	101	14	28	42	.297	.485	.352
vs. Left-Handed Batters			49	15	0	3	7	.306	.388	.346
vs. Right-Handed Batters			291	86	14	25	35	.296	.502	.353
Home	2-2	6.40	134	44	5	12	12	.328	.493	.381
Road	2-3	4.36	206	57	9	16	30	.277	.481	.333
Grass	4-5	5.24	311	94	13	26	39	.302	.492	.356
Artificial Turf	0-0	3.86	29	7	1	2	3	.241	.414	.313
Day	1-2	6.75	103	34	6	11	14	.330	.621	.391
Night	3-3	4.45	237	67	8	17	28	.283	.426	.335
April			0	0	0	0	0	.000	.000	.000
May			0	0	0	0	0	.000	.000	.000
June			0	0	0	0	0	.000	.000	.000
July	1-1	3.79	68	12	2	4	7	.176	.309	.222
August	1-3	7.12	127	44	8	10	13	.346	.606	.399
Sept./Oct.	2-1	4.17	145	45	4	14	22	.310	.462	.370
Leading Off Inn.			90	27	4	4	8	.300	.511	.330
Bases Empty			197	58	5	23	24	.294	.442	.371
Runners On			143	43	9	5	18	.301	.545	.325
Runners/Scor. Pos.			78	21	2	4	16	.269	.423	.306
Runners On/2 Out			61	15	2	5	12	.246	.377	.313
Scor. Pos./2 Out			38	8	1	4	10	.211	.316	.302
Late Inning Pressure			35	10	1	0	3	.286	.429	.286
Leading Off			13	3	0	0	1	.231	.308	.231
Bases Empty			28	8	0	0	3	.286	.357	.286
Runners On			7	2	1	0	0	.286	.714	.286
Runners/Scor. Pos.			2	2	1	0	0	1.000	2.500	1.000
First 9 Batters			123	33	4	9	20	.268	.423	.323
Second 9 Batters			109	41	6	8	11	.376	.624	.424
All Batters Thereafter			108	27	4	11	11	.250	.417	.314

Loves to face: Dan Meyer (0-for-17, 8 SO)
Hates to face: Wayne Tolleson (.667, 4-for-6, 1 HR)
Ground outs-to-air outs ratio: 1.44 last season (his highest since 1978), 1.30 for career. . . . Additional statistics: 9 double-play ground outs in 62 opportunities, 20 doubles, 1 triple allowed in 86.0 innings last season. . . . Allowed 9 first-inning runs in 15 starts last season. . . . Batting support: 4.00 runs per start. . . . Allowed one home run every 6.1 innings, 5th-worst average in the league (minimum: 15 GS). . . . Faced 36 batters in Late-Inning Pressure Situations without allowing a walk, highest total in either league last season. The Player Analysis record of 75 was set by teammate Scott McGregor in 1979. . . . Last A.L. Cy Young (1979) winner to have a winning record in the season following the award.

Bob Gibson
Milwaukee Brewers

	W–L	ERA	AB	H	HR	BB	SO	BA	SA	OBA
Season	6-7	3.90	331	86	10	49	53	.260	.405	.353
vs. Left-Handed Batters			142	35	6	22	19	.246	.423	.343
vs. Right-Handed Batters			189	51	4	27	34	.270	.392	.361
Home	2-2	3.97	174	48	4	20	35	.276	.414	.343
Road	4-5	3.83	157	38	6	29	18	.242	.395	.364
Grass	5-5	3.56	260	65	7	37	47	.250	.385	.339
Artificial Turf	1-2	5.21	71	21	3	12	6	.296	.479	.405
Day	1-3	4.78	114	33	6	18	17	.289	.482	.381
Night	5-4	3.43	217	53	4	31	36	.244	.364	.339
April	3-1	3.86	51	17	1	10	8	.333	.490	.435
May	2-0	1.23	75	14	1	11	15	.187	.240	.287
June	1-3	5.40	58	16	4	6	8	.276	.517	.344
July	0-1	3.46	44	10	1	8	10	.227	.318	.340
August	0-2	4.42	68	17	2	6	9	.250	.412	.311
Sept./Oct.	0-0	7.56	35	12	1	8	3	.343	.543	.467
Leading Off Inn.			69	19	3	10	11	.275	.493	.367
Bases Empty			173	47	6	27	31	.272	.439	.373
Runners On			158	39	4	22	22	.247	.367	.332
Runners/Scor. Pos.			103	28	4	12	17	.272	.437	.336
Runners On/2 Out			64	11	3	8	13	.172	.328	.264
Scor. Pos./2 Out			45	9	3	3	9	.200	.422	.250
Late Inning Pressure			135	30	6	19	24	.222	.407	.321
Leading Off			34	11	3	4	7	.324	.676	.395
Bases Empty			88	22	4	10	18	.250	.466	.333
Runners On			47	8	2	9	6	.170	.298	.298
Runners/Scor. Pos.			33	7	2	5	4	.212	.394	.308
First 9 Batters			251	65	6	36	34	.259	.386	.348
Second 9 Batters			70	17	4	11	18	.243	.457	.349
All Batters Thereafter			10	4	0	2	1	.400	.500	.500

Loves to face: Ernie Whitt (0-for-10, 3 SO)
Hates to face: Alvin Davis (.571, 4-for-7, 2 HR)
Ground outs-to-air outs ratio: 1.15 last season, 0.93 for career. . . . Additional statistics: 15 double-play ground outs in 82 opportunities (6th-highest rate in A.L.), 16 doubles, 1 triple allowed in 92.1 innings last season. . . . Has allowed only two triples in facing 1,061 batters in his three-year career. . . . Season turned sour on June 2, when he began a string of 25 relief appearances in which he was scored on in 17, and picked up six losses. . . . Walked at least one batter in 30 of 40 relief games. . . . Opponents' batting average with runners on base has declined each season since his rookie year of '83 (.270, .248, .247), while the average with the bases empty has risen (.209, .226, .272). . . . What's in a name? Ask Darrell Evans—he's the only man to have homered off both Bob Gibsons.

Mark Gubicza
Kansas City Royals

	W–L	ERA	AB	H	HR	BB	SO	BA	SA	OBA
Season	14-10	4.06	671	160	14	77	99	.238	.368	.319
vs. Left-Handed Batters			379	96	9	41	56	.253	.391	.329
vs. Right-Handed Batters			292	64	5	36	43	.219	.339	.305
Home	7-5	3.47	331	74	5	35	49	.224	.332	.303
Road	7-5	4.61	340	86	9	42	50	.253	.403	.334
Grass	5-2	3.32	235	55	3	27	36	.234	.345	.313
Artificial Turf	9-8	4.49	436	105	11	50	63	.241	.381	.322
Day	2-3	4.37	175	44	4	21	25	.251	.400	.330
Night	12-7	3.95	496	116	10	56	74	.234	.357	.315
April	0-1	3.75	47	11	1	5	7	.234	.362	.308
May	1-2	5.57	91	27	0	12	11	.297	.374	.377
June	5-1	3.10	140	27	4	22	29	.193	.300	.302
July	1-1	3.70	100	28	0	3	12	.280	.400	.302
August	3-2	3.89	129	28	3	17	20	.217	.349	.311
Sept./Oct.	4-3	4.63	164	39	6	18	20	.238	.421	.319
Leading Off Inn.			172	40	5	17	16	.233	.372	.302
Bases Empty			401	93	10	45	56	.232	.372	.311
Runners On			270	67	4	32	43	.248	.363	.330
Runners/Scor. Pos.			148	41	3	21	23	.277	.392	.369
Runners On/2 Out			103	27	1	15	13	.262	.417	.372
Scor. Pos./2 Out			69	15	1	11	11	.217	.333	.349
Late Inning Pressure			49	14	2	7	9	.286	.469	.375
Leading Off			15	1	1	1	4	.067	.267	.125
Bases Empty			37	8	2	5	6	.216	.405	.310
Runners On			12	6	0	2	3	.500	.667	.571
Runners/Scor. Pos.			4	1	0	2	3	.250	.500	.500
First 9 Batters			228	50	4	28	38	.219	.338	.307
Second 9 Batters			223	49	1	25	36	.220	.300	.298
All Batters Thereafter			220	61	9	24	25	.277	.468	.352

Loves to face: Rick Manning (.071, 1-for-14)
Hates to face: Paul Householder (.750, 3-for-4)
Ground outs-to-air outs ratio: 1.38 last season, 1.51 for career. . . . Additional statistics: 14 double-play ground outs in 139 opportunities, 29 doubles, 8 triples (5th-most in A.L.) allowed in 177.1 innings last season. . . . Allowed 14 first-inning runs in 28 starts last season. . . . Batting support: 4.57 runs per start. . . . Ranked 10th in A.L. with an average of 8.12 hits per nine innings. . . . Allowed one home run per 12.7 innings last season, 8th-best rate in A.L. last season. . . . Grass-field ERA ranked 7th in A.L. . . . Opponents have only four hits in 24 career at bats with the bases loaded (.167). . . . Two-year composite batting average of opposing batters in Late-Inning Pressure Situations with runners on base: .394. . . . Career home run averages: one for every 91 at bats at Royals Stadium, one per 31 AB in road games.

Ron Guidry
New York Yankees

	W–L	ERA	AB	H	HR	BB	SO	BA	SA	OBA
Season	22-6	3.27	980	243	28	42	143	.248	.392	.277
vs. Left-Handed Batters			184	39	8	8	28	.212	.348	.241
vs. Right-Handed Batters			796	204	20	34	115	.256	.402	.285
Home	13-2	2.82	524	132	12	22	78	.252	.382	.280
Road	9-4	3.77	456	111	16	20	65	.243	.404	.273
Grass	19-6	3.29	890	225	26	40	132	.253	.400	.283
Artificial Turf	3-0	3.00	90	18	2	2	11	.200	.311	.217
Day	10-0	2.42	290	64	7	12	48	.221	.372	.249
Night	12-6	3.63	690	179	21	30	95	.259	.400	.288
April	1-3	4.26	118	29	6	4	20	.246	.424	.264
May	4-0	2.41	147	29	4	6	20	.197	.333	.227
June	4-0	2.11	176	39	2	5	20	.222	.295	.243
July	4-1	3.83	184	45	3	10	21	.245	.353	.281
August	3-1	2.08	148	40	2	5	23	.270	.372	.292
Sept./Oct.	6-1	4.76	207	61	11	12	39	.295	.546	.332
Leading Off Inn.			253	70	8	12	35	.277	.439	.309
Bases Empty			619	154	16	27	93	.249	.381	.280
Runners On			361	89	12	15	50	.247	.410	.271
Runners/Scor. Pos.			181	44	8	11	31	.243	.442	.275
Runners On/2 Out			143	33	5	6	21	.231	.392	.262
Scor. Pos./2 Out			76	18	3	4	14	.237	.421	.275
Late Inning Pressure			104	28	1	3	14	.269	.356	.290
Leading Off			28	8	0	1	2	.286	.321	.310
Bases Empty			70	19	1	1	9	.271	.357	.282
Runners On			34	9	0	2	5	.265	.353	.306
Runners/Scor. Pos.			13	6	0	2	3	.462	.692	.533
First 9 Batters			282	54	9	15	55	.191	.330	.232
Second 9 Batters			278	78	6	14	38	.281	.406	.310
All Batters Thereafter			420	111	13	13	50	.264	.424	.285

Loves to face: Willie Upshaw (.091, 2-for-22)
Hates to face: Darrell Evans (2-for-2, 2 HR)
Ground outs-to-air outs ratio: 0.89 last season, 0.90 for career. . . . Additional statistics: 30 double-play ground outs in 160 opportunities (3d-highest rate in A.L.), 47 doubles (5th-most in A.L.), 5 triples allowed in 259.0 innings last season. . . . Ranked 2d among A.L. pitchers with an average of 7.84 innings per start. . . . Total of 80 extra-base hits allowed was 6th-highest in A.L. . . . Allowed 12 first-inning runs in 33 starts last season. . . . Batting support: 5.58 runs per start, 5th-highest average in A.L. (minimum: 15 GS). . . . Ranked 3d in A.L. with an average of 1.46 walks per nine innings. . . . Opposing batters have hit .310 in Late-Inning Pressure Situations over the past five seasons, 7th-highest in A.L. during that time (minimum: 100 hits). . . . Won seven consecutive starts, June 17–July 20, his longest streak since an 11-gamer in '79.

Moose Haas
Milwaukee Brewers

	W–L	ERA	AB	H	HR	BB	SO	BA	SA	OBA
Season	8-8	3.84	634	165	21	25	78	.260	.410	.287
vs. Left-Handed Batters			334	87	10	15	37	.260	.389	.291
vs. Right-Handed Batters			300	78	11	10	41	.260	.433	.283
Home	6-3	3.42	403	103	12	14	59	.256	.402	.280
Road	2-5	4.58	231	62	9	11	19	.268	.424	.299
Grass	8-6	3.83	541	137	18	23	69	.253	.405	.283
Artificial Turf	0-2	3.91	93	28	3	2	9	.301	.441	.309
Day	3-4	3.45	275	71	7	13	31	.258	.385	.291
Night	5-4	4.14	359	94	14	12	47	.262	.429	.284
April	1-2	2.48	114	25	2	6	13	.219	.342	.256
May	4-0	2.67	125	32	3	3	14	.256	.400	.273
June	2-1	1.97	117	23	2	4	18	.197	.274	.220
July	0-2	8.74	98	32	10	3	11	.327	.684	.343
August	1-1	5.40	68	20	1	3	9	.294	.382	.333
Sept./Oct.	0-2	3.90	112	33	3	6	13	.295	.411	.328
Leading Off Inn.			169	51	7	3	27	.302	.485	.318
Bases Empty			410	97	14	9	56	.237	.383	.255
Runners On			224	68	7	16	22	.304	.460	.343
Runners/Scor. Pos.			107	33	2	13	12	.308	.467	.368
Runners On/2 Out			76	16	3	7	5	.211	.368	.277
Scor. Pos./2 Out			46	10	2	6	2	.217	.391	.308
Late Inning Pressure			55	17	4	3	4	.309	.636	.345
Leading Off			16	8	4	1	1	.500	1.438	.529
Bases Empty			42	11	4	1	4	.262	.643	.279
Runners On			13	6	0	2	0	.462	.615	.533
Runners/Scor. Pos.			8	4	0	2	0	.500	.750	.600
First 9 Batters			236	59	8	5	31	.250	.369	.263
Second 9 Batters			209	49	5	7	26	.234	.364	.260
All Batters Thereafter			189	57	8	13	21	.302	.513	.345

Loves to face: Frank White (.096, 5-for-52)
Hates to face: Omar Moreno (.667, 4-for-6, 1 HR)
Ground outs-to-air outs ratio: 1.23 last season, 1.01 for career. . . . Additional statistics: 15 double-play ground outs in 126 opportunities, 20 doubles, 6 triples allowed in 161.2 innings last season. . . . Allowed 12 first-inning runs in 26 starts last season. . . . Batting support: 4.46 runs per start. . . . Led A.L. with an average of 1.39 walks per nine innings. . . . Watch him bear down on leadoff hitters: career strikeout average is 13 percent higher against the first batter in each inning than against all subsequent batters. . . . Career average of 2.68 strikeouts per walk vs. right-handed batters, 1.50 SO per BB vs. left-handers. . . . Opposing batters have hit .314 in Late-Inning Pressure Situations over the past five seasons, 5th-highest in A.L. during that time (minimum: 100 hits).

Greg Harris

Texas Rangers	W–L	ERA	AB	H	HR	BB	SO	BA	SA	OBA
Season	5-4	2.47	397	74	7	43	111	.186	.290	.273
vs. Left-Handed Batters			206	36	4	21	58	.175	.286	.257
vs. Right-Handed Batters			191	38	3	22	53	.199	.293	.290
Home	4-2	2.68	202	37	5	17	56	.183	.327	.260
Road	1-2	2.25	195	37	2	26	55	.190	.251	.286
Grass	4-3	2.15	348	57	6	35	99	.164	.264	.249
Artificial Turf	1-1	4.97	49	17	1	8	12	.347	.469	.431
Day	1-1	4.32	92	20	2	12	24	.217	.337	.308
Night	4-3	1.94	305	54	5	31	87	.177	.275	.262
April	0-0	1.74	33	5	1	4	7	.152	.303	.263
May	0-1	2.18	69	10	1	8	23	.145	.246	.244
June	2-0	2.49	92	19	1	6	18	.207	.304	.257
July	1-2	2.81	55	8	1	9	12	.145	.236	.277
August	1-0	1.61	78	15	2	9	34	.192	.295	.284
Sept./Oct.	1-1	3.93	70	17	1	7	17	.243	.343	.312
Leading Off Inn.			95	10	0	7	30	.105	.116	.175
Bases Empty			238	40	3	24	70	.168	.248	.256
Runners On			159	34	4	19	41	.214	.352	.298
Runners/Scor. Pos.			89	17	1	15	20	.191	.258	.302
Runners On/2 Out			71	9	0	9	21	.127	.197	.225
Scor. Pos./2 Out			46	4	0	7	13	.087	.130	.208
Late Inning Pressure			193	42	5	20	52	.218	.347	.298
Leading Off			50	5	0	4	19	.100	.100	.167
Bases Empty			121	23	2	12	36	.190	.289	.269
Runners On			72	19	3	8	16	.264	.444	.346
Runners/Scor. Pos.			43	10	1	6	10	.233	.349	.327
First 9 Batters			339	64	5	37	94	.189	.292	.275
Second 9 Batters			56	10	2	6	15	.179	.286	.270
All Batters Thereafter			2	0	0	0	2	.000	.000	.000

Loves to face: Brett Butler (.100, 1-for-10)
Hates to face: Phil Bradley (.800, 4-for-5)
Ground outs-to-air outs ratio: 1.55 last season, 1.36 for career. . . . Additional statistics: 10 double-play ground outs in 79 opportunities, 12 doubles, 4 triples allowed in 113.0 innings last year. . . . Rate of 5.89 hits per nine innings was 2d-lowest among A.L. relievers (minimum: 30 relief games); rate of 8.84 strikeouts was 3d-highest. . . . Led A.L. relievers with 111 strikeouts. . . . Set *Player Analysis* record with .175 on-base average leading off innings last year (minimum: 100 leadoff batters faced). . . . Opponents have .162 career average with runners in scoring position and two outs, 4th-lowest in past 11 years (minimum: 150 batters faced). . . . Rumor has it that he may one day pitch both left- and right-handed; Tony Mullane did that in majors before 1900, and Bert Campaneris (yes, the same guy) did it in a minor-league game in 1962.

Neal Heaton

Cleveland Indians	W–L	ERA	AB	H	HR	BB	SO	BA	SA	OBA
Season	9-17	4.90	819	244	19	80	82	.298	.443	.362
vs. Left-Handed Batters			161	49	2	16	20	.304	.435	.367
vs. Right-Handed Batters			658	195	17	64	62	.296	.445	.361
Home	7-5	3.55	446	121	11	42	49	.271	.388	.337
Road	2-12	6.63	373	123	8	38	33	.330	.509	.391
Grass	8-15	4.77	680	201	15	67	76	.296	.432	.361
Artificial Turf	1-2	5.56	139	43	4	13	6	.309	.496	.370
Day	4-4	3.86	307	90	4	30	31	.293	.381	.359
Night	5-13	5.51	512	154	15	50	51	.301	.480	.364
April	1-1	2.10	113	32	0	10	4	.283	.398	.341
May	2-3	3.49	142	31	3	18	15	.218	.380	.305
June	1-5	9.62	129	45	4	17	7	.349	.519	.432
July	1-3	4.63	135	41	3	11	17	.304	.452	.356
August	3-2	3.47	176	53	5	14	25	.301	.415	.352
Sept./Oct.	1-3	7.62	124	42	4	10	14	.339	.508	.394
Leading Off Inn.			202	61	6	19	16	.302	.480	.362
Bases Empty			439	144	11	47	44	.328	.487	.397
Runners On			380	100	8	33	38	.263	.392	.322
Runners/Scor. Pos.			201	51	5	21	19	.254	.393	.322
Runners On/2 Out			156	42	4	20	18	.269	.436	.360
Scor. Pos./2 Out			93	21	2	14	9	.226	.376	.339
Late Inning Pressure			73	23	3	9	6	.315	.548	.393
Leading Off			22	7	2	1	1	.318	.727	.348
Bases Empty			48	17	2	4	4	.354	.583	.415
Runners On			25	6	1	5	2	.240	.480	.355
Runners/Scor. Pos.			13	2	1	5	0	.154	.385	.368
First 9 Batters			287	76	7	26	35	.265	.411	.322
Second 9 Batters			255	81	5	27	22	.318	.451	.391
All Batters Thereafter			277	87	7	27	25	.314	.469	.377

Loves to face: Roy Smalley (.071, 1-for-14, 4 SO)
Hates to face: Gary Roenicke (.478, 11-for-23, 3 HR)
Ground outs-to-air outs ratio: 1.07 last season, 0.89 for career. . . . Additional statistics: 21 double-play ground outs in 182 opportunities, 48 doubles (tied for 3d-most in A.L.), 7 triples (tied for 6th-most in A.L.) allowed in 207.2 innings last season. . . . Allowed 21 first-inning runs in 33 starts last season. . . . Batting support: 3.91 runs per start, 8th-lowest average in A.L. (minimum: 15 GS). . . . Led majors with 12 road-game losses last season. . . . Opposing batters hit 65 points higher with the bases empty than with runners on base, 3d-largest difference in A.L. in '85 (minimum: 100 AB in both situations). . . . Has walked only one leadoff batter in 74 innings in Late-Inning Pressure Situations, 4th-best career average in the 11-year history of *The Player Analysis* (minimum: 50 BFP).

Tom Henke

Toronto Blue Jays	W–L	ERA	AB	H	HR	BB	SO	BA	SA	OBA
Season	3-3	2.03	141	29	4	8	42	.206	.312	.245
vs. Left-Handed Batters			80	18	4	4	23	.225	.387	.262
vs. Right-Handed Batters			61	11	0	4	19	.180	.213	.224
Home	0-2	2.61	73	16	3	5	19	.219	.356	.266
Road	3-1	1.40	68	13	1	3	23	.191	.265	.222
Grass	2-0	0.00	42	4	0	1	15	.095	.095	.116
Artificial Turf	1-3	3.00	99	25	4	7	27	.253	.404	.296
Day	1-1	1.59	42	11	1	4	13	.262	.357	.313
Night	2-2	2.20	99	18	3	4	29	.182	.293	.214
April			0	0	0	0	0	.000	.000	.000
May			0	0	0	0	0	.000	.000	.000
June			0	0	0	0	0	.000	.000	.000
July	2-0	0.00	12	0	0	1	4	.000	.000	.077
August	1-1	1.53	63	13	1	4	21	.206	.286	.250
Sept./Oct.	0-2	2.95	66	16	3	3	17	.242	.394	.271
Leading Off Inn.			31	8	0	1	8	.258	.290	.281
Bases Empty			82	17	1	3	25	.207	.268	.235
Runners On			59	12	3	5	17	.203	.373	.258
Runners/Scor. Pos.			25	6	1	3	5	.240	.360	.300
Runners On/2 Out			25	6	1	2	10	.240	.400	.296
Scor. Pos./2 Out			11	3	0	1	2	.273	.273	.333
Late Inning Pressure			97	20	3	5	29	.206	.330	.245
Leading Off			23	6	0	0	6	.261	.304	.261
Bases Empty			61	14	1	2	19	.230	.311	.254
Runners On			36	6	2	3	10	.167	.361	.231
Runners/Scor. Pos.			9	2	0	2	0	.222	.222	.364
First 9 Batters			135	28	4	7	40	.207	.319	.243
Second 9 Batters			6	1	0	1	2	.167	.167	.286
All Batters Thereafter			0	0	0	0	0	.000	.000	.000

Loves to face: Julio Cruz (0-for-7, 3 SO)
Hates to face: Carlton Fisk (.750, 3-for-4)
Ground outs-to-air outs ratio: 0.65 last season, 0.84 for career. . . . Additional statistics: 2 double-play ground outs in 35 opportunities, 3 doubles, 0 triples allowed in 40.0 innings last season. . . . Has faced 215 right-handed batters without allowing a home run, 3d-highest career total over past 11 years. He has allowed five home runs in 186 at bats vs. left-handers. . . . Ranked 2d in A.L. last season with 27.9 strikeouts per 100 batters faced in Late-Inning Pressure Situations; best was Best—Karl Best of Seattle, that is—with 28.3. . . . Many don't realize how long Henke has been around. He made his major-league debut on September 10, 1982; the winning pitcher in that game was Gaylord Perry.

Willie Hernandez

Detroit Tigers	W–L	ERA	AB	H	HR	BB	SO	BA	SA	OBA
Season	8-10	2.70	391	82	13	14	76	.210	.353	.236
vs. Left-Handed Batters			105	18	1	2	19	.171	.229	.193
vs. Right-Handed Batters			286	64	12	12	57	.224	.399	.252
Home	6-4	2.15	209	35	7	7	45	.167	.301	.196
Road	2-6	3.38	182	47	6	7	31	.258	.412	.281
Grass	7-10	2.92	341	71	12	14	68	.208	.358	.239
Artificial Turf	1-0	1.26	50	11	1	0	8	.220	.320	.216
Day	5-2	1.94	143	25	2	6	28	.175	.266	.204
Night	3-8	3.18	248	57	11	8	48	.230	.403	.255
April	2-0	2.08	44	8	0	2	9	.182	.227	.208
May	1-1	1.29	72	10	0	2	14	.139	.181	.160
June	1-2	2.14	73	14	3	3	12	.192	.342	.231
July	1-1	2.25	77	21	3	2	14	.273	.416	.288
August	2-5	7.13	75	22	5	4	13	.293	.587	.329
Sept./Oct.	1-1	1.29	50	7	2	1	14	.140	.280	.157
Leading Off Inn.			88	18	1	1	16	.205	.307	.213
Bases Empty			233	44	9	5	48	.189	.339	.209
Runners On			158	38	4	9	28	.241	.373	.273
Runners/Scor. Pos.			86	24	2	6	12	.279	.419	.309
Runners On/2 Out			79	17	0	6	14	.215	.278	.271
Scor. Pos./2 Out			48	12	0	4	6	.250	.313	.308
Late Inning Pressure			241	50	11	7	43	.207	.369	.231
Leading Off			54	9	1	0	10	.167	.241	.167
Bases Empty			152	27	8	2	29	.178	.342	.194
Runners On			89	23	3	5	14	.258	.416	.292
Runners/Scor. Pos.			48	14	1	4	5	.292	.438	.333
First 9 Batters			369	77	11	13	75	.209	.339	.233
Second 9 Batters			22	5	2	1	1	.227	.591	.292
All Batters Thereafter			0	0	0	0	0	.000	.000	.000

Loves to face: Pete O'Brien (0-for-15, 4 SO)
Hates to face: Bill Stein (.571, 4-for-7)
Ground outs-to-air outs ratio: 0.60 last season (8th-lowest in A.L.), 1.14 for career. . . . Additional statistics: 5 double-play ground outs in 74 opportunities, 13 doubles, 2 triples allowed in 106.2 innings last season. . . . Led A.L. pitchers with 10 relief losses. . . . Average of 1.18 walks per nine innings was 2d-lowest among A.L. relief pitchers (minimum: 30 relief games). . . . Allowed 11 home runs in Late-Inning Pressure Situations last season, one short of the *Player Analysis* record, set by Bob Lacey in 1977. Five of the homers came in extra innings; no other A.L. pitcher allowed more than two. . . . Average of 37.1 air outs every 100 batters faced was 2d-highest in A.L. last season (minimum: 200 BFP). . . . Even in an alleged "bad year," still led A.L. in lowest batting average vs. left-handers (.171).

Ted Higuera

Milwaukee Brewers	W–L	ERA	AB	H	HR	BB	SO	BA	SA	OBA
Season	15-8	3.90	793	186	22	63	127	.235	.373	.290
vs. Left-Handed Batters			127	30	3	10	27	.236	.378	.293
vs. Right-Handed Batters			666	156	19	53	100	.234	.372	.289
Home	7-4	5.44	338	86	14	32	53	.254	.450	.316
Road	8-4	2.78	455	100	8	31	74	.220	.316	.271
Grass	11-7	4.33	629	153	19	49	102	.243	.391	.297
Artificial Turf	4-1	2.35	164	33	3	14	25	.201	.305	.262
Day	3-3	5.84	171	43	8	16	17	.251	.450	.313
Night	12-5	3.38	622	143	14	47	110	.230	.352	.284
April	0-1	6.08	49	12	2	5	8	.245	.408	.304
May	3-2	3.57	129	25	1	15	25	.194	.279	.276
June	1-2	7.27	103	28	3	6	15	.272	.456	.306
July	4-1	3.89	165	37	7	10	29	.224	.394	.267
August	4-0	3.14	163	47	3	12	20	.288	.417	.335
Sept./Oct.	3-2	2.49	184	37	6	15	30	.201	.326	.267
Leading Off Inn.			208	49	6	16	32	.236	.404	.290
Bases Empty			503	120	15	39	83	.239	.390	.295
Runners On			290	66	7	24	44	.228	.345	.282
Runners/Scor. Pos.			141	37	4	16	24	.262	.404	.321
Runners On/2 Out			125	26	2	10	22	.208	.320	.267
Scor. Pos./2 Out			65	16	2	8	11	.246	.400	.329
Late Inning Pressure			147	39	4	8	22	.265	.361	.303
Leading Off			40	12	3	2	5	.300	.575	.333
Bases Empty			90	27	3	6	12	.300	.422	.344
Runners On			57	12	1	2	10	.211	.263	.237
Runners/Scor. Pos.			22	4	0	2	5	.182	.182	.250
First 9 Batters			251	48	4	26	52	.191	.299	.268
Second 9 Batters			233	53	9	19	34	.227	.408	.284
All Batters Thereafter			309	85	9	18	41	.275	.408	.313

Loves to face: Rickey Henderson (0-for-9)
Hates to face: Scott Fletcher (.545, 6-for-11)
Ground outs-to-air outs ratio: 0.82 last season, his first in majors. . . . Additional statistics: 12 double-play ground outs in 138 opportunities, 32 doubles, 6 triples allowed in 212.1 innings last season. . . . Allowed 13 first-inning runs in 30 starts last season. . . . Batting support: 4.43 runs per start. . . . Led A.L. rookies in wins; 2d in majors to 20-game winner Tom Browning. . . . Highest winning percentage in majors (.652) among pitchers for teams with losing records (minimum: 10 wins). . . . Ranked 5th in A.L. with 7.88 hits allowed per nine innings. . . . Road-game ERA ranked 4th in A.L. . . . Allowed one home run for every 24 at bats at County Stadium, one per 57 at bats in road games. . . . Started and won 6 one-run games, most in the A.L.; his ERA in those games was 2.00.

Burt Hooton

Texas Rangers	W–L	ERA	AB	H	HR	BB	SO	BA	SA	OBA
Season	5-8	5.23	501	149	18	40	62	.297	.489	.346
vs. Left-Handed Batters			264	78	13	28	37	.295	.527	.359
vs. Right-Handed Batters			237	71	5	12	25	.300	.447	.331
Home	2-3	4.75	260	73	9	24	37	.281	.462	.338
Road	3-5	5.77	241	76	9	16	25	.315	.519	.355
Grass	4-7	5.40	446	135	17	39	55	.303	.504	.355
Artificial Turf	1-1	3.86	55	14	1	1	7	.255	.364	.268
Day	0-1	10.80	37	14	4	4	5	.378	.784	.429
Night	5-7	4.82	464	135	14	36	57	.291	.466	.339
April	0-0	4.26	24	7	1	2	3	.292	.417	.346
May	2-1	2.53	121	28	2	4	14	.231	.372	.254
June	1-1	5.65	119	34	7	11	22	.286	.571	.346
July	2-3	5.83	121	39	4	10	12	.322	.496	.368
August	0-3	7.77	103	37	3	11	11	.359	.524	.414
Sept./Oct.	0-0	5.40	13	4	1	2	0	.308	.615	.400
Leading Off Inn.			125	37	4	6	13	.296	.472	.328
Bases Empty			291	88	11	20	31	.302	.509	.347
Runners On			210	61	7	20	31	.290	.462	.345
Runners/Scor. Pos.			119	33	2	13	15	.277	.378	.336
Runners On/2 Out			77	16	1	11	15	.208	.286	.307
Scor. Pos./2 Out			52	12	1	9	9	.231	.308	.344
Late Inning Pressure			20	8	0	1	1	.400	.500	.429
Leading Off			6	2	0	1	0	.333	.333	.429
Bases Empty			13	5	0	1	1	.385	.538	.429
Runners On			7	3	0	0	0	.429	.429	.429
Runners/Scor. Pos.			1	0	0	0	0	.000	.000	.000
First 9 Batters			222	59	9	20	29	.266	.477	.325
Second 9 Batters			163	52	5	8	20	.319	.515	.345
All Batters Thereafter			116	38	4	12	13	.328	.474	.388

Loves to face: Rudy Law (.111, 1-for-9)
Hates to face: Dwight Evans (.750, 3-for-4, 3 2B)
Ground outs-to-air outs ratio: 1.28 last season, 1.01 for career. . . . Additional statistics: 10 double-play ground outs in 100 opportunities, 34 doubles, 4 triples allowed in 124.0 innings last season. . . . Average of 5.35 innings per start was 8th-lowest among A.L. pitchers (minimum: 15 GS). . . . Allowed 13 first-inning runs in 20 starts last season. . . . Batting support: 4.00 runs per start. . . . ERA of 5.23 was 7th-highest among A.L. pitchers with at least 15 starts. . . . Opposing batters have hit .337 in Late-Inning Pressure Situations over the past four seasons. . . . Compiled a 2.65 ERA in nine relief appearances. . . . Opposing batters have hit .220 with two outs and runners in scoring position over the past nine seasons.

Charlie Hough

Texas Rangers	W–L	ERA	AB	H	HR	BB	SO	BA	SA	OBA
Season	14-16	3.31	920	198	23	83	141	.215	.338	.283
vs. Left-Handed Batters			495	112	11	42	77	.226	.343	.290
vs. Right-Handed Batters			425	86	12	41	64	.202	.332	.275
Home	8-6	3.52	430	97	12	36	70	.226	.367	.289
Road	6-10	3.13	490	101	11	47	71	.206	.312	.278
Grass	12-12	3.35	726	156	19	64	117	.215	.343	.282
Artificial Turf	2-4	3.15	194	42	4	19	24	.216	.320	.289
Day	3-3	3.79	207	45	7	21	29	.217	.357	.293
Night	11-13	3.17	713	153	16	62	112	.215	.332	.280
April	1-0	2.94	116	21	2	16	24	.181	.259	.291
May	3-4	3.44	196	45	5	14	28	.230	.357	.277
June	1-6	4.17	190	49	5	19	24	.258	.374	.325
July	4-1	2.63	136	22	3	15	24	.162	.243	.260
August	5-1	2.16	178	35	4	13	28	.197	.343	.249
Sept./Oct.	0-4	5.00	104	26	4	6	13	.250	.442	.298
Leading Off Inn.			244	56	8	12	26	.230	.398	.277
Bases Empty			604	127	15	36	87	.210	.334	.262
Runners On			316	71	8	47	54	.225	.345	.321
Runners/Scor. Pos.			184	40	6	26	35	.217	.337	.307
Runners On/2 Out			123	21	3	24	24	.171	.293	.306
Scor. Pos./2 Out			78	15	2	14	14	.192	.308	.315
Late Inning Pressure			115	27	3	10	21	.235	.374	.302
Leading Off			33	7	1	1	3	.212	.455	.257
Bases Empty			78	18	2	3	10	.231	.385	.268
Runners On			37	9	1	7	11	.243	.351	.364
Runners/Scor. Pos.			24	5	1	4	7	.208	.333	.321
First 9 Batters			262	56	6	35	40	.214	.332	.309
Second 9 Batters			286	49	10	17	42	.171	.315	.220
All Batters Thereafter			372	93	7	31	59	.250	.360	.311

Loves to face: Dan Meyer (.059, 1-for-17)
Hates to face: Bill Schroeder (.667, 4-for-6, 2 HR)
Ground outs-to-air outs ratio: 1.11 last season, 1.05 for career. . . . Additional statistics: 20 double-play ground outs in 157 opportunities, 36 doubles, 4 triples allowed in 250.1 innings last season. . . . Lasted 7.36 innings per start, 4th among A.L. pitchers. . . . Batting support: 3.62 runs per start, 4th-lowest average in A.L. (minimum: 15 GS). . . . Ranked 2d in A.L. with an average of 7.12 hits per nine innings. . . . Knuckleball stats: The following have faced Hough and the Niekros at least 10 times each over past 11 seasons: Dave Collins (.384 composite BA), Lonnie Smith (.384), Ken Griffey (.319), Bill Buckner (.284), Larry Herndon (.268), Larry Parrish (.265), Ted Simmons (.250), Dave Winfield (.247), Dave Kingman (.244), Brett Butler (.239), Steve Henderson (.235), Dane Iorg (.234), Darrell Evans (.222), Bob Boone (.197), George Vukovich (.175).

Jay Howell

Oakland As	W–L	ERA	AB	H	HR	BB	SO	BA	SA	OBA
Season	9-8	2.85	375	98	5	31	68	.261	.341	.316
vs. Left-Handed Batters			201	51	1	20	36	.254	.313	.318
vs. Right-Handed Batters			174	47	4	11	32	.270	.374	.314
Home	9-3	2.61	223	58	1	19	41	.260	.314	.318
Road	0-5	3.20	152	40	4	12	27	.263	.382	.313
Grass	9-7	2.63	334	83	5	28	61	.249	.332	.306
Artificial Turf	0-1	5.00	41	15	0	3	7	.366	.415	.400
Day	3-1	1.59	126	29	1	13	28	.230	.270	.300
Night	6-7	3.52	249	69	4	18	40	.277	.378	.325
April	0-1	1.46	46	10	1	5	10	.217	.326	.288
May	3-1	2.89	73	23	1	9	9	.315	.411	.390
June	4-1	1.07	88	15	0	6	17	.170	.193	.227
July	2-1	3.21	60	23	1	7	10	.383	.467	.441
August	0-1	5.00	31	5	0	1	8	.161	.226	.188
Sept./Oct.	0-3	4.82	77	22	2	3	14	.286	.403	.313
Leading Off Inn.			77	16	0	5	11	.208	.221	.256
Bases Empty			182	49	3	11	31	.269	.363	.311
Runners On			193	49	2	20	37	.254	.321	.321
Runners/Scor. Pos.			113	30	0	15	21	.265	.292	.346
Runners On/2 Out			79	11	1	11	14	.139	.190	.244
Scor. Pos./2 Out			50	8	0	8	10	.160	.160	.276
Late Inning Pressure			299	77	4	21	54	.258	.338	.305
Leading Off			66	13	0	0	10	.197	.212	.197
Bases Empty			157	40	2	6	28	.255	.338	.282
Runners On			142	37	2	15	26	.261	.338	.327
Runners/Scor. Pos.			84	23	0	11	15	.274	.298	.350
First 9 Batters			346	91	5	27	62	.263	.344	.315
Second 9 Batters			25	4	0	4	6	.160	.200	.276
All Batters Thereafter			4	3	0	0	0	.750	1.000	.750

Loves to face: Andre Thornton (0-for-10, 2 SO)
Hates to face: George Bell (.800, 4-for-5, 1 2B, 1 HR)
Ground outs-to-air outs ratio: 0.95 last season, 1.08 for career. . . . Additional statistics: 8 double-play ground outs in 101 opportunities, 13 doubles, 1 triple allowed in 98.0 innings last season. . . . Has walked only two leadoff batters in 129 innings in Late-Inning Pressure Situations, lowest career average in 11 years of *The Player Analysis* (minimum: 100 BFP). 0-for-66 mark last season was 3d-best single season during that period. . . Difference between set-up and stopper roles in bullpen? Howell faced 12 more batters in 1984 than in '85, but faced 108 more batters in Late-Inning Pressure Situations in '85. . . . Irony of Howell's spectacular opponents' batting average with two outs and runners on base is that the man he replaced, Bill Caudill, set the *Player Analysis* record last season with .098 for Toronto (minimum: 50 AB).

Bruce Hurst

Boston Red Sox	W–L	ERA	AB	H	HR	BB	SO	BA	SA	OBA
Season	11-13	4.51	890	243	31	70	189	.273	.439	.327
vs. Left-Handed Batters			153	43	5	12	39	.281	.425	.337
vs. Right-Handed Batters			737	200	26	58	150	.271	.442	.325
Home	6-8	4.66	415	118	14	28	81	.284	.448	.331
Road	5-5	4.39	475	125	17	42	108	.263	.432	.323
Grass	11-12	4.47	774	214	25	58	162	.276	.430	.327
Artificial Turf	0-1	4.78	116	29	6	12	27	.250	.500	.323
Day	3-6	5.44	343	102	12	23	58	.297	.458	.341
Night	8-7	3.97	547	141	19	47	131	.258	.428	.318
April	1-1	4.96	138	43	1	9	18	.312	.406	.354
May	0-3	8.69	82	29	5	8	15	.354	.585	.402
June	2-3	5.86	115	36	5	10	26	.313	.513	.367
July	4-1	2.57	182	42	5	10	43	.231	.374	.27[illegible]
August	2-2	4.02	173	41	5	13	36	.237	.382	.298
Sept./Oct.	2-3	4.22	200	52	10	20	51	.260	.470	.327
Leading Off Inn.			216	61	6	22	43	.282	.426	.35[illegible]
Bases Empty			521	135	17	49	109	.259	.415	.324
Runners On			369	108	14	21	80	.293	.474	.33[illegible]
Runners/Scor. Pos.			193	49	6	12	55	.254	.399	.299
Runners On/2 Out			143	40	5	11	35	.280	.483	.335
Scor. Pos./2 Out			89	24	2	8	25	.270	.416	.337
Late Inning Pressure			119	44	7	9	18	.370	.647	.419
Leading Off			33	11	1	2	5	.333	.485	.37[illegible]
Bases Empty			70	25	5	6	9	.357	.643	.408
Runners On			49	19	2	3	9	.388	.653	.434
Runners/Scor. Pos.			23	7	1	3	7	.304	.565	.407
First 9 Batters			277	82	9	26	70	.296	.462	.356
Second 9 Batters			252	54	8	24	47	.214	.377	.282
All Batters Thereafter			361	107	14	20	72	.296	.465	.336

Loves to face: Eddie Murray (.100, 2-for-20)
Hates to face: Tom Brunansky (.688, 11-for-16, 1 HR)
Ground outs-to-air outs ratio: 1.07 last season, 1.13 for career. . . . Additional statistics: 17 double-play ground outs in 184 opportunities, 45 doubles (tied for 8th-most in A.L.), 5 triples allowed in 229.1 innings last season. . . . Total of 81 extra-base hits allowed was 5th-highest in A.L. . . . Allowed 16 first-inning runs in 31 starts last season. . . . Batting support: 6.00 runs per start, 3d-highest average in A.L. (minimum: 15 GS). . . . Ranked 2d in A.L. with an average of 7.42 strikeouts per nine innings. . . . Opponents' career batting average of .319 in Late-Inning Pressure Situations is two points short of the highest mark in *Player Analysis* history, held by Tom Murphy (minimum: 100 hits). . . . Has allowed 20 triples in his career, only two to left-handed batters.

Danny Jackson

Kansas City Royals	W–L	ERA	AB	H	HR	BB	SO	BA	SA	OBA
Season	14-12	3.42	801	209	7	76	114	.261	.361	.328
vs. Left-Handed Batters			158	43	1	18	32	.272	.367	.350
vs. Right-Handed Batters			643	166	6	58	82	.258	.359	.322
Home	6-5	3.38	384	97	2	29	46	.253	.352	.308
Road	8-7	3.46	417	112	5	47	68	.269	.369	.345
Grass	6-5	3.44	321	92	2	39	51	.287	.364	.365
Artificial Turf	8-7	3.40	480	117	5	37	63	.244	.358	.302
Day	3-5	4.26	266	75	2	27	49	.282	.417	.349
Night	11-7	3.01	535	134	5	49	65	.250	.333	.318
April	1-0	1.53	104	22	0	13	15	.212	.298	.299
May	3-2	5.51	136	42	1	20	15	.309	.390	.399
June	2-2	2.45	106	22	3	11	12	.208	.321	.294
July	4-2	2.74	164	39	1	12	29	.238	.317	.292
August	2-2	3.55	132	36	0	8	30	.273	.379	.317
Sept./Oct.	2-4	4.39	159	48	2	12	13	.302	.434	.353
Leading Off Inn.			205	47	2	15	28	.229	.332	.288
Bases Empty			471	121	4	43	72	.257	.350	.326
Runners On			330	88	3	33	42	.267	.376	.332
Runners/Scor. Pos.			183	45	1	21	27	.246	.355	.321
Runners On/2 Out			137	28	0	9	24	.204	.299	.253
Scor. Pos./2 Out			85	19	0	4	16	.224	.341	.258
Late Inning Pressure			94	28	0	8	12	.298	.426	.353
Leading Off			24	4	0	3	4	.167	.208	.259
Bases Empty			58	17	0	5	7	.293	.397	.349
Runners On			36	11	0	3	5	.306	.472	.359
Runners/Scor. Pos.			18	7	0	3	4	.389	.500	.476
First 9 Batters			256	58	3	26	43	.227	.324	.300
Second 9 Batters			255	64	2	23	35	.251	.349	.322
All Batters Thereafter			290	87	2	27	36	.300	.403	.360

Loves to face: Kirby Puckett (0-for-13, 12 ground outs)
Hates to face: Kent Hrbek (.438, 7-for-16, 1 HR)
Ground outs-to-air outs ratio: 1.41 last season, 1.47 for career (1.75 at Royals Stadium, 1.23 in road games). . . . Additional statistics: 26 double-play ground outs in 169 opportunities, 39 doubles, 10 triples (tied for 3d-most in A.L.) allowed in 208.0 innings last season. . . . Allowed 12 first-inning runs in 32 starts last season. . . . Batting support: 3.78 runs per start, 5th-lowest average in A.L. (minimum: 15 GS). . . . Gave up one home run every 29.7 innings, best rate in A.L. last season. . . . Allowed only six stolen bases in 14 attempts in '85; two in four with Sundberg catching. . . . Has allowed only four home runs in 146.2 career innings at Royals Stadium. . . . Walked 15 of 222 leadoff batters last season, 15 of 80 the year before. . . . Tied World Series record by striking out in five consecutive at bats; last A.L. batter to do so was The Mick in 1953.

Bob James

Chicago White Sox	W–L	ERA	AB	H	HR	BB	SO	BA	SA	OBA
Season	8-7	2.13	399	90	5	23	88	.226	.303	.268
vs. Left-Handed Batters			195	46	1	14	44	.236	.297	.283
vs. Right-Handed Batters			204	44	4	9	44	.216	.309	.253
Home	6-3	2.65	207	49	3	15	46	.237	.324	.286
Road	2-4	1.55	192	41	2	8	42	.214	.281	.248
Grass	8-4	2.08	344	78	4	19	81	.227	.299	.268
Artificial Turf	0-3	2.45	55	12	1	4	7	.218	.327	.271
Day	1-1	2.30	120	28	3	5	23	.233	.358	.262
Night	7-6	2.06	279	62	2	18	65	.222	.280	.271
April	1-0	4.97	53	18	1	5	11	.340	.472	.390
May	0-2	1.23	53	10	1	3	18	.189	.264	.232
June	2-0	0.72	87	16	1	6	17	.184	.253	.234
July	1-1	2.16	31	6	0	1	7	.194	.194	.219
August	2-2	2.95	76	18	0	4	14	.237	.289	.289
Sept./Oct.	2-2	1.93	99	22	2	4	21	.222	.323	.248
Leading Off Inn.			79	16	2	6	18	.203	.316	.267
Bases Empty			203	41	2	14	41	.202	.276	.257
Runners On			196	49	3	9	47	.250	.332	.280
Runners/Scor. Pos.			115	29	2	8	27	.252	.348	.295
Runners On/2 Out			91	20	1	5	27	.220	.286	.260
Scor. Pos./2 Out			60	13	1	4	17	.217	.300	.266
Late Inning Pressure			258	59	4	17	54	.229	.318	.275
Leading Off			49	12	2	5	10	.245	.429	.315
Bases Empty			124	26	2	10	24	.210	.306	.269
Runners On			134	33	2	7	30	.246	.328	.281
Runners/Scor. Pos.			85	20	1	6	17	.235	.318	.281
First 9 Batters			380	88	5	21	84	.232	.313	.272
Second 9 Batters			19	2	0	2	4	.105	.105	.190
All Batters Thereafter			0	0	0	0	0	.000	.000	.000

Loves to face: Jesse Barfield (0-for-6, 4 SO)
Hates to face: Rance Mulliniks (3-for-3)
Ground outs-to-air outs ratio: 0.78 last season, 1.03 for career. . . . Additional statistics: 8 double-play ground outs in 93 opportunities, 16 doubles, 0 triples allowed in 110.0 innings last season. . . . Ranked 4th among A.L. relief pitchers with a 2.13 ERA last season (minimum: 30 relief games). . . . Average of 1.88 walks per nine innings was 5th-lowest among that group. . . . Career average of 8.37 strikeouts per nine innings ranks 6th among active pitchers (minimum: 250 SO). . . . Opponents' batting average in Late-Inning Pressure Situations, year by year starting with 1982: .300, .275, .265, .229. Batters faced in LIP situations during those seasons: 10, 82, 190, 287. . . . Has allowed four grand-slam home runs over the past four seasons.

Tommy John

Angels/As	W–L	ERA	AB	H	HR	BB	SO	BA	SA	OBA
Season	4-10	5.53	354	117	9	28	25	.331	.486	.379
vs. Left-Handed Batters			84	26	1	6	9	.310	.393	.352
vs. Right-Handed Batters			270	91	8	22	16	.337	.515	.387
Home	1-5	4.03	147	43	2	8	10	.293	.408	.331
Road	3-5	6.70	207	74	7	20	15	.357	.541	.411
Grass	3-9	5.03	289	90	6	23	22	.311	.453	.363
Artificial Turf	1-1	8.31	65	27	3	5	3	.415	.631	.451
Day	1-4	5.40	145	48	3	8	11	.331	.469	.365
Night	3-6	5.61	209	69	6	20	14	.330	.498	.388
April	1-1	4.73	57	18	2	7	3	.316	.526	.385
May	1-3	4.82	72	24	1	5	9	.333	.444	.380
June	0-0	4.26	26	9	0	3	5	.346	.385	.414
July	1-0	0.00	24	4	0	0	2	.167	.208	.200
August	1-1	5.06	89	30	3	6	2	.337	.506	.379
Sept./Oct.	0-5	9.15	86	32	3	7	4	.372	.581	.411
Leading Off Inn.			89	29	3	5	4	.326	.517	.362
Bases Empty			204	62	6	13	10	.304	.471	.349
Runners On			150	55	3	15	15	.367	.507	.418
Runners/Scor. Pos.			97	30	2	13	12	.309	.454	.383
Runners On/2 Out			65	20	0	9	10	.308	.338	.400
Scor. Pos./2 Out			45	11	0	8	9	.244	.267	.370
Late Inning Pressure			27	10	1	1	0	.370	.630	.379
Leading Off			9	3	0	0	0	.333	.444	.333
Bases Empty			20	6	1	1	0	.300	.500	.333
Runners On			7	4	0	0	0	.571	1.000	.500
Runners/Scor. Pos.			3	2	0	0	0	.667	1.000	.500
First 9 Batters			164	61	2	14	14	.372	.482	.418
Second 9 Batters			117	36	3	9	4	.308	.479	.357
All Batters Thereafter			73	20	4	5	7	.274	.507	.325

Loves to face: Ernie Whitt (.077, 1-for-13, 10 ground outs)
Hates to face: John Shelby (.700, 7-for-10, 1 HR)
Ground outs-to-air outs ratio: 2.11 last season, 2.47 for career; over past 11 years only Doug Corbett, Doug Sisk, and Ray Fontenot have higher ratios (minimum: 1,000 batters faced). . . . Additional statistics: 11 double-play ground outs in 59 opportunities (4th-highest rate in A.L.), 24 doubles, 2 triples allowed in 86.1 innings last season. . . . Average of 4.69 innings per start was 2d-lowest among A.L. pitchers (minimum: 15 GS). . . . Allowed 6 first-inning runs in 17 starts last season. . . . Batting support: 3.24 runs per start, lowest average in A.L. (minimum: 15 GS). . . . ERA of 5.53 was 4th-highest among A.L. pitchers with at least 15 starts. . . . Average of 2.61 strikeouts per nine innings was lowest among that group. . . . Opponents' batting average was highest in majors (minimum: 200 batters faced).

Mike Jones
Kansas City Royals

	W–L	ERA	AB	H	HR	BB	SO	BA	SA	OBA
Season	3-3	4.78	241	62	6	39	32	.257	.411	.353
vs. Left-Handed Batters			72	21	3	15	10	.292	.472	.404
vs. Right-Handed Batters			169	41	3	24	22	.243	.385	.330
Home	2-2	5.01	123	31	4	20	13	.252	.423	.349
Road	1-1	4.55	118	31	2	19	19	.263	.398	.357
Grass	1-1	4.18	89	24	1	14	13	.270	.382	.362
Artificial Turf	2-2	5.13	152	38	5	25	19	.250	.428	.348
Day	1-1	4.95	77	20	1	13	12	.260	.442	.355
Night	2-2	4.70	164	42	5	26	20	.256	.396	.352
April	0-1	0.96	33	5	1	5	6	.152	.303	.263
May	0-0	5.87	30	8	0	6	5	.267	.433	.368
June	1-1	6.43	53	16	2	10	7	.302	.491	.406
July	1-0	1.54	39	8	0	6	4	.205	.231	.304
August	0-0	6.75	53	15	3	6	7	.283	.509	.350
Sept./Oct.	1-1	6.75	33	10	0	6	3	.303	.424	.400
Leading Off Inn.			51	14	1	10	4	.275	.373	.393
Bases Empty			115	30	4	21	15	.261	.400	.375
Runners On			126	32	2	18	17	.254	.421	.333
Runners/Scor. Pos.			77	21	1	13	9	.273	.390	.354
Runners On/2 Out			60	14	1	12	5	.233	.433	.361
Scor. Pos./2 Out			41	11	1	8	3	.268	.463	.388
Late Inning Pressure			54	13	3	9	4	.241	.426	.349
Leading Off			14	3	0	3	1	.214	.214	.353
Bases Empty			29	10	3	8	2	.345	.655	.486
Runners On			25	3	0	1	2	.120	.160	.154
Runners/Scor. Pos.			13	2	0	1	2	.154	.154	.214
First 9 Batters			185	47	6	30	24	.254	.422	.348
Second 9 Batters			49	12	0	6	8	.245	.347	.327
All Batters Thereafter			7	3	0	3	0	.429	.571	.600

Loves to face: Julio Cruz (0-for-9)
Hates to face: Alvin Davis (.625, 5-for-8, 2 HR)
Ground outs-to-air outs ratio: 0.69 last season (1.37 vs. left-handed batters, 0.52 vs. right-handers), 0.66 for career. . . . Additional statistics: 2 double-play ground outs in 59 opportunities (3d-lowest rate in A.L.), 13 doubles, 3 triples allowed in 64.0 innings last season. . . . Career total of 25 games finished is 3d-highest among active pitchers without a save. . . . Has faced 22 batters with the bases loaded in his career, and only nine runs have resulted, the 6th-lowest ratio in *Player Analysis* history. . . . Career average of 9.00 extra-base hits allowed per 100 batters faced is 8th-highest among active pitchers (minimum: 75 XBH). . . . Made his only start of the 1985 season on the final day, a few hours after Royals clinched division title. He was not included on the post-season roster.

Jimmy Key
Toronto Blue Jays

	W–L	ERA	AB	H	HR	BB	SO	BA	SA	OBA
Season	14-6	3.00	794	188	22	50	85	.237	.384	.282
vs. Left-Handed Batters			157	28	4	12	31	.178	.306	.233
vs. Right-Handed Batters			637	160	18	38	54	.251	.403	.295
Home	10-3	2.66	479	110	12	27	54	.230	.370	.271
Road	4-3	3.54	315	78	10	23	31	.248	.406	.299
Grass	4-3	3.75	277	72	10	21	29	.260	.433	.313
Artificial Turf	10-3	2.62	517	116	12	29	56	.224	.358	.265
Day	3-2	3.25	208	52	7	15	28	.250	.423	.302
Night	11-4	2.92	586	136	15	35	57	.232	.370	.275
April	0-2	2.41	72	19	2	9	10	.264	.444	.354
May	3-0	2.87	112	22	3	9	15	.196	.330	.254
June	3-0	2.17	165	34	2	10	19	.206	.297	.250
July	3-2	3.20	171	42	7	8	15	.246	.444	.276
August	2-2	3.93	136	42	2	6	9	.309	.412	.340
Sept./Oct.	3-0	3.35	138	29	6	8	17	.210	.399	.253
Leading Off Inn.			214	49	9	10	21	.229	.430	.263
Bases Empty			518	126	14	26	57	.243	.390	.279
Runners On			276	62	8	24	28	.225	.373	.287
Runners/Scor. Pos.			149	31	4	17	16	.208	.322	.285
Runners On/2 Out			118	31	2	10	12	.263	.398	.331
Scor. Pos./2 Out			66	16	2	7	5	.242	.364	.324
Late Inning Pressure			70	15	1	8	8	.214	.271	.291
Leading Off			19	4	1	3	3	.211	.368	.318
Bases Empty			42	13	1	5	4	.310	.405	.383
Runners On			28	2	0	3	4	.071	.071	.156
Runners/Scor. Pos.			10	1	0	1	0	.100	.100	.167
First 9 Batters			281	65	6	19	40	.231	.377	.284
Second 9 Batters			253	60	8	13	23	.237	.391	.274
All Batters Thereafter			260	63	8	18	22	.242	.385	.287

Loves to face: Dave Winfield (0-for-11, 10 ground outs)
Hates to face: Rickey Henderson (.462, 6-for-13, 3 HR)
Also loves to face: Ron Kittle (0-for-12, 4 SO)—get in line, Jimmy. . . . Ground outs-to-air outs ratio: 1.48 last season, 1.47 for career. . . . Additional statistics: 21 double-play ground outs in 114 opportunities (5th-highest rate in A.L.), 43 doubles, 4 triples allowed in 212.2 innings last season. . . . Allowed 14 first-inning runs in 32 starts last season. . . . Batting support: 4.66 runs per start. . . . Ranked 6th in A.L. with an average of 7.96 hits allowed per nine innings, 5th with an average of 2.12 walks per nine innings. . . . Home-game ERA was 2d-lowest in A.L. last season. . . . Opponents' career batting average of .118 with bases loaded (2-for-17). . . . Thirty-six A.L. pitchers started 30 or more games; Key and Saberhagen are the only two who did not lose two consecutive starts.

Bruce Kison
Boston Red Sox

	W–L	ERA	AB	H	HR	BB	SO	BA	SA	OBA
Season	5-3	4.11	358	98	9	32	56	.274	.413	.332
vs. Left-Handed Batters			187	62	6	23	20	.332	.519	.403
vs. Right-Handed Batters			171	36	3	9	36	.211	.298	.251
Home	2-0	4.35	125	38	2	15	17	.304	.432	.373
Road	3-3	3.98	233	60	7	17	39	.258	.403	.310
Grass	4-2	4.16	263	74	5	27	41	.281	.399	.345
Artificial Turf	1-1	3.96	95	24	4	5	15	.253	.453	.297
Day	2-1	4.29	80	19	3	11	8	.238	.413	.333
Night	3-2	4.06	278	79	6	21	48	.284	.414	.332
April	0-0	6.75	6	2	0	3	0	.333	.500	.556
May	1-1	2.75	77	18	2	5	11	.234	.325	.280
June	2-1	5.70	125	40	3	11	21	.320	.488	.374
July	0-0	4.30	56	15	2	4	11	.268	.464	.317
August	0-1	2.13	44	12	0	4	6	.273	.318	.333
Sept./Oct.	2-0	3.95	50	11	2	5	7	.220	.380	.286
Leading Off Inn.			83	30	2	6	10	.361	.470	.404
Bases Empty			175	60	2	13	23	.343	.451	.392
Runners On			183	38	7	19	33	.208	.377	.278
Runners/Scor. Pos.			110	23	5	14	18	.209	.409	.291
Runners On/2 Out			76	20	3	8	10	.263	.447	.333
Scor. Pos./2 Out			54	15	2	8	4	.278	.481	.371
Late Inning Pressure			45	9	1	3	8	.200	.289	.250
Leading Off			12	3	0	0	2	.250	.250	.250
Bases Empty			30	4	0	1	7	.133	.133	.161
Runners On			15	5	1	2	1	.333	.600	.412
Runners/Scor. Pos.			11	3	0	2	0	.273	.364	.385
First 9 Batters			157	45	4	16	18	.287	.439	.349
Second 9 Batters			111	26	3	9	24	.234	.369	.298
All Batters Thereafter			90	27	2	7	14	.300	.422	.347

Loves to face: Cal Ripken (.071, 1-for-14, 6 SO)
Hates to face: Jorge Orta (.833, 5-for-6, 1 HR)
Also hates to face: Ozzie Guillen (4-for-4). . . . Ground outs-to-air outs ratio: 1.31 last season, 1.31 for career. . . . Additional statistics: 11 double-play ground outs in 87 opportunities, 19 doubles, 2 triples allowed in 92.0 innings last season. . . . Opponents batted 135 points higher with the bases empty than with runners on base last year, largest such difference in A.L. (minimum: 100 AB each way). . . . One of the most lopsided left/right breakdowns over past 11 years (lefties: batting .283, slugging .446; righties: batting .223, slugging .327); last year's 121-point differential marked the third time in the past five years that the batting averages have been more than 100 points apart. . . . Explain this: last season, his first in Fenway Park, was first of his career in which he allowed more home runs in road games than home games.

Bill Krueger
Oakland As

	W–L	ERA	AB	H	HR	BB	SO	BA	SA	OBA
Season	9-10	4.52	597	165	13	69	56	.276	.409	.351
vs. Left-Handed Batters			123	39	3	16	10	.317	.439	.397
vs. Right-Handed Batters			474	126	10	53	46	.266	.401	.338
Home	4-6	4.56	310	87	7	40	32	.281	.400	.363
Road	5-4	4.48	287	78	6	29	24	.272	.418	.338
Grass	9-8	4.56	503	142	12	61	48	.282	.414	.359
Artificial Turf	0-2	4.30	94	23	1	8	8	.245	.383	.304
Day	6-5	3.89	307	89	5	31	26	.290	.394	.355
Night	3-5	5.16	290	76	8	38	30	.262	.424	.346
April	2-2	3.82	123	24	2	18	11	.195	.285	.298
May	2-3	4.35	170	55	5	14	14	.324	.482	.373
June	1-2	9.98	66	22	1	10	7	.333	.455	.423
July	3-2	3.95	108	31	1	11	8	.287	.398	.355
August	0-1	6.75	37	11	1	8	2	.297	.486	.422
Sept./Oct.	1-0	2.39	93	22	3	8	14	.237	.387	.291
Leading Off Inn.			140	48	5	20	9	.343	.514	.429
Bases Empty			322	88	7	41	27	.273	.407	.357
Runners On			275	77	6	28	29	.280	.411	.343
Runners/Scor. Pos.			148	44	4	20	14	.297	.453	.374
Runners On/2 Out			108	29	3	16	11	.269	.417	.363
Scor. Pos./2 Out			68	19	2	11	8	.279	.456	.380
Late Inning Pressure			29	6	0	2	1	.207	.276	.258
Leading Off			10	2	0	0	0	.200	.300	.200
Bases Empty			25	4	0	1	1	.160	.240	.192
Runners On			4	2	0	1	0	.500	.500	.600
Runners/Scor. Pos.			2	1	0	0	0	.500	.500	.500
First 9 Batters			229	66	3	30	19	.288	.393	.366
Second 9 Batters			197	49	3	19	26	.249	.396	.321
All Batters Thereafter			171	50	7	20	11	.292	.444	.363

Loves to face: Rich Dauer (.056, 1-for-18)
Hates to face: Gary Gaetti (.625, 5-for-8, 2 HR)
Ground outs-to-air outs ratio: 1.03 last season, 1.17 for career (0.51 in Late-Inning Pressure Situations, 1.25 otherwise). . . . Additional statistics: 16 double-play ground outs in 135 opportunities, 34 doubles, 3 triples allowed in 151.1 innings last season. . . . Allowed 17 first-inning runs in 23 starts last season. . . . Batting support: 5.52 runs per start, 6th-highest average in A.L. (minimum: 15 GS). . . . Average of 3.33 strikeouts per nine innings was 3d-lowest among A.L. pitchers with at least 15 starts. . . . Career total of 63 starts is 2d-highest among pitchers without a complete-game shutout. . . . Has faced 344 left-handed batters in his career without allowing a triple. . . . Career average of 13.1 walks for every 100 leadoff batters is 4th-highest among active A.L. pitchers (minimum: 50 BB).

Dennis Lamp

Toronto Blue Jays	W–L	ERA	AB	H	HR	BB	SO	BA	SA	OBA
Season	11-0	3.32	388	96	7	27	68	.247	.338	.292
vs. Left-Handed Batters			172	41	3	15	24	.238	.320	.292
vs. Right-Handed Batters			216	55	4	12	44	.255	.352	.293
Home	6-0	3.02	158	42	4	13	29	.266	.386	.316
Road	5-0	3.52	230	54	3	14	39	.235	.304	.275
Grass	5-0	4.08	165	39	3	11	29	.236	.315	.281
Artificial Turf	6-0	2.73	223	57	4	16	39	.256	.354	.300
Day	4-0	2.91	126	29	3	8	23	.230	.325	.272
Night	7-0	3.52	262	67	4	19	45	.256	.344	.302
April	2-0	1.42	44	9	0	5	9	.205	.227	.280
May	2-0	2.89	66	14	0	6	11	.212	.242	.274
June	1-0	5.28	56	15	1	3	10	.268	.429	.295
July	1-0	4.79	85	25	3	3	16	.294	.424	.311
August	1-0	1.37	66	15	1	4	9	.227	.303	.271
Sept./Oct.	4-0	3.86	71	18	2	6	13	.254	.352	.312
Leading Off Inn.			82	18	1	7	19	.220	.256	.281
Bases Empty			205	52	2	13	35	.254	.307	.298
Runners On			183	44	5	14	33	.240	.372	.286
Runners/Scor. Pos.			115	28	3	9	22	.243	.374	.285
Runners On/2 Out			81	15	3	7	16	.185	.321	.250
Scor. Pos./2 Out			57	12	2	4	12	.211	.351	.262
Late Inning Pressure			115	22	1	7	21	.191	.235	.236
Leading Off			31	4	0	0	7	.129	.129	.129
Bases Empty			76	15	0	3	14	.197	.211	.228
Runners On			39	7	1	4	7	.179	.282	.250
Runners/Scor. Pos.			24	4	1	1	4	.167	.292	.192
First 9 Batters			315	77	5	19	53	.244	.327	.283
Second 9 Batters			67	19	2	8	12	.284	.418	.355
All Batters Thereafter			6	0	0	0	3	.000	.000	.000

Loves to face: Ben Oglivie (0-for-10)
Hates to face: Bob Boone (.400, 16-for-40, 3 HR)
Ground outs-to-air outs ratio: 2.62 last season (3d-highest in A.L.), 2.38 for career. . . . Additional statistics: 14 double-play ground outs in 88 opportunities, 10 doubles, 2 triples allowed in 105.2 innings last season. . . . Average of 39.0 ground outs per 100 batters faced was 2d-highest in A.L. last season (minimum: 200 BFP). . . . Set all-time major-league record for relief wins without a loss (11). Previous high: eight wins, by Lew Burdette, Nig Cuppy, Sandy Consuegra, Bob Grim, Grant Jackson, Emil Kush, George Mullin, Charlie Root, and Rube Waddell. . . . Allowed 10 steals in 12 attempts last season; only apprehended thieves: Ozzie Guillen and Reggie Jackson. . . . Difference in Lamp between last season and a year earlier was his ability to handle left-handed hitters: a less than brilliant .311 batting average in 1984, a shining .238 last season.

Gary Lavelle

Toronto Blue Jays	W–L	ERA	AB	H	HR	BB	SO	BA	SA	OBA
Season	5-7	3.10	252	54	5	36	50	.214	.302	.310
vs. Left-Handed Batters			91	20	3	16	21	.220	.330	.330
vs. Right-Handed Batters			161	34	2	20	29	.211	.286	.298
Home	2-1	1.13	109	17	0	11	27	.156	.193	.231
Road	3-6	4.65	143	37	5	25	23	.259	.385	.367
Grass	3-6	4.86	115	29	4	23	20	.252	.374	.374
Artificial Turf	2-1	1.60	137	25	1	13	30	.182	.241	.252
Day	3-2	3.48	109	23	3	16	25	.211	.303	.310
Night	2-5	2.81	143	31	2	20	25	.217	.301	.311
April	0-0	5.68	24	7	0	3	6	.292	.333	.357
May	2-0	0.68	43	5	0	8	11	.116	.163	.255
June	1-2	2.30	50	10	1	12	12	.200	.280	.355
July	0-4	4.32	63	17	1	8	5	.270	.349	.352
August	1-0	4.32	33	8	2	0	8	.242	.424	.242
Sept./Oct.	1-1	2.92	39	7	1	5	8	.179	.282	.267
Leading Off Inn.			56	11	1	5	11	.196	.286	.262
Bases Empty			132	26	3	15	27	.197	.280	.279
Runners On			120	28	2	21	23	.233	.325	.343
Runners/Scor. Pos.			72	11	0	17	17	.153	.194	.308
Runners On/2 Out			54	15	1	12	8	.278	.370	.409
Scor. Pos./2 Out			37	6	0	11	7	.162	.189	.354
Late Inning Pressure			153	35	3	27	30	.229	.314	.343
Leading Off			33	7	1	4	4	.212	.303	.297
Bases Empty			75	16	2	10	16	.213	.293	.306
Runners On			78	19	1	17	14	.244	.333	.375
Runners/Scor. Pos.			45	9	0	14	10	.200	.267	.383
First 9 Batters			250	54	5	34	50	.216	.304	.308
Second 9 Batters			2	0	0	2	0	.000	.000	.500
All Batters Thereafter			0	0	0	0	0	.000	.000	.000

Loves to face: Dave Kingman (.143, 2-for-14, 5 SO)
Hates to face: Lee Lacy (.423, 11-for-26, 1 HR)
Ground outs-to-air outs ratio: 1.57 last season, 1.61 for career (2.25 vs. left-handed batters, 1.42 vs. right-handers). . . . Additional statistics: 9 double-play ground outs in 63 opportunities, 3 doubles, 2 triples allowed in 72.2 innings last season. . . . Average of 6.69 hits per nine innings was 5th-lowest among A.L. relievers (minimum: 30 relief games). . . . Career average of one extra-base hit allowed per 33.4 at bats by left-handed batters is 3d-lowest in 11 years of *The Player Analysis* (minimum: 250 AB). . . . Tied Brian Fisher for A.L. lead with eight save set-ups (see Oakland essay). . . . Opponents' batting average in Late-Inning Pressure Situations was his lowest in the past 11 seasons. . . . Career average of 2.87 strikeouts per walk vs. left-handed batters, 1.48 vs. right-handers.

Mark Langston

Seattle Mariners	W–L	ERA	AB	H	HR	BB	SO	BA	SA	OBA
Season	7-14	5.47	479	122	22	91	72	.255	.451	.375
vs. Left-Handed Batters			79	18	3	14	17	.228	.392	.344
vs. Right-Handed Batters			400	104	19	77	55	.260	.463	.380
Home	4-5	5.43	217	59	6	31	30	.272	.410	.368
Road	3-9	5.50	262	63	16	60	42	.240	.485	.380
Grass	2-7	6.02	187	49	13	42	29	.262	.535	.394
Artificial Turf	5-7	5.12	292	73	9	49	43	.250	.397	.362
Day	3-1	2.96	98	22	2	16	16	.224	.316	.333
Night	4-13	6.16	381	100	20	75	56	.262	.486	.385
April	3-2	2.75	131	29	4	22	15	.221	.366	.333
May	2-3	4.94	88	19	5	18	16	.216	.420	.355
June	0-1	8.31	19	7	1	3	3	.368	.632	.455
July	0-1	5.79	18	6	1	1	4	.333	.611	.368
August	2-4	5.61	125	33	6	25	13	.264	.464	.388
Sept./Oct.	0-3	9.25	98	28	5	22	21	.286	.510	.413
Leading Off Inn.			112	25	4	23	15	.223	.357	.356
Bases Empty			257	65	16	55	36	.253	.486	.385
Runners On			222	57	6	36	36	.257	.410	.363
Runners/Scor. Pos.			119	29	2	27	18	.244	.387	.383
Runners On/2 Out			94	28	4	16	15	.298	.521	.405
Scor. Pos./2 Out			60	20	2	12	11	.333	.567	.444
Late Inning Pressure			13	2	0	3	2	.154	.154	.313
Leading Off			4	0	0	0	1	.000	.000	.000
Bases Empty			9	1	0	1	1	.111	.111	.200
Runners On			4	1	0	2	1	.250	.250	.500
Runners/Scor. Pos.			2	1	0	2	0	.500	.500	.750
First 9 Batters			170	42	4	36	35	.247	.376	.385
Second 9 Batters			160	44	9	28	20	.275	.500	.379
All Batters Thereafter			149	36	9	27	17	.242	.483	.358

Loves to face: Wade Boggs (0-for-9)
Hates to face: Julio Franco (.556, 5-for-9)
Ground outs-to-air outs ratio: 1.13 last season, 1.03 for career (1.91 in Late-Inning Pressure Situations, 0.97 unpressured). . . . Additional statistics: 13 double-play ground outs in 117 opportunities, 22 doubles, 3 triples allowed in 126.2 innings last season. . . . Allowed 20 first-inning runs in 24 starts last season. . . . Batting support: 3.96 runs per start, 9th-lowest average in A.L. (minimum: 15 GS). . . . Ranked among the league "leaders" in quite a few categories (minimum for all: 15 GS), most of which he'd just as soon forget: led in walks per nine innings with 6.47; had the 3d-worst home-run rate with one homer every 5.8 innings; had the 6th-highest ERA at 5.47; and lasted 5.28 innings per start to stand 6th-lowest among the league's starters. . . . His career walk rate (5.35 per nine innings) is 4th-highest among active pitchers (minimum: 200 BB).

Luis Leal

Toronto Blue Jays	W–L	ERA	AB	H	HR	BB	SO	BA	SA	OBA
Season	3-6	5.75	271	82	13	24	33	.303	.528	.361
vs. Left-Handed Batters			136	43	6	13	13	.316	.522	.368
vs. Right-Handed Batters			135	39	7	11	20	.289	.533	.353
Home	2-2	5.40	143	39	6	10	23	.273	.503	.321
Road	1-4	6.16	128	43	7	14	10	.336	.555	.404
Grass	1-2	5.32	99	33	6	7	10	.333	.556	.376
Artificial Turf	2-4	5.98	172	49	7	17	23	.285	.512	.352
Day	2-2	5.73	126	32	6	11	17	.254	.500	.314
Night	1-4	5.77	145	50	7	13	16	.345	.552	.400
April	2-1	3.13	115	24	5	8	13	.209	.400	.260
May	0-2	7.88	69	24	2	8	8	.348	.522	.420
June	1-3	8.24	87	34	6	8	12	.391	.701	.439
July			0	0	0	0	0	.000	.000	.000
August			0	0	0	0	0	.000	.000	.000
Sept./Oct.			0	0	0	0	0	.000	.000	.000
Leading Off Inn.			73	23	4	3	8	.315	.575	.342
Bases Empty			159	47	7	16	17	.296	.497	.364
Runners On			112	35	6	8	16	.313	.571	.357
Runners/Scor. Pos.			60	22	3	7	10	.367	.633	.417
Runners On/2 Out			46	15	2	2	8	.326	.522	.354
Scor. Pos./2 Out			25	10	1	1	4	.400	.600	.423
Late Inning Pressure			9	4	2	2	1	.444	1.222	.545
Leading Off			3	2	1	1	1	.667	2.000	.750
Bases Empty			5	3	2	1	1	.600	2.000	.667
Runners On			4	1	0	1	0	.250	.250	.400
Runners/Scor. Pos.			2	1	0	1	0	.500	.500	.667
First 9 Batters			111	33	3	11	18	.297	.468	.367
Second 9 Batters			106	29	2	7	13	.274	.396	.316
All Batters Thereafter			54	20	8	6	2	.370	.907	.433

Loves to face: Fred Lynn (.053, 1-for-19)
Hates to face: Wade Boggs (.500, 10-for-20, 1 HR)
Ground outs-to-air outs ratio: 0.99 last season, 0.84 for career. . . . Additional statistics: 8 double-play ground outs in 47 opportunities, 18 doubles, 2 triples allowed in 67.1 innings last season. . . . Allowed 13 first-inning runs in 14 starts last season. . . . Batting support: 4.00 runs per start. . . . Highest opponents' slugging average in majors in '85 (minimum: 200 batters faced). . . . Allowed 11 extra-base hits in 54 at bats in Late-Inning Pressure Situations in 1984. . . . Failed to complete five innings in half of his 14 starts, including early showers in each of his last four starts before being banished to Syracuse, where he won six of eight decisions. . . . Entering last season, opposing batters had a career batting average of .205 with two outs and runners in scoring position.

Charlie Leibrandt

Kansas City Royals	W–L	ERA	AB	H	HR	BB	SO	BA	SA	OBA
Season	17-9	2.69	900	223	17	68	108	.248	.356	.301
vs. Left-Handed Batters			204	51	4	12	29	.250	.348	.294
vs. Right-Handed Batters			696	172	13	56	79	.247	.358	.303
Home	9-2	2.56	403	99	6	29	50	.246	.352	.297
Road	8-7	2.79	497	124	11	39	58	.249	.358	.303
Grass	5-5	3.25	354	98	10	25	36	.277	.415	.322
Artificial Turf	12-4	2.34	546	125	7	43	72	.229	.317	.287
Day	3-2	1.85	169	45	4	10	19	.266	.385	.306
Night	14-7	2.88	731	178	13	58	89	.244	.349	.299
April	3-0	1.69	118	28	1	5	16	.237	.322	.268
May	2-3	3.35	167	40	5	14	8	.240	.383	.295
June	1-2	3.34	117	28	1	15	20	.239	.291	.326
July	4-1	3.96	154	43	4	10	15	.279	.396	.321
August	3-1	2.40	175	43	4	14	24	.246	.389	.305
Sept./Oct.	4-2	1.43	169	41	2	10	25	.243	.325	.285
Leading Off Inn.			233	64	4	15	20	.275	.378	.319
Bases Empty			535	143	10	39	61	.267	.374	.317
Runners On			365	80	7	29	47	.219	.329	.277
Runners/Scor. Pos.			206	46	2	18	22	.223	.296	.286
Runners On/2 Out			156	33	5	15	19	.212	.353	.289
Scor. Pos./2 Out			105	23	2	9	9	.219	.314	.293
Late Inning Pressure			91	26	4	10	14	.286	.484	.363
Leading Off			27	8	1	2	1	.296	.444	.345
Bases Empty			61	16	2	6	8	.262	.426	.328
Runners On			30	10	2	4	6	.333	.600	.429
Runners/Scor. Pos.			14	4	1	3	1	.286	.500	.444
First 9 Batters			271	64	3	22	31	.236	.310	.292
Second 9 Batters			268	65	5	21	28	.243	.347	.299
All Batters Thereafter			361	94	9	25	49	.260	.396	.308

Loves to face: Ruppert Jones (0-for-9)
Hates to face: Jim Gantner (.833, 5-for-6)
Ground outs-to-air outs ratio: 1.27 last season, 1.21 for career. . . . Additional statistics: 21 double-play ground outs in 168 opportunities, 34 doubles, 6 triples allowed in 237.2 innings last season. . . . Ranked 10th among A.L. pitchers with an average of 7.20 innings per start. . . . Allowed 7 first-inning runs in 33 starts, 2d-lowest rate in A.L. last season (minimum: 15 GS). . . . Batting support: 4.58 runs per start. . . . Allowed one home run every 14.0 innings last season, 6th-best rate in A.L. last season. . . . Home-game ERA was lowest in A.L. in '85. He had the lowest day-game ERA in majors as well. . . . Relief appearance in final game of 1985 A.L. playoffs was his first since September 30, 1982, when he pitched an inning of relief to defeat San Diego while pitching for Cincinnati.

Tim Lollar

White Sox/Red Sox	W–L	ERA	AB	H	HR	BB	SO	BA	SA	OBA
Season	8-10	4.62	560	140	19	98	105	.250	.427	.361
vs. Left-Handed Batters			120	25	3	17	34	.208	.342	.309
vs. Right-Handed Batters			440	115	16	81	71	.261	.450	.375
Home	5-3	4.07	287	70	11	50	60	.244	.439	.355
Road	3-7	5.25	273	70	8	48	45	.256	.414	.368
Grass	7-10	4.89	525	133	18	93	99	.253	.434	.365
Artificial Turf	1-0	0.90	35	7	1	5	6	.200	.314	.300
Day	3-5	4.43	245	56	10	50	55	.229	.404	.361
Night	5-5	4.77	315	84	9	48	50	.267	.444	.361
April	1-1	5.18	93	25	3	17	18	.269	.441	.378
May	0-1	3.93	69	17	2	12	16	.246	.435	.366
June	1-2	3.41	106	28	4	22	20	.264	.443	.385
July	2-2	8.53	76	25	5	10	16	.329	.632	.398
August	1-3	3.48	111	23	1	18	16	.207	.315	.318
Sept./Oct.	3-1	4.45	105	22	4	19	19	.210	.362	.336
Leading Off Inn.			131	31	2	26	26	.237	.374	.367
Bases Empty			289	75	9	67	60	.260	.446	.402
Runners On			271	65	10	31	45	.240	.406	.313
Runners/Scor. Pos.			158	32	1	23	27	.203	.285	.296
Runners On/2 Out			114	27	3	14	20	.237	.360	.320
Scor. Pos./2 Out			67	13	0	13	12	.194	.254	.325
Late Inning Pressure			38	13	1	10	6	.342	.658	.480
Leading Off			9	4	0	4	2	.444	1.000	.615
Bases Empty			16	5	0	7	4	.313	.688	.542
Runners On			22	8	1	3	2	.364	.636	.423
Runners/Scor. Pos.			14	7	0	3	1	.500	.714	.556
First 9 Batters			236	60	8	36	58	.254	.424	.352
Second 9 Batters			181	44	6	31	27	.243	.392	.354
All Batters Thereafter			143	36	5	31	20	.252	.476	.383

Loves to face: Lee Lacy (.125, 2-for-16)
Hates to face: Paul Householder (.421, 8-for-19, 3 HR)
Ground outs-to-air outs ratio: 0.87 last season, 0.81 for career. . . . Additional statistics: 15 double-play ground outs in 123 opportunities, 32 doubles, 5 triples allowed in 150.0 innings last season. . . . Allowed 9 first-inning runs in 23 starts last season. . . . Batting support: 4.70 runs per start. . . . Average of 5.88 walks per nine innings was highest among A.L. pitchers (minimum: 15 GS). . . . Opposing batters have a career batting average of .203 with two outs and runners in scoring position. . . . Had a 1-0 record with a 5.21 ERA in 11 relief appearances last season. . . . Has allowed 86 career home runs, but only 11 to left-handed batters. . . . Drove in 19 of 36 base runners from scoring position during his final two seasons in N.L.

Aurelio Lopez

Detroit Tigers	W–L	ERA	AB	H	HR	BB	SO	BA	SA	OBA
Season	3-7	4.80	328	82	15	41	53	.250	.436	.330
vs. Left-Handed Batters			147	33	3	23	28	.224	.306	.324
vs. Right-Handed Batters			181	49	12	18	25	.271	.541	.335
Home	2-3	4.90	245	62	12	21	43	.253	.437	.307
Road	1-4	4.50	83	20	3	20	10	.241	.434	.387
Grass	3-4	4.46	293	73	13	33	48	.249	.423	.321
Artificial Turf	0-3	7.45	35	9	2	8	5	.257	.543	.391
Day	0-3	4.94	92	25	3	9	8	.272	.413	.330
Night	3-4	4.74	236	57	12	32	45	.242	.445	.330
April	0-1	4.50	44	9	2	3	8	.205	.341	.250
May	0-1	2.38	84	19	3	12	9	.226	.345	.313
June	1-3	5.87	62	18	3	7	4	.290	.484	.366
July	0-2	6.97	41	9	2	4	14	.220	.439	.289
August	2-0	2.41	61	11	0	9	15	.180	.279	.282
Sept./Oct.	0-0	13.50	36	16	5	6	3	.444	.944	.524
Leading Off Inn.			69	17	2	7	15	.246	.406	.325
Bases Empty			175	40	8	17	35	.229	.423	.301
Runners On			153	42	7	24	18	.275	.451	.361
Runners/Scor. Pos.			93	29	5	16	11	.312	.516	.391
Runners On/2 Out			69	19	2	10	7	.275	.406	.367
Scor. Pos./2 Out			48	13	2	6	4	.271	.438	.352
Late Inning Pressure			140	32	6	23	28	.229	.393	.339
Leading Off			33	7	0	4	8	.212	.242	.316
Bases Empty			82	18	3	8	17	.220	.366	.297
Runners On			58	14	3	15	11	.241	.431	.392
Runners/Scor. Pos.			36	11	2	10	7	.306	.500	.447
First 9 Batters			280	70	14	38	45	.250	.454	.336
Second 9 Batters			43	10	1	3	7	.233	.302	.277
All Batters Thereafter			5	2	0	0	1	.400	.600	.400

Loves to face: Tom Brunansky (0-for-15)
Hates to face: Ernie Whitt (.429, 6-for-14, 3 HR)
Ground outs-to-air outs ratio: 0.65 last season (9th-lowest in A.L.), 0.65 for career. . . . Additional statistics: 5 double-play ground outs in 80 opportunities, 12 doubles, 2 triples allowed in 86.1 innings last season. . . . Allowed 50 runs in relief last season, 4th-highest total in A.L. . . . Career winning percentage of .640 (57–32) ranks 2d among active pitchers with at least 50 wins. . . . Right-handed batters averaged one home run every 15.1 at bats last year, 2d-worst rate in majors. Average of one extra-base hit per 7.9 at bats by right-handers was also 2d-worst (minimum: 200 BFP). . . . One of three pitchers to allow a grand-slam home run in each of the past three seasons. The others: Bob James and Phil Niekro. . . . Opposing batters had hit .167 in Late-Inning Pressure Situations with runners in scoring position in three years prior to last season's disaster.

Urbano Lugo

California Angels	W–L	ERA	AB	H	HR	BB	SO	BA	SA	OBA
Season	3-4	3.69	314	86	10	29	42	.274	.436	.341
vs. Left-Handed Batters			178	56	5	19	28	.315	.478	.382
vs. Right-Handed Batters			136	30	5	10	14	.221	.382	.287
Home	1-1	3.07	149	38	5	11	22	.255	.396	.317
Road	2-3	4.29	165	48	5	18	20	.291	.473	.362
Grass	2-3	3.84	255	71	8	24	36	.278	.439	.347
Artificial Turf	1-1	3.00	59	15	2	5	6	.254	.424	.313
Day	2-2	3.74	125	31	1	11	24	.248	.360	.317
Night	1-2	3.65	189	55	9	18	18	.291	.487	.357
April	0-0	0.00	7	2	0	1	1	.286	.286	.375
May	0-0	1.08	35	12	1	3	3	.343	.457	.395
June	3-1	2.10	112	24	4	6	18	.214	.393	.258
July	0-2	6.33	104	32	4	11	13	.308	.500	.381
August	0-1	8.10	11	3	0	3	2	.273	.455	.429
Sept./Oct.	0-0	2.84	45	13	1	5	5	.289	.400	.373
Leading Off Inn.			79	22	4	6	15	.278	.506	.345
Bases Empty			181	54	8	22	26	.298	.486	.383
Runners On			133	32	2	7	16	.241	.368	.280
Runners/Scor. Pos.			76	15	1	4	11	.197	.329	.241
Runners On/2 Out			50	8	0	2	6	.160	.200	.192
Scor. Pos./2 Out			30	5	0	1	4	.167	.200	.194
Late Inning Pressure			22	6	2	3	3	.273	.591	.360
Leading Off			8	4	1	1	1	.500	1.000	.556
Bases Empty			16	6	2	1	2	.375	.813	.412
Runners On			6	0	0	2	1	.000	.000	.250
Runners/Scor. Pos.			5	0	0	2	1	.000	.000	.286
First 9 Batters			147	39	4	10	21	.265	.408	.325
Second 9 Batters			109	30	3	10	16	.275	.422	.333
All Batters Thereafter			58	17	3	9	5	.293	.534	.391

Loves to face: George Bell (0-for-6)
Hates to face: Rance Mulliniks (.714, 5-for-7)
Ground outs-to-air outs ratio: 0.79 last season, his first in majors. . . . Additional statistics: 7 double-play ground outs in 59 opportunities, 17 doubles, 2 triples allowed in 83.0 innings last season. . . . Allowed 7 first-inning runs in 10 starts last season. . . . Batting support: 4.30 runs per start. . . . Has allowed one home run per 22.6 at bats with the bases empty, 8th-highest rate in the last 11 years (minimum: 200 PA). . . . Angels won seven consecutive games that he started, June 16–July 14. . . . ERA of 4.42 in 10 starts, 2.08 in 10 relief appearances. All of his decisions were as a starter. . . . Won both starts he made against the White Sox, with a 1.93 ERA in those games. . . . Where in hell are the Angels getting all these young pitchers? Witt, Romanick, McCaskill, Clements, Lugo, and Kipper are all children of the '60s.

Rick Lysander

Minnesota Twins	W–L	ERA	AB	H	HR	BB	SO	BA	SA	OBA
Season	0-2	6.05	236	72	3	22	26	.305	.415	.362
vs. Left-Handed Batters			108	34	3	10	12	.315	.491	.370
vs. Right-Handed Batters			128	38	0	12	14	.297	.352	.355
Home	0-0	3.25	96	22	0	12	8	.229	.271	.315
Road	0-2	8.37	140	50	3	10	18	.357	.514	.395
Grass	0-2	7.30	98	30	3	8	13	.306	.480	.355
Artificial Turf	0-0	5.20	138	42	0	14	13	.304	.370	.366
Day	0-1	8.44	69	25	2	7	11	.362	.522	.416
Night	0-1	5.20	167	47	1	15	15	.281	.371	.339
April	0-1	6.43	28	9	0	3	3	.321	.429	.387
May	0-0	6.16	75	25	1	9	10	.333	.480	.400
June	0-0	5.65	53	15	0	3	4	.283	.340	.316
July	0-1	6.00	47	15	1	3	7	.319	.404	.360
August	0-0	13.50	4	0	0	2	0	.000	.000	.333
Sept./Oct.	0-0	4.91	29	8	1	2	2	.276	.448	.323
Leading Off Inn.			49	17	1	5	6	.347	.429	.407
Bases Empty			111	34	1	9	11	.306	.378	.358
Runners On			125	38	2	13	15	.304	.448	.364
Runners/Scor. Pos.			80	27	2	8	10	.338	.525	.389
Runners On/2 Out			48	17	0	5	8	.354	.417	.415
Scor. Pos./2 Out			34	13	0	3	6	.382	.471	.432
Late Inning Pressure			32	11	1	3	3	.344	.656	.400
Leading Off			6	2	0	2	0	.333	.500	.500
Bases Empty			13	5	0	2	1	.385	.538	.467
Runners On			19	6	1	1	2	.316	.737	.350
Runners/Scor. Pos.			14	4	1	0	2	.286	.786	.286
First 9 Batters			194	60	2	19	24	.309	.423	.367
Second 9 Batters			41	12	1	3	2	.293	.390	.341
All Batters Thereafter			1	0	0	0	0	.000	.000	.000

Loves to face: Dave Collins (0-for-5, 3 SO)
Hates to face: Wade Boggs (.538, 7-for-13)
Ground outs-to-air outs ratio: 2.50 last season (4th-highest in A.L.), 2.05 for career. . . . Additional statistics: 12 double-play ground outs in 58 opportunities (highest rate in A.L.), 9 doubles, 4 triples allowed in 61.0 innings last season. . . . Allowed one home run per 29.3 relief innings, 4th-lowest average in A.L. (minimum: 30 relief games). . . . Rate of 3.53 strikeouts per nine innings was 3d-lowest among that same group. . . . Has allowed only two home runs at the Metrodome in three seasons with the Twins, compared to 11 in road games during that time. . . . Has faced 324 right-handed batters without allowing a home run since throwing a gopher ball to Larry Parrish on September 5, 1983.

Dennis Martinez

Baltimore Orioles	W–L	ERA	AB	H	HR	BB	SO	BA	SA	OBA
Season	13-11	5.15	706	203	29	63	68	.288	.472	.349
vs. Left-Handed Batters			388	106	14	45	41	.273	.459	.344
vs. Right-Handed Batters			318	97	15	18	27	.305	.487	.354
Home	5-6	6.11	299	90	13	22	35	.301	.468	.354
Road	8-5	4.49	407	113	16	41	33	.278	.474	.345
Grass	9-10	5.29	586	169	23	57	53	.288	.461	.353
Artificial Turf	4-1	4.45	120	34	6	6	15	.283	.525	.323
Day	4-4	3.97	219	61	6	16	18	.279	.429	.332
Night	9-7	5.69	487	142	23	47	50	.292	.491	.356
April	2-1	3.79	70	17	2	6	11	.243	.400	.295
May	2-2	4.60	123	39	6	11	9	.317	.528	.372
June	2-2	4.55	105	27	2	14	8	.257	.371	.341
July	1-2	7.45	128	43	6	7	16	.336	.539	.375
August	4-0	4.08	108	28	7	8	14	.259	.519	.322
Sept./Oct.	2-4	5.74	172	49	6	17	10	.285	.442	.356
Leading Off Inn.			181	49	7	10	19	.271	.425	.316
Bases Empty			435	122	16	33	49	.280	.451	.341
Runners On			271	81	13	30	19	.299	.506	.360
Runners/Scor. Pos.			150	43	9	22	13	.287	.527	.355
Runners On/2 Out			113	28	6	13	8	.248	.434	.336
Scor. Pos./2 Out			73	21	5	9	7	.288	.534	.366
Late Inning Pressure			59	17	1	4	7	.288	.424	.328
Leading Off			17	4	0	0	3	.235	.353	.235
Bases Empty			39	11	1	3	7	.282	.462	.333
Runners On			20	6	0	1	0	.300	.350	.318
Runners/Scor. Pos.			12	4	0	1	0	.333	.333	.357
First 9 Batters			266	74	11	24	24	.278	.474	.339
Second 9 Batters			232	67	7	23	19	.289	.427	.355
All Batters Thereafter			208	62	11	16	25	.298	.519	.354

Loves to face: Rich Gedman (0-for-15)
Hates to face: Steve Henderson (.538, 7-for-13)
Ground outs-to-air outs ratio: 1.05 last season, 1.16 for career. . . . Additional statistics: 15 double-play ground outs in 129 opportunities, 35 doubles, 4 triples allowed in 180.0 innings last season. . . . Allowed 26 first-inning runs (tied for 2d-most in A.L.) in 31 starts last season. . . . Batting support: 6.16 runs per start, highest average in A.L. (minimum: 15 GS). . . . ERA of 5.15 was 8th-highest among A.L. pitchers with at least 15 starts. . . . Career total of 108 wins ranks 3d among active pitchers with ERAs above 4.00. . . . Knocked out of 10 games before 5th inning last season. Orioles starters had 47 such games; 13 other A.L. teams averaged 38. . . . In his career, has thrown 14 double-play ground balls in 48 batters faced with the bases loaded and less than two outs.

Tippy Martinez

Baltimore Orioles	W–L	ERA	AB	H	HR	BB	SO	BA	SA	OBA
Season	3-3	5.40	268	70	8	37	47	.261	.407	.346
vs. Left-Handed Batters			106	21	1	8	25	.198	.311	.250
vs. Right-Handed Batters			162	49	7	29	22	.302	.469	.404
Home	2-1	3.73	157	39	4	20	28	.248	.382	.331
Road	1-2	7.76	111	31	4	17	19	.279	.441	.366
Grass	3-1	5.16	233	61	7	30	40	.262	.403	.341
Artificial Turf	0-2	7.00	35	9	1	7	7	.257	.429	.381
Day	2-2	4.18	90	22	1	12	15	.244	.333	.330
Night	1-1	6.02	178	48	7	25	32	.270	.444	.354
April	1-1	5.23	45	16	2	3	8	.356	.600	.388
May	0-1	3.86	49	13	1	5	9	.265	.367	.333
June	0-0	6.39	47	13	1	8	7	.277	.362	.375
July	1-0	5.40	37	10	3	7	4	.270	.541	.370
August	0-0	6.23	27	3	0	10	6	.111	.185	.351
Sept./Oct.	1-1	5.40	63	15	1	4	13	.238	.349	.284
Leading Off Inn.			56	13	3	7	10	.232	.464	.317
Bases Empty			128	32	4	19	22	.250	.422	.347
Runners On			140	38	4	18	25	.271	.393	.346
Runners/Scor. Pos.			81	24	3	13	15	.296	.444	.378
Runners On/2 Out			68	18	4	8	10	.265	.456	.342
Scor. Pos./2 Out			42	13	3	6	7	.310	.548	.396
Late Inning Pressure			81	19	3	14	12	.235	.407	.347
Leading Off			18	4	1	3	3	.222	.389	.333
Bases Empty			38	11	2	7	4	.289	.500	.400
Runners On			43	8	1	7	8	.186	.326	.300
Runners/Scor. Pos.			26	4	0	5	6	.154	.192	.290
First 9 Batters			226	60	7	33	39	.265	.407	.354
Second 9 Batters			37	9	1	4	6	.243	.405	.317
All Batters Thereafter			5	1	0	0	2	.200	.400	.200

Loves to face: Tom Paciorek (0-for-10, 6 SO)
Hates to face: Dave Henderson (.714, 5-for-7, 2 HR)
Ground outs-to-air outs ratio: 2.19 last season (highest in his career, 7th-highest in A.L.), 1.59 for career. . . . Additional statistics: 8 double-play ground outs in 74 opportunities, 11 doubles, 2 triples allowed in 70.0 innings last season. . . . Allowed 48 runs in relief in '85, 5th-highest total in A.L. . . . Opposing right-handed batters hit 104 points higher than left-handers, 2d-largest difference in A.L. (minimum: 100 AB each way). . . . Last season was fourth in past six years that opposing left-handers have hit below .200. . . . Faced only 96 batters in Late-Inning Pressure Situations last season, fewest since '75, when he split his time between Syracuse of the International League and the New York Yankees. . . . Opposing batters have a career batting average of .178 in LIP with runners in scoring position.

Mike Mason

Texas Rangers	W–L	ERA	AB	H	HR	BB	SO	BA	SA	OBA
Season	8-15	4.83	710	212	22	73	92	.299	.461	.362
vs. Left-Handed Batters			154	43	4	19	17	.279	.416	.356
vs. Right-Handed Batters			556	169	18	54	75	.304	.473	.363
Home	4-6	4.99	339	104	15	28	46	.307	.487	.359
Road	4-9	4.69	371	108	7	45	46	.291	.437	.364
Grass	7-13	4.90	608	185	21	60	75	.304	.474	.365
Artificial Turf	1-2	4.45	102	27	1	13	17	.265	.382	.345
Day	3-5	4.37	180	51	5	20	25	.283	.411	.358
Night	5-10	4.98	530	161	17	53	67	.304	.477	.363
April	2-2	4.63	94	25	4	12	17	.266	.436	.355
May	2-2	5.18	135	43	7	9	13	.319	.556	.351
June	1-3	4.66	116	34	4	11	16	.293	.474	.352
July	0-3	5.45	130	43	2	15	8	.331	.462	.397
August	0-2	4.24	70	19	1	11	9	.271	.400	.370
Sept./Oct.	3-3	4.53	165	48	4	15	29	.291	.412	.350
Leading Off Inn.			171	54	8	18	16	.316	.567	.384
Bases Empty			397	113	14	39	41	.285	.476	.352
Runners On			313	99	8	34	51	.316	.441	.374
Runners/Scor. Pos.			169	47	5	25	28	.278	.402	.356
Runners On/2 Out			124	42	2	16	19	.339	.427	.418
Scor. Pos./2 Out			72	20	1	12	11	.278	.347	.388
Late Inning Pressure			37	10	1	9	5	.270	.459	.426
Leading Off			10	2	0	3	3	.200	.200	.429
Bases Empty			23	5	0	5	4	.217	.304	.379
Runners On			14	5	1	4	1	.357	.714	.500
Runners/Scor. Pos.			5	2	0	4	1	.400	.600	.667
First 9 Batters			271	78	4	33	48	.288	.402	.359
Second 9 Batters			250	71	9	18	22	.284	.456	.332
All Batters Thereafter			189	63	9	22	22	.333	.550	.403

Loves to face: Gary Gaetti (.067, 1-for-15, 5 SO)
Hates to face: Ron Kittle (.545, 6-for-11, 3 HR)
Ground outs-to-air outs ratio: 1.02 last season, 1.18 for career. . . . Additional statistics: 16 double-play ground outs in 160 opportunities, 35 doubles, 7 triples (tied for 6th-most in A.L.) allowed in 179.0 innings last season. . . . Allowed 13 first-inning runs in 30 starts last season. . . . Batting support: 4.03 runs per start. . . . Average of 10.66 hits per nine innings was 7th-highest among A.L. pitchers with at least 15 starts. . . . Home run by Alejandro Sanchez on July 20 last season was the only one ever hit against Mason in Late-Inning Pressure Situations. Mason has faced 174 batters in LIP. . . . Winning percentage of .378 over past two seasons is 2d-lowest in majors among pitchers with at least 50 starts during that time.

Kirk McCaskill

California Angels	W–L	ERA	AB	H	HR	BB	SO	BA	SA	OBA
Season	12-12	4.70	732	189	23	64	102	.258	.408	.319
vs. Left-Handed Batters			407	113	11	39	46	.278	.420	.339
vs. Right-Handed Batters			325	76	12	25	56	.234	.394	.295
Home	7-4	4.58	373	93	16	23	52	.249	.440	.295
Road	5-8	4.82	359	96	7	41	50	.267	.376	.343
Grass	11-11	4.91	655	172	22	58	92	.263	.418	.324
Artificial Turf	1-1	3.00	77	17	1	6	10	.221	.325	.277
Day	4-4	4.68	255	67	9	17	40	.263	.439	.310
Night	8-8	4.71	477	122	14	47	62	.256	.392	.324
April			0	0	0	0	0	.000	.000	.000
May	0-3	6.30	120	33	7	14	17	.275	.483	.353
June	2-2	3.60	136	34	1	11	23	.250	.346	.304
July	4-2	4.38	156	46	1	13	13	.295	.385	.351
August	3-2	3.52	166	33	7	12	25	.199	.349	.261
Sept./Oct.	3-3	6.13	154	43	7	14	24	.279	.494	.335
Leading Off Inn.			184	49	3	15	19	.266	.364	.325
Bases Empty			442	102	10	37	65	.231	.348	.293
Runners On			290	87	13	27	37	.300	.500	.358
Runners/Scor. Pos.			165	42	5	13	27	.255	.394	.304
Runners On/2 Out			101	26	6	10	14	.257	.475	.336
Scor. Pos./2 Out			60	11	2	7	11	.183	.300	.279
Late Inning Pressure			54	18	2	1	4	.333	.500	.357
Leading Off			15	4	0	0	2	.267	.333	.267
Bases Empty			36	10	1	1	4	.278	.417	.297
Runners On			18	8	1	0	0	.444	.667	.474
Runners/Scor. Pos.			9	5	1	0	0	.556	.889	.556
First 9 Batters			239	66	9	24	35	.276	.431	.347
Second 9 Batters			238	52	4	18	30	.218	.324	.271
All Batters Thereafter			255	71	10	22	37	.278	.467	.337

Loves to face: Brook Jacoby (.100, 1-for-10, 5 SO)
Hates to face: Kirk Gibson (.545, 6-for-11, 4 HR)
Ground outs-to-air outs ratio: 1.09 last season, his first in majors. . . . Additional statistics: 22 double-play ground outs in 158 opportunities, 31 doubles, 5 triples allowed in 189.2 innings last season. . . . Allowed 26 first-inning runs (tied for 2d-most in A.L.) in 29 starts last season. . . . Allowed eight first-inning home runs, most in A.L. . . . Batting support: 4.86 runs per start. . . . Finished 3d among major-league rookies in wins and innings, behind Tom Browning and Ted Higuera, meaning he had the most among right-handers. . . . Once and for all: he did *not* play in the NHL. But he was the leading scorer (28 goals in 32 games) as a sophomore center on an awful University of Vermont team (9–23–2), and a 4th-round draft choice of the Winnipeg Jets in 1981, selected before a pretty fair goalie, John Vanbiesbrouck of the New York Rangers.

Steve McCatty

Oakland As	W–L	ERA	AB	H	HR	BB	SO	BA	SA	OBA
Season	4-4	5.57	332	95	10	41	36	.286	.440	.368
vs. Left-Handed Batters			148	41	4	23	16	.277	.446	.379
vs. Right-Handed Batters			184	54	6	18	20	.293	.435	.359
Home	0-4	5.79	149	47	4	20	11	.315	.443	.398
Road	4-0	5.40	183	48	6	21	25	.262	.437	.344
Grass	3-4	5.10	277	79	7	34	29	.285	.412	.364
Artificial Turf	1-0	8.10	55	16	3	7	7	.291	.582	.391
Day	2-3	6.85	179	58	5	20	14	.324	.480	.394
Night	2-1	4.17	153	37	5	21	22	.242	.392	.339
April	1-0	7.36	36	10	1	6	2	.278	.472	.400
May	1-2	7.45	81	24	4	13	6	.296	.506	.385
June	2-1	3.78	124	32	2	12	11	.258	.371	.328
July	0-1	9.39	37	16	2	2	4	.432	.649	.462
August	0-0	2.70	38	9	0	3	9	.237	.289	.310
Sept./Oct.	0-0	6.23	16	4	1	5	4	.250	.438	.429
Leading Off Inn.			73	20	1	7	10	.274	.370	.346
Bases Empty			169	46	3	20	20	.272	.396	.356
Runners On			163	49	7	21	16	.301	.485	.381
Runners/Scor. Pos.			100	32	4	18	11	.320	.460	.418
Runners On/2 Out			66	14	3	6	10	.212	.394	.278
Scor. Pos./2 Out			42	9	1	5	7	.214	.310	.298
Late Inning Pressure			33	10	1	6	3	.303	.485	.410
Leading Off			8	2	0	1	0	.250	.250	.333
Bases Empty			17	6	0	3	2	.353	.529	.450
Runners On			16	4	1	3	1	.250	.438	.368
Runners/Scor. Pos.			11	4	1	2	1	.364	.636	.462
First 9 Batters			176	48	6	29	23	.273	.438	.381
Second 9 Batters			102	32	2	9	8	.314	.441	.366
All Batters Thereafter			54	15	2	3	5	.278	.444	.328

Loves to face: Rick Dempsey (.045, 1-for-22)
Hates to face: Fred Lynn (.464, 13-for-28, 4 HR)
Ground outs-to-air outs ratio: 0.88 last season, 0.74 for career. . . . Additional statistics: 11 double-play ground outs in 89 opportunities, 13 doubles, 4 triples allowed in 85.2 innings last season. . . . Has faced 2,323 batters with runners on base and never balked, 2d-highest total among active pitchers. . . . Walked Ruppert Jones last April 13 to force in a run for first time in his career (91 batters faced with bases loaded). . . . Career average of 13.8 strikeouts per 100 batters faced with two outs and runners in scoring position. But with runners in scoring position and less than two outs—when he really needs it—his average is only 7.9 SOs per 100 batters. . . . Has completed only four of his last 65 starts, three of them in a row (including two shutouts) during the 1984 season.

Bob McClure

Milwaukee Brewers	W–L	ERA	AB	H	HR	BB	SO	BA	SA	OBA
Season	4-1	4.31	332	91	10	30	57	.274	.440	.338
vs. Left-Handed Batters			96	23	3	7	18	.240	.365	.295
vs. Right-Handed Batters			236	68	7	23	39	.288	.470	.355
Home	3-1	4.53	195	57	8	16	35	.292	.492	.346
Road	1-0	4.00	137	34	2	14	22	.248	.365	.327
Grass	4-1	4.28	306	82	10	29	53	.268	.438	.335
Artificial Turf	0-0	4.76	26	9	0	1	4	.346	.462	.370
Day	1-0	4.76	140	42	6	12	20	.300	.507	.364
Night	3-1	4.01	192	49	4	18	37	.255	.391	.319
April	0-0	0.00	32	6	0	2	7	.188	.250	.235
May	1-0	8.04	63	17	5	6	13	.270	.635	.333
June	1-0	4.05	50	12	1	6	6	.240	.380	.345
July	1-1	2.70	51	16	0	5	13	.314	.392	.362
August	0-0	9.72	36	14	2	7	3	.389	.639	.488
Sept./Oct.	1-0	2.84	100	26	2	4	15	.260	.360	.295
Leading Off Inn.			75	20	0	2	10	.267	.360	.295
Bases Empty			178	51	3	12	31	.287	.399	.339
Runners On			154	40	7	18	26	.260	.487	.337
Runners/Scor. Pos.			86	24	4	14	14	.279	.547	.373
Runners On/2 Out			69	20	4	10	12	.290	.565	.388
Scor. Pos./2 Out			39	13	2	8	8	.333	.641	.447
Late Inning Pressure			68	19	0	4	11	.279	.368	.319
Leading Off			18	5	0	1	4	.278	.444	.316
Bases Empty			39	14	0	3	8	.359	.462	.405
Runners On			29	5	0	1	3	.172	.241	.200
Runners/Scor. Pos.			15	2	0	1	1	.133	.200	.188
First 9 Batters			242	63	7	25	39	.260	.413	.332
Second 9 Batters			84	24	3	5	17	.286	.452	.333
All Batters Thereafter			6	4	0	0	1	.667	1.333	.667

Loves to face: Kent Hrbek (0-for-10, 3 SO)
Hates to face: Gary Gaetti (.462, 6-for-13, 3 HR)
Ground outs-to-air outs ratio: 0.97 last season, 0.79 for career. . . . Additional statistics: 11 double-play ground outs in 73 opportunities, 19 doubles, 3 triples allowed in 85.2 innings last season. . . . Pitched three or more innings in relief 13 times last season, tying him for 4th in A.L., behind Sammy Stewart (18), Stu Cliburn (16), and Nate Snell (15). . . . 7th among active pitchers with 21 career balks, one per 83 batters faced with runners on—more than four times the 1985 A.L. average. . . . Career average of one extra-base hit per 22.4 at bats by opposing left-handers is 5th-lowest in *Player Analysis* history (minimum: 750 AB). . . . Saved three games in 16 days during final month last season, after having only one save in previous 1,819 days. . . . Has not allowed a home run in Late-Inning Pressure Situations with runners on base since 1979.

Scott McGregor

Baltimore Orioles	W–L	ERA	AB	H	HR	BB	SO	BA	SA	OBA
Season	14-14	4.81	800	226	34	65	86	.283	.470	.334
vs. Left-Handed Batters			177	46	12	7	19	.260	.520	.286
vs. Right-Handed Batters			623	180	22	58	67	.289	.456	.347
Home	8-6	4.14	395	111	19	24	48	.281	.463	.318
Road	6-8	5.45	405	115	15	41	38	.284	.477	.349
Grass	13-10	4.32	668	182	29	52	74	.272	.452	.322
Artificial Turf	1-4	7.55	132	44	5	13	12	.333	.561	.395
Day	4-1	2.66	177	35	6	17	14	.198	.333	.268
Night	10-13	5.52	623	191	28	48	72	.307	.509	.353
April	1-2	5.40	77	24	4	9	8	.312	.545	.375
May	2-2	5.97	114	28	7	8	9	.246	.491	.295
June	3-2	2.36	161	44	3	12	16	.273	.360	.318
July	3-2	5.13	153	43	6	10	17	.281	.490	.319
August	1-4	8.88	104	38	5	13	14	.365	.548	.441
Sept./Oct.	4-2	3.70	191	49	9	13	22	.257	.461	.304
Leading Off Inn.			205	62	8	13	22	.302	.463	.344
Bases Empty			482	136	22	33	46	.282	.469	.329
Runners On			318	90	12	32	40	.283	.472	.341
Runners/Scor. Pos.			157	45	4	20	18	.287	.446	.351
Runners On/2 Out			129	30	5	16	21	.233	.395	.317
Scor. Pos./2 Out			67	15	2	12	9	.224	.373	.342
Late Inning Pressure			72	22	1	6	8	.306	.417	.359
Leading Off			22	7	0	2	5	.318	.318	.375
Bases Empty			49	12	0	3	6	.245	.265	.288
Runners On			23	10	1	3	2	.435	.739	.500
Runners/Scor. Pos.			12	5	0	2	1	.417	.583	.500
First 9 Batters			268	80	13	27	28	.299	.496	.354
Second 9 Batters			251	76	12	17	26	.303	.514	.349
All Batters Thereafter			281	70	9	21	32	.249	.406	.300

Loves to face: Mark Brouhard (.053, 1-for-19)
Hates to face: Larry Herndon (.476, 10-for-21, 3 HR)
Ground outs-to-air outs ratio: 0.65 last season (a career low), 0.80 for career. . . . Additional statistics: 22 double-play ground outs in 157 opportunities, 38 doubles, 5 triples allowed in 204.0 innings last year. . . . Allowed 27 first-inning runs (most in majors) in 34 starts. . . . Batting support: 4.91 runs per start. . . . Allowed one home run every 6.0 innings, 4th-worst rate among A.L. starters (minimum: 15 GS). Left-handed batters hit one every 14.8 at bats, highest rate in majors against a regular starter. . . . Day-game ERA was 4th-lowest in A.L. last season. . . . Career average of 2.05 walks per nine innings ranks 7th among active pitchers (minimum: 250 innings). . . . Opponents have .373 career batting average with the bases loaded. . . . Knocked out of 11 starts before fifth inning last year, 2d-most in A.L.

Donnie Moore
California Angels

	W–L	ERA	AB	H	HR	BB	SO	BA	SA	OBA
Season	8-8	1.92	384	91	9	21	72	.237	.336	.275
vs. Left-Handed Batters			200	40	2	13	41	.200	.270	.247
vs. Right-Handed Batters			184	51	7	8	31	.277	.408	.307
Home	5-3	1.01	196	44	0	12	34	.224	.260	.268
Road	3-5	2.92	188	47	9	9	38	.250	.415	.283
Grass	7-7	1.92	330	78	6	18	63	.236	.324	.274
Artificial Turf	1-1	1.93	54	13	3	3	9	.241	.407	.281
Day	1-2	3.13	120	32	4	9	19	.267	.392	.315
Night	7-6	1.39	264	59	5	12	53	.223	.311	.256
April	1-1	1.20	55	12	0	5	7	.218	.218	.283
May	2-0	0.54	59	12	0	3	14	.203	.220	.238
June	1-2	2.87	60	15	4	2	13	.250	.467	.270
July	3-1	1.26	52	12	0	2	10	.231	.327	.259
August	0-3	2.51	54	15	2	5	8	.278	.407	.339
Sept./Oct.	1-1	2.67	104	25	3	4	20	.240	.356	.269
Leading Off Inn.			81	21	3	3	22	.259	.395	.286
Bases Empty			197	53	6	8	38	.269	.396	.298
Runners On			187	38	3	13	34	.203	.273	.252
Runners/Scor. Pos.			105	23	3	8	19	.219	.343	.270
Runners On/2 Out			88	16	1	8	13	.182	.250	.250
Scor. Pos./2 Out			54	10	1	5	7	.185	.296	.254
Late Inning Pressure			267	68	7	13	47	.255	.363	.287
Leading Off			59	16	2	1	16	.271	.407	.283
Bases Empty			141	41	5	3	26	.291	.433	.306
Runners On			126	27	2	10	21	.214	.286	.268
Runners/Scor. Pos.			72	16	2	7	13	.222	.347	.284
First 9 Batters			356	84	9	18	66	.236	.337	.271
Second 9 Batters			28	7	0	3	6	.250	.321	.323
All Batters Thereafter			0	0	0	0	0	.000	.000	.000

Loves to face: Lonnie Smith (.111, 1-for-9, 3 SO)
Hates to face: John Shelby & Mike Young (.750, both 3-for-4)
Ground outs-to-air outs ratio: 0.86 last season, 1.15 for career. ... Additional statistics: 5 double-play ground outs in 92 opportunities (10th-lowest rate in A.L.), 9 doubles, 1 triple allowed in 103.0 innings last season. ... Allowed one home run every 13.7 innings last season, 6th-lowest rate in A.L. in '85. ... Led A.L. relievers with a 1.92 ERA last season (minimum: 30 relief games). ... Opposing right-handed batters hit 77 points higher than left-handers, 4th-largest difference in A.L. (minimum: 100 AB vs. each). ... Saved more games in '85 (31) than in nine previous years (28). Why was he baseball's best kept secret? Among his former teammates were Darold Knowles, Bruce Sutter, Willie Hernandez, Bill Caudill, Mark Littell, Pedro Borbon, Rollie Fingers, Gene Garber, Al Hrabosky, Doug Corbett, Terry Forster, and Dennis Lamp.

Mike Moore
Seattle Mariners

	W–L	ERA	AB	H	HR	BB	SO	BA	SA	OBA
Season	17-10	3.46	933	230	18	70	155	.247	.360	.300
vs. Left-Handed Batters			514	116	9	43	87	.226	.337	.285
vs. Right-Handed Batters			419	114	9	27	68	.272	.389	.319
Home	8-5	3.18	506	130	11	40	83	.257	.374	.312
Road	9-5	3.79	427	100	7	30	72	.234	.344	.285
Grass	7-3	3.56	324	78	6	21	59	.241	.352	.287
Artificial Turf	10-7	3.41	609	152	12	49	96	.250	.365	.307
Day	4-4	3.25	276	64	6	15	53	.232	.348	.278
Night	13-6	3.55	657	166	12	55	102	.253	.365	.309
April	2-2	8.00	112	38	1	12	12	.339	.446	.398
May	2-2	1.74	150	33	2	12	36	.220	.300	.276
June	2-0	2.93	54	11	1	9	9	.204	.315	.317
July	3-2	2.55	178	38	3	9	23	.213	.337	.253
August	3-2	2.75	202	48	5	11	37	.238	.356	.284
Sept./Oct.	5-2	4.09	237	62	6	17	38	.262	.388	.310
Leading Off Inn.			242	53	6	15	41	.219	.364	.265
Bases Empty			573	130	11	48	97	.227	.342	.291
Runners On			360	100	7	22	58	.278	.389	.314
Runners/Scor. Pos.			185	49	3	14	30	.265	.362	.306
Runners On/2 Out			162	46	5	11	27	.284	.407	.329
Scor. Pos./2 Out			92	27	3	7	13	.293	.424	.343
Late Inning Pressure			112	25	0	10	21	.223	.277	.288
Leading Off			30	4	0	4	4	.133	.133	.235
Bases Empty			69	14	0	9	12	.203	.217	.304
Runners On			43	11	0	1	9	.256	.372	.261
Runners/Scor. Pos.			16	4	0	1	4	.250	.313	.263
First 9 Batters			280	73	5	20	45	.261	.379	.309
Second 9 Batters			260	67	7	17	48	.258	.392	.307
All Batters Thereafter			393	90	6	33	62	.229	.326	.288

Loves to face: Steve Balboni (.071, 1-for-14, 7 SO)
Hates to face: Doug DeCinces (.536, 15-for-28, 6 HR)
Ground outs-to-air outs ratio: 1.22 last season, 1.23 for career. ... Additional statistics: 19 double-play ground outs in 157 opportunities, 38 doubles, 7 triples allowed in 247.0 innings last season. ... Ranked 8th among A.L. pitchers with an average of 7.25 innings per start. ... Allowed 14 first-inning runs in 34 starts last season. ... Batting support: 4.38 runs per start. ... Only pitcher in the 11-year history of The Player Analysis to face more than 200 batters in Late-Inning Pressure Situations and not allow a home run. Moore has faced 296. ... Opponents' batting average with runners on base has been higher than with the bases empty in each of his four seasons. 1985 ROB average (.278) was a career low. Career averages: .308 with runners on, .241 with bases empty.

Jack Morris
Detroit Tigers

	W–L	ERA	AB	H	HR	BB	SO	BA	SA	OBA
Season	16-11	3.33	944	212	21	110	191	.225	.340	.307
vs. Left-Handed Batters			533	119	11	68	108	.223	.341	.310
vs. Right-Handed Batters			411	93	10	42	83	.226	.338	.302
Home	5-5	4.49	402	100	14	48	80	.249	.388	.330
Road	11-6	2.51	542	112	7	62	111	.207	.304	.289
Grass	13-9	3.72	790	188	20	93	154	.238	.362	.320
Artificial Turf	3-2	1.42	154	24	1	17	37	.156	.227	.240
Day	4-3	4.33	258	59	8	29	45	.229	.391	.314
Night	12-8	2.95	686	153	13	81	146	.223	.321	.304
April	3-2	2.16	145	30	0	16	34	.207	.283	.282
May	3-3	2.34	182	38	4	28	38	.209	.308	.321
June	3-0	5.31	163	44	8	17	25	.270	.472	.348
July	3-1	2.66	151	36	3	17	29	.238	.331	.314
August	2-2	4.12	142	29	2	18	28	.204	.303	.290
Sept./Oct.	2-3	3.56	161	35	4	14	37	.217	.335	.278
Leading Off Inn.			240	60	8	23	48	.250	.413	.316
Bases Empty			549	123	13	70	115	.224	.350	.314
Runners On			395	89	8	40	76	.225	.327	.297
Runners/Scor. Pos.			205	49	4	30	39	.239	.356	.329
Runners On/2 Out			176	37	4	19	38	.210	.330	.294
Scor. Pos./2 Out			95	20	1	17	21	.211	.326	.336
Late Inning Pressure			151	35	2	17	24	.232	.325	.306
Leading Off			37	13	1	3	5	.351	.541	.400
Bases Empty			76	22	2	10	11	.289	.461	.372
Runners On			75	13	0	7	13	.173	.187	.238
Runners/Scor. Pos.			37	7	0	5	4	.189	.216	.273
First 9 Batters			280	63	4	27	74	.225	.321	.296
Second 9 Batters			264	54	5	41	47	.205	.299	.311
All Batters Thereafter			400	95	12	42	70	.238	.380	.311

Loves to face: Mike Easler (.071, 1-for-14, 6 SO)
Hates to face: Jim Rice (.385, 20-for-52, 3 HR)
Ground outs-to-air outs ratio: 0.98 last season, 1.21 for career. ... Additional statistics: 21 double-play ground outs in 182 opportunities, 32 doubles, 7 triples (tied for 6th-most in A.L.) allowed in 257.0 innings last season. ... Ranked 7th among A.L. pitchers with an average of 7.34 innings per start. ... Allowed 20 first-inning runs in 35 starts last season. ... Batting support: 4.63 runs per start. ... Ranked 4th in A.L. with averages of 7.42 hits and 6.69 strikeouts per nine innings. ... Tied Tom Seaver for A.L. lead with 11 road-game wins. ... ERA on artificial turf was lowest in majors last season. ... Winning pitcher in consecutive starts only twice in '85. ... Since 1980, has allowed 2 hits in 30 at bats with two outs and the bases loaded. ... Only pitcher to win 100 games during the 1980s; he has 102. Ron Guidry ranks 2d with 95.

Gene Nelson
Chicago White Sox

	W–L	ERA	AB	H	HR	BB	SO	BA	SA	OBA
Season	10-10	4.26	557	144	23	67	101	.259	.456	.344
vs. Left-Handed Batters			257	64	10	31	43	.249	.440	.334
vs. Right-Handed Batters			300	80	13	36	58	.267	.470	.353
Home	7-6	3.46	295	69	8	35	55	.234	.397	.322
Road	3-4	5.26	262	75	15	32	46	.286	.523	.369
Grass	10-9	4.15	508	127	20	62	92	.250	.441	.339
Artificial Turf	0-1	5.56	49	17	3	5	9	.347	.612	.407
Day	2-1	4.26	93	25	4	17	21	.269	.452	.378
Night	8-9	4.26	464	119	19	50	80	.256	.457	.337
April	1-1	5.79	35	12	2	10	5	.343	.543	.489
May	2-0	2.08	59	9	1	9	10	.153	.237	.265
June	1-2	2.25	72	14	3	11	21	.194	.347	.318
July	2-2	4.78	110	34	5	7	24	.309	.573	.367
August	2-3	6.48	138	41	6	13	14	.297	.522	.357
Sept./Oct.	2-2	3.66	143	34	6	17	27	.238	.427	.323
Leading Off Inn.			138	46	9	12	19	.333	.645	.403
Bases Empty			320	94	17	33	51	.294	.538	.367
Runners On			237	50	6	34	50	.211	.346	.315
Runners/Scor. Pos.			140	29	1	26	31	.207	.300	.339
Runners On/2 Out			96	15	1	18	16	.156	.219	.289
Scor. Pos./2 Out			62	10	0	14	12	.161	.177	.316
Late Inning Pressure			82	21	4	19	21	.256	.463	.408
Leading Off			23	7	2	4	7	.304	.609	.429
Bases Empty			49	14	3	8	13	.286	.571	.397
Runners On			33	7	1	11	8	.212	.303	.422
Runners/Scor. Pos.			21	5	1	10	6	.238	.381	.500
First 9 Batters			291	70	12	44	62	.241	.419	.348
Second 9 Batters			162	46	7	12	27	.284	.525	.341
All Batters Thereafter			104	28	4	11	12	.269	.452	.339

Loves to face: George Wright (.067, 1-for-15)
Hates to face: Cal Ripken (.700, 7-for-10, 2 HR)
Ground outs-to-air outs ratio: 1.18 last season, 1.32 for career. ... Additional statistics: 11 double-play ground outs in 118 opportunities, 27 doubles, 7 triples (tied for 6th-most in A.L.) allowed in 145.2 innings last season. ... Batting support: 4.50 runs per start. ... Allowed 5 first-inning runs in 18 starts, 6th-lowest rate in A.L. last season (minimum: 15 GS). ... Allowed one home run every 6.3 innings, 7th-worst average among that group. Career average of one home run allowed every 7.02 innings is 8th-highest among active pitchers (minimum: 20 HR). ... Opponents' career batting average of .250 on grass, .303 on artificial surfaces. ... Opponents' batting averages with runners in scoring position, year by year since 1983: .353, .250, .207.

Phil Niekro

New York Yankees	W–L	ERA	AB	H	HR	BB	SO	BA	SA	OBA
Season	16-12	4.09	829	203	29	120	149	.245	.409	.341
vs. Left-Handed Batters			440	115	17	74	65	.261	.432	.366
vs. Right-Handed Batters			389	88	12	46	84	.226	.383	.311
Home	9-5	3.85	412	98	12	66	73	.238	.396	.344
Road	7-7	4.34	417	105	17	54	76	.252	.422	.338
Grass	13-11	4.37	663	166	24	100	126	.250	.421	.348
Artificial Turf	3-1	3.00	166	37	5	20	23	.223	.361	.310
Day	7-3	4.04	307	76	10	46	51	.248	.407	.346
Night	9-9	4.12	522	127	19	74	98	.243	.410	.337
April	3-2	5.04	118	30	3	16	27	.254	.398	.343
May	3-1	2.92	130	24	5	23	18	.185	.323	.307
June	1-4	7.76	109	34	5	16	20	.312	.550	.394
July	3-1	2.31	139	32	4	15	23	.230	.338	.310
August	3-1	3.53	135	32	6	18	26	.237	.415	.325
Sept./Oct.	3-3	4.21	198	51	6	32	35	.258	.439	.364
Leading Off Inn.			209	54	4	22	24	.258	.383	.332
Bases Empty			481	116	19	63	76	.241	.424	.330
Runners On			348	87	10	57	73	.250	.388	.355
Runners/Scor. Pos.			198	49	6	42	52	.247	.394	.374
Runners On/2 Out			137	35	2	32	36	.255	.365	.396
Scor. Pos./2 Out			90	23	0	26	27	.256	.322	.422
Late Inning Pressure			58	17	5	10	8	.293	.586	.397
Leading Off			17	6	2	2	1	.353	.706	.421
Bases Empty			36	12	5	5	4	.333	.806	.415
Runners On			22	5	0	5	4	.227	.227	.370
Runners/Scor. Pos.			13	3	0	3	2	.231	.231	.375
First 9 Batters			263	61	11	29	53	.232	.426	.307
Second 9 Batters			250	65	5	41	45	.260	.396	.364
All Batters Thereafter			316	77	13	50	51	.244	.405	.349

Loves to face: Dave Henderson (0-for-9, 3 SO)
Hates to face: Harold Baines (.667, 6-for-9, 2 HR)
Ground outs-to-air outs ratio: 0.99 last season, 1.09 for career. ... Additional statistics: 27 double-play ground outs in 173 opportunities, 37 doubles, 6 triples allowed in 220.0 innings last season. ... Allowed 19 first-inning runs in 33 starts. ... Batting support: 4.70 runs per start. ... Ranked 8th in A.L. with 6.10 strikeouts per nine innings. ... Only pitcher to allow more than three hits to Hanshin Tigers superstar Randy Bass in his lacklustre career in the States. Bass was 7-for-11 with a homer off Phil. ... All-time major-league leader in wild pitches (207). ... Gained 300th career win in 5th try, the first 300-game winner not to succeed on his first attempt since Early Wynn needed eight (one an extra-inning relief appearance) in 1962–63. Gaylord Perry, Steve Carlton, and Tom Seaver all won on first tries, as did Warren Spahn in '61.

Al Nipper

Boston Red Sox	W–L	ERA	AB	H	HR	BB	SO	BA	SA	OBA
Season	9-12	4.06	614	157	14	82	85	.256	.396	.350
vs. Left-Handed Batters			299	82	8	48	31	.274	.421	.378
vs. Right-Handed Batters			315	75	6	34	54	.238	.371	.322
Home	5-6	3.34	355	91	7	35	51	.256	.389	.327
Road	4-6	5.05	259	66	7	47	34	.255	.405	.379
Grass	7-8	4.03	473	122	11	52	65	.258	.400	.338
Artificial Turf	2-4	4.14	141	35	3	30	20	.248	.383	.385
Day	2-1	4.41	129	37	1	20	17	.287	.426	.388
Night	7-11	3.97	485	120	13	62	68	.247	.388	.339
April	0-1	6.43	60	18	2	7	6	.300	.550	.382
May	1-4	5.03	141	36	5	21	16	.255	.440	.361
June	3-1	3.38	136	34	5	14	21	.250	.404	.320
July	3-0	2.25	73	15	0	11	13	.205	.247	.310
August	0-4	5.48	86	24	1	12	13	.279	.419	.392
Sept./Oct.	2-2	2.76	118	30	1	17	16	.254	.331	.346
Leading Off Inn.			148	40	4	19	23	.270	.459	.368
Bases Empty			341	88	8	47	53	.258	.411	.358
Runners On			273	69	6	35	32	.253	.377	.340
Runners/Scor. Pos.			144	38	2	21	16	.264	.389	.360
Runners On/2 Out			110	24	1	14	17	.218	.300	.312
Scor. Pos./2 Out			60	17	1	11	7	.283	.433	.403
Late Inning Pressure			68	17	3	5	9	.250	.441	.307
Leading Off			19	6	2	2	2	.316	.737	.381
Bases Empty			43	12	3	3	6	.279	.558	.340
Runners On			25	5	0	2	3	.200	.240	.250
Runners/Scor. Pos.			10	1	0	1	2	.100	.100	.167
First 9 Batters			186	44	6	30	29	.237	.430	.353
Second 9 Batters			183	43	3	27	24	.235	.333	.344
All Batters Thereafter			245	70	5	25	32	.286	.416	.352

Loves to face: Bob Kearney (0-for-12, 3 SO)
Hates to face: Ken Griffey (.667, 6-for-9, 1 HR)
Ground outs-to-air outs ratio: 1.25 last season, 1.15 for career. ... Additional statistics: 18 double-play ground outs in 137 opportunities, 34 doubles, 5 triples allowed in 220.0 innings last season. ... Allowed 9 first-inning runs in 25 starts, 10th-lowest rate in A.L. last season (minimum: 15 GS). ... Batting support: 4.08 runs per start. ... Career total of 51 starts is 2d-highest among pitchers without a complete-game shutout. ... Opponents' overall batting average has decreased in each season (.293, .257, .256) while average with runners in scoring position has increased (.125, .239, .264). ... Lost four consecutive starts twice last season. ... Let's not feel too sorry for another pitcher trapped in Fenway. Career ERAs: 3.20 at home, 4.75 on the road.

Dickie Noles

Texas Rangers	W–L	ERA	AB	H	HR	BB	SO	BA	SA	OBA
Season	4-8	5.06	447	129	11	33	59	.289	.418	.346
vs. Left-Handed Batters			233	79	5	21	29	.339	.468	.398
vs. Right-Handed Batters			214	50	6	12	30	.234	.364	.287
Home	2-4	5.11	230	68	6	18	31	.296	.430	.357
Road	2-4	5.00	217	61	5	15	28	.281	.406	.333
Grass	4-7	5.03	413	117	10	28	55	.283	.402	.336
Artificial Turf	0-1	5.40	34	12	1	5	4	.353	.618	.450
Day	2-1	2.78	123	31	1	10	14	.252	.309	.308
Night	2-7	6.00	324	98	10	23	45	.302	.460	.360
April	2-1	2.08	91	16	1	8	8	.176	.253	.242
May	0-5	5.06	109	32	4	8	18	.294	.450	.358
June	1-0	5.51	70	25	0	6	11	.357	.429	.408
July	1-0	3.09	42	9	2	4	7	.214	.405	.298
August	0-2	6.95	94	29	2	7	10	.309	.436	.369
Sept./Oct.	0-0	11.74	41	18	2	0	5	.439	.659	.439
Leading Off Inn.			106	31	3	5	15	.292	.434	.324
Bases Empty			247	63	7	20	33	.255	.389	.313
Runners On			200	66	4	13	26	.330	.455	.385
Runners/Scor. Pos.			123	44	3	9	17	.358	.496	.410
Runners On/2 Out			84	27	1	8	10	.321	.405	.400
Scor. Pos./2 Out			58	19	1	6	8	.328	.431	.391
Late Inning Pressure			45	10	2	6	6	.222	.400	.314
Leading Off			15	3	1	0	1	.200	.400	.200
Bases Empty			34	6	1	3	4	.176	.294	.243
Runners On			11	4	1	3	2	.364	.727	.500
Runners/Scor. Pos.			4	0	0	2	1	.000	.000	.333
First 9 Batters			220	56	4	18	31	.255	.377	.317
Second 9 Batters			156	52	6	8	20	.333	.506	.381
All Batters Thereafter			71	21	1	7	8	.296	.352	.359

Loves to face: Dave Kingman (.091, 3-for-33, 11 SO)
Hates to face: Lonnie Smith (.600, 9-for-15, 3 BB)
Ground outs-to-air outs ratio: 1.42 last season, 1.19 for career. ... Additional statistics: 12 double-play ground outs in 82 opportunities, 19 doubles, 3 triples allowed in 110.1 innings last season. ... Allowed 3 first-inning runs in 13 starts last season. ... Batting support: 3.85 runs per start. ... Opposing left-handed batters hit 105 points higher than right-handers, 3d-largest difference in A.L. last season (minimum: 100 AB vs. each). ... Opponents' career batting average of .298 with runners in scoring position. ... Has never had a winning record in seven years in the majors. ... Spelling of last name in Esperanto is identical to that of ex-major leaguer Darold Knowles. There's no mistaking their abilities: Knowles had 27 saves in 1970, Noles has seven in his career.

Edwin Nunez

Seattle Mariners	W–L	ERA	AB	H	HR	BB	SO	BA	SA	OBA
Season	7-3	3.09	337	79	13	34	58	.234	.401	.302
vs. Left-Handed Batters			152	32	7	22	21	.211	.388	.309
vs. Right-Handed Batters			185	47	6	12	37	.254	.411	.296
Home	5-2	2.11	158	36	4	14	26	.228	.348	.289
Road	2-1	3.97	179	43	9	20	32	.240	.447	.313
Grass	1-1	3.86	148	35	8	16	28	.236	.453	.307
Artificial Turf	6-2	2.49	189	44	5	18	30	.233	.360	.298
Day	1-1	3.79	69	19	4	7	14	.275	.493	.338
Night	6-2	2.90	268	60	9	27	44	.224	.377	.293
April	1-0	1.08	55	9	2	8	11	.164	.273	.270
May	1-0	5.91	47	15	1	8	7	.319	.489	.418
June	1-0	1.90	81	16	2	8	7	.198	.309	.264
July	2-1	3.07	58	14	4	3	11	.241	.466	.274
August	1-1	4.82	37	12	0	4	5	.324	.432	.390
Sept./Oct.	1-1	4.11	59	13	4	3	17	.220	.492	.258
Leading Off Inn.			70	17	2	7	8	.243	.386	.312
Bases Empty			171	35	7	18	32	.205	.374	.280
Runners On			166	44	6	16	26	.265	.428	.324
Runners/Scor. Pos.			99	27	4	11	19	.273	.455	.336
Runners On/2 Out			73	16	3	8	10	.219	.356	.296
Scor. Pos./2 Out			49	10	2	7	7	.204	.347	.304
Late Inning Pressure			156	36	7	16	21	.231	.410	.301
Leading Off			30	10	2	4	3	.333	.600	.412
Bases Empty			77	18	5	7	10	.234	.494	.298
Runners On			79	18	2	9	11	.228	.329	.303
Runners/Scor. Pos.			53	12	2	7	9	.226	.377	.311
First 9 Batters			319	75	13	33	56	.235	.404	.304
Second 9 Batters			18	4	0	1	2	.222	.333	.263
All Batters Thereafter			0	0	0	0	0	.000	.000	.000

Loves to face: Dwayne Murphy (0-for-7, 4 SO)
Hates to face: Tony Armas & Ken Griffey (both 3-for-3, 1 HR)
Ground outs-to-air outs ratio: 0.60 last season (7th-lowest in A.L.), 0.74 for career. ... Additional statistics: 6 double-play ground outs in 83 opportunities, 11 doubles, 3 triples allowed in 90.1 innings last season. ... Allowed 13 home runs in relief, tied for 3d-most in A.L. ... Allowed only one hit in 15 at bats with the bases loaded last season. ... Opponents' career batting average of .179 with two outs and runners in scoring position. ... Set Mariners club record with 24.0 consecutive shutout innings (June 9–July 9). ... Gave up home runs to the only two batters he faced on Sept. 20 at Texas, blowing one-run lead in the bottom of the ninth for his first loss of the season. ... Batting averages of opposing left-handed batters, year by year since 1982: .316, .286, .238, .211.

Bob Ojeda

Boston Red Sox	W–L	ERA	AB	H	HR	BB	SO	BA	SA	OBA
Season	9-11	4.00	608	166	11	48	102	.273	.396	.327
vs. Left-Handed Batters			127	40	2	6	25	.315	.449	.346
vs. Right-Handed Batters			481	126	9	42	77	.262	.383	.322
Home	4-7	3.50	377	99	7	27	74	.263	.385	.313
Road	5-4	4.80	231	67	4	21	28	.290	.416	.349
Grass	7-11	4.01	536	145	11	43	94	.271	.396	.324
Artificial Turf	2-0	3.86	72	21	0	5	8	.292	.403	.346
Day	1-3	4.19	135	37	3	10	24	.274	.356	.324
Night	8-8	3.94	473	129	8	38	78	.273	.408	.328
April	2-1	2.25	42	10	0	12	8	.238	.286	.407
May	0-0	4.50	36	12	0	4	6	.333	.444	.415
June	2-2	2.93	174	48	3	9	26	.276	.402	.315
July	1-3	7.52	82	25	3	4	18	.305	.451	.333
August	1-2	5.40	107	37	4	7	11	.346	.551	.383
Sept./Oct.	3-3	3.11	167	34	1	12	33	.204	.281	.256
Leading Off Inn.			153	46	3	7	19	.301	.438	.335
Bases Empty			360	100	6	17	50	.278	.403	.312
Runners On			248	66	5	31	52	.266	.387	.346
Runners/Scor. Pos.			138	39	3	24	29	.283	.435	.386
Runners On/2 Out			98	20	2	14	24	.204	.327	.304
Scor. Pos./2 Out			60	14	2	13	14	.233	.433	.370
Late Inning Pressure			90	24	1	15	13	.267	.367	.371
Leading Off			23	8	1	1	1	.348	.478	.375
Bases Empty			56	16	1	2	5	.286	.393	.310
Runners On			34	8	0	13	8	.235	.324	.447
Runners/Scor. Pos.			23	4	0	12	6	.174	.261	.457
First 9 Batters			245	64	4	21	53	.261	.371	.319
Second 9 Batters			171	55	4	13	26	.322	.485	.373
All Batters Thereafter			192	47	3	14	23	.245	.349	.296

Loves to face: Vance Law (.067, 1-for-15)
Hates to face: Enos Cabell (.556, 5-for-9, 1 HR)
Ground outs-to-air outs ratio: 1.03 last season, 0.96 for career. . . . Additional statistics: 16 double-play ground outs in 131 opportunities, 30 doubles, 6 triples allowed in 157.2 innings last season. . . . Allowed 10 first-inning runs in 22 starts. . . . Batting support: 3.82 runs per start, 6th-lowest average in A.L. (minimum: 15 GS). . . . Experienced under pressure: faced 27 batters with the bases loaded last season, most in major leagues. Acquitted himself well: 4-for-23, four walks, no extra-base hits. . . . Went 7–10 with a 4.32 ERA in 22 starts; 2–1, one save, 1.50 ERA in 17 relief appearances. . . . Mets have done well trading for young A.L. pitchers (Darling, Terrell, Lynch), but haven't gotten much from Boston. They've acquired six pitchers from the Sox in their history, and the six (including Tracy Stallard and Galen Cisco) went 50–108 for the Mets.

Randy O'Neal

Detroit Tigers	W–L	ERA	AB	H	HR	BB	SO	BA	SA	OBA
Season	5-5	3.24	342	82	8	36	52	.240	.365	.310
vs. Left-Handed Batters			191	45	4	18	30	.236	.340	.298
vs. Right-Handed Batters			151	37	4	18	22	.245	.397	.326
Home	1-2	4.73	125	36	5	10	15	.288	.480	.329
Road	4-3	2.47	217	46	3	26	37	.212	.300	.300
Grass	4-5	3.43	297	75	8	31	44	.253	.387	.320
Artificial Turf	1-0	2.08	45	7	0	5	8	.156	.222	.240
Day	1-3	2.80	124	33	1	18	23	.266	.347	.347
Night	4-2	3.51	218	49	7	18	29	.225	.376	.288
April			0	0	0	0	0	.000	.000	.000
May			0	0	0	0	0	.000	.000	.000
June	3-1	2.16	119	23	3	13	23	.193	.294	.271
July	2-2	3.68	107	25	1	12	15	.234	.336	.320
August	0-2	3.55	48	17	0	8	6	.354	.375	.424
Sept./Oct.	0-0	4.26	68	17	4	3	8	.250	.529	.274
Leading Off Inn.			88	20	3	9	16	.227	.375	.306
Bases Empty			214	44	6	22	32	.206	.350	.283
Runners On			128	38	2	14	20	.297	.391	.353
Runners/Scor. Pos.			80	23	1	11	13	.288	.363	.347
Runners On/2 Out			52	14	1	7	9	.269	.365	.356
Scor. Pos./2 Out			37	10	1	7	7	.270	.378	.386
Late Inning Pressure			23	7	1	2	3	.304	.478	.360
Leading Off			7	1	0	1	2	.143	.143	.250
Bases Empty			17	4	1	1	2	.235	.412	.278
Runners On			6	3	0	1	1	.500	.667	.571
Runners/Scor. Pos.			5	2	0	1	1	.400	.600	.500
First 9 Batters			165	38	7	15	27	.230	.400	.296
Second 9 Batters			104	25	0	11	15	.240	.327	.308
All Batters Thereafter			73	19	1	10	10	.260	.342	.345

Loves to face: Bill Buckner (0-for-3, 2 SO)
Hates to face: Rickey Henderson (.375, 3-for-8, 2 HR)
Ground outs-to-air outs ratio: 1.38 last season, 1.41 for career. . . . Additional statistics: 11 double-play ground outs in 67 opportunities, 17 doubles, 1 triple allowed in 94.1 innings last season. . . . Allowed 4 first-inning runs in 12 starts last season. . . . Batting support: 4.17 runs per start. . . . Only American League rookie to compile an ERA under 4.00 as a starting pitcher last season (minimum: 50 IP). . . . Had a 5–1 record with a 2.31 ERA in first seven starts, 0–4 and 5.01 in next five. He was then sent to the bullpen for the rest of the season. . . . Opponents' career batting averages: .212 with bases empty, .277 with runners on base, .286 with runners in scoring position; .294 in day games, .207 in night games. . . . Two-year average of 2.00 strikeouts per walk in night games, 1.09 in day games.

Steve Ontiveros

Oakland As	W–L	ERA	AB	H	HR	BB	SO	BA	SA	OBA
Season	1-3	1.93	259	45	4	19	36	.174	.259	.234
vs. Left-Handed Batters			134	29	2	11	13	.216	.321	.277
vs. Right-Handed Batters			125	16	2	8	23	.128	.192	.187
Home	0-3	2.06	148	23	3	9	21	.155	.250	.203
Road	1-0	1.74	111	22	1	10	15	.198	.270	.274
Grass	0-3	2.20	212	38	4	17	33	.179	.269	.245
Artificial Turf	1-0	0.68	47	7	0	2	3	.149	.213	.184
Day	0-0	0.69	82	9	1	5	9	.110	.159	.159
Night	1-3	2.59	177	36	3	14	27	.203	.305	.268
April			0	0	0	0	0	.000	.000	.000
May			0	0	0	0	0	.000	.000	.000
June	0-0	0.68	44	7	0	3	7	.159	.205	.208
July	1-1	0.95	62	8	0	1	6	.129	.161	.141
August	0-0	0.82	75	11	1	10	10	.147	.200	.247
Sept./Oct.	0-2	4.87	78	19	3	5	13	.244	.423	.306
Leading Off Inn.			56	12	2	5	8	.214	.375	.279
Bases Empty			138	27	3	11	20	.196	.312	.265
Runners On			121	18	1	8	16	.149	.198	.198
Runners/Scor. Pos.			58	8	1	7	13	.138	.207	.224
Runners On/2 Out			48	9	0	6	8	.188	.229	.278
Scor. Pos./2 Out			28	6	0	6	6	.214	.250	.353
Late Inning Pressure			126	20	1	10	18	.159	.206	.221
Leading Off			31	7	1	3	4	.226	.355	.294
Bases Empty			74	13	1	7	11	.176	.257	.247
Runners On			52	7	0	3	7	.135	.135	.182
Runners/Scor. Pos.			20	4	0	3	6	.200	.200	.304
First 9 Batters			235	42	4	19	30	.179	.272	.244
Second 9 Batters			24	3	0	0	6	.125	.125	.125
All Batters Thereafter			0	0	0	0	0	.000	.000	.000

Loves to face: Nelson Simmons (0-for-5)
Hates to face: Kirk Gibson (.750, 3-for-4, 1 HR)
Ground outs-to-air outs ratio: 1.53 last season, his first in majors. . . . Additional statistics: 10 double-play ground outs in 65 opportunities, 8 doubles, 1 triple allowed in 74.2 innings last season. . . . Ranked 2d among A.L. relief pitchers with a 1.93 ERA last season (minimum: 30 relief games). Average of 5.42 hits per nine innings was lowest among that group, contributing to his league-low opponents' batting and slugging averages. . . . Set A.L. *Player Analysis* record for batting average by opposing right-handed hitters. Major-league record since 1975 (.124) was set by J.R. Richard in 1980. . . . Opponents' batting average with runners in scoring position was the lowest in the majors since 1982 (minimum: 50 PA). . . . Had eight saves, finishing 3d among major-league rookies, behind Roger McDowell and Brian Fisher.

Dan Petry

Detroit Tigers	W–L	ERA	AB	H	HR	BB	SO	BA	SA	OBA
Season	15-13	3.36	875	190	24	81	109	.217	.346	.285
vs. Left-Handed Batters			487	108	13	59	52	.222	.347	.306
vs. Right-Handed Batters			388	82	11	22	57	.211	.345	.258
Home	7-9	3.60	479	102	18	52	58	.213	.365	.291
Road	8-4	3.05	396	88	6	29	51	.222	.323	.278
Grass	14-11	3.47	768	166	24	72	96	.216	.354	.284
Artificial Turf	1-2	2.51	107	24	0	9	13	.224	.290	.291
Day	7-4	3.03	321	71	5	27	40	.221	.324	.285
Night	8-9	3.54	554	119	19	54	69	.215	.359	.285
April	4-1	2.90	119	27	2	4	15	.227	.328	.256
May	4-2	3.45	168	38	6	15	20	.226	.393	.293
June	1-3	2.77	168	34	5	15	17	.202	.321	.268
July	2-4	4.57	169	38	7	17	25	.225	.402	.298
August	2-1	2.29	141	30	0	13	20	.213	.262	.279
Sept./Oct.	2-2	4.20	110	23	4	17	12	.209	.355	.315
Leading Off Inn.			227	41	5	18	33	.181	.300	.241
Bases Empty			564	112	13	50	71	.199	.317	.266
Runners On			311	78	11	31	38	.251	.399	.319
Runners/Scor. Pos.			170	47	5	21	17	.276	.418	.356
Runners On/2 Out			133	36	6	19	20	.271	.466	.362
Scor. Pos./2 Out			81	26	4	11	12	.321	.543	.402
Late Inning Pressure			121	16	2	14	14	.132	.207	.222
Leading Off			38	1	0	1	4	.026	.026	.051
Bases Empty			95	10	1	5	10	.105	.158	.150
Runners On			26	6	1	9	4	.231	.385	.429
Runners/Scor. Pos.			11	2	0	8	1	.182	.182	.526
First 9 Batters			281	66	11	24	45	.235	.388	.297
Second 9 Batters			260	61	5	25	25	.235	.362	.306
All Batters Thereafter			334	63	8	32	39	.189	.299	.259

Loves to face: Charlie Moore (.037, 1-for-27)
Hates to face: Willie Upshaw (.452, 14-for-31, 3 HR)
Ground outs-to-air outs ratio: 1.22 last season, 1.47 for career. . . . Additional statistics: 24 double-play ground outs in 124 opportunities (2d-highest rate in A.L.), 35 doubles, 3 triples allowed in 238.2 innings last season. . . . Allowed 23 first-inning runs (tied for 9th-most in A.L.) in 34 starts last season. . . . Batting support: 4.00 runs per start. . . . Ranked 3d in A.L. with 7.16 hits per nine innings. . . . Tied for 2d in A.L. with nine home-game losses. . . . Opponents' batting averages in Late-Inning Pressure Situations, year by year since 1983: .345, .277, .132. . . . Opponents' overall batting average was lowest of his career, while average with runners in scoring position was his highest since '79. . . . One of two major-league pitchers to win at least 15 games in each of past four seasons. The other: teammate Jack Morris.

Dan Quisenberry

Kansas City Royals	W–L	ERA	AB	H	HR	BB	SO	BA	SA	OBA
Season	8-9	2.37	508	142	8	16	54	.280	.376	.301
vs. Left-Handed Batters			271	86	4	14	17	.317	.435	.350
vs. Right-Handed Batters			237	56	4	2	37	.236	.308	.244
Home	6-3	2.30	285	76	6	9	23	.267	.379	.291
Road	2-6	2.47	223	66	2	7	31	.296	.372	.315
Grass	2-6	2.12	192	59	0	7	27	.307	.349	.328
Artificial Turf	6-3	2.51	316	83	8	9	27	.263	.392	.284
Day	3-3	2.72	144	42	3	4	16	.292	.375	.313
Night	5-6	2.23	364	100	5	12	38	.275	.376	.296
April	2-2	3.45	71	25	1	3	8	.352	.465	.387
May	1-1	2.21	69	12	0	2	7	.174	.246	.192
June	1-1	2.53	87	28	2	4	6	.322	.437	.352
July	0-2	3.09	98	31	2	2	13	.316	.408	.330
August	2-2	0.81	81	18	2	4	11	.222	.321	.256
Sept./Oct.	2-1	2.42	102	28	1	1	9	.275	.363	.282
Leading Off Inn.			105	31	3	0	7	.295	.457	.295
Bases Empty			254	74	6	3	25	.291	.417	.300
Runners On			254	68	2	13	29	.268	.335	.303
Runners/Scor. Pos.			157	35	2	13	25	.223	.287	.282
Runners On/2 Out			118	29	1	6	17	.246	.314	.288
Scor. Pos./2 Out			75	15	1	6	16	.200	.267	.268
Late Inning Pressure			325	90	5	11	36	.277	.366	.302
Leading Off			63	21	1	0	4	.333	.460	.333
Bases Empty			156	44	3	1	19	.282	.391	.287
Runners On			169	46	2	10	17	.272	.343	.315
Runners/Scor. Pos.			108	27	2	10	15	.250	.324	.317
First 9 Batters			477	135	8	12	49	.283	.386	.300
Second 9 Batters			31	7	0	4	5	.226	.226	.314
All Batters Thereafter			0	0	0	0	0	.000	.000	.000

Loves to face: Julio Franco (0-for-12)
Hates to face: Kent Hrbek (.571, 8-for-14, 2 HR)
Ground outs-to-air outs ratio: 1.98 last season, 2.33 for career. . . . Additional statistics: 14 double-play ground outs in 106 opportunities, 19 doubles, 3 triples allowed in 129.0 innings last year. . . . Tony Armas is the only player to have three career homers off him. . . . Led A.L. pitchers with 84 games, to become 5th three-time leader in A.L. history. Others: Firpo Marberry (6), Ed Walsh (5), Bob Feller (3), and Wilbur Wood (3). . . . Ranked 7th among A.L. relievers with 2.37 ERA last year (minimum: 30 relief games). . . . Faced 105 leadoff batters in Late-Inning Pressure Situations without allowing a walk, 3d-highest total in *Player Analysis* history, but 16 short of record he set in '83. . . . Career average of 1.18 walks per nine innings leads active pitchers (minimum: 250 innings).

Dennis Rasmussen

New York Yankees	W–L	ERA	AB	H	HR	BB	SO	BA	SA	OBA
Season	3-5	3.98	380	97	10	42	63	.255	.405	.327
vs. Left-Handed Batters			98	25	3	7	18	.255	.408	.305
vs. Right-Handed Batters			282	72	7	35	45	.255	.404	.334
Home	2-2	5.08	167	46	6	21	28	.275	.449	.353
Road	1-3	3.14	213	51	4	21	35	.239	.371	.307
Grass	2-3	3.95	304	83	8	32	51	.273	.421	.339
Artificial Turf	1-2	4.09	76	14	2	10	12	.184	.342	.281
Day	1-2	4.35	185	50	4	22	34	.270	.411	.344
Night	2-3	3.63	195	47	6	20	29	.241	.400	.311
April	0-1	2.84	73	21	1	6	12	.288	.411	.338
May	2-1	3.12	123	24	2	12	17	.195	.325	.263
June	0-2	4.68	99	33	4	13	18	.333	.505	.407
July	1-1	5.21	66	11	2	9	13	.167	.333	.273
August			0	0	0	0	0	.000	.000	.000
Sept./Oct.	0-0	6.75	19	8	1	2	3	.421	.632	.476
Leading Off Inn.			94	25	4	11	13	.266	.468	.343
Bases Empty			235	50	7	28	40	.213	.370	.297
Runners On			145	47	3	14	23	.324	.462	.376
Runners/Scor. Pos.			73	23	2	8	11	.315	.479	.368
Runners On/2 Out			56	20	2	7	11	.357	.518	.429
Scor. Pos./2 Out			33	11	2	4	5	.333	.576	.405
Late Inning Pressure			32	9	1	3	4	.281	.375	.343
Leading Off			8	1	0	2	1	.125	.125	.300
Bases Empty			21	6	1	3	2	.286	.429	.375
Runners On			11	3	0	0	2	.273	.273	.273
Runners/Scor. Pos.			2	1	0	0	0	.500	.500	.500
First 9 Batters			152	39	4	21	28	.257	.441	.339
Second 9 Batters			121	30	2	9	22	.248	.372	.305
All Batters Thereafter			107	28	4	12	13	.262	.393	.333

Loves to face: Lance Parrish (0-for-10, 3 SO)
Hates to face: Tom Brookens (.600, 6-for-10, 1 HR)
Ground outs-to-air outs ratio: 0.87 last season, 0.81 for career. . . . Additional statistics: 11 double-play ground outs in 78 opportunities, 15 doubles, 6 triples allowed in 101.2 innings last season. . . . Allowed 9 first-inning runs in 16 starts in '85. Allowed two in 24 starts in 1984. . . . Batting support: 4.63 runs per start. . . . Has allowed seven hits, including four grand-slam homers, and three walks to the 16 batters he has faced with the bases loaded. . . . Career total of 41 starts is 9th-highest among pitchers without a complete-game shutout. . . . Opposing batters hit 111 points higher with runners on base than with the bases empty, 2d-largest difference in A.L. last season (minimum: 100 AB in both situations). Career averages: .275 with men on base, .219 with the bases empty.

Jerry Reed

Cleveland Indians	W–L	ERA	AB	H	HR	BB	SO	BA	SA	OBA
Season	3-5	4.11	273	67	12	19	37	.245	.418	.298
vs. Left-Handed Batters			135	39	7	8	10	.289	.496	.329
vs. Right-Handed Batters			138	28	5	11	27	.203	.341	.268
Home	1-2	3.45	117	26	4	6	16	.222	.342	.256
Road	2-3	4.61	156	41	8	13	21	.263	.474	.328
Grass	2-4	3.47	226	52	10	13	29	.230	.381	.270
Artificial Turf	1-1	8.10	47	15	2	6	8	.319	.596	.418
Day	2-1	2.01	80	18	1	6	15	.225	.288	.287
Night	1-4	5.04	193	49	11	13	22	.254	.472	.302
April			0	0	0	0	0	.000	.000	.000
May			0	0	0	0	0	.000	.000	.000
June			0	0	0	0	0	.000	.000	.000
July	0-3	5.22	120	33	3	6	16	.275	.400	.315
August	0-1	4.66	73	19	5	3	6	.260	.479	.289
Sept./Oct.	3-1	2.28	80	15	4	10	15	.188	.388	.280
Leading Off Inn.			63	9	3	3	5	.143	.317	.194
Bases Empty			166	36	9	10	21	.217	.404	.270
Runners On			107	31	3	9	16	.290	.439	.339
Runners/Scor. Pos.			57	17	2	7	12	.298	.456	.362
Runners On/2 Out			47	10	2	4	11	.213	.340	.275
Scor. Pos./2 Out			24	6	1	3	9	.250	.375	.333
Late Inning Pressure			78	22	4	8	11	.282	.487	.345
Leading Off			19	6	2	0	2	.316	.684	.316
Bases Empty			49	12	3	3	6	.245	.449	.288
Runners On			29	10	1	5	5	.345	.552	.429
Runners/Scor. Pos.			14	5	1	4	2	.357	.571	.474
First 9 Batters			184	37	7	17	30	.201	.348	.273
Second 9 Batters			64	21	4	2	6	.328	.578	.358
All Batters Thereafter			25	9	1	0	1	.360	.520	.333

Loves to face: Frank White (0-for-5, 2 SO)
Hates to face: Phil Bradley (2-for-2, 1 HR)
Ground outs-to-air outs ratio: 1.19 last season, 1.28 for career. . . . Additional statistics: 7 double-play ground outs in 50 opportunities, 9 doubles, 1 triple allowed in 72.1 innings last season. . . . Opponents' career batting averages: .248 with bases empty, .291 with runners on base, .300 with runners in scoring position. . . . Opposing left-handed batters have hit .308, right-handers .233. . . . Record of 0–3, 4.97 ERA in five starts last season; 3–2, eight saves, 3.64 ERA in 28 relief appearances. . . . Opponents' average on artificial surfaces last season was the *lowest* of his four seasons in majors. Career averages: .248 on grass fields, .344 on artificial turf.

Dave Righetti

New York Yankees	W–L	ERA	AB	H	HR	BB	SO	BA	SA	OBA
Season	12-7	2.78	398	96	5	45	92	.241	.327	.316
vs. Left-Handed Batters			112	22	1	18	32	.196	.277	.308
vs. Right-Handed Batters			286	74	4	27	60	.259	.346	.320
Home	9-1	2.24	208	48	2	23	56	.231	.298	.307
Road	3-6	3.38	190	48	3	22	36	.253	.358	.326
Grass	12-6	2.77	356	82	5	43	84	.230	.323	.312
Artificial Turf	0-1	2.79	42	14	0	2	8	.333	.357	.356
Day	7-2	1.70	160	37	0	21	36	.231	.263	.317
Night	5-5	3.48	238	59	5	24	56	.248	.370	.316
April	1-1	1.84	55	16	0	6	10	.291	.309	.361
May	2-3	1.80	71	12	1	8	12	.169	.296	.250
June	2-2	6.88	69	18	3	13	16	.261	.493	.378
July	2-1	1.84	57	16	0	3	17	.281	.298	.311
August	4-0	1.17	80	14	1	9	22	.175	.225	.256
Sept./Oct.	1-0	3.57	66	20	0	6	15	.303	.348	.361
Leading Off Inn.			73	15	2	9	21	.205	.342	.293
Bases Empty			187	41	4	22	47	.219	.321	.301
Runners On			211	55	1	23	45	.261	.332	.329
Runners/Scor. Pos.			133	34	0	13	26	.256	.323	.315
Runners On/2 Out			101	23	1	14	24	.228	.297	.322
Scor. Pos./2 Out			66	14	0	10	13	.212	.242	.316
Late Inning Pressure			268	67	3	30	63	.250	.321	.323
Leading Off			51	11	1	4	14	.216	.333	.273
Bases Empty			126	30	3	14	29	.238	.333	.314
Runners On			142	37	0	16	34	.261	.310	.331
Runners/Scor. Pos.			94	25	0	8	22	.266	.319	.317
First 9 Batters			363	85	4	37	89	.234	.309	.303
Second 9 Batters			35	11	1	8	3	.314	.514	.442
All Batters Thereafter			0	0	0	0	0	.000	.000	.000

Loves to face: Reggie Jackson (.056, 1-for-18, 8 SO)
Hates to face: Cliff Johnson (.462, 6-for-13)
Ground outs-to-air outs ratio: 1.06 last season, 1.02 for career. . . . Additional statistics: 12 double-play ground outs in 97 opportunities, 15 doubles, 2 triples allowed in 107.0 innings last season. . . . Tied Cincinnati's John Franco for major-league lead with 12 relief wins. . . . Most decisions (19) among major-league relievers last season. . . . Has finished 80.6 percent of his relief appearances, 2d-highest career average among active pitchers. The leader: Dan Quisenberry (89.4). . . . Career rate of 25.6 strikeouts per 100 left-handed batters faced is a *Player Analysis* record (minimum: 100 SO vs. LHP). . . . Batting average by left-handers (.202) is 5th-lowest in majors since 1975 (minimum: 400 BFP). . . . Only pitcher to have fanned Wade Boggs six times in his career, including the final out of his 1983 no-hitter.

Jose Rijo
Oakland As

	W–L	ERA	AB	H	HR	BB	SO	BA	SA	OBA
Season	6-4	3.53	238	57	6	28	65	.239	.382	.322
vs. Left-Handed Batters			125	35	5	19	38	.280	.488	.379
vs. Right-Handed Batters			113	22	1	9	27	.195	.265	.254
Home	2-1	3.65	93	23	1	8	27	.247	.344	.314
Road	4-3	3.46	145	34	5	20	38	.234	.407	.327
Grass	5-2	3.51	188	43	4	24	50	.229	.356	.319
Artificial Turf	1-2	3.65	50	14	2	4	15	.280	.480	.333
Day	3-1	5.51	62	17	1	11	16	.274	.452	.392
Night	3-3	2.85	176	40	5	17	49	.227	.358	.295
April			0	0	0	0	0	.000	.000	.000
May			0	0	0	0	0	.000	.000	.000
June			0	0	0	0	0	.000	.000	.000
July			0	0	0	0	0	.000	.000	.000
August	2-1	1.61	75	11	3	10	23	.147	.307	.247
Sept./Oct.	4-3	4.57	163	46	3	18	42	.282	.417	.357
Leading Off Inn.			60	23	4	7	13	.383	.700	.448
Bases Empty			133	32	5	15	36	.241	.436	.318
Runners On			105	25	1	13	29	.238	.314	.328
Runners/Scor. Pos.			73	18	1	8	21	.247	.315	.329
Runners On/2 Out			39	7	1	9	10	.179	.308	.333
Scor. Pos./2 Out			29	6	1	6	8	.207	.345	.343
Late Inning Pressure			30	8	1	3	7	.267	.400	.333
Leading Off			10	5	1	2	2	.500	.900	.583
Bases Empty			19	6	1	2	5	.316	.526	.381
Runners On			11	2	0	1	2	.182	.182	.250
Runners/Scor. Pos.			7	2	0	0	2	.286	.286	.286
First 9 Batters			90	20	1	17	32	.222	.322	.346
Second 9 Batters			82	19	3	4	20	.232	.427	.276
All Batters Thereafter			66	18	2	7	13	.273	.409	.342

Loves to face: Lonnie Smith (0-for-7, 4 SO)
Hates to face: Rickey Henderson (3-for-3, 3 BB)
Ground outs-to-air outs ratio: 0.65 last season (10th-lowest in A.L.), 0.91 for career. . . . Additional statistics: 1 double-play ground out in 43 opportunities, 16 doubles, 0 triples allowed in 63.2 innings last season. . . . Career average of 2.38 strikeouts per walk in night games, 1.00 in day games. . . . Opponents' career batting average of .304 in Late-Inning Pressure Situations, .263 in nonpressure situations. . . . Opponents' career batting average of .342 leading off innings is the highest among active pitchers (minimum: 100 PA). . . . Career average of one extra-base hit allowed per 21.5 at bats (and 1 HR per 78.7) with runners on base, when the extra bases can do more damage; one XBH per 9.6 at bats (and 1 HR per 31.3) with bases empty.

Ron Romanick
California Angels

	W–L	ERA	AB	H	HR	BB	SO	BA	SA	OBA
Season	14-9	4.11	751	210	29	62	64	.280	.449	.334
vs. Left-Handed Batters			410	115	16	35	31	.280	.461	.333
vs. Right-Handed Batters			341	95	13	27	33	.279	.434	.334
Home	8-3	3.54	392	108	18	33	33	.276	.454	.331
Road	6-6	4.73	359	102	11	29	31	.284	.443	.337
Grass	14-5	3.49	636	171	27	53	49	.269	.442	.323
Artificial Turf	0-4	7.90	115	39	2	9	15	.339	.487	.391
Day	5-2	2.54	229	62	3	22	21	.271	.354	.333
Night	9-7	4.81	522	148	26	40	43	.284	.490	.334
April	2-1	3.96	102	33	4	14	6	.324	.480	.402
May	4-1	3.14	158	38	6	9	13	.241	.418	.276
June	2-2	2.38	158	41	2	11	17	.259	.335	.316
July	5-0	2.97	130	30	6	9	6	.231	.408	.277
August	0-2	10.71	89	36	3	14	8	.404	.607	.467
Sept./Oct.	1-3	5.16	114	32	8	5	14	.281	.544	.322
Leading Off Inn.			193	62	9	11	14	.321	.528	.358
Bases Empty			445	129	20	32	31	.290	.485	.339
Runners On			306	81	9	30	33	.265	.395	.327
Runners/Scor. Pos.			171	44	2	17	21	.257	.333	.312
Runners On/2 Out			129	36	4	15	15	.279	.419	.354
Scor. Pos./2 Out			84	21	1	8	10	.250	.345	.315
Late Inning Pressure			58	15	2	3	4	.259	.448	.295
Leading Off			17	5	1	0	2	.294	.588	.294
Bases Empty			43	10	2	2	4	.233	.419	.267
Runners On			15	5	0	1	0	.333	.533	.375
Runners/Scor. Pos.			8	3	0	1	0	.375	.750	.444
First 9 Batters			245	67	5	23	25	.273	.388	.333
Second 9 Batters			245	72	13	18	18	.294	.510	.343
All Batters Thereafter			261	71	11	21	21	.272	.448	.325

Loves to face: Dave Kingman (0-for-18, 4 SO)
Hates to face: Lance Parrish (.714, 5-for-7, 1 HR)
Ground outs-to-air outs ratio: 0.88 last season, 0.87 for career. . . . Additional statistics: 22 double-play ground outs in 154 opportunities, 30 doubles, 5 triples allowed in 195.0 innings last season. . . . Allowed 25 first-inning runs (tied for 4th-most in A.L.) in 31 starts last season. . . . Batting support: 4.81 runs per start. . . . Average of 2.95 strikeouts per nine innings was 2d-lowest among A.L. pitchers with at least 15 starts. . . . Day-game ERA was 3d-lowest in A.L. last season. . . . Career: has walked only one leadoff batter in 51 innings in Late-Inning Pressure Situations. . . . But can he win the big one? Won only one of his last 10 starts in Angels' pennant drive last season, two of his last 10 starts in 1984 pennant race.

Ramon Romero
Cleveland Indians

	W–L	ERA	AB	H	HR	BB	SO	BA	SA	OBA
Season	2-3	6.58	250	69	13	38	38	.276	.484	.381
vs. Left-Handed Batters			76	21	2	10	16	.276	.382	.356
vs. Right-Handed Batters			174	48	11	28	22	.276	.529	.391
Home	2-1	4.22	121	29	4	13	18	.240	.364	.313
Road	0-2	8.91	129	40	9	25	20	.310	.597	.438
Grass	2-2	6.41	228	62	11	35	35	.272	.469	.377
Artificial Turf	0-1	8.44	22	7	2	3	3	.318	.636	.423
Day	1-1	4.66	76	19	4	12	15	.250	.447	.360
Night	1-2	7.40	174	50	9	26	23	.287	.500	.390
April	0-0	54.00	1	1	0	1	0	1.000	1.000	1.000
May			0	0	0	0	0	.000	.000	.000
June			0	0	0	0	0	.000	.000	.000
July	1-1	4.65	117	27	6	13	17	.231	.410	.313
August	1-2	7.89	86	25	5	16	9	.291	.512	.413
Sept./Oct.	0-0	7.94	46	16	2	8	12	.348	.609	.456
Leading Off Inn.			61	16	4	8	7	.262	.492	.348
Bases Empty			139	40	11	19	17	.288	.576	.381
Runners On			111	29	2	19	21	.261	.369	.381
Runners/Scor. Pos.			68	19	0	15	14	.279	.338	.419
Runners On/2 Out			40	7	1	8	11	.175	.275	.313
Scor. Pos./2 Out			26	6	0	7	9	.231	.269	.394
Late Inning Pressure			11	2	1	0	0	.182	.455	.182
Leading Off			3	0	0	0	0	.000	.000	.000
Bases Empty			10	2	1	0	0	.200	.500	.200
Runners On			1	0	0	0	0	.000	.000	.000
Runners/Scor. Pos.			1	0	0	0	0	.000	.000	.000
First 9 Batters			119	35	9	20	19	.294	.597	.404
Second 9 Batters			83	19	2	14	13	.229	.349	.350
All Batters Thereafter			48	15	2	4	6	.313	.438	.377

Loves to face: Rich Gedman (0-for-7, 4 SO)
Hates to face: Rickey Henderson (.750, 3-for-4, 2 HR)
Ground outs-to-air outs ratio: 0.81 last season, 0.84 for career. . . . Additional statistics: 5 double-play ground outs in 59 opportunities, 11 doubles, 1 triple allowed in 64.1 innings last season. . . . Allowed 7 first-inning runs in 10 starts last season. . . . Batting support: 3.90 runs per start. . . . ERA of 9.42 in nine relief appearances last season. . . . Remember what they used to say about Catfish Hunter? Well, Romero has allowed an average of one home run per 56.5 at bats with runners on base, one per 13.2 at bats with the bases empty. Home run rate with the bases empty is 5th-worst in *Player Analysis* history (minimum: 150 PA). . . . Allowed at least one home run in seven consecutive starts (July 12 to Aug. 18). . . . Did not last past the fifth inning in any of his five starts on the road last season.

Dave Rozema
Texas Rangers

	W–L	ERA	AB	H	HR	BB	SO	BA	SA	OBA
Season	3-7	4.19	348	100	10	22	42	.287	.420	.332
vs. Left-Handed Batters			191	50	6	13	16	.262	.393	.311
vs. Right-Handed Batters			157	50	4	9	26	.318	.452	.359
Home	1-4	4.27	209	61	7	11	31	.292	.431	.329
Road	2-3	4.08	139	39	3	11	11	.281	.403	.338
Grass	3-7	4.48	325	94	10	21	40	.289	.431	.335
Artificial Turf	0-0	2.97	23	6	0	1	2	.261	.261	.262
Day	0-3	15.55	56	26	3	6	4	.464	.732	.516
Night	3-4	2.57	292	74	7	16	38	.253	.360	.296
April	1-3	4.07	95	24	3	4	8	.253	.379	.283
May	1-0	5.79	36	13	1	0	1	.361	.556	.361
June	1-2	5.68	84	31	1	6	11	.369	.440	.418
July	0-2	3.86	91	25	3	10	9	.275	.440	.353
August	0-0	0.00	9	1	0	0	3	.111	.111	.111
Sept./Oct.	0-0	2.00	33	6	2	2	10	.182	.364	.229
Leading Off Inn.			75	19	2	3	6	.253	.373	.282
Bases Empty			191	48	3	8	25	.251	.330	.281
Runners On			157	52	7	14	17	.331	.529	.391
Runners/Scor. Pos.			98	30	4	11	13	.306	.500	.378
Runners On/2 Out			58	14	1	4	5	.241	.345	.290
Scor. Pos./2 Out			37	9	0	4	4	.243	.297	.317
Late Inning Pressure			92	30	3	6	8	.326	.500	.364
Leading Off			21	4	0	1	3	.190	.238	.227
Bases Empty			56	16	0	2	7	.286	.321	.310
Runners On			36	14	3	4	1	.389	.778	.439
Runners/Scor. Pos.			19	6	1	4	1	.316	.632	.417
First 9 Batters			242	75	7	12	29	.310	.459	.346
Second 9 Batters			76	18	2	9	9	.237	.316	.318
All Batters Thereafter			30	7	1	1	4	.233	.367	.258

Loves to face: Tom Paciorek (.056, 1-for-18, 4 SO)
Hates to face: Pat Tabler (.556, 5-for-9, 2 HR)
Ground outs-to-air outs ratio: 1.91 last season, 1.77 for career. . . . Additional statistics: 10 double-play ground outs in 87 opportunities, 12 doubles, 2 triples allowed in 88.0 innings last season. . . . Opponents are 0-for-17 with the bases loaded over past two years (one walk, one sacrifice fly). . . . Record of 2-2, 2.88 ERA in four starts; 1-5, seven saves, 4.71 ERA in 30 relief appearances. . . . Opponents' batting averages in Late-Inning Pressure Situations, year by year since 1982: .133, .167, .222, .326. . . . Opponents have batted over .300 with runners in scoring position in each of the last three seasons. . . . Career average of 2.10 walks per nine innings ranks 10th among active pitchers (minimum: 250 innings).

Vern Ruhle

Cleveland Indians	W–L	ERA	AB	H	HR	BB	SO	BA	SA	OBA
Season	2-10	4.32	492	139	16	30	54	.283	.417	.324
vs. Left-Handed Batters			256	69	7	17	28	.270	.395	.314
vs. Right-Handed Batters			236	70	9	13	26	.297	.441	.335
Home	1-3	3.81	211	53	9	12	27	.251	.422	.290
Road	1-7	4.71	281	86	7	18	27	.306	.413	.349
Grass	1-9	4.21	413	116	13	27	45	.281	.414	.324
Artificial Turf	1-1	4.87	79	23	3	3	9	.291	.430	.321
Day	1-4	4.88	222	63	9	10	22	.284	.441	.313
Night	1-6	3.88	270	76	7	20	32	.281	.396	.332
April	1-2	3.50	72	20	2	6	8	.278	.389	.333
May	0-0	1.64	37	6	0	1	3	.162	.216	.200
June	0-1	8.16	61	24	3	4	5	.393	.590	.424
July	1-4	5.56	141	43	5	7	15	.305	.447	.342
August	0-2	3.22	84	20	2	8	9	.238	.345	.301
Sept./Oct.	0-1	3.20	97	26	4	4	14	.268	.423	.294
Leading Off Inn.			124	32	4	4	13	.258	.395	.287
Bases Empty			299	77	8	15	34	.258	.368	.297
Runners On			193	62	8	15	20	.321	.492	.363
Runners/Scor. Pos.			101	33	4	13	14	.327	.495	.390
Runners On/2 Out			78	20	4	9	8	.256	.449	.333
Scor. Pos./2 Out			42	10	3	9	5	.238	.476	.373
Late Inning Pressure			63	17	2	7	4	.270	.381	.338
Leading Off			22	7	2	0	0	.318	.591	.318
Bases Empty			49	14	2	3	3	.286	.429	.327
Runners On			14	3	0	4	1	.214	.214	.368
Runners/Scor. Pos.			7	2	0	4	1	.286	.286	.500
First 9 Batters			275	70	7	20	30	.255	.371	.308
Second 9 Batters			137	34	4	5	16	.248	.350	.273
All Batters Thereafter			80	35	5	5	8	.438	.688	.465

Loves to face: Paul Householder (0-for-11, 4 SO)
Hates to face: Hal McRae (.556, 15-for-27, 2 HR)
Ground outs-to-air outs ratio: 1.22 last season, 1.37 for career. . . . Additional statistics: 11 double-play ground outs in 95 opportunities, 16 doubles, 1 triple allowed in 125.0 innings last season. . . . Average of 5.06 innings per start was 3d-lowest among A.L. pitchers (minimum: 15 GS). . . . Allowed 11 first-inning runs in 16 starts last season. . . . Pitched fewer than five innings in seven of his 16 starts. . . . Batting support: 3.25 runs per start, 2d-lowest average in A.L. (minimum: 15 GS). . . . Career: has walked only four leadoff batters in 193 innings in Late-Inning Pressure Situations. . . . Career average of 2.16 strikeouts per walk in day games, 1.47 in night games. . . . Worst winning percentage (3–19, .136) in the majors over the past two seasons (minimum: 10 decisions).

Jeff Russell

Texas Rangers	W–L	ERA	AB	H	HR	BB	SO	BA	SA	OBA
Season	3-6	7.55	262	85	10	27	44	.324	.527	.388
vs. Left-Handed Batters			146	47	5	17	24	.322	.534	.390
vs. Right-Handed Batters			116	38	5	10	20	.328	.517	.385
Home	1-4	8.33	157	56	7	11	29	.357	.580	.400
Road	2-2	6.49	105	29	3	16	15	.276	.448	.371
Grass	3-5	6.95	239	76	9	21	41	.318	.519	.375
Artificial Turf	0-1	14.40	23	9	1	6	3	.391	.609	.500
Day	0-0	3.86	26	8	2	1	6	.308	.615	.333
Night	3-6	8.02	236	77	8	26	38	.326	.517	.393
April			0	0	0	0	0	.000	.000	.000
May			0	0	0	0	0	.000	.000	.000
June			0	0	0	0	0	.000	.000	.000
July			0	0	0	0	0	.000	.000	.000
August	1-4	8.20	118	42	5	12	14	.356	.559	.418
Sept./Oct.	2-2	7.07	144	43	5	15	30	.299	.500	.363
Leading Off Inn.			66	27	1	3	5	.409	.500	.435
Bases Empty			138	47	5	11	18	.341	.522	.397
Runners On			124	38	5	16	26	.306	.532	.378
Runners/Scor. Pos.			69	21	2	12	12	.304	.493	.393
Runners On/2 Out			50	18	2	5	10	.360	.560	.418
Scor. Pos./2 Out			31	12	1	4	5	.387	.581	.457
Late Inning Pressure			12	2	0	1	5	.167	.250	.231
Leading Off			4	2	0	0	1	.500	.750	.500
Bases Empty			9	2	0	0	3	.222	.333	.222
Runners On			3	0	0	1	2	.000	.000	.250
Runners/Scor. Pos.			3	0	0	1	2	.000	.000	.250
First 9 Batters			106	33	5	9	18	.311	.509	.371
Second 9 Batters			89	30	3	12	13	.337	.573	.417
All Batters Thereafter			67	22	2	6	13	.328	.493	.373

Loves to face: Alfredo Griffin (.125, 1-for-8)
Hates to face: Jim Presley (2-for-2, 1 HR)
Ground outs-to-air outs ratio: 1.20 last season, 0.94 for career. . . . Additional statistics: 4 double-play ground outs in 62 opportunities, 19 doubles, 2 triples allowed in 62.0 innings last season. . . . Allowed 8 first-inning runs in 13 starts last season. . . . Batting support: 4.46 runs per start. . . . 2d-highest opponents' slugging average in majors last season (minimum: 200 batters faced). . . . Failed to pitch into the seventh inning in 10 of his 13 starts. . . . Career ERA of 67.50 vs. Toronto. . . . Batting averages of opposing left-handers, year by year since 1983: .233, .281, .322. . . . Has allowed only one home run in 141 career plate appearances in Late-Inning Pressure Situations. . . . Opponents' career LIP batting average is .189.

Bret Saberhagen

Kansas City Royals	W–L	ERA	AB	H	HR	BB	SO	BA	SA	OBA
Season	20-6	2.87	876	211	19	38	158	.241	.357	.271
vs. Left-Handed Batters			501	121	14	28	91	.242	.363	.280
vs. Right-Handed Batters			375	90	5	10	67	.240	.349	.260
Home	10-3	2.80	472	111	8	22	80	.235	.337	.267
Road	10-3	2.95	404	100	11	16	78	.248	.381	.276
Grass	9-2	2.55	357	85	10	13	73	.238	.370	.265
Artificial Turf	11-4	3.09	519	126	9	25	85	.243	.349	.276
Day	1-2	4.88	109	31	1	9	19	.284	.376	.339
Night	19-4	2.60	767	180	18	29	139	.235	.355	.261
April	2-2	3.65	97	28	0	4	9	.289	.351	.317
May	3-1	3.41	126	29	3	5	14	.230	.365	.258
June	2-1	2.83	155	39	3	12	30	.252	.355	.302
July	5-1	2.05	178	39	6	4	35	.219	.354	.240
August	4-0	2.64	115	28	2	3	28	.243	.357	.261
Sept./Oct.	4-1	3.05	205	48	5	10	42	.234	.361	.266
Leading Off Inn.			233	57	7	10	37	.245	.386	.276
Bases Empty			563	143	15	23	107	.254	.387	.284
Runners On			313	68	4	15	51	.217	.304	.248
Runners/Scor. Pos.			154	35	1	10	23	.227	.312	.263
Runners On/2 Out			135	26	4	4	20	.193	.326	.216
Scor. Pos./2 Out			74	12	1	4	14	.162	.230	.205
Late Inning Pressure			106	25	5	6	21	.236	.396	.277
Leading Off			32	6	2	1	5	.188	.375	.212
Bases Empty			83	20	5	4	15	.241	.446	.276
Runners On			23	5	0	2	6	.217	.217	.280
Runners/Scor. Pos.			8	0	0	2	2	.000	.000	.200
First 9 Batters			271	63	2	11	51	.232	.303	.263
Second 9 Batters			268	63	4	11	49	.235	.332	.264
All Batters Thereafter			337	85	13	16	58	.252	.421	.283

Loves to face: Reggie Jackson (0-for-17, 6 SO)
Hates to face: Craig Gerber (.750, 6-for-8)
Ground outs-to-air outs ratio: 1.14 last season, 1.18 for career. . . . Additional statistics: 13 double-play ground outs in 145 opportunities, 33 doubles, 6 triples allowed in 235.1 innings last season. . . . Allowed 8 first-inning runs in 32 starts, 5th-lowest rate in A.L. (minimum: 15 GS). . . . Has not allowed a first-inning home run in his last 38 regular-season starts. Allowed five 9th-inning homers in '85, most by any starter in majors. . . . Batting support: 4.50 runs per start. . . . Career average of 1.69 walks per nine innings ranks 3d among active pitchers (minimum: 250 innings). . . . Saberhagen popped up George Bell with bases loaded in first inning of A.L.C.S. Game 7. The last batter he'd faced with bags full was Brian Downing on Sept. 18, 1984, who bounced into a double play. . . . Youngest pitcher ever to start Game 7 of World Series.

Luis Sanchez

California Angels	W–L	ERA	AB	H	HR	BB	SO	BA	SA	OBA
Season	2-0	5.72	237	67	9	27	34	.283	.498	.354
vs. Left-Handed Batters			115	36	5	17	20	.313	.530	.396
vs. Right-Handed Batters			122	31	4	10	14	.254	.467	.313
Home	2-0	7.66	91	28	6	10	13	.308	.560	.379
Road	0-0	4.62	146	39	3	17	21	.267	.459	.339
Grass	2-0	6.54	169	51	7	17	25	.302	.538	.363
Artificial Turf	0-0	3.86	68	16	2	10	9	.235	.397	.333
Day	0-0	6.14	84	25	3	11	12	.298	.536	.375
Night	2-0	5.49	153	42	6	16	22	.275	.477	.343
April	0-0	14.04	36	13	3	9	4	.361	.694	.478
May			0	0	0	0	0	.000	.000	.000
June	1-0	2.70	14	4	0	0	4	.286	.286	.286
July	0-0	4.58	76	22	2	7	8	.289	.474	.349
August	1-0	4.94	85	19	4	11	13	.224	.435	.316
Sept./Oct.	0-0	2.84	26	9	0	0	5	.346	.615	.333
Leading Off Inn.			50	12	1	5	7	.240	.360	.309
Bases Empty			122	31	3	14	19	.254	.402	.336
Runners On			115	36	6	13	15	.313	.600	.374
Runners/Scor. Pos.			65	23	3	11	9	.354	.662	.430
Runners On/2 Out			55	20	3	5	4	.364	.691	.417
Scor. Pos./2 Out			37	16	2	5	0	.432	.784	.500
Late Inning Pressure			43	9	2	4	9	.209	.395	.277
Leading Off			12	2	1	1	2	.167	.417	.231
Bases Empty			27	5	1	4	6	.185	.296	.290
Runners On			16	4	1	0	3	.250	.563	.250
Runners/Scor. Pos.			7	2	0	0	1	.286	.429	.286
First 9 Batters			174	51	6	18	28	.293	.506	.357
Second 9 Batters			55	14	3	6	5	.255	.473	.328
All Batters Thereafter			8	2	0	3	1	.250	.500	.455

Loves to face: Dwight Evans (0-for-15)
Hates to face: Rick Manning (.833, 5-for-6)
Ground outs-to-air outs ratio: 1.16 last season, 1.22 for career. . . . Additional statistics: 8 double-play ground outs in 52 opportunities, 14 doubles, 5 triples allowed in 61.1 innings last season. . . . Has allowed 32 career home runs: 22 at Anaheim Stadium and only 10 in road games. . . . Pitched three innings or more in nine of 26 appearances last season, compared to nine times in previous 88 appearances. . . . Percentage of pitching done in Late-Inning Pressure Situations dropped from 71% during 1983–84 to 18% last season. . . . Opponents' career batting average is .275 with two outs and runners in scoring position. . . . One of five A.L. relievers to allow three home runs in one game last season. The company evokes no images of Cooperstown past, present, or future: Bob Fallon, Len Whitehouse, Jeff Kaiser, and Alan Fowlkes.

Bill Scherrer

Detroit Tigers	W–L	ERA	AB	H	HR	BB	SO	BA	SA	OBA
Season	3-2	4.36	250	62	10	41	46	.248	.384	.354
vs. Left-Handed Batters			105	21	3	15	27	.200	.286	.306
vs. Right-Handed Batters			145	41	7	26	19	.283	.455	.387
Home	2-0	2.97	121	29	3	19	23	.240	.331	.338
Road	1-2	5.79	129	33	7	22	23	.256	.434	.368
Grass	3-2	4.40	227	58	9	37	42	.256	.392	.360
Artificial Turf	0-0	4.05	23	4	1	4	4	.174	.304	.296
Day	0-0	2.93	112	32	2	15	19	.286	.357	.367
Night	3-2	5.40	138	30	8	26	27	.217	.406	.343
April	0-1	9.64	19	5	2	2	5	.263	.632	.364
May	0-0	3.27	41	9	0	8	8	.220	.220	.347
June	0-0	3.31	54	7	3	9	8	.130	.296	.254
July	1-0	4.76	20	5	0	4	4	.250	.300	.375
August	2-0	1.93	48	7	1	10	12	.146	.229	.293
Sept./Oct.	0-1	6.91	68	29	4	8	9	.426	.618	.474
Leading Off Inn.			56	14	2	6	10	.250	.393	.323
Bases Empty			133	31	5	16	25	.233	.376	.315
Runners On			117	31	5	25	21	.265	.393	.393
Runners/Scor. Pos.			77	18	5	23	14	.234	.429	.408
Runners On/2 Out			53	10	2	17	8	.189	.302	.394
Scor. Pos./2 Out			39	5	2	16	7	.128	.282	.393
Late Inning Pressure			90	25	4	15	14	.278	.444	.383
Leading Off			24	9	0	1	3	.375	.417	.400
Bases Empty			50	14	1	5	8	.280	.400	.345
Runners On			40	11	3	10	6	.275	.500	.423
Runners/Scor. Pos.			31	7	3	9	5	.226	.516	.405
First 9 Batters			198	48	7	35	36	.242	.364	.356
Second 9 Batters			45	12	3	4	8	.267	.489	.327
All Batters Thereafter			7	2	0	2	2	.286	.286	.444

Loves to face: Ruppert Jones (.125, 1-for-8, 5 SO)
Hates to face: Alan Wiggins (.500, 5-for-10)
Ground outs-to-air outs ratio: 1.10 last season, 1.36 for career. . . . Additional statistics: 4 double-play ground outs in 55 opportunities, 4 doubles, 0 triples allowed in 66.0 innings last season. . . . Issued 13 intentional walks to lead the A.L. last season. . . . If all batters were left-handed, this guy would be Cy Young: Opposing right-handers hit 83 points higher than left-handers, 3d-largest difference in A.L. last season (minimum: 100 AB vs. each). . . . Has faced 357 lefty swingers in his career without allowing a triple. . . . Career average of one extra-base hit allowed every 39.5 at bats by left-handers is 2d-best in 11-year history of *The Player Analysis* (minimum: 250 AB). The leader: Jesse Orosco (one XBH every 40.3 AB). . . . Appeared in 48 games in relief last season without a save, highest total in A.L.; Jeff Dedmon led N.L. with 60.

Dave Schmidt

Texas Rangers	W–L	ERA	AB	H	HR	BB	SO	BA	SA	OBA
Season	7-6	3.15	329	81	6	22	46	.246	.350	.292
vs. Left-Handed Batters			168	39	3	11	25	.232	.369	.278
vs. Right-Handed Batters			161	42	3	11	21	.261	.329	.306
Home	4-2	2.83	179	42	3	8	25	.235	.335	.266
Road	3-4	3.55	150	39	3	14	21	.260	.367	.321
Grass	6-4	3.03	259	61	3	13	35	.236	.328	.271
Artificial Turf	1-2	3.63	70	20	3	9	11	.286	.429	.363
Day	1-0	2.77	50	12	0	2	7	.240	.300	.269
Night	6-6	3.22	279	69	6	20	39	.247	.358	.296
April	1-1	3.38	45	10	1	2	9	.222	.333	.255
May	1-1	2.25	28	5	0	2	3	.179	.179	.233
June	1-0	0.77	43	9	1	1	6	.209	.302	.227
July	1-1	1.98	46	9	0	2	6	.196	.217	.229
August	1-1	4.97	51	18	0	5	6	.353	.431	.404
Sept./Oct.	2-2	4.03	116	30	4	10	16	.259	.431	.315
Leading Off Inn.			77	16	0	2	10	.208	.273	.228
Bases Empty			186	43	5	8	23	.231	.355	.263
Runners On			143	38	1	14	23	.266	.343	.327
Runners/Scor. Pos.			98	22	1	10	16	.224	.337	.291
Runners On/2 Out			68	18	0	6	14	.265	.324	.324
Scor. Pos./2 Out			46	11	0	4	8	.239	.326	.300
Late Inning Pressure			120	27	1	7	20	.225	.292	.266
Leading Off			28	7	0	1	5	.250	.321	.276
Bases Empty			65	15	0	1	9	.231	.277	.242
Runners On			55	12	1	6	11	.218	.309	.290
Runners/Scor. Pos.			37	8	1	6	8	.216	.351	.318
First 9 Batters			257	61	3	17	36	.237	.311	.284
Second 9 Batters			42	16	3	3	6	.381	.714	.413
All Batters Thereafter			30	4	0	2	4	.133	.167	.188

Loves to face: Ben Oglivie (0-for-14)
Hates to face: Spike Owen (.778, 7-for-9, 1 HR)
Ground outs-to-air outs ratio: 1.57 last season, 1.50 for career. . . . Additional statistics: 9 double-play ground outs in 51 opportunities, 12 doubles, 2 triples allowed in 85.2 innings last season. . . . Average of 1.87 walks per nine innings was 4th-lowest among A.L. relief pitchers (minimum: 30 relief games). . . . Allowed one home run every 31.3 relief innings, 3d-lowest average among that group. . . . Has finished 71.7 percent of his relief appearances, 9th-highest career average among active pitchers (minimum: 50 GF). . . . Holds *Player Analysis* career marks for lowest on-base average by opposing batters leading off innings (.238) and lowest walk rate to leadoff batters: 1.6 for every 100 batters faced (minimums: 250 BFP). . . . Career strikeout averages: one per 5.8 batters in Late-Inning Pressure Situations, one per 8.3 batters when unpressured.

Ken Schrom

Minnesota Twins	W–L	ERA	AB	H	HR	BB	SO	BA	SA	OBA
Season	9-12	4.99	603	164	28	59	74	.272	.476	.333
vs. Left-Handed Batters			321	91	15	36	32	.283	.470	.350
vs. Right-Handed Batters			282	73	13	23	42	.259	.482	.313
Home	7-7	5.42	406	107	21	35	56	.264	.493	.318
Road	2-5	4.10	197	57	7	24	18	.289	.442	.363
Grass	2-4	4.65	155	50	5	19	17	.323	.465	.392
Artificial Turf	7-8	5.10	448	114	23	40	57	.254	.480	.312
Day	3-4	5.23	166	49	7	9	21	.295	.506	.328
Night	6-8	4.90	437	115	21	50	53	.263	.465	.335
April	1-2	6.38	94	25	5	7	6	.266	.500	.314
May	2-2	5.72	115	34	7	6	15	.296	.557	.331
June	4-1	1.93	140	27	3	15	19	.193	.293	.266
July	1-6	8.04	129	44	7	13	17	.341	.581	.396
August	0-1	4.50	57	15	2	8	11	.263	.439	.354
Sept./Oct.	1-0	4.26	68	19	4	10	6	.279	.515	.363
Leading Off Inn.			153	42	6	20	17	.275	.484	.358
Bases Empty			386	103	19	38	41	.267	.482	.333
Runners On			217	61	9	21	33	.281	.465	.333
Runners/Scor. Pos.			120	33	6	9	18	.275	.483	.307
Runners On/2 Out			89	21	3	10	15	.236	.427	.313
Scor. Pos./2 Out			51	11	2	5	9	.216	.431	.286
Late Inning Pressure			57	6	1	4	9	.105	.158	.164
Leading Off			18	3	1	2	1	.167	.333	.250
Bases Empty			47	6	1	4	7	.128	.191	.196
Runners On			10	0	0	0	2	.000	.000	.000
Runners/Scor. Pos.			5	0	0	0	1	.000	.000	.000
First 9 Batters			230	57	7	18	34	.248	.409	.299
Second 9 Batters			191	62	13	23	26	.325	.581	.392
All Batters Thereafter			182	45	8	18	14	.247	.451	.312

Loves to face: Spike Owen (0-for-17)
Hates to face: Jim Gantner (.611, 11-for-18, 1 HR)
Ground outs-to-air outs ratio: 0.82 last season, 0.85 for career. . . . Additional statistics: 8 double-play ground outs in 106 opportunities, 33 doubles, 3 triples allowed in 160.2 innings last season. . . . Allowed 19 first-inning runs in 26 starts last season. . . . Batting support: 4.00 runs per start. . . . Allowed one home run every 5.7 innings, 2d-worst average among A.L. pitchers (minimum: 15 GS). . . . Glad to leave Minnesota? Allowed 21 home runs at the Metrodome in 1985, one short of the *Player Analysis* record for home games, set by Gaylord Perry with Seattle in '82. . . . Has faced 978 batters in road games without allowing a triple. . . . Has faced 75 batters in his career in Late-Inning Pressure Situations with runners on base, and has not allowed an extra-base hit. . . . Career average of 1.70 strikeouts per walk in day games, 0.86 in night games.

Don Schulze

Cleveland Indians	W–L	ERA	AB	H	HR	BB	SO	BA	SA	OBA
Season	4-10	6.01	397	128	10	19	37	.322	.466	.357
vs. Left-Handed Batters			228	81	6	9	15	.355	.496	.379
vs. Right-Handed Batters			169	47	4	10	22	.278	.426	.328
Home	2-6	4.61	236	70	5	9	20	.297	.411	.327
Road	2-4	8.12	161	58	5	10	17	.360	.547	.400
Grass	3-9	6.05	352	116	10	17	30	.330	.480	.363
Artificial Turf	1-1	5.73	45	12	0	2	7	.267	.356	.313
Day	1-3	7.67	153	54	3	4	7	.353	.490	.381
Night	3-7	5.17	244	74	7	15	30	.303	.451	.342
April	2-0	5.06	89	27	2	6	6	.303	.449	.357
May	1-4	6.04	123	38	4	7	12	.309	.480	.351
June	0-3	11.57	58	25	2	2	3	.431	.603	.443
July			0	0	0	0	0	.000	.000	.000
August			0	0	0	0	0	.000	.000	.000
Sept./Oct.	1-3	4.64	127	38	2	4	16	.299	.402	.323
Leading Off Inn.			98	37	2	4	10	.378	.551	.408
Bases Empty			212	70	5	8	22	.330	.472	.357
Runners On			185	58	5	11	15	.314	.459	.356
Runners/Scor. Pos.			106	35	4	9	6	.330	.509	.383
Runners On/2 Out			64	17	1	4	4	.266	.375	.329
Scor. Pos./2 Out			39	11	1	3	1	.282	.410	.364
Late Inning Pressure			37	9	1	3	3	.243	.405	.300
Leading Off			9	2	0	1	1	.222	.444	.300
Bases Empty			19	7	1	2	1	.368	.684	.429
Runners On			18	2	0	1	2	.111	.111	.158
Runners/Scor. Pos.			10	1	0	1	1	.100	.100	.182
First 9 Batters			167	53	5	4	18	.317	.455	.333
Second 9 Batters			134	44	4	7	12	.328	.507	.366
All Batters Thereafter			96	31	1	8	7	.323	.427	.383

Loves to face: Donnie Scott (0-for-9)
Hates to face: Jim Gantner (4-for-4, 1 HR)
Ground outs-to-air outs ratio: 1.64 last season, 1.52 for career. . . . Additional statistics: 9 double-play ground outs in 92 opportunities, 25 doubles, 1 triple allowed in 94.1 innings last season. . . . Average of 5.15 innings per start was 5th-lowest among A.L. pitchers (minimum: 15 GS). . . . Allowed 4 first-inning runs in 18 starts, tied for 3d-lowest rate in A.L. last season (minimum: 15 GS). . . . Batting support: 4.44 runs per start. . . . ERA of 6.01 was 2d-highest among A.L. pitchers with at least 15 starts. . . . Average of 12.21 hits per nine innings was highest among same group. . . . Left-handers' .355 batting average was highest in A.L. . . . Opposing hitters have a career .318 batting average. Only one pitcher active last season has faced as many batters (892) and allowed an average above .300: Mike Morgan (.302).

Tom Seaver

Chicago White Sox	W–L	ERA	AB	H	HR	BB	SO	BA	SA	OBA
Season	16-11	3.17	901	223	22	69	134	.248	.374	.304
vs. Left-Handed Batters			466	116	10	44	84	.249	.363	.314
vs. Right-Handed Batters			435	107	12	25	50	.246	.386	.293
Home	5-6	4.35	393	106	11	40	56	.270	.415	.337
Road	11-5	2.26	508	117	11	29	78	.230	.343	.278
Grass	15-8	3.31	791	198	19	61	124	.250	.373	.306
Artificial Turf	1-3	2.17	110	25	3	8	10	.227	.382	.289
Day	5-3	2.80	273	68	6	19	44	.249	.377	.306
Night	11-8	3.32	628	155	16	50	90	.247	.373	.303
April	2-0	3.76	104	26	4	10	15	.250	.423	.313
May	3-3	2.54	169	40	4	16	19	.237	.396	.303
June	2-3	3.79	158	42	2	15	26	.266	.354	.339
July	4-2	2.47	186	38	4	9	29	.204	.312	.244
August	1-1	4.33	134	34	4	10	19	.254	.388	.315
Sept./Oct.	4-2	2.72	150	43	4	9	26	.287	.400	.325
Leading Off Inn.			229	48	6	18	35	.210	.332	.273
Bases Empty			570	133	16	35	90	.233	.368	.282
Runners On			331	90	6	34	44	.272	.384	.340
Runners/Scor. Pos.			192	42	3	27	31	.219	.307	.313
Runners On/2 Out			150	44	2	19	18	.293	.393	.384
Scor. Pos./2 Out			100	25	1	15	16	.250	.330	.359
Late Inning Pressure			119	30	2	17	18	.252	.378	.353
Leading Off			32	3	0	4	7	.094	.094	.194
Bases Empty			79	16	2	9	16	.203	.329	.284
Runners On			40	14	0	8	2	.350	.475	.471
Runners/Scor. Pos.			23	10	0	7	1	.435	.565	.576
First 9 Batters			278	70	9	21	42	.252	.399	.306
Second 9 Batters			273	66	5	16	43	.242	.348	.289
All Batters Thereafter			350	87	8	32	49	.249	.374	.314

Loves to face: Reggie Jackson (.100, 2-for-20, 9 SO)
Hates to face: Cal Ripken (.471, 8-for-17, 3 HR)
Ground outs-to-air outs ratio: 1.33 last season, 1.08 for career. . . . Additional statistics: 20 double-play ground outs in 147 opportunities, 40 doubles, 4 triples allowed in 238.2 innings last season. . . . Allowed 25 first-inning runs (tied for 4th-most in A.L.) in 33 starts. . . . Batting support: 4.06 runs per start. . . . Tied Jack Morris for A.L. lead with 11 road-game wins. Road-game ERA ranked 2d to Dave Stieb. . . . Enters 1986 season with 61 career shutouts, 7th-highest total in history. Could pass Warren Spahn (63) and Eddie Plank (64) by season's end. All-time leader: Walter Johnson (110). . . . Ranked 2d in A.L. with a 2.66 ERA vs. teams that won at least half their games last season. Won nine, lost eight of those games. . . . Has not allowed a home run in Late-Inning Pressure Situations with runners on base since August 21, 1979, when Rusty Staub clocked one.

Jim Slaton

California Angels	W–L	ERA	AB	H	HR	BB	SO	BA	SA	OBA
Season	6-10	4.37	570	162	22	63	60	.284	.470	.355
vs. Left-Handed Batters			303	90	10	41	29	.297	.479	.379
vs. Right-Handed Batters			267	72	12	22	31	.270	.461	.325
Home	2-4	3.96	292	78	13	30	27	.267	.455	.334
Road	4-6	4.82	278	84	9	33	33	.302	.486	.376
Grass	3-9	4.66	444	127	19	54	41	.286	.477	.361
Artificial Turf	3-1	3.34	126	35	3	9	19	.278	.444	.331
Day	2-0	2.76	125	38	2	9	15	.304	.416	.351
Night	4-10	4.82	445	124	20	54	45	.279	.485	.356
April	3-0	2.45	104	21	4	7	12	.202	.346	.252
May	1-3	5.08	131	41	4	18	12	.313	.481	.397
June	0-3	3.03	104	25	2	19	10	.240	.365	.349
July	0-3	7.65	90	35	4	8	6	.389	.622	.439
August	1-1	4.19	76	22	4	5	12	.289	.553	.337
Sept./Oct.	1-0	4.96	65	18	4	6	8	.277	.508	.338
Leading Off Inn.			144	43	6	16	10	.299	.472	.369
Bases Empty			323	94	18	41	36	.291	.502	.373
Runners On			247	68	4	22	24	.275	.429	.331
Runners/Scor. Pos.			127	33	2	16	15	.260	.425	.336
Runners On/2 Out			98	31	2	14	11	.316	.490	.402
Scor. Pos./2 Out			59	16	1	12	8	.271	.424	.394
Late Inning Pressure			34	7	1	5	3	.206	.353	.325
Leading Off			12	4	1	1	0	.333	.667	.385
Bases Empty			22	6	1	3	3	.273	.500	.385
Runners On			12	1	0	2	0	.083	.083	.214
Runners/Scor. Pos.			5	1	0	2	0	.200	.200	.429
First 9 Batters			230	59	8	21	31	.257	.430	.319
Second 9 Batters			192	52	6	21	19	.271	.432	.340
All Batters Thereafter			148	51	8	21	10	.345	.581	.427

Loves to face: Rickey Henderson (.050, 1-for-20)
Hates to face: Pat Sheridan (.857, 6-for-7)
Ground outs-to-air outs ratio: 0.99 last season, 0.95 for career. . . . Additional statistics: 21 double-play ground outs in 119 opportunities, 34 doubles, 3 triples allowed in 148.1 innings last season. . . . Allowed 12 first-inning runs in 24 starts last season. . . . Batting support: 3.96 runs per start, 9th-lowest average in A.L. (minimum: 15 GS). . . . Allowed one home run every 6.7 innings, 10th-highest average among that group. . . . Opposing batters have hit for a lower average in Late-Inning Pressure Situations than unpressured in each of the past nine seasons. Composites during that time: .224 in LIP, .282 in nonpressure at bats. . . . Lost seven games without a win from May 29 through July 22, one short of the longest losing streak of his career (1975).

Bob Shirley

New York Yankees	W–L	ERA	AB	H	HR	BB	SO	BA	SA	OBA
Season	5-5	2.64	411	103	5	26	55	.251	.333	.293
vs. Left-Handed Batters			146	31	1	8	30	.212	.267	.250
vs. Right-Handed Batters			265	72	4	18	25	.272	.370	.316
Home	5-1	1.86	248	56	2	16	34	.226	.302	.272
Road	0-4	3.92	163	47	3	10	21	.288	.380	.324
Grass	5-5	2.54	399	99	5	24	49	.248	.328	.288
Artificial Turf	0-0	6.75	12	4	0	2	6	.333	.500	.429
Day	2-2	3.78	131	35	2	6	23	.267	.344	.297
Night	3-3	2.14	280	68	3	20	32	.243	.329	.290
April	0-1	4.22	43	12	0	3	6	.279	.279	.326
May	0-0	0.00	3	0	0	0	0	.000	.000	.000
June	2-1	3.14	110	27	3	8	11	.245	.364	.297
July	1-1	4.26	77	23	0	3	11	.299	.377	.321
August	0-1	1.09	87	19	1	7	14	.218	.287	.268
Sept./Oct.	2-1	1.80	91	22	1	5	13	.242	.341	.281
Leading Off Inn.			100	29	1	6	9	.290	.360	.330
Bases Empty			227	55	3	16	24	.242	.330	.292
Runners On			184	48	2	10	31	.261	.337	.293
Runners/Scor. Pos.			117	24	1	6	22	.205	.248	.236
Runners On/2 Out			74	17	0	4	13	.230	.257	.269
Scor. Pos./2 Out			53	12	0	3	10	.226	.226	.268
Late Inning Pressure			88	20	0	8	11	.227	.273	.289
Leading Off			24	6	0	0	2	.250	.292	.250
Bases Empty			50	10	0	1	4	.200	.260	.216
Runners On			38	10	0	7	7	.263	.289	.370
Runners/Scor. Pos.			29	5	0	6	5	.172	.172	.306
First 9 Batters			248	65	2	18	43	.262	.335	.309
Second 9 Batters			102	26	3	5	9	.255	.392	.290
All Batters Thereafter			61	12	0	3	3	.197	.230	.231

Loves to face: Rudy Law (.071, 1-for-14)
Hates to face: Reid Nichols (.714, 5-for-7, 1 HR)
Ground outs-to-air outs ratio: 0.84 last season, 1.02 for career. . . . Additional statistics: 8 double-play ground outs in 93 opportunities, 17 doubles, 1 triple allowed in 109.0 innings last season. . . . Ranked 6th among A.L. relief pitchers with a 2.27 ERA last season (minimum: 30 relief games). . . . Allowed one home run every 31.7 relief innings last season, 2d-best average among that group. . . . Faced a single batter in eight different relief appearances, allowing two hits and two walks in those games. . . . Has allowed 105 career home runs: 97 (one per 38 AB) vs. right-handed batters, only eight (one per 143 AB) vs. left-handers. Career batting averages: lefties, .219; righties, .277. . . . Has allowed 13 hits in the last 25 opposing at bats with the bases loaded.

Roy Smith

Cleveland Indians	W–L	ERA	AB	H	HR	BB	SO	BA	SA	OBA
Season	1-4	5.34	262	84	8	17	28	.321	.492	.359
vs. Left-Handed Batters			131	43	6	10	8	.328	.542	.371
vs. Right-Handed Batters			131	41	2	7	20	.313	.443	.348
Home	1-3	3.62	149	45	2	8	12	.302	.430	.338
Road	0-1	7.92	113	39	6	9	16	.345	.575	.387
Grass	1-3	5.01	231	73	7	13	26	.316	.481	.351
Artificial Turf	0-1	8.10	31	11	1	4	2	.355	.581	.417
Day	0-1	10.38	67	30	3	4	8	.448	.716	.472
Night	1-3	4.01	195	54	5	13	20	.277	.415	.321
April			0	0	0	0	0	.000	.000	.000
May			0	0	0	0	0	.000	.000	.000
June	0-0	2.70	42	12	0	2	5	.286	.357	.311
July			0	0	0	0	0	.000	.000	.000
August	1-2	4.17	143	40	4	7	15	.280	.427	.312
Sept./Oct.	0-2	9.77	77	32	4	8	8	.416	.688	.471
Leading Off Inn.			64	17	3	4	6	.266	.422	.309
Bases Empty			146	43	4	9	16	.295	.466	.335
Runners On			116	41	4	8	12	.353	.526	.388
Runners/Scor. Pos.			63	19	2	6	7	.302	.413	.351
Runners On/2 Out			48	15	0	6	6	.313	.354	.389
Scor. Pos./2 Out			32	9	0	4	5	.281	.313	.361
Late Inning Pressure			27	9	1	1	2	.333	.519	.357
Leading Off			8	3	0	1	0	.375	.375	.444
Bases Empty			18	6	1	1	1	.333	.611	.368
Runners On			9	3	0	0	1	.333	.333	.333
Runners/Scor. Pos.			3	1	0	0	1	.333	.333	.333
First 9 Batters			93	34	3	4	11	.366	.548	.380
Second 9 Batters			77	25	3	9	6	.325	.506	.391
All Batters Thereafter			92	25	2	4	11	.272	.424	.309

Loves to face: Lou Whitaker (.083, 1-for-12)
Hates to face: Nelson (3-for-3, 2 HR) & Ted (.800, 4-for-5) Simmons
Ground outs-to-air outs ratio: 0.55 last season (5th-lowest in A.L.), 0.49 for career. . . . Additional statistics: 3 double-play ground outs in 51 opportunities, 15 doubles, 3 triples allowed in 62.1 innings last season. . . . Allowed 7 first-inning runs in 11 starts last season. . . . Batting support: 5.64 runs per start. . . . Career average of one home run allowed every 6.76 innings is 6th-highest among active pitchers (minimum: 20 HR). . . . Has allowed 15 home runs in 330 at bats vs. left-handed batters, 4th-worst rate in *Player Analysis* history, behind Brad Havens, Tom Walker, and Pete Ladd (minimum: 10 HR). . . . Lost four games without a win and compiled a 7.45 ERA over his last six starts.

Mike Smithson

Minnesota Twins	W–L	ERA	AB	H	HR	BB	SO	BA	SA	OBA
Season	15-14	4.34	978	264	25	78	127	.270	.418	.331
vs. Left-Handed Batters			570	164	19	36	69	.288	.467	.333
vs. Right-Handed Batters			408	100	6	42	58	.245	.350	.329
Home	8-6	4.34	460	122	12	37	66	.265	.407	.327
Road	7-8	4.35	518	142	13	41	61	.274	.429	.335
Grass	5-6	4.04	373	102	8	33	42	.273	.426	.338
Artificial Turf	10-8	4.54	605	162	17	45	85	.268	.413	.327
Day	5-5	3.15	361	92	5	23	49	.255	.363	.305
Night	10-9	5.06	617	172	20	55	78	.279	.451	.346
April	3-2	2.72	147	33	4	11	16	.224	.347	.292
May	1-2	7.96	154	52	7	13	18	.338	.571	.387
June	2-3	4.36	123	33	4	9	18	.268	.439	.331
July	5-0	3.18	192	47	2	15	28	.245	.333	.308
August	1-4	4.69	149	44	1	16	24	.295	.396	.369
Sept./Oct.	3-3	3.88	213	55	7	14	23	.258	.437	.310
Leading Off Inn.			254	63	4	18	30	.248	.390	.308
Bases Empty			590	154	12	46	80	.261	.393	.326
Runners On			388	110	13	32	47	.284	.456	.339
Runners/Scor. Pos.			215	61	9	21	25	.284	.479	.348
Runners On/2 Out			160	40	6	13	28	.250	.438	.314
Scor. Pos./2 Out			99	23	4	8	18	.232	.404	.303
Late Inning Pressure			73	21	1	9	7	.288	.438	.373
Leading Off			20	9	1	4	3	.450	.900	.560
Bases Empty			39	16	1	6	4	.410	.667	.500
Runners On			34	5	0	3	3	.147	.176	.216
Runners/Scor. Pos.			18	3	0	2	1	.167	.222	.250
First 9 Batters			293	69	6	27	42	.235	.362	.313
Second 9 Batters			309	84	7	15	45	.272	.417	.316
All Batters Thereafter			376	111	12	36	40	.295	.463	.357

Loves to face: Tony Armas (.077, 2-for-26)
Hates to face: Pete O'Brien (.545, 6-for-11, 3 HR)
Ground outs-to-air outs ratio: 1.24 last season, 1.21 for career. . . . Additional statistics: 21 double-play ground outs in 182 opportunities, 48 doubles (tied for 3d-most in A.L.), 11 triples (tied for most in A.L.) allowed in 257.0 innings last season. . . . Total of 84 extra-base hits allowed was tied for major-league lead. . . . Allowed 57 extra-base hits to left-handed batters, equalling the *Player Analysis* record he set in 1984. . . . Allowed 19 home runs to lefties last season, most in majors. . . . Allowed 14 first-inning runs in 37 starts last season. . . . Batting support: 4.38 runs per start. . . . Hit 15 batters with pitches, highest total in either league since 1975, when Pete Broberg hit 16. . . . Career total of 114 starts is highest among active pitchers without a relief appearance.

Nate Snell

Baltimore Orioles	W–L	ERA	AB	H	HR	BB	SO	BA	SA	OBA
Season	3-2	2.69	385	100	4	30	41	.260	.345	.314
vs. Left-Handed Batters			181	50	3	14	12	.276	.376	.327
vs. Right-Handed Batters			204	50	1	16	29	.245	.319	.303
Home	2-0	1.88	201	51	3	13	21	.254	.338	.302
Road	1-2	3.59	184	49	1	17	20	.266	.353	.327
Grass	3-1	2.44	327	83	4	24	34	.254	.343	.306
Artificial Turf	0-1	4.11	58	17	0	6	7	.293	.362	.359
Day	2-1	3.02	180	51	2	15	19	.283	.361	.340
Night	1-1	2.43	205	49	2	15	22	.239	.332	.291
April	0-1	1.15	58	12	1	5	5	.207	.293	.281
May	0-0	2.67	92	18	0	7	10	.196	.272	.253
June	2-0	1.33	80	21	0	6	8	.263	.300	.314
July	1-0	3.86	38	11	0	1	6	.289	.316	.308
August	0-1	2.61	36	11	1	5	2	.306	.417	.390
Sept./Oct.	0-0	5.09	81	27	2	6	10	.333	.494	.375
Leading Off Inn.			89	22	2	2	7	.247	.371	.264
Bases Empty			207	51	2	12	17	.246	.324	.291
Runners On			178	49	2	18	24	.275	.371	.340
Runners/Scor. Pos.			103	31	1	14	14	.301	.417	.381
Runners On/2 Out			66	13	0	7	14	.197	.258	.274
Scor. Pos./2 Out			43	10	0	5	8	.233	.279	.313
Late Inning Pressure			61	16	1	6	11	.262	.328	.328
Leading Off			16	3	1	1	4	.188	.375	.235
Bases Empty			42	10	1	1	9	.238	.333	.256
Runners On			19	6	0	5	2	.316	.316	.458
Runners/Scor. Pos.			8	2	0	4	1	.250	.250	.500
First 9 Batters			287	81	4	25	31	.282	.380	.342
Second 9 Batters			91	19	0	5	9	.209	.264	.247
All Batters Thereafter			7	0	0	0	1	.000	.000	.000

Loves to face: Dave Winfield (0-for-3, 2 SO)
Hates to face: Bill Buckner (.571, 4-for-7, 1 HR)
Ground outs-to-air outs ratio: 2.12 last season (10th-highest in A.L.), 2.00 for career. . . . Additional statistics: 12 double-play ground outs in 100 opportunities, 15 doubles, 3 triples allowed in 100.1 innings last season. . . . Allowed one home run every 25.1 relief innings, 5th-lowest average among A.L. pitchers (minimum: 30 relief games). . . . Average of 39.2 ground outs per 100 batters faced was 2d-highest in A.L. last season (minimum: 200 BFP). The leader: Juan Agosto (42.7). . . . G/A ratio of 1.74 vs. left-handed batters, 3.45 vs. right-handers last season. . . . Pitched three or more innings of relief 15 times in '85, 3d-highest total in A.L. All five saves and two of his three wins came in those games. . . . Has faced 31 career batters in Late-Inning Pressure Situations with runners on base without allowing an extra-base hit.

Dan Spillner

Chicago White Sox	W–L	ERA	AB	H	HR	BB	SO	BA	SA	OBA
Season	4-3	3.44	338	83	10	33	41	.246	.411	.310
vs. Left-Handed Batters			124	26	5	11	15	.210	.427	.272
vs. Right-Handed Batters			214	57	5	22	26	.266	.402	.332
Home	1-2	5.36	176	52	7	15	22	.295	.517	.351
Road	3-1	1.69	162	31	3	18	19	.191	.296	.268
Grass	4-3	3.91	279	72	9	29	35	.258	.444	.326
Artificial Turf	0-0	1.50	59	11	1	4	6	.186	.254	.234
Day	2-2	3.10	74	15	4	4	7	.203	.378	.244
Night	2-1	3.53	264	68	6	29	34	.258	.420	.328
April	0-1	1.42	19	3	1	4	2	.158	.316	.292
May	0-0	5.19	35	10	0	2	2	.286	.429	.324
June	2-0	2.16	93	22	2	7	10	.237	.366	.287
July	0-2	5.68	48	13	2	4	8	.271	.458	.327
August	2-0	3.98	79	21	3	6	8	.266	.481	.318
Sept./Oct.	0-0	2.89	64	14	2	10	11	.219	.375	.320
Leading Off Inn.			79	20	4	4	9	.253	.481	.289
Bases Empty			201	45	8	13	24	.224	.428	.271
Runners On			137	38	2	20	17	.277	.387	.363
Runners/Scor. Pos.			83	25	1	17	11	.301	.410	.408
Runners On/2 Out			59	15	1	11	6	.254	.356	.371
Scor. Pos./2 Out			40	11	1	9	6	.275	.400	.408
Late Inning Pressure			62	23	4	12	7	.371	.661	.473
Leading Off			18	6	1	1	3	.333	.611	.368
Bases Empty			37	13	4	5	3	.351	.757	.429
Runners On			25	10	0	7	4	.400	.520	.531
Runners/Scor. Pos.			17	6	0	6	3	.353	.471	.522
First 9 Batters			273	65	7	25	35	.238	.385	.299
Second 9 Batters			59	15	3	8	6	.254	.475	.343
All Batters Thereafter			6	3	0	0	0	.500	1.000	.500

Loves to face: Jesse Barfield (0-for-11, 6 SO)
Hates to face: Dave Winfield (.409, 9-for-22, 2 HR)
Ground outs-to-air outs ratio: 0.97 last season (1.92 in Late-Inning Pressure Situations), 0.90 for career. . . . Additional statistics: 9 double-play ground outs in 63 opportunities, 16 doubles, 5 triples allowed in 91.2 innings last season. . . . Used as pinch-hitter for Harold Baines in 9th inning of blowout game last July 7. Interesting, because Spillner has struck out in 56.2 percent of his career at bats, the highest rate of any active player (minimum: 50 SO). And, since he walked batting for Baines, that stat remains unchanged. . . . Opposing batters have hit over .300 in Late-Inning Pressure Situations in each of the past three seasons. His composite average (.355) is highest in majors during that time (minimum: 250 AB). . . . Opposing batters have hit .324 with runners in scoring position over the past three seasons, 2d-highest to Dickie Noles during that span.

Bob Stanley

Boston Red Sox	W–L	ERA	AB	H	HR	BB	SO	BA	SA	OBA
Season	6-6	2.87	321	76	7	30	46	.237	.355	.303
vs. Left-Handed Batters			161	40	4	20	23	.248	.354	.324
vs. Right-Handed Batters			160	36	3	10	23	.225	.356	.279
Home	3-2	3.21	157	41	2	12	20	.261	.350	.314
Road	3-4	2.56	164	35	5	18	26	.213	.360	.292
Grass	4-4	2.97	261	59	6	26	41	.226	.341	.296
Artificial Turf	2-2	2.40	60	17	1	4	5	.283	.417	.333
Day	4-2	2.56	133	26	3	10	15	.195	.286	.253
Night	2-4	3.12	188	50	4	20	31	.266	.404	.336
April	0-2	1.40	90	17	1	5	14	.189	.244	.232
May	1-0	3.71	66	19	3	8	7	.288	.515	.368
June	2-1	2.63	44	7	1	8	10	.159	.273	.278
July	2-2	1.54	41	8	0	6	4	.195	.268	.306
August	1-1	5.03	80	25	2	3	11	.313	.438	.337
Sept./Oct.			0	0	0	0	0	.000	.000	.000
Leading Off Inn.			71	18	5	3	12	.254	.507	.284
Bases Empty			175	35	6	9	33	.200	.337	.239
Runners On			146	41	1	21	13	.281	.377	.370
Runners/Scor. Pos.			98	30	1	17	11	.306	.439	.400
Runners On/2 Out			60	15	0	11	5	.250	.300	.384
Scor. Pos./2 Out			43	13	0	10	4	.302	.372	.444
Late Inning Pressure			218	45	5	22	34	.206	.317	.278
Leading Off			51	11	4	2	9	.216	.490	.245
Bases Empty			128	23	5	7	25	.180	.320	.222
Runners On			90	22	0	15	9	.244	.311	.345
Runners/Scor. Pos.			57	15	0	13	7	.263	.368	.387
First 9 Batters			254	60	6	28	36	.236	.366	.311
Second 9 Batters			63	15	1	2	10	.238	.317	.269
All Batters Thereafter			4	1	0	0	0	.250	.250	.250

Loves to face: Dave Collins (0-for-20)
Hates to face: Greg Walker (.833, 5-for-6, 2 HR)
Ground outs-to-air outs ratio: 1.58 last season (lowest of his career), 2.35 for career. . . . Additional statistics: 11 double-play ground outs in 78 opportunities, 13 doubles, 2 triples allowed in 87.2 innings last season. . . . Has finished 71.8 percent of his relief appearances, 8th-highest career average among active pitchers (minimum: 50 GF). . . . Has made 272 relief appearances since his last start (Sept. 1, 1981). . . . Pitched 69% of his time in Late-Inning Pressure Situations last season, highest mark of his nine-year career, and responded with lowest single-season opponents' batting average in LIP. . . . Opposing batters have hit for a higher average with runners on base than with the bases empty in seven of nine seasons, missing by a single hit in each of the other years (1977 and 1983).

Dave Stewart

Texas Rangers	W–L	ERA	AB	H	HR	BB	SO	BA	SA	OBA
Season	0-6	5.42	315	86	13	37	64	.273	.476	.351
vs. Left-Handed Batters			164	53	6	25	24	.323	.524	.408
vs. Right-Handed Batters			151	33	7	12	40	.219	.424	.285
Home	0-2	7.43	144	40	6	17	30	.278	.479	.356
Road	0-4	3.80	171	46	7	20	34	.269	.474	.347
Grass	0-4	5.64	257	68	11	32	51	.265	.459	.346
Artificial Turf	0-2	4.40	58	18	2	5	13	.310	.552	.375
Day	0-3	3.45	58	14	2	8	12	.241	.345	.343
Night	0-3	5.89	257	72	11	29	52	.280	.506	.353
April	0-2	6.52	42	13	1	5	9	.310	.429	.383
May	0-1	5.40	47	13	3	6	8	.277	.574	.358
June	0-1	3.29	49	8	0	5	14	.163	.265	.241
July	0-0	6.55	43	11	3	6	6	.256	.488	.340
August	0-1	4.91	82	25	4	9	16	.305	.561	.376
Sept./Oct.	0-1	6.75	52	16	2	6	11	.308	.481	.390
Leading Off Inn.			73	27	4	5	9	.370	.575	.410
Bases Empty			166	51	5	13	25	.307	.476	.365
Runners On			149	35	8	24	39	.235	.477	.337
Runners/Scor. Pos.			92	21	5	16	26	.228	.467	.336
Runners On/2 Out			66	11	2	6	20	.167	.364	.236
Scor. Pos./2 Out			45	6	0	4	15	.133	.222	.204
Late Inning Pressure			72	20	3	11	7	.278	.486	.369
Leading Off			19	7	1	2	0	.368	.632	.429
Bases Empty			46	11	1	3	3	.239	.391	.286
Runners On			26	9	2	8	4	.346	.654	.486
Runners/Scor. Pos.			16	5	2	7	2	.313	.750	.500
First 9 Batters			236	59	9	26	52	.250	.445	.328
Second 9 Batters			55	19	1	8	10	.345	.436	.422
All Batters Thereafter			24	8	3	3	2	.333	.875	.407

Loves to face: Warren Cromartie (0-for-4, 1 SO)
Hates to face: Reggie Smith (.600, 3-for-5)
Figures above are for A.L. only.... Ground outs-to-air outs ratio: 0.86 last season, 0.87 for career.... Additional statistics: 5 double-play ground outs in 79 opportunities, 15 doubles, 5 triples allowed in 85.2 innings last season.... Including appearances with both Rangers and Phillies, left-handers batted .329, right-handers .213 against him; that 116-point disparity was the 6th-largest in the major leagues (minimum: 100 AB each way).... Winning percentage of .259 (7–20) over the past two seasons is 5th-lowest in majors (minimum: 10 decisions).... Opponents' batting average with two outs and runners in scoring position, year by year since 1981: .143, .261, .156, .163, .128.... Unusual stat for a fly-ball pitcher: Opponents have hit for a lower average on grass than on artificial surfaces in each of the last four seasons.

Sammy Stewart

Baltimore Orioles	W–L	ERA	AB	H	HR	BB	SO	BA	SA	OBA
Season	5-7	3.61	476	117	15	66	77	.246	.387	.336
vs. Left-Handed Batters			230	58	6	43	36	.252	.413	.367
vs. Right-Handed Batters			246	59	9	23	41	.240	.362	.304
Home	2-2	3.41	268	64	9	48	48	.239	.373	.354
Road	3-5	3.88	208	53	6	18	29	.255	.404	.310
Grass	5-6	3.59	421	102	14	62	67	.242	.385	.338
Artificial Turf	0-1	3.77	55	15	1	4	10	.273	.400	.317
Day	1-2	4.65	118	34	5	14	12	.288	.458	.358
Night	4-5	3.28	358	83	10	52	65	.232	.363	.329
April	1-1	2.05	77	15	3	9	13	.195	.338	.279
May	0-0	4.24	59	14	2	7	6	.237	.339	.304
June	1-2	5.94	59	18	1	15	5	.305	.424	.447
July	1-1	2.15	104	22	4	14	24	.212	.365	.305
August	2-0	2.96	89	20	2	9	13	.225	.360	.296
Sept./Oct.	0-3	5.75	88	28	3	12	16	.318	.489	.396
Leading Off Inn.			100	29	7	14	18	.290	.560	.377
Bases Empty			239	55	9	29	37	.230	.393	.316
Runners On			237	62	6	37	40	.262	.380	.355
Runners/Scor. Pos.			152	41	2	26	27	.270	.368	.366
Runners On/2 Out			104	26	4	22	21	.250	.433	.381
Scor. Pos./2 Out			76	21	2	16	19	.276	.434	.402
Late Inning Pressure			144	39	4	19	24	.271	.382	.355
Leading Off			32	10	2	6	8	.313	.594	.421
Bases Empty			76	18	3	8	15	.237	.408	.318
Runners On			68	21	1	11	9	.309	.353	.395
Runners/Scor. Pos.			41	14	0	9	5	.341	.341	.442
First 9 Batters			335	82	9	43	60	.245	.376	.328
Second 9 Batters			122	30	6	17	16	.246	.434	.338
All Batters Thereafter			19	5	0	6	1	.263	.263	.440

Loves to face: Hal McRae (.095, 2-for-21)
Hates to face: Bobby Clark (.571, 4-for-7, 2 HR)
Ground outs-to-air outs ratio: 1.11 last season, 1.03 for career.... Additional statistics: 14 double-play ground outs in 119 opportunities, 18 doubles, 2 triples allowed in 129.2 innings last season.... Allowed 55 runs in relief in '85, 2d-highest total in A.L.... Led all major-league relievers with 65 walks, but none in 24 bases-loaded situations (the most bases-loaded situations without a walk by any major leaguer last year). They were too busy hitting him: 9-for-23 with the bags full.... Who's afraid of green monsters? Not this guy: Has allowed only one home run in 37.2 innings at Fenway (to Tony Perez in 1980).... Had allowed 41 of his 66 home runs at Memorial Stadium.... Opposing right-handed batters have never hit .250 or better, left-handers haven't hit below .250 since 1980.... Can be discreet: has walked Don Mattingly more than any other pitcher (5 times).

Dave Stieb

Toronto Blue Jays	W–L	ERA	AB	H	HR	BB	SO	BA	SA	OBA
Season	14-13	2.48	966	206	22	96	167	.213	.320	.290
vs. Left-Handed Batters			560	111	10	63	73	.198	.286	.281
vs. Right-Handed Batters			406	95	12	33	94	.234	.367	.302
Home	8-6	2.96	421	104	12	37	66	.247	.371	.312
Road	6-7	2.12	545	102	10	59	101	.187	.281	.273
Grass	5-5	2.22	414	76	9	51	75	.184	.285	.276
Artificial Turf	9-8	2.68	552	130	13	45	92	.236	.346	.301
Day	4-6	3.69	363	91	10	31	59	.251	.386	.316
Night	10-7	1.80	603	115	12	65	108	.191	.280	.274
April	1-2	2.93	118	27	3	15	17	.229	.347	.326
May	4-1	1.69	149	27	3	16	34	.181	.262	.265
June	3-2	1.51	167	28	2	17	30	.168	.240	.245
July	2-1	2.03	174	40	3	13	21	.230	.333	.289
August	2-3	3.80	167	36	6	15	31	.216	.371	.292
Sept./Oct.	2-4	3.04	191	48	5	20	34	.251	.361	.324
Leading Off Inn.			245	57	7	28	37	.233	.376	.319
Bases Empty			577	117	17	62	89	.203	.329	.287
Runners On			389	89	5	34	78	.229	.306	.294
Runners/Scor. Pos.			206	41	1	20	50	.199	.262	.274
Runners On/2 Out			157	30	1	12	37	.191	.236	.257
Scor. Pos./2 Out			97	18	1	6	27	.186	.258	.240
Late Inning Pressure			143	39	2	16	22	.273	.392	.350
Leading Off			38	7	0	4	7	.184	.263	.262
Bases Empty			85	19	2	8	13	.224	.365	.290
Runners On			58	20	0	8	9	.345	.431	.433
Runners/Scor. Pos.			33	14	0	6	5	.424	.576	.525
First 9 Batters			289	60	3	27	54	.208	.280	.287
Second 9 Batters			286	65	6	26	51	.227	.325	.293
All Batters Thereafter			391	81	13	43	62	.207	.345	.290

Loves to face: Andre Robertson (0-for-13)
Hates to face: Tony Phillips (.556, 5-for-9)
Ground outs-to-air outs ratio: 1.15 last season, 1.14 for career.... Additional statistics: 19 double-play ground outs in 215 opportunities, 33 doubles, 2 triples allowed in 265.0 innings last season.... 5th in A.L. with 7.36 innings per start.... Allowed 8 first-inning runs in 36 starts, tied for 3d-lowest rate in A.L. (minimum: 15 GS).... Batting support: 4.44 runs per start.... Led A.L. pitchers with 7.00 hits per nine innings.... Only pitcher with 100 starts since 1982 and an ERA below 3.00.... Opposing batters have hit below .200 with two outs and runners in scoring position in three of the past five seasons.... Some hard-luck stats: compiled a 1.73 ERA in 19 starts vs. teams that finished at or above .500, but went just 7–6.... Starting pitcher in 15 one-run games; his record in them was 1–6, with a 2.42 ERA.

Don Sutton

As/Angels	W–L	ERA	AB	H	HR	BB	SO	BA	SA	OBA
Season	15-10	3.86	875	221	25	59	107	.253	.385	.298
vs. Left-Handed Batters			442	108	13	32	63	.244	.373	.294
vs. Right-Handed Batters			433	113	12	27	44	.261	.397	.303
Home	8-3	3.31	429	101	6	30	47	.235	.324	.284
Road	7-7	4.43	446	120	19	29	60	.269	.444	.312
Grass	13-6	3.33	698	167	18	44	82	.239	.355	.283
Artificial Turf	2-4	6.21	177	54	7	15	25	.305	.503	.358
Day	8-1	3.01	331	77	8	21	39	.233	.350	.278
Night	7-9	4.39	544	144	17	38	68	.265	.406	.310
April	2-2	6.38	100	30	5	17	16	.300	.500	.402
May	1-3	6.44	147	41	4	11	22	.279	.408	.325
June	4-0	1.62	161	34	2	5	15	.211	.280	.234
July	2-1	3.51	165	47	3	7	18	.285	.382	.314
August	4-1	2.47	164	34	3	9	19	.207	.323	.246
Sept./Oct.	2-3	4.42	138	35	8	10	17	.254	.478	.304
Leading Off Inn.			223	54	6	12	24	.242	.372	.281
Bases Empty			541	134	17	36	62	.248	.390	.295
Runners On			334	87	8	23	45	.260	.377	.304
Runners/Scor. Pos.			169	44	3	16	22	.260	.361	.316
Runners On/2 Out			151	34	2	15	21	.225	.298	.295
Scor. Pos./2 Out			85	19	0	11	14	.224	.247	.313
Late Inning Pressure			63	19	1	2	4	.302	.397	.323
Leading Off			19	7	0	2	0	.368	.421	.429
Bases Empty			44	17	1	2	3	.386	.523	.413
Runners On			19	2	0	0	1	.105	.105	.105
Runners/Scor. Pos.			10	1	0	0	0	.100	.100	.100
First 9 Batters			286	66	8	19	45	.231	.371	.278
Second 9 Batters			288	81	12	16	36	.281	.455	.317
All Batters Thereafter			301	74	5	24	26	.246	.332	.300

Loves to face: Rod Carew (.059, 1-for-17)
Hates to face: Kent Hrbek (.563, 9-for-16, 1 HR)
Ground outs-to-air outs ratio: 0.73 last season, 0.89 for career.... Additional statistics: 13 double-play ground outs in 144 opportunities, 41 doubles, 0 triples allowed in 226.0 innings last season.... Allowed 15 first-inning runs in 34 starts last season.... Batting support: 4.68 runs per start.... Ranked 9th in A.L. with an average of 2.35 walks per nine innings.... Grass-field ERA ranked 8th in A.L.... Enters 1986 season with a career total of 672 games started, 4th-highest in history. Should pass Pud Galvin (682) and Gaylord Perry (690); no shot at all-time leader, Cy Young (818).... Ranks 6th among active pitchers with 174 complete games, but won't make 200: he has completed only two of his last 72 starts.... Opposing batters have hit for a higher average with runners on base than with bases empty in 10 of the past 11 seasons.

Bill Swift
Seattle Mariners

	W-L	ERA	AB	H	HR	BB	SO	BA	SA	OBA
Season	6-10	4.77	470	131	8	48	55	.279	.398	.350
vs. Left-Handed Batters			260	80	7	30	24	.308	.485	.383
vs. Right-Handed Batters			210	51	1	18	31	.243	.290	.307
Home	2-6	5.67	243	73	5	21	25	.300	.440	.361
Road	4-4	3.88	227	58	3	27	30	.256	.352	.339
Grass	3-4	4.84	169	45	3	22	22	.266	.385	.356
Artificial Turf	3-6	4.74	301	86	5	26	33	.286	.405	.346
Day	1-1	4.07	97	29	1	8	12	.299	.392	.352
Night	5-9	4.95	373	102	7	40	43	.273	.399	.349
April			0	0	0	0	0	.000	.000	.000
May			0	0	0	0	0	.000	.000	.000
June	2-1	4.08	105	26	0	9	12	.248	.362	.304
July	1-4	6.14	125	43	1	12	14	.344	.456	.400
August	1-3	4.18	124	32	3	17	11	.258	.363	.361
Sept./Oct.	2-2	4.75	116	30	4	10	18	.259	.405	.323
Leading Off Inn.			120	36	4	11	14	.300	.492	.359
Bases Empty			272	76	6	18	31	.279	.415	.329
Runners On			198	55	2	30	24	.278	.374	.376
Runners/Scor. Pos.			126	34	1	21	18	.270	.365	.375
Runners On/2 Out			73	25	1	17	10	.342	.438	.478
Scor. Pos./2 Out			50	15	0	13	8	.300	.380	.462
Late Inning Pressure			45	10	1	5	3	.222	.333	.314
Leading Off			15	7	1	2	1	.467	.800	.529
Bases Empty			31	7	1	4	1	.226	.387	.333
Runners On			14	3	0	1	2	.214	.214	.267
Runners/Scor. Pos.			10	1	0	1	2	.100	.100	.182
First 9 Batters			184	51	3	16	25	.277	.386	.335
Second 9 Batters			146	39	3	17	19	.267	.418	.352
All Batters Thereafter			140	41	2	15	11	.293	.393	.367

Loves to face: Lonnie Smith (0-for-11, 4 SO)
Hates to face: Harold Baines (.538, 7-for-13, 1 HR)
Ground outs-to-air outs ratio: 2.26 last season (5th-highest in A.L.), his first in majors.... Additional statistics: 14 double-play ground outs in 91 opportunities, 26 doubles, 3 triples allowed in 120.2 innings last season.... Average of 5.41 innings per start was 10th-lowest among A.L. pitchers (minimum: 15 GS).... Allowed 22 first-inning runs in 21 starts last season.... Batting support: 4.05 runs per start. Second player, first pitcher chosen in June 1984 free-agent draft. Only first-round choice from that draft to make an impact to date is 12th pick Oddibe McDowell. ... Logical successor to the throne of Bannister and others? See page 77.... Allowed seven of his eight home runs during a 26-inning stretch, from August 23–September 14.... Did not complete any of his 21 starts, but came within one batter of a complete-game loss to New York on August 23.

Frank Tanana
Rangers/Tigers

	W-L	ERA	AB	H	HR	BB	SO	BA	SA	OBA
Season	12-14	4.27	834	220	28	57	159	.264	.430	.310
vs. Left-Handed Batters			150	34	7	6	31	.227	.447	.253
vs. Right-Handed Batters			684	186	21	51	128	.272	.427	.323
Home	8-8	4.84	425	113	19	33	64	.266	.456	.316
Road	4-6	3.67	409	107	9	24	95	.262	.403	.304
Grass	11-11	4.19	732	189	27	49	138	.258	.430	.304
Artificial Turf	1-3	4.85	102	31	1	8	21	.304	.431	.354
Day	5-5	4.90	269	75	8	19	54	.279	.457	.331
Night	7-9	3.98	565	145	20	38	105	.257	.418	.300
April	0-3	8.20	79	30	4	5	13	.380	.595	.414
May	1-2	4.15	131	29	6	9	24	.221	.420	.270
June	2-2	5.17	126	38	5	10	17	.302	.500	.350
July	2-3	3.00	161	38	4	13	43	.236	.373	.297
August	2-2	3.48	162	39	4	8	34	.241	.377	.273
Sept./Oct.	5-2	4.06	175	46	5	12	28	.263	.417	.311
Leading Off Inn.			217	59	5	9	39	.272	.419	.301
Bases Empty			531	135	19	22	101	.254	.418	.285
Runners On			303	85	9	35	58	.281	.452	.351
Runners/Scor. Pos.			179	44	4	23	43	.246	.385	.322
Runners On/2 Out			124	34	2	17	24	.274	.419	.362
Scor. Pos./2 Out			81	17	1	9	20	.210	.321	.289
Late Inning Pressure			64	17	3	7	12	.266	.453	.338
Leading Off			20	6	1	1	4	.300	.500	.333
Bases Empty			52	14	3	2	10	.269	.500	.296
Runners On			12	3	0	5	2	.250	.250	.471
Runners/Scor. Pos.			8	2	0	2	2	.250	.250	.400
First 9 Batters			270	69	8	22	52	.256	.407	.307
Second 9 Batters			268	75	10	19	55	.280	.478	.329
All Batters Thereafter			296	76	10	16	52	.257	.409	.296

Loves to face: Wayne Gross (.050, 1-for-20)
Hates to face: Greg Gagne (.667, 4-for-6, 1 HR)
Ground outs-to-air outs ratio: 1.20 last season, 1.00 for career. ... Additional statistics: 16 double-play ground outs in 145 opportunities, 43 doubles, 6 triples allowed in 215.0 innings last season.... Total of 77 extra-base hits allowed was 8th-highest in A.L. ... Allowed 13 first-inning runs in 33 starts last season. ... Batting support: 4.21 runs per start.... Ranked 5th in A.L. with 6.66 strikeouts per nine innings—his highest mark since 1977, when he fanned 205 batters.... Ratio of 5.17 strikeouts per walk vs. left-handed batters was highest in A.L. last season (minimum: 25 SO).... Losingest pitcher in majors during the 1980s, with a 56–78 record.... Has faced 74 batters with two outs and the bases loaded without allowing an extra-base hit since he was tagged for a two-out grand slam by Charlie Spikes in 1976.

Walt Terrell
Detroit Tigers

	W-L	ERA	AB	H	HR	BB	SO	BA	SA	OBA
Season	15-10	3.85	865	221	9	95	130	.255	.350	.330
vs. Left-Handed Batters			502	124	2	47	64	.247	.323	.309
vs. Right-Handed Batters			363	97	7	48	66	.267	.388	.357
Home	9-2	2.86	441	95	3	45	63	.215	.293	.293
Road	6-8	4.94	424	126	6	50	67	.297	.410	.367
Grass	13-7	3.39	715	172	3	81	97	.241	.309	.320
Artificial Turf	2-3	6.21	150	49	6	14	33	.327	.547	.377
Day	3-3	4.67	244	65	2	24	35	.266	.352	.330
Night	12-7	3.55	621	156	7	71	95	.251	.349	.330
April	2-0	3.86	111	29	0	14	16	.261	.351	.339
May	4-1	3.86	147	38	3	14	30	.259	.367	.321
June	3-2	4.11	131	34	2	14	10	.260	.366	.327
July	1-3	4.21	172	34	1	16	27	.198	.279	.272
August	3-1	2.91	175	47	1	20	31	.269	.331	.342
Sept./Oct.	2-3	4.36	129	39	2	17	16	.302	.434	.392
Leading Off Inn.			214	46	1	26	33	.215	.299	.303
Bases Empty			478	115	6	59	81	.241	.343	.325
Runners On			387	106	3	36	49	.274	.359	.335
Runners/Scor. Pos.			197	52	1	22	27	.264	.350	.330
Runners On/2 Out			155	43	1	15	19	.277	.342	.345
Scor. Pos./2 Out			88	19	0	10	11	.216	.273	.303
Late Inning Pressure			88	26	3	12	13	.295	.443	.386
Leading Off			24	7	1	4	2	.292	.417	.414
Bases Empty			54	14	2	9	11	.259	.370	.375
Runners On			34	12	1	3	2	.353	.559	.405
Runners/Scor. Pos.			10	4	1	3	1	.400	.700	.538
First 9 Batters			272	64	1	28	45	.235	.309	.306
Second 9 Batters			264	76	2	27	40	.288	.386	.355
All Batters Thereafter			329	81	6	40	45	.246	.356	.329

Loves to face: Mike Stenhouse (0-for-10)
Hates to face: Dave Kingman (.556, 5-for-9)
Ground outs-to-air outs ratio: 1.53 last season, 1.42 for career. ... Additional statistics: 27 double-play ground outs in 207 opportunities, 41 doubles, 7 triples (tied for 6th-most in A.L.) allowed in 229.0 innings last season.... Allowed 18 first-inning runs in 34 starts in '85.... Batting support: 4.59 runs per start.... Allowed one home run per 25.4 innings last season, 2d-best rate in A.L. last season.... Career home run averages: one per 108 at bats vs. left-handed batters, one per 47 AB vs. right-handers.... Home-game ERA was 7th-lowest in A.L. last season.... Career record of 7–12 in day games, 28–22 in night games.... Walked Julio Franco with the bases loaded in first A.L. start, the only time in his major-league career that he has walked in a run. He has faced 43 batters with the bases loaded.

Roy Thomas
Seattle Mariners

	W-L	ERA	AB	H	HR	BB	SO	BA	SA	OBA
Season	7-0	3.36	326	66	8	48	70	.202	.316	.303
vs. Left-Handed Batters			148	26	3	31	22	.176	.284	.319
vs. Right-Handed Batters			178	40	5	17	48	.225	.343	.288
Home	3-0	3.54	138	26	5	19	26	.188	.341	.290
Road	4-0	3.23	188	40	3	29	44	.213	.298	.312
Grass	3-0	3.54	174	39	3	25	39	.224	.316	.315
Artificial Turf	4-0	3.18	152	27	5	23	31	.178	.316	.289
Day	3-0	0.66	43	4	0	5	11	.093	.116	.184
Night	4-0	3.83	283	62	8	43	59	.219	.346	.320
April			0	0	0	0	0	.000	.000	.000
May	0-0	5.40	17	5	2	5	1	.294	.706	.417
June	3-0	2.91	81	20	3	9	17	.247	.395	.330
July	2-0	4.18	82	15	3	10	22	.183	.329	.271
August	0-0	4.19	66	13	0	13	11	.197	.242	.325
Sept./Oct.	2-0	1.88	80	13	0	11	19	.163	.200	.261
Leading Off Inn.			80	21	3	4	14	.263	.400	.298
Bases Empty			191	36	4	15	38	.188	.283	.255
Runners On			135	30	4	33	32	.222	.363	.360
Runners/Scor. Pos.			79	21	1	27	22	.266	.367	.425
Runners On/2 Out			57	7	2	14	15	.123	.246	.296
Scor. Pos./2 Out			37	5	0	12	12	.135	.162	.347
Late Inning Pressure			65	10	1	12	18	.154	.246	.286
Leading Off			17	5	0	1	3	.294	.412	.333
Bases Empty			40	6	0	4	10	.150	.225	.227
Runners On			25	4	1	8	8	.160	.280	.364
Runners/Scor. Pos.			15	3	1	7	4	.200	.400	.455
First 9 Batters			228	48	6	36	54	.211	.329	.311
Second 9 Batters			91	18	2	12	15	.198	.308	.302
All Batters Thereafter			7	0	0	0	1	.000	.000	.000

Loves to face: Chet Lemon (0-for-6, 4 SO)
Hates to face: Cal Ripken (.583, 7-for-12, 1 HR)
Ground outs-to-air outs ratio: 1.40 last season, 1.26 for career. ... Additional statistics: 10 double-play ground outs in 78 opportunities, 11 doubles, 1 triple allowed in 93.2 innings last season.... Average of 6.34 hits per nine innings was 3d-lowest among A.L. relief pitchers (minimum: 30 relief games).... Allowed 48 walks, tied for 3d-most among A.L. relievers.... Has never made an error in 174 major-league games. Record for consecutive errorless games by a pitcher is 385 by Paul Lindblad.... Seven wins without a loss would have been one short of the pre-1985 record. See comments on Dennis Lamp.... Home run by Daryl Boston on June 12 was the only one he has allowed in Late-Inning Pressure Situations with runners on base. He has faced 177 batters in LIP.

Rick Thompson
Cleveland Indians

	W–L	ERA	AB	H	HR	BB	SO	BA	SA	OBA
Season	3-8	6.30	314	95	8	48	30	.303	.462	.398
vs. Left-Handed Batters			125	38	4	19	4	.304	.488	.390
vs. Right-Handed Batters			189	57	4	29	26	.302	.444	.404
Home	1-6	8.13	138	44	6	23	15	.319	.529	.416
Road	2-2	4.93	176	51	2	25	15	.290	.409	.385
Grass	2-7	7.32	249	78	7	41	22	.313	.490	.412
Artificial Turf	1-1	2.60	65	17	1	7	8	.262	.354	.342
Day	3-3	4.79	126	28	2	17	13	.222	.325	.318
Night	0-5	7.51	188	67	6	31	17	.356	.553	.451
April	0-0	0.00	2	0	0	0	0	.000	.000	.000
May	1-2	3.38	73	19	0	7	7	.260	.301	.329
June	1-0	3.74	77	21	2	12	7	.273	.390	.380
July	1-2	9.31	41	15	1	6	1	.366	.463	.469
August	0-2	17.00	45	19	5	8	3	.422	.933	.509
Sept./Oct.	0-2	5.95	76	21	0	15	12	.276	.421	.389
Leading Off Inn.			55	15	0	8	7	.273	.345	.385
Bases Empty			131	35	3	15	16	.267	.412	.356
Runners On			183	60	5	33	14	.328	.497	.427
Runners/Scor. Pos.			128	43	2	26	13	.336	.508	.442
Runners On/2 Out			77	21	2	17	6	.273	.468	.411
Scor. Pos./2 Out			57	16	2	13	6	.281	.544	.423
Late Inning Pressure			113	36	3	19	9	.319	.460	.416
Leading Off			22	7	0	4	3	.318	.364	.444
Bases Empty			47	14	1	7	6	.298	.404	.400
Runners On			66	22	2	12	3	.333	.500	.427
Runners/Scor. Pos.			43	14	1	7	2	.326	.512	.407
First 9 Batters			269	78	4	38	27	.290	.409	.382
Second 9 Batters			41	13	2	8	3	.317	.585	.429
All Batters Thereafter			4	4	2	2	0	1.000	2.750	1.000

Loves to face: Dwight Evans (0-for-6, 5 SO)
Hates to face: Don Baylor (.667, 2-for-3, 1 HR)
Ground outs-to-air outs ratio: 2.24 last season (4th-highest in A.L.), his first in majors. ... Additional statistics: 17 double-play ground outs in 96 opportunities (7th-highest rate in A.L.), 18 doubles, 4 triples allowed in 80.0 innings last season. ... Allowed 63 runs, most among A.L. relief pitchers last season. ... Relief ERA of 6.30 was 2d-highest among A.L. pitchers with at least 30 relief appearances. ... Made 15 consecutive relief appearances without a strikeout, from July 6 through August 26. ... Things were looking up when he fanned Tony Armas to end the streak at 73 batters on August 29. Then the sky fell: Thompson allowed 11 runs in that game, highest single-game total in either league last season. No excuses: all runs were earned.

Mike Trujillo
Boston Red Sox

	W–L	ERA	AB	H	HR	BB	SO	BA	SA	OBA
Season	4-4	4.82	350	112	7	23	19	.320	.440	.365
vs. Left-Handed Batters			173	53	2	16	12	.306	.428	.361
vs. Right-Handed Batters			177	59	5	7	7	.333	.452	.369
Home	2-1	4.71	174	54	2	13	10	.310	.414	.365
Road	2-3	4.93	176	58	5	10	9	.330	.466	.365
Grass	2-4	5.43	300	100	6	21	19	.333	.460	.380
Artificial Turf	2-0	1.42	50	12	1	2	0	.240	.320	.269
Day	1-1	5.65	179	57	7	15	11	.318	.486	.372
Night	3-3	3.95	171	55	0	8	8	.322	.392	.357
April	0-1	9.35	34	12	4	3	3	.353	.765	.395
May	0-0	6.48	36	13	0	3	2	.361	.361	.410
June	1-0	1.08	30	5	0	1	1	.167	.167	.194
July	1-1	5.23	87	32	2	7	3	.368	.540	.417
August	1-1	3.18	75	26	0	0	3	.347	.427	.355
Sept./Oct.	1-1	4.71	88	24	1	9	7	.273	.352	.347
Leading Off Inn.			74	25	1	9	2	.338	.459	.410
Bases Empty			167	59	2	14	7	.353	.455	.410
Runners On			183	53	5	9	12	.290	.426	.323
Runners/Scor. Pos.			98	30	4	7	7	.306	.480	.346
Runners On/2 Out			80	24	4	7	6	.300	.500	.364
Scor. Pos./2 Out			51	15	3	5	3	.294	.529	.357
Late Inning Pressure			41	14	0	3	4	.341	.415	.400
Leading Off			11	3	0	0	1	.273	.455	.273
Bases Empty			24	9	0	0	3	.375	.458	.400
Runners On			17	5	0	3	1	.294	.353	.400
Runners/Scor. Pos.			8	3	0	2	0	.375	.500	.500
First 9 Batters			182	54	4	15	14	.297	.407	.350
Second 9 Batters			96	31	1	6	4	.323	.427	.369
All Batters Thereafter			72	27	2	2	1	.375	.542	.400

Loves to face: Roy Smalley (0-for-5)
Hates to face: Bob Kearney (3-for-3)
Ground outs-to-air outs ratio: 1.96 last season, his first in majors. ... Additional statistics: 12 double-play ground outs in 78 opportunities, 17 doubles, 2 triples allowed in 84.0 innings last season. ... Strikeout percentage vs. right-handed batters (3.7%) was lowest in either league since 1982 (minimum: 100 BFP). The *Player Analysis* record (2.8%) was set in 1978 by Tom Hausman. ... Opposing batters hit 63 points higher with the bases empty than with runners on base, 4th-largest difference in A.L. last season (minimum: 100 AB in both situations). ... In battle of Latin Generalissimos, Franco (the one that's still alive) has three hits in six at bats vs. Trujillo. He was also hit by a missile—er, pitch. (The original Trujillo was assassinated in 1961 by a band of Seven Tough Dominicans.)

Ed Vande Berg
Seattle Mariners

	W–L	ERA	AB	H	HR	BB	SO	BA	SA	OBA
Season	2-1	3.72	259	71	4	31	34	.274	.394	.350
vs. Left-Handed Batters			118	29	1	15	16	.246	.331	.333
vs. Right-Handed Batters			141	42	3	16	18	.298	.447	.365
Home	0-1	4.31	125	38	2	15	18	.304	.448	.383
Road	2-0	3.22	134	33	2	16	16	.246	.343	.320
Grass	1-0	4.21	97	25	1	11	10	.258	.351	.327
Artificial Turf	1-1	3.43	162	46	3	20	24	.284	.420	.364
Day	0-0	1.17	49	7	1	8	10	.143	.224	.276
Night	2-1	4.47	210	64	3	23	24	.305	.433	.369
April	0-0	1.08	31	6	0	3	6	.194	.226	.270
May	0-0	1.38	51	18	0	5	4	.353	.451	.404
June	0-0	5.27	51	12	1	7	6	.235	.333	.328
July	1-1	8.10	43	15	1	3	4	.349	.558	.391
August	1-0	1.93	34	10	1	7	5	.294	.441	.415
Sept./Oct.	0-0	4.05	49	10	1	6	9	.204	.327	.291
Leading Off Inn.			48	12	0	5	9	.250	.333	.333
Bases Empty			108	30	1	10	13	.278	.398	.345
Runners On			151	41	3	21	21	.272	.391	.354
Runners/Scor. Pos.			96	24	2	15	13	.250	.375	.342
Runners On/2 Out			57	12	0	11	8	.211	.281	.338
Scor. Pos./2 Out			40	6	0	7	5	.150	.200	.277
Late Inning Pressure			83	23	1	18	17	.277	.398	.408
Leading Off			14	3	0	4	5	.214	.214	.421
Bases Empty			27	8	0	6	6	.296	.444	.441
Runners On			56	15	1	12	11	.268	.375	.391
Runners/Scor. Pos.			34	8	1	9	7	.235	.353	.386
First 9 Batters			241	64	4	30	34	.266	.373	.345
Second 9 Batters			18	7	0	1	0	.389	.667	.421
All Batters Thereafter			0	0	0	0	0	.000	.000	.000

Loves to face: Dave Lopes (0-for-5)
Hates to face: Mike Heath (.714, 5-for-7, 1 HR)
Ground outs-to-air outs ratio: 1.68 last season, 1.47 for career. ... Additional statistics: 10 double-play ground outs in 76 opportunities, 13 doubles, 3 triples allowed in 67.2 innings last season. ... Ranked 2d among A.L. pitchers with 76 appearances. ... Hands-down champion for the 1985 Don't Blink Award: in 18 of his appearances, he faced a single batter; next highest total by an A.L. reliever was eight, by Pat Clements and Bob Shirley. Vande Berg only finished four of those 18 games. ... Career batting averages: .229 by opposing left-handed hitters, .291 by right-handers. ... Percentage of pitching done in Late-Inning Pressure Situations in each of his four seasons, starting with 1982: 69%, 49%, 18%, 35%.

Frank Viola
Minnesota Twins

	W–L	ERA	AB	H	HR	BB	SO	BA	SA	OBA
Season	18-14	4.09	979	262	26	68	135	.268	.410	.315
vs. Left-Handed Batters			216	62	7	11	30	.287	.454	.325
vs. Right-Handed Batters			763	200	19	57	105	.262	.397	.312
Home	9-6	3.68	487	130	9	27	62	.267	.402	.304
Road	9-8	4.50	492	132	17	41	73	.268	.417	.325
Grass	8-4	4.06	338	86	10	29	52	.254	.391	.314
Artificial Turf	10-10	4.11	641	176	16	39	83	.275	.420	.315
Day	4-5	5.08	272	79	9	23	35	.290	.474	.341
Night	14-9	3.73	707	183	17	45	100	.259	.385	.305
April	3-2	3.86	148	35	4	8	20	.236	.358	.274
May	3-2	4.73	166	47	2	17	21	.283	.404	.357
June	3-2	3.79	143	39	5	7	15	.273	.434	.307
July	1-3	5.49	158	45	7	18	17	.285	.468	.356
August	3-2	3.02	174	51	2	7	26	.293	.420	.317
Sept./Oct.	5-3	3.86	190	45	6	11	36	.237	.379	.277
Leading Off Inn.			248	63	7	17	38	.254	.391	.302
Bases Empty			583	147	13	43	95	.252	.384	.304
Runners On			396	115	13	25	40	.290	.447	.332
Runners/Scor. Pos.			198	64	7	18	20	.323	.480	.377
Runners On/2 Out			166	49	5	9	18	.295	.446	.335
Scor. Pos./2 Out			95	32	2	8	10	.337	.463	.394
Late Inning Pressure			54	11	0	5	9	.204	.259	.271
Leading Off			17	5	0	1	3	.294	.353	.333
Bases Empty			39	8	0	2	7	.205	.256	.244
Runners On			15	3	0	3	2	.200	.267	.333
Runners/Scor. Pos.			6	1	0	2	0	.167	.167	.375
First 9 Batters			293	72	7	25	57	.246	.386	.306
Second 9 Batters			284	77	9	21	36	.271	.426	.318
All Batters Thereafter			402	113	10	22	42	.281	.415	.319

Loves to face: Reggie Jackson (.071, 1-for-14, 5 SO)
Hates to face: Darryl Motley (.421, 8-for-19, 3 HR)
Ground outs-to-air outs ratio: 0.79 last season, 0.79 for career. ... Additional statistics: 17 double-play ground outs in 191 opportunities, 51 doubles (2d-most in A.L.), 5 triples allowed in 250.2 innings last season. ... Total of 82 extra-base hits allowed was 3d-highest in A.L. ... Allowed 25 first-inning runs (tied for 4th-most in A.L.) in 36 starts last season. ... Batting support: 4.11 runs per start. ... Winning pitcher in 23.4 percent (18 of 77) of his team's victories last season, highest average in A.L. ... Has allowed 92 home runs to left-handers during his four seasons in majors, tying Floyd Bannister for highest total during that time. ... 3d-winningest pitcher born during the 1960s (47 career wins). ... Has retired the leadoff hitter in 54 of 76 innings in Late-Inning Pressure Situations during his career (71%).

Pete Vuckovich

Milwaukee Brewers	W–L	ERA	AB	H	HR	BB	SO	BA	SA	OBA
Season	6-10	5.51	450	134	16	48	55	.298	.464	.374
vs. Left-Handed Batters			225	70	4	23	24	.311	.422	.376
vs. Right-Handed Batters			225	64	12	25	31	.284	.507	.371
Home	4-4	4.13	220	62	7	24	28	.282	.436	.352
Road	2-6	6.91	230	72	9	24	27	.313	.491	.393
Grass	6-8	4.81	346	103	10	37	42	.298	.434	.371
Artificial Turf	0-2	8.03	104	31	6	11	13	.298	.567	.381
Day	1-4	7.40	87	30	1	10	13	.345	.460	.414
Night	5-6	5.09	363	104	15	38	42	.287	.466	.364
April	1-0	4.50	89	24	4	4	11	.270	.438	.309
May	0-2	13.50	26	13	1	4	3	.500	.692	.563
June	1-3	6.55	96	30	2	8	12	.313	.500	.377
July	3-2	3.30	110	25	4	16	12	.227	.373	.331
August	1-3	4.85	119	36	4	14	15	.303	.445	.385
Sept./Oct.	0-0	32.40	10	6	1	2	2	.600	1.000	.667
Leading Off Inn.			109	30	4	10	12	.275	.422	.347
Bases Empty			250	75	9	24	30	.300	.456	.373
Runners On			200	59	7	24	25	.295	.475	.374
Runners/Scor. Pos.			108	32	5	15	12	.296	.528	.389
Runners On/2 Out			83	25	2	12	9	.301	.482	.402
Scor. Pos./2 Out			53	16	2	7	4	.302	.547	.403
Late Inning Pressure			30	10	1	1	2	.333	.467	.355
Leading Off			8	2	1	0	1	.250	.625	.250
Bases Empty			18	7	1	0	2	.389	.556	.389
Runners On			12	3	0	1	0	.250	.333	.308
Runners/Scor. Pos.			6	1	0	0	0	.167	.167	.167
First 9 Batters			180	58	5	15	23	.322	.461	.378
Second 9 Batters			153	38	7	20	18	.248	.431	.348
All Batters Thereafter			117	38	4	13	14	.325	.513	.402

Loves to face: Lance Parrish (.050, 1-for-20, 8 SO)
Hates to face: Lou Whitaker (.522, 12-for-23, 2 HR)
Ground outs-to-air outs ratio: 1.18 last season, 1.35 for career. . . . Additional statistics: 10 double-play ground outs in 101 opportunities, 19 doubles, 4 triples allowed in 112.2 innings last season. . . . Average of 5.12 innings per start was 4th-lowest among A.L. pitchers (minimum: 15 GS). . . . Allowed 17 first-inning runs in 22 starts last season. . . . Batting support: 4.59 runs per start. . . . ERA of 5.51 was 5th-highest among A.L. pitchers with at least 15 starts. . . . Home run allowed to Phil Bradley on July 6, 1985 was first vs. Vuckovich in Late-Inning Pressure Situations since 1979. . . . Reached the eighth inning only once in 22 starts last season, a complete-game victory over Seattle on July 6.

Tom Waddell

Cleveland Indians	W–L	ERA	AB	H	HR	BB	SO	BA	SA	OBA
Season	8-6	4.87	422	104	20	39	53	.246	.453	.309
vs. Left-Handed Batters			203	56	12	27	19	.276	.502	.361
vs. Right-Handed Batters			219	48	8	12	34	.219	.406	.258
Home	7-3	4.76	238	56	13	19	27	.235	.450	.288
Road	1-3	5.03	184	48	7	20	26	.261	.457	.335
Grass	8-5	5.00	336	81	16	33	42	.241	.446	.306
Artificial Turf	0-1	4.37	86	23	4	6	11	.267	.477	.319
Day	3-3	4.79	156	39	7	11	15	.250	.468	.294
Night	5-3	4.92	266	65	13	28	38	.244	.444	.318
April	0-2	5.74	62	18	3	4	6	.290	.532	.333
May	1-1	2.25	55	12	1	9	15	.218	.327	.323
June	1-1	1.69	37	7	1	1	6	.189	.297	.205
July	3-1	4.57	81	21	3	9	7	.259	.457	.330
August	2-1	4.02	116	25	7	8	11	.216	.414	.264
Sept./Oct.	1-0	10.38	71	21	5	8	8	.296	.620	.375
Leading Off Inn.			90	26	4	10	9	.289	.489	.360
Bases Empty			225	59	11	18	23	.262	.471	.320
Runners On			197	45	9	21	30	.228	.431	.297
Runners/Scor. Pos.			115	31	6	17	22	.270	.496	.353
Runners On/2 Out			82	15	3	13	13	.183	.354	.295
Scor. Pos./2 Out			55	11	3	10	10	.200	.418	.323
Late Inning Pressure			121	32	4	9	17	.264	.438	.313
Leading Off			23	8	1	2	1	.348	.565	.400
Bases Empty			59	16	3	5	2	.271	.508	.328
Runners On			62	16	1	4	15	.258	.371	.299
Runners/Scor. Pos.			42	13	0	4	12	.310	.405	.362
First 9 Batters			258	59	11	31	39	.229	.422	.308
Second 9 Batters			96	22	1	3	5	.229	.313	.253
All Batters Thereafter			68	23	8	5	9	.338	.765	.387

Loves to face: Darryl Motley (0-for-7, 4 SO)
Hates to face: Gorman Thomas (.750, 3-for-4, 1 HR)
Ground outs-to-air outs ratio: 0.52 last season (3d-highest in A.L.), 0.53 for career. . . . Additional statistics: 4 double-play ground outs in 87 opportunities (7th-lowest rate in A.L. last season), 25 doubles, 1 triple allowed in 112.2 innings last season. . . . Has faced 405 left-handed batters in his career without allowing a triple. . . . Career average of one home run allowed every 6.55 innings is 5th-highest among active pitchers (minimum: 20 HR). . . . Average of 39.1 air outs per 100 batters faced was highest in A.L. last season (minimum: 200 BFP). . . . Opponents' career batting average in Late-Inning Pressure Situations (.220) is 2d-lowest among active A.L. pitchers (minimum: 300 PA). Mike Boddicker is lowest at .198. . . . Allowed 61 runs last season, highest total in the majors among pitchers who did not allow an unearned run.

Curt Wardle

Twins/Indians	W–L	ERA	AB	H	HR	BB	SO	BA	SA	OBA
Season	8-9	6.18	447	127	20	62	84	.284	.519	.369
vs. Left-Handed Batters			129	40	5	19	28	.310	.581	.397
vs. Right-Handed Batters			318	87	15	43	56	.274	.494	.358
Home	6-2	4.73	218	55	7	32	48	.252	.431	.345
Road	2-7	7.71	229	72	13	30	36	.314	.603	.393
Grass	7-7	6.99	307	94	14	40	47	.306	.560	.382
Artificial Turf	1-2	4.62	140	33	6	22	37	.236	.429	.341
Day	0-4	6.30	119	37	4	10	19	.311	.529	.364
Night	8-5	6.14	328	90	16	52	65	.274	.515	.371
April	0-0	5.56	40	9	2	6	7	.225	.400	.326
May	1-2	4.86	63	17	3	12	19	.270	.492	.390
June	0-0	2.57	23	5	1	6	4	.217	.391	.379
July	0-1	7.71	58	18	3	4	17	.310	.534	.355
August	5-2	6.06	124	32	6	22	16	.258	.500	.365
Sept./Oct.	2-4	7.29	139	46	5	12	21	.331	.597	.381
Leading Off Inn.			97	21	2	18	22	.216	.381	.339
Bases Empty			228	54	6	38	50	.237	.404	.348
Runners On			219	73	14	24	34	.333	.639	.392
Runners/Scor. Pos.			132	40	8	13	22	.303	.583	.351
Runners On/2 Out			84	21	3	6	16	.250	.512	.308
Scor. Pos./2 Out			51	9	1	4	11	.176	.314	.236
Late Inning Pressure			79	23	5	11	21	.291	.608	.378
Leading Off			19	3	1	4	7	.158	.421	.304
Bases Empty			43	8	1	8	15	.186	.349	.314
Runners On			36	15	4	3	6	.417	.917	.462
Runners/Scor. Pos.			25	10	3	0	5	.400	.960	.400
First 9 Batters			249	62	7	36	59	.249	.410	.346
Second 9 Batters			118	38	7	12	18	.322	.593	.382
All Batters Thereafter			80	27	6	14	7	.338	.750	.423

Loves to face: Kirk Gibson (0-for-6, 4 SO)
Hates to face: Don Mattingly (.625, 5-for-8, 1 HR)
Ground outs-to-air outs ratio: 0.57 last season (6th-lowest in A.L.), 0.57 for career. . . . Additional statistics: 7 double-play ground outs in 116 opportunities, 31 doubles, 7 triples allowed in 115.0 innings last season (highest rate of extra-base hits per 100 at bats in majors among pitchers facing 200 batters). . . . Allowed 3 first-inning runs in 12 starts last season. . . . Batting support: 6.17 runs per start. . . . Average of 8.35 strikeouts per nine innings was 5th-highest among A.L. relief pitchers (minimum: 30 relief games). . . . Career average of one home run allowed every 5.41 innings is highest among active pitchers (minimum: 20 HR). . . . Opponents' slugging average with runners on base was the highest in *Player Analysis* history (minimum: 150 AB).

Chris Welsh

Texas Rangers	W–L	ERA	AB	H	HR	BB	SO	BA	SA	OBA
Season	2-5	4.13	320	101	11	25	31	.316	.491	.371
vs. Left-Handed Batters			109	25	1	7	14	.229	.294	.276
vs. Right-Handed Batters			211	76	10	18	17	.360	.592	.419
Home	2-1	3.44	137	42	6	9	11	.307	.496	.358
Road	0-4	4.68	183	59	5	16	20	.322	.486	.381
Grass	2-3	4.05	249	78	10	19	25	.313	.494	.368
Artificial Turf	0-2	4.41	71	23	1	6	6	.324	.479	.385
Day	0-2	4.41	67	20	2	5	7	.299	.507	.342
Night	2-3	4.05	253	81	9	20	24	.320	.486	.379
April			0	0	0	0	0	.000	.000	.000
May	0-0	1.93	18	5	0	0	1	.278	.278	.278
June	1-2	3.07	55	15	3	5	8	.273	.491	.339
July	1-0	1.91	113	32	2	12	9	.283	.416	.357
August	0-3	8.84	98	38	4	5	12	.388	.622	.423
Sept./Oct.	0-0	3.86	36	11	2	3	1	.306	.472	.375
Leading Off Inn.			70	18	4	3	7	.257	.471	.297
Bases Empty			163	52	5	11	19	.319	.485	.366
Runners On			157	49	6	14	12	.312	.497	.377
Runners/Scor. Pos.			96	28	5	9	5	.292	.500	.349
Runners On/2 Out			74	25	2	7	6	.338	.486	.410
Scor. Pos./2 Out			51	17	2	6	2	.333	.510	.404
Late Inning Pressure			19	5	1	2	2	.263	.421	.333
Leading Off			4	1	1	1	0	.250	1.000	.400
Bases Empty			12	3	1	1	2	.250	.500	.308
Runners On			7	2	0	1	0	.286	.286	.375
Runners/Scor. Pos.			4	1	0	1	0	.250	.250	.400
First 9 Batters			179	56	7	14	19	.313	.464	.374
Second 9 Batters			95	30	3	6	8	.316	.537	.356
All Batters Thereafter			46	15	1	5	4	.326	.500	.392

Loves to face: Ron Kittle (0-for-6)
Hates to face: Cal Ripken (4-for-4)
Ground outs-to-air outs ratio: 1.32 last season, 1.56 for career. . . . Additional statistics: 7 double-play ground outs in 67 opportunities, 19 doubles, 2 triples allowed in 76.1 innings last season. . . . Career average of 3.43 strikeouts per nine innings is 9th-lowest among active pitchers (minimum: 250 innings). . . . Right-handers' .360 batting average was highest in majors; the 131-point disparity between righties' and lefties' batting averages was largest in A.L. (minimum: 100 AB each way). . . . Has allowed 43 home runs in major-league career, but only six to left-handers. . . . Has a 14–17 record with a 4.46 ERA in 46 career starts; 2–4, 3.97 with no saves in 47 relief appearances. . . . Has not pitched a complete game in 24 starts since June 12, 1982. . . . Only six pitchers active last season have more relief appearances without a save.

Ed Whitson

New York Yankees	W–L	ERA	AB	H	HR	BB	SO	BA	SA	OBA
Season	10-8	4.88	650	201	19	43	89	.309	.469	.350
vs. Left-Handed Batters			376	117	11	19	41	.311	.481	.342
vs. Right-Handed Batters			274	84	8	24	48	.307	.453	.362
Home	4-2	4.08	274	83	7	13	39	.303	.456	.336
Road	6-6	5.48	376	118	12	30	50	.314	.479	.361
Grass	8-6	4.66	539	167	16	36	75	.310	.473	.352
Artificial Turf	2-2	5.93	111	34	3	7	14	.306	.450	.342
Day	2-4	5.74	234	79	10	11	27	.338	.543	.364
Night	8-4	4.44	416	122	9	32	62	.293	.428	.343
April	0-3	4.43	89	27	5	6	10	.303	.528	.344
May	1-2	7.54	101	40	4	8	10	.396	.594	.441
June	2-1	1.86	110	25	0	4	18	.227	.273	.252
July	3-1	3.19	129	35	2	10	11	.271	.388	.319
August	2-0	7.42	132	45	6	7	23	.341	.583	.373
Sept./Oct.	2-1	5.95	89	29	2	8	17	.326	.461	.381
Leading Off Inn.			156	42	1	17	25	.269	.372	.345
Bases Empty			361	101	8	31	53	.280	.413	.340
Runners On			289	100	11	12	36	.346	.540	.364
Runners/Scor. Pos.			139	48	4	7	17	.345	.525	.359
Runners On/2 Out			109	32	5	6	15	.294	.514	.330
Scor. Pos./2 Out			58	16	3	4	9	.276	.500	.323
Late Inning Pressure			25	6	1	1	5	.240	.440	.269
Leading Off			7	1	0	0	2	.143	.143	.143
Bases Empty			18	4	0	0	5	.222	.333	.222
Runners On			7	2	1	1	0	.286	.714	.375
Runners/Scor. Pos.			1	0	0	1	0	.000	.000	.500
First 9 Batters			251	71	4	14	40	.283	.367	.320
Second 9 Batters			220	66	6	13	26	.300	.473	.336
All Batters Thereafter			179	64	9	16	23	.358	.609	.410

Loves to face: Ted Simmons (.111, 3-for-27)
Hates to face: Kirby Puckett (.625, 5-for-8)
Ground outs-to-air outs ratio: 0.97 last season, 0.94 for career. . . . Additional statistics: 14 double-play ground outs in 151 opportunities, 37 doubles, 5 triples allowed in 158.2 innings last season. . . . Average of 5.29 innings per start was 7th-lowest among A.L. pitchers (minimum: 15 GS). . . . Led A.L. pitchers in early-round knockouts last season. No, not that kind of knockout; we mean that he lasted less than five innings in 12 starts last year. . . . Allowed 13 first-inning runs in 30 starts last season. . . . Batting support: 5.93 runs per start, 4th-highest average in A.L. (minimum: 15 GS). . . . A real marshmallow: Average of 11.40 hits per nine innings was 4th-highest among A.L. pitchers with at least 15 starts.

Frank Wills

Seattle Mariners	W–L	ERA	AB	H	HR	BB	SO	BA	SA	OBA
Season	5-11	6.00	458	122	18	68	67	.266	.437	.359
vs. Left-Handed Batters			258	74	10	43	38	.287	.469	.387
vs. Right-Handed Batters			200	48	8	25	29	.240	.395	.323
Home	3-4	5.35	252	63	9	39	38	.250	.397	.352
Road	2-7	6.83	206	59	9	29	29	.286	.485	.368
Grass	2-6	7.63	177	53	8	22	26	.299	.503	.369
Artificial Turf	3-5	5.03	281	69	10	46	41	.246	.395	.353
Day	1-4	5.65	132	35	5	27	18	.265	.417	.384
Night	4-7	6.15	326	87	13	41	49	.267	.445	.349
April			0	0	0	0	0	.000	.000	.000
May			0	0	0	0	0	.000	.000	.000
June	3-1	5.00	97	23	2	19	16	.237	.340	.356
July	1-3	4.81	139	33	7	25	20	.237	.432	.353
August	0-2	6.75	99	28	4	11	15	.283	.485	.357
Sept./Oct.	1-5	7.76	123	38	5	13	16	.309	.480	.371
Leading Off Inn.			108	27	3	22	17	.250	.370	.377
Bases Empty			255	62	9	40	44	.243	.392	.348
Runners On			203	60	9	28	23	.296	.493	.373
Runners/Scor. Pos.			115	30	6	19	14	.261	.487	.350
Runners On/2 Out			66	14	5	10	5	.212	.455	.325
Scor. Pos./2 Out			47	8	3	8	5	.170	.383	.304
Late Inning Pressure			41	14	0	6	5	.341	.415	.408
Leading Off			11	3	0	2	0	.273	.364	.385
Bases Empty			21	7	0	3	1	.333	.381	.417
Runners On			20	7	0	3	4	.350	.450	.400
Runners/Scor. Pos.			11	3	0	3	2	.273	.364	.375
First 9 Batters			178	48	11	29	29	.270	.494	.374
Second 9 Batters			156	36	4	18	22	.231	.365	.309
All Batters Thereafter			124	38	3	21	16	.306	.444	.399

Loves to face: Oddibe McDowell (0-for-9)
Hates to face: Jerry Willard (.625, 5-for-8, 1 HR)
Ground outs-to-air outs ratio: 1.02 last season, 0.94 for career. . . . G/A ratio of 1.37 vs. left-handed batters, 0.73 vs. right-handers last season. . . . Additional statistics: 8 double-play ground outs in 120 opportunities, 22 doubles, 1 triple allowed in 123.0 innings last season. . . . Allowed 17 first-inning runs in 18 starts last season. . . . Batting support: 4.33 runs per start. . . . ERA of 6.00 was 3d-highest among A.L. pitchers with at least 15 starts. . . . Has faced 379 right-handed batters in his career without allowing a triple. . . . Career batting averages: .280 (one extra-base hit per 10.0 at bats) by opposing left-handed hitters; .249 (one XBH per 15.3 AB) by right-handers. . . . Lost eight of nine starts (with no decision in the other) following four wins in his first five decisions.

Mike Witt

California Angels	W–L	ERA	AB	H	HR	BB	SO	BA	SA	OBA
Season	15-9	3.56	938	228	22	98	180	.243	.360	.316
vs. Left-Handed Batters			520	137	11	52	81	.263	.375	.332
vs. Right-Handed Batters			418	91	11	46	99	.218	.342	.296
Home	8-5	3.38	461	114	14	51	82	.247	.369	.322
Road	7-4	3.75	477	114	8	47	98	.239	.352	.309
Grass	13-8	3.65	804	195	19	91	152	.243	.358	.320
Artificial Turf	2-1	3.03	134	33	3	7	28	.246	.373	.289
Day	5-2	3.93	261	57	6	26	56	.218	.345	.293
Night	10-7	3.42	677	171	16	72	124	.253	.366	.325
April	1-3	3.18	140	27	4	20	22	.193	.307	.294
May	1-2	3.48	128	33	1	12	24	.258	.344	.315
June	4-1	2.82	169	41	4	13	33	.243	.367	.297
July	2-1	3.26	168	41	3	22	32	.244	.351	.340
August	4-0	2.87	143	37	4	15	30	.259	.392	.329
Sept./Oct.	3-2	5.51	190	49	6	16	39	.258	.389	.317
Leading Off Inn.			236	62	6	27	47	.263	.360	.338
Bases Empty			549	132	11	56	111	.240	.341	.313
Runners On			389	96	11	42	69	.247	.388	.320
Runners/Scor. Pos.			203	49	4	29	38	.241	.330	.332
Runners On/2 Out			153	38	4	15	26	.248	.392	.320
Scor. Pos./2 Out			93	22	1	12	20	.237	.301	.330
Late Inning Pressure			113	23	4	19	22	.204	.336	.318
Leading Off			32	11	2	6	7	.344	.531	.447
Bases Empty			66	14	2	14	15	.212	.333	.350
Runners On			47	9	2	5	7	.191	.340	.269
Runners/Scor. Pos.			20	3	1	4	3	.150	.350	.292
First 9 Batters			279	63	2	34	61	.226	.301	.311
Second 9 Batters			278	68	9	24	51	.245	.367	.305
All Batters Thereafter			381	97	11	40	68	.255	.399	.327

Loves to face: Jerry Hairston (0-for-10)
Hates to face: Carney Lansford (.467, 7-for-15)
Ground outs-to-air outs ratio: 1.59 last season, 1.54 for career. . . . Additional statistics: 26 double-play ground outs in 202 opportunities, 30 doubles, 7 triples (tied for 6th-most in A.L.) allowed in 250.0 innings last season. . . . Allowed 12 first-inning runs in 35 starts, 7th-lowest rate in A.L. last season (minimum: 15 GS). . . . Batting support: 4.11 runs per start. . . . 2d-winningest pitcher born during the 1960s (53 career wins), behind Fernando (78). . . . Ranked 6th in A.L. with an average of 6.48 strikeouts per nine innings. . . . Consistently excellent in Late-Inning Pressure Situations. Opponents' batting, year by year since 1981: .233, .227, .218, .209, .204. . . . Failed to survive fourth inning in consecutive starts against Cleveland during late-season pennant chase (September 22 and 27).

Matt Young

Seattle Mariners	W–L	ERA	AB	H	HR	BB	SO	BA	SA	OBA
Season	12-19	4.91	858	242	23	76	136	.282	.416	.344
vs. Left-Handed Batters			148	39	1	14	39	.264	.304	.335
vs. Right-Handed Batters			710	203	22	62	97	.286	.439	.346
Home	8-8	3.85	507	132	13	46	92	.260	.383	.326
Road	4-11	6.56	351	110	10	30	44	.313	.464	.371
Grass	3-7	7.91	225	73	7	23	29	.324	.498	.393
Artificial Turf	9-12	3.96	633	169	16	53	107	.267	.387	.327
Day	2-5	5.23	172	50	4	16	26	.291	.419	.356
Night	10-14	4.83	686	192	19	60	110	.280	.415	.341
April	1-3	5.82	82	24	2	10	11	.293	.463	.368
May	3-2	3.27	125	28	2	5	22	.224	.312	.254
June	3-4	5.44	173	49	4	19	23	.283	.393	.369
July	0-2	5.72	162	50	7	16	30	.309	.481	.371
August	2-3	4.25	114	30	3	8	25	.263	.404	.311
Sept./Oct.	3-5	4.88	202	61	5	18	25	.302	.436	.362
Leading Off Inn.			219	65	3	12	26	.297	.402	.336
Bases Empty			506	135	11	36	83	.267	.393	.319
Runners On			352	107	12	40	53	.304	.449	.378
Runners/Scor. Pos.			191	62	8	32	28	.325	.497	.421
Runners On/2 Out			145	49	9	24	18	.338	.552	.442
Scor. Pos./2 Out			89	33	7	22	9	.371	.629	.504
Late Inning Pressure			96	27	0	11	12	.281	.313	.367
Leading Off			28	8	0	3	2	.286	.286	.355
Bases Empty			68	16	0	6	8	.235	.235	.297
Runners On			28	11	0	5	4	.393	.500	.514
Runners/Scor. Pos.			16	3	0	5	2	.188	.250	.409
First 9 Batters			292	77	6	23	43	.264	.377	.324
Second 9 Batters			261	80	8	29	38	.307	.467	.379
All Batters Thereafter			305	85	9	24	55	.279	.410	.333

Loves to face: Wade Boggs (0-for-14)
Hates to face: Dave Kingman (.714, 5-for-7, 3 HR, 2 BB)
Ground outs-to-air outs ratio: 1.80 last season, 1.63 for career. . . . Additional statistics: 19 double-play ground outs in 175 opportunities, 34 doubles, 6 triples allowed in 218.1 innings last season. . . . Allowed 25 first-inning runs (tied for 4th-most in A.L.) in 35 starts last season. . . . Batting support: 4.43 runs per start. . . . Young is the only major-league pitcher to have faced Boggs more than 10 times without allowing a hit. . . . Led A.L. with 19 losses, highest total since 1980, when Oakland's Brian Kingman lost 20. . . . Allowed major-league leading total of 33 hits with two outs and runners in scoring position last season. . . . Career average of one extra-base hit allowed every 28.3 at bats by left-handed batters is 2d-lowest in 11-year history of *The Player Analysis* (minimum: 250 AB).

Baltimore Orioles

	W–L	ERA	AB	H	HR	BB	SO	BA	SA	OBA
Season	83-78	4.38	5491	1480	160	568	793	.270	.416	.338
vs. Left-Handers			2502	658	65	289	351	.263	.410	.339
vs. Right-Handers			2989	822	95	279	442	.275	.420	.338
Home	45-36	4.19	2853	754	87	297	431	.264	.405	.335
Road	38-42	4.58	2638	726	73	271	362	.275	.428	.342
Grass	72-66	4.30	4713	1259	141	489	679	.267	.412	.336
Artificial Turf	11-12	4.87	778	221	19	79	114	.284	.441	.352
Day	22-23	4.42	1550	436	44	151	206	.281	.432	.346
Night	61-55	4.36	3941	1044	116	417	587	.265	.409	.335
April	12-7	3.90	620	159	15	74	96	.256	.390	.335
May	14-12	4.20	859	223	25	84	111	.260	.404	.324
June	11-15	4.62	912	260	17	102	109	.285	.394	.355
July	14-14	4.44	961	244	29	95	144	.254	.406	.323
August	16-11	4.51	910	250	31	92	145	.275	.430	.344
Sept./Oct.	16-19	4.42	1229	344	43	121	188	.280	.451	.345
Leading Off Inn.			1327	356	48	99	174	.268	.433	.322
Bases Empty			3082	799	90	282	430	.259	.406	.325
Runners On			2409	681	70	286	363	.283	.429	.355
Runners/Scor. Pos.			1404	397	38	211	238	.283	.426	.368
Runners On/2 Out			996	251	29	131	167	.252	.383	.342
Scor. Pos./2 Out			659	172	21	103	119	.261	.405	.362
Late Inning Pressure			838	221	20	103	128	.264	.381	.343
Leading Off			209	53	7	24	38	.254	.411	.333
Bases Empty			486	116	12	44	77	.239	.366	.305
Runners On			352	105	8	59	51	.298	.401	.391
Runners/Scor. Pos.			206	59	3	48	33	.286	.359	.408
First 9 Batters			2629	709	75	277	418	.270	.413	.339
Second 9 Batters			1559	437	45	160	199	.280	.433	.349
All Batters Thereafter			1303	334	40	131	176	.256	.401	.324

Starting pitchers: 60–60, 4.70 ERA
Relief pitchers: 23–18, 3.74 ERA

Ground outs-to-air outs ratio: 1.06. . . . Opponents grounded into one double play for every 8.25 opportunities, 3d-highest rate in A.L. . . . One of three A.L. teams not to lose more than four consecutive road games last season. The others: Detroit and Kansas City. . . . Starting pitchers compiled a 4.70 ERA at Memorial Stadium. Only one A.L. team's starters had a higher home-game figure: Texas (4.95). . . . Allowed 117 first-inning runs, 2d-highest total in majors, behind Seattle (130). . . . Lost 11 games in which they led after seven innings, tying Kansas City and San Francisco for 2d-highest total in majors, behind Toronto (13). . . . How they used their bullpen: Aase accounted for 25% of Baltimore's Late-Inning Pressure pitching; Stewart, 18%; Tippy Martinez, 10%; Snell, 7%.

Boston Red Sox

	W–L	ERA	AB	H	HR	BB	SO	BA	SA	OBA
Season	81-81	4.06	5619	1487	130	540	913	.265	.397	.331
vs. Left-Handers			2381	637	46	249	358	.268	.388	.337
vs. Right-Handers			3238	850	84	291	555	.263	.403	.326
Home	43-37	4.02	2846	773	64	246	475	.272	.403	.331
Road	38-44	4.09	2773	714	66	294	438	.257	.390	.331
Grass	67-69	4.17	4741	1275	112	446	782	.269	.400	.333
Artificial Turf	14-12	3.47	878	212	18	94	131	.241	.379	.319
Day	27-27	4.52	1880	512	45	186	292	.272	.402	.339
Night	54-54	3.83	3739	975	85	354	621	.261	.394	.327
April	9-11	4.29	735	192	15	74	125	.261	.385	.331
May	12-14	3.85	867	226	19	92	146	.261	.381	.337
June	17-10	4.01	923	250	24	86	148	.271	.412	.333
July	14-12	4.26	899	238	28	81	160	.265	.412	.325
August	8-21	4.36	1001	287	18	93	139	.287	.418	.350
Sept./Oct.	21-13	3.70	1194	294	26	114	195	.246	.374	.313
Leading Off Inn.			1340	363	28	117	199	.271	.395	.334
Bases Empty			3104	815	67	294	506	.263	.388	.330
Runners On			2515	672	63	246	407	.267	.407	.332
Runners/Scor. Pos.			1435	379	32	173	252	.264	.402	.340
Runners On/2 Out			1039	252	27	115	186	.243	.379	.322
Scor. Pos./2 Out			670	171	17	96	116	.255	.403	.351
Late Inning Pressure			967	277	28	119	141	.286	.438	.365
Leading Off			243	72	9	17	31	.296	.457	.342
Bases Empty			552	148	21	45	80	.268	.433	.327
Runners On			415	129	7	74	61	.311	.446	.411
Runners/Scor. Pos.			249	77	3	61	41	.309	.458	.438
First 9 Batters			2394	642	53	273	441	.268	.399	.345
Second 9 Batters			1531	383	36	129	231	.250	.386	.311
All Batters Thereafter			1694	462	41	138	241	.273	.403	.329

Starting pitchers: 62–62, 4.12 ERA
Relief pitchers: 19–19, 3.86 ERA

Ground outs-to-air outs ratio: 1.20. . . . Starters pitched an average of 6.73 innings per game, highest in A.L. . . . Only one A.L. team allowed fewer home runs last season: Kansas City (103). Red Sox have not allowed the league's fewest home runs since 1953. . . . Allowed only 12 home runs with two or more runners on base, fewest in the A.L. . . . Had A.L.'s 2d-lowest ERA on artificial turf. . . . Here's a weird combination: the Sox won all 39 home games in which they led after eight innings, but lost all eight games at Fenway that were tied after eight. Some things can't be explained; they just *are*. . . . How they used their bullpen: Stanley accounted for 22% of Boston's Late-Inning Pressure pitching; Crawford, 13%; Ojeda, 10%; Clear, 7%; Kison, 4%, Trujillo, 4%.

California Angels

	W–L	ERA	AB	H	HR	BB	SO	BA	SA	OBA
Season	90-72	3.91	5531	1453	171	514	767	.263	.414	.326
vs. Left-Handers			2679	739	81	275	351	.276	.427	.342
vs. Right-Handers			2852	714	90	239	416	.250	.402	.311
Home	49-30	3.71	2758	705	93	236	363	.256	.405	.316
Road	41-42	4.11	2773	748	78	278	404	.270	.423	.336
Grass	76-57	3.91	4542	1182	145	430	620	.260	.411	.325
Artificial Turf	14-15	3.91	989	271	26	84	147	.274	.429	.332
Day	30-20	3.65	1694	439	41	142	248	.259	.391	.318
Night	60-52	4.02	3837	1014	130	372	519	.264	.424	.330
April	14-7	3.76	733	182	24	83	79	.248	.390	.322
May	12-13	3.83	846	235	22	75	107	.278	.411	.335
June	15-12	2.74	936	223	20	87	137	.238	.356	.304
July	16-11	4.23	921	264	21	91	98	.287	.430	.354
August	16-13	4.58	984	260	39	102	164	.264	.442	.334
Sept./Oct.	17-16	4.23	1111	289	45	76	182	.260	.443	.309
Leading Off Inn.			1339	366	43	118	178	.273	.421	.334
Bases Empty			3151	824	104	299	431	.262	.416	.328
Runners On			2380	629	67	215	336	.264	.411	.323
Runners/Scor. Pos.			1308	337	31	141	212	.258	.391	.324
Runners On/2 Out			995	266	31	92	147	.267	.424	.332
Scor. Pos./2 Out			611	152	14	69	102	.249	.378	.328
Late Inning Pressure			989	250	31	96	139	.253	.399	.320
Leading Off			255	75	10	20	42	.294	.467	.348
Bases Empty			582	155	21	49	87	.266	.426	.325
Runners On			407	95	10	47	52	.233	.361	.312
Runners/Scor. Pos.			227	54	6	36	34	.238	.396	.338
First 9 Batters			2702	697	69	247	402	.258	.390	.321
Second 9 Batters			1532	396	52	136	199	.258	.420	.318
All Batters Thereafter			1297	360	50	131	166	.278	.458	.345

Starting pitchers: 62–56, 4.15 ERA
Relief pitchers: 28–16, 3.38 ERA

Ground outs-to-air outs ratio: 1.13. . . . Opponents grounded into one double play for every 7.22 opportunities, highest rate in majors. . . . Had A.L.'s lowest ERA during the month of June. . . . Rookie pitchers accounted for 379 of California's 1,457.1 innings (26.0%), highest total in A.L. last season. . . . Only team in majors not to allow an extra-inning home run last season. . . . One of two A.L. teams not to lose more than five consecutive games in '85. The other: Kansas City. . . . One of two A.L. teams not to lose more than three consecutive *home* games last season. The other: Toronto. . . . How they used their bullpen: Moore accounted for 26% of California's Late-Inning Pressure pitching; Cliburn, 19%; Clements, 9%; Corbett, 7%; Sanchez, 4%.

Chicago White Sox

	W–L	ERA	AB	H	HR	BB	SO	BA	SA	OBA
Season	85-77	4.07	5509	1411	161	569	1023	.256	.406	.327
vs. Left-Handers			2092	539	58	192	382	.258	.403	.322
vs. Right-Handers			3417	872	103	377	641	.255	.407	.331
Home	45-36	4.04	2789	709	83	313	551	.254	.406	.331
Road	40-41	4.10	2720	702	78	256	472	.258	.406	.323
Grass	76-62	4.10	4725	1209	142	500	907	.256	.406	.329
Artificial Turf	9-15	3.86	784	202	19	69	116	.258	.403	.319
Day	24-19	3.88	1475	372	43	148	280	.252	.399	.322
Night	61-58	4.13	4034	1039	118	421	743	.258	.408	.329
April	9-8	4.23	586	160	17	74	99	.273	.418	.353
May	13-13	3.28	826	190	18	94	174	.230	.362	.310
June	13-14	3.85	945	246	25	106	173	.260	.396	.338
July	14-12	4.24	916	235	28	88	175	.257	.412	.322
August	14-17	5.11	1070	285	39	101	177	.266	.443	.334
Sept./Oct.	22-13	3.66	1166	295	34	106	225	.253	.400	.316
Leading Off Inn.			1336	338	43	109	233	.253	.422	.315
Bases Empty			3195	787	91	285	603	.246	.397	.312
Runners On			2314	624	70	284	420	.270	.418	.347
Runners/Scor. Pos.			1352	328	32	207	269	.243	.373	.338
Runners On/2 Out			972	233	24	147	187	.240	.361	.343
Scor. Pos./2 Out			636	141	14	115	133	.222	.335	.344
Late Inning Pressure			935	242	29	112	175	.259	.407	.340
Leading Off			236	54	8	24	56	.229	.390	.303
Bases Empty			553	128	15	58	116	.231	.369	.308
Runners On			382	114	14	54	59	.298	.463	.384
Runners/Scor. Pos.			234	71	10	44	31	.303	.491	.411
First 9 Batters			2746	663	65	281	542	.241	.370	.314
Second 9 Batters			1428	378	44	147	273	.265	.422	.336
All Batters Thereafter			1335	370	52	141	208	.277	.461	.346

Starting pitchers: 60–58, 4.31 ERA
Relief pitchers: 25–19, 3.51 ERA

Ground outs-to-air outs ratio: 1.09. . . . Highest strikeout total in A.L. since 1970, when Cleveland Indians pitchers fanned 1,076 batters. The Sox had not led the league since 1953. . . . Remember Sandy Consuegra? . . . Had A.L.'s highest ERA during the month of August. . . . Lost eight consecutive home games, June 20–July 1, longest streak in majors last season. . . . Used two of the three youngest pitchers in the majors last season: Ed Correa (19 at season's end) and Joel Davis (20). Oakland's Jose Rijo was the 2d-youngest. . . . How they used their bullpen: James accounted for 26% of Chicago's Late-Inning Pressure pitching; Nelson, 10%; Agosto, 9%; Gleaton, 7%; Wehrmeister, 5%; Spillner, 4%.

Cleveland Indians

	W–L	ERA	AB	H	HR	BB	SO	BA	SA	OBA
Season	60-102	4.92	5540	1556	170	547	702	.281	.438	.346
vs. Left-Handers			2319	681	67	224	276	.294	.447	.355
vs. Right-Handers			3221	875	103	323	426	.272	.432	.340
Home	38-43	4.17	2830	751	76	246	357	.265	.402	.324
Road	22-59	5.72	2710	805	94	301	345	.297	.476	.368
Grass	53-85	4.84	4737	1321	141	463	604	.279	.431	.343
Artificial Turf	7-17	5.42	803	235	29	84	98	.293	.482	.362
Day	22-35	4.94	1989	576	51	197	222	.290	.434	.354
Night	38-67	4.91	3551	980	119	350	480	.276	.441	.342
April	7-13	4.38	680	190	17	73	74	.279	.418	.347
May	9-17	3.75	874	224	20	79	118	.256	.381	.319
June	7-19	5.32	909	267	25	92	111	.294	.447	.359
July	9-19	4.79	944	252	29	86	130	.267	.416	.334
August	14-15	5.07	979	271	43	104	107	.277	.461	.345
Sept./Oct.	14-19	5.83	1154	352	36	113	162	.305	.487	.367
Leading Off Inn.			1303	347	36	113	161	.266	.414	.329
Bases Empty			3036	825	93	272	389	.272	.426	.336
Runners On			2504	731	77	275	313	.292	.454	.357
Runners/Scor. Pos.			1446	425	46	204	201	.294	.462	.371
Runners On/2 Out			1029	268	28	142	147	.260	.412	.353
Scor. Pos./2 Out			661	172	19	111	102	.260	.418	.371
Late Inning Pressure			837	234	24	105	99	.280	.419	.358
Leading Off			207	63	8	19	19	.304	.483	.368
Bases Empty			468	135	16	41	49	.288	.449	.351
Runners On			369	99	8	64	50	.268	.382	.365
Runners/Scor. Pos.			221	63	6	55	29	.285	.416	.405
First 9 Batters			2813	757	83	302	383	.269	.419	.339
Second 9 Batters			1512	430	43	139	171	.284	.433	.347
All Batters Thereafter			1215	369	44	106	148	.304	.491	.361

Starting pitchers: 41–73 (fewest wins in A.L.), 5.22 ERA (highest in majors)
Relief pitchers: 19–29 (most losses in A.L.), 4.37 ERA
Ground outs-to-air outs ratio: 1.03. . . . Opponents grounded into one double play per 10.08 opportunities, 3d-lowest rate in A.L. . . . Highest ERA in A.L. since 1956, when Washington Senators compiled a 5.33 mark. That team had some pretty fair starting pitchers, though: Chuck Stobbs, Pedro Ramos, and Camilo Pascual. . . . Starting pitchers compiled a 6.68 ERA in road games; their 6.12 ERA during the month of September was highest by any team in any month (excluding October). . . . Only team in majors not to win three consecutive road games last season. . . . How they used their bullpen: Thompson accounted for 14% of Cleveland's Late-Inning Pressure pitching; Waddell, 14%; Easterly, 10%; Ruhle, 7%; Clark, 5%; Barkley, 5%; Van Ohlen, 4%.

Detroit Tigers

	W–L	ERA	AB	H	HR	BB	SO	BA	SA	OBA
Season	84-77	3.78	5462	1313	141	556	943	.240	.373	.311
vs. Left-Handers			2604	614	51	290	433	.236	.347	.311
vs. Right-Handers			2858	699	90	266	510	.245	.397	.310
Home	44-37	3.96	2814	666	93	287	461	.237	.384	.307
Road	40-40	3.59	2648	647	48	269	482	.244	.362	.314
Grass	73-63	3.82	4638	1112	126	472	785	.240	.371	.310
Artificial Turf	11-14	3.59	824	201	15	84	158	.244	.382	.312
Day	28-26	3.86	1817	451	35	175	301	.248	.369	.314
Night	56-51	3.75	3645	862	106	381	642	.236	.375	.309
April	11-7	3.71	617	144	10	54	108	.233	.345	.294
May	14-12	3.21	873	209	20	99	142	.239	.355	.316
June	16-11	3.88	913	214	31	97	122	.234	.380	.309
July	12-16	3.91	946	220	23	93	181	.233	.364	.303
August	16-13	3.51	981	232	15	105	192	.236	.341	.308
Sept./Oct.	15-18	4.34	1132	294	42	108	198	.260	.432	.325
Leading Off Inn.			1343	299	28	116	240	.223	.350	.286
Bases Empty			3231	732	89	298	582	.227	.366	.294
Runners On			2231	581	52	258	361	.260	.383	.334
Runners/Scor. Pos.			1243	342	29	186	200	.275	.406	.360
Runners On/2 Out			975	247	22	133	167	.253	.375	.345
Scor. Pos./2 Out			592	156	14	102	99	.264	.400	.374
Late Inning Pressure			996	220	32	112	172	.221	.350	.301
Leading Off			258	54	3	19	46	.209	.271	.269
Bases Empty			624	129	21	50	111	.207	.338	.270
Runners On			372	91	11	62	61	.245	.371	.349
Runners/Scor. Pos.			201	52	7	50	27	.259	.398	.399
First 9 Batters			2541	620	76	264	486	.244	.385	.314
Second 9 Batters			1436	346	28	145	230	.241	.364	.312
All Batters Thereafter			1485	347	37	147	227	.234	.362	.303

Starting pitchers: 67–56, 3.64 ERA
Relief pitchers: 17–21, 4.21 ERA
Ground outs-to-air outs ratio: 1.04. . . . Had A.L.'s lowest road-game ERA. . . . Right-handed pitchers started 139 games, highest total in A.L. Only left-handed starters: Tanana and Mickey Mahler, both acquired during the 1985 season. But opposing left-handed batters hit .236, the lowest mark in the league. . . . Lost seven games in which they led after eight innings (2d-highest total in majors last season), after posting perfect 87–0 mark in such games a year earlier. . . . Allowed 158 multi-run innings last season, only three more than Toronto, the A.L. leader. . . . How they used their bullpen: Hernandez accounted for 22% of Detroit's Late-Inning Pressure pitching; Lopez, 15%; Scherrer, 10%; Bair, 3%.

Kansas City Royals

	W–L	ERA	AB	H	HR	BB	SO	BA	SA	OBA
Season	91-71	3.49	5582	1433	103	463	846	.257	.374	.315
vs. Left-Handers			2087	547	46	192	321	.262	.386	.324
vs. Right-Handers			3495	886	57	271	525	.254	.367	.309
Home	50-32	3.36	2915	735	43	236	410	.252	.362	.310
Road	41-39	3.63	2667	698	60	227	436	.262	.388	.320
Grass	32-29	3.39	2055	547	42	169	339	.266	.383	.322
Artificial Turf	59-42	3.54	3527	886	61	294	507	.251	.369	.310
Day	18-25	4.23	1512	420	32	141	252	.278	.423	.340
Night	73-46	3.22	4070	1013	71	322	594	.249	.356	.305
April	11-8	2.61	680	168	6	54	94	.247	.338	.303
May	14-13	3.94	903	236	20	83	98	.261	.390	.324
June	12-14	3.64	891	229	17	106	152	.257	.365	.337
July	17-10	3.56	939	247	17	64	146	.263	.368	.312
August	15-12	3.64	951	251	20	74	174	.264	.403	.317
Sept./Oct.	22-14	3.36	1218	302	23	82	182	.248	.371	.297
Leading Off Inn.			1370	353	32	90	167	.258	.394	.307
Bases Empty			3186	825	64	242	478	.259	.381	.314
Runners On			2396	608	39	221	368	.254	.364	.315
Runners/Scor. Pos.			1359	348	17	160	218	.256	.357	.330
Runners On/2 Out			1017	235	19	102	150	.231	.352	.306
Scor. Pos./2 Out			638	146	9	77	107	.229	.329	.318
Late Inning Pressure			1053	292	24	90	168	.277	.408	.336
Leading Off			264	73	8	12	35	.277	.428	.308
Bases Empty			609	168	19	42	96	.276	.430	.325
Runners On			444	124	5	48	72	.279	.378	.350
Runners/Scor. Pos.			264	71	4	46	53	.269	.371	.378
First 9 Batters			2585	658	46	218	414	.255	.365	.312
Second 9 Batters			1504	370	17	126	221	.246	.348	.308
All Batters Thereafter			1493	405	40	119	211	.271	.417	.326

Starting pitchers: 75–54 (most wins in A.L.), 3.43 ERA
Relief pitchers: 16–17, 3.66 ERA
Ground outs-to-air outs ratio: 1.27 (highest in A.L.). . . . Relievers lost only one game after September 1. . . . Regular starting rotation (Black, Gubicza, Jackson, Leibrandt, and Saberhagen) started all but four games. Combined total of 158 starts was one short of all-time A.L. record for starts by a five-man group, set in 1970 by the Baltimore Orioles. . . . Royals were only four games above .500 in games not started by Saberhagen. . . . Left-handed pitchers started 99 games, highest total in majors. . . . Led A.L. with 15 losses in games in which they led after six innings. . . . How they used their bullpen: Quisenberry accounted for 29% of Kansas City's Late-Inning Pressure pitching; Beckwith, 15%; Jones, 6%; LaCoss, 5%; Farr, 4%. . . . Only one relief appearance lasted a single batter: June 26, when Quisenberry allowed an immediate game-winning single to Roy Smalley.

Milwaukee Brewers

	W–L	ERA	AB	H	HR	BB	SO	BA	SA	OBA
Season	71-90	4.39	5577	1510	175	499	777	.271	.424	.331
vs. Left-Handers			2416	659	76	241	291	.273	.427	.338
vs. Right-Handers			3161	851	99	258	486	.269	.422	.326
Home	40-40	4.48	2874	792	86	254	424	.276	.427	.334
Road	31-50	4.30	2703	718	89	245	353	.266	.421	.329
Grass	64-71	4.33	4686	1262	146	417	666	.269	.419	.330
Artificial Turf	7-19	4.72	891	248	29	82	111	.278	.450	.339
Day	16-35	5.00	1811	518	63	163	231	.286	.443	.345
Night	55-55	4.11	3766	992	112	336	546	.263	.415	.325
April	8-11	3.23	642	156	16	46	77	.243	.377	.293
May	13-11	4.49	813	210	22	78	121	.258	.410	.323
June	12-15	4.37	907	228	30	78	136	.251	.415	.313
July	11-17	4.54	969	277	38	96	134	.286	.459	.347
August	15-13	4.20	979	267	28	94	133	.273	.414	.339
Sept./Oct.	12-23	5.00	1267	372	41	107	176	.294	.446	.351
Leading Off Inn.			1348	372	44	91	179	.276	.455	.324
Bases Empty			3201	853	106	244	451	.266	.426	.323
Runners On			2376	657	69	255	326	.277	.422	.343
Runners/Scor. Pos.			1340	366	38	179	192	.273	.426	.350
Runners On/2 Out			1014	257	31	116	151	.253	.403	.334
Scor. Pos./2 Out			625	164	23	82	95	.262	.442	.353
Late Inning Pressure			1017	291	34	101	147	.286	.445	.349
Leading Off			262	85	16	15	43	.324	.603	.361
Bases Empty			597	179	22	43	87	.300	.477	.348
Runners On			420	112	12	58	60	.267	.400	.351
Runners/Scor. Pos.			245	62	7	44	38	.253	.392	.358
First 9 Batters			2724	742	80	243	405	.272	.417	.331
Second 9 Batters			1478	385	52	132	202	.260	.424	.325
All Batters Thereafter			1375	383	43	124	170	.279	.439	.339

Starting pitchers: 53–68, 4.30 ERA
Relief pitchers: 18–22, 4.63 ERA (highest in majors)
Ground outs-to-air outs ratio: 1.04 (3d-lowest in A.L.). . . . Allowed most home runs in A.L. for first time in team's history. Led majors with 34 home runs allowed in Late-Inning Pressure Situations. . . . Everyone who called George Bamberger the Einstein of pitching on April 28, take two giant steps backward. That was the day on which Milwaukee led the league with a 2.76 ERA. . . . Committed only four balks last season, tying California and Atlanta for the lowest total in the majors. . . . How they used their bullpen: Fingers accounted for 14% of Milwaukee's Late-Inning Pressure pitching; Gibson, 14%; Searage, 8%; McClure, 6%; Ladd, 3%; Waits, 2%.

Minnesota Twins

	W–L	ERA	AB	H	HR	BB	SO	BA	SA	OBA
Season	77-85	4.48	5473	1468	164	462	767	.268	.424	.326
vs. Left-Handers			2516	709	78	201	342	.282	.446	.334
vs. Right-Handers			2957	759	86	261	425	.257	.405	.318
Home	49-35	4.21	2912	759	83	233	438	.261	.415	.316
Road	28-50	4.79	2561	709	81	229	329	.277	.434	.336
Grass	24-35	4.22	1913	511	52	169	245	.267	.406	.327
Artificial Turf	53-50	4.62	3560	957	112	293	522	.269	.434	.325
Day	23-25	4.63	1636	446	46	136	233	.273	.432	.326
Night	54-60	4.41	3837	1022	118	326	534	.266	.420	.325
April	11-9	3.83	651	150	17	54	82	.230	.355	.292
May	10-16	5.68	923	269	32	95	135	.291	.477	.359
June	12-13	4.46	830	224	30	66	105	.270	.443	.325
July	13-15	4.77	965	270	32	79	137	.280	.437	.334
August	12-16	3.82	942	256	15	72	146	.272	.384	.322
Sept./Oct.	19-16	4.26	1162	299	38	96	162	.257	.428	.313
Leading Off Inn.			1317	342	24	110	185	.260	.389	.320
Bases Empty			3160	814	73	246	467	.258	.396	.314
Runners On			2313	654	91	216	300	.283	.463	.341
Runners/Scor. Pos.			1341	387	57	137	184	.289	.478	.346
Runners On/2 Out			959	251	39	90	142	.262	.446	.330
Scor. Pos./2 Out			610	161	24	65	94	.264	.438	.340
Late Inning Pressure			807	190	19	73	131	.235	.369	.303
Leading Off			204	46	3	22	31	.225	.328	.310
Bases Empty			493	111	7	35	79	.225	.333	.281
Runners On			314	79	12	38	52	.252	.427	.335
Runners/Scor. Pos.			199	50	10	26	35	.251	.462	.336
First 9 Batters			2479	646	64	249	419	.261	.406	.328
Second 9 Batters			1423	393	46	100	174	.276	.439	.324
All Batters Thereafter			1571	429	54	113	174	.273	.438	.323

Starting pitchers: 65–68, 4.48 ERA
Relief pitchers: 12–17 (fewest wins in majors), 4.47 ERA
Ground outs-to-air outs ratio: 1.05. . . . Opponents grounded into one double play for every 10.17 opportunities, 2d-lowest rate in A.L. . . . Led the A.L. in complete games (41) for the first time since 1967, when they won their last of four CG titles over a six-year period. . . . Relievers allowed only one home run during the month of August. . . . Lost 10 of 28 road games in which they led after six innings, highest total in A.L. . . . Only team in A.L. to win every home game in which it led after seven innings. . . . How they used their bullpen: Davis accounted for 20% of Minnesota's Late-Inning Pressure pitching; Eufemia, 9%; Filson, 8%; Howe, 4%; Lysander, 4%.

New York Yankees

	W–L	ERA	AB	H	HR	BB	SO	BA	SA	OBA
Season	97-64	3.69	5459	1373	157	518	907	.252	.391	.316
vs. Left-Handers			2294	580	75	258	363	.253	.398	.328
vs. Right-Handers			3165	793	82	260	544	.251	.385	.307
Home	58-22	3.24	2737	670	67	250	471	.245	.369	.308
Road	39-42	4.15	2722	703	90	268	436	.258	.412	.324
Grass	84-53	3.63	4677	1177	132	440	791	.252	.388	.315
Artificial Turf	13-11	4.01	782	196	25	78	116	.251	.403	.317
Day	38-20	3.55	1998	499	55	195	348	.250	.388	.316
Night	59-44	3.76	3461	874	102	323	559	.253	.392	.316
April	6-12	3.97	613	164	20	55	101	.268	.411	.325
May	18-8	3.54	845	196	24	84	121	.232	.369	.301
June	13-14	3.72	943	238	27	82	157	.252	.389	.312
July	18-10	3.59	915	227	21	80	131	.248	.368	.308
August	20-8	3.45	972	245	28	89	178	.252	.392	.314
Sept./Oct.	22-12	3.91	1171	303	37	128	219	.259	.412	.332
Leading Off Inn.			1322	343	37	119	197	.259	.398	.323
Bases Empty			3166	775	95	287	523	.245	.386	.310
Runners On			2293	598	62	231	384	.261	.397	.324
Runners/Scor. Pos.			1257	316	32	157	228	.251	.385	.325
Runners On/2 Out			954	240	29	122	178	.252	.398	.336
Scor. Pos./2 Out			585	137	14	90	115	.234	.361	.336
Late Inning Pressure			946	242	23	99	180	.256	.368	.327
Leading Off			233	60	5	20	40	.258	.361	.319
Bases Empty			543	141	15	41	99	.260	.383	.314
Runners On			403	101	8	58	81	.251	.347	.343
Runners/Scor. Pos.			229	57	2	41	47	.249	.323	.359
First 9 Batters			2657	624	63	257	508	.235	.353	.301
Second 9 Batters			1458	387	39	134	216	.265	.407	.326
All Batters Thereafter			1344	362	55	127	183	.269	.447	.333

Starting pitchers: 71–44, 4.03 ERA
Relief pitchers: 26–20, 2.91 ERA (lowest in A.L.)
Ground outs-to-air outs ratio: 0.93 (2d-lowest in majors). . . . Opponents grounded into one double play for every 7.88 opportunities, 2d-highest rate in A.L. . . . Relievers compiled a 2.40 ERA at Yankee Stadium, and a 1.87 ERA during the month of August, when their starters lost only four games, the fewest by any A.L. team's starters during any full month last season. . . . Of the 17 pitchers they used last season, 10 pitched for N.L. teams immediately before joining the Yankees; two others had pitched in the N.L. earlier in their careers. . . . How they used their bullpen: Righetti accounted for 29% of New York's Late-Inning Pressure pitching; Fisher, 16%; Bordi, 12%; Shirley, 10%; Allen, 2%. . . . Yogi and Billy used relievers to face a single batter 27 times, 3d-highest total in majors.

Oakland A's

	W–L	ERA	AB	H	HR	BB	SO	BA	SA	OBA
Season	77-85	4.39	5609	1451	172	607	785	.259	.412	.331
vs. Left-Handers			2303	600	67	247	317	.261	.411	.333
vs. Right-Handers			3306	851	105	360	468	.257	.413	.330
Home	43-36	3.82	2791	684	71	307	391	.245	.375	.321
Road	34-49	4.98	2818	767	101	300	394	.272	.450	.341
Grass	67-67	4.17	4642	1172	141	517	651	.252	.399	.328
Artificial Turf	10-18	5.53	967	279	31	90	134	.289	.478	.348
Day	37-24	4.05	2111	532	53	222	282	.252	.386	.325
Night	40-61	4.60	3498	919	119	385	503	.263	.429	.335
April	9-12	5.41	708	184	31	97	99	.260	.459	.350
May	13-12	5.05	888	248	29	102	119	.279	.444	.355
June	17-10	3.78	966	237	20	109	144	.245	.361	.322
July	13-14	3.84	926	253	18	87	110	.273	.394	.336
August	15-14	3.30	998	219	30	101	147	.219	.367	.291
Sept./Oct.	10-23	5.25	1123	310	44	111	166	.276	.458	.339
Leading Off Inn.			1329	361	43	123	168	.272	.432	.337
Bases Empty			3123	803	101	311	428	.257	.417	.327
Runners On			2486	648	71	296	357	.261	.407	.336
Runners/Scor. Pos.			1383	368	40	222	219	.266	.411	.360
Runners On/2 Out			1033	240	27	157	146	.232	.372	.334
Scor. Pos./2 Out			640	141	13	123	103	.220	.339	.346
Late Inning Pressure			919	225	21	101	138	.245	.360	.319
Leading Off			230	62	7	23	25	.270	.400	.336
Bases Empty			532	136	11	48	75	.256	.376	.317
Runners On			387	89	10	53	63	.230	.339	.321
Runners/Scor. Pos.			206	54	3	40	42	.262	.340	.378
First 9 Batters			2952	726	74	350	465	.246	.381	.326
Second 9 Batters			1543	418	53	142	204	.271	.444	.334
All Batters Thereafter			1114	307	45	115	116	.276	.451	.343

Starting pitchers: 54–61, 4.77 ERA
Relief pitchers: 23–24, 3.80 ERA
Ground outs-to-air outs ratio: 0.91 (lowest in majors). . . . Opponents grounded into one double play for every 10.69 opportunities, lowest rate in A.L. . . . Starters pitched an average of 5.65 innings per game, lowest average in A.L.; Atlanta had lowest mark in majors (5.56). . . . Complete games, year by year starting with 1980: 94 (most in A.L. since 1946), 60 (despite the strike), 42, 22, 15, 10 (fewest in A.L.). . . . Had A.L.'s lowest ERA during the month of August, 2d-highest after that. . . . Lost all six road games tied after eight innings. . . . How they used their bullpen: Howell accounted for 31% of Oakland's Late-Inning Pressure pitching; Atherton, 17%; Ontiveros, 13%; McCatty, 4%; Mura, 3%; Langford, 2%. . . . Relief pitchers worked three or more innings 57 times, 2d-highest total in majors, behind Baltimore (65).

Seattle Mariners

	W–L	ERA	AB	H	HR	BB	SO	BA	SA	OBA
Season	74-88	4.68	5496	1456	154	637	868	.265	.407	.343
vs. Left-Handers			2256	591	59	291	350	.262	.404	.348
vs. Right-Handers			3240	865	95	346	518	.267	.409	.340
Home	42-41	4.13	2901	751	78	316	448	.259	.393	.335
Road	32-47	5.30	2595	705	76	321	420	.272	.423	.352
Grass	24-36	5.61	1984	547	62	247	332	.276	.432	.355
Artificial Turf	50-52	4.16	3512	909	92	390	536	.259	.393	.336
Day	18-19	3.80	1218	297	26	139	208	.244	.360	.323
Night	56-69	4.94	4278	1159	128	498	660	.271	.420	.349
April	9-12	5.49	716	200	19	103	97	.279	.426	.372
May	11-14	3.87	862	229	21	91	155	.266	.397	.335
June	16-11	4.59	913	234	21	120	133	.256	.381	.345
July	12-16	4.90	960	256	33	98	150	.267	.429	.334
August	11-17	4.28	944	247	25	114	147	.262	.399	.347
Sept./Oct.	15-18	5.00	1101	290	35	111	186	.263	.411	.332
Leading Off Inn.			1292	330	31	136	194	.255	.389	.329
Bases Empty			3028	744	80	333	494	.246	.381	.324
Runners On			2468	712	74	304	374	.288	.439	.365
Runners/Scor. Pos.			1445	417	44	223	224	.289	.445	.378
Runners On/2 Out			1020	280	41	148	155	.275	.438	.372
Scor. Pos./2 Out			671	187	26	117	101	.279	.446	.392
Late Inning Pressure			797	186	15	107	139	.233	.338	.327
Leading Off			196	48	5	26	32	.245	.372	.336
Bases Empty			460	96	9	59	79	.209	.311	.303
Runners On			337	90	6	48	60	.267	.374	.359
Runners/Scor. Pos.			195	48	5	40	33	.246	.364	.373
First 9 Batters			2829	729	79	338	482	.258	.398	.339
Second 9 Batters			1419	394	38	161	210	.278	.425	.354
All Batters Thereafter			1248	333	37	138	176	.267	.408	.340

Starting pitchers: 52–80 (most losses in majors), 5.13 ERA
Relief pitchers: 22–8 (fewest losses in majors), 4.37 ERA
Ground outs-to-air outs ratio: 1.27 (2d-highest in A.L.). . . . Set an A.L. record with 18 balks, and also became first team ever to lead the league for three consecutive seasons. . . . Used 21 different pitchers, highest total in majors last season. . . . Allowed only 15 home runs in Late-Inning Pressure Situations, lowest total in A.L. . . . Only A.L. team to win every road game in which it led after eight innings. . . . Relievers lost only three road games last season. . . . How they used their bullpen: Nunez accounted for 19% of Seattle's Late-Inning Pressure pitching; Vande Berg, 11%; Thomas, 8%; Long, 5%. . . . Manager Chuck Cottier called on relievers to face a single batter 38 times, the highest total in the A.L.

Texas Rangers

	W–L	ERA	AB	H	HR	BB	SO	BA	SA	OBA
Season	62-99	4.56	5503	1479	173	501	863	.269	.426	.331
vs. Left-Handers			2508	685	78	243	380	.273	.436	.338
vs. Right-Handers			2995	794	95	258	483	.265	.418	.326
Home	37-43	4.64	2831	768	102	225	466	.271	.438	.327
Road	25-56	4.47	2672	711	71	276	397	.266	.414	.336
Grass	55-81	4.65	4688	1257	154	412	743	.268	.428	.329
Artificial Turf	7-18	4.03	815	222	19	89	120	.272	.415	.345
Day	11-25	4.77	1199	323	40	124	188	.269	.430	.339
Night	51-74	4.50	4304	1156	133	377	675	.269	.425	.329
April	7-12	4.26	647	161	20	60	103	.249	.382	.317
May	10-17	3.98	900	229	30	60	134	.254	.421	.301
June	11-17	4.28	961	264	28	83	148	.275	.428	.333
July	11-16	4.70	928	248	31	101	114	.267	.429	.342
August	9-18	5.04	928	268	26	90	155	.289	.450	.353
Sept./Oct.	14-19	4.93	1139	309	38	107	209	.271	.433	.335
Leading Off Inn.			1329	357	42	81	177	.269	.425	.314
Bases Empty			3165	815	91	240	462	.258	.407	.314
Runners On			2338	664	82	261	401	.284	.453	.353
Runners/Scor. Pos.			1371	365	47	179	241	.266	.425	.344
Runners On/2 Out			971	254	23	122	175	.262	.394	.348
Scor. Pos./2 Out			629	153	13	88	115	.243	.358	.338
Late Inning Pressure			866	222	23	85	159	.256	.401	.324
Leading Off			225	49	5	16	45	.218	.347	.276
Bases Empty			541	126	9	38	97	.233	.346	.287
Runners On			325	96	14	47	62	.295	.492	.382
Runners/Scor. Pos.			192	47	7	38	43	.245	.417	.363
First 9 Batters			2814	731	79	266	487	.260	.407	.326
Second 9 Batters			1532	419	57	127	213	.273	.452	.330
All Batters Thereafter			1157	329	37	108	163	.284	.438	.346

Starting pitchers: 46-77, 4.94 ERA
Relief pitchers: 16-22, 3.82 ERA
Ground outs-to-air outs ratio: 1.22.... Starting pitchers had 6-17 record with a 6.52 ERA during the month of August.... The Rangers have not pitched a road-game shutout since August 28, 1984 vs. Kansas City.... Used 14 different starting pitchers last season, as many as the total number of pitchers used by Kansas City and Detroit.... Allowed 35 home runs with two or more runners on base, highest total in majors.... News flash from Elias Time Warp Dept.: Jon Matlack pitched for Texas in 1982, Jim Bibby in 1984.... How they used their bullpen: Harris accounted for 22% of Texas's Late-Inning Pressure pitching; Schmidt, 13%; Rozema, 10%; Stewart, 9%; Henry, 6%; Welsh, 2%.

Toronto Blue Jays

	W–L	ERA	AB	H	HR	BB	SO	BA	SA	OBA
Season	99-62	3.29	5406	1312	147	484	823	.243	.375	.306
vs. Left-Handers			2459	602	69	264	343	.245	.381	.317
vs. Right-Handers			2947	710	78	220	480	.241	.371	.296
Home	54-26	2.93	2711	624	78	223	427	.230	.366	.290
Road	45-36	3.66	2695	688	69	261	396	.255	.385	.322
Grass	35-28	3.81	2071	531	55	211	299	.256	.387	.325
Artificial Turf	64-34	2.97	3335	781	92	273	524	.234	.368	.294
Day	33-24	3.68	1935	478	58	183	304	.247	.392	.313
Night	66-38	3.07	3471	834	89	301	519	.240	.366	.302
April	13-7	3.28	682	164	19	71	104	.240	.374	.315
May	17-8	3.86	837	207	27	84	140	.247	.392	.318
June	16-13	3.51	963	238	24	92	136	.247	.386	.311
July	18-10	2.71	954	231	22	74	126	.242	.362	.297
August	17-10	3.38	895	225	23	59	133	.251	.373	.299
Sept./Oct.	18-14	3.09	1075	247	32	104	184	.230	.367	.299
Leading Off Inn.			1324	329	40	122	186	.248	.403	.315
Bases Empty			3168	759	87	287	459	.240	.373	.306
Runners On			2238	553	60	197	364	.247	.378	.306
Runners/Scor. Pos.			1197	292	26	128	216	.244	.361	.311
Runners On/2 Out			953	227	20	90	173	.238	.346	.307
Scor. Pos./2 Out			578	135	11	57	108	.234	.332	.306
Late Inning Pressure			1010	261	29	110	168	.258	.385	.331
Leading Off			249	58	8	24	42	.233	.369	.300
Bases Empty			583	148	18	55	104	.254	.386	.319
Runners On			427	113	11	55	64	.265	.384	.347
Runners/Scor. Pos.			223	64	6	38	30	.287	.426	.387
First 9 Batters			2727	658	60	260	473	.241	.360	.308
Second 9 Batters			1408	342	42	117	197	.243	.382	.303
All Batters Thereafter			1271	312	45	107	153	.245	.400	.304

Starting pitchers: 64-42 (fewest losses in A.L.), 3.32 ERA (lowest in A.L.)
Relief pitchers: 35-20 (most wins in majors), 3.27 ERA
Ground outs-to-air outs ratio: 1.09.... Led A.L. in ERA for first time in team's history, marking the 11th time in 17 seasons that the A.L. leader has reached the playoffs.... How to win a pennant: fill-in starters Tom Filer, Ron Musselman, and Steve Davis compiled an 8-2 record with a 3.74 ERA in 18 starts; Blue Jays also won all eight of their no-decision starts.... Lost eight games in which they led after eight innings, highest total in majors last season.... How they used their bullpen: Lavelle accounted for 16% of Toronto's Late-Inning Pressure pitching; Caudill, 14%; Lamp, 11%; Acker, 10%; Henke, 9%.... Relief pitchers worked three or more innings only 31 times, 2d-lowest total in A.L., behind Chicago (26).

American League

	W–L	ERA	AB	H	HR	BB	SO	BA	SA	OBA
Season	1132-1132	4.14	77257	20182	2178	7465	11777	.261	.406	.327
vs. Left-Handers			33416	8841	916	3456	4858	.265	.408	.333
vs. Right-Handers			43841	11341	1262	4009	6919	.259	.404	.322
Home	637-494	3.92	39562	10141	1104	3669	6113	.256	.396	.320
Road	494-637	4.38	37695	10041	1074	3796	5664	.266	.415	.334
Grass	803-803	4.20	54812	14362	1591	5382	8443	.262	.406	.329
Artificial Turf	329-329	4.02	22445	5820	587	2083	3334	.259	.405	.324
Day	347-347	4.20	23825	6299	632	2302	3595	.264	.406	.330
Night	785-785	4.12	53432	13883	1546	5163	8182	.260	.406	.326
April	136-136	4.03	9310	2374	246	972	1338	.255	.391	.326
May	180-180	4.04	12116	3131	329	1200	1821	.258	.400	.326
June	188-188	4.04	12912	3352	339	1306	1911	.260	.396	.328
July	193-193	4.18	13143	3462	370	1213	1936	.263	.406	.327
August	198-198	4.16	13534	3563	380	1290	2137	.263	.409	.328
Sept./Oct.	237-237	4.34	16242	4300	514	1484	2634	.265	.422	.327
Leading Off Inn.			18619	4856	519	1544	2638	.261	.409	.321
Bases Empty			43996	11170	1231	3920	6703	.254	.397	.318
Runners On			33261	9012	947	3545	5074	.271	.416	.338
Runners/Scor. Pos.			18881	5067	509	2507	3094	.268	.412	.347
Runners On/2 Out			13927	3501	390	1707	2271	.251	.392	.336
Scor. Pos./2 Out			8805	2188	232	1295	1509	.248	.385	.348
Late Inning Pressure			12977	3353	352	1413	2084	.258	.392	.332
Leading Off			3271	852	102	281	525	.260	.408	.322
Bases Empty			7623	1916	216	648	1236	.251	.389	.313
Runners On			5354	1437	136	765	848	.268	.396	.357
Runners/Scor. Pos.			3091	829	79	607	516	.268	.401	.382
First 9 Batters			37592	9602	966	3825	6325	.255	.390	.325
Second 9 Batters			20763	5478	592	1895	2940	.264	.413	.327
All Batters Thereafter			18902	5102	620	1745	2512	.270	.428	.332

Ground outs-to-air outs ratio: 1.09 (12 percent lower than N.L.).... Royals pitchers were hitless in 18 at bats in the 1985 World Series. A.L. hurlers are now hitless in their last 49 World Series at bats, and have only one hit in 73 at bats since 1977—an RBI single by Tim Stoddard in 1979.... In five World Series using the DH, National League DHs have hit .320, American League DHs .221.... League total of 360 complete games was lowest since 1966, three seasons before expansion to 12 teams.... Starting pitchers lasted an average of 6.17 innings in the A.L., 6.28 innings in the N.L.... Left-handed pitchers started 33.6 percent of A.L. games last season, 31.0 percent of N.L. games. Winning percentage of left-handed A.L. starters (.515) was slightly lower than that of N.L. lefties (.518); even less of a difference between the leagues when comparing winning percentages of right-handed starters: .4923 in the A.L., .4918 in the N.L.

National League

Rick Aguilera

New York Mets	W–L	ERA	AB	H	HR	BB	SO	BA	SA	OBA
Season	10-7	3.24	457	118	8	37	74	.258	.370	.314
vs. Left-Handed Batters			224	54	3	22	37	.241	.330	.310
vs. Right-Handed Batters			233	64	5	15	37	.275	.408	.317
Home	3-2	2.14	169	37	1	12	35	.219	.272	.271
Road	7-5	3.91	288	81	7	25	39	.281	.427	.339
Grass	5-2	1.93	252	56	3	18	48	.222	.302	.274
Artificial Turf	5-5	4.99	205	62	5	19	26	.302	.454	.361
Day	1-2	4.45	117	32	3	16	22	.274	.444	.360
Night	9-5	2.80	340	86	5	21	52	.253	.344	.297
April			0	0	0	0	0	.000	.000	.000
May			0	0	0	0	0	.000	.000	.000
June	1-2	4.73	54	15	1	7	8	.278	.407	.361
July	3-1	0.89	139	25	1	10	23	.180	.259	.240
August	2-2	6.21	114	39	3	8	20	.342	.482	.376
Sept./Oct.	4-2	2.95	150	39	3	12	23	.260	.373	.317
Leading Off Inn.			118	27	4	7	16	.229	.381	.272
Bases Empty			277	67	6	21	41	.242	.361	.298
Runners On			180	51	2	16	33	.283	.383	.338
Runners/Scor. Pos.			107	28	0	10	24	.262	.318	.320
Runners On/2 Out			82	23	0	8	15	.280	.317	.344
Scor. Pos./2 Out			54	13	0	6	12	.241	.241	.317
Late Inning Pressure			29	3	0	3	6	.103	.103	.188
Leading Off			8	1	0	1	1	.125	.125	.222
Bases Empty			21	1	0	2	3	.048	.048	.130
Runners On			8	2	0	1	3	.250	.250	.333
Runners/Scor. Pos.			5	1	0	1	3	.200	.200	.333
First 9 Batters			163	42	1	15	33	.258	.350	.324
Second 9 Batters			152	34	4	10	19	.224	.336	.270
All Batters Thereafter			142	42	3	12	22	.296	.430	.348

Loves to face: Tim Raines (.071, 1-for-14)
Hates to face: Terry Francona (.714, 5-for-7)
Ground outs-to-air outs ratio: 0.95 last season, his first in majors. . . . Additional statistics: 8 double-play ground outs in 80 opportunities, 23 doubles, 2 triples allowed in 122.1 innings last season. . . . Allowed 8 first-inning runs in 19 starts last season. . . . Batting support: 3.47 runs per start. . . . Led N.L. pitchers with 0.89 ERA during July. . . . Batting average of .278 was highest among N.L. pitchers (minimum: 20 AB), and contributed to Mets' staff leading N.L. pitchers in batting. . . . Had a record of 4–4 with a 3.68 ERA when facing an opposing club for the first time, 6–3 record with a 2.92 ERA in subsequent meetings. . . . Brought up specifically to start May 21 game vs. San Diego, which was rained out. He returned to minors unused, but was recalled again in June, and was winning pitcher in relief in his first game with Mets.

Larry Andersen

Philadelphia Phillies	W–L	ERA	AB	H	HR	BB	SO	BA	SA	OBA
Season	3-3	4.32	285	78	5	26	50	.274	.393	.340
vs. Left-Handed Batters			123	38	2	18	17	.309	.415	.403
vs. Right-Handed Batters			162	40	3	8	33	.247	.377	.287
Home	3-0	3.21	161	41	2	11	31	.255	.354	.306
Road	0-3	5.81	124	37	3	15	19	.298	.444	.380
Grass	0-2	5.65	61	19	2	6	9	.311	.443	.373
Artificial Turf	3-1	3.99	224	59	3	20	41	.263	.379	.331
Day	0-0	1.83	74	16	0	5	14	.216	.338	.266
Night	3-3	5.23	211	62	5	21	36	.294	.412	.364
April	0-1	3.60	40	10	0	2	7	.250	.375	.286
May	1-1	5.09	72	19	2	4	13	.264	.431	.303
June	1-0	2.08	62	16	1	3	11	.258	.339	.299
July	1-1	16.20	16	7	1	5	3	.438	.750	.591
August	0-0	6.52	41	14	1	6	9	.341	.439	.426
Sept./Oct.	0-0	2.40	54	12	0	6	7	.222	.278	.311
Leading Off Inn.			59	17	0	5	5	.288	.322	.354
Bases Empty			141	40	2	10	20	.284	.390	.336
Runners On			144	38	3	16	30	.264	.396	.344
Runners/Scor. Pos.			97	24	2	14	16	.247	.361	.345
Runners On/2 Out			57	12	1	8	13	.211	.316	.318
Scor. Pos./2 Out			42	8	1	7	8	.190	.286	.306
Late Inning Pressure			154	46	3	7	28	.299	.429	.329
Leading Off			36	12	0	2	3	.333	.361	.368
Bases Empty			86	28	1	3	12	.326	.442	.348
Runners On			68	18	2	4	16	.265	.412	.306
Runners/Scor. Pos.			39	9	1	4	8	.231	.333	.302
First 9 Batters			270	72	5	26	48	.267	.381	.337
Second 9 Batters			15	6	0	0	2	.400	.600	.400
All Batters Thereafter			0	0	0	0	0	.000	.000	.000

Loves to face: Ryne Sandberg (0-for-14, 3 SO)
Hates to face: Wally Backman (.625, 5-for-8)
Ground outs-to-air outs ratio: 1.75 last season, 1.12 for career. . . . G/A ratios, year by year since '79: 0.54, 0.92, 0.91, 0.86, 1.23, 1.75. . . . Additional statistics: 4 double-play ground outs in 72 opportunities (8th-lowest rate in N.L.), 13 doubles, 3 triples allowed in 73.0 innings last season. . . . Season debut vs. Houston on April 12 foretold a disappointing year. Entered in the sixth inning with 3–1 lead and the tying runs on base. By end of inning, Phillies trailed 7–3, with four runs charged to Andersen in his one-third of an inning. His ERA after one game? 108.00. . . . First home run he allowed in majors was grand-slam by Terry Crowley in 1977, the only four-run job that he has allowed in eight seasons (47 bases-loaded at bats). . . . Relief ERA of 4.32 was 8th-highest among N.L. pitchers with at least 30 relief games.

Joaquin Andujar

St. Louis Cardinals	W–L	ERA	AB	H	HR	BB	SO	BA	SA	OBA
Season	21-12	3.40	1019	265	15	82	112	.260	.362	.321
vs. Left-Handed Batters			494	148	6	44	41	.300	.405	.357
vs. Right-Handed Batters			525	117	9	38	71	.223	.322	.286
Home	9-9	3.06	534	133	7	43	55	.249	.337	.310
Road	12-3	3.81	485	132	8	39	57	.272	.390	.333
Grass	8-1	4.12	292	85	5	24	30	.291	.418	.349
Artificial Turf	13-11	3.13	727	180	10	58	82	.248	.340	.309
Day	5-6	5.19	330	85	8	33	43	.258	.403	.327
Night	16-6	2.58	689	180	7	49	69	.261	.343	.318
April	4-0	2.61	146	35	2	8	17	.240	.329	.293
May	5-1	3.18	155	44	2	8	17	.284	.387	.325
June	4-2	1.86	176	37	1	9	25	.210	.256	.249
July	4-2	2.30	201	52	2	20	17	.259	.323	.330
August	3-2	4.95	161	42	3	24	17	.261	.404	.366
Sept./Oct.	1-5	5.76	180	55	5	13	19	.306	.478	.352
Leading Off Inn.			261	73	2	14	29	.280	.375	.321
Bases Empty			586	155	8	44	71	.265	.365	.321
Runners On			433	110	7	38	41	.254	.358	.320
Runners/Scor. Pos.			239	65	4	28	24	.272	.389	.350
Runners On/2 Out			181	50	3	18	13	.276	.376	.345
Scor. Pos./2 Out			112	27	1	15	9	.241	.321	.331
Late Inning Pressure			110	23	2	19	9	.209	.327	.336
Leading Off			30	8	2	2	4	.267	.567	.313
Bases Empty			62	13	2	11	5	.210	.371	.329
Runners On			48	10	0	8	4	.208	.271	.345
Runners/Scor. Pos.			30	6	0	8	3	.200	.267	.385
First 9 Batters			307	80	3	23	40	.261	.332	.319
Second 9 Batters			298	79	3	22	40	.265	.356	.317
All Batters Thereafter			414	106	9	37	32	.256	.389	.325

Loves to face: Brett Butler (.077, 1-for-13)
Hates to face: Paul Householder (.556, 5-for-9)
Ground outs-to-air outs ratio: 1.29 last season, 1.36 for career. . . . Additional statistics: 32 double-play ground outs in 202 opportunities, 51 doubles (2d-most in N.L.), 4 triples allowed in 269.2 innings last season. . . . Ranked 7th among N.L. pitchers with an average of 7.10 innings per start. . . . Allowed 15 first-inning runs in 38 starts last season. . . . Batting support: 4.89 runs per start, 5th-highest average in N.L. (minimum: 15 GS). . . . Has never allowed a grand-slam in majors (106 bases-loaded at bats). Could *that* be why he went berserk in the Series after walking Jim Sundberg to bring up Bye-Bye Balboni with the bases loaded? He got himself ejected, but protected his record. . . . Career record vs. N.L. East: 61–42, .590; vs. N.L. West: 49–59, .454. . . . Only pitcher so far to defeat Dwight Gooden twice.

Len Barker

Atlanta Braves	W–L	ERA	AB	H	HR	BB	SO	BA	SA	OBA
Season	2-9	6.35	292	84	10	37	47	.288	.449	.367
vs. Left-Handed Batters			162	49	7	24	24	.302	.500	.392
vs. Right-Handed Batters			130	35	3	13	23	.269	.385	.336
Home	2-6	5.92	204	59	4	25	34	.289	.407	.368
Road	0-3	7.36	88	25	6	12	13	.284	.545	.366
Grass	2-8	7.09	243	74	9	33	38	.305	.477	.388
Artificial Turf	0-1	3.21	49	10	1	4	9	.204	.306	.259
Day	0-2	16.20	43	18	4	6	3	.419	.767	.490
Night	2-7	5.10	249	66	6	31	44	.265	.394	.346
April	0-1	3.77	53	11	0	3	12	.208	.283	.250
May	1-3	4.08	106	27	2	13	13	.255	.368	.333
June			0	0	0	0	0	.000	.000	.000
July	0-0	12.15	28	12	2	3	2	.429	.679	.469
August	1-2	8.10	57	18	2	8	15	.316	.474	.400
Sept./Oct.	0-3	10.13	48	16	4	10	5	.333	.646	.458
Leading Off Inn.			64	20	2	13	9	.313	.453	.429
Bases Empty			151	43	5	21	23	.285	.437	.372
Runners On			141	41	5	16	24	.291	.461	.363
Runners/Scor. Pos.			82	27	4	10	14	.329	.549	.400
Runners On/2 Out			55	15	3	7	9	.273	.491	.365
Scor. Pos./2 Out			35	9	2	5	7	.257	.457	.366
Late Inning Pressure			6	0	0	0	1	.000	.000	.000
Leading Off			2	0	0	0	0	.000	.000	.000
Bases Empty			6	0	0	0	1	.000	.000	.000
Runners On			0	0	0	0	0	.000	.000	.000
Runners/Scor. Pos.			0	0	0	0	0	.000	.000	.000
First 9 Batters			144	44	6	22	30	.306	.493	.399
Second 9 Batters			109	32	3	14	13	.294	.431	.371
All Batters Thereafter			39	8	1	1	4	.205	.333	.225

Loves to face: Glenn Wilson (0-for-9)
Hates to face: Mike Marshall (.500, 8-for-16, 3 HR)
Ground outs-to-air outs ratio: 1.15 last season, 1.17 for career. . . . Additional statistics: 4 double-play ground outs in 64 opportunities, 17 doubles, 0 triples allowed in 73.2 innings last season. . . . Average of 3.94 innings per start was lowest among N.L. pitchers (minimum: 15 GS). . . . Allowed 17 first-inning runs in 18 starts last season. . . . Batting support: 2.89 runs per start, 4th-lowest average in N.L. (minimum: 15 GS). . . . ERA of 6.35 was highest in the N.L. among pitchers who started at least 15 games. . . . 1985 Braves had the worst record (66–96) of any team that Barker has pitched for in the major leagues. That says a lot when you consider who his past employers have been: Texas, 1976–78; Cleveland, 1979–83. . . . Opponents' on-base percentage leading off innings (.429) was highest of his career, 91 points higher than his career rate.

Steve Bedrosian

Atlanta Braves	W–L	ERA	AB	H	HR	BB	SO	BA	SA	OBA
Season	7-15	3.83	778	198	17	111	134	.254	.373	.349
vs. Left-Handed Batters			385	109	13	66	43	.283	.444	.386
vs. Right-Handed Batters			393	89	4	45	91	.226	.303	.309
Home	4-5	3.46	367	100	9	41	66	.272	.387	.346
Road	3-10	4.16	411	98	8	70	68	.238	.360	.351
Grass	5-9	3.87	563	146	16	67	95	.259	.387	.338
Artificial Turf	2-6	3.75	215	52	1	44	39	.242	.335	.374
Day	3-8	3.82	275	66	4	52	52	.240	.360	.363
Night	4-7	3.84	503	132	13	59	82	.262	.380	.340
April	0-1	3.33	106	28	1	13	14	.264	.349	.342
May	2-2	2.41	139	35	4	14	27	.252	.396	.320
June	3-3	2.75	144	36	2	26	24	.250	.354	.366
July	0-4	6.14	111	29	4	21	21	.261	.441	.381
August	0-1	2.84	141	33	4	15	23	.234	.355	.306
Sept./Oct.	2-4	6.06	137	37	2	22	25	.270	.350	.377
Leading Off Inn.			197	51	4	23	28	.259	.386	.336
Bases Empty			460	110	8	55	84	.239	.350	.322
Runners On			318	88	9	56	50	.277	.406	.384
Runners/Scor. Pos.			196	46	5	40	38	.235	.337	.362
Runners On/2 Out			134	35	4	24	22	.261	.403	.385
Scor. Pos./2 Out			93	21	2	16	19	.226	.323	.351
Late Inning Pressure			29	12	0	3	2	.414	.448	.485
Leading Off			8	2	0	2	1	.250	.250	.400
Bases Empty			15	5	0	2	2	.333	.333	.444
Runners On			14	7	0	1	0	.500	.571	.533
Runners/Scor. Pos.			7	1	0	1	0	.143	.143	.250
First 9 Batters			287	63	8	37	57	.220	.355	.306
Second 9 Batters			284	72	4	39	51	.254	.335	.340
All Batters Thereafter			207	63	5	35	26	.304	.449	.415

Loves to face: Jody Davis (0-for-11, 6 SO)
Hates to face: Ray Knight (.529, 9-for-17, 2 HR)
Ground outs-to-air outs ratio: 1.04 last season, 0.88 for career. . . . Additional statistics: 17 double-play ground outs in 152 opportunities, 33 doubles, 4 triples allowed in 206.2 innings last season. . . . Average of 5.59 innings per start was 10th-lowest among N.L. pitchers (minimum: 15 GS). . . . Allowed 22 first-inning runs in 37 starts (tied for 7th-most in N.L.) last season. . . . Batting support: 3.73 runs per start. . . . Started 37 games last season without a complete game, breaking major-league record of 33 set by Milt Wilcox in 1984; Bedrock's longest outing was seven innings. Has career total of 46 starts without a complete game. . . . Led major leagues with 15 no-decisions in 1985. . . . Rate of 4.83 walks per nine innings was 6th-highest in N.L. (minimum: 15 starts). . . . Has faced 1,121 batters with runners on base, most by any active N.L. pitcher who has never balked.

Tom Browning

Cincinnati Reds	W–L	ERA	AB	H	HR	BB	SO	BA	SA	OBA
Season	20-9	3.55	987	242	29	73	155	.245	.384	.297
vs. Left-Handed Batters			148	33	1	11	32	.223	.277	.282
vs. Right-Handed Batters			839	209	28	62	123	.249	.403	.300
Home	10-6	4.11	506	134	14	38	70	.265	.403	.318
Road	10-3	2.98	481	108	15	35	85	.225	.364	.276
Grass	4-2	3.24	303	68	8	26	53	.224	.337	.285
Artificial Turf	16-7	3.69	684	174	21	47	102	.254	.405	.303
Day	5-3	4.09	354	88	9	34	62	.249	.387	.316
Night	15-6	3.24	633	154	20	39	93	.243	.382	.287
April	2-0	0.38	86	14	0	3	14	.163	.186	.189
May	2-4	4.07	157	43	4	13	22	.274	.389	.326
June	3-1	5.24	133	34	4	19	26	.256	.421	.349
July	2-3	4.25	184	44	8	10	21	.239	.413	.279
August	5-1	2.49	193	47	5	11	28	.244	.363	.283
Sept./Oct.	6-0	3.79	234	60	8	17	44	.256	.427	.311
Leading Off Inn.			256	61	9	15	37	.238	.371	.280
Bases Empty			612	152	17	38	103	.248	.366	.296
Runners On			375	90	12	35	52	.240	.413	.300
Runners/Scor. Pos.			175	47	10	26	20	.269	.520	.351
Runners On/2 Out			165	35	5	17	25	.212	.364	.286
Scor. Pos./2 Out			86	23	5	14	10	.267	.535	.370
Late Inning Pressure			71	16	1	6	9	.225	.324	.286
Leading Off			17	4	0	3	3	.235	.235	.350
Bases Empty			36	10	0	5	5	.278	.278	.366
Runners On			35	6	1	1	4	.171	.371	.194
Runners/Scor. Pos.			14	3	1	1	1	.214	.571	.267
First 9 Batters			310	64	5	25	67	.206	.303	.267
Second 9 Batters			308	89	9	21	44	.289	.432	.332
All Batters Thereafter			369	89	15	27	44	.241	.412	.293

Loves to face: Jerry Mumphrey (0-for-9)
Hates to face: Ron Cey (.417, 5-for-12, 2 2B, 2 HR)
Ground outs-to-air outs ratio: 0.64 last season (7th-lowest in N.L.), 0.64 for career. . . . Additional statistics: 18 double-play ground outs in 180 opportunities, 48 doubles (tied for 3d-most in N.L.), 1 triple allowed in 261.1 innings last season. . . . Total of 78 extra-base hits allowed was 3d-highest in N.L. . . . Set N.L. *Player Analysis* record with 72 extra-base hits allowed to right-handed batters. . . . Allowed 10 first-inning runs in 38 starts, 4th-lowest rate in N.L. last season (minimum: 15 GS). . . . Batting support: 4.79 runs per start, 10th-highest average in N.L. (minimum: 15 GS). . . . First major-league rookie to win 20 games since Bob Grim in 1954. . . . April ERA (0.38) was 2d-lowest in N.L. . . . Tied for N.L. lead in losses in May (4); led N.L. in wins for August (5) and September (6). . . . 17 hits as batter ranked third among N.L. pitchers.

Vida Blue

San Francisco Giants	W–L	ERA	AB	H	HR	BB	SO	BA	SA	OBA
Season	8-8	4.47	479	115	17	80	103	.240	.411	.348
vs. Left-Handed Batters			75	15	2	8	18	.200	.307	.286
vs. Right-Handed Batters			404	100	15	72	85	.248	.431	.359
Home	6-2	4.44	285	61	14	44	56	.214	.407	.317
Road	2-6	4.50	194	54	3	36	47	.278	.418	.392
Grass	8-6	4.36	440	106	15	71	97	.241	.407	.346
Artificial Turf	0-2	5.56	39	9	2	9	6	.231	.462	.375
Day	5-1	3.56	277	58	12	42	58	.209	.394	.311
Night	3-7	5.81	202	57	5	38	45	.282	.436	.398
April	2-0	0.00	13	3	0	2	3	.231	.308	.333
May	0-1	13.50	16	6	1	6	4	.375	.750	.545
June	2-1	2.30	113	22	1	19	26	.195	.265	.311
July	1-2	6.46	59	21	2	8	10	.356	.593	.433
August	0-2	5.64	113	28	4	19	28	.248	.398	.353
Sept./Oct.	3-2	4.05	165	35	9	26	32	.212	.430	.320
Leading Off Inn.			116	29	3	19	22	.250	.405	.360
Bases Empty			263	61	8	55	54	.232	.395	.367
Runners On			216	54	9	25	49	.250	.431	.324
Runners/Scor. Pos.			107	31	5	14	18	.290	.486	.363
Runners On/2 Out			97	23	5	15	21	.237	.423	.339
Scor. Pos./2 Out			52	12	3	8	10	.231	.423	.333
Late Inning Pressure			24	5	1	5	8	.208	.375	.333
Leading Off			6	1	1	3	3	.167	.667	.444
Bases Empty			18	3	1	3	7	.167	.389	.286
Runners On			6	2	0	2	1	.333	.333	.444
Runners/Scor. Pos.			4	1	0	2	0	.250	.250	.429
First 9 Batters			203	48	7	42	45	.236	.409	.367
Second 9 Batters			152	38	5	21	24	.250	.414	.343
All Batters Thereafter			124	29	5	17	34	.234	.411	.322

Loves to face: Terry Harper (.095, 2-for-21)
Hates to face: Jack Clark (.800, 4-for-5, 2 HR)
Ground outs-to-air outs ratio: 0.89 last season, 0.92 for career. . . . Additional statistics: 7 double-play ground outs in 91 opportunities, 29 doubles, 1 triple allowed in 131.0 innings last season. . . . Allowed 6 first-inning runs in 20 starts, 10th-lowest rate in N.L. last season (minimum: 15 GS). . . . Batting support: 4.80 runs per start, 8th-highest average in N.L. (minimum: 15 GS). . . . Walked 5.50 batters per nine innings, most among N.L. pitchers who started at least 15 games. . . . Struck out in *only* 40 percent of his at bats last season, bringing his career rate down to 52.03 percent. Among players with 100 or more career strikeouts, only Joaquin Andujar (52.04) and Blue have fanned on more than half of their at bats. Now that Joaquin will not bat (another argument against the DH?), Blue has a clear field to take the lead.

Warren Brusstar

Chicago Cubs	W–L	ERA	AB	H	HR	BB	SO	BA	SA	OBA
Season	4-3	6.05	298	87	8	36	34	.292	.453	.368
vs. Left-Handed Batters			124	35	2	18	14	.282	.419	.372
vs. Right-Handed Batters			174	52	6	18	20	.299	.477	.365
Home	3-0	6.69	143	46	4	19	18	.322	.490	.400
Road	1-3	5.49	155	41	4	17	16	.265	.419	.339
Grass	4-2	5.59	222	64	6	24	25	.288	.441	.361
Artificial Turf	0-1	7.50	76	23	2	12	9	.303	.487	.389
Day	3-2	5.36	186	54	4	20	23	.290	.430	.358
Night	1-1	7.36	112	33	4	16	11	.295	.491	.385
April	0-0	0.00	15	4	0	2	0	.267	.267	.353
May	0-1	6.75	37	10	1	8	5	.270	.405	.413
June	1-0	3.21	55	13	1	5	8	.236	.400	.300
July	1-0	6.95	90	27	1	8	12	.300	.433	.363
August	2-2	5.40	87	27	3	9	8	.310	.471	.364
Sept./Oct.	0-0	21.60	14	6	2	4	1	.429	1.000	.556
Leading Off Inn.			64	12	2	7	7	.188	.359	.278
Bases Empty			153	39	3	13	12	.255	.379	.317
Runners On			145	48	5	23	22	.331	.531	.417
Runners/Scor. Pos.			96	31	3	20	19	.323	.479	.421
Runners On/2 Out			59	18	1	11	11	.305	.424	.423
Scor. Pos./2 Out			45	13	1	9	10	.289	.400	.407
Late Inning Pressure			99	28	1	9	11	.283	.384	.349
Leading Off			27	5	1	3	5	.185	.407	.267
Bases Empty			64	16	1	4	7	.250	.359	.294
Runners On			35	12	0	5	4	.343	.429	.439
Runners/Scor. Pos.			22	9	0	5	2	.409	.500	.519
First 9 Batters			268	76	6	32	31	.284	.425	.362
Second 9 Batters			30	11	2	4	3	.367	.700	.429
All Batters Thereafter			0	0	0	0	0	.000	.000	.000

Loves to face: Steve Sax (0-for-11)
Hates to face: Bill Russell (.421, 8-for-19)
Ground outs-to-air outs ratio: 1.12 last season (lowest of his career), 1.75 for career. . . . Additional statistics: 5 double-play ground outs in 76 opportunities, 16 doubles, 4 triples allowed in 74.1 innings last season. . . . Relief ERA of 6.05 was 2d-highest among N.L. pitchers with at least 30 relief games. . . . Career total of 340 relief appearances ranks 6th among active pitchers who have never started a game. . . . Career winning percentage (28–16, .636) ranks 7th among active pitchers with 20 or more wins. . . . Allowed two grand-slam homers last season. Opponents have hit .340 (17-for-50) with the bases loaded since 1982. . . . Two longest outings of the season (3.1 and 3.2 innings) came on consecutive days immediately prior to the All-Star break.

Tim Burke

Montreal Expos	W–L	ERA	AB	H	HR	BB	SO	BA	SA	OBA
Season	9-4	2.39	421	86	9	44	87	.204	.309	.288
vs. Left-Handed Batters			186	47	3	30	28	.253	.360	.355
vs. Right-Handed Batters			235	39	6	14	59	.166	.268	.233
Home	4-3	2.88	178	40	4	17	42	.225	.365	.296
Road	5-1	2.05	243	46	5	27	45	.189	.267	.283
Grass	2-0	1.90	147	27	4	14	28	.184	.286	.271
Artificial Turf	7-4	2.67	274	59	5	30	59	.215	.321	.298
Day	1-0	2.01	179	31	4	20	38	.173	.268	.261
Night	8-4	2.70	242	55	5	24	49	.227	.339	.309
April	0-0	3.00	43	11	1	7	9	.256	.395	.353
May	1-0	1.84	53	10	0	3	13	.189	.245	.232
June	3-0	0.96	64	13	1	5	13	.203	.297	.282
July	1-0	1.21	69	10	1	12	11	.145	.203	.277
August	3-2	2.08	74	13	2	5	18	.176	.297	.238
Sept./Oct.	1-2	4.35	118	29	4	12	23	.246	.381	.328
Leading Off Inn.			95	28	4	12	16	.295	.474	.380
Bases Empty			230	50	6	21	48	.217	.335	.291
Runners On			191	36	3	23	39	.188	.277	.285
Runners/Scor. Pos.			136	20	2	20	31	.147	.243	.265
Runners On/2 Out			86	16	1	12	19	.186	.244	.300
Scor. Pos./2 Out			67	9	1	11	16	.134	.209	.275
Late Inning Pressure			202	39	5	23	38	.193	.302	.288
Leading Off			51	15	3	8	8	.294	.510	.400
Bases Empty			119	25	4	13	25	.210	.345	.299
Runners On			83	14	1	10	13	.169	.241	.274
Runners/Scor. Pos.			59	7	1	9	11	.119	.220	.246
First 9 Batters			373	73	9	43	81	.196	.308	.288
Second 9 Batters			48	13	0	1	6	.271	.313	.294
All Batters Thereafter			0	0	0	0	0	.000	.000	.000

Loves to face: Ken Landreaux (0-for-5, 2 SO)
Hates to face: Pedro Guerrero (.750, 3-for-4, 1 HR)
Ground outs-to-air outs ratio: 1.87 last season, his first in majors. . . . Additional statistics: 11 double-play ground outs in 85 opportunities, 17 doubles, 0 triples allowed in 120.1 innings last season. . . . ERA of 1.90 on grass fields was 3d-lowest in N.L. . . . ERA of 2.36 was lowest among major-league rookies (minimum: 100 IP). . . . Led N.L. with 78 appearances (N.L. record for a rookie) and 120.1 relief innings. . . . First rookie pitcher to lead N.L. in games since Jack Baldschun in 1961. . . . Nine relief wins last season were tied for 2d-most in the N.L. . . . Allowed 6.43 hits per nine innings last season, 2d-best rate among N.L. relievers (minimum: 30 games). . . . Set Expos record with eight consecutive wins to start the season. . . . 1985 breakdown: 8–0, 1.56 ERA through Aug. 17; 1–4, 4.08 ERA after.

Jeff Calhoun

Houston Astros	W–L	ERA	AB	H	HR	BB	SO	BA	SA	OBA
Season	2-5	2.54	230	56	2	24	47	.243	.313	.313
vs. Left-Handed Batters			58	9	1	5	16	.155	.207	.215
vs. Right-Handed Batters			172	47	1	19	31	.273	.349	.346
Home	2-3	2.83	128	31	1	9	25	.242	.297	.290
Road	0-2	2.20	102	25	1	15	22	.245	.333	.339
Grass	0-0	0.54	51	7	0	10	12	.137	.196	.279
Artificial Turf	2-5	3.26	179	49	2	14	35	.274	.346	.323
Day	0-1	3.00	45	12	0	5	11	.267	.333	.333
Night	2-4	2.44	185	44	2	19	36	.238	.308	.307
April	0-0	4.91	27	9	1	4	5	.333	.444	.419
May	0-1	3.18	42	12	0	2	5	.286	.333	.318
June	0-0	0.00	12	1	0	3	3	.083	.083	.250
July	1-0	1.26	50	10	0	5	13	.200	.200	.273
August	0-2	1.93	37	10	0	5	8	.270	.405	.349
Sept./Oct.	1-2	3.12	62	14	1	5	13	.226	.323	.284
Leading Off Inn.			55	10	0	4	12	.182	.218	.237
Bases Empty			127	31	0	10	31	.244	.299	.299
Runners On			103	25	2	14	16	.243	.330	.328
Runners/Scor. Pos.			63	17	1	9	12	.270	.365	.351
Runners On/2 Out			42	10	2	8	7	.238	.429	.360
Scor. Pos./2 Out			32	6	1	5	7	.188	.344	.297
Late Inning Pressure			117	31	1	13	23	.265	.333	.336
Leading Off			31	4	0	2	6	.129	.194	.182
Bases Empty			71	17	0	5	16	.239	.310	.289
Runners On			46	14	1	8	7	.304	.370	.400
Runners/Scor. Pos.			30	9	1	6	5	.300	.400	.405
First 9 Batters			208	49	2	21	44	.236	.298	.303
Second 9 Batters			22	7	0	3	3	.318	.455	.400
All Batters Thereafter			0	0	0	0	0	.000	.000	.000

Loves to face: Kevin McReynolds (0-for-4, 3 SO)
Hates to face: Johnny Ray (3-for-3, 2 2B)
Ground outs-to-air outs ratio: 1.34 last season, 1.35 for career. . . . Additional statistics: 13 double-play ground outs in 52 opportunities (2d-highest rate in N.L.), 8 doubles, 1 triple allowed in 63.2 innings last season. . . . Ranked 10th among N.L. relief pitchers with a 2.54 ERA (minimum: 30 relief games). . . . Sept. 27 home run by Dave Parker is the only extra-base hit allowed to an opposing left-handed batter in 84 career plate appearances. Opponents' career slugging average is .176 by left-handed batters, .320 by right-handers. . . . Has pitched longer than three innings only once in his career (4 IP vs. Cincinnati on May 12). Has never been charged with more than two runs in any of 53 major-league games. . . . Opponents' career batting average of .167 (6-for-36) with two outs and runners in scoring position.

Rick Camp

Atlanta Braves	W–L	ERA	AB	H	HR	BB	SO	BA	SA	OBA
Season	4-6	3.95	494	130	8	61	49	.263	.358	.348
vs. Left-Handed Batters			253	68	1	39	20	.269	.328	.364
vs. Right-Handed Batters			241	62	7	22	29	.257	.390	.331
Home	1-5	5.74	258	75	6	38	28	.291	.407	.384
Road	3-1	2.13	236	55	2	23	21	.233	.305	.307
Grass	1-5	4.89	370	105	7	47	34	.284	.384	.368
Artificial Turf	3-1	1.51	124	25	1	14	15	.202	.282	.288
Day	1-0	1.89	124	27	2	9	7	.218	.298	.269
Night	3-6	4.67	370	103	6	52	42	.278	.378	.373
April	0-3	5.73	49	17	2	4	4	.347	.551	.396
May	1-0	2.49	85	20	1	11	9	.235	.282	.323
June	1-0	2.49	78	18	0	11	11	.231	.269	.333
July	0-2	4.15	95	27	2	10	6	.284	.389	.349
August	0-1	5.48	88	23	2	11	7	.261	.375	.343
Sept./Oct.	2-0	4.07	99	25	1	14	12	.253	.354	.362
Leading Off Inn.			102	29	5	16	9	.284	.461	.387
Bases Empty			236	66	7	28	22	.280	.432	.361
Runners On			258	64	1	33	27	.248	.291	.337
Runners/Scor. Pos.			163	44	1	25	18	.270	.313	.368
Runners On/2 Out			119	36	1	12	17	.303	.361	.371
Scor. Pos./2 Out			80	26	1	10	12	.325	.363	.407
Late Inning Pressure			148	42	1	17	19	.284	.365	.357
Leading Off			37	12	1	3	4	.324	.432	.375
Bases Empty			81	26	1	5	9	.321	.432	.368
Runners On			67	16	0	12	10	.239	.284	.346
Runners/Scor. Pos.			33	11	0	12	6	.333	.364	.489
First 9 Batters			397	102	7	50	35	.257	.350	.344
Second 9 Batters			87	26	0	9	14	.299	.368	.371
All Batters Thereafter			10	2	1	2	0	.200	.600	.333

Loves to face: Tony Pena (.071, 1-for-14)
Hates to face: Johnny Ray (.500, 8-for-16)
Ground outs-to-air outs ratio: 1.99 last season, 1.88 for career (2.46 vs. left-handed batters, 1.52 vs. right-handers). . . . Additional statistics: 24 double-play ground outs in 132 opportunities (7th-highest rate in N.L.), 23 doubles, 0 triples allowed in 127.2 innings last season. . . . Faced more batters in relief (523) than any pitcher in N.L. last season. . . . Career total of 65 games started, highest among active pitchers without a complete-game shutout. . . . Game-tying home run with two outs in 18th inning, July 4 vs. Mets, came off lefty Tom Gorman, but he always hit left-handers (.082 career) better than right-handers (.071). . . . Had a chance to tie the game again with two on in the 19th, this time against right-hander Ron Darling, but struck out to end game at 3:55 a.m.; then the fireworks show started.

Bill Campbell

St. Louis Cardinals	W–L	ERA	AB	H	HR	BB	SO	BA	SA	OBA
Season	5-3	3.50	239	55	5	21	41	.230	.326	.294
vs. Left-Handed Batters			97	22	1	14	13	.227	.299	.321
vs. Right-Handed Batters			142	33	4	7	28	.232	.345	.275
Home	1-1	3.64	110	26	3	8	19	.236	.336	.292
Road	4-2	3.38	129	29	2	13	22	.225	.318	.297
Grass	2-1	2.21	69	11	0	5	11	.159	.203	.224
Artificial Turf	3-2	4.09	170	44	5	16	30	.259	.376	.323
Day	2-0	5.26	98	23	4	14	19	.235	.388	.339
Night	3-3	2.33	141	32	1	7	22	.227	.284	.260
April	0-1	5.79	38	11	1	5	8	.289	.447	.378
May	1-0	0.00	47	7	0	2	3	.149	.149	.184
June	1-0	8.38	39	13	1	4	4	.333	.487	.395
July	0-1	3.24	28	7	1	2	5	.250	.393	.290
August	2-1	3.18	41	8	1	1	11	.195	.268	.209
Sept./Oct.	1-0	2.13	46	9	1	7	10	.196	.283	.315
Leading Off Inn.			56	14	1	2	8	.250	.393	.276
Bases Empty			130	29	2	6	22	.223	.315	.257
Runners On			109	26	3	15	19	.239	.339	.333
Runners/Scor. Pos.			82	18	3	13	14	.220	.354	.323
Runners On/2 Out			47	7	1	5	11	.149	.213	.245
Scor. Pos./2 Out			35	6	1	5	7	.171	.257	.293
Late Inning Pressure			60	13	0	6	11	.217	.267	.290
Leading Off			18	4	0	1	2	.222	.333	.263
Bases Empty			41	9	0	2	6	.220	.268	.256
Runners On			19	4	0	4	5	.211	.263	.346
Runners/Scor. Pos.			12	2	0	3	4	.167	.250	.333
First 9 Batters			222	52	4	20	40	.234	.324	.300
Second 9 Batters			17	3	1	1	1	.176	.353	.222
All Batters Thereafter			0	0	0	0	0	.000	.000	.000

Loves to face: Chili Davis (0-for-9, 3 SO)
Hates to face: Pete Rose (.571, 4-for-7)
Ground outs-to-air outs ratio: 1.25 last season, 1.33 for career. . . . Additional statistics: 3 double-play ground outs in 52 opportunities (9th-lowest rate in N.L.), 8 doubles, 0 triples allowed in 64.1 innings last season. . . . Opponents have hit for a higher average with runners on base than with bases empty in each of last five seasons. . . . Yearly batting averages of opposing left-handed batters since 1983: .265, .250, .227. . . . Opponents' batting averages with runners in scoring position since '83: .280, .255, .220. . . . Pitched to 11 batters with bases loaded last season, allowed only one single. . . . Over 11 years of *The Player Analysis* opponents have batted .199 (50-for-251) with two outs and runners in scoring position in Late-Inning Pressure Situations. . . . Allowed 10 steals in 11 attempts last season.

Steve Carlton

Philadelphia Phillies	W–L	ERA	AB	H	HR	BB	SO	BA	SA	OBA
Season	1-8	3.33	338	84	6	53	48	.249	.358	.349
vs. Left-Handed Batters			43	10	0	4	5	.233	.256	.298
vs. Right-Handed Batters			295	74	6	49	43	.251	.373	.357
Home	1-3	1.22	156	32	2	19	19	.205	.288	.290
Road	0-5	5.29	182	52	4	34	29	.286	.418	.398
Grass	0-2	4.10	96	23	3	17	18	.240	.385	.354
Artificial Turf	1-6	3.02	242	61	3	36	30	.252	.347	.348
Day	0-3	5.08	132	44	3	19	17	.333	.470	.414
Night	1-5	2.31	206	40	3	34	31	.194	.286	.308
April	0-2	3.24	93	24	0	15	11	.258	.312	.361
May	1-2	1.23	106	22	2	13	17	.208	.311	.292
June	0-3	3.09	84	22	2	14	8	.262	.357	.367
July			0	0	0	0	0	.000	.000	.000
August			0	0	0	0	0	.000	.000	.000
Sept./Oct.	0-1	8.16	55	16	2	11	12	.291	.527	.409
Leading Off Inn.			80	25	3	15	10	.313	.488	.421
Bases Empty			174	45	3	29	24	.259	.356	.365
Runners On			164	39	3	24	24	.238	.360	.333
Runners/Scor. Pos.			90	20	2	18	13	.222	.344	.349
Runners On/2 Out			65	16	1	12	12	.246	.369	.364
Scor. Pos./2 Out			41	8	1	10	7	.195	.341	.353
Late Inning Pressure			12	2	0	4	0	.167	.167	.375
Leading Off			3	2	0	1	0	.667	.667	.750
Bases Empty			4	2	0	2	0	.500	.500	.667
Runners On			8	0	0	2	0	.000	.000	.200
Runners/Scor. Pos.			5	0	0	2	0	.000	.000	.286
First 9 Batters			126	23	1	17	23	.183	.302	.280
Second 9 Batters			123	35	5	17	17	.285	.431	.371
All Batters Thereafter			89	26	0	19	8	.292	.337	.413

Loves to face: Chris Chambliss (.067, 1-for-15)
Hates to face: Keith Hernandez (.328, 11-for-43, 2 HR)
Ground outs-to-air outs ratio: 0.96 last season, 1.08 for career. . . . Additional statistics: 11 double-play ground outs in 88 opportunities, 17 doubles, 1 triple allowed in 92.0 innings last season. . . . Allowed 8 first-inning runs in 16 starts in '85. . . . Batting support: 2.44 runs per start, 2d-lowest average in N.L. (minimum: 15 GS). . . . Led N.L. with 1.23 ERA in May. . . . Placed on disabled list for first time in major-league career on June 21. . . . Career total of 81 balks is more than triple the total of any active pitcher except Phil Niekro (37) and Jerry Koosman (29). . . . Rate of 5.18 walks per nine innings was 3d-highest among N.L. pitchers (minimum: 15 GS). . . . Last 16 home runs allowed have been to right-handed batters. Last homer by a lefty off Lefty: Darryl Strawberry on June 20, 1984. . . . 49 wins short of Warren Spahn's career record for left-handers, 363.

Bobby Castillo

Los Angeles Dodgers	W–L	ERA	AB	H	HR	BB	SO	BA	SA	OBA
Season	2-2	5.43	256	59	9	41	57	.230	.402	.337
vs. Left-Handed Batters			104	22	2	14	28	.212	.356	.303
vs. Right-Handed Batters			152	37	7	27	29	.243	.434	.359
Home	2-0	4.38	141	30	4	13	33	.213	.348	.284
Road	0-2	6.68	115	29	5	28	24	.252	.470	.393
Grass	2-1	5.11	212	50	7	33	46	.236	.392	.339
Artificial Turf	0-1	6.94	44	9	2	8	11	.205	.455	.327
Day	2-1	3.42	96	18	1	20	26	.188	.292	.331
Night	0-1	6.70	160	41	8	21	31	.256	.469	.341
April	0-0	10.80	21	8	0	2	5	.381	.619	.417
May	1-1	3.71	63	12	2	11	15	.190	.349	.311
June	1-0	6.63	74	21	2	14	10	.284	.419	.400
July	0-0	5.40	18	2	1	2	3	.111	.278	.200
August	0-0	3.86	24	2	1	4	11	.083	.250	.214
Sept./Oct.	0-1	4.80	56	14	3	8	13	.250	.464	.344
Leading Off Inn.			54	7	1	8	19	.130	.204	.242
Bases Empty			143	28	2	16	35	.196	.280	.277
Runners On			113	31	7	25	22	.274	.558	.404
Runners/Scor. Pos.			76	22	5	12	15	.289	.605	.378
Runners On/2 Out			58	17	3	14	15	.293	.586	.431
Scor. Pos./2 Out			45	14	2	7	11	.311	.600	.404
Late Inning Pressure			23	7	1	6	7	.304	.522	.448
Leading Off			5	1	0	1	2	.200	.200	.333
Bases Empty			13	4	0	2	5	.308	.385	.400
Runners On			10	3	1	4	2	.300	.700	.500
Runners/Scor. Pos.			7	3	1	3	1	.429	1.000	.600
First 9 Batters			175	40	8	25	41	.229	.429	.325
Second 9 Batters			66	13	1	12	15	.197	.273	.321
All Batters Thereafter			15	6	0	4	1	.400	.667	.526

Loves to face: Steve Kemp (.040, 1-for-25)
Hates to face: Dale Murphy (.615, 8-for-13, 2 HR)
Ground outs-to-air outs ratio: 0.95 last season, 0.92 for career. . . . Additional statistics: 4 double-play ground outs in 58 opportunities, 13 doubles, 2 triples allowed in 68.0 innings last season. . . . Relief ERA of 5.89 was 3d-highest among N.L. pitchers (minimum: 30 relief games). . . . Definition of mop-up man: At one point last season the Dodgers lost 19 consecutive games in which he appeared in relief, and he was the pitcher of record in none of them. . . . Definition of a screwball-pitcher: opposing left-handers have a career batting average of .228, right-handers .262. . . . Faced a greater number of left-handed batters than right-handers in each of his three seasons in A.L., but in only one of six seasons in N.L. . . . Career home runs allowed: one per 76 at bats in Late-Inning Pressure Situations; one per 33 nonpressure AB.

Don Carman

Philadelphia Phillies	W–L	ERA	AB	H	HR	BB	SO	BA	SA	OBA
Season	9-4	2.08	292	52	6	38	87	.178	.274	.273
vs. Left-Handed Batters			87	19	1	5	21	.218	.299	.269
vs. Right-Handed Batters			205	33	5	33	66	.161	.263	.275
Home	6-0	1.05	141	20	2	16	38	.142	.213	.231
Road	3-4	3.09	151	32	4	22	49	.212	.331	.311
Grass	2-2	2.29	64	11	2	8	25	.172	.281	.257
Artificial Turf	7-2	2.03	228	41	4	30	62	.180	.272	.278
Day	2-2	2.49	73	14	2	9	24	.192	.329	.271
Night	7-2	1.95	219	38	4	29	63	.174	.256	.274
April	0-0	0.00	23	6	0	2	2	.261	.261	.333
May	0-0	1.42	40	5	0	5	11	.125	.175	.213
June	2-1	2.95	60	9	4	7	20	.150	.350	.235
July	1-2	4.00	63	15	1	9	17	.238	.349	.338
August	3-1	1.32	43	6	0	8	11	.140	.209	.275
Sept./Oct.	3-0	1.02	63	11	1	7	26	.175	.238	.257
Leading Off Inn.			68	14	3	9	23	.206	.353	.299
Bases Empty			165	29	4	20	57	.176	.267	.269
Runners On			127	23	2	18	30	.181	.283	.278
Runners/Scor. Pos.			70	15	0	13	15	.214	.300	.326
Runners On/2 Out			59	12	2	11	12	.203	.390	.338
Scor. Pos./2 Out			39	9	0	8	9	.231	.359	.375
Late Inning Pressure			197	31	3	24	67	.157	.239	.250
Leading Off			47	9	2	5	20	.191	.319	.269
Bases Empty			117	18	2	13	45	.154	.222	.244
Runners On			80	13	1	11	22	.163	.263	.258
Runners/Scor. Pos.			45	9	0	7	12	.200	.311	.296
First 9 Batters			286	51	6	38	86	.178	.276	.275
Second 9 Batters			6	1	0	0	1	.167	.167	.167
All Batters Thereafter			0	0	0	0	0	.000	.000	.000

Loves to face: Mariano Duncan (0-for-3, 3 SO)
Hates to face: Gary Carter (.750, 3-for-4, 1 HR)
Ground outs-to-air outs ratio: 0.65 last season (8th-lowest in N.L.), 0.61 for career. . . . Additional statistics: 6 double-play ground outs in 69 opportunities, 6 doubles, 2 triples allowed in 86.1 innings last season. . . . Allowed 5.42 hits per nine innings last season, best rate among N.L. relievers (minimum: 30 games). . . . Ranked 3d among same group in ERA (2.08) and strikeouts per nine innings (9.07). . . . Tied for 2d in N.L. with nine relief wins. . . . Opponents' career batting averages: .170 with bases empty, .213 with runners on base, .236 with runners in scoring position, .265 with runners in scoring position and two outs. . . . Opponents' career batting average of .163 in Late-Inning Pressure Situations is the lowest in 11-year history of *The Player Analysis* (minimum: 200 LIP batters faced).

Danny Cox

St. Louis Cardinals	W–L	ERA	AB	H	HR	BB	SO	BA	SA	OBA
Season	18-9	2.88	901	226	19	64	131	.251	.382	.300
vs. Left-Handed Batters			432	114	7	32	53	.264	.382	.313
vs. Right-Handed Batters			469	112	12	32	78	.239	.382	.288
Home	10-4	2.30	486	122	8	27	70	.251	.364	.288
Road	8-5	3.54	415	104	11	37	61	.251	.402	.313
Grass	4-3	3.91	193	51	2	17	25	.264	.373	.327
Artificial Turf	14-6	2.60	708	175	17	47	106	.247	.384	.292
Day	5-2	1.87	298	67	3	23	40	.225	.315	.282
Night	13-7	3.40	603	159	16	41	91	.264	.415	.309
April	1-1	2.75	73	18	1	5	10	.247	.370	.291
May	5-0	2.49	188	42	8	14	28	.223	.410	.277
June	3-2	1.91	175	40	5	12	27	.229	.343	.279
July	3-3	3.19	160	44	0	8	22	.275	.363	.308
August	2-2	4.14	157	45	3	14	21	.287	.420	.343
Sept./Oct.	4-1	2.93	148	37	2	11	23	.250	.378	.302
Leading Off Inn.			232	62	4	19	32	.267	.405	.323
Bases Empty			546	143	11	43	80	.262	.394	.318
Runners On			355	83	8	21	51	.234	.363	.272
Runners/Scor. Pos.			185	41	2	16	39	.222	.324	.275
Runners On/2 Out			160	35	3	14	26	.219	.338	.286
Scor. Pos./2 Out			95	22	2	10	19	.232	.368	.311
Late Inning Pressure			62	19	1	5	7	.306	.468	.353
Leading Off			16	9	1	3	2	.563	.938	.632
Bases Empty			30	14	1	4	4	.467	.700	.529
Runners On			32	5	0	1	3	.156	.250	.176
Runners/Scor. Pos.			20	3	0	0	3	.150	.300	.143
First 9 Batters			275	77	5	26	53	.280	.422	.340
Second 9 Batters			281	57	10	17	38	.203	.352	.247
All Batters Thereafter			345	92	4	21	40	.267	.374	.309

Loves to face: Dave Concepcion (.095, 2-for-21)
Hates to face: Denny Walling (.526, 10-for-19)
Ground outs-to-air outs ratio: 1.30 last season, 1.43 for career. . . . Additional statistics: 19 double-play ground outs in 146 opportunities, 45 doubles (6th-most in N.L.), 8 triples (tied for 7th-most in N.L.) allowed in 241.0 innings last season. . . . Total of 72 extra-base hits allowed was 5th-highest in N.L. . . . Allowed 25 first-inning runs (tied for 2d-most in N.L.) in 35 starts last season. . . . Batting support: 4.29 runs per start. . . . Led N.L. with 1.87 ERA in day games. . . . Opponents' batting average leading off in Late-Inning Pressure Situations was the highest in the majors last season (minimum: 10 AB). Opponents' career batting averages in LIP situations: .164 with runners on base, .345 with the bases empty. . . . Breakdown of 1985 record was typical of the Cardinals: 12–2 vs. teams below .500, 6–7 vs. teams above .500.

Ron Darling

New York Mets	W–L	ERA	AB	H	HR	BB	SO	BA	SA	OBA
Season	16-6	2.90	909	214	21	114	167	.235	.360	.321
vs. Left-Handed Batters			461	111	8	56	77	.241	.354	.323
vs. Right-Handed Batters			448	103	13	58	90	.230	.366	.320
Home	9-5	3.09	554	138	12	56	107	.249	.379	.319
Road	7-1	2.62	355	76	9	58	60	.214	.330	.325
Grass	13-6	3.07	731	182	16	88	139	.249	.373	.331
Artificial Turf	3-0	2.28	178	32	5	26	28	.180	.303	.284
Day	3-3	4.45	234	64	10	33	36	.274	.457	.361
Night	13-3	2.40	675	150	11	81	131	.222	.326	.307
April	1-0	2.25	99	18	2	11	23	.182	.313	.264
May	3-1	2.58	172	45	3	11	36	.262	.360	.310
June	2-1	2.09	144	30	4	20	32	.208	.319	.307
July	4-2	4.85	156	48	5	28	21	.308	.481	.412
August	3-1	1.66	156	33	3	25	26	.212	.321	.320
Sept./Oct.	3-1	3.83	182	40	4	19	29	.220	.346	.292
Leading Off Inn.			227	45	4	27	49	.198	.291	.289
Bases Empty			525	131	16	66	97	.250	.402	.336
Runners On			384	83	5	48	70	.216	.302	.302
Runners/Scor. Pos.			211	41	3	32	40	.194	.280	.296
Runners On/2 Out			175	37	2	24	33	.211	.297	.307
Scor. Pos./2 Out			109	21	2	19	23	.193	.294	.313
Late Inning Pressure			115	32	2	19	17	.278	.400	.381
Leading Off			31	8	0	3	4	.258	.355	.324
Bases Empty			66	19	2	11	10	.288	.455	.390
Runners On			49	13	0	8	7	.265	.327	.368
Runners/Scor. Pos.			31	7	0	6	5	.226	.290	.351
First 9 Batters			267	63	5	44	56	.236	.326	.346
Second 9 Batters			280	55	5	29	57	.196	.314	.272
All Batters Thereafter			362	96	11	41	54	.265	.420	.340

Loves to face: Tommy Herr (.048, 1-for-21)
Hates to face: Jeff Stone (.435, 10-for-23)
Ground outs-to-air outs ratio: 1.18 last season, 1.17 for career. . . . Additional statistics: 23 double-play ground outs in 183 opportunities, 44 doubles (7th-most in N.L.), 3 triples allowed in 248.0 innings last season. . . . Ranked 8th among N.L. pitchers with an average of 7.06 innings per start. . . . Allowed 10 first-inning runs in 35 starts, 8th-lowest rate in N.L. last season (minimum: 15 GS). . . . Batting support: 4.11 runs per start. . . . ERA of 2.62 in road games was 3d-lowest in N.L. . . . Led N.L. pitchers with 47 assists and 73 total chances. . . . Walked 114 batters last season, most by N.L. pitcher since J.R. Richard (141 in '78). . . . Picked off seven runners last year, tying Ray Fontenot for N.L. lead. . . . First "number-two" pitcher in Mets' history to have a season record of 10 games above .500.

Mark Davis

San Francisco Giants	W–L	ERA	AB	H	HR	BB	SO	BA	SA	OBA
Season	5-12	3.54	407	89	13	41	131	.219	.346	.294
vs. Left-Handed Batters			114	21	3	7	39	.184	.316	.231
vs. Right-Handed Batters			293	68	10	34	92	.232	.358	.317
Home	4-5	3.71	189	43	7	20	59	.228	.376	.308
Road	1-7	3.39	218	46	6	21	72	.211	.321	.282
Grass	5-9	4.04	281	66	10	28	89	.235	.377	.309
Artificial Turf	0-3	2.48	126	23	3	13	42	.183	.278	.262
Day	3-8	4.55	239	57	9	27	75	.238	.393	.321
Night	2-4	2.20	168	32	4	14	56	.190	.280	.255
April	1-1	1.76	53	8	2	3	23	.151	.283	.196
May	1-2	2.87	55	13	1	6	21	.236	.327	.323
June	1-2	2.16	88	18	1	8	29	.205	.284	.278
July	0-1	3.63	63	18	2	8	14	.286	.397	.366
August	1-1	3.71	59	10	3	7	19	.169	.339	.254
Sept./Oct.	1-5	6.38	89	22	4	9	25	.247	.427	.323
Leading Off Inn.			84	17	3	14	28	.202	.345	.323
Bases Empty			227	39	6	27	84	.172	.273	.266
Runners On			180	50	7	14	47	.278	.439	.332
Runners/Scor. Pos.			96	26	3	11	28	.271	.427	.343
Runners On/2 Out			80	18	5	4	22	.225	.450	.271
Scor. Pos./2 Out			44	9	2	3	12	.205	.364	.255
Late Inning Pressure			242	46	9	26	81	.190	.331	.277
Leading Off			50	9	3	11	16	.180	.360	.339
Bases Empty			139	20	4	18	54	.144	.237	.252
Runners On			103	26	5	8	27	.252	.456	.313
Runners/Scor. Pos.			57	13	2	5	18	.228	.421	.290
First 9 Batters			370	80	12	38	122	.216	.338	.292
Second 9 Batters			33	6	1	3	9	.182	.364	.270
All Batters Thereafter			4	3	0	0	0	.750	1.000	.750

Loves to face: Terry Kennedy (.053, 1-for-19, 10 SO)
Hates to face: Bruce Berenyi (.750, 3-for-4, 1 2B)
Ground outs-to-air outs ratio: 1.24 last season, 0.87 for career. . . . Additional statistics: 5 double-play ground outs in 93 opportunities (7th-lowest rate in N.L.), 11 doubles, 1 triple allowed in 114.1 innings last season. . . . Led major leagues with 11 relief losses. . . . Struck out 10.44 batters per nine innings last season, highest rate among N.L. relievers (minimum: 30 games). . . . Batting average of opposing left-handers (.184) was the lowest of career. Career batting averages: left-handers .209, right-handers .271. . . . Opponents' career batting average of .192 in Late-Inning Pressure Situations is 2d-lowest since we've been keeping track (minimum: 200 PA). . . . Has allowed three grand-slam home runs in only 39 batters faced with the bases loaded.

Bill Dawley

Houston Astros	W–L	ERA	AB	H	HR	BB	SO	BA	SA	OBA
Season	5-3	3.56	293	76	7	37	48	.259	.372	.338
vs. Left-Handed Batters			132	34	3	15	16	.258	.364	.333
vs. Right-Handed Batters			161	42	4	22	32	.261	.379	.342
Home	1-2	3.95	149	36	4	22	26	.242	.369	.333
Road	4-1	3.15	144	40	3	15	22	.278	.375	.344
Grass	2-0	3.86	87	27	1	11	11	.310	.402	.384
Artificial Turf	3-3	3.43	206	49	6	26	37	.238	.359	.319
Day	2-1	3.63	87	24	1	11	16	.276	.379	.357
Night	3-2	3.53	206	52	6	26	32	.252	.369	.331
April	0-1	6.75	28	9	1	12	3	.321	.464	.512
May	1-1	3.05	72	16	2	7	11	.222	.347	.288
June	0-0	5.14	56	19	2	6	8	.339	.500	.403
July	0-0	7.20	18	6	1	1	1	.333	.556	.368
August	1-0	0.93	37	9	1	6	9	.243	.378	.341
Sept./Oct.	3-1	2.28	82	17	0	5	16	.207	.232	.250
Leading Off Inn.			70	21	2	8	11	.300	.429	.372
Bases Empty			158	35	3	15	26	.222	.316	.289
Runners On			135	41	4	22	22	.304	.437	.391
Runners/Scor. Pos.			90	26	2	19	14	.289	.400	.398
Runners On/2 Out			58	17	2	12	10	.293	.431	.414
Scor. Pos./2 Out			46	14	2	10	8	.304	.457	.429
Late Inning Pressure			108	26	3	22	20	.241	.352	.366
Leading Off			33	11	1	3	7	.333	.455	.389
Bases Empty			69	16	1	7	14	.232	.304	.303
Runners On			39	10	2	15	6	.256	.436	.455
Runners/Scor. Pos.			23	5	1	14	3	.217	.348	.500
First 9 Batters			260	67	6	35	43	.258	.369	.342
Second 9 Batters			33	9	1	2	5	.273	.394	.306
All Batters Thereafter			0	0	0	0	0	.000	.000	.000

Loves to face: Jeff Leonard (.091, 1-for-11, 5 SO)
Hates to face: Tony Gwynn (.714, 5-for-7)
Ground outs-to-air outs ratio: 0.82 last season, 0.79 for career. . . . Additional statistics: 8 double-play ground outs in 74 opportunities, 12 doubles, 0 triples allowed in 81.0 innings last season. . . . Career winning percentage (22–13, .629) ranks 8th among active pitchers with 20 or more wins. . . . Houston lost 15 consecutive games in which he appeared (May 26 to July 30). . . . Opponents' batting averages, year by year since 1983: .185, .234, .259. . . . Batting average by left-handed batters in 1984 was the same as last season, but right-handers improved 47 points on their '84 mark. . . . Opponents' career batting averages: .214 with bases empty, .245 with runners on base, .257 with runners in scoring position. Opponents collected six hits in 14 at bats with the bases loaded last season.

Ken Dayley

St. Louis Cardinals	W–L	ERA	AB	H	HR	BB	SO	BA	SA	OBA
Season	4-4	2.76	247	65	2	18	62	.263	.360	.311
vs. Left-Handed Batters			80	25	1	4	21	.313	.400	.341
vs. Right-Handed Batters			167	40	1	14	41	.240	.341	.297
Home	3-1	2.38	130	34	2	8	29	.262	.377	.300
Road	1-3	3.16	117	31	0	10	33	.265	.342	.323
Grass	1-2	2.21	73	15	0	6	27	.205	.247	.266
Artificial Turf	3-2	3.00	174	50	2	12	35	.287	.408	.330
Day	3-3	3.10	107	30	0	12	27	.280	.318	.350
Night	1-1	2.48	140	35	2	6	35	.250	.393	.279
April	0-0	1.17	29	8	0	3	3	.276	.379	.344
May	0-0	0.79	41	9	0	2	12	.220	.244	.256
June	2-0	5.65	58	17	1	2	11	.293	.466	.306
July	1-0	0.00	24	3	0	2	10	.125	.125	.192
August	0-1	1.35	52	16	0	7	12	.308	.404	.390
Sept./Oct.	1-3	5.56	43	12	1	2	14	.279	.395	.311
Leading Off Inn.			53	13	0	3	18	.245	.302	.286
Bases Empty			122	30	2	7	35	.246	.352	.287
Runners On			125	35	0	11	27	.280	.368	.333
Runners/Scor. Pos.			77	21	0	10	14	.273	.338	.348
Runners On/2 Out			52	16	0	3	9	.308	.462	.345
Scor. Pos./2 Out			35	11	0	3	5	.314	.429	.368
Late Inning Pressure			164	47	1	15	45	.287	.366	.346
Leading Off			39	10	0	2	15	.256	.282	.293
Bases Empty			83	22	1	6	26	.265	.337	.315
Runners On			81	25	0	9	19	.309	.395	.378
Runners/Scor. Pos.			45	15	0	8	9	.333	.422	.434
First 9 Batters			237	62	1	16	61	.262	.350	.306
Second 9 Batters			10	3	1	2	1	.300	.600	.417
All Batters Thereafter			0	0	0	0	0	.000	.000	.000

Loves to face: Graig Nettles (0-for-3, 3 SO)
Hates to face: Pete Rose (.556, 5-for-9)
Ground outs-to-air outs ratio: 2.00 last season, 1.07 for career. . . . Additional statistics: 8 double-play ground outs in 61 opportunities, 14 doubles, 2 triples allowed in 65.1 innings last season. . . . Opposing left-handers have batted over .300 in each of four years in majors. Career averages: .317 by opposing left-handers, .273 by right-handers. . . . Career strikeout percentages: one per 4.4 batters faced in Late-Inning Pressure Situations, one per 7.4 batters when unpressured. . . . Faced 142 leadoff batters without allowing a home run, highest total in majors last year. . . . Cardinals' bullpen had 9–3 record from Sept. 1 to season's end; Dayley had all three losses. . . . Saved only one game after August 28, the date of Todd Worrell's first appearance, but had two in Championship Series, including one in Game Six.

Jeff Dedmon

Atlanta Braves	W–L	ERA	AB	H	HR	BB	SO	BA	SA	OBA
Season	6-3	4.08	318	84	5	49	41	.264	.368	.363
vs. Left-Handed Batters			144	33	1	35	22	.229	.319	.380
vs. Right-Handed Batters			174	51	4	14	19	.293	.408	.347
Home	2-2	3.53	162	45	2	21	22	.278	.389	.362
Road	4-1	4.64	156	39	3	28	19	.250	.346	.364
Grass	5-3	4.54	254	70	4	44	35	.276	.386	.383
Artificial Turf	1-0	2.41	64	14	1	5	6	.219	.297	.275
Day	3-2	6.43	108	33	2	25	10	.306	.435	.436
Night	3-1	2.95	210	51	3	24	31	.243	.333	.322
April			0	0	0	0	0	.000	.000	.000
May	2-0	2.70	55	10	2	6	7	.182	.309	.258
June	2-0	0.55	52	10	0	10	8	.192	.250	.323
July	0-1	5.17	67	21	0	9	7	.313	.418	.395
August	1-1	5.27	50	14	2	8	9	.280	.420	.379
Sept./Oct.	1-1	6.08	94	29	1	16	10	.309	.404	.414
Leading Off Inn.			67	20	0	9	8	.299	.388	.390
Bases Empty			149	40	2	16	24	.268	.369	.343
Runners On			169	44	3	33	17	.260	.367	.379
Runners/Scor. Pos.			115	33	1	30	10	.287	.391	.432
Runners On/2 Out			67	13	1	11	4	.194	.299	.308
Scor. Pos./2 Out			54	12	1	9	3	.222	.352	.333
Late Inning Pressure			104	27	1	21	12	.260	.346	.384
Leading Off			27	9	0	3	3	.333	.407	.400
Bases Empty			56	17	0	8	9	.304	.393	.391
Runners On			48	10	1	13	3	.208	.292	.377
Runners/Scor. Pos.			32	7	0	11	3	.219	.250	.419
First 9 Batters			285	77	5	45	35	.270	.382	.370
Second 9 Batters			33	7	0	4	6	.212	.242	.297
All Batters Thereafter			0	0	0	0	0	.000	.000	.000

Loves to face: Hubie Brooks (0-for-9)
Hates to face: Tim Raines (.750, 3-for-4, 1 2B, 1 HR)
Ground outs-to-air outs ratio: 2.89 last season (4th-highest in N.L.), 2.83 for career. . . . Additional statistics: 17 double-play ground outs in 94 opportunities (8th-highest rate in N.L.), 12 doubles, 3 triples allowed in 86.0 innings last season. . . . Opponents' career batting average of .314 in Late-Inning Pressure Situations is the highest against any active N.L. pitcher (minimum: 200 PA), but he has allowed only one home run in 249 batters faced in such situations. . . . Has never allowed a home run to lead off an inning (160 leadoff batters faced). . . . Career average of 1.50 strikeouts per walk in night games, 0.68 in day games. . . . Had 60 relief appearances without a save, the highest total in the majors last season.

Jose DeLeon

Pittsburgh Pirates	W–L	ERA	AB	H	HR	BB	SO	BA	SA	OBA
Season	2-19	4.70	597	138	15	89	149	.231	.357	.332
vs. Left-Handed Batters			285	79	7	51	47	.277	.414	.389
vs. Right-Handed Batters			312	59	8	38	102	.189	.304	.278
Home	2-9	3.97	340	73	5	49	97	.215	.312	.317
Road	0-10	5.68	257	65	10	40	52	.253	.416	.351
Grass	0-5	4.82	137	30	5	19	35	.219	.350	.310
Artificial Turf	2-14	4.67	460	108	10	70	114	.235	.359	.338
Day	1-5	3.86	185	39	6	30	40	.211	.357	.323
Night	1-14	5.09	412	99	9	59	109	.240	.357	.336
April	0-3	4.67	104	26	2	15	35	.250	.346	.345
May	0-4	6.27	122	32	1	20	35	.262	.344	.361
June	2-3	3.11	134	24	5	16	30	.179	.351	.267
July	0-4	5.84	92	20	3	14	16	.217	.348	.324
August	0-1	6.00	56	13	2	12	11	.232	.411	.377
Sept./Oct.	0-4	3.20	89	23	2	12	22	.258	.371	.350
Leading Off Inn.			144	38	3	23	34	.264	.382	.369
Bases Empty			330	71	6	60	86	.215	.321	.339
Runners On			267	67	9	29	63	.251	.401	.322
Runners/Scor. Pos.			154	39	8	22	34	.253	.455	.343
Runners On/2 Out			104	15	3	10	31	.144	.279	.219
Scor. Pos./2 Out			63	9	3	9	18	.143	.333	.250
Late Inning Pressure			68	22	2	9	17	.324	.500	.397
Leading Off			17	9	0	2	2	.529	.588	.579
Bases Empty			37	14	1	5	9	.378	.568	.452
Runners On			31	8	1	4	8	.258	.419	.333
Runners/Scor. Pos.			15	5	1	3	3	.333	.667	.421
First 9 Batters			218	45	4	32	65	.206	.307	.312
Second 9 Batters			194	48	4	21	41	.247	.366	.319
All Batters Thereafter			185	45	7	36	43	.243	.405	.366

Loves to face: George Foster (.182, 4-for-22, 11 SO)
Hates to face: Wally Backman (.421, 8-for-19)
Ground outs-to-air outs ratio: 0.75 last season, 0.83 for career. . . . Additional statistics: 7 double-play ground outs in 148 opportunities (4th-lowest rate in N.L.), 20 doubles, 5 triples allowed in 162.2 innings last season. . . . Batting support: 2.32 runs per start, lowest average in either league (minimum: 15 GS). . . . Struck out 8.24 batters per nine innings, 3d-highest rate in N.L. . . . Eleven-game losing streak (started June 19, still going) was longest in majors in '85. All-time record (not limited to one season) is 23 by Cliff Curtis of the 1911 Braves. Former Mets pitcher Craig Anderson lost 19 straight to end his career; he hasn't pitched since 1964, but he's only nine months older than Phil Niekro, and the record is there for him to shoot at if he decides to make a comeback.

John Denny

Philadelphia Phillies	W–L	ERA	AB	H	HR	BB	SO	BA	SA	OBA
Season	11-14	3.82	893	252	15	83	123	.282	.392	.342
vs. Left-Handed Batters			456	130	6	50	53	.285	.388	.356
vs. Right-Handed Batters			437	122	9	33	70	.279	.396	.328
Home	4-10	4.02	479	138	7	42	59	.288	.397	.343
Road	7-4	3.59	414	114	8	41	64	.275	.386	.341
Grass	4-2	3.03	253	64	6	22	40	.253	.364	.315
Artificial Turf	7-12	4.14	640	188	9	61	83	.294	.403	.353
Day	5-2	4.21	235	63	6	26	31	.268	.426	.337
Night	6-12	3.68	658	189	9	57	92	.287	.380	.344
April	1-2	4.03	119	39	1	12	12	.328	.412	.383
May	1-3	4.78	171	48	3	17	17	.281	.386	.344
June	3-0	3.03	140	41	2	9	29	.293	.371	.344
July	0-3	3.63	129	34	2	13	18	.264	.364	.329
August	3-3	3.28	175	49	3	13	23	.280	.423	.325
Sept./Oct.	3-3	4.14	159	41	4	19	24	.258	.390	.339
Leading Off Inn.			219	63	2	17	27	.288	.365	.342
Bases Empty			492	138	8	43	67	.280	.392	.342
Runners On			401	114	7	40	56	.284	.392	.343
Runners/Scor. Pos.			217	55	6	32	33	.253	.378	.339
Runners On/2 Out			174	52	5	20	22	.299	.431	.371
Scor. Pos./2 Out			109	32	4	17	13	.294	.440	.389
Late Inning Pressure			60	15	1	6	10	.250	.367	.313
Leading Off			16	5	1	0	2	.313	.625	.313
Bases Empty			34	10	1	2	6	.294	.471	.333
Runners On			26	5	0	4	4	.192	.231	.290
Runners/Scor. Pos.			19	4	0	2	3	.211	.211	.273
First 9 Batters			258	71	2	33	45	.275	.349	.357
Second 9 Batters			275	78	0	17	43	.284	.356	.327
All Batters Thereafter			360	103	13	33	35	.286	.450	.343

Loves to face: Bill Almon (.083, 3-for-36, 13 SO)
Hates to face: Steve Kemp (.444, 8-for-18)
Ground outs-to-air outs ratio: 2.46 last season (9th-highest in N.L.), 2.20 for career. . . . Additional statistics: 28 double-play ground outs in 196 opportunities, 31 doubles, 11 triples (2d-most in N.L.) allowed in 230.2 innings last season. . . . Ranked 9th among N.L. pitchers with an average of 6.99 innings per start. . . . Allowed 19 first-inning runs in 33 starts last season. . . . Batting support: 4.33 runs per start. . . . Tied for N.L. lead in home losses with 10, but it's on to Riverfront in '86. . . . Sorry to see Rusty retire: Staub was 1-for-19 (.053) in his career vs. Denny. . . . Batting average of opposing right-handed batters (.279) is his highest since 1975. Career average: .246. . . . It certainly wasn't his performance against the Reds last season that inspired the trade: he was 0–3 in four starts, with 7.40 ERA and .316 batting average allowed.

Carlos Diaz

Los Angeles Dodgers	W–L	ERA	AB	H	HR	BB	SO	BA	SA	OBA
Season	6-3	2.61	304	70	7	18	73	.230	.352	.272
vs. Left-Handed Batters			64	13	2	0	14	.203	.313	.203
vs. Right-Handed Batters			240	57	5	18	59	.238	.363	.290
Home	4-2	1.54	129	27	3	6	31	.209	.302	.244
Road	2-1	3.45	175	43	4	12	42	.246	.389	.293
Grass	4-3	2.32	207	47	5	13	51	.227	.343	.273
Artificial Turf	2-0	3.24	97	23	2	5	22	.237	.371	.272
Day	1-2	3.65	96	24	4	6	27	.250	.438	.294
Night	5-1	2.14	208	46	3	12	46	.221	.313	.262
April	2-0	2.25	44	9	2	2	13	.205	.364	.239
May	0-0	3.27	43	14	1	7	8	.326	.488	.412
June	0-0	0.00	21	3	0	0	6	.143	.143	.143
July	0-0	0.96	33	5	1	2	8	.152	.333	.200
August	1-2	4.50	57	15	0	1	13	.263	.316	.276
Sept./Oct.	3-1	2.73	106	24	3	6	25	.226	.358	.268
Leading Off Inn.			74	18	1	4	17	.243	.338	.282
Bases Empty			180	47	3	6	41	.261	.367	.285
Runners On			124	23	4	12	32	.185	.331	.255
Runners/Scor. Pos.			64	13	3	11	14	.203	.406	.316
Runners On/2 Out			57	9	2	6	15	.158	.281	.238
Scor. Pos./2 Out			27	3	1	6	7	.111	.222	.273
Late Inning Pressure			77	18	2	6	20	.234	.351	.289
Leading Off			22	6	1	1	5	.273	.409	.304
Bases Empty			49	15	2	1	13	.306	.490	.320
Runners On			28	3	0	5	7	.107	.107	.242
Runners/Scor. Pos.			19	2	0	5	7	.105	.105	.292
First 9 Batters			263	60	5	16	64	.228	.338	.271
Second 9 Batters			40	10	2	2	9	.250	.450	.286
All Batters Thereafter			1	0	0	0	0	.000	.000	.000

Loves to face: Juan Samuel (0-for-6, 3 SO)
Hates to face: George Foster (4-for-4)
Ground outs-to-air outs ratio: 1.64 last season, 1.39 for career. . . . Additional statistics: 4 double-play ground outs in 51 opportunities, 10 doubles, 3 triples allowed in 79.1 innings in '85. . . . Allowed 2.04 walks per nine innings last year, 4th-best rate among N.L. relievers (minimum: 30 games). . . . Faced 65 left-handed batters last season without allowing a walk, highest N.L. total in *Player Analysis* history. . . . Opposing batters hit 76 points higher with the bases empty than with runners on base, largest difference in N.L. (minimum: 100 AB in each situation). . . . Finished 21 games last season without recording a save, highest total in N.L. since Gary Ross finished 29 games without a save for the 1973 Padres. . . . Has never committed an error in 160 games in majors; N.L. record for consecutive errorless games by pitcher is Ron Reed's 297.

Frank DiPino

Houston Astros	W–L	ERA	AB	H	HR	BB	SO	BA	SA	OBA
Season	3-7	4.03	278	69	7	43	49	.248	.381	.350
vs. Left-Handed Batters			64	22	2	12	7	.344	.500	.442
vs. Right-Handed Batters			214	47	5	31	42	.220	.346	.321
Home	2-3	4.26	114	27	2	20	21	.237	.351	.358
Road	1-4	3.86	164	42	5	23	28	.256	.402	.344
Grass	1-2	3.00	100	27	3	15	18	.270	.440	.359
Artificial Turf	2-5	4.59	178	42	4	28	31	.236	.348	.344
Day	0-1	6.32	61	15	3	7	9	.246	.426	.319
Night	3-6	3.43	217	54	4	36	40	.249	.369	.358
April	1-2	4.63	40	10	1	6	6	.250	.350	.340
May	0-2	3.55	47	12	1	11	5	.255	.319	.397
June	0-0	3.48	37	8	0	6	7	.216	.297	.326
July	0-2	2.65	61	13	2	4	12	.213	.361	.262
August	0-0	5.79	37	11	0	9	6	.297	.351	.426
Sept./Oct.	2-1	4.80	56	15	3	7	13	.268	.554	.364
Leading Off Inn.			64	15	1	8	9	.234	.359	.319
Bases Empty			152	32	2	19	25	.211	.303	.298
Runners On			126	37	5	24	24	.294	.476	.406
Runners/Scor. Pos.			80	23	2	19	19	.288	.438	.417
Runners On/2 Out			48	16	2	12	10	.333	.521	.467
Scor. Pos./2 Out			34	10	1	10	10	.294	.441	.455
Late Inning Pressure			128	39	4	22	22	.305	.445	.409
Leading Off			29	7	1	5	5	.241	.379	.353
Bases Empty			69	16	2	12	15	.232	.362	.346
Runners On			59	23	2	10	7	.390	.542	.479
Runners/Scor. Pos.			34	13	0	9	6	.382	.441	.500
First 9 Batters			253	58	5	42	48	.229	.344	.340
Second 9 Batters			25	11	2	1	1	.440	.760	.462
All Batters Thereafter			0	0	0	0	0	.000	.000	.000

Loves to face: Ron Cey (0-for-10)
Hates to face: Candy Maldonado (.714, 5-for-7)
Ground outs-to-air outs ratio: 1.12 last season, 1.16 for career. . . . Additional statistics: 10 double-play ground outs in 68 opportunities, 16 doubles, 0 triples allowed in 76.0 innings last season. . . . Compare last season (above) to 1984's .226 with runners on base, .300 with the bases empty. . . . Yearly batting averages of opposing left-handed batters since 1983: .149, .211, .344. Career batting averages: left-handers .227, right-handers .250. . . . Opponents have batted .370 (10-for-27, 4 walks) with the bases loaded over past two seasons. . . . Had never made an error in 118 major league games before 1985, but ruined that record on his first chance of season, making a wild pickoff throw on May 3. Current leader among pitchers for most games in majors without making an error: Roy Thomas, 174.

Dave Dravecky

San Diego Padres	W–L	ERA	AB	H	HR	BB	SO	BA	SA	OBA
Season	13-11	2.93	802	200	18	57	105	.249	.354	.299
vs. Left-Handed Batters			90	24	1	7	24	.267	.322	.320
vs. Right-Handed Batters			712	176	17	50	81	.247	.358	.296
Home	6-3	2.97	358	86	11	25	54	.240	.355	.292
Road	7-8	2.91	444	114	7	32	51	.257	.354	.305
Grass	9-7	3.06	583	149	15	40	73	.256	.364	.304
Artificial Turf	4-4	2.61	219	51	3	17	32	.233	.329	.287
Day	5-3	3.39	262	65	9	25	34	.248	.393	.314
Night	8-8	2.72	540	135	9	32	71	.250	.335	.292
April	0-2	3.38	61	16	3	5	8	.262	.459	.318
May	4-0	2.19	129	26	1	17	20	.202	.287	.295
June	4-2	1.40	159	34	4	10	26	.214	.308	.259
July	0-2	2.43	149	35	3	11	22	.235	.349	.284
August	3-2	2.98	165	45	1	6	21	.273	.327	.302
Sept./Oct.	2-3	6.15	139	44	6	8	8	.317	.460	.354
Leading Off Inn.			206	49	4	15	27	.238	.325	.290
Bases Empty			483	124	10	37	61	.257	.358	.310
Runners On			319	76	8	20	44	.238	.348	.283
Runners/Scor. Pos.			152	38	2	17	23	.250	.329	.324
Runners On/2 Out			139	32	4	7	23	.230	.374	.267
Scor. Pos./2 Out			72	17	1	7	14	.236	.347	.304
Late Inning Pressure			64	19	4	8	7	.297	.516	.375
Leading Off			18	10	2	1	2	.556	.944	.579
Bases Empty			35	16	3	4	4	.457	.771	.513
Runners On			29	3	1	4	3	.103	.207	.212
Runners/Scor. Pos.			12	1	0	4	2	.083	.083	.313
First 9 Batters			268	64	5	23	46	.239	.340	.299
Second 9 Batters			257	60	7	18	30	.233	.342	.284
All Batters Thereafter			277	76	6	16	29	.274	.379	.313

Loves to face: Greg Brock (0-for-10)
Hates to face: Dave Lopes (.750, 6-for-8, 2 HR)
Ground outs-to-air outs ratio: 1.18 last season, 1.06 for career. . . . Additional statistics: 20 double-play ground outs in 160 opportunities, 28 doubles, 1 triple allowed in 214.2 innings last season. . . . Allowed 13 first-inning runs in 31 starts last season. . . . Batting support: 3.55 runs per start. . . . June ERA of 1.40 was 2d-lowest in N.L. . . . Had league's 8th-best ERA on artificial turf. . . . Opponents' batting average leading off in Late-Inning Pressure Situations was 2d-highest in the majors last season (minimum: 10 AB). . . . 1985 was a year of streaks: lost his first two games and then won four, lost two, won four, lost three, won three, lost three, won two, lost his season finale. . . . ERA dropped as low as 1.99 in early July, but he never took the league lead in that category. That trophy had been long since retired.

Dennis Eckersley

Chicago Cubs	W–L	ERA	AB	H	HR	BB	SO	BA	SA	OBA
Season	11-7	3.08	634	145	15	19	117	.229	.352	.254
vs. Left-Handed Batters			322	83	11	11	39	.258	.416	.284
vs. Right-Handed Batters			312	62	4	8	78	.199	.285	.223
Home	5-2	3.45	263	60	7	7	64	.228	.338	.250
Road	6-5	2.82	371	85	8	12	53	.229	.361	.256
Grass	5-4	3.24	350	79	9	11	76	.226	.337	.251
Artificial Turf	6-3	2.88	284	66	6	8	41	.232	.370	.258
Day	7-3	2.99	356	81	8	9	78	.228	.323	.248
Night	4-4	3.21	278	64	7	10	39	.230	.388	.261
April	3-1	1.85	122	26	2	2	23	.213	.303	.226
May	3-2	3.29	152	34	4	5	32	.224	.336	.252
June	1-2	3.55	141	29	0	5	20	.206	.284	.243
July	0-0	1.50	66	15	2	2	12	.227	.364	.250
August	1-0	1.50	24	6	0	0	4	.250	.292	.250
Sept./Oct.	3-2	4.73	129	35	7	5	26	.271	.496	.296
Leading Off Inn.			169	46	7	4	23	.272	.444	.289
Bases Empty			420	102	9	10	76	.243	.355	.262
Runners On			214	43	6	9	41	.201	.346	.238
Runners/Scor. Pos.			115	26	5	9	21	.226	.443	.283
Runners On/2 Out			96	19	2	5	22	.198	.333	.245
Scor. Pos./2 Out			57	14	1	5	10	.246	.386	.317
Late Inning Pressure			58	17	1	2	10	.293	.448	.323
Leading Off			16	7	0	1	0	.438	.563	.471
Bases Empty			35	11	1	1	5	.314	.457	.351
Runners On			23	6	0	1	5	.261	.435	.280
Runners/Scor. Pos.			11	3	0	1	3	.273	.545	.308
First 9 Batters			214	42	2	8	48	.196	.266	.224
Second 9 Batters			211	52	7	5	38	.246	.384	.271
All Batters Thereafter			209	51	6	6	31	.244	.407	.267

Loves to face: Jack Clark (0-for-10, 5 SO)
Hates to face: Tim Corcoran (.524, 11-for-21)
Ground outs-to-air outs ratio: 0.84 last season, 0.69 for career. . . . Additional statistics: 7 double-play ground outs in 90 opportunities, 25 doubles, 4 triples allowed in 169.1 innings last season. . . . Allowed 7 first-inning runs in 25 starts, 7th-lowest rate in N.L. last season (minimum: 15 GS). . . . Batting support: 4.04 runs per start. . . . Pitched to no decision in seven starts with an ERA of 2.30 in those games. . . . Led majors with a ratio of 6.16 strikeouts per walk last season, and set *Player Analysis* record with a 9.75 mark vs. right-handed batters (minimum: 50 SO). . . . Opposing left-handers hit .258, lowest mark against him since 1976; righties' mark of .199 was lowest since 1977. Career breakdown: left-handers .273, right-handers .222.

Sid Fernandez

New York Mets	W–L	ERA	AB	H	HR	BB	SO	BA	SA	OBA
Season	9-9	2.80	596	108	14	80	180	.181	.302	.279
vs. Left-Handed Batters			92	15	2	7	40	.163	.326	.222
vs. Right-Handed Batters			504	93	12	73	140	.185	.298	.289
Home	5-4	2.67	252	44	6	34	90	.175	.290	.272
Road	4-5	2.89	344	64	8	46	90	.186	.311	.284
Grass	7-5	2.65	406	73	8	60	127	.180	.288	.284
Artificial Turf	2-4	3.11	190	35	6	20	53	.184	.332	.268
Day	3-1	2.34	172	32	1	33	45	.186	.238	.316
Night	6-8	2.99	424	76	13	47	135	.179	.328	.263
April			0	0	0	0	0	.000	.000	.000
May	1-1	1.82	86	12	1	16	25	.140	.233	.275
June	1-3	3.48	109	27	2	13	34	.248	.376	.325
July	1-2	2.73	120	22	3	17	36	.183	.308	.285
August	2-2	2.78	114	21	2	14	44	.184	.281	.273
Sept./Oct.	4-1	2.92	167	26	6	20	41	.156	.299	.251
Leading Off Inn.			151	21	3	24	56	.139	.258	.261
Bases Empty			382	66	12	47	121	.173	.322	.267
Runners On			214	42	2	33	59	.196	.266	.300
Runners/Scor. Pos.			131	26	1	19	36	.198	.252	.294
Runners On/2 Out			91	16	0	16	27	.176	.198	.299
Scor. Pos./2 Out			63	11	0	11	20	.175	.206	.297
Late Inning Pressure			44	8	2	4	13	.182	.364	.250
Leading Off			12	2	2	1	4	.167	.667	.231
Bases Empty			35	5	2	3	10	.143	.343	.211
Runners On			9	3	0	1	3	.333	.444	.400
Runners/Scor. Pos.			4	2	0	0	2	.500	.750	.500
First 9 Batters			201	27	2	31	71	.134	.219	.250
Second 9 Batters			202	42	4	27	56	.208	.322	.302
All Batters Thereafter			193	39	8	22	53	.202	.368	.286

Loves to face: Ozzie Virgil (0-for-13, 3 SO)
Hates to face: Jeff Leonard (3-for-3, 1 HR)
Ground outs-to-air outs ratio: 0.53 last season (4th-lowest in N.L.), 0.50 for career. . . . Additional statistics: 10 double-play ground outs in 92 opportunities, 28 doubles, 1 triple allowed in 170.1 innings last season. . . . Allowed 7 first-inning runs in 26 starts, 5th-lowest rate in N.L. last season (minimum: 15 GS). . . . Batting support: 4.04 runs per start. . . . Led majors in strikeouts (9.51) and hits (5.71) per nine innings. . . . Strikeout percentage vs. left-handed batters (40.0) was 2d-highest in majors over past 11 years. The record is 40.5, by John Candelaria in 1983. . . . Career total of 42 starts is 8th-highest among active pitchers without a complete-game shutout. . . . Opponents are hitless in 10 at bats with the bases loaded since he joined Mets. . . . Breakdown of 1985 record: 7–2 vs. teams below .500, 2–7 vs. teams above .500.

Ray Fontenot

Chicago Cubs	W–L	ERA	AB	H	HR	BB	SO	BA	SA	OBA
Season	6-10	4.36	602	177	23	45	70	.294	.462	.342
vs. Left-Handed Batters			77	14	1	9	18	.182	.247	.264
vs. Right-Handed Batters			525	163	22	36	52	.310	.493	.354
Home	2-6	5.18	354	109	13	28	37	.308	.477	.358
Road	4-4	3.22	248	68	10	17	33	.274	.440	.320
Grass	3-10	4.78	489	149	21	38	55	.305	.489	.354
Artificial Turf	3-0	2.67	113	28	2	7	15	.248	.345	.289
Day	2-8	4.84	429	128	18	36	43	.298	.485	.352
Night	4-2	3.20	173	49	5	9	27	.283	.405	.317
April	0-0	1.59	19	4	1	3	3	.211	.368	.318
May	0-1	4.35	81	19	2	6	8	.235	.383	.284
June	2-2	2.40	107	28	4	6	17	.262	.467	.298
July	2-2	2.90	149	40	3	11	22	.268	.369	.319
August	1-3	5.35	142	44	6	12	8	.310	.486	.364
Sept./Oct.	1-2	8.74	104	42	7	7	12	.404	.635	.441
Leading Off Inn.			143	41	4	16	19	.287	.434	.358
Bases Empty			350	100	14	28	43	.286	.463	.339
Runners On			252	77	9	17	27	.306	.460	.347
Runners/Scor. Pos.			153	47	8	11	16	.307	.529	.349
Runners On/2 Out			103	34	3	10	12	.330	.495	.389
Scor. Pos./2 Out			72	23	2	7	7	.319	.500	.380
Late Inning Pressure			81	28	3	6	5	.346	.481	.391
Leading Off			20	8	2	3	2	.400	.750	.478
Bases Empty			45	16	3	3	3	.356	.578	.396
Runners On			36	12	0	3	2	.333	.361	.385
Runners/Scor. Pos.			20	6	0	1	1	.300	.350	.333
First 9 Batters			270	68	8	23	42	.252	.381	.310
Second 9 Batters			189	61	11	8	17	.323	.550	.348
All Batters Thereafter			143	48	4	14	11	.336	.497	.395

Loves to face: Tim Raines (.143, 1-for-7, 3 SO)
Hates to face: Bob Horner (.800, 4-for-5, 1 HR)
Ground outs-to-air outs ratio: 3.12 last season (3d-highest in N.L.), 2.53 for career. . . . Additional statistics: 22 double-play ground outs in 121 opportunities (7th-highest rate in N.L.), 22 doubles, 5 triples allowed in 154.2 innings last season. . . . Allowed 9 first-inning runs in 23 starts last season. . . . Batting support: 4.17 runs per start. . . . Average of 10.30 hits per nine innings was 4th-highest among N.L. pitchers (minimum: 15 starts). . . . Goodbye Yankee Stadium, hello Wrigley Field. Quote from last year's *Analyst*: "Allowed eight home runs in 169.1 innings, 2d-best in A.L. (in 1984)." In 1985, he allowed 23 home runs in 154.2 innings, the highest rate among N.L. pitchers (minimum: 15 GS). Cubs' record was 2–14 in games in which he allowed a home run. . . . Picked seven runners off base last year, tying Ron Darling for N.L. lead.

Bob Forsch

St. Louis Cardinals	W–L	ERA	AB	H	HR	BB	SO	BA	SA	OBA
Season	9-6	3.90	512	132	11	47	48	.258	.377	.322
vs. Left-Handed Batters			203	49	0	17	13	.241	.296	.299
vs. Right-Handed Batters			309	83	11	30	35	.269	.430	.337
Home	5-3	3.54	275	65	2	21	22	.236	.320	.294
Road	4-3	4.33	237	67	9	26	26	.283	.443	.354
Grass	3-1	3.63	127	31	5	15	12	.244	.370	.324
Artificial Turf	6-5	4.00	385	101	6	32	36	.262	.379	.321
Day	3-6	5.12	248	75	7	29	20	.302	.448	.376
Night	6-0	2.85	264	57	4	18	28	.216	.311	.269
April	2-1	2.45	67	18	1	5	3	.269	.433	.319
May	2-1	4.84	89	25	6	7	6	.281	.506	.330
June	0-2	5.74	57	14	0	12	8	.246	.298	.386
July	0-0	3.00	26	10	0	3	4	.385	.423	.448
August	2-1	4.13	107	24	3	6	9	.224	.374	.265
Sept./Oct.	3-1	3.38	166	41	1	14	18	.247	.307	.309
Leading Off Inn.			133	28	4	10	13	.211	.346	.271
Bases Empty			319	79	8	25	30	.248	.376	.304
Runners On			193	53	3	22	18	.275	.378	.350
Runners/Scor. Pos.			104	33	1	12	7	.317	.404	.385
Runners On/2 Out			77	16	0	10	6	.208	.247	.299
Scor. Pos./2 Out			47	14	0	6	3	.298	.340	.377
Late Inning Pressure			25	10	1	3	0	.400	.520	.483
Leading Off			8	4	1	1	0	.500	.875	.556
Bases Empty			14	7	1	2	0	.500	.714	.563
Runners On			11	3	0	1	0	.273	.273	.385
Runners/Scor. Pos.			6	2	0	0	0	.333	.333	.333
First 9 Batters			223	57	3	25	20	.256	.341	.329
Second 9 Batters			161	46	4	14	18	.286	.441	.347
All Batters Thereafter			128	29	4	8	10	.227	.359	.277

Loves to face: Leon Durham (.048, 1-for-21, 1 HR)
Hates to face: Darryl Strawberry (.429, 3-for-7, 3 HR)
Ground outs-to-air outs ratio: 1.17 last season, 1.51 for career. . . . Additional statistics: 12 double-play ground outs in 97 opportunities, 22 doubles, 3 triples allowed in 136.0 innings last season. . . . Allowed 11 first-inning runs in 19 starts last season. . . . Batting support: 4.74 runs per start. . . . Average of 3.18 strikeouts per nine innings was 5th-lowest among N.L. pitchers (minimum: 15 GS). . . . Faced 30 batters in Late-Inning Pressure Situations without a strikeout, 2d-highest total in N.L. last season; Greg Booker faced two more. . . . Did not allow a home run to a left-handed batter in 203 at bats, 5th-highest total in *Player Analysis* history. Last lefty to homer off Forsch: Dan Driessen, Sept. 27, 1984. . . . One of two pitchers ever to smack an extra-base hit off Gooden: Forsch and Fernando own doubles off Doc.

Terry Forster

Atlanta Braves	W–L	ERA	AB	H	HR	BB	SO	BA	SA	OBA
Season	2-3	2.28	221	49	7	28	37	.222	.357	.307
vs. Left-Handed Batters			71	16	2	11	12	.225	.366	.329
vs. Right-Handed Batters			150	33	5	17	25	.220	.353	.296
Home	1-0	1.85	141	28	5	16	26	.199	.348	.280
Road	1-3	3.10	80	21	2	12	11	.263	.375	.351
Grass	2-1	2.20	177	36	7	22	29	.203	.367	.289
Artificial Turf	0-2	2.61	44	13	0	6	8	.295	.318	.380
Day	1-1	1.80	55	13	0	13	9	.236	.273	.371
Night	1-2	2.44	166	36	7	15	28	.217	.386	.282
April	0-1	1.42	47	9	1	5	4	.191	.277	.269
May	0-0	1.80	39	9	2	2	9	.231	.385	.268
June	0-1	0.68	44	6	0	7	8	.136	.136	.255
July	1-0	4.50	44	13	1	3	8	.295	.455	.333
August	1-1	3.00	29	6	3	5	3	.207	.517	.314
Sept./Oct.	0-0	4.15	18	6	0	6	5	.333	.556	.500
Leading Off Inn.			51	5	0	1	8	.098	.137	.115
Bases Empty			120	22	2	14	19	.183	.267	.269
Runners On			101	27	5	14	18	.267	.465	.350
Runners/Scor. Pos.			59	18	3	12	13	.305	.508	.411
Runners On/2 Out			50	16	4	7	4	.320	.580	.404
Scor. Pos./2 Out			29	10	2	7	4	.345	.552	.472
Late Inning Pressure			119	29	5	11	18	.244	.412	.308
Leading Off			27	2	0	1	4	.074	.111	.107
Bases Empty			74	14	1	5	11	.189	.257	.241
Runners On			45	15	4	6	7	.333	.667	.412
Runners/Scor. Pos.			24	10	3	5	4	.417	.833	.517
First 9 Batters			209	46	6	27	35	.220	.349	.308
Second 9 Batters			12	3	1	1	2	.250	.500	.286
All Batters Thereafter			0	0	0	0	0	.000	.000	.000

Loves to face: Bill Madlock (.083, 1-for-12, 4 SO)
Hates to face: Gary Carter (.538, 7-for-13)
Ground outs-to-air outs ratio: 2.74 last season (5th-highest in N.L.), 2.06 for career. . . . Additional statistics: 6 double-play ground outs in 44 opportunities, 9 doubles, 0 triples allowed in 59.1 innings last season. . . . Ranked 6th among N.L. relievers with a 2.28 ERA (minimum: 30 relief games). . . . Opponents' on-base average leading off innings (.115) was a *Player Analysis* record (minimum: 50 PA). . . . Opposing batters hit 84 points higher with runners on base than with the bases empty, 5th-largest difference in N.L. (minimum: 100 AB in each situation). . . . Did not allow more than two earned runs in any game last season, but was usually used in short spurts; he pitched through the batting order only seven times. . . . According to *The Baseball Register*, he has gained only five pounds over the past 15 years.

John Franco

Cincinnati Reds	W–L	ERA	AB	H	HR	BB	SO	BA	SA	OBA
Season	12-3	2.18	354	83	5	40	61	.234	.322	.313
vs. Left-Handed Batters			85	15	1	4	15	.176	.224	.222
vs. Right-Handed Batters			269	68	4	36	46	.253	.353	.340
Home	7-0	1.25	196	39	1	21	38	.199	.270	.279
Road	5-3	3.48	158	44	4	19	23	.278	.386	.356
Grass	4-2	2.91	78	18	3	7	13	.231	.359	.294
Artificial Turf	8-1	1.98	276	65	2	33	48	.236	.312	.318
Day	5-3	3.86	104	29	3	11	17	.279	.462	.348
Night	7-0	1.52	250	54	2	29	44	.216	.264	.299
April	0-1	3.38	9	4	1	4	1	.444	.778	.615
May	2-0	3.77	54	16	1	7	11	.296	.407	.371
June	2-0	1.10	60	10	0	7	9	.167	.200	.254
July	5-0	2.00	59	11	0	7	10	.186	.220	.273
August	2-0	0.30	104	22	0	9	17	.212	.231	.281
Sept./Oct.	1-2	5.19	68	20	3	6	13	.294	.529	.351
Leading Off Inn.			89	25	3	9	9	.281	.438	.347
Bases Empty			206	48	3	21	38	.233	.345	.304
Runners On			148	35	2	19	23	.236	.291	.325
Runners/Scor. Pos.			90	22	1	16	12	.244	.300	.361
Runners On/2 Out			67	15	0	12	11	.224	.239	.342
Scor. Pos./2 Out			47	12	0	10	8	.255	.277	.386
Late Inning Pressure			275	61	4	26	48	.222	.313	.290
Leading Off			74	20	2	4	8	.270	.405	.308
Bases Empty			169	39	2	12	31	.231	.331	.282
Runners On			106	22	2	14	17	.208	.283	.303
Runners/Scor. Pos.			64	12	1	12	9	.188	.266	.321
First 9 Batters			332	79	5	38	61	.238	.331	.317
Second 9 Batters			22	4	0	2	0	.182	.182	.250
All Batters Thereafter			0	0	0	0	0	.000	.000	.000

Loves to face: Von Hayes (0-for-8, 3 SO)
Hates to face: Bill Doran (.857, 6-for-7)
Ground outs-to-air outs ratio: 1.99 last season, 1.78 for career. . . . Additional statistics: 8 double-play ground outs in 73 opportunities, 10 doubles, 3 triples allowed in 99.0 innings last season. . . . Faced 313 batters in Late-Inning Pressure situations last season, highest total in N.L. . . . Led N.L. pitchers with 0.30 ERA during August, after tying for league lead with five wins in July. Season total of 11 relief wins was highest in N.L. . . . Ranked 4th among N.L. relief pitchers with a 2.18 ERA for season (minimum: 30 relief games). . . . Only home run allowed to a left-handed batter was a game-winner to Darryl Strawberry in Franco's season debut on April 13. . . . First Reds pitcher since Rawly Eastwick in 1976 to reach double-figures in both wins and saves with an ERA below 2.50.

George Frazier

Chicago Cubs	W-L	ERA	AB	H	HR	BB	SO	BA	SA	OBA
Season	7-8	6.39	294	88	11	52	46	.299	.466	.409
vs. Left-Handed Batters			140	43	5	24	20	.307	.486	.413
vs. Right-Handed Batters			154	45	6	28	26	.292	.448	.404
Home	5-4	6.64	162	46	9	21	23	.284	.500	.376
Road	2-4	6.11	132	42	2	31	23	.318	.424	.445
Grass	5-6	6.27	217	62	9	34	32	.286	.452	.390
Artificial Turf	2-2	6.75	77	26	2	18	14	.338	.506	.458
Day	5-6	6.89	193	57	9	30	26	.295	.477	.398
Night	2-2	5.47	101	31	2	22	20	.307	.446	.427
April	1-0	11.57	21	8	1	2	2	.381	.571	.435
May	2-1	5.59	38	12	0	8	6	.316	.447	.447
June	1-1	3.77	54	14	3	11	11	.259	.537	.385
July	1-2	3.05	70	15	0	12	9	.214	.214	.337
August	2-1	8.83	76	27	3	9	12	.355	.526	.424
Sept./Oct.	0-3	11.57	35	12	4	10	6	.343	.686	.489
Leading Off Inn.			63	16	2	12	5	.254	.381	.373
Bases Empty			147	45	6	24	19	.306	.483	.410
Runners On			147	43	5	28	27	.293	.449	.407
Runners/Scor. Pos.			92	27	2	26	16	.293	.424	.445
Runners On/2 Out			64	17	1	12	11	.266	.406	.390
Scor. Pos./2 Out			47	14	1	11	7	.298	.468	.431
Late Inning Pressure			127	40	8	27	14	.315	.535	.436
Leading Off			34	10	2	6	2	.294	.500	.400
Bases Empty			73	23	4	12	5	.315	.507	.419
Runners On			54	17	4	15	9	.315	.574	.457
Runners/Scor. Pos.			31	8	2	13	4	.258	.484	.467
First 9 Batters			276	81	10	50	45	.293	.460	.407
Second 9 Batters			18	7	1	2	1	.389	.556	.429
All Batters Thereafter			0	0	0	0	0	.000	.000	.000

Loves to face: Phil Garner (.091, 1-for-11, 3 SO)
Hates to face: Mark Bailey (.800, 4-for-5)
Ground outs-to-air outs ratio: 1.77 last season, 1.52 for career. . . . Additional statistics: 8 double-play ground outs in 79 opportunities, 14 doubles, 1 triple allowed in 76.0 innings last season. . . . ERA of 6.39 was highest among N.L. relievers (mimimum: 30 relief games). . . . Also had highest rate of walks per nine innings among same group (6.16). Walked more batters than he struck out for the first time in his career. . . . Career total of 311 relief appearances ranks 9th among active pitchers who have never started a game. . . . Opponents' overall batting average (.299) was the highest of his career. . . . Yearly batting averages of opposing left-handed batters since 1983: .190, .264, .307. . . . Opponents have .349 career batting average (22-for-63) with the bases loaded.

Gene Garber

Atlanta Braves	W-L	ERA	AB	H	HR	BB	SO	BA	SA	OBA
Season	6-6	3.61	371	98	8	25	66	.264	.375	.313
vs. Left-Handed Batters			195	48	3	12	33	.246	.349	.293
vs. Right-Handed Batters			176	50	5	13	33	.284	.403	.335
Home	4-4	3.42	215	61	4	11	39	.284	.381	.322
Road	2-2	3.86	156	37	4	14	27	.237	.365	.302
Grass	4-5	3.36	300	81	5	15	56	.270	.360	.309
Artificial Turf	2-1	4.58	71	17	3	10	10	.239	.437	.329
Day	1-1	4.50	109	30	5	6	17	.275	.468	.319
Night	5-5	3.25	262	68	3	19	49	.260	.336	.311
April	1-0	5.40	27	8	3	1	7	.296	.630	.321
May	0-0	4.96	64	17	2	2	7	.266	.391	.299
June	0-3	6.30	39	15	0	6	5	.385	.436	.457
July	0-0	1.23	53	12	1	4	13	.226	.340	.281
August	4-2	3.63	83	22	0	3	13	.265	.313	.299
Sept./Oct.	1-1	2.63	105	24	2	9	21	.229	.343	.289
Leading Off Inn.			92	21	0	2	15	.228	.261	.253
Bases Empty			217	60	4	7	36	.276	.373	.305
Runners On			154	38	4	18	30	.247	.377	.324
Runners/Scor. Pos.			97	27	2	13	22	.278	.381	.360
Runners On/2 Out			68	15	1	10	14	.221	.309	.321
Scor. Pos./2 Out			45	10	0	9	9	.222	.267	.352
Late Inning Pressure			168	47	3	20	29	.280	.381	.361
Leading Off			46	10	0	2	7	.217	.217	.265
Bases Empty			109	28	1	4	16	.257	.321	.296
Runners On			59	19	2	16	13	.322	.492	.461
Runners/Scor. Pos.			43	14	1	12	10	.326	.442	.464
First 9 Batters			329	86	7	20	59	.261	.374	.307
Second 9 Batters			42	12	1	5	7	.286	.381	.362
All Batters Thereafter			0	0	0	0	0	.000	.000	.000

Loves to face: Johnnie LeMaster (.080, 2-for-25)
Hates to face: Tim Flannery (.500, 7-for-14)
Ground outs-to-air outs ratio: 2.70 last season (6th-highest in N.L.), 2.15 for career. . . . Additional statistics: 10 double-play ground outs in 74 opportunities, 15 doubles, 1 triple allowed in 97.1 innings last season. . . . Has walked the leadoff batter in only five of 410 innings over the past five seasons (league average: once every 13 innings). . . . Losing pitcher in three straight relief appearances (June 1, 11, 13) for first time in his 16-year career. . . . Finished 31 games last season but had only one save, in season finale. . . . Has faced 1,210 right-handed batters without allowing a triple since Ivan DeJesus connected for one on July 11, 1979. . . . Vested member in the I Yielded A Homer To Don Kessinger Association, 14 members strong. Garber joined in his first major-league game in 1969. Associates include Tom Seaver, Juan Marichal, and Sal Campisi.

Scott Garrelts

San Francisco Giants	W-L	ERA	AB	H	HR	BB	SO	BA	SA	OBA
Season	9-6	2.30	384	76	2	58	106	.198	.253	.306
vs. Left-Handed Batters			169	39	1	20	37	.231	.302	.314
vs. Right-Handed Batters			215	37	1	38	69	.172	.214	.300
Home	7-4	2.26	202	39	1	35	58	.193	.238	.318
Road	2-2	2.34	182	37	1	23	48	.203	.269	.291
Grass	9-6	2.35	319	61	2	50	88	.191	.248	.304
Artificial Turf	0-0	2.04	65	15	0	8	18	.231	.277	.315
Day	9-5	2.16	234	41	1	43	65	.175	.222	.309
Night	0-1	2.54	150	35	1	15	41	.233	.300	.301
April	0-0	2.51	45	7	0	5	8	.156	.222	.250
May	2-3	1.06	64	12	0	14	24	.188	.219	.333
June	0-0	0.36	85	13	1	10	24	.153	.188	.242
July	3-0	2.66	72	12	0	8	21	.167	.208	.247
August	3-0	2.35	60	15	0	10	13	.250	.333	.361
Sept./Oct.	1-3	6.43	58	17	1	11	16	.293	.379	.414
Leading Off Inn.			90	22	1	9	18	.244	.333	.320
Bases Empty			204	39	1	20	56	.191	.250	.270
Runners On			180	37	1	38	50	.206	.256	.342
Runners/Scor. Pos.			110	22	1	31	30	.200	.264	.372
Runners On/2 Out			79	12	0	21	17	.152	.165	.337
Scor. Pos./2 Out			55	6	0	16	14	.109	.109	.319
Late Inning Pressure			228	45	1	41	65	.197	.246	.319
Leading Off			55	13	0	6	9	.236	.291	.311
Bases Empty			120	21	0	14	33	.175	.217	.267
Runners On			108	24	1	27	32	.222	.278	.370
Runners/Scor. Pos.			68	16	1	25	18	.235	.294	.427
First 9 Batters			349	73	2	55	91	.209	.269	.320
Second 9 Batters			35	3	0	3	15	.086	.086	.158
All Batters Thereafter			0	0	0	0	0	.000	.000	.000

Loves to face: Dale Murphy (.091, 1-for-11, 5 SO)
Hates to face: Brad Komminsk (.571, 4-for-7, 1 HR)
Ground outs-to-air outs ratio: 1.51 last season, 1.17 for career. . . . Additional statistics: 6 double-play ground outs in 90 opportunities, 11 doubles, 2 triples allowed in 105.2 innings last season. . . . Tied for 2d in N.L. with nine relief wins last season. . . . His last 11 wins have all occurred in day games. Hasn't won a night game since Sept. 25, 1983. . . . Ranked 7th among N.L. relief pitchers with a 2.30 ERA (minimum: 30 relief games). . . . Career rate of one extra-base hit allowed per 28.6 at bats by left-handed batters is 5th-lowest in majors over past 11 years (minimum: 250 AB). . . . Opponents' batting average dropped from 1984 to '85 in every *Player Analysis* category except leading off innings, which rose 33 points. . . . Only one other Giants pitcher had a winning record: Greg Minton, 5–4.

Dwight Gooden

New York Mets	W-L	ERA	AB	H	HR	BB	SO	BA	SA	OBA
Season	24-4	1.53	986	198	13	69	268	.201	.270	.254
vs. Left-Handed Batters			567	115	3	44	134	.203	.249	.260
vs. Right-Handed Batters			419	83	10	25	134	.198	.298	.246
Home	13-2	1.50	508	97	9	31	143	.191	.268	.237
Road	11-2	1.56	478	101	4	38	125	.211	.272	.271
Grass	18-3	1.40	736	146	11	47	208	.198	.269	.246
Artificial Turf	6-1	1.92	250	52	2	22	60	.208	.272	.276
Day	11-3	1.97	463	99	7	29	109	.214	.285	.259
Night	13-1	1.15	523	99	6	40	159	.189	.256	.250
April	3-1	1.38	130	21	2	10	34	.162	.215	.220
May	4-2	2.14	172	38	3	10	55	.221	.314	.264
June	4-0	1.41	180	40	3	15	45	.222	.289	.284
July	5-0	1.66	149	26	3	12	39	.174	.275	.241
August	4-1	2.45	166	40	2	9	46	.241	.307	.280
Sept./Oct.	4-0	0.34	189	33	0	13	49	.175	.212	.228
Leading Off Inn.			255	50	7	24	74	.196	.310	.265
Bases Empty			625	133	11	48	166	.213	.299	.269
Runners On			361	65	2	21	102	.180	.219	.228
Runners/Scor. Pos.			174	25	1	13	60	.144	.184	.205
Runners On/2 Out			152	24	0	11	49	.158	.178	.215
Scor. Pos./2 Out			83	11	0	7	34	.133	.145	.200
Late Inning Pressure			151	35	2	14	41	.232	.298	.295
Leading Off			38	9	1	4	11	.237	.342	.310
Bases Empty			91	23	2	9	25	.253	.352	.320
Runners On			60	12	0	5	16	.200	.217	.258
Runners/Scor. Pos.			33	2	0	4	12	.061	.061	.158
First 9 Batters			287	55	3	20	80	.192	.261	.244
Second 9 Batters			285	59	5	21	83	.207	.288	.264
All Batters Thereafter			414	84	5	28	105	.203	.263	.255

Loves to face: Tim Wallach (.053, 1-for-19, 11 SO)
Hates to face: Claudell Washington (.571, 5-for-7, 1 HR)
Ground outs-to-air outs ratio: 1.01 last season, 0.96 for career. . . . Additional statistics: 21 double-play ground outs in 174 opportunities, 23 doubles, 3 triples allowed in 276.2 innings last season. . . . Led N.L. pitchers with an average of 7.90 innings per start. . . . Allowed 9 first-inning runs in 35 starts last season. . . . Batting support: 4.89 runs per start, 6th-highest average in N.L. (minimum: 15 GS). . . . Seventh pitcher in major-league history to lead both leagues in wins, ERA, and strikeouts in same season. Others: Walter Johnson, Grover Alexander, Dazzy Vance, Lefty Grove, Hal Newhouser, and Sandy Koufax. . . . First pitcher since Steve Carlton in 1972 to lead his league in both innings pitched and ERA. . . . And he can hit. Tied for league lead in hits among pitchers (21). . . . Over his last nine starts (from Aug. 20) he drove in as many runs as he allowed—8.

Rich Gossage

San Diego Padres	W–L	ERA	AB	H	HR	BB	SO	BA	SA	OBA
Season	5-3	1.82	283	64	1	17	52	.226	.272	.269
vs. Left-Handed Batters			131	33	1	8	23	.252	.313	.291
vs. Right-Handed Batters			152	31	0	9	29	.204	.237	.250
Home	4-2	1.30	119	23	0	5	23	.193	.227	.230
Road	1-1	2.23	164	41	1	12	29	.250	.305	.296
Grass	5-2	1.96	211	44	1	13	37	.209	.242	.256
Artificial Turf	0-1	1.40	72	20	0	4	15	.278	.361	.308
Day	0-1	3.18	85	22	1	5	14	.259	.353	.293
Night	5-2	1.28	198	42	0	12	38	.212	.237	.258
April	1-0	1.98	45	8	0	1	6	.178	.178	.213
May	0-1	2.65	64	17	1	4	16	.266	.359	.304
June	0-0	1.23	51	10	0	6	8	.196	.314	.276
July	1-1	1.15	57	13	0	3	8	.228	.246	.262
August			0	0	0	0	0	.000	.000	.000
Sept./Oct.	3-1	2.00	66	16	0	3	14	.242	.242	.271
Leading Off Inn.			67	11	0	1	18	.164	.194	.188
Bases Empty			168	34	0	7	37	.202	.226	.239
Runners On			115	30	1	10	15	.261	.339	.310
Runners/Scor. Pos.			60	16	1	5	10	.267	.383	.304
Runners On/2 Out			51	12	1	6	6	.235	.333	.316
Scor. Pos./2 Out			32	9	1	3	5	.281	.438	.343
Late Inning Pressure			228	47	0	14	42	.206	.237	.250
Leading Off			54	11	0	1	13	.204	.241	.218
Bases Empty			139	27	0	5	29	.194	.209	.222
Runners On			89	20	0	9	13	.225	.281	.290
Runners/Scor. Pos.			47	11	0	5	8	.234	.319	.296
First 9 Batters			276	63	1	15	51	.228	.275	.267
Second 9 Batters			7	1	0	2	1	.143	.143	.333
All Batters Thereafter			0	0	0	0	0	.000	.000	.000

Loves to face: Jeff Leonard (0-for-10, 6 SO)
Hates to face: Kevin Bass (.750, 3-for-4)
Ground outs-to-air outs ratio: 0.67 last season (9th-lowest in N.L.), 0.82 for career. . . . Additional statistics: 9 double-play ground outs in 62 opportunities, 6 doubles, 2 triples allowed in 79.0 innings last season. . . . Led N.L. relief pitchers with a 1.82 ERA (minimum: 30 relief games). . . . Allowed 1.94 walks per nine innings last season, 2d-best rate among same group. . . . Faced 247 batters in Late-Inning Pressure Situations without allowing a home run last season, the 3d-highest total over past 11 years. The record: 337, by Dale Murray in 1975. . . . Strikeouts per nine innings since 1980: 9.36, 9.19, 9.87, 9.27, 7.39, 5.92. Last year's rate was his lowest since 1976, the year that the White Sox, managed by Paul Richards, had him in the starting rotation. Goose went 9–17, the Sox went 64–97, and the manager's job went to Bob Lemon.

Jim Gott

San Francisco Giants	W–L	ERA	AB	H	HR	BB	SO	BA	SA	OBA
Season	7-10	3.88	567	144	10	51	78	.254	.377	.315
vs. Left-Handed Batters			294	72	4	33	37	.245	.357	.321
vs. Right-Handed Batters			273	72	6	18	41	.264	.399	.307
Home	4-4	2.32	285	63	4	22	49	.221	.326	.276
Road	3-6	5.60	282	81	6	29	29	.287	.429	.352
Grass	5-6	3.07	398	93	6	32	57	.234	.337	.289
Artificial Turf	2-4	5.91	169	51	4	19	21	.302	.473	.372
Day	5-6	3.24	414	97	9	36	55	.234	.357	.295
Night	2-4	5.79	153	47	1	15	23	.307	.431	.367
April	1-0	2.87	57	13	1	6	5	.228	.316	.297
May	1-2	2.52	145	31	2	12	18	.214	.297	.277
June	1-3	5.68	74	25	1	6	12	.338	.432	.378
July	1-3	4.45	113	29	3	9	18	.257	.372	.311
August	1-2	4.23	104	25	2	12	14	.240	.433	.319
Sept./Oct.	2-0	4.42	74	21	1	6	11	.284	.459	.338
Leading Off Inn.			145	38	4	13	22	.262	.407	.327
Bases Empty			332	81	5	28	52	.244	.364	.305
Runners On			235	63	5	23	26	.268	.396	.328
Runners/Scor. Pos.			141	36	3	20	18	.255	.397	.339
Runners On/2 Out			94	22	2	12	12	.234	.372	.321
Scor. Pos./2 Out			63	14	1	10	10	.222	.349	.329
Late Inning Pressure			28	10	0	4	2	.357	.429	.438
Leading Off			8	2	0	1	0	.250	.250	.333
Bases Empty			18	7	0	1	2	.389	.500	.421
Runners On			10	3	0	3	0	.300	.300	.462
Runners/Scor. Pos.			7	1	0	3	0	.143	.143	.400
First 9 Batters			213	57	3	15	30	.268	.390	.313
Second 9 Batters			188	42	2	20	24	.223	.309	.299
All Batters Thereafter			166	45	5	16	24	.271	.440	.335

Loves to face: U.L. Washington (.071, 1-for-14)
Hates to face: Leon Durham (.571, 4-for-7)
Ground outs-to-air outs ratio: 1.23 last season, 1.31 for career. . . . Additional statistics: 10 double-play ground outs in 108 opportunities, 36 doubles (tied for 10th-most in N.L.), 2 triples allowed in 148.1 innings last season. . . . Allowed 17 first-inning runs in 26 starts last season. . . . Batting support: 3.81 runs per start. . . . Only pitcher to hit three home runs last season. . . . Pitched two complete games last season, and failed to retire more than three batters in the start following each one. . . . Giants lost 14 of 16 games that he started from May 19 to Aug. 25. . . . Finished season with a three-game winning streak. . . . Had the misfortune of being one of three pitchers to face Gooden in three games last season, but beat him on Aug. 31 to break Dr. K's 14-game winning streak.

Kevin Gross

Philadelphia Phillies	W–L	ERA	AB	H	HR	BB	SO	BA	SA	OBA
Season	15-13	3.41	773	194	11	81	151	.251	.361	.326
vs. Left-Handed Batters			426	103	4	50	84	.242	.354	.329
vs. Right-Handed Batters			347	91	7	31	67	.262	.369	.322
Home	8-4	2.99	363	89	2	33	79	.245	.344	.308
Road	7-9	3.79	410	105	9	48	72	.256	.376	.340
Grass	3-6	5.66	199	62	7	22	39	.312	.467	.386
Artificial Turf	12-7	2.71	574	132	4	59	112	.230	.324	.305
Day	7-5	3.44	332	77	6	28	72	.232	.352	.295
Night	8-8	3.39	441	117	5	53	79	.265	.367	.348
April	2-2	3.18	61	15	0	5	17	.246	.344	.299
May	1-4	4.50	118	34	1	10	22	.288	.381	.344
June	3-1	2.29	145	35	2	9	27	.241	.352	.299
July	4-1	2.59	150	37	2	15	25	.247	.333	.326
August	3-1	3.78	127	34	4	18	24	.268	.425	.359
Sept./Oct.	2-4	4.27	172	39	2	24	36	.227	.337	.320
Leading Off Inn.			198	46	1	17	37	.232	.323	.296
Bases Empty			446	114	7	42	92	.256	.361	.327
Runners On			327	80	4	39	59	.245	.361	.324
Runners/Scor. Pos.			194	48	3	25	42	.247	.376	.329
Runners On/2 Out			131	23	3	15	30	.176	.321	.260
Scor. Pos./2 Out			89	13	2	11	24	.146	.292	.240
Late Inning Pressure			78	22	0	13	14	.282	.372	.380
Leading Off			22	7	0	3	1	.318	.500	.400
Bases Empty			46	15	0	4	6	.326	.457	.380
Runners On			32	7	0	9	8	.219	.250	.381
Runners/Scor. Pos.			22	3	0	5	8	.136	.182	.286
First 9 Batters			287	75	4	28	63	.261	.352	.327
Second 9 Batters			236	59	4	27	49	.250	.390	.341
All Batters Thereafter			250	60	3	26	39	.240	.344	.309

Loves to face: Mitch Webster (0-for-12)
Hates to face: Pedro Guerrero (.600, 9-for-15)
Ground outs-to-air outs ratio: 0.99 last season, 1.27 for career. . . . Additional statistics: 13 double-play ground outs in 168 opportunities, 32 doubles, 10 triples (tied for 3d-most in N.L.) allowed in 205.2 innings last season. . . . Allowed 9 first-inning runs in 31 starts, 9th-lowest rate in N.L. (minimum: 15 GS). . . . Batting support: 3.35 runs per start, 8th-lowest average in N.L. (minimum: 15 GS). . . . Had N.L.'s 9th-best ERA on artificial turf. . . . Allowed one home run every 18.7 innings, 8th-best average in N.L. last season. . . . Opponents' batting average in Late-Inning Pressure Situations has been at least 30 points higher than overall batting average in each of his three seasons. Career averages: .262 overall, .329 in LIP. . . . Pitched well against good teams last year: 12–8 vs. teams above .500, 3–5 vs. teams below .500.

Cecilio Guante

Pittsburgh Pirates	W–L	ERA	AB	H	HR	BB	SO	BA	SA	OBA
Season	4-6	2.72	393	84	5	40	92	.214	.328	.293
vs. Left-Handed Batters			152	44	3	24	23	.289	.447	.394
vs. Right-Handed Batters			241	40	2	16	69	.166	.253	.222
Home	2-0	2.25	197	39	4	18	45	.198	.315	.271
Road	2-6	3.23	196	45	1	22	47	.230	.342	.314
Grass	1-2	2.51	118	26	0	11	33	.220	.305	.295
Artificial Turf	3-4	2.82	275	58	5	29	59	.211	.338	.291
Day	0-4	2.67	120	25	2	16	28	.208	.350	.299
Night	4-2	2.75	273	59	3	24	64	.216	.319	.289
April	0-0	2.70	62	14	2	3	17	.226	.403	.262
May	1-0	1.37	65	12	0	9	13	.185	.262	.293
June	0-1	1.84	48	5	0	5	14	.104	.146	.185
July	2-2	2.66	88	20	1	7	23	.227	.307	.292
August	0-2	5.79	54	14	1	11	10	.259	.426	.391
Sept./Oct.	1-1	2.66	76	19	1	5	15	.250	.395	.305
Leading Off Inn.			95	23	2	5	23	.242	.379	.287
Bases Empty			230	52	3	16	57	.226	.339	.288
Runners On			163	32	2	24	35	.196	.313	.298
Runners/Scor. Pos.			100	20	1	21	25	.200	.320	.331
Runners On/2 Out			82	14	0	14	19	.171	.268	.292
Scor. Pos./2 Out			56	10	0	12	15	.179	.286	.324
Late Inning Pressure			201	43	3	25	40	.214	.323	.306
Leading Off			53	10	1	4	9	.189	.264	.246
Bases Empty			129	29	2	9	27	.225	.333	.281
Runners On			72	14	1	16	13	.194	.306	.344
Runners/Scor. Pos.			43	9	1	14	10	.209	.349	.397
First 9 Batters			344	73	4	36	82	.212	.331	.292
Second 9 Batters			46	11	1	4	9	.239	.326	.314
All Batters Thereafter			3	0	0	0	1	.000	.000	.000

Loves to face: George Foster (0-for-10, 4 SO)
Hates to face: Bo Diaz (.571, 4-for-7)
Ground outs-to-air outs ratio: 0.64 last season (6th-lowest in N.L.), 0.71 for career. . . . Additional statistics: 6 double-play ground outs in 74 opportunities, 18 doubles, 6 triples allowed in 109.0 innings last season. . . . Opponents' career batting average is .115 (3-for-26) with the bases full. With bases loaded and two outs, they're 0-for-13. . . . Opponents' career batting averages suggest he's ready to be a stopper: .246 with the bases empty, .210 with runners on base, .185 with runners in scoring position (.130 with two outs), .213 in Late-Inning Pressure Situations; even so, he saved only four games in 10 opportunities after the Pirates traded Al Holland. . . . Pitched three or more innings in 11 relief appearances last season, tied for 2d-highest total in N.L. . . . Yearly batting average of opposing right-handed batters since 1983: .270, .175, .166.

Bill Gullickson

Montreal Expos	W–L	ERA	AB	H	HR	BB	SO	BA	SA	OBA
Season	14-12	3.52	691	187	8	47	68	.271	.363	.315
vs. Left-Handed Batters			362	102	3	33	30	.282	.362	.338
vs. Right-Handed Batters			329	85	5	14	38	.258	.365	.288
Home	10-2	1.65	348	77	2	22	40	.221	.284	.265
Road	4-10	5.75	343	110	6	25	28	.321	.443	.365
Grass	2-6	5.80	193	62	4	12	13	.321	.456	.362
Artificial Turf	12-6	2.77	498	125	4	35	55	.251	.327	.296
Day	9-2	2.00	286	64	2	20	24	.224	.297	.272
Night	5-10	4.75	405	123	6	27	44	.304	.410	.345
April	3-2	4.08	106	29	1	6	10	.274	.358	.307
May	3-3	3.16	138	37	1	6	14	.268	.391	.303
June	1-0	0.00	16	3	0	4	1	.188	.188	.333
July	3-2	2.60	133	35	1	12	16	.263	.316	.324
August	3-2	3.26	150	42	1	6	15	.280	.347	.304
Sept./Oct.	1-3	5.06	148	41	4	13	12	.277	.419	.329
Leading Off Inn.			179	59	3	10	18	.330	.430	.365
Bases Empty			403	110	5	20	48	.273	.357	.309
Runners On			288	77	3	27	20	.267	.372	.322
Runners/Scor. Pos.			177	47	3	18	14	.266	.395	.320
Runners On/2 Out			125	32	0	12	12	.256	.336	.321
Scor. Pos./2 Out			87	23	0	10	7	.264	.356	.340
Late Inning Pressure			48	12	0	6	3	.250	.333	.333
Leading Off			15	4	0	0	1	.267	.267	.267
Bases Empty			31	9	0	3	1	.290	.323	.353
Runners On			17	3	0	3	2	.176	.353	.300
Runners/Scor. Pos.			11	1	0	2	2	.091	.182	.231
First 9 Batters			237	67	2	16	30	.283	.388	.325
Second 9 Batters			227	54	2	14	22	.238	.308	.280
All Batters Thereafter			227	66	4	17	16	.291	.392	.337

Loves to face: Danny Heep (.050, 1-for-20)
Hates to face: Wally Backman (.409, 9-for-22)
Ground outs-to-air outs ratio: 0.88 last season, 0.91 for career. . . . Additional statistics: 13 double-play ground outs in 127 opportunities, 34 doubles, 3 triples allowed in 181.1 innings last season. . . . Allowed 25 first-inning runs (tied for 2d-most in N.L.) in 29 starts last season. . . . Batting support: 3.55 runs per start. . . . Led N.L. in extra-base hits allowed in 1983 and '84. . . . Had league's 3d-best day-game ERA; only Gooden won more day games. . . . If you can't hit him, have him join you: Pete Rose career vs. Gullickson: .192 (10-for-52, 1 home run). . . . Opponents batted for a lower average in home games than in road games in each of his seven seasons with the Expos. His career records: 45–21 at Olympic Stadium, 27–40 elsewhere. . . . Won his only two starts at Riverfront last season.

Atlee Hammaker

San Francisco Giants	W–L	ERA	AB	H	HR	BB	SO	BA	SA	OBA
Season	5-12	3.74	651	161	17	47	100	.247	.386	.295
vs. Left-Handed Batters			105	23	2	3	17	.219	.333	.239
vs. Right-Handed Batters			546	138	15	44	83	.253	.396	.305
Home	2-3	3.39	342	79	11	19	64	.231	.365	.268
Road	3-9	4.15	309	82	6	28	36	.265	.408	.324
Grass	3-6	3.63	480	116	17	33	77	.242	.392	.288
Artificial Turf	2-6	4.06	171	45	0	14	23	.263	.368	.314
Day	2-5	3.39	366	82	11	24	63	.224	.347	.270
Night	3-7	4.23	285	79	6	23	37	.277	.435	.327
April	0-2	3.86	87	22	4	5	14	.253	.483	.290
May	1-2	2.25	118	27	0	11	19	.229	.271	.290
June	2-4	4.34	138	34	4	13	19	.246	.399	.307
July	0-1	2.37	69	13	2	3	18	.188	.348	.219
August	1-1	4.03	116	31	3	3	15	.267	.371	.283
Sept./Oct.	1-2	5.10	123	34	4	12	15	.276	.447	.341
Leading Off Inn.			171	42	3	5	24	.246	.374	.267
Bases Empty			397	101	13	25	66	.254	.418	.299
Runners On			254	60	4	22	34	.236	.335	.290
Runners/Scor. Pos.			141	38	3	13	21	.270	.426	.317
Runners On/2 Out			108	23	2	14	17	.213	.296	.303
Scor. Pos./2 Out			65	16	2	10	11	.246	.385	.347
Late Inning Pressure			34	7	1	5	3	.206	.294	.308
Leading Off			10	2	0	2	1	.200	.200	.333
Bases Empty			23	6	1	4	2	.261	.391	.370
Runners On			11	1	0	1	1	.091	.091	.167
Runners/Scor. Pos.			2	0	0	0	0	.000	.000	.000
First 9 Batters			239	49	8	16	49	.205	.331	.254
Second 9 Batters			231	69	4	18	26	.299	.446	.344
All Batters Thereafter			181	43	5	13	25	.238	.381	.286

Loves to face: Andre Dawson (.059, 1-for-17)
Hates to face: Dale Murphy (.542, 13-for-24, 4 HR)
Ground outs-to-air outs ratio: 1.51 last season, 1.39 for career. . . . Additional statistics: 12 double-play ground outs in 114 opportunities, 25 doubles, 7 triples allowed in 170.2 innings last season. . . . Allowed 16 first-inning runs in 29 starts last season. . . . Batting support: 3.38 runs per start, 9th-lowest average in N.L. (minimum: 15 GS). . . . Career average of 1.95 walks per nine innings ranks 4th among active pitchers (minimum: 500 innings). . . . Career average of one walk per 44.0 leadoff batters faced ranks 3d among active pitchers (minimum: 500 BFP). . . . Opponents' career batting averages: left-handers .189, right-handers .266. . . . Shut-out of the Reds on June 17 was his only complete game in his last 40 starts. . . . Has a record of 8–17 since his disastrous appearance in the 1983 All-Star Game.

Andy Hawkins

San Diego Padres	W–L	ERA	AB	H	HR	BB	SO	BA	SA	OBA
Season	18-8	3.15	859	229	18	65	69	.267	.395	.317
vs. Left-Handed Batters			413	111	9	40	29	.269	.402	.332
vs. Right-Handed Batters			446	118	9	25	40	.265	.388	.303
Home	10-6	3.14	474	128	12	35	35	.270	.409	.318
Road	8-2	3.16	385	101	6	30	34	.262	.377	.316
Grass	14-7	3.14	649	170	15	45	49	.262	.391	.309
Artificial Turf	4-1	3.17	210	59	3	20	20	.281	.405	.342
Day	7-4	3.02	300	83	9	28	27	.277	.427	.334
Night	11-4	3.22	559	146	9	37	42	.261	.377	.308
April	4-0	2.70	97	21	3	3	9	.216	.371	.238
May	6-0	2.72	168	47	5	7	19	.280	.440	.309
June	1-2	3.71	159	45	2	20	11	.283	.396	.368
July	2-1	3.16	100	30	1	10	6	.300	.440	.357
August	3-1	2.72	155	40	2	9	12	.258	.342	.295
Sept./Oct.	2-4	3.60	180	46	5	16	12	.256	.383	.313
Leading Off Inn.			230	67	9	11	19	.291	.496	.326
Bases Empty			528	147	14	28	47	.278	.430	.317
Runners On			331	82	4	37	22	.248	.338	.317
Runners/Scor. Pos.			198	44	2	26	18	.222	.278	.300
Runners On/2 Out			131	24	0	17	4	.183	.221	.282
Scor. Pos./2 Out			90	16	0	13	4	.178	.200	.288
Late Inning Pressure			80	24	4	13	1	.300	.500	.398
Leading Off			25	7	2	2	1	.280	.560	.333
Bases Empty			56	19	3	6	1	.339	.571	.403
Runners On			24	5	1	7	0	.208	.333	.387
Runners/Scor. Pos.			13	3	0	5	0	.231	.231	.444
First 9 Batters			273	65	4	20	37	.238	.344	.288
Second 9 Batters			261	73	6	19	17	.280	.418	.328
All Batters Thereafter			325	91	8	26	15	.280	.418	.332

Loves to face: Mookie Wilson (0-for-13, 5 SO)
Hates to face: Johnny Ray (.632, 12-for-19)
Ground outs-to-air outs ratio: 1.00 last season, 1.00 for career. . . . Additional statistics: 23 double-play ground outs in 162 opportunities, 42 doubles (8th-most in N.L.), 7 triples allowed in 228.2 innings last season. . . . Total of 67 extra-base hits allowed was 9th-highest in N.L. . . . Allowed 15 first-inning runs in 33 starts last season. . . . Batting support: 4.52 runs per start. . . . Won his first 10 starts. Record of 11–0 after 12 starts. . . . Led N.L. with six wins in May. . . . Average of 2.72 strikeouts per nine innings was 2d-lowest among N.L. pitchers who started at least 15 games. . . . Career average of one home run allowed per 33.6 at bats in day games, 61.8 at bats in night games. . . . Opponents' batting average with runners in scoring position was the lowest of his career.

Orel Hershiser

Los Angeles Dodgers	W–L	ERA	AB	H	HR	BB	SO	BA	SA	OBA
Season	19-3	2.03	870	179	8	68	157	.206	.272	.267
vs. Left-Handed Batters			477	106	3	39	72	.222	.289	.281
vs. Right-Handed Batters			393	73	5	29	85	.186	.252	.249
Home	11-0	1.08	463	74	4	39	96	.160	.207	.231
Road	8-3	3.22	407	105	4	29	61	.258	.346	.308
Grass	15-2	1.81	672	126	8	52	134	.188	.254	.251
Artificial Turf	4-1	2.82	198	53	0	16	23	.268	.333	.319
Day	4-2	2.87	323	76	6	19	59	.235	.341	.283
Night	15-1	1.57	547	103	2	49	98	.188	.232	.257
April	3-0	1.86	98	16	0	7	19	.163	.214	.219
May	2-0	1.59	151	31	1	11	40	.205	.285	.268
June	2-2	4.26	115	30	2	7	13	.261	.357	.303
July	4-1	2.16	154	32	1	17	26	.208	.266	.289
August	2-0	1.86	142	32	1	13	19	.225	.289	.302
Sept./Oct.	6-0	1.22	210	38	3	13	40	.181	.238	.227
Leading Off Inn.			228	50	3	16	39	.219	.298	.276
Bases Empty			542	110	4	35	101	.203	.258	.258
Runners On			328	69	4	33	56	.210	.296	.281
Runners/Scor. Pos.			173	37	2	25	33	.214	.306	.307
Runners On/2 Out			132	27	3	16	25	.205	.333	.291
Scor. Pos./2 Out			83	19	2	13	16	.229	.386	.333
Late Inning Pressure			86	15	2	8	18	.174	.279	.260
Leading Off			24	6	2	4	4	.250	.625	.357
Bases Empty			61	12	2	5	13	.197	.344	.269
Runners On			25	3	0	3	5	.120	.120	.241
Runners/Scor. Pos.			14	1	0	2	2	.071	.071	.188
First 9 Batters			292	57	2	25	64	.195	.260	.262
Second 9 Batters			279	60	3	18	53	.215	.280	.263
All Batters Thereafter			299	62	3	25	40	.207	.278	.276

Loves to face: Dave Concepcion (0-for-15)
Hates to face: Bob Brenly (.308, 4-for-13, 2 HR)
Led N.L. with .864 winning percentage. Who was last Dodgers pitcher to lead league? Answer later. . . . .Ground outs-to-air outs ratio: 2.21 last season, 2.47 for career. . . . Additional statistics: 25 double-play ground outs in 160 opportunities, 26 doubles, 4 triples allowed in 239.2 innings last season. . . . Allowed 14 first-inning runs in 34 starts last season. . . . Batting support: 4.50 runs per start. . . . Allowed one home run per 30.0 innings, best rate in majors last season. . . . Career average of one extra-base hit allowed per 23.6 at bats by right-handed batters is 8th-best in past 11 seasons (minimum: 250 AB). . . . His three losses were the only games all season in which he allowed more than three earned runs. . . . Had major leagues' best record (13–2) in games against teams with winning records. . . . Last L.A. pitcher to lead N.L. in W–L Pct. was Rick Rhoden in 1976.

Joe Hesketh

Montreal Expos	W–L	ERA	AB	H	HR	BB	SO	BA	SA	OBA
Season	10-5	2.49	562	125	10	45	113	.222	.331	.279
vs. Left-Handed Batters			93	20	1	7	17	.215	.269	.270
vs. Right-Handed Batters			469	105	9	38	96	.224	.343	.281
Home	6-3	2.30	285	65	4	23	64	.228	.326	.285
Road	4-2	2.69	277	60	6	22	49	.217	.336	.273
Grass	2-0	1.55	101	21	1	6	17	.208	.297	.250
Artificial Turf	8-5	2.71	461	104	9	39	96	.226	.338	.285
Day	3-3	2.83	203	48	2	14	33	.236	.345	.284
Night	7-2	2.30	359	77	8	31	80	.214	.323	.276
April	2-1	2.84	69	15	0	4	15	.217	.275	.260
May	3-1	1.26	148	26	4	9	37	.176	.311	.223
June	0-1	2.78	130	31	2	14	21	.238	.323	.308
July	3-1	2.62	127	31	3	10	27	.244	.331	.299
August	2-1	3.86	88	22	1	8	13	.250	.420	.313
Sept./Oct.			0	0	0	0	0	.000	.000	.000
Leading Off Inn.			148	27	1	11	21	.182	.236	.239
Bases Empty			362	73	6	30	71	.202	.287	.263
Runners On			200	52	4	15	42	.260	.410	.309
Runners/Scor. Pos.			106	24	2	5	29	.226	.340	.257
Runners On/2 Out			88	24	2	9	14	.273	.466	.340
Scor. Pos./2 Out			53	14	2	4	10	.264	.472	.316
Late Inning Pressure			44	14	0	6	10	.318	.432	.400
Leading Off			11	2	0	3	3	.182	.273	.357
Bases Empty			25	8	0	4	7	.320	.520	.414
Runners On			19	6	0	2	3	.316	.316	.381
Runners/Scor. Pos.			13	4	0	2	3	.308	.308	.400
First 9 Batters			198	44	1	19	44	.222	.278	.289
Second 9 Batters			202	40	8	7	33	.198	.366	.225
All Batters Thereafter			162	41	1	19	36	.253	.352	.330

Loves to face: Terry Kennedy (0-for-3, 3 SO)
Hates to face: Gary Carter (.800, 4-for-5, 1 HR)
Ground outs-to-air outs ratio: 1.07 last season, 1.09 for career. ... Additional statistics: 10 double-play ground outs in 93 opportunities, 29 doubles, 1 triple allowed in 155.1 innings last season. ... Allowed 12 first-inning runs in 25 starts last season. ... Batting support: 3.68 runs per start. ... ERA of 1.26 during month of May was 2d-best in N.L. ... Sixth in N.L. in ERA when his season ended on August 23, but fell 6.2 innings short of qualifying for ranking among leaders. ... Career total of 800 batters faced without hitting one with a pitch (4th-highest total among active pitchers). ... Opponents' career batting averages: .241 with runners on base, .216 with the bases empty. ... Has allowed only one home run (to Jose Cruz) in 131 career plate appearances by opposing left-handers.

Al Holland

Phillies/Pirates	W–L	ERA	AB	H	HR	BB	SO	BA	SA	OBA
Season	1-4	3.45	226	53	5	21	48	.235	.372	.295
vs. Left-Handed Batters			69	17	2	5	18	.246	.377	.286
vs. Right-Handed Batters			157	36	3	16	30	.229	.369	.299
Home	0-2	2.29	140	26	3	10	33	.186	.321	.238
Road	1-2	5.40	86	27	2	11	15	.314	.453	.380
Grass	1-2	4.05	47	13	2	7	7	.277	.426	.364
Artificial Turf	0-2	3.28	179	40	3	14	41	.223	.358	.276
Day	1-2	2.05	76	17	1	8	17	.224	.303	.298
Night	0-2	4.20	150	36	4	13	31	.240	.407	.293
April	0-1	1.50	41	6	0	6	7	.146	.195	.245
May	1-1	1.96	63	11	1	3	9	.175	.254	.209
June	0-2	5.79	73	22	1	10	23	.301	.466	.381
July	0-0	3.95	49	14	3	2	9	.286	.531	.314
August			0	0	0	0	0	.000	.000	.000
Sept./Oct.			0	0	0	0	0	.000	.000	.000
Leading Off Inn.			53	12	1	3	16	.226	.358	.268
Bases Empty			128	28	4	10	35	.219	.359	.275
Runners On			98	25	1	11	13	.255	.388	.319
Runners/Scor. Pos.			60	16	1	11	10	.267	.417	.360
Runners On/2 Out			47	12	0	4	6	.255	.362	.314
Scor. Pos./2 Out			30	9	0	4	5	.300	.433	.382
Late Inning Pressure			105	31	2	9	18	.295	.438	.348
Leading Off			25	7	0	1	7	.280	.360	.308
Bases Empty			54	18	2	4	12	.333	.500	.379
Runners On			51	13	0	5	6	.255	.373	.316
Runners/Scor. Pos.			35	9	0	5	6	.257	.400	.341
First 9 Batters			202	48	5	18	45	.238	.381	.295
Second 9 Batters			24	5	0	3	3	.208	.292	.296
All Batters Thereafter			0	0	0	0	0	.000	.000	.000

Loves to face: Steve Yeager (.176, 3-for-17, 4 SO)
Hates to face: Bill Buckner (.308, 4-for-13, 1 HR)
Figures above are for N.L. only. ... Ground outs-to-air outs ratio: 0.45 last season (3d-lowest in majors), 0.66 for career. ... Additional statistics: 5 double-play ground outs in 57 opportunities, 19 doubles, 0 triples allowed in 87.0 innings last season. ... 1985 combined-league averages: .196 with bases empty, .259 with runners on base. ... Opponents' career batting averages of .228 in Late-Inning Pressure Situations, .219 with runners in scoring position. ... Allowed five home runs in 62.2 innings in the N.L. last season, four home runs in 24.1 innings for California. ... Strikeout percentage of 26.6 per 100 plate appearances vs. left-handed batters since '83 is 2d-highest in majors during that period (minimum: 75 SO). ... More good news for the Angels: Highest K-rate vs. lefties from 1983–85 belongs to John Candelaria (36.2 per 100 PA).

Rick Honeycutt

Los Angeles Dodgers	W–L	ERA	AB	H	HR	BB	SO	BA	SA	OBA
Season	8-12	3.42	541	141	9	49	67	.261	.388	.321
vs. Left-Handed Batters			73	16	0	6	14	.219	.329	.272
vs. Right-Handed Batters			468	125	9	43	53	.267	.397	.329
Home	5-6	2.70	296	70	3	22	43	.236	.338	.288
Road	3-6	4.35	245	71	6	27	24	.290	.449	.359
Grass	6-8	2.80	381	89	6	31	54	.234	.357	.290
Artificial Turf	2-4	5.08	160	52	3	18	13	.325	.463	.392
Day	1-3	4.39	108	28	4	13	18	.259	.481	.339
Night	7-9	3.20	433	113	5	36	49	.261	.365	.316
April	1-1	2.25	68	12	1	4	8	.176	.265	.222
May	2-4	2.21	138	35	3	14	20	.254	.362	.320
June	2-2	3.91	92	22	1	8	16	.239	.359	.307
July	1-2	6.23	77	30	1	8	7	.390	.597	.442
August	1-3	4.43	78	20	3	8	7	.256	.423	.326
Sept./Oct.	1-0	2.92	88	22	0	7	9	.250	.341	.299
Leading Off Inn.			141	38	1	9	15	.270	.404	.318
Bases Empty			327	83	4	23	40	.254	.364	.305
Runners On			214	58	5	26	27	.271	.425	.344
Runners/Scor. Pos.			110	35	2	21	12	.318	.473	.415
Runners On/2 Out			93	30	2	14	11	.323	.495	.411
Scor. Pos./2 Out			53	17	0	12	5	.321	.415	.446
Late Inning Pressure			27	5	0	3	4	.185	.259	.267
Leading Off			9	3	0	1	1	.333	.444	.400
Bases Empty			20	4	0	1	3	.200	.250	.238
Runners On			7	1	0	2	1	.143	.286	.333
Runners/Scor. Pos.			4	1	0	1	0	.250	.500	.400
First 9 Batters			232	45	4	20	28	.194	.310	.261
Second 9 Batters			186	59	3	18	24	.317	.462	.370
All Batters Thereafter			123	37	2	11	15	.301	.423	.358

Loves to face: Brad Komminsk (0-for-15)
Hates to face: Jack Clark (.545, 6-for-11, 2 HR)
Ground outs-to-air outs ratio: 2.02 last season, 1.92 for career. ... Additional statistics: 17 double-play ground outs in 95 opportunities (10th-highest rate in N.L.), 34 doubles, 4 triples allowed in 142.0 innings last season. ... Average of 5.30 innings per start was 5th-lowest among N.L. pitchers (minimum: 15 GS). ... Allowed 11 first-inning runs in 25 starts last season. ... Batting support: 3.72 runs per start. ... Opposing left-handers batted .264 in his six years in the A.L., but only .204 in his three years with the Dodgers. ... Triple by Ken Oberkfell on June 28 last season was first vs. Honeycutt by a lefty batter since Mickey Rivers hit one on July 2, 1980. ... Opponents' batting average of .125 (3-for-24) with the bases loaded since 1983. ... Opponents' batting average in Late-Inning Pressure Situations was also under .200 in '84.

Ricky Horton

St. Louis Cardinals	W–L	ERA	AB	H	HR	BB	SO	BA	SA	OBA
Season	3-2	2.91	334	84	5	34	59	.251	.353	.324
vs. Left-Handed Batters			105	23	0	7	19	.219	.238	.270
vs. Right-Handed Batters			229	61	5	27	40	.266	.406	.347
Home	1-0	3.03	135	35	2	12	27	.259	.385	.318
Road	2-2	2.83	199	49	3	22	32	.246	.332	.327
Grass	0-0	0.63	50	12	0	7	10	.240	.280	.361
Artificial Turf	3-2	3.35	284	72	5	27	49	.254	.366	.316
Day	0-1	3.03	113	30	2	13	22	.265	.416	.357
Night	3-1	2.85	221	54	3	21	37	.244	.321	.306
April	0-0	0.96	29	4	0	1	8	.138	.172	.161
May	0-1	0.63	52	12	0	6	11	.231	.288	.310
June	0-0	5.79	39	14	1	5	8	.359	.462	.435
July	0-1	3.00	41	10	1	6	8	.244	.341	.347
August	2-0	4.50	84	23	2	8	13	.274	.429	.337
Sept./Oct.	1-0	2.55	89	21	1	8	11	.236	.337	.306
Leading Off Inn.			79	21	0	6	19	.266	.354	.318
Bases Empty			193	46	4	11	38	.238	.363	.279
Runners On			141	38	1	23	21	.270	.340	.376
Runners/Scor. Pos.			96	28	1	19	14	.292	.354	.408
Runners On/2 Out			64	16	0	12	8	.250	.297	.377
Scor. Pos./2 Out			43	13	0	11	4	.302	.372	.455
Late Inning Pressure			89	23	0	16	16	.258	.315	.383
Leading Off			24	9	0	2	3	.375	.542	.423
Bases Empty			49	17	0	3	7	.347	.449	.385
Runners On			40	6	0	13	9	.150	.150	.382
Runners/Scor. Pos.			27	5	0	11	4	.185	.185	.436
First 9 Batters			227	54	4	29	42	.238	.339	.328
Second 9 Batters			76	22	1	5	13	.289	.408	.333
All Batters Thereafter			31	8	0	0	4	.258	.323	.258

Loves to face: Mookie Wilson (0-for-10, 3 SO)
Hates to face: Johnny Ray (.571, 8-for-14)
Ground outs-to-air outs ratio: 1.51 last season, 1.32 for career. ... Additional statistics: 6 double-play ground outs in 66 opportunities, 15 doubles, 2 triples allowed in 89.2 innings last season. ... Opponents' career batting averages: left-handers .228, right-handers .288. Of 19 career home runs vs. Horton, 17 have been hit by right-handed batters. Only lefties to connect against Horton are both Mets: Hernandez and Strawberry. ... Career vs. New York: 1–0, 1.72 ERA in 12 games. ... Opponents' career batting average of .143 (3-for-21) with the bases loaded. ... Has never allowed a home run in Late-Inning Pressure Situations (133 career LIP batters faced). ... Did not reach the seventh inning in any of his three starts last season. Has pitched one complete game in 21 career starts.

Ken Howell

Los Angeles Dodgers	W–L	ERA	AB	H	HR	BB	SO	BA	SA	OBA
Season	4-7	3.77	317	66	8	35	85	.208	.312	.287
vs. Left-Handed Batters			151	28	1	17	36	.185	.245	.268
vs. Right-Handed Batters			166	38	7	18	49	.229	.373	.304
Home	1-4	4.17	165	36	4	21	37	.218	.327	.306
Road	3-3	3.32	152	30	4	14	48	.197	.296	.265
Grass	3-5	4.04	240	50	6	27	60	.208	.317	.288
Artificial Turf	1-2	2.95	77	16	2	8	25	.208	.299	.282
Day	3-1	1.42	105	15	2	15	31	.143	.219	.250
Night	1-6	5.13	212	51	6	20	54	.241	.358	.306
April	0-1	2.84	51	12	0	8	18	.235	.255	.339
May	2-1	3.14	49	7	3	8	17	.143	.347	.263
June	2-1	3.07	49	6	1	4	15	.122	.184	.189
July	0-1	2.77	47	9	1	3	12	.191	.277	.240
August	0-1	3.09	45	13	1	1	7	.289	.400	.304
Sept./Oct.	0-2	6.41	76	19	2	11	16	.250	.382	.345
Leading Off Inn.			71	19	4	8	18	.268	.493	.342
Bases Empty			169	32	4	20	48	.189	.290	.275
Runners On			148	34	4	15	37	.230	.338	.301
Runners/Scor. Pos.			82	23	2	12	18	.280	.378	.372
Runners On/2 Out			65	17	1	4	15	.262	.354	.304
Scor. Pos./2 Out			36	9	0	4	9	.250	.278	.325
Late Inning Pressure			204	45	5	27	54	.221	.319	.312
Leading Off			46	11	2	7	16	.239	.413	.340
Bases Empty			101	23	2	16	28	.228	.317	.333
Runners On			103	22	3	11	26	.214	.320	.289
Runners/Scor. Pos.			54	14	1	8	12	.259	.333	.355
First 9 Batters			297	61	8	33	77	.205	.313	.285
Second 9 Batters			20	5	0	2	8	.250	.300	.318
All Batters Thereafter			0	0	0	0	0	.000	.000	.000

Loves to face: Chili Davis (0-for-4, 3 SO)
Hates to face: Mike Schmidt (.600, 3-for-5, 1 HR)
Ground outs-to-air outs ratio: 1.07 last season, 1.13 for career. . . . Additional statistics: 3 double-play ground outs in 69 opportunities (3d-lowest rate in N.L.), 9 doubles, 0 triples allowed in 86.0 innings last season. . . . Collected 11 of Dodgers' first 22 saves last season, but only one of their last 14. . . . Pitched only two innings in N.L.C.S. after allowing 13 earned runs in his final 12.2 innings of work during the regular season. . . . Longest outing of the season was 3.2 innings vs. the Giants on April 24. . . . Lopsided lefty/righty breakdown for second straight year, but in different directions. Career averages: left-handers .249, right-handers .213. Career average of 4.24 strikeouts per walk vs. right-handed batters. . . . Danny Heep homer on June 3 is the only one surrendered to a left-handed batter in his career.

LaMarr Hoyt

San Diego Padres	W–L	ERA	AB	H	HR	BB	SO	BA	SA	OBA
Season	16-8	3.47	805	210	20	20	83	.261	.386	.280
vs. Left-Handed Batters			430	123	11	12	29	.286	.412	.303
vs. Right-Handed Batters			375	87	9	8	54	.232	.357	.252
Home	9-5	4.08	455	127	14	12	56	.279	.420	.298
Road	7-3	2.70	350	83	6	8	27	.237	.343	.256
Grass	11-6	3.65	600	156	16	16	71	.260	.390	.279
Artificial Turf	5-2	2.92	205	54	4	4	12	.263	.376	.280
Day	5-3	3.38	265	68	7	9	29	.257	.400	.283
Night	11-5	3.51	540	142	13	11	54	.263	.380	.278
April	2-2	4.09	129	33	2	1	16	.256	.372	.262
May	3-2	3.55	142	35	2	8	10	.246	.359	.288
June	5-0	2.05	162	36	5	4	25	.222	.340	.241
July	3-1	2.74	173	42	4	4	16	.243	.370	.258
August	0-3	9.82	89	39	5	2	8	.438	.652	.451
Sept./Oct.	3-0	2.03	110	25	2	1	8	.227	.318	.241
Leading Off Inn.			208	47	9	5	20	.226	.394	.248
Bases Empty			532	124	12	12	59	.233	.346	.251
Runners On			273	86	8	8	24	.315	.465	.333
Runners/Scor. Pos.			139	41	3	7	13	.295	.417	.327
Runners On/2 Out			125	40	2	3	14	.320	.448	.336
Scor. Pos./2 Out			74	20	1	3	8	.270	.405	.299
Late Inning Pressure			96	20	2	3	7	.208	.323	.232
Leading Off			25	2	1	1	4	.080	.200	.115
Bases Empty			73	13	2	3	6	.178	.288	.211
Runners On			23	7	0	0	1	.304	.435	.304
Runners/Scor. Pos.			12	3	0	0	0	.250	.417	.250
First 9 Batters			269	67	7	5	34	.249	.357	.264
Second 9 Batters			255	69	6	6	22	.271	.400	.288
All Batters Thereafter			281	74	7	9	27	.263	.402	.286

Loves to face: U.L. Washington (.091, 2-for-22)
Hates to face: Mike Marshall (.571, 4-for-7, 1 HR)
Ground outs-to-air outs ratio: 1.02 last season, 1.22 for career. . . . Additional statistics: 14 double-play ground outs in 115 opportunities, 31 doubles, 5 triples allowed in 210.1 innings last season. . . . Allowed 18 first-inning runs in 31 starts last season. . . . Batting support: 4.48 runs per start. . . . Turning point of his season: May 20, Hoyt vs. Gooden, bottom of the first, bases loaded, none out. Hoyt, 2–4, got Gary Carter to hit into a double play on a 3–0 pitch, and shut out the Mets to start an 11-game winning streak that included 3 shutouts and 7 complete games. . . . Career average of 1.65 walks per nine innings ranks 2d among active pitchers (minimum: 500 innings). . . . Opponents have hit for a higher average with runners on than with bases empty in every season of his career except '82, when the marks were .2658 and .2663.

Charles Hudson

Philadelphia Phillies	W–L	ERA	AB	H	HR	BB	SO	BA	SA	OBA
Season	8-13	3.78	746	188	23	74	122	.252	.412	.319
vs. Left-Handed Batters			377	103	9	41	45	.273	.419	.344
vs. Right-Handed Batters			369	85	14	33	77	.230	.404	.293
Home	3-5	3.86	361	93	14	28	56	.258	.440	.310
Road	5-8	3.70	385	95	9	46	66	.247	.384	.326
Grass	1-4	4.70	179	51	6	21	25	.285	.486	.358
Artificial Turf	7-9	3.49	567	137	17	53	97	.242	.388	.306
Day	4-2	2.91	204	35	7	26	37	.172	.319	.264
Night	4-11	4.15	542	153	16	48	85	.282	.446	.340
April	0-2	3.97	44	13	1	7	5	.295	.386	.396
May	1-3	2.91	117	17	4	9	17	.145	.316	.206
June	2-2	4.13	130	37	3	11	22	.285	.454	.336
July	2-1	4.83	132	40	4	11	27	.303	.492	.357
August	2-3	3.89	174	46	7	15	29	.264	.454	.323
Sept./Oct.	1-2	3.20	149	35	4	21	22	.235	.336	.327
Leading Off Inn.			184	42	2	15	20	.228	.283	.286
Bases Empty			438	101	15	41	71	.231	.390	.296
Runners On			308	87	8	33	51	.282	.442	.350
Runners/Scor. Pos.			183	42	4	27	33	.230	.383	.322
Runners On/2 Out			128	30	2	15	23	.234	.383	.315
Scor. Pos./2 Out			86	18	1	12	17	.209	.349	.306
Late Inning Pressure			105	26	3	11	14	.248	.362	.319
Leading Off			30	6	0	0	4	.200	.200	.200
Bases Empty			75	14	1	4	9	.187	.253	.228
Runners On			30	12	2	7	5	.400	.633	.514
Runners/Scor. Pos.			16	5	1	7	3	.313	.563	.522
First 9 Batters			269	62	7	28	51	.230	.372	.304
Second 9 Batters			206	54	7	23	38	.262	.422	.335
All Batters Thereafter			271	72	9	23	33	.266	.443	.321

Loves to face: Bob Dernier (.042, 1-for-24)
Hates to face: Dale Murphy (.538, 7-for-13, 4 HR)
Ground outs-to-air outs ratio: 0.85 last season, 0.88 for career. . . . Additional statistics: 11 double-play ground outs in 156 opportunities, 34 doubles, 8 triples (tied for 7th-most in N.L.) allowed in 193.0 innings last season. . . . Total of 65 extra-base hits allowed was 10th-highest in N.L. . . . Allowed 13 first-inning runs in 26 starts last season. . . . Batting support: 4.88 runs per start, 8th-highest average in N.L. (minimum: 15 GS). . . . Allowed one home run per 8.4 innings, 7th-worst rate among N.L. pitchers (minimum: 15 GS). . . . Has allowed only one career walk to leadoff batters in 60 innings in Late-Inning Pressure Situations. Opponents have a career batting average of .150 (9-for-60) in such situations.

Tom Hume

Cincinnati Reds	W–L	ERA	AB	H	HR	BB	SO	BA	SA	OBA
Season	3-5	3.26	290	65	7	35	50	.224	.341	.313
vs. Left-Handed Batters			116	29	2	23	13	.250	.371	.371
vs. Right-Handed Batters			174	36	5	12	37	.207	.322	.270
Home	1-0	3.35	142	36	3	21	20	.254	.401	.348
Road	2-5	3.19	148	29	4	14	30	.196	.284	.279
Grass	2-3	3.43	77	17	3	5	15	.221	.338	.286
Artificial Turf	1-2	3.20	213	48	4	30	35	.225	.343	.322
Day	2-2	2.88	126	25	3	16	22	.198	.286	.299
Night	1-3	3.55	164	40	4	19	28	.244	.384	.324
April	0-2	2.35	26	3	0	4	7	.115	.192	.281
May	1-0	4.73	51	11	1	6	12	.216	.373	.298
June	0-0	3.32	70	17	4	5	7	.243	.429	.293
July	0-1	2.25	44	11	0	7	8	.250	.318	.346
August	1-0	5.00	34	11	0	3	5	.324	.382	.395
Sept./Oct.	1-2	2.37	65	12	2	10	11	.185	.277	.293
Leading Off Inn.			69	13	1	5	13	.188	.304	.263
Bases Empty			167	38	4	19	29	.228	.341	.314
Runners On			123	27	3	16	21	.220	.341	.312
Runners/Scor. Pos.			71	16	0	10	13	.225	.296	.325
Runners On/2 Out			56	14	1	10	10	.250	.411	.364
Scor. Pos./2 Out			40	11	0	7	6	.275	.400	.383
Late Inning Pressure			132	30	5	11	24	.227	.364	.297
Leading Off			36	8	0	1	9	.222	.278	.282
Bases Empty			83	19	3	8	16	.229	.373	.312
Runners On			49	11	2	3	8	.224	.347	.269
Runners/Scor. Pos.			25	6	0	2	5	.240	.240	.296
First 9 Batters			272	60	6	32	46	.221	.320	.308
Second 9 Batters			18	5	1	3	4	.278	.667	.381
All Batters Thereafter			0	0	0	0	0	.000	.000	.000

Loves to face: Alan Ashby (.095, 2-for-21)
Hates to face: Jose Cruz (.415, 17-for-41)
Ground outs-to-air outs ratio: 1.35 last season, 1.34 for career. . . . Additional statistics: 12 double-play ground outs in 59 opportunities (3d-highest rate in N.L.), 5 doubles, 4 triples allowed in 80.0 innings last season. . . . Career total of 48 games started, 5th-highest among active pitchers without a complete-game shutout. All but eight of those starts were during the 1970s. . . . Opponents' overall batting average (.224) was the lowest of his career. . . . Batting average of opposing right-handers has been lower than that of lefties in each of his nine seasons with the Reds. Career averages: left-handers .298, right-handers .246. . . . Has lost his first two decisions in each of the last four seasons. Sounds like a natural for the Houston Astros.

Joe Johnson

Atlanta Braves	W–L	ERA	AB	H	HR	BB	SO	BA	SA	OBA
Season	4-4	4.10	333	95	9	24	34	.285	.435	.336
vs. Left-Handed Batters			156	45	5	11	18	.288	.455	.331
vs. Right-Handed Batters			177	50	4	13	16	.282	.418	.340
Home	0-2	6.06	142	44	7	9	15	.310	.542	.348
Road	4-2	2.70	191	51	2	15	19	.267	.356	.327
Grass	2-4	4.88	268	86	8	22	25	.321	.489	.375
Artificial Turf	2-0	1.40	65	9	1	2	9	.138	.215	.164
Day	3-0	2.77	102	29	1	7	9	.284	.392	.336
Night	1-4	4.68	231	66	8	17	25	.286	.455	.336
April			0	0	0	0	0	.000	.000	.000
May			0	0	0	0	0	.000	.000	.000
June			0	0	0	0	0	.000	.000	.000
July	0-0	2.08	48	11	0	2	3	.229	.250	.260
August	2-0	2.43	141	39	1	9	11	.277	.355	.325
Sept./Oct.	2-4	6.56	144	45	8	13	20	.313	.576	.370
Leading Off Inn.			83	22	0	5	7	.265	.325	.307
Bases Empty			194	54	3	13	18	.278	.412	.327
Runners On			139	41	6	11	16	.295	.468	.348
Runners/Scor. Pos.			90	24	3	10	15	.267	.400	.337
Runners On/2 Out			59	18	4	6	8	.305	.559	.369
Scor. Pos./2 Out			46	13	2	6	7	.283	.435	.365
Late Inning Pressure			17	4	0	1	1	.235	.235	.278
Leading Off			6	4	0	0	0	.667	.667	.667
Bases Empty			12	4	0	0	0	.333	.333	.333
Runners On			5	0	0	1	1	.000	.000	.167
Runners/Scor. Pos.			2	0	0	1	1	.000	.000	.333
First 9 Batters			122	31	3	8	18	.254	.393	.308
Second 9 Batters			114	38	3	9	10	.333	.491	.381
All Batters Thereafter			97	26	3	7	6	.268	.423	.317

Loves to face: Ron Cey (0-for-7)
Hates to face: Mike Marshall (.667, 4-for-6, 1 HR)
Ground outs-to-air outs ratio: 1.27 last season, his first in majors. . . . Additional statistics: 9 double-play ground outs in 65 opportunities, 15 doubles, 4 triples allowed in 85.2 innings last season. . . . Allowed 6 first-inning runs in 14 starts last season. . . . Batting support: 4.29 runs per start. . . . Faced seven batters with the bases loaded last season, and no runs scored, the highest total in either league since 1981. . . . Won his first four decisions, lost his last four. . . . Had an ERA of 1.59 in his victories, 8.41 in his losses. . . . Allowed one home run over his first 60 innings, eight homers over his last 25.2 innings. . . . Did not last to the fifth inning in three of his last five starts. . . . Believe it or not, he is the first Joe Johnson ever to play major-league baseball.

Kurt Kepshire

St. Louis Cardinals	W–L	ERA	AB	H	HR	BB	SO	BA	SA	OBA
Season	10-9	4.75	588	155	16	71	67	.264	.391	.339
vs. Left-Handed Batters			269	81	9	29	22	.301	.454	.363
vs. Right-Handed Batters			319	74	7	42	45	.232	.339	.320
Home	6-5	5.25	280	86	7	33	24	.307	.450	.378
Road	4-4	4.34	308	69	9	38	43	.224	.338	.305
Grass	3-0	3.08	191	40	5	21	26	.209	.304	.285
Artificial Turf	7-9	5.63	397	115	11	50	41	.290	.433	.365
Day	6-4	4.25	322	80	8	34	35	.248	.366	.317
Night	4-5	5.37	266	75	8	37	32	.282	.421	.366
April	1-3	7.32	83	28	1	4	7	.337	.422	.360
May	1-1	4.98	79	17	1	15	10	.215	.316	.333
June	3-1	3.09	128	29	6	11	19	.227	.391	.284
July	3-1	3.63	153	39	2	17	17	.255	.340	.329
August	2-2	5.40	97	25	3	14	7	.258	.423	.348
Sept./Oct.	0-1	7.30	48	17	3	10	7	.354	.563	.466
Leading Off Inn.			153	38	6	18	12	.248	.399	.327
Bases Empty			371	85	12	37	45	.229	.361	.299
Runners On			217	70	4	34	22	.323	.442	.403
Runners/Scor. Pos.			113	39	2	22	14	.345	.460	.430
Runners On/2 Out			80	20	2	15	8	.250	.388	.368
Scor. Pos./2 Out			41	7	1	10	5	.171	.268	.333
Late Inning Pressure			44	15	2	3	7	.341	.477	.383
Leading Off			13	3	1	0	2	.231	.462	.231
Bases Empty			29	10	2	3	5	.345	.552	.406
Runners On			15	5	0	0	2	.333	.333	.333
Runners/Scor. Pos.			5	3	0	0	1	.600	.600	.600
First 9 Batters			233	64	5	32	27	.275	.386	.357
Second 9 Batters			187	42	5	20	27	.225	.364	.297
All Batters Thereafter			168	49	6	19	13	.292	.429	.362

Loves to face: George Foster (0-for-9, 5 SO)
Hates to face: Rick Schu (.571, 4-for-7, 1 HR)
Ground outs-to-air outs ratio: 0.90 last season, 0.91 for career. . . . Additional statistics: 17 double-play ground outs in 125 opportunities, 21 doubles, 3 triples allowed in 153.1 innings last season. . . . Average of 5.07 innings per start was 3d-lowest among N.L. pitchers (minimum: 15 GS). . . . Allowed 24 first-inning runs (4th-most in N.L.) in 29 starts last season. . . . Batting support: 4.93 runs per start, 4th-highest average in N.L. (minimum: 15 GS). . . . ERA was 4th-highest among N.L. pitchers who started at least 15 games. . . . Career total of 1,124 batters faced without hitting one with a pitch is 2d-highest among active pitchers. . . . Knocked out of the box before end of 3d inning in five of his final eight starts of season. As a result, Herzog dropped him from Cardinals' 25-player post-season roster.

Bob Knepper

Houston Astros	W–L	ERA	AB	H	HR	BB	SO	BA	SA	OBA
Season	15-13	3.55	935	253	21	54	131	.271	.412	.310
vs. Left-Handed Batters			115	30	3	5	21	.261	.409	.287
vs. Right-Handed Batters			820	223	18	49	110	.272	.412	.313
Home	5-8	3.51	479	133	9	22	64	.278	.399	.311
Road	10-5	3.58	456	120	12	32	67	.263	.425	.308
Grass	6-1	2.77	233	58	5	16	33	.249	.369	.298
Artificial Turf	9-12	3.81	702	195	16	38	98	.278	.426	.314
Day	4-2	3.26	178	42	4	11	30	.236	.365	.279
Night	11-11	3.62	757	211	17	43	101	.279	.423	.317
April	1-0	2.88	90	21	3	8	19	.233	.378	.296
May	4-0	4.32	134	40	4	13	21	.299	.507	.358
June	3-4	3.14	170	43	2	13	18	.253	.347	.312
July	0-4	3.79	159	45	5	10	22	.283	.465	.322
August	3-2	3.33	195	53	4	7	28	.272	.395	.293
Sept./Oct.	4-3	3.75	187	51	3	3	23	.273	.390	.285
Leading Off Inn.			241	74	6	10	33	.307	.465	.337
Bases Empty			561	150	15	21	76	.267	.417	.295
Runners On			374	103	6	33	55	.275	.404	.330
Runners/Scor. Pos.			209	56	4	26	29	.268	.388	.341
Runners On/2 Out			158	41	3	18	25	.259	.373	.343
Scor. Pos./2 Out			103	25	2	12	17	.243	.350	.333
Late Inning Pressure			68	21	3	4	8	.309	.515	.347
Leading Off			21	10	2	1	4	.476	.810	.500
Bases Empty			47	16	3	1	5	.340	.574	.354
Runners On			21	5	0	3	3	.238	.381	.333
Runners/Scor. Pos.			8	0	0	1	2	.000	.000	.111
First 9 Batters			313	74	4	16	46	.236	.342	.275
Second 9 Batters			294	83	8	20	38	.282	.449	.329
All Batters Thereafter			328	96	9	18	47	.293	.445	.325

Loves to face: Greg Brock (.071, 1-for-14)
Hates to face: Marvell Wynne (.556, 5-for-9, 1 HR)
Ground outs-to-air outs ratio: 1.48 last season, 1.27 for career. . . . Additional statistics: 24 double-play ground outs in 171 opportunities, 53 doubles (most in majors), 8 triples allowed in 241.0 innings last season. . . . Total of 82 extra-base hits allowed was highest in N.L. . . . Set N.L. *Player Analysis* records with 47 doubles and 72 extra-base hits allowed to right-handed batters. . . . Batting support: 4.05 runs per start (37 GS). . . . Allowed 119 runs, tying Rick Rhoden for most in N.L.; first Houston pitcher ever to lead the league. . . . April 7, 1984 saw two historic events: Dwight Gooden's major-league debut, and the only homer by a lefty off Knepper in 607 innings in the Astrodome, by Darryl Strawberry. . . . Three home runs by opposing left-handed batters last season equalled the *highest* total of his career. . . . Losingest pitcher in the N.L. during the 1980s (59–77 for the decade).

Jerry Koosman

Philadelphia Phillies	W–L	ERA	AB	H	HR	BB	SO	BA	SA	OBA
Season	6-4	4.62	387	107	14	34	60	.276	.455	.336
vs. Left-Handed Batters			47	15	0	0	8	.319	.426	.333
vs. Right-Handed Batters			340	92	14	34	52	.271	.459	.337
Home	4-3	4.61	224	63	9	19	36	.281	.473	.339
Road	2-1	4.64	163	44	5	15	24	.270	.429	.333
Grass	0-0	5.59	37	10	3	4	6	.270	.568	.341
Artificial Turf	6-4	4.52	350	97	11	30	54	.277	.443	.336
Day	1-0	4.82	107	28	7	11	20	.262	.523	.325
Night	5-4	4.54	280	79	7	23	40	.282	.429	.341
April	1-1	4.21	111	39	2	6	18	.351	.459	.385
May			0	0	0	0	0	.000	.000	.000
June	2-0	1.48	103	18	1	10	18	.175	.272	.246
July	3-1	5.65	112	31	6	8	19	.277	.545	.333
August	0-2	9.82	61	19	5	10	5	.311	.590	.405
Sept./Oct.			0	0	0	0	0	.000	.000	.000
Leading Off Inn.			94	27	4	11	14	.287	.500	.362
Bases Empty			233	66	6	17	33	.283	.451	.337
Runners On			154	41	8	17	27	.266	.461	.335
Runners/Scor. Pos.			84	20	6	12	17	.238	.476	.327
Runners On/2 Out			60	10	1	7	11	.167	.217	.254
Scor. Pos./2 Out			36	5	1	5	8	.139	.222	.244
Late Inning Pressure			26	7	1	1	4	.269	.538	.286
Leading Off			7	3	0	0	2	.429	.857	.429
Bases Empty			19	6	0	0	3	.316	.526	.316
Runners On			7	1	1	1	1	.143	.571	.222
Runners/Scor. Pos.			6	1	1	1	1	.167	.667	.250
First 9 Batters			143	42	7	19	31	.294	.503	.378
Second 9 Batters			118	33	3	10	14	.280	.390	.336
All Batters Thereafter			126	32	4	5	15	.254	.460	.286

Loves to face: Vince Coleman (0-for-11)
Hates to face: Johnnie LeMaster (.636, 7-for-11)
Ground outs-to-air outs ratio: 0.79 last season, 1.12 for career. . . . Additional statistics: 6 double-play ground outs in 79 opportunities, 19 doubles, 4 triples allowed in 99.1 innings last season. . . . Average of 5.35 innings per start was 7th-lowest among N.L. pitchers (minimum: 15 GS). . . . Allowed 23 first-inning runs (tied for 5th-most in N.L.) in just 18 starts last season. . . . Batting support: 5.11 runs per start, 2d-highest average in N.L. (minimum: 15 GS). . . . June ERA of 1.48 was 4th-lowest in N.L. . . . Allowed one home run per 7.1 innings, 2d-worst rate among N.L. pitchers (minimum: 15 GS). . . . Of the last 51 home runs vs. Koosman, only one was hit by a left-handed batter: by Rick Manning, July 24, 1983. . . . Oldest pitcher in the N.L. last season. Pitched his final game at the age of 42 years, 7 months, 29 days.

Mike Krukow

San Francisco Giants	W–L	ERA	AB	H	HR	BB	SO	BA	SA	OBA
Season	8-11	3.38	739	176	19	49	150	.238	.373	.287
vs. Left-Handed Batters			385	109	10	28	75	.283	.442	.333
vs. Right-Handed Batters			354	67	9	21	75	.189	.299	.237
Home	6-5	2.24	430	95	8	29	98	.221	.328	.270
Road	2-6	5.06	309	81	11	20	52	.262	.437	.311
Grass	8-5	2.80	555	127	16	36	115	.229	.366	.277
Artificial Turf	0-6	5.21	184	49	3	13	35	.266	.397	.318
Day	6-4	2.75	453	107	10	28	95	.236	.362	.282
Night	2-7	4.40	286	69	9	21	55	.241	.392	.295
April	2-0	0.53	126	27	1	6	28	.214	.286	.256
May	2-3	2.79	150	26	4	11	31	.173	.320	.235
June	1-2	6.14	114	32	5	7	13	.281	.465	.325
July	1-3	4.54	166	47	6	10	35	.283	.446	.324
August	2-2	2.92	143	33	2	11	33	.231	.336	.284
Sept./Oct.	0-1	4.22	40	11	1	4	10	.275	.425	.333
Leading Off Inn.			190	53	7	7	43	.279	.479	.308
Bases Empty			455	114	10	20	87	.251	.385	.284
Runners On			284	62	9	29	63	.218	.356	.292
Runners/Scor. Pos.			179	35	7	22	48	.196	.363	.283
Runners On/2 Out			122	22	5	18	27	.180	.344	.296
Scor. Pos./2 Out			86	15	4	13	22	.174	.360	.290
Late Inning Pressure			104	17	0	12	17	.163	.212	.250
Leading Off			28	7	0	3	4	.250	.321	.323
Bases Empty			68	11	0	5	11	.162	.191	.219
Runners On			36	6	0	7	6	.167	.250	.302
Runners/Scor. Pos.			21	3	0	7	3	.143	.238	.357
First 9 Batters			238	49	6	9	51	.206	.361	.240
Second 9 Batters			229	62	9	17	47	.271	.437	.319
All Batters Thereafter			272	65	4	23	52	.239	.331	.301

Loves to face: Darryl Strawberry (.059, 1-for-17, 8 SO)
Hates to face: Gerald Perry (.833, 5-for-6, 2 HR)
Ground outs-to-air outs ratio: 0.90 last season (lowest of his career), 1.25 for career. . . . Additional statistics: 13 double-play ground outs in 110 opportunities, 35 doubles, 4 triples allowed in 194.2 innings last season. . . . Ranked 10th among N.L. pitchers with an average of 6.95 innings per start. . . . Allowed 16 first-inning runs in 28 starts last season. . . . Batting support: 2.89 runs per start, 2d-lowest average in N.L. (minimum: 15 GS). . . . Ranked 3d in N.L. in ERA during April. . . . Good hitter: one of three N.L. pitchers with five extra-base hits last season. The others: Jim Gott and John Tudor. . . . Giants had a .500 record in games he started last season. . . . Record of 0–1 with five no-decisions in games following his six complete games.

Jeff Lahti

St. Louis Cardinals	W–L	ERA	AB	H	HR	BB	SO	BA	SA	OBA
Season	5-2	1.84	251	63	3	26	41	.251	.355	.321
vs. Left-Handed Batters			86	22	0	14	7	.256	.337	.360
vs. Right-Handed Batters			165	41	3	12	34	.248	.364	.299
Home	3-1	1.33	93	18	0	5	10	.194	.269	.235
Road	2-1	2.18	158	45	3	21	31	.285	.405	.369
Grass	1-0	1.86	70	18	2	7	11	.257	.400	.325
Artificial Turf	4-2	1.84	181	45	1	19	30	.249	.337	.320
Day	2-0	2.53	126	37	3	16	21	.294	.444	.373
Night	3-2	1.24	125	26	0	10	20	.208	.264	.267
April	0-0	4.15	21	9	0	3	3	.429	.476	.500
May	0-0	2.89	35	10	1	3	2	.286	.457	.342
June	0-0	2.70	51	12	1	4	12	.235	.412	.291
July	1-0	0.00	24	2	0	1	5	.083	.083	.120
August	1-2	2.04	64	18	1	7	12	.281	.375	.352
Sept./Oct.	3-0	0.56	56	12	0	8	7	.214	.286	.313
Leading Off Inn.			50	12	2	3	8	.240	.420	.283
Bases Empty			119	32	2	6	19	.269	.370	.304
Runners On			132	31	1	20	22	.235	.341	.336
Runners/Scor. Pos.			92	15	0	15	18	.163	.228	.280
Runners On/2 Out			58	14	1	13	9	.241	.397	.380
Scor. Pos./2 Out			46	8	0	11	7	.174	.283	.333
Late Inning Pressure			158	39	1	14	25	.247	.310	.308
Leading Off			34	6	1	0	5	.176	.265	.176
Bases Empty			81	21	1	2	11	.259	.321	.277
Runners On			77	18	0	12	14	.234	.299	.337
Runners/Scor. Pos.			52	8	0	9	10	.154	.212	.279
First 9 Batters			235	56	2	24	40	.238	.328	.309
Second 9 Batters			16	7	1	2	1	.438	.750	.500
All Batters Thereafter			0	0	0	0	0	.000	.000	.000

Loves to face: Mookie Wilson (0-for-11)
Hates to face: Thad Bosley (.800, 4-for-5)
Ground outs-to-air outs ratio: 1.89 last season, 1.79 for career. . . . Additional statistics: 16 double-play ground outs in 57 opportunities, 13 doubles, 2 triples allowed in 68.1 innings last season. . . . Saved six games in July (tied for second-most in N.L.). . . . Ranked 2d among N.L. relief pitchers with a 1.84 ERA (minimum: 30 relief games). . . . Made 10 relief appearances last season in which he faced a single batter, most in N.L. . . . Opponents' career batting averages: .241 with bases empty, .237 with runners on base, .208 with runners in scoring position. . . . Last home run allowed to a left-handed batter: by Dave Parker, Aug. 20, 1984. . . . Winning pitcher in two consecutive relief appearances (September 21 and 23) for the first time in his career.

Dave LaPoint

San Francisco Giants	W–L	ERA	AB	H	HR	BB	SO	BA	SA	OBA
Season	7-17	3.57	800	215	18	74	122	.269	.398	.329
vs. Left-Handed Batters			106	28	4	3	14	.264	.406	.284
vs. Right-Handed Batters			694	187	14	71	108	.269	.396	.335
Home	2-10	3.09	424	106	10	41	72	.250	.366	.315
Road	5-7	4.13	376	109	8	33	50	.290	.434	.345
Grass	3-13	3.38	561	143	14	52	88	.255	.381	.316
Artificial Turf	4-4	4.05	239	72	4	22	34	.301	.435	.359
Day	4-9	2.92	423	113	9	34	67	.267	.381	.320
Night	3-8	4.29	377	102	9	40	55	.271	.416	.339
April	0-4	2.22	104	27	3	10	15	.260	.356	.322
May	2-1	1.77	126	25	1	19	17	.198	.286	.303
June	1-2	3.67	161	42	5	9	25	.261	.398	.300
July	2-2	3.86	112	34	1	11	17	.304	.393	.366
August	2-2	3.94	124	33	3	9	23	.266	.419	.313
Sept./Oct.	0-6	5.49	173	54	5	16	25	.312	.491	.365
Leading Off Inn.			199	60	5	17	31	.302	.477	.356
Bases Empty			460	124	12	38	75	.270	.420	.325
Runners On			340	91	6	36	47	.268	.368	.333
Runners/Scor. Pos.			187	43	2	29	26	.230	.294	.326
Runners On/2 Out			137	32	1	18	15	.234	.292	.323
Scor. Pos./2 Out			89	18	0	16	10	.202	.225	.324
Late Inning Pressure			81	25	5	9	13	.309	.519	.378
Leading Off			23	10	0	2	3	.435	.435	.480
Bases Empty			49	16	3	7	6	.327	.510	.411
Runners On			32	9	2	2	7	.281	.531	.324
Runners/Scor. Pos.			10	1	0	2	2	.100	.100	.250
First 9 Batters			253	69	4	22	42	.273	.403	.329
Second 9 Batters			247	66	3	27	36	.267	.348	.338
All Batters Thereafter			300	80	11	25	44	.267	.433	.321

Loves to face: Steve Yeager (.091, 1-for-11, 6 SO)
Hates to face: Lee Lacy (.419, 13-for-31, 2 HR)
Ground outs-to-air outs ratio: 1.38 last season, 1.33 for career. . . . Additional statistics: 19 double-play ground outs in 166 opportunities, 25 doubles, 12 triples (most in majors) allowed in 206.2 innings last season. . . . Allowed 11 triples to right-handed batters, one short of N.L. *Player Analysis* record set by Randy Jones in 1979. . . . Allowed 18 first-inning runs in 31 starts last season. . . . Batting support: 3.06 runs per start, 5th-lowest average in N.L. (minimum: 15 GS). . . . Ranked 4th in N.L. in ERA during May. . . . Lost five of his first six decisions with an ERA of 1.85 during that period. . . . Lost his last six starts of the season. . . . Tied for N.L. lead with 10 losses in home games. . . . Had misfortune to make 26 of his 31 starts, and get 20 of his 24 decisions, against teams that finished above .500. He lost 16 of those 20 decisions.

Bill Laskey

Giants/Expos	W–L	ERA	AB	H	HR	BB	SO	BA	SA	OBA
Season	5-16	4.91	583	165	19	53	60	.283	.449	.342
vs. Left-Handed Batters			296	82	8	36	26	.277	.419	.351
vs. Right-Handed Batters			287	83	11	17	34	.289	.481	.331
Home	2-8	5.59	276	84	9	21	30	.304	.467	.353
Road	3-8	4.35	307	81	10	32	30	.264	.433	.331
Grass	3-7	3.39	302	76	9	31	30	.252	.394	.318
Artificial Turf	2-9	6.68	281	89	10	22	30	.317	.509	.367
Day	2-5	4.53	199	53	3	17	17	.266	.387	.321
Night	3-11	5.11	384	112	16	36	43	.292	.482	.352
April	0-3	3.10	86	24	0	9	7	.279	.419	.347
May	1-2	5.16	86	24	3	6	10	.279	.407	.323
June	0-5	3.34	116	26	4	7	16	.224	.371	.260
July	4-1	3.03	143	36	3	17	9	.252	.385	.331
August	0-3	8.55	83	26	4	8	9	.313	.542	.370
Sept./Oct.	0-2	10.67	69	29	5	6	9	.420	.696	.481
Leading Off Inn.			149	42	6	9	16	.282	.463	.323
Bases Empty			351	89	11	32	37	.254	.413	.316
Runners On			232	76	8	21	23	.328	.504	.379
Runners/Scor. Pos.			147	48	5	16	15	.327	.497	.386
Runners On/2 Out			98	28	1	10	10	.286	.357	.352
Scor. Pos./2 Out			72	19	1	8	7	.264	.347	.338
Late Inning Pressure			31	6	0	2	1	.194	.226	.235
Leading Off			13	2	0	0	0	.154	.154	.154
Bases Empty			30	5	0	1	1	.167	.200	.194
Runners On			1	1	0	1	0	1.000	1.000	.667
Runners/Scor. Pos.			0	0	0	0	0	.000	.000	.000
First 9 Batters			219	63	6	23	28	.288	.443	.355
Second 9 Batters			209	65	10	17	18	.311	.536	.362
All Batters Thereafter			155	37	3	13	14	.239	.342	.294

Loves to face: Steve Sax (.120, 3-for-25)
Hates to face: Dale Murphy (.524, 11-for-21, 5 HR)
Ground outs-to-air outs ratio: 1.24 last season, 0.83 for career. . . . Additional statistics: 13 double-play ground outs in 110 opportunities, 36 doubles (tied for 10th-most in N.L.), 2 triples allowed in 148.1 innings last season. . . . Average of 5.55 innings per start was 9th-lowest among N.L. pitchers (minimum: 15 GS). . . . Allowed 15 first-inning runs in 26 starts last season. . . . Batting support: 3.15 runs per start, 6th-lowest average in N.L. (minimum: 15 GS). . . . Led N.L. with five losses in June. . . . Alan Wiggins and Lee Lacy have a combined record of one hit in 33 at bats against Laskey. Too bad they're in Baltimore. . . . ERA was 3d-highest among N.L. pitchers who started at least 15 games. . . . Won one of 13 decisions against teams that finished above .500. . . . Opposing batters have career average of .143 (5-for-35) with the bases loaded.

Craig Lefferts

San Diego Padres	W–L	ERA	AB	H	HR	BB	SO	BA	SA	OBA
Season	7-6	3.35	307	75	7	30	48	.244	.375	.311
vs. Left-Handed Batters			89	17	1	8	20	.191	.270	.255
vs. Right-Handed Batters			218	58	6	22	28	.266	.417	.333
Home	4-1	3.86	158	37	5	16	28	.234	.392	.305
Road	3-5	2.77	149	38	2	14	20	.255	.356	.317
Grass	6-1	3.00	237	53	5	25	42	.224	.350	.298
Artificial Turf	1-5	4.67	70	22	2	5	6	.314	.457	.355
Day	3-1	1.67	94	20	2	4	20	.213	.340	.242
Night	4-5	4.15	213	55	5	26	28	.258	.390	.339
April	1-0	1.59	20	3	0	3	2	.150	.250	.261
May	0-2	5.93	52	13	2	5	6	.250	.442	.310
June	3-0	2.04	60	12	1	4	8	.200	.317	.250
July	2-2	3.44	73	21	1	3	7	.288	.370	.316
August	1-1	3.07	54	15	0	8	13	.278	.370	.371
Sept./Oct.	0-1	3.38	48	11	3	7	12	.229	.438	.327
Leading Off Inn.			73	18	4	5	8	.247	.425	.295
Bases Empty			172	41	4	16	21	.238	.366	.303
Runners On			135	34	3	14	27	.252	.385	.320
Runners/Scor. Pos.			84	26	3	7	12	.310	.500	.359
Runners On/2 Out			64	17	2	7	9	.266	.406	.338
Scor. Pos./2 Out			42	13	2	3	5	.310	.524	.356
Late Inning Pressure			155	39	2	15	23	.252	.342	.316
Leading Off			40	9	2	2	4	.225	.375	.262
Bases Empty			94	22	2	8	12	.234	.319	.294
Runners On			61	17	0	7	11	.279	.377	.348
Runners/Scor. Pos.			35	13	0	4	4	.371	.486	.425
First 9 Batters			293	70	6	28	48	.239	.362	.304
Second 9 Batters			14	5	1	2	0	.357	.643	.438
All Batters Thereafter			0	0	0	0	0	.000	.000	.000

Loves to face: Dave Parker (0-for-14, 4 SO)
Hates to face: R.J. Reynolds (.800, 4-for-5)
Ground outs-to-air outs ratio: 0.73 last season, 0.80 for career. . . . Additional statistics: 3 double-play ground outs in 63 opportunities, 19 doubles, 0 triples allowed in 83.1 innings last season. . . . Career total of 318 left-handed batters faced without allowing a triple. . . . Pitched more than two innings in only three of his 60 appearances. Longest outing of last season was three innings. . . . Opponents' career batting averages: .256 with bases empty, .216 with runners on base, .207 with runners in scoring position. . . . For the third straight year opponents hit for a higher average on artificial surfaces than on grass. Career averages: .290 (1–7, 4.04 ERA) on the rug, .217 (12–7, 2.36 ERA) on natural surfaces. Why should the ground cover matter for a fly-ball pitcher?

Gary Lucas

Montreal Expos	W–L	ERA	AB	H	HR	BB	SO	BA	SA	OBA
Season	6-2	3.19	251	63	6	24	31	.251	.375	.314
vs. Left-Handed Batters			70	19	2	4	11	.271	.414	.311
vs. Right-Handed Batters			181	44	4	20	20	.243	.359	.315
Home	3-0	2.97	142	34	4	9	15	.239	.359	.281
Road	3-2	3.49	109	29	2	15	16	.266	.394	.355
Grass	2-0	2.19	47	12	2	6	2	.255	.404	.340
Artificial Turf	4-2	3.42	204	51	4	18	29	.250	.368	.308
Day	4-1	3.00	70	18	2	8	8	.257	.371	.325
Night	2-1	3.26	181	45	4	16	23	.249	.376	.310
April			0	0	0	0	0	.000	.000	.000
May	0-0	5.06	19	5	0	3	1	.263	.316	.364
June	2-0	1.62	62	13	2	3	7	.210	.323	.242
July	1-2	3.60	61	20	0	4	7	.328	.459	.369
August	1-0	5.40	52	16	2	5	11	.308	.462	.368
Sept./Oct.	2-0	2.08	57	9	2	9	5	.158	.281	.269
Leading Off Inn.			61	16	3	2	11	.262	.492	.286
Bases Empty			148	39	4	7	19	.264	.426	.297
Runners On			103	24	2	17	12	.233	.301	.336
Runners/Scor. Pos.			64	18	2	14	9	.281	.391	.400
Runners On/2 Out			40	7	1	4	5	.175	.250	.250
Scor. Pos./2 Out			27	6	1	4	3	.222	.333	.323
Late Inning Pressure			109	33	3	11	14	.303	.440	.364
Leading Off			28	6	1	1	7	.214	.357	.241
Bases Empty			65	19	1	3	10	.292	.431	.324
Runners On			44	14	2	8	4	.318	.455	.415
Runners/Scor. Pos.			29	8	2	8	4	.276	.483	.421
First 9 Batters			240	61	6	23	31	.254	.383	.317
Second 9 Batters			11	2	0	1	0	.182	.182	.250
All Batters Thereafter			0	0	0	0	0	.000	.000	.000

Loves to face: Johnnie LeMaster (0-for-11)
Hates to face: Rafael Santana (.800, 4-for-5)
Ground outs-to-air outs ratio: 1.15 last season, 1.44 for career. . . . Additional statistics: 6 double-play ground outs in 56 opportunities, 11 doubles, 1 triple allowed in 67.2 innings last season. . . . Has allowed only eight career walks to leadoff batters in 257 innings in Late-Inning Pressure Situations. Overall mark of one walk per 29.4 leadoff batters ranks 5th among active pitchers (minimum: 500 BFP). . . . Opponents' career batting average of .214 (15-for-70) with the bases loaded. . . . Three-game winning streak (twice) last season was one short of his career high. . . . Three of his six wins last season were against St. Louis (career record of 6–7 vs. Cardinals). . . . Opponents' LIP batting average with runners on base rose from career-best .160 in 1984 to career-worst .318.

Ed Lynch

New York Mets	W–L	ERA	AB	H	HR	BB	SO	BA	SA	OBA
Season	10-8	3.44	735	188	19	27	65	.256	.392	.281
vs. Left-Handed Batters			369	101	12	11	27	.274	.436	.295
vs. Right-Handed Batters			366	87	7	16	38	.238	.347	.268
Home	5-4	2.70	387	89	8	12	38	.230	.344	.254
Road	5-4	4.31	348	99	11	15	27	.284	.445	.311
Grass	7-5	2.85	537	128	11	17	48	.238	.350	.262
Artificial Turf	3-3	5.14	198	60	8	10	17	.303	.505	.332
Day	4-2	3.54	291	68	8	10	23	.234	.378	.257
Night	6-6	3.38	444	120	11	17	42	.270	.401	.297
April	0-1	3.92	76	16	3	3	9	.211	.447	.241
May	3-2	2.58	174	41	5	5	15	.236	.368	.257
June	1-2	3.05	143	35	3	6	9	.245	.364	.272
July	4-0	2.48	112	30	2	5	9	.268	.375	.299
August	2-2	3.34	137	39	3	4	10	.285	.401	.301
Sept./Oct.	0-1	6.75	93	27	3	4	13	.290	.441	.323
Leading Off Inn.			183	40	6	10	13	.219	.350	.263
Bases Empty			458	119	13	18	31	.260	.397	.289
Runners On			277	69	6	9	34	.249	.383	.268
Runners/Scor. Pos.			139	30	2	7	15	.216	.331	.245
Runners On/2 Out			130	31	2	8	20	.238	.338	.283
Scor. Pos./2 Out			72	15	1	6	12	.208	.278	.269
Late Inning Pressure			36	10	2	1	2	.278	.528	.289
Leading Off			10	4	2	1	0	.400	1.000	.455
Bases Empty			26	9	2	1	1	.346	.654	.370
Runners On			10	1	0	0	1	.100	.200	.091
Runners/Scor. Pos.			3	0	0	0	0	.000	.000	.000
First 9 Batters			255	63	2	12	33	.247	.325	.280
Second 9 Batters			236	64	7	9	21	.271	.445	.298
All Batters Thereafter			244	61	10	6	11	.250	.410	.266

Loves to face: Dave Concepcion (.059, 1-for-17)
Hates to face: Jeff Stone (.600, 6-for-10, 1 3B, 2 HR)
Ground outs-to-air outs ratio: 0.81 last season, 0.95 for career. . . . Additional statistics: 7 double-play ground outs in 117 opportunities, 33 doubles, 5 triples allowed in 191.0 innings last season. . . . Allowed 8 first-inning runs in 29 starts, 6th-lowest rate in N.L. last season (minimum: 15 GS). . . . Batting support: 4.07 runs per start. . . . Allowed 1.27 walks per nine innings, 3d-lowest rate in N.L. Career average of 1.95 ranks 5th among active pitchers (minimum: 500 innings). . . . Average of 3.06 strikeouts per nine innings was 4th-lowest among N.L. pitchers who started at least 15 games. . . . Average of 35.9 air outs per 100 batters faced was 2d-highest in N.L. last season (minimum: 200 BFP). . . . Not exactly a salary drive, Ed: he was 7–1 on June 14, 1984, and lost his last 7 starts; 10–5 on August 12, 1985, but winless in his last 8 starts.

Rick Mahler

Atlanta Braves	W–L	ERA	AB	H	HR	BB	SO	BA	SA	OBA
Season	17-15	3.48	1014	272	24	79	107	.268	.401	.321
vs. Left-Handed Batters			543	142	7	38	54	.262	.372	.308
vs. Right-Handed Batters			471	130	17	41	53	.276	.435	.335
Home	8-5	3.27	513	131	12	38	57	.255	.382	.307
Road	9-10	3.69	501	141	12	41	50	.281	.421	.335
Grass	11-11	3.12	730	191	17	60	81	.262	.385	.317
Artificial Turf	6-4	4.42	284	81	7	19	26	.285	.444	.330
Day	7-5	3.42	397	109	12	29	33	.275	.423	.322
Night	10-10	3.51	617	163	12	50	74	.264	.387	.320
April	5-0	1.64	140	30	2	8	13	.214	.307	.257
May	3-4	4.01	198	51	4	16	16	.258	.394	.312
June	3-3	3.53	187	53	8	16	26	.283	.460	.337
July	4-1	3.17	192	55	3	11	23	.286	.396	.325
August	2-4	4.57	160	47	4	14	15	.294	.419	.354
Sept./Oct.	0-3	3.75	137	36	3	14	14	.263	.416	.331
Leading Off Inn.			255	62	10	21	22	.243	.427	.301
Bases Empty			627	168	14	40	66	.268	.408	.312
Runners On			387	104	10	39	41	.269	.390	.335
Runners/Scor. Pos.			210	53	5	25	28	.252	.367	.328
Runners On/2 Out			167	46	4	25	19	.275	.383	.370
Scor. Pos./2 Out			104	25	2	18	12	.240	.337	.352
Late Inning Pressure			84	20	2	9	7	.238	.357	.312
Leading Off			23	5	1	3	1	.217	.348	.308
Bases Empty			59	14	1	4	4	.237	.339	.286
Runners On			25	6	1	5	3	.240	.400	.367
Runners/Scor. Pos.			11	3	0	3	2	.273	.364	.429
First 9 Batters			321	89	8	20	44	.277	.414	.320
Second 9 Batters			315	84	9	30	32	.267	.403	.331
All Batters Thereafter			378	99	7	29	31	.262	.389	.313

Loves to face: Craig Reynolds (.087, 2-for-23)
Hates to face: Jason Thompson (.529, 9-for-17, 2 HR)
Ground outs-to-air outs ratio: 1.67 last season, 1.59 for career. . . . Additional statistics: 33 double-play ground outs in 181 opportunities (6th-highest rate in N.L.), 47 doubles (5th-most in N.L.), 8 triples (tied for 7th-most in N.L.) allowed in 266.2 innings last season. . . . Total of 79 extra-base hits allowed was 2d-highest in N.L. . . . Allowed 18 first-inning runs in 39 starts last season. . . . Batting support: 4.72 runs per start. In his first six starts Braves averaged 7.83 runs. . . . Fielded nine double plays in '85, most by an N.L. pitcher since Rick Reuschel's nine in '79. . . . One of two N.L. pitchers to drive in three game-winning runs. The other: Rick Rhoden. . . . Led N.L. with five wins in April. . . . One of three pitchers for teams with losing records last season to win 10 or more games against teams above the .500 mark. The others: Kevin Gross and Shane Rawley.

Ron Mathis

Houston Astros	W–L	ERA	AB	H	HR	BB	SO	BA	SA	OBA
Season	3-5	6.04	283	83	7	27	34	.293	.459	.352
vs. Left-Handed Batters			128	32	1	15	11	.250	.375	.322
vs. Right-Handed Batters			155	51	6	12	23	.329	.529	.379
Home	3-3	5.04	176	47	3	13	25	.267	.386	.316
Road	0-2	7.82	107	36	4	14	9	.336	.579	.410
Grass	0-2	7.58	81	28	3	11	7	.346	.580	.419
Artificial Turf	3-3	5.47	202	55	4	16	27	.272	.411	.324
Day	1-2	7.41	72	23	2	8	5	.319	.528	.383
Night	2-3	5.60	211	60	5	19	29	.284	.436	.342
April	1-1	5.02	54	14	1	5	13	.259	.444	.322
May	2-0	2.84	73	17	1	3	9	.233	.301	.266
June	0-2	6.10	79	23	2	10	3	.291	.494	.363
July	0-2	8.71	47	16	1	6	5	.340	.511	.415
August			0	0	0	0	0	.000	.000	.000
Sept./Oct.	0-0	14.29	30	13	2	3	4	.433	.700	.485
Leading Off Inn.			66	23	2	7	8	.348	.606	.411
Bases Empty			152	43	4	14	19	.283	.480	.343
Runners On			131	40	3	13	15	.305	.435	.362
Runners/Scor. Pos.			81	25	1	8	10	.309	.420	.355
Runners On/2 Out			57	15	3	6	5	.263	.474	.344
Scor. Pos./2 Out			37	10	1	5	3	.270	.432	.357
Late Inning Pressure			31	10	0	6	3	.323	.419	.432
Leading Off			8	5	0	1	0	.625	.875	.667
Bases Empty			14	6	0	1	1	.429	.643	.467
Runners On			17	4	0	5	2	.235	.235	.409
Runners/Scor. Pos.			11	2	0	4	1	.182	.182	.400
First 9 Batters			157	46	6	18	19	.293	.497	.362
Second 9 Batters			76	22	1	4	9	.289	.408	.317
All Batters Thereafter			50	15	0	5	6	.300	.420	.375

Loves to face: Hubie Brooks (0-for-5)
Hates to face: Mike Fitzgerald (3-for-3)
Ground outs-to-air outs ratio: 1.05 last season, his first in majors. . . . Additional statistics: 2 double-play ground outs in 56 opportunities (2d-lowest rate in N.L.), 14 doubles, 6 triples allowed in 70.0 innings last season. . . . Opposing right-handed batters hit 79 points higher than opposing left-handers, largest difference in N.L. last season (minimum: 100 AB vs. each). . . . Faced only three batters in his first major-league inning in April. Nothing unusual, you say? Well, that inning left him with a career opponents' on-base average of 1.000. After allowing back-to-back singles to Stone and Samuel, he picked them both off base. Von Hayes followed with a walk only to be caught stealing, Ashby to Doran. . . . 1985 breakdown: 3–3, 4.44 ERA as a starter; 0–2, 9.26 ERA, one save in relief. . . . Allowed at least one run in 10 of his 13 relief appearances.

Roger McDowell

New York Mets	W–L	ERA	AB	H	HR	BB	SO	BA	SA	OBA
Season	6-5	2.83	470	108	9	37	70	.230	.332	.286
vs. Left-Handed Batters			226	53	2	16	24	.235	.319	.287
vs. Right-Handed Batters			244	55	7	21	46	.225	.344	.286
Home	5-3	2.11	257	58	7	18	28	.226	.350	.276
Road	1-2	3.66	213	50	2	19	42	.235	.310	.298
Grass	6-4	2.46	364	81	9	26	50	.223	.335	.273
Artificial Turf	0-1	4.08	106	27	0	11	20	.255	.321	.331
Day	3-3	4.10	220	53	4	21	34	.241	.355	.307
Night	3-2	1.72	250	55	5	16	36	.220	.312	.267
April	2-0	4.38	48	15	1	4	8	.313	.458	.365
May	3-1	2.08	86	12	0	6	14	.140	.151	.204
June	0-2	4.11	63	19	2	9	12	.302	.492	.389
July	0-1	2.82	89	22	3	6	13	.247	.382	.295
August	1-1	2.91	77	15	3	5	10	.195	.325	.241
Sept./Oct.	0-0	2.12	107	25	0	7	13	.234	.290	.278
Leading Off Inn.			118	29	1	8	10	.246	.297	.294
Bases Empty			285	66	2	17	43	.232	.295	.277
Runners On			185	42	7	20	27	.227	.389	.300
Runners/Scor. Pos.			94	23	4	19	18	.245	.426	.365
Runners On/2 Out			78	16	3	7	10	.205	.333	.271
Scor. Pos./2 Out			42	8	2	6	9	.190	.333	.292
Late Inning Pressure			260	55	3	23	34	.212	.292	.274
Leading Off			67	15	1	6	3	.224	.299	.288
Bases Empty			166	39	1	8	24	.235	.307	.270
Runners On			94	16	2	15	10	.170	.266	.279
Runners/Scor. Pos.			57	9	0	14	9	.158	.193	.315
First 9 Batters			382	86	8	30	62	.225	.325	.280
Second 9 Batters			82	18	1	4	8	.220	.305	.264
All Batters Thereafter			6	4	0	3	0	.667	1.167	.778

Loves to face: Glenn Hubbard (0-for-7)
Hates to face: Keith Moreland (.556, 5-for-9, 1 HR)
Ground outs-to-air outs ratio: 3.16 last season (2d-highest in N.L.), his first in majors. . . . Additional statistics: 11 double-play ground outs in 88 opportunities, 19 doubles, 1 triple allowed in 127.1 innings last season. . . . Record of 5–0 with two saves in his first 11 relief appearances last season. . . . May ERA of 2.08 was lowest on Mets' staff. . . . Ranked 8th among N.L. relief pitchers with a 2.38 ERA (minimum: 30 relief games). . . . Faced 291 batters in Late-Inning Pressure Situations last season, 3d-highest total in N.L. . . . Led major-league rookies with 17 saves, and had five set-ups as well (see Oakland essay). . . . Pete Rose had three hits in three at bats vs. McDowell. . . . Opponents' batting average of .143 (1-for-7) with the bases loaded. . . . Pitched three or more innings in 16 relief appearances last season, highest total in N.L.

Andy McGaffigan

Cincinnati Reds	W–L	ERA	AB	H	HR	BB	SO	BA	SA	OBA
Season	3-3	3.72	356	88	4	30	83	.247	.346	.309
vs. Left-Handed Batters			207	57	2	21	40	.275	.357	.342
vs. Right-Handed Batters			149	31	2	9	43	.208	.329	.263
Home	3-2	3.36	219	52	2	17	52	.237	.320	.295
Road	0-1	4.33	137	36	2	13	31	.263	.387	.331
Grass	0-1	5.00	74	21	2	6	17	.284	.446	.338
Artificial Turf	3-2	3.42	282	67	2	24	66	.238	.319	.302
Day	2-1	3.89	154	38	2	12	40	.247	.344	.301
Night	1-2	3.60	202	50	2	18	43	.248	.347	.315
April			0	0	0	0	0	.000	.000	.000
May			0	0	0	0	0	.000	.000	.000
June			0	0	0	0	0	.000	.000	.000
July	0-0	0.00	21	4	0	0	5	.190	.333	.227
August	1-2	4.26	173	46	2	13	39	.266	.364	.321
Sept./Oct.	2-1	3.68	162	38	2	17	39	.235	.327	.307
Leading Off Inn.			90	26	2	8	17	.289	.389	.347
Bases Empty			212	51	2	14	41	.241	.321	.288
Runners On			144	37	2	16	42	.257	.382	.340
Runners/Scor. Pos.			87	23	1	11	29	.264	.356	.360
Runners On/2 Out			58	14	1	6	18	.241	.414	.323
Scor. Pos./2 Out			39	10	1	5	13	.256	.385	.356
Late Inning Pressure			15	3	0	1	1	.200	.267	.250
Leading Off			4	0	0	1	0	.000	.000	.200
Bases Empty			11	1	0	1	1	.091	.182	.167
Runners On			4	2	0	0	0	.500	.500	.500
Runners/Scor. Pos.			4	2	0	0	0	.500	.500	.500
First 9 Batters			123	36	4	11	33	.293	.439	.351
Second 9 Batters			117	26	0	9	28	.222	.299	.289
All Batters Thereafter			116	26	0	10	22	.224	.293	.286

Loves to face: Jerry Mumphrey (.063, 1-for-16, 6 SO)
Hates to face: Ryne Sandberg (.556, 5-for-9)
Ground outs-to-air outs ratio: 1.05 last season, 1.07 for career. . . . Additional statistics: 4 double-play ground outs in 68 opportunities, 17 doubles, 3 triples allowed in 94.1 innings last season. . . . Allowed 9 first-inning runs in 15 starts last season. . . . Batting support: 3.73 runs per start. . . . Opponents' batting average of .200 (4-for-20) with the bases loaded. He has never allowed an extra-base hit with the bases full. . . . Large disparity in 1985 lefty/righty breakdown is not indicative of his past performance. Career batting averages: left-handers .246, right-handers .245. . . . Won his last two decisions last season, equalling longest single-season winning streak of his career. . . . Career at Olympic Stadium: 1–2, 2.22 ERA in 10 games.

Larry McWilliams

Pittsburgh Pirates	W–L	ERA	AB	H	HR	BB	SO	BA	SA	OBA
Season	7-9	4.70	492	139	9	62	52	.283	.429	.369
vs. Left-Handed Batters			76	25	2	6	10	.329	.500	.393
vs. Right-Handed Batters			416	114	7	56	42	.274	.416	.365
Home	3-5	5.86	225	70	7	24	24	.311	.493	.381
Road	4-4	3.80	267	69	2	38	28	.258	.375	.359
Grass	2-4	4.24	159	45	1	23	17	.283	.403	.384
Artificial Turf	5-5	4.92	333	94	8	39	35	.282	.441	.361
Day	1-3	3.12	101	30	1	15	7	.297	.386	.403
Night	6-6	5.11	391	109	8	47	45	.279	.440	.360
April	2-1	4.37	93	25	1	9	6	.269	.366	.346
May	1-2	5.82	66	20	1	6	8	.303	.500	.378
June	1-3	3.03	111	24	2	17	11	.216	.342	.323
July	1-1	4.91	108	34	1	13	13	.315	.426	.390
August	0-1	12.27	31	12	2	9	4	.387	.742	.524
Sept./Oct.	2-1	3.86	83	24	2	8	10	.289	.446	.352
Leading Off Inn.			117	37	2	13	11	.316	.479	.389
Bases Empty			259	80	5	27	27	.309	.475	.383
Runners On			233	59	4	35	25	.253	.378	.354
Runners/Scor. Pos.			132	37	3	23	13	.280	.432	.388
Runners On/2 Out			99	25	2	19	10	.253	.394	.388
Scor. Pos./2 Out			62	18	2	14	5	.290	.452	.436
Late Inning Pressure			31	9	1	7	2	.290	.419	.421
Leading Off			6	1	0	2	1	.167	.167	.375
Bases Empty			15	4	0	4	1	.267	.267	.421
Runners On			16	5	1	3	1	.313	.563	.421
Runners/Scor. Pos.			8	2	0	3	1	.250	.375	.455
First 9 Batters			213	55	4	30	28	.258	.404	.352
Second 9 Batters			160	47	3	20	16	.294	.438	.380
All Batters Thereafter			119	37	2	12	8	.311	.462	.383

Loves to face: Glenn Hubbard (.059, 1-for-17, 5 SO)
Hates to face: Willie McGee (.400, 10-for-25, 1 HR)
Ground outs-to-air outs ratio: 0.99 last season, 1.16 for career. . . . Additional statistics: 11 double-play ground outs in 113 opportunities, 39 doubles (9th-most in N.L.), 3 triples allowed in 126.1 innings last season. . . . Average of 5.53 innings per start was 8th-lowest among N.L. pitchers (minimum: 15 GS). . . . Allowed 9 first-inning runs in 19 starts last season. . . . Batting support: 4.58 runs per start. . . . ERA of 4.70 in '85 was highest of any pitcher who was under 3.00 in '84 (minimum: 162 innings in '84), except for Alejandro Pena. . . . Opponents batted .571 (8-for-14) with the bases loaded last season. . . . One of two pitchers who has had two hits off Dwight Gooden; the other: Dick Ruthven. Career batting average for pitchers vs. Dr. K is .118 (15-for-127); only three pitchers have been able to sacrifice against him.

Greg Minton

San Francisco Giants	W–L	ERA	AB	H	HR	BB	SO	BA	SA	OBA
Season	5-4	3.54	360	98	6	54	37	.272	.372	.364
vs. Left-Handed Batters			139	49	1	31	10	.353	.432	.462
vs. Right-Handed Batters			221	49	5	23	27	.222	.335	.294
Home	3-2	1.80	145	34	2	16	12	.234	.331	.305
Road	2-2	4.76	215	64	4	38	25	.298	.400	.402
Grass	4-3	3.41	272	72	6	36	27	.265	.379	.346
Artificial Turf	1-1	3.97	88	26	0	18	10	.295	.352	.415
Day	2-2	2.45	164	42	3	17	14	.256	.366	.324
Night	3-2	4.44	196	56	3	37	23	.286	.378	.394
April	1-1	4.91	31	11	1	6	1	.355	.548	.459
May	0-0	1.65	60	18	0	7	5	.300	.400	.368
June	0-0	3.00	73	13	1	9	11	.178	.247	.268
July	1-1	3.00	61	12	1	6	11	.197	.262	.265
August	1-1	6.55	46	18	0	9	3	.391	.478	.491
Sept./Oct.	2-1	3.91	89	26	3	17	6	.292	.416	.398
Leading Off Inn.			75	23	3	11	8	.307	.453	.395
Bases Empty			176	48	4	20	23	.273	.409	.347
Runners On			184	50	2	34	14	.272	.337	.378
Runners/Scor. Pos.			132	37	2	28	9	.280	.356	.396
Runners On/2 Out			80	23	2	16	4	.288	.400	.406
Scor. Pos./2 Out			62	16	2	14	2	.258	.387	.395
Late Inning Pressure			192	52	5	32	21	.271	.396	.372
Leading Off			42	14	2	8	5	.333	.500	.440
Bases Empty			95	28	3	14	14	.295	.442	.385
Runners On			97	24	2	18	7	.247	.351	.359
Runners/Scor. Pos.			66	18	2	16	4	.273	.409	.405
First 9 Batters			341	90	5	50	36	.264	.355	.355
Second 9 Batters			19	8	1	4	1	.421	.684	.500
All Batters Thereafter			0	0	0	0	0	.000	.000	.000

Loves to face: Terry Puhl (0-for-14)
Hates to face: Dave Parker (.588, 10-for-17)
Also hates to face: Darryl Strawberry (.800, 4-for-5, 1 HR).... Ground outs-to-air outs ratio: 2.22 last season, 2.41 for career.... Additional statistics: 13 double-play ground outs in 92 opportunities, 14 doubles, 2 triples allowed in 96.2 innings last season.... Averaged 3.44 strikeouts per nine innings, 4th-lowest among N.L. relievers (minimum: 30 relief games).... Opposing left-handed batters hit 131 points higher than right-handers, 2d-largest difference in N.L. last season (minimum: 100 AB vs. each).... Career average of one home run allowed per 28.9 innings is 4th-best among active pitchers (minimum: 250 innings).... Walked 18 batters intentionally last season, highest total in majors.... Has allowed 18 home runs in Late-Inning Pressure Situations over past four seasons, but faced 669 batters in LIP from 1979–81 without allowing a home run.

Tom Niedenfuer

Los Angeles Dodgers	W–L	ERA	AB	H	HR	BB	SO	BA	SA	OBA
Season	7-9	2.71	386	86	6	24	102	.223	.321	.268
vs. Left-Handed Batters			201	45	5	16	48	.224	.363	.284
vs. Right-Handed Batters			185	41	1	8	54	.222	.276	.250
Home	2-3	2.75	223	56	3	8	57	.251	.345	.279
Road	5-6	2.66	163	30	3	16	45	.184	.288	.254
Grass	5-5	2.71	295	69	3	14	73	.234	.315	.269
Artificial Turf	2-4	2.70	91	17	3	10	29	.187	.341	.265
Day	2-4	3.18	124	26	3	6	29	.210	.331	.246
Night	5-5	2.49	262	60	3	18	73	.229	.317	.278
April	1-0	3.95	49	13	0	2	10	.265	.367	.283
May	0-2	1.65	57	10	1	5	20	.175	.263	.238
June	1-0	1.62	59	11	0	2	20	.186	.203	.213
July	3-1	2.08	59	11	1	3	11	.186	.288	.226
August	1-1	0.48	66	11	0	4	22	.167	.227	.225
Sept./Oct.	1-5	5.70	96	30	4	8	19	.313	.490	.365
Leading Off Inn.			91	12	1	4	27	.132	.220	.177
Bases Empty			231	48	3	13	56	.208	.299	.253
Runners On			155	38	3	11	46	.245	.355	.290
Runners/Scor. Pos.			97	23	1	8	31	.237	.351	.287
Runners On/2 Out			68	13	0	7	22	.191	.279	.267
Scor. Pos./2 Out			48	11	0	6	15	.229	.354	.315
Late Inning Pressure			245	60	4	19	66	.245	.355	.300
Leading Off			55	8	0	4	18	.145	.236	.217
Bases Empty			139	34	2	9	34	.245	.367	.295
Runners On			106	26	2	10	32	.245	.340	.305
Runners/Scor. Pos.			67	15	1	8	21	.224	.328	.299
First 9 Batters			352	74	6	21	92	.210	.307	.255
Second 9 Batters			34	12	0	3	10	.353	.471	.405
All Batters Thereafter			0	0	0	0	0	.000	.000	.000

Loves to face: Johnny Ray (0-for-11, 4 SO)
Hates to face: Wally Backman (.800, 4-for-5)
Ground outs-to-air outs ratio: 0.47 last season (4th-lowest in N.L.), 0.54 for career.... Additional statistics: 2 double-play ground outs in 67 opportunities (lowest rate in N.L.), 18 doubles, 1 triple allowed in 106.1 innings last season.... Ranked 3d in N.L. with nine relief losses last season.... Average of 4.25 strikeouts per walk was highest among N.L. relievers (minimum: 30 relief games).... Career average of one extra-base hit allowed per 33.3 at bats by right-handed batters is 2d-lowest in 11-year history of *The Player Analysis* (minimum: 250 AB).... Opposing batters have hit .151 on artificial turf over the past three seasons, lowest average in majors during that time (minimum: 150 AB).... First pitcher to lose his team's last two post-season games since Deacon Phillippe in the first World Series, 1903.

Joe Niekro

Houston Astros	W–L	ERA	AB	H	HR	BB	SO	BA	SA	OBA
Season	9-12	3.72	799	197	21	99	117	.247	.357	.329
vs. Left-Handed Batters			380	103	9	61	36	.271	.379	.369
vs. Right-Handed Batters			419	94	12	38	81	.224	.337	.289
Home	2-5	4.15	338	86	7	43	54	.254	.358	.334
Road	7-7	3.41	461	111	14	56	63	.241	.356	.325
Grass	6-3	2.80	297	67	12	33	37	.226	.367	.310
Artificial Turf	3-9	4.27	502	130	9	66	80	.259	.351	.340
Day	2-2	4.46	142	37	9	12	21	.261	.472	.318
Night	7-10	3.57	657	160	12	87	96	.244	.332	.331
April	1-3	2.23	115	24	1	19	15	.209	.235	.314
May	1-2	3.35	144	34	4	19	32	.236	.347	.323
June	4-2	3.76	161	45	3	17	15	.280	.366	.363
July	2-1	2.66	158	36	4	19	25	.228	.335	.306
August	1-2	4.91	158	39	8	14	22	.247	.443	.306
Sept./Oct.	0-2	7.63	63	19	1	11	8	.302	.413	.395
Leading Off Inn.			203	50	6	18	28	.246	.369	.311
Bases Empty			465	124	16	49	71	.267	.400	.339
Runners On			334	73	5	50	46	.219	.296	.316
Runners/Scor. Pos.			191	44	4	38	30	.230	.335	.348
Runners On/2 Out			151	32	2	33	24	.212	.285	.364
Scor. Pos./2 Out			102	22	2	25	19	.216	.314	.385
Late Inning Pressure			75	21	5	10	11	.280	.493	.368
Leading Off			22	5	2	1	2	.227	.500	.261
Bases Empty			48	12	4	6	9	.250	.500	.345
Runners On			27	9	1	4	2	.333	.481	.406
Runners/Scor. Pos.			19	5	0	4	2	.263	.316	.375
First 9 Batters			242	58	6	37	45	.240	.351	.340
Second 9 Batters			257	62	3	25	36	.241	.304	.309
All Batters Thereafter			300	77	12	37	36	.257	.407	.336

Loves to face: George Vukovich (0-for-11)
Hates to face: Lonnie Smith (.382, 13-for-34, 1 HR)
Figures above are for N.L. only.... Ground outs-to-air outs ratio: 1.01 last season, 1.12 for career.... Additional statistics: 15 double-play ground outs in 156 opportunities, 22 doubles, 2 triples allowed in 225.1 innings last season.... Allowed 21 first-inning runs (10th-most in N.L.) in 35 starts last season.... Batting support: 4.11 runs per start.... Pitched to no decision in 11 starts for Houston with an ERA of 2.63 in those games.... Career at Yankee Stadium: 1–2, 5.95 ERA in seven games.... Allowed 24 homers last season (combined league total), his most since 1970, when he allowed 28 playing his home games in Tiger Stadium. One home run for every 35 at bats vs. left-handed batters last season; one for every 71 AB over previous ten seasons.... It's been 17 years since the Cubs traded Niekro for Dick Selma.

Jesse Orosco

New York Mets	W–L	ERA	AB	H	HR	BB	SO	BA	SA	OBA
Season	8-6	2.73	295	66	6	34	68	.224	.315	.303
vs. Left-Handed Batters			60	12	0	3	15	.200	.200	.238
vs. Right-Handed Batters			235	54	6	31	53	.230	.345	.318
Home	3-3	2.45	141	37	3	13	31	.262	.369	.323
Road	5-3	2.98	154	29	3	21	37	.188	.266	.285
Grass	5-4	3.58	194	49	5	24	41	.253	.371	.333
Artificial Turf	3-2	1.26	101	17	1	10	27	.168	.208	.243
Day	4-3	2.15	106	24	2	14	20	.226	.321	.317
Night	4-3	3.08	189	42	4	20	48	.222	.312	.295
April	1-1	2.08	46	9	0	7	12	.196	.239	.302
May	0-1	2.53	44	11	0	2	12	.250	.250	.283
June	0-2	3.86	61	21	1	7	11	.344	.492	.412
July	1-0	4.91	40	7	1	4	10	.175	.250	.250
August	2-0	0.00	38	5	0	1	7	.132	.158	.150
Sept./Oct.	4-2	2.95	66	13	4	13	16	.197	.379	.329
Leading Off Inn.			56	13	1	8	10	.232	.357	.328
Bases Empty			131	31	3	15	28	.237	.359	.315
Runners On			164	35	3	19	40	.213	.280	.293
Runners/Scor. Pos.			102	19	1	17	26	.186	.235	.300
Runners On/2 Out			66	14	3	11	13	.212	.348	.325
Scor. Pos./2 Out			44	6	1	10	10	.136	.205	.296
Late Inning Pressure			227	50	4	28	57	.220	.308	.306
Leading Off			43	9	1	6	10	.209	.372	.306
Bases Empty			101	22	2	13	26	.218	.337	.307
Runners On			126	28	2	15	31	.222	.286	.305
Runners/Scor. Pos.			80	16	0	14	20	.200	.225	.319
First 9 Batters			282	63	6	34	68	.223	.319	.306
Second 9 Batters			13	3	0	0	0	.231	.231	.231
All Batters Thereafter			0	0	0	0	0	.000	.000	.000

Loves to face: Garry Templeton (.071, 1-for-14)
Hates to face: Chili Davis (.615, 8-for-13, 1 HR)
Ground outs-to-air outs ratio: 0.72 last season, 0.91 for career.... Additional statistics: 6 double-play ground outs in 84 opportunities, 9 doubles, 0 triples allowed in 79.0 innings last season.... Did not allow an extra-base hit to a left-handed batter in 60 at bats last season, seven short of his N.L. *Player Analysis* mark set in '84. Last XBH by an opposing lefty: a double by Chris Chambliss on July 19, 1983.... Career average of one XBH allowed per 40.3 at bats by left-handers is lowest in *Player Analysis* history (minimum: 250 AB).... Opponents' had one hit in 19 at bats with the bases loaded last season.... Career total of 940 batters faced at Shea Stadium without allowing a triple.... Opponents' batting average with runners on base has been lower than with bases empty in each of last five seasons. Career averages: .203 with runners on base, .223 with bases empty.

David Palmer

Montreal Expos	W–L	ERA	AB	H	HR	BB	SO	BA	SA	OBA
Season	7-10	3.71	511	128	5	67	106	.250	.317	.340
vs. Left-Handed Batters			268	71	1	34	58	.265	.325	.348
vs. Right-Handed Batters			243	57	4	33	48	.235	.309	.331
Home	4-9	4.18	301	77	3	40	62	.256	.329	.347
Road	3-1	3.05	210	51	2	27	44	.243	.300	.329
Grass	0-1	2.70	91	18	2	16	23	.198	.264	.318
Artificial Turf	7-9	3.96	420	110	3	51	83	.262	.329	.345
Day	3-2	3.09	126	28	2	17	24	.222	.302	.319
Night	4-8	3.93	385	100	3	50	82	.260	.322	.346
April	1-2	4.50	58	11	2	6	10	.190	.328	.277
May	2-3	2.31	142	30	1	9	31	.211	.282	.258
June	3-1	2.31	143	33	1	19	36	.231	.287	.323
July	0-3	8.34	98	35	1	18	15	.357	.418	.457
August	0-0	4.50	10	4	0	0	1	.400	.400	.455
Sept./Oct.	1-1	3.18	60	15	0	15	13	.250	.283	.395
Leading Off Inn.			124	26	0	14	27	.210	.234	.290
Bases Empty			274	66	1	35	58	.241	.292	.327
Runners On			237	62	4	32	48	.262	.346	.354
Runners/Scor. Pos.			139	35	1	26	29	.252	.295	.373
Runners On/2 Out			105	29	2	12	24	.276	.371	.356
Scor. Pos./2 Out			69	18	1	10	16	.261	.304	.363
Late Inning Pressure			23	6	0	1	6	.261	.348	.320
Leading Off			5	0	0	1	2	.000	.000	.167
Bases Empty			12	4	0	1	3	.333	.333	.385
Runners On			11	2	0	0	3	.182	.364	.250
Runners/Scor. Pos.			1	0	0	0	0	.000	.000	.500
First 9 Batters			185	43	1	27	46	.232	.270	.330
Second 9 Batters			174	48	1	21	32	.276	.333	.357
All Batters Thereafter			152	37	3	19	28	.243	.355	.331

Loves to face: Ozzie Smith (.045, 1-for-22)
Hates to face: Joe Orsulak (.833, 5-for-6)
Ground outs-to-air outs ratio: 2.65 last season (7th-highest in N.L.), 2.12 for career. . . . Additional statistics: 12 double-play ground outs in 121 opportunities, 11 doubles, 4 triples allowed in 135.2 innings last season. . . . Allowed 14 first-inning runs in 23 starts last season. . . . Batting support: 3.35 runs per start, 7th-lowest average in N.L. (minimum: 15 GS). . . . G/A ratio of 4.37 vs. right-handed batters was the highest in *Player Analysis* history. . . . Set career-high marks last season in games started, innings pitched, and strikeouts. . . . 1985 was the first odd-numbered year in which he saw major-league action since 1979; elbow operations forced him to miss the 1981 and '83 seasons. . . . Career: has faced 243 batters in Late-Inning Pressure Situations, allowed only two LIP home runs.

Pascual Perez

Atlanta Braves	W–L	ERA	AB	H	HR	BB	SO	BA	SA	OBA
Season	1-13	6.14	387	115	10	57	57	.297	.455	.386
vs. Left-Handed Batters			212	64	6	36	28	.302	.467	.400
vs. Right-Handed Batters			175	51	4	21	29	.291	.440	.369
Home	1-8	6.99	192	59	5	28	30	.307	.438	.392
Road	0-5	5.33	195	56	5	29	27	.287	.472	.381
Grass	1-11	6.75	275	84	8	37	41	.305	.465	.387
Artificial Turf	0-2	4.71	112	31	2	20	16	.277	.429	.383
Day	1-2	5.76	103	30	2	12	12	.291	.466	.371
Night	0-11	6.27	284	85	8	45	45	.299	.451	.392
April	0-3	6.33	82	24	3	14	12	.293	.402	.392
May	0-2	8.10	38	9	2	13	4	.237	.474	.431
June	0-0	2.25	34	10	0	1	8	.294	.382	.314
July	1-3	7.79	76	26	3	4	11	.342	.553	.378
August	0-0	3.38	22	7	0	5	3	.318	.364	.444
Sept./Oct.	0-5	5.94	135	39	2	20	19	.289	.459	.378
Leading Off Inn.			99	36	5	5	17	.364	.596	.394
Bases Empty			204	60	5	23	27	.294	.456	.366
Runners On			183	55	5	34	30	.301	.454	.407
Runners/Scor. Pos.			111	28	3	29	20	.252	.360	.399
Runners On/2 Out			69	19	2	15	7	.275	.435	.412
Scor. Pos./2 Out			46	9	0	13	6	.196	.239	.373
Late Inning Pressure			14	6	0	0	2	.429	.500	.400
Leading Off			5	3	0	0	1	.600	.600	.600
Bases Empty			9	4	0	0	1	.444	.444	.444
Runners On			5	2	0	0	1	.400	.600	.333
Runners/Scor. Pos.			0	0	0	0	0	.000	.000	.000
First 9 Batters			171	54	7	21	26	.316	.503	.387
Second 9 Batters			144	39	3	21	19	.271	.444	.364
All Batters Thereafter			72	22	0	15	12	.306	.361	.427

Loves to face: Ozzie Virgil (0-for-12, 5 SO)
Hates to face: Leon Durham (.429, 9-for-21, 6 HR)
Also hates to face: Graig Nettles (.750, 6-for-8, 1 HR). . . . Ground outs-to-air outs ratio: 1.41 last season, 1.65 for career. . . . Additional statistics: 6 double-play ground outs in 100 opportunities, 27 doubles, 2 triples allowed in 95.1 innings last season. . . . Average of 4.33 innings per start was 2d-lowest among N.L. pitchers (minimum: 15 GS). . . . Allowed 16 first-inning runs in 22 starts last season. . . . Batting support: 3.82 runs per start. . . . ERA was 2d-highest among N.L. pitchers who started at least 15 games. . . . Has allowed only one career walk to leadoff batters in 65 innings in Late-Inning Pressure Situations. . . . Disappeared within five innings in 12 of his 22 starts, the most early exits in the league. . . . Braves had a record of 0–10 in games in which he allowed a home run.

Ted Power

Cincinnati Reds	W–L	ERA	AB	H	HR	BB	SO	BA	SA	OBA
Season	8-6	2.70	286	65	2	45	42	.227	.297	.331
vs. Left-Handed Batters			125	28	1	24	12	.224	.320	.349
vs. Right-Handed Batters			161	37	1	21	30	.230	.280	.317
Home	4-3	2.15	162	36	1	23	21	.222	.278	.317
Road	4-3	3.44	124	29	1	22	21	.234	.323	.349
Grass	3-2	4.35	75	20	1	14	12	.267	.387	.374
Artificial Turf	5-4	2.12	211	45	1	31	30	.213	.265	.316
Day	4-1	2.22	85	22	0	18	13	.259	.329	.387
Night	4-5	2.91	201	43	2	27	29	.214	.284	.306
April	0-1	3.86	25	6	1	5	4	.240	.400	.387
May	0-0	1.50	35	2	0	7	6	.057	.057	.209
June	1-1	1.35	48	9	1	7	9	.188	.271	.291
July	1-0	1.32	47	11	0	6	7	.234	.255	.321
August	3-2	7.15	49	18	0	8	7	.367	.531	.448
Sept./Oct.	3-2	2.38	82	19	0	12	9	.232	.268	.326
Leading Off Inn.			58	10	0	12	4	.172	.224	.314
Bases Empty			134	26	1	21	19	.194	.239	.303
Runners On			152	39	1	24	23	.257	.349	.356
Runners/Scor. Pos.			92	21	1	18	14	.228	.326	.345
Runners On/2 Out			67	18	1	10	8	.269	.373	.372
Scor. Pos./2 Out			45	10	1	9	7	.222	.333	.352
Late Inning Pressure			214	54	2	31	28	.252	.332	.344
Leading Off			46	9	0	6	2	.196	.261	.288
Bases Empty			100	24	1	14	10	.240	.300	.333
Runners On			114	30	1	17	18	.263	.360	.353
Runners/Scor. Pos.			62	14	1	14	10	.226	.339	.359
First 9 Batters			272	63	2	43	41	.232	.305	.335
Second 9 Batters			14	2	0	2	1	.143	.143	.250
All Batters Thereafter			0	0	0	0	0	.000	.000	.000

Loves to face: Garry Maddox (0-for-11)
Hates to face: Glenn Hubbard (.636, 7-for-11)
Ground outs-to-air outs ratio: 0.71 last season, 0.79 for career. . . . Additional statistics: 8 double-play ground outs in 85 opportunities, 12 doubles, 1 triple allowed in 80.0 innings last season. . . . Led N.L. with seven saves in September. . . . Career average of one extra-base hit allowed per 23.9 at bats by right-handed batters is 7th-lowest in 11-year history of *The Player Analysis* (minimum: 250 AB). . . . Opponents' career batting averages: left-handers .296, right-handers .225. . . . Made four appearances last season in which he faced only one batter, and was credited with a save in each one. . . . Pitched as many as three innings only three times last season, all in extra-inning games. . . . Pitched 20.1 consecutive shutout innings spanning 16 games (2–0, 10 saves) from June 13 to July 24.

Joe Price

Cincinnati Reds	W–L	ERA	AB	H	HR	BB	SO	BA	SA	OBA
Season	2-2	3.90	244	59	10	23	52	.242	.414	.301
vs. Left-Handed Batters			57	19	2	5	6	.333	.509	.375
vs. Right-Handed Batters			187	40	8	18	46	.214	.385	.279
Home	1-0	4.76	134	37	7	16	21	.276	.470	.349
Road	1-2	2.93	110	22	3	7	31	.200	.345	.242
Grass	0-2	4.08	67	18	2	5	14	.269	.433	.307
Artificial Turf	2-0	3.83	177	41	8	18	38	.232	.407	.299
Day	0-0	4.20	53	12	3	8	6	.226	.434	.317
Night	2-2	3.81	191	47	7	15	46	.246	.408	.297
April	0-0	2.70	10	1	1	1	3	.100	.400	.167
May	1-0	3.05	74	14	1	9	22	.189	.297	.274
June	1-1	4.87	83	24	4	6	13	.289	.482	.330
July	0-1	5.40	60	18	4	6	8	.300	.550	.358
August	0-0	0.00	17	2	0	1	6	.118	.118	.167
Sept./Oct.			0	0	0	0	0	.000	.000	.000
Leading Off Inn.			54	12	2	7	15	.222	.389	.311
Bases Empty			143	32	7	8	33	.224	.413	.265
Runners On			101	27	3	15	19	.267	.416	.347
Runners/Scor. Pos.			57	16	2	13	10	.281	.439	.387
Runners On/2 Out			39	7	2	5	9	.179	.333	.273
Scor. Pos./2 Out			27	5	2	5	6	.185	.407	.313
Late Inning Pressure			27	6	1	3	5	.222	.333	.300
Leading Off			5	0	0	3	2	.000	.000	.375
Bases Empty			14	1	1	3	2	.071	.286	.235
Runners On			13	5	0	0	3	.385	.385	.385
Runners/Scor. Pos.			9	3	0	0	2	.333	.333	.333
First 9 Batters			133	28	2	16	35	.211	.293	.291
Second 9 Batters			66	20	5	4	11	.303	.621	.333
All Batters Thereafter			45	11	3	3	6	.244	.467	.286

Loves to face: Brad Komminsk (0-for-10, 4 SO)
Hates to face: Jim Morrison (.692, 9-for-13)
Ground outs-to-air outs ratio: 0.44 last season (lowest in N.L.), 0.65 for career. . . . Additional statistics: 3 double-play ground outs in 59 opportunities (6th-lowest rate in N.L.), 12 doubles, 0 triples allowed in 64.2 innings last season. . . . Right-handed opponents' career batting average of .244 is two points higher than left-handers' despite large variation in last season's breakdown. Career home run averages: one allowed per 71 at bats by lefties, one per 34 AB by righties. . . . Yearly batting averages in Late-Inning Pressure situations since 1983: .222, .185, .222. . . . Opponents' career batting average of .222 (14-for-63) with the bases loaded. . . . Career record of 24–25 as a starter, 11–4 in relief. . . . Tied N.L. record for relief pitchers by striking out six consecutive batters vs. Phillies (who else?) on May 8.

Shane Rawley

Philadelphia Phillies	W–L	ERA	AB	H	HR	BB	SO	BA	SA	OBA
Season	13-8	3.31	755	188	16	81	106	.249	.359	.321
vs. Left-Handed Batters			91	21	2	11	14	.231	.319	.320
vs. Right-Handed Batters			664	167	14	70	92	.252	.364	.322
Home	6-6	3.44	376	94	9	46	51	.250	.372	.332
Road	7-2	3.17	379	94	7	35	55	.248	.346	.311
Grass	2-2	3.57	221	53	5	20	32	.240	.344	.305
Artificial Turf	11-6	3.20	534	135	11	61	74	.253	.365	.328
Day	2-5	5.37	262	79	10	28	36	.302	.477	.366
Night	11-3	2.30	493	109	6	53	70	.221	.296	.298
April	3-0	1.82	93	20	1	11	8	.215	.269	.298
May	1-3	5.40	108	34	2	17	13	.315	.472	.402
June	1-3	3.72	72	17	3	6	16	.236	.403	.295
July	2-0	1.99	165	36	2	16	28	.218	.285	.290
August	4-0	1.72	166	34	1	17	27	.205	.241	.277
Sept./Oct.	2-2	6.31	151	47	7	14	14	.311	.523	.371
Leading Off Inn.			188	42	3	18	31	.223	.293	.295
Bases Empty			437	114	9	44	60	.261	.373	.330
Runners On			318	74	7	37	46	.233	.340	.310
Runners/Scor. Pos.			174	35	2	30	28	.201	.270	.314
Runners On/2 Out			144	38	4	20	19	.264	.389	.358
Scor. Pos./2 Out			84	19	1	18	12	.226	.286	.369
Late Inning Pressure			59	16	3	6	11	.271	.458	.338
Leading Off			17	7	1	2	4	.412	.647	.474
Bases Empty			34	13	3	2	8	.382	.706	.417
Runners On			25	3	0	4	3	.120	.120	.241
Runners/Scor. Pos.			10	1	0	3	1	.100	.100	.308
First 9 Batters			260	67	6	35	42	.258	.381	.349
Second 9 Batters			230	51	4	18	35	.222	.317	.276
All Batters Thereafter			265	70	6	28	29	.264	.374	.332

Loves to face: Billy Sample (.067, 1-for-15)
Hates to face: Jody Davis (.438, 7-for-16, 2 HR)
Ground outs-to-air outs ratio: 1.55 last season, 1.32 for career. . . . Additional statistics: 18 double-play ground outs in 131 opportunities, 31 doubles, 2 triples allowed in 198.2 innings last season. . . . Allowed 26 first-inning runs (most in N.L.) in 31 starts last season. . . . Batting support: 4.58 runs per start. . . . July ERA of 1.99 was 7th-lowest in N.L. . . . Had league's 6th-best night-game ERA. . . . Acquitted himself well despite having 16 of his 21 decisions come against teams that finished above .500: he was 10–6 against the good teams, 3–2 against the bad. . . . Opponents' batting averages leading off innings (.223) and with runners in scoring position (.201) were by far the lowest of his career. . . . Career home run averages: one for every 114 at bats vs left-handed batters, one per 54 AB vs. right-handers.

Jeff Reardon

Montreal Expos	W–L	ERA	AB	H	HR	BB	SO	BA	SA	OBA
Season	2-8	3.18	325	68	7	26	67	.209	.295	.269
vs. Left-Handed Batters			181	38	4	16	30	.210	.287	.274
vs. Right-Handed Batters			144	30	3	10	37	.208	.306	.263
Home	2-5	3.27	153	32	1	15	26	.209	.255	.284
Road	0-3	3.11	172	36	6	11	41	.209	.331	.255
Grass	0-2	4.30	93	25	5	4	17	.269	.452	.299
Artificial Turf	2-6	2.78	232	43	2	22	50	.185	.233	.258
Day	1-3	2.65	126	26	2	14	21	.206	.286	.286
Night	1-5	3.52	199	42	5	12	46	.211	.302	.258
April	1-0	1.26	50	8	0	5	9	.160	.180	.236
May	1-1	0.93	68	11	0	3	19	.162	.176	.197
June	0-2	4.91	57	16	2	5	12	.281	.386	.339
July	0-1	4.50	24	6	3	0	3	.250	.625	.250
August	0-2	6.57	47	10	1	8	11	.213	.319	.339
Sept./Oct.	0-2	3.00	79	17	1	5	13	.215	.291	.259
Leading Off Inn.			75	12	2	3	13	.160	.267	.192
Bases Empty			193	36	4	11	38	.187	.259	.230
Runners On			132	32	3	15	29	.242	.348	.322
Runners/Scor. Pos.			76	21	1	13	16	.276	.355	.385
Runners On/2 Out			67	13	2	9	20	.194	.299	.289
Scor. Pos./2 Out			42	8	1	7	13	.190	.262	.306
Late Inning Pressure			236	50	4	24	49	.212	.280	.286
Leading Off			51	8	1	3	11	.157	.216	.204
Bases Empty			132	24	1	9	29	.182	.205	.234
Runners On			104	26	3	15	20	.250	.375	.347
Runners/Scor. Pos.			60	18	1	13	10	.300	.400	.427
First 9 Batters			311	63	7	24	65	.203	.283	.261
Second 9 Batters			14	5	0	2	2	.357	.571	.438
All Batters Thereafter			0	0	0	0	0	.000	.000	.000

Loves to face: Andy Van Slyke (.071, 1-for-14)
Hates to face: Eddie Milner (.750, 3-for-4, 1 HR)
Ground outs-to-air outs ratio: 0.70 last season (10th-lowest in N.L.), 0.58 for career. . . . Additional statistics: 3 double-play ground outs in 52 opportunities (9th-lowest rate in N.L.), 5 doubles, 1 triple allowed in 87.2 innings last season. . . . Career average of 2.47 strikeouts per walk in night games, 1.72 in day games. . . . Lost his last seven decisions, longest losing streak of his career. . . . Winning percentage of .200 (2–8) is lowest ever by a league leader in saves. . . . Opponents' career batting averages: left-handers .234, right-handers .208. . . . September injury may have determined outcome of N.L. East race last season. Missed three-game St. Louis sweep (September 20–22) in which Montreal bullpen blew late-inning leads in each game.

Rick Reuschel

Pittsburgh Pirates	W–L	ERA	AB	H	HR	BB	SO	BA	SA	OBA
Season	14-8	2.27	710	153	7	52	138	.215	.293	.271
vs. Left-Handed Batters			321	72	3	26	37	.224	.308	.283
vs. Right-Handed Batters			389	81	4	26	101	.208	.280	.261
Home	13-3	2.14	414	86	4	28	79	.208	.290	.258
Road	1-5	2.45	296	67	3	24	59	.226	.297	.288
Grass	1-2	2.42	195	42	3	15	41	.215	.287	.277
Artificial Turf	13-6	2.22	515	111	4	37	97	.216	.295	.268
Day	2-4	2.52	273	55	5	23	49	.201	.293	.268
Night	12-4	2.12	437	98	2	29	89	.224	.293	.273
April			0	0	0	0	0	.000	.000	.000
May	1-0	0.66	46	8	0	4	5	.174	.239	.250
June	4-1	2.79	156	37	1	9	30	.237	.314	.277
July	3-2	3.07	157	38	1	16	30	.242	.299	.316
August	2-4	2.35	171	39	0	17	29	.228	.304	.298
Sept./Oct.	4-1	1.58	180	31	5	6	44	.172	.272	.202
Leading Off Inn.			187	38	2	7	33	.203	.273	.236
Bases Empty			455	96	5	20	89	.211	.290	.246
Runners On			255	57	2	32	49	.224	.298	.312
Runners/Scor. Pos.			144	32	0	24	26	.222	.285	.335
Runners On/2 Out			108	22	0	17	23	.204	.259	.317
Scor. Pos./2 Out			66	17	0	13	14	.258	.333	.388
Late Inning Pressure			106	27	2	9	18	.255	.368	.313
Leading Off			29	9	0	0	4	.310	.379	.310
Bases Empty			64	17	2	2	10	.266	.406	.288
Runners On			42	10	0	7	8	.238	.310	.347
Runners/Scor. Pos.			22	6	0	6	2	.273	.409	.429
First 9 Batters			235	54	1	13	50	.230	.298	.274
Second 9 Batters			214	49	3	17	40	.229	.313	.289
All Batters Thereafter			261	50	3	22	48	.192	.272	.254

Loves to face: Buddy Bell (0-for-9)
Hates to face: Lee Mazzilli (.370, 17-for-46, 3 HR)
Ground outs-to-air outs ratio: 2.42 last season (10th-highest in N.L.), 2.15 for career. . . . Additional statistics: 17 double-play ground outs in 128 opportunities, 30 doubles, 2 triples allowed in 194.0 innings last season. . . . Ranked 5th among N.L. pitchers with an average of 7.27 innings per start. . . . Allowed 12 first-inning runs in 26 starts last season. . . . Batting support: 3.69 runs per start. . . . Won 13 home games last season to rank 2d in N.L. to John Tudor (14). ERA in home games was 2.14. The only other pitcher to win 13 games in a season at Three Rivers Stadium is Doc Ellis, 1971. . . . Led N.L. pitchers in fielding last season (64 total chances without an error). . . . Allowed only one home run per 27.7 innings, 2d-best rate in N.L. last season. . . . Came closer to 20-win season than you might think: In six no-decisions he had an ERA of 1.58.

Jerry Reuss

Los Angeles Dodgers	W–L	ERA	AB	H	HR	BB	SO	BA	SA	OBA
Season	14-10	2.92	808	210	13	58	84	.260	.365	.310
vs. Left-Handed Batters			103	29	2	4	10	.282	.369	.308
vs. Right-Handed Batters			705	181	11	54	74	.257	.365	.310
Home	6-4	2.41	352	86	7	23	30	.244	.347	.293
Road	8-6	3.32	456	124	6	35	54	.272	.379	.323
Grass	10-7	2.86	573	146	12	41	53	.255	.366	.305
Artificial Turf	4-3	3.06	235	64	1	17	31	.272	.362	.322
Day	4-2	2.45	262	66	4	21	30	.252	.355	.306
Night	10-8	3.15	546	144	9	37	54	.264	.370	.312
April	1-3	4.85	110	34	0	11	11	.309	.391	.369
May	2-2	2.76	122	29	2	5	13	.238	.336	.273
June	3-1	2.36	155	34	4	6	15	.219	.355	.248
July	2-1	3.74	132	37	3	10	12	.280	.386	.333
August	4-1	1.17	137	34	1	9	18	.248	.328	.293
Sept./Oct.	2-2	3.38	152	42	3	17	15	.276	.395	.347
Leading Off Inn.			207	50	1	13	25	.242	.314	.293
Bases Empty			486	128	6	28	43	.263	.368	.303
Runners On			322	82	7	30	41	.255	.360	.313
Runners/Scor. Pos.			173	39	5	20	24	.225	.364	.295
Runners On/2 Out			139	38	5	13	13	.273	.424	.335
Scor. Pos./2 Out			83	19	3	12	6	.229	.398	.325
Late Inning Pressure			54	15	1	4	5	.278	.352	.323
Leading Off			17	6	0	0	1	.353	.353	.353
Bases Empty			34	10	1	2	2	.294	.382	.333
Runners On			20	5	0	2	3	.250	.300	.318
Runners/Scor. Pos.			7	3	0	2	3	.429	.571	.556
First 9 Batters			273	75	4	25	25	.275	.388	.332
Second 9 Batters			274	66	3	13	32	.241	.332	.279
All Batters Thereafter			261	69	6	20	27	.264	.375	.317

Loves to face: Mike Fitzgerald (.111, 1-for-9)
Hates to face: Von Hayes (.556, 5-for-9, 1 HR)
Ground outs-to-air outs ratio: 1.67 last season, 1.91 for career. . . . Additional statistics: 21 double-play ground outs in 162 opportunities, 36 doubles (tied for 10th-most in N.L.), 5 triples allowed in 212.2 innings last season. . . . Allowed 22 first-inning runs (tied for 7th-most in N.L.) in 33 starts last season. . . . Batting support: 4.03 runs per start. . . . Total of 192 career wins is 4th-highest in baseball history among pitchers who never won 20 in a season. The leaders: Milt Pappas (209), Larry French (197), and Curt Simmons (193). . . . August ERA was 3d-lowest in N.L. . . . Had league's 5th-best day-game ERA. . . . Either very good or very bad: 1.21 ERA in his wins, 7.03 ERA in his losses. . . . Opponents were hitless in 13 at bats with the bases loaded last season. Has not walked a man with the bases loaded in 82 chances since 1978.

Rick Rhoden

Pittsburgh Pirates	W–L	ERA	AB	H	HR	BB	SO	BA	SA	OBA
Season	10-15	4.47	859	254	18	69	128	.296	.433	.352
vs. Left-Handed Batters			431	132	6	35	53	.306	.425	.360
vs. Right-Handed Batters			428	122	12	34	75	.285	.442	.345
Home	7-9	4.42	477	144	9	38	66	.302	.434	.358
Road	3-6	4.53	382	110	9	31	62	.288	.432	.345
Grass	2-4	3.88	234	66	4	17	35	.282	.419	.333
Artificial Turf	8-11	4.69	625	188	14	52	93	.301	.438	.359
Day	3-7	4.46	324	92	9	28	54	.284	.457	.350
Night	7-8	4.48	535	162	9	41	74	.303	.419	.354
April	1-3	4.66	121	42	2	13	11	.347	.471	.415
May	3-2	3.07	161	44	3	10	15	.273	.404	.320
June	1-2	6.26	113	35	2	8	20	.310	.434	.355
July	0-5	3.86	157	44	2	9	28	.280	.408	.327
August	3-1	3.53	144	39	3	11	30	.271	.396	.331
Sept./Oct.	2-2	5.98	163	50	6	18	24	.307	.491	.376
Leading Off Inn.			210	74	11	12	24	.352	.600	.387
Bases Empty			483	144	13	33	69	.298	.455	.343
Runners On			376	110	5	36	59	.293	.404	.364
Runners/Scor. Pos.			219	67	4	25	40	.306	.438	.390
Runners On/2 Out			167	49	3	16	27	.293	.425	.372
Scor. Pos./2 Out			102	30	2	14	20	.294	.422	.400
Late Inning Pressure			70	24	1	10	15	.343	.514	.425
Leading Off			17	7	1	3	3	.412	.765	.500
Bases Empty			33	13	1	5	8	.394	.697	.474
Runners On			37	11	0	5	7	.297	.351	.381
Runners/Scor. Pos.			29	7	0	3	7	.241	.310	.313
First 9 Batters			284	82	6	23	48	.289	.426	.346
Second 9 Batters			273	79	6	18	42	.289	.429	.336
All Batters Thereafter			302	93	6	28	38	.308	.444	.372

Loves to face: Chris Brown (.111, 1-for-9, 4 SO)
Hates to face: John Denny (.714, 5-for-7)
Ground outs-to-air outs ratio: 1.58 last season, 1.36 for career. ... Additional statistics: 14 double-play ground outs in 163 opportunities, 48 doubles (tied for 3d-most in N.L.), 8 triples (tied for 7th-most in N.L.) allowed in 213.1 innings last season. ... Total of 74 extra-base hits allowed was 4th-highest in N.L. ... Allowed 23 first-inning runs (tied for 5th-most in N.L.) in 35 starts last season. ... Batting support: 3.60 runs per start. ... Tied for N.L. lead with five losses in July. ... One of two N.L. pitchers to drive in three game-winning runs. ... Batting average of opposing right-handers (.285) was his highest in 11 years of *The Player Analysis*. ... Allowed 11 home runs to leadoff batters last season, tied for most in majors. ... One of five N.L. pitchers to start at least 30 games in each of the last four seasons.

Bert Roberge

Montreal Expos	W–L	ERA	AB	H	HR	BB	SO	BA	SA	OBA
Season	3-3	3.44	250	58	5	22	34	.232	.356	.299
vs. Left-Handed Batters			116	30	1	15	13	.259	.379	.353
vs. Right-Handed Batters			134	28	4	7	21	.209	.336	.248
Home	0-1	2.97	135	29	2	9	17	.215	.333	.269
Road	3-2	3.98	115	29	3	13	17	.252	.383	.333
Grass	2-0	5.06	42	12	1	2	5	.286	.452	.318
Artificial Turf	1-3	3.14	208	46	4	20	29	.221	.337	.296
Day	1-1	4.21	97	26	3	7	9	.268	.433	.330
Night	2-2	2.98	153	32	2	15	25	.209	.307	.280
April	0-1	1.64	39	8	1	7	5	.205	.308	.340
May	1-0	3.09	45	11	0	1	7	.244	.356	.261
June			0	0	0	0	0	.000	.000	.000
July	0-0	1.59	43	12	0	1	4	.279	.302	.295
August	2-0	2.55	63	12	2	6	11	.190	.349	.261
Sept./Oct.	0-2	7.16	60	15	2	7	7	.250	.433	.338
Leading Off Inn.			59	12	0	5	8	.203	.237	.277
Bases Empty			143	30	1	12	23	.210	.266	.280
Runners On			107	28	4	10	11	.262	.477	.325
Runners/Scor. Pos.			77	20	3	8	11	.260	.519	.329
Runners On/2 Out			49	13	2	6	4	.265	.490	.345
Scor. Pos./2 Out			37	9	2	5	4	.243	.541	.333
Late Inning Pressure			98	22	3	7	17	.224	.357	.283
Leading Off			24	7	0	4	3	.292	.333	.414
Bases Empty			62	12	1	4	13	.194	.274	.254
Runners On			36	10	2	3	4	.278	.500	.333
Runners/Scor. Pos.			25	7	1	3	4	.280	.480	.357
First 9 Batters			239	55	3	20	34	.230	.331	.295
Second 9 Batters			11	3	2	2	0	.273	.909	.385
All Batters Thereafter			0	0	0	0	0	.000	.000	.000

Loves to face: Gary Carter (0-for-5)
Hates to face: Tim Flannery (.667, 4-for-6)
Ground outs-to-air outs ratio: 1.04 last season (lowest of his career), 1.23 for career. ... Additional statistics: 3 double-play ground outs in 42 opportunities, 10 doubles, 3 triples allowed in 68.0 innings last season. ... Balked five times last season; no other major-league reliever had more than two. ... Has never committed an error in 50 chances in the major leagues, 3d-highest total among active errorless pitchers. ... Opponents' career batting averages: .205 with bases empty, .278 with runners on base; left-handers .217, right-handers .259. ... Has allowed only one home run in 368 career plate appearances by opposing left-handed batters: August 18, 1985, by Tommy Herr. ... Opponents' career batting average of .204 in Late-Inning Pressure Situations is 5th-lowest in *Player Analysis* history (minimum: 300 PA).

Don Robinson

Pittsburgh Pirates	W–L	ERA	AB	H	HR	BB	SO	BA	SA	OBA
Season	5-11	3.87	372	95	6	42	65	.255	.363	.334
vs. Left-Handed Batters			165	40	0	24	30	.242	.291	.339
vs. Right-Handed Batters			207	55	6	18	35	.266	.420	.330
Home	3-2	3.07	171	46	2	11	31	.269	.368	.317
Road	2-9	4.56	201	49	4	31	34	.244	.358	.348
Grass	1-4	6.63	75	17	1	13	16	.227	.333	.341
Artificial Turf	4-7	3.18	297	78	5	29	49	.263	.370	.332
Day	3-3	5.24	138	38	3	18	24	.275	.420	.359
Night	2-8	3.10	234	57	3	24	41	.244	.329	.319
April	1-0	3.27	39	6	0	8	8	.154	.231	.298
May	1-0	2.25	60	13	1	5	10	.217	.317	.277
June	0-3	4.63	96	29	2	9	12	.302	.448	.374
July	0-2	7.56	35	9	0	7	10	.257	.343	.381
August	2-5	4.78	106	34	3	10	16	.321	.453	.379
Sept./Oct.	1-1	0.00	36	4	0	3	9	.111	.111	.179
Leading Off Inn.			86	15	0	9	12	.174	.244	.260
Bases Empty			204	47	2	17	40	.230	.328	.296
Runners On			168	48	4	25	25	.286	.405	.378
Runners/Scor. Pos.			105	30	4	22	15	.286	.457	.409
Runners On/2 Out			75	18	3	8	14	.240	.373	.313
Scor. Pos./2 Out			49	11	3	7	9	.224	.408	.321
Late Inning Pressure			138	33	2	18	26	.239	.341	.335
Leading Off			31	5	0	5	4	.161	.226	.297
Bases Empty			74	17	1	7	14	.230	.324	.313
Runners On			64	16	1	11	12	.250	.359	.360
Runners/Scor. Pos.			41	10	1	9	6	.244	.366	.380
First 9 Batters			248	62	5	31	46	.250	.375	.338
Second 9 Batters			92	19	1	4	16	.207	.272	.240
All Batters Thereafter			32	14	0	7	3	.438	.531	.538

Loves to face: Gary Carter (.068, 3-for-44)
Hates to face: Ozzie Virgil (.467, 7-for-15, 2 HR)
Ground outs-to-air outs ratio: 1.15 last season, 0.89 for career. ... Additional statistics: 10 double-play ground outs in 80 opportunities, 22 doubles, 0 triples allowed in 95.1 innings last season. ... Led N.L. with five losses in August. ... Did not allow a home run to a left-handed batter in 165 at bats, 2d-highest total in N.L. last season. ... Let's talk about his batting. Career averages: .261 overall (same as Manny Trillo), .282 with runners on base, .375 (3-for-8) with the bases loaded. Has hit for a higher average against left-handers (.307) than against right-handers (.238), but five of his six career home runs have been hit off righties. ... RDI% of .379 from scoring position since 1980 is 3d-highest in majors during that time, if you lower the minimum to 25 RRFs to allow his inclusion. He ranks behind Butch Davis (.390) and Tim Lollar (.386).

Ron Robinson

Cincinnati Reds	W–L	ERA	AB	H	HR	BB	SO	BA	SA	OBA
Season	7-7	3.99	413	107	11	32	76	.259	.402	.311
vs. Left-Handed Batters			215	65	5	17	27	.302	.447	.353
vs. Right-Handed Batters			198	42	6	15	49	.212	.354	.266
Home	4-4	3.86	203	54	5	16	33	.266	.389	.323
Road	3-3	4.12	210	53	6	16	43	.252	.414	.300
Grass	2-1	2.70	135	31	5	13	26	.230	.378	.291
Artificial Turf	5-6	4.65	278	76	6	19	50	.273	.414	.321
Day	2-2	3.71	101	26	3	5	17	.257	.436	.287
Night	5-5	4.08	312	81	8	27	59	.260	.391	.319
April			0	0	0	0	0	.000	.000	.000
May	0-0	2.16	30	5	1	0	8	.167	.300	.167
June	3-0	2.03	44	8	1	6	5	.182	.250	.269
July	2-2	5.81	124	37	4	9	24	.298	.516	.343
August	0-1	3.75	45	12	2	7	8	.267	.422	.377
Sept./Oct.	2-4	3.71	170	45	3	10	31	.265	.371	.304
Leading Off Inn.			101	26	2	6	15	.257	.406	.299
Bases Empty			240	61	5	18	53	.254	.392	.306
Runners On			173	46	6	14	23	.266	.416	.318
Runners/Scor. Pos.			103	29	5	8	16	.282	.466	.328
Runners On/2 Out			75	20	3	6	10	.267	.427	.321
Scor. Pos./2 Out			50	13	3	3	8	.260	.480	.302
Late Inning Pressure			55	11	1	3	8	.200	.309	.241
Leading Off			18	2	0	0	1	.111	.222	.111
Bases Empty			43	7	1	2	6	.163	.302	.200
Runners On			12	4	0	1	2	.333	.333	.385
Runners/Scor. Pos.			7	4	0	0	2	.571	.571	.571
First 9 Batters			214	47	3	22	44	.220	.299	.292
Second 9 Batters			114	34	5	2	21	.298	.526	.308
All Batters Thereafter			85	26	3	8	11	.306	.494	.366

Loves to face: Paul Runge (0-for-7, 3 SO)
Hates to face: Ken Landreaux & Mike Scioscia (.467, 7-for-15 vs. each)
Ground outs-to-air outs ratio: 1.05 last season, 1.10 for career. ... Additional statistics: 7 double-play ground outs in 74 opportunities, 30 doubles, 5 triples allowed in 108.1 innings last season. ... Allowed 6 first-inning runs in 12 starts last season. ... Batting support: 3.17 runs per start. ... Record of 4–6, 4.83 ERA as a starter; 3–1, 2.27 ERA in relief. ... Career record of 0–4, 4.83 ERA in seven games against Los Angeles. ... Opponents' career batting average of .175 (11-for-63) in Late-Inning Pressure Situations. ... Has retired the leadoff batter in 19 of 21 career LIP innings. ... Won his first five decisions last season, then followed with a six-game losing streak. ... Opponents' career batting average of .214 (3-for-14) with the bases loaded.

Dave Rucker

Philadelphia Phillies	W–L	ERA	AB	H	HR	BB	SO	BA	SA	OBA
Season	3-2	4.31	298	83	6	40	41	.279	.426	.361
vs. Left-Handed Batters			72	15	1	7	11	.208	.347	.268
vs. Right-Handed Batters			226	68	5	33	30	.301	.451	.390
Home	3-2	4.33	203	54	3	24	31	.266	.394	.338
Road	0-0	4.26	95	29	3	16	10	.305	.495	.409
Grass	0-0	4.67	65	21	2	11	5	.323	.508	.418
Artificial Turf	3-2	4.21	233	62	4	29	36	.266	.403	.345
Day	1-0	3.77	55	16	2	7	9	.291	.455	.375
Night	2-2	4.43	243	67	4	33	32	.276	.420	.358
April			0	0	0	0	0	.000	.000	.000
May	1-0	3.38	52	10	1	12	9	.192	.365	.338
June	0-1	3.21	52	12	1	8	8	.231	.365	.328
July	0-0	9.00	39	16	2	3	4	.410	.718	.467
August	1-0	2.95	73	19	1	7	11	.260	.370	.325
Sept./Oct.	1-1	4.91	82	26	1	10	9	.317	.415	.379
Leading Off Inn.			63	16	0	10	12	.254	.349	.356
Bases Empty			147	39	2	20	24	.265	.408	.361
Runners On			151	44	4	20	17	.291	.444	.362
Runners/Scor. Pos.			92	25	3	17	13	.272	.413	.365
Runners On/2 Out			59	12	1	12	7	.203	.322	.338
Scor. Pos./2 Out			40	9	1	10	5	.225	.375	.380
Late Inning Pressure			61	17	3	10	10	.279	.508	.375
Leading Off			15	4	0	1	2	.267	.400	.313
Bases Empty			33	9	1	4	6	.273	.455	.351
Runners On			28	8	2	6	4	.286	.571	.400
Runners/Scor. Pos.			18	5	1	6	3	.278	.556	.440
First 9 Batters			216	57	6	31	31	.264	.444	.353
Second 9 Batters			58	18	0	5	7	.310	.397	.364
All Batters Thereafter			24	8	0	4	3	.333	.333	.429

Loves to face: Graig Nettles (0-for-10)
Hates to face: Dale Murphy (5-for-5) & Bob Horner (4-for-4, 1 HR)
Ground outs-to-air outs ratio: 1.38 last season (2.45 in Late-Inning Pressure Situations), 1.32 for career. . . . Additional statistics: 10 double-play ground outs in 78 opportunities, 16 doubles, 5 triples allowed in 79.1 innings last season. . . . Pitched three or more innings in six relief appearances last season, most on Phillies' staff. . . . Opponents' career batting averages: .223 (one extra-base hit per 20 at bats) vs. left-handers, .281 (one XBH per 14 AB) vs. right-handers. . . . Opposing batters have a career batting average of .217 with two outs and runners in scoring position. . . . Right place, wrong time: Rucker played for the 1983 Tigers and 1984 Cardinals, the season before each reached the World Series. . . . If Philadelphia trades him, take the Phillies plus the points.

Dick Ruthven

Chicago Cubs	W–L	ERA	AB	H	HR	BB	SO	BA	SA	OBA
Season	4-7	4.53	344	103	6	37	26	.299	.439	.362
vs. Left-Handed Batters			186	61	4	18	14	.328	.484	.378
vs. Right-Handed Batters			158	42	2	19	12	.266	.386	.343
Home	3-2	3.94	186	56	3	17	11	.301	.425	.354
Road	1-5	5.26	158	47	3	20	15	.297	.456	.370
Grass	4-4	4.16	270	83	6	25	20	.307	.452	.362
Artificial Turf	0-3	5.75	74	20	0	12	6	.270	.392	.360
Day	4-5	3.75	280	82	4	26	21	.293	.418	.347
Night	0-2	8.22	64	21	2	11	5	.328	.531	.421
April	0-1	5.06	17	4	0	4	1	.235	.353	.381
May	1-3	3.33	105	34	1	6	8	.324	.410	.351
June	2-2	5.67	103	27	1	17	6	.262	.398	.358
July	1-1	4.87	85	24	4	9	10	.282	.506	.351
August	0-0	3.52	34	14	0	1	1	.412	.529	.429
Sept./Oct.			0	0	0	0	0	.000	.000	.000
Leading Off Inn.			82	31	2	10	4	.378	.549	.446
Bases Empty			169	54	2	21	13	.320	.438	.395
Runners On			175	49	4	16	13	.280	.440	.330
Runners/Scor. Pos.			89	21	4	12	8	.236	.449	.308
Runners On/2 Out			67	16	1	6	6	.239	.373	.301
Scor. Pos./2 Out			39	8	1	5	3	.205	.359	.295
Late Inning Pressure			15	6	0	1	1	.400	.400	.438
Leading Off			4	3	0	1	0	.750	.750	.800
Bases Empty			7	4	0	1	0	.571	.571	.625
Runners On			8	2	0	0	1	.250	.250	.250
Runners/Scor. Pos.			4	1	0	0	1	.250	.250	.250
First 9 Batters			148	46	2	11	12	.311	.412	.356
Second 9 Batters			111	26	2	14	9	.234	.342	.313
All Batters Thereafter			85	31	2	12	5	.365	.612	.434

Loves to face: Jeff Leonard (.091, 2-for-22)
Hates to face: Steve Braun (.667, 6-for-9, 1 HR)
Ground outs-to-air outs ratio: 1.35 last season, 1.39 for career. . . . Additional statistics: 11 double-play ground outs in 95 opportunities, 22 doubles, 4 triples allowed in 87.1 innings last season. . . . Average of 5.31 innings per start was 6th-lowest among N.L. pitchers (minimum: 15 GS). . . . Allowed 8 first-inning runs in 15 starts last season. . . . Batting support: 3.40 runs per start, 10th-lowest average in N.L. (minimum: 15 GS). . . . Rate of 2.68 strikeouts per nine innings was lowest among N.L. pitchers (minimum: 15 starts), and rate of 10.61 hits per nine innings was 3d-highest among same group. . . . A survivor: career total of 123 wins, most among active pitchers with ERAs above 4.00. . . . One of two pitchers who has had two hits off Dwight Gooden; the other: Larry McWilliams. Ruthven also has one of the three walks that Dr. K has issued to pitchers.

Nolan Ryan

Houston Astros	W–L	ERA	AB	H	HR	BB	SO	BA	SA	OBA
Season	10-12	3.80	856	205	12	95	209	.239	.339	.318
vs. Left-Handed Batters			415	102	5	45	97	.246	.337	.317
vs. Right-Handed Batters			441	103	7	50	112	.234	.340	.319
Home	7-3	3.14	487	107	3	43	118	.220	.287	.281
Road	3-9	4.72	369	98	9	52	91	.266	.407	.363
Grass	3-4	5.54	214	65	7	24	45	.304	.481	.375
Artificial Turf	7-8	3.30	642	140	5	71	164	.218	.291	.299
Day	4-0	2.49	160	33	3	16	44	.206	.313	.282
Night	6-12	4.10	696	172	9	79	165	.247	.345	.326
April	2-1	2.80	130	26	3	4	28	.200	.323	.222
May	3-1	2.56	156	29	1	19	48	.186	.244	.287
June	3-3	4.24	158	45	2	14	33	.285	.392	.341
July	0-4	4.91	150	35	4	23	37	.233	.387	.343
August	1-2	4.30	139	34	2	19	40	.245	.317	.333
Sept./Oct.	1-1	4.13	123	36	0	16	23	.293	.374	.371
Leading Off Inn.			212	57	2	27	46	.269	.368	.351
Bases Empty			489	115	6	51	119	.235	.319	.311
Runners On			367	90	6	44	90	.245	.365	.326
Runners/Scor. Pos.			223	52	2	34	65	.233	.305	.325
Runners On/2 Out			146	28	0	18	42	.192	.233	.289
Scor. Pos./2 Out			98	22	0	12	34	.224	.286	.309
Late Inning Pressure			123	29	4	7	30	.236	.374	.287
Leading Off			31	7	0	4	10	.226	.258	.314
Bases Empty			76	17	2	4	21	.224	.316	.280
Runners On			47	12	2	3	9	.255	.468	.296
Runners/Scor. Pos.			26	6	1	2	6	.231	.346	.258
First 9 Batters			262	66	3	34	68	.252	.355	.338
Second 9 Batters			271	55	0	28	69	.203	.255	.275
All Batters Thereafter			323	84	9	33	72	.260	.396	.337

Loves to face: U.L. Washington (0-for-12, 7 SO)
Hates to face: Howard Johnson (3-for-3)
Ground outs-to-air outs ratio: 1.31 last season, 1.10 for career. . . . Additional statistics: 16 double-play ground outs in 172 opportunities, 33 doubles, 8 triples (tied for 7th-most in N.L.) allowed in 232.0 innings last season. . . . Allowed 17 first-inning runs in 35 starts last season. . . . Batting support: 3.86 runs per start. . . . ERA of 2.49 in day games was 6th-lowest in N.L. . . . Walked the leadoff batter in 27 innings, highest total in N.L. last season, but a far cry from his *Player Analysis* record of 60, set in 1977. . . . Pitched to no decision in 13 of his 35 starts, tied for 2d-most in N.L. . . . Opponents' career batting average of .199 in Late-Inning Pressure Situations is 4th-lowest in *Player Analysis* history (minimum: 300 PA). . . . Eight-game losing streak (June 22–Aug. 18) matched the longest of his career (1975 with Angels).

Randy St. Claire

Montreal Expos	W–L	ERA	AB	H	HR	BB	SO	BA	SA	OBA
Season	5-3	3.93	260	69	3	26	25	.265	.362	.333
vs. Left-Handed Batters			116	32	2	15	12	.276	.388	.356
vs. Right-Handed Batters			144	37	1	11	13	.257	.340	.314
Home	1-1	4.85	115	33	1	17	13	.287	.374	.383
Road	4-2	3.23	145	36	2	9	12	.248	.352	.290
Grass	3-0	4.29	77	18	2	3	7	.234	.325	.263
Artificial Turf	2-3	3.78	183	51	1	23	18	.279	.377	.361
Day	2-0	5.12	73	19	3	2	10	.260	.384	.289
Night	3-3	3.47	187	50	0	24	15	.267	.353	.349
April			0	0	0	0	0	.000	.000	.000
May	0-0	2.25	15	2	1	0	0	.133	.467	.133
June	2-1	2.81	62	17	0	4	8	.274	.355	.318
July	1-1	2.29	73	19	0	9	4	.260	.301	.345
August	1-0	4.80	56	14	1	5	6	.250	.321	.311
Sept./Oct.	1-1	7.07	54	17	1	8	7	.315	.463	.403
Leading Off Inn.			61	15	0	3	3	.246	.295	.292
Bases Empty			142	37	2	10	11	.261	.359	.314
Runners On			118	32	1	16	14	.271	.364	.356
Runners/Scor. Pos.			72	20	1	12	9	.278	.417	.376
Runners On/2 Out			50	13	0	11	6	.260	.320	.393
Scor. Pos./2 Out			34	10	0	8	5	.294	.382	.429
Late Inning Pressure			81	20	0	14	6	.247	.321	.358
Leading Off			22	4	0	1	0	.182	.227	.217
Bases Empty			48	13	0	4	2	.271	.333	.327
Runners On			33	7	0	10	4	.212	.303	.395
Runners/Scor. Pos.			20	4	0	7	2	.200	.350	.407
First 9 Batters			231	59	3	21	22	.255	.355	.319
Second 9 Batters			29	10	0	5	3	.345	.414	.441
All Batters Thereafter			0	0	0	0	0	.000	.000	.000

Loves to face: Jim Morrison (.125, 1-for-8)
Hates to face: Ron Oester (3-for-3)
Ground outs-to-air outs ratio: 1.32 last season, 1.33 for career. . . . Additional statistics: 10 double-play ground outs in 59 opportunities, 10 doubles, 3 triples allowed in 68.2 innings last season. . . . Average of 3.28 strikeouts per nine innings was 2d-lowest among N.L. relief pitchers (minimum: 30 relief games). . . . Salary negotiation must be tough when you share the bullpen with Jeff Reardon and Tim Burke. Career total of 46 relief appearances; has finished 18 games, but has no saves. . . . Career totals: 10 strikeouts and two walks in day games, 19 SOs and 26 BBs in night games. . . . But he has faced 250 batters in night games, and has not allowed a home run; he has surrendered home runs to three of the 82 batters he's faced in day games.

Scott Sanderson

Chicago Cubs	W–L	ERA	AB	H	HR	BB	SO	BA	SA	OBA
Season	5-6	3.12	439	100	13	27	80	.228	.405	.268
vs. Left-Handed Batters			251	61	10	20	37	.243	.470	.296
vs. Right-Handed Batters			188	39	3	7	43	.207	.319	.231
Home	3-3	3.25	253	58	11	17	50	.229	.435	.274
Road	2-3	2.96	186	42	2	10	30	.226	.366	.261
Grass	4-4	2.57	342	77	11	23	69	.225	.398	.270
Artificial Turf	1-2	5.13	97	23	2	4	11	.237	.433	.262
Day	4-3	2.85	316	73	11	19	65	.231	.408	.270
Night	1-3	3.86	123	27	2	8	15	.220	.398	.265
April	1-1	2.65	62	15	1	4	17	.242	.419	.284
May	2-0	2.03	161	35	7	6	25	.217	.391	.246
June	1-2	2.18	110	17	2	9	24	.155	.291	.215
July	1-1	3.21	51	14	1	4	7	.275	.431	.310
August	0-2	9.95	55	19	2	4	7	.345	.636	.383
Sept./Oct.			0	0	0	0	0	.000	.000	.000
Leading Off Inn.			119	30	3	5	16	.252	.437	.282
Bases Empty			290	66	10	16	55	.228	.431	.268
Runners On			149	34	3	11	25	.228	.356	.269
Runners/Scor. Pos.			85	18	3	5	16	.212	.365	.237
Runners On/2 Out			68	14	2	5	10	.206	.368	.260
Scor. Pos./2 Out			42	8	2	2	8	.190	.381	.227
Late Inning Pressure			44	6	0	2	8	.136	.136	.174
Leading Off			14	2	0	0	2	.143	.143	.143
Bases Empty			36	4	0	0	7	.111	.111	.158
Runners On			8	2	0	0	1	.250	.250	.250
Runners/Scor. Pos.			5	1	0	0	1	.200	.200	.200
First 9 Batters			155	34	7	8	36	.219	.439	.255
Second 9 Batters			134	35	5	9	22	.261	.455	.299
All Batters Thereafter			150	31	1	10	22	.207	.327	.255

Loves to face: Darryl Strawberry (0-for-9)
Hates to face: Pete Rose (.393, 22-for-56, 1 HR)
Ground outs-to-air outs ratio: 0.96 last season, 0.80 for career. … Additional statistics: 5 double-play ground outs in 62 opportunities, 19 doubles, 10 triples (tied for 3d-most in N.L.) allowed in 121.0 innings last season. … Allowed 13 first-inning runs in 19 starts last season. … Batting support: 4.37 runs per start. … Has allowed only four career walks to leadoff batters in 115 innings in Late-Inning Pressure Situations. … Opponents' on-base average in Late-Inning Pressure Situations last season was lowest in N.L. since 1976 (minimum: 40 PA). … Opposing batters have hit below .200 with two outs and runners in scoring position in four of his eight seasons in majors. Career average: .208.

Dan Schatzeder

Montreal Expos	W–L	ERA	AB	H	HR	BB	SO	BA	SA	OBA
Season	3-5	3.80	390	101	13	31	64	.259	.426	.311
vs. Left-Handed Batters			59	13	0	4	12	.220	.237	.266
vs. Right-Handed Batters			331	88	13	27	52	.266	.459	.319
Home	2-2	3.08	228	54	9	11	38	.237	.395	.270
Road	1-3	4.81	162	47	4	20	26	.290	.469	.366
Grass	1-3	5.19	98	26	2	9	15	.265	.429	.327
Artificial Turf	2-2	3.33	292	75	11	22	49	.257	.425	.306
Day	3-3	4.47	200	51	9	9	30	.255	.455	.286
Night	0-2	3.12	190	50	4	22	34	.263	.395	.336
April	0-0	7.50	48	16	5	1	7	.333	.708	.333
May	2-1	2.84	101	28	2	5	12	.277	.386	.311
June	0-2	3.16	89	16	1	6	18	.180	.247	.229
July	0-1	3.60	36	9	1	6	5	.250	.417	.357
August	0-0	3.00	13	5	1	1	2	.385	.769	.429
Sept./Oct.	1-1	3.81	103	27	3	12	20	.262	.447	.339
Leading Off Inn.			100	32	2	10	11	.320	.440	.382
Bases Empty			231	66	10	20	36	.286	.494	.343
Runners On			159	35	3	11	28	.220	.327	.266
Runners/Scor. Pos.			92	21	2	8	20	.228	.337	.282
Runners On/2 Out			56	10	0	6	10	.179	.232	.258
Scor. Pos./2 Out			36	7	0	6	7	.194	.250	.310
Late Inning Pressure			33	9	1	3	2	.273	.424	.333
Leading Off			10	3	0	1	0	.300	.400	.364
Bases Empty			25	6	1	2	1	.240	.400	.296
Runners On			8	3	0	1	1	.375	.500	.444
Runners/Scor. Pos.			5	2	0	1	1	.400	.400	.500
First 9 Batters			176	43	4	16	29	.244	.369	.306
Second 9 Batters			129	36	5	9	21	.279	.481	.321
All Batters Thereafter			85	22	4	6	14	.259	.459	.308

Loves to face: Tony Gwynn (0-for-9)
Hates to face: Bill Doran (.538, 7-for-13)
Ground outs-to-air outs ratio: 1.17 last season, 0.74 for career. … Additional statistics: 12 double-play ground outs in 78 opportunities, 20 doubles, 3 triples allowed in 104.1 innings last season. … Allowed 1 first-inning run in 15 starts, lowest rate in N.L. last season (minimum: 15 GS). … Batting support: 3.73 runs per start. … Allowed one home run per 8.0 innings, 6th-highest rate among N.L. pitchers (minimum: 15 GS). … Opposing batters hit 66 points higher with the bases empty than with runners on base last season, 3d-largest difference in N.L. (minimum: 100 AB in both situations). … Career batting average of opposing left-handed hitters (.257) is higher than that of right-handers (.239). … Opposing batters have hit .205 with two outs and runners in scoring position. … Excellent hitter: career batting average of .326 with runners in scoring position.

Mike Scott

Houston Astros	W–L	ERA	AB	H	HR	BB	SO	BA	SA	OBA
Season	18-8	3.29	827	194	20	80	137	.235	.363	.302
vs. Left-Handed Batters			429	93	3	43	61	.217	.289	.289
vs. Right-Handed Batters			398	101	17	37	76	.254	.442	.317
Home	11-2	2.18	425	83	7	35	74	.195	.296	.259
Road	7-6	4.60	402	111	13	45	63	.276	.433	.347
Grass	4-3	3.46	249	60	7	25	41	.241	.361	.310
Artificial Turf	14-5	3.22	578	134	13	55	96	.232	.363	.299
Day	4-2	5.96	180	50	8	23	31	.278	.489	.359
Night	14-6	2.60	647	144	12	57	106	.223	.328	.286
April	1-1	2.39	99	22	1	8	16	.222	.293	.278
May	1-1	4.78	102	28	4	12	23	.275	.431	.345
June	4-2	2.47	183	37	5	15	24	.202	.317	.263
July	4-1	2.06	126	30	3	8	25	.238	.413	.295
August	4-2	2.72	150	32	3	14	17	.213	.313	.279
Sept./Oct.	4-1	5.40	167	45	4	23	32	.269	.419	.358
Leading Off Inn.			206	37	6	23	31	.180	.286	.265
Bases Empty			511	118	13	45	71	.231	.370	.294
Runners On			316	76	7	35	66	.241	.351	.315
Runners/Scor. Pos.			172	44	5	22	40	.256	.395	.337
Runners On/2 Out			133	25	4	18	26	.188	.323	.285
Scor. Pos./2 Out			83	18	3	11	17	.217	.386	.309
Late Inning Pressure			65	7	1	8	9	.108	.169	.205
Leading Off			21	2	1	1	5	.095	.238	.136
Bases Empty			52	7	1	6	8	.135	.212	.224
Runners On			13	0	0	2	1	.000	.000	.133
Runners/Scor. Pos.			3	0	0	1	0	.000	.000	.250
First 9 Batters			287	67	6	26	57	.233	.348	.299
Second 9 Batters			268	70	3	29	44	.261	.362	.332
All Batters Thereafter			272	57	11	25	36	.210	.379	.276

Loves to face: Manny Trillo (.045, 1-for-22)
Hates to face: Pete Rose (.417, 15-for-36)
Ground outs-to-air outs ratio: 1.03 last season, 1.26 for career. … Additional statistics: 15 double-play ground outs in 159 opportunities, 36 doubles (tied for 10th-most in N.L.), 5 triples allowed in 221.2 innings last season. … Allowed 11 first-inning runs in 35 starts last season. … Batting support: 5.03 runs per start, 3d-highest average in N.L. (minimum: 15 GS). … ERA of 2.18 in home games was 7th-lowest in N.L. … Drove in 11 runs last season, most of any N.L. pitcher. … Did not allow a hit in 13 at bats in Late-Inning Pressure Situations with runners on base, the highest total since 1976, when Bo McLaughlin set the N.L. *Player Analysis* record (18 hitless AB). … Won 11 games (against five losses) vs. teams that finished the season with winning records. Only three pitchers won more: Hershiser, Gooden, and Gross.

Steve Shields

Atlanta Braves	W–L	ERA	AB	H	HR	BB	SO	BA	SA	OBA
Season	1-2	5.16	269	86	9	32	29	.320	.454	.390
vs. Left-Handed Batters			152	55	5	15	17	.362	.500	.420
vs. Right-Handed Batters			117	31	4	17	12	.265	.393	.353
Home	1-1	4.79	162	52	7	12	18	.321	.488	.367
Road	0-1	5.74	107	34	2	20	11	.318	.402	.422
Grass	1-1	5.51	203	68	8	18	22	.335	.488	.387
Artificial Turf	0-1	4.15	66	18	1	14	7	.273	.348	.400
Day	1-0	5.29	65	21	3	7	10	.323	.523	.384
Night	0-2	5.12	204	65	6	25	19	.319	.431	.392
April			0	0	0	0	0	.000	.000	.000
May			0	0	0	0	0	.000	.000	.000
June	1-2	4.19	140	37	6	15	17	.264	.414	.335
July	0-0	5.59	37	12	1	5	4	.324	.486	.395
August			0	0	0	0	0	.000	.000	.000
Sept./Oct.	0-0	6.86	92	37	2	12	8	.402	.500	.467
Leading Off Inn.			65	18	1	2	7	.277	.323	.299
Bases Empty			147	38	4	11	18	.259	.367	.314
Runners On			122	48	5	21	11	.393	.557	.473
Runners/Scor. Pos.			80	33	3	19	8	.413	.575	.510
Runners On/2 Out			49	17	1	10	7	.347	.469	.458
Scor. Pos./2 Out			36	12	1	9	5	.333	.472	.467
Late Inning Pressure			25	8	2	2	2	.320	.640	.357
Leading Off			8	2	1	0	0	.250	.625	.250
Bases Empty			19	5	1	0	1	.263	.474	.263
Runners On			6	3	1	2	1	.500	1.167	.556
Runners/Scor. Pos.			4	3	1	2	1	.750	1.750	.714
First 9 Batters			154	47	4	20	18	.305	.429	.382
Second 9 Batters			73	23	4	7	8	.315	.479	.375
All Batters Thereafter			42	16	1	5	3	.381	.500	.447

Loves to face: Gary Redus (0-for-5)
Hates to face: Mike Scioscia (.800, 4-for-5)
Ground outs-to-air outs ratio: 1.78 last season, his first in majors. … Additional statistics: 5 double-play ground outs in 65 opportunities (5th-highest in N.L.), 9 doubles, 0 triples allowed in 68.0 innings last season. … Opposing batters hit 134 points higher with runners on base than with the bases empty, the largest difference in the N.L. … First pitcher in the 11-year history of *The Player Analysis* to retire fewer than half the batters he faced with runners in scoring position. His opponents' on-base average eclipses the 10-year-old *Player Analysis* record of .496 held by Blue Moon Odom. … Opposing left-handed batters hit 97 points higher than right-handers, 5th-largest difference in N.L. (minimum: 100 AB vs. each).

Eric Show

San Diego Padres	W–L	ERA	AB	H	HR	BB	SO	BA	SA	OBA
Season	12-11	3.09	871	212	27	87	141	.243	.387	.314
vs. Left-Handed Batters			464	133	16	54	46	.287	.453	.362
vs. Right-Handed Batters			407	79	11	33	95	.194	.312	.259
Home	6-5	3.52	396	91	17	42	69	.230	.394	.305
Road	6-6	2.72	475	121	10	45	72	.255	.381	.321
Grass	9-8	3.54	597	145	24	61	104	.243	.402	.315
Artificial Turf	3-3	2.10	274	67	3	26	37	.245	.354	.311
Day	3-5	3.16	277	70	9	23	50	.253	.401	.317
Night	9-6	3.06	594	142	18	64	91	.239	.380	.313
April	2-1	2.93	97	21	4	7	17	.216	.361	.269
May	2-1	3.63	132	31	3	19	27	.235	.402	.329
June	2-3	3.38	147	34	5	17	26	.231	.395	.319
July	1-2	3.83	151	41	4	17	27	.272	.391	.351
August	2-2	2.50	155	40	6	9	17	.258	.419	.299
Sept./Oct.	3-2	2.47	189	45	5	18	27	.238	.354	.303
Leading Off Inn.			223	55	11	18	31	.247	.444	.303
Bases Empty			525	135	19	51	80	.257	.415	.325
Runners On			346	77	8	36	61	.223	.344	.297
Runners/Scor. Pos.			165	34	3	24	30	.206	.321	.303
Runners On/2 Out			147	30	3	22	27	.204	.299	.316
Scor. Pos./2 Out			81	14	1	16	18	.173	.247	.316
Late Inning Pressure			85	19	2	8	10	.224	.388	.287
Leading Off			26	7	2	1	4	.269	.538	.296
Bases Empty			60	12	2	5	7	.200	.350	.262
Runners On			25	7	0	3	3	.280	.480	.345
Runners/Scor. Pos.			8	0	0	2	1	.000	.000	.182
First 9 Batters			288	70	8	21	64	.243	.361	.297
Second 9 Batters			278	61	11	22	42	.219	.392	.282
All Batters Thereafter			305	81	8	44	35	.266	.407	.357

Loves to face: Steve Sax (0-for-18)
Hates to face: Darryl Strawberry (.500, 9-for-18, 3 HR)
Ground outs-to-air outs ratio: 0.82 last season, 1.01 for career. . . . Additional statistics: 20 double-play ground outs in 172 opportunities, 32 doubles, 6 triples allowed in 233.0 innings last season. . . . Total of 65 extra-base hits allowed was 10th-highest in N.L. . . . Batting support: 3.83 runs per start. . . . September ERA of 1.37 was 4th-lowest in N.L. . . . Had league's 4th-best ERA on artificial turf. . . . Allowed 11 home runs to leadoff batters last season, tied for most in majors. . . . Opposing right-handed batters have hit below .200 in three of past four seasons. . . . Compiled a 3.61 ERA in 23 starts vs. teams that finished season with winning records, but won only four of those games. . . . Interesting pattern as a batter: career average of .263 (three HR in 76 AB) in day games; .136 (one HR in 77 AB) in night games.

Doug Sisk

New York Mets	W–L	ERA	AB	H	HR	BB	SO	BA	SA	OBA
Season	4-5	5.30	296	86	3	40	26	.291	.389	.379
vs. Left-Handed Batters			134	41	2	19	9	.306	.403	.392
vs. Right-Handed Batters			162	45	1	21	17	.278	.377	.368
Home	1-1	5.04	125	38	2	11	12	.304	.360	.370
Road	3-4	5.48	171	48	1	29	14	.281	.409	.385
Grass	3-3	3.29	215	59	2	20	20	.274	.335	.342
Artificial Turf	1-2	11.29	81	27	1	20	6	.333	.531	.465
Day	2-1	4.33	145	44	2	16	15	.303	.407	.380
Night	2-4	6.21	151	42	1	24	11	.278	.371	.377
April	1-1	4.86	67	19	0	13	6	.284	.343	.407
May	0-1	15.63	30	12	3	2	1	.400	.800	.438
June	1-3	5.85	76	18	0	8	8	.237	.316	.310
July	0-0	3.07	64	21	0	5	7	.328	.406	.386
August	0-0	4.70	31	9	0	6	2	.290	.323	.405
Sept./Oct.	2-0	1.17	28	7	0	6	2	.250	.286	.382
Leading Off Inn.			61	13	0	9	8	.213	.262	.314
Bases Empty			133	35	0	18	14	.263	.323	.355
Runners On			163	51	3	22	12	.313	.442	.398
Runners/Scor. Pos.			106	37	3	15	11	.349	.519	.430
Runners On/2 Out			68	20	0	8	4	.294	.353	.368
Scor. Pos./2 Out			46	14	0	6	3	.304	.370	.385
Late Inning Pressure			130	39	1	19	11	.300	.362	.393
Leading Off			31	5	0	4	3	.161	.161	.257
Bases Empty			68	19	0	8	6	.279	.309	.355
Runners On			62	20	1	11	5	.323	.419	.432
Runners/Scor. Pos.			39	14	1	6	5	.359	.513	.444
First 9 Batters			239	68	2	31	22	.285	.368	.369
Second 9 Batters			56	17	1	9	4	.304	.464	.409
All Batters Thereafter			1	1	0	0	0	1.000	1.000	1.000

Loves to face: Ivan DeJesus (0-for-11, 10 ground outs)
Hates to face: Milt Thompson (.800, 4-for-5)
Ground outs-to-air outs ratio: 2.38 last season, 2.76 for career. . . . Additional statistics: 7 double-play ground outs in 87 opportunities, 14 doubles, 3 triples allowed in 73.0 innings last season. . . . Relief ERA of 5.30 was 4th-highest among N.L. pitchers (minimum: 30 relief games). . . . Allowed most hits (10.60) and fewest strikeouts (3.21) per nine innings among that group. . . . Career average of 3.24 strikeouts per nine innings is 5th-lowest among active pitchers (minimum: 250 innings). . . . Career average of 3.28 walks per strikeout vs. left-handed batters is highest in *Player Analysis* history (minimum: 25 BB). Other Mets mediocrities in the top five: Hank Webb (2.43), Charlie Williams (2.19), and Rick Ownbey (2.06). . . . Career average of one home run allowed per 43.9 innings is lowest among active pitchers (minimum: 250 innings).

Bryn Smith

Montreal Expos	W–L	ERA	AB	H	HR	BB	SO	BA	SA	OBA
Season	18-5	2.91	831	193	12	41	127	.232	.330	.268
vs. Left-Handed Batters			415	100	1	17	52	.241	.313	.268
vs. Right-Handed Batters			416	93	11	24	75	.224	.346	.268
Home	11-2	2.32	404	85	4	25	62	.210	.287	.256
Road	7-3	3.52	427	108	8	16	65	.253	.370	.280
Grass	6-3	3.23	302	74	7	13	46	.245	.364	.274
Artificial Turf	12-2	2.74	529	119	5	28	81	.225	.310	.264
Day	6-1	3.43	244	59	7	11	25	.242	.377	.270
Night	12-4	2.71	587	134	5	30	102	.228	.310	.267
April	3-0	2.57	102	23	3	2	15	.225	.353	.236
May	2-1	2.45	113	29	2	3	17	.257	.354	.276
June	4-2	3.89	171	43	1	10	17	.251	.327	.293
July	3-1	1.74	168	35	1	4	37	.208	.286	.225
August	3-0	3.11	142	32	4	8	22	.225	.366	.272
Sept./Oct.	3-1	3.68	135	31	1	14	19	.230	.311	.300
Leading Off Inn.			216	60	3	12	33	.278	.394	.316
Bases Empty			507	117	7	24	83	.231	.333	.266
Runners On			324	76	5	17	44	.235	.324	.272
Runners/Scor. Pos.			190	49	5	8	28	.258	.389	.286
Runners On/2 Out			129	31	3	10	19	.240	.357	.295
Scor. Pos./2 Out			86	21	3	6	13	.244	.395	.293
Late Inning Pressure			52	8	1	3	8	.154	.231	.200
Leading Off			15	4	1	1	1	.267	.467	.313
Bases Empty			37	6	1	2	6	.162	.243	.205
Runners On			15	2	0	1	2	.133	.200	.188
Runners/Scor. Pos.			5	1	0	1	1	.200	.200	.333
First 9 Batters			268	56	4	10	46	.209	.306	.237
Second 9 Batters			269	62	4	16	44	.230	.327	.273
All Batters Thereafter			294	75	4	15	37	.255	.354	.292

Loves to face: Gary Matthews (.040, 1-for-25)
Hates to face: Tony Perez (4-for-4, 2 2B, 1 HR)
Ground outs-to-air outs ratio: 1.86 last season, 1.67 for career. . . . Additional statistics: 21 double-play ground outs in 147 opportunities, 33 doubles, 6 triples allowed in 222.1 innings last season. . . . Allowed 16 first-inning runs in 32 starts last season. . . . Batting support: 5.44 runs per start, highest average in N.L. (minimum: 15 GS). . . . Allowed 1.66 walks per nine innings, 5th-lowest rate in N.L. . . . Allowed one home run per 18.5 innings, 9th-lowest average in N.L. in '85. . . . Career home run averages: one allowed per 24 at bats in Late-Inning Pressure Situations; one per 67 at bats when unpressured. . . . Fattened up on the weak sisters last year: 4–4 vs. teams above .500, but 14–1 vs. teams below .500. He was 5–0 vs. Cubs, 4–0 vs. Braves, 4–0 vs. Phillies, 1–1 vs. Pirates; that's the most wins by any major leaguer against teams from the netherworld.

Dave Smith

Houston Astros	W–L	ERA	AB	H	HR	BB	SO	BA	SA	OBA
Season	9-5	2.27	293	69	3	17	40	.235	.300	.279
vs. Left-Handed Batters			116	27	1	8	11	.233	.302	.286
vs. Right-Handed Batters			177	42	2	9	29	.237	.299	.274
Home	7-4	2.65	187	44	3	13	27	.235	.321	.284
Road	2-1	1.59	106	25	0	4	13	.236	.264	.270
Grass	2-1	1.59	63	13	0	3	8	.206	.222	.242
Artificial Turf	7-4	2.45	230	56	3	14	32	.243	.322	.289
Day	2-0	0.00	30	5	0	2	2	.167	.233	.219
Night	7-5	2.60	263	64	3	15	38	.243	.308	.286
April	3-1	0.59	53	9	0	0	12	.170	.189	.170
May	1-1	3.07	59	17	1	3	8	.288	.356	.333
June	0-1	1.64	37	3	0	5	7	.081	.135	.190
July	1-0	1.64	38	9	0	1	1	.237	.263	.256
August	2-2	6.57	52	17	2	5	8	.327	.481	.379
Sept./Oct.	2-0	0.60	54	14	0	3	4	.259	.315	.298
Leading Off Inn.			54	14	0	3	10	.259	.278	.310
Bases Empty			127	31	1	8	20	.244	.283	.294
Runners On			166	38	2	9	20	.229	.313	.267
Runners/Scor. Pos.			110	23	2	9	12	.209	.309	.267
Runners On/2 Out			73	13	0	4	10	.178	.205	.221
Scor. Pos./2 Out			52	9	0	4	6	.173	.212	.232
Late Inning Pressure			222	51	3	12	30	.230	.302	.272
Leading Off			43	11	0	3	6	.256	.279	.319
Bases Empty			103	26	1	5	15	.252	.301	.294
Runners On			119	25	2	7	15	.210	.303	.254
Runners/Scor. Pos.			75	15	2	7	7	.200	.307	.268
First 9 Batters			287	68	2	17	40	.237	.293	.281
Second 9 Batters			6	1	1	0	0	.167	.667	.167
All Batters Thereafter			0	0	0	0	0	.000	.000	.000

Loves to face: Dave Parker (0-for-11)
Hates to face: Andre Dawson (.571, 8-for-14, 2 HR)
Ground outs-to-air outs ratio: 1.25 last season, 1.40 for career. . . . Additional statistics: 8 double-play ground outs in 72 opportunities, 8 doubles, 1 triple allowed in 79.1 innings last season. . . . Allowed 1.93 walks per nine innings last season, best rate among N.L. relievers (minimum: 30 relief games). . . . Ranked 5th in the same group with a 2.27 ERA. . . . Career average of one home run allowed per 27.7 innings is 6th-lowest among active pitchers (minimum: 250 innings). . . . Seven of his 27 saves were in games in which he faced only one batter, highest total in the majors. . . . Opposing batters have hit below .200 with two outs and runners in scoring position in four of his six seasons in majors. Career average: .191.

Lee Smith

Chicago Cubs	W–L	ERA	AB	H	HR	BB	SO	BA	SA	OBA
Season	7-4	3.04	360	87	9	32	112	.242	.381	.305
vs. Left-Handed Batters			192	51	4	17	50	.266	.401	.324
vs. Right-Handed Batters			168	36	5	15	62	.214	.357	.283
Home	3-3	4.09	202	48	8	15	67	.238	.416	.292
Road	4-1	1.69	158	39	1	17	45	.247	.335	.320
Grass	5-3	3.50	273	66	8	22	80	.242	.392	.300
Artificial Turf	2-1	1.57	87	21	1	10	32	.241	.345	.320
Day	3-3	3.67	224	55	8	18	73	.246	.415	.303
Night	4-1	1.98	136	32	1	14	39	.235	.324	.307
April	0-0	0.84	38	7	0	1	18	.184	.263	.225
May	3-0	2.78	86	23	1	9	22	.267	.337	.333
June	0-2	3.45	53	13	2	9	15	.245	.415	.355
July	2-2	3.10	78	20	2	10	29	.256	.436	.341
August	1-0	3.45	59	14	2	2	15	.237	.441	.262
Sept./Oct.	1-0	4.26	46	10	2	1	13	.217	.348	.234
Leading Off Inn.			74	22	2	4	22	.297	.446	.342
Bases Empty			178	45	4	15	62	.253	.371	.314
Runners On			182	42	5	17	50	.231	.390	.295
Runners/Scor. Pos.			109	19	2	11	38	.174	.284	.248
Runners On/2 Out			74	14	3	9	23	.189	.392	.277
Scor. Pos./2 Out			50	6	2	4	18	.120	.260	.185
Late Inning Pressure			276	68	8	27	92	.246	.406	.315
Leading Off			53	17	2	4	17	.321	.509	.379
Bases Empty			130	34	4	12	47	.262	.400	.329
Runners On			146	34	4	15	45	.233	.411	.302
Runners/Scor. Pos.			93	15	1	9	36	.161	.258	.233
First 9 Batters			352	85	8	29	112	.241	.375	.300
Second 9 Batters			8	2	1	3	0	.250	.625	.455
All Batters Thereafter			0	0	0	0	0	.000	.000	.000

Loves to face: Andy Van Slyke (0-for-15)
Hates to face: Bo Diaz (.600, 6-for-10)
Also loves to face: Steve Braun (0-for-9). . . . Ground outs-to-air outs ratio: 1.19 last season, 1.25 for career (1.47 at Wrigley, 1.07 on the road). . . . Additional statistics: 13 double-play ground outs in 88 opportunities, 15 doubles, 4 triples allowed in 97.2 innings last season. . . . Allowed 24 extra-base hits in Late-Inning Pressure Situations, highest total in either league last season. . . . Led N.L. with seven saves during the month of July. . . . Struck out 10.32 batters per nine innings last season, 2d-highest rate among N.L. relievers (minimum: 30 games). . . . Faced 308 batters in Late-Inning Pressure Situations last season, 2d-highest total in N.L. . . . Career average of 2.72 strikeouts per walk in day games, 1.84 in night games. . . . Strikeout percentage vs. right-handed batters (33.5%) was 6th-highest in *Player Analysis* history (minimum: 50 SO).

Lary Sorensen

Chicago Cubs	W–L	ERA	AB	H	HR	BB	SO	BA	SA	OBA
Season	3-7	4.26	314	86	8	24	34	.274	.427	.331
vs. Left-Handed Batters			143	47	4	15	10	.329	.517	.390
vs. Right-Handed Batters			171	39	4	9	24	.228	.351	.281
Home	1-5	5.17	153	44	8	10	18	.288	.510	.333
Road	2-2	3.48	161	42	0	14	16	.261	.348	.330
Grass	3-5	4.40	226	60	8	16	27	.265	.434	.320
Artificial Turf	0-2	3.91	88	26	0	8	7	.295	.409	.361
Day	2-5	4.75	214	59	8	17	27	.276	.458	.333
Night	1-2	3.29	100	27	0	7	7	.270	.360	.327
April	0-0	6.00	11	3	0	1	3	.273	.364	.333
May	1-1	6.75	43	15	1	6	5	.349	.558	.431
June	0-0	2.25	45	13	0	4	5	.289	.378	.360
July	2-1	5.82	65	16	1	3	7	.246	.369	.300
August	0-4	6.04	87	26	6	6	9	.299	.563	.340
Sept./Oct.	0-1	0.48	63	13	0	4	5	.206	.254	.254
Leading Off Inn.			76	15	0	3	10	.197	.276	.238
Bases Empty			181	49	5	8	22	.271	.420	.313
Runners On			133	37	3	16	12	.278	.436	.355
Runners/Scor. Pos.			83	26	3	13	7	.313	.482	.404
Runners On/2 Out			69	21	2	9	7	.304	.522	.392
Scor. Pos./2 Out			46	16	2	8	2	.348	.587	.455
Late Inning Pressure			72	22	0	7	7	.306	.389	.375
Leading Off			22	5	0	1	4	.227	.364	.261
Bases Empty			46	13	0	2	6	.283	.348	.327
Runners On			26	9	0	5	1	.346	.462	.452
Runners/Scor. Pos.			18	8	0	4	0	.444	.500	.545
First 9 Batters			244	60	3	19	25	.246	.348	.309
Second 9 Batters			62	23	4	5	9	.371	.694	.418
All Batters Thereafter			8	3	1	0	0	.375	.750	.375

Loves to face: Graig Nettles (.143, 5-for-35)
Hates to face: Claudell Washington (.448, 13-for-29, 1 HR)
Ground outs-to-air outs ratio: 2.06 last season, 1.48 for career. . . . Additional statistics: 7 double-play ground outs in 53 opportunities, 18 doubles, 3 triples allowed in 82.1 innings last season. . . . Average of 3.63 strikeouts per nine innings was 5th-lowest among N.L. relief pitchers (minimum: 30 relief games). . . . Career average of 2.08 walks per nine innings ranks 8th among active pitchers (minimum: 500 innings). . . . Pitched three or more innings in seven relief appearances last season, most on Cubs' staff. . . . Opposing batters have hit .353 in Late-Inning Pressure Situations since 1982, the highest average by far in the majors over the past four seasons (minimum: 300 AB). . . . Opposing left-handed batters hit 101 points higher than right-handers, 4th-largest difference in N.L. last season.

Zane Smith

Atlanta Braves	W–L	ERA	AB	H	HR	BB	SO	BA	SA	OBA
Season	9-10	3.80	531	135	4	80	85	.254	.354	.354
vs. Left-Handed Batters			81	23	0	8	24	.284	.309	.348
vs. Right-Handed Batters			450	112	4	72	61	.249	.362	.356
Home	2-5	4.46	278	75	3	36	44	.270	.388	.354
Road	7-5	3.15	253	60	1	44	41	.237	.316	.355
Grass	6-7	3.61	387	95	3	53	57	.245	.344	.340
Artificial Turf	3-3	4.31	144	40	1	27	28	.278	.382	.392
Day	2-2	2.41	132	31	0	22	20	.235	.326	.348
Night	7-8	4.27	399	104	4	58	65	.261	.363	.357
April	2-1	3.00	62	14	0	7	10	.226	.274	.300
May	0-3	9.98	67	28	2	9	13	.418	.672	.487
June	2-0	1.73	127	28	1	20	24	.220	.276	.327
July	2-3	2.41	134	27	1	20	22	.201	.313	.310
August	0-1	5.06	20	6	0	4	2	.300	.450	.417
Sept./Oct.	3-2	4.93	121	32	0	20	14	.264	.331	.378
Leading Off Inn.			127	37	1	20	17	.291	.409	.392
Bases Empty			281	72	2	45	39	.256	.356	.361
Runners On			250	63	2	35	46	.252	.352	.347
Runners/Scor. Pos.			158	38	1	29	31	.241	.367	.356
Runners On/2 Out			103	24	0	15	26	.233	.291	.342
Scor. Pos./2 Out			70	13	0	11	19	.186	.257	.296
Late Inning Pressure			54	7	0	9	9	.130	.130	.254
Leading Off			15	4	0	4	2	.267	.267	.421
Bases Empty			35	5	0	5	6	.143	.143	.250
Runners On			19	2	0	4	3	.105	.105	.261
Runners/Scor. Pos.			9	2	0	4	2	.222	.222	.462
First 9 Batters			255	63	1	47	38	.247	.329	.365
Second 9 Batters			147	43	3	20	28	.293	.456	.377
All Batters Thereafter			129	29	0	13	19	.225	.287	.306

Loves to face: Cesar Cedeno (0-for-11)
Hates to face: Steve Garvey (.556, 5-for-9)
Ground outs-to-air outs ratio: 2.41 last season, 2.21 for career (3.06 in Atlanta, 1.67 in road games). . . . Additional statistics: 23 double-play ground outs in 120 opportunities (4th-highest rate in N.L.), 29 doubles, 6 triples allowed in 147.0 innings last season. . . . Allowed 8 first-inning runs in 18 starts last season. . . . Batting support: 3.67 runs per start. . . . June ERA of 1.73 was 6th-lowest in N.L. . . . Average of 4.90 walks per nine innings was 5th-highest among N.L. pitchers (minimum: 15 GS). . . . Career average of one home run allowed per 33.4 innings is 2d-lowest among active pitchers (minimum: 250 innings). Has faced 360 batters in road games, and allowed only one home run. . . . Has faced 77 batters in Late-Inning Pressure Situations in two-year career without allowing an extra-base hit.

Mario Soto

Cincinnati Reds	W–L	ERA	AB	H	HR	BB	SO	BA	SA	OBA
Season	12-15	3.58	927	196	30	104	214	.211	.361	.290
vs. Left-Handed Batters			454	95	17	63	91	.209	.370	.304
vs. Right-Handed Batters			473	101	13	41	123	.214	.353	.276
Home	6-8	4.23	461	100	14	59	109	.217	.371	.304
Road	6-7	2.95	466	96	16	45	105	.206	.352	.275
Grass	3-5	3.07	288	57	9	25	66	.198	.340	.262
Artificial Turf	9-10	3.81	639	139	21	79	148	.218	.371	.302
Day	7-3	2.66	332	61	9	35	89	.184	.304	.259
Night	5-12	4.11	595	135	21	69	125	.227	.393	.307
April	4-1	1.50	163	31	2	15	36	.190	.270	.257
May	3-2	3.56	151	26	4	22	33	.172	.298	.274
June	1-4	4.79	154	35	6	20	33	.227	.429	.311
July	2-4	3.57	200	48	7	22	47	.240	.405	.317
August	0-4	4.36	157	35	6	13	32	.223	.376	.285
Sept./Oct.	2-0	4.18	102	21	5	12	33	.206	.392	.287
Leading Off Inn.			239	59	9	21	47	.247	.444	.308
Bases Empty			590	128	19	54	127	.217	.363	.285
Runners On			337	68	11	50	87	.202	.359	.298
Runners/Scor. Pos.			204	37	6	36	54	.181	.328	.293
Runners On/2 Out			145	24	3	19	44	.166	.283	.262
Scor. Pos./2 Out			96	16	1	16	30	.167	.250	.286
Late Inning Pressure			115	28	3	14	19	.243	.383	.323
Leading Off			32	9	0	0	6	.281	.406	.281
Bases Empty			71	18	1	7	12	.254	.366	.321
Runners On			44	10	2	7	7	.227	.409	.327
Runners/Scor. Pos.			25	5	1	5	4	.200	.320	.323
First 9 Batters			291	53	8	24	89	.182	.299	.242
Second 9 Batters			281	63	11	32	54	.224	.395	.300
All Batters Thereafter			355	80	11	48	71	.225	.386	.319

Loves to face: Howard Johnson (0-for-11, 5 SO)
Hates to face: Tommy Herr (.440, 11-for-25)
Ground outs-to-air outs ratio: 0.88 last season, 0.84 for career. . . . Additional statistics: 10 double-play ground outs in 161 opportunities, 33 doubles, 8 triples (tied for 7th-most in N.L.) allowed in 256.2 innings last season. . . . Total of 71 extra-base hits allowed was 6th-highest in N.L. . . . Ranked 6th among N.L. pitchers with an average of 7.13 innings per start. . . . Allowed 11 first-inning runs in 36 starts last season. . . . Batting support: 3.69 runs per start. . . . Allowed an N.L.-high 30 homers; Reds were 6–14 when Soto allowed at least one home run. . . . Eight-game losing streak (June 9–July 18) was the longest of his career. . . . One of five N.L. pitchers to start at least 30 games in each of the last four seasons. . . . Knee-jerk platooners beware: Opposing right-handers have hit for a higher average than left-handers each year since '83.

Tim Stoddard
San Diego Padres

	W–L	ERA	AB	H	HR	BB	SO	BA	SA	OBA
Season	1-6	4.65	234	63	3	37	42	.269	.380	.366
vs. Left-Handed Batters			98	28	1	19	14	.286	.367	.395
vs. Right-Handed Batters			136	35	2	18	28	.257	.390	.344
Home	0-3	2.48	100	20	0	13	15	.200	.270	.289
Road	1-3	6.68	134	43	3	24	27	.321	.463	.421
Grass	1-5	3.63	167	41	1	28	29	.246	.335	.352
Artificial Turf	0-1	7.63	67	22	2	9	13	.328	.493	.403
Day	1-1	5.18	98	27	2	16	17	.276	.388	.377
Night	0-5	4.29	136	36	1	21	25	.265	.375	.358
April	0-1	4.50	14	3	1	1	1	.214	.500	.267
May	0-1	7.00	42	14	1	7	8	.333	.524	.429
June	0-1	2.76	57	12	0	9	7	.211	.246	.313
July	1-3	2.63	46	10	0	13	9	.217	.239	.390
August	0-0	7.11	53	16	1	6	10	.302	.472	.367
Sept./Oct.	0-0	6.23	22	8	0	1	7	.364	.455	.391
Leading Off Inn.			57	17	0	5	9	.298	.439	.355
Bases Empty			114	31	0	14	21	.272	.351	.352
Runners On			120	32	3	23	21	.267	.408	.379
Runners/Scor. Pos.			76	22	2	20	14	.289	.421	.429
Runners On/2 Out			56	13	0	15	12	.232	.286	.394
Scor. Pos./2 Out			38	8	0	14	10	.211	.263	.423
Late Inning Pressure			78	29	1	16	7	.372	.526	.474
Leading Off			23	11	0	3	1	.478	.739	.538
Bases Empty			40	15	0	4	3	.375	.525	.432
Runners On			38	14	1	12	4	.368	.526	.510
Runners/Scor. Pos.			29	11	0	12	3	.379	.448	.548
First 9 Batters			218	58	3	33	38	.266	.385	.360
Second 9 Batters			16	5	0	4	4	.313	.313	.450
All Batters Thereafter			0	0	0	0	0	.000	.000	.000

Loves to face: Lee Mazzilli (0-for-6, all air outs)
Hates to face: Hubie Brooks (.750, 3-for-4, 1 HR)
Ground outs-to-air outs ratio: 0.96 last season, 1.23 for career. ... Additional statistics: 5 double-play ground outs in 50 opportunities, 13 doubles, 2 triples allowed in 60.0 innings last season. ... Quiz question: In what year and with what team did Stoddard make his big-league debut? Answer below. ... Relief ERA of 4.65 was 5th-highest among N.L. pitchers (minimum: 30 relief games). ... Career total of 332 relief appearances ranks 8th among active pitchers who have never started a game. ... Losing pitcher in three consecutive relief appearances (July 24, 26, 31) for the first time in his 9-year career. ... Padres lost 16 of first 18 games in which he appeared, 15 of last 17. ... Answer: Stoddard made his major-league debut in 1975 with the White Sox.

John Stuper
Cincinnati Reds

	W–L	ERA	AB	H	HR	BB	SO	BA	SA	OBA
Season	8-5	4.55	383	116	8	37	38	.303	.405	.358
vs. Left-Handed Batters			174	56	2	24	13	.322	.408	.396
vs. Right-Handed Batters			209	60	6	13	25	.287	.402	.324
Home	4-3	6.34	183	63	5	16	19	.344	.492	.389
Road	4-2	3.11	200	53	3	21	19	.265	.325	.330
Grass	3-0	2.34	123	29	1	9	12	.236	.285	.284
Artificial Turf	5-5	5.74	260	87	7	28	26	.335	.462	.392
Day	1-2	2.67	122	30	0	8	17	.246	.279	.288
Night	7-3	5.51	261	86	8	29	21	.330	.464	.390
April	3-1	4.32	96	27	2	6	12	.281	.385	.324
May	2-3	5.34	115	33	2	16	8	.287	.391	.366
June	1-1	6.59	58	21	3	5	6	.362	.569	.400
July	0-0	4.85	53	17	0	6	6	.321	.340	.383
August	0-0	0.00	14	4	0	0	3	.286	.286	.286
Sept./Oct.	2-0	2.08	47	14	1	4	3	.298	.383	.346
Leading Off Inn.			91	32	2	11	7	.352	.429	.422
Bases Empty			207	53	4	25	24	.256	.333	.336
Runners On			176	63	4	12	14	.358	.489	.385
Runners/Scor. Pos.			91	34	3	8	7	.374	.538	.396
Runners On/2 Out			65	19	2	7	7	.292	.477	.361
Scor. Pos./2 Out			37	10	1	5	3	.270	.486	.357
Late Inning Pressure			20	6	0	2	2	.300	.350	.364
Leading Off			6	3	0	0	0	.500	.500	.500
Bases Empty			12	4	0	0	1	.333	.417	.333
Runners On			8	2	0	2	1	.250	.250	.400
Runners/Scor. Pos.			6	1	0	2	1	.167	.167	.375
First 9 Batters			212	61	1	21	27	.288	.335	.345
Second 9 Batters			103	32	5	8	8	.311	.515	.354
All Batters Thereafter			68	23	2	8	3	.338	.456	.408

Loves to face: Phil Garner (0-for-10)
Hates to face: Tim Raines (.647, 11-for-17, 1 HR)
Ground outs-to-air outs ratio: 1.33 last season, 1.34 for career. ... Additional statistics: 13 double-play ground outs in 99 opportunities, 13 doubles, 1 triple allowed in 99.0 innings last season. ... Allowed 11 first-inning runs in 13 starts last season. ... Batting support: 5.15 runs per start. ... Opposing batters hit 102 points higher with runners on base than with the bases empty, 3d-largest difference in N.L. (minimum: 100 AB in each situation). Career averages: .278 with runners on base, .276 with the bases empty. ... Opposing left-handers have hit above .300 in each of his four big-league seasons. ... Has allowed four hits in five at bats with the bases loaded since 1984. ... Opponents' batting average with runners in scoring position (.374) was the 10th-highest in *Player Analysis* history (minimum: 100 PA).

Rick Sutcliffe
Chicago Cubs

	W–L	ERA	AB	H	HR	BB	SO	BA	SA	OBA
Season	8-8	3.18	495	119	12	44	102	.240	.364	.304
vs. Left-Handed Batters			244	66	5	21	45	.270	.410	.331
vs. Right-Handed Batters			251	53	7	23	57	.211	.319	.279
Home	4-2	3.44	203	46	7	21	37	.227	.369	.300
Road	4-6	3.00	292	73	5	23	65	.250	.360	.307
Grass	7-4	3.11	331	74	10	34	65	.224	.363	.299
Artificial Turf	1-4	3.35	164	45	2	10	37	.274	.366	.314
Day	4-5	3.86	270	67	8	27	51	.248	.385	.317
Night	4-3	2.40	225	52	4	17	51	.231	.338	.289
April	3-2	1.66	148	34	0	9	29	.230	.277	.274
May	2-2	3.21	107	23	3	9	22	.215	.383	.280
June	2-2	1.62	138	28	3	10	28	.203	.312	.260
July	1-1	7.13	75	25	4	12	19	.333	.533	.427
August			0	0	0	0	0	.000	.000	.000
Sept./Oct.	0-1	9.82	27	9	2	4	4	.333	.556	.406
Leading Off Inn.			125	32	2	7	25	.256	.368	.295
Bases Empty			301	73	7	19	57	.243	.369	.292
Runners On			194	46	5	25	45	.237	.356	.321
Runners/Scor. Pos.			118	23	3	24	31	.195	.314	.327
Runners On/2 Out			85	18	3	15	22	.212	.341	.330
Scor. Pos./2 Out			58	7	1	15	19	.121	.190	.301
Late Inning Pressure			64	15	3	2	11	.234	.406	.258
Leading Off			17	7	1	0	4	.412	.647	.412
Bases Empty			40	11	2	1	7	.275	.475	.293
Runners On			24	4	1	1	4	.167	.292	.200
Runners/Scor. Pos.			11	2	0	1	3	.182	.182	.250
First 9 Batters			159	47	5	11	39	.296	.459	.341
Second 9 Batters			133	25	1	20	28	.188	.241	.297
All Batters Thereafter			203	47	6	13	35	.232	.369	.280

Loves to face: Darryl Strawberry (0-for-13, 6 SO)
Hates to face: Joe Orsulak (.727, 8-for-11)
Ground outs-to-air outs ratio: 1.03 last season, 0.85 for career. ... Additional statistics: 7 double-play ground outs in 87 opportunities, 23 doubles, 1 triple allowed in 130.0 innings last season. ... Allowed 17 first-inning runs in 20 starts last season. ... Batting support: 3.70 runs per start. ... Career batting average of .625 (5-for-8) with the bases loaded. ... No Cy Young Award winner since Fernando Valenzuela in 1981 has had a winning percentage above .500 in the season following the award. ... Opponents' batting average with runners in scoring position was the lowest of his career. ... Opponents were hitless in eight at bats with the bases loaded last season.

Bruce Sutter
Atlanta Braves

	W–L	ERA	AB	H	HR	BB	SO	BA	SA	OBA
Season	7-7	4.48	341	91	13	29	52	.267	.437	.328
vs. Left-Handed Batters			161	39	5	18	17	.242	.366	.322
vs. Right-Handed Batters			180	52	8	11	35	.289	.500	.333
Home	6-5	5.91	185	58	8	19	27	.314	.492	.385
Road	1-2	2.95	156	33	5	10	25	.212	.372	.257
Grass	6-7	5.74	251	75	12	24	38	.299	.498	.366
Artificial Turf	1-0	1.40	90	16	1	5	14	.178	.267	.219
Day	1-3	4.20	114	28	5	8	18	.246	.439	.301
Night	6-4	4.63	227	63	8	21	34	.278	.436	.341
April	1-0	1.42	40	4	1	2	7	.100	.200	.163
May	1-1	4.02	61	15	1	4	11	.246	.328	.303
June	2-2	4.30	87	24	3	7	11	.276	.448	.326
July	3-1	2.57	56	15	1	6	9	.268	.357	.339
August	0-2	8.53	52	16	5	3	9	.308	.712	.351
Sept./Oct.	0-1	6.97	45	17	2	7	5	.378	.556	.462
Leading Off Inn.			75	22	2	7	14	.293	.440	.354
Bases Empty			179	49	6	16	36	.274	.447	.337
Runners On			162	42	7	13	16	.259	.426	.318
Runners/Scor. Pos.			93	27	6	11	8	.290	.516	.370
Runners On/2 Out			67	12	3	6	7	.179	.328	.257
Scor. Pos./2 Out			39	8	3	6	3	.205	.436	.326
Late Inning Pressure			218	61	10	19	28	.280	.468	.342
Leading Off			44	14	2	7	8	.318	.523	.412
Bases Empty			104	33	5	12	20	.317	.529	.388
Runners On			114	28	5	7	8	.246	.412	.298
Runners/Scor. Pos.			69	17	4	7	5	.246	.449	.329
First 9 Batters			322	88	12	29	50	.273	.444	.337
Second 9 Batters			19	3	1	0	2	.158	.316	.158
All Batters Thereafter			0	0	0	0	0	.000	.000	.000

Loves to face: Jerry Mumphrey (.077, 2-for-26, 6 SO)
Hates to face: Mike Fitzgerald (.750, 3-for-4, 1 2B, 1 HR)
Ground outs-to-air outs ratio: 1.32 last season, 1.95 for career. ... Additional statistics: 4 double-play ground outs in 79 opportunities (5th-lowest rate in N.L.), 15 doubles, 2 triples allowed in 88.1 innings last season. ... Relief ERA of 4.48 was 6th-highest among N.L. pitchers (minimum: 30 relief games). ... Allowed 13 home runs, tying Mark Davis for highest total among N.L. relief pitchers. ... Tied N.L. *Player Analysis* record with 10 home runs allowed in Late-Inning Pressure Situations, set ten years earlier by the one and only Oscar Zamora. ... Career total of 607 relief appearances without a start ranks 2d among active pitchers. ... Opponents' batting average with runners in scoring position was the highest of his career.

Kent Tekulve

Pirates/Phillies	W–L	ERA	AB	H	HR	BB	SO	BA	SA	OBA
Season	4-10	3.57	287	74	5	30	40	.258	.359	.330
vs. Left-Handed Batters			128	38	2	12	12	.297	.398	.366
vs. Right-Handed Batters			159	36	3	18	28	.226	.327	.302
Home	3-4	4.12	155	42	3	18	18	.271	.381	.349
Road	1-6	2.97	132	32	2	12	22	.242	.333	.308
Grass	0-4	4.34	68	18	2	10	13	.265	.397	.363
Artificial Turf	4-6	3.32	219	56	3	20	27	.256	.347	.320
Day	2-3	3.62	103	25	3	11	13	.243	.330	.322
Night	2-7	3.54	184	49	2	19	27	.266	.375	.335
April	1-0	4.91	41	10	1	7	5	.244	.366	.367
May	2-1	2.19	40	9	1	5	4	.225	.325	.304
June	1-1	2.51	55	11	1	3	7	.200	.327	.241
July	0-5	6.92	54	19	1	7	7	.352	.463	.429
August	0-2	3.38	33	11	0	4	2	.333	.455	.405
Sept./Oct.	0-1	2.12	64	14	1	4	15	.219	.266	.265
Leading Off Inn.			67	18	1	2	4	.269	.343	.300
Bases Empty			150	40	2	9	16	.267	.340	.313
Runners On			137	34	3	21	24	.248	.380	.348
Runners/Scor. Pos.			81	19	2	17	16	.235	.383	.360
Runners On/2 Out			67	17	1	12	15	.254	.388	.367
Scor. Pos./2 Out			47	11	1	10	12	.234	.362	.368
Late Inning Pressure			184	51	4	22	21	.277	.391	.354
Leading Off			46	12	1	0	2	.261	.326	.277
Bases Empty			101	29	2	5	10	.287	.366	.327
Runners On			83	22	2	17	11	.265	.422	.382
Runners/Scor. Pos.			47	14	1	13	7	.298	.468	.435
First 9 Batters			271	68	4	29	38	.251	.343	.326
Second 9 Batters			16	6	1	1	2	.375	.625	.412
All Batters Thereafter			0	0	0	0	0	.000	.000	.000

Loves to face: Terry Puhl (.067, 1-for-15)
Hates to face: Chili Davis (.714, 5-for-7)
Ground outs-to-air outs ratio: 2.48 last season (8th-highest in N.L.), 2.35 for career. . . . Additional statistics: 7 double-play ground outs in 62 opportunities, 10 doubles, 2 triples allowed in 75.2 innings last season. . . . Has not committed an error in 277 consecutive games, 20 shy of N.L. record for a pitcher held by Ron Reed. . . . Lost five games during July to tie for most in N.L.; also saved six games that month to tie for 2d-most. . . . Ten losses in relief ranked second in the league. . . . Career total of 780 relief appearances without a start leads all active pitchers, and ranks second in history to Sparky Lyle's 899. . . . Faced 47 leadoff batters without a walk in Late-Inning Pressure Situations, highest total in N.L. last season. . . . Opposing left-handed batters have outhit right-handers in each of past four seasons. During that time: left-handers .280, right-handers .220.

Mark Thurmond

San Diego Padres	W–L	ERA	AB	H	HR	BB	SO	BA	SA	OBA
Season	7-11	3.97	529	154	9	44	57	.291	.395	.347
vs. Left-Handed Batters			92	23	0	10	13	.250	.304	.327
vs. Right-Handed Batters			437	131	9	34	44	.300	.414	.351
Home	3-5	2.99	255	68	2	17	30	.267	.337	.313
Road	4-6	4.96	274	86	7	27	27	.314	.449	.377
Grass	5-8	3.40	387	109	7	30	39	.282	.390	.334
Artificial Turf	2-3	5.66	142	45	2	14	18	.317	.408	.380
Day	1-3	4.42	216	64	6	20	21	.296	.435	.356
Night	6-8	3.63	313	90	3	24	36	.288	.367	.340
April	0-2	3.57	86	25	0	7	6	.291	.337	.340
May	2-0	4.12	69	15	3	4	5	.217	.377	.257
June	1-4	6.45	86	27	2	9	5	.314	.477	.394
July	0-1	6.17	52	19	0	5	6	.365	.423	.421
August	3-0	0.98	99	27	1	9	15	.273	.323	.333
Sept./Oct.	1-4	4.19	137	41	3	10	20	.299	.431	.345
Leading Off Inn.			136	38	5	4	21	.279	.404	.300
Bases Empty			314	90	6	10	32	.287	.376	.311
Runners On			215	64	3	34	25	.298	.423	.392
Runners/Scor. Pos.			121	37	2	27	17	.306	.455	.429
Runners On/2 Out			90	29	2	19	12	.322	.489	.445
Scor. Pos./2 Out			63	21	2	15	9	.333	.540	.468
Late Inning Pressure			64	16	0	4	12	.250	.344	.294
Leading Off			16	3	0	1	6	.188	.188	.235
Bases Empty			39	9	0	1	7	.231	.282	.250
Runners On			25	7	0	3	5	.280	.440	.357
Runners/Scor. Pos.			14	4	0	3	4	.286	.500	.412
First 9 Batters			247	76	7	20	26	.308	.453	.359
Second 9 Batters			171	39	2	11	15	.228	.310	.276
All Batters Thereafter			111	39	0	13	16	.351	.396	.424

Loves to face: Kevin Bass (.143, 3-for-21, 4 SO)
Hates to face: Rick Schu (.800, 4-for-5)
Ground outs-to-air outs ratio: 1.36 last season, 1.38 for career. . . . Additional statistics: 16 double-play ground outs in 123 opportunities, 22 doubles, 3 triples allowed in 138.1 innings last season. . . . Allowed 18 first-inning runs in 23 starts. . . . Batting support: 3.57 runs per start. . . . August ERA of 0.98 was 2d-lowest in N.L. . . . Lost a lot of friends this past year: Joaquin Andujar, David Green, and Al Oliver, all now American Leaguers, had a combined career batting record of 0-for-36 against Thurmond. . . . Average of 10.02 hits per nine innings was 3d-highest among N.L. starters (minimum: 15 GS). . . . Opponents' batting averages with runners in scoring position, year by year since 1983: .169, .201, .306. . . . Was 0–4 vs. Giants; he's the first to lose four games to a 100-game loser since Barry Lersch was 0–4 vs. the '71 Padres.

Jay Tibbs

Cincinnati Reds	W–L	ERA	AB	H	HR	BB	SO	BA	SA	OBA
Season	10-16	3.92	826	216	14	83	98	.262	.377	.326
vs. Left-Handed Batters			431	115	5	46	44	.267	.390	.336
vs. Right-Handed Batters			395	101	9	37	54	.256	.362	.315
Home	5-7	3.66	406	104	8	37	52	.256	.367	.315
Road	5-9	4.19	420	112	6	46	46	.267	.386	.336
Grass	0-7	5.03	225	58	4	24	25	.258	.378	.325
Artificial Turf	10-9	3.51	601	158	10	59	73	.263	.376	.326
Day	3-6	4.48	248	64	6	21	23	.258	.391	.313
Night	7-10	3.69	578	152	8	62	75	.263	.370	.332
April	0-4	4.35	153	39	1	16	22	.255	.359	.324
May	3-3	6.19	142	42	4	21	11	.296	.423	.377
June	1-2	2.95	140	35	2	14	12	.250	.357	.316
July	0-2	11.81	22	7	2	4	1	.318	.682	.423
August	3-4	1.64	180	39	1	11	27	.217	.306	.259
Sept./Oct.	3-1	4.04	189	54	4	17	25	.286	.402	.345
Leading Off Inn.			209	55	4	18	30	.263	.378	.322
Bases Empty			466	114	8	52	71	.245	.367	.320
Runners On			360	102	6	31	27	.283	.389	.333
Runners/Scor. Pos.			191	55	1	23	17	.288	.361	.351
Runners On/2 Out			146	37	2	14	14	.253	.329	.319
Scor. Pos./2 Out			94	22	0	9	10	.234	.266	.301
Late Inning Pressure			54	16	1	11	6	.296	.481	.415
Leading Off			16	6	0	1	4	.375	.563	.412
Bases Empty			28	9	0	5	6	.321	.536	.424
Runners On			26	7	1	6	0	.269	.423	.406
Runners/Scor. Pos.			12	5	0	4	0	.417	.500	.563
First 9 Batters			269	68	4	31	38	.253	.357	.326
Second 9 Batters			270	63	6	19	31	.233	.337	.284
All Batters Thereafter			287	85	4	33	29	.296	.432	.364

Loves to face: Mike Scioscia (0-for-11)
Hates to face: Bob Dernier (.714, 5-for-7)
Ground outs-to-air outs ratio: 1.56 last season, 1.53 for career. . . . Additional statistics: 25 double-play ground outs in 179 opportunities, 33 doubles, 10 triples (tied for 3d-most in N.L.) allowed in 218.0 innings last season. . . . Allowed 21 first-inning runs (9th-most in N.L.) in 34 starts last season. . . . Batting support: 4.12 runs per start. . . . Dig in, boys: career total of 1,331 batters faced without hitting one with a pitch is highest among active pitchers. . . . Four losses in April tied Dave LaPoint for league lead. . . . August ERA of 1.64 was 5th-lowest in N.L. . . . Did not lose a game after August 26, winning his last four decisions. . . . Career trends: Walk rate increases by 55 percent in Late-Inning Pressure Situations; strikeout rate decreases by 30 percent. . . . Opponents' career batting average of .167 (4-for-24) with the bases loaded.

Steve Trout

Chicago Cubs	W–L	ERA	AB	H	HR	BB	SO	BA	SA	OBA
Season	9-7	3.39	525	142	8	63	44	.270	.358	.347
vs. Left-Handed Batters			67	18	1	8	8	.269	.373	.347
vs. Right-Handed Batters			458	124	7	55	36	.271	.356	.347
Home	6-2	3.39	298	81	5	38	24	.272	.359	.354
Road	3-5	3.39	227	61	3	25	20	.269	.357	.337
Grass	7-4	3.57	397	109	6	48	29	.275	.363	.352
Artificial Turf	2-3	2.86	128	33	2	15	15	.258	.344	.331
Day	6-4	3.42	342	92	6	42	31	.269	.360	.347
Night	3-3	3.33	183	50	2	21	13	.273	.355	.346
April	4-1	1.51	129	30	2	10	9	.233	.318	.291
May	1-0	3.06	70	17	0	6	4	.243	.286	.299
June	2-2	2.73	97	27	0	12	11	.278	.299	.358
July	1-1	5.12	73	22	4	10	4	.301	.493	.386
August	0-0	1.00	29	6	0	5	3	.207	.207	.324
Sept./Oct.	1-3	5.79	127	40	2	20	13	.315	.441	.400
Leading Off Inn.			127	35	3	19	11	.276	.386	.374
Bases Empty			293	79	6	35	25	.270	.365	.350
Runners On			232	63	2	28	19	.272	.349	.343
Runners/Scor. Pos.			117	31	1	17	8	.265	.350	.345
Runners On/2 Out			87	15	1	17	4	.172	.241	.308
Scor. Pos./2 Out			50	9	0	10	3	.180	.200	.317
Late Inning Pressure			30	12	0	2	4	.400	.600	.438
Leading Off			9	3	0	0	1	.333	.556	.333
Bases Empty			20	6	0	0	4	.300	.450	.300
Runners On			10	6	0	2	0	.600	.900	.667
Runners/Scor. Pos.			5	2	0	2	0	.400	.600	.571
First 9 Batters			187	39	1	24	13	.209	.235	.297
Second 9 Batters			176	53	3	23	17	.301	.409	.383
All Batters Thereafter			162	50	4	16	14	.309	.444	.365

Loves to face: Brad Komminsk (0-for-14)
Hates to face: Steve Kemp (.727, 8-for-11, 1 HR)
Ground outs-to-air outs ratio: 3.72 last season (5th-highest in *Player Analysis* history), 2.03 for career. . . . Additional statistics: 22 double-play ground outs in 136 opportunities, 18 doubles, 2 triples allowed in 140.2 innings last season. . . . Allowed 8 first-inning runs in 24 starts last season. . . . Batting support: 4.79 runs per start, 9th-highest average in N.L. (minimum: 15 GS). . . . Unlikeliest home run of '85 season: Terry Kennedy's 2d-inning blast on July 22—the first Trout allowed to a left-handed batter in 489 innings since July 9, 1982, and the first he allowed in first three innings of a game since July 10, 1983. . . . Average of 45.3 ground outs per 100 batters faced is 2d-highest N.L. season rate in *Player Analysis* history (minimum: 200 BFP). Greg Minton set the league record (45.5) in 1979. . . . 1985 breakdown: 7–1 vs. teams below .500, 2–6 vs. teams above .500.

John Tudor

St. Louis Cardinals	W–L	ERA	AB	H	HR	BB	SO	BA	SA	OBA
Season	21-8	1.93	1001	209	14	49	169	.209	.285	.249
vs. Left-Handed Batters			148	30	2	7	44	.203	.264	.244
vs. Right-Handed Batters			853	179	12	42	125	.210	.288	.249
Home	14-2	1.49	549	108	6	19	95	.197	.262	.226
Road	7-6	2.47	452	101	8	30	74	.223	.312	.275
Grass	4-4	2.00	243	47	2	13	44	.193	.247	.239
Artificial Turf	17-4	1.91	758	162	12	36	125	.214	.297	.252
Day	8-2	2.09	345	73	4	14	52	.212	.275	.246
Night	13-6	1.85	656	136	10	35	117	.207	.290	.250
April	0-3	3.08	103	24	2	5	13	.233	.320	.288
May	1-4	4.19	146	35	5	11	19	.240	.418	.292
June	6-0	1.34	163	30	3	8	26	.184	.258	.222
July	5-1	1.09	181	39	0	3	33	.215	.238	.232
August	3-0	1.74	168	35	2	12	35	.208	.268	.261
Sept./Oct.	6-0	1.34	240	46	2	10	43	.192	.254	.224
Leading Off Inn.			273	53	3	6	41	.194	.282	.217
Bases Empty			675	140	10	23	119	.207	.287	.237
Runners On			326	69	4	26	50	.212	.279	.272
Runners/Scor. Pos.			170	38	4	14	25	.224	.318	.282
Runners On/2 Out			152	32	2	18	21	.211	.270	.298
Scor. Pos./2 Out			89	21	2	10	8	.236	.326	.313
Late Inning Pressure			110	26	2	5	17	.236	.327	.270
Leading Off			32	6	1	0	4	.188	.313	.188
Bases Empty			86	19	2	1	12	.221	.314	.230
Runners On			24	7	0	4	5	.292	.375	.393
Runners/Scor. Pos.			11	3	0	2	3	.273	.273	.385
First 9 Batters			300	56	3	17	59	.187	.233	.234
Second 9 Batters			308	63	6	12	51	.205	.295	.235
All Batters Thereafter			393	90	5	20	59	.229	.316	.270

Loves to face: Ron Cey (.071, 1-for-14)
Hates to face: Rick Cerone (.462, 6-for-13, 1 HR)
Ground outs-to-air outs ratio: 1.01 last season, 0.87 for career. ... Additional statistics: 19 double-play ground outs in 135 opportunities, 28 doubles, 3 triples allowed in 275.0 innings last season. ... Ranked 3d among N.L. pitchers with an average of 7.64 innings per start. ... Allowed 14 first-inning runs in 36 starts last season. ... Batting support: 4.44 runs per start. ... Ten shutouts over a span of 23 starts from June 8 to Sept. 26; previously had only four shutouts in 137 career starts. ... Most shutouts by an N.L. lefty since Sandy Koufax (11 in 1963). ... Allowed one home run per 19.6 innings, 5th-best average in N.L. last season. ... Won 12 of 13 decisions against sub-.500 teams. ... Lasted only 2.1 innings in Game 7 of the World Series, his earliest shower (and bloodiest) since July 18, 1982. Against the Kansas City Royals.

Lee Tunnell

Pittsburgh Pirates	W–L	ERA	AB	H	HR	BB	SO	BA	SA	OBA
Season	4-10	4.01	502	126	11	57	74	.251	.369	.327
vs. Left-Handed Batters			248	68	4	38	26	.274	.375	.372
vs. Right-Handed Batters			254	58	7	19	48	.228	.362	.281
Home	2-4	4.24	279	69	6	32	38	.247	.369	.323
Road	2-6	3.70	223	57	5	25	36	.256	.368	.333
Grass	1-4	3.86	94	25	3	6	13	.266	.372	.310
Artificial Turf	3-6	4.05	408	101	8	51	61	.248	.368	.331
Day	2-4	4.73	154	43	3	19	18	.279	.390	.356
Night	2-6	3.70	348	83	8	38	56	.239	.359	.314
April	0-2	3.21	48	9	0	9	9	.188	.271	.328
May	0-3	5.87	61	20	2	9	6	.328	.492	.414
June	0-0	8.31	19	6	0	2	0	.316	.421	.381
July	1-2	3.30	112	26	3	11	19	.232	.339	.298
August	0-2	3.62	120	27	3	7	15	.225	.350	.268
Sept./Oct.	3-1	3.96	142	38	3	19	25	.268	.380	.352
Leading Off Inn.			131	36	1	10	14	.275	.351	.326
Bases Empty			301	72	4	29	45	.239	.326	.306
Runners On			201	54	7	28	29	.269	.433	.358
Runners/Scor. Pos.			110	31	4	24	15	.282	.427	.404
Runners On/2 Out			75	18	3	17	13	.240	.387	.380
Scor. Pos./2 Out			46	11	2	14	7	.239	.391	.417
Late Inning Pressure			39	8	2	5	9	.205	.359	.295
Leading Off			11	1	0	3	2	.091	.091	.286
Bases Empty			29	4	1	5	7	.138	.241	.265
Runners On			10	4	1	0	2	.400	.700	.400
Runners/Scor. Pos.			1	0	0	0	0	.000	.000	.000
First 9 Batters			197	43	3	16	28	.218	.325	.277
Second 9 Batters			180	49	4	24	26	.272	.400	.356
All Batters Thereafter			125	34	4	17	20	.272	.392	.361

Loves to face: George Foster (.053, 1-for-19)
Hates to face: Terry Harper (.667, 4-for-6)
Ground outs-to-air outs ratio: 1.78 last season, 1.80 for career. ... Additional statistics: 10 double-play ground outs in 104 opportunities, 18 doubles, 4 triples allowed in 132.1 innings last season. ... Allowed 13 first-inning runs in 23 starts last season. ... Batting support: 3.87 runs per start. ... Opponents' career batting averages: .281 with runners on base, .245 with the bases empty, .360 (9-for-25) with the bases loaded. ... Lost last five decisions in 1984, first six decisions last season. ... Won three consecutive starts in September. ... Opponents' overall batting average (.251) was the lowest of his career. ... Allowed only one earned run in 15.0 innings against Houston last season. ... Career average of 2.07 strikeouts per walk vs. right-handed batters, 0.83 vs. left-handers.

Fernando Valenzuela

Los Angeles Dodgers	W–L	ERA	AB	H	HR	BB	SO	BA	SA	OBA
Season	17-10	2.45	986	211	14	101	208	.214	.292	.286
vs. Left-Handed Batters			163	38	3	14	35	.233	.344	.291
vs. Right-Handed Batters			823	173	11	87	173	.210	.282	.285
Home	7-5	2.09	475	96	5	49	108	.202	.263	.274
Road	10-5	2.79	511	115	9	52	100	.225	.319	.296
Grass	12-8	2.15	716	149	8	79	159	.208	.274	.286
Artificial Turf	5-2	3.30	270	62	6	22	49	.230	.341	.285
Day	6-5	3.18	337	67	8	30	76	.199	.309	.265
Night	11-5	2.06	649	144	6	71	132	.222	.284	.296
April	2-3	0.21	145	22	1	9	35	.152	.207	.206
May	3-2	3.38	163	39	1	20	39	.239	.307	.314
June	2-3	3.99	147	38	3	18	29	.259	.367	.337
July	5-0	1.24	176	31	1	20	35	.176	.233	.260
August	4-1	3.23	180	43	7	12	39	.239	.378	.285
Sept./Oct.	1-1	2.77	175	38	1	22	31	.217	.257	.303
Leading Off Inn.			255	50	3	21	53	.196	.263	.257
Bases Empty			599	114	7	62	133	.190	.260	.267
Runners On			387	97	7	39	75	.251	.341	.313
Runners/Scor. Pos.			206	47	4	29	41	.228	.306	.313
Runners On/2 Out			168	37	2	22	38	.220	.292	.311
Scor. Pos./2 Out			101	19	2	17	25	.188	.248	.305
Late Inning Pressure			138	23	1	15	23	.167	.210	.245
Leading Off			40	5	0	2	3	.125	.125	.167
Bases Empty			93	13	1	10	13	.140	.194	.223
Runners On			45	10	0	5	10	.222	.244	.288
Runners/Scor. Pos.			25	6	0	2	4	.240	.280	.276
First 9 Batters			282	54	4	28	73	.191	.252	.266
Second 9 Batters			272	62	6	32	59	.228	.342	.308
All Batters Thereafter			432	95	4	41	76	.220	.287	.284

Loves to face: Wally Backman (0-for-16, 5 SO)
Hates to face: Dwight Gooden (.375, 6-for-16, 5 for his last 7)
Ground outs-to-air outs ratio: 1.21 last season, 1.39 for career. ... Additional statistics: 21 double-play ground outs in 187 opportunities, 33 doubles, 1 triple allowed in 272.1 innings last season. ... Ranked 2d among N.L. pitchers with an average of 7.78 innings per start. ... Allowed 7 first-inning runs in 35 starts, 2d-lowest rate in N.L. last season (minimum: 15 GS), and a tremendous improvement over 1984: 24 first-inning runs in 34 starts. ... Batting support: 4.20 runs per start. ... Set major-league record with 41 innings without an earned run at the start of a season. April ERA of 0.21 was best in the majors, but not the best start of his career: Fernando had an April ERA of 0.20 in his rookie season (1981). ... Defeated every opposing N.L. club last season with the exception of Montreal. ... Dodgers have lost 49 of his last 90 starts.

Bob Welch

Los Angeles Dodgers	W–L	ERA	AB	H	HR	BB	SO	BA	SA	OBA
Season	14-4	2.31	626	141	16	35	96	.225	.359	.272
vs. Left-Handed Batters			327	70	3	17	52	.214	.291	.254
vs. Right-Handed Batters			299	71	13	18	44	.237	.435	.291
Home	9-3	2.70	370	89	12	21	64	.241	.381	.285
Road	5-1	1.78	256	52	4	14	32	.203	.328	.254
Grass	10-3	2.52	459	108	14	26	75	.235	.377	.284
Artificial Turf	4-1	1.76	167	33	2	9	21	.198	.311	.240
Day	4-1	1.87	165	40	3	7	20	.242	.352	.287
Night	10-3	2.47	461	101	13	28	76	.219	.362	.267
April	0-0	0.00	19	5	0	1	4	.263	.368	.300
May			0	0	0	0	0	.000	.000	.000
June	1-1	3.65	95	24	4	5	12	.253	.421	.290
July	5-0	1.56	145	27	4	7	20	.186	.331	.232
August	3-2	2.42	163	32	3	12	29	.196	.325	.254
Sept./Oct.	5-1	2.39	204	53	5	10	31	.260	.377	.304
Leading Off Inn.			159	36	8	11	19	.226	.396	.276
Bases Empty			400	97	14	17	56	.243	.408	.273
Runners On			226	44	2	18	40	.195	.274	.270
Runners/Scor. Pos.			128	23	0	15	23	.180	.234	.272
Runners On/2 Out			104	19	0	8	25	.183	.221	.254
Scor. Pos./2 Out			70	12	0	7	15	.171	.214	.256
Late Inning Pressure			50	11	0	2	4	.220	.280	.250
Leading Off			13	1	0	1	0	.077	.077	.143
Bases Empty			33	6	0	2	2	.182	.182	.229
Runners On			17	5	0	0	2	.294	.471	.294
Runners/Scor. Pos.			6	2	0	0	1	.333	.667	.333
First 9 Batters			190	40	8	14	39	.211	.395	.263
Second 9 Batters			187	47	0	12	27	.251	.316	.314
All Batters Thereafter			249	54	8	9	30	.217	.365	.246

Loves to face: Darryl Strawberry (0-for-14, 8 SO)
Hates to face: Pete Rose (.415, 22-for-53)
Ground outs-to-air outs ratio: 1.06 last season, 0.86 for career. ... Additional statistics: 6 double-play ground outs in 104 opportunities (9th-lowest rate in N.L.), 18 doubles, 9 triples (6th-most in N.L.) allowed in 167.1 innings last season. ... Ranked 4th among N.L. pitchers with an average of 7.28 innings per start. ... Allowed 7 first-inning runs in 23 starts last season. ... Batting support: 4.65 runs per start. ... ERA of 1.76 on artificial surfaces was the lowest in N.L. ... Allowed 1.88 walks per nine innings, 6th-lowest rate in N.L. ... Dodgers won all five games in which he did not get a decision. ... Long ball did not hurt him last season: Dodgers had a 12–1 record in games in which he allowed a home run. ... Has allowed more career home runs at Dodger Stadium (54), a decided pitchers' park, than in road games (44).

Frank Williams
San Francisco Giants

	W–L	ERA	AB	H	HR	BB	SO	BA	SA	OBA
Season	2-4	4.19	269	65	5	35	54	.242	.349	.338
vs. Left-Handed Batters			117	40	2	20	19	.342	.504	.436
vs. Right-Handed Batters			152	25	3	15	35	.164	.230	.259
Home	1-2	1.82	136	23	2	17	32	.169	.228	.268
Road	1-2	7.02	133	42	3	18	22	.316	.474	.408
Grass	2-3	3.59	190	41	2	26	38	.216	.274	.318
Artificial Turf	0-1	5.75	79	24	3	9	16	.304	.532	.385
Day	1-3	3.67	151	31	3	20	34	.205	.311	.307
Night	1-1	4.88	118	34	2	15	20	.288	.398	.377
April	0-1	8.44	25	9	0	4	4	.360	.520	.448
May	0-0	3.38	26	3	1	5	9	.115	.231	.281
June	2-1	3.63	67	20	2	9	14	.299	.418	.372
July			0	0	0	0	0	.000	.000	.000
August	0-2	8.22	58	15	1	8	9	.259	.362	.368
Sept./Oct.	0-0	1.67	93	18	1	9	18	.194	.280	.280
Leading Off Inn.			67	16	0	5	14	.239	.284	.292
Bases Empty			156	37	2	14	36	.237	.327	.316
Runners On			113	28	3	21	18	.248	.381	.364
Runners/Scor. Pos.			65	18	2	13	9	.277	.446	.386
Runners On/2 Out			52	14	2	15	7	.269	.500	.449
Scor. Pos./2 Out			33	10	1	10	5	.303	.545	.477
Late Inning Pressure			110	22	1	15	26	.200	.255	.299
Leading Off			32	8	0	2	9	.250	.281	.294
Bases Empty			74	14	1	6	21	.189	.270	.259
Runners On			36	8	0	9	5	.222	.222	.370
Runners/Scor. Pos.			20	2	0	8	4	.100	.100	.345
First 9 Batters			245	57	4	32	50	.233	.322	.332
Second 9 Batters			24	8	1	3	4	.333	.333	.393
All Batters Thereafter			0	0	0	0	0	.000	.000	.000

Loves to face: Dave Concepcion (.071, 1-for-14)
Hates to face: Dave Parker (.600, 6-for-10, 1 HR)
Ground outs-to-air outs ratio: 1.59 last season, 1.95 for career. . . . Additional statistics: 5 double-play ground outs in 49 opportunities, 12 doubles, 1 triple allowed in 73.0 innings last season. . . . Relief ERA of 4.19 was 10th-highest among N.L. pitchers with at least 30 relief appearances. . . . Opposing left-handed batters hit 178 points higher than opposing right-handers, largest difference in N.L. last season (minimum: 100 AB vs. each). . . . Career average of one extra-base hit allowed per 40.3 at bats by right-handed batters is lowest in 11-year history of *The Player Analysis* (minimum: 250 AB). . . . Career total of 424 right-handed batters faced without allowing a triple. . . . Opponents' career batting averages: .217 with runners on base, .237 with the bases empty.

Jim Winn
Pittsburgh Pirates

	W–L	ERA	AB	H	HR	BB	SO	BA	SA	OBA
Season	3-6	5.23	290	77	4	31	22	.266	.334	.340
vs. Left-Handed Batters			146	42	2	14	10	.288	.349	.350
vs. Right-Handed Batters			144	35	2	17	12	.243	.319	.329
Home	0-1	4.50	103	25	1	13	12	.243	.301	.325
Road	3-5	5.66	187	52	3	18	10	.278	.353	.348
Grass	1-2	8.10	64	16	1	10	3	.250	.297	.360
Artificial Turf	2-4	4.42	226	61	3	21	19	.270	.345	.333
Day	0-3	5.46	113	30	1	11	11	.265	.319	.341
Night	3-3	5.09	177	47	3	20	11	.266	.345	.338
April			0	0	0	0	0	.000	.000	.000
May	1-0	3.46	47	9	1	3	2	.191	.255	.240
June	1-3	3.16	98	25	2	5	5	.255	.367	.298
July	0-0	9.35	38	13	0	7	1	.342	.395	.444
August	0-2	9.00	48	16	0	9	7	.333	.354	.431
Sept./Oct.	1-1	4.96	59	14	1	7	7	.237	.288	.328
Leading Off Inn.			71	20	1	7	3	.282	.338	.354
Bases Empty			163	41	2	11	8	.252	.307	.303
Runners On			127	36	2	20	14	.283	.370	.383
Runners/Scor. Pos.			73	19	0	15	7	.260	.329	.389
Runners On/2 Out			49	14	1	7	8	.286	.408	.375
Scor. Pos./2 Out			32	7	0	6	5	.219	.313	.342
Late Inning Pressure			44	14	0	6	4	.318	.341	.412
Leading Off			11	2	0	3	1	.182	.182	.400
Bases Empty			21	5	0	3	1	.238	.238	.360
Runners On			23	9	0	3	3	.391	.435	.462
Runners/Scor. Pos.			12	4	0	2	1	.333	.417	.429
First 9 Batters			173	43	2	23	17	.249	.301	.343
Second 9 Batters			85	23	0	4	4	.271	.318	.300
All Batters Thereafter			32	11	2	4	1	.344	.563	.417

Loves to face: Terry Puhl (0-for-5)
Hates to face: Dave Lopes (.571, 4-for-7)
Ground outs-to-air outs ratio: 1.44 last season, 1.51 for career. . . . Additional statistics: 7 double-play ground outs in 68 opportunities, 8 doubles, 0 triples allowed in 75.2 innings last season. . . . Hey, Greg Kite, Granville Waiters, and Bill Wennington! Here's baseball's version of garbage time: Pirates had a record of 2-22 in games in which Winn appeared in relief. . . . Opponents' career batting averages: .229 on grass, .277 on artificial surfaces. . . . Record of 2-2, 4.08 ERA as a starter last season; 1-4, 6.50 ERA as a reliever. . . . Allowed only one home run over his last 57.2 innings last season. . . . Batting averages of opposing left-handed batters, year by year since 1983: .200, .219, .288. . . . Has walked five of 13 career batters faced with the bases loaded. In his debut season (1983) he faced four batters with the bases full, walking three and allowing one hit.

Todd Worrell
St. Louis Cardinals

	W–L	ERA	AB	H	HR	BB	SO	BA	SA	OBA
Season	3-0	2.91	79	17	2	7	17	.215	.405	.273
vs. Left-Handed Batters			31	6	1	1	11	.194	.419	.219
vs. Right-Handed Batters			48	11	1	6	10	.229	.396	.304
Home	2-0	4.38	45	9	1	4	11	.200	.400	.255
Road	1-0	0.96	34	8	1	3	6	.235	.412	.297
Grass	0-0	2.08	16	3	1	2	5	.188	.438	.278
Artificial Turf	3-0	3.12	63	14	1	5	12	.222	.397	.271
Day	1-0	4.15	33	9	1	5	8	.273	.515	.368
Night	2-0	2.08	46	8	1	2	9	.174	.326	.200
April			0	0	0	0	0	.000	.000	.000
May			0	0	0	0	0	.000	.000	.000
June			0	0	0	0	0	.000	.000	.000
July			0	0	0	0	0	.000	.000	.000
August	0-0	0.00	6	1	0	0	0	.167	.167	.167
Sept./Oct.	3-0	3.15	73	16	2	7	17	.219	.425	.280
Leading Off Inn.			18	5	1	1	2	.278	.556	.316
Bases Empty			42	10	2	3	5	.238	.500	.289
Runners On			37	7	0	4	12	.189	.297	.256
Runners/Scor. Pos.			28	5	0	3	9	.179	.321	.242
Runners On/2 Out			17	1	0	2	5	.059	.118	.158
Scor. Pos./2 Out			16	1	0	1	4	.063	.125	.118
Late Inning Pressure			53	12	1	5	10	.226	.415	.288
Leading Off			13	3	0	1	2	.231	.308	.286
Bases Empty			32	7	1	2	5	.219	.438	.265
Runners On			21	5	0	3	5	.238	.381	.320
Runners/Scor. Pos.			16	3	0	3	4	.188	.375	.300
First 9 Batters			78	17	2	6	17	.218	.410	.267
Second 9 Batters			1	0	0	1	0	.000	.000	.500
All Batters Thereafter			0	0	0	0	0	.000	.000	.000

Loves to face: Pete Rose (0-for-2, 2 SO)
Hates to face: Ryne Sandberg (.500, 2-for-4)
Ground outs-to-air outs ratio: 0.88 last season, his first in majors. . . . Additional statistics: 2 double-play ground outs in 14 opportunities, 5 doubles, 2 triples allowed in 21.2 innings last season. . . . Tied World Series record with six consecutive strikeouts in Game Five. . . . Struck out only four batters over his last nine innings of work in the regular season. Walked only one batter during that time. . . . Longest outing of the season was 2.1 innings (faced 11 batters). . . . Beat the Expos twice, hurling 5.1 scoreless innings in the process. . . . Cardinals won nine of the last ten regular-season games in which he appeared. . . . Call him Mr. Experience: 17 games, 21.2 innings in the regular season; seven games, 11 innings of post-season play.

Floyd Youmans
Montreal Expos

	W–L	ERA	AB	H	HR	BB	SO	BA	SA	OBA
Season	4-3	2.45	277	57	3	49	54	.206	.285	.325
vs. Left-Handed Batters			175	38	1	28	34	.217	.269	.324
vs. Right-Handed Batters			102	19	2	21	20	.186	.314	.328
Home	0-2	2.38	119	21	2	21	24	.176	.277	.303
Road	4-1	2.51	158	36	1	28	30	.228	.291	.342
Grass	2-1	2.57	82	22	1	13	11	.268	.366	.365
Artificial Turf	2-2	2.41	195	35	2	36	43	.179	.251	.309
Day	2-1	2.50	146	33	2	24	24	.226	.322	.331
Night	2-2	2.41	131	24	1	25	30	.183	.244	.318
April			0	0	0	0	0	.000	.000	.000
May			0	0	0	0	0	.000	.000	.000
June			0	0	0	0	0	.000	.000	.000
July	1-0	2.31	41	9	1	8	12	.220	.366	.347
August	0-1	1.37	99	19	1	12	18	.192	.283	.279
Sept./Oct.	3-2	3.23	137	29	1	29	24	.212	.263	.349
Leading Off Inn.			69	13	0	10	16	.188	.203	.291
Bases Empty			157	33	0	25	33	.210	.274	.322
Runners On			120	24	3	24	21	.200	.300	.329
Runners/Scor. Pos.			76	12	2	18	15	.158	.250	.313
Runners On/2 Out			59	12	3	8	10	.203	.390	.320
Scor. Pos./2 Out			42	8	2	8	9	.190	.357	.320
Late Inning Pressure			33	9	1	7	7	.273	.394	.400
Leading Off			7	1	0	3	3	.143	.286	.400
Bases Empty			19	4	0	6	5	.211	.263	.400
Runners On			14	5	1	1	2	.357	.571	.400
Runners/Scor. Pos.			10	2	0	2	2	.200	.200	.400
First 9 Batters			103	19	0	18	28	.184	.194	.309
Second 9 Batters			91	18	0	19	15	.198	.275	.336
All Batters Thereafter			83	20	3	12	11	.241	.410	.333

Loves to face: Andy Van Slyke (0-for-11)
Hates to face: Dan Driessen (.600, 3-for-5)
Ground outs-to-air outs ratio: 0.93 last season, his first in majors. . . . Additional statistics: 5 double-play ground outs in 58 opportunities, 7 doubles, 3 triples allowed in 77.0 innings last season. . . . Allowed 3 first-inning runs in 12 starts last season. . . . Batting support: 3.75 runs per start. . . . Pitched to no decision in seven starts with an ERA of 1.91 in those games. . . . August ERA of 1.37 was 4th-lowest in N.L. . . . Third-youngest pitcher in N.L. last season, behind Gooden and Bob Kipper. . . . Opponents were hitless in seven at bats with the bases loaded. . . . Longest outing of the season was 7.1 innings. . . . Only home run allowed to a left-handed batter in 206 plate appearances was to Willie McGee in Youmans's big-league debut.

Atlanta Braves

	W–L	ERA	AB	H	HR	BB	SO	BA	SA	OBA
Season	66-96	4.19	5579	1512	134	642	776	.271	.403	.347
vs. Left-Handers			2630	734	61	334	327	.279	.412	.359
vs. Right-Handers			2949	778	73	308	449	.264	.394	.336
Home	32-49	4.46	2964	832	80	309	429	.281	.417	.350
Road	34-47	3.91	2615	680	54	333	347	.260	.387	.344
Grass	46-74	4.38	4230	1175	113	468	585	.278	.413	.351
Artificial Turf	20-22	3.63	1349	337	21	174	191	.250	.369	.336
Day	24-27	3.97	1699	455	41	203	212	.268	.411	.347
Night	42-69	4.29	3880	1057	93	439	564	.272	.399	.348
April	9-10	3.49	640	154	15	61	86	.241	.356	.307
May	10-16	4.34	873	232	23	94	120	.266	.409	.337
June	14-14	3.17	951	246	23	121	146	.259	.375	.342
July	11-15	4.17	941	260	19	98	129	.276	.405	.344
August	11-17	4.31	937	258	25	96	125	.275	.410	.344
Sept./Oct.	11-24	5.26	1237	362	29	172	170	.293	.436	.382
Leading Off Inn.			1325	363	34	131	169	.274	.412	.342
Bases Empty			3068	821	69	304	428	.268	.401	.336
Runners On			2511	691	65	338	348	.275	.405	.361
Runners/Scor. Pos.			1533	423	38	264	239	.276	.402	.378
Runners On/2 Out			1054	277	30	157	150	.263	.398	.363
Scor. Pos./2 Out			709	177	17	127	110	.250	.364	.367
Late Inning Pressure			992	266	24	112	130	.268	.388	.344
Leading Off			249	67	5	25	31	.269	.357	.338
Bases Empty			582	155	10	45	80	.266	.366	.323
Runners On			410	111	14	67	50	.271	.420	.371
Runners/Scor. Pos.			237	71	9	58	34	.300	.451	.432
First 9 Batters			3144	836	81	365	470	.266	.399	.343
Second 9 Batters			1440	400	35	166	203	.278	.413	.352
All Batters Thereafter			995	276	18	111	103	.277	.399	.353

Starting pitchers: 39–68 (fewest wins in majors), 4.22 ERA
Relief pitchers: 27–28, 4.20 ERA
Ground outs-to-air outs ratio: 1.67 (highest in majors). . . . Opponents grounded into one double play for every 7.30 opportunities, 2d-highest rate in N.L. . . . Had N.L.'s highest ERA for sixth time in past 14 seasons, but for first time since 1979. . . . Walked 642 batters, highest total in N.L. since 1977. . . . Allowed five or more runs in 22 innings last season, highest total in N.L. . . . Year-by-year record in games started by Barker, McMurtry, or Perez, starting with 1983: 43–31, 39–41, 10–36. . . . Right-handed pitchers started 144 games, highest total in N.L. Only left-handed starter: Zane Smith. . . . How they used their bullpen: Sutter accounted for 21% of Atlanta's Late-Inning Pressure pitching; Garber, 17%; Camp, 15%; Forster, 11%; Dedmon, 11%.

Cincinnati Reds

	W–L	ERA	AB	H	HR	BB	SO	BA	SA	OBA
Season	89-72	3.71	5426	1347	131	535	910	.248	.376	.315
vs. Left-Handers			2147	552	41	251	309	.257	.376	.334
vs. Right-Handers			3279	795	90	284	601	.242	.376	.302
Home	47-34	3.99	2815	725	65	285	456	.258	.388	.325
Road	42-38	3.41	2611	622	66	250	454	.238	.363	.304
Grass	22-25	3.57	1545	361	44	139	267	.234	.362	.295
Artificial Turf	67-47	3.77	3881	986	87	396	643	.254	.381	.322
Day	32-24	3.82	1875	457	46	189	327	.244	.375	.312
Night	57-48	3.65	3551	890	85	346	583	.251	.376	.316
April	10-10	2.91	637	147	11	59	110	.231	.336	.296
May	14-12	4.62	875	219	19	104	142	.250	.365	.325
June	15-11	3.69	883	213	25	97	131	.241	.386	.313
July	13-13	4.00	888	231	27	84	142	.260	.414	.325
August	15-14	3.03	974	239	16	78	173	.245	.348	.303
Sept./Oct.	22-12	3.84	1169	298	33	113	212	.255	.392	.320
Leading Off Inn.			1335	343	37	118	203	.257	.396	.318
Bases Empty			3164	758	75	288	560	.240	.361	.304
Runners On			2262	589	56	247	350	.260	.397	.329
Runners/Scor. Pos.			1266	335	33	178	198	.265	.404	.346
Runners On/2 Out			962	227	23	115	167	.236	.368	.319
Scor. Pos./2 Out			613	146	15	90	105	.238	.372	.337
Late Inning Pressure			1022	249	21	111	154	.244	.359	.318
Leading Off			263	65	3	21	35	.247	.361	.308
Bases Empty			589	141	11	59	91	.239	.360	.311
Runners On			433	108	10	52	63	.249	.358	.328
Runners/Scor. Pos.			243	59	5	41	35	.243	.342	.348
First 9 Batters			2684	637	50	283	509	.237	.339	.309
Second 9 Batters			1377	359	42	108	211	.261	.414	.313
All Batters Thereafter			1365	351	39	144	190	.257	.410	.327

Starting pitchers: 58–56, 3.84 ERA
Relief pitchers: 31–16 (most wins in N.L.), 3.37 ERA
Ground outs-to-air outs ratio: 1.02 (2d-lowest in N.L.). . . . Relievers did not allow a home run in 69.1 innings during the month of August. . . . Reds were only team in majors to win every home game in which it led after six innings. . . . Had N.L.'s highest ERA during the month of May. . . . Opposing batters hit nearly 21 points higher with runners on base than with the bases empty, the 3d-largest bulge in the N.L. last season, after two consecutive seasons with the largest gaps (33 points in 1983, 25 in 1984). . . . Rookie pitchers accounted for 405.2 of Cincinnati's 1,451.1 innings (28.0%), 2d-highest percentage in the majors (Browning represents nearly two-thirds of that total). . . . How they used their bullpen: Franco accounted for 27% of Cincinnati's Late-Inning Pressure pitching; Power, 22%; Hume, 13%; Robinson, 5%; Stuper, 2%.

Chicago Cubs

	W–L	ERA	AB	H	HR	BB	SO	BA	SA	OBA
Season	77-84	4.16	5513	1492	156	519	820	.271	.420	.333
vs. Left-Handers			2251	633	55	216	310	.281	.432	.343
vs. Right-Handers			3262	859	101	303	510	.263	.413	.326
Home	41-39	4.71	2868	797	104	274	445	.278	.447	.341
Road	36-45	3.56	2645	695	52	245	375	.263	.392	.325
Grass	55-58	4.28	3935	1076	128	375	595	.273	.430	.337
Artificial Turf	22-26	3.84	1578	416	28	144	225	.264	.396	.324
Day	48-57	4.38	3650	1006	119	344	552	.276	.434	.337
Night	29-27	3.72	1863	486	37	175	268	.261	.395	.326
April	12-6	2.16	582	135	7	38	105	.232	.323	.280
May	15-11	3.60	894	228	21	70	138	.255	.385	.311
June	12-16	3.06	924	216	16	91	147	.234	.364	.303
July	13-14	4.61	924	261	27	91	141	.282	.433	.348
August	10-18	5.04	1004	305	36	103	123	.304	.484	.367
Sept./Oct.	15-19	5.44	1185	347	49	126	166	.293	.476	.360
Leading Off Inn.			1326	361	38	116	177	.272	.429	.333
Bases Empty			3143	846	85	263	465	.269	.414	.329
Runners On			2370	646	71	256	355	.273	.429	.340
Runners/Scor. Pos.			1387	354	50	202	229	.255	.428	.341
Runners On/2 Out			1022	253	31	137	167	.248	.414	.339
Scor. Pos./2 Out			674	157	21	108	115	.233	.393	.341
Late Inning Pressure			1017	283	27	110	190	.278	.423	.350
Leading Off			252	75	10	25	44	.298	.496	.363
Bases Empty			579	156	17	54	107	.269	.409	.336
Runners On			438	127	10	56	83	.290	.441	.368
Runners/Scor. Pos.			255	64	3	44	57	.251	.357	.355
First 9 Batters			2945	755	71	311	504	.256	.389	.328
Second 9 Batters			1384	407	53	112	181	.294	.470	.346
All Batters Thereafter			1184	330	32	96	135	.279	.440	.332

Starting pitchers: 49–61, 4.01 ERA
Relief pitchers: 28–23, 4.50 ERA (highest in N.L.)
Ground outs-to-air outs ratio: 1.40 (2d-highest in majors). . . . Relievers compiled a 5.12 ERA at Wrigley Field. . . . Allowed 156 home runs, highest total in N.L. since 1977. . . . Had N.L.'s lowest ERA during the month of April, including a 1.94 composite by starting pitchers. Had league's highest marks in August and in September (5.52). . . . For the second consecutive season, the only N.L. team to win every road game in which it led after *seven* innings. That streak extends 70 wins, back to July 29, 1983. . . . Even more stunning: the Cubs have won 127 consecutive road games in which they led after *eight* innings, dating back to October 2, 1981. . . . How they used their bullpen: Smith accounted for 27% of Chicago's Late-Inning Pressure pitching; Frazier, 14%; Brusstar, 9%; Sorensen, 7%; Meridith, 5%.

Houston Astros

	W–L	ERA	AB	H	HR	BB	SO	BA	SA	OBA
Season	83-79	3.66	5486	1393	119	543	909	.254	.375	.321
vs. Left-Handers			2102	523	32	246	300	.249	.344	.326
vs. Right-Handers			3384	870	87	297	609	.257	.394	.318
Home	44-37	3.51	2829	698	47	250	489	.247	.349	.307
Road	39-42	3.82	2657	695	72	293	420	.262	.402	.335
Grass	28-20	3.51	1590	406	45	171	234	.255	.396	.328
Artificial Turf	55-59	3.72	3896	987	74	372	675	.253	.366	.318
Day	23-13	3.88	1202	300	39	116	205	.250	.405	.315
Night	60-66	3.60	4284	1093	80	427	704	.255	.366	.322
April	10-10	3.06	651	147	14	67	118	.226	.329	.295
May	14-12	3.58	879	221	20	93	168	.251	.370	.324
June	14-15	3.55	971	241	18	96	127	.248	.359	.318
July	8-18	3.90	917	246	22	92	154	.268	.411	.336
August	14-12	3.82	874	224	23	86	153	.256	.386	.320
Sept./Oct.	23-12	3.86	1194	314	22	109	189	.263	.380	.324
Leading Off Inn.			1332	357	32	125	206	.268	.401	.333
Bases Empty			3106	790	72	267	503	.254	.380	.315
Runners On			2380	603	47	276	406	.253	.368	.328
Runners/Scor. Pos.			1405	356	27	208	255	.253	.362	.342
Runners On/2 Out			987	223	20	141	177	.226	.329	.327
Scor. Pos./2 Out			661	152	13	101	129	.230	.334	.336
Late Inning Pressure			1016	256	28	115	168	.252	.374	.330
Leading Off			257	67	8	24	48	.261	.393	.326
Bases Empty			595	145	16	53	111	.244	.360	.310
Runners On			421	111	12	62	57	.264	.394	.356
Runners/Scor. Pos.			250	61	7	52	34	.244	.352	.367
First 9 Batters			2707	667	53	288	474	.246	.359	.319
Second 9 Batters			1416	371	23	125	233	.262	.373	.320
All Batters Thereafter			1363	355	43	130	202	.260	.409	.325

Starting pitchers: 59–52, 3.76 ERA
Relief pitchers: 24–27, 3.45 ERA
Ground outs-to-air outs ratio: 1.18. . . . Opponents grounded into one double play for every 8.60 opportunities, 3d-highest rate in N.L. . . . Led league with 69 wild pitches, highest N.L. total since 1975. . . . Used seven different rookie pitchers last season, tying Chicago Cubs for most in the majors. . . . Only two N.L. teams allowed fewer home runs in home games, but Houston's total of 72 allowed on the road was highest in the N.L. . . . Lost 14 games in which they led after six innings, twice as many as in '84. . . . How they used their bullpen: Smith accounted for 20% of Houston's Late-Inning Pressure pitching; DiPino, 13%; Dawley, 12%; Calhoun, 12%; Solano, 2%.

Los Angeles Dodgers

	W–L	ERA	AB	H	HR	BB	SO	BA	SA	OBA
Season	95-67	2.96	5465	1280	102	462	979	.234	.341	.295
vs. Left-Handers			1768	390	22	143	315	.221	.311	.279
vs. Right-Handers			3697	890	80	319	664	.241	.355	.302
Home	48-33	2.59	2787	615	54	213	525	.221	.319	.277
Road	47-34	3.36	2678	665	48	249	454	.248	.363	.312
Grass	71-49	2.85	4064	930	80	340	746	.229	.333	.290
Artificial Turf	24-18	3.30	1401	350	22	122	233	.250	.363	.309
Day	28-24	3.03	1755	403	42	148	334	.230	.354	.291
Night	67-43	2.93	3710	877	60	314	645	.236	.334	.296
April	11-10	2.62	684	149	4	53	136	.218	.297	.272
May	12-14	3.00	878	211	16	87	184	.240	.349	.307
June	15-10	3.66	853	208	19	67	139	.244	.356	.300
July	20-7	2.65	889	197	19	79	142	.222	.341	.287
August	16-11	2.46	907	204	17	65	168	.225	.330	.279
Sept./Oct.	21-15	3.24	1254	311	27	111	210	.248	.356	.310
Leading Off Inn.			1358	304	25	103	240	.224	.331	.282
Bases Empty			3251	736	52	237	574	.226	.324	.281
Runners On			2214	544	50	225	405	.246	.365	.313
Runners/Scor. Pos.			1225	307	30	167	228	.251	.381	.333
Runners On/2 Out			968	237	21	113	194	.245	.370	.325
Scor. Pos./2 Out			597	143	12	92	119	.240	.360	.342
Late Inning Pressure			968	219	18	97	212	.226	.323	.298
Leading Off			245	53	5	23	52	.216	.327	.286
Bases Empty			568	129	10	51	116	.227	.324	.293
Runners On			400	90	8	46	96	.225	.323	.305
Runners/Scor. Pos.			226	56	5	35	56	.248	.367	.342
First 9 Batters			2631	594	57	232	544	.226	.339	.289
Second 9 Batters			1433	356	22	115	245	.248	.352	.306
All Batters Thereafter			1401	330	23	115	190	.236	.333	.294

Starting pitchers: 73–42, 2.71 ERA (lowest in majors)
Relief pitchers: 22–25, 3.82 ERA
Ground outs-to-air outs ratio: 1.40. . . . Led N.L. in ERA for 13th time in the past 23 years, and in shutouts (21, highest total in N.L. since 1974) for the 12th time during that period. . . . First team in either league with an ERA below 3.00 since 1976 (with the exception of the shortened 1981 season). . . . Allowed only 44 second-inning runs, lowest single-inning total (excluding ninth innings) in majors. . . . Starters compiled a 2.28 ERA at Dodger Stadium. . . . Only team in majors not to lose more than three consecutive road games last season. . . . Left-handed pitchers started 95 games, highest total in N.L. . . . How they used their bullpen: Niedenfuer accounted for 25% of Los Angeles's Late-Inning Pressure pitching; Howell, 22%; Diaz, 8%; Howe, 4%; Castillo, 3%.

Montreal Expos

	W–L	ERA	AB	H	HR	BB	SO	BA	SA	OBA
Season	84-77	3.55	5456	1346	99	509	870	.247	.354	.312
vs. Left-Handers			2298	598	25	240	321	.260	.344	.329
vs. Right-Handers			3158	748	74	269	549	.237	.361	.299
Home	44-37	3.23	2730	645	45	250	446	.236	.336	.302
Road	40-40	3.87	2726	701	54	259	424	.257	.372	.321
Grass	23-19	3.76	1430	364	35	119	211	.255	.378	.313
Artificial Turf	61-58	3.47	4026	982	64	390	659	.244	.346	.311
Day	38-24	3.46	2064	499	44	186	285	.242	.356	.305
Night	46-53	3.60	3392	847	55	323	585	.250	.353	.316
April	12-8	3.72	654	163	13	56	100	.249	.356	.307
May	15-12	2.77	901	215	12	52	155	.239	.342	.281
June	16-12	3.09	944	221	11	93	158	.234	.314	.302
July	13-14	3.02	950	239	14	95	155	.252	.340	.320
August	15-11	3.76	880	215	20	72	137	.244	.374	.303
Sept./Oct.	13-20	4.74	1127	293	29	141	165	.260	.393	.343
Leading Off Inn.			1346	350	24	110	193	.260	.366	.318
Bases Empty			3143	764	57	257	517	.243	.349	.302
Runners On			2313	582	42	252	353	.252	.361	.324
Runners/Scor. Pos.			1410	353	28	187	243	.250	.366	.335
Runners On/2 Out			986	237	18	118	161	.240	.351	.323
Scor. Pos./2 Out			663	160	14	97	115	.241	.357	.341
Late Inning Pressure			1019	234	19	115	179	.230	.330	.311
Leading Off			257	57	6	29	45	.222	.327	.306
Bases Empty			617	138	9	55	114	.224	.308	.290
Runners On			402	96	10	60	65	.239	.363	.342
Runners/Scor. Pos.			252	56	5	50	46	.222	.329	.355
First 9 Batters			2914	686	50	292	513	.235	.336	.307
Second 9 Batters			1418	367	27	117	201	.259	.372	.314
All Batters Thereafter			1124	293	22	100	156	.261	.379	.321

Starting pitchers: 58–56, 3.54 ERA
Relief pitchers: 26–21, 3.55 ERA
Ground outs-to-air outs ratio: 1.27. . . . Starting pitchers compiled a 5.10 ERA after September 1, highest in the N.L. . . . Rookie pitchers accounted for 435.1 of Montreal's 1,457 innings (29.9%), highest percentage in the majors. Hesketh, Youmans, and Burke combined for a 23–12 record, with a 2.45 ERA in 352.2 innings. . . . Starting pitchers allowed one home run per 16.5 innings, relievers one per 12.1 innings. . . . How they used their bullpen: Reardon accounted for 23% of Montreal's Late-Inning Pressure pitching; Burke, 20%; Lucas, 11%; Roberge, 9%; St. Claire, 8%; O'Connor, 4%. . . . Reardon and Burke had four saves apiece in games in which they faced a single batter. . . . Relief pitchers worked three or more innings 37 times, highest total in N.L.

New York Mets

	W–L	ERA	AB	H	HR	BB	SO	BA	SA	OBA
Season	98-64	3.11	5520	1306	111	515	1039	.237	.348	.302
vs. Left-Handers			2395	584	38	199	391	.244	.344	.302
vs. Right-Handers			3125	722	73	316	648	.231	.351	.303
Home	51-30	2.71	2788	647	58	212	545	.232	.338	.287
Road	47-34	3.52	2732	659	53	303	494	.241	.358	.318
Grass	73-41	2.69	3931	910	81	338	757	.231	.337	.293
Artificial Turf	25-23	4.16	1589	396	30	177	282	.249	.376	.326
Day	36-25	3.40	2084	515	46	199	363	.247	.363	.313
Night	62-39	2.93	3436	791	65	316	676	.230	.339	.296
April	12-6	2.98	613	134	9	68	117	.219	.321	.299
May	15-10	3.07	844	195	18	70	178	.231	.338	.291
June	11-18	3.95	990	263	21	97	181	.266	.393	.331
July	21-7	2.88	999	238	23	93	171	.238	.360	.305
August	17-11	3.00	918	219	20	81	175	.239	.349	.299
Sept./Oct.	22-12	2.79	1156	257	20	106	217	.222	.320	.288
Leading Off Inn.			1350	287	28	137	265	.213	.316	.288
Bases Empty			3241	765	71	288	601	.236	.353	.301
Runners On			2279	541	40	227	438	.237	.341	.305
Runners/Scor. Pos.			1284	301	21	159	275	.234	.336	.315
Runners On/2 Out			989	217	16	110	193	.219	.308	.298
Scor. Pos./2 Out			611	126	10	82	141	.206	.290	.300
Late Inning Pressure			1126	271	20	125	198	.241	.333	.316
Leading Off			277	64	7	29	42	.231	.343	.304
Bases Empty			658	161	13	61	116	.245	.348	.309
Runners On			468	110	7	64	82	.235	.312	.325
Runners/Scor. Pos.			282	62	2	51	58	.220	.280	.334
First 9 Batters			2588	618	42	268	516	.239	.338	.311
Second 9 Batters			1488	336	29	124	271	.226	.340	.287
All Batters Thereafter			1444	352	40	123	252	.244	.375	.303

Starting pitchers: 76–40 (fewest losses in majors), 2.84 ERA
Relief pitchers: 22–24, 3.86 ERA
Ground outs-to-air outs ratio: 1.12. . . . Issued fewest intentional walks in N.L. (36). . . . Starters pitched an average of 6.74 innings per game, highest average in majors. . . . Relievers compiled a 5.10 ERA on artificial turf. . . . Had N.L.'s highest ERA during the month of June. . . . Only team in majors with two pitchers who allowed 10 runs in a game last season: Calvin Schiraldi and Joe Sambito. Both had their disasters in the same game, the 26–7 rout by the Phillies. Both are history. . . . How they used their bullpen: McDowell accounted for 23% of New York's Late-Inning Pressure pitching; Orosco, 20%; Sisk, 12%; Gorman, 6%. . . . Davey Johnson used relievers to face a single batter only 11 times, 2d-lowest N.L. total behind Chicago (9).

Phila. Phillies

	W–L	ERA	AB	H	HR	BB	SO	BA	SA	OBA
Season	75-87	3.68	5506	1424	115	596	899	.259	.384	.331
vs. Left-Handers			2036	547	29	224	292	.269	.385	.344
vs. Right-Handers			3470	877	86	372	607	.253	.384	.324
Home	41-40	3.50	2842	724	57	287	452	.255	.381	.323
Road	34-47	3.88	2664	700	58	309	447	.263	.387	.340
Grass	14-28	4.12	1396	374	42	156	232	.268	.413	.342
Artificial Turf	61-59	3.54	4110	1050	73	440	667	.255	.374	.328
Day	26-26	3.89	1731	437	49	184	298	.252	.401	.324
Night	49-61	3.59	3775	987	66	412	601	.261	.376	.335
April	8-11	3.22	655	182	6	71	88	.278	.357	.348
May	9-17	3.78	866	211	17	100	127	.244	.373	.319
June	15-12	2.83	903	218	20	80	166	.241	.363	.306
July	13-14	4.22	916	254	23	92	155	.277	.422	.348
August	16-12	3.44	957	247	22	101	153	.258	.387	.328
Sept./Oct.	14-21	4.30	1209	312	27	152	210	.258	.391	.340
Leading Off Inn.			1318	332	19	130	199	.252	.347	.321
Bases Empty			3050	782	62	300	502	.256	.379	.326
Runners On			2456	642	53	296	397	.261	.390	.337
Runners/Scor. Pos.			1444	349	33	227	251	.242	.369	.337
Runners On/2 Out			1050	252	25	146	178	.240	.379	.334
Scor. Pos./2 Out			694	152	16	117	128	.219	.350	.333
Late Inning Pressure			1014	253	24	122	187	.250	.378	.328
Leading Off			258	71	5	18	43	.275	.391	.325
Bases Empty			591	153	11	45	110	.259	.374	.313
Runners On			423	100	13	77	77	.236	.383	.347
Runners/Scor. Pos.			260	62	8	60	49	.238	.396	.370
First 9 Batters			2740	682	55	334	515	.249	.370	.331
Second 9 Batters			1357	362	25	121	221	.267	.387	.329
All Batters Thereafter			1409	380	35	141	163	.270	.408	.334

Starting pitchers: 53–61, 3.76 ERA
Relief pitchers: 22–26, 3.50 ERA
Ground outs-to-air outs ratio: 1.24. . . . Opponents grounded into one double play for every 10.08 opportunities, 2d-lowest rate in N.L. . . . Had N.L.'s lowest ERA during the month of June. . . . Won eight consecutive road games from August 17 through September 3, longest streak in majors last season. . . . How they used their bullpen: Carman accounted for 19% of Philadelphia's Late-Inning Pressure pitching; Tekulve, 17%; Andersen, 14%; Rucker, 6%; Shipanoff, 5%. . . . The Phillies had three of the five oldest pitchers in the National League last season: Koosman, Carlton, and Tekulve. (The other two were Joe Niekro and Nolan Ryan).

Pittsburgh Pirates

	W–L	ERA	AB	H	HR	BB	SO	BA	SA	OBA
Season	57-104	3.97	5504	1406	107	584	962	.255	.377	.329
vs. Left-Handers			2299	632	34	261	325	.275	.381	.350
vs. Right-Handers			3205	774	73	323	637	.241	.374	.313
Home	35-45	3.84	2786	701	53	280	509	.252	.375	.321
Road	22-59	4.11	2718	705	54	304	453	.259	.380	.337
Grass	11-31	4.13	1422	361	28	151	259	.254	.366	.329
Artificial Turf	46-73	3.92	4082	1045	79	433	703	.256	.381	.329
Day	14-41	4.13	1870	479	46	211	308	.256	.392	.336
Night	43-63	3.89	3634	927	61	373	654	.255	.370	.325
April	6-12	4.12	626	157	12	80	117	.251	.379	.338
May	9-17	4.17	879	224	16	95	138	.255	.379	.329
June	9-18	3.70	939	229	17	91	166	.244	.363	.312
July	8-19	4.13	925	244	18	94	170	.264	.381	.335
August	8-20	4.00	944	251	18	108	164	.266	.393	.343
Sept./Oct.	17-18	3.82	1191	301	26	116	207	.253	.371	.320
Leading Off Inn.			1335	358	25	112	207	.268	.393	.328
Bases Empty			3137	772	54	271	554	.246	.362	.309
Runners On			2367	634	53	313	408	.268	.397	.354
Runners/Scor. Pos.			1391	387	36	239	245	.278	.422	.382
Runners On/2 Out			1029	260	22	149	196	.253	.385	.353
Scor. Pos./2 Out			655	173	14	120	127	.264	.400	.384
Late Inning Pressure			1107	296	20	129	212	.267	.390	.344
Leading Off			267	74	2	32	46	.277	.375	.359
Bases Empty			608	162	11	56	121	.266	.393	.332
Runners On			499	134	9	73	91	.269	.387	.358
Runners/Scor. Pos.			296	79	6	59	50	.267	.409	.380
First 9 Batters			2814	688	49	304	548	.244	.361	.320
Second 9 Batters			1478	386	28	140	231	.261	.380	.326
All Batters Thereafter			1212	332	30	140	183	.274	.411	.352

Starting pitchers: 42–72 (tied for most losses in N.L.), 3.99 ERA
Relief pitchers: 15–32 (fewest wins, most losses in N.L.), 3.94 ERA
Ground outs-to-air outs ratio: 1.26. . . . Opponents grounded into one double play for every 11.11 opportunities, lowest rate in majors. . . . Did not win three consecutive games until September 18–20. The last team to play an entire season without a three-game winning streak: the 1952 Pirates. . . . That's what happens when you have two announcers, an actor, a trainer, and guys named Clem, Clyde, and Catfish on the same roster. . . . Starting pitchers completed only one of 42 starts on grass fields. . . . Lost 19 road games in a row from July 23 through August 30, the longest N.L. streak since 1963, when the Mets lost 22 straight road games, a modern major-league record. . . . How they used their bullpen: Guante accounted for 18% of Pittsburgh's Late-Inning Pressure pitching; Candelaria, 13%; Robinson, 13%; Holland, 9%; Clements, 7%; Scurry, 5%; Winn, 4%.

San Diego Padres

	W–L	ERA	AB	H	HR	BB	SO	BA	SA	OBA
Season	83-79	3.40	5447	1399	127	443	727	.257	.380	.313
vs. Left-Handers			2132	573	50	192	239	.269	.396	.329
vs. Right-Handers			3315	826	77	251	488	.249	.370	.303
Home	44-37	3.46	2741	690	77	210	382	.252	.384	.306
Road	39-42	3.34	2706	709	50	233	345	.262	.376	.321
Grass	64-56	3.45	4050	1028	107	326	550	.254	.381	.311
Artificial Turf	19-23	3.27	1397	371	20	117	177	.266	.376	.321
Day	26-29	3.66	1832	485	57	157	256	.265	.414	.323
Night	57-50	3.27	3615	914	70	286	471	.253	.363	.308
April	10-9	3.01	609	140	13	37	72	.230	.338	.275
May	17-9	3.66	869	214	23	80	125	.246	.392	.310
June	17-13	3.21	991	245	24	93	132	.247	.377	.314
July	10-16	3.35	910	244	16	78	115	.268	.379	.325
August	14-13	3.19	919	252	17	65	127	.274	.380	.321
Sept./Oct.	15-19	3.82	1149	304	34	90	156	.265	.395	.319
Leading Off Inn.			1370	351	49	83	178	.256	.416	.302
Bases Empty			3237	827	78	218	427	.255	.378	.305
Runners On			2210	572	49	225	300	.259	.382	.325
Runners/Scor. Pos.			1218	324	23	165	174	.266	.379	.347
Runners On/2 Out			961	239	18	119	136	.249	.361	.335
Scor. Pos./2 Out			605	152	10	93	94	.251	.362	.356
Late Inning Pressure			1092	274	25	116	161	.251	.375	.322
Leading Off			286	79	13	20	47	.276	.462	.326
Bases Empty			672	169	19	50	97	.251	.379	.304
Runners On			420	105	6	66	64	.250	.369	.347
Runners/Scor. Pos.			233	66	2	53	35	.283	.395	.406
First 9 Batters			2746	690	62	239	457	.251	.372	.311
Second 9 Batters			1369	339	36	92	145	.248	.377	.297
All Batters Thereafter			1332	370	29	112	125	.278	.399	.334

Starting pitchers: 67–51, 3.33 ERA
Relief pitchers: 16–28, 3.54 ERA
Ground outs-to-air outs ratio: 1.02 (lowest in N.L.). . . . First team in baseball history to defend a league title without two pitchers who started 30 games each during the championship season: San Diego lost Tim Lollar and Ed Whitson. . . . Walked the fewest batters in N.L. for first time in team's history. . . . Also had league's fewest strikeouts and wild pitches (23). . . . Allowed five or more runs in only five innings last season, lowest total in either league. . . . September ERA of 5.60 was highest by any N.L. team during any month last season. . . . How they used their bullpen: Gossage accounted for 20% of San Diego's Late-Inning Pressure pitching; Lefferts, 14%; McCullers, 9; Jackson, 4%; DeLeon, 4%. . . . Relief pitchers worked three or more innings only 20 times, the lowest total in the majors.

St. Louis Cardinals

	W–L	ERA	AB	H	HR	BB	SO	BA	SA	OBA
Season	101-61	3.10	5468	1343	98	453	798	.246	.354	.305
vs. Left-Handers			2047	543	27	181	263	.265	.362	.324
vs. Right-Handers			3421	800	71	272	535	.234	.348	.293
Home	54-27	2.73	2757	660	39	192	386	.239	.337	.290
Road	47-34	3.49	2711	683	59	261	412	.252	.370	.319
Grass	27-15	2.97	1404	330	25	126	217	.235	.333	.302
Artificial Turf	74-46	3.15	4064	1013	73	327	581	.249	.360	.306
Day	36-28	3.49	2198	545	45	214	317	.248	.364	.316
Night	65-33	2.85	3270	798	53	239	481	.244	.346	.297
April	8-11	3.52	643	170	10	49	76	.264	.369	.321
May	16-10	3.02	892	216	23	75	117	.242	.376	.301
June	19-8	3.07	913	217	20	68	142	.238	.346	.290
July	17-9	2.31	857	207	6	66	122	.242	.303	.297
August	17-11	3.66	972	248	19	95	148	.255	.378	.322
Sept./Oct.	24-12	3.11	1191	285	20	100	193	.239	.351	.300
Leading Off Inn.			1377	335	24	87	193	.243	.362	.291
Bases Empty			3276	789	65	212	496	.241	.353	.289
Runners On			2192	554	33	241	302	.253	.354	.326
Runners/Scor. Pos.			1267	325	19	173	187	.257	.356	.341
Runners On/2 Out			938	216	12	117	122	.230	.323	.320
Scor. Pos./2 Out			595	135	7	87	75	.227	.318	.329
Late Inning Pressure			961	246	14	111	156	.256	.353	.335
Leading Off			248	65	7	14	42	.262	.411	.302
Bases Empty			558	150	12	40	86	.269	.382	.318
Runners On			403	96	2	71	70	.238	.313	.357
Runners/Scor. Pos.			247	57	2	56	43	.231	.320	.374
First 9 Batters			2609	638	38	250	446	.245	.342	.311
Second 9 Batters			1380	331	32	98	194	.240	.362	.290
All Batters Thereafter			1479	374	28	105	158	.253	.366	.306

Starting pitchers: 79–46 (most wins in majors), 3.21 ERA
Relief pitchers: 22–15 (fewest losses in N.L.), 2.85 ERA (lowest in majors)
Ground outs-to-air outs ratio: 1.21. . . . Opponents grounded into one double play for every 7.23 opportunities, highest rate in N.L. . . . Relievers compiled a 1.38 ERA during the month of May, and won nine of 11 decisions during September. . . . Fewest losses in N.L. (tied with Reds) in games in which they led after six innings, for third consecutive season. . . . Have won 91 consecutive home games in which they led after eight innings, dating back to September 24, 1983. . . . How they used their bullpen: Dayley accounted for 17% of St. Louis's Late-Inning Pressure pitching; Lahti, 16%; Horton, 10%; Allen, 6%; Campbell, 6%; Worrell, 5%. . . . Whitey used relievers to face a single batter 39 times last season, highest total in majors.

San Francisco Giants

	W–L	ERA	AB	H	HR	BB	SO	BA	SA	OBA
Season	62-100	3.61	5448	1348	125	572	985	.247	.374	.319
vs. Left-Handers			1848	485	36	190	304	.262	.386	.331
vs. Right-Handers			3600	863	89	382	681	.240	.368	.313
Home	38-43	2.96	2797	641	67	279	549	.229	.346	.299
Road	24-57	4.32	2651	707	58	293	436	.267	.403	.340
Grass	51-69	3.36	4102	984	102	433	759	.240	.364	.312
Artificial Turf	11-31	4.39	1346	364	23	139	226	.270	.404	.339
Day	39-52	3.25	3091	732	74	314	573	.237	.359	.307
Night	23-48	4.09	2357	616	51	258	412	.261	.393	.334
April	7-12	2.53	627	151	12	56	108	.241	.364	.303
May	10-16	2.67	846	185	13	97	158	.219	.317	.300
June	10-20	3.48	1029	245	25	97	189	.238	.354	.302
July	13-14	3.65	892	228	20	83	157	.256	.379	.318
August	11-14	4.36	850	219	19	90	161	.258	.391	.328
Sept./Oct.	11-24	4.45	1204	320	36	149	212	.266	.420	.347
Leading Off Inn.			1334	351	34	114	233	.263	.409	.323
Bases Empty			3114	752	72	292	584	.241	.374	.309
Runners On			2334	596	53	280	401	.255	.374	.332
Runners/Scor. Pos.			1366	349	34	208	240	.255	.387	.346
Runners On/2 Out			1009	236	26	152	171	.234	.355	.338
Scor. Pos./2 Out			660	149	17	115	117	.226	.344	.343
Late Inning Pressure			1100	247	24	153	241	.225	.326	.320
Leading Off			274	74	7	38	50	.270	.372	.361
Bases Empty			646	137	14	73	152	.212	.308	.296
Runners On			454	110	10	80	89	.242	.352	.351
Runners/Scor. Pos.			266	60	5	69	51	.226	.327	.375
First 9 Batters			2853	681	59	324	574	.239	.355	.318
Second 9 Batters			1382	363	34	135	215	.263	.402	.327
All Batters Thereafter			1213	304	32	113	196	.251	.386	.313

Starting pitchers: 39–72 (fewest wins, tied for most losses in N.L.), 3.79 ERA
Relief pitchers: 23–28, 3.26 ERA
Ground outs-to-air outs ratio: 1.27. . . . Opponents grounded into one double play for every 9.88 opportunities, 3d-lowest rate in N.L. . . . Had N.L.'s lowest ERA during the month of May. . . . Here's a tip for your runs-by-innings pool: the Giants allowed only 46 runs in third inning last season, 2d-lowest single-inning total by any team in majors (ninth innings don't count). . . . Lost 11 home games in which they led after six innings, highest total in either league since 1982, when Atlanta lost 12. . . . One of two N.L. teams not to lose more than three consecutive home games last season. The other: Cincinnati. . . . How they used their bullpen: Davis accounted for 22% of San Francisco's Late-Inning Pressure pitching; Garrelts, 21%; Minton, 18%; Williams, 10%; Jeffcoat, 1%.

National League

	W–L	ERA	AB	H	HR	BB	SO	BA	SA	OBA
Season	971-971	3.59	65818	16596	1424	6373	10674	.252	.374	.319
vs. Left-Handers			25953	6794	450	2677	3696	.262	.374	.330
vs. Right-Handers			39865	9802	974	3696	6978	.246	.374	.311
Home	519-451	3.47	33704	8375	746	3041	5613	.248	.369	.311
Road	451-519	3.71	32114	8221	678	3332	5061	.256	.379	.326
Grass	486-486	3.54	33099	8299	830	3142	5412	.251	.376	.317
Artificial Turf	485-485	3.64	32719	8297	594	3231	5262	.254	.372	.321
Day	371-371	3.71	25051	6313	648	2465	4030	.252	.386	.319
Night	600-600	3.52	40767	10283	776	3908	6644	.252	.366	.318
April	115-115	3.11	7621	1829	126	695	1233	.240	.344	.304
May	156-156	3.52	10496	2571	221	1017	1750	.245	.366	.312
June	167-167	3.37	11291	2762	239	1091	1824	.245	.363	.312
July	160-160	3.57	11008	2849	234	1045	1753	.259	.381	.324
August	164-164	3.66	11136	2881	252	1040	1807	.259	.385	.322
Sept./Oct.	209-209	4.04	14266	3704	352	1485	2307	.260	.390	.330
Leading Off Inn.			16106	4092	369	1366	2463	.254	.381	.315
Bases Empty			37930	9402	812	3197	6211	.248	.369	.309
Runners On			27888	7194	612	3176	4463	.258	.381	.332
Runners/Scor. Pos.			16196	4163	372	2377	2764	.257	.383	.346
Runners On/2 Out			11955	2874	262	1574	2012	.240	.362	.332
Scor. Pos./2 Out			7737	1822	166	1229	1375	.235	.354	.343
Late Inning Pressure			12434	3094	264	1416	2188	.249	.363	.326
Leading Off			3133	811	78	298	525	.259	.385	.326
Bases Empty			7263	1796	153	642	1301	.247	.359	.311
Runners On			5171	1298	111	774	887	.251	.368	.347
Runners/Scor. Pos.			3047	753	59	628	548	.247	.360	.370
First 9 Batters			33375	8172	667	3490	6070	.245	.359	.317
Second 9 Batters			16922	4377	386	1453	2551	.259	.386	.317
All Batters Thereafter			15521	4047	371	1430	2053	.261	.392	.324

Ground outs-to-air outs ratio: 1.24 (14 percent higher than the American League). . . . There has been only one no-hitter thrown in the N.L. over the past four seasons, by Bob Forsch in 1983. This is the first time since 1956–57 that no N.L. pitcher has tossed a no-hitter for two consecutive seasons. The modern league record of four complete seasons in a row was set more than 50 years ago: 64 months elapsed between no-hitters by Carl Hubbell on May 8, 1929 and Paul Dean on September 21, 1934. . . . Who gets called for more balks, left-handed pitchers or right-handers? National League umpires called 33 balks against southpaws last season, or one for every 885 batters they faced; right-handers were called for 87 balks, or one for every 513 batters. . . . Had only five fewer one-run games (317) than the American League (322), which played 161 more games overall.

V
Rankings Section

Rankings Section

The Rankings Section consists of a series of lists ranking players in a wide variety of batting and pitching categories. Players are ranked in 24 batting categories and 24 pitching categories ranging from the simple (batting average, for example) to the more esoteric (like percentage of runners driven in from third base with less than two out).

The exact number of plate appearances required to qualify for ranking in each category varies. The number of eligible players for each ranking is determined by the number of players in each league who had 200 or more plate appearances, or who faced 250 or more batters. In the American League, the 158 players and 131 pitchers with the most plate appearances or batters faced in a given category are eligible for ranking; in the National League, the top 134 batters and 115 pitchers are eligible. (If there is a tie for the final position, all tied players are included.)

The intent here is to rank all players who qualify as at least semiregulars for the season. To do this properly, it is necessary to look at the number of plate appearances in each specific situation. Rance Mulliniks and Garth Iorg platooned at third base for Toronto last year, and both can be considered as at least "semiregulars." But the vast majority of Mulliniks's plate appearances were against right-handers, and Iorg's were mostly against left-handers. Mulliniks was one of the 158 batters who faced righties most often, so he is ranked there, but he failed to meet this qualification against lefties, so he is not ranked in that category. Iorg, of course, is ranked against lefties but not against righties.

The material in this section is generally based on the categories used in the Batter and Pitcher Sections. If any of the breakdowns are unfamiliar, detailed descriptions can be found in the introductions to the Batter and Pitcher Sections.

Batting Average vs. Left-Handed Pitchers

American League

1. Rickey Henderson	NY	.361	41. Tim Hulett	CHI	.296	81. Bobby Grich	CAL	.265	121. Fred Lynn	BAL	.242
2. Juan Beniquez	CAL	.356	42. Dave Engle	MIN	.295	82. Larry Herndon	DET	.265	122. Dale Berra	NY	.241
3. Kirby Puckett	MIN	.356	43. Ron Washington	MIN	.294	83. Al Cowens	SEA	.264	123. Earnest Riles	MIL	.241
4. Wade Boggs	BOS	.347	44. Tony Fernandez	TOR	.294	84. Rod Carew	CAL	.264	124. Alvin Davis	SEA	.239
5. Jim Presley	SEA	.344	45. Lonnie Smith	KC	.293	85. Brian Downing	CAL	.262	125. Carney Lansford	OAK	.237
6. Harold Baines	CHI	.341	46. Mike Young	BAL	.293	86. Bob Boone	CAL	.259	126. Ron Kittle	CHI	.236
7. Tony Armas	BOS	.336	47. Willie Wilson	KC	.293	87. Dick Schofield	CAL	.259	127. Roy Smalley	MIN	.236
7. Floyd Rayford	BAL	.336	48. Bill Buckner	BOS	.291	88. Jim Rice	BOS	.258	128. Hal McRae	KC	.233
9. Bruce Bochte	OAK	.333	49. Tom Brookens	DET	.290	89. Tony Bernazard	CLE	.258	129. Greg Walker	CHI	.230
10. Brett Butler	CLE	.332	50. Buddy Bell	TEX	.289	90. Lloyd Moseby	TOR	.256	130. Lou Whitaker	DET	.228
11. Cliff Johnson	TOR	.330	51. Don Mattingly	NY	.288	91. Kent Hrbek	MIN	.256	131. Pete O'Brien	TEX	.225
12. George Brett	KC	.330	52. Don Slaught	TEX	.287	92. Spike Owen	SEA	.256	132. Bobby Meacham	NY	.225
13. Jim Gantner	MIL	.329	53. Julio Franco	CLE	.286	93. Darryl Motley	KC	.255	133. Kirk Gibson	DET	.224
14. Alfredo Griffin	OAK	.326	53. Eddie Murray	BAL	.286	94. Don Baylor	NY	.254	134. Reggie Jackson	CAL	.221
15. Mike Brown	CAL	.325	55. Mike Heath	OAK	.285	95. Mark Brouhard	MIL	.253	135. Steve Balboni	KC	.220
16. Rick Dempsey	BAL	.325	56. Charlie Moore	MIL	.285	96. Wayne Tolleson	TEX	.253	136. Dave Collins	OAK	.218
17. Paul Molitor	MIL	.324	57. Tom Paciorek	CHI	.282	97. George Bell	TOR	.252	137. Jim Sundberg	KC	.217
18. Rob Picciolo	OAK	.323	58. Dave Meier	MIN	.282	98. Carlton Fisk	CHI	.251	138. Onix Concepcion	KC	.217
19. Chet Lemon	DET	.322	58. Reid Nichols	CHI	.282	99. Dave Winfield	NY	.251	139. Butch Wynegar	NY	.216
20. Steve Henderson	OAK	.321	60. Gary Pettis	CAL	.281	100. Damaso Garcia	TOR	.251	140. Tom Brunansky	MIN	.214
21. Cecil Cooper	MIL	.321	61. Mickey Hatcher	MIN	.280	101. Dusty Baker	OAK	.250	141. Ben Oglivie	MIL	.213
22. Andre Robertson	NY	.320	61. Dave Henderson	SEA	.280	101. Julio Cruz	CHI	.250	141. Ernie Whitt	TOR	.213
23. Cecil Fielder	TOR	.319	63. Fritz Connally	BAL	.279	101. Donnie Hill	OAK	.250	143. Mickey Tettleton	OAK	.213
24. Willie Randolph	NY	.315	64. Curtis Wilkerson	TEX	.279	101. Randy Ready	MIL	.250	144. Ozzie Guillen	CHI	.211
25. Alan Wiggins	BAL	.314	65. Mike Easler	BOS	.277	101. Alan Trammell	DET	.250	145. Gorman Thomas	SEA	.211
26. Lee Lacy	BAL	.313	66. Brook Jacoby	CLE	.277	106. Joe Carter	CLE	.248	146. Gary Roenicke	BAL	.209
27. Pat Tabler	CLE	.312	67. Benny Ayala	CLE	.275	107. Frank White	KC	.247	147. Darrell Evans	DET	.208
28. Garth Iorg	TOR	.310	68. Willie Upshaw	TOR	.275	108. Rich Dauer	BAL	.247	148. Jackie Gutierrez	BOS	.206
29. Toby Harrah	TEX	.310	69. Marty Barrett	BOS	.274	109. Luis Salazar	CHI	.246	149. Gary Gaetti	MIN	.206
30. Jesse Barfield	TOR	.309	70. Cal Ripken	BAL	.272	110. Larry Parrish	TEX	.245	150. Tim Teufel	MIN	.200
31. Ted Simmons	MIL	.307	71. Mike Davis	OAK	.271	111. Rich Gedman	BOS	.244	151. Dwayne Murphy	OAK	.197
32. Billy Sample	NY	.307	72. Dwight Evans	BOS	.271	112. Dave Kingman	OAK	.244	152. Bob Kearney	SEA	.196
33. Lance Parrish	DET	.305	73. Carmen Castillo	CLE	.270	113. Doug DeCinces	CAL	.244	153. Ed Romero	MIL	.192
34. Paul Householder	MIL	.304	73. Tim Laudner	MIN	.270	113. Greg Gagne	MIN	.244	154. Lynn Jones	KC	.172
35. Glenn Hoffman	BOS	.304	75. Steve Lyons	BOS	.269	115. Alan Bannister	TEX	.244	155. George Wright	TEX	.172
36. Gary Ward	TEX	.301	76. Barbaro Garbey	DET	.268	115. Oddibe McDowell	TEX	.244	156. Chris Bando	CLE	.169
37. Robin Yount	MIL	.300	77. Andre Thornton	CLE	.268	115. John Shelby	BAL	.244	157. Domingo Ramos	SEA	.145
38. Scott Fletcher	CHI	.298	78. Phil Bradley	SEA	.267	118. Ken Griffey	NY	.243	158. Buck Martinez	TOR	.138
38. Alejandro Sanchez	DET	.298	79. Steve Buechele	TEX	.267	119. Bobby Clark	MIL	.243			
40. Ivan Calderon	SEA	.296	80. Jeff Burroughs	TOR	.266	120. Jack Perconte	SEA	.242			

National League

1. Mike Brown	PIT	.356	35. Mariano Duncan	LA	.286	69. Darryl Strawberry	NY	.256	103. Ron Cey	CHI	.221
2. Willie McGee	STL	.348	36. Dan Driessen	SF	.284	70. Tim Wallach	MTL	.256	104. John Russell	PHI	.221
3. Pete Rose	CIN	.347	37. Mike Schmidt	PHI	.284	71. Jeff Leonard	SF	.255	105. Terry Harper	ATL	.221
4. Tom Paciorek	NY	.337	38. Tom Herr	STL	.283	72. Garry Templeton	SD	.254	106. Graig Nettles	SD	.216
5. Dale Murphy	ATL	.333	39. Rick Schu	PHI	.280	73. Johnny Ray	PIT	.253	107. Jose Uribe	SF	.216
5. Chris Speier	CHI	.333	40. Dave Parker	CIN	.279	74. Mike Scioscia	LA	.253	108. Joe Orsulak	PIT	.215
7. Tony Perez	CIN	.331	41. Bill Madlock	LA	.278	75. Kurt Bevacqua	SD	.253	109. Steve Sax	LA	.215
8. Gary Carter	NY	.329	42. Glenn Davis	HOU	.278	76. Marvell Wynne	PIT	.252	110. Sixto Lezcano	PIT	.215
9. Jack Clark	STL	.324	43. Bill Almon	PIT	.277	77. Buddy Bell	CIN	.250	111. Brad Komminsk	ATL	.214
10. Mitch Webster	MTL	.322	44. Jose Cruz	HOU	.277	77. Paul Zuvella	ATL	.250	112. Jim Wohlford	MTL	.213
11. Cesar Cedeno	STL	.319	45. Ron Oester	CIN	.277	79. Chili Davis	SF	.248	113. Alan Knicely	PHI	.212
12. Bill Russell	LA	.318	46. Ryne Sandberg	CHI	.276	80. Carmelo Martinez	SD	.247	114. David Green	SF	.211
13. Keith Hernandez	NY	.315	47. Andre Dawson	MTL	.275	81. Vance Law	MTL	.245	115. Tom Nieto	STL	.210
14. Keith Moreland	CHI	.315	48. Tim Raines	MTL	.275	82. Dave Concepcion	CIN	.244	116. Chris Brown	SF	.209
15. Kevin Bass	HOU	.311	49. Bruce Bochy	SD	.274	83. Ken Oberkfell	ATL	.243	117. Rob Deer	SF	.209
16. Hubie Brooks	MTL	.310	50. Garry Maddox	PHI	.272	84. Gary Redus	CIN	.242	118. Claudell Washington	ATL	.206
17. Alex Trevino	SF	.308	51. Dickie Thon	HOU	.272	85. Jerry Mumphrey	HOU	.241	119. Steve Yeager	LA	.202
17. Joel Youngblood	SF	.308	52. George Foster	NY	.271	86. Rafael Ramirez	ATL	.240	120. George Hendrick	PIT	.202
19. Pedro Guerrero	LA	.304	53. Phil Garner	HOU	.268	87. Dave Lopes	CHI	.239	121. John Christensen	NY	.200
20. Bill Doran	HOU	.300	54. Len Dykstra	NY	.268	88. Juan Samuel	PHI	.239	122. Rick Cerone	ATL	.198
21. Enos Cabell	LA	.298	55. Leon Durham	CHI	.268	89. Ozzie Virgil	PHI	.238	123. Dave Anderson	LA	.194
21. Jerry Royster	SD	.298	56. Jim Morrison	PIT	.266	90. Larry Bowa	NY	.238	124. Steve Jeltz	PHI	.194
23. Bob Horner	ATL	.298	57. Danny Heep	NY	.265	91. Mike Fitzgerald	MTL	.237	125. Bob Brenly	SF	.193
23. Ozzie Smith	STL	.298	57. Rafael Santana	NY	.265	92. Vince Coleman	STL	.237	126. Luis Aguayo	PHI	.190
25. Nick Esasky	CIN	.298	59. Tito Landrum	STL	.265	93. Jody Davis	CHI	.235	127. U.L. Washington	MTL	.190
26. Steve Garvey	SD	.297	60. Sammy Khalifa	PIT	.264	93. Jim Pankovits	HOU	.235	128. Bruce Benedict	ATL	.190
27. Mookie Wilson	NY	.295	61. Eric Davis	CIN	.264	95. Bo Diaz	CIN	.233	129. Ken Landreaux	LA	.186
28. Terry Puhl	HOU	.294	62. R.J. Reynolds	PIT	.261	96. Candy Maldonado	LA	.232	130. Greg Brock	LA	.176
29. Mark Bailey	HOU	.290	63. Jason Thompson	PIT	.260	97. Gary Matthews	CHI	.232	131. Kelvin Chapman	NY	.172
30. Bob Dernier	CHI	.288	64. Kevin McReynolds	SD	.260	98. Von Hayes	PHI	.229	132. Howard Johnson	NY	.156
31. Alan Ashby	HOU	.288	65. Ray Knight	NY	.259	99. Glenn Hubbard	ATL	.229	133. Wally Backman	NY	.122
32. Tony Gwynn	SD	.288	66. Dan Gladden	SF	.259	100. Manny Trillo	SF	.229	134. Andy Van Slyke	STL	.111
33. Mike Marshall	LA	.287	66. Terry Kennedy	SD	.259	101. Terry Pendleton	STL	.228			
34. Glenn Wilson	PHI	.287	68. Tony Pena	PIT	.258	102. Paul Runge	ATL	.222			

Batting Average vs. Right-Handed Pitchers

American League

1. Wade Boggs	BOS	.377	41. Ken Griffey	NY	.284	81. Dwight Evans	BOS	.260	121. Larry Herndon	DET	.233
2. Don Mattingly	NY	.348	42. Hal McRae	KC	.282	82. Bryan Little	CHI	.258	122. Bobby Grich	CAL	.232
3. George Brett	KC	.337	43. Lee Lacy	BAL	.282	83. Jim Sundberg	KC	.258	123. Mike Heath	OAK	.232
4. Wayne Tolleson	TEX	.335	44. Mickey Hatcher	MIN	.282	84. Ted Simmons	MIL	.257	124. Carlton Fisk	CHI	.231
5. Ron Hassey	NY	.324	45. Dusty Baker	OAK	.281	85. Kirby Puckett	MIN	.256	125. Cliff Johnson	TOR	.230
6. Rich Gedman	BOS	.314	46. Ivan Calderon	SEA	.281	86. Mike Easler	BOS	.256	126. Butch Wynegar	NY	.229
7. Kirk Gibson	DET	.314	46. Gary Ward	TEX	.281	87. George Vukovich	CLE	.255	127. Paul Householder	MIL	.228
8. Ben Oglivie	MIL	.312	48. Cecil Cooper	MIL	.280	88. Tom Brunansky	MIN	.255	128. Dave Henderson	SEA	.227
9. Phil Bradley	SEA	.312	49. Tony Bernazard	CLE	.280	89. Willie Randolph	NY	.253	129. Ron Kittle	CHI	.225
10. Alvin Davis	SEA	.308	50. Jesse Barfield	TOR	.277	90. Al Oliver	TOR	.253	130. Jackie Gutierrez	BOS	.225
11. Mark Salas	MIN	.307	51. Don Slaught	TEX	.277	91. Steve Balboni	KC	.252	131. Tony Armas	BOS	.224
12. Earnest Riles	MIL	.306	52. Willie Upshaw	TOR	.276	92. Mike Pagliarulo	NY	.252	132. Mike Stenhouse	MIN	.224
13. Jim Rice	BOS	.304	53. Fred Lynn	BAL	.275	93. Ernie Whitt	TOR	.252	133. Andre Thornton	CLE	.221
14. Eddie Murray	BAL	.303	54. Jorge Orta	KC	.274	94. Rudy Law	CHI	.252	134. Bill Schroeder	MIL	.221
15. Bill Buckner	BOS	.302	55. Brook Jacoby	CLE	.273	95. Pat Tabler	CLE	.252	135. Jim Gantner	MIL	.220
16. Mike Hargrove	CLE	.302	56. Willie Wilson	KC	.272	96. Jim Dwyer	BAL	.250	136. Buddy Bell	TEX	.219
17. Brett Butler	CLE	.302	57. Jack Perconte	SEA	.272	96. Tim Hulett	CHI	.250	137. Dan Pasqua	NY	.218
18. Rance Mulliniks	TOR	.299	58. Greg Walker	CHI	.270	96. Larry Parrish	TEX	.250	138. Gorman Thomas	SEA	.217
19. Damaso Garcia	TOR	.299	59. Larry Sheets	BAL	.270	99. Jim Presley	SEA	.249	139. Donnie Scott	SEA	.217
20. Carney Lansford	OAK	.296	60. Alan Wiggins	BAL	.269	100. Frank White	KC	.249	140. Don Baylor	NY	.215
21. Lou Whitaker	DET	.295	61. Joe Carter	CLE	.268	101. Johnny Grubb	DET	.248	141. Rick Manning	MIL	.214
22. Donnie Hill	OAK	.295	62. Mickey Tettleton	OAK	.267	102. Toby Harrah	TEX	.248	141. Bobby Meacham	NY	.214
23. Jerry Willard	CLE	.294	63. Al Cowens	SEA	.266	103. Randy Bush	MIN	.248	143. Len Matuszek	TOR	.212
24. Mike Davis	OAK	.293	64. Juan Beniquez	CAL	.266	104. Dwayne Murphy	OAK	.247	144. Greg Gagne	MIN	.211
25. Harold Baines	CHI	.293	64. Robin Yount	MIL	.266	105. Gary Pettis	CAL	.247	145. Tom Brookens	DET	.211
26. Rickey Henderson	NY	.292	66. Glenn Hoffman	BOS	.265	106. Alfredo Griffin	OAK	.246	146. Oscar Gamble	CHI	.207
27. Ed Romero	MIL	.289	67. Gary Gaetti	MIN	.265	107. Luis Salazar	CHI	.244	147. Charlie Moore	MIL	.204
28. Kent Hrbek	MIN	.289	68. Bob Kearney	SEA	.264	108. Doug DeCinces	CAL	.243	148. Scott Fletcher	CHI	.203
29. Bruce Bochte	OAK	.289	69. Brian Downing	CAL	.264	109. Bob Boone	CAL	.243	149. Rick Dempsey	BAL	.200
30. Julio Franco	CLE	.289	70. Steve Lyons	BOS	.263	110. Chet Lemon	DET	.242	150. Dick Schofield	CAL	.199
31. Floyd Rayford	BAL	.288	71. Roy Smalley	MIN	.263	111. Lonnie Smith	KC	.240	151. George Wright	TEX	.199
32. Tim Teufel	MIN	.288	72. Reggie Jackson	CAL	.262	112. Pat Sheridan	KC	.240	152. Darryl Motley	KC	.198
33. George Bell	TOR	.288	73. Marty Barrett	BOS	.262	113. Ruppert Jones	CAL	.239	153. Onix Concepcion	KC	.197
34. Dave Winfield	NY	.287	74. Lance Parrish	DET	.261	114. Daryl Boston	CHI	.237	154. Steve Buechele	TEX	.194
35. Ozzie Guillen	CHI	.287	75. Alan Trammell	DET	.261	115. Oddibe McDowell	TEX	.237	155. Rob Wilfong	CAL	.194
36. Tony Fernandez	TOR	.286	76. Dave Collins	OAK	.260	116. Nelson Simmons	DET	.236	156. Dave Bergman	DET	.178
37. Cal Ripken	BAL	.286	77. Mike Young	BAL	.260	117. Dave Kingman	OAK	.236	157. Duane Walker	TEX	.175
38. Rod Carew	CAL	.285	78. Lloyd Moseby	TOR	.260	118. Wayne Gross	BAL	.235	158. Rich Dauer	BAL	.173
39. Pete O'Brien	TEX	.285	79. Darrell Evans	DET	.260	119. Bobby Jones	TEX	.234			
40. Paul Molitor	MIL	.285	80. Spike Owen	SEA	.260	120. Curtis Wilkerson	TEX	.234			

National League

1. Willie McGee	STL	.356	35. Vince Coleman	STL	.282	69. George Foster	NY	.258	103. Enos Cabell	LA	.240
2. Tim Raines	MTL	.340	36. Andy Van Slyke	STL	.281	70. Alan Knicely	PHI	.257	104. Rick Schu	PHI	.239
3. Thad Bosley	CHI	.337	37. Bill Doran	HOU	.280	71. Carmelo Martinez	SD	.256	105. Mitch Webster	MTL	.238
4. Tony Gwynn	SD	.331	38. Ken Landreaux	LA	.279	72. Dave Concepcion	CIN	.255	106. Dan Gladden	SF	.237
5. Dave Parker	CIN	.327	39. Terry Puhl	HOU	.278	73. Steve Kemp	PIT	.255	107. Gary Matthews	CHI	.236
6. Pedro Guerrero	LA	.327	40. Chili Davis	SF	.277	74. Paul Zuvella	ATL	.254	108. Ron Cey	CHI	.235
7. Wally Backman	NY	.324	41. Alan Ashby	HOU	.276	75. Pete Rose	CIN	.253	109. Jeff Leonard	SF	.235
8. Mike Brown	PIT	.322	42. Wayne Krenchicki	CIN	.276	76. Rafael Ramirez	ATL	.253	110. Glenn Hubbard	ATL	.234
9. Joe Orsulak	PIT	.316	43. Von Hayes	PHI	.276	77. Rafael Santana	NY	.252	111. Dan Driessen	SF	.234
10. Milt Thompson	ATL	.315	44. Vance Law	MTL	.275	78. Ron Roenicke	SF	.252	112. Jason Thompson	PIT	.233
11. Ryne Sandberg	CHI	.315	45. Juan Samuel	PHI	.275	79. Billy Hatcher	CHI	.252	113. Jody Davis	CHI	.232
12. Jose Cruz	HOU	.315	46. Steve Garvey	SD	.274	80. Bob Horner	ATL	.252	114. Larry Bowa	NY	.231
13. Tom Herr	STL	.313	47. Mike Schmidt	PHI	.274	81. Hubie Brooks	MTL	.251	115. Bob Brenly	SF	.230
14. Mike Scioscia	LA	.307	48. Graig Nettles	SD	.274	82. Tim Francona	MTL	.251	116. Darrell Porter	STL	.228
15. Dave Lopes	CHI	.306	49. Greg Brock	LA	.274	83. Mark Bailey	HOU	.250	117. Sammy Khalifa	PIT	.227
16. Steve Sax	LA	.305	50. Bill Madlock	LA	.273	83. Gary Carter	NY	.250	118. Rick Cerone	ATL	.225
17. Keith Moreland	CHI	.305	51. David Green	SF	.270	83. Len Dykstra	NY	.250	119. Mariano Duncan	LA	.224
18. Keith Hernandez	NY	.303	52. Glenn Wilson	PHI	.270	83. Ozzie Virgil	PHI	.250	120. Gerald Perry	ATL	.223
19. Max Venable	CIN	.302	53. Denny Walling	HOU	.270	83. Joel Youngblood	SF	.250	121. Kevin McReynolds	SD	.223
20. Ron Oester	CIN	.302	54. Shawon Dunston	CHI	.268	88. Bo Diaz	CIN	.249	122. Manny Trillo	SF	.222
21. Mike Marshall	LA	.296	55. Phil Garner	HOU	.267	89. George Hendrick	PIT	.248	123. Scot Thompson	MTL	.216
22. Garry Templeton	SD	.295	56. Cesar Cedeno	STL	.267	90. Tom Foley	PHI	.248	124. Tim Corcoran	PHI	.215
23. Tim Flannery	SD	.294	57. Glenn Davis	HOU	.267	91. Chris Chambliss	ATL	.246	125. Brad Wellman	SF	.214
24. Jerry Mumphrey	HOU	.293	58. Ozzie Smith	STL	.266	92. Andre Dawson	MTL	.246	126. Bruce Benedict	ATL	.207
25. R.J. Reynolds	PIT	.292	59. Craig Reynolds	HOU	.265	93. Brad Komminsk	ATL	.246	127. Buddy Bell	CIN	.206
26. Chris Brown	SF	.292	60. Howard Johnson	NY	.263	94. Tony Pena	PIT	.246	128. Chris Speier	CHI	.204
27. Darryl Strawberry	NY	.291	61. Gary Redus	CIN	.263	95. Jose Uribe	SF	.245	129. Dave Anderson	LA	.201
28. Claudell Washington	ATL	.290	62. Terry Kennedy	SD	.262	96. Terry Pendleton	STL	.245	130. Doug Frobel	MTL	.193
29. Terry Harper	ATL	.288	63. Tim Wallach	MTL	.262	97. Jim Morrison	PIT	.244	131. Mike Fitzgerald	MTL	.192
30. Leon Durham	CHI	.287	64. Jeff Stone	PHI	.261	98. Nick Esasky	CIN	.243	132. Steve Jeltz	PHI	.187
31. Dale Murphy	ATL	.286	65. Jack Clark	STL	.261	99. Bob Dernier	CHI	.242	133. Mike Jorgensen	STL	.186
32. Danny Heep	NY	.284	66. Mookie Wilson	NY	.261	100. Kevin Bass	HOU	.241	134. Marvell Wynne	PIT	.181
33. Johnny Ray	PIT	.283	67. Eddie Milner	CIN	.259	101. Herm Winningham	MTL	.241			
34. Ken Oberkfell	ATL	.283	68. Greg Gross	PHI	.258	102. Tom Nieto	STL	.240			

Slugging Average vs. Left-Handed Pitchers

American League

#	Player	Tm	Avg	#	Player	Tm	Avg	#	Player	Tm	Avg	#	Player	Tm	Avg
1.	Rickey Henderson	NY	.656	41.	Darryl Motley	KC	.478	81.	Lonnie Smith	KC	.414	121.	Greg Gagne	MIN	.354
2.	Floyd Rayford	BAL	.650	42.	Ron Washington	MIN	.471	82.	Tony Fernandez	TOR	.412	122.	Dick Schofield	CAL	.354
3.	Tony Armas	BOS	.636	43.	Jim Rice	BOS	.470	83.	Willie Wilson	KC	.409	123.	Gary Gaetti	MIN	.349
4.	Bruce Bochte	OAK	.611	44.	Lee Lacy	BAL	.470	84.	Julio Franco	CLE	.408	124.	Rich Gedman	BOS	.348
5.	Dave Engle	MIN	.581	45.	Dave Winfield	NY	.470	85.	Bill Buckner	BOS	.404	125.	Ken Griffey	NY	.346
6.	Jim Presley	SEA	.573	46.	Darrell Evans	DET	.467	86.	Kent Hrbek	MIN	.402	126.	Dale Berra	NY	.345
7.	Don Mattingly	NY	.568	46.	Hal McRae	KC	.467	87.	Alfredo Griffin	OAK	.401	127.	Mickey Tettleton	OAK	.344
8.	Chet Lemon	DET	.564	48.	Harold Baines	CHI	.465	88.	Reggie Jackson	CAL	.398	128.	Marty Barrett	BOS	.341
9.	Lance Parrish	DET	.563	49.	Toby Harrah	TEX	.465	89.	Luis Salazar	CHI	.398	129.	Damaso Garcia	TOR	.333
10.	Carmen Castillo	CLE	.557	50.	Carlton Fisk	CHI	.464	90.	Mark Brouhard	MIL	.398	129.	Roy Smalley	MIN	.333
11.	Cecil Fielder	TOR	.551	51.	Benny Ayala	CLE	.464	91.	Dusty Baker	OAK	.396	131.	Gary Pettis	CAL	.331
12.	Mike Brown	CAL	.550	52.	Paul Molitor	MIL	.464	92.	Curtis Wilkerson	TEX	.395	132.	Bob Boone	CAL	.326
13.	George Brett	KC	.550	53.	George Bell	TOR	.463	93.	Lloyd Moseby	TOR	.393	133.	Lou Whitaker	DET	.324
14.	Mike Young	BAL	.547	54.	Willie Upshaw	TOR	.462	94.	Joe Carter	CLE	.391	134.	Ernie Whitt	TOR	.320
15.	Jesse Barfield	TOR	.541	55.	Brook Jacoby	CLE	.459	95.	Alan Wiggins	BAL	.390	135.	Bob Kearney	SEA	.320
16.	Juan Beniquez	CAL	.540	55.	Ron Kittle	CHI	.459	96.	Andre Robertson	NY	.390	136.	Julio Cruz	CHI	.319
17.	Alejandro Sanchez	DET	.536	57.	Steve Henderson	OAK	.457	97.	Greg Walker	CHI	.388	137.	Butch Wynegar	NY	.317
18.	Ivan Calderon	SEA	.535	58.	Jeff Burroughs	TOR	.455	98.	Rob Picciolo	OAK	.387	138.	Tony Bernazard	CLE	.313
19.	Larry Parrish	TEX	.532	59.	Gary Roenicke	BAL	.453	99.	Ben Oglivie	MIL	.387	139.	Tom Paciorek	CHI	.306
20.	Rick Dempsey	BAL	.529	60.	Robin Yount	MIL	.453	100.	Fritz Connally	BAL	.382	140.	Earnest Riles	MIL	.298
21.	Kirby Puckett	MIN	.525	61.	Jim Sundberg	KC	.452	101.	Buddy Bell	TEX	.382	141.	Pete O'Brien	TEX	.296
22.	Glenn Hoffman	BOS	.519	62.	Andre Thornton	CLE	.451	102.	Scott Fletcher	CHI	.381	142.	Dave Collins	OAK	.287
23.	Dwight Evans	BOS	.518	63.	Doug DeCinces	CAL	.449	103.	Tom Brunansky	MIN	.379	143.	Bobby Clark	MIL	.286
24.	Gary Ward	TEX	.511	64.	Frank White	KC	.446	104.	Fred Lynn	BAL	.379	144.	Donnie Hill	OAK	.284
25.	Eddie Murray	BAL	.502	65.	Bobby Grich	CAL	.442	105.	Mickey Hatcher	MIN	.379	145.	Rod Carew	CAL	.283
26.	Ted Simmons	MIL	.500	66.	Wade Boggs	BOS	.441	106.	John Shelby	BAL	.378	146.	Jackie Gutierrez	BOS	.278
27.	Cecil Cooper	MIL	.498	67.	Dave Henderson	SEA	.439	107.	Billy Sample	NY	.377	147.	Jack Perconte	SEA	.273
28.	Gorman Thomas	SEA	.493	68.	Cliff Johnson	TOR	.438	108.	Dwayne Murphy	OAK	.374	148.	Alan Bannister	TEX	.268
29.	Don Baylor	NY	.492	69.	Cal Ripken	BAL	.436	109.	Jim Gantner	MIL	.372	149.	Bobby Meacham	NY	.267
30.	Mike Heath	OAK	.490	70.	Oddibe McDowell	TEX	.431	110.	Dave Meier	MIN	.372	150.	Tim Teufel	MIN	.267
31.	Paul Householder	MIL	.487	71.	Brett Butler	CLE	.430	111.	Randy Ready	MIL	.369	151.	Buck Martinez	TOR	.264
31.	Tim Laudner	MIN	.487	72.	Tim Hulett	CHI	.428	112.	Charlie Moore	MIL	.366	152.	Onix Concepcion	KC	.255
33.	Al Cowens	SEA	.486	73.	Steve Buechele	TEX	.427	113.	Mike Easler	BOS	.364	153.	Ozzie Guillen	CHI	.244
34.	Mike Davis	OAK	.484	74.	Don Slaught	TEX	.426	114.	Alan Trammell	DET	.364	154.	Ed Romero	MIL	.242
34.	Larry Herndon	DET	.484	75.	Kirk Gibson	DET	.424	115.	Carney Lansford	OAK	.359	155.	Chris Bando	CLE	.236
36.	Phil Bradley	SEA	.483	76.	Steve Balboni	KC	.421	116.	Steve Lyons	BOS	.358	156.	George Wright	TEX	.221
36.	Dave Kingman	OAK	.483	77.	Barbaro Garbey	DET	.420	117.	Rich Dauer	BAL	.358	157.	Domingo Ramos	SEA	.200
38.	Brian Downing	CAL	.483	78.	Reid Nichols	CHI	.419	118.	Alvin Davis	SEA	.358	158.	Lynn Jones	KC	.195
39.	Tom Brookens	DET	.481	79.	Pat Tabler	CLE	.416	119.	Wayne Tolleson	TEX	.356				
40.	Garth Iorg	TOR	.480	80.	Willie Randolph	NY	.414	120.	Spike Owen	SEA	.356				

National League

#	Player	Tm	Avg	#	Player	Tm	Avg	#	Player	Tm	Avg	#	Player	Tm	Avg
1.	Eric Davis	CIN	.604	35.	Carmelo Martinez	SD	.452	69.	Bob Brenly	SF	.377	103.	Dan Gladden	SF	.320
2.	Jack Clark	STL	.597	36.	Dave Parker	CIN	.443	70.	Terry Kennedy	SD	.374	104.	U.L. Washington	MTL	.316
3.	Mitch Webster	MTL	.578	37.	Ron Cey	CHI	.443	71.	Bob Dernier	CHI	.373	105.	Garry Templeton	SD	.316
4.	Willie McGee	STL	.571	38.	Tim Raines	MTL	.438	72.	Tom Herr	STL	.373	106.	Chili Davis	SF	.314
5.	Gary Carter	NY	.566	39.	Mark Bailey	HOU	.435	73.	Kevin McReynolds	SD	.370	107.	Dave Anderson	LA	.313
6.	Glenn Davis	HOU	.563	40.	Ryne Sandberg	CHI	.434	74.	R.J. Reynolds	PIT	.369	108.	Paul Zuvella	ATL	.309
7.	Pedro Guerrero	LA	.556	41.	Graig Nettles	SD	.433	75.	Phil Garner	HOU	.368	109.	Alan Knicely	PHI	.308
8.	Bob Horner	ATL	.553	42.	Bill Almon	PIT	.431	76.	Gary Redus	CIN	.367	110.	Marvell Wynne	PIT	.306
9.	Kevin Bass	HOU	.553	43.	Mariano Duncan	LA	.429	77.	Claudell Washington	ATL	.365	111.	Jim Wohlford	MTL	.306
10.	Dale Murphy	ATL	.552	44.	Jerry Royster	SD	.425	78.	John Christensen	NY	.365	112.	Rafael Santana	NY	.301
11.	Rob Deer	SF	.522	45.	Leon Durham	CHI	.425	78.	Bill Russell	LA	.365	113.	Howard Johnson	NY	.299
12.	Nick Esasky	CIN	.518	46.	Tom Paciorek	NY	.424	80.	Candy Maldonado	LA	.363	114.	Terry Pendleton	STL	.298
13.	Chris Speier	CHI	.515	47.	Tim Wallach	MTL	.423	81.	Buddy Bell	CIN	.361	115.	Jose Uribe	SF	.296
14.	Andre Dawson	MTL	.515	48.	Ray Knight	NY	.418	82.	Dave Concepcion	CIN	.359	116.	Jerry Mumphrey	HOU	.293
15.	Tony Perez	CIN	.508	49.	Keith Hernandez	NY	.415	83.	Sammy Khalifa	PIT	.356	117.	Ken Oberkfell	ATL	.287
16.	Darryl Strawberry	NY	.506	50.	John Russell	PHI	.411	84.	Paul Runge	ATL	.356	118.	Luis Aguayo	PHI	.286
17.	Steve Garvey	SD	.502	51.	Alan Ashby	HOU	.409	85.	Tony Gwynn	SD	.351	119.	Manny Trillo	SF	.282
18.	Cesar Cedeno	STL	.496	52.	Pete Rose	CIN	.408	86.	Bo Diaz	CIN	.350	120.	Glenn Hubbard	ATL	.278
19.	Mike Brown	PIT	.492	53.	Bill Madlock	LA	.405	87.	Jason Thompson	PIT	.350	120.	Steve Sax	LA	.278
20.	Mike Marshall	LA	.490	54.	Jose Cruz	HOU	.405	88.	Jim Morrison	PIT	.349	122.	David Green	SF	.275
21.	Mookie Wilson	NY	.490	55.	Gary Matthews	CHI	.402	89.	Mike Scioscia	LA	.345	123.	Rick Cerone	ATL	.275
22.	Jeff Leonard	SF	.489	56.	Chris Brown	SF	.400	90.	Tony Pena	PIT	.344	124.	George Hendrick	PIT	.273
23.	Glenn Wilson	PHI	.485	57.	Enos Cabell	LA	.398	91.	Sixto Lezcano	PIT	.342	125.	Mike Fitzgerald	MTL	.268
24.	Ozzie Smith	STL	.484	58.	Terry Harper	ATL	.395	92.	Vince Coleman	STL	.341	126.	Tom Nieto	STL	.255
25.	Mike Schmidt	PHI	.484	59.	Tito Landrum	STL	.394	93.	Ken Landreaux	LA	.339	127.	Greg Brock	LA	.255
26.	Alex Trevino	SF	.481	60.	Garry Maddox	PHI	.386	94.	Ron Oester	CIN	.338	128.	Steve Yeager	LA	.245
27.	Rick Schu	PHI	.477	61.	Juan Samuel	PHI	.386	95.	Von Hayes	PHI	.338	129.	Joe Orsulak	PIT	.231
28.	Hubie Brooks	MTL	.476	62.	Ozzie Virgil	PHI	.385	96.	Johnny Ray	PIT	.335	130.	Steve Jeltz	PHI	.226
29.	Jody Davis	CHI	.470	63.	Kurt Bevacqua	SD	.385	97.	Jim Pankovits	HOU	.330	131.	Bruce Benedict	ATL	.224
30.	George Foster	NY	.468	63.	Joel Youngblood	SF	.385	98.	Danny Heep	NY	.327	132.	Kelvin Chapman	NY	.188
31.	Dave Lopes	CHI	.467	65.	Vance Law	MTL	.384	99.	Larry Bowa	NY	.325	133.	Wally Backman	NY	.153
32.	Bruce Bochy	SD	.466	66.	Dickie Thon	HOU	.383	100.	Brad Komminsk	ATL	.324	134.	Andy Van Slyke	STL	.148
33.	Bill Doran	HOU	.461	67.	Terry Puhl	HOU	.382	101.	Rafael Ramirez	ATL	.323				
34.	Keith Moreland	CHI	.460	68.	Dan Driessen	SF	.379	102.	Len Dykstra	NY	.321				

Slugging Average vs. Right-Handed Pitchers

American League

#	Player	Team	Avg	#	Player	Team	Avg	#	Player	Team	Avg	#	Player	Team	Avg
1.	George Brett	KC	.604	41.	Larry Sheets	BAL	.457	81.	Larry Parrish	TEX	.397	121.	Pat Tabler	CLE	.344
2.	Ron Hassey	NY	.580	42.	Ben Oglivie	MIL	.455	82.	Jorge Orta	KC	.396	122.	Donnie Scott	SEA	.344
3.	Don Mattingly	NY	.567	43.	Jim Presley	SEA	.450	83.	Wayne Tolleson	TEX	.390	123.	Marty Barrett	BOS	.343
4.	Kirk Gibson	DET	.557	44.	Ken Griffey	NY	.450	84.	Dave Kingman	OAK	.389	124.	Ed Romero	MIL	.342
5.	Darrell Evans	DET	.535	45.	Lloyd Moseby	TOR	.449	85.	Nelson Simmons	DET	.389	125.	Bobby Grich	CAL	.340
6.	Rich Gedman	BOS	.534	46.	Lance Parrish	DET	.447	86.	Chet Lemon	DET	.389	126.	Tim Hulett	CHI	.339
7.	Eddie Murray	BAL	.534	47.	Rickey Henderson	NY	.447	87.	Don Baylor	NY	.387	127.	Mike Stenhouse	MIN	.333
8.	Jesse Barfield	TOR	.533	48.	Tony Armas	BOS	.445	88.	Alan Trammell	DET	.387	128.	Larry Herndon	DET	.331
9.	Pete O'Brien	TEX	.517	49.	Willie Upshaw	TOR	.439	89.	Andre Thornton	CLE	.386	129.	Bill Schroeder	MIL	.331
10.	Reggie Jackson	CAL	.516	50.	Floyd Rayford	BAL	.438	90.	Ozzie Guillen	CHI	.384	130.	Juan Beniquez	CAL	.329
11.	Ivan Calderon	SEA	.504	51.	Robin Yount	MIL	.437	91.	Paul Molitor	MIL	.383	131.	Oscar Gamble	CHI	.329
12.	Phil Bradley	SEA	.503	52.	Doug DeCinces	CAL	.437	92.	Tony Fernandez	TOR	.378	132.	Alan Wiggins	BAL	.326
13.	Carlton Fisk	CHI	.500	53.	Gary Gaetti	MIN	.436	93.	Spike Owen	SEA	.378	133.	Butch Wynegar	NY	.324
14.	Lou Whitaker	DET	.498	54.	Cecil Cooper	MIL	.436	94.	Lee Lacy	BAL	.377	134.	Willie Randolph	NY	.323
15.	Steve Balboni	KC	.498	55.	Al Cowens	SEA	.436	95.	Glenn Hoffman	BOS	.375	135.	Tom Brookens	DET	.322
16.	Wade Boggs	BOS	.495	56.	Tony Bernazard	CLE	.435	95.	Paul Householder	MIL	.375	136.	Len Matuszek	TOR	.322
17.	Jim Rice	BOS	.494	57.	Hal McRae	KC	.435	97.	Mike Hargrove	CLE	.374	137.	Buddy Bell	TEX	.321
18.	Mike Young	BAL	.491	58.	Mike Easler	BOS	.433	98.	Donnie Hill	OAK	.370	138.	Kirby Puckett	MIN	.320
19.	George Bell	TOR	.489	59.	Brett Butler	CLE	.432	99.	Dave Henderson	SEA	.370	139.	Dick Schofield	CAL	.320
20.	Fred Lynn	BAL	.485	60.	Oddibe McDowell	TEX	.431	100.	Bob Kearney	SEA	.370	140.	Steve Buechele	TEX	.319
21.	Mike Davis	OAK	.485	61.	Gorman Thomas	SEA	.431	101.	Julio Franco	CLE	.368	141.	Gary Pettis	CAL	.319
22.	Cal Ripken	BAL	.484	62.	Dwight Evans	BOS	.430	102.	George Vukovich	CLE	.367	142.	Bob Boone	CAL	.314
23.	Greg Walker	CHI	.483	63.	Don Slaught	TEX	.421	103.	Bobby Jones	TEX	.367	143.	Rick Dempsey	BAL	.312
24.	Tom Brunansky	MIN	.481	64.	Jerry Willard	CLE	.421	104.	Rudy Law	CHI	.367	144.	Duane Walker	TEX	.310
25.	Alvin Davis	SEA	.478	65.	Roy Smalley	MIN	.418	105.	Jack Perconte	SEA	.365	145.	Jim Gantner	MIL	.306
26.	Dusty Baker	OAK	.472	66.	Joe Carter	CLE	.418	106.	Rod Carew	CAL	.365	146.	Alfredo Griffin	OAK	.302
27.	Mark Salas	MIN	.472	67.	Earnest Riles	MIL	.414	107.	Mike Heath	OAK	.365	147.	Greg Gagne	MIN	.289
28.	Ron Kittle	CHI	.472	68.	Bruce Bochte	OAK	.414	108.	Darryl Motley	KC	.365	148.	Rick Manning	MIL	.286
29.	Ernie Whitt	TOR	.472	69.	Wayne Gross	BAL	.413	109.	Dave Collins	OAK	.363	149.	Curtis Wilkerson	TEX	.281
30.	Dave Winfield	NY	.471	70.	Brook Jacoby	CLE	.411	110.	Mickey Hatcher	MIN	.359	150.	Jackie Gutierrez	BOS	.270
31.	Bill Buckner	BOS	.470	71.	Luis Salazar	CHI	.410	111.	Al Oliver	TOR	.359	151.	Bobby Meacham	NY	.265
32.	Harold Baines	CHI	.468	72.	Dwayne Murphy	OAK	.410	112.	Steve Lyons	BOS	.359	152.	Dave Bergman	DET	.259
32.	Mike Pagliarulo	NY	.468	73.	Cliff Johnson	TOR	.409	113.	Ted Simmons	MIL	.356	153.	George Wright	TEX	.253
34.	Kent Hrbek	MIN	.464	74.	Willie Wilson	KC	.408	114.	Mickey Tettleton	OAK	.353	154.	Charlie Moore	MIL	.252
35.	Randy Bush	MIN	.464	75.	Johnny Grubb	DET	.405	115.	Bryan Little	CHI	.352	155.	Onix Concepcion	KC	.240
36.	Carney Lansford	OAK	.463	76.	Damaso Garcia	TOR	.402	116.	Jim Sundberg	KC	.349	156.	Rob Wilfong	CAL	.240
37.	Rance Mulliniks	TOR	.462	77.	Jim Dwyer	BAL	.401	117.	Pat Sheridan	KC	.349	157.	Scott Fletcher	CHI	.218
38.	Dan Pasqua	NY	.459	78.	Frank White	KC	.401	118.	Daryl Boston	CHI	.349	158.	Rich Dauer	BAL	.205
39.	Tim Teufel	MIN	.458	79.	Gary Ward	TEX	.400	119.	Toby Harrah	TEX	.346				
40.	Ruppert Jones	CAL	.458	80.	Brian Downing	CAL	.399	120.	Lonnie Smith	KC	.344				

National League

#	Player	Team	Avg	#	Player	Team	Avg	#	Player	Team	Avg	#	Player	Team	Avg
1.	Dave Parker	CIN	.601	35.	Terry Puhl	HOU	.437	69.	Johnny Ray	PIT	.392	103.	Brad Komminsk	ATL	.331
2.	Darryl Strawberry	NY	.591	36.	Tony Gwynn	SD	.436	70.	Craig Reynolds	HOU	.391	104.	Joel Youngblood	SF	.329
3.	Pedro Guerrero	LA	.585	37.	Darrell Porter	STL	.436	71.	Jason Thompson	PIT	.391	105.	Rick Schu	PHI	.324
4.	Mike Schmidt	PHI	.551	38.	Keith Moreland	CHI	.434	72.	David Green	SF	.389	106.	Herm Winningham	MTL	.323
5.	Dale Murphy	ATL	.533	39.	Dave Lopes	CHI	.432	73.	Ken Oberkfell	ATL	.387	107.	Jose Uribe	SF	.322
6.	Ryne Sandberg	CHI	.527	40.	Phil Garner	HOU	.428	74.	Hubie Brooks	MTL	.385	108.	Dave Concepcion	CIN	.319
7.	Mike Marshall	LA	.526	41.	Carmelo Martinez	SD	.425	75.	Milt Thompson	ATL	.381	109.	Greg Gross	PHI	.313
8.	Thad Bosley	CHI	.526	42.	Alan Knicely	PHI	.425	76.	Jody Davis	CHI	.379	110.	Terry Pendleton	STL	.309
9.	Mike Brown	PIT	.521	43.	Von Hayes	PHI	.421	77.	Bo Diaz	CIN	.379	111.	Ozzie Smith	STL	.309
10.	Greg Brock	LA	.494	44.	Bill Doran	HOU	.418	78.	Mark Bailey	HOU	.375	112.	Pete Rose	CIN	.306
11.	Tim Raines	MTL	.491	45.	Mitch Webster	MTL	.418	79.	Mookie Wilson	NY	.372	113.	Sammy Khalifa	PIT	.305
12.	Andy Van Slyke	STL	.481	46.	Ron Roenicke	SF	.417	80.	Buddy Bell	CIN	.371	114.	Rafael Santana	NY	.303
13.	Leon Durham	CHI	.477	47.	Graig Nettles	SD	.417	80.	Terry Kennedy	SD	.371	115.	Paul Zuvella	ATL	.303
14.	Bob Horner	ATL	.472	48.	Howard Johnson	NY	.417	82.	Kevin McReynolds	SD	.371	116.	Enos Cabell	LA	.299
15.	Claudell Washington	ATL	.472	49.	Vance Law	MTL	.414	83.	Ron Oester	CIN	.370	117.	Mike Fitzgerald	MTL	.298
16.	Alan Ashby	HOU	.472	50.	Ken Landreaux	LA	.414	84.	Tony Pena	PIT	.367	118.	Mariano Duncan	LA	.297
17.	Willie McGee	STL	.468	51.	Glenn Davis	HOU	.413	85.	Tom Foley	PHI	.362	119.	Bob Dernier	CHI	.296
18.	Gary Redus	CIN	.466	52.	Terry Harper	ATL	.413	86.	Steve Kemp	PIT	.361	120.	Tom Nieto	STL	.295
19.	Tim Wallach	MTL	.461	53.	Andre Dawson	MTL	.412	87.	Eddie Milner	CIN	.360	121.	Larry Bowa	NY	.291
20.	Jack Clark	STL	.459	54.	Denny Walling	HOU	.410	88.	Dan Gladden	SF	.358	122.	Manny Trillo	SF	.291
21.	Juan Samuel	PHI	.457	55.	Wally Backman	NY	.409	89.	Jeff Leonard	SF	.355	123.	Rick Cerone	ATL	.283
22.	Chris Brown	SF	.457	56.	Gary Matthews	CHI	.407	90.	Tim Flannery	SD	.352	124.	Gerald Perry	ATL	.279
23.	George Foster	NY	.455	57.	R.J. Reynolds	PIT	.407	91.	Chris Chambliss	ATL	.351	125.	Chris Speier	CHI	.276
24.	Ozzie Virgil	PHI	.451	58.	Billy Hatcher	CHI	.407	92.	Dan Driessen	SF	.344	126.	Doug Frobel	MTL	.272
25.	Max Venable	CIN	.442	59.	Garry Templeton	SD	.407	93.	Jim Morrison	PIT	.341	127.	Brad Wellman	SF	.271
26.	Danny Heep	NY	.441	60.	Wayne Krenchicki	CIN	.405	94.	Kevin Bass	HOU	.341	128.	Dave Anderson	LA	.266
26.	Keith Hernandez	NY	.441	61.	Glenn Wilson	PHI	.400	95.	Rafael Ramirez	ATL	.338	129.	Tim Corcoran	PHI	.264
28.	Jose Cruz	HOU	.441	62.	Bill Madlock	LA	.400	96.	George Hendrick	PIT	.338	130.	Scot Thompson	MTL	.252
29.	Jerry Mumphrey	HOU	.441	63.	Cesar Cedeno	STL	.398	97.	Terry Francona	MTL	.337	131.	Mike Jorgensen	STL	.245
30.	Tom Herr	STL	.440	64.	Ron Cey	CHI	.397	98.	Jeff Stone	PHI	.335	132.	Marvell Wynne	PIT	.235
31.	Chili Davis	SF	.439	65.	Bob Brenly	SF	.396	99.	Steve Sax	LA	.334	133.	Bruce Benedict	ATL	.233
32.	Mike Scioscia	LA	.439	66.	Steve Garvey	SD	.396	100.	Len Dykstra	NY	.333	134.	Steve Jeltz	PHI	.216
33.	Gary Carter	NY	.438	67.	Shawon Dunston	CHI	.395	101.	Glenn Hubbard	ATL	.332				
33.	Nick Esasky	CIN	.438	68.	Joe Orsulak	PIT	.392	102.	Vince Coleman	STL	.332				

Home Run Percentage vs. Left-Handed Pitchers

American League

1.	Floyd Rayford	BAL	8.57	40.	Dave Winfield	NY	4.65	81.	Tom Brookens	DET	2.47	121.	Wade Boggs	BOS	0.94
2.	Gorman Thomas	SEA	8.55	42.	Jim Rice	BOS	4.64	81.	Rich Dauer	BAL	2.47	122.	Damaso Garcia	TOR	0.91
3.	Larry Parrish	TEX	8.51	43.	Larry Herndon	DET	4.52	83.	Oddibe McDowell	TEX	2.44	123.	Billy Sample	NY	0.88
4.	Carmen Castillo	CLE	7.83	44.	Rick Dempsey	BAL	4.46	83.	John Shelby	BAL	2.44	124.	Greg Gagne	MIN	0.79
5.	Darrell Evans	DET	7.50	45.	Jesse Barfield	TOR	4.35	85.	Luis Salazar	CHI	2.34	125.	Mickey Hatcher	MIN	0.76
6.	Bruce Bochte	OAK	7.41	45.	Paul Householder	MIL	4.35	86.	Carney Lansford	OAK	2.29	126.	Bob Boone	CAL	0.74
7.	Dave Kingman	OAK	7.39	47.	Ivan Calderon	SEA	4.23	87.	Alvin Davis	SEA	2.27	126.	Tim Teufel	MIN	0.74
8.	Dwight Evans	BOS	7.06	48.	Ted Simmons	MIL	4.22	87.	Dave Henderson	SEA	2.27	128.	Willie Wilson	KC	0.61
9.	Gary Roenicke	BAL	6.98	49.	Jeff Burroughs	TOR	4.20	89.	Greg Walker	CHI	2.19	129.	Alfredo Griffin	OAK	0.53
10.	Don Mattingly	NY	6.82	50.	Kirk Gibson	DET	4.12	90.	Alan Trammell	DET	2.17	130.	Brett Butler	CLE	0.52
11.	Ron Kittle	CHI	6.76	51.	Steve Buechele	TEX	4.00	91.	Julio Franco	CLE	2.04	131.	Chris Bando	CLE	0.00
12.	Dave Engle	MIN	6.67	52.	Gary Ward	TEX	3.98	92.	Pat Tabler	CLE	1.95	131.	Alan Bannister	TEX	0.00
12.	Rickey Henderson	NY	6.67	53.	Al Cowens	SEA	3.57	93.	Ken Griffey	NY	1.87	131.	Marty Barrett	BOS	0.00
14.	Mike Young	BAL	6.63	54.	Reggie Jackson	CAL	3.54	94.	Kirby Puckett	MIN	1.83	131.	Buddy Bell	TEX	0.00
15.	Tony Armas	BOS	6.43	55.	Toby Harrah	TEX	3.52	95.	Cliff Johnson	TOR	1.79	131.	Tony Bernazard	CLE	0.00
16.	Tim Laudner	MIN	6.09	56.	Dusty Baker	OAK	3.47	96.	Bill Buckner	BOS	1.74	131.	Rod Carew	CAL	0.00
16.	Jim Sundberg	KC	6.09	57.	Juan Beniquez	CAL	3.45	97.	Reid Nichols	CHI	1.71	131.	Bobby Clark	MIL	0.00
18.	Lance Parrish	DET	5.96	57.	Buck Martinez	TOR	3.45	98.	Mickey Tettleton	OAK	1.64	131.	Onix Concepcion	KC	0.00
19.	Alejandro Sanchez	DET	5.95	59.	Gary Gaetti	MIN	3.43	99.	Rob Picciolo	OAK	1.61	131.	Julio Cruz	CHI	0.00
20.	Cecil Fielder	TOR	5.80	60.	Bobby Grich	CAL	3.40	100.	Steve Lyons	BOS	1.49	131.	Tony Fernandez	TOR	0.00
21.	Don Baylor	NY	5.70	61.	Mike Heath	OAK	3.31	101.	Rich Gedman	BOS	1.48	131.	Jim Gantner	MIL	0.00
22.	Frank White	KC	5.42	62.	Joe Carter	CLE	3.11	102.	Fritz Connally	BAL	1.47	131.	Ozzie Guillen	CHI	0.00
23.	Chet Lemon	DET	5.37	63.	Bob Kearney	SEA	3.09	102.	Ron Washington	MIN	1.47	131.	Jackie Gutierrez	BOS	0.00
24.	Hal McRae	KC	5.33	64.	Kent Hrbek	MIN	3.02	104.	Butch Wynegar	NY	1.44	131.	Donnie Hill	OAK	0.00
25.	George Brett	KC	5.24	65.	Lee Lacy	BAL	3.01	105.	Steve Henderson	OAK	1.43	131.	Lynn Jones	KC	0.00
26.	Andre Thornton	CLE	5.23	66.	Lloyd Moseby	TOR	2.99	105.	Lonnie Smith	KC	1.43	131.	Bobby Meacham	NY	0.00
27.	Mike Davis	OAK	5.16	67.	Cal Ripken	BAL	2.97	107.	Lou Whitaker	DET	1.38	131.	Charlie Moore	MIL	0.00
28.	George Bell	TOR	5.14	67.	Don Slaught	TEX	2.97	108.	Dick Schofield	CAL	1.36	131.	Tom Paciorek	CHI	0.00
29.	Phil Bradley	SEA	5.11	69.	Willie Upshaw	TOR	2.92	109.	Dave Meier	MIN	1.28	131.	Jack Perconte	SEA	0.00
30.	Jim Presley	SEA	5.10	70.	Benny Ayala	CLE	2.90	110.	Tim Hulett	CHI	1.26	131.	Gary Pettis	CAL	0.00
31.	Glenn Hoffman	BOS	5.06	70.	Barbaro Garbey	DET	2.90	111.	Mark Brouhard	MIL	1.20	131.	Domingo Ramos	SEA	0.00
32.	Mike Brown	CAL	5.00	72.	Cecil Cooper	MIL	2.87	112.	Scott Fletcher	CHI	1.19	131.	Earnest Riles	MIL	0.00
33.	Darryl Motley	KC	4.97	73.	Paul Molitor	MIL	2.79	112.	Randy Ready	MIL	1.19	131.	Ed Romero	MIL	0.00
34.	Eddie Murray	BAL	4.93	74.	Harold Baines	CHI	2.76	114.	Pete O'Brien	TEX	1.18	131.	Roy Smalley	MIN	0.00
35.	Carlton Fisk	CHI	4.92	75.	Tom Brunansky	MIN	2.75	115.	Mike Easler	BOS	1.16	131.	Wayne Tolleson	TEX	0.00
36.	Steve Balboni	KC	4.88	76.	Ben Oglivie	MIL	2.67	116.	Dale Berra	NY	1.15	131.	Alan Wiggins	BAL	0.00
37.	Brook Jacoby	CLE	4.86	76.	Ernie Whitt	TOR	2.67	116.	Dave Collins	OAK	1.15	131.	Curtis Wilkerson	TEX	0.00
38.	Dwayne Murphy	OAK	4.76	76.	Robin Yount	MIL	2.67	118.	Spike Owen	SEA	1.11	131.	George Wright	TEX	0.00
39.	Doug DeCinces	CAL	4.72	79.	Fred Lynn	BAL	2.61	119.	Willie Randolph	NY	1.10				
40.	Brian Downing	CAL	4.65	80.	Garth Iorg	TOR	2.50	120.	Andre Robertson	NY	1.00				

National League

1.	Eric Davis	CIN	9.43	35.	Cesar Cedeno	STL	3.70	69.	Hubie Brooks	MTL	2.14	103.	Dan Gladden	SF	0.68
2.	Rob Deer	SF	8.96	36.	John Christensen	NY	3.53	70.	Terry Kennedy	SD	2.04	104.	Johnny Ray	PIT	0.59
3.	Glenn Davis	HOU	8.33	36.	Ray Knight	NY	3.53	71.	Greg Brock	LA	1.96	105.	Garry Templeton	SD	0.56
4.	Darryl Strawberry	NY	7.05	38.	Glenn Wilson	PHI	3.51	72.	Alan Knicely	PHI	1.92	106.	Enos Cabell	LA	0.55
5.	Pedro Guerrero	LA	6.67	39.	Dave Parker	CIN	3.48	72.	Alex Trevino	SF	1.92	107.	Phil Garner	HOU	0.45
5.	Mitch Webster	MTL	6.67	40.	Ken Landreaux	LA	3.39	74.	Garry Maddox	PHI	1.75	108.	Wally Backman	NY	0.00
7.	Jack Clark	STL	6.47	41.	Tim Raines	MTL	3.37	75.	Kevin McReynolds	SD	1.73	108.	Bruce Benedict	ATL	0.00
8.	Bob Horner	ATL	6.21	42.	Willie McGee	STL	3.33	76.	Mike Brown	PIT	1.69	108.	Larry Bowa	NY	0.00
9.	Andre Dawson	MTL	5.99	43.	Kurt Bevacqua	SD	3.30	77.	Jerry Royster	SD	1.66	108.	Kelvin Chapman	NY	0.00
10.	Gary Carter	NY	5.94	44.	Ryne Sandberg	CHI	3.29	78.	Brad Komminsk	ATL	1.65	108.	Vince Coleman	STL	0.00
11.	Ron Cey	CHI	5.74	45.	Ozzie Virgil	PHI	3.28	79.	Luis Aguayo	PHI	1.59	108.	Bob Dernier	CHI	0.00
12.	Bruce Bochy	SD	5.48	46.	Mark Bailey	HOU	3.23	79.	Claudell Washington	ATL	1.59	108.	Bo Diaz	CIN	0.00
13.	Dale Murphy	ATL	5.46	47.	Leon Durham	CHI	3.15	81.	Gary Redus	CIN	1.56	108.	Len Dykstra	NY	0.00
14.	Dave Lopes	CHI	5.43	48.	Alan Ashby	HOU	3.03	82.	Tom Herr	STL	1.42	108.	Mike Fitzgerald	MTL	0.00
15.	Bob Brenly	SF	5.26	48.	Rick Schu	PHI	3.03	83.	Buddy Bell	CIN	1.39	108.	Danny Heep	NY	0.00
16.	Mike Marshall	LA	5.10	50.	Dave Anderson	LA	2.99	84.	Tony Pena	PIT	1.32	108.	George Hendrick	PIT	0.00
17.	Nick Esasky	CIN	4.96	51.	Candy Maldonado	LA	2.98	85.	Joel Youngblood	SF	1.28	108.	Steve Jeltz	PHI	0.00
17.	Jeff Leonard	SF	4.96	51.	Tim Wallach	MTL	2.98	86.	U.L. Washington	MTL	1.27	108.	Sammy Khalifa	PIT	0.00
19.	Gary Matthews	CHI	4.88	53.	Mookie Wilson	NY	2.68	87.	Terry Pendleton	STL	1.17	108.	Jerry Mumphrey	HOU	0.00
20.	Tony Perez	CIN	4.84	54.	Jim Pankovits	HOU	2.61	88.	Keith Hernandez	NY	1.15	108.	Tom Nieto	STL	0.00
21.	Carmelo Martinez	SD	4.82	55.	Dave Concepcion	CIN	2.56	89.	Mike Scioscia	LA	1.15	108.	Ken Oberkfell	ATL	0.00
22.	George Foster	NY	4.79	56.	Von Hayes	PHI	2.55	90.	Rick Cerone	ATL	1.10	108.	Ron Oester	CIN	0.00
23.	Terry Harper	ATL	4.65	57.	Juan Samuel	PHI	2.54	91.	Tom Paciorek	NY	1.09	108.	Joe Orsulak	PIT	0.00
24.	Kevin Bass	HOU	4.57	58.	Bill Madlock	LA	2.53	92.	Dan Driessen	SF	1.05	108.	Terry Puhl	HOU	0.00
25.	Chris Brown	SF	4.55	59.	Vance Law	MTL	2.52	93.	Tony Gwynn	SD	0.98	108.	Rafael Ramirez	ATL	0.00
25.	Chris Speier	CHI	4.55	60.	Dickie Thon	HOU	2.47	94.	Chili Davis	SF	0.95	108.	R.J. Reynolds	PIT	0.00
27.	Jody Davis	CHI	4.35	61.	Jason Thompson	PIT	2.44	95.	Jim Wohlford	MTL	0.93	108.	Pete Rose	CIN	0.00
28.	Steve Garvey	SD	4.31	62.	Keith Moreland	CHI	2.42	96.	David Green	SF	0.92	108.	Bill Russell	LA	0.00
29.	John Russell	PHI	4.21	63.	Bill Doran	HOU	2.30	96.	Jim Morrison	PIT	0.92	108.	Rafael Santana	NY	0.00
30.	Graig Nettles	SD	4.12	64.	Jose Cruz	HOU	2.27	98.	Marvell Wynne	PIT	0.90	108.	Andy Van Slyke	STL	0.00
31.	Howard Johnson	NY	3.90	64.	Tito Landrum	STL	2.27	99.	Jose Uribe	SF	0.80	108.	Steve Yeager	LA	0.00
32.	Mike Schmidt	PHI	3.87	66.	Paul Runge	ATL	2.22	100.	Manny Trillo	SF	0.76	108.	Paul Zuvella	ATL	0.00
33.	Sixto Lezcano	PIT	3.80	67.	Mariano Duncan	LA	2.20	101.	Glenn Hubbard	ATL	0.69				
34.	Ozzie Smith	STL	3.73	68.	Bill Almon	PIT	2.19	101.	Steve Sax	LA	0.69				

Home Run Percentage vs. Right-Handed Pitchers

American League

#	Player	Team	Pct
1.	Darrell Evans	DET	8.05
2.	Carlton Fisk	CHI	7.78
3.	Ron Kittle	CHI	6.93
4.	Dan Pasqua	NY	6.77
5.	Reggie Jackson	CAL	6.63
6.	Fred Lynn	BAL	6.44
7.	Steve Balboni	KC	6.42
8.	Mike Young	BAL	5.95
9.	Ron Hassey	NY	5.94
10.	Gorman Thomas	SEA	5.72
11.	Tony Armas	BOS	5.71
11.	Tom Brunansky	MIN	5.71
13.	George Brett	KC	5.57
14.	Ruppert Jones	CAL	5.54
15.	Eddie Murray	BAL	5.53
16.	Larry Sheets	BAL	5.47
17.	Jesse Barfield	TOR	5.42
18.	Kirk Gibson	DET	5.35
19.	Oddibe McDowell	TEX	5.30
20.	Mike Pagliarulo	NY	5.17
21.	Jim Rice	BOS	5.06
22.	Ernie Whitt	TOR	5.04
23.	Pete O'Brien	TEX	4.95
24.	Jim Presley	SEA	4.84
25.	Greg Walker	CHI	4.78
26.	Lance Parrish	DET	4.77
27.	Wayne Gross	BAL	4.69
28.	Doug DeCinces	CAL	4.67
29.	Cal Ripken	BAL	4.55
29.	Andre Thornton	CLE	4.55
31.	Dusty Baker	OAK	4.52
32.	Randy Bush	MIN	4.50
33.	Rich Gedman	BOS	4.41
34.	Don Mattingly	NY	4.38
35.	George Bell	TOR	4.33
36.	Cliff Johnson	TOR	4.28
37.	Don Baylor	NY	4.23
38.	Lou Whitaker	DET	4.09
39.	Dave Kingman	OAK	4.09
40.	Mike Davis	OAK	4.08
41.	Darryl Motley	KC	4.05
42.	Duane Walker	TEX	3.97
43.	Bobby Jones	TEX	3.91
44.	Luis Salazar	CHI	3.85
45.	Dave Winfield	NY	3.83
46.	Kent Hrbek	MIN	3.81
47.	Dwight Evans	BOS	3.80
48.	Roy Smalley	MIN	3.80
49.	Harold Baines	CHI	3.78
50.	Carney Lansford	OAK	3.70
51.	Phil Bradley	SEA	3.66
52.	Gary Gaetti	MIN	3.64
53.	Ivan Calderon	SEA	3.60
54.	Larry Parrish	TEX	3.57
55.	Mike Easler	BOS	3.54
56.	Hal McRae	KC	3.53
57.	Alvin Davis	SEA	3.48
58.	Robin Yount	MIL	3.48
59.	Dwayne Murphy	OAK	3.46
60.	Brian Downing	CAL	3.45
60.	Nelson Simmons	DET	3.45
62.	Frank White	KC	3.27
63.	Rickey Henderson	NY	3.27
63.	Johnny Grubb	DET	3.27
65.	Paul Householder	MIL	3.26
66.	Lloyd Moseby	TOR	3.14
67.	Joe Carter	CLE	3.05
68.	Willie Upshaw	TOR	3.03
69.	Jim Dwyer	BAL	3.02
70.	Tim Teufel	MIN	3.01
71.	Ben Oglivie	MIL	3.01
72.	Dave Henderson	SEA	2.97
73.	Tony Bernazard	CLE	2.96
74.	Rance Mulliniks	TOR	2.91
75.	Al Cowens	SEA	2.88
76.	Mike Stenhouse	MIN	2.87
77.	Oscar Gamble	CHI	2.86
78.	Mike Heath	OAK	2.81
79.	Jerry Willard	CLE	2.78
80.	Floyd Rayford	BAL	2.74
81.	Chet Lemon	DET	2.72
82.	Bill Buckner	BOS	2.71
83.	Bruce Bochte	OAK	2.70
84.	Mark Salas	MIN	2.65
85.	Brook Jacoby	CLE	2.61
86.	Rick Dempsey	BAL	2.44
87.	Ken Griffey	NY	2.42
88.	Bobby Grich	CAL	2.41
89.	Cecil Cooper	MIL	2.37
90.	Al Oliver	TOR	2.35
91.	Dave Bergman	DET	2.22
92.	Bill Schroeder	MIL	2.21
93.	Alan Trammell	DET	2.14
94.	Steve Buechele	TEX	2.08
95.	Don Slaught	TEX	2.07
96.	Dick Schofield	CAL	2.06
97.	George Vukovich	CLE	2.04
98.	Gary Ward	TEX	1.92
99.	Donnie Scott	SEA	1.91
100.	Spike Owen	SEA	1.91
101.	Butch Wynegar	NY	1.76
102.	Larry Herndon	DET	1.74
103.	Buddy Bell	TEX	1.69
104.	Earnest Riles	MIL	1.63
105.	Damaso Garcia	TOR	1.57
105.	Toby Harrah	TEX	1.57
107.	Pat Sheridan	KC	1.56
108.	Bob Kearney	SEA	1.44
109.	Daryl Boston	CHI	1.40
110.	Jim Gantner	MIL	1.39
111.	Jorge Orta	KC	1.39
112.	Ted Simmons	MIL	1.38
113.	Len Matuszek	TOR	1.37
114.	Wade Boggs	BOS	1.36
115.	Marty Barrett	BOS	1.35
116.	Mickey Tettleton	OAK	1.33
117.	Steve Lyons	BOS	1.32
118.	Lonnie Smith	KC	1.30
119.	Tim Hulett	CHI	1.27
120.	Paul Molitor	MIL	1.26
121.	Bob Boone	CAL	1.23
122.	Lee Lacy	BAL	1.23
123.	Jim Sundberg	KC	1.19
124.	Jackie Gutierrez	BOS	1.12
125.	Bryan Little	CHI	1.10
126.	Rudy Law	CHI	1.10
127.	Dave Collins	OAK	1.03
128.	Rob Wilfong	CAL	1.02
129.	Brett Butler	CLE	1.01
130.	Glenn Hoffman	BOS	1.00
131.	Donnie Hill	OAK	0.98
132.	Onix Concepcion	KC	0.96
133.	Willie Randolph	NY	0.95
134.	Tom Brookens	DET	0.93
135.	Juan Beniquez	CAL	0.84
136.	George Wright	TEX	0.83
137.	Pat Tabler	CLE	0.80
138.	Willie Wilson	KC	0.68
139.	Mickey Hatcher	MIN	0.64
140.	Greg Gagne	MIN	0.60
141.	Rod Carew	CAL	0.59
142.	Jack Perconte	SEA	0.57
143.	Rick Manning	MIL	0.55
144.	Tony Fernandez	TOR	0.54
145.	Julio Franco	CLE	0.45
146.	Wayne Tolleson	TEX	0.42
147.	Mike Hargrove	CLE	0.38
148.	Bobby Meacham	NY	0.34
149.	Gary Pettis	CAL	0.33
150.	Ozzie Guillen	CHI	0.25
151.	Alfredo Griffin	OAK	0.23
152.	Rich Dauer	BAL	0.00
152.	Scott Fletcher	CHI	0.00
152.	Charlie Moore	MIL	0.00
152.	Kirby Puckett	MIN	0.00
152.	Ed Romero	MIL	0.00
152.	Alan Wiggins	BAL	0.00
152.	Curtis Wilkerson	TEX	0.00

National League

#	Player	Team	Pct
1.	Darryl Strawberry	NY	7.59
2.	Mike Schmidt	PHI	6.85
3.	Pedro Guerrero	LA	6.82
4.	Dale Murphy	ATL	6.24
5.	Dave Parker	CIN	6.22
6.	Greg Brock	LA	5.65
6.	Gary Carter	NY	5.65
8.	Mike Marshall	LA	5.54
9.	Bob Horner	ATL	5.28
10.	Nick Esasky	CIN	5.15
11.	Ozzie Virgil	PHI	4.93
12.	Alan Ashby	HOU	4.88
13.	Ryne Sandberg	CHI	4.60
14.	George Foster	NY	4.55
15.	Darrell Porter	STL	4.46
16.	Jack Clark	STL	4.29
17.	Tim Wallach	MTL	4.24
18.	Claudell Washington	ATL	4.18
19.	Gary Matthews	CHI	4.17
20.	Mitch Webster	MTL	4.10
21.	Leon Durham	CHI	4.10
22.	Thad Bosley	CHI	4.00
23.	Bob Brenly	SF	3.99
24.	Ron Cey	CHI	3.97
25.	Glenn Davis	HOU	3.88
26.	Carmelo Martinez	SD	3.74
27.	Andre Dawson	MTL	3.59
28.	Alan Knicely	PHI	3.54
29.	Andy Van Slyke	STL	3.51
30.	Chris Brown	SF	3.42
31.	Gary Redus	CIN	3.39
32.	Dave Lopes	CHI	3.28
33.	Jody Davis	CHI	3.27
34.	Jason Thompson	PIT	3.23
35.	Graig Nettles	SD	3.21
36.	Chili Davis	SF	3.19
37.	Danny Heep	NY	3.15
38.	Kevin McReynolds	SD	3.07
39.	Juan Samuel	PHI	3.00
40.	Mark Bailey	HOU	2.88
41.	Buddy Bell	CIN	2.86
42.	Bo Diaz	CIN	2.82
43.	Terry Harper	ATL	2.81
44.	Mike Brown	PIT	2.74
45.	Jeff Leonard	SF	2.73
46.	Ron Roenicke	SF	2.61
47.	Jerry Mumphrey	HOU	2.57
48.	Howard Johnson	NY	2.56
49.	Mike Fitzgerald	MTL	2.53
50.	Bill Doran	HOU	2.49
51.	Cesar Cedeno	STL	2.48
52.	Wayne Krenchicki	CIN	2.45
53.	Keith Moreland	CHI	2.38
54.	Ken Landreaux	LA	2.36
55.	Denny Walling	HOU	2.33
56.	Bill Madlock	LA	2.25
57.	Chris Chambliss	ATL	2.24
58.	Jim Morrison	PIT	2.22
59.	Von Hayes	PHI	2.18
60.	David Green	SF	2.16
61.	Hubie Brooks	MTL	2.15
62.	Keith Hernandez	NY	2.10
63.	Phil Garner	HOU	2.06
64.	Tony Pena	PIT	2.03
65.	Dan Driessen	SF	2.01
66.	Joel Youngblood	SF	1.97
67.	Kevin Bass	HOU	1.88
68.	Glenn Wilson	PHI	1.83
69.	Terry Kennedy	SD	1.82
70.	Steve Garvey	SD	1.80
71.	Mike Scioscia	LA	1.75
72.	Dan Gladden	SF	1.69
73.	Vance Law	MTL	1.67
74.	Billy Hatcher	CHI	1.63
75.	Terry Puhl	HOU	1.59
76.	Shawon Dunston	CHI	1.46
77.	Tom Foley	PHI	1.43
78.	Johnny Ray	PIT	1.42
79.	Glenn Hubbard	ATL	1.36
80.	Garry Templeton	SD	1.36
81.	Rafael Ramirez	ATL	1.33
82.	R.J. Reynolds	PIT	1.33
83.	Jeff Stone	PHI	1.30
84.	Tom Herr	STL	1.30
85.	Dave Anderson	LA	1.30
86.	George Hendrick	PIT	1.27
87.	Tim Raines	MTL	1.26
88.	Jose Cruz	HOU	1.23
89.	Craig Reynolds	HOU	1.23
90.	Mookie Wilson	NY	1.06
91.	Rick Schu	PHI	1.06
92.	Rick Cerone	ATL	1.05
93.	Gerald Perry	ATL	1.02
94.	Ken Oberkfell	ATL	1.01
95.	Steve Kemp	PIT	0.96
96.	Tony Gwynn	SD	0.96
97.	Doug Frobel	MTL	0.88
98.	Sammy Khalifa	PIT	0.86
99.	Brad Komminsk	ATL	0.85
100.	Terry Francona	MTL	0.78
101.	Terry Pendleton	STL	0.77
102.	Herm Winningham	MTL	0.75
103.	Willie McGee	STL	0.75
104.	Dave Concepcion	CIN	0.74
105.	Eddie Milner	CIN	0.74
106.	Chris Speier	CHI	0.66
107.	Enos Cabell	LA	0.65
108.	Manny Trillo	SF	0.63
109.	Jose Uribe	SF	0.57
110.	Pete Rose	CIN	0.56
111.	Len Dykstra	NY	0.56
112.	Mariano Duncan	LA	0.53
113.	Marvell Wynne	PIT	0.44
114.	Rafael Santana	NY	0.30
115.	Tim Flannery	SD	0.29
116.	Bob Dernier	CHI	0.28
117.	Ron Oester	CIN	0.26
118.	Wally Backman	NY	0.26
119.	Vince Coleman	STL	0.24
120.	Bruce Benedict	ATL	0.00
120.	Larry Bowa	NY	0.00
120.	Tim Corcoran	PHI	0.00
120.	Greg Gross	PHI	0.00
120.	Steve Jeltz	PHI	0.00
120.	Mike Jorgensen	STL	0.00
120.	Tom Nieto	STL	0.00
120.	Joe Orsulak	PIT	0.00
120.	Steve Sax	LA	0.00
120.	Ozzie Smith	STL	0.00
120.	Milt Thompson	ATL	0.00
120.	Scot Thompson	MTL	0.00
120.	Max Venable	CIN	0.00
120.	Brad Wellman	SF	0.00
120.	Paul Zuvella	ATL	0.00

Batting Average, Day Games

American League

#	Player	Team	Avg	#	Player	Team	Avg	#	Player	Team	Avg	#	Player	Team	Avg
1.	Juan Beniquez	CAL	.368	41.	Lonnie Smith	KC	.295	81.	Bob Boone	CAL	.264	121.	John Wathan	KC	.232
2.	Wade Boggs	BOS	.360	42.	Dave Kingman	OAK	.293	82.	Alan Trammell	DET	.263	122.	Mike Young	BAL	.231
3.	Don Mattingly	NY	.346	43.	Fred Lynn	BAL	.292	83.	Cal Ripken	BAL	.263	123.	Larry Sheets	BAL	.231
4.	Jim Rice	BOS	.342	44.	Marty Barrett	BOS	.292	84.	Steve Henderson	OAK	.263	123.	Nelson Simmons	DET	.231
5.	Ron Hassey	NY	.341	45.	Chet Lemon	DET	.291	85.	Tony Bernazard	CLE	.262	125.	Gary Ward	TEX	.230
6.	Darrell Evans	DET	.338	46.	Mickey Tettleton	OAK	.289	86.	Willie Randolph	NY	.260	126.	Buddy Bell	TEX	.228
7.	Ken Griffey	NY	.335	47.	Kirby Puckett	MIN	.289	87.	Steve Balboni	KC	.260	127.	Roy Smalley	MIN	.228
8.	Mickey Hatcher	MIN	.333	48.	Ruppert Jones	CAL	.288	88.	Scott Fletcher	CHI	.259	128.	Carlton Fisk	CHI	.224
9.	Floyd Rayford	BAL	.330	49.	Damaso Garcia	TOR	.288	89.	Johnny Grubb	DET	.259	129.	Gary Roenicke	BAL	.224
10.	Carney Lansford	OAK	.327	50.	Eddie Murray	BAL	.288	90.	Brook Jacoby	CLE	.258	130.	Dave Henderson	SEA	.223
11.	Rickey Henderson	NY	.326	51.	Barbaro Garbey	DET	.288	90.	Mike Stenhouse	MIN	.258	131.	Greg Walker	CHI	.222
11.	Tim Hulett	CHI	.326	52.	Jesse Barfield	TOR	.287	92.	Daryl Boston	CHI	.258	132.	Andre Thornton	CLE	.221
13.	Ben Oglivie	MIL	.325	53.	Steve Lyons	BOS	.285	93.	John Shelby	BAL	.258	133.	Bobby Meacham	NY	.220
14.	Mike Hargrove	CLE	.324	54.	Dwayne Murphy	OAK	.284	94.	Jim Gantner	MIL	.255	134.	Dave Collins	OAK	.219
15.	Donnie Hill	OAK	.322	55.	George Brett	KC	.284	95.	Lloyd Moseby	TOR	.254	135.	Dick Schofield	CAL	.218
16.	Jerry Willard	CLE	.321	56.	George Bell	TOR	.284	96.	Pat Sheridan	KC	.253	136.	Bobby Grich	CAL	.218
17.	Phil Bradley	SEA	.319	56.	Ozzie Guillen	CHI	.284	97.	Rick Dempsey	BAL	.253	137.	Alan Wiggins	BAL	.217
18.	Rudy Law	CHI	.316	58.	Tim Teufel	MIN	.283	98.	Dwight Evans	BOS	.252	138.	Jim Sundberg	KC	.215
19.	Spike Owen	SEA	.316	59.	Earnest Riles	MIL	.283	99.	Frank White	KC	.252	139.	George Wright	TEX	.215
20.	Rance Mulliniks	TOR	.315	59.	Lou Whitaker	DET	.283	100.	Mike Heath	OAK	.252	140.	Jim Dwyer	BAL	.214
20.	Jim Presley	SEA	.315	61.	Rich Gedman	BOS	.282	101.	Tom Brookens	DET	.250	141.	Jackie Gutierrez	BOS	.210
22.	Pat Tabler	CLE	.313	62.	Tony Fernandez	TOR	.282	101.	Cecil Cooper	MIL	.250	142.	Larry Herndon	DET	.208
23.	Harold Baines	CHI	.312	63.	Wayne Tolleson	TEX	.281	101.	Doug DeCinces	CAL	.250	143.	Ed Romero	MIL	.208
24.	Al Cowens	SEA	.312	64.	Willie Wilson	KC	.280	101.	Mike Easler	BOS	.250	144.	Pete O'Brien	TEX	.206
25.	Don Slaught	TEX	.308	65.	Dave Winfield	NY	.280	101.	Garth Iorg	TOR	.250	145.	Oddibe McDowell	TEX	.203
26.	Bruce Bochte	OAK	.306	66.	Larry Parrish	TEX	.278	106.	Bob Kearney	SEA	.250	146.	Bill Schroeder	MIL	.200
27.	Julio Franco	CLE	.306	67.	Mike Davis	OAK	.277	107.	Kirk Gibson	DET	.249	146.	Gorman Thomas	SEA	.200
28.	Bill Buckner	BOS	.305	68.	Jeff Burroughs	TOR	.274	108.	Lance Parrish	DET	.249	146.	Butch Wynegar	NY	.200
29.	Tony Armas	BOS	.304	69.	Brian Downing	CAL	.274	109.	Reggie Jackson	CAL	.248	149.	Alejandro Sanchez	DET	.194
29.	Randy Bush	MIN	.304	70.	Cliff Johnson	TOR	.274	110.	Willie Upshaw	TOR	.247	150.	Domingo Ramos	SEA	.185
31.	Mark Salas	MIN	.304	71.	Ted Simmons	MIL	.272	111.	Gary Gaetti	MIN	.247	151.	Darryl Motley	KC	.184
32.	Curtis Wilkerson	TEX	.303	72.	Glenn Hoffman	BOS	.272	112.	Ernie Whitt	TOR	.245	152.	Greg Gagne	MIN	.183
33.	Rod Carew	CAL	.302	73.	Toby Harrah	TEX	.271	113.	Don Baylor	NY	.243	153.	Julio Cruz	CHI	.179
34.	Brett Butler	CLE	.301	74.	Jack Perconte	SEA	.270	114.	Luis Salazar	CHI	.239	154.	Otis Nixon	CLE	.179
35.	Alvin Davis	SEA	.298	75.	Lee Lacy	BAL	.268	115.	Tom Brunansky	MIN	.237	155.	Onix Concepcion	KC	.173
36.	Paul Molitor	MIL	.298	76.	Kent Hrbek	MIN	.268	116.	George Vukovich	CLE	.237	156.	Ron Kittle	CHI	.173
37.	Alfredo Griffin	OAK	.298	77.	Dusty Baker	OAK	.268	117.	Robin Yount	MIL	.236	157.	Rich Dauer	BAL	.169
38.	Paul Householder	MIL	.298	78.	Jorge Orta	KC	.267	118.	Charlie Moore	MIL	.235	158.	Rob Wilfong	CAL	.133
39.	Gary Pettis	CAL	.297	79.	Ivan Calderon	SEA	.267	118.	Mike Pagliarulo	NY	.235	159.	Len Matuszek	TOR	.125
40.	Wayne Gross	BAL	.297	79.	Joe Carter	CLE	.267	120.	Hal McRae	KC	.235	160.	Chris Bando	CLE	.092

National League

#	Player	Team	Avg	#	Player	Team	Avg	#	Player	Team	Avg	#	Player	Team	Avg
1.	Mitch Webster	MTL	.368	35.	Shawon Dunston	CHI	.286	69.	Dan Gladden	SF	.263	103.	Jeff Leonard	SF	.235
2.	Tim Raines	MTL	.365	35.	Keith Hernandez	NY	.286	70.	Ozzie Virgil	PHI	.261	104.	Terry Harper	ATL	.235
3.	Greg Gross	PHI	.349	37.	Eddie Milner	CIN	.285	71.	Ron Cey	CHI	.260	105.	Sal Butera	MTL	.234
4.	Dave Parker	CIN	.349	38.	Ken Landreaux	LA	.284	72.	Jack Clark	STL	.260	106.	Brad Wellman	SF	.231
5.	Willie McGee	STL	.348	39.	Pete Rose	CIN	.284	73.	Greg Brock	LA	.260	107.	Herm Winningham	MTL	.229
6.	Mike Brown	PIT	.338	40.	Glenn Wilson	PHI	.282	74.	Chili Davis	SF	.258	108.	Vince Coleman	STL	.228
7.	Claudell Washington	ATL	.336	41.	Brad Komminsk	ATL	.281	75.	Kevin Bass	HOU	.258	109.	Steve Kemp	PIT	.227
8.	Andre Dawson	MTL	.332	42.	Tony Gwynn	SD	.281	75.	Alan Knicely	PHI	.258	110.	Manny Trillo	SF	.227
9.	Thad Bosley	CHI	.328	43.	Dave Lopes	CHI	.281	77.	Billy Hatcher	CHI	.258	111.	Tom Nieto	STL	.225
10.	Tom Herr	STL	.326	43.	Jim Morrison	PIT	.281	78.	Gary Redus	CIN	.258	112.	Dave Anderson	LA	.224
11.	Jeff Stone	PHI	.325	45.	Bill Madlock	LA	.280	79.	Johnny Ray	PIT	.256	112.	Candy Maldonado	LA	.224
12.	Wayne Krenchicki	CIN	.324	46.	Hubie Brooks	MTL	.280	80.	Bob Dernier	CHI	.256	114.	Alex Trevino	SF	.223
13.	Mark Bailey	HOU	.321	47.	Rafael Ramirez	ATL	.280	81.	Bill Russell	LA	.253	115.	Tony Pena	PIT	.222
14.	Keith Moreland	CHI	.312	48.	Mariano Duncan	LA	.280	82.	Terry Kennedy	SD	.253	116.	Chris Speier	CHI	.221
15.	Tony Perez	CIN	.311	49.	Joel Youngblood	SF	.279	83.	Jerry Mumphrey	HOU	.252	117.	Richie Hebner	CHI	.220
15.	Darryl Strawberry	NY	.311	50.	Glenn Davis	HOU	.278	84.	Dave Concepcion	CIN	.250	118.	John Russell	PHI	.219
17.	Jerry Royster	SD	.310	51.	Pedro Guerrero	LA	.277	84.	U.L. Washington	MTL	.250	119.	Nick Esasky	CIN	.218
18.	Bill Doran	HOU	.308	52.	Graig Nettles	SD	.277	86.	Gary Matthews	CHI	.249	120.	Bob Brenly	SF	.213
19.	Dale Murphy	ATL	.308	53.	Terry Pendleton	STL	.277	87.	Bill Almon	PIT	.247	121.	Sammy Khalifa	PIT	.213
20.	Joe Orsulak	PIT	.306	54.	Tim Flannery	SD	.276	87.	Vance Law	MTL	.247	122.	Gerald Perry	ATL	.211
21.	Garry Templeton	SD	.304	55.	Larry Bowa	NY	.275	89.	Mike Fitzgerald	MTL	.247	123.	David Green	SF	.210
22.	Mike Scioscia	LA	.303	56.	Jason Thompson	PIT	.273	90.	Len Dykstra	NY	.247	124.	Carmelo Martinez	SD	.207
23.	Bob Horner	ATL	.302	57.	Garry Maddox	PHI	.273	91.	Von Hayes	PHI	.246	125.	Rafael Santana	NY	.204
24.	Ryne Sandberg	CHI	.301	58.	Mookie Wilson	NY	.270	92.	Ron Oester	CIN	.246	126.	Bruce Benedict	ATL	.204
25.	Jose Cruz	HOU	.299	59.	Gary Carter	NY	.270	93.	Chris Brown	SF	.243	127.	Tom Foley	PHI	.202
26.	Juan Samuel	PHI	.299	60.	Dickie Thon	HOU	.269	94.	Jody Davis	CHI	.242	128.	Ron Roenicke	SF	.194
27.	Enos Cabell	LA	.297	61.	Dan Driessen	SF	.269	95.	Steve Garvey	SD	.241	129.	Ray Knight	NY	.191
28.	Terry Francona	MTL	.296	62.	Tim Wallach	MTL	.268	96.	Mike Marshall	LA	.240	130.	Ken Oberkfell	ATL	.189
29.	Mike Schmidt	PHI	.292	63.	George Foster	NY	.267	97.	Howard Johnson	NY	.239	131.	Darrell Porter	STL	.185
30.	Phil Garner	HOU	.291	63.	Ozzie Smith	STL	.267	98.	Jose Uribe	SF	.238	132.	Glenn Hubbard	ATL	.175
31.	Steve Sax	LA	.291	65.	Cesar Cedeno	STL	.266	99.	Rick Schu	PHI	.238	133.	Rob Deer	SF	.174
32.	Danny Heep	NY	.289	66.	Wally Backman	NY	.265	100.	Andy Van Slyke	STL	.238	134.	Buddy Bell	CIN	.162
33.	Paul Zuvella	ATL	.288	67.	Tim Corcoran	PHI	.265	101.	Kevin McReynolds	SD	.237	135.	Steve Lake	CHI	.158
34.	Leon Durham	CHI	.287	68.	Gary Woods	CHI	.263	102.	R.J. Reynolds	PIT	.236	136.	Marvell Wynne	PIT	.149

Batting Average, Night Games

American League

#	Player	Team	AVG	#	Player	Team	AVG	#	Player	Team	AVG	#	Player	Team	AVG
1.	Wade Boggs	BOS	.371	41.	Tony Bernazard	CLE	.280	81.	Bryan Little	CHI	.255	121.	Doug DeCinces	CAL	.241
2.	George Brett	KC	.354	42.	Juan Beniquez	CAL	.279	82.	Alan Trammell	DET	.255	122.	Bob Boone	CAL	.241
3.	Garth Iorg	TOR	.348	43.	Julio Franco	CLE	.279	83.	Rick Dempsey	BAL	.255	123.	Bob Kearney	SEA	.241
4.	Wayne Tolleson	TEX	.320	44.	Damaso Garcia	TOR	.278	83.	Cliff Johnson	TOR	.255	124.	Buddy Bell	TEX	.240
5.	Brett Butler	CLE	.317	45.	Glenn Hoffman	BOS	.278	85.	Scott Fletcher	CHI	.255	125.	Rudy Law	CHI	.240
6.	Cecil Cooper	MIL	.313	46.	Lou Whitaker	DET	.278	86.	Steve Lyons	BOS	.254	126.	Gary Pettis	CAL	.239
7.	Don Mattingly	NY	.311	47.	Willie Wilson	KC	.277	87.	Jim Gantner	MIL	.254	127.	Paul Householder	MIL	.239
8.	Rickey Henderson	NY	.309	48.	Ron Hassey	NY	.275	88.	Reggie Jackson	CAL	.254	128.	Larry Parrish	TEX	.238
9.	Harold Baines	CHI	.308	49.	Larry Sheets	BAL	.274	89.	Alfredo Griffin	OAK	.254	129.	Steve Balboni	KC	.238
10.	Kirk Gibson	DET	.306	50.	Ted Simmons	MIL	.273	90.	Fred Lynn	BAL	.254	130.	Rick Manning	MIL	.238
11.	Gary Ward	TEX	.304	51.	Greg Walker	CHI	.272	91.	Tim Hulett	CHI	.252	131.	Butch Wynegar	NY	.237
12.	Alan Wiggins	BAL	.303	52.	Dave Winfield	NY	.272	92.	Marty Barrett	BOS	.252	132.	Darryl Motley	KC	.235
13.	Rich Gedman	BOS	.302	53.	Don Slaught	TEX	.272	93.	Jim Sundberg	KC	.252	133.	Ken Griffey	NY	.234
14.	Lee Lacy	BAL	.301	54.	Roy Smalley	MIN	.272	94.	Ron Kittle	CHI	.251	134.	Carmen Castillo	CLE	.234
15.	Eddie Murray	BAL	.300	55.	Ben Oglivie	MIL	.271	95.	Tim Teufel	MIN	.251	135.	Tom Brookens	DET	.231
16.	Floyd Rayford	BAL	.299	56.	George Bell	TOR	.271	96.	Chet Lemon	DET	.251	136.	Charlie Moore	MIL	.231
17.	Robin Yount	MIL	.298	57.	Rod Carew	CAL	.271	97.	Al Cowens	SEA	.251	137.	Mickey Tettleton	OAK	.227
18.	Mark Salas	MIN	.298	58.	Dave Collins	OAK	.270	98.	Bobby Grich	CAL	.251	138.	Curtis Wilkerson	TEX	.225
19.	Paul Molitor	MIL	.296	59.	Ed Romero	MIL	.270	99.	Mike Heath	OAK	.249	139.	Rob Wilfong	CAL	.224
20.	Bill Buckner	BOS	.296	60.	Toby Harrah	TEX	.270	100.	George Vukovich	CLE	.249	140.	Don Baylor	NY	.223
21.	John Shelby	BAL	.295	61.	Ozzie Guillen	CHI	.269	101.	Luis Salazar	CHI	.248	141.	Jackie Gutierrez	BOS	.222
22.	Phil Bradley	SEA	.294	62.	Dusty Baker	OAK	.269	102.	Frank White	KC	.248	142.	Dick Schofield	CAL	.220
23.	Ivan Calderon	SEA	.293	63.	Mike Easler	BOS	.268	103.	Gary Gaetti	MIN	.246	143.	Gorman Thomas	SEA	.219
24.	Tony Fernandez	TOR	.293	64.	Hal McRae	KC	.268	104.	Jeff Burroughs	TOR	.246	144.	Bobby Meacham	NY	.217
25.	Mike Davis	OAK	.292	65.	Dwight Evans	BOS	.268	105.	Dave Henderson	SEA	.246	145.	Daryl Boston	CHI	.217
26.	Randy Ready	MIL	.291	66.	Jorge Orta	KC	.266	105.	Oddibe McDowell	TEX	.246	146.	Rich Dauer	BAL	.217
27.	Mike Young	BAL	.291	67.	Jim Rice	BOS	.265	107.	Ernie Whitt	TOR	.245	147.	Gary Roenicke	BAL	.215
28.	Willie Upshaw	TOR	.291	68.	Donnie Hill	OAK	.264	108.	Lonnie Smith	KC	.245	148.	Pat Sheridan	KC	.214
29.	Jesse Barfield	TOR	.291	69.	Jim Presley	SEA	.264	109.	Tom Brunansky	MIN	.243	149.	Onix Concepcion	KC	.213
30.	Cal Ripken	BAL	.289	70.	Jack Perconte	SEA	.262	110.	Tony Armas	BOS	.243	150.	Randy Bush	MIN	.212
31.	Bruce Bochte	OAK	.288	71.	Larry Herndon	DET	.262	111.	Nelson Simmons	DET	.243	151.	Wayne Gross	BAL	.209
32.	Kirby Puckett	MIN	.288	72.	Bill Schroeder	MIL	.261	112.	Spike Owen	SEA	.243	152.	Darrell Evans	DET	.207
33.	Earnest Riles	MIL	.287	73.	Lloyd Moseby	TOR	.261	113.	Andre Thornton	CLE	.242	153.	Dave Kingman	OAK	.205
34.	Lance Parrish	DET	.286	74.	Mickey Hatcher	MIN	.261	114.	Jerry Willard	CLE	.242	154.	Steve Buechele	TEX	.205
35.	Pete O'Brien	TEX	.285	75.	Mike Hargrove	CLE	.260	115.	Barbaro Garbey	DET	.242	155.	Julio Cruz	CHI	.205
36.	Alvin Davis	SEA	.284	76.	Jim Dwyer	BAL	.260	116.	Mike Pagliarulo	NY	.242	156.	Ruppert Jones	CAL	.205
37.	Willie Randolph	NY	.284	77.	Joe Carter	CLE	.259	117.	Greg Gagne	MIN	.242	157.	Dwayne Murphy	OAK	.202
38.	Rance Mulliniks	TOR	.284	78.	Brian Downing	CAL	.259	118.	Carlton Fisk	CHI	.242	158.	George Wright	TEX	.181
39.	Brook Jacoby	CLE	.283	79.	Pat Tabler	CLE	.256	119.	Carney Lansford	OAK	.242				
40.	Kent Hrbek	MIN	.283	80.	Tim Laudner	MIN	.256	120.	Donnie Scott	SEA	.241				

National League

#	Player	Team	AVG	#	Player	Team	AVG	#	Player	Team	AVG	#	Player	Team	AVG
1.	Willie McGee	STL	.356	35.	Tim Flannery	SD	.284	69.	Len Dykstra	NY	.259	103.	Marvell Wynne	PIT	.236
2.	Pedro Guerrero	LA	.340	36.	Johnny Ray	PIT	.283	69.	Rick Schu	PHI	.259	104.	Rafael Ramirez	ATL	.234
3.	Tony Perez	CIN	.339	37.	Bill Doran	HOU	.282	71.	Jim Pankovits	HOU	.258	105.	Paul Zuvella	ATL	.234
4.	Tony Gwynn	SD	.335	38.	Ozzie Smith	STL	.281	72.	Glenn Hubbard	ATL	.258	106.	Alan Knicely	PHI	.233
5.	Mike Brown	PIT	.329	39.	Mookie Wilson	NY	.280	73.	Darryl Strawberry	NY	.257	107.	Kevin McReynolds	SD	.232
6.	Keith Hernandez	NY	.322	40.	Terry Harper	ATL	.279	74.	George Hendrick	PIT	.255	108.	Ray Knight	NY	.232
7.	Ron Oester	CIN	.318	41.	Wally Backman	NY	.278	75.	Pete Rose	CIN	.255	109.	Bob Brenly	SF	.230
8.	Mike Marshall	LA	.316	42.	Vance Law	MTL	.277	76.	Tim Wallach	MTL	.254	110.	Mariano Duncan	LA	.229
9.	Ryne Sandberg	CHI	.313	43.	Andy Van Slyke	STL	.276	77.	Bo Diaz	CIN	.254	111.	Mitch Webster	MTL	.229
10.	Ken Oberkfell	ATL	.309	44.	Leon Durham	CHI	.275	78.	Graig Nettles	SD	.253	112.	Candy Maldonado	LA	.227
11.	R.J. Reynolds	PIT	.308	45.	Carmelo Martinez	SD	.274	79.	Bob Horner	ATL	.253	113.	Tom Nieto	STL	.225
12.	Chris Brown	SF	.307	46.	Danny Heep	NY	.274	80.	Dave Concepcion	CIN	.253	114.	Jason Thompson	PIT	.224
13.	Cesar Cedeno	STL	.305	47.	Steve Sax	LA	.274	81.	Claudell Washington	ATL	.253	115.	Dan Driessen	SF	.224
14.	Steve Garvey	SD	.303	48.	Garry Templeton	SD	.273	82.	Terry Francona	MTL	.251	116.	Garry Maddox	PHI	.224
15.	Milt Thompson	ATL	.302	49.	Kevin Bass	HOU	.272	83.	Bob Dernier	CHI	.250	117.	Manny Trillo	SF	.221
16.	Jose Cruz	HOU	.300	50.	Bill Madlock	LA	.272	83.	Sammy Khalifa	PIT	.250	118.	Dan Gladden	SF	.219
17.	David Green	SF	.299	51.	Glenn Wilson	PHI	.271	85.	Darrell Porter	STL	.250	119.	John Russell	PHI	.217
18.	Dale Murphy	ATL	.297	52.	Von Hayes	PHI	.271	86.	Terry Puhl	HOU	.248	120.	Gerald Perry	ATL	.216
19.	Joe Orsulak	PIT	.297	53.	Mike Schmidt	PHI	.270	87.	Gary Redus	CIN	.248	121.	Terry Pendleton	STL	.215
20.	Keith Moreland	CHI	.296	54.	Glenn Davis	HOU	.269	88.	U.L. Washington	MTL	.248	122.	Gary Matthews	CHI	.215
21.	Jack Clark	STL	.295	55.	Denny Walling	HOU	.269	89.	Jeff Leonard	SF	.248	123.	Jody Davis	CHI	.214
22.	Mike Scioscia	LA	.293	56.	Tom Foley	PHI	.267	90.	Greg Brock	LA	.248	124.	Rick Cerone	ATL	.212
23.	Dave Parker	CIN	.293	57.	Steve Kemp	PIT	.266	91.	Juan Samuel	PHI	.247	125.	Greg Gross	PHI	.208
24.	Luis Aguayo	PHI	.292	58.	Terry Kennedy	SD	.266	92.	Mark Bailey	HOU	.247	126.	Andre Dawson	MTL	.207
25.	Tim Raines	MTL	.292	59.	Jerry Royster	SD	.265	93.	Dickie Thon	HOU	.245	127.	Brad Komminsk	ATL	.201
26.	Vince Coleman	STL	.291	60.	Hubie Brooks	MTL	.263	94.	Herm Winningham	MTL	.244	128.	Bruce Benedict	ATL	.200
27.	Gary Carter	NY	.287	61.	George Foster	NY	.262	95.	Howard Johnson	NY	.243	129.	Mike Fitzgerald	MTL	.188
28.	Alan Ashby	HOU	.287	61.	Craig Reynolds	HOU	.262	96.	Jeff Stone	PHI	.241	130.	Steve Jeltz	PHI	.186
29.	Tom Herr	STL	.287	63.	Tony Pena	PIT	.261	97.	Buddy Bell	CIN	.240	131.	Ron Cey	CHI	.185
30.	Bill Almon	PIT	.286	64.	Ken Landreaux	LA	.261	98.	Ozzie Virgil	PHI	.240	132.	Tim Corcoran	PHI	.184
30.	Nick Esasky	CIN	.286	65.	Enos Cabell	LA	.261	99.	Eddie Milner	CIN	.239	133.	Dave Anderson	LA	.184
32.	Chili Davis	SF	.285	66.	Phil Garner	HOU	.261	100.	Jim Morrison	PIT	.239	134.	Chris Chambliss	ATL	.165
33.	Rafael Santana	NY	.284	67.	Tito Landrum	STL	.260	101.	Wayne Krenchicki	CIN	.238				
34.	Jerry Mumphrey	HOU	.284	68.	Joel Youngblood	SF	.259	102.	Jose Uribe	SF	.236				

Batting Average, Grass Surfaces

American League

#	Player	Team	Avg	#	Player	Team	Avg	#	Player	Team	Avg	#	Player	Team	Avg
1	Wade Boggs	BOS	.363	41	Robin Yount	MIL	.285	81	Al Cowens	SEA	.262	121	Onix Concepcion	KC	.240
2	Don Mattingly	NY	.328	42	Glenn Hoffman	BOS	.284	82	Lou Whitaker	DET	.262	122	Tim Teufel	MIN	.239
3	Wayne Tolleson	TEX	.324	43	Tony Phillips	OAK	.284	83	Ed Romero	MIL	.262	123	Larry Parrish	TEX	.239
4	Juan Beniquez	CAL	.322	44	Gary Ward	TEX	.284	84	Chet Lemon	DET	.261	124	Mickey Hatcher	MIN	.237
5	Ron Hassey	NY	.320	45	Ken Griffey	NY	.283	85	Tim Hulett	CHI	.260	125	Mike Pagliarulo	NY	.237
6	Phil Bradley	SEA	.320	46	Jesse Barfield	TOR	.282	86	Frank White	KC	.260	126	Oddibe McDowell	TEX	.237
7	Harold Baines	CHI	.319	47	Dave Winfield	NY	.282	87	Mike Easler	BOS	.259	127	Jackie Gutierrez	BOS	.237
8	Rickey Henderson	NY	.316	48	Alvin Davis	SEA	.280	88	Rick Dempsey	BAL	.257	128	Charlie Moore	MIL	.237
9	Kirk Gibson	DET	.312	49	Ted Simmons	MIL	.279	89	Jerry Hairston	CHI	.256	129	Lloyd Moseby	TOR	.236
10	Billy Sample	NY	.311	50	Carney Lansford	OAK	.278	90	Brook Jacoby	CLE	.256	130	Dave Kingman	OAK	.235
11	Bruce Bochte	OAK	.309	51	Marty Barrett	BOS	.278	91	Greg Walker	CHI	.255	131	Scott Fletcher	CHI	.234
12	Rich Gedman	BOS	.308	52	Pete O'Brien	TEX	.275	92	Mickey Tettleton	OAK	.255	132	Jim Sundberg	KC	.234
13	George Brett	KC	.306	53	John Shelby	BAL	.275	93	Curtis Wilkerson	TEX	.255	133	Gary Roenicke	BAL	.233
14	Julio Franco	CLE	.306	54	Rod Carew	CAL	.275	94	Mike Heath	OAK	.255	134	Carmen Castillo	CLE	.232
15	Paul Molitor	MIL	.306	55	Ernie Whitt	TOR	.274	95	Larry Sheets	BAL	.254	135	Jim Dwyer	BAL	.231
16	Brett Butler	CLE	.306	56	Alfredo Griffin	OAK	.274	96	Doug DeCinces	CAL	.254	136	Andre Thornton	CLE	.230
17	Jack Perconte	SEA	.306	57	Randy Ready	MIL	.272	97	Bob Boone	CAL	.253	137	Dwayne Murphy	OAK	.229
18	Floyd Rayford	BAL	.305	58	Mike Brown	CAL	.272	98	Gary Pettis	CAL	.252	138	Ron Kittle	CHI	.228
19	George Bell	TOR	.305	59	Jerry Willard	CLE	.272	99	Johnny Grubb	DET	.252	139	Carlton Fisk	CHI	.225
20	Jim Rice	BOS	.304	60	Tony Fernandez	TOR	.271	100	Steve Balboni	KC	.251	140	Don Baylor	NY	.225
21	Mike Hargrove	CLE	.303	61	Kirby Puckett	MIN	.271	101	Dave Collins	OAK	.251	141	Ruppert Jones	CAL	.223
22	Bill Buckner	BOS	.302	62	Fred Lynn	BAL	.269	102	Reggie Jackson	CAL	.251	142	Darryl Motley	KC	.221
23	Reid Nichols	CHI	.299	63	Tony Armas	BOS	.269	103	Brian Downing	CAL	.251	143	Butch Wynegar	NY	.220
24	Earnest Riles	MIL	.297	64	Willie Randolph	NY	.268	104	Wayne Gross	BAL	.250	144	Daryl Boston	CHI	.217
25	Lee Lacy	BAL	.296	65	Rudy Law	CHI	.268	105	Luis Salazar	CHI	.249	145	Steve Buechele	TEX	.216
26	Cecil Cooper	MIL	.296	66	Damaso Garcia	TOR	.268	106	Paul Householder	MIL	.248	146	Bobby Meacham	NY	.214
27	Don Slaught	TEX	.295	66	Rance Mulliniks	TOR	.268	107	Jim Gantner	MIL	.247	147	Dick Schofield	CAL	.213
28	Eddie Murray	BAL	.294	68	Donnie Hill	OAK	.268	108	Gorman Thomas	SEA	.247	148	Dan Pasqua	NY	.208
29	Lonnie Smith	KC	.294	69	Steve Lyons	BOS	.267	109	Otis Nixon	CLE	.247	149	Dave Henderson	SEA	.203
30	Ben Oglivie	MIL	.293	70	Bryan Little	CHI	.267	110	George Vukovich	CLE	.247	150	Tom Brunansky	MIN	.200
31	Steve Henderson	OAK	.293	71	Dwight Evans	BOS	.267	111	Larry Herndon	DET	.245	151	Rick Manning	MIL	.199
32	Tony Bernazard	CLE	.291	72	Joe Carter	CLE	.267	112	Darrell Evans	DET	.245	152	Rich Dauer	BAL	.198
33	Willie Wilson	KC	.289	73	Toby Harrah	TEX	.266	113	Gary Gaetti	MIN	.244	153	Rob Wilfong	CAL	.196
34	Pat Tabler	CLE	.288	74	Willie Upshaw	TOR	.265	114	Nelson Simmons	DET	.244	154	Oscar Gamble	CHI	.193
35	Lance Parrish	DET	.287	75	Alan Trammell	DET	.264	115	Bill Schroeder	MIL	.243	155	Julio Cruz	CHI	.188
36	Ozzie Guillen	CHI	.287	76	Jim Presley	SEA	.264	116	Bobby Grich	CAL	.242	156	George Wright	TEX	.182
37	Mike Davis	OAK	.286	77	Roy Smalley	MIN	.264	117	Tom Brookens	DET	.241	157	Jack Howell	CAL	.169
38	Cal Ripken	BAL	.286	78	Barbaro Garbey	DET	.263	118	Buddy Bell	TEX	.241	158	Chris Bando	CLE	.132
39	Alan Wiggins	BAL	.286	79	Cliff Johnson	TOR	.263	119	Hal McRae	KC	.241				
39	Mike Young	BAL	.286	80	Dusty Baker	OAK	.262	120	Kent Hrbek	MIN	.240				

National League

#	Player	Team	Avg	#	Player	Team	Avg	#	Player	Team	Avg	#	Player	Team	Avg
1	Jack Clark	STL	.392	35	Bill Russell	LA	.288	69	Jerry Royster	SD	.256	103	Rick Cerone	ATL	.230
2	Jason Thompson	PIT	.349	36	Mookie Wilson	NY	.287	70	Vance Law	MTL	.255	104	Von Hayes	PHI	.227
3	Willie McGee	STL	.345	37	Andre Dawson	MTL	.284	71	Terry Pendleton	STL	.255	105	Joe Orsulak	PIT	.226
4	Bill Doran	HOU	.328	38	Ken Landreaux	LA	.284	72	George Foster	NY	.253	106	Bruce Benedict	ATL	.225
5	Milt Thompson	ATL	.326	39	Keith Hernandez	NY	.283	73	Scot Thompson	MTL	.253	106	Ron Oester	CIN	.225
6	Craig Reynolds	HOU	.326	40	Hubie Brooks	MTL	.282	73	Herm Winningham	MTL	.253	108	Howard Johnson	NY	.223
7	Thad Bosley	CHI	.323	41	Mike Schmidt	PHI	.282	75	Eddie Milner	CIN	.250	109	Brad Komminsk	ATL	.223
8	Mike Scioscia	LA	.323	42	R.J. Reynolds	PIT	.281	75	Ron Roenicke	SF	.250	110	Candy Maldonado	LA	.222
9	Tony Gwynn	SD	.323	43	Kevin Bass	HOU	.281	77	Bob Dernier	CHI	.249	111	Gerald Perry	ATL	.220
10	Keith Moreland	CHI	.320	44	Claudell Washington	ATL	.281	78	Greg Brock	LA	.249	112	Kevin McReynolds	SD	.220
10	Denny Walling	HOU	.320	45	Chris Brown	SF	.277	79	Johnny Ray	PIT	.248	113	Manny Trillo	SF	.219
12	Ryne Sandberg	CHI	.319	46	Danny Heep	NY	.276	80	Ron Cey	CHI	.248	114	Bob Brenly	SF	.218
13	Mark Bailey	HOU	.318	47	Dwight Gooden	NY	.275	81	Alex Trevino	SF	.248	115	Chris Chambliss	ATL	.217
14	U.L. Washington	MTL	.311	48	Wally Backman	NY	.275	82	Alan Ashby	HOU	.247	116	Glenn Davis	HOU	.214
15	Leon Durham	CHI	.307	49	Joel Youngblood	SF	.274	83	Graig Nettles	SD	.244	117	Ray Knight	NY	.214
16	Dickie Thon	HOU	.307	50	Garry Templeton	SD	.273	84	Dave Concepcion	CIN	.244	118	Steve Yeager	LA	.213
17	Darryl Strawberry	NY	.306	51	Shawon Dunston	CHI	.273	85	Kurt Bevacqua	SD	.243	119	Tony Pena	PIT	.212
18	Tim Raines	MTL	.304	52	Carmelo Martinez	SD	.270	86	Len Dykstra	NY	.243	120	Paul Runge	ATL	.209
19	Pedro Guerrero	LA	.304	53	Terry Harper	ATL	.269	87	Bob Bailor	LA	.242	121	Richie Hebner	CHI	.209
20	Tom Herr	STL	.302	54	Tim Wallach	MTL	.267	88	Glenn Hubbard	ATL	.240	122	Bill Almon	PIT	.208
21	Cesar Cedeno	STL	.301	54	Glenn Wilson	PHI	.267	89	Mariano Duncan	LA	.240	123	Gary Redus	CIN	.205
22	Dave Parker	CIN	.301	56	Bob Horner	ATL	.267	90	Jeff Leonard	SF	.240	124	Dave Anderson	LA	.199
23	Mike Marshall	LA	.298	57	Larry Bowa	NY	.267	91	Jody Davis	CHI	.239	125	Rick Schu	PHI	.195
24	Nick Esasky	CIN	.297	57	Dave Lopes	CHI	.267	92	Chris Speier	CHI	.238	126	Buddy Bell	CIN	.178
25	Phil Garner	HOU	.296	59	Rafael Ramirez	ATL	.266	93	Terry Kennedy	SD	.238	127	Rob Deer	SF	.174
26	Tom Paciorek	NY	.296	60	Jose Cruz	HOU	.266	94	Rafael Santana	NY	.238	128	Sammy Khalifa	PIT	.173
27	Enos Cabell	LA	.296	61	Pete Rose	CIN	.263	95	Dan Gladden	SF	.237	129	Darrell Porter	STL	.165
28	Bill Madlock	LA	.295	62	Chili Davis	SF	.263	96	Andy Van Slyke	STL	.235	130	Ozzie Virgil	PHI	.164
29	Dale Murphy	ATL	.294	63	Ozzie Smith	STL	.262	97	Jose Uribe	SF	.235	131	John Christensen	NY	.159
30	Ken Oberkfell	ATL	.294	64	Dan Driessen	SF	.262	98	David Green	SF	.233	132	Marvell Wynne	PIT	.155
31	Gary Carter	NY	.293	65	Juan Samuel	PHI	.262	99	Jeff Stone	PHI	.232	133	Kelvin Chapman	NY	.152
32	Jerry Mumphrey	HOU	.293	66	Gary Matthews	CHI	.262	100	Brad Wellman	SF	.231	134	Tom Foley	PHI	.151
33	Steve Garvey	SD	.293	67	Vince Coleman	STL	.259	101	Paul Zuvella	ATL	.230				
34	Tim Flannery	SD	.289	68	Steve Sax	LA	.257	102	Billy Hatcher	CHI	.230				

Batting Average, Artificial Surfaces

American League

#	Player	Team	AVG	#	Player	Team	AVG	#	Player	Team	AVG	#	Player	Team	AVG
1.	Wade Boggs	BOS	.389	41.	Dave Meier	MIN	.288	81.	Dave Engle	MIN	.252	121.	Greg Gagne	MIN	.228
2.	Mark Funderburk	MIN	.378	42.	Phil Bradley	SEA	.287	81.	Jim Sundberg	KC	.252	122.	Ken Griffey	NY	.225
3.	Brook Jacoby	CLE	.374	43.	Jim Gantner	MIL	.286	83.	Dave Collins	OAK	.250	123.	Luis Salazar	CHI	.224
4.	Lou Whitaker	DET	.371	43.	Chet Lemon	DET	.286	83.	Oddibe McDowell	TEX	.250	124.	Ernie Whitt	TOR	.224
5.	Donnie Hill	OAK	.354	45.	Pat Sheridan	KC	.283	83.	Jorge Orta	KC	.250	125.	Jim Rice	BOS	.224
6.	George Brett	KC	.352	46.	Jim Presley	SEA	.283	83.	Wayne Tolleson	TEX	.250	126.	Darryl Motley	KC	.223
7.	Scott Fletcher	CHI	.351	47.	Willie Upshaw	TOR	.282	87.	Gary Gaetti	MIN	.248	127.	Ken Phelps	SEA	.221
8.	Garth Iorg	TOR	.347	48.	Bill Buckner	BOS	.282	88.	Tony Armas	BOS	.246	128.	Tom Brookens	DET	.218
9.	Brett Butler	CLE	.340	48.	Cecil Cooper	MIL	.282	89.	Steve Lyons	BOS	.245	129.	Juan Beniquez	CAL	.217
10.	Cecil Fielder	TOR	.327	50.	Spike Owen	SEA	.281	90.	Randy Ready	MIL	.244	129.	Bob Boone	CAL	.217
11.	Rance Mulliniks	TOR	.318	51.	Mike Easler	BOS	.278	91.	Harold Baines	CHI	.244	129.	Rich Gedman	BOS	.217
12.	Brian Downing	CAL	.317	52.	Gary Pettis	CAL	.277	92.	Butch Wynegar	NY	.244	132.	Barry Bonnell	SEA	.215
13.	Willie Randolph	NY	.313	53.	Andre Thornton	CLE	.275	93.	Donnie Scott	SEA	.244	133.	Charlie Moore	MIL	.214
14.	Eddie Murray	BAL	.312	54.	Greg Walker	CHI	.275	94.	Bobby Grich	CAL	.244	133.	Rudy Law	MIL	.214
15.	Tim Hulett	CHI	.311	55.	Tim Teufel	MIN	.273	95.	Lynn Jones	KC	.242	135.	Doug DeCinces	CAL	.210
16.	Larry Sheets	BAL	.311	56.	Lloyd Moseby	TOR	.273	95.	Ted Simmons	MIL	.242	136.	Buddy Bell	TEX	.209
17.	Rickey Henderson	NY	.308	57.	Hal McRae	KC	.273	97.	Frank White	KC	.241	137.	Mike Young	BAL	.208
18.	Paul Householder	MIL	.306	58.	Ruppert Jones	CAL	.271	98.	Dwight Evans	BOS	.240	138.	Rudy Law	CHI	.207
19.	Mickey Hatcher	MIN	.306	59.	Willie Wilson	KC	.271	98.	Dave Winfield	NY	.240	139.	Lance Parrish	DET	.204
20.	Mark Salas	MIN	.304	60.	Carney Lansford	OAK	.270	100.	Bobby Meacham	NY	.240	140.	Marty Barrett	BOS	.202
21.	Carlton Fisk	CHI	.302	61.	Al Cowens	SEA	.268	100.	George Wright	TEX	.240	141.	Mike Hargrove	CLE	.200
22.	Gary Ward	TEX	.302	62.	Lee Lacy	BAL	.268	102.	Jack Perconte	SEA	.239	141.	Don Slaught	TEX	.200
23.	Dusty Baker	OAK	.302	63.	Don Baylor	NY	.266	103.	Steve Balboni	KC	.239	143.	Gorman Thomas	SEA	.199
24.	Tony Fernandez	TOR	.302	64.	Tom Brunansky	MIN	.265	104.	Larry Herndon	DET	.238	144.	Domingo Ramos	SEA	.198
25.	Jeff Burroughs	TOR	.300	65.	Dave Henderson	SEA	.265	104.	Ron Kittle	CHI	.238	145.	Curtis Wilkerson	TEX	.197
26.	Rod Carew	CAL	.299	66.	Darrell Evans	DET	.263	104.	Fred Lynn	BAL	.238	146.	Buddy Biancalana	KC	.195
27.	Kent Hrbek	MIN	.299	67.	Jerry Willard	CLE	.262	107.	Bob Kearney	SEA	.237	147.	Len Matuszek	TOR	.195
28.	Kirby Puckett	MIN	.298	68.	John Wathan	KC	.262	108.	Lonnie Smith	KC	.236	148.	Julio Franco	CLE	.194
29.	Don Mattingly	NY	.298	69.	Reggie Jackson	CAL	.260	109.	Rick Dempsey	BAL	.235	149.	Tony Bernazard	CLE	.193
30.	Omar Moreno	KC	.296	70.	Cal Ripken	BAL	.258	110.	Earnest Riles	MIL	.235	150.	Greg Pryor	KC	.188
31.	Larry Parrish	TEX	.295	71.	Al Oliver	TOR	.257	111.	Joe Carter	CLE	.234	151.	Ozzie Guillen	CHI	.182
32.	Ivan Calderon	SEA	.294	72.	Paul Molitor	MIL	.257	112.	Dane Iorg	KC	.233	152.	Onix Concepcion	KC	.178
33.	Jesse Barfield	TOR	.294	73.	George Bell	TOR	.255	113.	Glenn Hoffman	BOS	.233	153.	Wayne Gross	BAL	.171
34.	Ron Washington	MIN	.293	74.	Mike Pagliarulo	NY	.255	114.	Randy Bush	MIN	.231	154.	Ron Hassey	NY	.167
35.	Toby Harrah	TEX	.292	75.	Roy Smalley	MIN	.254	114.	Mike Heath	OAK	.231	155.	Kirk Gibson	DET	.160
36.	Alvin Davis	SEA	.292	76.	Dick Schofield	CAL	.254	114.	Mike Stenhouse	MIN	.231	156.	Buck Martinez	TOR	.138
37.	Tim Laudner	MIN	.290	77.	Cliff Johnson	TOR	.253	117.	Bruce Bochte	OAK	.230	157.	Jackie Gutierrez	BOS	.137
38.	Mike Davis	OAK	.290	78.	Alfredo Griffin	OAK	.253	118.	George Vukovich	CLE	.230	158.	Harold Reynolds	SEA	.134
39.	Damaso Garcia	TOR	.290	78.	Dwayne Murphy	OAK	.253	119.	Pete O'Brien	TEX	.229				
40.	Rick Manning	MIL	.289	80.	Dave Kingman	OAK	.252	120.	Alan Trammell	DET	.229				

National League

#	Player	Team	AVG	#	Player	Team	AVG	#	Player	Team	AVG	#	Player	Team	AVG
1.	Lee Mazzilli	PIT	.365	35.	Jeff Stone	PHI	.280	69.	Dan Gladden	SF	.260	103.	Terry Pendleton	STL	.234
2.	Keith Hernandez	NY	.364	36.	Howard Johnson	NY	.280	70.	Sammy Khalifa	PIT	.259	104.	Bo Diaz	CIN	.234
3.	Pedro Guerrero	LA	.359	37.	Tito Landrum	STL	.280	71.	Bill Madlock	LA	.259	105.	Herm Winningham	MTL	.231
4.	Tony Perez	CIN	.358	38.	Mike Marshall	LA	.279	72.	Tim Wallach	MTL	.257	106.	Dan Driessen	SF	.229
5.	Willie McGee	STL	.356	39.	Glenn Wilson	PHI	.277	73.	Greg Brock	LA	.257	107.	Denny Gonzalez	PIT	.229
6.	Mike Brown	PIT	.333	40.	Von Hayes	PHI	.276	74.	George Hendrick	PIT	.257	108.	Bob Brenly	SF	.228
6.	Steve Sax	LA	.333	41.	Terry Puhl	HOU	.275	75.	Mookie Wilson	NY	.256	109.	John Russell	PHI	.227
8.	Terry Kennedy	SD	.331	42.	Ozzie Virgil	PHI	.275	76.	Phil Garner	HOU	.256	110.	Leon Durham	CHI	.226
9.	Tim Raines	MTL	.326	43.	Rick Schu	PHI	.275	77.	Dave Concepcion	CIN	.255	111.	Ken Landreaux	LA	.226
10.	Ron Oester	CIN	.323	44.	Mike Schmidt	PHI	.275	78.	Eddie Milner	CIN	.255	112.	Marvell Wynne	PIT	.225
11.	Joe Orsulak	PIT	.322	45.	Ryne Sandberg	CHI	.275	79.	Mariano Duncan	LA	.255	113.	Greg Gross	PHI	.224
12.	Dale Murphy	ATL	.318	46.	Keith Moreland	CHI	.274	80.	Chris Brown	SF	.254	113.	Mike Scioscia	LA	.224
13.	Dave Parker	CIN	.317	47.	Kevin McReynolds	SD	.273	81.	Craig Reynolds	HOU	.254	115.	Derrel Thomas	PHI	.224
14.	Dave Lopes	CHI	.316	48.	Gary Redus	CIN	.272	82.	Gary Carter	NY	.253	116.	Jim Pankovits	HOU	.222
15.	Jose Cruz	HOU	.315	49.	Terry Francona	MTL	.271	83.	Jim Morrison	PIT	.252	117.	Dickie Thon	HOU	.221
16.	Garry Templeton	SD	.308	50.	Vince Coleman	STL	.271	84.	Terry Harper	ATL	.250	118.	Tim Corcoran	PHI	.221
17.	Max Venable	CIN	.306	51.	Jerry Mumphrey	HOU	.270	84.	Mitch Webster	MTL	.250	119.	Darryl Strawberry	NY	.219
18.	Alan Ashby	HOU	.306	52.	Vance Law	MTL	.270	86.	Steve Garvey	SD	.249	120.	Sal Butera	MTL	.216
19.	Glenn Davis	HOU	.304	53.	Wayne Krenchicki	CIN	.269	87.	Steve Kemp	PIT	.248	121.	Steve Jeltz	PHI	.215
20.	Graig Nettles	SD	.302	54.	Andy Van Slyke	STL	.269	88.	Darrell Porter	STL	.248	122.	Mike Jorgensen	STL	.214
21.	Tom Herr	STL	.302	55.	Bill Doran	HOU	.268	89.	Denny Walling	HOU	.248	123.	Jody Davis	CHI	.212
22.	Rafael Santana	NY	.301	56.	Wally Backman	NY	.268	90.	Mark Bailey	HOU	.246	124.	Ken Oberkfell	ATL	.211
23.	Tony Gwynn	SD	.300	56.	Bob Horner	ATL	.268	91.	Jose Uribe	SF	.245	125.	U.L. Washington	MTL	.210
24.	Bill Almon	PIT	.299	58.	Bob Dernier	CHI	.266	92.	Jeff Leonard	SF	.244	126.	Glenn Hubbard	ATL	.209
25.	Luis Aguayo	PHI	.293	59.	Claudell Washington	ATL	.265	93.	Nick Esasky	CIN	.244	127.	Jim Wohlford	MTL	.208
26.	Danny Heep	NY	.291	60.	Sid Bream	PIT	.265	94.	Andre Dawson	MTL	.243	128.	Carmelo Martinez	SD	.205
27.	Chili Davis	SF	.290	61.	Juan Samuel	PHI	.265	95.	Enos Cabell	LA	.242	129.	Jason Thompson	PIT	.203
28.	Tom Foley	PHI	.287	62.	Pete Rose	CIN	.265	96.	Manny Trillo	SF	.240	130.	Sixto Lezcano	PIT	.200
29.	Cesar Cedeno	STL	.286	63.	Tim Flannery	SD	.264	97.	Jack Clark	STL	.239	130.	Rafael Ramirez	ATL	.200
30.	George Foster	NY	.285	64.	Hubie Brooks	MTL	.264	98.	Dave Van Gorder	CIN	.238	132.	Doug Frobel	MTL	.197
31.	Johnny Ray	PIT	.284	65.	Kevin Bass	HOU	.263	99.	Brad Komminsk	ATL	.237	133.	Ron Cey	CHI	.193
32.	R.J. Reynolds	PIT	.282	65.	Garry Maddox	PHI	.263	100.	Buddy Bell	CIN	.236	134.	Mike Fitzgerald	MTL	.188
33.	Alan Knicely	PHI	.281	67.	Tony Pena	PIT	.262	101.	Tom Nieto	STL	.236	135.	Gary Matthews	CHI	.184
34.	Ozzie Smith	STL	.281	68.	Joel Youngblood	SF	.260	102.	Shawon Dunston	CHI	.235				

Batting Average, Home Games

American League

1. Wade Boggs	BOS	.418	41. Don Slaught	TEX	.293	81. Jim Presley	SEA	.264	121. Bob Boone	CAL	.235
2. Garth Iorg	TOR	.378	42. Pete O'Brien	TEX	.292	82. Donnie Scott	SEA	.263	122. Rick Dempsey	BAL	.235
3. George Brett	KC	.368	43. Ken Griffey	NY	.292	83. Willie Randolph	NY	.262	123. Tom Brookens	DET	.233
4. Wayne Tolleson	TEX	.354	44. Cal Ripken	BAL	.289	84. Gary Gaetti	MIN	.261	124. Greg Gagne	MIN	.232
5. Jim Rice	BOS	.350	45. Tony Armas	BOS	.289	85. Luis Salazar	CHI	.260	125. Dave Collins	OAK	.232
6. Gary Ward	TEX	.344	46. Toby Harrah	TEX	.289	86. Lloyd Moseby	TOR	.258	125. Mike Stenhouse	MIN	.232
7. Don Mattingly	NY	.336	47. Chet Lemon	DET	.288	87. Ed Romero	MIL	.258	127. George Vukovich	CLE	.231
8. Rich Gedman	BOS	.335	48. Alan Trammell	DET	.287	88. Alfredo Griffin	OAK	.257	128. Lonnie Smith	KC	.231
9. Earnest Riles	MIL	.332	49. Jesse Barfield	TOR	.286	89. Larry Herndon	DET	.256	129. Gary Pettis	CAL	.231
10. Ron Hassey	NY	.330	50. Pat Sheridan	KC	.286	90. Glenn Hoffman	BOS	.256	129. Andre Thornton	CLE	.231
11. Brett Butler	CLE	.329	51. Dave Winfield	NY	.285	91. Ruppert Jones	CAL	.256	131. Darryl Motley	KC	.230
12. Juan Beniquez	CAL	.327	52. Cecil Cooper	MIL	.285	92. George Bell	TOR	.255	132. Johnny Grubb	DET	.228
13. Pat Tabler	CLE	.326	53. Al Cowens	SEA	.284	93. Charlie Moore	MIL	.254	133. Buddy Bell	TEX	.226
14. Kirby Puckett	MIN	.324	54. Ted Simmons	MIL	.283	94. Tom Brunansky	MIN	.254	134. Wayne Gross	BAL	.225
15. Paul Molitor	MIL	.323	55. Harold Baines	CHI	.283	95. Alan Wiggins	BAL	.253	135. Scott Fletcher	CHI	.225
16. Floyd Rayford	BAL	.322	56. Lance Parrish	DET	.280	96. Steve Balboni	KC	.253	136. Curtis Wilkerson	TEX	.225
17. Bryan Little	CHI	.320	57. Ozzie Guillen	CHI	.279	97. Tim Hulett	CHI	.251	137. Ernie Whitt	TOR	.223
18. Ben Oglivie	MIL	.319	58. Rod Carew	CAL	.279	98. Jack Perconte	SEA	.251	138. Dave Kingman	OAK	.223
19. Rance Mulliniks	TOR	.316	59. Mike Young	BAL	.278	99. Randy Bush	MIN	.250	139. Dick Schofield	CAL	.219
20. Mark Salas	MIN	.315	60. Dwight Evans	BOS	.277	99. Bobby Grich	CAL	.250	140. Steve Buechele	TEX	.218
21. Bruce Bochte	OAK	.314	61. Larry Sheets	BAL	.276	99. Steve Henderson	OAK	.250	141. Larry Parrish	TEX	.218
22. Kent Hrbek	MIN	.312	62. Mike Davis	OAK	.276	99. Cliff Johnson	TOR	.250	142. Rick Manning	MIL	.218
23. Kirk Gibson	DET	.311	63. Tim Teufel	MIN	.276	99. Gary Roenicke	BAL	.250	143. Reggie Jackson	CAL	.218
24. Robin Yount	MIL	.309	64. Marty Barrett	BOS	.275	99. Jim Sundberg	KC	.250	144. Don Baylor	NY	.216
25. Lee Lacy	BAL	.308	65. Willie Wilson	KC	.275	105. Mike Easler	BOS	.249	145. Dwayne Murphy	OAK	.215
26. Julio Franco	CLE	.306	66. Jorge Orta	KC	.275	106. Dave Henderson	SEA	.249	146. Jackie Gutierrez	BOS	.214
27. Tony Fernandez	TOR	.306	67. Spike Owen	SEA	.274	107. Roy Smalley	MIN	.249	147. Jim Dwyer	BAL	.212
28. Phil Bradley	SEA	.305	68. Jerry Willard	CLE	.272	108. Dusty Baker	OAK	.248	148. Bill Schroeder	MIL	.212
29. Rickey Henderson	NY	.305	69. Fred Lynn	BAL	.272	109. Mickey Tettleton	OAK	.245	149. Gorman Thomas	SEA	.207
30. Damaso Garcia	TOR	.303	70. Rudy Law	CHI	.271	110. John Shelby	BAL	.245	150. Rob Wilfong	CAL	.205
31. Carney Lansford	OAK	.302	71. Nelson Simmons	DET	.271	111. Mike Heath	OAK	.244	151. Carlton Fisk	CHI	.203
32. Mike Hargrove	CLE	.302	72. Brook Jacoby	CLE	.271	112. Darrell Evans	DET	.244	152. Onix Concepcion	KC	.201
33. Tony Bernazard	CLE	.301	73. Donnie Hill	OAK	.268	113. Frank White	KC	.242	153. Butch Wynegar	NY	.196
34. Mickey Hatcher	MIN	.299	74. Lou Whitaker	DET	.267	114. Mike Pagliarulo	NY	.242	154. Rich Dauer	BAL	.178
35. Bill Buckner	BOS	.299	75. Joe Carter	CLE	.267	115. Ron Kittle	CHI	.241	155. Daryl Boston	CHI	.175
36. Ivan Calderon	SEA	.297	76. Hal McRae	KC	.267	116. Brian Downing	CAL	.241	156. Bobby Meacham	NY	.169
37. Willie Upshaw	TOR	.297	77. Greg Walker	CHI	.266	117. Barbaro Garbey	DET	.239	157. George Wright	TEX	.158
38. Eddie Murray	BAL	.296	78. Oddibe McDowell	TEX	.266	117. Paul Householder	MIL	.239	158. Chris Bando	CLE	.140
39. Jeff Burroughs	TOR	.294	79. Doug DeCinces	CAL	.264	119. Jim Gantner	MIL	.238	159. Julio Cruz	CHI	.140
40. Alvin Davis	SEA	.293	80. Steve Lyons	BOS	.264	120. Bob Kearney	SEA	.238			

National League

1. Joe Orsulak	PIT	.370	35. Mike Brown	PIT	.296	69. Chris Brown	SF	.266	103. Kevin McReynolds	SD	.235
2. Tony Perez	CIN	.369	36. Tom Foley	PHI	.296	70. Chili Davis	SF	.265	103. Rafael Santana	NY	.235
3. Thad Bosley	CHI	.361	37. Rafael Ramirez	ATL	.294	70. John Russell	PHI	.265	105. Marvell Wynne	PIT	.234
4. Cesar Cedeno	STL	.355	38. Glenn Wilson	PHI	.292	72. Gary Matthews	CHI	.264	106. Terry Kennedy	SD	.233
5. Willie McGee	STL	.353	39. Bill Madlock	LA	.292	73. Mark Bailey	HOU	.263	107. Dan Driessen	SF	.233
6. Tim Raines	MTL	.346	40. Johnny Ray	PIT	.291	73. Bruce Benedict	ATL	.263	108. Dan Gladden	SF	.232
7. Bill Almon	PIT	.345	41. Gary Redus	CIN	.289	75. Vance Law	MTL	.263	109. Jack Clark	STL	.231
8. Keith Moreland	CHI	.340	42. Danny Heep	NY	.288	76. George Foster	NY	.262	110. Craig Reynolds	HOU	.230
9. Leon Durham	CHI	.331	42. Jerry Royster	SD	.288	77. Ron Cey	CHI	.261	111. Nick Esasky	CIN	.230
10. Mookie Wilson	NY	.329	44. Von Hayes	PHI	.288	78. Denny Walling	HOU	.260	112. Billy Hatcher	CHI	.229
11. Milt Thompson	ATL	.326	45. Luis Aguayo	PHI	.287	79. Wally Backman	NY	.259	113. Howard Johnson	NY	.229
12. Tony Gwynn	SD	.326	46. Terry Harper	ATL	.286	80. Graig Nettles	SD	.258	114. Terry Pendleton	STL	.228
13. Bill Russell	LA	.326	47. Steve Garvey	SD	.284	81. Jim Morrison	PIT	.258	115. Bob Brenly	SF	.227
14. Terry Puhl	HOU	.325	48. Keith Hernandez	NY	.284	82. Tim Wallach	MTL	.257	116. Gerald Perry	ATL	.226
15. Glenn Davis	HOU	.317	49. Bill Doran	HOU	.283	83. Pete Rose	CIN	.255	117. Steve Sax	LA	.226
16. Pedro Guerrero	LA	.311	50. Dave Lopes	CHI	.282	84. Darrell Porter	STL	.255	118. Brad Wellman	SF	.226
17. Jose Cruz	HOU	.310	51. Garry Templeton	SD	.281	85. Jody Davis	CHI	.255	119. Chris Speier	CHI	.223
18. Wayne Krenchicki	CIN	.309	52. Hubie Brooks	MTL	.281	86. Sammy Khalifa	PIT	.255	120. Rick Cerone	ATL	.219
19. Dave Parker	CIN	.308	53. Larry Bowa	NY	.280	87. Ozzie Virgil	PHI	.252	121. Jose Uribe	SF	.214
20. Jerry Mumphrey	HOU	.305	54. Jeff Stone	PHI	.280	88. Greg Brock	LA	.251	122. Paul Zuvella	ATL	.209
21. Vince Coleman	STL	.305	55. Mike Schmidt	PHI	.279	89. Kevin Bass	HOU	.250	123. David Green	SF	.207
22. Ryne Sandberg	CHI	.304	56. Terry Francona	MTL	.279	89. Glenn Hubbard	ATL	.250	124. Brad Komminsk	ATL	.204
23. Ron Oester	CIN	.304	57. Bob Dernier	CHI	.278	91. Andre Dawson	MTL	.249	125. Steve Jeltz	PHI	.202
24. Tom Herr	STL	.303	58. Claudell Washington	ATL	.277	92. Juan Samuel	PHI	.248	126. Jason Thompson	PIT	.200
25. Mike Marshall	LA	.303	59. Steve Kemp	PIT	.275	93. Ken Landreaux	LA	.247	126. Manny Trillo	SF	.200
26. Ken Oberkfell	ATL	.301	60. Carmelo Martinez	SD	.273	93. Eddie Milner	CIN	.247	128. Ray Knight	NY	.197
27. Bo Diaz	CIN	.301	61. Tim Flannery	SD	.273	95. Tony Pena	PIT	.246	129. Candy Maldonado	LA	.194
28. Andy Van Slyke	STL	.301	62. Phil Garner	HOU	.272	96. Buddy Bell	CIN	.246	130. Herm Winningham	MTL	.191
29. R.J. Reynolds	PIT	.300	63. Dave Concepcion	CIN	.271	97. Tom Nieto	STL	.244	131. Dickie Thon	HOU	.190
30. Shawon Dunston	CHI	.299	64. Joel Youngblood	SF	.271	98. George Hendrick	PIT	.242	132. Dave Anderson	LA	.189
31. Dale Murphy	ATL	.299	65. Bob Horner	ATL	.269	99. Garry Maddox	PHI	.241	133. Tim Corcoran	PHI	.183
32. Ozzie Smith	STL	.298	66. Enos Cabell	LA	.269	100. Mariano Duncan	LA	.240	134. Mike Fitzgerald	MTL	.166
33. Darryl Strawberry	NY	.298	67. Rick Schu	PHI	.269	101. Jeff Leonard	SF	.239			
34. Mike Scioscia	LA	.297	68. Gary Carter	NY	.266	102. Len Dykstra	NY	.239			

Batting Average, Road Games

American League

1. Steve Henderson	OAK	.351	41. Lee Lacy	BAL	.277	81. Lloyd Moseby	TOR	.259	121. Mike Pagliarulo	NY	.238
2. Harold Baines	CHI	.335	42. Rance Mulliniks	TOR	.276	82. Mickey Tettleton	OAK	.257	122. Gary Ward	TEX	.235
3. Rickey Henderson	NY	.322	43. Paul Molitor	MIL	.276	83. George Vukovich	CLE	.257	123. Bobby Grich	CAL	.234
4. Wade Boggs	BOS	.322	43. Gary Pettis	CAL	.276	84. Willie Upshaw	TOR	.257	123. Larry Herndon	DET	.234
5. John Shelby	BAL	.320	45. Cal Ripken	BAL	.275	85. Marty Barrett	BOS	.257	125. Steve Balboni	KC	.233
6. Alan Wiggins	BAL	.316	46. Mike Easler	BOS	.275	86. Joe Carter	CLE	.256	126. Dave Henderson	SEA	.233
7. Don Mattingly	NY	.311	47. Tony Fernandez	TOR	.274	87. Rich Gedman	BOS	.256	127. Gary Gaetti	MIN	.232
8. Cecil Cooper	MIL	.301	48. Rick Dempsey	BAL	.273	88. Frank White	KC	.256	128. Luis Salazar	CHI	.232
9. Donnie Hill	OAK	.300	49. Ivan Calderon	SEA	.273	89. Mike Heath	OAK	.256	129. Jim Rice	BOS	.232
10. Bill Buckner	BOS	.299	49. Paul Householder	MIL	.273	90. Fred Lynn	BAL	.255	130. Alan Trammell	DET	.230
11. George Brett	KC	.298	51. Carlton Fisk	CHI	.272	91. Toby Harrah	TEX	.254	131. Julio Cruz	CHI	.230
12. Eddie Murray	BAL	.298	52. Jim Gantner	MIL	.271	92. Butch Wynegar	NY	.252	132. Tom Brunansky	MIN	.229
13. Mike Davis	OAK	.296	53. Julio Franco	CLE	.271	93. Hal McRae	KC	.252	133. Jeff Burroughs	TOR	.226
14. Brett Butler	CLE	.295	54. Dave Collins	OAK	.270	94. Dave Kingman	OAK	.252	134. Randy Bush	MIN	.224
15. Phil Bradley	SEA	.294	55. Ron Hassey	NY	.270	95. Darrell Evans	DET	.251	135. Rich Dauer	BAL	.224
16. Glenn Hoffman	BOS	.293	56. Mike Young	BAL	.269	96. Kirby Puckett	MIN	.251	136. Doug DeCinces	CAL	.224
17. George Bell	TOR	.293	57. Cliff Johnson	TOR	.269	97. Carney Lansford	OAK	.250	137. Gorman Thomas	SEA	.223
18. Jesse Barfield	TOR	.292	58. Mike Hargrove	CLE	.269	97. Greg Walker	CHI	.250	138. Jackie Gutierrez	BOS	.222
19. Floyd Rayford	BAL	.291	59. Jerry Willard	CLE	.268	99. Dwight Evans	BOS	.249	139. Carmen Castillo	CLE	.221
20. Lou Whitaker	DET	.291	60. Roy Smalley	MIN	.267	100. Dwayne Murphy	OAK	.249	140. Steve Buechele	TEX	.220
21. Jim Presley	SEA	.288	61. Ozzie Guillen	CHI	.267	101. Al Cowens	SEA	.249	141. Dick Schofield	CAL	.219
22. Willie Randolph	NY	.286	62. Lance Parrish	DET	.267	102. Bob Kearney	SEA	.248	142. Greg Gagne	MIN	.219
23. Dusty Baker	OAK	.286	63. Daryl Boston	CHI	.267	103. Tony Bernazard	CLE	.248	143. Rick Manning	MIL	.217
24. Reggie Jackson	CAL	.285	64. Garth Iorg	TOR	.266	104. Rudy Law	CHI	.247	144. Ron Kittle	CHI	.217
25. Tim Hulett	CHI	.285	65. Dave Winfield	NY	.266	105. Buddy Bell	TEX	.247	145. Pat Tabler	CLE	.215
26. Larry Parrish	TEX	.285	66. Don Slaught	TEX	.265	105. Larry Sheets	BAL	.247	146. George Wright	TEX	.215
27. Brian Downing	CAL	.284	67. Randy Ready	MIL	.265	107. Tony Armas	BOS	.245	147. Darryl Motley	KC	.214
28. Jim Dwyer	BAL	.283	68. Ben Oglivie	MIL	.265	108. Chet Lemon	DET	.245	148. Oddibe McDowell	TEX	.212
29. Scott Fletcher	CHI	.283	69. Ernie Whitt	TOR	.265	109. Tim Teufel	MIN	.244	149. Charlie Moore	MIL	.211
30. Alfredo Griffin	OAK	.283	70. Kirk Gibson	DET	.264	110. Don Baylor	NY	.244	150. Ruppert Jones	CAL	.211
31. Lonnie Smith	KC	.283	71. Steve Lyons	BOS	.264	110. Ed Romero	MIL	.244	151. Onix Concepcion	KC	.206
32. Barbaro Garbey	DET	.282	72. Bobby Meacham	NY	.264	112. Wayne Gross	BAL	.243	152. Nelson Simmons	DET	.203
33. Rod Carew	CAL	.281	73. Ted Simmons	MIL	.264	113. Pete O'Brien	TEX	.243	153. Domingo Ramos	SEA	.196
34. Alvin Davis	SEA	.281	74. Wayne Tolleson	TEX	.262	114. Robin Yount	MIL	.242	154. Tim Laudner	MIN	.188
35. Willie Wilson	KC	.281	75. Damaso Garcia	TOR	.260	115. Andre Thornton	CLE	.242	155. Gary Roenicke	BAL	.183
36. Mark Salas	MIN	.280	75. Mickey Hatcher	MIN	.260	116. Tom Brookens	DET	.241	156. Rob Wilfong	CAL	.178
37. Juan Beniquez	CAL	.279	75. Curtis Wilkerson	TEX	.260	117. Jim Sundberg	KC	.240	157. Pat Sheridan	KC	.176
38. Jack Perconte	SEA	.277	78. Jorge Orta	KC	.259	118. Kent Hrbek	MIN	.240	158. Bryan Little	CHI	.170
39. Bruce Bochte	OAK	.277	79. Bob Boone	CAL	.259	119. Earnest Riles	MIL	.239			
40. Brook Jacoby	CLE	.277	80. Ken Griffey	NY	.259	120. Spike Owen	SEA	.238			

National League

1. Mike Brown	PIT	.364	35. Juan Samuel	PHI	.280	69. Terry Francona	MTL	.258	103. Carmelo Martinez	SD	.233
2. Willie McGee	STL	.353	36. Rafael Santana	NY	.279	70. Mike Fitzgerald	MTL	.258	104. Mookie Wilson	NY	.232
3. Jack Clark	STL	.332	37. Steve Garvey	SD	.279	71. Glenn Wilson	PHI	.257	105. Steve Kemp	PIT	.231
4. Keith Hernandez	NY	.331	38. Milt Thompson	ATL	.276	72. Dan Driessen	SF	.255	106. Glenn Davis	HOU	.231
5. Pedro Guerrero	LA	.330	39. Claudell Washington	ATL	.275	73. Candy Maldonado	LA	.255	107. Vince Coleman	STL	.231
6. Steve Sax	LA	.329	40. Chili Davis	SF	.275	74. Ozzie Smith	STL	.254	108. Bob Dernier	CHI	.230
7. Dave Parker	CIN	.316	41. Chris Brown	SF	.275	75. Jerry Mumphrey	HOU	.254	109. Andy Van Slyke	STL	.225
8. Craig Reynolds	HOU	.314	42. Tony Perez	CIN	.275	76. Dan Gladden	SF	.254	110. Sammy Khalifa	PIT	.219
9. Dickie Thon	HOU	.308	43. Jerry Royster	SD	.275	77. Howard Johnson	NY	.254	111. Jim Pankovits	HOU	.216
10. Tony Gwynn	SD	.307	44. Mike Schmidt	PHI	.275	78. Brad Komminsk	ATL	.254	112. George Hendrick	PIT	.215
11. Ryne Sandberg	CHI	.307	45. Enos Cabell	LA	.275	79. Alan Ashby	HOU	.252	113. Bob Brenly	SF	.214
12. Dale Murphy	ATL	.302	45. Danny Heep	NY	.275	80. Tony Pena	PIT	.252	114. Gary Matthews	CHI	.214
13. Tom Herr	STL	.301	47. Pete Rose	CIN	.273	81. Greg Brock	LA	.251	115. Rick Cerone	ATL	.214
14. Mike Scioscia	LA	.295	48. Keith Moreland	CHI	.272	82. Terry Pendleton	STL	.251	116. Glenn Hubbard	ATL	.213
15. Tim Raines	MTL	.295	49. Luis Aguayo	PHI	.269	83. Jim Morrison	PIT	.250	117. Dave Anderson	LA	.209
16. Gary Carter	NY	.295	50. Vance Law	MTL	.268	84. Manny Trillo	SF	.249	118. Gary Redus	CIN	.207
17. Terry Kennedy	SD	.292	51. Joel Youngblood	SF	.268	85. Jeff Stone	PHI	.248	119. Tom Nieto	STL	.206
18. Bill Doran	HOU	.291	52. Len Dykstra	NY	.268	86. Mariano Duncan	LA	.247	120. Jody Davis	CHI	.206
19. Jose Cruz	HOU	.291	53. R.J. Reynolds	PIT	.267	87. Chris Chambliss	ATL	.244	121. Bill Almon	PIT	.206
20. Nick Esasky	CIN	.290	54. Mark Bailey	HOU	.267	88. Terry Harper	ATL	.242	121. Ron Cey	CHI	.206
21. Mitch Webster	MTL	.290	55. Bob Horner	ATL	.265	89. Jeff Leonard	SF	.242	123. Rafael Ramirez	ATL	.206
22. U.L. Washington	MTL	.289	56. Graig Nettles	SD	.265	90. Ken Oberkfell	ATL	.241	124. Shawon Dunston	CHI	.204
23. Jason Thompson	PIT	.289	57. George Foster	NY	.264	91. Rick Schu	PHI	.241	125. Bo Diaz	CIN	.201
24. Tim Flannery	SD	.288	58. Chris Speier	CHI	.264	92. Ozzie Virgil	PHI	.241	126. Gerald Perry	ATL	.198
25. Kevin Bass	HOU	.287	59. Phil Garner	HOU	.264	93. Von Hayes	PHI	.240	127. Darrell Porter	STL	.196
26. Herm Winningham	MTL	.287	60. Jose Uribe	SF	.263	94. Joe Orsulak	PIT	.239	128. Buddy Bell	CIN	.194
27. Wally Backman	NY	.286	61. Tim Wallach	MTL	.263	95. Sid Bream	PIT	.239	129. Bill Russell	LA	.193
28. Ken Landreaux	LA	.286	62. Andre Dawson	MTL	.261	96. Tito Landrum	STL	.239	130. Tom Foley	PHI	.193
29. Ron Oester	CIN	.285	62. Eddie Milner	CIN	.261	97. Leon Durham	CHI	.239	131. Larry Bowa	NY	.187
30. Dave Lopes	CHI	.285	64. Hubie Brooks	MTL	.260	98. Ray Knight	NY	.236	132. Marvell Wynne	PIT	.179
31. Mike Marshall	LA	.284	65. Johnny Ray	PIT	.259	99. Garry Maddox	PHI	.236	133. Steve Jeltz	PHI	.175
32. Garry Templeton	SD	.283	66. Bill Madlock	LA	.259	100. Cesar Cedeno	STL	.234	134. Doug Frobel	MTL	.175
33. David Green	SF	.283	67. Darryl Strawberry	NY	.259	101. Dave Concepcion	CIN	.233	135. John Russell	PHI	.162
34. Denny Walling	HOU	.280	68. Greg Gross	PHI	.258	102. Kevin McReynolds	SD	.233	136. Bruce Benedict	ATL	.150

Slugging Average, Home Games

American League

1. George Brett	KC	.628	41. Lloyd Moseby	TOR	.466	81. Willie Wilson	KC	.417	121. Steve Henderson	OAK	.365
2. Don Mattingly	NY	.616	42. Bruce Bochte	OAK	.466	82. Toby Harrah	TEX	.417	122. Tim Hulett	CHI	.364
3. Garth Iorg	TOR	.588	43. Carlton Fisk	CHI	.465	83. Larry Herndon	DET	.417	123. Rick Dempsey	BAL	.358
4. Kirk Gibson	DET	.580	44. Al Cowens	SEA	.464	84. Mike Pagliarulo	NY	.416	124. Charlie Moore	MIL	.349
5. Jeff Burroughs	TOR	.576	45. Harold Baines	CHI	.463	85. Luis Salazar	CHI	.413	125. Bob Kearney	SEA	.344
6. Wade Boggs	BOS	.566	46. Carney Lansford	OAK	.463	86. Wayne Tolleson	TEX	.410	126. Jim Sundberg	KC	.340
7. Jesse Barfield	TOR	.565	47. Oddibe McDowell	TEX	.463	87. Dave Kingman	OAK	.410	127. Rod Carew	CAL	.338
8. Tony Armas	BOS	.555	48. Lance Parrish	DET	.463	88. Steve Buechele	TEX	.409	128. Lonnie Smith	KC	.338
9. Ivan Calderon	SEA	.550	49. Ron Kittle	CHI	.462	89. Roy Smalley	MIN	.408	129. Dwayne Murphy	OAK	.335
10. Rich Gedman	BOS	.540	50. Reggie Jackson	CAL	.462	90. Mike Heath	OAK	.407	130. Dick Schofield	CAL	.333
11. Jim Rice	BOS	.540	51. Alvin Davis	SEA	.461	91. Rudy Law	CHI	.406	131. Jack Perconte	SEA	.332
12. Gary Ward	TEX	.539	52. Hal McRae	KC	.461	92. Ernie Whitt	TOR	.406	132. Greg Gagne	MIN	.331
13. Mike Young	BAL	.537	53. Rickey Henderson	NY	.459	93. Brian Downing	CAL	.406	133. Bill Schroeder	MIL	.327
14. Darrell Evans	DET	.533	54. Randy Bush	MIN	.456	94. Alan Trammell	DET	.405	134. Mike Stenhouse	MIN	.326
15. Phil Bradley	SEA	.526	55. Nelson Simmons	DET	.451	95. Dave Henderson	SEA	.403	135. Jim Gantner	MIL	.322
16. Robin Yount	MIL	.523	56. Jim Presley	SEA	.449	96. John Shelby	BAL	.402	136. Donnie Hill	OAK	.321
17. Eddie Murray	BAL	.515	57. Cliff Johnson	TOR	.448	97. Lee Lacy	BAL	.396	137. George Vukovich	CLE	.321
18. Wayne Gross	BAL	.510	58. Tony Fernandez	TOR	.445	98. Darryl Motley	KC	.396	138. Ed Romero	MIL	.313
19. Gary Roenicke	BAL	.509	59. Pat Tabler	CLE	.445	99. Julio Franco	CLE	.394	139. Jim Dwyer	BAL	.310
20. Mark Salas	MIN	.507	60. Donnie Scott	SEA	.444	100. Larry Sheets	BAL	.394	140. Buddy Bell	TEX	.310
21. Dave Winfield	NY	.507	61. Tom Brunansky	MIN	.439	101. Mickey Hatcher	MIN	.393	141. Mickey Tettleton	OAK	.309
22. Doug DeCinces	CAL	.505	62. Lou Whitaker	DET	.439	102. Jerry Willard	CLE	.390	142. Alan Wiggins	BAL	.308
23. Fred Lynn	BAL	.502	63. Ted Simmons	MIL	.438	103. Joe Carter	CLE	.389	143. Gary Pettis	CAL	.302
24. Steve Balboni	KC	.497	64. Don Slaught	TEX	.436	104. Glenn Hoffman	BOS	.388	144. Alfredo Griffin	OAK	.298
25. Mike Davis	OAK	.492	65. Gorman Thomas	SEA	.434	105. Johnny Grubb	DET	.386	145. Rick Manning	MIL	.297
26. Ben Oglivie	MIL	.488	66. Bill Buckner	BOS	.433	106. Dusty Baker	OAK	.385	146. Rob Wilfong	CAL	.295
27. Pete O'Brien	TEX	.487	67. Don Baylor	NY	.433	107. Spike Owen	SEA	.383	147. Butch Wynegar	NY	.285
28. Kent Hrbek	MIN	.487	68. Tony Bernazard	CLE	.431	108. Tom Brookens	DET	.379	148. Dave Collins	OAK	.284
29. Floyd Rayford	BAL	.486	69. Cecil Cooper	MIL	.430	109. Steve Lyons	BOS	.378	149. Jackie Gutierrez	BOS	.267
30. Dwight Evans	BOS	.483	70. George Bell	TOR	.430	110. Larry Parrish	TEX	.378	150. Onix Concepcion	KC	.264
31. Rance Mulliniks	TOR	.483	71. Bryan Little	CHI	.430	111. Mike Easler	BOS	.377	151. Curtis Wilkerson	TEX	.263
32. Cal Ripken	BAL	.482	72. Brett Butler	CLE	.429	112. Frank White	KC	.377	152. Bob Boone	CAL	.258
33. Greg Walker	CHI	.481	73. Kirby Puckett	MIN	.429	113. Ozzie Guillen	CHI	.377	153. Scott Fletcher	CHI	.246
34. Willie Upshaw	TOR	.479	74. Brook Jacoby	CLE	.426	114. Jorge Orta	KC	.373	154. Rich Dauer	BAL	.238
35. Ruppert Jones	CAL	.478	75. Gary Gaetti	MIN	.425	115. Barbaro Garbey	DET	.373	155. Daryl Boston	CHI	.237
36. Ken Griffey	NY	.477	76. Earnest Riles	MIL	.425	116. Bobby Grich	CAL	.371	156. George Wright	TEX	.215
37. Chet Lemon	DET	.473	77. Damaso Garcia	TOR	.423	117. Mike Hargrove	CLE	.367	157. Bobby Meacham	NY	.212
38. Ron Hassey	NY	.470	78. Tim Teufel	MIN	.421	118. Willie Randolph	NY	.367	158. Julio Cruz	CHI	.186
39. Juan Beniquez	CAL	.467	78. Andre Thornton	CLE	.421	119. Marty Barrett	BOS	.366	159. Chris Bando	CLE	.180
40. Paul Molitor	MIL	.467	80. Pat Sheridan	KC	.418	120. Paul Householder	MIL	.366			

National League

1. Leon Durham	CHI	.595	35. Joe Orsulak	PIT	.451	69. Greg Brock	LA	.388	103. Dave Concepcion	CIN	.333
2. Darryl Strawberry	NY	.585	36. Bill Doran	HOU	.450	70. Ozzie Smith	STL	.388	103. Tim Flannery	SD	.333
3. Ryne Sandberg	CHI	.560	37. Shawon Dunston	CHI	.449	71. Vince Coleman	STL	.387	105. Dan Driessen	SF	.332
4. Bob Horner	ATL	.553	38. Jerry Mumphrey	HOU	.445	72. Graig Nettles	SD	.387	106. Glenn Hubbard	ATL	.328
5. Tony Perez	CIN	.544	39. George Foster	NY	.444	73. Bill Russell	LA	.384	107. Gerald Perry	ATL	.321
6. Cesar Cedeno	STL	.543	40. Tom Foley	PHI	.443	74. Danny Heep	NY	.381	108. Craig Reynolds	HOU	.319
7. Dale Murphy	ATL	.539	41. Wayne Krenchicki	CIN	.443	75. Mark Bailey	HOU	.380	109. David Green	SF	.319
8. Mike Marshall	LA	.536	42. Mookie Wilson	NY	.441	76. Ron Oester	CIN	.378	110. Ken Landreaux	LA	.318
9. Thad Bosley	CHI	.536	43. Gary Carter	NY	.437	77. Rick Schu	PHI	.377	111. Rick Cerone	ATL	.318
10. Dave Parker	CIN	.535	44. Terry Harper	ATL	.431	78. Keith Hernandez	NY	.375	112. Brad Komminsk	ATL	.315
11. Luis Aguayo	PHI	.529	45. Tim Wallach	MTL	.430	79. Larry Bowa	NY	.374	113. Mariano Duncan	LA	.313
12. Tim Raines	MTL	.529	46. Jody Davis	CHI	.429	80. Phil Garner	HOU	.371	114. Terry Pendleton	STL	.313
13. Bill Almon	PIT	.522	46. Tom Herr	STL	.429	81. Denny Walling	HOU	.370	115. Tom Nieto	STL	.307
14. Keith Moreland	CHI	.517	48. Hubie Brooks	MTL	.428	82. Jeff Leonard	SF	.370	116. Jose Uribe	SF	.306
15. Mike Schmidt	PHI	.513	49. R.J. Reynolds	PIT	.427	83. Jason Thompson	PIT	.367	117. Pete Rose	CIN	.301
16. Gary Matthews	CHI	.504	50. Ozzie Virgil	PHI	.425	84. Howard Johnson	NY	.367	118. Dickie Thon	HOU	.298
17. Pedro Guerrero	LA	.498	51. Tony Gwynn	SD	.424	85. Mike Scioscia	LA	.366	119. Marvell Wynne	PIT	.297
18. Andy Van Slyke	STL	.497	52. Milt Thompson	ATL	.421	86. Steve Kemp	PIT	.363	120. Bruce Benedict	ATL	.295
19. Carmelo Martinez	SD	.496	53. Bill Madlock	LA	.420	87. Dan Gladden	SF	.362	121. Chris Speier	CHI	.295
20. Glenn Davis	HOU	.494	54. Andre Dawson	MTL	.419	88. Kevin McReynolds	SD	.360	122. Len Dykstra	NY	.294
21. Von Hayes	PHI	.493	55. Chris Brown	SF	.419	89. Terry Kennedy	SD	.358	123. George Hendrick	PIT	.282
22. Mike Brown	PIT	.490	56. Vance Law	MTL	.409	90. Garry Maddox	PHI	.357	124. Candy Maldonado	LA	.272
23. John Russell	PHI	.487	57. Jack Clark	STL	.409	91. Jeff Stone	PHI	.357	125. Brad Wellman	SF	.269
24. Bo Diaz	CIN	.485	58. Johnny Ray	PIT	.406	92. Bob Dernier	CHI	.352	126. Rafael Santana	NY	.265
25. Ron Cey	CHI	.483	59. Chili Davis	SF	.406	93. Enos Cabell	LA	.352	127. Steve Jeltz	PHI	.263
26. Gary Redus	CIN	.481	60. Nick Esasky	CIN	.403	94. Eddie Milner	CIN	.350	128. Steve Sax	LA	.255
27. Willie McGee	STL	.473	61. Kevin Bass	HOU	.402	95. Jim Morrison	PIT	.348	129. Manny Trillo	SF	.252
28. Darrell Porter	STL	.471	62. Rafael Ramirez	ATL	.401	96. Sammy Khalifa	PIT	.345	130. Herm Winningham	MTL	.247
29. Buddy Bell	CIN	.466	63. Bob Brenly	SF	.400	97. Terry Francona	MTL	.344	131. Mike Fitzgerald	MTL	.245
29. Jerry Royster	SD	.466	64. Claudell Washington	ATL	.398	98. Billy Hatcher	CHI	.339	132. Dave Anderson	LA	.236
31. Dave Lopes	CHI	.466	65. Jose Cruz	HOU	.396	99. Ray Knight	NY	.339	133. Paul Zuvella	ATL	.235
32. Terry Puhl	HOU	.455	66. Juan Samuel	PHI	.394	100. Joel Youngblood	SF	.336	134. Tim Corcoran	PHI	.211
33. Steve Garvey	SD	.454	67. Garry Templeton	SD	.393	101. Tony Pena	PIT	.336			
34. Glenn Wilson	PHI	.452	68. Ken Oberkfell	ATL	.392	102. Wally Backman	NY	.335			

Slugging Average, Road Games

American League

1.	Rickey Henderson	NY	.561	41.	Brian Downing	CAL	.446	81.	Luis Salazar	CHI	.395	121.	Jack Perconte	SEA	.349
2.	Floyd Rayford	BAL	.555	42.	Mike Easler	BOS	.444	82.	Mark Salas	MIN	.395	122.	Wayne Gross	BAL	.348
3.	George Brett	KC	.540	43.	Glenn Hoffman	BOS	.440	83.	Lonnie Smith	KC	.395	122.	Willie Randolph	NY	.348
4.	Ron Hassey	NY	.539	44.	Al Cowens	SEA	.440	84.	Kent Hrbek	MIN	.394	124.	Nelson Simmons	DET	.347
5.	Eddie Murray	BAL	.531	45.	Dave Winfield	NY	.439	85.	Gary Gaetti	MIN	.393	125.	Curtis Wilkerson	TEX	.345
6.	George Bell	TOR	.523	46.	Randy Bush	MIN	.439	85.	Carney Lansford	OAK	.393	126.	Wayne Tolleson	TEX	.345
7.	Jim Presley	SEA	.522	47.	Hal McRae	KC	.439	87.	Jorge Orta	KC	.392	127.	Rudy Law	CHI	.343
8.	Don Mattingly	NY	.521	48.	Jim Rice	BOS	.434	88.	Cliff Johnson	TOR	.391	128.	Tony Fernandez	TOR	.341
9.	Carlton Fisk	CHI	.511	49.	Brett Butler	CLE	.434	89.	Lloyd Moseby	TOR	.389	129.	Ozzie Guillen	CHI	.340
10.	Reggie Jackson	CAL	.511	50.	Joe Carter	CLE	.430	90.	Barbaro Garbey	DET	.388	130.	Kirby Puckett	MIN	.339
11.	Jesse Barfield	TOR	.511	51.	Darryl Motley	KC	.429	91.	Alan Wiggins	BAL	.388	131.	Mike Hargrove	CLE	.338
12.	Darrell Evans	DET	.506	51.	Greg Walker	CHI	.429	92.	Randy Ready	MIL	.388	132.	Gary Ward	TEX	.338
13.	Larry Parrish	TEX	.500	53.	Rich Gedman	BOS	.428	93.	Tim Hulett	CHI	.385	133.	Gary Pettis	CAL	.337
14.	Lance Parrish	DET	.495	54.	Dwight Evans	BOS	.428	94.	Garth Iorg	TOR	.385	134.	Steve Lyons	BOS	.337
15.	Larry Sheets	BAL	.494	55.	Rance Mulliniks	TOR	.427	95.	Ken Griffey	NY	.383	135.	Jim Gantner	MIL	.332
16.	Mike Young	BAL	.491	56.	Don Baylor	NY	.427	96.	Donnie Hill	OAK	.379	136.	Damaso Garcia	TOR	.330
17.	Dusty Baker	OAK	.489	57.	Brook Jacoby	CLE	.426	97.	Doug DeCinces	CAL	.379	136.	Mickey Hatcher	MIN	.330
18.	Jim Dwyer	BAL	.483	58.	Carmen Castillo	CLE	.425	98.	George Vukovich	CLE	.378	138.	Earnest Riles	MIL	.329
19.	Cecil Cooper	MIL	.481	59.	Jim Sundberg	KC	.425	99.	Jerry Willard	CLE	.378	139.	Dick Schofield	CAL	.329
20.	Tony Armas	BOS	.481	60.	Dave Kingman	OAK	.424	100.	Tony Bernazard	CLE	.378	140.	Marty Barrett	BOS	.320
21.	Ernie Whitt	TOR	.479	61.	Lee Lacy	BAL	.421	101.	Tim Teufel	MIN	.376	141.	Bobby Meacham	NY	.316
22.	Mike Davis	OAK	.478	62.	Ruppert Jones	CAL	.421	102.	Dave Henderson	SEA	.373	142.	Jeff Burroughs	TOR	.311
23.	Ivan Calderon	SEA	.475	63.	Alvin Davis	SEA	.420	103.	Bob Boone	CAL	.372	143.	Greg Gagne	MIN	.305
24.	Steve Henderson	OAK	.474	64.	Pete O'Brien	TEX	.419	104.	Bobby Grich	CAL	.372	144.	Steve Buechele	TEX	.303
25.	Lou Whitaker	DET	.474	65.	Willie Upshaw	TOR	.419	105.	Tom Brookens	DET	.372	145.	Rick Manning	MIL	.296
26.	Ron Kittle	CHI	.472	66.	Bruce Bochte	OAK	.414	106.	Ted Simmons	MIL	.368	146.	Ed Romero	MIL	.293
27.	Harold Baines	CHI	.471	67.	Mike Heath	OAK	.410	107.	Julio Franco	CLE	.368	147.	Rich Dauer	BAL	.290
28.	Phil Bradley	SEA	.469	68.	Chet Lemon	DET	.409	108.	Bob Kearney	SEA	.366	148.	Pat Tabler	CLE	.285
29.	Gorman Thomas	SEA	.468	69.	Dave Collins	OAK	.407	109.	Juan Beniquez	CAL	.365	149.	Jackie Gutierrez	BOS	.278
30.	John Shelby	BAL	.466	69.	Don Slaught	TEX	.407	110.	Scott Fletcher	CHI	.365	150.	Tim Laudner	MIN	.271
31.	Mike Pagliarulo	NY	.465	71.	Gary Roenicke	BAL	.404	111.	Toby Harrah	TEX	.364	151.	Domingo Ramos	SEA	.268
32.	Bill Buckner	BOS	.461	72.	Daryl Boston	CHI	.400	112.	Alfredo Griffin	OAK	.363	152.	George Wright	TEX	.263
33.	Paul Householder	MIL	.461	73.	Willie Wilson	KC	.399	113.	Buddy Bell	TEX	.361	153.	Pat Sheridan	KC	.259
34.	Kirk Gibson	DET	.458	74.	Oddibe McDowell	TEX	.399	114.	Paul Molitor	MIL	.361	154.	Julio Cruz	CHI	.257
35.	Tom Brunansky	MIN	.457	75.	Fred Lynn	BAL	.398	115.	Spike Owen	SEA	.358	155.	Charlie Moore	MIL	.239
36.	Cal Ripken	BAL	.456	76.	Ben Oglivie	MIL	.398	115.	Butch Wynegar	NY	.358	156.	Bryan Little	CHI	.239
37.	Steve Balboni	KC	.456	77.	Wade Boggs	BOS	.398	117.	Alan Trammell	DET	.356	157.	Rob Wilfong	CAL	.233
38.	Dwayne Murphy	OAK	.456	78.	Mickey Tettleton	OAK	.396	118.	Larry Herndon	DET	.355	158.	Onix Concepcion	KC	.229
39.	Frank White	KC	.455	79.	Andre Thornton	CLE	.396	119.	Robin Yount	MIL	.354				
40.	Rick Dempsey	BAL	.454	80.	Roy Smalley	MIN	.396	120.	Rod Carew	CAL	.353				

National League

1.	Pedro Guerrero	LA	.665	35.	Dave Lopes	CHI	.424	69.	David Green	SF	.371	103.	Dave Concepcion	CIN	.328
2.	Jack Clark	STL	.599	36.	Denny Walling	HOU	.421	70.	Darrell Porter	STL	.370	104.	Manny Trillo	SF	.326
3.	Dave Parker	CIN	.567	37.	Bill Doran	HOU	.421	71.	Rick Schu	PHI	.369	105.	Ken Oberkfell	ATL	.325
4.	Mike Schmidt	PHI	.549	38.	Howard Johnson	NY	.418	72.	R.J. Reynolds	PIT	.369	106.	Jose Uribe	SF	.325
5.	Dale Murphy	ATL	.539	39.	Chili Davis	SF	.417	73.	Jody Davis	CHI	.368	107.	Dave Anderson	LA	.322
6.	Gary Carter	NY	.534	40.	Mark Bailey	HOU	.416	74.	Mariano Duncan	LA	.366	108.	Garry Maddox	PHI	.321
7.	Mike Brown	PIT	.533	41.	Alan Ashby	HOU	.414	75.	Len Dykstra	NY	.362	109.	Bill Almon	PIT	.321
8.	Darryl Strawberry	NY	.532	42.	Jeff Leonard	SF	.413	76.	Garry Templeton	SD	.362	110.	Ray Knight	NY	.319
9.	Willie McGee	STL	.529	43.	U.L. Washington	MTL	.412	77.	Keith Moreland	CHI	.359	111.	Jeff Stone	PHI	.314
10.	Nick Esasky	CIN	.521	44.	Mookie Wilson	NY	.411	78.	Jerry Royster	SD	.359	112.	Von Hayes	PHI	.308
11.	Mitch Webster	MTL	.511	45.	Dickie Thon	HOU	.408	79.	Joel Youngblood	SF	.358	113.	Shawon Dunston	CHI	.301
12.	Claudell Washington	ATL	.507	46.	Steve Garvey	SD	.408	80.	Jerry Mumphrey	HOU	.357	114.	Terry Pendleton	STL	.300
13.	Mike Marshall	LA	.494	47.	Chris Speier	CHI	.406	81.	George Hendrick	PIT	.355	115.	Glenn Hubbard	ATL	.300
14.	Greg Brock	LA	.489	48.	Tom Herr	STL	.405	82.	Cesar Cedeno	STL	.354	116.	Milt Thompson	ATL	.299
15.	Keith Hernandez	NY	.481	49.	Vance Law	MTL	.401	83.	Wally Backman	NY	.353	117.	John Russell	PHI	.293
16.	Ken Landreaux	LA	.479	50.	Hubie Brooks	MTL	.401	84.	Enos Cabell	LA	.353	118.	Joe Orsulak	PIT	.291
17.	Juan Samuel	PHI	.476	51.	Candy Maldonado	LA	.400	85.	Terry Francona	MTL	.352	119.	Sammy Khalifa	PIT	.290
18.	George Foster	NY	.476	52.	Luis Aguayo	PHI	.397	86.	Johnny Ray	PIT	.348	120.	Jim Pankovits	HOU	.284
19.	Craig Reynolds	HOU	.468	53.	Glenn Wilson	PHI	.397	87.	Leon Durham	CHI	.347	121.	Bo Diaz	CIN	.284
20.	Tim Wallach	MTL	.468	54.	Herm Winningham	MTL	.393	88.	Tim Flannery	SD	.347	122.	Vince Coleman	STL	.283
21.	Andre Dawson	MTL	.467	55.	Tony Gwynn	SD	.392	89.	Ron Oester	CIN	.344	123.	Bob Dernier	CHI	.280
22.	Mike Scioscia	LA	.467	56.	Jason Thompson	PIT	.390	90.	Eddie Milner	CIN	.343	124.	Greg Gross	PHI	.280
23.	Chris Brown	SF	.463	57.	Andy Van Slyke	STL	.390	91.	Mike Fitzgerald	MTL	.341	125.	Buddy Bell	CIN	.279
24.	Glenn Davis	HOU	.457	58.	Terry Kennedy	SD	.387	91.	Tito Landrum	STL	.341	126.	Rafael Ramirez	ATL	.270
25.	Bob Horner	ATL	.455	59.	Tony Pena	PIT	.387	93.	Brad Komminsk	ATL	.341	127.	Doug Frobel	MTL	.263
26.	Jose Cruz	HOU	.453	60.	Bill Madlock	LA	.384	94.	Ron Cey	CHI	.340	128.	Tom Nieto	STL	.254
27.	Graig Nettles	SD	.453	61.	Bob Brenly	SF	.381	95.	Rafael Santana	NY	.340	129.	Tom Foley	PHI	.244
28.	Ryne Sandberg	CHI	.453	62.	Terry Harper	ATL	.381	96.	Jim Morrison	PIT	.339	130.	Rick Cerone	ATL	.237
29.	Danny Heep	NY	.451	63.	Kevin McReynolds	SD	.380	97.	Ozzie Smith	STL	.337	131.	Larry Bowa	NY	.234
30.	Kevin Bass	HOU	.451	64.	Steve Sax	LA	.378	98.	Steve Kemp	PIT	.336	132.	Bill Russell	LA	.229
31.	Ozzie Virgil	PHI	.439	65.	Tony Perez	CIN	.375	99.	Gary Matthews	CHI	.335	133.	Marvell Wynne	PIT	.223
32.	Phil Garner	HOU	.429	66.	Dan Driessen	SF	.372	100.	Pete Rose	CIN	.335	134.	Gerald Perry	ATL	.208
33.	Sid Bream	PIT	.424	67.	Chris Chambliss	ATL	.372	101.	Gary Redus	CIN	.333	135.	Bruce Benedict	ATL	.177
34.	Tim Raines	MTL	.424	67.	Carmelo Martinez	SD	.372	102.	Dan Gladden	SF	.331	136.	Steve Jeltz	PHI	.175

Batting Average with Runners On Base

American League

#	Player	Tm	Avg	#	Player	Tm	Avg	#	Player	Tm	Avg	#	Player	Tm	Avg
1.	Wade Boggs	BOS	.387	41.	Brian Downing	CAL	.300	81.	Dusty Baker	OAK	.267	121.	Steve Buechele	TEX	.247
2.	George Brett	KC	.367	42.	Brook Jacoby	CLE	.297	82.	Ernie Whitt	TOR	.266	122.	Buddy Bell	TEX	.247
3.	Eddie Murray	BAL	.361	43.	Mickey Hatcher	MIN	.297	83.	Don Baylor	NY	.265	123.	Willie Randolph	NY	.246
4.	Bruce Bochte	OAK	.342	44.	Mike Young	BAL	.296	84.	Ron Hassey	NY	.264	124.	Jerry Willard	CLE	.246
5.	Rickey Henderson	NY	.337	45.	Earnest Riles	MIL	.296	85.	Alan Trammell	DET	.264	125.	Doug DeCinces	CAL	.245
6.	Harold Baines	CHI	.337	46.	Alfredo Griffin	OAK	.296	86.	Alvin Davis	SEA	.264	126.	Daryl Boston	CHI	.244
7.	Carney Lansford	OAK	.333	47.	Lance Parrish	DET	.295	87.	Tim Teufel	MIN	.263	127.	Jack Perconte	SEA	.243
7.	Alan Wiggins	BAL	.333	48.	Jim Rice	BOS	.294	87.	Wayne Tolleson	TEX	.263	128.	Jorge Orta	KC	.242
9.	Bill Buckner	BOS	.330	49.	Willie Upshaw	TOR	.293	89.	Gary Pettis	CAL	.262	129.	Darryl Motley	KC	.242
10.	Mike Hargrove	CLE	.330	50.	Nelson Simmons	DET	.291	90.	Kent Hrbek	MIN	.262	130.	Barbaro Garbey	DET	.241
11.	Steve Henderson	OAK	.329	51.	Randy Ready	MIL	.291	91.	Al Cowens	SEA	.262	131.	George Vukovich	CLE	.240
12.	Ben Oglivie	MIL	.328	52.	Cal Ripken	BAL	.291	92.	Steve Balboni	KC	.262	132.	Al Oliver	TOR	.240
13.	Brett Butler	CLE	.328	53.	Darrell Evans	DET	.290	93.	Ivan Calderon	SEA	.261	133.	Greg Gagne	MIN	.239
14.	Cliff Johnson	TOR	.327	54.	Ted Simmons	MIL	.289	94.	Jim Presley	SEA	.261	134.	Butch Wynegar	NY	.237
15.	Rance Mulliniks	TOR	.326	55.	Gary Ward	TEX	.289	95.	Gary Roenicke	BAL	.260	135.	Curtis Wilkerson	TEX	.234
16.	Donnie Hill	OAK	.325	56.	Rod Carew	CAL	.288	96.	Rudy Law	CHI	.260	136.	Gary Gaetti	MIN	.234
17.	Mark Salas	MIN	.323	57.	Scott Fletcher	CHI	.287	97.	Fred Lynn	BAL	.260	137.	Tom Brunansky	MIN	.232
18.	Kirby Puckett	MIN	.323	58.	Carlton Fisk	CHI	.287	98.	Jeff Burroughs	TOR	.259	138.	Tony Armas	BOS	.232
19.	Cecil Cooper	MIL	.322	59.	Ruppert Jones	CAL	.287	99.	Mike Easler	BOS	.258	139.	Mike Pagliarulo	NY	.231
20.	Floyd Rayford	BAL	.322	60.	Roy Smalley	MIN	.286	100.	Dwight Evans	BOS	.258	140.	Rick Manning	MIL	.229
21.	Toby Harrah	TEX	.322	61.	Greg Walker	CHI	.285	101.	Onix Concepcion	KC	.258	141.	Glenn Hoffman	BOS	.229
22.	Robin Yount	MIL	.321	62.	Tony Fernandez	TOR	.283	102.	Tim Hulett	CHI	.258	142.	Dave Kingman	OAK	.226
23.	Don Mattingly	NY	.321	63.	Damaso Garcia	TOR	.283	103.	Spike Owen	SEA	.257	143.	Randy Bush	MIN	.223
24.	Kirk Gibson	DET	.320	64.	Jim Dwyer	BAL	.282	104.	Bob Boone	CAL	.257	144.	Tom Brookens	DET	.223
25.	Rich Gedman	BOS	.317	65.	Tony Bernazard	CLE	.281	105.	Pete O'Brien	TEX	.255	145.	Charlie Moore	MIL	.222
26.	Juan Beniquez	CAL	.313	66.	Ken Griffey	NY	.281	106.	Luis Salazar	CHI	.255	146.	Dick Schofield	CAL	.218
27.	Lou Whitaker	DET	.312	67.	Dave Winfield	NY	.281	107.	Bobby Grich	CAL	.255	147.	Dwayne Murphy	OAK	.215
28.	Lee Lacy	BAL	.312	68.	Frank White	KC	.281	108.	Larry Parrish	TEX	.254	148.	Larry Herndon	DET	.212
29.	Phil Bradley	SEA	.311	69.	Mike Davis	OAK	.280	109.	Jim Sundberg	KC	.254	149.	Gorman Thomas	SEA	.208
30.	Lloyd Moseby	TOR	.309	70.	Jesse Barfield	TOR	.279	110.	Chet Lemon	DET	.253	150.	Rich Dauer	BAL	.202
31.	Willie Wilson	KC	.307	71.	Don Slaught	TEX	.279	111.	Steve Lyons	BOS	.253	151.	Ron Kittle	CHI	.193
32.	Hal McRae	KC	.307	72.	Ozzie Guillen	CHI	.278	111.	Bill Schroeder	MIL	.253	152.	Oddibe McDowell	TEX	.192
33.	Rick Dempsey	BAL	.305	73.	Mike Heath	OAK	.275	113.	Rob Wilfong	CAL	.253	153.	Pat Sheridan	KC	.183
34.	Garth Iorg	TOR	.304	74.	Larry Sheets	BAL	.274	114.	George Bell	TOR	.253	154.	Wayne Gross	BAL	.175
35.	Mike Stenhouse	MIN	.303	75.	Joe Carter	CLE	.273	115.	Bobby Meacham	NY	.252	155.	Julio Cruz	CHI	.172
36.	Pat Tabler	CLE	.302	75.	Bryan Little	CHI	.273	116.	Jim Gantner	MIL	.251	156.	Jackie Gutierrez	BOS	.168
37.	Julio Franco	CLE	.301	77.	Reggie Jackson	CAL	.271	117.	Marty Barrett	BOS	.251	157.	George Wright	TEX	.159
38.	Ed Romero	MIL	.301	78.	Bob Kearney	SEA	.270	118.	Mickey Tettleton	OAK	.250	158.	Chris Bando	CLE	.115
39.	Dave Collins	OAK	.300	79.	Andre Thornton	CLE	.267	119.	Lonnie Smith	KC	.249				
39.	Paul Molitor	MIL	.300	80.	Dave Henderson	SEA	.267	120.	Paul Householder	MIL	.248				

National League

#	Player	Tm	Avg	#	Player	Tm	Avg	#	Player	Tm	Avg	#	Player	Tm	Avg
1.	Tony Perez	CIN	.378	35.	Tim Raines	MTL	.290	69.	Von Hayes	PHI	.265	103.	Jeff Stone	PHI	.235
2.	Willie McGee	STL	.360	36.	Denny Walling	HOU	.289	70.	Gary Matthews	CHI	.264	103.	Andy Van Slyke	STL	.235
3.	Tom Herr	STL	.357	37.	Greg Brock	LA	.288	71.	Steve Garvey	SD	.264	105.	Paul Zuvella	ATL	.235
4.	Cesar Cedeno	STL	.354	38.	Carmelo Martinez	SD	.288	72.	Tim Wallach	MTL	.264	106.	Bob Dernier	CHI	.233
5.	Terry Puhl	HOU	.351	39.	Terry Kennedy	SD	.288	73.	Mike Schmidt	PHI	.264	107.	Herm Winningham	MTL	.233
6.	Tim Flannery	SD	.349	40.	Gary Carter	NY	.288	74.	Phil Garner	HOU	.262	108.	Rick Schu	PHI	.232
7.	Mike Scioscia	LA	.348	41.	Andre Dawson	MTL	.287	75.	Nick Esasky	CIN	.260	109.	George Hendrick	PIT	.230
8.	Mark Bailey	HOU	.343	42.	Jason Thompson	PIT	.286	76.	Kevin Bass	HOU	.259	110.	Gary Redus	CIN	.230
9.	Dave Parker	CIN	.337	42.	Dickie Thon	HOU	.286	77.	Bob Horner	ATL	.258	111.	Len Dykstra	NY	.228
10.	Tony Gwynn	SD	.337	42.	Joel Youngblood	SF	.286	78.	Mitch Webster	MTL	.253	112.	Bruce Benedict	ATL	.227
11.	Keith Moreland	CHI	.329	45.	Jack Clark	STL	.283	79.	Chris Speier	CHI	.253	112.	Candy Maldonado	LA	.227
12.	Dale Murphy	ATL	.324	46.	Alan Ashby	HOU	.282	80.	Vince Coleman	STL	.253	114.	Howard Johnson	NY	.227
13.	Terry Francona	MTL	.317	47.	Jim Morrison	PIT	.282	81.	Dan Gladden	SF	.252	115.	Ray Knight	NY	.226
14.	Keith Hernandez	NY	.317	48.	Steve Sax	LA	.281	82.	Mariano Duncan	LA	.250	116.	John Russell	PHI	.223
15.	Garry Templeton	SD	.314	49.	Kevin McReynolds	SD	.281	82.	Vance Law	MTL	.250	117.	Gerald Perry	ATL	.223
16.	Chris Brown	SF	.313	50.	Rafael Ramirez	ATL	.279	82.	Terry Pendleton	STL	.250	118.	Brad Komminsk	ATL	.223
16.	Danny Heep	NY	.313	51.	Graig Nettles	SD	.279	85.	Buddy Bell	CIN	.246	119.	Steve Jeltz	PHI	.220
18.	Jerry Royster	SD	.311	52.	George Foster	NY	.276	86.	Terry Harper	ATL	.246	120.	Ozzie Virgil	PHI	.218
19.	Jose Cruz	HOU	.311	53.	Wayne Krenchicki	CIN	.276	87.	Eddie Milner	CIN	.245	121.	Mike Fitzgerald	MTL	.217
20.	Wally Backman	NY	.311	54.	Pete Rose	CIN	.275	88.	Garry Maddox	PHI	.244	122.	Glenn Hubbard	ATL	.216
21.	Jerry Mumphrey	HOU	.310	55.	Ryne Sandberg	CHI	.274	89.	Jeff Leonard	SF	.243	123.	Kurt Bevacqua	SD	.215
22.	Glenn Davis	HOU	.309	56.	Leon Durham	CHI	.274	90.	Rick Cerone	ATL	.243	124.	Mookie Wilson	NY	.214
23.	R.J. Reynolds	PIT	.308	57.	Dave Lopes	CHI	.273	91.	Bill Almon	PIT	.242	125.	Marvell Wynne	PIT	.214
24.	Tito Landrum	STL	.306	58.	Bo Diaz	CIN	.271	92.	David Green	SF	.241	126.	Sammy Khalifa	PIT	.211
25.	Ron Oester	CIN	.305	59.	Claudell Washington	ATL	.271	93.	Ken Landreaux	LA	.241	127.	Dave Concepcion	CIN	.211
26.	Mike Marshall	LA	.304	60.	Craig Reynolds	HOU	.270	94.	Chili Davis	SF	.240	128.	Dan Driessen	SF	.211
27.	Pedro Guerrero	LA	.304	61.	Bill Madlock	LA	.270	95.	Tony Pena	PIT	.239	129.	Tom Foley	PHI	.210
28.	Darryl Strawberry	NY	.303	62.	Manny Trillo	SF	.269	96.	Ron Cey	CHI	.239	130.	Jody Davis	CHI	.206
29.	U.L. Washington	MTL	.299	63.	Shawon Dunston	CHI	.268	97.	Ken Oberkfell	ATL	.239	131.	Darrell Porter	STL	.206
30.	Bill Doran	HOU	.297	64.	Glenn Wilson	PHI	.268	98.	Bob Brenly	SF	.238	132.	Larry Bowa	NY	.204
31.	Enos Cabell	LA	.296	65.	Juan Samuel	PHI	.267	99.	Steve Kemp	PIT	.237	133.	Chris Chambliss	ATL	.203
32.	Ozzie Smith	STL	.295	66.	Tom Nieto	STL	.267	100.	Rafael Santana	NY	.236	134.	Dave Anderson	LA	.165
33.	Hubie Brooks	MTL	.294	67.	Jose Uribe	SF	.266	101.	Joe Orsulak	PIT	.236	135.	Tim Corcoran	PHI	.143
34.	Mike Brown	PIT	.292	68.	Johnny Ray	PIT	.266	102.	Sid Bream	PIT	.236				

Batting Average in Pressure Situations

American League

#	Player	Team	Avg	#	Player	Team	Avg	#	Player	Team	Avg	#	Player	Team	Avg
1.	Mike Stenhouse	MIN	.424	41.	Joe Carter	CLE	.296	81.	Marty Barrett	BOS	.253	121.	Rod Carew	CAL	.214
2.	Curtis Wilkerson	TEX	.417	42.	Gary Gaetti	MIN	.292	82.	Tom Brookens	DET	.250	121.	Pat Tabler	CLE	.214
3.	Wade Boggs	BOS	.395	43.	Cal Ripken	BAL	.292	82.	Al Cowens	SEA	.250	123.	Alan Trammell	DET	.213
4.	Jim Sundberg	KC	.382	44.	Jesse Barfield	TOR	.291	82.	Bobby Jones	TEX	.250	124.	Randy Ready	MIL	.212
5.	Ozzie Guillen	CHI	.370	45.	Tony Bernazard	CLE	.291	85.	Ted Simmons	MIL	.247	125.	Mike Pagliarulo	NY	.212
6.	Rich Gedman	BOS	.362	46.	Brian Downing	CAL	.290	86.	Dave Kingman	OAK	.247	126.	Lance Parrish	DET	.210
7.	George Bell	TOR	.359	47.	Rudy Law	CHI	.289	87.	Roy Smalley	MIN	.246	127.	Oddibe McDowell	TEX	.208
8.	Cecil Cooper	MIL	.356	48.	Kent Hrbek	MIN	.288	88.	Ben Oglivie	MIL	.245	128.	Tim Teufel	MIN	.206
9.	Harold Baines	CHI	.355	49.	Carlton Fisk	CHI	.286	89.	Mike Davis	OAK	.244	129.	Jorge Orta	KC	.206
10.	Wayne Tolleson	TEX	.353	50.	Butch Wynegar	NY	.283	89.	Dave Winfield	NY	.244	130.	Julio Franco	CLE	.200
11.	Jerry Willard	CLE	.347	51.	Glenn Hoffman	BOS	.282	91.	Tom Brunansky	MIN	.243	130.	Rance Mulliniks	TOR	.200
12.	Dusty Baker	OAK	.345	51.	Chet Lemon	DET	.282	92.	Mike Easler	BOS	.241	130.	John Shelby	BAL	.200
13.	Jim Dwyer	BAL	.344	51.	Hal McRae	KC	.282	92.	Charlie Moore	MIL	.241	133.	Brett Butler	CLE	.195
14.	Bruce Bochte	OAK	.338	54.	Steve Henderson	OAK	.281	92.	Gary Ward	TEX	.241	134.	Daryl Boston	CHI	.194
15.	Bill Buckner	BOS	.333	55.	Don Baylor	NY	.276	95.	Cliff Johnson	TOR	.241	135.	Tony Armas	BOS	.194
15.	Eddie Murray	BAL	.333	55.	Rickey Henderson	NY	.276	96.	George Vukovich	CLE	.241	136.	Dwayne Murphy	OAK	.192
15.	Ed Romero	MIL	.333	57.	Bill Schroeder	MIL	.276	97.	Juan Beniquez	CAL	.239	137.	Alfredo Griffin	OAK	.191
18.	Toby Harrah	TEX	.328	58.	Donnie Hill	OAK	.273	97.	Willie Upshaw	TOR	.239	137.	Robin Yount	MIL	.191
19.	Don Slaught	TEX	.328	59.	Scott Fletcher	CHI	.270	99.	Dave Bergman	DET	.237	139.	Bobby Meacham	NY	.190
20.	Jack Perconte	SEA	.327	59.	Ron Hassey	NY	.270	99.	Lloyd Moseby	TOR	.237	140.	Larry Herndon	DET	.187
21.	Jerry Hairston	CHI	.326	61.	Bobby Grich	CAL	.270	99.	Rob Wilfong	CAL	.237	141.	Carney Lansford	OAK	.185
22.	Kirby Puckett	MIN	.325	62.	Luis Salazar	CHI	.269	102.	Larry Sheets	BAL	.235	141.	Ken Phelps	SEA	.185
23.	Garth Iorg	TOR	.323	62.	Lou Whitaker	DET	.269	103.	Lonnie Smith	KC	.234	143.	Wayne Gross	BAL	.184
24.	Mark Salas	MIN	.319	64.	Floyd Rayford	BAL	.268	104.	Tim Hulett	CHI	.231	144.	Randy Bush	MIN	.182
25.	Bob Boone	CAL	.316	65.	Damaso Garcia	TOR	.267	104.	Fred Lynn	BAL	.231	144.	Donnie Scott	SEA	.182
26.	Steve Balboni	KC	.314	66.	Dave Collins	OAK	.265	106.	Brook Jacoby	CLE	.229	146.	Jim Presley	SEA	.179
27.	Don Mattingly	NY	.313	66.	Pat Sheridan	KC	.265	107.	Jeff Burroughs	TOR	.229	147.	Johnny Grubb	DET	.179
27.	Frank White	KC	.313	68.	Jim Rice	BOS	.263	107.	Willie Randolph	NY	.229	148.	Jackie Gutierrez	BOS	.172
29.	Paul Molitor	MIL	.312	69.	Larry Parrish	TEX	.261	109.	Barbaro Garbey	DET	.227	149.	Rick Dempsey	BAL	.171
30.	George Brett	KC	.311	69.	Gary Pettis	CAL	.261	109.	Ken Griffey	NY	.227	150.	Dick Schofield	CAL	.167
31.	Dave Henderson	SEA	.311	71.	Julio Cruz	CHI	.259	111.	Jerry Narron	CAL	.226	151.	Pete O'Brien	TEX	.160
32.	Paul Householder	MIL	.308	71.	Alvin Davis	SEA	.259	112.	Dwight Evans	BOS	.225	152.	Spike Owen	SEA	.156
32.	Alan Wiggins	BAL	.308	71.	Doug DeCinces	CAL	.259	113.	Andre Thornton	CLE	.224	153.	George Wright	TEX	.155
34.	Tony Fernandez	TOR	.305	74.	Greg Walker	CHI	.259	114.	Mike Heath	OAK	.222	154.	Gorman Thomas	SEA	.154
35.	Phil Bradley	SEA	.304	75.	Mickey Tettleton	OAK	.258	114.	Mike Young	BAL	.222	155.	Rick Manning	MIL	.150
35.	Mike Hargrove	CLE	.304	76.	Kirk Gibson	DET	.257	116.	Ernie Whitt	TOR	.220	156.	Ron Kittle	CHI	.149
37.	Dave Henderson	SEA	.300	77.	Jim Gantner	MIL	.256	117.	Mickey Hatcher	MIN	.218	157.	Lynn Jones	KC	.147
38.	Willie Wilson	KC	.298	78.	Buddy Bell	TEX	.255	118.	Earnest Riles	MIL	.217	158.	Reggie Jackson	CAL	.136
39.	Bob Kearney	SEA	.297	79.	Steve Lyons	BOS	.254	119.	Ruppert Jones	CAL	.216	159.	Nelson Simmons	DET	.129
40.	Lee Lacy	BAL	.297	80.	Darrell Evans	DET	.254	120.	Darryl Motley	KC	.215				

National League

#	Player	Team	Avg	#	Player	Team	Avg	#	Player	Team	Avg	#	Player	Team	Avg
1.	Milt Thompson	ATL	.415	35.	Cesar Cedeno	STL	.298	69.	Eddie Milner	CIN	.254	103.	Jose Uribe	SF	.208
2.	Dave Parker	CIN	.385	36.	Dave Lopes	CHI	.296	69.	Marvell Wynne	PIT	.254	104.	Bill Doran	HOU	.208
3.	Ron Oester	CIN	.382	37.	Dale Murphy	ATL	.296	71.	Terry Pendleton	STL	.253	105.	Glenn Hubbard	ATL	.204
4.	Thad Bosley	CHI	.373	38.	Mike Marshall	LA	.296	72.	Carmelo Martinez	SD	.253	106.	Dan Gladden	SF	.202
5.	Ryne Sandberg	CHI	.368	39.	Hubie Brooks	MTL	.295	73.	Tim Flannery	SD	.250	107.	Manny Trillo	SF	.200
6.	Steve Kemp	PIT	.362	40.	Terry Kennedy	SD	.294	73.	Greg Gross	PHI	.250	107.	Denny Walling	HOU	.200
7.	Keith Hernandez	NY	.354	41.	Wally Backman	NY	.292	73.	Gary Redus	CIN	.250	107.	Herm Winningham	MTL	.200
8.	Chris Brown	SF	.351	42.	Rafael Ramirez	ATL	.292	73.	U.L. Washington	MTL	.250	110.	Kevin McReynolds	SD	.198
9.	Tim Raines	MTL	.348	43.	Phil Garner	HOU	.292	77.	Mark Bailey	HOU	.245	111.	Tony Pena	PIT	.196
10.	Tony Gwynn	SD	.347	44.	Ron Roenicke	SF	.290	78.	Vince Coleman	STL	.243	112.	Ray Knight	NY	.196
11.	Bill Madlock	LA	.344	45.	Pete Rose	CIN	.290	79.	Graig Nettles	SD	.242	113.	Doug Frobel	MTL	.194
12.	Tony Perez	CIN	.343	46.	Gary Carter	NY	.289	79.	Johnny Ray	PIT	.242	114.	Andy Van Slyke	STL	.190
13.	Bill Almon	PIT	.341	47.	Terry Harper	ATL	.286	81.	Rick Schu	PHI	.239	115.	Gary Matthews	CHI	.189
14.	Chris Speier	CHI	.340	48.	Vance Law	MTL	.282	82.	Gerald Perry	ATL	.238	116.	Brad Komminsk	ATL	.188
15.	Jack Clark	STL	.333	49.	Jose Cruz	HOU	.279	82.	Craig Reynolds	HOU	.238	117.	Bob Brenly	SF	.187
15.	Dan Driessen	SF	.333	50.	Howard Johnson	NY	.279	84.	Darryl Strawberry	NY	.237	118.	Darrell Porter	STL	.186
15.	Lee Mazzilli	PIT	.333	51.	Jeff Leonard	SF	.278	85.	Rafael Santana	NY	.237	119.	Sixto Lezcano	PIT	.184
15.	Jerry Royster	SD	.333	51.	Juan Samuel	PHI	.278	86.	Chili Davis	SF	.235	120.	Mariano Duncan	LA	.183
19.	Bob Horner	ATL	.325	51.	Mookie Wilson	NY	.278	87.	Richie Hebner	CHI	.234	121.	Ken Oberkfell	ATL	.181
20.	Willie McGee	STL	.321	54.	Jerry Mumphrey	HOU	.277	87.	Jim Morrison	PIT	.234	122.	Garry Maddox	PHI	.178
21.	Kevin Bass	HOU	.319	55.	Von Hayes	PHI	.277	89.	Steve Garvey	SD	.233	123.	Chris Chambliss	ATL	.176
22.	Mike Schmidt	PHI	.318	56.	Sammy Khalifa	PIT	.271	90.	Rick Cerone	ATL	.233	124.	Mitch Webster	MTL	.171
23.	Kurt Bevacqua	SD	.316	57.	Tom Foley	PHI	.271	91.	Wayne Krenchicki	CIN	.231	125.	Tim Corcoran	PHI	.167
24.	Alan Ashby	HOU	.314	58.	Danny Heep	NY	.269	92.	Ozzie Smith	STL	.230	125.	George Hendrick	PIT	.167
25.	Tom Herr	STL	.314	59.	Bo Diaz	CIN	.268	93.	Joel Youngblood	SF	.226	127.	Scot Thompson	MTL	.164
26.	Tito Landrum	STL	.313	59.	Garry Templeton	SD	.268	94.	Jason Thompson	PIT	.222	128.	Greg Brock	LA	.164
27.	David Green	SF	.311	61.	Ken Landreaux	LA	.267	95.	Ozzie Virgil	PHI	.218	129.	Bruce Benedict	ATL	.147
28.	Keith Moreland	CHI	.311	62.	Ron Cey	CHI	.266	96.	Joe Orsulak	PIT	.215	130.	George Foster	NY	.132
29.	Glenn Wilson	PHI	.311	63.	Enos Cabell	LA	.263	97.	Candy Maldonado	LA	.214	131.	Glenn Davis	HOU	.122
30.	Pedro Guerrero	LA	.306	63.	Bob Dernier	CHI	.263	98.	Claudell Washington	ATL	.213	132.	Jody Davis	CHI	.120
31.	R.J. Reynolds	PIT	.302	65.	Andre Dawson	MTL	.259	99.	Nick Esasky	CIN	.211	133.	Buddy Bell	CIN	.091
32.	Luis Aguayo	PHI	.300	66.	Leon Durham	CHI	.256	99.	Mike Fitzgerald	MTL	.211	133.	Gary Rajsich	SF	.091
32.	Terry Whitfield	LA	.300	67.	Terry Francona	MTL	.254	101.	Dave Concepcion	CIN	.210	135.	Rob Deer	SF	.079
34.	Steve Sax	LA	.299	67.	Mike Scioscia	LA	.254	102.	Tim Wallach	MTL	.209				

Home Run Percentage in Pressure Situations

American League

1.	Darrell Evans	DET	13.43	40.	Rich Gedman	BOS	4.35	80.	Barbaro Garbey	DET	2.27	113.	Julio Cruz	CHI	0.00
2.	Ivan Calderon	SEA	10.00	42.	Jerry Willard	CLE	4.08	82.	Buddy Bell	TEX	2.13	113.	Alvin Davis	SEA	0.00
3.	Steve Balboni	KC	9.30	43.	Harold Baines	CHI	3.95	82.	Ron Kittle	CHI	2.13	113.	Tony Fernandez	TOR	0.00
4.	Bobby Jones	TEX	9.09	43.	Rickey Henderson	NY	3.95	82.	Mark Salas	MIN	2.13	113.	Scott Fletcher	CHI	0.00
4.	Eddie Murray	BAL	9.09	45.	George Bell	TOR	3.85	85.	Wayne Tolleson	TEX	1.96	113.	Julio Franco	CLE	0.00
6.	Andre Thornton	CLE	8.96	46.	Ben Oglivie	MIL	3.77	86.	Paul Householder	MIL	1.92	113.	Bobby Grich	CAL	0.00
7.	Don Baylor	NY	7.89	47.	Ken Phelps	SEA	3.70	86.	Tim Hulett	CHI	1.92	113.	Alfredo Griffin	OAK	0.00
7.	Jim Rice	BOS	7.89	48.	Jim Sundberg	KC	3.64	86.	Luis Salazar	CHI	1.92	113.	Ozzie Guillen	CHI	0.00
9.	Dwight Evans	BOS	7.87	49.	Johnny Grubb	DET	3.57	89.	Doug DeCinces	CAL	1.85	113.	Jackie Gutierrez	BOS	0.00
10.	Dave Kingman	OAK	7.79	50.	Ted Simmons	MIL	3.53	89.	Cliff Johnson	TOR	1.85	113.	Jerry Hairston	CHI	0.00
11.	Fred Lynn	BAL	7.69	51.	Dave Winfield	NY	3.49	89.	Carney Lansford	OAK	1.85	113.	Mike Hargrove	CLE	0.00
12.	Floyd Rayford	BAL	7.32	52.	Bill Buckner	BOS	3.45	92.	Donnie Hill	OAK	1.82	113.	Mickey Hatcher	MIN	0.00
13.	Tom Brunansky	MIN	7.14	52.	Bill Schroeder	MIL	3.45	93.	Roy Smalley	MIN	1.75	113.	Steve Henderson	OAK	0.00
14.	Greg Walker	CHI	7.06	54.	Ernie Whitt	TOR	3.39	94.	Don Slaught	TEX	1.72	113.	Garth Iorg	TOR	0.00
15.	Cal Ripken	BAL	6.94	55.	Mickey Tettleton	OAK	3.23	95.	Steve Lyons	BOS	1.69	113.	Reggie Jackson	CAL	0.00
16.	Dusty Baker	OAK	6.90	56.	Jim Dwyer	BAL	3.13	96.	George Brett	KC	1.64	113.	Lynn Jones	KC	0.00
17.	Dave Henderson	SEA	6.76	57.	Bruce Bochte	OAK	3.08	97.	Tony Armas	BOS	1.61	113.	Rudy Law	CHI	0.00
18.	Phil Bradley	SEA	6.52	57.	Gary Gaetti	MIN	3.08	98.	Tim Teufel	MIN	1.59	113.	Bobby Meacham	NY	0.00
18.	Larry Parrish	TEX	6.52	59.	Randy Ready	MIL	3.03	99.	Darryl Motley	KC	1.54	113.	Charlie Moore	MIL	0.00
20.	Carlton Fisk	CHI	6.49	59.	Mike Stenhouse	MIN	3.03	99.	Gorman Thomas	SEA	1.54	113.	Lloyd Moseby	TOR	0.00
21.	Jerry Narron	CAL	6.45	61.	Jorge Orta	KC	2.94	101.	Ken Griffey	NY	1.52	113.	Spike Owen	SEA	0.00
22.	Jesse Barfield	TOR	6.33	62.	Jeff Burroughs	TOR	2.86	102.	Willie Upshaw	TOR	1.49	113.	Jack Perconte	SEA	0.00
23.	Don Mattingly	NY	6.25	63.	Joe Carter	CLE	2.82	103.	Kent Hrbek	MIN	1.37	113.	Gary Pettis	CAL	0.00
24.	Donnie Scott	SEA	6.06	64.	Daryl Boston	CHI	2.78	104.	Damaso Garcia	TOR	1.33	113.	Willie Randolph	NY	0.00
25.	Ruppert Jones	CAL	5.88	64.	Mike Heath	OAK	2.78	104.	Larry Herndon	DET	1.33	113.	Earnest Riles	MIL	0.00
25.	Larry Sheets	BAL	5.88	64.	Dick Schofield	CAL	2.78	106.	Paul Molitor	MIL	1.30	113.	Ed Romero	MIL	0.00
27.	Mike Pagliarulo	NY	5.77	67.	Bob Kearney	SEA	2.70	107.	Jim Presley	SEA	1.28	113.	John Shelby	BAL	0.00
28.	Oddibe McDowell	TEX	5.66	68.	Pete O'Brien	TEX	2.67	108.	Jim Gantner	MIL	1.22	113.	Pat Sheridan	KC	0.00
28.	Butch Wynegar	NY	5.66	69.	Dave Bergman	DET	2.63	109.	Brook Jacoby	CLE	1.20	113.	Nelson Simmons	DET	0.00
30.	Mike Young	BAL	5.56	69.	Wayne Gross	BAL	2.63	109.	Kirby Puckett	MIN	1.20	113.	Lonnie Smith	KC	0.00
31.	Kirk Gibson	DET	5.41	71.	Glenn Hoffman	BOS	2.56	111.	Cecil Cooper	MIL	1.15	113.	Pat Tabler	CLE	0.00
31.	Ron Hassey	NY	5.41	71.	Chet Lemon	DET	2.56	111.	Mike Easler	BOS	1.15	113.	Alan Trammell	DET	0.00
33.	Hal McRae	KC	5.13	71.	Lou Whitaker	DET	2.56	113.	Marty Barrett	BOS	0.00	113.	George Vukovich	CLE	0.00
33.	Dwayne Murphy	OAK	5.13	74.	Rick Manning	MIL	2.50	113.	Juan Beniquez	CAL	0.00	113.	Alan Wiggins	BAL	0.00
35.	Al Cowens	SEA	5.00	74.	Rance Mulliniks	TOR	2.50	113.	Wade Boggs	BOS	0.00	113.	Rob Wilfong	CAL	0.00
36.	Lance Parrish	DET	4.94	74.	Frank White	KC	2.50	113.	Bob Boone	CAL	0.00	113.	Curtis Wilkerson	TEX	0.00
37.	Toby Harrah	TEX	4.92	77.	Rick Dempsey	BAL	2.44	113.	Tom Brookens	DET	0.00	113.	Willie Wilson	KC	0.00
38.	Lee Lacy	BAL	4.69	78.	Tony Bernazard	CLE	2.33	113.	Brett Butler	CLE	0.00	113.	George Wright	TEX	0.00
39.	Mike Davis	OAK	4.65	79.	Gary Ward	TEX	2.30	113.	Rod Carew	CAL	0.00	113.	Robin Yount	MIL	0.00
40.	Brian Downing	CAL	4.35	80.	Randy Bush	MIN	2.27	113.	Dave Collins	OAK	0.00				

National League

1.	Darryl Strawberry	NY	10.17	34.	Jack Clark	STL	3.33	68.	David Green	SF	1.64	92.	Doug Frobel	MTL	0.00
2.	Pedro Guerrero	LA	9.68	36.	Tim Wallach	MTL	3.30	70.	Gerald Perry	ATL	1.59	92.	Steve Garvey	SD	0.00
3.	Bob Horner	ATL	8.75	37.	Carmelo Martinez	SD	3.16	70.	R.J. Reynolds	PIT	1.59	92.	Greg Gross	PHI	0.00
4.	Alan Ashby	HOU	8.57	38.	Tito Landrum	STL	3.13	72.	Steve Sax	LA	1.49	92.	George Hendrick	PIT	0.00
5.	Mike Schmidt	PHI	7.95	39.	Graig Nettles	SD	3.03	73.	Jose Cruz	HOU	1.47	92.	Steve Kemp	PIT	0.00
6.	Nick Esasky	CIN	7.89	40.	Dan Driessen	SF	2.90	73.	George Foster	NY	1.47	92.	Sammy Khalifa	PIT	0.00
7.	Thad Bosley	CHI	7.84	41.	Jerry Royster	SD	2.78	75.	Jason Thompson	PIT	1.39	92.	Brad Komminsk	ATL	0.00
8.	Dave Lopes	CHI	7.41	42.	Jody Davis	CHI	2.67	76.	Manny Trillo	SF	1.33	92.	Wayne Krenchicki	CIN	0.00
9.	Candy Maldonado	LA	7.14	43.	Rob Deer	SF	2.63	77.	Claudell Washington	ATL	1.25	92.	Ken Landreaux	LA	0.00
10.	Cesar Cedeno	STL	7.02	43.	Mike Fitzgerald	MTL	2.63	78.	Keith Hernandez	NY	1.22	92.	Vance Law	MTL	0.00
11.	Howard Johnson	NY	6.56	43.	Sixto Lezcano	PIT	2.63	78.	Garry Templeton	SD	1.22	92.	Gary Matthews	CHI	0.00
12.	Chris Speier	CHI	6.38	46.	Bill Doran	HOU	2.60	80.	Terry Kennedy	SD	1.18	92.	Lee Mazzilli	PIT	0.00
13.	Glenn Wilson	PHI	5.83	47.	Ozzie Virgil	PHI	2.56	81.	Terry Pendleton	STL	1.15	92.	Kevin McReynolds	SD	0.00
14.	Mitch Webster	MTL	5.71	48.	Chili Davis	SF	2.47	81.	Ozzie Smith	STL	1.15	92.	Eddie Milner	CIN	0.00
15.	Mike Marshall	LA	5.63	48.	Andre Dawson	MTL	2.47	83.	Tim Raines	MTL	1.12	92.	Jerry Mumphrey	HOU	0.00
16.	Mookie Wilson	NY	5.56	50.	Bill Almon	PIT	2.44	83.	Rafael Ramirez	ATL	1.12	92.	Ken Oberkfell	ATL	0.00
17.	Ron Cey	CHI	5.06	50.	Glenn Davis	HOU	2.44	85.	Jeff Leonard	SF	1.11	92.	Ron Oester	CIN	0.00
18.	Terry Whitfield	LA	5.00	50.	Bo Diaz	CIN	2.44	85.	Bill Madlock	LA	1.11	92.	Joe Orsulak	PIT	0.00
19.	Leon Durham	CHI	4.88	53.	Darrell Porter	STL	2.33	85.	Keith Moreland	CHI	1.11	92.	Tony Perez	CIN	0.00
20.	Gary Carter	NY	4.82	54.	Garry Maddox	PHI	2.22	88.	Dan Gladden	SF	1.06	92.	Gary Rajsich	SF	0.00
21.	Bob Brenly	SF	4.67	54.	Herm Winningham	MTL	2.22	89.	Jose Uribe	SF	1.04	92.	Johnny Ray	PIT	0.00
22.	Ryne Sandberg	CHI	4.60	56.	Ray Knight	NY	2.17	90.	Dave Concepcion	CIN	1.00	92.	Craig Reynolds	HOU	0.00
23.	Juan Samuel	PHI	4.44	57.	Chris Brown	SF	2.13	91.	Hubie Brooks	MTL	0.95	92.	Ron Roenicke	SF	0.00
24.	Jim Morrison	PIT	4.26	57.	Von Hayes	PHI	2.13	92.	Wally Backman	NY	0.00	92.	Pete Rose	CIN	0.00
25.	Kevin Bass	HOU	4.17	57.	Richie Hebner	CHI	2.13	92.	Buddy Bell	CIN	0.00	92.	Rafael Santana	NY	0.00
25.	Phil Garner	HOU	4.17	60.	Tony Gwynn	SD	2.11	92.	Bruce Benedict	ATL	0.00	92.	Rick Schu	PHI	0.00
25.	Dave Parker	CIN	4.17	61.	Tom Foley	PHI	2.08	92.	Kurt Bevacqua	SD	0.00	92.	Milt Thompson	ATL	0.00
28.	Mark Bailey	HOU	4.08	62.	Tony Pena	PIT	2.06	92.	Enos Cabell	LA	0.00	92.	Scot Thompson	MTL	0.00
28.	Dale Murphy	ATL	4.08	63.	Chris Chambliss	ATL	1.96	92.	Rick Cerone	ATL	0.00	92.	Andy Van Slyke	STL	0.00
30.	Terry Harper	ATL	3.90	64.	Joel Youngblood	SF	1.89	92.	Vince Coleman	STL	0.00	92.	Denny Walling	HOU	0.00
31.	Danny Heep	NY	3.85	65.	Glenn Hubbard	ATL	1.85	92.	Tim Corcoran	PHI	0.00	92.	U.L. Washington	MTL	0.00
32.	Willie McGee	STL	3.70	66.	Mike Scioscia	LA	1.69	92.	Bob Dernier	CHI	0.00	92.	Marvell Wynne	PIT	0.00
33.	Tom Herr	STL	3.49	67.	Mariano Duncan	LA	1.67	92.	Tim Flannery	SD	0.00				
34.	Luis Aguayo	PHI	3.33	68.	Greg Brock	LA	1.64	92.	Terry Francona	MTL	0.00				

% of Runners Driven in from Scoring Position, Pressure Situations

American League

#	Player	Tm	Pct	#	Player	Tm	Pct	#	Player	Tm	Pct	#	Player	Tm	Pct
1.	Eddie Murray	BAL	.636	40.	Spike Owen	SEA	.364	78.	Rob Wilfong	CAL	.273	124.	Jesse Barfield	TOR	.176
2.	Bill Stein	TEX	.625	40.	Kirby Puckett	MIN	.364	84.	Reggie Jackson	CAL	.267	124.	Ozzie Guillen	CHI	.176
3.	Steve Henderson	OAK	.615	40.	Mike Stenhouse	MIN	.364	84.	Ruppert Jones	CAL	.267	126.	Joe Carter	CLE	.174
4.	Butch Wynegar	NY	.600	45.	Barbaro Garbey	DET	.357	86.	Charlie Moore	MIL	.261	126.	Rickey Henderson	NY	.174
5.	Curtis Wilkerson	TEX	.556	45.	Jerry Narron	CAL	.357	87.	Chris Bando	CLE	.250	128.	Randy Bush	MIN	.167
6.	Bob Boone	CAL	.526	45.	Jim Sundberg	KC	.357	87.	Buddy Bell	TEX	.250	128.	Brett Butler	CLE	.167
7.	Don Baylor	NY	.500	48.	Bill Buckner	BOS	.353	87.	Julio Franco	CLE	.250	128.	Jim Gantner	MIL	.167
7.	Rich Gedman	BOS	.500	48.	Dave Collins	OAK	.353	87.	Carney Lansford	OAK	.250	128.	Larry Herndon	DET	.167
7.	Cliff Johnson	TOR	.500	48.	Bobby Grich	CAL	.353	87.	Rick Manning	MIL	.250	128.	Lee Lacy	BAL	.167
7.	Ben Oglivie	MIL	.500	48.	Mike Heath	OAK	.353	87.	Reid Nichols	CHI	.250	128.	Rudy Law	CHI	.167
11.	Jim Rice	BOS	.458	48.	Steve Lyons	BOS	.353	87.	Floyd Rayford	BAL	.250	134.	Steve Balboni	KC	.160
12.	Jim Dwyer	BAL	.455	53.	Tom Brunansky	MIN	.350	87.	Cal Ripken	BAL	.250	135.	Dwight Evans	BOS	.154
13.	Bobby Meacham	NY	.444	54.	Kent Hrbek	MIN	.348	87.	John Shelby	BAL	.250	135.	George Vukovich	CLE	.154
14.	Dave Winfield	NY	.440	55.	Harold Baines	CHI	.333	87.	Alan Trammell	DET	.250	137.	Mike Davis	OAK	.150
15.	Al Cowens	SEA	.438	55.	Barry Bonnell	SEA	.333	87.	Gary Ward	TEX	.250	138.	Jeff Burroughs	TOR	.143
16.	Julio Cruz	CHI	.429	55.	Rod Carew	CAL	.333	98.	Darryl Motley	KC	.240	139.	Alvin Davis	SEA	.136
17.	Ted Simmons	MIL	.424	55.	Tony Fernandez	TOR	.333	99.	Doug DeCinces	CAL	.235	139.	Lonnie Smith	KC	.136
18.	George Brett	KC	.421	55.	Hal McRae	KC	.333	100.	Gorman Thomas	SEA	.231	141.	Gary Gaetti	MIN	.133
18.	Lloyd Moseby	TOR	.421	55.	Willie Wilson	KC	.333	100.	Ernie Whitt	TOR	.231	141.	Jim Presley	SEA	.133
20.	Randy Ready	MIL	.417	55.	Mike Young	BAL	.333	102.	Juan Beniquez	CAL	.227	143.	Dave Bergman	DET	.125
21.	Don Mattingly	NY	.407	55.	Robin Yount	MIL	.333	103.	Wade Boggs	BOS	.226	143.	Johnny Grubb	DET	.125
22.	George Bell	TOR	.400	63.	Greg Walker	CHI	.321	104.	Tony Armas	BOS	.222	145.	Mike Easler	BOS	.118
22.	Tom Brookens	DET	.400	64.	Jerry Willard	CLE	.318	104.	Kirk Gibson	DET	.222	145.	Paul Householder	MIL	.118
22.	Dave Engle	MIN	.400	65.	Tony Bernazard	CLE	.308	104.	Mike Hargrove	CLE	.222	145.	Brook Jacoby	CLE	.118
22.	Toby Harrah	TEX	.400	65.	Brian Downing	CAL	.308	104.	Ed Romero	MIL	.222	145.	Tim Teufel	MIN	.118
22.	Glenn Hoffman	BOS	.400	65.	Lance Parrish	DET	.308	104.	Luis Salazar	CHI	.222	149.	Dane Iorg	KC	.111
22.	Chet Lemon	DET	.400	65.	Andre Thornton	CLE	.308	104.	Wayne Tolleson	TEX	.222	149.	Lynn Jones	KC	.111
22.	Alan Wiggins	BAL	.400	69.	Dusty Baker	OAK	.304	110.	Alfredo Griffin	OAK	.216	149.	Dwayne Murphy	OAK	.111
29.	Cecil Cooper	MIL	.391	69.	Roy Smalley	MIN	.304	111.	Fred Lynn	BAL	.214	149.	George Wright	TEX	.111
30.	Darrell Evans	DET	.385	71.	Ken Phelps	SEA	.300	111.	Pete O'Brien	TEX	.214	153.	Dave Kingman	OAK	.105
30.	Scott Fletcher	CHI	.385	71.	Willie Upshaw	TOR	.300	111.	Willie Randolph	NY	.214	153.	Oddibe McDowell	TEX	.105
32.	Phil Bradley	SEA	.375	71.	Frank White	KC	.300	114.	Jerry Hairston	CHI	.211	155.	Marty Barrett	BOS	.100
32.	Carlton Fisk	CHI	.375	74.	Paul Molitor	MIL	.294	114.	Mickey Hatcher	MIN	.211	155.	Wayne Gross	BAL	.100
32.	Donnie Hill	OAK	.375	75.	Jorge Orta	KC	.286	114.	Dave Henderson	SEA	.211	155.	John Wathan	KC	.100
32.	Mike Pagliarulo	NY	.375	75.	Earnest Riles	MIL	.286	117.	Jackie Gutierrez	BOS	.200	158.	Tim Hulett	CHI	.000
32.	Larry Parrish	TEX	.375	77.	Mark Salas	MIN	.278	117.	Bobby Jones	TEX	.200	158.	Jack Perconte	SEA	.000
32.	Tony Phillips	OAK	.375	78.	Rance Mulliniks	TOR	.273	117.	Tom Paciorek	CHI	.200	158.	Alejandro Sanchez	DET	.000
32.	Bill Schroeder	MIL	.375	78.	Dick Schofield	CAL	.273	117.	Gary Pettis	CAL	.200	158.	Donnie Scott	SEA	.000
39.	Damaso Garcia	TOR	.370	78.	Larry Sheets	BAL	.273	121.	Bruce Bochte	OAK	.188				
40.	Ken Griffey	NY	.364	78.	Pat Tabler	CLE	.273	122.	Rick Miller	BOS	.182				
40.	Ron Hassey	NY	.364	78.	Lou Whitaker	DET	.273	122.	Don Slaught	TEX	.182				

National League

#	Player	Tm	Pct	#	Player	Tm	Pct	#	Player	Tm	Pct	#	Player	Tm	Pct
1.	Jose Cruz	HOU	.533	36.	Gary Carter	NY	.320	64.	Scot Thompson	MTL	.250	106.	Ron Cey	CHI	.176
2.	Vince Coleman	STL	.526	36.	Mike Schmidt	PHI	.320	72.	Bob Brenly	SF	.242	106.	Tim Flannery	SD	.176
3.	Gerald Perry	ATL	.471	36.	Tim Wallach	MTL	.320	73.	Cesar Cedeno	STL	.240	108.	Ken Oberkfell	ATL	.174
4.	Mark Bailey	HOU	.462	39.	Andre Dawson	MTL	.316	73.	Johnny Ray	PIT	.240	109.	Chris Chambliss	ATL	.167
5.	Ron Roenicke	SF	.455	39.	Dan Driessen	SF	.316	75.	Dave Lopes	CHI	.238	109.	Kevin McReynolds	SD	.167
6.	Keith Moreland	CHI	.439	41.	Chris Brown	SF	.314	75.	R.J. Reynolds	PIT	.238	109.	Jim Morrison	PIT	.167
7.	Dave Parker	CIN	.438	42.	Dave Concepcion	CIN	.313	75.	Jason Thompson	PIT	.238	109.	Ron Oester	CIN	.167
8.	Steve Braun	STL	.417	43.	Bill Doran	HOU	.310	78.	Gary Matthews	CHI	.235	109.	Ozzie Smith	STL	.167
8.	Ryne Sandberg	CHI	.417	44.	Al Oliver	LA	.308	78.	Manny Trillo	SF	.235	114.	Tim Raines	MTL	.158
10.	Rick Cerone	ATL	.400	45.	Bill Madlock	LA	.306	80.	Dan Gladden	SF	.233	114.	Marvell Wynne	PIT	.158
10.	Phil Garner	HOU	.400	45.	Glenn Wilson	PHI	.306	81.	Ozzie Virgil	PHI	.231	116.	Buddy Bell	CIN	.154
10.	Darrell Porter	STL	.400	47.	Kurt Bevacqua	SD	.304	81.	U.L. Washington	MTL	.231	116.	Bob Dernier	CHI	.154
10.	Rafael Ramirez	ATL	.400	47.	Hubie Brooks	MTL	.304	83.	Mike Fitzgerald	MTL	.222	116.	Steve Kemp	PIT	.154
14.	Terry Francona	MTL	.391	49.	Tony Pena	PIT	.290	83.	Doug Frobel	MTL	.222	119.	Garry Templeton	SD	.136
14.	Willie McGee	STL	.391	50.	Tom Foley	PHI	.286	83.	Wayne Krenchicki	CIN	.222	120.	Jeff Leonard	SF	.125
16.	Chili Davis	SF	.385	50.	Danny Heep	NY	.286	83.	Tony Perez	CIN	.222	121.	Mariano Duncan	LA	.111
17.	Dale Murphy	ATL	.379	50.	Terry Kennedy	SD	.286	83.	Jim Wohlford	MTL	.222	121.	Ray Knight	NY	.111
17.	Juan Samuel	PHI	.379	50.	Darryl Strawberry	NY	.286	88.	Jody Davis	CHI	.217	121.	Milt Thompson	ATL	.111
19.	Pedro Guerrero	LA	.368	54.	Terry Pendleton	STL	.280	89.	Terry Harper	ATL	.214	124.	Greg Brock	LA	.100
20.	Eddie Milner	CIN	.364	55.	Brian Harper	STL	.273	89.	Howard Johnson	NY	.214	124.	Tito Landrum	STL	.100
21.	David Green	SF	.357	55.	Rusty Staub	NY	.273	89.	Bill Russell	LA	.214	124.	Mookie Wilson	NY	.100
22.	Richie Hebner	CHI	.350	55.	Joel Youngblood	SF	.273	89.	Mike Scioscia	LA	.214	127.	Mike Brown	PIT	.083
23.	Tony Gwynn	SD	.346	58.	Tom Herr	STL	.267	93.	Lee Mazzilli	PIT	.211	127.	Sammy Khalifa	PIT	.083
24.	Carmelo Martinez	SD	.344	59.	Vance Law	MTL	.265	93.	Jose Uribe	SF	.211	127.	Herm Winningham	MTL	.083
25.	Sid Bream	PIT	.333	60.	Jerry Mumphrey	HOU	.263	93.	Andy Van Slyke	STL	.211	130.	Sixto Lezcano	PIT	.071
25.	Jack Clark	STL	.333	61.	Pete Rose	CIN	.261	96.	Wally Backman	NY	.200	131.	Brad Komminsk	ATL	.067
25.	Bo Diaz	CIN	.333	62.	Tim Corcoran	PHI	.259	96.	Glenn Davis	HOU	.200	132.	Craig Reynolds	HOU	.056
25.	Leon Durham	CHI	.333	63.	Bob Horner	ATL	.258	96.	Graig Nettles	SD	.200	133.	Darren Daulton	PHI	.000
25.	George Foster	NY	.333	64.	Kevin Bass	HOU	.250	96.	Steve Sax	LA	.200	133.	George Hendrick	PIT	.000
25.	Steve Garvey	SD	.333	64.	Enos Cabell	LA	.250	96.	Claudell Washington	ATL	.200	133.	Ken Landreaux	LA	.000
25.	Keith Hernandez	NY	.333	64.	Nick Esasky	CIN	.250	101.	Von Hayes	PHI	.194	133.	Garry Maddox	PHI	.000
25.	Mike Marshall	LA	.333	64.	Mike Jorgensen	STL	.250	102.	Glenn Hubbard	ATL	.188	133.	Candy Maldonado	LA	.000
25.	Joe Orsulak	PIT	.333	64.	Tom Nieto	STL	.250	102.	Rafael Santana	NY	.188	133.	Denny Walling	HOU	.000
25.	Chris Speier	CHI	.333	64.	Gary Redus	CIN	.250	104.	Greg Gross	PHI	.182	133.	Paul Zuvella	ATL	.000
25.	Terry Whitfield	LA	.333	64.	Jerry Royster	SD	.250	104.	Rick Schu	PHI	.182				

On Base Average Leading Off the Inning

American League

#	Player	Tm	Avg	#	Player	Tm	Avg	#	Player	Tm	Avg	#	Player	Tm	Avg
1.	Wade Boggs	BOS	.468	41.	Eddie Murray	BAL	.350	81.	Kirby Puckett	MIN	.320	121.	Dusty Baker	OAK	.282
2.	Willie Randolph	NY	.448	42.	Otis Nixon	CLE	.348	82.	John Shelby	BAL	.317	122.	Don Slaught	TEX	.280
3.	George Brett	KC	.426	43.	Mike Davis	OAK	.348	83.	Rich Gedman	BOS	.315	123.	Pat Tabler	CLE	.278
4.	Rickey Henderson	NY	.418	44.	Mike Easler	BOS	.347	84.	Mike Pagliarulo	NY	.314	124.	Doug DeCinces	CAL	.276
5.	Kirk Gibson	DET	.412	45.	Gary Pettis	CAL	.345	85.	Buddy Biancalana	KC	.314	125.	Daryl Boston	CHI	.276
6.	Toby Harrah	TEX	.409	46.	Tony Armas	BOS	.344	86.	Jackie Gutierrez	BOS	.313	126.	Julio Cruz	CHI	.274
7.	Johnny Grubb	DET	.408	47.	Bruce Bochte	OAK	.344	86.	Cal Ripken	BAL	.313	127.	Ozzie Guillen	CHI	.274
8.	Mickey Tettleton	OAK	.396	48.	Ken Griffey	NY	.341	86.	Larry Sheets	BAL	.313	128.	Lee Lacy	BAL	.274
9.	Jerry Willard	CLE	.395	49.	Darrell Evans	DET	.341	89.	Rich Dauer	BAL	.313	129.	Luis Salazar	CHI	.273
10.	Dave Winfield	NY	.389	50.	Alan Wiggins	BAL	.341	89.	Willie Upshaw	TOR	.313	130.	Gary Gaetti	MIN	.271
11.	Alvin Davis	SEA	.389	51.	Larry Herndon	DET	.340	91.	Willie Wilson	KC	.312	131.	Larry Parrish	TEX	.271
12.	Carmen Castillo	CLE	.383	51.	Earnest Riles	MIL	.340	92.	Jim Sundberg	KC	.311	132.	Carlton Fisk	CHI	.270
13.	Jim Rice	BOS	.383	53.	Julio Franco	CLE	.339	93.	Jim Presley	SEA	.311	132.	Frank White	KC	.270
14.	Mike Hargrove	CLE	.382	54.	Wayne Gross	BAL	.339	94.	Donnie Hill	OAK	.309	134.	Dave Bergman	DET	.269
15.	Buddy Bell	TEX	.382	55.	Floyd Rayford	BAL	.338	95.	Barbaro Garbey	DET	.309	134.	Jim Gantner	MIL	.269
16.	Dwight Evans	BOS	.377	56.	Jack Perconte	SEA	.336	96.	Randy Bush	MIN	.308	134.	Bob Kearney	SEA	.269
17.	Paul Molitor	MIL	.377	57.	Chet Lemon	DET	.336	97.	Greg Walker	CHI	.307	134.	Mark Salas	MIN	.269
18.	Brian Downing	CAL	.374	58.	Phil Bradley	SEA	.336	98.	Ernie Whitt	TOR	.306	138.	Andre Thornton	CLE	.269
19.	Glenn Hoffman	BOS	.373	59.	Juan Beniquez	CAL	.333	99.	Bobby Meacham	NY	.306	139.	Alfredo Griffin	OAK	.268
20.	Reid Nichols	CHI	.373	59.	Steve Buechele	TEX	.333	100.	Rudy Law	CHI	.306	140.	Pete O'Brien	TEX	.265
21.	Gary Ward	TEX	.373	59.	Jim Dwyer	BAL	.333	101.	Steve Lyons	BOS	.305	141.	Garth Iorg	TOR	.265
22.	Spike Owen	SEA	.373	59.	Steve Henderson	OAK	.333	102.	Dick Schofield	CAL	.303	141.	Darryl Motley	KC	.265
23.	Marty Barrett	BOS	.372	59.	Reggie Jackson	CAL	.333	103.	Steve Balboni	KC	.302	143.	Greg Gagne	MIN	.260
24.	Cecil Cooper	MIL	.371	59.	Dwayne Murphy	OAK	.333	104.	Ed Romero	MIL	.302	144.	Rob Wilfong	CAL	.260
25.	Ron Hassey	NY	.369	59.	Lonnie Smith	KC	.333	105.	Dave Kingman	OAK	.301	145.	Ted Simmons	MIL	.257
26.	Jorge Orta	KC	.368	66.	Bobby Grich	CAL	.331	106.	Don Baylor	NY	.298	146.	Tom Brookens	DET	.252
27.	Rod Carew	CAL	.366	67.	Kent Hrbek	MIN	.331	106.	Tim Hulett	CHI	.298	147.	Carney Lansford	OAK	.250
28.	Lou Whitaker	DET	.365	68.	Tony Bernazard	CLE	.331	108.	Dave Collins	OAK	.297	148.	Charlie Moore	MIL	.243
29.	Hal McRae	KC	.365	69.	Harold Baines	CHI	.330	109.	Scott Fletcher	CHI	.296	149.	Cliff Johnson	TOR	.237
30.	Tim Teufel	MIN	.361	70.	Rick Dempsey	BAL	.330	110.	Butch Wynegar	NY	.296	150.	Rick Manning	MIL	.235
31.	Wayne Tolleson	TEX	.360	71.	Ben Oglivie	MIL	.330	111.	Alan Trammell	DET	.296	151.	Lance Parrish	DET	.235
32.	Rance Mulliniks	TOR	.357	72.	Paul Householder	MIL	.329	112.	Damaso Garcia	TOR	.296	152.	Nelson Simmons	DET	.230
33.	Don Mattingly	NY	.356	73.	George Bell	TOR	.329	113.	Ron Kittle	CHI	.295	153.	Robin Yount	MIL	.227
34.	Tony Fernandez	TOR	.355	74.	Mike Young	BAL	.328	114.	Bill Buckner	BOS	.295	154.	Domingo Ramos	SEA	.224
35.	Gorman Thomas	SEA	.353	75.	Fred Lynn	BAL	.327	115.	Joe Carter	CLE	.294	155.	George Wright	TEX	.215
36.	Lloyd Moseby	TOR	.352	76.	Al Cowens	SEA	.327	115.	Ruppert Jones	CAL	.294	156.	Mickey Hatcher	MIN	.205
37.	Mike Heath	OAK	.352	77.	Bob Boone	CAL	.325	117.	Tom Brunansky	MIN	.291	157.	Onix Concepcion	KC	.203
38.	Jesse Barfield	TOR	.352	78.	Curtis Wilkerson	TEX	.324	118.	George Vukovich	CLE	.287	158.	Mike Stenhouse	MIN	.196
39.	Brett Butler	CLE	.352	79.	Oddibe McDowell	TEX	.324	119.	Dave Henderson	SEA	.286	159.	Pat Sheridan	KC	.184
40.	Roy Smalley	MIN	.350	80.	Brook Jacoby	CLE	.322	119.	Gary Roenicke	BAL	.286				

National League

#	Player	Tm	Avg	#	Player	Tm	Avg	#	Player	Tm	Avg	#	Player	Tm	Avg
1.	Mike Brown	PIT	.446	35.	Vance Law	MTL	.359	69.	Mike Marshall	LA	.321	103.	Enos Cabell	LA	.279
2.	Jack Clark	STL	.436	36.	Jose Cruz	HOU	.357	70.	Leon Durham	CHI	.321	104.	Rafael Ramirez	ATL	.279
3.	Paul Zuvella	ATL	.429	37.	Herm Winningham	MTL	.355	71.	Rafael Santana	NY	.320	105.	Chris Speier	CHI	.279
4.	Pedro Guerrero	LA	.427	38.	Keith Moreland	CHI	.355	72.	Tim Flannery	SD	.320	106.	Tom Nieto	STL	.278
5.	Tim Corcoran	PHI	.422	39.	Hubie Brooks	MTL	.354	73.	Steve Garvey	SD	.320	107.	Steve Kemp	PIT	.276
6.	Ryne Sandberg	CHI	.417	40.	Steve Sax	LA	.354	74.	Carmelo Martinez	SD	.319	108.	Gary Matthews	CHI	.275
7.	Darrell Porter	STL	.415	41.	Ozzie Virgil	PHI	.354	75.	Mark Bailey	HOU	.317	109.	Garry Templeton	SD	.275
8.	Mitch Webster	MTL	.412	42.	Ozzie Smith	STL	.353	76.	Luis Aguayo	PHI	.315	110.	Steve Jeltz	PHI	.273
9.	Dale Murphy	ATL	.408	43.	Greg Gross	PHI	.353	77.	Nick Esasky	CIN	.313	111.	Miguel Dilone	SD	.271
10.	Glenn Hubbard	ATL	.404	44.	Vince Coleman	STL	.351	78.	Kevin Bass	HOU	.311	112.	George Foster	NY	.269
11.	Dave Concepcion	CIN	.400	45.	Jeff Stone	PHI	.350	79.	Chili Davis	SF	.308	113.	Bob Brenly	SF	.267
12.	Joel Youngblood	SF	.394	46.	Gary Redus	CIN	.350	80.	Dan Gladden	SF	.308	114.	Alan Ashby	HOU	.267
13.	Tony Gwynn	SD	.393	47.	Eddie Milner	CIN	.347	81.	Bob Dernier	CHI	.307	115.	Cesar Cedeno	STL	.265
14.	Tim Raines	MTL	.391	48.	Brad Komminsk	ATL	.344	82.	Dave Anderson	LA	.307	116.	Denny Walling	HOU	.263
15.	Bill Almon	PIT	.391	49.	Alan Knicely	PHI	.341	82.	R.J. Reynolds	PIT	.307	117.	Terry Pendleton	STL	.263
16.	Ken Oberkfell	ATL	.390	50.	Tony Perez	CIN	.340	84.	Ron Cey	CHI	.306	118.	Dickie Thon	HOU	.263
17.	Bill Madlock	LA	.388	51.	Shawon Dunston	CHI	.339	85.	Wally Backman	NY	.304	119.	Jody Davis	CHI	.261
18.	Joe Orsulak	PIT	.387	52.	Bruce Benedict	ATL	.333	85.	Craig Reynolds	HOU	.304	119.	John Russell	PHI	.261
19.	Keith Hernandez	NY	.385	52.	Chris Brown	SF	.333	87.	Terry Harper	ATL	.302	121.	Marvell Wynne	PIT	.260
20.	Mike Scioscia	LA	.384	52.	Tom Foley	PHI	.333	88.	Mariano Duncan	LA	.298	122.	Sammy Khalifa	PIT	.259
21.	Dave Lopes	CHI	.384	52.	Von Hayes	PHI	.333	89.	Buddy Bell	CIN	.295	123.	Larry Bowa	NY	.259
22.	Milt Thompson	ATL	.383	52.	Bob Horner	ATL	.333	90.	Manny Trillo	SF	.294	124.	Jeff Leonard	SF	.258
23.	Mookie Wilson	NY	.378	52.	Candy Maldonado	LA	.333	91.	Jerry Mumphrey	HOU	.294	125.	Garry Maddox	PHI	.254
24.	Dan Driessen	SF	.378	58.	Bill Doran	HOU	.332	92.	Johnny Ray	PIT	.293	126.	Jim Morrison	PIT	.241
25.	Thad Bosley	CHI	.375	59.	Ron Oester	CIN	.331	93.	Kevin McReynolds	SD	.289	127.	Greg Brock	LA	.238
25.	Gary Carter	NY	.375	60.	Andy Van Slyke	STL	.331	94.	Billy Hatcher	CHI	.288	128.	Ken Landreaux	LA	.236
27.	Tom Herr	STL	.374	61.	Len Dykstra	NY	.330	95.	Tony Pena	PIT	.288	129.	Ray Knight	NY	.231
28.	Dave Parker	CIN	.373	62.	Tim Wallach	MTL	.329	95.	Gerald Perry	ATL	.288	130.	Brad Wellman	SF	.227
29.	Pete Rose	CIN	.372	63.	Claudell Washington	ATL	.327	97.	Danny Heep	NY	.286	131.	Jose Uribe	SF	.227
30.	Mike Schmidt	PHI	.367	64.	Jerry Royster	SD	.326	97.	Howard Johnson	NY	.286	132.	Bo Diaz	CIN	.224
31.	Glenn Wilson	PHI	.365	65.	Juan Samuel	PHI	.325	99.	Mike Fitzgerald	MTL	.284	133.	Andre Dawson	MTL	.223
32.	Willie McGee	STL	.364	66.	Darryl Strawberry	NY	.324	100.	Jason Thompson	PIT	.282	134.	Terry Kennedy	SD	.216
33.	Glenn Davis	HOU	.363	67.	Graig Nettles	SD	.323	101.	George Hendrick	PIT	.281	135.	Rick Cerone	ATL	.200
34.	Rick Schu	PHI	.362	68.	Phil Garner	HOU	.323	102.	David Green	SF	.280	136.	Terry Francona	MTL	.197

Batting Average with Runners in Scoring Position

American League

#	Player	Team	Avg	#	Player	Team	Avg	#	Player	Team	Avg	#	Player	Team	Avg
1.	Steve Henderson	OAK	.426	41.	Alfredo Griffin	OAK	.303	81.	Lance Parrish	DET	.274	121.	Randy Bush	MIN	.234
2.	Wade Boggs	BOS	.392	42.	Greg Gagne	MIN	.303	82.	Tony Armas	BOS	.274	122.	Mark Salas	MIN	.234
3.	Alan Wiggins	BAL	.388	43.	Phil Bradley	SEA	.302	83.	Jim Presley	SEA	.273	123.	Chet Lemon	DET	.230
4.	Rance Mulliniks	TOR	.381	44.	Bruce Bochte	OAK	.300	84.	Tim Teufel	MIN	.272	124.	Ernie Whitt	TOR	.229
5.	Eddie Murray	BAL	.370	44.	Dave Engle	MIN	.300	85.	Luis Salazar	CHI	.272	125.	Tom Brunansky	MIN	.227
6.	Jim Dwyer	BAL	.362	44.	Tony Fernandez	TOR	.300	86.	Tom Brookens	DET	.271	125.	Ron Hassey	NY	.227
7.	Cliff Johnson	TOR	.355	44.	Ed Romero	MIL	.300	87.	Ken Griffey	NY	.269	125.	Jerry Willard	CLE	.227
8.	Brett Butler	CLE	.351	48.	Ben Oglivie	MIL	.299	88.	Jim Sundberg	KC	.268	128.	Charlie Moore	MIL	.223
9.	Harold Baines	CHI	.346	49.	Gary Roenicke	BAL	.298	89.	Willie Upshaw	TOR	.267	129.	Wayne Tolleson	TEX	.222
10.	Jim Rice	BOS	.341	50.	Cecil Cooper	MIL	.298	90.	Donnie Scott	SEA	.267	129.	Curtis Wilkerson	TEX	.222
11.	George Brett	KC	.340	51.	Bob Kearney	SEA	.295	91.	Kent Hrbek	MIN	.264	131.	Steve Balboni	KC	.220
12.	Pat Tabler	CLE	.340	52.	Willie Wilson	KC	.295	92.	Jorge Orta	KC	.263	131.	Ruppert Jones	CAL	.220
13.	Donnie Hill	OAK	.337	53.	Mickey Hatcher	MIN	.295	93.	Marty Barrett	BOS	.262	133.	Dave Kingman	OAK	.219
14.	Carlton Fisk	CHI	.336	54.	Lou Whitaker	DET	.293	94.	Mike Pagliarulo	NY	.262	134.	Willie Randolph	NY	.218
15.	Toby Harrah	TEX	.329	55.	Earnest Riles	MIL	.292	95.	Tony Bernazard	CLE	.262	135.	Rick Manning	MIL	.216
16.	Garth Iorg	TOR	.329	56.	Julio Franco	CLE	.292	96.	Glenn Hoffman	BOS	.260	136.	Dick Schofield	CAL	.214
17.	Cal Ripken	BAL	.327	57.	Dave Henderson	SEA	.291	97.	Bobby Meacham	NY	.260	136.	Butch Wynegar	NY	.214
18.	Ivan Calderon	SEA	.327	58.	Mike Young	BAL	.291	98.	Floyd Rayford	BAL	.259	138.	Mickey Tettleton	OAK	.212
19.	Jerry Hairston	CHI	.324	59.	Reggie Jackson	CAL	.289	99.	Carney Lansford	OAK	.259	139.	Dwayne Murphy	OAK	.211
20.	Mike Heath	OAK	.322	60.	Frank White	KC	.289	100.	Pete O'Brien	TEX	.257	140.	Larry Parrish	TEX	.210
21.	Mike Hargrove	CLE	.321	61.	Rick Dempsey	BAL	.289	101.	Ron Kittle	CHI	.256	141.	Barbaro Garbey	DET	.210
22.	Bill Buckner	BOS	.320	62.	Nelson Simmons	DET	.288	102.	Dusty Baker	OAK	.256	142.	Bill Schroeder	MIL	.209
23.	Bryan Little	CHI	.319	63.	Rickey Henderson	NY	.288	103.	Rob Wilfong	CAL	.255	143.	Oddibe McDowell	TEX	.207
24.	Kirby Puckett	MIN	.318	64.	Jeff Burroughs	TOR	.286	104.	Steve Buechele	TEX	.255	144.	Alan Trammell	DET	.207
25.	Rich Gedman	BOS	.317	65.	Greg Walker	CHI	.285	104.	Jack Perconte	SEA	.255	145.	Darryl Motley	KC	.207
26.	Gary Ward	TEX	.317	66.	Ted Simmons	MIL	.284	106.	Doug DeCinces	CAL	.254	146.	Paul Householder	MIL	.205
27.	Don Mattingly	NY	.316	67.	Steve Lyons	BOS	.283	107.	Onix Concepcion	KC	.254	147.	Lonnie Smith	KC	.202
28.	Dave Winfield	NY	.316	68.	Jesse Barfield	TOR	.281	108.	Don Slaught	TEX	.253	148.	Wayne Gross	BAL	.200
29.	Hal McRae	KC	.314	69.	Gary Pettis	CAL	.281	109.	Bob Boone	CAL	.250	149.	Daryl Boston	CHI	.196
30.	Dave Collins	OAK	.313	70.	Don Baylor	NY	.281	109.	Tim Hulett	CHI	.250	150.	Tim Laudner	MIN	.191
31.	Lee Lacy	BAL	.313	71.	Paul Molitor	MIL	.280	111.	Mike Easler	BOS	.248	151.	Larry Herndon	DET	.186
32.	Rod Carew	CAL	.313	72.	Mike Davis	OAK	.280	112.	Joe Carter	CLE	.244	152.	Julio Cruz	CHI	.183
33.	Brian Downing	CAL	.311	73.	Spike Owen	SEA	.280	113.	Roy Smalley	MIN	.242	153.	Dwight Evans	BOS	.177
34.	Andre Thornton	CLE	.309	74.	Lloyd Moseby	TOR	.279	114.	George Vukovich	CLE	.241	154.	Pat Sheridan	KC	.173
35.	Al Cowens	SEA	.308	75.	Robin Yount	MIL	.278	115.	Fred Lynn	BAL	.240	155.	George Wright	TEX	.163
36.	Damaso Garcia	TOR	.308	76.	Juan Beniquez	CAL	.278	116.	Bobby Grich	CAL	.240	156.	Gorman Thomas	SEA	.162
36.	Kirk Gibson	DET	.308	77.	Larry Sheets	BAL	.276	117.	Buddy Bell	TEX	.238	157.	Chris Bando	CLE	.130
38.	Scott Fletcher	CHI	.306	78.	Darrell Evans	DET	.276	118.	Jim Gantner	MIL	.238	158.	Jackie Gutierrez	BOS	.099
39.	Ozzie Guillen	CHI	.305	79.	Alvin Davis	SEA	.275	119.	Brook Jacoby	CLE	.237				
40.	Rudy Law	CHI	.304	80.	George Bell	TOR	.275	120.	Gary Gaetti	MIN	.235				

National League

#	Player	Team	Avg	#	Player	Team	Avg	#	Player	Team	Avg	#	Player	Team	Avg
1.	Jerry Royster	SD	.396	35.	Terry Kennedy	SD	.296	69.	Juan Samuel	PHI	.268	102.	Carmelo Martinez	SD	.231
2.	Willie McGee	STL	.391	36.	Gary Redus	CIN	.294	70.	Ozzie Smith	STL	.268	104.	Manny Trillo	SF	.229
3.	Tony Perez	CIN	.388	37.	Terry Francona	MTL	.293	71.	Kevin Bass	HOU	.267	105.	Mariano Duncan	LA	.227
4.	Dave Parker	CIN	.360	38.	Von Hayes	PHI	.291	71.	Dave Lopes	CHI	.267	105.	Darrell Porter	STL	.227
5.	Tim Flannery	SD	.356	39.	Bill Madlock	LA	.290	71.	Tony Pena	PIT	.267	107.	Jeff Leonard	SF	.226
6.	Bo Diaz	CIN	.352	40.	Steve Garvey	SD	.289	74.	Eddie Milner	CIN	.263	108.	Vance Law	MTL	.224
7.	Cesar Cedeno	STL	.349	41.	Alan Knicely	PHI	.289	75.	Mitch Webster	MTL	.261	109.	Gary Matthews	CHI	.224
8.	Chris Brown	SF	.337	42.	Tom Nieto	STL	.288	76.	Rafael Ramirez	ATL	.260	110.	Bob Brenly	SF	.216
9.	Keith Moreland	CHI	.335	43.	Glenn Wilson	PHI	.287	77.	Wayne Krenchicki	CIN	.259	111.	Dan Gladden	SF	.214
10.	Tom Herr	STL	.333	44.	Leon Durham	CHI	.286	78.	Rick Cerone	ATL	.258	112.	Larry Bowa	NY	.211
10.	Dickie Thon	HOU	.333	44.	Nick Esasky	CIN	.286	79.	Terry Pendleton	STL	.256	112.	Ken Oberkfell	ATL	.211
12.	Gary Carter	NY	.331	44.	George Hendrick	PIT	.286	80.	Bruce Benedict	ATL	.255	112.	Joe Orsulak	PIT	.211
12.	Andre Dawson	MTL	.331	47.	Jack Clark	STL	.285	81.	Terry Harper	ATL	.254	115.	Steve Jeltz	PHI	.208
14.	Jose Cruz	HOU	.331	48.	George Foster	NY	.284	81.	Brad Komminsk	ATL	.254	116.	Rafael Santana	NY	.208
15.	Garry Templeton	SD	.330	49.	Ryne Sandberg	CHI	.284	83.	Bob Horner	ATL	.252	117.	Bob Dernier	CHI	.208
16.	Darryl Strawberry	NY	.330	50.	Vince Coleman	STL	.283	84.	Pedro Guerrero	LA	.250	118.	Len Dykstra	NY	.207
17.	Dale Murphy	ATL	.329	51.	Greg Brock	LA	.283	85.	Mookie Wilson	NY	.246	119.	Dave Concepcion	CIN	.206
18.	Wally Backman	NY	.324	52.	Tito Landrum	STL	.283	86.	Ron Cey	CHI	.246	120.	Sammy Khalifa	PIT	.205
19.	Mike Scioscia	LA	.324	53.	Kurt Bevacqua	SD	.282	87.	Phil Garner	HOU	.245	121.	Chili Davis	SF	.204
20.	Denny Walling	HOU	.322	54.	Mike Schmidt	PHI	.282	88.	Chris Chambliss	ATL	.244	121.	Candy Maldonado	LA	.204
21.	Mike Brown	PIT	.317	55.	Ray Knight	NY	.281	89.	Andy Van Slyke	STL	.244	123.	Howard Johnson	NY	.200
22.	Glenn Davis	HOU	.316	56.	Graig Nettles	SD	.280	90.	Craig Reynolds	HOU	.241	123.	Steve Kemp	PIT	.200
23.	Hubie Brooks	MTL	.314	57.	Bill Doran	HOU	.278	91.	Mike Fitzgerald	MTL	.238	125.	Herm Winningham	MTL	.197
24.	Keith Hernandez	NY	.312	58.	Jerry Mumphrey	HOU	.277	91.	Glenn Hubbard	ATL	.238	126.	Dan Driessen	SF	.196
25.	Dave Van Gorder	CIN	.311	59.	Danny Heep	NY	.276	91.	Jim Morrison	PIT	.238	127.	Dave Anderson	LA	.185
26.	Kevin McReynolds	SD	.311	59.	Joel Youngblood	SF	.276	94.	Tim Raines	MTL	.237	128.	John Russell	PHI	.184
27.	Steve Sax	LA	.310	61.	Tim Wallach	MTL	.275	95.	Garry Maddox	PHI	.236	129.	David Green	SF	.182
28.	Jason Thompson	PIT	.308	62.	Claudell Washington	ATL	.274	95.	Ozzie Virgil	PHI	.236	130.	Jeff Stone	PHI	.176
29.	Mark Bailey	HOU	.308	63.	Jose Uribe	SF	.271	97.	Marvell Wynne	PIT	.235	131.	Ken Landreaux	LA	.168
30.	Chris Speier	CHI	.302	64.	Tony Gwynn	SD	.270	98.	Rick Schu	PHI	.235	132.	Gerald Perry	ATL	.164
31.	U.L. Washington	MTL	.300	65.	Enos Cabell	LA	.270	99.	Shawon Dunston	CHI	.233	133.	Jody Davis	CHI	.161
32.	R.J. Reynolds	PIT	.298	66.	Ron Oester	CIN	.269	100.	Bill Almon	PIT	.232	134.	Tim Corcoran	PHI	.141
33.	Johnny Ray	PIT	.296	66.	Pete Rose	CIN	.269	100.	Tom Foley	PHI	.232				
34.	Mike Marshall	LA	.296	68.	Sid Bream	PIT	.268	102.	Buddy Bell	CIN	.231				

Batting Average with Runners in Scoring Position and Two Outs

American League

1. Jim Dwyer	BAL	.440	40. Ted Simmons	MIL	.293	81. Bruce Bochte	OAK	.243	121. Dwight Evans	BOS	.211
2. Al Oliver	TOR	.423	41. Bill Buckner	BOS	.292	81. Darryl Motley	KC	.243	122. Mike Easler	BOS	.211
3. Alan Wiggins	BAL	.421	42. Len Matuszek	TOR	.292	83. Nelson Simmons	DET	.242	122. Kent Hrbek	MIN	.211
4. George Brett	KC	.396	44. Julio Franco	CLE	.286	84. Phil Bradley	SEA	.242	124. Larry Herndon	DET	.209
5. Rudy Law	CHI	.379	44. Butch Wynegar	NY	.286	85. Toby Harrah	TEX	.241	125. Ed Romero	MIL	.208
6. Mike Stenhouse	MIN	.375	46. Jim Presley	SEA	.284	85. Reggie Jackson	CAL	.241	125. Pat Tabler	CLE	.208
7. Wade Boggs	BOS	.373	47. Tim Teufel	MIN	.282	87. Tony Bernazard	CLE	.241	127. Greg Gagne	MIN	.206
8. Harold Baines	CHI	.370	48. Darrell Evans	DET	.280	87. Rod Carew	CAL	.241	128. Rick Dempsey	BAL	.205
9. Rance Mulliniks	TOR	.361	49. Floyd Rayford	BAL	.278	89. Alvin Davis	SEA	.239	128. Larry Parrish	TEX	.205
10. Gary Roenicke	BAL	.357	50. Marty Barrett	BOS	.274	90. Jerry Hairston	CHI	.238	130. Oddibe McDowell	TEX	.200
11. Gary Pettis	CAL	.356	50. Dave Henderson	SEA	.274	91. Wayne Tolleson	TEX	.237	130. Dwayne Murphy	OAK	.200
12. Don Mattingly	NY	.354	52. Dusty Baker	OAK	.273	92. Jack Perconte	SEA	.236	130. Mark Salas	MIN	.200
13. Eddie Murray	BAL	.347	52. Cal Ripken	BAL	.273	93. Bob Boone	CAL	.236	133. Gary Gaetti	MIN	.197
14. Carney Lansford	OAK	.344	52. Rob Wilfong	CAL	.273	94. Alfredo Griffin	OAK	.235	134. Fred Lynn	BAL	.196
14. Luis Salazar	CHI	.344	55. Don Baylor	NY	.271	94. Brook Jacoby	CLE	.235	135. Alan Trammell	DET	.194
16. Damaso Garcia	TOR	.339	56. Ben Oglivie	MIL	.268	96. Jeff Burroughs	TOR	.231	136. Randy Bush	MIN	.194
17. Donnie Hill	OAK	.333	57. Paul Molitor	MIL	.264	96. Tim Laudner	MIN	.231	137. Steve Balboni	KC	.192
17. Garth Iorg	TOR	.333	58. Robin Yount	MIL	.262	96. Lloyd Moseby	TOR	.231	138. Dave Kingman	OAK	.188
17. Spike Owen	SEA	.333	59. Dave Engle	MIN	.259	99. Barbaro Garbey	DET	.229	139. Julio Cruz	CHI	.182
17. Frank White	KC	.333	60. Mike Davis	OAK	.258	100. Willie Wilson	KC	.228	139. Rich Dauer	BAL	.182
21. Kirby Puckett	MIN	.328	61. Willie Upshaw	TOR	.258	101. Ruppert Jones	CAL	.227	141. Ron Hassey	NY	.179
22. Jesse Barfield	TOR	.328	62. Greg Walker	CHI	.257	101. Roy Smalley	MIN	.227	141. Don Slaught	TEX	.179
22. Jim Rice	BOS	.328	63. Jim Sundberg	KC	.256	103. Cecil Cooper	MIL	.227	143. Pete O'Brien	TEX	.179
24. Carlton Fisk	CHI	.328	64. Tim Hulett	CHI	.255	104. Larry Sheets	BAL	.226	144. Tom Brunansky	MIN	.176
25. Al Cowens	SEA	.327	65. Kirk Gibson	DET	.255	105. Curtis Wilkerson	TEX	.225	145. Ozzie Guillen	CHI	.172
26. Cliff Johnson	TOR	.327	65. Andre Thornton	CLE	.255	106. Juan Beniquez	CAL	.222	146. Gorman Thomas	SEA	.164
27. Dave Winfield	NY	.324	67. Bobby Meacham	NY	.254	107. Joe Carter	CLE	.220	147. George Wright	TEX	.159
28. Tony Fernandez	TOR	.324	68. Tony Armas	BOS	.250	107. Ken Griffey	NY	.220	148. Jerry Willard	CLE	.156
29. Tom Brookens	DET	.321	68. Johnny Grubb	DET	.250	107. Charlie Moore	MIL	.220	149. Chris Bando	CLE	.154
30. Mike Heath	OAK	.319	68. Mickey Hatcher	MIN	.250	110. Onix Concepcion	KC	.220	150. Buddy Bell	TEX	.152
31. Steve Buechele	TEX	.318	68. Rickey Henderson	NY	.250	111. Doug DeCinces	CAL	.218	151. Bobby Jones	TEX	.143
32. Earnest Riles	MIL	.315	68. Glenn Hoffman	BOS	.250	111. Jim Gantner	MIL	.218	152. Dick Schofield	CAL	.140
33. Rich Gedman	BOS	.308	68. Ron Kittle	CHI	.250	113. Daryl Boston	CHI	.217	153. Pat Sheridan	KC	.136
34. Bob Kearney	SEA	.304	68. Steve Lyons	BOS	.250	113. Lonnie Smith	KC	.217	153. Mickey Tettleton	OAK	.136
35. Brian Downing	CAL	.302	75. George Vukovich	CLE	.246	115. Chet Lemon	DET	.215	155. Willie Randolph	NY	.111
36. Gary Ward	TEX	.300	76. Bobby Grich	CAL	.246	115. Mike Young	BAL	.215	155. Ernie Whitt	TOR	.111
37. Dave Collins	OAK	.297	77. Hal McRae	KC	.245	117. George Bell	TOR	.215	157. Jackie Gutierrez	BOS	.079
38. Lou Whitaker	DET	.297	78. Lee Lacy	BAL	.245	118. Mike Hargrove	CLE	.214	158. Rick Manning	MIL	.071
39. Scott Fletcher	CHI	.296	79. Brett Butler	CLE	.244	119. Jorge Orta	KC	.213			
40. Mike Pagliarulo	NY	.293	80. Lance Parrish	DET	.244	120. Paul Householder	MIL	.212			

National League

1. Jerry Royster	SD	.417	35. Craig Reynolds	HOU	.292	69. Glenn Wilson	PHI	.241	100. John Russell	PHI	.200
2. Mike Brown	PIT	.407	36. Mark Bailey	HOU	.286	70. U.L. Washington	MTL	.240	104. Nick Esasky	CIN	.196
3. Kurt Bevacqua	SD	.400	36. Leon Durham	CHI	.286	71. Terry Francona	MTL	.239	105. Bill Almon	PIT	.194
4. Willie McGee	STL	.377	36. Denny Walling	HOU	.286	72. Dan Gladden	SF	.237	106. Darrell Porter	STL	.192
5. Chris Brown	SF	.373	39. Rafael Ramirez	ATL	.281	73. Mookie Wilson	NY	.235	107. Mariano Duncan	LA	.189
6. Andre Dawson	MTL	.370	40. Terry Harper	ATL	.279	74. Jerry Mumphrey	HOU	.233	108. Manny Trillo	SF	.184
7. Dale Murphy	ATL	.365	41. Bill Doran	HOU	.279	75. Jim Morrison	PIT	.231	109. Carmelo Martinez	SD	.183
8. Gary Redus	CIN	.357	41. Jason Thompson	PIT	.279	76. Graig Nettles	SD	.230	110. Chili Davis	SF	.182
9. Mike Marshall	LA	.343	43. Joel Youngblood	SF	.276	77. Jose Uribe	SF	.226	110. Tito Landrum	STL	.182
10. Mike Scioscia	LA	.340	44. Wally Backman	NY	.273	78. Jack Clark	STL	.226	110. Alex Trevino	SF	.182
11. Tim Flannery	SD	.333	44. Sid Bream	PIT	.273	79. Claudell Washington	ATL	.225	113. Ron Oester	CIN	.179
11. Johnny Ray	PIT	.333	44. Mitch Webster	MTL	.273	80. Vance Law	MTL	.224	114. Jeff Stone	PHI	.179
11. Garry Templeton	SD	.333	47. Gary Carter	NY	.271	81. Terry Kennedy	SD	.224	115. Jeff Leonard	SF	.175
14. Darryl Strawberry	NY	.326	48. Cesar Cedeno	STL	.270	82. Tim Raines	MTL	.220	116. Chris Chambliss	ATL	.174
15. Hubie Brooks	MTL	.325	48. R.J. Reynolds	PIT	.270	83. Jim Pankovits	HOU	.217	116. Bob Dernier	CHI	.174
16. Kevin Bass	HOU	.323	48. Rick Schu	PHI	.270	84. Bob Horner	ATL	.217	116. Paul Zuvella	ATL	.174
16. Vince Coleman	STL	.323	51. Ozzie Smith	STL	.269	85. Mike Schmidt	PHI	.215	119. Glenn Davis	HOU	.173
18. Bo Diaz	CIN	.320	52. Bill Madlock	LA	.268	86. Tom Foley	PHI	.214	120. Luis Aguayo	PHI	.167
19. Jose Cruz	HOU	.317	52. Ryne Sandberg	CHI	.268	86. Ray Knight	NY	.214	121. Rafael Santana	NY	.161
20. Tony Perez	CIN	.316	54. Ken Oberkfell	ATL	.267	88. Steve Sax	LA	.213	122. Gary Matthews	CHI	.160
21. Steve Garvey	SD	.310	55. Len Dykstra	NY	.265	89. Von Hayes	PHI	.212	123. Buddy Bell	CIN	.152
21. Dave Lopes	CHI	.310	56. George Hendrick	PIT	.263	89. Tony Pena	PIT	.212	123. Dave Concepcion	CIN	.152
23. Dave Parker	CIN	.310	57. Danny Heep	NY	.259	89. Tim Wallach	MTL	.212	125. Terry Puhl	HOU	.150
24. Bruce Benedict	ATL	.308	57. Steve Jeltz	PHI	.259	92. Phil Garner	HOU	.212	126. Sammy Khalifa	PIT	.147
24. Alan Knicely	PHI	.308	59. Pedro Guerrero	LA	.259	93. Dan Driessen	SF	.211	127. Brad Komminsk	ATL	.143
24. Dickie Thon	HOU	.308	60. Wayne Krenchicki	CIN	.257	94. Greg Brock	LA	.211	128. Ken Landreaux	LA	.140
27. Keith Moreland	CHI	.306	60. Tom Nieto	STL	.257	95. Enos Cabell	LA	.209	129. Gerald Perry	ATL	.138
28. George Foster	NY	.305	62. Terry Pendleton	STL	.257	95. Joe Orsulak	PIT	.209	130. Tim Corcoran	PHI	.133
29. Mike Fitzgerald	MTL	.304	63. Eddie Milner	CIN	.256	97. Howard Johnson	NY	.208	131. Herm Winningham	MTL	.125
30. Tom Herr	STL	.303	64. Glenn Hubbard	ATL	.255	98. Steve Kemp	PIT	.207	132. Ozzie Virgil	PHI	.120
30. Pete Rose	CIN	.303	65. Tony Gwynn	SD	.255	98. Andy Van Slyke	STL	.207	133. Jody Davis	CHI	.111
32. Kevin McReynolds	SD	.303	66. Rick Cerone	ATL	.250	100. Bob Brenly	SF	.200	134. Dave Anderson	LA	.097
33. Juan Samuel	PHI	.300	66. Ron Cey	CHI	.250	100. David Green	SF	.200	135. Candy Maldonado	LA	.074
34. Keith Hernandez	NY	.296	66. Marvell Wynne	PIT	.250	100. Garry Maddox	PHI	.200			

Batting Average with Runners On Base and Two Outs

American League

1. Harold Baines	CHI	.391	41. Roy Smalley	MIN	.288	81. Mike Davis	OAK	.250
2. George Brett	KC	.388	42. Marty Barrett	BOS	.287	81. Glenn Hoffman	BOS	.250
3. Wade Boggs	BOS	.373	43. Al Cowens	SEA	.286	81. Bobby Meacham	NY	.250
4. Mike Stenhouse	MIN	.368	43. Toby Harrah	TEX	.286	84. Alvin Davis	SEA	.247
5. Carmen Castillo	CLE	.353	43. Tim Teufel	MIN	.286	85. Mike Heath	OAK	.247
6. Bruce Bochte	OAK	.349	46. Lance Parrish	DET	.285	85. Jack Perconte	SEA	.247
7. Mark Salas	MIN	.348	47. Ben Oglivie	MIL	.283	87. Ken Griffey	NY	.246
8. Rance Mulliniks	TOR	.348	48. Damaso Garcia	TOR	.283	88. Paul Householder	MIL	.246
9. Eddie Murray	BAL	.345	49. Brett Butler	CLE	.282	88. Ron Pagliarulo	NY	.246
10. Cliff Johnson	TOR	.338	50. Robin Yount	MIL	.280	90. Andre Thornton	CLE	.245
11. Jim Dwyer	BAL	.333	51. Dave Henderson	SEA	.278	91. Scott Fletcher	CHI	.244
11. Donnie Hill	OAK	.333	51. Bill Schroeder	MIL	.278	92. Darryl Motley	KC	.242
11. Garth Iorg	TOR	.333	53. Paul Molitor	MIL	.277	93. Kent Hrbek	MIN	.242
11. Kirby Puckett	MIN	.333	54. Spike Owen	SEA	.277	94. Lloyd Moseby	TOR	.241
11. Gary Roenicke	BAL	.333	55. Cal Ripken	BAL	.276	95. Lee Lacy	BAL	.240
11. Alan Wiggins	BAL	.333	56. Bob Kearney	SEA	.273	95. Jorge Orta	KC	.240
17. Frank White	KC	.329	57. Julio Franco	CLE	.272	97. Jim Gantner	MIL	.239
18. Carney Lansford	OAK	.327	57. Brook Jacoby	CLE	.272	98. Willie Upshaw	TOR	.238
19. Jesse Barfield	TOR	.326	57. Jim Rice	BOS	.272	99. Nelson Simmons	DET	.236
19. Tony Fernandez	TOR	.326	60. Onix Concepcion	KC	.270	100. Johnny Grubb	DET	.235
21. Steve Buechele	TEX	.324	61. Kirk Gibson	DET	.269	100. Chet Lemon	DET	.235
22. Bill Buckner	BOS	.316	62. Ed Romero	MIL	.268	102. Cecil Cooper	MIL	.235
23. Rich Gedman	BOS	.315	63. Dusty Baker	OAK	.268	103. Don Slaught	TEX	.234
24. Earnest Riles	MIL	.309	64. Phil Bradley	SEA	.265	104. Jim Sundberg	KC	.233
25. Don Baylor	NY	.307	65. Ted Simmons	MIL	.264	105. Mike Young	BAL	.231
26. Brian Downing	CAL	.307	66. Daryl Boston	CHI	.263	106. Bob Boone	CAL	.230
27. Dave Winfield	NY	.306	66. Rickey Henderson	NY	.263	107. Tony Bernazard	CLE	.230
28. Dave Collins	OAK	.305	66. Larry Sheets	BAL	.263	108. Larry Herndon	DET	.230
29. Tim Hulett	CHI	.301	69. Hal McRae	KC	.263	109. Rick Dempsey	BAL	.229
29. Gary Pettis	CAL	.301	70. Greg Walker	CHI	.262	110. Pat Tabler	CLE	.228
31. Carlton Fisk	CHI	.301	71. Barbaro Garbey	DET	.260	111. Bobby Grich	CAL	.227
32. Floyd Rayford	BAL	.298	71. Reggie Jackson	CAL	.260	112. Larry Parrish	TEX	.227
33. Don Mattingly	NY	.298	73. Mickey Hatcher	MIN	.259	113. Alfredo Griffin	OAK	.223
33. Al Oliver	TOR	.298	73. Luis Salazar	CHI	.259	114. Mike Easler	BOS	.223
35. Ruppert Jones	CAL	.297	75. Dwight Evans	BOS	.259	115. George Vukovich	CLE	.221
36. Butch Wynegar	NY	.295	76. Darrell Evans	DET	.259	116. Lonnie Smith	KC	.216
37. Lou Whitaker	DET	.294	77. Gary Ward	TEX	.257	117. Alan Trammell	DET	.216
38. Tom Brookens	DET	.293	78. Jim Presley	SEA	.257	118. Doug DeCinces	CAL	.215
39. Juan Beniquez	CAL	.288	79. Rudy Law	CHI	.255	118. Dwayne Murphy	OAK	.215
40. Wayne Tolleson	TEX	.288	80. Joe Carter	CLE	.253	120. Rod Carew	CAL	.214

121. Charlie Moore	MIL	.213
122. Willie Wilson	KC	.213
123. Steve Balboni	KC	.211
124. Jeff Burroughs	TOR	.211
125. Tony Armas	BOS	.208
126. Pete O'Brien	TEX	.207
127. Dave Kingman	OAK	.203
128. Dave Engle	MIN	.200
128. Greg Gagne	MIN	.200
128. Steve Lyons	BOS	.200
128. Gorman Thomas	SEA	.200
132. Tom Brunansky	MIN	.199
133. Fred Lynn	BAL	.196
134. Rob Wilfong	CAL	.194
135. Curtis Wilkerson	TEX	.193
136. Mike Hargrove	CLE	.190
137. Ozzie Guillen	CHI	.190
138. Tim Laudner	MIN	.189
139. George Bell	TOR	.188
140. Ron Hassey	NY	.185
141. Ron Kittle	CHI	.183
142. Mickey Tettleton	OAK	.182
143. Gary Gaetti	MIN	.180
144. Jerry Hairston	CHI	.179
145. Randy Bush	MIN	.178
146. Rich Dauer	BAL	.167
146. Oddibe McDowell	TEX	.167
146. Dick Schofield	CAL	.167
149. Willie Randolph	NY	.165
150. Ernie Whitt	TOR	.164
151. Buddy Bell	TEX	.163
151. Rick Manning	MIL	.163
153. George Wright	TEX	.153
154. Jerry Willard	CLE	.152
155. Wayne Gross	BAL	.147
156. Chris Bando	CLE	.132
157. Julio Cruz	CHI	.128
158. Jackie Gutierrez	BOS	.125

National League

1. Chris Brown	SF	.392	35. Jim Morrison	PIT	.286	69. Greg Brock	LA	.247
2. Tim Flannery	SD	.380	36. Kevin Bass	HOU	.284	70. Vance Law	MTL	.247
3. Jerry Royster	SD	.359	37. Danny Heep	NY	.283	71. Cesar Cedeno	STL	.246
4. Dave Lopes	CHI	.357	38. Kevin McReynolds	SD	.281	72. Jack Clark	STL	.245
5. R.J. Reynolds	PIT	.353	39. Joel Youngblood	SF	.279	73. Dan Gladden	SF	.244
6. Mike Scioscia	LA	.351	40. Terry Harper	ATL	.279	73. Glenn Hubbard	ATL	.244
6. Mark Bailey	HOU	.350	41. Leon Durham	CHI	.276	75. Gary Matthews	CHI	.243
7. Mike Brown	PIT	.350	41. Pete Rose	CIN	.276	75. John Russell	PHI	.243
9. Tom Herr	STL	.347	43. Tim Raines	MTL	.275	77. Eddie Milner	CIN	.242
10. Willie McGee	STL	.333	44. Juan Samuel	PHI	.273	78. David Green	SF	.239
11. Mike Marshall	LA	.330	45. Wally Backman	NY	.272	79. Bo Diaz	CIN	.238
12. Tony Gwynn	SD	.330	46. Brad Komminsk	ATL	.270	79. Howard Johnson	NY	.238
13. Dale Murphy	ATL	.330	47. Jerry Mumphrey	HOU	.270	81. Nick Esasky	CIN	.236
14. Andre Dawson	MTL	.329	48. Claudell Washington	ATL	.266	82. Dan Driessen	SF	.235
15. Len Dykstra	NY	.326	49. Vince Coleman	STL	.264	83. Gary Redus	CIN	.234
16. Dave Parker	CIN	.322	49. Ozzie Smith	STL	.264	84. Paul Zuvella	ATL	.233
17. Hubie Brooks	MTL	.319	51. Terry Francona	MTL	.263	85. Gary Carter	NY	.231
18. Jose Cruz	HOU	.316	51. Carmelo Martinez	SD	.263	85. Terry Kennedy	SD	.231
19. Alan Knicely	PHI	.316	53. Bill Madlock	LA	.261	85. Wayne Krenchicki	CIN	.231
20. George Foster	NY	.313	54. Denny Walling	HOU	.260	85. Ron Oester	CIN	.231
20. Johnny Ray	PIT	.313	55. Ryne Sandberg	CHI	.258	85. Marvell Wynne	PIT	.231
22. Tony Perez	CIN	.308	56. Steve Jeltz	PHI	.256	90. Glenn Davis	HOU	.229
22. Darryl Strawberry	NY	.308	57. Bob Brenly	SF	.254	91. Rick Cerone	ATL	.228
24. Bill Doran	HOU	.304	58. Chili Davis	SF	.253	91. Terry Pendleton	STL	.228
24. Garry Templeton	SD	.304	59. Bruce Benedict	ATL	.250	93. Ron Cey	CHI	.226
26. Keith Hernandez	NY	.303	59. Sid Bream	PIT	.250	94. Phil Garner	HOU	.225
27. Keith Moreland	CHI	.301	59. Greg Gross	PHI	.250	94. Herm Winningham	MTL	.225
28. Craig Reynolds	HOU	.300	59. Tom Nieto	STL	.250	96. Tito Landrum	STL	.222
28. Dickie Thon	HOU	.300	59. Ken Oberkfell	ATL	.250	97. Bob Horner	ATL	.221
30. Pedro Guerrero	LA	.299	59. Mitch Webster	MTL	.250	98. Graig Nettles	SD	.221
31. Rafael Ramirez	ATL	.293	59. Glenn Wilson	PHI	.250	99. Jose Uribe	SF	.220
32. Kurt Bevacqua	SD	.289	66. Jason Thompson	PIT	.248	100. Joe Orsulak	PIT	.217
33. Rick Schu	PHI	.288	66. Tim Wallach	MTL	.248	101. Steve Kemp	PIT	.216
34. Enos Cabell	LA	.288	68. Steve Garvey	SD	.247	102. Jeff Leonard	SF	.214

103. Bill Almon	PIT	.213
104. Terry Puhl	HOU	.212
104. Manny Trillo	SF	.212
106. Buddy Bell	CIN	.212
106. George Hendrick	PIT	.212
108. Jeff Stone	PHI	.211
109. Garry Maddox	PHI	.209
110. Tony Pena	PIT	.206
111. Von Hayes	PHI	.198
112. Rafael Santana	NY	.198
113. Mariano Duncan	LA	.197
114. Mike Schmidt	PHI	.196
115. Mookie Wilson	NY	.196
116. Mike Fitzgerald	MTL	.195
117. Steve Sax	LA	.193
117. Andy Van Slyke	STL	.193
119. Bob Dernier	CHI	.191
120. Shawon Dunston	CHI	.176
121. Chris Chambliss	ATL	.171
121. Ken Landreaux	LA	.171
123. Sammy Khalifa	PIT	.170
123. Ray Knight	NY	.170
125. Larry Bowa	NY	.167
126. Gerald Perry	ATL	.159
127. Darrell Porter	STL	.154
128. Tom Foley	PHI	.152
129. Dave Anderson	LA	.140
130. Tim Corcoran	PHI	.139
131. Jody Davis	CHI	.137
132. Ozzie Virgil	PHI	.130
133. Dave Concepcion	CIN	.125
134. Candy Maldonado	LA	.100
135. Rob Deer	SF	.073

% of Runners Driven in from Scoring Position

American League

1. Steve Henderson	OAK	.474
2. Rance Mulliniks	TOR	.440
3. Bryan Little	CHI	.433
4. Eddie Murray	BAL	.428
5. Pat Tabler	CLE	.407
6. Ben Oglivie	MIL	.404
7. Don Mattingly	NY	.400
8. Cliff Johnson	TOR	.395
9. Cal Ripken	BAL	.378
10. Hal McRae	KC	.376
11. Scott Fletcher	CHI	.373
12. Donnie Hill	OAK	.373
13. Randy Ready	MIL	.373
14. Wade Boggs	BOS	.372
15. Dave Winfield	NY	.372
16. Mike Hargrove	CLE	.371
17. Bill Buckner	BOS	.370
18. Brian Downing	CAL	.369
19. Cecil Cooper	MIL	.364
19. Gary Roenicke	BAL	.364
21. Harold Baines	CHI	.362
22. George Brett	KC	.358
23. Andre Thornton	CLE	.356
24. Kirby Puckett	MIN	.350
25. Rich Gedman	BOS	.344
26. Toby Harrah	TEX	.343
27. Mike Davis	OAK	.342
28. Robin Yount	MIL	.340
29. Alan Wiggins	BAL	.339
30. Kirk Gibson	DET	.337
31. Carlton Fisk	CHI	.333
31. John Shelby	BAL	.333
33. Mike Heath	OAK	.330
34. Jim Rice	BOS	.330
35. Larry Sheets	BAL	.330
36. Don Baylor	NY	.330
37. Kent Hrbek	MIN	.329
38. Damaso Garcia	TOR	.329
39. Ed Romero	MIL	.328
40. Bobby Jones	TEX	.327
41. Dave Collins	OAK	.325
42. Al Cowens	SEA	.325
43. Jim Dwyer	BAL	.324
44. Alfredo Griffin	OAK	.322
45. Julio Franco	CLE	.320
46. Pete O'Brien	TEX	.319
47. Bruce Bochte	OAK	.319
48. Rick Dempsey	BAL	.318
49. Earnest Riles	MIL	.317
50. Ron Kittle	CHI	.316
51. Rudy Law	CHI	.315
52. Mike Pagliarulo	NY	.314
53. Reggie Jackson	CAL	.314
54. Al Oliver	TOR	.314
55. Jorge Orta	KC	.310
56. Ken Griffey	NY	.308
57. Jesse Barfield	TOR	.306
58. Lou Whitaker	DET	.306
59. Ted Simmons	MIL	.305
60. Rod Carew	CAL	.305
61. Luis Salazar	CHI	.303
61. Gary Ward	TEX	.303
63. Dave Kingman	OAK	.303
64. Greg Walker	CHI	.302
65. Mickey Hatcher	MIN	.300
66. Randy Bush	MIN	.299
67. Darrell Evans	DET	.299
68. Tim Teufel	MIN	.298
69. Ron Hassey	NY	.298
70. Doug DeCinces	CAL	.297
71. Dusty Baker	OAK	.294
72. Carney Lansford	OAK	.293
73. Mike Young	BAL	.293
74. Don Slaught	TEX	.293
75. Brett Butler	CLE	.292
76. Willie Upshaw	TOR	.291
77. Garth Iorg	TOR	.291
78. Jeff Burroughs	TOR	.290
79. Frank White	KC	.289
80. George Bell	TOR	.289
81. Nelson Simmons	DET	.288
82. Lloyd Moseby	TOR	.288
83. Dave Henderson	SEA	.288
84. Glenn Hoffman	BOS	.287
85. Brook Jacoby	CLE	.286
85. Lance Parrish	DET	.286
87. Tony Fernandez	TOR	.285
88. Fred Lynn	BAL	.285
89. Tony Bernazard	CLE	.282
89. Willie Wilson	KC	.282
91. Paul Molitor	MIL	.281
92. Phil Bradley	SEA	.281
93. Ivan Calderon	SEA	.281
94. Bob Boone	CAL	.278
95. Bobby Grich	CAL	.277
96. Joe Carter	CLE	.275
97. Johnny Grubb	DET	.275
98. Jim Presley	SEA	.274
99. Alvin Davis	SEA	.273
99. Roy Smalley	MIN	.273
101. Rickey Henderson	NY	.272
102. Tim Hulett	CHI	.269
103. Barbaro Garbey	DET	.268
103. Ernie Whitt	TOR	.268
105. Spike Owen	SEA	.268
105. Jerry Willard	CLE	.268
107. Alan Trammell	DET	.266
108. Ruppert Jones	CAL	.265
109. Bobby Meacham	NY	.263
110. Marty Barrett	BOS	.263
111. Tom Brookens	DET	.263
112. Tom Brunansky	MIN	.262
113. Lee Lacy	BAL	.262
114. Tony Armas	BOS	.255
115. Chris Bando	CLE	.255
115. Bill Schroeder	MIL	.255
117. Charlie Moore	MIL	.252
118. Larry Parrish	TEX	.252
119. Buddy Bell	TEX	.250
119. Mike Easler	BOS	.250
121. Chet Lemon	DET	.248
122. Gary Pettis	CAL	.248
123. Mike Brown	CAL	.245
124. Jim Gantner	MIL	.245
125. Dave Engle	MIN	.242
126. Greg Gagne	MIN	.239
127. George Vukovich	CLE	.238
128. Gorman Thomas	SEA	.237
129. Dwight Evans	BOS	.236
130. Dwayne Murphy	OAK	.235
131. Darryl Motley	KC	.235
132. Donnie Scott	SEA	.233
133. Juan Beniquez	CAL	.230
133. Ozzie Guillen	CHI	.230
135. Jim Sundberg	KC	.230
136. Rick Manning	MIL	.230
137. Willie Randolph	NY	.229
138. Curtis Wilkerson	TEX	.227
139. Rob Wilfong	CAL	.226
140. Butch Wynegar	NY	.225
141. Mark Salas	MIN	.223
142. Lonnie Smith	KC	.223
143. Floyd Rayford	BAL	.214
144. Larry Herndon	DET	.213
145. Gary Gaetti	MIN	.211
146. Steve Balboni	KC	.210
147. Dick Schofield	CAL	.210
148. Pat Sheridan	KC	.210
149. Oddibe McDowell	TEX	.206
150. Onix Concepcion	KC	.205
151. Tim Laudner	MIN	.204
152. Steve Lyons	BOS	.204
153. Steve Buechele	TEX	.200
154. Bob Kearney	SEA	.190
155. Jack Perconte	SEA	.190
156. Paul Householder	MIL	.188
157. Mickey Tettleton	OAK	.183
158. Wayne Tolleson	TEX	.179
159. Daryl Boston	CHI	.176
160. Jackie Gutierrez	BOS	.175
161. Julio Cruz	CHI	.174
162. George Wright	TEX	.172
163. Wayne Gross	BAL	.118

National League

1. Bo Diaz	CIN	.433
2. Tom Herr	STL	.409
3. Jose Cruz	HOU	.406
4. Tony Perez	CIN	.403
5. Jerry Royster	SD	.383
6. Darryl Strawberry	NY	.369
7. Dave Parker	CIN	.369
8. Kurt Bevacqua	SD	.364
9. Dave Van Gorder	CIN	.362
10. Keith Hernandez	NY	.360
11. Willie McGee	STL	.355
12. Hubie Brooks	MTL	.355
12. Denny Walling	HOU	.355
14. Danny Heep	NY	.349
15. Keith Moreland	CHI	.349
16. R.J. Reynolds	PIT	.346
17. Tim Flannery	SD	.336
18. Glenn Wilson	PHI	.336
19. Jerry Mumphrey	HOU	.336
20. Dale Murphy	ATL	.335
21. Richie Hebner	CHI	.333
22. Johnny Ray	PIT	.331
23. Pete Rose	CIN	.331
23. Garry Templeton	SD	.331
25. Andre Dawson	MTL	.330
26. Mike Fitzgerald	MTL	.329
27. Jack Clark	STL	.327
28. Chris Brown	SF	.325
29. Mike Scioscia	LA	.323
30. Tom Nieto	STL	.323
31. Dave Lopes	CHI	.322
32. Alan Knicely	PHI	.321
33. Leon Durham	CHI	.318
34. Mike Marshall	LA	.318
35. Dickie Thon	HOU	.317
36. Bob Horner	ATL	.315
37. Jason Thompson	PIT	.313
38. Mark Bailey	HOU	.313
38. Gary Carter	NY	.313
40. Chris Chambliss	ATL	.310
41. George Foster	NY	.309
42. Steve Garvey	SD	.309
43. Terry Kennedy	SD	.308
43. Steve Sax	LA	.308
45. Mike Brown	PIT	.307
46. Glenn Davis	HOU	.306
47. Tim Wallach	MTL	.305
48. Cesar Cedeno	STL	.305
49. Gary Redus	CIN	.304
49. Chris Speier	CHI	.304
51. Sammy Khalifa	PIT	.303
52. Mitch Webster	MTL	.302
53. Ray Knight	NY	.301
54. Nick Esasky	CIN	.301
55. Terry Pendleton	STL	.300
56. Pedro Guerrero	LA	.298
57. Dan Gladden	SF	.297
58. Graig Nettles	SD	.297
59. Mike Schmidt	PHI	.296
60. Chili Davis	SF	.296
61. Terry Francona	MTL	.293
62. Terry Harper	ATL	.293
63. Kevin McReynolds	SD	.292
64. Bill Doran	HOU	.291
65. Enos Cabell	LA	.291
66. Phil Garner	HOU	.288
67. Garry Maddox	PHI	.286
68. Rafael Ramirez	ATL	.285
69. Tony Gwynn	SD	.283
70. Ryne Sandberg	CHI	.283
71. Von Hayes	PHI	.282
72. Tom Foley	PHI	.281
73. Andy Van Slyke	STL	.281
74. Ozzie Smith	STL	.278
75. Darrell Porter	STL	.275
76. Juan Samuel	PHI	.275
77. Kevin Bass	HOU	.275
78. Wayne Krenchicki	CIN	.273
79. Gary Matthews	CHI	.269
80. Carmelo Martinez	SD	.266
81. Buddy Bell	CIN	.265
81. Claudell Washington	ATL	.265
83. Bill Madlock	LA	.265
84. Vince Coleman	STL	.262
85. Bruce Benedict	ATL	.261
86. Tony Pena	PIT	.260
87. Greg Brock	LA	.259
88. U.L. Washington	MTL	.259
89. Bob Brenly	SF	.256
90. Howard Johnson	NY	.256
91. Ken Landreaux	LA	.255
92. Ken Oberkfell	ATL	.254
93. Bill Almon	PIT	.253
94. Eddie Milner	CIN	.252
95. Wally Backman	NY	.250
96. Jeff Leonard	SF	.248
97. Tim Raines	MTL	.248
98. George Hendrick	PIT	.247
99. Tito Landrum	STL	.245
100. Brad Komminsk	ATL	.243
101. Joel Youngblood	SF	.243
102. Mookie Wilson	NY	.241
103. Glenn Hubbard	ATL	.240
104. Tim Corcoran	PHI	.238
105. Ron Oester	CIN	.236
106. Rick Cerone	ATL	.235
107. Dan Driessen	SF	.234
108. Bob Dernier	CHI	.233
109. Ozzie Virgil	PHI	.231
110. Dave Concepcion	CIN	.229
111. Len Dykstra	NY	.229
111. Steve Kemp	PIT	.229
113. Ron Cey	CHI	.227
114. Jody Davis	CHI	.227
115. Shawon Dunston	CHI	.224
116. Steve Jeltz	PHI	.222
116. Craig Reynolds	HOU	.222
118. Mariano Duncan	LA	.215
119. Jim Morrison	PIT	.215
120. Herm Winningham	MTL	.213
121. Vance Law	MTL	.212
122. David Green	SF	.209
123. Manny Trillo	SF	.208
124. Candy Maldonado	LA	.203
125. Dave Anderson	LA	.203
126. Rafael Santana	NY	.203
127. Joe Orsulak	PIT	.202
128. Jose Uribe	SF	.200
129. Rick Schu	PHI	.198
130. Larry Bowa	NY	.197
131. John Russell	PHI	.182
132. Marvell Wynne	PIT	.175
133. Gerald Perry	ATL	.145
134. Jeff Stone	PHI	.103

% of Runners Driven in from Third with Less than Two Out

American League

1. Mike Hargrove	CLE	.857
2. Pat Tabler	CLE	.840
3. Rod Carew	CAL	.824
4. Nelson Simmons	DET	.818
5. Dusty Baker	OAK	.813
6. Cecil Cooper	MIL	.805
7. Jorge Orta	KC	.800
8. Eddie Murray	BAL	.794
9. Ken Griffey	NY	.788
10. Bobby Jones	TEX	.786
11. Ben Oglivie	MIL	.786
12. Steve Henderson	OAK	.765
13. Bryan Little	CHI	.750
13. Hal McRae	KC	.750
13. Rance Mulliniks	TOR	.750
13. Cal Ripken	BAL	.750
13. Willie Wilson	KC	.750
18. Lee Lacy	BAL	.742
19. Fred Lynn	BAL	.739
20. Lou Whitaker	DET	.737
21. Bill Buckner	BOS	.735
22. Don Mattingly	NY	.732
23. Toby Harrah	TEX	.731
24. Ernie Whitt	TOR	.727
25. Rick Dempsey	BAL	.722
25. Robin Yount	MIL	.722
27. Pete O'Brien	TEX	.714
27. Kirby Puckett	MIN	.714
29. Brian Downing	CAL	.700
29. Jerry Hairston	CHI	.700
29. Cliff Johnson	TOR	.700
29. Len Matuszek	TOR	.700
33. Tim Teufel	MIN	.696
34. Ron Hassey	NY	.692
35. Joe Carter	CLE	.688
35. Dave Collins	OAK	.688
37. Buddy Bell	TEX	.684
37. Rickey Henderson	NY	.684
39. Alfredo Griffin	OAK	.683
40. Larry Sheets	BAL	.682
41. Doug DeCinces	CAL	.679
42. Wade Boggs	BOS	.677
42. Alan Trammell	DET	.677
44. Don Baylor	NY	.676
45. George Brett	KC	.676
46. Brook Jacoby	CLE	.674
47. Harold Baines	CHI	.667
47. Bruce Bochte	OAK	.667
47. Scott Fletcher	CHI	.667
47. Kirk Gibson	DET	.667
47. Roy Smalley	MIN	.667
47. Willie Upshaw	TOR	.667
53. Kent Hrbek	MIN	.659
54. Dave Winfield	NY	.648
55. Jim Gantner	MIL	.640
56. Ron Washington	MIN	.636
57. Earnest Riles	MIL	.632
58. Alvin Davis	SEA	.625
58. Ruppert Jones	CAL	.625
60. Al Cowens	SEA	.621
61. Dave Kingman	OAK	.619
62. Randy Bush	MIN	.615
62. Alan Wiggins	BAL	.615
64. Andre Thornton	CLE	.613
65. George Vukovich	CLE	.611
66. Mike Heath	OAK	.600
66. Bill Schroeder	MIL	.600
66. Jerry Willard	CLE	.600
66. Mike Young	BAL	.600
70. Mike Davis	OAK	.593
71. Ivan Calderon	SEA	.588
71. Chet Lemon	DET	.588
71. Spike Owen	SEA	.588
71. Lance Parrish	DET	.588
75. Tom Brunansky	MIN	.585
76. Julio Franco	CLE	.585
77. Onix Concepcion	KC	.583
77. Dane Iorg	KC	.583
79. Mike Easler	BOS	.581
80. George Bell	TOR	.576
80. Damaso Garcia	TOR	.576
80. Willie Randolph	NY	.576
83. Brett Butler	CLE	.571
83. Larry Parrish	TEX	.571
83. Don Slaught	TEX	.571
86. Glenn Hoffman	BOS	.563
86. Tim Hulett	CHI	.563
86. Jack Perconte	SEA	.563
89. Donnie Hill	OAK	.560
90. Bobby Meacham	NY	.559
91. Paul Molitor	MIL	.556
92. Jim Rice	BOS	.551
93. Dave Henderson	SEA	.550
93. Ron Kittle	CHI	.550
93. Rudy Law	CHI	.550
96. Mickey Hatcher	MIN	.545
97. Tony Bernazard	CLE	.538
97. Jim Dwyer	BAL	.538
99. Lloyd Moseby	TOR	.531
99. Jim Presley	SEA	.531
101. Gary Pettis	CAL	.526
102. Gary Gaetti	MIN	.520
103. Bob Boone	CAL	.519
103. Rich Gedman	BOS	.519
105. Carlton Fisk	CHI	.514
106. Tony Armas	BOS	.500
106. Steve Balboni	KC	.500
106. Phil Bradley	SEA	.500
106. Tom Brookens	DET	.500
106. Mike Brown	CAL	.500
106. Steve Buechele	TEX	.500
106. Jeff Burroughs	TOR	.500
106. Dwight Evans	BOS	.500
106. Barbaro Garbey	DET	.500
106. Paul Householder	MIL	.500
106. Steve Lyons	BOS	.500
106. Dwayne Murphy	OAK	.500
106. Luis Salazar	CHI	.500
106. Jim Sundberg	KC	.500
106. Mickey Tettleton	OAK	.500
106. Gary Ward	TEX	.500
122. Ted Simmons	MIL	.487
123. Gorman Thomas	SEA	.486
124. Marty Barrett	BOS	.484
124. Darrell Evans	DET	.484
126. Greg Walker	CHI	.483
127. Lonnie Smith	KC	.481
128. Bobby Grich	CAL	.478
128. Darryl Motley	KC	.478
130. Charlie Moore	MIL	.476
131. Mike Pagliarulo	NY	.474
132. Floyd Rayford	BAL	.467
132. Dick Schofield	CAL	.467
132. Donnie Scott	SEA	.467
135. Greg Gagne	MIN	.462
135. Pat Sheridan	KC	.462
137. Reid Nichols	CHI	.455
137. Domingo Ramos	SEA	.455
137. Mark Salas	MIN	.455
140. Jesse Barfield	TOR	.444
141. Carney Lansford	OAK	.440
142. Ozzie Guillen	CHI	.438
143. Dave Engle	MIN	.429
144. Jackie Gutierrez	BOS	.421
145. Tony Fernandez	TOR	.419
146. Buck Martinez	TOR	.400
146. Oddibe McDowell	TEX	.400
146. John Shelby	BAL	.400
149. Reggie Jackson	CAL	.393
150. Curtis Wilkerson	TEX	.385
150. Butch Wynegar	NY	.385
152. Frank White	KC	.375
153. Juan Beniquez	CAL	.364
154. George Wright	TEX	.333
155. Rich Dauer	BAL	.300
156. Tim Laudner	MIN	.286
157. Larry Herndon	DET	.278
158. Bob Kearney	SEA	.167

National League

1. Bo Diaz	CIN	.917
2. Tony Perez	CIN	.857
3. Richie Hebner	CHI	.846
3. Jerry Mumphrey	HOU	.846
5. Steve Kemp	PIT	.818
6. Keith Hernandez	NY	.805
7. Luis Aguayo	PHI	.800
7. Dan Gladden	SF	.800
7. Dave Van Gorder	CIN	.800
10. Jerry Royster	SD	.786
11. Claudell Washington	ATL	.769
12. Ron Oester	CIN	.760
13. Tom Herr	STL	.734
14. Tim Flannery	SD	.733
15. Howard Johnson	NY	.722
15. Jason Thompson	PIT	.722
17. Hubie Brooks	MTL	.714
17. Enos Cabell	LA	.714
17. Tom Foley	PHI	.714
20. Jose Cruz	HOU	.710
21. Jim Wohlford	MTL	.700
22. Bob Horner	ATL	.697
23. Chris Chambliss	ATL	.692
24. Jody Davis	CHI	.684
24. Steve Garvey	SD	.684
24. Danny Heep	NY	.684
27. Denny Walling	HOU	.680
28. Ken Landreaux	LA	.679
29. Kurt Bevacqua	SD	.667
29. Graig Nettles	SD	.667
31. Willie McGee	STL	.658
32. Mike Schmidt	PHI	.657
33. Gary Carter	NY	.656
33. Pete Rose	CIN	.656
35. Garry Templeton	SD	.654
36. Glenn Wilson	PHI	.651
37. Wally Backman	NY	.650
38. Gary Matthews	CHI	.647
38. Tom Nieto	STL	.647
40. Andy Van Slyke	STL	.645
41. Bill Madlock	LA	.643
41. Kevin McReynolds	SD	.643
41. Manny Trillo	SF	.643
44. Bill Doran	HOU	.636
44. Sammy Khalifa	PIT	.636
44. Ray Knight	NY	.636
47. Keith Moreland	CHI	.634
48. Chili Davis	SF	.630
49. Von Hayes	PHI	.629
50. Dave Parker	CIN	.628
51. Terry Francona	MTL	.625
52. Glenn Davis	HOU	.619
52. Mike Fitzgerald	MTL	.619
54. Terry Pendleton	STL	.614
55. Mike Brown	PIT	.611
55. Ozzie Smith	STL	.611
55. Herm Winningham	MTL	.611
58. Jack Clark	STL	.609
59. Thad Bosley	CHI	.600
59. Tim Corcoran	PHI	.600
59. Len Dykstra	NY	.600
59. Nick Esasky	CIN	.600
59. Terry Puhl	HOU	.600
59. Johnny Ray	PIT	.600
59. Tim Wallach	MTL	.600
66. Rafael Ramirez	ATL	.591
67. Phil Garner	HOU	.586
68. Dave Concepcion	CIN	.583
68. Shawon Dunston	CHI	.583
68. Leon Durham	CHI	.583
68. Wayne Krenchicki	CIN	.583
68. R.J. Reynolds	PIT	.583
68. Rick Schu	PHI	.583
74. Dan Driessen	SF	.576
75. Bill Almon	PIT	.571
75. Cesar Cedeno	STL	.571
75. Rick Cerone	ATL	.571
75. Dave Lopes	CHI	.571
75. Garry Maddox	PHI	.571
75. Chris Speier	CHI	.571
75. Ozzie Virgil	PHI	.571
82. Mike Marshall	LA	.568
82. Pedro Guerrero	LA	.567
84. Tony Gwynn	SD	.565
84. Ryne Sandberg	CHI	.565
86. Buddy Bell	CIN	.563
86. George Hendrick	PIT	.563
88. Vince Coleman	STL	.550
88. Darrell Porter	STL	.550
90. Bruce Benedict	ATL	.545
90. Bob Dernier	CHI	.545
90. Steve Lake	CHI	.545
90. Jeff Leonard	SF	.545
90. Joe Orsulak	PIT	.545
90. Tony Pena	PIT	.545
90. Mike Scott	HOU	.545
90. Darryl Strawberry	NY	.545
98. Mike Scioscia	LA	.542
99. Dale Murphy	ATL	.538
100. Chris Brown	SF	.526
101. Terry Kennedy	SD	.523
102. Terry Harper	ATL	.520
103. Juan Samuel	PHI	.519
104. George Foster	NY	.517
105. Mark Bailey	HOU	.500
105. Greg Brock	LA	.500
105. David Green	SF	.500
105. Brad Komminsk	ATL	.500
105. Tim Raines	MTL	.500
105. Craig Reynolds	HOU	.500
105. Scot Thompson	MTL	.500
105. Dickie Thon	HOU	.500
105. Joel Youngblood	SF	.500
114. Carmelo Martinez	SD	.484
115. Steve Sax	LA	.483
116. Kevin Bass	HOU	.480
117. Bob Brenly	SF	.478
118. Andre Dawson	MTL	.475
119. Dave Anderson	LA	.467
120. Rafael Santana	NY	.464
121. Eddie Milner	CIN	.450
122. Ken Oberkfell	ATL	.444
123. Glenn Hubbard	ATL	.440
124. Mookie Wilson	NY	.438
125. Larry Bowa	NY	.417
126. Ron Cey	CHI	.409
127. Rob Deer	SF	.400
127. Gary Redus	CIN	.400
127. Marvell Wynne	PIT	.400
130. Mariano Duncan	LA	.385
131. Jim Morrison	PIT	.381
132. Vance Law	MTL	.367
133. Billy Hatcher	CHI	.364
134. Jose Uribe	SF	.333

Opponents' Batting Average

American League

#	Player	Team	AVG
1.	Steve Ontiveros	OAK	.174
2.	Greg Harris	TEX	.186
3.	Roy Thomas	SEA	.202
4.	Bill Caudill	TOR	.209
5.	Willie Hernandez	DET	.210
6.	Dave Stieb	TOR	.213
7.	Gary Lavelle	TOR	.214
8.	Charlie Hough	TEX	.215
9.	Brian Fisher	NY	.216
10.	Dan Petry	DET	.217
11.	Joe Cowley	NY	.224
12.	Jack Morris	DET	.225
13.	Mark Clear	BOS	.225
14.	Bob James	CHI	.226
15.	Roger Clemens	BOS	.228
16.	Ron Davis	MIN	.230
17.	Keith Atherton	OAK	.231
18.	Edwin Nunez	SEA	.234
19.	Ted Higuera	MIL	.235
20.	Bob Stanley	BOS	.237
21.	Jimmy Key	TOR	.237
22.	Donnie Moore	CAL	.237
23.	Ken Dixon	BAL	.237
24.	Tim Birtsas	OAK	.238
25.	Mark Gubicza	KC	.238
26.	Bert Blyleven	MIN	.239
27.	Jose Rijo	OAK	.239
28.	Randy O'Neal	DET	.240
29.	Bret Saberhagen	KC	.241
30.	Stu Cliburn	CAL	.241
31.	Dave Righetti	NY	.241
32.	Jim Clancy	TOR	.241
33.	Britt Burns	CHI	.242
34.	Mike Witt	CAL	.243
35.	Phil Niekro	NY	.245
36.	Jerry Reed	CLE	.245
37.	Dan Spillner	CHI	.246
38.	Sammy Stewart	BAL	.246
39.	Dave Schmidt	TEX	.246
40.	Tom Waddell	CLE	.246
41.	Mike Moore	SEA	.247
42.	Dennis Lamp	TOR	.247
43.	Tom Seaver	CHI	.248
44.	Charlie Leibrandt	KC	.248
45.	Ron Guidry	NY	.248
46.	Bill Scherrer	DET	.248
47.	Frank Eufemia	MIN	.250
47.	Tim Lollar	BOS	.250
47.	Aurelio Lopez	DET	.250
50.	Bob Shirley	NY	.251
51.	Pete Filson	MIN	.251
52.	Don Sutton	CAL	.253
53.	Rich Bordi	NY	.253
54.	Danny Darwin	MIL	.254
55.	Mark Langston	SEA	.255
56.	Dennis Rasmussen	NY	.255
57.	Walt Terrell	DET	.255
58.	Storm Davis	BAL	.256
59.	Al Nipper	BOS	.256
60.	Joel Davis	CHI	.256
61.	Mike Jones	KC	.257
62.	Don Aase	BAL	.258
63.	Kirk McCaskill	CAL	.258
64.	Gene Nelson	CHI	.259
65.	Chris Codiroli	OAK	.259
66.	Juan Berenguer	DET	.259
67.	Nate Snell	BAL	.260
68.	Bob Gibson	MIL	.260
69.	Moose Haas	MIL	.260
70.	Danny Jackson	KC	.261
71.	Tippy Martinez	BAL	.261
72.	Dennis Boyd	BOS	.261
73.	Jay Howell	OAK	.261
74.	Floyd Bannister	CHI	.262
75.	John Candelaria	CAL	.262
76.	Jamie Easterly	CLE	.264
77.	Frank Tanana	DET	.264
78.	Doyle Alexander	TOR	.266
79.	Frank Wills	SEA	.266
80.	Frank Viola	MIN	.268
81.	Jim Acker	TOR	.268
82.	Bud Black	KC	.268
83.	Joe Beckwith	KC	.269
84.	Mike Smithson	MIN	.270
85.	Ray Burris	MIL	.272
86.	Ken Schrom	MIN	.272
87.	Dave Stewart	TEX	.273
88.	Bob Ojeda	BOS	.273
89.	Bruce Hurst	BOS	.273
90.	Bruce Kison	BOS	.274
91.	Urbano Lugo	CAL	.274
92.	Bob McClure	MIL	.274
93.	Ed Vande Berg	SEA	.274
94.	Jaime Cocanower	MIL	.274
95.	Ramon Romero	CLE	.276
96.	Bill Krueger	OAK	.276
97.	Bill Swift	SEA	.279
98.	Dan Quisenberry	KC	.280
99.	Ron Romanick	CAL	.280
100.	Matt Young	SEA	.282
101.	Scott McGregor	BAL	.283
102.	Vern Ruhle	CLE	.283
103.	Luis Sanchez	CAL	.283
104.	Curt Wardle	CLE	.284
105.	Jim Slaton	CAL	.284
106.	Mike Boddicker	BAL	.286
107.	Steve McCatty	OAK	.286
108.	Dave Rozema	DET	.287
109.	Dennis Martinez	BAL	.288
110.	Steve Crawford	BOS	.289
111.	Dickie Noles	TEX	.289
112.	John Butcher	MIN	.289
113.	Keith Creel	CLE	.296
114.	Mike Flanagan	BAL	.297
115.	Burt Hooton	TEX	.297
116.	Pete Vuckovich	MIL	.298
117.	Neal Heaton	CLE	.298
118.	Mike Mason	TEX	.299
119.	Rick Thompson	CLE	.303
120.	Luis Leal	TOR	.303
121.	Rick Lysander	MIN	.305
122.	Salome Barojas	SEA	.305
123.	Ed Whitson	NY	.309
124.	Bryan Clark	CLE	.311
125.	Chris Welsh	TEX	.316
126.	Jim Beattie	SEA	.316
127.	Mike Trujillo	BOS	.320
128.	Roy Smith	CLE	.321
129.	Don Schulze	CLE	.322
130.	Jeff Russell	TEX	.324
131.	Tommy John	OAK	.331

National League

#	Player	Team	AVG
1.	Don Carman	PHI	.178
2.	Sid Fernandez	NY	.181
3.	Scott Garrelts	SF	.198
4.	Dwight Gooden	NY	.201
5.	Tim Burke	MTL	.204
6.	Orel Hershiser	LA	.206
7.	Floyd Youmans	MTL	.206
8.	Ken Howell	LA	.208
9.	John Tudor	STL	.209
10.	Jeff Reardon	MTL	.209
11.	Mario Soto	CIN	.211
12.	Cecilio Guante	PIT	.214
13.	Fernando Valenzuela	LA	.214
14.	Rick Reuschel	PIT	.215
15.	Mark Davis	SF	.219
16.	Terry Forster	ATL	.222
17.	Joe Hesketh	MTL	.222
18.	Tom Niedenfuer	LA	.223
19.	Jesse Orosco	NY	.224
20.	Tom Hume	CIN	.224
21.	Bob Welch	LA	.225
22.	Rich Gossage	SD	.226
23.	Ted Power	CIN	.227
24.	Scott Sanderson	CHI	.228
25.	Dennis Eckersley	CHI	.229
26.	Roger McDowell	NY	.230
27.	Bill Campbell	STL	.230
28.	Carlos Diaz	LA	.230
29.	Bobby Castillo	LA	.230
30.	Jose DeLeon	PIT	.231
31.	Bert Roberge	MTL	.232
32.	Bryn Smith	MTL	.232
33.	John Franco	CIN	.234
34.	Al Holland	PIT	.235
35.	Mike Scott	HOU	.235
36.	Ron Darling	NY	.235
37.	Dave Smith	HOU	.235
38.	Mike Krukow	SF	.238
39.	Nolan Ryan	HOU	.239
40.	Vida Blue	SF	.240
41.	Rick Sutcliffe	CHI	.240
42.	Frank Williams	SF	.242
43.	Lee Smith	CHI	.242
44.	Joe Price	CIN	.242
45.	Eric Show	SD	.243
46.	Jeff Calhoun	HOU	.243
47.	Craig Lefferts	SD	.244
48.	Tom Browning	CIN	.245
49.	Joe Niekro	HOU	.247
50.	Andy McGaffigan	CIN	.247
51.	Atlee Hammaker	SF	.247
52.	Frank DiPino	HOU	.248
53.	Steve Carlton	PHI	.249
54.	Shane Rawley	PHI	.249
55.	Dave Dravecky	SD	.249
56.	David Palmer	MTL	.250
57.	Danny Cox	STL	.251
58.	Kevin Gross	PHI	.251
59.	Jeff Lahti	STL	.251
59.	Gary Lucas	MTL	.251
59.	Lee Tunnell	PIT	.251
62.	Ricky Horton	STL	.251
63.	Charles Hudson	PHI	.252
64.	Jim Gott	SF	.254
65.	Zane Smith	ATL	.254
66.	Steve Bedrosian	ATL	.254
67.	Don Robinson	PIT	.255
68.	Ed Lynch	NY	.256
69.	Bob Forsch	STL	.258
70.	Kent Tekulve	PHI	.258
71.	Rick Aguilera	NY	.258
72.	Dan Schatzeder	MTL	.259
73.	Ron Robinson	CIN	.259
74.	Bill Dawley	HOU	.259
75.	Jerry Reuss	LA	.260
76.	Joaquin Andujar	STL	.260
77.	Rick Honeycutt	LA	.261
78.	LaMarr Hoyt	SD	.261
79.	Jay Tibbs	CIN	.262
80.	Rick Camp	ATL	.263
80.	Ken Dayley	STL	.263
82.	Kurt Kepshire	STL	.264
83.	Jeff Dedmon	ATL	.264
83.	Gene Garber	ATL	.264
85.	Randy St. Claire	MTL	.265
86.	Jim Winn	PIT	.266
87.	Andy Hawkins	SD	.267
88.	Bruce Sutter	ATL	.267
89.	Rick Mahler	ATL	.268
90.	Dave LaPoint	SF	.269
91.	Tim Stoddard	SD	.269
92.	Steve Trout	CHI	.270
93.	Bob Knepper	HOU	.271
94.	Bill Gullickson	MTL	.271
95.	Greg Minton	SF	.272
96.	Larry Andersen	PHI	.274
97.	Lary Sorensen	CHI	.274
98.	Jerry Koosman	PHI	.276
99.	Dave Rucker	PHI	.279
100.	John Denny	PHI	.282
101.	Larry McWilliams	PIT	.283
102.	Bill Laskey	MTL	.283
103.	Joe Johnson	ATL	.285
104.	Len Barker	ATL	.288
105.	Doug Sisk	NY	.291
106.	Mark Thurmond	SD	.291
107.	Warren Brusstar	CHI	.292
108.	Ron Mathis	HOU	.293
109.	Ray Fontenot	CHI	.294
110.	Rick Rhoden	PIT	.296
111.	Pascual Perez	ATL	.297
112.	George Frazier	CHI	.299
113.	Dick Ruthven	CHI	.299
114.	John Stuper	CIN	.303
115.	Steve Shields	ATL	.320

Opponents' Slugging Average

American League

#	Player	Team	Avg
1.	Steve Ontiveros	OAK	.259
2.	Mark Clear	BOS	.275
3.	Brian Fisher	NY	.277
4.	Greg Harris	TEX	.290
5.	Roger Clemens	BOS	.299
6.	Gary Lavelle	TOR	.302
7.	Bob James	CHI	.303
8.	Roy Thomas	SEA	.316
9.	Dave Stieb	TOR	.320
10.	Dave Righetti	NY	.327
11.	Stu Cliburn	CAL	.332
12.	Bob Shirley	NY	.333
13.	Donnie Moore	CAL	.336
14.	Dennis Lamp	TOR	.338
15.	Charlie Hough	TEX	.338
16.	Jack Morris	DET	.340
17.	Jay Howell	OAK	.341
18.	Bill Caudill	TOR	.344
19.	Nate Snell	BAL	.345
20.	Rich Bordi	NY	.346
21.	Dan Petry	DET	.346
22.	Dave Schmidt	TEX	.350
23.	Walt Terrell	DET	.350
24.	Bert Blyleven	MIN	.353
25.	Willie Hernandez	DET	.353
26.	Bob Stanley	BOS	.355
27.	Charlie Leibrandt	KC	.356
28.	Jaime Cocanower	MIL	.357
29.	Bret Saberhagen	KC	.357
30.	Mike Moore	SEA	.360
31.	Mike Witt	CAL	.360
32.	Danny Jackson	KC	.361
33.	Randy O'Neal	DET	.365
34.	Mark Gubicza	KC	.368
35.	Jim Acker	TOR	.371
36.	Don Aase	BAL	.373
37.	Ted Higuera	MIL	.373
38.	Tom Seaver	CHI	.374
39.	Storm Davis	BAL	.376
40.	Dan Quisenberry	KC	.376
41.	Jamie Easterly	CLE	.376
42.	Ron Davis	MIN	.377
43.	Jose Rijo	OAK	.382
44.	Bill Scherrer	DET	.384
45.	Jimmy Key	TOR	.384
46.	Don Sutton	CAL	.385
47.	Mike Boddicker	BAL	.385
48.	Joel Davis	CHI	.386
49.	Sammy Stewart	BAL	.387
50.	Britt Burns	CHI	.387
51.	Ron Guidry	NY	.392
52.	Ken Dixon	BAL	.394
53.	Ed Vande Berg	SEA	.394
54.	Al Nipper	BOS	.396
55.	Doyle Alexander	TOR	.396
56.	Bob Ojeda	BOS	.396
57.	Dennis Boyd	BOS	.397
58.	Bud Black	KC	.398
59.	Bill Swift	SEA	.398
60.	Joe Beckwith	KC	.399
61.	Edwin Nunez	SEA	.401
62.	Pete Filson	MIN	.402
63.	Chris Codiroli	OAK	.403
64.	Bob Gibson	MIL	.405
65.	Dennis Rasmussen	NY	.405
66.	Tippy Martinez	BAL	.407
67.	Kirk McCaskill	CAL	.408
68.	Bill Krueger	OAK	.409
69.	Phil Niekro	NY	.409
70.	Steve Crawford	BOS	.409
71.	Frank Viola	MIN	.410
72.	Moose Haas	MIL	.410
73.	Mike Jones	KC	.411
74.	Dan Spillner	CHI	.411
75.	Joe Cowley	NY	.412
76.	Bruce Kison	BOS	.413
77.	Jim Clancy	TOR	.414
78.	Tim Birtsas	OAK	.415
79.	Frank Eufemia	MIN	.415
80.	Rick Lysander	MIN	.415
81.	Matt Young	SEA	.416
82.	Vern Ruhle	CLE	.417
83.	Jerry Reed	CLE	.418
84.	Mike Smithson	MIN	.418
85.	Dickie Noles	TEX	.418
86.	Juan Berenguer	DET	.419
87.	Dave Rozema	TEX	.420
88.	John Candelaria	CAL	.423
89.	Keith Atherton	OAK	.425
90.	Tim Lollar	BOS	.427
91.	Frank Tanana	DET	.430
92.	Danny Darwin	MIL	.432
93.	Aurelio Lopez	DET	.436
94.	Urbano Lugo	CAL	.436
95.	Frank Wills	SEA	.437
96.	Bruce Hurst	BOS	.439
97.	Steve McCatty	OAK	.440
97.	Bob McClure	MIL	.440
99.	Mike Trujillo	BOS	.440
100.	Neal Heaton	CLE	.443
101.	Floyd Bannister	CHI	.445
102.	Ron Romanick	CAL	.449
103.	Mark Langston	SEA	.451
104.	Tom Waddell	CLE	.453
105.	John Butcher	MIN	.455
106.	Salome Barojas	SEA	.455
107.	Gene Nelson	CHI	.456
108.	Mike Mason	TEX	.461
109.	Ray Burris	MIL	.461
110.	Rick Thompson	CLE	.462
111.	Pete Vuckovich	MIL	.464
112.	Keith Creel	CLE	.466
113.	Don Schulze	CLE	.466
114.	Ed Whitson	NY	.469
115.	Jim Beattie	SEA	.469
116.	Scott McGregor	BAL	.470
117.	Bryan Clark	CLE	.470
118.	Jim Slaton	CAL	.470
119.	Dennis Martinez	BAL	.472
120.	Ken Schrom	MIN	.476
121.	Dave Stewart	TEX	.476
122.	Ramon Romero	CLE	.484
123.	Mike Flanagan	BAL	.485
124.	Tommy John	OAK	.486
125.	Burt Hooton	TEX	.489
126.	Chris Welsh	TEX	.491
127.	Roy Smith	CLE	.492
128.	Luis Sanchez	CAL	.498
129.	Curt Wardle	CLE	.519
130.	Jeff Russell	TEX	.527
131.	Luis Leal	TOR	.528

National League

#	Player	Team	Avg
1.	Scott Garrelts	SF	.253
2.	Dwight Gooden	NY	.270
3.	Rich Gossage	SD	.272
4.	Orel Hershiser	LA	.272
5.	Don Carman	PHI	.274
6.	John Tudor	STL	.285
7.	Floyd Youmans	MTL	.285
8.	Fernando Valenzuela	LA	.292
9.	Rick Reuschel	PIT	.293
10.	Jeff Reardon	MTL	.295
11.	Ted Power	CIN	.297
12.	Dave Smith	HOU	.300
13.	Sid Fernandez	NY	.302
14.	Tim Burke	MTL	.309
15.	Ken Howell	LA	.312
16.	Jeff Calhoun	HOU	.313
17.	Jesse Orosco	NY	.315
18.	David Palmer	MTL	.317
19.	Tom Niedenfuer	LA	.321
20.	John Franco	CIN	.322
21.	Bill Campbell	STL	.326
22.	Cecilio Guante	PIT	.328
23.	Bryn Smith	MTL	.330
24.	Joe Hesketh	MTL	.331
25.	Roger McDowell	NY	.332
26.	Jim Winn	PIT	.334
27.	Nolan Ryan	HOU	.339
28.	Tom Hume	CIN	.341
29.	Andy McGaffigan	CIN	.346
30.	Mark Davis	SF	.346
31.	Frank Williams	SF	.349
32.	Dennis Eckersley	CHI	.352
33.	Carlos Diaz	LA	.352
34.	Ricky Horton	STL	.353
35.	Zane Smith	ATL	.354
36.	Dave Dravecky	SD	.354
37.	Jeff Lahti	STL	.355
38.	Bert Roberge	MTL	.356
39.	Joe Niekro	HOU	.357
40.	Jose DeLeon	PIT	.357
41.	Terry Forster	ATL	.357
42.	Steve Carlton	PHI	.358
43.	Steve Trout	CHI	.358
44.	Rick Camp	ATL	.358
45.	Kent Tekulve	PHI	.359
46.	Shane Rawley	PHI	.359
47.	Bob Welch	LA	.359
48.	Ron Darling	NY	.360
49.	Ken Dayley	STL	.360
50.	Kevin Gross	PHI	.361
51.	Mario Soto	CIN	.361
52.	Randy St. Claire	MTL	.362
53.	Joaquin Andujar	STL	.362
54.	Mike Scott	HOU	.363
55.	Don Robinson	PIT	.363
56.	Bill Gullickson	MTL	.363
57.	Rick Sutcliffe	CHI	.364
58.	Jerry Reuss	LA	.365
59.	Jeff Dedmon	ATL	.368
60.	Lee Tunnell	PIT	.369
61.	Rick Aguilera	NY	.370
62.	Al Holland	PIT	.372
63.	Bill Dawley	HOU	.372
64.	Greg Minton	SF	.372
65.	Steve Bedrosian	ATL	.373
66.	Mike Krukow	SF	.373
67.	Gary Lucas	MTL	.375
68.	Craig Lefferts	SD	.375
69.	Gene Garber	ATL	.375
70.	Jay Tibbs	CIN	.377
71.	Bob Forsch	STL	.377
72.	Jim Gott	SF	.377
73.	Tim Stoddard	SD	.380
74.	Lee Smith	CHI	.381
75.	Frank DiPino	HOU	.381
76.	Danny Cox	STL	.382
77.	Tom Browning	CIN	.384
78.	Atlee Hammaker	SF	.386
79.	LaMarr Hoyt	SD	.386
80.	Eric Show	SD	.387
81.	Rick Honeycutt	LA	.388
82.	Doug Sisk	NY	.389
83.	Kurt Kepshire	STL	.391
84.	Ed Lynch	NY	.392
85.	John Denny	PHI	.392
86.	Larry Andersen	PHI	.393
87.	Andy Hawkins	SD	.395
88.	Mark Thurmond	SD	.395
89.	Dave LaPoint	SF	.398
90.	Rick Mahler	ATL	.401
91.	Ron Robinson	CIN	.402
92.	Bobby Castillo	LA	.402
93.	John Stuper	CIN	.405
94.	Scott Sanderson	CHI	.405
95.	Vida Blue	SF	.411
96.	Charles Hudson	PHI	.412
97.	Bob Knepper	HOU	.412
98.	Joe Price	CIN	.414
99.	Dan Schatzeder	MTL	.426
100.	Dave Rucker	PHI	.426
101.	Lary Sorensen	CHI	.427
102.	Larry McWilliams	PIT	.429
103.	Rick Rhoden	PIT	.433
104.	Joe Johnson	ATL	.435
105.	Bruce Sutter	ATL	.437
106.	Dick Ruthven	CHI	.439
107.	Len Barker	ATL	.449
108.	Bill Laskey	MTL	.449
109.	Warren Brusstar	CHI	.453
110.	Steve Shields	ATL	.454
111.	Jerry Koosman	PHI	.455
111.	Pascual Perez	ATL	.455
113.	Ron Mathis	HOU	.459
114.	Ray Fontenot	CHI	.462
115.	George Frazier	CHI	.466

Opponents' Home Run Percentage

American League

1.	Mark Clear	BOS	0.50	34.	Joel Davis	CHI	2.17	67.	Ted Higuera	MIL	2.77	100.	Tim Birtsas	OAK	3.45
2.	Danny Jackson	KC	0.87	35.	Bret Saberhagen	KC	2.17	68.	Doyle Alexander	TOR	2.78	101.	Bruce Hurst	BOS	3.48
3.	Nate Snell	BAL	1.04	36.	Bill Krueger	OAK	2.18	69.	Salome Barojas	SEA	2.82	102.	Phil Niekro	NY	3.50
4.	Walt Terrell	DET	1.04	37.	Jim Acker	TOR	2.18	70.	Keith Creel	CLE	2.83	103.	Pete Filson	MIN	3.50
5.	Brian Fisher	NY	1.12	37.	Bob Stanley	BOS	2.18	71.	Ron Guidry	NY	2.86	104.	Pete Vuckovich	MIL	3.56
6.	Bob Shirley	NY	1.22	39.	Jack Morris	DET	2.22	71.	Don Sutton	CAL	2.86	105.	Bill Caudill	TOR	3.56
7.	Bob James	CHI	1.25	40.	Dave Stieb	TOR	2.28	73.	Dave Rozema	TEX	2.87	106.	Burt Hooton	TEX	3.59
8.	Dave Righetti	NY	1.26	41.	Al Nipper	BOS	2.28	74.	John Butcher	MIN	2.90	107.	Floyd Bannister	CHI	3.72
9.	Rick Lysander	MIN	1.27	42.	Neal Heaton	CLE	2.32	75.	Ed Whitson	NY	2.92	108.	Ray Burris	MIL	3.73
10.	Rich Bordi	NY	1.33	43.	Randy O'Neal	DET	2.34	76.	Ron Davis	MIN	2.93	109.	Luis Sanchez	CAL	3.80
11.	Jay Howell	OAK	1.33	44.	Donnie Moore	CAL	2.34	77.	Dan Spillner	CHI	2.96	110.	Jeff Russell	TEX	3.82
12.	Jaime Cocanower	MIL	1.35	45.	Mike Witt	CAL	2.35	78.	Tippy Martinez	BAL	2.99	111.	Edwin Nunez	SEA	3.86
13.	Roger Clemens	BOS	1.37	46.	Tom Seaver	CHI	2.44	79.	Steve McCatty	OAK	3.01	112.	Jim Slaton	CAL	3.86
14.	Stu Cliburn	CAL	1.39	47.	Joe Beckwith	KC	2.45	79.	Bob McClure	MIL	3.01	113.	Ron Romanick	CAL	3.86
15.	Steve Crawford	BOS	1.40	48.	Roy Thomas	SEA	2.45	81.	Bob Gibson	MIL	3.02	114.	Frank Wills	SEA	3.93
16.	Steve Ontiveros	OAK	1.54	49.	Dickie Noles	TEX	2.46	82.	Britt Burns	CHI	3.05	115.	Bill Scherrer	DET	4.00
17.	Ed Vande Berg	SEA	1.54	50.	Jamie Easterly	CLE	2.47	83.	Roy Smith	CLE	3.05	116.	Danny Darwin	MIL	4.08
18.	Dan Quisenberry	KC	1.57	51.	Dennis Boyd	BOS	2.49	84.	Jim Beattie	SEA	3.06	117.	Dennis Martinez	BAL	4.11
19.	Storm Davis	BAL	1.63	52.	Mike Jones	KC	2.49	85.	Jim Clancy	TOR	3.09	118.	Mike Flanagan	BAL	4.12
20.	Mike Boddicker	BAL	1.64	53.	Charlie Hough	TEX	2.50	86.	Mike Mason	TEX	3.10	119.	Dave Stewart	TEX	4.13
21.	Bill Swift	SEA	1.70	54.	Bruce Kison	BOS	2.51	87.	Frank Eufemia	MIN	3.13	120.	Gene Nelson	CHI	4.13
22.	Greg Harris	TEX	1.76	55.	Don Schulze	CLE	2.52	88.	Kirk McCaskill	CAL	3.14	121.	Scott McGregor	BAL	4.25
23.	Dennis Lamp	TOR	1.80	56.	Jose Rijo	OAK	2.52	89.	Sammy Stewart	BAL	3.15	122.	Jerry Reed	CLE	4.40
24.	Bob Ojeda	BOS	1.81	57.	Tommy John	OAK	2.54	90.	Urbano Lugo	CAL	3.18	123.	Keith Atherton	OAK	4.40
25.	Dave Schmidt	TEX	1.82	58.	Rick Thompson	CLE	2.55	91.	Bryan Clark	CLE	3.19	124.	Curt Wardle	CLE	4.47
26.	Don Aase	BAL	1.86	59.	Mike Smithson	MIN	2.56	92.	Juan Berenguer	DET	3.24	125.	Aurelio Lopez	DET	4.57
27.	Charlie Leibrandt	KC	1.89	60.	Chris Codiroli	OAK	2.61	93.	Vern Ruhle	CLE	3.25	126.	Mark Langston	SEA	4.59
28.	Mike Moore	SEA	1.93	61.	John Candelaria	CAL	2.62	94.	Ken Dixon	BAL	3.29	127.	Ken Schrom	MIN	4.64
29.	Gary Lavelle	TOR	1.98	62.	Dennis Rasmussen	NY	2.63	95.	Moose Haas	MIL	3.31	128.	Tom Waddell	CLE	4.74
30.	Mike Trujillo	BOS	2.00	63.	Frank Viola	MIN	2.66	96.	Willie Hernandez	DET	3.32	129.	Luis Leal	TOR	4.80
31.	Bert Blyleven	MIN	2.08	64.	Matt Young	SEA	2.68	97.	Frank Tanana	DET	3.36	130.	Joe Cowley	NY	4.93
32.	Mark Gubicza	KC	2.09	65.	Dan Petry	DET	2.74	98.	Tim Lollar	BOS	3.39	131.	Ramon Romero	CLE	5.20
33.	Bud Black	KC	2.11	66.	Jimmy Key	TOR	2.77	99.	Chris Welsh	TEX	3.44				

National League

1.	Rich Gossage	SD	0.35	30.	Tom Niedenfuer	LA	1.55	59.	Shane Rawley	PHI	2.12	88.	Bob Welch	LA	2.56
2.	Scott Garrelts	SF	0.52	31.	Jeff Dedmon	ATL	1.57	60.	Tim Burke	MTL	2.14	89.	Mike Krukow	SF	2.57
3.	Ted Power	CIN	0.70	32.	Jerry Reuss	LA	1.61	61.	Bob Forsch	STL	2.15	90.	Pascual Perez	ATL	2.58
4.	Zane Smith	ATL	0.75	33.	Don Robinson	PIT	1.61	62.	Jeff Reardon	MTL	2.15	91.	Ed Lynch	NY	2.59
5.	Ken Dayley	STL	0.81	34.	Rick Camp	ATL	1.62	63.	Gene Garber	ATL	2.16	92.	Atlee Hammaker	SF	2.61
6.	Jeff Calhoun	HOU	0.87	35.	Rick Honeycutt	LA	1.66	64.	Steve Bedrosian	ATL	2.19	93.	Joe Niekro	HOU	2.63
7.	Orel Hershiser	LA	0.92	36.	Greg Minton	SF	1.67	65.	Lee Tunnell	PIT	2.19	94.	Ron Robinson	CIN	2.66
8.	David Palmer	MTL	0.98	37.	John Denny	PHI	1.68	66.	Al Holland	PIT	2.21	95.	Warren Brusstar	CHI	2.68
9.	Rick Reuschel	PIT	0.99	38.	Jay Tibbs	CIN	1.69	67.	Dave Dravecky	SD	2.24	96.	Joe Johnson	ATL	2.70
10.	Doug Sisk	NY	1.01	39.	Mark Thurmond	SD	1.70	68.	Bob Knepper	HOU	2.25	97.	Kurt Kepshire	STL	2.72
11.	Dave Smith	HOU	1.02	40.	Kent Tekulve	PHI	1.74	69.	Dave LaPoint	SF	2.25	98.	Tom Browning	CIN	2.94
12.	Floyd Youmans	MTL	1.08	41.	Dick Ruthven	CHI	1.74	70.	Craig Lefferts	SD	2.28	99.	Scott Sanderson	CHI	2.96
13.	Andy McGaffigan	CIN	1.12	42.	Rick Aguilera	NY	1.75	71.	Carlos Diaz	LA	2.30	100.	Charles Hudson	PHI	3.08
14.	Randy St. Claire	MTL	1.15	43.	Larry Andersen	PHI	1.75	72.	Ron Darling	NY	2.31	101.	Eric Show	SD	3.10
15.	Bill Gullickson	MTL	1.16	44.	Jim Gott	SF	1.76	73.	Sid Fernandez	NY	2.35	102.	Terry Forster	ATL	3.17
16.	Jeff Lahti	STL	1.20	45.	Steve Carlton	PHI	1.78	74.	Dennis Eckersley	CHI	2.37	103.	Mark Davis	SF	3.19
17.	Cecilio Guante	PIT	1.27	46.	Joe Hesketh	MTL	1.78	75.	Rick Mahler	ATL	2.37	104.	Mario Soto	CIN	3.24
18.	Tim Stoddard	SD	1.28	47.	Larry McWilliams	PIT	1.83	76.	Bill Dawley	HOU	2.39	105.	Bill Laskey	MTL	3.26
19.	Dwight Gooden	NY	1.32	48.	Frank Williams	SF	1.86	77.	Gary Lucas	MTL	2.39	106.	Dan Schatzeder	MTL	3.33
20.	Jim Winn	PIT	1.38	49.	Roger McDowell	NY	1.91	78.	Tom Hume	CIN	2.41	107.	Steve Shields	ATL	3.35
21.	John Tudor	STL	1.40	50.	Bert Roberge	MTL	2.00	79.	Mike Scott	HOU	2.42	108.	Len Barker	ATL	3.42
22.	Nolan Ryan	HOU	1.40	51.	Dave Rucker	PHI	2.01	80.	Rick Sutcliffe	CHI	2.42	109.	Bobby Castillo	LA	3.52
23.	John Franco	CIN	1.41	52.	Jesse Orosco	NY	2.03	81.	Ron Mathis	HOU	2.47	110.	Vida Blue	SF	3.55
24.	Fernando Valenzuela	LA	1.42	53.	Don Carman	PHI	2.05	82.	LaMarr Hoyt	SD	2.48	111.	Jerry Koosman	PHI	3.62
25.	Kevin Gross	PHI	1.42	54.	John Stuper	CIN	2.09	83.	Lee Smith	CHI	2.50	112.	George Frazier	CHI	3.74
26.	Bryn Smith	MTL	1.44	55.	Bill Campbell	STL	2.09	84.	Jose DeLeon	PIT	2.51	113.	Bruce Sutter	ATL	3.81
27.	Joaquin Andujar	STL	1.47	56.	Andy Hawkins	SD	2.10	85.	Frank DiPino	HOU	2.52	114.	Ray Fontenot	CHI	3.82
28.	Ricky Horton	STL	1.50	56.	Rick Rhoden	PIT	2.10	86.	Ken Howell	LA	2.52	115.	Joe Price	CIN	4.10
29.	Steve Trout	CHI	1.52	58.	Danny Cox	STL	2.11	87.	Lary Sorensen	CHI	2.55				

Opponents' Extra Base Hits per 100 At Bats

American League

1. Brian Fisher	NY	3.64	34. Rick Lysander	MIN	6.78	67. Steve McCatty	OAK	8.13	100. Jose Rijo	OAK	9.24
2. Gary Lavelle	TOR	3.97	35. Charlie Hough	TEX	6.85	68. Bob Gibson	MIL	8.16	101. Frank Eufemia	MIN	9.38
3. Mark Clear	BOS	4.00	36. Bob Stanley	BOS	6.85	69. Dennis Rasmussen	NY	8.16	102. Ed Whitson	NY	9.38
4. Roger Clemens	BOS	4.12	37. Dave Rozema	TEX	6.90	70. Ron Guidry	NY	8.16	103. Tim Birtsas	OAK	9.40
5. Dennis Lamp	TOR	4.90	38. Danny Jackson	KC	6.99	71. Bud Black	KC	8.20	104. John Butcher	MIN	9.54
6. Donnie Moore	CAL	4.95	39. Dan Petry	DET	7.09	72. Joe Cowley	NY	8.33	105. Rick Thompson	CLE	9.55
7. Steve Ontiveros	OAK	5.02	40. Ron Davis	MIN	7.11	73. Bill Krueger	OAK	8.38	106. Scott McGregor	BAL	9.63
8. Jay Howell	OAK	5.07	41. Doyle Alexander	TOR	7.14	74. Frank Viola	MIN	8.38	107. Dennis Martinez	BAL	9.63
9. Bob James	CHI	5.26	42. Willie Hernandez	DET	7.16	75. Juan Berenguer	DET	8.38	108. Bob McClure	MIL	9.64
10. Jim Acker	TOR	5.30	43. Joel Davis	CHI	7.22	76. Bruce Kison	BOS	8.38	109. John Candelaria	CAL	9.74
11. Dave Righetti	NY	5.53	44. Tom Seaver	CHI	7.33	77. Steve Crawford	BOS	8.40	110. Mark Langston	SEA	9.81
12. Bob Shirley	NY	5.60	45. Matt Young	SEA	7.34	78. Chris Codiroli	OAK	8.51	111. Tommy John	OAK	9.89
13. Bill Scherrer	DET	5.60	46. Sammy Stewart	BAL	7.35	79. Ron Romanick	CAL	8.52	112. Roy Smith	CLE	9.92
14. Jaime Cocanower	MIL	5.62	47. Dickie Noles	TEX	7.38	80. Ken Dixon	BAL	8.57	113. Ray Burris	MIL	10.00
15. Nate Snell	BAL	5.71	48. Moose Haas	MIL	7.41	81. Mike Smithson	MIN	8.59	113. Tim Lollar	BOS	10.00
16. Greg Harris	TEX	5.79	49. Mike Trujillo	BOS	7.43	82. Al Nipper	BOS	8.63	113. Ramon Romero	CLE	10.00
17. Stu Cliburn	CAL	5.82	50. Don Aase	BAL	7.45	83. Pete Vuckovich	MIL	8.67	113. Chris Welsh	TEX	10.00
18. Rich Bordi	NY	5.85	51. Don Sutton	CAL	7.54	84. Phil Niekro	NY	8.69	117. Jim Clancy	TOR	10.10
19. Dave Stieb	TOR	5.90	52. Pete Filson	MIN	7.55	85. Jimmy Key	TOR	8.69	118. Keith Creel	CLE	10.12
20. Dan Quisenberry	KC	5.91	53. Ted Higuera	MIL	7.57	86. Bryan Clark	CLE	8.76	119. Floyd Bannister	CHI	10.17
21. Jamie Easterly	CLE	6.04	54. Mark Gubicza	KC	7.60	87. Aurelio Lopez	DET	8.84	120. Gene Nelson	CHI	10.23
22. Dave Schmidt	TEX	6.08	55. Randy O'Neal	DET	7.60	88. Jim Beattie	SEA	8.84	121. Mike Flanagan	BAL	10.29
23. Roy Thomas	SEA	6.13	56. Ed Vande Berg	SEA	7.72	89. Salome Barojas	SEA	8.92	122. Jim Slaton	CAL	10.35
24. Mike Witt	CAL	6.29	57. Bob Ojeda	BOS	7.73	90. Frank Wills	SEA	8.95	123. Keith Atherton	OAK	10.36
25. Bill Caudill	TOR	6.32	58. Tippy Martinez	BAL	7.84	91. Mike Mason	TEX	9.01	124. Dave Stewart	TEX	10.48
26. Charlie Leibrandt	KC	6.33	59. Britt Burns	CHI	7.86	92. Neal Heaton	CLE	9.04	125. Ken Schrom	MIN	10.61
27. Jack Morris	DET	6.36	60. Bill Swift	SEA	7.87	93. Don Schulze	CLE	9.07	126. Tom Waddell	CLE	10.90
28. Mike Boddicker	BAL	6.42	61. Joe Beckwith	KC	7.88	94. Bruce Hurst	BOS	9.10	127. Burt Hooton	TEX	11.18
29. Walt Terrell	DET	6.59	62. Edwin Nunez	SEA	8.01	95. Danny Darwin	MIL	9.11	128. Luis Sanchez	CAL	11.81
30. Bret Saberhagen	KC	6.62	63. Storm Davis	BAL	8.02	96. Mike Jones	KC	9.13	129. Jeff Russell	TEX	11.83
31. Bert Blyleven	MIN	6.69	64. Dennis Boyd	BOS	8.04	97. Dan Spillner	CHI	9.17	130. Luis Leal	TOR	12.18
32. Vern Ruhle	CLE	6.71	65. Jerry Reed	CLE	8.06	98. Frank Tanana	DET	9.23	131. Curt Wardle	CLE	12.98
33. Mike Moore	SEA	6.75	66. Kirk McCaskill	CAL	8.06	99. Urbano Lugo	CAL	9.24			

National League

1. Rich Gossage	SD	3.18	30. Roger McDowell	NY	6.17	59. LaMarr Hoyt	SD	6.96	88. Ron Robinson	CIN	8.23
2. Scott Garrelts	SF	3.91	31. Tim Burke	MTL	6.18	60. Bob Forsch	STL	7.03	89. Frank DiPino	HOU	8.27
3. David Palmer	MTL	3.91	32. Nolan Ryan	HOU	6.19	61. Steve Carlton	PHI	7.10	90. Ray Fontenot	CHI	8.31
4. Dwight Gooden	NY	3.96	33. Rick Camp	ATL	6.28	62. Joe Hesketh	MTL	7.12	91. Joe Johnson	ATL	8.41
5. Jeff Reardon	MTL	4.00	34. Jeff Dedmon	ATL	6.29	63. Jeff Lahti	STL	7.17	92. Jim Gott	SF	8.47
6. Dave Smith	HOU	4.10	35. John Denny	PHI	6.38	63. Gary Lucas	MTL	7.17	93. Craig Lefferts	SD	8.47
7. Jim Winn	PIT	4.14	36. Mark Thurmond	SD	6.43	65. Bert Roberge	MTL	7.20	94. Rick Rhoden	PIT	8.61
8. Orel Hershiser	LA	4.37	37. Gene Garber	ATL	6.47	66. Sid Fernandez	NY	7.21	95. Rick Honeycutt	LA	8.69
9. John Tudor	STL	4.50	38. Tom Niedenfuer	LA	6.48	67. Rick Aguilera	NY	7.22	96. Charles Hudson	PHI	8.71
10. Floyd Youmans	MTL	4.69	39. Bill Dawley	HOU	6.48	68. Terry Forster	ATL	7.24	97. Bob Knepper	HOU	8.77
11. Jeff Calhoun	HOU	4.78	40. Shane Rawley	PHI	6.49	69. Rick Sutcliffe	CHI	7.27	98. Bruce Sutter	ATL	8.80
12. Don Carman	PHI	4.79	41. Bill Gullickson	MTL	6.51	70. Ken Dayley	STL	7.29	99. George Frazier	CHI	8.84
13. Fernando Valenzuela	LA	4.87	42. Lee Tunnell	PIT	6.57	71. Zane Smith	ATL	7.34	100. Joe Price	CIN	9.02
14. John Franco	CIN	5.08	43. Carlos Diaz	LA	6.58	72. Larry Andersen	PHI	7.37	101. Dave Rucker	PHI	9.06
14. Jesse Orosco	NY	5.08	44. Ricky Horton	STL	6.59	73. Mike Scott	HOU	7.38	102. Dan Schatzeder	MTL	9.23
16. Ted Power	CIN	5.24	45. Jerry Reuss	LA	6.68	74. Cecilio Guante	PIT	7.38	103. Lary Sorensen	CHI	9.24
17. Steve Trout	CHI	5.33	46. Steve Shields	ATL	6.69	75. Eric Show	SD	7.46	104. Len Barker	ATL	9.25
18. Ken Howell	LA	5.36	46. Frank Williams	SF	6.69	76. Ron Darling	NY	7.48	105. Al Holland	PIT	9.29
19. Bill Campbell	STL	5.44	48. Jose DeLeon	PIT	6.70	77. Atlee Hammaker	SF	7.53	106. Dick Ruthven	CHI	9.30
20. Rick Reuschel	PIT	5.49	49. Andy McGaffigan	CIN	6.74	77. Don Robinson	PIT	7.53	107. Bobby Castillo	LA	9.38
21. Joe Niekro	HOU	5.51	50. Doug Sisk	NY	6.76	79. Mario Soto	CIN	7.66	108. Warren Brusstar	CHI	9.40
22. Tom Hume	CIN	5.52	51. Kurt Kepshire	STL	6.80	80. Tim Stoddard	SD	7.69	109. Ron Mathis	HOU	9.54
23. John Stuper	CIN	5.74	52. Kevin Gross	PHI	6.86	81. Ed Lynch	NY	7.76	110. Jerry Koosman	PHI	9.56
24. Dave Dravecky	SD	5.86	53. Bob Welch	LA	6.87	82. Lee Smith	CHI	7.78	111. Scott Sanderson	CHI	9.57
25. Kent Tekulve	PHI	5.92	54. Joaquin Andujar	STL	6.87	83. Rick Mahler	ATL	7.79	112. Bill Laskey	MTL	9.78
26. Greg Minton	SF	6.11	55. Dave LaPoint	SF	6.88	84. Andy Hawkins	SD	7.80	113. Vida Blue	SF	9.81
27. Bryn Smith	MTL	6.14	56. Jay Tibbs	CIN	6.90	85. Mike Krukow	SF	7.85	114. Pascual Perez	ATL	10.08
28. Mark Davis	SF	6.14	57. Dennis Eckersley	CHI	6.94	86. Tom Browning	CIN	7.90	115. Larry McWilliams	PIT	10.37
29. Randy St. Claire	MTL	6.15	58. Steve Bedrosian	ATL	6.94	87. Danny Cox	STL	7.99			

Opponents' Batting Average, Left-Handed Batters

American League

#	Name	Team	Avg	#	Name	Team	Avg	#	Name	Team	Avg	#	Name	Team	Avg
1.	Willie Hernandez	DET	.171	34.	Ray Burris	MIL	.236	67.	Matt Young	SEA	.264	100.	Jim Slaton	CAL	.297
2.	Greg Harris	TEX	.175	35.	Ted Higuera	MIL	.236	68.	Doyle Alexander	TOR	.264	101.	Keith Creel	CLE	.298
3.	Roy Thomas	SEA	.176	36.	Don Aase	BAL	.238	69.	Bud Black	KC	.267	102.	Joe Beckwith	KC	.299
4.	Jimmy Key	TOR	.178	37.	Dennis Lamp	TOR	.238	70.	Vern Ruhle	CLE	.270	103.	Steve Crawford	BOS	.301
5.	Dave Righetti	NY	.196	38.	Bob McClure	MIL	.240	71.	Jamie Easterly	CLE	.270	104.	Floyd Bannister	CHI	.301
6.	Tippy Martinez	BAL	.198	39.	Pat Clements	CAL	.240	72.	Danny Darwin	MIL	.270	105.	Rick Thompson	CLE	.304
7.	Dave Stieb	TOR	.198	40.	Britt Burns	CHI	.240	73.	Danny Jackson	KC	.272	106.	Neal Heaton	CLE	.304
8.	Donnie Moore	CAL	.200	41.	Bret Saberhagen	KC	.242	74.	Pete Filson	MIN	.273	107.	Juan Berenguer	DET	.305
8.	Bill Scherrer	DET	.200	42.	Mark Clear	BOS	.244	75.	Dennis Martinez	BAL	.273	108.	Mike Trujillo	BOS	.306
10.	Tim Lollar	BOS	.208	43.	Don Sutton	CAL	.244	76.	Al Nipper	BOS	.274	109.	Bill Swift	SEA	.308
11.	Dan Spillner	CHI	.210	44.	Ed Vande Berg	SEA	.246	77.	Tom Waddell	CLE	.276	110.	Jim Acker	TOR	.308
12.	Edwin Nunez	SEA	.211	45.	Bob Gibson	MIL	.246	78.	Nate Snell	BAL	.276	111.	Rich Bordi	NY	.309
13.	Ron Guidry	NY	.212	46.	Walt Terrell	DET	.247	79.	Steve McCatty	OAK	.277	112.	Curt Wardle	CLE	.310
14.	Bob Shirley	NY	.212	47.	Roger Clemens	BOS	.248	80.	Kirk McCaskill	CAL	.278	113.	Pete Vuckovich	MIL	.311
15.	Juan Agosto	CHI	.214	48.	Bill Caudill	TOR	.248	81.	Mike Mason	TEX	.279	114.	Ed Whitson	NY	.311
16.	Steve Ontiveros	OAK	.216	49.	Chris Codiroli	OAK	.248	82.	Jose Rijo	OAK	.280	115.	Luis Sanchez	CAL	.313
17.	Gary Lavelle	TOR	.220	50.	Bob Stanley	BOS	.248	83.	Ron Romanick	CAL	.280	116.	Jim Beattie	SEA	.313
18.	Tim Birtsas	OAK	.221	51.	Tom Seaver	CHI	.249	84.	Bruce Hurst	BOS	.281	117.	Urbano Lugo	CAL	.315
19.	Dan Petry	DET	.222	52.	Gene Nelson	CHI	.249	85.	Ken Schrom	MIN	.283	118.	Rick Lysander	MIN	.315
20.	Jack Morris	DET	.223	53.	Charlie Leibrandt	KC	.250	86.	Frank Wills	SEA	.287	119.	Bob Ojeda	BOS	.315
21.	Aurelio Lopez	DET	.224	54.	Jim Clancy	TOR	.251	87.	Frank Viola	MIN	.287	120.	Luis Leal	TOR	.316
22.	Brian Fisher	NY	.225	55.	Sammy Stewart	BAL	.252	88.	Jaime Cocanower	MIL	.288	121.	Rollie Fingers	MIL	.317
23.	Mike Moore	SEA	.226	56.	Mark Gubicza	KC	.253	89.	Mike Smithson	MIN	.288	122.	Bill Krueger	OAK	.317
24.	Ken Dixon	BAL	.226	57.	Jay Howell	OAK	.254	90.	Joel Davis	CHI	.288	123.	Dan Quisenberry	KC	.317
25.	Charlie Hough	TEX	.226	58.	Frank Eufemia	MIN	.255	91.	Doug Bair	DET	.289	124.	Jeff Russell	TEX	.322
26.	Frank Tanana	DET	.227	59.	Keith Atherton	OAK	.258	91.	Jerry Reed	CLE	.289	125.	Salome Barojas	SEA	.323
27.	Joe Cowley	NY	.228	60.	Bert Blyleven	MIN	.258	93.	Richard Dotson	CHI	.290	126.	Dave Stewart	TEX	.323
28.	Chris Welsh	TEX	.229	61.	Storm Davis	BAL	.258	94.	John Butcher	MIN	.290	127.	Roy Smith	CLE	.328
29.	Dennis Boyd	BOS	.231	62.	Scott McGregor	BAL	.260	95.	Stu Cliburn	CAL	.291	128.	Mike Warren	OAK	.329
30.	Dave Schmidt	TEX	.232	63.	Moose Haas	MIL	.260	96.	Rick Langford	OAK	.294	129.	Bruce Kison	BOS	.332
31.	Ron Davis	MIN	.233	64.	Phil Niekro	NY	.261	97.	Ron Musselman	TOR	.294	130.	Dickie Noles	TEX	.339
32.	Randy O'Neal	DET	.236	65.	Dave Rozema	TEX	.262	98.	Mike Boddicker	BAL	.294	131.	Don Schulze	CLE	.355
33.	Bob James	CHI	.236	66.	Mike Witt	CAL	.263	99.	Burt Hooton	TEX	.295				

National League

#	Name	Team	Avg	#	Name	Team	Avg	#	Name	Team	Avg	#	Name	Team	Avg
1.	Sid Fernandez	NY	.163	30.	Jeff Dedmon	ATL	.229	59.	Danny Cox	STL	.264	88.	Eric Show	SD	.287
2.	Roy Jackson	SD	.169	31.	Scott Garrelts	SF	.231	60.	Dave LaPoint	SF	.264	89.	Frank Pastore	CIN	.288
3.	John Franco	CIN	.176	31.	Shane Rawley	PHI	.231	61.	David Palmer	MTL	.265	90.	Jim Winn	PIT	.288
4.	Ray Fontenot	CHI	.182	33.	Dave Smith	HOU	.233	62.	Lee Smith	CHI	.266	91.	Joe Johnson	ATL	.288
5.	Mark Davis	SF	.184	34.	Fernando Valenzuela	LA	.233	63.	Dave Dravecky	SD	.267	92.	Cecilio Guante	PIT	.289
6.	Ken Howell	LA	.185	35.	Roger McDowell	NY	.235	64.	Jay Tibbs	CIN	.267	93.	Terry Leach	NY	.291
7.	Jeff Heathcock	HOU	.190	36.	Ron Darling	NY	.241	65.	Jay Baller	CHI	.268	94.	Kent Tekulve	PHI	.297
8.	Craig Lefferts	SD	.191	37.	Bryn Smith	MTL	.241	66.	Andy Hawkins	SD	.269	95.	Joaquin Andujar	STL	.300
9.	Vida Blue	SF	.200	38.	Rick Aguilera	NY	.241	67.	Rick Camp	ATL	.269	96.	Kurt Kepshire	STL	.301
10.	John Tudor	STL	.203	39.	Bob Forsch	STL	.241	68.	Rick Sutcliffe	CHI	.270	97.	Pascual Perez	ATL	.302
11.	Dwight Gooden	NY	.203	40.	Kevin Gross	PHI	.242	69.	Joe Niekro	HOU	.271	98.	Ron Robinson	CIN	.302
12.	Dave Rucker	PHI	.208	41.	Bruce Sutter	ATL	.242	70.	Charles Hudson	PHI	.273	99.	Len Barker	ATL	.302
13.	Mario Soto	CIN	.209	42.	Don Robinson	PIT	.242	71.	Ed Lynch	NY	.274	100.	Doug Sisk	NY	.306
14.	Jeff Reardon	MTL	.210	43.	Scott Sanderson	CHI	.243	72.	Lee Tunnell	PIT	.274	101.	Rick Rhoden	PIT	.306
15.	Bobby Castillo	LA	.212	44.	Jim Gott	SF	.245	73.	Andy McGaffigan	CIN	.275	102.	George Frazier	CHI	.307
16.	Bob Welch	LA	.214	45.	Nolan Ryan	HOU	.246	74.	Randy St. Claire	MTL	.276	103.	Larry Andersen	PHI	.309
17.	Joe Hesketh	MTL	.215	46.	Gene Garber	ATL	.246	75.	Bill Laskey	MTL	.277	104.	Derek Botelho	CHI	.311
18.	Mike Scott	HOU	.217	47.	Tom Hume	CIN	.250	76.	Jose DeLeón	PIT	.277	105.	Ken Dayley	STL	.313
19.	Floyd Youmans	MTL	.217	47.	Ron Mathis	HOU	.250	77.	Ed Wojna	SD	.279	106.	Steve Rogers	MTL	.314
20.	Don Carman	PHI	.218	47.	Mark Thurmond	SD	.250	78.	Bob Walk	PIT	.281	107.	John Stuper	CIN	.322
21.	Atlee Hammaker	SF	.219	50.	Rich Gossage	SD	.252	79.	Jerry Reuss	LA	.282	108.	Dick Ruthven	CHI	.328
21.	Ricky Horton	STL	.219	51.	Tim Burke	MTL	.253	80.	Bill Gullickson	MTL	.282	109.	Lary Sorensen	CHI	.329
23.	Rick Honeycutt	LA	.219	52.	Jeff Lahti	STL	.256	81.	Warren Brusstar	CHI	.282	110.	Charlie Kerfeld	HOU	.329
24.	Orel Hershiser	LA	.222	53.	Mike Bielecki	PIT	.257	82.	Steve Bedrosian	ATL	.283	111.	Larry McWilliams	PIT	.329
25.	Tom Browning	CIN	.223	54.	Bill Dawley	HOU	.258	82.	Mike Krukow	SF	.283	112.	Frank Williams	SF	.342
26.	Tom Niedenfuer	LA	.224	55.	Dennis Eckersley	CHI	.258	84.	Zane Smith	ATL	.284	113.	Craig McMurtry	ATL	.344
27.	Ted Power	CIN	.224	56.	Bert Roberge	MTL	.259	85.	John Denny	PHI	.285	114.	Greg Minton	SF	.353
28.	Rick Reuschel	PIT	.224	57.	Bob Knepper	HOU	.261	86.	Tim Stoddard	SD	.286	115.	Steve Shields	ATL	.362
29.	Bill Campbell	STL	.227	58.	Rick Mahler	ATL	.262	87.	LaMarr Hoyt	SD	.286				

Opponents' Batting Average, Right-Handed Batters

American League

1.	Steve Ontiveros	OAK	.128	35.	Dave Stieb	TOR	.234	69.	Moose Haas	MIL	.260
2.	Bill Caudill	TOR	.179	36.	Ted Higuera	MIL	.234	69.	Mark Langston	SEA	.260
3.	Greg Harris	TEX	.199	37.	Jim Acker	TOR	.234	71.	Dave Schmidt	TEX	.261
4.	Charlie Hough	TEX	.202	38.	Dan Quisenberry	KC	.236	72.	Don Sutton	CAL	.261
5.	Jerry Reed	CLE	.203	39.	Danny Darwin	MIL	.238	73.	Jamie Easterly	CLE	.261
6.	Juan Berenguer	DET	.204	40.	Al Nipper	BOS	.238	74.	Tim Lollar	BOS	.261
7.	Roger Clemens	BOS	.204	41.	Sammy Stewart	BAL	.240	75.	Bob Ojeda	BOS	.262
8.	Brian Fisher	NY	.207	42.	Bret Saberhagen	KC	.240	76.	Frank Viola	MIN	.262
9.	Stu Cliburn	CAL	.207	42.	Frank Wills	SEA	.240	77.	Bill Krueger	OAK	.266
10.	Rich Bordi	NY	.209	44.	Pete Filson	MIN	.241	78.	Dan Spillner	CHI	.266
11.	Mark Clear	BOS	.211	45.	Tim Birtsas	OAK	.242	79.	Gene Nelson	CHI	.267
11.	Bruce Kison	BOS	.211	46.	Britt Burns	CHI	.242	80.	Walt Terrell	DET	.267
11.	Mike Warren	OAK	.211	47.	Mike Jones	KC	.243	81.	Doyle Alexander	TOR	.268
14.	Keith Atherton	OAK	.211	48.	Bill Swift	SEA	.243	82.	Bud Black	KC	.269
15.	Gary Lavelle	TOR	.211	49.	Randy O'Neal	DET	.245	83.	Jim Slaton	CAL	.270
16.	Dan Petry	DET	.211	50.	Mike Smithson	MIN	.245	84.	Bob Gibson	MIL	.270
17.	Bert Blyleven	MIN	.212	50.	Nate Snell	BAL	.245	85.	Jay Howell	OAK	.270
18.	Joel Davis	CHI	.215	52.	Frank Eufemia	MIN	.246	86.	Aurelio Lopez	DET	.271
19.	Bob James	CHI	.216	53.	Tom Seaver	CHI	.246	87.	Chris Codiroli	OAK	.271
20.	Mike Witt	CAL	.218	54.	Joe Beckwith	KC	.246	88.	Bruce Hurst	BOS	.271
21.	Dave Stewart	TEX	.219	55.	Charlie Leibrandt	KC	.247	89.	Bob Shirley	NY	.272
22.	Mark Gubicza	KC	.219	56.	Ken Dixon	BAL	.251	90.	Frank Tanana	DET	.272
22.	Tom Waddell	CLE	.219	57.	Jimmy Key	TOR	.251	91.	Mike Moore	SEA	.272
24.	Joe Cowley	NY	.220	58.	Storm Davis	BAL	.252	92.	Curt Wardle	CLE	.274
25.	Urbano Lugo	CAL	.221	59.	Floyd Bannister	CHI	.253	93.	Mike Boddicker	BAL	.275
26.	Willie Hernandez	DET	.224	60.	Edwin Nunez	SEA	.254	94.	Steve Crawford	BOS	.276
27.	Roy Thomas	SEA	.225	61.	Luis Sanchez	CAL	.254	94.	Ramon Romero	CLE	.276
28.	Bob Stanley	BOS	.225	62.	Dennis Lamp	TOR	.255	96.	Donnie Moore	CAL	.277
29.	Phil Niekro	NY	.226	63.	Dennis Rasmussen	NY	.255	97.	Bryan Clark	CLE	.278
30.	Jack Morris	DET	.226	64.	Ron Guidry	NY	.256	97.	Don Schulze	CLE	.278
31.	Ron Davis	MIN	.228	65.	Danny Jackson	KC	.258	99.	Ron Romanick	CAL	.279
32.	Jim Clancy	TOR	.230	66.	Dave Righetti	NY	.259	100.	Don Aase	BAL	.279
33.	Dickie Noles	TEX	.234	67.	Ken Schrom	MIN	.259	101.	Bill Scherrer	DET	.283
34.	Kirk McCaskill	CAL	.234	68.	Jaime Cocanower	MIL	.259	102.	Dave Von Ohlen	CLE	.283

103.	John Candelaria	CAL	.284
104.	Pete Vuckovich	MIL	.284
105.	Matt Young	SEA	.286
106.	John Butcher	MIN	.286
107.	Bob McClure	MIL	.288
108.	Luis Leal	TOR	.289
109.	Scott McGregor	BAL	.289
110.	Salome Barojas	SEA	.292
111.	Geoff Zahn	CAL	.292
112.	Steve McCatty	OAK	.293
113.	Mike Flanagan	BAL	.296
114.	Neal Heaton	CLE	.296
115.	Vern Ruhle	CLE	.297
116.	Rick Lysander	MIN	.297
117.	Ed Vande Berg	SEA	.298
118.	Burt Hooton	TEX	.300
119.	Dennis Boyd	BOS	.300
120.	Rick Thompson	CLE	.302
121.	Tippy Martinez	BAL	.302
122.	Mike Mason	TEX	.304
123.	Dennis Martinez	BAL	.305
124.	Ed Whitson	NY	.307
125.	Ray Burris	MIL	.313
126.	Roy Smith	CLE	.313
127.	Dave Rozema	TEX	.318
128.	Jim Beattie	SEA	.319
129.	Curt Young	OAK	.331
130.	Mike Trujillo	BOS	.333
131.	Tommy John	OAK	.337
132.	Rick Waits	MIL	.357
133.	Chris Welsh	TEX	.360

National League

1.	Don Carman	PHI	.161	30.	Joaquin Andujar	STL	.223	59.	Gary Lucas	MTL	.243
2.	Frank Williams	SF	.164	31.	Mickey Mahler	MTL	.223	60.	Bobby Castillo	LA	.243
3.	Tim Burke	MTL	.166	32.	Bryn Smith	MTL	.224	61.	Larry Andersen	PHI	.247
4.	Cecilio Guante	PIT	.166	33.	Joe Hesketh	MTL	.224	62.	Dave Dravecky	SD	.247
5.	Scott Garrelts	SF	.172	34.	Joe Niekro	HOU	.224	63.	Vida Blue	SF	.248
6.	Sid Fernandez	NY	.185	35.	Roger McDowell	NY	.225	64.	Jeff Lahti	STL	.248
7.	Orel Hershiser	LA	.186	36.	Kent Tekulve	PHI	.226	65.	Zane Smith	ATL	.249
8.	Jose DeLeon	PIT	.189	37.	Steve Bedrosian	ATL	.226	66.	Tom Browning	CIN	.249
9.	Mike Krukow	SF	.189	38.	Lary Sorensen	CHI	.228	67.	Steve Carlton	PHI	.251
10.	Eric Show	SD	.194	39.	Lee Tunnell	PIT	.228	68.	Shane Rawley	PHI	.252
11.	Dwight Gooden	NY	.198	40.	Ken Howell	LA	.229	69.	Atlee Hammaker	SF	.253
12.	Dennis Eckersley	CHI	.199	41.	Al Holland	PIT	.229	70.	John Franco	CIN	.253
13.	Rich Gossage	SD	.204	42.	Jesse Orosco	NY	.230	71.	Mike Scott	HOU	.254
14.	Tom Hume	CIN	.207	43.	Ted Power	CIN	.230	72.	Jay Tibbs	CIN	.256
15.	Scott Sanderson	CHI	.207	44.	Ron Darling	NY	.230	73.	Jerry Reuss	LA	.257
16.	Andy McGaffigan	CIN	.208	45.	Charles Hudson	PHI	.230	74.	Randy St. Claire	MTL	.257
17.	Rick Reuschel	PIT	.208	46.	Kurt Kepshire	STL	.232	75.	Tim Camp	ATL	.257
18.	Jeff Reardon	MTL	.208	47.	LaMarr Hoyt	SD	.232	76.	Tim Stoddard	SD	.257
19.	John Tudor	STL	.210	48.	Mark Davis	SF	.232	77.	Bill Gullickson	MTL	.258
20.	Fernando Valenzuela	LA	.210	49.	Bill Campbell	STL	.232	78.	Bill Dawley	HOU	.261
21.	Rick Sutcliffe	CHI	.211	50.	Nolan Ryan	HOU	.234	79.	Kevin Gross	PHI	.262
22.	Ron Robinson	CIN	.212	51.	David Palmer	MTL	.235	80.	Jim Gott	SF	.264
23.	Mario Soto	CIN	.214	52.	Dave Smith	HOU	.237	81.	Andy Hawkins	SD	.265
24.	Joe Price	CIN	.214	53.	Bob Welch	LA	.237	82.	Don Robinson	PIT	.266
25.	Lee Smith	CHI	.214	54.	Carlos Diaz	LA	.238	83.	Dick Ruthven	CHI	.266
26.	Frank DiPino	HOU	.220	55.	Ed Lynch	NY	.238	84.	Dan Schatzeder	MTL	.266
27.	Terry Forster	ATL	.220	56.	Danny Cox	STL	.239	85.	Craig Lefferts	SD	.266
28.	Tom Niedenfuer	LA	.222	57.	Ken Dayley	STL	.240	86.	Ricky Horton	STL	.266
29.	Greg Minton	SF	.222	58.	Jim Winn	PIT	.243	87.	Rick Honeycutt	LA	.267

88.	Bob Forsch	STL	.269
89.	Dave LaPoint	SF	.269
90.	Jerry Koosman	PHI	.271
91.	Steve Trout	CHI	.271
92.	Bob Knepper	HOU	.272
93.	Jeff Calhoun	HOU	.273
94.	Larry McWilliams	PIT	.274
95.	Rick Aguilera	NY	.275
96.	Rick Mahler	ATL	.276
97.	Doug Sisk	NY	.278
98.	John Denny	PHI	.279
99.	Joe Johnson	ATL	.282
100.	Gene Garber	ATL	.284
101.	Rick Rhoden	PIT	.285
102.	Tom Gorman	NY	.287
103.	John Stuper	CIN	.287
104.	Bruce Sutter	ATL	.289
105.	Bill Laskey	MTL	.289
106.	Pascual Perez	ATL	.291
107.	George Frazier	CHI	.292
108.	Jeff Dedmon	ATL	.293
109.	John Candelaria	PIT	.297
110.	Warren Brusstar	CHI	.299
111.	Mark Thurmond	SD	.300
112.	Dave Rucker	PHI	.301
113.	Steve Engel	CHI	.308
114.	Ray Fontenot	CHI	.310
115.	Ron Mathis	HOU	.329

Opponents' Slugging Average, Left-Handed Batters

American League

1.	Willie Hernandez	DET	.229	34.	Ron Guidry	NY	.348	67.	Bill Caudill	TOR	.407	100.	Dickie Noles	TEX	.468
2.	Mark Clear	BOS	.256	35.	Charlie Leibrandt	KC	.348	68.	Sammy Stewart	BAL	.413	101.	Frank Wills	SEA	.469
3.	Bob Shirley	NY	.267	36.	Frank Eufemia	MIN	.353	69.	Doyle Alexander	TOR	.416	102.	Ken Schrom	MIN	.470
4.	Donnie Moore	CAL	.270	37.	Bob Stanley	BOS	.354	70.	Mike Mason	TEX	.416	103.	Keith Creel	CLE	.473
5.	Dave Righetti	NY	.277	38.	Bert Blyleven	MIN	.362	71.	Pete Filson	MIN	.418	104.	Richard Dotson	CHI	.477
6.	Roy Thomas	SEA	.284	39.	Tom Seaver	CHI	.363	72.	Kirk McCaskill	CAL	.420	105.	Urbano Lugo	CAL	.478
7.	Bill Scherrer	DET	.286	40.	Bret Saberhagen	KC	.363	73.	Steve Crawford	BOS	.421	106.	Joe Beckwith	KC	.478
7.	Dave Stieb	TOR	.286	41.	Bud Black	KC	.364	74.	Al Nipper	BOS	.421	107.	Jim Slaton	CAL	.479
9.	Greg Harris	TEX	.286	42.	Bob McClure	MIL	.365	75.	Pete Vuckovich	MIL	.422	108.	Jim Beattie	SEA	.480
10.	Brian Fisher	NY	.289	43.	Jaime Cocanower	MIL	.365	76.	Bob Gibson	MIL	.423	109.	Ron Musselman	TOR	.480
11.	Chris Welsh	TEX	.294	44.	Danny Jackson	KC	.367	77.	Bruce Hurst	BOS	.425	110.	Ed Whitson	NY	.481
12.	Jamie Easterly	CLE	.296	45.	Dave Schmidt	TEX	.369	78.	Dan Spillner	CHI	.427	111.	Bill Swift	SEA	.485
13.	Roger Clemens	BOS	.297	46.	Don Sutton	CAL	.373	79.	Mike Trujillo	BOS	.428	112.	Rollie Fingers	MIL	.485
14.	Bob James	CHI	.297	47.	Mike Witt	CAL	.375	80.	Ray Burris	MIL	.431	113.	Jose Rijo	OAK	.488
15.	Matt Young	SEA	.304	48.	Nate Snell	BAL	.376	81.	Phil Niekro	NY	.432	113.	Rick Thompson	CLE	.488
16.	Jimmy Key	TOR	.306	49.	Ted Higuera	MIL	.378	82.	Stu Cliburn	CAL	.432	115.	Rick Lysander	MIN	.491
17.	Aurelio Lopez	DET	.306	50.	Ken Dixon	BAL	.378	83.	Neal Heaton	CLE	.435	116.	Rick Langford	OAK	.495
18.	Tippy Martinez	BAL	.311	51.	Tim Birtsas	OAK	.379	84.	Dan Quisenberry	KC	.435	117.	Don Schulze	CLE	.496
19.	Jay Howell	OAK	.313	52.	Ron Davis	MIN	.379	85.	Keith Atherton	OAK	.436	118.	Jerry Reed	CLE	.496
20.	Juan Agosto	CHI	.316	53.	Chris Codiroli	OAK	.380	86.	Bill Krueger	OAK	.439	119.	Tom Waddell	CLE	.502
21.	Dennis Lamp	TOR	.320	54.	Pat Clements	CAL	.380	87.	Gene Nelson	CHI	.440	120.	Salome Barojas	SEA	.516
22.	Steve Ontiveros	OAK	.321	55.	Edwin Nunez	SEA	.388	88.	Rich Bordi	NY	.442	121.	Bruce Kison	BOS	.519
23.	Walt Terrell	DET	.323	56.	Moose Haas	MIL	.389	89.	Steve McCatty	OAK	.446	122.	Scott McGregor	BAL	.520
24.	Gary Lavelle	TOR	.330	57.	Jim Acker	TOR	.390	90.	Frank Tanana	DET	.447	123.	Luis Leal	TOR	.522
25.	Ed Vande Berg	SEA	.331	58.	Mark Gubicza	KC	.391	91.	Juan Berenguer	DET	.448	124.	Dave Stewart	TEX	.524
26.	Dennis Boyd	BOS	.334	59.	Dave Rozema	TEX	.393	92.	Bob Ojeda	BOS	.449	125.	Burt Hooton	TEX	.527
27.	Mike Moore	SEA	.337	60.	Storm Davis	BAL	.394	93.	Frank Viola	MIN	.454	126.	Luis Sanchez	CAL	.530
28.	Randy O'Neal	DET	.340	61.	Vern Ruhle	CLE	.395	94.	Doug Bair	DET	.456	127.	Jeff Russell	TEX	.534
29.	Jack Morris	DET	.341	62.	Jim Clancy	TOR	.396	95.	Dennis Martinez	BAL	.459	128.	Roy Smith	CLE	.542
30.	Tim Lollar	BOS	.342	63.	Britt Burns	CHI	.396	96.	Danny Darwin	MIL	.459	129.	Floyd Bannister	CHI	.548
31.	Charlie Hough	TEX	.343	64.	Joe Cowley	NY	.399	97.	Ron Romanick	CAL	.461	130.	Curt Wardle	CLE	.581
32.	Don Aase	BAL	.345	65.	Joel Davis	CHI	.404	98.	John Butcher	MIN	.463	131.	Mike Warren	OAK	.776
33.	Dan Petry	DET	.347	66.	Mike Boddicker	BAL	.405	99.	Mike Smithson	MIN	.467				

National League

1.	Roy Jackson	SD	.221	30.	Roger McDowell	NY	.319	59.	Jerry Reuss	LA	.369	88.	Dennis Eckersley	CHI	.416
2.	John Franco	CIN	.224	31.	Shane Rawley	PHI	.319	60.	Mario Soto	CIN	.370	89.	Bill Laskey	MTL	.419
3.	Ricky Horton	STL	.238	32.	Jeff Dedmon	ATL	.319	61.	Tom Hume	CIN	.371	90.	Charles Hudson	PHI	.419
4.	Ken Howell	LA	.245	33.	Ted Power	CIN	.320	62.	Rick Mahler	ATL	.372	91.	Warren Brusstar	CHI	.419
5.	Ray Fontenot	CHI	.247	34.	Dave Dravecky	SD	.322	63.	Ron Mathis	HOU	.375	92.	Rick Rhoden	PIT	.425
6.	Dwight Gooden	NY	.249	35.	David Palmer	MTL	.325	63.	Lee Tunnell	PIT	.375	93.	Charlie Kerfeld	HOU	.425
7.	John Tudor	STL	.264	36.	Sid Fernandez	NY	.326	65.	Joe Niekro	HOU	.379	94.	Greg Minton	SF	.432
8.	Floyd Youmans	MTL	.269	37.	Rick Camp	ATL	.328	66.	Bert Roberge	MTL	.379	95.	Ed Lynch	NY	.436
9.	Joe Hesketh	MTL	.269	38.	Rick Honeycutt	LA	.329	67.	Danny Cox	STL	.382	96.	Mike Krukow	SF	.442
10.	Craig Lefferts	SD	.270	39.	Rick Aguilera	NY	.330	68.	Jay Baller	CHI	.382	97.	Terry Leach	NY	.443
11.	Tom Browning	CIN	.277	40.	Atlee Hammaker	SF	.333	69.	Frank Pastore	CIN	.388	98.	Steve Bedrosian	ATL	.444
12.	Jeff Reardon	MTL	.287	41.	Jeff Lahti	STL	.337	70.	Randy St. Claire	MTL	.388	99.	Ron Robinson	CIN	.447
13.	Mike Scott	HOU	.289	42.	Nolan Ryan	HOU	.337	71.	John Denny	PHI	.388	100.	Cecilio Guante	PIT	.447
14.	Orel Hershiser	LA	.289	43.	Fernando Valenzuela	LA	.344	72.	Jay Tibbs	CIN	.390	101.	Eric Show	SD	.453
15.	Bob Welch	LA	.291	44.	Dave Rucker	PHI	.347	73.	Kent Tekulve	PHI	.398	102.	Ed Wojna	SD	.453
16.	Don Robinson	PIT	.291	45.	Gene Garber	ATL	.349	74.	Ken Dayley	STL	.400	103.	Kurt Kepshire	STL	.454
17.	Bob Forsch	STL	.296	46.	Jim Winn	PIT	.349	75.	Lee Smith	CHI	.401	104.	Joe Johnson	ATL	.455
18.	Jeff Heathcock	HOU	.298	47.	Ron Darling	NY	.354	76.	Andy Hawkins	SD	.402	105.	Pascual Perez	ATL	.467
19.	Don Carman	PHI	.299	48.	Kevin Gross	PHI	.354	77.	Doug Sisk	NY	.403	106.	Scott Sanderson	CHI	.470
20.	Bill Campbell	STL	.299	49.	Bobby Castillo	LA	.356	78.	Mike Bielecki	PIT	.404	107.	Dick Ruthven	CHI	.484
21.	Dave Smith	HOU	.302	50.	Jim Gott	SF	.357	79.	Joaquin Andujar	STL	.405	108.	George Frazier	CHI	.486
22.	Scott Garrelts	SF	.302	51.	Andy McGaffigan	CIN	.357	80.	Dave LaPoint	SF	.406	109.	Len Barker	ATL	.500
23.	Mark Thurmond	SD	.304	52.	Tim Burke	MTL	.360	81.	Steve Rogers	MTL	.407	109.	Larry McWilliams	PIT	.500
24.	Vida Blue	SF	.307	53.	Bill Gullickson	MTL	.362	82.	John Stuper	CIN	.408	109.	Steve Shields	ATL	.500
25.	Rick Reuschel	PIT	.308	54.	Tom Niedenfuer	LA	.363	83.	Bob Knepper	HOU	.409	112.	Frank Williams	SF	.504
26.	Zane Smith	ATL	.309	55.	Bill Dawley	HOU	.364	84.	Rick Sutcliffe	CHI	.410	113.	Lary Sorensen	CHI	.517
27.	Rich Gossage	SD	.313	56.	Bruce Sutter	ATL	.366	85.	LaMarr Hoyt	SD	.412	114.	Derek Botelho	CHI	.556
28.	Bryn Smith	MTL	.313	57.	Bob Walk	PIT	.367	86.	Jose DeLeon	PIT	.414	115.	Craig McMurtry	ATL	.594
29.	Mark Davis	SF	.316	58.	Tim Stoddard	SD	.367	87.	Larry Andersen	PHI	.415				

Opponents' Slugging Average, Right-Handed Batters

American League

#	Player	Team	Avg
1.	Steve Ontiveros	OAK	.192
2.	Stu Cliburn	CAL	.263
3.	Brian Fisher	NY	.266
4.	Rich Bordi	NY	.270
5.	Gary Lavelle	TOR	.286
6.	Mark Clear	BOS	.289
7.	Bill Swift	SEA	.290
8.	Bill Caudill	TOR	.293
9.	Greg Harris	TEX	.293
10.	Bruce Kison	BOS	.298
11.	Roger Clemens	BOS	.302
12.	Dan Quisenberry	KC	.308
13.	Bob James	CHI	.309
14.	Nate Snell	BAL	.319
15.	Dave Schmidt	TEX	.329
16.	Charlie Hough	TEX	.332
17.	Jack Morris	DET	.338
18.	Mark Gubicza	KC	.339
19.	Bert Blyleven	MIN	.340
20.	Jerry Reed	CLE	.341
21.	Joe Beckwith	KC	.341
22.	Mike Witt	CAL	.342
23.	Roy Thomas	SEA	.343
24.	Dan Petry	DET	.345
25.	Dave Righetti	NY	.346
26.	Jaime Cocanower	MIL	.349
27.	Bret Saberhagen	KC	.349
28.	Mike Smithson	MIN	.350
29.	Rick Lysander	MIN	.352
30.	Dennis Lamp	TOR	.352
31.	Jim Acker	TOR	.354
32.	Storm Davis	BAL	.355
33.	Bob Stanley	BOS	.356
34.	Charlie Leibrandt	KC	.358
35.	Danny Jackson	KC	.359
36.	Mike Boddicker	BAL	.360
36.	Mike Warren	OAK	.360
38.	Sammy Stewart	BAL	.362
39.	Joel Davis	CHI	.364
40.	Dickie Noles	TEX	.364
41.	Dave Stieb	TOR	.367
42.	Bob Shirley	NY	.370
43.	Al Nipper	BOS	.371
44.	Ted Higuera	MIL	.372
45.	Jay Howell	OAK	.374
46.	Ron Davis	MIN	.374
47.	Doyle Alexander	TOR	.375
48.	Urbano Lugo	CAL	.382
49.	Bob Ojeda	BOS	.383
50.	Phil Niekro	NY	.383
51.	Juan Berenguer	DET	.383
52.	Dave Von Ohlen	CLE	.383
53.	Mike Jones	KC	.385
54.	Britt Burns	CHI	.385
55.	Tom Seaver	CHI	.386
56.	Walt Terrell	DET	.388
57.	Mike Moore	SEA	.389
58.	Bob Gibson	MIL	.392
59.	Kirk McCaskill	CAL	.394
60.	Pete Filson	MIN	.395
61.	Frank Wills	SEA	.395
62.	Steve Crawford	BOS	.397
63.	Frank Viola	MIN	.397
64.	Don Sutton	CAL	.397
65.	Randy O'Neal	DET	.397
66.	Willie Hernandez	DET	.399
67.	Bill Krueger	OAK	.401
68.	Dan Spillner	CHI	.402
69.	Ron Guidry	NY	.402
70.	Don Aase	BAL	.403
71.	Jimmy Key	TOR	.403
72.	Danny Darwin	MIL	.404
73.	Dennis Rasmussen	NY	.404
74.	Tom Waddell	CLE	.406
75.	Bud Black	KC	.407
76.	Donnie Moore	CAL	.408
77.	Salome Barojas	SEA	.408
78.	Edwin Nunez	SEA	.411
79.	Ken Dixon	BAL	.413
80.	Jamie Easterly	CLE	.414
81.	Keith Atherton	OAK	.417
82.	Bryan Clark	CLE	.420
83.	Tim Birtsas	OAK	.423
84.	Floyd Bannister	CHI	.423
85.	Dave Stewart	TEX	.424
86.	Don Schulze	CLE	.426
87.	Frank Tanana	DET	.427
88.	Joe Cowley	NY	.428
89.	Chris Codiroli	OAK	.430
90.	Moose Haas	MIL	.433
91.	Ron Romanick	CAL	.434
92.	Jim Clancy	TOR	.435
92.	Steve McCatty	OAK	.435
94.	Matt Young	SEA	.439
95.	Vern Ruhle	CLE	.441
96.	Bruce Hurst	BOS	.442
97.	Roy Smith	CLE	.443
98.	Rick Thompson	CLE	.444
99.	Neal Heaton	CLE	.445
100.	John Butcher	MIN	.446
101.	Ed Vande Berg	SEA	.447
102.	Burt Hooton	TEX	.447
103.	Tim Lollar	BOS	.450
104.	Mike Trujillo	BOS	.452
105.	Dave Rozema	TEX	.452
106.	Ed Whitson	NY	.453
107.	Bill Scherrer	DET	.455
108.	Scott McGregor	BAL	.456
109.	Jim Beattie	SEA	.458
110.	John Candelaria	CAL	.459
111.	Rick Waits	MIL	.460
112.	Jim Slaton	CAL	.461
113.	Mark Langston	SEA	.463
114.	Frank Eufemia	MIN	.467
114.	Luis Sanchez	CAL	.467
116.	Tippy Martinez	BAL	.469
117.	Gene Nelson	CHI	.470
118.	Bob McClure	MIL	.470
119.	Mike Mason	TEX	.473
120.	Dennis Boyd	BOS	.478
121.	Ken Schrom	MIN	.482
122.	Geoff Zahn	CAL	.485
123.	Dennis Martinez	BAL	.487
124.	Curt Wardle	CLE	.494
125.	Ray Burris	MIL	.497
126.	Mike Flanagan	BAL	.502
127.	Pete Vuckovich	MIL	.507
128.	Tommy John	OAK	.515
129.	Ramon Romero	CLE	.529
130.	Luis Leal	TOR	.533
131.	Aurelio Lopez	DET	.541
132.	Chris Welsh	TEX	.592
133.	Curt Young	OAK	.690

National League

#	Player	Team	Avg
1.	Scott Garrelts	SF	.214
2.	Frank Williams	SF	.230
3.	Rich Gossage	SD	.237
4.	Orel Hershiser	LA	.252
5.	Cecilio Guante	PIT	.253
6.	Don Carman	PHI	.263
7.	Tim Burke	MTL	.268
8.	Tom Niedenfuer	LA	.276
9.	Ted Power	CIN	.280
10.	Rick Reuschel	PIT	.280
11.	Fernando Valenzuela	LA	.282
12.	Dennis Eckersley	CHI	.285
13.	John Tudor	STL	.288
14.	Sid Fernandez	NY	.298
15.	Dwight Gooden	NY	.298
16.	Mike Krukow	SF	.299
16.	Dave Smith	HOU	.299
18.	Steve Bedrosian	ATL	.303
19.	Jose DeLeon	PIT	.304
20.	Jeff Reardon	MTL	.306
21.	David Palmer	MTL	.309
22.	Eric Show	SD	.312
23.	Rick Sutcliffe	CHI	.319
24.	Scott Sanderson	CHI	.319
25.	Jim Winn	PIT	.319
26.	Tom Hume	CIN	.322
27.	Joaquin Andujar	STL	.322
28.	Kent Tekulve	PHI	.327
29.	Andy McGaffigan	CIN	.329
30.	Greg Minton	SF	.335
31.	Joe Niekro	HOU	.337
32.	Mickey Mahler	MTL	.338
33.	Kurt Kepshire	STL	.339
34.	Nolan Ryan	HOU	.340
35.	Randy St. Claire	MTL	.340
36.	Ken Dayley	STL	.341
37.	Joe Hesketh	MTL	.343
38.	Roger McDowell	NY	.344
39.	Jesse Orosco	NY	.345
40.	Bill Campbell	STL	.345
41.	Frank DiPino	HOU	.346
42.	Bryn Smith	MTL	.346
43.	Ed Lynch	NY	.347
44.	Jeff Calhoun	HOU	.349
45.	Lary Sorensen	CHI	.351
46.	Mario Soto	CIN	.353
47.	John Franco	CIN	.353
48.	Terry Forster	ATL	.353
49.	Ron Robinson	CIN	.354
50.	Steve Trout	CHI	.356
51.	Lee Smith	CHI	.357
52.	LaMarr Hoyt	SD	.357
53.	Dave Dravecky	SD	.358
54.	Mark Davis	SF	.358
55.	Gary Lucas	MTL	.359
56.	Jay Tibbs	CIN	.362
57.	Lee Tunnell	PIT	.362
58.	Zane Smith	ATL	.362
59.	Carlos Diaz	LA	.363
60.	Jeff Lahti	STL	.364
61.	Shane Rawley	PHI	.364
62.	Jerry Reuss	LA	.365
63.	Bill Gullickson	MTL	.365
64.	Ron Darling	NY	.366
65.	Kevin Gross	PHI	.369
66.	Al Holland	PIT	.369
67.	Steve Carlton	PHI	.373
68.	Ken Howell	LA	.373
69.	Larry Andersen	PHI	.377
69.	Doug Sisk	NY	.377
71.	Bill Dawley	HOU	.379
72.	Danny Cox	STL	.382
73.	Joe Price	CIN	.385
74.	Dick Ruthven	CHI	.386
75.	Andy Hawkins	SD	.388
76.	Tim Stoddard	SD	.390
77.	Rick Camp	ATL	.390
78.	Atlee Hammaker	SF	.396
79.	John Denny	PHI	.396
80.	Dave LaPoint	SF	.396
81.	Rick Honeycutt	LA	.397
82.	Jim Gott	SF	.399
83.	John Stuper	CIN	.402
84.	Tom Browning	CIN	.403
85.	Gene Garber	ATL	.403
86.	Charles Hudson	PHI	.404
87.	Ricky Horton	STL	.406
88.	Rick Aguilera	NY	.408
89.	Jeff Dedmon	ATL	.408
90.	Bob Knepper	HOU	.412
91.	Mark Thurmond	SD	.414
92.	Larry McWilliams	PIT	.416
93.	Craig Lefferts	SD	.417
94.	Joe Johnson	ATL	.418
95.	Don Robinson	PIT	.420
96.	Bob Forsch	STL	.430
97.	Vida Blue	SF	.431
98.	Bobby Castillo	LA	.434
99.	Bob Welch	LA	.435
100.	Rick Mahler	ATL	.435
101.	Pascual Perez	ATL	.440
102.	Rick Rhoden	PIT	.442
103.	Mike Scott	HOU	.442
104.	George Frazier	CHI	.448
105.	Dave Rucker	PHI	.451
106.	Jerry Koosman	PHI	.459
107.	Dan Schatzeder	MTL	.459
108.	Tom Gorman	NY	.460
109.	Warren Brusstar	CHI	.477
110.	Bill Laskey	MTL	.481
111.	Ray Fontenot	CHI	.493
112.	Bruce Sutter	ATL	.500
113.	John Candelaria	PIT	.525
114.	Ron Mathis	HOU	.529
115.	Steve Engel	CHI	.546

Opponents' Home Run Percentage, Left-Handed Batters

American League

#	Name	Team	Pct		#	Name	Team	Pct		#	Name	Team	Pct		#	Name	Team	Pct
1.	Mark Clear	BOS	0.00		34.	Mike Moore	SEA	1.75		67.	Ken Dixon	BAL	2.68		100.	Ray Burris	MIL	3.61
1.	Jamie Easterly	CLE	0.00		35.	Mike Boddicker	BAL	1.77		68.	Bill Swift	SEA	2.69		101.	Dave Stewart	TEX	3.66
1.	Frank Eufemia	MIN	0.00		36.	Pete Vuckovich	MIL	1.78		69.	Kirk McCaskill	CAL	2.70		102.	Keith Atherton	OAK	3.68
4.	Walt Terrell	DET	0.40		37.	Dave Schmidt	TEX	1.79		69.	Steve McCatty	OAK	2.70		103.	Richard Dotson	CHI	3.74
5.	Roger Clemens	BOS	0.50		37.	Dave Stieb	TOR	1.79		71.	Pete Filson	MIN	2.73		104.	Phil Niekro	NY	3.86
6.	Jay Howell	OAK	0.50		39.	Greg Harris	TEX	1.94		72.	Vern Ruhle	CLE	2.73		105.	Curt Wardle	CLE	3.88
7.	Bob James	CHI	0.51		40.	Jim Clancy	TOR	1.96		73.	Rick Lysander	MIN	2.78		105.	Frank Wills	SEA	3.88
8.	Danny Jackson	KC	0.63		40.	Charlie Leibrandt	KC	1.96		74.	Bret Saberhagen	KC	2.79		107.	Gene Nelson	CHI	3.89
9.	Matt Young	SEA	0.68		40.	Ron Musselman	TOR	1.96		75.	Urbano Lugo	CAL	2.81		108.	Britt Burns	CHI	3.90
10.	Bob Shirley	NY	0.68		43.	Roy Thomas	SEA	2.03		76.	Bill Scherrer	DET	2.86		109.	Ron Romanick	CAL	3.90
11.	Ed Vande Berg	SEA	0.85		44.	Aurelio Lopez	DET	2.04		77.	Ed Whitson	NY	2.93		110.	Rollie Fingers	MIL	3.96
12.	Jaime Cocanower	MIL	0.86		45.	Jack Morris	DET	2.06		78.	Don Sutton	CAL	2.94		111.	Jose Rijo	OAK	4.00
13.	Dave Righetti	NY	0.89		46.	Chris Codiroli	OAK	2.09		79.	Juan Berenguer	DET	2.96		112.	Dan Spillner	CHI	4.03
14.	Chris Welsh	TEX	0.92		47.	Randy O'Neal	DET	2.09		80.	Moose Haas	MIL	2.99		113.	Danny Darwin	MIL	4.07
15.	Tippy Martinez	BAL	0.94		48.	Mike Witt	CAL	2.12		81.	Pat Clements	CAL	3.00		114.	Floyd Bannister	CHI	4.11
16.	Willie Hernandez	DET	0.95		49.	Dickie Noles	TEX	2.15		82.	Keith Creel	CLE	3.05		115.	Bob Gibson	MIL	4.23
17.	Donnie Moore	CAL	1.00		49.	Tom Seaver	CHI	2.15		83.	John Butcher	MIN	3.06		116.	Ron Guidry	NY	4.35
18.	Juan Agosto	CHI	1.02		51.	Doug Bair	DET	2.22		84.	Doyle Alexander	TOR	3.11		116.	Luis Sanchez	CAL	4.35
19.	Steve Crawford	BOS	1.09		51.	Charlie Hough	TEX	2.22		85.	Bob McClure	MIL	3.13		118.	Luis Leal	TOR	4.41
20.	Bud Black	KC	1.14		53.	Ted Higuera	MIL	2.36		86.	Dave Rozema	TEX	3.14		119.	Bill Caudill	TOR	4.42
21.	Brian Fisher	NY	1.16		54.	Mark Gubicza	KC	2.37		87.	Tim Birtsas	OAK	3.16		120.	Joe Cowley	NY	4.44
21.	Mike Trujillo	BOS	1.16		55.	Don Aase	BAL	2.38		88.	Rick Thompson	CLE	3.20		121.	Joe Beckwith	KC	4.46
23.	Neal Heaton	CLE	1.24		56.	Rich Bordi	NY	2.42		89.	Bruce Kison	BOS	3.21		122.	Roy Smith	CLE	4.58
24.	Joel Davis	CHI	1.28		57.	Bill Krueger	OAK	2.44		90.	Salome Barojas	SEA	3.23		123.	Rick Langford	OAK	4.59
25.	Jim Acker	TOR	1.37		58.	Bob Stanley	BOS	2.48		91.	Frank Viola	MIN	3.24		124.	Edwin Nunez	SEA	4.61
26.	Dan Quisenberry	KC	1.48		59.	Tim Lollar	BOS	2.50		92.	Bruce Hurst	BOS	3.27		125.	Frank Tanana	DET	4.67
27.	Steve Ontiveros	OAK	1.49		60.	Jimmy Key	TOR	2.55		93.	Gary Lavelle	TOR	3.30		126.	Ken Schrom	MIN	4.67
28.	Bob Ojeda	BOS	1.57		61.	Ron Davis	MIN	2.59		94.	Jim Slaton	CAL	3.30		127.	Burt Hooton	TEX	4.92
29.	Nate Snell	BAL	1.66		62.	Mike Mason	TEX	2.60		95.	Jim Beattie	SEA	3.33		128.	Jerry Reed	CLE	5.19
30.	Storm Davis	BAL	1.67		62.	Sammy Stewart	BAL	2.61		95.	Mike Smithson	MIN	3.33		129.	Tom Waddell	CLE	5.91
31.	Dennis Boyd	BOS	1.70		64.	Don Schulze	CLE	2.63		97.	Stu Cliburn	CAL	3.38		130.	Scott McGregor	BAL	6.78
32.	Bert Blyleven	MIN	1.71		65.	Dan Petry	DET	2.67		98.	Jeff Russell	TEX	3.42		131.	Mike Warren	OAK	11.76
33.	Dennis Lamp	TOR	1.74		66.	Al Nipper	BOS	2.68		99.	Dennis Martinez	BAL	3.61					

National League

#	Name	Team	Pct		#	Name	Team	Pct		#	Name	Team	Pct		#	Name	Team	Pct
1.	Bob Forsch	STL	0.00		30.	Bob Welch	LA	0.92		59.	Doug Sisk	NY	1.49		88.	Jose DeLeon	PIT	2.46
1.	Rick Honeycutt	LA	0.00		31.	Rick Reuschel	PIT	0.93		60.	Gene Garber	ATL	1.54		89.	Tom Niedenfuer	LA	2.49
1.	Ricky Horton	STL	0.00		32.	Kevin Gross	PHI	0.94		61.	Kent Tekulve	PHI	1.56		90.	LaMarr Hoyt	SD	2.56
1.	Roy Jackson	SD	0.00		33.	Andy McGaffigan	CIN	0.97		62.	Warren Brusstar	CHI	1.61		91.	Mike Krukow	SF	2.60
1.	Jeff Lahti	STL	0.00		34.	Tim Stoddard	SD	1.02		62.	Tim Burke	MTL	1.61		92.	Bob Knepper	HOU	2.61
1.	Don Robinson	PIT	0.00		35.	Bill Campbell	STL	1.03		62.	Lee Tunnell	PIT	1.61		93.	Mark Davis	SF	2.63
1.	Zane Smith	ATL	0.00		36.	Joe Hesketh	MTL	1.08		65.	Danny Cox	STL	1.62		93.	Larry McWilliams	PIT	2.63
1.	Mark Thurmond	SD	0.00		37.	Dave Dravecky	SD	1.11		66.	Larry Andersen	PHI	1.63		95.	Vida Blue	SF	2.67
9.	Bryn Smith	MTL	0.24		38.	Craig Lefferts	SD	1.12		67.	Frank Williams	SF	1.71		96.	Bill Laskey	MTL	2.70
10.	David Palmer	MTL	0.37		39.	Don Carman	PHI	1.15		68.	Tom Hume	CIN	1.72		97.	Mike Bielecki	PIT	2.75
11.	Rick Camp	ATL	0.40		39.	John Stuper	CIN	1.15		68.	Randy St. Claire	MTL	1.72		98.	Lary Sorensen	CHI	2.80
12.	Dwight Gooden	NY	0.53		41.	Jay Tibbs	CIN	1.16		70.	Ron Darling	NY	1.74		99.	Pascual Perez	ATL	2.83
13.	Floyd Youmans	MTL	0.57		42.	Steve Rogers	MTL	1.16		71.	Fernando Valenzuela	LA	1.84		100.	Bruce Sutter	ATL	3.11
14.	Scott Garrelts	SF	0.59		43.	John Franco	CIN	1.18		72.	Atlee Hammaker	SF	1.90		101.	Craig McMurtry	ATL	3.13
15.	Orel Hershiser	LA	0.63		44.	Nolan Ryan	HOU	1.20		73.	Bobby Castillo	LA	1.92		102.	Joe Johnson	ATL	3.21
16.	Ken Howell	LA	0.66		45.	Joaquin Andujar	STL	1.21		74.	Jerry Reuss	LA	1.94		103.	Ed Lynch	NY	3.25
17.	Tom Browning	CIN	0.68		46.	Ken Dayley	STL	1.25		75.	Cecilio Guante	PIT	1.97		104.	Steve Shields	ATL	3.29
18.	Jeff Dedmon	ATL	0.69		46.	Frank Pastore	CIN	1.25		76.	Rick Sutcliffe	CHI	2.05		105.	Kurt Kepshire	STL	3.35
19.	Mike Scott	HOU	0.70		48.	Terry Leach	NY	1.27		77.	Lee Smith	CHI	2.08		106.	Steve Bedrosian	ATL	3.38
20.	Greg Minton	SF	0.72		49.	Rick Mahler	ATL	1.29		78.	Dick Ruthven	CHI	2.15		107.	Dennis Eckersley	CHI	3.42
21.	Rich Gossage	SD	0.76		50.	Ray Fontenot	CHI	1.30		79.	Sid Fernandez	NY	2.17		108.	Eric Show	SD	3.45
22.	Ron Mathis	HOU	0.78		51.	John Denny	PHI	1.32		80.	Andy Hawkins	SD	2.18		109.	Ed Wojna	SD	3.49
22.	Bob Walk	PIT	0.78		52.	Rick Aguilera	NY	1.34		81.	Shane Rawley	PHI	2.20		110.	George Frazier	CHI	3.57
24.	Ted Power	CIN	0.80		53.	John Tudor	STL	1.35		82.	Jeff Reardon	MTL	2.21		111.	Mario Soto	CIN	3.74
25.	Jay Baller	CHI	0.81		54.	Jim Gott	SF	1.36		83.	Bill Dawley	HOU	2.27		112.	Dave LaPoint	SF	3.77
26.	Bill Gullickson	MTL	0.83		55.	Charlie Kerfeld	HOU	1.37		84.	Ron Robinson	CIN	2.33		113.	Scott Sanderson	CHI	3.98
27.	Bert Roberge	MTL	0.86		55.	Jim Winn	PIT	1.37		85.	Joe Niekro	HOU	2.37		114.	Len Barker	ATL	4.32
27.	Dave Smith	HOU	0.86		57.	Dave Rucker	PHI	1.39		86.	Jeff Heathcock	HOU	2.38		115.	Derek Botelho	CHI	4.44
29.	Roger McDowell	NY	0.88		58.	Rick Rhoden	PIT	1.39		87.	Charles Hudson	PHI	2.39					

Opponents' Home Run Percentage, Right-Handed Batters

American League

1. Stu Cliburn	CAL	0.00	35. Walt Terrell	DET	1.93	69. Mike Trujillo	BOS	2.82	103. Urbano Lugo	CAL	3.68
1. Rick Lysander	MIN	0.00	36. Bob James	CHI	1.96	70. Jimmy Key	TOR	2.83	104. Kirk McCaskill	CAL	3.69
3. Rich Bordi	NY	0.47	37. Burt Hooton	TEX	2.11	71. Dan Petry	DET	2.84	105. Donnie Moore	CAL	3.80
4. Bill Swift	SEA	0.48	37. Bill Krueger	OAK	2.11	72. Ted Higuera	MIL	2.85	106. Ron Romanick	CAL	3.81
5. Nate Snell	BAL	0.49	39. Bob Gibson	MIL	2.12	73. Jim Acker	TOR	2.86	107. Vern Ruhle	CLE	3.81
6. Mark Clear	BOS	0.88	39. Rick Thompson	CLE	2.12	73. Bill Caudill	TOR	2.86	108. Pete Filson	MIN	3.83
7. Danny Jackson	KC	0.93	41. Ed Vande Berg	SEA	2.13	75. Britt Burns	CHI	2.87	109. Ray Burris	MIL	3.87
8. Joe Beckwith	KC	0.95	42. Mike Moore	SEA	2.15	76. Ed Whitson	NY	2.92	110. Frank Wills	SEA	4.00
9. Brian Fisher	NY	1.09	43. Jay Howell	OAK	2.30	77. Dave Stieb	TOR	2.96	111. Ken Dixon	BAL	4.06
10. Gary Lavelle	TOR	1.24	44. Dan Spillner	CHI	2.34	78. Tommy John	OAK	2.96	112. Danny Darwin	MIL	4.09
11. Don Aase	BAL	1.30	45. Bryan Clark	CLE	2.37	79. Bob McClure	MIL	2.97	113. Willie Hernandez	DET	4.20
12. Bret Saberhagen	KC	1.33	45. Don Schulze	CLE	2.37	80. Frank Tanana	DET	3.07	114. Tippy Martinez	BAL	4.32
13. Dave Righetti	NY	1.40	47. Bud Black	KC	2.38	81. Geoff Zahn	CAL	3.08	115. Gene Nelson	CHI	4.33
14. Mike Boddicker	BAL	1.46	48. Jack Morris	DET	2.43	82. Phil Niekro	NY	3.08	116. Jim Clancy	TOR	4.35
15. Mike Smithson	MIN	1.47	48. Doyle Alexander	TOR	2.43	83. Matt Young	SEA	3.10	117. Jim Slaton	CAL	4.49
16. Bob Shirley	NY	1.51	50. Roger Clemens	BOS	2.47	84. Chris Codiroli	OAK	3.23	118. Ken Schrom	MIN	4.61
17. Roy Smith	CLE	1.53	51. Dennis Rasmussen	NY	2.48	85. Mike Mason	TEX	3.24	119. Dave Stewart	TEX	4.64
18. Greg Harris	TEX	1.57	52. Frank Viola	MIN	2.49	86. Edwin Nunez	SEA	3.24	120. Dennis Martinez	BAL	4.72
19. Rick Waits	MIL	1.59	53. Salome Barojas	SEA	2.50	87. Ron Davis	MIN	3.25	120. Curt Wardle	CLE	4.72
20. Storm Davis	BAL	1.60	54. Ron Guidry	NY	2.51	88. Steve McCatty	OAK	3.26	122. Chris Welsh	TEX	4.74
21. Steve Ontiveros	OAK	1.60	55. Dave Rozema	TEX	2.55	89. Luis Sanchez	CAL	3.28	123. Mark Langston	SEA	4.75
22. Dave Von Ohlen	CLE	1.67	56. Neal Heaton	CLE	2.58	90. Joel Davis	CHI	3.31	124. Mike Flanagan	BAL	4.81
23. Dan Quisenberry	KC	1.69	57. Bert Blyleven	MIN	2.60	91. Dennis Boyd	BOS	3.51	125. Bill Scherrer	DET	4.83
24. Mark Gubicza	KC	1.71	58. Mike Warren	OAK	2.63	92. Tim Birtsas	OAK	3.52	126. Keith Atherton	OAK	4.93
25. Steve Crawford	BOS	1.72	58. Mike Witt	CAL	2.63	93. Bruce Hurst	BOS	3.53	127. Luis Leal	TOR	5.19
26. Bruce Kison	BOS	1.75	60. Randy O'Neal	DET	2.65	94. Scott McGregor	BAL	3.53	128. Pete Vuckovich	MIL	5.33
27. Mike Jones	KC	1.78	61. John Butcher	MIN	2.70	95. Juan Berenguer	DET	3.59	129. Joe Cowley	NY	5.60
28. Dennis Lamp	TOR	1.85	61. John Candelaria	CAL	2.70	96. Jamie Easterly	CLE	3.61	130. Frank Eufemia	MIN	5.74
29. Dave Schmidt	TEX	1.86	63. Tom Seaver	CHI	2.76	97. Jerry Reed	CLE	3.62	131. Ramon Romero	CLE	6.32
30. Charlie Leibrandt	KC	1.87	64. Don Sutton	CAL	2.77	98. Floyd Bannister	CHI	3.64	132. Aurelio Lopez	DET	6.63
31. Bob Ojeda	BOS	1.87	65. Jim Beattie	SEA	2.78	98. Tim Lollar	BOS	3.64	133. Curt Young	OAK	9.15
32. Bob Stanley	BOS	1.88	66. Dickie Noles	TEX	2.80	100. Tom Waddell	CLE	3.65			
33. Jaime Cocanower	MIL	1.89	67. Roy Thomas	SEA	2.81	101. Sammy Stewart	BAL	3.66			
34. Al Nipper	BOS	1.90	68. Charlie Hough	TEX	2.82	102. Moose Haas	MIL	3.67			

National League

1. Rich Gossage	SD	0.00	30. Joaquin Andujar	STL	1.71	59. Pascual Perez	ATL	2.29	88. Don Robinson	PIT	2.90
2. Scott Garrelts	SF	0.47	31. Jeff Lahti	STL	1.82	60. Jeff Dedmon	ATL	2.30	89. Ron Darling	NY	2.90
3. Tom Niedenfuer	LA	0.54	32. Larry Andersen	PHI	1.85	61. Frank DiPino	HOU	2.34	90. Rick Camp	ATL	2.90
4. Jeff Calhoun	HOU	0.58	33. Kent Tekulve	PHI	1.89	61. Lary Sorensen	CHI	2.34	91. Lee Smith	CHI	2.98
5. Ken Dayley	STL	0.60	34. Al Holland	PIT	1.91	63. Sid Fernandez	NY	2.38	92. Ron Robinson	CIN	3.03
6. Doug Sisk	NY	0.62	34. Mickey Mahler	MTL	1.91	64. Dwight Gooden	NY	2.39	93. Terry Forster	ATL	3.33
7. Ted Power	CIN	0.62	36. Ed Lynch	NY	1.91	65. Dave Dravecky	SD	2.39	94. Tom Browning	CIN	3.34
8. Randy St. Claire	MTL	0.69	37. Joe Hesketh	MTL	1.92	66. LaMarr Hoyt	SD	2.40	95. Mark Davis	SF	3.41
9. Cecilio Guante	PIT	0.83	38. Rick Honeycutt	LA	1.92	67. Don Carman	PHI	2.44	96. Warren Brusstar	CHI	3.45
10. Zane Smith	ATL	0.89	39. Frank Williams	SF	1.97	68. Bill Dawley	HOU	2.48	97. Bob Forsch	STL	3.56
11. Steve Bedrosian	ATL	1.02	40. Kevin Gross	PHI	2.02	69. Mike Krukow	SF	2.54	98. Rick Mahler	ATL	3.61
12. Rick Reuschel	PIT	1.03	40. Dave LaPoint	SF	2.02	70. Tim Burke	MTL	2.55	99. Vida Blue	SF	3.71
13. Dave Smith	HOU	1.13	42. Andy Hawkins	SD	2.02	70. Jesse Orosco	NY	2.55	100. Charles Hudson	PHI	3.79
14. Dick Ruthven	CHI	1.27	43. Steve Carlton	PHI	2.03	72. Danny Cox	STL	2.56	101. Bill Laskey	MTL	3.83
15. Orel Hershiser	LA	1.27	44. John Denny	PHI	2.06	73. Jose DeLeon	PIT	2.56	102. Ron Mathis	HOU	3.87
16. Dennis Eckersley	CHI	1.28	44. Mark Thurmond	SD	2.06	74. Bryn Smith	MTL	2.64	103. George Frazier	CHI	3.90
17. Fernando Valenzuela	LA	1.34	46. Carlos Diaz	LA	2.08	75. Eric Show	SD	2.70	104. Dan Schatzeder	MTL	3.93
18. Andy McGaffigan	CIN	1.34	46. Jeff Reardon	MTL	2.08	76. Atlee Hammaker	SF	2.75	105. Tom Gorman	NY	4.00
19. Jim Winn	PIT	1.39	48. Shane Rawley	PHI	2.11	77. Mario Soto	CIN	2.75	106. Jerry Koosman	PHI	4.12
20. John Tudor	STL	1.41	49. Rick Aguilera	NY	2.15	78. Craig Lefferts	SD	2.75	107. Ray Fontenot	CHI	4.19
21. Tim Stoddard	SD	1.47	50. Ricky Horton	STL	2.18	79. Lee Tunnell	PIT	2.76	108. Ken Howell	LA	4.22
22. John Franco	CIN	1.49	51. Kurt Kepshire	STL	2.19	80. Rick Sutcliffe	CHI	2.79	109. Mike Scott	HOU	4.27
23. Bill Gullickson	MTL	1.52	52. Bob Knepper	HOU	2.20	81. Rick Rhoden	PIT	2.80	110. Joe Price	CIN	4.28
24. Steve Trout	CHI	1.53	53. Jim Gott	SF	2.20	82. Bill Campbell	STL	2.82	111. Bob Welch	LA	4.35
25. Jerry Reuss	LA	1.56	54. Gary Lucas	MTL	2.21	83. Gene Garber	ATL	2.84	112. John Candelaria	PIT	4.43
26. Nolan Ryan	HOU	1.59	55. Dave Rucker	PHI	2.21	84. Joe Niekro	HOU	2.86	113. Bruce Sutter	ATL	4.44
27. Scott Sanderson	CHI	1.60	56. Joe Johnson	ATL	2.26	85. Roger McDowell	NY	2.87	114. Bobby Castillo	LA	4.61
28. David Palmer	MTL	1.65	57. Greg Minton	SF	2.26	86. John Stuper	CIN	2.87	115. Steve Engel	CHI	5.41
29. Larry McWilliams	PIT	1.68	58. Jay Tibbs	CIN	2.28	87. Tom Hume	CIN	2.87			

Opponents' Batting Average, Day Games

American League

#	Player	Team	Avg		#	Player	Team	Avg		#	Player	Team	Avg		#	Player	Team	Avg
1.	Steve Ontiveros	OAK	.110		34.	Bruce Kison	BOS	.238		67.	Randy O'Neal	DET	.266		100.	Dan Quisenberry	KC	.292
2.	Willie Hernandez	DET	.175		35.	Mark Clear	BOS	.239		68.	Charlie Leibrandt	KC	.266		101.	Neal Heaton	CLE	.293
3.	Bill Caudill	TOR	.195		36.	Tippy Martinez	BAL	.244		69.	Walt Terrell	DET	.266		102.	Ken Dixon	BAL	.294
4.	Bob Stanley	BOS	.195		37.	Phil Niekro	NY	.248		70.	Donnie Moore	CAL	.267		103.	Ken Schrom	MIN	.295
5.	Scott McGregor	BAL	.198		38.	Urbano Lugo	CAL	.248		71.	Bob Shirley	NY	.267		104.	Ray Burris	MIL	.297
6.	Dan Spillner	CHI	.203		39.	Roger Clemens	BOS	.248		72.	Gene Nelson	CHI	.269		105.	Bruce Hurst	BOS	.297
7.	Stu Cliburn	CAL	.206		40.	Tom Seaver	CHI	.249		73.	Don Aase	BAL	.269		106.	Luis Sanchez	CAL	.298
8.	Joe Cowley	NY	.207		41.	Jim Beattie	SEA	.250		74.	Dennis Rasmussen	NY	.270		107.	Chris Welsh	TEX	.299
9.	Gary Lavelle	TOR	.211		41.	Bert Blyleven	MIN	.250		75.	Ron Romanick	CAL	.271		108.	Bill Swift	SEA	.299
10.	Rich Bordi	NY	.212		41.	Jimmy Key	TOR	.250		76.	Aurelio Lopez	DET	.272		109.	Joe Beckwith	KC	.300
11.	Tim Birtsas	OAK	.212		41.	Ramon Romero	CLE	.250		77.	Jim Acker	TOR	.272		109.	Mike LaCoss	KC	.300
12.	Greg Harris	TEX	.217		41.	Tom Waddell	CLE	.250		78.	Bob Ojeda	BOS	.274		109.	Bob McClure	MIL	.300
12.	Charlie Hough	TEX	.217		46.	Dave Stieb	TOR	.251		79.	Jose Rijo	OAK	.274		112.	Jaime Cocanower	MIL	.301
14.	Keith Atherton	OAK	.218		47.	Jim Clancy	TOR	.251		80.	Edwin Nunez	SEA	.275		113.	Mike Boddicker	BAL	.302
15.	Mike Witt	CAL	.218		48.	Mark Gubicza	KC	.251		81.	Ron Musselman	TOR	.276		114.	Jim Slaton	CAL	.304
16.	Britt Burns	CHI	.218		49.	Ted Higuera	MIL	.251		82.	Dennis Martinez	BAL	.279		115.	Frank Eufemia	MIN	.308
17.	Ron Guidry	NY	.221		50.	Dickie Noles	TEX	.252		83.	Frank Tanana	DET	.279		116.	Curt Wardle	CLE	.311
18.	Richard Dotson	CHI	.221		51.	Luis Leal	TOR	.254		84.	Brian Fisher	NY	.279		117.	Storm Davis	BAL	.313
19.	Dan Petry	DET	.221		52.	Mike Smithson	MIN	.255		85.	Danny Jackson	KC	.282		118.	Jamie Easterly	CLE	.315
20.	Rick Thompson	CLE	.222		53.	Mike Warren	OAK	.255		86.	Mike Mason	TEX	.283		119.	Bryan Clark	CLE	.317
21.	Mark Langston	SEA	.224		54.	Floyd Bannister	CHI	.255		86.	Nate Snell	BAL	.283		120.	Mike Trujillo	BOS	.318
22.	Jerry Reed	CLE	.225		55.	Doyle Alexander	TOR	.256		88.	Steve Crawford	BOS	.283		121.	Juan Berenguer	DET	.320
23.	Chris Codiroli	OAK	.228		56.	Steve Mura	OAK	.257		89.	Vern Ruhle	CLE	.284		122.	Steve McCatty	OAK	.324
24.	Tim Lollar	BOS	.229		57.	Moose Haas	MIL	.258		90.	Bret Saberhagen	KC	.284		123.	Mike Flanagan	BAL	.330
25.	Jack Morris	DET	.229		58.	Danny Darwin	MIL	.258		90.	Dave Von Ohlen	CLE	.284		124.	Tommy John	OAK	.331
26.	Jay Howell	OAK	.230		59.	Mike Jones	KC	.260		92.	Bill Scherrer	DET	.286		125.	Ed Whitson	NY	.338
26.	Dennis Lamp	TOR	.230		60.	Joel Davis	CHI	.260		93.	Al Nipper	BOS	.287		126.	Rick Waits	MIL	.341
28.	Pete Filson	MIN	.231		61.	Bud Black	KC	.261		94.	Sammy Stewart	BAL	.288		127.	Pete Vuckovich	MIL	.345
29.	Dave Righetti	NY	.231		62.	Kirk McCaskill	CAL	.263		95.	Bob Gibson	MIL	.289		128.	Pete Ladd	MIL	.347
30.	Mike Moore	SEA	.232		63.	Keith Creel	CLE	.264		96.	Bill Krueger	OAK	.290		129.	Don Schulze	CLE	.353
31.	Don Sutton	CAL	.233		64.	Dennis Boyd	BOS	.264		97.	John Butcher	MIN	.290		130.	Rick Lysander	MIN	.362
32.	Bob James	CHI	.233		65.	Curt Young	OAK	.265		98.	Frank Viola	MIN	.290		131.	Ray Searage	MIL	.379
33.	Doug Bair	DET	.235		66.	Frank Wills	SEA	.265		99.	Matt Young	SEA	.291					

National League

#	Player	Team	Avg		#	Player	Team	Avg		#	Player	Team	Avg		#	Player	Team	Avg
1.	Ken Howell	LA	.143		30.	Jesse Orosco	NY	.226		59.	Tom Gorman	NY	.253		88.	Lary Sorensen	CHI	.276
2.	Charles Hudson	PHI	.172		31.	Dennis Eckersley	CHI	.228		60.	Eric Show	SD	.253		89.	Bill Dawley	HOU	.276
3.	Tim Burke	MTL	.173		32.	Scott Sanderson	CHI	.231		61.	Dan Schatzeder	MTL	.255		90.	Andy Hawkins	SD	.277
4.	Scott Garrelts	SF	.175		33.	Kevin Gross	PHI	.232		62.	Greg Minton	SF	.256		91.	Mike Scott	HOU	.278
5.	Mario Soto	CIN	.184		34.	Ed Lynch	NY	.234		63.	LaMarr Hoyt	SD	.257		92.	John Franco	CIN	.279
6.	Sid Fernandez	NY	.186		35.	Jim Gott	SF	.234		64.	Ron Robinson	CIN	.257		93.	Lee Tunnell	PIT	.279
7.	Bobby Castillo	LA	.188		36.	Bill Campbell	STL	.235		65.	Joaquin Andujar	STL	.258		94.	Ken Dayley	STL	.280
8.	Don Carman	PHI	.192		37.	Zane Smith	ATL	.235		66.	Jay Tibbs	CIN	.258		95.	Steve Engel	CHI	.282
9.	Tom Hume	CIN	.198		38.	Orel Hershiser	LA	.235		67.	Rich Gossage	SD	.259		96.	Rick Rhoden	PIT	.284
10.	Fernando Valenzuela	LA	.199		39.	Bob Knepper	HOU	.236		67.	Ted Power	CIN	.259		97.	Joe Johnson	ATL	.284
11.	Rick Reuschel	PIT	.201		40.	Mike Krukow	SF	.236		69.	Rick Honeycutt	LA	.259		98.	Jay Baller	CHI	.290
12.	Frank Williams	SF	.205		41.	Joe Hesketh	MTL	.236		70.	Joe Niekro	HOU	.261		99.	Warren Brusstar	CHI	.290
13.	Nolan Ryan	HOU	.206		42.	Mark Davis	SF	.238		71.	Jerry Koosman	PHI	.262		100.	Pascual Perez	ATL	.291
14.	Jeff Reardon	MTL	.206		43.	Steve Bedrosian	ATL	.240		72.	Ricky Horton	STL	.265		101.	Dick Ruthven	CHI	.293
15.	Cecilio Guante	PIT	.208		44.	Roger McDowell	NY	.241		73.	Jim Winn	PIT	.265		102.	Jeff Lahti	STL	.294
16.	Vida Blue	SF	.209		45.	Bryn Smith	MTL	.242		74.	Bill Laskey	MTL	.266		103.	Frank Pastore	CIN	.294
17.	Tom Niedenfuer	LA	.210		46.	Bob Welch	LA	.242		75.	Dave LaPoint	SF	.267		104.	George Frazier	CHI	.295
18.	Jose DeLeon	PIT	.211		47.	Kent Tekulve	PHI	.243		76.	Reggie Patterson	CHI	.267		105.	Mark Thurmond	SD	.296
19.	Mickey Mahler	MTL	.211		48.	Lee Smith	CHI	.246		77.	Bert Roberge	MTL	.268		106.	Larry McWilliams	PIT	.297
20.	John Tudor	STL	.212		49.	Bruce Sutter	ATL	.246		78.	John Denny	PHI	.268		107.	Ray Fontenot	CHI	.298
21.	Craig Lefferts	SD	.213		50.	John Stuper	CIN	.246		79.	Jeff Heathcock	HOU	.269		108.	Shane Rawley	PHI	.302
22.	Dwight Gooden	NY	.214		51.	Andy McGaffigan	CIN	.247		80.	Steve Trout	CHI	.269		109.	Ron Meridith	CHI	.302
23.	Rick Camp	ATL	.218		52.	Dave Dravecky	SD	.248		81.	Rick Aguilera	NY	.274		110.	Bob Forsch	STL	.302
24.	David Palmer	MTL	.222		53.	Rick Sutcliffe	CHI	.248		81.	Ron Darling	NY	.274		111.	Doug Sisk	NY	.303
25.	Al Holland	PIT	.224		54.	Kurt Kepshire	STL	.248		83.	Rick Mahler	ATL	.275		112.	Jeff Dedmon	ATL	.306
26.	Bill Gullickson	MTL	.224		55.	Tom Browning	CIN	.249		84.	Terry Leach	NY	.275		113.	Derek Botelho	CHI	.314
27.	Atlee Hammaker	SF	.224		56.	Mike Bielecki	PIT	.250		85.	Gene Garber	ATL	.275		114.	Steve Rogers	MTL	.317
28.	Danny Cox	STL	.225		56.	Carlos Diaz	LA	.250		86.	Don Robinson	PIT	.275		115.	Steve Carlton	PHI	.333
29.	Floyd Youmans	MTL	.226		58.	Jerry Reuss	LA	.252		87.	Tim Stoddard	SD	.276					

Opponents' Batting Average, Night Games

American League

#	Name	Team	Avg	#	Name	Team	Avg	#	Name	Team	Avg	#	Name	Team	Avg
1.	Brian Fisher	NY	.167	34.	Dennis Rasmussen	NY	.241	67.	Bruce Hurst	BOS	.258	100.	Mike Boddicker	BAL	.280
2.	Greg Harris	TEX	.177	35.	Aurelio Lopez	DET	.242	68.	Frank Viola	MIN	.259	101.	Dave Stewart	TEX	.280
3.	Dave Stieb	TOR	.191	36.	Steve McCatty	OAK	.242	69.	Ron Guidry	NY	.259	102.	Rick Lysander	MIN	.281
4.	Steve Ontiveros	OAK	.203	37.	Bob Shirley	NY	.243	70.	Ray Burris	MIL	.259	103.	Vern Ruhle	CLE	.281
5.	Charlie Hough	TEX	.215	38.	Phil Niekro	NY	.243	71.	Dennis Boyd	BOS	.260	104.	Rich Bordi	NY	.282
6.	Dan Petry	DET	.215	39.	Charlie Leibrandt	KC	.244	72.	Jaime Cocanower	MIL	.262	105.	Mike Flanagan	BAL	.283
7.	Roger Clemens	BOS	.216	40.	Bob Gibson	MIL	.244	73.	Moose Haas	MIL	.262	106.	Ron Romanick	CAL	.284
8.	Bill Caudill	TOR	.217	41.	Tom Waddell	CLE	.244	74.	Bill Krueger	OAK	.262	107.	Bruce Kison	BOS	.284
9.	Ken Dixon	BAL	.217	42.	Tom Seaver	CHI	.247	75.	Mark Langston	SEA	.262	108.	Pete Vuckovich	MIL	.287
10.	Juan Agosto	CHI	.218	43.	Dave Schmidt	TEX	.247	76.	Floyd Bannister	CHI	.263	109.	Ramon Romero	CLE	.287
11.	Roy Thomas	SEA	.219	44.	Al Nipper	BOS	.247	77.	Ken Schrom	MIN	.263	110.	John Butcher	MIN	.288
12.	Juan Berenguer	DET	.220	45.	Dave Righetti	NY	.248	78.	Stu Cliburn	CAL	.264	111.	Burt Hooton	TEX	.291
13.	Bob James	CHI	.222	46.	Tim Birtsas	OAK	.248	79.	Don Sutton	CAL	.265	112.	Urbano Lugo	CAL	.291
14.	Jack Morris	DET	.223	47.	Britt Burns	CHI	.249	80.	Jim Acker	TOR	.265	113.	Steve Crawford	BOS	.291
15.	Donnie Moore	CAL	.223	48.	Danny Jackson	KC	.250	81.	Bob Stanley	BOS	.266	114.	Dennis Martinez	BAL	.292
16.	Edwin Nunez	SEA	.224	49.	Walt Terrell	DET	.251	82.	Tim Lollar	BOS	.267	115.	Ed Whitson	NY	.293
17.	Randy O'Neal	DET	.225	50.	Danny Darwin	MIL	.252	83.	Frank Wills	SEA	.267	116.	Rollie Fingers	MIL	.296
18.	Pat Clements	CAL	.227	51.	Mike Witt	CAL	.253	84.	John Candelaria	CAL	.269	117.	Neal Heaton	CLE	.301
19.	Jose Rijo	OAK	.227	52.	Mike Moore	SEA	.253	85.	Tippy Martinez	BAL	.270	118.	Dickie Noles	TEX	.302
20.	Willie Hernandez	DET	.230	53.	Dave Rozema	TEX	.253	86.	Doyle Alexander	TOR	.271	119.	Don Schulze	CLE	.303
21.	Ted Higuera	MIL	.230	54.	Jerry Reed	CLE	.254	87.	Chris Codiroli	OAK	.272	120.	Mike Mason	TEX	.304
22.	Ron Davis	MIN	.230	55.	Don Aase	BAL	.254	88.	Bud Black	KC	.272	121.	Ed Vande Berg	SEA	.305
23.	Sammy Stewart	BAL	.232	56.	Joel Davis	CHI	.254	89.	Bob Ojeda	BOS	.273	122.	Scott McGregor	BAL	.307
24.	Jimmy Key	TOR	.232	57.	Bob McClure	MIL	.255	90.	Mike Stanton	CHI	.273	123.	Bryan Clark	CLE	.309
25.	Bert Blyleven	MIN	.234	58.	Dennis Lamp	TOR	.256	91.	Bill Swift	SEA	.273	124.	Keith Creel	CLE	.309
26.	Mark Gubicza	KC	.234	59.	Kirk McCaskill	CAL	.256	92.	Curt Wardle	CLE	.274	125.	Chris Welsh	TEX	.320
27.	Jim Clancy	TOR	.234	60.	Joe Beckwith	KC	.256	93.	Luis Sanchez	CAL	.275	126.	Mike Trujillo	BOS	.322
28.	Bret Saberhagen	KC	.235	61.	Mike Jones	KC	.256	94.	Dan Quisenberry	KC	.275	127.	Jeff Russell	TEX	.326
29.	Joe Cowley	NY	.237	62.	Gene Nelson	CHI	.256	95.	Roy Smith	CLE	.277	128.	Salome Barojas	SEA	.328
30.	Keith Atherton	OAK	.237	63.	Frank Tanana	DET	.257	96.	Jay Howell	OAK	.277	129.	Tommy John	OAK	.330
31.	Storm Davis	BAL	.237	64.	Rick Langford	OAK	.257	97.	Jim Slaton	CAL	.279	130.	Jim Beattie	SEA	.338
32.	Jamie Easterly	CLE	.238	65.	Pete Filson	MIN	.257	98.	Mike Smithson	MIN	.279	131.	Rick Thompson	CLE	.356
33.	Nate Snell	BAL	.239	66.	Dan Spillner	CHI	.258	99.	Matt Young	SEA	.280				

National League

#	Name	Team	Avg	#	Name	Team	Avg	#	Name	Team	Avg	#	Name	Team	Avg
1.	Don Carman	PHI	.174	30.	Bill Campbell	STL	.227	58.	Dave Dravecky	SD	.250	88.	John Candelaria	PIT	.275
2.	Sid Fernandez	NY	.179	31.	Tim Burke	MTL	.227	60.	Bill Dawley	HOU	.252	89.	Dave Rucker	PHI	.276
3.	Floyd Youmans	MTL	.183	32.	Bryn Smith	MTL	.228	61.	Bob Walk	PIT	.252	90.	Atlee Hammaker	SF	.277
4.	Orel Hershiser	LA	.188	33.	Tom Niedenfuer	LA	.229	62.	Rick Aguilera	NY	.253	91.	Bruce Sutter	ATL	.278
5.	Dwight Gooden	NY	.189	34.	Rod Scurry	PIT	.230	63.	Bobby Castillo	LA	.256	92.	Doug Sisk	NY	.278
6.	Mark Davis	SF	.190	35.	Dennis Eckersley	CHI	.230	64.	Craig Lefferts	SD	.258	93.	Rick Camp	ATL	.278
7.	Steve Carlton	PHI	.194	36.	Rick Sutcliffe	CHI	.231	65.	Gene Garber	ATL	.260	94.	Bob Knepper	HOU	.279
8.	John Tudor	STL	.207	37.	Scott Garrelts	SF	.233	66.	Ron Robinson	CIN	.260	95.	Larry McWilliams	PIT	.279
9.	Jeff Lahti	STL	.208	38.	Lee Smith	CHI	.235	67.	David Palmer	MTL	.260	96.	Kurt Kepshire	STL	.282
10.	Bert Roberge	MTL	.209	39.	Jeff Calhoun	HOU	.238	68.	Zane Smith	ATL	.261	97.	Jerry Koosman	PHI	.282
11.	Jeff Reardon	MTL	.211	40.	Lee Tunnell	PIT	.239	69.	Rick Honeycutt	LA	.261	98.	Vida Blue	SF	.282
12.	Rich Gossage	SD	.212	41.	Eric Show	SD	.239	70.	Andy Hawkins	SD	.261	99.	Charles Hudson	PHI	.282
13.	Ted Power	CIN	.214	42.	Al Holland	PIT	.240	71.	Joaquin Andujar	STL	.261	100.	Ray Fontenot	CHI	.283
14.	Joe Hesketh	MTL	.214	43.	Jose DeLeon	PIT	.240	72.	Steve Bedrosian	ATL	.262	101.	Ron Mathis	HOU	.284
15.	Bob Forsch	STL	.216	44.	Ken Howell	LA	.241	73.	LaMarr Hoyt	SD	.263	102.	Joe Johnson	ATL	.286
16.	John Franco	CIN	.216	45.	Mike Krukow	SF	.241	74.	Jay Tibbs	CIN	.263	103.	Greg Minton	SF	.286
17.	Cecilio Guante	PIT	.216	46.	Jeff Dedmon	ATL	.243	75.	Dan Schatzeder	MTL	.263	104.	John Denny	PHI	.287
18.	Terry Forster	ATL	.217	47.	Tom Browning	CIN	.243	76.	Danny Cox	STL	.264	105.	Mark Thurmond	SD	.288
19.	Bob Welch	LA	.219	48.	Dave Smith	HOU	.243	77.	Jerry Reuss	LA	.264	106.	Frank Williams	SF	.288
20.	Scott Sanderson	CHI	.220	49.	Joe Niekro	HOU	.244	78.	Rick Mahler	ATL	.264	107.	Bill Laskey	MTL	.292
21.	Roger McDowell	NY	.220	50.	Don Robinson	PIT	.244	79.	Tim Stoddard	SD	.265	108.	Larry Andersen	PHI	.294
22.	Shane Rawley	PHI	.221	51.	Tom Hume	CIN	.244	80.	Len Barker	ATL	.265	109.	Pascual Perez	ATL	.299
23.	Carlos Diaz	LA	.221	52.	Ricky Horton	STL	.244	81.	Kevin Gross	PHI	.265	110.	Rick Rhoden	PIT	.303
24.	Fernando Valenzuela	LA	.222	53.	Joe Price	CIN	.246	82.	Jim Winn	PIT	.266	111.	Bill Gullickson	MTL	.304
25.	Ron Darling	NY	.222	54.	Nolan Ryan	HOU	.247	83.	Kent Tekulve	PHI	.266	112.	Jim Gott	SF	.307
25.	Jesse Orosco	NY	.222	55.	Andy McGaffigan	CIN	.248	84.	Randy St. Claire	MTL	.267	113.	Steve Shields	ATL	.319
27.	Mike Scott	HOU	.223	56.	Gary Lucas	MTL	.249	85.	Ed Lynch	NY	.270	114.	Craig McMurtry	ATL	.324
28.	Rick Reuschel	PIT	.224	57.	Frank DiPino	HOU	.249	86.	Dave LaPoint	SF	.271	115.	John Stuper	CIN	.330
29.	Mario Soto	CIN	.227	58.	Ken Dayley	STL	.250	87.	Steve Trout	CHI	.273				

Opponents' Batting Average, Grass Surfaces

American League

1. Greg Harris	TEX	.164	34. Mike Moore	SEA	.241	67. Dan Spillner	CHI	.258	100. Dickie Noles	TEX	.283
2. Steve Ontiveros	OAK	.179	35. Rich Bordi	NY	.241	68. Frank Tanana	DET	.258	101. Curt Young	OAK	.284
3. Dave Stieb	TOR	.184	35. Tom Waddell	CLE	.241	69. Dennis Boyd	BOS	.259	102. Steve McCatty	OAK	.285
4. Steve Mura	OAK	.206	37. Sammy Stewart	BAL	.242	70. Jimmy Key	TOR	.260	103. Jim Slaton	CAL	.286
5. Willie Hernandez	DET	.208	38. Mike Witt	CAL	.243	71. Ray Burris	MIL	.260	104. Danny Jackson	KC	.287
6. Brian Fisher	NY	.211	39. Ted Higuera	MIL	.243	72. John Candelaria	CAL	.261	105. Dennis Martinez	BAL	.288
7. Pat Clements	CAL	.212	40. Tim Birtsas	OAK	.245	73. Tippy Martinez	BAL	.262	106. Dave Rozema	TEX	.289
8. Charlie Hough	TEX	.215	41. Roger Clemens	BOS	.245	74. Mark Langston	SEA	.262	107. Neal Heaton	CLE	.296
9. Dan Petry	DET	.216	42. Joel Davis	CHI	.246	75. Juan Berenguer	DET	.262	108. Pete Vuckovich	MIL	.298
10. Juan Agosto	CHI	.217	43. Ken Dixon	BAL	.247	76. Kirk McCaskill	CAL	.263	109. Frank Wills	SEA	.299
11. Joe Cowley	NY	.218	44. Danny Darwin	MIL	.248	77. Jamie Easterly	CLE	.264	110. Keith Creel	CLE	.300
12. Keith Atherton	OAK	.223	45. Bob Shirley	NY	.248	78. Dave Stewart	TEX	.265	111. Luis Sanchez	CAL	.302
13. Roy Thomas	SEA	.224	46. Jay Howell	OAK	.249	79. Floyd Bannister	CHI	.265	112. Mike Flanagan	BAL	.302
14. Bob Stanley	BOS	.226	47. Aurelio Lopez	DET	.249	80. Bill Swift	SEA	.266	113. Burt Hooton	TEX	.303
15. Mark Clear	BOS	.226	48. Storm Davis	BAL	.250	81. Bob McClure	MIL	.268	114. Mike Mason	TEX	.304
16. Bob James	CHI	.227	49. Bob Gibson	MIL	.250	82. Ron Romanick	CAL	.269	115. Steve Crawford	BOS	.305
17. Jose Rijo	OAK	.229	49. Gene Nelson	CHI	.250	83. Bob Ojeda	BOS	.271	116. Doyle Alexander	TOR	.306
18. Richard Dotson	CHI	.229	49. Mike Warren	OAK	.250	84. Jim Clancy	TOR	.271	117. Curt Wardle	CLE	.306
19. Jerry Reed	CLE	.230	52. Tom Seaver	CHI	.250	85. Ramon Romero	CLE	.272	118. Dan Quisenberry	KC	.307
20. Dave Righetti	NY	.230	53. Phil Niekro	NY	.250	86. Scott McGregor	BAL	.272	119. Ed Whitson	NY	.310
21. Rick Langford	OAK	.232	54. Bud Black	KC	.251	87. Dennis Rasmussen	NY	.273	120. Tommy John	OAK	.311
22. Mark Gubicza	KC	.234	55. Randy O'Neal	DET	.253	88. Mike Smithson	MIN	.273	121. Rick Thompson	CLE	.313
23. Dave Schmidt	TEX	.236	56. Don Aase	BAL	.253	89. Doug Corbett	CAL	.274	121. Chris Welsh	TEX	.313
24. Dennis Lamp	TOR	.236	57. Ron Guidry	NY	.253	90. Bruce Hurst	BOS	.276	123. Roy Smith	CLE	.316
24. Donnie Moore	CAL	.236	58. Moose Haas	MIL	.253	91. Charlie Leibrandt	KC	.277	124. Jeff Russell	TEX	.318
26. Edwin Nunez	SEA	.236	59. Tim Lollar	BOS	.253	92. Urbano Lugo	CAL	.278	125. Ken Schrom	MIN	.323
27. Bert Blyleven	MIN	.237	60. Nate Snell	BAL	.254	93. Jaime Cocanower	MIL	.279	126. Rick Waits	MIL	.323
28. Jack Morris	DET	.238	61. Frank Viola	MIN	.254	94. Mike Boddicker	BAL	.280	127. Matt Young	SEA	.324
29. Bret Saberhagen	KC	.238	62. Bill Scherrer	DET	.256	95. Vern Ruhle	CLE	.281	128. Bryan Clark	CLE	.325
30. Don Sutton	CAL	.239	63. Chris Codiroli	OAK	.256	96. Bruce Kison	BOS	.281	129. Don Schulze	CLE	.330
31. Stu Cliburn	CAL	.239	64. Dave Von Ohlen	CLE	.257	97. Marty Bystrom	NY	.281	130. Mike Trujillo	BOS	.333
32. Britt Burns	CHI	.240	65. John Butcher	MIN	.257	98. Bill Krueger	OAK	.282	131. Ray Searage	MIL	.376
33. Walt Terrell	DET	.241	66. Al Nipper	BOS	.258	99. Rollie Fingers	MIL	.282			

National League

1. Sid Fernandez	NY	.180	30. Dennis Eckersley	CHI	.226	59. Ron Darling	NY	.249	88. Mark Thurmond	SD	.282
2. Tim Burke	MTL	.184	31. Don Robinson	PIT	.227	60. Bill Laskey	MTL	.252	89. Rick Rhoden	PIT	.282
3. Mickey Mahler	MTL	.184	32. Carlos Diaz	LA	.227	61. Jesse Orosco	NY	.253	90. Larry McWilliams	PIT	.283
4. Orel Hershiser	LA	.188	33. Mike Krukow	SF	.229	62. John Denny	PHI	.253	91. Rick Camp	ATL	.284
5. Scott Garrelts	SF	.191	34. Ron Robinson	CIN	.230	63. Jerry Reuss	LA	.255	92. Charles Hudson	PHI	.285
6. John Tudor	STL	.193	35. John Franco	CIN	.231	64. Dave LaPoint	SF	.255	93. George Frazier	CHI	.286
7. David Palmer	MTL	.198	36. Rick Honeycutt	LA	.234	65. Dave Dravecky	SD	.256	94. Tom Brennan	LA	.288
8. Mario Soto	CIN	.198	37. Jim Gott	SF	.234	66. Jay Tibbs	CIN	.258	94. Warren Brusstar	CHI	.288
9. Dwight Gooden	NY	.198	38. Tom Niedenfuer	LA	.234	67. Steve Bedrosian	ATL	.259	96. Luis DeLeon	SD	.290
10. Terry Forster	ATL	.203	39. Jeff Heathcock	HOU	.234	68. LaMarr Hoyt	SD	.260	97. Joaquin Andujar	STL	.291
11. Joe Hesketh	MTL	.208	40. Mark Davis	SF	.235	69. Rick Mahler	ATL	.262	98. Jay Baller	CHI	.291
12. Fernando Valenzuela	LA	.208	41. Bob Welch	LA	.235	70. Andy Hawkins	SD	.262	99. Steve Engel	CHI	.294
13. Ken Howell	LA	.208	42. John Stuper	CIN	.236	71. Danny Cox	STL	.264	100. Derek Botelho	CHI	.295
14. Rich Gossage	SD	.209	43. Bobby Castillo	LA	.236	72. Greg Minton	SF	.265	101. Ron Meridith	CHI	.297
15. Kurt Kepshire	STL	.209	44. Ed Lynch	NY	.238	73. Reggie Patterson	CHI	.265	102. Bruce Sutter	ATL	.299
16. Lance McCullers	SD	.213	45. Steve Carlton	PHI	.240	74. Dan Schatzeder	MTL	.265	103. Nolan Ryan	HOU	.304
17. Rick Reuschel	PIT	.215	46. Shane Rawley	PHI	.240	75. Lary Sorensen	CHI	.265	104. Len Barker	ATL	.305
18. Frank Williams	SF	.216	47. Vida Blue	SF	.241	76. Lee Tunnell	PIT	.266	105. Ray Fontenot	CHI	.305
19. Jose DeLeon	PIT	.219	48. Mike Scott	HOU	.241	77. Ted Power	CIN	.267	106. Ed Wojna	SD	.305
20. Cecilio Guante	PIT	.220	49. Tom Gorman	NY	.241	78. Terry Leach	NY	.268	107. Pascual Perez	ATL	.305
21. Tom Hume	CIN	.221	50. Atlee Hammaker	SF	.242	79. Floyd Youmans	MTL	.268	108. Dick Ruthven	CHI	.307
22. Rick Aguilera	NY	.222	51. Lee Smith	CHI	.242	80. Jeff Reardon	MTL	.269	109. Bill Dawley	HOU	.310
22. Roy Jackson	SD	.222	52. Eric Show	SD	.243	81. Frank DiPino	HOU	.270	110. Kevin Gross	PHI	.312
24. Roger McDowell	NY	.223	53. Roger Mason	SF	.243	81. Gene Garber	ATL	.270	111. Steve Howe	LA	.321
25. Rick Sutcliffe	CHI	.224	54. Bob Forsch	STL	.244	83. Doug Sisk	NY	.274	112. Joe Johnson	ATL	.321
26. Craig Lefferts	SD	.224	55. Bryn Smith	MTL	.245	84. Steve Trout	CHI	.275	113. Bill Gullickson	MTL	.321
27. Tom Browning	CIN	.224	56. Zane Smith	ATL	.245	85. Jeff Dedmon	ATL	.276	114. Steve Shields	ATL	.335
28. Scott Sanderson	CHI	.225	57. Tim Stoddard	SD	.246	86. Craig McMurtry	ATL	.279	115. Ron Mathis	HOU	.346
29. Joe Niekro	HOU	.226	58. Bob Knepper	HOU	.249	87. Dennis Powell	LA	.281			

Opponents' Batting Average, Artificial Surfaces

American League

1.	Jack Morris	DET	.156	34.	Ron Davis	MIN	.238	67.	Ron Musselman	TOR	.259	100.	Bob Ojeda	BOS	.292
2.	Roy Thomas	SEA	.178	35.	Mike Trujillo	BOS	.240	68.	Pete Filson	MIN	.260	101.	Nate Snell	BAL	.293
3.	Gary Lavelle	TOR	.182	36.	Donnie Moore	CAL	.241	69.	Rick Thompson	CLE	.262	102.	Storm Davis	BAL	.295
4.	Dennis Rasmussen	NY	.184	37.	Mark Gubicza	KC	.241	70.	Dan Quisenberry	KC	.263	103.	Bob Gibson	MIL	.296
5.	Roger Clemens	BOS	.184	38.	Brian Fisher	NY	.241	71.	Jamie Easterly	CLE	.264	104.	Pete Ladd	MIL	.298
6.	Dan Spillner	CHI	.186	39.	Bret Saberhagen	KC	.243	72.	Mike Mason	TEX	.265	105.	Pete Vuckovich	MIL	.298
7.	Ken Dixon	BAL	.188	40.	Bert Blyleven	MIN	.243	73.	Matt Young	SEA	.267	106.	Moose Haas	MIL	.301
8.	Tom Filer	TOR	.189	41.	Karl Best	SEA	.244	74.	Tom Waddell	CLE	.267	106.	Brian Snyder	SEA	.301
9.	Tim Birtsas	OAK	.191	42.	Danny Jackson	KC	.244	75.	Mike Smithson	MIN	.268	108.	Frank Tanana	DET	.304
10.	Bill Caudill	TOR	.199	43.	Bill Krueger	OAK	.245	76.	Doug Bair	DET	.269	109.	Rick Lysander	MIN	.304
11.	Ron Guidry	NY	.200	44.	Frank Wills	SEA	.246	77.	Sammy Stewart	BAL	.273	110.	Don Sutton	CAL	.305
12.	Ted Higuera	MIL	.201	45.	Juan Berenguer	DET	.246	78.	Frank Eufemia	MIN	.273	111.	Ed Whitson	NY	.306
13.	Robert Long	SEA	.202	46.	Mike Witt	CAL	.246	79.	Chris Codiroli	OAK	.273	112.	Salome Barojas	SEA	.308
14.	Dennis Burtt	MIN	.204	47.	Mark Portugal	MIN	.247	80.	Steve Mura	OAK	.275	113.	Neal Heaton	CLE	.309
14.	Mark Huismann	KC	.204	48.	Stu Cliburn	CAL	.247	81.	Frank Viola	MIN	.275	114.	Danny Darwin	MIL	.310
16.	Jim Clancy	TOR	.209	49.	Al Nipper	BOS	.248	82.	Keith Atherton	OAK	.276	115.	Dave Stewart	TEX	.310
17.	Steve Crawford	BOS	.210	50.	Doyle Alexander	TOR	.249	82.	Dennis Boyd	BOS	.276	116.	John Butcher	MIN	.313
18.	Charlie Hough	TEX	.216	51.	Mike Moore	SEA	.250	84.	Jack Lazorko	SEA	.278	117.	Steve Howe	MIN	.316
19.	Bob James	CHI	.218	52.	Floyd Bannister	CHI	.250	84.	Jim Slaton	CAL	.278	118.	Mike Boddicker	BAL	.319
20.	Willie Hernandez	DET	.220	52.	Bruce Hurst	BOS	.250	86.	Bud Black	KC	.279	119.	Jerry Reed	CLE	.319
21.	Kirk McCaskill	CAL	.221	52.	Mike Jones	KC	.250	87.	Jose Rijo	OAK	.280	120.	Geoff Zahn	CAL	.321
22.	Phil Niekro	NY	.223	52.	Mark Langston	SEA	.250	87.	Mike Stanton	CHI	.280	121.	Chris Welsh	TEX	.324
23.	Dan Petry	DET	.224	56.	Jim Beattie	SEA	.253	89.	Dennis Martinez	BAL	.283	122.	Walt Terrell	DET	.327
24.	Jimmy Key	TOR	.224	56.	Tom Henke	TOR	.253	89.	Bob Stanley	BOS	.283	123.	Scott McGregor	BAL	.333
25.	Jim Acker	TOR	.226	58.	Bruce Kison	BOS	.253	91.	Ed Vande Berg	SEA	.284	124.	Ron Romanick	CAL	.339
26.	Tom Seaver	CHI	.227	59.	Urbano Lugo	CAL	.254	92.	Luis Leal	TOR	.285	125.	Greg Harris	TEX	.347
27.	Charlie Leibrandt	KC	.229	60.	Ken Schrom	MIN	.254	93.	Don Aase	BAL	.286	125.	Gene Nelson	CHI	.347
28.	Steve Davis	TOR	.232	61.	Burt Hooton	TEX	.255	93.	Joel Davis	CHI	.286	127.	Rich Bordi	NY	.350
29.	Edwin Nunez	SEA	.233	62.	Britt Burns	CHI	.256	93.	Dave Schmidt	TEX	.286	128.	Mike LaCoss	KC	.358
30.	Luis Sanchez	CAL	.235	63.	Dennis Lamp	TOR	.256	93.	Bill Swift	SEA	.286	129.	Rick Langford	OAK	.367
31.	Dave Stieb	TOR	.236	64.	Steve Farr	KC	.256	97.	Dave Geisel	SEA	.288	130.	Tommy John	OAK	.415
32.	Curt Wardle	CLE	.236	65.	Jaime Cocanower	MIL	.258	98.	Steve McCatty	OAK	.291	131.	Ray Burris	MIL	.417
33.	Joe Beckwith	KC	.237	65.	Joe Cowley	NY	.258	99.	Vern Ruhle	CLE	.291				

National League

1.	Jesse Orosco	NY	.168	30.	Mike Scott	HOU	.232	59.	Kent Tekulve	PHI	.256	88.	Randy St. Claire	MTL	.279
2.	Bruce Sutter	ATL	.178	31.	Dennis Eckersley	CHI	.232	60.	Dan Schatzeder	MTL	.257	89.	Andy Hawkins	SD	.281
3.	Floyd Youmans	MTL	.179	32.	Dave Dravecky	SD	.233	61.	Steve Trout	CHI	.258	90.	Larry McWilliams	PIT	.282
4.	Ron Darling	NY	.180	33.	Jose DeLeon	PIT	.235	62.	Bill Campbell	STL	.259	91.	Rick Mahler	ATL	.285
5.	Don Carman	PHI	.180	34.	John Franco	CIN	.236	63.	Joe Niekro	HOU	.259	92.	Charlie Kerfeld	HOU	.287
6.	Mark Davis	SF	.183	35.	Frank DiPino	HOU	.236	64.	Pat Clements	PIT	.261	92.	Julio Solano	HOU	.287
7.	Sid Fernandez	NY	.184	36.	Carlos Diaz	LA	.237	65.	David Palmer	MTL	.262	94.	Ken Dayley	STL	.287
8.	Jeff Reardon	MTL	.185	36.	Scott Sanderson	CHI	.237	66.	Bob Forsch	STL	.262	95.	Kurt Kepshire	STL	.290
9.	Tom Niedenfuer	LA	.187	38.	Andy McGaffigan	CIN	.238	67.	Mickey Mahler	MTL	.263	96.	Neil Allen	STL	.291
10.	Bob Welch	LA	.198	39.	Bill Dawley	HOU	.238	67.	Don Robinson	PIT	.263	97.	John Denny	PHI	.294
11.	Rick Camp	ATL	.202	40.	Dave Shipanoff	PHI	.239	69.	Jay Tibbs	CIN	.263	98.	Greg Minton	SF	.295
12.	Dwight Gooden	NY	.208	41.	Lee Smith	CHI	.241	70.	Atlee Hammaker	SF	.263	98.	Lary Sorensen	CHI	.295
13.	Cecilio Guante	PIT	.211	42.	Charles Hudson	PHI	.242	71.	Larry Andersen	PHI	.263	100.	Rick Rhoden	PIT	.301
14.	Ted Power	CIN	.213	43.	Steve Bedrosian	ATL	.242	72.	LaMarr Hoyt	SD	.263	101.	Dave LaPoint	SF	.301
15.	John Tudor	STL	.214	44.	Jeff Heathcock	HOU	.243	73.	Bob Walk	PIT	.265	102.	Jim Gott	SF	.302
16.	Tim Burke	MTL	.215	44.	Dave Smith	HOU	.243	74.	Dave Rucker	PHI	.266	103.	Rick Aguilera	NY	.302
17.	Rod Scurry	PIT	.216	46.	Eric Show	SD	.245	75.	Mike Krukow	SF	.266	104.	Ed Lynch	NY	.303
18.	Rick Reuschel	PIT	.216	47.	Danny Cox	STL	.247	76.	Orel Hershiser	LA	.268	105.	Frank Williams	SF	.304
19.	Mario Soto	CIN	.218	48.	Lee Tunnell	PIT	.248	77.	Jim Winn	PIT	.270	106.	Frank Pastore	CIN	.310
20.	Nolan Ryan	HOU	.218	49.	Joaquin Andujar	STL	.248	78.	Ron Mathis	HOU	.272	107.	John Candelaria	PIT	.311
21.	Bert Roberge	MTL	.221	50.	Ray Fontenot	CHI	.248	79.	Jerry Reuss	LA	.272	108.	Bill Laskey	MTL	.317
22.	Al Holland	PIT	.223	51.	Jeff Lahti	STL	.249	80.	Ron Robinson	CIN	.273	109.	Mark Thurmond	SD	.317
23.	Bryn Smith	MTL	.225	52.	Gary Lucas	MTL	.250	81.	Jeff Calhoun	HOU	.274	110.	Steve Rogers	MTL	.320
24.	Tom Hume	CIN	.225	53.	Bill Gullickson	MTL	.251	82.	Rick Sutcliffe	CHI	.274	111.	Rick Honeycutt	LA	.325
25.	Joe Hesketh	MTL	.226	54.	Steve Carlton	PHI	.252	83.	Pascual Perez	ATL	.277	112.	Doug Sisk	NY	.333
26.	Jay Baller	CHI	.227	55.	Shane Rawley	PHI	.253	84.	Jerry Koosman	PHI	.277	113.	John Stuper	CIN	.335
27.	Fernando Valenzuela	LA	.230	56.	Ricky Horton	STL	.254	85.	Mike Bielecki	PIT	.277	114.	Rocky Childress	PHI	.336
28.	Kevin Gross	PHI	.230	57.	Tom Browning	CIN	.254	86.	Bob Knepper	HOU	.278	115.	George Frazier	CHI	.338
29.	Joe Price	CIN	.232	58.	Roger McDowell	NY	.255	86.	Zane Smith	ATL	.278				

Opponents' Batting Average, Home Games

American League

#	Pitcher	Team	AVG
1.	Steve Ontiveros	OAK	.155
2.	Willie Hernandez	DET	.167
3.	Pat Clements	CAL	.173
4.	Greg Harris	TEX	.183
5.	Roy Thomas	SEA	.188
6.	Bill Caudill	TOR	.189
7.	Jim Clancy	TOR	.199
8.	Jim Acker	TOR	.204
9.	Keith Atherton	OAK	.209
10.	Jamie Easterly	CLE	.212
11.	Dan Petry	DET	.213
12.	Walt Terrell	DET	.215
13.	Joe Cowley	NY	.216
14.	Mark Gubicza	KC	.224
15.	Donnie Moore	CAL	.224
16.	Juan Agosto	CHI	.226
17.	Charlie Hough	TEX	.226
18.	Bob Shirley	NY	.226
19.	Rich Bordi	NY	.227
20.	Edwin Nunez	SEA	.228
21.	Ron Davis	MIN	.230
22.	Jimmy Key	TOR	.230
23.	Chris Codiroli	OAK	.231
23.	Dave Righetti	NY	.231
25.	Frank Eufemia	MIN	.233
26.	Storm Davis	BAL	.234
27.	Gene Nelson	CHI	.234
28.	Britt Burns	CHI	.234
29.	Richard Dotson	CHI	.234
30.	Dave Schmidt	TEX	.235
31.	Bret Saberhagen	KC	.235
32.	Tom Waddell	CLE	.235
33.	Don Sutton	CAL	.235
34.	Brian Fisher	NY	.236
35.	Bob James	CHI	.237
36.	Phil Niekro	NY	.238
37.	Bert Blyleven	MIN	.239
38.	Sammy Stewart	BAL	.239
39.	Tim Birtsas	OAK	.239
40.	Ramon Romero	CLE	.240
40.	Bill Scherrer	DET	.240
42.	Stu Cliburn	CAL	.242
43.	Floyd Bannister	CHI	.243
44.	Doyle Alexander	TOR	.243
45.	Tim Lollar	BOS	.244
46.	Jim Beattie	SEA	.244
47.	Charlie Leibrandt	KC	.246
48.	Danny Darwin	MIL	.246
49.	Joel Davis	CHI	.246
49.	Ken Dixon	BAL	.246
51.	Dave Stieb	TOR	.247
52.	Mike Witt	CAL	.247
53.	Tippy Martinez	BAL	.248
54.	Jack Morris	DET	.249
55.	Joe Beckwith	KC	.249
56.	Kirk McCaskill	CAL	.249
57.	Roger Clemens	BOS	.250
57.	Mike Warren	OAK	.250
57.	Frank Wills	SEA	.250
60.	Ray Burris	MIL	.251
61.	Vern Ruhle	CLE	.251
62.	Ron Guidry	NY	.252
63.	Mike Jones	KC	.252
64.	Curt Wardle	CLE	.252
65.	Don Aase	BAL	.252
66.	Danny Jackson	KC	.253
67.	Aurelio Lopez	DET	.253
68.	Nate Snell	BAL	.254
69.	Ted Higuera	MIL	.254
70.	Urbano Lugo	CAL	.255
71.	Moose Haas	MIL	.256
72.	Pete Filson	MIN	.256
73.	Al Nipper	BOS	.256
74.	Mike Moore	SEA	.257
75.	Jay Howell	OAK	.260
76.	Matt Young	SEA	.260
77.	Bob Stanley	BOS	.261
78.	Bob Ojeda	BOS	.263
79.	Ken Schrom	MIN	.264
80.	Steve Farr	KC	.264
81.	Mike Smithson	MIN	.265
82.	Dennis Lamp	TOR	.266
83.	Frank Tanana	DET	.266
84.	Dan Quisenberry	KC	.267
85.	Frank Viola	MIN	.267
86.	Jim Slaton	CAL	.267
87.	Dennis Boyd	BOS	.267
88.	Tom Seaver	CHI	.270
89.	Mike Boddicker	BAL	.270
90.	Neal Heaton	CLE	.271
91.	Mark Langston	SEA	.272
92.	Luis Leal	TOR	.273
93.	Dennis Rasmussen	NY	.275
94.	Ron Romanick	CAL	.276
95.	Bob Gibson	MIL	.276
96.	Jaime Cocanower	MIL	.277
97.	Bud Black	KC	.278
98.	Dave Stewart	TEX	.278
99.	Bill Krueger	OAK	.281
100.	Burt Hooton	TEX	.281
101.	Scott McGregor	BAL	.281
102.	Pete Vuckovich	MIL	.282
103.	Salome Barojas	SEA	.283
104.	Bruce Hurst	BOS	.284
105.	Juan Berenguer	DET	.286
106.	Randy O'Neal	DET	.288
107.	Dave Rozema	TEX	.292
108.	Bob McClure	MIL	.292
109.	Tommy John	OAK	.293
110.	Dan Spillner	CHI	.295
111.	Dickie Noles	TEX	.296
112.	Don Schulze	CLE	.297
113.	John Butcher	MIN	.300
114.	Bill Swift	SEA	.300
115.	Curt Young	OAK	.301
116.	Dennis Martinez	BAL	.301
117.	Roy Smith	CLE	.302
118.	Ed Whitson	NY	.303
119.	Bruce Kison	BOS	.304
119.	Ed Vande Berg	SEA	.304
121.	John Candelaria	CAL	.305
122.	Chris Welsh	TEX	.307
123.	Mike Mason	TEX	.307
124.	Keith Creel	CLE	.310
124.	Mike Trujillo	BOS	.310
126.	Bryan Clark	CLE	.312
127.	Steve McCatty	OAK	.315
128.	Rick Thompson	CLE	.319
129.	Steve Crawford	BOS	.326
130.	Mike Flanagan	BAL	.328
131.	Jeff Russell	TEX	.357

National League

#	Pitcher	Team	AVG
1.	Don Carman	PHI	.142
2.	Orel Hershiser	LA	.160
3.	Frank Williams	SF	.169
4.	Sid Fernandez	NY	.175
5.	Floyd Youmans	MTL	.176
6.	Al Holland	PIT	.186
7.	Dwight Gooden	NY	.191
8.	Scott Garrelts	SF	.193
9.	Rich Gossage	SD	.193
10.	Mike Scott	HOU	.195
11.	John Tudor	STL	.197
12.	Cecilio Guante	PIT	.198
13.	Terry Forster	ATL	.199
14.	John Franco	CIN	.199
15.	Fernando Valenzuela	LA	.202
16.	Steve Carlton	PHI	.205
17.	Rick Reuschel	PIT	.208
18.	Jeff Reardon	MTL	.209
19.	Carlos Diaz	LA	.209
20.	Bryn Smith	MTL	.210
21.	Bobby Castillo	LA	.213
22.	Vida Blue	SF	.214
23.	Jose DeLeon	PIT	.215
24.	Bert Roberge	MTL	.215
25.	Mario Soto	CIN	.217
26.	Ken Howell	LA	.218
27.	Rick Aguilera	NY	.219
28.	Nolan Ryan	HOU	.220
29.	Mike Krukow	SF	.221
30.	Jim Gott	SF	.221
31.	Bill Gullickson	MTL	.221
32.	Ted Power	CIN	.222
33.	Tim Burke	MTL	.225
34.	Roger McDowell	NY	.226
35.	Rick Sutcliffe	CHI	.227
36.	Mark Davis	SF	.228
37.	Joe Hesketh	MTL	.228
38.	Dennis Eckersley	CHI	.228
39.	Scott Sanderson	CHI	.229
40.	Eric Show	SD	.230
41.	Ed Lynch	NY	.230
42.	Atlee Hammaker	SF	.231
43.	Craig Lefferts	SD	.234
44.	Greg Minton	SF	.234
45.	Dave Smith	HOU	.235
46.	Bill Campbell	STL	.236
47.	Bob Forsch	STL	.236
48.	Rick Honeycutt	LA	.236
49.	Frank DiPino	HOU	.237
49.	Dan Schatzeder	MTL	.237
51.	Andy McGaffigan	CIN	.237
52.	Lee Smith	CHI	.238
53.	Gary Lucas	MTL	.239
54.	Dave Dravecky	SD	.240
55.	Bob Welch	LA	.241
56.	Bill Dawley	HOU	.242
57.	Jeff Calhoun	HOU	.242
58.	Jerry Reuss	LA	.244
59.	Kevin Gross	PHI	.245
60.	Lee Tunnell	PIT	.247
61.	Joaquin Andujar	STL	.249
62.	Ron Darling	NY	.249
63.	Dave LaPoint	SF	.250
63.	Shane Rawley	PHI	.250
65.	Danny Cox	STL	.251
66.	Tom Niedenfuer	LA	.251
67.	Tom Hume	CIN	.254
68.	Joe Niekro	HOU	.254
69.	Larry Andersen	PHI	.255
70.	Rick Mahler	ATL	.255
71.	David Palmer	MTL	.256
72.	Jay Tibbs	CIN	.256
73.	Charles Hudson	PHI	.258
74.	Ricky Horton	STL	.259
75.	Ken Dayley	STL	.262
76.	Jesse Orosco	NY	.262
77.	Tom Browning	CIN	.265
78.	Ron Robinson	CIN	.266
79.	Dave Rucker	PHI	.266
80.	Mark Thurmond	SD	.267
81.	Ron Mathis	HOU	.267
82.	Don Robinson	PIT	.269
83.	Zane Smith	ATL	.270
84.	Andy Hawkins	SD	.270
85.	Kent Tekulve	PHI	.271
86.	Steve Trout	CHI	.272
87.	Steve Bedrosian	ATL	.272
88.	Joe Price	CIN	.276
89.	Bob Knepper	HOU	.278
90.	Jeff Dedmon	ATL	.278
91.	LaMarr Hoyt	SD	.279
92.	Jerry Koosman	PHI	.281
93.	Steve Engel	CHI	.282
94.	Gene Garber	ATL	.284
95.	George Frazier	CHI	.284
96.	Randy St. Claire	MTL	.287
97.	Lary Sorensen	CHI	.288
98.	John Denny	PHI	.288
99.	Len Barker	ATL	.289
100.	Rick Camp	ATL	.291
101.	Ron Meridith	CHI	.297
102.	Dick Ruthven	CHI	.301
103.	Rick Rhoden	PIT	.302
104.	Doug Sisk	NY	.304
105.	Bill Laskey	MTL	.304
106.	Kurt Kepshire	STL	.307
107.	Pascual Perez	ATL	.307
108.	Ray Fontenot	CHI	.308
109.	Joe Johnson	ATL	.310
110.	Larry McWilliams	PIT	.311
111.	Bruce Sutter	ATL	.314
112.	Steve Shields	ATL	.321
113.	Warren Brusstar	CHI	.322
114.	Frank Pastore	CIN	.322
115.	John Stuper	CIN	.344

Opponents' Batting Average, Road Games

American League

#	Pitcher	Team	Avg	#	Pitcher	Team	Avg	#	Pitcher	Team	Avg	#	Pitcher	Team	Avg
1.	Dave Stieb	TOR	.187	34.	Ron Guidry	NY	.243	66.	Bruce Hurst	BOS	.263	100.	Rick Thompson	CLE	.290
2.	Brian Fisher	NY	.188	35.	Mark Clear	BOS	.244	68.	Jim Clancy	TOR	.263	101.	Bob Ojeda	BOS	.290
3.	Greg Harris	TEX	.190	36.	Rollie Fingers	MIL	.246	69.	Steve Crawford	BOS	.265	102.	Urbano Lugo	CAL	.291
4.	Dan Spillner	CHI	.191	37.	Ed Vande Berg	SEA	.246	70.	Joel Davis	CHI	.265	103.	Mike Mason	TEX	.291
5.	Steve Ontiveros	OAK	.198	38.	Bret Saberhagen	KC	.248	71.	Nate Snell	BAL	.266	104.	Dan Quisenberry	KC	.296
6.	Roger Clemens	BOS	.203	39.	Jimmy Key	TOR	.248	72.	Luis Sanchez	CAL	.267	105.	Walt Terrell	DET	.297
7.	Charlie Hough	TEX	.206	40.	Bob McClure	MIL	.248	73.	Don Aase	BAL	.267	106.	Rick Langford	OAK	.299
8.	Jack Morris	DET	.207	41.	Charlie Leibrandt	KC	.249	74.	Kirk McCaskill	CAL	.267	107.	Jamie Easterly	CLE	.300
9.	Randy O'Neal	DET	.212	42.	Britt Burns	CHI	.250	75.	Frank Viola	MIN	.268	108.	Joe Beckwith	KC	.301
10.	Roy Thomas	SEA	.213	42.	Donnie Moore	CAL	.250	76.	Moose Haas	MIL	.268	109.	Doyle Alexander	TOR	.301
11.	Bob Stanley	BOS	.213	44.	Phil Niekro	NY	.252	77.	Danny Jackson	KC	.269	110.	Mike Boddicker	BAL	.301
12.	Bob James	CHI	.214	45.	Dave Righetti	NY	.253	78.	Dave Stewart	TEX	.269	111.	Jim Slaton	CAL	.302
13.	Ted Higuera	MIL	.220	46.	Dennis Boyd	BOS	.253	79.	Don Sutton	CAL	.269	112.	Ray Burris	MIL	.306
14.	John Candelaria	CAL	.221	47.	Mark Gubicza	KC	.253	80.	Jaime Cocanower	MIL	.271	113.	Vern Ruhle	CLE	.306
15.	Ken Dixon	BAL	.221	48.	Sammy Stewart	BAL	.255	81.	Bill Krueger	OAK	.272	114.	Ron Musselman	TOR	.309
16.	Dan Petry	DET	.222	49.	Al Nipper	BOS	.255	82.	Mike Smithson	MIN	.274	115.	Bryan Clark	CLE	.310
17.	Juan Berenguer	DET	.230	50.	Bill Swift	SEA	.256	83.	Jeff Russell	TEX	.276	116.	Ramon Romero	CLE	.310
18.	Tom Seaver	CHI	.230	51.	Keith Atherton	OAK	.256	84.	John Butcher	MIN	.276	117.	Pete Vuckovich	MIL	.313
19.	Joe Cowley	NY	.230	52.	Bill Scherrer	DET	.256	85.	Floyd Bannister	CHI	.277	118.	Matt Young	SEA	.313
20.	Ron Davis	MIN	.231	53.	Tim Lollar	BOS	.256	86.	Mike Flanagan	BAL	.277	119.	Ed Whitson	NY	.314
21.	Bill Caudill	TOR	.231	54.	Bruce Kison	BOS	.258	87.	Storm Davis	BAL	.278	120.	Curt Wardle	CLE	.314
22.	Mike Moore	SEA	.234	55.	Bud Black	KC	.258	88.	Dennis Martinez	BAL	.278	121.	Burt Hooton	TEX	.315
23.	Jose Rijo	OAK	.234	56.	Willie Hernandez	DET	.258	89.	Tippy Martinez	BAL	.279	122.	Rick Waits	MIL	.322
24.	Dennis Lamp	TOR	.235	57.	Gary Lavelle	TOR	.259	90.	Dave Rozema	TEX	.281	123.	Chris Welsh	TEX	.322
25.	Tim Birtsas	OAK	.237	58.	Dave Schmidt	TEX	.260	91.	Dickie Noles	TEX	.281	124.	Mike Trujillo	BOS	.330
26.	Bert Blyleven	MIN	.239	59.	Danny Darwin	MIL	.261	92.	Chris Codiroli	OAK	.284	125.	Neal Heaton	CLE	.330
27.	Mike Witt	CAL	.239	60.	Dave Von Ohlen	CLE	.261	93.	Scott McGregor	BAL	.284	126.	Jim Acker	TOR	.333
28.	Dennis Rasmussen	NY	.239	60.	Tom Waddell	CLE	.261	94.	Rich Bordi	NY	.284	127.	Luis Leal	TOR	.336
29.	Stu Cliburn	CAL	.240	62.	Frank Tanana	DET	.262	95.	Ron Romanick	CAL	.284	128.	Rick Lysander	MIN	.357
29.	Edwin Nunez	SEA	.240	63.	Steve McCatty	OAK	.262	96.	Gene Nelson	CHI	.286	129.	Tommy John	OAK	.357
31.	Mark Langston	SEA	.240	64.	Mike Jones	KC	.263	97.	Frank Wills	SEA	.286	130.	Don Schulze	CLE	.360
32.	Bob Gibson	MIL	.242	65.	Jerry Reed	CLE	.263	98.	Bob Shirley	NY	.288	131.	Jim Beattie	SEA	.430
33.	Pete Filson	MIN	.243	66.	Jay Howell	OAK	.263	99.	Ken Schrom	MIN	.289				

National League

#	Pitcher	Team	Avg	#	Pitcher	Team	Avg	#	Pitcher	Team	Avg	#	Pitcher	Team	Avg
1.	Tom Niedenfuer	LA	.184	30.	Rick Camp	ATL	.233	59.	Eric Show	SD	.255	88.	Mike Scott	HOU	.276
2.	Sid Fernandez	NY	.186	31.	Ted Power	CIN	.234	60.	Craig Lefferts	SD	.255	89.	Bill Dawley	HOU	.278
3.	Jesse Orosco	NY	.188	32.	Roger McDowell	NY	.235	61.	Lee Tunnell	PIT	.256	90.	Jim Winn	PIT	.278
4.	Tim Burke	MTL	.189	33.	LaMarr Hoyt	SD	.237	62.	Frank DiPino	HOU	.256	91.	Vida Blue	SF	.278
5.	Tom Hume	CIN	.196	34.	Zane Smith	ATL	.237	62.	Kevin Gross	PHI	.256	92.	John Franco	CIN	.278
6.	Ken Howell	LA	.197	35.	Gene Garber	ATL	.237	64.	Dave Dravecky	SD	.257	93.	Doug Sisk	NY	.281
7.	Joe Price	CIN	.200	36.	Steve Bedrosian	ATL	.238	65.	Orel Hershiser	LA	.258	94.	Rick Aguilera	NY	.281
8.	Bob Welch	LA	.203	37.	Rod Scurry	PIT	.240	66.	Bob Walk	PIT	.258	95.	Rick Mahler	ATL	.281
9.	Scott Garrelts	SF	.203	38.	Joe Niekro	HOU	.241	67.	Larry McWilliams	PIT	.258	96.	Bob Forsch	STL	.283
10.	Mario Soto	CIN	.206	39.	Kent Tekulve	PHI	.242	68.	Lary Sorensen	CHI	.261	97.	Ed Lynch	NY	.284
11.	Jeff Reardon	MTL	.209	40.	David Palmer	MTL	.243	69.	Mike Krukow	SF	.262	98.	Jeff Lahti	STL	.285
12.	Mark Davis	SF	.211	41.	Don Robinson	PIT	.244	70.	Andy Hawkins	SD	.262	99.	Steve Carlton	PHI	.286
13.	Dwight Gooden	NY	.211	42.	Jeff Calhoun	HOU	.245	71.	Andy McGaffigan	CIN	.263	100.	Pascual Perez	ATL	.287
14.	Bruce Sutter	ATL	.212	43.	Carlos Diaz	LA	.246	72.	Bob Knepper	HOU	.263	101.	Jim Gott	SF	.287
15.	Don Carman	PHI	.212	44.	Ricky Horton	STL	.246	73.	Bill Laskey	MTL	.264	102.	Rick Rhoden	PIT	.288
16.	Mickey Mahler	MTL	.212	45.	Charles Hudson	PHI	.247	74.	Warren Brusstar	CHI	.265	103.	Rick Honeycutt	LA	.290
17.	Ron Darling	NY	.214	46.	Lee Smith	CHI	.247	75.	Ken Dayley	STL	.265	104.	Dave LaPoint	SF	.290
18.	Joe Hesketh	MTL	.217	47.	Shane Rawley	PHI	.248	76.	John Stuper	CIN	.265	105.	Dan Schatzeder	MTL	.290
19.	John Tudor	STL	.223	48.	Randy St. Claire	MTL	.248	77.	Atlee Hammaker	SF	.265	106.	Dick Ruthven	CHI	.297
20.	Kurt Kepshire	STL	.224	49.	Jeff Heathcock	HOU	.248	78.	Nolan Ryan	HOU	.266	107.	Greg Minton	SF	.298
21.	Tom Browning	CIN	.225	50.	Jeff Dedmon	ATL	.250	79.	Gary Lucas	MTL	.266	108.	Larry Andersen	PHI	.298
22.	Bill Campbell	STL	.225	50.	Rich Gossage	SD	.250	80.	Jay Tibbs	CIN	.267	109.	Dave Rucker	PHI	.305
23.	Fernando Valenzuela	LA	.225	50.	Rick Sutcliffe	CHI	.250	81.	Joe Johnson	ATL	.267	110.	Mark Thurmond	SD	.314
24.	Jay Baller	CHI	.225	53.	Danny Cox	STL	.251	82.	Steve Trout	CHI	.269	111.	Frank Williams	SF	.316
25.	Scott Sanderson	CHI	.226	54.	Bobby Castillo	LA	.252	83.	Jerry Koosman	PHI	.270	112.	Steve Shields	ATL	.318
26.	Rick Reuschel	PIT	.226	54.	Bert Roberge	MTL	.252	84.	Jerry Reuss	LA	.272	113.	George Frazier	CHI	.318
27.	Floyd Youmans	MTL	.228	56.	Ron Robinson	CIN	.252	85.	Joaquin Andujar	STL	.272	114.	Bill Gullickson	MTL	.321
28.	Dennis Eckersley	CHI	.229	57.	Jose DeLeon	PIT	.253	86.	Ray Fontenot	CHI	.274	115.	Tim Stoddard	SD	.321
29.	Cecilio Guante	PIT	.230	58.	Bryn Smith	MTL	.253	87.	John Denny	PHI	.275	116.	Ron Mathis	HOU	.336

Opponents' Batting Average with Runners On Base

American League

1. Steve Ontiveros	OAK	.149	34. Bert Blyleven	MIN	.246	67. Floyd Bannister	CHI	.269	100. Pete Vuckovich	MIL	.295
2. Joe Cowley	NY	.189	35. Ron Guidry	NY	.247	68. Mike Boddicker	BAL	.270	101. Frank Wills	SEA	.296
3. Bill Caudill	TOR	.200	36. Chris Codiroli	OAK	.247	69. John Candelaria	CAL	.271	102. Randy O'Neal	DET	.297
4. Donnie Moore	CAL	.203	37. Mike Witt	CAL	.247	70. Tippy Martinez	BAL	.271	103. Dennis Martinez	BAL	.299
5. Keith Atherton	OAK	.204	38. Bob Gibson	MIL	.247	71. Ed Vande Berg	SEA	.272	104. Keith Creel	CLE	.300
6. Bruce Kison	BOS	.208	39. Britt Burns	CHI	.247	72. Tom Seaver	CHI	.272	104. Kirk McCaskill	CAL	.300
7. Gene Nelson	CHI	.211	40. Mark Gubicza	KC	.248	73. Walt Terrell	DET	.274	106. Steve McCatty	OAK	.301
8. Greg Harris	TEX	.214	41. Bob James	CHI	.250	74. Bud Black	KC	.274	107. Mike Flanagan	BAL	.301
9. Brian Fisher	NY	.214	41. Phil Niekro	NY	.250	75. Aurelio Lopez	DET	.275	108. Storm Davis	BAL	.303
10. Tim Birtsas	OAK	.216	43. Dan Petry	DET	.251	76. Nate Snell	BAL	.275	109. Moose Haas	MIL	.304
11. Ron Davis	MIN	.217	44. Al Nipper	BOS	.253	77. Jim Slaton	CAL	.275	110. Matt Young	SEA	.304
12. Bret Saberhagen	KC	.217	45. Jay Howell	OAK	.254	78. Doyle Alexander	TOR	.276	111. Rick Lysander	MIN	.304
13. Roger Clemens	BOS	.218	46. Mike Jones	KC	.254	79. Dan Spillner	CHI	.277	112. Steve Crawford	BOS	.304
14. Charlie Leibrandt	KC	.219	47. Mark Langston	SEA	.257	80. Mike Moore	SEA	.278	113. Jeff Russell	TEX	.306
15. Pete Filson	MIN	.222	48. Bob McClure	MIL	.260	80. Bill Swift	SEA	.278	114. Juan Berenguer	DET	.307
16. Roy Thomas	SEA	.222	49. Jim Acker	TOR	.260	82. Ray Burris	MIL	.280	115. Chris Welsh	TEX	.312
17. Mark Clear	BOS	.224	50. Don Sutton	CAL	.260	83. Bill Krueger	OAK	.280	116. Luis Leal	TOR	.313
18. Jimmy Key	TOR	.225	51. Dave Righetti	NY	.261	84. Frank Tanana	DET	.281	117. Luis Sanchez	CAL	.313
19. Charlie Hough	TEX	.225	52. Bob Shirley	NY	.261	85. Bob Stanley	BOS	.281	118. Don Schulze	CLE	.314
20. Jack Morris	DET	.225	53. Ken Dixon	BAL	.261	86. Ken Schrom	MIN	.281	119. Mike Mason	TEX	.316
21. Ted Higuera	MIL	.228	54. Ramon Romero	CLE	.261	87. Scott McGregor	BAL	.283	120. John Butcher	MIN	.317
22. Tom Waddell	CLE	.228	55. Sammy Stewart	BAL	.262	88. Mike Smithson	MIN	.284	121. Rick Waits	MIL	.321
23. Dave Stieb	TOR	.229	56. Jamie Easterly	CLE	.263	89. Danny Darwin	MIL	.285	122. Vern Ruhle	CLE	.321
24. Gary Lavelle	TOR	.233	56. Neal Heaton	CLE	.263	90. Salome Barojas	SEA	.286	123. Dennis Rasmussen	NY	.324
25. Dave Stewart	TEX	.235	58. Ron Romanick	CAL	.265	90. Frank Eufemia	MIN	.286	124. Rick Thompson	CLE	.328
26. Jim Clancy	TOR	.235	59. Bill Scherrer	DET	.265	92. Rich Bordi	NY	.287	125. Dickie Noles	TEX	.330
27. Jose Rijo	OAK	.238	60. Edwin Nunez	SEA	.265	93. Joe Beckwith	KC	.288	126. Dave Rozema	TEX	.331
28. Tim Lollar	BOS	.240	61. Dennis Boyd	BOS	.266	94. Mike Trujillo	BOS	.290	127. Curt Wardle	CLE	.333
29. Dennis Lamp	TOR	.240	62. Dave Schmidt	TEX	.266	95. Jerry Reed	CLE	.290	128. Ed Whitson	NY	.346
30. Willie Hernandez	DET	.241	63. Bob Ojeda	BOS	.266	96. Don Aase	BAL	.290	129. Bryan Clark	CLE	.347
31. Urbano Lugo	CAL	.241	64. Danny Jackson	KC	.267	97. Frank Viola	MIN	.290	130. Roy Smith	CLE	.353
32. Jaime Cocanower	MIL	.245	65. Dan Quisenberry	KC	.268	98. Burt Hooton	TEX	.290	131. Tommy John	OAK	.367
33. Stu Cliburn	CAL	.246	66. Joel Davis	CHI	.268	99. Bruce Hurst	BOS	.293	132. Jim Beattie	SEA	.398

National League

1. Dwight Gooden	NY	.180	30. Bryn Smith	MTL	.235	59. Ted Power	CIN	.257	88. Mark Davis	SF	.278
2. Don Carman	PHI	.181	31. Jeff Lahti	STL	.235	60. Andy McGaffigan	CIN	.257	89. Lary Sorensen	CHI	.278
3. Carlos Diaz	LA	.185	32. Atlee Hammaker	SF	.236	61. Bruce Sutter	ATL	.259	90. Ken Dayley	STL	.280
4. Tim Burke	MTL	.188	33. John Franco	CIN	.236	62. Joe Hesketh	MTL	.260	90. Dick Ruthven	CHI	.280
5. Bob Welch	LA	.195	34. Rick Sutcliffe	CHI	.237	63. Jeff Dedmon	ATL	.260	92. Charles Hudson	PHI	.282
6. Sid Fernandez	NY	.196	35. Steve Carlton	PHI	.238	64. Rich Gossage	SD	.261	93. Rick Aguilera	NY	.283
7. Cecilio Guante	PIT	.196	36. Dave Dravecky	SD	.238	65. David Palmer	MTL	.262	93. Jay Tibbs	CIN	.283
8. Floyd Youmans	MTL	.200	37. Bill Campbell	STL	.239	66. Bert Roberge	MTL	.262	95. Jim Winn	PIT	.283
9. Dennis Eckersley	CHI	.201	38. Tom Browning	CIN	.240	67. Larry Andersen	PHI	.264	96. John Denny	PHI	.284
10. Mario Soto	CIN	.202	39. Mike Scott	HOU	.241	68. Ron Robinson	CIN	.266	97. Don Robinson	PIT	.286
11. Scott Garrelts	SF	.206	40. Jeff Reardon	MTL	.242	69. Jerry Koosman	PHI	.266	98. Len Barker	ATL	.291
12. Orel Hershiser	LA	.210	41. Jeff Calhoun	HOU	.243	70. Tim Stoddard	SD	.267	99. Dave Rucker	PHI	.291
13. John Tudor	STL	.212	42. Kevin Gross	PHI	.245	71. Terry Forster	ATL	.267	100. George Frazier	CHI	.293
14. Jesse Orosco	NY	.213	43. Tom Niedenfuer	LA	.245	71. Joe Price	CIN	.267	101. Rick Rhoden	PIT	.293
15. Ron Darling	NY	.216	44. Nolan Ryan	HOU	.245	73. Bill Gullickson	MTL	.267	102. Frank DiPino	HOU	.294
16. Mike Krukow	SF	.218	45. Gene Garber	ATL	.247	74. Dave LaPoint	SF	.268	103. Joe Johnson	ATL	.295
17. Joe Niekro	HOU	.219	46. Andy Hawkins	SD	.248	75. Jim Gott	SF	.268	104. Mark Thurmond	SD	.298
18. Tom Hume	CIN	.220	47. Frank Williams	SF	.248	76. Lee Tunnell	PIT	.269	105. Pascual Perez	ATL	.301
19. Dan Schatzeder	MTL	.220	48. Rick Camp	ATL	.248	77. Rick Mahler	ATL	.269	106. Bill Dawley	HOU	.304
20. Eric Show	SD	.223	49. Kent Tekulve	PHI	.248	78. Ricky Horton	STL	.270	107. Ron Mathis	HOU	.305
21. Rick Reuschel	PIT	.224	50. Ed Lynch	NY	.249	79. Rick Honeycutt	LA	.271	108. Ray Fontenot	CHI	.306
22. Roger McDowell	NY	.227	51. Vida Blue	SF	.250	80. Randy St. Claire	MTL	.271	109. Doug Sisk	NY	.313
23. Scott Sanderson	CHI	.228	52. Fernando Valenzuela	LA	.251	81. Steve Trout	CHI	.272	110. LaMarr Hoyt	SD	.315
24. Dave Smith	HOU	.229	53. Jose DeLeon	PIT	.251	82. Greg Minton	SF	.272	111. Kurt Kepshire	STL	.323
25. Ken Howell	LA	.230	54. Craig Lefferts	SD	.252	83. Bobby Castillo	LA	.274	112. Bill Laskey	MTL	.328
26. Lee Smith	CHI	.231	55. Zane Smith	ATL	.252	84. Bob Forsch	STL	.275	113. Warren Brusstar	CHI	.331
27. Shane Rawley	PHI	.233	56. Larry McWilliams	PIT	.253	85. Bob Knepper	HOU	.275	114. John Stuper	CIN	.358
28. Gary Lucas	MTL	.233	57. Joaquin Andujar	STL	.254	86. Steve Bedrosian	ATL	.277	115. Steve Shields	ATL	.393
29. Danny Cox	STL	.234	58. Jerry Reuss	LA	.255	87. Craig McMurtry	ATL	.277			

Opponents' Batting Average with Bases Empty

American League

#	Pitcher	Team	Avg	#	Pitcher	Team	Avg	#	Pitcher	Team	Avg	#	Pitcher	Team	Avg
1.	Greg Harris	TEX	.168	34.	Bill Scherrer	DET	.233	67.	Frank Tanana	DET	.254	100.	Bryan Clark	CLE	.277
2.	Juan Agosto	CHI	.179	35.	Tom Seaver	CHI	.233	68.	Keith Atherton	OAK	.255	101.	Bob Ojeda	BOS	.278
3.	Richard Dotson	CHI	.184	36.	Bert Blyleven	MIN	.234	69.	John Candelaria	CAL	.255	102.	Bill Swift	SEA	.279
4.	Roy Thomas	SEA	.188	37.	Roger Clemens	BOS	.234	70.	Dickie Noles	TEX	.255	103.	Ed Whitson	NY	.280
5.	Willie Hernandez	DET	.189	38.	Danny Darwin	MIL	.235	71.	Tim Birtsas	OAK	.255	104.	Dennis Martinez	BAL	.280
6.	Steve Ontiveros	OAK	.196	39.	Moose Haas	MIL	.237	72.	Floyd Bannister	CHI	.257	105.	Scott McGregor	BAL	.282
7.	Gary Lavelle	TOR	.197	40.	Curt Wardle	CLE	.237	73.	Danny Jackson	KC	.257	106.	Mike Mason	TEX	.285
8.	Dan Petry	DET	.199	41.	Stu Cliburn	CAL	.237	74.	Vern Ruhle	CLE	.258	107.	Rick Langford	OAK	.286
9.	Bob Stanley	BOS	.200	42.	Ted Higuera	MIL	.239	75.	Al Nipper	BOS	.258	108.	Bob McClure	MIL	.287
10.	Bob James	CHI	.202	43.	Britt Burns	CHI	.239	76.	Dennis Boyd	BOS	.258	109.	Ramon Romero	CLE	.288
11.	Dave Stieb	TOR	.203	44.	Mike Witt	CAL	.240	77.	Bruce Hurst	BOS	.259	110.	Curt Young	OAK	.288
12.	Edwin Nunez	SEA	.205	45.	Walt Terrell	DET	.241	78.	Doyle Alexander	TOR	.259	111.	Ron Romanick	CAL	.290
13.	Randy O'Neal	DET	.206	46.	Jose Rijo	OAK	.241	79.	Tim Lollar	BOS	.260	112.	Jim Slaton	CAL	.291
14.	Pat Clements	CAL	.207	47.	Phil Niekro	NY	.241	80.	Mike Jones	KC	.261	113.	Dan Quisenberry	KC	.291
15.	Charlie Hough	TEX	.210	48.	Bob Shirley	NY	.242	81.	Mike Smithson	MIN	.261	114.	Keith Creel	CLE	.292
16.	Dennis Rasmussen	NY	.213	49.	Frank Wills	SEA	.243	82.	Tom Waddell	CLE	.262	115.	Gene Nelson	CHI	.294
17.	Jerry Reed	CLE	.217	50.	Jimmy Key	TOR	.243	83.	Bud Black	KC	.264	116.	Mike Flanagan	BAL	.294
18.	Brian Fisher	NY	.217	51.	Jim Clancy	TOR	.245	84.	Jamie Easterly	CLE	.264	117.	Roy Smith	CLE	.295
19.	Bill Caudill	TOR	.219	52.	Mike Warren	OAK	.246	85.	Matt Young	SEA	.267	118.	Luis Leal	TOR	.296
20.	Dave Righetti	NY	.219	53.	Joe Cowley	NY	.246	86.	Ray Burris	MIL	.267	119.	Urbano Lugo	CAL	.298
21.	Storm Davis	BAL	.221	54.	Nate Snell	BAL	.246	87.	Ken Schrom	MIN	.267	120.	Pete Vuckovich	MIL	.300
22.	Don Aase	BAL	.222	55.	Don Sutton	CAL	.248	88.	Rick Thompson	CLE	.267	121.	Mike Boddicker	BAL	.300
23.	Ken Dixon	BAL	.223	56.	Jim Beattie	SEA	.248	89.	Charlie Leibrandt	KC	.267	122.	Burt Hooton	TEX	.302
24.	Dan Spillner	CHI	.224	57.	Joel Davis	CHI	.248	90.	Chris Codiroli	OAK	.268	123.	Tommy John	OAK	.304
25.	Jack Morris	DET	.224	58.	Ron Guidry	NY	.249	91.	Donnie Moore	CAL	.269	124.	Jaime Cocanower	MIL	.307
26.	Mike Moore	SEA	.227	59.	Joe Beckwith	KC	.250	92.	Jay Howell	OAK	.269	125.	Dave Stewart	TEX	.307
27.	Juan Berenguer	DET	.227	59.	Tippy Martinez	BAL	.250	93.	John Butcher	MIN	.271	126.	Chris Welsh	TEX	.319
28.	Rich Bordi	NY	.228	61.	Dave Rozema	TEX	.251	94.	Steve Crawford	BOS	.272	127.	Neal Heaton	CLE	.328
29.	Aurelio Lopez	DET	.229	62.	Frank Viola	MIN	.252	94.	Bob Gibson	MIL	.272	128.	Don Schulze	CLE	.330
30.	Sammy Stewart	BAL	.230	63.	Mark Langston	SEA	.253	96.	Steve McCatty	OAK	.272	129.	Jeff Russell	TEX	.341
31.	Kirk McCaskill	CAL	.231	64.	Dennis Lamp	TOR	.254	97.	Bill Krueger	OAK	.273	130.	Bruce Kison	BOS	.343
32.	Dave Schmidt	TEX	.231	65.	Bret Saberhagen	KC	.254	98.	Pete Filson	MIN	.275	131.	Mike Trujillo	BOS	.353
33.	Mark Gubicza	KC	.232	66.	Luis Sanchez	CAL	.254	99.	Jim Acker	TOR	.276				

National League

#	Pitcher	Team	Avg	#	Pitcher	Team	Avg	#	Pitcher	Team	Avg	#	Pitcher	Team	Avg
1.	Mark Davis	SF	.172	30.	Scott Sanderson	CHI	.228	59.	Ron Darling	NY	.250	87.	Kent Tekulve	PHI	.267
2.	Sid Fernandez	NY	.173	31.	Kurt Kepshire	STL	.229	60.	Mike Krukow	SF	.251	89.	Bob Knepper	HOU	.267
3.	Don Carman	PHI	.176	32.	Don Robinson	PIT	.230	61.	Jim Winn	PIT	.252	90.	Rick Mahler	ATL	.268
4.	Terry Forster	ATL	.183	33.	Charles Hudson	PHI	.231	62.	Lee Smith	CHI	.253	91.	Jeff Dedmon	ATL	.268
5.	Jeff Reardon	MTL	.187	34.	Bryn Smith	MTL	.231	63.	Bill Laskey	MTL	.254	92.	Dave LaPoint	SF	.270
6.	Ken Howell	LA	.189	35.	Mike Scott	HOU	.231	64.	Rick Honeycutt	LA	.254	93.	Steve Trout	CHI	.270
7.	Fernando Valenzuela	LA	.190	36.	Roger McDowell	NY	.232	65.	Ron Robinson	CIN	.254	94.	Lary Sorensen	CHI	.271
8.	Scott Garrelts	SF	.191	37.	Vida Blue	SF	.232	66.	Atlee Hammaker	SF	.254	95.	Greg Minton	SF	.273
9.	Ted Power	CIN	.194	38.	John Franco	CIN	.233	67.	Warren Brusstar	CHI	.255	96.	Bill Gullickson	MTL	.273
10.	Bobby Castillo	LA	.196	39.	LaMarr Hoyt	SD	.233	68.	Bob Walk	PIT	.255	97.	Bruce Sutter	ATL	.274
11.	Joe Hesketh	MTL	.202	40.	Nolan Ryan	HOU	.235	69.	Kevin Gross	PHI	.256	98.	Gene Garber	ATL	.276
12.	Rich Gossage	SD	.202	41.	Jesse Orosco	NY	.237	70.	John Stuper	CIN	.256	99.	Joe Johnson	ATL	.278
13.	Orel Hershiser	LA	.203	42.	Frank Williams	SF	.237	71.	Zane Smith	ATL	.256	100.	Andy Hawkins	SD	.278
14.	John Tudor	STL	.207	43.	Ricky Horton	STL	.238	72.	Dave Dravecky	SD	.257	101.	Rick Camp	ATL	.280
15.	Tom Niedenfuer	LA	.208	44.	Craig Lefferts	SD	.238	73.	Eric Show	SD	.257	102.	John Denny	PHI	.280
16.	Bert Roberge	MTL	.210	45.	Steve Bedrosian	ATL	.239	74.	Steve Shields	ATL	.259	103.	Ron Mathis	HOU	.283
17.	Floyd Youmans	MTL	.210	46.	Lee Tunnell	PIT	.239	75.	Steve Carlton	PHI	.259	104.	Jerry Koosman	PHI	.283
18.	Frank DiPino	HOU	.211	47.	Andy McGaffigan	CIN	.241	76.	Ed Lynch	NY	.260	105.	Larry Andersen	PHI	.284
19.	Rick Reuschel	PIT	.211	48.	David Palmer	MTL	.241	77.	Randy St. Claire	MTL	.261	106.	Len Barker	ATL	.285
20.	Dwight Gooden	NY	.213	49.	Rick Aguilera	NY	.242	78.	Shane Rawley	PHI	.261	107.	Ray Fontenot	CHI	.286
21.	Jose DeLeon	PIT	.215	50.	Bob Welch	LA	.243	79.	Carlos Diaz	LA	.261	108.	Dan Schatzeder	MTL	.286
22.	Mario Soto	CIN	.217	51.	Rick Sutcliffe	CHI	.243	80.	Jay Baller	CHI	.262	109.	Mark Thurmond	SD	.287
23.	Tim Burke	MTL	.217	52.	Dennis Eckersley	CHI	.243	80.	Danny Cox	STL	.262	110.	Pascual Perez	ATL	.294
24.	Al Holland	PIT	.219	53.	Jim Gott	SF	.244	82.	Doug Sisk	NY	.263	111.	Rick Rhoden	PIT	.298
25.	Bill Dawley	HOU	.222	54.	Jeff Calhoun	HOU	.244	83.	Jerry Reuss	LA	.263	112.	Jeff Heathcock	HOU	.305
26.	Bill Campbell	STL	.223	55.	Dave Smith	HOU	.244	84.	Gary Lucas	MTL	.264	113.	George Frazier	CHI	.306
27.	Joe Price	CIN	.224	56.	Jay Tibbs	CIN	.245	85.	Joaquin Andujar	STL	.265	114.	Larry McWilliams	PIT	.309
28.	Cecilio Guante	PIT	.226	57.	Bob Forsch	STL	.248	86.	Dave Rucker	PHI	.265	115.	Dick Ruthven	CHI	.320
29.	Tom Hume	CIN	.228	58.	Tom Browning	CIN	.248	87.	Joe Niekro	HOU	.267				

Opponents' Home Run Percentage with Runners On Base

American League

#	Pitcher	Team	Pct.
1.	Jaime Cocanower	MIL	0.43
2.	Dave Righetti	NY	0.47
3.	Steve Crawford	BOS	0.54
4.	Bob Stanley	BOS	0.68
5.	Dave Schmidt	TEX	0.70
6.	Walt Terrell	DET	0.78
7.	Dan Quisenberry	KC	0.79
8.	Mike Boddicker	BAL	0.79
9.	Mark Clear	BOS	0.80
10.	Steve Ontiveros	OAK	0.83
11.	Danny Jackson	KC	0.91
12.	Jose Rijo	OAK	0.95
13.	Bill Swift	SEA	1.01
14.	Jay Howell	OAK	1.04
15.	Bob Shirley	NY	1.09
16.	Nate Snell	BAL	1.12
17.	Stu Cliburn	CAL	1.20
18.	Rich Bordi	NY	1.27
19.	Bret Saberhagen	KC	1.28
20.	Dave Stieb	TOR	1.29
21.	Dan Spillner	CHI	1.46
22.	Mark Gubicza	KC	1.48
23.	Urbano Lugo	CAL	1.50
24.	Bob James	CHI	1.53
25.	Randy O'Neal	DET	1.56
26.	Mike Jones	KC	1.59
27.	Rick Lysander	MIN	1.60
28.	Donnie Moore	CAL	1.60
29.	Jim Slaton	CAL	1.62
30.	Gary Lavelle	TOR	1.67
31.	Brian Fisher	NY	1.73
32.	Ramon Romero	CLE	1.80
33.	Tom Seaver	CHI	1.81
34.	Keith Creel	CLE	1.82
35.	Bert Blyleven	MIN	1.86
36.	Chris Codiroli	OAK	1.86
37.	Rick Waits	MIL	1.89
38.	Charlie Leibrandt	KC	1.92
39.	Mike Moore	SEA	1.94
40.	Ed Vande Berg	SEA	1.99
41.	Tommy John	OAK	2.00
41.	Dickie Noles	TEX	2.00
43.	Bob Ojeda	BOS	2.02
44.	Jack Morris	DET	2.03
45.	Dennis Rasmussen	NY	2.07
46.	Neal Heaton	CLE	2.11
47.	Roger Clemens	BOS	2.11
47.	Storm Davis	BAL	2.11
49.	Bill Krueger	OAK	2.18
50.	Al Nipper	BOS	2.20
51.	Doyle Alexander	TOR	2.28
52.	Bud Black	KC	2.29
53.	Don Sutton	CAL	2.40
54.	Ted Higuera	MIL	2.41
55.	Greg Harris	TEX	2.52
56.	Bob Gibson	MIL	2.53
56.	Willie Hernandez	DET	2.53
56.	Charlie Hough	TEX	2.53
56.	Gene Nelson	CHI	2.53
56.	Sammy Stewart	BAL	2.53
61.	John Candelaria	CAL	2.54
62.	Mike Mason	TEX	2.56
63.	Joel Davis	CHI	2.68
64.	Mark Langston	SEA	2.70
64.	Don Schulze	CLE	2.70
66.	Joe Beckwith	KC	2.72
67.	Dennis Lamp	TOR	2.73
67.	Rick Thompson	CLE	2.73
67.	Mike Trujillo	BOS	2.73
70.	Ray Burris	MIL	2.76
71.	Jerry Reed	CLE	2.80
72.	Mike Witt	CAL	2.83
73.	Tippy Martinez	BAL	2.86
74.	Dennis Boyd	BOS	2.87
75.	Phil Niekro	NY	2.87
76.	Jimmy Key	TOR	2.90
77.	Ron Romanick	CAL	2.94
78.	Don Aase	BAL	2.96
78.	Jim Acker	TOR	2.96
80.	Roy Thomas	SEA	2.96
81.	Frank Tanana	DET	2.97
82.	Jim Beattie	SEA	3.01
83.	Tim Birtsas	OAK	3.03
84.	Ken Dixon	BAL	3.10
85.	Moose Haas	MIL	3.13
86.	Jamie Easterly	CLE	3.16
87.	Frank Viola	MIN	3.28
88.	Ron Davis	MIN	3.29
89.	Ron Guidry	NY	3.32
90.	Juan Berenguer	DET	3.33
90.	Burt Hooton	TEX	3.33
92.	Mike Smithson	MIN	3.35
93.	Matt Young	SEA	3.41
94.	Roy Smith	CLE	3.45
95.	Pete Vuckovich	MIL	3.50
96.	Dan Petry	DET	3.54
97.	Pete Filson	MIN	3.59
98.	Edwin Nunez	SEA	3.61
99.	Tim Lollar	BOS	3.69
100.	Jim Clancy	TOR	3.74
101.	Scott McGregor	BAL	3.77
102.	Bruce Hurst	BOS	3.79
103.	Ed Whitson	NY	3.81
104.	Chris Welsh	TEX	3.82
105.	Bruce Kison	BOS	3.83
106.	Bill Caudill	TOR	4.00
107.	Jeff Russell	TEX	4.03
108.	Britt Burns	CHI	4.06
109.	Vern Ruhle	CLE	4.15
110.	Ken Schrom	MIN	4.15
111.	Bill Scherrer	DET	4.27
112.	Steve McCatty	OAK	4.29
113.	Frank Wills	SEA	4.43
114.	Dave Rozema	TEX	4.46
115.	Kirk McCaskill	CAL	4.48
116.	Joe Cowley	NY	4.50
117.	Bob McClure	MIL	4.55
118.	Tom Waddell	CLE	4.57
119.	Aurelio Lopez	DET	4.58
120.	Danny Darwin	MIL	4.70
121.	Salome Barojas	SEA	4.76
121.	Frank Eufemia	MIN	4.76
123.	Dennis Martinez	BAL	4.80
124.	Keith Atherton	OAK	4.84
125.	Bryan Clark	CLE	4.96
126.	Floyd Bannister	CHI	5.14
127.	Luis Sanchez	CAL	5.22
128.	John Butcher	MIN	5.33
129.	Luis Leal	TOR	5.36
130.	Dave Stewart	TEX	5.37
131.	Mike Flanagan	BAL	6.29
132.	Curt Wardle	CLE	6.39

National League

#	Pitcher	Team	Pct.
1.	Ken Dayley	STL	0.00
2.	Rick Camp	ATL	0.39
3.	Dwight Gooden	NY	0.55
4.	Scott Garrelts	SF	0.56
5.	Ted Power	CIN	0.66
6.	Ricky Horton	STL	0.71
7.	Jeff Lahti	STL	0.76
8.	Rick Reuschel	PIT	0.78
9.	Zane Smith	ATL	0.80
10.	Randy St. Claire	MTL	0.85
11.	Steve Trout	CHI	0.86
12.	Rich Gossage	SD	0.87
13.	Bob Welch	LA	0.88
14.	Sid Fernandez	NY	0.93
15.	Bill Gullickson	MTL	1.04
16.	Greg Minton	SF	1.09
17.	Rick Aguilera	NY	1.11
18.	Dave Smith	HOU	1.20
19.	Andy Hawkins	SD	1.21
20.	Orel Hershiser	LA	1.22
21.	Kevin Gross	PHI	1.22
22.	Cecilio Guante	PIT	1.23
22.	John Tudor	STL	1.23
24.	Ron Darling	NY	1.30
25.	Rick Rhoden	PIT	1.33
26.	John Franco	CIN	1.35
27.	Andy McGaffigan	CIN	1.39
28.	Mark Thurmond	SD	1.40
29.	Joe Niekro	HOU	1.50
30.	Bryn Smith	MTL	1.54
31.	Bob Forsch	STL	1.55
32.	Tim Burke	MTL	1.57
33.	Don Carman	PHI	1.57
33.	Atlee Hammaker	SF	1.57
33.	Jim Winn	PIT	1.57
36.	Bob Knepper	HOU	1.60
37.	Joaquin Andujar	STL	1.62
38.	Nolan Ryan	HOU	1.63
39.	Jay Tibbs	CIN	1.67
40.	David Palmer	MTL	1.69
41.	Larry McWilliams	PIT	1.72
42.	John Denny	PHI	1.75
43.	Dave LaPoint	SF	1.76
44.	Jeff Dedmon	ATL	1.78
45.	Fernando Valenzuela	LA	1.81
46.	Steve Carlton	PHI	1.83
46.	Jesse Orosco	NY	1.83
48.	Doug Sisk	NY	1.84
49.	Kurt Kepshire	STL	1.84
50.	Dan Schatzeder	MTL	1.89
51.	Tom Niedenfuer	LA	1.94
52.	Jeff Calhoun	HOU	1.94
52.	Gary Lucas	MTL	1.94
54.	Joe Hesketh	MTL	2.00
55.	Scott Sanderson	CHI	2.01
56.	Larry Andersen	PHI	2.08
57.	Jim Gott	SF	2.13
58.	Ed Lynch	NY	2.17
59.	Jerry Reuss	LA	2.17
60.	Kent Tekulve	PHI	2.19
61.	Shane Rawley	PHI	2.20
62.	Mike Scott	HOU	2.22
63.	Craig Lefferts	SD	2.22
64.	Danny Cox	STL	2.25
65.	Lary Sorensen	CHI	2.26
66.	Jeff Reardon	MTL	2.27
66.	John Stuper	CIN	2.27
68.	Dick Ruthven	CHI	2.29
69.	Ron Mathis	HOU	2.29
70.	Eric Show	SD	2.31
71.	Rick Honeycutt	LA	2.34
72.	Don Robinson	PIT	2.38
73.	Tom Hume	CIN	2.44
74.	Tim Stoddard	SD	2.50
74.	Floyd Youmans	MTL	2.50
76.	Dave Dravecky	SD	2.51
77.	Rick Sutcliffe	CHI	2.58
78.	Rick Mahler	ATL	2.58
79.	Gene Garber	ATL	2.60
79.	Charles Hudson	PHI	2.60
81.	Dave Rucker	PHI	2.65
82.	Frank Williams	SF	2.65
83.	Ken Howell	LA	2.70
84.	Pascual Perez	ATL	2.73
85.	Lee Smith	CHI	2.75
86.	Bill Campbell	STL	2.75
87.	Dennis Eckersley	CHI	2.80
88.	Steve Bedrosian	ATL	2.83
89.	LaMarr Hoyt	SD	2.93
90.	Bill Dawley	HOU	2.96
91.	Craig McMurtry	ATL	2.97
91.	Joe Price	CIN	2.97
93.	Mike Krukow	SF	3.17
94.	Tom Browning	CIN	3.20
95.	Carlos Diaz	LA	3.23
96.	Mario Soto	CIN	3.26
97.	Jose DeLeon	PIT	3.37
98.	George Frazier	CHI	3.40
99.	Warren Brusstar	CHI	3.45
99.	Bill Laskey	MTL	3.45
101.	Ron Robinson	CIN	3.47
102.	Lee Tunnell	PIT	3.48
103.	Len Barker	ATL	3.55
104.	Ray Fontenot	CHI	3.57
105.	Bert Roberge	MTL	3.74
106.	Roger McDowell	NY	3.78
107.	Mark Davis	SF	3.89
108.	Frank DiPino	HOU	3.97
109.	Steve Shields	ATL	4.10
110.	Vida Blue	SF	4.17
111.	Joe Johnson	ATL	4.32
112.	Bruce Sutter	ATL	4.32
113.	Terry Forster	ATL	4.95
114.	Jerry Koosman	PHI	5.19
115.	Bobby Castillo	LA	6.19

Opponents' Home Run Percentage Bases Empty

American League

1.	Brian Fisher	NY	0.54	34.	Dave Righetti	NY	2.14	67.	Dave Schmidt	TEX	2.69	100. Frank Tanana DET 3.58
2.	Don Aase	BAL	0.65	35.	Joe Beckwith	KC	2.17	68.	Jimmy Key	TOR	2.70	101. Pete Vuckovich MIL 3.60
3.	Juan Agosto	CHI	0.81	35.	Bill Krueger	OAK	2.17	69.	Floyd Bannister	CHI	2.74	102. Jeff Russell TEX 3.62
4.	Pat Clements	CAL	0.83	35.	Steve Ontiveros	OAK	2.17	70.	Roy Smith	CLE	2.74	103. Keith Creel CLE 3.65
5.	Danny Jackson	KC	0.85	35.	Matt Young	SEA	2.17	71.	Randy O'Neal	DET	2.80	104. Dennis Martinez BAL 3.68
6.	Roger Clemens	BOS	0.90	39.	Bill Swift	SEA	2.21	72.	Tom Seaver	CHI	2.81	105. Danny Darwin MIL 3.69
7.	Nate Snell	BAL	0.97	40.	Ed Whitson	NY	2.22	73.	Dickie Noles	TEX	2.83	106. Jose Rijo OAK 3.76
8.	Dennis Lamp	TOR	0.98	41.	Bert Blyleven	MIN	2.22	74.	Tommy John	OAK	2.94	106. Bill Scherrer DET 3.76
9.	Bob James	CHI	0.99	42.	Frank Viola	MIN	2.23	75.	Dave Stieb	TOR	2.95	108. Sammy Stewart BAL 3.77
10.	Bruce Kison	BOS	1.14	43.	Dennis Boyd	BOS	2.23	76.	Dennis Rasmussen	NY	2.98	109. Burt Hooton TEX 3.78
11.	Mike Trujillo	BOS	1.20	44.	Kirk McCaskill	CAL	2.26	77.	Ted Higuera	MIL	2.98	110. Tim Birtsas OAK 3.79
12.	Walt Terrell	DET	1.26	45.	Gary Lavelle	TOR	2.27	78.	Dave Stewart	TEX	3.01	111. Willie Hernandez DET 3.86
13.	Greg Harris	TEX	1.26	46.	Rick Thompson	CLE	2.29	79.	Donnie Moore	CAL	3.05	112. Phil Niekro NY 3.95
14.	Storm Davis	BAL	1.29	47.	Dan Petry	DET	2.30	80.	Chris Welsh	TEX	3.07	113. Dan Spillner CHI 3.98
15.	Jim Acker	TOR	1.32	48.	Steve Crawford	BOS	2.31	81.	Doyle Alexander	TOR	3.10	114. Keith Atherton OAK 4.00
16.	Bob Shirley	NY	1.32	49.	Al Nipper	BOS	2.35	82.	Jim Beattie	SEA	3.11	115. Edwin Nunez SEA 4.09
17.	Rich Bordi	NY	1.37	50.	Jaime Cocanower	MIL	2.36	83.	Tim Lollar	BOS	3.11	116. Ray Burris MIL 4.33
18.	John Butcher	MIN	1.38	50.	Don Schulze	CLE	2.36	84.	Bill Caudill	TOR	3.13	117. Luis Leal TOR 4.40
19.	Bryan Clark	CLE	1.54	52.	Dan Quisenberry	KC	2.36	84.	Tippy Martinez	BAL	3.13	118. Urbano Lugo CAL 4.42
20.	Stu Cliburn	CAL	1.55	53.	Jack Morris	DET	2.37	86.	Don Sutton	CAL	3.14	119. Ron Romanick CAL 4.49
21.	Dave Rozema	TEX	1.57	54.	Mike Boddicker	BAL	2.40	87.	Chris Codiroli	OAK	3.17	120. Scott McGregor BAL 4.56
22.	Jay Howell	OAK	1.65	55.	Britt Burns	CHI	2.44	88.	Juan Berenguer	DET	3.18	121. Aurelio Lopez DET 4.57
23.	Bob Ojeda	BOS	1.67	56.	Luis Sanchez	CAL	2.46	89.	Richard Dotson	CHI	3.20	122. Tom Waddell CLE 4.89
24.	Bob McClure	MIL	1.69	57.	Charlie Hough	TEX	2.48	90.	Bruce Hurst	BOS	3.26	123. Ken Schrom MIN 4.92
25.	Jamie Easterly	CLE	1.72	58.	Mark Gubicza	KC	2.49	91.	Ken Dixon	BAL	3.41	124. Joe Cowley NY 5.19
26.	Steve McCatty	OAK	1.78	59.	Neal Heaton	CLE	2.51	92.	Moose Haas	MIL	3.41	125. Gene Nelson CHI 5.31
27.	Joel Davis	CHI	1.82	60.	Mike Flanagan	BAL	2.54	93.	Bob Stanley	BOS	3.43	126. Jerry Reed CLE 5.42
28.	Charlie Leibrandt	KC	1.87	61.	Ron Guidry	NY	2.58	94.	Pete Filson	MIN	3.43	127. Jim Slaton CAL 5.57
29.	Mike Moore	SEA	1.92	62.	Curt Wardle	CLE	2.63	95.	Bob Gibson	MIL	3.47	128. Mike Warren OAK 6.14
30.	Bud Black	KC	1.98	63.	Bret Saberhagen	KC	2.66	96.	Mike Jones	KC	3.48	129. Mark Langston SEA 6.23
31.	Mike Witt	CAL	2.00	64.	Vern Ruhle	CLE	2.68	97.	Mike Mason	TEX	3.53	130. Ramon Romero CLE 7.91
32.	Mike Smithson	MIN	2.03	65.	John Candelaria	CAL	2.68	98.	Frank Wills	SEA	3.53	131. Curt Young OAK 8.47
33.	Roy Thomas	SEA	2.09	65.	Jim Clancy	TOR	2.68	99.	Rick Langford	OAK	3.57	

National League

1.	Jeff Calhoun	HOU	0.00	30.	Dave Rucker	PHI	1.36	59.	Steve Trout	CHI	2.05	88. Rick Rhoden PIT 2.69
1.	Rich Gossage	SD	0.00	31.	Joaquin Andujar	STL	1.37	60.	Shane Rawley	PHI	2.06	89. Gary Lucas MTL 2.70
1.	Doug Sisk	NY	0.00	32.	Bryn Smith	MTL	1.38	61.	Dave Dravecky	SD	2.07	90. Steve Shields ATL 2.72
1.	Floyd Youmans	MTL	0.00	33.	Bobby Castillo	LA	1.40	62.	Ricky Horton	STL	2.07	91. Lary Sorensen CHI 2.76
5.	David Palmer	MTL	0.36	34.	Randy St. Claire	MTL	1.41	62.	Jeff Reardon	MTL	2.07	92. Tom Browning CIN 2.78
6.	Scott Garrelts	SF	0.49	35.	Larry Andersen	PHI	1.42	64.	Ron Robinson	CIN	2.08	93. Ed Lynch NY 2.84
7.	Bert Roberge	MTL	0.70	35.	Bob Walk	PIT	1.42	65.	Dennis Eckersley	CHI	2.14	94. Rick Camp ATL 2.97
8.	Roger McDowell	NY	0.70	37.	John Franco	CIN	1.46	66.	Rick Aguilera	NY	2.17	95. Vida Blue SF 3.04
9.	Zane Smith	ATL	0.71	38.	John Tudor	STL	1.48	67.	Mike Krukow	SF	2.20	96. Ron Darling NY 3.05
10.	Orel Hershiser	LA	0.74	39.	Jim Gott	SF	1.51	68.	Rick Mahler	ATL	2.23	97. Al Holland PIT 3.13
11.	Ted Power	CIN	0.75	40.	Bill Campbell	STL	1.54	69.	Lee Smith	CHI	2.25	98. Bill Laskey MTL 3.13
12.	Dave Smith	HOU	0.79	41.	Joe Johnson	ATL	1.55	70.	LaMarr Hoyt	SD	2.26	99. Sid Fernandez NY 3.14
13.	Andy McGaffigan	CIN	0.94	42.	Kevin Gross	PHI	1.57	71.	Greg Minton	SF	2.27	100. Mario Soto CIN 3.22
14.	Don Robinson	PIT	0.98	43.	John Denny	PHI	1.63	72.	Jesse Orosco	NY	2.29	101. Kurt Kepshire STL 3.23
15.	Rick Reuschel	PIT	1.10	44.	Joe Hesketh	MTL	1.66	73.	Craig Lefferts	SD	2.33	102. Atlee Hammaker SF 3.27
16.	Fernando Valenzuela	LA	1.17	45.	Carlos Diaz	LA	1.67	73.	Rick Sutcliffe	CHI	2.33	103. Len Barker ATL 3.31
17.	Dick Ruthven	CHI	1.18	45.	Terry Forster	ATL	1.67	75.	Ken Howell	LA	2.37	104. Bruce Sutter ATL 3.35
18.	Rick Honeycutt	LA	1.22	47.	Jay Tibbs	CIN	1.72	76.	Tom Hume	CIN	2.40	105. Charles Hudson PHI 3.42
19.	Nolan Ryan	HOU	1.23	48.	Steve Carlton	PHI	1.72	77.	Don Carman	PHI	2.42	106. Joe Niekro HOU 3.44
19.	Jim Winn	PIT	1.23	49.	Steve Bedrosian	ATL	1.74	78.	Pascual Perez	ATL	2.45	107. Scott Sanderson CHI 3.45
21.	Jerry Reuss	LA	1.23	50.	Dwight Gooden	NY	1.76	79.	Bob Forsch	STL	2.51	108. Bob Welch LA 3.50
22.	Bill Gullickson	MTL	1.24	51.	Jose DeLeon	PIT	1.82	80.	Mike Scott	HOU	2.54	109. Eric Show SD 3.62
23.	Frank Williams	SF	1.28	52.	Gene Garber	ATL	1.84	81.	Jerry Koosman	PHI	2.58	110. Ray Fontenot CHI 4.00
24.	Tom Niedenfuer	LA	1.30	53.	Bill Dawley	HOU	1.90	82.	Tim Burke	MTL	2.61	111. George Frazier CHI 4.08
25.	Cecilio Guante	PIT	1.30	54.	Mark Thurmond	SD	1.91	82.	Dave LaPoint	SF	2.61	112. Dan Schatzeder MTL 4.33
26.	Frank DiPino	HOU	1.32	55.	Larry McWilliams	PIT	1.93	84.	Ron Mathis	HOU	2.63	113. Jeff Heathcock HOU 4.69
27.	Lee Tunnell	PIT	1.33	56.	John Stuper	CIN	1.93	85.	Mark Davis	SF	2.64	114. Joe Price CIN 4.90
28.	Kent Tekulve	PHI	1.33	57.	Warren Brusstar	CHI	1.96	86.	Andy Hawkins	SD	2.65	115. Jay Baller CHI 5.56
29.	Jeff Dedmon	ATL	1.34	58.	Danny Cox	STL	2.01	87.	Bob Knepper	HOU	2.67	

Opponents' On Base Average Leading Off the Inning

American League

#	Pitcher	Tm	Avg	#	Pitcher	Tm	Avg	#	Pitcher	Tm	Avg	#	Pitcher	Tm	Avg
1.	Greg Harris	TEX	.175	34.	Danny Darwin	MIL	.288	67.	Moose Haas	MIL	.318	100.	Jim Clancy	TOR	.353
2.	Jerry Reed	CLE	.194	34.	Danny Jackson	KC	.288	68.	John Butcher	MIN	.318	101.	Stu Cliburn	CAL	.356
3.	Willie Hernandez	DET	.213	36.	Dan Spillner	CHI	.289	69.	Charlie Leibrandt	KC	.319	101.	Mark Langston	SEA	.356
4.	Dave Schmidt	TEX	.228	37.	Joel Davis	CHI	.289	70.	Dave Stieb	TOR	.319	103.	Ron Romanick	CAL	.358
5.	Pete Filson	MIN	.231	38.	Ted Higuera	MIL	.290	71.	Joe Beckwith	KC	.321	104.	Ken Schrom	MIN	.358
6.	Richard Dotson	CHI	.232	39.	Dave Righetti	NY	.293	72.	Bill Scherrer	DET	.323	105.	Jamie Easterly	CLE	.359
7.	Dan Petry	DET	.241	40.	Juan Berenguer	DET	.293	73.	Dickie Noles	TEX	.324	106.	Bill Swift	SEA	.359
8.	Rick Langford	OAK	.254	41.	Doyle Alexander	TOR	.295	74.	Aurelio Lopez	DET	.325	107.	Tom Waddell	CLE	.360
9.	Jay Howell	OAK	.256	42.	Bob McClure	MIL	.295	75.	Kirk McCaskill	CAL	.325	108.	Tommy John	OAK	.362
10.	Gary Lavelle	TOR	.262	43.	Bill Caudill	TOR	.295	76.	Burt Hooton	TEX	.328	109.	Neal Heaton	CLE	.362
11.	Jimmy Key	TOR	.263	44.	Dan Quisenberry	KC	.295	77.	Mike Flanagan	BAL	.330	110.	Tim Birtsas	OAK	.366
12.	Nate Snell	BAL	.264	45.	Chris Welsh	TEX	.297	78.	Bob Shirley	NY	.330	111.	Bob Gibson	MIL	.367
13.	Mike Moore	SEA	.265	46.	Roy Thomas	SEA	.298	79.	Phil Niekro	NY	.332	111.	Tim Lollar	BOS	.367
14.	Storm Davis	BAL	.267	47.	Frank Tanana	DET	.301	80.	Don Aase	BAL	.333	113.	Al Nipper	BOS	.368
15.	Bill James	CHI	.267	48.	Mark Gubicza	KC	.302	80.	Salome Barojas	SEA	.333	114.	Jim Slaton	CAL	.369
16.	Juan Agosto	CHI	.268	49.	Frank Viola	MIN	.302	80.	Ed Vande Berg	SEA	.333	115.	Mike Boddicker	BAL	.370
17.	Rich Bordi	NY	.268	50.	Brian Fisher	NY	.302	83.	Bob Ojeda	BOS	.335	116.	Jim Beattie	SEA	.372
18.	Ray Burris	MIL	.268	51.	Walt Terrell	DET	.303	84.	Matt Young	SEA	.336	117.	Frank Wills	SEA	.377
19.	Britt Burns	CHI	.269	52.	Randy O'Neal	DET	.306	85.	Mike Witt	CAL	.338	118.	Sammy Stewart	BAL	.377
20.	Tom Seaver	CHI	.273	53.	Mike Smithson	MIN	.308	86.	Curt Wardle	CLE	.339	119.	Mike Mason	TEX	.384
21.	Bret Saberhagen	KC	.276	54.	Steve Crawford	BOS	.309	87.	Chris Codiroli	OAK	.340	120.	Rick Thompson	CLE	.385
22.	Charlie Hough	TEX	.277	55.	Roy Smith	CLE	.309	88.	Keith Atherton	OAK	.341	121.	Mike Jones	KC	.393
23.	Ken Dixon	BAL	.277	56.	Luis Sanchez	CAL	.309	89.	Luis Leal	TOR	.342	122.	Jaime Cocanower	MIL	.398
24.	Pat Clements	CAL	.278	57.	Ron Guidry	NY	.309	90.	Floyd Bannister	CHI	.342	123.	Gene Nelson	CHI	.403
25.	Steve Ontiveros	OAK	.279	58.	Bud Black	KC	.312	91.	Roger Clemens	BOS	.343	124.	Bruce Kison	BOS	.404
26.	Don Sutton	CAL	.281	59.	Edwin Nunez	SEA	.312	91.	Dennis Rasmussen	NY	.343	125.	Rick Lysander	MIN	.407
27.	Dennis Lamp	TOR	.281	60.	Keith Creel	CLE	.313	93.	Scott McGregor	BAL	.344	126.	Don Schulze	CLE	.408
28.	Dave Rozema	TEX	.282	61.	John Candelaria	CAL	.315	94.	Urbano Lugo	CAL	.345	127.	Mike Trujillo	BOS	.410
29.	Bert Blyleven	MIN	.283	62.	Jack Morris	DET	.316	94.	Ed Whitson	NY	.345	128.	Dave Stewart	TEX	.410
30.	Bob Stanley	BOS	.284	63.	Joe Cowley	NY	.316	96.	Steve McCatty	OAK	.346	129.	Bill Krueger	OAK	.429
31.	Donnie Moore	CAL	.286	64.	Dennis Martinez	BAL	.316	97.	Pete Vuckovich	MIL	.347	130.	Jeff Russell	TEX	.435
32.	Dennis Boyd	BOS	.286	65.	Bryan Clark	CLE	.317	98.	Ramon Romero	CLE	.348	131.	Jose Rijo	OAK	.448
33.	Vern Ruhle	CLE	.287	65.	Tippy Martinez	BAL	.317	99.	Bruce Hurst	BOS	.351	132.	Jim Acker	TOR	.456

National League

#	Pitcher	Tm	Avg	#	Pitcher	Tm	Avg	#	Pitcher	Tm	Avg	#	Pitcher	Tm	Avg
1.	Tom Niedenfuer	LA	.177	30.	Scott Sanderson	CHI	.282	59.	Dave Smith	HOU	.310	88.	Nolan Ryan	HOU	.351
2.	Rich Gossage	SD	.188	31.	Ken Dayley	STL	.286	60.	Joe Niekro	HOU	.311	89.	Bruce Sutter	ATL	.354
3.	Jeff Reardon	MTL	.192	31.	Gary Lucas	MTL	.286	61.	Joe Price	CIN	.311	90.	Larry Andersen	PHI	.354
4.	John Tudor	STL	.217	33.	Charles Hudson	PHI	.286	61.	Bob Walk	PIT	.311	91.	Jim Winn	PIT	.354
5.	Rick Reuschel	PIT	.236	34.	Cecilio Guante	PIT	.287	63.	Ted Power	CIN	.314	92.	Tim Stoddard	SD	.355
6.	Jeff Calhoun	HOU	.237	35.	Dennis Eckersley	CHI	.289	63.	Doug Sisk	NY	.314	93.	Dave Rucker	PHI	.356
7.	Lary Sorensen	CHI	.238	36.	Ron Darling	NY	.289	65.	Bryn Smith	MTL	.316	94.	Dave LaPoint	SF	.356
8.	Joe Hesketh	MTL	.239	37.	Dave Dravecky	SD	.290	66.	Ricky Horton	STL	.318	95.	Ray Fontenot	CHI	.358
9.	Bobby Castillo	LA	.242	38.	David Palmer	MTL	.290	67.	Rick Honeycutt	LA	.318	96.	Vida Blue	SF	.360
10.	LaMarr Hoyt	SD	.248	39.	Floyd Youmans	MTL	.291	68.	Frank DiPino	HOU	.319	97.	Jerry Koosman	PHI	.362
11.	Gene Garber	ATL	.253	40.	Frank Williams	SF	.292	69.	Scott Garrelts	SF	.320	98.	Bill Gullickson	MTL	.365
12.	Fernando Valenzuela	LA	.257	41.	Randy St. Claire	MTL	.292	70.	Joaquin Andujar	STL	.321	99.	Jose DeLeon	PIT	.369
13.	Don Robinson	PIT	.260	42.	Jerry Reuss	LA	.293	71.	Jay Tibbs	CIN	.322	100.	Bill Dawley	HOU	.372
14.	Sid Fernandez	NY	.261	43.	Jeff Heathcock	HOU	.293	72.	Danny Cox	STL	.323	101.	George Frazier	CHI	.373
15.	Ed Lynch	NY	.263	44.	Roger McDowell	NY	.294	73.	Bill Laskey	MTL	.323	102.	Steve Trout	CHI	.374
16.	Tom Hume	CIN	.263	45.	Shane Rawley	PHI	.295	74.	Mark Davis	SF	.323	103.	Tim Burke	MTL	.380
17.	Mike Scott	HOU	.265	46.	Craig Lefferts	SD	.295	75.	Lee Tunnell	PIT	.326	104.	Dan Schatzeder	MTL	.382
18.	Dwight Gooden	NY	.265	47.	Rick Sutcliffe	CHI	.295	76.	Andy Hawkins	SD	.326	105.	Rick Camp	ATL	.387
19.	Atlee Hammaker	SF	.267	48.	Kevin Gross	PHI	.296	77.	Jim Gott	SF	.327	106.	Rick Rhoden	PIT	.387
20.	Al Holland	PIT	.268	49.	Steve Shields	ATL	.299	78.	Kurt Kepshire	STL	.327	107.	Larry McWilliams	PIT	.389
21.	Bob Forsch	STL	.271	50.	Don Carman	PHI	.299	79.	Jesse Orosco	NY	.328	108.	Jeff Dedmon	ATL	.390
22.	Rick Aguilera	NY	.272	51.	Ron Robinson	CIN	.299	80.	Steve Bedrosian	ATL	.336	109.	Zane Smith	ATL	.392
23.	Bill Campbell	STL	.276	52.	Kent Tekulve	PHI	.300	81.	Bob Knepper	HOU	.337	110.	Pascual Perez	ATL	.394
24.	Orel Hershiser	LA	.276	52.	Mark Thurmond	SD	.300	82.	John Denny	PHI	.342	111.	Greg Minton	SF	.395
25.	Bob Welch	LA	.276	54.	Rick Mahler	ATL	.301	82.	Ken Howell	LA	.342	112.	Ron Mathis	HOU	.411
26.	Bert Roberge	MTL	.277	55.	Eric Show	SD	.303	82.	Lee Smith	CHI	.342	113.	Steve Carlton	PHI	.421
27.	Warren Brusstar	CHI	.278	56.	Joe Johnson	ATL	.307	85.	Terry Leach	NY	.345	114.	John Stuper	CIN	.422
28.	Tom Browning	CIN	.280	57.	Mario Soto	CIN	.308	86.	John Franco	CIN	.347	115.	Len Barker	ATL	.429
29.	Carlos Diaz	LA	.282	58.	Mike Krukow	SF	.308	86.	Andy McGaffigan	CIN	.347	116.	Dick Ruthven	CHI	.446

Opponents' Batting Average with Runners in Scoring Position

American League

1. Joe Cowley	NY	.148	35. Ray Burris	MIL	.243	69. Doyle Alexander	TOR	.268	103. Curt Wardle	CLE	.303
2. Gary Lavelle	TOR	.153	36. Ron Guidry	NY	.243	70. Mike Flanagan	BAL	.269	104. Jeff Russell	TEX	.304
3. Roger Clemens	BOS	.167	37. Dennis Lamp	TOR	.243	71. Tom Waddell	CLE	.270	105. Dave Rozema	TEX	.306
4. Keith Atherton	OAK	.181	38. Mark Langston	SEA	.244	72. Rich Bordi	NY	.270	105. Bob Stanley	BOS	.306
5. Greg Harris	TEX	.191	39. Frank Tanana	DET	.246	73. Sammy Stewart	BAL	.270	105. Mike Trujillo	BOS	.306
6. Keith Creel	CLE	.197	40. Danny Jackson	KC	.246	74. Bill Swift	SEA	.270	108. Don Aase	BAL	.308
7. Urbano Lugo	CAL	.197	40. Mike Warren	OAK	.246	75. Bob Gibson	MIL	.272	108. Moose Haas	MIL	.308
8. Dave Stieb	TOR	.199	42. Ken Dixon	BAL	.246	76. Jim Clancy	TOR	.273	110. Tommy John	OAK	.309
9. Pete Filson	MIN	.202	43. Jose Rijo	OAK	.247	76. Jim Jones	KC	.273	111. Steve Crawford	BOS	.311
10. Tim Lollar	BOS	.203	44. Bert Blyleven	MIN	.247	76. Edwin Nunez	SEA	.273	112. Aurelio Lopez	DET	.312
11. Britt Burns	CHI	.205	45. Phil Niekro	NY	.247	79. Ken Schrom	MIN	.275	113. Dennis Rasmussen	NY	.315
12. Bob Shirley	NY	.205	46. Stu Cliburn	CAL	.248	80. Dan Petry	DET	.276	114. Steve McCatty	OAK	.320
13. Gene Nelson	CHI	.207	47. Ed Vande Berg	SEA	.250	81. Mark Gubicza	KC	.277	115. Frank Viola	MIN	.323
14. Jimmy Key	TOR	.208	48. Danny Darwin	MIL	.251	82. Burt Hooton	TEX	.277	116. Matt Young	SEA	.325
15. Bruce Kison	BOS	.209	49. Joe Beckwith	KC	.252	83. Mike Mason	TEX	.278	117. Vern Ruhle	CLE	.327
16. Tim Birtsas	OAK	.216	49. Bob James	CHI	.252	84. Willie Hernandez	DET	.279	118. Doug Bair	DET	.328
17. Charlie Hough	TEX	.217	51. Dennis Boyd	BOS	.252	84. Bob McClure	MIL	.279	118. Ray Searage	MIL	.328
18. Tom Seaver	CHI	.219	52. Neal Heaton	CLE	.254	86. Frank Eufemia	MIN	.279	120. Storm Davis	BAL	.329
19. Donnie Moore	CAL	.219	53. Bruce Hurst	BOS	.254	86. Ramon Romero	CLE	.279	121. John Butcher	MIN	.330
20. Dan Quisenberry	KC	.223	54. Kirk McCaskill	CAL	.255	88. Bob Ojeda	BOS	.283	122. Don Schulze	CLE	.330
21. Charlie Leibrandt	KC	.223	55. Dave Righetti	NY	.256	89. Mike Smithson	MIN	.284	123. Rick Thompson	CLE	.336
22. Dave Schmidt	TEX	.224	56. Ron Romanick	CAL	.257	90. Pete Ladd	MIL	.286	124. Rick Lysander	MIN	.338
23. Jaime Cocanower	MIL	.226	57. Jim Acker	TOR	.259	91. Scott McGregor	BAL	.287	125. Rick Waits	MIL	.344
24. Bret Saberhagen	KC	.227	58. Jim Slaton	CAL	.260	92. Dennis Martinez	BAL	.287	126. Juan Berenguer	DET	.345
25. Dave Stewart	TEX	.228	59. Don Sutton	CAL	.260	93. Randy O'Neal	DET	.288	127. Ed Whitson	NY	.345
26. Ron Davis	MIN	.229	60. Frank Wills	SEA	.261	94. Chris Codiroli	OAK	.290	128. Mike Stanton	CHI	.350
27. Bill Caudill	TOR	.233	61. Ted Higuera	MIL	.262	95. Bud Black	KC	.291	129. Luis Sanchez	CAL	.354
28. Mark Clear	BOS	.233	62. Al Nipper	BOS	.264	96. Chris Welsh	TEX	.292	130. Dickie Noles	TEX	.358
29. Bill Scherrer	DET	.234	63. Walt Terrell	DET	.264	97. Tippy Martinez	BAL	.296	131. Bryan Clark	CLE	.375
30. Mike Boddicker	BAL	.237	64. Salome Barojas	SEA	.265	97. Pete Vuckovich	MIL	.296	131. Mike LaCoss	KC	.375
31. Floyd Bannister	CHI	.239	64. Jamie Easterly	CLE	.265	99. Bill Krueger	OAK	.297	133. Jim Beattie	SEA	.415
31. Jack Morris	DET	.239	66. Mike Moore	SEA	.265	100. Nate Snell	BAL	.301			
33. Brian Fisher	NY	.240	67. Jay Howell	OAK	.265	101. Dan Spillner	CHI	.301			
34. Mike Witt	CAL	.241	68. Roy Thomas	SEA	.266	102. Roy Smith	CLE	.302			

National League

1. Dwight Gooden	NY	.144	30. Jerry Reuss	LA	.225	59. Bryn Smith	MTL	.258	88. Don Robinson	PIT	.286
2. Tim Burke	MTL	.147	31. Dennis Eckersley	CHI	.226	60. Bert Roberge	MTL	.260	89. Jeff Dedmon	ATL	.287
3. Floyd Youmans	MTL	.158	32. Joe Hesketh	MTL	.226	61. Jim Winn	PIT	.260	90. Frank DiPino	HOU	.288
4. Jeff Lahti	STL	.163	33. Fernando Valenzuela	LA	.228	62. Rick Aguilera	NY	.262	91. Jay Tibbs	CIN	.288
5. Lee Smith	CHI	.174	34. Ted Power	CIN	.228	63. Andy McGaffigan	CIN	.264	92. Bill Dawley	HOU	.289
6. Bob Welch	LA	.180	34. Dan Schatzeder	MTL	.228	64. Steve Trout	CHI	.265	93. Bobby Castillo	LA	.289
7. Mario Soto	CIN	.181	36. Charles Hudson	PHI	.230	65. Bill Gullickson	MTL	.266	93. Tim Stoddard	SD	.289
8. Jesse Orosco	NY	.186	37. Dave LaPoint	SF	.230	66. Al Holland	PIT	.267	95. Vida Blue	SF	.290
9. Ron Darling	NY	.194	38. Joe Niekro	HOU	.230	66. Jon Johnson	ATL	.267	96. Bruce Sutter	ATL	.290
10. Rick Sutcliffe	CHI	.195	39. Nolan Ryan	HOU	.233	68. Bob Knepper	HOU	.268	97. Ricky Horton	STL	.292
11. Mike Krukow	SF	.196	40. Kent Tekulve	PHI	.235	69. Tom Browning	CIN	.269	98. George Frazier	CHI	.293
12. Sid Fernandez	NY	.198	41. Steve Bedrosian	ATL	.235	70. Atlee Hammaker	SF	.270	99. LaMarr Hoyt	SD	.295
13. Scott Garrelts	SF	.200	42. John Candelaria	PIT	.235	71. Jeff Calhoun	HOU	.270	100. Craig McMurtry	ATL	.302
13. Cecilio Guante	PIT	.200	43. Dick Ruthven	CHI	.236	72. Rick Camp	ATL	.270	101. Mark Thurmond	SD	.306
15. Shane Rawley	PHI	.201	44. Tom Niedenfuer	LA	.237	73. Mark Davis	SF	.271	102. Rick Rhoden	PIT	.306
16. Carlos Diaz	LA	.203	45. Jerry Koosman	PHI	.238	74. Dave Rucker	PHI	.272	103. Ray Fontenot	CHI	.307
17. Eric Show	SD	.206	46. Zane Smith	ATL	.241	75. Joaquin Andujar	STL	.272	104. Ron Mathis	HOU	.309
18. Dave Smith	HOU	.209	47. John Franco	CIN	.244	76. Ken Dayley	STL	.273	105. Craig Lefferts	SD	.310
19. Scott Sanderson	CHI	.212	48. Roger McDowell	NY	.245	77. Jeff Reardon	MTL	.276	106. Lary Sorensen	CHI	.313
20. Orel Hershiser	LA	.214	49. Larry Andersen	PHI	.247	78. Frank Williams	SF	.277	107. Bob Forsch	STL	.317
21. Don Carman	PHI	.214	49. Kevin Gross	PHI	.247	79. Randy St. Claire	MTL	.278	108. Rick Honeycutt	LA	.318
22. Ed Lynch	NY	.216	51. Dave Dravecky	SD	.250	80. Gene Garber	ATL	.278	109. Warren Brusstar	CHI	.323
23. Bill Campbell	STL	.220	52. David Palmer	MTL	.252	81. Larry McWilliams	PIT	.280	110. Bill Laskey	MTL	.327
24. Danny Cox	STL	.222	53. Pascual Perez	ATL	.252	81. Greg Minton	SF	.280	111. Len Barker	ATL	.329
25. Steve Carlton	PHI	.222	54. Rick Mahler	ATL	.252	83. Ken Howell	LA	.280	112. Kurt Kepshire	STL	.345
25. Andy Hawkins	SD	.222	55. Jose DeLeon	PIT	.253	84. Joe Price	CIN	.281	113. Doug Sisk	NY	.349
25. Rick Reuschel	PIT	.222	56. John Denny	PHI	.253	85. Gary Lucas	MTL	.281	114. John Stuper	CIN	.374
28. John Tudor	STL	.224	57. Jim Gott	SF	.255	86. Ron Robinson	CIN	.282	115. Steve Shields	ATL	.413
29. Tom Hume	CIN	.225	58. Mike Scott	HOU	.256	87. Lee Tunnell	PIT	.282			

Opponents' Batting Average in Pressure Situations

American League

1. Ken Schrom	MIN	.105	34. Aurelio Lopez	DET	.229	67. Dwayne Henry	TEX	.264	100. Ken Dixon	BAL	.295
2. Dan Petry	DET	.132	35. Bob James	CHI	.229	68. Tom Waddell	CLE	.264	100. Walt Terrell	DET	.295
3. Robert Long	SEA	.150	36. Gary Lavelle	TOR	.229	69. Ted Higuera	MIL	.265	102. Danny Jackson	KC	.298
4. Roy Thomas	SEA	.154	37. Chris Codiroli	OAK	.229	69. Mike LaCoss	KC	.265	103. Don Sutton	CAL	.302
5. Steve Ontiveros	OAK	.159	38. Edwin Nunez	SEA	.231	71. Frank Tanana	DET	.266	104. Steve Crawford	BOS	.302
6. Britt Burns	CHI	.171	39. Jack Morris	DET	.232	72. Bob Ojeda	BOS	.267	105. Joe Beckwith	KC	.303
7. Juan Agosto	CHI	.172	40. Frank Eufemia	MIN	.234	72. Jose Rijo	OAK	.267	106. Steve McCatty	OAK	.303
7. Doug Bair	DET	.172	41. Tippy Martinez	BAL	.235	74. Ron Guidry	NY	.269	107. Doug Corbett	CAL	.304
9. Karl Best	SEA	.178	42. Charlie Hough	TEX	.235	75. Vern Ruhle	CLE	.270	108. Scott McGregor	BAL	.306
10. Bert Blyleven	MIN	.188	43. Bret Saberhagen	KC	.236	76. Mike Mason	TEX	.270	109. Dave Wehrmeister	CHI	.306
11. Dennis Lamp	TOR	.191	44. Jaime Cocanower	MIL	.238	77. Sammy Stewart	BAL	.271	110. Moose Haas	MIL	.309
12. Bruce Kison	BOS	.200	45. Mike Jones	KC	.241	78. Steve Howe	MIN	.273	111. Jim Acker	TOR	.310
13. Mike Witt	CAL	.204	46. Keith Atherton	OAK	.242	78. Dave Stieb	TOR	.273	112. Joel Davis	CHI	.313
14. Frank Viola	MIN	.204	47. Jerry Gleaton	CHI	.243	80. Danny Darwin	MIL	.276	112. Ron Musselman	TOR	.313
15. Jim Slaton	CAL	.206	47. Don Schulze	CLE	.243	81. Dan Quisenberry	KC	.277	114. Neal Heaton	CLE	.315
16. Tom Henke	TOR	.206	49. Don Aase	BAL	.244	82. Ed Vande Berg	SEA	.277	115. Rick Thompson	CLE	.319
17. Bob Stanley	BOS	.206	50. Ray Burris	MIL	.246	83. Bill Scherrer	DET	.278	116. Steve Farr	KC	.325
18. Willie Hernandez	DET	.207	51. Pete Filson	MIN	.247	83. Dave Stewart	TEX	.278	117. Dave Rozema	TEX	.326
19. Luis Sanchez	CAL	.209	52. Mike Boddicker	BAL	.247	85. Bob McClure	MIL	.279	118. Jeff Barkley	CLE	.333
20. Ron Davis	MIN	.211	53. John Butcher	MIN	.248	86. Dennis Rasmussen	NY	.281	118. Kirk McCaskill	CAL	.333
20. Storm Davis	BAL	.211	54. Juan Berenguer	DET	.250	86. Matt Young	SEA	.281	120. Doyle Alexander	TOR	.336
22. Brian Fisher	NY	.213	54. Bill Caudill	TOR	.250	88. Jerry Reed	CLE	.282	121. Rich Bordi	NY	.340
23. Jimmy Key	TOR	.214	54. Al Nipper	BOS	.250	89. Mike Stanton	CHI	.283	122. Mike Trujillo	BOS	.341
24. Greg Harris	TEX	.218	54. Dave Righetti	NY	.250	90. Mike Flanagan	BAL	.286	122. Frank Wills	SEA	.341
25. Stu Cliburn	CAL	.222	58. Tom Seaver	CHI	.252	90. Mark Gubicza	KC	.286	124. Tim Lollar	BOS	.342
25. Bob Gibson	MIL	.222	59. Jamie Easterly	CLE	.253	90. Charlie Leibrandt	KC	.286	125. Rick Lysander	MIN	.344
25. Dickie Noles	TEX	.222	60. Bud Black	KC	.253	93. Mike Smithson	MIN	.288	126. Dennis Boyd	BOS	.345
25. Bill Swift	SEA	.222	61. Donnie Moore	CAL	.255	94. Rollie Fingers	MIL	.288	127. Floyd Bannister	CHI	.348
29. Mike Moore	SEA	.223	62. Gene Nelson	CHI	.256	95. Dennis Martinez	BAL	.288	128. Ray Searage	MIL	.350
30. Joe Cowley	NY	.224	63. Jay Howell	OAK	.258	96. Pete Ladd	MIL	.290	129. Bruce Hurst	BOS	.370
31. Dave Schmidt	TEX	.225	64. Ron Romanick	CAL	.259	97. Curt Wardle	CLE	.291	130. Dan Spillner	CHI	.371
32. Pat Clements	CAL	.226	65. Bryan Clark	CLE	.262	98. Phil Niekro	NY	.293	131. Dave Von Ohlen	CLE	.500
33. Bob Shirley	NY	.227	66. Nate Snell	BAL	.262	99. Mark Clear	BOS	.294			

National League

1. Rick Aguilera	NY	.103	30. Jesse Orosco	NY	.220	59. Jeff Lahti	STL	.247	88. Larry McWilliams	PIT	.290
2. Mike Scott	HOU	.108	31. Ken Howell	LA	.221	60. Randy St. Claire	MTL	.247	89. Dennis Eckersley	CHI	.293
3. Zane Smith	ATL	.130	32. Lance McCullers	SD	.221	61. Charles Hudson	PHI	.248	90. Al Holland	PIT	.295
4. Jack O'Connor	MTL	.135	33. John Franco	CIN	.222	62. John Denny	PHI	.250	91. Jay Tibbs	CIN	.296
5. Scott Sanderson	CHI	.136	34. Dave Shipanoff	PHI	.222	62. Bill Gullickson	MTL	.250	92. Dave Dravecky	SD	.297
6. Bryn Smith	MTL	.154	35. Eric Show	SD	.224	62. Mark Thurmond	SD	.250	93. Larry Andersen	PHI	.299
7. Don Carman	PHI	.157	36. Bert Roberge	MTL	.224	65. Craig Lefferts	SD	.252	94. Andy Hawkins	SD	.300
8. Gene Walter	SD	.161	37. Tom Browning	CIN	.225	66. Ted Power	CIN	.252	94. Doug Sisk	NY	.300
9. Mike Krukow	SF	.163	38. Todd Worrell	STL	.226	67. Rick Reuschel	PIT	.255	96. Gary Lucas	MTL	.303
10. Fernando Valenzuela	LA	.167	39. Tom Hume	CIN	.227	68. Roy Jackson	SD	.255	97. Frank DiPino	HOU	.305
11. Orel Hershiser	LA	.174	40. Jay Baller	CHI	.228	69. Ricky Horton	STL	.258	98. Lary Sorensen	CHI	.306
12. Sid Fernandez	NY	.182	41. Dave Smith	HOU	.230	70. Jeff Dedmon	ATL	.260	99. Ron Meridith	CHI	.306
13. Mark Davis	SF	.190	42. Dwight Gooden	NY	.232	71. Jeff Calhoun	HOU	.265	100. Danny Cox	STL	.306
14. Tim Burke	MTL	.193	43. John Candelaria	PIT	.233	72. Greg Minton	SF	.271	101. Dave LaPoint	SF	.309
15. Bill Laskey	MTL	.194	44. Carlos Diaz	LA	.234	73. Shane Rawley	PHI	.271	102. Bob Knepper	HOU	.309
16. Scott Garrelts	SF	.197	45. Rick Sutcliffe	CHI	.234	74. Dan Schatzeder	MTL	.273	103. George Frazier	CHI	.315
17. Ron Robinson	CIN	.200	46. Nolan Ryan	HOU	.236	74. Floyd Youmans	MTL	.273	104. Joe Hesketh	MTL	.318
18. Frank Williams	SF	.200	47. John Tudor	STL	.236	76. Kent Tekulve	PHI	.277	104. Jim Winn	PIT	.318
19. Lee Tunnell	PIT	.205	48. Rick Mahler	ATL	.238	77. Ed Lynch	NY	.278	106. Ron Mathis	HOU	.323
20. Atlee Hammaker	SF	.206	49. Don Robinson	PIT	.239	77. Jerry Reuss	LA	.278	107. Jose DeLeon	PIT	.324
21. Rich Gossage	SD	.206	50. Greg Booker	SD	.240	79. Ron Darling	NY	.278	108. Pat Clements	PIT	.324
22. LaMarr Hoyt	SD	.208	51. Bill Dawley	HOU	.241	80. Dave Rucker	PHI	.279	109. Kurt Kepshire	STL	.341
23. Joaquin Andujar	STL	.209	52. Mario Soto	CIN	.243	81. Gene Garber	ATL	.280	110. Rick Rhoden	PIT	.343
24. Rod Scurry	PIT	.210	53. Terry Forster	ATL	.244	82. Bruce Sutter	ATL	.280	111. Ray Fontenot	CHI	.346
25. Roger McDowell	NY	.212	54. Steve Howe	LA	.244	83. Joe Niekro	HOU	.280	112. Jim Gott	SF	.357
26. Jeff Reardon	MTL	.212	55. Tom Niedenfuer	LA	.245	84. Kevin Gross	PHI	.282	113. Tim Stoddard	SD	.372
27. Cecilio Guante	PIT	.214	56. Neil Allen	STL	.245	85. Warren Brusstar	CHI	.283	114. Luis DeLeon	SD	.378
28. Bill Campbell	STL	.217	57. Lee Smith	CHI	.246	86. Rick Camp	ATL	.284	115. Steve Trout	CHI	.400
29. Bob Welch	LA	.220	58. Tom Gorman	NY	.247	87. Ken Dayley	STL	.287	116. Steve Bedrosian	ATL	.414

Strikeout Percentage in Pressure Situations

American League

1. Karl Best SEA 28.26	34. Mike Witt CAL 16.42	67. Danny Darwin MIL 12.73	99. Jimmy Key TOR 9.76
2. Tom Henke TOR 27.88	35. Bruce Kison BOS 16.33	68. Tom Waddell CLE 12.69	101. Scott McGregor BAL 9.64
3. Brian Fisher NY 24.28	36. Ed Vande Berg SEA 16.19	69. Jerry Reed CLE 12.64	102. Bryan Clark CLE 9.62
4. Ron Davis MIN 24.16	37. Nate Snell BAL 16.18	70. Tippy Martinez BAL 12.50	103. Chris Codiroli OAK 9.47
5. Greg Harris TEX 23.96	38. Donnie Moore CAL 16.10	70. Bill Scherrer DET 12.50	104. Rollie Fingers MIL 9.26
6. Roy Thomas SEA 23.38	39. Mark Gubicza KC 16.07	72. Bud Black KC 12.36	105. Pete Filson MIN 9.21
7. Curt Wardle CLE 22.34	40. Bill Caudill TOR 15.92	73. Mike Stanton CHI 12.28	105. Dan Spillner CHI 9.21
8. Britt Burns CHI 21.84	41. Gary Lavelle TOR 15.87	74. Walt Terrell DET 12.26	107. Pete Ladd MIL 9.09
9. Mike LaCoss KC 21.82	42. Joe Cowley NY 15.79	75. Jaime Cocanower MIL 12.24	108. Mike Trujillo BOS 8.89
10. Robert Long SEA 21.74	43. Dave Schmidt TEX 15.27	76. Doyle Alexander TOR 12.12	109. Ron Musselman TOR 8.57
11. Joe Beckwith KC 20.81	44. Frank Viola MIN 15.25	77. Rich Bordi NY 11.90	110. Dennis Boyd BOS 8.54
12. Dave Righetti NY 20.66	45. Bert Blyleven MIN 15.09	78. Edwin Nunez SEA 11.86	111. Mike Flanagan BAL 8.33
13. Doug Bair DET 20.59	46. Juan Berenguer DET 15.00	79. Al Nipper BOS 11.84	111. Rick Lysander MIN 8.33
14. Dave Wehrmeister CHI 20.37	47. Bob Gibson MIL 14.91	80. Frank Eufemia MIN 11.76	113. Mike Smithson MIN 8.14
15. Ray Searage MIL 20.21	48. Bob McClure MIL 14.86	80. Tim Lollar BOS 11.76	113. Dave Stewart TEX 8.14
16. Dwayne Henry TEX 20.00	49. Don Aase BAL 14.75	80. Phil Niekro NY 11.76	115. Dave Rozema TEX 8.00
16. Jose Rijo OAK 20.00	50. Jerry Gleaton CHI 14.63	80. Dickie Noles TEX 11.76	116. Don Schulze CLE 7.50
18. Gene Nelson CHI 19.81	51. Ken Schrom MIN 14.29	84. Bob Ojeda BOS 11.71	117. Jim Slaton CAL 7.32
19. Luis Sanchez CAL 19.15	52. Jamie Easterly CLE 14.14	85. Juan Agosto CHI 11.65	118. Kirk McCaskill CAL 7.14
20. Bob James CHI 18.82	53. Ted Higuera MIL 14.10	85. Danny Jackson KC 11.65	118. Steve McCatty OAK 7.14
21. Keith Atherton OAK 18.78	54. Storm Davis BAL 13.95	87. Dennis Rasmussen NY 11.43	120. Neal Heaton CLE 6.98
22. Steve Farr KC 18.75	54. Sammy Stewart BAL 13.95	88. John Butcher MIN 11.21	121. Jim Acker TOR 6.96
23. Joel Davis CHI 18.42	56. Jack Morris DET 13.87	88. Stu Cliburn CAL 11.21	122. Moose Haas MIL 6.90
23. Bret Saberhagen KC 18.42	57. Mike Boddicker BAL 13.79	90. Dennis Martinez BAL 10.94	123. Ron Romanick CAL 6.45
25. Floyd Bannister CHI 17.50	58. Bob Stanley BOS 13.71	91. Matt Young SEA 10.91	124. Jeff Barkley CLE 6.38
26. Dennis Lamp TOR 17.07	59. Bruce Hurst BOS 13.64	92. Bob Shirley NY 10.78	125. Rick Thompson CLE 6.34
27. Willie Hernandez DET 16.86	60. Charlie Leibrandt KC 13.46	93. Dan Quisenberry KC 10.53	126. Mike Jones KC 6.06
28. Mike Moore SEA 16.80	61. Ray Burris MIL 13.43	94. Mike Mason TEX 10.42	127. Don Sutton CAL 5.97
29. Aurelio Lopez DET 16.77	62. Dave Stieb TOR 13.33	95. Dan Petry DET 10.37	128. Bill Swift SEA 5.77
30. Charlie Hough TEX 16.67	63. Steve Ontiveros OAK 13.14	96. Frank Wills SEA 10.00	129. Vern Ruhle CLE 5.63
31. Steve Crawford BOS 16.56	64. Mark Clear BOS 12.99	97. Pat Clements CAL 9.90	130. Steve Howe MIN 5.56
32. Jay Howell OAK 16.46	65. Ron Guidry NY 12.96	98. Ken Dixon BAL 9.80	131. Dave Von Ohlen CLE 2.78
33. Frank Tanana DET 16.44	66. Tom Seaver CHI 12.77	99. Doug Corbett CAL 9.76	

National League

1. Jack O'Connor MTL 31.82	30. Cecilio Guante PIT 17.32	58. Dave LaPoint SF 14.29	88. Dave Dravecky SD 9.46
2. Lee Smith CHI 29.87	31. Larry Andersen PHI 17.28	58. Bryn Smith MTL 14.29	89. Jeff Dedmon ATL 9.30
3. Don Carman PHI 29.39	32. Ron Meridith CHI 17.24	58. Mario Soto CIN 14.29	90. Greg Minton SF 9.09
4. Mark Davis SF 28.83	33. Jeff Calhoun HOU 17.16	62. Frank DiPino HOU 14.10	91. Jay Tibbs CIN 8.96
5. Sid Fernandez NY 27.08	34. Rich Gossage SD 17.00	63. Ron Robinson CIN 13.79	92. George Frazier CHI 8.75
6. Gene Walter SD 25.71	35. Todd Worrell STL 16.95	64. Terry Forster ATL 13.74	93. Jerry Reuss LA 8.47
7. Tom Niedenfuer LA 24.63	36. Scott Sanderson CHI 16.67	65. Luis DeLeon SD 13.46	94. Lary Sorensen CHI 8.24
8. Ken Dayley STL 24.59	36. Rick Sutcliffe CHI 16.67	66. Zane Smith ATL 13.43	95. Ron Mathis HOU 8.11
9. Dwight Gooden NY 24.40	38. Tom Hume CIN 16.44	67. Dave Rucker PHI 13.33	96. Jim Winn PIT 7.84
10. Carlos Diaz LA 23.53	39. Shane Rawley PHI 16.42	68. Craig Lefferts SD 13.22	97. Atlee Hammaker SF 7.69
11. Scott Garrelts SF 23.47	40. Don Robinson PIT 16.35	69. Dave Shipanoff PHI 12.73	97. Bob Welch LA 7.69
12. Rod Scurry PIT 23.19	41. Tim Burke MTL 16.10	70. Tom Gorman NY 12.66	99. Rick Mahler ATL 7.45
13. Ken Howell LA 22.98	42. Bert Roberge MTL 15.74	71. Joe Niekro HOU 12.64	100. Doug Sisk NY 7.24
14. John Candelaria PIT 22.89	43. Dennis Eckersley CHI 15.63	72. Dave Smith HOU 12.61	101. Tim Stoddard SD 7.07
15. Jesse Orosco NY 22.27	44. Rick Reuschel PIT 15.52	73. Steve Trout CHI 12.50	102. Pat Clements PIT 7.06
16. Nolan Ryan HOU 21.90	45. Bill Campbell STL 15.49	74. Ron Darling NY 12.41	103. LaMarr Hoyt SD 7.00
17. Jay Baller CHI 21.54	46. John Franco CIN 15.34	75. Mike Scott HOU 12.33	104. Joaquin Andujar STL 6.72
18. Roy Jackson SD 21.43	47. Al Holland PIT 15.25	76. Charles Hudson PHI 11.76	105. Randy St. Claire MTL 6.12
19. Jose DeLeon PIT 20.99	48. Kevin Gross PHI 14.89	77. Tom Browning CIN 11.69	106. Steve Bedrosian ATL 6.06
20. Lee Tunnell PIT 20.45	49. John Tudor STL 14.66	78. Roger McDowell NY 11.68	107. Jim Gott SF 5.88
21. Lance McCullers SD 20.37	50. Steve Howe LA 14.58	79. Bruce Sutter ATL 11.38	108. Neil Allen STL 5.63
22. Frank Williams SF 20.16	50. Kurt Kepshire STL 14.58	80. Gary Lucas MTL 11.29	109. Ray Fontenot CHI 5.62
23. Joe Hesketh MTL 19.23	52. Gene Garber ATL 14.57	81. Rick Camp ATL 11.11	110. Bill Gullickson MTL 5.45
24. Orel Hershiser LA 18.56	53. Ricky Horton STL 14.49	82. Ted Power CIN 11.07	111. Dan Schatzeder MTL 5.41
25. Jeff Reardon MTL 18.49	54. John Denny PHI 14.49	83. Bob Knepper HOU 10.96	112. Larry McWilliams PIT 5.26
26. Rick Aguilera NY 18.18	55. Fernando Valenzuela LA 14.47	84. Eric Show SD 10.64	113. Ed Lynch NY 5.13
27. Rick Rhoden PIT 18.07	56. Bill Dawley HOU 14.39	85. Warren Brusstar CHI 10.09	114. Bill Laskey MTL 2.78
28. Floyd Youmans MTL 17.50	57. Jeff Lahti STL 14.37	86. Danny Cox STL 9.86	115. Andy Hawkins SD 1.05
29. Mark Thurmond SD 17.39	58. Mike Krukow SF 14.29	86. Kent Tekulve PHI 9.86	116. Greg Booker SD 0.00

VI
Single Season and Career Leaders

Single Season and Career Leaders

The Single Season and Career Leaders section lists, for a variety of batting and pitching categories, the top 25 performers since we began *The Player Analysis* in 1975.

When we began our analysis of play-by-play data from every game, we had a dual purpose: we recognized the value of the information for immediate use, and we knew we were accumulating and building a valuable resource for future study as well. This section gives us a chance to take stock of the results from our unparalleled files—files representing more than a million and a half plate appearances.

The leader categories for this section were chosen both for significance and for general interest (however quirky). The single season bests listed here provide an important context for evaluating the performances throughout this book. The career lists do considerably more; they combine eleven years' worth of statistics, and provide the definitive look at situational statistics since 1975.

Minimum qualifiers for most batting categories are expressed in hits rather than in the equivalent number of plate appearances. As a general rule, the number of hits is one third the number of at bats of the qualifying range, if you're more comfortable thinking about it in those terms.

In dealing with last season's statistics in the Ranking Section of this book, we used a more inclusive level for rankings qualification: the equivalent of 200 plate appearances. The levels used here are more stringent, corresponding more to everyday play than part-time or "semiregular" status.

In the pitching categories, it should not be too surprising that relievers dominate. They allow consistently lower batting averages than starters for a variety of reasons, not only in traditional statistics but in these situational statistics as well. We have tried to set qualifying levels that are meaningful for both starters and relievers; the levels are the equivalent of about one and a half seasons as a full-time starter, or three as a primary reliever.

Bear in mind that *The Player Analysis* began in 1975. For the vast majority of active players, this poses no obstacle to calling these "career" statistics. In some cases, the missing information is very minor (67 at bats out of Jim Rice's career; a little under 500 from George Brett's); in the case of a Pete Rose or Tony Perez, obviously, a larger chunk is missing. We'd love to be able to fill in the gaps; we'd also love to know how Lou Gehrig hit with runners in scoring position in late-inning pressure. Maybe someday . . .

CAREER BATTING AVERAGE VS. LEFT-HANDED PITCHERS

Min. 150 Hits

Keith Moreland	.320
Bob Watson	.318
Rickey Henderson	.317
Paul Molitor	.316
Jim Rice	.316
Buddy Bell	.314
Lee Lacy	.311
Rod Carew	.310
Julio Franco	.310
Bill Madlock	.309
Ron LeFlore	.309
Hal McRae	.307
Ellis Valentine	.307
John Castino	.307
Carney Lansford	.306
Gary Matthews	.305
Steve Henderson	.305
Willie Wilson	.305
Jack Clark	.304
Wayne Nordhagen	.304
Dave Cash	.304
Lou Piniella	.303
Gary Ward	.303
Dwight Evans	.303
Brett Butler	.303

CAREER SLUGGING AVERAGE VS. LEFT-HANDED PITCHERS

Min. 200 Total Bases

Mike Schmidt	.570
Ellis Valentine	.562
Jim Rice	.539
Jack Clark	.539
George Foster	.538
Dwight Evans	.533
Johnny Bench	.531
Dave Winfield	.529
Lance Parrish	.526
Ron Cey	.522
Dale Murphy	.521
Dave Kingman	.520
Gary Carter	.518
Hal McRae	.515
Cliff Johnson	.514
Bill Robinson	.513
Don Mattingly	.512
Tom Brunansky	.512
Pedro Guerrero	.512
Bob Horner	.510
Eric Soderholm	.509
Gary Ward	.506
Mike Ivie	.505
Richie Zisk	.505
Bob Watson	.504

CAREER HOME RUN PCT. VS. LEFT-HANDED PITCHERS

Min. 20 Home Runs

Dave Kingman	7.53
Mike Schmidt	6.93
Ron Kittle	6.86
Ron Cey	6.73
Gorman Thomas	6.19
Tom Brunansky	6.10
Ellis Valentine	6.07
Johnny Bench	6.03
Bob Horner	6.01
George Foster	5.95
Lance Parrish	5.95
Gene Tenace	5.90
John Wockenfuss	5.85
Dale Murphy	5.69
Cliff Johnson	5.43
Dave Winfield	5.36
Jim Rice	5.33
Pedro Guerrero	5.32
Greg Luzinski	5.25
Eric Soderholm	5.25
Gary Roenicke	5.23
Gary Carter	5.22
Jack Clark	5.21
Otto Velez	5.18
Larry Hisle	5.10

CAREER STRIKEOUT PCT. VS. LEFT-HANDED PITCHERS

Min. 500 PA

Ted Sizemore	2.90
Dave Cash	3.05
Tim Foli	3.08
Bob Bailor	3.41
Manny Sanguillen	3.48
Felix Millan	3.49
Doug Flynn	4.69
Rennie Stennett	4.72
Rich Dauer	4.96
Pete Rose	5.06
Bob Boone	5.08
Mickey Hatcher	5.08
Bucky Dent	5.09
Don Kessinger	5.30
Bruce Benedict	5.39
Mario Guerrero	5.46
Rob Andrews	5.48
Bill Russell	5.48
Jerry Terrell	5.54
Steve Nicosia	5.71
Willie Randolph	5.72
Bill Buckner	5.81
Eric Soderholm	6.03
Jim Essian	6.13
Alan Wiggins	6.16

CAREER BATTING AVERAGE VS. RIGHT-HANDED PITCHERS

Min. 250 Hits

Wade Boggs	.373
Rod Carew	.341
Tony Gwynn	.338
Don Mattingly	.337
George Brett	.334
Al Oliver	.326
Lyman Bostock	.325
Cecil Cooper	.313
Willie McGee	.312
Dave Parker	.311
Jose Cruz	.311
Pedro Guerrero	.309
Fred Lynn	.308
Bill Madlock	.307
Thurman Munson	.306
Bake McBride	.306
Ken Griffey	.305
Mike Easler	.305
Mickey Rivers	.305
Keith Hernandez	.304
Wally Backman	.304
Tim Raines	.303
Steve Garvey	.302
Terry Puhl	.301
Jerry Mumphrey	.301

CAREER SLUGGING AVERAGE VS. RIGHT-HANDED PITCHERS

Min. 300 Total Bases

George Brett	.554
Darryl Strawberry	.545
Reggie Smith	.539
Mike Schmidt	.538
Fred Lynn	.533
Willie Stargell	.532
Don Mattingly	.530
Greg Walker	.522
Reggie Jackson	.521
Jim Rice	.517
Bob Horner	.515
Pedro Guerrero	.514
Eddie Murray	.513
Cecil Cooper	.512
Alvin Davis	.509
Dave Parker	.507
Kirk Gibson	.504
Leon Durham	.500
Oscar Gamble	.498
Kent Hrbek	.497
Wade Boggs	.495
Willie Aikens	.494
Mike Easler	.492
Greg Luzinski	.490
Mel Hall	.489

CAREER HOME RUN PCT. VS. RIGHT-HANDED PITCHERS

Min. 40 Home Runs

Mike Schmidt	7.00
Ron Kittle	6.67
Darryl Strawberry	6.57
Dave Kingman	6.45
Reggie Jackson	6.33
Bob Horner	6.21
Willie Stargell	6.19
Steve Balboni	6.12
Reggie Smith	5.99
Gorman Thomas	5.86
Tony Armas	5.79
Oscar Gamble	5.67
Graig Nettles	5.60
Jason Thompson	5.36
Dale Murphy	5.28
Andre Thornton	5.23
Eddie Murray	5.20
Jesse Barfield	5.19
Greg Walker	5.11
John Mayberry	5.09
Jim Rice	5.05
Greg Luzinski	5.03
George Foster	5.00
Willie Aikens	4.96
Rick Monday	4.93

CAREER STRIKEOUT PCT. VS. RIGHT-HANDED PITCHERS

Min. 750 PA

Felix Millan	3.29
Bill Buckner	3.82
Johnny Ray	3.84
Tony Gwynn	4.09
Dave Cash	4.30
Larry Bowa	5.04
Greg Gross	5.15
Ken Oberkfell	5.16
Jack Brohamer	5.17
Mike Squires	5.17
Ozzie Smith	5.22
Rich Dauer	5.31
Wade Boggs	5.33
Al Oliver	5.37
Terry Francona	5.39
Rusty Staub	5.40
George Brett	5.44
Mike Scioscia	5.54
Pete Rose	5.59
Tom Poquette	5.72
Don Mattingly	5.77
Bill Madlock	5.87
Craig Reynolds	5.88
Dan Meyer	5.95
Bob Bailor	5.98

SINGLE-SEASON BATTING AVERAGE VS. LEFT-HANDED PITCHERS

Min. 40 Hits

Rennie Stennett, 1977	.435
Sixto Lezcano, 1979	.411
Steve Henderson, 1979	.395
Mike Vail, 1979	.395
Ken Griffey, 1976	.393
Bill Buckner, 1978	.389
Paul Molitor, 1979	.387
Brian Downing, 1979	.386
Chet Lemon, 1984	.384
Keith Moreland, 1983	.382
Buddy Bell, 1977	.382
Rico Carty, 1975	.381
Don Baylor, 1975	.380
Jack Clark, 1980	.380
Jeff Leonard, 1984	.380
Jose Cardenal, 1975	.379
Lee Lacy, 1980	.379
Gary Carter, 1977	.378
Ken Singleton, 1977	.373
Joe Charboneau, 1980	.373
Dwight Evans, 1975	.372
Jeff Burroughs, 1978	.372
Rod Carew, 1977	.371
Bill Madlock, 1983	.371
Eddie Murray, 1982	.370

SINGLE-SEASON BATTING AVERAGE VS. RIGHT-HANDED PITCHERS

Min. 75 Hits

George Brett, 1980	.437
Wade Boggs, 1983	.398
Rod Carew, 1977	.398
Rod Carew, 1975	.379
Wade Boggs, 1985	.377
Tony Gwynn, 1984	.371
Oscar Gamble, 1979	.370
Cecil Cooper, 1980	.365
Fred Lynn, 1979	.364
Willie Wilson, 1982	.360
Rod Carew, 1983	.358
Bill Madlock, 1975	.357
Mike Easler, 1980	.357
Wade Boggs, 1982	.356
Wade Boggs, 1984	.356
Willie McGee, 1985	.356
Rod Carew, 1982	.355
Al Oliver, 1979	.353
Miguel Dilone, 1980	.353
Keith Hernandez, 1979	.353
George Brett, 1979	.352
Al Oliver, 1980	.351
Don Mattingly, 1984	.351
Fred Lynn, 1975	.350
Al Oliver, 1976	.349

SINGLE-SEASON BATTING AVERAGE IN HOME GAMES

Min. 75 Hits

Wade Boggs, 1985	.418
Rod Carew, 1977	.401
Juan Beniquez, 1984	.399
Wade Boggs, 1983	.397
George Brett, 1980	.391
Rod Carew, 1975	.387
Fred Lynn, 1979	.386
Al Oliver, 1980	.385
Hal McRae, 1976	.382
Miguel Dilone, 1980	.378
Tony Gwynn, 1984	.376
Mike Easler, 1984	.375
George Brett, 1979	.373
Bill Buckner, 1977	.372
Jim Rice, 1979	.369
Fred Lynn, 1975	.368
George Brett, 1985	.368
Dave Parker, 1977	.368
George Brett, 1976	.367
Dave Parker, 1978	.367
Keith Hernandez, 1984	.366
George Brett, 1975	.362
Gary Matthews, 1977	.362
Jim Rice, 1978	.361
Tim Foli, 1979	.360

SINGLE-SEASON BATTING AVERAGE IN ROAD GAMES

Min. 75 Hits

George Brett, 1980	.388
Cecil Cooper, 1980	.386
Rod Carew, 1977	.374
Johnny Ray, 1984	.370
Rod Carew, 1975	.369
Don Mattingly, 1984	.364
Brian Downing, 1979	.360
Bob Watson, 1975	.358
Mickey Rivers, 1977	.358
Bill Madlock, 1975	.357
Ken Singleton, 1977	.354
Ben Oglivie, 1980	.353
Willie McGee, 1985	.353
Keith Hernandez, 1979	.350
Dave Winfield, 1984	.349
Enos Cabell, 1984	.348
Al Oliver, 1978	.348
Robin Yount, 1982	.347
Rod Carew, 1980	.347
Bob Bailor, 1977	.347
Rod Carew, 1976	.346
Jose Cruz, 1984	.344
Bill Buckner, 1980	.343
Ray Knight, 1983	.342
George Foster, 1977	.342

CAREER HOME RUN PCT. IN HOME GAMES

Min. 25 Home Runs

Bob Horner	8.00
Jesse Barfield	6.97
Mike Schmidt	6.95
Dave Kingman	6.71
Ron Kittle	6.59
Oscar Gamble	6.31
Willie Stargell	6.26
Greg Luzinski	6.25
Dale Murphy	6.09
Gorman Thomas	5.92
Reggie Jackson	5.91
George Foster	5.65
Jim Rice	5.61
Rick Monday	5.48
Andre Thornton	5.48
Gary Alexander	5.46
Reggie Smith	5.34
Graig Nettles	5.34
Champ Summers	5.31
Dwight Evans	5.26
Fred Lynn	5.11
Ron Cey	5.10
Cliff Johnson	5.09
Tony Armas	5.06
Greg Brock	4.94

CAREER HOME RUN PCT. IN ROAD GAMES

Min. 25 Home Runs

Darryl Strawberry	7.17
Mike Schmidt	7.01
Ron Kittle	6.90
Dave Kingman	6.83
Steve Balboni	6.65
Gorman Thomas	6.00
Tom Brunansky	5.92
Reggie Jackson	5.75
Pedro Guerrero	5.70
Tony Armas	5.36
Willie Stargell	5.35
Willie Aikens	5.29
Gary Roenicke	5.18
Eddie Murray	5.16
Jack Clark	5.11
Gene Tenace	5.08
Reggie Smith	5.06
Johnny Bench	5.05
Willie McCovey	5.00
George Foster	4.99
Bobby Bonds	4.93
Lance Parrish	4.92
John Mayberry	4.90
Nick Esasky	4.85
Cliff Johnson	4.82

CAREER BATTING AVERAGE IN HOME GAMES

Min. 200 Hits

Wade Boggs	.383
George Brett	.347
Rod Carew	.334
Tony Gwynn	.332
Al Oliver	.326
Jim Rice	.325
Kirby Puckett	.325
Kent Hrbek	.324
Don Mattingly	.322
Dave Parker	.322
Lyman Bostock	.318
Fred Lynn	.315
Bill Madlock	.312
Ryne Sandberg	.311
Thurman Munson	.311
Mike Easler	.310
Carney Lansford	.309
Hal McRae	.308
Pat Tabler	.308
Steve Garvey	.307
Bill Buckner	.307
Leon Durham	.307
Julio Franco	.307
Lou Brock	.306
Willie McGee	.305

CAREER BATTING AVERAGE IN ROAD GAMES

Min. 200 Hits

Rod Carew	.328
Don Mattingly	.324
Wade Boggs	.317
Tony Gwynn	.317
Willie McGee	.310
Cecil Cooper	.308
Mickey Rivers	.308
Pedro Guerrero	.308
Lyman Bostock	.305
Bob Watson	.305
Bill Madlock	.304
Manny Sanguillen	.303
Dave Winfield	.302
Keith Hernandez	.299
Ken Griffey	.299
Willie Wilson	.298
Rickey Henderson	.297
Thurman Munson	.297
Gene Richards	.297
Cal Ripken	.297
Ken Singleton	.296
Tim Raines	.295
Jose Cruz	.295
Eddie Murray	.295
Andre Dawson	.294

CAREER BATTING AVERAGE WITH RUNNERS ON BASE

Min. 200 Hits

Wade Boggs	.358
Rod Carew	.348
Tony Gwynn	.346
George Brett	.328
Dave Parker	.326
Lyman Bostock	.326
Don Mattingly	.322
Thurman Munson	.321
Cecil Cooper	.319
Garry Templeton	.317
Pete Rose	.317
Bill Madlock	.317
Keith Hernandez	.316
Al Oliver	.316
Steve Garvey	.313
Bill Buckner	.312
Pedro Guerrero	.311
Eddie Murray	.309
Mike Easler	.309
Kent Hrbek	.308
Bruce Bochte	.308
Jim Rice	.308
Fred Lynn	.307
Ken Griffey	.307
Manny Sanguillen	.307

SINGLE-SEASON BATTING AVERAGE WITH RUNNERS ON BASE

Min. 75 Hits

Rod Carew, 1977	.422
Tony Gwynn, 1984	.406
George Brett, 1980	.400
Garry Templeton, 1979	.388
Wade Boggs, 1985	.387
Fred Lynn, 1979	.387
Keith Hernandez, 1979	.383
Dave Parker, 1978	.383
Garry Templeton, 1977	.378
Rod Carew, 1975	.377
Mickey Rivers, 1977	.373
Bill Madlock, 1975	.370
Manny Sanguillen, 1975	.370
Bill Madlock, 1976	.368
Hal McRae, 1976	.368
George Brett, 1985	.367
Hal McRae, 1982	.366
Pete Rose, 1975	.366
Fred Lynn, 1975	.365
Ken Griffey, 1976	.362
Cecil Cooper, 1980	.362
Eddie Murray, 1985	.361
Dave Parker, 1976	.360
Willie McGee, 1985	.360
Don Mattingly, 1984	.359

CAREER BATTING AVERAGE WITH RUNNERS IN SCORING POSITION

Min. 100 Hits

Wade Boggs	.371
Rod Carew	.345
Tony Gwynn	.339
Don Mattingly	.334
Pat Tabler	.331
Thurman Munson	.329
Lyman Bostock	.324
Kent Hrbek	.323
George Brett	.323
Willie McGee	.323
Al Oliver	.323
Pete Rose	.322
Dane Iorg	.321
Broderick Perkins	.318
Bill Madlock	.318
Rennie Stennett	.315
Jim Rice	.315
Lou Piniella	.314
Cecil Cooper	.313
Lamar Johnson	.312
Julio Franco	.311
Steve Garvey	.310
Keith Hernandez	.310
Bake McBride	.309
Dave Parker	.309

SINGLE-SEASON BATTING AVERAGE WITH RUNNERS IN SCORING POSITION

Min. 50 Hits

George Brett, 1980	.466
Cecil Cooper, 1980	.421
Tony Gwynn, 1984	.418
Bill Madlock, 1976	.414
Ken Griffey, 1976	.412
Pete Rose, 1975	.412
Don Mattingly, 1984	.405
Fred Lynn, 1975	.400
Mickey Rivers, 1977	.400
Kent Hrbek, 1982	.398
Wade Boggs, 1985	.392
Robin Yount, 1982	.392
Joe Morgan, 1976	.391
Willie McGee, 1985	.391
Hal McRae, 1982	.383
Rod Carew, 1977	.382
Bake McBride, 1980	.380
Bill Robinson, 1977	.380
Garry Templeton, 1977	.379
Thurman Munson, 1975	.376
Rod Carew, 1978	.375
Ted Simmons, 1983	.375
Dave Winfield, 1979	.371
Eddie Murray, 1985	.370
Dave Parker, 1976	.369

CAREER BATTING AVERAGE WITH 2 OUTS AND RUNNERS ON BASE

Min. 75 Hits

Wade Boggs	.353
Tony Gwynn	.335
Larry Hisle	.321
Thurman Munson	.320
Dave Parker	.312
Al Oliver	.311
Garry Templeton	.309
Cecil Cooper	.308
Keith Hernandez	.307
Larry Biittner	.307
Bill Madlock	.304
Jose Cardenal	.304
Harold Baines	.303
Rico Carty	.303
Willie McGee	.302
George Brett	.302
Rod Carew	.301
Gene Richards	.301
Lyman Bostock	.301
Darryl Strawberry	.301
Steve Garvey	.300
Dane Iorg	.297
Oscar Gamble	.297
Jose Cruz	.295
Willie Montanez	.295

SINGLE-SEASON BATTING AVERAGE WITH 2 OUTS AND RUNNERS ON BASE

Min. 30 Hits

Barry Bonnell, 1977	.437
Lee Lacy, 1984	.432
Al Oliver, 1980	.424
Bruce Bochte, 1982	.418
Ted Simmons, 1983	.404
Sixto Lezcano, 1979	.402
Garry Templeton, 1979	.400
Rod Carew, 1977	.398
Harold Baines, 1985	.391
Greg Gross, 1975	.390
Lee Mazzilli, 1979	.390
Larry Parrish, 1979	.388
Rod Carew, 1975	.388
Joe Rudi, 1976	.386
Frank Taveras, 1978	.386
Rennie Stennett, 1975	.383
Larry Hisle, 1978	.379
Steve Garvey, 1979	.377
Rod Carew, 1978	.376
Garry Templeton, 1977	.376
Steve Kemp, 1980	.375
Pete Rose, 1979	.373
Wade Boggs, 1985	.373
Lee Mazzilli, 1978	.372
Willie Montanez, 1976	.371

CAREER BATTING AVERAGE WITH 2 OUTS & RUNNERS IN SCORING POSITION

Min. 50 Hits

Wade Boggs	.352
Larry Hisle	.332
Kent Hrbek	.331
Thurman Munson	.325
Al Oliver	.320
Dane Iorg	.317
Tony Gwynn	.315
Willie McGee	.308
Lamar Johnson	.307
Lyman Bostock	.304
Gene Richards	.303
Lou Piniella	.303
John Castino	.302
Bill Madlock	.302
George Brett	.302
Gary Ward	.302
Jose Morales	.301
Steve Garvey	.299
Rod Carew	.299
Cecil Cooper	.298
Pete Rose	.297
Steve Kemp	.295
Rennie Stennett	.294
Rusty Staub	.293
Dave Parker	.293

SINGLE-SEASON BATTING AVERAGE WITH 2 OUTS & RUNNERS IN SCORING POSITION

Min. 20 Hits

Kent Hrbek, 1982	.466
Bruce Bochte, 1982	.457
Al Oliver, 1980	.446
Rod Carew, 1975	.440
Ted Simmons, 1983	.437
George Foster, 1981	.426
Chris Speier, 1978	.426
Rod Carew, 1978	.414
Cecil Cooper, 1980	.414
Rod Carew, 1977	.412
Lee Mazzilli, 1978	.412
Joe Rudi, 1976	.410
Lyman Bostock, 1978	.407
Dave Winfield, 1979	.407
Mike Ivie, 1979	.404
Larry Hisle, 1978	.403
Lee Lacy, 1984	.400
Rusty Staub, 1976	.397
Pete Rose, 1975	.395
Barry Bonnell, 1977	.393
Gene Tenace, 1975	.390
Frank Taveras, 1978	.390
Larry Bowa, 1978	.388
Willie Stargell, 1975	.385
Rico Carty, 1975	.385

CAREER BATTING AVERAGE IN LATE-INNING PRESSURE SITUATIONS

Min. 50 Hits

Wade Boggs	.356
Tony Gwynn	.344
Tim Raines	.340
George Brett	.332
Garth Iorg	.329
George Bell	.327
Eddie Murray	.324
Cal Ripken	.324
Joe Lefebvre	.322
Ken Griffey	.320
Don Mattingly	.319
Cecil Cooper	.317
Mickey Hatcher	.316
Pedro Guerrero	.314
Ron LeFlore	.312
Mike Easler	.310
Lloyd Moseby	.309
Thurman Munson	.309
Mickey Rivers	.309
Jose Cardenal	.309
Mike Ivie	.308
Tom Paciorek	.308
Bo Diaz	.307
Thad Bosley	.306
Eric Soderholm	.305

SINGLE-SEASON BATTING AVERAGE IN LATE-INNING PRESSURE SITUATIONS

Min. 25 Hits

Manny Trillo, 1981	.466
Bill Madlock, 1975	.464
Mickey Rivers, 1977	.439
George Brett, 1976	.433
Steve Kemp, 1979	.429
Ken Griffey, 1975	.423
Tom Paciorek, 1976	.419
Mike Easler, 1984	.416
Scot Thompson, 1979	.413
Cecil Cooper, 1982	.412
Lloyd Moseby, 1983	.410
Luis Salazar, 1981	.408
Bill Buckner, 1984	.403
Chris Chambliss, 1981	.403
Rick Manning, 1983	.402
Cal Ripken, 1984	.398
Bill Buckner, 1978	.397
Wade Boggs, 1985	.395
Rickey Henderson, 1983	.391
Dale Murphy, 1984	.391
Rico Carty, 1976	.389
Ken Singleton, 1977	.388
Eddie Murray, 1983	.386
Dave Parker, 1985	.385
Steve Garvey, 1975	.384

CAREER HOME RUN PCT. IN LATE-INNING PRESSURE SITUATIONS

Min. 10 Home Runs

Gary Alexander	7.80
Steve Balboni	7.39
Dave Kingman	6.99
Eddie Murray	6.94
Craig Kusick	6.78
Tony Armas	6.70
Darryl Strawberry	6.67
Pedro Guerrero	6.56
Andre Thornton	6.40
Mike Schmidt	6.01
Graig Nettles	5.84
Oscar Gamble	5.57
Reggie Smith	5.56
Reggie Jackson	5.51
Bernie Carbo	5.41
Richie Zisk	5.32
Greg Walker	5.26
Willie Stargell	5.25
George Foster	5.21
Cliff Johnson	5.15
Kirk Gibson	5.15
Pat Putnam	5.14
Lance Parrish	5.08
Tom Brunansky	5.08
Dwight Evans	5.04

CAREER BATTING AVG. IN LATE-INNING PRESSURE SITUATIONS WITH RUNNERS IN SCORING POSITION

Min. 25 Hits

Eric Soderholm	.429
Eddie Murray	.407
Wade Boggs	.397
Cal Ripken	.371
Chili Davis	.361
Willie Montanez	.355
Lee May	.352
Pete Rose	.348
Oscar Gamble	.343
Ken Griffey	.342
Thurman Munson	.341
Rickey Henderson	.339
Bruce Bochte	.337
Mike Ivie	.333
Reggie Smith	.333
Willie McGee	.333
Dave Chalk	.333
Cesar Geronimo	.330
Rick Cerone	.329
Rod Carew	.328
Julio Cruz	.325
Dave Cash	.325
Dave Collins	.325
Dane Iorg	.324
Lou Piniella	.323

CAREER BATTING AVERAGE IN LATE-INNING PRESSURE SITUATIONS WITH RUNNERS ON BASE

Min. 25 Hits

Wade Boggs	.387
Eddie Murray	.379
Dickie Thon	.375
Mike Ivie	.370
Garth Iorg	.363
Thad Bosley	.356
George Bell	.353
Kevin Bass	.351
Eric Soderholm	.348
Manny Mota	.342
U.L. Washington	.340
Bo Diaz	.339
Bill Buckner	.337
Jose Cardenal	.335
Reggie Smith	.333
Cal Ripken	.333
Dave Rader	.333
George Bell	.331
Dane Iorg	.331
Thurman Munson	.331
Pete Rose	.331
Joe Torre	.329
H. Pat Kelly	.326
Tim Raines	.326
Willie Montanez	.326

SINGLE-SEASON BATTING AVERAGE IN LATE-INNING PRESSURE SITUATIONS WITH RUNNERS ON BASE

Min. 10 Hits

Rance Mulliniks, 1984	.684
Eddie Murray, 1985	.567
Bill Buckner, 1984	.563
Rowland Office, 1975	.536
Rusty Staub, 1981	.536
Jack Clark, 1984	.526
Ron Oester, 1981	.524
Pedro Guerrero, 1980	.520
Manny Trillo, 1981	.520
Carl Yastrzemski, 1975	.500
Ken Griffey, 1975	.500
Bernie Carbo, 1976	.500
Mickey Rivers, 1977	.500
Ken Singleton, 1977	.500
Pete Rose, 1977	.500
Barry Foote, 1979	.500
Glenn Adams, 1979	.500
Dan Ford, 1983	.500
Rick Manning, 1983	.486
Cesar Geronimo, 1976	.485
Toby Harrah, 1985	.481
Larry Biittner, 1975	.480
Greg Gross, 1982	.480
Johnnie LeMaster, 1982	.480
Jose Cardenal, 1978	.476

CAREER BATTING AVERAGE IN LATE-INNING PRESSURE SITUATIONS WITH 2 OUTS AND RUNNERS ON BASE

Min. 15 Hits

Garth Iorg	.474
Eric Soderholm	.429
Wade Boggs	.417
Marty Perez	.405
Eddie Murray	.394
Mike Ivie	.387
Dave Rader	.383
Thurman Munson	.365
Willie McGee	.364
Steve Henderson	.360
Alan Trammell	.356
Oscar Gamble	.355
Tim Raines	.355
Dickie Thon	.354
Glenn Adams	.345
George Brett	.345
Dane Iorg	.344
H. Pat Kelly	.344
Ed Ott	.343
Manny Sanguillen	.341
Pete Rose	.333
Ken Griffey	.333
U.L. Washington	.333
Dave Revering	.333
Rico Carty	.333

CAREER BATTING AVG. IN LATE-INNING PRESSURE SITUATIONS WITH 2 OUTS AND RUNNERS IN SCORING POSITION

Min. 10 Hits

Eric Soderholm	.444
Chili Davis	.438
Marty Perez	.435
Eddie Murray	.424
Jim Norris	.417
Rusty Staub	.405
Dickie Thon	.400
Wade Boggs	.394
Cesar Geronimo	.391
Thurman Munson	.387
Oscar Gamble	.381
Pete Rose	.375
Willie Horton	.373
Lloyd Moseby	.371
Tony Gwynn	.370
Jose Cruz	.369
Ernie Whitt	.367
Kent Hrbek	.367
Bo Diaz	.367
Steve Henderson	.356
Willie McGee	.354
Lee May	.352
Mike Ivie	.349
George Brett	.348
Frank White	.345

HIGHEST CAREER GROUND OUTS-TO-AIR OUTS RATIO

Min. 1,000 PA

Wally Backman	2.42
Gary Pettis	2.35
Juan Bonilla	2.17
Steve Henderson	2.04
Willie McGee	2.02
Duane Kuiper	2.02
Billy North	2.02
Alan Wiggins	2.01
Kirby Puckett	2.01
Tony Gwynn	2.01
Steve Carlton	1.96
Gene Richards	1.91
Rod Carew	1.89
Steve Sax	1.89
Ron LeFlore	1.82
Miguel Dilone	1.82
Wayne Tolleson	1.81
Garry Templeton	1.80
Pete Rose	1.79
Jerry Mumphrey	1.77
Mookie Wilson	1.74
Julio Cruz	1.73
Lyman Bostock	1.73
Claudell Washington	1.72
Lou Brock	1.69

LOWEST CAREER GROUND OUTS-TO-AIR OUTS RATIO

Min. 1,000 PA

Gary Redus	0.60
Jim Dwyer	0.62
Gene Tenace	0.63
Andre Thornton	0.65
Joe Morgan	0.65
Don Baylor	0.65
Steve Balboni	0.66
Darrell Evans	0.67
Mike Schmidt	0.69
Richie Hebner	0.70
Buck Martinez	0.70
Dave Revering	0.72
Howard Johnson	0.73
Dave Kingman	0.73
Bobby Murcer	0.73
Ron Kittle	0.74
Randy Bush	0.74
Tom Brunansky	0.74
Tim Laudner	0.75
Dave Henderson	0.75
Jerry White	0.75
Tony Solaita	0.75
Jim Wynn	0.76
Greg Luzinski	0.76
Gorman Thomas	0.76

CAREER BATTING AVERAGE IN DAY GAMES

Min. 100 Hits

Wade Boggs	.355
Rod Carew	.347
Willie McGee	.343
Don Mattingly	.329
Tony Gwynn	.322
Tim Raines	.318
Paul Molitor	.317
Bake McBride	.316
Ken Griffey	.315
Al Oliver	.315
Dave Parker	.314
George Brett	.314
Thad Bosley	.313
Lyman Bostock	.313
Jerry Grote	.312
Thurman Munson	.311
Jose Morales	.311
Reggie Smith	.310
Gene Richards	.309
Carney Lansford	.309
Lonnie Smith	.309
Tony Pena	.308
Bill Madlock	.307
Tom Paciorek	.307
Andre Dawson	.307

CAREER BATTING AVERAGE IN NIGHT GAMES

Min. 100 Hits

Wade Boggs	.349
Tony Gwynn	.326
Rod Carew	.324
George Brett	.321
Don Mattingly	.320
Pedro Guerrero	.316
Cecil Cooper	.311
Lyman Bostock	.310
Mickey Rivers	.309
Bill Madlock	.308
Willie Wilson	.306
Al Oliver	.306
Rick Peters	.305
Keith Hernandez	.304
Jim Rice	.303
Manny Sanguillen	.303
Mike Easler	.301
Steve Garvey	.301
Jeff Stone	.301
Dave Parker	.300
Pete Rose	.300
Thurman Munson	.300
Rickey Henderson	.299
Kirby Puckett	.299
Jose Cruz	.296

CAREER BATTING AVERAGE ON GRASS SURFACES

Min. 150 Hits

Wade Boggs	.354
Rod Carew	.331
Tony Gwynn	.329
Don Mattingly	.326
Al Oliver	.318
Lyman Bostock	.313
Keith Hernandez	.312
Willie McGee	.311
Bill Madlock	.310
Steve Garvey	.308
Cecil Cooper	.307
Willie Wilson	.306
Thurman Munson	.306
Jim Rice	.306
Bob Watson	.305
Ryne Sandberg	.305
Pedro Guerrero	.303
Bill Doran	.302
Andre Dawson	.300
Jose Cardenal	.300
Reggie Smith	.300
Bill Buckner	.300
Fred Lynn	.299
Eddie Murray	.299
Rickey Henderson	.298

CAREER BATTING AVERAGE ON ARTIFICIAL TURF

Min. 150 Hits

George Brett	.345
Rod Carew	.333
Kent Hrbek	.317
Al Bumbry	.314
Alan Trammell	.313
Pedro Guerrero	.313
Mickey Rivers	.312
Jim Gantner	.312
Dave Parker	.311
Von Joshua	.311
Lee Lacy	.310
Mike Easler	.308
Willie McGee	.306
Bill Madlock	.306
Cecil Cooper	.306
Ken Griffey	.305
Hal McRae	.304
Bake McBride	.301
Mickey Hatcher	.301
Bruce Bochte	.301
Buddy Bell	.301
Garry Templeton	.300
Pete Rose	.300
Kirby Puckett	.300
Chris Chambliss	.300

SINGLE-SEASON BATTING AVERAGE ON GRASS SURFACES

Min. 60 Hits

George Brett, 1980	.396
Rod Carew, 1977	.393
Pete Rose, 1979	.373
Ray Knight, 1983	.370
Ken Griffey, 1976	.368
Rod Carew, 1975	.367
Keith Hernandez, 1979	.366
Wade Boggs, 1983	.364
Wade Boggs, 1985	.363
Cecil Cooper, 1980	.363
Oscar Gamble, 1979	.362
Pat Sheridan, 1984	.358
Dan Gladden, 1984	.357
Wade Boggs, 1982	.354
Juan Beniquez, 1984	.352
Bill Buckner, 1978	.351
Fred Lynn, 1979	.350
Tony Gwynn, 1984	.349
Don Mattingly, 1984	.348
Glenn Adams, 1977	.346
Al Oliver, 1975	.346
Miguel Dilone, 1980	.345
Richie Zisk, 1982	.345
Willie Wilson, 1980	.345
Keith Hernandez, 1984	.344

SINGLE-SEASON BATTING AVERAGE ON ARTIFICIAL TURF

Min. 60 Hits

Bill Madlock, 1975	.398
George Brett, 1980	.386
Hal McRae, 1976	.382
George Brett, 1979	.369
George Brett, 1976	.367
Keith Hernandez, 1985	.364
George Brett, 1978	.357
Lee Lacy, 1980	.356
Willie McGee, 1985	.356
George Brett, 1981	.356
Greg Gross, 1983	.356
Pete Rose, 1976	.354
Bake McBride, 1976	.354
George Brett, 1975	.352
Bill Madlock, 1981	.352
George Brett, 1985	.352
Mike Easler, 1980	.349
Kent Hrbek, 1984	.349
Willie Wilson, 1982	.349
Pete Rose, 1981	.348
Joe Morgan, 1975	.347
Pete LaCock, 1978	.347
Garry Maddox, 1976	.347
Rennie Stennett, 1977	.346
Tommy Herr, 1983	.346

CAREER ON-BASE AVERAGE LEADING OFF INNINGS

Min. 200 PA

Wade Boggs	.442
Tony Gwynn	.405
Rickey Henderson	.399
Rod Carew	.392
Willie Randolph	.389
Mike Schmidt	.389
Pepe Mangual	.384
Greg Gross	.382
Mike Hargrove	.382
Tony Solaita	.382
Bryan Little	.380
Bobby Grich	.379
Pedro Guerrero	.377
Bob Stinson	.377
Tim Raines	.377
Keith Hernandez	.376
Jack Clark	.376
Johnny Grubb	.375
Gene Tenace	.375
Otto Velez	.375
Bernie Carbo	.374
Bobby Bonds	.374
Joe Morgan	.372
Rick Peters	.372
Marty Barrett	.372

SINGLE-SEASON ON-BASE AVERAGE LEADING OFF INNINGS

Min. 100 PA

Rod Carew, 1982	.523
Andre Thornton, 1975	.519
Carlton Fisk, 1977	.504
Wade Boggs, 1983	.494
Toby Harrah, 1981	.491
Joe Morgan, 1975	.470
Wade Boggs, 1985	.468
Ken Griffey, 1977	.466
Willie Randolph, 1980	.457
Hal McRae, 1977	.456
Mike Hargrove, 1977	.453
Mitchell Page, 1977	.452
Cal Ripken, 1984	.452
Willie Randolph, 1985	.448
Jose Cruz, 1979	.448
Richie Zisk, 1981	.447
Johnny Grubb, 1976	.443
John Stearns, 1977	.442
Mike Schmidt, 1979	.441
Bobby Grich, 1976	.441
Jose Cruz, 1976	.440
Tommy Herr, 1983	.439
Jack Clark, 1985	.436
Mike Hargrove, 1979	.434
Ken Singleton, 1977	.433

CAREER WALK PCT. LEADING OFF INNINGS

Min. 25 Walks

Jim Wynn	19.71
Gene Tenace	15.78
Joe Morgan	15.34
Bernie Carbo	15.05
Gary Pettis	15.00
Pepe Mangual	14.76
Jerry Hairston	14.68
Rickey Henderson	14.66
Otto Velez	14.55
Glenn Borgmann	14.35
Willie Randolph	14.16
Tommy Hutton	14.00
Joe Ferguson	13.84
Dave Anderson	13.78
Mike Hargrove	13.67
Billy North	13.62
Bud Harrelson	13.56
Dwayne Murphy	13.51
Bryan Little	13.43
Lee Mazzilli	13.39
Toby Harrah	13.33
Merv Rettenmund	13.27
Tony Solaita	13.16
Rick Peters	12.97
Steve Braun	12.96

SINGLE-SEASON WALK PCT. LEADING OFF INNINGS

Min. 15 Walks

Jim Wynn, 1975	23.85
Lee Mazzilli, 1982	22.97
Lee Mazzilli, 1983	22.50
Joe Morgan, 1975	22.00
Gene Tenace, 1977	21.43
Dwayne Murphy, 1981	21.43
Andre Thornton, 1975	21.30
Carlton Fisk, 1977	21.17
Bernie Carbo, 1975	21.05
Jerry Hairston, 1984	20.55
Mike Scioscia, 1985	20.54
Gary Matthews, 1984	19.82
Toby Harrah, 1981	19.81
Steve Kemp, 1981	19.74
Toby Harrah, 1985	19.71
Johnny Briggs, 1975	19.15
Gene Tenace, 1979	19.05
Mike Hargrove, 1977	18.95
Willie Randolph, 1980	18.78
Darrell Porter, 1975	18.75
Willie Randolph, 1981	18.75
Tommy Herr, 1985	18.69
Greg Luzinski, 1981	18.35
Jim Wynn, 1976	18.18
Reggie Smith, 1977	18.18

CAREER BATTING AVERAGE WITH BASES LOADED

Min. 15 Hits

Pat Tabler	.611
Eddie Murray	.445
Miguel Dilone	.436
Biff Pocoroba	.435
Bill Madlock	.430
Rick Bosetti	.429
Lou Brock	.423
Leon Durham	.421
Ken Singleton	.417
Ellis Valentine	.417
Rico Carty	.404
Lee May	.402
Jay Johnstone	.400
Oscar Gamble	.392
Larry Hisle	.389
Rod Carew	.388
Willie McGee	.385
Mickey Hatcher	.385
Richie Zisk	.382
Bill Russell	.380
Jim Gantner	.380
Steve Garvey	.379
Wade Boggs	.378
Lee Stanton	.375
Champ Summers	.375

CAREER RRF RATIO (PER PA) WITH BASES LOADED

Min. 30 RRF

Pat Tabler	1.27
Eddie Murray	1.14
John Milner	1.10
Dane Iorg	1.09
Biff Pocoroba	1.06
Terry Crowley	1.05
Mike Cubbage	1.04
Kent Hrbek	1.04
Leon Durham	1.04
Dale Berra	1.02
Steve Garvey	1.00
Rico Carty	1.00
Lee Stanton	1.00
Roy Howell	0.99
Oscar Gamble	0.99
H. Pat Kelly	0.98
Bill Madlock	0.98
Joe Rudi	0.98
Reggie Jackson	0.98
Jose Cruz	0.97
John Wockenfuss	0.96
Rod Carew	0.96
Lee May	0.95
Howard Johnson	0.95
Ted Simmons	0.95

CAREER WALK PCT. WITH BASES LOADED

Min. 10 Walks

Oscar Gamble	17.65
Mike Hargrove	17.48
Sixto Lezcano	17.12
Pete Rose	16.52
Gene Tenace	16.09
Joe Morgan	14.55
Gary Roenicke	14.47
Darrell Porter	14.29
Dwight Evans	13.91
Jeff Burroughs	12.90
Brian Downing	12.17
Carl Yastrzemski	12.15
Ruppert Jones	11.96
Dan Driessen	11.76
Bobby Murcer	11.58
Gorman Thomas	11.50
Ken Singleton	11.48
Darrell Evans	10.24
Dusty Baker	10.16
Dave Lopes	9.90
Dave Winfield	9.86
Butch Wynegar	9.82
Rick Dempsey	9.71
Fred Lynn	9.70
Toby Harrah	9.59

CAREER STRIKEOUT PCT. WITH BASES LOADED

Min. 50 PA

Ozzie Smith	1.05
Rico Carty	1.43
Jim Spencer	1.89
Biff Pocoroba	1.92
Jerry Morales	2.02
Craig Reynolds	2.60
Terry Puhl	2.99
Dave Cash	3.03
Ken Oberkfell	3.39
Dusty Baker	3.91
Lyman Bostock	3.92
Ellis Valentine	4.00
Jose Cardenal	4.00
Doug Flynn	4.08
Bo Diaz	4.11
Bill Madlock	4.12
Bill Buckner	4.13
Bruce Benedict	4.17
Rich Dauer	4.35
Jose Cruz	4.55
Frank Taveras	4.62
Lenny Randle	4.62
Larry Bowa	4.81
Al Cowens	4.90
Pete Rose	5.22

CAREER PCT. OF RUNNERS DRIVEN IN FROM SCORING POSITION

Min. 100 RRF

Don Mattingly	.373
Dane Iorg	.362
Kent Hrbek	.360
Wade Boggs	.356
Thurman Munson	.352
Cecil Cooper	.350
Broderick Perkins	.349
Al Oliver	.349
Rusty Staub	.349
George Brett	.348
Keith Hernandez	.347
Rod Carew	.346
Ted Simmons	.345
Dave Parker	.343
Pat Tabler	.342
Lou Piniella	.341
Rico Carty	.340
Mike Hargrove	.340
Eddie Murray	.339
Larry Hisle	.338
Dave Winfield	.337
Steve Garvey	.336
Bill Buckner	.335
Bill Madlock	.334
Leon Durham	.334

SINGLE-SEASON PCT. OF RUNNERS DRIVEN IN FROM SCORING POSITION

Min. 50 RRF

George Brett, 1980	.507
Bill Buckner, 1981	.476
Cecil Cooper, 1980	.470
Bill Madlock, 1976	.448
Dave Parker, 1976	.430
Eddie Murray, 1985	.428
Bill Buckner, 1978	.427
Richie Hebner, 1980	.422
Cecil Cooper, 1976	.420
Bake McBride, 1980	.419
Buddy Bell, 1984	.418
John Milner, 1976	.412
Rod Carew, 1977	.411
Ted Simmons, 1983	.410
Tommy Herr, 1985	.409
Rod Carew, 1975	.408
Joe Morgan, 1978	.408
Joe Morgan, 1976	.408
Pat Tabler, 1985	.407
Kent Hrbek, 1984	.405
Hal McRae, 1982	.402
Bill Madlock, 1979	.401
Eddie Murray, 1982	.401
Don Mattingly, 1985	.400
Jose Cruz, 1985	.400

CAREER PCT. OF RUNNERS DRIVEN IN FROM SCORING POSITION IN LATE-INNING PRESSURE SITUATIONS

Min. 20 RRF

Eddie Milner	.442
Eddie Murray	.439
Eric Soderholm	.427
Tony Gwynn	.417
Jim Essian	.403
Carmelo Martinez	.397
Jim Norris	.392
Pedro Guerrero	.389
Pete LaCock	.379
Ozzie Virgil	.371
Don Mattingly	.369
Wade Boggs	.369
Mike Hargrove	.369
Bo Diaz	.367
Rico Carty	.364
Bill Melton	.361
Rusty Staub	.357
Reggie Smith	.354
Chili Davis	.354
Ellis Valentine	.352
Rick Cerone	.351
Willie McGee	.350
Jose Cruz	.350
Oscar Gamble	.349
Ted Simmons	.347

SINGLE-SEASON RDI OPPORTUNITIES FROM SCORING POSITION

Tony Perez, 1975	268
Don Baylor, 1979	257
Johnny Bench, 1975	246
George Foster, 1976	245
Julio Franco, 1985	244
George Foster, 1977	243
Keith Moreland, 1985	238
Jerry Morales, 1975	236
Bob Watson, 1976	236
Lance Parrish, 1983	235
Tommy Herr, 1985	232
Greg Luzinski, 1975	230
Thurman Munson, 1976	229
Cecil Cooper, 1983	229
Jim Rice, 1975	228
Jim Rice, 1984	228
Willie Montanez, 1975	227
Steve Garvey, 1978	227
Rusty Staub, 1978	227
Willie Horton, 1979	226
Thurman Munson, 1975	224
Al Oliver, 1980	223
Steve Garvey, 1982	223
Dave Winfield, 1985	223
Butch Wynegar, 1977	222

CAREER PCT. OF RUNNERS DRIVEN IN FROM 3RD BASE WITH LESS THAN 2 OUTS

Min. 40 RRF

Broderick Perkins	.753
Don Mattingly	.739
Rico Carty	.722
Ed Kranepool	.720
Tony Solaita	.719
Rod Carew	.719
Pat Tabler	.716
Kevin McReynolds	.710
Manny Sanguillen	.695
Wade Boggs	.694
Dave Winfield	.694
Al Oliver	.692
Jerry Hairston	.691
Mike Hargrove	.689
Tony Gwynn	.688
Rusty Staub	.686
George Brett	.684
Pete Rose	.684
Keith Hernandez	.683
Mike Davis	.682
Cal Ripken	.678
Bill Madlock	.677
Fred Lynn	.675
Steve Kemp	.673
Robin Yount	.671

SINGLE-SEASON PCT. OF RUNNERS DRIVEN IN FROM 3RD BASE WITH LESS THAN 2 OUTS

Min. 15 RRF

Rod Carew, 1983	.900
Toby Harrah, 1981	.889
Elliott Maddox, 1978	.875
Bill Madlock, 1976	.868
Dave Revering, 1979	.857
Kevin McReynolds, 1984	.852
Al Oliver, 1983	.846
Jerry Mumphrey, 1985	.846
Paul Molitor, 1978	.842
Dave Bergman, 1984	.842
Pat Tabler, 1985	.840
George Brett, 1980	.838
Richie Hebner, 1976	.833
Rich Dauer, 1978	.833
Denny Walling, 1978	.833
Brian Downing, 1982	.833
Alan Wiggins, 1984	.833
Buddy Bell, 1984	.829
Jerry Remy, 1982	.826
Gene Richards, 1981	.818
Toby Harrah, 1982	.818
Don Kessinger, 1975	.815
Lou Whitaker, 1983	.815
Luis Salazar, 1982	.813
Ed Kranepool, 1976	.810

CAREER PCT. OF RUNNERS DRIVEN IN FROM 1ST BASE

Min. 30 RRF

Willie Stargell	.110
Alvin Davis	.106
Darryl Strawberry	.100
Mike Schmidt	.095
Dave Kingman	.095
Greg Luzinski	.092
Larry Hisle	.091
Don Mattingly	.091
Hal McRae	.091
Dale Murphy	.091
George Brett	.090
Ron Kittle	.090
Bob Horner	.089
Reggie Jackson	.088
Fred Lynn	.087
Oscar Gamble	.086
Bill Robinson	.086
Dave Parker	.085
Clint Hurdle	.085
Steve Balboni	.085
Greg Walker	.085
Lance Parrish	.083
Glenn Wilson	.083
Gorman Thomas	.083
Harold Baines	.082

SINGLE-SEASON RUNNERS DRIVEN IN FROM 1ST BASE

Hal McRae, 1982	36
George Foster, 1977	31
Jim Rice, 1978	29
Don Mattingly, 1985	29
Greg Luzinski, 1977	28
Alvin Davis, 1984	28
Keith Hernandez, 1979	27
Jim Rice, 1983	25
Fred Lynn, 1979	24
Steve Garvey, 1979	24
Dave Kingman, 1984	24
Jeff Burroughs, 1977	23
Ron Cey, 1977	23
Jim Rice, 1979	23
Tony Armas, 1980	23
Tony Perez, 1980	23
Mike Schmidt, 1983	23
Eddie Murray, 1985	23
Fred Lynn, 1975	22
Johnny Bench, 1975	22
Bob Watson, 1977	22
Dave Parker, 1978	22
Gorman Thomas, 1978	22
Mike Schmidt, 1979	22
Robin Yount, 1982	22

CAREER OPP. BATTING AVERAGE VS. LEFT-HANDED BATTERS		CAREER OPP. HOME RUN PCT. VS. LEFT-HANDED BATTERS		CAREER OPP. WALK PCT. VS. LEFT-HANDED BATTERS		CAREER OPP. STRIKEOUT PCT. VS. LEFT-HANDED BATTERS	
Min. 400 PA		*Min. 400 PA*		*Min. 400 PA*		*Min. 100 Strikeouts*	
Jesse Orosco	.179	Mickey Lolich	0.46	Steve Howe	2.86	Dave Righetti	25.57
Rod Scurry	.197	Dave Smith	0.52	Gary Nolan	3.23	Mark Davis	25.19
Pat Underwood	.201	Joe Sambito	0.53	Scott McGregor	3.91	Nolan Ryan	24.51
Bob Lacey	.201	Bruce Berenyi	0.58	Dan Quisenberry	4.52	John Candelaria	23.48
Dave Righetti	.202	Greg Minton	0.62	Dick Bosman	4.75	Jesse Orosco	23.18
Willie Hernandez	.207	Jim Crawford	0.64	Tom Burgmeier	4.80	Joe Sambito	22.94
John Candelaria	.208	Doug Sisk	0.69	Dave Tomlin	5.02	Dwight Gooden	22.91
Nolan Ryan	.209	Bob Shirley	0.70	Jim Kaat	5.13	Al Holland	22.85
Mark Davis	.209	Dwight Gooden	0.70	Jon Matlack	5.14	Rod Scurry	22.61
Dwight Gooden	.214	Orel Hershiser	0.72	Will McEnaney	5.42	John Tudor	22.53
Mike Norris	.216	Bob Knepper	0.72	Frank Tanana	5.42	Steve Carlton	22.02
John Fulgham	.216	Gary Lavelle	0.77	John Candelaria	5.45	Bob James	21.76
Joe Sambito	.217	Paul Mirabella	0.77	Ed Lynch	5.49	Tippy Martinez	21.55
John Henry Johnson	.218	Jeff Lahti	0.80	Bret Saberhagen	5.50	Willie Hernandez	20.94
Al Holland	.218	Donnie Moore	0.81	Bud Black	5.60	Mike Flanagan	20.93
Larry Gura	.218	Roger Clemens	0.81	Randy Jones	5.63	Gary Lavelle	20.88
Bruce Sutter	.218	Jerry Reuss	0.86	John Tudor	5.67	Frank Tanana	20.82
Bob Shirley	.219	Shane Rawley	0.88	Pedro Borbon	5.69	Bill Caudill	20.80
Dave Dravecky	.220	Jim Acker	0.91	Ron Guidry	5.70	John Hiller	20.42
Dave Smith	.221	Jay Howell	0.93	Dennis Boyd	5.74	Bob Knepper	20.38
Tippy Martinez	.222	Walt Terrell	0.93	Larry Gura	5.82	Rich Gossage	19.92
Steve Carlton	.222	Pedro Borbon	0.94	Glenn Abbott	5.86	John Henry Johnson	19.77
Tom Burgmeier	.223	Andy Hassler	0.95	Gary Ross	5.89	Bob Ojeda	19.72
Bill Dawley	.224	Dave Dravecky	0.97	Don Schulze	5.89	Bob Shirley	19.70
Mario Soto	.224	Jesse Orosco	0.99	Tommy John	5.91	Mark Clear	19.58

CAREER OPP. BATTING AVERAGE VS. RIGHT-HANDED BATTERS		CAREER OPP. HOME RUN PCT. VS. RIGHT-HANDED BATTERS		CAREER OPP. WALK PCT. VS. RIGHT-HANDED BATTERS		CAREER OPP. STRIKEOUT PCT. VS. RIGHT-HANDED BATTERS	
Min. 600 PA		*Min. 600 PA*		*Min. 600 PA*		*Min. 150 Strikeouts*	
Jose DeLeon	.181	Doug Sisk	0.57	Dan Quisenberry	2.00	Dwight Gooden	34.42
Dwight Gooden	.185	Mark Fidrych	0.63	LaMarr Hoyt	2.97	Jose DeLeon	29.18
J.R. Richard	.190	Steve Howe	0.65	Gary Nolan	3.51	J.R. Richard	26.06
Rich Gossage	.194	Rick Lysander	0.70	Bret Saberhagen	3.80	Lee Smith	25.47
Orel Hershiser	.196	Zane Smith	0.79	Larry Andersen	4.17	Cecilio Guante	24.81
Tom Niedenfuer	.198	Alejandro Pena	0.82	Bob Stanley	4.26	Skip Lockwood	24.68
Luis DeLeon	.198	J.R. Richard	0.98	Ferguson Jenkins	4.52	Jeff Reardon	24.52
Mario Soto	.201	Dave Heaverlo	1.00	Lary Sorensen	4.53	Victor Cruz	24.38
Mark Littell	.202	Cecilio Guante	1.03	Luis DeLeon	4.64	Mario Soto	23.97
Sid Fernandez	.203	Kent Tekulve	1.03	Dick Bosman	4.65	Tom Niedenfuer	23.92
Eric Show	.205	Danny Jackson	1.06	Fernando Arroyo	4.69	Mark Clear	23.82
Victor Cruz	.206	Dave Frost	1.09	Jim Barr	4.73	Luis DeLeon	23.60
Jeff Reardon	.208	Tom Niedenfuer	1.11	Ed Lynch	4.73	Rich Gossage	23.55
Andy Messersmith	.209	Mike Barlow	1.14	Tom Hausman	4.96	Nolan Ryan	23.46
Cecilio Guante	.211	Ted Power	1.15	Andy McGaffigan	4.97	Mark Littell	22.95
Mike Armstrong	.211	Greg Minton	1.18	Dennis Leonard	5.00	Bill Caudill	22.80
Skip Lockwood	.213	Bret Saberhagen	1.20	Roger Erickson	5.08	Ron Davis	22.63
Nolan Ryan	.213	Terry Forster	1.22	Rick Langford	5.10	Steve Bedrosian	22.48
Dan Warthen	.213	Pablo Torrealba	1.24	Rick Wise	5.12	Greg Harris	21.43
Jim Kern	.214	Ed Farmer	1.24	Scott Sanderson	5.13	Sid Fernandez	21.38
Steve Bedrosian	.215	Mark Littell	1.26	Moose Haas	5.16	Bruce Sutter	21.20
Bob Stoddard	.216	Dave Tomlin	1.28	Mike Caldwell	5.19	Orel Hershiser	21.05
Juan Berenguer	.218	Dale Murray	1.31	Doug Bird	5.20	Rod Scurry	20.78
Bill Caudill	.219	Dave Smith	1.33	Bill Gullickson	5.20	John Hiller	20.66
Mark Clear	.220	Jim Kern	1.33	Bill Lee	5.22	Enrique Romo	20.60

SINGLE-SEASON OPP. BATTING AVERAGE VS. LEFT-HANDED BATTERS

Min. 125 PA

Bill Dawley, 1983	.142
Bob Lacey, 1977	.146
Mark Clear, 1984	.147
Dave Smith, 1984	.152
Nolan Ryan, 1981	.153
Ron Guidry, 1978	.156
Bob Shirley, 1978	.156
Larry McWilliams, 1983	.156
Matt Young, 1983	.158
Gary Lavelle, 1984	.158
Bill Scherrer, 1983	.158
Rich Wortham, 1979	.159
Larry Gura, 1983	.159
Tom Burgmeier, 1980	.159
Mike Caldwell, 1978	.160
Sid Monge, 1979	.161
Andy Hassler, 1980	.162
Larry Gura, 1978	.164
Bob Knepper, 1981	.164
Gene Garber, 1978	.165
Mike Flanagan, 1982	.167
Tim Lollar, 1982	.170
Bruce Sutter, 1979	.170
Willie Hernandez, 1984	.173
John Candelaria, 1975	.173

SINGLE-SEASON OPP. BATTING AVERAGE VS. RIGHT-HANDED BATTERS

Min. 175 PA

J.R. Richard, 1980	.124
Dave LaRoche, 1976	.139
Rich Gossage, 1977	.140
Mario Soto, 1980	.147
Hank Webb, 1975	.156
Mark Clear, 1979	.157
Don Carman, 1985	.161
Jim Kern, 1979	.161
Jeff Reardon, 1984	.161
Aurelio Lopez, 1983	.162
Tom Niedenfuer, 1983	.162
Luis DeLeon, 1982	.163
Sid Monge, 1978	.164
Frank Williams, 1985	.164
Frank Williams, 1984	.166
Tim Burke, 1985	.166
Cecilio Guante, 1985	.166
Jose DeLeon, 1984	.168
Dwight Gooden, 1984	.170
J.R. Richard, 1978	.171
Rich Gossage, 1978	.171
Scott Garrelts, 1985	.172
John D'Acquisto, 1978	.174
Skip Lockwood, 1976	.175
Eric Show, 1982	.175

CAREER OPP. BATTING AVERAGE IN HOME GAMES

Min. 500 PA

Dwight Gooden	.191
Mike Armstrong	.196
J.R. Richard	.197
Nolan Ryan	.199
Orel Hershiser	.203
Jose DeLeon	.205
Mario Soto	.205
Joe Cowley	.209
Rich Gossage	.210
Bill Dawley	.210
Al Holland	.214
Skip Lockwood	.217
Joe Sambito	.218
Bret Saberhagen	.218
Craig Lefferts	.219
Jeff Reardon	.220
Mark Littell	.220
Sammy Stewart	.220
Mark Langston	.220
Bob Apodaca	.221
Dave Righetti	.221
Steve Carlton	.221
Mark Gubicza	.221
Jeff Lahti	.221
Jesse Orosco	.222

CAREER OPP. BATTING AVERAGE IN ROAD GAMES

Min. 500 PA

Tom Niedenfuer	.198
Sid Fernandez	.202
Mark Littell	.203
Jesse Orosco	.204
John Fulgham	.208
Dwight Gooden	.212
Rich Gossage	.214
Steve Bedrosian	.214
Bruce Sutter	.215
Cecilio Guante	.217
Rod Scurry	.218
Mario Soto	.219
Greg Harris	.219
Jeff Reardon	.222
John Martin	.222
Lee Smith	.223
J.R. Richard	.223
Dan Warthen	.224
Nolan Ryan	.224
Andy Messersmith	.226
Luis DeLeon	.226
Dave Stieb	.226
Mark Clear	.227
Don Gullett	.227
Fernando Valenzuela	.227

CAREER OPP. BATTING AVERAGE ON GRASS SURFACES

Min. 500 PA

J.R. Richard	.195
Sid Fernandez	.196
Dwight Gooden	.199
Danny Frisella	.199
Orel Hershiser	.206
Greg Harris	.206
Mark Littell	.211
Nolan Ryan	.211
Dan Warthen	.213
Mario Soto	.216
Rich Gossage	.216
Craig Lefferts	.217
Andy Messersmith	.221
Frank Williams	.221
Tom Seaver	.222
Dave Righetti	.222
Bill Laxton	.222
Tom Gorman	.223
Brent Strom	.223
Mike Armstrong	.223
Joe Cowley	.224
Al Holland	.224
Jeff Reardon	.224
Tom Waddell	.225
Juan Berenguer	.226

CAREER OPP. BATTING AVERAGE ON ARTIFICIAL TURF

Min. 500 PA

Mike Norris	.194
Rich Gossage	.200
Steve Bedrosian	.210
Mario Soto	.210
Nolan Ryan	.211
Mark Littell	.212
Jose DeLeon	.214
Bill Dawley	.215
J.R. Richard	.215
Lee Smith	.216
Jim Kern	.218
Jeff Reardon	.218
Al Holland	.222
Frank LaCorte	.222
Fernando Valenzuela	.223
Mark Langston	.223
Joe Sambito	.224
Bruce Sutter	.225
Joe Hesketh	.225
Eric Show	.226
Ron Darling	.226
Rod Scurry	.226
Len Barker	.226
Andy McGaffigan	.227
Alejandro Pena	.227

CAREER OPP. BATTING AVERAGE IN DAY GAMES

Min. 250 PA

Nolan Ryan	.198
Mario Soto	.199
Rich Gossage	.212
Mark Littell	.214
Steve Bedrosian	.216
Al Hrabosky	.216
Rod Scurry	.217
Bruce Berenyi	.217
Tim Lollar	.219
Andy Messersmith	.221
Rollie Fingers	.222
Steve Busby	.222
Jose DeLeon	.223
Dave Stewart	.225
Fernando Valenzuela	.225
Jesse Orosco	.225
Orel Hershiser	.225
Bruce Sutter	.225
J.R. Richard	.226
Dave Righetti	.226
Tom Seaver	.227
Ken Brett	.227
Britt Burns	.228
Skip Lockwood	.228
Jim Palmer	.230

CAREER OPP. BATTING AVERAGE IN NIGHT GAMES

Min. 250 PA

Dwight Gooden	.183
Sid Fernandez	.196
J.R. Richard	.205
Jesse Orosco	.208
Orel Hershiser	.208
Mark Littell	.210
Jeff Reardon	.211
Rich Gossage	.212
Jose DeLeon	.212
Jeff Lahti	.214
Joe Hesketh	.214
Nolan Ryan	.215
Mario Soto	.217
Luis DeLeon	.217
Bill Dawley	.218
Mike Norris	.218
Al Holland	.218
Bert Roberge	.219
Tim Conroy	.222
Cecilio Guante	.222
Aurelio Lopez	.222
Joe Sambito	.222
Ken Dixon	.222
Mark Clear	.223
Jim Kern	.223

CAREER OPP. BATTING AVERAGE IN LATE-INNING PRESSURE SITUATIONS

Min. 400 PA

Bill Dawley	.197
Nolan Ryan	.199
Jesse Orosco	.208
J.R. Richard	.209
Rich Gossage	.211
Mario Soto	.213
Cecilio Guante	.213
Steve Bedrosian	.214
Mark Littell	.214
Mike Witt	.215
Fernando Valenzuela	.221
Jeff Reardon	.221
Sid Monge	.221
Don Stanhouse	.222
Skip Lockwood	.224
Frank LaCorte	.224
Aurelio Lopez	.224
John Candelaria	.226
Dave Tobik	.226
Al Holland	.228
Rod Scurry	.228
Tom Niedenfuer	.228
Bill Caudill	.228
Jack Morris	.229
Dan Schatzeder	.229

SINGLE-SEASON OPP. BATTING AVERAGE IN LATE-INNING PRESSURE SITUATIONS

Min. 150 PA

Dave LaRoche, 1976	.142
Tom Niedenfuer, 1983	.146
Don Carman, 1985	.157
Tom Seaver, 1976	.163
Ron Davis, 1981	.166
Fernando Valenzuela, 1985	.167
Dennis Eckersley, 1977	.168
Bill Dawley, 1983	.169
Rich Gossage, 1977	.169
Aurelio Lopez, 1979	.173
Nolan Ryan, 1976	.174
Bill Caudill, 1982	.175
Manny Sarmiento, 1978	.176
Willie Hernandez, 1984	.176
Ed Farmer, 1979	.177
Skip Lockwood, 1976	.179
J.R. Richard, 1976	.179
Steve Bedrosian, 1982	.181
Frank Tanana, 1976	.181
Neil Allen, 1984	.182
Steve Carlton, 1979	.183
Mark Littell, 1979	.184
Jeff Reardon, 1981	.184
Charlie Hough, 1976	.184
Tug McGraw, 1980	.184

CAREER OPP. HOME RUN PCT. IN LATE-INNING PRESSURE SITUATIONS

Min. 400 PA

Dave J. Schmidt	0.39
Steve Comer	0.61
Fernando Valenzuela	0.66
Jim Todd	0.71
Jeff Lahti	0.74
Dave A. Roberts	0.75
Doug Sisk	0.75
Don Stanhouse	0.84
Bill Gullickson	0.91
Steve Howe	0.95
Dale Murray	0.96
Randy Jones	0.98
Clay Carroll	1.00
Dave Giusti	1.04
Darold Knowles	1.09
Scott Sanderson	1.11
Pete Vuckovich	1.12
Tommy John	1.12
Dickie Noles	1.13
Jay Howell	1.14
Manny Sarmiento	1.14
Greg Minton	1.16
Woody Fryman	1.20
Vida Blue	1.21
Gary Lavelle	1.23

CAREER OPP. STRIKEOUT PCT. IN LATE-INNING PRESSURE SITUATIONS

Min. 100 Strikeouts

Mark Davis	25.32
Nolan Ryan	23.59
Steve Bedrosian	22.99
Bill Caudill	22.87
Rich Gossage	22.73
Mark Clear	22.72
Skip Lockwood	22.56
Mark Littell	22.26
Rod Scurry	21.84
Lee Smith	21.57
John Hiller	21.46
Jesse Orosco	21.28
Victor Cruz	21.13
Tom Niedenfuer	20.85
Frank DiPino	20.17
Dave Righetti	20.11
Bruce Sutter	19.99
Ron Davis	19.94
Bob James	19.86
Dave LaRoche	19.59
Jim Kern	19.51
Al Holland	19.51
Steve Carlton	19.41
Tim Stoddard	19.32
Jay Howell	19.30

CAREER OPP. BATTING AVERAGE IN LATE-INNING PRESSURE SITUATIONS WITH RUNNERS ON BASE

Min. 150 PA

Kevin Saucier	.160
Dave Dravecky	.166
Dave Tobik	.177
Cecilio Guante	.188
Steve McCatty	.197
Steve Bedrosian	.197
Nolan Ryan	.201
Bill Dawley	.201
Mike Witt	.202
Ernie Camacho	.203
Jesse Orosco	.203
Jack Morris	.206
Sid Monge	.209
Danny Frisella	.210
Dock Ellis	.211
Bill Caudill	.212
Aurelio Lopez	.212
Randy Lerch	.213
Bill Greif	.213
Tom Niedenfuer	.214
Tippy Martinez	.216
Fernando Valenzuela	.217
Dave Campbell	.217
Doug Sisk	.218
Joe Niekro	.219

SINGLE-SEASON OPP. BATTING AVERAGE IN LATE-INNING PRESSURE SITUATIONS WITH RUNNERS ON BASE

Min. 60 PA

Frank Tanana, 1976	.116
Joe Sambito, 1981	.121
Dave LaRoche, 1976	.128
Jim Kern, 1976	.128
Dave Tobik, 1979	.130
Bill Greif, 1976	.130
Joaquin Andujar, 1978	.133
Nolan Ryan, 1978	.134
Steve Bedrosian, 1982	.136
Kevin Saucier, 1981	.140
George Frazier, 1982	.143
Mike Torrez, 1975	.143
Tug McGraw, 1980	.146
Dave Dravecky, 1984	.148
Andy Hassler, 1980	.148
George Frazier, 1983	.149
Tom Niedenfuer, 1983	.150
Jeff Reardon, 1981	.151
Jesse Orosco, 1983	.152
Richard Dotson, 1984	.153
Dave Tobik, 1982	.154
Jon Matlack, 1978	.154
Bill Dawley, 1984	.156
Tippy Martinez, 1976	.156
Keith Atherton, 1985	.157

CAREER OPP. HOME RUN PCT. IN LATE-INNING PRESSURE SITUATIONS WITH RUNNERS ON BASE

Min. 150 PA

Bill Lee	0.00
Steve Comer	0.00
Charlie Williams	0.00
Mark Lee	0.00
Ken Kravec	0.00
Kevin Saucier	0.00
Joaquin Andujar	0.28
Doyle Alexander	0.30
Fernando Valenzuela	0.31
Dave J. Schmidt	0.40
Dave Tomlin	0.41
Dave A. Roberts	0.45
Steve Howe	0.46
Tim Stoddard	0.48
Vern Ruhle	0.49
Greg Minton	0.56
Pete Vuckovich	0.62
Craig Lefferts	0.63
Bill Gullickson	0.68
Roy Thomas	0.69
Randy Lerch	0.71
Bill Bonham	0.73
Rick Mahler	0.79
Doug Sisk	0.79
Don Stanhouse	0.80

CAREER OPP. STRIKEOUT PCT. IN LATE-INNING PRESSURE SITUATIONS WITH RUNNERS ON BASE

Min. 40 Strikeouts

Ken Howell	24.19
Mark Clear	24.06
Bill Caudill	23.10
Skip Lockwood	21.50
Nolan Ryan	21.43
Mark Littell	21.19
Tom Niedenfuer	20.67
Steve Bedrosian	20.63
Rod Scurry	20.53
Lee Smith	20.06
John Hiller	20.00
Dave LaRoche	19.85
Victor Cruz	19.80
Doug Bair	19.66
Ron Davis	19.65
Tim Stoddard	19.61
Rich Gossage	19.40
Dave Righetti	19.27
Al Holland	19.21
Bob James	19.14
Jesse Orosco	18.71
Tippy Martinez	18.63
Bruce Sutter	18.62
John D'Acquisto	18.58
Rudy May	18.54

CAREER OPP. BATTING AVERAGE WITH RUNNERS ON BASE

Min. 500 PA

Dwight Gooden	.198
Jesse Orosco	.203
Cecilio Guante	.210
Jeff Reardon	.215
Craig Lefferts	.216
Bill Caudill	.216
Orel Hershiser	.217
Mario Soto	.218
Rod Scurry	.219
Ron Darling	.219
Bruce Sutter	.220
Tom Niedenfuer	.223
Lee Smith	.224
J.R. Richard	.224
Rich Gossage	.224
Mark Littell	.225
Nolan Ryan	.225
Mark Clear	.226
Steve Bedrosian	.226
Jim Kern	.227
Al Holland	.227
Victor Cruz	.228
Jose DeLeon	.228
Bob Apodaca	.230
Dave Dravecky	.230

SINGLE-SEASON OPP. BATTING AVERAGE WITH RUNNERS ON BASE

Min. 175 PA

John D'Acquisto, 1978	.155
Gene Garber, 1978	.160
Jesse Orosco, 1984	.167
Bill Caudill, 1980	.173
Jesse Orosco, 1983	.175
Rich Gossage, 1977	.175
Willie Hernandez, 1984	.176
Al Holland, 1983	.177
Charlie Hough, 1976	.177
Lee Smith, 1983	.178
Dwight Gooden, 1985	.180
Doug Bair, 1978	.181
Tippy Martinez, 1983	.181
Sid Monge, 1979	.182
Bruce Sutter, 1977	.182
Jose DeLeon, 1983	.185
Hal Dues, 1978	.185
Rich Gossage, 1975	.186
Don Sutton, 1980	.186
Mark Clear, 1984	.187
Mario Soto, 1982	.188
Tim Burke, 1985	.188
Tom Seaver, 1981	.189
Aurelio Lopez, 1983	.189
Joe Cowley, 1985	.189

CAREER OPP. BATTING AVERAGE WITH RUNNERS IN SCORING POSITION

Min. 300 PA

Cecilio Guante	.185
Dwight Gooden	.187
Lee Smith	.196
Bob Apodaca	.199
Jesse Orosco	.200
Ron Darling	.203
Steve Bedrosian	.204
Rich Gossage	.205
Mario Soto	.206
Steve Busby	.206
Craig Lefferts	.207
Jeff Lahti	.208
Stan Thomas	.213
Tippy Martinez	.216
Nolan Ryan	.217
Orel Hershiser	.218
Al Holland	.219
J.R. Richard	.219
Tom Seaver	.220
Bob Welch	.220
Jeff Reardon	.221
Mark Clear	.222
Sid Monge	.222
Victor Cruz	.223
Andy Messersmith	.223

SINGLE-SEASON OPP. BATTING AVERAGE WITH RUNNERS IN SCORING POSITION

Min. 125 PA

Rich Gossage, 1978	.143
Dwight Gooden, 1985	.144
Tim Burke, 1985	.147
Joe Cowley, 1985	.148
Tom Hilgendorf, 1975	.149
John Candelaria, 1977	.149
Cecilio Guante, 1983	.151
Don Sutton, 1980	.153
Gene Garber, 1982	.156
Bob Lacey, 1977	.157
Tom Hausman, 1975	.159
Rich Gossage, 1977	.159
Steve McCatty, 1981	.161
Tom Seaver, 1981	.163
Bill Campbell, 1977	.165
Joaquin Andujar, 1978	.167
Mario Soto, 1980	.167
Steve McCatty, 1982	.169
Frank Tanana, 1977	.170
Jim Kern, 1976	.171
Mark Clear, 1981	.171
Aurelio Lopez, 1983	.171
Aurelio Lopez, 1979	.172
Mike Willis, 1977	.173
Dave Stewart, 1983	.173

CAREER OPP. BATTING AVERAGE WITH 2 OUTS AND RUNNERS ON BASE

Min. 250 PA

Dwight Gooden	.165
Jose DeLeon	.172
Bill Caudill	.177
Victor Cruz	.190
Pete Filson	.194
Jesse Orosco	.195
Pat Dobson	.196
Bruce Sutter	.200
Mario Soto	.200
Orel Hershiser	.201
J.R. Richard	.202
Tom Niedenfuer	.203
Rollie Fingers	.204
Dave Smith	.204
Bob Welch	.205
Craig McMurtry	.205
Ed Glynn	.205
Jeff Reardon	.206
Mark Littell	.207
Rich Gossage	.207
Charlie Williams	.208
Dave Stewart	.209
Bud Black	.209
Al Nipper	.211
Dave Dravecky	.212

SINGLE-SEASON OPP. BATTING AVERAGE WITH 2 OUTS AND RUNNERS ON BASE

Min. 100 PA

Bill Caudill, 1980	.103
Pat Dobson, 1976	.115
Jerry Ujdur, 1982	.122
John Tudor, 1984	.143
Ed Whitson, 1984	.143
Jose DeLeon, 1985	.144
Bob Forsch, 1978	.147
Eduardo Rodriguez, 1976	.149
Sparky Lyle, 1978	.149
Dan Warthen, 1975	.149
Bill Campbell, 1977	.149
Frank Tanana, 1977	.150
Fred Norman, 1978	.152
Scott Garrelts, 1985	.152
Tom Seaver, 1981	.153
Scott Sanderson, 1980	.154
Luis Tiant, 1978	.155
Britt Burns, 1981	.155
Steve Bedrosian, 1983	.156
Gene Nelson, 1985	.156
Rick Rhoden, 1984	.157
Dave Stieb, 1981	.157
Bill Gullickson, 1982	.157
Randy Lerch, 1979	.158
Dwight Gooden, 1985	.158

CAREER OPP. BATTING AVERAGE WITH 2 OUTS AND RUNNERS IN SCORING POSITION

Min. 150 PA

Cecilio Guante	.130
Dwight Gooden	.158
Keith Atherton	.162
Greg Harris	.162
Bob Apodaca	.165
Jose DeLeon	.168
Dave Stewart	.170
Lee Smith	.173
Victor Cruz	.175
Craig Lefferts	.175
Jesse Orosco	.178
J.R. Richard	.185
Steve Busby	.186
Bill Caudill	.187
Bob Welch	.187
Mario Soto	.191
Dave Smith	.191
Tippy Martinez	.191
Rich Gossage	.195
Enrique Romo	.197
Doug Rau	.197
Dan Warthen	.197
Pat Dobson	.197
Dave Dravecky	.198
John Candelaria	.198

SINGLE-SEASON OPP. BATTING AVERAGE WITH 2 OUTS AND RUNNERS IN SCORING POSITION

Min. 75 PA

Dan Warthen, 1975	.100
John Tudor, 1984	.110
Luis Tiant, 1978	.113
Bill Gullickson, 1982	.118
Rich Gossage, 1978	.119
Ed Whitson, 1984	.119
Doug Corbett, 1980	.127
Frank Tanana, 1977	.130
Fred Norman, 1978	.130
Dwight Gooden, 1985	.133
Pat Dobson, 1976	.133
Tim Burke, 1985	.134
Frank Tanana, 1976	.135
Bill Campbell, 1977	.136
Tom Seaver, 1981	.138
Dave Freisleben, 1976	.143
Doug Rau, 1977	.143
Rick Langford, 1977	.143
Eduardo Rodriguez, 1976	.145
Juan Eichelberger, 1981	.145
Tippy Martinez, 1984	.145
Richard Dotson, 1984	.146
Kevin Gross, 1985	.146
J.R. Richard, 1979	.147
J.R. Richard, 1977	.147

SINGLE-SEASON DOUBLES ALLOWED

Dennis Leonard, 1978	62
Bruce Hurst, 1984	60
Rick Sutcliffe, 1983	58
Jim Barr, 1977	57
Jim Clancy, 1983	57
Bill Gullickson, 1983	56
Scott McGregor, 1983	55
John Montefusco, 1975	54
Dennis Leonard, 1980	54
Steve Rogers, 1983	54
Wilbur Wood, 1975	53
Mike Torrez, 1983	53
Ron Guidry, 1983	53
Doyle Alexander, 1984	53
Bob Knepper, 1985	53
Ron Reed, 1975	52
Larry Christenson, 1977	52
Steve Carlton, 1977	52
Mike Flanagan, 1978	52
Jerry Koosman, 1980	52
Dave Stieb, 1983	52
Dennis Boyd, 1985	52
Luis Tiant, 1975	51
Jim Kaat, 1975	51
Randy Jones, 1978	51

SINGLE-SEASON TRIPLES ALLOWED

Larry Christenson, 1976	17
Paul Thormodsgard, 1977	16
Jim Barr, 1975	14
Jim Kaat, 1977	14
Jim Barr, 1977	14
Dave Goltz, 1977	14
Craig Swan, 1979	14
Randy Jones, 1979	14
Rick Sutcliffe, 1984	14
Ray Burris, 1976	13
Rick Reuschel, 1976	13
Luis Tiant, 1979	13
Dick Ruthven, 1980	13
Steve Carlton, 1980	13
Rich Gale, 1982	13
Tommy John, 1982	13
Mike Smithson, 1983	13
John Montefusco, 1975	12
Jim Kaat, 1976	12
Ken Holtzman, 1976	12
Ray Burris, 1978	12
Roger Erickson, 1979	12
Bob Forsch, 1979	12
Doc Medich, 1980	12
Mike Krukow, 1980	12

SINGLE-SEASON EXTRA-BASE HITS ALLOWED

Phil Niekro, 1979	97
Dennis Leonard, 1978	94
Dennis Leonard, 1980	92
Rick Sutcliffe, 1983	92
LaMarr Hoyt, 1984	91
Jerry Garvin, 1977	90
Wilbur Wood, 1975	89
Jim Barr, 1977	89
Dan Petry, 1983	89
Jim Clancy, 1983	88
Ferguson Jenkins, 1979	87
Luis Tiant, 1975	86
Ferguson Jenkins, 1975	86
Scott McGregor, 1983	86
Bruce Hurst, 1984	86
Charlie Hough, 1984	86
Dennis Eckersley, 1977	85
Matt Keough, 1982	85
Frank Viola, 1983	85
Mike Caldwell, 1983	85
Ron Guidry, 1983	85
LaMarr Hoyt, 1983	85
Doyle Alexander, 1984	85
Dennis Eckersley, 1982	84
Mike Smithson, 1985	84

CAREER OPP. EXTRA-BASE HIT PCT.

Min. 1,000 PA

Steve Howe	3.72
Dwight Gooden	4.31
Orel Hershiser	4.53
Alejandro Pena	4.74
Tom Niedenfuer	4.75
Doug Sisk	4.77
Greg Minton	4.78
Gary Lavelle	5.08
Mark Fidrych	5.13
Nolan Ryan	5.20
Rich Gossage	5.21
Jim Kern	5.24
Jesse Orosco	5.25
J.R. Richard	5.28
Lee Smith	5.40
Mark Littell	5.40
David Palmer	5.46
Neil Allen	5.49
Clay Carroll	5.56
Jerry Reuss	5.58
Kent Tekulve	5.58
Dave Righetti	5.59
Joe Niekro	5.66
Dan Quisenberry	5.66
Fernando Valenzuela	5.72

HIGHEST CAREER GROUND OUTS-TO-AIR OUTS RATIO

Min. 1,000 PA

Doug Corbett	3.06
Doug Sisk	2.76
Ray Fontenot	2.53
Tommy John	2.47
Orel Hershiser	2.47
Greg Minton	2.41
Jim Todd	2.39
Jaime Cocanower	2.38
Dennis Lamp	2.38
Bob Stanley	2.35
Kent Tekulve	2.35
Dan Quisenberry	2.33
Jim Acker	2.24
John Denny	2.20
Bill Castro	2.17
Gene Garber	2.15
Rick Reuschel	2.15
Randy Jones	2.13
David Palmer	2.12
Terry Forster	2.06
Rick Lysander	2.05
Steve Trout	2.03
Chuck Rainey	2.01
Rick Matula	1.98
Dale Murray	1.96

LOWEST CAREER GROUND OUTS-TO-AIR OUTS RATIO

Min. 1,000 PA

Keith Atherton	0.48
Sid Fernandez	0.50
Tom Niedenfuer	0.54
Mike Armstrong	0.55
Jeff Reardon	0.58
Victor Cruz	0.59
Dave LaRoche	0.61
Chris Knapp	0.62
Bill Caudill	0.62
Juan Berenguer	0.63
Al Hrabosky	0.63
Tom Browning	0.64
Joe Price	0.65
Tim Conroy	0.65
Aurelio Lopez	0.65
Al Holland	0.66
Skip Lockwood	0.66
Luis Tiant	0.67
Dennis Eckersley	0.69
John Henry Johnson	0.69
Catfish Hunter	0.69
Buzz Capra	0.69
Dave Beard	0.70
Cecilio Guante	0.71
Manny Sarmiento	0.71

CAREER GROUND OUT PCT (PER 100 PA)

Min. 1,000 PA

Dan Quisenberry	43.8
Randy Jones	41.3
Tommy John	41.2
Doug Sisk	40.5
Bob Stanley	40.2
Bill Castro	40.0
Doug Corbett	39.9
Greg Minton	39.8
Dennis Lamp	39.4
Ray Fontenot	39.3
Kent Tekulve	39.0
Jim Todd	38.6
Orel Hershiser	38.4
Paul Hartzell	38.2
Jaime Cocanower	38.2
Fernando Arroyo	38.1
Rob Dressler	37.8
Clay Carroll	37.5
Rick Honeycutt	37.5
Dave Rozema	37.3
Rick Matula	37.3
John Denny	37.3
Mike Proly	37.1
Jerry Reuss	37.0
Rick Reuschel	36.9

CAREER AIR OUT PCT. (PER 100 PA)

Min. 1,000 PA

Keith Atherton	37.3
Gary Nolan	36.0
Catfish Hunter	35.8
John Martin	35.2
Tom Browning	35.2
Mike Armstrong	35.2
Luis Tiant	34.3
Scott McGregor	34.2
Manny Sarmiento	34.2
Tom Niedenfuer	34.1
Larry Gura	33.6
Dan Schatzeder	33.5
Chris Knapp	33.3
Joe Price	33.2
Grant Jackson	33.2
Dennis Eckersley	33.1
Pete Filson	33.1
Steve McCatty	33.1
Jeff Reardon	33.0
Sid Fernandez	33.0
Ron Romanick	32.9
Brian Kingman	32.9
Craig Swan	32.9
Al Hrabosky	32.8
Bill Laskey	32.8

CAREER OPP. ON-BASE AVERAGE LEADING OFF INNINGS

Min. 250 PA

Dave J. Schmidt	.238
Dan Quisenberry	.242
Mike Armstrong	.248
Dwight Gooden	.251
Rich Gossage	.256
Brad Havens	.259
John Martin	.261
Dave Tobik	.262
Tom Niedenfuer	.264
Gene Garber	.268
Tug McGraw	.269
Greg Harris	.269
Steve Howe	.269
Gary Nolan	.272
Darold Knowles	.273
Rod Scurry	.273
Frank Tanana	.273
Doug Corbett	.274
Gary Lucas	.275
Jimmy Key	.275
LaMarr Hoyt	.275
Pete Filson	.276
Bret Saberhagen	.277
Joe Sambito	.277
Mario Soto	.277

SINGLE-SEASON OPP. ON-BASE AVERAGE LEADING OFF INNINGS

Min. 100 PA

Greg Harris, 1985	.175
Dan Quisenberry, 1984	.188
Vern Ruhle, 1983	.191
Randy Martz, 1981	.202
Joe Price, 1983	.212
Dan Quisenberry, 1983	.215
Dave J. Schmidt, 1982	.217
John Tudor, 1985	.217
Rich Gossage, 1978	.219
Mike Armstrong, 1982	.220
Dan Schatzeder, 1984	.221
Don Sutton, 1975	.221
Dennis Eckersley, 1977	.223
Pat Underwood, 1982	.223
Ken Forsch, 1979	.223
Bob Forsch, 1977	.224
Marty Pattin, 1976	.224
Ron Guidry, 1981	.224
Vern Ruhle, 1981	.224
Francisco Barrios, 1979	.225
John Martin, 1981	.229
Ron Reed, 1978	.230
Mario Soto, 1981	.231
Bob Knepper, 1981	.231
Bill Gullickson, 1980	.231

CAREER OPP. WALK PCT. LEADING OFF INNINGS

Min. 250 PA

Dave J. Schmidt	1.61
Dan Quisenberry	2.07
Gene Garber	2.27
Atlee Hammaker	2.27
Gary Nolan	2.49
Kevin Kobel	3.02
Gary Lucas	3.40
Ron Reed	3.54
Mark Fidrych	3.55
Steve Howe	3.57
LaMarr Hoyt	3.65
Gary Ross	3.88
Pedro Borbon	3.95
Scott Sanderson	3.98
Mark Thurmond	4.02
Jim Barr	4.05
Dave Rozema	4.07
Tommy John	4.09
Roger Erickson	4.16
Ferguson Jenkins	4.27
Rick Reuschel	4.27
Ed Lynch	4.31
Frank Tanana	4.37
Mike Smithson	4.37
Dennis Eckersley	4.46

SINGLE-SEASON OPP. WALK PCT. LEADING OFF INNINGS

Min. 100 PA

Gene Garber, 1982	0.00
Dan Quisenberry, 1983	0.00
Dan Quisenberry, 1985	0.00
Rick Langford, 1982	0.41
Jim Barr, 1982	0.78
Tom Hausman, 1980	0.82
Bob Forsch, 1980	0.89
Dave J. Schmidt, 1982	0.94
Ron Reed, 1978	1.00
Mike Smithson, 1983	1.29
Gaylord Perry, 1981	1.29
Ferguson Jenkins, 1976	1.38
Glenn Abbott, 1983	1.45
Roger Clemens, 1984	1.45
Ron Guidry, 1981	1.49
Bob Shirley, 1980	1.50
Rick Rhoden, 1983	1.60
Atlee Hammaker, 1982	1.62
Gary Nolan, 1976	1.64
Roger Erickson, 1982	1.67
Atlee Hammaker, 1983	1.68
Dan Quisenberry, 1982	1.68
Dennis Eckersley, 1982	1.70
Dan Quisenberry, 1984	1.71
Dennis Eckersley, 1984	1.73

CAREER OPP. BATTING AVERAGE WITH BASES LOADED

Min. 50 PA

Jesse Orosco	.114
Ed Figueroa	.147
Doug Rau	.152
Dave LaRoche	.159
Eric Show	.163
Dave Lemanczyk	.167
Bruce Berenyi	.169
Keith Atherton	.171
Tippy Martinez	.177
Tom House	.179
Ed Halicki	.185
Dave LaPoint	.185
Butch Metzger	.188
Tom Griffin	.188
Craig Swan	.189
Steve Bedrosian	.190
Jim Palmer	.193
Mike Moore	.196
Wayne Twitchell	.196
Mike Stanton	.197
Bob Lacey	.197
Tom Underwood	.197
Jim Rooker	.200
Fred Breining	.200
Eduardo Rodriguez	.203

CAREER BASES LOADED BATTERS FACED WITHOUT ALLOWING A GRAND-SLAM HOME RUN

Jim Kern	139
Pat Zachry	128
Joaquin Andujar	124
Mike Krukow	118
Jim Palmer	105
Danny Darwin	98
Al Hrabosky	96
Andy Hassler	93
Jesse Jefferson	91
Ed Figueroa	82
Jesse Orosco	81
Bob Welch	78
Richard Dotson	77
Bruce Berenyi	76
Don Hood	74
Rawly Eastwick	73
Mike Stanton	73
Joe Price	72
Roger Erickson	71
Renie Martin	70
Roy Thomas	70
Doug Corbett	70
Luis Leal	67
Dave LaPoint	65
Eddie Solomon	65

CAREER OPP. WALK PCT. WITH BASES LOADED

Min. 50 PA

Rick Mahler	0.00
Dave Heaverlo	0.81
Vern Ruhle	1.05
Steve McCatty	1.10
Steve Trout	1.20
Dave Tobik	1.43
John Tudor	1.64
Mike G. Marshall	1.64
Fred Breining	1.72
Larry Christenson	1.79
Ferguson Jenkins	1.82
Jim Umbarger	1.82
Mike Garman	1.82
Butch Metzger	1.82
Dennis Eckersley	1.83
Will McEnaney	1.89
Mike Parrott	1.89
Paul Reuschel	1.92
Steve Howe	1.92
Ed Vande Berg	1.96
Matt Young	1.96
Paul Splittorff	2.00
Dock Ellis	2.00
Ed Lynch	2.00
Bill Castro	2.02

CAREER OPP. STRIKEOUT PCT. WITH BASES LOADED

Min. 15 Strikeouts

Nolan Ryan	28.23
John Hiller	28.13
Bruce Berenyi	27.63
Mark Littell	26.51
Al Holland	25.30
Dave LaRoche	25.20
Jeff Reardon	25.00
Rich Gossage	24.56
Mario Soto	24.55
Steve Carlton	23.86
Bill Caudill	23.23
Ron Guidry	23.17
Sammy Stewart	22.76
Tom Seaver	22.76
Tippy Martinez	22.67
Frank Tanana	22.58
Mike Krukow	22.03
Jim Kern	21.58
Dave Tobik	21.43
Tim Stoddard	21.18
Wayne Twitchell	21.13
Terry Forster	21.11
Mark Clear	21.02
Joe Sambito	20.73
Bruce Sutter	20.71

VII
Batter-Pitcher Matchups

Batter-Pitcher Matchups

The Batter-Pitcher Matchup section lists, for ten selected players, their performances against every pitcher or batter they have faced for at least five at bats in their careers. These statistics include all regular season appearances since the start of the 1975 season.

Earl Weaver used to keep them on index cards. Dave Johnson maintains his on a PC. But until the past few years the public was largely unaware of the importance many managers place on specific matchup statistics in setting a lineup. The stats do not even out over the long run, and the differences can be massive: according to Weaver, Boog Powell was two for sixty-one against Mickey Lolich, and last year we noted Ned Yost's ten for twelve with two homers against Tommy John (quite a performance for a lifetime .212 hitter!). In this section, we expand the "Loves to Face" and "Hates to Face" matchups listed in the Batter and Pitcher Sections to take a look at the career performances of some

of the most extraordinary players in the game.

The ten players selected here are five pitchers and five batters, five National Leaguers and five American Leaguers. Now you can see in detail just how few pitchers really give Wade Boggs trouble. Or if anyone has a book on Don Mattingly yet. Does a super pitcher like Dwight Gooden make everyone hit like Buddy Biancalana? What kind of hitters are effective against a ground-ball pitcher like Dan Quisenberry or Bruce Sutter? Has John Tudor changed his style of pitching since moving to the National League, and is that reflected in the types of hitters who have hit him? For the first time ever, you have the answers to these questions.

We hope you find this information interesting and useful. We intend to make it a regular feature of the *Analyst,* so, to the fans of Dale Murphy, Kirk Gibson, and Fernando Valenzuela, we say, take heart. There's always next year.

Wade Boggs

Pitcher	AB	H	2B	3B	HR	BB	SO	BA	SA	OBA	Pitcher	AB	H	2B	3B	HR	BB	SO	BA	SA	OBA
Glenn Abbott	9	5	1	0	0	0	1	.556	.667	.556	Dennis Lamp	9	2	0	0	0	1	0	.222	.222	.300
Jim Acker	8	4	1	0	0	2	0	.500	.625	.600	Rick Langford	6	1	1	0	0	2	1	.167	.333	.375
Doyle Alexander	26	9	4	0	0	3	1	.346	.500	.400	Mark Langston	9	0	0	0	0	3	2	.000	.000	.250
Bud Anderson	6	4	1	0	1	3	0	.667	1.333	.778	Luis Leal	20	10	1	1	2	0		.500	.800	.545
Luis Aponte	5	2	0	0	1	0	0	.400	1.000	.400	Charlie Leibrandt	14	7	1	0	1	1	0	.500	.786	.533
Mike Armstrong	9	7	0	0	0	0	1	.778	.778	.778	Dennis Leonard	11	2	1	0	0	1	0	.182	.273	.250
Keith Atherton	8	4	2	0	1	2	1	.500	1.125	.545	Aurelio Lopez	7	5	0	0	0	3	0	.714	.714	.800
Doug Bair	9	4	1	0	1	1	1	.444	.889	.500	Urbano Lugo	6	2	0	0	0	1	0	.333	.333	.429
Floyd Bannister	17	6	1	0	0	2	2	.353	.412	.421	Rick Lysander	13	7	2	0	0	1	0	.538	.692	.571
Len Barker	8	3	0	0	0	2	0	.375	.375	.500	Dennis Martinez	25	9	6	0	0	1	2	.360	.600	.385
Salome Barojas	6	2	1	0	0	1	0	.333	.500	.429	Tippy Martinez	11	1	0	0	0	1	1	.091	.091	.167
Jim Beattie	23	5	1	1	0	3	3	.217	.348	.308	Mike Mason	9	2	0	0	0	3	1	.222	.333	.417
Joe Beckwith	11	3	0	0	0	1	3	.273	.273	.333	Jon Matlack	6	3	0	0	1	1	1	.500	.500	.571
Juan Berenguer	21	9	2	0	0	3	1	.429	.524	.500	Kirk McCaskill	9	2	0	0	0	0	1	.222	.222	.222
Bud Black	14	4	0	0	0	1	1	.286	.286	.333	Steve McCatty	10	5	0	0	1	5	1	.500	.800	.667
Bert Blyleven	19	6	1	0	0	1	1	.316	.368	.350	Bob McClure	26	9	1	0	1	1	2	.346	.385	.393
Mike Boddicker	24	10	0	0	0	3	1	.417	.417	.500	Scott McGregor	18	4	0	0	0	0	1	.222	.222	.222
Tom Burgmeier	6	2	0	1	0	0	0	.333	.667	.333	Doc Medich	9	0	0	0	0	2	1	.000	.000	.182
Britt Burns	23	11	0	0	0	3	2	.478	.478	.538	Paul Mirabella	5	2	0	0	0	2	1	.400	.400	.571
Ray Burris	7	2	1	0	0	0	0	.286	.429	.286	John Montefusco	6	2	0	0	0	2	0	.333	.333	.500
John Butcher	27	11	1	0	0	3	0	.407	.444	.467	Mike Moore	16	6	1	0	0	5	2	.375	.438	.500
Marty Bystrom	6	3	1	0	0	0	0	.500	.667	.500	Jack Morris	26	8	1	0	0	5	5	.308	.346	.419
Mike Caldwell	10	2	1	0	0	0	1	.200	.300	.200	Dale Murray	6	3	1	0	0	2	1	.500	.667	.625
Ernie Camacho	6	3	0	0	0	0	0	.500	.500	.500	Gene Nelson	8	2	0	0	1	1	0	.250	.625	.333
Bobby Castillo	11	2	0	0	0	3	0	.182	.182	.357	Phil Niekro	12	4	1	0	0	2	3	.333	.417	.429
Bill Caudill	10	5	1	0	0	2	3	.500	.600	.583	Dickie Noles	11	7	2	0	0	1	1	.636	.818	.667
Jim Clancy	16	8	1	0	0	5	0	.500	.563	.619	Jim Palmer	5	3	0	0	0	1	0	.600	.600	.667
Bryan Clark	14	4	0	0	0	2	3	.286	.286	.375	Gaylord Perry	16	5	0	1	0	1	0	.313	.438	.353
Pat Clements	5	1	0	0	0	0	0	.200	.200	.200	Dan Petry	27	6	1	0	0	11	4	.222	.259	.447
Jaime Cocanower	15	3	2	0	0	5	0	.200	.333	.400	Chuck Porter	11	7	3	0	0	0	0	.636	.909	.636
Chris Codiroli	22	9	3	0	0	5	0	.409	.545	.483	Dan Quisenberry	16	2	0	0	0	0	0	.125	.125	.125
Steve Comer	5	1	0	0	0	0	0	.200	.200	.200	Dennis Rasmussen	10	4	0	0	0	0	1	.400	.400	.400
Doug Corbett	5	2	0	0	0	0	0	.400	.400	.400	Eric Rasmussen	6	4	0	1	0	0	0	.667	1.000	.667
Joe Cowley	15	4	1	0	0	3	1	.267	.333	.350	Shane Rawley	14	2	0	0	0	1	1	.143	.143	.133
Keith Creel	7	1	0	0	0	0	0	.143	.143	.143	Steve Renko	9	6	1	0	1	0	0	.667	1.111	.667
Danny Darwin	24	6	1	0	1	4	2	.250	.417	.357	Dave Righetti	21	4	2	0	0	3	6	.190	.286	.292
Ron Davis	6	4	0	0	0	2	1	.667	.667	.750	Jose Rijo	5	3	1	0	0	1	0	.600	.800	.667
Storm Davis	23	5	2	0	0	4	5	.217	.304	.333	Ron Romanick	13	6	2	0	0	1	0	.462	.615	.500
Ken Dixon	13	4	1	0	0	2	2	.308	.385	.400	Ramon Romero	6	1	0	0	0	2	1	.167	.167	.375
Richard Dotson	19	6	1	0	1	5	0	.316	.526	.458	Dave Rozema	9	4	1	1	0	1	0	.444	.778	.500
Jamie Easterly	16	8	2	0	0	0	1	.500	.625	.500	Bret Saberhagen	6	4	1	1	1	1	1	.667	1.667	.714
Steve Farr	10	5	0	0	0	1	1	.500	.500	.545	Luis Sanchez	11	7	2	1	0	1	1	.636	1.000	.667
Pete Filson	8	1	1	0	0	1	1	.125	.250	.222	Bill Scherrer	5	4	0	0	1	0	0	.800	.800	.833
Mike Flanagan	11	3	0	0	0	0	0	.273	.273	.273	Dave J. Schmidt	5	1	0	0	0	1	0	.200	.200	.333
Ray Fontenot	6	3	0	0	0	1	0	.500	.500	.571	Ken Schrom	9	6	0	0	0	0	0	.667	.667	.700
Ken Forsch	12	1	0	0	0	0	1	.083	.083	.083	Tom Seaver	23	9	2	0	1	2	0	.391	.609	.440
George Frazier	10	2	0	0	0	0	1	.200	.200	.200	Bob Shirley	12	2	1	0	1	3	3	.167	.250	.231
Bob L. Gibson	6	1	0	0	0	1	0	.167	.167	.286	Jim Slaton	20	8	2	0	0	3	1	.400	.500	.478
Jim Gott	10	2	0	0	0	2	1	.200	.200	.333	Roy Smith	6	2	0	0	0	2	0	.333	.333	.500
Mark Gubicza	19	7	4	0	0	6	3	.368	.579	.520	Mike Smithson	20	7	0	1	0	2	2	.350	.450	.435
Ron Guidry	36	9	1	0	0	1	2	.250	.278	.270	Nate Snell	7	2	0	0	0	0	0	.286	.286	.286
Larry Gura	10	1	0	0	0	2	0	.100	.100	.250	Larry Sorensen	18	5	0	0	0	3	0	.278	.278	.381
Moose Haas	31	11	3	0	0	6	0	.355	.452	.447	Dan Spillner	9	3	2	0	0	2	0	.333	.556	.417
Brad Havens	9	3	1	0	0	2	1	.333	.444	.455	Paul Splittorff	11	2	0	0	0	1	4	.182	.182	.250
Neal Heaton	20	5	0	0	1	4	1	.250	.400	.375	Dave Stewart	6	3	2	0	0	0	3	.500	.833	.500
Gorman Heimueller	6	2	0	0	1	1	0	.333	.833	.429	Sammy Stewart	14	3	0	0	0	0	0	.214	.214	.214
Willie Hernandez	6	3	0	0	2	0	0	.500	.500	.625	Dave Stieb	23	5	0	0	0	9	1	.217	.217	.438
Ted Higuera	7	4	1	0	0	1	1	.571	.714	.625	Bob Stoddard	13	3	0	1	0	0	0	.231	.385	.231
Ed Hodge	6	3	1	0	0	0	1	.500	.667	.500	Tim Stoddard	5	3	0	0	0	1	0	.600	.600	.667
Rick Honeycutt	14	4	0	0	0	1	0	.286	.286	.333	Rick Sutcliffe	16	5	0	0	0	1	2	.313	.313	.353
Charlie Hough	37	13	3	0	0	3	3	.351	.432	.400	Don Sutton	25	5	2	0	0	3	5	.200	.280	.286
Jay Howell	14	4	0	0	0	2	1	.286	.286	.375	Bill Swaggerty	8	5	0	0	0	0	0	.625	.625	.667
LaMarr Hoyt	14	7	1	0	0	0	0	.500	.571	.500	Bill Swift	6	4	1	0	0	0	1	.667	.833	.667
Danny Jackson	7	1	0	0	0	2	1	.143	.143	.333	Frank Tanana	12	3	1	0	1	1	2	.250	.583	.308
Roy Lee Jackson	9	2	0	0	0	1	0	.222	.222	.300	Tom Tellmann	7	7	2	0	1	2	0	1.000	1.714	1.000
Bob James	6	2	0	0	0	1	1	.333	.333	.429	Walt Terrell	14	5	2	0	0	1	0	.357	.500	.357
Tommy John	10	5	1	0	0	4	0	.500	.600	.583	Roy Thomas	8	4	0	0	1	0	1	.500	.875	.444
Mike Jones	10	3	0	0	0	0	0	.300	.300	.300	Rick Thompson	6	2	0	0	0	1	0	.333	.333	.429
Odell Jones	7	3	1	0	0	0	1	.429	.571	.429	Jerry Ujdur	8	4	0	0	0	0	0	.500	.500	.500
Matt Keough	11	6	2	0	1	0	0	.545	1.000	.500	Tom Underwood	9	2	0	0	0	0	2	.222	.222	.222
Jimmy Key	9	4	2	0	0	0	1	.444	.667	.444	Ed Vande Berg	16	5	1	0	0	3	2	.313	.375	.421
Bruce Kison	15	7	2	2	0	4	0	.467	.867	.579	Frank Viola	30	9	0	0	0	3	2	.300	.300	.364
Jerry Koosman	11	3	1	0	0	1	0	.273	.364	.333	Pete Vuckovich	14	6	0	0	0	1	0	.429	.429	.467
Bill Krueger	21	4	1	0	0	1	2	.190	.238	.227	Tom Waddell	5	1	1	0	0	0	0	.200	.400	.333
Pete Ladd	5	0	0	0	0	0	1	.000	.000	.167	Curt Wardle	9	4	1	1	0	1	1	.444	.778	.545

Wade Boggs continued

Pitcher	AB	H	2B	3B	HR	BB	SO	BA	SA	OBA	Pitcher	AB	H	2B	3B	HR	BB	SO	BA	SA	OBA
Mike Warren	11	3	0	0	0	0	0	.273	.273	.250	Frank Wills	10	4	1	0	0	1	2	.400	.500	.455
Ed Whitson	10	5	1	0	0	2	0	.500	.600	.583	Mike Witt	14	6	1	0	0	3	2	.429	.500	.529
Milt Wilcox	24	8	2	0	0	4	0	.333	.417	.429	Matt Young	14	0	0	0	0	3	2	.000	.000	.222
Al Williams	15	4	0	0	0	0	0	.267	.267	.267											

Pedro Guerrero

Pitcher	AB	H	2B	3B	HR	BB	SO	BA	SA	OBA	Pitcher	AB	H	2B	3B	HR	BB	SO	BA	SA	OBA
Doyle Alexander	8	1	0	0	0	1	0	.125	.125	.222	Mike LaCoss	27	9	2	0	2	2	2	.333	.630	.379
Neil Allen	24	6	1	0	2	5	3	.250	.542	.379	Jeff Lahti	10	6	1	0	0	3	2	.600	.700	.692
Larry Andersen	10	3	0	0	2	0	0	.300	.900	.300	Dave LaPoint	14	5	0	0	1	6	1	.357	.571	.550
Joaquin Andujar	24	7	1	0	1	8	5	.292	.458	.485	Bill Laskey	33	8	2	0	1	3	5	.242	.394	.316
Doug Bair	9	3	1	1	1	0	3	.333	1.000	.333	Gary Lavelle	13	4	0	0	1	2	2	.308	.538	.400
Len Barker	10	1	0	0	0	0	4	.100	.100	.100	Charlie Lea	22	5	1	0	1	3	2	.227	.409	.320
Jim Barr	11	5	3	0	2	0	0	.455	1.273	.455	Mark Lee	5	2	1	0	0	0	0	.400	.600	.400
Steve Bedrosian	22	4	0	0	0	1	5	.182	.182	.217	Craig Lefferts	7	1	0	0	0	2	2	.143	.143	.333
Bruce Berenyi	21	5	1	0	1	4	8	.238	.429	.360	Randy Lerch	7	1	0	0	0	1	1	.143	.143	.250
Vida Blue	19	5	0	0	1	3	5	.263	.421	.364	John Littlefield	5	0	0	0	0	0	0	.000	.000	.000
Tommy Boggs	13	5	0	0	0	0	0	.385	.385	.385	Tim Lollar	23	6	0	0	2	3	5	.261	.522	.346
Fred Breining	27	8	3	0	2	2	7	.296	.630	.345	Gary Lucas	13	2	1	0	1	3	2	.154	.462	.313
Tony Brizzolara	6	2	0	0	2	0	2	.333	1.333	.333	Ed Lynch	24	10	3	0	0	1	2	.417	.542	.440
Tom Browning	12	4	0	0	2	3	0	.333	.833	.467	Mike Madden	7	4	0	0	0	0	0	.571	.714	.667
Warren Brusstar	5	3	1	0	0	1	0	.600	.800	.667	Rick Mahler	30	10	1	0	2	3	4	.333	.567	.382
Ray Burris	10	3	1	0	1	1	0	.300	.700	.364	John Martin	8	0	0	0	0	1	0	.000	.000	.111
Marty Bystrom	15	4	1	0	0	2	3	.267	.333	.353	Renie Martin	13	4	1	0	1	2	1	.308	.615	.400
Rick Camp	23	9	2	0	1	4	2	.391	.609	.464	Silvio Martinez	10	2	0	0	0	2	1	.200	.200	.333
Bill Campbell	12	3	0	0	1	0	5	.250	.500	.250	Randy Martz	9	2	0	0	0	2	2	.222	.222	.364
John Candelaria	27	7	1	1	3	2	4	.259	.704	.300	Rick Matula	6	2	0	0	0	0	1	.333	.333	.333
Steve Carlton	30	8	3	0	2	1	4	.267	.567	.290	Andy McGaffigan	15	6	1	0	0	0	5	.400	.467	.400
Floyd Chiffer	9	0	0	0	0	0	2	.000	.000	.000	Tug McGraw	7	3	0	0	1	0	2	.429	.857	.429
Larry Christenson	16	5	1	0	2	2	4	.313	.750	.389	Craig McMurtry	22	7	0	0	1	2	2	.318	.455	.375
Danny Cox	10	4	1	1	0	1	3	.400	.700	.455	Larry McWilliams	30	8	3	0	0	2	12	.267	.367	.313
John Curtis	13	3	0	0	1	0	4	.231	.462	.286	Greg Minton	21	7	0	0	2	4	1	.333	.619	.440
Mark Davis	15	3	0	0	0	1	1	.200	.200	.250	John Montefusco	16	3	0	0	1	0	6	.188	.375	.188
Bill Dawley	11	4	0	0	1	1	3	.364	.636	.417	Donnie Moore	6	2	0	0	1	1	1	.333	.833	.429
Jeff Dedmon	9	5	0	0	0	0	0	.556	.556	.556	Paul Moskau	16	4	0	0	0	3	4	.250	.250	.350
Luis DeLeon	19	3	1	0	1	1	4	.158	.368	.182	Steve Mura	12	5	0	0	0	5	5	.417	.417	.556
John Denny	20	4	1	0	0	4	2	.200	.250	.333	Joe Niekro	52	20	3	1	4	5	5	.385	.712	.433
Frank DiPino	9	3	1	0	1	2	0	.333	.778	.455	Phil Niekro	29	10	0	0	3	1	3	.345	.655	.367
Dave Dravecky	31	9	1	1	2	3	5	.290	.581	.353	Dickie Noles	15	3	0	0	0	2	2	.200	.200	.294
Dennis Eckersley	9	0	0	0	0	0	2	.000	.000	.000	Jesse Orosco	7	2	0	0	0	1	1	.286	.286	.375
Juan Eichelberger	28	7	1	0	1	0	5	.250	.393	.241	Bob Owchinko	7	2	0	1	1	0	2	.286	1.000	.286
Pete Falcone	13	6	2	0	2	3	6	.462	1.077	.563	David Palmer	6	1	0	0	0	3	2	.167	.167	.444
Sid Fernandez	9	1	0	0	0	0	2	.111	.111	.111	Frank Pastore	32	5	1	0	0	3	4	.156	.188	.222
Bob Forsch	37	10	0	1	0	1	6	.270	.324	.289	Pascual Perez	31	9	3	1	2	2	5	.290	.645	.333
Terry Forster	5	3	0	0	0	0	0	.600	.600	.600	Gaylord Perry	15	4	0	0	0	1	1	.267	.267	.313
Alan Fowlkes	5	3	1	0	1	0	1	.600	1.400	.600	Ted Power	8	3	0	0	0	0	1	.375	.375	.500
Rich Gale	5	2	1	0	0	4	2	.400	.600	.700	Joe Price	15	3	0	0	1	4	6	.200	.400	.368
Gene Garber	20	7	1	0	0	6	2	.350	.400	.500	Mike Proly	10	3	0	0	1	0	0	.300	.600	.300
Scott Garrelts	10	2	0	0	0	1	2	.200	.200	.273	Charlie Puleo	17	5	1	0	2	1	4	.294	.706	.368
Dwight Gooden	20	3	1	0	2	3	10	.150	.500	.261	Chuck Rainey	6	4	0	0	1	1	1	.667	1.167	.714
Mark Grant	5	2	1	0	0	0	0	.400	.600	.400	Eric Rasmussen	6	0	0	0	0	1	0	.000	.000	.250
Mike Griffin	6	4	0	0	0	0	0	.667	.667	.667	Shane Rawley	13	3	0	0	0	0	3	.231	.231	.231
Tom Griffin	7	0	0	0	0	1	1	.000	.000	.125	Jeff Reardon	10	2	0	0	1	2	1	.200	.500	.333
Kevin Gross	15	9	1	0	1	3	3	.600	.867	.667	Ron Reed	13	6	1	0	3	0	2	.462	1.231	.462
Cecilio Guante	5	1	0	0	0	0	0	.200	.200	.200	Rick Reuschel	9	3	2	0	0	0	1	.333	.556	.333
Bill Gullickson	26	9	5	0	1	2	3	.346	.654	.393	Rick Rhoden	42	14	0	1	2	2	2	.333	.524	.364
Atlee Hammaker	10	5	1	0	0	0	3	.500	.600	.500	George Riley	7	3	0	0	0	0	1	.429	.429	.429
Preston Hanna	7	3	0	0	0	0	0	.429	.429	.375	Allen Ripley	13	3	0	0	0	2	3	.231	.231	.333
Greg Harris	7	3	0	0	0	1	2	.429	.429	.556	Don Robinson	20	4	1	0	0	4	4	.200	.250	.333
Tom Hausman	8	1	0	0	0	0	4	.125	.125	.125	Ron Robinson	11	3	0	0	1	2	4	.273	.545	.385
Andy Hawkins	24	9	1	0	3	2	0	.375	.792	.423	Steve Rogers	26	13	2	0	1	1	2	.500	.692	.519
Al Holland	15	4	1	0	1	2	3	.267	.533	.353	Vern Ruhle	19	4	0	1	1	2	2	.211	.474	.286
Scott Holman	6	2	1	0	0	0	1	.333	.500	.286	Jeff Russell	12	6	0	1	1	0	0	.500	.917	.462
LaMarr Hoyt	10	2	0	0	1	1	0	.200	.200	.273	Dick Ruthven	21	6	1	1	2	1	5	.286	.714	.318
Charles Hudson	15	7	1	1	0	1	2	.467	.667	.500	Nolan Ryan	37	11	1	0	2	5	9	.297	.486	.395
Tom Hume	21	7	1	1	0	1	1	.333	.476	.364	Joe Sambito	9	2	0	0	0	2	2	.222	.222	.364
Ferguson Jenkins	19	8	0	1	1	3	6	.421	.684	.458	Scott Sanderson	30	9	4	0	1	2	4	.300	.533	.333
Randy Jones	8	2	0	0	0	0	1	.250	.250	.250	Manny Sarmiento	6	3	0	0	0	1	2	.500	1.000	.625
Kurt Kepshire	8	3	2	0	0	2	1	.375	.625	.500	Dan Schatzeder	18	6	1	1	1	2	2	.333	.556	.350
Bob Knepper	48	16	2	0	2	3	10	.333	.500	.373	Mike Scott	38	9	3	1	1	4	8	.237	.447	.302
Jerry Koosman	9	2	0	0	0	1	1	.222	.222	.300	Rod Scurry	6	2	1	0	0	0	3	.333	.500	.333
Mike Krukow	44	12	2	0	2	5	10	.273	.455	.360	Tom Seaver	26	10	1	0	0	1	6	.385	.423	.407
Frank LaCorte	13	6	0	0	1	2	3	.462	.769	.533	Bob Shirley	12	5	2	0	0	0	1	.417	.583	.385

Pedro Guerrero continued

Pitcher	AB	H	2B	3B	HR	BB	SO	BA	SA	OBA	Pitcher	AB	H	2B	3B	HR	BB	SO	BA	SA	OBA
Eric Show	26	5	1	0	1	3	5	.192	.346	.300	Walt Terrell	11	3	0	0	1	0	2	.273	.545	.273
Doug Sisk	10	2	0	0	0	0	1	.200	.200	.200	Mark Thurmond	24	5	0	0	1	2	3	.208	.333	.269
Bryn Smith	25	10	3	0	0	3	8	.400	.520	.464	Jay Tibbs	8	2	0	0	1	2	2	.250	.625	.400
Dave Smith	14	3	1	0	0	0	2	.214	.286	.214	Dick Tidrow	7	2	0	0	0	0	0	.286	.286	.286
Lee Smith	14	1	0	0	0	0	5	.071	.071	.071	Mike Torrez	13	4	3	0	0	0	3	.308	.538	.286
Julio Solano	7	3	0	0	2	1	0	.429	1.286	.500	Steve Trout	15	6	0	1	0	1	3	.400	.533	.438
Eddie Solomon	7	4	0	0	0	0	0	.571	.571	.625	John Tudor	15	6	0	0	0	1	1	.400	.400	.412
Lary Sorensen	6	2	1	0	0	0	1	.333	.500	.429	Lee Tunnell	9	2	0	0	1	1	3	.222	.556	.300
Mario Soto	54	18	3	0	2	4	15	.333	.500	.383	Pete Vuckovich	6	2	0	0	0	0	0	.333	.333	.333
Tim Stoddard	5	2	0	0	0	1	1	.400	.400	.500	Bob Walk	11	2	0	0	0	0	2	.182	.182	.182
John Stuper	24	9	2	0	1	2	4	.375	.583	.423	Chris Welsh	6	2	0	0	1	0	1	.333	.833	.429
Rick Sutcliffe	6	4	0	1	0	3	0	.667	1.000	.727	Ed Whitson	36	11	2	0	1	1	7	.306	.444	.324
Bruce Sutter	19	8	1	0	1	2	4	.421	.632	.476	Rick Wise	8	2	0	0	0	1	0	.250	.250	.250
Don Sutton	17	3	1	1	0	2	3	.176	.353	.263	Pat Zachry	7	1	1	0	0	0	1	.143	.286	.143
Kent Tekulve	22	8	2	0	1	1	2	.364	.591	.391											

Don Mattingly

Pitcher	AB	H	2B	3B	HR	BB	SO	BA	SA	OBA	Pitcher	AB	H	2B	3B	HR	BB	SO	BA	SA	OBA
Don Aase	5	4	1	0	1	0	0	.800	1.600	.800	Bill Krueger	8	2	1	0	0	0	0	.250	.375	.250
Jim Acker	9	2	0	0	0	1	0	.222	.222	.300	Pete Ladd	7	1	0	0	0	1	2	.143	.143	.250
Doyle Alexander	27	7	1	0	2	0	1	.259	.519	.259	Dennis Lamp	6	3	0	1	0	1	1	.500	.833	.571
Keith Atherton	8	4	0	0	1	1	0	.500	.875	.556	Mark Langston	16	6	2	1	1	2	0	.375	.813	.444
Floyd Bannister	17	6	2	0	2	1	0	.353	.824	.389	Luis Leal	10	4	0	0	1	0	0	.400	.700	.400
Salome Barojas	13	3	0	0	1	0	1	.231	.462	.231	Charlie Leibrandt	14	2	0	0	1	1	0	.143	.357	.200
Jim Beattie	19	6	2	0	1	1	2	.316	.579	.350	Tim Lollar	9	3	2	0	0	1	0	.333	.556	.364
Juan Berenguer	6	1	0	0	0	0	0	.167	.167	.167	Aurelio Lopez	7	0	0	0	0	0	0	.000	.000	.000
Karl Best	5	2	0	0	0	0	0	.400	.400	.400	Dennis Martinez	16	4	0	0	1	0	0	.250	.438	.235
Bud Black	18	5	1	0	2	0	1	.278	.667	.278	Tippy Martinez	7	1	0	0	0	1	1	.143	.143	.250
Bert Blyleven	9	5	1	1	0	2	2	.556	.889	.615	Mike Mason	12	2	1	0	0	0	0	.167	.250	.154
Mike Boddicker	21	6	2	0	0	0	5	.286	.381	.286	Steve McCatty	12	4	0	0	0	1	0	.333	.333	.385
Dennis Boyd	21	7	2	0	0	0	5	.333	.429	.333	Bob McClure	10	4	0	0	0	1	2	.400	.400	.455
Mark Brown	6	2	1	0	0	0	0	.333	.500	.333	Scott McGregor	17	9	3	0	2	3	0	.529	1.059	.545
Britt Burns	10	3	0	0	3	0	0	.300	1.200	.300	Mike Moore	6	2	0	0	1	1	1	.333	.833	.429
Ray Burris	16	4	1	0	0	3	0	.250	.313	.368	Jack Morris	16	5	2	0	0	1	2	.313	.438	.353
John Butcher	9	5	2	1	0	0	0	.556	1.000	.500	Gene Nelson	7	3	1	0	1	0	0	.429	1.000	.429
Mike Caldwell	15	9	1	1	0	1	1	.600	.800	.625	Al Nipper	14	6	0	0	0	1	1	.429	.429	.467
John Candelaria	5	0	0	0	0	0	2	.000	.000	.000	Dickie Noles	9	5	1	0	1	1	1	.556	1.000	.600
Jim Clancy	13	5	2	0	1	0	2	.385	.769	.357	Edwin Nunez	6	2	0	0	1	1	2	.333	.833	.429
Bryan Clark	9	3	0	0	1	3	1	.333	.667	.538	Bob Ojeda	16	6	2	0	0	0	3	.375	.500	.353
Mark Clear	8	1	0	0	0	3	0	.125	.125	.364	Randy O'Neal	10	4	2	0	1	0	0	.400	.900	.400
Roger Clemens	8	4	0	0	0	0	1	.500	.500	.500	Dan Petry	27	13	1	1	1	1	2	.481	.704	.500
Jaime Cocanower	7	2	1	0	0	1	1	.286	.429	.375	Chuck Porter	11	3	2	0	0	1	1	.273	.455	.333
Chris Codiroli	18	8	0	1	2	1	1	.444	.889	.474	Dan Quisenberry	9	3	1	0	0	1	0	.333	.444	.400
Tim Conroy	8	3	0	0	0	1	2	.375	.375	.444	Ron Romanick	17	5	2	0	1	2	0	.294	.588	.368
Glen Cook	6	3	2	0	0	0	0	.500	.833	.500	Ramon Romero	5	2	0	0	1	1	0	.400	1.000	.500
Doug Corbett	9	4	1	0	0	0	0	.444	.556	.444	Dave Rozema	9	5	1	0	1	0	0	.556	1.000	.556
Steve Crawford	11	4	1	0	0	0	0	.364	.455	.364	Bret Saberhagen	16	4	0	0	0	0	0	.250	.250	.250
John Curtis	7	2	0	0	0	1	0	.286	.286	.375	Luis Sanchez	7	2	1	0	1	0	1	.286	.857	.286
Danny Darwin	16	6	2	0	0	0	0	.375	.500	.375	Dave J. Schmidt	6	1	0	0	0	0	0	.167	.167	.167
Ron Davis	5	2	0	0	1	1	1	.400	1.000	.500	Ken Schrom	13	3	0	0	0	2	0	.231	.231	.333
Storm Davis	15	2	0	0	0	3	0	.133	.133	.278	Don Schulze	6	1	0	0	0	0	0	.167	.167	.167
Ken Dixon	8	3	2	0	0	0	1	.375	.625	.333	Tom Seaver	8	2	0	0	0	0	0	.250	.250	.250
Richard Dotson	7	3	0	1	0	0	1	.429	.714	.429	Jim Slaton	12	6	1	0	1	1	0	.500	.833	.538
Jamie Easterly	10	3	1	0	0	1	0	.300	.400	.364	Roy Smith	6	4	1	0	1	1	0	.667	1.333	.625
Dennis Eckersley	7	1	0	0	0	0	0	.143	.143	.143	Mike Smithson	28	6	3	0	0	0	1	.214	.321	.200
Pete Filson	17	4	0	0	1	4	1	.235	.412	.381	Lary Sorensen	8	3	0	0	0	0	0	.375	.375	.375
Rollie Fingers	6	1	1	0	0	0	0	.167	.333	.167	Dan Spillner	5	1	0	0	0	1	0	.200	.200	.286
Mike Flanagan	12	3	2	0	0	0	2	.250	.417	.231	Bob Stanley	16	5	0	0	1	1	1	.313	.500	.353
Dave Geisel	7	2	0	0	0	0	0	.286	.286	.286	Dave Stewart	9	5	1	0	0	1	1	.556	.667	.600
Jerry Don Gleaton	5	4	1	0	0	0	0	.800	1.000	.800	Sammy Stewart	12	3	0	0	0	5	0	.250	.250	.471
Jim Gott	5	1	0	0	0	1	0	.200	.200	.286	Dave Stieb	33	12	4	0	2	0	3	.364	.667	.364
Mark Gubicza	12	5	2	0	0	1	1	.417	.583	.400	Rick Sutcliffe	5	3	0	0	1	2	0	.600	1.200	.714
Moose Haas	14	4	1	0	0	1	0	.286	.357	.333	Don Sutton	6	1	1	0	0	0	0	.167	.333	.167
Neal Heaton	16	5	1	0	1	2	0	.313	.563	.389	Bill Swaggerty	9	2	0	0	0	0	0	.222	.222	.222
Willie Hernandez	10	4	0	0	1	1	1	.400	.400	.455	Bill Swift	7	1	0	0	0	0	0	.143	.143	.143
Ted Higuera	8	0	0	0	0	0	3	.000	.000	.000	Frank Tanana	19	6	3	0	1	2	1	.316	.632	.381
Charlie Hough	17	5	2	0	0	2	1	.294	.412	.368	Tom Tellmann	9	4	1	0	0	0	0	.444	.778	.444
LaMarr Hoyt	7	2	0	0	0	1	0	.286	.286	.375	Roy Thomas	7	1	0	0	0	0	0	.143	.143	.143
Bruce Hurst	36	5	2	0	0	1	3	.139	.194	.162	John Tudor	9	1	0	0	1	1	1	.111	.444	.200
Roy Lee Jackson	6	3	1	0	0	0	0	.500	.667	.500	Frank Viola	15	3	2	0	0	0	1	.200	.333	.200
Mike Jeffcoat	8	2	0	0	0	0	0	.250	.250	.333	Tom Waddell	7	1	0	0	0	0	0	.143	.143	.143
Tommy John	14	4	0	0	1	1	1	.286	.500	.313	Rick Waits	8	1	0	0	0	0	0	.125	.125	.125
Jimmy Key	16	4	1	0	0	0	3	.250	.313	.235	Curt Wardle	8	5	2	0	1	0	0	.625	1.250	.667

Don Mattingly   continued

Pitcher	AB	H	2B	3B	HR	BB	SO	BA	SA	OBA	Pitcher	AB	H	2B	3B	HR	BB	SO	BA	SA	OBA
Mike Warren	8	4	1	0	1	2	0	.500	1.000	.600	Mike Witt	10	2	0	0	1	2	2	.200	.500	.333
Chris Welsh	5	0	0	0	0	3	1	.000	.000	.375	Matt Young	15	3	1	0	0	1	3	.200	.267	.250
Len Whitehouse	5	2	0	0	0	0	0	.400	.400	.400	Geoff Zahn	12	6	1	0	2	0	0	.500	1.083	.500

Willie McGee

Pitcher	AB	H	2B	3B	HR	BB	SO	BA	SA	OBA	Pitcher	AB	H	2B	3B	HR	BB	SO	BA	SA	OBA
Rick Aguilera	5	1	0	0	0	0	0	.200	.200	.200	Mike Krukow	20	5	1	0	0	0	0	.250	.300	.250
Larry Andersen	11	4	0	0	0	0	0	.364	.364	.364	Mike LaCoss	6	2	1	0	0	0	2	.333	.500	.333
Len Barker	15	5	2	0	0	0	3	.333	.467	.333	Dave LaPoint	12	2	1	1	0	2	4	.167	.417	.286
Jim Barr	7	4	0	1	0	0	0	.571	.857	.571	Bill Laskey	22	5	1	0	0	1	2	.227	.273	.261
Steve Bedrosian	11	4	0	0	0	2	1	.364	.364	.462	Gary Lavelle	9	2	0	0	0	0	4	.222	.222	.222
Bruce Berenyi	15	6	0	0	0	0	2	.400	.400	.400	Charlie Lea	20	5	0	0	0	4	1	.250	.250	.375
Jim Bibby	5	1	0	0	0	0	0	.200	.200	.200	Craig Lefferts	10	3	0	1	0	1	1	.300	.700	.300
Doug Bird	6	1	0	0	0	0	1	.167	.167	.167	Tim Lollar	18	1	0	0	0	2	7	.056	.056	.150
Rich Bordi	6	3	1	0	0	1	0	.500	.667	.571	Gary Lucas	6	2	0	0	0	1	1	.333	.333	.429
Fred Breining	17	4	0	0	0	0	0	.235	.235	.235	Ed Lynch	29	7	0	1	0	0	0	.241	.310	.241
Tom Browning	6	2	1	0	1	0	2	.333	1.000	.333	Mike Madden	7	3	1	0	0	1	0	.429	.571	.500
Warren Brusstar	10	2	1	0	0	0	1	.200	.300	.200	Rick Mahler	21	6	2	1	0	3	1	.286	.476	.375
Tim Burke	5	1	0	0	0	0	1	.200	.200	.200	Renie Martin	11	3	0	0	0	2	3	.273	.273	.385
Ray Burris	9	3	0	0	0	0	2	.333	.333	.333	Andy McGaffigan	14	3	0	1	0	1	1	.214	.357	.267
Marty Bystrom	16	4	1	0	0	0	1	.250	.313	.250	Craig McMurtry	15	7	1	1	0	4	2	.467	.667	.579
Rick Camp	18	7	1	0	0	0	1	.389	.444	.389	Larry McWilliams	25	10	2	2	1	2	2	.400	.760	.429
Bill Campbell	15	4	1	0	0	0	2	.267	.333	.267	Greg Minton	15	5	0	0	0	0	1	.333	.333	.333
John Candelaria	21	3	0	0	1	1	5	.143	.286	.182	Donnie Moore	8	4	0	0	0	0	2	.500	.500	.500
Steve Carlton	38	9	1	0	0	2	15	.237	.263	.275	Tom Niedenfuer	10	2	0	0	0	0	2	.200	.200	.200
Don Carman	7	1	0	1	0	0	4	.143	.429	.143	Joe Niekro	34	9	2	0	1	1	5	.265	.412	.286
Pat Clements	5	3	0	0	0	0	0	.600	.600	.600	Phil Niekro	10	1	0	0	0	1	1	.100	.100	.182
Ron Darling	17	6	1	0	0	1	3	.353	.412	.389	Dickie Noles	9	2	0	0	1	0	0	.222	.556	.222
Bill Dawley	6	1	0	0	0	0	0	.167	.167	.167	Jesse Orosco	22	5	0	0	1	2	9	.227	.364	.280
Jeff Dedmon	5	1	0	0	0	0	0	.200	.200	.200	David Palmer	19	7	0	0	0	1	1	.368	.368	.400
Jose DeLeon	19	6	0	0	0	0	3	.316	.316	.316	Frank Pastore	16	7	0	2	0	1	1	.438	.688	.471
Luis DeLeon	7	2	0	0	0	0	1	.286	.286	.286	Alejandro Pena	5	1	1	0	0	0	0	.200	.400	.200
John Denny	33	13	1	0	0	1	1	.394	.424	.412	Pascual Perez	12	4	0	0	0	0	1	.333	.333	.333
Frank DiPino	10	4	1	0	0	0	4	.400	.500	.400	Ted Power	10	5	0	1	0	1	2	.500	.700	.545
Carlos Diaz	10	6	0	0	1	0	1	.600	.900	.600	Joe Price	12	4	1	0	2	1	5	.333	.917	.385
Dave Dravecky	13	3	1	0	0	1	4	.231	.308	.286	Charlie Puleo	14	7	1	1	0	0	0	.500	.714	.500
Dennis Eckersley	17	8	1	0	0	0	0	.471	.529	.471	Chuck Rainey	22	6	1	2	1	0	2	.273	.636	.273
Steve Engel	9	6	1	0	1	0	2	.667	1.111	.667	Shane Rawley	17	6	0	1	0	1	5	.353	.471	.389
Pete Falcone	9	3	0	1	0	1	1	.333	.556	.400	Jeff Reardon	18	2	0	0	0	1	4	.111	.111	.158
Sid Fernandez	9	3	1	1	0	1	1	.333	.667	.400	Ron Reed	7	3	0	0	0	0	1	.429	.429	.429
Ray Fontenot	12	3	1	0	0	0	4	.250	.333	.250	Rick Reuschel	13	5	2	0	0	0	2	.385	.538	.385
Terry Forster	9	3	0	0	0	0	2	.333	.333	.333	Jerry Reuss	29	10	2	0	0	1	7	.345	.414	.355
John Franco	6	2	0	1	0	0	1	.333	.667	.333	Rick Rhoden	41	17	3	1	0	2	6	.415	.537	.442
George Frazier	5	1	0	1	0	0	0	.200	.600	.200	Allen Ripley	5	0	0	0	0	0	0	.000	.000	.000
Woody Fryman	6	1	0	1	0	0	0	.167	.500	.167	Don Robinson	24	9	2	0	1	3	3	.375	.583	.464
Brent Gaff	8	3	1	0	0	0	1	.375	.500	.375	Jeff Robinson	9	2	2	0	0	0	0	.222	.444	.300
Rich Gale	6	4	0	1	0	1	0	.667	1.000	.714	Ron Robinson	6	2	0	0	0	0	1	.333	.333	.333
Gene Garber	17	7	0	0	0	1	1	.412	.412	.421	Steve Rogers	44	13	2	0	0	5	3	.295	.341	.367
Dwight Gooden	23	11	0	0	0	1	3	.478	.478	.500	Dave Rucker	7	2	0	0	0	0	2	.286	.286	.286
Tom Gorman	11	2	0	0	0	0	1	.182	.182	.182	Vern Ruhle	9	0	0	0	0	0	0	.000	.000	.000
Jim Gott	5	1	0	0	0	0	0	.200	.200	.200	Dick Ruthven	15	5	1	2	0	0	3	.333	.667	.313
Kevin Gross	19	8	0	0	1	0	4	.421	.579	.421	Nolan Ryan	25	7	0	1	0	0	6	.280	.360	.280
Cecilio Guante	13	3	0	0	0	0	2	.231	.231	.231	Scott Sanderson	28	13	3	0	1	2	1	.464	.679	.484
Bill Gullickson	51	13	4	1	1	0	9	.255	.431	.255	Manny Sarmiento	6	2	0	0	0	1	1	.333	.333	.429
Atlee Hammaker	17	7	0	0	0	1	4	.412	.588	.421	Dan Schatzeder	18	6	0	1	0	1	4	.333	.333	.368
Andy Hawkins	20	7	0	0	0	2	4	.350	.350	.409	Bill Scherrer	5	2	1	0	0	0	1	.400	.800	.400
Willie Hernandez	9	1	0	0	0	0	1	.111	.111	.111	Mike Scott	18	11	0	0	0	1	0	.611	.611	.632
Orel Hershiser	14	5	0	1	0	0	1	.357	.500	.357	Rod Scurry	8	2	0	1	0	1	3	.250	.500	.400
Al Holland	11	3	0	0	2	1	2	.273	.818	.333	Tom Seaver	8	3	0	0	0	0	1	.375	.375	.375
Scott Holman	5	0	0	0	0	0	0	.000	.000	.000	Eric Show	22	6	2	0	0	1	5	.273	.364	.304
Rick Honeycutt	12	3	0	0	0	0	4	.250	.250	.250	Doug Sisk	8	3	0	0	0	2	0	.375	.375	.500
Burt Hooton	6	3	0	0	0	0	3	.500	.500	.500	Bryn Smith	25	6	0	0	0	0	3	.240	.240	.240
Steve Howe	7	2	0	0	0	0	2	.286	.286	.286	Dave Smith	8	2	1	0	0	0	0	.250	.375	.250
Ken Howell	6	2	0	0	0	0	1	.333	.333	.333	Lee Smith	15	4	1	0	0	3	3	.267	.333	.389
LaMarr Hoyt	9	5	0	1	0	0	0	.556	.778	.556	Zane Smith	5	2	1	0	1	0	0	.400	1.200	.400
Charles Hudson	29	7	0	0	0	1	4	.241	.241	.267	Mario Soto	20	4	0	0	0	3	3	.200	.200	.292
Tom Hume	10	3	0	0	0	2	3	.300	.300	.417	Dave Stewart	6	0	0	0	0	1	2	.000	.000	.143
Bob James	9	3	0	1	0	0	2	.333	.556	.333	Rick Sutcliffe	8	2	0	0	0	0	3	.250	.250	.250
Ferguson Jenkins	14	5	0	0	0	1	1	.357	.357	.400	Craig Swan	13	1	1	0	0	0	3	.077	.154	.077
Jim Kern	6	0	0	0	0	0	0	.000	.000	.000	Kent Tekulve	10	2	0	0	0	1	2	.200	.400	.250
Bob Knepper	32	5	1	0	0	0	9	.156	.188	.152	Walt Terrell	14	1	1	0	0	1	1	.071	.143	.133
Jerry Koosman	23	13	1	2	0	0	3	.565	.783	.565	Mark Thurmond	14	4	1	0	0	1	2	.286	.357	.333

Willie McGee continued

Pitcher	AB	H	2B	3B	HR	BB	SO	BA	SA	OBA
Jay Tibbs	19	6	1	0	0	0	2	.316	.368	.316
Mike Torrez	6	2	0	0	0	0	0	.333	.333	.333
Steve Trout	28	7	0	2	0	1	5	.250	.393	.276
John Tudor	8	2	0	0	0	0	2	.250	.250	.250
Lee Tunnell	18	3	0	0	0	1	1	.167	.167	.211
Fernando Valenzuela	24	7	1	0	0	1	5	.292	.333	.320

Pitcher	AB	H	2B	3B	HR	BB	SO	BA	SA	OBA
Bob Walk	7	3	0	0	0	0	0	.429	.429	.429
Bob Welch	24	7	1	1	0	0	2	.292	.417	.292
Frank Williams	5	1	0	0	0	1	0	.200	.200	.333
Jim Winn	6	1	1	0	0	1	1	.167	.333	.286
Floyd Youmans	9	3	1	0	1	1	1	.333	.778	.400
Pat Zachry	7	3	1	0	0	0	2	.429	.571	.429

Eddie Murray

Pitcher	AB	H	2B	3B	HR	BB	SO	BA	SA	OBA
Don Aase	26	10	1	0	2	4	4	.385	.654	.467
Glenn Abbott	38	7	1	0	4	5	7	.184	.526	.279
Doyle Alexander	41	6	0	0	2	5	8	.146	.293	.239
Larry Andersen	11	3	0	0	1	0	1	.273	.545	.273
Bud Anderson	5	2	1	0	0	1	0	.400	.600	.500
Luis Aponte	5	3	0	0	0	0	0	.600	.600	.600
Mike Armstrong	10	2	0	0	1	1	2	.200	.500	.273
Fernando Arroyo	15	4	1	0	1	1	4	.267	.533	.313
Keith Atherton	5	2	0	0	1	1	1	.400	1.000	.500
Jerry Augustine	31	10	2	0	3	1	2	.323	.677	.344
Doug Bair	10	0	0	0	0	0	2	.000	.000	.000
Steve Baker	9	1	0	0	0	2	4	.111	.111	.250
Floyd Bannister	31	7	3	0	1	9	5	.226	.419	.400
Len Barker	43	13	4	0	0	0	11	.302	.395	.295
Mike Barlow	8	3	0	0	3	0	0	.375	1.500	.375
Salome Barojas	12	7	1	0	1	2	2	.583	.917	.643
Jim Barr	11	6	0	0	0	3	0	.545	.545	.643
Francisco Barrios	12	3	0	0	0	0	0	.250	.250	.250
Dave Beard	8	3	0	0	1	4	2	.375	.750	.583
Jim Beattie	39	13	0	0	1	7	5	.333	.410	.417
Joe Beckwith	5	2	0	0	0	1	1	.400	.400	.429
Juan Berenguer	16	4	1	0	1	1	3	.250	.500	.294
Jim Bibby	7	2	1	0	0	0	1	.286	.429	.286
Jack Billingham	17	3	0	0	1	2	4	.176	.353	.263
Doug Bird	12	3	0	0	0	0	2	.250	.250	.250
Tim Birtsas	6	3	1	0	0	1	1	.500	.667	.571
Bud Black	13	3	0	0	0	2	1	.231	.231	.333
Vida Blue	13	8	0	0	0	0	1	.615	.615	.615
Bert Blyleven	34	12	2	0	0	3	8	.353	.412	.405
Mark Bomback	7	2	0	0	0	0	0	.286	.286	.286
Rich Bordi	7	3	1	0	0	0	0	.429	.571	.429
Dennis Boyd	26	4	2	0	1	4	5	.154	.346	.258
Tom Brennan	11	5	0	0	0	0	0	.455	.455	.455
Ken Brett	13	3	1	0	0	1	0	.231	.308	.286
Tom Burgmeier	22	4	0	0	1	4	2	.182	.318	.308
Britt Burns	34	15	0	1	3	2	4	.441	.765	.472
Ray Burris	10	3	0	0	0	2	0	.300	.300	.385
Tom Buskey	8	4	1	0	0	0	0	.500	.625	.500
John Butcher	36	10	2	0	1	1	2	.278	.417	.289
Jeff Byrd	6	2	0	0	0	0	0	.333	.333	.286
Mike Caldwell	36	11	2	0	5	5	6	.306	.778	.390
Bill Campbell	12	1	0	0	0	1	3	.083	.083	.154
Tom Candiotti	6	3	0	0	1	1	0	.500	1.000	.500
Bobby Castillo	13	3	0	0	3	2	6	.231	.923	.333
Bill Castro	10	2	1	0	0	3	1	.200	.300	.333
Bill Caudill	5	2	0	0	1	3	1	.400	1.000	.625
Jim Clancy	48	12	1	0	1	9	5	.250	.333	.368
Bryan Clark	8	2	0	0	1	1	1	.250	.250	.333
Mark Clear	19	5	0	0	4	7	7	.263	.263	.391
Pat Clements	5	1	1	0	0	0	0	.200	.400	.200
Reggie Cleveland	16	3	0	0	1	2	0	.188	.375	.278
David Clyde	10	5	0	0	0	0	1	.500	.500	.455
Jaime Cocanower	18	7	1	0	0	1	3	.389	.444	.421
Jim Colborn	14	3	1	0	2	2	3	.214	.500	.313
Joe Coleman	6	0	0	0	0	0	1	.000	.000	.000
Steve Comer	30	7	2	0	1	1	6	.233	.400	.281
Tim Conroy	7	4	0	0	1	3	0	.571	1.000	.700
Doug Corbett	6	2	0	0	1	0	2	.333	.833	.333
Joe Cowley	14	1	0	0	1	3	2	.071	.286	.235
Jim Crawford	9	3	1	0	0	0	1	.333	.444	.333
Steve Crawford	6	4	2	0	0	0	1	.667	1.000	.667
Victor Cruz	11	5	1	0	0	0	1	.455	.545	.455
Danny Darwin	29	8	0	0	1	1	1	.276	.448	.300

Pitcher	AB	H	2B	3B	HR	BB	SO	BA	SA	OBA
Ron Davis	28	13	3	0	3	0	6	.464	.893	.464
John Denny	12	2	1	0	0	3	6	.167	.250	.333
Adrian Devine	5	2	1	0	0	0	2	.400	.600	.400
Pat Dobson	9	6	0	0	2	0	1	.667	1.333	.667
Richard Dotson	38	12	2	0	3	7	8	.316	.605	.413
Dick Drago	13	2	0	0	0	0	4	.154	.154	.143
Rob Dressler	8	2	1	0	0	0	0	.250	.375	.250
Jamie Easterly	11	4	2	0	0	4	0	.364	.545	.500
Dennis Eckersley	41	14	2	0	3	1	4	.341	.610	.357
Butch Edge	5	2	2	0	0	0	1	.400	.800	.400
Dock Ellis	14	6	3	0	0	1	2	.429	.643	.467
Roger Erickson	39	12	4	0	0	4	7	.308	.410	.372
Ed Farmer	10	2	1	0	1	3	1	.200	.600	.385
Ed Figueroa	26	5	1	0	2	3	5	.192	.462	.276
Tom Filer	5	1	0	0	1	0	2	.200	.800	.200
Pete Filson	8	2	0	0	1	1	1	.250	.625	.333
Rollie Fingers	5	3	2	0	0	1	0	.600	1.000	.667
Al Fitzmorris	5	1	0	0	0	2	0	.200	.200	.429
Ray Fontenot	9	2	0	0	0	0	0	.222	.222	.222
Ken Forsch	25	6	1	0	1	0	5	.240	.400	.240
George Frazier	7	1	0	0	0	1	0	.143	.143	.250
Dave Frost	26	7	2	0	2	1	9	.269	.577	.296
Rich Gale	28	8	2	0	1	5	5	.286	.464	.394
Wayne Garland	13	4	1	0	2	3	5	.308	.846	.438
Jerry Garvin	19	4	2	0	0	1	2	.211	.316	.286
Bob L. Gibson	18	3	0	0	1	7	3	.167	.333	.370
Ed Glynn	9	2	0	0	0	2	1	.222	.222	.364
Dave Goltz	28	8	0	0	0	4	6	.286	.286	.364
Rich Gossage	20	4	1	0	0	5	5	.200	.250	.360
Jim Gott	7	3	0	0	1	0	0	.429	.429	.500
Steve Grilli	6	2	0	0	0	0	1	.333	.333	.333
Mark Gubicza	9	3	3	0	0	1	1	.333	.667	.400
Ron Guidry	68	16	4	0	3	4	14	.235	.426	.278
Don Gullett	8	2	0	0	1	1	1	.250	.625	.333
Larry Gura	56	19	2	0	5	6	6	.339	.643	.403
Moose Haas	43	14	2	0	2	9	4	.326	.512	.442
Dave Hamilton	6	1	1	0	0	0	1	.167	.333	.167
Paul Hartzell	28	6	1	0	1	2	3	.214	.357	.267
Andy Hassler	18	5	1	0	0	5	2	.278	.333	.435
Neal Heaton	18	7	1	0	0	6	0	.389	.444	.542
Dave Heaverlo	5	1	0	0	0	0	1	.200	.200	.200
Gorman Heimueller	5	2	0	0	1	1	0	.400	1.000	.500
Willie Hernandez	8	0	0	0	0	2	2	.000	.000	.200
Kevin Hickey	5	5	0	0	1	0	0	1.000	1.600	1.000
Ted Higuera	7	4	1	0	1	1	1	.571	1.143	.625
John Hiller	11	3	2	0	1	1	4	.273	.727	.308
Rick Honeycutt	17	8	4	0	1	0	1	.471	.706	.474
Don Hood	13	1	0	0	1	0	2	.077	.308	.071
Charlie Hough	23	5	2	0	0	4	4	.217	.304	.333
Jay Howell	17	5	1	0	0	1	4	.294	.353	.333
LaMarr Hoyt	26	11	1	0	3	3	0	.423	.808	.483
Al Hrabosky	6	2	0	0	0	1	0	.333	.333	.429
Phil Huffman	6	1	0	0	1	2	1	.167	.667	.375
Catfish Hunter	18	8	3	1	1	1	1	.444	.889	.474
Bruce Hurst	20	2	0	0	1	1	3	.100	.250	.143
Danny Jackson	11	3	2	0	1	3	3	.273	.455	.333
Darrell Jackson	8	5	0	0	1	0	0	.625	1.000	.625
Roy Lee Jackson	8	4	2	1	0	2	1	.500	1.000	.600
Jesse Jefferson	23	5	4	0	0	3	7	.217	.391	.308
Ferguson Jenkins	27	5	2	0	1	5	6	.185	.370	.313
Tommy John	38	13	2	0	3	5	2	.342	.632	.419
John Henry Johnson	13	2	1	1	0	2	0	.154	.385	.250
Tom Johnson	8	2	1	0	0	0	1	.250	.375	.250

Eddie Murray continued

Pitcher	AB	H	2B	3B	HR	BB	SO	BA	SA	OBA
Mike Jones	7	0	0	0	0	2	1	.000	.000	.222
Odell Jones	9	2	1	0	0	2	3	.222	.333	.364
Curt Kaufman	6	2	1	0	0	0	2	.333	.500	.333
Matt Keough	25	9	1	0	2	1	3	.360	.640	.370
Jim Kern	13	4	1	0	0	0	4	.308	.385	.357
Jimmy Key	7	0	0	0	0	0	1	.000	.000	.000
Brian Kingman	18	5	0	0	1	4	1	.278	.444	.409
Bruce Kison	13	5	0	0	0	3	0	.385	.385	.471
Chris Knapp	11	2	0	0	1	2	1	.182	.455	.308
Jerry Koosman	21	9	2	0	0	0	1	.429	.524	.429
Ken Kravec	24	7	0	0	0	2	1	.292	.292	.370
Bill Krueger	17	4	3	0	0	4	2	.235	.412	.381
Jack Kucek	6	0	0	0	0	0	0	.000	.000	.000
Bob Lacey	12	5	1	1	1	1	3	.417	.917	.462
Mike LaCoss	5	1	1	0	0	0	0	.200	.400	.200
Pete Ladd	5	3	0	0	2	1	0	.600	1.800	.667
Lerrin LaGrow	6	2	1	0	1	1	0	.333	1.000	.429
Dennis Lamp	15	5	0	0	4	1	0	.333	.333	.474
Rick Langford	57	20	2	0	4	4	4	.351	.596	.387
Mark Langston	5	3	2	1	0	4	1	.600	1.400	.778
Dave LaRoche	16	5	1	0	2	0	3	.313	.750	.294
Luis Leal	17	5	1	0	1	4	2	.294	.529	.409
Bill Lee	12	5	1	0	1	2	0	.417	.750	.467
Charlie Leibrandt	10	4	2	0	1	3	3	.400	.900	.538
Dave Lemanczyk	28	10	0	0	1	3	3	.357	.464	.406
Dennis Leonard	43	15	4	0	4	4	3	.349	.721	.417
Randy Lerch	6	2	0	0	0	0	0	.333	.333	.333
Paul Lindblad	6	2	0	0	0	1	2	.333	.333	.429
Aurelio Lopez	24	9	2	0	3	5	3	.375	.833	.483
Sparky Lyle	14	3	0	0	0	1	1	.214	.214	.267
Keith MacWhorter	6	2	0	1	0	0	1	.333	.833	.333
Mike G. Marshall	12	3	1	0	1	0	3	.250	.583	.308
Renie Martin	8	3	2	0	0	1	2	.375	.625	.444
Alfredo Martinez	8	3	0	0	1	0	0	.375	.750	.375
Mike Mason	11	2	1	0	0	1	2	.182	.273	.308
Jon Matlack	28	9	3	0	1	3	5	.321	.536	.387
Rudy May	12	2	0	0	0	0	3	.167	.167	.167
Steve McCatty	33	9	2	0	3	8	10	.273	.606	.405
Bob McClure	25	9	2	0	1	4	2	.360	.560	.467
Byron McLaughlin	14	1	0	0	0	0	5	.071	.071	.071
Joey McLaughlin	12	6	2	1	1	2	1	.500	1.083	.571
Doc Medich	10	2	1	0	0	1	1	.200	.300	.273
Dyar Miller	8	2	1	0	0	1	1	.250	.375	.333
Steve Mingori	6	1	1	0	0	0	0	.167	.333	.167
Paul Mirabella	12	4	0	0	0	3	3	.333	.333	.467
Paul Mitchell	12	4	1	0	2	1	1	.333	.917	.385
Sid Monge	11	4	0	0	1	3	2	.364	.636	.500
John Montague	13	6	2	0	0	3	4	.462	.615	.563
John Montefusco	5	1	1	0	0	0	0	.200	.400	.200
Balor Moore	10	4	0	0	1	2	0	.400	.700	.500
Mike Moore	30	6	0	0	0	3	5	.200	.200	.273
Angel Moreno	5	2	2	0	0	1	0	.400	.800	.500
Mike Morgan	17	2	0	1	0	3	5	.118	.235	.286
Jack Morris	66	17	2	0	4	8	16	.258	.470	.333
Tom Murphy	8	3	0	0	1	0	1	.375	.750	.375
Gene Nelson	24	3	2	0	1	1	8	.125	.333	.160
Phil Niekro	7	4	1	0	0	3	0	.571	.714	.700
Al Nipper	17	8	2	0	1	1	3	.471	.765	.500
Dickie Noles	6	1	0	0	0	1	1	.167	.167	.286
Mike Norris	32	8	0	0	3	2	6	.250	.531	.294
Edwin Nunez	5	1	0	0	0	0	1	.200	.200	.200
Jack O'Connor	14	6	0	0	2	1	2	.429	.857	.467
Bob Ojeda	33	6	2	0	1	2	5	.182	.333	.229
Randy O'Neal	7	0	0	0	0	1	0	.000	.000	.125
Bob Owchinko	18	3	0	0	0	1	1	.167	.167	.211
Mike Parrott	19	7	1	1	1	4	2	.368	.684	.500
Marty Pattin	7	5	1	1	0	0	0	.714	1.143	.714
Mike Paxton	19	10	2	0	2	4	2	.526	.947	.609
Gaylord Perry	34	10	1	0	0	2	2	.294	.324	.333
Dan Petry	53	16	2	0	3	6	4	.302	.509	.373
Dick Pole	10	2	0	0	1	3	2	.200	.500	.385
Chuck Porter	5	1	0	0	0	0	0	.200	.200	.200
Mike Proly	11	4	1	1	2	2	0	.364	1.182	.462
Dan Quisenberry	17	7	0	1	1	1	2	.412	.706	.421
Chuck Rainey	12	3	0	0	1	1	2	.250	.500	.308

Pitcher	AB	H	2B	3B	HR	BB	SO	BA	SA	OBA
Dennis Rasmussen	9	2	0	0	0	3	2	.222	.222	.417
Shane Rawley	28	11	2	0	1	6	2	.393	.571	.500
Pete Redfern	16	6	1	0	0	2	2	.375	.438	.421
Ron Reed	5	2	1	0	0	0	1	.400	.600	.400
Win Remmerswaal	8	3	2	0	0	1	1	.375	.625	.444
Steve Renko	34	8	1	0	0	9	6	.235	.265	.395
Andy Replogle	9	1	0	0	0	0	3	.111	.111	.111
Paul Reuschel	5	4	0	0	0	0	1	.800	.800	.800
Dave Righetti	31	12	1	0	1	0	1	.387	.516	.387
Jose Rijo	5	1	1	0	0	1	2	.200	.400	.333
Allen Ripley	11	2	0	0	1	1	1	.182	.455	.250
Dave A. Roberts	11	3	1	0	1	1	1	.273	.636	.333
Eduardo Rodriguez	12	4	1	0	0	1	2	.333	.417	.385
Jose Roman	5	1	0	0	1	0	0	.200	.800	.200
Ron Romanick	18	5	1	0	1	1	3	.278	.500	.316
Enrique Romo	5	2	0	0	1	1	1	.400	1.000	.500
Dave Rozema	29	7	1	0	2	1	2	.241	.483	.258
Dave Rucker	5	0	0	0	0	0	1	.000	.000	.000
Vern Ruhle	13	4	0	1	0	0	0	.308	.462	.308
Nolan Ryan	16	7	0	0	1	1	5	.438	.625	.444
Bret Saberhagen	8	4	1	0	0	2	0	.500	.625	.600
Luis Sanchez	6	2	0	0	1	6	0	.333	.833	.667
Dan Schatzeder	6	0	0	0	0	1	0	.000	.000	.125
Dave J. Schmidt	16	4	0	0	0	1	3	.250	.250	.294
Ken Schrom	27	8	0	0	3	2	2	.296	.630	.345
Ron Schueler	5	2	0	0	1	1	3	.400	1.000	.500
Don Schulze	6	3	0	0	0	0	0	.500	.500	.571
Tom Seaver	18	2	0	0	0	1	8	.111	.111	.158
Gary Serum	5	3	1	1	0	2	0	.600	1.200	.714
Bob Shirley	6	3	1	0	0	0	0	.500	.667	.500
Jim Slaton	54	11	2	0	4	7	5	.204	.463	.281
Mike Smithson	31	11	1	1	3	4	8	.355	.742	.417
Lary Sorensen	45	16	0	0	1	4	2	.356	.422	.400
Elias Sosa	6	1	0	0	0	0	0	.167	.167	.167
Dan Spillner	23	9	1	0	1	8	1	.391	.565	.548
Paul Splittorff	44	11	0	0	1	2	2	.250	.318	.283
Bob Stanley	39	16	5	0	2	5	4	.410	.692	.477
Mike Stanton	8	4	1	0	0	1	0	.500	.625	.500
Randy Stein	6	3	1	0	0	0	1	.500	.667	.500
Dave Stewart	10	3	0	0	0	2	1	.300	.300	.417
Dave Stieb	48	15	1	0	5	7	5	.313	.646	.400
Bob Stoddard	7	0	0	0	0	0	2	.000	.000	.000
Steve Stone	16	4	0	0	1	2	2	.250	.250	.294
Rick Sutcliffe	20	8	3	0	2	6	7	.400	.850	.538
Don Sutton	31	9	3	0	1	6	3	.290	.484	.395
Bob Sykes	15	3	1	0	0	1	0	.200	.267	.250
Frank Tanana	69	18	4	0	4	3	15	.261	.493	.292
Tom Tellmann	9	3	1	0	0	2	1	.333	.444	.455
Roy Thomas	7	2	0	0	0	3	0	.286	.286	.545
Luis Tiant	32	5	0	0	3	2	5	.156	.438	.206
Dick Tidrow	14	3	1	0	0	1	5	.214	.286	.250
Dave Tobik	18	4	1	0	1	3	3	.222	.278	.263
Jackson Todd	10	3	0	0	2	0	1	.300	.900	.300
Jim Todd	8	4	0	0	1	2	0	.500	.875	.600
Mike Torrez	36	8	0	0	2	10	4	.222	.389	.383
Bill Travers	27	8	1	0	0	1	3	.296	.333	.321
Steve Trout	22	3	1	0	0	1	2	.136	.182	.174
John Tudor	23	10	2	0	1	3	1	.435	.652	.500
Jerry Ujdur	11	0	0	0	0	2	1	.000	.000	.154
Pat Underwood	8	3	0	0	0	1	1	.375	.375	.444
Tom Underwood	38	12	1	0	0	6	3	.316	.342	.409
Ed Vande Berg	13	7	1	0	1	1	1	.538	.846	.571
John Verhoeven	9	1	0	0	1	1	2	.111	.444	.200
Frank Viola	27	6	1	0	0	3	5	.222	.259	.323
Pete Vuckovich	27	11	1	1	1	0	3	.407	.630	.407
Tom Waddell	5	2	1	0	0	2	1	.400	.600	.500
Rick Waits	41	15	1	1	2	3	5	.366	.585	.400
Curt Wardle	9	4	0	0	2	2	2	.444	1.111	.545
Mike Warren	5	2	1	0	0	2	0	.400	.600	.571
Bill Wegman	5	3	0	0	1	0	0	.600	1.200	.600
Ed Whitson	7	1	0	0	0	0	1	.143	.143	.143
Milt Wilcox	50	17	3	0	6	4	7	.340	.760	.386
Al Williams	12	2	0	0	1	1	4	.167	.167	.214
Mike Willis	5	2	1	0	0	1	0	.400	.600	.500
Jim Willoughby	6	2	0	0	0	0	0	.333	.333	.333

Eddie Murray continued

Pitcher	AB	H	2B	3B	HR	BB	SO	BA	SA	OBA	Pitcher	AB	H	2B	3B	HR	BB	SO	BA	SA	OBA
Rick Wise	27	7	2	0	1	0	3	.259	.444	.259	Kip Young	6	2	0	0	0	0	2	.333	.333	.333
Mike Witt	27	10	5	1	2	10	2	.370	.852	.553	Matt Young	14	3	0	0	0	3	1	.214	.214	.389
Rich Wortham	18	2	0	0	1	4	3	.111	.278	.273	Geoff Zahn	43	14	5	0	5	2	4	.326	.791	.356
Curt Young	5	0	0	0	0	1	0	.000	.000	.167											

Dwight Gooden

Batter	AB	H	2B	3B	HR	BB	SO	BA	SA	OBA	Batter	AB	H	2B	3B	HR	BB	SO	BA	SA	OBA
Dave Anderson	8	2	0	0	0	0	5	.250	.250	.250	Vance Law	6	1	0	0	1	2	3	.167	.667	.375
Joaquin Andujar	12	1	0	0	0	0	8	.083	.083	.083	Jeff Leonard	8	0	0	0	0	0	7	.000	.000	.000
Alan Ashby	11	2	0	0	0	0	0	.182	.182	.182	Bryan Little	7	1	0	0	0	2	2	.143	.143	.333
Mark Bailey	7	2	0	0	1	1	2	.286	.714	.375	Dave Lopes	7	0	0	0	0	1	0	.000	.000	.125
Bob Bailor	5	1	0	0	0	0	0	.200	.200	.200	Bill Madlock	6	2	0	0	0	1	0	.333	.333	.429
Kevin Bass	17	4	0	0	0	0	4	.235	.235	.235	Mike A. Marshall	11	1	0	0	0	2	5	.091	.091	.231
Dale Berra	7	1	0	0	0	2	1	.143	.143	.333	Carmelo Martinez	6	2	1	0	0	2	1	.333	.500	.500
Thad Bosley	9	1	0	0	0	0	5	.111	.111	.111	Gary Matthews	18	4	1	0	0	6	9	.222	.278	.400
Larry Bowa	16	3	0	0	0	3	0	.188	.188	.316	Lee Mazzilli	9	3	0	0	0	3	1	.333	.333	.500
Steve Braun	8	0	0	0	0	0	3	.000	.000	.000	Willie McGee	23	11	0	0	0	1	3	.478	.478	.500
Bob Brenly	8	1	0	0	0	1	6	.125	.125	.222	Kevin McReynolds	11	2	1	0	1	0	5	.182	.545	.182
Greg Brock	14	3	0	0	1	0	7	.214	.429	.214	Eddie Milner	12	0	0	0	0	0	2	.000	.000	.000
Hubie Brooks	7	3	0	0	0	0	1	.429	.429	.500	Keith Moreland	26	7	0	0	0	0	5	.269	.269	.269
Bobby Brown	9	1	1	0	0	0	2	.111	.222	.100	Jim Morrison	6	0	0	0	0	0	4	.000	.000	.000
Chris Brown	7	1	0	0	0	1	3	.143	.143	.250	Jerry Mumphrey	19	3	0	0	0	1	8	.158	.158	.200
Enos Cabell	6	3	0	0	0	0	1	.500	.500	.500	Dale Murphy	7	0	0	0	0	1	5	.000	.000	.125
Gary Carter	13	4	0	0	0	0	4	.308	.308	.308	Graig Nettles	14	2	0	0	1	1	7	.143	.357	.200
Cesar Cedeno	9	1	1	0	0	0	3	.111	.222	.111	Ken Oberkfell	6	1	0	0	0	2	2	.167	.167	.375
Ron Cey	21	5	2	0	0	5	9	.238	.333	.385	Ron Oester	16	3	0	0	0	0	3	.188	.188	.188
Chris Chambliss	5	2	0	0	1	1	0	.400	1.000	.500	Joe Orsulak	5	2	0	0	0	0	0	.400	.400	.400
Jack Clark	15	3	0	0	2	2	6	.200	.600	.294	Dave Parker	16	3	0	0	0	2	3	.188	.188	.278
Vince Coleman	19	4	1	0	0	1	3	.211	.263	.250	Tony Pena	13	1	0	0	0	0	7	.077	.077	.077
Dave Concepcion	8	0	0	0	0	0	5	.000	.000	.000	Terry Pendleton	21	4	1	0	0	1	3	.190	.238	.227
Tim Corcoran	13	3	0	0	0	1	2	.231	.231	.286	Darrell Porter	18	2	1	1	0	0	4	.111	.278	.158
Jose Cruz	20	3	2	0	0	2	4	.150	.250	.227	Terry Puhl	12	2	0	0	0	0	0	.167	.167	.167
Darren Daulton	5	0	0	0	0	1	3	.000	.000	.167	Tim Raines	18	4	1	0	0	4	3	.222	.278	.364
Chili Davis	14	7	1	0	0	1	5	.500	.571	.533	Rafael Ramirez	5	1	0	0	0	1	1	.200	.200	.333
Glenn Davis	6	1	0	0	1	0	1	.167	.667	.286	Johnny Ray	17	2	0	0	0	0	2	.118	.118	.118
Jody Davis	24	6	1	0	1	0	7	.250	.417	.250	Gary Redus	5	0	0	0	0	0	3	.000	.000	.000
Andre Dawson	21	6	1	0	0	0	8	.286	.476	.286	Craig Reynolds	20	5	0	0	0	0	0	.250	.250	.250
Bob Dernier	23	3	1	1	0	4	5	.130	.261	.259	R.J. Reynolds	9	3	0	0	0	1	2	.333	.333	.400
Bill Doran	21	9	3	1	0	3	7	.429	.667	.500	Ron Roenicke	5	2	0	0	0	0	2	.400	.400	.400
Dan Driessen	24	7	1	0	0	2	4	.292	.333	.346	Pete Rose	20	6	0	0	0	2	0	.300	.300	.364
Mariano Duncan	9	0	0	0	0	0	4	.000	.000	.000	Dick Ruthven	7	2	0	0	0	1	4	.286	.286	.375
Leon Durham	27	7	2	0	0	1	5	.259	.333	.286	Argenis Salazar	10	1	0	0	0	0	3	.100	.100	.100
Mike Fitzgerald	5	0	0	0	0	0	3	.000	.000	.000	Juan Samuel	20	3	1	1	0	0	11	.150	.300	.150
Tim Flannery	7	3	0	0	0	1	1	.429	.429	.500	Ryne Sandberg	36	10	1	1	0	1	7	.278	.361	.297
Tom Foley	15	2	1	0	0	1	5	.133	.200	.188	Steve Sax	21	5	0	0	0	0	4	.238	.238	.238
Terry Francona	6	1	0	0	0	1	1	.167	.167	.286	Mike Schmidt	15	3	1	0	1	3	5	.200	.467	.333
Doug Frobel	7	2	0	0	0	0	4	.286	.286	.286	Mike Scioscia	16	3	1	0	1	1	2	.188	.438	.235
Phil Garner	10	2	0	0	0	2	3	.200	.200	.333	Lonnie Smith	11	4	0	0	0	3	1	.364	.364	.500
Steve Garvey	17	7	3	0	0	0	3	.412	.588	.412	Ozzie Smith	20	5	0	0	0	4	0	.250	.250	.375
Dan Gladden	10	2	0	0	0	2	4	.200	.200	.333	Chris Speier	8	5	0	0	0	3	1	.625	.625	.727
Denny Gonzalez	9	0	0	0	0	0	6	.000	.000	.000	Jeff Stone	18	4	0	1	0	0	7	.222	.333	.222
Jim Gott	5	0	0	0	0	0	5	.000	.000	.000	Garry Templeton	13	1	0	0	0	2	5	.077	.077	.200
Greg Gross	9	2	0	0	0	1	0	.222	.222	.300	Jason Thompson	12	2	0	0	0	2	3	.167	.167	.286
Pedro Guerrero	20	3	1	0	2	3	10	.150	.500	.261	Manny Trillo	11	3	1	0	0	0	1	.273	.364	.273
Brad Gulden	5	1	0	0	0	1	1	.200	.200	.333	John Tudor	5	1	0	0	0	0	1	.200	.200	.200
Bill Gullickson	6	0	0	0	0	0	4	.000	.000	.000	Jose Uribe	10	1	0	0	0	0	2	.100	.100	.100
Tony Gwynn	16	2	0	1	0	1	1	.125	.250	.176	Fernando Valenzuela	13	1	1	0	0	0	4	.077	.154	.077
Terry Harper	6	0	0	0	0	0	2	.000	.000	.000	Andy Van Slyke	26	9	1	0	0	3	5	.346	.385	.414
Billy Hatcher	9	2	0	0	0	0	1	.222	.222	.222	Ozzie Virgil	12	2	0	0	0	0	6	.167	.167	.167
Von Hayes	18	4	1	0	0	3	2	.222	.278	.333	Duane Walker	8	3	2	0	0	3	3	.375	.625	.545
Richie Hebner	10	1	0	0	0	2	4	.100	.100	.250	Tim Wallach	19	1	0	0	0	0	11	.053	.053	.100
Tommy Herr	27	4	1	0	0	2	3	.148	.185	.200	Denny Walling	12	4	1	0	1	3	1	.333	.667	.467
Glenn Hubbard	7	1	0	0	1	0	1	.143	.571	.143	Claudell Washington	7	4	1	1	1	2	0	.571	1.429	.667
Steve Jeltz	5	0	0	0	0	0	1	.000	.000	.000	Brad Wellman	6	2	0	0	0	0	0	.333	.333	.333
Mike Jorgensen	8	3	0	0	0	1	2	.375	.375	.444	Terry Whitfield	13	1	0	0	0	0	9	.077	.077	.077
Terry Kennedy	14	3	0	0	0	1	6	.214	.214	.267	Alan Wiggins	10	2	0	0	0	0	1	.200	.200	.200
Alan Knicely	5	0	0	0	0	0	5	.000	.000	.000	Glenn Wilson	8	2	0	0	0	0	4	.250	.250	.250
Wayne Krenchicki	13	5	0	0	0	1	2	.385	.385	.429	Herm Winningham	7	0	0	0	0	0	3	.000	.000	.000
Lee Lacy	7	1	1	0	0	0	3	.143	.286	.143	Marvell Wynne	15	0	0	0	0	0	5	.000	.000	.000
Steve Lake	5	0	0	0	0	2	2	.000	.000	.000	Joel Youngblood	10	2	0	0	0	0	3	.200	.200	.200
Ken Landreaux	18	5	0	1	0	1	4	.278	.389	.316											

Ron Guidry

Batter	AB	H	2B	3B	HR	BB	SO	BA	SA	OBA	Batter	AB	H	2B	3B	HR	BB	SO	BA	SA	OBA
Willie Aikens	23	2	1	0	1	3	9	.087	.261	.192	Butch Davis	9	2	0	0	2	0	1	.222	.889	.222
Gary Alexander	13	5	0	0	1	2	4	.385	.615	.438	Dick Davis	16	6	0	0	0	0	2	.375	.375	.375
Jamie Allen	10	1	0	0	0	0	2	.100	.100	.100	Mike Davis	18	2	1	0	0	0	6	.111	.167	.111
Gary Allenson	24	3	0	0	0	3	10	.125	.125	.222	Doug DeCinces	61	15	5	0	5	7	8	.246	.574	.333
Bill Almon	23	7	1	0	0	0	5	.304	.348	.304	Rick Dempsey	48	12	1	1	1	4	7	.250	.375	.315
Dell Alston	8	0	0	0	0	0	4	.000	.000	.000	Bucky Dent	5	2	0	0	0	1	0	.400	.400	.500
Jim Anderson	13	4	1	0	0	3	2	.308	.385	.438	Bo Diaz	8	2	0	0	0	1	0	.250	.250	.333
Tony Armas	43	11	0	1	2	1	15	.256	.442	.267	Miguel Dilone	26	6	1	0	0	0	6	.231	.269	.231
Doug Ault	18	2	0	0	0	1	4	.111	.111	.158	Tom Donohue	5	1	0	0	0	1	2	.200	.200	.333
Benny Ayala	28	9	3	0	0	2	4	.321	.429	.367	Brian Downing	33	9	1	0	1	9	6	.273	.394	.419
Bob Bailey	6	0	0	0	0	1	0	.000	.000	.143	Denny Doyle	5	3	0	0	0	1	0	.600	.600	.667
Bob Bailor	30	11	2	1	0	3	2	.367	.500	.424	Taylor Duncan	14	3	1	0	0	1	1	.214	.286	.267
Harold Baines	28	7	1	0	0	2	3	.250	.286	.300	Jim Dwyer	7	2	1	0	0	0	1	.286	.429	.286
Dusty Baker	10	0	0	0	0	1	1	.000	.000	.091	Jerry Dybzinski	7	0	0	0	0	1	3	.000	.000	.125
Steve Balboni	19	4	1	0	1	0	2	.211	.421	.211	Duffy Dyer	5	1	0	0	0	0	2	.200	.200	.200
Chris Bando	20	5	2	0	0	1	4	.250	.350	.273	Mike Easler	14	4	2	0	0	0	8	.286	.429	.267
Sal Bando	20	3	0	0	1	2	3	.150	.300	.227	Dave Edler	7	1	0	0	0	1	2	.143	.143	.250
Alan Bannister	51	11	0	0	0	4	12	.216	.216	.273	Dave Edwards	19	7	1	0	0	0	3	.368	.421	.368
Jesse Barfield	25	6	1	1	1	3	5	.240	.480	.310	Mike Edwards	10	1	1	0	0	1	1	.100	.200	.182
Marty Barrett	17	2	1	0	0	1	1	.118	.176	.158	Johnny Ellis	18	5	3	0	0	0	4	.278	.444	.278
Don Baylor	26	6	1	0	0	4	5	.231	.269	.333	Dave Engle	34	10	5	0	1	2	5	.294	.529	.333
Mark Belanger	22	5	2	0	1	3	7	.227	.455	.320	Jim Essian	19	5	2	0	1	3	4	.263	.526	.364
Buddy Bell	62	16	6	2	1	6	5	.258	.468	.319	Dwight Evans	61	21	8	1	4	7	15	.344	.705	.412
George Bell	19	8	3	1	0	0	2	.421	.684	.421	Lenny Faedo	12	6	1	0	0	0	0	.500	.583	.500
Kevin Bell	7	2	0	0	0	0	4	.286	.286	.286	Tony Fernandez	6	2	1	0	0	0	0	.333	.500	.333
Juan Beniquez	38	6	1	0	0	1	6	.158	.184	.179	Mike Fischlin	23	6	2	0	0	0	5	.261	.348	.261
Tony Bernazard	24	6	3	0	0	2	4	.250	.375	.308	Carlton Fisk	59	14	5	0	3	8	12	.237	.475	.328
Juan Bernhardt	7	2	0	0	0	1	0	.286	.286	.375	Scott Fletcher	19	6	1	0	0	3	4	.316	.368	.409
Kurt Bevacqua	11	0	0	0	0	0	2	.000	.000	.000	Tim Foli	10	2	0	0	0	0	1	.200	.200	.200
Bruce Bochte	29	10	1	0	0	1	2	.345	.379	.367	Dan Ford	41	10	4	0	0	4	11	.244	.341	.311
Wade Boggs	36	9	1	0	0	1	2	.250	.278	.270	Julio Franco	19	8	1	0	1	1	4	.421	.632	.450
Bobby Bonds	11	2	0	0	1	4	5	.182	.455	.400	Tito Fuentes	15	4	0	1	1	0	0	.267	.600	.267
Barry Bonnell	23	6	1	0	1	2	3	.261	.435	.320	Gary Gaetti	41	6	1	0	1	2	11	.146	.244	.182
Bob Boone	15	6	2	0	0	1	1	.400	.533	.412	Greg Gagne	7	0	0	0	0	0	1	.000	.000	.000
Glenn Borgmann	12	1	0	0	0	3	4	.083	.083	.250	Jim Gantner	23	7	1	0	0	1	0	.304	.348	.333
Rick Bosetti	17	6	1	1	0	0	5	.353	.529	.353	Barbaro Garbey	15	5	0	0	1	0	0	.333	.533	.333
Lyman Bostock	11	5	1	0	0	0	1	.455	.545	.455	Damaso Garcia	34	10	0	1	0	0	2	.294	.353	.294
Phil Bradley	12	6	0	0	1	1	2	.500	.750	.538	Kiko Garcia	20	4	0	0	0	1	10	.200	.200	.238
Steve Braun	5	0	0	0	0	1	0	.000	.000	.167	Ralph Garr	9	1	0	0	0	0	3	.111	.222	.111
George Brett	45	13	0	0	2	5	4	.289	.422	.353	Kirk Gibson	15	2	0	0	1	1	6	.133	.333	.188
Tom Brookens	42	11	3	0	1	4	12	.262	.405	.319	Luis Gomez	5	1	0	0	0	0	0	.200	.200	.200
Mark Brouhard	21	4	1	0	0	1	8	.190	.238	.227	Gary Gray	5	0	0	0	0	0	2	.000	.000	.000
Darrell Brown	12	2	0	0	0	0	2	.167	.167	.167	Bobby Grich	40	12	4	0	3	5	10	.300	.625	.370
Tom Brunansky	39	11	2	0	3	4	6	.282	.564	.349	Tom Grieve	5	0	0	0	0	1	1	.000	.000	.167
Steve Brye	5	0	0	0	0	0	2	.000	.000	.000	Alfredo Griffin	41	11	0	0	0	0	7	.268	.268	.268
Bill Buckner	15	4	1	0	0	0	1	.267	.333	.267	Wayne Gross	11	1	0	0	0	1	3	.091	.091	.167
Al Bumbry	40	11	2	1	0	3	6	.275	.375	.326	Johnny Grubb	7	1	0	0	0	0	4	.143	.143	.143
Rick Burleson	39	10	2	0	0	3	12	.256	.308	.310	Mario Guerrero	18	5	0	0	1	0	4	.278	.278	.316
Jeff Burroughs	19	5	0	0	2	3	4	.263	.579	.364	Jackie Gutierrez	16	2	1	1	0	0	1	.125	.313	.125
Sal Butera	12	2	1	0	0	1	1	.167	.250	.231	Jerry Hairston	5	0	0	0	0	0	2	.000	.000	.000
Brett Butler	15	9	0	0	0	2	2	.600	.600	.611	Mike Hargrove	39	13	0	0	0	4	5	.333	.333	.400
Enos Cabell	13	3	1	0	1	0	1	.231	.538	.231	Toby Harrah	56	12	3	0	1	7	6	.214	.321	.297
Ivan Calderon	5	0	0	0	0	0	1	.000	.000	.000	Ron Hassey	7	3	1	0	0	1	1	.429	.571	.500
Bert Campaneris	16	4	0	0	0	4	2	.250	.250	.400	Mickey Hatcher	30	6	2	0	1	1	3	.200	.367	.226
Rod Carew	34	4	0	1	0	4	6	.118	.176	.211	Von Hayes	9	3	1	0	0	1	1	.333	.444	.400
Joe Carter	10	4	1	0	2	0	1	.400	1.100	.400	Mike Heath	36	12	5	1	0	2	4	.333	.528	.359
Rico Carty	14	4	1	0	0	1	0	.286	.357	.333	Richie Hebner	12	3	0	0	0	0	1	.250	.250	.250
Carmen Castillo	18	1	0	0	0	0	5	.056	.056	.056	Dave Henderson	26	7	2	1	1	2	6	.269	.538	.310
Marty Castillo	12	2	0	0	0	0	4	.167	.167	.167	Rickey Henderson	34	9	1	0	2	7	9	.265	.471	.390
John Castino	48	17	3	0	0	4	7	.354	.417	.404	Steve Henderson	22	10	1	0	2	2	4	.455	.773	.500
Rick Cerone	16	8	1	0	0	0	1	.500	.563	.500	Leo Hernandez	6	1	0	0	0	1	1	.167	.167	.286
Dave Chalk	16	5	0	0	0	0	7	.313	.313	.313	Larry Herndon	33	11	2	0	1	1	5	.333	.485	.353
Joe Charboneau	5	1	0	0	0	1	0	.200	.200	.333	Donnie Hill	9	3	1	0	0	1	3	.333	.444	.400
Bobby Clark	18	2	0	0	1	1	3	.111	.278	.158	Marc Hill	6	3	0	0	0	1	1	.500	.500	.500
Dave Collins	9	2	0	0	0	0	0	.222	.222	.222	Larry Hisle	19	3	0	0	2	2	5	.158	.474	.238
Onix Concepcion	10	3	0	0	1	0	1	.300	.600	.300	Butch Hobson	29	8	0	0	1	1	8	.276	.379	.290
Cecil Cooper	45	13	2	0	3	1	3	.289	.533	.304	Glenn Hoffman	23	4	0	1	1	0	6	.174	.391	.174
Al Cowens	58	17	7	1	1	1	10	.293	.500	.300	Willie Horton	28	5	1	0	0	3	7	.179	.214	.258
Larry Cox	9	2	0	0	1	2	2	.222	.222	.273	Tim Hosley	6	1	0	0	0	2	1	.167	.167	.375
Ted Cox	11	0	0	0	0	0	5	.000	.000	.000	Dave Hostetler	7	4	1	0	0	1	0	.571	.714	.625
Julio Cruz	39	11	1	0	1	4	6	.282	.385	.341	Roy Howell	21	2	0	0	0	1	5	.095	.095	.136
Todd Cruz	15	1	0	0	0	2	6	.067	.067	.176	Kent Hrbek	31	7	1	0	1	2	5	.226	.355	.273
Paul Dade	15	4	0	0	0	0	5	.267	.267	.235	Terry Humphrey	8	3	0	0	0	0	1	.375	.375	.375
Rich Dauer	49	7	0	0	0	2	4	.143	.143	.164	Garth Iorg	36	8	4	0	0	0	5	.222	.333	.222
Alvin Davis	10	2	0	0	0	0	2	.200	.200	.200	Reggie Jackson	30	7	0	0	2	1	7	.233	.433	.250

Ron Guidry continued

Batter	AB	H	2B	3B	HR	BB	SO	BA	SA	OBA
Ron Jackson	49	11	4	1	0	7	9	.224	.347	.321
Brook Jacoby	14	4	0	0	0	1	0	.286	.286	.333
Bobby Johnson	5	0	0	0	0	0	2	.000	.000	.000
Cliff Johnson	42	7	2	0	0	2	9	.167	.214	.205
Lamar Johnson	35	9	1	0	1	4	3	.257	.371	.325
Lynn Jones	19	4	1	0	0	3	3	.211	.263	.318
Ruppert Jones	18	3	1	0	0	0	5	.167	.222	.167
Ed Jurak	6	3	2	0	0	1	0	.500	.833	.571
Bob Kearney	14	4	0	0	0	2	4	.286	.286	.375
Steve Kemp	56	13	3	1	1	3	14	.232	.375	.283
Fred Kendall	5	3	0	0	0	0	0	.600	.600	.600
Don Kessinger	7	4	0	0	0	1	2	.571	.571	.625
Bruce Kimm	9	3	1	0	0	0	3	.333	.444	.333
Dave Kingman	18	3	0	0	0	1	5	.167	.167	.211
Ron Kittle	17	5	1	0	1	2	6	.294	.529	.368
Mickey Klutts	6	3	1	0	1	1	0	.500	1.167	.571
Duane Kuiper	18	7	0	1	0	1	1	.389	.500	.421
Rusty Kuntz	26	6	1	0	0	3	7	.231	.269	.310
Craig Kusick	21	8	0	0	1	5	5	.381	.524	.500
Lee Lacy	13	3	0	1	0	0	3	.231	.385	.231
Ken Landreaux	20	6	0	0	1	1	2	.300	.450	.333
Carney Lansford	40	16	1	1	0	1	6	.400	.475	.415
Tim Laudner	18	3	0	0	1	1	7	.167	.333	.211
Rudy Law	11	4	0	0	0	0	1	.364	.364	.364
Vance Law	20	4	0	0	0	2	5	.200	.200	.273
Ron LeFlore	61	13	3	1	2	2	13	.213	.393	.238
Chet Lemon	53	15	6	0	0	8	12	.283	.396	.397
Sixto Lezcano	18	6	1	0	1	2	3	.333	.556	.400
Dave Lopes	20	4	1	0	1	0	2	.200	.400	.190
Carlos Lopez	17	2	1	0	0	0	5	.118	.176	.118
Greg Luzinski	31	8	2	0	1	6	11	.258	.419	.378
Fred Lynn	36	9	3	1	0	2	7	.250	.389	.275
Pete Mackanin	13	2	1	0	0	1	3	.154	.231	.214
Jim Maler	6	1	0	0	0	0	3	.167	.167	.167
Rick Manning	40	3	2	0	0	2	11	.075	.125	.116
Jerry Martin	6	1	0	0	0	0	2	.167	.167	.167
Buck Martinez	29	4	0	0	0	2	6	.138	.138	.194
Lee May	33	8	4	0	1	2	4	.242	.455	.286
Milt May	9	0	0	0	0	1	3	.000	.000	.100
John Mayberry	20	2	0	0	1	1	9	.100	.250	.143
Oddibe McDowell	7	0	0	0	0	1	2	.000	.000	.125
Dave McKay	23	4	2	0	0	1	13	.174	.261	.208
Hal McRae	45	12	4	0	2	4	7	.267	.489	.320
Dave Meier	12	5	1	1	0	1	1	.417	.667	.462
Mario Mendoza	13	4	2	0	0	0	2	.308	.462	.308
Dan Meyer	11	5	0	1	0	0	1	.455	.636	.455
Larry Milbourne	26	3	0	0	0	0	5	.115	.115	.115
Rick Miller	35	8	0	0	0	2	8	.229	.229	.270
Paul Molitor	52	14	2	0	0	2	14	.269	.308	.296
Don Money	32	9	3	0	1	1	7	.281	.469	.303
Willie Montanez	5	1	0	0	0	0	2	.200	.200	.200
Alvin Moore	12	1	0	0	0	1	2	.083	.083	.154
Charlie Moore	42	9	0	0	1	3	3	.214	.286	.261
Kelvin Moore	6	1	0	0	0	0	2	.167	.167	.167
Andres Mora	9	2	2	0	0	0	1	.222	.444	.222
Jerry Morales	6	2	0	0	0	1	2	.333	.333	.429
Jose Morales	24	9	1	0	0	2	4	.375	.417	.423
Jim Morrison	23	3	1	0	2	0	7	.130	.435	.125
Lloyd Moseby	24	8	1	0	1	0	3	.333	.500	.333
Darryl Motley	19	5	0	1	0	0	1	.263	.526	.263
Dwayne Murphy	33	7	0	1	2	6	13	.212	.455	.325
Eddie Murray	68	16	4	0	3	4	14	.235	.426	.278
Larry Murray	8	0	0	0	0	1	4	.000	.000	.111
Bill Nahorodny	14	4	1	0	0	1	3	.286	.357	.333
Jeff Newman	22	4	1	0	0	2	5	.182	.227	.250
Reid Nichols	18	1	0	0	0	1	4	.056	.056	.105
Wayne Nordhagen	30	10	1	1	0	2	4	.333	.433	.364
Nelson Norman	5	1	0	0	0	1	1	.200	.200	.333
Jim Norris	6	1	0	0	0	1	2	.167	.167	.286
Willie Norwood	20	3	0	0	1	1	5	.150	.300	.190
Mike O'Berry	5	2	0	0	0	1	1	.400	.400	.500
Pete O'Brien	22	6	0	0	0	0	2	.273	.273	.273
Ben Oglivie	29	5	0	0	1	3	4	.172	.276	.250
Al Oliver	28	6	1	0	0	1	6	.214	.250	.241
Jorge Orta	21	3	0	0	0	2	3	.143	.143	.217
Amos Otis	28	6	1	0	0	1	4	.214	.250	.241
Spike Owen	11	2	1	0	0	1	2	.182	.273	.250
Tom Paciorek	42	10	4	0	2	2	17	.238	.476	.273
Mitchell Page	22	1	0	0	0	0	9	.045	.045	.045
Stan Papi	7	1	0	0	0	1	2	.143	.143	.250
Lance Parrish	75	18	2	0	6	3	20	.240	.507	.269
Larry Parrish	22	7	0	0	5	2	3	.318	1.000	.375
Fred Patek	15	1	0	0	0	0	4	.067	.067	.067
Jack Perconte	10	1	0	0	0	1	2	.100	.100	.182
Marty Perez	9	3	1	0	0	1	1	.333	.444	.400
Tony Perez	19	7	3	1	1	1	8	.368	.789	.400
Rick Peters	18	2	0	0	0	0	5	.111	.111	.111
Gary Pettis	8	5	0	1	0	0	1	.625	.875	.625
Tony Phillips	28	12	1	0	1	0	3	.429	.571	.429
Rob Picciolo	15	3	0	0	1	0	1	.200	.400	.200
Tom Poquette	7	3	1	0	0	0	2	.429	.571	.429
Darrell Porter	20	7	1	0	1	0	5	.350	.550	.350
Jim Presley	9	0	0	0	0	0	0	.000	.000	.000
Ron Pruitt	17	3	0	0	1	1	5	.176	.353	.222
Greg Pryor	34	8	0	0	1	2	1	.235	.324	.278
Kirby Puckett	11	4	0	1	0	0	1	.364	.545	.417
Pat Putnam	12	4	2	0	0	0	1	.333	.500	.333
Domingo Ramos	10	4	2	0	0	0	0	.400	.600	.400
Bob Randall	30	6	0	0	0	3	4	.200	.200	.273
Lenny Randle	5	1	0	0	0	2	0	.200	.200	.429
Floyd Rayford	8	3	1	0	1	0	0	.375	.875	.375
Randy Ready	7	2	0	0	0	0	1	.286	.286	.286
Jerry Remy	36	6	0	0	0	2	4	.167	.167	.211
Merv Rettenmund	14	4	1	0	0	1	4	.286	.357	.333
Dave Revering	14	3	0	1	0	2	3	.214	.429	.313
Craig Reynolds	12	4	0	0	0	0	1	.333	.333	.333
Kevin Rhomberg	5	2	0	0	0	1	1	.400	.400	.500
Jim Rice	69	24	2	1	5	6	15	.348	.623	.400
Cal Ripken	23	8	4	1	0	5	4	.348	.609	.448
Bombo Rivera	22	4	1	0	0	3	9	.182	.227	.280
Mickey Rivers	22	7	0	1	0	3	3	.318	.409	.400
Leon Roberts	21	6	3	0	2	2	6	.286	.714	.348
Aurelio Rodriguez	35	8	1	0	1	1	4	.229	.343	.250
Gary Roenicke	42	10	0	0	3	5	8	.238	.452	.306
Ron Roenicke	8	0	0	0	0	0	2	.000	.000	.000
Ed Romero	27	10	3	0	0	1	4	.370	.481	.393
Dave Rosello	9	2	0	0	0	0	3	.222	.222	.222
Joe Rudi	25	3	1	0	0	0	10	.120	.160	.120
Lenn Sakata	14	3	0	0	0	1	4	.214	.214	.267
Billy Sample	36	10	3	0	0	0	1	.278	.361	.278
Manny Sanguillen	11	3	1	0	1	0	0	.273	.636	.273
Dick Schofield	11	4	2	1	0	1	0	.364	.727	.417
George Scott	12	4	1	0	0	1	5	.333	.417	.385
Rodney Scott	6	1	0	0	0	0	1	.167	.167	.167
John Shelby	15	3	0	0	1	0	3	.200	.400	.200
Ted Simmons	29	9	5	1	0	1	2	.310	.552	.333
Ken Singleton	54	9	3	0	1	4	10	.167	.278	.224
Ted Sizemore	6	0	0	0	0	0	0	.000	.000	.000
Dave Skaggs	6	1	0	0	0	2	0	.167	.167	.375
Don Slaught	15	4	0	0	0	1	2	.267	.267	.294
Roy Smalley	41	5	3	0	0	6	11	.122	.195	.234
Eric Soderholm	17	4	2	0	2	3	0	.235	.706	.333
Tony Solaita	5	0	0	0	0	0	4	.000	.000	.000
Jim Spencer	6	2	0	0	2	0	1	.333	1.333	.333
Mike Squires	7	1	0	0	0	0	1	.143	.143	.143
Steve Staggs	5	0	0	0	0	0	4	.000	.000	.167
Mickey Stanley	25	6	2	0	1	0	5	.240	.440	.240
Lee Stanton	5	0	0	0	0	2	3	.000	.000	.286
Dave Stapleton	32	5	1	0	0	2	5	.156	.188	.206
Rusty Staub	42	11	1	0	0	0	7	.262	.286	.262
Dave Stegman	13	5	0	0	2	0	2	.385	.846	.385
Bill Stein	22	3	0	0	1	0	7	.136	.273	.136
Marc Sullivan	6	1	0	0	0	1	3	.167	.167	.286
Jim Sundberg	55	15	2	2	1	3	9	.273	.436	.310
Pat Tabler	19	6	2	0	0	2	1	.316	.421	.364
Jerry Terrell	12	3	0	0	0	1	2	.250	.250	.308
Tim Teufel	6	1	0	0	0	1	0	.167	.167	.286
Gorman Thomas	37	10	2	0	2	4	10	.270	.486	.357
Jason Thompson	31	8	0	0	1	2	9	.258	.355	.303
Dickie Thon	5	1	0	0	0	0	1	.200	.200	.200

Ron Guidry   continued

Batter	AB	H	2B	3B	HR	BB	SO	BA	SA	OBA
Andre Thornton	38	5	1	0	2	8	9	.132	.316	.277
Wayne Tolleson	25	9	1	0	0	0	6	.360	.400	.360
Rusty Torres	8	0	0	0	0	2	4	.000	.000	.182
Alan Trammell	60	18	3	0	0	8	9	.300	.350	.382
Jim Tyrone	9	2	0	0	0	1	4	.222	.222	.300
Willie Upshaw	22	2	0	0	0	1	8	.091	.091	.130
Mike Vail	8	1	0	0	0	0	4	.125	.125	.125
Bobby Valentine	5	1	1	0	0	1	0	.200	.400	.333
Jesus Vega	15	2	0	0	0	1	7	.133	.133	.188
Otto Velez	22	6	1	1	0	4	5	.273	.409	.385
Tom Veryzer	20	7	2	0	0	1	5	.350	.450	.381
Mark Wagner	7	2	0	1	0	1	3	.286	.571	.375
Greg Walker	6	0	0	0	0	0	3	.000	.000	.000
Gary Ward	55	20	4	0	4	3	7	.364	.655	.397
Claudell Washington	9	1	0	0	0	0	3	.111	.111	.111
Ron Washington	26	9	1	3	0	0	4	.346	.615	.333
U.L. Washington	23	4	0	0	0	2	6	.174	.174	.240
John Wathan	24	6	0	0	0	3	5	.250	.250	.333
Bob Watson	7	2	1	1	0	0	6	.286	.714	.286
Lou Whitaker	48	10	4	0	1	7	9	.208	.354	.309

Batter	AB	H	2B	3B	HR	BB	SO	BA	SA	OBA
Frank White	45	11	2	1	3	2	9	.244	.533	.277
Ernie Whitt	7	2	0	0	1	0	2	.286	.714	.286
Alan Wiggins	8	2	1	0	0	0	1	.250	.375	.250
Curtis Wilkerson	11	4	1	1	0	1	3	.364	.636	.417
Bump Wills	36	8	1	0	0	3	7	.222	.250	.282
Glenn Wilson	16	4	3	1	0	1	2	.250	.563	.294
Willie Wilson	46	10	2	0	1	1	9	.217	.326	.234
John Wockenfuss	45	6	1	0	1	5	13	.133	.222	.220
Jim Wohlford	10	1	0	0	0	2	2	.100	.100	.250
Larry Wolfe	11	2	0	0	0	2	3	.182	.182	.308
Al Woods	8	0	0	0	0	1	1	.000	.000	.111
Gary Woods	5	2	1	0	0	0	1	.400	.600	.400
George Wright	28	3	1	0	0	1	6	.107	.143	.138
Butch Wynegar	25	3	0	0	0	3	4	.120	.120	.214
Carl Yastrzemski	47	11	0	1	3	2	4	.234	.468	.260
Ned Yost	14	3	0	0	2	0	3	.214	.643	.214
Mike Young	14	6	4	0	0	1	2	.429	.714	.467
Robin Yount	54	14	5	1	1	0	10	.259	.444	.255
Joe Zdeb	5	3	0	0	0	0	1	.600	.600	.600
Richie Zisk	40	10	1	1	1	4	5	.250	.400	.311

Dan Quisenberry

Batter	AB	H	2B	3B	HR	BB	SO	BA	SA	OBA
Glenn Adams	6	2	2	0	0	0	0	.333	.667	.333
Willie Aikens	5	1	0	0	0	0	0	.200	.200	.200
Bill Almon	5	1	0	0	0	0	1	.200	.200	.200
Jim Anderson	9	2	1	0	1	0	2	.222	.667	.222
Tony Armas	30	11	1	0	3	0	3	.367	.700	.355
Bob Bailor	5	0	0	0	0	0	1	.000	.000	.000
Harold Baines	16	5	1	0	0	1	1	.313	.375	.353
Chris Bando	5	1	0	0	0	0	1	.200	.200	.200
Sal Bando	5	1	0	0	0	0	1	.200	.200	.200
Alan Bannister	7	1	1	0	0	0	1	.143	.286	.143
Jesse Barfield	6	1	0	0	0	0	2	.167	.167	.167
Marty Barrett	13	3	0	0	0	0	1	.231	.231	.231
Don Baylor	21	6	0	0	1	0	1	.286	.429	.286
Buddy Bell	19	4	1	0	0	1	1	.211	.263	.250
George Bell	10	1	0	0	1	0	2	.100	.400	.100
Juan Beniquez	13	3	0	0	0	0	3	.231	.231	.231
Dave Bergman	5	0	0	0	0	0	0	.000	.000	.000
Tony Bernazard	17	2	0	0	0	0	3	.118	.118	.118
Bruce Bochte	23	7	2	0	0	2	2	.304	.391	.360
Wade Boggs	16	2	0	0	0	0	0	.125	.125	.125
Barry Bonnell	13	6	1	0	0	0	1	.462	.538	.462
Bob Boone	9	3	0	0	0	0	0	.333	.333	.333
Phil Bradley	8	2	0	0	1	0	0	.250	.625	.250
Tom Brookens	14	2	0	0	0	0	1	.143	.143	.143
Tom Brunansky	14	2	0	0	0	1	3	.143	.143	.200
Bill Buckner	7	1	0	0	0	0	0	.143	.143	.143
Al Bumbry	14	3	0	0	0	0	0	.214	.214	.214
Rick Burleson	13	1	0	0	0	0	0	.077	.077	.077
Jeff Burroughs	8	1	0	0	0	0	1	.125	.125	.125
Randy Bush	9	2	1	0	0	0	0	.222	.333	.222
Brett Butler	5	3	0	0	0	0	0	.600	.600	.600
Enos Cabell	5	1	0	0	0	0	0	.200	.200	.200
Rod Carew	19	5	1	0	1	2	0	.263	.474	.333
Manny Castillo	5	1	0	0	0	0	0	.200	.200	.200
John Castino	11	2	0	0	0	0	1	.182	.182	.182
Rick Cerone	8	3	0	0	0	0	3	.375	.375	.333
Darnell Coles	6	1	0	0	0	0	0	.167	.167	.167
Dave Collins	12	3	0	0	0	0	1	.250	.250	.231
Cecil Cooper	19	9	0	0	2	0	1	.474	.789	.474
Al Cowens	20	4	0	0	0	1	1	.200	.200	.227
Rodney Craig	6	1	0	0	0	0	0	.167	.167	.167
Terry Crowley	9	2	1	0	0	1	0	.222	.333	.300
Julio Cruz	16	5	1	0	0	1	1	.313	.375	.353
Todd Cruz	6	0	0	0	0	0	0	.000	.000	.000
Mike Cubbage	5	0	0	0	0	0	1	.000	.000	.000
Rich Dauer	10	2	2	0	0	0	0	.200	.400	.200
Alvin Davis	10	3	1	0	0	0	0	.300	.400	.300
Mike Davis	18	5	0	0	0	1	3	.278	.278	.316
Doug DeCinces	20	2	0	0	0	1	2	.100	.100	.143

Batter	AB	H	2B	3B	HR	BB	SO	BA	SA	OBA
Rick Dempsey	5	1	0	0	0	1	0	.200	.200	.333
Bucky Dent	9	1	0	0	0	0	0	.111	.111	.111
Miguel Dilone	6	0	0	0	0	0	0	.000	.000	.000
Brian Downing	21	3	0	0	1	0	2	.143	.286	.143
Jim Dwyer	13	2	0	0	0	2	0	.154	.154	.250
Jerry Dybzinski	7	2	1	0	0	0	2	.286	.429	.286
Mike Easler	11	3	0	0	1	0	2	.273	.545	.273
Dave Engle	13	1	0	0	0	0	2	.077	.077	.077
Jim Essian	7	3	1	0	0	0	0	.429	.571	.429
Darrell Evans	8	1	0	0	0	2	1	.125	.125	.300
Dwight Evans	21	8	1	0	0	4	2	.381	.429	.480
Tony Fernandez	6	1	1	0	0	0	0	.167	.333	.167
Carlton Fisk	21	9	1	1	1	0	2	.429	.714	.409
Tim Foli	5	0	0	0	0	0	0	.000	.000	.000
Dan Ford	15	4	1	0	0	0	1	.267	.333	.267
Julio Franco	12	0	0	0	0	0	1	.000	.000	.000
Gary Gaetti	13	3	1	0	0	0	2	.231	.308	.231
Oscar Gamble	17	8	0	0	2	1	1	.471	.471	.526
Jim Gantner	16	1	0	0	0	1	0	.063	.063	.118
Damaso Garcia	18	3	1	0	0	0	1	.167	.222	.167
Rich Gedman	17	5	1	0	0	0	2	.294	.353	.294
Kirk Gibson	23	6	0	0	2	1	3	.261	.522	.280
Gary Gray	7	1	0	0	0	0	3	.143	.143	.143
Bobby Grich	22	7	0	0	1	0	1	.318	.455	.318
Ken Griffey	12	3	1	0	0	0	0	.250	.333	.250
Alfredo Griffin	19	4	0	0	0	1	0	.211	.211	.250
Wayne Gross	21	7	0	1	0	0	2	.333	.429	.333
Johnny Grubb	14	3	0	0	0	0	4	.214	.214	.214
Jerry Hairston	17	5	3	0	0	2	4	.294	.471	.368
Garry Hancock	11	3	0	0	0	0	0	.273	.273	.250
Mike Hargrove	17	5	0	0	0	0	0	.294	.294	.294
Larry Harlow	8	2	0	0	0	0	0	.250	.250	.250
Toby Harrah	14	3	1	0	0	1	1	.214	.286	.267
Ron Hassey	12	2	0	0	0	0	2	.167	.167	.167
Mickey Hatcher	13	7	1	0	0	1	0	.538	.615	.571
Von Hayes	5	1	0	0	0	0	0	.200	.200	.200
Mike Heath	18	4	0	1	0	1	4	.222	.333	.263
Richie Hebner	7	3	0	0	0	0	0	.429	.429	.429
Dave Henderson	13	4	1	1	0	0	2	.308	.538	.308
Rickey Henderson	20	5	0	0	1	3	4	.250	.400	.333
Steve Henderson	11	1	0	0	0	0	3	.091	.091	.091
Larry Herndon	16	3	0	0	0	0	3	.188	.188	.188
Glenn Hoffman	8	1	1	0	0	0	2	.125	.250	.125
Dave Hostetler	7	1	0	0	0	0	2	.143	.143	.143
Roy Howell	11	4	0	0	0	0	0	.364	.364	.364
Kent Hrbek	14	8	2	0	2	1	0	.571	1.143	.563
Garth Iorg	6	1	0	0	0	0	0	.167	.167	.167
Reggie Jackson	19	4	0	0	1	4	3	.211	.368	.348
Ron Jackson	5	0	0	0	0	0	0	.000	.000	.000

Dan Quisenberry continued

Batter	AB	H	2B	3B	HR	BB	SO	BA	SA	OBA
Cliff Johnson	16	7	0	0	0	0	1	.438	.438	.412
Howard Johnson	8	2	0	0	0	0	0	.250	.250	.250
Lamar Johnson	9	1	0	0	0	0	1	.111	.111	.111
Randy S. Johnson	6	2	0	0	0	0	1	.333	.333	.333
Ruppert Jones	8	4	0	0	1	0	1	.500	.875	.500
Steve Kemp	22	7	1	0	0	0	1	.318	.364	.318
Dave Kingman	9	3	0	0	0	0	1	.333	.333	.333
Ron Kittle	15	4	0	0	1	0	3	.267	.467	.267
Mickey Klutts	5	1	1	0	0	0	0	.200	.400	.200
Wayne Krenchicki	5	0	0	0	0	0	0	.000	.000	.000
Carney Lansford	23	4	2	0	0	0	1	.174	.261	.167
Rudy Law	15	3	0	0	0	0	2	.200	.200	.200
Rick Leach	5	2	1	0	0	0	0	.400	.600	.400
Ron LeFlore	8	2	0	0	0	0	0	.250	.250	.250
Chet Lemon	20	7	0	1	0	0	2	.350	.450	.381
Dave Lopes	13	3	1	1	0	0	0	.231	.462	.231
John Lowenstein	14	5	0	0	0	0	0	.357	.357	.333
Greg Luzinski	12	3	0	0	0	0	3	.250	.250	.250
Fred Lynn	21	5	1	0	0	4	2	.238	.286	.346
Rick Manning	18	3	2	0	0	0	0	.167	.278	.167
Don Mattingly	9	3	1	0	0	1	0	.333	.444	.400
John Mayberry	6	3	2	0	1	0	0	.500	1.333	.500
Bake McBride	5	2	0	0	0	0	0	.400	.400	.400
Dave McKay	5	2	1	0	0	0	0	.400	.600	.400
Dan Meyer	17	3	1	1	0	0	0	.176	.353	.176
Larry Milbourne	16	4	1	0	0	0	0	.250	.313	.250
Rick Miller	21	9	0	1	0	0	2	.429	.524	.429
Paul Molitor	17	3	0	0	1	0	4	.176	.353	.176
Don Money	9	4	0	0	0	0	0	.444	.444	.444
Charlie Moore	19	5	0	0	1	0	1	.263	.421	.263
Jim Morrison	5	2	1	0	0	0	1	.400	.600	.500
Lloyd Moseby	20	10	1	0	0	2	0	.500	.550	.545
John Moses	5	3	0	0	0	0	0	.600	.600	.600
Rance Mulliniks	17	5	0	0	0	0	2	.294	.294	.294
Jerry Mumphrey	6	2	0	0	0	3	1	.333	.333	.556
Bobby Murcer	7	0	0	0	0	1	0	.000	.000	.125
Dwayne Murphy	20	3	0	0	1	1	4	.150	.300	.190
Eddie Murray	17	7	0	1	1	1	2	.412	.706	.421
Jerry Narron	5	1	0	0	0	0	2	.200	.200	.167
Ricky Nelson	6	2	0	0	0	0	0	.333	.333	.333
Graig Nettles	12	3	1	0	0	0	0	.250	.333	.250
Jeff Newman	5	0	0	0	0	0	0	.000	.000	.000
Jim Norris	5	1	0	0	0	0	0	.200	.200	.200
Pete O'Brien	13	4	0	0	1	0	0	.308	.538	.308
Ben Oglivie	12	6	0	0	2	3	0	.500	1.000	.600
Al Oliver	6	1	1	0	0	0	0	.167	.333	.167
Jorge Orta	7	3	0	0	0	0	0	.429	.429	.429
Spike Owen	8	2	0	0	0	0	0	.250	.250	.250
Tom Paciorek	16	6	1	0	1	0	2	.375	.625	.375
Mitchell Page	8	1	0	0	0	0	1	.125	.125	.125
Mike Pagliarulo	6	3	0	0	0	0	2	.500	.500	.500
Lance Parrish	28	5	2	0	0	0	6	.179	.250	.179
Larry Parrish	11	1	1	0	0	0	2	.091	.182	.083
Jack Perconte	9	2	1	0	0	0	0	.222	.333	.222
Tony Perez	15	3	0	0	0	0	2	.200	.200	.200
Broderick Perkins	5	1	0	0	0	0	0	.200	.200	.200
Rick Peters	8	2	0	0	0	2	1	.250	.250	.400
Ken Phelps	7	2	0	0	1	0	0	.286	.714	.286
Tony Phillips	10	3	1	1	0	1	1	.300	.600	.364

Batter	AB	H	2B	3B	HR	BB	SO	BA	SA	OBA
Rob Picciolo	5	1	0	0	0	0	0	.200	.200	.200
Hosken Powell	9	3	0	0	0	0	2	.333	.333	.333
Kirby Puckett	6	2	0	0	0	0	0	.333	.333	.333
Pat Putnam	16	8	4	0	1	1	0	.500	.938	.529
Lenny Randle	6	2	0	0	0	0	0	.333	.333	.333
Willie Randolph	15	3	1	0	0	0	0	.200	.267	.200
Jerry Remy	16	5	0	0	0	0	0	.313	.313	.313
Dave Revering	5	2	0	0	0	1	1	.400	.400	.500
Jim Rice	31	6	1	0	0	0	4	.194	.226	.188
Mike Richardt	9	3	0	0	0	0	0	.333	.333	.333
Cal Ripken	14	4	0	0	1	0	1	.286	.500	.267
Mickey Rivers	7	1	0	0	0	1	1	.143	.143	.250
Dave W. Roberts	5	0	0	0	0	0	1	.000	.000	.000
Gary Roenicke	7	0	0	0	0	1	2	.000	.000	.125
Ed Romero	5	0	0	0	0	0	1	.000	.000	.000
Joe Rudi	6	2	1	0	0	0	0	.333	.500	.333
Lenn Sakata	5	3	0	0	0	0	1	.600	.600	.600
Luis Salazar	5	1	0	1	0	0	0	.200	.600	.200
Billy Sample	11	3	0	0	0	0	0	.273	.273	.273
Daryl Sconiers	6	2	0	0	0	0	2	.333	.333	.333
John Shelby	8	0	0	0	0	0	1	.000	.000	.000
Ted Simmons	10	4	0	0	1	1	1	.400	.700	.455
Joe Simpson	7	1	0	0	0	0	0	.143	.143	.250
Ken Singleton	15	3	0	0	1	3	2	.200	.400	.316
Roy Smalley	23	7	3	0	0	0	3	.304	.435	.304
Mike Squires	14	4	1	0	0	0	0	.286	.357	.286
Fred Stanley	5	0	0	0	0	0	0	.000	.000	.000
Dave Stapleton	11	2	0	0	0	0	0	.182	.182	.182
Champ Summers	5	1	0	0	1	0	0	.200	.800	.200
Jim Sundberg	16	3	0	0	0	1	3	.188	.188	.235
Rick Sweet	5	0	0	0	0	1	0	.000	.000	.167
Pat Tabler	7	1	0	0	0	0	0	.143	.143	.143
Tim Teufel	5	0	0	0	0	0	0	.000	.000	.000
Gorman Thomas	20	9	1	0	1	2	1	.450	.650	.500
Andre Thornton	16	3	0	0	1	1	1	.188	.375	.235
Wayne Tolleson	6	1	0	0	0	0	0	.167	.167	.167
Alan Trammell	28	7	3	0	1	2	2	.250	.464	.290
Willie Upshaw	15	7	1	0	0	0	1	.467	.533	.467
Otto Velez	6	2	1	0	0	0	1	.333	.500	.333
George Vukovich	8	3	0	0	0	0	2	.375	.375	.375
Greg Walker	15	4	1	0	0	1	1	.267	.333	.313
Gary Ward	18	2	1	0	0	0	3	.111	.167	.111
Ron Washington	7	1	0	0	0	0	1	.143	.143	.143
Lou Whitaker	25	12	6	0	0	2	2	.480	.720	.500
Ernie Whitt	15	5	0	0	1	1	0	.333	.533	.375
Rob Wilfong	11	2	1	0	0	1	0	.182	.273	.250
Curtis Wilkerson	5	1	0	0	0	0	0	.200	.200	.200
Jerry Willard	5	3	0	0	1	1	0	.600	1.200	.667
Bump Wills	7	3	0	0	0	0	0	.429	.429	.429
Glenn Wilson	6	1	0	0	0	0	0	.167	.167	.167
Dave Winfield	16	2	0	0	0	0	5	.125	.125	.125
John Wockenfuss	8	1	0	0	0	1	0	.125	.125	.222
Al Woods	7	0	0	0	0	0	0	.000	.000	.000
George Wright	16	6	1	0	0	0	0	.375	.438	.375
Butch Wynegar	12	4	0	0	0	0	0	.333	.333	.308
Carl Yastrzemski	16	3	0	0	0	1	1	.188	.188	.235
Mike Young	7	4	2	0	1	0	1	.571	1.286	.571
Robin Yount	17	8	0	1	1	2	3	.471	.765	.526
Richie Zisk	10	2	1	0	0	0	1	.200	.300	.200

Bruce Sutter

Batter	AB	H	2B	3B	HR	BB	SO	BA	SA	OBA
Bill Almon	6	0	0	0	0	0	3	.000	.000	.000
Dave Anderson	6	2	0	0	0	0	1	.333	.333	.333
Rob Andrews	6	0	0	0	0	1	0	.000	.000	.143
Alan Ashby	7	1	0	0	0	2	1	.143	.143	.333
Wally Backman	5	0	0	0	0	1	0	.000	.000	.167
Mark Bailey	7	1	1	0	0	0	4	.143	.286	.143
Bob Bailor	8	1	0	0	0	0	1	.125	.125	.125
Dusty Baker	23	4	0	0	1	1	3	.174	.304	.208
Kevin Bass	11	3	0	0	0	0	0	.273	.273	.273
Johnny Bench	19	4	0	0	1	1	3	.211	.368	.250

Batter	AB	H	2B	3B	HR	BB	SO	BA	SA	OBA
Bruce Benedict	13	0	0	0	0	0	2	.000	.000	.000
Dave Bergman	7	1	0	0	0	1	2	.143	.143	.250
Dale Berra	13	0	0	0	0	1	3	.000	.000	.071
Kurt Bevacqua	10	2	0	0	0	0	1	.200	.200	.200
Bruce Boisclair	7	0	0	0	0	0	4	.000	.000	.000
Juan Bonilla	11	1	0	0	0	0	1	.091	.091	.091
Bob Boone	14	0	0	0	0	3	5	.000	.000	.176
Thad Bosley	5	3	0	0	0	0	1	.600	.600	.600
Larry Bowa	33	5	2	0	0	1	1	.152	.212	.176
Bob Brenly	10	2	0	0	0	1	2	.200	.200	.273

Bruce Sutter continued

Batter	AB	H	2B	3B	HR	BB	SO	BA	SA	OBA
Dan Briggs	5	0	0	0	0	0	2	.000	.000	.000
Greg Brock	6	1	0	0	0	2	2	.167	.167	.375
Lou Brock	15	2	1	1	0	0	6	.133	.333	.133
Hubie Brooks	20	2	0	0	0	0	2	.100	.100	.100
Bill Buckner	13	3	0	0	0	0	1	.231	.231	.231
Jeff Burroughs	7	2	0	0	0	1	2	.286	.286	.333
Enos Cabell	14	3	1	0	0	0	2	.214	.286	.214
Gary Carter	42	16	1	1	3	8	5	.381	.667	.480
Dave Cash	20	4	1	0	0	2	3	.200	.250	.273
Cesar Cedeno	12	5	2	0	0	1	3	.417	.583	.462
Ron Cey	31	8	0	0	0	2	12	.258	.258	.324
Chris Chambliss	18	4	0	0	1	3	1	.222	.389	.333
Darrell Chaney	12	3	0	1	0	0	5	.250	.417	.250
Jack Clark	23	5	0	0	1	5	4	.217	.348	.357
Dave Collins	5	1	0	0	0	0	2	.200	.200	.167
Dave Concepcion	29	6	0	0	1	4	3	.207	.310	.294
Tim Corcoran	6	0	0	0	0	0	0	.000	.000	.000
Warren Cromartie	29	5	1	0	1	0	4	.172	.310	.167
Hector Cruz	11	1	0	0	1	0	6	.091	.364	.091
Jose Cruz	19	3	0	0	0	2	1	.158	.158	.238
Chili Davis	11	2	0	1	0	1	2	.182	.364	.250
Dick Davis	5	1	1	0	0	0	2	.200	.400	.200
Jody Davis	13	3	1	0	0	1	2	.231	.308	.286
Andre Dawson	45	7	2	0	0	5	12	.156	.200	.235
Ivan DeJesus	10	3	2	0	0	0	3	.300	.500	.300
Bob Dernier	8	1	1	0	0	1	2	.125	.250	.222
Bo Diaz	12	5	1	0	0	1	4	.417	.500	.462
Bill Doran	9	3	0	0	1	1	2	.333	.667	.400
Dan Driessen	31	5	1	0	0	3	10	.161	.194	.235
Leon Durham	15	7	0	0	3	1	2	.467	1.067	.500
Duffy Dyer	6	2	0	0	0	1	2	.333	.333	.429
Mike Easler	18	6	1	0	0	2	1	.333	.389	.400
Nick Esasky	7	2	0	0	2	2	4	.286	1.143	.444
Darrell Evans	19	8	1	2	0	0	2	.421	.684	.400
Bill Fahey	6	2	0	0	0	0	0	.333	.333	.333
Joe Ferguson	7	3	0	0	1	1	1	.429	.857	.500
Tim Flannery	14	3	0	0	0	1	1	.214	.214	.313
Doug Flynn	15	6	0	0	0	0	1	.400	.400	.400
Tim Foli	18	4	2	0	0	1	1	.222	.333	.263
George Foster	37	11	1	0	1	2	7	.297	.405	.333
Terry Francona	9	3	0	0	1	1	1	.333	.667	.400
Doug Frobel	5	1	0	0	0	0	3	.200	.200	.200
Phil Garner	19	4	1	0	2	2	4	.211	.579	.286
Wayne Garrett	10	1	1	0	0	1	2	.100	.200	.182
Steve Garvey	28	4	1	0	1	2	3	.143	.286	.200
Cesar Geronimo	16	2	0	0	0	2	4	.125	.125	.222
Fernando Gonzalez	6	1	1	0	0	0	1	.167	.333	.167
Ken Griffey	11	4	0	0	1	0	5	.364	.636	.364
Greg Gross	20	4	0	0	0	3	0	.200	.200	.304
Pedro Guerrero	19	8	1	0	1	2	4	.421	.632	.476
Tony Gwynn	8	3	0	0	0	0	0	.375	.375	.375
Von Hayes	14	6	0	0	0	0	1	.429	.429	.429
Richie Hebner	26	7	1	0	2	2	5	.269	.538	.321
Danny Heep	14	2	0	0	0	0	1	.143	.143	.143
Ken Henderson	5	2	0	0	1	0	1	.400	1.000	.400
Steve Henderson	20	6	0	0	3	1	5	.300	.750	.333
George Hendrick	15	6	1	1	0	0	4	.400	.600	.400
Keith Hernandez	33	15	0	2	0	7	6	.455	.576	.550
Larry Herndon	15	1	1	0	0	0	8	.067	.133	.067
Marc Hill	6	0	0	0	0	0	3	.000	.000	.000
Ron Hodges	14	1	0	0	0	1	5	.071	.071	.133
Bob Horner	13	4	2	0	0	0	4	.308	.462	.308
Art Howe	8	4	0	0	0	2	0	.500	.500	.600
Glenn Hubbard	10	2	0	0	0	4	2	.200	.200	.429
Tommy Hutton	9	0	0	0	0	0	1	.000	.000	.100
Dane Iorg	11	2	0	0	0	0	5	.182	.182	.182
Mike Ivie	9	4	2	0	0	0	3	.444	.667	.444
Jay Johnstone	16	4	1	0	0	1	3	.250	.313	.294
Ruppert Jones	9	2	0	0	1	3	3	.222	.556	.417
Mike Jorgensen	13	1	0	0	0	2	1	.077	.077	.200
Junior Kennedy	8	2	0	0	0	0	1	.250	.250	.250
Terry Kennedy	15	5	0	0	1	3	1	.333	.533	.444
Don Kessinger	7	2	0	0	0	0	1	.286	.286	.286
Dave Kingman	16	3	0	0	0	0	4	.188	.188	.188
Ray Knight	15	2	0	0	0	2	7	.133	.133	.235
Ed Kranepool	17	3	1	0	0	1	1	.176	.235	.222
Wayne Krenchicki	8	1	0	0	0	0	1	.125	.125	.125
Lee Lacy	15	1	0	0	0	0	7	.067	.067	.067
Rafael Landestoy	6	2	0	1	0	0	0	.333	.667	.333
Ken Landreaux	17	6	1	0	1	1	0	.353	.588	.368
Joe Lefebvre	13	5	1	0	1	1	3	.385	.692	.400
Johnnie LeMaster	12	1	0	0	0	0	2	.083	.083	.083
Jeff Leonard	19	7	1	0	0	0	4	.368	.421	.368
Sixto Lezcano	14	4	0	1	0	0	3	.286	.429	.286
Dave Lopes	10	3	1	1	0	0	3	.300	.900	.300
Mike Lum	8	4	1	0	0	1	1	.500	1.000	.555
Greg Luzinski	14	2	1	0	0	1	7	.143	.214	.176
Elliott Maddox	13	4	0	0	0	0	6	.308	.308	.308
Garry Maddox	31	3	1	0	0	3	7	.097	.129	.171
Bill Madlock	29	5	2	0	0	1	2	.172	.241	.226
Mike A. Marshall	9	4	0	0	0	1	1	.444	.444	.500
Jerry Martin	8	1	0	0	0	0	3	.125	.125	.125
Carmelo Martinez	5	2	0	0	0	0	0	.400	.400	.400
Gary Matthews	35	7	0	0	0	0	8	.200	.200	.194
Len Matuszek	9	3	1	0	1	1	0	.333	.778	.364
Milt May	12	4	2	0	0	2	0	.333	.500	.429
Lee Mazzilli	31	7	1	1	0	4	7	.226	.323	.314
Bake McBride	22	3	1	0	1	0	9	.136	.182	.174
Tim McCarver	7	1	1	0	0	1	0	.143	.286	.250
Willie McCovey	7	1	0	0	0	3	3	.143	.143	.400
Kevin McReynolds	8	1	1	0	0	0	2	.125	.250	.125
Sam Mejias	5	3	1	0	1	0	0	.600	1.400	.600
Felix Millan	5	1	0	0	0	0	1	.200	.200	.200
Brad Mills	5	1	0	0	0	0	1	.200	.200	.200
Eddie Milner	8	2	0	0	0	2	1	.250	.250	.400
John Milner	10	0	0	0	0	1	3	.000	.000	.083
Rick Monday	15	2	0	0	0	0	8	.133	.133	.133
Willie Montanez	18	8	0	1	0	0	4	.444	.722	.444
Jerry Morales	8	0	0	0	0	0	1	.000	.000	.111
Jose Morales	6	2	0	0	0	0	2	.333	.667	.333
Keith Moreland	21	8	1	0	0	1	2	.381	.429	.409
Omar Moreno	20	5	1	0	0	2	9	.250	.300	.304
Joe Morgan	19	5	2	1	0	5	2	.263	.474	.417
Jim Morrison	5	0	0	0	0	0	1	.000	.000	.167
Jerry Mumphrey	26	2	1	0	0	2	6	.077	.115	.143
Dale Murphy	21	6	1	1	2	1	7	.286	.714	.318
Joe Nolan	7	1	0	0	0	1	1	.143	.143	.250
Billy North	5	0	0	0	0	2	2	.000	.000	.286
Ken Oberkfell	12	4	0	1	0	1	1	.333	.500	.385
Ron Oester	12	2	2	0	0	2	3	.167	.333	.286
Rowland Office	15	3	0	0	0	0	4	.200	.200	.200
Al Oliver	17	5	0	0	0	2	0	.294	.294	.368
Ed Ott	12	2	0	0	0	2	7	.167	.167	.286
Dave Parker	28	8	1	0	2	6	7	.286	.536	.412
Larry Parrish	25	5	2	0	0	3	6	.200	.280	.286
Tony Pena	19	6	0	1	0	2	4	.316	.421	.381
Tony Perez	22	4	1	0	1	2	2	.182	.364	.250
Broderick Perkins	11	2	0	0	0	0	2	.182	.182	.182
Mike Phillips	16	2	0	0	1	0	3	.125	.313	.125
Biff Pocoroba	7	1	0	0	0	0	2	.143	.143	.143
Terry Puhl	17	4	0	0	0	3	0	.235	.235	.333
Tim Raines	18	5	0	0	0	0	4	.278	.278	.263
Rafael Ramirez	14	2	0	0	0	1	1	.143	.143	.200
Lenny Randle	5	0	0	0	0	0	3	.000	.000	.000
Johnny Ray	17	4	1	0	1	1	1	.235	.471	.278
Gary Redus	6	4	3	1	0	0	1	.667	1.500	.667
Ken Reitz	21	5	0	0	1	1	2	.238	.381	.273
Craig Reynolds	9	2	0	0	1	0	1	.222	.444	.222
R.J. Reynolds	6	1	0	0	0	0	1	.167	.167	.167
Gene Richards	19	6	2	0	0	2	4	.316	.421	.381
Bill Robinson	11	3	0	0	0	1	4	.273	.545	.333
Ron Roenicke	9	2	1	0	0	0	0	.222	.333	.222
Pete Rose	33	9	0	0	0	2	3	.273	.333	.333
Jerry Royster	20	3	0	0	0	2	3	.150	.150	.217
Bill Russell	18	6	0	0	0	1	3	.333	.500	.429
Luis Salazar	12	2	1	0	0	1	3	.167	.250	.231
Juan Samuel	12	1	0	0	0	0	9	.083	.083	.083
Ryne Sandberg	17	6	2	0	0	0	3	.353	1.000	.353
Steve Sax	13	5	0	0	0	1	0	.385	.538	.429
Mike Schmidt	45	10	3	0	2	3	10	.222	.422	.271